GREAT BOOKS OF THE WESTERN WORLD

28. GILBERT
    GALILEO
    HARVEY

29. CERVANTES

30. FRANCIS BACON

31. DESCARTES
    SPINOZA

32. MILTON

33. PASCAL

34. NEWTON
    HUYGENS

35. LOCKE
    BERKELEY
    HUME

36. SWIFT
    STERNE

37. FIELDING

38. MONTESQUIEU
    ROUSSEAU

39. ADAM SMITH

40. GIBBON I

41. GIBBON II

42. KANT

43. AMERICAN STATE
    PAPERS
    THE FEDERALIST
    J. S. MILL

44. BOSWELL

45. LAVOISIER
    FOURIER
    FARADAY

46. HEGEL

47. GOETHE

48. MELVILLE

49. DARWIN

50. MARX
    ENGELS

51. TOLSTOY

52. DOSTOEVSKY

53. WILLIAM JAMES

54. FREUD

GREAT BOOKS
OF THE WESTERN WORLD

ROBERT MAYNARD HUTCHINS, *EDITOR IN CHIEF*

41.

GIBBON: II

THE DECLINE AND FALL
OF THE
ROMAN EMPIRE

VOLUME II

BY EDWARD GIBBON

WILLIAM BENTON, *Publisher*

ENCYCLOPÆDIA BRITANNICA, INC.

CHICAGO · LONDON · TORONTO · GENEVA · SYDNEY · TOKYO · MANILA

THE UNIVERSITY OF CHICAGO

The Great Books
is published with the editorial advice of the faculties
of The University of Chicago

CONTENTS: VOLUME TWO

CHAPTERS XLI—LXXI

Contents

XLVII. *Theological History of the Doctrine of the Incarnation. The Human and Divine Nature of Christ. Enmity of the Patriarchs of Alexandria and Constantinople. St. Cyril and Nestorius. Third General Council of Ephesus. Heresy of Eutyches. Fourth General Council of Chalcedon. Civil and Ecclesiastical Discord. Intolerance of Justinian. The Three Chapters. The Monothelite Controversy. State of the Oriental Sects. I. The Nestorians. II. The Jacobites. III. The Maronites. IV. The Armenians. V. The Abyssinians*

XLVIII. *Plan of the Last Two Quarto Volumes. Succession and Characters of the Greek Emperors of Constantinople, from the Time of Heraclius to the Latin Conquest*

Contents

Contents

Contents

LX. *Schism of the Greeks and Latins. State of Constantinople. Revolt of the Bulgarians. Isaac Angelus
Dethroned by His Brother Alexius. Origin of the
Fourth Crusade. Alliance of the French and Venetians with the Son of Isaac. Their Naval Expedition to Constantinople. The Two Sieges and Final
Conquest of the City by the Latins*

LXI. *Partition of the Empire by the French and Venetians. Five Latin Emperors of the Houses of Flanders and Courtenay. Their Wars against the Bulgarians and Greeks. Weakness and Poverty of the Latin
Empire. Recovery of Constantinople by the Greeks.
General Consequences of the Crusades*

DIGRESSION ON THE FAMILY OF COURTENAY

LXV. *Elevation of Timour or Tamerlane to the Throne of Samarcand. His Conquests in Persia, Georgia, Tartary, Russia, India, Syria, and Anatolia. His Turkish War. Defeat and Captivity of Bajazet. Death of Timour. Civil War of the Sons of Bajazet. Restoration of the Turkish Monarchy by Mahomet the First. Siege of Constantinople by Amurath the Second*

LXVI. *Applications of the Eastern Emperors to the Popes. Visits to the West, of John the First, Manuel, and John the Second, Palæologus. Union of the Greek and Latin Churches, Promoted by the Council of Basil, and Concluded at Ferrara and Florence. State of Literature at Constantinople. Its Revival in Italy by the Greek Fugitives. Curiosity and Emulation of the Latins*

Contents

NOTES: Chapters XLI—LXXI, p. 599

MAPS, p. 797

INDEX, p. 807

CHAPTER XLI

Conquests of Justinian in the West. Character and first Campaigns of Belisarius. He invades and subdues the Vandal Kingdom of Africa. His Triumph. The Gothic War. He recovers Sicily, Naples, and Rome. Siege of Rome by the Goths. Their Retreat and Losses. Surrender of Ravenna. Glory of Belisarius. His domestic Shame and Misfortunes.

WHEN Justinian ascended the throne, about fifty years after the fall of the Western Empire, the kingdoms of the Goths and Vandals had obtained a solid, and, as it might seem, a legal establishment both in Europe and Africa. The titles which Roman victory had inscribed were erased with equal justice by the sword of the barbarians; and their successful rapine derived a more venerable sanction from time, from treaties, and from oaths of fidelity, already repeated by a second or third generation of obedient subjects. Experience and Christianity had refuted the superstitious hope that Rome was founded by the gods to reign for ever over the nations of the earth. But the proud claim of perpetual and indefeasible dominion, which her soldiers could no longer maintain, was firmly asserted by her statesmen and lawyers, whose opinions have been sometimes revived and propagated in the modern schools of jurisprudence. After Rome herself had been stripped of the Imperial purple, the princes of Constantinople assumed the sole and sacred sceptre of the monarchy; demanded, as their rightful inheritance, the provinces which had been subdued by the consuls or possessed by the Cæsars; and feebly aspired to deliver their faithful subjects of the West from the usurpation of heretics and barbarians. The execution of this splendid design was in some degree reserved for Justinian. During the five first years of his reign he reluctantly waged a costly and unprofitable war against the Persians, till his pride submitted to his ambition, and he purchased, at the price of four hundred and forty thousand pounds sterling, the benefit of a precarious truce, which, in the language of both nations, was dignified with the appellation of the *endless* peace. The safety of the East enabled the emperor to employ his forces against the Vandals; and the internal state of Africa afforded an honourable motive, and promised a powerful support to the Roman arms.[1]

According to the testament of the founder, the African kingdom had lineally descended to Hilderic, the eldest of the Vandal princes. A mild disposition inclined the son of a tyrant, the grandson of a conqueror, to prefer the counsels of clemency and peace, and his accession was marked by the salutary edict which restored two hundred bishops to their churches, and allowed the free profession of the Athanasian creed.[2] But the catholics accepted with cold and transient gratitude a favour so inadequate to their pretensions, and the virtues of Hilderic offended the prejudices of his countrymen. The Arian clergy presumed to insinuate that he had renounced the faith, and the soldiers more loudly complained that he had degenerated from the courage, of his ancestors. His ambassadors were suspected of a secret and disgraceful negotiation in the Byzantine court; and his general, the Achilles,[3] as he was named, of the Vandals, lost a battle against the naked and disorderly Moors. The public discontent was exasperated by Gelimer, whose age, descent, and military fame gave him an apparent title to the succession: he assumed, with the consent of the nation, the reins of government, and his unfortunate sovereign sunk without a struggle from the throne to a dungeon, where he was strictly guarded with a faithful counsellor, and his unpopular nephew the Achilles of the Vandals. But the indulgence which Hilderic had shown to his catholic subjects had powerfully recommended him to the favour of Justinian, who, for the benefit of his own sect, could acknowledge the use and justice of religious toleration: their alliance, while the nephew of Justin remained in a private station, was cemented by the mutual exchange of gifts and letters, and the emperor Justinian asserted the cause of royalty and friendship. In two successive embassies he admonished the usurper to repent of his treason, or to abstain, at least, from any further violence which might provoke the displeasure of God and of the Romans, to reverence the laws of kindred and succession, and to suffer an infirm old man peaceably to end his days either on the throne of Carthage or in the palace of Constantinople. The passions or even the prudence of Gelimer compelled him to reject these requests, which were urged in the haughty tone of menace and command; and he justified his ambition in a language rarely spoken in the Byzantine court, by alleging the right of a free people to remove or punish their chief magistrate who had failed in the execution of the kingly office. After his fruitless expostulation, the captive monarch was more rigorously treated, his nephew was deprived of his eyes, and the cruel Vandal, confident in his strength and distance, derided the vain threats and slow preparations of the emperor of the East. Justinian resolved to deliver or revenge his friend, Gelimer to maintain his usurpation; and the war was preceded, according to the practice of civilised nations, by the most solemn protestations that each party was sincerely desirous of peace.

The report of an African war was grateful only to the vain and idle populace of Constantinople, whose poverty exempted them from tribute, and whose cowardice was seldom exposed to military service. But the wiser citizens, who judged of the future by the past, revolved in their memory the immense loss, both of men and money, which the empire had sustained in the expedition of Basiliscus. The troops, which, after five laborious campaigns, had been recalled from the Persian frontier, dreaded the sea, the climate, and the arms of an unknown enemy. The ministers of the finances computed, as far as they might compute, the demands of an African war, the taxes which must be found and levied to supply those insatiate demands, and the danger lest their own lives, or at least their lucrative employments, should be made

responsible for the deficiency of the supply. Inspired by such selfish motives (for we may not suspect him of any zeal for the public good), John of Cappadocia ventured to oppose in full council the inclinations of his master. He confessed that a victory of such importance could not be too dearly purchased; but he represented in a grave discourse the certain difficulties and the uncertain event. "You undertake," said the præfect, "to besiege Carthage: by land the distance is not less than one hundred and forty days' journey; on the sea, a whole year[4] must elapse before you can receive any intelligence from your fleet. If Africa should be reduced, it cannot be preserved without the additional conquest of Sicily and Italy. Success will impose the obligation of new labours; a single misfortune will attract the barbarians into the heart of your exhausted empire." Justinian felt the weight of this salutary advice; he was confounded by the unwonted freedom of an obsequious servant; and the design of the war would perhaps have been relinquished, if his courage had not been revived by a voice which silenced the doubts of profane reason. "I have seen a vision," cried an artful or fanatic bishop of the East. "It is the will of heaven, O emperor! that you should not abandon your holy enterprise for the deliverance of the African church. The God of battles will march before your standard, and disperse your enemies, who are the enemies of his Son." The emperor might be tempted, and his counsellors were constrained, to give credit to this seasonable revelation; but they derived more rational hope from the revolt which the adherents of Hilderic of Athanasius had already excited on the borders of the Vandal monarchy. Pudentius, an African subject, had privately signified his loyal intentions, and a small military aid restored the province of Tripoli to the obedience of the Romans. The government of Sardinia had been intrusted to Godas, a valiant barbarian: he suspended the payment of tribute, disclaimed his allegiance to the usurper, and gave audience to the emissaries of Justinian, who found him master of that fruitful island, at the head of his guards, and proudly invested with the ensigns of royalty. The forces of the Vandals were diminished by discord and suspicion; the Roman armies were animated by the spirit of Belisarius, one of those heroic names which are familiar to every age and to every nation.

The Africanus of new Rome was born, and perhaps educated, among the Thracian peasants,[5] without any of those advantages which had formed the virtues of the elder and younger Scipio—a noble origin, liberal studies, and the emulation of a free state. The silence of a loquacious secretary may be admitted to prove that the youth of Belisarius could not afford any subject of praise: he served, most assuredly with valour and reputation, among the private guards of Justinian; and when his patron became emperor, the domestic was promoted to military command. After a bold inroad into Persarmenia, in which his glory was shared by a colleague, and his progress was checked by an enemy, Belisarius repaired to the important station of Dara, where he first accepted the service of Procopius, the faithful companion, and diligent historian, of his exploits.[6] The Mirranes of Persia advanced with forty thousand of her best troops, to raze the fortifications of Dara; and signified the day and the hour on which the citizens should prepare a bath for his refreshment after the toils of victory. He encountered an adversary equal to himself, by the new title of General of the East; his superior in the science of war, but much inferior in the number and quality of his troops, which amounted only to twenty-five thousand Romans and strangers, relaxed in their discipline, and humbled by recent disasters. As the level plain of Dara refused all shelter to stratagem and ambush, Belisarius protected his front with a deep trench, which was prolonged at first in perpendicular, and afterwards in parallel, lines, to cover the wings of cavalry advantageously posted to command the flanks and rear of the enemy. When the Roman centre was shaken, their well-timed and rapid charge decided the conflict: the standard of Persia fell; the *immortals* fled; the infantry threw away their bucklers, and eight thousand of the vanquished were left on the field of battle. In the next campaign Syria was invaded on the side of the desert; and Belisarius, with twenty thousand men, hastened from Dara to the relief of the province. During the whole summer the designs of the enemy were baffled by his skilful dispositions: he pressed their retreat, occupied each night their camp of the preceding day, and would have secured a bloodless victory, if he could have resisted the impatience of his own troops. Their valiant promise was faintly supported in the hour of battle; the right wing was exposed by the treacherous or cowardly desertion of the Christian Arabs; the Huns, a veteran band of eight hundred warriors, were oppressed by superior numbers; the flight of the Isaurians was intercepted; but the Roman infantry stood firm on the left;

for Belisarius himself, dismounting from his horse, showed them that intrepid despair was their only safety. They turned their backs to the Euphrates, and their faces to the enemy: innumerable arrows glanced without effect from the compact and shelving order of their bucklers; an impenetrable line of pikes was opposed to the repeated assaults of the Persian cavalry; and after a resistance of many hours, the remaining troops were skilfully embarked under the shadow of the night. The Persian commander retired with disorder and disgrace, to answer a strict account of the lives of so many soldiers which he had consumed in a barren victory. But the fame of Belisarius was not sullied by a defeat in which he alone had saved his army from the consequences of their own rashness: the approach of peace relieved him from the guard of the eastern frontier, and his conduct in the sedition of Constantinople amply discharged his obligations to the emperor. When the African war became the topic of popular discourse and secret deliberation, each of the Roman generals was apprehensive, rather than ambitious, of the dangerous honour; but as soon as Justinian had declared his preference of superior merit, their envy was rekindled by the unanimous applause which was given to the choice of Belisarius. The temper of the Byzantine court may encourage a suspicion that the hero was darkly assisted by the intrigues of his wife, the fair and subtle Antonina, who alternately enjoyed the confidence, and incurred the hatred, of the empress Theodora. The birth of Antonina was ignoble; she descended from a family of charioteers; and her chastity had been stained with the foulest reproach. Yet she reigned with long and absolute power over the mind of her illustrious husband; and if Antonina disdained the merit of conjugal fidelity, she expressed a manly friendship to Belisarius, whom she accompanied with undaunted resolution in all the hardships and dangers of a military life.[7]

The preparations for the African war were not unworthy of the last contest between Rome and Carthage. The pride and flower of the army consisted of the guards of Belisarius, who, according to the pernicious indulgence of the times, devoted themselves, by a particular oath of fidelity, to the service of their patron. Their strength and stature, for which they had been curiously selected, the goodness of their horses and armour, and the assiduous practice of all the exercises of war, enabled them to act whatever their courage might prompt; and their courage was exalted by the social honour of their rank, and the personal ambition of favour and fortune. Four hundred of the bravest of the Heruli marched under the banner of the faithful and active Pharas; their untractable valour was more highly prized than the tame submission of the Greeks and Syrians; and of such importance was it deemed to procure a reinforcement of six hundred Massagetæ, or Huns, that they were allured by fraud and deceit to engage in a naval expedition. Five thousand horse and ten thousand foot were embarked at Constantinople for the conquest of Africa; but the infantry, for the most part levied in Thrace and Isauria, yielded to the more prevailing use and reputation of the cavalry; and the Scythian bow was the weapon on which the armies of Rome were now reduced to place their principal dependence. From a laudable desire to assert the dignity of his theme, Procopius defends the soldiers of his own time against the morose critics, who confined that respectable name to the heavy-armed warriors of antiquity, and maliciously observed that the word *archer* is introduced by Homer[8] as a term of contempt. "Such contempt might perhaps be due to the naked youths who appeared on foot in the fields of Troy, and, lurking behind a tombstone, or the shield of a friend, drew the bowstring to their breast,[9] and dismissed a feeble and lifeless arrow. But our archers (pursues the historian) are mounted on horses, which they manage with admirable skill; their head and shoulders are protected by a casque or buckler; they wear greaves of iron on their legs, and their bodies are guarded by a coat of mail. On their right side hangs a quiver, a sword on their left, and their hand is accustomed to wield a lance or javelin in closer combat. Their bows are strong and weighty; they shoot in every possible direction, advancing, retreating, to the front, to the rear, or to either flank; and as they are taught to draw the bowstring not to the breast, but to the right ear, firm indeed must be the armour that can resist the rapid violence of their shaft." Five hundred transports, navigated by twenty thousand mariners of Egypt, Cilicia, and Ionia, were collected in the harbour of Constantinople. The smallest of these vessels may be computed at thirty, the largest at five hundred, tons; and the fair average will supply an allowance, liberal, but not profuse, of about one hundred thousand tons,[10] for the reception of thirty-five thousand soldiers and sailors, of five thousand horses, of arms, engines, and military stores, and of a sufficient stock of water and provisions for a voyage, perhaps, of three months. The proud galleys which

in former ages swept the Mediterranean with so many hundred oars had long since disappeared; and the fleet of Justinian was escorted only by ninety-two light brigantines, covered from the missile weapons of the enemy, and rowed by two thousand of the brave and robust youth of Constantinople. Twenty-two generals are named, most of whom were afterwards distinguished in the wars of Africa and Italy; but the supreme command, both by land and sea, was delegated to Belisarius alone, with a boundless power of acting according to his discretion, as if the emperor himself were present. The separation of the naval and military professions is at once the effect and the cause of the modern improvements in the science of navigation and maritime war.

In the seventh year of the reign of Justinian, and about the time of the summer solstice, the whole fleet of six hundred ships was ranged in martial pomp before the gardens of the palace. The patriarch pronounced his benediction, the emperor signified his last commands, the general's trumpet gave the signal of departure, and every heart, according to its fears or wishes, explored with anxious curiosity the omens of misfortune and success. The first halt was made at Perinthus or Heraclea, where Belisarius waited five days to receive some Thracian horses, a military gift of his sovereign. From thence the fleet pursued their course through the midst of the Propontis; but as they struggled to pass the Straits of the Hellespont, an unfavourable wind detained them four days at Abydus, where the general exhibited a memorable lesson of firmness and severity. Two of the Huns, who in a drunken quarrel had slain one of their fellow-soldiers, were instantly shown to the army suspended on a lofty gibbet. The national indignity was resented by their countrymen, who disclaimed the servile laws of the empire, and asserted the free privilege of Scythia, where a small fine was allowed to expiate the hasty sallies of intemperance and anger. Their complaints were specious, their clamours were loud, and the Romans were not averse to the example of disorder and impunity. But the rising sedition was appeased by the authority and eloquence of the general, and he represented to the assembled troops the obligation of justice, the importance of discipline, the rewards of piety and virtue, and the unpardonable guilt of murder, which, in his apprehension, was aggravated rather than excused by the vice of intoxication.[11] In the navigation from the Hellespont to Peloponnesus, which the Greeks after the siege of

Troy had performed in four days,[12] the fleet of Belisarius was guided in their course by his master-galley, conspicuous in the day by the redness of the sails, and in the night by the torches blazing from the mast-head. It was the duty of the pilots, as they steered between the islands and turned the capes of Malea and Tænarium, to preserve the just order and regular intervals of such a multitude of ships; as the wind was fair and moderate, their labours were not unsuccessful, and the troops were safely disembarked at Methone on the Messenian coast, to repose themselves for awhile after the fatigues of the sea. In this place they experienced how avarice, invested with authority, may sport with the lives of thousands which are bravely exposed for the public service. According to military practice, the bread or biscuit of the Romans was twice prepared in the oven, and the diminution of one-fourth was cheerfully allowed for the loss of weight. To gain this miserable profit, and to save the expense of wood, the præfect, John of Cappadocia, had given orders that the flour should be slightly baked by the same fire which warmed the baths of Constantinople; and when the sacks were opened, a soft and mouldy paste was distributed to the army. Such unwholesome food, assisted by the heat of the climate and season, soon produced an epidemical disease which swept away five hundred soldiers. Their health was restored by the diligence of Belisarius, who provided fresh bread at Methone, and boldly expressed his just and humane indignation: the emperor heard his complaint; the general was praised, but the minister was not punished. From the port of Methone the pilots steered along the western coast of Peloponnesus, as far as the isle of Zacynthus or Zante, before they undertook the voyage (in their eyes a most arduous voyage) of one hundred leagues over the Ionian Sea. As the fleet was surprised by a calm, sixteen days were consumed in the slow navigation; and even the general would have suffered the intolerable hardship of thirst, if the ingenuity of Antonina had not preserved the water in glass bottles, which she buried deep in the sand in a part of the ship impervious to the rays of the sun. At length the harbour of Caucana,[13] on the southern side of Sicily, afforded a secure and hospitable shelter. The Gothic officers, who governed the island in the name of the daughter and grandson of Theodoric, obeyed their imprudent orders to receive the troops of Justinian like friends and allies; provisions were liberally supplied, the cavalry was remounted,[14] and

Procopius soon returned from Syracuse with correct information of the state and designs of the Vandals. His intelligence determined Belisarius to hasten his operations, and his wise impatience was seconded by the winds. The fleet lost sight of Sicily, passed before the isle of Malta, discovered the capes of Africa, ran along the coast with a strong gale from the north-east, and finally cast anchor at the promontory of Caput Vada, about five days' journey to the south of Carthage.[15]

If Gelimer had been informed of the approach of the enemy, he must have delayed the conquest of Sardinia for the immediate defence of his person and kingdom. A detachment of five thousand soldiers and one hundred and twenty galleys would have joined the remaining forces of the Vandals; and the descendant of Genseric might have surprised and oppressed a fleet of deep-laden transports incapable of action, and of light brigantines that seem only qualified for flight. Belisarius had secretly trembled when he overheard his soldiers in the passage emboldening each other to confess their apprehensions. If they were once on shore, they hoped to maintain the honour of their arms; but if they should be attacked at sea, they did not blush to acknowledge that they wanted courage to contend at the same time with the winds, the waves, and the barbarians.[16] The knowledge of their sentiments decided Belisarius to seize the first opportunity of landing them on the coast of Africa; and he prudently rejected, in a council of war, the proposal of sailing with the fleet and army into the port of Carthage. Three months after their departure from Constantinople, the men and horses, the arms and military stores, were safely disembarked; and five soldiers were left as a guard on board each of the ships, which were disposed in the form of a semicircle. The remainder of the troops occupied a camp on the sea-shore, which they fortified, according to ancient discipline, with a ditch and rampart; and the discovery of a source of fresh water, while it allayed the thirst, excited the superstitious confidence of the Romans. The next morning some of the neighbouring gardens were pillaged; and Belisarius, after chastising the offenders, embraced the slight occasion, but the decisive moment, of inculcating the maxims of justice, moderation, and genuine policy. "When I first accepted the commission of subduing Africa, I depended much less," said the general, "on the numbers, or even the bravery of my troops, than upon the friendly disposition of the natives, and their immortal hatred to the

Vandals. You alone can deprive me of this hope: if you continue to extort by rapine what might be purchased for a little money, such acts of violence will reconcile these implacable enemies, and unite them in a just and holy league against the invaders of their country." These exhortations were enforced by a rigid discipline, of which the soldiers themselves soon felt and praised the salutary effects. The inhabitants, instead of deserting their houses or hiding their corn, supplied the Romans with a fair and liberal market, the civil officers of the province continued to exercise their functions in the name of Justinian, and the clergy, from motives of conscience and interest, assiduously laboured to promote the cause of a catholic emperor. The small town of Sullecte,[17] one day's journey from the camp, had the honour of being foremost to open her gates and to resume her ancient allegiance; the larger cities of Leptis and Adrumetum imitated the example of loyalty as soon as Belisarius appeared; and he advanced without opposition as far as Grasse, a palace of the Vandal kings, at the distance of fifty miles from Carthage. The weary Romans indulged themselves in the refreshment of shady groves, cool fountains, and delicious fruits; and the preference which Procopius allows to these gardens over any that he had seen, either in the East or West, may be ascribed either to the taste or the fatigue of the historian. In three generations prosperity and a warm climate had dissolved the hardy virtue of the Vandals, who insensibly became the most luxurious of mankind. In their villas and gardens, which might deserve the Persian name of *Paradise*,[18] they enjoyed a cool and elegant repose; and, after the daily use of the bath, the barbarians were seated at a table profusely spread with the delicacies of the land and sea. Their silken robes, loosely flowing after the fashion of the Medes, were embroidered with gold; love and hunting were the labours of their life, and their vacant hours were amused by pantomimes, chariot-races, and the music and dances of the theatre.

In a march of ten or twelve days the vigilance of Belisarius was constantly awake and active against his unseen enemies, by whom, in every place and at every hour, he might be suddenly attacked. An officer of confidence and merit, John the Armenian, led the vanguard of three hundred horse, six hundred Massagetæ covered at a certain distance the left flank, and the whole fleet, steering along the coast, seldom lost sight of the army, which moved each day about twelve miles, and lodged in the evening in strong camps or in friendly towns. The near approach of the Romans to Carthage filled the mind of Gelimer with anxiety and terror. He prudently wished to protract the war till his brother, with his veteran troops, should return from the conquest of Sardinia; and he now lamented the rash policy of his ancestors, who, by destroying the fortifications of Africa, had left him only the dangerous resource of risking a battle in the neighbourhood of his capital. The Vandal conquerors, from their original number of fifty thousand, were multiplied, without including their women and children, to one hundred and sixty thousand fighting men; and such forces, animated with valour and union, might have crushed at their first landing the feeble and exhausted bands of the Roman general. But the friends of the captive king were more inclined to accept the invitations than to resist the progress of Belisarius; and many a proud barbarian disguised his aversion to war under the more specious name of his hatred to the usurper. Yet the authority and promises of Gelimer collected a formidable army, and his plans were concerted with some degree of military skill. An order was despatched to his brother Ammatas to collect all the forces of Carthage, and to encounter the van of the Roman army at the distance of ten miles from the city: his nephew Gibamund with two thousand horse was destined to attack their left, when the monarch himself, who silently followed, should charge their rear in a situation which excluded them from the aid or even the view of their fleet. But the rashness of Ammatas was fatal to himself and his country. He anticipated the hour of the attack, outstripped his tardy followers, and was pierced with a mortal wound after he had slain with his own hand twelve of his boldest antagonists. His Vandals fled to Carthage; the highway, almost ten miles, was strewed with dead bodies; and it seemed incredible that such multitudes could be slaughtered by the swords of three hundred Romans. The nephew of Gelimer was defeated, after a slight combat, by the six hundred Massagetæ: they did not equal the third part of his numbers, but each Scythian was fired by the example of his chief, who gloriously exercised the privilege of his family by riding foremost and alone to shoot the first arrow against the enemy. In the meanwhile Gelimer himself, ignorant of the event, and misguided by the windings of the hills, inadvertently passed the Roman army, and reached the scene of action where Ammatas had fallen. He wept the fate of his brother and of Carthage, charged with irresistible fury the advancing squadrons, and might have pursued, and perhaps decided the victory, if he had not wasted those inestimable moments in the discharge of a vain though pious duty to the dead. While his spirit was broken by this mournful office, he heard the trumpet of Belisarius, who, leaving Antonina and his infantry in the camp, pressed forwards with his guards and the remainder of the cavalry to rally his flying troops, and to restore the fortune of the day. Much room could not be found in this disorderly battle for the talents of a general; but the king fled before the hero, and the Vandals, accustomed only to a Moorish enemy, were incapable of withstanding the arms and discipline of the Romans. Gelimer retired with hasty steps towards the desert of Numidia; but he had soon the consolation of learning that his private orders for the execution of Hilderic and his captive friends had been faithfully obeyed. The tyrant's revenge was useful only to his enemies. The death of a lawful prince excited the compassion of his people; his life might have perplexed the victorious Romans; and the lieutenant of Justinian, by a crime of which he was innocent, was relieved from the painful alternative of forfeiting his honour or relinquishing his conquests.

As soon as the tumult had subsided, the several parts of the army informed each other of the accidents of the day; and Belisarius pitched his camp on the field of victory, to which the tenth mile-stone from Carthage had applied the Latin appellation of *Decimus*. From a wise suspicion of the stratagems and resources of the Vandals, he marched the next day in order of battle, halted in the evening before the gates of Carthage, and allowed a night of repose, that he might not in darkness and disorder expose the city to the licence of the soldiers, or the soldiers themselves to the secret ambush of the city. But as the fears of Belisarius were the result of calm and intrepid reason, he was soon satisfied that he might confide, without danger, in the peaceful and friendly aspect of the capital. Carthage blazed, with innumerable torches, the signals of the public joy; the chain was removed that guarded the entrance of the port, the gates were thrown open, and the people with acclamations of gratitude hailed and invited their Roman deliverers. The defeat of the Vandals and the freedom of Africa were announced to the city on the eve of St. Cyprian, when the churches were already adorned and illuminated for the festival of the martyr, whom three centuries of superstition had almost raised to a local deity. The Arians, conscious that their reign had expired, resigned the temple to the catholics, who rescued their saint from profane hands, performed the holy rites, and loudly proclaimed the creed of Athanasius and Justinian. One awful hour reversed the fortunes of the contending parties. The suppliant Vandals, who had so lately indulged the vices of conquerors, sought an humble refuge in the sanctuary of the church; while the merchants of the East were delivered from the deepest dungeon of the palace by their affrighted keeper, who implored the protection of his captives, and showed them, through an aperture in the wall, the sails of the Roman fleet. After their separation from the army, the naval commanders had proceeded with slow caution along the coast till they reached the Hermæan promontory, and obtained the first intelligence of the victory of Belisarius. Faithful to his instructions, they would have cast anchor about twenty miles from Carthage, if the more skilful seamen had not represented the perils of the shore and the signs of an impending tempest. Still ignorant of the revolution, they declined, however, the rash attempt of forcing the chain of the port; and the adjacent harbour and suburb of Mandracium were insulted only by the rapine of a private officer who disobeyed and deserted his leaders. But the imperial fleet, advancing with a fair wind, steered through the narrow entrance of the Goletta, and occupied in the deep and capacious lake of Tunis a secure station about five miles from the capital.[19] No sooner was Belisarius informed of their arrival than he despatched orders that the greatest part of the mariners should be immediately landed, to join the triumph, and to swell the apparent numbers of the Romans. Before he allowed them to enter the gates of Carthage, he exhorted them, in a discourse worthy of himself and the occasion, not to disgrace the glory of their arms; and to remember that the Vandals had been the tyrants, but that *they* were the deliverers, of the Africans, who must now be respected as the voluntary and affectionate subjects of their common sovereign. The Romans marched through the streets in close ranks, prepared for battle if an enemy had appeared: the strict order maintained by the general imprinted on their minds the duty of obedience; and in an age in which custom and impunity almost sanctified the abuse of conquest, the genius of one man repressed the passions of a victorious army. The voice of menace and complaint was silent; the trade of Carthage was not interrupted; while Africa changed her master and her government, the shops continued open and busy; and the soldiers, after sufficient guards had been posted, modestly departed to the houses which were allotted for their reception. Belisarius fixed his residence in the palace, seated himself on the throne of Genseric, accepted and distributed the barbaric spoil, granted their lives to the suppliant Vandals, and laboured to repair the damage which the suburb of Mandracium had sustained in the preceding night. At supper he entertained his principal officers with the form and magnificence of a royal banquet.[20] The victor was respectfully served by the captive officers of the household; and in the moments of festivity, when the impartial spectators applauded the fortune and merit of Belisarius, his envious flatterers secretly shed their venom on every word and gesture which might alarm the suspicions of a jealous monarch. One day was given to these pompous scenes, which may not be despised as useless if they attracted the popular veneration; but the active mind of Belisarius, which in the pride of victory could suppose a defeat, had already resolved that the Roman empire in Africa should not depend on the chance of arms or the favour of the people. The fortifications of Carthage had alone been exempted from the general proscription; but in the reign of ninety-five years they were suffered to decay by the thoughtless and indolent Vandals. A wiser conqueror restored, with incredible despatch, the walls and ditches of the city. His liberality encouraged the workmen; the soldiers, the mariners, and the citizens vied with each other in the salutary labour; and Gelimer, who had feared to trust his person in an open town, beheld with astonishment and despair the rising strength of an impregnable fortress.

That unfortunate monarch, after the loss of his capital, applied himself to collect the remains of an army scattered, rather than destroyed, by the preceding battle, and the hopes of pillage attracted some Moorish bands to the standard of Gelimer. He encamped in the fields of Bulla, four days' journey from Carthage; insulted the capital, which he deprived of the use of an aqueduct; proposed a high reward for the head of every Roman; affected to spare the persons and property of his African subjects; and secretly negotiated with the Arian sectaries and the confederate Huns. Under these circumstances the conquest of Sardinia served only to aggravate his distress: he reflected, with the

deepest anguish, that he had wasted in that useless enterprise five thousand of his bravest troops, and he read, with grief and shame, the victorious letters of his brother Zano, who expressed a sanguine confidence that the king, after the example of their ancestors, had already chastised the rashness of the Roman invader. "Alas! my brother," replied Gelimer, "Heaven has declared against our unhappy nation. While you have subdued Sardinia, we have lost Africa. No sooner did Belisarius appear with a handful of soldiers, than courage and prosperity deserted the cause of the Vandals. Your nephew Gibamund, your brother Ammatas, have been betrayed to death by the cowardice of their followers. Our horses, our ships, Carthage itself, and all Africa, are in the power of the enemy. Yet the Vandals still prefer an ignominious repose, at the expense of their wives and children, their wealth and liberty. Nothing now remains except the field of Bulla, and the hope of your valour. Abandon Sardinia; fly to our relief; restore our empire, or perish by our side." On the receipt of this epistle Zano imparted his grief to the principal Vandals, but the intelligence was prudently concealed from the natives of the island. The troops embarked in one hundred and twenty galleys at the port of Cagliari, cast anchor the third day on the confines of Mauritania, and hastily pursued their march to join the royal standard in the camp of Bulla. Mournful was the interview: the two brothers embraced; they wept in silence; no questions were asked of the Sardinian victory; no inquiries were made of the African misfortunes: they saw before their eyes the whole extent of their calamities, and the absence of their wives and children afforded a melancholy proof that either death or captivity had been their lot. The languid spirit of the Vandals was at length awakened and united by the entreaties of their king, the example of Zano, and the instant danger which threatened their monarchy and religion. The military strength of the nation advanced to battle, and such was the rapid increase, that, before their army reached Tricameron, about twenty miles from Carthage, they might boast, perhaps with some exaggeration, that they surpassed, in a tenfold proportion, the diminutive powers of the Romans. But these powers were under the command of Belisarius, and, as he was conscious of their superior merit, he permitted the barbarians to surprise him at an unseasonable hour. The Romans were instantly under arms; a rivulet covered their front; the cavalry formed the first line, which Belisarius supported in the centre at the head of five hundred guards; the infantry, at some distance, was posted in the second line; and the vigilance of the general watched the separate station and ambiguous faith of the Massagetæ, who secretly reserved their aid for the conquerors. The historian has inserted, and the reader may easily supply, the speeches[21] of the commanders, who, by arguments the most opposite to their situation, inculcated the importance of victory and the contempt of life. Zano, with the troops which had followed him to the conquest of Sardinia, was placed in the centre, and the throne of Genseric might have stood, if the multitude of Vandals had imitated their intrepid resolution. Casting away their lances and missile weapons, they drew their swords and expected the charge; the Roman cavalry thrice passed the rivulet, they were thrice repulsed, and the conflict was firmly maintained till Zano fell and the standard of Belisarius was displayed. Gelimer retreated to his camp, the Huns joined the pursuit, and the victors despoiled the bodies of the slain. Yet no more than fifty Romans and eight hundred Vandals were found on the field of battle; so inconsiderable was the carnage of a day which extinguished a nation and transferred the empire of Africa. In the evening Belisarius led his infantry to the attack of the camp, and the pusillanimous flight of Gelimer exposed the vanity of his recent declarations, that to the vanquished death was a relief, life a burden, and infamy the only object of terror. His departure was secret, but, as soon as the Vandals discovered that their king had deserted them, they hastily dispersed, anxious only for their personal safety, and careless of every object that is dear or valuable to mankind. The Romans entered the camp without resistance, and the wildest scenes of disorder were veiled in the darkness and confusion of the night. Every barbarian who met their swords was inhumanly massacred: their widows and daughters, as rich heirs or beautiful concubines, were embraced by the licentious soldiers; and avarice itself was almost satiated with the treasures of gold and silver, the accumulated fruits of conquest or economy in a long period of prosperity and peace. In this frantic search the troops, even of Belisarius, forgot their caution and respect. Intoxicated with lust and rapine, they explored, in small parties or alone, the adjacent fields, the woods, the rocks, and the caverns that might possibly conceal any desirable prize; laden with booty, they deserted their ranks, and wandered,

without a guide, on the high road to Carthage, and, if the flying enemies had dared to return, very few of the conquerors would have escaped. Deeply sensible of the disgrace and danger, Belisarius passed an apprehensive night on the field of victory; at the dawn of day he planted his standard on a hill, recalled his guards and veterans, and gradually restored the modesty and obedience of the camp. It was equally the concern of the Roman general to subdue the hostile, and to save the prostrate, barbarian; and the suppliant Vandals, who could be found only in churches, were protected by his authority, disarmed, and separately confined, that they might neither disturb the public peace nor become the victims of popular revenge. After despatching a light detachment to tread the footsteps of Gelimer, he advanced, with his whole army, about ten days' march, as far as Hippo Regius, which no longer possessed the relics of St. Augustin.[22] The season, and the certain intelligence that the Vandal had fled to the inaccessible country of the Moors, determined Belisarius to relinquish the vain pursuit, and to fix his winter quarters at Carthage. From thence he despatched his principal lieutenant to inform the emperor that in the space of three months he had achieved the conquest of Africa.

Belisarius spoke the language of truth. The surviving Vandals yielded, without resistance, their arms and their freedom; the neighbourhood of Carthage submitted to his presence, and the more distant provinces were successively subdued by the report of his victory. Tripoli was confirmed in her voluntary allegiance; Sardinia and Corsica surrendered to an officer who carried instead of a sword the head of the valiant Zano; and the isles of Majorca, Minorca, and Yvica consented to remain an humble appendage of the African kingdom. Cæsarea, a royal city, which in looser geography may be confounded with the modern Algiers, was situate thirty days' march to the westward of Carthage; by land the road was infested by the Moors, but the sea was open, and the Romans were now masters of the sea. An active and discreet tribune sailed as far as the Straits, where he occupied Septem or Ceuta,[23] which rises opposite to Gibraltar on the African coast; that remote place was afterwards adorned and fortified by Justinian, and he seems to have indulged the vain ambition of extending his empire to the Columns of Hercules. He received the messengers of victory at the time when he was preparing to publish the Pandects of the Roman law, and the devout or jealous emperor celebrated the divine goodness, and confessed in silence the merit of his successful general.[24] Impatient to abolish the temporal and spiritual tyranny of the Vandals, he proceeded without delay to the full establishment of the catholic church. Her jurisdiction, wealth, and immunities, perhaps the most essential part of episcopal religion, were restored and amplified with a liberal hand; the Arian worship was suppressed, the Donatist meetings were proscribed,[25] and the synod of Carthage, by the voice of two hundred and seventeen bishops,[26] applauded the just measure of pious retaliation. On such an occasion it may not be presumed that many orthodox prelates were absent; but the comparative smallness of their number, which in ancient councils had been twice or even thrice multiplied, most clearly indicates the decay both of the church and state. While Justinian approved himself the defender of the faith, he entertained an ambitious hope that his victorious lieutenant would speedily enlarge the narrow limits of his dominion to the space which they occupied before the invasion of the Moors and Vandals; and Belisarius was instructed to establish five *dukes* or commanders in the convenient stations of Tripoli, Leptis, Cirta, Cæsarea, and Sardinia, and to compute the military force of *palatines* or *borderers* that might be sufficient for the defence of Africa. The kingdom of the Vandals was not unworthy of the presence of a Prætorian præfect; and four consulars, three presidents, were appointed to administer the seven provinces under his civil jurisdiction. The number of their subordinate officers, clerks, messengers, or assistants, was minutely expressed: three hundred and ninety-six for the præfect himself, fifty for each of his vicegerents; and the rigid definition of their fees and salaries was more effectual to confirm the right than to prevent the abuse. These magistrates might be oppressive, but they were not idle, and the subtle questions of justice and revenue were infinitely propagated under the new government, which professed to revive the freedom and equity of the Roman republic. The conqueror was solicitous to extract a prompt and plentiful supply from his African subjects, and he allowed them to claim, even in the third degree and from the collateral line, the houses and lands of which their families had been unjustly despoiled by the Vandals. After the departure of Belisarius, who acted by a high and special commission, no ordinary provision was made for a master-general of the forces; but the office of Prætorian præfect was intrusted to a

soldier; the civil and military powers were united, according to the practice of Justinian, in the chief governor; and the representative of the emperor in Africa, as well as in Italy, was soon distinguished by the appellation of Exarch.[27]

Yet the conquest of Africa was imperfect till her former sovereign was delivered, either alive or dead, into the hands of the Romans. Doubtful of the event, Gelimer had given secret orders that a part of his treasure should be transported to Spain, where he hoped to find a secure refuge at the court of the king of the Visigoths. But these intentions were disappointed by accident, treachery, and the indefatigable pursuit of his enemies, who intercepted his flight from the sea-shore, and chased the unfortunate monarch, with some faithful followers, to the inaccessible mountain of Papua,[28] in the inland country of Numidia. He was immediately besieged by Pharas, an officer whose truth and sobriety were the more applauded, as such qualities could seldom be found among the Heruli, the most corrupt of the barbarian tribes. To his vigilance Belisarius had intrusted this important charge; and, after a bold attempt to scale the mountain, in which he lost an hundred and ten soldiers, Pharas expected, during a winter siege, the operation of distress and famine on the mind of the Vandal king. From the softest habits of pleasure, from the unbounded command of industry and wealth, he was reduced to share the poverty of the Moors,[29] supportable only to themselves by their ignorance of a happier condition. In their rude hovels of mud and hurdles, which confined the smoke and excluded the light, they promiscuously slept on the ground, perhaps on a sheepskin, with their wives, their children, and their cattle. Sordid and scanty were their garments; the use of bread and wine was unknown, and their oaten or barley cakes, imperfectly baked in the ashes, were devoured almost in a crude state by the hungry savages. The health of Gelimer must have sunk under these strange and unwonted hardships, from whatsoever cause they had been endured; but his actual misery was embittered by the recollection of past greatness, the daily insolence of his protectors, and the just apprehension that the light and venal Moors might be tempted to betray the rights of hospitality. The knowledge of his situation dictated the humane and friendly epistle of Pharas. "Like yourself," said the chief of the Heruli, "I am an illiterate barbarian, but I speak the language of plain sense and an honest heart. Why will you persist in hopeless obstinacy? Why will you ruin yourself, your family, and nation? The love of freedom and abhorrence of slavery? Alas! my dearest Gelimer, are you not already the worst of slaves, the slave of the vile nation of the Moors? Would it not be preferable to sustain at Constantinople a life of poverty and servitude, rather than to reign the undoubted monarch of the mountain of Papua? Do you think it a disgrace to be the subject of Justinian? Belisarius is his subject, and we ourselves, whose birth is not inferior to your own, are not ashamed of our obedience to the Roman emperor. That generous prince will grant you a rich inheritance of lands, a place in the senate, and the dignity of patrician: such are his gracious intentions, and you may depend with full assurance on the word of Belisarius. So long as Heaven has condemned us to suffer, patience is a virtue; but if we reject the proffered deliverance, it degenerates into blind and stupid despair." "I am not insensible," replied the king of the Vandals, "how kind and rational is your advice. But I cannot persuade myself to become the slave of an unjust enemy, who has deserved my implacable hatred. *Him* I had never injured either by word or deed; yet he has sent against me, I know not from whence, a certain Belisarius, who has cast me headlong from the throne into this abyss of misery. Justinian is a man; he is a prince; does he not dread for himself a similar reverse of fortune? I can write no more; my grief oppresses me. Send me, I beseech you, my dear Pharas, send me a lyre,[30] a sponge, and a loaf of bread." From the Vandal messenger, Pharas was informed of the motives of this singular request. It was long since the king of Africa had tasted bread, a defluxion had fallen on his eyes, the effect of fatigue or incessant weeping, and he wished to solace the melancholy hours by singing to the lyre the sad story of his own misfortunes. The humanity of Pharas was moved: he sent the three extraordinary gifts; but even his humanity prompted him to redouble the vigilance of his guard, that he might sooner compel his prisoner to embrace a resolution advantageous to the Romans, but salutary to himself. The obstinacy of Gelimer at length yielded to reason and necessity; the solemn assurances of safety and honourable treatment were ratified in the emperor's name by the ambassador of Belisarius, and the king of the Vandals descended from the mountain. The first public interview was in one of the suburbs of Carthage; and when the royal captive accosted his conqueror, he burst into a fit of laughter. The crowd might naturally believe that extreme grief had deprived Gelimer of his senses; but in this mournful state unseasonable mirth insinuated to more intelligent observers that the vain and transitory scenes of human greatness are unworthy of a serious thought.[31]

Their contempt was soon justified by a new example of a vulgar truth—that flattery adheres to power, and envy to superior merit. The chiefs of the Roman army presumed to think themselves the rivals of an hero. Their private despatches maliciously affirmed that the conqueror of Africa, strong in his reputation and the public love, conspired to seat himself on the throne of the Vandals. Justinian listened with too patient an ear; and his silence was the result of jealousy rather than of confidence. An honourable alternative, of remaining in the province or of returning to the capital, was indeed submitted to the discretion of Belisarius; but he wisely concluded, from intercepted letters and the knowledge of his sovereign's temper, that he must either resign his head, erect his standard, or confound his enemies by his presence and submission. Innocence and courage decided his choice: his guards, captives, and treasures were diligently embarked; and so prosperous was the navigation, that his arrival at Constantinople preceded any certain account of his departure from the port of Carthage. Such unsuspecting loyalty removed the apprehensions of Justinian: envy was silenced and inflamed by the public gratitude; and the third Africanus obtained the honours of a triumph, a ceremony which the city of Constantine had never seen, and which ancient Rome, since the reign of Tiberius, had reserved for the *auspicious* arms of the Cæsars.[32] From the palace of Belisarius the procession was conducted through the principal streets to the hippodrome; and this memorable day seemed to avenge the injuries of Genseric and to expiate the shame of the Romans. The wealth of nations was displayed, the trophies of martial or effeminate luxury; rich armour, golden thrones, and the chariots of state which had been used by the Vandal queen; the massy furniture of the royal banquet, the splendour of precious stones, the elegant forms of statues and vases, the more substantial treasure of gold, and the holy vessels of the Jewish temple, which, after their long peregrination, were respectfully deposited in the Christian church of Jerusalem. A long train of the noblest Vandals reluctantly exposed their lofty stature and manly countenance. Gelimer slowly advanced: he was clad in a purple robe, and still maintained the majesty of a king. Not a tear escaped from his eyes, not a sigh was heard; but his pride or piety derived some secret consolation from the words of Solomon,[33] which he repeatedly pronounced, VANITY! VANITY! ALL IS VANITY! Instead of ascending a triumphal car drawn by four horses or elephants, the modest conqueror marched on foot at the head of his brave companions: his prudence might decline an honour too conspicuous for a subject; and his magnanimity might justly disdain what had been so often sullied by the vilest of tyrants. The glorious procession entered the gate of the hippodrome; was saluted by the acclamations of the senate and people; and halted before the throne where Justinian and Theodora were seated to receive the homage of the captive monarch and the victorious hero. They both performed the customary adoration; and falling prostrate on the ground, respectfully touched the footstool of a prince who had not unsheathed his sword, and of a prostitute who had danced on the theatre: some gentle violence was used to bend the stubborn spirit of the grandson of Genseric; and however trained to servitude, the genius of Belisarius must have secretly rebelled. He was immediately declared consul for the ensuing year, and the day of his inauguration resembled the pomp of a second triumph: his curule chair was borne aloft on the shoulders of captive Vandals; and the spoils of war, gold cups, and rich girdles, were profusely scattered among the populace.

But the purest reward of Belisarius was in the faithful execution of a treaty for which his honour had been pledged to the king of the Vandals. The religious scruples of Gelimer, who adhered to the Arian heresy, were incompatible with the dignity of senator or patrician: but he received from the emperor an ample estate in the province of Galatia, where the abdicated monarch retired, with his family and friends, to a life of peace, of affluence, and perhaps of content.[34] The daughters of Hilderic were entertained with the respectful tenderness due to their age and misfortune; and Justinian and Theodora accepted the honour of educating and enriching the female descendants of the great Theodosius. The bravest of the Vandal youth were distributed into five squadrons of cavalry, which adopted the name of their benefactor, and supported in the Persian wars the glory of their ancestors. But these rare exceptions, the reward of birth or valour, are insufficient to explain the fate of a nation whose numbers, before a short and bloodless war, amounted to more than six hundred thousand persons. After the exile of their king and nobles, the servile crowd might purchase their safety by adjuring their character, religion, and language; and their degenerate posterity would be insensibly mingled with the common herd of African subjects. Yet even in the present age, and in the heart of the Moorish tribes, a curious traveller has discovered the white complexion and long flaxen hair of a northern race;[35] and it was formerly believed that the boldest of the Vandals fled beyond the power, or even the knowledge, of the Romans, to enjoy their solitary freedom on the shores of the Atlantic ocean.[36] Africa had been their empire, it became their prison; nor could they entertain a hope, or even a wish, of returning to the banks of the Elbe, where their brethren, of a spirit less adventurous, still wandered in their native forests. It was impossible for cowards to surmount the barriers of unknown seas and hostile barbarians; it was impossible for brave men to expose their nakedness and defeat before the eyes of their countrymen, to describe the kingdoms which they had lost, and to claim a share of the humble inheritance which, in a happier hour, they had almost unanimously renounced.[37] In the country between the Elbe and the Oder several populous villages of Lusatia are inhabited by the Vandals: they still preserve their language, their customs, and the purity of their blood; support, with some impatience, the Saxon or Prussian yoke; and serve, with secret and voluntary allegiance, the descendant of their ancient kings, who in his garb and present fortune is confounded with the meanest of his vassals.[38] The name and situation of this unhappy people might indicate their descent from one common stock with the conquerors of Africa. But the use of a Sclavonian dialect more clearly represents them as the last remnant of the new colonies who succeeded to the genuine Vandals, already scattered or destroyed in the age of Procopius.[39]

If Belisarius had been tempted to hesitate in his allegiance, he might have urged, even against the emperor himself, the indispensable duty of saving Africa from an enemy more barbarous than the Vandals. The origin of the Moors is involved in darkness: they were ignorant of the use of letters.[40] Their limits cannot be precisely defined; a boundless continent was open to the Libyan shepherds; the change of seasons and pastures regulated their motions; and their rude huts and slender furniture were ransported with the same ease as their arms, heir families, and their cattle, which consisted of sheep, oxen, and camels.[41] During the vigour of the Roman power they observed a respectful distance from Carthage and the sea-shore; under the feeble reign of the Vandals they invaded the cities of Numidia, occupied the sea-coast from Tangier to Cæsarea, and pitched their camps, with impunity, in the fertile province of Pyzacium. The formidable strength and artful conduct of Belisarius secured the neutrality of the Moorish princes, whose vanity aspired to receive in the emperor's name the ensigns of their regal dignity.[42] They were astonished by the rapid event, and trembled in the presence of their conqueror. But his approaching departure soon relieved the apprehensions of a savage and superstitious people; the number of their wives allowed them to disregard the safety of their infant hostages; and when the Roman general hoisted sail in the port of Carthage, he heard the cries and almost beheld the flames of the desolated province. Yet he persisted in his resolution; and leaving only a part of his guards to reinforce the feeble garrisons, he intrusted the command of Africa to the eunuch Solomon,[43] who proved himself not unworthy to be the successor of Belisarius. In the first invasion some detachments, with two officers of merit, were surprised and intercepted; but Solomon speedily assembled his troops, marched from Carthage into the heart of the country, and in two great battles destroyed sixty thousand of the barbarians. The Moors depended on their multitude, their swiftness, and their inaccessible mountains; and the aspect and smell of their camels are said to have produced some confusion in the Roman cavalry.[44] But as soon as they were commanded to dismount, they derided this contemptible obstacle: as soon as the columns ascended the hills, the naked and disorderly crowd was dazzled by glittering arms and regular evolutions; and the menace of their female prophets was repeatedly fulfilled, that the Moors should be discomfited by a *beardless* antagonist. The victorious eunuch advanced thirteen days' journey from Carthage to besiege Mount Aurasius,[45] the citadel, and at the same time the garden, of Numidia. That range of hills, a branch of the great Atlas, contains, within a circumference of one hundred and twenty miles, a rare variety of soil and climate; the intermediate valleys and elevated plains abound with rich pastures, perpetual streams, and fruits of a delicious taste and uncommon magnitude. This fair solitude is decorated with the ruins of Lambesa, a Roman city, once the seat of a legion, and the residence of forty thousand inhabitants. The Ionic temple of Æsculapius is encompassed with Moorish huts; and the cattle now graze in the midst of an amphitheatre, under the shade of Corinthian columns. A sharp perpendicular rock rises above the level of the mountain, where the African princes deposited their wives and treasure; and a proverb is familiar to the Arabs, that the man may eat fire who dares to attack the craggy cliffs and inhospitable natives of Mount Aurasius. This hardy enterprise was twice attempted by the eunuch Solomon: from the first, he retreated with some disgrace; and in the second, his patience and provisions were almost exhausted; and he must again have retired, if he had not yielded to the impetuous courage of his troops, who audaciously scaled, to the astonishment of the Moors, the mountain, the hostile camp, and the summit of the Geminian rock. A citadel was erected to secure this important conquest, and to remind the barbarians of their defeat; and as Solomon pursued his march to the west, the long-lost province of Mauritanian Sitifi was again annexed to the Roman empire. The Moorish war continued several years after the departure of Belisarius; but the laurels which he resigned to a faithful lieutenant may be justly ascribed to his own triumph.

The experience of past faults, which may sometimes correct the mature age of an individual, is seldom profitable to the successive generations of mankind. The nations of antiquity, careless of each other's safety, were separately vanquished and enslaved by the Romans. This awful lesson might have instructed the barbarians of the West to oppose, with timely counsels and confederate arms, the unbounded ambition of Justinian. Yet the same error was repeated, the same consequences were felt, and the Goths, both of Italy and Spain, insensible of their approaching danger, beheld with indifference, and even with joy, the rapid downfall of the Vandals. After the failure of the royal line, Theudes, a valiant and powerful chief, ascended the throne of Spain, which he had formerly administered in the name of Theodoric and his infant grandson. Under his command the Visigoths besieged the fortress of Ceuta, on the African coast; but, while they spent the Sabbath-day in peace and devotion, the pious security of their camp was invaded by a sally from the town, and the king himself, with some difficulty and danger, escaped from the hands of a sacrilegious enemy.[46] It was not long before his pride and resentment were gratified by a suppliant embassy from the unfortunate Gelimer, who implored, in his distress, the aid of the Spanish monarch. But instead of sacrificing these unworthy passions to the dictates of generosity and prudence, Theudes amused the ambassadors till he was secretly informed of the loss of Carthage, and then dismissed them, with obscure and contemptuous advice, to seek in their native country a true knowledge of the state of the Vandals.[47] The long continuance of the Italian war delayed the punishment of the Visigoths, and the eyes of Theudes were closed before they tasted the fruits of his mistaken policy. After his death the sceptre of Spain was disputed by a civil war. The weaker candidate solicited the protection of Justinian, and ambitiously subscribed a treaty of alliance which deeply wounded the independence and happiness of his country. Several cities, both on the ocean and the Mediterranean, were ceded to the Roman troops, who afterwards refused to evacuate those pledges, as it should seem, either of safety or payment; and as they were fortified by perpetual supplies from Africa, they maintained their impregnable stations for the mischievous purpose of inflaming the civil and religious factions of the barbarians. Seventy years elapsed before this painful thorn could be extirpated from the bosom of the monarchy; and as long as the emperors retained any share of these remote and useless possessions, their vanity might number Spain in the list of their provinces, and the successors of Alaric in the rank of their vassals.[48]

The error of the Goths who reigned in Italy was less excusable than that of their Spanish brethren, and their punishment was still more immediate and terrible. From a motive of private revenge, they enabled their most dangerous enemy to destroy their most valuable ally. A sister of the great Theodoric had been given in marriage to Thrasimond the African king:[49] on this occasion the fortress of Lilybæum,[50] in Sicily, was resigned to the Vandals, and the princess Amalafrida was attended by a martial train of one thousand nobles and five thousand Gothic soldiers, who signalised their valour in the Moorish wars. Their merit was over-rated by themselves, and perhaps neglected by the Vandals: they viewed the country with envy, and the conquerors with disdain; but their real or fictitious conspiracy was prevented by a massacre; the Goths were oppressed, and the captivity of Amalafrida was soon followed by her secret and suspicious death. The eloquent pen of Cassiodorus was employed to reproach the Vandal court with the cruel violation of every social and public duty; but the vengeance which he threatened in the name of his sovereign might be derided with impunity as long as Africa was protected by the sea, and the Goths were destitute of a navy. In the blind impotence of grief and indignation they joyfully saluted the approach of the Romans, entertained the fleet of Belisarius in the ports of Sicily, and were speedily delighted or alarmed by the surprising intelligence that their revenge was executed beyond the measure of their hopes, or perhaps of their wishes. To their friendship the emperor was indebted for the kingdom of Africa, and the Goths might reasonably think that they were entitled to resume the possession of a barren rock, so recently separated as a nuptial gift from the island of Sicily. They were soon undeceived by the haughty mandate of Belisarius, which excited their tardy and unavailing repentance. "The city and promontory of Lilybæum," said the Roman general, "belonged to the Vandals, and I claim them by the right of conquest. Your submission may deserve the favour of the emperor; your obstinacy will provoke his displeasure, and must kindle a war that can terminate only in your utter ruin. If you compel us to take up arms, we shall contend, not to regain the possession of a single city, but to deprive you of all the provinces which you unjustly withhold from their lawful sovereign.' A nation of two hundred thousand soldiers might have smiled at the vain menace of Justinian and his lieutenant; but a spirit of discord and disaffection prevailed in Italy, and the Goths supported with reluctance the indignity of a female reign.[51]

The birth of Amalasontha, the regent and queen of Italy,[52] united the two most illustrious families of the barbarians. Her mother, the sister of Clovis, was descended from the long-haired kings of the *Merovingian* race,[53] and the regal succession of the *Amali* was illustrated in the eleventh generation by her father, the great Theodoric, whose merit might have ennobled a plebeian origin. The sex of his daughter excluded her from the Gothic throne; but his vigilant tenderness for his family and his people discovered the last heir of the royal line, whose ancestors had taken refuge in Spain, and the fortunate Eutharic was suddenly exalted to the rank of a consul and a prince. He enjoyed only a short time the charms of Amalasontha and the hopes of the succession; and his widow, after the death of her husband and father, was left the guardian of her son Athalaric and the kingdom of Italy. At the age of about twenty-eight years, the endowments of her mind and person had attained their perfect maturity. Her beauty, which, in the apprehension of Theodora herself, might have disputed the conquest of an emperor, was animated by manly sense, activity, and resolution. Education and experience had cultivated her talents; her philosophic studies were exempt from vanity; and, though she expressed herself with equal elegance and ease in the Greek, the Latin, and the Gothic tongue, the daughter of Theodoric maintained in her counsels a discreet and impenetrable silence. By a faithful imitation of the virtues, she revived the prosperity of his reign; while she strove, with pious care, to expiate the faults and to obliterate the darker memory of his declining age. The children of Boethius and Symmachus were restored to their paternal inheritance; her extreme lenity never consented to inflict any corporal or pecuniary penalties on her Roman subjects; and she generously despised the clamours of the Goths, who, at the end of forty years, still considered the people of Italy as their slaves or their enemies. Her salutary measures were directed by the wisdom and celebrated by the eloquence of Cassiodorus; she solicited and deserved the friendship of the emperor; and the kingdoms of Europe respected, both in peace and war, the majesty of the Gothic throne. But the future happiness of the queen of Italy depended on the education of her son, who was destined, by his birth, to support the different and almost incompatible characters of the chief of a barbarian camp and the first magistrate of a civilised nation. From the age of ten years[54] Athalaric was diligently instructed in the arts and sciences either useful or ornamental for a Roman prince, and three venerable Goths were chosen to instil the principles of honour and virtue into the mind of their young king. But the pupil who is insensible of the benefits must abhor the restraints of education; and the solicitude of the queen, which affection rendered anxious and severe, offended the untractable nature of her son and his subjects. On a solemn festival, when the Goths were assembled in the palace of Ravenna, the royal youth escaped from his mother's apartment, and, with tears of pride and anger, complained of a blow which his stubborn disobedience had provoked her to inflict. The barbarians resented the indignity which had been offered to their king, accused the regent of conspiring against his life and crown, and imperiously demanded that the grandson of Theodoric should be rescued from the dastardly discipline of women and pedants, and educated, like a valiant Goth, in the society of his equals and the glorious ignorance of his ancestors. To this rude clamour, importunately urged as the voice of the nation, Amalasontha was compelled to yield her reason and the dearest wishes of her heart. The king of Italy was abandoned to wine, to women, and to rustic sports; and the indiscreet contempt of the ungrateful youth betrayed the mischievous designs of his favourites and her enemies. Encompassed with domestic foes, she entered into a secret negotiation with the emperor Justinian, obtained the assurance of a friendly reception, and had actually deposited at Dyrrachium, in Epirus, a treasure of forty thousand pounds of gold. Happy would it have been for her fame and safety if she had calmly retired from barbarous faction to the peace and splendour of Constantinople. But the mind of Amalasontha was inflamed by ambition and revenge; and while her ships lay at anchor in the port, she waited for the success of a crime which her passions excused or applauded as an act of justice. Three of the most dangerous malcontents had been separately removed, under the pretence of trust and command, to the frontiers of Italy: they were assassinated by her private emissaries; and the blood of these noble Goths rendered the queen-mother absolute in the court of Ravenna, and justly odious to a free people. But if she had lamented the disorders of her son, she soon wept his irreparable loss; and the death of Athalaric, who, at the age of sixteen, was consumed by premature intemperance, left her destitute of any firm support or legal authority. Instead of submitting to the laws of her country, which held as a fundamental maxim that the succession could never pass from the lance to the distaff, the daughter of Theodoric conceived the impracticable design of sharing, with one of her cousins, the regal title, and of reserving in her own hands the substance of supreme power. He received the proposal with profound respect and affected gratitude; and the eloquent Cassiodorus announced to the senate and the emperor that Amalasontha and Theodatus had ascended the throne of Italy. His birth (for his mother was the sister of Theodoric) might be considered as an imperfect title; and the choice of Amalasontha was more strongly directed by her contempt of his avarice and pusillanimity, which had deprived him of the love of the Italians and the esteem of the barbarians. But Theodatus was exasperated by the contempt which he deserved: her justice had repressed and reproached the oppression which he exercised against his Tuscan neighbours; and the principal Goths, united by common guilt and resentment, conspired to instigate his slow and timid disposition. The letters of congratulation were scarcely dispatched before the queen of Italy was imprisoned in a small island of the lake of Bolsena,[55] where, after a short confinement, she was strangled in the bath, by the order or with the connivance of the new king, who instructed his turbulent subjects to shed the blood of their sovereigns.

Justinian beheld with joy the dissensions of the Goths, and the mediation of an ally concealed and promoted the ambitious views of the conqueror. His ambassadors, in their public audience, demanded the fortress of Lilybæum, ten barbarian fugitives, and a just compensation for the pillage of a small town on the Illyrian borders; but they secretly negotiated with Theodatus to betray the province of Tuscany, and tempted Amalasontha to extricate herself from danger and perplexity by a free surrender of the kingdom of Italy. A false and servile epistle was subscribed by the reluctant hand of the captive queen; but the confession of the Roman senators who were sent to Constantinople revealed the truth of her deplorable situation, and Justinian, by the voice of a new ambassador, most powerfully interceded for her life and liberty. Yet the secret instructions of the same minister were adapted to serve the cruel jealousy of Theodora, who dreaded the presence and superior charms of a rival: he prompted, with artful and ambiguous hints, the execution of a crime so useful to the Romans,[56] received the intelligence of her death with grief and indignation, and denounced, in his master's name, immortal war against the perfidious assassin. In Italy, as well as in Africa, the guilt of a usurper appeared to justify the arms of Justinian; but the forces which he prepared were insufficient for the subversion of a mighty kingdom, if their feeble numbers had not been multiplied by the name, the spirit, and the conduct of a hero. A chosen troop of guards, who served on horseback and were armed with lances and bucklers, attended the person of Belisarius; his cavalry was composed of two hundred Huns, three hundred Moors, and four thousand *confederates*, and the infantry consisted only of three thousand Isaurians. Steering the same course as in his former expedition, the Roman consul cast anchor before Catana, in Sicily, to survey the strength of the island, and to decide whether he should attempt the conquest or peaceably pursue his voyage for the African coast. He found a fruitful land and a friendly people. Notwithstanding the decay of agriculture, Sicily still supplied the granaries of Rome; the farmers were graciously exempted from the oppression of military quarters; and the Goths, who trusted the defence of the island to the inhabitants, had some reason to complain that their confidence was ungratefully betrayed. Instead of soliciting and expecting the aid of the king of Italy, they yielded to the first summons a cheerful obedience; and this province, the first fruits of the Punic wars, was again, after a long separation, united to the Roman empire.[57] The Gothic garrison of Palermo, which alone attempted to resist, was reduced, after a short siege, by a singular stratagem. Belisarius introduced his ships into the deepest recess of the harbour; their boats were laboriously hoisted with ropes and pulleys to the top-mast head, and he filled them with archers, who, from that superior station, commanded the ramparts of the city. After this easy though successful campaign, the conqueror entered Syracuse in triumph, at the head of his victorious bands, distributing gold medals to the people, on the day which so gloriously terminated the year of the consulship. He passed the winter season in the palace of ancient kings, amidst the ruins of a Grecian colony which once extended to a circumference of two-and-twenty miles;[58] but in the spring, about the festival of Easter, the prosecution of his designs was interrupted by a dangerous revolt of the African forces. Carthage was saved by the presence of Belisarius, who suddenly landed with a thousand guards. Two thousand soldiers of doubtful faith returned to the standard of their old commander, and he marched, without hesitation, above fifty miles, to seek an enemy whom he affected to pity and despise. Eight thousand rebels trembled at his approach; they were routed at the first onset by the dexterity of their master, and this ignoble victory would have restored the peace of Africa, if the conqueror had not been hastily recalled to Sicily to appease a sedition which was kindled during his absence in his own camp.[59] Disorder and disobedience were the common malady of the times: the genius to command and the virtue to obey resided only in the mind of Belisarius.

Although Theodatus descended from a race of heroes, he was ignorant of the art and averse to the dangers of war. Although he had studied the writings of Plato and Tully, philosophy was incapable of purifying his mind from the basest passions, avarice and fear. He had purchased a sceptre by ingratitude and murder: at the first menace of an enemy he degraded his own majesty, and that of a nation which already disdained their unworthy sovereign. Astonished by the recent example of Gelimer, he saw himself dragged in chains through the streets of Constantinople: the terrors which Belisarius inspired were heightened by the eloquence of Peter, the Byzantine ambassador; and that bold and subtle advocate persuaded him to sign a treaty too ignominious to become the foundation of a lasting peace. It was stipulated that in the acclamations of the Roman people the name of the emperor should be always proclaimed before that of the Gothic king; and that, as often as the statue of Theodatus was erected in brass or marble, the divine image of Justinian should be placed on its right hand. Instead of conferring, the king of Italy was reduced to solicit, the honours of the senate; and the consent of the emperor was made indispensable before he could execute, against a priest or senator, the sentence either of death or confiscation. The feeble monarch resigned the possession of Sicily; offered, as the annual mark of his dependence, a crown of gold of the weight of three hundred pounds; and promised to supply, at the requisition of his sovereign, three thousand Gothic auxiliaries for the service of the empire. Satisfied with these extraordinary concessions, the successful agent of Justinian hastened his journey to Constantinople; but no sooner had he reached the Alban villa[60] than he was recalled by the anxiety of Theodatus; and the dialogue which passed between the king and the ambassador deserves to be represented in its original simplicity. "Are you of opinion that the emperor will ratify this treaty? *Perhaps.* If he refuses, what consequence will ensue? *War.* Will such a war be just or reasonable? *Most assuredly: every one should act according to his character.* What is your meaning? *You are a philosopher —Justinian is emperor of the Romans: it would ill become the disciple of Plato to shed the blood of thousands in his private quarrel: the successor of Augustus should vindicate his rights, and recover by arms the ancient provinces of his empire.*" This reasoning might not convince, but it was sufficient to alarm and subdue the weakness of Theodatus; and he soon descended to his last

offer, that for the poor equivalent of a pension of forty-eight thousand pounds sterling he would resign the kingdom of the Goths and Italians, and spend the remainder of his days in the innocent pleasures of philosophy and agriculture. Both treaties were intrusted to the hands of the ambassador, on the frail security of an oath not to produce the second till the first had been positively rejected. The event may be easily foreseen: Justinian required and accepted the abdication of the Gothic king. His indefatigable agent returned from Constantinople to Ravenna with ample instructions, and a fair epistle, which praised the wisdom and generosity of the royal philosopher, granted his pension, with the assurance of such honours as a subject and a catholic might enjoy, and wisely referred the final execution of the treaty to the presence and authority of Belisarius. But in the interval of suspense two Roman generals, who had entered the province of Dalmatia, were defeated and slain by the Gothic troops. From blind and abject despair, Theodatus capriciously rose to groundless and fatal presumption,[61] and dared to receive, with menace and contempt, the ambassador of Justinian, who claimed his promise, solicited the allegiance of his subjects, and boldly asserted the inviolable privilege of his own character. The march of Belisarius dispelled this visionary pride; and as the first campaign[62] was employed in the reduction of Sicily, the invasion of Italy is applied by Procopius to the second year of the GOTHIC WAR.[63]

After Belisarius had left sufficient garrisons in Palermo and Syracuse, he embarked his troops at Messina, and landed them, without resistance, on the opposite shores of Rhegium. A Gothic prince, who had married the daughter of Theodatus, was stationed with an army to guard the entrance of Italy; but he imitated without scruple the example of a sovereign faithless to his public and private duties. The perfidious Ebermor deserted with his followers to the Roman camp, and was dismissed to enjoy the servile honours of the Byzantine court.[64] From Rhegium to Naples the fleet and army of Belisarius, almost always in view of each other, advanced near three hundred miles along the sea-coast. The people of Bruttium, Lucania, and Campania, who abhorred the name and religion of the Goths, embraced the specious excuse that their ruined walls were incapable of defence: the soldiers paid a just equivalent for a plentiful market; and curiosity alone interrupted the peaceful occupations of the husbandman or artificer. Naples, which has swelled to a great and populous capital, long cherished the language and manners of a Grecian colony;[65] and the choice of Virgil had ennobled this elegant retreat, which attracted the lovers of repose and study from the noise, the smoke, and the laborious opulence of Rome.[66] As soon as the place was invested by sea and land, Belisarius gave audience to the deputies of the people, who exhorted him to disregard a conquest unworthy of his arms, to seek the Gothic king in a field of battle, and, after his victory, to claim, as the sovereign of Rome, the allegiance of the dependent cities. "When I treat with my enemies," replied the Roman chief with a haughty smile, "I am more accustomed to give than to receive counsel; but I hold in one hand inevitable ruin, and in the other peace and freedom, such as Sicily now enjoys." The impatience of delay urged him to grant the most liberal terms; his honour secured their performance: but Naples was divided into two factions; and the Greek democracy was inflamed by their orators, who with much spirit and some truth represented to the multitude that the Goths would punish their defection, and that Belisarius himself must esteem their loyalty and valour. Their deliberations, however, were not perfectly free: the city was commanded by eight hundred barbarians, whose wives and children were detained at Ravenna as the pledge of their fidelity; and even the Jews, who were rich and numerous, resisted, with desperate enthusiasm, the intolerant laws of Justinian. In a much later period the circumference of Naples[67] measured only two thousand three hundred and sixty-three paces:[68] the fortifications were defended by precipices or the sea; when the aqueducts were intercepted, a supply of water might be drawn from wells and fountains; and the stock of provisions was sufficient to consume the patience of the besiegers. At the end of twenty days that of Belisarius was almost exhausted, and he had reconciled himself to the disgrace of abandoning the siege, that he might march, before the winter season, against Rome and the Gothic king. But his anxiety was relieved by the bold curiosity of an Isaurian, who explored the dry channel of an aqueduct, and secretly reported that a passage might be perforated to introduce a file of armed soldiers into the heart of the city. When the work had been silently executed, the humane general risked the discovery of his secret by a last and fruitless admonition of the impending danger. In the darkness of the night four hundred Romans entered the aqueduct, raised themselves by a rope, which they fastened to an olive-tree, into the house or garden of a solitary matron, sounded their trumpets, surprised the sentinels, and gave admittance to their companions, who on all sides scaled the walls and burst open the gates of the city. Every crime which is punished by social justice was practised as the rights of war: the Huns were distinguished by cruelty and sacrilege, and Belisarius alone appeared in the streets and churches of Naples to moderate the calamities which he predicted. "The gold and silver," he repeatedly exclaimed, "are the just rewards of your valour. But spare the inhabitants; they are Christians, they are suppliants, they are now your fellow-subjects. Restore the children to their parents, the wives to their husbands; and show them by your generosity of what friends they have obstinately deprived themselves." The city was saved by the virtue and authority of its conqueror;[69] and when the Neapolitans returned to their houses, they found some consolation in the secret enjoyment of their hidden treasures. The barbarian garrison enlisted in the service of the emperor; Apulia and Calabria, delivered from the odious presence of the Goths, acknowledged his dominion; and the tusks of the Calydonian boar, which were still shown at Beneventum, are curiously described by the historian of Belisarius.[70]

The faithful soldiers and citizens of Naples had expected their deliverance from a prince who remained the inactive and almost indifferent spectator of their ruin. Theodatus secured his person within the walls of Rome, while his cavalry advanced forty miles on the Appian way, and encamped in the Pomptine marshes; which, by a canal of nineteen miles in length, had been recently drained and converted into excellent pastures.[71] But the principal forces of the Goths were dispersed in Dalmatia, Venetia, and Gaul; and the feeble mind of their king was confounded by the unsuccessful event of a divination which seemed to presage the downfall of his empire[72] The most abject slaves have arraigned the guilt or weakness of an unfortunate master. The character of Theodatus was rigorously scrutinised by a free and idle camp of barbarians, conscious of their privilege and power: he was declared unworthy of his race, his nation, and his throne; and their general Vitiges, whose valour had been signalised in the Illyrian war, was raised with unanimous applause on the bucklers of his companions. On the first rumour the abdicated monarch fled from the justice of his country, but he was pursued by private revenge. A Goth, whom he had injured in his love, overtook Theodatus on the Flaminian way, and, regardless of his unmanly cries, slaughtered him as he lay prostrate on the ground, like a victim (says the historian) at the foot of the altar. The choice of the people is the best and purest title to reign over them: yet such is the prejudice of every age, that Vitiges impatiently wished to return to Ravenna, where he might seize, with the reluctant hand of the daughter of Amalasontha, some faint shadow of hereditary right. A national council was immediately held, and the new monarch reconciled the impatient spirit of the barbarians to a measure of disgrace which the misconduct of his predecessor rendered wise and indispensable. The Goths consented to retreat in the presence of a victorious enemy, to delay till the next spring the operations of offensive war, to summon their scattered forces, to relinquish their distant possessions, and to trust even Rome itself to the faith of its inhabitants. Leuderis, an aged warrior, was left in the capital with four thousand soldiers; a feeble garrison, which might have seconded the zeal, though it was incapable of opposing the wishes, of the Romans. But a momentary enthusiasm of religion and patriotism was kindled in their minds. They furiously exclaimed that the apostolic throne should no longer be profaned by the triumph or toleration of Arianism; that the tombs of the Cæsars should no longer be trampled by the savages of the North; and, without reflecting that Italy must sink into a province of Constantinople, they fondly hailed the restoration of a Roman emperor as a new era of freedom and prosperity. The deputies of the pope and clergy, of the senate and people, invited the lieutenant of Justinian to accept their voluntary allegiance, and to enter the city, whose gates would be thrown open for his reception. As soon as Belisarius had fortified his new conquests, Naples and Cumæ, he advanced about twenty miles to the banks of the Vulturnus, contemplated the decayed grandeur of Capua, and halted at the separation of the Latin and Appian ways. The work of the censor, after the incessant use of nine centuries, still preserved its primæval beauty, and not a flaw could be discovered in the large polished stones of which that solid though narrow road was so firmly compacted.[73] Belisarius, however, preferred the Latin way, which, at a distance from the sea and the marshes, skirted in a space of one hundred and twenty miles along the foot of the mountains. His enemies had disappeared: when he made his entrance through the Asinarian gate the garrison departed without molestation along the Flaminian way; and the city, after sixty years' servitude, was delivered from the yoke of the barbarians. Leuderis alone, from a motive of pride or discontent, refused to accompany the fugitives; and the Gothic chief, himself a trophy of the victory, was sent with the keys of Rome to the throne of the emperor Justinian.[74]

The first days, which coincided with the old Saturnalia, were devoted to mutual congratulations and the public joy; and the catholics prepared to celebrate without a rival the approaching festival of the nativity of Christ. In the familiar conversation of a hero the Romans acquired some notion of the virtues which history ascribed to their ancestors; they were edified by the apparent respect of Belisarius for the successor of St. Peter, and his rigid discipline secured in the midst of war the blessings of tranquillity and justice. They applauded the rapid success of his arms, which overran the adjacent country as far as Narni, Perusia, and Spoleto; but they trembled, the senate, the clergy, and the unwarlike people, as soon as they understood that he had resolved, and would speedily be reduced, to sustain a siege against the powers of the Gothic monarchy. The designs of Vitiges were executed during the winter season with diligence and effect. From their rustic habitations, from their distant garrisons, the Goths assembled at Ravenna for the defence of their country; and such were their numbers, that, after an army had been detached for the relief of Dalmatia, one hundred and fifty thousand fighting men marched under the royal standard. According to the degrees of rank or merit, the Gothic king distributed arms and horses, rich gifts, and liberal promises: he moved along the Flaminian way, declined the useless sieges of Perusia and Spoleto, respected the impregnable rock of Narni, and arrived within two miles of Rome at the foot of the Milvian bridge. The narrow passage was fortified with a tower, and Belisarius had computed the value of the twenty days which must be lost in the construction of another bridge. But the consternation of the soldiers of the tower, who either fled or deserted, disappointed his hopes, and betrayed his person into the most imminent danger. At the head of one thousand horse the Roman general sallied from the Flaminian gate to mark the ground of an advantageous position, and to survey the camp of the barbarians; but while he still believed them on the other side of the Tiber, he was suddenly encompassed and assaulted by their innumerable squadrons. The fate of Italy depended on his life; and the deserters pointed to the conspicuous horse, a bay[75] with a white face, which he rode on that memorable day. "Aim at the bay horse," was the universal cry. Every bow was bent, every javelin was directed, against that fatal object, and the command was repeated and obeyed by thousands who were ignorant of its real motive. The bolder barbarians advanced to the more honourable combat of swords and spears; and the praise of an enemy has graced the fall of Visandus, the standard-bearer,[76] who maintained his foremost station, till he was pierced with thirteen wounds, perhaps by the hand of Belisarius himself. The Roman general was strong, active, and dexterous: on every side he discharged his weighty and mortal strokes: his faithful guards imitated his valour and defended his person; and the Goths, after the loss of a thousand men, fled before the arms of a hero. They were rashly pursued to their camp; and the Romans, oppressed by multitudes, made a gradual and at length a precipitate retreat to the gates of the city: the gates were shut against the fugitives; and the public terror was increased by the report that Belisarius was slain. His countenance was indeed disfigured by sweat, dust, and blood; his voice was hoarse, his strength was almost exhausted; but his unconquerable spirit still remained; he imparted that spirit to his desponding companions; and their last desperate charge was felt by the flying barbarians as if a new army, vigorous and entire, had been poured from the city. The Flaminian gate was thrown open to a *real* triumph; but it was not before Belisarius had visited every post and provided for the public safety that he could be persuaded by his wife and friends to taste the needful refreshments of food and sleep. In the more improved state of the art of war a general is seldom required, or even permitted, to display the personal prowess of a soldier, and the example of Belisarius may be added to the rare examples of Henry IV., of Pyrrhus, and of Alexander.

After this first and unsuccessful trial of their enemies, the whole army of the Goths passed the Tiber, and formed the siege of the city, which continued above a year, till their final departure. Whatever fancy may conceive, the severe compass of the geographer defines the circumference of Rome within a line of twelve miles and three hundred and forty-five paces; and that circumference, except in the Vatican,

has invariably been the same from the triumph of Aurelian to the peaceful but obscure reign of the modern popes.[77] But in the day of her greatness the space within her walls was crowded with habitations and inhabitants, and the populous suburbs, that stretched along the public roads, were darted like so many rays from one common centre. Adversity swept away these extraneous ornaments, and left naked and desolate a considerable part even of the seven hills. Yet Rome in its present state could send into the field above thirty thousand males of a military age;[78] and, notwithstanding the want of discipline and exercise, the far greater part, inured to the hardships of poverty, might be capable of bearing arms for the defence of their country and religion. The prudence of Belisarius did not neglect this important resource. His soldiers were relieved by the zeal and diligence of the people, who watched while *they* slept, and laboured while *they* reposed: he accepted the voluntary service of the bravest and most indigent of the Roman youth; and the companies of townsmen sometimes represented in a vacant post the presence of the troops which had been drawn away to more essential duties. But his just confidence was placed in the veterans who had fought under his banner in the Persian and African wars; and although that gallant band was reduced to five thousand men, he undertook, with such contemptible numbers, to defend a circle of twelve miles against an army of one hundred and fifty thousand barbarians. In the walls of Rome, which Belisarius constructed or restored, the materials of ancient architecture may be discerned;[79] and the whole fortification was completed, except in a chasm still extant between the Pincian and Flaminian gates, which the prejudices of the Goths and Romans left under the effectual guard of St. Peter the apostle.[80]

The battlements or bastions were shaped in sharp angles; a ditch, broad and deep, protected the foot of the rampart; and the archers on the rampart were assisted by military engines; the *balista*, a powerful cross-bow, which darted short but massy arrows; the *onagri*, or wild asses, which, on the principle of a sling, threw stones and bullets of an enormous size.[81] A chain was drawn across the Tiber; the arches of the aqueducts were made impervious, and the mole or sepulchre of Hadrian[82] was converted, for the first time, to the uses of a citadel. That venerable structure, which contained the ashes of the Antonines, was a circular turret rising from a quadrangular basis: it was covered with the white marble of Paros, and decorated by the statues of gods and heroes; and the lover of the arts must read with a sigh that the works of Praxiteles or Lysippus were torn from their lofty pedestals, and hurled into the ditch on the heads of the besiegers.[83] To each of his lieutenants Belisarius assigned the defence of a gate, with the wise and peremptory instruction that, whatever might be the alarm, they should steadily adhere to their respective posts, and trust their general for the safety of Rome. The formidable host of the Goths was insufficient to embrace the ample measure of the city: of the fourteen gates, seven only were invested from the Praenestine to the Flaminian way; and Vitiges divided his troops into six camps, each of which was fortified with a ditch and rampart. On the Tuscan side of the river a seventh encampment was formed in the field or circus of the Vatican, for the important purpose of commanding the Milvian bridge and the course of the Tiber; but they approached with devotion the adjacent church of St. Peter; and the threshold of the holy apostles was respected during the siege by a Christian enemy. In the ages of victory, as often as the senate decreed some distant conquest, the consul denounced hostilities by unbarring, in solemn pomp, the gates of the temple of Janus.[84] Domestic war now rendered the admonition superfluous, and the ceremony was superseded by the establishment of a new religion. But the brazen temple of Janus was left standing in the forum; of a size sufficient only to contain the statue of the god, five cubits in height, of a human form, but with two faces directed to the east and west. The double gates were likewise of brass; and a fruitless effort to turn them on their rusty hinges revealed the scandalous secret that some Romans were still attached to the superstition of their ancestors.

Eighteen days were employed by the besiegers to provide for all the instruments of attack which antiquity had invented. Fascines were prepared to fill the ditches, scaling-ladders to ascend the walls. The largest trees of the forest supplied the timbers of four battering-rams: their heads were armed with iron; they were suspended by ropes, and each of them was worked by the labour of fifty men. The lofty wooden turrets moved on wheels or rollers, and formed a spacious platform of the level of the rampart. On the morning of the nineteenth day a general attack was made from the Praenestine gate to the Vatican: seven Gothic columns, with their military engines, advanced to the assault; and the Romans, who lined the ramparts, listened with doubt and anxiety to the cheerful assurances of their commander. As soon as the enemy approached the ditch, Belisarius himself drew the first arrow; and such was his strength and dexterity, that he transfixed the foremost of the barbarian leaders.

A shout of applause and victory was re-echoed along the wall. He drew a second arrow, and the stroke was followed with the same success and the same acclamation. The Roman general then gave the word that the archers should aim at the teams of oxen; they were instantly covered with mortal wounds; the towers which they drew remained useless and immovable, and a single moment disconcerted the laborious projects of the king of the Goths. After this disappointment Vitiges still continued, or feigned to continue, the assault of the Salarian gate, that he might divert the attention of his adversary, while his principal forces more strenuously attacked the Praenestine gate and the sepulchre of Hadrian, at the distance of three miles from each other. Near the former, the double walls of the Vivarium[85] were low or broken; the fortifications of the latter were feebly guarded: the vigour of the Goths was excited by the hope of victory and spoil; and if a single post had given way, the Romans, and Rome itself, were irrecoverably lost. This perilous day was the most glorious in the life of Belisarius. Amidst tumult and dismay, the whole plan of the attack and defence was distinctly present to his mind; he observed the changes of each instant, weighed every possible advantage, transported his person to the scenes of danger, and communicated his spirit in calm and decisive orders. The contest was fiercely maintained from the morning to the evening; the Goths were repulsed on all sides; and each Roman might boast that he had vanquished thirty barbarians, if the strange disproportion of numbers were not counterbalanced by the merit of one man. Thirty thousand Goths, according to the confession of their own chiefs, perished in this bloody action; and the multitude of the wounded was equal to that of the slain. When they advanced to the assault, their close disorder suffered not a javelin to fall without effect; and as they retired, the populace of the city joined the pursuit, and slaughtered, with impunity, the backs of their flying enemies. Belisarius instantly sallied from the gates; and while the soldiers chanted his name and victory, the hostile engines of war were reduced to ashes. Such was the loss and consternation of the Goths, that from this day the siege of Rome degenerated into a tedious and indolent blockade; and they were incessantly harassed by the Roman general, who, in frequent skirmishes, destroyed above five thousand of their bravest troops. Their cavalry was unpractised in the use of the bow; their archers served on foot; and this divided force was incapable of contending with their adversaries, whose lances and arrows, at a distance or at hand, were alike formidable. The consummate skill of Belisarius embraced the favourable opportunities; and as he chose the ground and the moment, as he pressed the charge or sounded the retreat,[86] the squadrons which he detached were seldom unsuccessful. These partial advantages diffused an impatient ardour among the soldiers and people, who began to feel the hardships of a siege, and to disregard the dangers of a general engagement. Each plebeian conceived himself to be a hero, and the infantry, who, since the decay of discipline, were rejected from the line of battle, aspired to the ancient honours of the Roman legion. Belisarius praised the spirit of his troops, condemned their presumption, yielded to their clamours, and prepared the remedies of a defeat, the possibility of which he alone had courage to suspect. In the quarter of the Vatican the Romans prevailed; and if the irreparable moments had not been wasted in the pillage of the camp, they might have occupied the Milvian bridge, and charged in the rear of the Gothic host. On the other side of the Tiber, Belisarius advanced from the Pincian and Salarian gates. But his army, four thousand soldiers perhaps, was lost in a spacious plain; they were encompassed and oppressed by fresh multitudes, who continually relieved the broken ranks of the barbarians. The valiant leaders of the infantry were unskilled to conquer; they died: the retreat (a hasty retreat) was covered by the prudence of the general, and the victors started back with affright from the formidable aspect of an armed rampart. The reputation of Belisarius was unsullied by a defeat; and the vain confidence of the Goths was not less serviceable to his designs than the repentance and modesty of the Roman troops.

From the moment that Belisarius had determined to sustain a siege, his assiduous care provided Rome against the danger of famine, more dreadful than the Gothic arms. An extraordinary supply of corn was imported from Sicily: the harvests of Campania and Tuscany were forcibly swept for the use of the city; and the rights of private property were infringed by the strong plea of the public safety. It might easily be foreseen that the enemy would intercept the aqueducts; and the cessation of the water-mills was the first inconvenience, which was speedily removed by mooring large vessels, and fixing mill-stones in the current of the river. The stream was soon embarrassed by the trunks of trees, and polluted with dead bodies; yet so effectual were the precautions of the Roman general, that the waters of the Tiber still continued to give motion to the mills and drink to the inhabitants: the more distant quarters were supplied from domestic wells; and a besieged city might support, without impatience, the privation of her public baths. A large portion of Rome, from the Prænestine gate to the church of St. Paul, was never invested by the Goths; their excursions were restrained by the activity of the Moorish troops: the navigation of the Tiber, and the Latin, Appian, and Ostian ways, were left free and unmolested for the introduction of corn and cattle, or the retreat of the inhabitants who sought a refuge in Campania or Sicily. Anxious to relieve himself from a useless and devouring multitude, Belisarius issued his peremptory orders for the instant departure of the women, the children, and slaves; required his soldiers to dismiss their male and female attendants; and regulated their allowance that one moiety should be given in provisions and the other in money. His foresight was justified by the increase of the public distress as soon as the Goths had occupied two important posts in the neighbourhood of Rome. By the loss of the port, or, as it is now called, the city of Porto, he was deprived of the country on the right of the Tiber and the best communication with the sea; and he reflected with grief and anger that three hundred men, could he have spared such a feeble band, might have defended its impregnable works. Seven miles from the capital, between the Appian and the Latin ways, two principal aqueducts crossing, and again crossing each other, enclosed within their solid and lofty arches a fortified space,[87] where Vitiges established a camp of seven thousand Goths to intercept the convoys of Sicily and Campania. The granaries of Rome were insensibly exhausted; the adjacent country had been wasted with fire and sword; such scanty supplies as might yet be obtained by hasty excursions were the reward of valour and the purchase of wealth; the forage of the horses and the bread of the soldiers never failed; but in the last months of the siege the people was exposed to the miseries of scarcity, unwholesome food,[88] and contagious disorders. Belisarius saw and pitied their sufferings; but he had foreseen, and he watched, the decay of their loyalty and the progress of their discontent. Adversity had awakened the Romans from the dreams of grandeur and freedom, and taught them the humiliating lesson that it was of small moment to the real happiness whether the name of their master was derived from the Gothic or the Latin language. The lieutenant of Justinian listened to their just complaints, but he rejected with disdain the idea of flight or capitulation; repressed their clamorous impatience for battle; amused them with the prospect of sure and speedy relief; and secured himself and the city from the effects of their despair or treachery. Twice in each month he changed the station of the officers to whom custody of the gates was committed: the various precautions of patrols, watch-words, lights, and music, were repeatedly employed to discover whatever passed on the ramparts; outguards were posted beyond the ditch, and the trusty vigilance of dogs supplied the more doubtful fidelity of mankind. A letter was intercepted which assured the king of the Goths that the Asinarian gate, adjoining to the Lateran church, should be secretly opened to his troops. On the proof or suspicion of treason several senators were banished, and the pope Sylverius was summoned to attend the representative of his sovereign at his headquarters in the Pincian palace.[89] The ecclesiastics, who followed their bishop, were detained in the first or second apartment,[90] and he alone was admitted to the presence of Belisarius. The conqueror of Rome and Carthage was modestly seated at the feet of Antonina, who reclined on a stately couch: the general was silent, but the voice of reproach and menace issued from the mouth of his imperious wife. Accused by credible witnesses, and the evidence of his own subscription, the successor of St. Peter was despoiled of his pontifical ornaments, clad in the mean habit of a monk, and embarked, without delay, for a distant exile in the East. At the emperor's command, the clergy of Rome proceeded to the choice of a new bishop, and, after a solemn invocation of the Holy Ghost, elected the deacon Vigilius, who had purchased the papal throne by a bribe of two hundred pounds of gold. The profit, and consequently the guilt, of this simony was imputed to Belisarius: but the hero obeyed the orders of his wife; Antonina served the passions of the empress; and Theodora lavished her treasures in the vain hope of obtaining a pontiff hostile or indifferent to the council of Chalcedon.[91]

The epistle of Belisarius to the emperor announced his victory, his danger, and his resolution. "According to your commands, we have entered the dominions of the Goths, and reduced to your obedience Sicily, Campania, and the city of Rome; but the loss of these conquests will be more disgraceful than their acquisition was glorious. Hitherto we have successfully fought against the multitudes of the barbarians, but their multitudes may finally prevail. Victory is the gift of Providence, but the reputation of kings and generals depends on the success or the failure of their designs. Permit me to speak with freedom: if you wish that we should live, send us subsistence; if you desire that we should conquer, send us arms, horses, and men. The Romans have received us as friends and deliverers: but in our present distress, *they* will be either betrayed by their confidence, or we shall be oppressed by *their* treachery and hatred. For myself, my life is consecrated to your service: it is yours to reflect whether my death in this situation will contribute to the glory and prosperity of your reign." Perhaps that reign would have been equally prosperous if the peaceful master of the East had abstained from the conquest of Africa and Italy: but as Justinian was ambitious of fame, he made some efforts, they were feeble and languid, to support and rescue his victorious general. A reinforcement of sixteen hundred Sclavonians and Huns was led by Martin and Valerian; and as they had reposed during the winter season in the harbours of Greece, the strength of the men and horses was not impaired by the fatigues of a sea-voyage; and they distinguished their valour in the first sally against the besiegers. About the time of the summer solstice, Euthalius landed at Terracina with large sums of money for the payment of the troops: he cautiously proceeded along the Appian way, and this convoy entered Rome through the gate Capena,[92] while Belisarius, on the other side, diverted the attention of the Goths by a vigorous and successful skirmish. These seasonable aids, the use and reputation of which were dexterously managed by the Roman general, revived the courage, or at least the hopes, of the soldiers and people. The historian Procopius was despatched with an important commission to collect the troops and provisions which Campania could furnish or Constantinople had sent; and the secretary of Belisarius was soon followed by Antonina herself,[93] who boldly traversed the posts of the enemy, and returned with the Oriental succours to the relief of her husband and the besieged city. A fleet of three thousand Isaurians cast anchor in the bay of Naples, and afterwards at Ostia. Above two thousand horse, of whom a part were Thracians, landed at Tarentum; and, after the junction of five hundred soldiers of Campania, and a train of waggons laden with wine and flour, they directed their march on the Appian way from Capua to the neighbourhood of Rome. The forces that arrived by land and sea were united at the mouth of the Tiber. Antonina convened a council of war: it was resolved to surmount, with sails and oars, the adverse stream of the river; and the Goths were apprehensive of disturbing, by any rash hostilities, the negotiation to which Belisarius had craftily listened. They credulously believed that they saw no more than the vanguard of a fleet and army which already covered the Ionian Sea and the plains of Campania; and the illusion was supported by the haughty language of the Roman general when he gave audience to the ambassadors of Vitiges. After a specious discourse to vindicate the justice of his cause, they declared that, for the sake of peace, they were disposed to renounce the possession of Sicily. "The emperor is not less generous," replied his lieutenant, with a disdainful smile; "in return for a gift which you no longer possess, he presents you with an ancient province of the empire; he resigns to the Goths the sovereignty of the British island." Belisarius rejected with equal firmness and contempt the offer of a tribute; but he allowed the Gothic ambassadors to seek their fate from the mouth of Justinian himself, and consented, with seeming reluctance, to a truce of three months, from the winter solstice to the equinox of spring. Prudence might not safely trust either the oaths or hostages of the barbarians, but the conscious superiority of the Roman chief was expressed in the distribution of his troops. As soon as fear or hunger compelled the Goths to evacuate Alba, Porto, and Centumcellæ, their place was instantly supplied; the garrisons of Narni, Spoleto, and Perusia were reinforced, and the seven camps of the besiegers were gradually encompassed with the calamities of a siege. The prayers and pilgrimage of Datius, bishop of Milan, were not without effect; and he obtained one thousand Thracians and Isaurians to assist the revolt of Liguria against her Arian tyrant. At the same time, John the Sanguinary,[94] the nephew of Vitalian, was detached with two thousand chosen horse, first to Alba on the Fucine lake, and afterwards to the frontiers of Picenum on the Hadriatic Sea. "In that prov-

ince," said Belisarius, "the Goths have deposited their families and treasures, without a guard or the suspicion of danger. Doubtless they will violate the truce: let them feel your presence before they hear of your motions. Spare the Italians; suffer not any fortified places to remain hostile in your rear; and faithfully reserve the spoil for an equal and common partition. It would not be reasonable," he added, with a laugh, "that, whilst we are toiling to the destruction of the drones, our more fortunate brethren should rifle and enjoy the honey."

The whole nation of the Ostrogoths had been assembled for the attack, and was almost entirely consumed in the siege of Rome. If any credit be due to an intelligent spectator, one-third at least of their enormous host was destroyed in frequent and bloody combats under the walls of the city. The bad fame and pernicious qualities of the summer air might already be imputed to the decay of agriculture and population, and the evils of famine and pestilence were aggravated by their own licentiousness and the unfriendly disposition of the country. While Vitiges struggled with his fortune, while he hesitated between shame and ruin, his retreat was hastened by domestic alarms. The king of the Goths was informed by trembling messengers that John the Sanguinary spread the devastations of war from the Apennine to the Hadriatic; that the rich spoils and innumerable captives of Picenum were lodged in the fortifications of Rimini; and that this formidable chief had defeated his uncle, insulted his capital, and seduced, by secret correspondence, the fidelity of his wife, the imperious daughter of Amalasontha. Yet, before he retired, Vitiges made a last effort either to storm or to surprise the city. A secret passage was discovered in one of the aqueducts; two citizens of the Vatican were tempted by bribes to intoxicate the guards of the Aurelian gate; an attack was meditated on the walls beyond the Tiber, in a place which was not fortified with towers; and the barbarians advanced, with torches and scaling-ladders, to the assault of the Pincian gate. But every attempt was defeated by the intrepid vigilance of Belisarius and his band of veterans, who, in the most perilous moments, did not regret the absence of their companions; and the Goths, alike destitute of hope and subsistence, clamorously urged their departure before the truce should expire, and the Roman cavalry should again be united. One year and nine days after the commencement of the siege, an army so lately strong and triumphant burnt their tents, and tumultuously repassed the Milvian bridge. They repassed not with impunity; their thronging multitudes, oppressed in a narrow passage, were driven headlong into the Tiber by their own fears and the pursuit of the enemy, and the Roman general, sallying from the Pincian gate, inflicted a severe and disgraceful wound on their retreat. The slow length of a sickly and desponding host was heavily dragged along the Flaminian way, from whence the barbarians were sometimes compelled to deviate, lest they should encounter the hostile garrisons that guarded the high road to Rimini and Ravenna. Yet so powerful was this flying army, that Vitiges spared ten thousand men for the defence of the cities which he was most solicitous to preserve, and detached his nephew Uraias, with an adequate force, for the chastisement of rebellious Milan. At the head of his principal army he besieged Rimini, only thirty-three miles distant from the Gothic capital. A feeble rampart and a shallow ditch were maintained by the skill and valour of John the Sanguinary, who shared the danger and fatigue of the meanest soldier, and emulated, on a theatre less illustrious, the military virtues of his great commander. The towers and battering-engines of the barbarians were rendered useless, their attacks were repulsed, and the tedious blockade, which reduced the garrison to the last extremity of hunger, afforded time for the union and march of the Roman forces. A fleet, which had surprised Ancona, sailed along the coast of the Hadriatic to the relief of the besieged city. The eunuch Narses landed in Picenum with two thousand Heruli and five thousand of the bravest troops of the East. The rock of the Apennine was forced, ten thousand veterans moved round the foot of the mountains, under the command of Belisarius himself, and a new army, whose encampment blazed with innumerable lights, *appeared* to advance along the Flaminian way. Overwhelmed with astonishment and despair, the Goths abandoned the siege of Rimini, their tents, their standards, and their leaders; and Vitiges, who gave or followed the example of flight, never halted till he found a shelter within the walls and morasses of Ravenna.

To these walls, and to some fortresses destitute of any mutual support, the Gothic monarchy was now reduced. The provinces of Italy had embraced the party of the emperor, and his army, gradually recruited to the number of twenty thousand men, must have achieved an easy and rapid conquest if their invincible powers had not been weakened by the discord of the Roman chiefs. Before the end of the siege, an act of blood, ambiguous and indiscreet, sullied the fair fame of Belisarius. Presidius, a loyal Italian, as he fled from Ravenna to Rome, was rudely stopped by Constantine, the military governor of Spoleto, and despoiled, even in a church, of two daggers, richly inlaid with gold and precious stones. As soon as the public danger had subsided, Presidius complained of the loss and injury; his complaint was heard, but the order of restitution was disobeyed by the pride and avarice of the offender. Exasperated by the delay, Presidius boldly arrested the general's horse as he passed through the forum, and, with the spirit of a citizen, demanded the common benefit of the Roman laws. The honour of Belisarius was engaged: he summoned a council, claimed the obedience of his subordinate officer, and was provoked, by an insolent reply, to call hastily for the presence of his guards. Constantine, viewing their entrance as the signal of death, drew his sword, and rushed on the general, who nimbly eluded the stroke and was protected by his friends, while the desperate assassin was disarmed, dragged into a neighbouring chamber, and executed, or rather murdered, by the guards, at the arbitrary command of Belisarius.[95] In this hasty act of violence the guilt of Constantine was no longer remembered; the despair and death of that valiant officer were secretly imputed to the revenge of Antonina; and each of his colleagues, conscious of the same rapine, was apprehensive of the same fate. The fear of a common enemy suspended the effects of their envy and discontent, but, in the confidence of approaching victory, they instigated a powerful rival to oppose the conqueror of Rome and Africa. From the domestic service of the palace and the administration of the private revenue, Narses the eunuch was suddenly exalted to the head of an army, and the spirit of a hero, who afterwards equalled the merit and glory of Belisarius, served only to perplex the operations of the Gothic war. To his prudent counsels the relief of Rimini was ascribed by the leaders of the discontented faction, who exhorted Narses to assume an independent and separate command. The epistle of Justinian had indeed enjoined his obedience to the general, but the dangerous exception, "as far as may be advantageous to the public service," reserved some freedom of judgment to the discreet favourite, who had so lately departed from the *sacred* and familiar conversation of his sovereign. In the exercise of this doubtful right the eunuch perpetually dissented from the opinions of Belisarius, and, after yielding with reluctance to the siege of Urbino, he deserted his colleague in the night, and marched away to the conquest of the Æmilian province. The fierce and formidable bands of the Heruli were attached to the person of Narses;[96] ten thousand Romans and confederates were persuaded to march under his banners; every malcontent embraced the fair opportunity of revenging his private or imaginary wrongs; and the remaining troops of Belisarius were divided and dispersed from the garrisons of Sicily to the shores of the Hadriatic. His skill and perseverance overcame every obstacle: Urbino was taken, the sieges of Fæsulæ, Orvieto, and Auximum were undertaken, and vigorously prosecuted, and the eunuch Narses was at length recalled to the domestic cares of the palace. All dissensions were healed, and all opposition was subdued, by the temperate authority of the Roman general, to whom his enemies could not refuse their esteem; and Belisarius inculcated the salutary lesson that the forces of the state should compose one body and be animated by one soul. But in the interval of discord the Goths were permitted to breathe; an important season was lost, Milan was destroyed, and the northern provinces of Italy were afflicted by an inundation of the Franks.

When Justinian first meditated the conquest of Italy, he sent ambassadors to the kings of the Franks, and adjured them, by the common ties of alliance and religion, to join in the holy enterprise against the Arians. The Goths, as their wants were more urgent, employed a more effectual mode of persuasion, and vainly strove, by the gift of lands and money, to purchase the friendship, or at least the neutrality, of a light and perfidious nation.[97] But the arms of Belisarius and the revolt of the Italians had no sooner shaken the Gothic monarchy, than Theodebert of Austrasia, the most powerful and warlike of the Merovingian kings, was persuaded to succour their distress by an indirect and seasonable aid. Without expecting the consent of their sovereign, ten thousand Burgundians, his recent subjects, descended from the Alps, and joined the troops which Vitiges had sent to chastise the revolt of Milan. After an obstinate siege the capital of Liguria was reduced by famine, but no capitulation could be obtained, except for the safe retreat of the Roman garrison. Datius, the orthodox bishop, who had seduced his countrymen to rebellion[98] and ruin, escaped to the luxury and honours of the Byzantine court;[99] but the clergy, perhaps the Arian clergy, were slaughtered at the foot of their own altars by the defenders of the catholic faith. Three hundred thousand males were *reported* to be slain;[100] the female sex and the more precious spoil was resigned to the Burgundians; and the houses, or at least the walls, of Milan were levelled with the ground. The Goths, in their last moments, were revenged by the destruction of a city second only to Rome in size and opulence, in the splendour of its buildings, or the number of its inhabitants, and Belisarius sympathised alone in the fate of his deserted and devoted friends. Encouraged by this successful inroad, Theodebert himself, in the ensuing spring, invaded the plains of Italy with an army of one hundred thousand barbarians.[101] The king and some chosen followers were mounted on horseback and armed with lances; the infantry, without bows or spears, were satisfied with a shield, a sword, and a double-edged battleaxe, which in their hands became a deadly and unerring weapon. Italy trembled at the march of the Franks, and both the Gothic prince and the Roman general, alike ignorant of their designs, solicited with hope and terror the friendship of these dangerous allies. Till he had secured the passage of the Po on the bridge of Pavia, the grandson of Clovis dissembled his intentions, which he at length declared by assaulting, almost at the same instant, the hostile camps of the Romans and Goths. Instead of uniting their arms, they fled with equal precipitation, and the fertile though desolate provinces of Liguria and Æmilia were abandoned to a licentious host of barbarians, whose rage was not mitigated by any thoughts of settlement or conquest. Among the cites which they ruined, Genoa, not yet constructed of marble, is particularly enumerated; and the deaths of thousands, according to the regular practice of war, appear to have excited less horror than some idolatrous sacrifices of women and children which were performed with impunity in the camp of the most Christian king. If it were not a melancholy truth that the first and most cruel sufferings must be the lot of the innocent and helpless, history might exult in the misery of the conquerors, who, in the midst of riches, were left destitute of bread or wine, reduced to drink the waters of the Po, and to feed on the flesh of distempered cattle. The dysentery swept away one-third of their army, and the clamours of his subjects, who were impatient to pass the Alps, disposed Theodebert to listen with respect to the mild exhortations

f Belisarius. The memory of this inglorious and
estructive warfare was perpetuated on the
iedals of Gaul, and Justinian, without un-
heathing his sword, assumed the title of con-
ueror of the Franks. The Merovingian prince
vas offended by the vanity of the emperor; he
ffected to pity the fallen fortunes of the Goths;
nd his insidious offer of a fœderal union was
ortified by the promise or menace of descend-
ng from the Alps at the head of five hundred
housand men. His plans of conquest were
oundless, and perhaps chimerical. The king
f Austrasia threatened to chastise Justinian,
nd to march to the gates of Constantinople;[102]
ie was overthrown and slain[103] by a wild
ull,[104] as he hunted in the Belgic or German
orests.

As soon as Belisarius was delivered from his
oreign and domestic enemies, he seriously ap-
lied his forces to the final reduction of Italy.
n the siege of Osimo the general was nearly
ranspierced with an arrow, if the mortal stroke
ad not been intercepted by one of his guards,
vho lost in that pious office the use of his hand.
The Goths of Osimo, four thousand warriors,
vith those of Fæsulæ and the Cottian Alps,
vere among the last who maintained their in-
lependence; and their gallant resistance, which
ilmost tired the patience, deserved the esteem,
of the conqueror. His prudence refused to sub-
cribe the safe-conduct which they asked to
oin their brethren of Ravenna: but they saved,
oy an honourable capitulation, one moiety at
east of their wealth, with the free alternative of
etiring peaceably to their estates or enlisting to
erve the emperor in his Persian wars. The
nultitudes which yet adhered to the standard of
Vitiges far surpassed the number of the Roman
roops, but neither prayers nor defiance, nor
he extreme danger of his most faithful subjects,
ould tempt the Gothic king beyond the forti-
ications of Ravenna. These fortifications were
ndeed impregnable to the assaults of art or
violence, and when Belisarius invested the
apital he was soon convinced that famine only
could tame the stubborn spirit of the barbarians. The sea, the land, and the channels of the
Po were guarded by the vigilance of the Roman
general; and his morality extended the rights of
war to the practice of poisoning the waters[105]
and secretly firing the granaries[106] of a besieged
city.[107] While he pressed the blockade of Ravenna, he was surprised by the arrival of two
ambassadors from Constantinople, with a
treaty of peace, which Justinian had imprudently signed without deigning to consult the

author of his victory. By this disgraceful and
precarious agreement, Italy and the Gothic
treasure were divided, and the provinces beyond
the Po were left with the regal title to the successor of Theodoric. The ambassadors were
eager to accomplish their salutary commission;
the captive Vitiges accepted with transport the
unexpected offer of a crown; honour was less
prevalent among the Goths than the want and
appetite of food; and the Roman chiefs, who
murmured at the continuance of the war, professed implicit submission to the commands of
the emperor. If Belisarius had possessed only
the courage of a soldier, the laurel would have
been snatched from his hand by timid and
envious counsels; but in this decisive moment
he resolved, with the magnanimity of a statesman,
to sustain alone the danger and merit of generous disobedience. Each of his officers gave a
written opinion that the siege of Ravenna was
impracticable and hopeless; the general then
rejected the treaty of partition, and declared
his own resolution of leading Vitiges in chains
to the feet of Justinian. The Goths retired with
doubt and dismay; this peremptory refusal
deprived them of the only signature which they
could trust, and filled their minds with a just
apprehension that a sagacious enemy had discovered the full extent of their deplorable state.
They compared the fame and fortune of Belisarius with the weakness of their ill-fated king,
and the comparison suggested an extraordinary
project, to which Vitiges, with apparent resignation, was compelled to acquiesce. Partition
would ruin the strength, exile would disgrace
the honour, of the nation; but they offered
their arms, their treasures, and the fortifications
of Ravenna, if Belisarius would disclaim the
authority of a master, accept the choice of the
Goths, and assume, as he had deserved, the
kingdom of Italy. If the false lustre of a diadem
could have tempted the loyalty of a faithful
subject, his prudence must have foreseen the
inconstancy of the barbarians, and his rational
ambition would prefer the safe and honourable
station of a Roman general. Even the patience
and seeming satisfaction with which he entertained a proposal of treason might be susceptible of a malignant interpretation. But the
lieutenant of Justinian was conscious of his own
rectitude; he entered into a dark and crooked
path, as it might lead to the voluntary submission of the Goths; and his dexterous policy
persuaded them that he was disposed to comply
with their wishes, without engaging an oath or
a promise for the performance of a treaty

which he secretly abhorred. The day of the surrender of Ravenna was stipulated by the Gothic ambassadors; a fleet, laden with provisions, sailed as a welcome guest into the deepest recess of the harbour, the gates were opened to the fancied king of Italy, and Belisarius, without meeting an enemy, triumphantly marched through the streets of an impregnable city.[108] The Romans were astonished by their success; the multitudes of tall and robust barbarians were confounded by the image of their own patience; and the masculine females, spitting in the faces of their sons and husbands, most bitterly reproached them for betraying their dominion and freedom to these pigmies of the south, contemptible in their numbers, diminutive in their stature. Before the Goths could recover from the first surprise and claim the accomplishment of their doubtful hopes, the victor established his power in Ravenna beyond the danger of repentance and revolt. Vitiges, who perhaps had attempted to escape, was honourably guarded in his palace;[109] the flower of the Gothic youth was selected for the service of the emperor; the remainder of the people was dismissed to their peaceful habitations in the southern provinces, and a colony of Italians was invited to replenish the depopulated city. The submission of the capital was imitated in the towns and villages of Italy which had not been subdued or even visited by the Romans; and the independent Goths, who remained in arms at Pavia and Verona, were ambitious only to become the subjects of Belisarius. But his inflexible loyalty rejected, except as the substitute of Justinian, their oaths of allegiance, and he was not offended by the reproach of their deputies that he rather chose to be a slave than a king.

After the second victory of Belisarius, envy again whispered, Justinian listened, and the hero was recalled. "The remnant of the Gothic war was no longer worthy of his presence: a gracious sovereign was impatient to reward his services and to consult his wisdom; and he alone was capable of defending the East against the innumerable armies of Persia." Belisarius understood the suspicion, accepted the excuse, embarked at Ravenna his spoils and trophies, and proved by his ready obedience that such an abrupt removal from the government of Italy was not less unjust than it might have been indiscreet. The emperor received with honourable courtesy both Vitiges and his more noble consort; and as the king of the Goths conformed to the Athanasian faith, he obtained, with a rich inheritance of lands in Asia, the rank of senator and patrician.[110] Every spectator admired, without peril, the strength and stature of the young barbarians: they adored the majesty of the throne, and promised to shed their blood in the service of their benefactor. Justinian deposited in the Byzantine palace the treasures of the Gothic monarchy. A flattering senate was sometimes admitted to gaze on the magnificent spectacle, but it was enviously secluded from the public view; and the conqueror of Italy renounced without a murmur, perhaps without a sigh, the well-earned honours of a second triumph. His glory was, indeed, exalted above all external pomp; and the faint and hollow praises of the court were supplied, even in a servile age, by the respect and admiration of his country. Whenever he appeared in the streets and public places of Constantinople, Belisarius attracted and satisfied the eyes of the people. His lofty stature and majestic countenance fulfilled their expectations of a hero, the meanest of his fellow-citizens were emboldened by his gentle and gracious demeanour, and the martial train which attended his footsteps left his person more accessible than in a day of battle. Seven thousand horsemen, matchless for beauty and valour, were maintained in the service, and at the private expense, of the general.[111] Their prowess was always conspicuous in single combats or in foremost ranks, and both parties confessed that in the siege of Rome the guards of Belisarius had alone vanquished the barbarian host. Their numbers were continually augmented by the bravest and most faithful of the enemy; and his fortunate captives, the Vandals, the Moors, and the Goths, emulated the attachment of his domestic followers. By the union of liberality and justice he acquired the love of the soldiers, without alienating the affections of the people. The sick and wounded were relieved with medicines and money, and still more efficaciously by the healing visits and smiles of their commander. The loss of a weapon or a horse was instantly repaired, and each deed of valour was rewarded by the rich and honourable gifts of a bracelet or a collar, which were rendered more precious by the judgment of Belisarius. He was endeared to the husbandmen by the peace and plenty which they enjoyed under the shadow of his standard. Instead of being injured, the country was enriched by the march of the Roman armies; and such was the rigid discipline of their camp, that not an apple was gathered from the tree, not a path could be traced in the fields of corn. Belisarius was chaste and sober. In the licence of a military life, none could boast that they had seen him intoxicated with wine; the most beautiful captives of Gothic or Vandal race were offered to his embraces, but he turned aside from their charms, and the husband of Antonina was never suspected of violating the laws of conjugal fidelity. The spectator and historian of his exploits has observed that amidst the perils of war he was daring without rashness, prudent without fear, slow or rapid according to the exigencies of the moment; that in the deepest distress he was animated by real or apparent hope, but that he was modest and humble in the most prosperous fortune. By these virtues he equalled or excelled the ancient masters of the military art. Victory, by sea and land, attended his arms. He subdued Africa, Italy, and the adjacent islands; led away captives the successors of Genseric and Theodoric; filled Constantinople with the spoils of their palaces; and in the space of six years recovered half the provinces of the Western empire. In his fame and merit, in wealth and power, he remained without a rival, the first of the Roman subjects: the voice of envy could only magnify his dangerous importance, and the emperor might applaud his own discerning spirit, which had discovered and raised the genius of Belisarius.

It was the custom of the Roman triumphs that a slave should be placed behind the chariot, to remind the conqueror of the instability of fortune and the infirmities of human nature. Procopius, in his Anecdotes, has assumed that servile and ungrateful office. The generous reader may cast away the libel, but the evidence of facts will adhere to his memory; and he will reluctantly confess that the fame and even the virtue of Belisarius were polluted by the lust and cruelty of his wife, and that the hero deserved an appellation which may not drop from the pen of the decent historian. The mother of Antonina[112] was a theatrical prostitute, and both her father and grandfather exercised, at Thessalonica and Constantinople, the vile though lucrative profession of charioteers. In the various situations of their fortune she became the companion, the enemy, the servant, and the favourite of the empress Theodora: these loose and ambitious females had been connected by similar pleasures; they were separated by the jealousy of vice, and at length reconciled by the partnership of guilt. Before her marriage with Belisarius, Antonina had one husband and many lovers; Photius, the son of her former nuptials, was of an age to distinguish himself at the siege of Naples; and it was not till the autumn of her age and beauty[113] that she indulged a scandalous attachment to a Thracian youth. Theodosius had been educated in the Eunomian heresy; the African voyage was consecrated by the baptism and auspicious name of the first soldier who embarked, and the proselyte was adopted into the family of his spiritual parents,[114] Belisarius and Antonina. Before they touched the shores of Africa, this holy kindred degenerated into sensual love; and as Antonina soon overleaped the bounds of modesty and caution, the Roman general was alone ignorant of his own dishonour. During their residence at Carthage he surprised the two lovers in a subterraneous chamber, solitary, warm, and almost naked. Anger flashed from his eyes. "With the help of this young man," said the unblushing Antonina, "I was secreting our most precious effects from the knowledge of Justinian." The youth resumed his garments, and the pious husband consented to disbelieve the evidence of his own senses. From this pleasing and perhaps voluntary delusion, Belisarius was awakened at Syracuse by the officious information of Macedonia; and that female attendant, after requiring an oath for her security, produced two chamberlains who like herself had often beheld the adulteries of Antonina. A hasty flight into Asia saved Theodosius from the justice of an injured husband, who had signified to one of his guards the order of his death; but the tears of Antonina and her artful seductions assured the credulous hero of her innocence, and he stooped, against his faith and judgment, to abandon those imprudent friends who had presumed to accuse or doubt the chastity of his wife. The revenge of a guilty woman is implacable and bloody: the unfortunate Macedonia, with the two witnesses, were secretly arrested by the minister of her cruelty; their tongues were cut out, their bodies were hacked into small pieces, and their remains were cast into the sea of Syracuse. A rash though judicious saying of Constantine, "I would sooner have punished the adulteress than the boy," was deeply remembered by Antonina; and two years afterwards, when despair had armed that officer against his general, her sanguinary advice decided and hastened his execution. Even the indignation of Photius was not forgiven by his mother; the exile of her son prepared the recall of her lover, and Theodosius condescended to accept the pressing and humble invitation of the conqueror of Italy. In the absolute direction of his household, and in the important commissions of peace and war,[115] the favourite youth most rapidly acquired a fortune of four hundred thousand pounds sterling; and after their return to Constantinople the passion of Antonina at least continued ardent and unabated. But fear, devotion, and lassitude perhaps, inspired Theodosius with more serious thoughts. He dreaded the busy scandal of the capital, and the indiscreet fondness of the wife of Belisarius, escaped from her embraces, and, retiring to Ephesus, shaved his head and took refuge in the sanctuary of a monastic life. The despair of the new Ariadne could scarcely have been excused by the death of her husband. She wept, she tore her hair, she filled the palace with her cries; "she had lost the dearest of friends, a tender, a faithful, a laborious friend!" But her warm entreaties, fortified by the prayers of Belisarius, were insufficient to draw the holy monk from the solitude of Ephesus. It was not till the general moved forward for the Persian war that Theodosius could be tempted to return to Constantinople, and the short interval before the departure of Antonina herself was boldly devoted to love and pleasure.

A philosopher may pity and forgive the infirmities of female nature from which he receives no real injury; but contemptible is the husband who feels, and yet endures, his own infamy in that of his wife. Antonina pursued her son with implacable hatred, and the gallant Photius[116] was exposed to her secret persecutions in the camp beyond the Tigris. Enraged by his own wrongs and by the dishonour of his blood, he cast away in his turn the sentiments of nature, and revealed to Belisarius the turpitude of a woman who had violated all the duties of a mother and a wife. From the surprise and indignation of the Roman general, his former credulity appears to have been sincere: he embraced the knees of the son of Antonina, adjured him to remember his obligations rather than his birth, and confirmed at the altar their holy vows of revenge and mutual defence. The dominion of Antonina was impaired by absence; and when she met her husband on his return from the Persian confines, Belisarius, in his first and transient emotions, confined her person and threatened her life. Photius was more resolved to punish, and less prompt to pardon; he flew to Ephesus, extorted from a trusty eunuch of his mother the full confession of her guilt, arrested Theodosius and his treasures in the church of St. John the Apostle, and concealed his captives, whose execution was only delayed, in a secure and sequestered for-

tress of Cilicia. Such a daring outrage against public justice could not pass with impunity, and the cause of Antonina was espoused by the empress, whose favour she had deserved by the recent services of the disgrace of a præfect, and the exile and murder of a pope. At the end of the campaign Belisarius was recalled; he complied as usual with the Imperial mandate. His mind was not prepared for rebellion: his obedience, however adverse to the dictates of honour, was consonant to the wishes of his heart; and when he embraced his wife, at the command and perhaps in the presence of the empress, the tender husband was disposed to forgive or to be forgiven. The bounty of Theodora reserved for her companion a more precious favour. "I have found," she said, "my dearest patrician, a pearl of inestimable value; it has not yet been viewed by any mortal eye, but the sight and the possession of this jewel are destined for my friend." As soon as the curiosity and impatience of Antonina were kindled, the door of a bedchamber was thrown open, and she beheld her lover, whom the diligence of the eunuchs had discovered in his secret prison. Her silent wonder burst into passionate exclamations of gratitude and joy, and she named Theodora her queen, her benefactress, and her saviour. The monk of Ephesus was nourished in the palace with luxury and ambition; but instead of assuming, as he was promised, the command of the Roman armies, Theodosius expired in the first fatigues of an amorous interview. The grief of Antonina could only be assuaged by the sufferings of her son. A youth of consular rank and a sickly constitution was punished without a trial, like a malefactor and a slave; yet such was the constancy of his mind, that Photius sustained the tortures of the scourge and the rack without violating the faith which he had sworn to Belisarius. After this fruitless cruelty the son of Antonina, while his mother feasted with the empress, was buried in her subterraneous prisons, which admitted not the distinction of night and day. He twice escaped to the most venerable sanctuaries of Constantinople, the church of St. Sophia and of the Virgin; but his tyrants were insensible of religion as of pity, and the helpless youth, amidst the clamours of the clergy and people, was twice dragged from the altar to the dungeon. His third attempt was more successful. At the end of three years the prophet Zachariah, or some mortal friend, indicated the means of an escape: he eluded the spies and guards of the empress, reached the holy sepulchre of Jerusalem, embraced the profession of a monk, and the abbot Photius was employed, after the death of Justinian, to reconcile and regulate the churches of Egypt. The son of Antonina suffered all that an enemy can inflict; her patient husband imposed on himself the more exquisite misery of violating his promise and deserting his friend.

In the succeeding campaign Belisarius was again sent against the Persians: he saved the East, but he offended Theodora, and perhaps the emperor himself. The malady of Justinian had countenanced the rumour of his death; and the Roman general, on the supposition of that probable event, spoke the free language of a citizen and a soldier. His colleague Buzes, who concurred in the same sentiments, lost his rank, his liberty, and his health by the persecution of the empress; but the disgrace of Belisarius was alleviated by the dignity of his own character and the influence of his wife, who might wish to humble, but could not desire to ruin, the partner of her fortunes. Even his removal was coloured by the assurance that the sinking state of Italy would be retrieved by the single presence of its conqueror. But no sooner had he returned, alone and defenceless, than a hostile commission was sent to the East to seize his treasures and criminate his actions; the guards and veterans who followed his private banner were distributed among the chiefs of the army, and even the eunuchs presumed to cast lots for the partition of his martial domestics. When he passed with a small and sordid retinue through the streets of Constantinople, his forlorn appearance excited the amazement and compassion of the people. Justinian and Theodora received him with cold ingratitude, the servile crowd with insolence and contempt; and in the evening he retired with trembling steps to his deserted palace. An indisposition, feigned or real, had confined Antonina to her apartment; and she walked disdainfully silent in the adjacent portico, while Belisarius threw himself on his bed, and expected, in an agony of grief and terror, the death which he had so often braved under the walls of Rome. Long after sunset a messenger was announced from the empress: he opened with anxious curiosity the letter which contained the sentence of his fate. "You cannot be ignorant how much you have deserved my displeasure. I am not insensible of the services of Antonina. To her merits and intercession I have granted your life, and permit you to retain a part of your treasures, which might be justly forfeited to the state. Let your gratitude where it is due be displayed, not in words, but in your future behaviour." I know not how to believe or to relate the transports with which the hero is said to have received this ignominious pardon. He fell prostrate before his wife, he kissed the feet of his saviour, and he devoutly promised to live the grateful and submissive slave of Antonina. A fine of one hundred and twenty thousand pounds sterling was levied on the fortunes of Belisarius; and with the office of count, or master of the royal stables, he accepted the conduct of the Italian war. At his departure from Constantinople, his friends, and even the public, were persuaded that as soon as he regained his freedom he would renounce his dissimulation; and that his wife, Theodora, and perhaps the emperor himself, would be sacrificed to the just revenge of a virtuous rebel. Their hopes were deceived; and the unconquerable patience and loyalty of Belisarius appear either *below* or *above* the character of a MAN.[117]

CHAPTER XLII

State of the Barbaric World. Establishment of the Lombards on the Danube. Tribes and Inroads of the Sclavonians. Origin, Empire, and Embassies of the Turks. The Flight of the Avars. Chosroes I., or Nushirvan, King of Persia. His prosperous Reign and Wars with the Romans. The Colchian or Lazic War. The Æthiopians.

OUR estimate of personal merit is relative to the common faculties of mankind. The aspiring efforts of genius or virtue, either in active or speculative life, are measured not so much by their real elevation as by the height to which they ascend above the level of their age or country; and the same stature which in a people of giants would pass unnoticed, must appear conspicuous in a race of pigmies. Leonidas and his three hundred companions devoted their lives at Thermopylæ; but the education of the infant, the boy, and the man, had prepared and almost ensured this memorable sacrifice; and each Spartan would approve, rather than admire, an act of duty, of which himself and eight thousand of his fellow-citizens were equally capable.[1] The great Pompey might inscribe on his trophies that he had defeated in battle two millions of enemies, and reduced fifteen hundred cities from the lake Mæotis to the Red Sea;[2] but the fortune of Rome flew before his eagles; the nations were oppressed by their own fears; and the invincible legions which he commanded had been formed by the habits of conquest and the discipline of ages. In this view the character of Belisarius may be deservedly placed above the heroes of the ancient republics. His imperfections flowed from the contagion of the times; his virtues were his own, the free gift of nature or reflection; he raised himself without a master or a rival; and so inadequate were the arms committed to his hand, that his sole advantage was derived from the pride and presumption of his adversaries. Under his command, the subjects of Justinian often deserved to be called Romans; but the unwarlike appellation of Greeks was imposed as a term of reproach by the haughty Goths, who affected to blush that they must dispute the kingdom of Italy with a nation of tragedians, pantomimes, and pirates.[3] The climate of Asia has indeed been found less congenial than that of Europe to military spirit: those populous countries were enervated by luxury, despotism, and superstition, and the monks were more expensive and more numerous than the soldiers of the East. The regular force of the empire had once amounted to six hundred and forty-five thousand men: it was reduced, in the time of Justinian, to one hundred and fifty thousand; and this number, large as it may seem, was thinly scattered over the sea and land—in Spain and Italy, in Africa and Egypt, on the banks of the Danube, the coast of the Euxine, and the frontiers of Persia. The citizen was exhausted, yet the soldier was unpaid; his poverty was mischievously soothed by the privilege of rapine and indolence, and the tardy payments were detained and intercepted by the fraud of those agents who usurp, without courage or danger, the emoluments of war. Public and private distress recruited the armies of the state; but in the field, and still more in the presence of the enemy, their numbers were always defective. The want of national spirit was supplied by the precarious faith and disorderly service of barbarian mercenaries. Even military honour, which has often survived the loss of virtue and

freedom, was almost totally extinct. The generals, who were multiplied beyond the example of former times, laboured only to prevent the success or to sully the reputation of their colleagues; and they had been taught by experience that, if merit sometimes provoked the jealousy, error, or even guilt, would obtain the indulgence, of a gracious emperor.[4] In such an age the triumphs of Belisarius, and afterwards of Narses, shine with incomparable lustre; but they are encompassed with the darkest shades of disgrace and calamity. While the lieutenant of Justinian subdued the kingdoms of the Goths and Vandals, the emperor,[5] timid, though ambitious, balanced the forces of the barbarians, fomented their divisions by flattery and falsehood, and invited by his patience and liberality the repetition of injuries.[6] The keys of Carthage, Rome, and Ravenna were presented to their conqueror, while Antioch was destroyed by the Persians, and Justinian trembled for the safety of Constantinople.

Even the Gothic victories of Belisarius were prejudicial to the state, since they abolished the important barrier of the Upper Danube, which had been so faithfully guarded by Theodoric and his daughter. For the defence of Italy, the Goths evacuated Pannonia and Noricum, which they left in a peaceful and flourishing condition: the sovereignty was claimed by the emperor of the Romans; the actual possession was abandoned to the boldness of the first invader. On the opposite banks of the Danube, the plains of Upper Hungary and the Transylvanian hills were possessed, since the death of Attila, by the tribes of the Gepidæ, who respected the Gothic arms, and despised, not indeed the gold of the Romans, but the secret motive of their annual subsidies. The vacant fortifications of the river were instantly occupied by these barbarians; their standards were planted on the walls of Sirmium and Belgrade; and the ironical tone of their apology aggravated this insult on the majesty of the empire: "So extensive, O Cæsar, are your dominions, so numerous are your cities, that you are continually seeking for nations to whom, either in peace or war, you may relinquish these useless possessions. The Gepidæ are your brave and faithful allies, and, if they have anticipated your gifts, they have shown a just confidence in your bounty." Their presumption was excused by the mode of revenge which Justinian embraced. Instead of asserting the rights of a sovereign for the protection of his subjects, the emperor invited a strange people to invade and possess the Roman provinces between the Danube and the Alps; and the ambition of the Gepidæ was checked by the rising power and fame of the LOMBARDS.[7] This corrupt appellation has been diffused in the thirteenth century by the merchants and bankers, the Italian posterity of these savage warriors; but the original name of *Langobards* is expressive only of the peculiar length and fashion of their beards. I am not disposed either to question or to justify their Scandinavian origin,[8] nor to pursue the migrations of the Lombards through unknown regions and marvellous adventures. About the time of Augustus and Trajan, a ray of historic light breaks on the darkness of their antiquities, and they are discovered, for the first time, between the Elbe and the Oder. Fierce, beyond the example of the Germans, they delighted to propagate the tremendous belief that their heads were formed like the heads of dogs, and that they drank the blood of their enemies whom they vanquished in battle. The smallness of their numbers was recruited by the adoption of their bravest slaves; and alone, amidst their powerful neighbours, they defended by arms their high-spirited independence. In the tempests of the north, which overwhelmed so many names and nations, this little bark of the Lombards still floated on the surface; they gradually descended towards the south and the Danube, and at the end of four hundred years they again appear with their ancient valour and renown. Their manners were not less ferocious. The assassination of a royal guest was executed in the presence and by the command of the king's daughter, who had been provoked by some words of insult, and disappointed by his diminutive stature; and a tribute, the price of blood, was imposed on the Lombards by his brother, the king of the Heruli. Adversity revived a sense of moderation and justice, and the insolence of conquest was chastised by the signal defeat and irreparable dispersion of the Heruli, who were seated in the southern provinces of Poland.[9] The victories of the Lombards recommended them to the friendship of the emperors; and, at the solicitation of Justinian, they passed the Danube to reduce, according to their treaty, the cities of Noricum and the fortresses of Pannonia. But the spirit of rapine soon tempted them beyond these ample limits; they wandered along the coast of the Hadriatic as far as Dyrrachium, and presumed, with familiar rudeness, to enter the towns and houses of their Roman allies, and to seize the captives who had escaped from their audacious hands. These acts of hostility, the sallies, as it might be pretended, of some loose adventurers, were disowned by the nation, and excused by the emperor; but the arms of the Lombards were more seriously engaged by a contest of thirty years, which was terminated only by the extirpation of the Gepidæ. The hostile nations often pleaded their cause before the throne of Constantinople; and the crafty Justinian, to whom the barbarians were almost equally odious, pronounced a partial and ambiguous sentence, and dexterously protracted the war by slow and ineffectual succours. Their strength was formidable, since the Lombards, who sent into the field several *myriads* of soldiers, still claimed, as the weaker side, the protection of the Romans. Their spirit was intrepid; yet such is the uncertainty of courage, that the two armies were suddenly struck with a panic: they fled from each other, and the rival kings remained with their guards in the midst of an empty plain. A short truce was obtained; but their mutual resentment again kindled, and the remembrance of their shame rendered the next encounter more desperate and bloody. Forty thousand of the barbarians perished in the decisive battle which broke the power of the Gepidæ, transferred the fears and wishes of Justinian, and first displayed the character of Alboin, the youthful prince of the Lombards, and the future conqueror of Italy.[10]

The wild people who dwelt or wandered in the plains of Russia, Lithuania, and Poland, might be reduced, in the age of Justinian, under the two great families of the BULGARIANS[11] and the SCLAVONIANS. According to the Greek writers, the former, who touched the Euxine and the lake Mæotis, derived from the Huns their name or descent; and it is needless to renew the simple and well-known picture of Tartar manners. They were bold and dexterous archers, who drank the milk and feasted on the flesh of their fleet and indefatigable horses; whose flocks and herds followed, or rather guided, the motions of their roving camps; to whose inroads no country was remote or impervious, and who were practised in flight, though incapable of fear. The nation was divided into two powerful and hostile tribes, who pursued each other with fraternal hatred. They eagerly disputed the friendship or rather the gifts of the emperor; and the distinction which nature had fixed between the faithful dog and the rapacious wolf was applied by an ambassador who received only verbal instructions from the mouth of his illiterate prince.[12] The Bulgarians, of whatsoever species, were equally attracted by Roman wealth: they assumed a vague dominion over the Sclavonian name, and their rapid marches could only be stopped by the Baltic Sea, or the extreme cold and poverty of the north. But the same race of Sclavonians appears to have maintained, in every age, the possession of the same countries. Their numerous tribes, however distant or adverse, used one common language (it was harsh and irregular), and were known by the resemblance of their form, which deviated from the swarthy Tartar, and approached without attaining the lofty stature and fair complexion of the German. Four thousand six hundred villages[13] were scattered over the provinces of Russia and Poland, and their huts were hastily built of rough timber, in a country deficient both in stone and iron. Erected, or rather concealed, in the depth of forests, on the banks of rivers, or the edge of morasses, we may not perhaps, without flattery, compare them to the architecture of the beaver, which they resembled in a double issue, to the land and water, for the escape of the savage inhabitant, an animal less cleanly, less diligent, and less social, than that marvellous quadruped. The fertility of the soil, rather than the labour of the natives, supplied the rustic plenty of the Sclavonians. Their sheep and horned cattle were large and numerous, and the fields which they sowed with millet and panic[14] afforded, in the place of bread, a coarse and less nutritive food. The incessant rapine of their neighbours compelled them to bury this treasure in the earth; but on the appearance of a stranger it was freely imparted by a people whose unfavourable character is qualified by the epithets of chaste, patient, and hospitable. As their supreme god, they adored an invisible master of the thunder. The rivers and the nymphs obtained their subordinate honours, and the popular worship was expressed in vows and sacrifice. The Sclavonians disdained to obey a despot, a prince, or even a magistrate; but their experience was too narrow, their passions too headstrong, to compose a system of equal law or general defence. Some voluntary respect was yielded to age and valour; but each tribe or village existed as a separate republic, and all must be persuaded where none could be compelled. They fought on foot, almost naked, and, except an unwieldy shield, without any defensive armour: their weapons of offence were a bow, a quiver of small poisoned arrows, and a long rope, which they dexterously threw from a distance, and entangled their enemy in a running noose. In the field, the Sclavonian infantry was dangerous by their speed, agility, and hardiness: they swam, they dived, they remained under water, drawing their breath through a hollow cane; and a river or lake was often the scene of their unsuspected ambuscade. But these were the achievements of spies or stragglers: the military art was unknown to the Sclavonians; their name was obscure, and their conquests were inglorious.[15]

I have marked the faint and general outline of the Sclavonians and Bulgarians, without attempting to define their intermediate boundaries, which were not accurately known or respected by the barbarians themselves. Their importance was measured by their vicinity to the empire; and the level country of Moldavia and Wallachia was occupied by the Antes,[16] a Sclavonian tribe, which swelled the titles of Justinian with an epithet of conquest.[17] Against the Antes he erected the fortifications of the Lower Danube, and laboured to secure the alliance of a people seated in the direct channel of northern inundation, an interval of two hundred miles between the mountains of Transylvania and the Euxine Sea. But the Antes wanted power and inclination to stem the fury of the torrent: and the light-armed Sclavonians from a hundred tribes pursued with almost equal speed the footsteps of the Bulgarian horse. The payment of one piece of gold for each soldier procured a safe and easy retreat through the country of the Gepidæ, who commanded the passage of the Upper Danube.[18] The hopes or fears of the barbarians, their intestine union or discord, the accident of a frozen or shallow stream, the prospect of harvest or vintage, the prosperity or distress of the Romans, were the causes which produced the uniform repetition of annual visits,[19] tedious in the narrative, and destructive in the event. The same year, and possibly the same month, in which Ravenna surrendered, was marked by an invasion of the Huns or Bulgarians, so dreadful that it almost effaced the memory of their past inroads. They spread from the suburbs of Constantinople to the Ionian Gulf, destroyed thirty-two cities or castles, erased Potidæa, which Athens had built and Philip had besieged, and repassed the Danube, dragging at their horses' heels one hundred and twenty thousand of the subjects of Justinian. In a subsequent inroad they pierced the wall of the Thracian Chersonesus, extirpated the habitations and the inhabitants, boldly traversed the Hellespont, and returned to their companions laden with the spoils of Asia. Another party, which seemed a multitude in the eyes of the Romans, penetrated without opposition from the straits of Thermopylæ to the isthmus of

Corinth; and the last ruin of Greece has appeared an object too minute for the attention of history. The works which the emperor raised for the protection, but at the expense of his subjects, served only to disclose the weakness of some neglected part; and the walls, which by flattery had been deemed impregnable, were either deserted by the garrison or scaled by the barbarians. Three thousand Sclavonians, who insolently divided themselves into two bands, discovered the weakness and misery of a triumphant reign. They passed the Danube and the Hebrus, vanquished the Roman generals who dared to oppose their progress, and plundered with impunity the cities of Illyricum and Thrace, each of which had arms and numbers to overwhelm their contemptible assailants. Whatever praise the boldness of the Sclavonians may deserve, it is sullied by the wanton and deliberate cruelty which they are accused of exercising on their prisoners. Without distinction of rank or age or sex, the captives were impaled or flayed alive, or suspended between four posts and beaten with clubs till they expired, or enclosed in some spacious building and left to perish in the flames with the spoil and cattle which might impede the march of these savage victors.[20] Perhaps a more impartial narrative would reduce the number and qualify the nature of these horrid acts, and they might sometimes be excused by the cruel laws of retaliation. In the siege of Topirus,[21] whose obstinate defence had enraged the Sclavonians, they massacred fifteen thousand males, but they spared the women and children; the most valuable captives were always reserved for labour or ransom; the servitude was not rigorous, and the terms of their deliverance were speedy and moderate. But the subject, or the historian of Justinian, exhaled his just indignation in the language of complaint and reproach; and Procopius has confidently affirmed that in a reign of thirty-two years each *annual* inroad of the barbarians consumed two hundred thousand of the inhabitants of the Roman empire. The entire population of Turkish Europe, which nearly corresponds with the provinces of Justinian, would perhaps be incapable of supplying six millions of persons, the result of this incredible estimate.[22]

In the midst of these obscure calamities, Europe felt the shock of a revolution, which first revealed to the world the name and nation of the Turks. Like Romulus, the founder of that martial people was suckled by a she-wolf, who afterwards made him the father of a numerous progeny; and the representation of that animal in the banners of the Turks preserved the memory, or rather suggested the idea, of a fable which was invented, without any mutual intercourse, by the shepherds of Latium and those of Scythia. At the equal distance of two thousand miles from the Caspian, the Icy, the Chinese, and the Bengal seas, a ridge of mountains is conspicuous, the centre, and perhaps the summit, of Asia, which, in the language of different nations, has been styled Imaus, and Caf,[23] and Altai, and the Golden Mountains, and the Girdle of the Earth. The sides of the hills were productive of minerals; and the iron-forges,[24] for the purpose of war, were exercised by the Turks, the most despised portion of the slaves of the great khan of the Geougen. But their servitude could only last till a leader, bold and eloquent, should arise to persuade his countrymen that the same arms which they forged for their masters might become in their own hands the instruments of freedom and victory. They sallied from the mountain;[25] a sceptre was the reward of his advice; and the annual ceremony, in which a piece of iron was heated in the fire, and a smith's hammer was successively handled, by the prince and his nobles, recorded for ages the humble profession and rational pride of the Turkish nation. Bertezena, their first leader, signalised their valour and his own in successful combats against the neighbouring tribes; but when he presumed to ask in marriage the daughter of the great khan, the insolent demand of a slave and a mechanic was contemptuously rejected. The disgrace was expiated by a more noble alliance with a princess of China; and the decisive battle which almost extirpated the nation of the Geougen established in Tartary the new and more powerful empire of the Turks. They reigned over the north; but they confessed the vanity of conquest by their faithful attachment to the mountain of their fathers. The royal encampment seldom lost sight of Mount Altai, from whence the river Irtish descends to water the rich pastures of the Calmucks,[26] which nourish the largest sheep and oxen in the world. The soil is fruitful, and the climate mild and temperate: the happy region was ignorant of earthquake and pestilence; the emperor's throne was turned towards the east, and a golden wolf on the top of a spear seemed to guard the entrance of his tent. One of the successors of Bertezena was tempted by the luxury and superstition of China; but his design of building cities and temples was defeated by the simple wisdom of a barbarian counsellor. "The Turks," he said, "are not equal in number to one hundredth part of the inhabitants of China. If we balance their power, and elude their armies, it is because we wander without any fixed habitations in the exercise of war and hunting. Are we strong? we advance and conquer: are we feeble? we retire and are concealed. Should the Turks confine themselves within the walls of cities, the loss of a battle would be the destruction of their empire. The bonzes preach only patience, humility, and the renunciation of the world. Such O king! is not the religion of heroes." They entertained with less reluctance the doctrines of Zoroaster; but the greatest part of the nation acquiesced without inquiry in the opinions, or rather in the practice, of their ancestors. The honours of sacrifice were reserved for the supreme deity; they acknowledged in rude hymns their obligations to the air, the fire, the water, and the earth; and their priests derived some profit from the art of divination. Their unwritten laws were rigorous and impartial: theft was punished by a tenfold restitution; adultery, treason, and murder with death; and no chastisement could be inflicted too severe for the rare and inexpiable guilt of cowardice. As the subject nations marched under the standard of the Turks, their cavalry, both men and horses, were proudly computed by millions; one of their effective armies consisted of four hundred thousand soldiers, and in less than fifty years they were connected in peace and war with the Romans, the Persians, and the Chinese. In their northern limits some vestige may be discovered of the form and situation of Kamtchatka, of a people of hunters and fishermen, whose sledges were drawn by dogs, and whose habitations were buried in the earth. The Turks were ignorant of astronomy; but the observation taken by some learned Chinese, with a gnomon of eight feet, fixes the royal camp in the latitude of forty-nine degrees, and marks their extreme progress within three, or at least ten degrees of the polar circle.[27] Among their southern conquests the most splendid was that of the Nephthalites or White Huns, a polite and warlike people, who possessed the commercial cities of Bochara and Samarcand, who had vanquished the Persian monarch, and carried their victorious arms along the banks and perhaps to the mouth of the Indus. On the side of the west the Turkish cavalry advanced to the lake Mæotis. They passed that lake on the ice. The khan, who dwelt at the foot of Mount Altai, issued his commands for the siege of Bosphorus,[28] a city the voluntary subject of Rome, and whose

princes had formerly been the friends of Athens.[29] To the east the Turks invaded China, as often as the vigour of the government was relaxed: and I am taught to read in the history of the times that they mowed down their patient enemies like hemp or grass, and that the mandarins applauded the wisdom of an emperor who repulsed these barbarians with golden lances. This extent of savage empire compelled the Turkish monarch to establish three subordinate princes of his own blood, who soon forgot their gratitude and allegiance. The conquerors were enervated by luxury, which is always fatal except to an industrious people; the policy of China solicited the vanquished nations to resume their independence; and the power of the Turks was limited to a period of two hundred years. The revival of their name and dominion in the southern countries of Asia are the events of a later age; and the dynasties which succeeded to their native realms may sleep in oblivion, since *their* history bears no relation to the decline and fall of the Roman empire.[30]

In the rapid career of conquest the Turks attacked and subdued the nation of the Ogors or Varchonites on the banks of the river Til, which derived the epithet of Black from its dark water or gloomy forests.[31] The khan of the Ogors was slain with three hundred thousand of his subjects, and their bodies were scattered over the space of four days' journey: their surviving countrymen acknowledged the strength and mercy of the Turks; and a small portion, about twenty thousand warriors, preferred exile to servitude. They followed the well-known road of the Volga, cherished the error of the nations who confounded them with the AVARS, and spread the terror of that false, though famous appellation, which had not, however, saved its lawful proprietors from the yoke of the Turks.[32] After a long and victorious march the new Avars arrived at the foot of Mount Caucasus, in the country of the Alani[33] and Circassians, where they first heard of the splendour and weakness of the Roman empire. They humbly requested their confederate, the prince of the Alani, to lead them to this source of riches; and their ambassador, with the permission of the governor of Lazica, was transported by the Euxine Sea to Constantinople. The whole city was poured forth to behold with curiosity and terror the aspect of a strange people; their long hair, which hung in tresses down their backs, was gracefully bound with ribands, but the rest of their habit appeared to imitate the fashion of the Huns. When they were admitted to the audience of Justinian, Candish, the first of the ambassadors, addressed the Roman emperor in these terms: "You see before you, O mighty prince, the representatives of the strongest and most populous of nations, the invincible, the irresistible Avars. We are willing to devote ourselves to your service: we are able to vanquish and destroy all the enemies who now disturb your repose. But we expect, as the price of our alliance, as the reward of our valour, precious gifts, annual subsidies, and fruitful possessions." At the time of this embassy Justinian had reigned above thirty, he had lived above seventy-five years: his mind, as well as his body, was feeble and languid; and the conqueror of Africa and Italy, careless of the permanent interest of his people, aspired only to end his days in the bosom even of inglorious peace. In a studied oration, he imparted to the senate his resolution to dissemble the insult and to purchase the friendship of the Avars; and the whole senate, like the mandarins of China, applauded the incomparable wisdom and foresight of their sovereign. The instruments of luxury were immediately prepared to captivate the barbarians; silken garments, soft and splendid beds, and chains and collars incrusted with gold. The ambassadors, content with such liberal reception, departed from Constantinople, and Valentin, one of the emperor's guards, was sent with a similar character to their camp at the foot of Mount Caucasus. As their destruction or their success must be alike advantageous to the empire, he persuaded them to invade the enemies of Rome; and they were easily tempted, by gifts and promises, to gratify their ruling inclinations. These fugitives, who fled before the Turkish arms, passed the Tanais and Borysthenes, and boldly advanced into the heart of Poland and Germany, violating the law of nations and abusing the rights of victory. Before ten years had elapsed their camps were seated on the Danube and the Elbe, many Bulgarian and Sclavonian names were obliterated from the earth, and the remainder of their tribes are found, as tributaries and vassals, under the standard of the Avars. The chagan, the peculiar title of their king, still affected to cultivate the friendship of the emperor; and Justinian entertained some thoughts of fixing them in Pannonia, to balance the prevailing power of the Lombards. But the virtue or treachery of an Avar betrayed the secret enmity and ambitious designs of their countrymen; and they loudly complained of the timid, though jealous policy, of detaining their ambassadors and denying the arms which they

had been allowed to purchase in the capital of the empire.[34]

Perhaps the apparent change in the dispositions of the emperors may be ascribed to the embassy which was received from the conquerors of the Avars.[35] The immense distance which eluded their arms could not extinguish their resentment: the Turkish ambassadors pursued the footsteps of the vanquished to the Jaik, the Volga, Mount Caucasus, the Euxine, and Constantinople, and at length appeared before the successor of Constantine, to request that he would not espouse the cause of rebels and fugitives. Even commerce had some share in this remarkable negotiation: and the Sogdoites, who were now the tributaries of the Turks, embraced the fair occasion of opening, by the north of the Caspian, a new road for the importation of Chinese silk into the Roman empire. The Persian, who preferred the navigation of Ceylon, had stopped the caravans of Bochara and Samarcand: their silk was contemptuously burnt: some Turkish ambassadors died in Persia, with a suspicion of poison; and the great khan permitted his faithful vassal Maniach, the prince of the Sogdoites, to propose, at the Byzantine court, a treaty of alliance against their common enemies. Their splendid apparel and rich presents, the fruit of Oriental luxury, distinguished Maniach and his colleagues from the rude savages of the North: their letters, in the Scythian character and language, announced a people who had attained the rudiments of science:[36] they enumerated the conquests, they offered the friendship and military aid, of the Turks; and their sincerity was attested by direful imprecations (if they were guilty of falsehood) against their own head and the head of Disabul their master. The Greek prince entertained with hospitable regard the ambassadors of a remote and powerful monarch: the sight of silkworms and looms disappointed the hopes of the Sogdoites; the emperor renounced, or seemed to renounce, the fugitive Avars, but he accepted the alliance of the Turks: and the ratification of the treaty was carried by a Roman minister to the foot of Mount Altai. Under the successors of Justinian the friendship of the two nations was cultivated by frequent and cordial intercourse; the most favoured vassals were permitted to imitate the example of the great khan; and one hundred and six Turks, who on various occasions had visited Constantinople, departed at the same time for their native country. The duration and length of the journey from the Byzantine court to Mount Altai are not specified: it might have been difficult to mark a road through the nameless deserts, the mountains, rivers, and morasses of Tartary; but a curious account has been preserved of the reception of the Roman ambassadors at the royal camp. After they had been purified with fire and incense, according to a rite still practised under the sons of Zingis, they were introduced to the presence of Disabul. In a valley of the Golden Mountain they found the great khan in his tent, seated in a chair with wheels, to which a horse might be occasionally harnessed. As soon as they had delivered their presents, which were received by the proper officers, they exposed in a florid oration the wishes of the Roman emperor that victory might attend the arms of the Turks, that their reign might be long and prosperous, and that a strict alliance, without envy or deceit, might for ever be maintained between the two most powerful nations of the earth. The answer of Disabul corresponded with these friendly professions, and the ambassadors were seated by his side at a banquet which lasted the greatest part of the day: the tent was surrounded with silk hangings, and a Tartar liquor was served on the table which possessed at least the intoxicating qualities of wine. The entertainment of the succeeding day was more sumptuous; the silk hangings of the second tent were embroidered in various figures; and the royal seat, the cups, and the bases were of gold. A third pavilion was supported by columns of gilt wood; a bed of pure and massy gold was raised on four peacocks of the same metal: and before the entrance of the tent, dishes, basins, and statues of solid silver and admirable art were ostentatiously piled in waggons, the monuments of valour rather than of industry. When Disabul led his armies against the frontiers of Persia, his Roman allies followed many days the march of the Turkish camp, nor were they dismissed till they had enjoyed their precedency over the envoy of the Great King, whose loud and intemperate clamours interrupted the silence of the royal banquet. The power and ambition of Chosroes cemented the union of the Turks and Romans, who touched his dominions on either side: but those distant nations, regardless of each other, consulted the dictates of interest, without recollecting the obligations of oaths and treaties. While the successor of Disabul celebrated his father's obsequies, he was saluted by the ambassadors of the emperor Tiberius, who proposed an invasion of Persia, and sustained with firmness the angry and perhaps the just reproaches of that haughty barbarian. "You see

my ten fingers," said the great khan, and he applied them to his mouth. "You Romans speak with as many tongues, but they are tongues of deceit and perjury. To me you hold one language, to my subjects another; and the nations are successively deluded by your perfidious eloquence. You precipitate your allies into war and danger, you enjoy their labours, and you neglect your benefactors. Hasten your return, inform your master that a Turk is incapable of uttering or forgiving falsehood, and that he shall speedily meet the punishment which he deserves. While he solicits my friendship with flattering and hollow words, he is sunk to a confederate of my fugitive Varchonites. If I condescend to march against those contemptible slaves, they will tremble at the sound of our whips; they will be trampled, like a nest of ants, under the feet of my innumerable cavalry. I am not ignorant of the road which they have followed to invade your empire; nor can I be deceived by the vain pretence that Mount Caucasus is the impregnable barrier of the Romans. I know the course of the Dniester, the Danube, and the Hebrus; the most warlike nations have yielded to the arms of the Turks; and from the rising to the setting sun the earth is my inheritance." Notwithstanding this menace, a sense of mutual advantage soon renewed the alliance of the Turks and Romans: but the pride of the great khan survived his resentment; and when he announced an important conquest to his friend the emperor Maurice, he styled himself the master of the seven races and the lord of the seven climates of the world.[37]

Disputes have often arisen between the sovereigns of Asia for the title of king of the world, while the contest has proved that it could not belong to either of the competitors. The kingdom of the Turks was bounded by the Oxus or Gihon; and *Touran* was separated by that great river from the rival monarchy of *Iran*, or Persia, which in a smaller compass contained perhaps a larger measure of power and population. The Persians, who alternately invaded and repulsed the Turks and the Romans, were still ruled by the house of Sassan, which ascended the throne three hundred years before the accession of Justinian. His contemporary, Cabades, or Kobad, had been successful in war against the emperor Anastasius; but the reign of that prince was distracted by civil and religious troubles. A prisoner in the hands of his subjects, an exile among the enemies of Persia, he recovered his liberty by prostituting the honour of his wife, and regained his kingdom with the dangerous and mercenary aid of the barbarians who had slain his father. His nobles were suspicious that Kobad never forgave the authors of his expulsion, or even those of his restoration. The people was deluded and inflamed by the fanaticism of Mazdak,[38] who asserted the community of women[39] and the equality of mankind, whilst he appropriated the richest lands and most beautiful females to the use of his sectaries. The view of these disorders, which had been fomented by his laws and example,[40] embittered the declining age of the Persian monarch; and his fears were increased by the consciousness of his design to reverse the natural and customary order of succession in favour of his third and most favoured son, so famous under the names of Chosroes and Nushirvan. To render the youth more illustrious in the eyes of the nations, Kobad was desirous that he should be adopted by the emperor Justin: the hope of peace inclined the Byzantine court to accept this singular proposal; and Chosroes might have acquired a specious claim to the inheritance of his Roman parent. But the future mischief was diverted by the advice of the quæstor Proclus: a difficulty was started, whether the adoption should be performed as a civil or military rite;[41] the treaty was abruptly dissolved; and the sense of this indignity sunk deep into the mind of Chosroes, who had already advanced to the Tigris on his road to Constantinople. His father did not long survive the disappointment of his wishes: the testament of their deceased sovereign was read in the assembly of the nobles; and a powerful faction, prepared for the event, and regardless of the priority of age, exalted Chosroes to the throne of Persia. He filled that throne during a prosperous period of forty-eight years;[42] and the JUSTICE of Nushirvan is celebrated as the theme of immortal praise by the nations of the East.

But the justice of kings is understood by themselves, and even by their subjects, with an ample indulgence for the gratification of passion and interest. The virtue of Chosroes was that of a conqueror who, in the measures of peace and war, is excited by ambition and restrained by prudence; who confounds the greatness with the happiness of a nation, and calmly devotes the lives of thousands to the fame, or even the amusement, of a single man. In his domestic administration the just Nushirvan would merit in our feelings the appellation of a tyrant. His two elder brothers had been deprived of their fair expectations of the diadem: their future life, between the supreme rank and the condition of subjects, was anxious to themselves and formidable to their master: fear, as well as revenge, might tempt them to rebel; the slightest evidence of a conspiracy satisfied the author of their wrongs; and the repose of Chosroes was secured by the death of these unhappy princes, with their families and adherents. One guiltless youth was saved and dismissed by the compassion of a veteran general; and this act of humanity, which was revealed by his son, overbalanced the merit of reducing twelve nations to the obedience of Persia. The zeal and prudence of Mebodes had fixed the diadem on the head of Chosroes himself; but he delayed to attend the royal summons till he had performed the duties of a military review: he was instantly commanded to repair to the iron tripod which stood before the gate of the palace,[43] where it was death to relieve or approach the victim; and Mebodes languished several days before his sentence was pronounced by the inflexible pride and calm ingratitude of the son of Kobad. But the people, more especially in the East, is disposed to forgive, and even to applaud, the cruelty which strikes at the loftiest heads—at the slaves of ambition, whose voluntary choice has exposed them to live in the smiles, and to perish by the frown, of a capricious monarch. In the execution of the laws which he had no temptation to violate; in the punishment of crimes which attacked his own dignity, as well as the happiness of individuals; Nushirvan, or Chosroes, deserved the appellation of *just*. His government was firm, rigorous, and impartial. It was the first labour of his reign to abolish the dangerous theory of common or equal possessions: the lands and women which the sectaries of Mazdak had usurped were restored to their lawful owners; and the temperate chastisement of the fanatics or impostors confirmed the domestic rights of society. Instead of listening with blind confidence to a favourite minister, he established four viziers over the four great provinces of his empire—Assyria, Media, Persia, and Bactriana. In the choice of judges, præfects, and counsellors, he strove to remove the mask which is always worn in the presence of kings: he wished to substitute the natural order of talents for the accidental distinctions of birth and fortune; he professed, in specious language, his intention to prefer those men who carried the poor in their bosoms, and to banish corruption from the seat of justice, as dogs were excluded from the temples of the Magi. The code of laws of the first Artaxerxes was revived and published as the rule of the magistrates; but the assurance of speedy punishment was the best

security of their virtue. Their behaviour was inspected by a thousand eyes, their words were
overheard by a thousand ears, the secret or public agents of the throne; and the provinces,
from the Indian to the Arabian confines, were
enlightened by the frequent visits of a sovereign
who affected to emulate his celestial brother in
his rapid and salutary career. Education and
agriculture he viewed as the two objects most
deserving of his care. In every city of Persia, orphans and the children of the poor were maintained and instructed at the public expense; the
daughters were given in marriage to the richest
citizens of their own rank, and the sons, according to their different talents, were employed in
mechanic trades or promoted to more honourable service. The deserted villages were relieved
by his bounty; to the peasants and farmers who
were found incapable of cultivating their lands
he distributed cattle, seed, and the instruments
of husbandry; and the rare and inestimable
treasure of fresh water was parsimoniously
managed, and skilfully dispersed over the arid
territory of Persia.[44] The prosperity of that kingdom was the effect and the evidence of his virtues; his vices are those of Oriental despotism;
but in the long competition between Chosroes
and Justinian, the advantage, both of merit and
fortune, is almost always on the side of the barbarian.[45]

To the praise of justice Nushirvan united the
reputation of knowledge; and the seven Greek
philosophers who visited his court were invited
and deceived by the strange assurance that a
disciple of Plato was seated on the Persian
throne. Did they expect that a prince, strenuously exercised in the toils of war and government, should agitate, with dexterity like their
own, the abstruse and profound questions
which amused the leisure of the schools of
Athens? Could they hope that the precepts of
philosophy should direct the life and control
the passions of a despot whose infancy had been
taught to consider *his* absolute and fluctuating
will as the only rule of moral obligation?[46] The
studies of Chosroes were ostentatious and superficial; but his example awakened the curiosity
of an ingenious people, and the light of science
was diffused over the dominions of Persia.[47] At
Gondi Sapor, in the neighbourhood of the royal
city of Susa, an academy of physic was founded,
which insensibly became a liberal school of
poetry, philosophy, and rhetoric.[48] The annals
of the monarchy[49] were composed; and while
recent and authentic history might afford some
useful lessons both to the prince and people, the
darkness of the first ages was embellished by the
giants, the dragons, and the fabulous heroes of
Oriental romance.[50] Every learned or confident
stranger was enriched by the bounty and flattered by the conversation of the monarch: he
nobly rewarded a Greek physician[51] by the deliverance of three thousand captives; and the
sophists, who contended for his favour, were exasperated by the wealth and insolence of Ura-
nius, their more successful rival. Nushirvan believed, or at least respected, the religion of the
Magi; and some traces of persecution may be
discovered in his reign.[52] Yet he allowed himself freely to compare the tenets of the various
sects; and the theological disputes, in which he
frequently presided, diminished the authority
of the priest and enlightened the minds of the
people. At his command the most celebrated
writers of Greece and India were translated into the Persian language—a smooth and elegant
idiom, recommended by Mahomet to the use of
paradise, though it is branded with the epithets
of savage and unmusical by the ignorance and
presumption of Agathias.[53] Yet the Greek historian might reasonably wonder that it should
be found possible to execute an entire version
of Plato and Aristotle in a foreign dialect, which
had not been framed to express the spirit of
freedom and the subtleties of philosophic disquisition. And, if the reason of the Stagyrite
might be equally dark or equally intelligible in
every tongue, the dramatic art and verbal argu-
mentation of the disciple of Socrates[54] appear to
be indissolubly mingled with the grace and perfection of his Attic style. In the search of universal knowledge, Nushirvan was informed that
the moral and political fables of Pilpay, an ancient Brahman, were preserved with jealous
reverence among the treasures of the kings of
India. The physician Perozes was secretly despatched to the banks of the Ganges, with instructions to procure, at any price, the communication of this valuable work. His dexterity
obtained a transcript, his learned diligence accomplished the translation; and the fables of
Pilpay[55] were read and admired in the assembly
of Nushirvan and his nobles. The Indian original and the Persian copy have long since disappeared; but this venerable monument has
been saved by the curiosity of the Arabian caliphs, revived in the modern Persic, the Turkish,
the Syriac, the Hebrew, and the Greek idioms,
and transfused through successive versions into
the modern languages of Europe. In their present form, the peculiar character, the manners
and religion of the Hindoos, are completely

bliterated; and the intrinsic merit of the fables of Pilpay is far inferior to the concise elegance of Phædrus and the native graces of La Fontaine. Fifteen moral and political sentences are illustrated in a series of apologies; but the composition is intricate, the narrative prolix, and the precept obvious and barren. Yet the Brahman may assume the merit of *inventing* a pleasing fiction, which adorns the nakedness of truth, and alleviates, perhaps, to a royal ear, the harshness of instruction. With a similar design, to admonish kings that they are strong only in the strength of their subjects, the same Indians invented the game of chess, which was likewise introduced into Persia under the reign of Nushirvan.[56]

The son of Kobad found his kingdom involved in a war with the successor of Constantine; and the anxiety of his domestic situation inclined him to grant the suspension of arms which Justinian was impatient to purchase. Chosroes saw the Roman ambassadors at his feet. He accepted eleven thousand pounds of gold as the price of an *endless* or indefinite peace;[57] some mutual exchanges were regulated; the Persian assumed the guard of the gates of Caucasus, and the demolition of Dara was suspended on the condition that it should never be made the residence of the general of the East. This interval of repose had been solicited and was diligently improved by the ambition of the emperor: his African conquests were the first fruits of the Persian treaty; and the avarice of Chosroes was soothed by a large portion of the spoils of Carthage, which his ambassadors required in a tone of pleasantry and under the colour of friendship.[58] But the trophies of Belisarius disturbed the slumbers of the Great King; and he heard with astonishment, envy, and fear that Sicily, Italy, and Rome itself had been reduced in three rapid campaigns to the obedience of Justinian. Unpractised in the art of violating treaties, he secretly excited his bold and subtle vassal Almondar. That prince of the Saracens, who resided at Hira,[59] had not been included in the general peace, and still waged an obscure war against his rival Arethas, the chief of the tribe of Gassan, and confederate of the empire. The subject of this dispute was an extensive sheep-walk in the desert to the south of Palmyra. An immemorial tribute for the licence of pasture appeared to attest the rights of Almondar, while the Gassanite appealed to the Latin name of strata, a paved road, as an unquestionable evidence of the sovereignty and labours of the Romans.[60] The two monarchs supported the cause of their respective vassals;

and the Persian Arab, without expecting the event of a slow and doubtful arbitration, enriched his flying camp with the spoil and captives of Syria. Instead of repelling the arms, Justinian attempted to seduce the fidelity of Almondar, while he called from the extremities of the earth the nations of Æthiopia and Scythia to invade the dominions of his rival. But the aid of such allies was distant and precarious, and the discovery of this hostile correspondence justified the complaints of the Goths and Armenians, who implored, almost at the same time, the protection of Chosroes. The descendants of Arsaces, who were still numerous in Armenia, had been provoked to assert the last relics of national freedom and hereditary rank; and the ambassadors of Vitiges had secretly traversed the empire to expose the instant, and almost inevitable, danger of the kingdom of Italy. Their representations were uniform, weighty, and effectual. "We stand before your throne, the advocates of your interest as well as of our own. The ambitious and faithless Justinian aspires to be the sole master of the world. Since the endless peace, which betrayed the common freedom of mankind, that prince, your ally in words, your enemy in actions, has alike insulted his friends and foes, and has filled the earth with blood and confusion. Has he not violated the privileges of Armenia, the independence of Colchis, and the wild liberty of the Tzanian mountains? Has he not usurped, with equal avidity, the city of Bosphorus on the frozen Mæotis, and the vale of palm-trees on the shores of the Red Sea? The Moors, the Vandals, the Goths, have been successively oppressed, and each nation has calmly remained the spectator of their neighbour's ruin. Embrace, O king! the favourable moment; the East is left without defence, while the armies of Justinian and his renowned general are detained in the distant regions of the West. If you hesitate and delay, Belisarius and his victorious troops will soon return from the Tiber to the Tigris, and Persia may enjoy the wretched consolation of being the last devoured."[61] By such arguments, Chosroes was easily persuaded to imitate the example which he condemned; but the Persian, ambitious of military fame, disdained the inactive warfare of a rival who issued his sanguinary commands from the secure station of the Byzantine palace.

Whatever might be the provocations of Chosroes, he abused the confidence of treaties; and the just reproaches of dissimulation and falsehood could only be concealed by the lustre of his victories.[62] The Persian army, which had been assembled in the plains of Babylon, prudently declined the strong cities of Mesopotamia, and followed the western bank of the Euphrates, till the small though populous town of Dura presumed to arrest the progress of the Great King. The gates of Dura, by treachery and surprise, were burst open; and as soon as Chosroes had stained his scimitar with the blood of the inhabitants, he dismissed the ambassador of Justinian to inform his master in what place he had left the enemy of the Romans. The conqueror still affected the praise of humanity and justice; and as he beheld a noble matron with her infant rudely dragged along the ground, he sighed, he wept, and implored the divine justice to punish the author of these calamities. Yet the herd of twelve thousand captives was ransomed for two hundred pounds of gold; the neighbouring bishop of Sergiopolis pledged his faith for the payment, and in the subsequent year the unfeeling avarice of Chosroes exacted the penalty of an obligation which it was generous to contract and impossible to discharge. He advanced into the heart of Syria; but a feeble enemy, who vanished at his approach, disappointed him of the honour of victory; and as he could not hope to establish his dominion, the Persian king displayed in this inroad the mean and rapacious vices of a robber. Hierapolis, Berrhœa or Aleppo, Apamea and Chalcis, were successively besieged: they redeemed their safety by a ransom of gold or silver proportioned to their respective strength and opulence, and their new master enforced without observing the terms of capitulation. Educated in the religion of the Magi, he exercised, without remorse, the lucrative trade of sacrilege; and, after stripping of its gold and gems a piece of the true cross, he generously restored the naked relic to the devotion of the Christians of Apamea. No more than fourteen years had elapsed since Antioch was ruined by an earthquake; but the queen of the East, the new Theopolis, had been raised from the ground by the liberality of Justinian; and the increasing greatness of the buildings and the people already erased the memory of this recent disaster. On one side the city was defended by the mountain, on the other by the river Orontes; but the most accessible part was commanded by a superior eminence: the proper remedies were rejected, from the despicable fear of discovering its weakness to the enemy; and Germanus, the emperor's nephew, refused to trust his person and dignity within the walls of a besieged city. The people of Antioch had inherited the vain

and satirical genius of their ancestors: they wer elated by a sudden reinforcement of six thou sand soldiers; they disdained the offers of a easy capitulation, and their intemperate clam ours insulted from the ramparts the majesty o the Great King. Under his eye the Persian myr iads mounted with scaling-ladders to the as sault; the Roman mercenaries fled through th opposite gate of Daphne; and the generous as sistance of the youth of Antioch served only t aggravate the miseries of their country. A Chosroes, attended by the ambassadors of Jus tinian, was descending from the mountain, h affected, in a plaintive voice, to deplore the ob stinacy and ruin of that unhappy people; bu the slaughter still raged with unrelenting fury and the city, at the command of a barbariar was delivered to the flames. The cathedral o Antioch was indeed preserved by the avarice not the piety, of the conqueror: a more honour able exemption was granted to the church o St. Julian and the quarter of the town where th ambassadors resided; some distant streets wer saved by the shifting of the wind, and the wal still subsisted to protect, and soon to betray their new inhabitants. Fanaticism had deface the ornaments of Daphne; but Chosroes breatl ed a purer air amidst her groves and fountain and some idolaters in his train might sacrific with impunity to the nymphs of that elegant re treat. Eighteen miles below Antioch the rive Orontes falls into the Mediterranean. Th haughty Persian visited the term of his cor quests, and, after bathing alone in the sea, h offered a solemn sacrifice of thanksgiving to th sun, or rather to the Creator of the sun, whor the Magi adored. If this act of superstition o fended the prejudices of the Syrians, they wer pleased by the courteous and even eager atter tion with which he assisted at the games of th circus; and as Chosroes had heard that the *blı* faction was espoused by the emperor, his pe emptory command secured the victory of th *green* charioteer. From the discipline of his can the people derived more solid consolation, an they interceded in vain for the life of a soldie who had too faithfully copied the rapine of th just Nushirvan. At length, fatigued though ur satiated with the spoil of Syria, he slowly move to the Euphrates, formed a temporary bridge i the neighbourhood of Barbalissus, and define the space of three days for the entire passage his numerous host. After his return he founde at the distance of one day's journey from th palace of Ctesiphon, a new city, which perpe uated the joint names of Chosroes and of Ar tioch. The Syrian captives recognised the form and situation of their native abodes; baths and a stately circus were constructed for their use; and a colony of musicians and charioteers revived in Assyria the pleasures of a Greek capital. By the munificence of the royal founder, a liberal allowance was assigned to these fortunate exiles, and they enjoyed the singular privilege of bestowing freedom on the slaves whom they acknowledged as their kinsmen. Palestine and the holy wealth of Jerusalem were the next objects that attracted the ambition, or rather the avarice, of Chosroes. Constantinople and the palace of the Cæsars no longer appeared impregnable or remote; and his aspiring fancy already covered Asia Minor with the troops, and the Black Sea with the navies, of Persia.

These hopes might have been realised, if the conqueror of Italy had not been seasonably recalled to the defence of the East.[63] While Chosroes pursued his ambitious designs on the coast of the Euxine, Belisarius, at the head of an army without pay or discipline, encamped beyond the Euphrates, within six miles of Nisibis. He meditated, by a skilful operation, to draw the Persians from their impregnable citadel, and, improving his advantage in the field, either to intercept their retreat, or perhaps to enter the gates with the flying barbarians. He advanced one day's journey on the territories of Persia, reduced the fortress of Sisaurane, and sent the governor, with eight hundred chosen horsemen, to serve the emperor in his Italian wars. He detached Arethas and his Arabs, supported by twelve hundred Romans, to pass the Tigris, and to ravage the harvests of Assyria, a fruitful province, long exempt from the calamities of war. But the plans of Belisarius were disconcerted by the untractable spirit of Arethas, who neither returned to the camp, nor sent any intelligence of his motions. The Roman general was fixed in anxious expectation to the same spot; the time of action elapsed; the ardent sum of Mesopotamia inflamed with fevers the blood of his European soldiers; and the stationary troops and officers of Syria affected to tremble for the safety of their defenceless cities. Yet this diversion had already succeeded in forcing Chosroes to return with loss and precipitation; and if the skill of Belisarius had been seconded by discipline and valour, his success might have satisfied the sanguine wishes of the public, who required at his hands the conquest of Ctesiphon and the deliverance of the captives of Antioch. At the end of the campaign, he was recalled to Constantinople by an ungrateful court, but the dangers of the ensuing spring restored his confidence and command; and the hero, almost alone, was despatched, with the speed of post-horses, to repel, by his name and presence, the invasion of Syria. He found the Roman generals, among whom was a nephew of Justinian, imprisoned by their fears in the fortifications of Hierapolis. But instead of listening to their timid counsels, Belisarius commanded them to follow him to Europus, where he had resolved to collect his forces, and to execute whatever God should inspire him to achieve against the enemy. His firm attitude on the banks of the Euphrates restrained Chosroes from advancing towards Palestine; and he received with art and dignity the ambassadors, or rather spies, of the Persian monarch. The plain between Hierapolis and the river was covered with the squadrons of cavalry, six thousand hunters, tall and robust, who pursued their game without the apprehension of an enemy. On the opposite bank the ambassadors descried a thousand Armenian horse, who appeared to guard the passage of the Euphrates. The tent of Belisarius was of the coarsest linen, the simple equipage of a warrior who disdained the luxury of the East. Around his tent the nations who marched under his standard were arranged with skilful confusion. The Thracians and Illyrians were posted in the front, the Heruli and Goths in the centre; the prospect was closed by the Moors and Vandals, and their loose array seemed to multiply their numbers. Their dress was light and active; one soldier carried a whip, another a sword, a third a bow, a fourth, perhaps, a battle-axe, and the whole picture exhibited the intrepidity of the troops and the vigilance of the general. Chosroes was deluded by the address, and awed by the genius, of the lieutenant of Justinian. Conscious of the merit, and ignorant of the force, of his antagonist, he dreaded a decisive battle in a distant country, from whence not a Persian might return to relate the melancholy tale. The Great King hastened to repass the Euphrates; and Belisarius pressed his retreat, by affecting to oppose a measure so salutary to the empire, and which could scarcely have been prevented by an army of a hundred thousand men. Envy might suggest to ignorance and pride that the public enemy had been suffered to escape; but the African and Gothic triumphs are less glorious than this safe and bloodless victory, in which neither fortune, nor the valour of the soldiers, can subtract any part of the general's renown. The second removal of Belisarius from the Persian to the Italian war revealed the extent of his personal merit, which had corrected or supplied the want of discipline and courage. Fifteen generals, without concert or skill, led through the mountains of Armenia an army of thirty thousand Romans, inattentive to their signals, their ranks, and their ensigns. Four thousand Persians, entrenched in the camp of Dubis, vanquished, almost without a combat, this disorderly multitude; their useless arms were scattered along the road, and their horses sunk under the fatigue of their rapid flight. But the Arabs of the Roman party prevailed over their brethren; the Armenians returned to their allegiance; the cities of Dara and Edessa resisted a sudden assault and a regular siege, and the calamities of war were suspended by those of pestilence. A tacit or formal agreement between the two sovereigns protected the tranquillity of the Eastern frontier; and the arms of Chosroes were confined to the Colchian or Lazic war, which has been too minutely described by the historians of the times.[64]

The extreme length of the Euxine Sea,[65] from Constantinople to the mouth of the Phasis, may be computed as a voyage of nine days, and a measure of seven hundred miles. From the Iberian Caucasus, the most lofty and craggy mountains of Asia, that river descends with such oblique vehemence, that in a short space it is traversed by one hundred and twenty bridges. Nor does the stream become placid and navigable till it reaches the town of Sarapana, five days' journey from the Cyrus, which flows from the same hills, but in a contrary direction to the Caspian lake. The proximity of these rivers has suggested the practice, or at least the idea, of wafting the precious merchandise of India down the Oxus, over the Caspian, up the Cyrus, and with the current of the Phasis into the Euxine and Mediterranean seas. As it successively collects the streams of the plain of Colchis, the Phasis moves with diminished speed, though accumulated weight. At the mouth it is sixty fathoms deep and half a league broad, but a small woody island is interposed in the midst of the channel: the water, so soon as it has deposited an earthy or metallic sediment, floats on the surface of the waves, and is no longer susceptible of corruption. In a course of one hundred miles, forty of which are navigable for large vessels, the Phasis divides the celebrated region of Colchis,[66] or Mingrelia,[67] which, on three sides, is fortified by the Iberian and Armenian mountains, and whose maritime coast extends about two hundred miles from the neighbourhood of Trebizond to Dioscurias and the confines of Circassia. Both the soil and climate are relaxed by excessive moisture: twenty-eight rivers, besides the Phasis and his dependent streams, convey their waters to the sea; and the hollowness of the ground appears to indicate the subterraneous channels between the Euxine and the Caspian. In the fields where wheat or barley is sown, the earth is too soft to sustain the action of the plough; but the *gom*, a small grain, not unlike the millet or coriander seed, supplies the ordinary food of the people; and the use of bread is confined to the prince and his nobles. Yet the vintage is more plentiful than the harvest; and the bulk of the stems, as well as the quality of the wine, display the unassisted powers of nature. The same powers continually tend to overshadow the face of the country with thick forests: the timber of the hills, and the flax of the plains, contribute to the abundance of naval stores; the wild and tame animals, the horse, the ox, and the hog are remarkably prolific, and the name of the pheasant is expressive of his native habitation on the banks of the Phasis. The gold-mines to the south of Trebizond, which are still worked with sufficient profit, were a subject of national dispute between Justinian and Chosroes; and it is not unreasonable to believe that a vein of precious metal may be equally diffused through the circle of the hills, although these secret treasures are neglected by the laziness, or concealed by the prudence, of the Mingrelians. The waters, impregnated with particles of gold, are carefully strained through sheepskins or fleeces; but this expedient, the groundwork perhaps of a marvellous fable, affords a faint image of the wealth extracted from a virgin earth by the power and industry of ancient kings. Their silver palaces and golden chambers surpass our belief; but the fame of their riches is said to have excited the enterprising avarice of the Argonauts.[68] Tradition has affirmed, with some colour of reason, that Egypt planted on the Phasis a learned and polite colony,[69] which manufactured linen, built navies, and invented geographical maps. The ingenuity of the moderns has peopled with flourishing cities and nations the isthmus between the Euxine and the Caspian;[70] and a lively writer, observing the resemblance of climate, and, in his apprehension, of trade, has not hesitated to pronounce Colchis the Holland of antiquity.[71]

But the riches of Colchis shine only through the darkness of conjecture or tradition; and its genuine history presents a uniform scene of rudeness and poverty. If one hundred and thiry languages were spoken in the market of Dios-urias,[72] they were the imperfect idioms of so many savage tribes or families, sequestered from each other in the valleys of Mount Caucasus; and their separation, which diminished the importance, must have multiplied the number of their rustic capitals. In the present state of Mingrelia, a village is an assemblage of huts within a wooden fence; the fortresses are seated in the depth of forests; the princely town of Cyta, or Cotatis, consists of two hundred houses, and a stone edifice appertains only to the magnificence of kings. Twelve ships from Constantinople, and about sixty barks, laden with the fruits of industry, annually cast anchor on the coast; and the list of Colchian exports is much increased, since the natives had only slaves and hides to offer in exchange for the corn and salt which they purchased from the subjects of Justinian. Not a vestige can be found of the art, the knowledge, or the navigation of the ancient Colchians: few Greeks desired or dared to pursue the footsteps of the Argonauts; and even the marks of an Egyptian colony are lost on a nearer approach. The rite of circumcision is practised only by the Mahometans of the Euxine; and the curled hair and swarthy complexion of Africa no longer disfigure the most perfect of the human race. It is in the adjacent climates of Georgia, Mingrelia, and Circassia, that nature has placed, at least to our eyes, the model of beauty, in the shape of the limbs, the colour of the skin, the symmetry of the features, and the expression of the countenance.[73] According to the destination of the two sexes, the men seem formed for action, the women for love; and the perpetual supply of females from Mount Caucasus has purified the blood, and improved the breed, of the southern nations of Asia. The proper district of Mingrelia, a portion only of the ancient Colchis, has long sustained an exportation of twelve thousand slaves. The number of prisoners or criminals would be inadequate to the annual demand; but the common people are in a state of servitude to their lords; the exercise of fraud or rapine is unpunished in a lawless community; and the market is continually replenished by the abuse of civil and paternal authority. Such a trade,[74] which reduces the human species to the level of cattle, may tend to encourage marriage and population, since the multitude of children enriches their sordid and inhuman parent. But this source of impure wealth must inevitably poison the national manners, obliterate the sense of honour and virtue, and almost extinguish the instincts of nature:

the *Christians* of Georgia and Mingrelia are the most dissolute of mankind; and their children, who, in a tender age, are sold into foreign slavery, have already learned to imitate the rapine of the father and the prostitution of the mother. Yet, amidst the rudest ignorance, the untaught natives discover a singular dexterity both of mind and hand; and although the want of union and discipline exposes them to their more powerful neighbours, a bold and intrepid spirit has animated the Colchians of every age. In the host of Xerxes they served on foot; and their arms were a dagger or a javelin, a wooden casque, and a buckler of raw hides. But in their own country the use of cavalry has more generally prevailed: the meanest of the peasants disdain to walk; the martial nobles are possessed, perhaps, of two hundred horses; and above five thousand are numbered in the train of the prince of Mingrelia. The Colchian government has been always a pure and hereditary kingdom and the authority of the sovereign is only restrained by the turbulence of his subjects. Whenever they were obedient, he could lead a numerous army into the field; but some faith is requisite to believe that the single tribe of the Suanians was composed of two hundred thousand soldiers, or that the population of Mingrelia now amounts to four millions of inhabitants.[75]

It was the boast of the Colchians that their ancestors had checked the victories of Sesostris; and the defeat of the Egyptian is less incredible than his successful progress as far as the foot of Mount Caucasus. They sunk without any memorable effort under the arms of Cyrus, followed in distant wars the standard of the Great King, and presented him every fifth year with one hundred boys and as many virgins, the fairest produce of the land.[76] Yet he accepted this *gift* like the gold and ebony of India, the frankincense of the Arabs, or the negroes and ivory of Æthiopia: the Colchians were not subject to the dominion of a satrap, and they continued to enjoy the name as well as substance of national independence.[77] After the fall of the Persian empire, Mithridates, king of Pontus, added Colchis to the wide circle of his dominions on the Euxine; and when the natives presumed to request that his son might reign over them, he bound the ambitious youth in chains of gold, and delegated a servant in his place. In pursuit of Mithridates, the Romans advanced to the banks of the Phasis, and their galleys ascended the river till they reached the camp of Pompey and his legions.[78] But the senate, and afterwards the emperors, disdained to reduce that distant and useless conquest into the form of a province. The family of a Greek rhetorician was permitted to reign in Colchis and the adjacent kingdoms from the time of Mark Antony to that of Nero; and after the race of Polemo[79] was extinct, the eastern Pontus, which preserved his name, extended no farther than the neighbourhood of Trebizond. Beyond these limits the fortifications of Hyssus, of Apsarus, of the Phasis, of Dioscurias or Sebastopolis, and of Pityus, were guarded by sufficient detachments of horse and foot; and six princes of Colchis received their diadems from the lieutenants of Cæsar. One of these lieutenants, the eloquent and philosophic Arrian, surveyed and has described the Euxine coast under the reign of Hadrian. The garrison which he reviewed at the mouth of the Phasis consisted of four hundred chosen legionaries; the brick walls and towers, the double ditch, and the military engines on the rampart, rendered this place inaccessible to the barbarians; but the new suburbs which had been built by the merchants and veterans required in the opinion of Arrian some external defence.[80] As the strength of the empire was gradually impaired, the Romans stationed on the Phasis were either withdrawn or expelled; and the tribe of the Lazi,[81] whose posterity speak a foreign dialect and inhabit the sea-coast of Trezibond, imposed their name and dominion on the ancient kingdom of Colchis. Their independence was soon invaded by a formidable neighbour, who had acquired by arms and treaties the sovereignty of Iberia. The dependent king of Lazica received his sceptre at the hands of the Persian monarch, and the successors of Constantine acquiesced in this injurious claim, which was proudly urged as a right of immemorial prescription. In the beginning of the sixth century their influence was restored by the introduction of Christianity, which the Mingrelians still profess with becoming zeal, without understanding the doctrines or observing the precepts of their religion. After the decease of his father, Zathus was exalted to the regal dignity by the favour of the Great King; but the pious youth abhorred the ceremonies of the Magi, and sought in the palace of Constantinople an orthodox baptism, a noble wife, and the alliance of the emperor Justin. The king of Lazica was solemnly invested with the diadem, and his cloak and tunic of white silk, with a gold border, displayed in rich embroidery the figure of his new patron, who soothed the jealousy of the Persian court, and excused the revolt of Colchis, by the venerable names of hospitality and religion. The common interest of both empires imposed on the Colchians the duty of guarding the passes of Mount Caucasus, where a wall of sixty miles is now defended by the monthly service of the musketeers of Mingrelia.[82]

But this honourable connection was soon corrupted by the avarice and ambition of the Romans. Degraded from the rank of allies, the Lazi were incessantly reminded by words and actions of their dependent state. At the distance of a day's journey beyond the Apsarus they beheld the rising fortress of Petra,[83] which commanded the maritime country to the south of the Phasis. Instead of being protected by the valour, Colchis was insulted by the licentiousness of foreign mercenaries: the benefits of commerce were converted into base and vexatious monopoly; and Gubazes, the native prince, was reduced to a pageant of royalty by the superior influence of the officers of Justinian. Disappointed in their expectations of Christian virtue, the indignant Lazi reposed some confidence in the justice of an unbeliever. After a private assurance that their ambassadors should not be delivered to the Romans, they publicly solicited the friendship and aid of Chosroes. The sagacious monarch instantly discerned the use and importance of Colchis, and meditated a plan of conquest which was renewed at the end of a thousand years by Shah Abbas, the wisest and most powerful of his successors.[84] His ambition was fired by the hope of launching a Persian navy from the Phasis, of commanding the trade and navigation of the Euxine Sea, of desolating the coast of Pontus and Bithynia, of distressing, perhaps of attacking, Constantinople, and of persuading the barbarians of Europe to second his arms and counsels against the common enemy of mankind. Under the pretence of a Scythian war he silently led his troops to the frontiers of Iberia; the Colchian guides were prepared to conduct them through the woods and along the precipices of Mount Caucasus, and a narrow path was laboriously formed into a safe and spacious highway for the march of cavalry, and even of elephants. Gubazes laid his person and diadem at the feet of the king of Persia, his Colchians imitated the submission of their prince; and after the walls of Petra had been shaken, the Roman garrison prevented by a capitulation the impending fury of the last assault. But the Lazi soon discovered that their impatience had urged them to choose an evil more intolerable than the calamities which they strove to escape. The monopoly of salt and corn was effectually removed by the loss of those valuable commodities. The authority of a Roman legislator was succeeded by the pride of an Oriental despot, who beheld with equal disdain the slaves whom he had exalted, and the kings whom he had humbled before the footstool of his throne. The adoration of fire was introduced into Colchis by the zeal of the Magi, their intolerant spirit provoked the fervour of a Christian people, and the prejudice of nature or education was wounded by the impious practice of exposing the dead bodies of their parents on the summit of a lofty tower to the crows and vultures of the air.[85] Conscious of the increasing hatred which retarded the execution of his great designs, the just Nushirvan had secretly given orders to assassinate the king of the Lazi, to transplant the people into some distant land, and to fix a faithful and warlike colony on the banks of the Phasis. The watchful jealousy of the Colchians foresaw and averted the approaching ruin. Their repentance was accepted at Constantinople by the prudence, rather than the clemency, of Justinian; and he commanded Dagisteus, with seven thousand Romans and one thousand of the Zani, to expel the Persians from the coast of the Euxine.

The siege of Petra, which the Roman general with the aid of the Lazi immediately undertook, is one of the most remarkable actions of the age. The city was seated on a craggy rock, which hung over the sea, and communicated by a steep and narrow path with the land. Since the approach was difficult, the attack might be deemed impossible; the Persian conqueror had strengthened the fortifications of Justinian, and the places least inaccessible were covered by additional bulwarks. In this important fortress the vigilance of Chosroes had deposited a magazine of offensive and defensive arms sufficient for five times the number, not only of the garrison, but of the besiegers themselves. The stock of flour and salt provisions was adequate to the consumption of five years; the want of wine was supplied by vinegar, and a grain from whence a strong liquor was extracted; and a triple aqueduct eluded the diligence and even the suspicions of the enemy. But the firmest defence of Petra was placed in the valour of fifteen hundred Persians, who resisted the assaults of the Romans, whilst in a softer vein of earth a mine was secretly perforated. The Wall, supported by slender and temporary props, hung tottering in the air; but Dagisteus delayed the attack till he had secured a specific recompense, and the town was relieved before the return of his mes-

senger from Constantinople. The Persian garrison was reduced to four hundred men, of whom no more than fifty were exempt from sickness or wounds; yet such had been their inflexible perseverance, that they concealed their losses from the enemy by enduring without a murmur the sight and putrefying stench of the dead bodies of their eleven hundred companions. After their deliverance the breaches were hastily stopped with sandbags, the mine was replenished with earth, a new wall was erected on a frame of substantial timber, and a fresh garrison of three thousand men was stationed at Petra to sustain the labours of a second siege. The operations, both of the attack and defence, were conducted with skilful obstinacy; and each party derived useful lessons from the experience of their past faults. A battering-ram was invented, of light construction and powerful effect; it was transported and worked by the hands of forty soldiers; and as the stones were loosened by its repeated strokes, they were torn with long iron hooks from the wall. From those walls a shower of darts was incessantly poured on the heads of the assailants, but they were most dangerously annoyed by a fiery composition of sulphur and bitumen, which in Colchis might with some propriety be named the oil of Medea. Of six thousand Romans who mounted the scaling-ladders, their general Besas was first, a gallant veteran of seventy years of age: the courage of their leader, his fall, and extreme danger, animated the irresistible effort of his troops, and their prevailing numbers oppressed the strength, without subduing the spirit, of the Persian garrison. The fate of these valiant men deserves to be more distinctly noticed. Seven hundred had perished in the siege, two thousand three hundred survived to defend the breach. One thousand and seventy were destroyed with fire and sword in the last assault; and if seven hundred and thirty were made prisoners, only eighteen among them were found without the marks of honourable wounds. The remaining five hundred escaped into the citadel, which they maintained without any hopes of relief, rejecting the fairest terms of capitulation and service till they were lost in the flames. They died in obedience to the commands of their prince, and such examples of loyalty and valour might excite their countrymen to deeds of equal despair and more prosperous event. The instant demolition of the works of Petra confessed the astonishment and apprehension of the conqueror.

A Spartan would have praised and pitied the virtue of these heroic slaves; but the tedious warfare and alternate success of the Roman and Persian arms cannot detain the attention of posterity at the foot of Mount Caucasus. The advantages obtained by the troops of Justinian were more frequent and splendid; but the forces of the Great King were continually supplied till they amounted to eight elephants and seventy thousand men, including twelve thousand Scythian allies and above three thousand Dilemites, who descended by their free choice from the hills of Hyrcania, and were equally formidable in close or distant combat. The siege of Archæopolis, a name imposed or corrupted by the Greeks, was raised with some loss and precipitation, but the Persians occupied the passes of Iberia. Colchis was enslaved by their forts and garrisons, they devoured the scanty sustenance of the people, and the prince of the Lazi fled into the mountains. In the Roman camp faith and discipline were unknown, and the independent leaders, who were invested with equal power, disputed with each other the preeminence of vice and corruption. The Persians followed without a murmur the commands of a single chief, who implicitly obeyed the instructions of their supreme lord. Their general was distinguished among the heroes of the East by his wisdom in council and his valour in the field. The advanced age of Mermeroes, and the lameness of both his feet, could not diminish the activity of his mind or even of his body; and, whilst he was carried in a litter in the front of battle, he inspired terror to the enemy, and a just confidence to the troops, who under his banners were always successful. After his death the command devolved to Nacoragan, a proud satrap who, in a conference with the Imperial chiefs, had presumed to declare that he disposed of victory as absolutely as of the ring on his finger. Such presumption was the natural cause and forerunner of a shameful defeat. The Romans had been gradually repulsed to the edge of the sea-shore; and their last camp, on the ruins of the Grecian colony of Phasis, was defended on all sides by strong entrenchments, the river, and Euxine, and a fleet of galleys. Despair united their counsels and invigorated their arms; they withstood the assault of the Persians, and the flight of Nacoragan preceded or followed the slaughter of ten thousand of his bravest soldiers. He escaped from the Romans to fall into the hands of an unforgiving master, who severely chastised the error of his own choice: the unfortunate general was flayed alive, and his skin, stuffed into the human form, was exposed on a mountain—a dreadful warning to those who might hereafter be intrusted with the fame and fortune of Persia.[86] Yet the prudence of Chosroes insensibly relinquished the prosecution of the Colchian war, in the just persuasion that it is impossible to reduce, or at least to hold, a distant country against the wishes and efforts of its inhabitants. The fidelity of Gubazes sustained the most rigorous trials. He patiently endured the hardships of a savage life, and rejected with disdain the specious temptations of the Persian court. The king of the Lazi had been educated in the Christian religion; his mother was the daughter of a senator; during his youth he had served ten years a silentiary of the Byzantine palace,[87] and the arrears of an unpaid salary were a motive of attachment as well as of complaint. But the long continuance of his sufferings extorted from him a naked representation of the truth, and truth was an unpardonable libel on the lieutenants of Justinian, who, amidst the delays of a ruinous war, had spared his enemies and trampled on his allies. Their malicious information persuaded the emperor that his faithless vassal already meditated a second defection: an order was surprised to send him prisoner to Constantinople; a treacherous clause was inserted that he might be lawfully killed in case of resistance; and Gubazes, without arms or suspicion of danger, was stabbed in the security of a friendly interview. In the first moments of rage and despair, the Colchians would have sacrificed their country and religion to the gratification of revenge. But the authority and eloquence of the wiser few obtained a salutary pause: the victory of the Phasis restored the terror of the Roman arms, and the emperor was solicitous to absolve his own name from the imputation of so foul a murder. A judge of senatorial rank was commissioned to inquire into the conduct and death of the king of the Lazi. He ascended a stately tribunal, encompassed by the ministers of justice and punishment: in the presence of both nations this extraordinary cause was pleaded according to the forms of civil jurisprudence, and some satisfaction was granted to an injured people by the sentence and execution of the meaner criminals.[88]

In peace the king of Persia continually sought the pretences of a rupture, but no sooner had he taken up arms than he expressed his desire of a safe and honourable treaty. During the fiercest hostilities the two monarchs entertained a deceitful negotiation: and such was the superiority of Chosroes, that, whilst he treated the Roman ministers with insolence and contempt, he obtained the most unprecedented honours for his own ambassadors at the Imperial court. The successor of Cyrus assumed the majesty of the Eastern sun, and graciously permitted his younger brother Justinian to reign over the West with the pale and reflected splendour of the moon. This gigantic style was supported by the pomp and eloquence of Isdigune, one of the royal chamberlains. His wife and daughters, with a train of eunuchs and camels, attended the march of the ambassador; two satraps with golden diadems were numbered among his followers; he was guarded by five hundred horse, the most valiant of the Persians, and the Roman governor of Dara wisely refused to admit more than twenty of this martial and hostile caravan. When Isdigune had saluted the emperor and delivered his presents, he passed ten months at Constantinople without discussing any serious affairs. Instead of being confined in his palace, and receiving food and water from the hands of his keepers, the Persian ambassador, without spies or guards, was allowed to visit the capital, and the freedom of conversation and trade enjoyed by his domestics offended the prejudices of an age which rigorously practised the law of nations without confidence or courtesy.[89] By an unexampled indulgence, his interpreter, a servant below the notice of a Roman magistrate, was seated at the table of Justinian by the side of his master, and one thousand pounds of gold might be assigned for the expense of his journey and entertainment. Yet the repeated labours of Isdigune could procure only a partial and imperfect truce, which was always purchased with the treasures, and renewed at the solicitation, of the Byzantine court. Many years of fruitless desolation elapsed before Justinian and Chosroes were compelled by mutual lassitude to consult the repose of their declining age. At a conference held on the frontier, each party, without expecting to gain credit, displayed the power, the justice, and the pacific intentions of their respective sovereigns; but necessity and interest dictated the treaty of peace, which was concluded for a term of fifty years, diligently composed in the Greek and Persian languages, and attested by the seals of twelve interpreters. The liberty of commerce and religion was fixed and defined, the allies of the emperor and the Great King were included in the same benefits and obligations, and the most scrupulous precautions were provided to prevent or determine the accidental disputes that might arise on the confines of two hostile nations. After twenty years of destructive though feeble war, the limits still remained without alteration, and Chosroes was persuaded to renounce his dangerous claim to the possession or sovereignty of Colchis and its dependent states. Rich in the accumulated treasures of the East, he extorted from the Romans an annual payment of thirty thousand pieces of gold; and the smallness of the sum revealed the disgrace of a tribute in its naked deformity. In a previous debate, the chariot of Sesostris and the wheel of fortune were applied by one of the Ministers of Justinian, who observed that the reduction of Antioch and some Syrian cities had elevated beyond measure the vain and ambitious spirit of the barbarian. "You are mistaken," replied the modest Persian; "the king of kings, the lord of mankind, looks down with contempt on such petty acquisitions; and of the ten nations vanquished by his invincible arms, he esteems the Romans as the least formidable."[90] According to the Orientals, the empire of Nushirvan extended from Ferganah, in Transoxiana, to Yemen, or Arabia Felix. He subdued the rebels of Hyrcania, reduced the provinces of Cabul and Zablestan on the banks of the Indus, broke the power of the Euthalites, terminated by an honourable treaty the Turkish war, and admitted the daughter of the great khan into the number of his lawful wives. Victorious and respected among the princes of Asia, he gave audience, in his palace of Madain or Ctesiphon, to the ambassadors of the world. Their gifts or tributes, arms, rich garments, gems, slaves, or aromatics, were humbly presented at the foot of his throne; and he condescended to accept from the king of India ten quintals of the wood of aloes, a maid seven cubits in height, and a carpet softer than silk, the skin, as it was reported, of an extraordinary serpent.[91]

Justinian had been reproached for his alliance with the Æthiopians, as if he attempted to introduce a people of savage negroes into the system of civilised society. But the friends of the Roman empire, the Axumites or Abyssinians, may be always distinguished from the original natives of Africa.[92] The hand of nature has flattened the noses of the negroes, covered their heads with shaggy wool, and tinged their skin with inherent and indelible blackness. But the olive complexion of the Abyssinians, their hair, shape, and features, distinctly mark them as a colony of Arabs, and this descent is confirmed by the resemblance of language and manners, the report of an ancient emigration, and the narrow interval between the shores of the Red Sea. Christianity had raised that nation above the level of African barbarism;[93] their intercourse with Egypt and the successors of Constantine[94] had communicated the rudiments of the arts and sciences; their vessels traded to the isle of Ceylon,[95] and seven kingdoms obeyed the Negus or supreme prince of Abyssinia. The independence of the Homerites, who reigned in the rich and happy Arabia, was first violated by an Æthiopian conqueror: he drew his hereditary claim from the Queen of Sheba,[96] and his ambition was sanctified by religious zeal. The Jews, powerful and active in exile, had seduced the mind of Dunaan, prince of the Homerites. They urged him to retaliate the persecution inflicted by the Imperial laws on their unfortunate brethren; some Roman merchants were injuriously treated, and several Christians of Negra[97] were honoured with the crown of martyrdom.[98] The churches of Arabia implored the protection of the Abyssinian monarch. The Negus passed the Red Sea with a fleet and army, deprived the Jewish proselyte of his kingdom and life, and extinguished a race of princes who had ruled above two thousand years the sequestered region of myrrh and frankincense. The conqueror immediately announced the victory of the Gospel, requested an orthodox patriarch, and so warmly professed his friendship to the Roman empire, that Justinian was flattered by the hope of diverting the silk trade through the channel of Abyssinia, and of exciting the forces of Arabia against the Persian king. Nonnosus, descended from a family of ambassadors, was named by the emperor to execute this important commission. He wisely declined the shorter but more dangerous road through the sandy deserts of Nubia, ascended the Nile, embarked on the Red Sea, and safely landed at the African port of Adulis. From Adulis to the royal city of Axume is no more than fifty leagues in a direct line, but the winding passes of the mountains detained the ambassador fifteen days, and as he traversed the forests he saw, and vaguely computed, about five thousand wild elephants. The capital, according to his report, was large and populous; and the *village* of Axume is still conspicuous by the regal coronations, by the ruins of a Christian temple, and by sixteen or seventeen obelisks inscribed with Grecian characters.[99] But the Negus gave audience in the open field, seated on a lofty chariot, which was drawn by four elephants superbly caparisoned, and surrounded by his nobles and musicians. He was clad in a linen garment and cap, holding in his hand two javelins and a light shield; and, although his nakedness was imperfectly covered, he displayed the barbaric pomp of gold chains, collars, and bracelets, richly adorned with pearls and precious stones. The ambassador of Justinian knelt: the Negus raised him from the ground, embraced Nonnosus, kissed the seal, perused the letter, accepted the Roman alliance, and, brandishing his weapons, denounced implacable war against the worshippers of fire. But the proposal of the silk-trade was eluded; and notwithstanding the assurances, and perhaps the wishes, of the Abyssinians, these hostile menaces evaporated without effect. The Homerites were unwilling to abandon their aromatic groves, to explore a sandy desert, and to encounter, after all their fatigues, a formidable nation from whom they had never received any personal injuries. Instead of enlarging his conquests, the king of Æthiopia was incapable of defending his possessions. Abrahah, the slave of a Roman merchant of Adulis, assumed the sceptre of the Homerites; the troops of Africa were seduced by the luxury of the climate; and Justinian solicited the friendship of the usurper, who honoured with a slight tribute the supremacy of his prince. After a long series of prosperity the power of Abrahah was overthrown before the gates of Mecca, his children were despoiled by the Persian conqueror, and the Æthiopians were finally expelled from the continent of Asia. This narrative of obscure and remote events is not foreign to the decline and fall of the Roman empire. If a Christian power had been maintained in Arabia, Mahomet must have been crushed in his cradle, and Abyssinia would have prevented a revolution which has changed the civil and religious state of the world.[100]

CHAPTER XLIII

Rebellions of Africa. Restoration of the Gothic Kingdom by Totila. Loss and Recovery of Rome. Final Conquest of Italy by Narses. Extinction of the Ostrogoths. Defeat of the Franks and Alemanni. Last Victory, Disgrace, and Death of Belisarius. Death and Character of Justinian. Comet, Earthquakes, and Plague.

THE review of the nations from the Danube to the Nile has exposed, on every side, the weakness of the Romans; and our wonder is reasonably excited that they should presume to enlarge an empire whose ancient limits they were incapable of defending. But the wars, the conquests, and the triumphs of Justinian, are the feeble and pernicious efforts of old age, which exhaust the remains of strength and accelerate the decay of the powers of life. He exulted in the glorious act of restoring Africa and Italy to the republic; but the calamities which followed the departure of Belisarius betrayed the impotence of the conqueror, and accomplished the ruin of those unfortunate countries.

From his new acquisitions Justinian expected that his avarice, as well as his pride, should be richly gratified. A rapacious minister of the finances closely pursued the footsteps of Belisarius; and, as the old registers of tribute had been burnt by the Vandals, he indulged his fancy in a liberal calculation and arbitrary assessment of the wealth of Africa.[1] The increase of taxes, which were drawn away by a distant sovereign, and a general resumption of the patrimony of crown lands, soon dispelled the intoxication of the public joy: but the emperor was insensible to the modest complaints of the people till he was awakened and alarmed by the clamours of military discontent. Many of the Roman soldiers had married the widows and daughters of the Vandals. As their own, by the double right of conquest and inheritance, they claimed the estates which Genseric had assigned to his victorious troops. They heard with disdain the cold and selfish representations of their officers, that the liberality of Justinian had raised them from a savage or servile condition; that they were already enriched by the spoils of Africa, the treasure, the slaves, and the movables of the vanquished barbarians; and that the ancient and lawful patrimony of the emperors would be applied only to the support of that government on which their own safety

and reward must ultimately depend. The mutiny was secretly inflamed by a thousand soldiers, for the most part Heruli, who had imbibed the doctrines, and were instigated by the clergy, of the Arian sect; and the cause of perjury and rebellion was sanctified by the dispensing powers of fanaticism. The Arians deplored the ruin of their church, triumphant above a century in Africa; and they were justly provoked by the laws of the conqueror which interdicted the baptism of their children and the exercise of all religious worship. Of the Vandals chosen by Belisarius, the far greater part, in the honours of the Eastern service, forgot their country and religion. But a generous band of four hundred obliged the mariners when they were in sight of the isle of Lesbos, to alter their course: they touched on Peloponnesus, ran ashore on a desert coast of Africa, and boldly erected on Mount Aurasius the standard of independence and revolt. While the troops of the province disclaimed the commands of their superiors, a conspiracy was formed at Carthage against the life of Solomon, who filled with honour the place of Belisarius; and the Arians had piously resolved to sacrifice the tyrant at the foot of the altar during the awful mysteries of the festival of Easter. Fear or remorse restrained the daggers of the assassins, but the patience of Solomon emboldened their discontent, and at the end of ten days a furious sedition was kindled in the circus, which desolated Africa above ten years. The pillage of the city, and the indiscriminate slaughter of its inhabitants, were suspended only by darkness, sleep, and intoxication. The governor, with seven companions, among whom was the historian Procopius, escaped to Sicily. Two-thirds of the army were involved in the guilt of treason; and eight thousand insurgents, assembling in the field of Bulla, elected Stoza for their chief, a private soldier, who possessed in a superior degree the virtues of a rebel. Under the mask of freedom, his eloquence could lead, or at least impel, the passions of his equals. He raised himself to a level with Belisarius and the nephew of the emperor, by daring to encounter them in the field; and the victorious generals were compelled to acknowledge that Stoza deserved a purer cause and a more legitimate command. Vanquished in battle, he dexterously employed the arts of negotiation; a Roman army was seduced from their allegiance, and the chiefs who had trusted to his faithless promise were murdered by his order in a church of Numidia. When every resource, either of force or perfidy, was exhausted, Stoza, with some desperate Vandals, retired to the wilds of Mauritania, obtained the daughter of a barbarian prince, and eluded the pursuit of his enemies by the report of his death. The personal weight of Belisarius, the rank, the spirit, and the temper of Germanus, the emperor's nephew, and the vigour and success of the second administration of the eunuch Solomon, restored the modesty of the camp, and maintained for a while the tranquillity of Africa. But the vices of the Byzantine court were felt in that distant province; the troops complained that they were neither paid nor relieved; and as soon as the public disorders were sufficiently mature, Stoza was again alive, in arms, and at the gates of Carthage. He fell in a single combat, but he smiled in the agonies of death when he was informed that his own javelin had reached the heart of his antagonist. The example of Stoza, and the assurance that a fortunate soldier had been the first king, encouraged the ambition of Gontharis, and he promised, by a private treaty, to divide Africa with the Moors, if, with their dangerous aid, he should ascend the throne of Carthage. The feeble Areobindus, unskilled in the affairs of peace and war, was raised by his marriage with the niece of Justinian to the office of exarch. He was suddenly oppressed by a sedition of the guards, and his abject supplications, which provoked the contempt, could not move the pity, of the inexorable tyrant. After a reign of thirty days, Gontharis himself was stabbed at a banquet by the hand of Artaban; and it is singular enough that an Armenian prince of the royal family of Arsaces should re-establish at Carthage the authority of the Roman empire. In the conspiracy which unsheathed the dagger of Brutus against the life of Cæsar, every circumstance is curious and important to the eyes of posterity; but the guilt or merit of these loyal or rebellious assassins could interest only the contemporaries of Procopius, who, by their hopes and fears, their friendship or resentment, were personally engaged in the revolutions of Africa.[2]

That country was rapidly sinking into th state of barbarism from whence it had bee raised by the Phœnician colonies and Roma laws; and every step of intestine discord wa marked by some deplorable victory of savag man over civilised society. The Moors,[3] thoug ignorant of justice, were impatient of oppres sion: their vagrant life and boundless wilder ness disappointed the arms and eluded th chains of a conqueror; and experience ha shown that neither oaths nor obligations coul secure the fidelity of their attachment. Th victory of Mount Auras had awed them int momentary submission; but if they respecte the character of Solomon, they hated and de spised the pride and luxury of his two nephews Cyrus and Sergius, on whom their uncle ha imprudently bestowed the provincial govern ments of Tripoli and Pentapolis. A Mooris tribe encamped under the walls of Leptis, t renew their alliance and receive from the gov ernor the customary gifts. Fourscore of thei deputies were introduced as friends into th city; but, on the dark suspicion of a conspiracy they were massacred at the table of Sergius, an the clamour of arms and revenge was re-echoe through the valleys of Mount Atlas from bot the Syrtes to the Atlantic Ocean. A persona injury, the unjust execution or murder of hi brother, rendered Antalas the enemy of the Ro mans. The defeat of the Vandals had formerl signalised his valour; the rudiments of justic and prudence were still more conspicuous in a Moor; and, while he laid Adrumetum in ashes he calmly admonished the emperor that the peace of Africa might be secured by the recal of Solomon and his unworthy nephews. The exarch led forth his troops from Carthage; but at the distance of six days' journey, in the neigh bourhood of Tebeste,[4] he was astonished by the superior numbers and fierce aspect of the bar barians. He proposed a treaty, solicited a recon ciliation, and offered to bind himself by the most solemn oaths. "By what oaths can he bind himself?" interrupted the indignant Moors. "Will he swear by the Gospels, the divine books of the Christians? It was on those books that the faith of his nephew Sergius was pledged to eighty of our innocent and unfortunate breth ren. Before we trust them a second time, let us try their efficacy in the chastisement of perjury and the vindication of their own honour." Their honour was vindicated in the field of Tebeste by the death of Solomon and the total loss of his army. The arrival of fresh troops and more skilful commanders soon checked the insolence of the Moors; seventeen of their princes were slain in the same battle; and the doubtful and transient submission of their tribes was celebrated with lavish applause by the people of Constantinople. Successive inroads had reduced the province of Africa to one-third of the measure of Italy; yet the Roman emperors continued to reign above a century over Carthage and the fruitful coast of the Mediterranean. But the victories and the losses of Justinian were alike pernicious to mankind; and such was the desolation of Africa, that in many parts a stranger might wander whole days without meeting the face either of a friend or an enemy. The nation of the Vandals had disappeared: they once amounted to a hundred and sixty thousand warriors, without including the children, the women, or the slaves. Their numbers were infinitely surpassed by the number of the Moorish families extirpated in a relentless war; and the same destruction was retaliated on the Romans and their allies, who perished by the climate, their mutual quarrels, and the rage of the barbarians. When Procopius first landed, he admired the populousness of the cities and country, strenuously exercised in the labours of commerce and agriculture. In less than twenty years that busy scene was converted into a silent solitude; the wealthy citizens escaped to Sicily and Constantinople; and the secret historian has confidently affirmed that five millions of Africans were consumed by the wars and government of the emperor Justinian.[5]

The jealousy of the Byzantine court had not permitted Belisarius to achieve the conquest of Italy; and his abrupt departure revived the courage of the Goths,[6] who respected his genius, his virtue, and even the laudable motive which had urged the servant of Justinian to deceive and reject them. They had lost their king (an inconsiderable loss), their capital, their treasures, the provinces from Sicily to the Alps, and the military force of two hundred thousand barbarians, magnificently equipped with horses and arms. Yet all was not lost as long as Pavia was defended by one thousand Goths, inspired by a sense of honour, the love of freedom, and the memory of their past greatness. The supreme command was unanimously offered to the brave Uraias; and it was in his eyes alone that the disgrace of his uncle Vitiges could appear as a reason of exclusion. His voice inclined the election in favour of Hildibald, whose personal merit was recommended by the vain hope that his kinsman Theudes, the Spanish monarch, would support the common interest of the Gothic nation. The success of his arms in Liguria and Venetia seemed to justify their choice; but he soon declared to the world that he was incapable of forgiving or commanding his benefactor. The consort of Hildibald was deeply wounded by the beauty, the riches, and the pride of the wife of Uraias; and the death of that virtuous patriot excited the indignation of a free people. A bold assassin executed their sentence by striking off the head of Hildibald in the midst of a banquet; the Rugians, a foreign tribe, assumed the privilege of election; and Totila, the nephew of the late king, was tempted by revenge to deliver himself and the garrison of Trevigo into the hands of the Romans. But the gallant and accomplished youth was easily persuaded to prefer the Gothic throne before the service of Justinian; and, as soon as the palace of Pavia had been purified from the Rugian usurper, he reviewed the national force of five thousand soldiers, and generously undertook the restoration of the kingdom of Italy.

The successors of Belisarius, eleven generals of equal rank, neglected to crush the feeble and disunited Goths, till they were roused to action by the progress of Totila and the reproaches of Justinian. The gates of Verona were secretly opened to Artabazus, at the head of one hundred Persians in the service of the empire. The Goths fled from the city. At the distance of sixty furlongs the Roman generals halted to regulate the division of the spoil. While they disputed, the enemy discovered the real number of the victors: the Persians were instantly overpowered, and it was by leaping from the wall that Artabazus preserved a life which he lost in a few days by the lance of a barbarian who had defied him to single combat. Twenty thousand Romans encountered the forces of Totila near Faenza, and on the hills of Mugello of the Florentine territory. The ardour of freemen who fought to regain their country was opposed to the languid temper of mercenary troops, who were even destitute of the merits of strong and well-disciplined servitude. On the first attack they abandoned their ensigns, threw down their arms, and dispersed on all sides with an active speed which abated the loss, whilst it aggravated the shame, of their defeat. The king of the Goths, who blushed for the baseness of his enemies, pursued with rapid steps the path of honour and victory. Totila passed the Po, traversed the Apennine, suspended the important conquest of Ravenna, Florence, and Rome, and marched through the heart of Italy to form the siege, or rather the blockade, of Naples. The

Roman chiefs, imprisoned in their respective cities and accusing each other of the common disgrace, did not presume to disturb his enterprise. But the emperor, alarmed by the distress and danger of his Italian conquests, despatched to the relief of Naples a fleet of galleys and a body of Thracian and Armenian soldiers. They landed in Sicily, which yielded its copious stores of provisions; but the delays of the new commander, an unwarlike magistrate, protracted the sufferings of the besieged; and the succours which he dropped with a timid and tardy hand were successively intercepted by the armed vessels stationed by Totila in the Bay of Naples. The principal officer of the Romans was dragged, with a rope round his neck, to the foot of the wall, from whence, with a trembling voice, he exhorted the citizens to implore, like himself, the mercy of the conqueror. They requested a truce, with a promise of surrendering the city if no effectual relief should appear at the end of thirty days. Instead of *one* month, the audacious barbarian granted them *three*, in the just confidence that famine would anticipate the term of their capitulation. After the reduction of Naples and Cumæ, the provinces of Lucania, Apulia, and Calabria submitted to the king of the Goths. Totila led his army to the gates of Rome, pitched his camp at Tibur or Tivoli, within twenty miles of the capital, and calmly exhorted the senate and people to compare the tyranny of the Greeks with the blessings of the Gothic reign.

The rapid success of Totila may be partly ascribed to the revolution which three years' experience had produced in the sentiments of the Italians. At the command, or at least in the name, of a catholic emperor, the pope,[7] their spiritual father, had been torn from the Roman church, and either starved or murdered on a desolate island.[8] The virtues of Belisarius were replaced by the various or uniform vices of eleven chiefs at Rome, Ravenna, Florence, Perugia, Spoleto, etc., who abused their authority for the indulgence of lust or avarice. The improvement of the revenue was committed to Alexander, a subtle scribe, long practised in the fraud and oppression of the Byzantine schools, and whose name of *Psalliction*, the *scissars*,[9] was drawn from the dexterous artifice with which he reduced the size, without defacing the figure, of the gold coin. Instead of expecting the restoration of peace and industry, he imposed a heavy assessment on the fortunes of the Italians. Yet his present or future demands were less odious than a prosecution of arbitrary rigour against the persons and property of all those who, under the Gothic kings, had been concerned in the receipt and expenditure of the public money. The subjects of Justinian who escaped these partial vexations were oppressed by the irregular maintenance of the soldiers, whom Alexander defrauded and despised, and their hasty sallies in quest of wealth or subsistence provoked the inhabitants of the country to await or implore their deliverance from the virtues of a barbarian. Totila[10] was chaste and temperate, and none were deceived, either friends or enemies, who depended on his faith or his clemency. To the husbandmen of Italy the Gothic king issued a welcome proclamation, enjoining them to pursue their important labours, and to rest assured that, on the payment of the ordinary taxes, they should be defended by his valour and discipline from the injuries of war. The strong towns he successively attacked, and, as soon as they had yielded to his arms, he demolished the fortifications, to save the people from the calamities of a future siege, to deprive the Romans of the arts of defence, and to decide the tedious quarrel of the two nations by an equal and honourable conflict in the field of battle. The Roman captives and deserters were tempted to enlist in the service of a liberal and courteous adversary, the slaves were attracted by the firm and faithful promise that they should never be delivered to their masters; and from the thousand warriors of Pavia a new people, under the same appellation of Goths, was insensibly formed in the camp of Totila. He sincerely accomplished the articles of capitulation, without seeking or accepting any sinister advantage from ambiguous expressions or unforeseen events: the garrison of Naples had stipulated that they should be transported by sea; the obstinacy of the winds prevented their voyage, but they were generously supplied with horses, provisions, and a safe-conduct to the gates of Rome. The wives of the senators who had been surprised in the villas of Campania were restored without a ransom to their husbands; the violation of female chastity was inexorably chastised with death; and in the salutary regulation of the diet of the famished Neapolitans, the conqueror assumed the office of a humane and attentive physician. The virtues of Totila are equally laudable, whether they proceeded from true policy, religious principle, or the instinct of humanity. He often harangued his troops; and it was his constant theme that national vice and ruin are inseparably connected; that victory is the fruit of moral as well is military virtue; and that the prince, and even the people, are responsible for the crimes which they neglect to punish.

The return of Belisarius to save the country which he had subdued was pressed with equal vehemence by his friends and enemies, and the Gothic war was imposed as a trust or an exile on the veteran commander. A hero on the banks of the Euphrates, a slave in the palace of Constantinople, he accepted with reluctance the painful task of supporting his own reputation and retrieving the faults of his successors. The sea was open to the Romans; the ships and soldiers were assembled at Salona, near the palace of Diocletian; he refreshed and reviewed his troops at Pola in Istria, coasted round the head of the Hadriatic, entered the port of Ravenna, and despatched orders rather than supplies to the subordinate cities. His first public oration was addressed to the Goths and Romans, in the name of the emperor, who had suspended for a while the conquest of Persia and listened to the prayers of his Italian subjects. He gently touched on the causes and the authors of the recent disasters, striving to remove the fear of punishment for the past, and the hope of impunity for the future, and labouring with more zeal than success to unite all the members of his government in a firm league of affection and obedience. Justinian, his gracious master, was inclined to pardon and reward, and it was their interest, as well as duty, to reclaim their deluded brethren, who had been seduced by the arts of the usurper. Not a man was tempted to desert the standard of the Gothic king. Belisarius soon discovered that he was sent to remain the idle and impotent spectator of the glory of a young barbarian, and his own epistle exhibits a genuine and lively picture of the distress of a noble mind. "Most excellent prince, we are arrived in Italy, destitute of all the necessary implements of war—men, horses, arms, and money. In our late circuit through the villages of Thrace and Illyricum, we have collected with extreme difficulty about four thousand recruits, naked and unskilled in the use of weapons and the exercises of the camp. The soldiers already stationed in the province are discontented, fearful, and dismayed; at the sound of an enemy they dismiss their horses, and cast their arms on the ground. No taxes can be raised, since Italy is in the hands of the barbarians: the failure of payment has deprived us of the right of command, or even of admonition. Be assured, dread Sir, that the greater part of your troops have already deserted to the Goths.

If the war could be achieved by the presence of Belisarius alone, your wishes are satisfied; Belisarius is in the midst of Italy. But if you desire to conquer, far other preparations are requisite: without a military force the title of general is an empty name. It would be expedient to restore to my service my own veterans and domestic guards. Before I can take the field I must receive an adequate supply of light and heavy armed troops, and it is only with ready money that you can procure the indispensable aid of a powerful body of the cavalry of the Huns."[11] An officer in whom Belisarius confided was sent from Ravenna to hasten and conduct the succours, but the message was neglected, and the messenger was detained at Constantinople by an advantageous marriage. After his patience had been exhausted by delay and disappointment, the Roman general repassed the Hadriatic, and expected at Dyrrachium the arrival of the troops, which were slowly assembled among the subjects and allies of the empire. His powers were still inadequate to the deliverance of Rome, which was closely besieged by the Gothic king. The Appian way, a march of forty days, was covered by the barbarians; and as the prudence of Belisarius declined a battle, he preferred the safe and speedy navigation of five days from the coast of Epirus to the mouth of the Tiber.

After reducing, by force or treaty, the towns of inferior note in the midland provinces of Italy, Totila proceeded, not to assault, but to encompass and starve, the ancient capital. Rome was afflicted by the avarice, and guarded by the valour, of Bessas, a veteran chief of Gothic extraction, who filled, with a garrison of three thousand soldiers, the spacious circle of her venerable walls. From the distress of the people he extracted a profitable trade, and secretly rejoiced in the continuance of the siege. It was for his use that the granaries had been replenished; the charity of Pope Vigilius had purchased and embarked an ample supply of Sicilian corn, but the vessels which escaped the barbarians were seized by a rapacious governor, who imparted a scanty sustenance to the soldiers, and sold the remainder to the wealthy Romans. The medimnus, or fifth part of the quarter of wheat, was exchanged for seven pieces of gold; fifty pieces were given for an ox, a rare and accidental prize; the progress of famine enhanced this exorbitant value, and the mercenaries were tempted to deprive themselves of the allowance which was scarcely sufficient for the support of life. A tasteless and unwholesome mixture, in which the bran thrice exceeded the quantity of flour, appeased the hunger of the poor; they were gradually reduced to feed on dead horses, dogs, cats, and mice, and eagerly to snatch the grass and even the nettles which grew among the ruins of the city. A crowd of spectres, pale and emaciated, their bodies oppressed with disease and their minds with despair, surrounded the palace of the governor, urged, with unavailing truth, that it was the duty of a master to maintain his slaves, and humbly requested that he would provide for their subsistence, permit their flight, or command their immediate execution. Bessas replied, with unfeeling tranquillity, that it was impossible to feed, unsafe to dismiss, and unlawful to kill, the subjects of the emperor. Yet the example of a private citizen might have shown his countrymen that a tyrant cannot withhold the privilege of death. Pierced by the cries of five children, who vainly called on their father for bread, he ordered them to follow his steps, advanced with calm and silent despair to one of the bridges of the Tiber, and, covering his face, threw himself headlong into the stream, in the presence of his family and the Roman people. To the rich and pusillanimous, Bessas sold the permission of departure; but the greatest part of the fugitives expired on the public highways, or were intercepted by the flying parties of barbarians.[12] In the meanwhile the artful governor soothed the discontent, and revived the hopes, of the Romans, by the vague reports of the fleets and armies which were hastening to their relief from the extremities of the East. They derived more rational comfort from the assurance that Belisarius had landed at the *port*; and, without numbering his forces, they firmly relied on the humanity, the courage, and the skill of their great deliverer.

The foresight of Totila had raised obstacles worthy of such an antagonist. Ninety furlongs below the city, in the narrowest part of the river, he joined the two banks by strong and solid timbers in the form of a bridge, on which he erected two lofty towers, manned by the bravest of his Goths, and profusely stored with missile weapons and engines of offence. The approach of the bridge and towers was covered by a strong and massy chain of iron, and the chain, at either end, on the opposite sides of the Tiber, was defended by a numerous and chosen detachment of archers. But the enterprise of forcing these barriers and relieving the capital displays a shining example of the boldness and conduct of Belisarius. His cavalry advanced from the port along the public road to awe the motions and distract the attention of the enemy. His infantry and provisions were distributed in two hundred large boats, and each boat was shielded by a high rampart of thick planks pierced with many small holes for the discharge of missile weapons. In the front, two large vessels were linked together to sustain a floating castle, which commanded the towers of the bridge, and contained a magazine of fire, sulphur, and bitumen. The whole fleet, which the general led in person, was laboriously moved against the current of the river. The chain yielded to their weight, and the enemies who guarded the banks were either slain or scattered. As soon as they touched the principal barrier the fireship was instantly grappled to the bridge; one of the towers, with two hundred Goths, was consumed by the flames, the assailants shouted victory, and Rome was saved, if the wisdom of Belisarius had not been defeated by the misconduct of his officers. He had previously sent orders to Bessas to second his operations by a timely sally from the town, and he had fixed his lieutenant, Isaac, by a peremptory command, to the station of the port. But avarice rendered Bessas immovable, while the youthful ardour of Isaac delivered him into the hands of a superior enemy. The exaggerated rumour of his defeat was hastily carried to the ears of Belisarius: he paused, betrayed in that single moment of his life some emotions of surprise and perplexity, and reluctantly sounded a retreat to save his wife Antonina, his treasures, and the only harbour which he possessed on the Tuscan coast. The vexation of his mind produced an ardent and almost mortal fever, and Rome was left without protection to the mercy or indignation of Totila. The continuance of hostilities had embittered the national hatred; the Arian clergy was ignominiously driven from Rome, Pelagius, the archdeacon, returned without success from an embassy to the Gothic camp, and a Sicilian bishop, the envoy or nuncio of the pope, was deprived of both his hands for daring to utter falsehoods in the service of the church and state.

Famine had relaxed the strength and discipline of the garrison of Rome. They could derive no effectual service from a dying people, and the inhuman avarice of the merchant at length absorbed the vigilance of the governor. Four Isaurian sentinels, while their companions slept and their officers were absent, descended by a rope from the wall, and secretly proposed to the Gothic king to introduce his troops into the city. The offer was entertained with coldness and suspicion; they returned in safety; they twice repeated their visit: the place was twice examined; the conspiracy was known and disregarded; and no sooner had Totila consented to the attempt, than they unbarred the Asinarian gate and gave admittance to the Goths. Till the dawn of day they halted in order of battle, apprehensive of treachery or ambush; but the troops of Bessas, with their leader, had already escaped; and when the king was pressed to disturb their retreat, he prudently replied that no sight could be more grateful than that of a flying enemy. The patricians who were still possessed of horses, Decius, Basilius, etc., accompanied the governor; their brethren, among whom Olybrius, Orestes, and Maximus are named by the historian, took refuge in the church of St. Peter: but the assertion that only five hundred persons remained in the capital inspires some doubt of the fidelity either of his narrative or of his text. As soon as daylight had displayed the entire victory of the Goths, their monarch devoutly visited the tomb of the prince of the apostles; but while he prayed at the altar, twenty-five soldiers and sixty citizens were put to the sword in the vestibule of the temple. The archdeacon Pelagius [13] stood before him, with the Gospels in his hand. "O Lord, be merciful to your servant." "Pelagius," said Totila with an insulting smile, "your pride now condescends to become a suppliant." "I *am* a suppliant," replied the prudent archdeacon; "God has now made us your subjects, and, as your subjects, we are entitled to your clemency." At his humble prayer the lives of the Romans were spared; and the chastity of the maids and matrons was preserved inviolate from the passions of the hungry soldiers. But they were rewarded by the freedom of pillage, after the most precious spoils had been reserved for the royal treasury. The houses of the senators were plentifully stored with gold and silver; and the avarice of Bessas had laboured with so much guilt and shame for the benefit of the conqueror. In this revolution the sons and daughters of Roman consuls tasted the misery which they had spurned or relieved, wandered in tattered garments through the streets of the city, and begged their bread, perhaps without success, before the gates of their hereditary mansions. The riches of Rusticiana, the daughter of Symmachus and widow of Boethius, had been generously devoted to alleviate the calamities of famine. But the barbarians were exasperated by the report that she had prompted the people to overthrow the statues of the great Theodoric; and the life of that venerable matron would have been sacrificed to his memory, if Totila had not respected her birth, her virtues, and even the pious motive of her revenge. The next day he pronounced two orations, to congratulate and admonish his victorious Goths, and to reproach the senate, as the vilest of slaves, with their perjury, folly, and ingratitude; sternly declaring that their estates and honours were justly forfeited to the companions of his arms. Yet he consented to forgive their revolt; and the senators repaid his clemency by despatching circular letters to their tenants and vassals in the provinces of Italy, strictly to enjoin them to desert the standard of the Greeks, to cultivate their lands in peace, and to learn from their masters the duty of obedience to a Gothic sovereign. Against the city which had so long delayed the course of his victories he appeared inexorable: one-third of the walls, in different parts, were demolished by his command; fire and engines prepared to consume or subvert the most stately works of antiquity; and the world was astonished by the fatal decree that Rome should be changed into a pasture for cattle. The firm and temperate remonstrance of Belisarius suspended the execution; he warned the barbarian not to sully his fame by the destruction of those monuments which were the glory of the dead and the delight of the living; and Totila was persuaded, by the advice of an enemy, to preserve Rome as the ornament of his kingdom, or the fairest pledge of peace and reconciliation. When he had signified to the ambassadors of Belisarius his intention of sparing the city, he stationed an army at the distance of one hundred and twenty furlongs, to observe the motions of the Roman general. With the remainder of his forces he marched into Lucania and Apulia, and occupied on the summit of Mount Garganus [14] one of the camps of Hannibal. [15] The senators were dragged in his train, and afterwards confined in the fortresses of Campania; the citizens, with their wives and children, were dispersed in exile; and during forty days Rome was abandoned to desolate and dreary solitude. [16]

The loss of Rome was speedily retrieved by an action to which, according to the event, the public opinion would apply the names of rashness or heroism. After the departure of Totila, the Roman general sallied from the port at the head of a thousand horse, cut in pieces the enemy who opposed his progress, and visited with pity and reverence the vacant space of the *eternal* city. Resolved to maintain a station so conspicuous in the eyes of mankind, he summoned the greatest part of his troops to the standard which he erected on the Capitol: the old inhabitants were recalled by the love of their country and the hopes of food; and the keys of Rome were sent a second time to the emperor Justinian. The walls, as far as they had been demolished by the Goths, were repaired with rude and dissimilar materials; the ditch was restored; iron spikes [17] were profusely scattered in the highways to annoy the feet of the horses; and as new gates could not suddenly be procured, the entrance was guarded by a Spartan rampart of his bravest soldiers. At the expiration of twenty-five days Totila returned by hasty marches from Apulia to avenge the injury and disgrace. Belisarius expected his approach. The Goths were thrice repulsed in three general assaults; they lost the flower of their troops; the royal standard had almost fallen into the hands of the enemy, and the fame of Totila sunk, as it had risen, with the fortune of his arms. Whatever skill and courage could achieve had been performed by the Roman general: it remained only that Justinian should terminate, by a strong and seasonable effort, the war which he had ambitiously undertaken. The indolence, perhaps the impotence, of a prince who despised his enemies and envied his servants, protracted the calamities of Italy. After a long silence Belisarius was commanded to leave a sufficient garrison at Rome, and to transport himself into the province of Lucania, whose inhabitants, inflamed by catholic zeal, had cast away the yoke of their Arian conquerors. In this ignoble warfare the hero, invincible against the power of the barbarians, was basely vanquished by the delay, the disobedience, and the cowardice of his own officers. He reposed in his winter quarters of Crotona, in the full assurance that the two passes of the Lucanian hills were guarded by his cavalry. They were betrayed by treachery or weakness; and the rapid march of the Goths scarcely allowed time for the escape of Belisarius to the coast of Sicily. At length a fleet and army were assembled for the relief of Ruscianum, or Rossano,[18] a fortress sixty furlongs from the ruins of Sybaris, where the nobles of Lucania had taken refuge. In the first attempt the Roman forces were dissipated by a storm. In the second, they approached the shore; but they saw the hills covered with archers, the landing-place defended by a line of spears, and the king of the Goths impatient for battle. The conqueror of Italy retired with a sigh, and continued to languish, inglorious and inactive, till Antonina, who had been sent to Constantinople to solicit succours, obtained, after the death of the empress, the permission of his return.

The five last campaigns of Belisarius might abate the envy of his competitors, whose eyes had been dazzled and wounded by the blaze of his former glory. Instead of delivering Italy from the Goths, he had wandered like a fugitive along the coast, without daring to march into the country, or to accept the bold and repeated challenge of Totila. Yet in the judgment of the few who could discriminate counsels from events, and compare the instruments with the execution, he appeared a more consummate master of the art of war than in the season of his prosperity, when he presented two captive kings before the throne of Justinian. The valour of Belisarius was not chilled by age: his prudence was matured by experience; but the moral virtues of humanity and justice seem to have yielded to the hard necessity of the times. The parsimony or poverty of the emperor compelled him to deviate from the rule of conduct which had deserved the love and confidence of the Italians. The war was maintained by the oppression of Ravenna, Sicily, and all the faithful subjects of the empire; and the rigorous prosecution of Herodian provoked that injured or guilty officer to deliver Spoleto into the hands of the enemy. The avarice of Antonina, which had been sometimes diverted by love, now reigned without a rival in her breast. Belisarius himself had always understood that riches, in a corrupt age, are the support and ornament of personal merit. And it cannot be presumed that he should stain his honour for the public service without applying a part of the spoil to his private emolument. The hero had escaped the sword of the barbarians, but the dagger of conspiracy[19] awaited his return. In the midst of wealth and honours, Artaban, who had chastised the African tyrant, complained of the ingratitude of courts. He aspired to Præjecta, the emperor's niece, who wished to reward her deliverer; but the impediment of his previous marriage was asserted by the piety of Theodora. The pride of royal descent was irritated by flattery; and the service in which he gloried had proved him capable of bold and sanguinary deeds. The death of Justinian was resolved, but the conspirators delayed the execution till they could surprise Belisarius, disarmed and naked, in the palace of Constantinople. Not a hope could be entertained of shaking his long-tried fidelity; and they justly dreaded the revenge, or rather justice, of the veteran general, who might speedily assemble an army in Thrace to punish the assassins, and perhaps to enjoy the fruits of their crime. Delay afforded time for rash communications and honest confessions: Artaban and his accomplices were condemned by the senate, but the extreme clemency of Justinian detained them in the gentle confinement of the palace, till he pardoned their flagitious attempt against his throne and life. If the emperor forgave his enemies, he must cordially embrace a friend whose victories were alone remembered, and who was endeared to his prince by the recent circumstance of their common danger. Belisarius reposed from his toils, in the high station of general of the East and count of the domestics; and the older consuls and patricians respectfully yielded the precedency of rank to the peerless merit of the first of the Romans.[20] The first of the Romans still submitted to be the slave of his wife; but the servitude of habit and affection became less disgraceful when the death of Theodora had removed the baser influence of fear. Joannina their daughter and the sole heiress of their fortunes, was betrothed to Anastasius, the grandson, or rather the nephew, of the empress,[21] whose kind interposition forwarded the consummation of their youthful loves. But the power of Theodora expired, the parents of Joannina returned, and her honour, perhaps her happiness, were sacrificed to the revenge of an unfeeling mother, who dissolved the imperfect nuptials before they had been ratified by the ceremonies of the church.[22]

Before the departure of Belisarius, Perusia was besieged, and few cities were impregnable to the Gothic arms. Ravenna, Ancona, and Crotona still resisted the barbarians; and when Totila asked in marriage one of the daughters of France, he was stung by the just reproach that the king of Italy was unworthy of his title till it was acknowledged by the Roman people. Three thousand of the bravest soldiers had been left to defend the capital. On the suspicion of a monopoly, they massacred the governor, and announced to Justinian, by a deputation of the clergy, that, unless their offence was pardoned, and their arrears were satisfied, they should instantly accept the tempting offers of Totila. But the officer who succeeded to the command (his name was Diogenes) deserved their esteem and confidence; and the Goths, instead of finding an easy conquest, encountered a vigorous resistance from the soldiers and people, who patiently endured the loss of the port and of all maritime supplies. The siege of Rome would perhaps have been raised, if the liberality of Totila to the Isaurians had not encouraged some of their venal countrymen to copy the example of treason. In a dark night, while the Gothic trumpets sounded on another side, they silently opened the gate of St. Paul: the barbarians rushed into the city; and the flying garrison was intercepted before they could reach the harbour of Centumcellæ. A soldier trained in the school of Belisarius, Paul of Cilicia, retired with four hundred men to the mole of Hadrian. They repelled the Goths; but they felt the approach of famine; and their aversion to the taste of horse-flesh confirmed their resolution to risk the event of a desperate and decisive sally. But their spirit insensibly stooped to the offers of capitulation: they retrieved their arrears of pay, and preserved their arms and horses, by enlisting in the service of Totila; their chiefs, who pleaded a laudable attachment to their wives and children in the East, were dismissed with honour; and above four hundred enemies, who had taken refuge in the sanctuaries, were saved by the clemency of the victor. He no longer entertained a wish of destroying the edifices of Rome,[23] which he now respected as the seat of the Gothic kingdom: the senate and people were restored to their country; the means of subsistence were liberally provided; and Totila, in the robe of peace, exhibited the equestrian games of the circus. Whilst he amused the eyes of the multitude, four hundred vessels were prepared for the embarkation of his troops. The cities of Rhegium and Tarentum were reduced; he passed into Sicily, the object of his implacable resentment; and the island was stripped of its gold and silver, of the fruits of the earth, and of an infinite number of horses, sheep, and oxen. Sardinia and Corsica obeyed the fortune of Italy; and the sea-coast of Greece was visited by a fleet of three hundred galleys.[24] The Goths were landed in Corcyra and the ancient continent of Epirus; they advanced as far as Nicopolis, the trophy of Augustus, and Dodona,[25] once famous by the oracle of Jove. In every step of his victories the wise barbarian repeated to Justinian his desire of peace, applauded the concord of their predecessors, and offered to employ the Gothic arms in the service of the empire.

Justinian was deaf to the voice of peace, but he neglected the prosecution of war; and the indolence of his temper disappointed, in some degree, the obstinacy of his passions. From this salutary slumber the emperor was awakened by the pope Vigilius and the patrician Cethegus, who appeared before his throne, and adjured him, in the name of God and the people, to resume the conquest and deliverance of Italy. In the choice of the generals, caprice, as well as judgment, was shown. A fleet and army sailed for the relief of Sicily, under the conduct of Liberius; but his want of youth and experience were afterwards discovered, and before he touched the shores of the island he was overtaken by his successor. In the place of Liberius the conspirator Artaban was raised from a prison to military honours, in the pious presumption that gratitude would animate his valour and fortify his allegiance. Belisarius reposed in the shade of his laurels, but the command of the principal army was reserved for Germanus,[26] the emperor's nephew, whose rank and merit had been long depressed by the jealousy of the court. Theodora had injured him in the rights of a private citizen, the marriage of his children, and the testament of his brother; and although his conduct was pure and blameless, Justinian was displeased that he should be thought worthy of the confidence of the malcontents. The life of Germanus was a lesson of implicit obedience: he nobly refused to prostitute his name and character in the factions of the circus; the gravity of his manners was tempered by innocent cheerfulness; and his riches were lent without interest to indigent or deserving friends. His valour had formerly triumphed over the Sclavonians of the Danube and the rebels of Africa: the first report of his promotion revived the hopes of the Italians; and he was privately assured that a crowd of Roman deserters would abandon, on his approach, the standard of Totila. His second marriage with Malasontha, the grand-daughter of Theodoric, endeared Germanus to the Goths themselves; and they marched with reluctance against the father of a royal infant, the last offspring of the line of Amali.[27] A splendid allowance was assigned by the emperor: the general contributed his private fortune; his two sons were popular and active; and he surpassed, in the promptitude and success of his levies, the expectation of mankind. He was permitted to select some squadrons of Thracian cavalry: the veterans, as well as the youth of Constantinople and Europe, engaged their voluntary service; and as far as the heart of Germany, his fame and liberality attracted the aid of the barbarians. The Romans advanced to Sardica; an army of Sclavonians fled before their march; but within two days of their final departure the designs of Germanus were terminated by his malady and death. Yet the impulse which he had given to the Italian war still continued to act with energy and effect. The maritime towns, Ancona, Crotona, Centumcellæ, resisted the assaults of Totila. Sicily was reduced by the zeal of Artaban, and the Gothic navy was defeated near the coast of the Hadriatic. The two fleets were almost equal, forty-seven to fifty galleys: the victory was decided by the knowledge and dexterity of the Greeks; but the ships were so closely grappled that only twelve of the Goths escaped from this unfortunate conflict. They affected to depreciate an element in which they were unskilled; but their own experience confirmed the truth of a maxim, that the master of the sea will always acquire the dominion of the land.[28]

After the loss of Germanus, the nations were provoked to smile by the strange intelligence that the command of the Roman armies was given to a eunuch. But the eunuch Narses[29] is ranked among the few who have rescued that unhappy name from the contempt and hatred of mankind. A feeble, diminutive body concealed the soul of a statesman and a warrior. His youth had been employed in the management of the loom and distaff, in the cares of the household, and the service of female luxury; but while his hands were busy, he secretly exercised the faculties of a vigorous and discerning mind. A stranger to the schools and the camp, he studied in the palace to dissemble, to flatter, and to persuade; and as soon as he approached the person of the emperor, Justinian listened with surprise and pleasure to the manly counsels of his chamberlain and private treasurer.[30] The talents of Narses were tried and improved in frequent embassies: he led an army into Italy, acquired a practical knowledge of the war and the country, and presumed to strive with the genius of Belisarius. Twelve years after his return the eunuch was chosen to achieve the conquests which had been left imperfect by the first of the Roman generals. Instead of being dazzled by vanity or emulation, he seriously declared that, unless he were armed with an adequate force, he would never consent to risk his own glory and that of his sovereign. Justinian granted to the favourite what he might have denied to the hero: the Gothic war was rekindled from its ashes, and the preparations were not unworthy of the ancient majesty of the empire. The key of the public treasure was put into his hand to collect magazines, to levy soldiers, to purchase arms and horses, to discharge the arrears of pay, and to tempt the fidelity of the fugitives and deserters. The troops of Germanus were still in arms; they halted at Salona in the expectation of a new leader, and legions of subjects and allies were created by the well-known liberality of the eunuch Narses. The king of the Lombards [31] satisfied or surpassed the obligations of a treaty, by lending two thousand two hundred of his bravest warriors, who were followed by three thousand of their martial attendants. Three thousand Heruli fought on horseback under Philemuth, their native chief; and the noble Aratus, who adopted the manners and discipline of Rome, conducted a band of veterans of the same nation. Dagistheus was released from prison to command the Huns; and Kobad, the grandson and nephew of the Great King, was conspicuous by the regal tiara at the head of his faithful Persians, who had devoted themselves to the fortunes of their prince. [32] Absolute in the exercise of his authority, more absolute in the affection of his troops, Narses led a numerous and gallant army from Philippopolis to Salona, from whence he coasted the eastern side of the Hadriatic as far as the confines of Italy. His progress was checked. The East could not supply vessels capable of transporting such multitudes of men and horses. The Franks, who in the general confusion had usurped the greater part of the Venetian province, refused a free passage to the friends of the Lombards. The station of Verona was occupied by Teias with the flower of the Gothic forces; and that skilful commander had overspread the adjacent country with the fall of woods and the inundation of waters. [33] In this perplexity an officer of experience proposed a measure, secure by the appearance of rashness, that the Roman army should cautiously advance along the sea-shore, while the fleet preceded their march, and successively cast a bridge of boats over the mouths of the rivers, the Timavus, the Brenta, the Adige, and the Po, that fall into the Hadriatic to the north of Ravenna. Nine days he reposed in the city, collected the fragments of the Italian army, and marched towards Rimini to meet the defiance of an insulting enemy.

The prudence of Narses impelled him to speedy and decisive action. His powers were the last effort of the state; the cost of each day accumulated the enormous account, and the nations, untrained to discipline or fatigue, might be rashly provoked to turn their arms against each other, or against their benefactor.

The same considerations might have tempered the ardour of Totila. But he was conscious that the clergy and people of Italy aspired to a second revolution: he felt or suspected the rapid progress of treason, and he resolved to risk the Gothic kingdom on the chance of a day, in which the valiant would be animated by instant danger, and the disaffected might be awed by mutual ignorance. In his march from Ravenna the Roman general chastised the garrison of Rimini, traversed in a direct line the hills of Urbino, and re-entered the Flaminian way, nine miles beyond the perforated rock, an obstacle of art and nature which might have stopped or retarded his progress. [34] The Goths were assembled in the neighbourhood of Rome, they advanced without delay to seek a superior enemy, and the two armies approached each other at the distance of one hundred furlongs, between Tagina [35] and the sepulchres of the Gauls. [36] The haughty message of Narses was an offer not of peace, but of pardon. The answer of the Gothic king declared his resolution to die or conquer. "What day," said the messenger, "will you fix for the combat?" "The eighth day," replied Totila; but early the next morning he attempted to surprise a foe suspicious of deceit and prepared for battle. Ten thousand Heruli and Lombards, of approved valour and doubtful faith, were placed in the centre. Each of the wings was composed of eight thousand Romans; the right was guarded by the cavalry of the Huns, the left was covered by fifteen hundred chosen horse, destined, according to the emergencies of action, to sustain the retreat of their friends, or to encompass the flank of the enemy. From his proper station at the head of the right wing, the eunuch rode along the line, expressing by his voice and countenance the assurance of victory, exciting the soldiers of the emperor to punish the guilt and madness of a band of robbers, and exposing to their view gold chains, collars, and bracelets, the rewards of military virtue. From the event of a single combat they drew an omen of success; and they beheld with pleasure the courage of fifty archers, who maintained a small eminence against three successive attacks of the Gothic cavalry. At the distance only of two bow-shots the armies spent the morning in dreadful suspense, and the Romans tasted some necessary food without unloosening the cuirass from their breast or the bridle from their horses. Narses awaited the charge; and it was delayed by Totila till he had received his last succours of two thousand Goths. While he consumed the hours in fruitless treaty, the king exhibited in a narrow space the strength and agility of a warrior. His armour was enchased with gold; his purple banner floated with the wind: he cast his lance into the air, caught it with the right hand, shifted it to the left, threw himself backwards, recovered his seat, and managed a fiery steed in all the paces and evolutions of the equestrian school. As soon as the succours had arrived, he retired to his tent, assumed the dress and arms of a private soldier, and gave the signal of battle. The first line of cavalry advanced with more courage than discretion, and left behind them the infantry of the second line. They were soon engaged between the horns of a crescent, into which the adverse wings had been insensibly curved, and were saluted from either side by the volleys of four thousand archers. Their ardour, and even their distress, drove them forwards to a close and unequal conflict, in which they could only use their lances against an enemy equally skilled in all the instruments of war. A generous emulation inspired the Romans and their barbarian allies; and Narses, who calmly viewed and directed their efforts, doubted to whom he should adjudge the prize of superior bravery. The Gothic cavalry was astonished and disordered, pressed and broken; and the line of infantry, instead of presenting their spears or opening their intervals, were trampled under the feet of the flying horse. Six thousand of the Goths were slaughtered without mercy in the field of Tagina. Their prince, with five attendants, was overtaken by Asbad, of the race of the Gepidæ: "Spare the king of Italy," cried a loyal voice, and Asbad struck his lance through the body of Totila. The blow was instantly revenged by the faithful Goths: they transported their dying monarch seven miles beyond the scene of his disgrace, and his last moments were not embittered by the presence of an enemy. Compassion afforded him the shelter of an obscure tomb; but the Romans were not satisfied of their victory till they beheld the corpse of the Gothic king. His hat, enriched with gems, and his bloody robe, were presented to Justinian by the messengers of triumph.[37]

As soon as Narses had paid his devotions to the Author of victory and the blessed Virgin, his peculiar patroness,[38] he praised, rewarded, and dismissed the Lombards. The villages had been reduced to ashes by these valiant savages: they ravished matrons and virgins on the altar; their retreat was diligently watched by a strong detachment of regular forces, who prevented a repetition of the like disorders. The victorious eunuch pursued his march through Tuscany, accepted the submission of the Goths, heard the acclamations and often the complaints of the Italians, and encompassed the walls of Rome with the remainder of his formidable host. Round the wide circumference Narses assigned to himself and to each of his lieutenants a real or a feigned attack, while he silently marked the place of easy and unguarded entrance. Neither the fortifications of Hadrian's mole, nor of the port, could long delay the progress of the conqueror; and Justinian once more received the keys of Rome, which, under his reign, had been *five* times taken and recovered.[39] But the deliverance of Rome was the last calamity of the Roman people. The barbarian allies of Narses too frequently confounded the privileges of peace and war. The despair of the flying Goths found some consolation in sanguinary revenge; and three hundred youths of the noblest families, who had been sent as hostages beyond the Po, were inhumanly slain by the successor of Totila. The fate of the senate suggests an awful lesson of the vicissitude of human affairs. Of the senators whom Totila had banished from their country, some were rescued by an officer of Belisarius and transported from Campania to Sicily, while others were too guilty to confide in the clemency of Justinian, or too poor to provide horses for their escape to the sea-shore. Their brethren languished five years in a state of indigence and exile: the victory of Narses revived their hopes; but their premature return to the metropolis was prevented by the furious Goths, and all the fortresses of Campania were stained with patrician[40] blood. After a period of thirteen centuries the institution of Romulus expired; and if the nobles of Rome still assumed the title of senators, few subsequent traces can be discovered of a public council or constitutional order. Ascend six hundred years, and contemplate the kings of the earth soliciting an audience, as the slaves or freedmen of the Roman senate![41]

The Gothic war was yet alive. The bravest of the nation retired beyond the Po, and Teias was unanimously chosen to succeed and revenge their departed hero. The new king immediately sent ambassadors to implore, or rather to purchase, the aid of the Franks, and nobly lavished for the public safety the riches which had been deposited in the palace of Pavia. The residue of the royal treasure was guarded by his brother Aligern, at Cumæ in Campania; but the strong castle which Totila had fortified was closely besieged by the arms of Narses. From the Alps to the foot of Mount Vesuvius, the Gothic king by rapid and secret marches advanced to the relief of his brother, eluded the vigilance of the Roman chiefs, and pitched his camp on the banks of the Sarnus or *Draco*,[42] which flows from Nuceria into the bay of Naples. The river separated the two armies; sixty days were consumed in distant and fruitless combats, and Teias maintained this important post till he was deserted by his fleet and the hope of subsistence. With reluctant steps he ascended the *Lactarian* mount, where the physicians of Rome since the time of Galen had sent their patients for the benefit of the air and the milk.[43] But the Goths soon embraced a more generous resolution—to descend the hill, to dismiss their horses, and to die in arms and in the possession of freedom. The king marched at their head, bearing in his right hand a lance, and an ample buckler in his left: with the one he struck dead the foremost of the assailants, with the other he received the weapons which every hand was ambitious to aim against his life. After a combat of many hours, his left arm was fatigued by the weight of twelve javelins which hung from his shield. Without moving from his ground or suspending his blows, the hero called aloud on his attendants for a fresh buckler, but in the moment while his side was uncovered, it was pierced by a mortal dart. He fell; and his head, exalted on a spear, proclaimed to the nations that the Gothic kingdom was no more. But the example of his death served only to animate the companions who had sworn to perish with their leader. They fought till darkness descended on the earth. They reposed on their arms. The combat was renewed with the return of light, and maintained with unabated vigour till the evening of the second day. The repose of a second night, the want of water, and the loss of their bravest champions, determined the surviving Goths to accept the fair capitulation which the prudence of Narses was inclined to propose. They embraced the alternative of residing in Italy as the subjects and soldiers of Justinian, or departing with a portion of their private wealth in search of some independent country.[44] Yet the oath of fidelity or exile was alike rejected by one thousand Goths, who broke away before the treaty was signed, and boldly effected their retreat to the walls of Pavia. The spirit as well as the situation of Aligern prompted him to imitate rather than to bewail his brother: a strong and dexterous archer, he transpierced with a single arrow the armour and breast of his antagonist, and his military conduct defended Cumæ[45] above a year against the forces of the Romans. Their industry had scooped the Sibyl's cave[46] into a prodigious mine; combustible materials were introduced to consume the temporary props: the wall and the gate of Cumæ sunk into the cavern, but the ruins formed a deep and inaccessible precipice. On the fragment of a rock Aligern stood alone and unshaken, till he calmly surveyed the hopeless condition of his country, and judged it more honourable to be the friend of Narses than the slave of the Franks. After the death of Teias the Roman general separated his troops to reduce the cities of Italy; Lucca sustained a long and vigorous siege, and such was the humanity or the prudence of Narses, that the repeated perfidy of the inhabitants could not provoke him to exact the forfeit lives of their hostages. These hostages were dismissed in safety, and their grateful zeal at length subdued the obstinacy of their countrymen.[47]

Before Lucca had surrendered, Italy was overwhelmed by a new deluge of barbarians. A feeble youth, the grandson of Clovis, reigned over the Austrasians or Oriental Franks. The guardians of Theodebald entertained with coldness and reluctance the magnificent promises of the Gothic ambassadors. But the spirit of a martial people outstripped the timid counsels of the court: two brothers, Lothaire and Buccelin,[48] the dukes of the Alamanni, stood forth as the leaders of the Italian war, and seventy-five thousand Germans descended in the autumn from the Rhætian Alps into the plain of Milan. The vanguard of the Roman army was stationed near the Po under the conduct of Fulcaris, a bold Herulian, who rashly conceived that personal bravery was the sole duty and merit of a commander. As he marched without order or precaution along the Æmilian way, an ambuscade of Franks suddenly rose from the amphitheatre of Parma; his troops were surprised and routed, but their leader refused to fly, declaring to the last moment that death was less terrible than the angry countenance of Narses. The death of Fulcaris, and the retreat of the surviving chiefs, decided the fluctuating and rebellious temper of the Goths; they flew to the standard of their deliverers, and admitted them into the cities which still resisted the arms of the Roman general. The conqueror of Italy opened a free passage to the irresistible torrent of barbarians. They passed under the walls of Cesena, and answered by threats and reproaches the advice of Aligern, that the Gothic treasures could no longer repay the labour of an invasion. Two thousand Franks were destroyed by the skill and valour of Narses himself, who sallied from Rimini at the head of three hundred horse to chastise the licentious rapine of their march. On the confines of Samnium the two brothers divided their forces. With the right wing Buccelin assumed the spoil of Campania, Lucania, and Bruttium; with the left, Lothaire accepted the plunder of Apulia and Calabria. They followed the coast of the Mediterranean and the Hadriatic as far as Rhegium and Otranto, and the extreme lands of Italy were the term of their destructive progress. The Franks, who were Christians and catholics, contented themselves with simple pillage and occasional murder. But the churches which their piety had spared were stripped by the sacrilegious hands of the Alamanni, who sacrificed horses' heads to their native deities of the woods and rivers;[49] they melted or profaned the consecrated vessels, and the ruins of shrines and altars were stained with the blood of the faithful. Buccelin was actuated by ambition, and Lothaire by avarice. The former aspired to restore the Gothic kingdom; the latter, after a promise to his brother of speedy succours, returned by the same road to deposit his treasure beyond the Alps. The strength of their armies was already wasted by the change of climate and contagion of disease; the Germans revelled in the vintage of Italy, and their own intemperance avenged in some degree the miseries of a defenceless people.

At the entrance of the spring the Imperial troops who had guarded the cities assembled, to the number of eighteen thousand men, in the neighbourhood of Rome. Their winter hours had not been consumed in idleness. By the command and after the example of Narses, they repeated each day their military exercise on foot and on horseback, accustomed their ear to obey the sound of the trumpet, and practised the steps and evolutions of the Pyrrhic dance. From the straits of Sicily, Buccelin with thirty thousand Franks and Alamanni slowly moved towards Capua, occupied with a wooden tower the bridge of Casilinum, covered his right by the stream of the Vulturnus, and secured the rest of his encampment by a rampart of sharp stakes, and a circle of waggons whose wheels were buried in the earth. He impatiently expected the return of Lothaire; ignorant, alas! that his brother could never return, and that the chief and his army had been swept away by a strange disease[50] on the banks of the lake

Benacus, between Trent and Verona. The banners of Narses soon approached the Vulturnus, and the eyes of Italy were anxiously fixed on the event of this final contest. Perhaps the talents of the Roman general were most conspicuous in the calm operations which precede the tumult of a battle. His skilful movements intercepted the subsistence of the barbarian, deprived him of the advantage of the bridge and river, and in the choice of the ground and moment of action reduced him to comply with the inclination of his enemy. On the morning of the important day, when the ranks were already formed, a servant for some trivial fault was killed by his master, one of the leaders of the Heruli. The justice or passion of Narses was awakened: he summoned the offender to his presence, and without listening to his excuses gave the signal to the minister of death. If the cruel master had not infringed the laws of his nation, this arbitrary execution was not less unjust than it appears to have been imprudent. The Heruli felt the indignity; they halted: but the Roman general, without soothing their rage or expecting their resolution, called aloud, as the trumpets sounded, that, unless they hastened to occupy their place, they would lose the honour of the victory. His troops were disposed[51] in a long front; the cavalry on the wings; in the centre the heavy-armed foot; the archers and slingers in the rear. The Germans advanced in a sharp-pointed column of the form of a triangle or solid wedge. They pierced the feeble centre of Narses, who received them with a smile into the fatal snare, and directed his wings of cavalry insensibly to wheel on their flanks and encompass their rear. The host of the Franks and Alamanni consisted of infantry: a sword and buckler hung by their side, and they used as their weapons of offence a weighty hatchet and a hooked javelin, which were only formidable in close combat or at a short distance. The flower of the Roman archers, on horseback and in complete armour, skirmished without peril round this immovable phalanx, supplied by active speed the deficiency of number, and aimed their arrows against a crowd of barbarians who, instead of a cuirass and helmet, were covered by a loose garment of fur or linen. They paused, they trembled, their ranks were confounded, and in the decisive moment the Heruli, preferring glory to revenge, charged with rapid violence the head of the column. Their leader Sindbal, and Aligern the Gothic prince, deserved the prize of superior valour; and their example incited the victorious troops to achieve with swords and spears the destruction of the enemy. Buccelin and the greatest part of his army perished on the field of battle, in the waters of the Vulturnus, or by the hands of the enraged peasants; but it may seem incredible that a victory[52] which no more than five of the Alamanni survived could be purchased with the loss of fourscore Romans. Seven thousand Goths, the relics of the war, defended the fortress of Campsa till the ensuing spring; and every messenger of Narses announced the reduction of the Italian cities, whose names were corrupted by the ignorance or vanity of the Greeks.[53] After the battle of Casilinum Narses entered the capital; the arms and treasures of the Goths, the Franks, and the Alamanni were displayed; his soldiers, with garlands in their hands, chanted the praises of the conqueror; and Rome for the last time beheld the semblance of a triumph.

After a reign of sixty years the throne of the Gothic kings was filled by the exarchs of Ravenna, the representatives in peace and war of the emperor of the Romans. Their jurisdiction was soon reduced to the limits of a narrow province; but Narses himself, the first and most powerful of the exarchs, administered above fifteen years the entire kingdom of Italy. Like Belisarius, he had deserved the honours of envy, calumny, and disgrace: but the favourite eunuch still enjoyed the confidence of Justinian; or the leader of a victorious army awed and repressed the ingratitude of a timid court. Yet it was not by weak and mischievous indulgence that Narses secured the attachment of his troops. Forgetful of the past, and regardless of the future, they abused the present hour of prosperity and peace. The cities of Italy resounded with the noise of drinking and dancing: the spoils of victory were wasted in sensual pleasures; and nothing (says Agathias) remained unless to exchange their shields and helmets for the soft lute and the capacious hogshead.[54] In a manly oration, not unworthy of a Roman censor, the eunuch reproved these disorderly vices, which sullied their fame and endangered their safety. The soldiers blushed, and obeyed; discipline was confirmed; the fortifications were restored; a *duke* was stationed for the defence and military command of each of the principal cities;[55] and the eye of Narses pervaded the ample prospect from Calabria to the Alps. The remains of the Gothic nation evacuated the country, or mingled with the people: the Franks, instead of revenging the death of Buccelin, abandoned, without a struggle, their Italian

conquests; and the rebellious Sindbal, chief of the Heruli, was subdued, taken, and hung on a lofty gallows, by the inflexible justice of the exarch.[56] The civil state of Italy, after the agitation of a long tempest, was fixed by a pragmatic sanction, which the emperor promulgated at the request of the pope. Justinian introduced his own jurisprudence into the schools and tribunals of the West: he ratified the acts of Theodoric and his immediate successors, but every deed was rescinded and abolished which force had extorted or fear had subscribed under the usurpation of Totila. A moderate theory was framed to reconcile the rights of property with the safety of prescription, the claims of the state with the poverty of the people, and the pardon of offences with the interest of virtue and order of society. Under the exarchs of Ravenna, Rome was degraded to the second rank. Yet the senators were gratified by the permission of visiting their estates in Italy, and of approaching without obstacle the throne of Constantinople: the regulation of weights and measures was delegated to the pope and senate; and the salaries of lawyers and physicians, of orators and grammarians, were destined to preserve or rekindle the light of science in the ancient capital. Justinian might dictate benevolent edicts,[57] and Narses might second his wishes by the restoration of cities, and more especially of churches. But the power of kings is most effectual to destroy: and the twenty years of the Gothic war had consummated the distress and depopulation of Italy. As early as the fourth campaign, under the discipline of Belisarius himself, fifty thousand labourers died of hunger[58] in the narrow region of Picenum;[59] and a strict interpretation of the evidence of Procopius would swell the loss of Italy above the total sum of her present inhabitants.[60]

I desire to believe, but I dare not affirm, that Belisarius sincerely rejoiced in the triumph of Narses. Yet the consciousness of his own exploits might teach him to esteem, without jealousy, the merit of a rival; and the repose of the aged warrior was crowned by a last victory, which saved the emperor and the capital. The barbarians, who annually visited the provinces of Europe, were less discouraged by some accidental defeats than they were excited by the double hope of spoil and of subsidy. In the thirty-second winter of Justinian's reign the Danube was deeply frozen; Zabergan led the cavalry of the Bulgarians, and his standard was followed by a promiscuous multitude of Sclavonians. The savage chief passed, without opposition, the river and the mountains, spread his troops over Macedonia and Thrace, and advanced with no more than seven thousand horse to the long walls which should have defended the territory of Constantinople. But the works of man are impotent against the assaults of nature: a recent earthquake had shaken the foundations of the walls; and the forces of the empire were employed on the distant frontiers of Italy, Africa, and Persia. The seven *schools*,[61] or companies, of the guards or domestic troops had been augmented to the number of five thousand five hundred men, whose ordinary station was in the peaceful cities of Asia. But the places of the brave Armenians were insensibly supplied by lazy citizens, who purchased an exemption from the duties of civil life without being exposed to the dangers of military service. Of such soldiers few could be tempted to sally from the gates; and none could be persuaded to remain in the field, unless they wanted strength and speed to escape from the Bulgarians. The report of the fugitives exaggerated the numbers and fierceness of an enemy who had polluted holy virgins and abandoned new-born infants to the dogs and vultures; a crowd of rustics, imploring food and protection, increased the consternation of the city; and the tents of Zabergan were pitched at the distance of twenty miles,[62] on the banks of a small river which encircles Melanthias and afterwards falls into the Propontis.[63] Justinian trembled: and those who had only seen the emperor in his old age were pleased to suppose that he had *lost* the alacrity and vigour of his youth. By his command the vessels of gold and silver were removed from the churches in the neighbourhood, and even the suburbs, of Constantinople: the ramparts were lined with trembling spectators; the golden gate was crowded with useless generals and tribunes; and the senate shared the fatigues and the apprehensions of the populace.

But the eyes of the prince and people were directed to a feeble veteran, who was compelled by the public danger to resume the armour in which he had entered Carthage and defended Rome. The horses of the royal stables, of private citizens, and even of the circus, were hastily collected; the emulation of the old and young was roused by the name of Belisarius, and his first encampment was in the presence of a victorious enemy. His prudence, and the labour of the friendly peasants, secured, with a ditch and rampart, the repose of the night; innumerable fires and clouds of dust were artfully contrived to magnify the opinion of his

strength; his soldiers suddenly passed from despondency to presumption; and, while ten thousand voices demanded the battle, Belisarius dissembled his knowledge that in the hour of trial he must depend on the firmness of three hundred veterans. The next morning the Bulgarian cavalry advanced to the charge. But they heard the shouts of multitudes, they beheld the arms and discipline of the front; they were assaulted on the flanks by two ambuscades which rose from the woods; their foremost warriors fell by the hand of the aged hero and his guards; and the swiftness of their evolutions was rendered useless by the close attack and rapid pursuit of the Romans. In this action (so speedy was their flight) the Bulgarians lost only four hundred horse: but Constantinople was saved; and Zabergan, who felt the hand of a master, withdrew to a respectful distance. But his friends were numerous in the councils of the emperor, and Belisarius obeyed with reluctance the commands of envy and Justinian, which forbade him to achieve the deliverance of his country. On his return to the city, the people, still conscious of their danger, accompanied his triumph with acclamations of joy and gratitude, which were imputed as a crime to the victorious general. But when he entered the palace the courtiers were silent, and the emperor, after a cold and thankless embrace, dismissed him to mingle with the train of slaves. Yet so deep was the impression of his glory on the minds of men, that Justinian, in the seventy-seventh year of his age, was encouraged to advance near forty miles from the capital, and to inspect in person the restoration of the long wall. The Bulgarians wasted the summer in the plains of Thrace; but they were inclined to peace by the failure of their rash attempts on Greece and the Chersonesus. A menace of killing their prisoners quickened the payment of heavy ransoms; and the departure of Zabergan was hastened by the report that double-prowed vessels were built on the Danube to intercept his passage. The danger was soon forgotten; and a vain question, whether their sovereign had shown more wisdom or weakness, amused the idleness of the city.[64]

About two years after the last victory of Belisarius, the emperor returned from a Thracian journey of health, or business, or devotion. Justinian was afflicted by a pain in his head; and his private entry countenanced the rumour of his death. Before the third hour of the day, the bakers' shops were plundered of their bread, the houses were shut, and every citizen, with hope or terror, prepared for the impending tumult. The senators themselves, fearful and suspicious, were convened at the ninth hour; and the præfect received their commands to visit every quarter of the city and proclaim a general illumination for the recovery of the emperor's health. The ferment subsided; but every accident betrayed the impotence of the government and the factious temper of the people: the guards were disposed to mutiny as often as their quarters were changed, or their pay was withheld: the frequent calamities of fires and earthquakes afforded the opportunities of disorder; the disputes of the blues and greens, of the orthodox and heretics, degenerated into bloody battles; and, in the presence of the Persian ambassador, Justinian blushed for himself and for his subjects. Capricious pardon and arbitrary punishment embittered the irksomeness and discontent of a long reign: a conspiracy was formed in the palace; and, unless we are deceived by the names of Marcellus and Sergius, the most virtuous and the most profligate of the courtiers were associated in the same designs. They had fixed the time of the execution; their rank gave them access to the royal banquet; and their black slaves[65] were stationed in the vestibule and porticoes to announce the death of the tyrant, and to excite a sedition in the capital. But the indiscretion of an accomplice saved the poor remnant of the days of Justinian. The conspirators were detected and seized with daggers hidden under their garments; Marcellus died by his own hand, and Sergius was dragged from the sanctuary.[66] Pressed by remorse, or tempted by the hopes of safety, he accused two officers of the household of Belisarius, and torture forced them to declare that they had acted according to the secret instructions of their patron.[67] Posterity will not hastily believe that a hero who in the vigour of life had disdained the fairest offers of ambition and revenge should stoop to the murder of his prince, whom he could not long expect to survive. His followers were impatient to fly; but flight must have been supported by rebellion, and he had lived enough for nature and for glory. Belisarius appeared before the council with less fear than indignation: after forty years' service the emperor had prejudged his guilt; and injustice was sanctified by the presence and authority of the patriarch. The life of Belisarius was graciously spared, but his fortunes were sequestered; and, from December to July, he was guarded as a prisoner in his own palace. At length his innocence was acknowledged; his freedom and

honours were restored; and death, which might be hastened by resentment and grief, removed him from the world about eight months after his deliverance. The name of Belisarius can never die: but, instead of the funeral, the monuments, the statues, so justly due to his memory, I only read that his treasures, the spoils of the Goths and Vandals, were immediately confiscated by the emperor. Some decent portion was reserved, however, for the use of his widow: and as Antonina had much to repent, she devoted the last remains of her life and fortune to the foundation of a convent. Such is the simple and genuine narrative of the fall of Belisarius and the ingratitude of Justinian.[68] That he was deprived of his eyes, and reduced by envy to beg his bread, "Give a penny to Belisarius the general!" is a fiction of later times,[69] which has obtained credit, or rather favour, as a strange example of the vicissitudes of fortune.[70]

If the emperor could rejoice in the death of Belisarius, he enjoyed the base satisfaction only eight months, the last period of a reign of thirty-eight and a life of eighty-three years. It would be difficult to trace the character of a prince who is not the most conspicuous object of his own times: but the confessions of an enemy may be received as the safest evidence of his virtues. The resemblance of Justinian to the bust of Domitian is maliciously urged,[71] with the acknowledgment, however, of a well-proportioned figure, a ruddy complexion, and a pleasing countenance. The emperor was easy of access, patient of hearing, courteous and affable in discourse, and a master of the angry passions which rage with such destructive violence in the breast of a despot. Procopius praises his temper, to reproach him with calm and deliberate cruelty: but in the conspiracies which attacked his authority and person, a more candid judge will approve the justice, or admire the clemency, of Justinian. He excelled in the private virtues of chastity and temperance; but the impartial love of beauty would have been less mischievous than his conjugal tenderness for Theodora; and his abstemious diet was regulated, not by the prudence of a philosopher, but the superstition of a monk. His repasts were short and frugal: on solemn fasts he contented himself with water and vegetables; and such was his strength as well as fervour, that he frequently passed two days, and as many nights, without tasting any food. The measure of his sleep was not less rigorous: after the repose of a single hour, the body was awakened by the soul, and, to the astonishment of his chamberlains, Justinian walked or studied till the morning light. Such restless application prolonged his time for the acquisition of knowledge[72] and the despatch of business; and he might seriously deserve the reproach of confounding, by minute and preposterous diligence, the general order of his administration. The emperor professed himself a musician and architect, a poet and philosopher, a lawyer and theologian; and if he failed in the enterprise of reconciling the Christian sects, the review of the Roman jurisprudence is a noble monument of his spirit and industry. In the government of the empire he was less wise, or less successful: the age was unfortunate; the people was oppressed and discontented; Theodora abused her power; a succession of bad ministers disgraced his judgment; and Justinian was neither beloved in his life nor regretted at his death. The love of fame was deeply implanted in his breast, but he condescended to the poor ambition of titles, honours, and contemporary praise; and while he laboured to fix the admiration, he forfeited the esteem and affection, of the Romans. The design of the African and Italian wars was boldly conceived and executed; and his penetration discovered the talents of Belisarius in the camp, of Narses in the palace. But the name of the emperor is eclipsed by the names of his victorious generals; and Belisarius still lives to upbraid the envy and ingratitude of his sovereign. The partial favour of mankind applauds the genius of a conqueror who leads and directs his subjects in the exercise of arms. The characters of Philip the Second and of Justinian are distinguished by the cold ambition which delights in war, and declines the dangers of the field. Yet a colossal statue of bronze represented the emperor on horseback, preparing to march against the Persians in the habit and armour of Achilles. In the great square before the church of St. Sophia, this monument was raised on a brass column and a stone pedestal of seven steps; and the pillar of Theodosius, which weighed seven thousand four hundred pounds of silver, was removed from the same place by the avarice and vanity of Justinian. Future princes were more just or indulgent to *his* memory; the elder Andronicus, in the beginning of the fourteenth century, repaired and beautified his equestrian statue: since the fall of the empire it has been melted into cannon by the victorious Turks.[73]

I shall conclude this chapter with the comets, the earthquakes, and the plague, which astonished or afflicted the age of Justinian.

I. In the fifth year of his reign, and in the month of September, a comet[74] was seen during twenty days in the western quarter of the heavens, and which shot its rays into the north. Eight years afterwards, while the sun was in Capricorn, another comet appeared to follow in the Sagittary: the size was gradually increasing; the head was in the east, the tail in the west, and it remained visible above forty days. The nations, who gazed with astonishment, expected wars and calamities from their baleful influence; and these expectations were abundantly fulfilled. The astronomers dissembled their ignorance of the nature of these blazing stars, which they affected to represent as the floating meteors of the air; and few among them embraced the simple notion of Seneca and the Chaldæans, that they are only planets of a longer period and more eccentric motion.[75] Time and science have justified the conjectures and predictions of the Roman sage: the telescope has opened new worlds to the eyes of astronomers;[76] and, in the narrow space of history and fable, one and the same comet is already found to have visited the earth in *seven* equal revolutions of five hundred and seventy-five years. The *first*,[77] which ascends beyond the Christian era one thousand seven hundred and sixty-seven years, is coëval with Ogyges, the father of Grecian antiquity. And this appearance explains the tradition which Varro has preserved, that under his reign the planet Venus changed her colour, size, figure, and course; a prodigy without example either in past or succeeding ages.[78] The *second* visit, in the year eleven hundred and ninety-three, is darkly implied in the fable of Electra, the seventh of the Pleiads, who have been reduced to six since the time of the Trojan war. That nymph, the wife of Dardanus, was unable to support the ruin of her country: she abandoned the dances of her sister orbs, fled from the zodiac to the north pole, and obtained, from her dishevelled locks, the name of the *comet*. The *third* period expires in the year six hundred and eighteen, a date that exactly agrees with the tremendous comet of the Sibyl, and perhaps of Pliny, which arose in the West two generations before the reign of Cyrus. The *fourth* apparition, forty-four years before the birth of Christ, is of all others the most splendid and important. After the death of Cæsar, a long-haired star was conspicuous to Rome and to the nations during the games which were exhibited by young Octavian in honour of Venus and his uncle. The vulgar opinion, that it conveyed to heaven the divine soul of the dictator, was cherished and consecrated by the piety of a statesman; while his secret superstition referred the comet to the glory of his own times.[79] The *fifth* visit has been already ascribed to the fifth year of Justinian, which coincides with the five hundred and thirty-first of the Christian era. And it may deserve notice, that in this, as in the preceding instance, the comet was followed, though at a longer interval, by a remarkable paleness of the sun. The *sixth* return, in the year eleven hundred and six, is recorded by the chronicles of Europe and China: and in the first fervour of the Crusades, the Christians and the Mahometans might surmise, with equal reason, that it portended the destruction of the Infidels. The *seventh* phenomenon, of one thousand six hundred and eighty, was presented to the eyes of an enlightened age.[80] The philosophy of Bayle dispelled a prejudice which Milton's muse had so recently adorned, that the comet, "from its horrid hair shakes pestilence and war." [81] Its road in the heavens was observed with exquisite skill by Flamsteed and Cassini: and the mathematical science of Bernoulli, Newton, and Halley investigated the laws of its revolutions. At the *eighth* period, in the year two thousand three hundred and fifty-five, their calculations may perhaps be verified by the astronomers of some future capital in the Siberian or American wilderness.

II. The near approach of a comet may injure or destroy the globe which we inhabit; but the changes on its surface have been hitherto produced by the action of volcanoes and earthquakes.[82] The nature of the soil may indicate the countries most exposed to these formidable concussions, since they are caused by subterraneous fires, and such fires are kindled by the union and fermentation of iron and sulphur. But their times and effects appear to lie beyond the reach of human curiosity; and the philosopher will discreetly abstain from the prediction of earthquakes, till he has counted the drops of water that silently filtrate on the inflammable mineral, and measured the caverns which increase by resistance the explosion of the imprisoned air. Without assigning the cause, history will distinguish the periods in which these calamitous events have been rare or frequent, and will observe that this fever of the earth raged with uncommon violence during the reign of Justinian.[83] Each year is marked by the repetition of earthquakes, of such duration that Constantinople has been shaken above forty days; of such extent that the shock has been communicated to the whole surface of the globe, or at least of the Roman empire. An impulsive or vibratory motion was felt, enormous chasms were opened, huge and heavy bodies were discharged into the air, the sea alternately advanced and retreated beyond its ordinary bounds, and a mountain was torn from Libanus [84] and cast into the waves, where it protected, as a mole, the new harbour of Botrys[85] in Phœnicia. The stroke that agitates an ant-hill may crush the insect-myriads in the dust; yet truth must extort a confession that man has industriously laboured for his own destruction. The institution of great cities, which include a nation within the limits of a wall, almost realises the wish of Caligula that the Roman people had but one neck. Two hundred and fifty thousand persons are said to have perished in the earthquake of Antioch, whose domestic multitudes were swelled by the conflux of strangers to the festival of the Ascension. The loss of Berytus [86] was of smaller account, but of much greater value. That city, on the coast of Phœnicia, was illustrated by the study of the civil law, which opened the surest road to wealth and dignity: the schools of Berytus were filled with the rising spirits of the age, and many a youth was lost in the earthquake who might have lived to be the scourge or the guardian of his country. In these disasters the architect becomes the enemy of mankind. The hut of a savage, or the tent of an Arab, may be thrown down without injury to the inhabitant; and the Peruvians had reason to deride the folly of their Spanish conquerors, who with so much cost and labour erected their own sepulchres. The rich marbles of a patrician are dashed on his own head; a whole people is buried under the ruins of public and private edifices; and the conflagration is kindled and propagated by the innumerable fires which are necessary for the subsistence and manufactures of a great city. Instead of the mutual sympathy which might comfort and assist the distressed, they dreadfully experience the vices and passions which are released from the fear of punishment; the tottering houses are pillaged by intrepid avarice; revenge embraces the moment and selects the victim; and the earth often swallows the assassin, or the ravisher, in the consummation of their crimes. Superstition involves the present danger with invisible terrors; and if the image of death may sometimes be subservient to the virtue or repentance of individuals, an affrighted people is more forcibly moved to expect the end of the world, or to deprecate with servile homage the wrath of an avenging Deity.

III. Æthiopia and Egypt have been stigmatised in every age as the original source and
seminary of the plague.[87] In a damp, hot, stag-
nating air, this African fever is generated from
the putrefaction of animal substances, and
especially from the swarms of locusts, not less
destructive to mankind in their death than in
their lives. The fatal disease which depopulated
the earth in the time of Justinian and his successors [88] first appeared in the neighbourhood of
Pelusium, between the Serbonian bog and the
eastern channel of the Nile. From thence, tracing
as it went a double path, it spread to the East,
over Syria, Persia, and the Indies, and penetrated to the West, along the coast of Africa and
over the continent of Europe. In the spring of
the second year Constantinople, during three
or four months, was visited by the pestilence;
and Procopius, who observed its progress and
symptoms with the eyes of a physician,[89] has
emulated the skill and diligence of Thucydides
in the description of the plague of Athens.[90] The
infection was sometimes announced by the
visions of a distempered fancy, and the victim
despaired as soon as he had heard the menace
and felt the stroke of an invisible spectre. But
the greater number, in their beds, in the streets,
in their usual occupation, were surprised by a
slight fever; so slight, indeed, that neither the
pulse nor the colour of the patient gave any
signs of the approaching danger. The same, the
next, or the succeeding day, it was declared by
the swelling of the glands, particularly those of
the groin, of the armpits, and under the ear;
and when these buboes or tumours were opened,
they were found to contain a *coal*, or black substance, of the size of a lentil. If they came to a
just swelling and suppuration, the patient was
saved by this kind and natural discharge of the
morbid humour; but if they continued hard
and dry, a mortification quickly ensued, and
the fifth day was commonly the term of his life.
The fever was often accompanied with lethargy
or delirium; the bodies of the sick were covered
with black pustules or carbuncles, the symptoms of immediate death; and in the constitutions too feeble to produce an eruption, the
vomiting of blood was followed by a mortification
of the bowels. To pregnant women the plague
was generally mortal; yet one infant was drawn
alive from his dead mother, and three mothers
survived the loss of their infected fœtus. Youth
was the most perilous season, and the female
sex was less susceptible than the male; but
every rank and profession was attacked with
indiscriminate rage, and many of those who

escaped were deprived of the use of their speech,
without being secure from a return of the disorder.[91] The physicians of Constantinople were
zealous and skilful; but their art was baffled by
the various symptoms and pertinacious vehemence of the disease: the same remedies were
productive of contrary effects, and the event
capriciously disappointed their prognostics of
death or recovery. The order of funerals and
the right of sepulchres were confounded; those
who were left without friends or servants lay
unburied in the streets, or in their desolate
houses; and a magistrate was authorised to
collect the promiscuous heaps of dead bodies,
to transport them by land or water, and to inter
them in deep pits beyond the precincts of the
city. Their own danger and the prospect of
public distress awakened some remorse in the
minds of the most vicious of mankind: the confidence of health again revived their passions
and habits; but philosophy must disdain the
observation of Procopius, that the lives of such
men were guarded by the peculiar favour of
fortune or Providence. He forgot, or perhaps he
secretly recollected, that the plague had touched
the person of Justinian himself; but the abstemious diet of the emperor may suggest, as in
the case of Socrates, a more rational and honourable cause for his recovery.[92] During his
sickness the public consternation was expressed
in the habits of the citizens; and their idleness
and despondence occasioned a general scarcity
in the capital of the East.

Contagion is the inseparable symptom of the
plague; which, by mutual respiration, is transfused from the infected persons to the lungs and
stomach of those who approach them. While
philosophers believe and tremble, it is singular
that the existence of a real danger should have
been denied by a people most prone to vain and
imaginary terrors.[93] Yet the fellow-citizens of
Procopius were satisfied, by some short and
partial experience, that the infection could not
be gained by the closest conversation;[94] and
this persuasion might support the assiduity of
friends or physicians in the care of the sick,
whom inhuman prudence would have condemned to solitude and despair. But the fatal
security, like the predestination of the Turks,
must have aided the progress of the contagion;
and those salutary precautions to which Europe
is indebted for her safety were unknown to the
government of Justinian. No restraints were
imposed on the free and frequent intercourse of
the Roman provinces: from Persia to France
the nations were mingled and infected by wars

and emigrations; and the pestilential odour which lurks for years in a bale of cotton was imported, by the abuse of trade, into the most distant regions. The mode of its propagation is explained by the remark of Procopius himself, that it always spread from the sea-coast to the inland country: the most sequestered islands and mountains were successively visited; the places which had escaped the fury of its first passage were alone exposed to the contagion of the ensuing year. The winds might diffuse that subtle venom; but unless the atmosphere be previously disposed for its reception, the plague would soon expire in the cold or temperate climates of the earth. Such was the universal corruption of the air, that the pestilence which burst forth in the fifteenth year of Justinian was not checked or alleviated by any difference of the seasons. In time its first malignity was abated and dispersed; the disease alternately languished and revived; but it was not till the end of a calamitous period of fifty-two years that mankind recovered their health, or the air resumed its pure and salubrious quality. No facts have been preserved to sustain an account, or even a conjecture, of the numbers that perished in this extraordinary mortality. I only find that, during three months, five and at length ten thousand persons died each day at Constantinople; that many cities of the East were left vacant; and that in several districts of Italy the harvest and the vintage withered on the ground. The triple scourge of war, pestilence, and famine afflicted the subjects of Justinian; and his reign is disgraced by a visible decrease of the human species, which has never been repaired in some of the fairest countries of the globe.[95]

CHAPTER XLIV

Idea of the Roman Jurisprudence. The Laws of the Kings. The Twelve Tables of the Decemvirs. The Laws of the People. The Decrees of the Senate. The Edicts of the Magistrates and Emperors. Authority of the Civilians. Code, Pandects, Novels, and Institutes of Justinian: I. Rights of Persons. II. Rights of Things. III. Private Injuries and Actions. IV. Crimes and Punishments.

THE vain titles of the victories of Justinian are crumbled into dust, but the name of the legislator is inscribed on a fair and everlasting monument. Under his reign, and by his care, the civil jurisprudence was digested in the immortal works of the CODE, the PANDECTS, and the INSTITUTES:[1] the public reason of the Romans has been silently or studiously transfused into the domestic institutions of Europe,[2] and the laws of Justinian still command the respect or obedience of independent nations. Wise or fortunate is the prince who connects his own reputation with the honour and interest of a perpetual order of men. The defence of their founder is the first cause which in every age has exercised the zeal and industry of the civilians. They piously commemorate his virtues, dissemble or deny his failings, and fiercely chastise the guilt or folly of the rebels who presume to sully the majesty of the purple. The idolatry of love has provoked, as it usually happens, the rancour of opposition; the character of Justinian has been exposed to the blind vehemence of flattery and invective; and the injustice of a sect (the *Anti-Tribonians*) has refused all praise and merit to the prince, his ministers, and his laws.[3] Attached to no party, interested only for the truth and candour of history, and directed by the most temperate and skilful guides,[4] I enter with just diffidence on the subject of civil law, which has exhausted so many learned lives and clothed the walls of such spacious libraries. In a single, if possible in a short, chapter, I shall trace the Roman jurisprudence from Romulus to Justinian,[5] appreciate the labours of that emperor, and pause to contemplate the principles of a science so important to the peace and happiness of society. The laws of a nation form the most instructive portion of its history; and, although I have devoted myself to write the annals of a declining monarchy, I shall embrace the occasion to breathe the pure and invigorating air of the republic.

The primitive government of Rome[6] was composed with some political skill of an elective king, a council of nobles, and a general assembly of the people. War and religion were administered by the supreme magistrate, and he alone proposed the laws which were debated in the senate, and finally ratified or rejected by a majority of votes in the thirty *curiæ* or parishes of the city. Romulus, Numa, and Servius Tullius are celebrated as the most ancient legislators; and each of them claims his peculiar part in the threefold division of jurisprudence.[7] The laws of marriage, the education of children, and the authority of parents, which may seem to draw their origin from *nature* itself, are ascribed to the untutored wisdom of Romulus. The law of *nations* and of religious worship, which Numa introduced, was derived from his nocturnal converse with the nymph Egeria. The *civil* law is attributed to the experience of Servius; he balanced the rights and fortunes of the seven classes of citizens, and guarded by fifty new regulations the observance of contracts and the punishment of crimes. The state, which he had inclined towards a democracy, was changed by the last Tarquin into lawless despotism; and when the kingly office was abolished, the patricians engrossed the benefits of freedom. The royal laws became odious or obsolete, the mysterious deposit was silently preserved by the priests and nobles, and at the end of sixty years the citizens of Rome still complained that they were ruled by the arbitrary sentence of the magistrates. Yet the positive institutions of the kings had blended themselves with the public and private manners of the city; some fragments of that venerable jurisprudence[8] were compiled by the diligence of antiquarians;[9] and above twenty texts still speak the rudeness of the Pelasgic idiom of the Latins.[10]

I shall not repeat the well-known story of the Decemvirs,[11] who sullied by their actions the honour of inscribing on brass, or wood, or ivory, the TWELVE TABLES of the Roman laws.[12] They were dictated by the rigid and jealous spirit of an aristocracy which had yielded with reluctance to the just demands of the people. But the substance of the Twelve Tables was adapted to the state of the city, and the Romans had emerged from barbarism, since they were capable of studying and embracing the institutions of their more enlightened neighbours. A wise Ephesian was driven by envy from his native country: before he could reach the shores of Latium, he had observed the various forms of human nature and civil society; he imparted his knowledge to the legislators of Rome, and a statue was erected in the forum to the perpetual memory of Hermodorus.[13] The names and divisions of the copper money, the sole coin of the infant state, were of Dorian origin;[14] the harvests of Campania and Sicily relieved the wants of a people whose agriculture was often inter-

rupted by war and faction; and since the trade was established,[15] the deputies who sailed from the Tiber might return from the same harbours with a more precious cargo of political wisdom. The colonies of Great Greece had transported and improved the arts of their mother-country. Cumæ and Rhegium, Crotona and Tarentum, Agrigentum and Syracuse, were in the rank of the most flourishing cities. The disciples of Pythagoras applied philosophy to the use of government, the unwritten laws of Charondas accepted the aid of poetry and music,[16] and Zaleucus framed the republic of the Locrains, which stood without alteration above two hundred years.[17] From a similar motive of national pride, both Livy and Dionysius are willing to believe that the deputies of Rome visited Athens under the wise and splendid administration of Pericles, and the laws of Solon were transfused into the Twelve Tables. If such an embassy had indeed been received from the barbarians of Hesperia, the Roman name would have been familiar to the Greeks before the reign of Alexander,[18] and the faintest evidence would have been explored and celebrated by the curiosity of succeeding times. But the Athenian monuments are silent, nor will it seem credible that the patricians should undertake a long and perilous navigation to copy the purest model of a democracy. In the comparison of the tables of Solon with those of the Decemvirs, some casual resemblance may be found; some rules which nature and reason have revealed to every society; some proofs of a common descent from Egypt or Phœnicia.[19] But in all the great lines of public and private jurisprudence the legislators of Rome and Athens appear to be strangers or adverse to each other.

Whatever might be the origin or the merit of the Twelve Tables,[20] they obtained among the Romans that blind and partial reverence which the lawyers of every country delight to bestow on their municipal institutions. The study is recommended by Cicero[21] as equally pleasant and instructive. "They amuse the mind by the remembrance of old words, and the portrait of ancient manners; they inculcate the soundest principles of government and morals; and I am not afraid to affirm that the brief composition of the Decemvirs surpasses in genuine value the libraries of Grecian philosophy. How admirable," says Tully, with honest or affected prejudice, "is the wisdom of our ancestors! We alone are the masters of civil prudence, and our superiority is the more conspicuous if we deign to cast our eyes on the rude and almost ridiculous jurisprudence of Draco, of Solon, and of Lycurgus.'' The Twelve Tables were committed to the memory of the young and the meditation of the old; they were transcribed and illustrated with learned diligence: they had escaped the flames of the Gauls, they subsisted in the age of Justinian, and their subsequent loss has been imperfectly restored by the labours of modern critics.[22] But although these venerable monuments were considered as the rule of right and the fountain of justice,[23] they were overwhelmed by the weight and variety of new laws which, at the end of five centuries, became a grievance more intolerable than the vices of the city.[24] Three thousand brass plates, the acts of the senate and people, were deposited in the Capitol;[25] and some of the acts, as the Julian law against extortion, surpassed the number of a hundred chapters.[26] The Decemvirs had neglected to import the sanction of Zaleucus, which so long maintained the integrity of his republic. A Locrian who proposed any new law stood forth in the assembly of the people with a cord round his neck, and if the law was rejected the innovator was instantly strangled.

The Decemvirs had been named, and their tables were approved, by an assembly of the *centuries*, in which riches preponderated against numbers. To the first class of Romans, the proprietors of one hundred thousand pounds of copper,[27] ninety-eight votes were assigned, and only ninety-five were left for the six inferior classes, distributed according to their substance by the artful policy of Servius. But the tribunes soon established a more specious and popular maxim, that every citizen has an equal right to enact the laws which he is bound to obey. Instead of the *centuries*, they convened the *tribes*; and the patricians, after an impotent struggle, submitted to the decrees of an assembly in which their votes were confounded with those of the meanest plebeians. Yet as long as the tribes successively passed over narrow *bridges*,[28] and gave their voices aloud, the conduct of each citizen was exposed to the eyes and ears of his friends and countrymen. The insolvent debtor consulted the wishes of his creditor, the client would have blushed to oppose the views of his patron, the general was followed by his veterans, and the aspect of a grave magistrate was a living lesson to the multitude. A new method of secret ballot abolished the influence of fear and shame, of honour and interest; and the abuse of freedom accelerated the progress of anarchy and despotism.[29] The Romans had aspired to be equal, they were levelled by the equality of ser-

vitude, and the dictates of Augustus were patiently ratified by the formal consent of the tribes or centuries. Once, and once only, he experienced a sincere and strenuous opposition. His subjects had resigned all political liberty; they defended the freedom of domestic life. A law which enforced the obligation and strengthened the bonds of marriage was clamorously rejected; Propertius, in the arms of Delia, applauded the victory of licentious love; and the project of reform was suspended till a new and more tractable generation had arisen in the world.[30] Such an example was not necessary to instruct a prudent usurper of the mischief of popular assemblies; and their abolition, which Augustus had silently prepared, was accomplished without resistance, and almost without notice, on the accession of his successor.[31] Sixty thousand plebeian legislators, whom numbers made formidable and poverty secure, were supplanted by six hundred senators, who held their honours, their fortunes, and their lives by the clemency of the emperor. The loss of executive power was alleviated by the gift of legislative authority; and Ulpian might assert, after the practice of two hundred years, that the decrees of the senate obtained the force and validity of laws. In the times of freedom the resolves of the people had often been dictated by the passion or error of the moment: the Cornelian, Pompeian, and Julian laws were adapted by a single hand to the prevailing disorders; but the senate, under the reign of the Cæsars, was composed of magistrates and lawyers, and in questions of private jurisprudence the integrity of their judgment was seldom perverted by fear or interest.[32]

The silence or ambiguity of the laws was supplied by the occasional EDICTS of those magistrates who were invested with the *honours* of the state.[33] This ancient prerogative of the Roman kings was transferred in their respective offices to the consuls and dictators, the censors and prætors; and a similar right was assumed by the tribunes of the people, the ædiles, and the proconsuls. At Rome, and in the provinces, the duties of the subject and the intentions of the governor were proclaimed; and the civil jurisprudence was reformed by the annual edicts of the supreme judge, the prætor of the city. As soon as he ascended his tribunal, he announced by the voice of the crier, and afterwards inscribed on a white wall, the rules which he proposed to follow in the decision of doubtful cases, and the relief which his equity would afford from the precise rigour of ancient statutes. A principle of discretion more congenial to monarchy was introduced into the republic: the art of respecting the name and eluding the efficacy of the laws was improved by successive prætors; subtleties and fictions were invented to defeat the plainest meaning of the Decemvirs; and where the end was salutary, the means were frequently absurd. The secret or probable wish of the dead was suffered to prevail over the order of succession and the forms of testaments; and the claimant, who was excluded from the character of heir, accepted with equal pleasure from an indulgent prætor the possession of the goods of his late kinsman or benefactor. In the redress of private wrongs, compensations and fines were substituted to the obsolete rigour of the Twelve Tables; time and space were annihilated by fanciful suppositions; and the plea of youth, or fraud, or violence, annulled the obligation or excused the performance of an inconvenient contract. A jurisdiction thus vague and arbitrary was exposed to the most dangerous abuse; the substance, as well as the form of justice, were often sacrificed to the prejudices of virtue, the bias of laudable affection, and the grosser seductions of interest or resentment. But the errors or vices of each prætor expired with his annual office; such maxims alone as had been approved by reason and practice were copied by succeeding judges; the rule of proceeding was defined by the solution of new cases; and the temptations of injustice were removed by the Cornelian law, which compelled the prætor of the year to adhere to the letter and spirit of his first proclamation.[34] It was reserved for the curiosity and learning of Hadrian to accomplish the design which had been conceived by the genius of Cæsar; and the prætorship of Salvius Julian, an eminent lawyer, was immortalised by the composition of the PERPETUAL EDICT. This well-digested code was ratified by the emperor and the senate; the long divorce of law and equity was at length reconciled; and, instead of the Twelve Tables, the Perpetual Edict was fixed as the invariable standard of civil jurisprudence.[35]

From Augustus to Trajan, the modest Cæsars were content to promulgate their edicts in the various characters of a Roman magistrate; and in the decrees of the senate the *epistles* and *orations* of the prince were respectfully inserted. Hadrian[36] appears to have been the first who assumed without disguise the plenitude of legislative power. And this innovation, so agreeable to his active mind, was countenanced by the patience of the times and his long absence from the seat of government. The same policy was embraced by succeeding monarchs, and, according to the harsh metaphor of Tertullian, "the gloomy and intricate forest of ancient laws was cleared away by the axe of royal mandates and *constitutions*."[37] During four centuries, from Hadrian to Justinian, the public and private jurisprudence was moulded by the will of the sovereign, and few institutions, either human or divine, were permitted to stand on their former basis. The origin of Imperial legislation was concealed by the darkness of ages and the terrors of armed despotism; and a double fiction was propagated by the servility, or perhaps the ignorance, of the civilians who basked in the sunshine of the Roman and Byzantine courts. 1. To the prayer of the ancient Cæsars the people or the senate had sometimes granted a personal exemption from the obligation and penalty of particular statutes, and each indulgence was an act of jurisdiction exercised by the republic over the first of her citizens. His humble privilege was at length transformed into the prerogative of a tyrant; and the Latin expression of "released from the laws"[38] was supposed to exalt the emperor above *all* human restraints, and to leave his conscience and reason as the sacred measure of his conduct. 2. A similar dependence was implied in the decrees of the senate, which in every reign defined the titles and powers of an elective magistrate. But it was not before the ideas and even the language of the Romans had been corrupted that a *royal* law,[39] and an irrevocable gift of the people, were created by the fancy of Ulpian, or more probably of Tribonian himself;[40] and the origin of Imperial power, though false in fact and slavish in its consequence, was supported on a principle of freedom and justice. "The pleasure of the emperor has the vigour and effect of law, since the Roman people, by the royal law, have transferred to their prince the full extent of their own power and sovereignty."[41] The will of a single man, of a child, perhaps, was allowed to prevail over the wisdom of ages and the inclinations of millions, and the degenerate Greeks were proud to declare that in his hands alone the arbitrary exercise of legislation could be safely deposited. "What interest or passion," exclaims Theophilus in the court of Justinian, "can reach the calm and sublime elevation of the monarch? he is already master of the lives and fortunes of his subjects, and those who have incurred his displeasure are already numbered with the dead."[42] Disdaining the language of flattery, the historian may confess that in questions of private jurisprudence the absolute sovereign of a great empire can seldom be influenced by any personal considerations. Virtue, or even reason, will suggest to his impartial mind that he is the guardian of peace and equity, and that the interest of society is inseparably connected with his own. Under the weakest and most vicious reign, the seat of justice was filled by the wisdom and integrity of Papinian and Ulpian,[43] and the purest materials of the Code and Pandects are inscribed with the names of Caracalla and his ministers.[44] The tyrant of Rome was sometimes the benefactor of the provinces. A dagger terminated the crimes of Domitian; but the prudence of Nerva confirmed his acts, which in the joy of their deliverance, had been rescinded by an indignant senate.[45] Yet in the *rescripts*,[46] replies to the consultations of the magistrates, the wisest of princes might be deceived by a partial exposition of the case. And this abuse, which placed their hasty decisions on the same level with mature and deliberate acts of legislation, was ineffectually condemned by the sense and example of Trajan. The *rescripts* of the emperor, his *grants* and *decrees*, his *edicts* and *pragmatic sanctions*, were subscribed in purple ink,[47] and transmitted to the provinces as general or special laws, which the magistrates were bound to execute and the people to obey. But as their number continually multiplied, the rule of obedience became each day more doubtful and obscure, till the will of the sovereign was fixed and ascertained in the Gregorian, the Hermogenian, and the Theodosian codes. The two first, of which some fragments have escaped, were framed by two private lawyers to preserve the constitutions of the Pagan emperors from Hadrian to Constantine. The third, which is still extant, was digested in sixteen books by the order of the younger Theodosius to consecrate the laws of the Christian princes from Constantine to his own reign. But the three codes obtained an equal authority in the tribunals, and any act which was not included in the sacred deposit might be disregarded by the judge as spurious or obsolete.[48]

Among savage nations the want of letters is imperfectly supplied by the use of visible signs, which awaken attention and perpetuate the remembrance of any public or private transaction. The jurisprudence of the first Romans exhibited the scenes of a pantomime; the words were adapted to the gestures, and the slightest error or neglect in the *forms* of proceeding was sufficient to annul the *substance* of the fairest claim. The communion of the marriage-life was denoted by the necessary elements of fire and water;[49] and the divorced wife resigned the bunch of keys, by the delivery of which she had been invested with the government of the family. The manumission of a son or a slave was performed by turning him round with a gentle blow on the cheek; a work was prohibited by the casting of a stone; prescription was interrupted by the breaking of a branch; the clenched fist was the symbol of a pledge or deposit; the right hand was the gift of faith and confidence. The indenture of covenants was a broken straw; weights and scales were introduced into every payment; and the heir who accepted a testament was sometimes obliged to snap his fingers, to cast away his garments, and to leap and dance with real or affected transport.[50] If a citizen pursued any stolen goods into a neighbour's house, he concealed his nakedness with a linen towel, and hid his face with a mask or basin, lest he should encounter the eyes of a virgin or a matron.[51] In a civil action, the plaintiff touched the ear of his witness, seized his reluctant adversary by the neck, and implored, in solemn lamentation, the aid of his fellow-citizens. The two competitors grasped each other's hand as if they stood prepared for combat before the tribunal of the prætor; he commanded them to produce the object of the dispute; they went, they returned with measured steps, and a clod of earth was cast at his feet to represent the field for which they contended. This occult science of the words and actions of law was the inheritance of the pontiffs and patricians. Like the Chaldæan astrologers, they announced to their clients the days of business and repose; these important trifles were interwoven with the religion of Numa, and after the publication of the Twelve Tables the Roman people was still enslaved by the ignorance of judicial proceedings. The treachery of some plebeian officers at length revealed the profitable mystery; in a more enlightened age the legal actions were derided and observed, and the same antiquity which sanctified the practice, obliterated the use and meaning, of this primitive language.[52]

A more liberal art was cultivated, however, by the sages of Rome, who, in a stricter sense, may be considered as the authors of the civil law. The alteration of the idiom and manners of the Romans rendered the style of the Twelve Tables less familiar to each rising generation, and the doubtful passages were imperfectly explained by the study of legal antiquarians. To define the ambiguities, to circumscribe the latitude, to apply the principles, to extend the consequences, to reconcile the real or apparent contradictions, was a much nobler and more important task; and the province of legislation was silently invaded by the expounders of ancient statutes. Their subtle interpretations concurred with the equity of the prætor to reform the tyranny of the darker ages; however strange or intricate the means, it was the aim of artificial jurisprudence to restore the simple dictates of nature and reason, and the skill of private citizens was usefully employed to undermine the public institutions of their country. The revolution of almost one thousand years, from the Twelve Tables to the reign of Justinian, may be divided into three periods almost equal in duration, and distinguished from each other by the mode of instruction and the character of the civilians.[53] Pride and ignorance contributed, during the first period, to confine within narrow limits the science of the Roman law. On the public days of market or assembly the masters of the art were seen walking in the forum, ready to impart the needful advice to the meanest of their fellow-citizens, from whose votes, on a future occasion, they might solicit a grateful return. As their years and honours increased, they seated themselves at home on a chair or throne, to expect, with patient gravity, the visits of their clients, who at the dawn of day, from the town and country, began to thunder at their door. The duties of social life and the incidents of judicial proceeding were the ordinary subject of these consultations, and the verbal or written opinions of the *juris-consults* was framed according to the rules of prudence and law. The youths of their own order and family were permitted to listen; their children enjoyed the benefit of more private lessons, and the Mucian race was long renowned for the hereditary knowledge of the civil law. The second period, the learned and splendid age of jurisprudence, may be extended from the birth of Cicero to the reign of Severus Alexander. A system was formed, schools were instituted, books were composed, and both the living and the dead became subservient to the instruction of the student. The *tripartite* of Ælius Pætus, surnamed Catus, or the Cunning, was preserved as the oldest work of jurisprudence. Cato the censor derived some additional fame from his legal studies and those of his son; the kindred appellation of Mucius Scævola was illustrated by three sages of the law, but the perfection of the science was ascribed to Servius Sulpicius, their disciple, and the friend of Tully; and the long succession, which shone with equal lustre under the repub-

lic and under the Cæsars, is finally closed by the respectable characters of Papinian, of Paul, and of Ulpian. Their names, and the various titles of their productions, have been minutely preserved, and the example of Labeo may suggest some idea of their diligence and fecundity. That eminent lawyer of the Augustan age divided the year between the city and country, between business and composition, and four hundred books are enumerated as the fruit of his retirement. Of the collections of his rival Capito, the two hundred and fifty-ninth book is expressly quoted, and few teachers could deliver their opinions in less than a century of volumes. In the third period, between the reigns of Alexander and Justinian, the oracles of jurisprudence were almost mute. The measure of curiosity had been filled; the throne was occupied by tyrants and barbarians; the active spirits were diverted by religious disputes; and the professors of Rome, Constantinople, and Berytus, were humbly content to repeat the lessons of their more enlightened predecessors. From the slow advances and rapid decay of these legal studies, it may be inferred that they require a state of peace and refinement. From the multitude of voluminous civilians who fill the intermediate space, it is evident that such studies may be pursued, and such works may be performed, with a common share of judgment, experience, and industry. The genius of Cicero and Virgil was more sensibly felt, as each revolving age had been found incapable of producing a similar or a second; but the most eminent teachers of the law were assured of leaving disciples equal or superior to themselves in merit and reputation.

The jurisprudence which had been grossly adapted to the wants of the first Romans was polished and improved in the seventh century of the city by the alliance of Grecian philosophy. The Scævolas had been taught by use and experience; but Servius Sulpicius was the first civilian who established his art on a certain and general theory.[54] For the discernment of truth and falsehood he applied, as an infallible rule, the logic of Aristotle and the stoics, reduced particular cases to general principles, and diffused over the shapeless mass the light of order and eloquence. Cicero, his contemporary and friend, declined the reputation of a professed lawyer; but the jurisprudence of his country was adorned by his incomparable genius, which converts into gold every object that it touches. After the example of Plato, he composed a republic; and, for the use of his republic, a treatise of laws, in which he labours to deduce from a celestial ori-

gin the wisdom and justice of the Roman constitution. The whole universe, according to his
sublime hypothesis, forms one immense commonwealth: gods and men, who participate of
the same essence, are members of the same community; reason prescribes the law of nature and
nations; and all positive institutions, however
modified by accident or custom, are drawn
from the rule of right, which the Deity has inscribed on every virtuous mind. From these philosophical mysteries he mildly excludes the
sceptics who refuse to believe, and the epicu-
reans who are unwilling to act. The latter disdain the care of the republic: he advises them to
slumber in their shady gardens. But he humbly
entreats that the new Academy would be silent,
since her bold objections would too soon destroy
the fair and well-ordered structure of his lofty
system.[55] Plato, Aristotle, and Zeno he represents as the only teachers who arm and instruct
a citizen for the duties of social life. Of these, the
armour of the stoics[56] was found to be of the
firmest temper; and it was chiefly worn, both
for use and ornament, in the schools of jurisprudence. From the Portico the Roman civilians
learned to live, to reason, and to die: but they
imbibed in some degree the prejudices of the
sect; the love of paradox, the pertinacious habits of dispute, and a minute attachment to
words and verbal distinctions. The superiority
of *form* to *matter* was introduced to ascertain the
right of property: and the equality of crimes is
countenanced by an opinion of Trebatius,[57]
that he who touches the ear touches the whole
body; and that he who steals from a heap of
corn or a hogshead of wine, is guilty of the entire theft.[58]

Arms, eloquence, and the study of the civil
law promoted a citizen to the honours of the
Roman state; and the three professions were
sometimes more conspicuous by their union in
the same character. In the composition of the
edict a learned prætor gave a sanction and preference to his private sentiments; the opinion of
a censor or a consul was entertained with respect; and a doubtful interpretation of the laws
might be supported by the virtues or triumphs
of the civilian. The patrician arts were long protected by the veil of mystery; and in more enlightened times the freedom of inquiry established the general principles of jurisprudence.
Subtle and intricate cases were elucidated by
the disputes of the forum; rules, axioms, and
definitions[59] were admitted as the genuine dictates of reason; and the consent of the legal professors was interwoven into the practice of the

tribunals. But these interpreters could neither
enact nor execute the laws of the republic; and
the judges might disregard the authority of the
Scævolas themselves, which was often overthrown by the eloquence or sophistry of an ingenious pleader.[60] Augustus and Tiberius were
the first to adopt, as a useful engine, the science
of the civilians; and their servile labours accommodated the old system to the spirit and
views of despotism. Under the fair pretence of
securing the dignity of the art, the privilege of
subscribing legal and valid opinions was confined to the sages of senatorian or equestrian
rank, who had been previously approved by the
judgment of the prince; and this monopoly
prevailed till Hadrian restored the freedom of
the profession to every citizen conscious of his
abilities and knowledge. The discretion of the
prætor was now governed by the lessons of his
teachers; the judges were enjoined to obey the
comment as well as the text of the law; and the
use of codicils was a memorable innovation,
which Augustus ratified by the advice of the
civilians.[61]

The most absolute mandate could only require that the judges should agree with the
civilians, if the civilians agreed among themselves. But positive institutions are often the
result of custom and prejudice; laws and language are ambiguous and arbitrary; where
reason is incapable of pronouncing, the love of
argument is inflamed by the envy of rivals, the
vanity of masters, the blind attachment of their
disciples; and the Roman jurisprudence was
divided by the once famous sects of the *Proculians*
and *Sabinians*.[62] Two sages of the law, Ateius
Capito and Antistius Labeo,[63] adorned the
peace of the Augustan age: the former distinguished by the favour of his sovereign; the
latter more illustrious by his contempt of that
favour, and his stern though harmless opposition
to the tyrant of Rome. Their legal studies were
influenced by the various colours of their temper
and principles. Labeo was attached to the form
of the old republic; his rival embraced the more
profitable substance of the rising monarchy.
But the disposition of a courtier is tame and
submissive; and Capito seldom presumed to
deviate from the sentiments, or at least from the
words, of his predecessors; while the bold republican pursued his independent ideas without fear of paradox or innovations. The freedom
of Labeo was enslaved, however, by the rigour
of his own conclusions, and he decided, according to the letter of the law, the same questions
which his indulgent competitor resolved with a

latitude of equity more suitable to the common sense and feelings of mankind. If a fair exchange had been substituted to the payment of money, Capito still considered the transaction as a legal sale;[64] and he consulted nature for the age of puberty, without confining his definition to the precise period of twelve or fourteen years.[65] This opposition of sentiments was propagated in the writings and lessons of the two founders; the schools of Capito and Labeo maintained their inveterate conflict from the age of Augustus to that of Hadrian;[66] and the two sects derived their appellations from Sabinus and Proculus, their most celebrated teachers. The names of *Cassians* and *Pegasians* were likewise applied to the same parties; but, by a strange reverse, the popular cause was in the hands of Pegasus,[67] a timid slave of Domitian, while the favourite of the Cæsars was represented by Cassius,[68] who gloried in his descent from the patriotic assassin. By the perpetual edict the controversies of the sects were in a great measure determined. For that important work the emperor Hadrian preferred the chief of the Sabinians: the friends of monarchy prevailed; but the moderation of Salvius Julian insensibly reconciled the victors and the vanquished. Like the contemporary philosophers, the lawyers of the age of the Antonines disclaimed the authority of a master, and adopted from every system the most probable doctrines.[69] But their writings would have been less voluminous, had their choice been more unanimous. The conscience of the judge was perplexed by the number and weight of discordant testimonies, and every sentence that his passion or interest might pronounce was justified by the sanction of some venerable name. An indulgent edict of the younger Theodosius excused him from the labour of comparing and weighing their arguments. Five civilians, Caius, Papinian, Paul, Ulpian, and Modestinus, were established as the oracles of jurisprudence: a majority was decisive; but if their opinions were equally divided, a casting vote was ascribed to the superior wisdom of Papinian.[70]

When Justinian ascended the throne, the reformation of the Roman jurisprudence was an arduous but indispensable task. In the space of ten centuries the infinite variety of laws and legal opinions had filled many thousand volumes, which no fortune could purchase and no capacity could digest. Books could not easily be found; and the judges, poor in the midst of riches, were reduced to the exercise of their illiterate discretion. The subjects of the Greek provinces were ignorant of the language that disposed of their lives and properties; and the *barbarous* dialect of the Latins was imperfectly studied in the academies of Berytus and Constantinople. As an Illyrian soldier, that idiom was familiar to the infancy of Justinian; his youth had been instructed by the lessons of jurisprudence, and his Imperial choice selected the most learned civilians of the East, to labour with their sovereign in the work of reformation.[71] The theory of professors was assisted by the practice of advocates and the experience of magistrates; and the whole undertaking was animated by the spirit of Tribonian.[72] This extraordinary man, the object of so much praise and censure, was a native of Side in Pamphilia; and his genius, like that of Bacon, embraced, as his own, all the business and knowledge of the age. Tribonian composed, both in prose and verse, on a strange diversity of curious and abstruse subjects:[73] a double panegyric of Justinian and the Life of the philosopher Theodotus; the nature of happiness and the duties of government; Homer's catalogue and the four-and-twenty sorts of metre; the astronomical canon of Ptolemy; the changes of the months; the houses of the planets; and the harmonic system of the world. To the literature of Greece he added the use of the Latin tongue; the Roman civilians were deposited in his library and in his mind; and he most assiduously cultivated those arts which opened the road of wealth and preferment. From the bar of the prætorian præfects he raised himself to the honours of quæstor, of consul, and of master of the offices: the council of Justinian listened to his eloquence and wisdom; and envy was mitigated by the gentleness and affability of his manners. The reproaches of impiety and avarice have stained the virtues or the reputation of Tribonian. In a bigoted and persecuting court, the principal minister was accused of a secret aversion to the Christian faith, and was supposed to entertain the sentiments of an Atheist and a Pagan, which have been imputed, inconsistently enough, to the last philosophers of Greece. His avarice was more clearly proved and more sensibly felt. If he were swayed by gifts in the administration of justice, the example of Bacon will again occur; nor can the merit of Tribonian atone for his baseness, if he degraded the sanctity of his profession, and if laws were every day enacted, modified, or repealed, for the base consideration of his private emolument. In the sedition of Constantinople, his removal was granted to the clamours, perhaps to the just indignation, of the people: but the quæstor was speedily restored, and, till the hour of his death, he possessed, above twenty years, the favour and confidence of the emperor. His passive and dutiful submission has been honoured with the praise of Justinian himself, whose vanity was incapable of discerning how often that submission degenerated into the grossest adulation. Tribonian adored the virtues of his gracious master: the earth was unworthy of such a prince; and he affected a pious fear, that Justinian, like Elijah or Romulus, would be snatched into the air, and translated alive to the mansions of celestial glory.[74]

If Cæsar had achieved the reformation of the Roman law, his creative genius, enlightened by reflection and study, would have given to the world a pure and original system of jurisprudence. Whatever flattery might suggest, the emperor of the East was afraid to establish his private judgment as the standard of equity: in the possession of legislative power, he borrowed the aid of time and opinion; and his laborious compilations are guarded by the sages and legislators of past times. Instead of a statue cast in a simple mould by the hand of an artist, the works of Justinian represent a tesselated pavement of antique and costly, but too often of incoherent, fragments. In the first year of his reign, he directed the faithful Tribonian, and nine learned associates, to revise the ordinances of his predecessors, as they were contained, since the time of Hadrian, in the Gregorian, Hermogenian, and Theodosian codes, to purge the errors and contradictions, to retrench whatever was obsolete or superfluous, and to select the wise and salutary laws best adapted to the practice of the tribunals and the use of his subjects. The work was accomplished in fourteen months; and the twelve books or *tables*, which the new decemvirs produced, might be designed to imitate the labours of their Roman predecessors. The new CODE of Justinian was honoured with his name, and confirmed by his royal signature: authentic transcripts were multiplied by the pens of notaries and scribes; they were transmitted to the magistrates of the European, the Asiatic, and afterwards the African provinces; and the law of the empire was proclaimed on solemn festivals at the doors of churches. A more arduous operation was still behind—to extract the spirit of jurisprudence from the decisions and conjectures, the questions and disputes, of the Roman civilians. Seventeen lawyers, with Tribonian at their head, were appointed by the emperor to exercise an absolute jurisdiction over the works of

their predecessors. If they had obeyed his commands in ten years, Justinian would have been satisfied with their diligence; and the rapid composition of the DIGEST or PANDECTS[75] in three years will deserve praise or censure according to the merit of the execution. From the library of Tribonian they chose forty, the most eminent civilians of former times:[76] two thousand treatises were comprised in an abridgment of fifty books; and it has been carefully recorded that three millions of lines or sentences[77] were reduced, in this abstract, to the moderate number of one hundred and fifty thousand. The edition of this great work was delayed a month after that of the INSTITUTES; and it seemed reasonable that the elements should precede the digest of the Roman law. As soon as the emperor had approved their labours, he ratified, by his legislative power, the speculations of these private citizens: their commentaries on the Twelve Tables, the Perpetual Edict, the laws of the people, and the decrees of the senate, succeeded to the authority of the text; and the text was abandoned, as a useless, though venerable, relic of antiquity. The *Code*, the *Pandects*, and the *Institutes* were declared to be the legitimate system of civil jurisprudence; they alone were admitted in the tribunals, and they alone were taught in the academies, of Rome, Constantinople, and Berytus. Justinian addressed to the senate and provinces his *eternal oracles*: and his pride, under the mask of piety, ascribed the consummation of this great design to the support and inspiration of the Deity.

Since the emperor declined the fame and envy of original composition, we can only require at his hands method, choice, and fidelity —the humble, though indispensable, virtues of a compiler. Among the various combinations of ideas it is difficult to assign any reasonable preference; but, as the order of Justinian is different in his three works, it is possible that all may be wrong, and it is certain that two cannot be right. In the selection of ancient laws he seems to have viewed his predecessors without jealousy and with equal regard: the series could not ascend above the reign of Hadrian, and the narrow distinction of Paganism and Christianity, introduced by the superstition of Theodosius, had been abolished by the consent of mankind. But the jurisprudence of the Pandects is circumscribed within a period of a hundred years, from the Perpetual Edict to the death of Severus Alexander: the civilians who lived under the first Cæsars are seldom permitted to speak, and only three names can be attributed to the age of the republic. The favourite of Justinian (it has been fiercely urged) was fearful of encountering the light of freedom and the gravity of Roman sages. Tribonian condemned to oblivion the genuine and native wisdom of Cato, the Scævolas, and Sulpicius; while he invoked spirits more congenial to his own, the Syrians, Greeks, and Africans, who flocked to the Imperial court to study Latin as a foreign tongue, and jurisprudence as a lucrative profession. But the ministers of Justinian[78] were instructed to labour not for the curiosity of antiquarians, but for the immediate benefit of his subjects. It was their duty to select the useful and practical parts of the Roman law; and the writings of the old republicans, however curious or excellent, were no longer suited to the new system of manners, religion, and government. Perhaps, if the preceptors and friends of Cicero were still alive, our candour would acknowledge that, except in purity of language,[79] their intrinsic merit was excelled by the school of Papinian and Ulpian. The science of the laws is the slow growth of time and experience, and the advantage both of method and materials is naturally assumed by the most recent authors. The civilians of the reign of the Antonines had studied the works of their predecessors: their philosophic spirit had mitigated the rigour of antiquity, simplified the forms of proceeding, and emerged from the jealousy and prejudice of the rival sects. The choice of the authorities that compose the Pandects depended on the judgment of Tribonian; but the power of his sovereign could not absolve him from the sacred obligations of truth and fidelity. As the legislator of the empire, Justinian might repeal the acts of the Antonines, or condemn as seditious the free principles which were maintained by the last of the *Roman* lawyers.[80] But the existence of past facts is placed beyond the reach of despotism; and the emperor was guilty of fraud and forgery when he corrupted the integrity of their text, inscribed with their venerable names the words and ideas of his servile reign,[81] and suppressed by the hand of power the pure and authentic copies of their sentiments. The changes and interpolations of Tribonian and his colleagues are excused by the pretence of uniformity: but their cares have been insufficient, and the *antinomies*, or contradictions, of the Code and Pandects, still exercise the patience and subtlety of modern civilians.[82]

A rumour, devoid of evidence, has been propagated by the enemies of Justinian, that the jurisprudence of ancient Rome was reduced to ashes by the author of the Pandects, from the vain persuasion that it was now either false or superfluous. Without usurping an office so invidious, the emperor might safely commit to ignorance and time the accomplishment of this destructive wish. Before the invention of printing and paper, the labour and the materials of writing could be purchased only by the rich; and it may reasonably be computed that the price of books was a hundred-fold their present value.[83] Copies were slowly multiplied and cautiously renewed: the hopes of profit tempted the sacrilegious scribes to erase the characters of antiquity, and Sophocles or Tacitus were obliged to resign the parchment to missals, homilies, and the golden legend.[84] If such was the fate of the most beautiful compositions of genius, what stability could be expected for the dull and barren works of an obsolete science? The books of jurisprudence were interesting to few and entertaining to none; their value was connected with present use, and they sunk for ever as soon as that use was superseded by the innovations of fashion, superior merit, or public authority. In the age of peace and learning, between Cicero and the last of the Antonines, many losses had been already sustained, and some luminaries of the school or forum were known only to the curious by tradition and report. Three hundred and sixty years of disorder and decay accelerated the progress of oblivion; and it may fairly be presumed that, of the writings which Justinian is accused of neglecting, many were no longer to be found in the libraries of the East.[85] The copies of Papinian or Ulpian, which the reformer had proscribed, were deemed unworthy of future notice; the Twelve Tables and prætorian edict insensibly vanished; and the monuments of ancient Rome were neglected or destroyed by the envy and ignorance of the Greeks. Even the Pandects themselves have escaped with difficulty and danger from the common shipwreck, and criticism has pronounced that *all* the editions and manuscripts of the West are derived from one original.[86] It was transcribed at Constantinople in the beginning of the seventh century,[87] was successively transported by the accidents of war and commerce to Amalphi,[88] Pisa,[89] and Florence,[90] and is now deposited as a sacred relic[91] in the ancient palace of the republic.[92]

It is the first care of a reformer to prevent any future reformation. To maintain the text of the Pandects, the Institutes, and the Code, the use of ciphers and abbreviations was rigorously proscribed; and as Justinian recollected that the Perpetual Edict had been buried under the weight of commentators, he denounced the punishment of forgery against the rash civilians who should presume to interpret or pervert the will of their sovereign. The scholars of Accursius, of Bartolus, of Cujacius, should blush for their accumulated guilt, unless they dare to dispute his right of binding the authority of his successors and the native freedom of the mind. But the emperor was unable to fix his own inconstancy; and, while he boasted of renewing the exchange of Diomede, of transmuting brass into gold,[93] he discovered the necessity of purifying his gold from the mixture of baser alloy. Six years had not elapsed from the publication of the Code before he condemned the imperfect attempt by a new and more accurate edition of the same work, which he enriched with two hundred of his own laws and fifty decisions of the darkest and most intricate points of jurisprudence. Every year, or, according to Procopius, each day, of his long reign was marked by some legal innovation. Many of his acts were rescinded by himself; many were rejected by his successors; many have been obliterated by time; but the number of sixteen EDICTS, and one hundred and sixty-eight NOVELS,[94] has been admitted into the authentic body of the civil jurisprudence. In the opinion of a philosopher superior to the prejudices of his profession, these incessant, and for the most part trifling alterations, can be only explained by the venal spirit of a prince who sold without shame his judgments and his laws.[95] The charge of the secret historian is indeed explicit and vehement; but the sole instance which he produces may be ascribed to the devotion as well as to the avarice of Justinian. A wealthy bigot had bequeathed his inheritance to the church of Emesa, and its value was enhanced by the dexterity of an artist, who subscribed confessions of debt and promises of payment with the names of the richest Syrians. They pleaded the established prescription of thirty or forty years; but their defence was overruled by a retrospective edict, which extended the claims of the church to the term of a century—an edict so pregnant with injustice and disorder, that, after serving this occasional purpose, it was prudently abolished in the same reign.[96] If candour will acquit the emperor himself, and transfer the corruption to his wife and favourites, the suspicion of so foul a vice must still degrade the majesty of his laws; and the advocates of Justinian may acknowledge that such levity, whatsoever be the motive, is unworthy of a legislator and a man.

Monarchs seldom condescend to become the preceptors of their subjects; and some praise is due to Justinian, by whose command an ample system was reduced to a short and elementary treatise. Among the various institutes of the Roman law,[97] those of Caius [98] were the most popular in the East and West; and their use may be considered as an evidence of their merit. They were selected by the Imperial delegates, Tribonian, Theophilus, and Dorotheus; and the freedom and purity of the Antonines was incrusted with the coarser materials of a degenerate age. The same volume which introduced the youth of Rome, Constantinople, and Berytus to the gradual study of the Code and Pandects, is still precious to the historian, the philosopher, and the magistrate. The INSTITUTES of Justinian are divided into four books: they proceed, with no contemptible method, from, I. *Persons*, to, II. *Things*, and from things to, III. *Actions*; and the article IV., of *Private Wrongs*, is terminated by the principles of *Criminal Law*.

I. The distinction of ranks and *persons* is the firmest basis of a mixed and limited government. In France the remains of liberty are kept alive by the spirit, the honours, and even the prejudices of fifty thousand nobles.[99] Two hundred families supply, in lineal descent, the second branch of the English legislature, which maintains, between the king and commons, the balance of the constitution. A gradation of patricians and plebeians, of strangers and subjects, has supported the aristocracy of Genoa, Venice, and ancient Rome. The perfect equality of men is the point in which the extremes of democracy and despotism are confounded; since the majesty of the prince or people would be offended if any heads were exalted above the level of their fellow-slaves or fellow-citizens. In the decline of the Roman empire, the proud distinctions of the republic were gradually abolished, and the reason or instinct of Justinian completed the simple form of an absolute monarchy. The emperor could not eradicate the popular reverence which always waits on the possession of hereditary wealth or the memory of famous ancestors. He delighted to honour with titles and emoluments his generals, magistrates, and senators; and his precarious indulgence communicated some rays of their glory to the persons of their wives and children. But in the eye of the law all Roman citizens were equal, and all subjects of the empire were citizens of Rome. That inestimable character was degraded to an obsolete and empty name.

The voice of a Roman could no longer enact his laws, or create the annual ministers of his power: his constitutional rights might have checked the arbitrary will of a master; and the bold adventurer from Germany or Arabia was admitted, with equal favour, to the civil and military command, which the citizen alone had been once entitled to assume over the conquests of his fathers. The first Cæsars had scrupulously guarded the distinction of *ingenuous* and *servile* birth, which was decided by the condition of the mother; and the candour of the laws was satisfied if *her* freedom could be ascertained, during a single moment, between the conception and the delivery. The slaves who were liberated by a generous master immediately entered into the middle class of *libertines* or freedmen; but they could never be enfranchised from the duties of obedience and gratitude: whatever were the fruits of their industry, their patron and his family inherited the third part; or even the whole of their fortune if they died without children and without a testament. Justinian respected the rights of patrons; but his indulgence removed the badge of disgrace from the two inferior orders of freedmen: whoever ceased to be a slave obtained, without reserve or delay, the station of a citizen; and at length the dignity of an ingenuous birth, which nature had refused, was created, or supposed, by the omnipotence of the emperor. Whatever restraints of age, or forms, or numbers, had been formerly introduced to check the abuse of manumissions and the too rapid increase of vile and indigent Romans, he finally abolished; and the spirit of his laws promoted the extinction of domestic servitude. Yet the eastern provinces were filled, in the time of Justinian, with multitudes of slaves, either born or purchased for the use of their masters; and the price, from ten to seventy pieces of gold, was determined by their age, their strength, and their education.[100] But the hardships of this dependent state were continually diminished by the influence of government and religion; and the pride of a subject was no longer elated by his absolute dominion over the life and happiness of his bondsman.[101]

The law of nature instructs most animals to cherish and educate their infant progeny. The law of reason inculcates to the human species the returns of filial piety. But the exclusive, absolute, and perpetual dominion of the father over his children is peculiar to the Roman jurisprudence,[102] and seems to be coeval with the foundation of the city.[103] The paternal power was instituted or confirmed by Romulus himself; and, after the practice of three centuries, it was inscribed on the fourth table of the Decemvirs. In the forum, the senate, or the camp, the adult son of a Roman citizen enjoyed the public and private rights of a *person*: in his father's house he was a mere *thing*; confounded by the laws with the movables, the cattle, and the slaves, whom the capricious master might alienate or destroy without being responsible to any earthly tribunal. The hand which bestowed the daily sustenance might resume the voluntary gift, and whatever was acquired by the labour or fortune of the son was immediately lost in the property of the father. His stolen goods (his oxen or his children) might be recovered by the same action of theft;[104] and if either had been guilty of a trespass, it was in his own option to compensate the damage, or resign to the injured party the obnoxious animal. At the call of indigence or avarice, the master of a family could dispose of his children or his slaves. But the condition of the slave was far more advantageous, since he regained, by the first manumission, his alienated freedom: the son was again restored to his unnatural father; he might be condemned to servitude a second and a third time, and it was not till after the third sale and deliverance[105] that he was enfranchised from the domestic power which had been so repeatedly abused. According to his descretion, a father might chastise the real or imaginary faults of his children by stripes, by imprisonment, by exile, by sending them to the country to work in chains among the meanest of his servants. The majesty of a parent was armed with the power of life and death;[106] and the examples of such bloody executions, which were sometimes praised and never punished, may be traced in the annals of Rome, beyond the times of Pompey and Augustus. Neither age, nor rank, nor the consular office, nor the honours of a triumph, could exempt the most illustrious citizen from the bonds of filial subjection:[107] his own descendants were included in the family of their common ancestor; and the claims of adoption were not less sacred or less rigorous than those of nature. Without fear, though not without danger of abuse, the Roman legislators had reposed an unbounded confidence in the sentiments of paternal love; and the oppression was tempered by the assurance that each generation must succeed in its turn to the awful dignity of parent and master.

The first limitation of paternal power is ascribed to the justice and humanity of Numa; and the maid who, with *his* father's consent, had espoused a freeman, was protected from the disgrace of becoming the wife of a slave. In the first ages, when the city was pressed and often famished by her Latin and Tuscan neighbours, the sale of children might be a frequent practice; but as a Roman could not legally purchase the liberty of his fellow-citizen, the market must gradually fail, and the trade would be destroyed by the conquests of the republic. An imperfect right of property was at length communicated to sons; and the threefold distinction of *profectitious*, *adventitious*, and *professional* was ascertained by the jurisprudence of the Code and Pandects.[108] Of all that proceeded from the father he imparted only the use, and reserved the absolute dominion; yet, if his goods were sold, the filial portion was excepted, by a favourable interpretation, from the demands of the creditors. In whatever accrued by marriage, gift, or collateral succession, the property was secured to the son; but the father, unless he had been specially excluded, enjoyed the usufruct during his life. As a just and prudent reward of military virtue, the spoils of the enemy were acquired, possessed, and bequeathed by the soldier alone; and the fair analogy was extended to the emoluments of any liberal profession, the salary of public service, and the sacred liberality of the emperor or the empress. The life of a citizen was less exposed than his fortune to the abuse of paternal power. Yet his life might be adverse to the interest or passions of an unworthy father: the same crimes that flowed from the corruption, were more sensibly felt by the humanity of the Augustan age; and the cruel Erixo, who whipped his son till he expired, was saved by the emperor from the just fury of the multitude.[109] The Roman father, from the licence of servile dominion, was reduced to the gravity and moderation of a judge. The presence and opinion of Augustus confirmed the sentence of exile pronounced against an intentional parricide by the domestic tribunal of Arius. Hadrian transported to an island the jealous parent, who, like a robber, had seized the opportunity of hunting to assassinate a youth, the incestuous lover of his stepmother.[110] A private jurisdiction is repugnant to the spirit of monarchy; the parent was again reduced from a judge to an accuser; and the magistrates were enjoined by Severus Alexander to hear his complaints and execute his sentence. He could no longer take the life of a son without incurring the guilt and punishment of murder; and the pains of parricide, from which he had been excepted by the Pompeian law, were finally inflicted by the justice of Constantine.[111] The same protection was due to every period of existence; and reason must applaud the humanity of Paulus for imputing the crime of murder to the father who strangles, or starves, or abandons his new-born infant, or exposes him in a public place to find the mercy which he himself had denied. But the exposition of children was the prevailing and stubborn vice of antiquity: it was sometimes prescribed, often permitted, almost always practised with impunity by the nations who never entertained the Roman ideas of paternal power; and the dramatic poets, who appeal to the human heart, represent with indifference a popular custom which was palliated by the motives of economy and compassion.[112] If the father could subdue his own feelings, he might escape, though not the censure, at least the chastisement, of the laws; and the Roman empire was stained with the blood of infants, till such murders were included by Valentinian and his colleagues in the letter and spirit of the Cornelian law. The lessons of jurisprudence [113] and Christianity had been insufficient to eradicate this inhuman practice, till their gentle influence was fortified by the terrors of capital punishment.[114]

Experience has proved that savages are the tyrants of the female sex, and that the condition of women is usually softened by the refinements of social life. In the hope of a robust progeny, Lycurgus had delayed the season of marriage: it was fixed by Numa at the tender age of twelve years, that the Roman husband might educate to his will a pure and obedient virgin.[115] According to the custom of antiquity, he bought his bride of her parents, and she fulfilled the *coemption* by purchasing, with three pieces of copper, a just introduction to his house and household deities. A sacrifice of fruits was offered by the pontiffs in the presence of ten witnesses; the contracting parties were seated on the same sheepskin; they tasted a salt cake of *far*, or rice; and this *confarreation*,[116] which denoted the ancient food of Italy, served as an emblem of their mystic union of mind and body. But this union on the side of the woman was rigorous and unequal; and she renounced the name and worship of her father's house, to embrace a new servitude, decorated only by the title of adoption: a fiction of the law, neither rational nor elegant, bestowed on the mother of a family[117] (her proper appellation) the strange characters of sister to her own children and of daughter to her husband or master, who was invested with the plenitude of paternal

power. By his judgment or caprice her behaviour was approved, or censured, or chastised;
he exercised the jurisdiction of life and death;
and it was allowed that in the cases of adultery
or drunkenness [118] the sentence might be properly inflicted. She acquired and inherited for
the sole profit of her lord; and so clearly was
woman defined, not as a *person*, but as a *thing*,
that, if the original title were deficient, she
might be claimed, like other movables, by the
use and possession of an entire year. The inclination of the Roman husband discharged or
withheld the conjugal debt, so scrupulously
exacted by the Athenian and Jewish laws:[119]
but as polygamy was unknown, he could never
admit to his bed a fairer or more favoured
partner.

After the Punic triumphs the matrons of
Rome aspired to the common benefits of a free
and opulent republic; their wishes were gratified by the indulgence of fathers and lovers, and
their ambition was unsuccessfully resisted by
the gravity of Cato the Censor.[120] They declined
the solemnities of the old nuptials, defeated the
annual prescription by an absence of three days,
and, without losing their name or independence, subscribed the liberal and definite terms
of a marriage contract. Of their private fortunes
they communicated the use and secured the
property: the estates of a wife could neither be
alienated nor mortgaged by a prodigal husband;
their mutual gifts were prohibited by the jealousy of the laws; and the misconduct of either
party might afford, under another name, a
future subject for an action of theft. To this
loose and voluntary compact religious and civil
rites were no longer essential, and between
persons of a similar rank the apparent community of life was allowed as sufficient evidence
of their nuptials. The dignity of marriage was
restored by the Christians, who derived all
spiritual grace from the prayers of the faithful
and the benediction of the priest or bishop. The
origin, validity, and duties of the holy institution
were regulated by the tradition of the synagogue, the precepts of the Gospel, and the
canons of general or provincial synods;[121] and
the conscience of the Christians was awed by
the decrees and censures of their ecclesiastical
rulers. Yet the magistrates of Justinian were not
subject to the authority of the church; the emperor consulted the unbelieving civilians of
antiquity; and the choice of matrimonial laws
in the Code and Pandects is directed by the
earthly motives of justice, policy, and the
natural freedom of both sexes.[122]

Besides the agreement of the parties, the
essence of every rational contract, the Roman
marriage required the previous approbation of
the parents. A father might be forced by some
recent laws to supply the wants of a mature
daughter, but even his insanity was not generally allowed to supersede the necessity of his
consent. The causes of the dissolution of matrimony have varied among the Romans;[123] but
the most solemn sacrament, the confarreation
itself, might always be done away by rites of a
contrary tendency. In the first ages the father of
a family might sell his children, and his wife
was reckoned in the number of his children: the
domestic judge might pronounce the death of
the offender, or his mercy might expel her from
his bed and house; but the slavery of the wretched
female was hopeless and perpetual, unless he
asserted for his own convenience the manly
prerogative of divorce. The warmest applause
has been lavished on the virtue of the Romans,
who abstained from the exercise of this tempting privilege above five hundred years;[124] but
the same fact evinces the unequal terms of a
connection in which the slave was unable to renounce her tyrant, and the tyrant was unwilling
to relinquish his slave. When the Roman matrons
became the equal and voluntary companions of
their lords, a new jurisprudence was introduced, that marriage, like other partnerships,
might be dissolved by the abdication of one of
the associates. In three centuries of prosperity
and corruption, this principle was enlarged to
frequent practice and pernicious abuse. Passion,
interest, or caprice suggested daily motives for
the dissolution of marriage; a word, a sign, a
message, a letter, the mandate of a freedman,
declared the separation; the most tender of
human connections was degraded to a transient
society of profit or pleasure. According to the
various conditions of life, both sexes alternately
felt the disgrace and injury: an inconstant
spouse transferred her wealth to a new family,
abandoning a numerous, perhaps a spurious,
progeny to the paternal authority and care of
her late husband; a beautiful virgin might be
dismissed to the world, old, indigent, and
friendless; but the reluctance of the Romans,
when they were pressed to marriage by Augustus, sufficiently marks that the prevailing institutions were least favourable to the males. A
specious theory is confuted by this free and
perfect experiment, which demonstrates that
the liberty of divorce does not contribute to
happiness and virtue. The facility of separation
would destroy all mutual confidence, and in-

flame every trifling dispute: the minute difference between a husband and a stranger, which might so easily be removed, might still more easily be forgotten; and the matron who in five years can submit to the embraces of eight husbands must cease to reverence the chastity of her own person.[125]

Insufficient remedies followed with distant and tardy steps the rapid progress of the evil. The ancient worship of the Romans afforded a peculiar goddess to hear and reconcile the complaints of a married life; but her epithet of *Viriplaca*,[126] the appeaser of husbands, too clearly indicates on which side submission and repentance were always expected. Every act of a citizen was subject to the judgment of the *censors*; the first who used the privilege of divorce assigned at their command the motives of his conduct;[127] and a senator was expelled for dismissing his virgin spouse without the knowledge or advice of his friends. Whenever an action was instituted for the recovery of a marriage-portion, the *prætor*, as the guardian of equity, examined the cause and the characters, and gently inclined the scale in favour of the guiltless and injured party. Augustus, who united the powers of both magistrates, adopted their different modes of repressing or chastising the licence of divorce.[128] The presence of seven Roman witnesses was required for the validity of this solemn and deliberate act: if any adequate provocation had been given by the husband, instead of the delay of two years, he was compelled to refund immediately or in the space of six months; but if he could arraign the manners of his wife, her guilt or levity was expiated by the loss of the sixth of eighth part of her marriage-portion. The Christian princes were the first who specified the just causes of a private divorce; their institutions, from Constantine to Justinian, appear to fluctuate between the custom of the empire and the wishes of the church;[129] and the author of the Novels too frequently reforms the jurisprudence of the Code and Pandects. In the most rigorous laws a wife was condemned to support a gamester, a drunkard, or a libertine, unless he were guilty of homicide, poison, or sacrilege; in which cases the marriage, as it should seem, might have been dissolved by the hand of the executioner. But the sacred right of the husband was invariably maintained to deliver his name and family from the disgrace of adultery; the list of *mortal* sins, either male or female, was curtailed and enlarged by successive regulations, and the obstacles of incurable impotence, long absence,

and monastic profession, were allowed to rescind the matrimonial obligation. Whoever transgressed the permission of the law was subject to various and heavy penalties. The woman was stripped of her wealth and ornaments, without excepting the bodkin of her hair; if the man introduced a new bride into his bed, *her* fortune might be lawfully seized by the vengeance of his exiled wife. Forfeiture was sometimes commuted to a fine; the fine was sometimes aggravated by transportation to an island, or imprisonment in a monastery; the injured party was released from the bonds of marriage, but the offender, during life or a term of years, was disabled from the repetition of nuptials. The successor of Justinian yielded to the prayers of his unhappy subjects, and restored the liberty of divorce by mutual consent; the civilians were unanimous,[130] the theologians were divided,[131] and the ambiguous word which contains the precept of Christ is flexible to any interpretation that the wisdom of a legislator can demand.

The freedom of love and marriage was restrained among the Romans by natural and civil impediments. An instinct, almost innate and universal, appears to prohibit the incestuous commerce[132] of parents and children in the infinite series of ascending and descending generations. Concerning the oblique and collateral branches nature is indifferent, reason mute, and custom various and arbitrary. In Egypt the marriage of brothers and sisters was admitted without scruple or exception: a Spartan might espouse the daughter of his father; an Athenian, that of his mother; and the nuptials of an uncle with his niece were applauded at Athens as a happy union of the dearest relations. The profane lawgivers of Rome were never tempted by interest or superstition to multiply the forbidden degrees; but they inflexibly condemned the marriage of sisters and brothers, hesitated whether first-cousins should be touched by the same interdict, revered the parental character of aunts and uncles, and treated affinity and adoption as a just imitation of the ties of blood. According to the proud maxims of the republic, a legal marriage could only be contracted by free citizens; an honourable, at least an ingenuous, birth was required for the spouse of a senator: but the blood of kings could never mingle in legitimate nuptials with the blood of a Roman; and the name of Stranger degraded Cleopatra and Berenice[133] to live the *concubines* of Mark Antony and Titus.[134] This appellation, indeed, so injurious to the majesty, cannot without indulgence be applied to the manners, of these Oriental queens. A concubine, in the strict sense of the civilians, was a woman of servile or plebeian extraction, the sole and faithful companion of a Roman citizen, who continued in a state of celibacy. Her modest station, below the honours of a wife, above the infamy of a prostitute, was acknowledged and approved by the laws: from the age of Augustus to the tenth century the use of this secondary marriage prevailed both in the West and East; and the humble virtues of a concubine were often preferred to the pomp and insolence of a noble matron. In this connection the two Antonines, the best of princes and of men, enjoyed the comforts of domestic love; the example was imitated by many citizens impatient of celibacy, but regardful of their families. If at any time they desired to legitimate their natural children, the conversion was instantly performed by the celebration of their nuptials with a partner whose fruitfulness and fidelity they had already tried. By this epithet of *natural* the offspring of the concubine were distinguished from the spurious brood of adultery, prostitution, and incest, to whom Justinian reluctantly grants the necessary aliments of life; and these natural children alone were capable of succeeding to a sixth part of the inheritance of their reputed father. According to the rigour of law, bastards were entitled only to the name and condition of their mother, from whom they might derive the character of a slave, a stranger, or a citizen. The outcasts of every family were adopted, without reproach, as the children of the state.[135]

The relation of guardian and ward, or, in Roman words, of *tutor* and *pupil*, which covers so many titles of the Institutes and Pandects,[136] is of a very simple and uniform nature. The person and property of an orphan must always be trusted to the custody of some discreet friend. If the deceased father had not signified his choice, the *agnats*, or paternal kindred of the nearest degree, were compelled to act as the natural guardians: the Athenians were apprehensive of exposing the infant to the power of those most interested in his death; but an axiom of Roman jurisprudence has pronounced that the charge of tutelage should constantly attend the emolument of succession. If the choice of the father and the line of consanguinity afforded no efficient guardian, the failure was supplied by the nomination of the prætor of the city or the president of the province; but the person whom they named to this *public* office might be legally excused by insanity or blindness, by ignorance or inability, by previous enmity or adverse interest, by the number of children or guardianships with which he was already burthened, and by the immunities which were granted to the useful labours of magistrates, lawyers, physicians, and professors. Till the infant could speak and think, he was represented by the tutor, whose authority was finally determined by the age of puberty. Without his consent, no act of the pupil could bind himself to his own prejudice, though it might oblige others for his personal benefit. It is needless to observe that the tutor often gave security, and always rendered an account; and that the want of diligence or integrity exposed him to a civil and almost criminal action for the violation of his sacred trust. The age of puberty had been rashly fixed by the civilians at fourteen; but, as the faculties of the mind ripen more slowly than those of the body, a *curator* was interposed to guard the fortunes of a Roman youth from his own inexperience and headstrong passions. Such a trustee had been first instituted by the prætor to save the family from the blind havoc of a prodigal or madman; and the minor was compelled by the laws to solicit the same protection to give validity to his acts till he accomplished the full period of twenty-five years. Women were condemned to the perpetual tutelage of parents, husbands, or guardians; a sex created to please and obey was never supposed to have attained the age of reason and experience. Such at least was the stern and haughty spirit of the ancient law, which had been insensibly mollified before the time of Justinian.

II. The original right of property can only be justified by the accident or merit of prior occupancy; and on this foundation it is wisely established by the philosophy of the civilians.[137] The savage who hollows a tree, inserts a sharp stone into a wooden handle, or applies a string to an elastic branch, becomes in a state of nature the just proprietor of the canoe, the bow, or the hatchet. The materials were common to all; the new form, the produce of his time and simple industry, belongs solely to himself. His hungry brethren cannot, without a sense of their own injustice, extort from the hunter the game of the forest overtaken or slain by his personal strength and dexterity. If his provident care preserves and multiplies the tame animals, whose nature is tractable to the arts of education, he acquires a perpetual title to the use and service of their numerous progeny, which derives its existence from him alone. If he encloses and cultivates a field for their sustenance and his own, a barren waste is converted into a fertile soil; the seed, the manure, the labour, create a new value, and the rewards of harvest are painfully earned by the fatigues of the revolving year. In the successive states of society, the hunter, the shepherd, the husbandman, may defend their possessions by two reasons which forcibly appeal to the feelings of the human mind: that whatever they enjoy is the fruit of their own industry; and that every man who envies their felicity may purchase similar acquisitions by the exercise of similar diligence. Such, in truth, may be the freedom and plenty of a small colony cast on a fruitful island. But the colony multiplies, while the space still continues the same; the common rights, the equal inheritance of mankind, are engrossed by the bold and crafty; each field and forest is circumscribed by the landmarks of a jealous master; and it is the peculiar praise of the Roman jurisprudence that it asserts the claim of the first occupant to the wild animals of the earth, the air, and the waters. In the progress from primitive equity to final injustice, the steps are silent, the shades are almost imperceptible, and the absolute monopoly is guarded by positive laws and artificial reason. The active, insatiate principle of self-love can alone supply the arts of life and the wages of industry; and as soon as civil government and exclusive property have been introduced, they become necessary to the existence of the human race. Except in the singular institutions of Sparta, the wisest legislators have disapproved an agrarian law as a false and dangerous innovation. Among the Romans, the enormous disproportion of wealth surmounted the ideal restraints of a doubtful tradition and an obsolete statute—a tradition that the poorest follower of Romulus had been endowed with the perpetual inheritance of two *jugera*;[138] a statute which confined the richest citizen to the measure of five hundred jugera, or three hundred and twelve acres of land. The original territory of Rome consisted only of some miles of wood and meadow along the banks of the Tiber; and domestic exchange could add nothing to the national stock. But the goods of an alien or enemy were lawfully exposed to the first hostile occupier; the city was enriched by the profitable trade of war; and the blood of her sons was the only price that was paid for the Volscian sheep, the slaves of Britain, or the gems and gold of Asiatic kingdoms. In the language of ancient jurisprudence, which was corrupted and forgotten before the age of Justinian, these spoils were distinguished by the name of *manceps* or *mancipium*, taken with the hand; and whenever they were sold or *emancipated*, the purchaser required some assurance that they had been the property of an enemy, and not of a fellow-citizen.[139] A citizen could only forfeit his rights by apparent dereliction, and such dereliction of a valuable interest could not easily be presumed. Yet, according to the Twelve Tables, a prescription of one year for movables, and of two years for immovables, abolished the claim of the ancient master, if the actual possessor had acquired them by a fair transaction from the person whom he believed to be the lawful proprietor.[140] Such conscientious injustice, without any mixture of fraud or force, could seldom injure the members of a small republic; but the various periods of three, of ten, or of twenty years, determined by Justinian, are more suitable to the latitude of a great empire. It is only in the term of prescription that the distinction of real and personal fortune has been remarked by the civilians; and their general idea of property is that of simple, uniform, and absolute dominion. The subordinate exceptions of *use*, of *usufruct*,[141] of *servitudes*,[142] imposed for the benefit of a neighbour on lands and houses, are abundantly explained by the professors of jurisprudence. The claims of property, as far as they are altered by the mixture, the division, or the transformation of substances, are investigated with metaphysical subtlety by the same civilians.

The personal title of the first proprietor must be determined by his death; but the possession, without any appearance of change, is peaceably continued in his children, the associates of his toil, and the partners of his wealth. This natural inheritance has been protected by the legislators of every climate and age, and the father is encouraged to persevere in slow and distant improvements, by the tender hope that a long posterity will enjoy the fruits of his labour. The *principle* of hereditary succession is universal; but the *order* has been variously established by convenience or caprice, by the spirit of national institutions, or by some partial example which was originally decided by fraud or violence. The jurisprudence of the Romans appears to have deviated from the equality of nature much less than the Jewish,[143] the Athenian,[144] or the English institutions.[145] On the death of a citizen, all his descendants, unless they were already freed from his paternal power, were called to the inheritance of his possessions. The insolent prerogative of primogeniture was unknown; the two sexes were placed on a just level; all the sons and daughters were entitled to an equal portion of the patrimonial estate; and if any of the sons had been intercepted by a premature death, his person was represented, and his share was divided, by his surviving children. On the failure of the direct line, the right of succession must diverge to the collateral branches. The degrees of kindred [146] are numbered by the civilians, ascending from the last possessor to a common parent, and descending from the common parent to the next heir: my father stands in the first degree, my brother in the second, his children in the third, and the remainder of the series may be conceived by fancy, or pictured in a genealogical table. In this computation a distinction was made, essential to the laws and even the constitution of Rome: the *agnats*, or persons connected by a line of males, were called, as they stood in the nearest degree, to an equal partition; but a female was incapable of transmitting any legal claims; and the *cognats* of every rank, without excepting the dear relation of a mother and a son, were disinherited by the Twelve Tables, as strangers and aliens. Among the Romans a *gens* or lineage was united by a common *name* and domestic rites; the various *cognomens* or *surnames* of Scipio or Marcellus distinguished from each other the subordinate branches or families of the Cornelian or Claudian race: the default of the *agnats* of the same surname was supplied by the larger denomination of *gentiles*; and the vigilance of the laws maintained, in the same name, the perpetual descent of religion and property. A similar principle dictated the Voconian law,[147] which abolished the right of female inheritance. As long as virgins were given or sold in marriage, the adoption of the wife extinguished the hopes of the daughter. But the equal succession of independent matrons supported their pride and luxury, and might transport into a foreign house the riches of their fathers. While the maxims of Cato [148] were revered, they tended to perpetuate in each family a just and virtuous mediocrity: till female blandishments insensibly triumphed, and every salutary restraint was lost in the dissolute greatness of the republic. The rigour of the decemvirs was tempered by the equity of the prætors. Their edicts restored emancipated and posthumous children to the rights of nature; and upon the failure of the *agnats*, they preferred the blood of the *cognats* to the name of the gentiles, whose title and character were insensibly covered with oblivion. The reciprocal inheritance of mothers and sons was established in the Tertullian and Orphitian decrees by the humanity of the senate. A new and more impartial order was introduced by the novels of Justinian, who affected to revive the jurisprudence of the Twelve Tables. The lines of masculine and female kindred were confounded: the descending, ascending, and collateral series was accurately defined; and each degree, according to the proximity of blood and affection, succeeded to the vacant possessions of a Roman citizen.[149]

The order of succession is regulated by nature, or at least by the general and permanent reason of the lawgiver; but this order is frequently violated by the arbitrary and partial *wills*, which prolong the dominion of the testator beyond the grave.[150] In the simple state of society this last use or abuse of the right of property is seldom indulged; it was introduced at Athens by the laws of Solon, and the private testaments of the father of a family are authorised by the Twelve Tables. Before the time of the decemvirs,[151] a Roman citizen exposed his wishes and motives to the assembly of the thirty curiæ or parishes, and the general law of inheritance was suspended by an occasional act of the legislature. After the permission of the decemvirs, each private law-giver promulgated his verbal or written testament in the presence of five citizens, who represented the five classes of the Roman people; a sixth witness attested their concurrence; a seventh weighed the copper money, which was paid by an imaginary purchaser, and the estate was emancipated by a fictitious sale and immediate release. This singular ceremony,[152] which excited the wonder of the Greeks, was still practised in the age of Severus; but the prætors had already approved a more simple testament, for which they required the seals and signatures of seven witnesses, free from all legal exception, and purposely summoned for the execution of that important act. A domestic monarch, who reigned over the lives and fortunes of his children, might distribute their respective shares according to the degrees of their merit or his affection; his arbitrary displeasure chastised an unworthy son by the loss of his inheritance, and the mortifying preference of a stranger. But the experience of unnatural parents recommended some limitations of their testamentary powers. A son, or, by the laws of Justinian, even a daughter, could no longer be disinherited by their silence: they were compelled to name the criminal, and to specify the offence; and the justice of the emperor enumerated the sole causes that could justify such a violation of the first principles of nature and society.[153] Unless a legitimate portion, a fourth part, had been reserved for the children, they were entitled to institute an action or complaint of *inofficious* testament—to suppose that their father's understanding was impaired by sickness or age, and respectfully to appeal from his rigorous sentence to the deliberate wisdom of the magistrate. In the Roman jurisprudence an essential distinction was admitted between the inheritance and the legacies. The heirs who succeeded to the entire unity, or to any of the twelve fractions of the substance of the testator, represented his civil and religious character, asserted his rights, fulfilled his obligations, and discharged the gifts of friendship or liberality which his last will had bequeathed under the name of legacies. But as the imprudence or prodigality of a dying man might exhaust the inheritance, and leave only risk and labour to his successor, he was empowered to retain the *Falcidian* portion; to deduct, before the payment of the legacies, a clear fourth for his own emolument. A reasonable time was allowed to examine the proportion between the debts and the estate, to decide whether he should accept or refuse the testament; and if he used the benefit of an inventory, the demands of the creditors could not exceed the valuation of the effects. The last will of a citizen might be altered during his life, or rescinded after his death: the persons whom he named might die before him, or reject the inheritance, or be exposed to some legal disqualification. In the contemplation of these events, he was permitted to substitute second and third heirs, to replace each other according to the order of the testament; and the incapacity of a madman or an infant to bequeath his property might be supplied by a similar substitution.[154] But the power of the testator expired with the acceptance of the testament: each Roman of mature age and discretion acquired the absolute dominion of his inheritance, and the simplicity of the civil law was never clouded by the long and intricate entails which confine the happiness and freedom of unborn generations.

Conquest and the formalities of law established the use of *codicils*. If a Roman was surprised by death in a remote province of the empire, he addressed a short epistle to his legitimate or testamentary heir, who fulfilled with honour, or neglected with impunity, this last request, which the judges before the age of Augustus were not authorised to enforce. A codicil might be expressed in any mode or in any language, but the subscription of five witnesses must declare that it was the genuine composition of the author. His intention, however laudable, was sometimes illegal, and the invention of *fidei-commissa*, or trusts, arose from the struggle between natural justice and positive jurisprudence. A stranger of Greece or Africa might be the friend or benefactor of a childless Roman, but none, except a fellow-citizen, could act as his heir. The Voconian law, which abolished female succession, restrained the legacy or inheritance of a woman to the sum of one hundred thousand sesterces;[155] and an only daughter was condemned almost as an alien in her father's house. The zeal of friendship and parental affection suggested a liberal artifice: a qualified citizen was named in the testament, with a prayer of injunction that he would restore the inheritance to the person for whom it was truly intended. Various was the conduct of the trustees in this painful situation; they had sworn to observe the laws of their country, but honour prompted them to violate their oath; and, if they preferred their interest under the mask of patriotism, they forfeited the esteem of every virtuous mind. The declaration of Augustus relieved their doubts, gave a legal sanction to confidential testaments and codicils, and gently unravelled the forms and restraints of the republican jurisprudence.[156] But as the new practice of trusts degenerated into some abuse, the trustee was enabled, by the Trebellian and Pegasian decrees, to reserve one fourth of the estate, or to transfer on the head of the real heir all the debts and actions of the succession. The interpretation of testaments was strict and literal; but the language of *trusts* and codicils was delivered from the minute and technical accuracy of the civilians.[157]

III. The general duties of mankind are imposed by their public and private relations, but their specific *obligations* to each other can only be the effect of, 1, a promise; 2, a benefit; or 3, an injury; and when these obligations are ratified by law, the interested party may compel the performance by a judicial *action*. On this principle the civilians of every country have erected a similar jurisprudence, the fair conclusion of universal reason and justice.[158]

1. The goddess of *faith* (of human and social faith) was worshipped, not only in her temples, but in the lives of the Romans; and if that nation was deficient in the more amiable qualities of benevolence and generosity, they astonished the Greeks by their sincere and simple performance of the most burdensome engagements.[159] Yet among the same people, according

to the rigid maxims of the patricians and decemvirs, a *naked pact*, a promise, or even an oath, did not create any civil obligation, unless it was confirmed by the legal form of a *stipulation*. Whatever might be the etymology of the Latin word, it conveyed the idea of a firm and irrevocable contract, which was always expressed in the mode of a question and answer. Do you promise to pay me one hundred pieces of gold? was the solemn interrogation of Seius. I do promise—was the reply of Sempronius. The friends of Sempronius, who answered for his ability and inclination, might be separately sued at the option of Seius; and the benefit of partition, or order of reciprocal actions, insensibly deviated from the strict theory of stipulation. The most cautious and deliberate consent was justly required to sustain the validity of a gratuitous promise, and the citizen who might have obtained a legal security incurred the suspicion of fraud, and paid the forfeit of his neglect. But the ingenuity of the civilians successfully laboured to convert simple engagements into the form of solemn stipulations. The prætors, as the guardians of social faith, admitted every rational evidence of a voluntary and deliberate act, which in their tribunal produced an equitable obligation, and for which they gave an action and a remedy.[160]

2. The obligations of the second class, as they were contracted by the delivery of a thing, are marked by the civilians with the epithet of real.[161] A grateful return is due to the author of a benefit; and whoever is intrusted with the property of another has bound himself to the sacred duty of restitution. In the case of a friendly loan, the merit of generosity is on the side of the lender only; in a deposit, on the side of the receiver; but in a *pledge*, and the rest of the selfish commerce of ordinary life, the benefit is compensated by an equivalent, and the obligation to restore is variously modified by the nature of the transaction. The Latin language very happily expresses the fundamental difference between the *commodatum* and the *mutuum*, which our poverty is reduced to confound under the vague and common appellation of a loan. In the former, the borrower was obliged to restore the same individual thing with which he had been *accommodated* for the temporary supply of his wants; in the latter, it was destined for his use and consumption, and he discharged this *mutual* engagement by substituting the same specific value according to a just estimation of number, of weight, and of measure. In the contract of *sale*, the absolute

dominion is transferred to the purchaser, and he repays the benefit with an adequate sum of gold or silver, the price and universal standard of all earthly possessions. The obligation of another contract, that of *location*, is of a more complicated kind. Lands or houses, labour or talents, may be hired for a definite term; at the expiration of the time, the thing itself must be restored to the owner with an additional reward for the beneficial occupation and employment. In these lucrative contracts, to which may be added those of partnership and commissions, the civilians sometimes imagine the delivery of the object, and sometimes presume the consent of the parties. The substantial pledge has been refined into the invisible rights of a mortgage or *hypotheca*; and the agreement of sale for a certain price imputes, from that moment, the chances of gain or loss to the account of the purchaser. It may be fairly supposed that every man will obey the dictates of his interest; and if he accepts the benefit, he is obliged to sustain the expense, of the transaction. In this boundless subject, the historian may observe the *location* of land and money, the rent of the one and the interest of the other, as they materially affect the prosperity of agriculture and commerce. The landlord was often obliged to advance the stock and instruments of husbandry, and to content himself with a partition of the fruits. If the feeble tenant was oppressed by accident, contagion, or hostile violence, he claimed a proportionable relief from the equity of the laws: five years were the customary term, and no solid or costly improvements could be expected from a farmer who, at each moment, might be ejected by the sale of the estate.[162] Usury,[163] the inveterate grievance of the city, had been discouraged by the Twelve Tables,[164] and abolished by the clamours of the people. It was revived by their wants and idleness, tolerated by the discretion of the prætors, and finally determined by the Code of Justinian. Persons of illustrious rank were confined to the moderate profit of *four per cent.*; six was pronounced to be the ordinary and legal standard of interest; eight was allowed for the convenience of manufacturers and merchants; twelve was granted to nautical insurance, which the wiser ancients had not attempted to define; but, except in this perilous adventure, the practice of exorbitant usury was severely restrained.[165] The most simple interest was condemned by the clergy of the East and West;[166] but the sense of mutual benefit, which had triumphed over the laws of the republic, has resisted with equal firmness the decrees of the church, and even the prejudices of mankind.[167]

3. Nature and society impose the strict obligation of repairing an injury; and the sufferer by private injustice acquires a personal right and a legitimate action. If the property of another be intrusted to our care, the requisite degree of care may rise and fall according to the benefit which we derive from such temporary possession; we are seldom made responsible for inevitable accident, but the consequences of a voluntary fault must always be imputed to the author.[168] A Roman pursued and recovered his stolen goods by a civil action of theft; they might pass through a succession of pure and innocent hands, but nothing less than a prescription of thirty years could extinguish his original claim. They were restored by the sentence of the prætor, and the injury was compensated by double, or three-fold, or even quadruple damages, as the deed had been perpetrated by secret fraud or open rapine, as the robber had been surprised in the fact, or detected by a subsequent research. The Aquilian law [169] defended the living property of a citizen, his slaves and cattle, from the stroke of malice or negligence: the highest price was allowed that could be ascribed to the domestic animal at any moment of the year preceding his death; a similar latitude of thirty days was granted on the destruction of any other valuable effects. A personal injury is blunted or sharpened by the manners of the times and the sensibility of the individual: the pain or the disgrace of a word or blow cannot easily be appreciated by a pecuniary equivalent. The rude jurisprudence of the decemvirs had confounded all hasty insults, which did not amount to the fracture of a limb, by condemning the aggressor to the common penalty of twenty-five *asses*. But the same denomination of money was reduced, in three centuries, from a pound to the weight of half an ounce; and the insolence of a wealthy Roman indulged himself in the cheap amusement of breaking and satisfying the law of the Twelve Tables. Veratius ran through the streets striking on the face the inoffensive passengers, and his attendant purse-bearer immediately silenced their clamours by the legal tender of twenty-five pieces of copper, about the value of one shilling.[170] The equity of the prætors examined and estimated the distinct merits of each particular complaint. In the adjudication of civil damages, the magistrate assumed a right to consider the various circumstances of time and place, of age and dignity, which may aggravate the shame and sufferings of the injured person; but if he admitted the idea of a fine, a punishment, an example, he invaded the province, though perhaps he supplied the defects, of the criminal law.

The execution of the Alban dictator, who was dismembered by eight horses, is represented by Livy as the first and last instance of Roman cruelty in the punishment of the most atrocious crimes.[171] But this act of justice or revenge was inflicted on a foreign enemy in the heat of victory, and at the command of a single man. The Twelve Tables afford a more decisive proof of the national spirit, since they were framed by the wisest of the senate and accepted by the free voices of the people; yet these laws, like the statutes of Draco,[172] are written in characters of blood.[173] They approve the inhuman and unequal principle of retaliation; and the forfeit of an eye for an eye, a tooth for a tooth, a limb for a limb, is rigorously exacted, unless the offender can redeem his pardon by a fine of three hundred pounds of copper. The decemvirs distributed with much liberality the slighter chastisements of flagellation and servitude; and nine crimes of a very different complexion are adjudged worthy of death. 1. Any act of *treason* against the state, or of correspondence with the public enemy. The mode of execution was painful and ignominious: the head of the degenerate Roman was shrouded in a veil, his hands were tied behind his back, and, after he had been scourged by the lictor, he was suspended in the midst of the forum on a cross, or inauspicious tree. 2. Nocturnal meetings in the city, whatever might be the pretence—of pleasure, or religion, or the public good. 3. The murder of a citizen; for which the common feelings of mankind demand the blood of the murderer. Poison is still more odious than the sword or dagger; and we are surprised to discover, in two flagitious events, how early such subtle wickedness had infected the simplicity of the republic and the chaste virtues of the Roman matrons.[174] The parricide, who violated the duties of nature and gratitude, was cast into the river or the sea, enclosed in a sack; and a cock, a viper, a dog, and a monkey, were successively added as the most suitable companions.[175] Italy produces no monkeys; but the want could never be felt till the middle of the sixth century first revealed the guilt of a parricide.[176] 4. The malice of an *incendiary*. After the previous ceremony of whipping, he himself was delivered to the flames; and in this example alone our reason is tempted to applaud the justice of retaliation. 5. *Judicial perjury*. The corrupt or malicious witness was thrown headlong from the Tarpeian rock to expiate his falsehood, which was rendered still more fatal by the severity of the penal laws and the deficiency of written evidence. 6. The corruption of a judge, who accepted bribes to pronounce an iniquitous sentence. 7. Libels and satires, whose rude strains sometimes disturbed the peace of an illiterate city. The author was beaten with clubs, a worthy chastisement; but it is not certain that he was left to expire under the blows of the executioner.[177] 8. The nocturnal mischief of damaging or destroying a neighbour's corn. The criminal was suspended as a grateful victim to Ceres. But the sylvan deities were less implacable, and the extirpation of a more valuable tree was compensated by the moderate fine of twenty-five pounds of copper. 9. Magical incantations; which had power, in the opinion of the Latian shepherds, to exhaust the strength of an enemy, to extinguish his life, and to remove from their seats his deep-rooted plantations. The cruelty of the Twelve Tables against insolvent debtors still remains to be told; and I shall dare to prefer the literal sense of antiquity to the specious refinements of modern criticism.[178] After the judicial proof or confession of the debt, thirty days of grace were allowed before a Roman was delivered into the power of his fellow-citizen. In this private prison twelve ounces of rice were his daily food; he might be bound with a chain of fifteen pounds weight; and his misery was thrice exposed in the market-place, to solicit the compassion of his friends and countrymen. At the expiration of sixty days the debt was discharged by the loss of liberty or life; the insolvent debtor was either put to death or sold in foreign slavery beyond the Tiber: but, if several creditors were alike obstinate and unrelenting, they might legally dismember his body, and satiate their revenge by this horrid partition. The advocates for this savage law have insisted that it must strongly operate in deterring idleness and fraud from contracting debts which they were unable to discharge; but experience would dissipate this salutary terror, by proving that no creditor could be found to exact this unprofitable penalty of life or limb. As the manners of Rome were insensibly polished, the criminal code of the decemvirs was abolished by the humanity of accusers, witnesses, and judges; and impunity became the consequence of immoderate rigour. The Porcian and Valerian laws prohibited the magistrates from inflicting on a free citizen any capital, or even corporal, punishment; and the obsolete statutes of blood were artfully, and

perhaps truly, ascribed to the spirit, not of patrician, but of regal, tyranny.

In the absence of penal laws and the insufficiency of civil actions, the peace and justice of the city were imperfectly maintained by the private jurisdiction of the citizens. The malefactors who replenish our gaols are the outcasts of society, and the crimes for which they suffer may be commonly ascribed to ignorance, poverty, and brutal appetite. For the perpetration of similar enormities, a vile plebeian might claim and abuse the sacred character of a member of the republic; but on the proof or suspicion of guilt the slave or the stranger was nailed to a cross, and this strict and summary justice might be exercised without restraint over the greatest part of the populace of Rome. Each family contained a domestic tribunal, which was not confined, like that of the prætor, to the cognisance of external actions: virtuous principles and habits were inculcated by the discipline of education, and the Roman father was accountable to the state for the manners of his children, since he disposed without appeal of their life, their liberty, and their inheritance. In some pressing emergencies, the citizen was authorised to avenge his private or public wrongs. The consent of the Jewish, the Athenian, and the Roman laws, approved the slaughter of the nocturnal thief; though in open daylight a robber could not be slain without some previous evidence of danger and complaint. Whoever surprised an adulterer in his nuptial bed might freely exercise his revenge;[179] the most bloody or wanton outrage was excused by the provocation;[180] nor was it before the reign of Augustus that the husband was reduced to weigh the rank of the offender, or that the parent was condemned to sacrifice his daughter with her guilty seducer. After the expulsion of the kings, the ambitious Roman who should dare to assume their title or imitate their tyranny was devoted to the infernal gods: each of his fellow-citizens was armed with the sword of justice; and the act of Brutus, however repugnant to gratitude or prudence, had been already sanctified by the judgment of his country.[181] The barbarous practice of wearing arms in the midst of peace,[182] and the bloody maxims of honour, were unknown to the Romans; and during the two purest ages, from the establishment of equal freedom to the end of the Punic wars, the city was never disturbed by sedition, and rarely polluted with atrocious crimes. The failure of penal laws was more sensibly felt when every vice was inflamed by faction at home and dominion abroad. In the time of Cicero each private citizen enjoyed the privilege of anarchy—each minister of the republic was exalted to the temptations of regal power, and their virtues are entitled to the warmest praise as the spontaneous fruits of nature or philosophy. After a triennial indulgence of lust, rapine, and cruelty, Verres, the tyrant of Sicily, could only be sued for the pecuniary restitution of three hundred thousand pounds sterling; and such was the temper of the laws, the judges, and perhaps the accuser himself,[183] that, on refunding a thirteenth part of his plunder, Verres could retire to an easy and luxurious exile.[184]

IV. The first imperfect attempt to restore the proportion of crimes and punishments was made by the dictator Sylla, who, in the midst of his sanguinary triumph, aspired to restrain the licence rather than to oppress the liberty of the Romans. He gloried in the arbitrary proscription of four thousand seven hundred citizens.[185] But, in the character of a legislator, he respected the prejudices of the times; and instead of pronouncing a sentence of death against the robber or assassin, the general who betrayed an army or the magistrate who ruined a province, Sylla was content to aggravate the pecuniary damages by the penalty of exile, or, in more constitutional language, by the interdiction of fire and water. The Cornelian, and afterwards the Pompeian and Julian laws, introduced a new system of criminal jurisprudence;[186] and the emperors, from Augustus to Justinian, disguised their increasing rigour under the names of the original authors. But the invention and frequent use of *extraordinary pains* proceeded from the desire to extend and conceal the progress of despotism. In the condemnation of illustrious Romans, the senate was always prepared to confound, at the will of their masters, the judicial and legislative powers. It was the duty of the governors to maintain the peace of their province by the arbitrary and rigid administration of justice; the freedom of the city evaporated in the extent of empire, and the Spanish malefactor who claimed the privilege of a Roman was elevated by the command of Galba on a fairer and more lofty cross.[187] Occasional rescripts issued from the throne to decide the questions which, by their novelty or importance, appeared to surpass the authority and discernment of a proconsul. Transportation and beheading were reserved for honourable persons; meaner criminals were either hanged, or burnt, or buried in the mines, or exposed to the wild beasts of the amphitheatre. Armed robbers were pursued and extirpated as the enemies of society; the driving away horses or cattle was made a capital offence;[188] but simple theft was uniformly considered as a mere civil and private injury. The degrees of guilt and the modes of punishment were too often determined by the discretion of the rulers, and the subject was left in ignorance of the legal danger which he might incur by every action of his life.

A sin, a vice, a crime, are the objects of theology, ethics, and jurisprudence. Whenever their judgments agree, they corroborate each other; but as often as they differ, a prudent legislator appreciates the guilt and punishment according to the measure of social injury. On this principle the most daring attack on the life and property of a private citizen is judged less atrocious than the crime of treason or rebellion, which invades the *majesty* of the republic: the obsequious civilians unanimously pronounced that the republic is contained in the person of its chief, and the edge of the Julian law was sharpened by the incessant diligence of the emperors. The licentious commerce of the sexes may be tolerated as an impulse of nature, or forbidden as a source of disorder and corruption; but the fame, the fortunes, the family of the husband, are seriously injured by the adultery of the wife. The wisdom of Augustus, after curbing the freedom of revenge, applied to this domestic offence the animadversion of the laws; and the guilty parties, after the payment of heavy forfeitures and fines, were condemned to long or perpetual exile in two separate islands.[189] Religion pronounces an equal censure against the infidelity of the husband, but, as it is not accompanied by the same civil effects, the wife was never permitted to vindicate her wrongs;[190] and the distinction of simple or double adultery, so familiar and so important in the canon law, is unknown to the jurisprudence of the Code and Pandects. I touch with reluctance, and despatch with impatience, a more odious vice, of which modesty rejects the name, and nature abominates the idea. The primitive Romans were infected by the example of the Etruscans[191] and Greeks;[192] in the mad abuse of prosperity and power every pleasure that is innocent was deemed insipid; and the Scatinian law,[193] which had been extorted by an act of violence, was insensibly abolished by the lapse of time and the multitude of criminals. By this law the rape, perhaps the seduction, of an ingenuous youth was compensated as a personal injury by the poor damages of ten thousand sesterces, or fourscore pounds; the ravisher might be slain by the resistance or revenge of chastity; and I wish to believe that at Rome, as in Athens, the voluntary and effeminate deserter of his sex was degraded from the honours and the rights of a citizen.[194] But the practice of vice was not discouraged by the severity of opinion: the indelible stain of manhood was confounded with the more venial transgressions of fornication and adultery; nor was the licentious lover exposed to the same dishonour which he impressed on the male or female partner of his guilt. From Catullus to Juvenal,[195] the poets accuse and celebrate the degeneracy of the times; and the reformation of manners was feebly attempted by the reason and authority of the civilians, till the most virtuous of the Cæsars proscribed the sin against nature as a crime against society.[196]

A new spirit of legislation, respectable even in its error, arose in the empire with the religion of Constantine.[197] The laws of Moses were received as the divine original of justice, and the Christian princes adapted their penal statutes to the degrees of moral and religious turpitude. Adultery was first declared to be a capital offence: the frailty of the sexes was assimilated to poison or assassination, to sorcery or parricide; the same penalties were inflicted on the passive and active guilt of pæderasty; and all criminals, of free or servile condition, were either drowned, or beheaded, or cast alive into the avenging flames. The adulterers were spared by the common sympathy of mankind; but the lovers of their own sex were pursued by general and pious indignation: the impure manners of Greece still prevailed in the cities of Asia, and every vice was fomented by the celibacy of the monks and clergy. Justinian relaxed the punishment at least of female infidelity: the guilty spouse was only condemned to solitude and penance, and at the end of two years might be recalled to the arms of a forgiving husband. But the same emperor declared himself the implacable enemy of unmanly lust, and the cruelty of his persecution can scarcely be excused by the purity of his motives.[198] In defiance of every principle of justice, he stretched to past as well as future offences the operations of his edicts, with the previous allowance of a short respite for confession and pardon. A painful death was inflicted by the amputation of the sinful instrument, or the insertion of sharp reeds into the pores and tubes of most exquisite sensibility; and Justinian defended the propriety of the execution, since the criminals would have lost their hands had they been convicted of sacrilege. In this state of disgrace and agony two

bishops, Isaiah of Rhodes and Alexander of Diospolis, were dragged through the streets of Constantinople, while their brethren were admonished by the voice of a crier to observe this awful lesson, and not to pollute the sanctity of their character. Perhaps these prelates were innocent. A sentence of death and infamy was often founded on the slight and suspicious evidence of a child or a servant: the guilt of the green faction, of the rich, and of the enemies of Theodora, was presumed by the judges, and pæderasty became the crime of those to whom no crime could be imputed. A French philosopher[199] has dared to remark that whatever is secret must be doubtful, and that our natural horror of vice may be abused as an engine of tyranny. But the favourable persuasion of the same writer, that a legislator may confide in the taste and reason of mankind, is impeached by the unwelcome discovery of the antiquity and extent of the disease.[200]

The free citizens of Athens and Rome enjoyed in all criminal cases the invaluable privilege of being tried by their country.[201] 1. The administration of justice is the most ancient office of a prince: it was exercised by the Roman kings, and abused by Tarquin, who alone, without law or council, pronounced his arbitrary judgments. The first consuls succeeded to this regal prerogative; but the sacred right of appeal soon abolished the jurisdiction of the magistrates, and all public causes were decided by the supreme tribunal of the people. But a wild democracy, superior to the forms, too often disdains the essential principles, of justice; the pride of despotism was envenomed by plebeian envy; and the heroes of Athens might sometimes applaud the happiness of the Persian, whose fate depended on the caprice of a *single* tyrant. Some salutary restraints, imposed by the people on their own passions, were at once the cause and effect of the gravity and temperance of the Romans. The right of accusation was confined to the magistrates. A vote of the thirty-five tribes could inflict a fine; but the cognisance of all capital crimes was reserved by a fundamental law to the assembly of the centuries, in which the weight of influence and property was sure to preponderate. Repeated proclamations and adjournments were interposed, to allow time for prejudice and resentment to subside; the whole proceeding might be annulled by a seasonable omen or the opposition of a tribune, and such popular trials were commonly less formidable to innocence than they were favourable to guilt. But this union of the judicial and legislative powers left it doubtful whether the accused party was pardoned or acquitted; and, in the defence of an illustrious client, the orators of Rome and Athens address their arguments to the policy and benevolence, as well as to the justice, of their sovereign. 2. The task of convening the citizens for the trial of each offender became more difficult, as the citizens and the offenders continually multiplied, and the ready expedient was adopted of delegating the jurisdiction of the people to the ordinary magistrates or to extraordinary *inquisitors*. In the first ages these questions were rare and occasional. In the beginning of the seventh century of Rome they were made perpetual: four prætors were annually empowered to sit in judgment on the state offences of treason, extortion, peculation, and bribery; and Sylla added new prætors and new questions for those crimes which more directly injure the safety of individuals. By these *inquisitors* the trial was prepared and directed; but they could only pronounce the sentence of the majority of *judges*, who, with some truth and more prejudice, have been compared to the English juries.[202] To discharge this important though burdensome office, an annual list of ancient and respectable citizens was formed by the prætor. After many constitutional struggles, they were chosen in equal numbers from the senate, the equestrian order, and the people; four hundred and fifty were appointed for single questions, and the various rolls or *decuries* of judges must have contained the names of some thousand Romans, who represented the judicial authority of the state. In each particular cause a sufficient number was drawn from the urn; their integrity was guarded by an oath; the mode of ballot secured their independence; the suspicion of partiality was removed by the mutual challenges of the accuser and defendant; and the judges of Milo, by the retrenchment of fifteen on each side, were reduced to fifty-one voices or tablets, of acquittal, of condemnation, or of favourable doubt.[203] 3. In his civil jurisdiction the prætor of the city was truly a judge, and almost a legislator; but, as soon as he had prescribed the action of law, he often referred to a delegate the determination of the fact. With the increase of legal proceedings, the tribunal of the centumvirs, in which he presided, acquired more weight and reputation. But whether he acted alone or with the advice of his council, the most absolute powers might be trusted to a magistrate who was annually chosen by the votes of the people. The rules and precautions of freedom have required some explanation; the order of despotism is simple and inanimate. Before the age of Justinian, or perhaps of Diocletian, the decuries of Roman judges had sunk to an empty title; the humble advice of the assessors might be accepted or despised; and in each tribunal the civil and criminal jurisdiction was administered by a single magistrate, who was raised and disgraced by the will of the emperor.

A Roman accused of any capital crime might prevent the sentence of the law by voluntary exile or death. Till his guilt had been legally proved, his innocence was presumed and his person was free; till the votes of the last *century* had been counted and declared, he might peaceably secede to any of the allied cities of Italy, or Greece, or Asia.[204] His fame and fortunes were preserved, at least to his children, by this civil death; and he might still be happy in every rational and sensual enjoyment, if a mind accustomed to the ambitious tumult of Rome could support the uniformity and silence of Rhodes or Athens. A bolder effort was required to escape from the tyranny of the Cæsars; but this effort was rendered familiar by the maxims of the Stoics, the example of the bravest Romans, and the legal encouragements of suicide. The bodies of condemned criminals were exposed to public ignominy, and their children, a more serious evil, were reduced to poverty by the confiscation of their fortunes. But, if the victims of Tiberius and Nero anticipated the decree of the prince or senate, their courage and despatch were recompensed by the applause of the public, the decent honours of burial, and the validity of their testaments.[205] The exquisite avarice and cruelty of Domitian appears to have deprived the unfortunate of this last consolation, and it was still denied even by the clemency of the Antonines. A voluntary death, which, in the case of a capital offence, intervened between the accusation and the sentence, was admitted as a confession of guilt, and the spoils of the deceased were seized by the inhuman claims of the treasury.[206] Yet the civilians have always respected the natural right of a citizen to dispose of his life; and the posthumous disgrace invented by Tarquin[207] to check the despair of his subjects was never revived or imitated by succeeding tyrants. The powers of this world have indeed lost their dominion over him who is resolved on death, and his arm can only be restrained by the religious apprehension of a future state. Suicides are enumerated by Virgil among the unfortunate, rather than the guilty,[208] and the poetical fables of the infernal shades could not seriously influence the faith or practice of mankind. But the precepts of the Gospel or the church have at length imposed a pious servitude on the minds of Christians, and condemn them to expect, without a murmur, the last stroke of disease or the executioner.

The penal statutes form a very small proportion of the sixty-two books of the Code and Pandects, and in all judicial proceeding the life or death of a citizen is determined with less caution and delay than the most ordinary question of covenant or inheritance. This singular distinction, though something may be allowed for the urgent necessity of defending the peace of society, is derived from the nature of criminal and civil jurisprudence. Our duties to the state are simple and uniform; the law by which he is condemned is inscribed not only on brass or marble, but on the conscience of the offender, and his guilt is commonly proved by the testimony of a single fact. But our relations to each other are various and infinite; our obligations are created, annulled, and modified by injuries, benefits, and promises; and the interpretation of voluntary contracts and testaments, which are often dictated by fraud or ignorance, affords a long and laborious exercise to the sagacity of the judge. The business of life is multiplied by the extent of commerce and dominion, and the residence of the parties in the distant provinces of an empire is productive of doubt, delay, and inevitable appeals from the local to the supreme magistrate. Justinian, the Greek emperor of Constantinople and the East, was the legal successor of the Latian shepherd who had planted a colony on the banks of the Tiber. In a period of thirteen hundred years the laws had reluctantly followed the changes of government and man-

ners; and the laudable desire of conciliating ancient names with recent institutions destroyed the harmony, and swelled the magnitude, of the obscure and irregular system. The laws which excuse on any occasions the ignorance of their subjects, confess their own imperfections; the civil jurisprudence, as it was abridged by Justinian, still continued a mysterious science and a profitable trade, and the innate perplexity of the study was involved in tenfold darkness by the private industry of the practitioners. The expense of the pursuit sometimes exceeded the value of the prize, and the fairest rights were abandoned by the poverty or prudence of the claimants. Such costly justice might tend to abate the spirit of litigation, but the unequal pressure serves only to increase the influence of the rich, and to aggravate the misery of the poor. By these dilatory and expensive proceedings the wealthy pleader obtains a more certain advantage than he could hope from the accidental corruption of his judge. The experience of an abuse from which our own age and country are not perfectly exempt may sometimes provoke a generous indignation, and extort the hasty wish of exchanging our elaborate jurisprudence for the simple and summary decrees of a Turkish cadhi. Our calmer reflection will suggest that such forms and delays are necessary to guard the person and property of the citizen; that the discretion of the judge is the first engine of tyranny; and that the laws of a free people should foresee and determine every question that may probably arise in the exercise of power and the transactions of industry. But the government of Justinian united the evils of liberty and servitude, and the Romans were oppressed at the same time by the multiplicity of their laws and the arbitrary will of their master.

CHAPTER XLV

Reign of the Younger Justin. Embassy of the Avars. Their Settlement on the Danube. Conquest of Italy by the Lombards. Adoption and Reign of Tiberius. Of Maurice. State of Italy under the Lombards and the Exarchs Of Ravenna. Distress of Rome. Character and Pontificate of Gregory the First.

DURING the last years of Justinian, his infirm mind was devoted to heavenly contemplation, and he neglected the business of the lower world. His subjects were impatient of the long continuance of his life and

reign: yet all who were capable of reflection apprehended the moment of his death, which might involve the capital in tumult and the empire in civil war. Seven nephews[1] of the childless monarch, the sons or grandsons of his brother and sister, had been educated in the splendour of a princely fortune; they had been shown in high commands to the provinces and armies; their characters were known, their followers were zealous, and, as the jealousy of age postponed the declaration of a successor, they might expect with equal hopes the inheritance of their uncle. He expired in his palace, after a reign of thirty-eight years; and the decisive opportunity was embraced by the friends of Justin, the son of Vigilantia.[2] At the hour of midnight his domestics were awakened by an importunate crowd, who thundered at his door, and obtained admittance by revealing themselves to be the principal members of the senate. These welcome deputies announced the recent and momentous secret of the emperor's decease; reported, or perhaps invented, his dying choice of the best beloved and most deserving of his nephews; and conjured Justin to prevent the disorders of the multitude, if they should perceive, with the return of light, that they were left without a master. After composing his countenance to surprise, sorrow, and decent modesty, Justin, by the advice of his wife Sophia, submitted to the authority of the senate. He was conducted with speed and silence to the palace; the guards saluted their new sovereign; and the martial and religious rites of his coronation were diligently accomplished. By the hands of the proper officers he was invested with the Imperial garments, the red buskins, white tunic, and purple robe. A fortunate soldier, whom he instantly promoted to the rank of tribune, encircled his neck with a military collar; four robust youths exalted him on a shield; he stood firm and erect to receive the adoration of his subjects; and their choice was sanctified by the benediction of the patriarch, who imposed the diadem on the head of an orthodox prince. The hippodrome was already filled with innumerable multitudes; and no sooner did the emperor appear on his throne than the voices of the blue and the green factions were confounded in the same loyal acclamations. In the speeches which Justin addressed to the senate and people he promised to correct the abuses which had disgraced the age of his predecessor, displayed the maxims of a just and beneficent government, and declared that, on the approaching calends of January,[3] he would revive in his own person the name and liberality of a Roman consul. The immediate discharge of his uncle's debts exhibited a solid pledge of his faith and generosity: a train of porters, laden with bags of gold, advanced into the midst of the hippodrome, and the hopeless creditors of Justinian accepted this equitable payment as a voluntary gift. Before the end of three years his example was imitated and surpassed by the empress Sophia, who delivered many indigent citizens from the weight of debt and usury: an act of benevolence the best entitled to gratitude, since it relieves the most intolerable distress; but in which the bounty of a prince is the most liable to be abused by the claims of prodigality and fraud.[4]

On the seventh day of his reign Justin gave audience to the ambassadors of the Avars, and the scene was decorated to impress the barbarians with astonishment, veneration, and terror. From the palace gate, the spacious courts and long porticoes were lined with the lofty crests and gilt bucklers of the guards, who presented their spears and axes with more confidence than they would have shown in a field of battle. The officers who exercised the power, or attended the person, of the prince, were attired in their richest habits, and arranged according to the military and civil order of the hierarchy. When the veil of the sanctuary was withdrawn, the ambassadors beheld the emperor of the East on his throne, beneath a canopy, or dome, which was supported by four columns, and crowned with a winged figure of Victory. In the first emotions of surprise, they submitted to the servile adoration of the Byzantine court; but, as soon as they rose from the ground, Targetius, the chief of the embassy, expressed the freedom and pride of a barbarian. He extolled, by the tongue of his interpreter, the greatness of the chagan, by whose clemency the kingdoms of the South were permitted to exist, whose victorious subjects had traversed the frozen rivers of Scythia, and who now covered the banks of the Danube with innumerable tents. The late emperor had cultivated, with annual and costly gift, the friendship of a grateful monarch, and the enemies of Rome had respected the allies of the Avars. The same prudence would instruct the nephew of Justinian to imitate the liberality of his uncle, and to purchase the blessings of peace from an invincible people, who delighted and excelled in the exercise of war. The reply of the emperor was delivered in the same strain of haughty defiance, and he derived his confidence from the God of the Christians, the ancient glory of Rome, and the recent triumphs of Justinian. "The empire," said he, "abounds with men and horses, and arms sufficient to defend our frontiers and to chastise the barbarians. You offer aid, you threaten hostilities: we despise your enmity and your aid. The conquerors of the Avars solicit our alliance; shall we dread their fugitives and exiles?[5] The bounty of our uncle was granted to your misery, to your humble prayers. From us you shall receive a more important obligation, the knowledge of your own weakness. Retire from our presence; the lives of ambassadors are safe; and, if you return to implore our pardon, perhaps you will taste of our benevolence."[6] On the report of his ambassadors, the chagan was awed by the apparent firmness of a Roman emperor of whose character and resources he was ignorant. Instead of executing his threats against the Eastern empire, he marched into the poor and savage countries of Germany, which were subject to the dominion of the Franks. After two doubtful battles he consented to retire, and the Austrasian king relieved the distress of his camp with an immediate supply of corn and cattle.[7] Such repeated disappointments had chilled the spirit of the Avars, and their power would have dissolved away in the Sarmatian desert, if the alliance of Alboin, king of the Lombards, had not given a new object to their arms, and a lasting settlement to their wearied fortunes.

While Alboin served under his father's standard, he encountered in battle, and transpierced with his lance, the rival prince of the Gepidæ. The Lombards, who applauded such early prowess, requested his father, with unanimous acclamations, that the heroic youth, who had shared the dangers of the field, might be admitted to the feast of victory. "You are not unmindful," replied the inflexible Audoin, "of the wise customs of our ancestors. Whatever may be his merit, a prince is incapable of sitting at table with his father till he has received his arms from a foreign and royal hand." Alboin bowed with reverence to the institutions of his country, selected forty companions, and boldly visited the court of Turisund, king of the Gepidæ, who embraced and entertained, according to the laws of hospitality, the murderer of his son. At the banquet, whilst Alboin occupied the seat of the youth whom he had slain, a tender remembrance arose in the mind of Turisund. "How dear is that place—how hateful is that person!" were the words that escaped, with a sigh, from the indignant father. His grief exasperated the national resentment of the Gepidæ; and Cunimund, his surviving son, was provoked by wine, or fraternal affection, to the desire of vengeance. "The Lombards," said the rude barbarian, "resemble, in figure and in smell, the mares of our Sarmatian plains." And this insult was a coarse allusion to the white

bands which enveloped their legs. "Add another resemblance," replied an audacious Lombard; "you have felt how strongly they kick. Visit the plain of Asfeld, and seek for the bones of thy brother: they are mingled with those of the vilest animals." The Gepidæ, a nation of warriors, started from their seats, and the fearless Alboin, with his forty companions, laid their hands on their swords. The tumult was appeased by the venerable interposition of Turisund. He saved his own honour, and the life of his guest; and, after the solemn rites of investiture, dismissed the stranger in the bloody arms of his son, the gift of a weeping parent. Alboin returned in triumph; and the Lombards, who celebrated his matchless intrepidity, were compelled to praise the virtues of an enemy.[8] In this extraordinary visit he had probably seen the daughter of Cunimund, who soon after ascended the throne of the Gepidæ. Her name was Rosamond, an appellation expressive of female beauty, and which our own history or romance has consecrated to amorous tales. The king of the Lombards (the father of Alboin no longer lived) was contracted to the grand-daughter of Clovis; but the restraints of faith and policy soon yielded to the hope of possessing the fair Rosamond, and of insulting her family and nation. The arts of persuasion were tried without success; and the impatient lover, by force and stratagem, obtained the object of his desires. War was the consequence which he foresaw and solicited; but the Lombards could not long withstand the furious assault of the Gepidæ, who were sustained by a Roman army. And, as the offer of marriage was rejected with contempt, Alboin was compelled to relinquish his prey, and to partake of the disgrace which he had inflicted on the house of Cunimund.[9]

When a public quarrel is envenomed by private injuries, a blow that is not mortal or decisive can be productive only of a short truce, which allows the unsuccessful combatant to sharpen his arms for a new encounter. The strength of Alboin had been found unequal to the gratification of his love, ambition, and revenge: he condescended to implore the formidable aid of the chagan; and the arguments that he employed are expressive of the art and policy of the barbarians. In the attack of the Gepidæ he had been prompted by the just desire of extirpating a people whom their alliance with the Roman empire had rendered the common enemies of the nations, and the personal adversaries of the chagan. If the forces of the Avars and the Lombards should unite in this glorious quarrel, the victory was secure and the reward inestimable: the Danube, the Hebrus, Italy, and Constantinople would be exposed, without a barrier, to their invincible arms. But, if they hesitated or delayed to prevent the malice of the Romans, the same spirit which had insulted would pursue the Avars to the extremity of the earth. These specious reasons were heard by the chagan with coldness and disdain: he detained the Lombard ambassadors in his camp, protracted the negotiation, and by turns alleged his want of inclination, or his want of ability, to undertake this important enterprise. At length he signified the ultimate price of his alliance, that the Lombards should immediately present him with the tithe of their cattle; that the spoils and captives should be equally divided; but that the lands of the Gepidæ should become the sole patrimony of the Avars. Such hard conditions were eagerly accepted by the passions of Alboin; and, as the Romans were dissatisfied with the ingratitude and perfidy of the Gepidæ, Justin abandoned that incorrigible people to their fate, and remained the tranquil spectator of this unequal conflict. The despair of Cunimund was active and dangerous. He was informed that the Avars had entered his confines; but, on the strong assurance that after the defeat of the Lombards these foreign invaders would easily be repelled, he rushed forwards to encounter the implacable enemy of his name and family. But the courage of the Gepidæ could secure them no more than an honourable death. The bravest of the nation fell in the field of battle: the king of the Lombards contemplated with delight the head of Cunimund, and his skull was fashioned into a cup to satiate the hatred of the conqueror, or perhaps to comply with the savage custom of his country.[10] After this victory no farther obstacle could impede the progress of the confederates, and they faithfully executed the terms of their agreement. [11] The fair countries of Wallachia, Moldavia, Transylvania, and the parts of Hungary beyond the Danube, were occupied without resistance by a new colony of Scythians; and the Dacian empire of the chagans subsisted with splendour above two hundred and thirty years. The nation of the Gepidæ was dissolved; but, in the distribution of the captives, the slaves of the Avars were less fortunate than the companions of the Lombards, whose generosity adopted a valiant foe, and whose freedom was incompatible with cool and deliberate tyranny. One moiety of the spoil introduced into the camp of Alboin more wealth than a barbarian could readily compute. The fair Rosamond was persuaded or compelled to acknowledge the rights of her victorious lover; and the daughter of Cunimund appeared to forgive those crimes which might be imputed to her own irresistible charms.

The destruction of a mighty kingdom established the fame of Alboin. In the days of Charlemagne the Bavarians, the Saxons, and the other tribes of the Teutonic language, still repeated the songs which described the heroic virtues, the valour, liberality, and fortune of the king of the Lombards.[12] But his ambition was yet unsatisfied; and the conqueror of the Gepidæ turned his eyes from the Danube to the richer banks of the Po and the Tiber. Fifteen years had not elapsed since his subjects, the confederates of Narses, had visited the pleasant climate of Italy; the mountains, the rivers, the highways, were familiar to their memory; the report of their success, perhaps the view of their spoils, had kindled in the rising generation the flame of emulation and enterprise. Their hopes were encouraged by the spirit and eloquence of Alboin; and it is affirmed that he spoke to their senses by producing at the royal feast the fairest and most exquisite fruits that grew spontaneously in the garden of the world. No sooner had he erected his standard than the native strength of the Lombards was multiplied by the adventurous youth of Germany and Scythia. The robust peasantry of Noricum and Pannonia had resumed the manners of barbarians; and the names of the Gepidæ, Bulgarians, Sarmatians, and Bavarians may be distinctly traced in the provinces of Italy.[13] Of the Saxons, the old allies of the Lombards, twenty thousand warriors, with their wives and children, accepted the invitation of Alboin. Their bravery contributed to his success; but the accession or the absence of their numbers was not sensibly felt in the magnitude of his host. Every mode of religion was freely practised by its respective votaries. The king of the Lombards had been educated in the Arian heresy, but the catholics in their public worship were allowed to pray for his conversion; while the more stubborn barbarians sacrificed a she-goat, or perhaps a captive, to the gods of their fathers.[14] The Lombards and their confederates were united by their common attachment to a chief who excelled in all the virtues and vices of a savage hero; and the vigilance of Alboin provided an ample magazine of offensive and defensive arms for the use of the expedition. The portable wealth of the Lombards attended the march: their lands they cheerfully relinquished to the Avars, on the solemn promise, which was made and accepted without a smile, that if they failed in the conquest of Italy these voluntary exiles should be reinstated in their former possessions.

They might have failed if Narses had been the antagonist of the Lombards; and the veteran warriors, the associates of his Gothic victory, would have encountered with reluctance an enemy whom they dreaded and esteemed. But the weakness of the Byzantine court was subservient to the barbarian cause; and it was for the ruin of Italy that the emperor once listened to the complaints of his subjects. The virtues of Narses were stained with avarice; and in his provincial reign of fifteen years he accumulated a treasure of gold and silver which surpassed the modesty of a private fortune. His government was oppressive or unpopular, and the general discontent was expressed with freedom by the deputies of Rome. Before the throne of Justin they boldly declared that their Gothic servitude had been more tolerable than the despotism of a Greek eunuch; and that, unless their tyrant were instantly removed, they would consult their own happiness in the choice of a master. The apprehension of a revolt was urged by the voice of envy and detraction, which had so recently triumphed over the merit of Belisarius. A new exarch, Longinus, was appointed to supersede the conqueror of Italy; and the base motives of his recall were revealed in the insulting mandate of the empress Sophia, "that he should leave to *men* the exercise of arms, and return to his proper station among the maidens of the palace, where a distaff should be again placed in the hand of the eunuch." "I will spin her such a thread as she shall not easily unravel!" is said to have been the reply which indignation and conscious virtue extorted from the hero. Instead of attending, a slave and a victim, at the gate of the Byzantine palace, he retired to Naples, from whence (if any credit is due to the belief of the times) Narses invited the Lombards to chastise the ingratitude of the prince and people.[15] But the passions of the people are furious and changeable, and the Romans soon recollected the merits, or dreaded the resentment, of their victorious general. By the mediation of the pope, who undertook a special pilgrimage to Naples, their repentance was accepted; and Narses, assuming a milder aspect and a more dutiful language, consented to fix his residence in the Capitol. His death,[16] though in the extreme period of old age, was

unseasonable and premature, since *his* genius alone could have repaired the last and fatal error of his life. The reality, or the suspicion, of a conspiracy disarmed and disunited the Italians. The soldiers resented the disgrace, and bewailed the loss, of their general. They were ignorant of their new exarch; and Longinus was himself ignorant of the state of the army and the province. In the preceding years Italy had been desolated by pestilence and famine, and a disaffected people ascribed the calamities of nature to the guilt or folly of their rulers.[17]

Whatever might be the grounds of his security, Alboin neither expected nor encountered a Roman army in the field. He ascended the Julian Alps, and looked down with contempt and desire on the fruitful plains to which his victory communicated the perpetual appellation of LOMBARDY. A faithful chieftain and a select band were stationed at Forum Julii, the modern Friuli, to guard the passes of the mountains. The Lombards respected the strength of Pavia, and listened to the prayers of the Trevisans: their slow and heavy multitudes proceeded to occupy the palace and city of Verona; and Milan, now rising from her ashes, was invested by the powers of Alboin five months after his departure from Pannonia. Terror preceded his march: he found everywhere, or he left, a dreary solitude; and the pusillanimous Italians presumed, without a trial, that the stranger was invincible. Escaping to lakes, or rocks, or morasses, the affrighted crowds concealed some fragments of their wealth, and delayed the moment of their servitude. Paulinus, the patriarch of Aquileia, removed his treasures, sacred and profane, to the isle of Grado,[18] and his successors were adopted by the infant republic of Venice, which was continually enriched by the public calamities. Honoratus, who filled the chair of St. Ambrose, had credulously accepted the faithless offers of a capitulation; and the archbishop, with the clergy and nobles of Milan, were driven by the perfidy of Alboin to seek a refuge in the less accessible ramparts of Genoa. Along the maritime coast the courage of the inhabitants was supported by the facility of supply, the hopes of relief, and the power of escape; but, from the Trentine hills to the gates of Ravenna and Rome, the inland regions of Italy became, without a battle or a siege, the lasting patrimony of the Lombards. The submission of the people invited the barbarian to assume the character of a lawful sovereign, and the helpless exarch was confined to the office of announcing to the emperor Justin the rapid and irretrievable loss of his provinces and cities.[19] One city, which had been diligently fortified by the Goths, resisted the arms of a new invader; and, while Italy was subdued by the flying detachments of the Lombards, the royal camp was fixed above three years before the western gate of Ticinum, or Pavia. The same courage which obtains the esteem of a civilised enemy provokes the fury of a savage; and the impatient besieger had bound himself by a tremendous oath that age, and sex, and dignity should be confounded in a general massacre. The aid of famine at length enabled him to execute his bloody vow; but as Alboin entered the gate his horse stumbled, fell, and could not be raised from the ground. One of his attendants was prompted by compassion, or piety, to interpret this miraculous sign of the wrath of Heaven: the conqueror paused and relented; he sheathed his sword, and, peacefully reposing himself in the palace of Theodoric, proclaimed to the trembling multitude that they should live and obey. Delighted with the situation of a city which was endeared to his pride by the difficulty of the purchase, the prince of the Lombards disdained the ancient glories of Milan; and Pavia during some ages was respected as the capital of the kingdom of Italy.[20]

The reign of the founder was splendid and transient; and, before he could regulate his new conquests, Alboin fell a sacrifice to domestic treason and female revenge. In a palace near Verona, which had not been erected for the barbarians, he feasted the companions of his arms; intoxication was the reward of valour, and the king himself was tempted by appetite or vanity to exceed the ordinary measure of his intemperance. After draining many capacious bowls of Rhætian or Falernian wine he called for the skull of Cunimund, the noblest and most precious ornament of his sideboard. The cup of victory was accepted with horrid applause by the circle of the Lombard chiefs. "Fill it again with wine!" exclaimed the inhuman conqueror, "fill it to the brim! carry this goblet to the queen, and request in my name that she would rejoice with her father." In an agony of grief and rage, Rosamond had strength to utter, "Let the will of my lord be obeyed!" and, touching it with her lips, pronounced a silent imprecation that the insult should be washed away in the blood of Alboin. Some indulgence might be due to the resentment of a daughter, if she had not already violated the duties of a wife. Implacable in her enmity, or inconstant in her love, the queen of Italy had stooped from the throne to the arms of a subject, and Helmichis, the king's armour-bearer, was the secret minister of her pleasure and revenge. Against the proposal of the murder he could no longer urge the scruples of fidelity or gratitude; but Helmichis trembled when he revolved the danger as well as the guilt, when he recollected the matchless strength and intrepidity of a warrior whom he had so often attended in the field of battle. He pressed, and obtained, that one of the bravest champions of the Lombards should be associated to the enterprise; but no more than a promise of secrecy could be drawn from the gallant Peredeus, and the mode of seduction employed by Rosamond betrays her shameless insensibility both to honour and love. She supplied the place of one of her female attendants who was beloved by Peredeus, and contrived some excuse for darkness and silence till she could inform her companion that he had enjoyed the queen of the Lombards, and that his own death or the death of Alboin must be the consequence of such treasonable adultery. In this alternative he chose rather to be the accomplice than the victim of Rosamond,[21] whose undaunted spirit was incapable of fear or remorse. She expected and soon found a favourable moment, when the king, oppressed with wine, had retired from the table to his afternoon slumbers. His faithless spouse was anxious for his health and repose; the gates of the palace were shut, the arms removed, the attendants dismissed, and Rosamond, after lulling him to rest by her tender caresses, unbolted the chamber-door and urged the reluctant conspirators to the instant execution of the deed. On the first alarm the warrior started from his couch: his sword, which he attempted to draw, had been fastened to the scabbard by the hand of Rosamond; and a small stool, his only weapon, could not long protect him from the spears of the assassins. The daughter of Cunimund smiled in his fall: his body was buried under the staircase of the palace; and the grateful posterity of the Lombards revered the tomb and the memory of their victorious leader.

The ambitious Rosamond aspired to reign in the name of her lover; the city and palace of Verona were awed by her power; and a faithful band of her native Gepidæ was prepared to applaud the revenge and to second the wishes of their sovereign. But the Lombard chiefs, who fled in the first moments of consternation and disorder, had resumed their courage and collected their powers; and the nation, instead of submitting to her reign, demanded with unanimous cries that justice should be executed on the guilty spouse and the murderers of their king. She sought a refuge among the enemies of her country, and a criminal who deserved the abhorrence of mankind was protected by the selfish policy of the exarch. With her daughter, the heiress of the Lombard throne, her two lovers, her trusty Gepidæ, and the spoils of the palace of Verona, Rosamond descended the Adige and the Po, and was transported by a Greek vessel to the safe harbour of Ravenna. Longinus beheld with delight the charms and the treasures of the widow of Alboin: her situation and her past conduct might justify the most licentious proposals, and she readily listened to the passion of a minister who, even in the decline of the empire, was respected as the equal of kings. The death of a jealous lover was an easy and grateful sacrifice, and as Helmichis issued from the bath he received the deadly potion from the hand of his mistress. The taste of the liquor, its speedy operation, and his experience of the character of Rosamond, convinced him that he was poisoned; he pointed his dagger to her breast, compelled her to drain the remainder of the cup, and expired in a few minutes with the consolation that she could not survive to enjoy the fruits of her wickedness. The daughter of Alboin and Rosamond, with the richest spoils of the Lombards, was embarked for Constantinople: the surprising strength of Peredeus amused and terrified the Imperial court; his blindness and revenge exhibited an imperfect copy of the adventures of Samson. By the free suffrage of the nation in the assembly of Pavia, Clepho, one of their noblest chiefs, was elected as the successor of Alboin. Before the end of eighteen months the throne was polluted by a second murder: Clepho was stabbed by the hand of a domestic; the regal office was suspended above ten years during the minority of his son Autharis, and Italy was divided and oppressed by a ducal aristocracy of thirty tyrants.[22]

When the nephew of Justinian ascended the throne, he proclaimed a new era of happiness and glory. The annals of the second Justin[23] are marked with disgrace abroad and misery at home. In the West the Roman empire was afflicted by the loss of Italy, the desolation of Africa, and the conquests of the Persians. Injustice prevailed both in the capital and the provinces: the rich trembled for their property, the poor for their safety; the ordinary magistrates were ignorant or venal, the occasional remedies appear to have been arbitrary and violent, and the complaints of the people could

no longer be silenced by the splendid names of a legislator and a conqueror. The opinion which imputes to the prince all the calamities of his times may be countenanced by the historian as a serious truth or a salutary prejudice. Yet a candid suspicion will arise that the sentiments of Justin were pure and benevolent, and that he might have filled his station without reproach if the faculties of his mind had not been impaired by disease, which deprived the emperor of the use of his feet and confined him to the palace, a stranger to the complaints of the people and the vices of the government. The tardy knowledge of his own impotence determined him to lay down the weight of the diadem, and in the choice of a worthy substitute he showed some symptoms of a discerning and even magnanimous spirit. The only son of Justin and Sophia died in his infancy; their daughter Arabia was the wife of Baduarius,[23a] superintendent of the palace, and afterwards commander of the Italian armies, who vainly aspired to confirm the rights of marriage by those of adoption. While the empire appeared an object of desire, Justin was accustomed to behold with jealousy and hatred his brothers and cousins, the rivals of his hopes; nor could he depend on the gratitude of those who would accept the purple as a restitution rather than a gift. Of these competitors one had been removed by exile, and afterwards by death; and the emperor himself had inflicted such cruel insults on another, that he must either dread his resentment or despise his patience. This domestic animosity was refined into a generous resolution of seeking a successor, not in his family, but in the republic; and the artful Sophia recommended Tiberius,[24] his faithful captain of the guards, whose virtues and fortune the emperor might cherish as the fruit of his judicious choice. The ceremony of his elevation to the rank of Cæsar or Augustus was performed in the portico of the palace in the presence of the patriarch and the senate. Justin collected the remaining strength of his mind and body; but the popular belief that his speech was inspired by the Deity betrays a very humble opinion both of the man and of the times.[25] "You behold," said the emperor, "the ensigns of supreme power. You are about to receive them, not from my hand, but from the hand of God. Honour them, and from them you will derive honour. Respect the empress your mother; you are now her son; before, you were her servant. Delight not in blood; abstain from revenge; avoid those actions by which I have incurred the public hatred; and consult the experience, rather than the example, of your predecessor. As a man, I have sinned; as a sinner, even in this life, I have been severely punished: but these servants (and he pointed to his ministers), who have abused my confidence and inflamed my passions, will appear with me before the tribunal of Christ. I have been dazzled by the splendour of the diadem: be thou wise and modest; remember what you have been, remember what you are. You see around us your slaves and your children; with the authority, assume the tenderness of a parent. Love your people like yourself; cultivate the affections, maintain the discipline, of the army; protect the fortunes of the rich, relieve the necessities of the poor."[26] The assembly, in silence and in tears, applauded the counsels and sympathised with the repentance of their prince; the patriarch rehearsed the prayers of the church; Tiberius received the diadem on his knees; and Justin, who in his abdication appeared most worthy to reign, addressed the new monarch in the following words:—"If you consent, I live; if you command, I die: may the God of heaven and earth infuse into your heart whatever I have neglected or forgotten." The four last years of the emperor Justin were passed in tranquil obscurity: his conscience was no longer tormented by the remembrance of those duties which he was incapable of discharging, and his choice was justified by the filial reverence and gratitude of Tiberius.

Among the virtues of Tiberius,[27] his beauty (he was one of the tallest and most comely of the Romans) might introduce him to the favour of Sophia; and the widow of Justin was persuaded that she should preserve her station and influence under the reign of a second and more youthful husband. But if the ambitious candidate had been tempted to flatter and dissemble, it was no longer in his power to fulfil her expectations or his own promise. The factions of the hippodrome demanded with some impatience the name of their new empress; both the people and Sophia were astonished by the proclamation of Anastasia, the secret though lawful wife of the emperor Tiberius. Whatever could alleviate the disappointment of Sophia, imperial honours, a stately palace, a numerous household, was liberally bestowed by the piety of her adopted son; on solemn occasions he attended and consulted the widow of his benefactor, but her ambition disdained the vain semblance of royalty, and the respectful appellation of mother served to exasperate rather than appease the rage of an injured woman.

While she accepted and repaid with a courtly smile the fair expressions of regard and confidence, a secret alliance was concluded between the dowager empress and her ancient enemies; and Justinian, the son of Germanus, was employed as the instrument of her revenge. The pride of the reigning house supported with reluctance the dominion of a stranger: the youth was deservedly popular, his name after the death of Justin had been mentioned by a tumultuous faction, and his own submissive offer of his head, with a treasure of sixty thousand pounds, might be interpreted as an evidence of guilt, or at least of fear. Justinian received a free pardon and the command of the eastern army. The Persian monarch fled before his arms, and the acclamations which accompanied his triumph declared him worthy of the purple. His artful patroness had chosen the month of the vintage, while the emperor in a rural solitude was permitted to enjoy the pleasures of a subject. On the first intelligence of her designs he returned to Constantinople, and the conspiracy was suppressed by his presence and firmness. From the pomp and honours which she had abused, Sophia was reduced to a modest allowance; Tiberius dismissed her train, intercepted her correspondence, and committed to a faithful guard the custody of her person. But the services of Justinian were not considered by that excellent prince as an aggravation of his offences: after a mild reproof his treason and ingratitude were forgiven, and it was commonly believed that the emperor entertained some thoughts of contracting a double alliance with the rival of his throne. The voice of an angel (such a fable was propagated) might reveal to the emperor that he should always triumph over his domestic foes, but Tiberius derived a firmer assurance from the innocence and generosity of his own mind.

With the odious name of Tiberius he assumed the more popular appellation of Constantine, and imitated the purer virtues of the Antonines. After recording the vice or folly of so many Roman princes, it is pleasing to repose for a moment on a character conspicuous by the qualities of humanity, justice, temperance, and fortitude; to contemplate a sovereign affable in his palace, pious in the church, impartial on the seat of judgment, and victorious, at least by his generals, in the Persian war. The most glorious trophy of his victory consisted in a multitude of captives, whom Tiberius entertained, redeemed, and dismissed to their native homes with the charitable spirit of a Christian hero. The merit or misfortunes of his own subjects had a dearer claim to his beneficence, and he measured his bounty not so much by their expectations as by his own dignity. This maxim, however dangerous in a trustee of the public wealth, was balanced by a principle of humanity and justice, which taught him to abhor, as of the basest alloy, the gold that was extracted from the tears of the people. For their relief, as often as they had suffered by natural or hostile calamities, he was impatient to remit the arrears of the past or the demands of future taxes: he sternly rejected the servile offerings of his ministers, which were compensated by tenfold oppression; and the wise and equitable laws of Tiberius excited the praise and regret of succeeding times. Constantinople believed that the emperor had discovered a treasure; but his genuine treasure consisted in the practice of liberal economy, and the contempt of all vain and superfluous expense. The Romans of the East would have been happy if the best gift of heaven, a patriot king, had been confirmed as a proper and permanent blessing. But in less than four years after the death of Justin, his worthy successor sunk into a mortal disease, which left him only sufficient time to restore the diadem, according to the tenure by which he held it, to the most deserving of his fellow-citizens. He selected Maurice from the crowd—a judgment more precious than the purple itself: the patriarch and senate were summoned to the bed of the dying prince; he bestowed his daughter and the empire, and his last advice was solemnly delivered by the voice of the quæstor. Tiberius expressed his hope that the virtues of his son and successor would erect the noblest mausoleum to his memory. His memory was embalmed by the public affliction; but the most sincere grief evaporates in the tumult of a new reign, and the eyes and acclamations of mankind were speedily directed to the rising sun.

The emperor Maurice derived his origin from ancient Rome;[28] but his immediate parents were settled at Arabissus in Cappadocia, and their singular felicity preserved them alive to behold and partake the fortune of their *august* son. The youth of Maurice was spent in the profession of arms: Tiberius promoted him to the command of a new and favourite legion of twelve thousand confederates; his valour and conduct were signalised in the Persian war; and he returned to Constantinople to accept, as his just reward, the inheritance of the empire. Maurice ascended the throne at the mature age of forty-three years; and he reigned above twenty years over the East and over himself;[29] expelling from his mind the wild democracy of passions, and establishing (according to the quaint expression of Evagrius) a perfect aristocracy of reason and virtue. Some suspicion will degrade the testimony of a subject, though he protests that his secret praise should never reach the ear of his sovereign,[30] and some failings seem to place the character of Maurice below the purer merit of his predecessor. His cold and reserved demeanour might be imputed to arrogance; his justice was not always exempt from cruelty, nor his clemency from weakness; and his rigid economy too often exposed him to the reproach of avarice. But the rational wishes of an absolute monarch must tend to the happiness of his people: Maurice was endowed with sense and courage to promote that happiness, and his administration was directed by the principles and example of Tiberius. The pusillanimity of the Greeks had introduced so complete a separation between the offices of king and of general, that a private soldier, who had deserved and obtained the purple, seldom or never appeared at the head of his armies. Yet the emperor Maurice enjoyed the glory of restoring the Persian monarch to his throne; his lieutenants waged a doubtful war against the Avars of the Danube; and he cast an eye of pity, of ineffectual pity, on the abject and distressful state of his Italian provinces.

From Italy the emperors were incessantly tormented by tales of misery and demands of succour, which extorted the humiliating confession of their own weakness. The expiring dignity of Rome was only marked by the freedom and energy of her complaints: "If you are incapable," she said, "of delivering us from the sword of the Lombards, save us at least from the calamity of famine." Tiberius forgave the reproach, and relieved the distress: a supply of corn was transported from Egypt to the Tiber; and the Roman people, invoking the name, not of Camillus, but of St. Peter, repulsed the barbarians from their walls. But the relief was accidental, the danger was perpetual and pressing; and the clergy and senate, collecting the remains of their ancient opulence, a sum of three thousand pounds of gold, despatched the patrician Pamphronius to lay their gifts and their complaints at the foot of the Byzantine throne. The attention of the court, and the forces of the East, were diverted by the Persian war; but the justice of Tiberius applied the subsidy to the defence of the city; and he dismissed the patrician with his best advice, either to bribe the Lombard chiefs, or to purchase the aid of the kings of France. Notwithstanding this weak invention, Italy was still afflicted, Rome was again besieged, and the suburb of Classe, only three miles from Ravenna, was pillaged and occupied by the troops of a simple duke of Spoleto. Maurice gave audience to a second deputation of priests and senators: the duties and the menaces of religion were forcibly urged in the letters of the Roman pontiff; and his nuncio, the deacon Gregory, was alike qualified to solicit the powers either of heaven or of the earth. The emperor adopted, with stronger effect, the measures of his predecessor: some formidable chiefs were persuaded to embrace the friendship of the Romans; and one of them, a mild and faithful barbarian, lived and died in the service of the exarch: the passes of the Alps were delivered to the Franks; and the pope encouraged them to violate, without scruple, their oaths and engagements to the misbelievers. Childebert, the great-grandson of Clovis, was persuaded to invade Italy by the payment of fifty thousand pieces; but, as he had viewed with delight some Byzantine coin of the weight of one pound of gold, the king of Austrasia might stipulate that the gift should be rendered more worthy of his acceptance by a proper mixture of these respectable medals. The dukes of the Lombards had provoked by frequent inroads their powerful neighbours of Gaul. As soon as they were apprehensive of a just retaliation, they renounced their feeble and disorderly independence: the advantages of regal government, union, secrecy, and vigour, were unanimously confessed; and Autharis, the son of Clepho, had already attained the strength and reputation of a warrior. Under the standard of their new king, the conquerors of Italy withstood three successive invasions, one of which was led by Childebert himself, the last of the Merovingian race who descended from the Alps. The first expedition was defeated by the jealous animosity of the Franks and Alemanni. In the second they were vanquished in a bloody battle, with more loss and dishonour than they had sustained since the foundation of their monarchy. Impatient for revenge, they returned a third time with accumulated force, and Autharis yielded to the fury of the torrent. The troops and treasures of the Lombards were distributed in the walled towns between the Alps and the Apennine. A nation, less sensible of danger than of fatigue and delay, soon murmured against the folly of their twenty commanders; and the hot vapours of an Italian sun infected with disease those tramontane bodies which had already suffered the vicissitudes of intemperance and famine. The powers that were inadequate to the conquest, were more than sufficient for the desolation, of the country; nor could the trembling natives distinguish between their enemies and their deliverers. If the junction of the Merovingian and Imperial forces had been effected in the neighbourhood of Milan, perhaps they might have subverted the throne of the Lombards; but the Franks expected six days the signal of a flaming village, and the arms of the Greeks were idly employed in the reduction of Modena and Parma, which were torn from them after the retreat of their transalpine allies. The victorious Autharis asserted his claim to the dominion of Italy. At the foot of the Rhætian Alps, he subdued the resistance, and rifled the hidden treasures, of a sequestered island in the lake of Comum. At the extreme point of Calabria, he touched with his spear a column on the sea-shore of Rhegium, [31] proclaiming that ancient landmark to stand the immovable boundary of his kingdom. [32]

During a period of two hundred years Italy was unequally divided between the kingdom of the Lombards and the exarchate of Ravenna. The offices and professions which the jealousy of Constantine had separated were united by the indulgence of Justinian; and eighteen successive exarchs were invested, in the decline of the empire, with the full remains of civil, of military, and even of ecclesiastical power. Their immediate jurisdiction, which was afterwards consecrated as the patrimony of St. Peter, extended over the modern Romagna, the marshes or valleys of Ferrara and Commachio, [33] five maritime cities from Rimini to Ancona, and a second inland Pentapolis, between the Hadriatic coast and the hills of the Apennine. Three subordinate provinces, of Rome, of Venice, and of Naples, which were divided by hostile lands from the palace of Ravenna, acknowledged, both in peace and war, the supremacy of the exarch. The duchy of Rome appears to have included the Tuscan, Sabine, and Latin conquests of the first four hundred years of the city, and the limits may be distinctly traced along the coast, from Civita Vecchia to Terracina, and with the course of the Tiber from Ameria and Narni to the port of Ostia. The numerous islands from Grado to Chiozza composed the infant dominion of Venice; but the more accessible towns on the continent were overthrown by the Lombards, who beheld with impotent fury a new capital rising from the waves. The power of the dukes of Naples was circumscribed by the bay and the adjacent isles, by the hostile territory of Capua, and by the Roman colony of Amalphi,[34] whose industrious citizens, by the invention of the mariner's compass, have unveiled the face of the globe. The three islands of Sardinia, Corsica, and Sicily still adhered to the empire; and the acquisition of the farther Calabria removed the landmark of Autharis from the shore of Rhegium to the isthmus of Consentia. In Sardinia the savage mountaineers preserved the liberty and religion of their ancestors; but the husbandmen of Sicily were chained to their rich and cultivated soil. Rome was oppressed by the iron sceptre of the exarchs, and a Greek, perhaps a eunuch, insulted with impunity the ruins of the Capitol. But Naples soon acquired the privilege of electing her own dukes:[35] the independence of Amalphi was the fruit of commerce; and the voluntary attachment of Venice was finally ennobled by an equal alliance with the Eastern empire. On the map of Italy the measure of the exarchate occupies a very inadequate space, but it included an ample proportion of wealth, industry, and population. The most faithful and valuable subjects escaped from the barbarian yoke; and the banners of Pavia and Verona, of Milan and Padua, were displayed in their respective quarters by the new inhabitants of Ravenna. The remainder of Italy was possessed by the Lombards; and from Pavia, the royal seat, their kingdom was extended to the east, the north, and the west, as far as the confines of the Avars, the Bavarians, and the Franks of Austrasia and Burgundy. In the language of modern geography, it is now represented by the Terra Firma of the Venetian republic, Tyrol, the Milanese, Piedmont, the coast of Genoa, Mantua, Parma, and Modena, the grand duchy of Tuscany, and a large portion of the ecclesiastical state from Perugia to the Hadriatic. The dukes, and at length the princes, of Beneventum, survived the monarchy, and propagated the name of the Lombards. From Capua to Tarentum, they reigned near five hundred years over the greatest part of the present kingdom of Naples.[36]

In comparing the proportion of the victorious and the vanquished people, the change of language will afford the most probable inference. According to this standard it will appear that the Lombards of Italy, and the Visigoths of Spain, were less numerous than the Franks or Burgundians; and the conquerors of Gaul must yield, in their turn, to the multitude of Saxons and Angles who almost eradicated the idioms of Britain. The modern Italian has been insensibly formed by the mixture of nations: the awkwardness of the barbarians in the nice management of declensions and conjugations reduced them to the use of articles and auxiliary verbs; and many new ideas have been expressed by Teutonic appellations. Yet the principal stock of technical and familiar words is found to be of Latin derivation;[37] and, if we were sufficiently conversant with the obsolete, the rustic, and the municipal dialects of ancient Italy, we should trace the origin of many terms which might, perhaps, be rejected by the classic purity of Rome. A numerous army constitutes but a small nation, and the powers of the Lombards were soon diminished by the retreat of twenty thousand Saxons, who scorned a dependent situation, and returned, after many bold and perilous adventures, to their native country.[38] The camp of Alboin was of formidable extent, but the extent of a camp would be easily circumscribed within the limits of a city; and its martial inhabitants must be thinly scattered over the face of a large country. When Alboin descended from the Alps, he invested his nephew, the first duke of Friuli, with the command of the province and the people: but the prudent Gisulf would have declined the dangerous office, unless he had been permitted to choose, among the nobles of the Lombards, a sufficient number of families[39] to form a perpetual colony of soldiers and subjects. In the progress of conquest, the same option could not be granted to the dukes of Brescia or Bergamo, of Pavia or Turin, of Spoleto or Beneventum; but each of these, and each of their colleagues, settled in his appointed district with a band of followers who resorted to his standard in war and his tribunal in peace. Their attachment was free and honourable: resigning the gifts and benefits which they had accepted, they might emigrate with their families into the jurisdiction of another duke; but their absence from the kingdom was punished with death, as a crime of military desertion.[40] The posterity of the first conquerors struck a deeper root into the soil, which, by every motive of interest and honour, they were bound to defend. A Lombard was born the soldier of his king and his duke; and the civil assemblies of the nation displayed the banners, and assumed the appellation, of a regular army. Of this army the pay and the rewards were drawn from the conquered provinces; and the distribution, which was not effected till after the death of Alboin, is disgraced by the foul marks of injustice and rapine. Many of the most wealthy Ita-ians were slain or banished; the remainder were divided among the strangers, and a tributary obligation was imposed (under the name of hospitality) of paying to the Lombards a third part of the fruits of the earth. Within less than seventy years this artificial system was abolished by a more simple and solid tenure.[41] Either the Roman landlord was expelled by his strong and insolent guest, or the annual payment, a third of the produce, was exchanged by a more equitable transaction for an adequate proportion of landed property. Under these foreign masters, the business of agriculture, in the cultivation of corn, vines, and olives, was exercised with degenerate skill and industry by the labour of the slaves and natives. But the occupations of a pastoral life were more pleasing to the idleness of the barbarians. In the rich meadows of Venetia they restored and improved the breed of horses, for which that province had once been illustrious;[42] and the Italians beheld with astonishment a foreign race of oxen or buffaloes.[43] The depopulation of Lombardy, and the increase of forests, afforded an ample range for the pleasures of the chase.[44] That marvellous art which teaches the birds of the air to acknowledge the voice, and execute the commands, of their master had been unknown to the ingenuity of the Greeks and Romans.[45] Scandinavia and Scythia produce the boldest and most tractable falcons:[46] they were tamed and educated by the roving inhabitants, always on horseback and in the field. This favourite amusement of our ancestors was introduced by the barbarians into the Roman provinces: and the laws of Italy esteem the sword and the hawk as of equal dignity and importance in the hands of a noble Lombard.[47]

So rapid was the influence of climate and example, that the Lombards of the fourth generation surveyed with curiosity and affright the portraits of their savage forefathers.[48] Their heads were shaven behind, but the shaggy locks hung over their eyes and mouth, and a long beard represented the name and character of the nation. Their dress consisted of loose linen garments, after the fashion of the Anglo-Saxons, which were decorated, in their opinion, with broad stripes of variegated colours. The legs and feet were clothed in long hose and open sandals, and even in the security of peace a trusty sword was constantly girt to their side. Yet this strange apparel and horrid aspect often concealed a gentle and generous disposition; and as soon as the rage of battle had subsided, the captives and subjects were sometimes surprised by the humanity of the victor. The vices of the Lombards were the effect of passion, of ignorance, of intoxication; their virtues are the more laudable, as they were not affected by the hypocrisy of social manners, nor imposed by the rigid constraint of laws and education. I should not be apprehensive of deviating from my subject, if it were in my power to delineate the private life of the conquerors of Italy; and I shall relate with pleasure the adventurous gallantry of Autharis, which breathes the true spirit of chivalry and romance.[49] After the loss of his promised bride, a Merovingian princess, he sought in marriage the daughter of the king of Bavaria, and Garibald accepted the alliance of the Italian monarch. Impatient of the slow progress of negotiation, the ardent lover escaped from his palace and visited the court of Bavaria in the train of his own embassy. At the public audience the unknown stranger advanced to the throne, and informed Garibald that the ambassador was indeed the minister of state, but that he alone was the friend of Autharis, who had trusted him with the delicate commission of making a faithful report of the charms of his spouse. Theudelinda was summoned to undergo this important examination, and, after a pause of silent rapture, he hailed her as the queen of Italy, and humbly requested that, according to the custom of the nation, she would present a cup of wine to the first of her new subjects. By the command of her father she obeyed: Autharis received the cup in his turn, and, in restoring it to the princess, he secretly touched her hand, and drew his own finger over his face and lips. In the evening Theudelinda imparted to her nurse the indiscreet familiarity of the stranger, and was comforted by the assurance that such boldness could proceed only from the king her husband, who, by his beauty and courage, appeared worthy of her love. The ambassadors were dismissed: no sooner did they reach the confines of Italy than Autharis, raising himself on his horse, darted his battle-axe against a tree with incomparable strength and dexterity: "Such," said he to the astonished Bavarians, "such are the strokes of the king of the Lombards." On the approach of a French army, Garibald and his daughter took refuge in the dominions of their ally, and the marriage was consummated in the palace of Verona. At the end of one year it was dissolved by the death of Autharis; but the virtues of Theudelinda[50] had endeared her to the nation, and she was permitted to bestow, with her hand, the sceptre of the Italian kingdom.

From this fact, as well as from similar events,[51] it is certain that the Lombards possessed freedom to elect their sovereign, and sense to decline the frequent use of that dangerous privilege. The public revenue arose from the produce of land and the profits of justice. When the independent dukes agreed that Autharis should ascend the throne of his father, they endowed the regal office with a fair moiety of their respective domains. The proudest nobles aspired to the honours of servitude near the person of their prince; he rewarded the fidelity of his vassals by the precarious gift of pensions and *benefices*, and atoned for the injuries of war by the rich foundation of monasteries and churches. In peace a judge, a leader in war, he never usurped the powers of a sole and absolute legislator. The king of Italy convened the national assemblies in the palace, or more probably in the fields, of Pavia; his great council was composed of the persons most eminent by their birth and dignities; but the validity, as well as the execution, of their decrees depended on the approbation of the *faithful* people, the *fortunate* army of the Lombards. About fourscore years after the conquest of Italy their traditional customs were transcribed in Teutonic Latin,[52] and ratified by the consent of the prince and people; some new regulations were introduced, more suitable to their present condition; the example of Rotharis was imitated by the wisest of his successors: and the laws of the Lombards have been esteemed the least imperfect of the barbaric codes.[53] Secure by their courage in the possession of liberty, these rude and hasty legislators were incapable of balancing the powers of the constitution, or of discussing the nice theory of political government. Such crimes as threatened the life of the sovereign or the safety of the state were adjudged worthy of death; but their attention was principally confined to the defence of the person and property of the subject. According to the strange jurisprudence of the times, the guilt of blood might be redeemed by a fine; yet the high price of nine hundred pieces of gold declares a just sense of the value of a simple citizen. Less atrocious injuries, a wound, a fracture, a blow, an opprobrious word, were measured with scrupulous and almost ridiculous diligence; and the prudence of the legislator encouraged the ignoble practice of bartering honour and revenge for a pecuniary compensation. The ignorance of the Lombards in the state of Paganism or Christianity gave implicit credit to the malice and mischief of witchcraft: but the judges of the seventeenth century might

have been instructed and confounded by the wisdom of Rotharis, who derides the absurd superstition, and protects the wretched victims of popular or judicial cruelty.[54] The same spirit of a legislator superior to his age and country may be ascribed to Liutprand, who condemns while he tolerates the impious and inveterate abuse of duels,[55] observing, from his own experience, that the juster cause had often been oppressed by successful violence. Whatever merit may be discovered in the laws of the Lombards, they are the genuine fruit of the reason of the barbarians, who never admitted the bishops of Italy to a seat in their legislative councils. But the succession of their kings is marked with virtue and ability; the troubled series of their annals is adorned with fair intervals of peace, order, and domestic happiness; and the Italians enjoyed a milder and more equitable government than any of the other kingdoms which had been founded on the ruins of the Western empire.[56]

Amidst the arms of the Lombards, and under the despotism of the Greeks, we again inquire into the fate of Rome,[57] which had reached, about the close of the sixth century, the lowest period of her depression. By the removal of the seat of empire and the successive loss of the provinces, the sources of public and private opulence were exhausted: the lofty tree, under whose shade the nations of the earth had reposed, was deprived of its leaves and branches, and the sapless trunk was left to wither on the ground. The ministers of command and the messengers of victory no longer met on the Appian or Flaminian way, and the hostile approach of the Lombards was often felt and continually feared. The inhabitants of a potent and peaceful capital, who visit without an anxious thought the garden of the adjacent country, will faintly picture in their fancy the distress of the Romans: they shut or opened their gates with a trembling hand, beheld from the walls the flames of their houses, and heard the lamentations of their brethren, who were coupled together like dogs, and dragged away into distant slavery beyond the sea and the mountains. Such incessant alarms must annihilate the pleasures and interrupt the labours of a rural life; and the Campagna of Rome was speedily reduced to the state of a dreary wilderness, in which the land is barren, the waters are impure, and the air is infectious. Curiosity and ambition no longer attracted the nations to the capital of the world; but, if chance or necessity directed the steps of a wandering stranger, he contemplated with horror the vacancy and solitude of the city, and might be tempted to ask, where is the senate, and where are the people? In a season of excessive rains the Tiber swelled above its banks, and rushed with irresistible violence into the valleys of the seven hills. A pestilential disease arose from the stagnation of the deluge, and so rapid was the contagion that fourscore persons expired in an hour in the midst of a solemn procession which implored the mercy of Heaven.[58] A society in which marriage is encouraged and industry prevails soon repairs the accidental losses of pestilence and war; but, as the far greater part of the Romans was condemned to hopeless indigence and celibacy, the depopulation was constant and visible, and the gloomy enthusiasts might expect the approaching failure of the human race.[59] Yet the number of citizens still exceeded the measure of subsistence: their precarious food was supplied from the harvests of Sicily or Egypt, and the frequent repetition of famine betrays the inattention of the emperor to a distant province. The edifices of Rome were exposed to the same ruin and decay; the mouldering fabrics were easily overthrown by inundations, tempests, and earthquakes; and the monks, who had occupied the most advantageous stations, exulted in their base triumph over the ruins of antiquity.[60] It is commonly believed that pope Gregory the First attacked the temples and mutilated the statues of the city; that, by the command of the barbarian, the Palatine library was reduced to ashes, and that the history of Livy was the peculiar mark of his absurd and mischievous fanaticism. The writings of Gregory himself reveal his implacable aversion to the monuments of classic genius, and he points his severest censure against the profane learning of a bishop who taught the art of grammar, studied the Latin poets, and pronounced with the same voice the praises of Jupiter and those of Christ. But the evidence of his destructive rage is doubtful and recent: the Temple of Peace or the Theatre of Marcellus have been demolished by the slow operation of ages, and a formal proscription would have multiplied the copies of Virgil and Livy in the countries which were not subject to the ecclesiastical dictator.[61]

Like Thebes, or Babylon, or Carthage, the name of Rome might have been erased from the earth, if the city had not been animated by a vital principle, which again restored her to honour and dominion. A vague tradition was embraced, that two Jewish teachers, a tent-maker and a fisherman, had formerly been executed in the circus of Nero, and at the end of five hundred years their genuine or fictitious relics were adored as the Palladium of Christian Rome. The pilgrims of the East and West resorted to the holy threshold; but the shrines of the apostles were guarded by miracles and invisible terrors, and it was not without fear that the pious catholic approached the object of his worship. It was fatal to touch, it was dangerous to behold, the bodies of the saints; and those who, from the purest motives, presumed to disturb the repose of the sanctuary were affrighted by visions or punished with sudden death. The unreasonable request of an empress, who wished to deprive the Romans of their sacred treasure, the head of St. Paul, was rejected with the deepest abhorrence; and the pope asserted, most probably with truth, that a linen which had been sanctified in the neighbourhood of his body, or the filings of his chain, which it was sometimes easy and sometimes impossible to obtain, possessed an equal degree of miraculous virtue.[62] But the power as well as virtue of the apostles resided with living energy in the breast of their successors: and the chair of St. Peter was filled under the reign of Maurice by the first and greatest of the name of Gregory.[63] His grandfather Felix had himself been pope, and, as the bishops were already bound by the law of celibacy, his consecration must have been preceded by the death of his wife. The parents of Gregory, Sylvia and Gordian, were the noblest of the senate and the most pious of the church of Rome; his female relations were numbered among the saints and virgins, and his own figure, with those of his father and mother, were represented near three hundred years in a family portrait[64] which he offered to the monastery of St. Andrew. The design and colouring of this picture afford an honourable testimony that the art of painting was cultivated by the Italians of the sixth century; but the most abject ideas must be entertained of their taste and learning, since the epistles of Gregory, his sermons, and his dialogues, are the work of a man who was second in erudition to none of his contemporaries:[65] his birth and abilities had raised him to the office of præfect of the city, and he enjoyed the merit of renouncing the pomp and vanities of this world. His ample patrimony was dedicated to the foundation of seven monasteries,[66] one in Rome[67] and six in Sicily; and it was the wish of Gregory that he might be unknown in this life and glorious only in the next. Yet his devotion, and it might be sincere, pursued the path which would have been chosen by a crafty and ambitious statesman. The talents of Gregory, and the splendour which accompanied his retreat, rendered him dear and useful to the church, and implicit obedience has been always inculcated as the first duty of a monk. As soon as he had received the character of deacon, Gregory was sent to reside at the Byzantine court, the nuncio or minister of the apostolic see; and he boldly assumed, in the name of St. Peter, a tone of independent dignity which would have been criminal and dangerous in the most illustrious layman of the empire. He returned to Rome with a just increase of reputation, and, after a short exercise of the monastic virtues, he was dragged from the cloister to the papal throne by the unanimous voice of the clergy, the senate, and the people. He alone resisted, or seemed to resist, his own elevation; and his humble petition that Maurice would be pleased to reject the choice of the Romans could only serve to exalt his character in the eyes of the emperor and the public. When the fatal mandate was proclaimed, Gregory solicited the aid of some friendly merchants to convey him in a basket beyond the gates of Rome, and modestly concealed himself some days among the woods and mountains, till his retreat was discovered, as it is said, by a celestial light.

The pontificate of Gregory the *Great*, which lasted thirteen years, six months, and ten days, is one of the most edifying periods of the history of the church. His virtues, and even his faults, a singular mixture of simplicity and cunning, of pride and humility, of sense and superstition, were happily suited to his station and to the temper of the times. In his rival, the patriarch of Constantinople, he condemned the antichristian title of universal bishop, which the successor of St. Peter was too haughty to concede and too feeble to assume; and the ecclesiastical jurisdiction of Gregory was confined to the triple character of Bishop of Rome, Primate of Italy, and Apostle of the West. He frequently ascended the pulpit, and kindled, by his rude though pathetic eloquence, the congenial passions of his audience: the language of the Jewish prophets were interpreted and applied; and the minds of a people depressed by their present calamities were directed to the hopes and fears of the invisible world. His precepts and example defined the model of the Roman liturgy;[68] the distribution of the parishes, the calendar of festivals, the order of processions, the service of the priests and deacons, the variety and change of sacerdotal garments. Till the last days of his life

he officiated in the canon of the mass, which continued above three hours: the Gregorian chant[69] has preserved the vocal and instrumental music of the theatre, and the rough voices of the barbarians attempted to imitate the melody of the Roman school.[70] Experience had shown him the efficacy of these solemn and pompous rites to soothe the distress, to confirm the faith, to mitigate the fierceness, and to dispel the dark enthusiasm of the vulgar, and he readily forgave their tendency to promote the reign of priesthood and superstition. The bishops of Italy and the adjacent islands acknowledged the Roman pontiff as their special metropolitan. Even the existence, the union, or the translation of episcopal seats was decided by his absolute discretion: and his successful inroads into the provinces of Greece, of Spain, and of Gaul, might countenance the more lofty pretensions of succeeding popes. He interposed to prevent the abuses of popular elections; his jealous care maintained the purity of faith and discipline; and the apostolic shepherd assiduously watched over the faith and discipline of the subordinate pastors. Under his reign the Arians of Italy and Spain were reconciled to the catholic church, and the conquest of Britain reflects less glory on the name of Cæsar than on that of Gregory the First. Instead of six legions, forty monks were embarked for that distant island, and the pontiff lamented the austere duties which forbade him to partake the perils of their spiritual warfare. In less than two years he could announce to the archbishop of Alexandria that they had baptised the king of Kent with ten thousand of his Anglo-Saxons; and that the Roman missionaries, like those of the primitive church, were armed only with spiritual and supernatural powers. The credulity or the prudence of Gregory was always disposed to confirm the truths of religion by the evidence of ghosts, miracles, and resurrections;[71] and posterity has paid to *his* memory the same tribute which he freely granted to the virtue of his own or the preceding generation. The celestial honours have been liberally bestowed by the authority of the popes, but Gregory is the last of their own order whom they have presumed to inscribe in the calendar of saints.

Their temporal power insensibly arose from the calamities of the times; and the Roman bishops, who have deluged Europe and Asia with blood, were compelled to reign as the ministers of charity and peace. I. The church of Rome, as it has been formerly observed, was endowed with ample possessions in Italy, Sicily, and the more distant provinces; and her agents, who were commonly subdeacons, had acquired a civil and even criminal jurisdiction over their tenants and husbandmen. The successor of St. Peter administered his patrimony with the temper of a vigilant and moderate landlord;[72] and the epistles of Gregory are filled with salutary instructions to abstain from doubtful or vexatious lawsuits, to preserve the integrity of weights and measures, to grant every reasonable delay, and to reduce the capitation of the slaves of the glebe, who purchased the right of marriage by the payment of an arbitrary fine.[73] The rent or the produce of these estates was transported to the mouth of the Tiber, at the risk and expense of the pope: in the use of wealth he acted like a faithful steward of the church and the poor, and liberally applied to their wants the inexhaustible resources of abstinence and order. The voluminous account of his receipts and disbursements was kept above three hundred years in the Lateran, as the model of Christian economy. On the four great festivals he divided their quarterly allowance to the clergy, to his domestics, to the monasteries, the churches, the places of burial, the almshouses, and the hospitals of Rome, and the rest of the diocese. On the first day of every month he distributed to the poor, according to the season, their stated portion of corn, wine, cheese, vegetables, oil, fish, fresh provisions, clothes, and money; and his treasurers were continually summoned to satisfy, in his name, the extraordinary demands of indigence and merit. The instant distress of the sick and helpless, of strangers and pilgrims, was relieved by the bounty of each day and of every hour; nor would the pontiff indulge himself in a frugal repast till he had sent the dishes from his own table to some objects deserving of his compassion. The misery of the times had reduced the nobles and matrons of Rome to accept, without a blush, the benevolence of the church: three thousand virgins received their food and raiment from the hand of their benefactor; and many bishops of Italy escaped from the barbarians to the hospitable threshold of the Vatican. Gregory might justly be styled the Father of his country; and such was the extreme sensibility of his conscience, that, for the death of a beggar who had perished in the streets, he interdicted himself during several days from the exercise of sacerdotal functions. II. The misfortunes of Rome involved the apostolical pastor in the business of peace and war; and it might be doubtful to himself whether piety or ambition prompted him to supply the place of his absent sovereign. Gregory awakened the emperor from a long slumber; exposed the guilt or incapacity of the exarch and his inferior ministers; complained that the veterans were withdrawn from Rome for the defence of Spoleto; encouraged the Italians to guard their cities and altars; and condescended, in the crisis of danger, to name the tribunes and to direct the operations of the provincial troops. But the martial spirit of the pope was checked by the scruples of humanity and religion: the imposition of tribute, though it was employed in the Italian war, he freely condemned as odious and oppressive; whilst he protected, against the Imperial edicts, the pious cowardice of the soldiers who deserted a military for a monastic life. If we may credit his own declarations, it would have been easy for Gregory to exterminate the Lombards by their domestic factions, without leaving a king, a duke, or a count, to save that unfortunate nation from the vengeance of their foes. As a Christian bishop, he preferred the salutary offices of peace; his mediation appeased the tumult of arms; but he was too conscious of the arts of the Greeks and the passions of the Lombards to engage his sacred promise for the observance of the truce. Disappointed in the hope of a general and lasting treaty, he presumed to save his country without the consent of the emperor or the exarch. The sword of the enemy was suspended over Rome; it was averted by the mild eloquence and seasonable gifts of the pontiff, who commanded the respect of heretics and barbarians. The merits of Gregory were treated by the Byzantine court with reproach and insult; but in the attachment of a grateful people he found the purest reward of a citizen, and the best right of a sovereign.[74]

CHAPTER XLVI

Revolutions of Persia after the Death of the Chosroes or Nushirvan. His Son Hormouz, a Tyrant, is deposed. Usurpation of Bahram. Flight and Restoration of Chosroes II. His Gratitude to the Romans. The Chagan of the Avars. Revolt of the Army against Maurice. His Death. Tyranny of Phocas. Elevation of Heraclius. The Persian War. Chosroes subdues Syria, Egypt, and Asia Minor. Siege of Constantinople by the Persians and Avars. Persian Expeditions. Victories and Triumphs of Heraclius.

THE conflict of Rome and Persia was prolonged from the death of Crassus to the reign of Heraclius. An experience of seven hundred years might convince the rival nations of the impossibility of maintaining their conquests beyond the fatal limits of the Tigris and Euphrates. Yet the emulation of Trajan and Julian was awakened by the trophies of Alexander, and the sovereigns of Persia indulged the ambitious hope of restoring the empire of Cyrus.[1] Such extraordinary efforts of power and courage will always command the attention of posterity; but the events by which the fate of nations is not materially changed leave a faint impression on the page of history, and the patience of the reader would be exhausted by the repetition of the same hostilities, undertaken without cause, prosecuted without glory, and terminated without effect. The arts of negotiation, unknown to the simple greatness of the senate and the Cæsars, were assiduously cultivated by the Byzantine princes; and the memorials of their perpetual embassies[2] repeat, with the same uniform prolixity, the language of falsehood and declamation, the insolence of the barbarians, and the servile temper of the tributary Greeks. Lamenting the barren superfluity of materials, I have studied to compress the narrative of these uninteresting transactions: but the just Nushirvan is still applauded as the model of Oriental kings, and the ambition of his grandson Chosroes prepared the revolution of the East, which was speedily accomplished by the arms and the religion of the successors of Mohammed.

In the useless altercations that precede and justify the quarrels of princes, the Greeks and the barbarians accused each other of violating the peace which had been concluded between the two empires about four years before the death of Justinian. The sovereign of Persia and India aspired to reduce under his obedience the province of Yemen, or Arabia[3] Felix; the distant land of myrrh and frankincense, which had escaped, rather than opposed, the conquerors of the East. After the defeat of Abrahah under the walls of Mecca, the discord of his sons and brothers gave an easy entrance to the Persians: they chased the strangers of Abyssinia beyond the Red Sea; and a native prince of the ancient Homerites was restored to the throne as the vassal or viceroy of the great Nushirvan.[4] But the nephew of Justinian declared his resolution to avenge the injuries of his Christian ally the prince of Abyssinia, as they suggested a decent pretence to discontinue the annual *tribute*, which was poorly disguised by the name of pension. The churches of Persarmenia were oppressed by the intolerant spirit of the Magi; they secretly invoked the protector of the Christians, and, after the pious murder of their satraps, the rebels were avowed and supported as the brethren and subjects of the Roman emperor. The complaints of Nushirvan were disregarded by the Byzantine court; Justin yielded to the importunities of the Turks, who offered an alliance against the common enemy; and the Persian monarchy was threatened at the same instant by the united forces of Europe, of Æthiopia, and of Scythia. At the age of fourscore the sovereign of the East would perhaps have chosen the peaceful enjoyment of his glory and greatness; but as soon as war became inevitable he took the field with the alacrity of youth, whilst the aggressor trembled in the palace of Constantinople. Nushirvan or Chosroes conducted in person the siege of Dara; and although that important fortress had been left destitute of troops and magazines, the valour of the inhabitants resisted above five months the archers, the elephants, and the military engines of the Great King. In the meanwhile his general Adarman advanced from Babylon, traversed the desert, passed the Euphrates, insulted the suburbs of

Antioch, reduced to ashes the city of Apamea, and laid the spoils of Syria at the feet of his master, whose perseverance in the midst of winter at length subverted the bulwark of the East. But these losses, which astonished the provinces and the court, produced a salutary effect in the repentance and abdication of the emperor Justin: a new spirit arose in the Byzantine councils; and a truce of three years was obtained by the prudence of Tiberius. That seasonable interval was employed in the preparations of war; and the voice of rumour proclaimed to the world that from the distant countries of the Alps and the Rhine, from Scythia, Mæsia, Pannonia, Illyricum, and Isauria, the strength of the Imperial cavalry was reinforced with one hundred and fifty thousand soldiers. Yet the king of Persia, without fear or without faith, resolved to prevent the attack of the enemy; again passed the Euphrates, and, dismissing the ambassadors of Tiberius, arrogantly commanded them to await his arrival at Cæsarea, the metropolis of the Cappadocian provinces. The two armies encountered each other in the battle of Melitene: the barbarians, who darkened the air with a cloud of arrows, prolonged their line and extended their wings across the plain; while the Romans, in deep and solid bodies, expected to prevail in closer action by the weight of their swords and lances. A Scythian chief, who commanded their right wing, suddenly turned the flank of the enemy, attacked their rear-guard in the presence of Chosroes, penetrated to the midst of the camp, pillaged the royal tent, profaned the eternal fire, loaded a train of camels with the spoils of Asia, cut his way through the Persian host, and returned with songs of victory to his friends, who had consumed the day in single combats or ineffectual skirmishes. The darkness of the night and the separation of the Romans afforded the Persian monarch an opportunity of revenge; and one of their camps was swept away by a rapid and impetuous assault. But the review of his loss and the consciousness of his danger determined Chosroes to a speedy retreat: he burnt in his passage the vacant town of Melitene; and, without consulting the safety of his troops, boldly swam the Euphrates on the back of an elephant. After this unsuccessful campaign, the want of magazines, and perhaps some inroad of the Turks, obliged him to disband or divide his forces; the Romans were left masters of the field, and their general Justinian, advancing to the relief of the Persarmenian rebels, erected his standard on the banks of the Araxes. The great Pompey had formerly halted within three days' march of the Caspian:[5] that inland sea was explored for the first time by a hostile fleet,[6] and seventy thousand captives were transplanted from Hyrcania to the isle of Cyprus. On the return of spring Justinian descended into the fertile plains of Assyria; the flames of war approached the residence of Nushirvan; the indignant monarch sunk into the grave; and his last edict restrained his successors from exposing their person in a battle against the Romans. Yet the memory of this transient affront was lost in the glories of a long reign; and his formidable enemies, after indulging their dream of conquest, again solicited a short respite from the calamities of war.[7]

The throne of Chosroes Nushirvan was filled by Hormouz, or Hormisdas, the eldest or the most favoured of his sons. With the kingdoms of Persia and India, he inherited the reputation and example of his father, the service, in every rank, of his wise and valiant officers, and a general system of administration harmonised by time and political wisdom to promote the happiness of the prince and people. But the royal youth enjoyed a still more valuable blessing, the friendship of a sage who had presided over his education, and who always preferred the honour to the interest of his pupil, his interest to his inclination. In a dispute with the Greek and Indian philosophers, Buzurg[8] had once maintained that the most grievous misfortune of life is old age without the remembrance of virtue; and our candour will presume that the same principle compelled him during three years to direct the councils of the Persian empire. His zeal was rewarded by the gratitude and docility of Hormouz, who acknowledged himself more indebted to his preceptor than to his parent: but when age and labour had impaired the strength, and perhaps the faculties, of this prudent counsellor, he retired from court and abandoned the youthful monarch to his own passions and those of his favourites. By the fatal vicissitude of human affairs the same scenes were renewed at Ctesiphon which had been exhibited in Rome after the death of Marcus Antoninus. The ministers of flattery and corruption, who had been banished by the father, were recalled and cherished by the son; the disgrace and exile of the friends of Nushirvan established their tyranny; and virtue was driven by degrees from the mind of Hormouz, from his palace, and from the government of the state. The faithful agents, the eyes and ears of the king, informed him of the progress of disorder, that the provincial governors flew to their prey with the fierceness of lions and eagles, and that their rapine and injustice would teach the most loyal of his subjects to abhor the name and authority of their sovereign. The sincerity of this advice was punished with death; the murmurs of the cities were despised, their tumults were quelled by military execution; the intermediate powers between the throne and the people were abolished; and the childish vanity of Hormouz, who affected the daily use of the tiara, was fond of declaring that he alone would be the judge as well as the master of his kingdom. In every word and in every action the son of Nushirvan degenerated from the virtues of his father. His avarice defrauded the troops; his jealous caprice degraded the satraps; the palace, the tribunals, the waters of the Tigris, were stained with the blood of the innocent, and the tyrant exulted in the sufferings and execution of thirteen thousand victims. As the excuse of his cruelty, he sometimes condescended to observe that the fears of the Persians would be productive of hatred, and that their hatred must terminate in rebellion; but he forgot that his own guilt and folly had inspired the sentiments which he deplored, and prepared the event which he so justly apprehended. Exasperated by long and hopeless oppression, the provinces of Babylon, Susa, and Carmania erected the standard of revolt; and the princes of Arabia, India, and Scythia refused the customary tribute to the unworthy successor of Nushirvan. The arms of the Romans, in slow sieges and frequent inroads, afflicted the frontiers of Mesopotamia and Assyria: one of their generals professed himself the disciple of Scipio; and the soldiers were animated by a miraculous image of Christ, whose mild aspect should never have been displayed in the front of battle.[9] At the same time the eastern provinces of Persia were invaded by the great khan, who passed the Oxus at the head of three or four hundred thousand Turks. The imprudent Hormouz accepted their perfidious and formidable aid; the cities of Khorassan or Bactriana were commanded to open their gates; the march of the barbarians towards the mountains of Hyrcania revealed the correspondence of the Turkish and Roman arms; and their union must have subverted the throne of the house of Sassan.

Persia had been lost by a king; it was saved by a hero. After his revolt, Varanes or Bahram is stigmatised by the son of Hormouz as an ungrateful slave: the proud and ambiguous reproach of despotism, since he was truly descended from the ancient princes of Rei,[10] one of the seven families whose splendid, as well as

substantial, prerogatives exalted them above the heads of the Persian nobility.[11] At the siege of Dara the valour of Bahram was signalised under the eyes of Nushirvan, and both the father and son successively promoted him to the command of armies, the government of Media, and the superintendence of the palace. The popular prediction which marked him as the deliverer of Persia might be inspired by his past victories and extraordinary figure: the epithet *Giubin* is expressive of the quality of *dry wood*; he had the strength and stature of a giant; and his savage countenance was fancifully compared to that of a wild cat. While the nation trembled, while Hormouz disguised his terror by the name of suspicion, and his servants concealed their disloyalty under the mask of fear, Bahram alone displayed his undaunted courage and apparent fidelity: and as soon as he found that no more than twelve thousand soldiers would follow him against the enemy, he prudently declared that to this fatal number Heaven had reserved the honours of the triumph. The steep and narrow descent of the Pule Rudbar,[12] or Hyrcanian rock, is the only pass through which an army can penetrate into the territory of Rei and the plains of Media. From the commanding heights a band of resolute men might overwhelm with stones and darts the myriads of the Turkish host: their emperor and his son were transpierced with arrows; and the fugitives were left, without counsel or provisions, to the revenge of an injured people. The patriotism of the Persian general was stimulated by his affection for the city of his forefathers; in the hour of victory every peasant became a soldier, and every soldier a hero; and their ardour was kindled by the gorgeous spectacle of beds, and thrones, and tables of massy gold, the spoils of Asia and the luxury of the hostile camp. A prince of a less malignant temper could not easily have forgiven his benefactor; and the secret hatred of Hormouz was envenomed by a malicious report that Bahram had privately retained the most precious fruits of his Turkish victory. But the approach of a Roman army on the side of the Araxes compelled the implacable tyrant to smile and to applaud; and the toils of Bahram were rewarded with the permission of encountering a new enemy, by their skill and discipline more formidable than a Scythian multitude. Elated by his recent success, he despatched a herald with a bold defiance to the camp of the Romans, requesting them to fix a day of battle, and to choose whether they would pass the river themselves, or allow a free passage to the arms of the

Great King. The lieutenant of the emperor Maurice preferred the safer alternative; and this local circumstance, which would have enhanced the victory of the Persians, rendered their defeat more bloody and their escape more difficult. But the loss of his subjects, and the danger of his kingdom, were overbalanced in the mind of Hormouz by the disgrace of his personal enemy; and no sooner had Bahram collected and reviewed his forces than he received from a royal messenger the insulting gift of a distaff, a spinning-wheel, and a complete suit of female apparel. Obedient to the will of his sovereign, he showed himself to the soldiers in this unworthy disguise: they resented his ignominy and their own; a shout of rebellion ran through the ranks; and the general accepted their oath of fidelity and vows of revenge. A second messenger, who had been commanded to bring the rebel in chains, was trampled under the feet of an elephant, and manifestos were diligently circulated, exhorting the Persians to assert their freedom against an odious and contemptible tyrant. The defection was rapid and universal; his loyal slaves were sacrificed to the public fury; the troops deserted to the standard of Bahram; and the provinces again saluted the deliverer of his country.

As the passes were faithfully guarded, Hormouz could only compute the number of his enemies by the testimony of a guilty conscience, and the daily defection of those who, in the hour of his distress, avenged their wrongs or forgot their obligations. He proudly displayed the ensigns of royalty; but the city and palace of Modain had already escaped from the hand of the tyrant. Among the victims of his cruelty, Bindoes, a Sassanian prince, had been cast into a dungeon: his fetters were broken by the zeal and courage of a brother; and he stood before the king at the head of those trusty guards who had been chosen as the ministers of his confinement, and perhaps of his death. Alarmed by the hasty intrusion and bold reproaches of the captive, Hormouz looked round, but in vain, for advice or assistance; discovered that his strength consisted in the obedience of others; and patiently yielded to the single arm of Bindoes, who dragged him from the throne to the same dungeon in which he himself had been so lately confined. At the first tumult, Chosroes, the eldest of the sons of Hormouz, escaped from the city; he was persuaded to return by the pressing and friendly invitation of Bindoes, who promised to seat him on his father's throne, and who expected to reign under the name of an inexperi-enced youth. In the just assurance that his accomplices could neither forgive nor hope to be forgiven, and that every Persian might be trusted as the judge and enemy of the tyrant, he instituted a public trial without a precedent and without a copy in the annals of the East. The son of Nushirvan, who had requested to plead in his own defence, was introduced as a criminal into the full assembly of the nobles and satraps.[13] He was heard with decent attention as long as he expatiated on the advantages of order and obedience, the danger of innovation, and the inevitable discord of those who had encouraged each other to trample on their lawful and hereditary sovereign. By a pathetic appeal to their humanity he extorted that pity which is seldom refused to the fallen fortunes of a king; and while they beheld the abject posture and squalid appearance of the prisoner, his tears, his chains, and the marks of ignominious stripes, it was impossible to forget how recently they had adored the divine splendour of his diadem and purple. But an angry murmur arose in the assembly as soon as he presumed to vindicate his conduct, and to applaud the victories of his reign. He defined the duties of a king, and the Persian nobles listened with a smile of contempt; they were fired with indignation when he dared to vilify the character of Chosroes; and by the indiscreet offer of resigning the sceptre to the second of his sons, he subscribed his own condemnation and sacrificed the life of his innocent favourite. The mangled bodies of the boy and his mother were exposed to the people; the eyes of Hormouz were pierced with a hot needle; and the punishment of the father was succeeded by the coronation of his eldest son. Chosroes had ascended the throne without guilt, and his piety strove to alleviate the misery of the abdicated monarch; from the dungeon he removed Hormouz to an apartment of the palace, supplied with liberality the consolations of sensual enjoyment, and patiently endured the furious sallies of his resentment and despair. He might despise the resentment of a blind and unpopular tyrant, but the tiara was trembling on his head, till he could subvert the power, or acquire the friendship, of the great Bahram, who sternly denied the justice of a revolution in which himself and his soldiers, the true representatives of Persia, had never been consulted. The offer of a general amnesty, and of the second rank in his kingdom, was answered by an epistle from Bahram, friend of the gods, conqueror of men, and enemy of tyrants, the satrap of satraps, general of the Persian armies, and a prince adorned with the title of eleven virtues.[14] He commands Chosroes, the son of Hormouz, to shun the example and fate of his father, to confine the traitors who had been released from their chains, to deposit in some holy place the diadem which he had usurped, and to accept from his gracious benefactor the pardon of his faults and the government of a province. The rebel might not be proud, and the king most assuredly was not humble; but the one was conscious of his strength, the other was sensible of his weakness; and even the modest language of his reply still left room for treaty and reconciliation. Chosroes led into the field the slaves of the palace and the populace of the capital: they beheld with terror the banners of a veteran army; they were encompassed and surprised by the evolutions of the general; and the satraps who had deposed Hormouz received the punishment of their revolt, or expiated their first treason by a second and more criminal act of disloyalty. The life and liberty of Chosroes were saved, but he was reduced to the necessity of imploring aid or refuge in some foreign land; and the implacable Bindoes, anxious to secure an unquestionable title, hastily returned to the palace, and ended, with a bow-string, the wretched existence of the son of Nushirvan.[15]

While Chosroes despatched the preparations of his retreat, he deliberated with his remaining friends[16] whether he should lurk in the valleys of Mount Caucasus, or fly to the tents of the Turks, or solicit the protection of the emperor. The long emulation of the successors of Artaxerxes and Constantine increased his reluctance to appear as a suppliant in a rival court; but he weighed the forces of the Romans, and prudently considered that the neighbourhood of Syria would render his escape more easy and his succours more effectual. Attended only by his concubines and a troop of thirty guards, he secretly departed from the capital, followed the banks of the Euphrates, traversed the desert, and halted at the distance of ten miles from Circesium. About the third watch of the night the Roman præfect was informed of his approach, and he introduced the royal stranger to the fortress at the dawn of day. From thence the king of Persia was conducted to the more honourable residence of Hierapolis; and Maurice dissembled his pride, and displayed his benevolence, at the reception of the letters and ambassadors of the grandson of Nushirvan. They humbly represented the vicissitudes of fortune and the common interest of princes, exaggerated the ingratitude of Bahram, the agent of

the evil principle, and urged, with specious argument, that it was for the advantage of the Romans themselves to support the two monarchies which balance the world, the two great luminaries by whose salutary influence it is vivified and adorned. The anxiety of Chosroes was soon relieved by the assurance that the emperor had espoused the cause of justice and royalty; but Maurice prudently declined the expense and delay of his useless visit to Constantinople. In the name of his generous benefactor, a rich diadem was presented to the fugitive prince, with an inestimable gift of jewels and gold; a powerful army was assembled on the frontiers of Syria and Armenia, under the command of the valiant and faithful Narses;[17] and this general, of his own nation, and his own choice, was directed to pass the Tigris, and never to sheathe his sword till he had restored Chosroes to the throne of his ancestors. The enterprise, however splendid, was less arduous than it might appear. Persia had already repented of her fatal rashness, which betrayed the heir of the house of Sassan to the ambition of a rebellious subject: and the bold refusal of the Magi to consecrate his usurpation compelled Bahram to assume the sceptre, regardless of the laws and prejudices of the nation. The palace was soon distracted with conspiracy, the city with tumult, the provinces with insurrection; and the cruel execution of the guilty and the suspected served to irritate rather than subdue the public discontent. No sooner did the grandson of Nushirvan display his own and the Roman banners beyond the Tigris, than he was joined, each day, by the increasing multitudes of the nobility and people; and as he advanced, he received from every side the grateful offerings of the keys of his cities and the heads of his enemies. As soon as Modain was freed from the presence of the usurper, the loyal inhabitants obeyed the first summons of Mebodes at the head of only two thousand horse, and Chosroes accepted the sacred and precious ornaments of the palace as the pledge of their truth and a presage of his approaching success. After the junction of the Imperial troops, which Bahram vainly struggled to prevent, the contest was decided by two battles on the banks of the Zab and the confines of Media. The Romans, with the faithful subjects of Persia, amounted to sixty thousand, while the whole force of the usurper did not exceed forty thousand men: the two generals signalised their valour and ability; but the victory was finally determined by the prevalence of numbers and discipline. With the remnant of a broken army,

Bahram fled towards the eastern provinces of the Oxus: the enmity of Persia reconciled him to the Turks; but his days were shortened by poison, perhaps the most incurable of poisons, the stings of remorse and despair, and the bitter remembrance of lost glory. Yet the modern Persians still commemorate the exploits of Bahram; and some excellent laws have prolonged the duration of his troubled and transitory reign.

The restoration of Chosroes was celebrated with feasts and executions; and the music of the royal banquet was often disturbed by the groan of dying or mutilated criminals. A general pardon might have diffused comfort and tranquillity through a country which had been shaken by the late revolutions; yet, before the sanguinary temper of Chosroes is blamed, we should learn whether the Persians had not been accustomed either to dread the rigour or to despise the weakness of their sovereign. The revolt of Bahram and the conspiracy of the satraps were impartially punished by the revenge or justice of the conqueror; the merits of Bindoes himself could not purify his hand from the guilt of royal blood; and the son of Hormouz was desirous to assert his own innocence and to vindicate the sanctity of kings. During the vigour of the Roman power several princes were seated on the throne of Persia by the arms and the authority of the first Cæsars. But their new subjects were soon disgusted with the vices or virtues which they had imbibed in a foreign land; the instability of their dominion gave birth to a vulgar observation, that the choice of Rome was solicited and rejected with equal ardour by the capricious levity of Oriental slaves.[18] But the glory of Maurice was conspicuous in the long and fortunate reign of his *son* and his ally. A band of a thousand Romans, who continued to guard the person of Chosroes, proclaimed his confidence in the fidelity of the strangers; his growing strength enabled him to dismiss this unpopular aid, but he steadily professed the same gratitude and reverence to his adopted father; and, till the death of Maurice, the peace and alliance of the two empires were faithfully maintained. Yet the mercenary friendship of the Roman prince had been purchased with costly and important gifts; the strong cities of Martyropolis and Dara were restored, and the Persarmenians became the willing subjects of an empire whose eastern limit was extended, beyond the example of former times, as far as the banks of the Araxes and the neighbourhood of the Caspian. A pious hope was indulged that the church as well as the state might triumph in this revolution: but

if Chosroes had sincerely listened to the Christian bishops, the impression was erased by the zeal and eloquence of the Magi; if he was armed with philosophic indifference, he accommodated his belief, or rather his professions, to the various circumstances of an exile and a sovereign. The imaginary conversion of the king of Persia was reduced to a local and superstitious veneration for Sergius,[19] one of the saints of Antioch, who heard his prayers and appeared to him in dreams; he enriched the shrine with offerings of gold and silver, and ascribed to this invisible patron the success of his arms, and the pregnancy of Sira, a devout Christian and the best beloved of his wives.[20] The beauty of Sira, or Schirin,[21] her wit, her musical talents, are still famous in the history, or rather in the romances, of the East: her own name is expressive, in the Persian tongue, of sweetness and grace; and the epithet of *Parviz* alludes to the charms of her royal lover. Yet Sira never shared the passion which she inspired, and the bliss of Chosroes was tortured by a jealous doubt, that while he possessed her person she had bestowed her affections on a meaner favourite.[22]

While the majesty of the Roman name was revived in the East, the prospect of Europe is less pleasing and less glorious. By the departure of the Lombards and the ruin of the Gepidæ the balance of power was destroyed on the Danube; and the Avars spread their permanent dominion from the foot of the Alps to the sea-coast of the Euxine. The reign of Baian is the brightest era of their monarchy; their chagan, who occupied the rustic palace of Attila, appears to have imitated his character and policy;[23] but as the same scenes were repeated in a smaller circle, a minute representation of the copy would be devoid of the greatness and novelty of the original. The pride of the second Justin, of Tiberius, and Maurice was humbled by a proud barbarian, more prompt to inflict than exposed to suffer the injuries of war; and as often as Asia was threatened by the Persian arms, Europe was oppressed by the dangerous inroads or costly friendship of the Avars. When the Roman envoys approached the presence of the chagan, they were commanded to wait at the door of his tent till, at the end perhaps of ten or twelve days, he condescended to admit them. If the substance or the style of their message was offensive to his ear, he insulted, with real or affected fury, their own dignity and that of their prince; their baggage was plundered, and their lives were only saved by the promise of a richer present and a more respectful address. But *his* sacred ambassadors enjoyed and abused an unbounded licence in the midst of Constantinople: they urged, with importunate clamours, the increase of tribute, or the restitution of captives and deserters: and the majesty of the empire was almost equally degraded by a base compliance, or by the false and fearful excuses with which they eluded such insolent demands. The chagan had never seen an elephant; and his curiosity was excited by the strange, and perhaps fabulous, portrait of that wonderful animal. At his command, one of the largest elephants of the Imperial stables was equipped with stately caparisons, and conducted by a numerous train to the royal village in the plains of Hungary. He surveyed the enormous beast with surprise, with disgust, and possibly with terror; and smiled at the vain industry of the Romans, who in search of such useless rarities could explore the limits of the land and sea. He wished, at the expense of the emperor, to repose in a golden bed. The wealth of Constantinople, and the skilful diligence of her artists, were instantly devoted to the gratification of his caprice; but when the work was finished, he rejected with scorn a present so unworthy the majesty of a great king.[24] These were the casual sallies of his pride; but the avarice of the chagan was a more steady and tractable passion: a rich and regular supply of silk apparel, furniture, and plate introduced the rudiments of art and luxury among the tents of the Scythians; their appetite was stimulated by the pepper and cinnamon of India;[25] the annual subsidy or tribute was raised from fourscore to one hundred and twenty thousand pieces of gold; and, after each hostile interruption, the payment of the arrears, with exorbitant interest, was always made the first condition of the new treaty. In the language of a barbarian, without guile, the prince of the Avars affected to complain of the insincerity of the Greeks;[26] yet he was not inferior to the most civilised nations in the refinements of dissimulation and perfidy. As the successor of the Lombards, the chagan asserted his claim to the important city of Sirmium, the ancient bulwark of the Illyrian provinces.[27] The plains of the Lower Hungary were covered with the Avar horse; and a fleet of large boats was built in the Hercynian wood, to descend the Danube, and to transport into the Save the materials of a bridge. But as the strong garrison of Singidunum, which commanded the conflux of the two rivers, might have stopped their passage and baffled his designs, he dispelled their apprehensions by a solemn oath that his views were not hostile to the

empire. He swore by his sword, the symbol of the god of war, that he did not, as the enemy of Rome, construct a bridge upon the Save. "If I violate my oath," pursued the intrepid Baian, "may I myself, and the last of my nation, perish by the sword! May the heavens, and fire, the deity of the heavens, fall upon our heads! May the forests and mountains bury us in their ruins; and the Save, returning, against the laws of nature, to his source, overwhelm us in his angry waters!" After this barbarous imprecation he calmly inquired what oath was most sacred and venerable among the Christians; what guilt of perjury it was most dangerous to incur. The bishop of Singidunum presented the Gospel, which the chagan received with devout reverence. "I swear," said he, "by the God who has spoken in this holy book, that I have neither falsehood on my tongue nor treachery in my heart." As soon as he rose from his knees he accelerated the labour of the bridge, and despatched an envoy to proclaim what he no longer wished to conceal. "Inform the emperor," said the perfidious Baian, "that Sirmium is invested on every side. Advise his prudence to withdraw the citizens and their effects, and to resign a city which it is now impossible to relieve or defend." Without the hope of relief, the defence of Sirmium was prolonged above three years: the walls were still untouched; but famine was enclosed within the walls, till a merciful capitulation allowed the escape of the naked and hungry inhabitants. Singidunum, at the distance of fifty miles, experienced a more cruel fate: the buildings were razed, and the vanquished people was condemned to servitude and exile. Yet the ruins of Sirmium are no longer visible; the advantageous situation of Singidunum soon attracted a new colony of Sclavonians; and the conflux of the Save and Danube is still guarded by the fortifications of Belgrade, or the *White City*, so often and so obstinately disputed by the Christian and Turkish arms.[28] From Belgrade to the walls of Constantinople a line may be measured of six hundred miles: that line was marked with flames and with blood; the horses of the Avars were alternately bathed in the Euxine and the Hadriatic; and the Roman pontiff, alarmed by the approach of a more savage enemy,[29] was reduced to cherish the Lombards as the protectors of Italy. The despair of a captive whom his country refused to ransom disclosed to the Avars the invention and practice of military engines.[30] But in the first attempts they were rudely framed and awkwardly managed; and the resistance of

Diocletianopolis and Berœa, of Philippopolis and Adrianople, soon exhausted the skill and patience of the besiegers. The warfare of Baian was that of a Tartar; yet his mind was susceptible of a humane and generous sentiment: he spared Anchialus, whose salutary waters had restored the health of the best beloved of his wives; and the Romans confess that their starving army was fed and dismissed by the liberality of a foe. His empire extended over Hungary, Poland, and Prussia, from the mouth of the Danube to that of the Oder;[31] and his new subjects were divided and transplanted by the jealous policy of the conqueror.[32] The eastern regions of Germany, which had been left vacant by the emigration of the Vandals, were replenished with Sclavonian colonists; the same tribes are discovered in the neighbourhood of the Hadriatic and of the Baltic; and with the name of Baian himself, the Illyrian cities of Neyss and Lissa are again found in the heart of Silesia. In the disposition both of his troops and provinces the chagan exposed the vassals, whose lives he disregarded,[33] to the first assault; and the swords of the enemy were blunted before they encountered the native valour of the Avars.

The Persian alliance restored the troops of the East to the defence of Europe; and Maurice, who had supported ten years the insolence of the chagan, declared his resolution to march in person against the barbarians. In the space of two centuries none of the successors of Theodosius had appeared in the field; their lives were supinely spent in the palace of Constantinople; and the Greeks could no longer understand that the name of *emperor*, in its primitive sense, denoted the chief of the armies of the republic. The martial ardour of Maurice was opposed by the grave flattery of the senate, the timid superstition of the patriarch, and the tears of the empress Constantina; and they all conjured him to devolve on some meaner general the fatigues and perils of a Scythian campaign. Deaf to their advice and entreaty, the emperor boldly advanced[34] seven miles from the capital; the sacred ensign of the cross was displayed in the front, and Maurice reviewed with conscious pride the arms and numbers of the veterans who had fought and conquered beyond the Tigris. Anchialus was the last term of his progress by sea and land; he solicited without success a miraculous answer to his nocturnal prayers; his mind was confounded by the death of a favourite horse, the encounter of a wild boar, a storm of wind and rain, and the birth of a monstrous child; and he forgot that the best of

omens is to unsheathe our sword in the defence of our country.[35] Under the pretence of receiving the ambassadors of Persia, the emperor returned to Constantinople, exchanged the thoughts of war for those of devotion, and disappointed the public hope by his absence and the choice of his lieutenants. The blind partiality of fraternal love might excuse the promotion of his brother Peter, who fled with equal disgrace from the barbarians, from his own soldiers, and from the inhabitants of a Roman city. That city, if we may credit the resemblance of name and character, was the famous Azimuntium,[36] which had alone repelled the tempest of Attila. The example of her warlike youth was propagated to succeeding generations; and they obtained, from the first or the second Justin, an honourable privilege that their valour should be always reserved for the defence of their native country. The brother of Maurice attempted to violate this privilege, and to mingle a patriot band with the mercenaries of his camp; they retired to the church; he was not awed by the sanctity of the place; the people rose in their cause, the gates were shut, the ramparts were manned; and the cowardice of Peter was found equal to his arrogance and injustice. The military fame of Commentiolus[37] is the object of satire or comedy rather than of serious history, since he was even deficient in the vile and vulgar qualification of personal courage. His solemn counsels, strange evolutions, and secret orders, always supplied an apology for flight or delay. If he marched against the enemy, the pleasant valleys of Mount Hæmus opposed an insuperable barrier; but in his retreat he explored with fearless curiosity the most difficult and obsolete paths, which had almost escaped the memory of the oldest native. The only blood which he lost was drawn, in a real or affected malady, by the lancet of a surgeon; and his health, which felt with exquisite sensibility the approach of the barbarians, was uniformly restored by the repose and safety of the winter season. A prince who could promote and support this unworthy favourite must derive no glory from the accidental merit of his colleague Priscus.[38] In five successive battles, which seem to have been conducted with skill and resolution, seventeen thousand two hundred barbarians were made prisoners: near sixty thousand, with four sons of the chagan, were slain: the Roman general surprised a peaceful district of the Gepidæ, who slept under the protection of the Avars; and his last trophies were erected on the banks of the Danube and the Theiss. Since the death of Trajan the arms of the empire had not penetrated so deeply into the old Dacia; yet the success of Priscus was transient and barren, and he was soon recalled by the apprehension that Baian, with dauntless spirit and recruited forces, was preparing to avenge his defeat under the walls of Constantinople.[39]

The theory of war was not more familiar to the camps of Cæsar and Trajan than to those of Justinian and Maurice.[40] The iron of Tuscany or Pontus still received the keenest temper from the skill of the Byzantine workmen. The magazines were plentifully stored with every species of offensive and defensive arms. In the construction and use of ships, engines, and fortifications, the barbarians admired the superior ingenuity of a people whom they so often vanquished in the field. The science of tactics, the order, evolutions, and stratagems of antiquity, was transcribed and studied in the books of the Greeks and Romans. But the solitude or degeneracy of the provinces could no longer supply a race of men to handle those weapons, to guard those walls, to navigate those ships, and to reduce the theory of war into bold and successful practice. The genius of Belisarius and Narses had been formed without a master, and expired without a disciple. Neither honour, nor patriotism, nor generous superstition, could animate the lifeless bodies of slaves and strangers who had succeeded to the honours of the legions: it was in the camp alone that the emperor should have exercised a despotic command; it was only in the camp that his authority was disobeyed and insulted: he appeased and inflamed with gold the licentiousness of the troops; but their vices were inherent, their victories were accidental, and their costly maintenance exhausted the substance of a state which they were unable to defend. After a long and pernicious indulgence, the cure of this inveterate evil was undertaken by Maurice; but the rash attempt, which drew destruction on his own head, tended only to aggravate the disease. A reformer should be exempt from the suspicion of interest, and he must possess the confidence and esteem of those whom he proposes to reclaim. The troops of Maurice might listen to the voice of a victorious leader; they disdained the admonitions of statesmen and sophists; and when they received an edict which deducted from their pay the price of their arms and clothing, they execrated the avarice of a prince insensible of the dangers and fatigues from which he had escaped. The camps both of Asia and Europe were agitated with frequent and furious seditions;[41] the enraged soldiers of Edessa pursued with reproaches, with threats, with wounds, their trembling generals; they overturned the statues of the emperor, cast stones against the miraculous image of Christ, and either rejected the yoke of all civil and military laws, or instituted a dangerous model of voluntary subordination. The monarch, always distant and often deceived, was incapable of yielding or persisting, according to the exigence of the moment. But the fear of a general revolt induced him too readily to accept any act of valour, or any expression of loyalty, as an atonement for the popular offence; the new reform was abolished as hastily as it had been announced; and the troops, instead of punishment and restraint, were agreeably surprised by a gracious proclamation of immunities and rewards. But the soldiers accepted without gratitude the tardy and reluctant gifts of the emperor: their insolence was elated by the discovery of his weakness and their own strength, and their mutual hatred was inflamed beyond the desire of forgiveness or the hope of reconciliation. The historians of the times adopt the vulgar suspicion that Maurice conspired to destroy the troops whom he had laboured to reform; the misconduct and favour of Commentiolus are imputed to this malevolent design; and every age must condemn the inhumanity or avarice[42] of a prince who, by the trifling ransom of six thousand pieces of gold, might have prevented the massacre of twelve thousand prisoners in the hands of the chagan. In the just fervour of indignation, an order was signified to the army of the Danube that they should spare the magazines of the province, and establish their winter quarters in the hostile country of the Avars. The measure of their grievances was full: they pronounced Maurice unworthy to reign, expelled or slaughtered his faithful adherents, and under the command of Phocas, a simple centurion, returned by hasty marches to the neighbourhood of Constantinople. After a long series of legal succession, the military disorders of the third century were again revived; yet such was the novelty of the enterprise that the insurgents were awed by their own rashness. They hesitated to invest their favourite with the vacant purple; and while they rejected all treaty with Maurice himself, they held a friendly correspondence with his son Theodosius and with Germanus, the father-in-law of the royal youth. So obscure had been the former condition of Phocas, that the emperor was ignorant of the name and character of his rival; but as soon as he learned that the centurion, though bold in sedition, was timid in the face of danger, "Alas!" cried the desponding prince, "if he is a coward, he will surely be a murderer."

Yet if Constantinople had been firm and faithful, the murderer might have spent his fury against the walls; and the rebel army would have been gradually consumed or reconciled by the prudence of the emperor. In the games of the circus, which he repeated with unusual pomp, Maurice disguised with smiles of confidence the anxiety of his heart, condescended to solicit the applause of the *factions*, and flattered their pride by accepting from their respective tribunes a list of nine hundred *blues* and fifteen hundred *greens*, whom he affected to esteem as the solid pillars of his throne. Their treacherous or languid support betrayed his weakness and hastened his fall: the green faction were the secret accomplices of the rebels, and the blues recommended lenity and moderation in a contest with their Roman brethren. The rigid and parsimonious virtues of Maurice had long since alienated the hearts of his subjects: as he walked barefoot in a religious procession he was rudely assaulted with stones, and his guards were compelled to present their iron maces in the defence of his person. A fanatic monk ran through the streets with a drawn sword, denouncing against him the wrath and the sentence of God; and a vile plebeian, who represented his countenance and apparel, was seated on an ass and pursued by the imprecations of the multitude.[43] The emperor suspected the popularity of Germanus with the soldiers and citizens: he feared, he threatened, but he delayed to strike; the patrician fled to the sanctuary of the church; the people rose in his defence, the walls were deserted by the guards, and the lawless city was abandoned to the flames and rapine of a nocturnal tumult. In a small bark the unfortunate Maurice, with his wife and nine children, escaped to the Asiatic shore, but the violence of the wind compelled him to land at the church of St. Autonomus,[44] near Chalcedon, from whence he despatched Theodosius, his eldest son, to implore the gratitude and friendship of the Persian monarch. For himself, he refused to fly: his body was tortured with sciatic pains,[45] his mind was enfeebled by superstition; he patiently awaited the event of the revolution, and addressed a fervent and public prayer to the Almighty, that the punishment of his sins might be inflicted in this world rather than in a future life. After the abdication of Maurice, the two factions disputed the choice of an emperor; but the favourite of the blues was rejected by the

jealousy of their antagonists, and Germanus himself was hurried along by the crowds who rushed to the palace of Hebdomon, seven miles from the city, to adore the majesty of Phocas the centurion. A modest wish of resigning the purple to the rank and merit of Germanus was opposed by *his* resolution, more obstinate and equally sincere; the senate and clergy obeyed his summons; and as soon as the patriarch was assured of his orthodox belief, he consecrated the successful usurper in the church of St. John the Baptist. On the third day, amidst the acclamations of a thoughtless people, Phocas made his public entry in a chariot drawn by four white horses: the revolt of the troops was rewarded by a lavish donative, and the new sovereign, after visiting the palace, beheld from his throne the games of the hippodrome. In a dispute of precedency between the two factions, his partial judgment inclined in favour of the greens. "Remember that Maurice is still alive" resounded from the opposite side; and the indiscreet clamour of the blues admonished and stimulated the cruelty of the tyrant. The ministers of death were despatched to Chalcedon: they dragged the emperor from his sanctuary, and the five sons of Maurice were successively murdered before the eyes of their agonising parent. At each stroke, which he felt in his heart, he found strength to rehearse a pious ejaculation: "Thou art just, O Lord! and thy judgments are righteous." And such in the last moments was his rigid attachment to truth and justice, that he revealed to the soldiers the pious falsehood of a nurse who presented her own child in the place of a royal infant.[46] The tragic scene was finally closed by the execution of the emperor himself, in the twentieth year of his reign, and the sixty-third of his age. The bodies of the father and his five sons were cast into the sea; their heads were exposed at Constantinople to the insults or pity of the multitude; and it was not till some signs of putrefaction had appeared that Phocas connived at the private burial of these venerable remains. In that grave the faults and errors of Maurice were kindly interred. His fate alone was remembered; and at the end of twenty years, in the recital of the history of Theophylact, the mournful tale was interrupted by the tears of the audience.[47]

Such tears must have flowed in secret, and such compassion would have been criminal, under the reign of Phocas, who was peaceably acknowledged in the provinces of the East and West. The images of the emperor and his wife Leontia were exposed in the Lateran to the veneration of the clergy and senate of Rome, and afterwards deposited in the palace of the Cæsars, between those of Constantine and Theodosius. As a subject and a Christian, it was the duty of Gregory to acquiesce in the established government; but the joyful applause with which he salutes the fortune of the assassin has sullied, with indelible disgrace, the character of the saint. The successor of the apostles might have inculcated with decent firmness the guilt of blood and the necessity of repentance; he is content to celebrate the deliverance of the people and the fall of the oppressor; to rejoice that the piety and benignity of Phocas have been raised by Providence to the Imperial throne; to pray that his hands may be strengthened against all his enemies; and to express a wish, perhaps a prophecy, that, after a long and triumphant reign, he may be transferred from a temporal to an everlasting kingdom.[48] I have already traced the steps of a revolution so pleasing, in Gregory's opinion, both to heaven and earth; and Phocas does not appear less hateful in the exercise than in the acquisition of power. The pencil of an impartial historial has delineated the portrait of a monster;[49] his diminutive and deformed person, the closeness of his shaggy eyebrows, his red hair, his beardless chin, and his cheek disfigured and discoloured by a formidable scar. Ignorant of letters, of laws, and even of arms, he indulged in the supreme rank a more ample privilege of lust and drunkenness, and his brutal pleasures were either injurious to his subjects or disgraceful to himself. Without assuming the office of a prince, he renounced the profession of a soldier, and the reign of Phocas afflicted Europe with ignominious peace and Asia with desolating war. His savage temper was inflamed by passion, hardened by fear, exasperated by resistance or reproach. The flight of Theodosius to the Persian court had been intercepted by a rapid pursuit or a deceitful message: he was beheaded at Nice, and the last hours of the young prince were soothed by the comforts of religion and the consciousness of innocence. Yet his phantom disturbed the repose of the usurper; a whisper was circulated through the East that the son of Maurice was still alive; the people expected their avenger, and the widow and daughters of the late emperor would have adopted as their son and brother the vilest of mankind. In the massacre of the Imperial family,[50] the mercy, or rather the discretion, of Phocas had spared these unhappy females, and they were decently confined to a private house. But the spirit of the empress Constantina, still

mindful of her father, her husband, and her sons, aspired to freedom and revenge. At the dead of night she escaped to the sanctuary of St. Sophia, but her tears and the gold of her associate Germanus were insufficient to provoke an insurrection. Her life was forfeited to revenge, and even to justice; but the patriarch obtained and pledged an oath for her safety, a monastery was allotted for her prison, and the widow of Maurice accepted and abused the lenity of his assassin. The discovery or the suspicion of a second conspiracy dissolved the engagements, and rekindled the fury, of Phocas. A matron who commanded the respect and pity of mankind, the daughter, wife, and mother of emperors, was tortured like the vilest malefactor, to force a confession of her designs and associates; and the empress Constantina, with her three innocent daughters, was beheaded at Chalcedon, on the same ground which had been stained with the blood of her husband and five sons. After such an example, it would be superfluous to enumerate the names and sufferings of meaner victims. Their condemnation was seldom preceded by the forms of trial, and their punishment was embittered by the refinements of cruelty: their eyes were pierced, their tongues were torn from the root, the hands and feet were amputated; some expired under the lash, others in the flames, others again were transfixed with arrows, and a simple speedy death was mercy which they could rarely obtain. The hippodrome, the sacred asylum of the pleasures and the liberty of the Romans, was polluted with heads and limbs and mangled bodies; and the companions of Phocas were the most sensible that neither his favour nor their services could protect them from a tyrant, the worthy rival of the Caligulas and Domitians of the first age of the empire.[51]

A daughter of Phocas, his only child, was given in marriage to the patrician Crispus,[52] and the *royal* images of the bride and bridegroom were indiscreetly placed in the circus by the side of the emperor. The father must desire that his posterity should inherit the fruit of his crimes, but the monarch was offended by this premature and popular association; the tribunes of the green faction, who accused the officious error of their sculptors, were condemned to instant death; their lives were granted to the prayers of the people, but Crispus might reasonably doubt whether a jealous usurper could forget and pardon his involuntary competition. The green faction was alienated by the ingratitude of Phocas and the loss of their privileges:

every province of the empire was ripe for rebellion; and Heraclius, exarch of Africa, persisted above two years in refusing all tribute and obedience to the centurion who disgraced the throne of Constantinople. By the secret emissaries of Crispus and the senate, the independent exarch was solicited to save and to govern his country: but his ambition was chilled by age, and he resigned the dangerous enterprise to his son Heraclius, and to Nicetas, the son of Gregory, his friend and lieutenant. The powers of Africa were armed by the two adventurous youths: they agreed that the one should navigate the fleet from Carthage to Constantinople, that the other should lead an army through Egypt and Asia, and that the Imperial purple should be the reward of diligence and success. A faint rumour of their undertaking was conveyed to the ears of Phocas, and the wife and mother of the younger Heraclius were secured as the hostages of his faith; but the treacherous heart of Crispus extenuated the distant peril, the means of defence were neglected or delayed, and the tyrant supinely slept till the African navy cast anchor in the Hellespont. Their standard was joined at Abydus by the fugitives and exiles who thirsted for revenge: the ships of Heraclius, whose lofty masts were adorned with the holy symbols of religion,[53] steered their triumphant course through the Propontis; and Phocas beheld from the windows of the palace his approaching and inevitable fate. The green faction was tempted, by gifts and promises, to oppose a feeble and fruitless resistance to the landing of the Africans; but the people, and even the guards, were determined by the well-timed defection of Crispus, and the tyrant was seized by a private enemy, who boldly invaded the solitude of the palace. Stripped of the diadem and purple, clothed in a vile habit, and loaded with chains, he was transported in a small boat to the Imperial galley of Heraclius, who reproached him with the crimes of his abominable reign. "Wilt thou govern better?" were the last words of the despair of Phocas. After suffering each variety of insult and torture, his head was severed from his body, the mangled trunk was cast into the flames, and the same treatment was inflicted on the statues of the vain usurper and the seditious banner of the green faction. The voice of the clergy, the senate, and the people invited Heraclius to ascend the throne which he had purified from guilt and ignominy; after some graceful hesitation he yielded to their entreaties. His coronation was accompanied by that of his wife Eudoxia, and their posterity, till the fourth generation, continued to reign over the empire of the East. The voyage of Heraclius had been easy and prosperous; the tedious march of Nicetas was not accomplished before the decision of the contest, but he submitted without a murmur to the fortune of his friend, and his laudable intentions were rewarded with an equestrian statue and a daughter of the emperor. It was more difficult to trust the fidelity of Crispus, whose recent services were recompensed by the command of the Cappadocian army. His arrogance soon provoked, and seemed to excuse, the ingratitude of his new sovereign. In the presence of the senate, the son-in-law of Phocas was condemned to embrace the monastic life; and the sentence was justified by the weighty observation of Heraclius, that the man who had betrayed his father could never be faithful to his friend.[54]

Even after his death the republic was afflicted by the crimes of Phocas, which armed with a pious cause the most formidable of her enemies. According to the friendly and equal forms of the Byzantine and Persian courts, he announced his exaltation to the throne; and his ambassador Lilius, who had presented him with the heads of Maurice and his sons, was the best qualified to describe the circumstances of the tragic scene.[55] However it might be varnished by fiction or sophistry, Chosroes turned with horror from the assassin, imprisoned the pretended envoy, disclaimed the usurper, and declared himself the avenger of his father and benefactor. The sentiments of grief and resentment, which humanity would feel and honour would dictate, promoted on this occasion the interest of the Persian king, and his interest was powerfully magnified by the national and religious prejudices of the Magi and satraps. In a strain of artful adulation, which assumed the language of freedom, they presumed to censure the excess of his gratitude and friendship for the Greeks, a nation with whom it was dangerous to conclude either peace or alliance, whose superstition was devoid of truth and justice, and who must be incapable of any virtue since they could perpetrate the most atrocious of crimes, the impious murder of their sovereign.[56] For the crime of an ambitious centurion the nation which he oppressed was chastised with the calamities of war, and the same calamities, at the end of twenty years, were retaliated and redoubled on the heads of the Persians.[57] The general who had restored Chosroes to the throne still commanded in the East, and the name of Narses was the formidable sound with which the Assyrian mothers were accustomed to terrify their infants. It is not improbable that a native subject of Persia should encourage his master and his friend to deliver and possess the provinces of Asia. It is still more probable that Chosroes should animate his troops by the assurance that the sword which they dreaded the most would remain in its scabbard or be drawn in their favour. The hero could not depend on the faith of a tyrant, and the tyrant was conscious how little he deserved the obedience of a hero. Narses was removed from his military command; he reared an independent standard at Hierapolis, in Syria; he was betrayed by fallacious promises, and burnt alive in the market-place of Constantinople. Deprived of the only chief whom they could fear or esteem, the bands which he had led to victory were twice broken by the cavalry, trampled by the elephants, and pierced by the arrows of the barbarians; and a great number of the captives were beheaded on the field of battle by the sentence of the victor, who might justly condemn these seditious mercenaries as the authors or accomplices of the death of Maurice. Under the reign of Phocas, the fortifications of Merdin, Dara, Amida, and Edessa were successively besieged, reduced, and destroyed by the Persian monarch; he passed the Euphrates, occupied the Syrian cities, Hierapolis, Chalcis, and Berrhœa or Aleppo, and soon encompassed the walls of Antioch with his irresistible arms. The rapid tide of success discloses the decay of the empire, the incapacity of Phocas, and the disaffection of his subjects; and Chosroes provided a decent apology for their submission or revolt by an impostor who attended his camp as the son of Maurice[58] and the lawful heir of the monarchy.

The first intelligence from the East which Heraclius received[59] was that of the loss of Antioch; but the aged metropolis, so often overturned by earthquakes and pillaged by the enemy, could supply but a small and languid stream of treasure and blood. The Persians were equally successful and more fortunate in the sack of Cæsarea, the capital of Cappadocia; and as they advanced beyond the ramparts of the frontier, the boundary of ancient war, they found a less obstinate resistance and a more plentiful harvest. The pleasant vale of Damascus has been adorned in every age with a royal city: her obscure felicity has hitherto escaped the historian of the Roman empire: but Chosroes reposed his troops in the paradise of Damascus before he ascended the hills of Libanus or invaded the cities of the Phœnician coast.

The conquest of Jerusalem,[60] which had been meditated by Nushirvan, was achieved by the zeal and avarice of his grandson; the ruin of the proudest monument of Christianity was vehemently urged by the intolerant spirit of the Magi; and he could enlist for this holy warfare an army of six-and-twenty-thousand Jews, whose furious bigotry might compensate in some degree for the want of valour and discipline. After the reduction of Galilee and the region beyond the Jordan, whose resistance appears to have delayed the fate of the capital, Jerusalem itself was taken by assault. The sepulchre of Christ and the stately churches of Helena and Constantine were consumed, or at least damaged, by the flames; the devout offerings of three hundred years were rifled in one sacrilegious day; the patriarch Zachariah and the *true cross* were transported into Persia; and the massacre of ninety thousand Christians is imputed to the Jews and Arabs, who swelled the disorder of the Persian march. The fugitives of Palestine were entertained at Alexandria by the charity of John the archbishop, who is distinguished among a crowd of saints by the epithet of *almsgiver*:[61] and the revenues of the church, with a treasure of three hundred thousand pounds, were restored to the true proprietors, the poor of every country and every denomination. But Egypt itself, the only province which had been exempt since the time of Diocletian from foreign and domestic war, was again subdued by the successors of Cyrus. Pelusium, the key of that impervious country, was surprised by the cavalry of the Persians: they passed with impunity the innumerable channels of the Delta, and explored the long valley of the Nile from the pyramids of Memphis to the confines of Æthiopia. Alexandria might have been relieved by a naval force, but the archbishop and the præfect embarked for Cyprus; and Chosroes entered the second city of the empire, which still preserved a wealthy remnant of industry and commerce. His western trophy was erected, not on the walls of Carthage,[62] but in the neighbourhood of Tripoli: the Greek colonies of Cyrene were finally extirpated; and the conqueror, treading in the footsteps of Alexander, returned in triumph through the sands of the Libyan desert. In the same campaign another army advanced from the Euphrates to the Thracian Bosphorus; Chalcedon surrendered after a long siege, and a Persian camp was maintained above ten years in the presence of Constantinople. The seacoast of Pontus, the city of Ancyra, and the isle of Rhodes are enumerated among the last conquests of the Great King; and if Chosroes had possessed any maritime power, his boundless ambition would have spread slavery and desolation over the provinces of Europe.

From the long-disputed banks of the Tigris and Euphrates, the reign of the grandson of Nushirvan was suddenly extended to the Hellespont and the Nile, the ancient limits of the Persian monarchy. But the provinces, which had been fashioned by the habits of six hundred years to the virtues and vices of the Roman government, supported with reluctance the yoke of the barbarians. The idea of a republic was kept alive by the institutions, or at least by the writings, of the Greeks and Romans, and the subjects of Heraclius had been educated to pronounce the words of liberty and law. But it has always been the pride and policy of Oriental princes to display the titles and attributes of their omnipotence; to upbraid a nation of slaves with their true name and abject condition; and to enforce, by cruel and insolent threats, the rigour of their absolute commands. The Christians of the East were scandalised by the worship of fire and the impious doctrine of the two principles: the Magi were not less intolerant than the bishops; and the martyrdom of some native Persians who had deserted the religion of Zoroaster[63] was conceived to be the prelude of a fierce and general persecution. By the oppressive laws of Justinian the adversaries of the church were made the enemies of the state; the alliance of the Jews, Nestorians, and Jacobites had contributed to the success of Chosroes, and his partial favour to the sectaries provoked the hatred and fears of the catholic clergy. Conscious of their fear and hatred, the Persian conqueror governed his new subjects with an iron sceptre; and, as if he suspected the stability of his dominion, he exhausted their wealth by exorbitant tributes and licentious rapine; despoiled or demolished the temples of the East; and transported to his hereditary realms the gold, the silver, the precious marbles, the arts, and the artists of the Asiatic cities. In the obscure picture of the calamities of the empire[64] it is not easy to discern the figure of Chosroes himself, to separate his actions from those of his lieutenants, or to ascertain his personal merit in the general blaze of glory and magnificence. He enjoyed with ostentation the fruits of victory, and frequently retired from the hardships of war to the luxury of the palace. But, in the space of twenty-four years, he was deterred by superstition or resentment from approaching the gates of Ctesiphon: and his favourite residence of Artemita, or Dastagerd, was situate beyond the Tigris, about sixty miles to the north of the capital.[65] The adjacent pastures were covered with flocks and herds: the paradise or park was replenished with pheasants, peacocks, ostriches, roebucks, and wild boars; and the noble game of lions and tigers was sometimes turned loose for the bolder pleasures of the chase. Nine hundred and sixty elephants were maintained for the use or splendour of the Great King; his tents and baggage were carried into the field by twelve thousand great camels and eight thousand of a smaller size;[66] and the royal stables were filled with six thousand mules and horses, among whom the names of Shebdiz and Barid are renowned for their speed or beauty. Six thousand guards successively mounted before the palace gate; the service of the interior apartments was performed by twelve thousand slaves; and in the number of three thousand virgins, the fairest of Asia, some happy concubine might console her master for the age or the indifference of Sira. The various treasures of gold, silver, gems, silk, and aromatics were deposited in a hundred subterraneous vaults; and the chamber Badaverd denoted the accidental gift of the winds which had wafted the spoils of Heraclius into one of the Syrian harbours of his rival. The voice of flattery, and perhaps of fiction, is not ashamed to compute the thirty thousand rich hangings that adorned the walls; the forty thousand colums of silver, or more probably of marble, and plated wood, that supported the roof; and the thousand globes of gold suspended in the dome, to imitate the motions of the planets and the constellations of the zodiac.[67] While the Persian monarch contemplated the wonders of his art and power, he received an epistle from an obscure citizen of Mecca, inviting him to acknowledge Mohammed as the apostle of God. He rejected the invitation, and tore the epistle. "It is thus," exclaimed the Arabian prophet, "that God will tear the kingdom and reject the supplications of Chosroes"[68] Placed on the verge of the two great empires of the East, Mohammed observed with secret joy the progress of their mutual destruction; and in the midst of the Persian triumphs he ventured to foretell that, before many years should elapse, victory would again return to the banners of the Romans.[69]

At the time when this prediction is said to have been delivered, no prophecy could be more distant from its accomplishment, since the first twelve years of Heraclius announced the approaching dissolution of the empire. If the motives of Chosroes had been pure and honourable, he must have ended the quarrel with the death of Phocas, and he would have embraced, as his best ally, the fortunate African who had so generously avenged the injuries of his benefactor Maurice. The prosecution of the war revealed the true character of the barbarian; and the suppliant embassies of Heraclius to beseech his clemency, that he would spare the innocent, accept a tribute, and give peace to the world, were rejected with contemptuous silence or insolent menace. Syria, Egypt, and the provinces of Asia were subdued by the Persian arms; while Europe, from the confines of Istria to the long wall of Thrace, was oppressed by the Avars, unsatiated with the blood and rapine of the Italian war. They had coolly massacred their male captives in the sacred field of Pannonia; the women and children were reduced to servitude, and the noblest virgins were abandoned to the promiscuous lust of the barbarians. The amorous matron who opened the gates of Friuli passed a short night in the arms of her royal lover; the next evening Romilda was condemned to the embraces of twelve Avars; and, the third day, the Lombard princess was impaled in the sight of the camp, while the chagan observed, with a cruel smile, that such a husband was the fit recompense of her lewdness and perfidy.[70] By these implacable enemies Heraclius, on either side, was insulted and besieged: and the Roman empire was reduced to the walls of Constantinople, with the remnant of Greece, Italy, and Africa, and some maritime cities, from Tyre to Trebizond, of the Asiatic coast. After the loss of Egypt the capital was afflicted by famine and pestilence; and the emperor, incapable of resistance and hopeless of relief, had resolved to transfer his person and government to the more secure residence of Carthage. His ships were already laden with the treasures of the palace; but his flight was arrested by the patriarch, who armed the powers of religion in the defence of his country, led Heraclius to the altar of St. Sophia, and extorted a solemn oath that he would live and die with the people whom God had intrusted to his care. The chagan was encamped in the plains of Thrace; but he dissembled his perfidious designs, and solicited an interview with the emperor near the town of Heraclea. Their reconciliation was celebrated with equestrian games; the senate and people, in their gayest apparel, resorted to the festival of peace; and the Avars beheld, with envy and desire, the spectacle of Roman luxury. On a sudden the hippodrome was encompassed by the Scythian cavalry, who had pressed their secret and nocturnal march: the tremendous sound of the chagan's whip gave the signal of the assault; and Heraclius, wrapping his diadem round his arm, was saved, with extreme hazard, by the fleetness of his horse. So rapid was the pursuit, that the Avars almost entered the golden gate of Constantinople with the flying crowds:[71] but the plunder of the suburbs rewarded their treason, and they transported beyond the Danube two hundred and seventy thousand captives. On the shore of Chalcedon the emperor held a safer conference with a more honourable foe, who, before Heraclius descended from his galley, saluted with reverence and pity the majesty of the purple. The friendly offer of Sain, the Persian general, to conduct an embassy to the presence of the Great King was accepted with the warmest gratitude; and the prayer for pardon and peace was humbly presented by the prætorian præfect, the præfect of the city, and one of the first ecclesiastics of the patriarchal church.[72] But the lieutenant of Chosroes had fatally mistaken the intentions of his master. "It was not an embassy," said the tyrant of Asia, "it was the person of Heraclius, bound in chains, that he should have brought to the foot of my throne. I will never give peace to the emperor of Rome till he has abjured his crucified God and embraced the worship of the sun." Sain was flayed alive, according to the inhuman practice of his country; and the separate and rigorous confinement of the ambassadors violated the law of nations and the faith of an express stipulation. Yet the experience of six years at length persuaded the Persian monarch to renounce the conquest of Constantinople, and to specify the annual tribute or ransom of the Roman empire: a thousand talents of gold, a thousand talents of silver, a thousand silk robes, a thousand horses, and a thousand virgins. Heraclius subscribed these ignominious terms; but the time and space which he obtained to collect such treasures from the poverty of the East was industriously employed in the preparations of a bold and desperate attack.

Of the characters conspicuous in history, that of Heraclius is one of the most extraordinary and inconsistent. In the first and the last years of a long reign the emperor appears to be the slave of sloth, of pleasure, or of superstition; the careless and impotent spectator of the public calamities. But the languid mists of the morning and evening are separated by the brightness of the meridian sun: the Arcadius of the palace arose the Cæsar of the camp; and the honour of Rome and Heraclius was gloriously retrieved by the exploits and trophies of six adventurous campaigns. It was the duty of the Byzantine historians to have revealed the causes of his slumber and vigilance. At this distance we can only conjecture that he was endowed with more personal courage than political resolution: that he was detained by the charms, and perhaps the arts, of his niece Martina, with whom, after the death of Eudocia, he contracted an incestuous marriage;[73] and that he yielded to the base advice of the counsellors who urged, as a fundamental law, that the life of the emperor should never be exposed in the field.[74] Perhaps he was awakened by the last insolent demand of the Persian conqueror; but at the moment when Heraclius assumed the spirit of a hero, the only hopes of the Romans were drawn from the vicissitudes of fortune, which might threaten the proud prosperity of Chosroes, and must be favourable to those who had attained the lowest period of depression.[75] To provide for the expenses of war was the first care of the emperor; and for the purpose of collecting the tribute he was allowed to solicit the benevolence of the Eastern provinces. But the revenue no longer flowed in the usual channels; the credit of an arbitrary prince is annihilated by his power; and the courage of Heraclius was first displayed in daring to borrow the consecrated wealth of churches, under the solemn vow of restoring, with usury, whatever he had been compelled to employ in the service of religion and of the empire. The clergy themselves appear to have sympathised with the public distress; and the discreet patriarch of Alexandria, without admitting the precedent of sacrilege, assisted his sovereign by the miraculous and seasonable revelation of a secret treasure.[76] Of the soldiers who had conspired with Phocas, only two were found to have survived the stroke of time and of the barbarians;[77] the loss even of these seditious veterans was imperfectly supplied by the new levies of Heraclius; and the gold of the sanctuary united, in the same camp, the names, and arms, and languages of the East and West. He would have been content with the neutrality of the Avars; and his friendly entreaty that the chagan would act not as the enemy, but as the guardian of the empire, was accompanied with a more persuasive donative of two hundred thousand pieces of gold. Two days after the festival of Easter, the emperor, exchanging his purple for the simple garb of a penitent and warrior,[78] gave the signal of his departure. To the faith of the people Heraclius recommended his children; the civil and military powers were vested in the most deserving hands; and the discretion of the patriarch and senate was authorised to save or surrender the city, if they should be oppressed in his absence by the superior forces of the enemy.

The neighbouring heights of Chalcedon were covered with tents and arms; but if the new levies of Heraclius had been rashly led to the attack, the victory of the Persians in the sight of Constantinople might have been the last day of the Roman empire. As imprudent would it have been to advance into the provinces of Asia, leaving their innumerable cavalry to intercept his convoys, and continually to hang on the lassitude and disorder of his rear. But the Greeks were still masters of the sea; a fleet of galleys, transports, and store-ships was assembled in the harbour; the barbarians consented to embark; a steady wind carried them through the Hellespont; the western and southern coast of Asia Minor lay on their left hand; the spirit of their chief was first displayed in a storm; and even the eunuchs of his train were excited to suffer and to work by the example of their master. He landed his troops on the confines of Syria and Cilicia, in the gulf of Scanderoon, where the coast suddenly turns to the south;[79] and his discernment was expressed in the choice of this important post.[80] From all sides the scattered garrisons of the maritime cities and the mountains might repair with speed and safety to his Imperial standard. The natural fortifications of Cilicia protected and even concealed the camp of Heraclius, which was pitched near Issus, on the same ground where Alexander had vanquished the host of Darius. The angle which the emperor occupied was deeply indented into a vast semicircle of the Asiatic, Armenian, and Syrian provinces; and to whatsoever point of the circumference he should direct his attack, it was easy for him to dissemble his own motions, and to prevent those of the enemy. In the camp of Issus the Roman general reformed the sloth and disorder of the veterans, and educated the new recruits in the knowledge and practice of military virtue. Unfolding the miraculous image of Christ, he urged them to *revenge* the holy altars which had been profaned by the worshippers of fire; addressing them by the endearing appellations of sons and brethren, he deplored the public and private wrongs of the republic. The subjects of a monarch were persuaded that they fought in the cause of freedom, and a similar enthusiasm was communicated to the foreign mercenaries, who must have viewed with equal indifference the interest of Rome and of Persia. Heraclius himself, with the skill and patience of a centurion, inculcated the lessons of the school of tactics, and the soldiers were assiduously trained in the use of their weapons and the exercises and evolutions of the field. The cavalry and infantry, in light or heavy armour, were divided into two parties; the trumpets were fixed in the centre, and their signals directed the march, the charge, the retreat or pursuit, the direct or oblique order, the deep or extended phalanx, to represent in fictitious combat the operations of genuine war. Whatever hardship the emperor imposed on the troops, he inflicted with equal severity on himself; their labour, their diet, their sleep, were measured by the inflexible rules of discipline; and, without despising the enemy, they were taught to repose an implicit confidence in their own valour and the wisdom of their leader. Cilicia was soon encompassed with the Persian arms, but their cavalry hesitated to enter the defiles of Mount Taurus till they were circumvented by the evolutions of Heraclius, who insensibly gained their rear, whilst he appeared to present his front in order of battle. By a false motion, which seemed to threaten Armenia, he drew them against their wishes to a general action. They were tempted by the artful disorder of his camp; but when they advanced to combat, the ground, the sun, and the expectation of both armies were unpropitious to the barbarians: the Romans successfully repeated their tactics in a field of battle,[81] and the event of the day declared to the world that the Persians were not invincible, and that a hero was invested with the purple. Strong in victory and fame, Heraclius boldly ascended the heights of Mount Taurus, directed his march through the plains of Cappadocia, and established his troops for the winter season in safe and plentiful quarters on the banks of the river Halys.[82] His soul was superior to the vanity of entertaining Constantinople with an imperfect triumph; but the presence of the emperor was indispensably required to soothe the restless and rapacious spirit of the Avars.

Since the days of Scipio and Hannibal, no bolder enterprise has been attempted than that which Heraclius achieved for the deliverance of the empire.[83] He permitted the Persians to oppress for awhile the provinces, and to insult with impunity the capital of the East, while the Roman emperor explored his perilous way through the Black Sea,[84] and the mountains of Armenia, penetrated into the heart of Persia,[8t] and recalled the armies of the Great King to the defense of their bleeding country.

With a select band of five thousand soldiers, Heraclius sailed from Constantinople to Trebizond; assembled his forces which had wintered in the Pontic regions; and from the mouth of the Phasis to the Caspian Sea, encouraged his subjects and allies to march with the successor of Constantine under the faithful and victorious banner of the cross. When the legions of Lucullus and Pompey first passed the Euphrates, they blushed at their easy victory over the natives of Armenia. But the long experience of war had hardened the minds and bodies of that effeminate people; their zeal and bravery were approved in the service of a declining empire; they abhorred and feared the usurpation of the house of Sassan, and the memory of persecution envenomed their pious hatred of the enemies of Christ. The limits of Armenia. as it had been ceded to the emperor Maurice, extended as far as the Araxes: the river submitted to the indignity of a bridge,[86] and Heraclius, in the footsteps of Mark Antony, advanced towards the city of Tauris or Gandzaca,[87] the ancient and modern capital of one of the provinces of Media. At the head of forty thousand men, Chosroes himself had returned from some distant expedition to oppose the progress of the Roman arms; but he retreated on the approach of Heraclius, declining the generous alternative of peace or battle. Instead of half a million of inhabitants, which have been ascribed to Tauris under the reign of the Sophys, the city contained no more than three thousand houses; but the value of the royal treasures was enhanced by a tradition that they were the spoils of Crœsus, which had been transported by Cyrus from the citadel of Sardes. The rapid conquests of Heraclius were suspended only by the winter season; a motive of prudence or superstition[88] determined his retreat into the province of Albania, along the shores of the Caspian; and his tents were most probably pitched in the plains of Mogan,[89] the favourite encampment of Oriental princes. In the course of this successful inroad he signalised the zeal and revenge of a Christian emperor: at his command the soldiers extinguished the fire, and destroyed the temples, of the Magi; the statues of Chosroes, who aspired to divine honours, were abandoned to the flames; and the ruin of Thebarma or Ormia,[90] which had given birth to Zoroaster himself, made some atonement for the injuries of the holy sepulchre. A purer spirit of religion was shown in the relief and deliverance of fifty thousand captives. Heraclius was rewarded by their tears and grateful acclamations; but this wise measure, which spread the fame of his benevolence, diffused the murmurs of the Persians against the pride and obstinacy of their own sovereign.

Amidst the glories of the succeeding campaign, Heraclius is almost lost to our eyes, and to those of the Byzantine historians.[91] From the spacious and fruitful plains of Albania, the emperor appears to follow the chain of Hyrcanian mountains, to descend into the province of Media or Irak, and to carry his victorious arms as far as the royal cities of Casbin and Ispahan, which had never been approached by a Roman conqueror. Alarmed by the danger of his kingdom, the powers of Chosroes were already recalled from the Nile and the Bosphorus, and three formidable armies surrounded, in a distant and hostile land, the camp of the emperor. The Colchian allies prepared to desert his standard; and the fears of the bravest veterans were expressed, rather than concealed, by their desponding silence. "Be not terrified," said the intrepid Heraclius, "by the multitude of your foes. With the aid of Heaven, one Roman may triumph over a thousand barbarians. But if we devote our lives for the salvation of our brethren, we shall obtain the crown of martyrdom, and our immortal reward will be liberally paid by God and posterity." These magnanimous sentiments were supported by the vigour of his actions. He repelled the threefold attack of the Persians, improved the divisions of their chiefs, and, by a well-concerted train of marches, retreats, and successful actions, finally chased them from the field into the fortified cities of Media and Assyria. In the severity of the winter season, Sarbaraza deemed himself secure in the walls of Salban: he was surprised by the activity of Heraclius, who divided his troops, and performed a laborious march in the silence of the night. The flat roofs of the houses were defended with useless valour against the darts and torches of the Romans: the satraps and nobles of Persia, with their wives and children, and the flower of their martial youth, were either slain or made prisoners. The general escaped by a precipitate flight, but his golden armour was the prize of the conqueror; and the soldiers of Heraclius enjoyed the wealth and repose which they had so nobly deserved. On the return of spring, the emperor traversed in seven days the mountains of Curdistan, and passed without resistance the rapid stream of the Tigris. Op-

pressed by the weight of their spoils and captives, the Roman army halted under the walls of Amida; and Heraclius informed the senate of Constantinople of his safety and success, which they had already felt by the retreat of the besiegers. The bridges of the Euphrates were destroyed by the Persians; but as soon as the emperor had discovered a ford, they hastily retired to defend the banks of the Sarus,[92] in Cilicia. That river, an impetuous torrent, was about three hundred feet broad; the bridge was fortified with strong turrets; and the banks were lined with barbarian archers. After a bloody conflict, which continued till the evening, the Romans prevailed in the assault; and a Persian of gigantic size was slain and thrown into the Sarus by the hand of the emperor himself. The enemies were dispersed and dismayed; Heraclius pursued his march to Sebaste in Cappadocia; and at the expiration of three years, the same coast of the Euxine applauded his return from a long and victorious expedition.[93]

Instead of skirmishing on the frontier, the two monarchs who disputed the empire of the East aimed their desperate strokes at the heart of their rival. The military force of Persia was wasted by the marches and combats of twenty years, and many of the veterans, who had survived the perils of the sword and the climate, were still detained in the fortresses of Egypt and Syria. But the revenge and ambition of Chosroes exhausted his kingdom; and the new levies of subjects, strangers, and slaves, were divided into three formidable bodies.[94] The first army of fifty thousand men, illustrious by the ornament and title of the *golden spears*, was destined to march against Heraclius; the second was stationed to prevent his junction with the troops of his brother Theodorus; and the third was commanded to besiege Constantinople, and to second the operations of the chagan, with whom the Persian king had ratified a treaty of alliance and partition. Sarbar, the general of the third army, penetrated through the provinces of Asia to the well-known camp of Chalcedon, and amused himself with the destruction of the sacred and profane buildings of the Asiatic suburbs, while he impatiently waited the arrival of his Scythian friends on the opposite side of the Bosphorus. On the twenty-ninth of June, thirty thousand barbarians, the vanguard of the Avars, forced the long wall, and drove into the capital a promiscuous crowd of peasants, citizens, and soldiers. Fourscore thousand[95] of his native subjects, and of the vassal tribes of Gepidæ, Russians, Bulgarians, and Sclavonians, advanced under the standard of the chagan; a month was spent in marches and negotiations, but the whole city was invested on the thirty-first of July, from the suburbs of Pera and Galata to the Blachernæ and seven towers; and the inhabitants descried with terror the flaming signals of the European and Asiatic shores. In the meanwhile the magistrates of Constantinople repeatedly strove to purchase the retreat of the chagan; but their deputies were rejected and insulted; and he suffered the patricians to stand before his throne, while the Persian envoys, in silk robes, were seated by his side. "You see," said the haughty barbarian, "the proofs of my perfect union with the Great King; and his lieutenant is ready to send into my camp a select band of three thousand warriors. Presume no longer to tempt your master with a partial and inadequate ransom: your wealth and your city are the only presents worthy of my acceptance. For yourselves, I shall permit you to depart, each with an undergarment and a shirt; and, at my entreaty, my friend Sarbar will not refuse a passage through his lines. Your absent prince, even now a captive or a fugitive, has left Constantinople to its fate; nor can you escape the arms of the Avars and Persians, unless you could soar into air like birds, unless like fishes you could dive into the waves."[96] During ten successive days the capital was assaulted by the Avars, who had made some progress in the science of attack: they advanced to sap or batter the wall, under the cover of the impenetrable tortoise; their engines discharged a perpetual volley of stones and darts; and twelve lofty towers of wood exalted the combatants to the height of the neighbouring ramparts. But the senate and people were animated by the spirit of Heraclius, who had detached to their relief a body of twelve thousand cuirassiers; the powers of fire and mechanics were used with superior art and success in the defence of Constantinople; and the galleys, with two and three ranks of oars, commanded the Bosphorus, and rendered the Persians the idle spectators of the defeat of their allies. The Avars were repulsed; a fleet of Sclavonian canoes was destroyed in the harbour; the vassals of the chagan threatened to desert, his provisions were exhausted, and, after burning his engines, he gave the signal of a slow and formidable retreat. The devotion of the Romans ascribed this signal deliverance to the Virgin Mary; but the mother of Christ would surely have condemned their inhuman murder of the Persian envoys, who were entitled to the rights of humanity, if they were not protected by the laws of nations.[97]

After the division of his army, Heraclius prudently retired to the banks of the Phasis, from whence he maintained a defensive war against the fifty thousand gold spears of Persia. His anxiety was relieved by the deliverance of Constantinople; his hopes were confirmed by a victory of his brother Theodorus; and to the hostile league of Chosroes with the Avars, the Roman emperor opposed the useful and honourable alliance of the Turks. At his liberal invitation, the horde of Chozars[98] transported their tents from the plains of the Volga to the mountains of Georgia; Heraclius received them in the neighbourhood of Teflis, and the khan with his nobles dismounted from their horses, if we may credit the Greeks, and fell prostrate on the ground to adore the purple of the Cæsar. Such voluntary homage and important aid were entitled to the warmest acknowledgments, and the emperor, taking off his own diadem, placed it on the head of the Turkish prince, whom he saluted with a tender embrace and the appellation of son. After a sumptuous banquet he presented Ziebel with the plate and ornaments, the gold, the gems, and the silk which had been used at the Imperial table, and, with his own hand, distributed rich jewels and earrings to his new allies. In a secret interview he produced the portrait of his daughter Eudocia,[99] condescended to flatter the barbarian with the promise of a fair and *august* bride, obtained an immediate succour of forty thousand horse, and negotiated a strong diversion of the Turkish arms on the side of the Oxus.[100] The Persians, in their turn, retreated with precipitation; in the camp of Edessa Heraclius reviewed an army of seventy thousand Romans and strangers; and some months were successfully employed in the recovery of the cities of Syria, Mesopotamia, and Armenia, whose fortifications had been imperfectly restored. Sarbar still maintained the important station of Chalcedon, but the jealousy of Chosroes, or the artifice of Heraclius, soon alienated the mind of that powerful satrap from the service of his king and country. A messenger was intercepted with a real or fictitious mandate to the cadarigan, or second in command, directing him to send, without delay, to the throne the head of a guilty or unfortunate general. The despatches were transmitted to Sarbar himself, and, as soon as he read the sentence of his own death, he dexterously inserted the names of four hundred officers, assembled a military council, and asked the *cadarigan* whether he was prepared to execute the commands of their tyrant? The Persians unanimously declared that Chosroes had forfeited the sceptre; a separate treaty was concluded with the government of Constantinople; and if some considerations of honour or policy restrained Sarbar from joining the standard of Heraclius, the emperor was assured that he might prosecute without interruption his designs of victory and peace.

Deprived of his firmest support, and doubtful of the fidelity of his subjects, the greatness of Chosroes was still conspicuous in its ruins. The number of five hundred thousand may be interpreted as an Oriental metaphor to describe the men and arms, the horses and elephants, that covered Media and Assyria against the invasion of Heraclius. Yet the Romans boldly advanced from the Araxes to the Tigris, and the timid prudence of Rhazates was content to follow them by forced marches through a desolate country, till he received a peremptory mandate to risk the fate of Persia in a decisive battle. Eastward of the Tigris, at the end of the bridge of Mosul, the great Nineveh had formerly been erected:[101] the city, and even the ruins of the city, had long since disappeared;[102] the vacant space afforded a spacious field for the operations of the two armies. But these operations are neglected by the Byzantine historians, and, like the authors of epic poetry and romance, they ascribe the victory, not to the military conduct, but to the personal valour, of their favourite hero. On this memorable day Heraclius, on his horse Phallas, surpassed the bravest of his warriors; his lip was pierced with a spear, the steed was wounded in the thigh, but he carried his master safe and victorious through the triple phalanx of the barbarians. In the heat of the action three valiant chiefs were successively slain by the sword and lance of the emperor: among these was Rhazates himself; he fell like a soldier, but the sight of his head scattered grief and despair through the fainting ranks of the Persians. His armour of pure and massy gold, the shield of one hundred and twenty plates, the sword and belt, the saddle and cuirass, adorned the triumph of Heraclius; and if he had not been faithful to Christ and his mother, the champion of Rome might have offered the fourth *opime* spoils to the Jupiter of the Capitol.[103] In the battle of Nineveh, which was fiercely fought from daybreak to the eleventh hour, twenty-eight standards, besides those which might be broken or torn, were taken from the Persians; the greatest part of their army was cut in pieces; and the victors, concealing their own loss, passed the night on the field. They acknowledge that, on this occasion, it was less difficult to kill than to discomfit the soldiers of Chosroes; amidst the bodies of their friends, no more than two bow-shot from the enemy, the remnant of the Persian cavalry stood firm till the seventh hour of the night; about the eighth hour they retired to their unrifled camp, collected their baggage, and dispersed on all sides from the want of orders rather than of resolution. The diligence of Heraclius was not less admirable in the use of victory; by a march of forty-eight miles in four-and-twenty hours his vanguard occupied the bridges of the great and the lesser Zab, and the cities and palaces of Assyria were open for the first time to the Romans. By a just gradation of magnificent scenes they penetrated to the royal seat of Dastagerd, and, though much of the treasure had been removed and much had been expended, the remaining wealth appears to have exceeded their hopes, and even to have satiated their avarice. Whatever could not be easily transported they consumed with fire, that Chosroes might feel the anguish of those wounds which he had so often inflicted on the provinces of the empire; and justice might allow the excuse, if the desolation had been confined to the works of regal luxury—if national hatred, military licence, and religious zeal had not wasted with equal rage the habitations and the temples of the guiltless subject. The recovery of three hundred Roman standards and the deliverance of the numerous captives of Edessa and Alexandria reflect a purer glory on the arms of Heraclius. From the palace of Dastagerd he pursued his march within a few miles of Modain or Ctesiphon, till he was stopped, on the banks of the Arba, by the difficulty of the passage, the rigour of the season, and perhaps the fame of an impregnable capital. The return of the emperor is marked by the modern name of the city of Sherhzour: he fortunately passed Mount Zara before the snow, which fell incessantly thirty-four days; and the citizens of Gandzaca, or Tauris, were compelled to entertain his soldiers and their horses with an hospitable reception.[104]

When the ambition of Chosroes was reduced to the defence of his hereditary kingdom, the love of glory, or even the sense of shame, should have urged him to meet his rival in the field. In the battle of Nineveh his courage might have taught the Persians to vanquish, or he might have fallen with honour by the lance of a Roman emperor. The successor of Cyrus chose rather, at a secure distance, to expect the event, to assemble the relics of the defeat, and to retire by measured steps before the march of Heraclius, till he beheld with a sigh the once loved mansions of Dastagerd. Both his friends and enemies were persuaded that it was the intention of Chosroes to bury himself under the ruins of the city and palace: and as both might have been equally adverse to his flight, the monarch of Asia, with Sira and three concubines, escaped through a hole in the wall nine days before the arrival of the Romans. The slow and stately procession in which he showed himself to the prostrate crowd was changed to a rapid and secret journey; the first evening he lodged in the cottage of a peasant, whose humble door would scarcely give admittance to the Great King.[105] His superstition was subdued by fear: on the third day he entered with joy the fortifications of Ctesiphon; yet he still doubted of his safety till he had opposed the river Tigris to the pursuit of the Romans. The discovery of his flight agitated with terror and tumult the palace, the city, and the camp of Dastagerd: the satraps hesitated whether they had most to fear from their sovereign or the enemy; and the females of the harem were astonished and pleased by the sight of mankind, till the jealous husband of three thousand wives again confined them to a more distant castle. At his command the army of Dastagerd retreated to a new camp: the front was covered by the Arba and a line of two hundred elephants; the troops of the more distant provinces successively arrived; and the vilest domestics of the king and satraps were enrolled for the last defence of the throne. It was still in the power of Chosroes to obtain a reasonable peace; and he was repeatedly pressed by the messengers of Heraclius to spare the blood of his subjects, and to relieve a humane conqueror from the painful duty of carrying fire and sword through the fairest countries of Asia. But the pride of the Persian had not yet sunk to the level of his fortune; he derived a momentary confidence from the retreat of the emperor; he wept with impotent rage over the ruins of his Assyrian palaces; and disregarded too long the rising murmurs of the nation, who complained that their lives and fortunes were sacrificed to the obstinacy of an old man. That unhappy old man was himself tortured with the sharpest pains both of mind and body; and, in the consciousness of his approaching end, he resolved to fix the tiara on the head of Merdaza, the most favoured of his sons. But the will of Chosroes was no longer revered, and Siroes, who gloried in the rank and

merit of his mother Sira, had conspired with the malcontents to assert and anticipate the rights of primogeniture.[106] Twenty-two satraps, they styled themselves patriots, were tempted by the wealth and honours of a new reign: to the soldiers the heir of Chosroes promised an increase of pay; to the Christians, the free exercise of their religion; to the captives, liberty and rewards; and to the nation, instant peace and the reduction of taxes. It was determined by the conspirators that Siroes, with the ensigns of royalty, should appear in the camp; and if the enterprise should fail, his escape was contrived to the Imperial court. But the new monarch was saluted with unanimous acclamations; the flight of Chosroes (yet where could he have fled?) was rudely arrested, eighteen sons were massacred before his face, and he was thrown into a dungeon, where he expired on the fifth day. The Greeks and modern Persians minutely described how Chosroes was insulted, and famished, and tortured, by the command of an inhuman son, who so far surpassed the example of his father; but at the time of his death what tongue would relate the story of the parricide? what eye could penetrate into the *tower of darkness?* According to the faith and mercy of his Christian enemies, he sunk without hope into a still deeper abyss,[107] and it will not be denied that tyrants of every age and sect are the best entitled to such infernal abodes. The glory of the house of Sassan ended with the life of Chosroes; his unnatural son enjoyed only eight months the fruit of his crimes; and in the space of four years the regal title was assumed by nine candidates, who disputed, with the sword or dagger, the fragments of an exhausted monarchy. Every province and each city of Persia was the scene of independence, of discord, and of blood; and the state of anarchy prevailed about eight years longer, till the factions were silenced and united under the common yoke of the Arabian caliphs.[108]

As soon as the mountains became passable the emperor received the welcome news of the success of the conspiracy, the death of Chosroes, and the elevation of his eldest son to the throne of Persia. The authors of the revolution, eager to display their merits in the court or camp of Tauris, preceded the ambassadors of Siroes, who delivered the letters of their master to his *brother* the emperor of the Romans.[109] In the language of the usurpers of every age, he imputes his own crimes to the Deity, and, without degrading his equal majesty, he offers to reconcile the long discord of the two nations by a treaty of peace and alliance more durable than brass or iron. The conditions of the treaty were easily defined and faithfully executed. In the recovery of the standards and prisoners which had fallen into the hands of the Persians, the emperor imitated the example of Augustus; their care of the national dignity was celebrated by the poets of the times, but the decay of genius may be measured by the distance between Horace and George of Pisidia; the subjects and brethren of Heraclius were redeemed from persecution, slavery, and exile; but, instead of the Roman eagles, the true wood of the holy cross was restored to the importunate demands of the successor of Constantine. The victor was not ambitious of enlarging the weakness of the empire; the son of Chosroes abandoned without regret the conquests of his father; the Persians who evacuated the cities of Syria and Egypt were honourably conducted to the frontier; and a war which had wounded the vitals of the two monarchies produced no change in their external and relative situation. The return of Heraclius from Tauris to Constantinople was a perpetual triumph, and after the exploits of six glorious campaigns he peaceably enjoyed the sabbath of his toils. After a long impatience, the senate, the clergy, and the people went forth to meet their hero with tears and acclamations, with olive-branches and innumerable lamps; he entered the capital in a chariot drawn by four elephants, and, as soon as the emperor could disengage himself from the tumult of public joy, he tasted more genuine satisfaction in the embraces of his mother and his sons.[110]

The succeeding year was illustrated by a triumph of a very different kind, the restitution of the true cross to the holy sepulchre. Heraclius performed in person the pilgrimage of Jerusalem: the identity of the relic was verified by the discreet patriarch,[111] and this august ceremony has been commemorated by the annual festival of the exaltation of the cross. Before the emperor presumed to tread the consecrated ground he was instructed to strip himself of the diadem and purple, the pomp and vanity of the world; but in the judgment of his clergy, the persecution of the Jews was more easily reconciled with the precepts of the Gospel. He again ascended his throne to receive the congratulations of the ambassadors of France and India; and the fame of Moses, Alexander, and Hercules[112] was eclipsed, in the popular estimation, by the superior merit and glory of the great Heraclius. Yet the deliverer of the East was indigent and feeble. Of the Persian spoils the most valuable portion had been expended in the war, distributed to the soldiers, or buried, by an unlucky tempest, in the waves of the Euxine. The conscience of the emperor was oppressed by the obligation of restoring the wealth of the clergy, which he had borrowed for their own defence: a perpetual fund was required to satisfy these inexorable creditors; the provinces, already wasted by the arms and avarice of the Persians, were compelled to a second payment of the same taxes; and the arrears of a simple citizen, the treasurer of Damascus, were commuted to a fine of one hundred thousand pieces of gold. The loss of two hundred thousand soldiers,[113] who had fallen by the sword, was of less fatal importance than the decay of arts, agriculture, and population in this long and destructive war; and although a victorious army had been formed under the standard of Heraclius, the unnatural effort appears to have exhausted rather than exercised their strength. While the emperor triumphed at Constantinople or Jerusalem, an obscure town on the confines of Syria was pillaged by the Saracens, and they cut in pieces some troops who advanced to its relief; an ordinary and trifling occurrence, had it not been the prelude of a mighty revolution. These robbers were the apostles of Mohammed; their fanatic valour had emerged from the desert; and in the last eight years of his reign Heraclius lost to the Arabs the same provinces which he had rescued from the Persians.

CHAPTER XLVII

Theological History of the Doctrine of the Incarnation. The Human and Divine Nature of Christ. Enmity of the Patriarchs of Alexandria and Constantinople. St. Cyril and Nestorius. Third General Council of Ephesus. Heresy of Eutyches. Fourth General Council of Chalcedon. Civil and Ecclesiastical Discord. Intolerance of Justinian. The Three Chapters. The Monothelite Controversy. State of the Oriental Sects. I. The Nestorians. II. The Jacobites. III. The Maronites. IV. The Armenians. V. The Copts. VI. Abyssinians.

AFTER the extinction of paganism, the Christians in peace and piety might have enjoyed their solitary triumph. But the principle of discord was alive in their bosom, and they were more solicitous to explore the nature, than to practise the laws, of their founder. I have already observed that the disputes of the TRINITY were succeeded by those of the INCARNATION; alike scandalous to the church, alike pernicious to the state, still more minute in their origin, still more durable in their effects. It is my design to comprise in the present chapter a religious war of two hundred and fifty years, to represent the ecclesiastical and political schism of the Oriental sects, and to introduce their clamorous or sanguinary contests by a modest inquiry into the doctrines of the primitive church.[1]

I. A laudable regard for the honour of the first proselytes has countenanced the belief, the hope, the wish, that the Ebionites, or at least the Nazarenes, were distinguished only by their obstinate perseverance in the practise of the Mosaic rites. Their churches have disappeared, their books are obliterated: their obscure freedom might allow a latitude of faith, and the softness of their infant creed would be variously moulded by the zeal or prudence of three hundred years. Yet the most charitable criticism must refuse these sectaries any knowledge of the pure and proper divinity of Christ. Educated in the school of Jewish prophecy and prejudice, they had never been taught to elevate their hopes above a human and temporal Messiah.[2] If they had courage to hail their king when he appeared in a plebeian garb, their grosser apprehensions were incapable of discerning their God, who had studiously disguised his celestial character under the name and person of a mortal.[3] The familiar companions of Jesus of Nazareth conversed with their friend and countryman, who, in all the actions of rational and animal life, appeared of the same species with themselves. His progress from infancy to youth and manhood was marked by a regular increase in stature and wisdom; and after a painful agony of mind and body, he expired on the cross. He lived and died for the service of mankind: but the life and death of Socrates had likewise been devoted to the cause of religion and justice; and although the stoic or the hero may disdain the humble virtues of Jesus, the tears which he shed over his friend and country may be esteemed the purest evidence of his humanity. The miracles of the gospel could not astonish a people who held with intrepid faith the more splendid prodigies of the Mosaic law. The prophets of ancient days had cured diseases, raised the dead, divided the sea, stopped the sun, and ascended to heaven in a fiery chariot. And the metaphorical style of the Hebrews might ascribe to a saint and martyr the adoptive title of SON OF GOD.

Yet in the insufficient creed of the Nazarenes and the Ebionites a distinction is faintly noticed between the heretics, who confounded the generation of Christ in the common order of nature, and the less guilty schismatics, who revered the virginity of his mother and excluded the aid of an earthly father. The incredulity of the former was countenanced by the visible circumstances of his birth, the legal marriage of his reputed parents, Joseph and Mary, and his lineal claim to the kingdom of David and the inheritance of Judah. But the secret and authentic history has been recorded in several copies of the Gospel according to St. Matthew,[4] which these sectaries long preserved in the original Hebrew,[5] as the sole evidence of their faith. The natural suspicions of the husband, conscious of his own chastity, were dispelled by the assurance (in a dream) that his wife was pregnant of the Holy Ghost: and as this distant and domestic prodigy could not fall under the personal observation of the historian, he must have listened to the same voice which dictated to Isaiah the future conception of a virgin. The son of a virgin, generated by the ineffable operation of the Holy Spirit, was a creature without example or resemblance, superior in every attribute of mind and body to the children of Adam. Since the introduction of the Greek or Chaldean philosophy,[6] the Jews[7] were persuaded of the pre-existence, transmigration, and immortality of souls; and Providence was justified by a supposition that they were confined in their earthly prisons to expiate the stains which they had contracted in a former state.[8] But the degrees of purity and corruption are almost immeasurable. It might be fairly presumed that the most sublime and virtuous of human spirits was infused into the offspring of Mary and the Holy Ghost;[9] that his abasement was the result of his voluntary choice; and that the object of his mission was to purify, not his own, but the sins of the world. On his return to his native skies he received the immense reward of his obedience: the everlasting kingdom of the Messiah, which had been darkly foretold by the prophets, under the carnal images of peace, of conquest, and of dominion. Omnipotence could enlarge the human faculties of Christ to the extent of his celestial office. In the language of antiquity, the title of God has not been severely confined to the first parent; and his incomparable minister, his only begotten Son, might claim, without presumption, the religious, though secondary, worship of a subject world.

II. The seeds of the faith, which had slowly arisen in the rocky and ungrateful soil of Judea, were transplanted, in full maturity, to the happier climes of the Gentiles; and the strangers of Rome or Asia, who never beheld the manhood, were the more readily disposed to embrace the divinity, of Christ. The polytheist and the philosopher, the Greek and the barbarian, were alike accustomed to conceive a long succession, an infinite chain of angels, or demons, or deities, or æons, or emanations, issuing from the throne of light. Nor could it seem strange or incredible that the first of these æons, the Logos, or Word of God, of the same substance with the Father, should descend upon earth, to deliver the human race from vice and error, and to conduct them in the paths of life and immortality. But the prevailing doctrine of the eternity and inherent pravity of matter infected the primitive churches of the East. Many among the Gentile proselytes refused to believe that a celestial spirit, an undivided portion of the first essence, had been personally united with a mass of impure and contaminated flesh; and, in their zeal for the divinity, they piously abjured the humanity, of Christ. While his blood was still recent on Mount Calvary,[10] the Docetes, a numerous and learned sect of Asiatics, invented the phantastic system which was afterwards propagated by the Marcionites, the Manichæans, and the various names of the Gnostic heresy.[11] They denied the truth and authenticity of the gospels, as far as they relate the conception of Mary, the birth of Christ, and the thirty years that preceded the exercise of his ministry. He first appeared on the banks of the Jordan in the form of perfect manhood; but it was a form only, and not a substance; a human figure created by the hand of Omnipotence to imitate the faculties and actions of a man, and to impose a perpetual illusion on the senses of his friends and enemies. Articulate sounds vibrated on the ears of the disciples; but the image which was impressed on their optic nerve eluded the more stubborn evidence of the touch; and they enjoyed the spiritual, not the corporeal, presence of the Son of God. The rage of the Jews was idly wasted against an impassive phantom; and the mystic scenes of the passion and death, the resurrection and ascension of Christ, were represented on the theatre of Jerusalem for the benefit of mankind. If it were urged that such ideal mimicry, such incessant deception, was unworthy of the God of truth, the Docetes agreed with too many of their orthodox brethren in the justification of pious falsehood. In the system of the Gnostics the Jehovah of Israel, the Creator of this lower world, was a rebellious, or at least an ignorant, spirit. The Son of God descended upon earth to abolish his temple and his law; and, for the accomplishment of this salutary end, he dexterously transferred to his own person the hope and prediction of a temporal Messiah.

One of the most subtle disputants of the Manichæan school has pressed the danger and indecency of supposing that the God of the Christians, in the state of a human fœtus, emerged at the end of nine months from a female womb. The pious horror of his antagonists provoked them to disclaim all sensual circumstances of conception and delivery; to maintain that the divinity passed through Mary like a sunbeam through a plate of glass; and to assert that the seal of her virginity remained unbroken even at the moment when she became the mother of Christ. But the rashness of these concessions has encouraged a milder sentiment of those Docetes who taught, not that Christ was a phantom, but that he was clothed with an impassible and incorruptible body. Such, indeed, in the more orthodox system, he has acquired since his resurrection, and such he must have always possessed, if it were capable of pervading, without resistance or injury, the density of intermediate matter. Devoid of its most essential properties, it might be exempt from the attributes and infirmities of the flesh. A fœtus that could increase from an invisible point to its full maturity; a child that could attain the stature of perfect manhood, without deriving any nourishment from the ordinary sources, might continue to exist without repairing a daily waste by a daily supply of external matter. Jesus might share the repasts of his disciples without being subject to the calls of thirst or hunger; and his virgin purity was never sullied by the involuntary stains of sensual concupiscence. Of a body thus singularly constituted, a question would arise, by what means and of what materials it was originally framed; and our sounder theology is startled by an answer which was not peculiar to the Gnostics, that both the form and the substance proceeded from the divine essence. The idea of pure and absolute spirit is a refinement of modern philosophy: the incorporeal essence, ascribed by the ancients to human souls, celestial beings, and even the Deity himself, does not exclude the notion of extended space; and their imagination was satisfied with a subtle nature of air, or fire, or ether, incomparably more perfect than the grossness of the material world. If we define the place, we must describe the figure, of the Deity. Our experience, perhaps our vanity, represents the powers of reason and virtue under a human form. The Anthropomorphites, who swarmed among the monks of Egypt and the Catholics of Africa, could produce the express declaration of Scripture, that man was made after the image of his Creator.[12] The venerable Serapion, one of the saints of the Nitrian desert, relinquished, with many a tear, his darling prejudice; and bewailed, like an infant, his unlucky conversion, which had stolen away his God, and left his mind without any visible object of faith or devotion.[13]

III. Such were the fleeting shadows of the Docetes. A more substantial, though less simple hypothesis, was contrived by Cerinthus of Asia,[14] who dared to oppose the last of the apostles. Placed on the confines of the Jewish and Gentile world, he laboured to reconcile the Gnostic with the Ebionite, by confessing in the same Messiah the supernatural union of a man and a God; and this mystic doctrine was adopted with many fanciful improvements by Carpocrates, Basilides, and Valentine,[15] the heretics of the Egyptian school. In their eyes Jesus of Nazareth was a mere mortal, the legitimate son of Joseph and Mary: but he was the best and wisest of the human race, selected as the worthy instrument to restore upon earth the worship of the true and supreme Deity. When he was baptised in the Jordan, the Christ, the first of the æons, the Son of God himself, descended on Jesus in the form of a dove, to inhabit his mind and direct his actions during the allotted period of his ministry. When the Messiah was delivered into the hands of the Jews, the Christ, an immortal and impassible being, forsook his earthly tabernacle, flew back to the *pleroma* or world of spirits, and left the solitary Jesus to suffer, to complain, and to expire. But the justice and generosity of such a desertion are strongly questionable; and the fate of an innocent martyr, at first impelled, and at length abandoned, by his divine companion, might provoke the pity and indignation of the profane. Their murmurs were variously silenced by the sectaries who espoused and modified the double system of Cerinthus. It was alleged that, when Jesus was nailed to the cross, he was endowed with a miraculous apathy of mind and body, which rendered him insensible of his apparent sufferings. It was affirmed that these momentary, though real pangs, would be abundantly repaid by the temporal reign of a thousand years reserved for the Messiah in his kingdom of the new Jerusalem. It was insinuated that if he suffered, he deserved to suffer; that human nature is never absolutely perfect; and that the cross and passion might serve to expiate the venial transgressions of the son of Joseph, before his mysterious union with the Son of God.[16]

IV. All those who believe the immateriality of the soul, a specious and noble tenet, must confess, from their present experience, the incomprehensible union of mind and matter. A similar union is not inconsistent with a much higher, or even with the highest, degree of mental faculties; and the incarnation of an æon or archangel, the most perfect of created spirits, does not involve any positive contradiction or absurdity. In the age of religious freedom, which was determined by the council of Nice, the dignity of Christ was measured by private judgment according to the indefinite rule of

Scripture, or reason, or tradition. But when his pure and proper divinity had been established on the ruins of Arianism, the faith of the Catholics trembled on the edge of a precipice where it was impossible to recede, dangerous to stand, dreadful to fall; and the manifold inconveniences of their creed were aggravated by the sublime character of their theology. They hesitated to pronounce—*that* God himself, the second person of an equal and consubstantial trinity, was manifested in the flesh;[17] *that* a being who pervades the universe had been confined in the womb of Mary; *that* his eternal duration had been marked by the days, and months, and years of human existence; *that* the Almighty had been scourged and crucified; *that* his impassible essence had felt pain and anguish; *that* his omniscience was not exempt from ignorance; and *that* the source of life and immortality expired on Mount Calvary. These alarming consequences were affirmed with unblushing simplicity by Apollinaris,[18] bishop of Laodicea, and one of the luminaries of the church. The son of a learned grammarian, he was skilled in all the sciences of Greece; eloquence, erudition, and philosophy, conspicuous in the volumes of Apollinaris, were humbly devoted to the service of religion. The worthy friend of Athanasius, the worthy antagonist of Julian, he bravely wrestled with the Arians and Polytheists, and, though he affected the rigour of geometrical demonstration, his commentaries revealed the literal and allegorical sense of the Scriptures. A mystery which had long floated in the looseness of popular belief was defined by his perverse diligence in a technical form; and he first proclaimed the memorable words, "One incarnate nature of Christ," which are still re-echoed with hostile clamours in the churches of Asia, Egypt, and Æthiopia. He taught that the Godhead was united or mingled with the body of a man; and that the *Logos*, the eternal wisdom, supplied in the flesh the place and office of a human soul. Yet, as the profound doctor had been terrified at his own rashness, Apollinaris was heard to mutter some faint accents of excuse and explanation. He acquiesced in the old distinction of the Greek philosophers between the rational and sensitive soul of man; that he might reserve the *Logos* for intellectual functions, and employ the subordinate human principle in the meaner actions of animal life. With the moderate Docetes he revered Mary as the spiritual, rather than as the carnal, mother of Christ, whose body either came from heaven, impassible and incorruptible, or was absorbed, and as it were

transformed, into the essence of the Deity. The system of Apollinaris was strenuously encountered by the Asiatic and Syrian divines, whose schools are honoured by the names of Basil, Gregory, and Chrysostom, and tainted by those of Diodorus, Theodore, and Nestorius. But the person of the aged bishop of Laodicea, his character and dignity, remained inviolate; and his rivals, since we may not suspect them of the weakness of toleration, were astonished, perhaps, by the novelty of the argument, and diffident of the final sentence of the Catholic church. Her judgment at length inclined in their favour; the heresy of Apollinaris was condemned, and the separate congregations of his disciples were proscribed by the Imperial laws. But his principles were secretly entertained in the monasteries of Egypt, and his enemies felt the hatred of Theophilus and Cyril, the successive patriarchs of Alexandria.

V. The grovelling Ebionite and the fantastic Docete were rejected and forgotten: the recent zeal against the errors of Apollinaris reduced the Catholics to a seeming agreement with the double nature of Cerinthus. But instead of a temporary and occasional alliance, *they* established, and *we* still embrace, the substantial, indissoluble, and everlasting union of a perfect God with a perfect man, of the second person of the trinity with a reasonable soul and human flesh. In the beginning of the fifth century the *unity* of the *two natures* was the prevailing doctrine of the church. On all sides it was confessed that the mode of their co-existence could neither be represented by our ideas nor expressed by our language. Yet a secret and incurable discord was cherished between those who were most apprehensive of confounding, and those who were most fearful of separating, the divinity and the humanity of Christ. Impelled by religious frenzy, they fled with adverse haste from the error which they mutually deemed most destructive of truth and salvation. On either hand they were anxious to guard, they were jealous to defend, the union and the distinction of the two natures, and to invent such forms of speech, such symbols of doctrine, as were least susceptible of doubt or ambiguity. The poverty of ideas and language tempted them to ransack art and nature for every possible comparison, and each comparison misled their fancy in the explanation of an incomparable mystery. In the polemic microscope an atom is enlarged to a monster, and each party was skilful to exaggerate the absurd or impious conclusions that might be extorted from the principles of their adversaries. To escape from each other they wandered through many a dark and devious thicket, till they were astonished by the horrid phantoms of Cerinthus and Apollinaris, who guarded the opposite issues of the theological labyrinth. As soon as they beheld the twilight of sense and heresy, they started, measured back their steps, and were again involved in the gloom of impenetrable orthodoxy. To purge themselves from the guilt or reproach of damnable error, they disavowed their consequences, explained their principles, excused their indiscretions, and unanimously pronounced the sounds of concord and faith. Yet a latent and almost invisible spark still lurked among the embers of controversy: by the breath of prejudice and passion it was quickly kindled to a mighty flame, and the verbal disputes[19] of the Oriental sects have shaken the pillars of the church and state.

The name of CYRIL of Alexandria is famous in controversial story, and the title of *saint* is a mark that his opinions and his party have finally prevailed. In the house of his uncle, the archbishop Theophilus, he imbibed the orthodox lessons of zeal and dominion, and five years of his youth were profitably spent in the adjacent monasteries of Nitria. Under the tuition of the abbot Serapion, he applied himself to ecclesiastical studies with such indefatigable ardour, that in the course of *one* sleepless night he has perused the four gospels, the catholic epistles, and the epistle to the Romans. Origen he detested; but the writings of Clemens and Dionysius, of Athanasius and Basil, were continually in his hands: by the theory and practice of dispute, his faith was confirmed and his wit was sharpened; he extended round his cell the cobwebs of scholastic theology, and meditated the works of allegory and metaphysics, whose remains, in seven verbose folios, now peaceably slumber by the side of their rivals.[20] Cyril prayed and fasted in the desert, but his thoughts (it is the reproach of a friend[21]) were still fixed on the world; and the call of Theophilus, who summoned him to the tumult of cities and synods, was too readily obeyed by the aspiring hermit. With the approbation of his uncle he assumed the office and acquired the fame of a popular preacher. His comely person adorned the pulpit; the harmony of his voice resounded in the cathedral; his friends were stationed to lead or second the applause of the congregation;[22] and the hasty notes of the scribes preserved his discourses, which, in their effect, though not in their composition, might be compared with those of the Athenian orators. The death of Theophilus expanded and realised the hopes of his nephew. The clergy of Alexandria was divided; the soldiers and their general supported the claims of the archdeacon; but a resistless multitude, with voices and with hands, asserted the cause of their favourite; and after a period of thirty-nine years Cyril was seated on the throne of Athanasius.[23]

The prize was not unworthy of his ambition. At a distance from the court, and at the head of an immense capital, the patriarch, as he was now styled, of Alexandria had gradually usurped the state and authority of a civil magistrate. The public and private charities of the city were managed at his discretion; his voice inflamed or appeased the passions of the multitude; his commands were blindly obeyed by his numerous and fanatic *parabolani*,[24] familiarised in their daily office with scenes of death; and the præfects of Egypt were awed or provoked by the temporal power of these Christian pontiffs. Ardent in the prosecution of heresy, Cyril auspiciously opened his reign by oppressing the Novatians, the most innocent and harmless of the sectaries. The interdiction of their religious worship appeared in his eyes a just and meritorious act; and he confiscated their holy vessels, without apprehending the guilt of sacrilege. The toleration, and even the privileges of the Jews, who had multiplied to the number of forty thousand, were secured by the laws of the Cæsars and Ptolemies, and a long prescription of seven hundred years since the foundation of Alexandria. Without any legal sentence, without any royal mandate, the patriarch, at the dawn of day, led a seditious multitude to the attack of the synagogues. Unarmed and unprepared, the Jews were incapable of resistance; their houses of prayer were levelled with the ground, and the episcopal warrior, after rewarding his troops with the plunder of their goods, expelled from the city the remnant of the unbelieving nation. Perhaps he might plead the insolence of their prosperity, and their deadly hatred of the Christians, whose blood they had recently shed in a malicious or accidental tumult. Such crimes would have deserved the animadversion of the magistrate; but in this promiscuous outrage the innocent were confounded with the guilty, and Alexandria was impoverished by the loss of a wealthy and industrious colony. The zeal of Cyril exposed him to the penalties of the Julian law; but in a feeble government and a superstitious age he was secure of impunity, and even of praise. Orestes complained; but his just complaints were too quickly forgotten by the ministers of Theodosius, and too deeply remembered by a priest who affected to pardon, and continued to hate, the præfect of Egypt. As he passed through the streets his chariot was assaulted by a band of five hundred of the Nitrian monks; his guards fled from the wild beasts of the desert; his protestations that he was a Christian and a Catholic were answered by a volley of stones, and the face of Orestes was covered with blood. The loyal citizens of Alexandria hastened to his rescue; he instantly satisfied his justice and revenge against the monk by whose hand he had been wounded, and Ammonius expired under the rod of the lictor. At the command of Cyril his body was raised from the ground, and transported in solemn procession to the cathedral; the name of Ammonius was changed to that of Thaumasius, the *wonderful;* his tomb was decorated with the trophies of martyrdom; and the patriarch ascended the pulpit to celebrate the magnanimity of an assassin and a rebel. Such honours might incite the faithful to combat and die under the banners of the saint; and he soon prompted, or accepted, the sacrifice of a virgin, who professed the religion of the Greeks, and cultivated the friendship of Orestes. Hypatia, the daughter of Theon the mathematician,[25] was initiated in her father's studies; her learned comments have elucidated the geometry of Apollonius and Diophantus; and she publicly taught, both at Athens and Alexandria, the philosophy of Plato and Aristotle. In the bloom of beauty, and in the maturity of wisdom, the modest maid refused her lovers and instructed her disciples; the persons most illustrious for their rank or merit were impatient to visit the female philosopher; and Cyril beheld with a jealous eye the gorgeous train of horses and slaves who crowded the door of her academy. A rumour was spread among the Christians that the daughter of Theon was the only obstacle to the reconciliation of the præfect and the archbishop; and that obstacle was speedily removed. On a fatal day, in the holy season of Lent, Hypatia was torn from her chariot, stripped naked, dragged to the church, and inhumanly butchered by the hands of Peter the reader and a troop of savage and merciless fanatics: her flesh was scraped from her bones with sharp oyster-shells,[26] and her quivering limbs were delivered to the flames. The just progress of inquiry and punishment was stopped by seasonable gifts; but the murder of Hypatia has imprinted an indelible stain on the character and religion of Cyril of Alexandria.[27]

Superstition, perhaps, would more gently expiate the blood of a virgin than the banishment of a saint; and Cyril had accompanied his uncle to the iniquitous synod of the Oak. When the memory of Chrysostom was restored and consecrated, the nephew of Theophilus, at the head of a dying faction, still maintained the justice of his sentence; nor was it till after a tedious delay and an obstinate resistance that he yielded to the consent of the Catholic world.[28] His enmity to the Byzantine pontiffs[29] was a sense of interest, not a sally of passion: he envied their fortunate station in the sunshine of the Imperial court; and he dreaded their upstart ambition, which oppressed the metropolitans of Europe and Asia, invaded the provinces of Antioch and Alexandria, and measured their diocese by the limits of the empire. The long moderation of Atticus, the mild usurper of the throne of Chrysostom, suspended the animosities of the Eastern patriarchs; but Cyril was at length awakened by the exaltation of a rival more worthy of his esteem and hatred. After the short and troubled reign of Sisinnius, bishop of Constantinople, the factions of the clergy and people were appeased by the choice of the emperor, who, on this occasion, consulted the voice of fame, and invited the merit of a stranger. Nestorius,[30] a native of Germanicia and a monk of Antioch, was recommended by the austerity of his life and the eloquence of his sermons; but the first homily which he preached before the devout Theodosius betrayed the acrimony and impatience of his zeal. "Give me, O Cæsar!" he exclaimed, "give me the earth purged of heretics, and I will give you in exchange the kingdom of heaven. Exterminate with me the heretics, and with you I will exterminate the Persians." On the fifth day, as if the treaty had been already signed, the patriarch of Constantinople discovered, surprised, and attacked a secret conventicle of the Arians; they preferred death to submission; the flames that were kindled by their despair soon spread to the neighbouring houses, and the triumph of Nestorius was clouded by the name of *incendiary.* On either side of the Hellespont his episcopal vigour imposed a rigid formulary of faith and discipline— a chronological error concerning the festival of Easter was punished as an offence against the church and state. Lydia and Caria, Sardes and Miletus, were purified with the blood of the obstinate Quartodecimans; and the edict of the emperor, or rather of the patriarch, enumerates three-and-twenty degrees and denominations in the guilt and punishment of heresy.[31] But the sword of persecution which Nestorius so furiously wielded was soon turned against his own breast. Religion was the pretence; but, in the judgment of a contemporary saint, ambition was the genuine motive of episcopal warfare.[32]

In the Syrian school Nestorius had been taught to abhor the confusion of the two natures, and nicely to discriminate the humanity of his *master* Christ from the divinity of the *Lord* Jesus.[33] The Blessed Virgin he revered as the mother of Christ, but his ears were offended with the rash and recent title of mother of God,[34] which had been insensibly adopted since the origin of the Arian controversy. From the pulpit of Constantinople, a friend of the patriarch, and afterwards the patriarch himself, repeatedly preached against the use, or the abuse, of a word[35] unknown to the apostles, unauthorised by the church, and which could only tend to alarm the timorous, to mislead the simple, to amuse the profane, and to justify, by a seeming resemblance, the old genealogy of Olympus.[36] In his calmer moments Nestorius confessed that it might be tolerated or excused by the union of the two natures, and the communication of their *idioms:*[37] but he was exasperated by contradiction to disclaim the worship of a new-born, an infant Deity, to draw his inadequate similes from the conjugal or civil partnerships of life, and to describe the manhood of Christ as the robe, the instrument, the tabernacle of his Godhead. At these blasphemous sounds the pillars of the sanctuary were shaken. The unsuccessful competitors of Nestorius indulged their pious or personal resentment, the Byzantine clergy was secretly displeased with the intrusion of a stranger: whatever is superstitious or absurd might claim the protection of the monks; and the people was interested in the glory of their virgin patroness.[38] The sermons of the archbishop, and the service of the altar, were disturbed by seditious clamour; his authority and doctrine were renounced by separate congregations; every wind scattered round the empire the leaves of controversy; and the voice of the combatants on a sonorous theatre re-echoed in the cells of Palestine and Egypt. It was the duty of Cyril to enlighten the zeal and ignorance of his innumerable monks: in the school of Alexandria he had imbibed and professed the incarnation of one nature; and the successor of Athanasius consulted his pride and ambition when he rose in arms against another Arius, more formidable and more guilty, on the second throne of the hierarchy. After a short correspondence, in which the rival prelates disguised their hatred in the hollow language of respect and charity, the patriarch of Alexandria denounced to the prince and people, to the East and to the West, the damnable errors of the Byzantine pontiff. From the East, more especially from Antioch, he obtained the ambiguous counsels of toleration and silence, which were addressed to both parties while they favoured the cause of Nestorius. But the Vatican received with open arms the messengers of Egypt. The vanity of Celestine was flattered by the appeal; and the partial version of a monk decided the faith of the pope, who, with his Latin clergy, was ignorant of the language, the arts, and the theology of the Greeks. At the head of an Italian synod, Celestine weighed the merits of the cause, approved the creed of Cyril, condemned the sentiments and person of Nestorius, degraded the heretic from his episcopal dignity, allowed a respite of ten days for recantation and penance, and delegated to his enemy the execution of this rash and illegal sentence. But the patriarch of Alexandria, whilst he darted the thunders of a god, exposed the errors and passions of a mortal; and his twelve anathemas[39] still torture the orthodox slaves who adore the memory of a saint without forfeiting their allegiance to the synod of Chalcedon. These bold assertions are indelibly tinged with the colours of the Apollinarian heresy; but the serious, and perhaps the sincere, professions of Nestorius have satisfied the wiser and less partial theologians of the present times.[40]

Yet neither the emperor nor the primate of the East were disposed to obey the mandate of an Italian priest; and a synod of the Catholic, or rather of the Greek, church was unanimously demanded as the sole remedy that could appease or decide this ecclesiastical quarrel.[41] Ephesus, on all sides accessible by sea and land, was chosen for the place, the festival of Pentecost for the day, of the meeting; a writ of summons was despatched to each metropolitan, and a guard was stationed to protect and confine the fathers till they should settle the mysteries of heaven and the faith of the earth. Nestorius appeared not as a criminal, but as a judge; he depended on the weight rather than the number of his prelates, and his sturdy slaves from the baths of Zeuxippus were armed for every service of injury or defence. But his adversary Cyril was more powerful in the weapons both of the flesh and of the spirit. Disobedient to the letter, or at least to the meaning, of the royal summons, he was attended by fifty Egyptian bishops, who expected from their patriarch's nod the inspiration of the Holy Ghost. He had contracted an intimate alliance with Memnon bishop of Ephesus. The despotic primate of Asia disposed of the ready succours of thirty or forty episcopal votes: a crowd of peasants, the slaves of the church, was poured into the city to support with blows and clamours a metaphysical argument; and the people zealously asserted the honour of the Virgin, whose body reposed within the walls of Ephesus.[42] The fleet which had transported Cyril from Alexandria was laden with the riches of Egypt; and he disembarked a numerous body of mariners, slaves, and fanatics, enlisted with blind obedience under the banner of St. Mark and the mother of God. The fathers, and even the guards, of the council were awed by this martial array; the adversaries of Cyril and Mary were insulted in the streets or threatened in their houses; his eloquence and liberality made a daily increase in the number of his adherents; and the Egyptian soon computed that he might command the attendance and the voices of two hundred bishops.[43] But the author of the twelve anathemas foresaw and dreaded the opposition of John of Antioch, who, with a small though respectable train of metropolitans and divines, was advancing by slow journeys from the distant capital of the East. Impatient of a delay which he stigmatised as voluntary and culpable,[44] Cyril announced the opening of the synod sixteen days after the festival of Pentecost. Nestorius, who depended on the near approach of his Eastern friends, persisted, like his predecessor Chrysostom, to disclaim the jurisdiction, and to disobey the summons, of his enemies: they hastened his trial, and his accuser presided in the seat of judgment. Sixty-eight bishops, twenty-two of metropolitan rank, defended his cause by a modest and temperate protest: they were excluded from the councils of their brethren. Candidian, in the emperor's name, requested a delay of four days; the profane magistrate was driven with outrage and insult from the assembly of the saints. The whole of this momentous transaction was crowded into the compass of a summer's day: the bishops delivered their separate opinions; but the uniformity of style reveals the influence or the hand of a master, who has been accused of corrupting the public evidence of their acts and subscriptions.[45] Without a dissenting voice they recognised in the epistles of Cyril the Nicene creed and the doctrine of the fathers: but the partial extracts from the letters and homilies of Nestorius were interrupted by curses and anathemas; and the heretic was degraded from his episcopal and ecclesiastical dignity. The sentence, maliciously inscribed to the new Judas, was affixed and proclaimed in the streets of Ephesus: the weary prelates, as they issued from the church of the mother of God, were saluted as her champions; and her victory was celebrated by the illuminations, the songs, and the tumult of the night.

On the fifth day the triumph was clouded by the arrival and indignation of the Eastern bishops. In a chamber of the inn, before he had wiped the dust from his shoes, John of Antioch gave audience to Candidian the Imperial minister, who related his ineffectual efforts to prevent or to annul the hasty violence of the Egyptian. With equal haste and violence the Oriental synod of fifty bishops degraded Cyril and Memnon from their episcopal honours; condemned, in the twelve anathemas, the purest venom of the Apollinarian heresy; and described the Alexandrian primate as a monster, born and educated for the destruction of the church.[46] *His* throne was distant and inaccessible; but they instantly resolved to bestow on the flock of Ephesus the blessing of a faithful shepherd. By the vigilance of Memnon the churches were shut against them, and a strong garrison was thrown into the cathedral. The troops, under the command of Candidian, advanced to the assault; the outguards were routed and put to the sword, but the place was impregnable: the besiegers retired; their retreat was pursued by a vigorous sally; they lost their horses, and many of the soldiers were dangerously wounded with clubs and stones. Ephesus, the city of the Virgin, was defiled with rage and clamour, with sedition and blood; the rival synods darted anathemas and excommunications from their spiritual engines; and the court of Theodosius was perplexed by the adverse and contradictory narratives of the Syrian and Egyptian factions. During a busy period of three months the emperor tried every method, except the most effectual means of indifference and contempt, to reconcile this theological quarrel. He attempted to remove or intimidate the leaders by a common sentence of acquittal or condemnation; he invested his representatives at Ephesus with ample power and military force; he summoned from either party eight chosen deputies to a free and candid conference in the neighbourhood of the capital, far from the contagion of popular frenzy. But the Orientals refused to yield, and the Catholics, proud of their numbers and of their Latin allies, rejected all terms of union or toleration. The patience of the meek Theodosius was provoked, and he dissolved in anger this episcopal tumult, which at the distance of thirteen centuries assumes the venerable aspect of the third œcumenical council.[47] "God is my witness," said the pious prince, "that I am not the author of this confusion. His providence will discern and punish the guilty. Return to your provinces, and may your private virtues repair the mischief and scandal of your meeting." They returned to their provinces; but the same passions which had distracted the synod of Ephesus were diffused over the Eastern world. After three obstinate and equal campaigns, John of Antioch and Cyril of Alexandria condescended to explain and embrace: but their seeming re-union must be imputed rather to prudence than to reason, to the mutual lassitude rather than to the Christian charity of the patriarchs.

The Byzantine pontiff had instilled into the royal ear a baleful prejudice against the character and conduct of his Egyptian rival. An epistle of menace and invective,[48] which accompanied the summons, accused him as a busy, insolent, and envious priest, who perplexed the simplicity of the faith, violated the peace of the church and state, and, by his artful and separate addresses to the wife and sister of Theodosius, presumed to suppose, or to scatter, the seeds of discord in the Imperial family. At the stern command of his sovereign, Cyril had repaired to Ephesus, where he was resisted, threatened, and confined, by the magistrates in the interest of Nestorius and the Orientals, who assembled the troops of Lydia and Ionia to suppress the fanatic and disorderly train of the patriarch. Without expecting the royal licence, he escaped from his guards, precipitately embarked, deserted the imperfect synod, and retired to his episcopal fortress of safety and independence. But his artful emissaries, both in the court and city, successfully laboured to appease the resentment, and to conciliate the favour, of the emperor. The feeble son of Arcadius was alternately swayed by his wife and sister, by the eunuchs and women of the palace: superstition and avarice were their ruling passions; and the orthodox chiefs were assiduous in their endeavours to alarm the former and to gratify the latter. Constantinople and the suburbs were sanctified with frequent monasteries, and the holy abbots, Dalmatius and Eutyches,[49] had de-

voted their zeal and fidelity to the cause of Cyril, the worship of Mary, and the unity of Christ. From the first moment of their monastic life they had never mingled with the world, or trod the profane ground of the city. But in this awful moment of the danger of the church, their vow was superseded by a more sublime and indispensable duty. At the head of a long order of monks and hermits, who carried burning tapers in their hands, and chanted litanies to the mother of God, they proceeded from their monasteries to the palace. The people was edified and inflamed by this extraordinary spectacle, and the trembling monarch listened to the prayers and adjurations of the saints, who boldly pronounced that none could hope for salvation unless they embraced the person and the creed of the orthodox successor of Athanasius. At the same time every avenue of the throne was assaulted with gold. Under the decent names of *eulogies* and *benedictions*, the courtiers of both sexes were bribed according to the measure of their power and rapaciousness. But their incessant demands despoiled the sanctuaries of Constantinople and Alexandria; and the authority of the patriarch was unable to silence the just murmur of his clergy, that a debt of sixty thousand pounds had already been contracted to support the expense of this scandalous corruption.[50] Pulcheria, who relieved her brother from the weight of an empire, was the firmest pillar of orthodoxy; and so intimate was the alliance between the thunders of the synod and the whispers of the court, that Cyril was assured of success if he could displace one eunuch, and substitute another in the favour of Theodosius. Yet the Egyptian could not boast of a glorious or decisive victory. The emperor, with unaccustomed firmness, adhered to his promise of protecting the innocence of the Oriental bishops; and Cyril softened his anathemas, and confessed, with ambiguity and reluctance, a twofold nature of Christ, before he was permitted to satiate his revenge against the unfortunate Nestorius.[51]

The rash and obstinate Nestorius, before the end of the synod, was oppressed by Cyril, betrayed by the court, and faintly supported by his Eastern friends. A sentiment of fear or indignation prompted him, while it was yet time, to affect the glory of a voluntary abdication:[52] his wish, or at least his request, was readily granted; he was conducted with honour from Ephesus to his old monastery of Antioch; and, after a short pause, his successors, Maximian and Proclus, were acknowledged as the lawful bishops of Constantinople. But in the silence of his cell the degraded patriarch could no longer resume the innocence and security of a private monk. The past he regretted, he was discontented with the present, and the future he had reason to dread: the Oriental bishops successively disengaged their cause from his unpopular name, and each day decreased the number of the schismatics who revered Nestorius as the confessor of the faith. After a residence at Antioch of four years, the hand of Theodosius subscribed an edict[53] which ranked him with Simon the magician, proscribed his opinions and followers, condemned his writings to the flames, and banished his person first to Petra in Arabia, and at length to Oasis, one of the *islands* of the Libyan desert.[54] Secluded from the church and from the world, the exile was still pursued by the rage of bigotry and war. A wandering tribe of the Blemmyes or Nubians invaded his solitary prison: in their retreat they dismissed a crowd of useless captives; but no sooner had Nestorius reached the banks of the Nile, than he would gladly have escaped from a Roman and orthodox city to the milder servitude of the savages. His flight was punished as a new crime: the soul of the patriarch inspired the civil and ecclesiastical powers of Egypt; the magistrates, the soldiers, the monks, devoutly tortured the enemy of Christ and St. Cyril; and, as far as the confines of Æthiopia, the heretic was alternately dragged and recalled, till his aged body was broken by the hardships and accidents of these reiterated journeys. Yet his mind was still independent and erect; the president of Thebais was awed by his pastoral letters; he survived the Catholic tyrant of Alexandria, and, after sixteen years' banishment, the synod of Chalcedon would perhaps have restored him to the honours, or at least to the communion, of the church. The death of Nestorius prevented his obedience to their welcome summons;[55] and his disease might afford some colour to the scandalous report, that his tongue, the organ of blasphemy, had been eaten by the worms. He was buried in a city of Upper Egypt, known by the names of Chemnis, or Panopolis, or Akmim;[56] but the immortal malice of the Jacobites has persevered for ages to cast stones against his sepulchre, and to propagate the foolish tradition that it was never watered by the rain of heaven, which equally descends on the righteous and the ungodly.[57] Humanity may drop a tear on the fate of Nestorius; yet justice must observe that he suffered the persecution which he had approved and inflicted.[58]

The death of the Alexandrian primate, after a reign of thirty-two years, abandoned the Catholics to the intemperance of zeal and the abuse of victory.[59] The *monophysite* doctrine (one incarnate nature) was rigorously preached in the churches of Egypt and the monasteries of the East; the primitive creed of Apollinaris was protected by the sanctity of Cyril; and the name of EUTYCHES, his venerable friend, has been applied to the sect most adverse to the Syrian heresy of Nestorius. His rival Eutyches was the abbot, or archimandrite, or superior of three hundred monks; but the opinions of a simple and illiterate recluse might have expired in a cell where he had slept above seventy years if the resentment or indiscretion of Flavian, the Byzantine pontiff, had not exposed the scandal to the eyes of the Christian world. His domestic synod was instantly convened, their proceedings were sullied with clamour and artifice, and the aged heretic was surprised into a seeming confession that Christ had not derived his body from the substance of the Virgin Mary. From their partial decree Eutyches appealed to a general council; and his cause was vigorously asserted by his godson Chrysaphius, the reigning eunuch of the palace, and his accomplice Dioscorus, who had succeeded to the throne, the creed, the talents, and the vices of the nephew of Theophilus. By the special summons of Theodosius, the second synod of Ephesus was judiciously composed of ten metropolitans and ten bishops from each of the six dioceses of the Eastern empire: some exceptions of favour or merit enlarged the number to one hundred and thirty-five; and the Syrian Barsumas, as the chief and representative of the monks, was invited to sit and vote with the successors of the apostles. But the despotism of the Alexandrian patriarch again oppressed the freedom of debate; the same spiritual and carnal weapons were again drawn from the arsenals of Egypt; the Asiatic veterans, a band of archers, served under the orders of Dioscorus; and the more formidable monks, whose minds were inaccessible to reason or mercy, besieged the doors of the cathedral. The general and, as it should seem, the unconstrained voice of the fathers accepted the faith and even the anathemas of Cyril; and the heresy of the two natures was formally condemned in the persons and writings of the most learned Orientals. "May those who divide Christ be divided with the sword, may they be hewn in pieces, may they be burned alive!" were the charitable wishes of a Christian synod.[60] The innocence and sanctity of Eutyches were acknowledged without hesitation; but the prelates, more especially those of Thrace and Asia, were unwilling to depose their patriarch for the use or even the abuse of his lawful jurisdiction. They embraced the knees of Dioscorus, as he stood with a threatening aspect on the footstool of his throne, and conjured him to forgive the offences and to respect the dignity of his brother. "Do you mean to raise a sedition?" exclaimed the relentless tyrant. "Where are the officers?" At these words a furious multitude of monks and soldiers, with stakes, and swords, and chains, burst into the church: the trembling bishops hid themselves behind the altar or under the benches; and as they were not inspired with the zeal of martyrdom, they successively subscribed a blank paper, which was afterwards filled with the condemnation of the Byzantine pontiff. Flavian was instantly delivered to the wild beasts of this spiritual amphitheatre: the monks were stimulated by the voice and example of Barsumas to avenge the injuries of Christ: it is said that the patriarch of Alexandria reviled, and buffeted, and kicked, and trampled his brother of Constantinople:[61] it is certain that the victim, before he could reach the place of his exile, expired on the third day of the wounds and bruises which he had received at Ephesus. This second synod has been justly branded as a gang of robbers and assassins; yet the accusers of Dioscorus would magnify his violence, to alleviate the cowardice and inconstancy of their own behaviour.

The faith of Egypt had prevailed: but the vanquished party was supported by the same pope who encountered without fear the hostile rage of Attila and Genseric. The theology of Leo, his famous *tome* or epistle on the mystery of the incarnation, had been disregarded by the synod of Ephesus: his authority, and that of the Latin church, was insulted in his legates, who escaped from slavery and death to relate the melancholy tale of the tyranny of Dioscorus and the martyrdom of Flavian. His provincial synod annulled the irregular proceedings of Ephesus; but as this step was itself irregular, he solicited the convocation of a general council in the free and orthodox provinces of Italy. From his independent throne the Roman bishop spoke and acted without danger as the head of the Christians, and his dictates were obsequiously transcribed by Placidia and her son Valentinian, who addressed their Eastern colleague to restore the peace and unity of the church. But the pageant of Oriental royalty was moved with equal dexterity by the hand of the eunuch; and

Theodosius could pronounce, without hesitation, that the church was already peaceful and triumphant, and that the recent flame had been extinguished by the just punishment of the Nestorians. Perhaps the Greeks would be still involved in the heresy of the Monophysites, if the emperor's horse had not fortunately stumbled; Theodosius expired; his orthodox sister, Pulcheria, with a nominal husband, succeeded to the throne; Chrysaphius was burnt, Dioscorus was disgraced, the exiles were recalled, and the *tome* of Leo was subscribed by the Oriental bishops. Yet the pope was disappointed in his favourite project of a Latin council: he disdained to preside in the Greek synod which was speedily assembled at Nice in Bithynia; his legates required in a peremptory tone the presence of the emperor; and the weary fathers were transported to Chalcedon under the immediate eye of Marcian and the senate of Constantinople. A quarter of a mile from the Thracian Bosphorus the church of St. Euphemia was built on the summit of a gentle though lofty ascent: the triple structure was celebrated as a prodigy of art, and the boundless prospect of the land and sea might have raised the mind of a sectary to the contemplation of the God of the universe. Six hundred and thirty bishops were ranged in order in the nave of the church; but the patriarchs of the East were preceded by the legates, of whom the third was a simple priest; and the place of honour was reserved for twenty laymen of consular or senatorian rank. The gospel was ostentatiously displayed in the centre, but the rule of faith was defined by the papal and imperial ministers, who moderated the thirteen sessions of the council of Chalcedon.[62] Their partial interposition silenced the intemperate shouts and execrations which degraded the episcopal gravity; but, on the formal accusation of the legates, Dioscorus was compelled to descend from his throne to the rank of a criminal, already condemned in the opinion of his judges. The Orientals, less adverse to Nestorius than to Cyril, accepted the Romans as their deliverers: Thrace, and Pontus, and Asia, were exasperated against the murderer of Flavian, and the new patriarchs of Constantinople and Antioch secured their places by the sacrifice of their benefactor. The bishops of Palestine, Macedonia, and Greece were attached to the faith of Cyril; but in the face of the synod, in the heat of the battle, the leaders, with their obsequious train, passed from the right to the left wing, and decided the victory by this seasonable desertion. Of the seventeen suffragans who sailed from

Alexandria, four were tempted from their allegiance, and the thirteen, falling prostrate on the ground, implored the mercy of the council, with sighs and tears, and a pathetic declaration, that, if they yielded, they should be massacred, on their return to Egypt, by the indignant people. A tardy repentance was allowed to expiate the guilt or error of the accomplices of Dioscorus: but their sins were accumulated on his head; he neither asked nor hoped for pardon, and the moderation of those who pleaded for a general amnesty was drowned in the prevailing cry of victory and revenge. To save the reputation of his late adherents, some *personal* offences were skilfully detected; his rash and illegal excommunication of the pope, and his contumacious refusal (while he was detained a prisoner) to attend the summons of the synod. Witnesses were introduced to prove the special facts of his pride, avarice, and cruelty; and the fathers heard with abhorrence that the alms of the church were lavished on the female dancers, that his palace, and even his bath, was open to the prostitutes of Alexandria, and that the infamous Pansophia, or Irene, was publicly entertained as the concubine of the patriarch.[63]

For these scandalous offences Dioscorus was deposed by the synod and banished by the emperor; but the purity of his faith was declared in the presence, and with the tacit approbation, of the fathers. Their prudence supposed rather than pronounced the heresy of Eutyches, who was never summoned before their tribunal; and they sat silent and abashed when a bold Monophysite, casting at their feet a volume of Cyril, challenged them to anathematise in his person the doctrine of the saint. If we fairly peruse the acts of Chalcedon as they are recorded by the orthodox party,[64] we shall find that a great majority of the bishops embraced the simple unity of Christ; and the ambiguous concession that he was formed OF or FROM two natures might imply either their previous existence, or their subsequent confusion, or some dangerous interval between the conception of the man and the assumption of the God. The Roman theology, more positive and precise, adopted the term most offensive to the ears of the Egyptians, that Christ existed IN two natures; and this momentous particle[65] (which the memory, rather than the understanding, must retain) had almost produced a schism among the Catholic bishops. The *tome* of Leo had been respectfully, perhaps sincerely, subscribed; but they protested, in two successive debates, that it was neither expedient nor lawful to transgress the sacred landmarks

which had been fixed at Nice, Constantinople, and Ephesus, according to the rule of Scripture and tradition. At length they yielded to the importunities of their masters, but their infallible decree, after it had been ratified with deliberate votes and vehement acclamations, was overturned in the next session by the opposition of the legates and their Oriental friends. It was in vain that a multitude of episcopal voices repeated in chorus, "The definition of the fathers is orthodox and immutable! The heretics are now discovered! Anathema to the Nestorians! Let them depart from the synod! Let them repair to Rome."[66] The legates threatened, the emperor was absolute, and a committee of eighteen bishops prepared a new decree, which was imposed on the reluctant assembly. In the name of the fourth general council, the Christ in one person, but *in* two natures, was announced to the Catholic world: an invisible line was drawn between the heresy of Apollinaris and the faith of St. Cyril; and the road to paradise, a bridge as sharp as a razor, was suspended over the abyss by the master-hand of the theological artist. During ten centuries of blindness and servitude Europe received her religious opinions from the oracle of the Vatican; and the same doctrine, already varnished with the rust of antiquity, was admitted without dispute into the creed of the reformers, who disclaimed the supremacy of the Roman pontiff. The synod of Chalcedon still triumphs in the Protestant churches; but the ferment of controversy has subsided, and the most pious Christians of the present day are ignorant, or careless, of their own belief concerning the mystery of the incarnation.

Far different was the temper of the Greeks and Egyptians under the orthodox reigns of Leo and Marcian. Those pious emperors enforced with arms and edicts the symbol of their faith;[67] and it was declared by the conscience or honour of five hundred bishops, that the decrees of the synod of Chalcedon might be lawfully supported, even with blood. The Catholics observed with satisfaction that the same synod was odious both to the Nestorians and the Monophysites;[68] but the Nestorians were less angry, or less powerful, and the East was distracted by the obstinate and sanguinary zeal of the Monophysites. Jerusalem was occupied by an army of monks; in the name of the one incarnate nature, they pillaged, they burnt, they murdered; the sepulchre of Christ was defiled with blood; and the gates of the city were guarded in tumultuous rebellion against the troops of the emperor.

After the disgrace and exile of Dioscorus, the Egyptians still regretted their spiritual father, and detested the usurpation of his successor, who was introduced by the fathers of Chalcedon. The throne of Proterius was supported by a guard of two thousand soldiers; he waged a five years' war against the people of Alexandria; and on the first intelligence of the death of Marcian, he became the victim of their zeal. On the third day before the festival of Easter the patriarch was besieged in the cathedral, and murdered in the baptistery. The remains of his mangled corpse were delivered to the flames, and his ashes to the wind: and the deed was inspired by the vision of a pretended angel; an ambitious monk who, under the name of Timothy the Cat,[69] succeeded to the place and opinions of Dioscorus. This deadly superstition was inflamed on either side by the principle and the practice of retaliation: in the pursuit of a metaphysical quarrel many thousands[70] were slain, and the Christians of every degree were deprived of the substantial enjoyments of social life, and of the invisible gifts of baptism and the holy communion. Perhaps an extravagant fable of the times may conceal an allegorical picture of these fanatics, who tortured each other and themselves. "Under the consulship of Venantius and Celer," says a grave bishop, "the people of Alexandria, and all Egypt, were seized with a strange and diabolical frenzy: great and small, slaves and freedmen, monks and clergy, the natives of the land, who opposed the synod of Chalcedon, lost their speech and reason, barked like dogs, and tore, with their own teeth, the flesh from their hands and arms."[71]

The disorders of thirty years at length produced the famous HENOTICON[72] of the emperor Zeno, which in his reign, and in that of Anastasius, was signed by all the bishops of the East, under the penalty of degradation and exile if they rejected or infringed this salutary and fundamental law. The clergy may smile or groan at the presumption of a layman who defines the articles of faith; yet, if he stoops to the humiliating task, his mind is less infected by prejudice or interest, and the authority of the magistrate can only be maintained by the concord of the people. It is in ecclesiastical story that Zeno appears least contemptible; and I am not able to discern any Manichæan or Eutychian guilt in the generous saying of Anastasius, That it was unworthy of an emperor to persecute the worshippers of Christ and the citizens of Rome. The Henoticon was most pleasing to the Egyptians; yet the smallest blemish has not been descried

by the jealous and even jaundiced eyes of our orthodox schoolmen, and it accurately represents the Catholic faith of the incarnation, without adopting or disclaiming the peculiar terms or tenets of the hostile sects. A solemn anathema is pronounced against Nestorius and Eutyches; against all heretics by whom Christ is divided, or confounded, or reduced to a phantom. Without defining the number or the article of the word *nature*, the pure system of St. Cyril, the faith of Nice, Constantinople, and Ephesus, is respectfully confirmed; but, instead of bowing at the name of the fourth council, the subject is dismissed by the censure of all contrary doctrines, *if* any such have been taught either elsewhere or at Chalcedon. Under this ambiguous expression the friends and the enemies of the last synod might unite in a silent embrace. The most reasonable Christians acquiesced in this mode of toleration; but their reason was feeble and inconstant, and their obedience was despised as timid and servile by the vehement spirit of their brethren. On a subject which engrossed the thoughts and discourses of men, it was difficult to preserve an exact neutrality; a book, a sermon, a prayer, rekindled the flame of controversy; and the bonds of communion were alternately broken and renewed by the private animosity of the bishops. The space between Nestorius and Eutyches was filled by a thousand shades of language and opinion; the *acephali*[73] of Egypt, and the Roman pontiffs, of equal valour, though of unequal strength, may be found at the two extremities of the theological scale. The acephali, without a king or bishop, were separated above three hundred years from the patriarchs of Alexandria, who had accepted the communion of Constantinople, without exacting a formal condemnation of the synod of Chalcedon. For accepting the communion of Alexandria, without a formal approbation of the same synod, the patriarchs of Constantinople were anathematised by the popes. Their inflexible despotism involved the most orthodox of the Greek churches in this spiritual contagion, denied or doubted the validity of their sacraments,[74] and fomented, thirty-five years, the schism of the East and West, till they finally abolished the memory of four Byzantine pontiffs who had dared to oppose the supremacy of St. Peter.[75] Before that period the precarious truce of Constantinople and Egypt had been violated by the zeal of the rival prelates. Macedonius who was suspected of the Nestorian heresy, asserted, in disgrace and exile, the synod of Chalcedon, while the successor of Cyril would have purchased its overthrow with a bribe of two thousand pounds of gold.

In the fever of the times the sense, or rather the sound of a syllable, was sufficient to disturb the peace of an empire. The TRISAGION[76] (thrice holy), "Holy, holy, holy, Lord God of Hosts!" is supposed by the Greeks to be the identical hymn which the angels and cherubim eternally repeat before the throne of God, and which, about the middle of the fifth century, was miraculously revealed to the church of Constantinople. The devotion of Antioch soon added, "who was crucified for us!" and this grateful address, either to Christ alone, or to the whole Trinity, may be justified by the rules of theology, and has been gradually adopted by the Catholics of the East and West. But it had been imagined by a Monophysite bishop;[77] the gift of an enemy was at first rejected as a dire and dangerous blasphemy, and the rash innovation had nearly cost the emperor Anastasius his throne and his life.[78] The people of Constantinople was devoid of any rational principles of freedom; but they held, as a lawful cause of rebellion, the colour of a livery in the races, or the colour of a mystery in the schools. The Trisagion, with and without this obnoxious addition, was chanted in the cathedral by two adverse choirs, and, when their lungs were exhausted, they had recourse to the more solid arguments of sticks and stones; the aggressors were punished by the emperor, and defended by the patriarch; and the crown and mitre were staked on the event of this momentous quarrel. The streets were instantly crowded with innumerable swarms of men, women, and children; the legions of monks, in regular array, marched, and shouted, and fought at their head. "Christians! this is the day of martyrdom: let us not desert our spiritual father; anathema to the Manichæan tyrant! he is unworthy to reign." Such was the Catholic cry; and the galleys of Anastasius lay upon their oars before the palace, till the patriarch had pardoned his penitent, and hushed the waves of the troubled multitude. The triumph of Macedonius was checked by a speedy exile; but the zeal of his flock was again exasperated by the same question, "Whether one of the Trinity had been crucified?" On this momentous occasion the blue and green factions of Constantinople suspended their discord, and the civil and military powers were annihilated in their presence. The keys of the city, and the standards of the guards, were deposited in the forum of Constantine, the principal station and camp of the faithful. Day and night they were incessantly busied either in singing hymns to the honour of their God, or in pillaging and murdering the servants of their prince. The head of his favourite monk, the friend, as they styled him, of the enemy of the Holy Trinity, was borne aloft on a spear; and the fire-brands, which had been darted against heretical structures, diffused the undistinguishing flames over the most orthodox buildings. The statues of the emperor were broken, and his person was concealed in a suburb, till, at the end of three days, he dared to implore the mercy of his subjects. Without his diadem, and in the posture of a suppliant, Anastasius appeared on the throne of the circus. The Catholics, before his face, rehearsed their genuine Trisagion; they exulted in the offer which he proclaimed by the voice of a herald of abdicating the purple; they listened to the admonition, that, since *all* could not reign, they should previously agree in the choice of a sovereign: and they accepted the blood of two unpopular ministers, whom their master without hesitation condemned to the lions. These furious but transient seditions were encouraged by the success of Vitalian, who, with an army of Huns and Bulgarians, for the most part idolaters, declared himself the champion of the Catholic faith. In this pious rebellion he depopulated Thrace, besieged Constantinople, exterminated sixty-five thousand of his fellow-Christians, till he obtained the recall of the bishops, the satisfaction of the pope, and the establishment of the council of Chalcedon, an orthodox treaty, reluctantly signed by the dying Anastasius, and more faithfully performed by the uncle of Justinian. And such was the event of the *first* of the religious wars which have been waged in the name and by the disciples of the God of Peace.[79]

Justinian has been already seen in the various lights of a prince, a conqueror, and a lawgiver: the theologian[80] still remains, and it affords an unfavourable prejudice that his theology should form a very prominent feature of his portrait. The sovereign sympathised with his subjects in their superstitious reverence for living and departed saints: his Code, and more especially his Novels, confirm and enlarge the privileges of the clergy; and in every dispute between a monk and a layman, the partial judge was inclined to pronounce that truth and innocence and justice were always on the side of the church. In his public and private devotions the emperor was assiduous and exemplary; his prayers, vigils, and fasts displayed the austere penance of a monk; his fancy was amused by the hope or belief of personal inspiration; he had secured the patronage of the Virgin and St. Michael the archangel; and his recovery from a dangerous disease was ascribed to the miraculous succour of the holy martyrs Cosmas and Damian. The capital and the provinces of the East were decorated with the monuments of his religion;[81] and though the far greater part of these costly structures may be attributed to his taste or ostentation, the zeal of the royal architect was probably quickened by a genuine sense of love and gratitude towards his invisible benefactors. Among the titles of Imperial greatness the name of *Pious* was most pleasing to his ear; to promote the temporal and spiritual interest of the church was the serious business of his life; and the duty of father of his country was often sacrificed to that of defender of the faith. The controversies of the times were congenial to his temper and understanding; and the theological professors must inwardly deride the diligence of a stranger who cultivated their art and neglected his own. "What can ye fear," said a bold conspirator to his associates, "from your bigoted tyrant? Sleepless and unarmed he sits whole nights in his closet debating with reverend greybeards, and turning over the pages of ecclesiastical volumes."[82] The fruits of these lucubrations were displayed in many a conference, where Justinian might shine as the loudest and most subtle of the disputants; in many a sermon which, under the name of edicts and epistles, proclaimed to the empire the theology of their master. While the barbarians invaded the provinces, while the victorious legions marched under the banners of Belisarius and Narses, the successor of Trajan, unknown to the camp, was content to vanquish at the head of a synod. Had he invited to these synods a disinterested and rational spectator, Justinian might have learned "*that* religious controversy is the offspring of arrogance and folly; *that* true piety is most laudably expressed by silence and submission; *that* man, ignorant of his own nature, should not presume to scrutinise the nature of his God; and *that* it is sufficient for us to know that power and benevolence are the perfect attributes of the Deity."[83]

Toleration was not the virtue of the times, and indulgence to rebels has seldom been the virtue of princes. But when the prince descends to the narrow and peevish character of a disputant, he is easily provoked to supply the defect of argument by the plenitude of power, and to chastise without mercy the perverse blindness of those who wilfully shut their eyes against the light of demonstration. The reign of Justinian was a uniform yet various scene of persecution; and he appears to have surpassed his indolent predecessors, both in the contrivance of his laws and the rigour of their execution. The insufficient term of three months was assigned for the conversion or exile of all heretics;[84] and if he still connived at their precarious stay, they were deprived, under his iron yoke, not only of the benefits of society, but of the common birthright of men and Christians.

At the end of four hundred years the Montanists of Phrygia[85] still breathed the wild enthusiasm of perfection and prophecy which they had imbibed from their male and female apostles, the special organs of the Paraclete. On the approach of the Catholic priests and soldiers, they grasped with alacrity the crown of martyrdom; the conventicle and the congregation perished in the flames, but these primitive fanatics were not extinguished three hundred years after the death of their tyrant. Under the protection of the Gothic confederates, the church of the Arians at Constantinople had braved the severity of the laws: their clergy equalled the wealth and magnificence of the senate; and the gold and silver which were seized by the rapacious hand of Justinian might perhaps be claimed as the spoils of the provinces and the trophies of the barbarians. A secret remnant of pagans, who still lurked in the most refined and most rustic conditions of mankind, excited the indignation of the Christians, who were perhaps unwilling that any strangers should be the witnesses of their intestine quarrels. A bishop was named as the inquisitor of the faith, and his diligence soon discovered, in the court and city, the magistrates, lawyers, physicians, and sophists, who still cherished the superstition of the Greeks. They were sternly informed that they must choose without delay between the displeasure of Jupiter or Justinian, and that their aversion to the gospel could no longer be disguised under the scandalous mask of indifference or impiety. The patrician Photius perhaps alone was resolved to live and to die like his ancestors: he enfranchised himself with the stroke of a dagger, and left his tyrant the poor consolation of exposing with ignominy the lifeless corpse of the fugitive. His weaker brethren submitted to their earthly monarch, underwent the ceremony of baptism, and laboured, by their extraordinary zeal, to erase the suspicion, or to expiate the guilt, of idolatry. The native country of Homer, and the theatre of the Trojan war, still retained the last sparks of his mythology: by the care of the same bishop, seventy thousand pagans were detected and converted in Asia, Phrygia, Lydia, and Caria; ninety-six churches were built for the new proselytes; and linen vestments, bibles and liturgies, and vases of gold and silver, were supplied by the pious munificence of Justinian.[86] The Jews, who had been gradually stripped of their immunities, were oppressed by a vexatious law, which compelled them to observe the festival of Easter the same day on which it was celebrated by the Christians.[87] And they might complain with the more reason, since the Catholics themselves did not agree with the astronomical calculations of their sovereign: the people of Constantinople delayed the beginning of their Lent a whole week after it had been ordained by authority; and they had the pleasure of fasting seven days, while meat was exposed for sale by the command of the emperor. The Samaritans of Palestine[88] were a motley race, an ambiguous sect, rejected as Jews by the pagans, by the Jews as schismatics, and by the Christians as idolators. The abomination of the cross had already been planted on their holy mount of Garizim,[89] but the persecution of Justinian offered only the alternative of baptism or rebellion. They chose the latter: under the standard of a desperate leader they rose in arms, and retaliated their wrongs on the lives, the property, and the temples of a defenceless people. The Samaritans were finally subdued by the regular forces of the East: twenty thousand were slain, twenty thousand were sold by the Arabs to the infidels of Persia and India, and the remains of that unhappy nation atoned for the crime of treason by the sin of hypocrisy. It has been computed that one hundred thousand Roman subjects were extirpated in the Samaritan war,[90] which converted the once fruitful province into a desolate and smoking wilderness. But in the creed of Justinian the guilt of murder could not be applied to the slaughter of unbelievers; and he piously laboured to establish with fire and sword the unity of the Christian faith.[91]

With these sentiments, it was incumbent on him, at least, to be always in the right. In the first years of his administration he signalised his zeal as the disciple and patron of orthodoxy: the reconciliation of the Greeks and Latins established the *tome* of St. Leo as the creed of the emperor and the empire; the Nestorians and Eutychians were exposed, on either side, to the double edge of persecution; and the four synods, of Nice, Constantinople, Ephesus, and *Chalcedon*, were ratified by the code of a Catholic lawgiver.[92] But while Justinian strove to maintain

the uniformity of faith and worship, his wife Theodora, whose vices were not incompatible with devotion, had listened to the Monophysite teachers; and the open or clandestine enemies of the church revived and multiplied at the smile of their gracious patroness. The capital, the palace, the nuptial bed, were torn by spiritual discord; yet so doubtful was the sincerity of the royal consorts, that their seeming disagreement was imputed by many to a secret and mischievous confederacy against the religion and happiness of their people.[93] The famous dispute of the THREE CHAPTERS,[94] which has filled more volumes than it deserves lines, is deeply marked with this subtle and disingenuous spirit. It was now three hundred years since the body of Origen[95] had been eaten by the worms: his soul, of which he held the pre-existence, was in the hands of its Creator; but his writings were eagerly perused by the monks of Palestine. In these writings the piercing eye of Justinian descried more than ten metaphysical errors; and the primitive doctor, in the company of Pythagoras and Plato, was devoted by the clergy to the *eternity* of hell-fire, which he had presumed to deny. Under the cover of this precedent a treacherous blow was aimed at the council of Chalcedon. The fathers had listened without impatience to the praise of Theodore of Mopsuestia;[96] and their justice or indulgence had restored both Theodoret of Cyrrhus and Ibas of Edessa to the communion of the church. But the characters of these Oriental bishops were tainted with the reproach of heresy; the first had been the master, the two others were the friends, of Nestorius: their most suspicious passages were accused under the title of the *three chapters*; and the condemnation of their memory must involve the honour of a synod whose name was pronounced with sincere or affected reverence by the Catholic world. If these bishops, whether innocent or guilty, were annihilated in the sleep of death, they would not probably be awakened by the clamour which, after a hundred years, was raised over their grave. If they were already in the fangs of the demon, their torments could neither be aggravated nor assuaged by human industry. If in the company of saints and angels they enjoyed the rewards of piety, they must have smiled at the idle fury of the theological insects who still crawled on the surface of the earth. The foremost of these insects, the emperor of the Romans, darted his sting, and distilled his venom, perhaps without discerning the true motives of Theodora and her ecclesiastical faction. The victims were no longer subject to his power, and the vehement style of his edicts could only proclaim their damnation, and invite the clergy of the East to join in a full chorus of curses and anathemas. The East, with some hesitation, consented to the voice of her sovereign: the fifth general council, of three patriarchs and one hundred and sixty-five bishops, was held at Constantinople; and the authors, as well as the defenders of the three chapters, were separated from the communion of the saints, and solemnly delivered to the prince of darkness. But the Latin churches were more jealous of the honour of Leo and the synod of Chalcedon; and if they had fought as they usually did under the standard of Rome, they might have prevailed in the cause of reason and humanity. But their chief was a prisoner in the hands of the enemy; the throne of St. Peter, which had been disgraced by the simony, was betrayed by the cowardice, of Vigilius, who yielded, after a long and inconsistent struggle, to the despotism of Justinian and the sophistry of the Greeks. His apostasy provoked the indignation of the Latins, and no more than two bishops could be found who would impose their hands on his deacon and successor Pelagius. Yet the perseverance of the popes insensibly transferred to their adversaries the appellation of schismatics; the Illyrian, African, and Italian churches were oppressed by the civil and ecclesiastical powers, not without some effort of military force;[97] the distant barbarians transcribed the creed of the Vatican, and, in the period of a century, the schism of the three chapters expired in an obscure angle of the Venetian province.[98] But the religious discontent of the Italians had already promoted the conquests of the Lombards, and the Romans themselves were accustomed to suspect the faith, and to detest the government, of their Byzantine tyrant.

Justinian was neither steady nor consistent in the nice process of fixing his volatile opinions and those of his subjects. In his youth he was offended by the slightest deviation from the orthodox line; in his old age he transgressed the measure of temperate heresy, and the Jacobites, not less than the Catholics, were scandalised by his declaration that the body of Christ was incorruptible, and that his manhood was never subject to any wants and infirmities, the inheritance of our mortal flesh. This *fantastic* opinion was announced in the last edicts of Justinian; and at the moment of his seasonable departure, the clergy had refused to subscribe, the prince was prepared to persecute, and the people were resolved to suffer or resist. A bishop of Trèves, secure beyond the limits of his power, addressed the monarch of the East in the language of authority and affection. "Most gracious Justinian, remember your baptism and your creed. Let not your grey hairs be defiled with heresy. Recall your fathers from exile, and your followers from perdition. You cannot be ignorant that Italy and Gaul, Spain and Africa, already deplore your fall and anathematise your name. Unless, without delay, you destroy what you have taught; unless you exclaim with a loud voice, I have erred, I have sinned, anathema to Nestorius, anathema to Eutyches, you deliver your soul to the same flames in which *they* will eternally burn." He died and made no sign.[99] His death restored in some degree the peace of the church, and the reigns of his four successors, Justin, Tiberius, Maurice, and Phocas, are distinguished by a rare, though fortunate, vacancy in the ecclesiastical history of the East.[100]

The faculties of sense and reason are least capable of acting on themselves; the eye is most inaccessible to the sight, the soul to the thought; yet we think, and even feel, that *one will*, a sole principle of action, is essential to a rational and conscious being. When Heraclius returned from the Persian war, the orthodox hero consulted his bishops whether the Christ whom he adored, of one person but of two natures, was actuated by a single or a double will. They replied in the singular, and the emperor was encouraged to hope that the Jacobites of Egypt and Syria might be reconciled by the profession of a doctrine most certainly harmless and most probably true, since it was taught even by the Nestorians themselves.[101] The experiment was tried without effect, and the timid or vehement Catholics condemned even the semblance of a retreat in the presence of a subtle and audacious enemy. The orthodox (the prevailing) party devised new modes of speech, and argument, and interpretation: to either nature of Christ they speciously applied a proper and distinct energy; but the difference was no longer visible when they allowed that the human and the divine will were invariably the same.[102] The disease was attended with the customary symptoms; but the Greek clergy, as if satiate with the endless controversy of the incarnation, instilled a healing counsel into the ear of the prince and people. They delcared themselves MONOTHELITES (asserters of the unity of will), but they treated the words as new, the questions as superfluous; and recommended a religious silence as the most agreeable to the prudence and charity of the gospel. This law of silence was successively imposed by the *ecthesis* or exposition of Heraclius, the *type* or model of his grandson Constans;[103] and the Imperial edicts were subscribed with alacrity or reluctance by the four patriarchs of Rome, Constantinople, Alexandria, and Antioch. But the bishop and monks of Jerusalem sounded the alarm: in the language, or even in the silence, of the Greeks, the Latin churches detected a latent heresy; and the obedience of pope Honorius to the commands of his sovereign was retracted and censured by the bolder ignorance of his successors. They condemned the execrable and abominable heresy of the Monothelites, who revived the errors of Manes, Apollinaris, Eutyches, etc.; they signed the sentence of excommunication on the tomb of St. Peter; the ink was mingled with the sacramental wine, the blood of Christ; and no ceremony was omitted that could fill the superstitious mind with horror and affright. As the representative of the Western church, pope Martin and his Lateran synod anathematised the perfidious and guilty silence of the Greeks: one hundred and five bishops of Italy, for the most part the subjects of Constans, presumed to reprobate his wicked *type* and the impious *ecthesis* of his grandfather; and to confound the authors and their adherents with the twenty-one notorious heretics, the apostates from the church and the organs of the devil. Such an insult under the tamest reign could not pass with impunity. Pope Martin ended his days on the inhospitable shore of the Tauric Chersonesus, and his oracle, the abbot Maximus, was inhumanly chastised by the amputation of his tongue and his right hand.[104] But the same invincible spirit survived in their successors; and the triumph of the Latins avenged their recent defeat and obliterated the disgrace of the three chapters. The synods of Rome were confirmed by the sixth general council of Constantinople, in the palace and the presence of a new Constantine, a descendant of Heraclius. The royal convert converted the Byzantine pontiff and a majority of the bishops;[105] the dissenters, with their chief, Macarius of Antioch, were condemned to the spiritual and temporal pains of heresy; the East condescended to accept the lessons of the West; and the creed was finally settled which teaches the Catholics of every age that two wills or energies are harmonised in the person of Christ. The majesty of the pope and the Roman synod was represented by two priests, one deacon, and three bishops; but these obscure Latins had neither arms to compel, nor treasures to bribe, nor language to persuade; and I am ignorant by what arts they could determine the lofty emperor of the Greeks to abjure the catechism of his infancy, and to persecute the religion of his fathers. Perhaps the monks and people of Constantinople[106] were favourable to the Lateran creed, which is indeed the least reasonable of the two; and the suspicion is countenanced by the unnatural moderation of the Greek clergy, who appear in this quarrel to be conscious of their weakness. While the synod debated, a fanatic proposed a more summary decision, by raising a dead man to life: the prelates assisted at the trial; but the acknowledged failure may serve to indicate that the passions and prejudices of the multitude were not enlisted on the side of the Monothelites. In the next generation, when the son of Constantine was deposed and slain by the disciple of Macarius, they tasted the feast of revenge and dominion; the image or monument of the sixth council was defaced, and the original acts were committed to the flames. But in the second year their patron was cast headlong from the throne, the bishops of the East were released from their occasional conformity, the Roman faith was more firmly replanted by the orthodox successors of Bardanes, and the fine problems of the incarnation were forgotten in the more popular and visible quarrel of the worship of images.[107]

Before the end of the seventh century the creed of the incarnation, which had been defined at Rome and Constantinople, was uniformly preached in the remote islands of Britain and Ireland;[108] the same ideas were entertained, or rather the same words were repeated, by all the Christians whose liturgy was performed in the Greek or the Latin tongue. Their numbers and visible splendour bestowed an imperfect claim to the appellation of Catholics: but in the East they were marked with the less honourable name of *Melchites*, or Royalists;[109] of men whose faith, instead of resting on the basis of Scripture, reason, or tradition, had been established, and was still maintained, by the arbitrary power of a temporal monarch. Their adversaries might allege the words of the fathers of Constantinople who profess themselves the slaves of the king; and they might relate, with malicious joy, how the decrees of Chalcedon had been inspired and reformed by the emperor Marcian and his virgin bride. The prevailing faction will naturally inculate the duty of submission, nor is it less natural that dissenters should feel and assert the principles of freedom. Under the rod of persecution the Nestorians and Monophysites degenerated into rebels and fugitives; and the most ancient and useful allies of Rome were taught to consider the emperor not as the chief but as the enemy of the Christians. Language, the leading principle which unites or separates the tribes of mankind, soon discriminated the sectaries of the East by a peculiar and pepetual badge which abolished the means of intercourse and the hope or reconciliation. The long dominion of the Greeks, their colonies, and above all their eloquence, had propagated a language doubtless the most perfect that has been contrived by the art of man. Yet the body of the people, both in Syria and Egypt, still persevered in the use of their national idioms; with this difference, however, that the Coptic was confined to the rude and illiterate peasants of the Nile, while the Syriac,[110] from the mountains of Assyria to the Red Sea, was adapted to the higher topics of poetry and argument. Armenia and Abyssinia were infected by the speech or learning of the Greeks; and their barbaric tongues, which have been revived in the studies of modern Europe, were unintelligible to the inhabitants of the Roman empire. The Syriac and the Coptic, the Armenian and the Æthiopic, are consecrated in the service of their respective churches; and their theology is enriched by domestic versions[111] both of the scriptures and of the most popular fathers. After a period of thirteen hundred and sixty years, the spark of controversy, first kindled by a sermon of Nestorius, still burns in the bosom of the East, and the hostile communions still maintain the faith and discipline of their founders. In the most abject state of ignorance, poverty, and servitude, the Nestorians and Monophysites reject the spiritual supremacy of Rome, and cherish the toleration of their Turkish masters, which allows them to anathematise, on one hand, St. Cyril and the synod of Ephesus; on the other, pope Leo and the council of Chalcedon. The weight which they cast into the downfall of the Eastern empire demands our notice, and the reader may be amused with the various prospect of, I. The Nestorians; II. The Jacobites;[112] III. The Maronites; IV. The Armenians; V. The Copts; and VI. The Abyssinians. To the three former the Syriac is common; but of the latter, each is discriminated by the use of a national idiom. Yet the modern natives of Armenia and Abyssinia would be incapable of conversing with their ancestors; and the Christians of Egypt and Syria, who reject the religion, have adopted the language, of the Arabians. The lapse of time has seconded the sacerdotal arts; and in the East as well as in the West

the Deity is addressed in an obsolete tongue unknown to the majority of the congregation.

I. Both in his native and his episcopal province the heresy of the unfortunate Nestorius was speedily obliterated. The Oriental bishops, who at Ephesus had resisted to his face the arrogance of Cyril, were mollified by his tardy concessions. The same prelates, or their successors, subscribed, not without a murmur, the decrees of Chalcedon; the power of the Monophysites reconciled them with the Catholics in the conformity of passion, of interest, and, insensibly, of belief; and their last reluctant sigh was breathed in the defence of the three chapters. Their dissenting brethren, less moderate or more sincere, were crushed by the penal laws; and, as early as the reign of Justinian, it became difficult to find a church of Nestorians within the limits of the Roman empire. Beyond those limits they had discovered a new world in which they might hope for liberty and aspire to conquest. In Persia, notwithstanding the resistance of the Magi, Christianity had struck a deep root, and the nations of the East reposed under its salutary shade. The *catholic*, or primate, resided in the capital: in *his* synods, and in *their* dioceses, his metropolitans, bishops, and clergy represented the pomp and order of a regular hierarchy: they rejoiced in the increase of proselytes, who were converted from the Zendavesta to the Gospel, from the secular to the monastic life; and their zeal was stimulated by the presence of an artful and formidable enemy. The Persian church had been founded by the missionaries of Syria; and their language, discipline, and doctrine were closely interwoven with its original frame. The *catholics* were elected and ordained by their own suffragans; but their filial dependence on the patriarchs of Antioch is attested by the canons of the Oriental church.[113] In the Persian school of Edessa,[114] the rising generations of the faithful imbibed their theological idiom: they studied in the Syriac version the ten thousand volumes of Theodore of Mopsuestia; and they revered the apostolic faith and holy martyrdom of his disciple Nestorius, whose person and language were equally unknown to the nations beyond the Tigris. The first indelible lesson of Ibas, bishop of Edessa, taught them to execrate the *Egyptians*, who, in the synod of Ephesus, had impiously confounded the two natures of Christ. The flight of the masters and scholars, who were twice expelled from the Athens of Syria, dispersed a crowd of missionaries inflamed by the double zeal of religion and revenge. And the rigid unity of the

Monophysites, who, under the reigns of Zeno and Anastasius, had invaded the thrones of the East, provoked their antagonists in a land of freedom to avow a moral, rather than a physical, union of the two persons of Christ. Since the first preaching of the gospel the Sassanian kings beheld with an eye of suspicion a race of aliens and apostates who had embraced the religion, and who might favour the cause, of the hereditary foes of their country. The royal edicts had often prohibited their dangerous correspondence with the Syrian clergy: the progress of the schism was grateful to the jealous pride of Perozes, and he listened to the eloquence of an artful prelate, who painted Nestorius as the friend of Persia, and urged him to secure the fidelity of his Christian subjects by granting a just preference to the victims and enemies of the Roman tyrant. The Nestorians composed a large majority of the clergy and people: they were encouraged by the smile, and armed with the sword, of despotism; yet many of their weaker brethren were startled at the thought of breaking loose from the communion of the Christian world, and the blood of seven thousand seven hundred Monophysites or Catholics confirmed the uniformity of faith and discipline in the churches of Persia.[115] Their ecclesiastical institutions are distinguished by a liberal principle of reason, or at least of policy: the austerity of the cloister was relaxed and gradually forgotten: houses of charity were endowed for the education of orphans and foundlings; the law of celibacy, so forcibly recommended to the Greeks and Latins, was disregarded by the Persian clergy; and the number of the elect was multiplied by the public and reiterated nuptials of the priests, the bishops, and even the patriarch himself. To this standard of natural and religious freedom myriads of fugitives resorted from all the provinces of the Eastern empire; the narrow bigotry of Justinian was punished by the emigration of his most industrious subjects; they transported into Persia the arts both of peace and war: and those who deserved the favour were promoted in the service of a discerning monarch. The arms of Nushirvan, and his fiercer grandson, were assisted with advice, and money, and troops, by the desperate sectaries who still lurked in their native cities of the East: their zeal was rewarded with the gift of the Catholic churches; but when those cities and churches were recovered by Heraclius, their open profession of treason and heresy compelled them to seek a refuge in the realm of their foreign ally. But the seeming tranquillity of the Nestorians was often endangered and sometimes overthrown. They were involved in the common evils of Oriental despotism: their enmity to Rome could not always atone for their attachment to the gospel: and a colony of three hundred thousand Jacobites, the captives of Apamea and Antioch, was permitted to erect a hostile altar in the face of the *catholic* and in the sunshine of the court. In his last treaty Justinian introduced some conditions which tended to enlarge and fortify the toleration of Christianity in Persia. The emperor, ignorant of the rights of conscience, was incapable of pity or esteem for the heretics who denied the authority of the holy synods: but he flattered himself that they would gradually perceive the temporal benefits of union with the empire and the Church of Rome; and if he failed in exciting their gratitude, he might hope to provoke the jealousy of their sovereign. In a later age the Lutherans have been burnt at Paris and protected in Germany, by the superstition and policy of the most Christian king.

The desire of gaining souls for God and subjects for the church has excited in every age the diligence of the Christian priests. From the conquest of Persia, they carried their spiritual arms to the north, the east, and the south; and the simplicity of the gospel was fashioned and painted with the colours of the Syriac theology. In the sixth century, according to the report of a Nestorian traveller,[116] Christianity was successfully preached to the Bactrians, the Huns, the Persians, the Indians, the Persarmenians, the Medes, and the Elamites: the barbaric churches, from the Gulf of Persia to the Caspian Sea, were almost infinite; and their recent faith was conspicuous in the number and sanctity of their monks and martyrs. The pepper coast of Malabar and the isles of the ocean, Socotora and Ceylon, were peopled with an increasing multitude of Christians; and the bishops and clergy of those sequestered regions derived their ordination from the catholic of Babylon. In a subsequent age the zeal of the Nestorians overleaped the limits which had confined the ambition and curiosity both of the Greeks and Persians. The missionaries of Balch and Samarcand pursued without fear the footsteps of the roving Tartar, and insinuated themselves into the camps of the valleys of Imaus and the banks of the Selinga. They exposed a metaphysical creed to those illiterate shepherds: to those sanguinary warriors they recommended humanity and repose. Yet a khan, whose power they vainly magnified, is said to have received at their hands the rites of baptism and even of ordination; and the fame of *Prester* or *Presbyter* John[117] has long amused the credulity of Europe. The royal convert was indulged in the use of a portable altar; but he despatched an embassy to the patriarch to inquire how, in the season of Lent, he should abstain from animal food, and how he might celebrate the Eucharist in a desert that produced neither corn nor wine. In their progress by sea and land the Nestorians entered China by the port of Canton and the northern residence of Sigan. Unlike the senators of Rome, who assumed with a smile the characters of priests and augurs, the mandarins, who affect in public the reason of philosophers, are devoted in private to every mode of popular superstition. They cherished and they confounded the gods of Palestine and of India; but the propagation of Christianity awakened the jealousy of the state, and, after a short vicissitude of favour and persecution, the foreign sect expired in ignorance and oblivion.[118] Under the reign of the caliphs the Nestorian church was diffused from China to Jerusalem and Cyprus; and their numbers, with those of the Jacobites, were computed to surpass the Greek and Latin communions.[119] Twenty-five metropolitans or archbishops composed their hierarchy; but several of these were dispensed, by the distance and danger of the way, from the duty of personal attendance, on the easy condition that every six years they should testify their faith and obedience to the *catholic* or patriarch of Babylon, a vague appellation which has been successively applied to the royal seats of Seleucia, Ctesiphon, and Bagdad. These remote branches are long since withered; and the old patriarchal trunk[120] is now divided by the *Elijahs* of Mosul, the representatives almost in lineal descent of the genuine and primitive succession; the *Josephs* of Amida, who are reconciled to the church of Rome;[121] and the *Simeons* of Van or Ormia, whose revolt, at the head of forty thousand families, was promoted in the sixteenth century by the Sophis of Persia. The number of three hundred thousand is allowed for the whole body of the Nestorians, who, under the name of Chaldæans or Assyrians, are confounded with the most learned or the most powerful nation of Eastern antiquity.

According to the legend of antiquity, the gospel was preached in India by St. Thomas.[122] At the end of the ninth century his shrine, perhaps in the neighbourhood of Madras, was devoutly visited by the ambassadors of Alfred: and their return with a cargo of pearls and spices rewarded the zeal of the English monarch, who entertained the largest projects of trade and discovery.[123] When the Portuguese first opened the navigation of India, the Christians of St. Thomas had been seated for ages on the coast of Malabar, and the difference of their character and colour attested the mixture of a foreign race. In arms, in arts, and possibly in virtue, they excelled the natives of Hindostan; the husbandmen cultivated the palm tree, the merchants were enriched by the pepper trade, the soldiers preceded the *nairs* or nobles of Malabar, and their hereditary privileges were respected by the gratitude or the fear of the king of Cochin and the Zamorin himself. They acknowledged a Gentoo sovereign, but they were governed, even in temporal concerns, by the bishop of Angamala. He still asserted his ancient title of metropolitan of India, but his real jurisdiction was exercised in fourteen hundred churches, and he was intrusted with the care of two hundred thousand souls. Their religion would have rendered them the firmest and most cordial allies of the Portuguese; but the inquisitors soon discerned in the Christians of St. Thomas the unpardonable guilt of heresy and schism. Instead of owning themselves the subjects of the Roman pontiff, the spiritual and temporal monarch of the globe, they adhered, like their ancestors, to the communion of the Nestorian patriarch; and the bishops whom he ordained at Mosul traversed the dangers of the sea and land to reach their diocese on the coast of Malabar. In their Syriac liturgy the names of Theodore and Nestorius were piously commemorated: they united their adoration of the two persons of Christ; the title of Mother of God was offensive to their ear; and they measured with scrupulous avarice the honours of the Virgin Mary, whom the superstition of the Latins had *almost* exalted to the rank of a goddess. When her image was first presented to the disciples of St. Thomas they indignantly exclaimed, "We are Christians, not idolators!" and their simple devotion was content with the veneration of the cross. Their separation from the Western world had left them in ignorance of the improvements or corruptions of a thousand years; and their conformity with the faith and practice of the fifth century would equally disappoint the prejudices of a Papist or a Protestant. It was the first care of the ministers of Rome to intercept all correspondence with the Nestorian patriarch, and several of his bishops expired in the prisons of the holy office. The flock, without a shepherd, was assaulted by the power of the Portuguese, the arts of the Jesuits, and the zeal of Alexis de Menezes, archbishop of Goa, in his personal visitation of the coast of Malabar. The synod of Diamper, at which he presided, consummated the pious work of the re-union, and rigorously imposed the doctrine and discipline of the Roman church, without forgetting auricular confession, the strongest engine of ecclesiastical torture. The memory of Theodore and Nestorius was condemned, and Malabar was reduced under the dominion of the pope, of the primate, and of the Jesuits who invaded the see of Angamala or Cranganor. Sixty years of servitude and hypocrisy were patiently endured; but as soon as the Portuguese empire was shaken by the courage and industry of the Dutch, the Nestorians asserted with vigour and effect the religion of their fathers. The Jesuits were incapable of defending the power which they had abused; the arms of forty thousand Christians were pointed against their falling tyrants; and the Indian archdeacon assumed the character of bishop till a fresh supply of episcopal gifts and Syriac missionaries could be obtained from the patriarch of Babylon. Since the expulsion of the Portuguese the Nestorian creed is freely professed on the coast of Malabar. The trading companies of Holland and England are the friends of toleration; but if oppression be less mortifying than contempt, the Christians of St. Thomas have reason to complain of the cold and silent indifference of their brethren of Europe.[124]

II. The history of the Monophysites is less copious and interesting than that of the Nestorians. Under the reigns of Zeno and Anastasius their artful leaders surprised the ear of the prince, usurped the thrones of the East, and crushed on its native soil the school of the Syrians. The rule of the Monophysite faith was defined with exquisite discretion by Severus, patriarch of Antioch; he condemned, in the style of the Henoticon, the adverse heresies of Nestorius and Eutyches; maintained against the latter the reality of the body of Christ; and constrained the Greeks to allow that he was a liar who spoke truth.[125] But the approximation of ideas could not abate the vehemence of passion; each party was the more astonished that their blind antagonist could dispute on so trifling a difference; the tyrant of Syria enforced the belief of his creed, and his reign was polluted with the blood of three hundred and fifty monks, who were slain, not perhaps without provocation or resistance, under the walls of Apamea.[126] The successor of Anastasius replanted the orthodox

standard in the East; Severus fled into Egypt; and his friend, the eloquent Xenaias,[127] who had escaped from the Nestorians of Persia, was suffocated in his exile by the Melchites of Paphlagonia. Fifty-four bishops were swept from their thrones, eight hundred ecclesiastics were cast into prison,[128] and, notwithstanding the ambiguous favour of Theodora, the Oriental flocks, deprived of their shepherds, must insensibly have been either famished or poisoned. In this spiritual distress the expiring faction was revived, and united, and perpetuated by the labours of a monk; and the name of James Baradæus[129] has been preserved in the appellation of *Jacobites*, a familiar sound which may startle the ear of an English reader. From the holy confessors in their prison of Constantinople he received the powers of bishop of Edessa and apostle of the East, and the ordination of fourscore thousand bishops, priests, and deacons, is derived from the same inexhaustible source. The speed of the zealous missionary was promoted by the fleetest dromedaries of a devout chief of the Arabs; the doctrine and discipline of the Jacobites were secretly established in the dominions of Justinian; and each Jacobite was compelled to violate the laws and to hate the Roman legislator. The successors of Severus, while they lurked in convents or villages, while they sheltered their proscribed heads in the caverns of hermits or the tents of the Saracens, still asserted, as they now assert, their indefeasible right to the title, the rank, and the prerogatives of patriarch of Antioch: under the milder yoke of the infidels they reside about a league from Merdin, in the pleasant monastery of Zapharan, which they have embellished with cells, aqueducts, and plantations. The secondary, though honourable, place is filled by the *maphrian*, who, in his station at Mosul itself, defies the Nestorian *catholic* with whom he contests the primacy of the East. Under the patriarch and the maphrian one hundred and fifty archbishops and bishops have been counted in the different ages of the Jacobite church; but the order of the hierarchy is relaxed or dissolved, and the greater part of their dioceses is confined to the neighbourhood of the Euphrates and the Tigris. The cities of Aleppo and Amida, which are often visited by the patriarch, contain some wealthy merchants and industrious mechanics, but the multitude derive their scanty sustenance from their daily labour: and poverty, as well as superstition, may impose their excessive fasts—five annual lents, during which both the clergy and laity abstain not only from flesh or eggs, but even from the taste of wine, of oil, and of fish. Their present numbers are esteemed from fifty to fourscore thousand souls, the remnant of a populous church, which has gradually decreased under the oppression of twelve centuries. Yet in that long period some strangers of merit have been converted to the Monophysite faith, and a Jew was the father of Abulpharagius,[130] primate of the East, so truly eminent both in his life and death. In his life he was an elegant writer of the Syriac and Arabic tongues, a poet, physician, and historian, a subtle philosopher, and a moderate divine. In his death his funeral was attended by his rival the Nestorian patriarch, with a train of Greeks and Armenians, who forgot their disputes, and mingled their tears over the grave of an enemy. The sect which was honoured by the virtues of Abulpharagius appears, however, to sink below the level of their Nestorian brethren. The superstition of the Jacobites is more abject, their fasts more rigid,[131] their intestine divisions are more numerous, and their doctrines (as far as I can measure the degrees of nonsense) are more remote from the precincts of reason. Something may possibly be allowed for the rigour of the Monophysite theology, much more for the superior influence of the monastic order. In Syria, in Egypt, in Æthiopia, the Jacobite monks have ever been distinguished by the austerity of their penance and the absurdity of their legends. Alive or dead, they are worshipped as the favourites of the Deity; the crosier of bishop and patriarch is reserved for their venerable hands; and they assume the government of men while they are yet reeking with the habits and prejudices of the cloister.[132]

III. In the style of the Oriental Christians, the Monothelites of every age are described under the appellation of *Maronites*,[133] a name which has been insensibly transferred from a hermit to a monastery, from a monastery to a nation. Maron, a saint or savage of the fifth century, displayed his religious madness in Syria; the rival cities of Apamea and Emesa disputed his relics, a stately church was erected on his tomb, and six hundred of his disciples united their solitary cells on the banks of the Orontes. In the controversies of the incarnation they nicely threaded the orthodox line between the sects of Nestorius and Eutyches; but the unfortunate question of *one will* or operation in the two natures of Christ was generated by their curious leisure. Their proselyte, the emperor Heraclius, was rejected as a Maronite from the walls of Emesa; he found a refuge in the monastery of his brethren; and their theological lessons were repaid with the gift of a spacious and wealthy domain. The name and doctrine of this venerable school were propagated among the Greeks and Syrians, and their zeal is expressed by Macarius, patriarch of Antioch, who declared before the synod of Constantinople, that, sooner than subscribe the *two wills* of Christ, he would submit to be hewn piecemeal and cast into the sea.[134] A similar or a less cruel mode of persecution soon converted the unresisting subjects of the plain, while the glorious title of *Mardaites*,[135] or rebels, was bravely maintained by the hardy natives of Mount Libanus. John Maron, one of the most learned and popular of the monks, assumed the character of patriarch of Antioch; his nephew, Abraham, at the head of the Maronites, defended their civil and religious freedom against the tyrants of the East. The son of the orthodox Constantine pursued with pious hatred a people of soldiers, who might have stood the bulwark of his empire against the common foes of Christ and of Rome. An army of Greeks invaded Syria; the monastery of St. Maron was destroyed with fire; the bravest chieftains were betrayed and murdered, and twelve thousand of their followers were transplanted to the distant frontiers of Armenia and Thrace. Yet the humble nation of the Maronites has survived the empire of Constantinople, and they still enjoy, under their Turkish masters, a free religion and a mitigated servitude. Their domestic governors are chosen among the ancient nobility: the patriarch, in his monastery of Canobin, still fancies himself on the throne of Antioch; nine bishops compose his synod, and one hundred and fifty priests, who retain the liberty of marriage, are intrusted with the care of one hundred thousand souls. Their country extends from the ridge of Mount Libanus to the shores of Tripoli; and the gradual descent affords, in a narrow space, each variety of soil and climate, from the Holy Cedars, erect under the weight of snow,[136] to the vine, the mulberry, and the olive trees of the fruitful valley. In the twelfth century the Maronites, abjuring the Monothelite error, were reconciled to the Latin churches of Antioch and Rome,[137] and the same alliance has been frequently renewed by the ambition of the popes and the distress of the Syrians. But it may reasonably be questioned whether their union has ever been perfect or sincere; and the learned Maronites of the college of Rome have vainly laboured to absolve their ancestors from the guilt of heresy and schism.[138]

IV. Since the age of Constantine, the AR-

MENIANS[139] had signalised their attachment to the religion and empire of the Christians. The disorders of their country, and their ignorance of the Greek tongue, prevented their clergy from assisting at the synod of Chalcedon, and they floated eighty-four years[140] in a state of indifference or suspense, till their vacant faith was finally occupied by the missionaries of Julian of Halicarnassus,[141] who in Egypt, their common exile, had been vanquished by the arguments or the influence of his rival Severus, the Monophysite patriarch of Antioch. The Armenians alone are the pure disciples of Eutyches, an unfortunate parent, who has been renounced by the greater part of his spiritual progeny. They alone persevere in the opinion that the manhood of Christ was created, or existed without creation, of a divine and incorruptible substance. Their adversaries reproach them with the adoration of a phantom; and they retort the accusation, by deriding or execrating the blasphemy of the Jacobites, who impute to the Godhead the vile infirmities of the flesh, even the natural effects of nutrition and digestion. The religion of Armenia could not derive much glory from the learning or the power of its inhabitants. The royalty expired with the origin of their schism; and their Christian kings, who arose and fell in the thirteenth century on the confines of Cilicia, were the clients of the Latins and the vassals of the Turkish sultan of Iconium. The helpless nation has seldom been permitted to enjoy the tranquillity of servitude. From the earliest period to the present hour Armenia has been the theatre of perpetual war: the lands between Tauris and Erivan were dispeopled by the cruel policy of the Sophis; and myriads of Christian families were transplanted, to perish or to propagate in the distant provinces of Persia. Under the rod of oppression, the zeal of the Armenians is fervent and intrepid; they have often preferred the crown of martyrdom to the white turban of Mohammed; they devoutly hate the error and idolatry of the Greeks; and their transient union with the Latins is not less devoid of truth than the thousand bishops whom their patriarch offered at the feet of the Roman pontiff.[142] The *catholic*, or patriarch, of the Armenians resides in the monastery of Ekmiasin, three leagues from Erivan. Forty-seven archbishops, each of whom may claim the obedience of four or five suffragans, are consecrated by his hand; but the far greater part are only titular prelates, who dignify with their presence and service the simplicity of his court. As soon as they have performed the liturgy, they cultivate the garden; and our bishops will hear with surprise that the austerity of their life increases in just proportion to the elevation of their rank. In the fourscore thousand towns or villages of his spiritual empire, the patriarch receives a small and voluntary tax from each person above the age of fifteen; but the annual amount of six hundred thousand crowns is insufficient to supply the incessant demands of charity and tribute. Since the beginning of the last century the Armenians have obtained a large and lucrative share of the commerce of the East: in their return from Europe, the caravan usually halts in the neighbourhood of Erivan, the altars are enriched with the fruits of their patient industry; and the faith of Eutyches is preached in their recent congregations of Barbary and Poland.[143]

V. In the rest of the Roman empire the despotism of the prince might eradicate or silence the sectaries of an obnoxious creed. But the stubborn temper of the Egyptians maintained their opposition to the synod of Chalcedon, and the policy of Justinian condescended to expect and to seize the opportunity of discord. The Monophysite church of Alexandria[144] was torn by the disputes of the *corruptibles* and *incorruptibles*, and on the death of the patriarch the two factions upheld their respective candidates.[145] Gaian was the disciple of Julian, Theodosius had been the pupil of Severus: the claims of the former were supported by the consent of the monks and senators, the city and the province; the latter depended on the priority of his ordination, the favour of the empress Theodora, and the arms of the eunuch Narses, which might have been used in more honourable warfare. The exile of the popular candidate to Carthage and Sardinia inflamed the ferment of Alexandria; and after a schism of one hundred and seventy years, the *Gaianites* still revered the memory and doctrine of their founder. The strength of numbers and of discipline was tried in a desperate and bloody conflict; the streets were filled with the dead bodies of citizens and soldiers; the pious women, ascending the roofs of their houses, showered down every sharp or ponderous utensil on the heads of the enemy; and the final victory of Narses was owing to the flames with which he wasted the third capital of the Roman world. But the lieutenant of Justinian had not conquered in the cause of a heretic; Theodosius himself was speedily, though gently, removed; and Paul of Tanis, an orthodox monk, was raised to the throne of Athanasius. The powers of government were strained in his support; he might appoint or displace the dukes and tribunes of Egypt; the allowance of bread, which Diocletian had granted, was suppressed, the churches were shut, and a nation of schismatics was deprived at once of their spiritual and carnal food. In his turn, the tyrant was excommunicated by the zeal and revenge of the people; and none except his servile Melchites would salute him as a man, a Christian, or a bishop. Yet such is the blindness of ambition, that, when Paul was expelled on a charge of murder, he solicited, with a bribe of seven hundred pounds of gold, his restoration to the same station of hatred and ignominy. His successor Apollinaris entered the hostile city in military array, alike qualified for prayer or for battle. His troops, under arms, were distributed through the streets; the gates of the cathedral were guarded, and a chosen band was stationed in the choir to defend the person of their chief. He stood erect on his throne, and, throwing aside the upper garment of a warrior, suddenly appeared before the eyes of the multitude in the robes of patriarch of Alexandria. Astonishment held them mute; but no sooner had Apollinaris begun to read the tome of St. Leo, than a volley of curses, and invectives, and stones assaulted the odious minister of the emperor and the synod. A charge was instantly sounded by the successor of the apostles; the soldiers waded to their knees in blood; and two hundred thousand Christians are said to have fallen by the sword: an incredible account, even if it be extended from the slaughter of a day to the eighteen years of the reign of Apollinaris. Two succeeding patriarchs, Eulogius[146] and John,[147] laboured in the conversion of heretics with arms and arguments more worthy of their evangelical profession. The theological knowledge of Eulogius was displayed in many a volume, which magnified the errors of Eutyches and Severus, and attempted to reconcile the ambiguous language of St. Cyril with the orthodox creed of pope Leo and the fathers of Chalcedon. The bounteous alms of John the Eleemosynary were dictated by superstition, or benevolence, or policy. Seven thousand five hundred poor were maintained at his expense; on his accession he found eight thousand pounds of gold in the treasury of the church; he collected ten thousand from the liberality of the faithful; yet the primate could boast in his testament that he left behind him no more than the third part of the smallest of the silver coins. The churches of Alexandria were delivered to the Catholics, the religion of the Monophysites was proscribed in Egypt, and a law was revived which excluded the natives from the honours and emoluments of the state.

A more important conquest still remained, of the patriarch, the oracle and leader of the Egyptian church. Theodosius had resisted the threats and promises of Justinian with the spirit of an apostle or an enthusiast. "Such," replied the patriarch, "were the offers of the tempter when he showed the kingdoms of the earth. But my soul is far dearer to me than life or dominion. The churches are in the hands of a prince who can kill the body; but my conscience is my own; and in exile, poverty, or chains, I will steadfastly adhere to the faith of my holy predecessors, Athanasius, Cyril, and Dioscorus. Anathema to the tome of Leo and the synod of Chalcedon! Anathema to all who embrace their creed! Anathema to them now and for evermore! Naked came I out of my mother's womb, naked shall I descend into the grave. Let those who love God follow me and seek their salvation." After comforting his brethren, he embarked for Constantinople, and sustained, in six successive interviews, the almost irresistible weight of the royal presence. His opinions were favourably entertained in the palace and the city; the influence of Theodora assured him a safe-conduct and honourable dismission; and he ended his days, though not on the throne, yet in the bosom of his native country. On the news of his death, Apollinaris indecently feasted the nobles and the clergy; but his joy was checked by the intelligence of a new election; and while he enjoyed the wealth of Alexandria, his rivals reigned in the monasteries of Thebais, and were maintained by the voluntary oblations of the people. A perpetual succession of patriarchs arose from the ashes of Theodosius; and the Monophysite churches of Syria and Egypt were united by the name of Jacobites and the communion of the faith. But the same faith, which has been confined to a narrow sect of the Syrians, was diffused over the mass of the Egyptian or Coptic nation, who almost unanimously rejected the decrees of the synod of Chalcedon. A thousand years were now elapsed since Egypt had ceased to be a kingdom, since the conquerors of Asia and Europe had trampled on the ready necks of a people whose ancient wisdom and power ascends beyond the records of history. The conflict of zeal and persecution rekindled some sparks of their national spirit. They abjured, with a foreign heresy, the manners and language of the Greeks: every Melchite, in their eyes, was a stranger, every Jacobite a citizen; the alliance of marriage, the offices of humanity, were condemned as a deadly sin;

the natives renounced all allegiance to the emperor; and his orders, at a distance from Alexandria, were obeyed only under the pressure of military force. A generous effort might have redeemed the religion and liberty of Egypt, and her six hundred monasteries might have poured forth their myriads of holy warriors, for whom death should have no terrors since life had no comfort or delight. But experience has proved the distinction of active and passive courage; the fanatic who endures without a groan the torture of the rack or the stake, would tremble and fly before the face of an armed enemy. The pusillanimous temper of the Egyptians could only hope for a change of masters; the arms of Chosroes depopulated the land, yet under his reign the Jacobites enjoyed a short and precarious respite. The victory of Heraclius renewed and aggravated the persecution, and the patriarch again escaped from Alexandria to the desert. In his flight, Benjamin was encouraged by a voice which bade him expect, at the end of ten years, the aid of a foreign nation, marked like the Egyptians themselves with the ancient rite of circumcision. The character of these deliverers, and the nature of the deliverance, will be hereafter explained; and I shall step over the interval of eleven centuries to observe the present misery of the Jacobites of Egypt. The populous city of Cairo affords a residence, or rather a shelter, for their indigent patriarch and a remnant of ten bishops; forty monasteries have survived the inroads of the Arabs; and the progress of servitude and apostasy has reduced the Coptic nation to the despicable number of twenty-five or thirty thousand families;[148] a race of illiterate beggars, whose only consolation is derived from the superior wretchedness of the Greek patriarch and his diminutive congregation.[149]

VI. The Coptic patriarch, a rebel to the Cæsars, or a slave to the Caliphs, still gloried in the filial obedience of the kings of Nubia and Æthiopia. He repaid their homage by magnifying their greatness; and it was boldly asserted that they could bring into the field a hundred thousand horse, with an equal number of camels;[150] that their hand could pour or restrain the waters of the Nile;[151] and the peace and plenty of Egypt was obtained, even in this world, by the intercession of the patriarch. In exile at Constantinople, Theodosius recommended to his patroness the conversion of the black nations of Nubia, from the tropic of Cancer to the confines of Abyssinia.[152] Her design was suspected and emulated by the more orthodox emperor.

The rival missionaries, a Melchite and a Jacobite, embarked at the same time; but the empress, from a motive of love or fear, was more effectually obeyed; and the Catholic priest was detained by the president of Thebais, while the king of Nubia and his court were hastily baptised in the faith of Dioscorus. The tardy envoy of Justinian was received and dismissed with honour; but when he accused the heresy and treason of the Egyptians, the negro convert was instructed to reply that he would never abandon his brethren, the true believers, to the persecuting ministers of the synod of Chalcedon.[153] During several ages the bishops of Nubia were named and consecrated by the Jacobite patriarch of Alexandria: as late as the twelfth century Christianity prevailed; and some rites, some ruins, are still visible in the savage towns of Sennaar and Dongola.[154] But the Nubians at length executed their threats of returning to the worship of idols; the climate required the indulgence of polygamy, and they have finally preferred the triumph of the Koran to the abasement of the Cross. A metaphysical religion may appear too refined for the capacity of the negro race: yet a black or a parrot might be taught to repeat the *words* of the Chalcedonian or Monophysite creed.

Christianity was more deeply rooted in the Abyssinian empire; and, although the correspondence has been sometimes interrupted above seventy or a hundred years, the mother-church of Alexandria retains her colony in a state of perpetual pupilage. Seven bishops once composed the Æthiopic synod: had their number amounted to ten, they might have elected an independent primate; and one of their kings was ambitious of promoting his brother to the ecclesiastical throne. But the event was foreseen, the increase was denied; the episcopal office has been gradually confined to the *abuna*,[155] the head and author of the Abyssinian priesthood; the patriarch supplies each vacancy with an Egyptian monk; and the character of a stranger appears more venerable in the eyes of the people, less dangerous in those of the monarch. In the sixth century, when the schism of Egypt was confirmed, the rival chiefs, with their patrons Justinian and Theodora, strove to outstrip each other in the conquest of a remote and independent province. The industry of the empress was again victorious, and the pious Theodora has established in that sequestered church the faith and discipline of the Jacobites.[156] Encompassed on all sides by the enemies of their religion, the Æthiopians slept near a thousand years, forgetful of the world, by whom they were forgotten. They were awakened by the Portuguese, who, turning the southern promontory of Africa, appeared in India and the Red Sea, as if they had descended through the air from a distant planet. In the first moments of their interview, the subjects of Rome and Alexandria observed the resemblance rather than the difference of their faith; and each nation expected the most important benefits from an alliance with their Christian brethren. In their lonely situation the Æthiopians had almost relapsed into the savage life. Their vessels, which had traded to Ceylon, scarcely presumed to navigate the rivers of Africa; the ruins of Axume were deserted, the nation was scattered in villages, and the emperor, a pompous name, was content, both in peace and war, with the movable residence of a camp. Conscious of their own indigence, the Abyssinians had formed the rational project of importing the arts and ingenuity of Europe;[157] and their ambassadors at Rome and Lisbon were instructed to solicit a colony of smiths, carpenters, tilers, masons, printers, surgeons, and physicians, for the use of their country. But the public danger soon called for the instant and effectual aid of arms and soldiers, to defend an unwarlike people from the barbarians who ravaged the inland country, and the Turks and Arabs who advanced from the sea-coast in more formidable array. Æthiopia was saved by four hundred and fifty Portuguese, who displayed in the field the native valour of Europeans, and the artificial powers of the musket and cannon. In a moment of terror the emperor had promised to reconcile himself and his subjects to the Catholic faith; a Latin patriarch represented the supremacy of the pope;[158] the empire, enlarged in a tenfold proportion, was supposed to contain more gold than the mines of America; and the wildest hopes of avarice and zeal were built on the willing submission of the Christians of Africa.

But the vows which pain had extorted were forsworn on the return of health. The Abyssinians still adhered with unshaken constancy to the Monophysite faith; their languid belief was inflamed by the exercise of dispute; they branded the Latins with the names of Arians and Nestorians, and imputed the adoration of four gods to those who separated the two natures of Christ. Fremona, a place of worship, or rather of exile, was assigned to the Jesuit missionaries. Their skill in the liberal and mechanic arts, their theological learning, and the decency of their manners, inspired a barren esteem; but they were not endowed with the gift of miracles,[159] and they vainly solicited a reinforcement of European troops. The patience and dexterity of forty years at length obtained a more favourable audience, and two emperors of Abyssinia were persuaded that Rome could insure the temporal and everlasting happiness of her votaries. The first of these royal converts lost his crown and his life; and the rebel army was sanctified by the *abuna*, who hurled an anathema at the apostate and absolved his subjects from their oath of fidelity. The fate of Zadenghel was revenged by the courage and fortune of Susneus, who ascended the throne under the name of Segued, and more vigorously prosecuted the pious enterprise of his kinsman. After the amusement of some unequal combats between the Jesuits and his illiterate priests, the emperor declared himself a proselyte to the synod of Chalcedon, presuming that his clergy and people would embrace without delay the religion of their prince. The liberty of choice was succeeded by a law which imposed, under pain of death, the belief of the two natures of Christ: the Abyssinians were enjoined to work and to play on the Sabbath; and Segued, in the face of Europe and Africa, renounced his connection with the Alexandrian church. A Jesuit, Alphonso Mendez, the Catholic patriarch of Æthiopia, accepted, in the name of Urban VIII., the homage and abjuration of his penitent. "I confess," said the emperor on his knees, "I confess that the pope is the vicar of Christ, the successor of St. Peter, and the sovereign of the world. To him I swear true obedience, and at his feet I offer my person and kingdom." A similar oath was repeated by his son, his brother, the clergy, the nobles, and even the ladies of the court: the Latin patriarch was invested with honours and wealth; and his missionaries erected their churches or citadels in the most convenient stations of the empire. The Jesuits themselves deplore the fatal indiscretion of their chief, who forgot the mildness of the gospel and the policy of his order, to introduce with hasty violence the liturgy of Rome and the inquisition of Portugal. He condemned the ancient practice of circumcision, which health rather than superstition had first invented in the climate of Æthiopia.[160] A new baptism, a new ordination, was inflicted on the natives; and they trembled with horror when the most holy of the dead were torn from their graves, when the most illustrious of the living were excommunicated by a foreign priest. In the defence of their religion and liberty the Abyssinians rose in arms, with desperate but unsuccessful zeal. Five rebellions were extinguished in the blood of the insurgents: two abunas were slain in battle; whole legions were slaughtered in the field, or suffocated in their caverns; and neither merit, nor rank, nor sex, could save from an ignominious death the enemies of Rome. But the victorious monarch was finally subdued by the constancy of the nation, of his mother, of his son, and of his most faithful friends. Segued listened to the voice of pity, of reason, perhaps of fear: and his edict of liberty of conscience instantly revealed the tyranny and weakness of the Jesuits. On the death of his father, Basilides expelled the Latin patriarch, and restored to the wishes of the nation the faith and discipline of Egypt. The Monophysite churches resounded with a song of triumph, "that the sheep of Æthiopia were now delivered from the hyænas of the West;" and the gates of that solitary realm were for ever shut against the arts, the science, and the fanaticism of Europe.[161]

CHAPTER XLVIII

Plan of the last two [quarto] Volumes. Succession and Characters of the Greek Emperors of Constantinople, from the Time of Heraclius to the Latin Conquest.

I HAVE now deduced from Trajan to Constantine, from Constantine to Heraclius, the regular series of the Roman emperors; and faithfully exposed the prosperous and adverse fortunes of their reigns. Five centuries of the decline and fall of the empire have already elapsed; but a period of more than eight hundred years still separates me from the term of my labours, the taking of Constantinople by the Turks. Should I persevere in the same course, should I observe the same measure, a prolix and slender thread would be spun through many a volume, nor would the patient reader find an adequate reward of instruction or amusement. At every step, as we sink deeper in the decline and fall of the Eastern empire, the annals of each succeeding reign would impose a more ungrateful and melancholy task. These annals must continue to repeat a tedious and uniform tale of weakness and misery; the natural connection of causes and events would be broken by frequent and hasty transitions, and a minute accummulation of circumstances must destroy the light and effect of those general pictures which compose the use and ornament of a remote history. From the time of Heraclius the Byzantine theatre is contracted and darkened: the line of empire, which had been defined by the laws of Justinian and the arms of Belisarius, recedes on all sides from our view; the Roman name, the proper subject of our inquiries, is reduced to a narrow corner of Europe, to the lonely suburbs of Constantinople; and the fate of the Greek empire has been compared to that of the Rhine, which loses itself in the sands before its waters can mingle with the ocean. The scale of dominion is diminished to our view by the distance of time and place; nor is the loss of external splendour compensated by the nobler gifts of virtue and genius. In the last moments of her decay Constantinople was doubtless more opulent and populous than Athens at her most flourishing era, when a scanty sum of six thousand talents, or twelve hundred thousand pounds sterling, was possessed by twenty-one thousand male citizens of an adult age. But each of these citizens was a freeman who dared to assert the liberty of his thoughts, words, and actions; whose person and property were guarded by equal law; and who exercised his independent vote in the government of the republic. Their numbers seem to be multiplied by the strong and various discriminations of character; under the shield of freedom, on the wings of emulation and vanity, each Athenian aspired to the level of the national dignity; from this commanding eminence some chosen spirits soared beyond the reach of a vulgar eye; and the chances of superior merit in a great and populous kingdom, as they are proved by experience, would excuse the computation of imaginary millions. The territories of Athens, Sparta, and their allies, do not exceed a moderate province of France or England; but after the trophies of Salamis and Platæa, they expand in our fancy to the gigantic size of Asia, which had been trampled under the feet of the victorious Greeks. But the subjects of the Byzantine empire, who assume and dishonour the names both of Greeks and Romans, present a dead uniformity of abject vices, which are neither softened by the weakness of humanity nor animated by the vigour of memorable crimes. The freemen of antiquity might repeat with generous enthusiasm the sentence of Homer, "that on the first day of his servitude the captive is deprived of one half of his manly virtue." But the poet had only seen the effects of civil or domestic slavery, nor could he foretell that the second moiety of manhood must be annihilated by the spiritual despotism, which shackles not only the actions but even the thoughts of the prostrate votary. By this double yoke the Greeks were oppressed under the successors of Heraclius; the tyrant, a law of eternal justice, was degraded by the vices of his subjects; and on the throne, in the camp, in the schools, we search, perhaps with fruitless diligence, the names and characters that may deserve to be rescued from oblivion. Nor are the defects of the subject compensated by the skill and variety of the painters. Of a space of eight hundred years, the four first centuries are overspread with a cloud interrupted by some faint and broken rays of historic light: in the lives of the emperors, from Maurice to Alexius, Basil the Macedonian has alone been the theme of a separate work; and the absence, or loss, or imperfection of contemporary evidence, must be poorly supplied by the doubtful authority of more recent compilers. The four last centuries are exempt from the reproach of penury: and with the Comnenian family the historic muse of Constantinople again revives, but her apparel is gaudy, her motions are without elegance or grace. A succession of priests, or courtiers, treads in each other's footsteps in the same path of servitude and superstition: their views are narrow, their judgment is feeble or corrupt: and we close the volume of copious barrenness, still ignorant of the causes of events, the characters of the actors, and the manners of the times, which they celebrate or deplore. The observation which has been applied to a man may be extended to a whole people, that the energy of the sword is communicated to the pen; and it will be found by experience that the tone of history will rise or fall with the spirit of the age.

From these considerations I should have abandoned without regret the Greek slaves and their servile historians, had I not reflected that the fate of the Byzantine monarchy is *passively* connected with the most splendid and important revolutions which have changed the state of the world. The space of the lost provinces was immediately replenished with new colonies and rising kingdoms: the active virtues of peace and war deserted from the vanquished to the victorious nations; and it is in their origin and conquests, in their religion and government, that we must explore the causes and effects of the decline and fall of the Eastern empire. Nor will this scope of narrative, the riches and variety of these materials, be incompatible with the unity of design and composition. As, in his daily prayers, the Musulman of Fez or Delhi still turns his face towards the temple of Mecca, the historian's eye shall be always fixed on the city of Constantinople. The excursive line may embrace the wilds of Arabia and Tartary, but the circle will be ultimately reduced to the decreasing limit of the Roman monarchy.

On this principle I shall now establish the plan of the last two volumes of the present work. The first chapter will contain, in a regular series, the emperors who reigned at Constantinople during a period of six hundred years, from the days of Heraclius to the Latin conquest: a rapid abstract, which may be supported by a *general* appeal to the order and text of the original historians. In this introduction I shall confine myself to the revolutions of the throne, the succession of families, the personal characters of the Greek princes, the mode of their life and death, the maxims and influence of their domestic government, and the tendency of their reign to accelerate or suspend the downfall of the Eastern empire. Such a chronological review will serve to illustrate the various argument of the subsequent chapters; and each circumstance of the eventful story of the barbarians will adapt itself in a proper place to the Byzantine annals. The internal state of the empire, and the dangerous heresy of the Paulicians, which shook the East and enlightened the West, will be the subject of two separate chapters; but these inquiries must be postponed till our farther progress shall have opened the view of the world in the ninth and tenth centuries of the Christian era. After this foundation of Byzantine history, the following nations will pass before our eyes, and each will occupy the space to which it may be entitled by greatness or merit, or the degree of connection with the Roman world and the present age. I. The FRANKS; a general appellation which includes all the barbarians of France, Italy, and Germany, who were united by the sword and sceptre of Charlemagne. The persecution of images and their votaries separated Rome and Italy from the Byzantine throne, and prepared the restoration of the Roman empire in the West. II. The ARABS or SARACENS. Three ample chapters will be devoted to this curious and interesting object. In the first, after a picture of the country and its inhabitants, I shall investigate the character of Mohammed; the character, religion, and success of the prophet. In the second I shall lead the Arabs to the conquest of Syria, Egypt, and Africa, the provinces of the Roman empire; nor can I check their victorious career till they have overthrown the monarchies of Persia and Spain. In the third I shall inquire how Constantinople and Europe were saved by the luxury and arts, the division and decay, of the empire of the caliphs. A single chapter will include, III. The BULGARIANS, IV. HUNGARIANS, and V. RUSSIANS, who assaulted by sea or by land the provinces and the capital; but the last of these, so important in their present greatness, will excite some curiosity in their origin and infancy. VI. The NORMANS; or rather the private adventurers of that warlike people, who founded a powerful kingdom in Apulia and Sicily, shook the throne of Constantinople, displayed the trophies of chivalry, and almost realised the wonders of romance. VII. The LATINS; the subjects of the pope, the nations of the West, who enlisted under the banner of the cross for the recovery or relief of the holy sepulchre. The Greek emperors were terrified and preserved by the myriads of pilgrims who marched to Jerusalem with Godfrey of Bouillon and the peers of Christendom. The second and third crusades trod in the footsteps of the first: Asia and Europe were mingled in a sacred war of two hundred years; and the Christian powers were bravely resisted and finally expelled by Saladin and the Mamalukes of Egypt. In these memorable crusades a fleet and army of French and Venetians were diverted from Syria to the Thracian Bosphorus: they assaulted the capital, they subverted the Greek monarchy: and a dynasty of Latin princes was seated near threescore years on the throne of Constantine. VIII. The GREEKS themselves, during this period of captivity and exile, must be considered as a foreign nation; the enemies, and again the sovereigns of Constantinople. Misfortune had rekindled a spark of national virtue; and the Imperial series may be continued with some dignity from their restoration to the Turkish conquest. IX. The MOGULS and TARTARS. By the arms of Zingis and his descendants the globe was shaken from China to Poland and Greece: the sultans were overthrown: the caliphs fell, and the Cæsars trembled on their throne. The victories of Timour suspended above fifty years the final ruin of the Byzantine empire. X. I have already noticed the first appearance of the TURKS; and the names of the names of the fathers, of *Seljuk* and *Othman*, discriminate the two successive dynasties of the nation which

emerged in the eleventh century from the Scythian wilderness. The former established a potent and splendid kingdom from the banks of the Oxus to Antioch and Nice; and the first crusade was provoked by the violation of Jerusalem and the danger of Constantinople. From a humble origin the *Ottomans* arose the scourge and terror of Christendom. Constantinople was besieged and taken by Mohammed II., and his triumph annihilates the remnant, the image, the title, of the Roman empire in the East. The schism of the Greeks will be connected with their last calamities and the restoration of learning in the Western world. I shall return from the captivity of the new to the ruins of ancient ROME; and the venerable name, the interesting theme, will shed a ray of glory on the conclusion of my labours.

THE emperor Heraclius had punished a tyrant and ascended his throne; and the memory of his reign is perpetuated by the transient conquest and irreparable loss of the Eastern provinces. After the death of Eudocia, his first wife, he disobeyed the patriarch and violated the laws by his second marriage with his niece Martina; and the superstition of the Greeks beheld the judgment of Heaven in the diseases of the father and the deformity of his offspring. But the opinion of an illegitimate birth is sufficient to distract the choice and loosen the obedience of the people: the ambition of Martina was quickened by maternal love, and perhaps by the envy of a stepmother; and the aged husband was too feeble to withstand the arts of conjugal allurements. Constantine, his eldest son, enjoyed in a mature age the title of Augustus; but the weakness of his constitution required a colleague and a guardian, and he yielded with secret reluctance to the partition of the empire. The senate was summoned to the palace to ratify or attest the association of Heracleonas, the son of Martina: the imposition of the diadem was consecrated by the prayer and blessing of the patriarch; the senators and patricians adored the majesty of the great emperor and the partners of his reign; and as soon as the doors were thrown open they were hailed by the tumultuary but important voice of the soldiers. After an interval of five months the pompous ceremonies which formed the essence of the Byzantine state were celebrated in the cathedral and the hippodrome: the concord of the royal brothers was affectedly displayed by the younger leaning on the arm of the elder; and the name of Martina was mingled in the reluctant or venal acclamations of the people. Heraclius survived this association about two years: his last testimony declared his two sons the equal heirs of the Eastern empire, and commanded them to honour his widow Martina as their mother and their sovereign.

When Martina first appeared on the throne with the name and attributes of royalty, she was checked by a firm, though respectful, opposition; and the dying embers of freedom were kindled by the breath of superstitious prejudice. "We reverence," exclaimed the voice of a citizen, "we reverence the mother of our princes; but to those princes alone our obedience is due; and Constantine, the elder emperor, is of an age to sustain, in his own hands, the weight of the sceptre. Your sex is excluded by nature from the toils of government. How could you combat, how could you answer, the barbarians who, with hostile or friendly intentions, may approach the royal city? May Heaven avert from the Roman republic this national disgrace, which would provoke the patience of the slaves of Persia!" Martina descended from the throne with indignation, and sought a refuge in the female apartment of the palace. The reign of Constantine the Third lasted only one hundred and three days: he expired in the thirtieth year of his age, and although his life had been a long malady, a belief was entertained that poison had been the means, and his cruel stepmother the author, of his untimely fate. Martina reaped indeed the harvest of his death, and assumed the government in the name of the surviving emperor; but the incestuous widow of Heraclius was universally abhorred; the jealousy of the people was awakened, and the two orphans whom Constantine had left became the objects of the public care. It was in vain that the son of Martina, who was no more than fifteen years of age, was taught to declare himself the guardian of his nephews, one of whom he had presented at the baptismal font: it was in vain that he swore on the wood of the true cross to defend them against all their enemies. On his deathbed the late emperor had despatched a trusty servant to arm the troops and provinces of the East in the defence of his helpless children: the eloquence and liberality of Valentin had been successful, and from his camp of Chalcedon he boldly demanded the punishment of the assassins, and the restoration of the lawful heir. The licence of the soldiers, who devoured the grapes and drank the wine of their Asiatic vineyards, provoked the citizens of Constantinople against the domestic authors of their calamities, and the

dome of St. Sophia re-echoed, not with prayers and hymns, but with the clamours and imprecations of an enraged multitude. At their imperious command Heracleonas appeared in the pulpit with the eldest of the royal orphans; Constans alone was saluted as emperor of the Romans, and a crown of gold, which had been taken from the tomb of Heraclius, was placed on his head, with the solemn benediction of the patriarch. But, in the tumult of joy and indignation, the church was pillaged, the sanctuary was polluted by a promiscuous crowd of Jews and barbarians; and the Monothelite Pyrrhus, a creature of the empress, after dropping a protestation on the altar, escaped by a prudent flight from the zeal of the Catholics. A more serious and bloody task was reserved for the senate, who derived a temporary strength from the consent of the soldiers and people. The spirit of Roman freedom revived the ancient and awful examples of the judgment of tyrants, and the Imperial culprits were deposed and condemned as the authors of the death of Constantine. But the severity of the conscript fathers was stained by the indiscriminate punishment of the innocent and the guilty: Martina and Heracleonas were sentenced to the amputation, the former of her tongue, the latter of his nose; and after this cruel execution they consumed the remainder of their days in exile and oblivion. The Greeks who were capable of reflection might find some consolation for their servitude by observing the abuse of power when it was lodged for a moment in the hands of an aristocracy.

We shall imagine ourselves transported five hundred years backwards to the age of the Antonines if we listen to the oration which Constans II. pronounced in the twelfth year of his age before the Byzantine senate. After returning his thanks for the just punishment of the assassins who had intercepted the fairest hopes of his father's reign, "By the divine Providence," said the young emperor, "and by your righteous decree, Martina and her incestuous progeny have been cast headlong from the throne. Your majesty and wisdom have prevented the Roman state from degenerating into lawless tyranny. I therefore exhort and beseech you to stand forth as the counsellors and judges of the common safety." The senators were gratified by the respectful address and liberal donative of their sovereign; but these servile Greeks were unworthy and regardless of freedom; and in his mind the lesson of an hour was quickly erased by the prejudices of the age and the habits of despotism. He retained only a jealous fear lest the senate or people should one day invade the right of primogeniture, and seat his brother Theodosius on an equal throne. By the imposition of holy orders, the grandson of Heraclius was disqualified for the purple; but this ceremony, which seemed to profane the sacraments of the church, was insufficient to appease the suspicions of the tyrant, and the death of the deacon Theodosius could alone expiate the crime of his royal birth. His murder was avenged by the imprecations of the people, and the assassin, in the fulness of power, was driven from his capital into voluntary and perpetual exile. Constans embarked for Greece; and, as if he meant to retort the abhorrence which he deserved, he is said, from the imperial galley, to have spit against the walls of his native city. After passing the winter at Athens, he sailed to Tarentum in Italy, visited Rome, and concluded a long pilgrimage of disgrace and sacrilegious rapine by fixing his residence at Syracuse. But if Constans could fly from his people, he could not fly from himself. The remorse of his conscience created a phantom who pursued him by land and sea, by day and by night; and the visionary Theodosius, presenting to his lips a cup of blood, said, or seemed to say, "Drink, brother, drink"—a sure emblem of the aggravation of his guilt, since he had received from the hands of the deacon the mystic cup of the blood of Christ. Odious to himself and to mankind, Constans perished by domestic, perhaps by episcopal, treason in the capital of Sicily. A servant who waited in the bath, after pouring warm water on his head, struck him violently with the vase. He fell, stunned by the blow and suffocated by the water; and his attendants, who wondered at the tedious delay, beheld with indifference the corpse of their lifeless emperor. The troops of Sicily invested with the purple an obscure youth, whose inimitable beauty eluded, and it might easily elude, the declining art of the painters and sculptors of the age.

Constans had left in the Byzantine palace three sons, the eldest of whom had been clothed in his infancy with the purple. When the father summoned them to attend his person in Sicily, these precious hostages were detained by the Greeks, and a firm refusal informed him that they were the children of the state. The news of his murder was conveyed with almost supernatural speed from Syracuse to Constantinople; and Constantine, the eldest of his sons, inherited his throne without being the heir of the public hatred. His subjects contributed with zeal and alacrity to chastise the guilt and presumption of a province which had usurped the rights of the senate and people; the young emperor sailed from the Hellespont with a powerful fleet, and the legions of Rome and Carthage were assembled under his standard in the harbour of Syracuse. The defeat of the Sicilian tyrant was easy, his punishment just, and his beauteous head was exposed in the hippodrome; but I cannot applaud the clemency of a prince who, among a crowd of victims, condemned the son of a patrician for deploring with some bitterness the execution of a virtuous father. The youth was castrated: he survived the operation, and the memory of this indecent cruelty is preserved by the elevation of Germanus to the rank of a patriarch and saint. After pouring this bloody libation on his father's tomb, Constantine returned to his capital; and the growth of his young beard during the Sicilian voyage was announced, by the familiar surname of Pogonatus, to the Grecian world. But his reign, like that of his predecessor, was stained with fraternal discord. On his two brothers, Heraclius and Tiberius, he had bestowed the title of Augustus —an empty title, for they continued to languish, without trust or power, in the solitude of the palace. At their secret instigation the troops of the Anatolian *theme* or province approached the city on the Asiatic side, demanded for the royal brothers the partition or exercise of sovereignty, and supported their seditious claim by a theological argument. They were Christians, they cried, and orthodox Catholics, the sincere votaries of the holy and undivided Trinity. Since there are three equal persons in heaven, it is reasonable there should be three equal persons upon earth. The emperor invited these learned divines to a friendly conference, in which they might propose their arguments to the senate: they obeyed the summons, but the prospect of their bodies hanging on the gibbet in the suburb of Galata reconciled their companions to the unity of the reign of Constantine. He pardoned his brothers, and their names were still pronounced in the public acclamations; but on the repetition or suspicion of a similar offence, the obnoxious princes were deprived of their titles and noses, in the presence of the Catholic bishops who were assembled at Constantinople in the sixth general synod. In the close of his life Pogonatus was anxious only to establish the right of primogeniture: the heir of his two sons, Justinian and Heraclius, was offered on the shrine of St. Peter, as a symbol of their spiritual adoption by the pope; but the elder was alone exalted to the rank of Augustus, and the assurance of the empire.

After the decease of his father the inheritance of the Roman world devolved to Justinian II.; and the name of a triumphant lawgiver was dishonoured by the vices of a boy, who imitated his namesake only in the expensive luxury of building. His passions were strong; his understanding was feeble; and he was intoxicated with a foolish pride that his birth had given him the command of millions, of whom the smallest community would not have chosen him for their local magistrate. His favourite ministers were two beings the least susceptible of human sympathy, a eunuch and a monk; to the one he abandoned the palace, to the other the finances; the former corrected the emperor's mother with a scourge, the latter suspended the insolvent tributaries, with their heads downwards, over a slow and smoky fire. Since the days of Commodus and Caracalla the cruelty of the Roman princes had most commonly been the effect of their fear; but Justinian, who possessed some vigour of character, enjoyed the sufferings, and braved the revenge, of his subjects about ten years, till the measure was full of his crimes and of their patience. In a dark dungeon Leontius, a general of reputation, had groaned above three years, with some of the noblest and most deserving of the patricians: he was suddenly drawn forth to assume the government of Greece; and this promotion of an injured man was a mark of the contempt rather than of the confidence of his prince. As he was followed to the port by the kind offices of his friends, Leontius observed, with a sigh, that he was a victim adorned for sacrifice, and that inevitable death would pursue his footsteps. They ventured to reply that glory and empire might be the recompence of a generous resolution, that every order of men abhorred the reign of a monster, and that the hands of two hundred thousand patriots expected only the voice of a leader. The night was chosen for their deliverance; and in the first effort of the conspirators the præfect was slain and the prisons were forced open: the emissaries of Leontius proclaimed in every street, "Christians, to St. Sophia!" and the seasonable text of the patriarch, "This is the day of the Lord!" was the prelude of an inflammatory sermon. From the church the people adjourned to the hippodrome: Justinian, in whose cause not a sword had been drawn, was dragged before these tumultuary judges, and their clamours demanded the instant death of the tyrant. But Leontius, who was already

clothed with the purple, cast an eye of pity on the prostrate son of his own benefactor and of so many emperors. The life of Justinian was spared; the amputation of his nose, perhaps of his tongue, was imperfectly performed: the happy flexibility of the Greek language could impose the name of Rhinotmetus; and the mutilated tyrant was banished to Chersonæ in Crim-Tartary, a lonely settlement, where corn, wine, and oil were imported as foreign luxuries.

On the edge of the Scythian wilderness Justinian still cherished the pride of his birth, and the hope of his restoration. After three years' exile, he received the pleasing intelligence that his injury was avenged by a second revolution, and that Leontius in his turn had been dethroned and mutilated by the rebel Apsimar, who assumed the more respectable name of Tiberius. But the claim of lineal succession was still formidable to a plebeian usurper; and his jealousy was stimulated by the complaints and charges of the Chersonites, who beheld the vices of the tyrant in the spirit of the exile. With a band of followers, attached to his person by common hope or common despair, Justinian fled from the inhospitable shore to the horde of the Chozars, who pitched their tents between the Tanais and Borysthenes. The khan entertained with piety and respect the royal suppliant: Phanagoria, once an opulent city, on the Asiatic side of the lake Mæotis, was assigned for his residence; and every Roman prejudice was stifled in his marriage with the sister of the barbarian, who seems, however, from the name of Theodora, to have received the sacrament of baptism. But the faithless Chozar was soon tempted by the gold of Constantinople: and had not the design been revealed by the conjugal love of Theodora, her husband must have been assassinated or betrayed into the power of his enemies. After strangling, with his own hands, the two emissaries of the khan, Justinian sent back his wife to her brother, and embarked on the Euxine in search of new and more faithful allies. His vessel was assaulted by a violent tempest; and one of his pious companions advised him to deserve the mercy of God by a vow of general forgiveness if he should be restored to the throne. "Of forgiveness?" replied the intrepid tyrant: "may I perish this instant—may the Almighty whelm me in the waves, if I consent to spare a single head of my enemies!" He survived this impious menace, sailed into the mouth of the Danube, trusted his person in the royal village of the Bulgarians, and purchased the aid of Terbelis, a pagan conqueror, by the promise of his daughter, and a fair partition of the treasures of the empire. The Bulgarian kingdom extended to the confines of Thrace; and the two princes besieged Constantinople at the head of fifteen thousand horse. Apsimar was dismayed by the sudden and hostile apparition of his rival, whose head had been promised by the Chozar, and of whose evasion he was yet ignorant. After an absence of ten years the crimes of Justinian were faintly remembered, and the birth and misfortunes of their hereditary sovereign excited the pity of the multitude, ever discontented with the ruling powers; and by the active diligence of his adherents he was introduced into the city and palace of Constantine.

In rewarding his allies, and recalling his wife, Justinian displayed some sense of honour and gratitude; and Terbelis retired, after sweeping away a heap of gold coin which he measured with his Scythian whip. But never was vow more religiously performed than the sacred oath of revenge which he had sworn amidst the storms of the Euxine. The two usurpers, for I must reserve the name of tyrant for the conqueror, were dragged into the hippodrome, the one from his prison, the other from his palace. Before their execution Leontius and Apsimar were cast prostrate in chains beneath the throne of the emperor; and Justinian, planting a foot on each of their necks, contemplated above an hour the chariot race, while the inconstant people shouted, in the words of the Psalmist, "Thou shalt trample on the asp and basilisk, and on the lion and dragon shalt thou set thy foot!" The universal defection which he had once experienced might provoke him to repeat the wish of Caligula, that the Roman people had but one head. Yet I shall presume to observe that such a wish is unworthy of an ingenious tyrant, since his revenge and cruelty would have been extinguished by a single blow, instead of the slow variety of tortures which Justinian inflicted on the victims of his anger. His pleasures were inexhaustible: neither private virtue nor public service could expiate the guilt of active, or even passive, obedience to an established government; and, during the six years of his new reign, he considered the axe, the cord, and the rack as the only instruments of royalty. But his most implacable hatred was pointed against the Chersonites, who had insulted his exile and violated the laws of hospitality. Their remote situation afforded some means of defence, or at least of escape; and a grievous tax was imposed on Constantinople to supply the preparations of a fleet and army. "All are guilty, and all must perish," was the mandate of Justinian; and the bloody execution was intrusted to his favourite Stephen, who was recommended by the epithet of the Savage. Yet even the savage Stephen imperfectly accomplished the intentions of his sovereign. The slowness of his attack allowed the greater part of the inhabitants to withdraw into the country; and the minister of vengeance contented himself with reducing the youth of both sexes to a state of servitude, with roasting alive seven of the principal citizens, with drowning twenty in the sea, and with reserving forty-two in chains to receive their doom from the mouth of the emperor. In their return the fleet was driven on the rocky shores of Anatolia; and Justinian applauded the obedience of the Euxine, which had involved so many thousands of his subjects and enemies in a common shipwreck: but the tyrant was still insatiate of blood; and a second expedition was commanded to extirpate the remains of the proscribed colony. In the short interval the Chersonites had returned to their city, and were prepared to die in arms; the khan of the Chozars had renounced the cause of his odious brother; the exiles of every province were assembled in Tauris; and Bardanes, under the name of Philippicus, was invested with the purple. The Imperial troops, unwilling and unable to perpetrate the revenge of Justinian, escaped his displeasure by abjuring his allegiance; the fleet, under their new sovereign, steered back a more auspicious course to the harbours of Sinope and Constantinople; and every tongue was prompt to pronounce, every hand to execute, the death of the tyrant. Destitute of friends, he was deserted by his barbarian guards; and the stroke of the assassin was praised as an act of patriotism and Roman virtue. His son Tiberius had taken refuge in a church; his aged grandmother guarded the door; and the innocent youth, suspending round his neck the most formidable relics, embraced with one hand the altar, with the other the wood of the true cross. But the popular fury that dares to trample on superstition, is deaf to the cries of humanity; and the race of Heraclius was extinguished after a reign of one hundred years.

Between the fall of the Heraclian and the rise of the Isaurian dynasty, a short interval of six years is divided into three reigns. Bardanes, or Philippicus, was hailed at Constantinople as a hero who had delivered his country from a tyrant; and he might taste some moments of happiness in the first transports of sincere and universal joy. Justinian had left behind him an ample treasure, the fruit of cruelty and rapine: but this useful fund was soon and idly dissipated by his successor. On the festival of his birthday Philippicus entertained the multitude with the games of the hippodrome; from thence he paraded through the streets with a thousand banners and a thousand trumpets; refreshed himself in the baths of Zeuxippus, and, returning to the palace, entertained his nobles with a sumptuous banquet. At the meridian hour he withdrew to his chamber, intoxicated with flattery and wine, and forgetful that his example had made every subject ambitious, and that every ambitious subject was his secret enemy. Some bold conspirators introduced themselves in the disorder of the feast; and the slumbering monarch was surprised, bound, blinded, and deposed, before he was sensible of his danger. Yet the traitors were deprived of their reward; and the free voice of the senate and people promoted Artemius from the office of secretary to that of emperor: he assumed the title of Anastasius the Second, and displayed in a short and troubled reign the virtues both of peace and war. But after the extinction of the Imperial line the rule of obedience was violated, and every change diffused the seeds of new revolutions. In a mutiny of the fleet an obscure and reluctant officer of the revenue was forcibly invested with the purple; after some months of a naval war, Anastasius resigned the sceptre; and the conqueror, Theodosius the Third, submitted in his turn to the superior ascendant of Leo, the general and emperor of the Oriental troops. His two predecessors were permitted to embrace the ecclesiastical profession: the restless impatience of Anastasius tempted him to risk and to lose his life in a treasonable enterprise; but the last days of Theodosius were honourable and secure. The single sublime word, "HEALTH," which he inscribed on his tomb, expresses the confidence of philosophy or religion; and the fame of his miracles was long preserved among the people of Ephesus. This convenient shelter of the church might sometimes impose a lesson of clemency; but it may be questioned whether it is for the public interest to diminish the perils of unsuccessful ambition.

I have dwelt on the fall of a tyrant; I shall briefly represent the founder of a new dynasty, who is known to posterity by the invectives of his enemies, and whose public and private life is involved in the ecclesiastical story of the Iconoclasts. Yet in spite of the clamours of superstition, a favourable prejudice for the character of Leo the Isaurian may be reasonably drawn from the obscurity of his birth and the duration of his reign.—I. In an age of manly spirit the prospect of an Imperial reward would have kindled every energy of the mind, and produced a crowd of competitors as deserving as they were desirous to reign. Even in the corruption and debility of the modern Greeks the elevation of a plebeian from the last to the first rank of society supposes some qualifications above the level of the multitude. He would probably be ignorant and disdainful of speculative science; and, in the pursuit of fortune, he might absolve himself from the obligations of benevolence and justice; but to his character we may ascribe the useful virtues of prudence and fortitude, the knowledge of mankind, and the important art of gaining their confidence and directing their passions. It is agreed that Leo was a native of Isauria, and that Conon was his primitive name. The writers, whose awkward satire is praise, describe him as an itinerant pedlar, who drove an ass with some paltry merchandise to the country fairs; and foolishly relate that he met on the road some Jewish fortune-tellers, who promised him the Roman empire, on condition that he should abolish the worship of idols. A more probable account relates the migration of his father from Asia Minor to Thrace, where he exercised the lucrative trade of a grazier; and he must have acquired considerable wealth, since the first introduction of his son was procured by a supply of five hundred sheep to the Imperial camp. His first service was in the guards of Justinian, where he soon attracted the notice, and by degrees the jealousy, of the tyrant. His valour and dexterity were conspicuous in the Colchian war: from Anastasius he received the command of the Anatolian legions, and by the suffrage of the soldiers he was raised to the empire with the general applause of the Roman world.—II. In this dangerous elevation Leo the Third supported himself against the envy of his equals, the discontent of a powerful faction, and the assaults of his foreign and domestic enemies. The Catholics, who accuse his religious innovations, are obliged to confess that they were undertaken with temper and conducted with firmness. Their silence respects the wisdom of his administration and the purity of his manners. After a reign of twenty-four years he peaceably expired in the palace of Constantinople; and the purple which he had acquired was transmitted by the right of inheritance to the third generation.

In a long reign of thirty-four years the son and successor of Leo, Constantine the Fifth, surnamed Copronymus, attacked with less temperate zeal the images or idols of the church. Their votaries have exhausted the bitterness of religious gall in their portrait of this spotted panther, this antichrist, this flying dragon of the serpent's seed, who surpassed the vices of Elagabalus and Nero. His reign was a long butchery of whatever was most noble, or holy, or innocent, in his empire. In person, the emperor assisted at the execution of his victims, surveyed their agonies, listened to their groans, and indulged, without satiating, his appetite for blood: a plate of noses was accepted as a grateful offering, and his domestics were often scourged or mutilated by the royal hand. His surname was derived from his pollution of his baptismal font. The infant might be excused; but the manly pleasures of Copronymus degraded him below the level of a brute; his lust confounded the eternal distinction of sex and species, and he seemed to extract some unnatural delight from the objects most offensive to human sense. In his religion the Iconoclast was a Heretic, a Jew, a Mohammedan, a Pagan, and an Atheist; and his belief of an invisible power could be discovered only in his magic rites, human victims, and nocturnal sacrifices to Venus and the demons of antiquity. His life was stained with the most opposite vices, and the ulcers which covered his body anticipated before his death the sentiment of hell-tortures. Of these accusations, which I have so patiently copied, a part is refuted by its own absurdity; and in the private anecdotes of the life of princes, the lie is more easy as the detection is more difficult. Without adopting the pernicious maxim, that, where much is alleged, something must be true, I can however discern that Constantine the Fifth was dissolute and cruel. Calumny is more prone to exaggerate than to invent; and her licentious tongue is checked in some measure by the experience of the age and country to which she appeals. Of the bishops and monks, the generals and magistrates, who are said to have suffered under his reign, the numbers are recorded, the names were conspicuous, the execution was public, the mutilation visible and permanent. The Catholics hated the person and government of Copronymus; but even their hatred is a proof of their oppression. They dissembled the provocations which might excuse or justify his rigour, but even these provocations must gradually inflame his resentment and harden his temper in the use or the abuse of his despotism. Yet the character of the fifth Constantine was not devoid of merit, nor did his government always deserve the curses or the contempt of the Greeks. From the confession of his enemies I am informed of the restoration of an ancient aqueduct, of the redemption of two thousand five hundred captives, of the uncommon plenty of the times, and of the new colonies with which he repeopled Constantinople and the Thracian cities. They reluctantly praise his activity and courage; he was on horseback in the field at the head of his legions; and, although the fortune of his arms was various, he triumphed by sea and land, on the Euphrates and the Danube, in civil and barbarian war. Heretical praise must be cast into the scale to counterbalance the weight of orthodox invective. The Iconoclasts revered the virtues of the prince: forty years after his death they still prayed before the tomb of the saint. A miraculous vision was propagated by fanaticism or fraud: and the Christian hero appeared on a milk-white steed, brandishing his lance against the pagans of Bulgaria: "An absurd fable," says the Catholic historian, "since Copronymus is chained with the demons in the abyss of hell."

Leo the Fourth, the son of the fifth and the father of the sixth Constantine, was of a feeble constitution both of mind and body, and the principal care of his reign was the settlement of the succession. The association of the young Constantine was urged by the officious zeal of his subjects; and the emperor, conscious of his decay, complied, after a prudent hesitation, with their unanimous wishes. The royal infant, at the age of five years, was crowned with his mother Irene; and the national consent was ratified by every circumstance of pomp and solemnity that could dazzle the eyes or bind the conscience of the Greeks. An oath of fidelity was administered in the palace, the church, and the hippodrome, to the several orders of the state, who adjured the holy names of the son and mother of God. "Be witness, O Christ! that we will watch over the safety of Constantine the son of Leo, expose our lives in his service, and bear true allegiance to his person and posterity." They pledged their faith on the wood of the true cross, and the act of their engagement was deposited on the altar of St. Sophia. The first to swear, and the first to violate their oath, were the five sons of Copronymus by a second marriage; and the story of these princes is singular and tragic. The right of primogeniture excluded them from the throne; the injustice of their elder brother defrauded them of a legacy of about two millions sterling; some vain titles were not deemed a sufficient compensation for wealth and power; and they repeatedly conspired against their nephew, before and after the death of his father. Their first attempt was pardoned; for the second offence they were condemned to the ecclesiastical state; and for the third treason, Nicephorus, the eldest and most guilty, was deprived of his eyes, and his four brothers, Christopher, Nicetas, Anthimus, and Eudoxus, were punished, as a milder sentence, by the amputation of their tongues. After five years' confinement they escaped to the church of St. Sophia, and displayed a pathetic spectacle to the people. "Countrymen and Christians," cried Nicephorus for himself and his mute brethren, "behold the sons of your emperor, if you can still recognise our features in this miserable state. A life, an imperfect life, is all that the malice of our enemies has spared. It is now threatened, and we now throw ourselves on your compassion." The rising murmur might have produced a revolution had it not been checked by the presence of a minister, who soothed the unhappy princes with flattery and hope, and gently drew them from the sanctuary to the palace. They were speedily embarked for Greece, and Athens was allotted for the place of their exile. In this calm retreat, and in their helpless condition, Nicephorus and his brothers were tormented by the thirst of power, and tempted by a Sclavonian chief, who offered to break their prison and to lead them in arms, and in the purple, to the gates of Constantinople. But the Athenian people, ever zealous in the cause of Irene, prevented her justice or cruelty; and the five sons of Copronymus were plunged in eternal darkness and oblivion.

For himself, that emperor had chosen a barbarian wife, the daughter of the khan of the Chozars; but in the marriage of his heir he preferred an Athenian virgin, an orphan seventeen years old, whose sole fortune must have consisted in her personal accomplishments. The nuptials of Leo and Irene were celebrated with royal pomp; she soon acquired the love and confidence of a feeble husband, and in his testament he declared the empress guardian of the Roman world, and of their son Constantine the Sixth, who was no more than ten years of age. During his childhood, Irene most ably and assiduously discharged, in her public administration, the duties of a faithful mother; and her zeal in the restoration of images has deserved the name and honours of a saint, which she still occupies in the Greek calendar. But the emperor attained the maturity of youth; the maternal yoke became more grievous; and he listened to the favourites of his own age, who shared his pleasures, and were ambitious of sharing his power. Their reasons convinced him of his right, their praises of his ability, to reign; and he consented to reward the services of Irene by a perpetual banishment to the isle of Sicily. But her vigilance and penetration easily disconcerted their rash projects: a similar, or more severe, punishment was retaliated on themselves and their advisers; and Irene inflicted on the ungrateful prince the chastisement of a boy. After this contest the mother and the son were at the head of two domestic factions; and instead of mild influence and voluntary obedience, she held in chains a captive and an enemy. The empress was overthrown by the abuse of victory; the oath of fidelity, which she exacted to herself alone, was pronounced with reluctant murmurs; and the bold refusal of the Armenian guards encouraged a free and general declaration that Constantine the Sixth was the lawful emperor of the Romans. In this character he ascended his hereditary throne, and dismissed Irene to a life of solitude and repose. But her haughty spirit condescended to the arts of dissimulation: she flattered the bishops and eunuchs, revived the filial tenderness of the prince, regained his confidence, and betrayed his credulity. The character of Constantine was not destitute of sense or spirit; but his education had been studiously neglected; and his ambitious mother exposed to the public censure the vices which she had nourished and the actions which she had secretly advised: his divorce and second marriage offended the prejudices of the clergy, and by his imprudent rigour he forfeited the attachment of the Armenian guards. A powerful conspiracy was formed for the restoration of Irene; and the secret, though widely diffused, was faithfully kept above eight months, till the emperor, suspicious of his danger, escaped from Constantinople with the design of appealing to the provinces and armies. By this hasty flight the empress was left on the brink of the precipice; yet before she implored the mercy of her son, Irene addressed a private epistle to the friends whom she had placed about his person, with a menace, that unless *they* accomplished, *she* would reveal, their treason. Their fear rendered them intrepid; they seized the emperor on the Asiatic shore, and he was transported to the porphyry apartment of the palace, where he had first seen the light. In the mind of Irene ambition had stifled every sentiment of humanity and nature; and it was decreed in her bloody council that Constantine should be rendered incapable of the throne: her emissaries assaulted the sleeping prince, and stabbed their daggers with such violence and precipitation into his eyes as if they meant to execute a mortal sentence. An ambiguous passage of Theophanes persuaded the annalist of the church that death was the immediate consequence of this barbarous execution. The Catholics have been deceived or subdued by the authority of Baronius; and Protestant zeal has re-echoed the words of a cardinal, desirous, as it should seem, to favour the patroness of images. Yet the blind son of Irene survived many years, oppressed by the court and forgotten by the world: the Isaurian dynasty was silently extinguished; and the memory of Constantine was recalled only by the nuptials of his daughter Euphrosyne with the emperor Michael the Second.

The most bigoted orthodoxy has justly execrated the unnatural mother, who may not easily be paralleled in the history of crimes. To her bloody deed superstition has attributed a subsequent darkness of seventeen days, during which many vessels in mid-day were driven from their course, as if the sun, a globe of fire so vast and so remote, could sympathise with the atoms of a revolving planet. On earth, the crime of Irene was left five years unpunished; her reign was crowned with external splendour; and if she could silence the voice of conscience, she neither heard nor regarded the reproaches of mankind. The Roman world bowed to the government of a female; and as she moved through the streets of Constantinople the reins of four milk-white steeds were held by as many patricians, who marched on foot before the golden chariot of their queen. But these patricians were for the most part eunuchs; and their black ingratitude justified, on this occasion, the popular hatred and contempt. Raised, enriched, intrusted with the first dignities of the empire, they basely conspired against their benefactress; the great treasurer Nicephorus was secretly invested with the purple; her successor was introduced into the palace, and crowned at St. Sophia by the venal patriarch. In their first interview she recapitulated with dignity the revolutions of her life, gently accused the perfidy of Nicephorus, insinuated that he owed his life to her unsuspicious clemency, and, for the throne and treasures which she resigned, solicited a decent and honourable retreat. His avarice refused this modest compensation; and, in her exile on the isle of Lesbos, the empress earned a scanty subsistence by the labours of her distaff.

Many tyrants have reigned undoubtedly more criminal than Nicephorus, but none perhaps have more deeply incurred the universal abhorrence of their people. His character was stained with the three odious vices of hypocrisy, ingratitude, and avarice: his want of virtue was not redeemed by any superior talents, nor his want of talents by any pleasing qualifications. Unskilful and unfortunate in war, Nicephorus was vanquished by the Saracens and slain by the Bulgarians; and the advantage of his death overbalanced, in the public opinion, the destruction of a Roman army. His son and heir Stauracius escaped from the field with a mortal wound; yet six months of an expiring life were sufficient to refute his indecent, though popular declaration, that he would in all things avoid the example of his father. On the near prospect of his decease, Michael, the great master of the palace, and the husband of his sister Procopia, was named by every person of the palace and city, except by his envious brother. Tenacious of a sceptre now falling from his hand, he conspired against the life of his successor, and cherished the idea of changing to a democracy the Roman empire. But these rash projects served only to inflame the zeal of the people and to remove the scruples of the candidate: Michael the First accepted the purple, and before he sunk into the grave the son of Nicephorus implored the clemency of his new sovereign. Had Michael in an age of peace ascended an hereditary throne, he might have reigned and died the father of his people: but his mild virtues were adapted to the shade of private life, nor was he capable of controlling the ambition of his equals, or of resisting the arms of the victorious Bulgarians. While his want of ability and success exposed him to the contempt of the soldiers, the masculine spirit of his wife Procopia awakened their indignation. Even the Greeks of the ninth century were provoked by the insolence of a female who, in the front of the standards, presumed to direct their discipline and animate their valour; and their licentious clamours advised the new Semiramis to reverence the majesty of a Roman camp. After an unsuccessful campaign the emperor left, in their winter quarters of Thrace, a disaffected army under the command of his enemies; and their artful eloquence persuaded the soldiers to break the dominion of the eunuchs, to degrade the husband of Procopia, and to assert the right of a military election. They marched towards the capital: yet the clergy, the senate, and the people of Constantinople adhered to the cause of Michael; and the troops and treasures of Asia might have protracted the mischiefs of civil war. But his humanity (by the ambitious it will be termed his weakness) protested that not a drop of Christian blood should be shed in his quarrel, and his messengers presented the conquerors with the keys of the city and the palace. They were disarmed by his innocence and submission; his life and his eyes were spared; and the Imperial monk enjoyed the comforts of solitude and religion above thirty-two years after he had been stripped of the purple and separated from his wife.

A rebel, in the time of Nicephorus, the famous and unfortunate Bardanes, had once the curiosity to consult an Asiatic prophet, who, after prognosticating his fall, announced the fortunes of his three principal officers, Leo the Armenian, Michael the Phrygian, and Thomas the Cappadocian, the successive reigns of the two former, the fruitless and fatal enterprise of the third. This prediction was verified, or rather was produced, by the event. Ten years afterwards, when the Thracian camp rejected the husband of Procopia, the crown was presented to the same Leo, the first in military rank and the secret author of the mutiny. As he affected to hesitate, "With this sword," said his companion Michael, "I will open the gates of Constantinople to your Imperial sway, or instantly plunge it into your bosom, if you obstinately resist the just desires of your fellow-soldiers." The compliance of the Armenian was rewarded with the empire, and he reigned seven years and a half under the name of Leo the Fifth. Educated in a camp, and ignorant both of laws and letters, he introduced into his civil government the rigour and even cruelty of military discipline; but if his severity was sometimes dangerous to the innocent, it was always formidable to the guilty. His religious inconstancy was taxed by the epithet of Chameleon, but the Catholics have acknowledged, by the voice of a saint and confessors, that the life of the Iconoclast was useful to the republic. The zeal of his companion Michael was repaid with riches, honours, and military command; and his subordinate talents were beneficially employed in the public service. Yet the Phrygian was dissatisfied at receiving as a favour a scanty portion of the Imperial prize which he had bestowed on his equal; and his discontent, which sometimes evaporated in hasty discourse, at length assumed a more threatening and hostile aspect against a prince whom he represented as a cruel tyrant. That tyrant, however, repeatedly detected, warned, and dismissed the old companion of his arms, till fear and resentment prevailed over gratitude; and Michael, after a scrutiny into his actions and designs, was convicted of treason, and sentenced to be burnt alive in the furnace of the private baths. The devout humanity of the empress Theophano was fatal to her husband and family. A solemn day, the twenty-fifth of December, had been fixed for the execution: she urged that the anniversary of the Saviour's birth would be profaned by this inhuman spectacle, and Leo consented with reluctance to a decent respite. But on the vigil of the feast his sleepless anxiety prompted him to visit at the dead of night the chamber in which his enemy was confined: he beheld him released from his chain, and stretched on his gaoler's bed in a profound slumber: Leo was alarmed at these signs of security and intelligence; but though he retired with silent steps, his entrance and departure were noticed by a slave who lay concealed in a corner of the prison. Under the pretence of requesting the spiritual aid of a confessor, Michael informed the conspirators that their lives depended on his discretion, and that a few hours were left to assure their own safety, by the deliverance of their friend and country. On the great festivals a chosen band of priests and chanters was admitted into the palace by a private gate to sing matins in the chapel; and Leo, who regulated with the same strictness the discipline of the choir and of the camp, was seldom absent from these early devotions. In the ecclesiastical habit, but with swords under their robes, the conspirators mingled with the procession, lurked in the angles of the chapel, and expected, as a signal of murder, the intonation of the first psalm by the emperor himself. The imperfect light and the uniformity of dress, might have favoured his escape, while their assault was pointed against a harmless priest; but they soon discovered their mistake, and encompassed on all sides the royal victim. Without a weapon and without a friend, he grasped a weighty cross, and stood at bay against the hunters of his life; but as he asked for mercy, "This is the hour, not of mercy, but of vengeance," was the inexorable reply. The stroke of a well-aimed sword separated from his body the right arm and the cross, and Leo the Armenian was slain at the foot of the altar.

A memorable reverse of fortune was displayed in Michael the Second, who from a defect in his speech was surnamed the Stammerer. He was snatched from the fiery furnace to the sovereignty of an empire; and as in the tumult a smith could not readily be found, the fetters remained on his legs several hours after he was seated on the throne of the Cæsars. The royal blood which had been the price of his elevation was unprofitably spent; in the purple he retained the ignoble vices of his origin; and Michael lost his provinces with as supine indifference as if they had been the inheritance of his fathers. His title was disputed by Thomas, the last of the military triumvirate, who transported into Europe fourscore thousand barbarians from the banks of the Tigris and the shores of the Caspian. He formed the siege of Constantinople; but the capital was defended with spiritual and carnal weapons; a Bulgarian king assaulted the camp of the Orientals, and Thomas had the misfortune or the weakness to fall alive into the power of the conqueror. The hands and feet of the rebel were amputated; he was placed on an ass, and, amidst the insults of the people, was led through the streets, which he sprinkled with his blood. The depravation of manners, as savage as they were corrupt, is marked by the presence of the emperor himself. Deaf to the lamentations of a fellow-soldier, he incessantly pressed the discovery of more accomplices, till his curiosity was checked by the question of an honest or guilty minister: "Would you give credit to an enemy against the most faithful of your friends?" After the death of his first wife, the emperor, at the request of the senate, drew from her monastery Euphrosyne, the daughter of Constantine the Sixth. Her august birth might justify a stipulation in the marriage-contract that her children should equally share the empire with their elder brother. But the nuptials of Michael and Euphrosyne were barren; and she was content with the title of mother of Theophilus, his son and successor.

The character of Theophilus is a rare example in which religious zeal has allowed and perhaps magnified the virtues of a heretic and a persecutor. His valour was often felt by the enemies, and his justice by the subjects, of the monarchy; but the valour of Theophilus was rash and fruitless, and his justice arbitrary and cruel. He displayed the banner of the cross against the Saracens; but his five expeditions were concluded by a signal overthrow: Amorium, the native city of his ancestors, was levelled with the ground, and from his military toils he derived only the surname of the Unfortunate.

The wisdom of a sovereign is comprised in the institution of laws and the choice of magistrates, and, while he seems without action, his civil government revolves round his centre with the silence and order of the planetary system. But the justice of Theophilus was fashioned on the model of the Oriental despots, who, in personal and irregular acts of authority, consult the reason or passion of the moment, without measuring the sentence by the law, or the penalty by the offence. A poor woman threw herself at the emperor's feet to complain of a powerful neighbour, the brother of the empress, who had raised his palace-wall to such an inconvenient height, that her humble dwelling was excluded from light and air! On the proof of the fact, instead of granting, like an ordinary judge, sufficient or ample damages to the plaintiff, the sovereign adjudged to her use and benefit the palace and the ground. Nor was Theophilus content with this extravagant satisfaction: his zeal converted a civil trespass into a criminal act; and the unfortunate patrician was stripped and scourged in the public place of Constantinople. For some venial offences, some defect of equity or vigilance, the principal ministers, a præfect, a quæstor, a captain of the guards, were banished or mutilated, or scalded with boiling pitch, or burnt alive in the hippodrome; and as these dreadful examples might be the effects of error or caprice, they must have alienated from his service the best and wisest of the citizens. But the pride of the monarch was flattered in the exercise of power, or, as he thought, of virtue; and the people, safe in their obscurity, applauded the danger and debasement of their superiors. This extraordinary rigour was justified in some measure by its salutary consequences; since, after a scrutiny of seventeen days, not a complaint or abuse could be found in the court or city: and it might be alleged that the Greeks could be ruled only with a rod of iron, and that the public interest is the motive and law of the supreme judge. Yet in the crime, or the suspicion, of treason, that judge is of all others the most credulous and partial. Theophilus might inflict a tardy vengeance on the assassins of Leo and the saviours of his father; but he enjoyed the fruits of their crime; and his jealous tyranny sacrificed a brother and a prince to the future safety of his life. A Persian of the race of the Sassanides died in poverty and exile at Constantinople, leaving an only son, the issue of a plebeian marriage. At the age of twelve years the royal birth of Theophobus was revealed, and his merit was not unworthy of his birth. He was educated in the Byzantine palace, a Christian and a soldier; advanced with rapid steps in the career of fortune and glory; received the hand of the emperor's sister; and was promoted to the command of thirty thousand Persians, who, like his father, had fled from the Mohammedan conquerors. These troops, doubly infected with mercenary and fanatic vices, were desirous of revolting against their benefactor, and erecting the standard of their native king: but the loyal Theophobus rejected their offers, disconcerted their schemes, and escaped from their hands to the camp or palace of his royal brother. A generous confidence might have secured a faithful and able guardian for his wife and his infant son, to whom Theophilus, in the flower of his age, was compelled to leave the inheritance of the empire. But his jealousy was exasperated by envy and disease: he feared the dangerous virtues which might either support or oppress their infancy and weakness; and the dying emperor demanded the head of the Persian prince. With savage delight he recognised the familiar features of his brother: "Thou art no longer Theophobus," he said; and, sinking on his couch, he added, with a faltering voice, "Soon, too soon, I shall be no more Theophilus!"

The Russians, who have borrowed from the Greeks the greatest part of their civil and ecclesiastical policy, preserved, till the last century, a singular institution in the marriage of the Czar. They collected, not the virgins of every rank and of every province, a vain and romantic idea, but the daughters of the principal nobles, who awaited in the palace the choice of their sovereign. It is affirmed that a similar method was adopted in the nuptials of Theophilus. With a golden apple in his hand, he slowly walked between two lines of contending beauties: his eye was detained by the charms of Icasia, and, in the awkwardness of a first declaration, the prince could only observe, that in this world, women had been the cause of much evil; "And surely, sir," she pertly replied, "they have likewise been the occasion of much good." This affectation of unseasonable wit displeased the Imperial lover: he turned aside in disgust; Icasia concealed her mortification in a convent; and the modest silence of Theodora was rewarded with the golden apple. She deserved the love, but did not escape the severity, of her lord. From the palace garden he beheld a vessel deeply laden, and steering into the port: on the discovery that the precious cargo of Syrian luxury was the property of his wife, he

condemned the ship to the flames, with a sharp reproach, that her avarice had degraded the character of an empress into that of a merchant. Yet his last choice intrusted her with the guardianship of the empire and her son Michael, who was left an orphan in the fifth year of his age. The restoration of images, and the final extirpation of the Iconoclasts, has endeared her name to the devotion of the Greeks; but in the fervour of religious zeal Theodora entertained a grateful regard for the memory and salvation of her husband. After thirteen years of a prudent and frugal administration, she perceived the decline of her influence; but the second Irene imitated only the virtues of her predecessor. Instead of conspiring against the life or government of her son, she retired without a struggle, though not without a murmur, to the solitude of private life, deploring the ingratitude, the vices, and the inevitable ruin of the worthless youth.

Among the successors of Nero and Elagabalus we have not hitherto found the imitation of their vices, the character of a Roman prince who considered pleasure as the object of life, and virtue as the enemy of pleasure. Whatever might have been the maternal care of Theodora in the education of Michael the Third, her unfortunate son was a king before he was a man. If the ambitious mother laboured to check the progress of reason, she could not cool the ebullition of passion; and her selfish policy was justly repaid by the contempt and ingratitude of the headstrong youth. At the age of eighteen he rejected her authority, without feeling his own incapacity to govern the empire and himself. With Theodora all gravity and wisdom retired from the court; their place was supplied by the alternate dominion of vice and folly; and it was impossible, without forfeiting the public esteem, to acquire or preserve the favour of the emperor. The millions of gold and silver which had been accumulated for the service of the state were lavished on the vilest of men, who flattered his passions and shared his pleasures; and, in a reign of thirteen years, the richest of sovereigns was compelled to strip the palace and the churches of their precious furniture. Like Nero, he delighted in the amusements of the theatre, and sighed to be surpassed in the accomplishments in which he should have blushed to excel. Yet the studies of Nero in music and poetry betrayed some symptoms of a liberal taste; the more ignoble arts of the son of Theophilus were confined to the chariot-race of the hippodrome. The four factions which had agitated the peace, still amused the idleness, of the capital: for himself, the emperor assumed the blue livery: the three rival colours were distributed to his favourites, and in the vile though eager contention he forgot the dignity of his person and the safety of his dominions. He silenced the messenger of an invasion who presumed to divert his attention in the most critical moment of the race; and by his command the importunate beacons were extinguished that too frequently spread the alarm from Tarsus to Constantinople. The most skilful charioteers obtained the first place in his confidence and esteem; their merit was profusely rewarded; the emperor feasted in their houses, and presented their children at the baptismal font; and while he applauded his own popularity, he affected to blame the cold and stately reserve of his predecessors. The unnatural lusts which had degraded even the manhood of Nero were banished from the world; yet the strength of Michael was consumed by the indulgence of love and intemperance. In his midnight revels, when his passions were inflamed by wine, he was provoked to issue the most sanguinary commands; and if any feelings of humanity were left, he was reduced, with the return of sense, to approve the salutary disobedience of his servants. But the most extraordinary feature in the character of Michael is the profane mockery of the religion of his country. The superstition of the Greeks might indeed excite the smile of a philosopher; but his smile would have been rational and temperate, and he must have condemned the ignorant folly of a youth who insulted the objects of public veneration. A buffoon of the court was invested in the robes of the patriarch: his twelve metropolitans, among whom the emperor was ranked, assumed their ecclesiastical garments: they used or abused the sacred vessels of the altar; and in their bacchanalian feasts the holy communion was administered in a nauseous compound of vinegar and mustard. Nor were these impious spectacles concealed from the eyes of the city. On the day of a solemn festival, the emperor, with his bishops or buffoons, rode on asses through the streets, encountered the true patriarch at the head of his clergy, and, by their licentious shouts and obscene gestures, disordered the gravity of the Christian procession. The devotion of Michael appeared only in some offence to reason or piety: he received his theatrical crowns from the statue of the Virgin; and an Imperial tomb was violated for the sake of burning the bones of Constantine the Iconoclast. By this extravagant

conduct the son of Theophilus became as contemptible as he was odious: every citizen was impatient for the deliverance of his country; and even the favourites of the moment were apprehensive that a caprice might snatch away what a caprice had bestowed. In the thirtieth year of his age, and in the hour of intoxication and sleep, Michael the Third was murdered in his chamber by the founder of a new dynasty, whom the emperor had raised to an equality of rank and power.

The genealogy of Basil the Macedonian (if it be not the spurious offspring of pride and flattery) exhibits a genuine picture of the revolution of the most illustrious families. The Arsacides, the rivals of Rome, possessed the sceptre of the East near four hundred years: a younger branch of these Parthian kings continued to reign in Armenia, and their royal descendants survived the partition and servitude of that ancient monarchy. Two of these, Artabanus and Chlienes, escaped or retired to the court of Leo the First: his bounty seated them in a safe and hospitable exile in the province of Macedonia; Adrianople was their final settlement. During several generations they maintained the dignity of their birth; and their Roman patriotism rejected the tempting offers of the Persian and Arabian powers, who recalled them to their native country. But their splendour was insensibly clouded by time and poverty; and the father of Basil was reduced to a small farm, which he cultivated with his own hands: yet he scorned to disgrace the blood of the Arsacides by a plebeian alliance: his wife, a widow of Adrianople, was pleased to count among her ancestors the great Constantine; and their royal infant was connected by some dark affinity of lineage or country with the Macedonian Alexander. No sooner was he born than the cradle of Basil, his family, and his city, were swept away by an inundation of the Bulgarians: he was educated a slave in a foreign land; and in this severe discipline he acquired the hardiness of body and flexibility of mind which promoted his future elevation. In the age of youth or manhood he shared the deliverance of the Roman captives, who generously broke their fetters, marched through Bulgaria to the shores of the Euxine, defeated two armies of barbarians, embarked in the ships which had been stationed for their reception, and returned to Constantinople, from whence they were distributed to their respective homes. But the freedom of Basil was naked and destitute: his farm was ruined by the calamities of war: after his father's death his manual labour or service could no longer support a family of orphans; and he resolved to seek a more conspicuous theatre, in which every virtue and every vice may lead to the paths of greatness. The first night of his arrival at Constantinople, without friends or money, the weary pilgrim slept on the steps of the church of St. Diomede: he was fed by the casual hospitality of a monk; and was introduced to the service of a cousin and namesake of the emperor Theophilus, who, though himself of a diminutive person, was always followed by a train of tall and handsome domestics. Basil attended his patron to the government of Peloponnesus; eclipsed, by his personal merit, the birth and dignity of Theophilus, and formed a useful connection with a wealthy and charitable matron of Patras. Her spiritual or carnal love embraced the young adventurer, whom she adopted as her son. Danielis presented him with thirty slaves; and the produce of her bounty was expended in the support of his brothers, and the purchase of some large estates in Macedonia. His gratitude or ambition still attached him to the service of Theophilus; and a lucky accident recommended him to the notice of the court. A famous wrestler in the train of the Bulgarian ambassadors had defied, at the royal banquet, the boldest and most robust of the Greeks. The strength of Basil was praised; he accepted the challenge; and the barbarian champion was overthrown at the first onset. A beautiful but vicious horse was condemned to be hamstrung: it was subdued by the dexterity and courage of the servant of Theophilus; and his conqueror was promoted to an honourable rank in the Imperial stables. But it was impossible to obtain the confidence of Michael without complying with his vices; and his new favourite, the great chamberlain of the palace, was raised and supported by a disgraceful marriage with a royal concubine, and the dishonour of his sister, who succeeded to her place. The public administration had been abandoned to the Cæsar Bardas, the brother and enemy of Theodora; but the arts of female influence persuaded Michael to hate and to fear his uncle: he was drawn from Constantinople, under the pretence of a Cretan expedition, and stabbed in the tent of audience by the sword of the chamberlain, and in the presence of the emperor. About a month after this execution, Basil was invested with the title of Augustus and the government of the empire. He supported this unequal association till his influence was fortified by popular esteem. His life was endangered by the caprice of the em-

peror; and his dignity was profaned by a second colleague, who had rowed in the galleys. Yet the murder of his benefactor must be condemned as an act of ingratitude and treason; and the churches which he dedicated to the name of St. Michael were a poor and puerile expiation of his guilt.

The different ages of Basil the First may be compared with those of Augustus. The situation of the Greek did not allow him in his earliest youth to lead an army against his country, or to proscribe the noblest of her sons; but his aspiring genius stooped to the arts of a slave; he dissembled his ambition and even his virtues, and grasped, with the bloody hand of an assassin, the empire which he ruled with the wisdom and tenderness of a parent. A private citizen may feel his interest repugnant to his duty; but it must be from a deficiency of sense or courage that an absolute monarch can separate his happiness from his glory, or his glory from the public welfare. The life or panegyric of Basil has indeed been composed and published under the long reign of his descendants; but even their stability on the throne may be justly ascribed to the superior merit of their ancestor. In his character, his grandson Constantine has attempted to delineate a perfect image of royalty: but that feeble prince, unless he had copied a real model, could not easily have soared so high above the level of his own conduct or conceptions. But the most solid praise of Basil is drawn from the comparison of a ruined and a flourishing monarchy, that which he wrested from the dissolute Michael, and that which he bequeathed to the Macedonian dynasty. The evils which had been sanctified by time and example were corrected by his master-hand; and he revived, if not the national spirit, at least the order and majesty of the Roman empire. His application was indefatigable, his temper cool, his understanding vigorous and decisive; and in his practice he observed that rare and salutary moderation, which pursues each virtue, at an equal distance between the opposite vices. His military service had been confined to the palace; nor was the emperor endowed with the spirit or the talents of a warrior. Yet under his reign the Roman arms were again formidable to the barbarians. As soon as he had formed a new army by discipline and exercise, he appeared in person on the banks of the Euphrates, curbed the pride of the Saracens, and suppressed the dangerous though just revolt of the Manichæans. His indignation against a rebel who had long eluded his pursuit provoked him to wish and to pray that, by the grace of God, he might drive three arrows into the head of Chrysochir. That odious head, which had been obtained by treason rather than by valour, was suspended from a tree, and thrice exposed to the dexterity of the Imperial archer: a base revenge against the dead, more worthy of the times than of the character of Basil. But his principal merit was in the civil administration of the finances and of the laws. To replenish an exhausted treasury it was proposed to resume the lavish and ill-placed gifts of his predecessor: his prudence abated one moiety of the restitution; and a sum of twelve hundred thousand pounds was instantly procured to answer the most pressing demands, and to allow some space for the mature operations of economy. Among the various schemes for the improvement of the revenue, a new mode was suggested of capitation, or tribute, which would have too much depended on the arbitrary discretion of the assessors. A sufficient list of honest and able agents was instantly produced by the minister; but on the more careful scrutiny of Basil himself, only two could be found who might be safely intrusted with such dangerous powers; and they justified his esteem by declining his confidence. But the serious and successful diligence of the emperor established by degrees an equitable balance of property and payment, of receipt and expenditure; a peculiar fund was appropriated to each service; and a public method secured the interest of the prince and the property of the people. After reforming the luxury, he assigned two patrimonial estates to supply the decent plenty, of the Imperial table; the contributions of the subject were reserved for his defence; and the residue was employed in the embellishment of the capital and provinces. A taste for building, however costly, may deserve some praise and much excuse: from thence industry is fed, art is encouraged, and some object is attained of public emolument or pleasure: the use of a road, an aqueduct, or a hospital, is obvious and solid; and the hundred churches that arose by the command of Basil were consecrated to the devotion of the age. In the character of a judge he was assiduous and impartial, desirous to save, but not afraid to strike: the oppressors of the people were severely chastised; but his personal foes, whom it might be unsafe to pardon, were condemned, after the loss of their eyes, to a life of solitude and repentance. The change of language and manners demanded a revision of the obsolete jurisprudence of Justinian: the voluminous body of his Institutes, Pandects, Code, and Novels was digested under forty titles, in the Greek idiom; and the *Basilics*, which were improved and completed by his son and grandson, must be referred to the original genius of the founder of their race. This glorious reign was terminated by an accident in the chase. A furious stag entangled his horns in the belt of Basil, and raised him from his horse: he was rescued by an attendant, who cut the belt and slew the animal; but the fall, or the fever, exhausted the strength of the aged monarch, and he expired in the palace amidst the tears of his family and people. If he struck off the head of the faithful servant for presuming to draw his sword against his sovereign, the pride of despotism, which had lain dormant in his life, revived in the last moments of despair, when he no longer wanted or valued the opinion of mankind.

Of the four sons of the emperor, Constantine died before his father, whose grief and credulity were amused by a flattering impostor and a vain apparition. Stephen, the youngest, was content with the honours of a patriarch and a saint; both Leo and Alexander were alike invested with the purple, but the powers of government were solely exercised by the elder brother. The name of Leo the Sixth has been dignified with the title of *philosopher;* and the union of the prince and the sage, of the active and speculative virtues, would indeed constitute the perfection of human nature. But the claims of Leo are far short of this ideal excellence. Did he reduce his passions and appetites under the dominion of reason? His life was spent in the pomp of the palace, in the society of his wives and concubines; and even the clemency which he showed, and the peace which he strove to preserve, must be imputed to the softness and indolence of his character. Did he subdue his prejudices, and those of his subjects? His mind was tinged with the most puerile superstition; the influence of the clergy and the errors of the people were consecrated by his laws; and the oracles of Leo, which reveal, in prophetic style, the fates of the empire, are founded on the arts of astrology and divination. If we still inquire the reason of his sage appellation, it can only be replied, that the son of Basil was less ignorant than the greater part of his contemporaries in church and state; that his education had been directed by the learned Photius; and that several books of profane and ecclesiastical science were composed by the pen, or in the name, of the Imperial *philosopher*. But the reputation of his philosophy and religion was overthrown by a domestic vice, the repetition of his nuptials. The primitive ideas of the merit and holiness of celibacy were preached by the monks and entertained by the Greeks. Marriage was allowed as a necessary means for the propagation of mankind; after the death of either party the survivor might satisfy by a *second* union the weakness or the strength of the flesh; but a *third* marriage was censured as a state of legal fornication; and a *fourth* was a sin or scandal as yet unknown to the Christians of the East. In the beginning of his reign Leo himself had abolished the state of concubines, and condemned, without annulling, third marriages: but his patriotism and love soon compelled him to violate his own laws, and to incur the penance which in a similar case he had imposed on his subjects. In his first three alliances his nuptial bed was unfruitful; the emperor required a female companion, and the empire a legitimate heir. The beautiful Zoe was introduced into the palace as a concubine; and after a trial of her fecundity, and the birth of Constantine, her lover declared his intention of legitimating the mother and the child by the celebration of his fourth nuptials. But the patriarch Nicholas refused his blessing; the Imperial baptism of the young prince was obtained by a promise of separation; and the contumacious husband of Zoe was excluded from the communion of the faithful. Neither the fear of exile, nor the desertion of his brethren, nor the authority of the Latin church, nor the danger of failure or doubt in the succession to the empire, could bend the spirit of the inflexible monk. After the death of Leo he was recalled from exile to the civil and ecclesiastical administration; and the edict of union which was promulgated in the name of Constantine condemned the future scandal of fourth marriages, and left a tacit imputation on his own birth.

In the Greek language *purple* and *porphyry* are the same word: and as the colours of nature are invariable, we may learn that a dark deep red was the Tyrian dye which stained the purple of the ancients. An apartment of the Byzantine palace was lined with porphyry: it was reserved for the use of the pregnant empresses; and the royal birth of their children was expressed by the appellation of *porphyrogenite*, or born in the purple. Several of the Roman princes had been blessed with an heir; but this peculiar surname was first applied to Constantine the Seventh. His life and titular reign were of equal duration: but of fifty-four years six had elapsed before his father's death; and the son of Leo was ever the voluntary or reluctant subject of those who oppressed his weakness or abused his con-

fidence. His uncle Alexander, who had long been invested with the title of Augustus, was the first colleague and governor of the young prince but in a rapid career of vice and folly the brother of Leo already emulated the reputation of Michael; and when he was extinguished by a timely death, he entertained a project of castrating his nephew and leaving the empire to a worthless favourite. The succeeding years of the minority of Constantine were occupied by his mother Zoe, and a succession or council of seven regents, who pursued their interest, gratified their passions, abandoned the republic, supplanted each other, and finally vanished in the presence of a soldier. From an obscure origin Romanus Lecapenus had raised himself to the command of the naval armies; and in the anarchy of the times had deserved, or at least had obtained, the national esteem. With a victorious and affectionate fleet he sailed from the mouth of the Danube into the harbour of Constantinople, and was hailed as the deliverer of the people and the guardian of the prince. His supreme office was at first defined by the new appellation of father of the emperor; but Romanus soon disdained the subordinate powers of a minister, and assumed, with the titles of Cæsar and Augustus, the full independence of royalty, which he held near five-and-twenty years. His three sons, Christopher, Stephen, and Constantine, were successively adorned with the same honours, and the lawful emperor was degraded from the first to the fifth rank in this college of princes. Yet, in the preservation of his life and crown, he might still applaud his own fortune and the clemency of the usurper. The examples of ancient and modern history would have excused the ambition of Romanus: the powers and the laws of the empire were in his hand; the spurious birth of Constantine would have justified his exclusion; and the grave or the monastery was open to receive the son of the concubine. But Lecapenus does not appear to have possessed either the virtues or the vices of a tyrant. The spirit and activity of his private life dissolved away in the sunshine of the throne; and in his licentious pleasures he forgot the safety both of the republic and of his family. Of a mild and religious character, he respected the sanctity of oaths, the innocence of the youth, the memory of his parents, and the attachment of the people. The studious temper and retirement of Constantine disarmed the jealousy of power: his books and music, his pen and his pencil, were a constant source of amusement; and if he could improve a scanty allowance by the sale of his pictures, if their price was not enhanced by the name of the artist, he was endowed with a personal talent which few princes could employ in the hour of adversity.

The fall of Romanus was occasioned by his own vices and those of his children. After the decease of Christopher, his eldest son, the two surviving brothers quarreled with each other, and conspired against their father. At the hour of noon, when all strangers were regularly excluded from the palace, they entered his apartment with an armed force, and conveyed him, in the habit of a monk, to a small island in the Propontis, which was peopled by a religious community. The rumour of this domestic revolution excited a tumult in the city; but Porphyrogenitus alone, the true and lawful emperor, was the object of the public care; and the sons of Lecapenus were taught, by tardy experience, that they had achieved a guilty and perilous enterprise for the benefit of their rival. Their sister Helena, the wife of Constantine, revealed, or supposed, their treacherous design of assassinating her husband at the royal banquet. His loyal adherents were alarmed, and the two usurpers were prevented, seized, degraded from the purple, and embarked for the same island and monastery where their father had been so lately confined. Old Romanus met them on the beach with a sarcastic smile, and, after a just reproach of their folly and ingratitude, presented his Imperial colleagues with an equal share of his water and vegetable diet. In the fortieth year of his reign Constantine the Seventh obtained the possession of the Eastern world, which he ruled, or seemed to rule, near fifteen years. But he was devoid of that energy of character which could emerge into a life of action and glory; and the studies which had amused and dignified his leisure were incompatible with the serious duties of a sovereign. The emperor neglected the practice, to instruct his son Romanus in the theory, of government: while he indulged the habits of intemperance and sloth, he dropped the reins of the administration into the hands of Helena his wife; and, in the shifting scene of her favour and caprice, each minister was regretted in the promotion of a more worthless successor. Yet the birth and misfortunes of Constantine had endeared him to the Greeks; they excused his failings; they respected his learning, his innocence and charity, his love of justice; and the ceremony of his funeral was mourned with the unfeigned tears of his subjects. The body, according to ancient custom, lay in state in the vestibule of the palace; and the civil and military officers, the patricians, the senate, and the clergy approached in due order to adore and kiss the inanimate corpse of their sovereign. Before the procession moved towards the Imperial sepulchre, a herald proclaimed this awful admonition: "Arise, O king of the world, and obey the summons of the King of kings!"

The death of Constantine was imputed to poison; and his son Romanus, who derived that name from his maternal grandfather, ascended the throne of Constantinople. A prince who, at the age of twenty, could be suspected of anticipating his inheritance, must have been already lost in the public esteem; yet Romanus was rather weak than wicked; and the largest share of the guilt was transferred to his wife, Theophano, a woman of base origin, masculine spirit, and flagitious manners. The sense of personal glory and public happiness, the true pleasures of royalty, were unknown to the son of Constantine; and, while the two brothers, Nicephorus and Leo, triumphed over the Saracens, the hours which the emperor owed to his people were consumed in strenuous idleness. In the morning he visited the circus; at noon he feasted the senators; the greater part of the afternoon he spent in the *sphæristerium*, or tennis-court, the only theatre of his victories; from thence he passed over to the Asiatic side of the Bosphorus, hunted and killed four wild boars of the largest size, and returned to the palace, proudly content with the labours of the day. In strength and beauty he was conspicuous above his equals: tall and straight as a young cypress, his complexion was fair and florid, his eyes sparkling, his shoulders broad, his nose long and aquiline. Yet even these perfections were insufficient to fix the love of Theophano; and, after a reign of four years, she mingled for her husband the same deadly draught which she had composed for his father.

By his marriage with this impious woman Romanus the younger left two sons, Basil the Second and Constantine the Ninth, and two daughters, Theophano and Anne. The eldest sister was given to Otho the Second, emperor of the West; the younger became the wife of Wolodomir, great duke and apostle of Russia; and, by the marriage of her granddaughter with Henry the First, king of France, the blood of the Macedonians, and perhaps of the Arsacides, still flows in the veins of the Bourbon line. After the death of her husband the empress aspired to reign in the name of her sons, the elder of whom was five, and the younger only two years of age; but she soon felt the instability of a throne which was supported by a female who could not be esteemed, and two infants who could not be feared. Theophano looked around for a protector, and threw herself into the arms of the bravest soldier; her heart was capacious; but the deformity of the new favourite rendered it more probable that interest was the motive and excuse of her love. Nicephorus Phocas united, in the popular opinion, the double merit of a hero and a saint. In the former character his qualifications were genuine and splendid: the descendant of a race illustrious by their military exploits, he had displayed in every station and in every province the courage of a soldier and the conduct of a chief; and Nicephorus was crowned with recent laurels from the important conquest of the isle of Crete. His religion was of a more ambiguous cast; and his hair-cloth, his fasts, his pious idiom, and his wish to retire from the business of the world, were a convenient mask for his dark and dangerous ambition. Yet he imposed on a holy patriarch, by whose influence, and by a decree of the senate, he was intrusted, during the minority of the young princes, with the absolute and independent command of the Oriental armies. As soon as he had secured the leaders and the troops he boldly marched to Constantinople, trampled on his enemies, avowed his correspondence with the empress, and, without degrading her sons, assumed, with the title of Augustus, the pre-eminence of rank and the plenitude of power. But his marriage with Theophano was refused by the same patriarch who had placed the crown on his head: by his second nuptials he incurred a year of canonical penance; a bar of spiritual affinity was opposed to their celebration; and some evasion and perjury were required to silence the scruples of the clergy and people. The popularity of the emperor was lost in the purple: in a reign of six years he provoked the hatred of strangers and subjects, and the hypocrisy and avarice of the first Nicephorus were revived in his successor. Hypocrisy I shall never justify or palliate; but I will dare to observe that the odious vice of avarice is of all others most hastily arraigned, and most unmercifully condemned. In a private citizen our judgment seldom expects an accurate scrutiny into his fortune and expense; and in a steward of the public treasure frugality is always a virtue, and the increase of taxes too often an indispensable duty. In the use of his patrimony the generous temper of Nicephorus had been proved; and the revenue was strictly applied to the service of the state: each spring the emperor marched in person against the Saracens; and every Roman might compute the employment of his taxes in triumphs, conquests, and the security of the Eastern barrier.

Among the warriors who promoted his elevation and served under his standard, a noble and valiant Armenian had deserved and obtained the most eminent rewards. The stature of John Zimisces was below the ordinary standard; but this diminutive body was endowed with strength, beauty, and the soul of a hero. By the jealousy of the emperor's brother he was degraded from the office of general of the East to that of director of the posts, and his murmurs were chastised with disgrace and exile. But Zimisces was ranked among the numerous lovers of the empress: on her intercession he was permitted to reside at Chalcedon, in the neighbourhood of the capital: her bounty was repaid in his clandestine and amorous visits to the palace; and Theophano consented with alacrity to the death of an ugly and penurious husband. Some bold and trusty conspirators were concealed in her most private chambers: in the darkness of a winter night, Zimisces, with his principal companions, embarked in a small boat, traversed the Bosphorus, landed at the palace stairs, and silently ascended a ladder of ropes, which was cast down by the female attendants. Neither his own suspicions, nor the warnings of his friends, nor the tardy aid of his brother Leo, nor the fortress which he had erected in the palace, could protect Nicephorus from a domestic foe, at whose voice every door was opened to the assassins. As he slept on a bear-skin on the ground, he was roused by their noisy intrusion, and thirty daggers glittered before his eyes. It is doubtful whether Zimisces imbrued his hands in the blood of his sovereign; but he enjoyed the inhuman spectacle of revenge. The murder was protracted by insult and cruelty; and as soon as the head of Nicephorus was shown from the window, the tumult was hushed, and the Armenian was emperor of the East. On the day of his coronation he was stopped on the threshold of St. Sophia by the intrepid patriarch, who charged his conscience with the deed of treason and blood, and required, as a sign of repentance, that he should separate himself from his more criminal associate. This sally of apostolic zeal was not offensive to the prince, since he could neither love nor trust a woman who had repeatedly violated the most sacred obligations; and Theophano, instead of sharing his Imperial fortune, was dismissed with ignominy from his bed and palace. In their last interview she displayed a frantic and impotent rage, accused the ingratitude of her lover, assaulted, with words and blows, her son Basil, as he stood silent and submissive in the presence of a superior colleague, and avowed her own prostitution in proclaiming the illegitimacy of his birth. The public indignation was appeased by her exile and the punishment of the meaner accomplices: the death of an unpopular prince was forgiven; and the guilt of Zimisces was forgotten in the splendour of his virtues. Perhaps his profusion was less useful to the state than the avarice of Nicephorus; but his gentle and generous behaviour delighted all who approached his person; and it was only in the paths of victory that he trod in the footsteps of his predecessor. The greatest part of his reign was employed in the camp and the field: his personal valour and activity were signalised on the Danube and the Tigris, the ancient boundaries of the Roman world; and by his double triumph over the Russians and the Saracens he deserved the titles of saviour of the empire and conqueror of the East. In his last return from Syria he observed that the most fruitful lands of his new provinces were possessed by the eunuchs. "And is it for them," he exclaimed, with honest indignation, "that we have fought and conquered? Is it for them that we shed our blood and exhaust the treasures of our people?" The complaint was re-echoed to the palace, and the death of Zimisces is strongly marked with the suspicion of poison.

Under this usurpation, or regency, of twelve years, the two lawful emperors, Basil and Constantine, had silently grown to the age of manhood. Their tender years had been incapable of dominion: the respectful modesty of their attendance and salutation was due to the age and merit of their guardians: the childless ambition of those guardians had no temptation to violate their right of succession: their patrimony was ably and faithfully administered; and the premature death of Zimisces was a loss rather than a benefit to the sons of Romanus. Their want of experience detained them twelve years longer the obscure and voluntary pupils of a minister who extended his reign by persuading them to indulge the pleasures of youth, and to disdain the labours of government. In this silken web the weakness of Constantine was for ever entangled; but his elder brother felt the impulse of genius and the desire of action; he frowned, and the minister was no more. Basil was the acknowledged sovereign of Constantinople and the provinces of Europe; but Asia was oppressed by two veteran generals, Phocas and Sclerus, who, alternately friends and enemies, subjects and rebels, maintained their independence, and laboured to emulate the example of successful usurpation. Against these domestic enemies the son of Romanus first drew his sword, and they trembled in the presence of a lawful and high-spirited prince. The first, in the front of battle, was thrown from his horse by the stroke of poison or an arrow; the second, who had been twice loaded with chains, and twice invested with the purple, was desirous of ending in peace the small remainder of his days. As the aged suppliant approached the throne, with dim eyes and faltering steps, leaning on his two attendants, the emperor exclaimed, in the insolence of youth and power, "And is this the man who has so long been the object of our terror?" After he had confirmed his own authority and the peace of the empire, the trophies of Nicephorus and Zimisces would not suffer their royal pupil to sleep in the palace. His long and frequent expeditions against the Saracens were rather glorious than useful to the empire; but the final destruction of the kingdom of Bulgaria appears, since the time of Belisarius, the most important triumph of the Roman arms. Yet, instead of applauding their victorious prince, his subjects detested the rapacious and rigid avarice of Basil; and, in the imperfect narrative of his exploits, we can only discern the courage, patience, and ferociousness of a soldier. A vicious education, which could not subdue his spirit, had clouded his mind; he was ignorant of every science and the remembrance of his learned and feeble grandsire might encourage his real or affected contempt of laws and lawyers, of artists and arts. Of such a character, in such an age, superstition took a firm and lasting possession: after the first licence of his youth, Basil the Second devoted his life, in the palace and the camp, to the penance of a hermit, wore the monastic habit under his robes and armour, observed a vow of continence, and imposed on his appetites a perpetual abstinence from wine and flesh. In the sixty-eighth year of his age his martial spirit urged him to embark in person for a holy war against the Saracens of Sicily; he was prevented by death, and Basil, surnamed the Slayer of the Bulgarians, was dismissed from the world with the blessings of the clergy and the curses of the people. After his decease, his brother Constantine enjoyed about three years the power or rather the pleasures of royalty; and his only care was the settlement of the succession. He had enjoyed sixty-six years the title of Augustus; and the reign of the two brothers is the longest and most obscure of the Byzantine history.

A lineal succession of five emperors, in a period of one hundred and sixty years, had attached the loyalty of the Greeks to the Macedonian dynasty, which had been thrice respected by the usurpers of their power. After the death of Constantine the Ninth, the last male of the royal race, a new and broken scene presents itself, and the accumulated years of twelve emperors do not equal the space of his single reign. His elder brother had preferred his private chastity to the public interest, and Constantine himself had only three daughters—Eudocia, who took the veil, and Zoe and Theodora, who were preserved till a mature age in a state of ignorance and virginity. When their marriage was discussed in the council of their dying father, the cold or pious Theodora refused to give an heir to the empire, but her sister Zoe presented herself a willing victim at the altar. Romanus Argyrus, a patrician of a graceful person and fair reputation, was chosen for her husband, and, on his declining that honour, was informed that blindness or death was the second alternative. The motive of his reluctance was conjugal affection, but his faithful wife sacrificed her own happiness to his safety and greatness, and her entrance into a monastery removed the only bar to the Imperial nuptials. After the decease of Constantine the sceptre devolved to Romanus the Third; but his labours at home and abroad were equally feeble and fruitless; and the mature age, the forty-eight years of Zoe, were less favourable to the hopes of pregnancy than to the indulgence of pleasure. Her favourite chamberlain was a handsome Paphlagonian of the name of Michael, whose first trade had been that of a money-changer; and Romanus, either from gratitude or equity, connived at their criminal intercourse, or accepted a slight assurance of their innocence. But Zoe soon justified the Roman maxim, that every adulteress is capable of poisoning her husband; and the death of Romanus was instantly followed by the scandalous marriage and elevation of Michael the Fourth. The expectations of Zoe were, however, disappointed: instead of a vigorous and grateful lover, she had placed in her bed a miserable wretch, whose health and reason were impaired by epileptic fits, and whose conscience was tormented by despair and remorse. The most skilful physicians of the mind and body were summoned to his aid; and his hopes were amused by frequent pilgrimages to the baths, and to the tombs of the most popular saints; the monks applauded his penance, and, except restitution (but to whom should he have restored?), Michael sought every method of expiating his guilt. While he groaned and prayed in sackcloth and ashes, his brother, the eunuch John, smiled at his remorse, and enjoyed the harvest of a crime of which himself was the secret and most guilty author. His administration was only the art of satiating his avarice, and Zoe became a captive in the palace of her fathers and in the hands of her slaves. When he perceived the irretrievable decline of his brother's health, he introduced his nephew, another Michael, who derived his surname of Calaphates from his father's occupation in the careening of vessels: at the command of the eunuch, Zoe adopted for her son the son of a mechanic; and this fictitious heir was invested with the title and purple of the Cæsars in the presence of the senate and clergy. So feeble was the character of Zoe, that she was oppressed by the liberty and power which she recovered by the death of the Paphlagonian; and at the end of four days she placed the crown on the head of Michael the Fifth, who had protested with tears and oaths that he should ever reign the first and most obedient of her subjects. The only act of his short reign was his base ingratitude to his benefactors, the eunuch and the empress. The disgrace of the former was pleasing to the public; but the murmurs, and at length the clamours, of Constantinople deplored the exile of Zoe, the daughter of so many emperors; her vices were forgotten, and Michael was taught that there is a period in which the patience of the tamest slaves rises into fury and revenge. The citizens of every degree assembled in a formidable tumult which lasted three days; they besieged the palace, forced the gates, recalled their *mothers*, Zoe from her prison, Theodora from her monastery, and condemned the son of Calaphates to the loss of his eyes or of his life. For the first time the Greeks beheld with surprise the two royal sisters seated on the same throne, presiding in the senate, and giving audience to the ambassadors of the nations. But this singular union subsisted no more than two months; the two sovereigns, their tempers, interests, and adherents, were secretly hostile to each other; and as Theodora was still averse to marriage, the indefatigable Zoe, at the age of sixty, consented, for the public good, to sustain the embraces of a third husband, and the censures of the Greek church. His name and number were Constantine the Tenth, and the epithet of *Monomachus*, the single combatant, must have been expressive of his valour and victory in some public or private quarrel. But his health was broken by the tortures of the gout, and his dissolute reign was spent in the alternative of sickness and pleasure. A fair and noble widow had accompanied Constantine in his exile to the isle of Lesbos, and Sclerena gloried in the appellation of his mistress. After his marriage and elevation she was invested with the title and pomp of *Augusta*, and occupied a contiguous apartment in the palace. The lawful consort (such was the delicacy or corruption of Zoe) consented to this strange and scandalous partition; and the emperor appeared in public between his wife and his concubine. He survived them both; but the last measures of Constantine to change the order of succession were prevented by the more vigilant friends of Theodora; and after his decease, she resumed, with the general consent, the possession of her inheritance. In her name, and by the influence of four eunuchs, the Eastern world was peaceably governed about nineteen months; and as they wished to prolong their dominion, they persuaded the aged princess to nominate for her successor Michael the Sixth. The surname of *Stratioticus* declares his military profession; but the crazy and decrepit veteran could only see with the eyes, and execute with the hands, of his ministers. Whilst he ascended the throne, Theodora sunk into the grave—the last of the Macedonian or Basilian dynasty. I have hastily reviewed and gladly dismiss this shameful and destructive period of twenty-eight years, in which the Greeks, degraded below the common level of servitude, were transferred like a herd of cattle by the choice or caprice of two impotent females.

From this night of slavery, a ray of freedom, or at least of spirit, begins to emerge: the Greeks either preserved or revived the use of surnames, which perpetuate the fame of hereditary virtue: and we now discern the rise, succession, and alliances of the last dynasties of Constantinople and Trebizond. The *Comneni*, who upheld for a while the fate of the sinking empire, assumed the honour of a Roman origin: but the family had been long since transported from Italy to Asia. Their patrimonial estate was situate in the district of Castamona, in the neighbourhood of the Euxine; and one of their chiefs, who had already entered the paths of ambition, revisited with affection, perhaps with regret, the modest though honourable dwelling of his fathers. The first of their line was the illustrious Manuel, who, in the reign of the second Basil, contrib-

uted by war and treaty to appease the troubles of the East: he left in a tender age two sons, Isaac and John, whom, with the consciousness of desert, he bequeathed to the gratitude and favour of his sovereign. The noble youths were carefully trained in the learning of the monastery, the arts of the palace, and the exercises of the camp: and, from the domestic service of the guards, they were rapidly promoted to the command of provinces and armies. Their fraternal union doubled the force and reputation of the Comneni, and their ancient nobility was illustrated by the marriage of the two brothers, with a captive princess of Bulgaria, and the daughter of a patrician who had obtained the name of *Charon* from the number of enemies whom he had sent to the infernal shades. The soldiers had served with reluctant loyalty a series of effeminate masters; the elevation of Michael the Sixth was a personal insult to the more deserving generals; and their discontent was inflamed by the parsimony of the emperor and the insolence of the eunuchs. They secretly assembled in the sanctuary of St. Sophia, and the votes of the military synod would have been unanimous in favour of the old and valiant Catacalon, if the patriotism or modesty of the veteran had not suggested the importance of birth as well as merit in the choice of a sovereign. Isaac Comnenus was approved by general consent, and the associates separated without delay to meet in the plains of Phrygia at the head of their respective squadrons and detachments. The cause of Michael was defended in a single battle by the mercenaries of the imperial guard, who were aliens to the public interest, and animated only by a principle of honour and gratitude. After their defeat the fears of the emperor solicited a treaty, which was almost accepted by the moderation of the Comnenian. But the former was betrayed by his ambassadors, and the latter was prevented by his friends. The solitary Michael submitted to the voice of the people; the patriarch annulled their oath of allegiance; and as he shaved the head of the royal monk, congratulated his beneficial exchange of temporal royalty for the kingdom of heaven; an exchange, however, which the priest, on his own account, would probably have declined. By the hands of the same patriarch, Isaac Comnenus was solemnly crowned; the sword which he inscribed on his coins might be an offensive symbol if it implied his title by conquest; but this sword would have been drawn against the foreign and domestic enemies of the state. The decline of his health and vigour suspended the operation of active virtue; and the prospect of approaching death determined him to interpose some moments between life and eternity. But instead of leaving the empire as the marriage portion of his daughter, his reason and inclination concurred in the preference of his brother John, a soldier, a patriot, and the father of five sons, the future pillars of an hereditary succession. His first modest reluctance might be the natural dictates of discretion and tenderness, but his obstinate and successful perseverance, however it may dazzle with the show of virtue, must be censured as a criminal desertion of his duty, and a rare offence against his family and country. The purple which he had refused was accepted by Constantine Ducas, a friend of the Comnenian house, and whose noble birth was adorned with the experience and reputation of civil policy. In the monastic habit Isaac recovered his health, and survived two years his voluntary abdication. At the command of his abbot, he observed the rule of St. Basil, and executed the most servile offices of the convent: but his latent vanity was gratified by the frequent and respectful visits of the reigning monarch, who revered in his person the character of a benefactor and a saint.

If Constantine the Eleventh were indeed the subject most worthy of empire, we must pity the debasement of the age and nation in which he was chosen. In the labour of puerile declamations he sought, without obtaining, the crown of eloquence, more precious in his opinion than that of Rome; and in the subordinate functions of a judge he forgot the duties of a sovereign and a warrior. Far from imitating the patriotic indifference of the authors of his greatness, Ducas was anxious only to secure, at the expense of the republic, the power and prosperity of his children. His three sons, Michael the Seventh, Andronicus the First, and Constantine the Twelfth, were invested in a tender age with the equal title of Augustus; and the succession was speedily opened by their father's death. His widow, Eudocia, was intrusted with the administration; but experience had taught the jealousy of the dying monarch to protect his sons from the danger of her second nuptials; and her solemn engagement, attested by the principal senators, was deposited in the hands of the patriarch. Before the end of seven months, the wants of Eudocia or those of the state called aloud for the male virtues of a soldier; and her heart had already chosen Romanus Diogenes, whom she raised from the scaffold to the throne. The discovery of a treasonable attempt had ex-

posed him to the severity of the laws; his beauty and valour absolved him in the eyes of the empress; and Romanus, from a mild exile, was recalled on the second day to the command of the Oriental armies. Her royal choice was yet unknown to the public; and the promise which would have betrayed her falsehood and levity was stolen by a dexterous emissary from the ambition of the patriarch. Xiphilin at first alleged the sanctity of oaths and the sacred nature of a trust; but a whisper that his brother was the future emperor relaxed his scruples, and forced him to confess that the public safety was the supreme law. He resigned the important paper; and when his hopes were confounded by the nomination of Romanus, he could no longer regain his security, retract his declarations, nor oppose the second nuptials of the empress. Yet a murmur was heard in the palace; and the barbarian guards had raised their battleaxes in the cause of the house of Ducas, till the young princes were soothed by the tears of their mother and the solemn assurances of the fidelity of their guardian, who filled the imperial station with dignity and honour. Hereafter I shall relate his valiant but unsuccessful efforts to resist the progress of the Turks. His defeat and captivity inflicted a deadly wound on the Byzantine monarchy of the East; and after he was released from the chains of the sultan, he vainly sought his wife and his subjects. His wife had been thrust into a monastery, and the subjects of Romanus had embraced the rigid maxim of the civil law, that a prisoner in the hands of the enemy is deprived, as by the stroke of death, of all the public and private rights of a citizen. In the general consternation the Cæsar John asserted the indefeasible right of his three nephews: Constantinople listened to his voice: and the Turkish captive was proclaimed in the capital, and received on the frontier, as an enemy of the republic. Romanus was not more fortunate in domestic than in foreign war: the loss of two battles compelled him to yield, on the assurance of fair and honourable treatment; but his enemies were devoid of faith or humanity; and, after the cruel extinction of his sight, his wounds were left to bleed and corrupt, till in a few days he was relieved from a state of misery. Under the triple reign of the house of Ducas, the two younger brothers were reduced to the vain honours of the purple; but the eldest, the pusillanimous Michael, was incapable of sustaining the Roman sceptre; and his surname of *Parapinaces* denotes the reproach which he shared with an avaricious favourite, who enhanced the price and diminished the measure of wheat. In the school of Psellus, and after the example of his mother, the son of Eudocia made some proficiency in philosophy and rhetoric; but his character was degraded rather than ennobled by the virtues of a monk and the learning of a sophist. Strong in the contempt of their sovereign and their own esteem, two generals, at the head of the European and Asiatic legions, assumed the purple at Adrianople and Nice. Their revolt was in the same month; they bore the same name of Nicephorus; but the two candidates were distinguished by the surnames of Bryennius and Botaniates: the former in the maturity of wisdom and courage, the latter conspicuous only by the memory of his past exploits. While Botaniates advanced with cautious and dilatory steps, his active competitor stood in arms before the gates of Constantinople. The name of Bryennius was illustrious; his cause was popular; but his licentious troops could not be restrained from burning and pillaging a suburb; and the people, who would have hailed the rebel, rejected and repulsed the incendiary of his country. This change of the public opinion was favourable to Botaniates, who at length, with an army of Turks, approached the shores of Chalcedon. A formal invitation, in the name of the patriarch, the synod, and the senate, was circulated through the streets of Constantinople; and the general assembly, in the dome of St. Sophia, debated, with order and calmness, on the choice of their sovereign. The guards of Michael would have dispersed this unarmed multitude; but the feeble emperor, applauding his own moderation and clemency, resigned the ensigns of royalty, and was rewarded with the monastic habit, and the title of Archbishop of Ephesus. He left a son, a Constantine, born and educated in the purple; and a daughter of the house of Ducas illustrated the blood and confirmed the succession of the Comnenian dynasty.

John Comnenus, the brother of the emperor Isaac, survived in peace and dignity his generous refusal of the sceptre. By his wife Anne, a woman of masculine spirit and policy, he left eight children: the three daughters multiplied the Comnenian alliances with the noblest of the Greeks: of the five sons, Manuel was stopped by a premature death; Isaac and Alexius restored the Imperial greatness of their house, which was enjoyed without toil or danger by the two younger brethren, Adrian and Nicephorus. Alexius, the third and most illustrious of the brothers, was endowed by nature with the choicest gifts both of mind and body: they were cultivated by a liberal education, and exercised in the school of obedience and adversity. The youth was dismissed from the perils of the Turkish war by the paternal care of the emperor Romanus: but the mother of the Comneni, with her aspiring race, was accused of treason, and banished, by the sons of Ducas, to an island in the Propontis. The two brothers soon emerged into favour and action, fought by each other's side against the rebels and barbarians, and adhered to the emperor Michael, till he was deserted by the world and by himself. In his first interview with Botaniates, "Prince," said Alexius, with a noble frankness, "my duty rendered me your enemy; the decrees of God and of the people have made me your subject. Judge of my future loyalty by my past opposition." The successor of Michael entertained him with esteem and confidence: his valour was employed against three rebels, who disturbed the peace of the empire, or at least of the emperors. Ursel, Bryennius, and Basilacius were formidable by their numerous forces and military fame: they were successively vanquished in the field, and led in chains to the foot of the throne; and whatever treatment they might receive from a timid and cruel court, they applauded the clemency as well as the courage of their conqueror. But the loyalty of the Comneni was soon tainted by fear and suspicion; nor is it easy to settle between a subject and a despot the debt of gratitude which the former is tempted to claim by a revolt, and the latter to discharge by an executioner. The refusal of Alexius to march against a fourth rebel, the husband of his sister, destroyed the merit or memory of his past services: the favourites of Botaniates provoked the ambition which they apprehended and accused; and the retreat of the two brothers might be justified by the defence of their life or liberty. The women of the family were deposited in a sanctuary, respected by tyrants: the men, mounted on horseback, sallied from the city, and erected the standard of civil war. The soldiers who had been gradually assembled in the capital and the neighbourhood were devoted to the cause of a victorious and injured leader: the ties of common interest and domestic alliance secured the attachment of the house of Ducas; and the generous dispute of the Comneni was terminated by the decisive resolution of Isaac, who was the first to invest his younger brother with the name and ensigns of royalty. They returned to Constantinople, to threaten rather than besiege that impregnable fortress; but the fidelity of the guards was corrupted; a gate was surprised, and the fleet was occupied by the active courage of George Palæologus, who fought against his father, without foreseeing that he laboured for his posterity. Alexius ascended the throne; and his aged competitor disappeared in a monastery. An army of various nations was gratified with the pillage of the city; but the public disorders were expiated by the tears and fasts of the Comneni, who submitted to every penance compatible with the possession of the empire.

The life of the emperor Alexius has been delineated by a favourite daughter, who was inspired by a tender regard for his person and a laudable zeal to perpetuate his virtues. Conscious of the just suspicion of her readers, the princess Anna Comnena repeatedly protests that, besides her personal knowledge, she had searched the discourse and writings of the most respectable veterans: that, after an interval of thirty years, forgotten by and forgetful of the world, her mournful solitude was inaccessible to hope and fear; and that truth, the naked perfect truth, was more dear and sacred than the memory of her parent. Yet, instead of the simplicity of style and narrative which wins our belief, an elaborate affectation of rhetoric and science betrays in every page the vanity of a female author. The genuine character of Alexius is lost in a vague constellation of virtues; and the perpetual strain of panegyric and apology awakens our jealousy, to question the veracity of the historian and the merit of the hero. We cannot, however, refuse her judicious and important remark, that the disorders of the times were the misfortune and the glory of Alexius; and that every calamity which can afflict a declining empire was accumulated on his reign by the justice of Heaven and the vices of his predecessors. In the East, the victorious Turks had spread, from Persia to the Hellespont, the reign of the Koran and the Crescent: the West was invaded by the adventurous valour of the Normans; and, in the moments of peace, the Danube poured forth new swarms, who had gained, in the science of war, what they had lost in the ferociousness of manners. The sea was not less hostile than the land; and while the frontiers were assaulted by an open enemy, the palace was distracted with secret treason and conspiracy. On a sudden the banner of the Cross was displayed by the Latins; Europe was precipitated on Asia; and Constantinople had almost been swept away by this impetuous deluge. In the tempest, Alexius steered the Imperial vessel with dexterity and courage. At the head of his armies he was bold in action, skilful in stratagem, patient of fatigue, ready to improve his advantages, and rising from his defeats with inexhaustible vigour. The discipline of the camp was revived, and a new generation of men and soldiers was created by the example and the precepts of their leader. In his intercourse with the Latins, Alexius was patient and artful: his discerning eye pervaded the new system of an unknown world; and I shall hereafter describe the superior policy with which he balanced the interests and passions of the champions of the first crusade. In a long reign of thirty-seven years he subdued and pardoned the envy of his equals: the laws of public and private order were restored: the arts of wealth and science were cultivated: the limits of the empire were enlarged in Europe and Asia; and the Comnenian sceptre was transmitted to his children of the third and fourth generation. Yet the difficulties of the times betrayed some defects in his character; and have exposed his memory to some just or ungenerous reproach. The reader may possibly smile at the lavish praise which his daughter so often bestows on a flying hero: the weakness or prudence of his situation might be mistaken for a want of personal courage, and his political arts are branded by the Latins with the names of deceit and dissimulation. The increase of the male and female branches of his family adorned the throne, and secured the succession; but their princely luxury and pride offended the patricians, exhausted the revenue, and insulted the misery of the people. Anna is a faithful witness that his happiness was destroyed, and his health was broken, by the cares of a public life: the patience of Constantinople was fatigued by the length and severity of his reign; and before Alexius expired, he had lost the love and reverence of his subjects. The clergy could not forgive his application of the sacred riches to the defence of the state; but they applauded his theological learning and ardent zeal for the orthodox faith, which he defended with his tongue, his pen, and his sword. His character was degraded by the superstition of the Greeks; and the same inconsistent principle of human nature enjoined the emperor to found a hospital for the poor and infirm, and to direct the execution of a heretic, who was burnt alive in the square of St. Sophia. Even the sincerity of his moral and religious virtues was suspected by the persons who had passed their lives in his familiar confidence. In his last hours, when he was pressed by his wife Irene to alter the succession, he raised his head, and breathed a pious ejaculation on the vanity of this world. The indignant reply of the empress may be inscribed as an epitaph on his tomb, "You die, as you have lived—A HYPOCRITE!"

It was the wish of Irene to supplant the eldest of her surviving sons, in favour of her daughter the princess Anna, whose philosophy would not have refused the weight of a diadem. But the order of male succession was asserted by the friends of their country; the lawful heir drew the royal signet from the finger of his insensible or conscious father, and the empire obeyed the master of the palace. Anna Comnena was stimulated by ambition and revenge to conspire against the life of her brother, and, when the design was prevented by the fears or scruples of her husband, she passionately exclaimed that nature had mistaken the two sexes, and had endowed Bryennius with the soul of a woman. The two sons of Alexius, John and Isaac, maintained the fraternal concord, the hereditary virtue of their race, and the younger brother was content with the title of *Sebastocrator*, which approached the dignity without sharing the power of the emperor. In the same person the claims of primogeniture and merit were fortunately united; his swarthy complexion, harsh features, and diminutive stature had suggested the ironical surname of Calo-Johannes, or John the Handsome, which his grateful subjects more seriously applied to the beauties of his mind. After the discovery of her treason, the life and fortune of Anna were justly forfeited to the laws. Her life was spared by the clemency of the emperor; but he visited the pomp and treasures of her palace, and bestowed the rich confiscation on the most deserving of his friends. That respectable friend, Axuch, a slave of Turkish extraction, presumed to decline the gift, and to intercede for the criminal: his generous master applauded and imitated the virtue of his favourite, and the reproach or complaint of an injured brother was the only chastisement of the guilty princess. After this example of clemency, the remainder of his reign was never disturbed by conspiracy or rebellion: feared by his nobles, beloved by his people, John was never reduced to the painful necessity of punishing, or even of pardoning, his personal enemies. During his government of twenty-five years, the penalty of death was abolished in the Roman empire, a law of mercy most delightful to the humane theorist, but of which the practice, in a large and vicious community, is seldom consistent with the public safety. Severe to himself, indulgent to others, chaste, frugal, abstemious, the philosophic Marcus would not have disdained the artless virtues of his successor, derived from his heart, and not borrowed from the schools. He despised and moderated the stately magnificence of the Byzantine court, so oppressive to the people, so contemptible to the eye of reason. Under such a prince innocence had nothing to fear, and merit had everything to hope; and, without assuming the tyrannic office of a censor, he introduced a gradual though visible reformation in the public and private manners of Constantinople. The only defect of this accomplished character was the frailty of noble minds—the love of arms and military glory. Yet the frequent expeditions of John the Handsome may be justified, at least in their principle, by the necessity of repelling the Turks from the Hellespont and the Bosphorus. The sultan of Iconium was confined to his capital, the barbarians were driven to the mountains, and the maritime provinces of Asia enjoyed the transient blessings of their deliverance. From Constantinople to Antioch and Aleppo, he repeatedly marched at the head of a victorious army; and in the sieges and battles of this holy war, his Latin allies were astonished by the superior spirit and prowess of a Greek. As he began to indulge the ambitious hope of restoring the ancient limits of the empire, as he revolved in his mind the Euphrates and Tigris, the dominion of Syria, and the conquest of Jerusalem, the thread of his life and of the public felicity was broken by a singular accident. He hunted the wild boar in the valley of Anazarbus, and had fixed his javelin in the body of the furious animal; but in the struggle a poisoned arrow dropped from his quiver, and a slight wound in his hand, which produced a mortification, was fatal to the best and greatest of the Comnenian princes.

A premature death had swept away the two eldest sons of John the Handsome; of the two survivors, Isaac and Manuel, his judgment or affection preferred the younger; and the choice of their dying prince was ratified by the soldiers, who had applauded the valour of his favourite in the Turkish war. The faithful Axuch hastened to the capital, secured the person of Isaac in honourable confinement, and purchased, with a gift of two hundred pounds of silver, the leading ecclesiastics of St. Sophia, who possessed a decisive voice in the consecration of an emperor. With his veteran and affectionate troops, Manuel soon visited Constantinople; his brother acquiesced in the title of Sebastocrator; his subjects admired the lofty stature and martial graces of their new sovereign, and listened with credulity to the flattering promise that he blended the wisdom of age with the activity and vigour of youth. By the experience of his government they were taught that he emulated the spirit and shared the talents of his father, whose social virtues were buried in the grave. A reign of thirty-seven years is filled by a perpetual though various warfare against the Turks, the Christians, and the hordes of the wilderness beyond the Danube. The arms of Manuel were exercised on Mount Taurus, in the plains of Hungary, on the coast of Italy and Egypt, and on the seas of Sicily and Greece: the influence of his negotiations extended from Jerusalem to Rome and Russia; and the Byzantine monarchy for a while became an object of respect or terror to the powers of Asia and Europe. Educated in the silk and purple of the East, Manuel possessed the iron temper of a soldier, which cannot easily be paralleled, except in the lives of Richard the First of England, and of Charles the Twelfth of Sweden. Such was his strength and exercise in arms, that Raymond, surnamed the Hercules of Antioch, was incapable of wielding the lance and buckler of the Greek emperor. In a famous tournament he entered the lists on a fiery courser, and overturned in his first career two of the stoutest of the Italian knights. The first in the charge, the last in the retreat, his friends and his enemies alike trembled, the former for *his* safety, and the latter for their own. After posting an ambuscade in a wood, he rode forwards in search of some perilous adventure, accompanied only by his brother and the faithful Axuch, who refused to desert their sovereign. Eighteen horsemen, after a short combat, fled before them: but the numbers of the enemy increased; the march of the reinforcement was tardy and fearful, and Manuel, without receiving a wound, cut his way through a squadron of five hundred Turks. In a battle against the Hungarians, impatient of the slowness of his troops, he snatched a standard from the head of the column, and was the first, almost alone, who passed a bridge that separated him from the enemy. In the same country, after transporting his army beyond the Save, he sent back the boats, with an order, under pain of death, to their commander, that he should leave him to conquer or die on that hostile land. In the siege of Corfu, towing after him a captive galley, the emperor stood aloft on the poop, opposing against the volleys of darts and stones a large buckler and a flowing sail; nor could he have escaped inevitable death, had

not the Sicilian admiral enjoined his archers to respect the person of a hero. In one day he is said to have slain above forty of the barbarians with his own hand; he returned to the camp, dragging along four Turkish prisoners, whom he had tied to the rings of his saddle: he was ever the foremost to provoke or to accept a single combat; and the *gigantic* champions who encountered his arm were transpierced by the lance, or cut asunder by the sword, of the invincible Manuel. The story of his exploits, which appear as a model or a copy of the romances of chivalry, may induce a reasonable suspicion of the veracity of the Greeks: I will not, to vindicate their credit, endanger my own; yet I may observe that, in the long series of their annals, Manuel is the only prince who has been the subject of similar exaggeration. With the valour of a soldier he did not unite the skill or prudence of a general: his victories were not productive of any permanent or useful conquest; and his Turkish laurels were blasted in his last unfortunate campaign, in which he lost his army in the mountains of Pisidia, and owed his deliverance to the generosity of the sultan. But the most singular feature in the character of Manuel is the contrast and vicissitude of labour and sloth, of hardiness and effeminacy. In war he seemed ignorant of peace, in peace he appeared incapable of war. In the field he slept in the sun or in the snow, tired in the longest marches the strength of his men and horses, and shared with a smile the abstinence or diet of the camp. No sooner did he return to Constantinople, than he resigned himself to the arts and pleasures of a life of luxury: the expense of his dress, his table, and his palace surpassed the measure of his predecessors, and whole summer days were idly wasted in the delicious isles of the Propontis, in the incestuous love of his niece Theodora. The double cost of a warlike and dissolute prince exhausted the revenue and multiplied the taxes; and Manuel, in the distress of his last Turkish campaign, endured a bitter reproach from the mouth of a desperate soldier. As he quenched his thirst, he complained that the water of a fountain was mingled with Christian blood. "It is not the first time," exclaimed a voice from the crowd, "that you have drank, O emperor, the blood of your Christian subjects." Manuel Comnenus was twice married, to the virtuous Bertha or Irene of Germany, and to the beauteous Maria, a French or Latin princess of Antioch. The only daughter of his first wife was destined for Bela, an Hungarian prince, who was educated at

Constantinople under the name of Alexius; and the consummation of their nuptials might have transferred the Roman sceptre to a race of free and warlike barbarians. But as soon as Maria of Antioch had given a son and heir to the empire, the presumptive rights of Bela were abolished, and he was deprived of his promised bride; but the Hungarian prince resumed his name and the kingdom of his fathers, and displayed such virtues as might excite the regret and envy of the Greeks. The son of Maria was named Alexius; and at the age of ten years he ascended the Byzantine throne, after his father's decease had closed the glories of the Comnenian line.

The fraternal concord of the two sons of the great Alexius had been sometimes clouded by an opposition of interest and passion. By ambition, Isaac the Sebastocrator was excited to flight and rebellion, from whence he was reclaimed by the firmness and clemency of John the Handsome. The errors of Isaac, the father of the emperors of Trebizond, were short and venial; but John, the elder of his sons, renounced for ever his religion. Provoked by a real or imaginary insult of his uncle, he escaped from the Roman to the Turkish camp: his apostasy was rewarded with the sultan's daughter, the title of Chelebi, or noble, and the inheritance of a princely estate; and, in the fifteenth century, Mohammed the Second boasted of his Imperial descent from the Comnenian family. Andronicus, younger brother of John, son of Isaac, and grandson of Alexius Comnenus, is one of the most conspicuous characters of the age; and his genuine adventures might form the subject of a very singular romance. To justify the choice of three ladies of royal birth, it is incumbent on me to observe that their fortunate lover was cast in the best proportions of strength and beauty; and that the want of the softer graces was supplied by a manly countenance, a lofty stature, athletic muscles, and the air and deportment of a soldier. The preservation, in his old age, of health and vigour, was the reward of temperance and exercise. A piece of bread and a draught of water was often his sole and evening repast; and if he tasted of a wild boar or a stag, which he had roasted with his own hands, it was the well-earned fruit of a laborious chase. Dexterous in arms, he was ignorant of fear: his persuasive eloquence could bend to every situation and character of life: his style, though not his practice, was fashioned by the example of St. Paul; and, in every deed of mischief, he had a heart to resolve, a head to contrive, and a hand to execute. In his youth, after the death of the

emperor John, he followed the retreat of the Roman army; but, in the march through Asia Minor, design or accident tempted him to wander in the mountains: the hunter was encompassed by the Turkish huntsmen, and he remained some time a reluctant or willing captive in the power of the sultan. His virtues and vices recommended him to the favour of his cousin: he shared the perils and the pleasures of Manuel; and while the emperor lived in public incest with his niece Theodora, the affections of her sister Eudocia were seduced and enjoyed by Andronicus. Above the decencies of her sex and rank, she gloried in the name of his concubine; and both the palace and the camp could witness that she slept, or watched, in the arms of her lover. She accompanied him to his military command of Cilicia, the first scene of his valour and imprudence. He pressed, with active ardour, the siege of Mopsuestia: the day was employed in the boldest attacks; but the night was wasted in song and dance; and a band of Greek comedians formed the choicest part of his retinue. Andronicus was surprised by the sally of a vigilant foe; but, while his troops fled in disorder, his invincible lance transpierced the thickest ranks of the Armenians. On his return to the Imperial camp in Macedonia, he was received by Manuel with public smiles and a private reproof; but the duchies of Naissus, Braniseba, and Castoria were the reward or consolation of the unsuccessful general. Eudocia still attended his motions: at midnight their tent was suddenly attacked by her angry brothers, impatient to expiate her infamy in his blood: his daring spirit refused her advice, and the disguise of a female habit; and, boldly starting from his couch, he drew his sword, and cut his way through the numerous assassins. It was here that he first betrayed his ingratitude and treachery: he engaged in a treasonable correspondence with the king of Hungary and the German emperor; approached the royal tent at a suspicious hour with a drawn sword, and, under the mask of a Latin soldier, avowed an intention of revenge against a mortal foe; and imprudently praised the fleetness of his horse as an instrument of flight and safety. The monarch dissembled his suspicions; but, after the close of the campaign, Andronicus was arrested and strictly confined in a tower of the palace of Constantinople.

In this prison he was left above twelve years; a most painful restraint, from which the thirst of action and pleasure perpetually urged him to escape. Alone and pensive, he perceived some broken bricks in a corner of the chamber, and gradually widened the passage till he had explored a dark and forgotten recess. Into this hole he conveyed himself and the remains of his provisions, replacing the bricks in their former position, and erasing with care the footsteps of his retreat. At the hour of the customary visit, his guards were amazed by the silence and solitude of the prison, and reported, with shame and fear, his incomprehensible flight. The gates of the palace and city were instantly shut: the strictest orders were despatched into the provinces for the recovery of the fugitive; and his wife on the suspicion of a pious act, was basely imprisoned in the same tower. At the dead of night she beheld a spectre: she recognised her husband; they shared their provisions, and a son was the fruit of these stolen interviews, which alleviated the tediousness of their confinement. In the custody of a woman the vigilance of the keepers was insensibly relaxed, and the captive had accomplished his real escape, when he was discovered, brought back to Constantinople, and loaded with a double chain. At length he found the moment and the means of his deliverance. A boy, his domestic servant, intoxicated the guards, and obtained in wax the impression of the keys. By the diligence of his friends a similar key, with a bundle of ropes, was introduced into the prison in the bottom of a hogshead. Andronicus employed, with industry and courage, the instruments of his safety, unlocked the doors, descended from the tower, concealed himself all day among the bushes, and scaled in the night the garden-wall of the palace. A boat was stationed for his reception; he visited his own house, embraced his children, cast away his chain, mounted a fleet horse, and directed his rapid course towards the banks of the Danube. At Anchialus, in Thrace, an intrepid friend supplied him with horses and money: he passed the river, traversed with speed the desert of Moldavia and the Carpathian hills, and had almost reached the town of Halicz, in the Polish Russia, when he was intercepted by a party of Walachians, who resolved to convey their important captive to Constantinople. His presence of mind again extricated him from this danger. Under the pretence of sickness he dismounted in the night, and was allowed to step aside from the troop: he planted in the ground his long staff, clothed it with his cap and upper garment, and, stealing into the wood, left a phantom to amuse for some time the eyes of the Wallachians. From Halicz he was honourably conducted to Kiow, the residence of the great duke: the sub-

tle Greek soon obtained the esteem and confidence of Ieroslaus; his character could assume the manners of every climate, and the barbarians applauded his strength and courage in the chase of the elks and bears of the forest. In this northern region he deserved the forgiveness of Manuel, who solicited the Russian prince to join his arms in the invasion of Hungary. The influence of Andronicus achieved this important service: his private treaty was signed with a promise of fidelity on one side and of oblivion on the other, and he marched, at the head of the Russian cavalry, from the Borysthenes to the Danube. In his resentment Manuel had ever sympathised with the martial and dissolute character of his cousin, and his free pardon was sealed in the assault of Zemlin, in which he was second, and second only, to the valour of the emperor.

No sooner was the exile restored to freedom and his country than his ambition revived, at first to his own, and at length to the public misfortune. A daughter of Manuel was a feeble bar to the succession of the more deserving males of the Comnenian blood: her future marriage with the prince of Hungary was repugnant to the hopes or prejudices of the princes and nobles. But when an oath of allegiance was required to the presumptive heir, Andronicus alone asserted the honour of the Roman name, declined the unlawful engagement, and boldly protested against the adoption of a stranger. His patriotism was offensive to the emperor; but he spoke the sentiments of the people, and was removed from the royal presence by an honourable banishment, a second command of the Cilician frontier, with the absolute disposal of the revenues of Cyprus. In this station the Armenians again exercised his courage and exposed his negligence; and the same rebel, who baffled all his operations, was unhorsed, and almost slain by the vigour of his lance. But Andronicus soon discovered a more easy and pleasing conquest, the beautiful Philippa, sister of the empress Maria, and daughter of Raymond of Poitou, the Latin prince of Antioch. For her sake he deserted his station, and wasted the summer in balls and tournaments: to his love she sacrificed her innocence, her reputation, and the offer of an advantageous marriage. But the resentment of Manuel for this domestic affront interrupted his pleasures: Andronicus left the indiscreet princess to weep and to repent; and, with a band of desperate adventurers, undertook the pilgrimage of Jerusalem His birth, his martial renown, and professions of zeal announced him as the champion of the Cross: he soon captivated both the clergy and the king, and the Greek prince was invested with the lordship of Berytus, on the coast of Phœnicia. In his neighbourhood resided a young and handsome queen, of his own nation and family, great-granddaughter of the emperor Alexis, and widow of Baldwin the Third, king of Jerusalem. She visited and loved her kinsman. Theodora was the third victim of his amorous seduction, and her shame was more public and scandalous than that of her predecessors. The emperor still thirsted for revenge, and his subjects and allies of the Syrian frontier were repeatedly pressed to seize the person and put out the eyes of the fugitive. In Palestine he was no longer safe; but the tender Theodora revealed his danger and accompanied his flight. The queen of Jerusalem was exposed to the East, his obsequious concubine, and two illegitimate children were the living monuments of her weakness. Damascus was his first revenge, and, in the characters of the great Noureddin and his servant Saladin, the superstitious Greek might learn to revere the virtues of the Musulmans. As the friend of Noureddin he visited, most probably, Bagdad and the courts of Persia, and, after a long circuit round the Caspian Sea and the mountains of Georgia, he finally settled among the Turks of Asia Minor, the hereditary enemies of his country. The sultan of Colonia afforded an hospitable retreat to Andronicus, his mistress, and his band of outlaws: the debt of gratitude was paid by frequent inroads in the Roman province of Trebizond, and he seldom returned without an ample harvest of spoil and of Christian captives. In the story of his adventures he was fond of comparing himself to David, who escaped, by a long exile, the snares of the wicked. But the royal prophet (he presumed to add) was content to lurk on the borders of Judæa, to slay an Amalekite, and to threaten, in his miserable state, the life of the avaricious Nabal. The excursions of the Comnenian prince had a wider range, and he had spread over the Eastern world the glory of his name and religion. By a sentence of the Greek church, the licentious rover had been separated from the faithful; but even this excommunication may prove that he never abjured the profession of Christianity.

His vigilance had eluded or repelled the open and secret persecution of the emperor; but he was at length ensnared by the captivity of his female companion. The governor of Trebizond succeeded in his attempt to surprise the person of Theodora: the queen of Jerusalem and her two children were sent to Constantinople, and their loss embittered the tedious solitude of banishment. The fugitive implored and obtained a final pardon, with leave to throw himself at the feet of his sovereign, who was satisfied with the submission of this haughty spirit. Prostrate on the ground, he deplored with tears and groans the guilt of his past rebellion; nor would he presume to arise, unless some faithful subject would drag him to the foot of the throne by an iron chain with which he had secretly encircled his neck. This extraordinary penance excited the wonder and pity of the assembly: his sins were forgiven by the church and state; but the just suspicion of Manuel fixed his residence at a distance from the court, at Oenoe, a town of Pontus, surrounded with rich vineyards, and situate on the coast of the Euxine. The death of Manuel and the disorders of the minority soon opened the fairest field to his ambition. The emperor was a boy of twelve or fourteen years of age, without vigour, or wisdom, or experience: his mother, the empress Mary, abandoned her person and government to a favourite of the Comnenian name; and his sister, another Mary, whose husband, an Italian, was decorated with the title of Cæsar, excited a conspiracy, and at length an insurrection, against her odious stepmother. The provinces were forgotten, the capital was in flames, and a century of peace and order was overthrown in the vice and weakness of a few months. A civil war was kindled in Constantinople; the two factions fought a bloody battle in the square of the palace, and the rebels sustained a regular siege in the cathedral of St. Sophia. The patriarch laboured with honest zeal to heal the wounds of the republic, the most respectable patriots called aloud for a guardian and avenger, and every tongue repeated the praise of the talents and even the virtues of Andronicus. In his retirement he affected to revolve the solemn duties of his oath: "If the safety or honour of the Imperial family be threatened, I will reveal and oppose the mischief to the utmost of my power." His correspondence with the patriarch and patricians was seasoned with apt quotations from the Psalms of David and the Epistles of St. Paul; and he patiently waited till he was called to her deliverance by the voice of his country. In his march from Oenoe to Constantinople, his slender train insensibly swelled to a crowd and an army; his professions of religion and loyalty were mistaken for the language of his heart; and the simplicity of a foreign dress, which showed to advantage his majestic stature, displayed a lively image of his poverty and exile. All opposition sunk before him; he reached the straits of the Thracian Bosphorus; the Byzantine navy sailed from the harbour to receive and transport the saviour of the empire: the torrent was loud and irresistible, and the insects who had basked in the sunshine of royal favour disappeared at the blast of the storm. It was the first care of Andronicus to occupy the palace, to salute the emperor, to confine his mother, to punish her minister, and to restore the public order and tranquillity. He then visited the sepulchre of Manuel: the spectators were ordered to stand aloof, but, as he bowed in the attitude of prayer, they heard, or thought they heard, a murmur of triumph and revenge: "I no longer fear thee, my old enemy, who hast driven me a vagabond to every climate of the earth. Thou art safely deposited under a seven-fold dome, from whence thou canst never arise till the signal of the last trumpet. It is now my turn, and speedily will I trample on thy ashes and thy posterity." From his subsequent tyranny we may impute such feelings to the man and the moment; but it is not extremely probable that he gave an articulate sound to his secret thoughts. In the first months of his administration his designs were veiled by a fair semblance of hypocrisy, which could delude only the eyes of the multitude: the coronation of Alexius was performed with due solemnity, and his perfidious guardian, holding in his hands the body and blood of Christ, most fervently declared that he lived, and was ready to die, for the service of his beloved pupil. But his numerous adherents were instructed to maintain that the sinking empire must perish in the hands of a child; that the Romans could only be saved by a veteran prince, bold in arms, skilful in policy, and taught to reign by the long experience of fortune and mankind; and that it was the duty of every citizen to force the reluctant modesty of Andronicus to undertake the burden of the public care. The young emperor was himself constrained to join his voice to the general acclamation, and to solicit the association of a colleague, who instantly degraded him from the supreme rank, secluded his person, and verified the rash declaration of the patriarch, that Alexius might be considered as dead so soon as he was committed to the custody of his guardian. But his death was preceded by the imprisonment and execution of his mother. After blackening her reputation, and inflaming against her the passions of the multitude, the tyrant accused and tried the empress for a treasonable correspondence with the king of Hungary. His own son, a youth of honour and humanity, avowed his abhorrence of this flagitious act, and three of the judges had the merit of preferring their conscience to their safety; but the obsequious tribunal, without requiring any proof or hearing any defence, condemned the widow of Manuel, and her unfortunate son subscribed the sentence of her death. Maria was strangled, her corpse was buried in the sea, and her memory was wounded by the insult most offensive to female vanity, a false and ugly representation of her beauteous form. The fate of her son was not long deferred: he was strangled with a bowstring, and the tyrant, insensible to pity or remorse, after surveying the body of the innocent youth, struck it rudely with his foot. "Thy father," he cried, "was a *knave*, thy mother a *whore*, and thyself a *fool!*"

The Roman sceptre, the reward of his crimes, was held by Andronicus about three years and a half as the guardian or sovereign of the empire. His government exhibited a singular contrast of vice and virtue. When he listened to his passions, he was the scourge; when he consulted his reason, the father of his people. In the exercise of private justice he was equitable and rigorous; a shameful and pernicious venality was abolished, and the offices were filled with the most deserving candidates by a prince who had sense to choose and severity to punish. He prohibited the inhuman practice of pillaging the goods and persons of shipwrecked mariners; the provinces, so long the objects of oppression or neglect, revived in prosperity and plenty; and millions applauded the distant blessings of his reign, while he was cursed by the witnesses of his daily cruelties. The ancient proverb, that bloodthirsty is the man who returns from banishment to power, had been applied, with too much truth, to Marius and Tiberius, and was now verified for the third time in the life of Andronicus. His memory was stored with a black list of the enemies and rivals who had traduced his merit, opposed his greatness, or insulted his misfortunes; and the only comfort of his exile was the sacred hope and promise of revenge. The necessary extinction of the young emperor and his mother imposed the fatal obligation of extirpating the friends who hated, and might punish, the assassin; and the repetition of murder rendered him less willing and less able to forgive. A horrid narrative of the victims whom he sacrificed by poison or the sword, by the sea or the flames, would be less expressive of his cruelty than the appellation of the Halcyon-days, which was applied to a rare and bloodless week of repose: the tyrant strove to transfer on the laws and the judges some portion of his guilt, but the mask was fallen, and his subjects could no longer mistake the true author of their calamities. The noblest of the Greeks, more especially those who, by descent or alliance, might dispute the Comnenian inheritance, escaped from the monster's den: Nice or Prusa, Sicily or Cyprus, were their places of refuge; and as their flight was already criminal, they aggravated their offence by an open revolt and the Imperial title. Yet Andronicus resisted the daggers and swords of his most formidable enemies: Nice and Prusa were reduced and chastised; the Sicilians were content with the sack of Thessalonica; and the distance of Cyprus was not more propitious to the rebel than to the tyrant. His throne was subverted by a rival without a merit, and a people without arms. Isaac Angelus, a descendant in the female line from the great Alexius, was marked as a victim by the prudence or superstition of the emperor. In a moment of despair Angelus defended his life and liberty, slew the executioner, and fled to the church of St. Sophia. The sanctuary was insensibly filled with a curious and mournful crowd, who, in his fate, prognosticated their own. But their lamentations were soon turned to curses, and their curses to threats: they dared to ask, "Why do we fear? why do we obey? We are many, and he is one; our patience is the only bond of our slavery." With the dawn of day the city burst into a general sedition, the prisons were thrown open, the coldest and most servile were roused to the defence of their country, and Isaac, the second of the name, was raised from the sanctuary to the throne. Unconscious of his danger, the tyrant was absent —withdrawn from the toils of state, in the delicious islands of the Propontis. He had contracted an indecent marriage with Alice, or Agnes, daughter of Lewis the Seventh, of France, and relict of the unfortunate Alexius; and his society, more suitable to his temper than to his age, was composed of a young wife and a favourite concubine. On the first alarm he rushed to Constantinople, impatient for the blood of the guilty; but he was astonished by the silence of the palace, the tumult of the city, and the general desertion of mankind. Andronicus proclaimed a free pardon to his subjects; they neither desired nor would grant forgiveness: he offered to resign the crown to his son Manuel; but the virtues of the son could not expiate his father's crimes. The sea was still open for his retreat; but the news of the revolution had flown along the coast; when fear had ceased, obedience was no more; the Imperial galley was pursued and taken by an armed brigantine, and the tyrant was dragged to the presence of Isaac Angelus, loaded with fetters, and a long chain round his neck. His eloquence and the tears of his female companions pleaded in vain for his life; but, instead of the decencies of a legal execution, the new monarch abandoned the criminal to the numerous sufferers whom he had deprived of a father, a husband, or a friend. His teeth and hair, an eye and a hand, were torn from him, as a poor compensation for their loss; and a short respite was allowed, that he might feel the bitterness of death. Astride on a camel, without any danger of a rescue, he was carried through the city, and the basest of the populace rejoiced to trample on the fallen majesty of their prince. After a thousand blows and outrages, Andronicus was hung by the feet between two pillars that supported the statues of a wolf and a sow; and every hand that could reach the public enemy inflicted on his body some mark of ingenious or brutal cruelty, till two friendly or furious Italians, plunging their swords into his body, released him from all human punishment. In this long and painful agony, "Lord have mercy upon me!" and "Why will you bruise a broken reed?" were the only words that escaped from his mouth. Our hatred for the tyrant is lost in pity for the man; nor can we blame his pusillanimous resignation, since a Greek Christian was no longer master of his life.

I have been tempted to expatiate on the extraordinary character and adventures of Andronicus; but I shall here terminate the series of the Greek emperors since the time of Heraclius. The branches that sprang from the Comnenian trunk had insensibly withered, and the male line was continued only in the posterity of Andronicus himself, who, in the public confusion, usurped the sovereignty of Trebizond, so obscure in history, and so famous in romance. A private citizen of Philadelphia, Constantine Angelus, had emerged to wealth and honours by his marriage with the daughter of the emperor Alexius. His son Andronicus is conspicuous only by his cowardice. His grandson Isaac punished and succeeded the tyrant; but he was dethroned by his own vices and the ambition of his brother; and their discord introduced the Latins to the conquest of Constantinople, the first great period in the fall of the Eastern empire.

If we compute the number and duration of the reigns, it will be found that a period of six hundred years is filled by sixty emperors, including in the Augustan list some female sovereigns, and deducting some usurpers who were never acknowledged in the capital, and some princes who did not live to possess their inheritance. The average proportion will allow ten years for each emperor—far below the chronological rule of Sir Isaac Newton, who, from the experience of more recent and regular monarchies, has defined about eighteen or twenty years as the term of an ordinary reign. The Byzantine empire was most tranquil and prosperous when it could acquiesce in hereditary succession: five dynasties, the Heraclian, Isaurian, Amorian, Basilian, and Comnenian families, enjoyed and transmitted the royal patrimony during their respective series of five, four, three, six, and four generations; several princes number the years of their reign with those of their infancy; and Constantine the Seventh and his two grandsons occupy the space of an entire century. But in the intervals of the Byzantine dynasties the succession is rapid and broken, and the name of a successful candidate is speedily erased by a more fortunate competitor. Many were the paths that led to the summit of royalty: the fabric of rebellion was overthrown by the stroke of conspiracy, or undermined by the silent arts of intrigue: the favourites of the soldiers or people, of the senate or clergy, of the women and eunuchs, were alternately clothed with the purple: the means of their elevation were base, and their end was often contemptible or tragic. A being of the nature of man, endowed with the same faculties, but with a longer measure of existence, would cast down a smile of pity and contempt on the crimes and follies of human ambition, so eager, in a narrow span, to grasp at a precarious and short-lived enjoyment. It is thus that the experience of history exalts and enlarges the horizon of our intellectual view. In a composition of some days, in a perusal of some hours, six hundred years have rolled away, and the duration of a life or reign is contracted to a fleeting moment: the grave is ever beside the throne; the success of a criminal is almost instantly followed by the loss of his prize; and our immortal reason survives and disdains the sixty phantoms of kings who have passed before our eyes, and faintly dwell on our remembrance. The observation, that in every age and climate ambition has prevailed with the same commanding energy, may abate the surprise of a philosopher; but while he condemns the vanity, he may search the motive of this universal desire to obtain and hold the sceptre of dominion. To the greater part of the Byzantine series we cannot reasonably ascribe the love of fame and of mankind. The virtue alone of John Comnenus was beneficent and pure: the most illustrious of the princes who precede or follow that respectable name have trod with some dexterity and vigour the crooked and bloody paths of a selfish policy: in scrutinising the imperfect characters of Leo the Isaurian, Basil the First, and Alexius Comnenus, of Theophilus, the second Basil, and Manuel Comnenus, our esteem and censure are almost equally balanced; and the remainder of the Imperial crowd could only desire and expect to be forgotten by posterity. Was personal happiness the aim and object of their ambition? I shall not descant on the vulgar topics of the misery of kings; but I may surely observe that their condition, of all others, is the most pregnant with fear, and the least susceptible of hope. For these opposite passions a larger scope was allowed in the revolutions of antiquity than in the smooth and solid temper of the modern world, which cannot easily repeat either the triumph of Alexander or the fall of Darius. But the peculiar infelicity of the Byzantine princes exposed them to domestic perils, without affording any lively promise of foreign conquest. From the pinnacle of greatness Andronicus was precipitated by a death more cruel and shameful than that of the vilest malefactor; but the most glorious of his predecessors had much more to dread from their subjects than to hope from their enemies. The army was licentious without spirit, the nation turbulent without freedom: the barbarians of the East and West pressed on the monarchy, and the loss of the provinces was terminated by the final servitude of the capital.

The entire series of Roman emperors, from the first of the Cæsars to the last of the Constantines, extends above fifteen hundred years: and the term of dominion, unbroken by foreign conquest, surpasses the measure of the ancient monarchies—the Assyrians or Medes, the successors of Cyrus, or those of Alexander.

CHAPTER XLIX

Introduction, Worship, and Persecution of Images. Revolt of Italy and Rome. Temporal Dominion of the Popes. Conquest of Italy by the Franks. Establishment of Images. Character and Coronation of Charlemagne. Restoration and Decay of the Roman Empire in the West. Independence of Italy. Constitution of the Germanic Body.

In the connection of the church and state I have considered the former as subservient only, and relative, to the latter; a salutary maxim, if in fact as well as in narrative it had ever been held sacred. The oriental philosophy of the Gnostics, the dark abyss of predestination and grace, and the strange transformation of the Eucharist from the sign to the substance of Christ's body,[1] I have purposely abandoned to the curiosity of speculative divines. But I have reviewed with diligence and pleasure the objects of ecclesiastical history by which the decline and fall of the Roman empire were materially affected, the propagation of Christianity, the constitution of the Catholic church, the ruin of Paganism, and the sects that arose from the mysterious controversies concerning the Trinity and incarnation. At the head of this class we may justly rank the worship of images, so fiercely disputed in the eighth and ninth centuries; since a question of popular superstition produced the revolt of Italy, the temporal power of the popes, and the restoration of the Roman empire in the West.

The primitive Christians were possessed with an unconquerable repugnance to the use and abuse of images; and this aversion may be ascribed to their descent from the Jews, and their enmity to the Greeks. The Mosaic law had severely proscribed all representations of the Deity; and that precept was firmly established in the principles and practice of the chosen people. The wit of the Christian apologists was pointed against the foolish idolaters who bowed before the workmanship of their own hands: the images of brass and marble, which had *they* been endowed with sense and motion, should have started rather from the pedestal to adore the creative powers of the artist.[2] Perhaps some recent and imperfect converts of the Gnostic tribe might crown the statues of Christ and St. Paul with the profane honours which they paid to those of Aristotle and Pythagoras;[3] but the public religion of the Catholics was uniformly simple and spiritual; and the first notice of the use of pictures is in the censure of the council of Illiberis, three hundred years after the Christian æra. Under the successors of Constantine, in the peace and luxury of the triumphant church, the more prudent bishops condescended to indulge a visible superstition for the benefit of the multitude; and after the ruin of Paganism they were no longer restrained by the apprehension of an odious parallel. The first introduction of a symbolic worship was in the veneration of the cross and of relics. The saints and martyrs, whose intercession was implored, were seated on the right hand of God; but the gracious and often supernatural favours which, in the popular belief, were showered round their tomb, conveyed an unquestionable sanction of the devout pilgrims who visited, and touched, and kissed these lifeless remains, the memorials of their merits and sufferings.[4] But a memorial more interesting than the skull or the sandals of a departed worthy is the faithful copy of his person and features, delineated by the arts of painting or sculpture. In every age such copies, so congenial to human feelings, have been cherished by the zeal of private friendship or public esteem: the images of the Roman emperors were adored with civil and almost religious honours; a reverence less ostentatious, but more sincere, was applied to the statues of sages and patriots; and these profane virtues, these splendid sins, disappeared in the presence of the holy men who had died for their celestial and everlasting country. At first the experiment was made with caution and scruple; and the venerable pictures were discreetly allowed to instruct the ignorant, to awaken the cold, and to gratify the prejudices of the heathen proselytes. By a slow though inevitable progression the honours of the original were transferred to the copy: the devout Christian prayed before the image of a saint; and the Pagan rites of genuflexion, luminaries, and incense again stole into the Catholic church. The scruples of reason or piety were silenced by the strong evidence of visions and miracles; and the pictures which speak, and move, and bleed, must be endowed with a divine energy, and may be considered as the proper objects of religious adoration. The most audacious pencil might tremble in the rash attempt of defining by forms and colours the infinite Spirit, the eternal Father, who pervades and sustains the universe.[5] But the superstitious mind was more easily reconciled to paint and to worship the angels, and above all, the Son of God, under the human shape which on earth they have condescended to assume. The second person of the Trinity had been clothed with a real and mortal body; but that body had ascended into heaven: and had not some similitude been presented to the eyes of his disciples, the spiritual worship of Christ might have been obliterated by the visible relics and representations of the saints. A similar indulgence was requisite and propitious for the Virgin Mary: the place of her burial was unknown; and the assumption of her soul and body into heaven was adopted by the credulity of the Greeks and Latins. The use, and even the worship, of images was firmly established before the end of the sixth century: they were fondly cherished by the warm imagination of the Greeks and Asiatics: the Pantheon and Vatican were adorned with the emblems of a new superstition; but this semblance of idolatry was more coldly entertained by the rude barbarians and the Arian clergy of the West. The bolder forms of sculpture, in brass or marble, which peopled the temples of antiquity, were offensive to the fancy or conscience of the Christian Greeks; and a smooth surface of colours has ever been esteemed a more decent and harmless mode of imitation.[6]

The merit and effect of a copy depends on its resemblance with the original; but the primitive Christians were ignorant of the genuine features of the Son of God, his mother, and his apostles: the statue of Christ at Paneas, in Palestine,[7] was more probably that of some temporal saviour; the Gnostics and their profane monuments were reprobated, and the fancy of the Christian artists could only be guided by the clandestine imitation of some heathen model. In this distress a bold and dexterous invention assured at once the likeness of the image and the innocence of the worship. A new superstructure of fable was raised on the popular basis of a Syrian legend on the correspondence of Christ and Abgarus, so famous in the days of Eusebius, so reluctantly deserted by our modern advocates. The bishop of Cæsarea[8] records the epistle,[9] but he most strangely forgets the picture of Christ[10]—the perfect impression of his face on a linen, with which he gratified the faith of the royal stranger who had invoked his healing power, and offered the strong city of Edessa to protect him against the malice of the Jews. The ignorance of the primitive church is explained by the long imprisonment of the image in a niche of the wall, from whence, after an oblivion of five hundred years, it was released by some prudent bishop, and seasonably presented to the devotion of the times. Its first and most glorious exploit was the deliverance of the city from the arms of Chosroes Nushirvan; and it was soon revered as a pledge of the divine promise that Edessa should never be taken by a foreign enemy. It is true, indeed, that the text of Procopius ascribes the double deliverance of Edessa to the wealth and valour of her citizens, who purchased the absence and repelled the assaults of the Persian monarch. He was ignorant, the profane historian, of the testimony which he is compelled to deliver in the ecclesiastical page of Evagrius, that the Palladium was exposed on the rampart, and that the water which had been sprinkled on the holy face, instead of quenching, added new fuel to the flames of the besieged. After this important service the image of Edessa was preserved with respect and gratitude; and if the Armenians rejected the legend, the more credulous Greeks adored the similitude, which was not the work of any mortal pencil, but the immediate creation of the divine original. The style and sentiments of a Byzantine hymn will declare how far their worship was removed from the grossest idolatry. "How can we with mortal eyes contemplate this image, whose celestial splendour the host of heaven presumes not to behold? HE who dwells in heaven condescends this day to visit us by his venerable image; HE who is seated on the cherubim visits us this day by a picture, which the Father has delineated with his immaculate hand, which he has formed in an ineffable manner, and which we sanctify by adoring it with fear and love." Before the end of the sixth century these images, *made without hands* (in Greek it is a single word[11]), were propagated in the camps and cities of the Eastern empire;[12] they were the objects of worship, and the instruments of miracles; and in the hour of danger or tumult their venerable presence could revive the hope, rekindle the courage, or repress the fury of the Roman legions. Of these pictures the far greater part, the transcripts of a human pencil, could only pretend to a secondary likeness and improper title; but there were some of higher descent, who derived their resemblance from an immediate contact with the original, endowed for that purpose with a miraculous and prolific virtue. The most ambitious aspired from a filial to a fraternal relation with the image of Edessa; and such is the *veronica* of Rome, or Spain, or Jerusalem, which Christ in his agony and bloody sweat applied to his face, and delivered to a holy matron. The fruitful precedent was speedily transferred to the Virgin Mary, and the saints and martyrs. In the church of Diospolis, in Palestine, the features of the Mother of God[13] were deeply inscribed in a marble column: the East and West have been decorated by the pencil of St. Luke; and the Evangelist, who was perhaps a physician, has been forced to exercise the occupation of a painter, so profane and odious in the eyes of the primitive Christians. The Olympian Jove, created by the muse of Homer and the chisel of Phidias, might inspire a philosophic mind with momentary devotion; but these Catholic images were faintly and flatly delineated by monkish artists in the last degeneracy of taste and genius.[14]

The worship of images had stolen into the church by insensible degrees, and each petty step was pleasing to the superstitious mind, as productive of comfort and innocent of sin. But in the beginning of the eighth century, in the full magnitude of the abuse, the more timorous Greeks were awakened by an apprehension that, under the mask of Christianity, they had restored the religion of their fathers: they heard, with grief and impatience, the name of idolators—the incessant charge of the Jews and Mohammedans,[15] who derived from the Law and the Koran an immortal hatred to graven images and all relative worship. The servitude of the Jews might curb their zeal and depreciate their authority; but the triumphant Musulmans, who reigned at Damascus, and threatened Constantinople, cast into the scale of reproach the accumulated weight of truth and victory. The cities of Syria, Palestine, and Egypt had been fortified with the images of Christ, his mother, and his saints; and each city presumed on the hope or promise of miraculous defence. In a rapid conquest of ten years the Arabs subdued those cities and these images; and, in their opinion, the Lord of Hosts pronounced a decisive judgment between the adoration and contempt of these mute and inanimate idols. For a while Edessa had braved the Persian assaults; but the chosen city, the spouse of Christ, was involved in the common ruin; and his divine resemblance became the slave and trophy of the infidels. After a servitude of three hundred years, the Palladium was yielded to the devotion of Constantinople, for a ransom of twelve thousand pounds of silver, the redemption of two hundred Musulmans, and a perpetual truce for the territory of Edessa.[16] In this season of distress and dismay the eloquence of the monks was exercised in the defence of images; and they attempted to prove that the sin and schism of the greatest part of the Orientals had forfeited the favour and annihilated the virtue of these precious symbols. But they were now opposed by the murmurs of many simple or rational Christians, who appealed to the evidence of texts, of facts, and of the primitive times, and secretly desired the reformation of the church. As the worship of images had never been established by any general or positive law, its progress in the Eastern empire had been retarded, or accelerated, by the differences of men and manners, the local degrees of refinement, and the personal characters of the bishops. The splendid devotion was fondly cherished by the levity of the capital and the inventive genius of the Byzantine clergy; while the rude and remote districts of Asia were strangers to this innovation of sacred luxury. Many large congregations of Gnostics and Arians maintained, after their conversion, the simple worship which had preceded their separation; and the Armenians, the most warlike subjects of Rome, were not reconciled, in the twelfth century, to the sight of images.[17] These various denominations of men afforded a fund of prejudice and aversion, of small account in the villages of Anatolia or Thrace, but which, in the fortune of a soldier, a prelate, or a eunuch, might be often connected with the powers of the church and state.

Of such adventurers the most fortunate was the emperor Leo the Third,[18] who, from the mountains of Isauria, ascended the throne of the East. He was ignorant of sacred and profane letters: but his education, his reason, perhaps his intercourse with the Jews and Arabs, had inspired the martial peasant with a hatred of images; and it was held to be the duty of a prince to impose on his subjects the dictates of his own conscience. But in the outset of an unsettled reign, during ten years of toil and danger, Leo submitted to the meanness of hypocrisy, bowed before the idols which he despised, and satisfied the Roman pontiff with the annual professions of his orthodoxy and zeal. In the reformation of religion his first steps were moderate and cautious: he assembled a great council of senators and bishops, and enacted, with their consent, that all the images should be removed from the sanctuary and altar to a proper height in the churches, where they might be visible to the eyes, and inaccessible to the superstition, of the people. But it was impossible on either side to check the rapid though adverse impulse of veneration and abhorrence: in their lofty position the sacred images still edified their votaries and reproached the tyrant. He was himself provoked by resistance and invective; and his own party accused him of an imperfect discharge of his duty, and urged for his imitation the example of the Jewish king, who had broken without scruple the brazen serpent of the temple. By a second edict he proscribed the existence as well as the use of religious pictures; the churches of Constantinople and the provinces were cleansed from idolatry; the images of Christ, the Virgin, and the saints were demolished, or a smooth surface of plaster was spread over the walls of the edifice. The sect of the Iconoclasts was supported by the zeal and despotism of six emperors, and the East and West were involved in a noisy conflict of one hundred and twenty years. It was the design of Leo the Isaurian to pronounce the condemnation of images as an article of faith, and by the authority of a general council: but the convocation of such an assembly was reserved for his son Constantine;[19] and though it is stigmatised by triumphant bigotry as a meeting of fools and atheists, their own partial and mutilated acts betray many symptoms of reason and piety. The debates and decrees of many provincial synods introduced the summons of the general council which met in the suburbs of Constantinople, and was composed of the respectable number of three hundred and thirty-eight bishops of Europe and Anatolia; for the patriarchs of Antioch and Alexandria were the slaves of the caliph, and the Roman pontiff had withdrawn the churches of Italy and the West from the communion of the Greeks. This Byzantine synod assumed the rank and powers of the seventh general council; yet even this title was a recognition of the six preceding assemblies, which had laboriously built the structure of the Catholic faith. After a serious deliberation of six months, the three hundred and thirty-eight bishops pronounced and subscribed a unanimous decree, that all visible symbols of Christ, except in the Eucharist, were either blasphemous or heretical; that image-worship was a corruption of Christianity and a renewal of Paganism; that all such monuments of idolatry should be broken or erased; and that those who should refuse to deliver the objects of their private superstition were guilty of disobedience to the authority of the church and of the emperor. In their loud and loyal acclamations they celebrated the merits of their temporal redeemer; and to his zeal and justice they intrusted the execution of their spiritual censures. At Constantinople, as in the former councils, the will of the prince was the rule of episcopal faith; but on this occasion I am inclined to suspect that a large majority of the prelates sacrificed their secret conscience to the temptations of hope and fear. In the long night of superstition the Christians had wandered far away from the simplicity of the Gospel: nor was it easy for them to discern the clue, and tread back the mazes of the labyrinth. The worship of images was inseparably blended, at least to a pious fancy, with the Cross, the Virgin, the saints and their relics; the holy ground was involved in a cloud of miracles and visions; and the nerves of the mind, curiosity and scepticism, were benumbed by the habits of obedience and belief. Constantine himself is accused of indulging a royal licence to doubt, or deny, or deride the mysteries of the Catholics,[20] but they were deeply inscribed in the public and private creed of his bishops; and the boldest Iconoclast might assault with a secret horror the monuments of popular devotion, which were consecrated to the honour of his celestial patrons. In the reformation of the sixteenth century freedom and knowledge had expanded all the faculties of man: the thirst of innovation superseded the reverence of antiquity; and the vigour of Europe could disdain those phantoms which terrified the sickly and servile weakness of the Greeks.

The scandal of an abstract heresy can be only proclaimed to the people by the blast of the ecclesiastical trumpet; but the most ignorant can perceive, the most torpid must feel, the profanation and downfall of their visible deities. The first hostilities of Leo were directed against a lofty Christ on the vestibule, and above the gate, of the palace. A ladder had been planted for the assault, but it was furiously shaken by a crowd of zealots and women: they beheld, with pious transport, the ministers of sacrilege tumbling from on high and dashed against the pavement; and the honours of the ancient martyrs were prostituted to these criminals, who justly suffered for murder and rebellion.[21] The execution of the Imperial edicts was resisted by frequent tumults in Constantinople and the provinces: the person of Leo was endangered, his officers were massacred, and the popular enthusiasm was quelled by the strongest efforts of the civil and military power. Of the Archipelago, or Holy Sea, the numerous islands were filled with images and monks: their votaries abjured, without scruple, the enemy of Christ, his mother, and the saints; they armed a fleet of boats and galleys, displayed their consecrated banners, and boldly steered for the harbour of Constantinople, to place on the throne a new favourite of God and the people. They depended on the succour of a miracle: but their miracles were inefficient against the *Greek fire;* and, after the defeat and conflagration of their fleet, the naked islands were abandoned to the clemency or justice of the conqueror. The son of Leo, in the first year of his reign, had undertaken an expedition against the Saracens: during his absence the capital, the palace, and the purple were occupied by his kinsman Artavasdes, the ambitious champion of the orthodox faith. The worship of images was triumphantly restored: the patriarch renounced his dissimulation, or dissembled his sentiments: and the righteous claim of the usurper was acknowledged, both in the new and in ancient Rome. Constantine flew for refuge to his paternal mountains; but he descended at the head of the bold and affectionate Isaurians; and his final victory confounded the arms and predictions of the fanatics. His long reign was distracted with clamour, sedition, conspiracy, and mutual hatred and sanguinary revenge: the persecution of images was the motive or pretence of his adversaries; and, if they missed a temporal diadem, they were rewarded by the Greeks with the crown of martyrdom. In every act of open and clandestine treason the emperor felt the unforgiving enmity of the monks, the faithful slaves of the superstition to which they owed their riches and influence. They prayed, they preached, they absolved, they inflamed, they conspired; the solitude of Palestine poured forth a torrent of invective; and the pen of St. John Damascenus,[22] the last of the Greek fathers, devoted the tyrant's head, both in this world and the next.[23] I am not at leisure to examine how far the monks provoked, nor how much they have exaggerated, their real and pretended sufferings, nor how many lost their lives or limbs, their eyes or their beards, by the cruelty of the emperor. From the chastisement of individuals he proceeded to the abolition of the order; and, as it was wealthy and useless, his resentment might be stimulated by avarice, and justified by patriotism. The formidable name and mission of the *Dragon*,[24] his visitor-general, excited the terror and abhorrence of the *black* nation: the religious communities were dissolved, the buildings were converted into magazines or barracks; the lands, movables, and cattle were confiscated; and our modern precedents will support the charge, that much wanton or malicious havoc was exercised against the relics, and even the books, of the monasteries. With the habit and profession of monks, the public and private worship of images was rigorously proscribed; and it should seem that a solemn abjuration of idolatry was exacted from the subjects, or at least from the clergy, of the Eastern empire.[25]

The patient East abjured with reluctance her sacred images; they were fondly cherished, and vigorously defended, by the independent zeal of the Italians. In ecclesiastical rank and jurisdiction the patriarch of Constantinople and the pope of Rome were nearly equal. But the Greek prelate was a domestic slave under the eye of his master, at whose nod he alternately passed from the convent to the throne, and from the throne to the convent. A distant and dangerous station, amidst the barbarians of the West, excited the spirit and freedom of the Latin bishops. Their popular election endeared them to the Romans: the public and private indigence was relieved by their ample revenue; and the weakness or neglect of the emperors compelled them to consult, both in peace and war, the temporal safety of the city. In the school of adversity the priest insensibly imbibed the virtues and the ambition of a prince; the same character was assumed, the same policy was adopted, by the Italian, the Greek, or the Syrian, who ascended the chair of St. Peter; and, after the loss of her legions and provinces, the genius and fortune of the popes again restored the supremacy of Rome. It is agreed that in the eighth century their dominion was founded on rebellion, and that the rebellion was produced, and justified, by the heresy of the Iconoclasts; but the conduct of the second and third Gregory, in this memorable contest, is variously interpreted by the wishes of their friends and enemies. The Byzantine writers unanimously declare that, after a fruitless admonition, they pronounced the separation of the East and West, and deprived the sacrilegious tyrant of the revenue and sovereignty of Italy. Their excommunication is still more clearly expressed by the Greeks, who beheld the accomplishment of the paper triumphs; and as they are more strongly attached to their religion than to their country, they praise, instead of blaming, the zeal and orthodoxy of these apostolical men.[26] The modern champions of Rome are eager to accept the praise and the precedent: this great and glorious example of the deposition of royal heretics is celebrated by the cardinals Baronius and Bellarmine;[27] and if they are asked why the same thunders were not hurled against the Neros and Julians of antiquity? they reply, that the weakness of the primitive church was the sole cause of her patient loyalty.[28] On this occasion the effects of love and hatred are the same; and the zealous Protestants, who seek to kindle the indignation and to alarm the fears of princes and magistrates, expatiate on the insolence and treason of the two Gregories against their lawful sovereign.[29] They are defended only by the moderate Catholics, for the most part of the Gallican church,[30] who respect the saint without approving the sin. These common advocates of the crown and mitre circumscribe the truth of facts by the rule of equity, Scripture, and tradition, and appeal to the evidence of the Latins,[31] and the lives[32] and epistles of the popes themselves.

Two original epistles, from Gregory the Second to the emperor Leo, are still extant;[33] and if they cannot be praised as the most perfect models of eloquence and logic, they exhibit the portrait, or at least the mask, of the founder of the papal monarchy. "During ten pure and fortunate years," says Gregory to the emperor, "we have tasted the annual comfort of your royal letters, subscribed in purple ink with your own hand, the sacred pledges of your attachment to the orthodox creed of our fathers. How deplorable is the change! how tremendous the scandal! You now accuse the Catholics of idolatry; and, by the accusation, you betray your own impiety and ignorance. To this ignorance we are compelled to adapt the grossness of our style and arguments: the first elements of holy letters are sufficient for your confusion; and were you to enter a grammar-school, and avow yourself the enemy of our worship, the simple and pious children would be provoked to cast their horn-books at your head." After this decent salutation the pope attempts the usual distinction between the idols of antiquity and the Christian images. The former were the fanciful representations of phantoms or demons, at a time when the true God had not manifested his person in any visible likeness. The latter are the genuine forms of Christ, his mother, and his saints, who had approved, by a crowd of miracles, the innocence and merit of this relative worship. He must indeed have trusted to the ignorance of Leo, since he could assert the perpetual use of images from the apostolic age, and

their venerable presence in the six synods of the Catholic church. A more specious argument is drawn from present possession and recent practice: the harmony of the Christian world supersedes the demand of a general council; and Gregory frankly confesses that such assemblies can only be useful under the reign of an orthodox prince. To the impudent and inhuman Leo, more guilty than a heretic, he recommends peace, silence, and implicit obedience to his spiritual guides of Constantinople and Rome. The limits of civil and ecclesiastical powers are defined by the pontiff. To the former he appropriates the body; to the latter the soul: the sword of justice is in the hands of the magistrate: the more formidable weapon of excommunication is intrusted to the clergy; and in the exercise of their divine commission a zealous son will not spare his offending father: the successor of St. Peter may lawfully chastise the kings of the earth. "You assault us, O tyrant! with a carnal and military hand: unarmed and naked we can only implore the Christ, the prince of the heavenly host, that he will send unto you a devil for the destruction of your body and the salvation of your soul. You declare, with foolish arrogance, I will despatch my orders to Rome: I will break in pieces the image of St. Peter; and Gregory, like his predecessor Martin, shall be transported in chains and in exile to the foot of the imperial throne. Would to God that I might be permitted to tread in the footsteps of the holy Martin! but may the fate of Constans serve as a warning to the persecutors of the church! After his just condemnation by the bishops of Sicily, the tyrant was cut off in the fulness of his sins, by a domestic servant: the saint is still adored by the nations of Scythia, among whom he ended his banishment and his life. But it is our duty to live for the edification and support of the faithful people; nor are we reduced to risk our safety on the event of a combat. Incapable as you are of defending your Roman subjects, the maritime situation of the city may perhaps expose it to your depredation; but we can remove to the distance of four-and-twenty *stadia*,[34] to the first fortress of the Lombards, and then—you may pursue the winds. Are you ignorant that the popes are the bond of union, the mediators of peace between the East and West? The eyes of the nations are fixed on our humility; and they revere, as a God upon earth, the apostle St. Peter, whose image you threaten to destroy.[35] The remote and interior kingdoms of the West present their homage to Christ and his vicegerent; and we now prepare to visit one of their most powerful monarchs who desires to receive from our hands the sacrament of baptism.[36] The barbarians have submitted to the yoke of the Gospel, while you alone are deaf to the voice of the shepherd. These pious barbarians are kindled into rage: they thirst to avenge the persecution of the East. Abandon your rash and fatal enterprise; reflect, tremble, and repent. If you persist, we are innocent of the blood that will be spilt in the contest; may it fall on your own head!"

The first assault of Leo against the images of Constantinople had been witnessed by a crowd of strangers from Italy and the West, who related with grief and indignation the sacrilege of the emperor. But on the reception of his proscriptive edict they trembled for their domestic deities; the images of Christ and the Virgin, of the angels, martyrs, and saints, were abolished in all the churches of Italy; and a strong alternative was proposed to the Roman pontiff, the royal favour, as the price of his compliance, degradation and exile as the penalty of his disobedience. Neither zeal nor policy allowed him to hesitate; and the haughty strain in which Gregory addressed the emperor displays his confidence in the truth of his doctrine, or the powers of resistance. Without depending on prayers or miracles, he boldly armed against the public enemy, and his pastoral letters admonished the Italians of their danger and their duty.[37] At this signal, Ravenna, Venice, and the cities of the Exarchate and Pentapolis adhered to the cause of religion; their military force by sea and land consisted, for the most part, of the natives; and the spirit of patriotism and zeal was transfused into the mercenary strangers. The Italians swore to live and die in the defence of the pope and the holy images; the Roman people was devoted to their father, and even the Lombards were ambitious to share the merit and advantage of this holy war. The most treasonable act, but the most obvious revenge, was the destruction of the statues of Leo himself: the most effectual and pleasing measure of rebellion was the withholding of the tribute of Italy, and depriving him of a power which he had recently abused by the imposition of a new capitation.[38] A form of administration was preserved by the election of magistrates and governors; and so high was the public indignation, that the Italians were prepared to create an orthodox emperor, and to conduct him with a fleet and army to the palace of Constantinople. In that palace the Roman bishops, the second and third Gregory, were condemned as the authors of the revolt, and every attempt was made, either by fraud or force, to seize their persons and to strike at their lives. The city was repeatedly visited or assaulted by captains of the guards, and dukes and exarchs of high dignity or secret trust; they landed with foreign troops, they obtained some domestic aid, and the superstition of Naples may blush that her fathers were attached to the cause of heresy. But these clandestine or open attacks were repelled by the courage and vigilance of the Romans; the Greeks were overthrown and massacred, their leaders suffered an ignominious death, and the popes, however inclined to mercy, refused to intercede for these guilty victims. At Ravenna,[39] the several quarters of the city had long exercised a bloody and hereditary feud; in religious controversy they found a new aliment of faction: but the votaries of images were superior in numbers or spirit, and the exarch, who attempted to stem the torrent, lost his life in a popular sedition. To punish this flagitious deed, and restore his dominion in Italy, the emperor sent a fleet and army into the Hadriatic gulf. After suffering from the winds and waves much loss and delay, the Greeks made their descent in the neighbourhood of Ravenna: they threatened to depopulate the guilty capital, and to imitate, perhaps to surpass, the example of Justinian the Second, who had chastised a former rebellion by the choice and execution of fifty of the principal inhabitants. The women and clergy, in sackcloth and ashes, lay prostrate in prayer; the men were in arms for the defence of their country; the common danger had united the factions, and the event of a battle was preferred to the slow miseries of a siege. In a hard-fought day, as the two armies alternately yielded and advanced, a phantom was seen, a voice was heard, and Ravenna was victorious by the assurance of victory. The strangers retreated to their ships, but the populous seacoast poured forth a multitude of boats; the waters of the Po were so deeply infected with blood, that during six years the public prejudice abstained from the fish of the river; and the institution of an annual feast perpetuated the worship of images and the abhorrence of the Greek tyrant. Amidst the triumph of the Catholic arms, the Roman pontiff convened a synod of ninety-three bishops against the heresy of the Iconoclasts. With their consent, he pronounced a general excommunication against all who by word or deed should attack the tradition of the fathers and the images of the saints: in this sentence the emperor was tacitly involved [40] but the vote of a last and hopeless remonstrance may seem to imply that the anathema was yet suspended over his guilty head. No sooner had they confirmed their own safety, the worship of images, and the freedom of Rome and Italy, than the popes appear to have relaxed of their severity, and to have spared the relics of the Byzantine dominion. Their moderate counsels delayed and prevented the election of a new emperor, and they exhorted the Italians not to separate from the body of the Roman monarchy. The exarch was permitted to reside within the walls of Ravenna, a captive rather than a master; and till the Imperial coronation of Charlemagne, the government of Rome and Italy was exercised in the name of the successors of Constantine.[41]

The liberty of Rome, which had been oppressed by the arms and arts of Augustus, was rescued, after seven hundred and fifty years of servitude, from the persecution of Leo the Isaurian. By the Cæsars the triumphs of the consuls had been annihilated: in the decline and fall of the empire, the god Terminus, the sacred boundary, had insensibly receded from the ocean, the Rhine, the Danube, and the Euphrates; and Rome was reduced to her ancient territory from Viterbo to Terracina, and from Narni to the mouth of the Tiber.[42] When the kings were banished, the republic reposed on the firm basis which had been founded by their wisdom and virtue. Their perpetual jurisdiction was divided between two annual magistrates: the senate continued to exercise the powers of administration and counsel; and the legislative authority was distributed in the assemblies of the people by a well-proportioned scale of property and service. Ignorant of the arts of luxury, the primitive Romans had improved the science of government and war: the will of the community was absolute: the rights of individuals were sacred: one hundred and thirty thousand citizens were armed for defence or conquest; and a band of robbers and outlaws was moulded into a nation, deserving of freedom and ambitious of glory.[43] When the sovereignty of the Greek emperors was extinguished, the ruins of Rome presented the sad image of depopulation and decay: her slavery was a habit, her liberty an accident; the effect of superstition, and the object of her own amazement and terror. The last vestige of the substance, or even the forms, of the constitution, was obliterated from the practice and memory of the Romans; and they were devoid of knowledge, or virtue, again to build the fabric of a commonwealth. Their scanty remnant, the off-

spring of slaves and strangers, was despicable in the eyes of the victorious barbarians. As often as the Franks or Lombards expressed their most bitter contempt of a foe, they called him a Roman; "and in this name," says the bishop Liutprand, "we include whatever is base, whatever is cowardly, whatever is perfidious, the extremes of avarice and luxury, and every vice that can prostitute the dignity of human nature."[44] By the necessity of their situation, the inhabitants of Rome were cast into the rough model of a republican government: they were compelled to elect some judges in peace and some leaders in war: the nobles assembled to deliberate, and their resolves could not be executed without the union and consent of the multitude. The style of the Roman senate and people was revived,[45] but the spirit was fled; and their new independence was disgraced by the tumultuous conflict of licentiousness and oppression. The want of laws could only be supplied by the influence of religion, and their foreign and domestic counsels were moderated by the authority of the bishop. His alms, his sermons, his correspondence with the kings and prelates of the West, his recent services, their gratitude and oath, accustomed the Romans to consider him as the first magistrate or prince of the city. The Christian humility of the popes was not offended by the name of Dominus, or Lord; and their face and inscription are still apparent on the most ancient coins.[46] Their temporal dominion is now confirmed by the reverence of a thousand years; and their noblest title is the free choice of a people whom they had redeemed from slavery.

In the quarrels of ancient Greece, the holy people of Elis enjoyed a perpetual peace, under the protection of Jupiter, and in the exercise of the Olympic games.[47] Happy would it have been for the Romans if a similar privilege had guarded the patrimony of St. Peter from the calamities of war; if the Christians who visited the holy threshold would have sheathed their swords in the presence of the apostle and his successor. But this mystic circle could have been traced only by the want of a legislator and a sage: this pacific system was incompatible with the zeal and ambition of the popes: the Romans were not addicted, like the inhabitants of Elis, to the innocent and placid labours of agriculture; and the barbarians of Italy, though softened by the climate, were far below the Grecian states in the institutions of public and private life. A memorable example of repentance and piety was exhibited by Liutprand, king of the

Lombards. In arms, at the gate of the Vatican, the conqueror listened to the voice of Gregory the Second,[48] withdrew his troops, resigned his conquests, respectfully visited the church of St. Peter, and, after performing his devotions, offered his sword and dagger, his cuirass and mantle, his silver cross, and his crown of gold, on the tomb of the apostle. But this religious fervour was the illusion, perhaps the artifice, of the moment; the sense of interest is strong and lasting; the love of arms and rapine was congenial to the Lombards; and both the prince and people were irresistibly tempted by the disorders of Italy, the nakedness of Rome, and the unwarlike profession of her new chief. On the first edicts of the emperor, they declared themselves the champions of the holy images: Liutprand invaded the province of Romagna, which had already assumed that distinctive appellation; the Catholics of the Exarchate yielded without reluctance to his civil and military power; and a foreign enemy was introduced for the first time into the impregnable fortress of Ravenna. That city and fortress were speedily recovered by the active diligence and maritime forces of the Venetians; and those faithful subjects obeyed the exhortation of Gregory himself, in separating the personal guilt of Leo from the general cause of the Roman empire.[49] The Greeks were less mindful of the service than the Lombards of the injury: the two nations, hostile in their faith, were reconciled in a dangerous and unnatural alliance: the king and the exarch marched to the conquest of Spoleto and Rome; the storm evaporated without effect, but the policy of Liutprand alarmed Italy with a vexatious alternative of hostility and truce. His successor Astolphus declared himself the equal enemy of the emperor and the pope: Ravenna was subdued by force or treachery,[50] and this final conquest extinguished the series of the exarchs, who had reigned with a subordinate power since the time of Justinian and the ruin of the Gothic kingdom. Rome was summoned to acknowledge the victorious Lombard as her lawful sovereign; the annual tribute of a piece of gold was fixed as the ransom of each citizen, and the sword of destruction was unsheathed to exact the penalty of her disobedience. The Romans hesitated; they entreated; they complained; and the threatening barbarians were checked by arms and negotiations, till the popes had engaged the friendship of an ally and avenger beyond the Alps.[51]

In his distress the first Gregory had implored the aid of the hero of the age, of Charles Martel, who governed the French monarchy with the humble title of mayor or duke; and who, by his signal victory over the Saracens, had saved his country, and perhaps Europe, from the Mohammedan yoke. The ambassadors of the pope were received by Charles with decent reverence; but the greatness of his occupations, and the shortness of his life, prevented his interference in the affairs of Italy, except by a friendly and ineffectual mediation. His son Pepin, the heir of his power and virtues, assumed the office of champion of the Roman church; and the zeal of the French prince appears to have been prompted by the love of glory and religion. But the danger was on the banks of the Tiber, the succour on those of the Seine; and our sympathy is cold to the relation of distant misery. Amidst the tears of the city, Stephen the Third embraced the generous resolution of visiting in person the courts of Lombardy and France, to deprecate the injustice of his enemy, or to excite the pity and indignation of his friend. After soothing the public despair by litanies and orations, he undertook this laborious journey with the ambassadors of the French monarch and the Greek emperor. The king of the Lombards was inexorable; but his threats could not silence the complaints, nor retard the speed, of the Roman pontiff, who traversed the Pennine Alps, reposed in the abbey of St. Maurice, and hastened to grasp the right hand of his protector; a hand which was never lifted in vain, either in war or friendship. Stephen was entertained as the visible successor of the apostle; at the next assembly, the field of March or of May, his injuries were exposed to a devout and warlike nation, and he repassed the Alps, not as a suppliant, but as a conqueror, at the head of a French army, which was led by the king in person. The Lombards, after a weak resistance, obtained an ignominious peace, and swore to restore the possessions, and to respect the sanctity, of the Roman church. But no sooner was Astolphus delivered from the presence of the French arms, than he forgot his promise and resented his disgrace. Rome was again encompassed by his arms; and Stephen, apprehensive of fatiguing the zeal of his Transalpine allies, enforced his complaint and request by an eloquent letter in the name and person of St. Peter himself.[52] The apostle assures his adoptive sons, the king, the clergy, and the nobles of France, that, dead in the flesh, he is still alive in the spirit; that they now hear, and must obey, the voice of the founder and guardian of the Roman church; that the Virgin, the angels, the saints, and the

martyrs, and all the host of heaven, unanimously urge the request, and will confess the obligation; that riches, victory, and paradise will
crown their pious enterprise, and that eternal
damnation will be the penalty of their neglect,
if they suffer his tomb, his temple, and his people to fall into the hands of the perfidious Lombards. The second expedition of Pepin was not
less rapid and fortunate than the first: St. Peter
was satisfied, Rome was again saved, and Astolphus was taught the lessons of justice and sincerity by the scourge of a foreign master. After
this double chastisement, the Lombards languished about twenty years in a state of languor
and decay. But their minds were not yet humbled to their condition; and instead of affecting
the pacific virtues of the feeble, they peevishly
harassed the Romans with a repetition of claims,
evasions, and inroads, which they undertook
without reflection and terminated without glory.
On either side, their expiring monarchy was
pressed by the zeal and prudence of Pope Adrian
the First, the genius, the fortune, and greatness
of Charlemagne the son of Pepin; these heroes
of the church and state were united in public
and domestic friendship, and, while they trampled on the prostrate, they varnished their proceedings with the fairest colours of equity and
moderation.[53] The passes of the Alps and the
walls of Pavia were the only defence of the Lombards; the former were surprised, the latter
were invested, by the son of Pepin; and after a
blockade of two years, Desiderius, the last of
their native princes, surrendered his sceptre and
his capital. Under the dominion of a foreign
king, but in the possession of their national
laws, the Lombards became the brethren, rather than the subjects, of the Franks; who derived their blood, and manners, and language
from the same Germanic origin.[54]

The mutual obligations of the popes and the
Carlovingian family form the important link of
ancient and modern, of civil and ecclesiastical,
history. In the conquest of Italy, the champions
of the Roman church obtained a favourable occasion, a specious title, the wishes of the people,
the prayers and intrigues of the clergy. But the
most essential gifts of the popes to the Carlovingian race were the dignities of king of France[55]
and of patrician of Rome. I. Under the sacerdotal monarchy of St. Peter the nations began
to resume the practice of seeking, on the banks
of the Tiber, their kings, their laws, and the
oracles of their fate. The Franks were perplexed
between the name and substance of their government. All the powers of royalty were exercised by Pepin, mayor of the palace; and nothing, except the regal title, was wanting to his
ambition. His enemies were crushed by his valour; his friends were multiplied by his liberality; his father had been the saviour of Christendom; and the claims of personal merit were repeated and ennobled in a descent of four generations. The name and image of royalty was still
preserved in the last descendant of Clovis, the
feeble Childeric; but his obsolete right could
only be used as an instrument of sedition: the
nation was desirous of restoring the simplicity
of the constitution; and Pepin, a subject and a
prince, was ambitious to ascertain his own rank
and the fortune of his family. The mayor and
the nobles were bound, by an oath of fidelity,
to the royal phantom: the blood of Clovis was
pure and sacred in their eyes; and their common ambassadors addressed the Roman pontiff
to dispel their scruples or to absolve their
promise. The interest of Pope Zachary, the successor of the two Gregories, prompted him to
decide, and to decide in their favour: he pronounced that the nation might lawfully unite,
in the same person, the title and authority of
king; and that the unfortunate Childeric, a victim of the public safety, should be degraded,
shaved, and confined in a monastery for the remainder of his days. An answer so agreeable to
their wishes was accepted by the Franks, as the
opinion of a casuist, the sentence of a judge, or
the oracle of a prophet: the Merovingian race
disappeared from the earth; and Pepin was exalted on a buckler by the suffrage of a free people, accustomed to obey his laws and to march
under his standard. His coronation was twice
performed, with the sanction of the popes, by
their most faithful servant St. Boniface, the
apostle of Germany, and by the grateful hands
of Stephen the Third, who, in the monastery of
St. Denys, placed the diadem on the head of his
benefactor. The royal unction of the kings of
Israel was dexterously applied:[56] the successor
of St. Peter assumed the character of a divine
ambassador: a German chieftain was transformed into the Lord's anointed; and this Jewish rite has been diffused and maintained by the
superstition and vanity of modern Europe. The
Franks were absolved from their ancient oath;
but a dire anathema was thundered against
them and their posterity, if they should dare to
renew the same freedom of choice, or to elect a
king, except in the holy and meritorious race of
the Carlovingian princes. Without apprehending the future danger, these princes gloried in
their present security: the secretary of Charle-

magne affirms that the French sceptre was transferred by the authority of the popes;[57] and, in their boldest enterprises, they insist, with confidence, on this signal and successful act of temporal jurisdiction.

II. In the change of manners and language the patricians of Rome[58] were far removed from the senate of Romulus, or the palace of Constantine—from the free nobles of the republic, or the fictitious parents of the emperor. After the recovery of Italy and Africa by the arms of Justinian, the importance and danger of those remote provinces required the presence of a supreme magistrate; he was indifferently styled the exarch or the patrician; and these governors of Ravenna, who fill their place in the chronology of princes, extended their jurisdiction over the Roman city. Since the revolt of Italy and the loss of the Exarchate, the distress of the Romans had exacted some sacrifice of their independence. Yet, even in this act, they exercised the right of disposing of themselves; and the decrees of the senate and people successively invested Charles Martel and his posterity with the honours of patrician of Rome. The leaders of a powerful nation would have disdained a servile title and subordinate office; but the reign of the Greek emperors was suspended; and, in the vacancy of the empire, they derived a more glorious commission from the pope and the republic. The Roman ambassadors presented these patricians with the keys of the shrine of St. Peter, as a pledge and symbol of sovereignty; with a holy banner which it was their right and duty to unfurl in the defence of the church and the city.[59] In the time of Charles Martel and of Pepin, the interposition of the Lombard kingdom covered the freedom, while it threatened the safety, of Rome; and the *patriciate* represented only the title, the service, the alliance, of these distant protectors. The power and policy of Charlemagne annihilated an enemy and imposed a master. In his first visit to the capital he was received with all the honours which had formerly been paid to the exarch, the representative of the emperor; and these honours obtained some new decorations from the joy and gratitude of Pope Adrian the First.[60] No sooner was he informed of the sudden approach of the monarch, than he despatched the magistrates and nobles of Rome to meet him, with the banner, about thirty miles from the city. At the distance of one mile the Flaminian Way was lined with the *schools*, or national communities, of Greeks, Lombards, Saxons, etc.: the Roman youth was under arms; and the children of a

more tender age, with palms and olive branches in their hands, chanted the praises of their great deliverer. At the aspect of the holy crosses, and ensigns of the saints, he dismounted from his horse, led the procession of his nobles to the Vatican, and, as he ascended the stairs, devoutly kissed each step of the threshold of the apostles. In the portico, Adrian expected him at the head of his clergy: they embraced, as friends and equals: but in their march to the altar, the king or patrician assumed the right hand of the pope. Nor was the Frank content with these vain and empty demonstrations of respect. In the twenty-six years that elapsed between the conquest of Lombardy and his Imperial coronation, Rome, which had been delivered by the sword, was subject, as his own, to the sceptre of Charlemagne. The people swore allegiance to his person and family: in his name money was coined and justice was administered; and the election of the popes was examined and confirmed by his authority. Except an original and self-inherent claim of sovereignty, there was not any prerogative remaining which the title of emperor could add to the patrician of Rome.[61]

The gratitude of the Carlovingians was adequate to these obligations, and their names are consecrated as the saviours and benefactors of the Roman church. Her ancient patrimony of farms and houses was transformed by their bounty into the temporal dominion of cities and provinces; and the donation of the Exarchate was the first-fruits of the conquests of Pepin.[62] Astolphus with a sigh relinquished his prey; the keys and the hostages of the principal cities were delivered to the French ambassador; and, in his master's name, he presented them before the tomb of St. Peter. The ample measure of the Exarchate[63] might comprise all the provinces of Italy which had obeyed the emperor and his vicegerent; but its strict and proper limits were included in the territories of Ravenna, Bologna, and Ferrara: its inseparable dependency was the Pentapolis, which stretched along the Hadriatic from Rimini to Ancona, and advanced into the midland country as far as the ridges of the Apennine. In this transaction the ambition and avarice of the popes has been severely condemned. Perhaps the humility of a Christian priest should have rejected an earthly kingdom, which it was not easy for him to govern without renouncing the virtues of his profession. Perhaps a faithful subject, or even a generous enemy, would have been less impatient to divide the spoils of the barbarian; and if the emperor had intrusted Stephen to solicit in his name the restitution of the Exarchate, I will not absolve the pope from the reproach of treachery and falsehood. But in the rigid interpretation of the laws, every one may accept, without injury, whatever his benefactor can bestow without injustice. The Greek emperor had abdicated or forfeited his right to the Exarchate; and the sword of Astolphus was broken by the stronger sword of the Carlovingian. It was not in the cause of the Iconoclast that Pepin had exposed his person and army in a double expedition beyond the Alps: he possessed, and might lawfully alienate, his conquests: and to the importunities of the Greeks he piously replied that no human consideration should tempt him to resume the gift which he had conferred on the Roman pontiff for the remission of his sins and the salvation of his soul. The splendid donation was granted in supreme and absolute dominion, and the world beheld for the first time a Christian bishop invested with the prerogatives of a temporal prince—the choice of magistrates, the exercise of justice, the imposition of taxes, and the wealth of the palace of Ravenna. In the dissolution of the Lombard kingdom the inhabitants of the duchy of Spoleto[64] sought a refuge from the storm, shaved their heads after the Roman fashion, declared themselves the servants and subjects of St. Peter, and completed, by this voluntary surrender, the present circle of the ecclesiastical state. That mysterious circle was enlarged to an indefinite extent by the verbal or written donation of Charlemagne,[65] who, in the first transports of his victory, despoiled himself and the Greek emperor of the cities and islands which had formerly been annexed to the Exarchate. But in the cooler moments of absence and reflection he viewed with an eye of jealousy and envy the recent greatness of his ecclesiastic ally. The execution of his own and his father's promises was respectfully eluded: the king of the Franks and Lombards asserted the inalienable rights of the empire; and, in his life and death, Ravenna,[66] as well as Rome, was numbered in the list of his metropolitan cities. The sovereignty of the Exarchate melted away in the hands of the popes; they found in the archbishops of Ravenna a dangerous and domestic rival:[67] the nobles and people disdained the yoke of a priest; and in the disorders of the times they could only retain the memory of an ancient claim, which, in a more prosperous age, they have revived and realised.

Fraud is the resource of weakness and cunning; and the strong, though ignorant, barbarian was often entangled in the net of sacerdotal policy. The Vatican and Lateran were an arsenal and manufacture which, according to the occasion, have produced or concealed a various collection of false or genuine, of corrupt or suspicious acts, as they tended to promote the interest of the Roman church. Before the end of the eighth century some apostolical scribe, perhaps the notorious Isidore, composed the decretals and the donation of Constantine, the two magic pillars of the spiritual and temporal monarchy of the popes. This memorable donation was introduced to the world by an epistle of Adrian the First, who exhorts Charlemagne to imitate the liberality and revive the name of the great Constantine.[68] According to the legend, the first of the Christian emperors was healed of the leprosy, and purified in the waters of baptism, by St. Silvester, the Roman bishop; and never was physician more gloriously recompensed. His royal proselyte withdrew from the seat and patrimony of St. Peter; declared his resolution of founding a new capital in the East; and resigned to the popes the free and perpetual sovereignty of Rome, Italy, and the provinces of the West.[69] This fiction was productive of the most beneficial effects. The Greek princes were convicted of the guilt of usurpation; and the revolt of Gregory was the claim of his lawful inheritance. The popes were delivered from their debt of gratitude; and the nominal gifts of the Carlovingians were no more than the just and irrevocable restitution of a scanty portion of the ecclesiastical state. The sovereignty of Rome no longer depended on the choice of a fickle people; and the successors of St. Peter and Constantine were invested with the purple and prerogatives of the Cæsars. So deep was the ignorance and credulity of the times that the most absurd of fables was received with equal reverence in Greece and in France, and is still enrolled among the decrees of the canon law.[70] The emperors and the Romans were incapable of discerning a forgery that subverted their rights and freedom; and the only opposition proceeded from a Sabine monastery, which in the beginning of the twelfth century disputed the truth and validity of the donation of Constantine.[71] In the revival of letters and liberty this fictitious deed was transpierced by the pen of Laurentius Valla, the pen of an eloquent critic and a Roman patriot.[72] His contemporaries of the fifteenth century were astonished at his sacrilegious boldness; yet such is the silent and irresistible progress of reason, that before the end of the next age the fable was rejected by the contempt of historians[73] and poets,[74] and the acit or modest censure of the advocates of the Roman church.[75] The popes themselves have indulged a smile at the credulity of the vulgar;[76] but a false and obsolete title still sanctifies their reign; and by the same fortune which has attended the decretals and the Sibylline oracles, the edifice has subsisted after the foundations have been undermined.

While the popes established in Italy their freedom and dominion, the images, the first cause of their revolt, were restored in the Eastern empire.[77] Under the reign of Constantine the Fifth, the union of civil and ecclesiastical power had overthrown the tree, without extirpating the root, of superstition. The idols, for such they were now held, were secretly cherished by the order and the sex most prone to devotion; and the fond alliance of the monks and females obtained a final victory over the reason and authority of man. Leo the Fourth maintained with less rigour the religion of his father and grandfather; but his wife, the fair and ambitious Irene, had imbibed the zeal of the Athenians, the heirs of the idolatry, rather than the philosophy, of their ancestors. During the life of her husband these sentiments were inflamed by danger and dissimulation, and she could only labour to protect and promote some favourite monks whom she drew from their caverns and seated on the metropolitan thrones of the East. But as soon as she reigned in her own name and that of her son, Irene more seriously undertook the ruin of the Iconoclasts; and the first step of her future persecution was a general edict for liberty of conscience. In the restoration of the monks a thousand images were exposed to the public veneration; a thousand legends were invented of their sufferings and miracles. By the opportunities of death or removal the episcopal seats were judiciously filled; the most eager competitors for earthly or celestial favour anticipated and flattered the judgment of their sovereign; and the promotion of her secretary Tarasius gave Irene the patriarch of Constantinople, and the command of the Oriental church. But the decrees of a general council could only be repealed by a similar assembly:[78] the Iconoclasts whom she convened were bold in possession, and averse to debate; and the feeble voice of the bishops was reechoed by the more formidable clamour of the soldiers and people of Constantinople. The delay and intrigues of a year, the separation of the disaffected troops, and the choice of Nice for a second orthodox synod, removed these obstacles; and the episcopal conscience was again, after the Greek fashion, in the hands of the prince. No more than eighteen days were allowed for the consummation of this important work: the Iconoclasts appeared, not as judges, but as criminals or penitents: the scene was decorated by the legates of Pope Adrian and the Eastern patriarchs;[79] the decrees were framed by the president Tarasius, and ratified by the acclamations and subscriptions of three hundred and fifty bishops. They unanimously pronounced that the worship of images is agreeable to Scripture and reason, to the fathers and councils of the church: but they hesitate whether that worship be relative or direct; whether the Godhead and the figure of Christ be entitled to the same mode of adoration. Of this second Nicene council the acts are still extant; a curious monument of superstition and ignorance, of falsehood and folly. I shall only notice the judgment of the bishops, on the comparative merit of image-worship and morality. A monk had concluded a truce with the demon of fornication, on condition of interrupting his daily prayers to a picture that hung in his cell. His scruples prompted him to consult the abbot. "Rather than abstain from adoring Christ and his Mother in their holy images, it would be better for you," replied the casuist, "to enter every brothel, and visit every prostitute, in the city."[80] For the honour of orthodoxy, at least the orthodoxy of the Roman church, it is somewhat unfortunate that the two princes who convened the two councils of Nice are both stained with the blood of their sons. The second of these assemblies was approved and rigorously executed by the despotism of Irene, and she refused her adversaries the toleration which at first she had granted to her friends. During the five succeeding reigns, a period of thirty-eight years, the contest was maintained with unabated rage and various success between the worshippers and the breakers of the images; but I am not inclined to pursue with minute diligence the repetition of the same events. Nicephorus allowed a general liberty of speech and practice; and the only virtue of his reign is accused by the monks as the cause of his temporal and eternal perdition. Superstition and weakness formed the character of Michael the First, but the saints and images were incapable of supporting their votary on the throne. In the purple, Leo the Fifth asserted the name and religion of an Armenian; and the idols, with their seditious adherents, were condemned to a second exile. Their applause would have sanctified the murder of an impious tyrant, but his assassin and successor, the second Michael, was tainted from his birth with the Phrygian heresies; he attempted to mediate between the contending parties; and the intractable spirit of the Catholics insensibly cast him into the opposite scale. His moderation was guarded by timidity; but his son Theophilus, alike ignorant of fear and pity, was the last and most cruel of the Iconoclasts. The enthusiasm of the times ran strongly against them; and the emperors, who stemmed the torrent, were exasperated and punished by the public hatred. After the death of Theophilus the final victory of the images was achieved by a second female, his widow Theodora, whom he left the guardian of the empire. Her measures were bold and decisive. The fiction of a tardy repentance absolved the fame and the soul of her deceased husband; the sentence of the Iconoclast patriarch was commuted from the loss of his eyes to a whipping of two hundred lashes: the bishops trembled, the monks shouted, and the festival of orthodoxy preserves the annual memory of the triumph of the images. A single question yet remained, whether they are endowed with any proper and inherent sanctity; it was agitated by the Greeks of the eleventh century;[81] and as this opinion has the strongest recommendation of absurdity, I am surprised that it was not more explicitly decided in the affirmative. In the West Pope Adrian the First accepted and announced the decrees of the Nicene assembly, which is now revered by the Catholics as the seventh in rank of the general councils. Rome and Italy were docile to the voice of their father; but the greatest part of the Latin Christians were far behind in the race of superstition. The churches of France, Germany, England, and Spain steered a middle course between the adoration and the destruction of images, which they admitted into their temples, not as objects of worship, but as lively and useful memorials of faith and history. An angry book of controversy was composed and published in the name of Charlemagne:[82] under his authority a synod of three hundred bishops was assembled at Frankfort:[83] they blamed the fury of the Iconoclasts, but they pronounced a more severe censure against the superstition of the Greeks, and the decrees of their pretended council, which was long despised by the barbarians of the West.[84] Among them the worship of images advanced with a silent and insensible progress; but a large atonement is made for their hesitation and delay by the gross idolatry of the ages which precede the reformation, and of the countries, both in Europe and America, which are still immersed in the gloom of superstition.

It was after the Nicene synod, and under the reign of the pious Irene, that the popes consummated the separation of Rome and Italy, by the translation of the empire to the less orthodox Charlemagne. They were compelled to choose between the rival nations: religion was not the sole motive of their choice; and while they dissembled the failings of their friends, they beheld, with reluctance and suspicion, the Catholic virtues of their foes. The difference of language and manners had perpetuated the enmity of the two capitals; and they were alienated from each other by the hostile opposition of seventy years. In that schism the Romans had tasted of freedom, and the popes of sovereignty: their submission would have exposed them to the revenge of a jealous tyrant; and the revolution of Italy had betrayed the impotence, as well as the tyranny, of the Byzantine court. The Greek emperors had restored the images, but they had not restored the Calabrian estates[85] and the Illyrian diocese,[86] which the Iconoclasts had torn away from the successors of St. Peter; and Pope Adrian threatens them with a sentence of excommunication unless they speedily abjure this practical heresy.[87] The Greeks were now orthodox; but their religion might be tainted by the breath of the reigning monarch; the Franks were now contumacious; but a discerning eye might discern their approaching conversion, from the use, to the adoration, of images. The name of Charlemagne was stained by the polemic acrimony of his scribes; but the conqueror himself conformed, with the temper of a statesman, to the various practice of France and Italy. In his four pilgrimages or visits to the Vatican he embraced the popes in the communion of friendship and piety; knelt before the tomb, and consequently before the image, of the apostle; and joined, without scruple, in all the prayers and processions of the Roman liturgy. Would prudence or gratitude allow the pontiffs to renounce their benefactor? Had they a right to alienate his gift of the Exarchate? Had they power to abolish his government of Rome? The title of patrician was below the merit and greatness of Charlemagne; and it was only by reviving the Western empire that they could pay their obligations or secure their establishment. By this decisive measure they would finally eradicate the claims of the Greeks: from the debasement of a provincial town, the majesty of Rome would be restored; the Latin Christians would be united, under a supreme head, in their ancient metropolis; and the conquerors of the West would receive their crown from the successors of St. Peter. The Roman church would acquire a zealous and respectable advocate; and, under the shadow of the Carlovingian power, the bishop might exercise, with honour and safety, the government of the city.[88]

Before the ruin of Paganism in Rome the competition for a wealthy bishopric had often been productive of tumult and bloodshed. The people was less numerous, but the times were more savage, the prize more important, and the chair of St. Peter was fiercely disputed by the leading ecclesiastics who aspired to the rank of sovereign. The reign of Adrian the First[89] surpasses the measure of past or succeeding ages;[90] the walls of Rome, the sacred patrimony, the ruin of the Lombards, and the friendship of Charlemagne, were the trophies of his fame: he secretly edified the throne of his successors, and displayed in a narrow space the virtues of a great prince. His memory was revered; but in the next election, a priest of the Lateran, Leo the Third, was preferred to the nephew and the favourite of Adrian, whom he had promoted to the first dignities of the church. Their acquiescence or repentance disguised, above four years, the blackest intention of revenge, till the day of a procession, when a furious band of conspirators dispersed the unarmed multitude, and assaulted with blows and wounds the sacred person of the pope. But their enterprise on his life or liberty was disappointed, perhaps by their own confusion and remorse. Leo was left for dead on the ground: on his revival from the swoon, the effect of his loss of blood, he recovered his speech and sight; and this natural event was improved to the miraculous restoration of his eyes and tongue, of which he had been deprived, twice deprived, by the knife of the assassins.[91] From his prison he escaped to the Vatican: the duke of Spoleto hastened to his rescue, Charlemagne sympathised in his injury, and in his camp of Paderborn in Westphalia accepted, or solicited, a visit from the Roman pontiff. Leo repassed the Alps with a commission of counts and bishops, the guards of his safety and the judges of his innocence; and it was not without reluctance that the conqueror of the Saxons delayed till the ensuing year the personal discharge of this pious office. In his fourth and last pilgrimage he was received at Rome with the due honours of king and patrician: Leo was permitted to purge himself by oath of the crimes imputed to his charge: his enemies were silenced, and the sacrilegious attempt against his life was punished by the mild and insufficient penalty of exile. On the festival of Christmas, the last year of the eighth century, Charlemagne appeared in the church of St. Peter; and, to gratify the vanity of Rome, he had exchanged the simple dress of his country for the habit of a patrician.[92] After the celebration of the holy mysteries, Leo suddenly placed a precious crown on his head,[93] and the dome resounded with the acclamations of the people, "Long life and victory to Charles, the most pious Augustus, crowned by God the great and pacific emperor of the Romans!" The head and body of Charlemagne were consecrated by the royal unction: after the example of the Cæsars, he was saluted or adored by the pontiff: his coronation oath represents a promise to maintain the faith and privileges of the church; and the first-fruits were paid in his rich offerings to the shrine of the apostle. In his familiar conversation the emperor protested his ignorance of the intentions of Leo, which he would have disappointed by his absence on that memorable day. But the preparations of the ceremony must have disclosed the secret; and the journey of Charlemagne reveals his knowledge and expectation: he had acknowledged that the Imperial title was the object of his ambition, and a Roman synod had pronounced that it was the only adequate reward of his merit and services.[94]

The appellation of *great* has been often bestowed, and sometimes deserved, but CHARLE-MAGNE is the only prince in whose favour the title has been indissolubly blended with the name. That name, with the addition of *saint*, is inserted in the Roman calendar; and the saint, by a rare felicity, is crowned with the praises of the historians and philosophers of an enlightened age.[95] His *real* merit is doubtless enhanced by the barbarism of the nation and the times from which he emerged: but the *apparent* magnitude of an object is likewise enlarged by an unequal comparison; and the ruins of Palmyra derive a casual splendour from the nakedness of the surrounding desert. Without injustice to his fame, I may discern some blemishes in the sanctity and greatness of the restorer of the Western empire. Of his moral virtues, chastity is not the most conspicuous:[96] but the public happiness could not be materially injured by his nine wives or concubines, the various indulgence of meaner or more transient amours, the multitude of his bastards whom he bestowed on the church, and the long celibacy and licentious manners of his daughters,[97] whom the father was suspected of loving with too fond a passion. I shall be scarcely permitted to accuse the ambition of a conqueror; but in a day of equal retribution, the sons of his brother Carloman, the Merovingian princes of Aquitain, and the four thousand five hundred Saxons who were beheaded on the same spot, would have something to allege against the justice and humanity of Charlemagne. His treatment of the vanquished Saxons[98] was an abuse of the right of conquest; his laws were not less sanguinary than his arms, and, in the discussion of his motives, whatever is subtracted from bigotry must be imputed to temper. The sedentary reader is amazed by his incessant activity of mind and body; and his subjects and enemies were not less astonished at his sudden presence at the moment when they believed him at the most distant extremity of the empire; neither peace nor war, nor summer nor winter, were a season of repose; and our fancy cannot easily reconcile the annals of his reign with the geography of his expeditions. But this activity was a national, rather than a personal virtue: the vagrant life of a Frank was spent in the chase, in pilgrimage, in military adventures; and the journeys of Charlemagne were distinguished only by a more numerous train and a more important purpose. His military renown must be tried by the scrutiny of his troops, his enemies, and his actions. Alexander conquered with the arms of Philip, but the *two* heroes who preceded Charlemagne bequeathed him their name, their examples, and the companions of their victories. At the head of his veteran and superior armies he oppressed the savage or degenerate nations, who were incapable of confederating for their common safety; nor did he ever encounter an equal antagonist in numbers, in discipline, or in arms. The science of war has been lost and revived with the arts of peace; but his campaigns are not illustrated by any siege or battle of singular difficulty and success; and he might behold with envy the Saracen trophies of his grandfather. After his Spanish expedition his rear-guard was defeated in the Pyrenæan mountains; and the soldiers, whose situation was irretrievable, and whose valour was useless, might accuse, with their last breath, the want of skill or caution of their general.[99] I touch with reverence the laws of Charlemagne, so highly applauded by a respectable judge. They compose not a system, but a series, of occasional and minute edicts, for the correction of abuses, the reformation of manners, the economy of his farms, the care of his poultry, and even the sale of his eggs. He wished to improve the laws and the character of the Franks; and his attempts, however feeble and imperfect, are deserving of praise: the inveterate evils of the times were suspended or mollified by his government;[100] but in his institutions I can seldom discover the general views and the immortal spirit of a legislator, who survives himself for the benefit of posterity. The union and stability of his empire depended on the life of a single man: he imitated the dangerous practice of dividing his kingdoms among his sons; and, after his numerous diets, the whole constitution was left to fluctuate between the disorders of anarchy and despotism. His esteem for the piety and knowledge of the clergy tempted him to intrust that aspiring order with temporal dominion and civil jurisdiction; and his son Lewis, when he was stripped and degraded by the bishops, might accuse, in some measure, the imprudence of his father. His laws enforced the imposition of tithes, because the demons had proclaimed in the air that the default of payment had been the cause of the last scarcity.[101] The literary merits of Charlemagne are attested by the foundation of schools, the introduction of arts, the works which were published in his name, and his familiar connection with the subjects and strangers whom he invited to his court to educate both the prince and people. His own studies were tardy, laborious, and imperfect; if he spoke Latin, and understood Greek, he derived the rudiments of knowledge from conversation, rather than from books; and, in his mature age, the emperor strove to acquire the practice of writing, which every peasant now learns in his infancy.[102] The grammar and logic, the music and astronomy, of the times were only cultivated as the handmaids of superstition; but the curiosity of the human mind must ultimately tend to its improvement, and the encouragement of learning reflects the purest and most pleasing lustre on the character of Charlemagne.[103] The dignity of his person,[104] the length of his reign, the prosperity of his arms, the vigour of his government, and the reverence of distant nations, distinguish him from the royal crowd; and Europe dates a new era from his restoration of the Western empire.

That empire was not unworthy of its title,[105] and some of the fairest kingdoms of Europe were the patrimony or conquest of a prince who reigned at the same time in France, Spain, Italy, Germany, and Hungary.[106] I. The Roman province of Gaul had been transformed into the name and monarchy of FRANCE: but, in the decay of the Merovingian line, its limits were contracted by the independence of the *Britons* and the revolt of *Aquitain*. Charlemagne pursued and confined the Britons on the shores of the ocean; and that ferocious tribe, whose origin and language are so different from the French, was chastised by the imposition of tribute, hostages, and peace. After a long and evasive contest, the rebellion of the dukes of Aquitain was punished by the forfeiture of their province, their liberty, and their lives. Harsh and rigorous would have been such treatment of ambitious governors, who had too faithfully copied the mayors of the palace. But a recent discovery[107] has proved that these unhappy princes were the last and lawful heirs of the blood and sceptre of Clovis, a younger branch, from the brother of Dagobert, of the Merovingian house. Their ancient kingdom was reduced to the duchy of Gascogne, to the counties of Fesenzac and Armagnac, at the foot of the Pyrenees: their race was propagated till the beginning of the sixteenth century, and, after surviving their Carlovingian tyrants, they were reserved to feel the injustice or the favours of a third dynasty. By the re-union of Aquitain, France was enlarged to its present boundaries, with the additions of the Netherlands and Spain, as far as the Rhine. II. The Saracens had been expelled from France by the grandfather and father of Charlemagne; but they still possessed the greatest part of SPAIN, from the rock of Gibraltar to the Pyrenees. Amidst their civil divisions, an Arabian emir of Saragossa implored his protection in the diet of Paderborn. Charlemagne undertook the expedition, restored the emir, and without distinction of faith, impartially crushed the resistance of the Christians, and rewarded the obedience and service of the Mohammedans. In his absence he instituted the *Spanish march*,[108] which extended from the Pyrenees to the river Ebro: Barcelona was the residence of the French governor; he possessed the counties of *Rousillon* and *Catalonia*, and the infant kingdoms of *Navarre* and *Arragon* were subject to his jurisdiction. III. As king of the Lombards and patrician of Rome he reigned over the greatest part of ITALY,[109] a tract of a thousand miles from the Alps to the borders of Calabria. The duchy of *Beneventum*, a Lombard fief, had spread, at the expense of the Greeks, over the modern kingdom of Naples. But Arrechis, the reigning duke, refused to be included in the slavery of his country, assumed the independent title of prince, and opposed his sword to the Carlovingian monarchy. His defence was firm, his submission was not in-

glorious, and the emperor was content with an easy tribute, the demolition of his fortresses, and the acknowledgment, on his coins, of a supreme lord. The artful flattery of his son Grimoald added the appellation of father, but he asserted his dignity with prudence, and Beneventum insensibly escaped from the French yoke.[110] IV. Charlemagne was the first who united GERMANY under the same sceptre. The name of *Oriental France* is preserved in the circle of *Franconia;* and the people of *Hesse* and *Thuringia* were recently incorporated with the victors by the conformity of religion and government. The *Alemanni*, so formidable to the Romans, were the faithful vassals and confederates of the Franks, and their country was inscribed within the modern limits of *Alsace, Swabia*, and *Switzerland*. The *Bavarians*, with a similar indulgence of their laws and manners, were less patient of a master: the repeated treasons of Tasillo justified the abolition of their hereditary dukes, and their power was shared among the counts who judged and guarded that important frontier. But the north of Germany, from the Rhine and beyond the Elbe, was still hostile and Pagan; nor was it till after a war of thirty-three years that the Saxons bowed under the yoke of Christ and of Charlemagne. The idols and their votaries were extirpated; the foundation of eight bishoprics, of Munster, Osnaburgh, Paderborn, and Minden, of Bremen, Verden, Hildesheim, and Halberstadt, define, on either side of the Weser, the bounds of ancient Saxony; these episcopal seats were the first schools and cities of that savage land, and the religion and humanity of the children atoned, in some degree, for the massacre of the parents. Beyond the Elbe, the *Slavi*, or Sclavonians, of similar manners and various denominations, overspread the modern dominions of Prussia, Poland, and Bohemia, and some transient marks of obedience have tempted the French historian to extend the empire to the Baltic and the Vistula. The conquest or conversion of those countries is of a more recent age, but the first union of *Bohemia* with the Germanic body may be justly ascribed to the arms of Charlemagne. V. He retaliated on the Avars, or Huns of Pannonia, the same calamities which they had inflicted on the nations. Their rings, the wooden fortifications which encircled their districts and villages, were broken down by the triple effort of a French army that was poured into their country by land and water, through the Carpathian mountains and along the plain of the Danube. After a bloody conflict of eight years, the loss of some French generals was avenged by the slaughter of the most noble Huns: the relics of the nation submitted: the royal residence of the chagan was left desolate and unknown; and the treasures, the rapine of two hundred and fifty years, enriched the victorious troops, or decorated the churches, of Italy and Gaul.[111] After the reduction of Pannonia, the empire of Charlemagne was bounded only by the conflux of the Danube with the Theiss and the Save: the provinces of Istria, Liburnia, and Dalmatia were an easy though unprofitable accession; and it was an effect of his moderation that he left the maritime cities under the real or nominal sovereignty of the Greeks. But these distant possessions added more to the reputation than to the power of the Latin emperor; nor did he risk any ecclesiastical foundations to reclaim the barbarians from their vagrant life and idolatrous worship. Some canals of communication between the rivers, the Saône and the Meuse, the Rhine and the Danube, were faintly attempted.[112] Their execution would have vivified the empire; and more cost and labour were often wasted in the structure of a cathedral.

If we retrace the outlines of this geographical picture, it will be seen that the empire of the Franks extended, between east and west, from the Ebro to the Elbe or Vistula; between the north and south, from the duchy of Beneventum to the river Eyder, the perpetual boundary of Germany and Denmark. The personal and political importance of Charlemagne was magnified by the distress and division of the rest of Europe. The islands of Great Britain and Ireland were disputed by a crowd of princes of Saxon or Scottish origin; and, after the loss of Spain, the Christian and Gothic kingdom of Alphonso the Chaste was confined to the narrow range of the Asturian mountains. These petty sovereigns revered the power or virtue of the Carlovingian monarch, implored the honour and support of his alliance, and styled him their common parent, the sole and supreme emperor of the West.[113] He maintained a more equal intercourse with the caliph Harun al Rashid,[114] whose dominion stretched from Africa to India, and accepted from his ambassadors a tent, a water-clock, an elephant, and the keys of the Holy Sepulchre. It is not easy to conceive the private friendship of a Frank and an Arab, who were strangers to each other's person, and language, and religion: but their public correspondence was founded on vanity, and their remote situation left no room for a competition of interest. Two-thirds of the West-

ern empire of Rome were subject to Charlemagne, and the deficiency was amply supplied by his command of the inaccessible or invincible nations of Germany. But in the choice of his enemies we may be reasonably surprised that he so often preferred the poverty of the north to the riches of the south. The three-and-thirty campaigns laboriously consumed in the woods and morasses of Germany would have sufficed to assert the amplitude of his title by the expulsion of the Greeks from Italy and the Saracens from Spain. The weakness of the Greeks would have insured an easy victory: and the holy crusade against the Saracens would have been prompted by glory and revenge, and loudly justified by religion and policy. Perhaps, in his expeditions beyond the Rhine and the Elbe, he aspired to save his monarchy from the fate of the Roman empire, to disarm the enemies of civilised society, and to eradicate the seed of future emigrations. But it has been wisely observed, that, in a light of precaution, all conquest must be ineffectual, unless it could be universal, since the increasing circle must be involved in a larger sphere of hostility.[115] The subjugation of Germany withdrew the veil which had so long concealed the continent or islands of Scandinavia from the knowledge of Europe, and awakened the torpid courage of their barbarous natives. The fiercest of the Saxon idolaters escaped from the Christian tyrant to their brethren of the North; the Ocean and Mediterranean were covered with their piratical fleets; and Charlemagne beheld with a sigh the destructive progress of the Normans, who, in less than seventy years, precipitated the fall of his race and monarchy.

Had the pope and the Romans revived the primitive constitution, the titles of emperor and Augustus were conferred on Charlemagne for the term of his life; and his successors, on each vacancy, must have ascended the throne by a formal or tacit election. But the association of his son Lewis the Pious asserts the independent right of monarchy and conquest, and the emperor seems on this occasion to have foreseen and prevented the latent claims of the clergy. The royal youth was commanded to take the crown from the altar, and with his own hands to place it on his head, as a gift which he held from God, his father, and the nation.[116] The same ceremony was repeated, though with less energy, in the subsequent associations of Lothaire and Lewis the Second: the Carlovingian sceptre was transmitted from father to son in a lineal descent of four generations; and the amɔition of the popes was reduced to the empty ɦonour of crowning and anointing these heredi-ɫary princes, who were already invested with ɫheir power and dominions. The pious Lewis ɟurvived his brothers, and embraced the whole ɟmpire of Charlemagne; but the nations and ɫhe nobles, his bishops and his children, quickly ɖiscerned that this mighty mass was no longer ɪnspired by the same soul; and the foundations ɪwere undermined to the centre, while the exter-ɳal surface was yet fair and entire. After a war, ɔr battle, which consumed one hundred thou-ɟand Franks, the empire was divided by treaty ɓetween his three sons, who had violated every ɸilial and fraternal duty. The kingdoms of Ger-ɰany and France were for ever separated; the ɸrovinces of Gaul, between the Rhone and the Alps, the Meuse and the Rhine, were assigned, with Italy, to the Imperial dignity of Lothaire. In the partition of his share, Lorraine and Arles, ɫwo recent and transitory kingdoms, were be-ɟtowed on the younger children: and Lewis the Second, his eldest son, was content with the ɽealm of Italy, the proper and sufficient patri-ɰony of a Roman emperor. On his death, with-ɔut any male issue, the vacant throne was dis-ɸuted by his uncles and cousins and the popes ɰost dexterously seized the occasion of judging ɫhe claims and merits of the candidates, and of ɓestowing on the most obsequious, or most lib-ɟral, the Imperial office of advocate of the Ro-ɰan church. The dregs of the Carlovingian ɽace no longer exhibited any symptoms of vir-ɫue or power, and the ridiculous epithets of the *bald*, the *stammerer*, the *fat*, and the *simple*, dis-ɫinguished the tame and uniform features of a ɔrowd of kings alike deserving of oblivion. By ɫhe failure of the collateral branches the whole ɪnheritance devolved to Charles the Fat, the ɫast emperor of his family: his insanity author-ɪsed the desertion of Germany, Italy, and ɸrance: he was deposed in a diet, and solicited ɦis daily bread from the rebels by whose con-ɫempt his life and liberty had been spared. Ac-ɔording to the measure of their force, the gover-ɳors, the bishops, and the lords usurped the ɸragments of the falling empire; and some pre-ɸerence was shown to the female or illegitimate ɓlood of Charlemagne. Of the greater part, the ɫitle and possession were alike doubtful, and the ɰerit was adequate to the contracted scale of ɫheir dominions. Those who could appear with ɑn army at the gates of Rome were crowned em-ɸerors in the Vatican; but their modesty was ɰore frequently satisfied with the appellation ɔf kings of Italy: and the whole term of seventy-

four years may be deemed a vacancy, from the abdication of Charles the Fat to the establish-ment of Otho the First.

Otho[117] was of the noble race of the dukes of Saxony; and if he truly descended from Witi-kind, the adversary and proselyte of Charle-magne, the posterity of a vanquished people was exalted to reign over their conquerors. His father, Henry the Fowler, was elected, by the suffrage of the nation, to save and institute the kingdom of Germany. Its limits[118] were en-larged on every side by his son, the first and greatest of the Othos. A portion of Gaul, to the west of the Rhine, along the banks of the Meuse and the Moselle, was assigned to the Germans, by whose blood and language it has been tinged since the time of Cæsar and Tacitus. Between the Rhine, the Rhone, and the Alps, the suc-cessors of Otho acquired a vain supremacy over the broken kingdoms of Burgundy and Arles. In the North, Christianity was propagated by the sword of Otho, the conqueror and apostle of the Slavic nations of the Elbe and Oder: the march-es of Brandenburg and Sleswick were fortified with German colonies; and the king of Den-mark, the dukes of Poland and Bohemia, con-fessed themselves his tributary vassals. At the head of a victorious army he passed the Alps, subdued the kingdom of Italy, delivered the pope, and for ever fixed the Imperial crown in the name and nation of Germany. From that memorable era two maxims of public jurispru-dence were introduced by force and ratified by time. I. *That* the prince, who was elected in the German diet, acquired from that instant the subject kingdoms of Italy and Rome. II. But that he might not legally assume the titles of emperor and Augustus, till he had received the crown from the hands of the Roman pontiff.[119]

The imperial dignity of Charlemagne was announced to the East by the alteration of his style; and instead of saluting his fathers, the Greek emperors, he presumed to adopt the more equal and familiar appellation of bro-ther.[120] Perhaps in his connection with Irene he aspired to the name of husband: his embassy to Constantinople spoke the language of peace and friendship, and might conceal a treaty of marriage with that ambitious princess, who had renounced the most sacred duties of a mother. The nature, the duration, the probable conse-quences of such a union between two distant and dissonant empires, it is impossible to con-jecture; but the unanimous silence of the Latins may teach us to suspect that the report was in-vented by the enemies of Irene, to charge her with the guilt of betraying the church and state to the strangers of the West.[121] The French ambassadors were the spectators, and had nearly been the victims, of the conspiracy of Nicephorus, and the national hatred. Constantinople was exasperated by the treason and sacrilege of ancient Rome: a proverb, "That the Franks were good friends and bad neighbours," was in every one's mouth; but it was dangerous to provoke a neighbour who might be tempted to reiterate, in the church of St. Sophia, the ceremony of his Imperial coronation. After a tedious journey of circuit and delay, the ambassadors of Nicephorus found him in his camp, on the banks of the river Sala; and Charlemagne affected to confound their vanity by displaying, in a Franconian village, the pomp, or at least the pride, of the Byzantine palace.[122] The Greeks were successively led through four halls of audience: in the first they were ready to fall prostrate before a splendid personage in a chair of state, till he informed them that he was only a servant, the constable, or master of the horse, of the emperor. The same mistake and the same answer were repeated in the apartments of the count palatine, the steward, and the chamberlain; and their impatience was gradually heightened, till the doors of the presence-chamber were thrown open, and they beheld the genuine monarch on his throne, enriched with the foreign luxury which he despised, and encircled with the love and reverence of his victorious chiefs. A treaty of peace and alliance was concluded between the two empires, and the limits of the East and West were defined by the right of present possession. But the Greeks[123] soon forgot this humiliating equality, or remembered it only to hate the barbarians by whom it was extorted. During the short union of virtue and power, they respectfully saluted the *august* Charlemagne with the acclamations of *basileus*, and emperor of the Romans. As soon as these qualities were separated in the person of his pious son, the Byzantine letters were inscribed, "To the king, or, as he styles himself, the emperor, of the Franks and Lombards." When both the power and virtue were extinct, they despoiled Lewis the Second of his hereditary title, and, with the barbarous appellation of rex or *rega*, degraded him among the crowd of Latin princes. His reply[124] is expressive of his weakness: he proves, with some learning, that both in sacred and profane history the name of king is synonymous with the Greek word *basileus:* if, at Constantinople, it were assumed in a more exclusive and imperial sense, he claims from his ancestors, and from the pope, a just participation of the honours of the Roman purple. The same controversy was revived in the reign of the Othos; and their ambassador describes in lively colours the insolence of the Byzantine court.[125] The Greeks affected to despise the poverty and ignorance of the Franks and Saxons; and in their last decline refused to prostitute to the kings of Germany the title of Roman emperors.

These emperors, in the election of the popes, continued to exercise the powers which had been assumed by the Gothic and Grecian princes; and the importance of this prerogative increased with the temporal estate and spiritual jurisdiction of the Roman church. In the Christian aristocracy the principal members of the clergy still formed a senate to assist the administration, and to supply the vacancy, of the bishop. Rome was divided into twenty-eight parishes, and each parish was governed by a cardinal-priest, or presbyter—a title which, however common and modest in its origin, has aspired to emulate the purple of kings. Their number was enlarged by the association of the seven deacons of the most considerable hospitals, the seven palatine judges of the Lateran, and some dignitaries of the church. This ecclesiastical senate was directed by the seven cardinal-bishops of the Roman province, who were less occupied in the suburb dioceses of Ostia, Porto, Velitræ, Tusculum, Præneste, Tibur, and the Sabines, than by their weekly service in the Lateran, and their superior share in the honours and authority of the apostolic see. On the death of the pope these bishops recommended a successor to the suffrage of the college of cardinals,[126] and their choice was ratified or rejected by the applause or clamour of the Roman people. But the election was imperfect; nor could the pontiff be legally consecrated till the emperor, the advocate of the church, had graciously signified his approbation and consent. The royal commissioner examined on the spot the form and freedom of the proceedings; nor was it till after a previous scrutiny into the qualifications of the candidates that he accepted an oath of fidelity, and confirmed the donations which had successively enriched the patrimony of St. Peter. In the frequent schisms the rival claims were submitted to the sentence of the emperor; and in a synod of bishops he presumed to judge, to condemn, and to punish the crimes of a guilty pontiff. Otho the First imposed a treaty on the senate and people, who engaged to prefer the candidate most acceptable to his majesty:[127] his successors anticipated or prevented their choice: they bestowed the Roman benefice, like the bishoprics of Cologne or Bamberg, on their chancellors or preceptors; and whatever might be the merit of a Frank or Saxon, his name sufficiently attests the interposition of foreign power. These acts of prerogative were most speciously excused by the vices of a popular election. The competitor who had been excluded by the cardinals appealed to the passions or avarice of the multitude; the Vatican and the Lateran were stained with blood; and the most powerful senators, the marquises of Tuscany and the counts of Tusculum, held the apostolic see in a long and disgraceful servitude. The Roman pontiffs of the ninth and tenth centuries were insulted, imprisoned, and murdered by their tyrants; and such was their indigence, after the loss and usurpation of the ecclesiastical patrimonies, that they could neither support the state of a prince, nor exercise the charity of a priest.[128] The influence of two sister prostitutes, Marozia and Theodora, was founded on their wealth and beauty, their political and amorous intrigues: the most strenuous of their lovers were rewarded with the Roman mitre, and their reign[129] may have suggested to the darker ages[130] the fable[131] of a female pope.[132] The bastard son, the grandson, and the great-grandson of Marozia, a rare genealogy, were seated in the chair of St. Peter; and it was at the age of nineteen years that the second of these became the head of the Latin church. His youth and manhood were of a suitable complexion; and the nations of pilgrims could bear testimony to the charges that were urged against him in a Roman synod, and in the presence of Otho the Great. As John XII. had renounced the dress and decencies of his profession, the *soldier* may not perhaps be dishonoured by the wine which he drank, the blood that he spilt, the flames that he kindled, or the licentious pursuits of gaming and hunting. His open simony might be the consequence of distress; and his blasphemous invocation of Jupiter and Venus, if it be true, could not possibly be serious. But we read, with some surprise, that the worthy grandson of Marozia lived in public adultery with the matrons of Rome; that the Lateran palace was turned into a school for prostitution; and that his rapes of virgins and widows had deterred the female pilgrims from visiting the tomb of St. Peter, lest, in the devout act, they should be violated by his successor.[133] The Protestants have dwelt with malicious pleasure on these characters of antichrist; but to a philosophic eye the vices of the clergy are far less dangerous than their virtues.

After a long series of scandal the apostolic see was reformed and exalted by the austerity and zeal of Gregory VII. That ambitious monk devoted his life to the execution of two projects. I. To fix in the college of cardinals the freedom and independence of election, and for ever to abolish the right or usurpation of the emperors and the Roman people. II. To bestow and resume the Western empire as a fief or benefice[134] of the church, and to extend his temporal dominion over the kings and kingdoms of the earth. After a contest of fifty years the first of these designs was accomplished by the firm support of the ecclesiastical order, whose liberty was connected with that of their chief. But the second attempt, though it was crowned with some partial and apparent success, has been vigorously resisted by the secular power, and finally extinguished by the improvement of human reason.

In the revival of the empire of Rome neither the bishop nor the people could bestow on Charlemagne or Otho the provinces which were lost, as they had been won by the chance of arms. But the Romans were free to choose a master for themselves; and the powers which had been delegated to the patrician were irrevocably granted to the French and Saxon emperors of the West. The broken records of the times[135] preserve some remembrance of their palace, their mint, their tribunal, their edicts, and the sword of justice, which, as late as the thirteenth century, was derived from Cæsar to the præfect of the city.[136] Between the arts of the popes and the violence of the people this supremacy was crushed and annihilated. Content with the titles of emperor and Augustus, the successors of Charlemagne neglected to assert this local jurisdiction. In the hour of prosperity their ambition was diverted by more alluring objects; and in the decay and division of the empire they were oppressed by the defence of their hereditary provinces. Amidst the ruins of Italy the famous Marozia invited one of the usurpers to assume the character of her third husband; and Hugh king of Burgundy was introduced by her faction into the mole of Hadrian or castle of St. Angelo, which commands the principal bridge and entrance of Rome. Her son by the first marriage, Alberic, was compelled to attend at the nuptial banquet; but his reluctant and ungraceful service was chastised with a blow by his new father. The blow was productive of a revolution. "Romans," exclaimed the youth, "once you were the masters of the world, and these Burgundians the most abject of your slaves. They now reign, these voracious and brutal savages, and my injury is the commencement of your servitude."[137] The alarum-bell rang to arms in every quarter of the city: the Burgundians retreated with haste and shame; Marozia was imprisoned by her victorious son; and his brother, Pope John XI., was reduced to the exercise of his spiritual functions. With the title of prince, Alberic possessed above twenty years the government of Rome; and he is said to have gratified the popular prejudice by restoring the office, or at least the title, of consuls and tribunes. His son and heir Octavian assumed, with the pontificate, the name of John XII.: like his predecessor, he was provoked by the Lombard princes to seek a deliverer for the church and republic; and the services of Otho were rewarded with the Imperial dignity. But the Saxon was imperious, the Romans were impatient, the festival of the coronation was disturbed by the secret conflict of prerogative and freedom, and Otho commanded his sword-bearer not to stir from his person lest he should be assaulted and murdered at the foot of the altar.[138] Before he repassed the Alps, the emperor chastised the revolt of the people and the ingratitude of John XII. The pope was degraded in a synod; the præfect was mounted on an ass, whipped through the city, and cast into a dungeon; thirteen of the most guilty were hanged, others were mutilated or banished; and this severe processs was justified by the ancient laws of Theodosius and Justinian. The voice of fame has accused the second Otho of a perfidious and bloody act, the massacre of the senators, whom he had invited to his table under the fair semblance of hospitality and friendship.[139] In the minority of his son Otho the Third, Rome made a bold attempt to shake off the Saxon yoke, and the consul Crescentius was the Brutus of the republic. From the condition of a subject and an exile he twice rose to the command of the city, oppressed, expelled, and created the popes, and formed a conspiracy for restoring the authority of the Greek emperors. In the fortress of St. Angelo he maintained an obstinate siege, till the unfortunate consul was betrayed by a promise of safety: his body was suspended on a gibbet, and his head was exposed on the battlements of the castle. By a reverse of fortune, Otho, after separating his troops, was besieged three days, without food, in his palace, and a disgraceful escape saved him from the justice or fury of the Romans. The senator Ptolemy was the leader of the people, and the widow of Crescentius enjoyed the pleasure or the fame of revenging her husband by a poison which she administered to her Imperial lover. It was the design of Otho the Third to abandon the ruder countries of the North, to erect his throne in Italy, and to revive the institutions of the Roman monarchy. But his successors only once in their lives appeared on the banks of the Tiber to receive their crown in the Vatican.[140] Their absence was contemptible, their presence odious and formidable. They descended from the Alps at the head of their barbarians, who were strangers and enemies to the country; and their transient visit was a scene of tumult and bloodshed.[141] A faint remembrance of their ancestors still tormented the Romans; and they beheld with pious indignation the succession of Saxons, Franks, Swabians, and Bohemians, who usurped the purple and prerogatives of the Cæsars.

There is nothing perhaps more adverse to nature and reason than to hold in obedience remote countries and foreign nations in opposition to their inclination and interest. A torrent of barbarians may pass over the earth, but an extensive empire must be supported by a refined system of policy and oppression: in the centre an absolute power, prompt in action and rich in resources: a swift and easy communication with the extreme parts: fortifications to check the first effort of rebellion: a regular administration to protect and punish; and a well-disciplined army to inspire fear, without provoking discontent and despair. Far different was the situation of the German Cæsars, who were ambitious to enslave the kingdom of Italy. Their patrimonial estates were stretched along the Rhine, or scattered in the provinces; but this ample domain was alienated by the imprudence or distress of successive princes; and their revenue from minute and vexatious prerogative, was scarcely sufficient for the maintenance of their household. Their troops were formed by the legal or voluntary service of their feudal vassals, who passed the Alps with reluctance, assumed the licence of rapine and disorder, and capriciously deserted before the end of the campaign. Whole armies were swept away by the pestilential influence of the climate: the survivors brought back the bones of their princes and nobles;[142] and the effects of their own intemperance were often imputed to the treachery and malice of the Italians, who rejoiced at least in the calamities of the barbarians. This irregular tyranny might contend on equal terms with the petty tyrants of Italy; nor can the people, or the reader, be much interested in the event of the quarrel. But in the eleventh and twelfth centuries the Lombards rekindled the flame of industry and freedom, and the generous example was at length imitated by the republics of Tuscany. In the Italian cities a municipal government had never been totally abolished; and their first privileges were granted by the favour and policy of the emperors, who were desirous of erecting a plebeian barrier against the independence of the nobles. But their rapid progress, the daily extension of their power and pretensions, were founded on the numbers and spirit of these rising communities.[143] Each city filled the measure of her diocese or district: the jurisdiction of the counts and bishops, of the marquises and counts, was banished from the land; and the proudest nobles were persuaded or compelled to desert their solitary castles, and to embrace the more honourable character of freemen and magistrates. The legislative authority was inherent in the general assembly; but the executive powers were intrusted to three consuls, annually chosen from the three orders of *captains, valvassors,*[144] and commons, into which the republic was divided. Under the protection of equal law the labours of agriculture and commerce were gradually revived; but the martial spirit of the Lombards was nourished by the presence of danger; and as often as the bell was rung, or the standard[145] erected, the gates of the city poured forth a numerous and intrepid band, whose zeal in their own cause was soon guided by the use and discipline of arms. At the foot of these popular ramparts the pride of the Cæsars was overthrown; and the invincible genius of liberty prevailed over the two Frederics, the greatest princes of the middle age: the first, superior perhaps in military prowess; the second, who undoubtedly excelled in the softer accomplishments of peace and learning.

Ambitious of restoring the splendour of the purple, Frederic the First invaded the republics of Lombardy with the arts of a statesman, the valour of a soldier, and the cruelty of a tyrant. The recent discovery of the Pandects had renewed a science most favourable to despotism; and his venal advocates proclaimed the emperor the absolute master of the lives and properties of his subjects. His royal prerogatives, in a less odious sense, were acknowledged in the diet of Roncaglia, and the revenue of Italy was fixed at thirty thousand pounds of silver,[146] which were multiplied to an indefinite demand by the rapine of the fiscal officers. The obstinate cities were reduced by the terror or the force of his arms; his captives were delivered to the executioner, or shot from his military engines; and after the siege and surrender of Milan the buildings of that stately capital were razed to the ground, three hundred hostages were sent into Germany, and the inhabitants were dispersed in four villages, under the yoke of the inflexible conqueror.[147] But Milan soon rose from her ashes; and the league of Lombardy was cemented by distress: their cause was espoused by Venice, Pope Alexander the Third, and the Greek emperor: the fabric of oppression was overturned in a day; and in the treaty of Constance, Frederic subscribed, with some reservations, the freedom of four-and-twenty cities. His grandson contended with their vigour and maturity; but Frederic the Second[148] was endowed with some personal and peculiar advantages. His birth and education recommended him to the Italians; and in the implacable discord of the two factions the Ghibelins were attached to the emperor, while the Guelfs displayed the banner of liberty and the church. The court of Rome had slumbered when his father Henry the Sixth was permitted to unite with the empire the kingdoms of Naples and Sicily; and from these hereditary realms the son derived an ample and ready supply of troops and treasure. Yet Frederic the Second was finally oppressed by the arms of the Lombards and the thunders of the Vatican: his kingdom was given to a stranger, and the last of his family was beheaded at Naples on a public scaffold. During sixty years no emperor appeared in Italy, and the name was remembered only by the ignominious sale of the last relics of sovereignty.

The barbarian conquerors of the West were pleased to decorate their chief with the title of emperor; but it was not their design to invest him with the despotism of Constantine and Justinian. The persons of the Germans were free, their conquests were their own, and their national character was animated by a spirit which scorned the servile jurisprudence of the new or the ancient Rome. It would have been a vain and dangerous attempt to impose a monarch on the armed freemen, who were impatient of a magistrate; on the bold, who refused to obey; on the powerful, who aspired to command. The empire of Charlemagne and Otho was distributed among the dukes of the nations or provinces, the counts of the smaller districts, and the margraves of the marches or frontiers, who all united the civil and military authority as it had been delegated to the lieutenants of the first

Cæsars. The Roman governors, who for the most part were soldiers of fortune, seduced their mercenary legions, assumed the Imperial purple, and either failed or succeeded in their revolt, without wounding the power and unity of government. If the dukes, margraves, and counts of Germany were less audacious in their claims, the consequences of their success were more lasting and pernicious to the state. Instead of aiming at the supreme rank, they silently laboured to establish and appropriate their provincial independence. Their ambition was seconded by the weight of their estates and vassals, their mutual example and support, the common interest of the subordinate nobility, the change of princes and families, the minorities of Otho the Third and Henry the Fourth, the ambition of the popes, and the vain pursuit of the fugitive crowns of Italy and Rome. All the attributes of regal and territorial jurisdiction were gradually usurped by the commanders of the provinces; the right of peace and war, of life and death, of coinage and taxation, of foreign alliance and domestic economy. Whatever had been seized by violence was ratified by favour or distress, was granted as the price of a doubtful vote or a voluntary service; whatever had been granted to one could not without injury be denied to his successor or equal; and every act of local or temporary possession was insensibly moulded into the constitution of the Germanic kingdom. In every province the visible presence of the duke or count was interposed between the throne and the nobles; the subjects of the law became the vassals of a private chief; and the standard which *he* received from his sovereign was often raised against him in the field. The temporal power of the clergy was cherished and exalted by the superstition or policy of the Carlovingian and Saxon dynasties, who blindly depended on their moderation and fidelity; and the bishoprics of Germany were made equal in extent and privilege, superior in wealth and population, to the most ample states of the military order. As long as the emperors retained the prerogative of bestowing on every vacancy these ecclesiastic and secular benefices, their cause was maintained by the gratitude or ambition of their friends and favourites. But in the quarrel of the investitures they were deprived of their influence over the episcopal chapters; the freedom of election was restored, and the sovereign was reduced, by a solemn mockery, to his *first prayers*, the recommendation, once in his reign, to a single prebend in each church. The secular governors, in-

stead of being recalled at the will of a superior, could be degraded only by the sentence of their peers. In the first age of the monarchy the appointment of the son to the duchy or county of his father was solicited as a favour; it was gradually obtained as a custom, and extorted as a right: the lineal succession was often extended to the collateral or female branches; the states of the empire (their popular, and at length their legal, appellation) were divided and alienated by testament and sale; and all idea of a public trust was lost in that of a private and perpetual inheritance. The emperor could not even be enriched by the casualties of forfeiture and extinction: within the term of a year he was obliged to dispose of the vacant fief; and in the choice of the candidate it was his duty to consult either the general or the provincial diet.

After the death of Frederic the Second, Germany was left a monster with a hundred heads. A crowd of princes and prelates disputed the ruins of the empire: the lords of innumerable castles were less prone to obey than to imitate their superiors; and, according to the measure of their strength, their incessant hostilities received the name of conquest or robbery. Such anarchy was the inevitable consequence of the laws and manners of Europe; and the kingdoms of France and Italy were shivered into fragments by the violence of the same tempest. But the Italian cities and the French vassals were divided and destroyed, while the union of the Germans has produced, under the name of an empire, a great system of a federative republic. In the frequent and at last the perpetual institution of diets, a national spirit was kept alive, and the powers of a common legislature are still exercised by the three branches or colleges of the electors, the princes, and the free Imperial cities of Germany. I. Seven of the most powerful feudatories were permitted to assume, with a distinguished name and rank, the exclusive privilege of choosing the Roman emperor; and these electors were the king of Bohemia, the duke of Saxony, the margrave of Brandenburg, the count palatine of the Rhine, and the three archbishops of Mentz, of Trèves, and of Cologne. II. The college of princes and prelates purged themselves of a promiscuous multitude: they reduced to four representative votes the long series of independent counts, and excluded the nobles or equestrian order, sixty thousand of whom, as in the Polish diets, had appeared on horseback in the field of election. III. The pride of birth and dominion, of the sword and the mitre, wisely adopted the commons as the third branch of the legislature, and, in the progress of society, they were introduced about the same era into the national assemblies of France, England, and Germany. The Hanseatic League commanded the trade and navigation of the north: the confederates of the Rhine secured the peace and intercourse of the inland country; the influence of the cities has been adequate to their wealth and policy, and their negative still invalidates the acts of the two superior colleges of electors and princes.[149]

It is in the fourteenth century that we may view in the strongest light the state and contrast of the Roman empire of Germany, which no longer held, except on the borders of the Rhine and Danube, a single province of Trajan or Constantine. Their unworthy successors were the counts of Hapsburg, of Nassau, of Luxemburg, and of Schwartzenburg: the emperor Henry the Seventh procured for his son the crown of Bohemia, and his grandson Charles the Fourth was born among a people strange and barbarous in the estimation of the Germans themselves.[150] After the excommunication of Lewis of Bavaria, he received the gift or promise of the vacant empire from the Roman pontiffs, who, in the exile and captivity of Avignon, affected the dominion of the earth. The death of his competitors united the electoral college, and Charles was unanimously saluted king of the Romans, and future emperor, a title which in the same age was prostituted to the Cæsars of Germany and Greece. The German emperor was no more than the elective and impotent magistrate of an aristocracy of princes, who had not left him a village that he might call his own. His best prerogative was the right of presiding and proposing in the national senate, which was convened at his summons; and his native kingdom of Bohemia, less opulent than the adjacent city of Nuremberg, was the firmest seat of his power and the richest source of his revenue. The army with which he passed the Alps consisted of three hundred horse. In the cathedral of St. Ambrose, Charles was crowned with the *iron* crown, which tradition ascribed to the Lombard monarchy; but he was admitted only with a peaceful train; the gates of the city were shut upon him; and the king of Italy was held a captive by the arms of the Visconti, whom he confirmed in the sovereignty of Milan. In the Vatican he was again crowned with the *golden* crown of the empire; but, in obedience to a secret treaty, the Roman emperor immediately withdrew, without reposing a single night within the walls of Rome. The eloquent Petrarch,[151] whose fancy revived the visionary glories of the Capitol, deplores and upbraids the ignominious flight of the Bohemian; and even his contemporaries could observe that the sole exercise of his authority was in the lucrative sale of privileges and titles. The gold of Italy secured the election of his son; but such was the shameful poverty of the Roman emperor, that his person was arrested by a butcher in the streets of Worms, and was detained in the public inn as a pledge or hostage for the payment of his expenses.

From this humiliating scene let us turn to the apparent majesty of the same Charles in the diets of the empire. The golden bull, which fixes the Germanic constitution, is promulgated in the style of a sovereign and legislator. A hundred princes bowed before his throne, and exalted their own dignity by the voluntary honours which they yielded to their chief or minister. At the royal banquet the hereditary great officers, the seven electors, who in rank and title were equal to kings, performed their solemn and domestic service of the palace. The seals of the triple kingdom were borne in state by the archbishops of Mentz, Cologne, and Trèves, the perpetual arch-chancellors of Germany, Italy, and Arles. The great marshal, on horseback, exercised his function with a silver measure of oats, which he emptied on the ground, and immediately dismounted to regulate the order of the guests. The great steward, the count palatine of the Rhine, placed the dishes on the table. The great chamberlain, the margrave of Brandenburg, presented, after the repast, the golden ewer and basin, to wash. The king of Bohemia, as great cupbearer, was represented by the emperor's brother, the duke of Luxemburg and Brabant; and the procession was closed by the great huntsmen, who introduced a boar and a stag, with a loud chorus of horns and hounds.[152] Nor was the supremacy of the emperor confined to Germany alone: the hereditary monarchs of Europe confessed the pre-eminence of his rank and dignity: he was the first of the Christian princes, the temporal head of the great republic of the West:[153] to his person the title of majesty was long appropriated; and he disputed with the pope the sublime prerogative of creating kings and assembling councils. The oracle of the civil law, the learned Bartolus, was a pensioner of Charles the Fourth; and his school resounded with the doctrine that the Roman emperor was the rightful sovereign of the earth, from the rising to the setting sun. The contrary opinion was condemned, not as an error, but as a heresy, since even the Gospel had pronounced, "And there went forth a decree from Cæsar Augustus, that *all the world* should be taxed."[154]

If we annihilate the interval of time and space between Augustus and Charles, strong and striking will be the contrast between the two Cæsars: the Bohemian, who concealed his weakness under the mask of ostentation, and the Roman, who disguised his strength under the semblance of modesty. At the head of his victorious legions, in his reign over the sea and land, from the Nile and Euphrates to the Atlantic Ocean, Augustus professed himself the ser-vant of the state and the equal of his fellow citizens. The conqueror of Rome and her prov-inces assumed the popular and legal form of a censor, a consul, and a tribune. His will was the law of mankind, but in the declaration of his laws he borrowed the voice of the senate and people; and, from their decrees, their master accepted and renewed his temporary commis-sion to administer the republic. In his dress, his domestics,[155] his titles, in all the offices of social life, Augustus maintained the character of a private Roman; and his most artful flatter-ers respected the secret of his absolute and per-petual monarchy.

CHAPTER L

Description of Arabia and its Inhabitants. Birth, Character, and Doctrine of Mo-hammed. He preaches at Mecca. Flies to Medina. Propagates his Religion by the Sword. Voluntary or reluctant Submission of the Arabs. His Death and Suc-cessors. The Claims and Fortunes of Ali and his Descendants.

AFTER pursuing above six hundred years the fleeting Cæsars of Constantinople and Germany, I now descend, in the reign of Heraclius, on the eastern borders of the Greek monarchy. While the state was exhausted by the Persian war, and the church was dis-tracted by the Nestorian and Monophysite sects, Mohammed, with the sword in one hand and the Koran in the other, erected his throne on the ruins of Christianity and of Rome. The genius of the Arabian prophet, the manners of his na-tion, and the spirit of his religion, involve the causes of the decline and fall of the Eastern em-pire; and our eyes are curiously intent on one of the most memorable revolutions which have impressed a new and lasting character on the nations of the globe.[1]

In the vacant space between Persia, Syria, Egypt, and Æthiopia, the Arabian peninsula[2] may be conceived as a triangle of spacious but irregular dimensions. From the northern point of Beles,[3] on the Euphrates, a line of fifteen hun-dred miles is terminated by the Straits of Babel-mandeb and the land of frankincense. About half this length may be allowed for the middle breadth, from east to west, from Bassora to Suez, from the Persian Gulf to the Red Sea.[4] The sides of the triangle are gradually enlarged, and the southern basis presents a front of a thousand miles to the Indian Ocean. The entire surface of the peninsula exceeds in a fourfold proportion that of Germany or France, but the far greater part has been justly stigmatised with the epithets of the *stony* and the *sandy*. Even the wilds of Tartary are decked, by the hand of na-ture, with lofty trees and luxuriant herbage; and the lonesome traveller derives a sort of com-fort and society from the presence of vegetable life. But in the dreary waste of Arabia a bound-less level of sand is intersected by sharp and naked mountains; and the face of the desert, without shade or shelter, is scorched by the di-rect and intense rays of a tropical sun. Instead of refreshing breezes, the winds, particularly from the south-west diffuse a noxious and even deadly vapour; the hillocks of sand which they alternately raise and scatter are compared to the billows of the ocean, and whole caravans, whole armies, have been lost and buried in the whirlwind. The common benefits of water are an object of desire and contest; and such is the scarcity of wood, that some art is requisite to preserve and propagate the element of fire. Arabia is destitute of navigable rivers, which fertilise the soil, and convey its produce to the adjacent regions: the torrents that fall from the hills are imbibed by the thirsty earth: the rare and hardy plants, the tamarind or the acacia, that strike their roots into the clefts of the rocks, are nourished by the dews of the night: a scanty supply of rain is collected in cisterns and aque-ducts: the wells and springs are the secret treasure of the desert; and the pilgrim of Mecca,[5] after many a dry and sultry march, is disgusted by the taste of the waters which have rolled over a bed of sulphur or salt. Such is the general and genuine picture of the climate of Arabia. The experience of evil enhances the value of any local or partial enjoyments. A shady grove, a green pasture, a stream of fresh water, are sufficient to attract a colony of sedentary Arabs to the fortunate spots which can afford food and refreshment to themselves and their cattle, and which encourage their industry in the cultivation of the palm-tree and the vine. The high lands that border on the Indian Ocean are distinguished by their superior plenty of wood and water: the air is more temperate, the fruits are more delicious, the animals and the human race more numerous: the fertility of the soil invites and rewards the toil of the husbandman; and the peculiar gifts of frankincense[6] and coffee have attracted in different ages the merchants of the world. If it be compared with the rest of the peninsula, this sequestered region may truly deserve the appellation of the *happy*; and the splendid colouring of fancy and fiction has been suggested by contrast and countenanced by distance. It was for this earthly paradise that nature had reserved her choicest favours and her most curious workmanship: the incompatible blessings of luxury and innocence were ascribed to the natives: the soil was impregnated with gold[7] and gems, and both the land and sea were taught to exhale the odours of aromatic sweets. This division of the *sandy*, the *stony*, and the *happy*, so familiar to the Greeks and Latins, is unknown to the Arabians themselves; and it is singular enough, that a country whose language and inhabitants have ever been the same should scarcely retain a vestige of its ancient geography. The maritime districts of *Bahrein* and *Oman* are opposite to the realm of Persia. The kingdom of *Yemen* displays the limits, or at least the situation, of Arabia Felix: the name of *Neged* is extended over the inland space; and the birth of Mohammed has illustrated the province of *Hejaz* along the coast of the Red Sea.[8]

The measure of population is regulated by the means of subsistence; and the inhabitants of this vast peninsula might be out-numbered by the subjects of a fertile and industrious province. Along the shores of the Persian Gulf, of the ocean, and even of the Red Sea, the *Ichthyophagi*,[9] or fish-eaters, continued to wander in quest of their precarious food. In this primitive and abject state, which ill deserves the name of society, the human brute, without arts or laws, almost without sense or language, is poorly distinguished from the rest of the animal creation. Generations and ages might roll away in silent oblivion, and the helpless savage was restrained from multiplying his race by the wants and pursuits which confined his existence to the narrow margin of the sea-coast. But in an early period of antiquity the great body of the Arabs had emerged from this scene of misery; and as the naked wilderness could not maintain a people of hunters, they rose at once to the more secure and plentiful condition of the pastoral life. The same life is uniformly pursued by the roving tribes of the desert; and in the portrait of the modern *Bedoweens* we may trace the features of their ancestors,[10] who, in the age of Moses or Mohammed, dwelt under similar tents, and conducted their horses, and camels, and sheep to the same springs and the same pastures. Our toil is lessened, and our wealth is increased, by our dominion over the useful animals; and the Arabian shepherd had acquired the absolute possession of a faithful friend and a laborious slave.[11] Arabia, in the opinion of the naturalist, is the genuine and original country of the *horse*; the climate most propitious, not indeed to the size, but to the spirit and swiftness, of that generous animal. The merit of the Barb, the Spanish, and the English breed is derived from a mixture of Arabian blood:[12] the Bedoweens preserve, with superstitious care, the honours and the memory of the purest race: the males are sold at a high price, but the females are seldom alienated; and the birth of a noble foal was esteemed among the tribes as a subject of joy and mutual congratulation. These horses are educated in the tents, among the children of the Arabs, with a tender familiarity, which trains them in the habits of gentleness and attachment. They are accustomed only to walk and to gallop: their sensations are not blunted by the incessant abuse of the spur and the whip: their powers are reserved for the moments of flight and pursuit: but no sooner do they feel the touch of the hand or the stirrup, than they dart away with the swiftness of the wind; and if their friend be dismounted in the rapid career, they instantly stop till he has recovered his seat. In the sands of Africa and Arabia the *camel* is a sacred and precious gift. That strong and patient beast of burden can perform, without eating or drinking, a journey of several days; and a reservoir of fresh water is preserved in a large bag, a fifth stomach of the animal, whose body is imprinted with the marks of servitude: the larger breed is capable of transporting a weight of a thousand pounds; and the dromedary, of a lighter and more active frame, outstrips the fleetest courser in the race. Alive or dead, almost every part of the camel is serviceable to man: her milk is plentiful and nutritious: the young and tender flesh has the taste of veal:[13] a valuable salt is extracted from the urine: the dung supplies the deficiency of fuel; and the long hair, which falls each year and is renewed, is coarsely manufactured into the garments, the furniture, and the tents of the Bedoweens. In the rainy seasons they consume the rare and insufficient herbage of the desert: during the heats of summer and the scarcity of winter they remove their encampments to the sea-coast, the hills of Yemen, or the neighbourhood of the Euphrates, and have often extorted the dangerous licence of visiting the banks of the Nile and the villages of Syria and Palestine. The life of a wandering Arab is a life of danger and distress; and though sometimes, by rapine or exchange, he may appropriate the fruits of industry, a private citizen in Europe is in the possession of more solid and pleasing luxury than the proudest emir who marches in the field at the head of ten thousand horse.

Yet an essential difference may be found between the hordes of Scythia and the Arabian tribes; since many of the latter were collected into towns, and employed in the labours of trade and agriculture. A part of their time and industry was still devoted to the management of their cattle: they mingled, in peace and war, with their brethren of the desert; and the Bedoweens derived from their useful intercourse some supply of their wants, and some rudiments of art and knowledge. Among the forty-two cities of Arabia,[14] enumerated by Abulfeda, the most ancient and populous were situate in the *happy* Yemen: the towers of Saana,[15] and the marvellous reservoir of Merab,[16] were constructed by the kings of the Homerites; but their profane lustre was eclipsed by the prophetic glories of MEDINA,[17] and MECCA,[18] near the Red Sea, and at the distance from each other of two hundred and seventy miles. The last of these holy places was known to the Greeks under the name of Macoraba; and the termination of the word is expressive of its greatness, which has not indeed, in the most flourishing period, exceeded the size and populousness of Marseilles. Some latent motive, perhaps of superstition, must have impelled the founders in the choice of a most unpromising situation. They erected their habitations of mud or stone in a plain about two miles long and one mile broad, at the foot of three barren mountains: the soil is a rock; the water even of the holy well of Zemzem is bitter or brackish; the pastures are remote from the city; and grapes are transported above seventy miles from the gardens of Tayef. The fame and spirit of the Koreishites, who reigned in Mecca, were conspicuous among the Arabian tribes; but their ungrateful soil refused the labours of agriculture, and their position was favourable to the enterprises of trade. By the seaport of Gedda, at the distance only of forty miles, they maintained an easy correspondence with Abyssinia; and that Christian kingdom afforded the first refuge to the disciples of Mohammed. The treasures of Africa were conveyed over the peninsula to Gerrha or Katif, in the province of Bahrein, a city built, as it is said, of rock-salt, by the Chaldæan exiles;[19] and from thence, with the native pearls of the Persian Gulf, they were floated on rafts to the mouth of the Euphrates. Mecca is placed almost at an equal distance, a month's journey, between Yemen on the right and Syria on the left hand. The former was the winter, the latter the summer, station of her caravans; and their seasonable arrival relieved the ships of India from the tedious and troublesome navigation of the Red Sea. In the markets of Saana and Merab, in the harbours of Oman and Aden, the camels of the Koreishites were laden with a precious cargo of aromatics; a supply of corn and manufactures was purchased in the fairs of Bostra and Damascus; the lucrative exchange diffused plenty and riches in the streets of Mecca; and the noblest of her sons united the love of arms with the profession of merchandise.[20]

The perpetual independence of the Arabs has been the theme of praise among strangers and natives; and the arts of controversy transform this singular event into a prophecy and a miracle in favour of the posterity of Ismael.[21] Some exceptions, that can neither be dissembled nor eluded, render this mode of reasoning as indiscreet as it is superfluous; the kingdom of Yemen has been successively subdued by the Abyssinians, the Persians, the sultans of Egypt,[22] and the Turks:[23] the holy cities of Mecca and Medina have repeatedly bowed under a Scythian tyrant; and the Roman province of Arabia[24] embraced the peculiar wilderness in which Ismael and his sons must have pitched their tents in the face of their brethren. Yet these exceptions are temporary or local; the body of the nation has escaped the yoke of the most powerful monarchies: the arms of Sesostris and Cyrus, of Pompey and Trajan, could never achieve the conquest of Arabia; the present sovereign of the Turks[25] may exercise a shadow of jurisdiction, but his pride is reduced to solicit the friendship of a people whom it is dangerous to provoke and fruitless to attack. The obvious causes of their freedom are inscribed on the character and country of the Arabs. Many ages before Mohammed,[26] their intrepid valour had been severely felt by their neighbours in offensive and defensive war. The patient and active virtues of a soldier are insensibly nursed in the habits and discipline of a pastoral life. The care of the sheep and camels is abandoned to the women of the tribe; but the martial youth, under the banner of the emir, is ever on horseback, and in the field, to practise the exercise of the bow, the javelin, and the scymetar. The long memory of their independence is the firmest pledge of its perpetuity, and succeeding generations are animated to prove their descent and to maintain their inheritance. Their domestic feuds are suspended on the approach of a common enemy; and in their last hostilities against the Turks, the caravan of Mecca was attacked and pillaged by fourscore thousand of the confederates. When they advance to battle, the hope of victory is in the front; in the rear, the assurance of a retreat. Their horses and camels, who in eight or ten days can perform a march of four or five hundred miles, disappear before the conqueror; the secret waters of the desert elude his search; and his victorious troops are consumed with thirst, hunger, and fatigue in the pursuit of an invisible foe, who scorns his efforts, and safely reposes in the heart of the burning solitude. The arms and deserts of the Bedoweens are not only the safeguards of their own freedom, but the barriers also of the happy Arabia, whose inhabitants, remote from war, are enervated by the luxury of the soil and climate. The legions of Augustus melted away in disease and lassitude;[27] and it is only by a naval power that the reduction of Yemen has been successfully attempted. When Mohammed erected his holy standard,[28] that kingdom was a province of the Persian empire; yet seven princes of the Homerites still reigned in the mountains; and the vicegerent of Chosroes was tempted to forget his distant country and his unfortunate master. The historians of the age of Justinian represent the state of the independent Arabs, who were divided by interest or affection in the long quarrel of the East: the tribe of *Gassan* was allowed to encamp on the Syrian territory: the princes of *Hira* were permitted to form a city about forty miles to the southward of the ruins of Babylon. Their service in the field was speedy and vigorous; but their friendship was venal, their faith inconstant, their enmity capricious: it was an easier task to excite than to disarm these roving barbarians; and, in the familiar intercourse of war, they learned to see and to despise the splendid weakness both of Rome and of Persia. From Mecca to the Euphrates, the Arabian tribes[29] were confounded by the Greeks and Latins under the general appellation of SARACENS,[30] a name which every Christian mouth has been taught to pronounce with terror and abhorrence.

The slaves of domestic tyranny may vainly exult in their national independence: but the Arab is personally free; and he enjoys, in some degree, the benefits of society, without forfeiting the prerogatives of nature. In every tribe, superstition, or gratitude, or fortune has exalted a particular family above the heads of their equals. The dignities of sheick and emir invariably descend in this chosen race; but the order of succession is loose and precarious; and the most worthy or aged of the noble kinsmen are preferred to the simple though important office of composing disputes by their advice, and guiding valour by their example. Even a female of sense and spirit has been permitted to command the countrymen of Zenobia.[31] The momentary junction of several tribes produces an army; their more lasting union constitutes a nation; and the supreme chief, the emir of emirs, whose banner is displayed at their head, may deserve, in the eyes of strangers, the honours of the kingly name. If the Arabian princes abuse their power, they are quickly punished by the desertion of their subjects, who had been accustomed to a mild and parental jurisdiction. Their spirit is free, their steps are unconfined, the desert is open, and the tribes and families are held together by a mutual and voluntary compact. The softer natives of Yemen supported the pomp and majesty of a monarch; but if he could not leave his palace without endangering his life,[32] the active powers of government must have been devolved on his nobles and magistrates. The cities of Mecca and Medina present, in the heart of Asia, the form, or rather the substance, of a commonwealth. The grandfather of Mohammed, and his lineal ancestors, appear in foreign and domestic transactions as the princes of their country; but they reigned, like Pericles at Athens, or the Medici at Florence, by the opinion of their wisdom and integrity; their influence was divided with their patrimony; and the sceptre was transferred from the uncles of the prophet to a younger branch of the tribe of Koreish. On solemn occasions they convened the assembly of the people; and, since mankind must be either compelled or persuaded to obey, the use and reputation of oratory among the ancient Arabs is the clearest evidence of public freedom.[33] But their simple freedom was of a very different cast from the nice and artificial machinery of the Greek and Roman republics, in which each member possessed an undivided share of the civil and political rights of the community. In the more simple state of the Arabs, the nation is free, because each of her sons disdains a base submission to the will of a master. His breast is fortified with the austere virtues of courage, patience, and sobriety; the love of independence prompts him to exercise the habits of self-command; and the fear of dishonour guards him from the meaner apprehension of pain, of danger, and of death. The gravity and firmness of the mind is conspicuous in his outward demeanour: his speech is slow, weighty, and concise; he is seldom provoked to laughter; his only gesture is that of stroking his beard, the venerable symbol of manhood; and the sense of his own importance teaches him to accost his equals without levity, and his superiors without awe.[34] The liberty of the Saracens survived their conquests: the first caliphs indulged the bold and familiar language of their subjects: they ascended the pulpit to persuade and edify the congregation; nor was it before the seat of empire was removed to the Tigris that the Abbassides adopted the proud and pompous ceremonial of the Persian and Byzantine courts.

In the study of nations and men we may observe the causes that render them hostile or friendly to each other, that tend to narrow or enlarge, to mollify or exasperate, the social character. The separation of the Arabs from the rest of mankind has accustomed them to confound the ideas of stranger and enemy; and the poverty of the land has introduced a maxim of jurisprudence which they believe and practise to the present hour. They pretend that, in the division of the earth, the rich and fertile climates were assigned to the other branches of the human family; and that the posterity of the outlaw Ismael might recover, by fraud or force, the portion of inheritance of which he had been unjustly deprived. According to the remark of Pliny, the Arabian tribes are equally addicted to theft and merchandise: the caravans that traverse the desert are ransomed or pillaged; and their neighbours, since the remote times of Job and Sesostris,[35] have been the victims of their rapacious spirit. If a Bedoween discovers from afar a solitary traveller, he rides furiously against him, crying, with a loud voice, "Undress thyself, thy aunt (*my wife*) is without a garment." A ready submission entitles him to mercy; resistance will provoke the aggressor, and his own blood must expiate the blood which he presumes to shed in legitimate defence. A single robber, or a few associates, are branded with their genuine name; but the exploits of a numerous band assume the character of lawful and honourable war. The temper of a people thus armed against mankind was doubly inflamed by the domestic licence of rapine, murder, and revenge. In the constitution of Europe, the right of peace and war is now confined to a small, and the actual exercise to a much smaller, list of respectable potentates; but each Arab, with impunity and renown, might point his javelin against the life of his countrymen. The union of the nation consisted only in a vague resemblance of language and manners; and in each community the jurisdiction of the magistrate was mute and impotent. Of the time of ignorance which preceded Mohammed, seventeen hundred battles[36] are recorded by tradition: hostility was embittered with the rancour of civil faction: and the recital, in prose or verse, of an obsolete feud, was sufficient to rekindle the same passions among the descendants of the hostile tribes. In private life every man, at least every family, was the judge and avenger of its own cause. The nice sensibility of honour, which weighs the insult rather than the injury, sheds its deadly venom on the quarrels of the Arabs: the honour of their women, and of their *beards*, is most easily wounded; and indecent action, a contemptuous word, can be expiated only by the blood of the offender; and such is their patient inveteracy, that they expect whole months and years the opportunity of revenge. A fine or compensation for murder is familiar to the barbarians of every age: but in Arabia the kinsmen of the dead are at liberty to accept the atonement, or to exercise with their own hands the law of retaliation. The refined malice of the Arabs refuses even the head of the murderer, substitutes an innocent to the guilty person, and transfers the penalty to the best and most considerable of the race by whom they have been injured. If he falls by their hands, they are exposed in their turn to the danger of reprisals; the interest and principal of the bloody debt are accumulated: the individuals of either family lead a life of malice and suspicion, and fifty years may sometimes elapse before the account of vengeance be finally set-led.[37] This sanguinary spirit, ignorant of pity or forgiveness, has been moderated, however, by the maxims of honour, which require in every private encounter some decent equality of age and strength, of numbers and weapons. An annual festival of two, perhaps of four, months, was observed by the Arabs before the time of Mohammed, during which their swords were religiously sheathed both in foreign and domestic hostility; and this partial truce is more strongly expressive of the habits of an-archy and warfare.[38]

But the spirit of rapine and revenge was at-tempered by the milder influence of trade and literature. The solitary peninsula is encompass-ed by the most civilised nations of the ancient world; the merchant is the friend of mankind; and the annual caravans imported the first seeds of knowledge and politeness into the cities and even the camps of the desert. Whatever may be the pedigree of the Arabs, their lan-guage is derived from the same original stock with the Hebrew, the Syriac, and the Chaldæan tongues; the independence of the tribes was marked by their peculiar dialects;[39] but each, after their own, allowed a just preference to the pure and perspicuous idiom of Mecca. In Ara-bia, as well as in Greece, the perfection of lan-guage outstripped the refinement of manners; and her speech could diversify the fourscore names of honey, the two hundred of a serpent, the five hundred of a lion, the thousand of a sword, at a time when this copious dictionary was intrusted to the memory of an illiterate peo-ple. The monuments of the Homerites were in-scribed with an obsolete and mysterious charac-ter; but the Cufic letters, the groundwork of the present alphabet, were invented on the banks of the Euphrates; and the recent invention was taught at Mecca by a stranger who settled in that city after the birth of Mohammed. The arts of grammar, of metre, and of rhetoric were unknown to the free-born eloquence of the Arabians; but their penetration was sharp, their fancy luxuriant, their wit strong and senten-tious,[40] and their more elaborate compositions were addressed with energy and effect to the minds of their hearers. The genius and merit of a rising poet was celebrated by the applause of his own and the kindred tribes. A solemn ban-quet was prepared, and a chorus of women, striking their tymbals, and displaying the pomp of their nuptials, sung in the presence of their sons and husbands the felicity of their native tribe—that a champion had now appeared to vindicate their rights—that a herald had raised his voice to immortalise their renown. The dis-tant or hostile tribes resorted to an annual fair, which was abolished by the fanaticism of the first Moslems—a national assembly that must have contributed to refine and harmonise the barbarians. Thirty days were employed in the exchange, not only of corn and wine, but of elo-quence and poetry. The prize was disputed by the generous emulation of the bards; the vic-torious performance was deposited in the ar-chives of princes and emirs; and we may read in our own language the seven original poems which were inscribed in letters of gold, and sus-pended in the temple of Mecca.[41] The Arabian poets were the historians and moralists of the age; and if they sympathised with the preju-dices, they inspired and crowned the virtues, of their countrymen. The indissoluble union of generosity and valour was the darling theme of their song; and when they pointed their keenest satire against a despicable race, they affirmed, in the bitterness of reproach, that the men knew not how to give, nor the women to deny.[42] The same hospitality, which was practised by Abra-ham, and celebrated by Homer, is still renewed in the camps of the Arabs. The ferocious Bedo-weens, the terror of the desert, embrace, with-out inquiry or hesitation, the stranger who dares to confide in their honour and to enter their tent. His treatment is kind and respectful: he shares the wealth or the poverty of his host; and, after a needful repose, he is dismissed on his way with thanks, with blessings, and per-haps with gifts. The heart and hand are more largely expanded by the wants of a brother or a friend; but the heroic acts that could deserve the public applause must have surpassed the narrow measure of discretion and experience. A dispute had arisen, who among the citizens of Mecca was entitled to the prize of generosity; and a successive application was made to the three who were deemed most worthy of the trial. Abdallah, the son of Abbas, had under-taken a distant journey, and his foot was in the stirrup, when he heard the voice of a supplicant, "O son of the uncle of the apostle of God, I am a traveller, and in distress!" He instantly dis-mounted to present the pilgrim with his camel, her rich caparison, and a purse of four thousand pieces of gold, accepting only the sword, either for its intrinsic value, or as the gift of an hon-oured kinsman. The servant of Kais informed the second supplicant that his master was asleep: but he immediately added, "Here is a purse of seven thousand pieces of gold (it is all we have in the house), and here is an order that will entitle you to a camel and a slave;" the master, as soon as he awoke, praised and enfranchised his faithful steward, with a gentle reproof, that by respecting his slumbers he had stinted his bounty. The third of these heroes, the blind Arabah, at the hour of prayer, was supporting his steps on the shoulders of two slaves. "Alas!" he replied, "my coffers are empty! but these you may sell; if you refuse, I renounce them." At these words, pushing away the youths, he groped along the wall with his staff. The character of Hatem is the perfect model of Arabian virtue:[43] he was brave and liberal, an eloquent poet, and a successful robber: forty camels were roasted at his hospitable feasts; and at the prayer of a suppliant enemy he restored both the captives and the spoil. The freedom of his countrymen disdained the laws of justice; they proudly indulged the spontaneous impulse of pity and benevolence.

The religion of the Arabs,[44] as well as of the Indians, consisted in the worship of the sun, the moon, and the fixed stars; a primitive and specious mode of superstition. The bright luminaries of the sky display the visible image of a Deity: their number and distance convey to a philosophic, or even a vulgar, eye the idea of boundless space: the character of eternity is marked on these solid globes, that seem incapable of corruption or decay: the regularity of their motions may be ascribed to a principle of reason or instinct; and their real or imaginary influence encourages the vain belief that the earth and its inhabitants are the object of their peculiar care. The science of astronomy was cultivated at Babylon; but the school of the Arabs was a clear firmament and a naked plain. In their nocturnal marches they steered by the guidance of the stars; their names, and order, and daily station were familiar to the curiosity and devotion of the Bedoween; and he was taught by experience to divide in twenty-eight parts the zodiac of the moon, and to bless the constellations who refreshed with salutary rains the thirst of the desert. The reign of the heavenly orbs could not be extended beyond the visible sphere; and some metaphysical powers were necessary to sustain the transmigration of souls and the resurrection of bodies: a camel was left to perish on the grave, that he might serve his master in another life; and the invocation of departed spirits implies that they were still endowed with consciousness and power. I am ignorant, and I am careless, of the blind mythology of the barbarians—of the local deities, of

the stars, the air, and the earth, of their sex or titles, their attributes or subordination. Each tribe, each family, each independent warrior created and changed the rites and the object of his fantastic worship; but the nation, in every age, has bowed to the religion as well as to the language of Mecca. The genuine antiquity of the CAABA ascends beyond the Christian era: in describing the coast of the Red Sea the Greek historian Diodorus[45] has remarked, between the Thamudites and the Sabæans, a famous temple whose superior sanctity was revered by *all* the Arabians; the linen or silken veil, which is annually renewed by the Turkish emperor, was first offered by a pious king of the Homerites who reigned seven hundred years before the time of Mohammed.[46] A tent or a cavern might suffice for the worship of the savages, but an edifice of stone and clay has been erected in its place; and the art and power of the monarchs of the East have been confined to the simplicity of the original model.[47] A spacious portico encloses the quadrangle of the Caaba—a square chapel twenty-four cubits long, twenty-three broad, and twenty-seven high: a door and a window admit the light; the double roof is supported by three pillars of wood; a spout (now of gold) discharges the rain-water, and the well Zemzem is protected by a dome from accidental pollution. The tribe of Koreish, by fraud or force, had acquired the custody of the Caaba: the sacerdotal office devolved through four lineal descents to the grandfather of Mohammed; and the family of the Hashemites, from whence he sprung, was the most respectable and sacred in the eyes of their country.[48] The precincts of Mecca enjoyed the rights of sanctuary; and in the last month of each year the city and the temple were crowded with a long train of pilgrims, who presented their vows and offerings in the house of God. The same rites which are now accomplished by the faithful Musulman were invented and practised by the superstition of the idolaters. At an awful distance they cast away their garments: seven times with hasty steps they encircled the Caaba, and kissed the black stone: seven times they visited and adored the adjacent mountains: seven times they threw stones into the valley of Mina: and the pilgrimage was achieved, as at the present hour, by a sacrifice of sheep and camels, and the burial of their hair and nails in the consecrated ground. Each tribe either found or introduced in the Caaba their domestic worship: the temple was adorned, or defiled, with three hundred and sixty idols of men, eagles, lions, and antelopes;

nd most conspicuous was the statue of Hebal, f red agate, holding in his hand seven arrows without heads or feathers, the instruments and ymbols of profane divination. But this statue was a monument of Syrian arts: the devotion of he ruder ages was content with a pillar or a ablet; and the rocks of the desert were hewn nto gods or altars in imitation of the black tone[49] of Mecca, which is deeply tainted with he reproach of an idolatrous origin. From Ja-pan to Peru the use of sacrifice has universally prevailed; and the votary has expressed his gratitude or fear by destroying or consuming, n honour of the gods, the dearest and most precious of their gifts. The life of a man[50] is the most precious oblation to deprecate a public calamity: the altars of Phœnicia and Egypt, of Rome and Carthage, have been polluted with human gore: the cruel practice was long pre-served among the Arabs; in the third century a boy was annually sacrificed by the tribe of the Dumatians;[51] and a royal captive was piously slaughtered by the prince of the Saracens, the ally and soldier of the emperor Justinian.[52] A parent who drags his son to the altar exhibits he most painful and sublime effort of fanati-cism: the deed or the intention was sanctified by the example of saints and heroes; and the father of Mohammed himself was devoted by a rash vow, and hardly ransomed for the equiv-alent of a hundred camels. In the time of ig-norance the Arabs, like the Jews and Egyptians, abstained from the taste of swine's flesh;[53] they circumcised[54] their children at the age of puber-ty: the same customs, without the censure or the precept of the Koran, have been silently transmitted to their posterity and proselytes. It has been sagaciously conjectured that the artful legislator indulged the stubborn prejudices of his countrymen. It is more simple to believe that he adhered to the habits and opinions of his youth, without foreseeing that a practice congenial to the climate of Mecca might be-come useless or inconvenient on the banks of the Danube or the Volga.

Arabia was free: the adjacent kingdoms were shaken by the storms of conquest and tyranny, and the persecuted sects fled to the happy land where they might profess what they thought, and practise what they professed. The religions of the Sabians and Magians, of the Jews and Christians, were disseminated from the Persian Gulf to the Red Sea. In a remote period of an-tiquity Sabianism was diffused over Asia by the science of the Chaldæans[55] and the arms of the Assyrians. From the observations of two thou-sand years the priests and astronomers of Baby-lon[56] deduced the eternal laws of nature and providence. They adored the seven gods, or angels, who directed the course of the seven planets, and shed their irresistible influence on the earth. The attributes of the seven planets, with the twelve signs of the zodiac, and the twenty-four constellations of the northern and southern hemisphere, were represented by im-ages and talismans; the seven days of the week were dedicated to their respective deities; the Sabians prayed thrice each day; and the temple of the moon at Haran was the term of their pil-grimage.[57] But the flexible genius of their faith was always ready either to teach or to learn: in the tradition of the creation, the deluge, and the patriarchs, they held a singular agreement with their Jewish captives; they appealed to the se-cret books of Adam, Seth, and Enoch; and a slight infusion of the Gospel has transformed the last remnant of the Polytheists into the Chris-tians of St. John, in the territory of Bassora.[58] The altars of Babylon were overturned by the Magians; but the injuries of the Sabians were revenged by the sword of Alexander; Persia groaned above five hundred years under a for-eign yoke; and the purest disciples of Zoroaster escaped from the contagion of idolatry, and breathed with their adversaries the freedom of the desert.[59] Seven hundred years before the death of Mohammed the Jews were settled in Arabia; and a far greater multitude was expell-ed from the Holy Land in the wars of Titus and Hadrian. The industrious exiles aspired to liber-ty and power: they erected synagogues in the cities, and castles in the wilderness; and their Gentile converts were confounded with the children of Israel, whom they resembled in the outward mark of circumcision. The Christian missionaries were still more active and success-ful: the Catholics asserted their universal reign; the sects whom they oppressed successively re-tired beyond the limits of the Roman empire; the Marcionites and Manichæans dispersed their *fantastic* opinions and apocryphal gospels; the churches of Yemen, and the princes of Hira and Gassan, were instructed in a purer creed by the Jacobite and Nestorian bishops.[60] The liber-ty of choice was presented to the tribes: each Arab was free to elect or to compose his private religion; and the rude superstition of his house was mingled with the sublime theology of saints and philosophers. A fundamental article of faith was inculcated by the consent of the learned strangers; the existence of one supreme God, who is exalted above the powers of heaven and earth, but who has often revealed himself to mankind by the ministry of his angels and prophets, and whose grace or justice has interrupted, by seasonable miracles, the order of nature. The most rational of the Arabs acknowledged his power, though they neglected his worship;[61] and it was habit rather than conviction that still attached them to the relics of idolatry. The Jews and Christians were the people of the *Book*; the Bible was already translated into the Arabic language,[62] and the volume of the Old Testament was accepted by the concord of these implacable enemies. In the story of the Hebrew patriarchs the Arabs were pleased to discover the fathers of their nation. They applauded the birth and promises of Ismael; revered the faith and virtue of Abraham; traced his pedigree and their own to the creation of the first man, and imbibed with equal credulity the prodigies of the holy text, and the dreams and traditions of the Jewish rabbis.

The base and plebeian origin of Mohammed is an unskilful calumny of the Christians,[63] who exalt instead of degrading the merit of their adversary. His descent from Ismael was a national privilege or fable; but if the first steps of the pedigree[64] are dark and doubtful, he could produce many generations of pure and genuine nobility: he sprung from the tribe of Koreish and the family of Hashem, the most illustrious of the Arabs, the princes of Mecca, and the hereditary guardians of the Caaba. The grandfather of Mohammed was Abdol Motalleb, the son of Hashem, a wealthy and generous citizen, who relieved the distress of famine with the supplies of commerce. Mecca, which had been fed by the liberality of the father, was saved by the courage of a son. The kingdom of Yemen was subject to the Christian princes of Abyssinia: their vassal Abrahah was provoked by an insult to avenge the honour of the cross; and the holy city was invested by a train of elephants and an army of Africans. A treaty was proposed; and, in the first audience, the grandfather of Mohammed demanded the restitution of his cattle. "And why," said Abrahah, "do you not rather implore my clemency in favour of your temple, which I have threatened to destroy?" "Because," replied the intrepid chief, "the cattle is my own; the Caaba belongs to the gods, and *they* will defend their house from injury and sacrilege." The want of provisions, or the valour of the Koreish, compelled the Abyssinians to a disgraceful retreat: their discomfiture has been adorned with a miraculous flight of birds, who showered down stones on the heads of the infi-

dels; and the deliverance was long commemorated by the era of the elephant.[65] The glory of Abdol Motalleb was crowned with domestic happiness; his life was prolonged to the age of one hundred and ten years; and he became the father of six daughters and thirteen sons. His best beloved Abdallah was the most beautiful and modest of the Arabian youth; and in the first night, when he consummated his marriage with Amina, of the noble race of the Zahrites, two hundred virgins are said to have expired of jealousy and despair. Mohammed, the only son of Abdallah and Amina, was born at Mecca, four years after the death of Justinian, and two months after the defeat of the Abyssinians,[66] whose victory would have introduced into the Caaba the religion of the Christians. In his early infancy[67] he was deprived of his father, his mother, and his grandfather; his uncles were strong and numerous; and, in the division of the inheritance, the orphan's share was reduced to five camels and an Æthiopian maid-servant. At home and abroad, in peace and war, Abu Taleb, the most respectable of his uncles, was the guide and guardian of his youth; in his twenty-fifth year he entered into the service of Cadijah, a rich and noble widow of Mecca, who soon rewarded his fidelity with the gift of her hand and fortune. The marriage contract, in the simple style of antiquity, recites the mutual love of Mohammed and Cadijah; describes him as the most accomplished of the tribe of Koreish; and stipulates a dowry of twelve ounces of gold and twenty camels, which was supplied by the liberality of his uncle.[68] By this alliance the son of Abdallah was restored to the station of his ancestors; and the judicious matron was content with his domestic virtues, till, in the fortieth year of his age,[69] he assumed the title of a prophet, and proclaimed the religion of the Koran.

According to the tradition of his companions, Mohammed[70] was distinguished by the beauty of his person, an outward gift which is seldom despised, except by those to whom it has been refused. Before he spoke, the orator engaged on his side the affections of a public or private audience. They applauded his commanding presence, his majestic aspect, his piercing eye, his gracious smile, his flowing beard, his countenance that painted every sensation of the soul, and his gestures that enforced each expression of the tongue. In the familiar offices of life he scrupulously adhered to the grave and ceremonious politeness of his country: his respectful attention to the rich and powerful was dignified by his condescension and affability to the poorest citizens of Mecca: the frankness of his manner concealed the artifice of his views; and the habits of courtesy were imputed to personal friendship or universal benevolence. His memory was capacious and retentive; his wit easy and social; his imagination sublime; his judgment clear, rapid, and decisive. He possessed the courage both of thought and action; and, although his designs might gradually expand with his success, the first idea which he entertained of his divine mission bears the stamp of an original and superior genius. The son of Abdallah was educated in the bosom of the noblest race, in the use of the purest dialect of Arabia; and the fluency of his speech was corrected and enhanced by the practice of discreet and seasonable silence. With these powers of eloquence, Mohammed was an illiterate barbarian: his youth had never been instructed in the arts of reading and writing;[71] the common ignorance exempted him from shame or reproach, but he was reduced to a narrow circle of existence, and deprived of those faithful mirrors which reflect to our mind the minds of sages and heroes. Yet the book of nature and of man was open to his view; and some fancy has been indulged in the political and philosophical observations which are ascribed to the Arabian traveller.[72] He compares the nations and the religions of the earth; discovers the weakness of the Persian and Roman monarchies; beholds with pity and indignation the degeneracy of the times; and resolves to unite under one God and one king the invincible spirit and primitive virtues of the Arabs. Our more accurate inquiry will suggest, that, instead of visiting the courts, the camps, the temples of the East, the two journeys of Mohammed into Syria were confined to the fairs of Bostra and Damascus; that he was only thirteen years of age when he accompanied the caravan of his uncle; and that his duty compelled him to return as soon as he had disposed of the merchandise of Cadijah. In these hasty and superficial excursions the eye of genius might discern some objects invisible to his grosser companions; some seeds of knowledge might be cast upon a fruitful soil; but his ignorance of the Syriac language must have checked his curiosity; and I cannot perceive in the life or writings of Mohammed that his prospect was far extended beyond the limits of the Arabian world. From every region of that solitary world the pilgrims of Mecca were annually assembled by the calls of devotion and commerce: in the free concourse of multitudes, a simple citizen, in his native tongue, might study the political state and character of the tribes, the theory and practice of the Jews and Christians. Some useful strangers might be tempted, or forced, to implore the rights of hospitality; and the enemies of Mohammed have named the Jew, the Persian, and the Syrian monk, whom they accuse of lending their secret aid to the composition of the Koran.[73] Conversation enriches the understanding, but solitude is the school of genius; and the uniformity of a work denotes the hand of a single artist. From his earliest youth Mohammed was addicted to religious contemplation; each year, during the month of Ramadan, he withdrew from the world and from the arms of Cadijah: in the cave of Hera, three miles from Mecca,[74] he consulted the spirit of fraud or enthusiasm, whose abode is not in the heavens, but in the mind of the prophet. The faith which, under the name of *Islam*, he preached to his family and nation, is compounded of an eternal truth and a necessary fiction. THAT THERE IS ONLY ONE GOD, AND MOHAMMED IS THE APOSTLE OF GOD.

It is the boast of the Jewish apologists, that, while the learned nations of antiquity were deluded by the fables of polytheism, their simple ancestors of Palestine preserved the knowledge and worship of the true God. The moral attributes of Jehovah may not easily be reconciled with the standard of *human* virtue: his metaphysical qualities are darkly expressed; but each page of the Pentateuch and the Prophets is an evidence of his power: the unity of his name is inscribed on the first table of the law; and his sanctuary was never defiled by any visible image of the invisible essence. After the ruin of the temple, the faith of the Hebrew exiles was purified, fixed, and enlightened by the spiritual devotion of the synagogue; and the authority of Mohammed will not justify his perpetual reproach that the Jews of Mecca or Medina adored Ezra as the son of God.[75] But the children of Israel had ceased to be a people; and the religions of the world were guilty, at least in the eyes of the prophet, of giving sons, or daughters, or companions to the supreme God. In the rude idolatry of the Arabs the crime is manifest and audacious: the Sabians are poorly excused by the pre-eminence of the first planet, or intelligence, in their celestial hierarchy; and in the Magian system the conflict of the two principles betrays the imperfection of the conqueror. The Christians of the seventh century had insensibly relapsed into a semblance of paganism; their public and private vows were addressed to the relics and images that disgraced the temples of the East: the throne of the Almighty was darkened by a cloud of martyrs, and saints, and angels, the objects of popular veneration; and the Collyridian heretics, who flourished in the fruitful soil of Arabia, invested the Virgin Mary with the name and honours of a goddess.[76] The mysteries of the Trinity and Incarnation *appear* to contradict the principle of the divine unity. In their obvious sense, they introduce three equal deities, and transform the man Jesus into the substance of the Son of God:[77] an orthodox commentary will satisfy only a believing mind: intemperate curiosity and zeal had torn the veil of the sanctuary: and each of the Oriental sects was eager to confess that all, except themselves, deserved the reproach of idolatry and polytheism. The creed of Mohammed is free from suspicion or ambiguity; and the Koran is a glorious testimony to the unity of God. The prophet of Mecca rejected the worship of idols and men, of stars and planets, on the rational principle that whatever rises must set, that whatever is born must die, that whatever is corruptible must decay and perish.[78] In the Author of the universe his rational enthusiasm confessed and adored an infinite and eternal being, without form or place, without issue or similitude, present to our most secret thoughts, existing by the necessity of his own nature, and deriving from himself all moral and intellectual perfection. These sublime truths, thus announced in the language of the prophet,[79] are firmly held by his disciples, and defined with metaphysical precision by the interpreters of the Koran. A philosophic theist might subscribe the popular creed of the Mohammedans:[80] a creed too sublime perhaps for our present faculties. What object remains for the fancy, or even the understanding, when we have abstracted from the unknown substance all ideas of time and space, of motion and matter, of sensation and reflection? The first principle of reason and revelation was confirmed by the voice of Mohammed: his proselytes, from India to Morocco, are distinguished by the name of *Unitarians*; and the danger of idolatry has been prevented by the interdiction of images. The doctrine of eternal decrees and absolute predestination is strictly embraced by the Mohammedans; and they struggle with the common difficulties, *how* to reconcile the prescience of God with the freedom and responsibility of man; *how* to explain the permission of evil under the reign of infinite power and infinite goodness.

The God of nature has written his existence on all his works, and his law in the heart of man. To restore the knowledge of the one, and the practice of the other, has been the real or pretended aim of the prophets of every age: the liberality of Mohammed allowed to his predecessors the same credit which he claimed for himself; and the chain of inspiration was prolonged from the fall of Adam to the promulgation of the Koran.[81] During that period some rays of prophetic light had been imparted to one hundred and twenty-four thousand of the elect, discriminated by their respective measure of virtue and grace; three hundred and thirteen apostles were sent with a special commission to recall their country from idolatry and vice; one hundred and four volumes have been dictated by the Holy Spirit; and six legislators of transcendant brightness have announced to mankind the six successive revelations of various rites, but of one immutable religion. The authority and station of Adam, Noah, Abraham, Moses, Christ, and Mohammed, rise in just gradation above each other; but whosoever hates or rejects any one of the prophets is numbered with the infidels. The writings of the patriarchs were extant only in the apocryphal copies of the Greeks and Syrians:[82] the conduct of Adam had not entitled him to the gratitude or respect of his children; the seven precepts of Noah were observed by an inferior and imperfect class of the proselytes of the synagogue;[83] and the memory of Abraham was obscurely revered by the Sabians in his native land of Chaldæa: of the myriads of prophets, Moses and Christ alone lived and reigned; and the remnant of the inspired writings was comprised in the books of the Old and New Testament. The miraculous story of Moses is consecrated and embellished in the Koran;[84] and the captive Jews enjoy the secret revenge of imposing their own belief on the nations whose recent creeds they deride. For the author of Christianity, the Mohammedans are taught by the prophet to entertain a high and mysterious reverence.[85] "Verily, Christ Jesus, the son of Mary, is the apostle of God, and his word, which he conveyed unto Mary, and a Spirit proceeding from him: honourable in this world, and in the world to come; and one of those who approach near to the presence of God."[86] The wonders of the genuine and apocryphal gospels[87] are profusely heaped on his head; and the Latin church has not disdained to borrow from the Koran the immaculate conception[88] of his virgin mother. Yet Jesus was a mere mortal; and, at the day of judgment, his estimony will serve to condemn both the Jews, who reject him as a prophet, and the Christians, who adore him as the Son of God. The malice of his enemies aspersed his reputation, and conspired against his life; but their intention only was guilty; a phantom or a criminal was substituted on the cross; and the innocent saint was translated to the seventh heaven.[89] During six hundred years the Gospel was the way of truth and salvation; but the Christians insensibly forgot both the laws and the example of their founder; and Mohammed was instructed by the Gnostics to accuse the church, as well as the synagogue, of corrupting the integrity of the sacred text.[90] The piety of Moses and of Christ rejoiced in the assurance of a future Prophet, more illustrious than themselves: the evangelic promise of the *Paraclete*, or Holy Ghost, was prefigured in the name, and accomplished in the person, of Mohammed,[91] the greatest and the last of the apostles of God.

The communication of ideas requires a similitude of thought and language: the discourse of a philosopher would vibrate without effect on the ear of a peasant; yet how minute is the distance of *their* understandings, if it be compared with the contact of an infinite and a finite mind, with the word of God expressed by the tongue or the pen of a mortal? The inspiration of the Hebrew prophets, of the apostles and evangelists of Christ, might not be incompatible with the exercise of their reason and memory; and the diversity of their genius is strongly marked in the style and composition of the books of the Old and New Testament. But Mohammed was content with a character more humble, yet more sublime, of a simple editor; the substance of the Koran,[92] according to himself or his disciples, is uncreated and eternal; subsisting in the essence of the Deity, and inscribed with a pen of light on the table of his everlasting decrees. A paper copy, in a volume of silk and gems, was brought down to the lowest heaven by the angel Gabriel, who, under the Jewish economy, had indeed been despatched on the most important errands; and this trusty messenger successively revealed the chapters and verses to the Arabian prophet. Instead of a perpetual and perfect measure of the divine will, the fragments of the Koran were produced at the discretion of Mohammed; each revelation is suited to the emergencies of his policy or passion; and all contradiction is removed by the saving maxim that any text of Scripture is abrogated or modified by any subsequent passage. The word of God and of the apostle was dili-

gently recorded by his disciples on palm-leaves and the shoulder-bones of mutton; and the pages, without order or connection, were cast into a domestic chest in the custody of one of his wives. Two years after the death of Mohammed, the sacred volume was collected and published by his friend and successor Abubeker: the work was revised by the caliph Othman, in the thirtieth year of the Hegira; and the various editions of the Koran assert the same miraculous privilege of a uniform and incorruptible text. In the spirit of enthusiasm or vanity, the prophet rests the truth of his mission on the merit of his book; audaciously challenges both men and angels to imitate the beauties of a single page; and presumes to assert that God alone could dictate this incomparable performance.[93] This argument is most powerfully addressed to a devout Arabian, whose mind is attuned to faith and rapture; whose ear is delighted by the music of sounds; and whose ignorance is incapable of comparing the productions of human genius.[94] The harmony and copiousness of style will not reach, in a version, the European infidel: he will peruse with impatience the endless incoherent rhapsody of fable, and precept, and declamation, which seldom excites a sentiment or an idea, which sometimes crawls in the dust, and is sometimes lost in the clouds. The divine attributes exalt the fancy of the Arabian missionary; but his loftiest strains must yield to the sublime simplicity of the book of Job, composed in a remote age, in the same country, and in the same language.[95] If the composition of the Koran exceeds the faculties of a man, to what superior intelligence should we ascribe the Iliad of Homer, or the Philippics of Demosthenes? In all religions the life of the founder supplies the silence of his written revelation: the sayings of Mohammed were so many lessons of truth; his actions so many examples of virtue; and the public and private memorials were preserved by his wives and companions. At the end of two hundred years the *Sonna*, or oral law, was fixed and consecrated by the labours of Al Bochari, who discriminated seven thousand two hundred and seventy-five genuine traditions from a mass of three hundred thousand reports of a more doubtful or spurious character. Each day the pious author prayed in the temple of Mecca, and performed his ablutions with the water of Zemzem: the pages were successively deposited on the pulpit and the sepulchre of the apostle; and the work has been approved by the four orthodox sects of the Sonnites.[96]

The mission of the ancient prophets, of Moses and of Jesus, had been confirmed by many splendid prodigies; and Mohammed was repeatedly urged, by the inhabitants of Mecca and Medina, to produce a similar evidence of his divine legation; to call down from heaven the angel or the volume of his revelation, to create a garden in the desert, or to kindle a conflagration in the unbelieving city. As often as he is pressed by the demands of the Koreish, he involves himself in the obscure boast of vision and prophecy, appeals to the internal proofs of his doctrine, and shields himself behind the providence of God, who refuses those signs and wonders that would depreciate the merit of faith and aggravate the guilt of infidelity. But the modest or angry tone of his apologies betrays his weakness and vexation; and these passages of scandal established beyond suspicion the integrity of the Koran.[97] The votaries of Mohammed are more assured than himself of his miraculous gifts; and their confidence and credulity increase as they are farther removed from the time and place of his spiritual exploits. They believe or affirm that trees went forth to meet him; that he was saluted by stones; that water gushed from his fingers; that he fed the hungry, cured the sick, and raised the dead; that a beam groaned to him; that a camel complained to him; that a shoulder of mutton informed him of its being poisoned; and that both animate and inanimate nature were equally subject to the apostle of God.[98] His dream of a nocturnal journey is seriously described as a real and corporeal transaction. A mysterious animal, the Borak, conveyed him from the temple of Mecca to that of Jerusalem: with his companion Gabriel he successively ascended the seven heavens, and received and repaid the salutations of the patriarchs, the prophets, and the angels, in their respective mansions. Beyond the seventh heaven Mohammed alone was permitted to proceed; he passed the veil of unity, approached within two bow-shots of the throne, and felt a cold that pierced him to the heart, when his shoulder was touched by the hand of God. After this familiar though important conversation, he again descended to Jerusalem, remounted the Borak, returned to Mecca, and performed in the tenth part of a night the journey of many thousand years.[99] According to another legend, the apostle confounded in a national assembly the malicious challenge of the Koreish. His resistless word split asunder the orb of the moon: the obedient planet stooped from her station in the sky, accomplished the

seven revolutions round the Caaba, saluted Mohammed in the Arabian tongue, and, suddenly contracting her dimensions, entered at the collar, and issued forth through the sleeve, of his shirt.[100] The vulgar are amused with these marvellous tales; but the gravest of the Musulman doctors imitate the modesty of their master, and indulge a latitude of faith or interpretation.[101] They might speciously allege, that in preaching the religion it was needless to violate the harmony of nature; that a creed unclouded with mystery may be excused from miracles; and that the sword of Mohammed was not less potent than the rod of Moses.

The polytheist is oppressed and distracted by the variety of superstition: a thousand rites of Egyptian origin were interwoven with the essence of the Mosaic law; and the spirit of the Gospel had evaporated in the pageantry of the church. The prophet of Mecca was tempted by prejudice, or policy, or patriotism, to sanctify the rites of the Arabians, and the custom of visiting the holy stone of the Caaba. But the precepts of Mohammed himself inculcate a more simple and rational piety: prayer, fasting, and alms are the religious duties of a Musulman; and he is encouraged to hope that prayer will carry him half way to God, fasting will bring him to the door of his palace, and alms will gain him admittance.[102] I. According to the tradition of the nocturnal journey, the apostle, in his personal conference with the Deity, was commanded to impose on his disciples the daily obligation of fifty prayers. By the advice of Moses, he applied for an alleviation of this intolerable burden; the number was gradually reduced to five; without any dispensation of business or pleasure, or time or place: the devotion of the faithful is repeated at daybreak, at noon, in the afternoon, in the evening, and at the first watch of the night; and in the present decay of religious fervour, our travellers are edified by the profound humility and attention of the Turks and Persians. Cleanliness is the key of prayer: the frequent lustration of the hands, the face, and the body, which was practised of old by the Arabs, is solemnly enjoined by the Koran; and a permission is formally granted to supply with sand the scarcity of water. The words and attitudes of supplication, as it is performed either sitting, or standing, or prostrate on the ground, are prescribed by custom or authority; but the prayer is poured forth in short and fervent ejaculations; the measure of zeal is not exhausted by a tedious liturgy; and each Musulman for his own person is invested with the character of a priest. Among the theists, who reject the use of images, it has been found necessary to restrain the wanderings of the fancy, by directing the eye and the thought towards a *kebla* or visible point of the horizon. The prophet was at first inclined to gratify the Jews by the choice of Jerusalem; but he soon returned to a more natural partiality; and five times every day the eyes of the nations at Astracan, at Fez, at Delhi, are devoutly turned to the holy temple of Mecca. Yet every spot for the service of God is equally pure: the Mohammedans indifferently pray in their chamber or in the street. As a distinction from the Jews and Christians, the Friday in each week is set apart for the useful institution of public worship: the people is assembled in the mosch; and the imam, some respectable elder, ascends the pulpit, to begin the prayer and pronounce the sermon. But the Mohammedan religion is destitute of priesthood or sacrifice; and the independent spirit of fanaticism looks down with contempt on the ministers and the slaves of superstition. II. The voluntary[103] penance of the ascetics, the torment and glory of their lives, was odious to a prophet who censured in his companions a rash vow of abstaining from flesh, and women, and sleep; and firmly declared that he would suffer no monks in his religion.[104] Yet he instituted, in each year, a fast of thirty days; and strenuously recommended the observance as a discipline which purifies the soul and subdues the body, as a salutary exercise of obedience to the will of God and his apostle. During the month of Ramadan, from the rising to the setting of the sun, the Musulman abstains from eating, and drinking, and women, and baths, and perfumes; from all nourishment that can restore his strength, from all pleasure that can gratify his senses. In the revolution of the lunar year, the Ramadan coincides, by turns, with the winter cold and the summer heat; and the patient martyr, without assuaging his thirst with a drop of water, must expect the close of a tedious and sultry day. The interdiction of wine, peculiar to some orders of priests or hermits, is converted by Mohammed alone into a positive and general law;[105] and a considerable portion of the globe has abjured, at his command, the use of that salutary, though dangerous, liquor. These painful restraints are, doubtless, infringed by the libertine, and eluded by the hypocrite; but the legislator, by whom they are enacted, cannot surely be accused of alluring his proselytes by the indulgence of their sensual appetites. III. The charity of the Mohammedans descends to the animal creation; and the Koran repeatedly inculcates, not as a merit, but as a strict and indispensable duty, the relief of the indigent and unfortunate. Mohammed, perhaps, is the only lawgiver who has defined the precise measure of charity: the standard may vary with the degree and nature of property, as it consists either in money, in corn or cattle, in fruits or merchandise: but the Musulman does not accomplish the law, unless he bestows a *tenth* of his revenue; and if his conscience accuses him of fraud or extortion, the tenth, under the idea of restitution, is enlarged to a *fifth*.[106] Benevolence is the foundation of justice, since we are forbid to injure those whom we are bound to assist. A prophet may reveal the secrets of heaven and of futurity; but in his moral precepts he can only repeat the lessons of our own hearts.

The two articles of belief, and the four practical duties, of Islam, are guarded by rewards and punishments; and the faith of the Musulman is devoutly fixed on the event of the judgment and the last day. The prophet has not presumed to determine the moment of that awful catastrophe, though he darkly announces the signs, both in heaven and earth, which will precede the universal dissolution, when life shall be destroyed, and the order of creation shall be confounded in the primitive chaos. At the blast of the trumpet new worlds will start into being; angels, genii, and men will arise from the dead, and the human soul will again be united to the body. The doctrine of the resurrection was first entertained by the Egyptians;[107] and their mummies were embalmed, their pyramids were constructed, to preserve the ancient mansion of the soul during a period of three thousand years. But the attempt is partial and unavailing; and it is with a more philosophic spirit that Mohammed relies on the omnipotence of the Creator, whose word can re-animate the breathless clay, and collect the innumerable atoms that no longer retain their form or substance.[108] The intermediate state of the soul it is hard to decide; and those who most firmly believe her immaterial nature, are at a loss to understand how she can think or act without the agency of the organs of sense.

The re-union of the soul and body will be followed by the final judgment of mankind; and in his copy of the Magian picture, the prophet has too faithfully represented the forms of proceeding, and even the slow and successive operations, of an earthly tribunal. By his intolerant adversaries he is upbraided for extending, even to themselves, the hope of salvation; for asserting the blackest heresy, that every man who believes in God, and accomplishes good works, may expect in the last day a favourable sentence. Such rational indifference is ill adapted to the character of a fanatic; nor is it probable that a messenger from heaven should depreciate the value and necessity of his own revelation. In the idiom of the Koran,[109] the belief of God is inseparable from that of Mohammed: the good works are those which he has enjoined; and the two qualifications imply the profession of Islam, to which all nations and all sects are equally invited. The spiritual blindness, though excused by ignorance and crowned with virtue, will be scourged with everlasting torments; and the tears which Mohammed shed over the tomb of his mother, for whom he was forbidden to pray, display a striking contrast of humanity and enthusiasm.[110] The doom of the infidels is common: the measure of their guilt and punishment is determined by the degree of evidence which they have rejected, by the magnitude of the errors which they have entertained: the eternal mansions of the Christians, the Jews, the Sabians, the Magians, and the idolaters are sunk below each other in the abyss; and the lowest hell is reserved for the faithless hypocrites who have assumed the mask of religion. After the greater part of mankind has been condemned for their opinions, the true believers only will be judged by their actions. The good and evil of each Musulman will be accurately weighed in a real or allegorical balance; and a singular mode of compensation will be allowed for the payment of injuries: the aggressor will refund an equivalent of his own good actions, for the benefit of the person whom he has wronged; and if he should be destitute of any moral property, the weight of his sins will be loaded with an adequate share of the demerits of the sufferer. According as the shares of guilt or virtue shall preponderate, the sentence will be pronounced, and all, without distinction, will pass over the sharp and perilous bridge of the abyss; but the innocent, treading in the footsteps of Mohammed, will gloriously enter the gates of paradise, while the guilty will fall into the first and mildest of the seven hells. The term of expiation will vary from nine hundred to seven thousand years; but the prophet has judiciously promised that *all* his disciples, whatever may be their sins, shall be saved, by their own faith and his intercession, from eternal damnation. It is not surprising that superstition should act most powerfully on the fears of her votaries, since the human fancy can paint with more energy the misery than the bliss of a future life. With the two simple elements of darkness and fire we create a sensation of pain, which may be aggravated to an infinite degree by the idea of endless duration. But the same idea operates with an opposite effect on the continuity of pleasure; and too much of our present enjoyments is obtained from the relief, or the comparison, of evil. It is natural enough that an Arabian prophet should dwell with rapture on the groves, the fountains, and the rivers of paradise; but instead of inspiring the blessed inhabitants with a liberal taste for harmony and science, conversation and friendship, he idly celebrates the pearls and diamonds, the robes of silk, palaces of marble, dishes of gold, rich wines, artificial dainties, numerous attendants, and the whole train of sensual and costly luxury, which becomes insipid to the owner, even in the short period of this mortal life. Seventy-two *Houris*, or black-eyed girls, of resplendent beauty, blooming youth, virgin purity, and exquisite sensibility, will be created for the use of the meanest believer; a moment of pleasure will be prolonged to a thousand years, and his faculties will be increased a hundred fold, to render him worthy of his felicity. Notwithstanding a vulgar prejudice, the gates of heaven will be open to both sexes; but Mohammed has not specified the male companions of the female elect, lest he should either alarm the jealousy of their former husbands, or disturb their felicity by the suspicion of an everlasting marriage. This image of a carnal paradise has provoked the indignation, perhaps the envy, of the monks: they declaim against the impure religion of Mohammed; and his modest apologists are driven to the poor excuse of figures and allegories. But the sounder and more consistent party adhere, without shame, to the literal interpretation of the Koran: useless would be the resurrection of the body, unless it were restored to the possession and exercise of its worthiest faculties; and the union of sensual and intellectual enjoyment is requisite to complete the happiness of the double animal, the perfect man. Yet the joys of the Mohammedan paradise will not be confined to the indulgence of luxury and appetite; and the prophet has expressly declared that all meaner happiness will be forgotten and despised by the saints and martyrs, who shall be admitted to the beatitude of the divine vision.[111]

The first and most arduous conquests of Mohammed[112] were those of his wife, his servant, his pupil, and his friend;[113] since he presented himself as a prophet to those who were most conversant with his infirmities as a man. Yet Cadijah believed the words, and cherished the glory, of her husband; the obsequious and affectionate Zeid was tempted by the prospect of freedom; the illustrious Ali, the son of Abu Taleb, embraced the sentiments of his cousin with the spirit of a youthful hero; and the wealth, the moderation, the veracity of Abubeker, confirmed the religion of the prophet whom he was destined to succeed. By his persuasion ten of the most respectable citizens of Mecca were introduced to the private lessons of Islam; they yielded to the voice of reason and enthusiasm; they repeated the fundamental creed, 'there is but one God, and Mohammed is the apostle of God;" and their faith, even in this life, was rewarded with riches and honours, with the command of armies and the government of kingdoms. Three years were silently employed in the conversion of fourteen proselytes, the first-fruits of his mission; but in the fourth year he assumed the prophetic office, and, resolving to impart to his family the light of divine truth, he prepared a banquet, a lamb, as it is said, and a bowl of milk, for the entertainment of forty guests of the race of Hashem. "Friends and kinsmen," said Mohammed to the assembly, "I offer you, and I alone can offer, the most precious of gifts, the treasures of this world and of the world to come. God has commanded me to call you to his service. Who among you will support my burden? Who among you will be my companion and my vizir?"[114] No answer was returned, till the silence of astonishment, and doubt, and contempt was at length broken by the impatient courage of Ali, a youth in the fourteenth year of his age. "O prophet, I am the man: whosoever rises against thee, I will dash out his teeth, tear out his eyes, break his legs, rip up his belly. O prophet, I will be thy vizir over them." Mohammed accepted his offer with transport, and Abu Taleb was ironically exhorted to respect the superior dignity of his son. In a more serious tone, the father of Ali advised his nephew to relinquish his impracticable design. "Spare your remonstrances," replied the intrepid fanatic to his uncle and benefactor; "if they should place the sun on my right hand, and the moon on my left, they should not divert me from my course." He persevered ten years in the exercise of his mission; and the religion which has overspread the East and the West advanced with a slow and painful progress within the walls of Mecca. Yet Mohammed enjoyed the satisfaction of beholding the increase of his infant congregation of Unitarians, who revered him as a prophet, and to whom he seasonally dispensed the spiritual nourishment of the Koran. The number of proselytes may be esteemed by the absence of eighty-three men and eighteen women, who retired to Æthiopia in the seventh year of his mission; and his party was fortified by the timely conversion of his uncle Hamza, and of the fierce and inflexible Omar, who signalised in the cause of Islam same zeal which he had exerted for its destruction. Nor was the charity of Mohammed confined to the tribe of Koreish, or the precincts of Mecca: on solemn festivals, in the days of pilgrimage, he frequented the Caaba, accosted the strangers of every tribe, and urged, both in private converse and public discourse, the belief and worship of a sole Deity. Conscious of his reason and of his weakness, he asserted the liberty of conscience, and disclaimed the use of religious violence:[115] but he called the Arabs to repentance, and conjured them to remember the ancient idolaters of Ad and Thamud, whom the divine justice had swept away from the face of the earth.[116]

The people of Mecca were hardened in their unbelief by superstition and envy. The elders of the city, the uncles of the prophet, affected to despise the presumption of an orphan, the reformer of his country: the pious orations of Mohammed in the Caaba were answered by the clamours of Abu Taleb. "Citizens and pilgrims, listen not to the tempter, hearken not to his impious novelties. Stand fast in the worship of Al Lâta and Al Uzzah." Yet the son of Abdallah was ever dear to the aged chief: and he protected the fame and person of his nephew against the assaults of the Koreishites, who had long been jealous of the pre-eminence of the family of Hashem. Their malice was coloured with the pretence of religion: in the age of Job the crime of impiety was punished by the Arabian magistrate;[117] and Mohammed was guilty of deserting and denying the national deities. But so loose was the policy of Mecca, that the leaders of the Koreish, instead of accusing a criminal, were compelled to employ the measures of persuasion or violence. They repeatedly addressed Abu Taleb in the style of reproach and menace. "Thy nephew reviles our religion; he accuses our wise forefathers of ignorance and folly; silence him quickly, lest he kindle tumult and discord in the city. If he persevere, we shall draw our swords against him and his adherents, and thou wilt be responsible for the blood of thy fellow-citizens." The weight and moderation of Abu Taleb eluded the violence of religious faction; the most helpless or timid of the disciples retired to Æthiopia, and the prophet withdrew himself to various places of strength in the town and country. As he was still supported by his family, the rest of the tribe of Koreish engaged themselves to renounce all intercourse with the children of Hashem—neither to buy nor sell, neither to marry nor to give in marriage, but to pursue them with implacable enmity, till they should deliver the person of Mohammed to the justice of the gods. The decree was suspended in the Caaba before the eyes of the nation: the messengers of the Koreish pursued the Musulman exiles in the heart of Africa; they besieged the prophet and his most faithful followers, intercepted their water, and inflamed their mutual animosity by the retaliation of injuries and insults. A doubtful truce restored the appearances of concord, till the death of Abu Taleb abandoned Mohammed to the power of his enemies, at the moment when he was deprived of his domestic comforts by the loss of his faithful and generous Cadijah. Abu Sophian, the chief of the branch of Ommiyah, succeeded to the principality of the republic of Mecca. A zealous votary of the idols, a mortal foe of the line of Hashem, he convened an assembly of the Koreishites and their allies to decide the fate of the apostle. His imprisonment might provoke the despair of his enthusiasm; and the exile of an eloquent and popular fanatic would diffuse the mischief through the provinces of Arabia. His death was resolved; and they agreed that a sword from each tribe should be buried in his heart, to divide the guilt of his blood, and baffle the vengeance of the Hashemites. An angel or a spy revealed their conspiracy, and flight was the only resource of Mohammed.[118] At the dead of night, accompanied by his friend Abubeker, he silently escaped from his house: the assassins watched at the door; but they were deceived by the figure of Ali, who reposed on the bed, and was covered with the green vestment, of the apostle. The Koreish respected the piety of the heroic youth; but some verses of Ali, which are still extant, exhibit an interesting picture of his anxiety, his tenderness, and his religious confidence. Three days Mohammed and his companion were concealed in the cave of Thor, at the distance of a league from Mecca; and in the close of each evening they received from the son and daughter of Abubeker a secret supply of intelligence and food. The diligence of the Koreish explored every haunt in the neighbourhood of the city:

they arrived at the entrance of the cavern; bu the providential deceit of a spider's web and pigeon's nest is supposed to convince them tha the place was solitary and inviolate. "We ar only two," said the trembling Abubeker. "Ther is a third," replied the prophet; "it is God him self." No sooner was the pursuit abated than the two fugitives issued from the rock and mounte their camels: on the road to Medina they wer overtaken by the emissaries of the Koreish; the redeemed themselves with prayers and prom ises from their hands. In this eventful momen the lance of an Arab might have changed th history of the world. The flight of the prophe from Mecca to Medina has fixed the memorabl era of the *Hegira*,[119] which, at the end of twelv centuries, still discriminates the lunar years o the Mohammedan nations.[120]

The religion of the Koran might have per ished in its cradle had not Medina embraced wit faith and reverence the holy outcasts of Mecca Medina, or the *city*, known under the name o Yathreb before it was sanctified by the thron of the prophet, was divided between the tribe of the Charegites and the Awsites, whose hered itary feud was rekindled by the slightest prov ocations: two colonies of Jews, who boasted sacerdotal race, were their humble allies, and without converting the Arabs, they introduce the taste of science and religion, which distin guished Medina as the city of the Book. Some o her noblest citizens, in a pilgrimage to the Caa ba, were converted by the preaching of Mo hammed; on their return they diffused the be lief of God and his prophet, and the new alli ance was ratified by their deputies in two secre and nocturnal interviews on a hill in the sub urbs of Mecca. In the first, ten Charegites an two Awsites, united in faith and love, protested in the name of their wives, their children an their absent brethren, that they would for eve profess the creed and observe the precepts of th Koran. The second was a political association the first vital spark of the empire of the Sara cens.[121] Seventy-three men and two women o Medina held a solemn conference with Moham med, his kinsmen, and his disciples, and pledge themselves to each other by a mutual oath o fidelity. They promised, in the name of the city that if he should be banished they would re ceive him as a confederate, obey him as a leader and defend him to the last extremity, like thei wives and children. "But if you are recalled by your country," they asked with a flattering anxiety, "will you not abandon your new al lies?" "All things," replied Mohammed, with smile, "are now common between us; your blood is as my blood, your ruin as my ruin. We are bound to each other by the ties of honour and interest. I am your friend, and the enemy of your foes." "But if we are killed in your service, what," exclaimed the deputies of Medina, "will be our reward?" "PARADISE," replied the prophet. "Stretch forth thy hand." He stretched it forth, and they reiterated the oath of allegiance and fidelity. Their treaty was ratified by the people, who unanimously embraced the profession of Islam; they rejoiced in the exile of the apostle, but they trembled for his safety, and impatiently expected his arrival. After a perilous and rapid journey along the sea-coast, he halted at Koba, two miles from the city, and made his public entry into Medina, sixteen days after his flight from Mecca. Five hundred of the citizens advanced to meet him; he was hailed with acclamations of loyalty and devotion; Mohammed was mounted on a she-camel, an umbrella shaded his head, and a turban was unfurled before him to supply the deficiency of a standard. His bravest disciples, who had been scattered by the storm, assembled round his person; and the equal, though various, merit of the Moslems was distinguished by the names of *Mohagerians* and *Ansars*, the fugitives of Mecca, and the auxiliaries of Medina. To eradicate the seeds of jealousy, Mohammed judiciously coupled his principal followers with the rights and obligations of brethren; and when Ali found himself without a peer, the prophet tenderly declared that *he* would be the companion and brother of the noble youth. The expedient was crowned with success; the holy fraternity was respected in peace and war, and the two parties vied with each other in a generous emulation of courage and fidelity. Once only the concord was slightly ruffled by an accidental quarrel: a patriot of Medina arraigned the insolence of the strangers, but the hint of their expulsion was heard with abhorrence; and his own son most eagerly offered to lay at the apostle's feet the head of his father.

From his establishment at Medina, Mohammed assumed the exercise of the regal and sacerdotal office; and it was impious to appeal from a judge whose decrees were inspired by the divine wisdom. A small portion of ground, the patrimony of two orphans, was acquired by gift or purchase;[122] on that chosen spot he built a house and a mosch, more venerable in their rude simplicity than the palaces and temples of the Assyrian caliphs. His seal of gold, or silver, was inscribed with the apostolic title; when he prayed and preached in the weekly assembly, he leaned against the trunk of a palm tree; and it was long before he indulged himself in the use of a chair or pulpit of rough timber.[123] After a reign of six years fifteen hundred Moslems, in arms and in the field, renewed their oath of allegiance; and their chief repeated the assurance of protection till the death of the last member, or the final dissolution of the party. It was in the same camp that the deputy of Mecca was astonished by the attention of the faithful to the words and looks of the prophet, by the eagerness with which they collected his spittle, a hair that dropped on the ground, the refuse water of his lustrations, as if they participated in some degree of the prophetic virtue. "I have seen," said he, "the Chosroes of Persia and the Cæsar of Rome, but never did I behold a king among his subjects like Mohammed among his companions." The devout fervour of enthusiasm acts with more energy and truth than the cold and formal servility of courts.

In the state of nature every man has a right to defend, by force of arms, his person and his possessions; to repel, or even to prevent, the violence of his enemies, and to extend his hostilities to a reasonable measure of satisfaction and retaliation. In the free society of the Arabs, the duties of subject and citizen imposed a feeble restraint; and Mohammed, in the exercise of a peaceful and benevolent mission, had been despoiled and banished by the injustice of his countrymen. The choice of an independent people had exalted the fugitive of Mecca to the rank of a sovereign; and he was invested with the just prerogative of forming alliances, and of waging offensive or defensive war. The imperfection of human rights was supplied and armed by the plenitude of divine power: the prophet of Medina assumed, in his new revelations, a fiercer and more sanguinary tone, which proves that his former moderation was the effect of weakness:[124] the means of persuasion had been tried, the season of forbearance was elapsed, and he was now commanded to propagate his religion by the sword, to destroy the monuments of idolatry, and, without regarding the sanctity of days or months, to pursue the unbelieving nations of the earth. The same bloody precepts, so repeatedly inculcated in the Koran, are ascribed by the author to the Pentateuch and the Gospel. But the mild tenor of the evangelic style may explain an ambiguous text, that Jesus did not bring peace on the earth, but a sword: his patient and humble virtues should not be confounded with the intolerant zeal of princes and bishops, who have disgraced the name of his disciples. In the prosecution of religious war, Mohammed might appeal with more propriety to the example of Moses, of the Judges, and the kings of Israel. The military laws of the Hebrews are still more rigid than those of the Arabian legislator.[125] The Lord of hosts marched in person before the Jews: if a city resisted their summons, the males, without distinction, were put to the sword: the seven nations of Canaan were devoted to destruction; and neither repentance nor conversion could shield them from the inevitable doom, that no creature within their precincts should be left alive. The fair option of friendship, or submission, or battle, was proposed to the enemies of Mohammed. If they professed the creed of Islam, they were admitted to all the temporal and spiritual benefits of his primitive disciples, and marched under the same banner to extend the religion which they had embraced. The clemency of the prophet was decided by his interest: yet he seldom trampled on a prostrate enemy; and he seems to promise that on the payment of a tribute the least guilty of his unbelieving subjects might be indulged in their worship, or at least in their imperfect faith. In the first months of his reign he practised the lessons of holy warfare, and displayed his white banner before the gates of Medina: the martial apostle fought in person at nine battles or sieges;[126] and fifty enterprises of war were achieved in ten years by himself or his lieutenants. The Arab continued to unite the professions of a merchant and a robber; and his petty excursions for the defence or the attack of a caravan insensibly prepared his troops for the conquest of Arabia. The distribution of the spoil was regulated by a divine law:[127] the whole was faithfully collected in one common mass: a fifth of the gold and silver, the prisoners and cattle, the movables and immovables, was reserved by the prophet for pious and charitable uses; the remainder was shared in adequate portions by the soldiers who had obtained the victory or guarded the camp: the rewards of the slain devolved to their widows and orphans; and the increase of cavalry was encouraged by the allotment of a double share to the horse and to the man. From all sides the roving Arabs were allured to the standard of religion and plunder: the apostle sanctified the licence of embracing the female captives as their wives or concubines; and the enjoyment of wealth and beauty was a feeble type of the joys of paradise prepared for the valiant martyrs of the faith.

"The sword," says Mohammed, "is the key of heaven and of hell: a drop of blood shed in the cause of God, a night spent in arms, is of more avail than two months of fasting and prayer: whosoever falls in battle, his sins are forgiven: at the day of judgment his wounds shall be resplendent as vermilion, and odoriferous as musk; and the loss of his limbs shall be supplied by the wings of angels and cherubim." The intrepid souls of the Arabs were fired with enthusiasm: the picture of the invisible world was strongly painted on their imagination; and the death which they had always despised became an object of hope and desire. The Koran inculcates, in the most absolute sense, the tenets of fate and predestination, which would extinguish both industry and virtue, if the actions of man were governed by his speculative belief. Yet their influence in every age has exalted the courage of the Saracens and Turks. The first companions of Mohammed advanced to battle with a fearless confidence: there is no danger where there is no chance: they were ordained to perish in their beds; or they were safe and invulnerable amidst the darts of the enemy.[128]

Perhaps the Koreish would have been content with the flight of Mohammed, had they not been provoked and alarmed by the vengeance of an enemy who could intercept their Syrian trade as it passed and repassed through the territory of Medina. Abu Sophian himself, with only thirty or forty followers, conducted a wealthy caravan of a thousand camels; the fortune or dexterity of his march escaped the vigilance of Mohammed; but the chief of the Koreish was informed that the holy robbers were placed in ambush to await his return. He despatched a messenger to his brethren of Mecca, and they were roused, by the fear of losing their merchandise and their provisions, unless they hastened to his relief with the military force of the city. The sacred band of Mohammed was formed of three hundred and thirteen Moslems, of whom seventy-seven were fugitives, and the rest auxiliaries: they mounted by turns a train of seventy camels (the camels of Yathreb were formidable in war); but such was the poverty of his first disciples, that only two could appear on horseback in the field.[129] In the fertile and famous vale of Beder,[130] three stations from Medina, he was informed by his scouts of the caravan that approached on one side; of the Koreish, one hundred horse, eight hundred and fifty foot, who advanced on the other. After a short debate he sacrificed the prospect of wealth to the pursuit of glory and revenge; and a slight ntrenchment was formed to cover his troops, and a stream of fresh water that glided through he valley. "O God," he exclaimed as the numbers of the Koreish descended from the hills, "O God, if these are destroyed, by whom wilt thou be worshipped on the earth?—Courage, my children; close your ranks; discharge your arrows, and the day is your own." At these words he placed himself, with Abubeker, on a throne or pulpit,[131] and instantly demanded the succour of Gabriel and three thousand angels. His eye was fixed on the field of battle: the Musulmans fainted and were pressed: in that decisive moment the prophet started from his throne, mounted his horse, and cast a handful of sand into the air; "Let their faces be covered with confusion." Both armies heard the thunder of his voice: their fancy beheld the angelic warriors:[132] the Koreish trembled and fled: seventy of the bravest were slain; and seventy captives adorned the first victory of the faithful. The dead bodies of the Koreish were despoiled and insulted: two of the most obnoxious prisoners were punished with death; and the ransom of the others, four thousand drachms of silver, compensated in some degree the escape of the caravan. But it was in vain that the camels of Abu Sophian explored a new road through the desert and along the Euphrates: they were overtaken by the diligence of the Musulmans; and wealthy must have been the prize, if twenty thousand drachms could be set apart for the fifth of the apostle. The resentment of the public and private loss stimulated Abu Sophian to collect a body of three thousand men, seven hundred of whom were armed with cuirasses, and two hundred were mounted on horseback; three thousand camels attended his march; and his wife Henda, with fifteen matrons of Mecca, incessantly sounded their timbrels to animate the troops, and to magnify the greatness of Hobal, the most popular deity of the Caaba. The standard of God and Mohammed was upheld by nine hundred and fifty believers: the disproportion of numbers was not more alarming than in the field of Beder, and their presumption of victory prevailed against the divine and human sense of the apostle. The second battle was fought on Mount Ohud, six miles to the north of Medina:[133] the Koreish advanced in the form of a crescent; and the right wing of cavalry was led by Caled, the fiercest and most successful of the Arabian warriors. The troops of Mohammed were skilfully posted on the declivity of the hill; and their rear was guarded by a detachment of fifty archers. The weight of their charge impell-

ed and broke the centre of the idolaters: but in the pursuit they lost the advantage of their ground: the archers deserted their station: the Musulmans were tempted by the spoil, disobeyed their general, and disordered their ranks. The intrepid Caled, wheeling his cavalry on their flank and rear, exclaimed, with a loud voice, that Mohammed was slain. He was indeed wounded in the face with a javelin: two of his teeth were shattered with a stone; yet, in the midst of tumult and dismay, he reproached the infidels with the murder of a prophet; and blessed the friendly hand that stanched his blood, and conveyed him to a place of safety. Seventy martyrs died for the sins of the people; they fell, said the apostle, in pairs, each brother embracing his lifeless companion;[134] their bodies were mangled by the inhuman females of Mecca; and the wife of Abu Sophian tasted the entrails of Hamza, the uncle of Mohammed. They might applaud their superstition and satiate their fury; but the Musulmans soon rallied in the field, and the Koreish wanted strength or courage to undertake the siege of Medina. It was attacked the ensuing year by an army of ten thousand enemies; and this third expedition is variously named, from the *nations* which marched under the banner of Abu Sophian, from the *ditch* which was drawn before the city, and a camp of three thousand Musulmans. The prudence of Mohammed declined a general engagement: the valour of Ali was signalised in single combat; and the war was protracted twenty days, till the final separation of the confederates. A tempest of wind, rain, and hail overturned their tents; their private quarrels were fomented by an insidious adversary; and the Koreish, deserted by their allies, no longer hoped to subvert the throne, or to check the conquests, of their invincible exile.[135]

The choice of Jerusalem for the first kebla of prayer discovers the early propensity of Mohammed in favour of the Jews; and happy would it have been for their temporal interest had they recognized in the Arabian prophet the hope of Israel and the promised Messiah. Their obstinacy converted his friendship into implacable hatred, with which he pursued that unfortunate people to the last moment of his life; and in the double character of an apostle and a conqueror, his persecution was extended to both worlds.[136] The Kainoka dwelt at Medina under the protection of the city: he seized the occasion of an accidental tumult, and summoned them to embrace his religion or contend with him in battle. "Alas," replied the trembling Jews, "we are ignorant of the use of arms, but we persevere in the faith and worship of our fathers; why wilt thou reduce us to the necessity of a just defence?" The unequal conflict was terminated in fifteen days; and it was with extreme reluctance that Mohammed yielded to the importunity of his allies, and consented to spare the lives of the captives. But their riches were confiscated, their arms became more effectual in the hands of the Musulmans; and a wretched colony of seven hundred exiles was driven with their wives and children to implore a refuge on the confines of Syria. The Nadhirites were more guilty, since they conspired in a friendly interview to assassinate the prophet. He besieged their castle, three miles from Medina; but their resolute defence obtained an honourable capitulation; and the garrison, sounding their trumpets and beating their drums was permitted to depart with the honours of war. The Jews had excited and joined the war of the Koreish: no sooner had the *nations* retired from the *ditch*, than Mohammed, without laying aside his armour, marched on the same day to extirpate the hostile race of the children of Koraidha. After a resistance of twenty-five days they surrendered at discretion. They trusted to the intercession of their old allies of Medina: they could not be ignorant that fanaticism obliterates the feelings of humanity. A venerable elder, to whose judgment they appealed, pronounced the sentence of their death: seven hundred Jews were dragged in chains to the market-place of the city; they descended alive into the grave prepared for their execution and burial; and the apostle beheld with an inflexible eye the slaughter of his helpless enemies. Their sheep and camels were inherited by the Musulmans: three hundred cuirasses, five hundred pikes, a thousand lances, composed the most useful portion of the spoil. Six days' journey to the north-east of Medina, the ancient and wealthy town of Chaibar was the seat of the Jewish power in Arabia: the territory, a fertile spot in the desert, was covered with plantations and cattle, and protected by eight castles, some of which were esteemed of impregnable strength. The forces of Mohammed consisted of two hundred horse and fourteen hundred foot: in the succession of eight regular and painful sieges they were exposed to danger, and fatigue, and hunger; and the most undaunted chiefs despaired of the event. The apostle revived their faith and courage by the example of Ali, on whom he bestowed the surname of the Lion of God: perhaps we may believe that a Hebrew champion of gigantic sta-

ture was cloven to the chest by his irresistibl scimitar; but we cannot praise the modesty c romance, which represents him as tearing from its hinges the gate of a fortress and wielding th ponderous buckler in his left hand.[137] After th reduction of the castles the town of Chaiba submitted to the yoke. The chief of the trib was tortured, in the presence of Mohammed, t force a confession of his hidden treasure: th industry of the shepherds and husbandmen wa rewarded with a precarious toleration: the were permitted, so long as it should please th conqueror, to improve their patrimony, in equa shares, for *his* emolument and their own. Unde the reign of Omar, the Jews of Chaibar were transplanted to Syria; and the caliph allege the injunction of his dying master, that one an the true religion should be professed in his na tive land of Arabia.[138]

Five times each day the eyes of Mohammed were turned towards Mecca,[139] and he wa urged by the most sacred and powerful motive to revisit, as a conqueror, the city and the tem ple from whence he had been driven as an exile The Caaba was present to his waking and sleep ing fancy: an idle dream was translated int vision and prophecy; he unfurled the holy ban ner; and a rash promise of success too hastily dropped from the lips of the apostle. His march from Medina to Mecca displayed the peacefu and solemn pomp of a pilgrimage: seventy camels, chosen and bedecked for sacrifice, pre ceded the van; the sacred territory was respect ed; and the captives were dismissed withou ransom to proclaim his clemency and devotion But no sooner did Mohammed descend into the plain, within a day's journey of the city, than he exclaimed, "They have clothed themselves with the skins of tigers:" the numbers and resolution of the Koreish opposed his progress; and the roving Arabs of the desert might desert or betray a leader whom they had followed for the hopes of spoil. The intrepid fanatic sunk into a cool and cautious politician: he waived in the treaty his title of apostle of God; concluded with the Koreish and their allies a truce of ten years engaged to restore the fugitives of Mecca who should embrace his religion; and stipulated only, for the ensuing year, the humble privilege of entering the city as a friend, and of remaining three days to accomplish the rites of the pilgrimage. A cloud of shame and sorrow hung on the retreat of the Musulmans, and their disappointment might justly accuse the failure of a prophet who had so often appealed to the evidence of success. The faith and hope of the pilgrims were rekindled by the prospect of Mecca: their swords were sheathed: seven times in the footsteps of the apostle they encompassed the Caaba: the Koreish had retired to the hills, and Mohammed, after the customary sacrifice, evacuated the city on the fourth day. The people was edified by his devotion; the hostile chiefs were awed, or divided, or seduced; and both Caled and Amrou, the future conquerors of Syria and Egypt, most seasonably deserted the sinking cause of idolatry. The power of Mohammed was increased by the submission of the Arabian tribes; ten thousand soldiers were assembled for the conquest of Mecca; and the idolators, the weaker party, were easily convicted of violating the truce. Enthusiasm and discipline impelled the march, and preserved the secret, till the blaze of ten thousand fires proclaimed to the astonished Koreish the design, the approach, and the irresistible force of the enemy. The haughty Abu Sophian presented the keys of the city; admired the variety of arms and ensigns that passed before him in review; observed that the son of Abdallah had acquired a mighty kingdom; and confessed, under the scimitar of Omar, that he was the apostle of the true God. The return of Marius and Sulla was stained with the blood of the Romans: the revenge of Mohammed was stimulated by religious zeal, and his injured followers were eager to execute or to prevent the order of a massacre. Instead of indulging their passions and his own,[140] the victorious exile forgave the guilt, and united the factions, of Mecca. His troops in three divisions, marched into the city: eight-and-twenty of the inhabitants were slain by the sword of Caled; eleven men and six women were proscribed by the sentence of Mohammed; but he blamed the cruelty of his lieutenant; and several of the most obnoxious victims were indebted for their lives to his clemency or contempt. The chiefs of the Koreish were prostrate at his feet. "What mercy can you expect from the man whom you have wronged?" "We confide in the generosity of our kinsman." "And you shall not confide in vain: begone! you are safe, you are free." The people of Mecca deserved their pardon by the profession of Islam; and after an exile of seven years, the fugitive missionary was enthroned as the prince and prophet of his native country.[141] But the three hundred and sixty idols of the Caaba were ignominiously broken: the house of God was purified and adorned: as an example to future times, the apostle again fulfilled the duties of a pilgrim; and a perpetual law was enacted that no unbeliever should dare to set his foot on the territory of the holy city.[142]

The conquest of Mecca determined the faith and obedience of the Arabian tribes;[143] who, according to the vicissitudes of fortune, had obeyed, or disregarded, the eloquence or the arms of the prophet. Indifference for rites and opinions still marks the character of the Bedoweens; and they might accept, as loosely as they hold, the doctrine of the Koran. Yet an obstinate remnant still adhered to the religion and liberty of their ancestors, and the war of Honain derived a proper appellation from the *idols*, whom Mohammed had vowed to destroy, and whom the confederates of Tayef had sworn to defend.[144] Four thousand Pagans advanced with secrecy and speed to surprise the conqueror: they pitied and despised the supine negligence of the Koreish, but they depended on the wishes, and perhaps the aid, of a people who had so lately renounced their gods, and bowed beneath the yoke of their enemy. The banners of Medina and Mecca were displayed by the prophet; a crowd of Bedoweens increased the strength or numbers of the army, and twelve thousand Musulmans entertained a rash and sinful presumption of their invincible strength. They descended without precaution into the valley of Honain: the heights had been occupied by the archers and slingers of the confederates; their numbers were oppressed, their discipline was confounded, their courage was appalled, and the Koreish smiled at their impending destruction. The prophet, on his white mule, was encompassed by the enemies: he attempted to rush against their spears in search of a glorious death: ten of his faithful companions interposed their weapons and their breasts; three of these fell dead at his feet: "O my brethren," he repeatedly cried with sorrow and indignation, "I am the son of Abdallah, I am the apostle of truth! O man, stand fast in the faith! O God, send down thy succour!" His uncle Abbas, who, like the heroes of Homer, excelled in the loudness of his voice, made the valley resound with the recital of the gifts and promises of God: the flying Moslems returned from all sides to the holy standard; and Mohammed observed with pleasure that the furnace was again rekindled: his conduct and example restored the battle, and he animated his victorious troops to inflict a merciless revenge on the authors of their shame. From the field of Honain he marched without delay to the siege of Tayef, sixty miles to the south-east of Mecca, a fortress of strength, whose fertile lands produce the fruits of Syria in the midst of the Arabian desert. A friendly tribe, instructed (I know not how) in the art of sieges, supplied him with a train of battering-rams and military engines, with a body of five hundred artificers. But it was in vain that he offered freedom to the slaves of Tayef; that he violated his own laws by the extirpation of the fruit-trees; that the ground was opened by the miners; that the breach was assaulted by the troops. After a siege of twenty days the prophet sounded a retreat; but he retreated with a song of devout triumph, and affected to pray for the repentance and safety of the unbelieving city. The spoil of this fortunate expedition amounted to six thousand captives, twenty-four thousand camels, forty thousand sheep, and four thousand ounces of silver: a tribe who had fought at Honain redeemed their prisoners by the sacrifice of their idols: but Mohammed compensated the loss by resigning to the soldiers his fifth of the plunder, and wished, for their sake, that he possessed as many head of cattle as there were trees in the province of Tehama. Instead of chastising the disaffection of the Koreish, he endeavoured to cut out their tongues (his own expression), and to secure their attachment, by a superior measure of liberality: Abu Sophian alone was presented with three hundred camels and twenty ounces of silver; and Mecca was sincerely converted to the profitable religion of the Koran.

The *fugitives* and *auxiliaries* complained that they who had borne the burden were neglected in the season of victory. "Alas!" replied their artful leader, "suffer me to conciliate these recent enemies, these doubtful proselytes, by the gift of some perishable goods. To your guard I intrust my life and fortunes. You are the companions of my exile, of my kingdom, of my paradise." He was followed by the deputies of Tayef, who dreaded the repetition of a siege. "Grant us, O apostle of God! a truce of three years with the toleration of our ancient worship." "Not a month, not an hour." "Excuse us at least from the obligation of prayer." "Without prayer religion is of no avail." They submitted in silence: their temples were demolished, and the same sentence of destruction was executed on all the idols of Arabia. His lieutenants, on the shores of the Red Sea, the Ocean, and the Gulf of Persia, were saluted by the acclamations of a faithful people; and the ambassadors who knelt before the throne of Medina were as numerous (says the Arabian proverb) as the dates that fall from the maturity of a palm-tree. The nation submitted to the

God and the sceptre of Mohammed: the opprobrious name of tribute was abolished: the spontaneous or reluctant oblations of alms and tithes were applied to the service of religion; and one hundred and fourteen thousand Moslems accompanied the last pilgrimage of the apostle.[145]

When Heraclius returned in triumph from the Persian war, he entertained, at Emesa, one of the ambassadors of Mohammed, who invited the princes and nations of the earth to the profession of Islam. On this foundation the zeal of the Arabians has supposed the secret conversion of the Christian emperor: the vanity of the Greeks has feigned a personal visit of the prince of Medina, who accepted from the royal bounty a rich domain, and a secure retreat, in the province of Syria.[146] But the friendship of Heraclius and Mohammed was of short continuance: the new religion had inflamed rather than assuaged the rapacious spirit of the Saracens; and the murder of an envoy afforded a decent pretence for invading, with three thousand soldiers, the territory of Palestine, that extends to the eastward of the Jordan. The holy banner was intrusted to Zeid; and such was the discipline and enthusiasm of the rising sect, that the noblest chiefs served without reluctance under the slave of the prophet. On the event of his decease Jaafar and Abdallah were successively substituted to the command; and if the three should perish in the war, the troops were authorised to elect their general. The three leaders were slain in the battle of Muta,[147] the first military action which tried the valour of the Moslems against a foreign enemy. Zeid fell, like a soldier, in the foremost ranks: the death of Jaafar was heroic and memorable: he lost his right hand: he shifted the standard to his left: the left was severed from his body: he embraced the standard with his bleeding stumps, till he was transfixed to the ground with fifty honourable wounds. "Advance," cried Abdallah, who stepped into the vacant place, "advance with confidence: either victory or paradise is our own." The lance of a Roman decided the alternative; but the falling standard was rescued by Caled, the proselyte of Mecca: nine swords were broken in his hand; and his valour withstood and repulsed the superior numbers of the Christians. In the nocturnal council of the camp he was chosen to command: his skilful evolutions of the ensuing day secured either the victory or the retreat of the Saracens; and Caled is renowned among his brethren and his enemies by the glorious appellation of the *Sword of God*. In the pulpit, Mohammed described, with prophetic rapture, the crowns of the blessed martyrs; but in private he betrayed the feelings of human nature: he was surprised as he wept over the daughter of Zeid: "What do I see?" said the astonished votary. "You see," replied the apostle, "a friend who is deploring the loss of his most faithful friend." After the conquest of Mecca the sovereign of Arabia affected to prevent the hostile preparations of Heraclius; and solemnly proclaimed war against the Romans, without attempting to disguise the hardships and dangers of the enterprise.[148] The Moslems were discouraged: they alleged the want of money, or horses, or provisions; the season of harvest, and the intolerable heat of the summer: "Hell is much hotter," said the indignant prophet. He disdained to compel their service: but on his return he admonished the most guilty by an excommunication of fifty days. Their desertion enhanced the merit of Abubeker, Othman, and the faithful companions who devoted their lives and fortunes; and Mohammed displayed his banner at the head of ten thousand horse and twenty thousand foot. Painful indeed was the distress of the march: lassitude and thirst were aggravated by the scorching and pestilential winds of the desert: ten men rode by turns on the same camel; and they were reduced to the shameful necessity of drinking the water from the belly of that useful animal. In the midway, ten days' journey from Medina and Damascus, they reposed near the grove and fountain of Tabuc. Beyond that place Mohammed declined the prosecution of the war: he declared himself satisfied with the peaceful intentions, he was more probably daunted by the martial array, of the emperor of the East. But the active and intrepid Caled spread around the terror of his name; and the prophet received the submission of the tribes and cities, from the Euphrates to Ailah, at the head of the Red Sea. To his Christian subjects Mohammed readily granted the security of their persons, the freedom of their trade, the property of their goods, and the toleration of their worship.[149] The weakness of their Arabian brethren had restrained them from opposing his ambition; the disciples of Jesus were endeared to the enemy of the Jews; and it was the interest of a conqueror to propose a fair capitulation to the most powerful religion of the earth.

Till the age of sixty-three years the strength of Mohammed was equal to the temporal and spiritual fatigues of his mission. His epileptic fits, an absurd calumny of the Greeks, would be an object of pity rather than abhorrence;[150] but he seriously believed that he was poisoned at Chaibar by the revenge of a Jewish female.[151] During four years the health of the prophet declined; his infirmities increased; but his mortal disease was a fever of fourteen days, which deprived him by intervals of the use of reason. As soon as he was conscious of his danger, he edified his brethren by the humility of his virtue or penitence. "If there be any man," said the apostle from the pulpit, "whom I have unjustly scourged, I submit my own back to the lash of retaliation. Have I aspersed the reputation of a Musulman? let him proclaim my faults in the face of the congregation. Has any one been despoiled of his goods? the little that I possess shall compensate the principal and the interest of the debt." "Yes," replied a voice from the crowd, "I am entitled to three drachms of silver." Mohammed heard the complaint, satisfied the demand, and thanked his creditor for accusing him in this world rather than at the day of judgment. He beheld with temperate firmness the approach of death; enfranchised his slaves (seventeen men, as they are named, and eleven women); minutely directed the order of his funeral; and moderated the lamentations of his weeping friends, on whom he bestowed the benediction of peace. Till the third day before his death he regularly performed the function of public prayer: the choice of Abubeker to supply his place appeared to mark that ancient and faithful friend as his successor in the sacerdotal and regal office; but he prudently declined the risk and envy of a more explicit nomination. At a moment when his faculties were visibly impaired, he called for pen and ink to write, or, more properly, to dictate, a divine book, the sum and accomplishment of all his revelations: a dispute arose in the chamber whether he should be allowed to supersede the authority of the Koran; and the prophet was forced to reprove the indecent vehemence of his disciples. If the slightest credit may be afforded to the traditions of his wives and companions, he maintained, in the bosom of his family, and to the last moments of his life, the dignity of an apostle, and the faith of an enthusiast; described the visits of Gabriel, who bid an everlasting farewell to the earth; and expressed his lively confidence, not only of the mercy, but of the favour of the Supreme Being. In a familiar discourse he had mentioned his special prerogative, that the angel of death was not allowed to take his soul till he had respectfully asked the permission of the prophet. The request was granted; and Mohammed immediately fell into the agony of his dissolution: his head was reclined on the lap of Ayesha, the best beloved of all his wives; he fainted with the violence of pain; recovering his spirits, he raised his eyes towards the roof of the house, and, with a steady look, though a faltering voice, uttered the last broken, though articulate, words: "O God! . . . pardon my sins . . . Yes . . . I come . . . among my fellow citizens on high;" and thus peaceably expired on a carpet spread upon the floor. An expedition for the conquest of Syria was stopped by this mournful event: the army halted at the gates of Medina; the chiefs were assembled round their dying master. The city, more especially the house, of the prophet, was a scene of clamorous sorrow or silent despair: fanaticism alone could suggest a ray of hope and consolation. "How can he be dead, our witness, our intercessor, our mediator, with God? By God he is not dead: like Moses and Jesus, he is wrapt in a holy trance, and speedily will he return to his faithful people." The evidence of sense was disregarded; and Omar, unsheathing his scimitar, threatened to strike off the heads of the infidels who should dare to affirm that the prophet was no more. The tumult was appeased by the weight and moderation of Abubeker. "Is it Mohammed," said he to Omar and the multitude, "or the God of Mohammed, whom you worship? The God of Mohammed liveth for ever; but the apostle was a mortal like ourselves, and, according to his own prediction, he has experienced the common fate of mortality." He was piously interred by the hands of his nearest kinsman, on the same spot on which he expired:[152] Medina has been sanctified by the death and burial of Mohammed; and the innumerable pilgrims of Mecca often turn aside from the way, to bow, in voluntary devotion,[153] before the simple tomb of the prophet.[154]

At the conclusion of the life of Mohammed it may perhaps be expected that I should balance his faults and virtues, that I should decide whether the title of enthusiast or impostor more properly belongs to that extraordinary man. Had I been intimately conversant with the son of Abdallah, the task would still be difficult, and the success uncertain: at the distance of twelve centuries I darkly contemplate his shade through a cloud of religious incense; and could I truly delineate the portrait of an hour, the fleeting resemblance would not equally apply to the solitary of Mount Hera, to the preacher of Mecca, and to the conqueror of Arabia. The author of a mighty revolution appears to have

been endowed with a pious and contemplative disposition: so soon as marriage had raised him above the pressure of want, he avoided the paths of ambition and avarice; and till the age of forty he lived with innocence, and would have died without a name. The unity of God is an idea most congenial to nature and reason; and a slight conversation with the Jews and Christians would teach him to despise and detest the idolatry of Mecca. It was the duty of a man and a citizen to impart the doctrine of salvation, to rescue his country from the dominion of sin and error. The energy of a mind incessantly bent on the same object would convert a general obligation into a particular call; the warm suggestions of the understanding or the fancy would be felt as the inspirations of Heaven; the labour of thought would expire in rapture and vision; and the inward sensation, the invisible monitor, would be described with the form and attributes of an angel of God.[155] From enthusiasm to imposture the step is perilous and slippery; the demon of Socrates[156] affords a memorable instance how a wise man may deceive himself, how a good man may deceive others, how the conscience may slumber in a mixed and middle state between self-illusion and voluntary fraud. Charity may believe that the original motives of Mohammed were those of pure and genuine benevolence; but a human missionary is incapable of cherishing the obstinate unbelievers who reject his claims, despise his arguments, and persecute his life; he might forgive his personal adversaries, he may lawfully hate the enemies of God; the stern passion of pride and revenge were kindled in the bosom of Mohammed, and he sighed, like the prophet of Nineveh, for the destruction of the rebels whom he had condemned. The injustice of Mecca and the choice of Medina transformed the citizen into a prince, the humble preacher into the leader of armies; but his sword was consecrated by the example of the saints; and the same God who afflicts a sinful world with pestilence and earthquakes might inspire for their conversion or chastisement the valour of his servants. In the exercise of political government he was compelled to abate of the stern rigour of fanaticism, to comply in some measure with the prejudices and passions of his followers, and to employ even the vices of mankind as the instruments of their salvation. The use of fraud and perfidy, of cruelty and injustice, were often subservient to the propagation of the faith; and Mohammed commanded or approved the assassination of the Jews and idolaters who had escaped from he field of battle. By the repetition of such acts he character of Mohammed must have been gradually stained; and the influence of such pernicious habits would be poorly compensated by the practice of the personal and social virtues which are necessary to maintain the reputation of a prophet among his sectaries and friends. Of his last years ambition was the ruling passion; and a politician will suspect that he secretly smiled (the victorious impostor!) at the enthusiasm of his youth, and the credulity of his proselytes.[157] A philosopher will observe that *their* credulity and *his* success would tend more strongly to fortify the assurance of his divine mission, that his interest and religion were inseparably connected, and that his conscience would be soothed by the persuasion that he alone was absolved by the Deity from the obligation of positive and moral laws. If he retained any vestige of his native innocence, the sins of Mohammed may be allowed as an evidence of his sincerity. In the support of truth, the arts of fraud and fiction may be deemed less criminal; and he would have started at the foulness of the means, had he not been satisfied of the importance and justice of the end. Even in a conqueror or a priest I can surprise a word or action of unaffected humanity; and the decree of Mohammed, that, in the sale of captives, the mothers should never be separated from their children, may suspend, or moderate, the censure of the historian.[158]

The good sense of Mohammed[159] despised the pomp of royalty; the apostle of God submitted to the menial offices of the family; he kindled the fire, swept the floor, milked the ewes, and mended with his own hands his shoes and his woollen garment. Disdaining the penance and merit of a hermit, he observed, without effort or vanity, the abstemious diet of an Arab and a soldier. On solemn occasions he feasted his companions with rustic and hospitable plenty; but in his domestic life many weeks would elapse without a fire being kindled on the hearth of the prophet. The interdiction of wine was confirmed by his example; his hunger was appeased with a sparing allowance of barley-bread: he delighted in the taste of milk and honey; but his ordinary food consisted of dates and water. Perfumes and women were the two sensual enjoyments which his nature required, and his religion did not forbid; and Mohammed affirmed that the fervour of his devotion was increased by these innocent pleasures. The heat of the climate inflames the blood of the Arabs, and their libidinous complexion has been noticed by the writers of antiquity.[160] Their incontinence was regulated by the civil and religious laws of the Koran: their incestuous alliances were blamed: the boundless licence of polygamy was reduced to four legitimate wives or concubines; their rights both of bed and of dowry were equitably determined; the freedom of divorce was discouraged; adultery was condemned as a capital offence; and fornication, in either sex, was punished with a hundred stripes.[161] Such were the calm and rational precepts of the legislator; but in his private conduct Mohammed indulged the appetites of a man, and abused the claims of a prophet. A special revelation dispensed him from the laws which he had imposed on his nation; the female sex, without reserve, was abandoned to his desires; and this singular prerogative excited the envy rather than the scandal, the veneration rather than the envy, of the devout Musulmans. If we remember the seven hundred wives and three hundred concubines of the wise Solomon, we shall applaud the modesty of the Arabian, who espoused no more than seventeen or fifteen wives; eleven are enumerated who occupied at Medina their separate apartments round the house of the apostle, and enjoyed in their turns the favour of his conjugal society. What is singular enough, they were all widows, excepting only Ayesha, the daughter of Abubeker. *She* was doubtless a virgin, since Mohammed consummated his nuptials (such is the premature ripeness of the climate) when she was only nine years of age. The youth, the beauty, the spirit of Ayesha gave her a superior ascendant: she was beloved and trusted by the prophet; and, after his death, the daughter of Abubeker was long revered as the mother of the faithful. Her behaviour had been ambiguous and indiscreet: in a nocturnal march she was accidentally left behind, and in the morning Ayesha returned to the camp with a man. The temper of Mohammed was inclined to jealousy; but a divine revelation assured him of her innocence: he chastised her accusers, and published a law of domestic peace, that no woman should be condemned unless four male witnesses had seen her in the act of adultery.[162] In his adventures with Zeineb, the wife of Zeid, and with Mary, an Egyptian captive, the amorous prophet forgot the interest of his reputation. At the house of Zeid, his freedman and adopted son, he beheld, in a loose undress, the beauty of Zeineb, and burst forth into an ejaculation of devotion and desire. The servile, or grateful, freedman understood the hint, and yielded without hesitation

to the love of his benefactor. But as the filial relation had excited some doubt and scandal, the
angel Gabriel descended from heaven to ratify
the deed, to annul the adoption, and gently to
reprove the apostle for distrusting the indulgence of his God. One of his wives, Hafna, the
daughter of Omar, surprised him on her own
bed in the embraces of his Egyptian captive:
she promised secrecy and forgiveness: he swore
that he would renounce the possession of Mary.
Both parties forgot their engagements; and
Gabriel again descended with a chapter of the
Koran to absolve him from his oath, and to
exhort him freely to enjoy his captives and
concubines without listening to the clamours of
his wives. In a solitary retreat of thirty days he
laboured alone with Mary to fulfill the commands of the angel. When his love and revenge
were satiated, he summoned to his presence his
eleven wives, reproached their disobedience
and indiscretion, and threatened them with a
sentence of divorce, both in this world and in
the next—a dreadful sentence, since those who
had ascended the bed of a prophet were forever excluded from the hope of a second marriage. Perhaps the incontinence of Mohammed
may be palliated by the tradition of his natural
or preternatural gifts:[163] he united the manly
virtue of thirty of the children of Adam; and the
apostle might rival the thirteenth labour[164] of
the Grecian Hercules.[165] A more serious and
decent excuse may be drawn from his fidelity to
Cadijah. During the twenty-four years of their
marriage her youthful husband abstained from
the right of polygamy, and the pride or tenderness of the venerable matron was never insulted
by the society of a rival. After her death he
placed her in the rank of the four perfect wom-
en, with the sister of Moses, the mother of Jesus,
and Fatima, the best beloved of his daughters.
"Was she not old?" said Ayesha, with the insolence of a blooming beauty; "has not God given
you a better in her place?" "No, by God," said
Mohammed, with an effusion of honest gratitude, "there never can be a better! She believed
in me when men despised me; she relieved my
wants when I was poor and persecuted by the
world."[166]

In the largest indulgence of polygamy, the
founder of a religion and empire might aspire
to multiply the chances of a numerous posterity
and a lineal succession. The hopes of Mohammed were fatally disappointed. The virgin Ayesha, and his ten widows of mature age and approved fertility, were barren in his potent embraces. The four sons of Cadijah died in their
infancy. Mary, his Egyptian concubine, was endeared to him by the birth of Ibrahim. At the
end of fifteen months the prophet wept over his
grave; but he sustained with firmness the raillery of his enemies, and checked the adulation
or credulity of the Moslems by the assurance
that an eclipse of the sun was *not* occasioned by
the death of the infant. Cadijah had likewise
given him four daughters, who were married to
the most faithful of his disciples: the three eldest
died before their father; but Fatima, who possessed his confidence and love, became the wife
of her cousin Ali, and the mother of an illustrious progeny. The merit and misfortunes of Ali
and his descendants will lead me to anticipate,
in this place, the series of the Saracen caliphs, a
title which describes the commanders of the
faithful as the vicars and successors of the apostle of God.[167]

The birth, the alliance, the character of Ali,
which exalted him above the rest of his countrymen, might justify his claim to the vacant throne
of Arabia. The son of Abu Taleb was, in his own
right, the chief of the family of Hashem, and the
hereditary prince or guardian of the city and
temple of Mecca. The light of prophecy was extinct; but the husband of Fatima might expect
the inheritance and blessing of her father: the
Arabs had sometimes been patient of a female
reign; and the two grandsons of the prophet
had often been fondled in his lap, and shown in
his pulpit, as the hope of his age, and the chief
of the youth of paradise. The first of the true
believers might aspire to march before them in
this world and in the next; and if some were of
a graver and more rigid cast, the zeal and virtue
of Ali were never outstripped by any recent
proselyte. He united the qualifications of a poet,
a soldier, and a saint: his wisdom still breathes
in a collection of moral and religious sayings;[168]
and every antagonist, in the combats of the
tongue or of the sword, was subdued by his eloquence and valour. From the first hour of his
mission to the last rites of his funeral, the apostle
was never forsaken by a generous friend, whom
he delighted to name his brother, his vicegerent,
and the faithful Aaron of a second Moses. The
son of Abu Taleb was afterwards reproached
for neglecting to secure his interest by a solemn
declaration of his right, which would have silenced all competition, and sealed his succession by the decrees of Heaven. But the unsuspecting hero confided in himself: the jealousy
of empire, and perhaps the fear of opposition,
might suspend the resolutions of Mohammed;
and the bed of sickness was besieged by the art-

ful Ayesha, the daughter of Abubeker, and the enemy of Ali.

The silence and death of the prophet restored the liberty of the people; and his companions convened an assembly to deliberate on the choice of his successor. The hereditary claim and lofty spirit of Ali were offensive to an aristocracy of elders, desirous of bestowing and resuming the sceptre by a free and frequent election: the Koreish could never be reconciled to the proud pre-eminence of the line of Hashem: the ancient discord of the tribes was rekindled; the *fugitives* of Mecca and the *auxiliaries* of Medina asserted their respective merits; and the rash proposal of choosing two independent caliphs would have crushed in their infancy the religion and empire of the Saracens. The tumult was appeased by the disinterested resolution of Omar, who, suddenly renouncing his own pretensions, stretched forth his hand and declared himself the first subject of the mild and venerable Abubeker. The urgency of the moment, and the acquiescence of the people, might excuse this illegal and precipitate measure; but Omar himself confessed from the pulpit, that, if any Musulman should hereafter presume to anticipate the suffrage of his brethren, both the elector and the elected would be worthy of death.[169] After the simple inauguration of Abubeker, he was obeyed in Medina, Mecca, and the provinces of Arabia: the Hashemites alone declined the oath of fidelity; and their chief, in his own house, maintained above six months a sullen and independent reserve, without listening to the threats of Omar, who attempted to consume with fire the habitation of the daughter of the apostle. The death of Fatima, and the decline of his party, subdued the indignant spirit of Ali: he condescended to salute the commander of the faithful, accepted his excuse of the necessity of preventing their common enemies, and wisely rejected his courteous offer of abdicating the government of the Arabians. After a reign of two years the aged caliph was summoned by the angel of death. In his testament, with the tacit approbation of the companions, he bequeathed the sceptre to the firm and intrepid virtue of Omar. "I have no occasion," said the modest candidate, "for the place." "But the place has occasion for you," replied Abubeker; who expired with a fervent prayer that the God of Mohammed would ratify his choice, and direct the Musulmans in the way of concord and obedience. The prayer was not ineffectual, since Ali himself, in a life of privacy and prayer, professed to revere the superior worth and dignity of his rival, who comforted him for the loss of empire by the most flattering marks of confidence and esteem. In the twelfth year of his reign Omar received a mortal wound from the hand of an assassin: he rejected with equal impartiality the names of his son and of Ali, refused to load his conscience with the sins of his successor, and devolved on six of the most respectable companions the arduous task of electing a commander of the faithful. On this occasion Ali was again blamed by his friends[170] for submitting his right to the judgment of men, for recognising their jurisdiction by accepting a place among the six electors. He might have obtained their suffrage had he deigned to promise a strict and servile conformity, not only to the Koran and tradition, but likewise to the determinations of two *seniors*.[171] With these limitations, Othman, the secretary of Mohammed, accepted the government; nor was it till after the third caliph, twenty-four years after the death of the prophet, that Ali was invested by the popular choice with the regal and sacerdotal office. The manners of the Arabians retained their primitive simplicity, and the son of Abu Taleb despised the pomp and vanity of this world. At the hour of prayer he repaired to the mosch of Medina, clothed in a thin cotton gown, a coarse turban on his head, his slippers in one hand, and his bow in the other, instead of a walking-staff. The companions of the prophet and the chiefs of the tribe saluted their new sovereign, and gave him their right hands as a sign of fealty and allegiance.

The mischiefs that flow from the contests of ambition are usually confined to the times and countries in which they have been agitated. But the religious discord of the friends and enemies of Ali has been renewed in every age of the Hegira, and is still maintained in the immortal hatred of the Persians and Turks.[172] The former, who are branded with the appellation of *Shiites* or sectaries, have enriched the Mohammedan creed with a new article of faith; and if Mohammed be the apostle, his companion Ali is the vicar, of God. In their private converse, in their public worship, they bitterly execrate the three usurpers who intercepted his indefeasible right to the dignity of Imam and Caliph; and the name of Omar expresses in their tongue the perfect accomplishment of wickedness and impiety.[173] The *Sonnites*, who are supported by the general consent and orthodox tradition of the Musulmans, entertain a more impartial, or at least a more decent, opinion. They respect the memory of Abubeker, Omar, Othman, and Ali, the holy and legitimate successors of the prophet. But they assign the last and most humble place to the husband of Fatima, in the persuasion that the order of succession was determined by the degrees of sanctity.[174] An historian who balances the four caliphs with a hand unshaken by superstition will calmly pronounce that their manners were alike pure and exemplary; that their zeal was fervent, and probably sincere; and that, in the midst of riches and power, their lives were devoted to the practice of moral and religious duties. But the public virtues of Abubeker and Omar, the prudence of the first, the severity of the second, maintained the peace and prosperity of their reigns. The feeble temper and declining age of Othman were incapable of sustaining the weight of conquest and empire. He chose, and he was deceived; he trusted, and he was betrayed: the most deserving of the faithful became useless or hostile to his government, and his lavish bounty was productive only of ingratitude and discontent. The spirit of discord went forth in the provinces: their deputies assembled at Medina; and the Charegites, the desperate fanatics who disclaimed the yoke of subordination and reason, were confounded among the free-born Arabs, who demanded the redress of their wrongs and the punishment of their oppressors. From Cufa, from Bassora, from Egypt, from the tribes of the desert, they rose in arms, encamped about a league from Medina, and despatched a haughty mandate to their sovereign, requiring him to execute justice or to descend from the throne. His repentance began to disarm and disperse the insurgents; but their fury was rekindled by the arts of his enemies; and the forgery of a perfidious secretary was contrived to blast his reputation and precipitate his fall. The caliph had lost the only guard of his predecessors, the esteem and confidence of the Moslems: during a siege of six weeks his water and provisions were intercepted, and the feeble gates of the palace were protected only by the scruples of the more timorous rebels. Forsaken by those who had abused his simplicity, the helpless and venerable caliph expected the approach of death: the brother of Ayesha marched at the head of the assassins; and Othman, with the Koran in his lap, was pierced with a multitude of wounds. A tumultuous anarchy of five days was appeased by the inauguration of Ali: his refusal would have provoked a general massacre. In this painful situation he supported the becoming pride of the chief of the Hashemites; declared that he had rather serve than reign; rebuked the presumption of the strangers; and required the formal if not the voluntary assent of the chiefs of the nation. He has never been accused of prompting the assassin of Omar; though Persia indiscreetly celebrates the festival of that holy martyr. The quarrel between Othman and his subjects was assuaged by the early mediation of Ali; and Hassan, the eldest of his sons, was insulted and wounded in the defence of the caliph. Yet it is doubtful whether the father of Hassan was strenuous and sincere in his opposition to the rebels; and it is certain that he enjoyed the benefit of their crime. The temptation was indeed of such magnitude as might stagger and corrupt the most obdurate virtue. The ambitious candidate no longer aspired to the barren sceptre of Arabia; the Saracens had been victorious in the East and West; and the wealthy kingdoms of Persia, Syria, and Egypt were the patrimony of the commander of the faithful.

A life of prayer and contemplation had not chilled the martial activity of Ali; but in a mature age, after a long experience of mankind, he still betrayed in his conduct the rashness and indiscretion of youth. In the first days of his reign he neglected to secure, either by gifts or fetters, the doubtful allegiance of Telha and Zobeir, two of the most powerful of the Arabian chiefs. They escaped from Medina to Mecca, and from thence to Bassora; erected the standard of revolt; and usurped the government of Irak, or Assyria, which they had vainly solicited as the reward of their services. The mask of patriotism is allowed to cover the most glaring inconsistencies; and the enemies, perhaps the assassins, of Othman now demanded vengeance for his blood. They were accompanied in their flight by Ayesha, the widow of the prophet, who cherished to the last hour of her life an implacable hatred against the husband and the posterity of Fatima. The most reasonable Moslems were scandalised that the mother of the faithful should expose in a camp her person and character; but the superstitious crowd was confident that her presence would sanctify the justice and assure the success of their cause. At the head of twenty thousand of his loyal Arabs, and nine thousand valiant auxiliaries of Cufa, the caliph encountered and defeated the superior numbers of the rebels under the walls of Bassora. Their leaders, Telha and Zobeir, were slain in the first battle that stained with civil blood the arms of the Moslems. After passing through the ranks to animate the troops, Ayesha had chosen her post amidst the dangers of the field. In the heat of the action, seventy men who held the bridle of her camel were successively killed or wounded; and the cage, or litter, in which she sat was stuck with javelins and darts like the quills of a porcupine. The venerable captive sustained with firmness the reproaches of the conqueror, and was speedily dismissed to her proper station at the tomb of Mohammed, with the respect and tenderness that was still due to the widow of the apostle. After this victory, which was styled the Day of the Camel, Ali marched against a more formidable adversary; against Moawiyah, the son of Abu Sophian, who had assumed the title of caliph, and whose claim was supported by the forces of Syria and the interest of the house of Ommiyah. From the passage of Thapsacus, the plain of Siffin[175] extends along the Western bank of the Euphrates. On this spacious and level theatre the two competitors waged a desultory war of one hundred and ten days. In the course of ninety actions or skirmishes, the loss of Ali was estimated at twenty-five, that of Moawiyah at forty-five, thousand soldiers; and the list of the slain was dignified with the names of five-and-twenty veterans who had fought at Beder under the standard of Mohammed. In this sanguinary contest the lawful caliph displayed a superior character of valour and humanity. His troops were strictly enjoined to await the first onset of the enemy, to spare their flying brethren, and to respect the bodies of the dead, and the chastity of the female captives. He generously proposed to save the blood of the Moslems by a single combat; but his trembling rival declined the challenge as a sentence of inevitable death. The ranks of the Syrians were broken by the charge of a hero who was mounted on a piebald horse, and wielded with irresistible force his ponderous and two-edged sword. As often as he smote a rebel, he shouted the Allah Acbar, "God is victorious!" and in the tumult of a nocturnal battle he was heard to repeat four hundred times that tremendous exclamation. The prince of Damascus already meditated his flight but the certain victory was snatched from the grasp of Ali by the disobedience and enthusiasm of his troops. Their conscience was awed by the solemn appeal to the books of the Koran which Moawiyah exposed on the foremost lances; and Ali was compelled to yield to a disgraceful truce and an insidious compromise. He retreated with sorrow and indignation to Cufa; his party was discouraged; the distant provinces of Persia, of Yemen, and of Egypt were subdued or seduced by his crafty rival; and the stroke of fanaticism, which was aimed against the three chiefs of the nation, was fatal only to the cousin of Mohammed. In the temple of Mecca three Charegites or enthusiasts discoursed of the disorders of the church and state: they soon agreed that the deaths of Ali, of Moawiyah, and of his friend Amrou, the viceroy of Egypt, would restore the peace and unity of religion. Each of the assassins chose his victim, poisoned his dagger, devoted his life, and secretly repaired to the scene of action. Their resolution was equally desperate: but the first mistook the person of Amrou, and stabbed the deputy who occupied his seat; the prince of Damascus was dangerously hurt by the second; the lawful caliph, in the mosch of Cufa, received a mortal wound from the hand of the third. He expired in the sixty-third year of his age, and mercifully recommended to his children that they would despatch the murderer by a single stroke. The sepulchre of Ali[176] was concealed from the tyrants of the house of Ommiyah;[177] but in the fourth age of the Hegira, a tomb, a temple, a city, arose near the ruins of Cufa.[178] Many thousands of the Shiites repose in holy ground at the feet of the vicar of God; and the desert is vivified by the numerous and annual visits of the Persians, who esteem their devotion not less meritorious than the pilgrimage of Mecca.

The persecutors of Mohammed usurped the inheritance of his children; and the champions of idolatry became the supreme heads of his religion and empire. The opposition of Abu Sophian had been fierce and obstinate; his conversion was tardy and reluctant; his new faith was fortified by necessity and interest; he served, he fought, perhaps he believed; and the sins of the time of ignorance were expiated by the recent merits of the family of Ommiyah. Moawiyah, the son of Abu Sophian, and of the cruel Henda, was dignified in his early youth with the office or title of secretary of the prophet: the judgment of Omar intrusted him with the government of Syria; and he administered that important province above forty years, either in a subordinate or supreme rank. Without renouncing the fame of valour and liberality, he affected the reputation of humanity and moderation: a grateful people was attached to their benefactor; and the victorious Moslems were enriched with the spoils of Cyprus and Rhodes. The sacred duty of pursuing the assassins of Othman was the engine and pretence of his ambition. The bloody shirt of the martyr was exposed in the mosch of Damascus: the emir deplored the fate of his injured kinsman; and sixty thousand Syrians were engaged in his service by an oath of fidelity and revenge. Amrou, the conqueror of Egypt, himself an army, was the first who saluted the new monarch, and divulged the dangerous secret that the Arabian caliphs might be created elsewhere than in the city of the prophet.[179] The policy of Moawiyah eluded the valour of his rival; and, after the death of Ali, he negotiated the abdication of his son Hassan, whose mind was either above or below the government of the world, and who retired without a sigh from the palace of Cufa to a humble cell near the tomb of his grandfather. The aspiring wishes of the caliph were finally crowned by the important change of an elective to an hereditary kingdom. Some murmurs of freedom or fanaticism attested the reluctance of the Arabs, and four citizens of Medina refused the oath of fidelity; but the designs of Moawiyah were conducted with vigour and address; and his son Yezid, a feeble and dissolute youth, was proclaimed as the commander of the faithful and the successor of the apostle of God.

A familiar story is related of the benevolence of one of the sons of Ali. In serving at a table a slave had inadvertently dropped a dish of scalding broth on his master: the heedless wretch fell prostrate, to deprecate his punishment, and repeated a verse of the Koran: "Paradise is for those who command their anger:"—"I am not angry:"—"and for those who pardon offences:"—"I pardon your offence:"—"and for those who return good for evil:"—"I give you your liberty, and four hundred pieces of silver." With an equal measure of piety, Hosein, the younger brother of Hassan, inherited a remnant of his father's spirit, and served with honour against the Christians in the siege of Constantinople. The primogeniture of the line of Hashem, and the holy character of grandson of the apostle, had centered in his person, and he was at liberty to prosecute his claim against Yezid, the tyrant of Damascus, whose vices he despised, and whose title he had never deigned to acknowledge. A list was secretly transmitted from Cufa to Medina, of one hundred and forty thousand Moslems, who professed their attachment to his cause, and who were eager to draw their swords so soon as he should appear on the banks of the Euphrates. Against the advice of his wisest friends, he resolved to trust his person and family in the hands of a perfidious people. He traversed the desert of Arabia with a timorous retinue of women and children; but as he approached the confines of Irak he was alarmed

by the solitary or hostile face of the country, and suspected either the defection or ruin of his party. His fears were just: Obeidollah, the governor of Cufa, had extinguished the first sparks of an insurrection; and Hosein, in the plain of Kerbela, was encompassed by a body of five thousand horse, who intercepted his communication with the city and the river. He might still have escaped to a fortress in the desert that had defied the power of Cæsar and Chosroes, and confided in the fidelity of the tribe of Tai, which would have armed ten thousand warriors in his defence. In a conference with the chief of the enemy he proposed the option of three honourable conditions: that he should be allowed to return to Medina, or be stationed in a frontier garrison against the Turks, or safely conducted to the presence of Yezid. But the commands of the caliph, or his lieutenant, were stern and absolute; and Hosein was informed that he must either submit as a captive and a criminal to the commander of the faithful, or expect the consequences of his rebellion. "Do you think," replied he, "to terrify me with death?" And, during the short respite of a night, he prepared with calm and solemn resignation to encounter his fate. He checked the lamentations of his sister Fatima, who deplored the impending ruin of his house. "Our trust," said Hosein, "is in God alone. All things, both in heaven and earth, must perish and return to their Creator. My brother, my father, my mother, were better than me, and every Musulman has an example in the prophet." He pressed his friends to consult their safety by a timely flight: they unanimously refused to desert or survive their beloved master: and their courage was fortified by a fervent prayer and the assurance of paradise. On the morning of the fatal day, he mounted on horseback, with his sword in one hand and the Koran in the other: his generous band of martyrs consisted only of thirty-two horse and forty foot; but their flanks and rear were secured by the tent-ropes, and by a deep trench which they had filled with lighted faggots, according to the practice of the Arabs. The enemy advanced with reluctance, and one of their chiefs deserted, with thirty followers, to claim the partnership of inevitable death. In every close onset, or single combat, the despair of the Fatimites was invincible; but the surrounding multitudes galled them from a distance with a cloud of arrows, and the horses and men were successively slain: a truce was allowed on both sides for the hour of prayer; and the battle at length expired by the death of the last of the companions of

Hosein. Alone, weary, and wounded, he seated himself at the door of his tent. As he tasted a drop of water, he was pierced in the mouth with a dart; and his son and nephew, two beautiful youths, were killed in his arms. He lifted his hands to heaven—they were full of blood—and he uttered a funeral prayer for the living and the dead. In a transport of despair his sister issued from the tent, and adjured the general of the Cufians that he would not suffer Hosein to be murdered before his eyes: a tear trickled down his venerable beard; and the boldest of his soldiers fell back on every side as the dying hero threw himself among them. The remorseless Shamer, a name detested by the faithful, reproached their cowardice; and the grandson of Mohammed was slain with three-and-thirty strokes of lances and swords. After they had trampled on his body, they carried his head to the castle of Cufa, and the inhuman Obeidollah struck him on the mouth with a cane: "Alas," exclaimed an aged Musulman, "on these lips have I seen the lips of the apostle of God!" In a distant age and climate the tragic scene of the death of Hosein will awaken the sympathy of the coldest reader.[180] On the annual festival of his martyrdom, in the devout pilgrimage to his sepulchre, his Persian votaries abandon their souls to the religious frenzy of sorrow and indignation.[181]

When the sisters and children of Ali were brought in chains to the throne of Damascus, the caliph was advised to extirpate the enmity of a popular and hostile race, whom he had injured beyond the hope of reconciliation. But Yezid preferred the counsels of mercy; and the mourning family was honourably dismissed to mingle their tears with their kindred at Medina. The glory of martyrdom superseded the right of primogeniture; and the twelve IMAMS,[182] or pontiffs, of the Persian creed, are Ali, Hassan, Hosein, and the lineal descendants of Hosein to the ninth generation. Without arms, or treasures, or subjects, they successively enjoyed the veneration of the people, and provoked the jealousy of the reigning caliphs: their tombs, at Mecca or Medina, on the banks of the Euphrates, or in the province of Chorasan, are still visited by the devotion of their sect. Their names were often the pretence of sedition and civil war: but these royal saints despised the pomp of the world; submitted to the will of God and the injustice of man; and devoted their innocent lives to the study and practice of religion. The twelfth and last of the Imams, conspicuous by the title of *Mahadi*, or the Guide, surpassed the solitude and sanctity of his predecessors. He concealed himself in a cavern near Bagdad: the time and place of his death are unknown; and his votaries pretend that he still lives, and will appear before the day of judgment to overthrow the tyranny of Dejal, or the Antichrist.[183] In the lapse of two or three centuries, the posterity of Abbas, the uncle of Mohammed, had multiplied to the number of thirty-three thousand:[184] the race of Ali might be equally prolific: the meanest individual was above the first and greatest of princes; and the most eminent were supposed to excel the perfection of angels. But their adverse fortune, and the wide extent of the Musulman empire, allowed an ample scope for every bold and artful impostor who claimed affinity with the holy seed: the sceptre of the Almohades, in Spain and Afric; of the Fatimites, in Egypt and Syria;[185] of the Sultans of Yemen; and of the Sophis of Persia;[186] has been consecrated by this vague and ambiguous title. Under their reigns it might be dangerous to dispute the legitimacy of their birth; and one of the Fatimite caliphs silenced an indiscreet question by drawing his scimitar: "This," said Moez, "is my pedigree; and these," casting a handful of gold to his soldiers—"and these are my kindred and my children." In the various conditions of princes, or doctors, or nobles, or merchants, or beggars, a swarm of the genuine or fictitious descendants of Mohammed and Ali is honoured with the appellation of sheiks, or sherifs, or emirs. In the Ottoman empire they are distinguished by a green turban; receive a stipend from the treasury; are judged only by their chief; and, however debased by fortune or character, still assert the proud pre-eminence of their birth. A family of three hundred persons, the pure and orthodox branch of the caliph Hassan, is preserved without taint or suspicion in the holy cities of Mecca and Medina, and still retains, after the revolutions of twelve centuries, the custody of the temple and the sovereignty of their native land. The fame and merit of Mohammed would ennoble a plebeian race, and the ancient blood of the Koreish transcends the recent majesty of the kings of the earth.[187]

The talents of Mohammed are entitled to our applause; but his success has, perhaps, too strongly attracted our admiration. Are we surprised that a multitude of proselytes should embrace the doctrine and the passions of an eloquent fanatic? In the heresies of the church the same seduction has been tried and repeated from the time of the apostles to that of the reformers. Does it seem incredible that a private citizen should grasp the sword and the sceptre, subdue his native country, and erect a monarchy by his victorious arms? In the moving picture of the dynasties of the East, a hundred fortunate usurpers have arisen from a baser origin, surmounted more formidable obstacles, and filled a larger scope of empire and conquest. Mohammed was alike instructed to preach and to fight; and the union of these opposite qualities, while it enhanced his merit, contributed to his success: the operation of force and persuasion, of enthusiasm and fear, continually acted on each other, till every barrier yielded to their irresistible power. His voice invited the Arabs to freedom and victory, to arms and rapine, to the indulgence of their darling passions in this world and the other: the restraints which he imposed were requisite to establish the credit of the prophet, and to exercise the obedience of the people; and the only objection to his success was his rational creed of the unity and perfections of God. It is not the propagation, but the permanency of his religion, that deserves our wonder: the same pure and perfect impression which he engraved at Mecca and Medina is preserved, after the revolutions of twelve centuries, by the Indian, the African, and the Turkish proselytes of the Koran. If the Christian apostles, St. Peter or St. Paul, could return to the Vatican, they might possibly inquire the name of the Deity who is worshipped with such mysterious rites in that magnificent temple: at Oxford or Geneva they would experience less surprise; but it might still be incumbent on them to peruse the catechism of the church, and to study the orthodox commentators on their own writings and the words of their Master. But the Turkish dome of St. Sophia, with an increase of splendour and size, represents the humble tabernacle erected at Medina by the hands of Mohammed. The Mohammedans have uniformly withstood the temptation of reducing the object of their faith and devotion to a level with the senses and imagination of man. "I believe in one God, and Mohammed the apostle of God," is the simple and invariable profession of Islam. The intellectual image of the Deity has never been degraded by any visible idol; the honours of the prophet have never transgressed the measure of human virtue; and his living precepts have restrained the gratitude of his disciples within the bounds of reason and religion. The votaries of Ali have, indeed, consecrated the memory of their hero, his wife, and his children; and some of the Persian doctors pretend that the divine essence was incarnate in the person of the Imams; but their superstition is universally condemned by the Sonnites; and their impiety has afforded a seasonable warning against the worship of saints and martyrs. The metaphysical questions on the attributes of God, and the liberty of man, have been agitated in the schools of the Mohammedans as well as in those of the Christians; but among the former they have never engaged the passions of the people, or disturbed the tranquillity of the state. The cause of this important difference may be found in the separation or union of the regal and sacerdotal characters. It was the interest of the caliphs, the successors of the prophet and commanders of the faithful, to repress and discourage all religious innovations: the order, the discipline, the temporal and spiritual ambition of the clergy, are unknown to the Moslems; and the sages of the law are the guides of their conscience and the oracles of their faith. From the Atlantic to the Ganges the Koran is acknowledged as the fundamental code, not only of theology but of civil and criminal jurisprudence; and the laws which regulate the actions and the property of mankind are guarded by the infallible and immutable sanction of the will of God. This religious servitude is attended with some practical disadvantage; the illiterate legislator has been often misled by his own prejudices and those of his country; and the institutions of the Arabian desert may be ill adapted to the wealth and numbers of Ispahan and Constantinople. On these occasions the Cadhi respectfully places on his head the holy volume, and substitutes a dexterous interpretation more apposite to the principles of equity and the manners and policy of the times.

His beneficial or pernicious influence on the public happiness is the last consideration in the character of Mohammed. The most bitter or most bigoted of his Christian or Jewish foes will surely allow that he assumed a false commission to inculcate a salutary doctrine, less perfect only than their own. He piously supposed, as the basis of his religion, the truth and sanctity of *their* prior revelations, the virtues and miracles of their founders. The idols of Arabia were broken before the throne of God; the blood of human victims was expiated by prayer, and fasting, and alms, the laudable or innocent arts of devotion; and his rewards and punishments of a future life were painted by the images most congenial to an ignorant and carnal generation. Mohammed was, perhaps, incapable of dictatng a moral and political system for the use of his countrymen: but he breathed among the faithful a spirit of charity and friendship; recommended the practice of the social virtues; and checked, by his laws and precepts, the thirst of revenge, and the oppression of widows and orphans. The hostile tribes were united in faith and obedience, and the valour which had been idly spent in domestic quarrels was vigorously directed against a foreign enemy. Had the impulse been less powerful, Arabia, free at home, and formidable abroad, might have flourished under a succession of her native monarchs. Her sovereignty was lost by the extent and rapidity of conquest. The colonies of the nation were scattered over the East and West, and their blood was mingled with the blood of their converts and captives. After the reign of three caliphs, the throne was transported from Medina to the valley of Damascus and the banks of the Tigris; the holy cities were violated by impious war; Arabia was ruled by the rod of a subject, perhaps of a stranger; and the Bedoweens of the desert, awakening from their dream of dominion, resumed their old and solitary independence.[188]

CHAPTER LI

The Conquest of Persia, Syria, Egypt, Africa, and Spain, by the Arabs or Saracens. Empire of the Caliphs, or Successors of Mohammed. State of the Christians, etc., under their Government.

THE revolution of Arabia had not changed the character of the Arabs: the death of Mohammed was the signal of independence; and the hasty structure of his power and religion tottered to its foundations. A small and faithful band of his primitive disciples had listened to his eloquence, and shared his distress; had fled with the apostle from the persecution of Mecca, or had received the fugitive in the walls of Medina. The increasing myriads who acknowledged Mohammed as their king and prophet had been compelled by his arms, or allured by his prosperity. The polytheists were confounded by the simple idea of a solitary and invisible God; the pride of the Christians and Jews disdained the yoke of a mortal and contemporary legislator. Their habits of faith and obedience were not sufficiently confirmed; and many of the new converts regretted the venerable antiquity of the law of Moses; or the rites and mysteries of the Catholic church; or the idols, the sacrifices, the joyous festivals of their Pagan ancestors. The jarring interests and hereditary feuds of the Arabian tribes had not yet coalesced in a system of union and subordination; and the barbarians were impatient of the mildest and most salutary laws that curbed their passions or violated their customs. They submitted with reluctance to the religious precepts of the Koran, the abstinence from wine, the fast of the Ramadan, and the daily repetition of five prayers; and the alms and tithes which were collected for the treasury of Medina could be distinguished only by a name from the payment of a perpetual and ignominious tribute. The example of Mohammed had excited a spirit of fanaticism or imposture, and several of his rivals presumed to imitate the conduct, and defy the authority, of the living prophet. At the head of the *fugitives* and *auxiliaries*, the first caliph was reduced to the cities of Mecca, Medina, and Tayef; and perhaps the Koreish would have restored the idols of the Caaba, if their levity had not been checked by a seasonable reproof. "Ye men of Mecca, will ye be the last to embrace, and the first to abandon, the religion of Islam?" After exhorting the Moslems to confide in the aid of God and his apostle, Abubeker resolved, by a vigorous attack, to prevent the junction of the rebels. The women and children were safely lodged in the cavities of the mountains: the warriors, marching under eleven banners, diffused the terror of their arms; and the appearance of a military force revived and confirmed the loyalty of the faithful. The inconstant tribes accepted, with humble repentance, the duties of prayer, and fasting, and alms; and, after some examples of success and severity, the most daring apostates fell prostrate before the sword of the Lord and of Caled. In the fertile province of Yemanah,[1] between the Red Sea and the Gulf of Persia, in a city not inferior to Medina itself, a powerful chief, his name was Moseilama, had assumed the character of a prophet, and the tribe of Hanifa listened to his voice. A female prophetess was attracted by his reputation: the decencies of words and actions were spurned by these favourites of heaven;[2] and they employed several days in mystic and amorous converse. An obscure sentence of his Koran, or book, is yet extant;[3] and, in the pride of his mission, Moseilama condescended to offer a partition of the earth. The proposal was answered by Mohammed with contempt; but the rapid progress of the impostor awakened the fears of his successor: forty thousand Moslems were assembled under the standard of Caled; and the existence of their faith was resigned to the event of a decisive battle. In the first action they were repulsed with the loss of twelve hundred men; but the skill and perseverance of their general prevailed: their defeat was avenged by the slaughter of ten thousand infidels; and Moseilama himself was pierced by an Æthiopian slave with the same javelin which had mortally wounded the uncle of Mohammed. The various rebels of Arabia, without a chief or a cause, were speedily suppressed by the power and discipline of the rising monarchy; and the whole nation again professed, and more steadfastly held, the religion of the Koran. The ambition of the caliphs provided an immediate exercise for the restless spirit of the Saracens: their valour was united in the prosecution of a holy war; and their enthusiasm was equally confirmed by opposition and victory.

From the rapid conquests of the Saracens a presumption will naturally arise, that the first caliphs commanded in person the armies of the faithful, and sought the crown of martyrdom in the foremost ranks of the battle. The courage of Abubeker,[4] Omar,[5] and Othman[6] had indeed been tried in the persecution and wars of the prophet: and the personal assurance of paradise must have taught them to despise the pleasures and dangers of the present world. But they ascended the throne in a venerable or mature age; and esteemed the domestic cares of religion and justice the most important duties of a sovereign. Except the presence of Omar at the siege of Jerusalem, their longest expeditions were the frequent pilgrimage from Medina to Mecca; and they calmly received the tidings of victory as they prayed or preached before the sepulchre of the prophet. The austere and frugal measure of their lives was the effect of virtue or habit, and the pride of their simplicity insulted the vain magnificence of the kings of the earth. When Abubeker assumed the office of caliph, he enjoined his daughter Ayesha to take a strict account of his private patrimony, that it might be evident whether he were enriched or impoverished by the service of the state. He thought himself entitled to a stipend of three pieces of gold, with the sufficient maintenance of a single camel and a black slave; but on the Friday of each week he distributed the residue of his own and the public money, first to the most worthy, and then to the most indigent, of the Moslems. The remains of his wealth, a coarse garment and five pieces of gold, were delivered to his successor, who lamented with a modest sigh his own inability to equal such an admirable model. Yet the abstinence and humility of Omar were not inferior to the virtue of Abubeker; his food consisted of barley-bread or dates; his drink was water; he preached in a gown that was torn or tattered in twelve places; and a Persian satrap, who paid his homage to the conqueror, found him asleep among the beggars on the steps of the mosch of Medina. Economy is the source of liberality, and the increase of the revenue enabled Omar to establish a just and perpetual reward for the past and present services of the faithful. Careless of his own emolument, he assigned to Abbas, the uncle of the prophet, the first and most ample allowance of twenty-five thousand drachms or pieces of silver. Five thousand were allotted to each of the aged warriors, the relics of the field of Beder, and the last and meanest of the companions of Mohammed was distinguished by the annual reward of three thousand pieces. One thousand was the stipend of the veterans who had fought in the first battles against the Greeks and Persians; and the decreasing pay, as low as fifty pieces of silver, was adapted to the respective merit and seniority of the soldiers of Omar. Under his reign, and that of his predecessor, the conquerors of the East were the trusty servants of God and the people; the mass of the public treasure was consecrated to the expenses of peace and war; a prudent mixture of justice and bounty maintained the discipline of the Saracens, and they united, by a rare felicity, the despatch and execution of despotism with the equal and frugal maxims of a republican government. The heroic courage of Ali,[7] the consummate prudence of Moawiyah,[8] excited the emulation of their subjects; and the talents which had been exercised in the school of civil discord were more usefully applied to propagate the faith and dominion of the prophet. In the sloth and vanity of the palace of Damascus the succeeding princes of the house of Ommiyah were alike destitute of the qualifications of statesmen and of saints.[9] Yet the spoils of unknown nations were continually laid at the foot of their throne, and the uniform ascent of the

Arabian greatness must be ascribed to the spirit of the nation rather than the abilities of their chiefs. A large deduction must be allowed for the weakness of their enemies. The birth of Mohammed was fortunately placed in the most degenerate and disorderly period of the Persians, the Romans, and the barbarians of Europe: the empires of Trajan, or even of Constantine or Charlemagne, would have repelled the assault of the naked Saracens, and the torrent of fanaticism might have been obscurely lost in the sands of Arabia.

In the victorious days of the Roman republic it had been the aim of the senate to confine their councils and legions to a single war, and completely to suppress a first enemy before they provoked the hostilities of a second. These timid maxims of policy were disdained by the magnanimity or enthusiasm of the Arabian caliphs. With the same vigour and success they invaded the successors of Augustus and those of Artaxerxes; and the rival monarchies at the same instant became the prey of an enemy whom they had been so long accustomed to despise. In the ten years of the administration of Omar, the Saracens reduced to his obedience thirty-six thousand cities or castles, destroyed four thousand churches or temples of the unbelievers, and edified fourteen hundred moschs for the exercise of the religion of Mohammed. One hundred years after his flight from Mecca the arms and the reign of his successors extended from India to the Atlantic Ocean, over the various and distant provinces which may be comprised under the names of, I. Persia; II. Syria; III. Egypt; IV. Africa; and V. Spain. Under this general division I shall proceed to unfold these memorable transactions, despatching with brevity the remote and less interesting conquests of the East, and reserving a fuller narrative for those domestic countries which had been included within the pale of the Roman empire. Yet I must excuse my own defects by a just complaint of the blindness and insufficiency of my guides. The Greeks, so loquacious in controversy, have not been anxious to celebrate the triumphs of their enemies.[10] After a century of ignorance the first annals of the Musulmans were collected in a great measure from the voice of tradition.[11] Among the numerous productions of Arabic and Persian literature,[12] our interpreters have selected the imperfect sketches of a more recent age.[13] The art and genius of history have ever been unknown to the Asiatics;[14] they are ignorant of the laws of criticism; and our monkish chronicles of the same period may be compared to their most popular works, which are never vivified by the spirit of philosophy and freedom. The *Oriental library* of a Frenchman[15] would instruct the most learned mufti of the East; and perhaps the Arabs might not find in a single historian so clear and comprehensive a narrative of their own exploits as that which will be deduced in the ensuing sheets.

I. In the first year of the first caliph, his lieutenant Chaled, the Sword of God, and the scourge of the infidels, advanced to the banks of the Euphrates, and reduced the cities of Anbar and Hira. Westward of the ruins of Babylon, a tribe of sedentary Arabs had fixed themselves on the verge of the desert; and Hira was the seat of a race of kings who had embraced the Christian religion, and reigned above six hundred years under the shadow of the throne of Persia.[16] The last of the Mondars was defeated and slain by Chaled; his son was sent a captive to Medina; his nobles bowed before the successor of the prophet; the people was tempted by the example and success of their countrymen; and the caliph accepted as the first-fruits of foreign conquest an annual tribute of seventy thousand pieces of gold. The conquerors, and even their historians, were astonished by the dawn of their future greatness: "In the same year," says Elmacin, "Chaled fought many signal battles: an immense multitude of the infidels was slaughtered, and spoils infinite and innumerable were acquired by the victorious Moslems."[17] But the invincible Chaled was soon transferred to the Syrian war: the invasion of the Persian frontier was conducted by less active or less prudent commanders: the Saracens were repulsed with loss in the passage of the Euphrates; and, though they chastised the insolent pursuit of the Magians, their remaining forces still hovered in the desert of Babylon.

The indignation and fears of the Persians suspended for a moment their intestine divisions. By the unanimous sentence of the priests and nobles, their queen Arzema was deposed; the sixth of the transient usurpers who had risen and vanished in three or four years since the death of Chosroes and the retreat of Heraclius. Her tiara was placed on the head of Yezdegerd, the grandson of Chosroes; and the same era, which coincides with an astonomical period,[18] has recorded the fall of the Sassanian dynasty and the religion of Zoroaster.[19] The youth and inexperience of the prince—he was only fifteen years of age—declined a perilous encounter; the royal standard was delivered into the hands of his general Rustam; and a remnant of thirty thousand regular troops was swelled in truth, or in opinion, to one hundred and twenty thousand subjects, or allies, of the Great King. The Moslems, whose numbers were reinforced from twelve to thirty thousand, had pitched their camp in the plains of Cadesia:[20] and their line, though it consisted of fewer *men*, could produce more *soldiers*, than the unwieldy host of the infidels. I shall here observe what I must often repeat, that the charge of the Arabs was not, like that of the Greeks and Romans, the effort of a firm and compact infantry: their military force was chiefly formed of cavalry and archers; and the engagement, which was often interrupted and often renewed by single combats and flying skirmishes, might be protracted without any decisive event to the continuance of several days. The periods of the battle of Cadesia were distinguished by their peculiar appellations. The first, from the well-timed appearance of six thousand of the Syrian brethren, was denominated the day of *succour*. The day of *concussion* might express the disorder of one, or perhaps of both, of the contending armies. The third, a nocturnal tumult, received the whimsical name of the night of *barking*, from the discordant clamours, which were compared to the inarticulate sounds of the fiercest animals. The morning of the succeeding day determined the fate of Persia; and a seasonable whirlwind drove a cloud of dust against the faces of the unbelievers. The clangour of arms was re-echoed to the tent of Rustam, who, far unlike the ancient hero of his name, was gently reclining in a cool and tranquil shade, amidst the baggage of his camp, and the train of mules that were laden with gold and silver. On the sound of danger he started from his couch; but his flight was overtaken by a valiant Arab, who caught him by the foot, struck off his head, hoisted it on a lance, and, instantly returning to the field of battle, carried slaughter and dismay among the thickest ranks of the Persians. The Saracens confess a loss of seven thousand five hundred men; and the battle of Cadesia is justly described by the epithets of obstinate and atrocious.[21] The standard of the monarchy was overthrown and captured in the field—a leathern apron of a blacksmith who in ancient times had arisen the deliverer of Persia; but this badge of heroic poverty was disguised and almost concealed by a profusion of precious gems.[22] After this victory the wealthy province of Irak, or Assyria, submitted to the caliph, and his conquests were firmly established by the speedy foundation of Bassora,[23] a place which ever commands the trade and navigation of the Persians. At the distance of fourscore miles from the Gulf the Euphrates and Tigris unite in a broad and direct current, which is aptly styled the river of the Arabs. In the midway, between the junction and the mouth of these famous streams, the new settlement was planted on the western bank: the first colony was composed of eight hundred Moslems; but the influence of the situation soon reared a flourishing and populous capital. The air, though excessively hot, is pure and healthy; the meadows are filled with palm-trees and cattle; and one of the adjacent valleys has been celebrated among the four paradises or gardens of Asia. Under the first caliphs the jurisdiction of this Arabian colony extended over the southern provinces of Persia: the city has been sanctified by the tombs of the companions and martyrs; and the vessels of Europe still frequent the port of Bassora, as a convenient station and passage of the Indian trade.

After the defeat of Cadesia, a country intersected by rivers and canals might have opposed an insuperable barrier to the victorious cavalry; and the walls of Ctesiphon or Madayn, which had resisted the battering-rams of the Romans, would not have yielded to the darts of the Saracens. But the flying Persians were overcome by the belief that the last day of their religion and empire was at hand; the strongest posts were abandoned by treachery or cowardice; and the king, with a part of his family and treasures, escaped to Holwan, at the foot of the Median hills. In the third month after the battle, Said, the lieutenant of Omar, passed the Tigris without opposition; the capital was taken by assault; and the disorderly resistance of the people gave a keener edge to the sabres of the Moslems, who shouted with religious transport, "This is the white palace of Chosroes; this is the promise of the apostle of God!" The naked robbers of the desert were suddenly enriched beyond the measure of their hope or knowledge. Each chamber revealed a new treasure secreted with art, or ostentatiously displayed; the gold and silver, the various wardrobes and precious furniture, surpassed (says Abulfeda) the estimate of fancy or numbers; and another historian defines the untold and almost infinite mass by the fabulous computation of three thousands of thousands of thousands of pieces of gold.[24] Some minute though curious facts represent the contrast of riches and ignorance. From the remote islands of the Indian Ocean a large provision of camphire[25] had been imported, which is employed with a mixture of wax to illuminate the palaces of the East. Strangers to the name and properties of that odoriferous gum, the Saracens, mistaking it for salt, mingled the camphire in their bread, and were astonished at the bitterness of the taste. One of the apartments of the palace was decorated with a carpet of silk, sixty cubits in length, and as many in breadth: a paradise or garden was depictured on the ground; the flowers, fruits, and shrubs were imitated by the figures of the gold embroidery, and the colours of the precious stones; and the ample square was encircled by a variegated and verdant border. The Arabian general persuaded his soldiers to relinquish their claim, in the reasonable hope that the eyes of the caliph would be delighted with the splendid workmanship of nature and industry. Regardless of the merit of art and the pomp of royalty, the rigid Omar divided the prize among his brethren of Medina: the picture was destroyed; but such was the intrinsic value of the materials, that the share of Ali alone was sold for twenty thousand drams. A mule that carried away the tiara and cuirass, the belt and bracelets of Chosroes, was overtaken by the pursuers; the gorgeous trophy was presented to the commander of the faithful; and the gravest of the companions condescended to smile when they beheld the white beard, hairy arms, and uncouth figure of the veteran who was invested with the spoils of the Great King.[26] The sack of Ctesiphon was followed by its desertion and gradual decay. The Saracens disliked the air and situation of the place, and Omar was advised by his general to remove the seat of government to the Western side of the Euphrates. In every age the foundation and ruin of the Assyrian cities has been easy and rapid: the country is destitute of stone and timber; and the most solid structures[27] are composed of bricks baked in the sun, and joined by a cement of a native bitumen. The name of *Cufa*[28] describes an habitation of reeds and earth; but the importance of the new capital was supported by the numbers, wealth, and spirit of a colony of veterans; and their licentiousness was indulged by the wisest caliphs, who were apprehensive of provoking the revolt of a hundred thousand swords: "Ye men of Cufa," said Ali, who solicited their aid, "you have been always conspicuous by your valour. You conquered the Persian king and scattered his forces, till you had taken possession of his inheritance." This mighty conquest was achieved by the battles of Jalula and Nehavend. After the loss of the former, Yezdegerd fled from Hol-

wan, and concealed his shame and despair in the mountains of Farsistan, from whence Cyrus had descended with his equal and valiant companions. The courage of the nation survived that of the monarch: among the hills to the south of Ecbatana or Hamadan one hundred and fifty thousand Persians made a third and final stand for their religion and country; and the decisive battle of Nehavend was styled by the Arabs the victory of victories. If it be true that the flying general of the Persians was stopped and overtaken in a crowd of mules and camels laden with honey, the incident, however slight or singular, will denote the luxurious impediments of an Oriental army.[29]

The geography of Persia is darkly delineated by the Greeks and Latins; but the most illustrious of her cities appear to be more ancient than the invasion of the Arabs. By the reduction of Hamadan and Ispahan, of Caswin, Tauris, and Rei, they gradually approached the shores of the Caspian Sea: and the orators of Mecca might applaud the success and spirit of the faithful, who had already lost sight of the northern bear, and had almost transcended the bounds of the habitable world.[30] Again turning towards the West and the Roman empire, they repassed the Tigris over the bridge of Mosul, and, in the captive provinces of Armenia and Mesopotamia, embraced their victorious brethren of the Syrian army. From the palace of Madayn their Eastern progress was not less rapid or extensive. They advanced along the Tigris and the Gulf, penetrated through the passes of the mountains into the valley of Estachar or Persepolis, and profaned the last sanctuary of the Magian empire. The grandson of Chosroes was nearly surprised among the falling columns and mutilated figures—a sad emblem of the past and present fortune of Persia:[31] he fled with accelerated haste over the desert of Kirman, implored the aid of the warlike Segestans, and sought a humble refuge on the verge of the Turkish and Chinese power. But a victorious army is insensible of fatigue: the Arabs divided their forces in the pursuit of a timorous enemy; and the caliph Othman promised the government of Chorasan to the first general who should enter that large and populous country, the kingdom of the ancient Bactrians. The condition was accepted; the prize was deserved; the standard of Mohammed was planted on the walls of Herat, Merou, and Balch; and the successful leader neither halted nor reposed till his foaming cavalry had tasted the waters of the Oxus. In the public anarchy the independent governors of the cities and castles obtained their separate capitulations; the terms were granted or imposed by the esteem, the prudence, or the compassion of the victors; and a simple profession of faith established the distinction between a brother and a slave. After a noble defence, Harmozan, the prince or satrap of Ahwaz and Susa, was compelled to surrender his person and his state to the discretion of the caliph; and their interview exhibits a portrait of the Arabian manners. In the presence, and by the command, of Omar the gay barbarian was despoiled of his silken robes embroidered with gold, and of his tiara bedecked with rubies and emeralds: "Are you now sensible," said the conqueror to his naked captive, "are you now sensible of the judgment of God, and of the different rewards of infidelity and obedience?" "Alas!" replied Harmozan, "I feel them too deeply. In the days of our common ignorance we fought with the weapons of the flesh, and my nation was superior. God was then neuter: since he has espoused your quarrel, you have subverted our kingdom and religion." Oppressed by this painful dialogue, the Persian complained of intolerable thirst, but discovered some apprehension lest he should be killed whilst he was drinking a cup of water. "Be of good courage," said the caliph; "your life is safe till you have drunk this water:" the crafty satrap accepted the assurance, and instantly dashed the vase against the ground. Omar would have avenged the deceit, but his companions represented the sanctity of an oath; and the speedy conversion of Harmozan entitled him not only to a free pardon, but even to a stipend of two thousand pieces of gold. The administration of Persia was regulated by an actual survey of the people, the cattle, and the fruits of the earth;[32] and this monument, which attests the vigilance of the caliphs, might have instructed the philosophers of every age.[33]

The flight of Yezdegerd had carried him beyond the Oxus, and as far as the Jaxartes, two rivers[34] of ancient and modern renown, which descend from the mountains of India towards the Caspian Sea. He was hospitably entertained by Tarkhan, prince of Fargana,[35] a fertile province on the Jaxartes: the king of Samarcand, with the Turkish tribes of Sogdiana and Scythia, were moved by the lamentations and promises of the fallen monarch; and he solicited, by a suppliant embassy, the more solid and powerful friendship of the emperor of China.[36] The virtuous Taitsong,[37] the first of the dynasty of the Tang, may be justly compared with the Antonines of Rome: his people enjoyed the blessings of prosperity and peace; and his dominion was acknowledged by forty-four hordes of the barbarians of Tartary. His last garrisons of Cashgar and Khoten maintained a frequent intercourse with their neighbours of the Jaxartes and Oxus; a recent colony of Persians had introduced into China the astronomy of the Magi; and Taitsong might be alarmed by the rapid progress and dangerous vicinity of the Arabs. The influence, and perhaps the supplies, of China revived the hopes of Yezdegerd and the zeal of the worshippers of fire; and he returned with an army of Turks to conquer the inheritance of his fathers. The fortunate Moslems, without unsheathing their swords, were the spectators of his ruin and death. The grandson of Chosroes was betrayed by his servant, insulted by the seditious inhabitants of Merou, and oppressed, defeated, and pursued by his barbarian allies. He reached the banks of a river, and offered his rings and bracelets for an instant passage in a miller's boat. Ignorant or insensible of royal distress, the rustic replied that four drams of silver were the daily profit of his mill, and that he would not suspend his work unless the loss were repaid. In this moment of hesitation and delay the last of the Sassanian kings was overtaken and slaughtered by the Turkish cavalry, in the nineteenth year of his unhappy reign.[38] His son Firuz, a humble client of the Chinese emperor, accepted the station of captain of his guards; and the Magian worship was long preserved by a colony of loyal exiles in the province of Bucharia. His grandson inherited the regal name; but after a faint and fruitless enterprise he returned to China, and ended his days in the palace of Sigan. The male line of the Sassanides was extinct; but the female captives, the daughters of Persia, were given to the conquerors in servitude or marriage; and the race of the caliphs and imams was ennobled by the blood of their royal mothers.[39]

After the fall of the Persian kingdom, the river Oxus divided the territories of the Saracens and of the Turks. This narrow boundary was soon overleaped by the spirit of the Arabs; the governors of Chorasan extended their successive inroads; and one of their triumphs was adorned with the buskin of a Turkish queen, which she dropped in her precipitate flight beyond the hills of Bochara.[40] But the final conquest of Transoxiana,[41] as well as of Spain, was reserved for the glorious reign of the inactive Walid, and the name of Catibah, the camel-driver, declares the origin and merit of his successful lieutenant.

While one of his colleagues displayed the first Mohammedan banner on the banks of the Indus, the spacious regions between the Oxus, the Iaxartes, and the Caspian Sea were reduced by the arms of Catibah to the obedience of the prophet and of the caliph.[42] A tribute of two millions of pieces of gold was imposed on the infidels; their idols were burnt or broken; the Musulman chief pronounced a sermon in the new mosch of Carizme; after several battles the Turkish hordes were driven back to the desert; and the emperors of China solicited the friendship of the victorious Arabs. To their industry the prosperity of the province, the Sogdiana of the ancients, may in a great measure be ascribed; but the advantages of the soil and climate had been understood and cultivated since the reign of the Macedonian kings. Before the invasion of the Saracens, Carizme, Bochara, and Samarcand were rich and populous under the yoke of the shepherds of the north. These cities were surrounded with a double wall; and the exterior fortification, of a larger circumference, enclosed the fields and gardens of the adjacent district. The mutual wants of India and Europe were supplied by the diligence of the Sogdian merchants; and the inestimable art of transforming linen into paper has been diffused from the manufacture of Samarcand over the Western world.[43]

II. No sooner had Abubeker restored the unity of faith and government than he despatched a circular letter to the Arabian tribes. "In the name of the most merciful God, to the rest of the true believers. Health and happiness, and the mercy and blessing of God, be upon you. I praise the most high God, and I pray for his prophet Mohammed. This is to acquaint you that I intend to send the true believers into Syria[44] to take it out of the hands of the infidels. And I would have you know that the fighting for religion is an act of obedience to God." His messengers returned with the tidings of pious and martial ardour which they had kindled in every province; and the camp of Medina was successively filled with the intrepid bands of the Saracens, who panted for action, complained of the heat of the season and the scarcity of provisions, and accused with impatient murmurs the delays of the caliph. As soon as their numbers were complete, Abubeker ascended the hill, reviewed the men, the horses, and the arms, and poured forth a fervent prayer for the success of their undertaking. In person and on foot he accompanied the first day's march; and when the blushing leaders attempted to dismount, the caliph removed their scruples by a declaration that those who rode and those who walked in the service of religion were equally meritorious. His instructions[45] to the chiefs of the Syrian army were inspired by the warlike fanaticism which advances to seize and affects to despise the objects of earthly ambition. "Remember," said the successor of the prophet, "that you are always in the presence of God, on the verge of death, in the assurance of judgment, and the hope of paradise. Avoid injustice and oppression; consult with your brethren, and study to preserve the love and confidence of your troops. When you fight the battles of the Lord, acquit yourselves like men, without turning your backs; but let not your victory be stained with the blood of women or children. Destroy no palm-trees, nor burn any fields of corn. Cut down no fruit-trees, nor do any mischief to cattle, only such as you kill to eat. When you make any covenant or article, stand to it, and be as good as your word. As you go on, you will find some religious persons who live retired in monasteries, and propose to themselves to serve God that way: let them alone, and neither kill them nor destroy their monasteries:[46] and you will find another sort of people, that belong to the synagogue of Satan, who have shaven crowns;[47] be sure you cleave their skulls, and give them no quarter till they either turn Mohammedans or pay tribute." All profane or frivolous conversation, all dangerous recollection of ancient quarrels, was severely prohibited among the Arabs: in the tumult of a camp the exercises of religion were assiduously practised; and the intervals of action were employed in prayer, meditation, and the study of the Koran The abuse, or even the use, of wine was chastised by fourscore strokes on the soles of the feet, and in the fervour of their primitive zeal many secret sinners revealed their fault and solicited their punishment. After some hesitation, the command of the Syrian army was delegated to Abu Obeidah, one of the fugitives of Mecca, and companions of Mohammed; whose zeal and devotion were assuaged, without being abated, by the singular mildness and benevolence of his temper. But in all the emergencies of war the soldiers demanded the superior genius of Chaled; and whoever might be the choice of the prince, the *Sword of God* was both in fact and fame the foremost leader of the Saracens. He obeyed without reluctance; he was consulted without jealousy; and such was the spirit of the man, or rather of the times, that Chaled professed his readiness to serve under the banner of the faith, though it were in the hands of a child or an enemy. Glory and riches and dominion were indeed promised to the victorious Musulman; but he was carefully instructed, that, if the goods of this life were his only incitement, *they* likewise would be his only reward.

One of the fifteen provinces of Syria, the cultivated lands to the eastward of the Jordan had been decorated by Roman vanity with the name of *Arabia*;[48] and the first arms of the Saracens were justified by the semblance of a national right. The country was enriched by the various benefits of trade; by the vigilance of the emperors it was covered with a line of forts; and the populous cities of Gerasa, Philadelphia, and Bosra[49] were secure, at least from a surprise, by the solid structure of their walls. The last of these cities was the eighteenth station from Medina: the road was familiar to the caravans of Hejaz and Irak, who annually visited this plenteous market of the province and the desert: the perpetual jealousy of the Arabs had trained the inhabitants to arms; and twelve thousand horse could sally from the gates of Bosra, an appellation which signifies, in the Syriac language, a strong tower of defence. Encouraged by their first success against the open towns and flying parties of the borders, a detachment of four thousand Moslems presumed to summon and attack the fortress of Bosra. They were oppressed by the numbers of the Syrians; they were saved by the presence of Chaled, with fifteen hundred horse: he blamed the enterprise, restored the battle, and rescued his friend, the venerable Serjabil, who had vainly invoked the unity of God and the promises of the apostle. After a short repose the Moslems performed their ablutions with sand instead of water;[50] and the morning prayer was recited by Chaled before they mounted on horseback. Confident in their strength, the people of Bosra threw open their gates, drew their forces into the plain, and swore to die in the defence of their religion. But a religion of peace was incapable of withstanding the fanatic cry of "Fight, fight! Paradise, paradise!" that re-echoed in the ranks of the Saracens; and the uproar of the town, the ringing of bells,[51] and the exclamations of the priests and monks, increased the dismay and disorder of the Christians. With the loss of two hundred and thirty men, the Arabs remained masters of the field; and the ramparts of Bosra, in expectation of human or divine aid, were crowded with holy crosses and consecrated banners. The governor Romanus had recommended an early submission: despised by the people, and degraded from his office, he still retained the desire and opportunity of revenge. In a nocturnal interview he informed the enemy of a subterraneous passage from his house under the wall of the city; the son of the caliph, with a hundred volunteers, were committed to the faith of this new ally, and their successful intrepidity gave an easy entrance to their companions. After Chaled had imposed the terms of servitude and tribute, the apostate or convert avowed in the assembly of the people his meritorious treason: "I renounce your society," said Romanus, "both in this world and the world to come. And I deny him that was crucified, and whosoever worships him. And I choose God for my Lord, Islam for my faith, Mecca for my temple, the Moslems for my brethren, and Mohammed for my prophet; who was sent to lead us into the right way, and to exalt the true religion in spite of those who join partners with God."

The conquest of Bosra, four days' journey from Damascus,[52] encouraged the Arabs to besiege the ancient capital of Syria.[53] At some distance from the walls they encamped among the groves and fountains of that delicious territory,[54] and the usual option, of the Mohammedan faith, of tribute, or of war, was proposed to the resolute citizens, who had been lately strengthened by a reinforcement of five thousand Greeks. In the decline, as in the infancy of the military art, a hostile defiance was frequently offered and accepted by the generals themselves:[55] many a lance was shivered in the plain of Damascus, and the personal prowess of Chaled was signalised in the first sally of the besieged. After an obstinate combat he had overthrown and made prisoner one of the Christian leaders, a stout and worthy antagonist. He instantly mounted a fresh horse, the gift of the governor of Palmyra, and pushed forwards to the front of the battle. "Repose yourself for a moment," said his friend Derar, "and permit me to supply your place: you are fatigued with fighting with this dog." "O Derar," replied the indefatigable Saracen, "we shall rest in the world to come. He that labours to-day shall rest to-morrow." With the same unabated ardour Chaled answered, encountered, and vanquished a second champion; and the heads of his two captives, who refused to abandon their religion, were indignantly hurled into the midst of the city. The event of some general and partial actions reduced the Damascenes to a closer defence: but a messenger, whom they dropped from the walls, returned with the promise of speedy and powerful succour, and their tumultuous joy conveyed the intelligence to the camp of the Arabs. After some debate, it was resolved by the generals to raise, or rather to suspend, the siege of Damascus till they had given battle to the forces of the emperor. In the retreat Chaled would have chosen the more perilous station of the rear-guard; he modestly yielded to the wishes of Abu Obeidah. But in the hour of danger he flew to the rescue of his companion, who was rudely pressed by a sally of six thousand horse and ten thousand foot, and few among the Christians could relate at Damascus the circumstances of their defeat. The importance of the contest required the junction of the Saracens, who were dispersed on the frontiers of Syria and Palestine; and I shall transcribe one of the circular mandates which was addressed to Amrou, the future conqueror of Egypt: "In the name of the most merciful God: from Chaled to Amrou, health and happiness. Know that thy brethren the Moslems design to march to Aiznadin, where there is an army of seventy thousand Greeks, who purpose to come against us, *that they may extinguish the light of God with their mouths; but God preserveth his light in spite of the infidels.*[56] As soon therefore as this letter of mine shall be delivered to thy hands, come with those that are with thee to Aiznadin, where thou shalt find us if it please the most high God." The summons was cheerfully obeyed, and the forty-five thousand Moslems, who met on the same day, on the same spot, ascribed to the blessing of Providence the effects of their activity and zeal.

About four years after the triumphs of the Persian war the repose of Heraclius and the empire was again disturbed by a new enemy, the power of whose religion was more strongly felt than it was clearly understood by the Christians of the East. In his palace of Constantinople or Antioch he was awakened by the invasion of Syria, the loss of Bosra, and the danger of Damascus. An army of seventy thousand veterans, or new levies, was assembled at Hems or Emesa, under the command of his general Werdan:[57] and these troops, consisting chiefly of cavalry, might be indifferently styled either Syrians, or Greeks, or Romans: *Syrians*, from the place of their birth or warfare; *Greeks*, from the religion and language of their sovereign; and *Romans*, from the proud appellation which was still profaned by the successors of Constantine. On the plain of Aiznadin, as Werdan rode on a white mule decorated with gold chains, and surrounded with ensigns and standards, he was surprised by the near approach of a fierce and naked warrior, who had undertaken to view the state of the enemy. The adventurous valour of Derar was inspired, and has perhaps been adorned, by the enthusiasm of his age and country. The hatred of the Christians, the love of spoil, and the contempt of danger, were the ruling passions of the audacious Saracen; and the prospect of instant death could never shake his religious confidence, or ruffle the calmness of his resolution, or even suspend the frank and martial pleasantry of his humour. In the most hopeless enterprises he was bold, and prudent, and fortunate: after innumerable hazards, after being thrice a prisoner in the hands of the infidels, he still survived to relate the achievements, and to enjoy the rewards, of the Syrian conquest. On this occasion his single lance maintained a flying fight against thirty Romans, who were detached by Werdan; and, after killing or unhorsing seventeen of their number, Derar returned in safety to his applauding brethren. When his rashness was mildly censured by the general, he excused himself with the simplicity of a soldier. "Nay," said Derar, "I did not begin first: but they came out to take me, and I was afraid that God should see me turn my back: and indeed I fought in good earnest, and without doubt God assisted me against them; and had I not been apprehensive of disobeying your orders, I should not have come away as I did; and I perceive already that they will fall into our hands." In the presence of both armies a venerable Greek advanced from the ranks with a liberal offer of peace; and the departure of the Saracens would have been purchased by a gift to each soldier of a turban, a robe, and a piece of gold; ten robes and a hundred pieces to their leader; one hundred robes and a thousand pieces to the caliph. A smile of indignation expressed the refusal of Chaled. "Ye Christian dogs, you know your option; the Koran, the tribute, or the sword. We are a people whose delight is in war rather than in peace: and we despise your pitiful alms, since we shall be speedily masters of your wealth, your families, and your persons." Notwithstanding this apparent disdain, he was deeply conscious of the public danger: those who had been in Persia, and had seen the armies of Chosroes, confessed that they never beheld a more formidable array. From the superiority of the enemy the artful Saracen derived a fresh incentive of courage: "You see before you," said he, "the united force of the Romans; you cannot hope to escape, but you may conquer Syria in a single day. The event depends on your discipline and patience. Reserve yourselves till the evening. It was in the evening that the Prophet was accustomed to vanquish." During two successive engagements, his temperate firmness sustained the darts of the enemy and the murmurs of his troops. At length, when the spirits and quivers of the adverse line were almost exhausted, Chaled gave the signal of onset and victory. The remains of the Imperial army fled to Antioch, or Cæsarea, or Damascus; and the death of four hundred and seventy Moslems was compensated by the opinion that they had sent to hell above fifty thousand of the infidels. The spoil was inestimable; many banners and crosses of gold and silver, precious stones, silver and gold chains, and innumerable suits of the richest armour and apparel. The general distribution was postponed till Damascus should be taken; but the seasonable supply of arms became the instrument of new victories. The glorious intelligence was transmitted to the throne of the caliph; and the Arabian tribes, the coldest or most hostile to the prophet's mission, were eager and importunate to share the harvest of Syria.

The sad tidings were carried to Damascus by the speed of grief and terror; and the inhabitants beheld from their walls the return of the heroes of Aiznadin. Amrou led the van at the head of nine thousand horse: the bands of the Saracens succeeded each other in formidable review; and the rear was closed by Chaled in person, with the standard of the black eagle. To the activity of Derar he intrusted the commission of patrolling round the city with two thousand horse, of scouring the plain, and of intercepting all succour or intelligence. The rest of the Arabian chiefs were fixed in their respective stations before the seven gates of Damascus; and the siege was renewed with fresh vigour and confidence. The art, the labour, the military engines of the Greeks and Romans are seldom to be found in the simple, though successful, operations of the Saracens: it was sufficient for them to invest a city with arms rather than with trenches; to repel the sallies of the besieged; to attempt a stratagem or an assault; or to expect the progress of famine and discontent. Damascus would have acquiesced in the trial of Aiznadin, as a final and peremptory sentence between the emperor and the caliph: her courage was rekindled by the example and authority of Thomas, a noble Greek, illustrious in a private condition by the alliance of Heraclius.[58]

The tumult and illumination of the night proclaimed the design of the morning sally; and the Christian hero, who affected to despise the enthusiasm of the Arabs, employed the resource of a similar superstition. At the principal gate, in the sight of both armies, a lofty crucifix was erected; the bishop, with his clergy, accompanied the march, and laid the volume of the New Testament before the image of Jesus; and the contending parties were scandalised or edified by a prayer that the Son of God would defend his servants and vindicate his truth. The battle raged with incessant fury; and the dexterity of Thomas,[59] an incomparable archer, was fatal to the boldest Saracens, till their death was revenged by a female heroine. The wife of Aban, who had followed him to the holy war, embraced her expiring husband. "Happy," said she, "happy art thou, my dear: thou art gone to thy Lord, who first joined us together, and then parted us asunder. I will revenge thy death, and endeavour to the utmost of my power to come to the place where thou art, because I love thee. Henceforth shall no man ever touch me more, for I have dedicated myself to the service of God." Without a groan, without a tear, she washed the corpse of her husband, and buried him with the usual rites. Then grasping the manly weapons, which in her native land she was accustomed to wield, the intrepid widow of Aban sought the place where his murderer fought in the thickest of the battle. Her first arrow pierced the hand of his standard-bearer; her second wounded Thomas in the eye; and the fainting Christians no longer beheld their ensign or their leader. Yet the generous champion of Damascus refused to withdraw to his palace: his wound was dressed on the rampart; the fight was continued till the evening; and the Syrians rested on their arms. In the silence of the night, the signal was given by a stroke on the great bell; the gates were thrown open, and each gate discharged an impetuous column on the sleeping camp of the Saracens. Chaled was the first in arms: at the head of four hundred horse he flew to the post of danger, and the tears trickled down his iron cheeks as he uttered a fervent ejaculation: "O God, who never sleepest, look upon thy servants, and do not deliver them into the hands of their enemies." The valour and victory of Thomas were arrested by the presence of the *Sword of God*; with the knowledge of the peril, the Moslems recovered their ranks, and charged the assailants in the flank and rear. After the loss of thousands, the Christian general retreated with a sigh of despair, nd the pursuit of the Saracens was checked by he military engines of the rampart.

After a siege of seventy days,[60] the patience, nd perhaps the provisions, of the Damascenes vere exhausted; and the bravest of their chiefs ubmitted to the hard dictates of necessity. In he occurrences of peace and war, they had een taught to dread the fierceness of Chaled nd to revere the mild virtues of Abu Obeidah. At the hour of midnight one hundred chosen eputies of the clergy and people were intro- uced to the tent of that venerable commander. He received and dismissed them with courtesy. They returned with a written agreement, on the aith of a companion of Mohammed, that all ostilities should cease; that the voluntary emi- rants might depart in safety, with as much as hey could carry away of their effects; and that he tributary subjects of the caliph should enjoy heir lands and houses, with the use and pos- ession of seven churches. On these terms, the nost respectable hostages, and the gate nearest o his camp, were delivered into his hands: his oldiers imitated the moderation of their chief; nd he enjoyed the submissive gratitude of a eople whom he had rescued from destruction. But the success of the treaty had relaxed their igilance, and in the same moment the opposite quarter of the city was betrayed and taken by ssault. A party of a hundred Arabs had opened he eastern gate to a more inexorable foe. "No quarter," cried the rapacious and sanguinary Chaled, "no quarter to the enemies of the Lord:" his trumpets sounded, and a torrent of Christian blood was poured down the streets of Damascus. When he reached the church of St. Mary, he was astonished and provoked by the eaceful aspect of his companions; their swords vere in the scabbard, and they were surrounded y a multitude of priests and monks. Abu Obei- lah saluted the general: "God," said he, "has lelivered the city into my hands by way of sur- ender, and has saved the believers the trouble f fighting." "And am *I* not," replied the indig- ant Chaled, "am *I* not the lieutenant of the ommander of the faithful? Have I not taken he city by storm? The unbelievers shall perish y the sword. Fall on." The hungry and cruel Arabs would have obeyed the welcome com- nand; and Damascus was lost, if the benevo- ence of Abu Obeidah had not been supported y a decent and dignified firmness. Throwing imself between the trembling citizens and the nost eager of the barbarians, he adjured them, y the holy name of God, to respect his promise, o suspend their fury, and to wait the determi-

nation of their chiefs. The chiefs retired into the church of St. Mary; and after a vehement de- bate, Chaled submitted in some measure to the reason and authority of his colleague; who urged the sanctity of a covenant, the advantage as well as the honour which the Moslems would derive from the punctual performance of their word, and the obstinate resistance which they must encounter from the distrust and despair of the rest of the Syrian cities. It was agreed that the sword should be sheathed, that the part of Damascus which had surrendered to Abu Obeidah should be immediately entitled to the benefit of his capitulation, and that the final decision should be referred to the justice and wisdom of the caliph.[61] A large majority of the people accepted the terms of toleration and tribute; and Damascus is still peopled by twenty thousand Christians. But the valiant Thomas, and the free-born patriots who had fought under his banner, embraced the alternative of poverty and exile. In the adjacent meadow a numerous encampment was formed of priests and laymen, of soldiers and citizens, of women and children: they collected, with haste and terror, their most precious movables; and abandoned, with loud lamentations or silent anguish, their native homes and the pleasant banks of the Pharpar. The inflexible soul of Chaled was not touched by the spectacle of their distress: he disputed with the Damascenes the property of a maga- zine of corn; endeavoured to exclude the garri- son from the benefit of the treaty; consented, with reluctance, that each of the fugitives should arm himself with a sword, or a lance, or a bow; and sternly declared, that, after a respite of three days, they might be pursued and treated as the enemies of the Moslems.

The passion of a Syrian youth completed the ruin of the exiles of Damascus. A nobleman of the city, of the name of Jonas,[62] was betrothed to a wealthy maiden; but her parents delayed the consummation of his nuptials, and their daughter was persuaded to escape with the man whom she had chosen. They corrupted the nightly watchmen of the gate Keisan; the lover, who led the way, was encompassed by a squad- ron of Arabs; but his exclamation in the Greek tongue, "the bird is taken," admonished his mistress to hasten her return. In the presence of Chaled, and of death, the unfortunate Jonas professed his belief in one God and his apostle Mohammed; and continued, till the season of his martyrdom, to discharge the duties of a brave and sincere Musulman. When the city was taken, he flew to the monastery where Eudocia had taken refuge; but the lover was forgotten; the apostate was scorned; she preferred her religion to her country; and the justice of Chaled, though deaf to mercy, refused to detain by force a male or female inhabitant of Damascus. Four days was the general confined to the city by the obligation of the treaty and the urgent cares of his new conquest. His appetite for blood and rapine would have been extinguished by the hopeless computation of time and distance; but he listened to the importunities of Jonas, who assured him that the weary fugitives might yet be overtaken. At the head of four thousand horse, in the disguise of Christian Arabs, Chaled undertook the pursuit. They halted only for the moments of prayer; and their guide had a perfect knowledge of the country. For a long way the footsteps of the Damascenes were plain and conspicuous: they vanished on a sudden; but the Saracens were comforted by the assurance that the caravan had turned aside into the mountains, and must speedily fall into their hands. In traversing the ridges of the Libanus they endured intolerable hardships, and the sinking spirits of the veteran fanatics were supported and cheered by the unconquerable ardour of a lover. From a peasant of the country they were informed that the emperor had sent orders to the colony of exiles to pursue without delay the road of the sea-coast and of Constantinople, apprehensive, perhaps, that the soldiers and people of Antioch might be discouraged by the sight and the story of their sufferings. The Saracens were conducted through the territories of Gabala[63] and Laodicea, at a cautious distance from the walls of the cities; the rain was incessant, the night was dark, a single mountain separated them from the Roman army; and Chaled, ever anxious for the safety of his brethren, whispered an ominous dream in the ear of his companion. With the dawn of day the prospect again cleared, and they saw before them, in a pleasant valley, the tents of Damascus. After a short interval of repose and prayer Chaled divided his cavalry into four squadrons, committing the first to his faithful Derar, and reserving the last for himself. They successively rushed on the promiscuous multitude, insufficiently provided with arms, and already vanquished by sorrow and fatigue. Except a captive, who was pardoned and dismissed, the Arabs enjoyed the satisfaction of believing that not a Christian of either sex escaped the edge of their scimitars. The gold and silver of Damascus was scattered over the camp, and a royal wardrobe of three hundred load of silk might clothe an army of naked barbarians. In the tumult of the battle Jonas sought and found the object of his pursuit: but her resentment was inflamed by the last act of his perfidy; and as Eudocia struggled in his hateful embraces, she struck a dagger to her heart. Another female, the widow of Thomas, and the real or supposed daughter of Heraclius, was spared and released without a ransom; but the generosity of Chaled was the effect of his contempt; and the haughty Saracen insulted, by a message of defiance, the throne of the Cæsars. Chaled had penetrated above a hundred and fifty miles into the heart of the Roman province; he returned to Damascus with the same secrecy and speed. On the accession of Omar, the *Sword of God* was removed from the command; but the caliph, who blamed the rashness, was compelled to applaud the vigour and conduct of the enterprise.

Another expedition of the conquerors of Damascus will equally display their avidity and their contempt for the riches of the present world. They were informed that the produce and manufactures of the country were annually collected in the fair of Abyla,[64] about thirty miles from the city; that the cell of a devout hermit was visited at the same time by a multitude of pilgrims; and that the festival of trade and superstition would be ennobled by the nuptials of the daughter of the governor of Tripoli. Abdallah, the son of Jaafar, a glorious and holy martyr, undertook, with a banner of five hundred horse, the pious and profitable commission of despoiling the infidels. As he approached the fair of Abyla, he was astonished by the report of the mighty concourse of Jews and Christians, Greeks and Armenians, of natives of Syria and of strangers of Egypt, to the number of ten thousand, besides a guard of five thousand horse that attended the person of the bride. The Saracens paused: "For my own part," said Abdallah, "I *dare not* go back: our foes are many, our danger is great, but our reward is splendid and secure, either in this life or in the life to come. Let every man, according to his inclination, advance or retire." Not a Musulman deserted his standard. "Lead the way," said Abdallah to his Christian guide, "and you shall see what the companions of the prophet can perform." They charged in five squadrons; but after the first advantage of the surprise they were encompassed and almost overwhelmed by the multitude of their enemies; and their valiant band is fancifully compared to a white spot in the skin of a black camel.[65] About the hour of sunset when their weapons dropped from their hands, when they panted on the verge of eternity, they discovered an approaching cloud of dust, they heard the welcome sound of the *techir*,[66] and they soon perceived the standard of Chaled, who flew to their relief with the utmost speed of his cavalry. The Christians were broken by his attack, and slaughtered in their flight, as far as the river of Tripoli. They left behind them the various riches of the fair; the merchandises that were exposed for sale, the money that was brought for purchase, the gay decorations of the nuptials, and the governor's daughter, with forty of her female attendants. The fruits, provisions, and furniture, the money, plate, and jewels, were diligently laden on the backs of horses, asses, and mules; and the holy robbers returned in triumph to Damascus. The hermit, after a short and angry controversy with Chaled, declined the crown of martyrdom, and was left alive in the solitary scene of blood and devastation.

Syria,[67] one of the countries that have been improved by the most early cultivation, is not unworthy of the preference.[68] The heat of the climate is tempered by the vicinity of the sea and mountains, by the plenty of wood and water; and the produce of a fertile soil affords the subsistence, and encourages the propagation, of men and animals. From the age of David to that of Heraclius, the country was overspread with ancient and flourishing cities: the inhabitants were numerous and wealthy; and, after the slow ravage of despotism and superstition, after the recent calamities of the Persian war, Syria could still attract and reward the rapacious tribes of the desert. A plain, of ten days' journey, from Damascus to Aleppo and Antioch, is watered, on the western side, by the winding course of the Orontes. The hills of Libanus and Anti-Libanus are planted from north to south, between the Orontes and the Mediterranean; and the epithet of *hollow* (Cœlesyria) was applied to a long and fruitful valley, which is confined in the same direction by the two ridges of snowy mountains.[69] Among the cities which are enumerated by Greek and Oriental names in the geography and conquest of Syria, we may distinguish Emesa or Hems, Heliopolis or Baalbec, the former as the metropolis of the plain, the latter as the capital of the valley. Under the last of the Cæsars they were strong and populous; the turrets glittered from afar: an ample space was covered with public and private buildings; and the citizens were illustrious by their spirit, or at least by their pride; by their riches, or at least by their luxury. In the days of paganism, both Emesa and Heliopolis were addicted to the worship of Baal, or the sun; but the decline of their superstition and splendour has been marked by a singular variety of fortune. Not a vestige remains of the temple of Emesa, which was equalled in poetic style to the summits of Mount Libanus,[70] while the ruins of Baalbec, invisible to the writers of antiquity, excite the curiosity and wonder of the European traveller.[71] The measure of the temple is two hundred feet in length and one hundred in breadth: the front is adorned with a double portico of eight columns; fourteen may be counted on either side; and each column, forty-five feet in height, is composed of three massy blocks of stone or marble. The proportions and ornaments of the Corinthian order express the architecture of the Greeks: but as Baalbec has never been the seat of a monarch, we are at a loss to conceive how the expense of these magnificent structures could be supplied by private or municipal liberality.[72] From the conquest of Damascus the Saracens proceeded to Heliopolis and Emesa: but I shall decline the repetition of the sallies and combats which have been already shown on a larger scale. In the prosecution of the war their policy was not less effectual than their sword. By short and separate truces they dissolved the union of the enemy; accustomed the Syrians to compare their friendship with their enmity; familiarised the idea of their language, religion, and manners; and exhausted, by clandestine purchase, the magazines and arsenals of the cities which they returned to besiege. They aggravated the ransom of the more wealthy or the more obstinate; and Chalcis alone was taxed at five thousand ounces of gold, five thousand ounces of silver, two thousand robes of silk, and as many figs and olives as would load five thousand asses. But the terms of truce or capitulation were faithfully observed; and the lieutenant of the caliph, who had promised not to enter the walls of the captive Baalbec, remained tranquil and immovable in his tent till the jarring factions solicited the interposition of a foreign master. The conquest of the plain and valley of Syria was achieved in less than two years. Yet the commander of the faithful reproved the slowness of their progress; and the Saracens, bewailing their fault with tears of rage and repentance, called aloud on their chiefs to lead them forth to fight the battles of the Lord. In a recent action, under the walls of Emesa, an Arabian youth, the cousin of Chaled, was heard aloud to exclaim, "Methinks I see the black-eyed girls looking upon me; one of whom, should she appear in this world, all mankind would die for love of her. And I see in the hand of one of them a handkerchief of green silk and a cap of precious stones, and she beckons me, and calls out, Come hither quickly, for I love thee." With these words, charging the Christians, he made havoc wherever he went, till, observed at length by the governor of Hems, he was struck through with a javelin.

It was incumbent on the Saracens to exert the full powers of their valour and enthusiasm against the forces of the emperor, who was taught, by repeated losses, that the rovers of the desert had undertaken, and would speedily achieve, a regular and permanent conquest. From the provinces of Europe and Asia, fourscore thousand soldiers were transported by sea and land to Antioch and Cæsarea: the light troops of the army consisted of sixty thousand Christian Arabs of the tribe of Gassan. Under the banner of Jabalah, the last of their princes, they marched in the van; and it was a maxim of the Greeks, that, for the purpose of cutting diamond, a diamond was the most effectual. Heraclius withheld his person from the dangers of the field; but his presumption, or perhaps his despondency, suggested a peremptory order, that the fate of the province and the war should be decided by a single battle. The Syrians were attached to the standard of Rome and of the cross; but the noble, the citizen, the peasant, were exasperated by the injustice and cruelty of a licentious host, who oppressed them as subjects and despised them as strangers and aliens.[73] A report of these mighty preparations was conveyed to the Saracens in their camp of Emesa; and the chiefs, though resolved to fight, assembled a council: the faith of Abu Obeidah would have expected on the same spot the glory of martyrdom; the wisdom of Chaled advised an honourable retreat to the skirts of Palestine and Arabia, where they might await the succours of their friends and the attack of the unbelievers. A speedy messenger soon returned from the throne of Medina, with the blessings of Omar and Ali, the prayers of the widows of the prophet, and a reinforcement of eight thousand Moslems. In their way they overturned a detachment of Greeks; and when they joined at Yermuk the camp of their brethren, they found the pleasing intelligence that Chaled had already defeated and scattered the Christian Arabs of the tribe of Gassan. In the neighbourhood of Bosra, the springs of Mount Hermon descend in a torrent to the plain of Decapolis, or ten cities; and the Hieromax, a name which has been corrupted to Yermuk, is lost, after a short course, in the lake of Tiberias.[74] The banks of this obscure stream were illustrated by a long and bloody encounter. On this momentous occasion the public voice and the modesty of Abu Obeidah restored the command to the most deserving of the Moslems. Chaled assumed his station in the front, his colleague was posted in the rear, that the disorder of the fugitives might be checked by his venerable aspect, and the sight of the yellow banner which Mohammed had displayed before the walls of Chaibar. The last line was occupied by the sister of Derar, with the Arabian women who had enlisted in this holy war, who were accustomed to wield the bow and the lance, and who in a moment of captivity had defended, against the uncircumcised ravishers, their chastity and religion.[75] The exhortation of the generals was brief and forcible: "Paradise is before you, the devil and hell-fire in your rear." Yet such was the weight of the Roman cavalry that the right wing of the Arabs was broken and separated from the main body. Thrice did they retreat in disorder, and thrice were they driven back to the charge by the reproaches and blows of the women. In the intervals of action, Abu Obeidah visited the tents of his brethren, prolonged their repose by repeating at once the prayers of two different hours; bound up their wounds with his own hands, and administered the comfortable reflection that the infidels partook of their sufferings without partaking of their reward. Four thousand and thirty of the Moslems were buried in the field of battle; and the skill of the Armenian archers enabled seven hundred to boast that they had lost an eye in that meritorious service. The veterans of the Syrian war acknowledged that it was the hardest and most doubtful of the days which they had seen. But it was likewise the most decisive: many thousands of the Greeks and Syrians fell by the swords of the Arabs; many were slaughtered after the defeat, in the woods and mountains, many, by mistaking the ford, were drowned in the waters of the Yermuk; and however the loss may be magnified,[76] the Christian writers confess and bewail the bloody punishment of their sins.[77] Manuel, the Roman general, was either killed at Damascus, or took refuge in the monastery of Mount Sinai. An exile in the Byzantine court, Jabalah lamented the manners of Arabia, and his unlucky preference of the Christian cause.[78] He had once inclined to the profession of Islam; but in the pilgrimage of Mecca, Jabalah was provoked to strike one of his brethren, and fled with amazement from the stern and equal justice of the caliph. The victorious Saracens enjoyed at Damascus a month of pleasure and repose: the spoil was divided by the discretion of Abu Obeidah: an equal share was allotted to a soldier and to his horse, and a double portion was reserved for the noble coursers of the Arabian breed.

After the battle of Yermuk the Roman army no longer appeared in the field; and the Saracens might securely choose among the fortified towns of Syria the first object of their attack. They consulted the caliph whether they should march to Cæsarea or Jerusalem; and the advice of Ali determined the immediate siege of the latter. To a profane eye Jerusalem was the first or second capital of Palestine; but after Mecca and Medina, it was revered and visited by the devout Moslems as the temple of the Holy Land, which had been sanctified by the revelation of Moses, of Jesus, and of Mohammed himself. The son of Abu Sophian was sent with five thousand Arabs to try the first experiment of surprise or treaty; but on the eleventh day the town was invested by the whole force of Abu Obeidah. He addressed the customary summons to the chief commanders and people of Ælia.[79] "Health and happiness to every one that follows the right way! We require of you to testify that there is but one God, and that Mohammed is his apostle. If you refuse this, consent to pay tribute, and be under us forthwith. Otherwise I shall bring men against you who love death better than you do the drinking of wine or eating hog's flesh. Nor will I ever stir from you, if it please God, till I have destroyed those that fight for you, and made slaves of your children." But the city was defended on every side by deep valleys and steep ascents; since the invasion of Syria the walls and towers had been anxiously restored; the bravest of the fugitives of Yermuk had stopped in the nearest place of refuge; and in the defence of the sepulchre of Christ the natives and strangers might feel some sparks of the enthusiasm which so fiercely glowed in the bosoms of the Saracens. The siege of Jerusalem lasted four months; not a day was lost without some action of sally or assault; the military engines incessantly played from the ramparts; and the inclemency of the winter was still more painful and destructive to the Arabs. The Christians yielded at length to the perseverance of the besiegers. The patriarch Sophronius appeared on the walls, and by the voice of an interpreter demanded a conference. After a vain attempt to dissuade the lieutenant of the caliph from his impious enterprise, he proposed, in the name of the people, a fair capitulation, with this extraordinary clause, that the articles of security should be ratified by the authority and presence of Omar himself. The question was debated in the council of Medina; the sanctity of the place, and the advice of Ali, persuaded the caliph to gratify the wishes of his soldiers and enemies; and the simplicity of his journey is more illustrious than the royal pageants of vanity and oppression. The conqueror of Persia and Syria was mounted on a red camel, which carried, besides his person, a bag of corn, a bag of dates, a wooden dish, and a leathern bottle of water. Wherever he halted, the company, without distinction, was invited to partake of his homely fare, and the repast was consecrated by the prayer and exhortation of the commander of the faithful.[80] But in this expedition or pilgrimage his power was exercised in the administration of justice: he reformed the licentious polygamy of the Arabs, relieved the tributaries from extortion and cruelty, and chastised the luxury of the Saracens by despoiling them of their rich silks, and dragging them on their faces in the dirt. When he came within sight of Jerusalem, the caliph cried with a loud voice, "God is victorious: O Lord, give us an easy conquest!" and, pitching his tent of coarse hair, calmly seated himself on the ground. After signing the capitulation, he entered the city without fear or precaution, and courteously discoursed with the patriarch concerning its religious antiquities.[81] Sophronius bowed before his new master, and secretly muttered, in the words of Daniel, "The abomination of desolation is in the holy place."[82] At the hour of prayer they stood together in the church of the Resurrection; but the caliph refused to perform his devotions, and contented himself with praying on the steps of the church of Constantine. To the patriarch he disclosed his prudent and honourable motive. "Had I yielded," said Omar, "to your request, the Moslems of a future age would have infringed the treaty under colour of imitating my example." By his command the ground of the temple of Solomon was prepared for the foundation of a mosch;[83] and, during a residence of ten days, he regulated the present and future state of his Syrian conquests. Medina might be jealous lest the caliph should be detained by the sanctity of Jerusalem or the beauty of Damascus; her apprehensions were dispelled by his prompt and voluntary return to the tomb of the apostle.[84]

To achieve what yet remained of the Syrian war, the caliph had formed two separate armies; a chosen detachment, under Amrou and Yezid, was left in the camp of Palestine; while the larger division, under the standard of Abu Obeidah and Chaled, marched away to the north against Antioch and Aleppo. The latter of these, the Berœa of the Greeks, was not yet illustrious as the capital of a province or a kingdom; and the inhabitants, by anticipating their submission and pleading their poverty, obtained a moderate composition for their lives and religion. But the castle of Aleppo,[85] distinct from the city, stood erect on a lofty artificial mound: the sides were sharpened to a precipice, and faced with freestone; and the breadth of the ditch might be filled with water from the neighbouring springs. After the loss of three thousand men, the garrison was still equal to the defence; and Youkinna, their valiant and hereditary chief, had murdered his brother, a holy monk, for daring to pronounce the name of peace. In a siege of four or five months, the hardest of the Syrian war, great numbers of the Saracens were killed and wounded: their removal to the distance of a mile could not seduce the vigilance of Youkinna; nor could the Christians be terrified by the execution of three hundred captives, whom they beheaded before the castle wall. The silence, and at length the complaints, of Abu Obeidah informed the caliph that their hope and patience were consumed at the foot of this impregnable fortress. "I am variously affected," replied Omar, "by the difference of your success; but I charge you by no means to raise the siege of the castle. Your retreat would diminish the reputation of our arms, and encourage the infidels to fall upon you on all sides. Remain before Aleppo till God shall determine the event, and forage with your horse round the adjacent country." The exhortation of the commander of the faithful was fortified by a supply of volunteers from all the tribes of Arabia, who arrived in the camp on horses or camels. Among these was Dames, of a servile birth, but of gigantic size and intrepid resolution. The forty-seventh day of his service he proposed, with only thirty men, to make an attempt on the castle. The experience and testimony of Chaled recommended his offer; and Abu Obeidah admonished his brethren not to despise the baser origin of Dames, since he himself, could he relinquish the public care, would cheerfully serve under the banner of the slave.

His design was covered by the appearance of a retreat; and the camp of the Saracens was pitched about a league from Aleppo. The thirty adventurers lay in ambush at the foot of the hill; and Dames at length succeeded in his inquiries, though he was provoked by the ignorance of his Greek captives. "God curse these dogs," said the illiterate Arab, "what a strange barbarous language they speak!" At the darkest hour of the night he scaled the most accessible height, which he had diligently surveyed, a place where the stones were less entire, or the slope less perpendicular, or the guard less vigilant. Seven of the stoutest Saracens mounted on each other's shoulders, and the weight of the column was sustained on the broad and sinewy back of the gigantic slave. The foremost in this painful ascent could grasp and climb the lowest part of the battlements; they silently stabbed and cast down the sentinels; and the thirty brethren, repeating a pious ejaculation, "O apostle of God, help and deliver us!" were successively drawn up by the long folds of their turbans. With bold and cautious footsteps Dames explored the palace of the governor, who celebrated, in riotous merriment, the festival of his deliverance. From thence, returning to his companions, he assaulted on the inside the entrance of the castle. They overpowered the guard, unbolted the gate, let down the drawbridge, and defended the narrow pass, till the arrival of Chaled, with the dawn of day, relieved their danger and assured their conquest. Youkinna, a formidable foe, became an active and useful proselyte; and the general of the Saracens expressed his regard for the most humble merit, by detaining the army at Aleppo till Dames was cured of his honourable wounds. The capital of Syria was still covered by the castle of Aazaz and the iron bridge of the Orontes. After the loss of those important posts, and the defeat of the last of the Roman armies, the luxury of Antioch[86] trembled and obeyed. Her safety was ransomed with three hundred thousand pieces of gold; but the throne of the successors of Alexander, the seat of the Roman government in the East, which had been decorated by Cæsar with the titles of free, and holy. and inviolate, was degraded under the yoke of the caliphs to the secondary rank of a provincial town.[87]

In the life of Heraclius the glories of the Persian war are clouded on either hand by the disgrace and weakness of his more early and his later days. When the successors of Mohammed unsheathed the sword of war and religion, he was astonished at the boundless prospect of toil and danger; his nature was indolent, nor could the infirm and frigid age of the emperor be kindled to a second effort. The sense of shame, and the importunities of the Syrians, prevented his hasty departure from the scene of action; but the hero was no more; and the loss of Damascus and Jerusalem, the bloody fields of Aiznadin and Yermuk, may be imputed in some degree to the absence or misconduct of the sovereign. Instead of defending the sepulchre of Christ, he involved the church and state in a metaphysical controversy for the unity of his will; and while Heraclius crowned the offspring of his second nuptials, he was tamely stripped of the most valuable part of their inheritance. In the cathedral of Antioch, in the presence of the bishops, at the foot of the crucifix, he bewailed the sins of the prince and people; but his confession instructed the world that it was vain, and perhaps impious, to resist the judgment of God. The Saracens were invincible in fact, since they were invincible in opinion; and the desertion of Youkinna, his false repentance and repeated perfidy, might justify the suspicion of the emperor that he was encompassed by traitors and apostates who conspired to betray his person and their country to the enemies of Christ. In the hour of adversity his superstition was agitated by the omens and dreams of a falling crown; and after bidding an eternal farewell to Syria, he secretly embarked with a few attendants, and absolved the faith of his subjects.[88] Constantine, his eldest son, had been stationed with forty thousand men at Cæsarea, the civil metropolis of the three provinces of Palestine. But his private interest recalled him to the Byzantine court; and, after the flight of his father, he felt himself an unequal champion to the united force of the caliph. His vanguard was boldly attacked by three hundred Arabs and a thousand black slaves, who, in the depth of winter, had climbed the snowy mountains of Libanus, and who were speedily followed by the victorious squadrons of Chaled himself. From the north and south the troops of Antioch and Jerusalem advanced along the seashore till their banners were joined under the walls of the Phœnician cities: Tripoli and Tyre were betrayed; and a fleet of fifty transports, which entered without distrust the captive harbours, brought a seasonable supply of arms and provisions to the camp of the Saracens. Their labours were terminated by the unexpected surrender of Cæsarea: the Roman prince had embarked in the night;[89] and the defenceless citizens solicited their pardon with an offering of two hundred thousand pieces of gold. The remainder of the province, Ramlah, Ptolemais or Acre, Sichem or Neapolis, Gaza, Ascalon, Berytus, Sidon, Gabala, Laodicea, Apamea, Hierapolis, no longer presumed to dispute the will of the conqueror; and Syria bowed under the sceptre of the caliphs seven hundred years after Pompey had despoiled the last of the Macedonian kings.[90]

The sieges and battles of six campaigns had consumed many thousands of the Moslems. They died with the reputation and the cheerfulness of martyrs; and the simplicity of their faith may be expressed in the words of an Arabian youth, when he embraced, for the last time, his sister and mother: "It is not," said he, "the delicacies of Syria, or the fading delights of this world, that have prompted me to devote my life in the cause of religion. But I seek the favour of God and his apostles; and I have heard, from one of the companions of the prophet, that the spirits of the martyrs will be lodged in the crops of green birds, who shall taste the fruits, and drink of the rivers, of paradise. Farewell: we shall meet again among the groves and fountains which God has provided for his elect." The faithful captives might exercise a passive and more arduous resolution; and a cousin of Mohammed is celebrated for refusing, after an abstinence of three days, the wine and pork, the only nourishment that was allowed by the malice of the infidels. The frailty of some weaker brethren exasperated the implacable spirit of fanaticism; and the father of Amer deplored, in pathetic strains, the apostasy and damnation of a son, who had renounced the promises of God and the intercession of the prophet, to occupy, with the priests and deacons, the lowest mansions of hell. The more fortunate Arabs who survived the war and persevered in the faith were restrained by their abstemious leader from the abuse of prosperity. After a refreshment of three days Abu Obeidah withdrew his troops from the pernicious contagion of the luxury of Antioch, and assured the caliph that their religion and virtue could only be preserved by the hard discipline of poverty and labour. But the virtue of Omar, however rigorous to himself, was kind and liberal to his brethren. After a just tribute of praise and thanksgiving, he dropped a tear of compassion; and sitting down on the ground wrote an answer in which he mildly censured the severity of his lieutenant: "God," said the successor of the prophet, "has not forbidden the use of the good things of this world to faithful men, and such as have performed good works. Therefore you ought to have given them leave to rest themselves, and partake freely of those good things which the country affordeth. If any of the Saracens have no family in Arabia, they may marry in Syria; and whosoever of them wants any female slaves, he may purchase as many as he hath occasion for." The conquerors prepared to use, or to abuse, this gracious permission; but the year of their triumph was marked by a mortality of men and cattle, and twenty-five thousand Saracens were snatched away from the possession of Syria. The death of Abu Obeidah might be lamented by the Christians; but his brethren recollected that he was one of the ten elect whom the prophet had named as the heirs of paradise.[91] Chaled survived his brethren about three years; and the tomb of the Sword of God is shown in the neighbourhood of Emesa. His valour, which founded in Arabia and Syria the empire of the caliphs, was fortified by the opinion of a special providence; and as long as he wore a cap which had been blessed by Mohammed, he deemed himself invulnerable amidst the darts of the infidels.

The place of the first conquerors was supplied by a new generation of their children and countrymen: Syria became the seat and support of the house of Ommiyah; and the revenue, the soldiers, the ships of that powerful kingdom were consecrated to enlarge on every side the empire of the caliphs. But the Saracens despise a superfluity of fame; and their historians scarcely condescend to mention the subordinate conquests which are lost in the splendour and rapidity of their victorious career. To the *north* of Syria they passed Mount Taurus, and reduced to their obedience the province of Cilicia, with its capital Tarsus, the ancient monument of the Assyrian kings. Beyond a second ridge of the same mountains, they spread the flame of war, rather than the light of religion, as far as the shores of the Euxine and the neighbourhood of Constantinople. To the *east* they advanced to the banks and sources of the Euphrates and Tigris:[92] the long-disputed barrier of Rome and Persia was for ever confounded; the walls of Edessa and Amida, of Dara and Nisibis, which had resisted the arms and engines of Sapor or Nushirvan, were levelled in the dust; and the holy city of Abgarus might vainly produce the epistle or the image of Christ to an unbelieving conqueror. To the *west* the Syrian kingdom is bounded by the sea: and the ruin of Aradus, a small island or peninsula on the coast, was post-poned during ten years. But the hills of Libanus abounded in timber, the trade of Phœnicia was populous in mariners; and a fleet of seventeen hundred barks was equipped and manned by the natives of the desert. The Imperial navy of the Romans fled before them from the Pamphylian rocks to the Hellespont; but the spirit of the emperor, a grandson of Heraclius, had been subdued before the combat by a dream and a pun.[93] The Saracens rode masters of the sea; and the islands of Cyprus, Rhodes, and the Cyclades were successively exposed to their rapacious visits. Three hundred years before the Christian era, the memorable though fruitless siege of Rhodes,[94] by Demetrius, had furnished that maritime republic with the materials and the subject of a trophy. A gigantic statue of Apollo, or the sun, seventy cubits in height, was erected at the entrance of the harbour, a monument of the freedom and the arts of Greece. After standing fifty-six years, the colossus of Rhodes was overthrown by an earthquake; but the massy trunk, and huge fragments, lay scattered eight centuries on the ground, and are often described as one of the wonders of the ancient world. They were collected by the diligence of the Saracens, and sold to a Jewish merchant of Edessa, who is said to have laden nine hundred camels with the weight of the brass metal: an enormous weight, though we should include the hundred colossal figures,[95] and the three thousand statues, which adorned the prosperity of the city of the sun.

III. The conquest of Egypt may be explained by the character of the victorious Saracen, one of the first of his nation, in an age when the meanest of the brethren was exalted above his nature by the spirit of enthusiasm. The birth of Amrou was at once base and illustrious; his mother, a notorious prostitute, was unable to decide among the five of the Koreish; but the proof of resemblance adjudged the child to Aasi, the oldest of her lovers.[96] The youth of Amrou was impelled by the passions and prejudices of his kindred: his poetic genius was exercised in satirical verses against the person and doctrine of Mohammed; his dexterity was employed by the reigning faction to pursue the religious exiles who had taken refuge in the court of the Æthiopian king.[97] Yet he returned from this embassy a secret proselyte; his reason or his interest determined him to renounce the worship of idols; he escaped from Mecca with his friend Chaled; and the prophet of Medina enjoyed at the same moment the satisfaction of embracing the two firmest champions of his cause. The impatience of Amrou to lead the armies of the faithful was checked by the reproof of Omar, who advised him not to seek power and dominion, since he who is a subject to-day may be a prince to-morrow. Yet his merit was not overlooked by the two first successors of Mohammed; they were indebted to his arms for the conquest of Palestine; and in all the battles and sieges of Syria he united with the temper of a chief the valour of an adventurous soldier. In a visit to Medina the caliph expressed a wish to survey the sword which had cut down so many Christian warriors: the son of Aasi unsheathed a short and ordinary scimitar; and as he perceived the surprise of Omar, "Alas," said the modest Saracen, "the sword itself, without the arm of its master, is neither sharper nor more weighty than the sword of Pharezdak the poet."[98] After the conquest of Egypt he was recalled by the jealousy of the caliph Othman; but in the subsequent troubles, the ambition of a soldier, a statesman, and an orator, emerged from a private station. His powerful support, both in council and in the field, established the throne of the Ommiades; the administration and revenue of Egypt were restored by the gratitude of Moawiyah to a faithful friend who had raised himself above the rank of a subject; and Amrou ended his days in the palace and city which he had founded on the banks of the Nile. His dying speech to his children is celebrated by the Arabians as a model of eloquence and wisdom: he deplored the errors of his youth; but if the penitent was still infected by the vanity of a poet, he might exaggerate the venom and mischief of his impious compositions.[99]

From his camp in Palestine Amrou had surprised or anticipated the caliph's leave for the invasion of Egypt.[100] The magnanimous Omar trusted in his God and his sword, which had shaken the thrones of Chosroes and Cæsar: but when he compared the slender force of the Moslems with the greatness of the enterprise, he condemned his own rashness, and listened to his timid companions. The pride and the greatness of Pharaoh were familiar to the readers of the Koran; and a tenfold repetition of prodigies had been scarcely sufficient to effect, not the victory, but the flight, of six hundred thousand of the children of Israel: the cities of Egypt were many and populous; their architecture was strong and solid; the Nile, with its numerous branches, was alone an insuperable barrier; and the granary of the Imperial city would be obstinately defended by the Roman powers. In this perplexity the commander of the faithful resigned himself to the decision of chance, or, in his opinion, of Providence. At the head of only four thousand Arabs, the intrepid Amrou had marched away from his station of Gaza when he was overtaken by the messenger of Omar. "If you are still in Syria," said the ambiguous mandate, "retreat without delay; but if, at the receipt of this epistle, you have already reached the frontiers of Egypt, advance with confidence, and depend on the succour of God and of your brethren." The experience, perhaps the secret intelligence, of Amrou had taught him to suspect the mutability of courts; and he continued his march till his tents were unquestionably pitched on Egyptian ground. He there assembled his officers, broke the seal, perused the epistle, gravely inquired the name and situation of the place, and declared his ready obedience to the commands of the caliph. After a siege of thirty days he took possession of Farmah or Pelusium; and that key of Egypt, as it has been justly named, unlocked the entrance of the country as far as the ruins of Heliopolis and the neighbourhood of the modern Cairo.

On the western side of the Nile, at a small distance to the east of the Pyramids, at a small distance to the south of the Delta, Memphis, one hundred and fifty furlongs in circumference, displayed the magnificence of ancient kings. Under the reign of the Ptolemies and Cæsars, the seat of government was removed to the seacoast; the ancient capital was eclipsed by the arts and opulence of Alexandria; the palaces, and at length the temples, were reduced to a desolate and ruinous condition: yet, in the age of Augustus, and even in that of Constantine, Memphis was still numbered among the greatest and most populous of the provincial cities.[101] The banks of the Nile, in this place of the breadth of three thousand feet, were united by two bridges of sixty and of thirty boats, connected in the middle stream by the small island of Rouda, which was covered with gardens and habitations.[102] The eastern extremity of the bridge was terminated by the town of Babylon and the camp of a Roman legion, which protected the passage of the river and the second capital of Egypt. This important fortress, which might fairly be described as a part of Memphis or *Misrah*, was invested by the arms of the lieutenant of Omar: a reinforcement of four thousand Saracens soon arrived in his camp; and the military engines, which battered the walls, may be imputed to the art and labour of his Syrian allies. Yet the siege was protracted to seven months; and the rash invaders were encompassed and threatened by the inundation of the Nile.[103] Their last assault was bold and successful: they passed the ditch, which had been fortified with iron spikes, applied their scaling-ladders, entered the fortress with the shout of "God is victorious!" and drove the remnant of the Greeks to their boats and the isle of Rouda. The spot was afterwards recommended to the conqueror by the easy communication with the gulf and the peninsula of Arabia; the remains of Memphis were deserted; the tents of the Arabs were converted into permanent habitations; and the first mosch was blessed by the presence of fourscore companions of Mohammed.[104] A new city arose in their camp on the eastward bank of the Nile; and the contiguous quarters of Babylon and Fostat are confounded in their present decay by the appellation of Old Misrah, or Cairo, of which they form an extensive suburb. But the name of Cairo, the town of victory, more strictly belongs to the modern capital, which was founded in the tenth century by the Fatimite caliphs.[105] It has gradually receded from the river; but the continuity of buildings may be traced by an attentive eye from the monuments of Sesostris to those of Saladin.[106]

Yet the Arabs, after a glorious and profitable enterprise, must have retreated to the desert, had they not found a powerful alliance in the heart of the country. The rapid conquest of Alexander was assisted by the superstition and revolt of the natives; they abhorred their Persian oppressors, the disciples of the Magi, who had burnt the temples of Egypt, and feasted with sacrilegious appetite on the flesh of the god Apis.[107] After a period of ten centuries the same revolution was renewed by a similar cause; and in the support of an incomprehensible creed the zeal of the Coptic Christians was equally ardent. I have already explained the origin and progress of the Monophysite controversy, and the persecution of the emperors, which converted a sect into a nation, and alienated Egypt from their religion and government. The Saracens were received as the deliverers of the Jacobite church; and a secret and effectual treaty was opened during the siege of Memphis between a victorious army and a people of slaves. A rich and noble Egyptian, of the name of Mokawkas, had dissembled his faith to obtain the administration of his province: in the disorders of the Persian war he aspired to independence: the embassy of Mohammed ranked him among princes; but he declined, with rich gifts and ambiguous compliments, the proposal of a new religion.[108] The abuse of his trust exposed him to the re-

sentment of Heraclius: his submission was delayed by arrogance and fear; and his conscience was prompted by interest to throw himself on the favour of the nation and the support of the Saracens. In his first conference with Amrou he heard without indignation the usual option, of the Koran, the tribute, or the sword. "The Greeks," replied Mokawkas, "are determined to abide the determination of the sword; but with the Greeks I desire no communion, either in this world or in the next, and I abjure for ever the Byzantine tyrant, his synod of Chalcedon, and his Melchite slaves. For myself and my brethren, we are resolved to live and die in the profession of the gospel and unity of Christ. It is impossible for us to embrace the revelations of your prophet; but we are desirous of peace, and cheerfully submit to pay tribute and obedience to his temporal successors." The tribute was ascertained at two pieces of gold for the head of every Christian; but old men, monks, women, and children of both sexes under sixteen years of age, were exempted from this personal assessment: the Copts above and below Memphis swore allegiance to the caliph, and promised an hospitable entertainment of three days to every Musulman who should travel through their country. By this charter of security the ecclesiastical and civil tyranny of the Melchites was destroyed:[109] the anathemas of St. Cyril were thundered from every pulpit; and the sacred edifices, with the patrimony of the church, were restored to the national communion of the Jacobites, who enjoyed without moderation the moment of triumph and revenge. At the pressing summons of Amrou, their patriarch Benjamin emerged from his desert; and, after the first interview, the courteous Arab affected to declare that he had never conversed with a Christian priest of more innocent manners and a more venerable aspect.[110] In the march from Memphis to Alexandria the lieutenant of Omar intrusted his safety to the zeal and gratitude of the Egyptians: the roads and bridges were diligently repaired; and in every step of his progress he could depend on a constant supply of provisions and intelligence. The Greeks of Egypt, whose numbers could scarcely equal a tenth of the natives, were overwhelmed by the universal defection: they had ever been hated, they were no longer feared: the magistrate fled from his tribunal, the bishop from his altar; and the distant garrisons were surprised or starved by the surrounding multitudes. Had not the Nile afforded a safe and ready conveyance to the sea, not an individual could have escaped who by birth, or language, or office, or religion, was connected with their odious name.

By the retreat of the Greeks from the provinces of Upper Egypt a considerable force was collected in the island of Delta; the natural and artificial channels of the Nile afforded a succession of strong and defensible posts; and the road to Alexandria was laboriously cleared by the victory of the Saracens in two-and-twenty days of general or partial combat. In their annals of conquest the siege of Alexandria[111] is perhaps the most arduous and important enterprise. The first trading city in the world was abundantly replenished with the means of subsistence and defence. Her numerous inhabitants fought for the dearest of human rights, religion and property; and the enmity of the natives seemed to exclude them from the common benefit of peace and toleration. The sea was continually open; and if Heraclius had been awake to the public distress, fresh armies of Romans and barbarians might have been poured into the harbour to save the second capital of the empire. A circumference of ten miles would have scattered the forces of the Greeks, and favoured the stratagems of an active enemy; but the two sides of an oblong square were covered by the sea and the lake Maræotis, and each of the narrow ends exposed a front of no more than ten furlongs. The efforts of the Arabs were not inadequate to the difficulty of the attempt and value of the prize. From the throne of Medina the eyes of Omar were fixed on the camp and city: his voice excited to arms the Arabian tribes and the veterans of Syria; and the merit of a holy war was recommended by the peculiar fame and fertility of Egypt. Anxious for the ruin or expulsion of their tyrants, the faithful natives devoted their labours to the service of Amrou; some sparks of martial spirit were perhaps rekindled by the example of their allies; and the sanguine hopes of Mokawkas had fixed his sepulchre in the church of St. John of Alexandria. Eutychius, the patriarch, observes that the Saracens fought with the courage of lions; they repulsed the frequent and almost daily sallies of the besieged, and soon assaulted in their turn the walls and towers of the city. In every attack the sword, the banner of Amrou, glittered in the van of the Moslems. On a memorable day he was betrayed by his imprudent valour: his followers who had entered the citadel were driven back; and the general, with a friend and a slave, remained a prisoner in the hands of the Christians. When Amrou was conducted before the præfect, he remembered his dignity, and forgot his situation: a lofty demeanour and resolute language revealed the lieutenant of the caliph, and the battle-axe of a soldier was already raised to strike off the head of the audacious captive. His life was saved by the readiness of his slave, who instantly gave his master a blow on the face, and commanded him with an angry tone to be silent in the presence of his superiors. The credulous Greek was deceived: he listened to the offer of a treaty, and his prisoners were dismissed in the hope of a more respectable embassy, till the joyful acclamations of the camp announced the return of their general, and insulted the folly of the infidels. At length, after a siege of fourteen months,[112] and the loss of three-and-twenty thousand men, the Saracens prevailed: the Greeks embarked their dispirited and diminished numbers, and the standard of Mohammed was planted on the walls of the capital of Egypt. "I have taken," said Amrou to the caliph, "the great city of the West. It is impossible for me to enumerate the variety of its riches and beauty; and I shall content myself with observing that it contains four thousand palaces, four thousand baths, four hundred theatres or places of amusement, twelve thousand shops for the sale of vegetable food, and forty thousand tributary Jews. The town has been subdued by force of arms, without treaty or capitulation, and the Moslems are impatient to seize the fruits of their victory."[113] The commander of the faithful rejected with firmness the idea of pillage, and directed his lieutenant to reserve the wealth and revenue of Alexandria for the public service and the propagation of the faith: the inhabitants were numbered; a tribute was imposed; the zeal and resentment of the Jacobites were curbed, and the Melchites who submitted to the Arabian yoke were indulged in the obscure but tranquil exercise of their worship. The intelligence of this disgraceful and calamitous event afflicted the declining health of the emperor; and Heraclius died of a dropsy about seven weeks after the loss of Alexandria.[114] Under the minority of his grandson the clamours of the people deprived of their daily sustenance compelled the Byzantine court to undertake the recovery of the capital of Egypt. In the space of four years the harbour and fortifications of Alexandria were twice occupied by a fleet and army of Romans. They were twice expelled by the valour of Amrou, who was recalled by the domestic peril from the distant wars of Tripoli and Nubia. But the facility of the attempt, the repetition of the insult, and the obstinacy of the resistance, provoked him to swear that, if a third time he drove the infidels into the sea, he would render Alexandria as accessible on all sides as the house of a prostitute. Faithful to his promise, he dismantled several parts of the walls and towers; but the people was spared in the chastisement of the city, and the mosch of *Mercy* was erected on the spot where the victorious general had stopped the fury of his troops.

I should deceive the expectation of the reader if I passed in silence the fate of the Alexandrian library, as it is described by the learned Abulpharagius. The spirit of Amrou was more curious and liberal than that of his brethren, and in his leisure hours the Arabian chief was pleased with the conversation of John, the last disciple of Ammonius, and who derived the surname of *Philoponus* from his laborious studies of grammar and philosophy.[115] Emboldened by this familiar intercourse, Philoponus presumed to solicit a gift, inestimable in *his* opinion, contemptible in that of the barbarians—the royal library, which alone, among the spoils of Alexandria, had not been appropriated by the visit and the seal of the conqueror. Amrou was inclined to gratify the wish of the grammarian, but his rigid integrity refused to alienate the minutest object without the consent of the caliph: and the well-known answer of Omar was inspired by the ignorance of a fanatic. "If these writings of the Greeks agree with the book of God, they are useless and need not be preserved: if they disagree, they are pernicious and ought to be destroyed." The sentence was executed with blind obedience: the volumes of paper or parchment were distributed to the four thousand baths of the city; and such was their incredible multitude, that six months were barely sufficient for the consumption of this precious fuel. Since the Dynasties of Abulpharagius[116] have been given to the world in a Latin version, the tale has been repeatedly transcribed; and every scholar, with pious indignation, has deplored the irreparable shipwreck of the learning, the arts, and the genius of antiquity. For my own part, I am strongly tempted to deny both the fact and the consequences. The fact is indeed marvellous. "Read and wonder!" says the historian himself: and the solitary report of a stranger who wrote at the end of six hundred years on the confines of Media is overbalanced by the silence of two annalists of a more early date, both Christians, both natives of Egypt, and the most ancient of whom, the patriarch Eutychius, has amply described the conquest of Alexandria.[117] The rigid sentence of Omar is repugnant to the sound and orthodox precept of the Mohammedan casuists: they expressly declare that the religious books of the Jews and Christians, which are acquired by the right of war, should never be committed to the flames; and that the works of profane science, historians or poets, physicians or philosophers, may be lawfully applied to the use of the faithful.[118] A more destructive zeal may perhaps be attributed to the first successors of Mohammed; yet in this instance the conflagration would have speedily expired in the deficiency of materials. I shall not recapitulate the disasters of the Alexandrian library, the involuntary flame that was kindled by Cæsar in his own defence,[119] or the mischievous bigotry of the Christians, who studied to destroy the monuments of idolatry.[120] But if we gradually descend from the age of the Antonines to that of Theodosius, we shall learn from a chain of contemporary witnesses that the royal palace and the temple of Serapis no longer contained the four, or the seven, hundred thousand volumes which had been assembled by the curiosity and magnificence of the Ptolemies.[121] Perhaps the church and seat of the patriarchs might be enriched with a repository of books; but, if the ponderous mass of Arian and Monophysite controversy were indeed consumed in the public baths,[122] a philosopher may allow, with a smile, that it was ultimately devoted to the benefit of mankind. I sincerely regret the more valuable libraries which have been involved in the ruin of the Roman empire; but when I seriously compute the lapse of ages, the waste of ignorance, and the calamities of war, our treasures, rather than our losses, are the object of my surprise. Many curious and interesting facts are buried in oblivion: the three great historians of Rome have been transmitted to our hands in a mutilated state; and we are deprived of many pleasing compositions of the lyric, iambic, and dramatic poetry of the Greeks. Yet we should gratefully remember that the mischances of time and accident have spared the classic works to which the suffrage of antiquity[123] had adjudged the first place of genius and glory: the teachers of ancient knowledge, who are still extant, had perused and compared the writings of their predecessors;[124] nor can it fairly be presumed that any important truth, any useful discovery in art or nature, has been snatched away from the curiosity of modern ages.

In the administration of Egypt,[125] Amrou balanced the demands of justice and policy;

the interest of the people of the law, who were defended by God; and of the people of the alliance, who were protected by man. In the recent tumult of conquest and deliverance, the tongue of the Copts and the sword of the Arabs were most adverse to the tranquillity of the province. To the former, Amrou declared that faction and falsehood would be doubly chastised—by the punishment of the accusers, whom he should detest as his personal enemies, and by the promotion of their innocent brethren, whom their envy had laboured to injure and supplant. He excited the latter by the motives of religion and honour to sustain the dignity of their character, to endear themselves by a modest and temperate conduct to God and the caliph, to spare and protect a people who had trusted to their faith, and to content themselves with the legitimate and splendid rewards of their victory. In the management of the revenue he disapproved the simple but oppressive mode of a capitation, and preferred with reason a proportion of taxes deducted on every branch from the clear profits of agriculture and commerce. A third part of the tribute was appropriated to the annual repairs of the dykes and canals, so essential to the public welfare. Under his administration the fertility of Egypt supplied the dearth of Arabia; and a string of camels, laden with corn and provisions, covered almost without an interval the long road from Memphis to Medina.[126] But the genius of Amrou soon renewed the maritime communication which had been attempted or achieved by the Pharaohs, the Ptolemies, or the Cæsars; and a canal, at least eighty miles in length, was opened from the Nile to the Red Sea. This inland navigation, which would have joined the Mediterranean and the Indian Ocean, was soon discontinued as useless and dangerous: the throne was removed from Medina to Damascus, and the Grecian fleets might have explored a passage to the holy cities of Arabia.[127]

Of his new conquest the caliph Omar had an imperfect knowledge from the voice of fame and the legends of the Koran. He requested that his lieutenant would place before his eyes the realm of Pharaoh and the Amalekites; and the answer of Amrou exhibits a lively and not unfaithful picture of that singular country.[128] "O commander of the faithful, Egypt is a compound of black earth and green plants, between a pulverised mountain and a red sand. The distance from Syene to the sea is a month's journey for a horseman. Along the valley descends a river, on which the blessing of the Most High reposes both in the evening and morning, and which rises and falls with the revolutions of the sun and moon. When the annual dispensation of Providence unlocks the springs and fountains that nourish the earth, the Nile rolls his swelling and sounding waters through the realm of Egypt: the fields are overspread by the salutary flood; and the villages communicate with each other in their painted barks. The retreat of the inundation deposits a fertilising mud for the reception of the various seeds: the crowds of husbandmen who blacken the land may be compared to a swarm of industrious ants; and their native indolence is quickened by the lash of the taskmaster and the promise of the flowers and fruits of a plentiful increase. Their hope is seldom deceived; but the riches which they extract from the wheat, the barley, and the rice, the legumes, the fruit-trees, and the cattle, are unequally shared between those who labour and those who possess. According to the vicissitudes of the seasons, the face of the country is adorned with a *silver* wave, a verdant *emerald*, and the deep yellow of a *golden* harvest."[129] Yet this beneficial order is sometimes interrupted; and the long delay and sudden swell of the river in the first year of the conquest might afford some colour to an edifying fable. It is said that the annual sacrifice of a virgin[130] had been interdicted by the piety of Omar; and that the Nile lay sullen and inactive in his shallow bed, till the mandate of the caliph was cast into the obedient stream, which rose in a single night to the height of sixteen cubits. The admiration of the Arabs for their new conquest encouraged the license of their romantic spirit. We may read, in the gravest authors, that Egypt was crowded with twenty thousand cities or villages:[131] *that*, exclusive of the Greeks and Arabs, the Copts alone were found, on the assessment, six millions of tributary subjects,[132] or twenty millions of either sex and of every age: *that* three hundred millions of gold or silver were annually paid to the treasury of the caliph.[133] Our reason must be startled by these extravagant assertions; and they will become more palpable if we assume the compass and measure the extent of habitable ground: a valley from the tropic to Memphis seldom broader than twelve miles, and the triangle of the Delta, a flat surface of two thousand one hundred square leagues, compose a twelfth part of the magnitude of France.[134] A more accurate research will justify a more reasonable estimate. The three hundred millions, created by the error of a scribe, are reduced to the decent revenue of four millions three hundred thousand pieces of gold, of which nine hundred thousand were consumed by the pay of the soldiers.[135] Two authentic lists, of the present and of the twelfth century, are circumscribed within the respectable number of two thousand seven hundred villages and towns.[136] After a long residence at Cairo, a French consul has ventured to assign about four millions of Mohammedans, Christians, and Jews, for the ample, though not incredible, scope of the population of Egypt.[137]

IV. The conquest of Africa, from the Nile to the Atlantic Ocean,[138] was first attempted by the arms of the caliph Othman. The pious design was approved by the companions of Mohammed and the chiefs of the tribes; and twenty thousand Arabs marched from Medina, with the gifts and the blessing of the commander of the faithful. They were joined in the camp of Memphis by twenty thousand of their countrymen; and the conduct of the war was intrusted to Abdallah,[139] the son of Said and the foster-brother of the caliph, who had lately supplanted the conqueror and lieutenant of Egypt. Yet the favour of the prince, and the merit of his favourite, could not obliterate the guilt of his apostasy. The early conversion of Abdallah, and his skilful pen, had recommended him to the important office of transcribing the sheets of the Koran: he betrayed his trust, corrupted the text, derided the errors which he had made, and fled to Mecca to escape the justice, and expose the ignorance, of the apostle. After the conquest of Mecca he fell prostrate at the feet of Mohammed: his tears, and the entreaties of Othman, extorted a reluctant pardon; but the prophet declared that he had so long hesitated, to allow time for some zealous disciple to avenge his injury in the blood of the apostate. With apparent fidelity and effective merit he served the religion which it was no longer his interest to desert: his birth and talents gave him an honourable rank among the Koreish; and, in a nation of cavalry, Abdallah was renowned as the boldest and most dexterous horseman of Arabia. At the head of forty thousand Moslems he advanced from Egypt into the unknown countries of the West. The sands of Barca might be impervious to a Roman legion; but the Arabs were attended by their faithful camels; and the natives of the desert beheld without terror the familiar aspect of the soil and climate. After a painful march they pitched their tents before the walls of Tripoli,[140] a maritime city in which the *name*, the wealth, and the inhabitants of the province had gradually centred, and

which now maintains the third rank among the states of Barbary. A reinforcement of Greeks was surprised and cut in pieces on the seashore; but the fortifications of Tripoli resisted the first assaults; and the Saracens were tempted by the approach of the præfect Gregory[141] to relinquish the labours of the siege for the perils and the hopes of a decisive action. If his standard was followed by one hundred and twenty thousand men, the regular bands of the empire must have been lost in the naked and disorderly crowd of Africans and Moors, who formed the strength, or rather the numbers, of his host. He rejected with indignation the option of the Koran or the tribute; and during several days the two armies were fiercely engaged from the dawn of light to the hour of noon, when their fatigue and the excessive heat compelled them to seek shelter and refreshment in their respective camps. The daughter of Gregory, a maid of incomparable beauty and spirit, is said to have fought by his side: from her earliest youth she was trained to mount on horseback, to draw the bow, and to wield the scimitar; and the richness of her arms and apparel were conspicuous in the foremost ranks of the battle. Her hand, with a hundred thousand pieces of gold, was offered for the head of the Arabian general, and the youths of Africa were excited by the prospect of the glorious prize. At the pressing solicitation of his brethren, Abdallah withdrew his person from the field; but the Saracens were discouraged by the retreat of their leader, and the repetition of these equal or unsuccessful conflicts.

A noble Arabian, who afterwards became the adversary of Ali, and the father of a caliph, had signalised his valour in Egypt, and Zobeir[142] was the first who planted the scaling-ladder against the walls of Babylon. In the African war he was detached from the standard of Abdallah. On the news of the battle, Zobeir, with twelve companions, cut his way through the camp of the Greeks, and pressed forwards, without tasting either food or repose, to partake of the dangers of his brethren. He cast his eyes round the field: "Where," said he, "is our general?" "In his tent." "Is the tent a station for the general of the Moslems?" Abdallah represented with a blush the importance of his own life, and the temptation that was held forth by the Roman præfect. "Retort," said Zobeir, "on the infidels their ungenerous attempt. Proclaim through the ranks that the head of Gregory shall be repaid with his captive daughter, and the equal sum of one hundred thousand pieces of gold."

To the courage and discretion of Zobeir the lieutenant of the caliph intrusted the execution of his own stratagem, which inclined the long-disputed balance in favour of the Saracens. Supplying by activity and artifice the deficiency of numbers, a part of their forces lay concealed in their tents, while the remainder prolonged an irregular skirmish with the enemy till the sun was high in the heavens. On both sides they retired with fainting steps: their horses were unbridled, their armour was laid aside, and the hostile nations prepared, or seemed to prepare, for the refreshment of the evening, and the encounter of the ensuing day. On a sudden the charge was sounded; the Arabian camp poured forth a swarm of fresh and intrepid warriors; and the long line of the Greeks and Africans was surprised, assaulted, overturned, by new squadrons of the faithful, who, to the eye of fanaticism, might appear as a band of angels descending from the sky. The præfect himself was slain by the hand of Zobeir: his daughter, who sought revenge and death, was surrounded and made prisoner; and the fugitives involved in their disaster the town of Sufetula, to which they escaped from the sabres and lances of the Arabs. Sufetula was built one hundred and fifty miles to the south of Carthage: a gentle declivity is watered by a running stream, and shaded by a grove of juniper-trees; and, in the ruins of a triumphal arch, a portico, and three temples of the Corinthian order, curiosity may yet admire the magnificence of the Romans.[143] After the fall of this opulent city, the provincials and barbarians implored on all sides the mercy of the conqueror. His vanity or his zeal might be flattered by offers of tribute or professions of faith: but his losses, his fatigues, and the progress of an epidemical disease prevented a solid establishment; and the Saracens, after a campaign of fifteen months, retreated to the confines of Egypt, with the captives and the wealth of their African expedition. The caliph's fifth was granted to a favourite, on the nominal payment of five hundred thousand pieces of gold;[144] but the state was doubly injured by this fallacious transaction, if each foot-soldier had shared one thousand, and each horseman three thousand pieces, in the real division of the plunder. The author of the death of Gregory was expected to have claimed the most precious reward of the victory: from his silence it might be presumed that he had fallen in the battle, till the tears and exclamations of the præfect's daughter at the sight of Zobeir revealed the valour and modesty of that gallant soldier. The unfortunate virgin

was offered, and almost rejected, as a slave, by her father's murderer, who coolly declared that his sword was consecrated to the service of religion; and that he laboured for a recompense far above the charms of mortal beauty or the riches of this transitory life. A reward congenial to his temper was the honourable commission of announcing to the caliph Othman the success of his arms. The companions, the chiefs, and the people were assembled in the mosch of Medina, to hear the interesting narrative of Zobeir; and, as the orator forgot nothing except the merit of his own counsels and actions, the name of Abdallah was joined by the Arabians with the heroic names of Chaled and Amrou.[145]

The Western conquests of the Saracens were suspended near twenty years, till their dissensions were composed by the establishment of the house of Ommiyah; and the caliph Moawiyah was invited by the cries of the Africans themselves. The successors of Heraclius had been informed of the tribute which they had been compelled to stipulate with the Arabs; but instead of being moved to pity and relieve their distress, they imposed, as an equivalent or a fine, a second tribute of a similar amount. The ears of the Byzantine ministers were shut against the complaints of their poverty and ruin; their despair was reduced to prefer the dominion of a single master; and the extortions of the patriarch of Carthage, who was invested with civil and military power, provoked the sectaries, and even the Catholics, of the Roman province, to abjure the religion as well as the authority of their tyrants. The first lieutenant of Moawiyah acquired a just renown, subdued an important city, defeated an army of thirty thousand Greeks, swept away fourscore thousand captives, and enriched with their spoils the bold adventurers of Syria and Egypt.[146] But the title of conqueror of Africa is more justly due to his successor Akbah. He marched from Damascus at the head of ten thousand of the bravest Arabs; and the genuine force of the Moslems was enlarged by the doubtful aid and conversion of many thousand barbarians. It would be difficult, nor is it necessary, to trace the accurate line of the progress of Akbah. The interior regions have been peopled by the Orientals with fictitious armies and imaginary citadels. In the warlike province of Zab, or Numidia, fourscore thousand of the natives might assemble in arms; but the number of three hundred and sixty towns is incompatible with the ignorance or decay of husbandry;[147] and a circumference of three leagues will not be justified by the ruins of Erbe or Lambesa, the ancient metropolis of that inland country. As we approach the sea-coast, the well-known cities of Bugia[148] and Tangier[149] define the more certain limits of the Saracen victories. A remnant of trade still adheres to the commodious harbour of Bugia, which in a more prosperous age is said to have contained about twenty thousand houses; and the plenty of iron which is dug from the adjacent mountains might have supplied a braver people with the instruments of defence. The remote position and venerable antiquity of Tingi, or Tangier, have been decorated by the Greek and Arabian fables; but the figurative expressions of the latter, that the walls were constructed of brass, and that the roofs were covered with gold and silver, may be interpreted as the emblems of strength and opulence. The province of Mauritania Tingitana,[150] which assumed the name of the capital, had been imperfectly discovered and settled by the Romans; the five colonies were confined to a narrow pale, and the more southern parts were seldom explored except by the agents of luxury, who searched the forests for ivory and the citron-wood,[151] and the shores of the ocean for the purple shell-fish. The fearless Akbah plunged into the heart of the country, traversed the wilderness in which his successors erected the splendid capitals of Fez and Morocco,[152] and at length penetrated to the verge of the Atlantic and the great desert. The river Sus descends from the western sides of Mount Atlas, fertilises, like the Nile, the adjacent soil, and falls into the sea at a moderate distance from the Canary, or Fortunate, islands. Its banks were inhabited by the last of the Moors, a race of savages, without laws or discipline or religion: they were astonished by the strange and irresistible terrors of the Oriental arms; and as they possessed neither gold nor silver, the richest spoil was the beauty of the female captives, some of whom were afterwards sold for a thousand pieces of gold. The career, though not the zeal, of Akbah was checked by the prospect of a boundless ocean. He spurred his horse into the waves, and, raising his eyes to heaven, exclaimed with the tone of a fanatic, "Great God! if my course were not stopped by this sea, I would still go on, to the unknown kingdoms of the West, preaching the unity of thy holy name, and putting to the sword the rebellious nations who worship any other gods than thee."[153] Yet this Mohammedan Alexander, who sighed for new worlds, was unable to preserve his recent conquests. By the universal defection of the Greeks and Africans he was recalled from the shores of the Atlantic, and the surrounding multitudes left him only the resource of an honourable death. The last scene was dignified by an example of national virtue. An ambitious chief, who had disputed the command and failed in the attempt, was led about as a prisoner in the camp of the Arabian general. The insurgents had trusted to his discontent and revenge; he disdained their offers and revealed their designs. In the hour of danger the grateful Akbah unlocked his fetters and advised him to retire; he chose to die under the banner of his rival. Embracing as friends and martyrs, they unsheathed their scimitars, broke their scabbards, and maintained an obstinate combat till they fell by each other's side on the last of their slaughtered countrymen. The third general or governor of Africa, Zuheir, avenged and encountered the fate of his predecessor. He vanquished the natives in many battles; he was overthrown by a powerful army which Constantinople had sent to the relief of Carthage.

It had been the frequent practice of the Moorish tribes to join the invaders, to share the plunder, to profess the faith, and to revolt to their savage state of independence and idolatry on the first retreat or misfortune of the Moslems. The prudence of Akbah had proposed to found an Arabian colony in the heart of Africa; a citadel that might curb the levity of the barbarians, a place of refuge to secure, against the accidents of war, the wealth and the families of the Saracens. With this view, and under the modest title of the station of a caravan, he planted this colony in the fiftieth year of the Hegira. In its present decay, Cairoan[154] still holds the second rank in the kingdom of Tunis, from which it is distant about fifty miles to the south:[155] its inland situation, twelve miles westward of the sea, has protected the city from the Greek and Sicilian fleets. When the wild beasts and serpents were extirpated, when the forest, or rather wilderness, was cleared, the vestiges of a Roman town were discovered in a sandy plain: the vegetable food of Cairoan is brought from afar; and the scarcity of springs constrains the inhabitants to collect in cisterns and reservoirs a precarious supply of rain-water. These obstacles were subdued by the industry of Akbah; he traced a circumference of three thousand and six hundred paces, which he encompassed with a brick wall; in the space of five years the governor's palace was surrounded with a sufficient number of private habitations; a spacious mosch was supported by five hundred columns of granite, porphyry, and Numidian marble; and Cairoan became the seat of learning as well as of empire. But these were the glories of a later age; the new colony was shaken by the successive defeats of Akbah and Zuheir, and the western expeditions were again interrupted by the civil discord of the Arabian monarchy. The son of the valiant Zobeir maintained a war of twelve years, a siege of seven months, against the house of Ommiyah. Abdallah was said to unite the fierceness of the lion with the subtlety of the fox; but if he inherited the courage, he was devoid of the generosity, of his father.[156]

The return of domestic peace allowed the caliph Abdalmalek to resume the conquest of Africa; the standard was delivered to Hassan, governor of Egypt, and the revenue of that kingdom, with an army of forty thousand men, was consecrated to the important service. In the vicissitudes of war, the interior provinces had been alternately won and lost by the Saracens. But the sea-coast still remained in the hands of the Greeks; the predecessors of Hassan had respected the name and fortifications of Carthage; and the number of its defenders was recruited by the fugitives of Cabes and Tripoli. The arms of Hassan were bolder and more fortunate: he reduced and pillaged the metropolis of Africa; and the mention of scaling-ladders may justify the suspicion that he anticipated by a sudden assault the more tedious operations of a regular siege. But the joy of the conquerors was soon disturbed by the appearance of the Christian succours. The præfect and patrician John, a general of experience and renown, embarked at Constantinople the forces of the Eastern empire;[157] they were joined by the ships and soldiers of Sicily, and a powerful reinforcement of Goths[158] was obtained from the fears and religion of the Spanish monarch. The weight of the confederate navy broke the chain that guarded the entrance of the harbour; the Arabs retired to Cairoan, or Tripoli; the Christians landed; the citizens hailed the ensign of the cross, and the winter was idly wasted in the dream of victory or deliverance. But Africa was irrecoverably lost; the zeal and resentment of the commander of the faithful[159] prepared in the ensuing spring a more numerous armament by sea and land; and the patrician in his turn was compelled to evacuate the post and fortifications of Carthage. A second battle was fought in the neighbourhood of Utica: the Greeks and Goths were again defeated; and their timely embarkation saved them from the sword of Hassan, who had invested the slight and insufficient rampart of their camp. Whatever yet remained of Carthage was delivered to the flames, and the colony of Dido[160] and Cæsar lay desolate above two hundred years, till a part, perhaps a twentieth, of the old circumference was repeopled by the first of the Fatimite caliphs. In the beginning of the sixteenth century the second capital of the West was represented by a mosch, a college without students, twenty-five or thirty shops, and the huts of five hundred peasants, who, in their abject poverty, displayed the arrogance of the Punic senators. Even that paltry village was swept away by the Spaniards whom Charles the Fifth had stationed in the fortress of the Goletta. The ruins of Carthage have perished; and the place might be unknown if some broken arches of an aqueduct did not guide the footsteps of the inquisitive traveller.[161]

The Greeks were expelled, but the Arabians were not yet masters of the country. In the interior provinces the Moors or *Berbers*,[162] so feeble under the first Cæsars, so formidable to the Byzantine princes, maintained a disorderly resistance to the religion and power of the successors of Mohammed. Under the standard of their queen Cahina the independent tribes acquired some degree of union and discipline; and as the Moors respected in their females the character of a prophetess, they attacked the invaders with an enthusiasm similar to their own. The veteran bands of Hassan were inadequate to the defence of Africa: the conquests of an age were lost in a single day; and the Arabian chief, overwhelmed by the torrent, retired to the confines of Egypt, and expected, five years, the promised succours of the caliph. After the retreat of the Saracens, the victorious prophetess assembled the Moorish chiefs, and recommended a measure of strange and savage policy. "Our cities," said she, "and the gold and silver which they contain, perpetually attract the arms of the Arabs. These vile metals are not the objects of *our* ambition; we content ourselves with the simple productions of the earth. Let us destroy these cities; let us bury in their ruins those pernicious treasures; and when the avarice of our foes shall be destitute of temptation, perhaps they will cease to disturb the tranquillity of a warlike people." The proposal was accepted with unanimous applause. From Tangier to Tripoli the buildings, or at least the fortifications, were demolished, the fruit-trees were cut down, the means of subsistence were extirpated, a fertile and populous garden was changed into a desert, and the historians of a more recent period could discern the frequent traces of the prosperity and devastation of their ancestors. Such is the tale of the modern Arabians. Yet I strongly suspect that their ignorance of antiquity, the love of the marvellous, and the fashion of extolling the philosophy of barbarians, has induced them to describe, as one voluntary act, the calamities of three hundred years since the first fury of the Donatists and Vandals. In the progress of the revolt Cahina had most probably contributed her share of destruction; and the alarm of universal ruin might terrify and alienate the cities that had reluctantly yielded to her unworthy yoke. They no longer hoped, perhaps they no longer wished, the return of their Byzantine sovereigns: their present servitude was not alleviated by the benefits of order and justice; and the most zealous Catholic must prefer the imperfect truths of the Koran to the blind and rude idolatry of the Moors. The general of the Saracens was again received as the saviour of the province: the friends of civil society conspired against the savages of the land and the royal prophetess was slain in the first battle, which overturned the baseless fabric of her superstition and empire. The same spirit revived under the successor of Hassan: it was finally quelled by the activity of Musa and his two sons; but the number of the rebels may be presumed from that of three hundred thousand captives; sixty thousand of whom, the caliph's fifth, were sold for the profit of the public treasury. Thirty thousand of the barbarian youth were enlisted in the troops; and the pious labours of Musa, to inculcate the knowledge and practice of the Koran, accustomed the Africans to obey the apostle of God and the commander of the faithful. In their climate and government, their diet and habitation, the wandering Moors resembled the Bedoweens of the desert. With the religion they were proud to adopt the language, name, and origin of Arabs: the blood of the strangers and natives was insensibly mingled; and from the Euphrates to the Atlantic the same nation might seem to be diffused over the sandy plains of Asia and Africa. Yet I will not deny that fifty thousand tents of pure Arabians might be transported over the Nile, and scattered through the Libyan desert; and I am not ignorant that five of the Moorish tribes still retain their *barbarous* idiom, with the appellation and character of *white* Africans.[163]

V. In the progress of conquest from the north and south, the Goths and the Saracens encountered each other on the confines of Europe and Africa. In the opinion of the latter, the differenc of religion is a reasonable ground of enmity an warfare.[164]

As early as the time of Othman,[165] their pi ratical squadrons had ravaged the coast of An dalusia,[166] nor had they forgotten the relief o Carthage by the Gothic succours. In that age as well as in the present, the kings of Spain were possessed of the fortress of Ceuta; one of the Columns of Hercules, which is divided by a narrow strait from the opposite pillar or poin of Europe. A small portion of Mauritania wa still wanting to the African conquest; but Musa in the pride of victory, was repulsed from the walls of Ceuta, by the vigilance and courage o Count Julian, the general of the Goths. From his disappointment and perplexity Musa wa relieved by an unexpected message of the Christian chief, who offered his place, his person, and his sword to the successors of Mohammed, and solicited the disgraceful honour of introducing their arms into the heart of Spain.[167] If we inquire into the cause of his treachery, the Spaniards will repeat the popular story of his daughter Cava;[168] of a virgin who was seduced, or ravished, by her sovereign; of a father who sacrificed his religion and country to the thirst of revenge. The passions of princes have often been licentious and destructive; but this wellknown tale, romantic in itself, is indifferently supported by external evidence; and the history of Spain will suggest some motives of interest and policy more congenial to the breast of a veteran statesman.[169] After the decease or deposition of Witiza, his two sons were supplanted by the ambition of Roderic, a noble Goth, whose father, the duke or governor of a province, had fallen a victim to the preceding tyranny. The monarchy was still elective; but the sons of Witiza, educated on the steps of the throne, were impatient of a private station. Their resentment was the more dangerous, as it was varnished with the dissimulation of courts; their followers were excited by the remembrance of favours and the promise of a revolution; and their Uncle Oppas, archbishop of Toledo and Seville, was the first person in the church, and the second in the state. It is probable that Julian was involved in the disgrace of the unsuccessful faction; that he had little to hope and much to fear from the new reign; and that the imprudent king could not forget or forgive the injuries which Roderic and his family had sustained. The merit and influence of the count rendered him a useful or formidable subject; his estates were ample, his followers bold and numerous;

nd it was too fatally shown that, by his Anda-
usian and Mauritanian commands, he held in
his hand the keys of the Spanish monarchy. Too
eeble, however, to meet his sovereign in arms,
he sought the aid of a foreign power; and his
ash invitation of the Moors and Arabs produced the calamities of eight hundred years. In
his epistles, or in a personal interview, he revealed the wealth and nakedness of his country;
the weakness of an unpopular prince; the degeneracy of an effeminate people. The Goths
were no longer the victorious barbarians, who
had humbled the pride of Rome, despoiled the
queen of nations, and penetrated from the
Danube to the Atlantic Ocean. Secluded from
the world by the Pyrenæan mountains, the successors of Alaric had slumbered in a long peace;
the walls of the cities were mouldered into dust:
the youth had abandoned the exercise of arms;
and the presumption of their ancient renown
would expose them in a field of battle to the first
assault of the invaders. The ambitious Saracen
was fired by the ease and importance of the
attempt; but the execution was delayed till he
had consulted the commander of the faithful;
and his messenger returned with the permission
of Walid to annex the unknown kingdoms of
the West to the religion and throne of the
caliphs. In his residence of Tangier, Musa, with
secrecy and caution, continued his correspondence and hastened his preparations. But the remorse of the conspirators was soothed by the
fallacious assurance that he should content himself with the glory and spoil, without aspiring to
establish the Moslems beyond the sea that separates Africa from Europe.[170]

Before Musa would trust an army of the
faithful to the traitors and infidels of a foreign
land, he made a less dangerous trial of their
strength and veracity. One hundred Arabs, and
four hundred Africans, passed over, in four
vessels, from Tangier or Ceuta: the place of
their descent on the opposite shore of the strait
is marked by the name of Tarif their chief; and
the date of this memorable event[171] is fixed to
the month of Ramadan, of the ninety-first year
of the Hegira, to the month of July, seven hundred and forty-eight years from the Spanish era
of Cæsar,[172] seven hundred and ten after the
birth of Christ. From their first station, they
marched eighteen miles through a hilly country
to the castle and town of Julian;[173] on which (it
is still called Algezire) they bestowed the name
of the Green Island, from a verdant cape that
advances into the sea. Their hospitable entertainment, the Christians who joined their stan-

dard, their inroad into a fertile and unguarded
province, the richness of their spoil, and the
safety of their return, announced to their
brethren the most favourable omens of victory.
In the ensuing spring five thousand veterans
and volunteers were embarked under the command of Tarik, a dauntless and skilful soldier,
who surpassed the expectation of his chief; and
the necessary transports were provided by the
industry of their too faithful ally. The Saracens
landed [174] at the pillar or point of Europe; the
corrupt and familiar appellation of Gibraltar
(Gebel al Tarik) describes the mountain of Tarik;
and the entrenchments of his camp were the
first outline of those fortifications which, in the
hands of our countrymen, have resisted the art
and power of the house of Bourbon. The adjacent governors informed the court of Toledo
of the descent and progress of the Arabs; and
the defeat of his lieutenant Edeco, who had
been commanded to seize and bind the presumptuous strangers, admonished Roderic of
the magnitude of the danger. At the royal summons, the dukes and counts, the bishops and
nobles of the Gothic monarchy, assembled at
the head of their followers; and the title of King
of the Romans, which is employed by an Arabic
historian, may be excused by the close affinity
of language, religion, and manners, between
the nations of Spain. His army consisted of
ninety or a hundred thousand men; a formidable power, if their fidelity and discipline had
been adequate to their numbers. The troops of
Tarik had been augmented to twelve thousand
Saracens; but the Christian malcontents were
attracted by the influence of Julian, and a
crowd of Africans most greedily tasted the temporal blessings of the Koran. In the neighbourhood of Cadiz, the town of Xeres[175] has been
illustrated by the encounter which determined
the fate of the kingdom; the stream of the Gua-
dalete, which falls into the bay, divided the two
camps, and marked the advancing and retreating skirmishes of three successive and bloody
days. On the fourth day the two armies joined a
more serious and decisive issue; but Alaric
would have blushed at the sight of his unworthy
successor, sustaining on his head a diadem of
pearls, encumbered with a flowing robe of gold
and silken embroidery, and reclining on a litter
or arc of ivory drawn by two white mules. Notwithstanding the valour of the Saracens, they
fainted under the weight of multitudes, and the
plain of Xeres was overspread with sixteen
thousand of their dead bodies. "My brethren,"
said Tarik to his surviving companions, "the

enemy is before you, the sea is behind; whither would ye fly? Follow your general: I am resolved either to lose my life or to trample on the prostrate king of the Romans." Besides the resource of despair, he confided in the secret correspondence and nocturnal interviews of Count Julian with the sons and the brother of Witiza. The two princes and the archbishop of Toledo occupied the most important post: their well-timed defection broke the ranks of the Christians; each warrior was prompted by fear or suspicion to consult his personal safety; and the remains of the Gothic army were scattered or destroyed in the flight and pursuit of the three following days. Amidst the general disorder Roderic started from his car, and mounted Orelia, the fleetest of his horses; but he escaped from a soldier's death to perish more ignobly in the waters of the Bætis or Guadalquivir. His diadem, his robes, and his courser were found on the bank; but as the body of the Gothic prince was lost in the waves, the pride and ignorance of the caliph must have been gratified with some meaner head, which was exposed in triumph before the palace of Damascus. "And such," continues a valiant historian of the Arabs, "is the fate of those kings who withdraw themselves from a field of battle."[176]

Count Julian had plunged so deep into guilt and infamy, that his only hope was in the ruin of his country. After the battle of Xeres he recommended the most effectual measures to the victorious Saracen. "The king of the Goths is slain; their princes have fled before you, the army is routed, the nation is astonished. Secure with sufficient detachments the cities of Bætica; but in person, and without delay, march to the royal city of Toledo, and allow not the distracted Christians either time or tranquillity for the election of a new monarch." Tarik listened to his advice. A Roman captive and proselyte, who had been enfranchised by the caliph himself, assaulted Cordova with seven hundred horse: he swam the river, surprised the town, and drove the Christians into the great church, where they defended themselves above three months. Another detachment reduced the sea-coast of Bætica, which in the last period of the Moorish power has comprised in a narrow space the populous kingdom of Granada. The march of Tarik from the Bætis to the Tagus[177] was directed through the Sierra Morena, that separates Andalusia and Castille, till he appeared in arms under the walls of Toledo.[178] The most zealous of the Catholics had escaped with the relics of their saints; and if the gates

were shut, it was only till the victor had subscribed a fair and reasonable capitulation. The voluntary exiles were allowed to depart with their effects; seven churches were appropriated to the Christian worship; the archbishop and his clergy were at liberty to exercise their functions, the monks to practise or neglect their penance; and the Goths and Romans were left in all civil and criminal cases to the subordinate jurisdiction of their own laws and magistrates. But if the justice of Tarik protected the Christians, his gratitude and policy rewarded the Jews, to whose secret or open aid he was indebted for his most important acquisitions. Persecuted by the kings and synods of Spain, who had often pressed the alternative of banishment or baptism, that outcast nation embraced the moment of revenge: the comparison of their past and present state was the pledge of their fidelity; and the alliance between the disciples of Moses and of Mohammed was maintained till the final era of their common expulsion. From the royal seat of Toledo, the Arabian leader spread his conquests to the north, over the modern realms of Castille and Leon: but it is needless to enumerate the cities that yielded on his approach, or again to describe the table of emerald,[179] transported from the East by the Romans, acquired by the Goths among the spoils of Rome, and presented by the Arabs to the throne of Damascus. Beyond the Asturian mountains, the maritime town of Gijon was the term[180] of the lieutenant of Musa, who had performed, with the speed of a traveller, his victorious march, of seven hundred miles, from the rock of Gibraltar to the Bay of Biscay. The failure of land compelled him to retreat; and he was recalled to Toledo, to excuse his presumption of subduing a kingdom in the absence of his general. Spain, which, in a more savage and disorderly state, had resisted, two hundred years, the arms of the Romans, was overrun in a few months by those of the Saracens; and such was the eagerness of submission and treaty, that the governor of Cordova is recorded as the only chief who fell, without conditions, a prisoner into their hands. The cause of the Goths had been irrevocably judged in the field of Xeres; and, in the national dismay, each part of the monarchy declined a contest with the antagonist who had vanquished the united strength of the whole.[181] That strength had been wasted by two successive seasons of famine and pestilence; and the governors, who were impatient to surrender, might exaggerate the difficulty of collecting the provisions of a siege. To disarm

he Christians, superstition likewise contributed
er terrors: and the subtle Arab encouraged the
eport of dreams, omens, and prophecies, and of
he portraits of the destined conquerors of
Spain, that were discovered on breaking open
an apartment of the royal palace. Yet a spark
of the vital flame was still alive; some invincible
ugitives preferred a life of poverty and freedom
n the Asturian valleys; the hardy mountaineers
epulsed the slaves of the caliph; and the sword
of Pelagius has been transformed into the
sceptre of the Catholic kings.[182]

On the intelligence of this rapid success, the
applause of Musa degenerated into envy, and
he began, not to complain, but to fear, that
Tarik would leave him nothing to subdue. At
the head of ten thousand Arabs and eight thousand Africans, he passed over in person from
Mauritania to Spain: the first of his companions
were the noblest of the Koreish; his eldest son
was left in the command of Africa; the three
younger brethren were of an age and spirit to
second the boldest enterprises of their father. At
his landing in Algezire he was respectfully
entertained by Count Julian, who stifled his
inward remorse, and testified, both in words
and actions, that the victory of the Arabs had
not impaired his attachment to their cause.
Some enemies yet remained for the sword of
Musa. The tardy repentance of the Goths had
compared their own numbers and those of the
invaders; the cities from which the march of
Tarik had declined considered themselves as
impregnable; and the bravest patriots defended
the fortifications of Seville and Merida. They
were successively besieged and reduced by the
labour of Musa, who transported his camp from
the Bætis to the Anas, from the Guadalquivir to
the Guadiana. When he beheld the works of
Roman magnificence, the bridge, the aqueducts, the triumphal arches, and the theatre of
the ancient metropolis of Lusitania, "I should
imagine," said he to his four companions, "that
the human race must have united their art and
power in the foundation of this city: happy is
the man who shall become its master!" He
aspired to that happiness, but the Emeritus sustained on this occasion the honour of their
descent from the veteran legionaries of Augustus.[183] Disdaining the confinement of their
walls, they gave battle to the Arabs on the
plain; but an ambuscade rising from the shelter
of a quarry, or a ruin, chastised their indiscretion, and intercepted their return. The
wooden turrets of assault were rolled forwards
to the foot of the rampart; but the defence of

Merida was obstinate and long; and the *castle of
the martyrs* was a perpetual testimony of the
losses of the Moslems. The constancy of the besieged was at length subdued by famine and
despair; and the prudent victor disguised his
impatience under the names of clemency and
esteem. The alternative of exile or tribute was
allowed; the churches were divided between
the two religions; and the wealth of those who
had fallen in the siege, or retired to Gallicia,
was confiscated as the reward of the faithful.
In the midway between Merida and Toledo,
the lieutenant of Musa saluted the vicegerent
of the caliph, and conducted him to the palace
of the Gothic kings. Their first interview was
cold and formal; a rigid account was exacted of
the treasures of Spain: the character of Tarik
was exposed to suspicion and obloquy; and the
hero was imprisoned, reviled, and ignominiously scourged by the hand, or the command,
of Musa. Yet so strict was the discipline, so pure
the zeal, or so tame the spirit, of the primitive
Moslems, that after this public indignity Tarik
could serve and be trusted in the reduction of
the Tarragonese province. A mosch was erected
at Saragossa by the liberality of the Koreish:
the port of Barcelona was opened to the vessels
of Syria; and the Goths were pursued beyond
the Pyrenean mountains into their Gallic province of Septimania or Languedoc.[184] In the
church of St. Mary, at Carcassonne, Musa
found, but it is improbable that he left, seven
equestrian statues of massy silver; and from his
term or column of Narbonne, he returned on his
footsteps to the Gallician and Lusitanian shores
of the ocean. During the absence of the father,
his son Abdelaziz chastised the insurgents of
Seville, and reduced, from Malaga to Valentia,
the sea-coast of the Mediterranean: his original
treaty with the discreet and valiant Theodemir[185]
will represent the manners and policy of the
times. "*The conditions of peace agreed and sworn between Abdelaziz, the son of Musa, the son of Nassir,
and Theodemir prince of the Goths. In the name of
the most merciful God, Abdelaziz makes peace
on these conditions: that* Theodemir shall not
be disturbed in his principality, nor any injury
be offered to the life or property, the wives and
children, the religion and temples, of the Christians; *that* Theodemir shall freely deliver his
seven cities, Orihuela, Valentola, Alicant, Mola,
Vacasora, Bigerra (now Bejar), Ora (or Opta),
and Lorca; *that* he shall not assist or entertain
the enemies of the caliph, but shall faithfully
communicate his knowledge of their hostile designs; *that* himself, and each of the Gothic

nobles, shall annually pay one piece of gold, four measures of wheat, as many of barley, with a certain proportion of honey, oil, and vinegar; and that each of their vassals shall be taxed at one moiety of the said imposition. Given the fourth of Regeb, in the year of the Hegira ninety-four, and subscribed with the names of four Musulman witnesses."[186] Theodemir and his subjects were treated with uncommon lenity; but the rate of tribute appears to have fluctuated from a tenth to a fifth, according to the submission or obstinacy of the Christians.[187] In this revolution many partial calamities were inflicted by the carnal or religious passions of the enthusiasts: some churches were profaned by the new worship: some relics or images were confounded with idols: the rebels were put to the sword, and one town (an obscure place between Cordova and Seville) was razed to its foundations. Yet if we compare the invasion of Spain by the Goths, or its recovery by the kings of Castille and Arragon, we must applaud the moderation and discipline of the Arabian conquerors.

The exploits of Musa were performed in the evening of life, though he affected to disguise his age by colouring with a red powder the whiteness of his beard. But in the love of action and glory his breast was still fired with the ardour of youth; and the possession of Spain was considered only as the first step to the monarchy of Europe. With a powerful armament by sea and land he was preparing to repass the Pyrenees, to extinguish in Gaul and Italy the declining kingdoms of the Franks and Lombards, and to preach the unity of God on the altar of the Vatican. From thence, subduing the barbarians of Germany, he proposed to follow the course of the Danube from its source to the Euxine Sea, to overthrow the Greek or Roman empire of Constantinople, and, returning from Europe to Asia, to unite his new acquisitions with Antioch and the provinces of Syria.[188] But his vast enterprise, perhaps of easy execution, must have seemed extravagant to vulgar minds; and the visionary conqueror was soon reminded of his dependence and servitude. The friends of Tarik had effectually stated his services and wrongs: at the court of Damascus the proceedings of Musa were blamed, his intentions were suspected, and his delay in complying with the first invitation was chastised by a harsher and more peremptory summons. An intrepid messenger of the caliph entered his camp at Lugo in Gallicia, and in the presence of the Saracens and Christians arrested the bridle of his horse. His own loyalty, or that of his troops, inculcated the duty of obedience; and his disgrace was alleviated by the recall of his rival, and the permission of investing with his two governments his two sons, Abdallah and Abdelaziz. His long triumph from Ceuta to Damascus displayed the spoils of Afric and the treasures of Spain: four hundred Gothic nobles, with gold coronets and girdles, were distinguished in his train; and the number of male and female captives, selected for their birth or beauty, was computed at eighteen, or even at thirty, thousand persons. As soon as he reached Tiberias in Palestine, he was apprised of the sickness and danger of the caliph, by a private message from Soliman, his brother and presumptive heir, who wished to reserve for his own reign the spectacle of victory. Had Walid recovered, the delay of Musa would have been criminal: he pursued his march, and found an enemy on the throne. In his trial before a partial judge, against a popular antagonist, he was convicted of vanity and falsehood; and a fine of two hundred thousand pieces of gold either exhausted his poverty or proved his rapaciousness. The unworthy treatment of Tarik was revenged by a similar indignity; and the veteran commander, after a public whipping, stood a whole day in the sun before the palace gate, till he obtained a decent exile, under the pious name of a pilgrimage to Mecca. The resentment of the caliph might have been satiated with the ruin of Musa; but his fears demanded the extirpation of a potent and injured family. A sentence of death was intimated with secrecy and speed to the trusty servants of the throne both in Africa and Spain; and the forms, if not the substance, of justice were superseded in this bloody execution. In the mosch or palace of Cordova, Abdelaziz was slain by the swords of the conspirators; they accused their governor of claiming the honours of royalty; and his scandalous marriage with Egilona, the widow of Roderic, offended the prejudices both of the Christians and Moslems. By a refinement of cruelty, the head of the son was presented to the father, with an insulting question, whether he acknowledged the features of the rebel? "I know his features," he exclaimed with indignation: "I assert his innocence; and I imprecate the same, a juster fate, against the authors of his death." The age and despair of Musa raised him above the power of kings; and he expired at Mecca of the anguish of a broken heart. His rival was more favourably treated: his services were forgiven; and Tarik was permitted to mingle with the crowd of slaves.[189] I am ignorant whether Count Julian was rewarded with the death which he deserved indeed, though not from the hands of the Saracens; but the tale of their ingratitude to the sons of Witiza is disproved by the most unquestionable evidence. The two royal youths were reinstated in the private patrimony of their father; but on the decease of Eba, the elder, his daughter was unjustly despoiled of her portion by the violence of her uncle Sigebut. The Gothic maid pleaded her cause before the caliph Hashem, and obtained the restitution of her inheritance; but she was given in marriage to a noble Arabian, and their two sons, Isaac and Ibrahim, were received in Spain with the consideration that was due to their origin and riches.

A province is assimilated to the victorious state by the introduction of strangers and the imitative spirit of the natives; and Spain, which had been successively tinctured with Punic, and Roman, and Gothic blood, imbibed, in a few generations, the name and manners of the Arabs. The first conquerors, and the twenty successive lieutenants of the caliphs, were attended by a numerous train of civil and military followers, who preferred a distant fortune to a narrow home: the private and public interest was promoted by the establishment of faithful colonies; and the cities of Spain were proud to commemorate the tribe or country of their Eastern progenitors. The victorious though motley bands of Tarik and Musa asserted, by the name of *Spaniards*, their original claim of conquest; yet they allowed their brethren of Egypt to share their establishments of Murcia and Lisbon. The royal legion of Damascus was planted at Cordova; that of Emesa at Seville; that of Kinnisrin or Chalcis at Jaen; that of Palestine at Algezire and Medina Sidonia. The natives of Yemen and Persia were scattered round Toledo and the inland country, and the fertile seats of Granada were bestowed on ten thousand horsemen of Syria and Irak, the children of the purest and most noble of the Arabian tribes.[190] A spirit of emulation, sometimes beneficial, more frequently dangerous, was nourished by these hereditary factions. Ten years after the conquest, a map of the province was presented to the caliph: the seas, the rivers, and the harbours, the inhabitants and cities, the climate, the soil, and the mineral productions of the earth.[191] In the space of two centuries the gifts of nature were improved by the agriculture,[192] the manufactures, and the commerce of an industrious people; and the effects of their diligence have been magnified by the idleness of their fancy. The first of the Ommiades who reigned in Spain solicited the support of the Christians; and in his edict of peace and protection, he contents himself with a modest imposition of ten thousand ounces of gold, ten thousand pounds of silver, ten thousand horses, as many mules, one thousand cuirasses, with an equal number of helmets and lances.[193] The most powerful of his successors derived from the same kingdom the annual tribute of twelve millions and forty-five thousands dinars or pieces of gold, about six millions of sterling money;[194] a sum which, in the tenth century most probably surpassed the united revenues of the Christian monarchs. His royal seat of Cordova contained six hundred moschs, nine hundred baths, and two hundred thousand houses; he gave laws to eighty cities of the first, to three hundred of the second and third order; and the fertile banks of the Guadalquivir were adorned with twelve thousand villages and hamlets. The Arabs might exaggerate the truth, but they created, and they describe, the most prosperous era of the riches, the cultivation, and the populousness of Spain.[195]

The wars of the Moslems were sanctified by the prophet; but among the various precepts and examples of his life, the caliphs selected the lessons of toleration that might tend to disarm the resistance of the unbelievers. Arabia was the temple and patrimony of the God of Mohammed; but he beheld with less jealousy and affection the nations of the earth. The polytheists and idolaters, who were ignorant of his name, might be lawfully extirpated by his votaries;[196] but a wise policy supplied the obligation of justice; and after some acts of intolerant zeal, the Mohammedan conquerors of Hindostan have spared the pagodas of that devout and populous country. The disciples of Abraham, of Moses, and of Jesus were solemnly invited to accept the more *perfect* revelation of Mohammed; but if they preferred the payment of a moderate tribute, they were entitled to the freedom of conscience and religious worship.[197] In a field of battle, the forfeit lives of the prisoners were redeemed by the profession of *Islam;* the females were bound to embrace the religion of their masters, and a race of sincere proselytes was gradually multiplied by the education of the infant captives. But the millions of African and Asiatic converts, who swelled the native band of the faithful Arabs, must have been allured, rather than constrained, to declare their belief in one God and the apostle of God. By the repetition of a sentence and the loss of a fore-skin, the subject or the slave, the captive or the criminal, arose in a moment the free and equal companion of the victorious Moslems. Every sin was expiated, every engagement was dissolved: the vow of celibacy was superseded by the indulgence of nature; the active spirits who slept in the cloister were awakened by the trumpets of the Saracens; and in the convulsion of the world, every member of a new society ascended to the natural level of his capacity and courage. The minds of the multitude were tempted by the invisible as well as temporal blessings of the Arabian prophet; and charity will hope that many of his proselytes entertained a serious conviction of the truth and sanctity of his revelation. In the eyes of an inquisitive polytheist, it must appear worthy of the human and the divine nature. More pure than the system of Zoroaster, more liberal than the law of Moses, the religion of Mohammed might seem less inconsistent with reason than the creed of mystery and superstition which, in the seventh century, disgraced the simplicity of the Gospel.

In the extensive provinces of Persia and Africa, the national religion has been eradicated by the Mohammedan faith. The ambiguous theology of the Magi stood alone among the sects of the East: but the profane writings of Zoroaster[198] might, under the reverend name of Abraham, be dexterously connected with the chain of divine revelation. Their evil principle, the demon Ahriman, might be represented as the rival, or as the creature, of the God of light. The temples of Persia were devoid of images; but the worship of the sun and of fire might be stigmatised as a gross and criminal idolatry.[199] The milder sentiment was consecrated by the practice of Mohammed[200] and the prudence of the caliphs: the Magians or Ghebers were ranked with the Jews and Christians among the people of the written law;[201] and as late as the third century of the Hegira, the city of Herat will afford a lively contrast of private zeal and public toleration.[202] Under the payment of an annual tribute, the Mohammedan law secured to the Ghebers of Herat their civil and religious liberties: but the recent and humble mosch was overshadowed by the antique splendour of the adjoining temple of fire. A fanatic Imam deplored, in his sermons, the scandalous neighbourhood, and accused the weakness or indifference of the faithful. Excited by his voice, the people assembled in tumult; the two houses of prayer were consumed by the flames, but the vacant ground was immediately occupied by

the foundations of a new mosch. The injured Magi appealed to the sovereign of Chorasan; he promised justice and relief; when, behold four thousand citizens of Herat, of a grave character and mature age, unanimously swore that the idolatrous fane had *never* existed; the inquisition was silenced, and their conscience was satisfied (says the historian Mirchond[203]) with this holy and meritorious perjury.[204] But the greatest part of the temples of Persia were ruined by the insensible and general desertion of their votaries. It was *insensible*, since it is not accompanied with any memorial of time or place, of persecution or resistance. It was *general*, since the whole realm, from Shiraz to Samarcand, imbibed the faith of the Koran; and the preservation of the native tongue reveals the descent of the Mohammedans of Persia.[205] In the mountains and deserts an obstinate race of unbelievers adhered to the superstition of their fathers; and a faint tradition of the Magian theology is kept alive in the province of Kirman, along the banks of the Indus, among the exiles of Surat, and in the colony which, in the last century, was planted by Shaw Abbas at the gates of Ispahan. The chief pontiff has retired to Mount Elbourz, eighteen leagues from the city of Yezd: the perpetual fire (if it continue to burn) is inaccessible to the profane: but his residence is the school, the oracle, and the pilgrimage of the Ghebers, whose hard and uniform features attest the unmingled purity of their blood. Under the jurisdiction of their elders, eighty thousand families maintain an innocent and industrious life; their subsistence is derived from some curious manufactures and mechanic trades; and they cultivate the earth with the fervour of a religious duty. Their ignorance withstood the despotism of Shaw Abbas, who demanded with threats and tortures the prophetic books of Zoroaster; and this obscure remnant of the Magians is spared by the moderation or contempt of their present sovereigns.[206]

The Northern coast of Africa is the only land in which the light of the Gospel, after a long and perfect establishment, has been totally extinguished. The arts, which had been taught by Carthage and Rome, were involved in a cloud of ignorance; the doctrine of Cyprian and Augustin was no longer studied. Five hundred episcopal churches were overturned by the hostile fury of the Donatists, the Vandals, and the Moors. The zeal and numbers of the clergy declined; and the people, without discipline, or knowledge, or hope, submissively sunk under he yoke of the Arabian prophet. Within fifty years after the expulsion of the Greeks, a lieutenant of Africa informed the caliph that the tribute of the infidels was abolished by their conversion;[207] and, though he sought to disguise his fraud and rebellion, his specious pretence was drawn from the rapid and extensive progress of the Mohammedan faith. In the next age an extraordinary mission of five bishops was detached from Alexandria to Cairoan. They were ordained by the Jacobite patriarch to cherish and revive the dying embers of Christianity:[208] but the interposition of a foreign prelate, a stranger to the Latins, an enemy to the Catholics, supposes the decay and dissolution of the African hierarchy. It was no longer the time when the successor of St. Cyprian, at the head of a numerous synod, could maintain an equal contest with the ambition of the Roman pontiff. In the eleventh century the unfortunate priest who was seated on the ruins of Carthage implored the arms and the protection of the Vatican; and he bitterly complains that his naked body had been scourged by the Saracens, and that his authority was disputed by the four suffragans, the tottering pillars of his throne. Two epistles of Gregory the Seventh[209] are destined to soothe the distress of the Catholics and the pride of a Moorish prince. The pope assures the sultan that they both worship the same God, and may hope to meet in the bosom of Abraham; but the complaint that three bishops could no longer be found to consecrate a brother, announces the speedy and inevitable ruin of the episcopal order. The Christians of Africa and Spain had long since submitted to the practice of circumcision and the legal abstinence from wine and pork; and the name of *Mozarabes*[210] (adoptive Arabs) was applied to their civil or religious conformity.[211] About the middle of the twelfth century the worship of Christ and the succession of pastors were abolished along the coast of Barbary, and in the kingdoms of Cordova and Seville, of Valencia and Granada.[212] The throne of the Almohades, or Unitarians, was founded on the blindest fanaticism, and their extraordinary rigour might be provoked or justified by the recent victories and intolerant zeal of the princes of Sicily and Castille, of Arragon and Portugal. The faith of the Mozarabes was occasionally revived by the papal missionaries; and, on the landing of Charles the Fifth, some families of Latin Christians were encouraged to rear their heads at Tunis and Algiers. But the seed of the Gospel was quickly eradicated, and the long province from Tripoli to the Atlantic has lost all memory of the language and religion of Rome.[213]

After the revolution of eleven centuries the Jews and Christians of the Turkish empire enjoy the liberty of conscience which was granted by the Arabian caliphs. During the first age of the conquest they suspected the loyalty of the Catholics, whose name of Melchites betrayed their secret attachment to the Greek emperor, while the Nestorians and Jacobites, his inveterate enemies, approved themselves the sincere and voluntary friends of the Mohammedan government.[214] Yet this partial jealousy was healed by time and submission; the churches of Egypt were shared with the Catholics;[215] and all the Oriental sects were included in the common benefits of toleration. The rank, the immunities, the domestic jurisdiction of the patriarchs, the bishops, and the clergy, were protected by the civil magistrate: the learning of individuals recommended them to the employments of secretaries and physicians: they were enriched by the lucrative collection of the revenue; and their merit was sometimes raised to the command of cities and provinces. A caliph of the house of Abbas was heard to declare that the Christians were most worthy of trust in the administration of Persia. "The Moslems," said he, "will abuse their present fortune; the Magians regret their fallen greatness; and the Jews are impatient for their approaching deliverance."[216] But the slaves of despotism are exposed to the alternative of favour and disgrace. The captive churches of the East have been afflicted in every age by the avarice or bigotry of their rulers; and the ordinary and legal restraints must be offensive to the pride, or the zeal, of the Christians.[217] About two hundred years after Mohammed, they were separated from their fellow-subjects by a turban or girdle of a less honourable colour; instead of horses or mules, they were condemned to ride on asses, in the attitude of women. Their public and private buildings were measured by a diminutive standard; in the streets or the baths it is their duty to give way or bow down before the meanest of the people; and their testimony is rejected if it may tend to the prejudice of a true believer. The pomp of processions, the sound of bells or of psalmody, is interdicted in their worship; a decent reverence for the national faith is imposed on their sermons and conversations; and the sacrilegious attempt to enter a mosch, or to seduce a Musulman, will not be suffered to escape with impunity. In a time, however, of tranquillity and justice the Christians have never been compelled to renounce the Gospel, or to embrace the Koran; but the punishment of death is inflicted for the apostates who have professed and deserted the law of Mohammed. The martyrs of Cordova provoked the sentence of the cadhi by the public confession of their inconstancy, or their passionate invectives against the person and religion of the prophet.[218]

At the end of the first century of the Hegira the caliphs were the most potent and absolute monarchs of the globe. Their prerogative was not circumscribed, either in right or in fact, by the power of the nobles, the freedom of the commons, the privileges of the church, the votes of a senate, or the memory of a free constitution. The authority of the companions of Mohammed expired with their lives; and the chiefs or emirs of the Arabian tribes left behind in the desert the spirit of equality and independence. The regal and sacerdotal characters were united in the successors of Mohammed; and if the Koran was the rule of their actions, they were the supreme judges and interpreters of that divine book. They reigned by the right of conquest over the nations of the East, to whom the name of liberty was unknown, and who were accustomed to applaud in their tyrants the acts of violence and severity that were exercised at their own expense. Under the last of the Ommiades the Arabian empire extended two hundred days' journey from east to west, from the confines of Tartary and India to the shores of the Atlantic Ocean. And if we retrench the sleeve of the robe, as it is styled by their writers, the long and narrow province of Africa, the solid and compact dominion from Fargana to Aden, from Tarsus to Surat, will spread on every side to the measure of four or five months of the march of a caravan.[219] We should vainly seek the indissoluble union and easy obedience that pervaded the government of Augustus and the Antonines; but the progress of the Mohammedan religion diffused over this ample space a general resemblance of manners and opinions. The language and laws of the Koran were studied with equal devotion at Samarcand and Seville: the Moor and the Indian embraced as countrymen and brothers in the pilgrimage of Mecca; and the Arabian language was adopted as the popular idiom in all the provinces to the westward of the Tigris.[220]

CHAPTER LII

The Two Sieges of Constantinople by the Arabs. Their Invasion of France, and Defeat by Charles Martel. Civil War of the Ommiades and Abbassides. Learning of the Arabs. Luxury of the Caliphs. Naval Enterprises on Crete, Sicily, and Rome. Decay and Division of the Empire of the Caliphs. Defeats and Victories of the Greek Emperors.

WHEN the Arabs first issued from the desert they must have been surprised at the ease and rapidity of their own success. But when they advanced in the career of victory to the banks of the Indus and the summit of the Pyrenees, when they had repeatedly tried the edge of their scimitars and the energy of their faith, they might be equally astonished that any nation could resist their invincible arms, that any boundary should confine the dominion of the successor of the prophet. The confidence of soldiers and fanatics may indeed be excused, since the calm historian of the present hour, who strives to follow the rapid course of the Saracens, must study to explain by what means the church and state were saved from this impending, and, as it should seem, from this inevitable danger. The deserts of Scythia and Sarmatia might be guarded by their extent, their climate, their poverty, and the courage of the northern shepherds; China was remote and inaccessible; but the greatest part of the temperate zone was subject to the Mohammedan conquerors, the Greeks were exhausted by the calamities of war and the loss of their fairest provinces, and the barbarians of Europe might justly tremble at the precipitate fall of the Gothic monarchy. In this inquiry I shall unfold the events that rescued our ancestors of Britain, and our neighbours of Gaul, from the civil and religious yoke of the Koran; that protected the majesty of Rome, and delayed the servitude of Constantinople; that invigorated the defence of the Christians, and scattered among their enemies the seeds of division and decay.

Forty-six years after the flight of Mohammed

from Mecca his disciples appeared in arms under the walls of Constantinople.[1] They were animated by a genuine or fictitious saying of the prophet, that, to the first army which besieged the city of the Cæsars, their sins were forgiven: the long series of Roman triumphs would be meritoriously transferred to the conquerors of New Rome; and the wealth of nations was deposited in this well-chosen seat of royalty and commerce. No sooner had the caliph Moawiyah suppressed his rivals and established his throne, than he aspired to expiate the guilt of civil blood by the success and glory of this holy expedition;[2] his preparations by sea and land were adequate to the importance of the object; his standard was intrusted to Sophian, a veteran warrior, but the troops were encouraged by the example and presence of Yezid, the son and presumptive heir of the commander of the faithful. The Greeks had little to hope, nor had their enemies any reasons of fear, from the courage and vigilance of the reigning emperor, who disgraced the name of Constantine, and imitated only the inglorious years of his grandfather Heraclius. Without delay or opposition, the naval forces of the Saracens passed through the unguarded channel of the Hellespont, which even now, under the feeble and disorderly government of the Turks, is maintained as the natural bulwark of the capital.[3] The Arabian fleet cast anchor, and the troops were disembarked near the palace of Hebdomon, seven miles from the city. During many days, from the dawn of light to the evening, the line of assault was extended from the golden gate to the eastern promontory, and the foremost warriors were impelled by the weight and effort of the succeeding columns. But the besiegers had formed an insufficient estimate of the strength and resources of Constantinople. The solid and lofty walls were guarded by numbers and discipline: the spirit of the Romans was rekindled by the last danger of their religion and empire: the fugitives from the conquered provinces more successfully renewed the defence of Damascus and Alexandria; and the Saracens were dismayed by the strange and prodigious effects of artificial fire. This firm and effectual resistance diverted their arms to the more easy attempts of plundering the European and Asiatic coasts of the Propontis; and, after keeping the sea from the month of April to that of September, on the approach of winter they retreated fourscore miles from the capital, to the isle of Cyzicus, in which they had established their magazine of spoil and provisions. So patient was their perseverance, or so languid were their operations, that they repeated in the six following summers the same attack and retreat, with a gradual abatement of hope and vigour, till the mischances of shipwreck and disease, of the sword and of fire, compelled them to relinquish the fruitless enterprise. They might bewail the loss, or commemorate the martyrdom, of thirty thousand Moslems who fell in the siege of Constantinople; and the solemn funeral of Abu Ayub, or Job, excited the curiosity of the Christians themselves. That venerable Arab, one of the last of the companions of Mohammed, was numbered among the *ansars*, or auxiliaries, of Medina, who sheltered the head of the flying prophet. In his youth he fought, at Beder and Ohud, under the holy standard: in his mature age he was the friend and follower of Ali; and the last remnant of his strength and life was consumed in a distant and dangerous war against the enemies of the Koran. His memory was revered; but the place of his burial was neglected and unknown, during a period of seven hundred and eighty years, till the conquest of Constantinople by Mohammed the Second. A seasonable vision (for such are the manufacture of every religion) revealed the holy spot at the foot of the walls and the bottom of the harbour; and the mosch of Ayub has been deservedly chosen for the simple and martial inauguration of the Turkish sultans.[4]

The event of the siege revived, both in the East and West, the reputation of the Roman arms, and cast a momentary shade over the glories of the Saracens. The Greek ambassador was favourably received at Damascus, in a general council of the emirs of Koreish: a peace, or truce, of thirty years was ratified between the two empires; and the stipulation of an annual tribute, fifty horses of a noble breed, fifty slaves, and three thousand pieces of gold, degraded the majesty of the commander of the faithful.[5] The aged caliph was desirous of possessing his dominions, and ending his days, in tranquillity and repose: while the Moors and Indians trembled at his name, his palace and city of Damascus was insulted by the Mardaites, or Maronites, of Mount Libanus, the firmest barrier of the empire, till they were disarmed and transplanted by the suspicious policy of the Greeks.[6] After the revolt of Arabia and Persia, the house of Ommiyah[7] was reduced to the kingdom of Syria and Egypt: their distress and fear enforced their compliance with the pressing demands of the Christians; and the tribute was increased to a slave, a horse, and a thousand pieces of gold, for each of the three hundred and sixty-five days of the solar year. But as soon as the empire was again united by the arms and policy of Abdalmalek, he disclaimed a badge of servitude not less injurious to his conscience than to his pride; he discontinued the payment of the tribute; and the resentment of the Greeks was disabled from action by the mad tyranny of the second Justinian, the just rebellion of his subjects, and the frequent change of his antagonists and successors. Till the reign of Abdalmalek the Saracens had been content with the free possession of the Persian and Roman treasures in the coin of Chosroes and Cæsar. By the command of that caliph a national mint was established, both for silver and gold, and the inscription of the Dinar, though it might be censured by some timorous casuists, proclaimed the unity of the God of Mohammed.[8] Under the reign of the caliph Walid, the Greek language and characters were excluded from the accounts of the public revenue.[9] If this change was productive of the invention or familiar use of our present numerals, the Arabic or Indian ciphers, as they are commonly styled, a regulation of office has promoted the most important discoveries of arithmetic, algebra, and the mathematical sciences.[10]

Whilst the caliph Walid sat idle on the throne of Damascus, while his lieutenants achieved the conquest of Transoxiana and Spain, a third army of Saracens overspread the provinces of Asia Minor, and approached the borders of the Byzantine capital. But the attempt and disgrace of the second siege was reserved for his brother Soliman, whose ambition appears to have been quickened by a more active and martial spirit. In the revolutions of the Greek empire, after the tyrant Justinian had been punished and avenged, a humble secretary, Anastasius or Artemius, was promoted by chance or merit to the vacant purple. He was alarmed by the sound of war; and his ambassador returned from Damascus with the tremendous news that the Saracens were preparing an armament by sea and land, such as would transcend the experience of the past, or the belief of the present, age. The precautions of Anastasius were not unworthy of his station, or of the impending danger. He issued a peremptory mandate, that all persons who were not provided with the means of subsistence for a three years' siege should evacuate the city: the public granaries and arsenals were abundantly replenished; the walls were restored and strengthened; and the engines for casting stones, or darts, or fire, were stationed along the ramparts, or in the brigantines of war, of which an additional number was hastily constructed. To prevent is safer, as well as more honourable, than to repel an attack; and a design was meditated, above the usual spirit of the Greeks, of burning the naval stores of the enemy, the cypress timber that had been hewn in Mount Libanus, and was piled along the seashore of Phœnicia, for the service of the Egyptian fleet. This generous enterprise was defeated by the cowardice or treachery of the troops, who, in the new language of the empire, were styled of the *Obsequian Theme*.[11] They murdered their chief, deserted their standard in the isle of Rhodes, dispersed themselves over the adjacent continent, and deserved pardon or reward by investing with the purple a simple officer of the revenue. The name of Theodosius might recommend him to the senate and people; but after some months he sunk into a cloister, and resigned, to the firmer hand of Leo the Isaurian, the urgent defence of the capital and empire. The most formidable of the Saracens, Moslemah the brother of the caliph, was advancing at the head of one hundred and twenty thousand Arabs and Persians, the greater part mounted on horses or camels; and the successful sieges of Tyana, Amorium, and Pergamus were of sufficient duration to exercise their skill and to elevate their hopes. At the well-known passage of Abydus, on the Hellespont, the Mohammedan arms were transported, for the first time, from Asia to Europe. From thence, wheeling round the Thracian cities of the Propontis, Moslemah invested Constantinople on the land side, surrounded his camp with a ditch and rampart, prepared and planted his engines of assault, and declared, by words and actions, a patient resolution of expecting the return of seed-time and harvest, should the obstinacy of the besieged prove equal to his own. The Greeks would gladly have ransomed their religion and empire by a fine or assessment of a piece of gold on the head of each inhabitant of the city; but the liberal offer was rejected with disdain, and the presumption of Moslemah was exalted by the speedy approach and invincible force of the navies of Egypt and Syria. They are said to have amounted to eighteen hundred ships: the number betrays their inconsiderable size; and of the twenty stout and capacious vessels, whose magnitude impeded their progress, each was manned with no more than one hundred heavy-armed soldiers. This huge armada proceeded on a smooth sea, and with a gentle gale, towards the mouth of the Bosphorus; the surface of the strait was overshadowed, in the language of the Greeks, with a moving forest, and the same fatal night had been fixed by the Saracen chief for a general assault by sea and land. To allure the confidence of the enemy the emperor had thrown aside the chain that usually guarded the entrance of the harbour; but while they hesitated whether they should seize the opportunity or apprehend the snare, the ministers of destruction were at hand. The fire-ships of the Greeks were launched against them; the Arabs, their arms, and vessels, were involved in the same flames; the disorderly fugitives were dashed against each other or overwhelmed in the waves; and I no longer find a vestige of the fleet that had threatened to extirpate the Roman name. A still more fatal and irreparable loss was that of the caliph Soliman, who died of an indigestion,[12] in his camp near Kinnisrin or Chalcis in Syria, as he was preparing to lead against Constantinople the remaining forces of the East. The brother of Moslemah was succeeded by a kinsman and an enemy; and the throne of an active and able prince was degraded by the useless and pernicious virtues of a bigot. While he started and satisfied the scruples of a blind conscience, the siege was continued through the winter by the neglect, rather than by the resolution of the caliph Omar.[13] The winter proved uncommonly rigorous: above a hundred days the ground was covered with deep snow, and the natives of the sultry climes of Egypt and Arabia lay torpid and almost lifeless in their frozen camp. They revived on the return of spring; a second effort had been made in their favour, and their distress was relieved by the arrival of two numerous fleets laden with corn, and arms, and soldiers; the first from Alexandria, of four hundred transports and galleys; the second, of three hundred and sixty vessels, from the ports of Africa. But the Greek fires were again kindled, and, if the destruction was less complete, it was owing to the experience which had taught the Moslems to remain at a safe distance, or to the perfidy of the Egyptian mariners, who deserted with their ships to the emperor of the Christians. The trade and navigation of the capital were restored; and the produce of the fisheries supplied the wants, and even the luxury, of the inhabitants. But the calamities of famine and disease were soon felt by the troops of Moslemah, and, as the former was miserably assuaged, so the latter was dreadfully propagated, by the pernicious nutriment which hunger compelled them to extract from the most unclean or unnatural food. The

spirit of conquest, and even of enthusiasm, was extinct: the Saracens could no longer straggle beyond their lines, either single or in small parties, without exposing themselves to the merciless retaliation of the Thracian peasants. An army of Bulgarians was attracted from the Danube by the gifts and promises of Leo; and these savage auxiliaries made some atonement for the evils which they had inflicted on the empire by the defeat and slaughter of twenty-two thousand Asiatics. A report was dexterously scattered that the Franks, the unknown nations of the Latin world, were arming by sea and land in the defence of the Christian cause, and their formidable aid was expected with far different sensations in the camp and city. At length, after a siege of thirteen months,[14] the hopeless Moslemah received from the caliph the welcome permission of retreat. The march of the Arabian cavalry over the Hellespont and through the provinces of Asia was executed without delay or molestation; but an army of their brethren had been cut in pieces on the side of Bithynia, and the remains of the fleet were so repeatedly damaged by tempest and fire, that only five galleys entered the port of Alexandria to relate the tale of their various and almost incredible disasters.[15]

In the two sieges the deliverance of Constantinople may be chiefly ascribed to the novelty, the terrors, and the real efficacy of the *Greek fire*.[16] The important secret of compounding and directing this artificial flame was imparted by Callinicus, a native of Heliopolis in Syria, who deserted from the service of the caliph to that of the emperor.[17] The skill of a chemist and engineer was equivalent to the succour of fleets and armies; and this discovery or improvement of the military art was fortunately reserved for the distressful period when the degenerate Romans of the East were incapable of contending with the warlike enthusiasm and youthful vigour of the Saracens. The historian who presumes to analyse this extraordinary composition should suspect his own ignorance and that of his Byzantine guides, so prone to the marvellous, so careless, and, in this instance, so jealous of the truth. From their obscure, and perhaps fallacious hints, it should seem that the principal ingredient of the Greek fire was the *naphtha*,[18] or liquid bitumen, a light, tenacious, and inflammable oil,[19] which springs from the earth, and catches fire as soon as it comes in contact with the air. The naphtha was mingled, I know not by what methods or in what proportions, with sulphur and with the pitch that is extracted from evergreen firs.[20] From this mixture, which produced a thick smoke and a loud explosion, proceeded a fierce and obstinate flame, which not only rose in perpendicular ascent, but likewise burnt with equal vehemence in descent or lateral progress; instead of being extinguished, it was nourished and quickened by the element of water; and sand, urine, or vinegar, were the only remedies that could damp the fury of this powerful agent, which was justly denominated by the Greeks the *liquid*, or the *maritime*, fire. For the annoyance of the enemy, it was employed with equal effect by sea and land, in battles or in sieges. It was either poured from the rampart in large boilers, or launched in red-hot balls of stone and iron, or darted in arrows and javelins, twisted round with flax and tow, which had deeply imbibed the inflammable oil; sometimes it was deposited in fireships, the victims and instruments of a more ample revenge, and was most commonly blown through long tubes of copper, which were planted on the prow of a galley, and fancifully shaped into the mouths of savage monsters, that seemed to vomit a stream of liquid and consuming fire. This important art was preserved at Constantinople, as the palladium of the state: the galleys and *artillery* might occasionally be lent to the allies of Rome; but the composition of the Greek fire was concealed with the most jealous scruple, and the terror of the enemies was increased and prolonged by their ignorance and surprise. In the treatise of the administration of the empire, the royal author[21] suggests the answers and excuses that might best elude the indiscreet curiosity and importunate demands of the barbarians. They should be told that the mystery of the Greek fire had been revealed by an angel to the first and greatest of the Constantines, with a sacred injunction that this gift of Heaven, this peculiar blessing of the Romans, should never be communicated to any foreign nation: that the prince and subject were alike bound to religious silence under the temporal and spiritual penalties of treason and sacrilege; and that the impious attempt would provoke the sudden and supernatural vengeance of the God of the Christians. By these precautions the secret was confined, above four hundred years, to the Romans of the East; and at the end of the eleventh century, the Pisans, to whom every sea and every art were familiar, suffered the effects, without understanding the composition, of the Greek fire. It was at length either discovered or stolen by the Mohammedans; and, in the holy wars of Syria and Egypt, they retorted an invention, contrived against themselves, on the heads of the Christians. A knight, who despised the swords and lances of the Saracens, relates with heartfelt sincerity his own fears, and those of his companions, at the sight and sound of the mischievous engine that discharged a torrent of the Greek fire, the *feu Gregeois*, as it is styled by the more early of the French writers. It came flying through the air, says Joinville,[22] like a winged long-tailed dragon, about the thickness of a hogshead, with the report of thunder and the velocity of lightning; and the darkness of the night was dispelled by this deadly illumination. The use of the Greek, or, as it might now be called, of the Saracen fire, was continued to the middle of the fourteenth century,[23] when the scientific or casual compound of nitre, sulphur, and charcoal effected a new revolution in the art of war and the history of mankind.[24]

Constantinople and the Greek fire might exclude the Arabs from the eastern entrance of Europe; but in the West, on the side of the Pyrenees, the provinces of Gaul were threatened and invaded by the conquerors of Spain.[2] The decline of the French monarchy invited the attack of these insatiate fanatics. The descendants of Clovis had lost the inheritance of his martial and ferocious spirit; and their misfortune or demerit has affixed the epithet of *lazy* to the last kings of the Merovingian race.[26] They ascended the throne without power, and sunk into the grave without a name. A country palace, in the neighbourhood of Compiègne,[27] was allotted for their residence or prison: but each year, in the month of March or May, they were conducted in a waggon drawn by oxen to the assembly of the Franks, to give audience to foreign ambassadors and to ratify the acts of the mayor of the palace. That domestic officer was become the minister of the nation and the master of the prince. A public employment was converted into the patrimony of a private family: the elder Pepin left a king of mature years under the guardianship of his own widow and her child; and these feeble regents were forcibly dispossessed by the most active of his bastards. A government, half savage and half corrupt, was almost dissolved; and the tributary dukes, and provincial counts, and the territorial lords, were tempted to despise the weakness of the monarch and to imitate the ambition of the mayor. Among these independent chiefs, one of the boldest and most successful was Eudes, duke of Aquitain, who in the southern provinces of Gaul usurped the authority, and even the title of king. The Goths, the Gascons, and the

Franks assembled under the standard of this Christian hero: he repelled the first invasion of the Saracens; and Zama, lieutenant of the caliph, lost his army and his life under the walls of Toulouse. The ambition of his successors was stimulated by revenge; they repassed the Pyrenees with the means and the resolution of conquest. The advantageous situation which had recommended Narbonne[28] as the first Roman colony was again chosen by the Moslems: they claimed the province of Septimania or Languedoc as a just dependence of the Spanish monarchy: the vineyards of Gascony and the city of Bordeaux were possessed by the sovereign of Damascus and Samarcand; and the south of France, from the mouth of the Garonne to that of the Rhône, assumed the manners and religion of Arabia.

But these narrow limits were scorned by the spirit of Abdalrahman, or Abderame, who had been restored by the caliph Hashem to the wishes of the soldiers and people of Spain. That veteran and daring commander adjudged to the obedience of the prophet whatever yet remained of France or Europe; and prepared to execute the sentence, at the head of a formidable host, in the full confidence of surmounting all opposition, either of nature or of man. His first care was to suppress a domestic rebel, who commanded the most important passes of the Pyrenees: Munuza, a Moorish chief, had accepted the alliance of the duke of Aquitain; and Eudes, from a motive of private or public interest, devoted his beauteous daughter to the embraces of the African misbeliever. But the strongest fortresses of Cerdagne were invested by a superior force; the rebel was overtaken and slain in the mountains; and his widow was sent a captive to Damascus, to gratify the desires, or more probably the vanity, of the commander of the faithful. From the Pyrenees, Abderame proceeded without delay to the passage of the Rhône and the siege of Arles. An army of Christians attempted the relief of the city: the tombs of their leaders were yet visible in the thirteenth century; and many thousands of their dead bodies were carried down the rapid stream into the Mediterranean Sea. The arms of Abderame were not less successful on the side of the ocean. He passed without opposition the Garonne and Dordogne, which unite their waters in the gulf of Bordeaux; but he found, beyond those rivers, the camp of the intrepid Eudes, who had formed a second army and sustained a second defeat, so fatal to the Christians, that, according to their sad confession,

God alone could reckon the number of the slain. The victorious Saracen overran the provinces of Aquitain, whose Gallic names are disguised, rather than lost, in the modern appellations of Perigord, Saintonge, and Poitou: his standards were planted on the walls, or at least before the gates, of Tours and of Sens; and his detachments overspread the kingdom of Burgundy as far as the well-known cities of Lyons and Besançon. The memory of these devastations, for Abderame did not spare the country or the people, was long preserved by tradition; and the invasion of France by the Moors or Mohammedans affords the groundwork of those fables which have been so wildly disfigured in the romances of chivalry, and so elegantly adorned by the Italian muse. In the decline of society and art, the deserted cities could supply a slender booty to the Saracens; their richest spoil was found in the churches and monasteries, which they stripped of their ornaments and delivered to the flames: and the tutelar saints, both Hilary of Poitiers and Martin of Tours, forgot their miraculous powers in the defence of their own sepulchres.[29] A victorious line of march had been prolonged above a thousand miles from the rock of Gibraltar to the banks of the Loire; the repetition of an equal space would have carried the Saracens to the confines of Poland and the Highlands of Scotland; the Rhine is not more impassable than the Nile or Euphrates, and the Arabian fleet might have sailed without a naval combat into the mouth of the Thames. Perhaps the interpretation of the Koran would now be taught in the schools of Oxford, and her pulpits might demonstrate to a circumcised people the sanctity and truth of the revelation of Mohammed.[30]

From such calamities was Christendom delivered by the genius and fortune of one man. Charles, the illegitimate son of the elder Pepin, was content with the titles of mayor or duke of the Franks; but he deserved to become the father of a line of kings. In a laborious administration of twenty-four years he restored and supported the dignity of the throne, and the rebels of Germany and Gaul were successively crushed by the activity of a warrior who in the same campaign could display his banner on the Elbe, the Rhône, and the shores of the ocean. In the public danger he was summoned by the voice of his country; and his rival, the duke of Aquitain, was reduced to appear among the fugitives and suppliants. "Alas!" exclaimed the Franks, "what a misfortune! what an indignity! We have long heard of the name and conquests of the Arabs: we were apprehensive of their attack from the East; they have now conquered Spain, and invade our country on the side of the West. Yet their numbers and (since they have no buckler) their arms are inferior to our own." "If you follow my advice," replied the prudent mayor of the palace, "you will not interrupt their march, nor precipitate your attack. They are like a torrent, which it is dangerous to stem in its career. The thirst of riches, and the consciousness of success, redoubled their valour, and valour is of more avail than arms or numbers. Be patient till they have loaded themselves with the incumbrance of wealth. The possession of wealth will divide their counsels and assure your victory." This subtle policy is perhaps a refinement of the Arabian writers; and the situation of Charles will suggest a more narrow and selfish motive of procrastination; the secret desire of humbling the pride and wasting the provinces of the rebel duke of Aquitain. It is more probable that the delays of Charles were inevitable and reluctant. A standing army was unknown under the first and second race; more than half the kingdom was now in the hands of the Saracens: according to their respective situation, the Franks of Neustria and Austrasia were too conscious or too careless of the impending danger; and the voluntary aids of the Gepidæ and Germans were separated by a long interval from the standard of the Christian general. No sooner had he collected his forces than he sought and found the enemy in the centre of France, between Tours and Poitiers. His well-conducted march was covered by a range of hills, and Abderame appears to have been surprised by his unexpected presence. The nations of Asia, Africa, and Europe advanced with equal ardour to an encounter which would change the history of the world. In the six first days of desultory combat the horsemen and archers of the East maintained their advantage; but in the closer onset of the seventh day the Orientals were oppressed by the strength and stature of the Germans, who, with stout hearts and *iron* hands,[31] asserted the civil and religious freedom of their posterity. The epithet of *Martel*, the *hammer*, which had been added to the name of Charles, is expressive of his weighty and irresistible strokes: the valour of Eudes was excited by resentment and emulation; and their companions, in the eye of history, are the true Peers and Paladins of French chivalry. After a bloody field, in which Abderame was slain, the Saracens, in the close of the evening, retired to their camp. In the disorder and despair of the night

the various tribes of Yemen and Damascus, of Africa and Spain, were provoked to turn their arms against each other: the remains of their host were suddenly dissolved, and each *emir* consulted his safety by a hasty and separate retreat. At the dawn of day the stillness of a hostile camp was suspected by the victorious Christians: on the report of their spies they ventured to explore the riches of the vacant tents; but if we expect some celebrated relics, a small portion of the spoil was restored to the innocent and lawful owners. The joyful tidings were soon diffused over the Catholic world, and the monks of Italy could affirm and believe that three hundred and fifty, or three hundred and seventy-five, thousand of the Mohammedans had been crushed by the hammer of Charles,[32] while no more than fifteen hundred Christians were slain in the field of Tours. But this incredible tale is sufficiently disproved by the caution of the French general, who apprehended the snare and accidents of a pursuit, and dismissed his German allies to their native forests. The inactivity of a conqueror betrays the loss of strength and blood, and the most cruel execution is inflicted, not in the ranks of battle, but on the backs of a flying enemy. Yet the victory of the Franks was complete and final; Aquitain was recovered by the arms of Eudes; the Arabs never resumed the conquest of Gaul, and they were soon driven beyond the Pyrenees by Charles Martel and his valiant race.[33] It might have been expected that the saviour of Christendom would have been canonised, or at least applauded, by the gratitude of the clergy, who are indebted to his sword for their present existence. But in the public distress the mayor of the palace had been compelled to apply the riches, or at least the revenues, of the bishops and abbots to the relief of the state and the reward of the soldiers. His merits were forgotten, his sacrilege alone was remembered, and, in an epistle to a Carlovingian prince, a Gallic synod presumes to declare that his ancestor was damned; that on the opening of his tomb the spectators were affrighted by a smell of fire and the aspect of a horrid dragon; and that a saint of the times was indulged with a pleasant vision of the soul and body of Charles Martel burning, to all eternity, in the abyss of hell.[34]

The loss of an army, or a province, in the Western world was less painful to the court of Damascus than the rise and progress of a domestic competitor. Except among the Syrians, the caliphs of the house of Ommiyah had never been the objects of the public favour. The life of

Mohammed recorded their perseverance in idolatry and rebellion: their conversion had been reluctant, their elevation irregular and factious, and their throne was cemented with the most holy and noble blood of Arabia. The best of their race, the pious Omar, was dissatisfied with his own title: their personal virtues were insufficient to justify a departure from the order of succession; and the eyes and wishes of the faithful were turned towards the line of Hashem and the kindred of the apostle of God. Of these the Fatimites were either rash or pusillanimous; but the descendants of Abbas cherished, with courage and discretion, the hopes of their rising fortunes. From an obscure residence in Syria, they secretly despatched their agents and missionaries, who preached in the Eastern provinces their hereditary indefeasible right; and Mohammed, the son of Ali, the son of Abdallah, the son of Abbas, the uncle of the prophet, gave audience to the deputies of Chorasan, and accepted their free gift of four hundred thousand pieces of gold. After the death of Mohammed, the oath of allegiance was administered in the name of his son Ibrahim to a numerous band of votaries, who expected only a signal and a leader; and the governor of Chorasan continued to deplore his fruitless admonitions and the deadly slumber of the caliphs of Damascus, till he himself, with all his adherents, was driven from the city and palace of Meru by the rebellious arms of Abu Moslem.[35] That maker of kings, the author, as he is named, of the *call* of the Abbassides, was at length rewarded for his presumption of merit with the usual gratitude of courts. A mean, perhaps a foreign, extraction could not repress the aspiring energy of Abu Moslem. Jealous of his wives, liberal of his wealth, prodigal of his own blood and of that of others, he could boast with pleasure, and possibly with truth, that he had destroyed six hundred thousand of his enemies; and such was the intrepid gravity of his mind and countenance, that he was never seen to smile except on a day of battle. In the visible separation of parties, the *green* was consecrated to the Fatimites; the Ommiades were distinguished by the *white;* and the *black*, as the most adverse, was naturally adopted by the Abbassides. Their turbans and garments were stained with that gloomy colour: two black standards, on pike-staves nine cubits long, were borne aloft in the van of Abu Moslem; and their allegorical names of the *night* and the *shadow* obscurely represented the indissoluble union and perpetual succession of the line of Hashem. From the Indus to the Euphrates,

the East was convulsed by the quarrel of the white and the black factions: the Abbassides were most frequently victorious; but their public success was clouded by the personal misfortune of their chief. The court of Damascus, awakening from a long slumber, resolved to prevent the pilgrimage of Mecca, which Ibrahim had undertaken with a splendid retinue, to recommend himself at once to the favour of the prophet and of the people. A detachment of cavalry intercepted his march and arrested his person; and the unhappy Ibrahim, snatched away from the promise of untasted royalty, expired in iron fetters in the dungeons of Haran. His two younger brothers, Saffah and Almansor, eluded the search of the tyrant, and lay concealed at Cufa, till the zeal of the people and the approach of his Eastern friends allowed them to expose their persons to the impatient public. On Friday, in the dress of a caliph, in the colours of the sect, Saffah proceeded with religious and military pomp to the mosch: ascending the pulpit, he prayed and preached as the lawful successor of Mohammed; and, after his departure, his kinsmen bound a willing people by an oath of fidelity. But it was on the banks of the Zab, and not in the mosch of Cufa, that this important controversy was determined. Every advantage appeared to be on the side of the white faction: the authority of established government; an army of a hundred and twenty thousand soldiers, against a sixth part of that number; and the presence and merit of the caliph Mervan, the fourteenth and last of the house of Ommiyah. Before his accession to the throne he had deserved, by his Georgian warfare the honourable epithet of the ass of Mesopotamia;[36] and he might have been ranked among the greatest princes, had not, says Abulfeda, the eternal order decreed that moment for the ruin of his family; a decree against which all human prudence and fortitude must struggle in vain. The orders of Mervan were mistaken, or disobeyed: the return of his horse, from which he had dismounted on a necessary occasion, impressed the belief of his death; and the enthusiasm of the black squadrons was ably conducted by Abdallah, the uncle of his competitor. After an irretrievable defeat, the caliph escaped to Mosul; but the colours of the Abbassides were displayed from the rampart; he suddenly repassed the Tigris, cast a melancholy look on his palace of Haran, crossed the Euphrates, abandoned the fortifications of Damascus, and, without halting in Palestine, pitched his last and fatal camp at Busir, on the banks of the Nile.[37] His speed was urged by the incessant diligence of Abdallah, who in every step of the pursuit acquired strength and reputation: the remains of the white faction were finally vanquished in Egypt; and the lance, which terminated the life and anxiety of Mervan, was not less welcome perhaps to the unfortunate than to the victorious chief. The merciless inquisition of the conqueror eradicated the most distant branches of the hostile race: their bones were scattered, their memory was accursed, and the martyrdom of Hossein was abundantly revenged on the posterity of his tyrants. Fourscore of the Ommiades, who had yielded to the faith or clemency of their foes, were invited to a banquet at Damascus. The laws of hospitality were violated by a promiscuous massacre: the board was spread over their fallen bodies; and the festivity of the guests was enlivened by the music of their dying groans. By the event of the civil war the dynasty of the Abbassides was firmly established; but the Christians only could triumph in the mutual hatred and common loss of the disciples of Mohammed.[38]

Yet the thousands who were swept away by the sword of war might have been speedily retrieved in the succeeding generation, if the consequences of the revolution had not tended to dissolve the power and unity of the empire of the Saracens. In the proscription of the Ommiades, a royal youth of the name of Abdalrahman alone escaped the rage of his enemies, who hunted the wandering exile from the banks of the Euphrates to the valleys of Mount Atlas. His presence in the neighbourhood of Spain revived the zeal of the white faction. The name and cause of the Abbassides had been first vindicated by the Persians: the West had been pure from civil arms; and the servants of the abdicated family still held, by a precarious tenure, the inheritance of their lands and the offices of government. Strongly prompted by gratitude, indignation, and fear, they invited the grandson of the caliph Hashem to ascend the throne of his ancestors; and, in his desperate condition, the extremes of rashness and prudence were almost the same. The acclamations of the people saluted his landing on the coast of Andalusia; and, after a successful struggle, Abdalrahman established the throne of Cordova, and was the father of the Ommiades of Spain, who reigned above two hundred and fifty years from the Atlantic to the Pyrenees.[39] He slew in battle a lieutenant of the Abbassides, who had invaded his dominions with a fleet and army: the head of Ala, in salt and camphire, was suspended by a daring messenger before the palace of Mecca; and the caliph Almansor rejoiced in his safety, that he was removed by seas and lands from such a formidable adversary. Their mutual designs or declarations of offensive war evaporated without effect; but instead of opening a door to the conquest of Europe, Spain was dissevered from the trunk of the monarchy, engaged in perpetual hostility with the East, and inclined to peace and friendship with the Christian sovereigns of Constantinople and France. The example of the Ommiades was imitated by the real or fictitious progeny of Ali, the Edrissites of Mauritania, and the more powerful Fatimites of Africa and Egypt. In the tenth century the chair of Mohammed was disputed by three caliphs or commanders of the faithful, who reigned at Bagdad, Cairoan, and Cordova, excommunicated each other, and agreed only in a principle of discord, that a sectary is more odious and criminal than an unbeliever.[40]

Mecca was the patrimony of the line of Hashem, yet the Abbassides were never tempted to reside either in the birthplace or the city of the prophet. Damascus was disgraced by the choice and polluted with the blood, of the Ommiades; and, after some hesitation, Almansor, the brother and successor of Saffah, laid the foundations of Bagdad,[41] the Imperial seat of his posterity during a reign of five hundred years.[42] The chosen spot is on the eastern bank of the Tigris, about fifteen miles above the ruins of Modain: the double wall was of a circular form; and such was the rapid increase of a capital now dwindled to a provincial town, that the funeral of a popular saint might be attended by eight hundred thousand men and sixty thousand women of Bagdad and the adjacent villages. In this *city of peace*,[43] amidst the riches of the East, the Abbassides soon disdained the abstinence and frugality of the first caliphs, and aspired to emulate the magnificence of the Persian kings. After his wars and buildings, Almansor left behind him in gold and silver about thirty millions sterling;[44] and this treasure was exhausted in a few years by the vices or virtue of his children. His son Mahadi, in a single pilgrimage to Mecca, expended six millions of dinars of gold. A pious and charitable motive may sanctify the foundation of cisterns and caravanseras, which he distributed along a measured road of seven hundred miles; but his train of camels, laden with snow, could serve only to astonish the natives of Arabia, and to refresh the fruits and liquors of the royal banquet.[45] The courtiers would surely praise the liberality of his grandson Almamon, who gave away four-fifths of the income of a province, a sum of two millions four hundred thousand gold dinars, before he drew his foot from the stirrup. At the nuptials of the same prince a thousand pearls of the largest size were showered on the head of the bride,[46] and a lottery of lands and houses displayed the capricious bounty of fortune. The glories of the court were brightened rather than impaired in the decline of the empire, and a Greek ambassador might admire, or pity, the magnificence of the feeble Moctader. "The caliph's whole army," says the historian Abulfeda, "both horse and foot, was under arms, which together made a body of one hundred and sixty thousand men. His state officers, the favourite slaves, stood near him in splendid apparel, their belts glittering with gold and gems. Near them were seven thousand eunuchs, four thousand of them white, the remainder black. The porters or doorkeepers were in number seven hundred. Barges and boats, with the most superb decorations, were seen swimming upon the Tigris. Nor was the palace itself less splendid, in which were hung up thirty-eight thousand pieces of tapestry, twelve thousand five hundred of which were of silk embroidered with gold. The carpets on the floor were twenty-two thousand. A hundred lions were brought out, with a keeper to each lion.[47] Among the other spectacles of rare and stupendous luxury was a tree of gold and silver spreading into eighteen large branches, on which, and on the lesser boughs, sat a variety of birds made of the same precious metals, as well as the leaves of the tree. While the machinery affected spontaneous motions, the several birds warbled their natural harmony. Through this scene of magnificence the Greek ambassador was led by the vizir to the foot of the caliph's throne."[48] In the West the Ommiades of Spain supported with equal pomp the title of commander of the faithful. Three miles from Cordova, in honour of his favourite sultana, the third and greatest of the Abdalrahmans constructed the city, palace, and gardens of Zehra. Twenty-five years, and above three millions sterling, were employed by the founder: his liberal taste invited the artists of Constantinople, the most skilful sculptors and architects of the age; and the buildings were sustained or adorned by twelve hundred columns of Spanish and African, of Greek and Italian marble. The hall of audience was encrusted with gold and pearls, and a great basin in the centre was surrounded with the curious and costly figures of birds and quadrupeds. In a lofty pavilion of the gardens one of these basins and fountains, so delightful in a sultry climate, was replenished not with water, but with the purest quicksilver. The seraglio of Abdalrahman, his wives, concubines, and black eunuchs, amounted to six thousand three hundred persons: and he was attended to the field by a guard of twelve thousand horse, whose belts and scimitars were studded with gold.[49]

In a private condition our desires are perpetually repressed by poverty and subordination; but the lives and labours of millions are devoted to the service of a despotic prince, whose laws are blindly obeyed, and whose wishes are instantly gratified. Our imagination is dazzled by the splendid picture; and whatever may be the cool dictates of reason, there are few among us who would obstinately refuse a trial of the comforts and the cares of royalty. It may therefore be of some use to borrow the experience of the same Abdalrahman, whose magnificence has perhaps excited our admiration and envy, and to transcribe an authentic memorial which was found in the closet of the deceased caliph. "I have now reigned above fifty years in victory or peace; beloved by my subjects, dreaded by my enemies, and respected by my allies. Riches and honours, power and pleasure, have waited on my call, nor does any earthly blessing appear to have been wanting to my felicity. In this situation I have diligently numbered the days of pure and genuine happiness which have fallen to my lot: they amount to FOURTEEN:—O man! place not thy confidence in this present world!"[50] The luxury of the caliphs, so useless to their private happiness, relaxed the nerves, and terminated the progress, of the Arabian empire. Temporal and spiritual conquest had been the sole occupation of the first successors of Mohammed; and after supplying themselves with the necessaries of life, the whole revenue was scrupulously devoted to that salutary work. The Abbassides were impoverished by the multitude of their wants and their contempt of economy. Instead of pursuing the great object of ambition, their leisure, their affections, the powers of their mind, were diverted by pomp and pleasure: the rewards of valour were embezzled by women and eunuchs, and the royal camp was encumbered by the luxury of the palace. A similar temper was diffused among the subjects of the caliph. Their stern enthusiasm was softened by time and prosperity: they sought riches in the occupations of industry, fame in the pursuits of literature, and happiness in the tranquillity of domestic life. War was no longer the passion of the Saracens; and the increase of pay, the repetition of donatives, were insufficient to allure the posterity of those voluntary champions who had crowded to the standard of Abubeker and Omar for the hopes of spoil and of paradise.

Under the reign of the Ommiades the studies of the Moslems were confined to the interpretation of the Koran, and the eloquence and poetry of their native tongue. A people continually exposed to the dangers of the field must esteem the healing powers of medicine, or rather of surgery: but the starving physicians of Arabia murmured a complaint that exercise and temperance deprived them of the greatest part of their practice.[51] After their civil and domestic wars, the subjects of the Abbassides, awakening from this mental lethargy, found leisure and felt curiosity for the acquisition of profane science. This spirit was first encouraged by the caliph Almansor, who, besides his knowledge of the Mohammedan law, had applied himself with success to the study of astronomy. But when the sceptre devolved to Almamon, the seventh of the Abbassides, he completed the designs of his grandfather, and invited the Muses from their ancient seats. His ambassadors at Constantinople, his agents in Armenia, Syria, and Egypt, collected the volumes of Grecian science: at his command they were translated by the most skilful interpreters into the Arabic language: his subjects were exhorted assiduously to peruse these instructive writings; and the successor of Mohammed assisted with pleasure and modesty at the assemblies and disputations of the learned. "He was not ignorant," says Abulpharagius, "that *they* are the elect of God, his best and most useful servants, whose lives are devoted to the improvement of their rational faculties. The mean ambition of the Chinese or the Turks may glory in the industry of their hands or the indulgence of their brutal appetites. Yet these dexterous artists must view, with hopeless emulation, the hexagons and pyramids of the cells of a beehive:[52] these fortitudinous heroes are awed by the superior fierceness of the lions and tigers; and in their amorous enjoyments they are much inferior to the vigour of the grossest and most sordid quadrupeds. The teachers of wisdom are the true luminaries and legislators of a world, which, without their aid, would again sink in ignorance and barbarism."[53] The zeal and curiosity of Almamon were imitated by succeeding princes of the line of Abbas: their rivals, the Fatimites of Africa and the Ommiades of Spain, were the patrons of the

learned, as well as the commanders of the faithful; the same royal prerogative was claimed b their independent emirs of the provinces; an their emulation diffused the taste and the re wards of science from Samarcand and Bochar to Fez and Cordova. The vizir of a sultan con secrated a sum of two hundred thousand piece of gold to the foundation of a college at Bagdac which he endowed with an annual revenue fifteen thousand dinars. The fruits of instructio were communicated, perhaps at different time to six thousand disciples of every degree, fror the son of the noble to that of the mechanic: sufficient allowance was provided for the ind gent scholars; and the merit or industry of th professors was repaid with adequate stipend. In every city the productions of Arabic litera ture were copied and collected by the curiosit of the studious and the vanity of the rich. A pr vate doctor refused the invitation of the sulta of Bochara, because the carriage of his book would have required four hundred camels. Th royal library of the Fatimites consisted of or hundred thousand manuscripts, elegantly trar scribed and splendidly bound, which were len without jealousy or avarice, to the students Cairo. Yet this collection must appear mode ate, if we can believe that the Ommiades Spain had formed a library of six hundred tho sand volumes, forty-four of which were employ ed in the mere catalogue. Their capital, Co dova, with the adjacent towns of Malaga, A meria, and Murcia, had given birth to mo than three hundred writers, and above sevent public libraries were opened in the cities of th Andalusian kingdom. The age of Arabian learr ing continued about five hundred years, till th great eruption of the Moguls, and was coev with the darkest and most slothful period European annals; but since the sun of scienc has arisen in the West, it should seem that th Oriental studies have languished and declined.

In the libraries of the Arabians, as in those Europe, the far greater part of the innumerabl volumes were possessed only of local value imaginary merit.[55] The shelves were crowde with orators and poets, whose style was adapte to the taste and manners of their countryme with general and partial histories, which eac revolving generation supplied with a new ha vest of persons and events; with codes and con mentaries of jurisprudence which derived th authority from the law of the prophet; with th interpreters of the Koran, and orthodox trad tion: and with the whole theological tribe, pol mics, mystics, scholastics, and moralists, th first or the last of writers, according to the different estimates of sceptics or believers. The works of speculation or science may be reduced to the four classes of philosophy, mathematics, astronomy, and physic. The sages of Greece were translated and illustrated in the Arabic language, and some treatises, now lost in the original, have been recovered in the versions of the East,[56] which possessed and studied the writings of Aristotle and Plato, of Euclid and Apollonius, of Ptolemy, Hippocrates, and Galen.[57] Among the ideal systems which have varied with the fashion of the times, the Arabians adopted the philosophy of the Stagirite, alike intelligible or alike obscure for the readers of every age. Plato wrote for the Athenians, and his allegorical genius is too closely blended with the language and religion of Greece. After the fall of that religion, the Peripatetics, emerging from their obscurity, prevailed in the controversies of the Oriental sects, and their founder was long afterwards restored by the Mohammedans of Spain to the Latin schools.[58] The physics, both of the Academy and the Lycæum, as they are built, not on observation but on argument, have retarded the progress of real knowledge. The metaphysics of infinite or finite spirit have too often been enlisted in the service of superstition. But the human faculties are fortified by the art and practice of dialectics; the ten predicaments of Aristotle collect and methodise our ideas,[59] and his syllogism is the keenest weapon of dispute. It was dexterously wielded in the schools of the Saracens, but, as it is more effectual for the detection of error than for the investigation of truth, it is not surprising that new generations of masters and disciples should still revolve in the same circle of logical argument. The mathematics are distinguished by a peculiar privilege, that, in the course of ages, they may always advance and can never recede. But the ancient geometry, if I am not misinformed, was resumed in the same state by the Italians of the fifteenth century; and whatever may be the origin of the name, the science of algebra is ascribed to the Grecian Diophantus by the modest testimony of the Arabs themselves.[60] They cultivated with more success the sublime science of astronomy, which elevates the mind of man to disdain his diminutive planet and momentary existence. The costly instruments of observation were supplied by the caliph Almamon, and the land of the Chaldeans still afforded the same spacious level, and the same unclouded horizon. In the plains of Sinaar, and a second time in those of Cufa, his mathematicians accurately measured a degree of the great circle of the earth, and determined at twenty-four thousand miles the entire circumference of our globe.[61] From the reign of the Abbassides to that of the grandchildren of Tamerlane, the stars, without the aid of glasses, were diligently observed; and the astronomical tables of Bagdad, Spain, and Samarcand[62] correct some minute errors, without daring to renounce the hypothesis of Ptolemy, without advancing a step towards the discovery of the solar system. In the eastern courts, the truths of science could be recommended only by ignorance and folly, and the astronomer would have been disregarded, had he not debased his wisdom or honesty by the vain predictions of astrology.[63] But in the science of medicine the Arabians have been deservedly applauded. The names of Mesua and Geber, of Razis and Avicenna, are ranked with the Grecian masters; in the city of Bagdad eight hundred and sixty physicians were licensed to exercise their lucrative profession:[64] in Spain, the life of the Catholic princes was intrusted to the skill of the Saracens,[65] and the school of Salerno, their legitimate offspring, revived in Italy and Europe the precepts of the healing art.[66] The success of each professor must have been influenced by personal and accidental causes; but we may form a less fanciful estimate of their general knowledge of anatomy,[67] botany,[68] and chemistry,[69] the threefold basis of their theory and practice. A superstitious reverence for the dead confined both the Greeks and the Arabians to the dissection of apes and quadrupeds; the more solid and visible parts were known in the time of Galen, and the finer scrutiny of the human frame was reserved for the microscope and the injections of modern artists. Botany is an active science, and the discoveries of the torrid zone might enrich the herbal of Dioscorides with two thousand plants. Some traditionary knowledge might be secreted in the temples and monasteries of Egypt; much useful experience had been acquired in the practice of arts and manufactures; but the *science* of chemistry owes its origin and improvement to the industry of the Saracens. They first invented and named the alembic for the purposes of distillation, analysed the substances of the three kingdoms of nature, tried the distinction and affinities of alcalis and acids, and converted the poisonous minerals into soft and salutary medicines. But the most eager search of Arabian chemistry was the transmutation of metals, and the elixir of immortal health: the reason and the fortunes of thousands were evaporated in the crucibles of alchymy, and the consummation of the great work was promoted by the worthy aid of mystery, fable, and superstition.

But the Moslems deprived themselves of the principal benefits of a familiar intercourse with Greece and Rome, the knowledge of antiquity, the purity of taste, and the freedom of thought. Confident in the riches of their native tongue, the Arabians disdained the study of any foreign idiom. The Greek interpreters were chosen among their Christian subjects; they formed their translations sometimes on the original text, more frequently perhaps on a Syriac version: and in the crowd of astronomers and physicians there is no example of a poet, an orator, or even an historian, being taught to speak the language of the Saracens.[70] The mythology of Homer would have provoked the abhorrence of those stern fanatics: they possessed in lazy ignorance the colonies of the Macedonians, and the provinces of Carthage and Rome: the heroes of Plutarch and Livy were buried in oblivion; and the history of the world before Mohammed was reduced to a short legend of the patriarchs, the prophets, and the Persian kings. Our education in the Greek and Latin schools may have fixed in our minds a standard of exclusive taste; and I am not forward to condemn the literature and judgment of nations of whose language I am ignorant. Yet I *know* that the classics have much to teach, and I *believe* that the Orientals have much to learn: the temperate dignity of style, the graceful proportions of art, the forms of visible and intellectual beauty, the just delineation of character and passion, the rhetoric of narrative and argument, the regular fabric of epic and dramatic poetry.[71] The influence of truth and reason is of a less ambiguous complexion. The philosophers of Athens and Rome enjoyed the blessings, and asserted the rights, of civil and religious freedom. Their moral and political writings might have gradually unlocked the fetters of Eastern despotism, diffused a liberal spirit of inquiry and toleration, and encouraged the Arabian sages to suspect that their caliph was a tyrant, and their prophet an impostor.[72] The instinct of superstition was alarmed by the introduction even of the abstract sciences; and the more rigid doctors of the law condemned the rash and pernicious curiosity of Almamon.[73] To the thirst of martyrdom, the vision of paradise, and the belief of predestination, we must ascribe the invincible enthusiasm of the prince and people. And the sword of the Saracens became less for-

midable when their youth was drawn away from the camp to the college, when the armies of the faithful presumed to read and to reflect Yet the foolish vanity of the Greeks was jealous of their studies, and reluctantly imparted the sacred fire to the barbarians of the East.[74]

In the bloody conflict of the Ommiades and Abbassides the Greeks had stolen the opportunity of avenging their wrongs and enlarging their limits. But a severe retribution was exacted by Mohadi, the third caliph of the new dynasty who seized, in his turn, the favourable opportunity, while a woman and a child, Irene and Constantine, were seated on the Byzantine throne. An army of ninety-five thousand Persians and Arabs was sent from the Tigris to the Thracian Bosphorus, under the command of Harun,[75] or Aaron, the second son of the commander of the faithful. His encampment on the opposite heights of Chrysopolis, or Scutari, informed Irene, in her palace of Constantinople of the loss of her troops and provinces. With the consent or connivance of their sovereign, her ministers subscribed an ignominious peace; and the exchange of some royal gifts could not disguise the annual tribute of seventy thousand dinars of gold, which was imposed on the Roman empire. The Saracens had too rashly advanced into the midst of a distant and hostile land; their retreat was solicited by the promise of faithful guides and plentiful markets; and not a Greek had courage to whisper that their weary forces might be surrounded and destroyed in their necessary passage between a slippery mountain and the river Sangarius. Five years after this expedition, Harun ascended the throne of his father and his elder brother; the most powerful and vigorous monarch of his race, illustrious in the West as the ally of Charlemagne, and familiar to the most childish readers as the perpetual hero of the Arabian tales. His title to the name of *Al Rashid* (the *Just*) is sullied by the extirpation of the generous, perhaps the innocent, Barmecides: yet he could listen to the complaint of a poor widow who had been pillaged by his troops, and who dared, in a passage of the Koran, to threaten the inattentive despot with the judgment of God and posterity. His court was adorned with luxury and science; but, in a reign of three-and-twenty years, Harun repeatedly visited his provinces from Chorasan to Egypt; nine times he performed the pilgrimage of Mecca; eight times he invaded the territories of the Romans; and as often as they declined the payment of the tribute, they were taught to feel that a month of depredation was more costly than a year of submission. But when the unnatural mother of Constantine was deposed and banished, her successor, Nicephorus, resolved to obliterate this badge of servitude and disgrace. The epistle of the emperor to the caliph was pointed with an allusion to the game of chess, which had already spread from Persia to Greece. "The queen (he spoke of Irene) considered you as a rook, and herself as a pawn. That pusillanimous female submitted to pay a tribute, the double of which she ought to have exacted from the barbarians. Restore therefore the fruits of your injustice, or abide the determination of the sword." At these words the ambassadors cast a bundle of swords before the foot of the throne. The caliph smiled at the menace, and, drawing his scimitar, *samsamah*, a weapon of historic or fabulous renown, he cut asunder the feeble arms of the Greeks, without turning the edge or endangering the temper of his blade. He then dictated an epistle of tremendous brevity: "In the name of the most merciful God, Harun al Rashid, commander of the faithful, to Nicephorus, the Roman dog. I have read thy letter, O thou son of an unbelieving mother. Thou shalt not hear, thou shalt behold, my reply." It was written in characters of blood and fire on the plains of Phrygia; and the war-like celerity of the Arabs could only be checked by the arts of deceit and the show of repentance. The triumphant caliph retired, after the fatigues of the campaign, to his favourite palace of Racca on the Euphrates:[76] but the distance of five hundred miles, and the inclemency of the season, encouraged his adversary to violate the peace. Nicephorus was astonished by the bold and rapid march of the commander of the faithful, who repassed, in the depth of winter, the snows of Mount Taurus: his stratagems of policy and war were exhausted; and the perfidious Greek escaped with three wounds from a field of battle overspread with forty thousand of his subjects. Yet the emperor was ashamed of submission, and the caliph was resolved on victory. One hundred and thirty-five thousand regular soldiers received pay, and were inscribed in the military roll; and above three hundred thousand persons of every denomination marched under the black standard of the Abbassides. They swept the surface of Asia Minor far beyond Tyana and Ancyra, and invested the Pontic Heraclea,[77] once a flourishing state, now a paltry town; at that time capable of sustaining, in her antique walls, a month's siege against the forces of the East. The ruin was complete, the spoil was ample; but if Harun

had been conversant with Grecian story, he would have regretted the statue of Hercules, whose attributes, the club, the bow, the quiver, and the lion's hide, were sculptured in massy gold. The progress of desolation by sea and land, from the Euxine to the isle of Cyprus, compelled the emperor Nicephorus to retract his haughty defiance. In the new treaty, the ruins of Heraclea were left for ever as a lesson and a trophy: and the coin of the tribute was marked with the image and superscription of Harun and his three sons.[78] Yet this plurality of lords might contribute to remove the dishonour of the Roman name. After the death of their father, the heirs of the caliph were involved in civil discord, and the conqueror, the liberal Almamon, was sufficiently engaged in the restoration of domestic peace and the introduction of foreign science.

Under the reign of Almamon at Bagdad, of Michael the Stammerer at Constantinople, the islands of Crete[79] and Sicily were subdued by the Arabs. The former of these conquests is disdained by their own writers, who are ignorant of the fame of Jupiter and Minos, but it has not been overlooked by the Byzantine historians, who now begin to cast a clearer light on the affairs of their own times.[80] A band of Andalusian volunteers, discontented with the climate or government of Spain, explored the adventures of the sea; but as they sailed in no more than ten or twenty galleys, their warfare must be branded with the name of piracy. As the subjects and sectaries of the *white* party, they might lawfully invade the dominions of the *black* caliphs. A rebellious faction introduced them into Alexandria;[81] they cut in pieces both friends and foes, pillaged the churches and the moschs, sold above six thousand Christian captives, and maintained their station in the capital of Egypt, till they were oppressed by the forces and the presence of Almamon himself. From the mouth of the Nile to the Hellespont, the islands and sea-coasts both of the Greeks and Moslems were exposed to their depredations; they saw, they envied, they tasted the fertility of Crete, and soon returned with forty galleys to a more serious attack. The Andalusians wandered over the land fearless and unmolested; but when they descended with their plunder to the sea-shore, their vessels were in flames, and their chief, Abu Caab, confessed himself the author of the mischief. Their clamours accused his madness or treachery. "Of what do you complain?" replied the crafty emir. "I have brought you to a land flowing with milk and honey. Here is your true country; repose from your toils, and forget the barren place of your nativity." "And our wives and children?" "Your beauteous captives will supply the place of your wives, and in their embraces you will soon become the fathers of a new progeny." The first habitation was their camp, with a ditch and rampart in the bay of Suda; but an apostate monk led them to a more desirable position in the eastern parts; and the name of Candax, their fortress and colony, has been extended to the whole island, under the corrupt and modern appellation of *Candia*. The hundred cities of the age of Minos were diminished to thirty; and of these, only one, most probably Cydonia, had courage to retain the substance of freedom and the profession of Christianity. The Saracens of Crete soon repaired the loss of their navy; and the timbers of Mount Ida were launched into the main. During a hostile period, of one hundred and thirty-eight years, the princes of Constantinople attacked these licentious corsairs with fruitless curses and ineffectual arms.

The loss of Sicily[82] was occasioned by an act of superstitious rigour. An amorous youth, who had stolen a nun from her cloister, was sentenced by the emperor to the amputation of his tongue. Euphemius appealed to the reason and policy of the Saracens of Africa; and soon returned with the Imperial purple, a fleet of one hundred ships, and an army of seven hundred horse and ten thousand foot. They landed at Mazara, near the ruins of the ancient Selinus; but after some partial victories, Syracuse[83] was delivered by the Greeks, the apostate was slain before her walls, and his African friends were reduced to the necessity of feeding on the flesh of their own horses. In their turn they were relieved by a powerful reinforcement of their brethren of Andalusia; the largest and western part of the island was gradually reduced, and the commodious harbour of Palermo was chosen for the seat of the naval and military power of the Saracens. Syracuse preserved about fifty years the faith which she had sworn to Christ and to Cæsar. In the last and fatal siege her citizens displayed some remnant of the spirit which had formerly resisted the powers of Athens and Carthage. They stood above twenty days against the battering-rams and *catapultæ*, the mines and tortoises of the besiegers; and the place might have been relieved, if the mariners of the Imperial fleet had not been detained at Constantinople in building a church to the Virgin Mary. The deacon Theodosius, with the bishop and clergy, was dragged in chains from the altar to Palermo, cast into a subterraneous dungeon, and exposed to the hourly peril of death or apostasy. His pathetic, and not inelegant complaint, may be read as the epitaph of his country.[84] From the Roman conquest to this final calamity, Syracuse, now dwindled to the primitive isle of Ortygea, had insensibly declined. Yet the relics were still precious; the plate of the cathedral weighed five thousand pounds of silver; the entire spoil was computed at one million of pieces of gold (about four hundred thousand pounds sterling), and the captives must outnumber the seventeen thousand Christians who were transported from the sack of Tauromenium into African servitude. In Sicily the religion and language of the Greeks were eradicated; and such was the docility of the rising generation, that fifteen thousand boys were circumcised and clothed on the same day with the son of the Fatimite caliph. The Arabian squadrons issued from the harbours of Palermo, Biserta, and Tunis; a hundred and fifty towns of Calabria and Campania were attacked and pillaged, nor could the suburbs of Rome be defended by the name of the Cæsars and apostles. Had the Mohammedans been united, Italy must have fallen an easy and glorious accession to the empire of the prophet. But the caliphs of Bagdad had lost their authority in the West; the Aglabites and Fatimites usurped the provinces of Africa, their emirs of Sicily aspired to independence; and the design of conquest and dominion was degraded to a repetition of predatory inroads.[85]

In the sufferings of prostrate Italy the name of Rome awakens a solemn and mournful recollection. A fleet of Saracens from the African coast presumed to enter the mouth of the Tiber, and to approach a city which even yet, in her fallen state, was revered as the metropolis of the Christian world. The gates and ramparts were guarded by a trembling people; but the tombs and temples of St. Peter and St. Paul were left exposed in the suburbs of the Vatican and of the Ostian way. Their invisible sanctity had protected them against the Goths, the Vandals, and the Lombards; but the Arabs disdained both the Gospel and the legend; and their rapacious spirit was approved and animated by the precepts of the Koran. The Christian *idols* were stripped of their costly offerings; a silver altar was torn away from the shrine of St. Peter; and if the bodies or the buildings were left entire, their deliverance must be imputed to the haste rather than the scruples of the Saracens. In their course along the Appian way, they pillaged

Fundi and besieged Gaëta; but they had turned aside from the walls of Rome, and, by their divisions, the Capitol was saved from the yoke of the prophet of Mecca. The same danger still impended on the heads of the Roman people; and their domestic force was unequal to the assault of an African emir. They claimed the protection of their Latin sovereign; but the Carlovingian standard was overthrown by a detachment of the barbarians: they meditated the restoration of the Greek emperors; but the attempt was treasonable, and the succour remote and precarious.[86] Their distress appeared to receive some aggravation from the death of their spiritual and temporal chief; but the pressing emergency superseded the forms and intrigues of an election; and the unanimous choice of Pope Leo the Fourth[87] was the safety of the church and city. This pontiff was born a Roman; the courage of the first ages of the republic glowed in his breast; and, amidst the ruins of his country, he stood erect, like one of the firm and lofty columns that rear their heads above the fragments of the Roman forum. The first days of his reign were consecrated to the purification and removal of relics, to prayers and processions, and to all the solemn offices of religion, which served at least to heal the imagination and restore the hopes of the multitude. The public defence had been long neglected, not from the presumption of peace, but from the distress and poverty of the times. As far as the scantiness of his means and the shortness of his leisure would allow, the ancient walls were repaired by the command of Leo; fifteen towers, in the most accessible stations, were built or renewed; two of these commanded on either side the Tiber; and an iron chain was drawn across the stream to impede the ascent of a hostile navy. The Romans were assured of a short respite by the welcome news that the siege of Gaëta had been raised, and that a part of the enemy with their sacrilegious plunder had perished in the waves.

But the storm which had been delayed soon burst upon them with redoubled violence. The Aglabite,[88] who reigned in Africa, had inherited from his father a treasure and an army: a fleet of Arabs and Moors, after a short refreshment in the harbours of Sardinia, cast anchor before the mouth of the Tiber, sixteen miles from the city; and their discipline and numbers appeared to threaten, not a transient inroad, but a serious design of conquest and dominion. But the vigilance of Leo had formed an alliance with the vassals of the Greek empire, the free and maritime states of Gaëta, Naples, and Amalfi; and, in the hour of danger, their galleys appeared in the port of Ostia under the command of Cæsarius, the son of the Neapolitan duke, a noble and valiant youth, who had already vanquished the fleets of the Saracens. With his principal companions, Cæsarius was invited to the Lateran palace, and the dexterous pontiff affected to inquire their errand, and to accept with joy and surprise their providential succour. The city bands, in arms, attended their father to Ostia, where he reviewed and blessed his generous deliverers. They kissed his feet, received the communion with martial devotion, and listened to the prayer of Leo, that the same God who had supported St. Peter and St. Paul on the waves of the sea would strengthen the hands of his champions against the adversaries of his holy name. After a similar prayer, and with equal resolution, the Moslems advanced to the attack of the Christian galleys, which preserved their advantageous station along the coast. The victory inclined to the side of the allies, when it was less gloriously decided in their favour by a sudden tempest, which confounded the skill and courage of the stoutest mariners. The Christians were sheltered in a friendly harbour, while the Africans were scattered and dashed in pieces among the rocks and islands of a hostile shore. Those who escaped from shipwreck and hunger neither found nor deserved mercy at the hands of their implacable pursuers. The sword and the gibbet reduced the dangerous multitude of captives; and the remainder was more usefully employed to restore the sacred edifices which they had attempted to subvert. The pontiff, at the head of the citizens and allies, paid his grateful devotion at the shrines of the apostles; and, among the spoils of this naval victory, thirteen Arabian bows of pure and massy silver were suspended round the altar of the fisherman of Galilee. The reign of Leo the Fourth was employed in the defence and ornament of the Roman state. The churches were renewed and embellished: near four thousand pounds of silver were consecrated to repair the losses of St. Peter; and his sanctuary was decorated with a plate of gold of the weight of two hundred and sixteen pounds, embossed with the portraits of the pope and emperor, and encircled with a string of pearls. Yet this vain magnificence reflects less glory on the character of Leo than the paternal care with which he rebuilt the walls of Horta and Ameria; and transported the wandering inhabitants of Centumcellæ to his new foundation of Leopolis, twelve miles from the sea-shore.[89] By his liberality a colony of Corsicans, with their wives and children, was planted in the station of Porto at the mouth of the Tiber: the falling city was restored for their use, the fields and vineyards were divided among the new settlers: their first efforts were assisted by a gift of horses and cattle; and the hardy exiles, who breathed revenge against the Saracens, swore to live and die under the standard of St. Peter. The nations of the West and North who visited the threshold of the apostles had gradually formed the large and populous suburb of the Vatican, and their various habitations were distinguished, in the language of the times, as the *schools* of the Greeks and Goths, of the Lombards and Saxons. But this venerable spot was still open to sacrilegious insult: the design of enclosing it with walls and towers exhausted all that authority could command, or charity would supply: and the pious labour of four years was animated in every season and at every hour by the presence of the indefatigable pontiff. The love of fame, a generous but worldly passion, may be detected in the name of the *Leonine city*, which he bestowed on the Vatican; yet the pride of the dedication was tempered with Christian penance and humility. The boundary was trod by the bishop and his clergy, barefoot, in sackcloth and ashes; the songs of triumph were modulated to psalms and litanies; the walls were besprinkled with holy water; and the ceremony was concluded with a prayer, that, under the guardian care of the apostles and the angelic host, both the old and the new Rome might ever be preserved pure, prosperous, and impregnable.[90]

The emperor Theophilus, son of Michael the Stammerer, was one of the most active and high-spirited princes who reigned at Constantinople during the middle age. In offensive or defensive war he marched in person five times against the Saracens, formidable in his attack, esteemed by the enemy in his losses and defeats. In the last of these expeditions he penetrated into Syria, and besieged the obscure town of Sozopetra; the casual birthplace of the caliph Motassem, whose father Harun was attended in peace or war by the most favoured of his wives and concubines. The revolt of a Persian impostor employed at that moment the arms of the Saracen, and he could only intercede in favour of a place for which he felt and acknowledged some degree of filial affection. These solicitations determined the emperor to wound his pride in so sensible a part. Sozopetra was levelled with the ground, the Syrian prisoners were marked or mutilated with ignominious cruelty, and a thousand female captives were forced away from the adjacent territory. Among these a matron of the house of Abbas invoked, in an agony of despair, the name of Motassem; and the insults of the Greeks engaged the honour of her kinsman to avenge his indignity, and to answer her appeal. Under the reign of the two elder brothers, the inheritance of the youngest had been confined to Anatolia, Armenia, Georgia, and Circassia; this frontier station had exercised his military talents; and among his accidental claims to the name of *Octonary*,[91] the most meritorious are the *eight* battles which he gained or fought against the enemies of the Koran. In this personal quarrel, the troops of Irak, Syria, and Egypt were recruited from the tribes of Arabia and the Turkish hordes: his cavalry might be numerous, though we should deduct some myriads from the hundred and thirty thousand horses of the royal stables; and the expense of the armament was computed at four millions sterling, or one hundred thousand pounds of gold. From Tarsus, the place of assembly, the Saracens advanced in three divisions along the high road of Constantinople: Motassem himself commanded the centre, and the vanguard was given to his son Abbas, who, in the trial of the first adventures, might succeed with the more glory, or fail with the least reproach. In the revenge of his injury the caliph prepared to retaliate a similar affront. The father of Theophilus was a native of Amorium[92] in Phrygia: the original seat of the Imperial house had been adorned with privileges and monuments; and, whatever might be the indifference of the people, Constantinople itself was scarcely of more value in the eyes of the sovereign and his court. The name of AMORIUM was inscribed on the shields of the Saracens; and their three armies were again united under the walls of the devoted city. It had been proposed by the wisest counsellors to evacuate Amorium, to remove the inhabitants, and to abandon the empty structures to the vain resentment of the barbarians. The emperor embraced the more generous resolution of defending, in a siege and battle, the country of his ancestors. When the armies drew near, the front of the Mohammedan line appeared to a Roman eye more closely planted with spears and javelins; but the event of the action was not glorious on either side to the national troops. The Arabs were broken, but it was by the swords of thirty thousand Persians, who had obtained service and settlement in the Byzantine empire. The Greeks were repulsed and vanquished, but it vas by the arrows of the Turkish cavalry; and ıad not their bowstrings been damped and re-axed by the evening rain, very few of the Chris-ians could have escaped with the emperor from he field of battle. They breathed at Dorylæum, ıt the distance of three days; and Theophilus, eviewing his trembling squadrons, forgave the ommon flight both of the prince and people. ıfter this discovery of his weakness, he vainly ıoped to deprecate the fate of Amorium: the ınexorable caliph rejected with contempt his ırayers and promises, and detained the Roman ımbassadors to be the witnesses of his great re-venge. They had nearly been the witnesses of ıis shame. The vigorous assaults of fifty-five ıays were encountered by a faithful governor, ı veteran garrison, and a desperate people; and he Saracens must have raised the siege, if a ıomestic traitor had not pointed to the weakest ıart of the wall, a place which was decorated vith the statues of a lion and a bull. The vow ıf Motassem was accomplished with unrelent-ng rigour: tired, rather than satiated, with de-struction, he returned to his new palace of Sa-nara, in the neighbourhood of Bagdad, while he *unfortunate*[93] Theophilus implored the tardy ınd doubtful aid of his Western rival the em-peror of the Franks. Yet in the siege of Amorium ıbout seventy thousand Moslems had perished; heir loss had been revenged by the slaughter of hirty thousand Christians, and the sufferings ıf an equal number of captives, who were treat-ed as the most atrocious criminals. Mutual ıecessity could sometimes extort the exchange ır ransom of prisoners;[94] but in the national and eligious conflict of the two empires, peace was vithout confidence, and war without mercy. Quarter was seldom given in the field; those vho escaped the edge of the sword were con-lemned to hopeless servitude or exquisite tor-ture; and a Catholic emperor relates, with vis-ıble satisfaction, the execution of the Saracens ıf Crete, who were flayed alive, or plunged into caldrons of boiling oil.[95] To a point of honour Motassem had sacrificed a flourishing city, two hundred thousand lives, and the property of nillions. The same caliph descended from his horse, and dirtied his robe, to relieve the dis-tress of a decrepit old man, who, with his laden ıss, had tumbled into a ditch. On which of these actions did he reflect with the most pleasure when he was summoned by the angel of death?[96]

With Motassem, the eighth of the Abbassides, the glory of his family and nation expired. When the Arabian conquerors had spread them-selves over the East, and were mingled with the servile crowds of Persia, Syria, and Egypt, they insensibly lost the freeborn and martial virtues of the desert. The courage of the South is the artificial fruit of discipline and prejudice; the active power of enthusiasm had decayed, and the mercenary forces of the caliphs were re-cruited in those climates of the North, of which valour is the hardy and spontaneous produc-tion. Of the Turks[97] who dwelt beyond the Oxus and Jaxartes, the robust youths, either taken in war, or purchased in trade, were educated in the exercises of the field and the profession of the Mohammedan faith. The Turkish guards stood in arms round the throne of their bene-factor, and their chiefs usurped the dominion of the palace and the provinces. Motassem, the first author of this dangerous example, intro-duced into the capital above fifty thousand Turks: their licentious conduct provoked the public indignation, and the quarrels of the sol-diers and people induced the caliph to retire from Bagdad, and establish his own residence and the camp of his barbarian favourites at Sa-mara on the Tigris, about twelve leagues above the City of Peace.[98] His son Motawakkel was a jealous and cruel tyrant: odious to his subjects, he cast himself on the fidelity of the strangers, and these strangers, ambitious and apprehen-sive, were tempted by the rich promise of a revo-lution. At the instigation, or at least in the cause of his son, they burst into his apartment at the hour of supper, and the caliph was cut into seven pieces by the same swords which he had recently distributed among the guards of his life and throne. To this throne, yet streaming with a father's blood, Montasser was trium-phantly led; but in a reign of six months he found only the pangs of a guilty conscience. If he wept at the sight of an old tapestry which represented the crime and punishment of the son of Chosroes; if his days were abridged by grief and remorse, we may allow some pity to a parricide, who exclaimed, in the bitterness of death, that he had lost both this world and the world to come. After this act of treason, the en-signs of royalty, the garment and walking staff of Mohammed, were given and torn away by the foreign mercenaries, who in four years cre-ated, deposed, and murdered three commanders of the faithful. As often as the Turks were in-flamed by fear, or rage, or avarice, these ca-liphs were dragged by the feet, exposed naked to the scorching sun, beaten with iron clubs, and compelled to purchase, by the abdication of their dignity, a short reprieve of inevitable fate.[99] At length, however, the fury of the tempest was spent or diverted: the Abbassides returned to the less turbulent residence of Bagdad; the insolence of the Turks was curbed with a firmer and more skilful hand, and their numbers were divided and destroyed in foreign warfare. But the nations of the East had been taught to trample on the successors of the prophet; and the blessings of domestic peace were obtained by the relaxation of strength and discipline. So uniform are the mischiefs of military despotism, that I seem to repeat the story of the Prætorians of Rome.[100]

While the flame of enthusiasm was damped by the business, the pleasure, and the knowledge of the age, it burnt with concentrated heat in the breasts of the chosen few, the congenial spirits, who were ambitious of reigning either in this world or in the next. How carefully soever the book of prophecy had been sealed by the apostle of Mecca, the wishes, and (if we may profane the word) even the reason of fanaticism, might believe that, after the successive missions of Adam, Noah, Abraham, Moses, Jesus, and Mohammed, the same God, in the fulness of time, would reveal a still more perfect and permanent law. In the two hundred and seventy-seventh year of the Hegira, and in the neighbourhood of Cufa, an Arabian preacher of the name of Carmath assumed the lofty and incomprehensible style of the Guide, the Director, the Demonstration, the Word, the Holy Ghost, the Camel, the Herald of the Messiah, who had conversed with him in a human shape, and the representative of Mohammed the son of Ali, of St. John the Baptist, and of the angel Gabriel. In his mystic volume the precepts of the Koran were refined to a more spiritual sense; he relaxed the duties of ablution, fasting, and pilgrimage; allowed the indiscriminate use of wine and forbidden food; and nourished the fervour of his disciples by the daily repetition of fifty prayers. The idleness and ferment of the rustic crowd awakened the attention of the magistrates of Cufa; a timid persecution assisted the progress of the new sect; and the name of the prophet became more revered after his person had been withdrawn from the world. His twelve apostles dispersed themselves among the Bedoweens, "a race of men," says Abulfeda, "equally devoid of reason and of religion;" and the success of their preaching seemed to threaten Arabia with a new revolution. The Carmathians were ripe for rebellion, since they disclaimed the title of the house of Abbas, and abhorred the worldly pomp of the caliphs of Bagdad. They were susceptible of discipline, since they vowed a blind and absolute submission to their Imam, who was called to the prophetic office by the voice of God and the people. Instead of the legal tithes he claimed the fifth of their substance and spoil; the most flagitious sins were no more than the type of disobedience; and the brethren were united and concealed by an oath of secrecy.

After a bloody conflict they prevailed in the province of Bahrein, along the Persian Gulf far and wide the tribes of the desert were subject to the sceptre, or rather to the sword, of Abu Said and his son Abu Taher; and these rebellious imams could muster in the field a hundred and seven thousand fanatics. The mercenaries of the caliph were dismayed at the approach of an enemy who neither asked nor accepted quarter; and the difference between them in fortitude and patience is expressive of the change which three centuries of prosperity had effected in the character of the Arabians Such troops were discomfited in every action the cities of Racca and Baalbec, of Cufa and Bassora, were taken and pillaged; Bagdad was filled with consternation; and the caliph trembled behind the veils of his palace. In a daring inroad beyond the Tigris, Abu Taher advanced to the gates of the capital with no more than five hundred horse. By the special order of Moctader the bridges had been broken down and the person or head of the rebel was expected every hour by the commander of the faithful His lieutenant, from a motive of fear or pity apprised Abu Taher of his danger, and recommended a speedy escape. "Your master," said the intrepid Carmathian to the messenger, "is at the head of thirty thousand soldiers: three such men as these are wanting in his host:" at the same instant, turning to three of his companions, he commanded the first to plunge a dagger into his breast, the second to leap into the Tigris, and the third to cast himself headlong down a precipice. They obeyed without a murmur. "Relate," continued the imam, "what you have seen: before the evening your general shall be chained among my dogs." Before the evening the camp was surprised, and the menace was executed. The rapine of the Carmathians was sanctified by their aversion to the worship of Mecca: they robbed a caravan of pilgrims, and twenty thousand devout Moslems were abandoned on the burning sands to a death of hunger and thirst. Another year they suffered the pilgrims to proceed without interruption; but, in the festival of devotion, Abu Taher stormed the holy city, and trampled on the most venerable relics of the Mohammedan faith. Thirty thousand citizens and strangers were put to the sword; the sacred precincts were polluted by the burial of three thousand dead bodies; the well of Zemzem overflowed with blood; the golden spout was forced from its place; the veil of the Caaba was divided among these impious sectaries; and the black stone, the first monument of the nation, was borne away in triumph to their capital. After this deed of sacrilege and cruelty they continued to infest the confines of Irak, Syria, and Egypt: but the vital principle of enthusiasm had withered at the root. Their scruples of their avarice again opened the pilgrimage of Mecca, and restored the black stone of the Caaba; and it is needless to inquire into what factions they were broken, or by whose swords they were finally extirpated. The sect of the Carmathians may be considered as the second visible cause of the decline and fall of the empire of the caliphs.[101]

The third and most obvious cause was the weight and magnitude of the empire itself. The caliph Almamon might proudly assert that it was easier for him to rule the East and the West than to manage a chess-board of two feet square:[102] yet I suspect that in both those games he was guilty of many fatal mistakes; and I perceive that in the distant provinces the authority of the first and most powerful of the Abbassides was already impaired. The analogy of despotism invests the representative with the full majesty of the prince; the division and balance of powers might relax the habits of obedience, might encourage the passive subject to inquire into the origin and administration of civil government. He who is born in the purple is seldom worthy to reign; but the elevation of a private man, of a peasant perhaps, or a slave, affords a strong presumption of his courage and capacity. The viceroy of a remote kingdom aspires to secure the property and inheritance of his precarious trust; the nations must rejoice in the presence of their sovereign; and the command of armies and treasures are at once the object and the instrument of his ambition. A change was scarcely visible as long as the lieutenants of the caliph were content with their vicarious title; while they solicited for themselves or their sons a renewal of the Imperial grant, and still maintained on the coin and in the public prayers the name and prerogative of the commander of the faithful. But in the long and hereditary exercise of power they assumed the pride and attributes of royalty; the alternative of peace or war, of reward or punishment, depended solely on their will; and the

revenues of their government were reserved for local services or private magnificence. Instead of a regular supply of men and money, the successors of the prophet were flattered with the ostentatious gift of an elephant, or a cast of hawks, a suit of silk hangings, or some pounds of musk and amber.[103]

After the revolt of Spain from the temporal and spiritual supremacy of the Abbassides, the first symptoms of disobedience broke forth in the province of Africa. Ibrahim, the son of Aglab, the lieutenant of the vigilant and rigid Harun, bequeathed to the dynasty of the *Aglabites* the inheritance of his name and power. The indolence or policy of the caliphs dissembled the injury and loss, and pursued only with poison the founder of the *Edrisites*,[104] who erected the kingdom and city of Fez on the shores of the Western ocean.[105] In the East the first dynasty was that of the *Taherites*[106]—the posterity of the valiant Taher, who, in the civil wars of the sons of Harun, had served with too much zeal and success the cause of Almamon, the younger brother. He was sent into honourable exile, to command on the banks of the Oxus; and the independence of his successors, who reigned in Chorasan till the fourth generation, was palliated by their modest and respectful demeanour, the happiness of their subjects, and the security of their frontier. They were supplanted by one of those adventurers so frequent in the annals of the East, who left his trade of a brazier (from whence the name of *Soffarides*) for the profession of a robber. In a nocturnal visit to the treasure of the prince of Sistan, Jacob, the son of Leith, stumbled over a lump of salt, which he unwarily tasted with his tongue. Salt, among the Orientals, is the symbol of hospitality, and the pious robber immediately retired without spoil or damage. The discovery of this honourable behaviour recommended Jacob to pardon and trust; he led an army at first for his benefactor, at last for himself, subdued Persia, and threatened the residence of the Abbassides. On his march towards Bagdad the conqueror was arrested by a fever. He gave audience in bed to the ambassador of the caliph; and beside him on a table were exposed a naked scimitar, a crust of brown bread, and a bunch of onions. "If I die," said he, "your master is delivered from his fears. If I live, *this* must determine between us. If I am vanquished, I can return without reluctance to the homely fare of my youth." From the height where he stood, the descent would not have been so soft or harmless: a timely death secured his own repose and that of the caliph, who paid with the most lavish concessions the retreat of his brother Amrou to the palaces of Shiraz and Ispahan. The Abbassides were too feeble to contend, too proud to forgive: they invited the powerful dynasty of the *Samanides*, who passed the Oxus with ten thousand horse, so poor that their stirrups were of wood; so brave, that they vanquished the Soffarian army, eight times more numerous than their own. The captive Amrou was sent in chains, a grateful offering, to the court of Bagdad; and as the victor was content with the inheritance of Transoxiana and Chorasan, the realms of Persia returned for a while to the allegiance of the caliphs. The provinces of Syria and Egypt were twice dismembered by their Turkish slaves of the race of *Toulun* and *Ikshid*.[107] These barbarians, in religion and manners the countrymen of Mohammed, emerged from the bloody factions of the palace to a provincial command and an independent throne: their names became famous and formidable in their time; but the founders of these two potent dynasties confessed, either in words or actions, the vanity of ambition. The first on his deathbed implored the mercy of God to a sinner, ignorant of the limits of his own power: the second, in the midst of four hundred thousand soldiers and eight thousand slaves, concealed from every human eye the chamber where he attempted to sleep. Their sons were educated in the vices of kings; and both Egypt and Syria were recovered and possessed by the Abbassides during an interval of thirty years. In the decline of their empire, Mesopotamia, with the important cities of Mosul and Aleppo, was occupied by the Arabian princes of the tribe of *Hamadan*. The poets of their court could repeat, without a blush, that nature had formed their countenances for beauty, their tongues for eloquence, and their hands for liberality and valour: but the genuine tale of the elevation and reign of the *Hamadanites* exhibits a scene of treachery, murder, and parricide. At the same fatal period the Persian kingdom was again usurped by the dynasty of the *Bowides*, by the sword of three brothers, who, under various names, were styled the support and columns of the state, and who, from the Caspian sea to the ocean, would suffer no tyrants but themselves. Under their reign the language and genius of Persia revived, and the Arabs, three hundred and four years after the death of Mohammed, were deprived of the sceptre of the East.

Rahdi, the twentieth of the Abbassides, and the thirty-ninth of the successors of Moham-med, was the last who deserved the title of commander of the faithful;[108] the last (says Abulfeda) who spoke to the people or conversed with the learned; the last who, in the expense of his household, represented the wealth and magnificence of the ancient caliphs. After him, the lords of the Eastern world were reduced to the most abject misery, and exposed to the blows and insults of a servile condition. The revolt of the provinces circumscribed their dominions within the walls of Bagdad: but that capital still contained an innumerable multitude, vain of their past fortune, discontented with their present state, and oppressed by the demands of a treasury which had formerly been replenished by the spoil and tribute of nations. Their idleness was exercised by faction and controversy. Under the mask of piety, the rigid followers of Hanbal[109] invaded the pleasures of domestic life, burst into the houses of plebeians and princes, spilt the wine, broke the instruments, beat the musicians, and dishonoured, with infamous suspicions, the associates of every handsome youth. In each profession which allowed room for two persons, the one was a votary, the other an antagonist, of Ali; and the Abbassides were awakened by the clamorous grief of the sectaries, who denied their title, and cursed their progenitors. A turbulent people could only be repressed by a military force; but who could satisfy the avarice or assert the discipline of the mercenaries themselves? The African and the Turkish guards drew their swords against each other, and the chief commanders, the emirs al Omra,[110] imprisoned or deposed their sovereigns, and violated the sanctuary of the mosch and harem. If the caliphs escaped to the camp or court of any neighbouring prince, their deliverance was a change of servitude, till they were prompted by despair to invite the Bowides, the sultans of Persia, who silenced the factions of Bagdad by their irresistible arms. The civil and military powers were assumed by Moezaldowlat, the second of the three brothers, and a stipend of sixty thousand pounds sterling was assigned by his generosity for the private expense of the commander of the faithful. But on the fortieth day, at the audience of the ambassadors of Chorasan, and in the presence of a trembling multitude, the caliph was dragged from his throne to a dungeon, by the command of the stranger, and the rude hands of his Dilemites. His palace was pillaged, his eyes were put out, and the mean ambition of the Abbassides aspired to the vacant station of danger and disgrace. In the school of adversity the luxurious caliphs resumed the grave and abstemious virtues of the primitive times. Despoiled of their armour and silken robes, they fasted, they prayed, they studied the Koran and the tradition of the Sonnites: they performed, with zeal and knowledge, the functions of their ecclesiastical character. The respect of nations still waited on the successors of the apostle, the oracles of the law and conscience of the faithful; and the weakness or division of their tyrants sometimes restored the Abbassides to the sovereignty of Bagdad. But their misfortunes had been embittered by the triumph of the Fatimites, the real or spurious progeny of Ali. Arising from the extremity of Africa, these successful rivals extinguished, in Egypt and Syria, both the spiritual and temporal authority of the Abbassides; and the monarch of the Nile insulted the humble pontiff on the banks of the Tigris.

In the declining age of the caliphs, in the century which elapsed after the war of Theophilus and Motassem, the hostile transactions of the two nations were confined to some inroads by sea and land, the fruits of their close vicinity and indelible hatred. But when the Eastern world was convulsed and broken, the Greeks were roused from their lethargy by the hopes of conquest and revenge. The Byzantine empire, since the accession of the Basilian race, had reposed in peace and dignity; and they might encounter with their entire strength the front of some petty emir, whose rear was assaulted and threatened by his national foes of the Mohammedan faith. The lofty titles of the morning-star, and the death of the Saracens,[111] were applied in the public acclamations to Nicephorus Phocas, a prince as renowned in the camp as he was unpopular in the city. In the subordinate station of great domestic, or general of the East, he reduced the island of Crete, and extirpated the nest of pirates who had so long defied, with impunity, the majesty of the empire.[112] His military genius was displayed in the conduct and success of the enterprise, which had so often failed with loss and dishonour. The Saracens were confounded by the landing of his troops on safe and level bridges, which he cast from the vessels to the shore. Seven months were consumed in the siege of Candia; the despair of the native Cretans was stimulated by the frequent aid of their brethren of Africa and Spain; and, after the massy wall and double ditch had been stormed by the Greeks, a hopeless conflict was still maintained in the streets and houses of the city. The whole island was subdued in the capital, and a submissive people accepted, without resistance, the baptism of the conqueror.[113] Constantinople applauded the long-forgotten pomp of a triumph; but the Imperial diadem was the sole reward that could repay the service, or satisfy the ambition, of Nicephorus.

After the death of the younger Romanus, the fourth in lineal descent of the Basilian race, his widow Theophania successively married Nicephorus Phocas and his assassin John Zimisces, the two heroes of the age. They reigned as the guardians and colleagues of her infant sons; and the twelve years of their military command form the most splendid period of the Byzantine annals. The subjects and confederates whom they led to war appeared, at least in the eyes of an enemy, two hundred thousand strong; and of these about thirty thousand were armed with cuirasses:[114] a train of four thousand mules attended their march; and their evening camp was regularly fortified with an enclosure of iron spikes. A series of bloody and undecisive combats is nothing more than an anticipation of what would have been effected in a few years by the course of nature: but I shall briefly prosecute the conquests of the two emperors from the hills of Cappadocia to the desert of Bagdad. The sieges of Mopsuestia and Tarsus, in Cilicia, first exercised the skill and perseverance of their troops, on whom, at this moment, I shall not hesitate to bestow the name of Romans. In the double city of Mopsuestia, which is divided by the river Sarus, two hundred thousand Moslems were predestined to death or slavery,[115] a surprising degree of population, which must at least include the inhabitants of the dependent districts. They were surrounded and taken by assault; but Tarsus was reduced by the slow progress of famine; and no sooner had the Saracens yielded on honourable terms than they were mortified by the distant and unprofitable view of the naval succours of Egypt. They were dismissed with a safe-conduct to the confines of Syria: a part of the old Christians had quietly lived under their dominion; and the vacant habitations were replenished by a new colony. But the mosch was converted into a stable; the pulpit was delivered to the flames; many rich crosses of gold and gems, the spoil of Asiatic churches, were made a grateful offering to the piety or avarice of the emperor; and he transported the gates of Mopsuestia and Tarsus, which were fixed in the wall of Constantinople, an eternal monument of his victory. After they had forced and secured the narrow passes of Mount Amanus, the two Roman princes repeatedly carried their arms into the heart of Syria. Yet, instead of assaulting the walls of Antioch, the humanity or superstition of Nicephorus appeared to respect the ancient metropolis of the East: he contented himself with drawing round the city a line of circumvallation; left a stationary army; and instructed his lieutenant to expect, without impatience, the return of spring. But in the depth of winter, in a dark and rainy night, an adventurous subaltern, with three hundred soldiers, approached the rampart, applied his scaling-ladders, occupied two adjacent towers, stood firm against the pressure of multitudes, and bravely maintained his post till he was relieved by the tardy, though effectual, support of his reluctant chief. The first tumult of slaughter and rapine subsided; the rein of Cæsar and of Christ was restored; and the efforts of a hundred thousand Saracens, of the armies of Syria and the fleets of Africa, were consumed without effect before the walls of Antioch. The royal city of Aleppo was subject to Seifeddowlat, of the dynasty of Hamadan, who clouded his past glory by the precipitate retreat which abandoned his kingdom and capital to the Roman invaders. In his stately palace, that stood without the walls of Aleppo, they joyfully seized a well-furnished magazine of arms, a stable of fourteen hundred mules, and three hundred bags of silver and gold. But the walls of the city withstood the strokes of their battering-rams; and the besiegers pitched their tents on the neighbouring mountain of Jaushan. Their retreat exasperated the quarrel of the townsmen and mercenaries; the guard of the gates and ramparts was deserted; and, while they furiously charged each other in the market-place, they were surprised and destroyed by the sword of a common enemy. The male sex was exterminated by the sword; ten thousand youths were led into captivity; the weight of the precious spoil exceeded the strength and number of the beasts of burthen; the superfluous remainder was burnt; and, after a licentious possession of ten days, the Romans marched away from the naked and bleeding city. In their Syrian inroads they commanded the husbandmen to cultivate their lands, that they themselves, in the ensuing season, might reap the benefit: more than a hundred cities were reduced to obedience; and eighteen pulpits of the principal moschs were committed to the flames to expiate the sacrilege of the disciples of Mohammed. The classic names of Hierapolis, Apamea, and Emesa re-

vive for a moment in the list of conquest: the emperor Zimisces encamped in the paradise of Damascus, and accepted the ransom of a submissive people; and the torrent was only stopped by the impregnable fortress of Tripoli, on the sea-coast of Phœnicia. Since the days of Heraclius, the Euphrates, below the passage of Mount Taurus, had been impervious, and almost invisible, to the Greeks. The river yielded a free passage to the victorious Zimisces: and the historian may imitate the speed with which he overran the once famous cities of Samosata, Edessa, Martyropolis, Amida,[116] and Nisibis, the ancient limit of the empire in the neighbourhood of the Tigris. His ardour was quickened by the desire of grasping the virgin treasures of Ecbatana,[117] a well-known name, under which the Byzantine writer has concealed the capital of the Abbassides. The consternation of the fugitives had already diffused the terror of his name; but the fancied riches of Bagdad had already been dissipated by the avarice and prodigality of domestic tyrants. The prayers of the people, and the stern demands of the lieutenant of the Bowides, required the caliph to provide for the defence of the city. The helpless Mothi replied, that his arms, his revenues, and his provinces had been torn from his hands, and that he was ready to abdicate a dignity which he was unable to support. The emir was inexorable; the furniture of the palace was sold; and the paltry price of forty thousand pieces of gold was instantly consumed in private luxury. But the apprehensions of Bagdad were relieved by the retreat of the Greeks: thirst and hunger guarded the desert of Mesopotamia; and the emperor, satiated with glory, and laden with Oriental spoils, returned to Constantinople, and displayed, in his triumph, the silk, the aromatics, and three hundred myriads of gold and silver. Yet the powers of the East had been bent, not broken, by this transient hurricane. After the departure of the Greeks, the fugitive princes returned to their capitals; the subjects disclaimed their involuntary oaths of allegiance; the Moslems again purified their temples, and overturned the idols of the saints and martyrs; the Nestorians and Jacobites preferred a Saracen to an orthodox master; and the numbers and spirit of the Melchites were inadequate to the support of the church and state. Of these extensive conquests, Antioch, with the cities of Cilicia and the isle of Cyprus, was alone restored, a permanent and useful accession to the Roman empire.[118]

CHAPTER LIII

State of the Eastern Empire in the Tenth Century. Extent and Division. Wealth and Revenue. Palace of Constantinople. Titles and Offices. Pride and Power of the Emperors. Tactics of the Greeks, Arabs, and Franks. Loss of the Latin Tongue. Studies and Solitude of the Greeks.

A RAY of historic light seems to beam from the darkness of the tenth century. We open with curiosity and respect the royal volumes of Constantine Porphyrogenitus,[1] which he composed at a mature age for the instruction of his son, and which promise to unfold the state of the Eastern empire, both in peace and war, both at home and abroad. In the first of these works he minutely describes the pompous ceremonies of the church and palace of Constantinople, according to his own practice and that of his predecessors.[2] In the second he attempts an accurate survey of the provinces, the *themes*, as they were then denominated, both of Europe and Asia.[3] The system of Roman tactics, the discipline and order of the troops, and the military operations by land and sea, are explained in the third of these didactic collections, which may be ascribed to Constantine or his father Leo.[4] In the fourth, of the administration of the empire, he reveals the secrets of the Byzantine policy, in friendly or hostile intercourse with the nations of the earth. The literary labours of the age, the practical systems of law, agriculture, and history, might redound to the benefit of the subject, and the honour of the Macedonian princes. The sixty books of the *Basilics*,[5] the code and pandects of civil jurisprudence, were gradually framed in the three first reigns of that prosperous dynasty. The art of agriculture had amused the leisure, and exercised the pens, of the best and wisest of the ancients; and their chosen precepts are comprised in the twenty books of the *Geoponics*[6] of Constantine. At his command the historical examples of vice and virtue were methodised in fifty-three books,[7] and every citizen might apply to his contemporaries or himself the lesson or the warning of past times. From the august character of a legislator, the sovereign of the East descends to the more humble office of a teacher and a scribe; and if his successors and subjects were regardless of his paternal cares, *we* may inherit and enjoy the everlasting legacy.

A closer survey will indeed reduce the value of the gift and the gratitude of posterity: in the possession of these Imperial treasures we may still deplore our poverty and ignorance; and the fading glories of their authors will be obliterated by indifference or contempt. The Basilics will sink to a broken copy, a partial and mutilated version in the Greek language, of the laws of Justinian; but the sense of the old civilians is often superseded by the influence of bigotry: and the absolute prohibition of divorce, concubinage, and interest for money, enslaves the freedom of trade and the happiness of private life. In the historical book a subject of Constantine might admire the inimitable virtues of Greece and Rome: he might learn to what a pitch of energy and elevation the human character had formerly aspired. But a contrary effect must have been produced by a new edition of the lives of the saints, which the great logothete, or chancellor of the empire, was directed to prepare; and the dark fund of superstition was enriched by the fabulous and florid legends of Simon the *Metaphrast*.[8] The merits and miracles of the whole calendar are of less account in the eyes of a sage than the toil of a single husbandman, who multiplies the gifts of the Creator and supplies the food of his brethren. Yet the royal authors of the *Geoponics* were more seriously employed in expounding the precepts of the destroying art, which has been taught since the days of Xenophon[9] as the art of heroes and kings. But the *Tactics* of Leo and Constantine are mingled with the baser alloy of the age in which they lived. It was destitute of original genius; they implicitly transcribe the rules and maxims which had been confirmed by victories. It was unskilled in the propriety of style and method; they blindly confound the most distant and discordant institutions, the phalanx of Sparta and that of Macedon, the legions of Cato and Trajan, of Augustus and Theodosius. Even the use, or at least the importance, of these military rudiments may be fairly questioned: their general theory is dictated by reason; but the merit, as well as difficulty, consists in the application. The discipline of a soldier is formed by exercise rather than by study: the talents of a commander are appropriated to those calm, though rapid, minds, which nature produces to decide the fate of armies and nations: the former is the habit of a life, the latter the glance of a moment; and the battles won by lessons of tactics may be numbered with the epic poems created from the rules of criticism. The book of ceremonies is a recital, tedious yet imperfect, of the despicable pageantry which had infected the church and state since the gradual decay of the purity of the one and the power of the other. A review of the themes or provinces might promise such authentic and useful information as the curiosity of government only can obtain, instead of traditionary fables on the origin of the cities, and malicious epigrams on the vices of their inhabitants.[10] Such information the historian would have been pleased to record; nor should his silence be condemned if the most interesting objects, the population of the capital and provinces, the amount of taxes and revenues, the numbers of subjects and strangers who served under the Imperial standard, have been unnoticed by Leo the Philosopher and his son Constantine. His treatise of the public administration is stained with the same blemishes; yet it is discriminated by peculiar merit: the antiquities of the nations may be doubtful or fabulous; but the geography and manners of the barbaric world are delineated with curious accuracy. Of these nations the Franks alone were qualified to observe in their turn, and to describe, the metropolis of the East. The ambassador of the great Otho, a bishop of Cremona, has painted the state of Constantinople about the middle of the tenth century: his style is glowing, his narrative lively, his observation keen; and even the prejudices and passions of Liutprand are stamped with an original character of freedom and genius.[11] From this scanty fund of foreign and domestic materials I shall investigate the form and substance of the Byzantine empire; the provinces and wealth, the civil government and military force, the character and literature, of the Greeks in a period of six hundred years, from the reign of Heraclius to the successful invasion of the Franks or Latins.

After the final division between the sons of Theodosius, the swarms of the barbarians from Scythia and Germany overspread the provinces and extinguished the empire of ancient Rome. The weakness of Constantinople was concealed by extent of dominion; her limits were inviolate, or at least entire; and the kingdom of Justinian was enlarged by the splendid acquisition of Africa and Italy. But the possession of these new conquests was transient and precarious; and almost a moiety of the Eastern empire was torn away by the arms of the Saracens. Syria and Egypt were oppressed by the Arabian caliphs, and, after the reduction of Africa, their lieutenants invaded and subdued the Roman province which had been changed into the Gothic monarchy of Spain. The islands of the Mediterranean were not inaccessible to their naval powers; and it was from their extreme stations, the harbours of Crete and the fortresses of Cilicia, that the faithful or rebel emirs insulted the majesty of the throne and capital. The remaining provinces, under the obedience of the emperors, were cast into a new mould; and the jurisdiction of the presidents, the consulars, and the counts was superseded by the institution of the *themes*,[12] or military governments, which prevailed under the successors of Heraclius, and are described by the pen of the royal author. Of the twenty-nine themes, twelve in Europe and seventeen in Asia, the origin is obscure, the etymology doubtful or capricious, the limits were arbitrary and fluctuating; but some particular names that sound the most strangely to our ear were derived from the character and attributes of the troops that were maintained at the expense and for the guard of the respective divisions. The vanity of the Greek princes most eagerly grasped the shadow of conquest and the memory of lost dominion. A new Mesopotamia was created on the western side of the Euphrates; the appellation and prætor of Sicily were transferred to a narrow slip of Calabria; and a fragment of the duchy of Beneventum was promoted to the style and title of the theme of Lombardy. In the decline of the Arabian empire the successors of Constantine might indulge their pride in more solid advantages. The victories of Nicephorus, John Zimisces, and Basil the Second, revived the fame, and enlarged the boundaries, of the Roman name; the province of Cilicia, the metropolis of Antioch, the islands of Crete and Cyprus were restored to the allegiance of Christ and Cæsar; one-third of Italy was annexed to the throne of Constantinople, the kingdom of Bulgaria was destroyed, and the last sovereigns of the Macedonian dynasty extended their sway from the sources of the Tigris to the neighbourhood of Rome. In the eleventh century the prospect was again clouded by new enemies and new misfortunes; the relics of Italy were swept away by the Norman adventurers, and almost all the Asiatic branches were dissevered from the Ro-nan trunk by the Turkish conquerors. After these losses the emperors of the Comnenian family continued to reign from the Danube to Peloponnesus, and from Belgrade to Nice, Trebizond, and the winding stream of the Meander. The spacious provinces of Thrace, Macedonia, and Greece were obedient to their sceptre; the possession of Cyprus, Rhodes, and Crete was accompanied by the fifty islands of the Ægean or Holy Sea,[13] and the remnant of their empire transcends the measure of the largest of the European kingdoms.

The same princes might assert, with dignity and truth, that of all the monarchs of Christendom they possessed the greatest city,[14] the most ample revenue, the most flourishing and populous state. With the decline and fall of the empire the cities of the West had decayed and fallen; nor could the ruins of Rome, or the mud walls, wooden hovels, and narrow precincts of Paris and London, prepare the Latin stranger to contemplate the situation and extent of Constantinople, her stately palaces and churches, and the arts and luxury of an innumerable people. Her treasures might attract, but her virgin strength had repelled, and still promised to repel, the audacious invasion of the Persian and Bulgarian, the Arab and the Russian. The provinces were less fortunate and impregnable, and few districts, few cities, could be discovered which had not been violated by some fierce barbarian, impatient to despoil, because he was hopeless to possess. From the age of Justinian the Eastern empire was sinking below its former level; the powers of destruction were more active than those of improvement; and the calamities of war were embittered by the more permanent evils of civil and ecclesiastical tyranny. The captive who had escaped from the barbarians was often stripped and imprisoned by the ministers of his sovereign; the Greek superstition relaxed the mind by prayer, and emaciated the body by fasting; and the multitude of convents and festivals diverted many hands and many days from the temporal service of mankind. Yet the subjects of the Byzantine empire were still the most dexterous and diligent of nations; their country was blessed by nature with every advantage of soil, climate, and situation; and, in the support and restoration of the arts, their patient and peaceful temper was more useful than the warlike spirit and feudal anarchy of Europe. The provinces that still adhered to the empire were repeopled and enriched by the misfortunes of those which were irrecoverably lost. From the yoke of the caliphs, the Catholics of Syria, Egypt, and Africa retired to the allegiance of their prince, to the soceity of their brethren; the movable wealth, which eludes the search of oppression, accompanied and alleviated their exile, and Constantinople received into her bosom the fugitive trade of Alexandria and Tyre. The chiefs of Armenia and Scythia, who fled from hostile or religious persecution, were hospitably entertained; their followers were encouraged to build new cities and to cultivate waste lands; and many spots, both in Europe and Asia, preserved the name, the manners, or at least the memory, of these national colonies. Even the tribes of barbarians who had seated themselves in arms on the territory of the empire were gradually reclaimed to the laws of the church and state, and, as long as they were separated from the Greeks, their posterity supplied a race of faithful and obedient soldiers. Did we possess sufficient materials to survey the twenty-nine themes of the Byzantine monarchy, our curiosity might be satisfied with a chosen example: it is fortunate enough that the clearest light should be thrown on the most interesting province, and the name of PELOPONNESUS will awaken the attention of the classic reader.

As early as the eighth century, in the troubled reign of the Iconoclasts, Greece, and even Peloponnesus,[15] were overrun by some Sclavonian bands who outstripped the royal standard of Bulgaria. The strangers of old, Cadmus, and Danaus, and Pelops, had planted in that fruitful soil the seeds of policy and learning; but the savages of the north eradicated what yet remained of their sickly and withered roots. In this irruption the country and the inhabitants were transformed; the Grecian blood was contaminated; and the proudest nobles of Peloponnesus were branded with the names of foreigners and *slaves*. By the diligence of succeeding princes, the land was in some measure purified from the barbarians; and the humble remnant was bound by an oath of obedience, tribute, and military service, which they often renewed and often violated. The siege of Patras was formed by a singular concurrence of the Sclavonians of Peloponnesus and the Saracens of Africa. In their last distress a pious fiction of the approach of the prætor of Corinth revived the courage of the citizens. Their sally was bold and successful; the strangers embarked, the rebels submitted, and the glory of the day was ascribed to a phantom or a stranger, who fought in the foremost ranks under the character of St. Andrew the Apostle. The shrine which contained his relics was decorated with the trophies of victory, and the captive race was for ever devoted to the service and vassalage of the metropolitan church of Patras. By the revolt of two Sclavonian tribes in the neighbourhood of Helos and Lacedæmon, the peace of the peninsula was often disturbed. They sometimes insulted the weakness, and sometimes resisted the oppression, of the Byzantine government, till at length the approach of their hostile brethren extorted a golden bull to define the rights and obligations of the Ezzerites and Milengi, whose annual tribute was defined at twelve hundred pieces of gold. From these strangers the Imperial geographer has accurately distinguished a domestic and perhaps original race, who, in some degree, might derive their blood from the much-injured Helots. The liberality of the Romans, and especially of Augustus, had enfranchised the maritime cities from the dominion of Sparta; and the continuance of the same benefit ennobled them with the title of *Eleuthero*, or Free-Laconians.[16] In the time of Constantine Porphyrogenitus they had acquired the name of *Mainotes*, under which they dishonour the claim of liberty by the inhuman pillage of all that is shipwrecked on their rocky shores. Their territory, barren of corn but fruitful of olives, extended to the Cape of Malea: they accepted a chief or prince from the Byzantine prætor; and a light tribute of four hundred pieces of gold was the badge of their immunity rather than of their dependence. The freemen of Laconia assumed the character of Romans, and long adhered to the religion of the Greeks. By the zeal of the emperor Basil, they were baptised in the faith of Christ: but the altars of Venus and Neptune had been crowned by these rustic votaries five hundred years after they were proscribed in the Roman world. In the theme of Peloponnesus[17] forty cities were still numbered, and the declining state of Sparta, Argos, and Corinth may be suspended in the tenth century, at an equal distance, perhaps, between their antique splendour and their present desolation. The duty of military service, either in person or by substitute, was imposed on the lands or benefices of the province; a sum of five pieces of gold was assessed on each of the substantial tenants; and the same capitation was shared among several heads of inferior value. On the proclamation of an Italian war, the Peloponnesians excused themselves by a voluntary oblation of one hundred pounds of gold (four thousand pounds sterling), and a thousand horses with their arms and trappings. The churches and monasteries furnished their contingent; a sacrilegious profit

was extorted from the sale of ecclesiastical honours; and the indigent bishop of Leucadia[18] was made responsible for a pension of one hundred pieces of gold.[19]

But the wealth of the province, and the trust of the revenue, were founded on the fair and plentiful produce of trade and manufactures; and some symptoms of liberal policy may be traced in a law which exempts from all personal taxes the mariners of Peloponnesus, and the workmen in parchment and purple. This denomination may be fairly applied or extended to the manufactures of linen, woollen, and more especially of silk: the two former of which had flourished in Greece since the days of Homer; and the last was introduced perhaps as early as the reign of Justinian. These arts, which were exercised at Corinth, Thebes, and Argos, afforded food and occupation to a numerous people: the men, women, and children were distributed according to their age and strength; and if many of these were domestic slaves, their masters, who directed the work and enjoyed the profit, were of a free and honourable condition. The gifts which a rich and generous matron of Peloponnesus presented to the emperor Basil, her adopted son, were doubtless fabricated in the Grecian looms. Danielis bestowed a carpet of fine wool, of a pattern which imitated the spots of a peacock's tail, of a magnitude to overspread the floor of a new church, erected in the triple name of Christ, of Michael the archangel, and of the prophet Elijah. She gave six hundred pieces of silk and linen, of various use and denomination: the silk was painted with the Tyrian dye, and adorned by the labours of the needle; and the linen was so exquisitely fine, that an entire piece might be rolled in the hollow of a cane.[20] In his description of the Greek manufactures, an historian of Sicily discriminates their price, according to the weight and quality of the silk, the closeness of the texture, the beauty of the colours, and the taste and materials of the embroidery. A single, or even a double or treble thread was thought sufficient for ordinary sale; but the union of six threads composed a piece of stronger and more costly workmanship. Among the colours, he celebrates, with affectation of eloquence, the fiery blaze of the scarlet, and the softer lustre of the green. The embroidery was raised either in silk or gold: the more simple ornament of stripes or circles was surpassed by the nicer imitation of flowers: the vestments that were fabricated for the palace or the altar often glittered with precious stones; and the figures were delineated in strings of Oriental pearls.[21] Till the twelfth century, Greece alone, of all the countries of Christendom, was possessed of the insect who is taught by nature, and of the workmen who are instructed by art, to prepare this elegant luxury. But the secret had been stolen by the dexterity and diligence of the Arabs: the caliphs of the East and West scorned to borrow from the unbelievers their furniture and apparel; and two cities of Spain, Almeria and Lisbon, were famous for the manufacture, the use, and perhaps the exportation of silk. It was first introduced into Sicily by the Normans; and this emigration of trade distinguishes the victory of Roger from the uniform and fruitless hostilities of every age. After the sack of Corinth, Athens, and Thebes, his lieutenant embarked with a captive train of weavers and artificers of both sexes, a trophy glorious to their master and disgraceful to the Greek emperor.[22] The king of Sicily was not insensible of the value of the present; and, in the restitution of the prisoners, he excepted only the male and female manufacturers of Thebes and Corinth, who labour, says the Byzantine historian, under a barbarous lord, like the old Eretrians in the service of Darius.[23] A stately edifice, in the palace of Palermo, was erected for the use of this industrious colony;[24] and the art was propagated by their children and disciples to satisfy the increasing demand of the western world. The decay of the looms of Sicily may be ascribed to the troubles of the island and the competition of the Italian cities. In the year thirteen hundred and fourteen, Lucca alone, among her sister republics, enjoyed the lucrative monopoly.[25] A domestic revolution dispersed the manufacturers to Florence, Bologna, Venice, Milan, and even the countries beyond the Alps; and thirteen years after this event, the statutes of Modena enjoin the planting of mulberry-trees and regulate the duties on raw silk.[26] The northern climates are less propitious to the education of the silkworm; but the industry of France and England[27] is supplied and enriched by the productions of Italy and China.

I must repeat the complaint that the vague and scanty memorials of the times will not afford any just estimate of the taxes, the revenue, and the resources of the Greek empire. From every province of Europe and Asia the rivulets of gold and silver discharged into the Imperial reservoir a copious and perennial stream. The separation of the branches from the trunk increased the relative magnitude of Constantinople; and the maxims of despotism contracted the state to the capital, the capital to the palace, and the palace to the royal person. A Jewish traveller, who visited the East in the twelfth century, is lost in his admiration of the Byzantine riches. "It is here," says Benjamin of Tudela, "in the queen of cities, that the tributes of the Greek empire are annually deposited, and the lofty towers are filled with precious magazines of silk, purple, and gold. It is said that Constantinople pays each day to her sovereign twenty thousand pieces of gold, which are levied on the shops, taverns, and markets, on the merchants of Persia and Egypt, of Russia and Hungary, of Italy and Spain, who frequent the capital by sea and land."[28] In all pecuniary matters the authority of a Jew is doubtless respectable; but as the three hundred and sixty-five days would produce a yearly income exceeding seven millions sterling, I am tempted to retrench at least the numerous festivals of the Greek calendar. The mass of treasure that was saved by Theodora and Basil the Second will suggest a splendid, though indefinite, idea of their supplies and resources. The mother of Michael, before she retired to a cloister, attempted to check or expose the prodigality of her ungrateful son by a free and faithful account of the wealth which he inherited; one hundred and nine thousand pounds of gold and three hundred thousand of silver, the fruits of her own economy and that of her deceased husband.[29] The avarice of Basil is not less renowned than his valour and fortune: his victorious armies were paid and rewarded without breaking into the mass of two hundred thousand pounds of gold (about eight millions sterling), which he had buried in the subterraneous vaults of the palace.[30] Such accumulation of treasure is rejected by the theory and practice of modern policy; and we are more apt to compute the national riches by the use and abuse of the public credit. Yet the maxims of antiquity are still embraced by a monarch formidable to his enemies; by a republic respectable to her allies; and both have attained their respective ends of military power and domestic tranquillity.

Whatever might be consumed for the present wants or reserved for the future use of the state, the first and most sacred demand was for the pomp and pleasure of the emperor; and his discretion only could define the measure of his private expense. The princes of Constantinople were far removed from the simplicity of nature; yet, with the revolving seasons, they were led by taste or fashion to withdraw to a purer air from the smoke and tumult of the capital. They enjoyed, or affected to enjoy, the rustic festival of the vintage: their leisure was amused by the exercise of the chase and the calmer occupation of fishing; and in the summer heats they were shaded from the sun, and refreshed by the cooling breezes from the sea. The coasts and islands of Asia and Europe were covered with their magnificent villas; but instead of the modest art which secretly strives to hide itself and to decorate the scenery of nature, the marble structure of their gardens served only to expose the riches of the lord and the labours of the architect. The successive casualties of inheritance and forfeiture had rendered the sovereign proprietor of many stately houses in the city and suburbs, of which twelve were appropriated to the ministers of state; but the great palace,[31] the centre of the Imperial residence, was fixed during eleven centuries to the same position, between the hippodrome, the cathedral of St. Sophia, and the gardens, which descended by many a terrace to the shores of the Propontis. The primitive edifice of the first Constantine was a copy, or rival, of ancient Rome; the gradual improvements of his successors aspired to emulate the wonders of the old world,[32] and in the tenth century the Byzantine palace excited the admiration, at least of the Latins, by an unquestionable pre-eminence of strength, size, and magnificence.[33] But the toil and treasure of so many ages had produced a vast and irregular pile: each separate building was marked with the character of the times and of the founder; and the want of space might excuse the reigning monarch who demolished, perhaps with secret satisfaction, the works of his predecessors. The economy of the emperor Theophilus allowed a more free and ample scope for his domestic luxury and splendour. A favourite ambassador, who had astonished the Abbassides themselves by his pride and liberality, presented on his return the model of a palace which the caliph of Bagdad had recently constructed on the banks of the Tigris. The model was instantly copied and surpassed: the new buildings of Theophilus[34] were accompanied with gardens and with five churches, one of which was conspicuous for size and beauty: it was crowned with three domes, the roof of gilt brass reposed on columns of Italian marble, and the walls were incrusted with marbles of various colours. In the face of the church a semicircular portico, of the figure and name of the Greek *sigma*, was supported by fifteen columns of Phrygian marble, and the subterraneous vaults were of a similar construction. The

square before the sigma was decorated with a fountain, and the margin of the basin was lined and encompassed with plates of silver. In the beginning of each season the basin, instead of water, was replenished with the most exquisite fruits, which were abandoned to the populace for the entertainment of the prince. He enjoyed this tumultuous spectacle from a throne resplendent with gold and gems, which was raised by a marble staircase to the height of a lofty terrace. Below the throne were seated the officers of his guards, the magistrates, the chiefs of the factions of the circus; the inferior steps were occupied by the people, and the place below was covered with troops of dancers, singers, and pantomimes. The square was surrounded by the hall of justice, the arsenal, and the various offices of business and pleasure; and the *purple* chamber was named from the annual distribution of robes of scarlet and purple by the hand of the empress herself. The long series of the apartments was adapted to the seasons, and decorated with marble and porphyry, with painting, sculpture, and mosaics, with a profusion of gold, silver, and precious stones. His fanciful magnificence employed the skill and patience of such artists as the times could afford; but the taste of Athens would have despised their frivolous and costly labours; a golden tree, with its leaves and branches, which sheltered a multitude of birds warbling their artificial notes, and two lions of massy gold, and of the natural size, who looked and roared like their brethren of the forest. The successors of Theophilus, of the Basilian and Comnenian dynasties, were not less ambitious of leaving some memorial of their residence; and the portion of the palace most splendid and august was dignified with the title of the golden *triclinium*.[35] With becoming modesty the rich and noble Greeks aspired to imitate their sovereign, and when they passed through the streets on horseback, in their robes of silk and embroidery, they were mistaken by the children for kings.[36] A matron of Peloponnesus,[37] who had cherished the infant fortunes of Basil the Macedonian, was excited by tenderness or vanity to visit the greatness of her adopted son. In a journey of five hundred miles from Patras to Constantinople, her age or indolence declined the fatigue of a horse or carriage; the soft litter or bed of Danielis was transported on the shoulders of ten robust slaves, and, as they were relieved at easy distances, a band of three hundred was selected for the performance of this service. She was entertained in the Byzantine palace with filial reverence and the honours of a queen; and whatever might be the origin of her wealth, her gifts were not unworthy of the regal dignity. I have already described the fine and curious manufactures of Peloponnesus, of linen, silk, and woollen; but the most acceptable of her presents consisted in three hundred beautiful youths, of whom one hundred were eunuchs;[38] "for she was not ignorant," says the historian, "that the air of the palace is more congenial to such insects, than a shepherd's dairy to the flies of the summer." During her lifetime she bestowed the greater part of her estates in Peloponnesus, and her testament instituted Leo, the son of Basil, her universal heir. After the payment of the legacies, fourscore villas or farms were added to the Imperial domain, and three thousand slaves of Danielis were enfranchised by their new lord, and transplanted as a colony to the Italian coast. From this example of a private matron we may estimate the wealth and magnificence of the emperors. Yet our enjoyments are confined by a narrow circle, and, whatsoever may be its value, the luxury of life is possessed with more innocence and safety by the master of his own, than by the steward of the public, fortune.

In an absolute government, which levels the distinctions of noble and plebeian birth, the sovereign is the sole fountain of honour; and the rank, both in the palace and the empire, depends on the titles and offices which are bestowed and resumed by his arbitrary will. Above a thousand years, from Vespasian to Alexius Comnenus,[39] the *Cæsar* was the second person, or at least the second degree, after the supreme title of *Augustus* was more freely communicated to the sons and brothers of the reigning monarch. To elude without violating his promise to a powerful associate, the husband of his sister, and, without giving himself an equal, to reward the piety of his brother Isaac, the crafty Alexius interposed a new and supereminent dignity. The happy flexibility of the Greek tongue allowed him to compound the names of Augustus and Emperor (Sebastos and Autocrator), and the union produced the sonorous title of *Sebastocrator*. He was exalted above the Cæsar on the first step of the throne: the public acclamations repeated his name; and he was only distinguished from the sovereign by some peculiar ornaments of the head and feet. The emperor alone could assume the purple or red buskins, and the close diadem or tiara, which imitated the fashion of the Persian kings.[40] It was a high pyramidal cap of cloth or silk, al-

most concealed by a profusion of pearls and jewels: the crown was formed by a horizontal circle and two arches of gold: at the summit, the point of their intersection, was placed a globe or cross, and two strings or lappets of pearl depended on either cheek. Instead of red, the buskins of the Sebastocrator and Cæsar were green; and on their *open* coronets, or crowns, the precious gems were more sparingly distributed. Beside and below the Cæsar the fancy of Alexius created the *Panhypersebastos* and the *Protosebastos*, whose sound and signification will satisfy a Grecian ear. They imply a superiority and a priority above the simple name of Augustus; and this sacred and primitive title of the Roman prince was degraded to the kinsmen and servants of the Byzantine court. The daughter of Alexius applauds with fond complacency this artful gradation of hopes and honours; but the science of words is accessible to the meanest capacity; and this vain dictionary was easily enriched by the pride of his successors. To their favourite sons or brothers they imparted the more lofty appellation of Lord or *Despot*, which was illustrated with new ornaments and prerogatives, and placed immediately after the person of the emperor himself. The five titles of, 1. *Despot*; 2. *Sebastocrator*; 3. *Cæsar*; 4. *Panhypersebastos*; and, 5. *Protosebastos*; were usually confined to the princes of his blood: they were the emanations of his majesty; but as they exercised no regular functions, their existence was useless, and their authority precarious.

But in every monarchy the substantial powers of government must be divided and exercised by the ministers of the palace and treasury, the fleet and army. The titles alone can differ; and in the revolution of ages, the counts and præfects, the prætor and quæstor, insensibly descended, while their servants rose above their heads to the first honours of the state. 1. In a monarchy, which refers every object to the person of the prince, the care and ceremonies of the palace form the most respectable department. The *Curopalata*,[41] so illustrious in the age of Justinian, was supplanted by the *Protovestiare*, whose primitive functions were limited to the custody of the wardrobe. From thence his jurisdiction was extended over the numerous menials of pomp and luxury; and he presided with his silver wand at the public and private audience. 2. In the ancient system of Constantine, the name of *Logothete*, or accountant, was applied to the receivers of the finances: the principal officers were distinguished as the Logothetes of the domain, of the posts, the Army, the private and public treasure; and the *great Logothete*, the supreme guardian of the laws and revenues, is compared with the chancellor of the Latin monarchies.[42] His discerning eye pervaded the civil administration; and he was assisted, in due subordination, by the eparch or præfect of the city, the first secretary, and the keepers of the privy seal, the archives, and the red and purple ink which was reserved for the sacred signature of the emperor alone.[43] The introductor and interpreter of foreign ambassadors were the great *Chiauss*[44] and the *Dragoman*,[45] two names of Turkish origin, and which are still familiar to the Sublime Porte. 3. From the humble style and service of guards, the *Domestics* insensibly rose to the station of generals; the military themes of the East and West, the legions of Europe and Asia, were often divided, till the *great Domestic* was finally invested with the universal and absolute command of the land forces. The *Protostrator*, in his original functions was the assistant of the emperor when he mounted on horseback: he gradually became the lieutenant of the great Domestic in the field; and his jurisdiction extended over the stables, the cavalry, and the royal train of hunting and hawking. The *Stratopedarch* was the great judge of the camp: the *Protospathaire* commanded the guards; the *Constable*,[46] the *great Æteriarch*, and the *Acolyth*, were the separate chiefs of the Franks, the barbarians, and the Varangi, or English, the mercenary strangers, who, in the decay of the national spirit, formed the nerve of the Byzantine armies. 4. The naval powers were under the command of the *great Duke*; in his absence they obeyed the *great Drungaire* of the fleet; and, in *his* place, the *Emir*, or *Admiral*, a name of Saracen extraction,[47] but which has been naturalised in all the modern languages of Europe. Of these officers, and of many more whom it would be useless to enumerate, the civil and military hierarchy was framed. Their honours and emoluments, their dress and titles, their mutual salutations and respective pre-eminence, were balanced with more exquisite labour than would have fixed the constitution of a free people; and the code was almost perfect when this baseless fabric, the monument of pride and servitude, was for ever buried in the ruins of the empire.[48]

The most lofty titles, and the most humble postures, which devotion has applied to the Supreme Being, have been prostituted by flattery and fear to creatures of the same nature with ourselves. The mode of *adoration*,[49] of falling prostrate on the ground and kissing the feet of the emperor, was borrowed by Diocletian from Persian servitude; but it was continued and aggravated till the last age of the Greek monarchy. Excepting only on Sundays, when it was waived, from a motive of religious pride, this humiliating reverence was exacted from all who entered the royal presence, from the princes invested with the diadem and purple, and from the ambassadors who represented their independent sovereigns, the caliphs of Asia, Egypt, or Spain, the kings of France and Italy, and the Latin emperors of ancient Rome. In his transactions of business, Liutprand, bishop of Cremona,[50] asserted the free spirit of a Frank and the dignity of his master Otho. Yet his sincerity cannot disguise the abasement of his first audience. When he approached the throne, the birds of the golden tree began to warble their notes, which were accompanied by the roarings of the two lions of gold. With his two companions Liutprand was compelled to bow and to fall prostrate; and thrice he touched the ground with his forehead. He arose; but in the short interval the throne had been hoisted by an engine from the floor to the ceiling, the Imperial figure appeared in new and more gorgeous apparel, and the interview was concluded in haughty and majestic silence. In this honest and curious narrative the bishop of Cremona represents the ceremonies of the Byzantine court, which are still practised in the Sublime Porte, and which were preserved in the last age of the dukes of Muscovy or Russia. After a long journey by the sea and land, from Venice to Constantinople, the ambassador halted at the golden gate, till he was conducted by the formal officers to the hospitable palace prepared for his reception; but this palace was a prison, and his jealous keepers prohibited all social intercourse either with strangers or natives. At his first audience he offered the gifts of his master— slaves, and golden vases, and costly armour. The ostentatious payment of the officers and troops displayed before his eyes the riches of the empire: he was entertained at a royal banquet,[51] in which the ambassadors of the nations were marshalled by the esteem or contempt of the Greeks: from his own table, the emperor, as the most signal favour, sent the plates which he had tasted; and his favourites were dismissed with a robe of honour.[52] In the morning and evening of each day his civil and military servants attended their duty in the palace; their labour was repaid by the sight, perhaps by the smile, of their lord; his commands were signified by a nod or a sign: but all earthly greatness stood silent and submissive in his presence. In his regular or extraordinary processions through the capital, he unveiled his person to the public view: the rites of policy were connected with those of religion, and his visits to the principal churches were regulated by the festivals of the Greek calendar. On the eve of these processions the gracious or devout intention of the monarch was proclaimed by the heralds. The streets were cleared and purified; the pavement was strewed with flowers; the most precious furniture, the gold and silver plate and silken hangings, were displayed from the windows and balconies; and a severe discipline restrained and silenced the tumult of the populace. The march was opened by the military officers at the head of their troops: they were followed in long order by the magistrates and ministers of the civil government: the person of the emperor was guarded by his eunuchs and domestics, and at the church door he was solemnly received by the patriarch and his clergy. The task of applause was not abandoned to the rude and spontaneous voices of the crowd. The most convenient stations were occupied by the bands of the blue and green factions of the circus; and their furious conflicts, which had shaken the capital, were insensibly sunk to an emulation of servitude. From either side they echoed in responsive melody the praises of the emperor; their poets and musicians directed the choir, and long life[53] and victory were the burden of every song. The same acclamations were performed at the audience, the banquet, and the church, and as an evidence of boundless sway, they were repeated in the Latin,[54] Gothic, Persian, French, and even English language,[55] by the mercenaries who sustained the real or fictitious character of those nations. By the pen of Constantine Porphyrogenitus this science of form and flattery has been reduced into a pompous and trifling volume,[56] which the vanity of succeeding times might enrich with an ample supplement. Yet the calmer reflection of a prince would surely suggest that the same acclamations were applied to every character and every reign: and if he had risen from a private rank, he might remember that his own voice had been the loudest and most eager in applause, at the very moment when he envied the fortune, or conspired against the life, of his predecessor.[57]

The princes of the North, of the nations, says Constantine, without faith or fame, were ambitious of mingling their blood with the blood of the Cæsars, by their marriage with a royal virgin, or by the nuptials of their daughters with a Roman prince.[58] The aged monarch, in his instructions to his son, reveals the secret maxims of policy and pride, and suggests the most decent reasons for refusing these insolent and unreasonable demands. Every animal, says the discreet emperor, is prompted by nature to seek a mate among the animals of his own species; and the human species is divided into various tribes, by the distinction of language, religion, and manners. A just regard to the purity of descent preserves the harmony of public and private life; but the mixture of foreign blood is the fruitful source of disorder and discord. Such had ever been the opinion and practice of the sage Romans: their jurisprudence proscribed the marriage of a citizen and a stranger: in the days of freedom and virtue a senator would have scorned to match his daughter with a king: the glory of Mark Antony was sullied by an Egyptian wife:[59] and the emperor Titus was compelled, by popular censure, to dismiss with reluctance the reluctant Berenice.[60] This perpetual interdict was ratified by the fabulous sanction of the great Constantine. The ambassadors of the nations, more especially of the unbelieving nations, were solemnly admonished that such strange alliances had been condemned by the founder of the church and city. The irrevocable law was inscribed on the altar of St. Sophia; and the impious prince who should stain the majesty of the purple was excluded from the civil and ecclesiastical communion of the Romans. If the ambassadors were instructed by any false brethren in the Byzantine history, they might produce three memorable examples of the violation of this imaginary law: the marriage of Leo, or rather of his father Constantine the Fourth, with the daughter of the king of the Chazars, the nuptials of the grand-daughter of Romanus with a Bulgarian prince, and the union of Bertha of France or Italy with young Romanus, the son of Constantine Porphyrogenitus himself. To these objections three answers were prepared, which solved the difficulty and established the law. I. The deed and the guilt of Constantine Copronymus were acknowledged. The Isaurian heretic, who sullied the baptismal font and declared war against the holy images, had indeed embraced a barbarian wife. By this impious alliance he accomplished the measure of his crimes, and was devoted to the just censure of the church and of posterity. II. Romanus could not be alleged as a legitimate emperor; he was a plebeian usurper, ignorant of the laws, and regardless of the honour, of the monarchy. His son Christopher, the father of the bride, was the third in rank in the college of princes, at once the subject and the accomplice of a rebellious parent. The Bulgarians were sincere and devout Christians; and the safety of the empire, with the redemption of many thousand captives, depended on this preposterous alliance. Yet no consideration could dispense from the law of Constantine: the clergy, the senate, and the people disapproved the conduct of Romanus; and he was reproached, both in his life and death, as the author of the public disgrace. III. For the marriage of his own son with the daughter of Hugo, king of Italy, a more honourable defence is contrived by the wise Porphyrogenitus. Constantine, the great and holy, esteemed the fidelity and valour of the Franks;[61] and his prophetic spirit beheld the vision of their future greatness. They alone were excepted from the general prohibition: Hugo, king of France, was the lineal descendant of Charlemagne;[62] and his daughter, Bertha, inherited the prerogatives of her family and nation. The voice of truth and malice insensibly betrayed the fraud or error of the Imperial court. The patrimonial estate of Hugo was reduced from the monarchy of France to the simple county of Arles; though it was not denied that, in the confusion of the times, he had usurped the sovereignty of Provence, and invaded the kingdom of Italy. His father was a private noble; and if Bertha derived her female descent from the Carlovingian line, every step was polluted with illegitimacy or vice. The grandmother of Hugo was the famous Valdrada, the concubine, rather than the wife, of the second Lothair; whose adultery, divorce, and second nuptials had provoked against him the thunders of the Vatican. His mother, as she was styled, the great Bertha, was successively the wife of the Count of Arles and of the Marquis of Tuscany: France and Italy were scandalised by her gallantries; and, till the age of threescore, her lovers, of every degree, were the zealous servants of her ambition. The example of maternal incontinence was copied by the king of Italy; and the three favourite concubines of Hugo were decorated with the classic names of Venus, Juno, and Semele.[63] The daughter of Venus was granted to the solicitations of the Byzantine court: her name of Bertha was changed to that of Eudoxia; and she was wedded, or rather betrothed, to young Romanus, the future heir of the empire of the East. The consummation of this foreign alliance was suspended by the tender age of the two parties; and, at the end of five years, the union was dissolved by the death of the virgin spouse. The second wife of the emperor Romanus was a maiden of plebeian, but of Roman, birth; and their two daughters, Theophano and Anne, were given in marriage to the princes of the earth. The eldest was bestowed, as the pledge of peace, on the eldest son of the great Otho, who had solicited this alliance with arms and embassies. It might legally be questioned how far a Saxon was entitled to the privilege of the French nation; but every scruple was silenced by the fame and piety of a hero who had restored the empire of the West. After the death of her father-in-law and husband, Theophano governed Rome, Italy, and Germany, during the minority of her son, the third Otho; and the Latins have praised the virtues of an empress who sacrificed to a superior duty the remembrance of her country.[64] In the nuptials of her sister Anne, every prejudice was lost, and every consideration of dignity was superseded, by the stronger argument of necessity and fear. A Pagan of the North, Wolodomir, great prince of Russia, aspired to a daughter of the Roman purple; and his claim was enforced by the threats of war, the promise of conversion, and the offer of a powerful succour against a domestic rebel. A victim of her religion and country, the Grecian princess was torn from the palace of her fathers, and condemned to a savage reign and a hopeless exile on the banks of the Borysthenes, or in the neighbourhood of the Polar circle.[65] Yet the marriage of Anne was fortunate and fruitful: the daughter of her grandson Jeroslaus was recommended by her Imperial descent; and the king of France, Henry I., sought a wife on the last borders of Europe and Christendom.[66]

In the Byzantine palace the emperor was the first slave of the ceremonies which he imposed, of the rigid forms which regulated each word and gesture, besieged him in the palace, and violated the leisure of his rural solitude. But the lives and fortunes of millions hung on his arbitrary will; and the firmest minds, superior to the allurements of pomp and luxury, may be seduced by the more active pleasure of commanding their equals. The legislative and executive powers were centred in the person of the monarch, and the last remains of the authority of the senate were finally eradicated by Leo the Philosopher.[67] A lethargy of servitude had benumbed the minds of the Greeks: in the wildest tumults of rebellion they never aspired to the idea of a free constitution; and the private character of the prince was the only source and measure of their public happiness. Superstition riveted their chains; in the church of St. Sophia he was solemnly crowned by the patriarch; at the foot of the altar they pledged their passive and unconditional obedience to his government and family. On his side he engaged to abstain as much as possible from the capital punishments of death and mutilation; his orthodox creed was subscribed with his own hand, and he promised to obey the decrees of the seven synods and the canons of the holy church.[68] But the assurance of mercy was loose and indefinite: he swore, not to his people, but to an invisible judge; and except in the inexpiable guilt of heresy, the ministers of heaven were always prepared to preach the indefeasible right, and to absolve the venial transgressions, of their sovereign. The Greek ecclesiastics were themselves the subjects of the civil magistrate: at the nod of a tyrant the bishops were created, or transferred, or deposed, or punished with an ignominious death; whatever might be their wealth or influence, they could never succeed like the Latin clergy in the establishment of an independent republic; and the patriarch of Constantinople condemned, what he secretly envied, the temporal greatness of his Roman brother. Yet the exercise of boundless despotism is happily checked by the laws of nature and necessity. In proportion to his wisdom and virtue, the master of an empire is confined to the path of his sacred and laborious duty. In proportion to his vice and folly, he drops the sceptre too weighty for his hands; and the motions of the royal image are ruled by the imperceptible thread of some minister or favourite, who undertakes for his private interest to exercise the task of the public oppression. In some fatal moment the most absolute monarch may dread the reason or the caprice of a nation of slaves; and experience has proved that whatever is gained in the extent is lost in the safety and solidity of regal power.

Whatever titles a despot may assume, whatever claims he may assert, it is on the sword that he must ultimately depend to guard him against his foreign and domestic enemies. From the age of Charlemagne to that of the Crusades the world (for I overlook the remote monarchy of China) was occupied and disputed by the three great empires or nations of the Greeks, the Saracens, and the Franks. Their military strength may be ascertained by a comparison of their courage, their arts and riches, and their obedience to a supreme head, who might call into action all the energies of the state. The Greeks, far inferior to their rivals in the first, were superior to the Franks, and at least equal to the Saracens, in the second and third of these warlike qualifications.

The wealth of the Greeks enabled them to purchase the service of the poorer nations, and to maintain a naval power for the protection of their coasts and the annoyance of their enemies.[69] A commerce of mutual benefit exchanged the gold of Constantinople for the blood of the Sclavonians and Turks, the Bulgarians and Russians: their valour contributed to the victories of Nicephorus and Zimisces; and if a hostile people pressed too closely on the frontier, they were recalled to the defence of their country, and the desire of peace, by the well-managed attack of a more distant tribe.[70] The command of the Mediterranean, from the mouth of the Tanais to the Columns of Hercules, was always claimed, and often possessed, by the successors of Constantine. Their capital was filled with naval stores and dexterous artificers: the situation of Greece and Asia, the long coasts, deep gulfs, and numerous islands, accustomed their subjects to the exercise of navigation; and the trade of Venice and Amalfi supplied a nursery of seamen to the Imperial fleet.[71] Since the time of the Peloponnesian and Punic wars, the sphere of action had not been enlarged; and the science of naval architecture appears to have declined. The art of constructing those stupendous machines which displayed three, or six, or ten ranges of oars, rising above, or falling behind, each other, was unknown to the ship-builders of Constantinople, as well as to the mechanicians of modern days.[72] The *Dromones*,[73] or light galleys of the Byzantine empire, were content with two tier of oars; each tier was composed of five-and-twenty benches; and two rowers were seated on each bench, who plied their oars on either side of the vessel. To these we must add the captain or centurion, who, in time of action, stood erect with his armour-bearer on the poop, two steersmen at the helm, and two officers at the prow, the one to manage the anchor, the other to point and play against the enemy the tube of liquid fire. The whole crew, as in the infancy of the art, performed the double service of mariners and soldiers; they were provided with defensive and offensive arms—with bows and arrows, which they used from the upper deck; with long pikes, which they pushed through the port-holes of the lower tier. Sometimes, indeed, the ships of war were of a larger and more solid construction; and the labours of combat and navigation were more regularly divided between seventy soldiers and two hundred and thirty mariners. But for the most part they were of the light and manageable size; and as the cape of Malea in Peloponnesus was still clothed with its ancient terrors, an Imperial fleet was transported five miles over land across the Isthmus of Corinth.[74] The principles of maritime tactics had not undergone any change since the time of Thucydides: a squadron of galleys still advanced in a crescent, charged to the front, and strove to impel their sharp beaks against the feeble sides of their antagonists. A machine for casting stones and darts was built of strong timbers in the midst of the deck; and the operation of boarding was effected by a crane that hoisted baskets of armed men. The language of signals, so clear and copious in the naval grammar of the moderns, was imperfectly expressed by the various positions and colours of a commanding flag. In the darkness of the night the same orders to chase, to attack, to halt, to retreat, to break, to form, were conveyed by the lights of the leading galley. By land, the fire-signals were repeated from one mountain to another; a chain of eight stations commanded a space of five hundred miles; and Constantinople in a few hours was apprised of the hostile motions of the Saracens of Tarsus.[75] Some estimate may be formed of the power of the Greek emperors by the curious and minute detail of the armament which was prepared for the reduction of Crete. A fleet of one hundred and twelve galleys, and seventy-five vessels of the Pamphylian style, was equipped in the capital, the islands of the Ægean Sea, and the seaports of Asia, Macedonia, and Greece. It carried thirty-four thousand mariners, seven thousand three hundred and forty soldiers, seven hundred Russians, and five thousand and eighty-seven Mardaites, whose fathers had been transplanted from the mountains of Libanus. Their pay, most probably of a month, was computed at thirty-four centenaries of gold, about one hundred and thirty-six thousand pounds sterling. Our fancy is bewildered by the endless recapitulation of arms and engines, of clothes and linen, of bread for the men and forage for the horses, and of stores and utensils of every description, inadequate to the conquest of a petty island, but amply sufficient for the establishment of a flourishing colony.[76]

The invention of the Greek fire did not, like that of gunpowder, produce a total revolution in the art of war. To these liquid combustibles the city and empire of Constantine owed their deliverance; and they were employed in sieges and sea-fights with terrible effect. But they were either less improved, or less susceptible of improvement: the engines of antiquity, the catapultæ, balistæ, and battering-rams, were still of most frequent and powerful use in the attack and defence of fortifications; nor was the decision of battles reduced to the quick and heavy *fire* of a line of infantry, whom it were fruitless to protect with armour against a similar fire of their enemies. Steel and iron were still the common instruments of destruction and safety; and the helmets, cuirasses, and shields of the tenth century did not, either in form or substance, essentially differ from those which had covered the companions of Alexander or Achilles.[77] But instead of accustoming the modern Greeks, like the legionaries of old, to the constant and easy use of this salutary weight, their armour was laid aside in light chariots, which followed the march, till on the approach of an enemy, they resumed with haste and reluctance the unusual encumbrance. Their offensive weapons consisted of swords, battle-axes, and spears; but the Macedonian pike was shortened a fourth of its length, and reduced to the more convenient measure of twelve cubits or feet. The sharpness of the Scythian and Arabian arrows had been severely felt; and the emperors lament the decay of archery as a cause of the public misfortunes, and recommend, as an advice and a command, that the military youth, till the age of forty, should assiduously practise the exercise of the bow.[78] The *bands*, or regiments, were usually three hundred strong; and, as a medium between the extremes of four and sixteen, the footsoldiers of Leo and Constantine were formed eight deep; but the cavalry charged in four ranks, from the reasonable consideration that the weight of the front could not be increased by any pressure of the hindmost horses. If the ranks of the infantry or cavalry were sometimes doubled, this cautious array betrayed a secret distrust of the courage of the troops, whose numbers might swell the appearance of the line, but of whom only a chosen band would dare to encounter the spears and swords of the barbarians. The order of battle must have varied according to the ground, the object, and the adversary; but their ordinary disposition, in two lines and a reserve, presented a succession of hopes and resources most agreeable to the temper as well as the judgment of the Greeks.[79] In case of a repulse, the first line fell back into the intervals of the second; and the reserve, breaking into two divisions, wheeled round the flanks to improve the victory or cover the retreat. Whatever authority could enact was accomplished, at least in theory, by the camps and marches, the exercises and evolutions, the edicts and books, of the Byzantine monarch.[80] Whatever art could produce from the forge, the loom, or the laboratory, was abundantly supplied by the riches of the prince and the industry of his numerous workmen. But neither authority nor art could frame the most important machine, the soldier himself; and if the *ceremonies* of Constantine always suppose the safe and triumphal return of the emperor,[81] his *tactics* seldom soar above the means of escaping a defeat and procrastinating the war.[82] Notwithstanding some transient success, the Greeks were sunk in their own esteem and that of their neighbours. A cold hand and a loquacious tongue was the vulgar description of the nation; the author of the Tactics was besieged in his capital; and the last of the barbarians, who trembled at the name of the Saracens or Franks, could proudly exhibit the medals of gold and silver which they had extorted from the feeble sovereign of Constantinople. What spirit their government and character denied might have been inspired, in some degree, by the influence of religion; but the religion of the Greeks could only teach them to suffer and to yield. The emperor Nicephorus, who restored for a moment the discipline and glory of the Roman name, was desirous of bestowing the honours of martyrdom on the Christians who lost their lives in a holy war against the infidels. But this political law was defeated by the opposition of the patriarch, the bishops, and the principal senators; and they strenuously urged the canons of St. Basil, that all who were polluted by the bloody trade of a soldier should be separated, during three years, from the communion of the faithful.[83]

These scruples of the Greeks have been compared with the tears of the primitive Moslems when they were held back from battle; and this contrast of base superstition and high-spirited enthusiasm unfolds to a philosophic eye the history of the rival nations. The subjects of the last caliphs[84] had undoubtedly degenerated from the zeal and faith of the companions of the prophet. Yet their martial creed represented the Deity as the author of war;[85] the vital though latent spark of fanaticism still glowed in the heart of their religion, and among the Saracens who dwelt on the Christian borders it was frequently rekindled to a lively and active flame. Their regular force was formed of the valiant slaves who had been educated to guard the person and accompany the standard of their lord; but the Musulman people of Syria and Cilicia, of Africa and Spain, was awakened by the trumpet which proclaimed a holy war against the infidels. The rich were ambitious of death or victory in the cause of God; the poor were allured by the hopes of plunder; and the old, the infirm, and the women assumed their share of meritorious service by sending their substitutes, with arms and horses, into the field. These offensive and defensive arms were similar in strength and temper to those of the Romans, whom they far excelled in the management of the horse and the bow; the massy silver of their belts, their bridles, and their swords displayed the magnificence of a prosperous nation; and, except some black archers of the South, the Arabs disdained the naked bravery of their ancestors. Instead of waggons they were attended by a long train of camels, mules, and asses; the multitude of these animals, whom they bedecked with flags and streamers, appeared to swell the pomp and magnitude of their host, and the horses of the enemy were often disordered by the uncouth figure and odious smell of the camels of the East. Invincible by their patience of thirst and heat, their spirits were frozen by a winter's cold, and the consciousness of their propensity to sleep exacted the most rigorous precautions against the surprises of the night. Their order of battle was a long square of two deep solid lines; the first of archers, the second of cavalry. In their engagements by sea and land they sustained with patient firmness the fury of the attack, and seldom advanced to the charge till they could discern and oppress the lassitude of their foes. But if they were repulsed and broken, they knew not how to rally or renew the combat, and their dismay was heightened by the superstitious prejudice that God had declared himself on the side of their enemies. The decline and fall of the caliphs countenanced this fearful opinion, nor were there wanting, among the Mohammedans and Christians, some obscure prophecies[86] which prognosticated their alternate defeats. The unity of the Arabian empire was dissolved, but the independent fragments were equal to populous and powerful kingdoms, and in their naval and military armaments an emir of Aleppo or Tunis might command no despicable fund of skill, and industry, and treasure. In their transactions of peace and war with the Saracens, the princes of Constantinople too often felt that these barbarians had nothing barbarous in their discipline, and that, if they were destitute of original genius, they had been endowed with a quick spirit of curiosity and imitation. The model was indeed more perfect than the copy; their ships, and engines, and fortifications were of a less skilful construction; and they confess, without shame, that the same God who has given a tongue to the Arabian had more nicely fashioned the hands of the Chinese and the heads of the Greeks.[87]

A name of some German tribes between the Rhine and the Weser had spread its victorious influence over the greatest part of Gaul, Germany, and Italy; and the common appellation of FRANKS[88] was applied by the Greeks and Arabians to the Christians of the Latin church, the nations of the West, who stretched beyond *their* knowledge to the shores of the Atlantic Ocean. The vast body had been inspired and united by the soul of Charlemagne; but the division and degeneracy of his race soon annihilated the Imperial power, which would have rivalled the Cæsars of Byzantium, and revenged the indignities of the Christian name. The enemies no longer feared, nor could the subjects any longer trust, the application of a public revenue, the labours of trade and manufactures in the military service, the mutual aid of provinces and armies, and the naval squadrons which were regularly stationed from the mouth of the Elbe to that of the Tiber. In the beginning of the tenth century the family of Charlemagne had almost disappeared; his monarchy was broken into many hostile and independent states; the regal title was assumed by the most ambitious chiefs; their revolt was imitated in a long subordination of anarchy and discord; and the nobles of every province disobeyed their sovereign, oppressed their vassals, and exercised perpetual hostilities against their equals and neighbours. Their private wars, which overturned the fabric of government, fomented the martial spirit of the nation. In the system of modern Europe the power of the sword is possessed, at least in fact, by five or six mighty potentates; their operations are conducted on a distant frontier by an order of men who devote their lives to the study and practice of the military art: the rest of the country and community enjoys in the midst of war the tranquillity of peace, and is only made sensible of the change by the aggravation or decrease of the public taxes. In the disorders of the tenth and eleventh centuries every peasant was a soldier, and every village a fortification; each wood or valley was a scene of murder and rapine; and the lords of each castle were compelled to assume the char-

acter of princes and warriors. To their own courage and policy they boldly trusted for the safety of their family, the protection of their lands, and the revenge of their injuries; and, like the conquerors of a larger size, they were too apt to transgress the privilege of defensive war. The powers of the mind and body were hardened by the presence of danger and necessity of resolution: the same spirit refused to desert a friend and to forgive an enemy; and, instead of sleeping under the guardian care of the magistrate, they proudly disdained the authority of the laws. In the days of feudal anarchy the instruments of agriculture and art were converted into the weapons of bloodshed; the peaceful occupations of civil and ecclesiastical society were abolished or corrupted; and the bishop who exchanged his mitre for a helmet was more forcibly urged by the manners of the times than by the obligation of his tenure.[89]

The love of freedom and of arms was felt with conscious pride by the Franks themselves, and is observed by the Greeks with some degree of amazement and terror. "The Franks," says the emperor Constantine, "are bold and valiant to the verge of temerity; and their dauntless spirit is supported by the contempt of danger and death. In the field, and in close onset, they press to the front and rush headlong against the enemy, without deigning to compute either his numbers or their own. Their ranks are formed by the firm connections of consanguinity and friendship; and their martial deeds are prompted by the desire of saving or revenging their dearest companions. In their eyes a retreat is shameful flight, and flight is indelible infamy."[90] A nation endowed with such high and intrepid spirit must have been secure of victory if these advantages had not been counterbalanced by many weighty defects. The decay of their naval power left the Greeks and Saracens in possession of the sea for every purpose of annoyance and supply. In the age which preceded the institution of knighthood the Franks were rude and unskilful in the service of cavalry;[91] and in all perilous emergencies their warriors were so conscious of their ignorance, that they chose to dismount from their horses and fight on foot. Unpractised in the use of pikes or of missile weapons, they were encumbered by the length of their swords, the weight of their armour, the magnitude of their shields, and, if I may repeat the satire of the meagre Greeks, by their unwieldy intemperance. Their independent spirit disdained the yoke of subordination, and abandoned the standard of their chief if he attempted to keep the field beyond the term of their stipulation or service. On all sides they were open to the snares of an enemy less brave but more artful than themselves. They might be bribed, for the barbarians were venal; or surprised in the night, for they neglected the precautions of a close encampment or vigilant sentinels. The fatigues of a summer's campaign exhausted their strength and patience, and they sunk in despair if their voracious appetite was disappointed of a plentiful supply of wine and of food. This general character of the Franks was marked with some national and local shades, which I should ascribe to accident rather than to climate, but which were visible both to natives and to foreigners. An ambassador of the great Otho declared, in the palace of Constantinople, that the Saxons could dispute with swords better than with pens, and that they preferred inevitable death to the dishonour of turning their backs to an enemy.[92] It was the glory of the nobles of France that, in their humble dwellings, war and rapine were the only pleasure, the sole occupation, of their lives. They affected to deride the palaces, the banquets, the polished manners of the Italians, who in the estimate of the Greeks themselves had degenerated from the liberty and valour of the ancient Lombards.[93]

By the well-known edict of Caracalla, his subjects, from Britain to Egypt, were entitled to the name and privileges of Romans, and their national sovereign might fix his occasional or permanent residence in any province of their common country. In the division of the East and West an ideal unity was scrupulously preserved, and in their titles, laws, and statutes the successors of Arcadius and Honorius announced themselves as the inseparable colleagues of the same office, as the joint sovereigns of the Roman world and city, which were bounded by the same limits. After the fall of the Western monarchy the majesty of the purple resided solely in the princes of Constantinople, and of these Justinian was the first who, after a divorce of sixty years, regained the dominion of ancient Rome, and asserted, by the right of conquest, the august title of Emperor of the Romans.[94] A motive of vanity or discontent solicited one of his successors, Constans the Second, to abandon the Thracian Bosphorus and to restore the pristine honours of the Tiber: an extravagant project (exclaims the malicious Byzantine), as if he had despoiled a beautiful and blooming virgin, to enrich, or rather to expose, the deformity of a wrinkled and decrepit matron.[95] But the sword of the Lombards opposed his settlement in Italy; he entered Rome not as a conqueror, but as a fugitive, and, after a visit of twelve days, he pillaged and for ever deserted the ancient capital of the world.[96] The final revolt and separation of Italy was accomplished about two centuries after the conquests of Justinian, and from his reign we may date the gradual oblivion of the Latin tongue. That legislator had composed his Institutes, his Code, and his Pandects in a language which he celebrates as the proper and public style of the Roman government, the consecrated idiom of the palace and senate of Constantinople, of the camps and tribunals of the East.[97] But this foreign dialect was unknown to the people and soldiers of the Asiatic provinces, it was imperfectly understood by the greater part of the interpreters of the laws and the ministers of the state. After a short conflict, nature and habit prevailed over the obsolete institutions of human power: for the general benefit of his subjects Justinian promulgated his novels in the two languages, the several parts of his voluminous jurisprudence were successively translated,[98] the original was forgotten, the version was studied, and the Greek, whose intrinsic merit deserved indeed the preference, obtained a legal as well as popular establishment in the Byzantine monarchy. The birth and residence of succeeding princes estranged them from the Roman idiom; Tiberius by the Arabs,[99] and Maurice by the Italians,[100] are distinguished as the first of the Greek Cæsars, as the founders of a new dynasty and empire; the silent revolution was accomplished before the death of Heraclius, and the ruins of the Latin speech were darkly preserved in the terms of jurisprudence and the acclamations of the palace. After the restoration of the Western empire by Charlemagne and the Othos, the names of Franks and Latins acquired an equal signification and extent, and these haughty barbarians asserted, with some justice, their superior claim to the language and dominion of Rome. They insulted the aliens of the East who had renounced the dress and idiom of Romans, and their reasonable practice will justify the frequent appellation of Greeks.[101] But this contemptuous appellation was indignantly rejected by the prince and people to whom it is applied. Whatsoever changes had been introduced by the lapse of ages, they alleged a lineal and unbroken succession from Augustus and Constantine; and, in the lowest period of degeneracy and decay, the name of ROMANS adhered to the last fragments of the empire of Constantinople.[102]

While the government of the East was transacted in Latin, the Greek was the language of literature and philosophy, nor could the masters of this rich and perfect idiom be tempted to envy the borrowed learning and imitative taste of their Roman disciples. After the fall of Paganism, the loss of Syria and Egypt, and the extinction of the schools of Alexandria and Athens, the studies of the Greeks insensibly retired to some regular monasteries, and, above all, to the royal college of Constantinople, which was burnt in the reign of Leo the Isaurian.[103] In the pompous style of the age, the president of that foundation was named the Sun of Science; his twelve associates, the professors in the different arts and faculties, were the twelve signs of the zodiac; a library of thirty-six thousand five hundred volumes was open to their inquiries; and they could show an ancient manuscript of Homer, on a roll of parchment one hundred and twenty feet in length, the intestines, as it was fabled, of a prodigious serpent.[104] But the seventh and eighth centuries were a period of discord and darkness; the library was burnt, the college was abolished, the Iconoclasts are represented as the foes of antiquity, and a savage ignorance and contempt of letters has disgraced the princes of the Heraclean and Isaurian dynasties.[105]

In the ninth century we trace the first dawnings of the restoration of science.[106] After the fanaticism of the Arabs had subsided, the caliphs aspired to conquer the arts, rather than the provinces, of the empire: their liberal curiosity rekindled the emulation of the Greeks, brushed away the dust from their ancient libraries, and taught them to know and reward the philosophers, whose labours had been hitherto repaid by the pleasure of study and the pursuit of truth. The Cæsar Bardas, the uncle of Michael the Third, was the generous protector of letters, a title which alone has preserved his memory and excused his ambition. A particle of the treasures of his nephew was sometimes diverted from the indulgence of vice and folly; a school was opened in the palace of Magnaura, and the presence of Bardas excited the emulation of the masters and students. At their head was the philosopher Leo, archbishop of Thessalonica; his profound skill in astronomy and the mathematics was admired by the strangers of the East, and this occult science was magnified by vulgar credulity, which modestly supposes that all knowledge superior to its own must be the effect of inspiration or magic. At the pressing entreaty of the Cæsar, his friend, the celebrated Photius,[107] renounced the freedom of a secular and studious life, ascended the patriarchal throne, and was alternately excommunicated and absolved by the synods of the East and West. By the confession even of priestly hatred, no art or science, except poetry, was foreign to this universal scholar, who was deep in thought, indefatigable in reading, and eloquent in diction. Whilst he exercised the office of protospathaire, or captain of the guards, Photius was sent ambassador to the caliph of Bagdad.[108] The tedious hours of exile, perhaps of confinement, were beguiled by the hasty composition of his *Library*, a living monument of erudition and criticism. Two hundred and fourscore writers, historians, orators, philosophers, theologians, are reviewed without any regular method; he abridges their narrative or doctrine, appreciates their style and character, and judges even the fathers of the church with a discreet freedom which often breaks through the superstition of the times. The emperor Basil, who lamented the defects of his own education intrusted to the care of Photius his son and successor Leo the Philosopher, and the reign of that prince and of his son Constantine Porphyrogenitus forms one of the most prosperous eras of the Byzantine literature. By their munificence the treasures of antiquity were deposited in the Imperial library; by their pens, or those of their associates, they were imparted in such extracts and abridgments as might amuse the curiosity, without oppressing the indolence, of the public. Besides the *Basilics*, or code of laws, the arts of husbandry and war, of feeding or destroying the human species, were propagated with equal diligence; and the history of Greece and Rome was digested into fifty-three heads or titles, of which two only (of embassies, and of virtues and vices) have escaped the injuries of time. In every station the reader might contemplate the image of the past world, apply the lesson or warning of each page, and learn to admire, perhaps to imitate, the examples of a brighter period. I shall not expatiate on the works of the Byzantine Greeks, who, by the assiduous study of the ancients, have deserved, in some measure, the remembrance and gratitude of the moderns. The scholars of the present age may still enjoy the benefit of the philosophical commonplace-book of Stobæus, the grammatical and historic lexicon of Suidas, the Chiliads of Tzetzes, which comprise six hundred narratives in twelve thousand verses, and the commentaries on Homer of Eustathius archbishop of Thessalonica, who, from his horn of plenty, has poured the names and authorities of four hundred writers. From these originals, and from the numerous tribe of scholiasts and critics,[109] some estimate may be formed of the literary wealth of the twelfth century. Constantinople was enlightened by the genius of Homer and Demosthenes, of Aristotle and Plato; and in the enjoyment or neglect of our present riches we must envy the generation that could still peruse the history of Theopompus, the orations of Hyperides, the comedies of Menander,[110] and the odes of Alcæus and Sappho. The frequent labour of illustration attests not only the existence but the popularity of the Grecian classics; the general knowledge of the age may be deduced from the example of two learned females, the empress Eudocia and the princess Anna Comnena, who cultivated, in the purple, the arts of rhetoric and philosophy.[111] The vulgar dialect of the city was gross and barbarous: a more correct and elaborate style distinguished the discourse, or at least the compositions, of the church and palace, which sometimes affected to copy the purity of the Attic models.

In our modern education, the painful though necessary attainment of two languages which are no longer living may consume the time and damp the ardour of the youthful student. The poets and orators were long imprisoned in the barbarous dialects of our Western ancestors, devoid of harmony or grace; and their genius, without precept or example, was abandoned to the rude and native powers of their judgment and fancy. But the Greeks of Constantinople, after purging away the impurities of their vulgar speech, acquired the free use of their ancient language, the most happy composition of human art, and a familiar knowledge of the sublime masters who had pleased or instructed the first of nations. But these advantages only tend to aggravate the reproach and shame of a degenerate people. They held in their lifeless hands the riches of their fathers, without inheriting the spirit which had created and improved that sacred patrimony: they read, they praised, they compiled, but their languid souls seemed alike incapable of thought and action. In the revolution of ten centuries, not a single discovery was made to exalt the dignity or promote the happiness of mankind. Not a single idea has been added to the speculative systems of antiquity, and a succession of patient disciples became in their turn the dogmatic teachers of the next servile generation. Not a single composition of history, philosophy, or literature, has been saved from oblivion by the intrinsic beauties of style or sentiment, of original fancy, or

even of successful imitation. In prose, the least offensive of the Byzantine writers are absolved from censure by their naked and unpresuming simplicity: but the orators, most eloquent[112] in their own conceit, are the farthest removed from the models whom they affect to emulate. In every page our taste and reason are wounded by the choice of gigantic and obsolete words, a stiff and intricate phraseology, the discord of images, the childish play of false or unseasonable ornament, and the painful attempt to elevate themselves, to astonish the reader, and to involve a trivial meaning in the smoke of obscurity and exaggeration. Their prose is soaring to the vicious affectation of poetry: their poetry is sinking below the flatness and insipidity of prose. The tragic, epic, and lyric muses were silent and inglorious: the bards of Constantinople seldom rose above a riddle or epigram, a panegyric or tale; they forgot even the rules of prosody; and with the melody of Homer yet sounding in their ears, they confound all measure of feet and syllables in the impotent strains which have received the name of *political* or city verses.[113] The minds of the Greeks were bound in the fetters of a base and imperious superstition, which extends her dominion round the circle of profane science. Their understandings were bewildered in metaphysical controversy: in the belief of visions and miracles they had lost all principles of moral evidence, and their taste was vitiated by the homilies of the monks, an absurd medley of declamation and Scripture. Even these contemptible studies were no longer dignified by the abuse of superior talents: the leaders of the Greek church were humbly content to admire and copy the oracles of antiquity, nor did the schools or pulpit produce any rivals of the fame of Athanasius and Chrysostom.[114]

In all the pursuits of active and speculative life, the emulation of states and individuals is the most powerful spring of the efforts and improvements of mankind. The cities of ancient Greece were cast in the happy mixture of union and independence, which is repeated on a larger scale, but in a looser form, by the nations of modern Europe: the union of language, religion, and manners, which renders them the spectators and judges of each other's merit:[115] the independence of government and interest, which asserts their separate freedom, and excites them to strive for pre-eminence in the career of glory. The situation of the Romans was less favourable; yet in the early ages of the republic, which fixed the national character, a similar emulation was kindled among the states of Latium and Italy; and in the arts and sciences they aspired to equal or surpass their Grecian masters. The empire of the Cæsars undoubtedly checked the activity and progress of the human mind: its magnitude might indeed allow some scope for domestic competition; but when it was gradually reduced, at first to the East, and at last to Greece and Constantinople, the Byzantine subjects were degraded to an abject and languid temper, the natural effect of their solitary and insulated state. From the North they were oppressed by nameless tribes of barbarians, to whom they scarcely imparted the appellation of men. The language and religion of the more polished Arabs were an insurmountable bar to all social intercourse. The conquerors of Europe were their brethren in the Christian faith; but the speech of the Franks or Latins was unknown, their manners were rude, and they were rarely connected, in peace or war with the successors of Heraclius. Alone in the universe, the self-satisfied pride of the Greeks was not disturbed by the comparison of foreign merit; and it is no wonder if they fainted in the race, since they had neither competitors to urge their speed, nor judges to crown their victory. The nations of Europe and Asia were mingled by the expeditions to the Holy Land; and it is under the Comnenian dynasty that a faint emulation of knowledge and military virtue was rekindled in the Byzantine empire.

CHAPTER LIV

Origin and Doctrine of the Paulicians. Their Persecution by the Greek Emperors. Revolt in Armenia, etc. Transplantation into Thrace. Propagation in the West. The Seeds, Character, and Consequences of the Reformation.

IN the profession of Christianity the variety of national characters may be clearly distinguished. The natives of Syria and Egypt abandoned their lives to lazy and contemplative devotion: Rome again aspired to the dominion of the world; and the wit of the lively and loquacious Greeks was consumed in the disputes of metaphysical theology. The incomprehensible mysteries of the Trinity and Incarnation, instead of commanding their silent submission, were agitated in vehement and subtle controversies, which enlarged their faith at the expense, perhaps, of their charity and reason. From the council of Nice to the end of the seventh century, the peace and unity of the church was invaded by these spiritual wars; and so deeply did they affect the decline and fall of the empire, that the historian has too often been compelled to attend the synods, to explore the creeds, and to enumerate the sects, of this busy period of ecclesiastical annals. From the beginning of the eighth century to the last ages of the Byzantine empire the sound of controversy was seldom heard: curiosity was exhausted, zeal was fatigued, and in the decrees of six councils the articles of the Catholic faith had been irrevocably defined. The spirit of dispute, however vain and pernicious, requires some energy and exercise of the mental faculties; and the prostrate Greeks were content to fast, to pray, and to believe in blind obedience to the patriarch and his clergy. During a long dream of superstition the Virgin and the saints, their visions and miracles, their relics and images, were preached by the monks, and worshipped by the people; and the appellation of people might be extended, without injustice to the first ranks of civil society. At an unseasonable moment the Isaurian emperors attempted somewhat rudely to awaken their subjects: under their influence reason might obtain some proselytes, a far greater number was swayed by interest or fear; but the Eastern world embraced or deplored their visible deities, and the restoration of images was celebrated as the feast of orthodoxy. In this passive and unanimous state the ecclesiastical rulers were relieved from the toil, or deprived of the pleasure, of persecution. The Pagans had disappeared; the Jews were silent and obscure; the disputes with the Latins were rare and remote hostilities against a national enemy; and the sects of Egypt and Syria enjoyed a free toleration under the shadow of the Arabian caliphs. About the middle of the seventh century a branch of Manichæans was selected as the victims of spiritual tyranny: their patience was at length exasperated to despair and rebellion; and their exile has scattered over the West the seeds of reformation. These important events will justify some inquiry into the doctrine and story of the PAULICIANS[1] and, as they cannot plead for hemselves, our candid criticism will magnify he *good*, and abate or suspect the *evil*, that is eported by their adversaries.

The Gnostics, who had distracted the infancy, were oppressed by the greatness and authority of the church. Instead of emulating or surpassing the wealth, learning, and numbers of the Catholics, their obscure remnant vas driven from the capitals of the East and West, and confined to the villages and mountains along the borders of the Euphrates. Some vestige of the Marcionites may be detected in the fifth century;[2] but the numerous sects were finally lost in the odious name of the Manichæans: and these heretics, who presumed to reconcile the doctrines of Zoroaster and Christ, were pursued by the two religions with equal and unrelenting hatred. Under the grandson of Heraclius, in the neighbourhood of Samosata, more famous for the birth of Lucian than for the title of a Syrian kingdom, a reformer arose, esteemed by the *Paulicians* as the chosen messenger of truth. In his humble dwelling of Mananalis, Constantine entertained a deacon who returned from Syrian captivity, and received the inestimable gift of the New Testament, which was already concealed from the vulgar by the prudence of the Greek, and perhaps of the Gnostic, clergy.[3] These books became the measure of his studies and the rule of his faith; and the Catholics, who dispute his interpretation, acknowledge that his text was genuine and sincere. But he attached himself with peculiar devotion to the writings and character of St. Paul: the name of the Paulicians is derived by their enemies from some unknown and domestic teacher; but I am confident that they gloried in their affinity to the apostle of the Gentiles. His disciples, Titus, Timothy, Sylvanus, Tychichus, were represented by Constantine, and his fellow-labourers: the names of the apostolic churches were applied to the congregations which they assembled in Armenia and Cappadocia; and this innocent allegory revived the example and memory of the first ages. In the Gospel and the Epistles of St. Paul his faithful follower investigated the creed of primitive Christianity; and, whatever might be the success, a Protestant reader will applaud the spirit of the inquiry. But if the Scriptures of the Paulicians were pure, they were not perfect. Their founders rejected the two Epistles of St. Peter,[4] the apostle of the circumcision, whose dispute with their favourite for the observance of the law could not easily be forgiven.[5] They agreed with their Gnostic brethren in the universal contempt for the Old Testament, the books of Moses and the prophets, which have been consecrated by the decrees of the Catholic church. With equal boldness, and doubtless with more reason, Constantine, the new Sylvanus, disclaimed the visions which in so many bulky and splendid volumes had been published by the Oriental sects;[6] the fabulous productions of the Hebrew patriarchs and the sages of the East; the spurious gospels, epistles, and acts, which in the first age had overwhelmed the orthodox code; the theology of Manes, and the authors of the kindred heresies; and the thirty generations, or æons, which had been created by the fruitful fancy of Valentine. The Paulicians sincerely condemned the memory and opinions of the Manichæan sect, and complained of the injustice which impressed that invidious name on the simple votaries of St. Paul and of Christ.

Of the ecclesiastical chain, many links had been broken by the Paulician reformers; and their liberty was enlarged, as they reduced the number of masters at whose voice profane reason must bow to mystery and miracle. The early separation of the Gnostics had preceded the establishment of the Catholic worship; and against the gradual innovations of discipline and doctrine they were as strongly guarded by habit and aversion as by the silence of St. Paul and the evangelists. The objects which had been transformed by the magic of superstition appeared to the eyes of the Paulicians in their genuine and naked colours. An image made without hands was the common workmanship of a mortal artist, to whose skill alone the wood and canvas must be indebted for their merit or value. The miraculous relics were a heap of bones and ashes, destitute of life or virtue, or of any relation, perhaps, with the person to whom they were ascribed. The true and vivifying cross was a piece of sound or rotten timber; the body and blood of Christ, a loaf of bread and a cup of wine, the gifts of nature and the symbols of grace. The mother of God was degraded from her celestial honours and immaculate virginity; and the saints and angels were no longer solicited to exercise the laborious office of mediation in heaven and ministry upon earth. In the practice, or at least in the theory, of the sacraments, the Paulicians were inclined to abolish all visible objects of worship, and the words of the Gospel were, in their judgment, the baptism and communion of the faithful. They indulged a convenient latitude for the interpretation of Scripture: and as often as they were pressed by the literal sense, they could escape to the intricate mazes of figure and allegory. Their utmost diligence must have been employed to dissolve the connection between the Old and the New Testament; since they adored the latter as the oracles of God, and abhorred the former as the fabulous and absurd invention of men or demons. We cannot be surprised that they should have found in the Gospel the orthodox mystery of the Trinity: but instead of confessing the human nature and substantial sufferings of Christ, they amused their fancy with a celestial body that passed through the virgin like water through a pipe; with a fantastic crucifixion, that eluded the vain and impotent malice of the Jews. A creed thus simple and spiritual was not adapted to the genius of the times;[7] and the rational Christian, who might have been contented with the light yoke and easy burden of Jesus and his apostles, was justly offended that the Paulicians should dare to violate the unity of God, the first article of natural and revealed religion. Their belief and their trust was in the Father, of Christ, of the human soul, and of the invisible world. But they likewise held the eternity of matter; a stubborn and rebellious substance, the origin of a second principle, of an active being, who has created this visible world, and exercises his temporal reign till the final consummation of death and sin.[8] The appearances of moral and physical evil had established the two principles in the ancient philosophy and religion of the East, from whence this doctrine was transfused to the various swarms of the Gnostics. A thousand shades may be devised in the nature and character of *Ahriman*, from a rival god to a subordinate demon, from passion and frailty to pure and perfect malevolence: but, in spite of our efforts, the goodness and the power of Ormusd are placed at the opposite extremities of the line; and every step that approaches the one must recede in equal proportion from the other.[9]

The apostolic labours of Constantine-Sylvanus soon multiplied the number of his disciples, the secret recompense of spiritual ambition. The remnant of the Gnostic sects, and especially the Manichæans of Armenia, were united under his standard; many Catholics were converted or seduced by his arguments; and he preached with success in the regions of Pontus[10] and Cappadocia, which had long since imbibed the religion of Zoroaster. The Paulician teachers were distinguished only by

their Scriptural names, by the modest title of Fellow-pilgrims, by the austerity of their lives, their zeal or knowledge, and the credit of some extraordinary gifts of the Holy Spirit. But they were incapable of desiring, or at least of obtaining, the wealth and honours of the Catholic prelacy: such anti-Christian pride they bitterly censured: and even the rank of elders or presbyters was condemned as an institution of the Jewish synagogue. The new sect was loosely spread over the provinces of Asia Minor to the westward of the Euphrates; six of their principal congregations represented the churches to which St. Paul had addressed his epistles; and their founder chose his residence in the neighbourhood of Colonia,[11] in the same district of Pontus which had been celebrated by the altars of Bellona[12] and the miracles of Gregory.[13] After a mission of twenty-seven years, Sylvanus, who had retired from the tolerating government of the Arabs, fell a sacrifice to Roman persecution. The laws of the pious emperors, which seldom touched the lives of less odious heretics, proscribed without mercy or disguise the tenets, the books, and the persons of the Montanists and Manichæans: the books were delivered to the flames; and all who should presume to secrete such writings, or to profess such opinions, were devoted to an ignominious death.[14] A Greek minister, armed with legal and military powers, appeared at Colonia to strike the shepherd, and to reclaim, if possible, the lost sheep. By a refinement of cruelty, Simeon placed the unfortunate Sylvanus before a line of his disciples, who were commanded, as the price of their pardon and the proof of their repentance, to massacre their spiritual father. They turned aside from the impious office; the stones dropped from their filial hands; and of the whole number only one executioner could be found, a new David, as he is styled by the Catholics, who boldly overthrew the giant of heresy. This apostate, Justus was his name, again deceived and betrayed his unsuspecting brethren, and a new conformity to the acts of St. Paul may be found in the conversion of Simeon: like the apostle, he embraced the doctrine which he had been sent to persecute, renounced his honours and fortunes, and acquired among the Paulicians the fame of a missionary and a martyr. They were not ambitious of martyrdom,[15] but in a calamitous period of one hundred and fifty years their patience sustained whatever zeal could inflict; and power was insufficient to eradicate the obstinate vegetation of fanaticism and reason.

From the blood and ashes of the first victims a succession of teachers and congregations repeatedly arose: amidst their foreign hostilities they found leisure for domestic quarrels: they preached, they disputed, they suffered; and the virtues, the apparent virtues, of Sergius, in a pilgrimage of thirty-three years, are reluctantly confessed by the orthodox historians.[16] The native cruelty of Justinian the Second was stimulated by a pious cause; and he vainly hoped to extinguish, in a single conflagration, the name and memory of the Paulicians. By their primitive simplicity, their abhorrence of popular superstition, the Iconoclast princes might have been reconciled to some erroneous doctrines; but they themselves were exposed to the calumnies of the monks, and they chose to be the tyrants, lest they be accused as the accomplices, of the Manichæans. Such a reproach has sullied the clemency of Nicephorus, who relaxed in their favour the severity of the penal statutes, nor will his character sustain the honour of a more liberal motive. The feeble Michael the First, the rigid Leo the Armenian, were foremost in the race of persecution; but the prize must doubtless be adjudged to the sanguinary devotion of Theodora, who restored the images to the Oriental church. Her inquisitors explored the cities and mountains of the lesser Asia, and the flatterers of the empress have affirmed that, in a short reign, one hundred thousand Paulicians were extirpated by the sword, the gibbet, or the flames. Her guilt or merit has perhaps been stretched beyond the measure of truth: but if the account be allowed, it must be presumed that many simple Iconoclasts were punished under a more odious name; and that some who were driven from the church, unwillingly took refuge in the bosom of heresy.

The most furious and desperate of rebels are the sectaries of a religion long persecuted, and at length provoked. In a holy cause they are no longer susceptible of fear or remorse: the justice of their arms hardens them against the feelings of humanity; and they revenge their fathers' wrongs on the children of their tyrants. Such have been the Hussites of Bohemia and the Calvinists of France, and such, in the ninth century, were the Paulicians of Armenia and the adjacent provinces.[17] They were first awakened to the massacre of a governor and bishop, who exercised the Imperial mandate of converting or destroying the heretics; and the deepest recesses of Mount Argæus protected their independence and revenge. A more dangerous and consuming flame was kindled by the persecution of Theodora, and the revolt of Carbeas, a valiant Paulician, who commanded the guards of the general of the East. His father had been impaled by the Catholic inquisitors; and religion, or at least nature, might justify his desertion and revenge. Five thousand of his brethren were united by the same motives; they renounced the allegiance of anti-Christian Rome; a Saracen emir introduced Carbeas to the caliph; and the commander of the faithful extended his sceptre to the implacable enemy of the Greeks. In the mountains between Siwas and Trebizond he founded or fortified the city of Tephrice,[18] which is still occupied by a fierce and licentious people, and the neighbouring hills were covered with the Paulician fugitives, who now reconciled the use of the Bible and the sword. During more than thirty years Asia was afflicted by the calamities of foreign and domestic war: in their hostile inroads the disciples of St. Paul were joined with those of Mohammed; and the peaceful Christians, the aged parent and tender virgin, who were delivered into barbarous servitude, might justly accuse the intolerant spirit of their sovereign. So urgent was the mischief, so intolerable the shame, that even the dissolute Michael, the son of Theodora, was compelled to march in person against the Paulicians: he was defeated under the walls of Samosata; and the Roman emperor fled before the heretics whom his mother had condemned to the flames. The Saracens fought under the same banners, but the victory was ascribed to Carbeas; and the captive generals, with more than a hundred tribunes, were either released by his avarice or tortured by his fanaticism. The valour and ambition of Chrysocheir,[19] his successor, embraced a wider circle of rapine and revenge. In alliance with his faithful Moslems, he boldly penetrated into the heart of Asia; the troops of the frontier and the palace were repeatedly overthrown; the edicts of persecution were answered by the pillage of Nice and Nicomedia, of Ancyra and Ephesus; nor could the apostle St. John protect from violation his city and sepulchre. The cathedral of Ephesus was turned into a stable for mules and horses; and the Paulicians vied with the Saracens in their contempt and abhorrence of images and relics. It is not unpleasing to observe the triumph of rebellion over the same despotism which has disdained the prayers of an injured people. The emperor Basil, the Macedonian, was reduced to sue for peace, to offer a ransom for the captives, and to request, in the language of moderation and charity, that Chrysocheir would spare his fellow-Christians, and content himself with a royal donative of gold and silver and silk garments. "If the emperor," replied the insolent fanatic, "be desirous of peace, let him abdicate the East, and reign without molestation in the West. If he refuse, the servants of the Lord will precipitate him from the throne." The reluctant Basil suspended the treaty, accepted the defiance, and led his army into the land of heresy, which he wasted with fire and sword. The open country of the Paulicians was exposed to the same calamities which they had inflicted; but when he had explored the strength of Tephrice, the multitude of the barbarians, and the ample magazines of arms and provisions, he desisted with a sigh from the hopeless siege. On his return to Constantinople he laboured, by the foundation of convents and churches, to secure the aid of his celestial patrons, of Michael the archangel and the prophet Elijah; and it was his daily prayer that he might live to transpierce, with three arrows, the head of his impious adversary. Beyond his expectations, the wish was accomplished: after a successful inroad Chrysocheir was surprised and slain in his retreat; and the rebel's head was triumphantly presented at the foot of the throne. On the reception of this welcome trophy, Basil instantly called for his bow, discharged three arrows with unerring aim, and accepted the applause of the court, who hailed the victory of the royal archer. With Chrysocheir, the glory of the Paulicians faded and withered:[20] on the second expedition of the emperor, the impregnable Tephrice was deserted by the heretics, who sued for mercy or escaped to the borders. The city was ruined, but the spirit of independence survived in the mountains: the Paulicians defended, above a century, their religion and liberty, infested the Roman limits, and maintained their perpetual alliance with the enemies of the empire and the Gospel.

About the middle of the eighth century, Constantine, surnamed Copronymus by the worshippers of images, had made an expedition into Armenia, and found, in the cities of Melitene and Theodosiopolis, a great number of Paulicians, his kindred heretics. As a favour, or punishment, he transplanted them from the banks of the Euphrates to Constantinople and Thrace; and by this emigration their doctrine was introduced and diffused in Europe.[21] If the sectaries of the metropolis were soon mingled with the promiscuous mass, those of the country struck a deep root in a foreign soil. The Paulicians of Thrace resisted the storms of persecution, maintained a secret correspondence with their Armenian brethren, and gave aid and comfort to their preachers, who solicited, not without success, the infant faith of the Bulgarians.[22] In the tenth century they were restored and multiplied by a more powerful colony which John Zimisces[23] transported from the Chalybian hills to the valleys of Mount Hæmus. The Oriental clergy, who would have preferred the destruction, impatiently sighed for the absence, of the Manichæans: the warlike emperor had felt and esteemed their valour: their attachment to the Saracens was pregnant with mischief; but, on the side of the Danube, against the barbarians of Scythia, their service might be useful, and their loss would be desirable. Their exile in a distant land was softened by a free toleration: the Paulicians held the city of Philippopolis and the keys of Thrace; the Catholics were their subjects; the Jacobite emigrants their associates: they occupied a line of villages and castles in Macedonia and Epirus; and many native Bulgarians were associated to the communion of arms and heresy. As long as they were awed by power and treated with moderation, their voluntary bands were distinguished in the armies of the empire; and the courage of these *dogs*, ever greedy of war, ever thirsty of human blood, is noticed with astonishment, and almost with reproach, by the pusillanimous Greeks. The same spirit rendered them arrogant and contumacious: they were easily provoked by caprice or injury; and their privileges were often violated by the faithless bigotry of the government and clergy. In the midst of the Norman war, two thousand five hundred Manichæans deserted the standard of Alexius Comnenus,[24] and retired to their native homes. He dissembled till the moment of revenge; invited the chiefs to a friendly conference; and punished the innocent and guilty by imprisonment, confiscation, and baptism. In an interval of peace the emperor undertook the pious office of reconciling them to the church and state: his winter quarters were fixed at Philippopolis; and the thirteenth apostle, as he is styled by his pious daughter, consumed whole days and nights in theological controversy. His arguments were fortified, their obstinacy was melted, by the honours and rewards which he bestowed on the most eminent proselytes; and a new city, surrounded with gardens, enriched with immunities, and digni-

ed with his own name, was founded by
Alexius, for the residence of his vulgar converts.
The important station of Philippopolis was
wrested from their hands; the contumacious
leaders were secured in a dungeon, or banished
from their country; and their lives were
spared by the prudence, rather than the mercy,
of an emperor, at whose command a poor and
solitary heretic was burnt alive before the
church of St. Sophia.[25] But the proud hope of
eradicating the prejudices of a nation was
speedily overturned by the invincible zeal of
the Paulicians, who ceased to dissemble or refused to obey. After the departure and death of
Alexius they soon resumed their civil and religious laws. In the beginning of the thirteenth
century their pope or primate (a manifest corruption) resided on the confines of Bulgaria,
Croatia, and Dalmatia, and governed by his
vicars the filial congregations of Italy and
France.[26] From that era a minute scrutiny
might prolong and perpetuate the chain of
tradition. At the end of the last age the sect or
colony still inhabited the valleys of Mount
Hæmus, where their ignorance and poverty
were more frequently tormented by the Greek
clergy than by the Turkish government. The
modern Paulicians have lost all memory of
their origin; and their religion is disgraced by
the worship of the cross, and the practice of
bloody sacrifice, which some captives have imported from the wilds of Tartary.[27]

In the West the first teachers of the Mani-
hæan theology had been repulsed by the
people or suppressed by the prince. The favour
and success of the Paulicians in the eleventh
and twelfth centuries must be imputed to the
strong, though secret, discontent which armed
the most pious Christians against the church
of Rome. Her avarice was oppressive, her
despotism odious: less degenerate perhaps than
the Greeks in the worship of saints and images,
her innovations were more rapid and scandalous: she had rigorously defined and imposed
the doctrine of transubstantiation: the lives of
the Latin clergy were more corrupt, and the
Eastern bishops might pass for the successors
of the apostles if they were compared with the
lordly prelates who wielded by turns the
crosier, the sceptre, and the sword. Three different roads might introduce the Paulicians
into the heart of Europe. After the conversion
of Hungary the pilgrims who visited Jerusalem
might safely follow the course of the Danube:
in their journey and return they passed through
Philippopolis; and the sectaries, disguising

their name and heresy, might accompany the
French or German caravans to their respective
countries. The trade and dominion of Venice
pervaded the coast of the Adriatic, and the
hospitable republic opened her bosom to foreigners of every climate and religion. Under
the Byzantine standard the Paulicians were
often transported to the Greek provinces of
Italy and Sicily: in peace and war they freely
conversed with strangers and natives, and
their opinions were silently propagated in
Rome, Milan, and the kingdoms beyond the
Alps.[28] It was soon discovered that many thousand Catholics of every rank, and of either sex,
had embraced the Manichæan heresy; and
the flames which consumed twelve canons of
Orleans was the first act and signal of persecution. The Bulgarians,[29] a name so innocent in
its origin, so odious in its application, spread
their branches over the face of Europe. United
in common hatred of idolatry and Rome, they
were connected by a form of episcopal and
presbyterian government; their various sects
were discriminated by some fainter or darker
shades of theology; but they generally agreed
in the two principles—the contempt of the Old
Testament, and the denial of the body of Christ
either on the cross or in the eucharist. A confession of simple worship and blameless manners is extorted from their enemies; and so high
was their standard of perfection, that the increasing congregations were divided into two
classes of disciples, of those who practised and
of those who aspired. It was in the country of
the Albigeois,[30] in the southern provinces of
France, that the Paulicians were most deeply
implanted; and the same vicissitudes of martyrdom and revenge which had been displayed in
the neighbourhood of the Euphrates were repeated in the thirteenth century on the banks
of the Rhône. The laws of the Eastern emperors were revived by Frederic the Second.
The insurgents of Tephrice were represented by
the barons and cities of Languedoc: Pope Innocent III. surpassed the sanguinary fame
of Theodora. It was in cruelty alone that
her soldiers could equal the heroes of the
Crusades, and the cruelty of her priests was
far excelled by the founders of the Inquisition[31]—an office more adapted to confirm than
to refute the belief of an evil principle. The
visible assemblies of the Paulicians, or Albigeois, were extirpated by fire and sword; and
the bleeding remnant escaped by flight, con-
cealment, or Catholic conformity. But the invincible spirit which they had kindled still lived

and breathed in the Western world. In the state, in the church, and even in the cloister, a latent succession was preserved of the disciples of St. Paul, who protested against the tyranny of Rome, embraced the Bible as the rule of faith, and purified their creed from all the visions of the Gnostic theology. The struggles of Wickliff in England, of Huss in Bohemia, were premature and ineffectual; but the names of Zuinglius, Luther, and Calvin are pronounced with gratitude as the deliverers of nations.

A philosopher, who calculates the degree of their merit and the value of their reformation, will prudently ask from what articles of faith, *above* or *against* our reason, they have enfranchised the Christians; for such enfranchisement is doubtless a benefit so far as it may be compatible with truth and piety. After a fair discussion we shall rather be surprised by the timidity than scandalised by the freedom of our first reformers.[32] With the Jews, they adopted the belief and defence of all the Hebrew Scriptures, with all their prodigies, from the garden of Eden to the visions of the prophet Daniel; and they were bound, like the Catholics, to justify against the Jews the abolition of a divine law. In the great mysteries of the Trinity and Incarnation the reformers were severely orthodox: they freely adopted the theology of the four or the six first councils; and with the Athanasian creed they pronounced the eternal damnation of all who did not believe the Catholic faith. Transubstantiation, the invisible change of the bread and wine into the body and blood of Christ, is a tenet that may defy the power of argument and pleasantry; but instead of consulting the evidence of their senses, of their sight, their feeling, and their taste, the first Protestants were entangled in their own scruples, and awed by the words of Jesus in the institution of the sacrament. Luther maintained a *corporeal*, and Calvin a *real*, presence of Christ in the eucharist; and the opinion of Zuinglius, that it is no more than a spiritual communion, a simple memorial, has slowly prevailed in the reformed churches.[33] But the loss of one mystery was amply compensated by the stupendous doctrines of original sin, redemption, faith, grace, and predestination, which have been strained from the epistles of St. Paul. These subtle questions had most assuredly been prepared by the fathers and schoolmen; but the final improvement and popular use may be attributed to the first reformers, who enforced them as the absolute and essential terms of salvation. Hitherto the weight of supernatural belief inclines against the Protestants; and many a sober Christian would rather admit that a wafer is God than that God is a cruel and capricious tyrant.

Yet the services of Luther and his rivals are solid and important; and the philosopher must own his obligations to these fearless enthusiasts.[34] I. By their hands the lofty fabric of superstition, from the abuse of indulgences to the intercession of the Virgin, has been levelled with the ground. Myriads of both sexes of the monastic profession were restored to the liberty and labours of social life. A hierarchy of saints and angels, of imperfect and subordinate deities, were stripped of their temporal power and reduced to the enjoyment of celestial happiness: their images and relics were banished from the church; and the credulity of the people was no longer nourished with the daily repetition of miracles and visions. The imitation of paganism was supplied by a pure and spiritual worship of prayer and thanksgiving, the most worthy of man, the least unworthy of the Deity. It only remains to observe whether such sublime simplicity be consistent with popular devotion; whether the vulgar, in the absence of all visible objects, will not be inflamed by enthusiasm or insensibly subside in languor and indifference. II. The chain of authority was broken, which restrains the bigot from thinking as he pleases, and the slave from speaking as he thinks: the popes, fathers, and councils were no longer the supreme and infallible judges of the world; and each Christian was taught to acknowledge no law but the Scriptures, no interpreter but his own conscience. This freedom, however, was the consequence rather than the design of the Reformation. The patriot reformers were ambitious of succeeding the tyrants whom they had dethroned. They imposed with equal rigour their creeds and confessions; they asserted the right of the magistrate to punish heretics with death. The pious or personal animosity of Calvin proscribed in Servetus[35] the guilt of his own rebellion;[36] and the flames of Smithfield, in which he was afterwards consumed, had been kindled for the Anabaptists by the zeal of Cranmer.[37] The nature of the tiger was the same, but he was gradually deprived of his teeth and fangs. A spiritual and temporal kingdom was possessed by the Roman pontiff; the Protestant doctors were subjects of a humble rank, without revenue or jurisdiction. *His* decrees were consecrated by the antiquity of the Catholic church; *their* arguments and disputes were submitted to the people; and their appeal to private judgment was accepted, beyond their wishes, by curiosity and enthusiasm. Since the days of Luther and Calvin a secret reformation has been silently working in the bosom of the reformed churches; many weeds of prejudice were eradicated; and the disciples of Erasmus[38] diffused a spirit of freedom and moderation. The liberty of conscience has been claimed as a common benefit, an inalienable right:[39] the free governments of Holland[40] and England[41] introduced the practice of toleration; and the narrow allowance of the laws has been enlarged by the prudence and humanity of the times. In the exercise the mind has understood the limits of its powers, and the words and shadows that might amuse the child can no longer satisfy his manly reason. The volumes of controversy are overspread with cobwebs: the doctrine of a Protestant church is far removed from the knowledge or belief of its private members; and the forms of orthodoxy, the articles of faith, are subscribed with a sigh, or a smile, by the modern clergy. Yet the friends of Christianity are alarmed at the boundless impulse of inquiry and scepticism. The predictions of the Catholics are accomplished: the web of mystery is unravelled by the Armenians, Arians, and Socinians, whose numbers must not be computed from their separate congregations; and the pillars of Revelation are shaken by those men who preserve the name without the substance of religion, who indulge the licence without the temper of philosophy.[42]

CHAPTER LV

The Bulgarians. Origin, Migrations, and Settlement of the Hungarians. Their Inroads in the East and West. The Monarchy of Russia. Geography and Trade. Wars of the Russians against the Greek Empire. Conversion of the Barbarians.

UNDER the reign of Constantine, the grandson of Heraclius, the ancient barrier of the Danube, so often violated and so often restored, was irretrievably swept away by a new deluge of barbarians. Their progress was favoured by the caliphs, their unknown and accidental auxiliaries: the Roman legions were occupied in Asia; and after the loss of Syria, Egypt, and Africa, the Cæsars were twice reduced to the danger and disgrace of defending their capital against the Saracens. If, in the account of this interesting people, I have deviated from the strict and original line of my undertaking, the merit of the subject will hide my transgression, or solicit my excuse. In the East, in the West, in war, in religion, in science, in their prosperity, and in their decay, the Arabians press themselves on our curiosity: the first overthrow of the church and empire of the Greeks may be imputed to their arms; and the disciples of Mohammed still hold the civil and religious sceptre of the Oriental world. But the same labour would be unworthily bestowed on the swarms of savages who, between the seventh and the twelfth century, descended from the plains of Scythia, in transient inroad or perpetual emigration.[1] Their names are uncouth, their origins doubtful, their actions obscure, their superstition was blind, their valour brutal, and the uniformity of their public and private lives was neither softened by innocence nor refined by policy. The majesty of the Byzantine throne repelled and survived their disorderly attacks; the greater part of these barbarians has disappeared without leaving any memorial of their existence, and the despicable remnant continues, and may long continue, to groan under the dominion of a foreign tyrant. From the antiquities of, I. *Bulgarians*, II. *Hungarians*, and, III. *Russians*, I shall content myself with selecting such facts as yet deserve to be remembered. The conquests of the, IV. NORMANS, and the monarchy of the, V. TURKS, will naturally terminate in the memorable Crusades to the Holy Land and the double fall of the city and empire of Constantine.

I. In his march to Italy, Theodoric,[2] the Ostrogoth, had trampled on the arms of the Bulgarians. After this defeat the name and the nation are lost during a century and a half; and it may be suspected that the same or a similar appellation was revived by strange colonies from the Borysthenes, the Tanais, or the Volga. A king of the ancient Bulgaria[3] bequeathed to his five sons a last lesson of moderation and concord. It was received as youth has ever received the counsels of age and experience: the five princes buried their father; divided his subjects and cattle; forgot his advice; separated from each other; and wandered in quest of fortune, till we find the most adventurous in the heart of Italy, under the protection of the exarch of Ravenna.[4] But the stream of emigration was directed or impelled towards the capital. The modern Bulgaria, along the southern banks of the Danube, was stamped with the name and image which it was retained to the present hour: the new conquerors successively acquired, by war or treaty, the Roman provinces of Dardania, Thessaly, and the two Epirus';[5] the ecclesiastical supremacy was translated from the native city of Justinian; and, in their prosperous age, the obscure town of Lychnidus, or Achrida, was honoured with the throne of a king and a patriarch.[6] The unquestionable evidence of language attests the descent of the Bulgarians from the original stock of the Sclavonian, or more properly Slavonian, race;[7] and the kindred bands of Servians, Bosnians, Rascians, Croatians, Wallachians,[8] etc., followed either the standard or the example of the leading tribe. From the Euxine to the Adriatic, in the state of captives, or subjects, or allies, or enemies, of the Greek empire, they overspread the land; and the national appellation of the SLAVES[9] has been degraded by chance or malice from the signification of glory to that of servitude.[10] Among these colonies, the Chrobatians,[11] or Croats, who now attend the motions of an Austrian army, are the descendants of a mighty people, the conquerors and sovereigns of Dalmatia. The maritime cities, and of these the infant republic of Ragusa, implored the aid and instructions of the Byzantine court: they were advised by the magnanimous Basil to reserve a small acknowledgment of their fidelity to the Roman empire, and to appease, by an annual tribute, the wrath of these irresistible barbarians. The kingdom of Croatia was shared by eleven *Zoupans*, or feudatory lords; and their united forces were numbered at sixty thousand horse and one hundred thousand foot. A long sea-coast, indented with capacious harbours, covered with a string of islands, and almost in sight of the Italian shores, disposed both the natives and strangers to the practice of navigation. The boats or brigantines of the Croats were constructed after the fashion of the old Liburnians: one hundred and eighty vessels may excite the idea of a respectable navy; but our seamen will smile at the allowance of ten, or twenty, or forty men, for each of these ships of war. They were gradually converted to the more honourable service of commerce; yet the Sclavonian pirates were still frequent and dangerous; and it was not before the close of the tenth century that the freedom and sovereignty of the Gulf were effectually vindicated by the Venetian republic.[12] The ancestors of these Dalmatian kings were equally removed from the use and abuse of navigation: they dwelt in the White Croatia, in the inland regions of Silesia and Little Poland, thirty days' journey, according to the Greek computation, from the sea of darkness.

The glory of the Bulgarians[13] was confined to a narrow scope both of time and place. In the ninth and tenth centuries they reigned to the south of the Danube, but the more powerful nations that had followed their emigration repelled all return to the north and all progress to the west. Yet in the obscure catalogue of their exploits they might boast an honour which had hitherto been appropriated to the Goths, that of slaying in battle one of the successors of Augustus and Constantine. The emperor Nicephorus had lost his fame in the Arabian, he lost his life in the Sclavonian, war. In the first operations he advanced with boldness and success into the centre of Bulgaria, and burnt the *royal court*, which was probably no more than an edifice and village of timber. But while he searched the spoil and refused all offers of treaty, his enemies collected their spirits and their forces; the passes of retreat were insuperably barred, and the trembling Nicephorus was heard to exclaim, "Alas, alas! unless we could assume the wings of birds, we cannot hope to escape." Two days he waited his fate in the inactivity of despair, but, on the morning of the third, the Bulgarians surprised the camp, and the Roman prince, with the great officers of the empire, were slaughtered in their tents. The body of Valens had been saved from insult, but the head of Nicephorus was exposed on a spear, and his skull, enchased with gold, was often replenished in the feasts of victory. The Greeks bewailed the dishonour of the throne, but they acknowledged the just punishment of avarice and cruelty. This savage cup was deeply tinctured with the manners of the Scythian wilderness, but they were softened before the end of the same century by a peaceful intercourse with the Greeks, the possession of a cultivated region, and the introduction of the Christian worship. The nobles of Bulgaria were educated in the schools and palace of Constantinople, and Simeon,[14] a youth of the royal line, was instructed in the rhetoric of

Demosthenes and the logic of Aristotle. He relinquished the profession of a monk for that of a king and warrior, and in his reign of more than forty years Bulgaria assumed a rank among the civilised powers of the earth. The Greeks, whom he repeatedly attacked, derived a faint consolation from indulging themselves in the reproaches of perfidy and sacrilege. They purchased the aid of the pagan Turks, but Simeon, in a second battle, redeemed the loss of the first, at a time when it was esteemed a victory to elude the arms of that formidable nation. The Servians were overthrown, made captive, and dispersed; and those who visited the country before their restoration could discover no more than fifty vagrants, without women or children, who extorted a precarious subsistence from the chase. On classic ground, on the banks of the Achelöus, the Greeks were defeated: their horn was broken by the strength of the barbaric Hercules.[15] He formed the siege of Constantinople, and, in a personal conference with the emperor, Simeon imposed the conditions of peace. They met with the most jealous precautions: the royal galley was drawn close to an artificial and well-fortified platform, and the majesty of the purple was emulated by the pomp of the Bulgarian. "Are you a Christian?" said the humble Romanus; "It is your duty to abstain from the blood of your fellow-Christians. Has the thirst of riches seduced you from the blessings of peace? Sheathe your sword, open your hand, and I will satiate the utmost measure of your desires." The reconciliation was sealed by a domestic alliance; the freedom of trade was granted or restored; the first honours of the court were secured to the friends of Bulgaria, above the ambassadors of enemies or strangers;[16] and her princes were dignified with the high and invidious title of *Basileus*, or emperor. But this friendship was soon disturbed: after the death of Simeon the nations were again in arms, his feeble successors were divided and extinguished, and, in the beginning of the eleventh century, the second Basil, who was born in the purple, deserved the appellation of conqueror of the Bulgarians. His avarice was in some measure gratified by a treasure of four hundred thousand pounds sterling (ten thousand pounds weight of gold), which he found in the palace of Lychnidus. His cruelty inflicted a cool and exquisite vengeance on fifteen thousand captives who had been guilty of the defence of their country. They were deprived of sight, but to one of each hundred a single eye was left, that he might conduct his blind century to the presence of their king. Their king is said to have expired of grief and horror; the nation was awed by this terrible example; the Bulgarians were swept away from their settlements, and circumscribed within a narrow province; the surviving chiefs bequeathed to the children the advice of patience and the duty of revenge.

II. When the black swarm of Hungarians first hung over Europe, about nine hundred years after the Christian era, they were mistaken by fear and superstition for the Gog and Magog of the Scriptures, the signs and forerunners of the end of the world.[17] Since the introduction of letters they have explored their own antiquities with a strong and laudable impulse of patriotic curiosity.[18] Their rational criticism can no longer be amused with a vain pedigree of Attila and the Huns: but they complain that their primitive records have perished in the Tartar war; that the truth or fiction of their rustic songs is long since forgotten; and that the fragments of a rude chronicle[19] must be painfully reconciled with the contemporary though foreign intelligence of the Imperial geographer.[20] *Magyar* is the national and oriental denomination of the Hungarians; but, among the tribes of Scythia, they are distinguished by the Greeks under the proper and peculiar name of *Turks*, as the descendants of that mighty people who had conquered and reigned from China to the Volga. The Pannonian colony preserved a correspondence of trade and amity with the eastern Turks on the confines of Persia; and after a separation of three hundred and fifty years the missionaries of the king of Hungary discovered and visited their ancient country near the banks of the Volga. They were hospitably entertained by a people of pagans and savages who still bore the name of Hungarians; conversed in their native tongue, recollected a tradition of their long-lost brethren, and listened with amazement to the marvellous tale of their new kingdom and religion. The zeal of conversion was animated by the interest of consanguinity, and one of the greatest of their princes had formed the generous, though fruitless, design of replenishing the solitude of Pannonia by this domestic colony from the heart of Tartary.[21] From this primitive country they were driven to the West by the tide of war and emigration, by the weight of the more distant tribes, who at the same time were fugitives and conquerors. Reason or fortune directed their course towards the frontiers of the Roman empire; they halted in the usual stations along the banks of the great rivers; and in the territories of Moscow, Kiow, and Moldavia, some vestiges have been discovered of their temporary residence. In this long and various peregrination they could not always escape the dominion of the stronger, and the purity of their blood was improved or sullied by the mixture of a foreign race; from a motive of compulsion or choice, several tribes of the Chazars were associated to the standard of their ancient vassals, introduced the use of a second language, and obtained by their superior renown the most honourable place in the front of battle. The military force of the Turks and their allies marched in seven equal and artificial divisions: each division was formed of thirty thousand eight hundred and fifty-seven warriors, and the proportion of women, children, and servants supposes and requires at least a million of emigrants. Their public counsels were directed by seven *vayvods*, or hereditary chiefs; but the experience of discord and weakness recommended the more simple and vigorous administration of a single person. The sceptre, which had been declined by the modest Lebedias, was granted to the birth or merit of Almus and his son Arpad, and the authority of the supreme khan of the Chazars confirmed the engagement of the prince and people; of the people to obey his commands, of the prince to consult their happiness and glory.

With this narrative we might be reasonably content, if the penetration of modern learning had not opened a new and larger prospect of the antiquities of nations. The Hungarian language stands alone, and as it were insulated, among the Sclavonian dialects; but it bears a close and clear affinity to the idioms of the Fennic race,[22] of an obsolete and savage race, which formerly occupied the northern regions of Asia and Europe. The genuine appellation of *Ugri* or *Igours* is found on the western confines of China;[23] their migration to the banks of the Irtish is attested by Tartar evidence;[24] a similar name and language are detected in the southern parts of Siberia;[25] and the remains of the Fennic tribes are widely, though thinly, scattered from the sources of the Oby to the shores of Lapland.[26] The consanguinity of the Hungarians and Laplanders would display the powerful energy of climate on the children of a common parent; the lively contrast between the bold adventurers who are intoxicated with the wines of the Danube, and the wretched fugitives who are immersed beneath the snows of the polar circle. Arms and freedom have ever been the ruling, though too often the unsuccessful, passion of the Hungarians, who are endowed by nature with a vigorous constitution of soul and body.[27] Extreme cold has diminished the stature and congealed the faculties of the Laplanders; and the Arctic tribes, alone among the sons of men, are ignorant of war and unconscious of human blood: a happy ignorance, if reason and virtue were the guardians of their peace![28]

It is the observation of the Imperial author of the Tactics,[29] that all the Scythian hordes resembled each other in their pastoral and military life, that they all practised the same means of subsistence, and employed the same instruments of destruction. But he adds that the two nations of Bulgarians and Hungarians were superior to their brethren, and similar to each other, in the improvements, however rude, of their discipline and government: their visible likeness determines Leo to confound his friends and enemies in one common description; and the picture may be heightened by some strokes from their contemporaries of the tenth century. Except the merit and fame of military prowess, all that is valued by mankind appeared vile and contemptible to these barbarians, whose native fierceness was stimulated by the consciousness of numbers and freedom. The tents of the Hungarians were of leather, their garments of fur; they shaved their hair and scarified their faces: in speech they were slow, in action prompt, in treaty perfidious; and they shared the common reproach of barbarians, too ignorant to conceive the importance of truth, too proud to deny or palliate the breach of their most solemn engagements. Their simplicity has been praised; yet they abstained only from the luxury they had never known: whatever they saw they coveted; their desires were insatiate, and their sole industry was the hand of violence and rapine. By the definition of a pastoral nation I have recalled a long description of the economy, the warfare, and the government that prevail in that state of society; I may add, that to fishing as well as to the chase the Hungarians were indebted for a part of their subsistence; and since they *seldom* cultivated the ground, they must, at least in their new settlements, have sometimes practised a slight and unskilful husbandry. In their emigrations, perhaps in their expeditions, the host was accompanied by thousands of sheep and oxen, which increased the cloud of formidable dust, and afforded a constant and wholesome supply of milk and animal food. A plentiful command of forage was the first care of the general; and if the flocks and herds were secure of their pastures, the hardy warrior was alike insensible of danger and fatigue. The confusion of men and cattle that overspread the country exposed their camp to a nocturnal surprise, had not a still wider circuit been occupied by their light cavalry, perpetually in motion to discover and delay the approach of the enemy. After some experience of the Roman tactics, they adopted the use of the sword and spear, the helmet of the soldier, and the iron breastplate of his steed: but their native and deadly weapon was the Tartar bow: from the earliest infancy their children and servants were exercised in the double science of archery and horsemanship; their arm was strong; their aim was sure; and in the most rapid career they were taught to throw themselves backwards, and to shoot a volley of arrows into the air. In open combat, in secret ambush, in flight, or pursuit, they were equally formidable: an appearance of order was maintained in the foremost ranks, but their charge was driven forwards by the impatient pressure of succeeding crowds. They pursued, headlong and rash, with loosened reins and horrific outcries; but, if they fled, with real or dissembled fear, the ardour of a pursuing foe was checked and chastised by the same habits of irregular speed and sudden evolution. In the abuse of victory they astonished Europe, yet smarting from the wounds of the Saracen and the Dane: mercy they rarely asked, and more rarely bestowed: both sexes were accused as equally inaccessible to pity; and their appetite for raw flesh might countenance the popular tale that they drank the blood and feasted on the hearts of the slain. Yet the Hungarians were not devoid of those principles of justice and humanity which nature has implanted in every bosom. The licence of public and private injuries was restrained by laws and punishments; and in the security of an open camp, theft is the most tempting and most dangerous offence. Among the barbarians there were many whose spontaneous virtue supplied their laws and corrected their manners, who performed the duties, and sympathised with the affections, of social life.

After a long pilgrimage of flight or victory, the Turkish hordes approached the common limits of the French and Byzantine empires. Their first conquests and final settlements extended on either side of the Danube above Vienna, below Belgrade, and beyond the measure of the Roman province, or the modern kingdom of Hungary.[30] That ample and fertile land was loosely occupied by the Moravians, a Sclavonian name and tribe, which were driven by the invaders into the compass of a narrow province. Charlemagne had stretched a vague and nominal empire as far as the edge of Transylvania; but, after the failure of his legitimate line, the dukes of Moravia forgot their obedience and tribute to the monarchs of Oriental France. The bastard Arnulph was provoked to invite the arms of the Turks: they rushed through the real or figurative wall which his indiscretion had thrown open; and the king of Germany has been justly reproached as a traitor to the civil and ecclesiastical society of the Christians. During the life of Arnulph the Hungarians were checked by gratitude or fear; but in the infancy of his son Lewis they discovered and invaded Bavaria; and such was their Scythian speed, that in a single day a circuit of fifty miles was stripped and consumed. In the battle of Augsburg the Christians maintained their advantage till the seventh hour of the day: they were deceived and vanquished by the flying stratagems of the Turkish cavalry. The conflagration spread over the provinces of Bavaria, Swabia, and Franconia; and the Hungarians[31] promoted the reign of anarchy by forcing the stoutest barons to discipline their vassals and fortify their castles.

The origin of walled towns is ascribed to their calamitous period; nor could any distance be secure against an enemy, who, almost at the same instant, laid in ashes the Helvetian monastery of St. Gall, and the city of Bremen on the shores of the northern ocean. Above thirty years the Germanic empire, or kingdom, was subject to the ignominy of tribute; and resistance was disarmed by the menace, the serious and effectual menace, of dragging the women and children into captivity, and of slaughtering the males above the age of ten years. I have neither power nor inclination to follow the Hungarians beyond the Rhine; but I must observe with surprise that the southern provinces of France were blasted by the tempest, and that Spain, behind her Pyrenees, was astonished at the approach of these formidable strangers.[32] The vicinity of Italy had tempted their early inroads; but from their camp on the Brenta they beheld with some terror the apparent strength and populousness of the newdiscovered country. They requested leave to retire; their request was proudly rejected by the Italian king; and the lives of twenty thousand Christians paid the forfeit of his obstinacy and rashness. Among the cities of the West the royal

Pavia was conspicuous in fame and splendour; and the pre-eminence of Rome itself was only derived from the relics of the apostles. The Hungarians appeared; Pavia was in flames; forty-three churches were consumed; and, after the massacre of the people, they spared about two hundred wretches who had gathered some bushels of gold and silver (a vague exaggeration) from the smoking ruins of their country. In these annual excursions from the Alps to the neighbourhood of Rome and Capua, the churches that yet escaped resounded with a fearful litany: "Oh, save and deliver us from the arrows of the Hungarians!" But the saints were deaf or inexorable; and the torrent rolled forwards, till it was stopped by the extreme land of Calabria.[33] A composition was offered and accepted for the head of each Italian subject; and ten bushels of silver were poured forth in the Turkish camp. But falsehood is the natural antagonist of violence; and the robbers were defrauded both in the numbers of the assess· ment and the standard of the metal. On the side of the East the Hungarians were opposed in doubtful conflict by the equal arms of the Bulgarians, whose faith forbade an alliance with the pagans, and whose situation formed the barrier of the Byzantine empire. The barrier was overturned; the emperor of Constantinople beheld the waving banners of the Turks; and one of their boldest warriors presumed to strike a battle-axe into the golden gate. The arts and treasures of the Greeks diverted the assault; but the Hungarians might boast in their retreat that they had imposed a tribute on the spirit of Bulgaria and the majesty of the Cæsars.[34] The remote and rapid operations of the same campaign appear to magnify the power and numbers of the Turks; but their courage is most deserving of praise, since a light troop of three or four hundred horses would often attempt and execute the most daring inroads to the gates of Thessalonica and Constantinople. At this disastrous era of the ninth and tenth centuries, Europe was afflicted by a triple scourge from the North, the East, and the South: the Norman, the Hungarian, and the Saracen sometimes trod the same ground of desolation; and these savage foes might have been compared by Homer to the two lions growling over the carcase of a mangled stag.[35]

The deliverance of Germany and Christendom was achieved by the Saxon princes, Henry the Fowler and Otho the Great, who, in two memorable battles, forever broke the power of the Hungarians.[36] The valiant Henry was roused from a bed of sickness by the invasion of his country, but his mind was vigorous and his prudence successful. "My companions," said he, on the morning of the combat, "maintain your ranks, receive on your bucklers the first arrows of the pagans, and prevent their second discharge by the equal and rapid career of your lances." They obeyed and conquered; and the historical picture of the castles of Merseburgh expressed the features, or at least the character, of Henry, who, in an age of ignorance, intrusted to the finer arts the perpetuity of his name.[37] At the end of twenty years the children of the Turks who had fallen by his sword invaded the empire of his son, and their force is defined, in the lowest estimate, at one hundred thousand horse. They were invited by domestic faction; the gates of Germany were treacherously unlocked, and they spread, far beyond the Rhine and the Meuse, into the heart of Flanders. But the vigour and prudence of Otho dispelled the conspiracy; the princes were made sensible that, unless they were true to each other, their religion and country were irrecoverably lost, and the national powers were reviewed in the plains of Augsburg. They marched and fought in eight legions, according to the division of provinces and tribes: the first, second, and third were composed of Bavarians, the fourth of Franconians, the fifth of Saxons under the immediate command of the monarch, the sixth and seventh consisted of Swabians, and the eighth legion, of a thousand Bohemians, closed the rear of the host. The resources of discipline and valour were fortified by the arts of superstition, which, on this occasion, may deserve the epithets of generous and salutary. The soldiers were purified with a fast, the camp was blessed with the relics of saints and martyrs, and the Christian hero girded on his side the sword of Constantine, grasped the invincible spear of Charlemagne, and waved the banner of St. Maurice, the præfect of the Thebæan legion. But his firmest confidence was placed in the holy lance,[38] whose point was fashioned of the nails of the cross, and which his father had extorted from the king of Burgundy by the threats of war and the gift of a province. The Hungarians were expected in the front; they secretly passed the Lech, a river of Bavaria that falls into the Danube, turned the rear of the Christian army, plundered the baggage, and disordered the legions of Bohemia and Swabia. The battle was restored by the Franconians, whose duke, the valiant Conrad, was pierced with an arrow as he rested from his fatigues;

the Saxons fought under the eyes of their king, and his victory surpassed, in merit and importance, the triumphs of the last two hundred years. The loss of the Hungarians was still greater in the flight than in the action; they were encompassed by the rivers of Bavaria, and their past cruelties excluded them from the hope of mercy. Three captive princes were hanged at Ratisbon, the multitude of prisoners was slain or mutilated, and the fugitives who presumed to appear in the face of their country were condemned to everlasting poverty and disgrace.[39] Yet the spirit of the nation was humbled, and the most accessible passes of Hungary were fortified with a ditch and rampart. Adversity suggested the counsels of moderation and peace: the robbers of the West acquiesced in a sedentary life; and the next generation was taught, by a discerning prince, that far more might be gained by multiplying and exchanging the produce of a fruitful soil. The native race, with new colonies of Scythian or Sclavonian origin:[40] many thousands of robust and industrious captives had been imported from all the countries of Europe;[41] and after the marriage of Geisa with a Bavarian princess, he bestowed honours and estates on the nobles of Germany.[42] The son of Geisa was invested with the regal title, and the house of Arpad reigned three hundred years in the kingdom of Hungary. But the freeborn barbarians were not dazzled by the lustre of the diadem, and the people asserted their indefeasible right of choosing, deposing, and punishing the hereditary servant of the state.

III. The name of RUSSIANS[43] was first divulged, in the ninth century, by an embassy from Theophilus, emperor of the East, to the emperor of the West, Lewis, the son of Charlemagne. The Greeks were accompanied by the envoys of the great duke, or chagan, or *czar* of the Russians. In their journey to Constantinople they had traversed many hostile nations, and they hoped to escape the dangers of their return by requesting the French monarch to transport them by sea to their native country. A closer examination detected their origin: they were the brethren of the Swedes and Normans, whose name was already odious and formidable in France; and it might justly be apprehended that these Russian strangers were not the messengers of peace, but the emissaries of war. They were detained, while the Greeks were dismissed; and Lewis expected a more satisfactory account, that he might obey the laws of hos-

pitality or prudence according to the interest of both empires.[44] This Scandinavian origin of the people, or at least the princes, of Russia, may be confirmed and illustrated by the national annals[45] and the general history of the North. The Normans, who had so long been concealed by a veil of impenetrable darkness, suddenly burst forth in the spirit of naval and military enterprise. The vast, and, as it is said, the populous, regions of Denmark, Sweden, and Norway were crowded with independent chieftains and desperate adventurers, who sighed in the laziness of peace, and smiled in the agonies of death. Piracy was the exercise, the trade, the glory, and the virtue of the Scandinavian youth. Impatient of a bleak climate and narrow limits, they started from the banquet, grasped their arms, sounded their horn, ascended the vessels, and explored every coast that promised either spoil or settlement. The Baltic was the first scene of their naval achievements; they visited the eastern shores, the silent residence of Fennic and Sclavonian tribes; and the primitive Russians of the lake Ladoga paid a tribute, the skins of white squirrels, to these strangers, whom they saluted with the title of *Varangians*[46] or Corsairs. Their superiority in arms, discipline, and renown commanded the fear and reverence of the natives. In their wars against the more inland savages the Varangians condescended to serve as friends and auxiliaries, and gradually, by choice or conquest, obtained the dominion of a people whom they were qualified to protect. Their tyranny was expelled, their valour was again recalled, till at length Ruric, a Scandinavian chief, became the father of a dynasty which reigned above seven hundred years. His brothers extended his influence; the example of service and usurpation was imitated by his companions in the southern provinces of Russia; and their establishments, by the usual methods of war and assassination, were cemented into the fabric of a powerful monarchy.

As long as the descendants of Ruric were considered as aliens and conquerors, they ruled by the sword of the Varangians, distributed estates and subjects to their faithful captains, and supplied their numbers with fresh streams of adventurers from the Baltic coast.[47] But when the Scandinavian chiefs had struck a deep and permanent root into the soil, they mingled with the Russians in blood, religion, and language, and the first Waladimir had the merit of delivering his country from these foreign mercenaries. They had seated him on the throne; his riches were insufficient to satisfy their demands; but they listened to his pleasing advice, that they should seek, not a more grateful, but a more wealthy, master; that they should embark for Greece, where, instead of the skins of squirrels, silk and gold would be the recompense of their service. At the same time the Russian prince admonished his Byzantine ally to disperse and employ, to recompense and restrain, these impetuous children of the North. Contemporary writers have recorded the introduction, name, and character of the *Varangians*: each day they rose in confidence and esteem; the whole body was assembled at Constantinople to perform the duty of guards; and their strength was recruited by a numerous band of their countrymen from the island of Thule. On this occasion the vague appellation of Thule is applied to England; and the new Varangians were a colony of English and Danes who fled from the yoke of the Norman conqueror. The habits of pilgrimage and piracy had approximated the countries of the earth; these exiles were entertained in the Byzantine court; and they preserved, till the last age of the empire, the inheritance of spotless loyalty, and the use of the Danish or English tongue. With their broad and double-edged battle-axes on their shoulders, they attended the Greek emperor to the temple, the senate, and the hippodrome; he slept and feasted under their trusty guard; and the keys of the palace, the treasury, and the capital, were held by the firm and faithful hands of the Varangians.[48]

In the tenth century the geography of Scythia was extended far beyond the limits of ancient knowledge; and the monarchy of the Russians obtains a vast and conspicuous place in the map of Constantine.[49] The sons of Ruric were masters of the spacious province of Wolodomir, or Moscow; and, if they were confined on that side by the hordes of the East, their Western frontier in those early days was enlarged to the Baltic Sea and the country of the Prussians. Their northern reign ascended above the sixtieth degree of latitude, over the Hyperborean regions, which fancy had peopled with monsters, or clouded with eternal darkness. To the south they followed the course of the Borysthenes, and approached with that river the neighbourhood of the Euxine Sea. The tribes that dwelt, or wandered, in this ample circuit were obedient to the same conqueror, and insensibly blended into the same nation. The language of Russia is a dialect of the Sclavonian; but in the tenth century these two modes of speech were different from each other; and, as the Sclavonians prevailed in the South, it may be presumed that the original Russians of the North, the primitive subjects of the Varangian chief, were a portion of the Fennic race. With the emigration, union, or dissolution of the wandering tribes, the loose and indefinite picture of the Scythian desert has continually shifted. But the most ancient map of Russia affords some places which still retain their name and position; and the two capitals, Novogorod[50] and Kiow,[51] are coeval with the first age of the monarchy. Novogorod had not yet deserved the epithet of great, nor the alliance of the Hanseatic League, which diffused the streams of opulence and the principles of freedom. Kiow could not yet boast of three hundred churches, an innumerable people, and a degree of greatness and splendour which was compared with Constantinople by those who had never seen the residence of the Cæsars. In their origin the two cities were no more than camps or fairs, the most convenient stations in which the barbarians might assemble for the occasional business of war or trade. Yet even these assemblies announce some progress in the arts of society; a new breed of cattle was imported from the southern provinces; and the spirit of commercial enterprise pervaded the sea and land, from the Baltic to the Euxine, from the mouth of the Oder to the port of Constantinople. In the days of idolatry and barbarism the Sclavonic city of Julin was frequented and enriched by the Normans, who had prudently secured a free mart of purchase and exchange.[52] From this harbour, at the entrance of the Oder, the corsair, or merchant, sailed in forty-three days to the eastern shores of the Baltic, the most distant nations were intermingled, and the holy groves of Curland *are said* to have been decorated with *Grecian* and Spanish gold.[53] Between the sea and Novogorod an easy intercourse was discovered; in the summer, through a gulf, a lake, and a navigable river; in the winter season, over the hard and level surface of boundless snows. From the neighbourhood of that city the Russians descended the streams that fall into the Borysthenes; their canoes, of a single tree, were laden with slaves of every age, furs of every species, the spoil of their beehives, and the hides of their cattle; and the whole produce of the North was collected and discharged in the magazines of Kiow. The month of June was the ordinary season of the departure of the fleet: the timber of the canoes was framed into the oars and enches of the more solid and capacious boats; nd they proceeded without obstacle down the Borysthenes, as far as the seven or thirteen idges of rocks, which traverse the bed, and precipitate the waters, of the river. At the more shallow falls it was sufficient to lighten the vessels; but the deeper cataracts were impass-ible; and the mariners, who dragged their vessels and their slaves six miles over land, were exposed in this toilsome journey to the robbers of the desert.[54] At the first island below the falls, the Russians celebrated the festival of their escape: at a second, near the mouth of the river, hey repaired their shattered vessels for the longer and more perilous voyage of the Black Sea. If they steered along the coast, the Danube was accessible; with a fair wind they could reach in thirty-six or forty hours the opposite shores of Anatolia; and Constantinople ad-mitted the annual visit of the strangers of the North. They returned at the stated season with a rich cargo of corn, wine, and oil, the manu-factures of Greece, and the spices of India. Some of their countrymen resided in the capi-tal and provinces; and the national treaties protected the persons, effects, and privileges of the Russian merchant.[55]

But the same communication which had been opened for the benefit, was soon abused for the injury, of mankind. In a period of one hundred and ninety years the Russians made four attempts to plunder the treasures of Con-stantinople: the event was various, but the motive, the means, and the object were the same in these naval expeditions.[56] The Russian traders had seen the magnificence, and tasted the luxury, of the city of the Cæsars. A mar-vellous tale, and a scanty supply, excited the desires of their savage countrymen: they envied the gifts of nature which their climate denied; they coveted the works of art, which they were too lazy to imitate and too indigent to pur-chase; the Varangian princes unfurled the ban-ners of piratical adventure, and their bravest soldiers were drawn from the nations that dwelt in the northern isles of the ocean.[57] The image of their naval armaments was revived in the last century in the fleets of the Cosacks, which issued from the Borysthenes to navigate the same seas for a similar purpose.[58] The Greek appellation of *monoxyla*, or single canoes, might be justly applied to the bottom of their vessels. It was scooped out of the long stem of a beech or willow, but the slight and narrow foundation was raised and continued on either side with planks, till it attained the length of sixty and

the height of about twelve feet. These boats were built without a deck, but with two rud-ders and a mast; to move with sails and oars; and to contain from forty to seventy men, with their arms, and provisions of fresh water and salt fish. The first trial of the Russians was made with two hundred boats; but when the national force was exerted they might arm against Constantinople a thousand or twelve hundred vessels. Their fleet was not much in-ferior to the royal navy of Agamemnon, but it was magnified in the eyes of fear to ten or fifteen times the real proportion of its strength and numbers. Had the Greek emperors been endowed with foresight to discern, and vigour to prevent, perhaps they might have sealed with a maritime force the mouth of the Borys-thenes. Their indolence abandoned the coast of Anatolia to the calamities of a piratical war, which, after an interval of six hundred years, again infested the Euxine; but as long as the capital was respected, the sufferings of a distant province escaped the notice both of the prince and the historian. The storm, which had swept along from the Phasis and Trebizond, at length burst on the Bosphorus of Thrace; a strait of fifteen miles, in which the rude vessels of the Russian might have been stopped and destroyed by a more skilful adversary. In their first enterprise[59] under the princes of Kiow, they passed without opposition, and occupied the port of Constantinople in the absence of the emperor Michael, the son of Theophilus. Through a crowd of perils he landed at the palace stairs, and immediately repaired to a church of the Virgin Mary.[60] By the advice of the patriarch, her garment, a precious relic, was drawn from the sanctuary and dipped in the sea; and a seasonable tempest, which deter-mined the retreat of the Russians, was devoutly ascribed to the mother of God.[61] The silence of the Greeks may inspire some doubt of the truth, or at least of the importance, of the second at-tempt by Oleg, the guardian of the sons of Ruric.[62] A strong barrier of arms and fortifica-tions defended the Bosphorus: they were eluded by the usual expedient of drawing the boats over the isthmus; and this simple operation is described in the national chronicles as if the Russian fleet had sailed over dry land with a brisk and favourable gale. The leader of the third armament, Igor, the son of Ruric, had chosen a moment of weakness and decay, when the naval powers of the empire were employed against the Saracens. But if courage be not wanting, the instruments of defence are seldom deficient. Fifteen broken and decayed galleys were boldly launched against the enemy; but instead of the single tube of Greek fire usually planted on the prow, the sides and stern of each vessel were abundantly supplied with that liquid combustible. The engineers were dexterous; the weather was propitious; many thousand Russians, who chose rather to be drowned that burnt, leaped into the sea; and those who escaped to the Thracian shore were inhumanly slaughtered by the peasants and soldiers. Yet one third of the canoes escaped into shallow water; and the next spring Igor was again prepared to retrieve his disgrace and claim his revenge.[63] After a long peace, Jaroslaus, the great-grandson of Igor, resumed the same project of a naval invasion. A fleet, under the command of his son, was repulsed at the entrance of the Bosphorus, by the same artificial flames. But in the rashness of pursuit the vanguard of the Greeks was encompassed by an irresistible multitude of boats and men; their provision of fire was probably exhausted; and twenty-four galleys were either taken, sunk, or destroyed.[64]

Yet the threats or calamities of a Russian war were more frequently diverted by treaty than by arms. In these naval hostilities every disadvantage was on the side of the Greeks; their savage enemy afforded no mercy: his poverty promised no spoil; his impenetrable retreat deprived the conqueror of the hopes of revenge; and the pride or weakness of empire indulged an opinion that no honour could be gained or lost in the intercourse with barbarians. At first, their demands were high and inadmissible, three pounds of gold for each soldier or mariner of the fleet: the Russian youth adhered to the design of conquest and glory; but the counsels of moderation were recommended by the hoary sages. "Be content," they said, "with the liberal offers of Cæsar; is it not far better to obtain without a combat the possession of gold, silver, silks, and all the objects of our desires? Are we sure of victory? Can we conclude a treaty with the sea? We do not tread on the land; we float on the abyss of water, and a common death hangs over our heads."[65] The memory of these Arctic fleets, that seemed to descend from the polar circle, left a deep impression of terror on the Imperial city. By the vulgar of every rank it was asserted and believed that an equestrian statue in the square of Taurus was secretly inscribed with a prophecy, how the Russians, in the last days, should become masters of Constantinople.[66] In our own time, a Russian armament, instead of sailing from the Borysthenes, has circumnavigated the continent of Europe; and the Turkish capital has been threatened by a squadron of strong and lofty ships of war, each of which, with its naval science and thundering artillery, could have sunk or scattered a hundred canoes, such as those of their ancestors. Perhaps the present generation may yet behold the accomplishment of the prediction, of a rare prediction, of which the style is unambiguous and the date unquestionable.

By land the Russians were less formidable than by sea; and as they fought for the most part on foot, their irregular legions must often have been broken and overthrown by the cavalry of the Scythian hordes. Yet their growing towns, however slight and imperfect, presented a shelter to the subject, and a barrier to the enemy: the monarchy of Kiow, till a fatal partition, assumed the dominion of the North; and the nations from the Volga to the Danube were subdued or repelled by the arms of Swatoslaus,[67] the son of Igor, the son of Oleg, the son of Ruric. The vigour of his mind and body was fortified by the hardships of a military and savage life. Wrapped in a bear-skin, Swatoslaus usually slept on the ground, his head reclining on a saddle; his diet was coarse and frugal, and, like the heroes of Homer,[68] his meat (it was often horse-flesh) was broiled or roasted on the coals. The exercise of war gave stability and discipline to his army; and it may be presumed that no soldier was permitted to transcend the luxury of his chief. By an embassy from Nicephorus, the Greek emperor, he was moved to undertake the conquest of Bulgaria; and a gift of fifteen hundred pounds of gold was laid at his feet to defray the expense, or reward the toils, of the expedition. An army of sixty thousand men was assembled and embarked; they sailed from the Borysthenes to the Danube; their landing was effected on the Mæsian shore; and, after a sharp encounter, the swords of the Russians prevailed against the arrows of the Bulgarian horse. The vanquished king sunk into the grave; his children were made captive; and his dominions, as far as Mount Hæmus, were subdued or ravaged by the northern invaders. But instead of relinquishing his prey, and performing his engagements, the Varangian prince was more disposed to advance than to retire, and, had his ambition been crowned with success, the seat of empire in that early period might have been transferred to a more temperate and fruitful climate. Swatoslaus enjoyed and acknowledged the advantages of his new position, in which he could unite, by exchange or rapine, the various productions of the earth. By an easy navigation he might draw from Russia the native commodities of furs, wax, and hydromel: Hungary supplied him with a breed of horses and the spoils of the West; and Greece abounded with gold, silver, and the foreign luxuries which his poverty had affected to disdain. The bands of Patzinacites, Chazars, and Turks repaired to the standard of victory; and the ambassador of Nicephorus betrayed his trust, assumed the purple, and promised to share with his new allies the treasures of the Eastern world. From the banks of the Danube the Russian prince pursued his march as far as Adrianople; a formal summons to evacuate the Roman province was dismissed with contempt; and Swatoslaus fiercely replied that Constantinople might soon expect the presence of an enemy and a master.

Nicephorus could no longer expel the mischief which he had introduced; but his throne and wife were inherited by John Zimisces,[69] who, in a diminutive body, possessed the spirit and abilities of a hero. The first victory of his lieutenants deprived the Russians of their foreign allies, twenty-thousand of whom were either destroyed by the sword, or provoked to revolt, or tempted to desert. Thrace was delivered, but seventy thousand barbarians were still in arms; and the legions that had been recalled from the new conquests of Syria prepared, with the return of the spring, to march under the banners of a warlike prince, who declared himself the friend and avenger of the injured Bulgaria. The passes of Mount Hæmus had been left unguarded; they were instantly occupied; the Roman vanguard was formed of the *immortals* (a proud imitation of the Persian style); the emperor led the main body of ten thousand five hundred foot; and the rest of his forces followed in slow and cautious array, with the baggage and military engines. The first exploit of Zimisces was the reduction of Marcianopolis, or Peristhlaba,[70] in two days; the trumpets sounded; the walls were scaled; eight thousand five hundred Russians were put to the sword; and the sons of the Bulgarian king were rescued from an ignominious prison, and invested with a nominal diadem. After these repeated losses Swatoslaus retired to the strong post of Dristra, on the banks of the Danube, and was pursued by an enemy who alternately employed the arms of celerity and delay. The Byzantine galleys ascended the river; the legions completed a line of circumvallation; and

the Russian prince was encompassed, assaulted, and famished in the fortifications of the camp and city. Many deeds of valour were performed; several desperate sallies were attempted; nor was it till after a siege of sixty-five days that Swatoslaus yielded to his adverse fortune. The liberal terms which he obtained announce the prudence of the victor, who respected the valour and apprehended the despair of an unconquered mind. The great duke of Russia bound himself, by solemn imprecations, to relinquish all hostile designs; a safe passage was opened for his return; the liberty of trade and navigation was restored; a measure of corn was distributed to each of his soldiers; and the allowance of twenty-two thousand measures attests the loss and the remnant of the barbarians. After a painful voyage they again reached the mouth of the Borysthenes; but their provisions were exhausted; the season was unfavourable; they passed the winter on the ice; and before they could prosecute their march, Swatoslaus was surprised and oppressed by the neighbouring tribes, with whom the Greeks entertained a perpetual and useful correspondence.[71] Far different was the return of Zimisces, who was received in his capital like Camillus or Marius, the saviours of ancient Rome. But the merit of the victory was attributed by the pious emperor to the mother of God: and the image of the Virgin Mary, with the divine infant in her arms, was placed on a triumphal car, adorned with the spoils of war and the ensigns of Bulgarian royalty. Zimisces made his public entry on horseback; the diadem on his head, a crown of laurel in his hand; and Constantinople was astonished to applaud the martial virtues of her sovereign.[72]

Photius of Constantinople, a patriarch whose ambition was equal to his curiosity, congratulates himself and the Greek church on the conversion of the Russians.[73] Those fierce and bloody barbarians had been persuaded, by the voice of reason and religion, to acknowledge Jesus for their God, the Christian missionaries for their teachers, and the Romans for their friends and brethren. His triumph was transient and premature. In the various fortune of their piratical adventures, some Russian chiefs might allow themselves to be sprinkled with the waters of baptism; and a Greek bishop, with the name of metropolitan, might administer the sacraments in the church of Kiow to a congregation of slaves and natives. But the seed of the Gospel was sown on a barren soil: many were the apostates, the converts were few, and the baptism of Olga may be fixed as the era of Russian Christianity.[74] A female, perhaps of the basest origin, who could revenge the death and assume the sceptre of her husband Igor, must have been endowed with those active virtues which command the fear and obedience of barbarians. In a moment of foreign and domestic peace she sailed from Kiow to Constantinople, and the emperor Constantine Porphyrogenitus has described, with minute diligence, the ceremonial of her reception in his capital and palace. The steps, the titles, the salutations, the banquet, the presents, were exquisitely adjusted to gratify the vanity of the stranger, with due reverence to the superior majesty of the purple.[75] In the sacrament of baptism she received the venerable name of the empress Helena; and her conversion might be preceded or followed by her uncle, two interpreters, sixteen damsels of a higher, and eighteen of a lower rank, twenty-two domestics or ministers, and forty-four Russian merchants, who composed the retinue of the great princess Olga. After her return to Kiow and Novogorod, she firmly persisted in her new religion; but her labours in the propagation of the Gospel were not crowned with success; and both her family and nation adhered with obstinacy or indifference to the gods of their fathers. Her son Swatoslaus was apprehensive of the scorn and ridicule of his companions; and her grandson Wolodomir devoted his youthful zeal to multiply and decorate the monuments of ancient worship. The savage deities of the North were still propitiated with human sacrifices: in the choice of the victim a citizen was preferred to a stranger, a Christian to an idolater; and the father who defended his son from the sacerdotal knife was involved in the same doom by the rage of a fanatic tumult. Yet the lessons and example of the pious Olga had made a deep, though secret, impression on the minds of the prince and people: the Greek missionaries continued to preach, to dispute, and to baptise; and the ambassadors or merchants of Russia compared the idolatry of the woods with the elegant superstition of Constantinople. They had gazed with admiration on the dome of St. Sophia: the lively pictures of saints and martyrs, the riches of the altar, the number and vestments of the priests, the pomp and order of the ceremonies; they were edified by the alternate succession of devout silence and harmonious song; nor was it difficult to persuade them that a choir of angels descended each day from heaven to join in the devotion of the Christians.[76] But the conversion of Wolodomir was determined, or hastened, by his desire of a Roman bride. At the same time, and in the city of Cherson, the rites of baptism and marriage were celebrated by the Christian pontiff: the city he restored to the emperor Basil, the brother of his spouse; but the brazen gates were transported, as it is said, to Novogorod, and erected before the first church as a trophy of his victory and faith.[77] At his despotic command, Peroun, the god of thunder, whom he had so long adored, was dragged through the streets of Kiow, and twelve sturdy barbarians battered with clubs the misshapen image, which was indignantly cast into the waters of the Borysthenes. The edict of Wolodomir had proclaimed that all who should refuse the rites of baptism would be treated as the enemies of God and their prince; and the rivers were constantly filled with many thousands of obedient Russians, who acquiesced in the truth and excellence of a doctrine which had been embraced by the great duke and his boyars. In the next generation the relics of paganism were finally extirpated; but as the two brothers of Wolodomir had died without baptism, their bones were taken from the grave and sanctified by an irregular and posthumous sacrament.

In the ninth, tenth, and eleventh centuries of the Christian era the reign of the Gospel and of the church was extended over Bulgaria, Hungary, Bohemia, Saxony, Denmark, Norway, Sweden, Poland, and Russia.[78] The triumphs of apostolic zeal were repeated in the iron age of Christianity; and the northern and eastern regions of Europe submitted to a religion more different in theory than in practice from the worship of their native idols. A laudable ambition excited the monks both of Germany and Greece to visit the tents and huts of the barbarians: poverty, hardships, and dangers were the lot of the first missionaries; their courage was active and patient; their motive pure and meritorious; their present reward consisted in the testimony of their conscience and the respect of a grateful people; but the fruitful harvest of their toils was inherited and enjoyed by the proud and wealthy prelates of succeeding times. The first conversions were free and spontaneous: a holy life and an eloquent tongue were the only arms of the missionaries; but the domestic fables of the pagans were silenced by the miracles and visions of the strangers; and the favourable temper of the chiefs was accelerated by the dictates of vanity and interest. The leaders of nations, who were aluted with the titles of kings and saints,[79] held lawful and pious to impose the Catholic faith in their subjects and neighbours: the coast of the Baltic, from Holstein to the gulf of Finland, was invaded under the standard of the cross; and the reign of idolatry was closed by the conversion of Lithuania in the fourteenth century. Yet truth and candour must acknowledge that the conversion of the North imparted many temporal benefits both to the old and the new Christians. The rage of war, inherent to the human species, could not be healed by the evangelic precepts of charity and peace; and the ambition of Catholic princes has renewed in every age the calamities of hostile contention. But the admission of the barbarians into the pale of civil and ecclesiastical society delivered Europe from the depredations, by sea and land, of the Normans, the Hungarians, and the Russians, who learned to spare their brethren and cultivate their possessions.[80] The establishment of law and order was promoted by the influence of the clergy; and the rudiments of art and science were introduced into the savage countries of the globe. The liberal piety of the Russian princes engaged in their service the most skilful of the Greeks to decorate the cities and instruct the inhabitants: the dome and the paintings of St. Sophia were rudely copied in the churches of Kiow and Novogorod: the writings of the fathers were translated into the Sclavonic idiom; and three hundred noble youths were invited or compelled to attend the lessons of the college of Jaroslaus. It should appear that Russia might have derived an early and rapid improvement from her peculiar connection with the church and state of Constantinople, which in that age so justly despised the ignorance of the Latins. But the Byzantine nation was servile, solitary, and verging to a hasty decline: after the fall of Kiow the navigation of the Borysthenes was forgotten; the great princes of Wolodomir and Moscow were separated from the sea and Christendom; and the divided monarchy was oppressed by the ignominy and blindness of Tartar servitude.[81] The Sclavonic and Scandinavian kingdoms, which had been converted by the Latin missionaries, were exposed, it is true, to the spiritual jurisdiction and temporal claims of the popes;[82] but they were united, in language and religious worship with each other and with Rome; they imbibed the free and generous spirit of the European republic, and gradually shared the light of knowledge which arose on the western world.

CHAPTER LVI

The Saracens, Franks, and Greeks, in Italy. First Adventures and Settlement of the Normans. Character and Conquests of Robert Guiscard, Duke of Apulia. Deliverance of Sicily by his Brother Roger. Victories of Robert over the Emperors of the East and West. Roger, King of Sicily, invades Africa and Greece. The Emperor Manuel Comnenus. Wars of the Greeks and Normans. Extinction of the Normans.

THE three great nations of the world, the Greeks, the Saracens, and the Franks, encountered each other on the theatre of Italy.[1] The southern provinces, which now compose the kingdom of Naples, were subject, for the most part, to the Lombard dukes and princes of Beneventum[2]—so powerful in war, that they checked for a moment the genius of Charlemagne—so liberal in peace, that they maintained in their capital an academy of thirty-two philosophers and grammarians. The division of this flourishing state produced the rival principalities of Benevento, Salerno, and Capua; and the thoughtless ambition or revenge of the competitors invited the Saracens to the ruin of their common inheritance. During a calamitous period of two hundred years Italy was exposed to a repetition of wounds, which the invaders were not capable of healing by the union and tranquillity of a perfect conquest. Their frequent and almost annual squadrons issued from the port of Palermo, and were entertained with too much indulgence by the Christians of Naples: the more formidable fleets were prepared on the African coast; and even the Arabs of Andalusia were sometimes tempted to assist or oppose the Moslems of an adverse sect. In the revolution of human events a new ambuscade was concealed in the Caudine forks, the fields of Cannæ were bedewed a second time with the blood of the Africans, and the sovereign of Rome again attacked or defended the walls of Capua and Tarentum. A colony of Saracens had been planted at Bari, which commands the entrance of the Adriatic Gulf; and their impartial depredations provoked the resentment and conciliated the union of the two emperors. An offensive alliance was concluded between Basil the Macedonian, the first of his race, and Lewis the great-grandson of Charlemagne;[3] and each party supplied the deficiencies of his associate. It would have been imprudent in the Byzantine monarch to transport his stationary troops of Asia to an Italian campaign; and the Latin arms would have been insufficient if *his* superior navy had not occupied the mouth of the Gulf. The fortress of Bari was invested by the infantry of the Franks, and by the cavalry and galleys of the Greeks; and, after a defence of four years, the Arabian emir submitted to the clemency of Lewis, who commanded in person the operations of the siege. This important conquest had been achieved by the concord of the East and West; but their recent amity was soon embittered by the mutual complaints of jealousy and pride. The Greeks assumed as their own the merit of the conquest and the pomp of the triumph, extolled the greatness of their powers, and affected to deride the intemperance and sloth of the handful of barbarians who appeared under the banners of the Carlovingian prince. His reply is expressed with the eloquence of indignation and truth: "We confess the magnitude of your preparations," says the great-grandson of Charlemagne. "Your armies were indeed as numerous as a cloud of summer locusts, who darken the day, flap their wings, and, after a short flight, tumble weary and breathless to the ground. Like them, ye sunk after a feeble effort; ye were vanquished by your own cowardice, and withdrew from the scene of action to injure and despoil our Christian subjects of the Sclavonian coast. We were few in number, and why were we few? because, after a tedious expectation of your arrival, I had dismissed my host, and retained only a chosen band of warriors to continue the blockade of the city. If they indulged their hospitable feasts in the face of danger and death, did these feasts abate the vigour of their enterprise? Is it by your fasting that the walls of Bari have been overturned? Did not these valiant Franks, diminished as they were by languor and fatigue, intercept and vanquish the three most powerful emirs of the Saracens? and did not their defeat precipitate the fall of the city? Bari

is now fallen; Tarentum trembles; Calabri will be delivered; and, if we command the sea the island of Sicily may be rescued from th hands of the infidels. My brother" (a nam most offensive to the vanity of the Greek), "ac celerate your naval succours, respect your a lies, and distrust your flatterers."[4]

These lofty hopes were soon extinguished b the death of Lewis, and the decay of the Car lovingian house; and whoever might deserv the honour, the Greek emperors, Basil and hi son Leo, secured the advantage, of the reduc tion of Bari. The Italians of Apulia and Cala bria were persuaded or compelled to acknowl edge their supremacy, and an ideal line from Mount Garganus to the bay of Salerno leave the far greater part of the kingdom of Naple under the dominion of the Eastern empire. Be yond that line the dukes or republics of Amalfi and Naples, who had never forfeited their vo untary allegiance, rejoiced in the neighbour hood of their lawful sovereign; and Amalfi wa enriched by supplying Europe with the produc and manufactures of Asia. But the Lombard princes of Benevento, Salerno, and Capua were reluctantly torn from the communion o the Latin world, and too often violated thei oaths of servitude and tribute. The city of Bar rose to dignity and wealth as the metropolis o the new theme or province of Lombardy; th title of patrician, and afterwards the singula name of *Catapan*,[7] was assigned to the supreme governor; and the policy both of the church and state was modelled in exact subordinatio to the throne of Constantinople. As long as the sceptre was disputed by the princes of Italy their efforts were feeble and adverse; and the Greeks resisted or eluded the forces of Germany which descended from the Alps under the Im perial standard of the Othos. The first and greatest of those Saxon princes was compelled to relinquish the siege of Bari: the second, after the loss of his stoutest bishops and barons, es caped with honour from the bloody field o Crotona. On that day the scale of war was turned against the Franks by the valour of the Saracens.[8] These corsairs had indeed been driv en by the Byzantine fleets from the fortresses and coasts of Italy; but a sense of interest was more prevalent than superstition or resentment, and the caliph of Egypt had transported forty thousand Moslems to the aid of his Christian ally. The successors of Basil amused themselves with the belief that the conquest of Lombardy had been achieved, and was still preserved, by the justice of their laws, the virtues of their ministers, and the gratitude of a people whom they had rescued from anarchy and oppression. A series of rebellions might dart a ray of truth into the palace of Constantinople; and the illusions of flattery were dispelled by the easy and rapid success of the Norman adventurers.

The revolution of human affairs had produced in Apulia and Calabria a melancholy contrast between the age of Pythagoras and the tenth century of the Christian era. At the former period the coast of Great Greece (as it was then styled) was planted with free and opulent cities: these cities were peopled with soldiers, artists, and philosophers; and the military strength of Tarentum, Sybaris, or Crotona was not inferior to that of a powerful kingdom. At the second era these once flourishing provinces were clouded with ignorance, impoverished by tyranny, and depopulated by barbarian war: nor can we severely accuse the exaggeration of a contemporary, that a fair and ample district was reduced to the same desolation which had covered the earth after the general deluge.[9] Among the hostilities of the Arabs, the Franks, and the Greeks in the southern Italy, I shall select two or three anecdotes expressive of their national manners. 1. It was the amusement of the Saracens to profane, as well as to pillage, the monasteries and churches. At the siege of Salerno a Musulman chief spread his couch on the communion table, and on that altar sacrificed each night the virginity of a Christian nun. As he wrestled with a reluctant maid, a beam in the roof was accidentally or dexterously thrown down on his head; and the death of the lustful emir was imputed to the wrath of Christ, which was at length awakened to the defence of his faithful spouse.[10] 2. The Saracens besieged the cities of Beneventum and Capua; after a vain appeal to the successors of Charlemagne, the Lombards implored the clemency and aid of the Greek emperor.[11] A fearless citizen dropped from the walls, passed the intrenchments, accomplished his commission, and fell into the hands of the barbarians as he was returning with the welcome news. They commanded him to assist their enterprise, and deceive his countrymen, with the assurance that wealth and honours should be the reward of his falsehood, and that his sincerity would be punished with immediate death. He affected to yield, but as soon as he was conducted within hearing of the Christians on the rampart, "Friends and brethren," he cried with a loud voice, "be bold and patient; maintain the city; your sovereign is in-

formed of your distress, and your deliverers are at hand. I know my doom, and commit my wife and children to your gratitude." The rage of the Arabs confirmed his evidence; and the self-devoted patriot was transpierced with a hundred spears. He deserves to live in the memory of the virtuous, but the repetition of the same story in ancient and modern times may sprinkle some doubts on the reality of this generous deed.[12] 3. The recital of the third incident may provoke a smile amidst the horrors of war. Theobald, marquis of Camerino and Spoleto,[13] supported the rebels of Beneventum; and his wanton cruelty was not incompatible in that age with the character of a hero. His captives of the Greek nation or party were castrated without mercy, and the outrage was aggravated by a cruel jest, that he wished to present the emperor with a supply of eunuchs, the most precious ornaments of the Byzantine court. The garrison of a castle had been defeated in a sally, and the prisoners were sentenced to the customary operation. But the sacrifice was disturbed by the intrusion of a frantic female, who, with bleeding cheeks, dishevelled hair, and importunate clamours, compelled the marquis to listen to her complaint. "Is it thus," she cried, "ye magnanimous heroes, that ye wage war against women, against women who have never injured ye, and whose only arms are the distaff and the loom?" Theobald denied the charge, and protested that, since the Amazons, he had never heard of a female war. "And how," she furiously exclaimed, "can you attack us more directly, how can you wound us in a more vital part, than by robbing our husbands of what we most dearly cherish, the source of our joys, and the hope of our posterity? The plunder of our flocks and herds I have endured without a murmur, but this fatal injury, this irreparable loss, subdues my patience, and calls aloud on the justice of heaven and earth." A general laugh applauded her eloquence; the savage Franks, inaccessible to pity, were moved by her ridiculous, yet rational, despair; and with the deliverance of the captives she obtained the restitution of her effects. As she returned in triumph to the castle she was overtaken by a messenger, to inquire, in the name of Theobald, what punishment should be inflicted on her husband, were he again taken in arms? "Should such," she answered without hesitation, "be his guilt and misfortune, he has eyes, and a nose, and hands, and feet. These are his own, and these he may deserve to forfeit by his personal offences. But let my lord be pleased to spare what his little handmaid presumes to claim as her peculiar and lawful property."[14]

The establishment of the Normans in the kingdoms of Naples and Sicily[15] is an event most romantic in its origin, and in its consequences most important both to Italy and the Eastern empire. The broken provinces of the Greeks, Lombards, and Saracens were exposed to every invader, and every sea and land were invaded by the adventurous spirit of the Scandinavian pirates. After a long indulgence of rapine and slaughter, a fair and ample territory was accepted, occupied, and named, by the Normans of France: they renounced their gods for the God of the Christians;[16] and the dukes of Normandy acknowledged themselves the vassals of the successors of Charlemagne and Capet. The savage fierceness which they had brought from the snowy mountains of Norway was refined, without being corrupted, in a warmer climate; the companions of Rollo insensibly mingled with the natives; they imbibed the manners, language,[17] and gallantry of the French nation; and, in a martial age, the Normans might claim the palm of valour and glorious achievements. Of the fashionable superstitions, they embraced with ardour the pilgrimages of Rome, Italy, and the Holy Land. In this active devotion their minds and bodies were invigorated by exercise: danger was the incentive, novelty the recompense; and the prospect of the world was decorated by wonder, credulity, and ambitious hope. They confederated for their mutual defence; and the robbers of the Alps, who had been allured by the garb of a pilgrim, were often chastised by the arm of a warrior. In one of these pious visits to the cavern of Mount Garganus in Apulia, which had been sanctified by the apparition of the archangel Michael,[18] they were accosted by a stranger in the Greek habit, but who soon revealed himself as a rebel, a fugitive, and a mortal foe of the Greek empire. His name was Melo; a noble citizen of Bari, who, after an unsuccessful revolt was compelled to seek new allies and avengers of his country. The bold appearance of the Normans revived his hopes and solicited his confidence: they listened to the complaints, and still more to the promises, of the patriot. The assurance of wealth demonstrated the justice of his cause; and they viewed, as the inheritance of the brave, the fruitful land which was oppressed by effeminate tyrants. On their return to Normandy they kindled a spark of enterprise, and a small but intrepid band was freely associated for the deliverance of Apulia. They passed the Alps by separate roads, and in the disguise of pilgrims; but in the neighbourhood of Rome they were saluted by the chief of Bari, who supplied the more indigent with arms and horses, and instantly led them to the field of action. In the first conflict their valour prevailed; but in the second engagement they were overwhelmed by the numbers and military engines of the Greeks, and indignantly retreated with their faces to the enemy. The unfortunate Melo ended his life a suppliant at the court of Germany: his Norman followers, excluded from their native and their promised land, wandered among the hills and valleys of Italy, and earned their daily subsistence by the sword. To that formidable sword the princes of Capua, Beneventum, Salerno, and Naples alternately appealed in their domestic quarrels; the superior spirit and discipline of the Normans gave victory to the side which they espoused; and their cautious policy observed the balance of power, lest the preponderance of any rival state should render their aid less important and their service less profitable. Their first asylum was a strong camp in the depth of the marshes of Campania; but they were soon endowed by the liberality of the duke of Naples with a more plentiful and permanent seat. Eight miles from his residence, as a bulwark against Capua, the town of Aversa was built and fortified for their use; and they enjoyed as their own the corn and fruits, the meadows and groves, of that fertile district. The report of their success attracted every year new swarms of pilgrims and soldiers: the poor were urged by necessity; the rich were excited by hope; and the brave and active spirits of Normandy were impatient of ease and ambitious of renown. The independent standard of Aversa afforded shelter and encouragement to the outlaws of the province, to every fugitive who had escaped from the injustice or justice of his superiors; and these foreign associates were quickly assimilated in manners and language to the Gallic colony. The first leader of the Normans was Count Rainulf; and, in the origin of society, pre-eminence of rank is the reward and the proof of superior merit.[19]

Since the conquest of Sicily by the Arabs, the Grecian emperors had been anxious to regain that valuable possession; but their efforts, however strenuous, had been opposed by the distance and the sea. Their costly armaments, after a gleam of success, added new pages of calamity and disgrace to the Byzantine annals: twenty thousand of their best troops were lost in a single expedition; and the victorious Moslems erided the policy of a nation which intrusted unuchs not only with the custody of their vomen, but with the command of their men.[20] After a reign of two hundred years, the Saracens were ruined by their divisions.[21] The emir disclaimed the authority of the king of Tunis; the people rose against the emir; the cities were usurped by the chiefs; each meaner rebel was independent in his village or castle; and the weaker of two rival brothers implored the friendship of the Christians. In every service of danger the Normans were prompt and useful; and five hundred *knights*, or warriors on horseback, were enrolled by Arduin, the agent and interpreter of the Greeks, under the standard of Maniaces, governor of Lombardy. Before their landing the brothers were reconciled; the union of Sicily and Africa was restored; and the island was guarded to the water's edge. The Normans led the van, and the Arabs of Messina felt the valour of an untried foe. In a second action the emir of Syracuse was unhorsed and transpierced by the *iron arm* of William of Hauteville. In a third engagement his intrepid companions discomfited the host of sixty thousand Saracens, and left the Greeks no more than the labour of the pursuit; a splendid victory; but of which the pen of the historian may divide the merit with the lance of the Normans. It is, however, true, that they essentially promoted the success of Maniaces, who reduced thirteen cities, and the greater part of Sicily, under the obedience of the emperor. But his military fame was sullied by ingratitude and tyranny. In the division of the spoil the deserts of his brave auxiliaries were forgotten; and neither their avarice nor their pride could brook this injurious treatment. They complained by the mouth of their interpreter: their complaint was disregarded; their interpreter was scourged; the sufferings were *his*; the insult and resentment belonged to *those* whose sentiments he had delivered. Yet they dissembled till they had obtained, or stolen, a safe passage to the Italian continent: their brethren of Aversa sympathised in their indignation and the province of Apulia was invaded as the forfeit of the debt.[22] Above twenty years after the first emigration, the Normans took the field with no more than seven hundred horse and five hundred foot; and after the recall of the Byzantine legions[23] from the Sicilian war, their numbers are magnified to the amount of three-score thousand men. Their herald proposed the option of battle or retreat: "Of battle," was the unanimous cry of the Normans; and one of their stoutest warriors, with a stroke

of his fist, felled to the ground the horse of the Greek messenger. He was dismissed with a fresh horse; the insult was concealed from the Imperial troops; but in two successive battles they were more fatally instructed of the prowess of their adversaries. In the plains of Cannæ the Asiatics fled before the adventurers of France; the duke of Lombardy was made prisoner; the Apulians acquiesced in a new dominion; and the four places of Bari, Otranto, Brundusium, and Tarentum were alone saved in the shipwreck of the Grecian fortunes. From this era we may date the establishment of the Norman power, which soon eclipsed the infant colony of Aversa. Twelve counts[24] were chosen by the popular suffrage; and age, birth, and merit were the motives of their choice. The tributes of their peculiar districts were appropriated to their use; and each count erected a fortress in the midst of his lands, and at the head of his vassals. In the centre of the province the common habitation of Melphi was reserved as the metropolis and citadel of the republic; a house and separate quarter was allotted to each of the twelve counts; and the national concerns were regulated by this military senate. The first of his peers, their president and general, was entitled Count of Apulia; and this dignity was conferred on William of the iron arm, who, in the language of the age, is styled a lion in battle, a lamb in society, and an angel in council.[25] The manners of his countrymen are fairly delineated by a contemporary and national historian.[26] "The Normans," says Malaterra, "are a cunning and revengeful people; eloquence and dissimulation appear to be their hereditary qualities; they can stoop to flatter; but, unless they are curbed by the restraint of law, they indulge the licentiousness of nature and passion. Their princes affect the praise of popular munificence; the people observe the medium, or rather blend the extremes, of avarice and prodigality; and in their eager thirst of wealth and dominion, they despise whatever they possess, and hope whatever they desire. Arms and horses, the luxury of dress, the exercises of hunting and hawking[27] are the delight of the Normans; but, on pressing occasions, they can endure with incredible patience the inclemency of every climate, and the toil and abstinence of a military life."[28]

The Normans of Apulia were seated on the verge of the two empires, and, according to the policy of the hour, they accepted the investiture of their lands from the sovereigns of Germany or Constantinople. But the firmest title of these adventurers was the right to conquest; they neither loved nor trusted; they were neither trusted nor beloved; the contempt of the princes was mixed with fear, and the fear of the natives was mingled with hatred and resentment. Every object of desire, a horse, a woman, a garden, tempted and gratified the rapaciousness of the strangers,[29] and the avarice of their chiefs was only coloured by the more specious names of ambition and glory. The twelve counts were sometimes joined in a league of injustice; in their domestic quarrels they disputed the spoils of the people; the virtues of William were buried in his grave; and Drogo, his brother and successor, was better qualified to lead the valour, than to restrain the violence, of his peers. Under the reign of Constantine Monomachus, the policy, rather than benevolence, of the Byzantine court attempted to relieve Italy from this adherent mischief, more grievous than a flight of barbarians;[30] and Argyrus, the son of Melo, was invested for this purpose with the most lofty titles[31] and the most ample commission. The memory of his father might recommend him to the Normans, and he had already engaged their voluntary service to quell the revolt of Maniaces, and to avenge their own and the public injury. It was the design of Constantine to transplant this warlike colony from the Italian provinces to the Persian war, and the son of Melo distributed among the chiefs the gold and manufactures of Greece as the firstfruits of the Imperial bounty. But his arts were baffled by the sense and spirit of the conquerors of Apulia: his gifts, or at least his proposals, were rejected, and they unanimously refused to relinquish their possessions and their hopes for the distant prospect of Asiatic fortune. After the means of persuasion had failed, Argyrus resolved to compel or to destroy: the Latin powers were solicited against the common enemy, and an offensive alliance was formed of the pope and the two emperors of the East and West. The throne of St. Peter was occupied by Leo the Ninth, a simple saint,[32] of a temper most apt to deceive himself and the world, and whose venerable character would consecrate with the name of piety the measures least compatible with the practice of religion. His humanity was affected by the complaints, perhaps the calumnies, of an injured people; the impious Normans had interrupted the payment of tithes, and the temporal sword might be lawfully unsheathed against the sacrilegious robbers who were deaf to the censures of the church. As a German of noble birth and royal kindred, Leo had free access to the court and confidence of the emperor Henry the Third, and in search of arms and allies his ardent zeal transported him from Apulia to Saxony, from the Elbe to the Tiber. During these hostile preparations, Argyrus indulged himself in the use of secret and guilty weapons: a crowd of Normans became the victims of public or private revenge, and the valiant Drogo was murdered in a church. But his spirit survived in his brother Humphrey, the third count of Apulia. The assassins were chastised, and the son of Melo, overthrown and wounded, was driven from the field to hide his shame behind the walls of Bari, and to await the tardy succour of his allies.

But the power of Constantine was distracted by a Turkish war, the mind of Henry was feeble and irresolute, and the pope, instead of repassing the Alps with a German army, was accompanied only by a guard of seven hundred Swabians and some volunteers of Lorraine. In his long progress from Mantua to Beneventum a vile and promiscuous multitude of Italians was enlisted under the holy standard;[33] the priest and the robber slept in the same tent, the pikes and crosses were intermingled in the front, and the martial saint repeated the lessons of his youth in the order of march, of encampment, and of combat. The Normans of Apulia could muster in the field no more than three thousand horse, with a handful of infantry; the defection of the natives intercepted their provisions and retreat; and their spirit, incapable of fear, was chilled for a moment by superstitious awe. On the hostile approach of Leo, they knelt, without disgrace or reluctance, before their spiritual father. But the pope was inexorable; his lofty Germans affected to deride the diminutive stature of their adversaries; and the Normans were informed that death or exile was their only alternative. Flight they disdained, and, as many of them had been three days without tasting food, they embraced the assurance of a more easy and honourable death. They climbed the hill of Civitella, descended into the plain, and charged in three divisions the army of the pope. On the left, and in the centre, Richard count of Aversa, and Robert the famous Guiscard, attacked, broke, routed, and pursued the Italian multitudes, who fought without discipline and fled without shame. A harder trial was reserved for the valour of Count Humphrey, who led the cavalry of the right wing. The Germans[34] have been described as unskilful in the management of the horse and lance, but on foot they formed a strong and impenetrable phalanx, and neither man, nor steed, nor armour could resist the weight of their long and two-handed swords. After a severe conflict they were encompassed by the squadrons returning from the pursuit, and died in their ranks with the esteem of their foes and the satisfaction of revenge. The gates of Civitella were shut against the flying pope, and he was overtaken by the pious conquerors, who kissed his feet to implore his blessing and the absolution of their sinful victory. The soldiers beheld in their enemy and captive the vicar of Christ; and, though we may suppose the policy of the chiefs, it is probable that they were infected by the popular superstition. In the calm of retirement the well-meaning pope deplored the effusion of Christian blood which must be imputed to his account; he felt that he had been the author of sin and scandal; and, as his undertaking had failed, the indecency of his military character was universally condemned.[35] With these dispositions he listened to the offers of a beneficial treaty, deserted an alliance which he had preached as the cause of God, and ratified the past and future conquests of the Normans. By whatever hands they had been usurped, the provinces of Apulia and Calabria were a part of the donation of Constantine and the patrimony of St. Peter: the grant and the acceptance confirmed the mutual claims of the pontiff and the adventurers. They promised to support each other with spiritual and temporal arms; a tribute or quit-rent of twelve pence was afterwards stipulated for every ploughland, and since this memorable transaction the kingdom of Naples has remained above seven hundred years a fief of the Holy See.[36]

The pedigree of Robert Guiscard[37] is variously deduced from the peasants and the dukes of Normandy: from the peasants, by the pride and ignorance of a Grecian princess;[38] from the dukes, by the ignorance and flattery of the Italian subjects.[39] His genuine descent may be ascribed to the second or middle order of private nobility.[40] He sprang from a race of *valvassors* or *bannerets*, of the diocese of Coutances, in the Lower Normandy; the castle of Hauteville was their honourable seat; his father Tancred was conspicuous in the court and army of the duke, and his military service was furnished by ten soldiers or knights. Two marriages, of a rank not unworthy of his own, made him the father of twelve sons, who were educated at home by the impartial tenderness of his second wife. But a narrow patrimony was insufficient for this numerous and daring progeny; they saw around the neighborhood the mischiefs of poverty and discord, and resolved to seek in foreign wars a more glorious inheritance. Two only remained to perpetuate the race and cherish their father's age; their ten brothers, as they successively attained the vigour of manhood, departed from the castle, passed the Alps, and joined the Apulian camp of the Normans. The elder were prompted by native spirit: their success encouraged their younger brethren; and the three first in seniority, William, Drogo, and Humphrey, deserved to be the chiefs of their nation and the founders of the new republic. Robert was the eldest of the seven sons of the second marriage, and even the reluctant praise of his foes has endowed him with the heroic qualities of a soldier and a statesman. His lofty stature surpassed the tallest of his army; his limbs were cast in the true proportion of strength and gracefulness; and to the decline of life he maintained the patient vigour of health and the commanding dignity of his form. His complexion was ruddy, his shoulders were broad, his hair and beard were long and of a flaxen colour, his eyes sparkled with fire, and his voice, like that of Achilles, could impress obedience and terror amidst the tumult of battle. In the ruder ages of chivalry such qualifications are not below the notice of the poet or historian; they may observe that Robert, at once, and with equal dexterity, could wield in the right hand his sword, his lance in the left; that in the battle of Civitella he was thrice unhorsed, and that in the close of that memorable day he was adjudged to have borne away the prize of valour from the warriors of the two armies.[41] His boundless ambition was founded on the consciousness of superior worth; in the pursuit of greatness he was never arrested by the scruples of justice, and seldom moved by the feelings of humanity; though not insensible of fame, the choice of open or clandestine means was determined only by his present advantage. The surname of *Guiscard*[42] was applied to this master of political wisdom, which is too often confounded with the practice of dissimulation and deceit, and Robert is praised by the Apulian poet for excelling the cunning of Ulysses and the eloquence of Cicero. Yet these arts were disguised by an appearance of military frankness; in his highest fortune he was accessible and courteous to his fellow-soldiers; and while he indulged the prejudices of his new subjects, he affected in his dress and manners to maintain the ancient fashion of his country. He grasped with a rapacious, that he might distribute with a liberal, hand; his primitive indigence had taught the habits of frugality; the gain of a merchant was not below his attention; and his prisoners were tortured with slow and unfeeling cruelty to force a discovery of their secret treasure. According to the Greeks, he departed from Normandy with only five followers on horseback and thirty on foot; yet even this allowance appears too bountiful; the sixth son of Tancred of Hauteville passed the Alps as a pilgrim, and his first military band was levied among the adventurers of Italy. His brothers and countrymen had divided the fertile lands of Apulia, but they guarded their shares with the jealousy of avarice; the aspiring youth was driven forwards to the mountains of Calabria, and in his first exploits against the Greeks and the natives it is not easy to discriminate the hero from the robber. To surprise a castle or a convent, to ensnare a wealthy citizen, to plunder the adjacent villages for necessary food, were the obscure labours which formed and exercised the powers of his mind and body. The volunteers of Normandy adhered to his standard, and under his command, the peasants of Calabria assumed the name and character of Normans.

As the genius of Robert expanded with his fortune, he awakened the jealousy of his elder brother, by whom, in a transient quarrel, his life was threatened and his liberty restrained. After the death of Humphrey the tender age of his sons excluded them from the command; they were reduced to a private estate by the ambition of their guardian and uncle; and Guiscard was exalted on a buckler, and saluted count of Apulia and general of the republic. With an increase of authority and of force he resumed the conquest of Calabria, and soon aspired to a rank that should raise him for ever above the heads of his equals. By some acts of rapine or sacrilege he had incurred a papal excommunication: but Nicholas the Second was easily persuaded that the divisions of friends could terminate only in their mutual prejudice; that the Normans were the faithful champions of the Holy See; and it was safer to trust the alliance of a prince than the caprice of an aristocracy. A synod of one hundred bishops was convened at Melphi; and the count interrupted an important enterprise to guard the person and execute the decrees of the Roman pontiff. His gratitude and policy conferred on Robert and his posterity the ducal title,[43] with the investiture of Apulia, Calabria, and all the lands, both in Italy and Sicily, which his sword could rescue from the schismatic Greeks and the unbelieving Saracens.[44] This apostolic sanction might justify his arms: but the obedience of a

free and victorious people could not be transferred without their consent; and Guiscard dissembled his elevation till the ensuing campaign had been illustrated by the conquest of Consenza and Reggio. In the hour of triumph he assembled his troops and solicited the Normans to confirm by their suffrage the judgment of the vicar of Christ; the soldiers hailed with joyful acclamations their valiant duke; and the counts, his former equals, pronounced the oath of fidelity with hollow smiles and secret indignation. After this inauguration, Robert styled himself, "By the grace of God and St. Peter, duke of Apulia, Calabria, and hereafter of Sicily;" and it was the labour of twenty years to deserve and realise these lofty appellations. Such tardy progress, in a narrow space, may seem unworthy of the abilities of the chief and the spirit of the nation: but the Normans were few in number; their resources were scanty; their service was voluntary and precarious. The bravest designs of the duke were sometimes opposed by the free voice of his parliament of barons: the twelve counts of popular election conspired against his authority; and against their perfidious uncle the sons of Humphrey demanded justice and revenge. By his policy and vigour Guiscard discovered their plots, suppressed their rebellions, and punished the guilty with death or exile; but in these domestic feuds his years, and the national strength, were unprofitably consumed. After the defeat of his foreign enemies, the Greeks, Lombards, and Saracens, their broken forces retreated to the strong and populous cities of the sea-coast. They excelled in the arts of fortification and defence; the Normans were accustomed to serve on horseback in the field, and their rude attempts could only succeed by the efforts of persevering courage. The resistance of Salerno was maintained above eight months: the siege or blockade of Bari lasted near four years. In these actions the Norman duke was the foremost in every danger, in every fatigue the last and most patient. As he pressed the citadel of Salerno a huge stone from the rampart shattered one of his military engines, and by a splinter he was wounded in the breast. Before the gates of Bari he lodged in a miserable hut or barrack, composed of dry branches, and thatched with straw —a perilous station, on all sides open to the inclemency of the winter and the spears of the enemy.[45]

The Italian conquests of Robert correspond with the limits of the present kingdom of Naples; and the countries united by his arms have not been dissevered by the revolutions of seven hundred years.[46] The monarchy has been composed of the Greek provinces of Calabria and Apulia, of the Lombard principality of Salerno, the republic of Amalphi, and the inland dependencies of the large and ancient duchy of Beneventum. Three districts only were exempted from the common law of subjection—the first for ever, and the two last till the middle of the succeeding century. The city and immediate territory of Benevento had been transferred, by gift or exchange, from the German emperor to the Roman pontiff; and although this holy land was sometimes invaded, the name of St. Peter was finally more potent than the sword of the Normans. Their first colony of Aversa subdued and held the state of Capua, and her princes were reduced to beg their bread before the palace of their fathers. The dukes of Naples, the present metropolis, maintained the popular freedom under the shadow of the Byzantine empire. Among the new acquisitions of Guiscard the science of Salerno[47] and the trade of Amalphi[48] may detain for a moment the curiosity of the reader. I. Of the learned faculties jurisprudence implies the previous establishment of laws and property; and theology may perhaps be superseded by the full light of religion and reason. But the savage and the sage must alike implore the assistance of physic; and if *our* diseases are inflamed by luxury, the mischiefs of blows and wounds would be more frequent in the ruder ages of society. The treasures of Grecian medicine had been communicated to the Arabian colonies of Africa, Spain, and Sicily; and in the intercourse of peace and war a spark of knowledge had been kindled and cherished at Salerno, an illustrious city, in which the men were honest and the women beautiful.[49] A school, the first that arose in the darkness of Europe, was consecrated to the healing art: the conscience of monks and bishops was reconciled to that salutary and lucrative profession; and a crowd of patients of the most eminent rank and most distant climates invited or visited the physicians of Salerno. They were protected by the Norman conquerors; and Guiscard, though bred in arms, could discern the merit and value of a philosopher. After a pilgrimage of thirty-nine years, Constantine, an African Christian, returned from Bagdad, a master of the language and learning of the Arabians; and Salerno was enriched by the practice, the lessons, and the writings of the pupil of Avicenna. The school of medicine has long slept in the name of a university; but her precepts are abridged in a string of aphorisms, bound together in the Leonine verses, or Latin rhymes, of the twelfth century.[50] II. Seven miles to the west of Salerno, and thirty to the south of Naples, the obscure town of Amalphi displayed the power and rewards of industry. The land, however fertile, was of narrow extent; but the sea was accessible and open: the inhabitants first assumed the office of supplying the western world with the manufactures and productions of the East; and this useful traffic was the source of their opulence and freedom. The government was popular, under the administration of a duke and the supremacy of the Greek emperor. Fifty thousand citizens were numbered in the walls of Amalphi; nor was any city more abundantly provided with gold, silver, and the objects of precious luxury. The mariners who swarmed in her port excelled in the theory and practice of navigation and astronomy; and the discovery of the compass, which has opened the globe, is due to their ingenuity or good fortune. Their trade was extended to the coasts, or at least to the commodities, of Africa, Arabia, and India; and their settlements in Constantinople, Antioch, Jerusalem, and Alexandria acquired the privileges of independent colonies.[51] After three hundred years of prosperity Amalphi was oppressed by the arms of the Normans, and sacked by the jealousy of Pisa; but the poverty of one thousand fishermen is yet dignified by the remains of an arsenal, a cathedral, and the palaces of royal merchants.

Roger, the twelfth and last of the sons of Tancred, had been long detained in Normandy by his own and his father's age. He accepted the welcome summons; hastened to the Apulian camp; and deserved at first the esteem, and afterwards the envy, of his elder brother. Their valour and ambition were equal; but the youth, the beauty, the elegant manners, of Roger, engaged the disinterested love of the soldiers and people. So scanty was his allowance, for himself and forty followers, that he descended from conquest to robbery, and from robbery to domestic theft; and so loose were the notions of property, that, by his own historian, at his special command, he is accused of stealing horses from a stable at Melphi.[52] His spirit emerged from poverty and disgrace; from these base practices he rose to the merit and glory of a holy war; and the invasion of Sicily was seconded by the zeal and policy of his brother Guiscard. After the retreat of the Greeks, the *idolaters*, a most audacious reproach of the Catholics, had retrieved their losses and possessions; but the deliverance of the island, so vainly undertaken by the forces of the Eastern empire, was achieved by a small and private band of adventurers.[53] In the first attempt Roger braved, in an open boat, the real and fabulous dangers of Scylla and Charybdis; landed with only sixty soldiers on a hostile shore; drove the Saracens to the gates of Messina; and safely returned with the spoils of the adjacent country. In the fortress of Trani his active and patient courage were equally conspicuous. In his old age he related with pleasure that, by the distress of the siege, himself, and the countess his wife, had been reduced to a single cloak or mantle, which they wore alternately: that in a sally his horse had been slain, and he was dragged away by the Saracens; but that he owed his rescue to his good sword, and had retreated with his saddle on his back, lest the meanest trophy might be left in the hands of the miscreants. In the siege of Trani, three hundred Normans withstood and repulsed the forces of the island. In the field of Ceramio fifty thousand horse and foot were overthrown by one hundred and thirty-six Christian soldiers, without reckoning St. George, who fought on horseback in the foremost ranks. The captive banners, with four camels, were reserved for the successor of St. Peter; and had these barbaric spoils been exposed not in the Vatican, but in the Capitol, they might have revived the memory of the Punic triumphs. These insufficient numbers of the Normans most probably denote their knights, the soldiers of honourable and equestrian rank, each of whom was attended by five or six followers in the field;[54] yet, with the aid of this interpretation, and after every fair allowance on the side of valour, arms, and reputation, the discomfiture of so many myriads will reduce the prudent reader to the alternative of a miracle or a fable. The Arabs of Sicily derived a frequent and powerful succour from their countrymen of Africa: in the siege of Palermo the Norman cavalry was assisted by the galleys of Pisa; and, in the hour of action, the envy of the two brothers was sublimed to a generous and invincible emulation. After a war of thirty years,[55] Roger, with the title of great count, obtained the sovereignty of the largest and most fruitful island of the Mediterranean; and his administration displays a liberal and enlightened mind above the limits of his age and education. The Moslems were maintained in the free enjoyment of their religion and property:[56] a philosopher and physician of Mazara, of the race of Mohammed,

harangued the conqueror, and was invited to court; his geography of the seven climates was translated into Latin; and Roger, after a diligent perusal, preferred the work of the Arabian to the writings of the Grecian Ptolemy.[57] A remnant of Christian natives had promoted the success of the Normans: they were rewarded by the triumph of the cross. The island was restored to the jurisdiction of the Roman pontiff; new bishops were planted in the principal cities, and the clergy was satisfied by a liberal endowment of churches and monasteries. Yet the Catholic hero asserted the rights of the civil magistrate. Instead of resigning the investiture of benefices, he dexterously applied to his own profit the papal claims: the supremacy of the crown was secured and enlarged by the singular bull which declares the princes of Sicily hereditary and perpetual legates of the Holy See.[58]

To Robert Guiscard the conquest of Sicily was more glorious than beneficial: the possession of Apulia and Calabria was inadequate to his ambition; and he resolved to embrace or create the first occasion of invading, perhaps of subduing, the Roman empire of the East.[59] From his first wife, the partner of his humble fortunes, he had been divorced under the pretence of consanguinity; and her son Bohemond was destined to imitate, rather than to succeed, his illustrious father. The second wife of Guiscard was the daughter of the princes of Salerno; the Lombards acquiesced in the lineal succession of their son Roger; their five daughters were given in honourable nuptials,[60] and one of them was betrothed, in a tender age, to Constantine, a beautiful youth, the son and heir of the emperor Michael.[61] But the throne of Constantinople was shaken by a revolution: the Imperial family of Ducas was confined to the palace or the cloister; and Robert deplored and resented the disgrace of his daughter and the expulsion of his ally. A Greek, who styled himself the father of Constantine, soon appeared at Salerno, and related the adventures of his fall and flight. That unfortunate friend was acknowledged by the duke, and adorned with the pomp and titles of Imperial dignity: in his triumphal progress through Apulia and Calabria, Michael[62] was saluted with the tears and acclamations of the people; and pope Gregory the Seventh exhorted the bishops to preach, and the Catholics to fight, in the pious work of his restoration. His conversations with Robert were frequent and familiar; and their mutual promises were justified by the valour of the Normans and the treasures of the East. Yet this Michael, by he confession of the Greeks and Latins, was a pageant and an impostor; a monk who had fled from his convent, or a domestic who had served in the palace. The fraud had been contrived by the subtle Guiscard; and he trusted that, after his pretender had given a decent colour to his arms, he would sink, at the nod of the conqueror, into his primitive obscurity. But victory was the only argument that could determine the belief of the Greeks; and the ardour of the Latins was much inferior to their credulity: the Norman veterans wished to enjoy the harvest of their toils, and the unwarlike Italians trembled at the known and unknown dangers of a transmarine expedition. In his new levies Robert exerted the influence of gifts and promises, the terrors of civil and ecclesiastical authority; and some acts of violence might justify the reproach that age and infancy were pressed without distinction into the service of their unrelenting prince. After two years' incessant preparations the land and naval forces were assembled at Otranto, at the heel, or extreme promontory, of Italy; and Robert was accompanied by his wife, who fought by his side, his son Bohemond, and the representative of the emperor Michael. Thirteen hundred knights[63] of Norman race or discipline formed the sinews of the army, which might be swelled to thirty thousand[64] followers of every denomination. The men, the horses, the arms, the engines, the wooden towers covered with raw hides, were embarked on board one hundred and fifty vessels: the transports had been built in the ports of Italy, and the galleys were supplied by the alliance of the republic of Ragusa.

At the mouth of the Adriatic Gulf the shores of Italy and Epirus incline towards each other. The space between Brundusium and Durazzo, the Roman passage, is no more than one hundred miles;[65] at the last station of Otranto it is contracted to fifty;[66] and this narrow distance had suggested to Pyrrhus and Pompey the sublime or extravagant idea of a bridge. Before the general embarkation the Norman duke despatched Bohemond with fifteen galleys to seize or threaten the isle of Corfu, to survey the opposite coast, and to secure a harbour in the neighbourhood of Vallona for the landing of the troops. They passed and landed without perceiving an enemy; and this successful experiment displayed the neglect and decay of the naval power of the Greeks. The islands of Epirus and the maritime towns were subdued by the arms of the name of Robert, who led his fleet and army from Corfu (I use the modern

appellation) to the siege of Durazzo. That city, the western key of the empire, was guarded by ancient renown and recent fortifications, by George Palæologus, a patrician, victorious in the Oriental wars, and a numerous garrison of Albanians and Macedonians, who, in every age, have maintained the character of soldiers. In the prosecution of his enterprise the courage of Guiscard was assailed by every form of danger and mischance. In the most propitious season of the year, as his fleet passed along the coast, a storm of wind and snow unexpectedly arose; the Adriatic was swelled by the raging blast of the south, and a new shipwreck confirmed the old infamy of the Acroceraunian rocks.[67] The sails, the masts, and the oars were shattered or torn away; the sea and shore were covered with the fragments of vessels, with arms and dead bodies; and the greatest part of the provisions were either drowned or damaged. The ducal galley was laboriously rescued from the waves, and Robert halted seven days on the adjacent cape to collect the relics of his loss and revive the drooping spirits of his soldiers. The Normans were no longer the bold and experienced mariners who had explored the ocean from Greenland to Mount Atlas, and who smiled at the petty dangers of the Mediterranean. They had wept during the tempest; they were alarmed by the hostile approach of the Venetians, who had been solicited by the prayers and promises of the Byzantine court. The first day's action was not disadvantageous to Bohemond, a beardless youth,[68] who led the naval powers of his father. All night the galleys of the republic lay on their anchors in the form of a crescent; and the victory of the second day was decided by the dexterity of their evolutions, the station of their archers, the weight of their javelins, and the borrowed aid of the Greek fire. The Apulian and Ragusian vessels fled to the shore, several were cut from their cables and dragged away by the conqueror; and a sally from the town carried slaughter and dismay to the tents of the Norman duke. A seasonable relief was poured into Durazzo, and, as soon as the besiegers had lost the command of the sea, the islands and maritime towns withdrew from the camp the supply of tribute and provision. That camp was soon afflicted with a pestilential disease; five hundred knights perished by an inglorious death; and the list of burials (if all could obtain a decent burial) amounted to ten thousand persons. Under these calamities the mind of Guiscard alone was firm and invincible; and while he collected new forces from

Apulia and Sicily, he battered, or scaled, or sapped, the walls of Durazzo. But his industry and valour were encountered by equal valour and more perfect industry. A movable turret, of a size and capacity to contain five hundred soldiers, had been rolled forwards to the foot of the rampart; but the descent of the door or drawbridge was checked by an enormous beam, and the wooden structure was instantly consumed by artificial flames.

While the Roman empire was attacked by the Turks in the East, and the Normans in the West, the aged successor of Michael surrendered the sceptre to the hands of Alexius, an illustrious captain, and the founder of the Comnenian dynasty. The princess Anne, his daughter and historian, observes, in her affected style, that even Hercules was unequal to a double combat; and, on this principle, she approves a hasty peace with the Turks, which allowed her father to undertake in person the relief of Durazzo. On his accession, Alexius found the camp without soldiers, and the treasury without money; yet such were the vigour and activity of his measures, that in six months he assembled an army of seventy thousand men,[69] and performed a march of five hundred miles. His troops were levied in Europe and Asia, from Peloponnesus to the Black Sea; his majesty was displayed in the silver arms and rich trappings of the companies of horse-guards; and the emperor was attended by a train of nobles and princes, some of whom, in rapid succession, had been clothed with the purple, and were indulged by the lenity of the times in a life of affluence and dignity. Their youthful ardour might animate the multitude; but their love of pleasure and contempt of subordination were pregnant with disorder and mischief; and their importunate clamours for speedy and decisive action disconcerted the prudence of Alexius, who might have surrounded and starved the besieging army. The enumeration of provinces recalls a sad comparison of the past and present limits of the Roman world: the raw levies were drawn together in haste and terror; and the garrisons of Anatolia, or Asia Minor, had been purchased by the evacuation of the cities which were immediately occupied by the Turks. The strength of the Greek army consisted in the Varangians, the Scandinavian guards, whose numbers were recently augmented by a colony of exiles and volunteers from the British island of Thule. Under the yoke of the Norman conqueror, the Danes and English were oppressed and united; a band of adventurous youths resolved to desert

a land of slavery; the sea was open to their escape; and, in their long pilgrimage, they visited every coast that afforded any hope of liberty and revenge. They were entertained in the service of the Greek emperor; and their first station was in a new city on the Asiatic shore but Alexius soon recalled them to the defence of his person and palace; and bequeathed to his successors the inheritance of their faith and valour.[70] The name of a Norman invader revived the memory of their wrongs: the marched with alacrity against the national foe and panted to regain in Epirus the glory whic they had lost in the battle of Hastings. The Varangians were supported by some companie of Franks or Latins; and the rebels who had fled to Constantinople from the tyranny of Guiscar were eager to signalise their zeal and gratif their revenge. In this emergency the empero had not disdained the impure aid of the Pauli cians or Manichæans of Thrace and Bulgaria and these heretics united with the patience of martyrdom the spirit and discipline of activ valour.[71] The treaty with the sultan had procured a supply of some thousand Turks; and the arrows of the Scythian horse were oppose to the lances of the Norman cavalry. On th report and distant prospect of these formidabl numbers, Robert assembled a council of hi principal officers. "You behold," said he, "you danger: it is urgent and inevitable. The hills ar covered with arms and standards; and the em peror of the Greeks is accustomed to wars an triumphs. Obedience and union are our onl safety; and I am ready to yield the command t a more worthy leader." The vote and acclama tion, even of his secret enemies, assured him, i that perilous moment, of their esteem and con fidence; and the duke thus continued: "Let u trust in the rewards of victory, and depriv cowardice of the means of escape. Let us bur our vessels and our baggage, and give battle o this spot, as if it were the place of our nativit and our burial." The resolution was unani mously approved; and, without confining him self to his lines, Guiscard awaited in battle array the nearer approach of the enemy. Hi rear was covered by a small river; his righ wing extended to the sea; his left to the hills nor was he conscious, perhaps, that on the sam ground Cæsar and Pompey had formerly dis puted the empire of the world.[72]

Against the advice of his wisest captain Alexius resolved to risk the event of a genera action, and exhorted the garrison of Durazzo t assist their own deliverance by a well-time sally from the town. He marched in two columns to surprise the Normans before daybreak on two different sides: his light cavalry was scattered over the plain; the archers formed the second line; and the Varangians claimed the honours of the vanguard. In the first onset the battle-axes of the strangers made a deep and bloody impression on the army of Guiscard, which was now reduced to fifteen thousand men. The Lombards and Calabrians ignominiously turned their backs; they fled towards the river and the sea; but the bridge had been broken down to check the sally of the garrison, and the coast was lined with the Venetian galleys, who played their engines among the disorderly throng. On the verge of ruin, they were saved by the spirit and conduct of their chiefs. Gaita, the wife of Robert, is painted by the Greeks as a warlike Amazon, a second Pallas; less skilful in arts, but not less terrible in arms, than the Athenian goddess:[73] though wounded by an arrow, she stood her ground, and strove, by her exhortation and example, to rally the flying troops.[74] Her female voice was seconded by the more powerful voice and arm of the Norman duke, as calm in action as he was magnanimous in council: "Whither," he cried aloud, "whither do ye fly? Your enemy is implacable; and death is less grievous than servitude." The moment was decisive: as the Varangians advanced before the line, they discovered the nakedness of their flanks: the main battle of the duke, of eight hundred knights, stood firm and entire; they couched their lances, and the Greeks deplore the furious and irresistible shock of the French cavalry.[75] Alexius was not deficient in the duties of a soldier or a general; but he no sooner beheld the slaughter of the Varangians, and the flight of the Turks, than he despised his subjects, and despaired of his fortune. The princess Anne, who drops a tear on this melancholy event, is reduced to praise the strength and swiftness of her father's horse, and his vigorous struggle when he was almost overthrown by the stroke of a lance which had shivered the Imperial helmet. His desperate valour broke through a squadron of Franks who opposed his flight; and after wandering two days and as many nights in the mountains, he found some repose, of body, though not of mind, in the walls of Lychnidus. The victorious Robert reproached the tardy and feeble pursuit which had suffered the escape of so illustrious a prize: but he consoled his disappointment by the trophies and standards of the field, the wealth and luxury of the Byzantine camp, and the

glory of defeating an army five times more numerous than his own. A multitude of Italians had been the victims of their own fears; but only thirty of his knights were slain in this memorable day. In the Roman host, the loss of Greeks, Turks, and English amounted to five or six thousand:[76] the plain of Durazzo was stained with noble and royal blood; and the end of the impostor Michael was more honourable than his life.

It is more than probable that Guiscard was not afflicted by the loss of a costly pageant, which had merited only the contempt and derision of the Greeks. After their defeat they still persevered in the defence of Durazzo; and a Venetian commander supplied the place of George Palæologus, who had been imprudently called away from his station. The tents of the besiegers were converted into barracks, to sustain the inclemency of the winter; and in answer to the defiance of the garrison, Robert insinuated that his patience was at least equal to their obstinacy.[77] Perhaps he already trusted to his secret correspondence with a Venetian noble, who sold the city for a rich and honourable marriage. At the dead of night several rope-ladders were dropped from the walls; the light Calabrians ascended in silence; and the Greeks were awakened by the name and trumpets of the conqueror. Yet they defended the streets three days against an enemy already master of the rampart; and near seven months elapsed between the first investment and the final surrender of the place. From Durazzo the Norman duke advanced into the heart of Epirus or Albania; traversed the first mountains of Thessaly; surprised three hundred English in the city of Castoria; approached Thessalonica; and made Constantinople tremble. A more pressing duty suspended the prosecution of his ambitious designs. By shipwreck, pestilence, and the sword, his army was reduced to a third of the original numbers; and instead of being recruited from Italy, he was informed, by plaintive epistles, of the mischiefs and dangers which had been produced by his absence: the revolt of the cities and barons of Apulia; the distress of the pope; and the approach or invasion of Henry king of Germany. Highly presuming that his person was sufficient for the public safety, he repassed the sea in a single brigantine, and left the remains of the army under the command of his son and the Norman counts, exhorting Bohemond to respect the freedom of his peers, and the counts to obey the authority of their leader. The son of Guiscard trod in the footsteps of his father; and the two destroyers are compared by the Greeks to the caterpillar and the locust, the last of whom devours whatever has escaped the teeth of the former.[78] After winning two battles against the emperor, he descended into the plain of Thessaly, and besieged Larissa, the fabulous realm of Achilles,[79] which contained the treasure and magazines of the Byzantine camp. Yet a just praise must not be refused to the fortitude and prudence of Alexius, who bravely struggled with the calamities of the times. In the poverty of the state, he presumed to borrow the superfluous ornaments of the churches: the desertion of the Manichæans was supplied by some tribes of Moldavia: a reinforcement of seven thousand Turks replaced and revenged the loss of their brethren; and the Greek soldiers were exercised to ride, to draw the bow, and to the daily practice of ambuscades and evolutions. Alexius had been taught by experience that the formidable cavalry of the Franks on foot was unfit for action, and almost incapable of motion;[80] his archers were directed to aim their arrows at the horse rather than the man; and a variety of spikes and snares were scattered over the ground on which he might expect an attack. In the neighbourhood of Larissa the events of war were protracted and balanced. The courage of Bohemond was always conspicuous, and often successful; but his camp was pillaged by a stratagem of the Greeks; the city was impregnable; and the venal or discontented counts deserted his standard, betrayed their trusts, and enlisted in the service of the emperor. Alexius returned to Constantinople with the advantage, rather than the honour, of victory. After evacuating the conquests which he could no longer defend, the son of Guiscard embarked for Italy, and was embraced by a father who esteemed his merit, and sympathised in his misfortune.

Of the Latin princes, the allies of Alexius and enemies of Robert, the most prompt and powerful was Henry the Third or Fourth, king of Germany and Italy, and future emperor of the West. The epistle of the Greek monarch[81] to his brother is filled with the warmest professions of friendship, and the most lively desire of strengthening their alliance by every public and private tie. He congratulates Henry on his success in a just and pious war, and complains that the prosperity of his own empire is disturbed by the audacious enterprises of the Norman Robert. The list of his presents expresses the manners of the age—a radiated crown of gold, a cross set with pearls to hang on the breast, a case of relics with the names and titles of the saints, a vase of crystal, a vase of sardonyx, some balm, most probably of Mecca, and one hundred pieces of purple. To these he added a more solid present, of one hundred and forty-four thousand Byzantines of gold, with a farther assurance of two hundred and sixteen thousand, so soon as Henry should have entered in arms the Apulian territories, and confirmed by an oath the league against the common enemy. The German,[82] who was already in Lombardy at the head of an army and a faction, accepted these liberal offers and marched towards the south: his speed was checked by the sound of the battle of Durazzo; but the influence of his arms, or name, in the hasty return of Robert, was a full equivalent for the Grecian bribe. Henry was the sincere adversary of the Normans, the allies and vassals of Gregory the Seventh, his implacable foe. The long quarrel of the throne and mitre had been recently kindled by the zeal and ambition of that haughty priest:[83] the king and the pope had degraded each other; and each had seated a rival on the temporal or spiritual throne of his antagonist. After the defeat and death of his Swabian rebel, Henry descended into Italy, to assume the Imperial crown, and to drive from the Vatican the tyrant of the church.[84] But the Roman people adhered to the cause of Gregory: their resolution was fortified by supplies of men and money from Apulia; and the city was thrice ineffectually besieged by the king of Germany. In the fourth year he corrupted, as it is said, with Byzantine gold, the nobles of Rome, whose estates and castles had been ruined by the war. The gates, the bridges, and fifty hostages were delivered into his hands: the anti-pope, Clement the Third, was consecrated in the Lateran: the grateful pontiff crowned his protector in the Vatican; and the emperor Henry fixed his residence in the Capitol, as the lawful successor of Augustus and Charlemagne. The ruins of the Septizonium were still defended by the nephew of Gregory: the pope himself was invested in the castle of St. Angelo; and his last hope was in the courage and fidelity of his Norman vassal. Their friendship had been interrupted by some reciprocal injuries and complaints; but, on this pressing occasion, Guiscard was urged by the obligation of his oath, by his interest, more potent than oaths, by the love of fame, and his enmity to the two emperors. Unfurling the holy banner, he resolved to fly to the relief of the prince of the apostles: the most numerous of his armies, six thousand horse and thirty thousand foot, was instantly assembled;

nd his march from Salerno to Rome was animated by the public applause and the promise of the divine favour. Henry, invincible in sixty-six battles, trembled at his approach; recollected some indispensable affairs that required his presence in Lombardy; exhorted the Romans to persevere in their allegiance; and hastily retreated three days before the entrance of the Normans. In less than three years the son of Tancred of Hauteville enjoyed the glory of delivering the pope, and of compelling the two emperors, of the East and West, to fly before his victorious arms.[85] But the triumph of Robert was clouded by the calamities of Rome. By the aid of the friends of Gregory the walls had been perforated or scaled; but the Imperial faction was still powerful and active; on the third day the people rose in a furious tumult; and a hasty word of the conqueror, in his defence or revenge, was the signal of fire and pillage.[86] The Saracens of Sicily, the subjects of Roger, and auxiliaries of his brother, embraced this fair occasion of rifling and profaning the holy city of the Christians; many thousands of the citizens, in the sight and by the allies of their spiritual father, were exposed to violation, captivity, or death; and a spacious quarter of the city, from the Lateran to the Coliseum, was consumed by the flames, and devoted to perpetual solitude.[87] From a city where he was now hated, and might be no longer feared, Gregory retired to end his days in the palace of Salerno. The artful pontiff might flatter the vanity of Guiscard with the hope of a Roman or Imperial crown; but this dangerous measure, which would have inflamed the ambition of the Norman, must for ever have alienated the most faithful princes of Germany.

The deliverer and scourge of Rome might have indulged himself in a season of repose; but in the same year of the flight of the German emperor the indefatigable Robert resumed the design of his Eastern conquests. The zeal or gratitude of Gregory had promised to his valour the kingdoms of Greece and Asia;[88] his troops were assembled in arms, flushed with success, and eager for action. Their numbers, in the language of Homer, are compared by Anna to a swarm of bees;[89] yet the utmost and moderate limits of the powers of Guiscard have been already defined: they were contained in this second occasion in one hundred and twenty vessels, and, as the season was far advanced, the harbour of Brundusium[90] was preferred to the open road of Otranto. Alexius, apprehensive of a second attack, had assiduously laboured to restore the naval forces of the empire, and obtained from the republic of Venice an important succour of thirty-six transports, fourteen galleys, and nine galeots or ships of extraordinary strength and magnitude. Their services were liberally paid by the licence or monopoly of trade, a profitable gift of many shops and houses in the port of Constantinople, and a tribute to St. Mark, the more acceptable, as it was the produce of a tax on their rivals of Amalphi. By the union of the Greeks and Venetians the Adriatic was covered with a hostile fleet; but their own neglect, or the vigilance of Robert, the change of a wind, or the shelter of a mist, opened a free passage, and the Norman troops were safely disembarked on the coast of Epirus. With twenty strong and well-appointed galleys their intrepid duke immediately sought the enemy, and, though more accustomed to fight on horseback, he trusted his own life, and the lives of his brother and two sons, to the event of a naval combat. The dominion of the sea was disputed in three engagements, in sight of the isle of Corfu; in the two former the skill and numbers of the allies were superior; but in the third the Normans obtained a final and complete victory.[91] The light brigantines of the Greeks were scattered in ignominious flight; the nine castles of the Venetians maintained a more obstinate conflict; seven were sunk, two were taken; two thousand five hundred captives implored in vain the mercy of the victor; and the daughter of Alexius deplores the loss of thirteen thousand of his subjects or allies. The want of experience had been supplied by the genius of Guiscard; and each evening, when he had sounded a retreat, he calmly explored the causes of his repulse, and invented new methods how to remedy his own defects and to baffle the advantages of the enemy. The winter season suspended his progress; with the return of spring he again aspired to the conquest of Constantinople; but, instead of traversing the hills of Epirus, he turned his arms against Greece and the islands, where the spoils would repay the labour; and where the land and sea forces might pursue their joint operations with vigour and effect. But in the isle of Cephalonia his projects were fatally blasted by an epidemical disease: Robert himself, in the seventieth year of his age, expired in his tent, and a suspicion of poison was imputed, by public rumour, to his wife, or to the Greek emperor.[92] This premature death might allow a boundless scope for the imagination of his future exploits, and the event sufficiently declares that the Norman greatness was founded on his life.[93] Without the appearance of an enemy a victorious army dispersed or retreated in disorder and consternation, and Alexius, who had trembled for his empire, rejoiced in his deliverance. The galley which transported the remains of Guiscard was shipwrecked on the Italian shore, but the duke's body was recovered from the sea, and deposited in the sepulchre of Venusia,[94] a place more illustrious for the birth of Horace[95] than for the burial of the Norman heroes. Roger, his second son and successor, immediately sunk to the humble station of a duke of Apulia; the esteem or partiality of his father left the valiant Bohemond to the inheritance of his sword. The national tranquillity was disturbed by his claims, till the first crusade against the infidels of the East opened a more splendid field of glory and conquest.[96]

Of human life the most glorious or humble prospects are alike and soon bounded by the sepulchre. The male line of Robert Guiscard was extinguished, both in Apulia and at Antioch, in the second generation; but his younger brother became the father of a line of kings; and the son of the great count was endowed with the name, the conquests, and the spirit of the first Roger.[97] The heir of that Norman adventurer was born in Sicily, and at the age of only four years he succeeded to the sovereignty of the island, a lot which reason might envy could she indulge for a moment the visionary, though virtuous, wish of dominion. Had Roger been content with his fruitful patrimony, a happy and grateful people might have blessed their benefactor; and if a wise administration could have restored the prosperous times of the Greek colonies,[98] the opulence and power of Sicily alone might have equalled the widest scope that could be acquired and desolated by the sword of war. But the ambition of the great count was ignorant of these noble pursuits; it was gratified by the vulgar means of violence and artifice. He sought to obtain the undivided possession of Palermo, of which one moiety had been ceded to the elder branch; struggled to enlarge his Calabrian limits beyond the measure of former treaties; and impatiently watched the declining health of his cousin William of Apulia, the grandson of Robert. On the first intelligence of his premature death, Roger sailed from Palermo with seven galleys, cast anchor in the bay of Salerno, received, after ten days' negotiation, an oath of fidelity from the Norman capital, commanded the submission of the barons, and extorted a legal investiture from the reluctant

popes, who could not long endure either th friendship or enmity of a powerful vassal. Th sacred spot of Benevento was respectfull spared, as the patrimony of St. Peter; but th reduction of Capua and Naples completed th design of his uncle Guiscard; and the sole in heritance of the Norman conquests was po sessed by the victorious Roger. A conscious su periority of power and merit prompted him disdain the titles of duke and of count; and th isle of Sicily, with a third perhaps of the cont nent of Italy, might form the basis of a king dom[99] which would only yield to the monarchi of France and England. The chiefs of the natio who attended his coronation at Palermo migh doubtless pronounce under what name h should reign over them; but the example of Greek tyrant or a Saracen emir were insufficie to justify his regal character; and the nine kin of the Latin world[100] might disclaim their ne associate unless he were consecrated by the au thority of the supreme pontiff. The pride Anacletus was pleased to confer a title whic the pride of the Norman had stooped to soli it;[101] but his own legitimacy was attacked the adverse election of Innocent the Secon and while Anacletus sat in the Vatican, the su cessful fugitive was acknowledged by the na tions of Europe. The infant monarchy of Roge was shaken, and almost overthrown, by the un lucky choice of an ecclesiastical patron; and th sword of Lothaire the Second of Germany, th excommunications of Innocent, the fleets Pisa, and the zeal of St. Bernard, were unite for the ruin of the Sicilian robber. After a ga lant resistance the Norman prince was drive from the continent of Italy: a new duke Apulia was invested by the pope and the em peror, each of whom held one end of the go fanor, or flagstaff, as a token that they asserte their right, and suspended their quarrel. Bu such jealous friendship was of short and pr carious duration: the German armies soon var ished in disease and desertion:[102] the Apulia duke, with all his adherents was exterminate by a conqueror who seldom forgave either th dead or the living; like his predecessor Leo th Ninth, the feeble though haughty pontiff be came the captive and friend of the Norman and their reconciliation was celebrated by th eloquence of Bernard, who now revered th title and virtues of the king of Sicily.

As a penance for his impious war against th successor of St. Peter, that monarch might hav promised to display the banner of the cross, an he accomplished with ardour a vow so prop tious to his interest and revenge. The recent injuries of Sicily might provoke a just retaliation on the heads of the Saracens: the Normans, whose blood had been mingled with so many subject streams, were encouraged to remember and emulate the naval trophies of their fathers, and in the maturity of their strength they contended with the decline of an African power. When the Fatimite caliph departed for the conquest of Egypt, he rewarded the real merit and apparent fidelity of his servant Joseph with a gift of his royal mantle, and forty Arabian horses, his palace, with its sumptuous furniture, and the government of the kingdoms of Tunis and Algiers. The Zeirides,[103] the descendants of Joseph, forgot their allegiance and gratitude to a distant benefactor, grasped and abused the fruits of prosperity; and after running the little course of an Oriental dynasty, were now fainting in their own weakness. On the side of the land they were oppressed by the Almohades, the fanatic princes of Morocco, while the seacoast was open to the enterprise of the Greeks and Franks, who, before the close of the eleventh century, had extorted a ransom of two hundred thousand pieces of gold. By the first arms of Roger, the island or rock of Malta, which has been since ennobled by a military and religious colony, was inseparably annexed to the crown of Sicily. Tripoli,[104] a strong and maritime city, was the next object of his attack; and the slaughter of the males, the captivity of the females, might be justified by the frequent practice of the Moslems themselves. The capital of the Zeirides was named Africa from the country, and Mahadia[105] from the Arabian founder: it is strongly built on a neck of land, but the imperfection of the harbour is not compensated by the fertility of the adjacent plain. Mahadia was besieged by George the Sicilian admiral, with a fleet of one hundred and fifty galleys, amply provided with men and the instruments of mischief; the sovereign had fled, the Moorish governor refused to capitulate, declined the last and irresistible assault, and, secretly escaping with the Moslem inhabitants, abandoned the place and its treasures to the rapacious Franks. In successive expeditions the king of Sicily or his lieutenants reduced the cities of Tunis, Safax, Capsia, Bona, and a long tract of the seacoast;[106] the fortresses were garrisoned, the country was tributary, and a boast that it held Africa in subjection might be inscribed with some flattery on the sword of Roger.[107] After his death that sword was broken; and these transmarine possessions were neglected, evacuated, or lost, under the troubled reign of his successor.[108] The triumphs of Scipio and Belisarius have proved that the African continent is neither inaccessible nor invincible; yet the great princes and powers of Christendom have repeatedly failed in their armaments against the Moors, who may still glory in the easy conquest and long servitude of Spain.

Since the decease of Robert Guiscard the Normans had relinquished, above sixty years, their hostile designs against the empire of the East. The policy of Roger solicited a public and private union with the Greek princes, whose alliance would dignify his regal character: he demanded in marriage a daughter of the Comnenian family, and the first steps of the treaty seemed to promise a favourable event. But the contemptuous treatment of his ambassadors exasperated the vanity of the new monarch; and the insolence of the Byzantine court was expiated according to the laws of nations, by the sufferings of a guiltless people.[109] With a fleet of seventy galleys George the admiral of Sicily appeared before Corfu; and both the island and city were delivered into his hands by the disaffected inhabitants, who had yet to learn that a siege is still more calamitous than a tribute. In this invasion, of some moment in the annals of commerce, the Normans spread themselves by sea, and over the provinces of Greece; and the venerable age of Athens, Thebes, and Corinth, was violated by rapine and cruelty. Of the wrongs of Athens no memorial remains. The ancient walls which encompassed, without guarding, the opulence of Thebes, were scaled by the Latin Christians; but their sole use of the Gospel was to sanctify an oath that the lawful owners had not secreted any relic of their inheritance or industry. On the approach of the Normans the lower town of Corinth was evacuated: the Greeks retired to the citadel, which was seated on a lofty eminence, abundantly watered by the classic fountain of Pirene; an impregnable fortress, if the want of courage could be balanced by any advantages of art or nature. As soon as the besiegers had surmounted the labour (their sole labour) of climbing the hill, their general, from the commanding eminence, admired his own victory, and testified his gratitude to Heaven by tearing from the altar the precious image of Theodore the tutelary saint. The silk-weavers of both sexes, whom George transported to Sicily, composed the most valuable part of the spoil; and in comparing the skilful industry of the mechanic with the sloth and cowardice of the soldier, he was heard to exclaim that the distaff and loom were the only weapons which the Greeks were capable of using. The progress of this naval armament was marked by two conspicuous events, the rescue of the king of France and the insult of the Byzantine capital. In his return by sea from an unfortunate crusade, Louis the Seventh was intercepted by the Greeks, who basely violated the laws of honour and religion. The fortunate encounter of the Norman fleet delivered the royal captive; and after a free and honourable entertainment in the court of Sicily, Louis continued his journey to Rome and Paris.[110] In the absence of the emperor, Constantinople and the Hellespont were left without defence and without the suspicion of danger. The clergy and people, for the soldiers had followed the standard of Manuel, were astonished and dismayed at the hostile appearance of a line of galleys, which boldly cast anchor in the front of the Imperial city. The forces of the Sicilian admiral were inadequate to the siege or assault of an immense and populous metropolis; but George enjoyed the glory of humbling the Greek arrogance, and of marking the path of conquest to the navies of the West. He landed some soldiers to rifle the fruits of the royal gardens, and pointed with silver, or more probably with fire, the arrows which he discharged against the palace of the Cæsars.[111] This playful outrage of the pirates of Sicily, who had surprised an unguarded moment, Manuel affected to despise, while his martial spirit and the forces of the empire were awakened to revenge. The Archipelago and Ionian Sea were covered with his squadrons and those of Venice; but I know not by what favourable allowance of transports, victuallers, and pinnaces, our reason, or even our fancy, can be reconciled to the stupendous account of fifteen hundred vessels, which is proposed by a Byzantine historian. These operations were directed with prudence and energy: in his homeward voyage George lost nineteen of his galleys, which were separated and taken: after an obstinate defence Corfu implored the clemency of her lawful sovereign; nor could a ship, a soldier, of the Norman prince, be found, unless a captive, within the limits of the Eastern empire. The prosperity and the health of Roger were already in a declining state: while he listened in his palace of Palermo to the messengers of victory or defeat, the invincible Manuel, the foremost in every assault, was celebrated by the Greeks and Latins as the Alexander or Hercules of the age.

A prince of such a temper could not be satisfied with having repelled the insolence of a barbarian. It was the right and duty, it might be the interest and glory, of Manuel to restore the ancient majesty of the empire, to recover the provinces of Italy and Sicily, and to chastise this pretended king, the grandson of a Norman vassal.[112] The natives of Calabria were still attached to the Greek language and worship, which had been inexorably proscribed by the Latin clergy: after the loss of her dukes Apulia was chained as a servile appendage to the crown of Sicily: the founder of the monarchy had ruled by the sword; and his death had abated the fear, without healing the discontent, of his subjects: the feudal government was always pregnant with the seeds of rebellion; and a nephew of Roger himself invited the enemies of his family and nation. The majesty of the purple, and a series of Hungarian and Turkish wars, prevented Manuel from embarking his person in the Italian expedition. To the brave and noble Palæologus, his lieutenant, the Greek monarch intrusted a fleet and army: the siege of Bari was his first exploit; and, in every operation, gold as well as steel was the instrument of victory. Salerno, and some places along the western coast, maintained their fidelity to the Norman king; but he lost in two campaigns the greater part of his continental possessions; and the modest emperor, disdaining all flattery and falsehood, was content with the reduction of three hundred cities or villages of Apulia and Calabria, whose names and titles were inscribed on all the walls of the palace. The prejudices of the Latins were gratified by a genuine or fictitious donation under the seal of the German Cæsars;[113] but the successor of Constantine soon renounced this ignominious pretence, claimed the indefeasible dominion of Italy, and professed his design of chasing the barbarians beyond the Alps. By the artful speeches, liberal gifts, and unbounded promises of their Eastern ally, the free cities were encouraged to persevere in their generous struggle against the despotism of Frederic Barbarossa: the walls of Milan were rebuilt by the contributions of Manuel: and he poured, says the historian, a river of gold into the bosom of Ancona, whose attachment to the Greeks was fortified by the jealous enmity of the Venetians.[114] The situation and trade of Ancona rendered it an important garrison in the heart of Italy: it was twice besieged by the arms of Frederic; the Imperial forces were twice repulsed by the spirit of freedom; that spirit was animated by the ambassador of Constantinople; and the most intrepid patriots, the most faithful

ervants, were rewarded by the wealth and honours of the Byzantine court.[115] The pride of
Manuel disdained and rejected a barbarian colleague; his ambition was excited by the hope of
tripping the purple from the German usurpers,
and of establishing in the West as in the East his
awful title of sole emperor of the Romans. With
this view he solicited the alliance of the people
and the bishop of Rome. Several of the nobles
embraced the cause of the Greek monarch; the
splendid nuptials of his niece with Odo Frangipani secured the support of that powerful family,[116] and his royal standard or image was entertained with due reverence in the ancient
metropolis.[117] During the quarrel between Frederic and Alexander the Third, the pope twice
received in the Vatican the ambassadors of
Constantinople. They flattered his piety by the
long-promised union of the two churches,
tempted the avarice of his venal court, and exhorted the Roman pontiff to seize the just provocation, the favourable moment, to humble the
savage insolence of the Alemanni and to acknowledge the true representative of Constantine and Augustus.[118]

But these Italian conquests, this universal
reign, soon escaped from the hand of the Greek
emperor. His first demands were eluded by the
prudence of Alexander the Third, who paused
on this deep and momentous revolution;[119] nor
could the pope be seduced by a personal dispute
to renounce the perpetual inheritance of the
Latin name. After his re-union with Frederic,
he spoke a more peremptory language, confirmed the acts of his predecessors, excommunicated the adherents of Manuel, and pronounced
the final separation of the churches, or at least
the empires, of Constantinople and Rome.[120]
The free cities of Lombardy no longer remembered their foreign benefactor, and, without
preserving the friendship of Ancona, he soon
incurred the enmity of Venice.[121] By his own
avarice, or the complaints of his subjects, the
Greek emperor was provoked to arrest the persons, and confiscate the effects, of the Venetian
merchants. This violation of the public faith
exasperated a free and commercial people: one
hundred galleys were launched and armed in as
many days; they swept the coasts of Dalmatia
and Greece; but after some mutual wounds, the
war was terminated by an agreement, inglorious
to the empire, insufficient for the republic; and
a complete vengeance of these and of fresh injuries was reserved for the succeeding generation. The lieutenant of Manuel had informed
his sovereign that he was strong enough to quell

any domestic revolt of Apulia and Calabria:
but that his forces were inadequate to resist the
impending attack of the king of Sicily. His
prophecy was soon verified: the death of Palæologus devolved the command on several chiefs,
alike eminent in rank, alike defective in military
talents; the Greeks were oppressed by land and
sea; and a captive remnant that escaped the
swords of the Normans and Saracens abjured
all future hostility against the person or dominions of their conqueror.[122] Yet the king of Sicily
esteemed the courage and constancy of Manuel,
who had landed a second army on the Italian
shore: he respectfully addressed the new Justinian; solicited a peace or truce of thirty years;
accepted as a gift the regal title; and acknowledged himself the military vassal of the Roman
empire.[123] The Byzantine Cæsars acquiesced in
this shadow of dominion, without expecting,
perhaps without desiring, the service of a Norman army; and the truce of thirty years was not
disturbed by any hostilities between Sicily and
Constantinople. About the end of that period,
the throne of Manuel was usurped by an inhuman tyrant, who had deserved the abhorrence
of his country and mankind: the sword of William the Second, the grandson of Roger, was
drawn by a fugitive of the Comnenian race;
and the subjects of Andronicus might salute the
strangers as friends, since they detested their
sovereign as the worst of enemies. The Latin
historians[124] expatiate on the rapid progress of
the four counts who invaded Romania with a
fleet and army, and reduced many castles and
cities to the obedience of the king of Sicily. The
Greeks[125] accuse and magnify the wanton sacrilegious cruelties that were perpetrated in the
sack of Thessalonica, the second city of the empire. The former deplore the fate of those invincible but unsuspecting warriors who were
destroyed by the arts of a vanquished foe. The
latter applaud, in songs of triumph, the repeated victories of their countrymen on the sea of
Marmora or Propontis, on the banks of the
Strymon, and under the walls of Durazzo. A
revolution which punished the crimes of Andronicus had united against the Franks the zeal
and courage of the successful insurgents: ten
thousand were slain in battle; and Isaac Angelus, the new emperor, might indulge his vanity
or vengeance in the treatment of four thousand
captives. Such was the event of the last contest
between the Greeks and Normans: before the
expiration of twenty years the rival nations
were lost or degraded in foreign servitude; and
the successors of Constantine did not long sur-

vive to insult the fall of the Sicilian monarchy.

The sceptre of Roger successively devolved to his son and grandson: they might be confounded under the name of William: they are strongly discriminated by the epithets of the *bad* and the *good*; but these epithets, which appear to describe the perfection of vice and virtue, cannot strictly be applied to either of the Norman princes. When he was roused to arms by danger and shame, the first William did not degenerate from the valour of his race; but his temper was slothful; his manners were dissolute; his passions headstrong and mischievous; and the monarch is responsible, not only for his personal vices, but for those of Majo, the great admiral, who abused the confidence, and conspired against the life, of his benefactor. From the Arabian conquest, Sicily had imbibed a deep tincture of Oriental manners; the despotism, the pomp, and even the harem, of a sultan; and a Christian people was oppressed and insulted by the ascendant of the eunuchs, who openly professed, or secretly cherished, the religion of Mohammed. An eloquent historian of the times[126] has delineated the misfortunes of his country:[127] the ambition and fall of the ungrateful Majo; the revolt and punishment of his assassins; the imprisonment and deliverance of the king himself; the private feuds that arose from the public confusion; and the various forms of calamity and discord which afflicted Palermo, the island, and the continent, during the reign of William the First, and the minority of his son. The youth, innocence, and beauty of William the Second,[128] endeared him to the nation: the factions were reconciled; the laws were revived; and from the manhood to the premature death of that amiable prince, Sicily enjoyed a short season of peace, justice, and happiness, whose value was enhanced by the remembrance of the past and the dread of futurity. The legitimate male posterity of Tancred of Hauteville was extinct in the person of the second William; but his aunt, the daughter of Roger, had married the most powerful prince of the age; and Henry the Sixth, the son of Frederic Barbarossa, descended from the Alps, to claim the Imperial crown and the inheritance of his wife. Against the unanimous wish of a free people, this inheritance could only be acquired by arms; and I am pleased to transcribe the style and sense of the historian Falcandus, who writes at the moment, and on the spot, with the feelings of a patriot, and the prophetic eye of a statesman. "Constantia, the daughter of Sicily, nursed from her cradle in the plea-

sures and plenty, and educated in the arts and manners, of this fortunate isle, departed long since to enrich the barbarians with our treasures, and now returns, with her savage allies, to contaminate the beauties of her venerable parent. Already I behold the swarms of angry barbarians: our opulent cities, the places flourishing in a long peace, are shaken with fear, desolated by slaughter, consumed by rapine, and polluted by intemperance and lust. I see the massacre or captivity of our citizens, the rapes of our virgins and matrons.[129] In this extremity (he interrogates a friend) how must the Sicilians act? By the unanimous election of a king of valour and experience, Sicily and Calabria might yet be preserved;[130] for in the levity of the Apulians, ever eager for new revolutions, I can repose neither confidence nor hope.[131] Should Calabria be lost, the lofty towers, the numerous youth, and the naval strength of Messina,[132] might guard the passage against a foreign invader. If the savage Germans coalesce with the pirates of Messina; if they destroy with fire the fruitful region, so often wasted by the fires of Mount Ætna,[133] what resource will be left for the interior parts of the island, these noble cities which should never be violated by the hostile footsteps of a barbarian?[134] Catana has again been overwhelmed by an earthquake: the ancient virtue of Syracuse expires in poverty and solitude;[135] but Palermo is still crowned with a diadem, and her triple walls enclose the active multitudes of Christians and Saracens. If the two nations, under one king, can unite for their common safety, they may rush on the barbarians with invincible arms. But if the Saracens, fatigued by a repetition of injuries, should now retire and rebel; if they should occupy the castles of the mountains and sea-coast, the unfortunate Christians, exposed to a double attack, and placed as it were between the hammer and the anvil, must resign themselves to hopeless and inevitable servitude."[136] We must not forget that a priest here prefers his country to his religion: and that the Moslems, whose alliance he seeks, were still numerous and powerful in the state of Sicily.

The hopes, or at least the wishes, of Falcandus were at first gratified by the free and unanimous election of Tancred, the grandson of the first king, whose birth was illegitimate, but whose civil and military virtues shone without a blemish. During four years, the term of his life and reign, he stood in arms on the farthest verge of the Apulian frontier against the powers of Germany; and the restitution of a royal captive, of Constantia herself, without injury or ransom, may appear to surpass the most liberal measure of policy or reason. After his decease the kingdom of his widow and infant son fell without a struggle, and Henry pursued his victorious march from Capua to Palermo. The political balance of Italy was destroyed by his success; and if the pope and the free cities had consulted their obvious and real interest, they would have combined the powers of earth and heaven to prevent the dangerous union of the German empire with the kingdom of Sicily. But the subtle policy, for which the Vatican has so often been praised or arraigned, was on this occasion blind and inactive; and if it were true that Celestine the Third had kicked away the Imperial crown from the head of the prostrate Henry,[137] such an act of impotent pride could serve only to cancel an obligation and provoke an enemy. The Genoese, who enjoyed a beneficial trade and establishment in Sicily, listened to the promise of his boundless gratitude and speedy departure:[138] their fleet commanded the straits of Messina, and opened the harbour of Palermo; and the first act of his government was to abolish the privileges and to seize the property of these imprudent allies. The last hope of Falcandus was defeated by the discord of the Christians and Mohammedans: they fought in the capital: several thousands of the latter were slain, but their surviving brethren fortified the mountains, and disturbed above thirty years the peace of the island. By the policy of Frederic the Second, sixty thousand Saracens were transplanted to Nocera in Apulia. In their wars against the Roman church, the emperor and his son Mainfroy were strengthened and disgraced by the service of the enemies of Christ; and this national colony maintained their religion and manners in the heart of Italy till they were extirpated, at the end of the thirteenth century, by the zeal and revenge of the house of Anjou.[139] All the calamities which the prophetic orator had deplored were surpassed by the cruelty and avarice of the German conqueror. He violated the royal sepulchres, and explored the secret treasures of the palace, Palermo, and the whole kingdom; the pearls and jewels, however, precious, might be easily removed, but one hundred and sixty horses were laden with the gold and silver of Sicily.[140] The young king, his mother and sisters, and the nobles of both sexes, were separately confined in the fortresses of the Alps, and, on the slightest rumour of rebellion, the captives were deprived of life, of their eyes, or the hope of posterity. Constantia herself was touched with sympathy for the miseries of her country, and the heiress of the Norman line might struggle to check her despotic husband, and to save the patrimony of her new-born son, of an emperor so famous in the next age under the name of Frederic the Second. Ten years after this revolution, the French monarchs annexed to their crown the duchy of Normandy: the sceptre of her ancient dukes had been transmitted, by a granddaughter of William the Conqueror, to the house of Plantagenet; and the adventurous Normans, who had raised so many trophies in France, England, and Ireland, in Apulia, Sicily, and the East, were lost, either in victory or servitude, among the vanquished nations.

CHAPTER LVII

The Turks of the House of Seljuk. Their Revolt against Mahmud, Conqueror of Hindostan. Togrul subdues Persia, and protects the Caliphs. Defeat and Captivity of the Emperor Romanus Diogenes by Alp Arslan. Power and Magnificence of Malek Shah. Conquest of Asia Minor and Syria. State and Oppression of Jerusalem. Pilgrimages to the Holy Sepulchre.

FROM the isle of Sicily the reader must transport himself beyond the Caspian Sea to the original seat of the Turks or Turkmans, against whom the first crusade was principally directed. Their Scythian empire of the sixth century was long since dissolved, but the name was still famous among the Greeks and Orientals, and the fragments of the nation, each a powerful and independent people, were scattered over the desert from China to the Oxus and the Danube: the colony of Hungarians was admitted into the republic of Europe, and the thrones of Asia were occupied by slaves and soldiers of Turkish extraction. While Apulia and Sicily were subdued by the Norman lance, a swarm of these northern shepherds overspread the kingdoms of Persia; their princes of the race of Seljuk erected a splendid and solid empire from Samarcand to the confines of Greece and Egypt, and the Turks have maintained their dominion in Asia Minor till the victorious crescent has been planted on the dome of St. Sophia.

One of the greatest of the Turkish princes was Mamood or Mahmud,[1] the Gaznevide, who reigned in the eastern provinces of Persia one thousand years after the birth of Christ. His father Sebectagi was the slave of the slave of the slave of the commander of the faithful. But in this descent of servitude the first degree was merely titular, since it was filled by the sovereign of Transoxiana and Chorasan, who still paid a nominal allegiance to the caliph of Bagdad. The second rank was that of a minister of state, a lieutenant of the Samanides,[2] who broke, by his revolt, the bonds of political slavery. But the third step was a state of real and domestic servitude in the family of that rebel, from which Sebectagi, by his courage and dexterity, ascended to the supreme command of the city and province of Gazna[3] as the son-in-law and successor of his grateful master. The falling dynasty of the Samanides was at first protected, and at last overthrown, by their servants, and, in the public disorders, the fortune of Mahmud continually increased. For him the title of *Sultan*[4] was first invented; and his kingdom was enlarged from Transoxiana to the neighbourhood of Ispahan, from the shores of the Caspian to the mouth of the Indus. But the principal source of his fame and riches was the holy war which he waged against the Gentoos of Hindostan. In this foreign narrative I may not consume a page, and a volume would scarcely suffice to recapitulate the battles and sieges of his twelve expeditions. Never was the Musulman hero dismayed by the inclemency of the seasons, the height of the mountains, the breadth of the rivers, the barrenness of the desert, the multitudes of the enemy, or the formidable array of their elephants of war.[5] The sultan of Gazna surpassed the limits of the conquests of Alexander; after a march of three months, over the hills of Cashmir and Thibet, he reached the famous city of Kinoge,[6] on the Upper Ganges, and, in a naval combat on one of the branches of the Indus, he fought and vanquished four thousand boats of the natives. Delhi, Lahor, and Multan were compelled to open their gates; the fertile kingdom of Guzarat attracted his ambition and tempted his stay; and his avarice indulged the fruitless project of

discovering the golden and aromatic isles of the Southern Ocean. On the payment of a tribute the *rajahs* preserved their dominions, the people their lives and fortunes: but to the religion of Hindostan the zealous Musulman was cruel and inexorable; many hundred temples or pagodas were levelled with the ground, many thousand idols were demolished, and the servants of the prophet were stimulated and rewarded by the precious materials of which they were composed. The pagoda of Sumnat was situate on the promontory of Guzarat, in the neighbourhood of Diu, one of the last remaining possessions of the Portuguese.[7] It was endowed with the revenue of two thousand villages; two thousand Brahmins were consecrated to the service of the deity, whom they washed each morning and evening in water from the distant Ganges; the subordinate ministers consisted of three hundred musicians, three hundred barbers, and five hundred dancing girls, conspicuous for their birth or beauty. Three sides of the temple were protected by the ocean, the narrow isthmus was fortified by a natural or artificial precipice, and the city and adjacent country were peopled by a nation of fanatics. They confessed the sins and the punishment of Kinoge and Delhi; but if the impious stranger should presume to approach *their* holy precincts, he would surely be overwhelmed by a blast of the divine vengeance. By this challenge the faith of Mahmud was animated to a personal trial of the strength of this Indian deity. Fifty thousand of his worshippers were pierced by the spear of the Moslems; the walls were scaled, the sanctuary was profaned, and the conqueror aimed a blow of his iron mace at the head of the idol. The trembling Brahmins are said to have offered ten millions sterling for his ransom; and it was urged by the wisest counsellors that the destruction of a stone image would not change the hearts of the Gentoos, and that such a sum might be dedicated to the relief of the true believers. "Your reasons," replied the sultan, "are specious and strong; but never in the eyes of posterity shall Mahmud appear as a merchant of idols." He repeated his blows, and a treasure of pearls and rubies, concealed in the belly of the statue, explained in some degree the devout prodigality of the Brahmins. The fragments of the idol were distributed to Gazna, Mecca, and Medina. Bagdad listened to the edifying tale, and Mahmud was saluted by the caliph with the title of guardian of the fortune and faith of Mohammed.

From the paths of blood, and such is the his-

ory of nations, I cannot refuse to turn aside to
gather some flowers of science or virtue. The
name of Mahmud the Gaznevide is still venerable in the East: his subjects enjoyed the blessings of prosperity and peace; his vices were concealed by the veil of religion; and two familiar
examples will testify his justice and magnanimity. I. As he sat in the divan, an unhappy
subject bowed before the throne to accuse the
insolence of a Turkish soldier who had driven
him from his house and bed. "Suspend your
clamours," said Mahmud; "inform me of his
next visit, and ourself in person will judge and
punish the offender." The sultan followed his
guide, invested the house with his guards, and,
extinguishing the torches, pronounced the
death of the criminal, who had been seized in
the act of rapine and adultery. After the execution of his sentence the lights were rekindled,
Mahmud fell prostrate in prayer, and, rising
from the ground, demanded some homely fare,
which he devoured with the voraciousness of
hunger. The poor man, whose injury he had
avenged, was unable to suppress his astonishment and curiosity; and the courteous monarch
condescended to explain the motives of this
singular behaviour. "I had reason to suspect
that none, except one of my sons, could dare to
perpetrate such an outrage; and I extinguished
the lights that my justice might be blind and
inexorable. My prayer was a thanksgiving on
the discovery of the offender; and so painful
was my anxiety, that I had passed three days
without food since the first moment of your
complaint." II. The sultan of Gazna had declared war against the dynasty of the Bowides,
the sovereigns of the western Persia; he was
disarmed by an epistle of the sultana mother,
and delayed his invasion till the manhood of
her son.[8] "During the life of my husband," said
the artful regent, "I was ever apprehensive of
your ambition: he was a prince and a soldier
worthy of your arms. He is now no more; his
sceptre has passed to a woman and a child, and
you *dare not* attack their infancy and weakness.
How inglorious would be your conquest, how
shameful your defeat! and yet the event of war
is in the hand of the Almighty." Avarice was
the only defect that tarnished the illustrious
character of Mahmud; and never has that
passion been more richly satiated. The Orientals exceed the measure of credibility in the
account of millions of gold and silver, such as
the avidity of man has never accumulated; in
the magnitude of pearls, diamonds, and rubies,
such as have never been produced by the work-

manship of nature.[9] Yet the soil of Hindostan is
impregnated with precious minerals: her trade,
in every age, has attracted the gold and silver
of the world; and her virgin spoils were rifled
by the first of the Mohammedan conquerors.
His behaviour, in the last days of his life, evinces
the vanity of these possessions, so laboriously
won, so dangerously held, and so inevitably
lost. He surveyed the vast and various chambers of the treasury of Gazna; burst into tears;
and again closed the doors, without bestowing
any portion of the wealth which he could no
longer hope to preserve. The following day he
reviewed the state of his military force; one
hundred thousand foot, fifty-five thousand
horse, and thirteen hundred elephants of battle.[10] He again wept the instability of human
greatness; and his grief was embittered by the
hostile progress of the Turkmans, whom he had
introduced into the heart of his Persian kingdom.

In the modern depopulation of Asia the regular operation of government and agriculture is
confined to the neighbourhood of cities, and
the distant country is abandoned to the pastoral
tribes of Arabs, Curds, and *Turkmans*.[11] Of the
last-mentioned people, two considerable branches extend on either side of the Caspian Sea: the
western colony can muster forty thousand soldiers; the eastern, less obvious to the traveller,
but more strong and populous, has increased to
the number of one hundred thousand families.
In the midst of civilised nations they preserve
the manners of the Scythian desert, remove
their encampments with the change of seasons,
and feed their cattle among the ruins of palaces and temples. Their flocks and herds are
their only riches; their tents, either black or
white, according to the colour of the banner,
are covered with felt, and of a circular form;
their winter apparel is a sheepskin; a robe of
cloth or cotton their summer garment: the
features of the men are harsh and ferocious; the
countenance of their women is soft and pleasing. Their wandering life maintains the spirit
and exercise of arms; they fight on horseback;
and their courage is displayed in frequent contests with each other and with their neighbours.
For the licence of pasture they pay a slight
tribute to the sovereign of the land; but the
domestic jurisdiction is in the hands of the
chiefs and elders. The first emigration of the
Eastern Turkmans, the most ancient of their
race, may be ascribed to the tenth century of
the Christian era.[12] In the decline of the caliphs,
and the weakness of their lieutenants, the bar-

rier of the Jaxartes was often violated: in each invasion, after the victory or retreat of their countrymen, some wandering tribe, embracing the Mohammedan faith, obtained a free encampment in the spacious plains and pleasant climate of Transoxiana and Carizme. The Turkish slaves who aspired to the throne encouraged these emigrations, which recruited their armies, awed their subjects and rivals, and protected the frontier against the wilder natives of Turkestan; and this policy was abused by Mahmud the Gaznevide beyond the example of former times. He was admonished of his error by a chief of the race of Seljuk, who dwelt in the territory of Bochara. The sultan had inquired what supply of men he could furnish for military service. "If you send," replied Ismael, "one of these arrows into our camp, fifty thousand of your servants will mount on horseback." "And if that number," continued Mahmud, "should not be sufficient?" "Send this second arrow to the horde of Balik, and you will find fifty thousand more." "But," said the Gaznevide, dissembling his anxiety, "if I should stand in need of the whole force of your kindred tribes?" "Despatch my bow," was the last reply of Ismael, "and, as it is circulated around, the summons will be obeyed by two hundred thousand horse." The apprehension of such formidable friendship induced Mahmud to transport the most obnoxious tribes into the heart of Chorasan, where they would be separated from their brethren by the river Oxus, and enclosed on all sides by the walls of obedient cities. But the face of the country was an object of temptation rather than terror; and the vigour of government was relaxed by the absence and death of the sultan of Gazna. The shepherds were converted into robbers; the bands of robbers were collected into an army of conquerors; as far as Ispahan and the Tigris Persia was afflicted by their predatory inroads; and the Turkmans were not ashamed or afraid to measure their courage and numbers with the proudest sovereigns of Asia. Massoud, the son and successor of Mahmud, had too long neglected the advice of his wisest Omrahs. "Your enemies," they repeatedly urged, "were in their origin a swarm of ants; they are now little snakes; and, unless they be instantly crushed, they will acquire the venom and magnitude of serpents." After some alternatives of truce and hostility, after the repulse or partial success of his lieutenants, the sultan marched in person against the Turkmans, who attacked him on all sides with barbarous shouts and irregular onset. "Massoud," says the Per-

sian historian,[13] "plunged singly to oppose the torrent of gleaming arms, exhibiting such acts of gigantic force and valour as never king had before displayed. A few of his friends, roused by his words and actions, and that innate honour which inspires the brave, seconded their lord so well, that, wheresoever he turned his fatal sword, the enemies were mowed down or retreated before him. But now, when victory seemed to blow on his standard, misfortune was active behind it; for when he looked round he beheld almost his whole army, excepting that body he commanded in person, devouring the paths of flight." The Gaznevide was abandoned by the cowardice or treachery of some generals of the Turkish race; and this memorable day of Zendecan[14] founded in Persia the dynasty of the shepherd kings.[15]

The victorious Turkmans immediately proceeded to the election of a king; and, if the probable tale of a Latin historian[16] deserves any credit, they determined by lot the choice of their new master. A number of arrows were successively inscribed with the name of a tribe, a family, and a candidate; they were drawn from the bundle by the hand of a child, and the important prize was obtained by Togrul Beg, the son of Michael, the son of Seljuk, whose surname was immortalised in the greatness of his posterity. The sultan Mahmud, who valued himself on his skill in national genealogy, professed his ignorance of the family of Seljuk; yet the father of that race appears to have been a chief of power and renown.[17] For a daring intrusion into the harem of his prince, Seljuk was banished from Turkestan: with a numerous tribe of his friends and vassals he passed the Jaxartes, encamped in the neighbourhood of Samarcand, embraced the religion of Mohammed, and acquired the crown of martyrdom in a war against the infidels. His age, of a hundred and seven years, surpassed the life of his son, and Seljuk adopted the care of his two grandsons, Togrul and Jaafar, the eldest of whom, at the age of forty-five, was invested with the title of Sultan in the royal city of Nishabur. The blind determination of chance was justified by the virtues of the successful candidate. It would be superfluous to praise the valour of a Turk; and the ambition of Togrul[18] was equal to his valour. By his arms the Gaznevides were expelled from the eastern kingdoms of Persia, and gradually driven to the banks of the Indus, in search of a softer and more wealthy conquest. In the West he annihilated the dynasty of the Bowides; and the sceptre of Irak passed from he Persian to the Turkish nation. The princes who had felt, or who feared, the Seljukian arrows bowed their heads in the dust; by the conquest of Aderbijan, or Media, he approached the Roman confines; and the shepherd presumed to despatch an ambassador, or herald to demand the tribute and obedience of the emperor of Constantinople.[19] In his own dominions Togrul was the father of his soldiers and people; by a firm and equal administration Persia was relieved from the evils of anarchy; and the same hands which had been imbrued in blood became the guardians of justice and the public peace. The more rustic, perhaps the wisest, portion of the Turkmans[20] continued to dwell in the tents of their ancestors; and, from the Oxus to the Euphrates, these military colonies were protected and propagated by their native princes. But the Turks of the court and city were refined by business and softened by pleasure: they imitated the dress, language, and manners of Persia; and the royal palaces of Nishabur and Rei displayed the order and magnificence of a great monarchy. The most deserving of the Arabians and Persians were promoted to the honours of the state; and the whole body of the Turkish nation embraced with fervour and sincerity the religion of Mohammed. The northern swarms of barbarians who overspread both Europe and Asia have been irreconcilably separated by the consequences of a similar conduct. Among the Moslems, as among the Christians, their vague and local traditions have yielded to the reason and authority of the prevailing system, to the fame of antiquity, and the consent of nations. But the triumph of the Koran is more pure and meritorious as it was not assisted by any visible splendour of worship which might allure the pagans by some resemblance of idolatry. The first of the Seljukian sultans was conspicuous by his zeal and faith; each day he repeated the five prayers which are enjoined to the true believers; of each week the two first days were consecrated by an extraordinary fast; and in every city a mosch was completed before Togrul presumed to lay the foundations of a palace.[21]

With the belief of the Koran, the son of Seljuk imbibed a lively reverence for the successor of the prophet. But that sublime character was still disputed by the caliphs of Bagdad and Egypt, and each of the rivals was solicitous to prove his title in the judgment of the strong, though illiterate, barbarians. Mahmud the Gaznevide had declared himself in favour of the line of Abbas; and had treated with indignity the robe of honour which was presented by the Fatimite ambassador. Yet the ungrateful Hashemite had changed with the change of fortune; he applauded the victory of Zendecan, and named the Seljukian sultan his temporal vicegerent over the Moslem world. As Togrul executed and enlarged this important trust, he was called to the deliverance of the caliph Cayem, and obeyed the holy summons, which gave a new kingdom to his arms.[22] In the palace of Bagdad the commander of the faithful still slumbered, a venerable phantom. His servant or master, the prince of the Bowides, could no longer protect him from the insolence of meaner tyrants; and the Euphrates and Tigris were oppressed by the revolt of the Turkish and Arabian emirs. The presence of a conqueror was implored as a blessing; and the transient mischiefs of fire and sword were excused as the sharp but salutary remedies which alone could restore the health of the republic. At the head of an irresistible force the sultan of Persia marched from Hamadan: the proud were crushed, the prostrate were spared; the prince of the Bowides disappeared; the heads of the most obstinate rebels were laid at the feet of Togrul; and he inflicted a lesson of obedience on the people of Mosul and Bagdad. After the chastisement of the guilty, and the restoration of peace, the royal shepherd accepted the reward of his labours; and a solemn comedy represented the triumph of religious prejudice over barbarian power.[23] The Turkish sultan embarked on the Tigris, landed at the gate of Racca, and made his public entry on horseback. At the palace-gate he respectfully dismounted, and walked on foot, preceded by his emirs without arms. The caliph was seated behind his black veil: the black garment of the Abbassides was cast over his shoulders, and he held in his hand the staff of the apostle of God. The conqueror of the East kissed the ground, stood some time in a modest posture, and was led towards the throne by the vizir and an interpreter. After Togrul had seated himself on another throne his commission was publicly read, which declared him the temporal lieutenant of the vicar of the prophet. He was successively invested with seven robes of honour, and presented with seven slaves, the natives of the seven climates of the Arabian empire. His mystic veil was perfumed with musk; two crowns were placed on his head; two scimitars were girded to his side, as the symbols of a double reign over the East and West. After this inauguration the sultan was prevented from prostrating himself a second time; but he twice kissed the hand of the commander of the faithful, and his titles were proclaimed by the voice of heralds and the applause of the Moslems. In a second visit to Bagdad the Seljukian prince again rescued the caliph from his enemies; and devoutly, on foot, led the bridle of his mule from the prison to the palace. Their alliance was cemented by the marriage of Togrul's sister with the successor of the prophet. Without reluctance he had introduced a Turkish virgin into his harem; but Cayem proudly refused his daughter to the sultan, disdained to mingle the blood of the Hashemites with the blood of a Scythian shepherd; and protracted the negotiation many months, till the gradual diminution of his revenue admonished him that he was still in the hands of a master. The royal nuptials were followed by the death of Togrul himself;[24] as he left no children, his nephew Alp Arslan succeeded to the title and prerogatives of sultan; and his name, after that of the caliph, was pronounced in the public prayers of the Moslems. Yet in this revolution the Abbassides acquired a larger measure of liberty and power. On the throne of Asia the Turkish monarchs were less jealous of the domestic administration of Bagdad; and the commanders of the faithful were relieved from the ignominious vexations to which they had been exposed by the presence and poverty of the Persian dynasty.

Since the fall of the caliphs, the discord and degeneracy of the Saracens respected the Asiatic provinces of Rome; which, by the victories of Nicephorus, Zimisces, and Basil, had been extended as far as Antioch and the eastern boundaries of Armenia. Twenty-five years after the death of Basil, his successors were suddenly assaulted by an unknown race of barbarians, who united the Scythian valour with the fanaticism of new proselytes, and the art and riches of a powerful monarchy.[25] The myriads of Turkish horse overspread a frontier of six hundred miles from Tauris to Arzeroum, and the blood of one hundred and thirty thousand Christians was a grateful sacrifice to the Arabian prophet. Yet the arms of Togrul did not make any deep or lasting impression on the Greek empire. The torrent rolled away from the open country; the sultan retired without glory or success from the siege of an Armenian city; the obscure hostilities were continued or suspended with a vicissitude of events; and the bravery of the Macedonian legions renewed the fame of the conqueror of Asia.[26] The name of Alp Arslan, the valiant lion, is expressive of the popular idea of the perfection of man; and the successor of Togrul displayed the fierceness and generosity of the royal animal. He passed the Euphrates at the head of the Turkish cavalry, and entered Cæsarea, the metropolis of Cappadocia, to which he had been attracted by the fame and wealth of the temple of St. Basil. The solid structure resisted the destroyer: but he carried away the doors of the shrine incrusted with gold and pearls, and profaned the relics of the tutelar saint, whose mortal frailties were now covered by the venerable rust of antiquity. The final conquest of Armenia and Georgia was achieved by Alp Arslan. In Armenia, the title of a kingdom, and the spirit of a nation, were annihilated: the artificial fortifications were yielded by the mercenaries of Constantinople; by strangers without faith, veterans without pay or arms, and recruits without experience or discipline. The loss of this important frontier was the news of a day: and the Catholics were neither surprised nor displeased that a people so deeply infected with the Nestorian and Eutychian errors had been delivered by Christ and his mother into the hands of the infidels.[27] The woods and valleys of Mount Caucasus were more strenuously defended by the native Georgians,[28] or Iberians: but the Turkish sultan and his son Malek were indefatigable in this holy war: their captives were compelled to promise a spiritual, as well as temporal, obedience; and, instead of their collars and bracelets, an iron horse-shoe, a badge of ignominy, was imposed on the infidels who still adhered to the worship of their fathers. The change, however, was not sincere or universal; and, through ages of servitude, the Georgians have maintained the succession of their princes and bishops. But a race of men whom Nature has cast in her most perfect mould is degraded by poverty, ignorance, and vice; their profession, and still more their practice, of Christianity is an empty name, and if they have emerged from heresy, it is only because they are too illiterate to remember a metaphysical creed.[29]

The false or genuine magnanimity of Mahmud the Gaznevide was not imitated by Alp Arslan; and he attacked without scruple the Greek empress Eudocia and her children. His alarming progress compelled her to give herself and her sceptre to the hand of a soldier; and Romanus Diogenes was invested with the Imperial purple. His patriotism, and perhaps his pride, urged him from Constantinople within two months after his accession; and the next campaign he most scandalously took the field during the holy festival of Easter. In the palace, Diogenes was no more than the husband of Eudocia: in the camp, he was the emperor of the Romans, and he sustained that character with feeble resources and invincible courage. By his spirit and success, the soldiers were taught to act, the subjects to hope, and the enemies to fear. The Turks had penetrated into the heart of Phrygia; but the sultan himself had resigned to his emirs the prosecution of the war; and their numerous detachments were scattered over Asia in the security of conquest. Laden with spoil, and careless of discipline, they were separately surprised and defeated by the Greeks: the activity of the emperor seemed to multiply his presence; and while they heard of his expedition to Antioch, the enemy felt his sword on the hills of Trebizond. In three laborious campaigns the Turks were driven beyond the Euphrates: in the fourth and last, Romanus undertook the deliverance of Armenia. The desolation of the land obliged him to transport a supply of two months' provisions; and he marched forwards to the siege of Malazkerd,[30] an important fortress in the midway between the modern cities of Arzeroum and Van. His army amounted, at the least, to one hundred thousand men. The troops of Constantinople were reinforced by the disorderly multitudes of Phrygia and Cappadocia; but the real strength was composed of the subjects and allies of Europe, the legions of Macedonia, and the squadrons of Bulgaria; the Uzi, a Moldavian horde, who were themselves of the Turkish race;[31] and, above all, the mercenary and adventurous bands of French and Normans. Their lances were commanded by the valiant Ursel of Baliol, the kinsman or father of the Scottish kings,[32] and were allowed to excel in the exercise of arms, or, according to the Greek style, in the practice of the Pyrrhic dance.

On the report of this bold invasion, which threatened his hereditary dominions, Alp Arslan flew to the scene of action at the head of forty thousand horse.[33] His rapid and skilful evolutions distressed and dismayed the superior numbers of the Greeks; and in the defeat of Basilacius, one of their principal generals, he displayed the first example of his valour and clemency. The imprudence of the emperor has separated his forces after the reduction of Malazkerd. It was in vain that he attempted to recall the mercenary Franks: they refused to obey his summons; he disdained to await their return: the desertion of the Uzi filled his mind with anxiety and suspicion; and against the

most salutary advice he rushed forwards to speedy and decisive action. Had he listened to the fair proposals of the sultan, Romanus might have secured a retreat, perhaps a peace; but in these overtures he supposed the fear or weakness of the enemy, and his answer was conceived in the tone of insult and defiance. "If the barbarian wishes for peace, let him evacuate the ground which he occupies for the encampment of the Romans, and surrender his city and palace of Rei as a pledge of his sincerity." Alp Arslan smiled at the vanity of the demand, but he wept the death of so many faithful Moslems; and after a devout prayer, proclaimed a free permission to all who were desirous of retiring from the field. With his own hands he tied up his horse's tail, exchanged his bow and arrows for a mace and scimitar, clothed himself in a white garment, perfumed his body with musk, and declared that, if he were vanquished, that spot should be the place of his burial.[34] The sultan himself had affected to cast away his missile weapons; but his hopes of victory were placed in the arrows of the Turkish cavalry, whose squadrons were loosely distributed in the form of a crescent. Instead of the successive lines and reserves of the Grecian tactics, Romanus led his army in a single and solid phalanx, and pressed with vigour and impatience the artful and yielding resistance of the barbarians. In this desultory and fruitless combat he wasted the greater part of a summer's day, till prudence and fatigue compelled him to return to his camp. But a retreat is always perilous in the face of an active foe; and no sooner had the standard been turned to the rear than the phalanx was broken by the base cowardice, or the baser jealousy, of Andronicus, a rival prince, who disgraced his birth and the purple of the Cæsars.[35] The Turkish squadrons poured a cloud of arrows on this moment of confusion and lassitude; and the horns of their formidable crescent were closed in the rear of the Greeks. In the destruction of the army and pillage of the camp, it would be needless to mention the number of the slain or captives. The Byzantine writers deplore the loss of an inestimable pearl: they forgot to mention, that in this fatal day the Asiatic provinces of Rome were irretrievably sacrificed.

As long as a hope survived, Romanus attempted to rally and save the relics of his army. When the centre, the Imperial station, was left naked on all sides, and encompassed by the victorious Turks, he still, with desperate courage, maintained the fight till the close of day, at the head of the brave and faithful subjects who adhered to his standard. They fell around him; his horse was slain; the emperor was wounded; yet he stood alone and intrepid till he was oppressed and bound by the strength of multitudes. The glory of this illustrious prize was disputed by a slave and a soldier; a slave who had seen him on the throne of Constantinople, and a soldier whose extreme deformity had been excused on the promise of some signal service. Despoiled of his arms, his jewels, and his purple, Romanus spent a dreary and perilous night on the field of battle, amidst a disorderly crowd of the meaner barbarians. In the morning the royal captive was presented to Alp Arslan, who doubted of his fortune, till the identity of the person was ascertained by the report of his ambassadors, and by the more pathetic evidence of Basilacius, who embraced with tears the feet of his unhappy sovereign. The successor of Constantine, in a plebeian habit, was led into the Turkish divan and commanded to kiss the ground before the lord of Asia. He reluctantly obeyed; and Alp Arslan, starting from his throne, is said to have planted his foot on the neck of the Roman emperor.[36] But the fact is doubtful; and if, in this moment of insolence, the sultan complied with the national custom, the rest of his conduct has extorted the praise of his bigoted foes, and may afford a lesson to the most civilised ages. He instantly raised the royal captive from the ground; and thrice clasping his hand with tender sympathy, assured him that his life and dignity should be inviolate in the hands of a prince who had learned to respect the majesty of his equals and the vicissitudes of fortune. From the divan Romanus was conducted to an adjacent tent, where he was served with pomp and reverence by the officers of the sultan, who, twice each day, seated him in the place of honour at his own table. In a free and familiar conversation of eight days, not a word, not a look, of insult escaped from the conqueror; but he severely censured the unworthy subjects who had deserted their valiant prince in the hour of danger, and gently admonished his antagonist of some errors which he had committed in the management of the war. In the preliminaries of negotiation Alp Arslan asked him what treatment he expected to receive, and the calm indifference of the emperor displays the freedom of his mind. "If you are cruel," said he, "you will take my life; if you listen to pride, you will drag me at your chariot wheels; if you consult your interest, you will accept a ransom and re-

store me to my country." "And what," continued the sultan, "would have been your own behaviour had fortune smiled on your arms?" The reply of the Greek betrays a sentiment which prudence, and even gratitude, should have taught him to suppress. "Had I vanquished," he fiercely said, "I would have inflicted on thy body many a stripe." The Turkish conqueror smiled at the insolence of his captive; observed that the Christian law inculcated the love of enemies and forgiveness of injuries; and nobly declared that he would not imitate an example which he condemned. After mature deliberation, Alp Arslan dictated the terms of liberty and peace, a ransom of a million, an annual tribute of three hundred and sixty thousand pieces of gold,[37] the marriage of the royal children, and the deliverance of all the Moslems who were in the power of the Greeks. Romanus, with a sigh, subscribed this treaty, so disgraceful to the majesty of the empire: he was immediately invested with a Turkish robe of honour; his nobles and patricians were restored to their sovereign; and the sultan, after a courteous embrace, dismissed him with rich presents and a military guard. No sooner did he reach the confines of the empire than he was informed that the palace and provinces had disclaimed their allegiance to a captive; a sum of two hundred thousand pieces was painfully collected; and the fallen monarch transmitted this part of his ransom, with a sad confession of his impotence and disgrace. The generosity, or perhaps the ambition, of the sultan prepared to espouse the cause of his ally; but his designs were prevented by the defeat, imprisonment, and death of Romanus Diogenes.[38]

In the treaty of peace it does not appear that Alp Arslan extorted any province or city from the captive emperor; and his revenge was satisfied with the trophies of his victory, and the spoils of Anatolia, from Antioch to the Black Sea. The fairest part of Asia was subject to his laws: twelve hundred princes, or the sons of princes, stood before his throne; and two hundred thousand soldiers marched under his banners. The sultan disdained to pursue the fugitive Greeks; but he meditated the more glorious conquest of Turkestan, the original seat of the house of Seljuk. He moved from Bagdad to the banks of the Oxus; a bridge was thrown over the river; and twenty days were consumed in the passage of his troops. But the progress of the great king was retarded by the governor of Berzem; and Joseph the Carizmian presumed to defend his fortress against the powers of the

East. When he was produced a captive in the royal tent, the sultan, instead of praising his valour, severely reproached his obstinate folly; and the insolent replies of the rebel provoked a sentence, that he should be fastened to four stakes and left to expire in that painful situation. At this command the desperate Carizmian, drawing a dagger, rushed headlong towards the throne: the guards raised their battle-axes; their zeal was checked by Alp Arslan, the most skilful archer of the age: he drew his bow, but his foot slipped, the arrow glanced aside, and he received in his breast the dagger of Joseph, who was instantly cut in pieces. The wound was mortal; and the Turkish prince bequeathed a dying admonition to the pride of kings. "In my youth," said Alp Arslan, "I was advised by a sage to humble myself before God; to distrust my own strength; and never to despise the most contemptible foe. I have neglected these lessons; and my neglect has been deservedly punished. Yesterday, as from an eminence I beheld the numbers, the discipline, and the spirit of my armies, the earth seemed to tremble under my feet; and I said in my heart, Surely thou art the king of the world, the greatest and most invincible of warriors. These armies are no longer mine; and, in the confidence of my personal strength, I now fall by the hand of an assassin."[39] Alp Arslan possessed the virtues of a Turk and a Musulman; his voice and stature commanded the reverence of mankind; his face was shaded with long whiskers; and his ample turban was fashioned in the shape of a crown. The remains of the sultan were deposited in the tomb of the Seljukian dynasty; and the passenger might read and meditate this useful inscription:[40] "O YE WHO HAVE SEEN THE GLORY OF ALP ARSLAN EXALTED TO THE HEAVENS, REPAIR TO MARU, AND YOU WILL BEHOLD IT BURIED IN THE DUST." The annihilation of the inscription, and the tomb itself, more forcibly proclaims the instability of human greatness.

During the life of Alp Arslan his eldest son had been acknowledged as the future sultan of the Turks. On his father's death the inheritance was disputed by an uncle, a cousin, and a brother: they drew their scimitars and assembled their followers; and the triple victory of Malek Shah[41] established his own reputation and the right of primogeniture. In every age, and more especially in Asia, the thirst of power has inspired the same passions and occasioned the same disorders; but, from the long series of civil war, it would not be easy to extract a sentiment more pure and magnanimous than is contained in a saying of the Turkish prince. On the eve of the battle he performed his devotions at Thous, before the tomb of the Imam Riza. As the sultan rose from the ground he asked his vizir, Nizam, who had knelt beside him, what had been the object of his secret petition: "That your arms may be crowned with victory," was the prudent, and most probably the sincere, answer of the minister. "For my part," replied the generous Malek, "I implored the Lord of hosts that he would take from me my life and crown, if my brother be more worthy than myself to reign over the Moslems." The favourable judgment of Heaven was ratified by the caliph; and for the first time the sacred title of Commander of the Faithful was communicated to a barbarian. But this barbarian, by his personal merit and the extent of his empire, was the greatest prince of his age. After the settlement of Persia and Syria he marched at the head of innumerable armies to achieve the conquest of Turkestan which had been undertaken by his father. In his passage of the Oxus the boatmen, who had been employed in transporting some troops, complained that their payment was assigned on the revenues of Antioch. The sultan frowned at this preposterous choice; but he smiled at the artful flattery of his vizir. "It was not to postpone their reward that I selected those remote places, but to leave a memorial to posterity, that, under your reign, Antioch and the Oxus were subject to the same sovereign." But this description of his limits was unjust and parsimonious: beyond the Oxus he reduced to his obedience the cities of Bochara, Carizme, and Samarcand, and crushed each rebellious slave or independent savage who dared to resist. Malek passed the Sihon or Jaxartes, the last boundary of Persian civilisation: the hordes of Turkestan yielded to his supremacy: his name was inserted on the coins and in the prayers of Cashgar, a Tartar kingdom on the extreme borders of China. From the Chinese frontier he stretched his immediate jurisdiction of feudatory sway to the west and south, as far as the mountains of Georgia, the neighbourhood of Constantinople, the holy city of Jerusalem, and the spicy groves of Arabia Felix. Instead of resigning himself to the luxury of his harem, the shepherd king, both in peace and war, was in action and in the field. By the perpetual motion of the royal camp each province was successively blessed with his presence; and he is said to have perambulated twelve times the wide extent of his dominions, which surpassed the *Asi-*

atic reign of Cyrus and the caliphs. Of these expeditions the most pious and splendid was the pilgrimage of Mecca; the freedom and safety of the caravans were protected by his arms; the citizens and pilgrims were enriched by the profusion of his alms; and the desert was cheered by the places of relief and refreshment which he instituted for the use of his brethren. Hunting was the pleasure, and even the passion, of the sultan, and his train consisted of forty-seven thousand horses; but after the massacre of a Turkish chase, for each piece of game he bestowed a piece of gold on the poor, a slight atonement, at the expense of the people, for the cost and mischief of the amusement of kings. In the peaceful prosperity of his reign the cities of Asia were adorned with palaces and hospitals, with moschs and colleges: few departed from his divan without reward, and none without justice. The language and literature of Persia revived under the house of Seljuk;[42] and if Malek emulated the liberality of a Turk less potent than himself,[43] his palace might resound with the songs of a hundred poets. The sultan bestowed a more serious and learned care on the reformation of the calendar, which was affected by a general assembly of the astronomers of the East. By a law of the prophet the Moslems are confined to the irregular course of the lunar months; in Persia, since the age of Zoroaster, the revolution of the sun has been known and celebrated as an annual festival;[44] but after the fall of the Magian empire, the intercalation had been neglected; the fractions of minutes and hours were multiplied into days; and the date of the spring was removed from the sign of Aries to that of Pisces. The reign of Malek was illustrated by the Gelalæan era; and all errors, either past or future, were corrected by a computation of time, which surpasses the Julian, and approaches the accuracy of the Gregorian, style.[45]

In a period when Europe was plunged in the deepest barbarism, the light and splendour of Asia may be ascribed to the docility rather than the knowledge of the Turkish conquerors. An ample share of their wisdom and virtue is due to a Persian vizir, who ruled the empire under the reigns of Alp Arslan and his son. Nizam, one of the most illustrious ministers of the East, was honoured by the caliph as an oracle of religion and science; he was trusted by the sultan as the faithful vicegerent of his power and justice. After an administration of thirty years, the fame of the vizir, his wealth, and even his services, were transformed into crimes. He was overthrown by the insidious arts of a wom-

an and a rival; and his fall was hastened by a rash declaration, that his cap and inkhorn, the badges of his office, were connected by the divine decree with the throne and diadem of the sultan. At the age of ninety-three years the venerable statesman was dismissed by his master, accused by his enemies, and murdered by a fanatic: the last words of Nizam attested his innocence, and the remainder of Malek's life was short and inglorious. From Ispahan, the scene of this disgraceful transaction, the sultan moved to Bagdad, with the design of transplanting the caliph, and of fixing his own residence in the capital of the Moslem world. The feeble successor of Mohammed obtained a respite of ten days; and before the expiration of the term the barbarian was summoned by the angel of death. His ambassadors at Constantinople had asked in marriage a Roman princess; but the proposal was decently eluded, and the daughter of Alexius, who might herself have been the victim, expresses her abhorrence of this unnatural conjunction.[46] The daughter of the sultan was bestowed on the caliph Moctadi, with the imperious condition that, renouncing the society of his wives and concubines, he should for ever confine himself to this honourable alliance.

The greatness and unity of the Turkish empire expired in the person of Malek Shah. His vacant throne was disputed by his brother and his four sons; and, after a series of civil wars, the treaty which reconciled the surviving candidates confirmed a lasting separation in the Persian dynasty, the eldest and principal branch of the house of Seljuk. The three younger dynasties were those of Kerman, of Syria, and of Roum: the first of these commanded an extensive, though obscure,[47] dominion on the shores of the Indian Ocean;[48] the second expelled the Arabian princes of Aleppo and Damascus; and the third, our peculiar care, invaded the Roman provinces of Asia Minor. The generous policy of Malek contributed to their elevation: he allowed the princes of his blood, even those whom he had vanquished in the field, to seek new kingdoms worthy of their ambition; nor was he displeased that they should draw away the more ardent spirits who might have disturbed the tranquillity of his reign. As the supreme head of his family and nation, the great sultan of Persia commanded the obedience and tribute of his royal brethren: the thrones of Kerman and Nice, of Aleppo and Damascus, the Atabeks and emirs of Syria and Mesopotamia, erected their standards under the shadow of his sceptre:[49] and the hordes of Turkmans overspread the plains of the Western Asia. After the death of Malek the bands of union and subordination were relaxed and finally dissolved: the indulgence of the house of Seljuk invested their slaves with the inheritance of kingdoms; and, in the Oriental style, a crowd of princes arose from the dust of their feet.[50]

A prince of the royal line, Cutulmish, the son of Izrail, the son of Seljuk, had fallen in a battle against Alp Arslan: and the humane victor had dropped a tear over his grave. His five sons, strong in arms, ambitious of power, and eager for revenge, unsheathed their scimitars against the son of Alp Arslan. The two armies expected the signal, when the caliph, forgetful of the majesty which secluded him from vulgar eyes, interposed his venerable mediation. "Instead of shedding the blood of your brethren, your brethren both in descent and faith, unite your forces in a holy war against the Greeks, the enemies of God and his apostle." They listened to his voice; the sultan embraced his rebellious kinsmen; and the eldest, the valiant Soliman, accepted the royal standard, which gave him the free conquest and hereditary command of the provinces of the Roman empire, from Arzeroum to Constantinople and the unknown regions of the West.[51] Accompanied by his four brothers, he passed the Euphrates: the Turkish camp was soon seated in the neighbourhood of Kutaieh in Phrygia; and his flying cavalry laid waste the country as far as the Hellespont and the Black Sea. Since the decline of the empire the peninsula of Asia Minor had been exposed to the transient though destructive inroads of the Persians and Saracens; but the fruits of a lasting conquest were reserved for the Turkish sultan; and his arms were introduced by the Greeks, who aspired to reign on the ruins of their country. Since the captivity of Romanus, six years the feeble son of Eudocia had trembled under the weight of the Imperial crown, till the provinces of the East and West were lost in the same month by a double rebellion: of either chief Nicephorus was the common name; but the surnames of Bryennius and Botoniates distinguish the European and Asiatic candidates. Their reasons, or rather their promises, were weighed in the divan; and, after some hesitation, Soliman declared himself in favour of Botoniates, opened a free passage to his troops in their march from Antioch to Nice, and joined the banner of the crescent to that of the cross. After his ally had ascended the throne of Constantinople, the sultan was hospitably entertained in the suburb of Chrysopolis or Scutari; and a body of two thousand Turks was transported into Europe, to whose dexterity and courage the new emperor was indebted for the defeat and captivity of his rival Bryennius. But the conquest of Europe was dearly purchased by the sacrifice of Asia; Constantinople was deprived of the obedience and revenue of the provinces beyond the Bosphorus and Hellespont; and the regular progress of the Turks, who fortified the passes of the rivers and mountains, left not a hope of their retreat or expulsion. Another candidate implored the aid of the sultan: Melissenus, in his purple robes and red buskins, attended the motions of the Turkish camp; and the desponding cities were tempted by the summons of a Roman prince, who immediately surrendered them into the hands of the barbarians. These acquisitions were confirmed by a treaty of peace with the emperor Alexius; his fear of Robert compelled him to seek the friendship of Soliman; and it was not till after the sultan's death that he extended as far as Nicomedia, about sixty miles from Constantinople, the eastern boundary of the Roman world. Trebizond alone, defended on either side by the sea and mountains, preserved at the extremity of the Euxine the ancient character of a Greek colony, and the future destiny of a Christian empire.

Since the first conquests of the caliphs, the establishment of the Turks in Anatolia or Asia Minor was the most deplorable loss which the church and empire had sustained. By the propagation of the Moslem faith, Soliman deserved the name of *Gazi*, a holy champion; and his new kingdom of the Romans, or of *Roum*, was added to the tables of Oriental geography. It is described as extending from the Euphrates to Constantinople, from the Black Sea to the confines of Syria; pregnant with mines of silver and iron, of alum and copper, fruitful in corn and wine, and productive of cattle and excellent horses.[52] The wealth of Lydia, the arts of the Greeks, the splendour of the Augustan age, existed only in books and ruins, which were equally obscure in the eyes of the Scythian conquerors. Yet in the present decay Anatolia still contains *some* wealthy and populous cities; and, under the Byzantine empire, they were far more flourishing in numbers, size, and opulence. By the choice of the sultan, Nice, the metropolis of Bithynia, was preferred for his palace and fortress: the seat of the Seljukian dynasty of Roum was planted one hundred miles from Constantinople; and the divinity of Christ was denied and derided in the same temple in which it had been pronounced by the first general synod of the Catholics. The unity of God, and the mission of Mohammed, were preached in the moschs; the Arabian learning was taught in the schools; the Cadhis judged according to the law of the Koran; the Turkish manners and language prevailed in the cities; and Turkman camps were scattered over the plains and mountains of Anatolia. On the hard conditions of tribute and servitude, the Greek Christians might enjoy the exercise of their religion; but their most holy churches were profaned, their priests and bishops were insulted,[53] they were compelled to suffer the triumph of the *pagans* and the apostasy of their brethren, many thousand children were marked by the knife of circumcision, and many thousand captives were devoted to the service or the pleasures of their masters.[54] After the loss of Asia, Antioch still maintained her primitive allegiance to Christ and Cæsar; but the solitary province was separated from all Roman aid, and surrounded on all sides by the Mohammedan powers. The despair of Philaretus the governor prepared the sacrifice of his religion and loyalty, had not his guilt been prevented by his son, who hastened to the Nicene palace, and offered to deliver this valuable prize into the hands of Soliman. The ambitious sultan mounted on horseback, and in twelve nights (for he reposed in the day) performed a march of six hundred miles. Antioch was oppressed by the speed and secrecy of his enterprise; and the dependent cities, as far as Laodicea and the confines of Aleppo,[55] obeyed the example of the metropolis. From Laodicea to the Thracian Bosphorus, or arm of St. George, the conquests and reign of Soliman extended thirty days' journey in length, and in breadth about ten or fifteen, between the rocks of Lycia and the Black Sea.[56] The Turkish ignorance of navigation protected for a while the inglorious safety of the emperor; but no sooner had a fleet of two hundred ships been constructed by the hands of the captive Greeks, than Alexius trembled behind the walls of his capital. His plaintive epistles were dispersed over Europe to excite the compassion of the Latins, and to paint the danger, the weakness, and the riches of the city of Constantine.[57]

But the most interesting conquest of the Seljukian Turks was that of Jerusalem,[58] which soon became the theatre of nations. In their capitulation with Omar, the inhabitants had stipulated the assurance of their religion and property, but the articles were interpreted by a master against whom it was dangerous to dispute; and in the four hundred years of the reign of the caliphs the political climate of Jerusalem was exposed to the vicissitudes of storms and sunshine.[59] By the increase of proselytes and population the Mohammedans might excuse their usurpation of three-fourths of the city: but a peculiar quarter was reserved for the patriarch with his clergy and people; a tribute of two pieces of gold was the price of protection; and the sepulchre of Christ, with the church of the Resurrection, was still left in the hands of his votaries. Of these votaries the most numerous and respectable portion were strangers to Jerusalem; the pilgrimages to the Holy Land had been stimulated, rather than suppressed, by the conquest of the Arabs; and the enthusiasm which had always prompted these perilous journeys was nourished by the congenial passions of grief and indignation. A crowd of pilgrims from the East and West continued to visit the holy sepulchre and the adjacent sanctuaries, more especially at the festival of Easter; and the Greeks and Latins, the Nestorians and Jacobites, the Copts and Abyssinians, the Armenians and Georgians, maintained the chapels, the clergy, and the poor of their respective communions. The harmony of prayer in so many various tongues, the worship of so many nations in the common temple of their religion, might have afforded a spectacle of edification and peace; but the zeal of the Christian sects was embittered by hatred and revenge; and in the kingdom of a suffering Messiah, who had pardoned his enemies, they aspired to command and persecute their spiritual brethren. The preeminence was asserted by the spirit and numbers of the Franks, and the greatness of Charlemagne[60] protected both the Latin pilgrims and the Catholics of the East. The poverty of Carthage, Alexandria, and Jerusalem was relieved by the alms of that pious emperor, and many monasteries of Palestine were founded or restored by his liberal devotion. Harun Alrashid, the greatest of the Abbassides, esteemed in his Christian brother a similar supremacy of genius and power: their friendship was cemented by a frequent intercourse of gifts and embassies; and the caliph, without resigning the substantial dominion, presented the emperor with the keys of the holy sepulchre, and perhaps of the city of Jerusalem. In the decline of the Carlovingian monarchy the republic of Amalphi promoted the interest of trade and religion in the East. Her vessels transported the Latin pilgrims to the coasts of Egypt and Palestine, and deserved, by heir useful imports, the favour and alliance of the Fatimite caliphs:[61] an annual fair was instituted on Mount Calvary; and the Italian merchants founded the convent and hospital of St. John of Jerusalem, the cradle of the monastic and military order which has since reigned in the isles of Rhodes and of Malta. Had the Christian pilgrims been content to revere the tomb of a prophet, the disciples of Mohammed, instead of blaming, would have imitated, their piety; but these rigid *Unitarians* were scandalised by a worship which represents the birth, death, and resurrection of a God; the Catholic images were branded with the name of idols; and the Moslems smiled with indignation[62] at the miraculous flame which was kindled on the eve of Easter in the holy sepulchre.[63] This pious fraud, first devised in the ninth century,[64] was devoutly cherished by the Latin crusaders, and is annually repeated by the clergy of the Greek, Armenian, and Coptic sects,[65] who impose on the credulous spectators[66] for their own benefit and that of their tyrants. In every age a principle of toleration has been fortified by a sense of interest, and the revenue of the prince and his emir was increased each year by the expense and tribute of so many thousand strangers.

The revolution which transferred the sceptre from the Abbassides to the Fatimites was a benefit rather than an injury to the Holy Land. A sovereign resident in Egypt was more sensible of the importance of Christian trade; and the emirs of Palestine were less remote from the justice and power of the throne. But the third of these Fatimite caliphs was the famous Hakem,[67] a frantic youth, who was delivered by his impiety and despotism from the fear either of God or man, and whose reign was a wild mixture of vice and folly. Regardless of the most ancient customs of Egypt, he imposed on the women an absolute confinement; the restraint excited the clamours of both sexes; their clamours provoked his fury; a part of Old Cairo was delivered to the flames, and the guards and citizens were engaged many days in a bloody conflict. At first the caliph declared himself a zealous Musulman, the founder or benefactor of moschs and colleges: twelve hundred and ninety copies of the Koran were transcribed at his expense in letters of gold, and his edict extirpated the vineyards of the Upper Egypt. But his vanity was soon flattered by the hope of introducing a new religion; he aspired above the fame of a prophet, and styled himself the visible image of the Most High God, who, after nine apparitions on earth, was at length manifest in his royal person. At the name of Hakem, the lord of the living and the dead, every knee was bent in religious adoration; his mysteries were performed on a mountain near Cairo; sixteen thousand converts had signed his profession of faith; and at the present hour a free and warlike people, the Druses of Mount Libanus, are persuaded of the life and divinity of a madman and tyrant.[68] In his divine character Hakem hated the Jews and Christians, as the servants of his rivals, while some remains of prejudice or prudence still pleaded in favour of the law of Mohammed. Both in Egypt and Palestine his cruel and wanton persecution made some martyrs and many apostates; the common rights and special privileges of the sectaries were equally disregarded, and a general interdict was laid on the devotion of strangers and natives. The temple of the Christian world, the church of the Resurrection, was demolished to its foundations; the luminous prodigy of Easter was interrupted; and much profane labour was exhausted to destroy the cave in the rock which properly constitutes the holy sepulchre. At the report of this sacrilege the nations of Europe were astonished and afflicted; but, instead of arming in the defence of the Holy Land, they contented themselves with burning or banishing the Jews, as the secret advisers of the impious barbarian.[69] Yet the calamities of Jerusalem were in some measure alleviated by the inconstancy or repentance of Hakem himself; and the royal mandate was sealed for the restitution of the churches when the tyrant was assassinated by the emissaries of his sister. The succeeding caliphs resumed the maxims of religion and policy: a free toleration was again granted; with the pious aid of the emperor of Constantinople the holy sepulchre arose from its ruins; and, after a short abstinence, the pilgrims returned with an increase of appetite to the spiritual feast.[70] In the sea-voyage of Palestine the dangers were frequent, and the opportunities rare; but the conversion of Hungary opened a safe communication between Germany and Greece. The charity of St. Stephen, the apostle of his kingdom, relieved and conducted his itinerant brethren;[71] and from Belgrade to Antioch they traversed fifteen hundred miles of a Christian empire. Among the Franks the zeal of pilgrimage prevailed beyond the example of former times, and the roads were covered with multitudes of either sex and of every rank, who professed their contempt of life so soon as they should have kissed the tomb of their Redeemer. Princes and prelates abandoned the care of their dominions, and the numbers of these pious caravans were a prelude to the armies which marched in the ensuing age under the banner of the cross. About thirty years before the first crusade, the archbishop of Mentz, with the bishops of Utrecht, Bamberg, and Ratisbon, undertook this laborious journey from the Rhine to the Jordan, and the multitude of their followers amounted to seven thousand persons.

At Constantinople they were hospitably entertained by the emperor, but the ostentation of their wealth provoked the assault of the wild Arabs; they drew their swords with scrupulous reluctance, and sustained a siege in the village of Capernaum till they were rescued by the venal protection of the Fatimite emir. After visiting the holy places they embarked for Italy, but only a remnant of two thousand arrived in safety in their native land. Ingulphus, a secretary of William the Conqueror, was a companion of this pilgrimage; he observes that they sallied from Normandy thirty stout and well-appointed horsemen; but that they repassed the Alps twenty miserable palmers, with the staff in their hand, and the wallet at their back.[72]

After the defeat of the Romans the tranquillity of the Fatimite caliphs was invaded by the Turks.[73] One of the lieutenants of Malek Shah, Atsiz the Carizmian, marched into Syria at the head of a powerful army, and reduced Damascus by famine and the sword. Hems, and the other cities of the province, acknowledged the caliph of Bagdad and the sultan of Persia; and the victorious emir advanced without resistance to the banks of the Nile: the Fatimite was preparing to fly into the heart of Africa; but the negroes of his guard and the inhabitants of Cairo made a desperate sally, and repulsed the Turk from the confines of Egypt. In his retreat he indulged the licence of slaughter and rapine: the judge and notaries of Jerusalem were invited to his camp; and their execution was followed by the massacre of three thousand citizens. The cruelty or the defeat of Atsiz was soon punished by the sultan Toucush, the brother of Malek Shah, who, with a higher title and more formidable powers, asserted the dominion of Syria and Palestine. The house of Seljuk reigned about twenty years in Jerusalem;[74] but the hereditary command of the holy city and territory was intrusted or abandoned to the emir Ortok, the chief of a tribe of Turkmans, whose children, after their expulsion from Palestine, formed two dynasties on the borders of Armenia and Assyria.[75] The Oriental Christians and the Latin pilgrims deplored a revolution which, instead of the regular government and old alliance of the caliphs, imposed on their necks the iron yoke of the strangers of the North.[76] In his court and camp the great sultan had adopted in some degree the arts and manners of Persia; but the body of the Turkish nation, and more especially the pastoral tribes, still breathed the fierceness of the desert. From Nice to Jerusalem the western countries of Asia were a scene of foreign and domestic hostility; and the shepherds of Palestine, who held a precarious sway on a doubtful frontier, had neither leisure nor capacity to await the slow profits of commercial and religious freedom. The pilgrims, who, through innumerable perils, had reached the gates of Jerusalem, were the victims of private rapine or public oppression, and often sunk under the pressure of famine and disease, before they were permitted to salute the holy sepulchre. A spirit of native barbarism, or recent zeal, prompted the Turkmans to insult the clergy of every sect: the patriarch was dragged by the hair along the pavement and cast into a dungeon, to extort a ransom from the sympathy of his flock; and the divine worship in the church of the Resurrection was often disturbed by the savage rudeness of its masters. The pathetic tale excited the millions of the West to march under the standard of the cross to the relief of the Holy Land; and yet how trifling is the sum of these accumulated evils, if compared with the single act of the sacrilege of Hakem, which had been so patiently endured by the Latin Christians! A slighter provocation inflamed the more irascible temper of their descendants: a new spirit had arisen of religious chivalry and papal dominion; a nerve was touched of exquisite feeling; and the sensation vibrated to the heart of Europe.

CHAPTER LVIII

Origin and Numbers of the First Crusade. Characters of the Latin Princes. Their March to Constantinople. Policy of the Greek Emperor Alexius. Conquest of Nice, Antioch, and Jerusalem, by the Franks. Deliverance of the Holy Sepulchre. Godfrey of Bouillon, First King of Jerusalem. Institutions of the French or Latin Kingdom.

ABOUT twenty years after the conquest of Jerusalem by the Turks, the holy sepulchre was visited by a hermit of the name of Peter, a native of Amiens, in the province of Picardy[1] in France. His resentment and sympathy were excited by his own injuries and the oppression of the Christian name; he mingled his tears with those of the patriarch, and earnestly inquired if no hopes of relief could be entertained from the Greek emperors of the East. The patriarch exposed the vices and weakness of the successors of Constantine. "I will rouse," exclaimed the hermit, "the martial nations of Europe in your cause;" and Europe was obedient to the call of the hermit. The astonished patriarch dismissed him with epistles of credit and complaint; and no sooner did he land at Bari than Peter hastened to kiss the feet of the Roman pontiff. His stature was small, his appearance contemptible; but his eye was keen and lively, and he possessed that vehemence of speech which seldom fails to impart the persuasion of the soul.[2] He was born of a gentleman's family (for we must now adopt a modern idiom), and his military service was under the neighbouring counts of Boulogne, the heroes of the first crusade. But he soon relinquished the sword and the world; and if it be true that his wife, however noble, was aged and ugly, he might withdraw with the less reluctance from her bed to a convent, and at length to a hermitage. In this austere solitude his body was emaciated, his fancy was inflamed; whatever he wished, he believed; whatever he believed, he *saw* in dreams and revelations. From Jerusalem the pilgrim returned an accomplished fanatic; but as he excelled in the popular madness of the times, Pope Urban the Second received him as a prophet, applauded his glorious design, promised to support it in a general council, and encouraged him to proclaim the deliverance of the Holy Land. Invigorated by the approbation of the pontiff, his zealous missionary traversed, with speed and success, the provinces of Italy and France. His diet was abstemious, his prayers long and fervent, and the alms which he received with one hand, he distributed with the other: his head was bare, his feet naked, his meagre body was wrapped in a coarse garment; he bore and displayed a weighty crucifix; and the ass on which he rode was sanctified, in the public eye, by the service of the man of God. He preached to innumerable crowds in the churches, the streets, and the highways: the hermit entered with equal confidence the palace and the cottage; and the people, for all was people, was impetuously moved by his call to repentance and arms. When he painted the sufferings of the natives and pilgrims of Palestine, every heart was melted to compassion; every breast glowed with indignation when he challenged the warriors of the age to defend their brethren, and rescue their Saviour: his ignorance of art and language was compensated by sighs, and tears, and ejaculations; and Peter supplied the deficiency of reason by loud and frequent appeals to Christ and his mother, to the saints and angels of paradise, with whom he had personally conversed. The most perfect orator of Athens might have envied the success of his eloquence: the rustic enthusiast inspired the passions which he felt, and Christendom expected with impatience the counsels and decrees of the supreme pontiff.

The magnanimous spirit of Gregory the Seventh had already embraced the design of arming Europe against Asia; the ardour of his zeal and ambition still breathes in his epistles; from either side of the Alps fifty thousand Catholics had enlisted under the banner of St. Peter;[3] and his successor reveals *his* intention of marching at their head against the impious sectaries of Mohammed. But the glory or reproach of executing, though not in person, this holy enterprise, was reserved for Urban the the Second,[4] the most faithful of his disciples. He undertook the conquest of the East, whilst the larger portion of Rome was possessed and fortified by his rival Guibert of Ravenna, who contended with Urban for the name and honours of the pontificate. He attempted to unite the powers of the West, at a time when the princes were separated from the church, and the people from their princes, by the excommunication which himself and his predecessors had thundered against the emperor and the king of France. Philip the First of France supported with patience the censures which he had provoked by his scandalous life and adulterous marriage. Henry the Fourth of Germany asserted the right of investitures, the prerogative of confirming his bishops by the delivery of the ring and crosier. But the emperor's party was crushed in Italy by the arms of the Normans and the countess Mathilda; and the long quarrel had been recently envenomed by the revolt of his son Conrad and the shame of his wife,[5] who, in the synods of Constance and Placentia, confessed the manifold prostitutions to which she had been exposed by a husband regardless of her honour and his own.[6] So popular was the cause of Urban, so weighty was his influence, that the council which he summoned at Placentia[7] was composed of two hundred bishops of Italy, France, Burgundy, Swabia, and Bavaria. Four thousand of the clergy and thirty thousand of the laity attended this important meeting; and, as the most spacious cathedral would have been inadequate to the multitude, the session of seven days was held in a plain adjacent to the city. The ambassadors of the Greek emperor, Alexius Comnenus, were introduced to plead the distress of their sovereign, and the danger of Constantinople, which was divided only by a narrow sea from the victorious Turks, the common enemies of the Christian name. In their suppliant address they flattered the pride of the Latin princes; and, appealing at once to their policy and religion, exhorted them to repel the barbarians on the confines of Asia, rather than to expect them in the heart of Europe. At the sad tale of the misery and perils of their Eastern brethren the assembly burst into tears: the most eager champions declared their readiness to march; and the Greek ambassadors were dismissed with the assurance of a speedy and powerful succour.

The relief of Constantinople was included in the larger and most distant project of the deliverance of Jerusalem; but the prudent Urban adjourned the final decision to a second synod, which he proposed to celebrate in some city of France in the autumn of the same year. The short delay would propagate the flame of enthusiasm; and his firmest hope was in a nation of soldiers[8] still proud of the pre-eminence of their name, and ambitious to emulate their hero Charlemagne,[9] who, in the popular romance of Turpin,[10] had achieved the conquest of the Holy Land. A latent motive of affection or vanity might influence the choice of Urban: he was himself a native of France, a monk of Clugny, and the first of his countrymen who ascended the throne of St. Peter. The pope had illustrated his family and province; nor is there perhaps a more exquisite gratification than to revisit, in a conspicuous dignity, the humble and laborious scenes of our youth.

It may occasion some surprise that the Roman pontiff should erect, in the heart of France, the tribunal from whence he hurled his anathemas against the king; but our surprise will vanish so soon as we form a just estimate of a king of France of the eleventh century.[11] Philip the First was the great-grandson of Hugh Capet, the founder of the present race, who, in the decline of Charlemagne's posterity, added the regal title to his patrimonial estates of Paris and Orleans. In this narrow compass he was possessed of wealth and jurisdiction; but in the rest of France Hugh and his first descendants were no more than the feudal lords of about sixty dukes and counts, of independent and hereditary power,[12] who disdained the control of laws and legal assemblies, and whose disregard of their sovereign was revenged by the disobedience of their inferior vassals. At Clermont, in the territories of the count of Auvergne,[13] the pope might brave with impunity the resentment of Philip; and the council which he convened in that city was not less numerous or respectable than the synod of Placentia.[14] Besides his court and council of Roman cardinals, he was supported by thirteen archbishops and two hundred and twenty-five bishops; the number of mitred prelates was computed at four hundred; and the fathers of the church were blessed by the saints and enlightened by the doctors of the age. From the adjacent kingdoms a martial train of lords and knights of power and renown attended the council,[15] in high expectation of its resolves; and such was the ardour of zeal and curiosity, that the city was filled, and many thousands, in the month of November, erected their tents or huts in the open field. A session of eight days produced some useful or edifying canons for the reformation of manners; a severe censure was pronounced against the licence of private war; the Truce of God[16] was confirmed, a suspension of hostilities during four days of the week; women and priests were placed under the safeguard of the church; and a protection of three years was extended to husbandmen and merchants, the defenceless victims of military rapine. But a law, however venerable be the sanction, cannot suddenly transform the temper of the times; and the benevolent efforts of Urban deserve the less praise, since he laboured to appease some domestic quarrels that he might spread the flames of war from the Atlantic to the Euphrates. From the synod of Placentia the rumour of his great design had gone forth among the nations: the clergy on their return had preached in every diocese the merit and glory of the deliverance of the Holy Land; and when the pope ascended a lofty scaffold in the market-place of Clermont, his eloquence was addressed to a well-prepared and impatient audience. His topics were obvious, his exhortation was vehement, his success inevitable. The orator was interrupted by the shout of thousands, who with one voice, and in their rustic idiom, exclaimed aloud, "God wills it, God wills it!"[17] "It is indeed the will of God," replied the pope; "and let this memorable word, the inspiration surely of the Holy Spirit, be for ever adopted as your cry of battle, to animate the devotion and courage of the champions of Christ. His cross is the symbol of your salvation; wear it, a red, a bloody cross, as an external mark, on your breasts or shoulders, as a pledge of your sacred and irrevocable engagement." The proposal was joyfully accepted; great numbers, both of the clergy and laity, impressed on their garments the sign of the cross,[18] and solicited the pope to march at their head. This dangerous honour was declined by the more prudent successor of Gregory, who alleged the schism of the church, and the duties of his pastoral office, recommending to the faithful, who were disqualified by sex or profession, by age or infirmity, to aid with their prayers and alms the personal service of their robust brethren. The name and powers of his legate he devolved on Adhemar, bishop of Puy, the first who had received the cross at his hands. The foremost of the temporal chiefs was Raymond, count of Toulouse, whose ambassadors in the council excused the absence, and pledged the honour, of their master. After the confession and absolution of their sins, the champions of the cross were dismissed with a superfluous admonition to invite their countrymen and friends; and their departure for the Holy Land was fixed to the festival of the Assumption, the fifteenth of August, of the ensuing year.[19]

So familiar, and as it were so natural to man, is the practice of violence, that our indulgence allows the slightest provocation, the most disputable right, as a sufficient ground of national hostility. But the name and nature of a *holy war* demands a more rigorous scrutiny; nor can we hastily believe that the servants of the Prince of Peace would unsheathe the sword of destruction unless the motive were pure, the quarrel legitimate, and the necessity inevitable. The policy of an action may be determined from the tardy lessons of experience; but before we act, our conscience should be satisfied of the justice and propriety of our enterprise. In the age of the crusades, the Christians, both of the East and West, were persuaded of their lawfulness and merit; their arguments are clouded by the perpetual abuse of Scripture and rhetoric; but they seem to insist on the right of natural and religious defence, their peculiar title to the Holy Land, and the impiety of their Pagan and Mohammedan foes.[20] I. The right of a just defence may fairly include our civil and spiritual allies: it depends on the existence of danger; and that danger must be estimated by the twofold consideration of the malice and the power of our enemies. A pernicious tenet has been imputed to the Mohammedans, the duty of *extirpating* all other religions by the sword. This charge of ignorance and bigotry is refuted by the Koran, by the history of the Musulman conquerors, and by their public and legal toleration of the Christian worship. But it cannot be denied that the Oriental churches are depressed under their iron yoke; that, in peace and war, they assert a divine and indefeasible claim of universal empire; and that, in their orthodox creed, the unbelieving nations are continually threatened with the loss of religion or liberty. In the eleventh century the victorious arms of the Turks presented a real and urgent apprehension of these losses. They had subdued in less than thirty years the kingdoms of Asia, as far as Jerusalem and the Hellespont; and the Greek empire tottered on the verge of destruction. Besides an honest sympathy for their brethren, the Latins had a right and interest in the support of Constantinople, the most important barrier of the West; and the privilege of defence must reach to prevent, as well as to repel, an impending assault. But this salutary purpose might have been accomplished by a moderate succour; and our calmer reason must disclaim the innumerable hosts and remote operations which overwhelmed Asia and depopulated Europe. II. Palestine could add nothing to the strength or safety of the Latins; and fanaticism alone could pretend to justify the conquest of that distant and narrow province. The Christians affirmed that their inalienable title to the promised land had been sealed by the blood of their divine Saviour; it was their right and duty to rescue their inheritance from the unjust possessors, who profaned his sepulchre, and oppressed the pilgrimage of his disciples. Vainly would it be alleged that the pre-eminence of Jerusalem and the sanctity of Palestine have been abolished with the Mosaic law; that the God of the Christians is not a local deity, and that the recovery of Bethlehem or Calvary, his cradle or his tomb, will not atone for the violation of the moral precepts of the Gospel. Such arguments glance aside from the leaden shield of superstition; and the religious mind will not easily relinquish its hold on the sacred ground of mystery and miracle. III. But the holy wars which have been waged in every climate of the globe, from Egypt to Livonia, and from Peru to Hindostan, require the support of some more general and flexible tenet. It has been often supposed, and sometimes affirmed, that a difference of religion is a worthy cause of hostility; that obstinate unbelievers may be slain or subdued by the champions of the cross; and that grace is the sole fountain of dominion as well as of mercy. Above four hundred years before the first crusade, the eastern and western provinces of the Roman empire had been acquired about the same time, and in the same manner, by the barbarians of Germany and Arabia. Time and treaties had legitimated the conquests of the *Christian* Franks; but in the eyes of their subjects and neighbours the Mohammedan princes were still tyrants and usurpers, who, by the arms of war or rebellion, might be lawfully driven from their unlawful possession.[21]

As the manners of the Christians were relaxed, their discipline of penance[22] was enforced; and with the multiplication of sins the remedies were multiplied. In the primitive church a voluntary and open confession prepared the work of atonement. In the middle ages the bishops and priests interrogated the criminal, compelled him to account for his thoughts, words, and actions, and prescribed the terms of his reconciliation with God. But as this discretionary power might alternately be abused by indulgence and tyranny, a rule of discipline was framed to inform and regulate

the spiritual judges. This mode of legislation was invented by the Greeks; their *penitentials*[23] were translated, or imitated, in the Latin church; and in the time of Charlemagne the clergy of every diocese were provided with a code, which they prudently concealed from the knowledge of the vulgar. In this dangerous estimate of crimes and punishments each case was supposed, each difference was remarked, by the experience or penetration of the monks; some sins are enumerated which innocence could not have suspected, and others which reason cannot believe; and the more ordinary offences of fornication and adultery, of perjury and sacrilege, of rapine and murder, were expiated by a penance which, according to the various circumstances, was prolonged from forty days to seven years. During this term of mortification the patient was healed, the criminal was absolved, by a salutary regimen of fasts and prayers: the disorder of his dress was expressive of grief and remorse; and he humbly abstained from all the business and pleasure of social life. But the rigid execution of these laws would have depopulated the palace, the camp, and the city; the barbarians of the West believed and trembled; but nature often rebelled against principle; and the magistrate laboured without effect to enforce the jurisdiction of the priest. A liberal accomplishment of penance was indeed impracticable: the guilt of adultery was multiplied by daily repetition; that of homicide might involve the massacre of a whole people; each act was separately numbered; and, in those times of anarchy and vice, a modest sinner might easily incur a debt of three hundred years. His insolvency was relieved by a commutation or *indulgence*: a year of penance was appreciated at twenty-six *solidi*[24] of silver, about four pounds sterling, for the rich; at three solidi, or nine shillings, for the indigent: and these alms were soon appropriated to the use of the church, which derived from the redemption of sins an inexhaustible source of opulence and dominion. A debt of three hundred years, or twelve hundred pounds, was enough to impoverish a plentiful fortune; the scarcity of gold and silver was supplied by the alienation of land; and the princely donations of Pepin and Charlemagne are expressly given for the *remedy* of their soul. It is a maxim of the civil law, that whosoever cannot pay with his purse must pay with his body; and the practice of flagellation was adopted by the monks—a cheap though painful equivalent. By a fantastic arithmetic, a year of penance was taxed at three thousand lashes;[25] and such was the skill and patience of a famous hermit, St. Dominic of the Iron Cuirass,[26] that in six days he could discharge an entire century by a whipping of three hundred thousand stripes. His example was followed by many penitents of both sexes; and as a vicarious sacrifice was accepted, a sturdy disciplinarian might expiate on his own back the sins of his benefactors.[27] These compensations of the purse and the person introduced, in the eleventh century, a more honourable mode of satisfaction. The merit of military service against the Saracens of Africa and Spain had been allowed by the predecessors of Urban the Second. In the council of Clermont, that pope proclaimed a *plenary indulgence* to those who should enlist under the banner of the cross; the absolution of *all* their sins, and a full receipt for *all* that might be due of canonical penance.[28] The cold philosophy of modern times is incapable of feeling the impression that was made on a sinful and fanatic world. At the voice of their pastor, the robber, the incendiary, the homicide, arose by thousands to redeem their souls by repeating on the infidels the same deeds which they had exercised against their Christian brethren; and the terms of atonement were eagerly embraced by offenders of every rank and denomination. None were pure; none were exempt from the guilt and penalty of sin; and those who were the least amenable to the justice of God and the church were the best entitled to the temporal and eternal recompense of their pious courage. If they fell, the spirit of the Latin clergy did not hesitate to adorn their tomb with the crown of martyrdom;[29] and should they survive, they could expect without impatience the delay and increase of their heavenly reward. They offered their blood to the Son of God, who had laid down his life for their salvation: they took up the cross, and entered with confidence into the way of the Lord. His providence would watch over their safety; perhaps his visible and miraculous power would smooth the difficulties of their holy enterprise. The cloud and pillar of Jehovah had marched before the Israelites into the promised land. Might not the Christians more reasonably hope that the rivers would open for their passage; that the walls of the strongest cities would fall at the sound of their trumpets; and that the sun would be arrested in his mid-career to allow them time for the destruction of the infidels?

Of the chiefs and soldiers who marched to the holy sepulchre, I will dare to affirm that all were prompted by the spirit of enthusiasm, the belief of merit, the hope of reward, and the assurance of divine aid. But I am equally persuaded that in *many* it was not the sole, that in *some* it was not the leading, principle of action. The use and abuse of religion are feeble to stem, they are strong and irresistible to impel, the stream of national manners. Against the private wars of the barbarians, their bloody tournaments, licentious loves, and judicial duels, the popes and synods might ineffectually thunder. It is a more easy task to provoke the metaphysical disputes of the Greeks, to drive into the cloister the victims of anarchy or despotism, to sanctify the patience of slaves and cowards, or to assume the merit of the humanity and benevolence of modern Christians. War and exercise were the reigning passions of the Franks or Latins; they were enjoined, as a penance, to gratify those passions, to visit distant lands, and to draw their swords against the nations of the East. Their victory, or even their attempt, would immortalise the names of the intrepid heroes of the cross; and the purest piety could not be insensible to the most splendid prospect of military glory. In the petty quarrels of Europe they shed the blood of their friends and countrymen for the acquisition, perhaps, of a castle or a village. They could march with alacrity against the distant and hostile nations who were devoted to their arms; their fancy already grasped the golden sceptres of Asia; and the conquest of Apulia and Sicily by the Normans might exalt to royalty the hopes of the most private adventurer. Christendom, in her rudest state, must have yielded to the climate and cultivation of the Mohammedan countries; and their natural and artificial wealth had been magnified by the tales of pilgrims and the gifts of an imperfect commerce. The vulgar, both the great and small, were taught to believe every wonder, of lands flowing with milk and honey, of mines and treasures, of gold and diamonds, of palaces of marble and jasper, and of odoriferous groves of cinnamon and frankincense. In this earthly paradise each warrior depended on his sword to carve a plenteous and honourable establishment, which he measured only by the extent of his wishes.[30] Their vassals and soldiers trusted their fortunes to God and their master: the spoils of a Turkish emir might enrich the meanest follower of the camp; and the flavour of the wines, the beauty of the Grecian women,[31] were temptations more adapted to the nature, than to the profession, of the champions of the cross. The love of freedom was a powerful incitement to the multitudes who were oppressed by feudal or ecclesiastical tyranny. Under this holy sign, the peasants and burghers, who were attached to the servitude of the glebe, might escape from a haughty lord, and transplant themselves and their families to a land of liberty. The monk might release himself from the discipline of his convent, the debtor might suspend the accumulation of usury and the pursuit of his creditors, and outlaws and malefactors of every cast might continue to brave the laws and elude the punishment of their crimes.[32]

These motives were potent and numerous: when we have singly computed their weight on the mind of each individual, we must add the infinite series, the multiplying powers of example and fashion. The first proselytes became the warmest and most effectual missionaries of the cross: among their friends and countrymen they preached the duty, the merit, and the recompense of their holy vow, and the most reluctant hearers were insensibly drawn within the whirlpool of persuasion and authority. The martial youths were fired by the reproach or suspicion of cowardice; the opportunity of visiting with an army the sepulchre of Christ was embraced by the old and infirm, by women and children, who consulted rather their zeal than their strength; and those who in the evening had derided the folly of their companions were the most eager, the ensuing day, to tread in their footsteps. The ignorance which magnified the hopes, diminished the perils, of the enterprise. Since the Turkish conquest, the paths of pilgrimage were obliterated; the chiefs themselves had an imperfect notion of the length of the way and the state of their enemies; and such was the stupidity of the people, that, at the sight of the first city or castle beyond the limits of their knowledge, they were ready to ask whether that was not the Jerusalem, the term and object of their labours. Yet the more prudent of the crusaders, who were not sure that they should be fed from heaven with a shower of quails or manna, provided themselves with those precious metals which, in every country, are the representatives of every commodity. To defray, according to their rank, the expenses of the road, princes alienated their provinces, nobles their lands and castles, peasants their cattle and the instruments of husbandry. The value of property was depreciated by the eager competition of multitudes; while the price of arms and horses was raised to an exorbitant height

by the wants and impatience of the buyers.[33] Those who remained at home, with sense and money, were enriched by the epidemical disease: the sovereigns acquired at a cheap rate the domains of their vassals, and the ecclesiastical purchasers completed the payment by the assurance of their prayers. The cross, which was commonly sewed on the garment, in cloth or silk, was inscribed by some zealots on their skin: an hot iron, or indelible liquor, was applied to perpetuate the mark; and a crafty monk, who showed the miraculous impression on his breast, was repaid with the popular veneration and richest benefices of Palestine.[34]

The fifteenth of August had been fixed in the council of Clermont for the departure of the pilgrims; but the day was anticipated by the thoughtless and needy crowd of plebeians; and I shall briefly despatch the calamities which they inflicted and suffered before I enter on the more serious and successful enterprise of the chiefs. Early in the spring, from the confines of France and Lorraine, above sixty thousand of the populace of both sexes flocked round the first missionary of the crusade, and pressed him, with clamorous importunity, to lead them to the holy sepulchre. The hermit, assuming the character, without the talents or authority, of a general, impelled or obeyed the forward impulse of his votaries along the banks of the Rhine and Danube. Their wants and numbers soon compelled them to separate, and his lieutenant, Walter the Penniless, a valiant though needy soldier, conducted a vanguard of pilgrims, whose condition may be determined from the proportion of eight horsemen to fifteen thousand foot. The example and footsteps of Peter were closely pursued by another fanatic, the monk Godescal, whose sermons had swept away fifteen or twenty thousand peasants from the villages of Germany. Their rear was again pressed by a herd of two hundred thousand, the most stupid and savage refuse of the people, who mingled with their devotion a brutal licence of rapine, prostitution, and drunkenness. Some counts and gentlemen, at the head of three thousand horse, attended the motions of the multitude to partake in the spoil: but their genuine leaders (may we credit such folly?) were a goose and a goat, who were carried in the front, and to whom these worthy Christians ascribed an infusion of the divine spirit.[35] Of these, and of other bands of enthusiasts, the first and most easy warfare was against the Jews, the murderers of the Son of God. In the trading cities of the Moselle and the Rhine their colonies were numerous and rich, and they enjoyed, under the protection of the emperor and the bishops, the free exercise of their religion.[36] At Verdun, Trèves, Mentz, Spires, Worms, many thousands of that unhappy people were pillaged and massacred,[37] nor had they felt a more bloody stroke since the persecution of Hadrian. A remnant was saved by the firmness of their bishops, who accepted a feigned and transient conversion; but the more obstinate Jews opposed their fanaticism to the fanaticism of the Christians, barricadoed their houses, and, precipitating themselves, their families, and their wealth into the rivers or the flames, disappointed the malice, or at least the avarice, of their implacable foes.

Between the frontiers of Austria and the seat of the Byzantine monarchy the crusaders were compelled to traverse an interval of six hundred miles, the wild and desolate countries of Hungary[38] and Bulgaria. The soil is fruitful, and intersected with rivers; but it was then covered with morasses and forests, which spread to a boundless extent whenever man has ceased to exercise his dominion over the earth. Both nations had imbibed the rudiments of Christianity: the Hungarians were ruled by their native princes, the Bulgarians by a lieutenant of the Greek emperor; but, on the slightest provocation, their ferocious nature was rekindled, and ample provocation was afforded by the disorders of the first pilgrims. Agriculture must have been unskilful and languid among a people whose cities were built of reeds and timber, which were deserted in the summer season for the tents of hunters and shepherds. A scanty supply of provisions was rudely demanded, forcibly seized, and greedily consumed, and on the first quarrel the crusaders gave a loose to indignation and revenge. But their ignorance of the country, of war, and of discipline exposed them to every snare. The Greek præfect of Bulgaria commanded a regular force; at the trumpet of the Hungarian king, the eighth or the tenth of his martial subjects bent their bows and mounted on horseback; their policy was insidious, and their retaliation on these pious robbers was unrelenting and bloody.[39] About a third of the naked fugitives, and the hermit Peter was of the number, escaped to the Thracian mountains; and the emperor, who respected the pilgrimage and succour of the Latins, conducted them by secure and easy journeys to Constantinople, and advised them to await the arrival of their brethren. For a while they remembered their faults and losses, but no sooner

were they revived by the hospitable entertainment, than their venom was again inflamed; they stung their benefactor, and neither gardens, nor palaces, nor churches, were safe from their depredations. For his own safety, Alexius allured them to pass over to the Asiatic side of the Bosphorus; but their blind impetuosity soon urged them to desert the station which he had assigned, and to rush headlong against the Turks, who occupied the road of Jerusalem. The hermit, conscious of his shame, had withdrawn from the camp to Constantinople; and his lieutenant, Walter the Penniless, who was worthy of a better command, attempted without success to introduce some order and prudence among the herd of savages. They separated in quest of prey, and themselves fell an easy prey to the arts of the sultan. By a rumour that their foremost companions were rioting in the spoils of his capital, Soliman tempted the main body to descend into the plain of Nice: they were overwhelmed by the Turkish arrows, and a pyramid of bones[40] informed their companions of the place of their defeat. Of the first crusaders, three hundred thousand had already perished before a single city was rescued from the infidels, before their graver and more noble brethren had completed the preparations of their enterprise.[41]

None of the great sovereigns of Europe embarked their persons in the first crusade. The emperor Henry the Fourth was not disposed to obey the summons of the pope; Philip the First of France was occupied by his pleasures; William Rufus of England by a recent conquest; the kings of Spain were engaged in a domestic war against the Moors; and the northern monarchs of Scotland, Denmark,[42] Sweden, and Poland were yet strangers to the passions and interests of the South. The religious ardour was more strongly felt by the princes of the second order, who held an important place in the feudal system. Their situation will naturally cast under four distinct heads the review of their names and characters; but I may escape some needless repetition, by observing at once that courage and the exercise of arms are the common attribute of these Christian adventurers. I. The first rank both in war and council is justly due to Godfrey of Bouillon; and happy would it have been for the crusaders, if they had trusted themselves to the sole conduct of that accomplished hero, a worthy representative of Charlemagne, from whom he was descended in the female line. His father was of the noble race of the counts of Boulogne: Brabant, the lower province of Lorraine,[43] was the inheritance of his mother; and by the emperor's bounty he was himself invested with that ducal title, which has been improperly transferred to his lordship of Bouillon in the Ardennes.[44] In the service of Henry the Fourth he bore the great standard of the empire, and pierced with his lance the breast of Rodolph, the rebel king: Godfrey was the first who ascended the walls of Rome; and his sickness, his vow, perhaps his remorse for bearing arms against the pope, confirmed an early resolution of visiting the holy sepulchre not as a pilgrim, but a deliverer. His valour was matured by prudence and moderation; his piety, though blind, was sincere; and, in the tumult of a camp, he practised the real and fictitious virtues of a convent. Superior to the private factions of the chiefs, he reserved his enmity for the enemies of Christ; and though he gained a kingdom by the attempt, his pure and disinterested zeal was acknowledged by his rivals. Godfrey of Bouillon[45] was accompanied by his two brothers, by Eustace the elder, who had succeeded to the county of Boulogne, and by the younger, Baldwin, a character of more ambiguous virtue. The duke of Lorraine was alike celebrated on either side of the Rhine: from his birth and education, he was equally conversant with the French and Teutonic languages: the barons of France, Germany, and Lorraine assembled their vassals; and the confederate force that marched under his banner was composed of fourscore thousand foot and about ten thousand horse. II. In the parliament that was held at Paris, in the king's presence, about two months after the council of Clermont, Hugh, count of Vermandois, was the most conspicuous of the princes who assumed the cross. But the appellation of *the Great* was applied, not so much to his merit or possessions (though neither were contemptible), as to the royal birth of the brother of the king of France.[46] Robert, duke of Normandy, was the eldest son of William the Conqueror; but on his father's death he was deprived of the kingdom of England, by his own indolence and the activity of his brother Rufus. The worth of Robert was degraded by an excessive levity and easiness of temper: his cheerfulness seduced him to the indulgence of pleasure; his profuse liberality impoverished the prince and people; his indiscriminate clemency multiplied the number of offenders; and the amiable qualities of a private man became the essential defects of a sovereign. For the trifling sum of ten thousand marks he

mortgaged Normandy during his absence to the English usurper;[47] but his engagement and behaviour in the holy war announced in Robert a reformation of manners, and restored him in some degree to the public esteem. Another Robert was count of Flanders, a royal province, which, in this century, gave three queens to the thrones of France, England, and Denmark: he was surnamed the Sword and Lance of the Christians; but in the exploits of a soldier he sometimes forgot the duties of a general. Stephen, count of Chartres, of Blois, and of Troyes, was one of the richest princes of the age; and the number of his castles has been compared to the three hundred and sixty-five days of the year. His mind was improved by literature; and, in the council of the chiefs, the eloquent Stephen[48] was chosen to discharge the office of their president. These four were the principal leaders of the French, the Normans, and the pilgrims of the British isles: but the list of the barons who were possessed of three or four towns would exceed, says a contemporary, the catalogue of the Trojan war.[49] III. In the south of France the command was assumed by Adhemar, bishop of Puy, the pope's legate, and by Raymond count of St. Giles and Toulouse, who added the prouder titles of duke of Narbonne and marquis of Provence. The former was a respectable prelate, alike qualified for this world and the next. The latter was a veteran warrior, who had fought against the Saracens of Spain, and who consecrated his declining age, not only to the deliverance, but to the perpetual service, of the holy sepulchre. His experience and riches gave him a strong ascendant in the Christian camp, whose distress he was often able, and sometimes willing, to relieve. But it was easier for him to extort the praise of the Infidels than to preserve the love of his subjects and associates. His eminent qualities were clouded by a temper, haughty, envious, and obstinate; and, though he resigned an ample patrimony for the cause of God, his piety, in the public opinion, was not exempt from avarice and ambition.[50] A mercantile, rather than a martial, spirit prevailed among his *provincials*,[51] a common name, which included the natives of Auvergne and Languedoc,[52] the vassals of the kingdom of Burgundy or Arles. From the adjacent frontier of Spain he drew a band of hardy adventurers; as he marched through Lombardy, a crowd of Italians flocked to his standard, and his united force consisted of one hundred thousand horse and foot. If Raymond was the first to enlist and the last to depart, the delay may be excused by the greatness of his preparation and the promise of an everlasting farewell. IV. The name of Bohemond, the son of Robert Guiscard, was already famous by his double victory over the Greek emperor: but his father's will had reduced him to the principality of Tarentum, and the remembrance of his Eastern trophies, till he was awakened by the rumour and passage of the French pilgrims. It is in the person of this Norman chief that we may seek for the coolest policy and ambition, with a small allay of religious fanaticism. His conduct may justify a belief that he had secretly directed the design of the pope, which he affected to second with astonishment and zeal: at the siege of Amalphi his example and discourse inflamed the passions of a confederate army; he instantly tore his garment to supply crosses for the numerous candidates, and prepared to visit Constantinople and Asia at the head of ten thousand horse and twenty thousand foot. Several princes of the Norman race accompanied this veteran general; and his cousin Tancred[53] was the partner, rather than the servant, of the war. In the accomplished character of Tancred we discover all the virtues of a perfect knight,[54] the true spirit of chivalry, which inspired the generous sentiments and social offices of man far better than the base philosophy, or the baser religion, of the times.

Between the age of Charlemagne and that of the crusades, a revolution had taken place among the Spaniards, the Normans, and the French, which was gradually extended to the rest of Europe. The service of the infantry was degraded to the plebeians; the cavalry formed the strength of the armies; and the honourable name of *miles*, or soldier, was confined to the gentlemen[55] who served on horseback, and were invested with the character of knighthood. The dukes and counts, who had usurped the rights of sovereignty, divided the provinces among their faithful barons: the barons distributed among their vassals the fiefs or benefices of their jurisdiction; and these military tenants, the peers of each other and of their lord, composed the noble or equestrian order, which disdained to conceive the peasant or burgher as of the same species with themselves. The dignity of their birth was preserved by pure and equal alliances; their sons alone, who could produce four quarters or lines of ancestry, without spot or reproach, might legally pretend to the honour of knighthood; but a valiant plebeian was sometimes enriched and ennobled by the sword, and became the father of a new race. A single knight could impart, according to his judgment, the character which he received; and the warlike sovereigns of Europe derived more glory from this personal distinction than from the lustre of their diadem. This ceremony, of which some traces may be found in Tacitus and the woods of Germany,[56] was in its origin simple and profane: the candidate, after some previous trial, was invested with the sword and spurs; and his cheek or shoulder was touched with a slight blow, as an emblem of the last affront which it was lawful for him to endure. But superstition mingled in every public and private action of life: in the holy wars it sanctified the profession of arms; and the order of chivalry was assimilated in its rights and privileges to the sacred orders of priesthood. The bath and white garment of the novice were an indecent copy of the regeneration of baptism: his sword, which he offered on the altar, was blessed by the ministers of religion: his solemn reception was preceded by fasts and vigils; and he was created a knight in the name of God, of St. George, and of St. Michael the archangel. He swore to accomplish the duties of his profession; and education, example, and the public opinion were the inviolable guardians of his oath. As the champion of God and the ladies (I blush to unite such discordant names), he devoted himself to speak with truth; to maintain the right; to protect the distressed; to practise *courtesy*, a virtue less familiar to the ancients; to pursue the infidels; to despise the allurements of ease and safety; and to vindicate in every perilous adventure the honour of his character. The abuse of the same spirit provoked the illiterate knight to disdain the arts of industry and peace; to esteem himself the sole judge and avenger of his own injuries; and proudly to neglect the laws of civil society and military discipline. Yet the benefits of this institution, to refine the temper of barbarians, and to infuse some principles of faith, justice, and humanity, were strongly felt, and have been often observed. The asperity of national prejudice was softened; and the community of religion and arms spread a similar colour and generous emulation over the face of Christendom. Abroad in enterprise and pilgrimage, at home in martial exercise, the warriors of every country were perpetually associated; and impartial taste must prefer a Gothic tournament to the Olympic games of classic antiquity.[57] Instead of the naked spectacles which corrupted the manners of the Greeks, and banished from the stadium the virgins and matrons, the pompous decoration of the lists was crowned with the presence of chaste and high-born beauty, from whose hands the conqueror received the prize of his dexterity and courage. The skill and strength that were exerted in wrestling and boxing bear a distant and doubtful relation to the merit of a soldier; but the tournaments, as they were invented in France, and eagerly adopted both in the East and West, presented a lively image of the business of the field. The single combats, the general skirmish, the defence of a pass, or castle, were rehearsed as in actual service; and the contest, both in real and mimic war, was decided by the superior management of the horse and lance. The lance was the proper and peculiar weapon of the knight: his horse was of a large and heavy breed; but this charger, till he was roused by the approaching danger, was usually led by an attendant, and he quietly rode a pad or palfrey of a more easy pace. His helmet and sword, his greaves and buckler, it would be superfluous to describe; but I may remark, that, at the period of the crusades, the armour was less ponderous than in later times; and that, instead of a massy cuirass, his breast was defended by a hauberk or coat of mail. When their long lances were fixed in the rest, the warriors furiously spurred their horses against the foe; and the light cavalry of the Turks and Arabs could seldom stand against the direct and impetuous weight of their charge. Each knight was attended to the field by his faithful squire, a youth of equal birth and similar hopes; he was followed by his archers and men-at-arms, and four, or five, or six soldiers, were computed as the furniture of a complete *lance*. In the expeditions to the neighbouring kingdoms or the Holy Land, the duties of the feudal tenure no longer subsisted; the voluntary service of the knights and their followers was either prompted by zeal or attachment, or purchased with rewards and promises; and the numbers of each squadron were measured by the power, the wealth, and the fame of each independent chieftain. They were distinguished by his banner, his armorial coat, and his cry of war; and the most ancient families of Europe must seek in these achievements the origin and proof of their nobility. In this rapid portrait of chivalry I have been urged to anticipate on the story of the crusades, at once an effect and a cause of this memorable institution.[58]

Such were the troops, and such the leaders, who assumed the cross for the deliverance of the holy sepulchre. As soon as they were relieved by the absence of the plebeian multitude, they encouraged each other, by interviews and messages, to accomplish their vow, and hasten their departure. Their wives and sisters were desirous of partaking the danger and merit of the pilgrimage: their portable treasures were conveyed in bars of silver and gold; and the princes and barons were attended by their equipage of hounds and hawks to amuse their leisure and to supply their table. The difficulty of procuring subsistence for so many myriads of men and horses engaged them to separate their forces: their choice or situation determined the road; and it was agreed to meet in the neighbourhood of Constantinople, and from thence to begin their operations against the Turks. From the banks of the Meuse and the Moselle, Godfrey of Bouillon followed the direct way of Germany, Hungary, and Bulgaria; and, as long as he exercised the sole command, every step afforded some proof of his prudence and virtue. On the confines of Hungary he was stopped three weeks by a Christian people, to whom the name, or at least the abuse, of the cross was justly odious. The Hungarians still smarted with the wounds which they had received from the first pilgrims: in their turn they had abused the right of defence and retaliation; and they had reason to apprehend a severe revenge from a hero of the same nation, and who was engaged in the same cause. But, after weighing the motives and the events, the virtuous duke was content to pity the crimes and misfortunes of his worthless brethren; and his twelve deputies, the messengers of peace, requested in his name a free passage and an equal market. To remove their suspicions, Godfrey trusted himself, and afterwards his brother, to the faith of Carloman, king of Hungary, who treated them with a simple but hospitable entertainment: the treaty was sanctified by their common Gospel; and a proclamation, under pain of death, restrained the animosity and licence of the Latin soldiers. From Austria to Belgrade, they traversed the plains of Hungary, without enduring or offering an injury; and the proximity of Carloman, who hovered on their flanks with his numerous cavalry, was a precaution not less useful for their safety than for his own. They reached the banks of the Save; and no sooner had they passed the river than the king of Hungary restored the hostages, and saluted their departure with the fairest wishes for the success of their enterprise. With the same conduct and discipline Godfrey pervaded the woods of Bulgaria and the frontiers of Thrace; and might congratulate himself that he had almost reached the first term of his pilgrimage without drawing his sword against a Christian adversary. After an easy and pleasant journey through Lombardy, from Turin to Aquileia, Raymond and his provincials marched forty days through the savage country of Dalmatia[59] and Sclavonia. The weather was a perpetual fog; the land was mountainous and desolate; the natives were either fugitive or hostile: loose in their religion and government, they refused to furnish provisions or guides; murdered the stragglers; and exercised by night and day the vigilance of the count, who derived more security from the punishment of some captive robbers than from his interview and treaty with the prince of Scodra.[60] His march between Durazzo and Constantinople was harassed, without being stopped, by the peasants and soldiers of the Greek emperor; and the same faint and ambiguous hostility was prepared for the remaining chiefs, who passed the Adriatic from the coast of Italy. Bohemond had arms and vessels, and foresight and discipline; and his name was not forgotten in the provinces of Epirus and Thessaly. Whatever obstacles he encountered were surmounted by his military conduct and the valour of Tancred; and if the Norman prince affected to spare the Greeks, he gorged his soldiers with the full plunder of an heretical castle.[61] The nobles of France pressed forwards with the vain and thoughtless ardour of which their nation has been sometimes accused. From the Alps to Apulia the march of Hugh the Great, of the two Roberts, and of Stephen of Chartres, through a wealthy country, and amidst the applauding Catholics, was a devout or triumphant progress: they kissed the feet of the Roman pontiff; and the golden standard of St. Peter was delivered to the brother of the French monarch.[62] But in this visit of piety and pleasure then neglected to secure the season and the means of their embarkation: the winter was insensibly lost: their troops were scattered and corrupted in the towns of Italy. They separately accomplished their passage, regardless of safety or dignity; and within nine months from the feast of the Assumption, the day appointed by Urban, all the Latin princes had reached Constantinople. But the count of Vermandois was produced as a captive; his foremost vessels were scattered by a tempest; and his person, against the law of nations, was detained by the lieutenants of Alexius. Yet the arrival of Hugh had been announced by four-and-twenty knights in golden armour, who commanded the emperor to revere the general of the Latin Christians, the brother of the king of kings.[63]

In some Oriental tale I have read the fable of a shepherd who was ruined by the accomplishment of his own wishes: he had prayed for water; the Ganges was turned into his ground, and his flock and cottage were swept away by the inundation. Such was the fortune, or at least the apprehension, of the Greek emperor Alexius Comnenus, whose name has already appeared in this history, and whose conduct is so differently represented by his daughter Anna,[64] and by the Latin writers.[65] In the council of Placentia his ambassadors had solicited a moderate succour, perhaps of ten thousand soldiers; but he was astonished by the approach of so many potent chiefs and fanatic nations. The emperor fluctuated between hope and fear, between timidity and courage; but in the crooked policy which he mistook for wisdom, I cannot believe, I cannot discern, that he maliciously conspired against the life or honour of the French heroes. The promiscuous multitudes of Peter the Hermit were savage beasts, alike destitute of humanity and reason: nor was it possible for Alexius to prevent or deplore their destruction. The troops of Godfrey and his peers were less contemptible, but not less suspicious, to the Greek emperor. Their motives *might* be pure and pious; but he was equally alarmed by his knowledge of the ambitious Bohemond, and his ignorance of the Transalpine chiefs: the courage of the French was blind and headstrong; they might be tempted by the luxury and wealth of Greece, and elated by the view and opinion of their invincible strength; and Jerusalem might be forgotten in the prospect of Constantinople. After a long march and painful abstinence, the troops of Godfrey encamped in the plains of Thrace; they heard with indignation that their brother, the count of Vermandois, was imprisoned by the Greeks; and their reluctant duke was compelled to indulge them in some freedom of retaliation and rapine. They were appeased by the submission of Alexius: he promised to supply their camp; and as they refused, in the midst of winter, to pass the Bosphorus, their quarters were assigned among the gardens and palaces on the shores of that narrow sea. But an incurable jealousy still rankled in the minds of the two nations, who despised each other as slaves and barbarians. Ignorance is the ground of suspicion, and suspicion was inflamed into daily provocations: prejudice is blind, hunger is deaf; and Alexius is accused of a design to starve or assault the Latins in a dangerous post, on all sides encompassed with the waters.[66] Godfrey sounded his trumpets, burst the net, overspread the plain, and insulted the suburbs: but the gates of Constantinople were strongly fortified; the ramparts were lined with archers; and after a doubtful conflict, both parties listened to the voice of peace and religion. The gifts and promises of the emperor insensibly soothed the fierce spirit of the Western strangers; as a Christian warrior, he re-kindled their zeal for the prosecution of their holy enterprise, which he engaged to second with his troops and treasures. On the return of spring, Godfrey was persuaded to occupy a pleasant and plentiful camp in Asia; and no sooner had he passed the Bosphorus than the Greek vessels were suddenly recalled to the opposite shore. The same policy was repeated with the succeeding chiefs, who were swayed by the example, and weakened by the departure, of their foremost companions. By his skill and diligence Alexius prevented the union of any two of the confederate armies at the same moment under the walls of Constantinople; and before the feast of the Pentecost not a Latin pilgrim was left on the coast of Europe.

The same arms which threatened Europe might deliver Asia, and repel the Turks from the neighbouring shores of the Bosphorus and Hellespont. The fair provinces from Nice to Antioch were the recent patrimony of the Roman emperor; and his ancient and perpetual claim still embraced the kingdoms of Syria and Egypt. In his enthusiasm, Alexius indulged, or affected, the ambitious hope of leading his new allies to subvert the thrones of the East; but the calmer dictates of reason and temper dissuaded him from exposing his royal person to the faith of unknown and lawless barbarians. His prudence, or his pride, was content with extorting from the French princes an oath of homage and fidelity, and a solemn promise that they would either restore, or hold, their Asiatic conquests, as the humble and loyal vassals of the Roman empire. Their independent spirit was fired at the mention of their foreign and voluntary servitude: they successively yielded to the dexterous application of gifts and flattery; and the first proselytes became the most eloquent and effectual missionaries to multiply the companions of their shame. The pride of Hugh of Vermandois was soothed by the honours of his captivity; and in the brother of the French king the example of submission was prevalent and weighty. In the mind of Godfrey of Bouillon every human consideration was subordinate to the glory of God and the success of the crusade. He had firmly resisted the temptations of Bohemond and Raymond, who urged the attack and conquest of Constantinople. Alexius esteemed his virtues, deservedly named him the champion of the empire, and dignified his homage with the filial name and the rites of adoption.[67] The hateful Bohemond was received as a true and ancient ally; and if the emperor reminded him of former hostilities, it was only to praise the valour that he had displayed, and the glory that he had acquired, in the fields of Durazzo and Larissa. The son of Guiscard was lodged, and entertained, and served with Imperial pomp: one day, as he passed through the gallery of the palace, a door was carelessly left open to expose a pile of gold and silver, of silk and gems, of curious and costly furniture, that was heaped in seeming disorder from the floor to the roof of the chamber. "What conquests," exclaimed the ambitious miser, "might not be achieved by the possession of such a treasure?"—"It is your own," replied a Greek attendant, who watched the motions of his soul; and Bohemond, after some hesitation, condescended to accept this magnificent present. The Norman was flattered by the assurance of an independent principality; and Alexius eluded, rather than denied, his daring demand of the office of great domestic, or general of the East. The two Roberts, the son of the conqueror of England, and the kinsman of three queens,[68] bowed in their turn before the Byzantine throne. A private letter of Stephen of Chartres attests his admiration of the emperor, the most excellent and liberal of men, who taught him to believe that he was a favourite, and promised to educate and establish his youngest son. In his southern province, the count of St. Giles and Toulouse faintly recognised the supremacy of the king of France, a prince of a foreign nation and language. At the head of a hundred thousand men, he declared that he was the soldier and servant of Christ alone, and that the Greek might be satisfied with an equal treaty of alliance and friendship. His obstinate resistance enhanced the value and the price of his submission; and he shone, says the princess Anna, among the barbarians, as the sun amidst the stars of heaven. His disgust of the noise and insolence of the French, his suspicions of the designs of Bohemond, the emperor imparted to his faithful Raymond; and that aged statesman might clearly discern, that, however false in friendship, he was sincere in his enmity.[69] The spirit of chivalry was last subdued in the person of Tancred; and none could deem themselves dishonoured by the imitation of that gallant knight. He disdained the gold and flattery of the Greek monarch; assaulted in his presence an insolent patrician; escaped to Asia in the habit of a private soldier; and yielded with a sigh to the authority of Bohemond, and the interest of the Christian cause. The best and most ostensible reason was the impossibility of passing the sea and accomplishing their vow without the licence and the vessels of Alexius; but they cherished a secret hope, that, as soon as they trod the continent of Asia, their swords would obliterate their shame, and dissolve the engagement, which on his side might not be very faithfully performed. The ceremony of their homage was grateful to a people who had long since considered pride as the substitute of power. High on his throne the emperor sat mute and immovable: his majesty was adored by the Latin princes; and they submitted to kiss either his feet or his knees, an indignity which their own writers are ashamed to confess, and unable to deny.[70]

Private or public interest suppressed the murmurs of the dukes and counts; but a French baron (he is supposed to be Robert of Paris[71]) presumed to ascend the throne, and to place himself by the side of Alexius. The sage reproof of Baldwin provoked him to exclaim, in his barbarous idiom, "Who is this rustic, that keeps his seat while so many valiant captains are standing round him?" The emperor maintained his silence, dissembled his indignation, and questioned his interpreter concerning the meaning of the words, which he partly suspected from the universal language of gesture and countenance. Before the departure of the pilgrims he endeavoured to learn the name and condition of the audacious baron. "I am a Frenchman," replied Robert, "of the purest and most ancient nobility of my country. All that I know is, that there is a church in my neighbourhood,[72] the resort of those who are desirous of approving their valour in single combat. Till an enemy appears, they address their prayers to God and his saints. That church I have frequently visited, but never have I found an antagonist who dared to accept my defiance." Alexius dismissed the challenger with some prudent advice for his conduct in the Turkish warfare; and history repeats with pleasure this lively example of the manners of his age and country.

The conquest of Asia was undertaken and achieved by Alexander, with thirty-five thousand Macedonians and Greeks;[73] and his best hope was in the strength and discipline of his phalanx of infantry. The principal force of the crusaders consisted in their cavalry; and when that force was mustered in the plains of Bithynia, the knights and their martial attendants on horseback amounted to one hundred thousand fighting men, completely armed with the helmet and coat of mail. The value of these soldiers deserved a strict and authentic account; and the flower of European chivalry might furnish, in a first effort, this formidable body of heavy horse. A part of the infantry might be enrolled for the service of scouts, pioneers, and archers; but the promiscuous crowd were lost in their own disorder; and we depend not on the eyes or knowledge, but on the belief and fancy, of a chaplain of Count Baldwin,[74] in the estimate of six hundred thousand pilgrims able to bear arms, besides the priests and monks, the women and children, of the Latin camp. The reader starts; and before he is recovered from his surprise I shall add, on the same testimony, that, if all who took the cross had accomplished their vow, above SIX MILLIONS would have migrated from Europe to Asia. Under this oppression of faith I derive some relief from a more sagacious and thinking writer,[75] who, after the same review of the cavalry, accuses the credulity of the priest of Chartres, and even doubts whether the *Cisalpine* regions (in the geography of a Frenchman) were sufficient to produce and pour forth such incredible multitudes. The coolest scepticism will remember that of these religious volunteers great numbers never beheld Constantinople and Nice. Of enthusiasm the influence is irregular and transient: many were detained at home by reason or cowardice, by poverty or weakness; and many were repulsed by the obstacles of the way, the more insuperable as they were unforeseen to these ignorant fanatics. The savage countries of Hungary and Bulgaria were whitened with their bones: their vanguard was cut in pieces by the Turkish sultan; and the loss of the first adventure, by the sword, or climate, or fatigue, has already been stated at three hundred thousand men. Yet the myriads that survived, that marched, that pressed forwards on the holy pilgrimage, were a subject of astonishment to themselves and to the Greeks. The copious energy of her language sinks under the efforts of the princess Anna:[76] the images of locusts, of leaves and flowers, of the sands of the sea, or the stars of heaven, imperfectly represent what she had seen and heard; and the daughter of Alexius exclaims that Europe was loosened from its foundations, and hurled against Asia. The ancient hosts of Darius and Xerxes labour under the same doubt of a vague and indefinite magnitude; but I am inclined to believe that a larger number has never been contained within the lines of a single camp than at the siege of Nice, the first operation of the Latin princes. Their motives, their characters, and their arms, have been already displayed. Of their troops, the most numerous portion were natives of France: the Low Countries, the banks of the Rhine, and Apulia sent a powerful reinforcement: some bands of adventurers were drawn from Spain, Lombardy, and England;[77] and from the distant bogs and mountains of Ireland and Scotland[78] issued some naked and savage fanatics, ferocious at home, but unwarlike abroad. Had not superstition condemned the sacrilegious prudence of depriving the poorest or weakest Christian of the merit of the pilgrimage, the useless crowd, with mouths but without hands, might have been stationed in the Greek empire till their companions had opened and secured the way of the Lord. A small remnant of the pilgrims, who passed the Bosphorus, was permitted to visit the holy sepulchre. Their northern constitution was scorched by the rays, and infected by the vapours, of a Syrian sun. They consumed, with heedless prodigality, their stores of water and provision: their numbers exhausted the inland country: the sea was remote, the Greeks were unfriendly, and the Christians of every sect fled before the voracious and cruel rapine of their brethren. In the dire necessity of famine, they sometimes roasted and devoured the flesh of their infant or adult captives. Among the Turks and Saracens, the idolaters of Europe were rendered more odious by the name and reputation of cannibals; the spies, who introduced themselves into the kitchen of Bohemond, were shown several human bodies turning on the spit: and the artful Norman encouraged a report which increased at the same time the abhorrence and the terror of the infidels.[79]

I have expatiated with pleasure on the first steps of the crusaders, as they paint the manners and character of Europe: but I shall abridge the tedious and uniform narrative of their blind achievements, which were performed by strength and are described by ignorance. From their first station in the neighbourhood of Nicomedia, they advanced in suc-

cessive divisions; passed the contracted limit of the Greek empire; opened a road through the hills; and commenced, by the siege of his capital, their pious warfare against the Turkish sultan. His kingdom of Roum extended from the Hellespont to the confines of Syria, and barred the pilgrimage of Jerusalem: his name was Kilidge-Arslan, or Soliman,[80] of the race of Seljuk, and son of the first conqueror; and in the defence of a land which the Turks considered as their own, he deserved the praise of his enemies, by whom alone he is known to posterity. Yielding to the first impulse of the torrent, he deposited his family and treasure in Nice; retired to the mountains with fifty thousand horse; and twice descended to assault the camps or quarters of the Christian besiegers, which formed an imperfect circle of above six miles. The lofty and solid walls of Nice were covered by a deep ditch, and flanked by three hundred and seventy towers; and on the verge of Christendom the Moslems were trained in arms, and inflamed by religion. Before this city the French princes occupied their stations, and prosecuted their attacks without correspondence or subordination: emulation prompted their valour; but their valour was sullied by cruelty, and their emulation degenerated into envy and civil discord. In the siege of Nice the arts and engines of antiquity were employed by the Latins; the mine and the battering-ram, the tortoise, and the belfry or movable turret, artificial fire, and the *catapult* and *balist*, the sling, and the crossbow for the casting of stones and darts.[81] In the space of seven weeks much labour and blood were expended, and some progress, especially by Count Raymond, was made on the side of the besiegers. But the Turks could protract their resistance and secure their escape, as long as they were masters of the lake[82] Ascanius, which stretches several miles to the westward of the city. The means of conquest were supplied by the prudence and industry of Alexius; a great number of boats was transported on sledges from the sea to the lake; they were filled with the most dexterous of his archers; the flight of the sultana was intercepted; Nice was invested by land and water; and a Greek emissary persuaded the inhabitants to accept his master's protection, and to save themselves, by a timely surrender, from the rage of the savages of Europe. In the moment of victory, or at least of hope, the crusaders, thirsting for blood and plunder, were awed by the Imperial banner that streamed from the citadel; and Alexius guarded with jealous vigilance this important conquest. The murmurs of the chiefs were stifled by honour or interest; and after a halt of nine days they directed their march towards Phrygia under the guidance of a Greek general, whom they suspected of a secret connivance with the sultan. The consort and the principal servants of Soliman had been honourably restored without ransom; and the emperor's generosity to the *miscreants*[83] was interpreted as treason to the Christian cause.

Soliman was rather provoked than dismayed by the loss of his capital; he admonished his subjects and allies of this strange invasion of the Western barbarians; the Turkish emirs obeyed the call of loyalty or religion, the Turkman hordes encamped round his standard, and his whole force is loosely stated by the Christians at two hundred, or even three hundred and sixty thousand horse. Yet he patiently waited till they had left behind them the sea and the Greek frontier, and, hovering on the flanks, observed their careless and confident progress in two columns beyond the view of each other. Some miles before they could reach Dorylæum in Phrygia, the left, and least numerous, division was surprised and attacked, and almost oppressed, by the Turkish cavalry.[84] The heat of the weather, the clouds of arrows, and the barbarous onset overwhelmed the crusaders; they lost their order and confidence, and the fainting fight was sustained by the personal valour, rather than by the military conduct, of Bohemond, Tancred, and Robert of Normandy. They were revived by the welcome banners of duke Godfrey, who flew to their succour, with the count of Vermandois and sixty thousand horse, and was followed by Raymond of Toulouse, the bishop of Puy, and the remainder of the sacred army. Without a moment's pause they formed in new order, and advanced to a second battle. They were received with equal resolution, and, in their common disdain for the unwarlike people of Greece and Asia, it was confessed on both sides that the Turks and the Franks were the only nations entitled to the appellation of soldiers.[85] Their encounter was varied, and balanced by the contrast of arms and discipline: of the direct charge and wheeling evolutions, of the couched lance and the brandished javelin, of a weighty broadsword and a crooked sabre, of cumbrous armour and thin flowing robes, and of the long Tartar bow and the *arbalist*, or crossbow, a deadly weapon, yet unknown to the Orientals.[86] As long as the horses were fresh,

and the quivers full, Soliman maintained the advantage of the day, and four thousand Christians were pierced by the Turkish arrows. In the evening swiftness yielded to strength; on either side the numbers were equal, or at least as great as any ground could hold, or any generals could manage; but, in turning the hills, the last division of Raymond and his *provincials* was led, perhaps without design, on the rear of an exhausted enemy, and the long contest was determined. Besides a nameless and unaccounted multitude, three thousand *pagan* knights were slain in the battle and pursuit; the camp of Soliman was pillaged, and in the variety of precious spoil the curiosity of the Latins was amused with foreign arms and apparel, and the new aspect of dromedaries and camels. The importance of the victory was proved by the hasty retreat of the sultan: reserving ten thousand guards of the relics of his army, Soliman evacuated the kingdom of Roum, and hastened to implore the aid, and kindle the resentment, of his Eastern brethren. In a march of five thousand miles the crusaders traversed the Lesser Asia, through a wasted land and deserted towns, without finding either a friend or an enemy. The geographer[87] may trace the position of Dorylæum, Antioch of Pisidia, Iconium, Archelais, and Germanicia, and may compare those classic appellations with the modern names of Eskishehr the old city, Akshehr the white city, Cogni, Erekli, and Marash. As the pilgrims passed over a desert, where a draught of water is exchanged for silver, they were tormented by intolerable thirst, and on the banks of the first rivulet their haste and intemperance were still more pernicious to the disorderly throng. They climbed with toil and danger the steep and slippery sides of Mount Taurus; many of the soldiers cast away their arms to secure their footsteps; and had not terror preceded their van, the long and trembling file might have been driven down the precipice by a handful of resolute enemies. Two of their most respectable chiefs, the duke of Lorraine and the count of Toulouse, were carried in litters; Raymond was raised, as it is said, by miracle, from a hopeless malady; and Godfrey had been torn by a bear, as he pursued that rough and perilous chase in the mountains of Pisidia.

To improve the general consternation, the cousin of Bohemond and the brother of Godfrey were detached from the main army with their respective squadrons of five and of seven hundred knights. They overran in a rapid career the hills and sea-coast of Cilicia, from

Cogni to the Syrian gates; the Norman standard was first planted on the walls of Tarsus and Malmistra; but the proud injustice of Baldwin at length provoked the patient and generous Italian, and they turned their consecrated swords against each other in a private and profane quarrel. Honour was the motive, and fame the reward, of Tancred, but fortune smiled on the more selfish enterprise of his rival.[88] He was called to the assistance of a Greek or Armenian tyrant, who had been suffered, under the Turkish yoke, to reign over the Christians of Edessa. Baldwin accepted the character of his son and champion, but no sooner was he introduced into the city than he inflamed the people to the massacre of his father, occupied the throne and treasure, extended his conquests over the hills of Armenia and the plain of Mesopotamia, and founded the first principality of the Franks or Latins, which subsisted fifty-four years beyond the Euphrates.[89]

Before the Franks could enter Syria, the summer, and even the autumn, were completely wasted; the siege of Antioch, or the separation and repose of the army during the winter season, was strongly debated in their council; the love of arms and the holy sepulchre urged them to advance, and reason perhaps was on the side of resolution, since every hour of delay abates the fame and force of the invader, and multiplies the resources of defensive war. The capital of Syria was protected by the river Orontes, and the *iron bridge* of nine arches derives its name from the massy gates of the two towers which are constructed at either end. They were opened by the sword of the duke of Normandy; his victory gave entrance to three hundred thousand crusaders, an account which may allow some scope for losses and desertion, but which clearly detects much exaggeration in the review of Nice. In the description of Antioch[90] it is not easy to define a middle term between her ancient magnificence, under the successors of Alexander and Augustus, and the modern aspect of Turkish desolation. The Tetrapolis, or four cities, if they retained their name and position, must have left a large vacuity in a circumference of twelve miles; and that measure, as well as the number of four hundred towers, are not perfectly consistent with the five gates so often mentioned in the history of the siege. Yet Antioch must have still flourished as a great and populous capital. At the head of the Turkish emirs, Baghisian, a veteran chief, commanded in the place; his garrison was composed of six or seven thousand horse, and fifteen or twenty thousand foot; one hundred thousand Moslems are said to have fallen by the sword, and their numbers were probably inferior to the Greeks, Armenians, and Syrians, who had been no more than fourteen years the slaves of the house of Seljuk. From the remains of a solid and stately wall it appears to have arisen to the height of threescore feet in the valleys; and wherever less art and labour had been applied, the ground was supposed to be defended by the river, the morass, and the mountains. Notwithstanding these fortifications, the city had been repeatedly taken by the Persians, the Arabs, the Greeks, and the Turks; so large a circuit must have yielded many previous points of attack, and in a siege that was formed about the middle of October the vigour of the execution could alone justify the boldness of the attempt. Whatever strength and valour could perform in the field was abundantly discharged by the champions of the cross: in the frequent occasions of sallies, of forage, of the attack and defence of convoys, they were often victorious; and we can only complain that their exploits are sometimes enlarged beyond the scale of probability and truth. The sword of Godfrey[91] divided a Turk from the shoulder to the haunch, and one half of the infidel fell to the ground, while the other was transported by his horse to the city gate. As Robert of Normandy rode against his antagonist, "I devote thy head," he piously exclaimed, "to the demons of hell;" and that head was instantly cloven to the breast by the resistless stroke of his descending falchion. But the reality or the report of such gigantic prowess[92] must have taught the Moslems to keep within their walls, and against those walls of earth or stone the sword and the lance were unavailing weapons. In the slow and successive labours of a siege the crusaders were supine and ignorant, without skill to contrive, or money to purchase, or industry to use the artificial engines and implements of assault. In the conquest of Nice they had been powerfully assisted by the wealth and knowledge of the Greek emperor; his absence was poorly supplied by some Genoese and Pisan vessels that were attracted by religion or trade to the coast of Syria; the stores were scanty, the return precarious, and the communication difficult and dangerous. Indolence or weakness had prevented the Franks from investing the entire circuit, and the perpetual freedom of two gates relieved the wants and recruited the garrison of the city. At the end of seven months, after the ruin of their avalry and an enormous loss by famine, desertion, and fatigue, the progress of the crusaders was imperceptible, and their success remote, if the Latin Ulysses, the artful and ambitious Bohemond, had not employed the arms of cunning and deceit. The Christians of Antioch were numerous and discontented: Phirouz, a Syrian renegado, had acquired the favour of the emir and the command of three towers, and the merit of his repentance disguised to the Latins, and perhaps to himself, the foul design of perfidy and treason. A secret correspondence, for their mutual interest, was soon established between Phirouz and the prince of Tarento; and Bohemond declared in the council of the chiefs that he could deliver the city into their hands. But he claimed the sovereignty of Antioch as the reward of his service, and the proposal which had been rejected by the envy, was at length extorted from the distress, of his equals. The nocturnal surprise was executed by the French and Norman princes, who ascended in person the scaling-ladders that were thrown from the walls; their new proselyte, after the murder of his too scrupulous brother, embraced and introduced the servants of Christ, the army rushed through the gates, and the Moslems soon found that, although mercy was hopeless, resistance was impotent. But the citadel still refused to surrender, and the victors themselves were speedily encompassed and besieged by the innumerable forces of Kerboga, prince of Mosul, who, with twenty-eight Turkish emirs, advanced to the deliverance of Antioch. Five-and-twenty days the Christians spent on the verge of destruction, and the proud lieutenant of the caliph and the sultan left them only the choice of servitude or death.[93] In this extremity they collected the relics of their strength, sallied from the town, and in a single memorable day annihilated or dispersed the host of Turks and Arabians, which they might safely report to have consisted of six hundred thousand men.[94] Their supernatural allies I shall proceed to consider: the human causes of the victory of Antioch were the fearless despair of the Franks, and the surprise, the discord, perhaps the errors, of their unskilful and presumptuous adversaries. The battle is described with as much disorder as it was fought; but we may observe the tent of Kerboga, a movable and spacious palace, enriched with the luxury of Asia, and capable of holding above two thousand persons; we may distinguish his three thousand guards, who were cased, the horses as well as the men, in complete steel.

In the eventful period of the siege and defence of Antioch, the crusaders were alternately exalted by victory or sunk in despair; either swelled with plenty or emaciated with hunger. A speculative reasoner might suppose that their faith had a strong and serious influence on their practice; and that the soldiers of the cross, the deliverers of the holy sepulchre, prepared themselves by a sober and virtuous life for the daily contemplation of martyrdom. Experience blows away this charitable illusion; and seldom does the history of profane war display such scenes of intemperance and prostitution as were exhibited under the walls of Antioch. The grove of Daphne no longer flourished; but the Syrian air was still impregnated with the same vices; the Christians were seduced by every temptation[95] that nature either prompts or reprobates; the authority of the chiefs was despised; and sermons and edicts were alike fruitless against those scandalous disorders, not less pernicious to military discipline than repugnant to evangelic purity. In the first days of the siege and the possession of Antioch the Franks consumed with wanton and thoughtless prodigality the frugal subsistence of weeks and months: the desolate country no longer yielded a supply; and from that country they were at length excluded by the arms of the besieging Turks. Disease, the faithful companion of want, was envenomed by the rains of the winter, the summer heats, unwholesome food, and the close imprisonment of multitudes. The pictures of famine and pestilence are always the same, and always disgustful; and our imagination may suggest the nature of their sufferings and their resources. The remains of treasure or spoil were eagerly lavished in the purchase of the vilest nourishment: and dreadful must have been the calamities of the poor, since, after paying three marks of silver for a goat and fifteen for a lean camel,[96] the count of Flanders was reduced to beg a dinner, and duke Godfrey to borrow a horse. Sixty thousand horses had been reviewed in the camp; before the end of the siege they were diminished to two thousand, and scarcely two hundred fit for service could be mustered on the day of battle. Weakness of body and terror of mind extinguished the ardent enthusiasm of the pilgrims; and every motive of honour and religion was subdued by the desire of life.[97] Among the chiefs, three heroes may be found without fear or reproach: Godfrey of Bouillon was supported by his magnanimous piety; Bohemond by ambition and interest; and

Tancred declared, in the true spirit of chivalry, that, as long as he was at the head of forty knights, he would never relinquish the enterprise of Palestine. But the count of Toulouse and Provence was suspected of a voluntary indisposition; the duke of Normandy was recalled from the sea-shore by the censures of the church; Hugh the Great, though he led the vanguard of the battle, embraced an ambiguous opportunity of returning to France; and Stephen count of Chartres basely deserted the standard which he bore, and the council in which he presided. The soldiers were discouraged by the flight of William viscount of Melun, surnamed the *Carpenter*, from the weighty strokes of his axe; and the saints were scandalised by the fall of Peter the Hermit, who, after arming Europe against Asia, attempted to escape from the penance of a necessary fast. Of the multitude of recreant warriors, the names (says an historian) are blotted from the book of life; and the opprobrious epithet of the rope-dancers was applied to the deserters who dropped in the night from the walls of Antioch. The emperor Alexius,[98] who seemed to advance to the succour of the Latins, was dismayed by the assurance of their hopeless condition. They expected their fate in silent despair; oaths and punishments were tried without effect; and to rouse the soldiers to the defence of the walls, it was found necessary to set fire to their quarters.

For their salvation and victory they were indebted to the same fanaticism which had led them to the brink of ruin. In such a cause, and in such an army, visions, prophecies, and miracles were frequent and familiar. In the distress of Antioch, they were repeated with unusual energy and success: St. Ambrose had assured a pious ecclesiastic that two years of trial must precede the season of deliverance and grace; the deserters were stopped by the presence and reproaches of Christ himself; the dead had promised to arise and combat with their brethren; the Virgin had obtained the pardon of their sins; and their confidence was revived by a visible sign, the seasonable and splendid discovery of the HOLY LANCE. The policy of their chiefs has on this occasion been admired, and might surely be excused; but a pious fraud is seldom produced by the cool conspiracy of many persons; and a voluntary impostor might depend on the support of the wise and the credulity of the people. Of the diocese of Marseilles, there was a priest of low cunning and loose manners, and his name was Peter Bartholemy. He presented himself at the door

of the council-chamber, to disclose an apparition of St. Andrew, which had been thrice reiterated in his sleep, with a dreadful menace if he presumed to suppress the commands of heaven. "At Antioch," said the apostle, "in the church of my brother St. Peter, near the high altar, is concealed the steel head of the lance that pierced the side of our Redeemer. In three days, that instrument of eternal, and now of temporal, salvation, will be manifested to his disciples. Search, and ye shall find: bear it aloft in battle; and that mystic weapon shall penetrate the souls of the miscreants." The pope's legate, the bishop of Puy, affected to listen with coldness and distrust; but the revelation was eagerly accepted by Count Raymond, whom his faithful subject, in the name of the apostle, had chosen for the guardian of the holy lance. The experiment was resolved; and on the third day, after a due preparation of prayer and fasting, the priest of Marseilles introduced twelve trusty spectators, among whom were the count and his chaplain; and the church doors were barred against the impetuous multitude. The ground was opened in the appointed place; but the workmen, who relieved each other, dug to the depth of twelve feet without discovering the object of their search. In the evening, when Count Raymond had withdrawn to his post, and the weary assistants began to murmur, Bartholemy, in his shirt and without his shoes, boldly descended into the pit; the darkness of the hour and of the place enabled him to secrete and deposit the head of a Saracen lance; and the first sound, the first gleam, of the steel was saluted with a devout rapture. The holy lance was drawn from its recess, wrapped in a veil of silk and gold, and exposed to the veneration of the crusaders; their anxious suspense burst forth in a general shout of joy and hope, and the desponding troops were again inflamed with the enthusiasm of valour. Whatever had been the arts, and whatever might be the sentiments of the chiefs, they skilfully improved this fortunate revolution by every aid that discipline and devotion could afford. The soldiers were dismissed to their quarters with an injunction to fortify their minds and bodies for the approaching conflict, freely to bestow their last pittance on themselves and their horses, and to expect with the dawn of day the signal of victory. On the festival of St. Peter and St. Paul the gates of Antioch were thrown open: a martial psalm, "Let the Lord arise, and let his enemies be scattered!" was chanted by a procession of priests and monks; the battle array was mar-shalled in twelve divisions, in honour of the twelve apostles; and the holy lance, in the ab-sence of Raymond, was intrusted to the hands of his chaplain. The influence of this relic or trophy was felt by the servants, and perhaps by the enemies, of Christ;[99] and its potent energy was heightened by an accident, a stratagem, or a rumour, of a miraculous complexion. Three knights, in white garments and resplendent arms, either issued, or seemed to issue, from the hills: the voice of Adhemar, the pope's legate, proclaimed them as the martyrs St. George, St. Theodore, and St. Maurice: the tumult of bat-tle allowed no time for doubt or scrutiny; and the welcome apparition dazzled the eyes or the imagination of a fanatic army. In the season of danger and triumph the revelation of Bar-tholemy of Marseilles was unanimously as-serted; but as soon as the temporary service was accomplished, the personal dignity and liberal alms which the count of Toulouse derived from the custody of the holy lance provoked the envy, and awakened the reason, of his rivals. A Norman clerk presumed to sift, with a philo-sophic spirit, the truth of the legend, the cir-cumstances of the discovery, and the character of the prophet; and the pious Bohemond ascribed their deliverance to the merits and intercession of Christ alone. For a while the Provincials defended their national palladium with clam-ours and arms; and new visions condemned to death and hell the profane sceptics who pre-sumed to scrutinise the truth and merit of the discovery. The prevalence of incredulity com-pelled the author to submit his life and verac-ity to the judgment of God. A pile of dry fag-gots, four feet high and fourteen long, was erected in the midst of the camp; the flames burnt fiercely to the elevation of thirty cubits; and a narrow path of twelve inches was left for the perilous trial. The unfortunate priest of Marseilles traversed the fire with dexterity and speed; but his thighs and belly were scorched by the intense heat; he expired the next day; and the logic of believing minds will pay some regard to his dying protestations of innocence and truth. Some efforts were made by the Provin-cials to substitute a cross, a ring, or a tabernacle, in the place of the holy lance, which soon vanish-ed in contempt and oblivion.[100] Yet the revela-tion of Antioch is gravely asserted by succeeding historians: and such is the progress of credulity, that miracles, most doubtful on the spot and at the moment, will be received with implicit faith at a convenient distance of time and space.

The prudence or fortune of the Franks had delayed their invasion till the decline of the Turkish empire.[101] Under the manly govern-ment of the three first sultans, the kingdoms of Asia were united in peace and justice; and the innumerable armies which they led in person were equal in courage, and superior in disci-pline, to the barbarians of the West. But at the time of the crusade, the inheritance of Malek Shah was disputed by his four sons; their private ambition was insensible of the public danger; and, in the vicissitudes of their fortune, the royal vassals were ignorant, or regardless, of the true object of their allegiance. The twenty-eight emirs who marched with the standard of Kerboga were his rivals or enemies: their hasty levies were drawn from the towns and tents of Mesopotamia and Syria; and the Turkish vet-erans were employed or consumed in the civil wars beyond the Tigris. The caliph of Egypt embraced this opportunity of weakness and dis-cord to recover his ancient possessions; and his sultan Aphdal besieged Jerusalem and Tyre, expelled the children of Ortok, and restored in Palestine the civil and ecclesiastical authority of the Fatimites.[102] They heard with astonishment of the vast armies of Christians that had passed from Europe to Asia, and rejoiced in the sieges and battles which broke the power of the Turks, the adversaries of their sect and monarchy. But the same Christians were the enemies of the prophet; and from the over-throw of Nice and Antioch, the motive of their enterprise, which was gradually understood, would urge them forwards to the banks of the Jordan, or perhaps of the Nile. An intercourse of epistles and embassies, which rose and fell with the events of war, was maintained be-tween the throne of Cairo and the camp of the Latins; and their adverse pride was the result of ignorance and enthusiasm. The ministers of Egypt declared in a haughty, or insinuated in a milder, tone, that their sovereign, the true and lawful commander of the faithful, had res-cued Jerusalem from the Turkish yoke; and that the pilgrims, if they would divide their numbers, and lay aside their arms, should find a safe and hospitable reception at the sepulchre of Jesus. In the belief of their lost con-dition, the caliph Mostali despised their arms and imprisoned their deputies: the con-quest and victory of Antioch prompted him to solicit those formidable champions with gifts of horses and silk robes, of vases, and purses of gold and silver; and in his estimate of their merit or power the first place was assigned to

Bohemond, and the second to Godfrey. In either fortune, the answer of the crusaders was firm and uniform: they disdained to inquire into the private claims or possessions of the followers of Mohammed: whatsoever was his name or nation, the usurper of Jerusalem was their enemy; and instead of prescribing the mode and terms of their pilgrimage, it was only by a timely surrender of the city and province, their sacred right, that he could deserve their alliance, or deprecate their impending and irresistible attack.[103]

Yet this attack, when they were within the view and reach of their glorious prize, was suspended above ten months after the defeat of Kerboga. The zeal and courage of the crusaders were chilled in the moment of victory; and instead of marching to improve the consternation, they hastily dispersed to enjoy the luxury, of Syria. The causes of this strange delay may be found in the want of strength and subordination. In the painful and various service of Antioch the cavalry was annihilated; many thousands of every rank had been lost by famine, sickness, and desertion: the same abuse of plenty had been productive of a third famine; and the alternative of intemperance and distress had generated a pestilence which swept away above fifty thousand of the pilgrims. Few were able to command, and none were willing to obey: the domestic feuds, which had been stifled by common fear, were again renewed in acts, or at least in sentiments, of hostility; the fortune of Baldwin and Bohemond excited the envy of their companions; the bravest knights were enlisted for the defence of their new principalities; and Count Raymond exhausted his troops and treasures in an idle expedition into the heart of Syria. The winter was consumed in discord and disorder; a sense of honour and religion was rekindled in the spring; and the private soldiers, less susceptible of ambition and jealousy, awakened with angry clamours the indolence of their chiefs. In the month of May the relics of this mighty host proceeded from Antioch to Laodicea: about forty thousand Latins, of whom no more than fifteen hundred horse and twenty thousand foot were capable of immediate service. Their easy march was continued between Mount Libanus and the sea-shore: their wants were liberally supplied by the coasting traders of Genoa and Pisa; and they drew large contributions from the emirs of Tripoli, Tyre, Sidon, Acre, and Cæsarea, who granted a free passage and promised to follow the example of Jerusalem.

From Cæsarea they advanced into the midland country: their clerks recognised the sacred geography of Lydda, Ramla, Emmaus, and Bethlehem, and as soon as they descried the holy city, the crusaders forgot their toils and claimed their reward.[104]

Jerusalem has derived some reputation from the number and importance of her memorable sieges. It was not till after a long and obstinate contest that Babylon and Rome could prevail against the obstinacy of the people, the craggy ground that might supersede the necessity of fortifications, and the walls and towers that would have fortified the most accessible plain.[105] These obstacles were diminished in the age of the crusades. The bulwarks had been completely destroyed and imperfectly restored: the Jews, their nation and worship, were for ever banished: but nature is less changeable than man, and the site of Jerusalem, though somewhat softened and somewhat removed, was still strong against the assaults of an enemy. By the experience of a recent siege, and a three years' possession, the Saracens of Egypt had been taught to discern, and in some degree to remedy, the defects of a place which religion as well as honour forbade them to resign. Aladin, or Iftikhar, the caliph's lieutenant, was intrusted with the defence: his policy strove to restrain the native Christians by the dread of their own ruin and that of the holy sepulchre; to animate the Moslems by the assurance of temporal and eternal rewards. His garrison is said to have consisted of forty thousand Turks and Arabians; and if he could muster twenty thousand of the inhabitants, it must be confessed that the besieged were more numerous than the besieging army.[106] Had the diminished strength and numbers of the Latins allowed them to grasp the whole circumference of four thousands yards (about two English miles and a half[107]), to what useful purpose should they have descended into the valley of Ben Hinnom and torrent of Kedron,[108] or approached the precipices of the south and east, from whence they had nothing either to hope or fear? Their siege was more reasonably directed against the northern and western sides of the city. Godfrey of Bouillon erected his standard on the first swell of Mount Calvary: to the left, as far as St. Stephen's gate, the line of attack was continued by Tancred and the two Roberts; and Count Raymond established his quarters from the citadel to the foot of Mount Sion, which was no longer included within the precincts of the city. On the fifth day the cruaders made a general assault, in the fanatic ope of battering down the walls without en-ines, and of scaling them without ladders. By he dint of brutal force they burst the first arrier, but they were driven back with shame nd slaughter to the camp: the influence of ision and prophecy was deadened by the too requent abuse of those pious stratagems; and ime and labour were found to be the only neans of victory. The time of the siege was ndeed fulfilled in forty days, but they were orty days of calamity and anguish. A repetition f the old complaint of famine may be im-uted in some degree to the voracious or dis-rderly appetite of the Franks; but the stony oil of Jerusalem is almost destitute of water; he scanty springs and hasty torrents were dry n the summer season: nor was the thirst of the esiegers relieved, as in the city, by the arti-icial supply of cisterns and aqueducts. The ircumjacent country is equally destitute of rees for the uses of shade or building; but some arge beams were discovered in a cave by the rusaders: a wood near Sichem, the enchanted rove of Tasso,[109] was cut down: the necessary imber was transported to the camp by the vigour and dexterity of Tancred; and the en-ines were framed by some Genoese artists, who ad fortunately landed in the harbour of Jaffa. Two movable turrets were contructed at the xpense, and in the stations, of the duke of Lorraine and the count of Toulouse, and rolled orwards with devout labour, not to the most ccessible, but to the most neglected, parts of he fortification. Raymond's tower was reduced o ashes by the fire of the besieged, but his col-eague was more vigilant and successful; the nemies were driven by his archers from the -ampart; the drawbridge was let down; and on a Friday, at three in the afternoon, the day and 1our of the Passion, Godfrey of Bouillon stood victorious on the walls of Jerusalem. His ex-ample was followed on every side by the emula-ion of valour; and about four hundred and ixty years after the conquest of Omar, the holy city was rescued from the Mohammedan yoke. In the pillage of public and private wealth, the adventurers had agreed to respect the ex-lusive property of the first occupant; and the spoils of the great mosque, seventy lamps and massy vases of gold and silver, rewarded the diligence, and displayed the generosity, of Tancred. A bloody sacrifice was offered by his mistaken votaries to the God of the Christians: resistance might provoke, but neither age nor -ex could mollify, their implacable rage: they indulged themselves three days in a promiscu-ous massacre;[110] and the infection of the dead bodies produced an epidemical disease. After seventy thousand Moslems had been put to the sword, and the harmless Jews had been burnt in their synagogue, they could still reserve a multitude of captives whom interest or lassitude persuaded them to spare. Of these savage heroes of the cross, Tancred alone betrayed some sentiments of compassion; yet we may praise the more selfish lenity of Raymond, who granted a capitulation and safe-conduct to the garrison of the citadel.[111] The holy sepulchre was now free; and the bloody victors prepared to accomplish their vow. Bareheaded and bare-foot, with contrite hearts and in a humble pos-ture, they ascended the hill of Calvary, amidst the loud anthems of the clergy; kissed the stone which had covered the Saviour of the world; and bedewed with tears of joy and penitence the monument of their redemption. This union of the fiercest and most tender passions has been variously considered by two philosophers: by the one,[112] as easy and natural; by the other,[113] as absurd and incredible. Perhaps it is too rigorously applied to the same persons and the same hour: the example of the virtuous Godfrey awakened the piety of his companions; while they cleansed their bodies they purified their minds; nor shall I believe that the most ardent in slaughter and rapine were the fore-most in the procession to the holy sepulchre.

Eight days after this memorable event, which pope Urban did not live to hear, the Latin chiefs proceeded to the election of a king, to guard and govern their conquests in Palestine. Hugh the Great and Stephen of Chartres had retired with some loss of reputation, which they strove to regain by a second crusade and an honourable death. Baldwin was established at Edessa, and Bohemond at Antioch; and two Roberts, the duke of Normandy[114] and the count of Flanders, preferred their fair inheri-tance in the West to a doubtful competition or a barren sceptre. The jealousy and ambition of Raymond were condemned by his own followers, and the free, the just, the unanimous voice of the army proclaimed Godfrey of Bouillon the first and most worthy of the champions of Christendom. His magnanimity accepted a trust as full of danger as of glory; but in a city where his Saviour had been crowned with thorns, the devout pilgrim rejected the name and ensigns of royalty; and the founder of the kingdom of Jerusalem contented himself with the modest title of Defender and Baron of the

Holy Sepulchre. His government of a single year,[115] too short for the public happiness, was interrupted in the first fortnight by a summons to the field, by the approach of the vizir or sultan of Egypt, who had been too slow to prevent, but who was impatient to avenge, the loss of Jerusalem. His total overthrow in the battle of Ascalon sealed the establishment of the Latins in Syria, and signalised the valour of the French princes, who in this action bade a long farewell to the holy wars. Some glory might be derived from the prodigious inequality of numbers, though I shall not count the myriads of horse and foot on the side of the Fatimites; but, except three thousand Ethiopians or Blacks, who were armed with flails or scourges of iron, the barbarians of the South fled on the first onset, and afforded a pleasing comparison between the active valour of the Turks and the sloth and effeminacy of the natives of Egypt. After suspending before the holy sepulchre the sword and standard of the sultan, the new king (he deserves the title) embraced his departing companions, and could retain only with the gallant Tancred three hundred knights, and two thousand foot soldiers, for the defence of Palestine. His sovereignty was soon attacked by a new enemy, the only one against whom Godfrey was a coward. Adhemar, bishop of Puy, who excelled both in council and action, had been swept away in the last plague of Antioch: the remaining ecclesiastics preserved only the pride and avarice of their character; and their seditious clamours had required that the choice of a bishop should precede that of a king. The revenue and jurisdiction of the lawful patriarch were usurped by the Latin clergy: the exclusion of the Greeks and Syrians was justified by the reproach of heresy or schism;[116] and, under the iron yoke of their deliverers, the Oriental Christians regretted the tolerating government of the Arabian caliphs. Daimbert, archbishop of Pisa, had long been trained in the secret policy of Rome: he brought a fleet of his countrymen to the succour of the Holy Land, and was installed, without a competitor, the spiritual and temporal head of the church. The new patriarch[117] immediately grasped the sceptre which had been acquired by the toil and blood of the victorious pilgrims; and both Godfrey and Bohemond submitted to receive at his hands the investiture of their feudal possessions. Nor was this sufficient; Daimbert claimed the immediate property of Jerusalem and Jaffa; instead of a firm and generous refusal, the hero negotiated with the priest; a quarter of either

city was ceded to the church; and the modest bishop was satisfied with an eventual reversion of the rest, on the death of Godfrey without children, or on the future acquisition of a new seat at Cairo or Damascus.

Without this indulgence the conqueror would have almost been stripped of his infant kingdom, which consisted only of Jerusalem and Jaffa, with about twenty villages and towns of the adjacent country.[118] Within this narrow verge the Mohammedans were still lodged in some impregnable castles; and the husbandman, the trader, and the pilgrim were exposed to daily and domestic hostility. By the arms of Godfrey himself, and of the two Baldwins, his brother and cousin, who succeeded to the throne, the Latins breathed with more ease and safety; and at length they equalled, in the extent of their dominions, though not in the millions of their subjects, the ancient princes of Judah and Israel.[119] After the reduction of the maritime cities of Laodicea, Tripoli, Tyre, and Ascalon,[120] which were powerfully assisted by the fleets of Venice, Genoa, and Pisa, and even of Flanders and Norway,[121] the range of seacoast from Scanderoon to the borders of Egypt was possessed by the Christian pilgrims. If the prince of Antioch disclaimed his supremacy, the counts of Edessa and Tripoli owned themselves the vassals of the king of Jerusalem: the Latins reigned beyond the Euphrates; and the four cities of Hems, Hamah, Damascus, and Aleppo were the only relics of the Mohammedan conquests in Syria.[122] The laws and language, the manners and titles, of the French nation and Latin church, were introduced into these transmarine colonies. According to the feudal jurisprudence, the principal states and subordinate baronies descended in the line of male and female succession:[123] but the children of the first conquerors,[124] a motley and degenerate race, were dissolved by the luxury of the climate; the arrival of new crusaders from Europe was a doubtful hope and a casual event. The service of the feudal tenures[125] was performed by six hundred and sixty-six knights, who might expect the aid of two hundred more under the banner of the count of Tripoli; and each knight was attended to the field by four squires or archers on horseback.[126] Five thousand and seventy-five serjeants, most probably foot-soldiers, were supplied by the churches and cities; and the whole legal militia of the kingdom could not exceed eleven thousand men, a slender defence against the surrounding myriads of Saracens and Turks.[127] But the firmest

ery weapon in his defence,okokook

The Fifty-eighth Chapter — 403

bulwark of Jerusalem was founded on the knights of the Hospital of St. John,[128] and of the temple of Solomon;[129] on the strange association of a monastic and military life, which fanaticism might suggest, but which policy must approve. The flower of the nobility of Europe aspired to wear the cross, and to profess the vows, of these respectable orders; their spirit and discipline were immortal; and the speedy donation of twenty-eight thousand farms, or manors,[130] enabled them to support a regular force of cavalry and infantry for the defence of Palestine. The austerity of the convert soon evaporated in the exercise of arms: the world was scandalised by the pride, avarice, and corruption of these Christian soldiers; their claims of immunity and jurisdiction disturbed the harmony of the church and state; and the public peace was endangered by their jealous emulation. But in their most dissolute period the knights of the hospital and temple maintained their fearless and fanatic character: they neglected to live, but they were prepared to die, in the service of Christ; and the spirit of chivalry, the parent and offspring of the crusades, has been transplanted by this institution from the holy sepulchre to the isle of Malta.[131]

The spirit of freedom, which pervades the feudal institutions, was felt in its strongest energy by the volunteers of the cross, who elected for their chief the most deserving of his peers. Amidst the slaves of Asia, unconscious of the lesson or example, a model of political liberty was introduced; and the laws of the French kingdom are derived from the purest source of equality and justice. Of such laws, the first and indispensable condition is the assent of those whose obedience they require, and for whose benefit they are designed. No sooner had Godfrey of Bouillon accepted the office of supreme magistrate than he solicited the public and private advice of the Latin pilgrims who were the best skilled in the statutes and customs of Europe. From these materials, with the counsel and approbation of the patriarch and barons, of the clergy and laity, Godfrey composed the ASSISE OF JERUSALEM,[132] a precious monument of feudal jurisprudence. The new code, attested by the seals of the king, the patriarch, and the viscount of Jerusalem, was deposited in the holy sepulchre, enriched with the improvements of succeeding times, and respectfully consulted as often as any doubtful question arose in the tribunals of Palestine. With the kingdom and city all was lost;[133] the fragments of the written law were preserved by jealous tradition[134] and variable practice till the middle of the thirteenth century: the code was restored by the pen of John d'Ibelin, count of Jaffa, one of the principal feudatories;[135] and the final revision was accomplished in the year thirteen hundred and sixty-nine, for the use of the Latin kingdom of Cyprus.[136]

The justice and freedom of the constitution were maintained by two tribunals of unequal dignity, which were instituted by Godfrey of Bouillon after the conquest of Jerusalem. The king, in person, presided in the upper court, the court of the barons. Of these the four most conspicuous were the prince of Galilee, the lord of Sidon and Cæsarea, and the counts of Jaffa and Tripoli, who, perhaps with the constable and marshal,[137] were in a special manner the compeers and judges of each other. But all the nobles who held their lands immediately of the crown were entitled and bound to attend the king's court; and each baron exercised a similar jurisdiction in the subordinate assemblies of his own feudatories. The connection of lord and vassal was honourable and voluntary: reverence was due to the benefactor, protection to the dependent; but they mutually pledged their faith to each other; and the obligation on either side might be suspended by neglect or dissolved by injury. The cognisance of marriages and testaments was blended with religion, and usurped by the clergy: but the civil and criminal causes of the nobles, the inheritance and tenure of their fiefs, formed the proper occupation of the supreme court. Each member was the judge and guardian both of public and private rights. It was his duty to assert with his tongue and sword the lawful claims of the lord: but if an unjust superior presumed to violate the freedom or property of a vassal, the confederate peers stood forth to maintain his quarrel by word and deed. They boldly affirmed his innocence and his wrongs; demanded the restitution of his liberty and his lands; suspended, after a fruitless demand, their own service; rescued their brother from prison; and employed every weapon in his defence, without offering direct violence to the person of their lord, which was ever sacred in their eyes.[138] In their pleadings, replies, and rejoinders, the advocates of the court were subtle and copious; but the use of argument and evidence was often superseded by judicial combat; and the Assise of Jerusalem admits in many cases this barbarous institution, which has been slowly abolished by the laws and manners of Europe.

The trial by battle was established in all criminal cases which affected the life, or limb, or honour of any person; and in all civil transactions of or above the value of one mark of silver. It appears that in criminal cases the combat was the privilege of the accuser, who, except in a charge of treason, avenged his personal injury, or the death of those persons whom he had a right to represent; but wherever, from the nature of the charge, testimony could be obtained, it was necessary for him to produce witnesses of the fact. In civil cases the combat was not allowed as the means of establishing the claim of the demandant, but he was obliged to produce witnesses who had, or assumed to have, knowledge of the fact. The combat was then the privilege of the defendant, because he charged the witness with an attempt by perjury to take away his right. He came therefore to be in the same situation as the appellant in criminal cases. It was not, then, as a mode of proof that the combat was received, nor as making negative evidence (according to the supposition of Montesquieu);[139] but in every case the right to offer battle was founded on the right to pursue by arms the redress of an injury, and the judicial combat was fought on the same principle and with the same spirit as a private duel. Champions were only allowed to women, and to men maimed or past the age of sixty. The consequence of a defeat was death to the person accused, or to the champion or witness, as well as to the accuser himself; but in civil cases the demandant was punished with infamy and the loss of his suit, while his witness and champion suffered an ignominious death. In many cases it was in the option of the judge to award or to refuse the combat: but two are specified in which it was the inevitable result of the challenge; if a faithful vassal gave the lie to his compeer who unjustly claimed any portion of their lord's demesnes, or if an unsuccessful suitor presumed to impeach the judgment and veracity of the court. He might impeach them, but the terms were severe and perilous; in the same day he successfully fought *all* the members of the tribunal, even those who had been absent; a single defeat was followed by death and infamy, and where none could hope for victory it is highly probable that none would adventure the trial. In the Assise of Jerusalem, the legal subtlety of the count of Jaffa is more laudably employed to elude, than to facilitate, the judicial combat, which he derives from a principle of honour rather than of superstition.[140]

Among the causes which enfranchised the plebeians from the yoke of feudal tyranny, the institution of cities and corporations is one of the most powerful; and if those of Palestine are coeval with the first crusade, they may be ranked with the most ancient of the Latin world. Many of the pilgrims had escaped from their lords under the banner of the cross, and it was the policy of the French princes to tempt their stay by the assurance of the rights and privileges of freemen. It is expressly declared in the Assise of Jerusalem, that after instituting, for his knights and barons, the court of peers, in which he presided himself, Godfrey of Bouillon established a second tribunal, in which his person was represented by his viscount. The jurisdiction of this inferior court extended over the burgesses of the kingdom, and it was composed of a select number of the most discreet and worthy citizens, who were sworn to judge, according to the laws, of the actions and fortunes of their equals.[141] In the conquest and settlement of new cities, the example of Jerusalem was imitated by the kings and their great vassals, and above thirty similar corporations were founded before the loss of the Holy Land. Another class of subjects, the Syrians,[142] or Oriental Christians, were oppressed by the zeal of the clergy, and protected by the toleration of the state. Godfrey listened to their reasonable prayer that they might be judged by their own national laws. A third court was instituted for their use, of limited and domestic jurisdiction; the sworn members were Syrians, in blood, language, and religion, but the office of the president (in Arabic, of the *rais*) was sometimes exercised by the viscount of the city. At an immeasurable distance below the *nobles*, the *burgesses*, and the *strangers*, the Assise of Jerusalem condescends to mention the *villains* and *slaves*, the peasants of the land and the captives of war, who were almost equally considered as the objects of property. The relief or protection of these unhappy men was not esteemed worthy of the care of the legislator: but he diligently provides for the recovery, though not indeed for the punishment, of the fugitives. Like hounds or hawks, who had strayed from the lawful owner, they might be lost and claimed; the slave and falcon were of the same value, but three slaves or twelve oxen were accumulated to equal the price of the war-horse, and a sum of three hundred pieces of gold was fixed, in the age of chivalry, as the equivalent of the more noble animal.[143]

CHAPTER LIX

Preservation of the Greek Empire. Numbers, Passage, and Event of the Second and Third Crusades. St. Bernard. Reign of Saladin in Egypt and Syria. His Conquest of Jerusalem. Naval Crusades. Richard the First of England. Pope Innocent the Third; and the Fourth and Fifth Crusades. The Emperor Frederic the Second. Louis the Ninth of France; and the two last Crusades. Expulsion of the Latins or Franks by the Mamalukes.

IN a style less grave than that of history I should perhaps compare the emperor Alexius[1] to the jackal, who is said to follow the steps, and devour the leavings, of the lion. Whatever had been his fears and toils in the passage of the first crusade, they were amply recompensed by the subsequent benefits which he derived from the exploits of the Franks. His dexterity and vigilance secured their first conquest of Nice, and from this threatening station the Turks were compelled to evacuate the neighbourhood of Constantinople. While the crusaders, with blind valour, advanced into the midland countries of Asia, the crafty Greek improved the favourable occasion when the emirs of the sea-coast were recalled to the standard of the sultan. The Turks were driven from the isles of Rhodes and Chios: the cities of Ephesus and Smyrna, of Sardes, Philadelphia, and Laodicea, were restored to the empire, which Alexius enlarged from the Hellespont to the banks of the Mæander and the rocky shores of Pamphylia. The churches resumed their splendour, the towns were rebuilt and fortified, and the desert country was peopled with colonies of Christians, who were gently removed from the more distant and dangerous frontier. In these paternal cares we may forgive Alexius if he forgot the deliverance of the holy sepulchre; but by the Latins he was stigmatised with the foul reproach of treason and desertion. They had sworn fidelity and obedience to his throne, but *he* had promised to assist their enterprise in person, or, at least, with his troops and treasures; his base retreat dissolved their obligations; and the sword, which had been the instrument of their victory, was the pledge and title of their just independence. It does not appear that the emperor attempted to revive his obsolete claims over the kingdom of Jerusalem,[2] but the borders of Cilicia and Syria were more recent in his possession, and more accessible to his arms. The great army of the crusaders was annihilated or dispersed; the principality of Antioch was left without a head by the surprise and captivity of Bohemond; his ransom had oppressed him with a heavy debt, and his Norman followers were insufficient to repel the hostilities of the Greeks and Turks. In this distress Bohemond embraced a magnanimous resolution of leaving the defence of Antioch to his kinsman the faithful Tancred, of arming the West against the Byzantine empire, and of executing the design which he inherited from the lessons and example of his father Guiscard. His embarkation was clandestine, and, if we may credit a tale of the princess Anna, he passed the hostile sea closely secreted in a coffin.[3] But his reception in France was dignified by the public applause and his marriage with the king's daughter; his return was glorious, since the bravest spirits of the age enlisted under his veteran command; and he repassed the Adriatic at the head of five thousand horse and forty thousand foot, assembled from the most remote climates of Europe.[4] The strength of Durazzo and prudence of Alexius, the progress of famine and approach of winter, eluded his ambitious hopes, and the venal confederates were seduced from his standard. A treaty of peace[5] suspended the fears of the Greeks, and they were finally delivered by the death of an adversary whom neither oaths could bind, nor dangers could appall, nor prosperity could satiate. His children succeeded to the principality of Antioch, but the boundaries were strictly defined, the homage was clearly stipulated, and the cities of Tarsus and Malmistra were restored to the Byzantine emperors. Of the coast of Anatolia, they possessed the entire circuit from Trebizond to the Syrian gates. The Seljukian dynasty of Roum[6] was separated on all sides from the sea and their Musulman brethren; the power of the sultans was shaken by the victories and even the defeats of the Franks; and after the loss of Nice they removed their throne to Cogni or Iconium, an obscure and inland town above three hundred miles from Constantinople.[7] Instead of trembling for their capital, the Comnenian princes waged an offensive war against the Turks, and the first crusade prevented the fall of the declining empire.

In the twelfth century three great emigrations marched by land from the West to the relief of Palestine. The soldiers and pilgrims of Lombardy, France, and Germany were excited by the example and success of the first crusade.[8] Forty-eight years after the deliverance of the holy sepulchre, the emperor and the French king, Conrad the Third and Louis the Seventh, undertook the second crusade to support the falling fortunes of the Latins.[9] A grand division of the third crusade was led by the emperor Frederic Barbarossa,[10] who sympathised with his brothers of France and England in the common loss of Jerusalem. These three expeditions may be compared, in their resemblance of the greatness of numbers, their passage through the Greek empire, and the nature and event of their Turkish warfare; and a brief parallel may save the repetition of a tedious narrative. However splendid it may seem, a regular story of the crusades would exhibit the perpetual return of the same causes and effects, and the frequent attempts for the defence or recovery of the Holy Land would appear so many faint and unsuccessful copies of the original.

I. Of the swarms that so closely trod in the footsteps of the first pilgrims, the chiefs were equal in rank, though unequal in fame and merit, to Godfrey of Bouillon and his fellow adventurers. At their head were displayed the banners of the dukes of Burgundy, Bavaria, and Aquitain: the first a descendant of Hugh Capet, the second a father of the Brunswick line; the archbishop of Milan, a temporal prince, transported, for the benefit of the Turks, the treasures and ornaments of his church and palace; and the veteran crusaders, Hugh the Great and Stephen of Chartres, returned to consummate their unfinished vow. The huge and disorderly bodies of their followers moved forward in two columns; and if the first consisted of two hundred and sixty thousand persons, the second might possibly amount to sixty thousand horse and one hundred thousand foot.[11] The armies of the second crusade might have claimed the conquest of Asia; the nobles of France and Germany were animated by the presence of their sovereigns, and both the rank and personal characters of Conrad and Louis gave a dignity to their cause, and a discipline to their force, which might be vainly expected from the feudatory chiefs. The cavalry of the emperor and that of the king was each composed of seventy thousand knights and their immediate attendants in the field;[12] and if the light-armed troops, the peasant infantry, the women and children, the priests and monks, be rigorously excluded, the full account will scarcely be satisfied with four hundred thousand souls. The West, from Rome to Britain, was called into action; the kings of Poland and Bohemia obeyed the summons of Conrad; and it is affirmed by the Greeks and Latins, that, in the passage of a strait or river, the Byzantine agents, after a tale of nine hundred thousand, desisted from the endless and formidable computation.[13] In the third crusade, as the French and English preferred the navigation of the Mediterranean, the host of Frederic Barbarossa was less numerous. Fifteen thousand knights and as many squires were the flower of the German chivalry; sixty thousand horse and one hundred thousand foot were mustered by the emperor in the plains of Hungary; and after such repetitions we shall no longer be startled at the six hundred thousand pilgrims which credulity has ascribed to this last emigration.[14] Such extravagant reckonings prove only the astonishment of contemporaries, but their astonishment most strongly bears testimony to the existence of an enormous though indefinite multitude. The Greeks might applaud their superior knowledge of the arts and stratagems of war, but they confessed the strength and courage of the French cavalry and the infantry of the Germans;[15] and the strangers are described as an iron race, of gigantic stature who darted fire from their eyes, and spilt blood like water on the ground. Under the banners of Conrad a troop of females rode in the attitude and armour of men, and the chief of these Amazons, from her gilt spurs and buskins, obtained the epithet of the Golden-footed Dame.

II. The numbers and character of the strangers was an object of terror to the effeminate Greeks, and the sentiment of fear is nearly allied to that of hatred. This aversion was suspended or softened by the apprehension of the Turkish power; and the invectives of the Latins will not bias our more candid belief that the emperor Alexius dissembled their insolence, eluded their hostilities, counselled their rashness, and opened to their ardour the road of pilgrimage and conquest. But when the Turks had been driven from Nice and the seacoast, when the Byzantine princes no longer dreaded the distant sultans of Cogni, they felt with purer indignation the free and frequent passage of the Western barbarians, who violated the majesty and enangered the safety of the empire. The second and third crusades were undertaken under the reign of Manuel Comnenus and Isaac Angelus. Of the former, the passions were always impetuous, and often malevolent; and the natural union of a cowardly and a mischievous temper was exemplified in the latter, who, without merit or mercy, could punish a tyrant and occupy his throne. It was secretly, and perhaps tacitly resolved by the prince and people to destroy, or at least to discourage, the pilgrims by every species of injury and oppression; and their want of prudence and discipline continually afforded the pretence or the opportunity. The Western monarchs had stipulated a safe passage and fair market in the country of their Christian brethren; the treaty had been ratified by oaths and hostages; and the poorest soldier of Frederic's army was furnished with three marks of silver to defray his expenses on the road. But every engagement was violated by treachery and injustice; and the complaints of the Latins are attested by the honest confession of a Greek historian, who has dared to prefer truth to his country.[16] Instead of an hospitable reception, the gates of the cities, both in Europe and Asia, were closely barred against the crusaders; and the scanty pittance of food was let down in baskets from the walls. Experience or foresight might excuse this timid jealousy; but the common duties of humanity prohibited the mixture of chalk, or other poisonous ingredients, in the bread; and should Manuel be acquitted of any foul connivance, he is guilty of coining base money for the purpose of trading with the pilgrims. In every step of their march they were stopped or misled: the governors had private orders to fortify the passes and break down the bridges against them: the stragglers were pillaged and murdered: the soldiers and horses were pierced in the woods by arrows from an invisible hand; the sick were burnt in their beds; and the dead bodies were hung on gibbets along the highways. These injuries exasperated the champions of the cross, who were not endowed with evangelical patience; and the Byzantine princes, who had provoked the unequal conflict, promoted the embarkation and march of these formidable guests. On the verge of the Turkish frontier Barbarossa spared the guilty Philadelphia,[17] rewarded the hospitable Laodicea, and deplored the hard necessity that had stained his sword with any drops of Christian blood. In their intercourse with the monarchs of Germany and France, the pride of the Greeks was exposed to an anxious trial. They might boast that on the first interview the seat of Louis was a low stool beside the throne of Manuel;[18] but no sooner had the French king transported his army beyond the Bosphorus than he refused the offer of a second conference unless his brother would meet him on equal terms either on the sea or land. With Conrad and Frederic the ceremonial was still nicer and more difficult: like the successors of Constantine, they styled themselves emperors of the Romans,[19] and firmly maintained the purity of their title and dignity. The first of these representatives of Charlemagne would only converse with Manuel on horseback in the open field; the second, by passing the Hellespont rather than the Bosphorus, declined the view of Constantinople and its sovereign. An emperor who had been crowned at Rome was reduced in the Greek epistles to the humble appellation of *Rex*, or prince, of the Alemanni; and the vain and feeble Angelus affected to be ignorant of the name of one of the greatest men and monarchs of the age. While they viewed with hatred and suspicion the Latin pilgrims, the Greek emperors maintained a strict, though secret, alliance with the Turks and Saracens. Isaac Angelus complained that by his friendship for the great Saladin he had incurred the enmity of the Franks; and a mosque was founded at Constantinople for the public exercise of the religion of Mohammed.[20]

III. The swarms that followed the first crusade were destroyed in Anatolia by famine, pestilence, and the Turkish arrows; and the princes only escaped with some squadrons of horse to accomplish their lamentable pilgrimage. A just opinion may be formed of their knowledge and humanity; of their knowledge, from the design of subduing Persia and Chorasan in their way to Jerusalem; of their humanity, from the massacre of the Christian people, a friendly city, who came out to meet them with palms and crosses in their hands. The arms of Conrad and Louis were less cruel and imprudent; but the event of the second crusade was still more ruinous to Christendom; and the Greek Manuel is accused by his own subjects of giving seasonable intelligence to the sultan, and treacherous guides to the Latin princes. Instead of crushing the common foe by a double attack at the same time, but on different sides, the Germans were urged by emulation, and the French were retarded by jealousy. Louis had scarcely passed the Bosphorus when he was met by the returning emperor, who had lost the greatest part of his army in glorious, but unsuccessful, action, on the banks of the Mæander. The contrast of the pomp of his rival hastened the retreat of Conrad: the desertion of his independent vassals reduced him to his hereditary troops: and he borrowed some Greek vessels to execute by sea the pilgrimage of Palestine. Without studying the lessons of experience, or the nature of the war, the king of France advanced through the same country to a similar fate. The vanguard, which bore the royal banner and the oriflamme of St. Denys,[21] had doubled their march with rash and inconsiderate speed; and the rear, which the king commanded in person, no longer found their companions in the evening camp. In darkness and disorder, they were encompassed, assaulted, and overwhelmed by the innumerable hosts of Turks, who, in the art of war, were superior to the Christians of the twelfth century. Louis, who climbed a tree in the general discomfiture, was saved by his own valour and the ignorance of his adversaries; and with the dawn of day he escaped alive, but almost alone, to the camp of the vanguard. But instead of pursuing his expedition by land, he was rejoiced to shelter the relics of his army in the friendly seaport of Satalia. From thence he embarked for Antioch; but so penurious was the supply of Greek vessels that they could only afford room for his knights and nobles; and the plebeian crowd of infantry was left to perish at the foot of the Pamphylian hills. The emperor and the king embraced and wept at Jerusalem; their martial trains, the remnant of mighty armies, were joined to the Christian powers of Syria, and a fruitless siege of Damascus was the final effort of the second crusade. Conrad and Louis embarked for Europe with the personal fame of piety and courage; but the Orientals had braved these potent monarchs of the Franks, with whose names and military forces they had been so often threatened.[22] Perhaps they had still more to fear from the veteran genius of Frederic the First, who in his youth had served in Asia under his uncle Conrad. Forty campaigns in Germany and Italy had taught Barbarossa to command; and his soldiers, even the princes of the empire, were accustomed under his reign to obey. As soon as he lost sight of Philadelphia and Laodicea, the last cities of the Greek frontier, he plunged into the salt and barren desert, a land (says the historian) of horror and tribulation.[23] During twenty days every step of his fainting and sickly march was besieged by the innumerable hordes of Turkmans,[24] whose numbers and fury seemed after each defeat to multiply and inflame. The emperor continued to struggle and to suffer; and such was the measure of his calamities, that when he reached the gates of Iconium no more than one thousand knights were able to serve on horseback. By a sudden and resolute assault he defeated the guards, and stormed the capital, of the sultan,[25] who humbly sued for pardon and peace. The road was now open, and Frederic advanced in a career of triumph till he was unfortunately drowned in a petty torrent of Cilicia.[26] The remainder of his Germans was consumed by sickness and desertion; and the emperor's son expired with the greatest part of his Swabian vassals at the siege of Acre. Among the Latin heroes Godfrey of Bouillon and Frederic Barbarossa could alone achieve the passage of the Lesser Asia; yet even their success was a warning; and in the last and most experienced age of the crusades every nation preferred the sea to the toils and perils of an inland expedition.[27]

The enthusiasm of the first crusade is a natural and simple event, while hope was fresh, danger untried, and enterprise congenial to the spirit of the times. But the obstinate perseverance of Europe may indeed excite our pity and admiration; that no instruction should have been drawn from constant and adverse experience; that the same confidence should have repeatedly grown from the same failures; that six succeeding generations should have rushed headlong down the precipice that was open before them; and that men of every condition should have staked their public and private fortunes on the desperate adventure of possessing or recovering a tombstone two thousand miles from their country. In a period of two centuries after the council of Clermont, each spring and summer produced a new emigration of pilgrim warriors for the defence of the Holy Land; but the seven great armaments or crusades were excited by some impending or recent calamity: the nations were moved by the authority of their pontiffs and the example of their kings: their zeal was kindled, and their reason was silenced, by the voice of their holy orators; and among these, Bernard,[28] the monk, or the saint, may claim the most honourable place. About eight years before the first conquest of Jerusalem he was born of a noble family in Burgundy; at the age of three-and-twenty he buried himself in the monastery of Citeaux, then in the primitive fervour of the institution; at the end of two years he led forth her third colony, or daughter, to the valley of Clairvaux[29] in Champagne; and was content till the hour of his death, with the humble station of abbot of his own community. A philosophic age has abolished, with too liberal and indiscriminate disdain, the honours of these spiritual heroes. The meanest among them are distinguished by some energies of the mind; they were at least superior to their votaries and disciples; and, in the race of superstition, they attained the prize for which such numbers contended. In speech, in writing, in action, Bernard stood high above his rivals and contemporaries; his compositions are not devoid of wit and eloquence; and he seems to have preserved as much reason and humanity as may be reconciled with the character of a saint. In a secular life he would have shared the seventh part of a private inheritance; by a vow of poverty and penance, by closing his eyes against the visible world,[30] by the refusal of all ecclesiastical dignities, the abbot of Clairvaux became the oracle of Europe, and the founder of one hundred and sixty convents. Princes and pontiffs trembled at the freedom of his apostolical censures: France, England, and Milan consulted and obeyed his judgment in a schism of the church: the debt was repaid by the gratitude of Innocent the Second: and his successor, Eugenius the Third, was the friend and disciple of the holy Bernard. It was in the proclamation of the second crusade that he shone as the missionary and prophet of God, who called the nations to the defence of his holy sepulchre.[31] At the parliament of Vezelay he spoke before the king; and Louis the Seventh, with his nobles, received their crosses from his hand. The abbot of Clairvaux then marched to the less easy conquest of the emperor Conrad: a phlegmatic people, ignorant of his language, was transported by the pathetic vehemence of his tone and gestures; and his progress, from Constance to Cologne, was the triumph of eloquence and zeal. Bernard applauds his own success in the depopulation of Europe; affirms that cities and castles were emptied of their inhabitants; and computes that only one man was left behind for the consolation of seven widows.[32] The blind fanatics were desirous of electing him for their general; but the example of the hermit Peter was before his eyes; and while he assured the crusaders of the divine favour, he prudently declined a military command, in which failure and victory would have been almost equally disgraceful to his character.[33] Yet, after the calamitous event, the abbot of Clairvaux was loudly accused as a false prophet, the author of the public and private mourning; his enemies exulted, his friends blushed, and his apology was slow and unsatis-factory. He justifies his obedience to the commands of the pope; expatiates on the mysterious ways of Providence; imputes the misfortunes of the pilgrims to their own sins; and modestly insinuates that his mission had been approved by signs and wonders.[34] Had the fact been certain, the argument would be decisive; and his faithful disciples, who enumerate twenty or thirty miracles in a day, appeal to the public assemblies of France and Germany, in which they were performed.[35] At the present hour such prodigies will not obtain credit beyond the precincts of Clairvaux; but in the preternatural cures of the blind, the lame, and the sick, who were presented to the man of God, it is impossible for us to ascertain the separate shares of accident, of fancy, of imposture, and of fiction.

Omnipotence itself cannot escape the murmurs of its discordant votaries; since the same dispensation which was applauded as a deliverance in Europe, was deplored, and perhaps arraigned, as a calamity in Asia. After the loss of Jerusalem the Syrian fugitives diffused their consternation and sorrow: Bagdad mourned in the dust; the cadhi Beineddin of Damascus tore his beard in the caliph's presence; and the whole divan shed tears at his melancholy tale.[36] But the commanders of the faithful could only weep; they were themselves captives in the hands of the Turks: some temporal power was restored to the last age of the Abbassides; but their humble ambition was confined to Bagdad and the adjacent province. Their tyrants, the Seljukian sultans, had followed the common law of the Asiatic dynasties, the unceasing round of valour, greatness, discord, degeneracy, and decay: their spirit and power were unequal to the defence of religion; and, in his distant realm of Persia, the Christians were strangers to the name and the arms of Sangiar, the last hero of his race.[37] While the sultans were involved in the silken web of the harem, the pious task was undertaken by their slaves, the Atabeks,[38] a Turkish name, which, like the Byzantine patricians, may be translated by Father of the Prince. Ascansar, a valiant Turk, had been the favourite of Malek Shah, from whom he received the privilege of standing on the right hand of the throne; but, in the civil wars that ensued on the monarch's death, he lost his head and the government of Aleppo. His domestic emirs persevered in their attachment to his son Zenghi, who proved his first arms against the Franks in the defeat of Antioch: thirty campaigns in the service of the caliph and sultan established his military fame; and he was invested with the command of Mosul, as the only champion that could avenge the cause of the prophet. The public hope was not disappointed: after a siege of twenty-five days he stormed the city of Edessa, and recovered from the Franks their conquests beyond the Euphrates:[39] the martial tribes of Curdistan were subdued by the independent sovereign of Mosul and Aleppo: his soldiers were taught to behold the camp as their only country; they trusted to his liberality for their rewards; and their absent families were protected by the vigilance of Zenghi. At the head of these veterans his son Noureddin gradually united the Mohammedan powers, added the kingdom of Damascus to that of Aleppo, and waged a long and successful war against the Christians of Syria; he spread his ample reign from the Tigris to the Nile, and the Abbassides rewarded their faithful servant with all the titles and prerogatives of royalty. The Latins themselves were compelled to own the wisdom and courage, and even the justice and piety, of this implacable adversary.[40] In his life and government the holy warrior revived the zeal and simplicity of the first caliphs. Gold and silk were banished from his palace, the use of wine from his dominions; the public revenue was scrupulously applied to the public service; and the frugal household of Noureddin was maintained from his legitimate share of the spoil which he vested in the purchase of a private estate. His favourite sultana sighed for some female object of expense. "Alas," replied the king, "I fear God, and am no more than the treasurer of the Moslems. Their property I cannot alienate; but I still possess three shops in the city of Hems: these you may take; and these alone can I bestow." His chamber of justice was the terror of the great and the refuge of the poor. Some years after the sultan's death an oppressed subject called aloud in the streets of Damascus, "O Noureddin, Noureddin, where art thou now? Arise, arise, to pity and protect us!" A tumult was apprehended, and a living tyrant blushed or trembled at the name of a departed monarch.

By the arms of the Turks and Franks the Fatimites had been deprived of Syria. In Egypt the decay of their character and influence was still more essential. Yet they were still revered as the descendants and successors of the prophet; they maintained their invisible state in the palace of Cairo; and their person was seldom violated by the profane eyes of subjects or strangers. The Latin ambassadors[41] have described their own introduction through a series of gloomy passages and glittering porticoes: the scene was enlivened by the warbling of birds and the murmur of fountains: it was enriched by a display of rich furniture and rare animals; of the Imperial treasures, something was shown, and much was supposed; and the long order of unfolding doors was guarded by black soldiers and domestic eunuchs. The sanctuary of the presence chamber was veiled with a curtain; and the vizir, who conducted the ambassadors, laid aside his scimitar, and prostrated himself three times on the ground; the veil was then removed; and they beheld the commander of the faithful, who signified his pleasure to the first slave of the throne. But this slave was his master: the vizirs or sultans had usurped the supreme administration of Egypt; the claims of the rival candidates were decided by arms; and the name of the most worthy, of the strongest, was inserted in the royal patent of command. The factions of Dargham and Shawer alternately expelled each other from the capital and country; and the weaker side implored the dangerous protection of the sultan of Damascus, or the king of Jerusalem, the perpetual enemies of the sect and monarchy of the Fatimites. By his arms and religion the Turk was most formidable; but the Frank, in an easy direct march, could advance from Gaza to the Nile; while the intermediate situation of his realm compelled the troops of Noureddin to wheel round the skirts of Arabia, a long and painful circuit, which exposed them to thirst, fatigue, and the burning winds of the desert. The secret zeal and ambition of the Turkish prince aspired to reign in Egypt under the name of the Abbassides; but the restoration of the suppliant Shawer was the ostensible motive of the first expedition; and the success was intrusted to the emir Shiracouh, a valiant and veteran commander. Dargham was oppressed and slain; but the ingratitude, the jealousy, the just apprehensions, of his more fortunate rival, soon provoked him to invite the king of Jerusalem to deliver Egypt from his insolent benefactors. To this union the forces of Shiracouh were unequal: he relinquished the premature conquest; and the evacuation of Belbeis or Pelusium was the condition of his safe retreat. As the Turks defiled before the enemy, and their general closed the rear, with a vigilant eye, and a battle-axe in his hand, a Frank presumed to ask him if he were not afraid of an attack? "It is doubtless in your power to begin the attack," replied the intrepid emir; "but rest assured that not one of my soldiers will go to paradise till he as sent an infidel to hell." His report of the riches of the land, the effeminacy of the natives, and the disorders of the government, revived the hopes of Noureddin; the caliph of Bagdad applauded the pious design; and Shiracouh descended into Egypt a second time with twelve thousand Turks and eleven thousand Arabs. Yet his forces were still inferior to the confederate armies of the Franks and Saracens; and I can discern an unusual degree of military art in his passage of the Nile, his retreat into Thebais, his masterly evolutions in the battle of Babain, the surprise of Alexandria, and his marches and countermarches in the flats and valley of Egypt, from the tropic to the sea. His conduct was seconded by the courage of his troops, and on the eve of action a Mamaluke[42] exclaimed, "If we cannot wrest Egypt from the Christian dogs, why do we not renounce the honours and rewards of the sultan, and retire to labour with the peasants, or to spin with the females of the harem?" Yet, after all his efforts in the field,[43] after the obstinate defence of Alexandria[44] by his nephew Saladin, an honourable capitulation and retreat concluded the second enterprise of Shiracouh; and Noureddin reserved his abilities for a third and more propitious occasion. It was soon offered by the ambition and avarice of Amalric or Amaury, king of Jerusalem, who had imbibed the pernicious maxim that no faith should be kept with the enemies of God. A religious warrior, the great master of the hospital, encouraged him to proceed; the emperor of Constantinople either gave, or promised, a fleet to act with the armies of Syria; and the perfidious Christian, unsatisfied with spoil and subsidy, aspired to the conquest of Egypt. In this emergency the Moslems turned their eyes towards the sultan of Damascus; the vizir, whom danger encompassed on all sides, yielded to their unanimous wishes; and Noureddin seemed to be tempted by the fair offer of one third of the revenue of the kingdom. The Franks were already at the gates of Cairo; but the suburbs, the old city, were burnt on their approach; they were deceived by an insidious negotiation, and their vessels were unable to surmount the barriers of the Nile. They prudently declined a contest with the Turks in the midst of a hostile country; and Amaury retired into Palestine with the shame and reproach that always adhere to unsuccessful injustice. After this deliverance, Shiracouh was invested with a robe of honour, which he soon stained with the blood of the unfortunate Shawer. For a while the Turkish emirs condescended to hold the office of vizir; but this foreign conquest precipitated the fall of the Fatimites themselves; and the bloodless change was accomplished by a message and a word. The caliphs had been degraded by their own weakness and the tyranny of the vizirs: their subjects blushed when the descendant and successor of the prophet presented his naked hand to the rude gripe of a Latin ambassador; they wept when he sent the hair of his women, a sad emblem of their grief and terror, to excite the pity of the sultan of Damascus. By the command of Noureddin, and the sentence of the doctors, the holy names of Abubeker, Omar, and Othman were solemnly restored: the caliph Mosthadi, of Bagdad, was acknowledged in the public prayers as the true commander of the faithful; and the green livery of the sons of Ali was exchanged for the black colour of the Abbassides. The last of his race, the caliph Adhed, who survived only ten days, expired in happy ignorance of his fate: his treasures secured the loyalty of the soldiers, and silenced the murmurs of the sectaries; and in all subsequent revolutions Egypt has never departed from the orthodox tradition of the Moslems.[45]

The hilly country beyond the Tigris is occupied by the pastoral tribes of the Curds;[46] a people hardy, strong, savage, impatient of the yoke, addicted to rapine, and tenacious of the government of their national chiefs. The resemblance of name, situation, and manners, seems to identify them with the Carduchians of the Greeks;[47] and they still defend against the Ottoman Porte the antique freedom which they asserted against the successors of Cyrus. Poverty and ambition prompted them to embrace the profession of mercenary soldiers: the service of his father and uncle prepared the reign of the great Saladin;[48] and the son of Job or Ayub, a simple Curd, magnanimously smiled at his pedigree, which flattery deduced from the Arabian caliphs.[49] So unconscious was Noureddin of the impending ruin of his house, that he constrained the reluctant youth to follow his uncle Shiracouh into Egypt: his military character was established by the defence of Alexandria; and if we may believe the Latins, he solicited and obtained from the Christian general the *profane* honours of knighthood.[50] On the death of Shiracouh, the office of grand vizir was bestowed on Saladin, as the youngest and least powerful of the emirs; but with the advice of his father, whom he invited to Cairo, his genius obtained the ascendant over his equals, and attached the army to his person and interest. While Noureddin lived, these ambitious Curds were the most humble of his slaves; and the indiscreet murmurs of the divan were silenced by the prudent Ayub who loudly protested that at the command of the Sultan he himself would lead his son in chains to the foot of the throne. "Such language," he added in private, "was prudent and proper in an assembly of your rivals; but we are now above fear and obedience; and the threats of Noureddin shall not extort the tribute of a sugar-cane." His seasonable death relieved them from the odious and doubtful conflict: his son, a minor of eleven years of age, was left for a while to the emirs of Damascus; and the new lord of Egypt was decorated by the caliph with every title[51] that could sanctify his usurpation in the eyes of the people. Nor was Saladin long content with the possession of Egypt: he despoiled the Christians of Jerusalem, and the Atabeks of Damascus, Aleppo, and Diarbekir: Mecca and Medina acknowledged him for their temporal protector: his brother subdued the distant regions of Yemen, or the happy Arabia; and at the hour of his death his empire was spread from the African Tripoli to the Tigris, and from the Indian Ocean to the mountains of Armenia. In the judgment of his character, the reproaches of treason and ingratitude strike forcibly on *our* minds, impressed, as they are, with the principle and experience of law and loyalty. But his ambition may in some measure be excused by the revolutions of Asia,[52] which had erased every notion of legitimate succession; by the recent example of the Atabeks themselves; by his reverence to the son of his benefactor; his humane and generous behaviour to the collateral branches; by *their* incapacity and *his* merit; by the approbation of the caliph, the sole source of all legitimate power; and, above all, by the wishes and interest of the people, whose happiness is the first object of government. In *his* virtues, and in those of his patron, they admired the singular union of the hero and the saint; for both Noureddin and Saladin are ranked among the Mohammedan saints; and the constant meditation of the holy war appears to have shed a serious and sober colour over their lives and actions. The youth of the latter[53] was addicted to wine and women; but his aspiring spirit soon renounced the temptations of pleasure for the graver follies of fame and dominion: the garment of Saladin was a coarse woollen; water was his only drink; and, while he emulated the temperance, he surpassed the chastity, of his Arabian prophet. Both in faith and practice he was a rigid Musulman; he ever deplored that the defence of religion had

not allowed him to accomplish the pilgrimage of Mecca; but at the stated hours, five times each day, the sultan devoutly prayed with his brethren: the involuntary omission of fasting was scrupulously repaid; and his perusal of the Koran, on horseback between the approaching armies, may be quoted as a proof, however ostentatious, of piety and courage.[54] The superstitious doctrine of the sect of Shafei was the only study that he deigned to encourage: the poets were safe in his contempt; but all profane science was the object of his aversion; and a philosopher who had vented some speculative novelties was seized and strangled by the command of the royal saint. The justice of his divan was accessible to the meanest suppliant against himself and his ministers; and it was only for a kingdom that Saladin would deviate from the rule of equity. While the descendants of Seljuk and Zenghi held his stirrup and smoothed his garments, he was affable and patient with the meanest of his servants. So boundless was his liberality that he distributed twelve thousand horses at the siege of Acre; and at the time of his death no more than forty-seven drachms of silver and one piece of gold coin were found in the treasury; yet, in a martial reign, the tributes were diminished, and the wealthy citizens enjoyed, without fear or danger, the fruits of their industry. Egypt, Syria, and Arabia were adorned by the royal foundations of hospitals, colleges, and mosques; and Cairo was fortified with a wall and citadel; but his works were consecrated to public use;[55] nor did the sultan indulge himself in a garden or palace of private luxury. In a fanatic age, himself a fanatic, the genuine virtues of Saladin commanded the esteem of the Christians: the emperor of Germany gloried in his friendship;[56] the Greek emperor solicited his alliance;[57] and the conquest of Jerusalem diffused, and perhaps magnified, his fame both in the East and West.

During its short existence the kingdom of Jerusalem[58] was supported by the discord of the Turks and Saracens; and both the Fatimite caliphs and the sultans of Damascus were tempted to sacrifice the cause of their religion to the meaner considerations of private and present advantage. But the powers of Egypt, Syria, and Arabia were now united by a hero whom nature and fortune had armed against the Christians. All without now bore the most threatening aspect; and all was feeble and hollow in the internal state of Jerusalem. After the two first Baldwins, the brother and cousin of Godfrey of Bouillon, the sceptre devolved by female succession to Melisenda, daughter of the second Baldwin, and her husband Fulk, count of Anjou, the father, by a former marriage, of our English Plantagenets. Their two sons, Baldwin the Third and Amaury, waged a strenuous, and not unsuccessful, war against the infidels; but the son of Amaury, Baldwin the Fourth, was deprived, by the leprosy, a gift of the crusades, of the faculties both of mind and body. His sister Sybilla, the mother of Baldwin the Fifth, was his natural heiress: after the suspicious death of her child, she crowned her second husband, Guy of Lusignan, a prince of a handsome person, but of such base renown that his own brother Jeffrey was heard to exclaim, "Since they have made *him* a king, surely they would have made *me* a god!" The choice was generally blamed; and the most powerful vassal, Raymond count of Tripoli, who had been excluded from the succession and regency, entertained an implacable hatred against the king, and exposed his honour and conscience to the temptations of the sultan. Such were the guardians of the holy city; a leper, a child, a woman, a coward, and a traitor: yet its fate was delayed twelve years by some supplies from Europe, by the valour of the military orders, and by the distant or domestic avocations of their great enemy. At length, on every side, the sinking state was encircled and pressed by a hostile line; and the truce was violated by the Franks, whose existence it protected. A soldier of fortune, Reginald of Châtillon, had seized a fortress on the edge of the desert, from whence he pillaged the caravans, insulted Mohammed, and threatened the cities of Mecca and Medina. Saladin condescended to complain; rejoiced in the denial of justice; and at the head of fourscore thousand horse and foot invaded the Holy Land. The choice of Tiberias for his first siege was suggested by the count of Tripoli, to whom it belonged; and the king of Jerusalem was persuaded to drain his garrison,[59] and to arm his people, for the relief of that important place. By the advice of the perfidious Raymond the Christians were betrayed into a camp destitute of water: he fled on the first onset, with the curses of both nations:[60] Lusignan was overthrown, with the loss of thirty thousand men; and the wood of the true cross, a dire misfortune! was left in the power of the infidels. The royal captive was conducted to the tent of Saladin; and as he fainted with thirst and terror, the generous victor presented him with a cup of sherbet, cooled in snow, without suffering his companion, Reginald of Châtillon, to partake of this pledge of hospitality and pardon. "The person and dignity of a king," said the sultan, "are sacred; but this impious robber must instantly acknowledge the prophet, whom he has blasphemed, or meet the death which he has so often deserved." On the proud or conscientious refusal of the Christian warrior, Saladin struck him on the head with his scimitar, and Reginald was despatched by the guards.[61] The trembling Lusignan was sent to Damascus to an honourable prison and speedy ransom; but the victory was stained by the execution of two hundred and thirty knights of the hospital, the intrepid champions and martyrs of their faith. The kingdom was left without a head; and of the two grand masters of the military orders, the one was slain and the other was a prisoner. From all the cities, both of the seacoast and the inland country, the garrisons had been drawn away for this fatal field: Tyre and Tripoli alone could escape the rapid inroad of Saladin; and three months after the battle of Tiberias he appeared in arms before the gates of Jerusalem.[62]

He might expect that the siege of a city so venerable on earth and in heaven, so interesting to Europe and Asia, would rekindle the last sparks of enthusiasm; and that, of sixty thousand Christians, every man would be a soldier, and every soldier a candidate for martyrdom. But queen Sybilla trembled for herself and her captive husband; and the barons and knights, who had escaped from the sword and chains of the Turks, displayed the same factious and selfish spirit in the public ruin. The most numerous portion of the inhabitants was composed of the Greek and Oriental Christians, whom experience had taught to prefer the Mohammedan before the Latin yoke;[63] and the holy sepulchre attracted a base and needy crowd, without arms or courage, who subsisted only on the charity of the pilgrims. Some feeble and hasty efforts were made for the defence of Jerusalem: but in the space of fourteen days a victorious army drove back the sallies of the besieged, planted their engines, opened the wall to the breadth of fifteen cubits, applied their scaling-ladders, and erected on the breach twelve banners of the prophet and the sultan. It was in vain that a barefoot procession of the queen, the women, and the monks, implored the Son of God to save his tomb and his inheritance from impious violation. Their sole hope was in the mercy of the conqueror, and to the first suppliant deputation that mercy was sternly denied. "He had sworn to avenge the patience and long-suffering of the Moslems; the hour of forgiveness was elapsed, and the moment was now arrived to expiate, in blood, the innocent blood which had been spilt by Godfrey and the first crusaders." But a desperate and successful struggle of the Franks admonished the sultan that his triumph was not yet secure; he listened with reverence to a solemn adjuration in the name of the common Father of mankind; and a sentiment of human sympathy mollified the rigour of fanaticism and conquest. He consented to accept the city and to spare the inhabitants. The Greek and Oriental Christians were permitted to live under his dominion; but it was stipulated that in forty days all the Franks and Latins should evacuate Jerusalem and be safely conducted to the seaports of Syria and Egypt; that ten pieces of gold should be paid for each man, five for each woman, and one for every child; and that those who were unable to purchase their freedom should be detained in perpetual slavery. Of some writers it is a favourite and invidious theme to compare the humanity of Saladin with the massacre of the first crusade. The difference would be merely personal; but we should not forget that the Christians had offered to capitulate, and that the Mohammedans of Jerusalem sustained the last extremities of an assault and storm. Justice is indeed due to the fidelity with which the Turkish conqueror fulfilled the conditions of the treaty; and he may be deservedly praised for the glance of pity which he cast on the misery of the vanquished. Instead of a rigorous exaction of his debt, he accepted a sum of thirty thousand byzants for the ransom of seven thousand poor; two or three thousand more were dismissed by his gratuitous clemency; and the number of slaves was reduced to eleven or fourteen thousand persons. In his interview with the queen, his words, and even his tears, suggested the kindest consolations: his liberal alms were distributed among those who had been made orphans or widows by the fortune of war; and while the knights of the hospital were in arms against him he allowed their more pious brethren to continue, during the term of a year, the care and service of the sick. In these acts of mercy the virtue of Saladin deserves our admiration and love: he was above the necessity of dissimulation, and his stern fanaticism would have prompted him to dissemble, rather than to affect, this profane compassion for the enemies of the Koran. After Jerusalem had been delivered from the presence of the strangers, the sultan made his triumphant entry, his banners waving in the wind, and to the harmony of martial music. The great mosque of Omar, which had been converted into a church, was again consecrated to one God and his prophet Mohammed: the walls and pavement were purified with rose-water; and a pulpit, the labour of Noureddin, was erected in the sanctuary. But when the golden cross that glittered on the dome was cast down and dragged through the streets, the Christians of every sect uttered a lamentable groan, which was answered by the joyful shouts of the Moslems. In four ivory chests the patriarch had collected the crosses, the images, the vases, and the relics of the holy place; they were seized by the conqueror, who was desirous of presenting the caliph with the trophies of Christian idolatry. He was persuaded, however, to intrust them to the patriarch and prince of Antioch; and the pious pledge was redeemed by Richard of England, at the expense of fifty-two thousand byzants of gold.[64]

The nations might fear and hope the immediate and final expulsion of the Latins from Syria, which was yet delayed above a century after the death of Saladin.[65] In the career of victory he was first checked by the resistance of Tyre; the troops and garrisons, which had capitulated, were imprudently conducted to the same port: their numbers were adequate to the defence of the place; and the arrival of Conrad of Montferrat inspired the disorderly crowd with confidence and union. His father, a venerable pilgrim, had been made prisoner in the battle of Tiberias; but that disaster was unknown in Italy and Greece, when the son was urged by ambition and piety to visit the inheritance of his royal nephew, the infant Baldwin. The view of the Turkish banners warned him from the hostile coast of Jaffa; and Conrad was unanimously hailed as the prince and champion of Tyre, which was already besieged by the conqueror of Jerusalem. The firmness of his zeal, and perhaps his knowledge of a generous foe, enabled him to brave the threats of the sultan, and to declare that, should his aged parent be exposed before the walls, he himself would discharge the first arrow, and glory in his descent from a Christian martyr.[66] The Egyptian fleet was allowed to enter the harbour of Tyre; but the chain was suddenly drawn, and five galleys were either sunk or taken; a thousand Turks were slain in a sally; and Saladin, after burning his engines, concluded a glorious campaign by a disgraceful retreat to Damascus. He was soon assailed by a more formidable empest. The pathetic narratives, and even the ictures, that represented in lively colours the ervitude and profanation of Jerusalem, awak- ned the torpid sensibility of Europe: the em- peror Frederic Barbarossa, and the kings of France and England, assumed the cross; and he tardy magnitude of their armaments was inticipated by the maritime states of the Medi- erranean and the Ocean. The skilful and provi- lent Italians first embarked in the ships of Genoa, Pisa, and Venice. They were speedily followed by the most eager pilgrims of France, Normandy, and the Western Isles. The power- ul succour of Flanders, Frise, and Denmark illed near a hundred vessels; and the Northern warriors were distinguished in the field by a ofty stature and a ponderous battle-axe.[67] Their increasing multitudes could no longer be confined within the walls of Tyre, or remain obedient to the voice of Conrad. They pitied he misfortunes and revered the dignity of Lu- ignan, who was released from prison, perhaps o divide the army of the Franks. He proposed he recovery of Ptolemais, or Acre, thirty miles o the south of Tyre; and the place was first in- vested by two thousand horse and thirty thou- sand foot under his nominal command. I shall not expatiate on the story of this memorable siege, which lasted near two years, and con- sumed, in a narrow space, the forces of Europe and Asia. Never did the flame of enthusiasm burn with fiercer and more destructive rage; nor could the true believers, a common appella- tion, who consecrated their own martyrs, refuse some applause to the mistaken zeal and courage of their adversaries. At the sound of the holy trumpet the Moslems of Egypt, Syria, Arabia, and the Oriental provinces assembled under the servant of the prophet;[68] his camp was pitched and removed within a few miles of Acre; and he laboured night and day for the relief of his brethren and the annoyance of the Franks. Nine battles, not unworthy of the name, were fought in the neighbourhood of Mount Carmel, with such vicissitude of fortune, that in one at- tack the sultan forced his way into the city; that in one sally the Christians penetrated to the royal tent. By the means of divers and pigeons a regular correspondence was maintained with the besieged; and, as often as the sea was left open, the exhausted garrison was withdrawn, and a fresh supply was poured into the place. The Latin camp was thinned by famine, the sword, and the climate; but the tents of the dead were replenished with new pilgrims, who exaggerated the strength and speed of their approaching countrymen. The vulgar was as- tonished by the report that the pope himself, with an innumerable crusade, was advanced as far as Constantinople. The march of the em- peror filled the East with more serious alarms: the obstacles which he encountered in Asia, and perhaps in Greece, were raised by the policy of Saladin: his joy on the death of Barbarossa was measured by his esteem; and the Christians were rather dismayed than encouraged at the sight of the duke of Swabia and his way-worn remnant of five thousand Germans. At length, in the spring of the second year, the royal fleets of France and England cast anchor in the bay of Acre, and the siege was more vigorously prosecuted by the youthful emulation of the two kings, Philip Augustus and Richard Planta- genet. After every resource had been tried, and every hope was exhausted, the defenders of Acre submitted to their fate; a capitulation was granted, but their lives and liberties were taxed at the hard conditions of a ransom of two hun- dred thousand pieces of gold, the deliverance of one hundred nobles and fifteen hundred in- ferior captives, and the restoration of the wood of the holy cross. Some doubts in the agreement, and some delay in the execution, rekindled the fury of the Franks, and three thousand Mos- lems, almost in the sultan's view, were behead- ed by the command of the sanguinary Richard.[69] By the conquest of Acre the Latin powers ac- quired a strong town and a convenient har- bour; but the advantage was most dearly pur- chased. The minister and historian of Saladin computes, from the report of the enemy, that their numbers, at different periods, amounted to five or six hundred thousand; that more than one hundred thousand Christians were slain; that a far greater number was lost by disease or shipwreck; and that a small portion of this mighty host could return in safety to their native countries.[70]

Philip Augustus and Richard the First are the only kings of France and England who have fought under the same banners; but the holy service in which they were enlisted was inces- santly disturbed by their national jealousy; and the two factions which they protected in Pales- tine were more averse to each other than to the common enemy. In the eyes of the Orientals the French monarch was superior in dignity and power; and, in the emperor's absence, the Lat- ins revered him as their temporal chief.[71] His exploits were not adequate to his fame. Philip was brave, but the statesman predominated in his character; he was soon weary of sacrificing his health and interest on a barren coast: the surrender of Acre became the signal of his departure; nor could he justify this unpopular desertion by leaving the duke of Burgundy, with five hundred knights and ten thousand foot, for the service of the Holy Land. The king of England, though inferior in dignity, surpassed his rival in wealth and military renown;[72] and if heroism be confined to brutal and ferocious valour, Richard Plantagenet will stand high among the heroes of the age. The memory of *Coeur de Lion*, of the lion-hearted prince, was long dear and glorious to his English subjects; and at the distance of sixty years it was celebrated in proverbial sayings by the grandsons of the Turks and Saracens against whom he had fought: his tremendous name was employed by the Syrian mothers to silence their infants; and if a horse suddenly started from the way, his rider was wont to exclaim, "Dost thou think king Richard is in that bush?"[73] His cruelty to the Mohammedans was the effect of temper and zeal; but I cannot believe that a soldier, so free and fearless in the use of his lance, would have descended to whet a dagger against his valiant brother Conrad of Montferrat, who was slain at Tyre by some secret assassins.[74] After the surrender of Acre, and the departure of Philip, the king of England led the crusaders to the recovery of the sea-coast; and the cities of Cæsarea and Jaffa were added to the fragments of the kingdom of Lusignan. A march of one hundred miles from Acre to Ascalon was a great and perpetual battle of eleven days. In the disorder of his troops, Saladin remained on the field with seventeen guards, without lowering his standard, or suspending the sound of his brazen kettledrum: he again rallied and renewed the charge; and his preachers or heralds called aloud on the *Unitarians* manfully to stand up against the Christian idolaters. But the progress of these idolaters was irresistible; and it was only by demolishing the walls and buildings of Ascalon that the sultan could prevent them from occupying an important fortress on the confines of Egypt. During a severe winter the armies slept; but in the spring the Franks advanced within a day's march of Jerusalem, under the leading standard of the English king; and his active spirit intercepted a convoy, or caravan, of seven thousand camels. Saladin[75] had fixed his station in the holy city; but the city was struck with consternation and discord: he fasted; he prayed; he preached; he offered to share the dangers of the siege; but his Mamalukes, who remembered the fate of their companions at Acre, pressed the sultan, with loyal or seditious clamours, to reserve *his* person and *their* courage for the future defence of the religion and empire.[76] The Moslems were delivered by the sudden, or, as they deemed, the miraculous, retreat of the Christians;[77] and the laurel of Richard were blasted by the prudence, or envy, of his companions. The hero, ascending a hill, and veiling his face, exclaimed with an indignant voice, "Those who are unwilling to rescue, are unworthy to view, the sepulchre of Christ!" After his return to Acre, on the news that Jaffa was surprised by the sultan, he sailed with some merchant vessels, and leaped foremost on the beach: the castle was relieved by his presence; and sixty thousand Turks and Saracens fled before his arms. The discovery of his weakness provoked them to return in the morning; and they found him carelessly encamped before the gates with only seventeen knights and three hundred archers. Without counting their numbers, he sustained their charge; and we learn from the evidence of his enemies that the king of England, grasping his lance, rode furiously along their front, from the right to the left wing, without meeting an adversary who dared to encounter his career.[78] Am I writing the history of Orlando or Amadis?

During these hostilities a languid and tedious negotiation[79] between the Franks and Moslems was started, and continued, and broken, and again resumed, and again broken. Some acts of royal courtesy, the gift of snow and fruit, the exchange of Norway hawks and Arabian horses, softened the asperity of religious war; from the vicissitude of success the monarchs might learn to suspect that Heaven was neuter in the quarrel: nor, after the trial of each other, could either hope for a decisive victory.[80] The health both of Richard and Saladin appeared to be in a declining state; and they respectively suffered the evils of distant and domestic warfare: Plantagenet was impatient to punish a perfidious rival who had invaded Normandy in his absence; and the indefatigable sultan was subdued by the cries of the people, who was the victim, and of the soldiers, who were the instruments, of his martial zeal. The first demands of the king of England were the restitution of Jerusalem, Palestine, and the true cross; and he firmly declared that himself and his brother pilgrims would end their lives in the pious labour, rather than return to Europe with ignominy and remorse. But the conscience of Saladin refused, without some weighty compensation, to restore the idols, or promote the idolatry, of the

Christians: he asserted, with equal firmness, his religious and civil claim to the sovereignty of Palestine; descanted on the importance and sanctity of Jerusalem; and rejected all terms of the establishment, or partition, of the Latins. The marriage which Richard proposed, of his sister with the sultan's brother, was defeated by the difference of faith: the princess abhorred the embraces of a Turk; and Adel, or Saphadin, would not easily renounce a plurality of wives. A personal interview was declined by Saladin, who alleged their mutual ignorance of each other's language; and the negotiation was managed with much art and delay by their interpreters and envoys. The final agreement was equally disapproved by the zealots of both parties, by the Roman pontiff and the caliph of Bagdad. It was stipulated that Jerusalem and the holy sepulchre should be open, without tribute or vexation, to the pilgrimage of the Latin Christians; that, after the demolition of Ascalon, they should inclusively possess the seacoast from Jaffa to Tyre; that the count of Tripoli and the prince of Antioch should be comprised in the truce; and that, during three years and three months, all hostilities should cease. The principal chiefs of the two armies swore to the observance of the treaty; but the monarchs were satisfied with giving their word and their right hand; and the royal majesty was excused from an oath, which always implies some suspicion of falsehood and dishonour. Richard embarked for Europe, to see a long captivity and a premature grave; and the space of a few months concluded the life and glories of Saladin. The Orientals described his edifying death, which happened at Damascus; but they seem ignorant of the equal distribution of his alms along the three religions,[81] or of the display of a shroud, instead of a standard, to admonish the East of the instability of human greatness. The unity of empire was dissolved by his death; his sons were oppressed by the stronger arm of their uncle Saphadin; the hostile interests of the sultans of Egypt, Damascus, and Aleppo[82] were again revived; and the Franks or Latins stood, and breathed, and hoped, in their fortresses along the Syrian coast.

The noblest monument of a conqueror's fame, and of the terror which he inspired, is the Saladine tenth, a general tax, which was imposed on the laity and even the clergy of the Latin church for the service of the holy war. The practice was too lucrative to expire with the occasion; and this tribute became the foundation of all the tithes and tenths on ecclesiastical benefices which have been granted by the Roman pontiffs to Catholic sovereigns, or reserved for the immediate use of the apostolic see.[83] This pecuniary emolument must have tended to increase the interest of the popes in the recovery of Palestine: after the death of Saladin they preached the crusade by their epistles, their legates, and their missionaries; and the accomplishment of the pious work might have been expected from the zeal and talents of Innocent the Third.[84] Under that young and ambitious priest the successors of St. Peter attained the full meridian of their greatness: and in a reign of eighteen years exercised a despotic command over the emperors and kings, whom he raised and deposed; over the nations, whom an interdict of months or years deprived, for the offence of their rulers, of the exercise of Christian worship. In the council of the Lateran he acted as the ecclesiastical, almost as the temporal, sovereign of the East and West. It was at the feet of his legate that John of England surrendered his crown; and Innocent may boast of the two most signal triumphs over sense and humanity, the establishment of transubstantiation and the origin of the inquisition. At his voice two crusades, the fourth and the fifth, were undertaken; but, except a king of Hungary, the princes of the second order were at the head of the pilgrims; the forces were inadequate to the design, nor did the effects correspond with the hopes and wishes of the pope and the people. The fourth crusade was diverted from Syria to Constantinople; and the conquest of the Greek or Roman empire by the Latins will form the proper and important subject of the next chapter. In the fifth,[85] two hundred thousand Franks were landed at the eastern mouth of the Nile. They reasonably hoped that Palestine must be subdued in Egypt, the seat and storehouse of the sultan; and after a siege of sixteen months the Moslems deplored the loss of Damietta. But the Christian army was ruined by the pride and insolence of the legate Pelagius, who, in the pope's name, assumed the character of general; the sickly Franks were encompassed by the waters of the Nile and the Oriental forces; and it was by the evacuation of Damietta that they obtained a safe retreat, some concessions for the pilgrims, and the tardy restitution of the doubtful relic of the true cross. The failure may in some measure be ascribed to the abuse and multiplication of the crusades, which were preached at the same time against the pagans of Livonia, the Moors of Spain, the Albigeois of France, and the kings of Sicily of the Imperial family.[86] In these meritorious services the volunteers might acquire at home the same spiritual indulgence and a larger measure of temporal rewards; and even the popes, in their zeal against a domestic enemy, were sometimes tempted to forget the distress of their Syrian brethren. From the last age of the crusades they derived the occasional command of an army and revenue, and some deep reasoners have suspected that the whole enterprise, from the first synod of Placentia, was contrived and executed by the policy of Rome. The suspicion is not founded either in nature or in fact. The successors of St. Peter appear to have followed, rather than guided, the impulse of manners and prejudice; without much foresight of the seasons or cultivation of the soil, they gathered the ripe and spontaneous fruits of the superstition of the times. They gathered these fruits without toil or personal danger: in the council of the Lateran, Innocent the Third declared an ambiguous resolution of animating the crusaders by his example; but the pilot of the sacred vessel could not abandon the helm, nor was Palestine ever blessed with the presence of a Roman pontiff.[87]

The persons, the families, and estates of the pilgrims were under the immediate protection of the popes; and these spiritual patrons soon claimed the prerogative of directing their operations, and enforcing, by commands and censures, the accomplishment of their vow. Frederic the Second,[88] the grandson of Barbarossa, was successively the pupil, the enemy, and the victim of the church. At the age of twenty-one years, and in obedience to his guardian Innocent the Third, he assumed the cross; the same promise was repeated at his royal and imperial coronations, and his marriage with the heiress of Jerusalem for ever bound him to defend the kingdom of his son Conrad. But as Frederic advanced in age and authority, he repented of the rash engagements of his youth: his liberal sense and knowledge taught him to despise the phantoms of superstition and the crowns of Asia; he no longer entertained the same reverence for the successors of Innocent; and his ambition was occupied by the restoration of the Italian monarchy from Sicily to the Alps. But the success of this project would have reduced the popes to their primitive simplicity, and, after the delays and excuses of twelve years, they urged the emperor, with entreaties and threats, to fix the time and place of his departure for Palestine. In the harbours of Sicily and Apulia he prepared a fleet of one hundred galleys, and of one hundred vessels, that were framed to transport and land two thousand five hundred knights, with their horses and attendants; his vassals of Naples and Germany formed a powerful army, and the number of English crusaders was magnified to sixty thousand by the report of fame. But the inevitable or affected slowness of these mighty preparations consumed the strength and provisions of the more indigent pilgrims; the multitude was thinned by sickness and desertion, and the sultry summer of Calabria anticipated the mischiefs of a Syrian campaign. At length the emperor hoisted sail at Brundusium, with a fleet and army of forty thousand men; but he kept the sea no more than three days, and his hasty retreat, which was ascribed by his friends to a grievous indisposition, was accused by his enemies as a voluntary and obstinate disobedience. For suspending his vow was Frederic excommunicated by Gregory the Ninth; for presuming, the next year, to accomplish his vow, he was again excommunicated by the same pope.[89] While he served under the banner of the cross a crusade was preached against him in Italy; and after his return he was compelled to ask pardon for the injuries which he had suffered. The clergy and military orders of Palestine were previously instructed to renounce his communion and dispute his commands, and in his own kingdom the emperor was forced to consent that the orders of the camp should be issued in the name of God and of the Christian republic. Frederic entered Jerusalem in triumph, and with his own hands (for no priest would perform the office) he took the crown from the altar of the holy sepulchre. But the patriarch cast an interdict on the church which his presence had profaned; and the knights of the hospital and temple informed the sultan how easily he might be surprised and slain in his unguarded visit to the river Jordan. In such a state of fanaticism and faction, victory was hopeless and defence was difficult; but the conclusion of an advantageous peace may be imputed to the discord of the Mohammedans, and their personal esteem for the character of Frederic. The enemy of the church is accused of maintaining with the miscreants an intercourse of hospitality and friendship unworthy of a Christian; of despising the barrenness of the land; and of indulging a profane thought that if Jehovah had seen the kingdom of Naples, he never would have selected Palestine for the inheritance of his chosen people. Yet Frederic obtained from the sultan the restitution of Jerusalem, of Bethlehem and Nazareth, of Tyre and Sidon; the Latins were allow-ed to inhabit and fortify the city; an equal code of civil and religious freedom was ratified for the sectaries of Jesus and those of Mohammed; and while the former worshipped at the holy sepulchre, the latter might pray and preach in the mosque of the temple[90] from whence the prophet undertook his nocturnal journey to heaven. The clergy deplored this scandalous toleration, and the weaker Moslems were grad-ually expelled; but every rational object of the crusades was accomplished without bloodshed; the churches were restored, the monasteries were replenished, and, in the space of fifteen years, the Latins of Jerusalem exceeded the number of six thousand. This peace and pros-perity, for which they were ungrateful to their benefactor, was terminated by the irruption of the strange and savage hordes of Carizmians.[91] Flying from the arms of the Moguls, those shep-herds of the Caspian rolled headlong on Syria; and the union of the Franks with the sultans of Aleppo, Hems, and Damascus was insufficient to stem the violence of the torrent. Whatever stood against them was cut off by the sword or dragged into captivity; the military orders were almost exterminated in a single battle; and in the pillage of the city, in the profanation of the holy sepulchre, the Latins confess and regret the modesty and discipline of the Turks and Saracens.

Of the seven crusades, the two last were un-dertaken by Louis the Ninth, king of France, who lost his liberty in Egypt, and his life on the coast of Africa. Twenty-eight years after his death he was canonised at Rome, and sixty-five miracles were readily found and solemnly at-tested to justify the claim of the royal saint.[92] The voice of history renders a more honourable testi-mony, that he united the virtues of a king, a hero, and a man; that his martial spirit was tempered by the love of private and public jus-tice; and that Louis was the father of his people, the friend of his neighbours, and the terror of the infidels. Superstition alone, in all the extent of her baleful influence,[93] corrupted his under-standing and his heart; his devotion stooped to admire and imitate the begging friars of Francis and Dominic; he pursued with blind and cruel zeal the enemies of the faith; and the best of kings twice descended from his throne to seek the adventures of a spiritual knight-errant. A monkish historian would have been content to applaud the most despicable part of his charac-ter; but the noble and gallant Joinville,[94] who shared the friendship and captivity of Louis,

has traced with the pencil of nature the free por-trait of his virtues as well as of his failings. From this intimate knowledge we may learn to sus-pect the political views of depressing their great vassals, which are so often imputed to the royal authors of the crusades. Above all the princes of the middle ages Louis the Ninth successfully laboured to restore the prerogatives of the crown; but it was at home, and not in the East, that he acquired for himself and his posterity; his vow was the result of enthusiasm and sick-ness; and if he were the promoter, he was like-wise the victim, of this holy madness. For the invasion of Egypt, France was exhausted of her troops and treasures; he covered the sea of Cy-prus with eighteen hundred sails; the most modest enumeration amounts to fifty thousand men; and, if we might trust his own confession, as it is reported by Oriental vanity, he disem-barked nine thousand five hundred horse, and one hundred and thirty thousand foot, who per-formed their pilgrimage under the shadow of his power.[95]

In complete armour, the oriflamme waving before him, Louis leaped foremost on the beach; and the strong city of Damietta, which had cost his predecessors a siege of sixteen months, was abandoned on the first assault by the trembling Moslems. But Damietta was the first and the last of his conquests; and in the fifth and sixth crusades the same causes, almost on the same ground, were productive of similar calami-ties.[96] After a ruinous delay, which introduced into the camp the seeds of an epidemical dis-ease, the Franks advanced from the sea-coast towards the capital of Egypt, and strove to sur-mount the unseasonable inundation of the Nile which opposed their progress. Under the eye of their intrepid monarch, the barons and knights of France displayed their invincible contempt of danger and discipline; his brother, the count of Artois, stormed with inconsiderate valour the town of Massoura; and the carrier pigeons an-nounced to the inhabitants of Cairo that all was lost. But a soldier, who afterwards usurped the sceptre, rallied the flying troops: the main body of the Christians was far behind their van-guard, and Artois was overpowered and slain. A shower of Greek fire was incessantly poured on the invaders; the Nile was commanded by the Egyptian galleys, the open country by the Arabs; all provisions were intercepted; each day aggravated the sickness and famine; and about the same time a retreat was found to be necessary and impracticable. The Oriental writers confess that Louis might have escaped if he would have deserted his subjects: he was made prisoner, with the greatest part of his nobles; all who could not redeem their lives by service or ransom were inhumanly massacred, and the walls of Cairo were decorated with a circle of Christian heads.[97] The king of France was loaded with chains, but the generous victor, a great-grandson of the brother of Saladin, sent a robe of honour to his royal captive, and his deliverance, with that of his soldiers, was obtained by the restitution of Damietta[98] and the payment of four hundred thousand pieces of gold. In a soft and luxurious climate the degenerate children of the companions of Nouredin and Saladin were incapable of resisting the flower of European chivalry; they triumphed by the arms of their slaves or Mamalukes, the hardy natives of Tartary, who at a tender age had been purchased of the Syrian merchants, and were educated in the camp and palace of the sultan. But Egypt soon afforded a new example of the danger of prætorian bands; and the rage of these ferocious animals, who had been let loose on the strangers, was provoked to devour their benefactor. In the pride of conquest, Touran Shah, the last of his race, was murdered by his Mamalukes; and the most daring of the assassins entered the chamber of the captive king, with drawn scimitars, and their hands imbrued in the blood of their sultan. The firmness of Louis commanded their respect;[99] their avarice prevailed over cruelty and zeal, the treaty was accomplished, and the king of France, with the relics of his army, was permitted to embark for Palestine. He wasted four years within the walls of Acre, unable to visit Jerusalem, and unwilling to return without glory to his native country.

The memory of his defeat excited Louis, after sixteen years of wisdom and repose, to undertake the seventh and last of the crusades. His finances were restored, his kingdom was enlarged; a new generation of warriors had arisen, and he embarked with fresh confidence at the head of six thousand horse and thirty thousand foot. The loss of Antioch had provoked the enterprise; a wild hope of baptising the king of Tunis tempted him to steer for the African coast; and the report of an immense treasure reconciled his troops to the delay of their voyage to the Holy Land. Instead of a proselyte, he found a siege; the French panted and died on the burning sands; St. Louis expired in his tent; and no sooner had he closed his eyes than his son and successor gave the signal of the retreat.[100] "It is thus," says a lively writer, "that

a Christian king died near the ruins of Carthage, waging war against the sectaries of Mohammed, in a land to which Dido had introduced the deities of Syria."[101]

A more unjust and absurd constitution cannot be devised than that which condemns the natives of a country to perpetual servitude under the arbitrary dominion of strangers and slaves. Yet such has been the state of Egypt above five hundred years. The most illustrious sultans of the Baharite and Borgite dynasties[102] were themselves promoted from the Tartar and Circassian bands; and the four-and-twenty beys, or military chiefs, have ever been succeeded, not by their sons, but by their servants. They produce the great charter of their liberties, the treaty of Selim the First with the republic;[103] and the Othman emperor still accepts from Egypt a slight acknowledgment of tribute and subjection. With some breathing intervals of peace and order, the two dynasties are marked as a period of rapine and bloodshed;[104] but their throne, however shaken, reposed on the two pillars of discipline and valour; their sway extended over Egypt, Nubia, Arabia, and Syria; their Mamalukes were multiplied from eight hundred to twenty-five thousand horse; and their numbers were increased by a provincial militia of one hundred and seven thousand foot, and the occasional aid of sixty-six thousand Arabs.[105] Princes of such power and spirit could not long endure on their coast a hostile and independent nation; and if the ruin of the Franks was postponed about forty years, they were indebted to the cares of an unsettled reign, to the invasion of the Moguls, and to the occasional aid of some warlike pilgrims. Among these the English reader will observe the name of our first Edward, who assumed the cross in the lifetime of his father Henry. At the head of a thousand soldiers the future conqueror of Wales and Scotland delivered Acre from a siege; marched as far as Nazareth with an army of nine thousand men; emulated the fame of his uncle Richard; extorted, by his valour, a ten years' truce; and escaped, with a dangerous wound, from the dagger of a fanatic *assassin*.[106] Antioch,[107] whose situation had been less exposed to the calamities of the holy war, was finally occupied and ruined by Bondocdar, or Bibars, sultan of Egypt and Syria; the Latin principality was extinguished; and the first seat of the Christian name was dispeopled by the slaughter of seventeen, and the captivity of one hundred, thousand of her inhabitants. The maritime towns of Laodicea, Gabala, Tripoli, erytus, Sidon, Tyre, and Jaffa, and the strong-castles of the Hospitalers and Templars, successively fell; and the whole existence of the ranks was confined to the city and colony of t. John of Acre, which is sometimes described y the more classic title of Ptolemais.

After the loss of Jerusalem, Acre,[108] which is istant about seventy miles, became the metropolis of the Latin Christians, and was adorned with strong and stately buildings, with aqueucts, an artificial port, and a double wall. The opulation was increased by the incessant creams of pilgrims and fugitives; in the pauses f hostility the trade of the East and West was ttracted to this convenient station, and the market could offer the produce of every clime nd the interpreters of every tongue. But in this onflux of nations every vice was propagated nd practised: of all the disciples of Jesus and Mohammed, the male and female inhabitants f Acre were esteemed the most corrupt, nor ould the abuse of religion be corrected by the iscipline of law. The city had many sovereigns nd no government. The kings of Jerusalem and Cyprus, of the house of Lusignan, the princes of Antioch, the counts of Tripoli and Sidon, the reat masters of the hospital, the temple, and the Teutonic order, the republics of Venice, Genoa, nd Pisa, the pope's legate, the kings of France nd England, assumed an independent command; seventeen tribunals exercised the power f life and death; every criminal was protected n the adjacent quarter; and the perpetual jealusy of the nations often burst forth in acts of violence and blood. Some adventurers, who lisgraced the ensign of the cross, compensated heir want of pay by the plunder of the Mohammedan villages; nineteen Syrian merchants, who traded under the public faith, were despoiled and hanged by the Christians, and the

denial of satisfaction justified the arms of the sultan Khalil. He marched against Acre at the head of sixty thousand horse and one hundred and forty thousand foot; his train of artillery (if I may use the word) was numerous and weighty; the separate timbers of a single engine were transported in one hundred waggons; and the royal historian Abulfeda, who served with the troops of Hamah, was himself a spectator of the holy war. Whatever might be the vices of the Franks, their courage was rekindled by enthusiasm and despair; but they were torn by the discord of seventeen chiefs, and overwhelmed on all sides by the powers of the sultan. After a siege of thirty-three days the double wall was forced by the Moslems; the principal tower yielded to their engines; the Mamalukes made a general assault; the city was stormed, and death or slavery was the lot of sixty thousand Christians. The convent, or rather fortress, of the Templars resisted three days longer; but the great master was pierced with an arrow, and, of five hundred knights, only ten were left alive, less happy than the victims of the sword, if they lived to suffer on a scaffold in the unjust and cruel proscription of the whole order. The king of Jerusalem, the patriarch, and the great master of the hospital effected their retreat to the shore; but the sea was rough, the vessels were insufficient, and great numbers of the fugitives were drowned before they could reach the isle of Cyprus, which might comfort Lusignan for the loss of Palestine. By the command of the sultan the churches and fortifications of the Latin cities were demolished: a motive of avarice or fear still opened the holy sepulchre to some devout and defenceless pilgrims: and a mournful and solitary silence prevailed along the coast which had so long resounded with the WORLD'S DEBATE.[109]

CHAPTER LX

Schism of the Greeks and Latins. State of Constantinople. Revolt of the Bulgarians. Isaac Angelus dethroned by his Brother Alexius. Origin of the Fourth Crusade. Alliance of the French and Venetians with the Son of Isaac. Their Naval Expedition to Constantinople. The Two Sieges and Final Conquest of the City by the Latins.

THE restoration of the Western empire by Charlemagne was speedily followed by the separation of the Greek and Latin churches.[1] A religious and national animosity still divides the two largest communions of the

Christian world; and the schism of Constantinople, by alienating her most useful allies, and provoking her most dangerous enemies, has precipitated the decline and fall of the Roman empire in the East.

In the course of the present history the aversion of the Greeks for the Latins has been often visible and conspicuous. It was originally derived from the disdain of servitude, inflamed, after the time of Constantine, by the pride of equality or dominion, and finally exasperated by the preference which their rebellious subjects had given to the alliance of the Franks. In every age the Greeks were proud of their superiority in profane and religious knowledge: they had first received the light of Christianity; they had pronounced the decrees of the seven general councils; they alone possessed the language of Scripture and philosophy: nor should the barbarians, immersed in the darkness of the West,[2] presume to argue on the high and mysterious questions of theological science. Those barbarians despised in their turn the restless and subtle levity of the Orientals, the authors of every heresy, and blessed their own simplicity, which was content to hold the tradition of the apostolic church. Yet in the seventh century the synods of Spain, and afterwards of France, improved or corrupted the Nicene creed, on the mysterious subject of the third person of the Trinity.[3] In the long controversies of the East the nature and generation of the Christ had been scrupulously defined; and the well-known relation of father and son seemed to convey a faint image to the human mind. The idea of birth was less analogous to the Holy Spirit, who, instead of a divine gift or attribute, was considered by the Catholics as a substance, a person, a god; he was not begotten, but in the orthodox style he *proceeded*. Did he proceed from the Father alone, perhaps *by* the Son? or from the Father *and* the Son? The first of these opinions was asserted by the Greeks, the second by the Latins; and the addition to the Nicene creed of the word *filioque* kindled the flame of discord between the Oriental and the Gallic churches. In the origin of the dispute the Roman pontiffs affected a character of neutrality and moderation:[4] they condemned the innovation, but they acquiesced in the sentiment, of their Transalpine brethren: they seemed desirous of casting a veil of silence and charity over the superfluous research; and in the correspondence of Charlemagne and Leo the Third, the pope assumes the liberality of a statesman, and the prince descends to the passions and prejudices of a priest.[5] But the orthodoxy of Rome spontaneously obeyed the impulse of her temporal policy; and the *filioque*, which Leo wished to erase, was transcribed in the symbol and chanted in the liturgy of the Vatican. The

Nicene and Athanasian creeds are held as the Catholic faith, without which none can be saved; and both Papists and Protestants must now sustain and return the anathemas of the Greeks, who deny the procession of the Holy Ghost from the Son as well as from the Father. Such articles of faith are not susceptible of treaty; but the rules of discipline will vary in remote and independent churches; and the reason, even of divines, might allow that the difference is inevitable and harmless. The craft or superstition of Rome has imposed on her priests and deacons the rigid obligation of celibacy; among the Greeks it is confined to the bishops; the loss is compensated by dignity or annihilated by age; and the parochial clergy, the papas, enjoy the conjugal society of the wives whom they have married before their entrance into holy orders. A question concerning the *Azyms* was fiercely debated in the eleventh century, and the essence of the Eucharist was supposed in the East and West to depend on the use of leavened or unleavened bread. Shall I mention in a serious history the furious reproaches that were urged against the Latins, who for a long while remained on the defensive? They neglected to abstain, according to the apostolical decree, from things strangled, and from blood: they fasted, a Jewish observance, on the Saturday of each week: during the first week of Lent they permitted the use of milk and cheese;[6] their infirm monks were indulged in the taste of flesh; and animal grease was substituted for the want of vegetable oil: the holy chrism or unction in baptism was reserved to the episcopal order; the bishops, as the bridegrooms of their churches, were decorated with rings; their priests shaved their faces, and baptised by a single immersion. Such were the crimes which provoked the zeal of the patriarch of Constantinople, and which were justified with equal zeal by the doctors of the Latin church.[7]

Bigotry and national aversion are powerful magnifiers of every object of dispute; but the immediate cause of the schism of the Greeks may be traced in the emulation of the leading prelates, who maintained the supremacy of the old metropolis, superior to all, and of the reigning capital, inferior to none, in the Christian world. About the middle of the ninth century Photius,[8] an ambitious layman, the captain of the guards and principal secretary, was promoted by merit and favour to the more desirable office of patriarch of Constantinople. In science, even ecclesiastical science, he surpassed the clergy of the age; and the purity of his morals has never been impeached: but his ordination was hasty, his rise was irregular; and Ignatius, his abdicated predecessor, was yet supported by the public compassion and the obstinacy of his adherents. They appealed to the tribunal of Nicholas the First, one of the proudest and most aspiring of the Roman pontiffs, who embraced the welcome opportunity of judging and condemning his rival of the East. Their quarrel was embittered by a conflict of jurisdiction over the king and nation of the Bulgarians; nor was their recent conversion to Christianity of much avail to either prelate, unless he could number the proselytes among the subjects of his power. With the aid of his court the Greek patriarch was victorious; but in the furious contest he deposed in his turn the successor of St. Peter, and involved the Latin church in the reproach of heresy and schism. Photius sacrificed the peace of the world to a short and precarious reign: he fell with his patron, the Cæsar Bardas; and Basil the Macedonian performed an act of justice in the restoration of Ignatius, whose age and dignity had not been sufficiently respected. From his monastery, or prison, Photius solicited the favour of the emperor by pathetic complaints and artful flattery; and the eyes of his rival were scarcely closed when he was again restored to the throne of Constantinople. After the death of Basil he experienced the vicissitudes of courts and the ingratitude of a royal pupil: the patriarch was again deposed, and in his last solitary hours he might regret the freedom of a secular and studious life. In each revolution the breath, the nod, of the sovereign had been accepted by a submissive clergy; and a synod of three hundred bishops was always prepared to hail the triumph, or to stigmatise the fall, of the holy, or the execrable, Photius.[9] By a delusive promise of succour or reward, the popes were tempted to countenance these various proceedings; and the synods of Constantinople were ratified by their epistles or legates. But the court and the people, Ignatius and Photius, were equally adverse to their claims; their ministers were insulted or imprisoned; the procession of the Holy Ghost was forgotten; Bulgaria was for ever annexed to the Byzantine throne; and the schism was prolonged by their rigid censure of all the multiplied ordinations of an irregular patriarch. The darkness and corruption of the tenth century suspended the intercourse, without reconciling the minds, of the two nations. But when the Norman sword restored the churches of Apulia to the jurisdiction of Rome, the departing flock was warned, by a petulant epistle of the Greek patriarch, to avoid and abhor the errors of the Latins. The rising majesty of Rome could no longer brook the insolence of a rebel; and Michael Cerularius was excommunicated in the heart of Constantinople by the pope's legates. Shaking the dust from their feet, they deposited on the altar of St. Sophia a direful anathema,[10] which enumerates the seven mortal heresies of the Greeks, and devotes the guilty teachers, and their unhappy sectaries, to the eternal society of the devil and his angels. According to the emergencies of the church and state, a friendly correspondence was sometimes resumed; the language of charity and concord was sometimes affected; but the Greeks have never recanted their errors, the popes have never repealed their sentence; and from this thunderbolt we may date the consummation of the schism. It was enlarged by each ambitious step of the Roman pontiffs: the emperors blushed and trembled at the ignominious fate of their royal brethren of Germany; and the people was scandalised by the temporal power and military life of the Latin clergy.[11]

The aversion of the Greeks and Latins was nourished and manifested in the three first expeditions to the Holy Land. Alexius Comnenus contrived the absence at least of the formidable pilgrims: his successors, Manuel and Isaac Angelus, conspired with the Moslems for the ruin of the greatest princes of the Franks; and their crooked and malignant policy was seconded by the active and voluntary obedience of every order of their subjects. Of this hostile temper a large portion may doubtless be ascribed to the difference of language, dress, and manners, which severs and alienates the nations of the globe. The pride as well as the prudence of the sovereign was deeply wounded by the intrusion of foreign armies that claimed a right of traversing his dominions, and passing under the walls of his capital: his subjects were insulted and plundered by the rude strangers of the West: and the hatred of the pusillanimous Greeks was sharpened by secret envy of the bold and pious enterprises of the Franks. But these profane causes of national enmity were fortified and inflamed by the venom of religious zeal. Instead of a kind embrace, an hospitable reception from their Christian brethren of the East, every tongue was taught to repeat the names of schismatic and heretic, more odious to an orthodox ear than those of pagan and infidel: instead of being loved for the general conformity of faith and worship, they were abhorred for some rules of discipline, some questions of theology, in which themselves or their teachers might differ from the Oriental church. In the crusade of Louis the Seventh the Greek clergy washed and purified the altars which had been defiled by the sacrifice of a French priest. The companions of Frederic Barbarossa deplore the injuries which they endured, both in word and deed, from the peculiar rancour of the bishops and monks. Their prayers and sermons excited the people against the impious barbarians; and the patriarch is accused of declaring that the faithful might obtain the redemption of all their sins by the extirpation of the schismatics.[12] An enthusiast named Dorotheus alarmed the fears and restored the confidence of the emperor by a prophetic assurance that the German heretic, after assaulting the gate of Blachernes, would be made a signal example of the divine vengeance. The passage of these mighty armies were rare and perilous events; but the crusades introduced a frequent and familiar intercourse between the two nations, which enlarged their knowledge without abating their prejudices. The wealth and luxury of Constantinople demanded the productions of every climate: these imports were balanced by the art and labour of her numerous inhabitants; her situation invites the commerce of the world; and, in every period of her existence, that commerce has been in the hands of foreigners. After the decline of Amalphi, the Venetians, Pisans, and Genoese introduced their factories and settlements into the capital of the empire: their services were rewarded with honours and immunities; they acquired the possession of lands and houses, their families were multiplied by marriages with the natives, and, after the toleration of a Mohammedan mosque, it was impossible to interdict the churches of the Roman rite.[13] The two wives of Manuel Comnenus[14] were of the race of the Franks: the first, a sister-in-law of the emperor Conrad; the second, a daughter of the prince of Antioch: he obtained for his son Alexius a daughter of Philip Augustus king of France; and he bestowed his own daughter on a marquis of Montferrat, who was educated and dignified in the palace of Constantinople. The Greek encountered the arms, and aspired to the empire, of the West: he esteemed the valour, and trusted the fidelity, of the Franks;[15] their military talents were unfitly recompensed by the lucrative offices of judges and treasurers; the policy of Manuel had solicited the alliance of the pope; and the popular voice accused him of a partial bias to the nation and religion of the Latins.[16] During his reign and that of his successor Alexius, they were exposed at Constantinople to the reproach of foreigners, heretics, and favourites; and this triple guilt was severely expiated in the tumult which announced the return and elevation of Andronicus.[17] The people rose in arms: from the Asiatic shore the tyrant despatched his troops and galleys to assist the national revenge; and the hopeless resistance of the strangers served only to justify the rage and sharpen the daggers of the assassins. Neither age, nor sex, nor the ties of friendship or kindred, could save the victims of national hatred, and avarice, and religious zeal: the Latins were slaughtered in their houses and in the streets; their quarter was reduced to ashes; the clergy were burnt in their churches, and the sick in their hospitals; and some estimate may be formed of the slain from the clemency which sold above four thousand Christians in perpetual slavery to the Turks. The priests and monks were the loudest and most active in the destruction of the schismatics; and they chanted a thanksgiving to the Lord when the head of a Roman cardinal, the pope's legate, was severed from his body, fastened to the tail of a dog, and dragged, with savage mockery, through the city. The more diligent of the strangers had retreated, on the first alarm, to their vessels, and escaped through the Hellespont from the scene of blood. In their flight they burnt and ravaged two hundred miles of the sea-coast, inflicted a severe revenge on the guiltless subjects of the empire, marked the priests and monks as their peculiar enemies, and compensated, by the accumulation of plunder, the loss of their property and friends. On their return they exposed to Italy and Europe the wealth and weakness, the perfidy and malice of the Greeks, whose vices were painted as the genuine characters of heresy and schism. The scruples of the first crusaders had neglected the fairest opportunities of securing, by the possession of Constantinople, the way to the Holy Land: a domestic revolution invited, and almost compelled, the French and Venetians to achieve the conquest of the Roman empire of the East.

In the series of the Byzantine princes I have exhibited the hypocrisy and ambition, the tyranny and fall, of Andronicus, the last male of the Comnenian family who reigned at Constantinople. The revolution which cast him headlong from the throne saved and exalted Isaac Angelus,[18] who descended by the females

om the same Imperial dynasty. The successor
' a second Nero might have found it an easy
usk to deserve the esteem and affection of his
ubjects: they sometimes had reason to regret
ue administration of Andronicus. The sound
nd vigorous mind of the tyrant was capable of
iscerning the connection between his own and
ue public interest; and while he was feared by
ll who could inspire him with fear, the unsus-
ected people, and the remote provinces, might
less the inexorable justice of their master. But
is successor was vain and jealous of the su-
reme power, which he wanted courage and
bilities to exercise: his vices were pernicious,
is virtues (if he possessed any virtues) were
seless, to mankind; and the Greeks, who im-
uted their calamities to his negligence, denied
im the merit of any transient or accidental
enefits of the times. Isaac slept on the throne,
nd was awakened only by the sound of plea-
ure: his vacant hours were amused by come-
ians and buffoons, and even to these buffoons
ue emperor was an object of contempt: his
asts and buildings exceeded the examples of
oyal luxury: the number of his eunuchs and
omestics amounted to twenty thousand; and a
aily sum of four thousand pounds of silver
ould swell to four millions sterling the annual
xpense of his household and table. His poverty
as relieved by oppression; and the public dis-
ontent was inflamed by equal abuses in the
ollection and the application of the revenue.
Vhile the Greeks numbered the days of their
ervitude, a flattering prophet, whom he re-
arded with the dignity of patriarch, assured
im of a long and victorious reign of thirty-two
ears, during which he should extend his way
o Mount Libanus, and his conquests beyond
ue Euphrates. But his only step towards the
ccomplishment of the prediction was a splendid
nd scandalous embassy to Saladin,[19] to de-
1and the restitution of the holy sepulchre, and
o propose an offensive and defensive league
vith the enemy of the Christian name. In these
nworthy hands, of Isaac and his brother, the
emains of the Greek empire crumbled into
ust. The island of Cyprus, whose name excites
ne ideas of elegance and pleasure, was usurped
y his namesake, a Comnenian prince; and by
strange concatenation of events, the sword of
ur English Richard bestowed that kingdom on
he house of Lusignan, a rich compensation for
he loss of Jerusalem.

The honour of the monarchy and the safety
f the capital were deeply wounded by the re-
olt of the Bulgarians and Wallachians. Since
the victory of the second Basil, they had supported, above a hundred and seventy years, the
loose dominion of the Byzantine princes; but no
effectual measures had been adopted to impose
the yoke of laws and manners on these savage
tribes. By the command of Isaac, their sole
means of subsistence, their flocks and herds,
were driven away to contribute towards the
pomp of the royal nuptials; and their fierce
warriors were exasperated by the denial of
equal rank and pay in the military service. Peter
and Asan, two powerful chiefs, of the race of
the ancient kings,[20] asserted their own rights
and the national freedom: their demoniac impostors proclaimed to the crowd that their
glorious patron St. Demetrius had for ever deserted the cause of the Greeks: and the conflagration spread from the banks of the Danube to
the hills of Macedonia and Thrace. After some
faint efforts, Isaac Angelus and his brother
acquiesced in their independence; and the Imperial troops were soon discouraged by the
bones of their fellow-soldiers that were scattered
along the passes of Mount Hæmus. By the arms
and policy of John, or Joannices, the second
kingdom of Bulgaria was firmly established.
The subtle barbarian sent an embassy to Innocent the Third to acknowledge himself a genuine son of Rome in descent and religion,[21] and
humbly received from the pope the licence of
coining money, the royal title, and a Latin
archbishop or patriarch. The Vatican exulted
in the spiritual conquest of Bulgaria, the first
object of the schism; and if the Greeks could
have preserved the prerogatives of the church,
they would gladly have resigned the rights of
the monarchy.

The Bulgarians were malicious enough to
pray for the long life of Isaac Angelus, the surest
pledge of their freedom and prosperity. Yet
their chiefs could involve in the same indiscriminate contempt the family and nation of
the emperor. "In all the Greeks," said Asan to
his troops, "the same climate, and character,
and education, will be productive of the same
fruits. Behold my lance," continued the warrior, "and the long streamers that float in the
wind. They differ only in colour; they are
formed of the same silk, and fashioned by the
same workman; nor has the stripe that is stained
in purple any superior price or value above its
fellows."[22] Several of these candidates for the
purple successively rose and fell under the empire of Isaac: a general who had repelled the
fleets of Sicily was driven to revolt and ruin by
the ingratitude of the prince; and his luxurious

repose was disturbed by secret conspiracies and popular insurrections. The emperor was saved by accident, or the merit of his servants: for he was at length oppressed by an ambitious brother, who, for the hope of a precarious diadem, forgot the obligations of nature, of loyalty, and of friendship.[23] While Isaac in the Thracian valleys pursued the idle and solitary pleasures of the chase, his brother, Alexius Angelus, was invested with the purple by the unanimous suffrage of the camp: the capital and the clergy subscribed to their choice; and the vanity of the new sovereign rejected the name of his fathers for the lofty and royal appellation of the Comnenian race. On the despicable character of Isaac I have exhausted the language of contempt, and can only add that in a reign of eight years the baser Alexius[24] was supported by the masculine vices of his wife Euphrosyne. The first intelligence of his fall was conveyed to the late emperor by the hostile aspect and pursuit of the guards, no longer his own: he fled before them above fifty miles as far as Stagyra in Macedonia; but the fugitive, without an object or a follower, was arrested, brought back to Constantinople, deprived of his eyes, and confined in a lonesome tower, on a scanty allowance of bread and water. At the moment of the revolution, his son Alexius, whom he educated in the hope of empire, was twelve years of age. He was spared by the usurper, and reduced to attend his triumph both in peace and war; but as the army was encamped on the sea-shore, an Italian vessel facilitated the escape of the royal youth; and, in the disguise of a common sailor, he eluded the search of his enemies, passed the Hellespont, and found a secure refuge in the isle of Sicily. After saluting the threshold of the apostles, and imploring the protection of pope Innocent the Third, Alexius accepted the kind invitation of his sister Irene, the wife of Philip of Swabia, king of the Romans. But in his passage through Italy he heard that the flower of Western chivalry was assembled at Venice for the deliverance of the Holy Land; and a ray of hope was kindled in his bosom that their invincible swords might be employed in his father's restoration.

About ten or twelve years after the loss of Jerusalem, the nobles of France were again summoned to the holy war by the voice of a third prophet, less extravagant, perhaps, than Peter the Hermit, but far below St. Bernard in the merit of an orator and a statesman. An illiterate priest of the neighbourhood of Paris, Fulk of Neuilly,[25] forsook his parochial duty, to assume the more flattering character of a popular and itinerant missionary. The fame of his sanctity and miracles was spread over the land; he declaimed, with severity and vehemence, against the vices of the age; and his sermon, which he preached in the streets of Paris, converted the robbers, the usurers, the prostitute, and even the doctors and scholars of the university. No sooner did Innocent the Third ascend the chair of St. Peter than he proclaimed in Italy, Germany, and France, the obligation of a new crusade.[26] The eloquent pontiff described the ruin of Jerusalem, the triumph of the Pagans, and the shame of Christendom: his liberality proposed the redemption of sins, a plenary indulgence to all who should serve in Palestine, either a year in person, or two years by a substitute:[27] and among his legates and orators who blew the sacred trumpet, Fulk of Neuilly was the loudest and most successful. The situation of the principal monarchs was averse to the pious summons. The emperor Frederic the Second was a child; and his kingdom of Germany was disputed by the rival houses of Brunswick and Swabia, the memorable factions of the Guelphs and Ghibelines. Philip Augustus of France had performed, and could not be persuaded to renew, the perilous vow; but as he was not less ambitious of praise than of power, he cheerfully instituted a perpetual fund for the defence of the Holy Land. Richard of England was satiated with the glory and misfortunes of his first adventure, and he presumed to deride the exhortations of Fulk of Neuilly, who was not abashed in the presence of kings. "You advise me," said Plantagenet, "to dismiss my three daughters, pride, avarice, and incontinence: I bequeath them to the most deserving; my pride to the knights-templars, my avarice to the monks of Cisteaux, and my incontinence to the prelates." But the preacher was heard and obeyed by the great vassals, the princes of the second order; and Theobald, or Thibaut, count of Champagne, was the foremost in the holy race. The valiant youth, at the age of twenty-two years, was encouraged by the domestic examples of his father, who marched in the second crusade, and of his elder brother who had ended his days in Palestine with the title of King of Jerusalem: two thousand two hundred knights owed service and homage to his peerage:[28] the nobles of Champagne excelled in all the exercises of war;[29] and, by his marriage with the heiress of Navarre, Thibaut could draw a band of hardy Gascons from either side of the Pyrenæan mountains. His comanion in arms was Louis count of Blois and Chartres; like himself of regal lineage, for both the princes were nephews, at the same time, of the kings of France and England. In a crowd of prelates and barons, who imitated their zeal, I distinguish the birth and merit of Matthew of Montmorency; the famous Simon of Montfort, the scourge of the Albigeois; and a valiant noble, Jeffrey of Villehardouin,[30] marshal of Champagne,[31] who has condescended, in the rude idiom of his age and country,[32] to write or dictate[33] an original narrative of the councils and actions in which he bore a memorable part. At the same time, Baldwin count of Flanders, who had married the sister of Thibaut, assumed the cross at Bruges, with his brother Henry and the principal knights and citizens of that rich and industrious province.[34] The vow which the chiefs had pronounced in churches, they ratified in tournaments: the operations of the war were debated in full and frequent assemblies: and it was resolved to seek the deliverance of Palestine in Egypt, a country, since Saladin's death, which was almost ruined by famine and civil war. But the fate of so many royal armies displayed the toils and perils of a land expedition; and if the Flemings dwelt along the ocean, the French barons were destitute of ships and ignorant of navigation. They embraced the wise resolution of choosing six deputies or representatives, of whom Villehardouin was one, with a discretionary trust to direct the motions, and to pledge the faith, of the whole confederacy. The maritime states of Italy were alone possessed of the means of transporting the holy warriors with their arms and horses; and the six deputies proceeded to Venice to solicit, on motives of piety or interest, the aid of that powerful republic.

In the invasion of Italy by Attila, I have mentioned[35] the flight of the Venetians from the fallen cities of the continent, and their obscure shelter in the chain of islands that line the extremity of the Adriatic Gulf. In the midst of the waters, free, indigent, laborious, and inaccessible, they gradually coalesced into a republic: the first foundations of Venice were laid in the island of Rialto; and the annual election of the twelve tribunes was superseded by the permanent office of a duke or doge. On the verge of the two empires, the Venetians exult in the relief of primitive and perpetual independence.[36] Against the Latins their antique freedom has been asserted by the sword, and may be justified by the pen. Charlemagne himself resigned all claims of sovereignty to the islands of the Adri-

atic Gulf: his son Pepin was repulsed in the attacks of the *lagunas* or canals, too deep for the cavalry, and too shallow for the vessels; and in every age, under the German Cæsars, the lands of the republic have been clearly distinguished from the kingdom of Italy. But the inhabitants of Venice were considered by themselves, by strangers, and by their sovereigns, as an inalienable portion of the Greek empire:[37] in the ninth and tenth centuries the proofs of their subjection are numerous and unquestionable; and the vain titles, the servile honours, of the Byzantine court, so ambitiously solicited by their dukes, would have degraded the magistrates of a free people. But the bands of this dependence, which was never absolute or rigid, were imperceptibly relaxed by the ambition of Venice and the weakness of Constantinople. Obedience was softened into respect, privilege ripened into prerogative, and the freedom of domestic government was fortified by the independence of foreign dominion. The maritime cities of Istria and Dalmatia bowed to the sovereigns of the Adriatic; and when they armed against the Normans in the cause of Alexius, the emperor applied, not to the duty of his subjects, but to the gratitude and generosity of his faithful allies. The sea was their patrimony:[38] the western parts of the Mediterranean, from Tuscany to Gibraltar, were indeed abandoned to their rivals of Pisa and Genoa; but the Venetians acquired an early and lucrative share of the commerce of Greece and Egypt. Their riches increased with the increasing demand of Europe: their manufactures of silk and glass, perhaps the institution of their bank, are of high antiquity; and they enjoyed the fruits of their industry in the magnificence of public and private life. To assert her flag, to avenge her injuries, to protect the freedom of navigation, the republic could launch and man a fleet of a hundred galleys; and the Greeks, the Saracens, and the Normans were encountered by her naval arms. The Franks of Syria were assisted by the Venetians in the reduction of the seacoast; but their zeal was neither blind nor disinterested; and in the conquest of Tyre they shared the sovereignty of a city, the first seat of the commerce of the world. The policy of Venice was marked by the avarice of a trading, and the insolence of a maritime power; yet her ambition was prudent: nor did she often forget that, if armed galleys were the effect and safeguard, merchant vessels were the cause and supply, of her greatness. In her religion she avoided the schism of the Greeks, without yielding a servile obedience to the Roman pontiff; and a free intercourse with the infidels of every clime appears to have allayed betimes the fever of superstition. Her primitive government was a loose mixture of democracy and monarchy: the doge was elected by the votes of the general assembly; as long as he was popular and successful, he reigned with the pomp and authority of a prince; but in the frequent revolutions of the state, he was deposed, or banished, or slain, by the justice or injustice of the multitude. The twelfth century produced the first rudiments of the wise and jealous aristocracy, which has reduced the doge to a pageant, and the people to a cipher.[39]

When the six ambassadors of the French pilgrims arrived at Venice, they were hospitably entertained in the palace of St. Mark, by the reigning duke: his name was Henry Dandolo;[40] and he shone in the last period of human life as one of the most illustrious characters of the times. Under the weight of years, and after the loss of his eyes,[41] Dandolo retained a sound understanding and a manly courage; the spirit of a hero, ambitious to signalise his reign by some memorable exploits; and the wisdom of a patriot, anxious to build his fame on the glory and advantage of his country. He praised the bold enthusiasm and liberal confidence of the barons and their deputies: in such a cause, and with such associates, he should aspire, were he a private man, to terminate his life; but he was the servant of the republic, and some delay was requisite to consult, on this arduous business, the judgment of his colleagues. The proposal of the French was first debated by the six *sages* who had been recently appointed to control the administration of the doge: it was next disclosed to the forty members of the council of state; and finally communicated to the legislative assembly of four hundred and fifty representatives, who were annually chosen in the six quarters of the city. In peace and war the doge was still the chief of the republic; his legal authority was supported by the personal reputation of Dandolo; his arguments of public interest were balanced and approved; and he was authorised to inform the ambassadors of the following conditions of the treaty.[42] It was proposed that the crusaders should assemble at Venice on the feast of St. John of the ensuing year; that flat-bottomed vessels should be prepared for four thousand five hundred horses and nine thousand squires, with a number of ships sufficient for the embarkation of four thousand five hundred knights and twenty thousand foot: that

during a term of nine months they should be supplied with provisions, and transported to whatsoever coast the service of God and Christendom should require; and that the republic should join the armament with a squadron of fifty galleys. It was required that the pilgrims should pay, before their departure, a sum of eighty-five thousand marks of silver; and that all conquests, by sea and land, should be equally divided between the confederates. The terms were hard; but the emergency was pressing, and the French barons were not less profuse of money than of blood. A general assembly was convened to ratify the treaty: the stately chapel and place of St. Mark were filled with ten thousand citizens; and the noble deputies were taught a new lesson of humbling themselves before the majesty of the people. "Illustrious Venetians," said the marshal of Champagne, "we are sent by the greatest and most powerful barons of France to implore the aid of the masters of the sea for the deliverance of Jerusalem. They have enjoined us to fall prostrate at your feet; nor will we rise from the ground till you have promised to avenge with us the injuries of Christ." The eloquence of their words and tears,[43] their martial aspect and suppliant attitude, were applauded by a universal shout; as it were, says Jeffrey, by the sound of an earthquake. The venerable doge ascended the pulpit to urge their request by those motives of honour and virtue which alone can be offered to a popular assembly: the treaty was transcribed on parchment, attested with oaths and seals, mutually accepted by the weeping and joyful representatives of France and Venice, and despatched to Rome for the approbation of pope Innocent the Third. Two thousand marks were borrowed of the merchants for the first expense of the armament. Of the six deputies, two repassed the Alps to announce their success, while their four companions made a fruitless trial of the zeal and emulation of the republics of Genoa and Pisa.

The execution of the treaty was still opposed by unforeseen difficulties and delays. The marshal, on his return to Troyes, was embraced and approved by Thibaut count of Champagne, who had been unanimously chosen general of the confederates. But the health of that valiant youth already declined, and soon became hopeless; and he deplored the untimely fate which condemned him to expire, not in a field of battle, but on a bed of sickness. To his brave and numerous vassals the dying prince distributed his treasures: they swore in his presence to accomplish his vow and their own; but some there were, says the marshal, who accepted his gifts and forfeited their word. The more resolute champions of the cross held a parliament at Soissons for the election of a new general; but such was the incapacity, or jealousy, or reluctance, of the princes of France, that none could be found both able and willing to assume the conduct of the enterprise. They acquiesced in the choice of a stranger, of Boniface marquis of Montferrat, descended of a race of heroes, and himself of conspicuous fame in the wars and negotiations of the times;[44] nor could the piety or ambition of the Italian chief decline this honourable invitation. After visiting the French court, where he was received as a friend and kinsman, the marquis, in the church of Soissons, was invested with the cross of a pilgrim and the staff of a general; and immediately repassed the Alps, to prepare for the distant expedition of the East. About the festival of the Pentecost he displayed his banner, and marched towards Venice at the head of the Italians: he was preceded or followed by the counts of Flanders and Blois and the most respectable barons of France; and their numbers were swelled by the pilgrims of Germany,[45] whose object and motives were similar to their own. The Venetians had fulfilled, and even surpassed, their engagements: stables were constructed for the horses, and barracks for the troops; the magazines were abundantly replenished with forage and provisions; and the fleet of transports, ships, and galleys, was ready to hoist sail as soon as the republic had received the price of the freight and armament. But that price far exceeded the wealth of the crusaders who were assembled at Venice. The Flemings, whose obedience to their count was voluntary and precarious, had embarked in their vessels for the long navigation of the ocean and Mediterranean; and many of the French and Italians had preferred a cheaper and more convenient passage from Marseilles and Apulia to the Holy Land. Each pilgrim might complain that, after he had furnished his own contribution, he was made responsible for the deficiency of his absent brethren: the gold and silver plate of the chiefs, which they freely delivered to the treasury of St. Mark, was a generous but inadequate sacrifice; and after all their efforts, thirty-four thousand marks were still wanting to complete the stipulated sum. The obstacle was removed by the policy and patriotism of the doge, who proposed to the barons that, if they would join their arms in reducing some revolted cities of Dalmatia, he would expose his person in the holy war, and obtain from the republic a long indulgence, till some wealthy conquest should afford the means of satisfying the debt. After much scruple and hesitation, they chose rather to accept the offer than to relinquish the enterprise; and the first hostilities of the fleet and army were directed against Zara,[46] a strong city of the Sclavonian coast, which had renounced its allegiance to Venice, and implored the protection of the king of Hungary.[47] The crusaders burst the chain or boom of the harbour; landed their horses, troops, and military engines; and compelled the inhabitants, after a defence of five days, to surrender at discretion: their lives were spared, but the revolt was punished by the pillage of their houses and the demolition of their walls. The season was far advanced; the French and Venetians resolved to pass the winter in a secure harbour and plentiful country; but their repose was disturbed by national and tumultuous quarrels of the soldiers and mariners. The conquest of Zara had scattered the seeds of discord and scandal: the arms of the allies had been stained in their outset with the blood, not of infidels, but of Christians: the king of Hungary and his new subjects were themselves enlisted under the banner of the cross; and the scruples of the devout were magnified by the fear or lassitude of the reluctant pilgrims. The pope had excommunicated the false crusaders who had pillaged and massacred their brethren,[48] and only the marquis Boniface and Simon of Montfort escaped these spiritual thunders; the one by his absence from the siege, the other by his final departure from the camp. Innocent might absolve the simple and submissive penitents of France; but he was provoked by the stubborn reason of the Venetians, who refused to confess their guilt, to accept their pardon, or to allow, in their temporal concerns, the interposition of a priest.

The assembly of such formidable powers by sea and land had revived the hopes of young[49] Alexius, and both at Venice and Zara he solicited the arms of the crusaders for his own restoration and his father's[50] deliverance. The royal youth was recommended by Philip king of Germany; his prayers and presence excited the compassion of the camp, and his cause was embraced and pleaded by the marquis of Montferrat and the doge of Venice. A double alliance, and the dignity of Cæsar, had connected with the Imperial family the two elder brothers of Boniface;[51] he expected to derive a kingdom from the important service; and the more generous ambition of Dandolo was eager to secure the inestimable benefits of trade and dominion that might accrue to his country.[52] Their influence procured a favourable audience for the ambassadors of Alexius; and if the magnitude of his offers excited some suspicion, the motives and rewards which he displayed might justify the delay and diversion of those forces which had been consecrated to the deliverance of Jerusalem. He promised, in his own and his father's name, that, as soon as they should be seated on the throne of Constantinople, they would terminate the long schism of the Greeks, and submit themselves and their people to the lawful supremacy of the Roman church. He engaged to recompense the labours and merits of the crusaders by the immediate payment of two hundred thousand marks of silver; to accompany them in person to Egypt; or, if it should be judged more advantageous, to maintain, during a year, ten thousand men, and, during his life, five hundred knights, for the service of the Holy Land. These tempting conditions were accepted by the republic of Venice, and the eloquence of the doge and marquis persuaded the counts of Flanders, Blois, and St. Pol, with eight barons of France, to join in the glorious enterprise. A treaty of offensive and defensive alliance was confirmed by their oaths and seals; and each individual, according to his situation and character, was swayed by the hope of public or private advantage; by the honour of restoring an exiled monarch; or by the sincere and probable opinion that their efforts in Palestine would be fruitless and unavailing, and that the acquisition of Constantinople must precede and prepare the recovery of Jerusalem. But they were the chiefs or equals of a valiant band of freemen and volunteers, who thought and acted for themselves: the soldiers and clergy were divided; and, if a large majority subscribed to the alliance, the numbers and arguments of the dissidents were strong and respectable.[53] The boldest hearts were appalled by the report of the naval power and impregnable strength of Constantinople, and their apprehensions were disguised to the world, and perhaps to themselves, by the more decent objections of religion and duty. They alleged the sanctity of a vow which had drawn them from their families and homes to the rescue of the holy sepulchre; nor should the dark and crooked counsels of human policy divert them from a pursuit, the event of which was in the hands of the Almighty. Their first offence, the attack of Zara, had been severely

punished by the reproach of their conscience and the censures of the pope, nor would they again imbrue their hands in the blood of their fellow Christians. The apostle of Rome had pronounced; nor would they usurp the right of avenging with the sword the schism of the Greeks and the doubtful usurpation of the Byzantine monarch. On these principles or pretences many pilgrims, the most distinguished for their valour and piety, withdrew from the camp; and their retreat was less pernicious than the open or secret opposition of a discontented party that laboured, on every occasion, to separate the army and disappoint the enterprise.

Notwithstanding this defection, the departure of the fleet and army was vigorously pressed by the Venetians, whose zeal for the service of the royal youth concealed a just resentment to his nation and family. They were mortified by the recent preference which had been given to Pisa, the rival of their trade; they had a long arrear of debt and injury to liquidate with the Byzantine court; and Dandolo might not discourage the popular tale that he had been deprived of his eyes by the emperor Manuel, who perfidiously violated the sanctity of an ambassador. A similar armament, for ages, had not rode the Adriatic: it was composed of one hundred and twenty flat-bottomed vessels or *palanders* for the horses, two hundred and forty transports filled with men and arms, seventy store-ships laden with provisions, and fifty stout galleys well prepared for the encounter of an enemy.[54] While the wind was favourable, the sky serene, and the water smooth, every eye was fixed with wonder and delight on the scene of military and naval pomp which overspread the sea. The shields of the knights and squires, at once an ornament and a defence, were arranged on either side of the ships; the banners of the nations and families were displayed from the stern; our modern artillery was supplied by three hundred engines for casting stones and darts; the fatigues of the way were cheered with the sound of music; and the spirits of the adventurers were raised by the mutual assurance that forty thousand Christian heroes were equal to the conquest of the world.[55] In the navigation[56] from Venice and Zara the fleet was successfully steered by the skill and experience of the Venetian pilots: at Durazzo the confederates first landed on the territories of the Greek empire; the isle of Corfu afforded a station and repose; they doubled, without accident, the perilous cape of Malea, the southern point of

Peloponnesus or the Morea; made a descent in the islands of Negropont and Andros; and cast anchor at Abydus on the Asiatic side of the Hellespont. These preludes of conquest were easy and bloodless; the Greeks of the provinces, without patriotism or courage, were crushed by an irresistible force; the presence of the lawful heir might justify their obedience, and it was rewarded by the modesty and discipline of the Latins. As they penetrated through the Hellespont, the magnitude of their navy was compressed in a narrow channel, and the face of the waters was darkened with innumerable sails. They again expanded in the basin of the Propontis, and traversed that placid sea, till they approached the European shore at the abbey of St. Stephen, three leagues to the west of Constantinople. The prudent doge dissuaded them from dispersing themselves in a populous and hostile land; and, as their stock of provisions was reduced, it was resolved, in the season of harvest, to replenish their storeships in the fertile islands of the Propontis. With this resolution they directed their course; but a strong gale and their own impatience drove them to the eastward, and so near did they run to the shore and the city, that some volleys of stones and darts were exchanged between the ships and the rampart. As they passed along, they gazed with admiration on the capital of the East, or, as it should seem, of the earth, rising from her seven hills, and towering over the continents of Europe and Asia. The swelling domes and lofty spires of five hundred palaces and churches were gilded by the sun and reflected in the waters; the walls were crowded with soldiers and spectators, whose number they beheld, of whose temper they were ignorant; and each heart was chilled by the reflection that, since the beginning of the world, such an enterprise had never been undertaken by such a handful of warriors. But the momentary apprehension was dispelled by hope and valour; and every man, says the marshal of Champagne, glanced his eye on the sword or lance which he must speedily use in the glorious conflict.[57] The Latins cast anchor before Chalcedon; the mariners only were left in the vessels; the soldiers, horses, and arms were safely landed; and, in the luxury of an Imperial palace, the barons tasted the first fruits of their success. On the third day the fleet and army moved towards Scutari, the Asiatic suburb of Constantinople: a detachment of five hundred Greek horse was surprised and defeated by fourscore French knights; and in a halt of nine days the camp was plentifully supplied with forage and provisions.

In relating the invasion of a great empire, it may seem strange that I have not described the obstacles which should have checked the progress of the strangers. The Greeks, in truth, were an unwarlike people; but they were rich, industrious, and subject to the will of a single man; had that man been capable of fear when his enemies were at a distance, or of courage when they approached his person. The first rumour of his nephew's alliance with the French and Venetians was despised by the usurper Alexius: his flatterers persuaded him that in this contempt he was bold and sincere; and each evening, in the close of the banquet, he thrice discomfited the barbarians of the West. These barbarians had been justly terrified by the report of his naval power; and the sixteen hundred fishing-boats of Constantinople[58] could have manned a fleet to sink them in the Adriatic, or stop their entrance in the mouth of the Hellespont. But all force may be annihilated by the negligence of the prince and the venality of his ministers. The great duke or admiral made a scandalous, almost a public, auction of the sails, the masts, and the rigging; the royal forests were reserved for the more important purpose of the chase; and the trees, says Nicetas, were guarded by the eunuchs like the groves of religious worship.[59] From this dream of pride Alexius was awakened by the siege of Zara and the rapid advances of the Latins: as soon as he saw the danger was real, he thought it inevitable, and his vain presumption was lost in abject despondency and despair. He suffered these contemptible barbarians to pitch their camp in the sight of the palace, and his apprehensions were thinly disguised by the pomp and menace of a suppliant embassy. The sovereign of the Romans was astonished (his ambassadors were instructed to say) at the hostile appearance of the strangers. If these pilgrims were sincere in their vow for the deliverance of Jerusalem, his voice must applaud, and treasures should assist, their pious design; but should they dare to invade the sanctuary of empire, their numbers, were they ten times more considerable, should not protect them from his just resentment. The answer of the doge and barons was simple and magnanimous. "In the cause of honour and justice," they said, "we despise the usurper of Greece, his threats, and his offers. *Our* friendship and *his* allegiance are due to the lawful heir, to the young prince who is seated among us, and to his father the emperor Isaac, who has been deprived of his sceptre, his freedom, and his eyes by the crime of an ungrateful brother. Let that brother confess his guilt and implore forgiveness, and we ourselves will intercede that he may be permitted to live in affluence and security. But let him not insult us by a second message: our reply will be made in arms, in the palace of Constantinople."

On the tenth day of their encampment at Scutari the crusaders prepared themselves, as soldiers and as Catholics, for the passage of the Bosphorus. Perilous indeed was the adventure: the stream was broad and rapid; in a calm the current of the Euxine might drive down the liquid and unextinguishable fire of the Greeks, and the opposite shores of Europe were defended by seventy thousand horse and foot in formidable array. On this memorable day, which happened to be bright and pleasant, the Latins were distributed in six battles or divisions; the first, or vanguard, was led by the count of Flanders, one of the most powerful of the Christian princes in the skill and number of his crossbows. The four successive battles of the French were commanded by his brother Henry, the counts of St. Pol and Blois, and Matthew of Montmorency, the last of whom was honoured by the voluntary service of the marshal and nobles of Champagne. The sixth division, the rearguard and reserve of the army, was conducted by the marquis of Montferrat, at the head of the Germans and Lombards. The chargers, saddled, with their long caparisons dragging on the ground, were embarked in the flat *palanders*,[60] and the knights stood by the side of their horses, in complete armour, the helmets laced, and their lances in their hands. Their numerous train of *serjeants*[61] and archers occupied the transports, and each transport was towed by the strength and swiftness of a galley. The six divisions traversed the Bosphorus without encountering an enemy or an obstacle; to land the foremost was the wish, to conquer or die was the resolution, of every division and of every soldier. Jealous of the pre-eminence of danger, the knights in their heavy armour leaped into the sea when it rose as high as their girdle; the serjeants and archers were animated by their valour; and the squires, letting down the drawbridges of the palanders, led the horses to the shore. Before the squadrons could mount, and form, and couch their lances, the seventy thousand Greeks had vanished from their sight; the timid Alexius gave the example to his troops, and it was only by the plunder of his rich pavilions that the Latins were informed

that they had fought against an emperor. In the first consternation of the flying enemy, they resolved, by a double attack, to open the entrance of the harbour. The tower of Galata,[62] in the suburb of Pera, was attacked and stormed by the French, while the Venetians assumed the more difficult task of forcing the boom or chain that was stretched from that tower to the Byzantine shore. After some fruitless attempts their intrepid perseverance prevailed; twenty ships of war, the relics of the Grecian navy, were either sunk or taken; the enormous and massy links of iron were cut asunder by the shears or broken by the weight of the galleys;[e] and the Venetian fleet, safe and triumphant, rode at anchor in the port of Constantinople. By these daring achievements a remnant of twenty thousand Latins solicited the licence of besieging a capital which contained above four hundred thousand inhabitants,[64] able, though not willing, to bear arms in the defence of their country. Such an account would indeed suppose a population of near two millions: but whatever abatement may be required in the numbers of the Greeks, the *belief* of those numbers will equally exalt the fearless spirit of their assailants.

In the choice of the attack the French and Venetians were divided by their habits of life and warfare. The former affirmed with truth that Constantinople was most accessible on the side of the sea and the harbour. The latter might assert with honour that they had long enough trusted their lives and fortunes to a frail bark and a precarious element, and loudly demanded a trial of knighthood, a firm ground, and a close onset, either on foot or horseback. After a prudent compromise of employing the two nations by sea and land in the service best suited to their character, the fleet covering the army, they both proceeded from the entrance to the extremity of the harbour: the stone bridge of the river was hastily repaired; and the six battles of the French formed their encampment against the front of the capital, the basis of the triangle which runs about four miles from the port to the Propontis.[65] On the edge of a broad ditch, at the foot of a lofty rampart, they had leisure to contemplate the difficulties of their enterprise. The gates to the right and left of their narrow camp poured forth frequent sallies of cavalry and light infantry, which cut off their stragglers, swept the country of provisions, sounded the alarm five or six times in the course of each day, and compelled them to plant a palisade and sink an entrenchment for their immediate safety. In the supplies and con voys the Venetians had been too sparing, or the Franks too voracious: the usual complaints of hunger and scarcity were heard, and perhaps felt: their stock of flour would be exhausted in three weeks; and their disgust of salt meat tempted them to taste the flesh of their horses. The trembling usurper was supported by Theodore Lascaris, his son-in-law, a valiant youth, who aspired to save and to rule his country; the Greeks, regardless of that country, were awakened to the defence of their religion; but their firmest hope was in the strength and spirit of the Varangian guards, of the Danes and English, as they are named in the writers of the times.[66] After ten days' incessant labour the ground was levelled, the ditch filled, the approaches of the besiegers were regularly made, and two hundred and fifty engines of assault exercised their various powers to clear the rampart, to batter the walls, and to sap the foundations. On the first appearance of a breach the scaling-ladders were applied: the numbers that defended the vantage-ground repulsed and oppressed the adventurous Latins: but they admired the resolution of fifteen knights and serjeants, who had gained the ascent, and maintained their perilous station till they were precipitated or made prisoners by the Imperial guards. On the side of the harbour the naval attack was more successfully conducted by the Venetians; and that industrious people employed every resource that was known and practised before the invention of gunpowder. A double line, three bow-shots in front, was formed by the galleys and ships; and the swift motion of the former was supported by the weight and loftiness of the latter, whose decks, and poops, and turret, were the platforms of military engines, that discharged their shot over the head of the first line. The soldiers, who leaped from the galleys on shore, immediately planted and ascended their scaling-ladders, while the large ships, advancing more slowly into the intervals, and lowering a draw-bridge, opened a way through the air from their masts to the rampart. In the midst of the conflict the doge, a venerable and conspicuous form, stood aloft in complete armour on the prow of his galley. The great standard of St. Mark was displayed before him; his threats, promises, and exhortations urged the diligence of the rowers; his vessel was the first that struck; and Dandolo was the first warrior on the shore. The nations admired the magnanimity of the blind old man, without reflecting that his age and infirmities diminished the price of life and enhanced the value of immortal glory. On a sudden, by an invisible hand (for the standard-bearer was probably slain), the banner of the republic was fixed on the rampart: twenty-five towers were rapidly occupied; and, by the cruel expedient of fire, the Greeks were driven from the adjacent quarter. The doge had despatched the intelligence of his success, when he was checked by the danger of his confederates. Nobly declaring that he would rather die with the pilgrims than gain a victory by their destruction, Dandolo relinquished his advantage, recalled his troops, and hastened to the scene of action. He found the six weary diminutive *battles* of the French encompassed by sixty squadrons of the Greek cavalry, the least of which was more numerous than the largest of their divisions. Shame and despair had provoked Alexius to the last effort of a general sally; but he was awed by the firm order and manly aspect of the Latins; and, after skirmishing at a distance, withdrew his troops in the close of the evening. The silence or tumult of the night exasperated his fears; and the timid usurper, collecting a treasure of ten thousand pounds of gold, basely deserted his wife, his people, and his fortune; threw himself into a bark; stole through the Bosphorus; and landed in shameful safety in an obscure harbour of Thrace. As soon as they were apprised of his flight, the Greek nobles sought pardon and peace in the dungeon where the blind Isaac expected each hour the visit of the executioner. Again saved and exalted by the vicissitudes of fortune, the captive in his Imperial robes was replaced on the throne, and surrounded with prostrate slaves, whose real terror and affected joy he was incapable of discerning. At the dawn of day hostilities were suspended and the Latin chiefs were surprised by a message from the lawful and reigning emperor, who was impatient to embrace his son and to reward his generous deliverers.[67]

But these generous deliverers were unwilling to release their hostage till they had obtained from his father the payment, or at least the promise, of their recompense. They chose four ambassadors, Matthew of Montmorency, our historian the marshal of Champagne, and two Venetians, to congratulate the emperor. The gates were thrown open on their approach, the streets on both sides were lined with the battle-axes of the Danish and English guard: the presence-chamber glittered with gold and jewels, the false substitutes of virtue and power: by the side of the blind Isaac his wife was seated, the sister of the king of Hungary: and by her appearance, the noble matrons of Greece were drawn from their domestic retirement and mingled with the circle of senators and soldiers. The Latins, by the mouth of the marshal, spoke like men conscious of their merits, but who respected the work of their own hands; and the emperor clearly understood that his son's engagements with Venice and the pilgrims must be ratified without hesitation or delay. Withdrawing into a private chamber with the empress, a chamberlain, an interpreter, and the four ambassadors, the father of young Alexius inquired with some anxiety into the nature of his stipulations. The submission of the Eastern empire to the pope, the succour of the Holy Land, and a present contribution of two hundred thousand marks of silver.—"These conditions are weighty," was his prudent reply: "they are hard to accept, and difficult to perform. But no conditions can exceed the measure of your services and deserts." After this satisfactory assurance, the barons mounted on horseback and introduced the heir of Constantinople to the city and palace: his youth and marvellous adventures engaged every heart in his favour, and Alexius was solemnly crowned with his father in the dome of St. Sophia. In the first days of his reign, the people, already blessed with the restoration of plenty and peace, was delighted by the joyful catastrophe of the tragedy; and the discontent of the nobles, their regret, and their fears, were covered by the polished surface of pleasure and loyalty. The mixture of two discordant nations in the same capital might have been pregnant with mischief and danger; and the suburb of Galata, or Pera, was assigned for the quarters of the French and Venetians. But the liberty of trade and familiar intercourse was allowed between the friendly nations; and each day the pilgrims were tempted by devotion or curiosity to visit the churches and palaces of Constantinople. Their rude minds, insensible perhaps of the finer arts, were astonished by the magnificent scenery: and the poverty of their native towns enhanced the populousness and riches of the first metropolis of Christendom.[68] Descending from his state, young Alexius was prompted by interest and gratitude to repeat his frequent and familiar visits to his Latin allies; and in the freedom of the table the gay petulance of the French sometimes forgot the emperor of the East.[69] In their more serious conferences it was agreed that the re-union of the two churches must be the result of patience and time; but avarice was less tractable than zeal; and a large sum was instantly disbursed to appease the wants, and silence the importunity, of the crusaders.[70] Alexius was alarmed by the approaching hour of their departure: their absence might have relieved him from the engagement which he was yet incapable of performing; but his friends would have left him, naked and alone, to the caprice and prejudice of a perfidious nation. He wished to bribe their stay, the delay of a year, by undertaking to defray their expense, and to satisfy, in their name, the freight of the Venetian vessels. The offer was agitated in the council of the barons; and, after a repetition of their debates and scruples, a majority of votes again acquiesced in the advice of the doge and the prayer of the young emperor. At the price of sixteen hundred pounds of gold, he prevailed on the marquis of Montferrat to lead him with an army round the provinces of Europe; to establish his authority, and pursue his uncle, while Constantinople was awed by the presence of Baldwin and his confederates of France and Flanders. The expedition was successful: the blind emperor exulted in the success of his arms, and listened to the predictions of his flatterers, that the same Providence which had raised him from the dungeon to the throne would heal his gout, restore his sight, and watch over the long prosperity of his reign. Yet the mind of the suspicious old man was tormented by the rising glories of his son; nor could his pride conceal from his envy, that, while his own name was pronounced in faint and reluctant acclamations, the royal youth was the theme of spontaneous and universal praise.[71]

By the recent invasion the Greeks were awakened from a dream of nine centuries; from the vain presumption that the capital of the Roman empire was impregnable to foreign arms. The strangers of the West had violated the city, and bestowed the sceptre, of Constantine: their Imperial clients soon became as unpopular as themselves: the well-known vices of Isaac were rendered still more contemptible by his infirmities, and the young Alexius was hated as an apostate who had renounced the manners and religion of his country. His secret covenant with the Latins was divulged or suspected; the people, and especially the clergy, were devoutly attached to their faith and superstition; and every convent, and every shop, resounded with the danger of the church and the tyranny of the pope.[72] An empty treasury could ill supply the demands of regal luxury and foreign extortion: the Greeks refused to avert, by a general tax, the impending evils of servitude and pillage;

the oppression of the rich excited a more dangerous and personal resentment; and if the emperor melted the plate and despoiled the images of the sanctuary, he seemed to justify the complaints of heresy and sacrilege. During the absence of marquis Boniface and his Imperial pupil, Constantinople was visited with a calamity which might be justly imputed to the zeal and indiscretion of the Flemish pilgrims.[73] In one of their visits to the city they were scandalised by the aspect of a mosque or synagogue, in which one God was worshipped, without a partner or a son. Their effectual mode of controversy was to attack the infidels with the sword, and their habitation with fire: but the infidels, and some Christian neighbours, presumed to defend their lives and properties; and the flames which bigotry had kindled consumed the most orthodox and innocent structures. During eight days and nights the conflagration spread above a league in front, from the harbour to the Propontis, over the thickest and most populous regions of the city. It is not easy to count the stately churches and palaces that were reduced to a smoking ruin, to value the merchandise that perished in the trading streets, or to number the families that were involved in the common destruction. By this outrage, which the doge and the barons in vain affected to disclaim, the name of the Latins became still more unpopular; and the colony of that nation, above fifteen thousand persons, consulted their safety in a hasty retreat from the city to the protection of their standard in the suburb of Pera. The emperor returned in triumph; but the firmest and most dexterous policy would have been insufficient to steer him through the tempest which overwhelmed the person and government of that unhappy youth. His own inclination, and his father's advice, attached him to his benefactors; but Alexius hesitated between gratitude and patriotism, between the fear of his subjects and of his allies.[74] By his feeble and fluctuating conduct he lost the esteem and confidence of both; and, while he invited the marquis of Montferrat to occupy the palace, he suffered the nobles to conspire, and the people to arm, for the deliverance of their country. Regardless of his painful situation, the Latin chiefs repeated their demands, resented his delays, suspected his intentions, and exacted a decisive answer of peace or war. The haughty summons was delivered by three French knights and three Venetian deputies, who girded their swords, mounted their horses, pierced through the angry multitude, and entered, with a fearless countenance, the palace and presence of the Greek emperor. In a peremptory tone they recapitulated their services and his engagements; and boldly declared that, unless their just claims were fully and immediately satisfied, they should no longer hold him either as a sovereign or a friend. After this defiance, the first that had ever wounded an Imperial ear, they departed without betraying any symptoms of fear; but their escape from a servile palace and a furious city astonished the ambassadors themselves: and their return to the camp was the signal of mutual hostility.

Among the Greeks all authority and wisdom were overborne by the impetuous multitude, who mistook their rage for valour, their numbers for strength, and their fanaticism for the support and inspiration of Heaven. In the eyes of both nations Alexius was false and contemptible: the base and spurious race of the Angeli was rejected with clamorous disdain; and the people of Constantinople encompassed the senate to demand at their hands a more worthy emperor. To every senator, conspicuous by his birth or dignity, they successively presented the purple: by each senator the deadly garment was repulsed: the contest lasted three days; and we may learn from the historian Nicetas, one of the members of the assembly, that fear and weakness were the guardians of their loyalty. A phantom, who vanished in oblivion, was forcibly proclaimed by the crowd:[75] but the author of the tumult, and the leader of the war, was a prince of the house of Ducas; and his common appellation of Alexius must be discriminated by the epithet of Mourzoufle,[76] which in the vulgar idiom expressed the close junction of his black and shaggy eyebrows. At once a patriot and a courtier, the perfidious Mourzoufle, who was not destitute of cunning and courage, opposed the Latins both in speech and action, inflamed the passions and prejudices of the Greeks, and insinuated himself into the favour and confidence of Alexius, who trusted him with the office of great chamberlain, and tinged his buskins with the colours of royalty. At the dead of night he rushed into the bed-chamber with an affrighted aspect, exclaiming that the palace was attacked by the people and betrayed by the guards. Starting from his couch, the unsuspecting prince threw himself into the arms of his enemy, who had contrived his escape by a private staircase. But that staircase terminated in a prison: Alexius was seized, stripped, and loaded with chains; and, after tasting some days the bitterness of death, he was poisoned, or strangled, or beaten with clubs, at the command, and in the presence, of the tyrant. The emperor Isaac Angelus soon followed his son to the grave; and Mourzoufle, perhaps, might spare the superfluous crime of hastening the extinction of impotence and blindness.

The death of the emperors, and the usurpation of Mourzoufle, had changed the nature of the quarrel. It was no longer the disagreement of allies who overvalued their services, or neglected their obligations: the French and Venetians forgot their complaints against Alexius, dropped a tear on the untimely fate of their companion, and swore revenge against the perfidious nation who had crowned his assassin. Yet the prudent doge was still inclined to negotiate: he asked as a debt, a subsidy, or a fine, fifty thousand pounds of gold, about two millions sterling; nor would the conference have been abruptly broken if the zeal, or policy, of Mourzoufle had not refused to sacrifice the Greek church to the safety of the state.[77] Amidst the invectives of his foreign and domestic enemies, we may discern that he was not unworthy of the character which he had assumed, of the public champion: the second siege of Constantinople was far more laborious than the first; the treasury was replenished, and discipline was restored, by a severe inquisition into the abuses of the former reign; and Mourzoufle, an iron mace in his hand, visiting the posts, and affecting the port and aspect of a warrior, was an object of terror to his soldiers, at least, and to his kinsmen. Before and after the death of Alexius, the Greeks made two vigorous and well-conducted attempts to burn the navy in the harbour; but the skill and courage of the Venetians repulsed the fire-ships; and the vagrant flames wasted themselves without injury in the sea.[78] In a nocturnal sally the Greek emperor was vanquished by Henry, brother of the count of Flanders: the advantages of number and surprise aggravated the shame of his defeat: his buckler was found on the field of battle; and the Imperial standard,[79] a divine image of the Virgin, was presented, as a trophy and a relic, to the Cistercian monks, the disciples of St. Bernard. Near three months, without excepting the holy season of Lent, were consumed in skirmishes and preparations, before the Latins were ready or resolved for a general assault. The land fortifications had been found impregnable; and the Venetian pilots represented, that, on the shore of the Propontis, the anchorage was unsafe, and the ships must be driven by the current far away to the straits of the Hellespont;

a prospect not unpleasing to the reluctant pilgrims, who sought every opportunity of breaking the army. From the harbour, therefore, the assault was determined by the assailants and expected by the besieged; and the emperor had placed his scarlet pavilions on a neighbouring height, to direct and animate the efforts of his troops. A fearless spectator, whose mind could entertain the ideas of pomp and pleasure, might have admired the long array of two embattled armies, which extended above half a league, the one on the ships and galleys, the other on the walls and towers raised above the ordinary level by several stages of wooden turrets. Their first fury was spent in the discharge of darts, stones, and fire, from the engines; but the water was deep; the French were bold; the Venetians were skilful; they approached the walls; and a desperate conflict of swords, spears, and battle-axes, was fought on the trembling bridges that grappled the floating to the stable batteries. In more than a hundred places the assault was urged and the defence was sustained; till the superiority of ground and numbers finally prevailed, and the Latin trumpets sounded a retreat. On the ensuing days the attack was renewed with equal vigour and a similar event; and, in the night, the doge and the barons held a council, apprehensive only for the public danger: not a voice pronounced the words of escape or treaty; and each warrior, according to his temper, embraced the hope of victory or the assurance of a glorious death.[80] By the experience of the former siege the Greeks were instructed, but the Latins were animated; and the knowledge that Constantinople *might* be taken was of more avail than the local precautions which that knowledge had inspired for its defence. In the third assault two ships were linked together to double their strength; a strong north wind drove them on the shore; the bishops of Troyes and Soissons led the van; and the auspicious names of the *Pilgrim* and the *Paradise* resounded along the line.[81] The episcopal banners were displayed on the walls; a hundred marks of silver had been promised to the first adventurers; and if their reward was intercepted by death, their names have been immortalised by fame. Four towers were scaled; three gates were burst open; and the French knights, who might tremble on the waves, felt themselves invincible on horseback on the solid ground. Shall I relate that the thousands who guarded the emperor's person fled on the approach, and before the lance, of a single warrior? Their ignominious flight is attested by

eir countryman Nicetas: an army of phan-
ms marched with the French hero, and he
as magnified to a giant in the eyes of the
reeks.[82] While the fugitives deserted their
osts and cast away their arms, the Latins en-
red the city under the banners of their leaders:
ie streets and gates opened for their passage;
nd either design or accident kindled a third
onflagration, which consumed in a few hours
ie measure of three of the largest cities of
rance.[83] In the close of evening the barons
hecked their troops and fortified their stations:
iey were awed by the extent and populousness
f the capital, which might yet require the
ibour of a month, if the churches and palaces
vere conscious of their internal strength. But in
he morning a suppliant procession, with crosses
nd images, announced the submission of the
ireeks and deprecated the wrath of the con-
uerors: the usurper escaped through the golden
ate: the palaces of Blachernæ and Boucoleon
vere occupied by the count of Flanders and the
narquis of Montferrat; and the empire, which
till bore the name of Constantine and the title
f Roman, was subverted by the arms of the
_atin pilgrims.[84]

Constantinople had been taken by storm;
nd no restraints except those of religion and
iumanity were imposed on the conquerors by
he laws of war. Boniface, marquis of Mont-
errat, still acted as their general, and the
ireeks, who revered his name as that of their
uture sovereign, were heard to exclaim in a
amentable tone, "Holy marquis-king, have
nercy upon us!" His prudence or compassion
pened the gates of the city to the fugitives, and
ie exhorted the soldiers of the cross to spare the
ives of their fellow-Christians. The streams of
lood that flow down the pages of Nicetas may
e reduced to the slaughter of two thousand of
iis unresisting countrymen;[85] and the greater
art was massacred, not by the strangers, but
oy the Latins who had been driven from the
ity, and who exercised the revenge of a trium-
ohant faction. Yet of these exiles, some were less
nindful of injuries than of benefits; and Nicetas
iimself was indebted for his safety to the gen-
rosity of a Venetian merchant. Pope Innocent
he Third accuses the pilgrims of respecting, in
heir lust, neither age, nor sex, nor religious
orofession; and bitterly laments that the deeds
of darkness, fornication, adultery, and incest,
vere perpetrated in open day; and that noble
natrons and holy nuns were polluted by the
;rooms and peasants of the Catholic camp.[86]
t is indeed probable that the licence of victory

prompted and covered a multitude of sins: but
it is certain that the capital of the East contained a stock of venal or willing beauty sufficient to satiate the desires of twenty thousand
pilgrims, and female prisoners were no longer
subject to the right or abuse of domestic slavery.
The marquis of Montferrat was the patron of
discipline and decency: the count of Flanders
was the mirror of chastity: they had forbidden,
under pain of death, the rape of married women,
or virgins, or nuns; and the proclamation was
sometimes invoked by the vanquished[87] and
respected by the victors. Their cruelty and lust
were moderated by the authority of the chiefs
and feelings of the soldiers; for we are no longer
describing an irruption of the northern savages;
and however ferocious they might still appear,
time, policy, and religion had civilised the
manners of the French, and still more of the
Italians. But a free scope was allowed to their
avarice, which was glutted, even in the holy
week, by the pillage of Constantinople. The
right of victory, unshackled by any promise or
treaty, had confiscated the public and private
wealth of the Greeks; and every hand, according to its size and strength, might lawfully execute the sentence and seize the forfeiture. A
portable and universal standard of exchange
was found in the coined and uncoined metals of
gold and silver, which each captor, at home or
abroad, might convert into the possessions most
suitable to his temper and situation. Of the
treasures which trade and luxury had accumulated, the silks, velvets, furs, the gems, spices,
and rich movables, were the most precious, as
they could not be procured for money in the
ruder countries of Europe. An order of rapine
was instituted; nor was the share of each individual abandoned to industry or chance. Under
the tremendous penalties of perjury—excommunication and death—the Latins were bound
to deliver their plunder into the common stock;
three churches were selected for the deposit and
distribution of the spoil: a single share was
allotted to a foot soldier, two for a serjeant on
horseback, four to a knight, and larger proportions according to the rank and merit of the
barons and princes. For violating this sacred
engagement, a knight belonging to the count of
St. Paul was hanged with his shield and coat of
arms around his neck: his example might render
similar offenders more artful and discreet, but
avarice was more powerful than fear, and it is
generally believed that the secret far exceeded
the acknowledged plunder. Yet the magnitude
of the prize surpassed the largest scale of ex-

perience or expectation.[88] After the whole had been equally divided between the French and Venetians, fifty thousand marks were deducted to satisfy the debts of the former and the demands of the latter. The residue of the French amounted to four hundred thousand marks of silver,[89] about eight hundred thousand pounds sterling; nor can I better appreciate the value of that sum in the public and private transactions of the age than by defining it as seven times the annual revenue of the kingdom of England.[90]

In this great revolution we enjoy the singular felicity of comparing the narratives of Villehardouin and Nicetas, the opposite feelings of the marshal of Champagne and the Byzantine senator.[91] At the first view it should seem that the wealth of Constantinople was only transferred from one nation to another, and that the loss and sorrow of the Greeks is exactly balanced by the joy and advantage of the Latins. But in the miserable account of war the gain is never equivalent to the loss, the pleasure to the pain; the smiles of the Latins were transient and fallacious; the Greeks for ever wept over the ruins of their country, and their real calamities were aggravated by sacrilege and mockery. What benefits accrued to the conquerors from the three fires which annihilated so vast a portion of the buildings and riches of the city? What a stock of such things as could neither be used nor transported was maliciously or wantonly destroyed! How much treasure was idly wasted in gaming, debauchery, and riot! And what precious objects were bartered for a vile price by the impatience or ignorance of the soldiers, whose reward was stolen by the base industry of the last of the Greeks! These alone who had nothing to lose might derive some profit from the revolution; but the misery of the upper ranks of society is strongly painted in the personal adventures of Nicetas himself. His stately palace had been reduced to ashes in the second conflagration; and the senator, with his family and friends, found an obscure shelter in another house which he possessed near the church of St. Sophia. It was the door of this mean habitation that his friend the Venetian merchant guarded, in the disguise of a soldier, till Nicetas could save by a precipitate flight the relics of his fortune and the chastity of his daughter. In a cold wintry season these fugitives, nursed in the lap of prosperity, departed on foot; his wife was with child; the desertion of their slaves compelled them to carry their baggage on their own shoulders; and their women,

whom they placed in the centre, were exhorte to conceal their beauty with dirt, instead c adorning it with paint and jewels. Every ste was less painful than the taunts of the plebeians with whom they were now levelled; nor did th exiles breathe in safety till their mournful pil grimage was concluded at Selymbria, abov forty miles from the capital. On the way the overtook the patriarch, without attendance an almost without apparel, riding on an ass, an reduced to a state of apostolical poverty, which had it been voluntary, might perhaps have bee meritorious. In the meanwhile his desolat churches were profaned by the licentiousnes and party zeal of the Latins. After stripping th gems and pearls, they converted the chalice into drinking-cups; their tables, on which the gamed and feasted, were covered with the pic tures of Christ and the saints; and they trample under foot the most venerable objects of th Christian worship. In the cathedral of St. So phia the ample veil of the sanctuary was ren asunder for the sake of the golden fringe; an the altar, a monument of art and riches, wa broken in pieces and shared among the captors Their mules and horses were laden with th wrought silver and gilt carvings which the tore down from the doors and pulpit; and if th beasts stumbled under the burden, they wer stabbed by their impatient drivers, and th holy pavement streamed with their impur blood. A prostitute was seated on the throne o the patriarch; and that daughter of Belial, a she is styled, sung and danced in the church t ridicule the hymns and processions of the Ori entals. Nor were the repositories of the roya dead secure from violation: in the church of th Apostles the tombs of the emperors were rifled and it is said that after six centuries the corps of Justinian was found without any signs of de cay or putrefaction. In the streets the Frencl and Flemings clothed themselves and thei horses in painted robes and flowing head dresses of linen; and the coarse intemperance o their feasts[92] insulted the splendid sobriety of th East. To expose the arms of a people of scribe and scholars, they affected to display a pen, a inkhorn, and a sheet of paper, without discern ing that the instruments of science and valou were *alike* feeble and useless in the hands of th modern Greeks.

Their reputation and their language encour aged them, however, to despise the ignoranc and to overlook the progress of the Latins.[93] I the love of the arts the national difference wa still more obvious and real; the Greeks pre

served with reverence the works of their ancestors, which they could not imitate; and, in
the destruction of the statues of Constantinople,
we are provoked to join in the complaints and
invectives of the Byzantine historian.[94] We have
seen how the rising city was adorned by the
vanity and despotism of the Imperial founder:
in the ruins of paganism some gods and heroes
were saved from the axe of superstition; and
the forum and hippodrome were dignified with
the relics of a better age. Several of these
are described by Nicetas[95] in a florid and affected style; and from his descriptions I shall
select some interesting particulars. 1. The victorious charioteers were cast in bronze, at their
own, or the public, charge, and fitly placed in
the hippodrome: they stood aloft in their chariots wheeling round the goal: the spectators
could admire their attitude and judge of the resemblance; and of these figures, the most perfect might have been transported from the
Olympic stadium. 2. The sphinx, river-horse,
and crocodile, denote the climate and manufacture of Egypt and the spoils of that ancient
province. 3. The she-wolf suckling Romulus
and Remus, a subject alike pleasing to the *old*
and the *new* Romans, but which could rarely be
treated before the decline of the Greek sculpture. 4. An eagle holding and tearing a serpent
in his talons—a domestic monument of the
Byzantines, which they ascribed, not to a human artist, but to the magic power of the philosopher Apollonius, who, by this talisman, delivered the city from such venomous reptiles.
5. An ass and his driver, which were erected by
Augustus in his colony of Nicopolis, to commemorate a verbal omen of the victory of Actium. 6. An equestrian statue, which passed in
the vulgar opinion for Joshua, the Jewish conqueror, stretching out his hand to stop the
course of the descending sun. A more classical
tradition recognised the figures of Bellerophon
and Pegasus, and the free attitude of the steed
seemed to mark that he trod on air rather than
on the earth. 7. A square and lofty obelisk of
brass; the sides were embossed with a variety of
picturesque and rural scenes: birds singing,
rustics labouring or playing on their pipes,
sheep bleating, lambs skipping, the sea, and a
scene of fish and fishing, little naked Cupids
laughing, playing, and pelting each other with
apples, and on the summit a female figure
turning with the slightest breath, and thence
denominated *the wind's attendant*. 8. The Phrygian shepherd presenting to Venus the prize of
beauty, the apple of discord. 9. The incom-

parable statue of Helen, which is delineated by
Nicetas in the words of admiration and love:
her well-turned feet, snowy arms, rosy lips, be-
witching smiles, swimming eyes, arched eyebrows, the harmony of her shape, the lightness
of her drapery, and her flowing locks that
waved in the wind—a beauty that might have
moved her barbarian destroyers to pity and remorse. 10. The manly, or divine, form of Hercules,[96] as he was restored to life by the master-
hand of Lysippus, of such magnitude that his
thumb was equal to the waist, his leg to the
stature, of a common man:[97] his chest ample,
his shoulders broad, his limbs strong and mus-
cular, his hair curled, his aspect commanding.
Without his bow, or quiver, or club, his lion's
skin carelessly thrown over him, he was seated
on an osier basket, his right leg and arm stretched
to the utmost, his left knee bent and supporting
his elbow, his head reclining on his left hand,
his countenance indignant and pensive. 11. A
colossal statue of Juno, which had once adorned
her temple of Samos; the enormous head by
four yoke of oxen was laboriously drawn to the
palace. 12. Another colossus, of Pallas or Minerva, thirty feet in height, and representing
with admirable spirit the attributes and character of the martial maid. Before we accuse the
Latins, it is just to remark that this Pallas was
destroyed after the first siege by the fear and
superstition of the Greeks themselves.[98] The
other statues of brass which I have enumerated
were broken and melted by the unfeeling avarice of the crusaders: the cost and labour were
consumed in a moment; the soul of genius
evaporated in smoke, and the remnant of base
metal was coined into money for the payment
of the troops. Bronze is not the most durable of
monuments: from the marble forms of Phidias
and Praxiteles the Latins might turn aside with
stupid contempt;[99] but unless they were crushed
by some accidental injury, those useless stones
stood secure on their pedestals.[100] The most enlightened of the strangers, above the gross and
sensual pursuits of their countrymen, more
piously exercised the right of conquest in the
search and seizure of the relics of the saints.[101]
Immense was the supply of heads and bones,
crosses and images, that were scattered by this
revolution over the churches of Europe; and
such was the increase of pilgrimage and oblation, that no branch, perhaps, was more lucrative
plunder was imported from the East.[102] Of the
writings of antiquity many that still existed in
the twelfth century are now lost. But the pilgrims were not solicitous to save or transport

the volumes of an unknown tongue: the perishable substance of paper or parchment can only be preserved by the multiplicity of copies; the literature of the Greeks had almost centered in the metropolis; and, without computing the extent of our loss, we may drop a tear over the libraries that have perished in the triple fire of Constantinople.[103]

CHAPTER LXI

Partition of the Empire by the French and Venetians. Five Latin Emperors of the Houses of Flanders and Courtenay. Their Wars against the Bulgarians and Greeks. Weakness and Poverty of the Latin Empire. Recovery of Constantinople by the Greeks. General Consequences of the Crusades.

AFTER the death of the lawful princes, the French and Venetians, confident of justice and victory, agreed to divide and regulate their future possessions.[1] It was stipulated by treaty that twelve electors, six of either nation, should be nominated; that a majority should choose the emperor of the East; and that, if the votes were equal, the decision of chance should ascertain the successful candidate. To him, with all the titles and prerogatives of the Byzantine throne, they assigned the two palaces of Boucoleon and Blachernæ, with a fourth part of the Greek monarchy. It was defined that the three remaining portions should be equally shared between the republic of Venice and the barons of France; that each feudatory, with an honourable exception for the doge, should acknowledge and perform the duties of homage and military service to the supreme head of the empire; that the nation which gave an emperor should resign to their brethren the choice of a patriarch; and that the pilgrims, whatever might be their impatience to visit the Holy Land, should devote another year to the conquest and defence of the Greek provinces. After the conquest of Constantinople by the Latins, the treaty was confirmed and executed; and the first and most important step was the creation of an emperor. The six electors of the French nation were all ecclesiastics, the abbot of Loces, the archbishop elect of Acre in Palestine, and the bishops of Troyes, Soissons, Halberstadt, and Bethlehem, the last of whom exercised in the camp the office of pope's legate: their profession and knowledge were respectable; and as *they* could not be the objects, they were best qualified to be the authors, of the choice. The six Venetians were the principal servants of the state, and in this list the noble families of Querini and Contarini are still proud to discover their ancestors.

The twelve assembled in the chapel of the palace; and after the solemn invocation of the Holy Ghost, they proceeded to deliberate and vote. A just impulse of respect and gratitude prompted them to crown the virtues of the doge: his wisdom had inspired their enterprise; and the most youthful knights might envy and applaud the exploits of blindness and age. But the patriot Dandolo was devoid of all personal ambition, and fully satisfied that he had been judged worthy to reign. His nomination was overruled by the Venetians themselves: his countrymen, and perhaps his friends,[2] represented, with the eloquence of truth, the mischiefs that might arise to national freedom and the common cause from the union of two incompatible characters, of the first magistrate of a republic and the emperor of the East. The exclusion of the doge left room for the more equal merits of Boniface and Baldwin; and at their names all meaner candidates respectfully withdrew. The marquis of Montferrat was recommended by his mature age and fair reputation, by the choice of the adventurers, and the wishes of the Greeks; nor can I believe that Venice, the mistress of the sea, could be seriously apprehensive of a petty lord at the foot of the Alps.[3] But the count of Flanders was the chief of a wealthy and warlike people; he was valiant, pious, and chaste; in the prime of life, since he was only thirty-two years of age; a descendant of Charlemagne, a cousin of the king of France, and a compeer of the prelates and barons who had yielded with reluctance to the command of a foreigner. Without the chapel, these barons, with the doge and marquis at their head, expected the decision of the twelve electors. It was announced by the bishop of Soissons, in the name of his colleagues: "Ye have sworn to obey the prince whom we should choose: by our unanimous suffrage, Baldwin ount of Flanders and Hainault is now your sovereign, and the emperor of the East." He was saluted with loud applause, and the proclamation was re-echoed through the city by the joy of the Latins and the trembling adulation of the Greeks. Boniface was the first to kiss the hand of his rival, and to raise him on the buckler; and Baldwin was transported to the cathedral, and solemnly invested with the purple buskins. At the end of three weeks he was crowned by the legate, in the vacancy of a patriarch; but the Venetian clergy soon filled the chapter of St. Sophia, seated Thomas Morosini on the ecclesiastical throne, and employed every art to perpetuate in their own nation the honours and benefices of the Greek church.[4] Without delay the successor of Constantine instructed Palestine, France, and Rome, of this memorable revolution. To Palestine he sent, as a trophy, the gates of Constantinople, and the chain of the harbour;[5] and adopted, from the Assise of Jerusalem, the laws or customs best adapted to a French colony and conquest in the East. In his epistles the natives of France are encouraged to swell that colony, and to secure that conquest, to people a magnificent city and a fertile land, which will reward the labours both of the priest and the soldier. He congratulates the Roman pontiff on the restoration of his authority in the East; invites him to extinguish the Greek schism by his presence in a general council; and implores his blessing and forgiveness for the disobedient pilgrims. Prudence and dignity are blended in the answer of Innocent.[6] In the subversion of the Byzantine empire, he arraigns the vices of man, and adores the providence of God: the conquerors will be absolved or condemned by their future conduct; the validity of their treaty depends on the judgment of St. Peter; but he inculcates their most sacred duty of establishing a just subordination of obedience and tribute, from the Greeks to the Latins, from the magistrates to the clergy, and from the clergy to the pope.

In the division of the Greek provinces[7] the share of the Venetians was more ample than that of the Latin emperor. No more than one fourth was appropriated to his domain; a clear moiety of the remainder was reserved for Venice; and the other moiety was distributed among the adventurers of France and Lombardy. The venerable Dandolo was proclaimed despot of Romania, and invested after the Greek fashion with the purple buskins. He ended at Constantinople his long and glorious life; and if the prerogative was personal, the title was used by his successors till the middle of the fourteenth century, with the singular, though true, addition of lords of one fourth and a half of the Roman empire.[8] The doge, a slave of state, was seldom permitted to depart from the helm of the republic; but his place was supplied by the *bail*, or regent, who exercised a supreme jurisdiction over the colony of Venetians: they possessed three of the eight quarters of the city; and his independent tribunal was composed of six judges, four counsellors, two chamberlains, two fiscal advocates, and a constable. The long experience of the Eastern trade enabled them to select their portion with discernment: they had rashly accepted the dominion and defence of Adrianople; but it was the more reasonable aim of their policy to form a chain of factories, and cities, and islands, along the maritime coast, from the neighbourhood of Ragusa to the Hellespont and the Bosphorus. The labour and cost of such extensive conquests exhausted their treasury: they abandoned the maxims of government, adopted a feudal system, and contented themselves with the homage of their nobles[9] for the possessions which these private vassals undertook to reduce and maintain. And thus it was that the family of Sanut acquired the duchy of Naxos, which involved the greatest part of the archipelago. For the price of ten thousand marks the republic purchased of the marquis of Montferrat the fertile island of Crete or Candia with the ruins of a hundred cities;[10] but its improvement was stinted by the proud and narrow spirit of an aristocracy;[11] and the wisest senators would confess that the sea, not the land, was the treasury of St. Mark. In the moiety of the adventurers the marquis Boniface might claim the most liberal reward; and, besides the isle of Crete, his exclusion from the throne was compensated by the royal title and the provinces beyond the Hellespont. But he prudently exchanged that distant and difficult conquest for the kingdom of Thessalonica or Macedonia, twelve days' journey from the capital, where he might be supported by the neighbouring powers of his brother-in-law the king of Hungary. His progress was hailed by the voluntary or reluctant acclamations of the natives; and Greece, the proper and ancient Greece, again received a Latin conqueror,[12] who trod with indifference that classic ground. He viewed with a careless eye the beauties of the valley of Tempe; traversed with a cautious step the straits of Thermopylæ; occupied the unknown cities of Thebes, Athens, and Argos; and assaulted the fortifications of Corinth and Napoli,[13] which resisted his arms. The lots of the Latin pilgrims were regulated by chance, or choice, or subsequent exchange; and they abused, with intemperate joy, their triumph over the lives and fortunes of a great people. After a minute survey of the provinces, they weighed in the scales of avarice the revenue of each district, the advantage of the situation, and the ample or scanty supplies for the maintenance of soldiers and horses. Their presumption claimed and divided the long-lost dependencies of the Roman sceptre: the Nile and Euphrates rolled through their imaginary realms; and happy was the warrior who drew for his prize the palace of the Turkish sultan of Iconium.[14] I shall not descend to the pedigree of families and the rent-roll of estates, but I wish to specify that the counts of Blois and St. Pol were invested with the duchy of Nice and the lordship of Demotica:[15] the principal fiefs were held by the service of constable, chamberlain, cup-bearer, butler, and chief cook; and our historian, Jeffrey of Villehardouin, obtained a fair establishment on the banks of the Hebrus, and united the double office of marshal of Champagne and Romania. At the head of his knights and archers each baron mounted on horseback to secure the possession of his share, and their first efforts were generally successful. But the public force was weakened by their dispersion; and a thousand quarrels must arise under a law, and among men, whose sole umpire was the sword. Within three months after the conquest of Constantinople, the emperor and the king of Thessalonica drew their hostile followers into the field: they were reconciled by the authority of the doge, the advice of the marshal, and the firm freedom of their peers.[16]

Two fugitives, who had reigned at Constantinople, still asserted the title of emperor; and the subjects of their fallen throne might be moved to pity by the misfortunes of the elder Alexius, or excited to revenge by the spirit of Mourzoufle. A domestic alliance, a common interest, a similar guilt, and the merit of extinguishing his enemies, a brother and a nephew, induced the more recent usurper to unite with the former the relics of his power. Mourzoufle was received with smiles and honours in the camp of his father Alexius; but the wicked can never love, and should rarely trust, their fellow criminals: he was seized in the bath, deprived of his eyes, stripped of his troops and treasures, and

turned out to wander an object of horror and contempt to those who with more propriety could hate, and with more justice could punish, the assassin of the emperor Isaac and his son. As the tyrant, pursued by fear or remorse, was stealing over to Asia, he was seized by the Latins of Constantinople, and condemned, after an open trial, to an ignominious death. His judges debated the mode of execution, the axe, the wheel, or the stake; and it was resolved that Mourzoufle[17] should ascend the Theodosian column, a pillar of white marble of one hundred and forty-seven feet in height.[18] From the summit he was cast down headlong and dashed in pieces on the pavement, in the presence of innumerable spectators, who filled the forum of Taurus, and admired the accomplishment of an old prediction, which was explained by this singular event.[19] The fate of Alexius is less tragical: he was sent by the marquis a captive to Italy, and a gift to the king of the Romans; but he had not much to applaud his fortune if the sentence of imprisonment and exile were changed from a fortress in the Alps to a monastery in Asia. But his daughter, before the national calamity, had been given in marriage to a young hero, who continued the succession, and restored the throne, of the Greek princes.[20] The valour of Theodore Lascaris was signalised in the two sieges of Constantinople. After the flight of Mourzoufle, when the Latins were already in the city, he offered himself as their emperor to the soldiers and people; and his ambition, which might be virtuous, was undoubtedly brave. Could he have infused a soul into the multitude, they might have crushed the strangers under their feet: their abject despair refused his aid; and Theodore retired to breathe the air of freedom in Anatolia, beyond the immediate view and pursuit of the conquerors. Under the title, at first of despot, and afterwards of emperor, he drew to his standard the bolder spirits, who were fortified against slavery by the contempt of life; and, as every means was lawful for the public safety, implored without scruple the alliance of the Turkish sultan. Nice, where Theodore established his residence, Prusa and Philadelphia, Smyrna and Ephesus, opened their gates to their deliverer: he derived strength and reputation from his victories, and even from his defeats; and the successor of Constantine preserved a fragment of the empire from the banks of the Mæander to the suburbs of Nicomedia, and at length of Constantinople. Another portion, distant and obscure, was possessed by the lineal heir of the

Comneni, a son of the virtuous Manuel, a grandson of the tyrant Andronicus. His name was Alexius; and the epithet of great was applied perhaps to his stature, rather than to his exploits. By the indulgence of the Angeli, he was appointed governor or duke of Trebizond:[21] his birth gave him ambition, the revolution independence; and without changing his title, he reigned in peace from Sinope to the Phasis, along the coast of the Black Sea. His nameless son and successor is described as the vassal of the sultan, whom he served with two hundred lances: that Comnenian prince was no more than duke of Trebizond, and the title of emperor was first assumed by the pride and envy of the grandsom of Alexius. In the West a third fragment was saved from the common shipwreck by Michael, a bastard of the house of Angeli, who, before the revolution, had been known as an hostage, a soldier, and a rebel. His flight from the camp of the marquis Boniface secured his freedom; by his marriage with the governor's daughter he commanded the important place of Durazzo, assumed the title of despot, and founded a strong and conspicuous principality in Epirus, Ætolia, and Thessaly, which have ever been peopled by a warlike race. The Greeks, who had offered their service to their new sovereigns, were excluded by the haughty Latins[22] from all civil and military honours, as a nation born to tremble and obey. Their resentment prompted them to show that they might have been useful friends, since they could be dangerous enemies: their nerves were braced by adversity: whatever was learned or holy, whatever was noble or valiant, rolled away into the independent states of Trebizond, Epirus, and Nice; and a single patrician is marked by the ambiguous praise of attachment and loyalty to the Franks. The vulgar herd of the cities and the country would have gladly submitted to a mild and regular servitude; and the transient disorders of war would have been obliterated by some years of industry and peace. But peace was banished, and industry was crushed, in the disorders of the feudal system. The *Roman* emperors of Constantinople, if they were endowed with abilities, were armed with power for the protection of their subjects: their laws were wise, and their administration was simple. The Latin throne was filled by a titular prince, the chief, and often the servant, of his licentious confederates: the fiefs of the empire, from a kingdom to a castle, were held and ruled by the sword of the barons; and their discord, poverty, and ignorance extended the ramifications of tyranny to the most sequestered villages. The Greeks were oppressed by the double weight of the priest, who was invested with temporal power, and of the soldier, who was inflamed by fanatic hatred; and the insuperable bar of religion and language for ever separated the stranger and the native. As long as the crusaders were united at Constantinople, the memory of their conquest, and the terror of their arms, imposed silence on the captive land: their dispersion betrayed the smallness of their numbers and the defects of their discipline; and some failures and mischances revealed the secret that they were not invincible. As the fear of the Greeks abated, their hatred increased. They murmured; they conspired; and before a year of slavery had elapsed, they implored, or accepted, the succour of a barbarian, whose power they had felt, and whose gratitude they trusted.[23]

The Latin conquerors had been saluted with a solemn and early embassy from John, or Joannice, or Calo-John, the revolted chief of the Bulgarians and Wallachians. He deemed himself their brother, as the votary of the Roman pontiff, from whom he had received the regal title and a holy banner; and in the subversion of the Greek monarchy he might aspire to the name of their friend and accomplice. But Calo-John was astonished to find that the count of Flanders had assumed the pomp and pride of the successors of Constantine; and his ambassadors were dismissed with a haughty message, that the rebel must deserve a pardon by touching with his forehead the footstool of the Imperial throne. His resentment[24] would have exhaled in acts of violence and blood; his cooler policy watched the rising discontent of the Greeks, affected a tender concern for their sufferings, and promised that their first struggles for freedom should be supported by his person and kingdom. The conspiracy was propagated by national hatred, the firmest band of association and secrecy; the Greeks were impatient to sheathe their daggers in the breast of the victorious strangers; but the execution was prudently delayed till Henry, the emperor's brother, had transported the flower of his troops beyond the Hellespont. Most of the towns and villages of Thrace were true to the moment and the signal; and the Latins, without arms or suspicion, were slaughtered by the vile and merciless revenge of their slaves. From Demotica, the first scene of the massacre, the surviving vassals of the count of St. Pol escaped to Adrianople, but the French and Venetians, who occupied that city, were slain or expelled by the furious multitude; the garrisons that could effect their retreat fell back on each other towards the metropolis; and the fortresses, that separately stood against the rebels, were ignorant of each other's and of their sovereign's fate. The voice of fame and fear announced the revolt of the Greeks and the rapid approach of their Bulgarian ally; and Calo-John, not depending on the forces of his own kingdom, had drawn from the Scythian wilderness a body of fourteen thousand Comans, who drank, as it was said, the blood of their captives, and sacrificed the Christians on the altars of their gods.[25]

Alarmed by this sudden and growing danger, the emperor despatched a swift messenger to recall Count Henry and his troops; and had Baldwin expected the return of his gallant brother, with a supply of twenty thousand Armenians, he might have encountered the invader with equal numbers and a decisive superiority of arms and discipline. But the spirit of chivalry could seldom discriminate caution from cowardice, and the emperor took the field with a hundred and forty knights, and their train of archers and serjeants. The marshal, who dissuaded and obeyed, led the vanguard in their march to Adrianople; the main body was commanded by the count of Blois; the aged doge of Venice followed with the rear; and their scanty numbers were increased from all sides by the fugitive Latins. They undertook to besiege the rebels of Adrianople; and such was the pious tendency of the crusades, that they employed the holy week in pillaging the country for their subsistence, and in framing engines for the destruction of their fellow-Christians. But the Latins were soon interrupted and alarmed by the light cavalry of the Comans, who boldly skirmished to the edge of their imperfect lines; and a proclamation was issued by the marshal of Romania, that, on the trumpet's sound, the cavalry should mount and form; but that none, under pain of death, should abandon themselves to a desultory and dangerous pursuit. This wise injunction was first disobeyed by the count of Blois, who involved the emperor in his rashness and ruin. The Comans, of the Parthian or Tartar school, fled before their first charge; but after a career of two leagues, when the knights and their horses were almost breathless, they suddenly turned, rallied, and encompassed the heavy squadrons of the Franks. The count was slain on the field, the emperor was made prisoner; and if the one disdained to fly, if the other refused to yield, their personal bravery made a poor atonement for their ignorance or neglect of the duties of a general.[26]

Proud of his victory and his royal prize, the Bulgarian advanced to relieve Adrianople and achieve the destruction of the Latins. They must inevitably have been destroyed if the marshal of Romania had not displayed a cool courage and consummate skill, uncommon in all ages, but most uncommon in those times, when war was a passion rather than a science. His grief and fears were poured into the firm and faithful bosom of the doge; but in the camp he diffused an assurance of safety, which could only be realised by the general belief. All day he maintained his perilous station between the city and the barbarians; Villehardouin decamped in silence at the dead of night, and his masterly retreat of three days would have deserved the praise of Xenophon and the ten thousand. In the rear, the marshal supported the weight of the pursuit; in the front, he moderated the impatience of the fugitives, and wherever the Comans approached they were repelled by a line of impenetrable spears. On the third day the weary troops beheld the sea, the solitary town of Rodosto,[27] and their friends, who had landed from the Asiatic shore. They embraced, they wept; but they united their arms and counsels; and, in his brother's absence, Count Henry assumed the regency of the empire, at once in a state of childhood and caducity.[28] If the Comans withdrew from the summer heats, seven thousand Latins, in the hour of danger, deserted Constantinople, their brethren, and their vows. Some partial success was overbalanced by the loss of one hundred and twenty knights in the field of Rusium; and of the Imperial domain no more was left than the capital, with two or three adjacent fortresses on the shores of Europe and Asia. The king of Bulgaria was resistless and inexorable; and Calo-John respectfully eluded the demands of the pope, who conjured his new proselyte to restore peace and the emperor to the afflicted Latins. The deliverance of Baldwin was no longer, he said, in the power of man: that prince had died in prison, and the manner of his death is variously related by ignorance and credulity. The lovers of a tragic legend will be pleased to hear that the royal captive was tempted by the amorous queen of the Bulgarians; that his chaste refusal exposed him to the falsehood of a woman and the jealousy of a savage; that his hands and feet were severed from his body; that his bleeding trunk was cast among the carcases of dogs and horses; and that he breathed three days before he was devoured by the birds of prey.[29] About twenty years afterwards, in a wood of the Netherlands, a hermit announced himself as the true Baldwin, the emperor of Constantinople, and lawful sovereign of Flanders. He related the wonders of his escape, his adventures, and his penance, among a people prone to believe and to rebel; and, in the first transport, Flanders acknowledged her long-lost sovereign. A short examination before the French court detected the imposter, who was punished with an ignominious death; but the Flemings still adhered to the pleasing error, and the countess Jane is accused by the gravest historians of sacrificing to her ambition the life of an unfortunate father.[30]

In all civilised hostility a treaty is established for the exchange or ransom of prisoners; and if their captivity be prolonged, their condition is known, and they are treated according to their rank with humanity or honour. But the savage Bulgarian was a stranger to the laws of war; his prisons were involved in darkness and silence; and above a year elapsed before the Latins could be assured of the death of Baldwin, before his brother, the regent Henry, would consent to assume the title of emperor. His moderation was applauded by the Greeks as an act of rare and inimitable virtue. Their light and perfidious ambition was eager to seize or anticipate the moment of a vacancy, while a law of succession, the guardian both of the prince and people, was gradually defined and confirmed in the hereditary monarchies of Europe. In the support of the Eastern empire Henry was gradually left without an associate, as the heroes of the crusade retired from the world or from the war. The doge of Venice, the venerable Dandolo, in the fulness of years and glory sunk into the grave. The marquis of Montferrat was slowly recalled from the Peloponnesian war to the revenge of Baldwin and the defence of Thessalonica. Some nice disputes of feudal homage and service were reconciled in a personal interview between the emperor and the king; they were firmly united by mutual esteem and the common danger; and their alliance was sealed by the nuptials of Henry with the daughter of the Italian prince. He soon deplored the loss of his friend and father. At the persuasion of some faithful Greeks, Boniface made a bold and successful inroad among the hills of Rhodope; the Bulgarians fled on his approach; they assembled to harass his retreat. On the intelligence that his rear was attacked, without waiting for any defensive armour, he leaped on horseback, couched his lance, and drove the enemies before him; but in the rash pursuit he was pierced with a mortal wound, and the head of the king of Thessalonica was presented to Calo-John, who enjoyed the honours, without the merit, of victory. It is here, at this melancholy event, that the pen or the voice of Jeffrey of Villehardouin seems to drop or to expire;[31] and if he still exercised his military office of marshal of Romania, his subsequent exploits are buried in oblivion.[32] The character of Henry was not unequal to his arduous situation: in the siege of Constantinople, and beyond the Hellespont, he had deserved the fame of a valiant knight and a skilful commander, and his courage was tempered with a degree of prudence and mildness unknown to his impetuous brother. In the double war against the Greeks of Asia and the Bulgarians of Europe he was ever the foremost on shipboard or on horseback; and though he cautiously provided for the success of his arms, the drooping Latins were often roused by his example to save and to second their fearless emperor. But such efforts, and some supplies of men and money from France, were of less avail than the errors, the cruelty, and death of their most formidable adversary. When the despair of the Greek subjects invited Calo-John as their deliverer, they hoped that he would protect their liberty and adopt their laws; they were soon taught to compare the degrees of national ferocity, and to execrate the savage conqueror, who no longer dissembled his intention of dispeopling Thrace, of demolishing the cities, and of transplanting the inhabitants beyond the Danube. Many towns and villages of Thrace were already evacuated; a heap of ruins marked the place of Philippopolis, and a similar calamity was expected at Demotica and Adrianople by the first authors of the revolt. They raised a cry of grief and repentance to the throne of Henry; the emperor alone had the magnanimity to forgive and trust them. No more than four hundred knights, with their serjeants and archers, could be assembled under his banner; and with this slender force he fought and repulsed the Bulgarian, who, besides his infantry, was at the head of forty thousand horse. In this expedition Henry felt the difference between a hostile and a friendly country; the remaining cities were preserved by his arms, and the savage, with shame and loss, was compelled to relinquish his prey. The siege of Thessalonica was the last of the evils which Calo-John inflicted or suffered; he was stabbed in the night in his tent, and the general, perhaps the assassin, who found him weltering in his blood, ascribed the blow with general applause to the lance of St. Demetrius.[33] After several victories the prudence of Henry concluded an honourable peace with the successor of the tyrant, and with the Greek princes of Nice and Epirus. If he ceded some doubtful limits, an ample kingdom was reserved for himself and his feudatories; and his reign, which lasted only ten years, afforded a short interval of prosperity and peace. Far above the narrow policy of Baldwin and Boniface, he freely intrusted to the Greeks the most important offices of the state and army; and this liberality of sentiment and practice was the more seasonable, as the princes of Nice and Epirus had already learned to seduce and employ the mercenary valour of the Latins. It was the aim of Henry to unite and reward his deserving subjects of every nation and language; but he appeared less solicitous to accomplish the impracticable union of the two churches. Pelagius, the pope's legate, who acted as the sovereign of Constantinople, had interdicted the worship of the Greeks, and sternly imposed the payment of tithes, the double procession of the Holy Ghost, and a blind obedience to the Roman pontiff. As the weaker party, they pleaded the duties of conscience, and implored the rights of toleration: "Our bodies," they said, "are Cæsar's, but our souls belong only to God." The persecution was checked by the firmness of the emperor;[34] and if we can believe that the same prince was poisoned by the Greeks themselves, we must entertain a contemptible idea of the sense and gratitude of mankind. His valour was a vulgar attribute, which he shared with ten thousand knights: but Henry possessed the superior courage to oppose, in a superstitious age, the pride and avarice of the clergy. In the cathedral of St. Sophia he presumed to place his throne on the right hand of the patriarch; and this presumption excited the sharpest censure of pope Innocent the Third. By a salutary edict, one of the first examples of the laws of mortmain, he prohibited the alienation of fiefs; many of the Latins, desirous of returning to Europe, resigned their estates to the church for a spiritual or temporal reward; these holy lands were immediately discharged from military service, and a colony of soldiers would have been gradually transformed into a college of priests.[35]

The virtuous Henry died at Thessalonica in the defence of that kingdom, and of an infant, the son of his friend Boniface. In the two first emperors of Constantinople the male line of the counts of Flanders was extinct. But their sister Yolande was the wife of a French prince, the mother of a numerous progeny; and one of her daughters had married Andrew king of Hungary, a brave and pious champion of the cross. By seating him on the Byzantine throne, the barons of Romania would have acquired the forces of a neighbouring and warlike kingdom; but the prudent Andrew revered the laws of succession; and the princess Yolande, with her husband Peter of Courtenay, count of Auxerre, was invited by the Latins to assume the empire of the East. The royal birth of his father, the noble origin of his mother, recommended to the barons of France the first-cousin of their king. His reputation was fair, his possessions were ample, and, in the bloody crusade against the Albigeois, the soldiers and priests had been abundantly satisfied of his zeal and valour. Vanity might applaud the elevation of a French emperor of Constantinople; but prudence must pity, rather than envy, his treacherous and imaginary greatness. To assert and adorn his title, he was reduced to sell or mortgage the best of his patrimony. By these expedients, the liberality of his royal kinsman Philip Augustus, and the national spirit of chivalry, he was enabled to pass the Alps at the head of one hundred and forty knights, and five thousand five hundred serjeants and archers. After some hesitation, pope Honorius the Third was persuaded to crown the successor of Constantine: but he performed the ceremony in a church without the walls, lest he should seem to imply or to bestow any right of sovereignty over the ancient capital of the empire. The Venetians had engaged to transport Peter and his forces beyond the Adriatic, and the empress, with her four children, to the Byzantine palace; but they required, as the price of their service, that he should recover Durazzo from the despot of Epirus. Michael Angelus, or Comnenus, the first of his dynasty, had bequeathed the succession of his power and ambition to Theodore, his legitimate brother, who already threatened and invaded the establishments of the Latins. After discharging his debt by a fruitless assault, the emperor raised the siege to prosecute a long and perilous journey over land from Durazzo to Thessalonica. He was soon lost in the mountains of Epirus: the passes were fortified; his provisions exhausted; he was delayed and deceived by a treacherous negotiation; and, after Peter of Courtenay and the Roman legate had been arrested in a banquet, the French troops, without leaders or hopes, were eager to exchange their arms for the delusive promise of mercy and bread. The Vatican thundered; and the impious Theodore was threatened with the vengeance of earth and heaven; but the captive emperor and his soldiers were forgotten, and the reproaches of the pope are confined to the imprisonment of his legate. No sooner was he satisfied by the deliverance of the priest and a promise of spiritual obedience, than he pardoned and protected the despot of Epirus. His peremptory commands suspended the ardour of the Venetians and the king of Hungary; and it was only by a natural or untimely death[36] that Peter of Courtenay was released from his hopeless captivity.[37]

The long ignorance of his fate, and the presence of the lawful sovereign, of Yolande, his wife or widow, delayed the proclamation of a new emperor. Before her death, and in the midst of her grief, she was delivered of a son, who was named Baldwin, the last and most unfortunate of the Latin princes of Constantinople. His birth endeared him to the barons of Romania; but his childhood would have prolonged the troubles of a minority, and his claims were superseded by the elder claims of his brethren. The first of these, Philip of Courtenay, who derived from his mother the inheritance of Namur, had the wisdom to prefer the substance of a marquisate to the shadow of an empire; and on his refusal, Robert, the second of the sons of Peter and Yolande, was called to the throne of Constantinople. Warned by his father's mischance, he pursued his slow and secure journey through Germany and along the Danube: a passage was opened by his sister's marriage with the king of Hungary; and the emperor Robert was crowned by the patriarch in the cathedral of St. Sophia. But his reign was an era of calamity and disgrace; and the colony, as it was styled, of NEW FRANCE yielded on all sides to the Greeks of Nice and Epirus. After a victory, which he owed to his perfidy rather than his courage, Theodore Angelus entered the kingdom of Thessalonica; expelled the feeble Demetrius, the son of the marquis Boniface; erected his standard on the walls of Adrianople; and added, by his vanity, a third or a fourth name to the list of rival emperors. The relics of the Asiatic province were swept away by John Vataces, the son-in-law and successor of Theodore Lascaris, and who, in a triumphant reign of thirty-three years, displayed the virtues both of peace and war. Under his discipline, the swords of the French mercenaries were the most

effectual instrument of his conquests, and their desertion from the service of their country was at once a symptom and a cause of the rising ascendant of the Greeks. By the construction of a fleet he obtained the command of the Hellespont, reduced the islands of Lesbos and Rhodes, attacked the Venetians of Candia, and intercepted the rare and parsimonious succours of the West. Once, and once only, the Latin emperor sent an army against Vataces; and in the defeat of that army, the veteran knights, the last of the original conquerors, were left on the field of battle. But the success of a foreign enemy was less painful to the pusillanimous Robert than the insolence of his Latin subjects, who confounded the weakness of the emperor and of the empire. His personal misfortunes will prove the anarchy of the government and the ferociousness of the times. The amorous youth had neglected his Greek bride, the daughter of Vataces, to introduce into the palace a beautiful maid, of a private, though noble, family of Artois; and her mother had been tempted by the lustre of the purple to forfeit her engagements with a gentleman of Burgundy. His love was converted into rage; he assembled his friends, forced the palace gates, threw the mother into the sea, and inhumanly cut off the nose and lips of the wife or concubine of the emperor. Instead of punishing the offender, the barons avowed and applauded the savage deed,[38] which, as a prince and as a man, it was impossible that Robert should forgive. He escaped from the guilty city to implore the justice or compassion of the pope: the emperor was coolly exhorted to return to his station; before he could obey, he sunk under the weight of grief, shame, and impotent resentment.[39]

It was only in the age of chivalry that valour could ascend from a private station to the thrones of Jerusalem and Constantinople. The titular kingdom of Jerusalem had devolved to Mary, the daughter of Isabella and Conrad of Montferrat, and the grand-daughter of Almeric or Amaury. She was given to John of Brienne, of a noble family in Champagne, by the public voice, and the judgment of Philip Augustus, who named him as the most worthy champion of the Holy Land.[40] In the fifth crusade he led a hundred thousand Latins to the conquest of Egypt: by him the siege of Damietta was achieved; and the subsequent failure was justly ascribed to the pride and avarice of the legate. After the marriage of his daughter with Frederic the Second[41] he was provoked by the emperor's ingratitude to accept the command of the army of the church; and though advanced in life, and despoiled of royalty, the sword and spirit of John of Brienne were still ready for the service of Christendom. In the seven years of his brother's reign, Baldwin of Courtenay had not emerged from a state of childhood, and the barons of Romania felt the strong necessity of placing the sceptre in the hands of a man and a hero. The veteran king of Jerusalem might have disdained the name and office of regent; they agreed to invest him for his life with the title and prerogatives of emperor, on the sole condition that Baldwin should marry his second daughter, and succeed at a mature age to the throne of Constantinople. The expectation, both of the Greeks and Latins, was kindled by the renown, the choice, and the presence of John of Brienne; and they admired his martial aspect, his green and vigorous age of more than fourscore years, and his size and stature, which surpassed the common measure of mankind.[42] But avarice, and the love of ease, appear to have chilled the ardour of enterprise: his troops were disbanded, and two years rolled away without action or honour, till he was awakened by the dangerous alliance of Vataces emperor of Nice, and of Azan king of Bulgaria. They besieged Constantinople by sea and land, with an army of one hundred thousand men, and a fleet of three hundred ships of war; while the entire force of the Latin emperor was reduced to one hundred and sixty knights, and a small addition of serjeants and archers. I tremble to relate, that, instead of defending the city, the hero made a sally at the head of his cavalry; and that, of forty-eight squadrons of the enemy, no more than three escaped from the edge of his invincible sword. Fired by his example, the infantry and the citizens boarded the vessels that anchored close to the walls; and twenty-five were dragged in triumph into the harbour of Constantinople. At the summons of the emperor, the vassals and allies armed in her defence; broke through every obstacle that opposed their passage; and, in the succeeding year, obtained a second victory over the same enemies. By the rude poets of the age John of Brienne is compared to Hector, Roland, and Judas Maccabæus:[43] but their credit, and his glory, receives some abatement from the silence of the Greeks. The empire was soon deprived of the last of her champions; and the dying monarch was ambitious to enter paradise in the habit of a Franciscan friar.[44]

In the double victory of John of Brienne I cannot discover the name or exploits of his pupil Baldwin, who had attained the age of military service, and who succeeded to the imperial dignity on the decease of his adoptive father.[45] The royal youth was employed on a commission more suitable to his temper; he was sent to visit the Western courts, of the pope more especially, and of the king of France; to excite their pity by the view of his innocence and distress; and to obtain some supplies of men or money for the relief of the sinking empire. He thrice repeated these mendicant visits, in which he seemed to prolong his stay, and postpone his return; of the five-and-twenty years of his reign, a greater number were spent abroad than at home; and in no place did the emperor deem himself less free and secure than in his native country and his capital. On some public occasions, his vanity might be soothed by the title of Augustus, and by the honours of the purple; and at the general council of Lyons, when Frederic the Second was excommunicated and deposed, his Oriental colleague was enthroned on the right hand of the pope. But how often was the exile, the vagrant, the Imperial beggar, humbled with scorn, insulted with pity, and degraded in his own eyes and those of the nations! In his first visit to England he was stopped at Dover by a severe reprimand, that he should presume, without leave, to enter an independent kingdom. After some delay, Baldwin, however, was permitted to pursue his journey, was entertained with cold civility, and thankfully departed with a present of seven hundred marks.[46] From the avarice of Rome he could only obtain the proclamation of a crusade, and a treasure of indulgences: a coin whose currency was depreciated by too frequent and indiscriminate abuse. His birth and misfortunes recommended him to the generosity of his cousin Louis the Ninth; but the martial zeal of the saint was diverted from Constantinople to Egypt and Palestine; and the public and private poverty of Baldwin was alleviated, for a moment, by the alienation of the marquisate of Namur and the lordship of Courtenay, the last remains of his inheritance.[47] By such shameful or ruinous expedients he once more returned to Romania, with an army of thirty thousand soldiers, whose numbers were doubled in the apprehension of the Greeks. His first despatches to France and England announced his victories and his hopes: he had reduced the country round the capital to the distance of three days' journey; and if he succeeded against an important, though nameless, city (most probably Chiorli), the frontier would be safe and the passage accessible. But these expectations (if Baldwin was sincere) quickly vanished like a dream: the troops and treasures of France melted away in his unskilful hands: and the throne of the Latin emperor was protected by a dishonourable alliance with the Turks and Comans. To secure the former, he consented to bestow his niece on the unbelieving sultan of Cogni; to please the latter he complied with their pagan rites; a dog was sacrificed between the two armies; and the contracting parties tasted each other's blood, as a pledge of their fidelity.[48] In the palace, or prison, of Constantinople, the successor of Augustus demolished the vacant houses for winter-fuel, and stripped the lead from the churches for the daily expense of his family. Some usurious loans were dealt with a scanty hand by the merchants of Italy; and Philip, his son and heir, was pawned at Venice as the security for a debt.[49] Thirst, hunger, and nakedness are positive evils: but wealth is relative; and a prince, who would be rich in a private station, may be exposed by the increase of his wants to all the anxiety and bitterness of poverty.

But in this abject distress the emperor and empire were still possessed of an ideal treasure, which drew its fantastic value from the superstition of the Christian world. The merit of the true cross was somewhat impaired by its frequent division; and a long captivity among the infidels might shed some suspicion on the fragments that were produced in the East and West. But another relic of the Passion was preserved in the Imperial chapel of Constantinople; and the crown of thorns which had been placed on the head of Christ was equally precious and authentic. It had formerly been the practice of the Egyptian debtors to deposit, as a security, the mummies of their parents; and both their honour and religion were bound for the redemption of the pledge. In the same manner, and in the absence of the emperor, the barons of Romania borrowed the sum of thirteen thousand one hundred and thirty-four pieces of gold[50] on the credit of the holy crown: they failed in the performance of their contract; and a rich Venetian, Nicholas Querini, undertook to satisfy their impatient creditors, on condition that the relic should be lodged at Venice, to become his absolute property if it were not redeemed within a short and definite term. The barons apprised their sovereign of the hard treaty and impending loss; and as the empire could not afford a ransom of seven thousand pounds sterling, Baldwin was anxious to snatch the prize from the Venetians, and to vest it

with more honour and emolument in the hands of the most Christian king.[51] Yet the negotiation was attended with some delicacy. In the purchase of relics the saint would have started at the guilt of simony; but if the mode of expression were changed, he might lawfully repay the debt, accept the gift, and acknowledge the obligation. His ambassadors, two Dominicans, were despatched to Venice to redeem and receive the holy crown, which had escaped the dangers of the sea and the galleys of Vataces. On opening a wooden box they recognised the seals of the doge and barons, which were applied on a shrine of silver; and within this shrine the monument of the Passion was enclosed in a golden vase. The reluctant Venetians yielded to justice and power; the emperor Frederic granted a free and honourable passage; the court of France advanced as far as Troyes in Champagne to meet with devotion this inestimable relic: it was borne in triumph through Paris by the king himself, barefoot, and in his shirt; and a free gift of ten thousand marks of silver reconciled Baldwin to his loss. The success of this transaction tempted the Latin emperor to offer with the same generosity the remaining furniture of his chapel;[52] a large and authentic portion of the true cross; the baby-linen of the Son of God; the lance, the sponge, and the chain of his Passion; the rod of Moses; and part of the skull of St. John the Baptist. For the reception of these spiritual treasures twenty thousand marks were expended by St. Louis on a stately foundation, the holy chapel of Paris, on which the muse of Boileau has bestowed a comic immortality. The truth of such remote and ancient relics, which cannot be proved by any human testimony, must be admitted by those who believe in the miracles which they have performed. About the middle of the last age, an inveterate ulcer was touched and cured by a holy prickle of the holy crown:[53] the prodigy is attested by the most pious and enlightened Christians of France; nor will the fact be easily disproved, except by those who are armed with a general antidote against religious credulity.[54]

The Latins of Constantinople[55] were on all sides encompassed and pressed: their sole hope, the last delay of their ruin, was in the division of their Greek and Bulgarian enemies; and of this hope they were deprived by the superior arms and policy of Vataces emperor of Nice. From the Propontis to the rocky coast of Pamphylia, Asia was peaceful and prosperous under his reign; and the events of every campaign extended his influence in Europe. The strong cities of the hills of Macedonia and Thrace were rescued from the Bulgarians, and their kingdom was circumscribed by its present and proper limits along the southern banks of the Danube. The sole emperor of the Romans could no longer brook that a lord of Epirus, a Comnenian prince of the West, should presume to dispute or share the honours of the purple; and the humble Demetrius changed the colour of his buskins, and accepted with gratitude the appellation of despot. His own subjects were exasperated by his baseness and incapacity; they implored the protection of their supreme lord. After some resistance, the kingdom of Thessalonica was united to the empire of Nice; and Vataces reigned without a competitor from the Turkish borders to the Adriatic gulf. The princes of Europe revered his merit and power; and had he subscribed an orthodox creed, it should seem that the pope would have abandoned without reluctance the Latin throne of Constantinople. But the death of Vataces, the short and busy reign of Theodore his son, and the helpless infancy of his grandson John, suspended the restoration of the Greeks. In the next chapter I shall explain their domestic revolutions; in this place it will be sufficient to observe that the young prince was oppressed by the ambition of his guardian and colleague Michael Palæologus, who displayed the virtues and vices that belong to the founder of a new dynasty. The emperor Baldwin had flattered himself that he might recover some provinces or cities by an impotent negotiation. His ambassadors were dismissed from Nice with mockery and contempt. At every place which they named Palæologus alleged some special reason which rendered it dear and valuable in his eyes: in the one he was born; in another he had been first promoted to military command; and in a third he had enjoyed, and hoped long to enjoy, the pleasures of the chase. "And what then do you propose to give us?" said the astonished deputies. "Nothing," replied the Greek; "not a foot of land. If your master be desirous of peace, let him pay me, as an annual tribute, the sum which he receives from the trade and customs of Constantinople. On these terms I may allow him to reign. If he refuses, it is war. I am not ignorant of the art of war, and I trust the event to God and my sword."[56] An expedition against the despot of Epirus was the first prelude of his arms. If a victory was followed by a defeat, if the race of the Comneni or Angeli survived in those mountains his efforts and his reign, the captivity of Villehardouin prince of Achaia deprived the Latins of the most active and powerful vassal of their expiring monarchy. The republics of Venice and Genoa disputed, in the first of their naval wars, the command of the sea and the commerce of the East. Pride and interest attached the Venetians to the defence of Constantinople; their rivals were tempted to promote the designs of her enemies, and the alliance of the Genoese with the schismatic conqueror provoked the indignation of the Latin church.[57]

Intent on his great object, the emperor Michael visited in person and strengthened the troops and fortifications of Thrace. The remains of the Latins were driven from their last possessions: he assaulted without success the suburb of Galata, and corresponded with a perfidious baron, who proved unwilling, or unable, to open the gates of the metropolis. The next spring his favourite general, Alexius Strategopulus, whom he had decorated with the title of Cæsar, passed the Hellespont with eight hundred horse and some infantry[58] on a secret expedition. His instructions enjoined him to approach, to listen, to watch, but not to risk any doubtful or dangerous enterprise against the city. The adjacent territory between the Propontis and the Black Sea was cultivated by a hardy race of peasants and outlaws, exercised in arms, uncertain in their allegiance, but inclined by language, religion, and present advantage, to the party of the Greeks. They were styled the *volunteers*,[59] and by their free service the army of Alexius, with the regulars of Thrace and the Coman auxiliaries,[60] was augmented to the number of five-and-twenty thousand men. By the ardour of the volunteers, and by his own ambition, the Cæsar was stimulated to disobey the precise orders of his master, in the just confidence that success would plead his pardon and reward. The weakness of Constantinople and the distress and terror of the Latins were familiar to the observation of the volunteers; and they represented the present moment as the most propitious to surprise and conquest. A rash youth, the new governor of the Venetian colony, had sailed away with thirty galleys and the best of the French knights on a wild expedition to Daphnusia, a town on the Black Sea, at the distance of forty leagues, and the remaining Latins were without strength or suspicion. They were informed that Alexius had passed the Hellespont; but their apprehensions were lulled by the smallness of his original numbers, and their imprudence had not watched the subsequent increase of his army. If he left his main body to second and support his operations, he might advance unperceived in the night with a chosen detachment. While some applied scaling-ladders to the lowest part of the walls, they were secure of an old Greek who would introduce their companions through a subterraneous passage into his house; they could soon on the inside break an entrance through the golden gate, which had been long obstructed; and the conqueror would be in the heart of the city before the Latins were conscious of their danger. After some debate, the Cæsar resigned himself to the faith of the volunteers; they were trusty, bold, and successful; and, in describing the plan, I have already related the execution and success.[61] But no sooner had Alexius passed the threshold of the golden gate than he trembled at his own rashness; he paused, he deliberated, till the desperate volunteers urged him forwards by the assurance that in retreat lay the greatest and most inevitable danger. Whilst the Cæsar kept his regulars in firm array, the Comans dispersed themselves on all sides; an alarm was sounded, and the threats of fire and pillage compelled the citizens to a decisive resolution. The Greeks of Constantinople remembered their native sovereigns; the Genoese merchants their recent alliance and Venetian foes; every quarter was in arms; and the air resounded with a general acclamation of "Long life and victory to Michael and John, the august emperors of the Romans!" Their rival, Baldwin, was awakened by the sound; but the most pressing danger could not prompt him to draw his sword in the defence of a city which he deserted perhaps with more pleasure than regret: he fled from the palace to the seashore, where he descried the welcome sails of the fleet returning from the vain and fruitless attempt on Daphnusia. Constantinople was irrecoverably lost; but the Latin emperor and the principal families embarked on board the Venetian galleys, and steered for the isle of Eubœa, and afterwards for Italy, where the royal fugitive was entertained by the pope and Sicilian king with a mixture of contempt and pity. From the loss of Constantinople to his death he consumed thirteen years soliciting the Catholic powers to join in his restoration: the lesson had been familiar to his youth; nor was his last exile more indigent or shameful than his three former pilgrimages to the courts of Europe. His son Philip was the heir of an ideal empire; and the pretensions of *his* daughter Catherine were transported by her marriage, to Charles of Valois, the brother of Philip the Fair, king of France. The house of Courtenay was represented in the female line by successive alliances, till the title of emperor of Constantinople, too bulky and sonorous for a private name, modesty expired in silence and oblivion.[62]

After this narrative of the expeditions of the Latins to Palestine and Constantinople, I cannot dismiss the subject without revolving the general consequences on the countries that were the scene, and on the nations that were the actors, of these memorable crusades.[63] As soon as the arms of the Franks were withdrawn, the impression, though not the memory, was erased in the Mohammedan realms of Egypt and Syria. The faithful disciples of the prophet were never tempted by a profane desire to study the laws and languages of the idolaters; nor did the simplicity of their primitive manners receive the slightest alteration from their intercourse in peace and war with the unknown strangers of the West. The Greeks, who thought themselves proud, but who were only vain, showed a disposition somewhat less inflexible. In the efforts for the recovery of their empire they emulated the valour, discipline, and tactics of their antagonists. The modern literature of the West they might justly despise; but its free spirit would instruct them in the rights of man; and some institutions of public and private life were adopted from the French. The correspondence of Constantinople and Italy diffused the knowledge of the Latin tongue; and several of the fathers and classics were at length honoured with a Greek version.[64] But the national and religious prejudices of the Orientals were inflamed by persecution; and the reign of the Latins confirmed the separation of the two churches.

If we compare the era of the crusades, the Latins of Europe with the Greeks and Arabians, their respective degrees of knowledge, industry, and art, our rude ancestors must be content with the third rank in the scale of nations. Their successive improvement and present superiority may be ascribed to a peculiar energy of character, to an active and imitative spirit, unknown to their more polished rivals, who at that time were in a stationary or retrograde state. With such a disposition the Latins should have derived the most early and essential benefits from a series of events which opened to their eyes the prospect of the world, and introduced them to a long and frequent intercourse with the more cultivated regions of the East. The first and most obvious progress was in trade and manufactures, in the arts which are strongly prompted by the thirst of wealth, the calls of necessity, and the gratification of the sense or vanity. Among the crowd of unthinking fanatics a captive or a pilgrim might sometimes observe the superior refinements of Cairo and Constantinople: the first importer of windmills[65] was the benefactor of nations; and if such blessings are enjoyed without any grateful remembrance, history has condescended to notice the more apparent luxuries of silk and sugar, which were transported into Italy from Greece and Egypt. But the intellectual wants of the Latins were more slowly felt and supplied; the ardour of studious curiosity was awakened in Europe by different causes and more recent events; and, in the age of the crusaders, they viewed with careless indifference the literature of the Greeks and Arabians. Some rudiments of mathematical and medicinal knowledge might be imparted in practice and in figures; necessity might produce some interpreters for the grosser business of merchants and soldiers; but the commerce of the Orientals had not diffused the study and knowledge of their languages in the schools of Europe.[66] If a similar principle of religion repulsed the idiom of the Koran, it should have excited their patience and curiosity to understand the original text of the Gospel; and the same grammar would have unfolded the sense of Plato and the beauties of Homer. Yet, in a reign of sixty years, the Latins of Constantinople disdained the speech and learning of their subjects; and the manuscripts were the only treasures which the natives might enjoy without rapine or envy. Aristotle was indeed the oracle of the Western universities, but it was a barbarous Aristotle; and, instead of ascending to the fountain head, his Latin votaries humbly accepted a corrupt and remote version from the Jews and Moors of Andalusia. The principle of the crusades was a savage fanaticism; and the most important effects were analogous to the cause. Each pilgrim was ambitious to return with his sacred spoils, the relics of Greece and Palestine;[67] and each relic was preceded and followed by a train of miracles and visions. The belief of the Catholics was corrupted by new legends, their practice by new superstitions; and the establishment of the inquisition, the mendicant orders of monks and friars, the last abuse of indulgences, and the final progress of idolatry, flowed from the baleful fountain of the holy war. The active spirit of the Latins preyed on the vitals of their reason and religion; and if the ninth and tenth centuries were the times of darkness, the thirteenth and fourteenth were the age of absurdity and fable.

In the profession of Christianity, in the cultivation of a fertile land, the northern conquerors of the Roman empire insensibly mingled with the provincials and rekindled the embers of the arts of antiquity. Their settlements about the age of Charlemagne had acquired some degree of order and stability, when they were overwhelmed by new swarms of invaders, the Normans, Saracens,[68] and Hungarians, who replunged the western countries of Europe into their former state of anarchy and barbarism. About the eleventh century the second tempest had subsided by the expulsion or conversion of the enemies of Christendom: the tide of civilisation, which had so long ebbed, began to flow with a steady and accelerated course; and a fairer prospect was opened to the hopes and efforts of the rising generations. Great was the increase, and rapid the progress, during the two hundred years of the crusades; and some philosophers have applauded the propitious influence of these holy wars, which appear to me to have checked rather than forwarded the maturity of Europe.[69] The lives and labours of millions which were buried in the East would have been more profitably employed in the improvement of their native country: the accumulated stock of industry and wealth would have overflowed in navigation and trade; and the Latins would have been enriched and enlightened by a pure and friendly correspondence with the climates of the East. In one respect I can indeed perceive the accidental operation of the crusades, not so much in producing a benefit as in removing an evil. The larger portion of the inhabitants of Europe was chained to the soil, without freedom, or property, or knowledge; and the two orders of ecclesiastics and nobles, whose numbers were comparatively small, alone deserved the name of citizens and men. This oppressive system was supported by the arts of the clergy and the swords of the barons. The authority of the priests operated in the darker ages as a salutary antidote: they prevented the total extinction of letters, mitigated the fierceness of the times, sheltered the poor and defenceless, and preserved or revived the peace and order of civil society. But the independence, rapine, and discord of the feudal lords were unmixed with any semblance of good; and every hope of industry and improvement was crushed by the iron weight of the martial aristocracy. Among the causes that undermined that Gothic edifice, a conspicuous place must be allowed to the crusades. The estates of the barons were dissipated, and their race was often extinguished in these costly and perilous expeditions. Their poverty extorted from their pride those charters of freedom which unlocked the fetters of the slave, secured the farm of the peasant and the shop of the artificer, and gradually restored a substance and a soul to the most numerous and useful part of the community. The conflagration which destroyed the tall and barren trees of the forest gave air and scope to the vegetation of the smaller and nutritive plants of the soil.

Digression on the Family of Courtenay

THE purple of three emperors who have reigned at Constantinople will authorise or excuse a digression on the origin and singular fortunes of the house of COURTENAY,[70] in the three principal branches, I. Of Edessa; II. Of France; and III. Of England; of which the last only has survived the revolutions of eight hundred years.

I. Before the introduction of trade, which scatters riches, and of knowledge, which dispels prejudice, the prerogative of birth is most strongly felt and most humbly acknowledged. In every age the laws and manners of the Germans have discriminated the ranks of society: the dukes and counts who shared the empire of Charlemagne converted their office to an inheritance; and to his children each feudal lord bequeathed his honour and his sword. The proudest families are content to lose, in the darkness of the middle ages, the tree of their pedigree, which, however deep and lofty, must ultimately rise from a plebeian root; and their historians must descend ten centuries below the Christian era, before they can ascertain any lineal succession by the evidence of surnames, of arms, and of authentic records. With the first rays of light[71] we discern the nobility and opulence of Atho, a French knight: his nobility, in the rank and title of a nameless father; his opulence, in the foundation of the castle of Courtenay in the district of Gatinois, about fifty-six miles to the south of Paris. From the reign of Robert, the son of Hugh Capet, the barons of Courtenay are conspicuous among the immediate vassals of the crown; and Joscelin, the grandson of Atho and a noble dame, is enrolled among the heroes of the first crusade. A domestic alliance (their mothers were sisters) attached him to the standard of Baldwin of Bruges, the second count of Edessa; a princely fief, which he was worthy to receive and able to maintain, announces the number of his martial followers; and after the departure of his cousin, Joscelin himself was invested with the county of Edessa on both sides of the Euphrates. By economy in peace his territories were replenished with Latin and Syrian subjects; his magazines with corn, wine, and oil; his castles with gold and silver, with arms and horses. In a holy warfare of thirty years he was alternately a conqueror and a captive; but he died like a soldier, in a horse litter at the head of his troops; and his last glance beheld the flight of the Turkish invaders who had presumed on his age and infirmities. His son and successor, of the same name, was less deficient in valour than in vigilance; but he sometimes forgot that dominion is acquired and maintained by the same arts. He challenged the hostility of the Turks without securing the friendship of the prince of Antioch; and, amidst the peaceful luxury of Turbessel, in Syria,[72] Joscelin neglected the defence of the Christian frontier beyond the Euphrates. In his absence, Zenghi, the first of the Atabeks, besieged and stormed his capital, Edessa, which was feebly defended by a timorous and disloyal crowd of Orientals: the Franks were oppressed in a bold attempt for its recovery, and Courtenay ended his days in the prison of Aleppo. He still left a fair and ample patrimony. But the victorious Turks oppressed on all sides the weakness of a widow and orphan; and, for the equivalent of an annual pension, they resigned to the Greek emperor the charge of defending, and the shame of losing, the last relics of the Latin conquest. The countess-dowager of Edessa retired to Jerusalem with her two children: the daughter, Agnes, became the wife and mother of a king; the son, Joscelin the Third, accepted the office of seneschal, the first of the kingdom, and held his new estates in Palestine by the service of fifty knights. His name appears with honour in all the transactions of peace and war; but he finally vanishes in the fall of Jerusalem; and the name of Courtenay, in this branch of Edessa, was lost by the marriage of his two daughters with a French and a German baron.[73]

II. While Joscelin reigned beyond the Euphrates, his elder brother Milo, the son of Joscelin the son of Atho, continued, near the Seine, to possess the castle of their fathers, which was at length inherited by Rainaud, or Reginald, the youngest of his three sons. Examples of genius or virtue must be rare in the annals of the oldest families; and, in a remote age, their pride will embrace a deed of rapine and violence; such, however, as could not be perpetrated without some superiority of courage, or, at least, of power. A descendant of Reginald of Courtenay may blush for the public robber who stripped and imprisoned several merchants after they had satisfied the king's duties at Sens and Orleans. He will glory in the offence, since the bold offender could not be compelled to obedience and restitution till the regent and the count of Champagne prepared to march against him at the head of an army.[74] Reginald bestowed his estates on his eldest daughter, and his daughter on the seventh son of king Louis the Fat; and their marriage was crowned with a numerous offspring. We might expect that a private should have merged in a royal name; and that the descendants of Peter of France and Elizabeth of Courtenay would have enjoyed the title and honours of princes of the blood. But this legitimate claim was long neglected, and finally denied; and the causes of their disgrace will represent the story of this second branch. 1. Of all the families now extant, the most ancient, doubtless, and the most illustrious, is the house of France, which has occupied the same throne above eight hundred years, and descends, in a clear and lineal series of males, from the middle of the ninth century.[75] In the age of the crusades it was already revered both in the East and West. But from Hugh Capet to the marriage of Peter no more than five reigns or generations had elapsed; and so precarious was their title, that the eldest sons, as a necessary precaution, were previously crowned during the lifetime of their fathers. The peers of France have long maintained their precedency before the younger branches of the royal line, nor had the princes of the blood, in the twelfth century, acquired that hereditary lustre which is now diffused over the most remote candidates for the succession. 2. The barons of Courtenay must have stood high in their own estimation, and in that of the world, since they could impose on the son of a king the obligation of adopting for himself and all his descendants the name and arms of their daughter and his wife. In the marriage of an heiress with her inferior or her equal, such exchange was often required and allowed: but as they continued to diverge from the regal stem, the sons of Louis the Fat were insensibly confounded with their maternal ancestors; and the new Courtenays might deserve to forfeit the honours of their birth, which a motive of interest had tempted them to renounce. 3. The shame was far more permanent than the reward, and a momentary blaze was followed by a long darkness. The eldest son of these nuptials, Peter of Courtenay, had married, as I have already mentioned, the sister of the counts of Flanders, the two first emperors of Constantinople: he rashly accepted the invitation of the barons of Romania; his two sons, Robert and Baldwin, successively held and lost the remains of the Latin empire in the East, and the grand-daughter of Baldwin the Second again mingled her blood with the blood of France and of Valois. To support the expenses of a troubled and transitory reign, their patrimonial estates were mortgaged or sold; and the last emperors of Constantinople depended on the annual charity of Rome and Naples.

While the elder brothers dissipated their wealth in romantic adventures, and the castle of Courtenay was profaned by a plebeian owner, the younger branches of that adopted name were propagated and multiplied. But their splendour was clouded by poverty and time: after the decease of Robert, great butler of France, they descended from princes to barons; the next generations were confounded with the simple gentry; the descendants of Hugh Capet could no longer be visible in the rural lords of Tanlay and of Champignelles. The more adventurous embraced without dishonour the profession of a soldier: the least active and opulent might sink, like their cousins of the branch of Dreux, into the condition of peasants. Their royal descent in a dark period of four hundred years became each day more obsolete and ambiguous; and their pedigree, instead of being enrolled in the annals of the kingdom, must be painfully searched by the minute diligence of heralds and genealogists. It was not till the end of the sixteenth century, on the accession of a family almost as remote as their own, that the princely spirit of the Courtenays again revived; and the question of the nobility provoked them to assert the royalty of their blood. They appealed to the justice and compassion of Henry the Fourth; obtained a favourable opinion from twenty lawyers of Italy and Germany, and modestly compared themselves to the descendants of king David, whose prerogatives were not impaired by the lapse of ages or the trade of a carpenter.[76] But every ear was deaf, and every circumstance was adverse, to their lawful claims. The Bourbon kings were justified by the neglect of the Valois; the princes of the blood, more recent and lofty, disdained the alliance of this humble kindred: the parliament, without denying their proofs, eluded a dangerous precedent by an arbitrary distinction, and established St. Louis as the first father of the royal line.[77] A repetition of complaints and protests was repeatedly disregarded; and the hopeless pursuit was terminated in the present century by the death of the last male of the family.[78] Their painful and anxious situation was alleviated by the pride of conscious virtue: they sternly rejected the temptations of fortune and favour; and a dying Courtenay would have sacrificed his son if the youth could have renounced, for any temporal interest, the right and title of a legitimate prince of the blood of France.[79]

III. According to the old register of Ford Abbey, the Courtenays of Devonshire are descended from prince *Florus*, the second son of Peter, and the grandson of Louis the Fat.[80] This fable of the grateful or venal monks was too respectfully entertained by our antiquaries, Camden[81] and Dugdale:[82] but it is so clearly repugnant to truth and time, that the rational pride of the family now refuses to accept this imaginary founder. Their most faithful historians believe that, after giving his daughter to the king's son, Reginald of Courtenay abandoned his possessions in France, and obtained from the English monarch a second wife and a new inheritance. It is certain, at least, that Henry the Second distinguished in his camps and councils *a* Reginald, of the name and arms, and, as it may be fairly presumed, of the genuine race, of the Courtenays of France. The right of wardship enabled a feudal lord to reward his vassal with the marriage and estate of a noble heiress; and Reginald of Courtenay acquired a fair establishment in Devonshire, where his posterity has been seated above six hundred years.[83] From a Norman baron, Baldwin de Brioniis, who had been invested by the Conqueror, Hawise, the wife of Reginald, derived the honour of Okehampton, which was held by the service of ninety-three knights; and a female might claim the manly offices of hereditary viscount or sheriff, and of captain of the royal castle of Exeter. Their son Robert married the sister of the earl of Devon: at the end of a century, on the failure of the family of Rivers,[84] his great-grandson, Hugh the Second, succeeded to a title which was still considered as a territorial dignity; and twelve earls of Devonshire, of the name of Courtenay, have flourished in a period of two hundred and twenty years. They were ranked among the chief of the barons of the realm; nor was it till after a strenuous dispute that they yielded to the fief of Arundel the first place in the parliament of England: their alliances were contracted with the noblest families, the Veres, Despensers, St. Johns, Talbots, Bohuns, and even the Plantagenets themselves; and in a contest with John of Lancaster, a Courtenay, bishop of London, and afterwards archbishop of Canterbury, might be accused of profane confidence in the strength and number of his kindred. In peace the earls of Devon resided in their numerous castles and manors of the west: their ample revenue was appropriated to devotion and hospitality: and the epitaph of Edward, surnamed, from his misfortune, the *blind*, from his virtues, the *good*, earl, inculcates with much ingenuity a moral sentence, which may however be abused by thoughtless generosity. After a grateful commemoration of the fifty-five years of union and happiness which he enjoyed with Mabel his wife, the good earl thus speaks from the tomb:—

What we gave, we have;
What we spent, we had;
What we left, we lost.[85]

But their *losses*, in this sense, were far superior to their gifts and expenses; and their heirs, not less than the poor, were the objects of their paternal care. The sums which they paid for livery and seisin attest the greatness of their possessions; and several estates have remained in their family since the thirteenth and fourteenth centuries. In war the Courtenays of England fulfilled the duties, and deserved the honours of chivalry. They were often intrusted to levy and command the militia of Devonshire and Cornwall; they often attended their supreme lord to the borders of Scotland; and in foreign service, for a stipulated price, they sometimes maintained fourscore men-at-arms and as many archers. By sea and land they fought under the standard of the Edwards and Henries: their names are conspicuous in battles, in tournaments, and in the original list of the Order of the Garter; three brothers shared the Spanish victory of the Black Prince; and in the lapse of six generations the English Courtenays had learned to despise the nation and country from which they derived their origin. In the quarrel of the two Roses the earls of Devon adhered to the house of Lancaster, and three brothers successively died either in the field or on the scaffold. Their honours and estates were restored by Henry the Seventh: a daughter of Edward the Fourth was not disgraced by the nuptials of a Courtenay; their son, who was created marquis of Exeter, enjoyed the favour of his cousin Henry the Eighth; and in the camp of Cloth of Gold he broke a lance against the French monarch. But the favour of Henry was the prelude of disgrace; his disgrace was the signal of death; and of the victims of the jealous tyrant the marquis of Exeter is one of the most noble and guiltless. His son Edward lived a prisoner in the Tower, and died in exile at Padua; and the secret love of queen Mary, whom he slighted, perhaps for the princess Elizabeth, has shed a romantic colour on the story of this beautiful youth. The relics of his patrimony were conveyed into strange families by the marriages of his four aunts; and his personal honours, as if they had been legally extinct, were revived by the patents of succeeding princes. But there still survived a lineal descendant of Hugh the first earl of Devon, a younger branch of the Courtenays, who have been seated at Powderham Castle above four hundred years, from the reign of Edward the Third to the present hour. Their estates have been increased by the grant and improvement of lands in Ireland, and they have been recently restored to the honours of the peerage. Yet the Courtenays still retain the plaintive motto which asserts the innocence and deplores the fall of their ancient house.[86] While they sigh for past greatness, they are doubtless sensible of present blessings: in the long series of the Courtenay annals the most splendid era is likewise the most unfortunate; nor can an opulent peer of Britain be inclined to envy the emperors of Constantinople who wandered over Europe to solicit alms for the support of their dignity and the defence of their capital.

CHAPTER LXII

The Greek Emperors of Nice and Constantinople. Elevation and Reign of Michael Palæologus. His false Union with the Pope and the Latin Church. Hostile Designs of Charles of Anjou. Revolt of Sicily. War of the Catalans in Asia and Greece. Revolutions and Present State of Athens.

THE loss of Constantinople restored a momentary vigour to the Greeks. From their palaces the princes and nobles were driven into the field; and the fragments of the falling monarchy were grasped by the hands of the most vigorous or the most skilful candidates. In the long and barren pages of the Byzantine annals[1] it would not be an easy task to equal the two characters of Theodore Lascaris and John Ducas Vataces,[2] who replanted and upheld the Roman standard at Nice in Bithynia. The difference of their virtues was happily suited to the diversity of their situation. In his first efforts the fugitive Lascaris commanded only three cities and two thousand soldiers: his reign was the season of generous and active despair; in every military operation he staked his life and crown; and his enemies of the Hellespont and the Mæander were surprised by his celerity and subdued by his boldness. A victorious reign of eighteen years expanded the principality of Nice to the magnitude of an empire. The throne of his successor and son-in-law Vataces was founded on a more solid basis, a larger scope, and more plentiful resources; and it was the temper, as well as the interest, of Vataces to calculate the risk, to expect the moment, and to insure the success, of his ambitious designs. In the decline of the Latins I have briefly exposed the progress of the Greeks; the prudent and gradual advances of a conqueror who, in a reign of thirty-three years, rescued the provinces from national and foreign usurpers, till he pressed on all sides the Imperial city, a leafless and sapless trunk, which must fall at the first stroke of the axe. But his interior and peaceful administration is still more deserving of notice and praise.[3] The calamities of the times had wasted the numbers and the substance of the Greeks. the motives and the means of agriculture were extirpated; and the most fertile lands were left without cultivation or inhabitants. A portion of this vacant property was occupied and improved by the command, and for the benefit, of the emperor: a powerful hand and a vigilant eye supplied and surpassed, by a skilful management, the minute diligence of a private farmer: the royal domain became the garden and granary of Asia; and, without impoverishing the people, the sovereign acquired a fund of innocent and productive wealth. According to the nature of the soil, his lands were sown with corn or planted with vines; the pastures were filled with horses and oxen, with sheep and hogs; and when Vataces presented to the empress a crown of diamonds and pearls, he informed her, with a smile, that this precious ornament arose from the sale of the eggs of his innumerable poultry. The produce of his domain was applied to the maintenance of his palace and hospitals, the calls of dignity and benevolence: the lesson was still more useful than the revenue: the plough was restored to its ancient security and honour; and the nobles were taught to seek a sure and independent revenue from their estates, instead of adorning their splendid beggary by the oppression of the people, or (what is almost the same) by the favours of the court. The superfluous stock of corn and cattle was eagerly purchased by the Turks, with whom Vataces preserved a strict and sincere alliance; but he discouraged the importation of foreign manufactures, the costly silks of the East and the curious labours of the Italian looms. "The demands of nature and necessity," was he accustomed to say, "are indispensable; but the influence of fashion may rise and sink at the breath of a monarch;" and both his precept and example recommended simplicity of manners and the use of domestic industry. The education of youth and the revival of learning were the most serious objects of his care; and, without deciding the precedency, he pronounced with truth that a prince and a philosopher[4] are the two most eminent characters of human society. His first wife was Irene, the daughter of Theodore Lascaris, a woman more illustrious by her personal merit, the milder virtues of her sex, than by the blood of the Angeli and Comneni that flowed in her veins, and transmitted the inheritance of the empire. After her death he was contracted to Anne or Constance, a natural daughter of the emperor Frederic the Second; but as the bride had not attained the years of puberty, Vataces placed in his solitary bed an Italian damsel of her train; and his amorous weakness bestowed on the concubine the honours, though not the title, of lawful empress. His frailty was censured as a flagitious and damnable sin by the monks; and their rude invectives exercised and displayed the patience of the royal lover. A philosophic age may excuse a single vice, which was redeemed by a crowd of virtues; and in the review of his faults, and the more intemperate passions of Lascaris, the judgment of their contemporaries was softened by gratitude to the second founders of the empire.[5] The slaves of the Latins, without law or peace, applauded the happiness of their brethren who had resumed

their national freedom; and Vataces employed the laudable policy of convincing the Greeks of every dominion that it was their interest to be enrolled in the number of his subjects.

A strong shade of degeneracy is visible between John Vataces and his son Theodore; between the founder who sustained the weight, and the heir who enjoyed the splendour, of the Imperial crown.[6] Yet the character of Theodore was not devoid of energy; he had been educated in the school of his father, in the exercise of war and hunting: Constantinople was yet spared; but in the three years of a short reign he thrice led his armies into the heart of Bulgaria. His virtues were sullied by a choleric and suspicious temper: the first of these may be ascribed to the ignorance of control; and the second might naturally arise from a dark and imperfect view of the corruption of mankind. On a march in Bulgaria he consulted on a question of policy his principal ministers; and the Greek logothete, George Acropolita, presumed to offend him by the declaration of a free and honest opinion. The emperor half unsheathed his scimitar; but his more deliberate rage reserved Acropolita for a baser punishment. One of the first officers of the empire was ordered to dismount, stripped of his robes, and extended on the ground in the presence of the prince and army. In this posture he was chastised with so many and such heavy blows from the clubs of two guards or executioners, that, when Theodore commanded them to cease, the great logothete was scarcely able to arise and crawl away to his tent. After a seclusion of some days he was recalled by a peremptory mandate to his seat in council; and so dead were the Greeks to the sense of honour and shame, that it is from the narrative of the sufferer himself that we acquire the knowledge of his disgrace.[7] The cruelty of the emperor was exasperated by the pangs of sickness, the approach of a premature end, and the suspicion of poison and magic. The lives and fortunes, the eyes and limbs, of his kinsmen and nobles, were sacrificed to each sally of passion; and before he died, the son of Vataces might deserve from the people, or at least from the court, the appellation of tyrant. A matron of the family of the Palæologi had provoked his anger by refusing to bestow her beauteous daughter on the vile plebeian who was recommended by his caprice. Without regard to her birth or age, her body, as high as the neck was enclosed in a sack with several cats, who were pricked with pins to irritate their fury against their unfortunate fellow-captive.

In his last hours the emperor testified a wish to forgive and be forgiven, a just anxiety for the fate of John his son and successor, who, at the age of eight years, was condemned to the dangers of a long minority. His last choice instructed the office of guardian to the sanctity of the patriarch Arsenius, and to the courage of George Muzalon, the great domestic, who was equally distinguished by the royal favour and the public hatred. Since their connection with the Latins, the names and privileges of hereditary rank had insinuated themselves into the Greek monarchy; and the noble families[8] were provoked by the elevation of a worthless favourite, to whose influence they imputed the errors and calamities of the late reign. In the first council after the emperor's death, Muzalon, from a lofty throne, pronounced a laboured apology of his conduct and intentions: his modesty was subdued by a unanimous assurance of esteem and fidelity; and his most inveterate enemies were the loudest to salute him as the guardian and saviour of the Romans. Eight days were sufficient to prepare the execution of the conspiracy. On the ninth, the obsequies of the deceased monarch were solemnised in the cathedral of Magnesia,[9] an Asiatic city, where he expired, on the banks of the Hermus and at the foot of Mount Sipylus. The holy rites were interrupted by a sedition of the guards; Muzalon, his brothers, and his adherents, were massacred at the foot of the altar; and the absent patriarch was associated with a new colleague, with Michael Palæologus, the most illustrious, in birth and merit, of the Greek nobles.[10]

Of those who are proud of their ancestors the far greater part must be content with local or domestic renown, and few there are who dare trust the memorials of their family to the public annals of their country. As early as the middle of the eleventh century, the noble race of the Palæologi[11] stands high and conspicuous in the Byzantine history: it was the valiant George Palæologus who placed the father of the Comneni on the throne; and his kinsmen or descendants continue, in each generation, to lead the armies and councils of the state. The purple was not dishonoured by their alliance; and had the law of succession, and female succession, been strictly observed, the wife of Theodore Lascaris must have yielded to her elder sister, the mother of Michael Palæologus, who afterwards raised his family to the throne. In his person the splendour of birth was dignified by the merit of the soldier and statesman; in his early youth he was promoted to the office of

constable or commander of the French mercenaries: the private expense of a day never exceeded three pieces of gold; but his ambition was rapacious and profuse, and his gifts were doubled by the graces of his conversation and manners. The love of the soldiers and people excited the jealousy of the court; and Michael thrice escaped from the dangers in which he was involved by his own imprudence or that of his friends. I. Under the reign of Justice and Vataces, a dispute arose[12] between two officers, one of whom accused the other of maintaining the hereditary right of the Palæologi. The cause was decided, according to the new jurisprudence of the Latins, by single combat; the defendant was overthrown; but he persisted in declaring that himself alone was guilty, and that he had uttered these rash or treasonable speeches without the approbation or knowledge of his patron. Yet a cloud of suspicion hung over the innocence of the constable; he was still pursued by the whispers of malevolence, and a subtle courtier, the archbishop of Philadelphia, urged him to accept the judgment of God in the fiery proof of the ordeal.[13] Three days before the trial the patient's arm was enclosed in a bag, and secured by the royal signet; and it was incumbent on him to bear a red-hot ball of iron three times from the altar to the rails of the sanctuary, without artifice and without injury. Palæologus eluded the dangerous experiment with sense and pleasantry. "I am a soldier," said he, "and will boldly enter the lists with my accusers; but a layman, a sinner like myself, is not endowed with the gift of miracles. *Your* piety, most holy prelate, may deserve the interposition of Heaven, and from your hands I will receive the fiery globe, the pledge of my innocence." The archbishop started; the emperor smiled; and the absolution or pardon of Michael was approved by new rewards and new services. II. In the succeeding reign, as he held the government of Nice, he was secretly informed that the mind of the absent prince was poisoned with jealousy, and that death or blindness would be his final reward. Instead of awaiting the return and sentence of Theodore, the constable, with some followers, escaped from the city and the empire, and, though he was plundered by the Turkmans of the desert, he found an hospitable refuge in the court of the sultan. In the ambiguous state of an exile, Michael reconciled the duties of gratitude and loyalty: drawing his sword against the Tartars; admonishing the garrisons of the Roman limit; and promoting, by his influence, the restoration of peace, in which his pardon and recall were honourably included. III. While he guarded the West against the despot of Epirus, Michael was again suspected and condemned in the palace; and such was his loyalty or weakness, that he submitted to be led in chains above six hundred miles from Durazzo to Nice. The civility of the messenger alleviated his disgrace, the emperor's sickness dispelled his danger; and the last breath of Theodore, which recommended his infant son, at once acknowledged the innocence and the power of Palæologus.

But his innocence had been too unworthily treated, and his power was too strongly felt, to curb an aspiring subject in the fair field that was opened to his ambition.[14] In the council after the death of Theodore, he was the first to pronounce, and the first to violate, the oath of allegiance to Muzalon; and so dexterous was his conduct that he reaped the benefit, without incurring the guilt, or at least the reproach, of the subsequent massacre. In the choice of a regent he balanced the interests and passions of the candidates, turned their envy and hatred from himself against each other, and forced every competitor to own that, after his own claims, those of Palæologus were best entitled to the preference. Under the title of great duke, he accepted or assumed, during a long minority, the active powers of government; the patriarch was a venerable name, and the factious nobles were seduced or oppressed by the ascendant of his genius. The fruits of the economy of Vataces were deposited in a strong castle on the banks of the Hermus, in the custody of the faithful Varangians; the constable retained his command or influence over the foreign troops; he employed the guards to possess the treasure, and the treasure to corrupt the guards; and whatsoever might be the abuse of the public money, his character was above the suspicion of private avarice. By himself, or by his emissaries, he strove to persuade every rank of subjects that their own prosperity would rise in just proportion to the establishment of his authority. The weight of taxes was suspended, the perpetual theme of popular complaint; and he prohibited the trials by the ordeal and judicial combat. These barbaric institutions were already abolished or undermined in France[15] and England;[16] and the appeal to the sword offended the sense of a civilised,[17] and the temper of an unwarlike, people. For the future maintenance of their wives and children the veterans were grateful; the priest and the philosopher applauded his ardent zeal for the advancement of religion and learning; and his vague promise of rewarding merit was applied by every candidate to his own hopes. Conscious of the influence of the clergy, Michael successfully laboured to secure the suffrage of that powerful order. Their expensive journey from Nice to Magnesia afforded a decent and ample pretence: the leading prelates were tempted by the liberality of his nocturnal visits; and the incorruptible patriarch was flattered by the homage of his new colleague, who led his mule by the bridle into the town, and removed to a respectful distance the importunity of the crowd. Without renouncing his title by royal descent, Palæologus encouraged a free discussion into the advantages of elective monarchy; and his adherents asked, with the insolence of triumph, what patient would trust his health, or what merchant would abandon his vessel, to the *hereditary* skill of a physician or a pilot? The youth of the emperor, and the impending dangers of a minority, required the support of a mature and experienced guardian; of an associate raised above the envy of his equals, and invested with the name and prerogatives of royalty. For the interest of the prince and people, without any selfish views for himself or his family, the great duke consented to guard and instruct the son of Theodore: but he sighed for the happy moment when he might restore to his firmer hands the administration of his patrimony, and enjoy the blessings of a private station. He was first invested with the title and prerogatives of *despot*, which bestowed the purple ornaments and the second place in the Roman monarchy. It was afterwards agreed that John and Michael should be proclaimed as joint emperors, and raised on the buckler, but that the pre-eminence should be reserved for the birthright of the former. A mutual league of amity was pledged between the royal partners; and in case of a rupture, the subjects were bound, by their oath of allegiance, to declare themselves against the aggressor: an ambiguous name, the seed of discord and civil war. Palæologus was content; but on the day of the coronation, and in the cathedral of Nice, his zealous adherents most vehemently urged the just priority of his age and merit. The unseasonable dispute was eluded by postponing to a more convenient opportunity the coronation of John Lascaris; and he walked with a slight diadem in the train of his guardian, who alone received the Imperial crown from the hands of the patriarch. It was not without extreme reluctance that Arsenius abandoned the cause of his pupil; but the Varangians brandished their battle-axes; a sign of assent was extorted from the trembling youth; and some voices were heard, that the life of a child should no longer impede the settlement of the nation. A full harvest of honours and employments was distributed among his friends by the grateful Palæologus. In his own family he created a despot and two sebastocrators; Alexius Strategopulus was decorated with the title of Cæsar; and that veteran commander soon repaid the obligation by restoring Constantinople to the Greek emperor.

It was in the second year of his reign, while he resided in the palace and gardens of Nymphæum,[18] near Smyrna, that the first messenger arrived at the dead of night; and the stupendous intelligence was imparted to Michael, after he had been gently waked by the tender precaution of his sister Eulogia. The man was unknown or obscure; he produced no letters from the victorious Cæsar; nor could it easily be credited, after the defeat of Vataces and the recent failure of Palæologus himself, that the capital had been surprised by a detachment of eight hundred soldiers. As a hostage, the doubtful author was confined, with the assurance of death or an ample recompense; and the court was left some hours in the anxiety of hope and fear, till the messengers of Alexius arrived with the authentic intelligence, and displayed the trophies of the conquest, the sword and sceptre,[19] the buskins and bonnet,[20] of the usurper Baldwin, which he had dropped in his precipitate flight. A general assembly of the bishops, senators, and nobles was immediately convened, and never perhaps was an event received with more heartfelt and universal joy. In a studied oration the new sovereign of Constantinople congratulated his own and the public fortune. "There was a time," said he, "a far distant time, when the Roman empire extended to the Adriatic, the Tigris, and the confines of Æthiopia. After the loss of the provinces, our capital itself, in these last and calamitous days, has been wrested from our hands by the barbarians of the West. From the lowest ebb the tide of prosperity has again returned in our favour; but our prosperity was that of fugitives and exiles; and when we were asked which was the country of the Romans, we indicated with a blush the climate of the globe, and the quarter of the heavens. The divine Providence has now restored to our arms the city of Constantine, the sacred seat of religion and empire; and it will depend on our valour and conduct to render this important acquisition the pledge and omen of future victories."

So eager was the impatience of the prince and people, that Michael made his triumphal entry into Constantinople only twenty days after the expulsion of the Latins. The golden gate was thrown open at his approach; the devout conqueror dismounted from his horse; and a miraculous image of Mary the Conductress was borne before him, that the divine Virgin in person might appear to conduct him to the temple of her Son, the cathedral of St. Sophia. But after the first transport of devotion and pride, he sighed at the dreary prospect of solitude and ruin. The palace was defiled with smoke and dirt, and the gross intemperance of the Franks; whole streets had been consumed by fire, or were decayed by the injuries of time; the sacred and profane edifices were stripped of their ornaments; and, as if they were conscious of their approaching exile, the industry of the Latins had been confined to the work of pillage and destruction. Trade had expired under the pressure of anarchy and distress, and the numbers of inhabitants had decreased with the opulence of the city. It was the first care of the Greek monarch to reinstate the nobles in the palaces of their fathers, and the houses, or the ground which they occupied, were restored to the families that could exhibit a legal right of inheritance. But the far greater part was extinct or lost; the vacant property had devolved to the lord; he repeopled Constantinople by a liberal invitation to the provinces, and the brave *volunteers* were seated in the capital which had been recovered by their arms. The French barons and the principal families had retired with their emperor, but the patient and humble crowd of Latins was attached to the country, and indifferent to the change of masters. Instead of banishing the factories of the Pisans, Venetians, and Genoese, the prudent conqueror accepted their oaths of allegiance, encouraged their industry, confirmed their privileges, and allowed them to live under the jurisdiction of their proper magistrates. Of these nations the Pisans and Venetians preserved their respective quarters in the city; but the services and power of the Genoese deserved at the same time the gratitude and the jealousy of the Greeks. Their independent colony was first planted at the seaport town of Heraclea in Thrace. They were speedily recalled, and settled in the exclusive possession of the suburb of Galata, an advantageous post, in which they revived the commerce and insulted the majesty of the Byzantine empire.[21]

The recovery of Constantinople was cele-

brated as the era of a new empire; the conqueror, alone, and by the right of the sword, renewed his coronation in the church of St. Sophia; and the name and honours of John Lascaris, his pupil and lawful sovereign, were insensibly abolished. But his claims still lived in
the minds of the people, and the royal youth
must speedily attain the years of manhood and
ambition. By fear or conscience Palæologus was
restrained from dipping his hands in innocent
and royal blood; but the anxiety of a usurper
and a parent urged him to secure his throne by
one of those imperfect crimes so familiar to the
modern Greeks. The loss of sight incapacitated
the young prince for the active business of the
world: instead of the brutal violence of tearing
out his eyes, the visual nerve was destroyed by
the intense glare of a red-hot basin,[22] and John
Lascaris was removed to a distant castle, where
he spent many years in privacy and oblivion.
Such cool and deliberate guilt may seem incompatible with remorse; but if Michael could
trust the mercy of Heaven, he was not inaccessible to the reproaches and vengeance of mankind, which he had provoked by cruelty and
treason. His cruelty imposed on a servile court
the duties of applause or silence; but the clergy
had a right to speak in the name of their invisible Master, and their holy legions were led by
a prelate whose character was above the temptations of hope or fear. After a short abdication
of his dignity, Arsenius[23] had consented to
ascend the ecclesiastical throne of Constantinople, and to preside in the restoration of the
church. His pious simplicity was long deceived
by the arts of Palæologus, and his patience and
submission might soothe the usurper, and protect the safety of the young prince. On the news
of his inhuman treatment the patriarch unsheathed the spiritual sword, and superstition,
on this occasion, was enlisted in the cause of
humanity and justice. In a synod of bishops,
who were stimulated by the example of his zeal,
the patriarch pronounced a sentence of excommunication, though his prudence still repeated
the name of Michael in the public prayers. The
Eastern prelates had not adopted the dangerous
maxims of ancient Rome, nor did they presume
to enforce their censures by deposing princes or
absolving nations from their oaths of allegiance.
But the Christian who had been separated from
God and the church became an object of horror,
and, in a turbulent and fanatic capital, that
horror might arm the hand of an assassin, or inflame a sedition of the people. Palæologus felt
his danger, confessed his guilt, and deprecated

his judge: the act was irretrievable, the prize
was obtained; and the most rigorous penance,
which he solicited, would have raised the sinner
to the reputation of a saint. The unrelenting
patriarch refused to announce any means of
atonement or any hopes of mercy, and condescended only to pronounce that, for so great a
crime, great indeed must be the satisfaction.
"Do you require," said Michael, "that I should
abdicate the empire?" And at these words he
offered, or seemed to offer, the sword of state.
Arsenius eagerly grasped this pledge of sovereignty; but when he perceived that the emperor was unwilling to purchase absolution at
so dear a rate, he indignantly escaped to his
cell, and left the royal sinner kneeling and weeping before the door.[24]

The danger and scandal of this excommunication subsisted above three years, till the popular clamour was assuaged by time and repentance; till the brethren of Arsenius condemned his inflexible spirit, so repugnant to the
unbounded forgiveness of the Gospel. The emperor had artfully insinuated, that, if he were
still rejected at home, he might seek, in the Roman pontiff, a more indulgent judge; but it was
far more easy and effectual to find or to place
that judge at the head of the Byzantine church.
Arsenius was involved in a vague rumour of
conspiracy and disaffection; some irregular
steps in his ordination and government were
liable to censure; a synod deposed him from the
episcopal office; and he was transported under
a guard of soldiers to a small island of the Propontis. Before his exile he sullenly requested
that a strict account might be taken of the
treasures of the church; boasted that his sole
riches, three pieces of gold, had been earned by
transcribing the psalms; continued to assert the
freedom of his mind; and denied, with his last
breath, the pardon which was implored by the
royal sinner.[25] After some delay, Gregory,
bishop of Adrianople, was translated to the
Byzantine throne; but his authority was found
insufficient to support the absolution of the
emperor; and Joseph, a reverend monk, was
substituted to that important function. This
edifying scene was represented in the presence
of the senate and people; at the end of six years
the humble penitent was restored to the communion of the faithful; and humanity will rejoice that a milder treatment of the captive Lascaris was stipulated as a proof of his remorse.
But the spirit of Arsenius still survived in a
powerful faction of the monks and clergy, who
persevered above forty-eight years in an ob-

stinate schism. Their scruples were treated with tenderness and respect by Michael and his son, and the reconciliation of the Arsenites was the serious labour of the church and state. In the confidence of fanaticism, they had proposed to try their cause by a miracle; and when the two papers, that contained their own and the adverse cause, were cast into a fiery brazier, they expected that the Catholic verity would be respected by the flames. Alas! the two papers were indiscriminately consumed, and this unforeseen accident produced the union of a day, and renewed the quarrel of an age.[26] The final treaty displayed the victory of the Arsenites; the clergy abstained during forty days from all ecclesiastical functions; a slight penance was imposed on the laity, the body of Arsenius was deposited in the sanctuary, and in the name of the departed saint the prince and people were released from the sins of their fathers.[27]

The establishment of his family was the motive, or at least the pretence, of the crime of Palæologus; and he was impatient to confirm the succession, by sharing with his eldest son the honours of the purple. Andronicus, afterwards surnamed the Elder, was proclaimed and crowned emperor of the Romans in the fifteenth year of his age; and, from the first era of a prolix and inglorious reign, he held that august title nine years as the colleague, and fifty as the successor, of his father. Michael himself, had he died in a private station, would have been thought more worthy of the empire; and the assaults of his temporal and spiritual enemies left him few moments to labour for his own fame or the happiness of his subjects. He wrested from the Franks several of the noblest islands of the Archipelago—Lesbos, Chios, and Rhodes: his brother Constantine was sent to command in Malvasia and Sparta; and the eastern side of the Morea, from Argos and Napoli to Cape Tænarus, was repossessed by the Greeks. This effusion of Christian blood was loudly condemned by the patriarch; and the insolent priest presumed to interpose his fears and scruples between the arms of princes. But in the prosecution of these western conquests the countries beyond the Hellespont were left naked to the Turks; and their depredations verified the prophecy of a dying senator, that the recovery of Constantinople would be the ruin of Asia. The victories of Michael were achieved by his lieutenants; his sword rusted in the palace; and, in the transactions of the emperor with the popes and the king of Naples, his political arts were stained with cruelty and fraud.[28]

I. The Vatican was the most natural refuge of a Latin emperor who had been driven from his throne; and pope Urban the Fourth appeared to pity the misfortunes, and vindicate the cause, of the fugitive Baldwin. A crusade, with plenary indulgence, was preached by his command against the schismatic Greeks: he excommunicated their allies and adherents; solicited Louis the Ninth in favour of his kinsman; and demanded a tenth of the ecclesiastic revenues of France and England for the service of the holy war.[29] The subtle Greek, who watched the rising tempest of the West, attempted to suspend or soothe the hostility of the pope by suppliant embassies and respectful letters; but he insinuated that the establishment of peace must prepare the reconciliation and obedience of the Eastern church. The Roman court could not be deceived by so gross an artifice; and Michael was admonished that the repentance of the son should precede the forgiveness of the father; and that *faith* (an ambiguous word) was the only basis of friendship and alliance. After a long and affected delay, the approach of danger, and the importunity of Gregory the Tenth, compelled him to enter on a more serious negotiation: he alleged the example of the great Vataces; and the Greek clergy, who understood the intentions of their prince, were not alarmed by the first steps of reconciliation and respect. But when he pressed the conclusion of the treaty, they strenuously declared that the Latins, though not in name, were heretics in fact, and that they despised those strangers as the vilest and most despicable portion of the human race.[30] It was the task of the emperor to persuade, to corrupt, to intimidate the most popular ecclesiastics, to gain the vote of each individual, and alternately to urge the arguments of Christian charity and the public welfare. The texts of the fathers and the arms of the Franks were balanced in the theological and political scale; and without approving the addition to the Nicene creed, the most moderate were taught to confess that the two hostile propositions of proceeding from the Father BY the Son, and of proceeding from the Father AND the Son, might be reduced to a safe and Catholic sense.[31] The supremacy of the pope was a doctrine more easy to conceive, but more painful to acknowledge; yet Michael represented to his monks and prelates that they might submit to name the Roman bishop as the first of the patriarchs; and that their distance and discretion would guard the liberties of the Eastern church from the mischievous consequences of the right of appeal.

He protested that he would sacrifice his life and empire rather than yield the smallest point of orthodox faith or national independence; and this declaration was sealed and ratified by a golden bull. The patriarch Joseph withdrew to a monastery, to resign or resume his throne, according to the event of the treaty: the letters of union and obedience were subscribed by the emperor, his son Andronicus, and thirty-five archbishops and metropolitans, with their respective synods; and the episcopal list was multiplied by many dioceses which were annihilated under the yoke of the infidels. An embassy was composed of some trusty ministers and prelates: they embarked for Italy, with rich ornaments and rare perfumes, for the altar of St. Peter; and their secret orders authorised and recommended a boundless compliance. They were received in the general council of Lyons, by pope Gregory the Tenth, at the head of five hundred bishops.[32] He embraced with tears his long-lost and repentant children; accepted the oath of the ambassadors, who abjured the schism in the name of the two emperors; adorned the prelates with the ring and mitre; chanted in Greek and Latin the Nicene creed with the addition of *filioque;* and rejoiced in the union of the East and West, which had been reserved for his reign. To consummate this pious work, the Byzantine deputies were speedily followed by the pope's nuncios; and their instruction discloses the policy of the Vatican, which could not be satisfied with the vain title of supremacy. After viewing the temper of the prince and people, they were enjoined to absolve the schismatic clergy who should subscribe and swear their abjuration and obedience; to establish in all the churches the use of the perfect creed; to prepare the entrance of a cardinal legate, with the full powers and dignity of his office; and to instruct the emperor in the advantages which he might derive from the temporal protection of the Roman pontiff.[33]

But they found a country without a friend, a nation in which the names of Rome and Union were pronounced with abhorrence. The patriarch Joseph was indeed removed: his place was filled by Veccus, an ecclesiastic of learning and moderation; and the emperor was still urged by the same motives to persevere in the same professions. But in his private language Palæologus affected to deplore the pride, and to blame the innovations, of the Latins; and while he debased his character by this double hypocrisy, he justified and punished the opposition of his subjects. By the joint suffrage of the new and the ancient Rome, a sentence of excommunication was pronounced against the obstinate schismatics: the censures of the churches were executed by the sword of Michael; on the failure of persuasion, he tried the arguments of prison and exile, of whipping and mutilation—those touchstones, says an historian, of cowards and the brave. Two Greeks still reigned in Ætolia, Epirus, and Thessaly, with the appellation of despots: they had yielded to the sovereign of Constantinople, but they rejected the chains of the Roman pontiff, and supported their refusal by successful arms. Under their protection, the fugitive monks and bishops assembled in hostile synods, and retorted the name of heretic with the galling addition of apostate: the prince of Trebizond was tempted to assume the forfeit title of emperor; and even the Latins of Negropont, Thebes, Athens, and the Morea forgot the merits of the convert, to join, with open or clandestine aid, the enemies of Palæologus. His favourite generals, of his own blood and family successively deserted, or betrayed, the sacrilegious trust. His sister Eulogia, a niece, and two female cousins conspired against him; another niece, Mary queen of Bulgaria, negotiated his ruin with the sultan of Egypt; and, in the public eye, their treason was consecrated as the most sublime virtue.[34] To the pope's nuncios, who urged the consummation of the work, Palæologus exposed a naked recital of all that he had done and suffered for their sake. They were assured that the guilty sectaries, of both sexes and every rank, had been deprived of their honours, their fortunes, and their liberty; a spreading list of confiscation and punishment, which involved many persons the dearest to the emperor, or the best deserving of his favour. They were conducted to the prison, to behold four princes of the royal blood chained in the four corners, and shaking their fetters in an agony of grief and rage. Two of these captives were afterwards released; the one by submission, the other by death: but the obstinacy of their two companions was chastised by the loss of their eyes; and the Greeks, the least adverse to the union, deplore that cruel and inauspicious tragedy.[35] Persecutors must expect the hatred of those whom they oppress; but they commonly find some consolation in the testimony of their conscience, the applause of their party, and, perhaps, the success of their undertaking. But the hypocrisy of Michael, which was prompted only by political motives, must have forced him to hate himself, to despise his followers, and to esteem and envy the rebel champions by whom he was detested and despised. While his violence was abhorred at Constantinople, at Rome his slowness was arraigned, and his sincerity suspected; till at length pope Martin the Fourth excluded the Greek emperor from the pale of a church into which he was striving to reduce a schismatic people. No sooner had the tyrant expired than the union was dissolved and abjured by unanimous consent; the churches were purified; the penitents were reconciled; and his son Andronicus, after weeping the sins and errors of his youth, most piously denied his father the burial of a prince and a Christian.[36]

II. In the distress of the Latins the walls and towers of Constantinople had fallen to decay; they were restored and fortified by the policy of Michael, who deposited a plenteous store of corn and salt provisions, to sustain the siege which he might hourly expect from the resentment of the Western powers. Of these, the sovereign of the Two Sicilies was the most formidable neighbour; but as long as they were possessed by Mainfroy, the bastard of Frederic the Second, his monarchy was the bulwark, rather than the annoyance, of the Eastern empire. The usurper, though a brave and active prince, was sufficiently employed in the defence of his throne: his proscription by successive popes had separated Mainfroy from the common cause of the Latins; and the forces that might have besieged Constantinople were detained in a crusade against the domestic enemy of Rome. The prize of her avenger, the crown of the Two Sicilies, was won and worn by the brother of St. Louis, by Charles of Anjou and Provence, who led the chivalry of France on this holy expedition.[37] The disaffection of his Christian subjects compelled Mainfroy to enlist a colony of Saracens whom his father had planted in Apulia; and this odious succour will explain the defiance of the Catholic hero, who rejected all terms of accommodation. "Bear this message," said Charles, "to the sultan of Nocera, that God and the sword are umpire between us; and that he shall either send me to paradise, or I will send him to the pit of hell." The armies met; and though I am ignorant of Mainfroy's doom in the other world, in this he lost his friends, his kingdom, and his life, in the bloody battle of Benevento. Naples and Sicily were immediately peopled with a warlike race of French nobles; and their aspiring leader embraced the future conquest of Africa, Greece, and Palestine. The most specious reasons might point his first arms against the Byzantine empire; and Palæologus, diffident of his own strength, repeatedly appealed from the ambition of Charles to the humanity of St. Louis, who still preserved a just ascendant over the mind of his ferocious brother. For a while the attention of that brother was confined at home by the invasion of Conradin, the last heir of the Imperial house of Swabia: but the hapless boy sunk in the unequal conflict; and his execution on a public scaffold taught the rivals of Charles to tremble for their heads as well as their dominions. A second respite was obtained by the last crusade of St. Louis to the African coast; and the double motive of interest and duty urged the king of Naples to assist, with his powers and his presence, the holy enterprise. The death of St. Louis released him from the importunity of a virtuous censor: the king of Tunis confessed himself the tributary and vassal of the crown of Sicily; and the boldest of the French knights were free to enlist under his banner against the Greek empire. A treaty and a marriage united his interest with the house of Courtenay; his daughter Beatrice was promised to Philip, son and heir of the emperor Baldwin; a pension of six hundred ounces of gold was allowed for his maintenance; and his generous father distributed among his allies the kingdoms and provinces of the East, reserving only Constantinople, and one day's journey round the city, for the Imperial domain.[38] In this perilous moment Palæologus was the most eager to subscribe the creed, and implore the protection, of the Roman pontiff, who assumed, with propriety and weight, the character of an angel of peace, the common father of the Christians. By his voice the sword of Charles was chained in the scabbard; and the Greek ambassadors beheld him, in the pope's antechamber, biting his ivory sceptre in a transport of fury, and deeply resenting the refusal to enfranchise and consecrate his arms. He appears to have respected the disinterested mediation of Gregory the Tenth; but Charles was insensibly disgusted by the pride and partiality of Nicholas the Third; and his attachment to his kindred, the Ursini family, alienated the most strenuous champion from the service of the church. The hostile league against the Greeks, of Philip the Latin emperor, the king of the Two Sicilies, and the republic of Venice, was ripened into execution; and the election of Martin the Fourth, a French pope, gave a sanction to the cause. Of the allies, Philip supplied his name; Martin, a bull of excommunication; the Venetians, a squadron of forty galleys; and the formidable powers of

Charles consisted of forty counts, ten thousand men-at-arms, a numerous body of infantry, and a fleet of more than three hundred ships and transports. A distant day was appointed for assembling this mighty force in the harbour of Brindisi; and a previous attempt was risked with a detachment of three hundred knights, who invaded Albania and besieged the fortress of Belgrade. Their defeat might amuse with a triumph the vanity of Constantinople; but the more sagacious Michael, despairing of his arms, depended on the effects of a conspiracy; on the secret workings of a rat who gnawed the bow-string[39] of the Sicilian tyrant.

Among the proscribed adherents of the house of Swabia, John of Procida forfeited a small island of that name in the bay of Naples. His birth was noble, but his education was learned; and in the poverty of exile he was relieved by the practice of physic, which he had studied in the school of Salerno. Fortune had left him nothing to lose, except life; and to despise life is the first qualification of a rebel. Procida was endowed with the art of negotiation to enforce his reasons and disguise his motives; and in his various transactions with nations and men, he could persuade each party that he laboured solely for *their* interest. The new kingdoms of Charles were afflicted by every species of fiscal and military oppression;[40] and the lives and fortunes of his Italian subjects were sacrificed to the greatness of their master and the licentiousness of his followers. The hatred of Naples was repressed by his presence; but the looser government of his vicegerents excited the contempt, as well as the aversion, of the Sicilians: the island was roused to a sense of freedom by the eloquence of Procida; and he displayed to every baron his private interest in the common cause. In the confidence of foreign aid, he successively visited the courts of the Greek emperor, and of Peter king of Arragon,[41] who possessed the maritime countries of Valentia and Catalonia. To the ambitious Peter a crown was presented, which he might justly claim by his marriage with the sister of Mainfroy, and by the dying voice of Conradin, who from the scaffold had cast a ring to his heir and avenger. Palæologus was easily persuaded to divert his enemy from a foreign war by a rebellion at home; and a Greek subsidy of twenty-five thousand ounces of gold was most profitably applied to arm a Catalan fleet, which sailed under a holy banner to the specious attack of the Saracens of Africa. In the disguise of a monk or beggar, the indefatigable missionary of revolt flew from Constantinople to Rome, and from Sicily to Saragossa: the treaty was sealed with the signet of pope Nicholas himself, the enemy of Charles; and his deed of gift transferred the fiefs of St. Peter from the house of Anjou to that of Arragon. So widely diffused and so freely circulated, the secret was preserved above two years with impenetrable discretion; and each of the conspirators imbibed the maxim of Peter, who declared that he would cut off his left hand if it were conscious of the intentions of his right. The mine was prepared with deep and dangerous artifice; but it may be questioned whether the instant explosion of Palermo were the effect of accident or design.

On the vigil of Easter a procession of the disarmed citizens visited a church without the walls, and a noble damsel was rudely insulted by a French soldier.[42] The ravisher was instantly punished with death; and if the people was at first scattered by a military force, their numbers and fury prevailed: the conspirators seized the opportunity; the flame spread over the island, and eight thousand French were exterminated in a promiscuous massacre, which has obtained the name of the SICILIAN VESPERS.[43] From every city the banners of freedom and the church were displayed: the revolt was inspired by the presence or the soul of Procida; and Peter of Arragon, who sailed from the African coast to Palermo, was saluted as the king and saviour of the isle. By the rebellion of a people on whom he had so long trampled with impunity, Charles was astonished and confounded; and in the first agony of grief and devotion he was heard to exclaim, "O God! if thou hast decreed to humble me, grant me at least a gentle and gradual descent from the pinnacle of greatness!" His fleet and army, which already filled the seaports of Italy, were hastily recalled from the service of the Grecian war; and the situation of Messina exposed that town to the first storm of his revenge. Feeble in themselves, and yet hopeless of foreign succour, the citizens would have repented and submitted on the assurance of full pardon and their ancient privileges. But the pride of the monarch was already rekindled; and the most fervent entreaties of the legate could extort no more than a promise that he would forgive the remainder after a chosen list of eight hundred rebels had been yielded to his discretion. The despair of the Messinese renewed their courage: Peter of Arragon approached to their relief,[44] and his rival was driven back by the failure of provision and the terrors of the equinox to the Calabrian shore.

At the same moment the Catalan admiral, the famous Roger de Loria, swept the channel with an invincible squadron: the French fleet, more numerous in transports than in galleys, was either burnt or destroyed; and the same blow assured the independence of Sicily and the safety of the Greek empire. A few days before his death the emperor Michael rejoiced in the fall of an enemy whom he hated and esteemed; and perhaps he might be content with the popular judgment, that, had they not been matched with each other, Constantinople and Italy must speedily have obeyed the same master.[45] From this disastrous moment the life of Charles was a series of misfortunes: his capital was insulted, his son was made prisoner, and he sunk into the grave without recovering the isle of Sicily, which, after a war of twenty years, was finally severed from the throne of Naples, and transferred, as an independent kingdom, to a younger branch of the house of Arragon.[46]

I shall not, I trust, be accused of superstition; but I must remark that, even in this world, the natural order of events will sometimes afford the strong appearances of moral retribution. The first Palæologus had saved his empire by involving the kingdoms of the West in rebellion and blood; and from these seeds of discord uprose a generation of iron men, who assaulted and endangered the empire of his son. In modern times our debts and taxes are the secret poison which still corrodes the bosom of peace; but in the weak and disorderly government of the middle ages it was agitated by the present evil of the disbanded armies. Too idle to work, too proud to beg, the mercenaries were accustomed to a life of rapine: they could rob with more dignity and effect under a banner and a chief; and the sovereign, to whom their service was useless and their presence importunate, endeavoured to discharge the torrent on some neighbouring countries. After the peace of Sicily, many thousands of Genoese, *Catalans*,[47] etc., who had fought by sea and land under the standard of Anjou or Arragon, were blended into one nation by the resemblance of their manners and interest. They heard that the Greek provinces of Asia were invaded by the Turks: they resolved to share the harvest of pay and plunder; and Frederic king of Sicily most liberally contributed the means of their departure. In a warfare of twenty years a ship or a camp was become their country; arms were their sole profession and property; valour was the only virtue which they knew; their women had imbibed the fearless temper of their lovers

and husbands: it was reported that with a stroke of their broad-sword the Catalans could cleave a horseman and a horse; and the report itself was a powerful weapon. Roger de Flor was the most popular of their chiefs; and his personal merit overshadowed the dignity of his prouder rivals of Arragon. The offspring of a marriage between a German gentleman of the court of Frederic the Second and a damsel of Brindisi, Roger was successively a templar, an apostate, a pirate, and at length the richest and most powerful admiral of the Mediterranean. He sailed from Messina to Constantinople with eighteen galleys, four great ships, and eight thousand adventurers; and his previous treaty was faithfully accomplished by Andronicus the Elder, who accepted with joy and terror this formidable succour. A palace was allotted for his reception, and a niece of the emperor was given in marriage to the valiant stranger, who was immediately created great duke or admiral of Romania. After a decent repose he transported his troops over the Propontis, and boldly led them against the Turks: in two bloody battles thirty thousand of the Moslems were slain: he raised the siege of Philadelphia, and deserved the name of the deliverer of Asia. But after a short season of prosperity the cloud of slavery and ruin again burst on that unhappy province. The inhabitants escaped (says a Greek historian) from the smoke into the flames; and the hostility of the Turks was less pernicious than the friendship of the Catalans. The lives and fortunes which they had rescued they considered as their own: the willing or reluctant maid was saved from the race of circumcision for the embraces of a Christian soldier: the exaction of fines and supplies was enforced by licentious rapine and arbitrary executions; and, on the resistance of Magnesia, the great duke besieged a city of the Roman empire.[48] These disorders he excused by the wrongs and passions of a victorious army; nor would his own authority or person have been safe had he dared to punish his faithful followers, who were defrauded of the just and covenanted price of their services. The threats and complaints of Andronicus disclosed the nakedness of the empire. His golden bull had invited no more than five hundred horse and a thousand foot soldiers; yet the crowds of volunteers who migrated to the East had been enlisted and fed by his spontaneous bounty. While his bravest allies were content with three byzants or pieces of gold for the monthly pay, an ounce or even two ounces of gold were assigned to the Catalans, whose annual pension would thus amount to near a hundred pounds sterling: one of their chiefs had modestly rated at three hundred thousand crowns the value of his *future* merits; and above a million had been issued from the treasury for the maintenance of these costly mercenaries. A cruel tax had been imposed on the corn of the husbandmen: one-third was retrenched from the salaries of the public officers; and the standard of the coin was so shamefully debased, that of the four-and-twenty parts only five were of pure gold.[49] At the summons of the emperor, Roger evacuated a province which no longer supplied the materials of rapine; but he refused to disperse his troops; and while his style was respectful, his conduct was independent and hostile. He protested that, if the emperor should march against him, he would advance forty paces to kiss the ground before him; but in rising from this prostrate attitude Roger had a life and sword at the service of his friends. The great duke of Romania condescended to accept the title and ornaments of Cæsar; but he rejected the new proposal of the government of Asia with a subsidy of corn and money, on condition that he should reduce his troops to the harmless number of three thousand men. Assassination is the last resource of cowards. The Cæsar was tempted to visit the royal residence of Adrianople; in the apartment, and before the eyes, of the empress he was stabbed by the Alani guards; and, though the deed was imputed to their private revenge, his countrymen, who dwelt at Constantinople in the security of peace, were involved in the same proscription by the prince or people. The loss of their leader intimidated the crowd of adventurers, who hoisted the sails of flight, and were soon scattered round the coasts of the Mediterranean. But a veteran band of fifteen hundred Catalans or French stood firm in the strong fortress of Gallipoli on the Hellespont, displayed the banners of Arragon, and offered to revenge and justify their chief by an equal combat of ten or a hundred warriors. Instead of accepting this bold defiance, the emperor Michael, the son and colleague of Andronicus, resolved to oppress them with the weight of multitudes: every nerve was strained to form an army of thirteen thousand horse and thirty thousand foot, and the Propontis was covered with the ships of the Greeks and Genoese. In two battles by sea and land these mighty forces were encountered and overthrown by the despair and discipline of the Catalans: the young emperor fled to the palace, and an insufficient guard of light-horse was left for the protection of the open country. Victory renewed the hopes and numbers of the adventurers; every nation was blended under the name and standard of the *great company;* and three thousand Turkish proselytes deserted from the Imperial service to join this military association. In the possession of Gallipoli the Catalans intercepted the trade of Constantinople and the Black Sea, while they spread their devastations on either side of the Hellespont over the confines of Europe and Asia. To prevent their approach the greatest part of the Byzantine territory was laid waste by the Greeks themselves: the peasants and their cattle retired into the city; and myriads of sheep and oxen, for which neither place nor food could be procured, were unprofitably slaughtered on the same day. Four times the emperor Andronicus sued for peace, and four times he was inflexibly repulsed, till the want of provisions and the discord of the chiefs compelled the Catalans to evacuate the banks of the Hellespont and the neighbourhood of the capital. After their separation from the Turks, the remains of the great company pursued their march through Macedonia and Thessaly, to seek a new establishment in the heart of Greece.[50]

After some ages of oblivion Greece was awakened to new misfortunes by the arms of the Latins. In the two hundred and fifty years between the first and the last conquest of Constantinople that venerable land was disputed by a multitude of petty tyrants; without the comforts of freedom and genius, her ancient cities were again plunged in foreign and intestine war; and, if servitude be preferable to anarchy, they might repose with joy under the Turkish yoke. I shall not pursue the obscure and various dynasties that rose and fell on the continent or in the isles; but our silence on the fate of ATHENS[51] would argue a strange ingratitude to the first and purest school of liberal science and amusement. In the partition of the empire the principality of Athens and Thebes was assigned to Otho de la Roche, a noble warrior of Burgundy,[52] with the title of great duke,[53] which the Latins understood in their own sense, and the Greeks more foolishly derived from the age of Constantine.[54] Otho followed the standard of the marquis of Montferrat: the ample state which he acquired by a miracle of conduct or fortune,[55] was peaceably inherited by his son and two grandsons, till the family, though not the nation, was changed by the marriage of an heiress into the elder branch of the house of Brienne. The son of that marriage, Walter de Brienne, succeeded to the duchy of Athens; and, with the aid of some Catalan mercenaries, whom he invested with fiefs, reduced above thirty castles of the vassal or neighbouring lords. But when he was informed of the approach and ambition of the great company, he collected a force of seven hundred knights, six thousand four hundred horse, and eight thousand foot, and boldly met them on the banks of the river Cephisus in Bœotia. The Catalans amounted to no more than three thousand five hundred horse and four thousand foot; but the deficiency of numbers was compensated by stratagem and order. They formed round their camp an artificial inundation; the duke and his knights advanced without fear or precaution on the verdant meadow; their horses plunged into the bog, and he was cut in pieces, with the greatest part of the French cavalry. His family and nation were expelled; and his son Walter de Brienne, the titular duke of Athens, the tyrant of Florence, and the constable of France, lost his life in the field of Poitiers. Attica and Bœotia were the rewards of the victorious Catalans; they married the widows and daughters of the slain; and during fourteen years the great company was the terror of the Grecian states. Their factions drove them to acknowledge the sovereignty of the house of Arragon; and during the remainder of the fourteenth century Athens, as a government or an appanage, was successively bestowed by the kings of Sicily. After the French and Catalans, the third dynasty was that of the Accaioli, a family, plebeian at Florence, potent at Naples, and sovereign in Greece. Athens, which they embellished with new buildings, became the capital of a state that extended over Thebes, Argos, Corinth, Delphi, and a part of Thessaly; and their reign was finally determined by Mohammed the Second, who strangled the last duke, and educated his sons in the discipline and religion of the seraglio.

Athens,[56] though no more than the shadow of her former self, still contains about eight or ten thousand inhabitants: of these, three-fourths are Greeks in religion and language; and the Turks, who compose the remainder, have relaxed, in their intercourse with the citizens, somewhat of the pride and gravity of their national character. The olive-tree, the gift of Minerva, flourishes in Attica; nor has the honey of Mount Hymettus lost any part of its exquisite flavor:[57] but the languid trade is monopolised by strangers, and the agriculture of a barren land is abandoned to the vagrant Wallachians. The Athenians are still distinguished by the subtlety and acuteness of their understandings; but these qualities, unless ennobled by freedom and enlightened by study, will degenerate into a low and selfish cunning: and it is a proverbial saying of the country, "From the Jews of Thessalonica, the Turks of Negropont, and the Greeks of Athens, good Lord deliver us!" This artful people has eluded the tyranny of the Turkish bashaws by an expedient which alleviates their servitude and aggravates their shame. About the middle of the last century the Athenians chose for their protector the Kislar Aga, or chief black eunuch of the seraglio. This Æthiopian slave, who possesses the sultan's ear, condescends to accept the tribute of thirty thousand crowns: his lieutenant, the Waywode, whom he annually confirms, may reserve for his own about five or six thousand more; and such is the policy of the citizens, that they seldom fail to remove and punish an oppressive governor. Their private differences are decided by the archbishop, one of the richest prelates of the Greek church, since he possesses a revenue of one thousand pounds sterling; and by a tribunal of the eight *geronti* or elders, chosen in the eight quarters of the city: the noble families cannot trace their pedigree above three hundred years; but their principal members are distinguished by a grave demeanour, a fur cap, and the lofty appellation of *archon*. By some, who delight in the contrast, the modern language of Athens is represented as the most corrupt and barbarous of the seventy dialects of the vulgar Greek:[58] this picture is too darkly coloured; but it would not be easy, in the country of Plato and Demosthenes, to find a reader or a copy of their works. The Athenians walk with supine indifference among the glorious ruins of antiquity; and such is the debasement of their character, that they are incapable of admiring the genius of their predecessors.[59]

CHAPTER LXIII

Civil Wars, and Ruin of the Greek Empire. Reigns of Andronicus the Elder and Younger, and John Palæologus. Regency, Revolt, Reign, and Abdication of John Cantacuzene. Establishment of a Genoese Colony at Pera or Galata. Their Wars with the Empire and City of Constantinople.

THE long reign of Andronicus[1] the elder is chiefly memorable by the disputes of the Greek church, the invasion of the Catalans, and the rise of the Ottoman power. He is celebrated as the most learned and virtuous prince of the age; but such virtue, and such learning, contributed neither to the perfection of the individual nor to the happiness of society. A slave of the most abject superstition, he was surrounded on all sides by visible and invisible enemies; nor were the flames of hell less dreadful to his fancy than those of a Catalan or Turkish war. Under the reign of the Palæologi the choice of the patriarch was the most important business of the state; the heads of the Greek church were ambitious and fanatic monks; and their vices or virtues, their learning or ignorance, were equally mischievous or contemptible. By his intemperate discipline the patriarch Athanasius[2] excited the hatred of the clergy and people: he was heard to declare that the sinner should swallow the last dregs of the cup of penance; and the foolish tale was propagated of his punishing a sacrilegious ass that had tasted the lettuce of a convent garden. Driven from the throne by the universal clamour Athanasius composed before his retreat two papers of a very opposite cast. His public testament was in the tone of charity and resignation; the private codicil breathed the direst anathemas against the authors of his disgrace, whom he excluded for ever from the communion of the Holy Trinity, the angels, and the saints. This last paper he enclosed in an earthen pot, which was placed, by his order, on the top of one of the pillars in the dome of St. Sophia, in the distant hope of discovery and revenge. At the end of four years some youths, climbing by a ladder in search of pigeons' nests, detected the fatal secret; and, as Andronicus felt himself touched and bound by the excommunication, he trembled on the brink of the abyss which had been so treacherously dug under his feet. A synod of bishops was instantly convened to debate this important question: the rashness of these clandestine anathemas was generally condemned; but as the knot could be untied only by the same hand, as that hand was now deprived of the crosier, it appeared that this posthumous decree was irrevocable by any earthly power. Some faint testimonies of repentance and pardon were extorted from the author of the mischief; but the conscience of the emperor was still wounded, and he desired, with no less ardour than Athanasius himself, the restoration of a patriarch by whom alone he could be healed. At the dead of night a monk rudely knocked at the door of the royal bed-chamber, announcing a revelation of plague and famine, of inundations and earthquakes. Andronicus started from his bed and spent the night in prayer, till he felt, or thought that he felt, a slight motion of the earth. The emperor on foot led the bishops and monks to the cell of Athanasius; and, after a proper resistance, the saint, from whom this message had been sent, consented to absolve the prince and govern the church of Constantinople. Untamed by disgrace, and hardened by solitude, the shepherd was again odious to the flock, and his enemies contrived a singular, and, as it proved, a successful, mode of revenge. In the night they stole away the foot-stool or foot-cloth of his throne, which they secretly replaced with the decoration of a satirical picture. The emperor was painted with a bridle in his mouth, and Athanasius leading the tractable beast to the feet of Christ. The authors of the libel were detected and punished; but as their lives had been spared, the Christian priest in sullen indignation retired to his cell; and the eyes of Andronicus, which had been opened for a moment, were again closed by his successor.

If this transaction be one of the most curious and important of a reign of fifty years, I cannot at least accuse the brevity of my materials, since I reduce into some few pages the enormous folios of Pachymer,[3] Cantacuzene,[4] and Nicephorus Gregoras,[5] who have composed the prolix and languid story of the times. The name and situation of the emperor John Cantacuzene might inspire the most lively curiosity. His memorials of forty years extend from the revolt of the younger Andronicus to his own abdication of the empire; and it is observed that, like Moses and Cæsar, he was the principal actor in the scenes which he describes. But in this eloquent work we should vainly seek the sincerity of a hero or a penitent. Retired in a cloister from the vices and passions of the world, he presents not a confession, but an apology, of the life of an ambitious statesman. Instead of unfolding the true counsels and characters of men, he displays the smooth and specious surface of events, highly varnished with his own praises and those of his friends. Their motives are always pure; their ends always legitimate: they conspire and rebel without any views of interest; and the violence which they inflict or suffer is celebrated as the spontaneous effect of reason and virtue.

After the example of the first of the Palæologi, the elder Andronicus associated his son Michael to the honours of the purple; and from the age of eighteen to his premature death, that prince was acknowledged, above twenty-five years, as the second emperor of the Greeks.[6] At the head of an army he excited neither the fears of the enemy nor the jealousy of the court: his modesty and patience were never tempted to compute the years of his father; nor was that father compelled to repent of his liberality either by the virtues or vices of his son. The son of Michael was named Andronicus from his grandfather, to whose early favour he was introduced by that nominal resemblance. The blossoms of wit and beauty increased the fondness of the elder Andronicus; and, with the common vanity of age, he expected to realise in the second, the hope which had been disappointed in the first, generation. The boy was educated in the palace as an heir and a favourite; and in the oaths and acclamations of the people, the *august triad* was formed by the names of the father, the son, and the grandson. But the younger Andronicus was speedily corrupted by his infant greatness, while he beheld with puerile impatience the double obstacle that hung, and might long hang, over his rising ambition. It was not to acquire fame, or to diffuse happiness, that he so eagerly aspired: wealth and impunity were in his eyes the most precious attributes of a monarch; and his first indiscreet demand was the sovereignty of some rich and fertile island, where he might lead a life of independence and pleasure. The emperor was offended by the loud and frequent intemperance which disturbed his capital; the sums which his parsimony denied were supplied by the Genoese usurers of Pera; and the oppressive debt, which consoli-

dated the interest of a faction, could be discharged only by a revolution. A beautiful female, a matron in rank, a prostitute in manners, had instructed the younger Andronicus in the rudiments of love; but he had reason to suspect the nocturnal visits of a rival; and a stranger passing through the street was pierced by the arrows of his guards, who were placed in ambush at her door. That stranger was his brother, prince Manuel, who languished and died of his wound; and the emperor Michael, their common father, whose health was in a declining state, expired on the eighth day, lamenting the loss of both his children.[7] However guiltless in his intention, the younger Andronicus might impute a brother's and a father's death to the consequence of his own vices; and deep was the sigh of thinking and feeling men when they perceived, instead of sorrow and repentance, his ill-dissembled joy on the removal of two odious competitors. By these melancholy events, and the increase of his disorders, the mind of the elder emperor was gradually alienated; and, after many fruitless reproofs, he transferred on another grandson[8] his hopes and affection. The change was announced by the new oath of allegiance to the reigning sovereign, and the *person* whom he should appoint for his successor; and the acknowledged heir, after a repetition of insults and complaints, was exposed to the indignity of a public trial. Before the sentence, which would probably have condemned him to a dungeon or a cell, the emperor was informed that the palace courts were filled with the armed followers of his grandson; the judgment was softened to a treaty of reconciliation; and the triumphant escape of the prince encouraged the ardour of the younger faction.

Yet the capital, the clergy, and the senate adhered to the person, or at least to the government, of the old emperor; and it was only in the provinces, by flight, and revolt, and foreign succour, that the malcontents could hope to vindicate their cause and subvert his throne. The soul of the enterprise was the great domestic John Cantacuzene: the sally from Constantinople is the first date of his actions and memorials; and if his own pen be most descriptive of his patriotism, an unfriendly historian has not refused to celebrate the zeal and ability which he displayed in the service of the young emperor. That prince escaped from the capital under the pretence of hunting; erected his standard at Adrianople; and, in a few days, assembled fifty thousand horse and foot, whom neither honour nor duty could have armed against the barbarians. Such a force might have saved or commanded the empire; but their counsels were discordant, their motions were slow and doubtful, and their progress was checked by intrigue and negotiation. The quarrel of the two Andronici was protracted, and suspended, and renewed, during a ruinous period of seven years. In the first treaty the relics of the Greek empire were divided: Constantinople, Thessalonica, and the islands were left to the elder, while the younger acquired the sovereignty of the greatest part of Thrace, from Philippi to the Byzantine limit. By the second treaty he stipulated the payment of his troops, his immediate coronation, and an adequate share of the power and revenue of the state. The third civil war was terminated by the surprise of Constantinople, the final retreat of the old emperor, and the sole reign of his victorious grandson. The reasons of this delay may be found in the characters of the men and of the times. When the heir of the monarchy first pleaded his wrongs and his apprehensions, he was heard with pity and applause; and his adherents repeated on all sides the inconsistent promise that he would increase the pay of the soldiers and alleviate the burdens of the people. The grievances of forty years were mingled in his revolt; and the rising generation was fatigued by the endless prospect of a reign whose favourites and maxims were of other times. The youth of Andronicus had been without spirit, his age was without reverence: his taxes produced an annual revenue of five hundred thousand pounds; yet the richest of the sovereigns of Christendom was incapable of maintaining three thousand horse and twenty galleys, to resist the destructive progress of the Turks.[9] "How different," said the younger Andronicus, "is my situation from that of the son of Philip! Alexander might complain that his father would leave him nothing to conquer: alas! my grandsire will leave me nothing to lose." But the Greeks were soon admonished that the public disorders could not be healed by a civil war; and that their young favourite was not destined to be the saviour of a falling empire. On the first repulse his party was broken by his own levity, their intestine discord, and the intrigues of the ancient court, which tempted each malcontent to desert or betray the cause of rebellion. Andronicus the younger was touched with remorse, or fatigued with business, or deceived by negotiation: pleasure rather than power was his aim; and the licence of maintaining a thousand hounds, a thousand hawks, and a thousand huntsmen, was sufficient to sully his fame and disarm his ambition.

Let us now survey the catastrophe of this busy plot and the final situation of the principal actors.[10] The age of Andronicus was consumed in civil discord; and, amidst the events of war and treaty, his power and reputation continually decayed, till the fatal night in which the gates of the city and palace were opened without resistance to his grandson. His principal commander scorned the repeated warnings of danger; and, retiring to rest in the vain security of ignorance, abandoned the feeble monarch, with some priests and pages, to the terrors of a sleepless night. These terrors were quickly realised by the hostile shouts which proclaimed the titles and victory of Andronicus the younger; and the aged emperor, falling prostrate before an image of the Virgin, despatched a suppliant message to resign the sceptre and to obtain his life at the hands of the conqueror. The answer of his grandson was decent and pious; at the prayer of his friends the younger Andronicus assumed the sole administration; but the elder still enjoyed the name and pre-eminence of the first emperor, the use of the great palace, and a pension of twenty-four thousand pieces of gold, one half of which was assigned on the royal treasure and the other on the fishery of Constantinople. But his impotence was soon exposed to contempt and oblivion; the vast silence of the palace was disturbed only by the cattle and poultry of the neighbourhood, which roved with impunity through the solitary courts; and a reduced allowance of ten thousand pieces of gold[11] was all that he could ask and more than he could hope. His calamities were embittered by the gradual extinction of sight; his confinement was rendered each day more rigorous; and during the absence and sickness of his grandson, his inhuman keepers, by the threats of instant death, compelled him to exchange the purple for the monastic habit and profession. The monk *Antony* had renounced the pomp of the world: yet he had occasion for a coarse fur in the winter season; and as wine was forbidden by his confessor, and water by his physician, the sherbet of Egypt was his common drink. It was not without difficulty that the late emperor could procure three or four pieces to satisfy these simple wants; and if he bestowed the gold to relieve the more painful distress of a friend, the sacrifice is of some weight in the scale of humanity and religion. Four years after his abdication Andronicus, or Antony, expired in a cell, in the seventy-fourth year of his age: and the last strain of adulation could only promise a more splendid crown of glory in heaven than he had enjoyed upon earth.[12]

Nor was the reign of the younger, more glorious or fortunate than that of the elder, Andronicus.[13] He gathered the fruits of ambition; but the taste was transient and bitter: in the supreme station he lost the remains of his early popularity; and the defects of his character became still more conspicuous to the world. The public reproach urged him to march in person against the Turks; nor did his courage fail in the hour of trial; but a defeat and a wound were the only trophies of his expedition in Asia, which confirmed the establishment of the Ottoman monarchy. The abuses of the civil government attained their full maturity and perfection: his neglect of forms and the confusion of national dresses are deplored by the Greeks as the fatal symptoms of the decay of the empire. Andronicus was old before his time; the intemperance of youth had accelerated the infirmities of age; and after being rescued from a dangerous malady by nature, or physic, or the Virgin, he was snatched away before he had accomplished his forty-fifth year. He was twice married; and as the progress of the Latins in arms and arts had softened the prejudices of the Byzantine court, his two wives were chosen in the princely houses of Germany and Italy. The first, Agnes at home, Irene in Greece, was daughter of the duke of Brunswick. Her father[14] was a petty lord[15] in the poor and savage regions of the north of Germany;[16] yet he derived some revenue from his silver-mines;[17] and his family is celebrated by the Greeks as the most ancient and noble of the Teutonic name.[18] After the death of this childless princess, Andronicus sought in marriage Jane, the sister of the count of Savoy;[19] and his suit was preferred to that of the French king.[20] The count respected in his sister the superior majesty of a Roman empress: her retinue was composed of knights and ladies; she was regenerated and crowned in St. Sophia under the more orthodox appellation of Anne; and, at the nuptial feast, the Greeks and Italians vied with each other in the martial exercises of tilts and tournaments.

The empress Anne of Savoy survived her husband: their son, John Palæologus, was left an orphan and an emperor in the ninth year of his age; and his weakness was protected by the first and most deserving of the Greeks. The long and cordial friendship of his father for John Cantacuzene is alike honourable to the prince and the subject. It had been formed amidst the pleasures of their youth: their families were almost equally noble;[21] and the recent lustre of the purple was amply compensated by the energy of a private education. We have seen that the young emperor was saved by Cantacuzene from the power of his grandfather; and, after six years of civil war, the same favourite brought him back in triumph to the palace of Constantinople. Under the reign of Andronicus the younger, the great domestic ruled the emperor and the empire; and it was by his valour and conduct that the isle of Lesbos and the principality of Ætolia were restored to their ancient allegiance. His enemies confess that among the public robbers Cantacuzene alone was moderate and abstemious; and the free and voluntary account which he produces of his own wealth[22] may sustain the presumption that it was devolved by inheritance, and not accumulated by rapine. He does not indeed specify the value of his money, plate, and jewels, yet, after a voluntary gift of two hundred vases of silver, after much had been secreted by his friends and plundered by his foes, his forfeit treasures were sufficient for the equipment of a fleet of seventy galleys. He does not measure the size and number of his estates; but his granaries were heaped with an incredible store of wheat and barley; and the labour of a thousand yoke of oxen might cultivate, according to the practice of antiquity, about sixty-two thousand five hundred acres of arable land.[23] His pastures were stocked with two thousand five hundred brood mares, two hundred camels, three hundred mules, five hundred asses, five thousand horned cattle, fifty thousand hogs, and seventy thousand sheep:[24] a precious record of rural opulence in the last period of the empire, and in a land, most probably in Thrace, so repeatedly wasted by foreign and domestic hostility. The favour of Cantacuzene was above his fortune. In the moments of familiarity, in the hour of sickness, the emperor was desirous to level the distance between them, and pressed his friend to accept the diadem and purple. The virtue of the great domestic, which is attested by his own pen, resisted the dangerous proposal; but the last testament of Andronicus the younger named him the guardian of his son, and the regent of the empire.

Had the regent found a suitable return of obedience and gratitude, perhaps he would have acted with pure and zealous fidelity in the service of his pupil.[25] A guard of five hundred soldiers watched over his person and the palace; the funeral of the late emperor was decently performed, the capital was silent and submissive, and five hundred letters, which Cantacuzene despatched in the first month, informed the provinces of their loss and their duty. The prospect of a tranquil minority was blasted by the great duke or admiral Apocaucus; and to exaggerate *his* perfidy, the Imperial historian is pleased to magnify his own imprudence in raising him to that office against the advice of his more sagacious sovereign. Bold and subtle, rapacious and profuse, the avarice and ambition of Apocaucus were by turns subservient to each other, and his talents were applied to the ruin of his country. His arrogance was heightened by the command of a naval force and an impregnable castle, and under the mask of oaths and flattery he secretly conspired against his benefactor. The female court of the empress was bribed and directed; he encouraged Anne of Savoy to assert, by the law of nature, the tutelage of her son; the love of power was disguised by the anxiety of maternal tenderness; and the founder of the Palæologi had instructed his posterity to dread the example of a perfidious guardian. The patriarch John of Apri was a proud and feeble old man, encompassed by a numerous and hungry kindred. He produced an obsolete epistle of Andronicus, which bequeathed the prince and people to his pious care: the fate of his predecessor Arsenius prompted him to prevent, rather than punish, the crimes of a usurper; and Apocaucus smiled at the success of his own flattery when he beheld the Byzantine priest assuming the state and temporal claims of the Roman pontiff.[26] Between three persons so different in their station and character a private league was concluded: a shadow of authority was restored to the senate, and the people was tempted by the name of freedom. By this powerful confederacy the great domestic was assaulted at first with clandestine, at length with open arms. His prerogatives were disputed, his opinions slighted, his friends persecuted, and his safety was threatened both in the camp and city. In his absence on the public service he was accused of treason, proscribed as an enemy of the church and state, and delivered, with all his adherents, to the sword of justice, the vengeance of the people, and the power of the devil; his fortunes were confiscated, his aged mother was cast into prison, all his past services were buried in oblivion, and he was driven by injustice to perpetrate the crime of which he was accused.[27] From the review of his preceding conduct, Cantacuzene appears to have been guiltless of any treasonable designs; and the only suspicion of his innocence must arise from the vehemence of his protestations, and the sublime purity which he ascribes to his own virtue. While the empress and patriarch still affected the appearances of harmony, he repeatedly solicited the permission of retiring to a private, and even a monastic life. After he had been declared a public enemy it was his fervent wish to throw himself at the feet of the young emperor, and to receive without a murmur the stroke of the executioner: it was not without reluctance that he listened to the voice of reason, which inculcated the sacred duty of saving his family and friends, and proved that he could only save them by drawing the sword and assuming the Imperial title.

In the strong city of Demotica, his peculiar domain, the emperor John Cantacuzenus was invested with the purple buskins: his right leg was clothed by his noble kinsman, the left by the Latin chiefs, on whom he conferred the order of knighthood. But even in this act of revolt he was still studious of loyalty; and the titles of John Palæologus and Anne of Savoy were proclaimed before his own name and that of his wife Irene. Such vain ceremony is a thin disguise of rebellion; nor are there perhaps any *personal* wrongs that can authorise a subject to take arms against his sovereign: but the want of preparation and success may confirm the assurance of the usurper that this decisive step was the effect of necessity rather than of choice. Constantinople adhered to the young emperor; the king of Bulgaria was invited to the relief of Adrianople; the principal cities of Thrace and Macedonia, after some hesitation, renounced their obedience to the great domestic; and the leaders of the troops and provinces were induced by their private interest to prefer the loose dominion of a woman and a priest. The army of Cantacuzene, in sixteen divisions, was stationed on the banks of the Melas to tempt or intimidate the capital: it was dispersed by treachery or fear, and the officers, more especially the mercenary Latins, accepted the bribes and embraced the service of the Byzantine court. After this loss, the rebel emperor (he fluctuated between the two characters) took the road to Thessalonica with a chosen remnant; but he failed in his enterprise on that important place; and he was closely pursued by the great duke, his enemy Apocaucus, at the head of a superior power by sea and land. Driven from the coast, in his march, or rather flight, into the mountains of Servia, Cantacuzene assembled his troops to scrutinise those who were worthy and willing to accompany his broken fortunes.

A base majority bowed and retired; and his trusty band was diminished to two thousand, and at last to five hundred, volunteers. The cral,[28] or despot of the Servians, received him with generous hospitality; but the ally was insensibly degraded to a suppliant, a hostage, a captive; and, in this miserable dependence, he waited at the door of the barbarian, who could dispose of the life and liberty of a Roman emperor. The most tempting offers could not persuade the cral to violate his trust; but he soon inclined to the stronger side, and his friend was dismissed without injury to a new vicissitude of hopes and perils. Near six years the flame of discord burnt with various success and unabated rage; the cities were distracted by the faction of the nobles and the plebeians—the Cantacuzeni and Palæologi: and the Bulgarians, the Servians, and the Turks were invoked on both sides as the instruments of private ambition and the common ruin. The regent deplored the calamities of which he was the author and victim: and his own experience might dictate a just and lively remark on the different nature of foreign and civil war. "The former," said he, "is the external warmth of summer, always tolerable, and often beneficial; the latter is the deadly heat of a fever, which consumes without a remedy the vitals of the constitution."[29]

The introduction of barbarians and savages into the contests of civilised nations is a measure pregnant with shame and mischief, which the interest of the moment may compel, but which is reprobated by the best principles of humanity and reason. It is the practice of both sides to accuse their enemies of the guilt of the first alliances; and those who fail in their negotiations are loudest in their censure of the example which they envy and would gladly imitate. The Turks of Asia were less barbarous perhaps than the shepherds of Bulgaria and Servia, but their religion rendered them the implacable foes of Rome and Christianity. To acquire the friendship of their emirs, the two factions vied with each other in baseness and profusion: the dexterity of Cantacuzene obtained the preference: but the succour and victory were dearly purchased by the marriage of his daughter with an infidel, the captivity of many thousand Christians, and the passage of the Ottomans into Europe, the last and fatal stroke in the fall of the Roman empire. The inclining scale was decided in his favour by the death of Apocaucus, the just though singular retribution of his crimes. A crowd of nobles or plebeians whom he feared or hated had been seized by his orders in the capital and the provinces, and the old palace of Constantine was assigned for the place of their confinement. Some alterations in raising the walls and narrowing the cells had been ingeniously contrived to prevent their escape and aggravate their misery, and the work was incessantly pressed by the daily visits of the tyrant. His guards watched at the gate; and as he stood in the inner court to overlook the architects, without fear or suspicion, he was assaulted and laid breathless on the ground by two resolute prisoners of the Palæologian race,[30] who were armed with sticks and animated by despair. On the rumour of revenge and liberty, the captive multitude broke their fetters, fortified their prison, and exposed from the battlements the tyrant's head, presuming on the favour of the people and the clemency of the empress. Anne of Savoy might rejoice in the fall of a haughty and ambitious minister; but while she delayed to resolve or to act, the populace, more especially the mariners, were excited by the widow of the great duke to a sedition, an assault, and a massacre. The prisoners (of whom the far greater part were guiltless or inglorious of the deed) escaped to a neighbouring church: they were slaughtered at the foot of the altar; and in his death the monster was not less bloody and venomous than in his life. Yet his talents alone upheld the cause of the young emperor; and his surviving associates, suspicious of each other, abandoned the conduct of the war, and rejected the fairest terms of accommodation. In the beginning of the dispute the empress felt and complained that she was deceived by the enemies of Cantacuzene: the patriarch was employed to preach against the forgiveness of injuries; and her promise of immortal hatred was sealed by an oath under the penalty of excommunication.[31] But Anne soon learned to hate without a teacher: she beheld the misfortunes of the empire with the indifference of a stranger; her jealousy was exasperated by the competition of a rival empress; and on the first symptoms of a more yielding temper, she threatened the patriarch to convene a synod and degrade him from his office. Their incapacity and discord would have afforded the most decisive advantage; but the civil war was protracted by the weakness of both parties; and the moderation of Cantacuzene has not escaped the reproach of timidity and indolence. He successively recovered the provinces and cities; and the realm of his pupil was measured by the walls of Constantinople; but the metropolis alone counterbalanced the rest of the empire; nor could he attempt that important conquest till he had secured in his favour the public voice and a private correspondence. An Italian, of the name of Faccioati,[32] had succeeded to the office of great duke: the ships, the guards, and the golden gate were subject to his command; but his humble ambition was bribed to become the instrument of treachery; and the revolution was accomplished without danger or bloodshed. Destitute of the powers of resistance or the hope of relief, the inflexible Anne would have still defended the palace, and have smiled to behold the capital in flames rather than in the possession of a rival. She yielded to the prayers of her friends and enemies, and the treaty was dictated by the conqueror, who professed a loyal and zealous attachment to the son of his benefactor. The marriage of his daughter with John Palæologus was at length consummated; the hereditary right of the pupil was acknowledged, but the sole administration during ten years was vested in the guardian. Two emperors and three empresses were seated on the Byzantine throne; and a general amnesty quieted the apprehensions and confirmed the property of the most guilty subjects. The festival of the coronation and nuptials was celebrated with the appearances of concord and magnificence, and both were equally fallacious. During the late troubles the treasures of the state, and even the furniture of the palace, had been alienated or embezzled; the royal banquet was served in pewter or earthenware; and such was the proud poverty of the times, that the absence of gold and jewels was supplied by the paltry artifices of glass and gilt leather.[33]

I hasten to conclude the personal history of John Cantacuzene.[34] He triumphed and reigned; but his reign and triumph were clouded by the discontent of his own and the adverse faction. His followers might style the general amnesty an act of pardon for his enemies, and of oblivion for his friends: in his cause their estates had been forfeited or plundered; and as they wandered naked and hungry through the streets, they cursed the selfish generosity of a leader who, on the throne of the empire, might relinquish without merit his private inheritance.[35] The adherents of the empress blushed to hold their lives and fortunes by the precarious favour of a usurper, and the thirst of revenge was concealed by a tender concern for the succession, and even the safety, of her son. They were justly alarmed by a petition of the friends of Cantacuzene, that they might be released from their oath of allegiance to the Palæologi,

and intrusted with the defence of some cautionary towns; a measure supported with argument and eloquence, and which was rejected (says the Imperial historian) "by *my* sublime and almost incredible virtue." His repose was disturbed by the sound of plots and seditions, and he trembled lest the lawful prince should be stolen away by some foreign or domestic enemy, who would inscribe his name and his wrongs in the banners of rebellion. As the son of Andronicus advanced in the years of manhood he began to feel and to act for himself, and his rising ambition was rather stimulated than checked by the imitation of his father's vices. If we may trust his own professions, Cantacuzene laboured with honest industry to correct these sordid and sensual appetites, and to raise the mind of the young prince to a level with his fortune. In the Servian expedition the two emperors showed themselves in cordial harmony to the troops and provinces, and the younger colleague was initiated by the elder in the mysteries of war and government. After the conclusion of the peace, Palæologus was left at Thessalonica, a royal residence and a frontier station, to secure by his absence the peace of Constantinople, and to withdraw his youth from the temptations of a luxurious capital. But the distance weakened the powers of control, and the son of Andronicus was surrounded with artful or unthinking companions, who taught him to hate his guardian, to deplore his exile, and to vindicate his rights. A private treaty with the cral or despot of Servia was soon followed by an open revolt; and Cantacuzene, on the throne of the elder Andronicus, defended the cause of age and prerogative, which in his youth he had so vigorously attacked. At his request the empress-mother undertook the voyage of Thessalonica and the office of mediation: she returned without success; and unless Anne of Savoy was instructed by adversity, we may doubt the sincerity, or at least the fervour, of her zeal. While the regent grasped the sceptre with a firm and vigorous hand, she had been instructed to declare that the ten years of his legal administration would soon elapse; and that, after a full trial of the vanity of the world, the emperor Cantacuzene sighed for the repose of a cloister, and was ambitious only of a heavenly crown. Had these sentiments been genuine, his voluntary abdication would have restored the peace of the empire, and his conscience would have been relieved by an act of justice. Palæologus alone was responsible for his future government; and whatever might be his vices, they were surely less formidable than the calamities of a civil war, in which the barbarians and infidels were again invited to assist the Greeks in their mutual destruction. By the arms of the Turks, who now struck a deep and everlasting root in Europe, Cantacuzene prevailed in the third contest in which he had been involved, and the young emperor, driven from the sea and land, was compelled to take shelter among the Latins of the isle of Tenedos. His insolence and obstinacy provoked the victor to a step which must render the quarrel irreconcilable; and the association of his son Matthew, whom he invested with the purple, established the succession in the family of the Cantacuzeni. But Constantinople was still attached to the blood of her ancient princes, and this last injury accelerated the restoration of the rightful heir. A noble Genoese espoused the cause of Palæologus, obtained a promise of his sister, and achieved the revolution with two galleys and two thousand five hundred auxiliaries. Under the pretence of distress they were admitted into the lesser port; a gate was opened, and the Latin shout of "Long life and victory to the emperor John Palæologus!" was answered by a general rising in his favour. A numerous and loyal party yet adhered to the standard of Cantacuzene; but he asserts in his history (does he hope for belief?) that his tender conscience rejected the assurance of conquest; that, in free obedience to the voice of religion and philosophy, he descended from the throne, and embraced with pleasure the monastic habit and profession.[36] So soon as he ceased to be a prince, his successor was not unwilling that he should be a saint; the remainder of his life was devoted to piety and learning; in the cells of Constantinople and Mount Athos the monk Joasaph was respected as the temporal and spiritual father of the emperor; and if he issued from his retreat, it was as the minister of peace, to subdue the obstinacy and solicit the pardon of his rebellious son.[37]

Yet in the cloister the mind of Cantacuzene was still exercised by theological war. He sharpened a controversial pen against the Jews and Mohammedans;[38] and in every state he defended with equal zeal the divine light of Mount Thabor, a memorable question which consummates the religious follies of the Greeks. The fakirs of India[39] and the monks of the Oriental church were alike persuaded that, in total abstraction of the faculties of the mind and body, the purer spirit may ascend to the enjoyment and vision of the Deity. The opinion and practice of the monasteries of Mount Athos[40] will be best represented in the words of an abbot who flourished in the eleventh century. "When thou art alone in thy cell," says the ascetic teacher "shut thy door, and seat thyself in a corner raise thy mind above all things vain and transitory; recline thy beard and chin on thy breast turn thy eyes and thy thought towards the middle of thy belly, the region of the naval; and search the place of the heart, the seat of the soul. At first all will be dark and comfortless but if you persevere day and night, you will fee an ineffable joy; and no sooner has the soul discovered the place of the heart, than it is involved in a mystic and etherial light." This light, the production of a distempered fancy, the creature of an empty stomach and an empty brain, was adored by the Quietists as the pure and perfect essence of God himself; and as long as the folly was confined to Mount Athos, the simple solitaries were not inquisitive how the divine essence could be a *material* substance, or how an *immaterial* substance could be perceived by the eyes of the body. But in the reign of the younger Andronicus these monasteries were visited by Barlaam,[41] a Calabrian monk, who was equally skilled in philosophy and theology, who possessed the languages of the Greeks and Latins, and whose versatile genius could maintain their opposite creeds, according to the interest of the moment. The indiscretion of an ascetic revealed to the curious traveller the secrets of mental prayer; and Barlaam embraced the opportunity of ridiculing the Quietists, who placed the soul in the naval; of accusing the monks of Mount Athos of heresy and blasphemy. His attack compelled the more learned to renounce or dissemble the simple devotion of their brethren, and Gregory Palamas introduced a scholastic distinction between the essence and operation of God. His inaccessible essence dwells in the midst of an uncreated and eternal light; and this beatific vision of the saints had been manifested to the disciples on Mount Thabor in the transfiguration of Christ. Yet this distinction could not escape the reproach of polytheism; the eternity of the light of Thabor was fiercely denied, and Barlaam still charged the Palamites with holding two eternal substances, a visible and an invisible God. From the rage of the monks of Mount Athos, who threatened his life, the Calabrian retired to Constantinople, where his smooth and specious manners introduced him to the favour of the great domestic and the emperor. The court and the city were involved in this theological dispute, which flamed amidst the civil war; but the doctrine of Barlaam was disgraced by his flight and apostasy; the Palamites triumphed; and their adversary, the patriarch John of Apri, was deposed by the consent of the adverse factions of the state. In the character of emperor and theologian, Cantacuzene presided in the synod of the Greek church, which established, as an article of faith, the uncreated light of Mount Thabor: and, after so many insults, the reason of mankind was slightly wounded by the addition of a single absurdity. Many rolls of paper or parchment have been blotted; and the impenitent sectaries, who refused to subscribe the orthodox creed, were deprived of the honours of Christian burial; but in the next age the question was forgotten, nor can I learn that the axe or the faggot were employed for the extirpation of the Barlaamite heresy.[42]

For the conclusion of this chapter I have reserved the Genoese war, which shook the throne of Cantacuzene and betrayed the debility of the Greek empire. The Genoese, who, after the recovery of Constantinople, were seated in the suburb of Pera or Galata, received that honourable fief from the bounty of the emperor. They were indulged in the use of their laws and magistrates, but they submitted to the duties of vassals and subjects; the forcible word of *liegemen*[43] was borrowed from the Latin jurisprudence, and their *podestà*, or chief, before he entered on his office, saluted the emperor with loyal acclamations and vows of fidelity. Genoa sealed a firm alliance with the Greeks; and, in the case of a defensive war, a supply of fifty empty galleys, and a succour of fifty galleys completely armed and manned, was promised by the republic to the empire. In the revival of a naval force it was the aim of Michael Palæologus to deliver himself from a foreign aid; and his vigorous government contained the Genoese of Galata within those limits which the insolence of wealth and freedom provoked them to exceed. A sailor threatened that they should soon be masters of Constantinople, and slew the Greek who resented this national affront; and an armed vessel, after refusing to salute the palace, was guilty of some acts of piracy in the Black Sea. Their countrymen threatened to support their cause: but the long and open village of Galata was instantly surrounded by the Imperial troops; till, in the moment of the assault, the prostrate Genoese implored the clemency of their sovereign. The defenceless situation which secured their obedience exposed

them to the attack of their Venetian rivals, who, in the reign of the elder Andronicus, presumed to violate the majesty of the throne. On the approach of their fleets, the Genoese, with their families and effects, retired into the city; their empty habitations were reduced to ashes; and the feeble prince, who had viewed the destruction of his suburb, expressed his resentment, not by arms, but by ambassadors. This misfortune, however, was advantageous to the Genoese, who obtained, and imperceptibly abused, the dangerous licence of surrounding Galata with a strong wall, of introducing into the ditch the waters of the sea, of erecting lofty turrets, and of mounting a train of military engines on the rampart. The narrow bounds in which they had been circumscribed were insufficient for the growing colony; each day they acquired some addition of landed property, and the adjacent hills were covered with their villas and castles, which they joined and protected by new fortifications.[44] The navigation and trade of the Euxine was the patrimony of the Greek emperors, who commanded the narrow entrance, the gates, as it were, of that inland sea. In the reign of Michael Palæologus their prerogative was acknowledged by the sultan of Egypt, who solicited and obtained the liberty of sending an annual ship for the purchase of slaves in Circassia and the Lesser Tartary: a liberty pregnant with mischief to the Christian cause, since these youths were transformed by education and discipline into the formidable Mamalukes.[45] From the colony of Pera the Genoese engaged with superior advantage in the lucrative trade of the Black Sea, and their industry supplied the Greeks with fish and corn, two articles of food almost equally important to a superstitious people. The spontaneous bounty of nature appears to have bestowed the harvests of the Ukraine, the produce of a rude and savage husbandry; and the endless exportation of salt-fish and caviar is annually renewed by the enormous sturgeons that are caught at the mouth of the Don or Tanais, in their last station of the rich mud and shallow water of the Mæotis.[46] The waters of the Oxus, the Caspian, the Volga, and the Don opened a rare and laborious passage for the gems and spices of India; and after three months' march the caravans of Carizme met the Italian vessels in the harbours of Crimea.[47] These various branches of trade were monopolised by the diligence and power of the Genoese. Their rivals of Venice and Pisa were forcibly expelled; the natives were awed by the castles and cities which arose on the foundations of their humble factories; and their principal establishment of Caffa[48] was besieged without effect by the Tartar powers. Destitute of a navy, the Greeks were oppressed by these haughty merchants, who fed or famished Constantinople according to their interest. They proceeded to usurp the customs, the fishery, and even the toll, of the Bosphorus; and while they derived from these objects a revenue of two hundred thousand pieces of gold, a remnant of thirty thousand was reluctantly allowed to the emperor.[49] The colony of Pera or Galata acted, in peace and war, as an independent state; and, as it will happen in distant settlements, the Genoese podestà too often forgot that he was the servant of his own masters.

These usurpations were encouraged by the weakness of the elder Andronicus, and by the civil wars that afflicted his age and the minority of his grandson. The talents of Cantacuzene were employed to the ruin, rather than the restoration, of the empire; and after his domestic victory he was condemned to an ignominious trial, whether the Greeks or the Genoese should reign in Constantinople. The merchants of Pera were offended by his refusal of some contiguous lands, some commanding heights, which they proposed to cover with new fortifications; and in the absence of the emperor, who was detained at Damotica by sickness, they ventured to brave the debility of a female reign. A Byzantine vessel, which had presumed to fish at the mouth of the harbour, was sunk by these audacious strangers; the fishermen were murdered. Instead of suing for pardon, the Genoese demanded satisfaction; required, in a haughty strain, that the Greeks should renounce the exercise of navigation; and encountered with regular arms the first sallies of the popular indignation. They instantly occupied the debatable land; and by the labour of a whole people, of either sex and of every age, the wall was raised, and the ditch was sunk, with incredible speed. At the same time they attacked and burnt two Byzantine galleys; while the three others, the remainder of the Imperial navy, escaped from their hands: the habitations without the gates, or along the shore, were pillaged and destroyed; and the care of the regent, of the empress Irene, was confined to the preservation of the city. The return of Cantacuzene dispelled the public consternation: the emperor inclined to peaceful counsels; but he yielded to the obstinacy of his enemies, who rejected all reasonable terms, and to the ardour of his subjects, who threatened, in the style of Scripture, to

break them in pieces like a potter's vessel. Yet they reluctantly paid the taxes that he imposed for the construction of ships, and the expenses of the war; and as the two nations were masters, the one of the land, the other of the sea, Constantinople and Pera were pressed by the evils of a mutual siege. The merchants of the colony, who had believed that a few days would terminate the war, already murmured at their losses: the succours from their mother-country were delayed by the factions of Genoa; and the most cautious embraced the opportunity of a Rhodian vessel to remove their families and effects from the scene of hostility. In the spring, the Byzantine fleet, seven galleys and a train of smaller vessels, issued from the mouth of the harbour, and steered in a single line along the shore of Pera; unskilfully presenting their sides to the beaks of the adverse squadron. The crews were composed of peasants and mechanics; nor was their ignorance compensated by the native courage of barbarians: the wind was strong, the waves were rough; and no sooner did the Greeks perceive a distant and inactive enemy, than they leaped headlong into the sea, from a doubtful, to an inevitable, peril. The troops that marched to the attack of the lines of Pera were struck at the same moment with a similar panic; and the Genoese were astonished, and almost ashamed, at their double victory. Their triumphant vessels, crowned with flowers, and dragging after them the captive galleys, repeatedly passed and repassed before the palace: the only virtue of the emperor was patience; and the hope of revenge his sole consolation. Yet the distress of both parties interposed a temporary agreement; and the shame of the empire was disguised by a thin vein of dignity and power. Summoning the chiefs of the colony, Cantacuzene affected to despise the trivial object of the debate; and, after a mild reproof, most liberally granted the lands, which had been previously resigned to the seeming custody of his officers.[50]

But the emperor was soon solicited to violate the treaty, and to join his arms with the Venetians, the perpetual enemies of Genoa and her colonies. While he compared the reasons of peace and war, his moderation was provoked by a wanton insult of the inhabitants of Pera, who discharged from their rampart a large stone that fell in the midst of Constantinople. On his just complaint, they coldly blamed the imprudence of their engineer; but the next day the insult was repeated; and they exulted in a second proof that the royal city was not beyond he reach of their artillery. Cantacuzene instantly signed his treaty with the Venetians; but the weight of the Roman empire was scarcely felt in the balance of these opulent and powerful republics.[51] From the straits of Gibraltar to the mouth of the Tanais, their fleets encountered each other with various success; and a memorable battle was fought in the narrow sea, under the walls of Constantinople. It would not be an easy task to reconcile the accounts of the Greeks, the Venetians, and the Genoese;[52] and while I depend on the narrative of an impartial historian,[53] I shall borrow from each nation the facts that redound to their own disgrace and the honour of their foes. The Venetians, with their allies the Catalans, had the advantage of number; and their fleet, with the poor addition of eight Byzantine galleys, amounted to seventy-five sail: the Genoese did not exceed sixty-four; but in those times their ships of war were distinguished by the superiority of their size and strength. The names and families of their naval commanders, Pisani and Doria, are illustrious in the annals of their country; but the personal merit of the former was eclipsed by the fame and abilities of his rival. They engaged in tempestuous weather; and the tumultuary conflict was continued from the dawn to the extinction of light. The enemies of the Genoese applaud their prowess; the friends of the Venetians are dissatisfied with their behaviour; but all parties agree in praising the skill and boldness of the Catalans, who, with many wounds, sustained the brunt of the action. On the separation of the fleets, the event might appear doubtful; but the thirteen Genoese galleys that had been sunk or taken were compensated by a double loss of the allies; of fourteen Venetians, ten Catalans, and two Greeks; and even the grief of the conquerors expressed the assurance and habit of more decisive victories. Pisani confessed his defeat by retiring into a fortified harbour, from whence, under the pretext of the orders of the senate, he steered with a broken and flying squadron for the isle of Candia, and abandoned to his rivals the sovereignty of the sea. In a public epistle,[54] addressed to the doge and senate, Petrarch employs his eloquence to reconcile the maritime powers, the two luminaries of Italy. The orator celebrates the valour and victory of the Genoese, the first of men in the exercise of naval war: he drops a tear on the misfortunes of their Venetian brethren; but he exhorts them to pursue with fire and sword the base and perfidious Greeks; to purge the metropolis of the East from the heresy with which it was infected. Deserted by their friends, the Greeks were incapable of resistance; and three months after the battle the emperor Cantacuzene solicited and subscribed a treaty, which for ever banished the Venetians and Catalans, and granted to the Genoese a monopoly of trade, and almost a right of dominion. The Roman Empire (I smile in transcribing the name) might soon have sunk into a province of Genoa, if the ambition of the republic had not been checked by the ruin of her freedom and naval power. A long contest of one hundred and thirty years was determined by the triumph of Venice; and the factions of the Genoese compelled them to seek for domestic peace under the protection of a foreign lord, the duke of Milan, or the French king. Yet the spirit of commerce survived that of conquest; and the colony of Pera still awed the capital and navigated the Euxine, till it was involved by the Turks in the final servitude of Constantinople itself.

CHAPTER LXIV

Conquests of Zingis Khan and the Moguls from China to Poland. Escape of Constantinople and the Greeks. Origin of the Ottoman Turks in Bithynia. Reigns and Victories of Othman, Orchan, Amurath the First, and Bajazet the First. Foundation and Progress of the Turkish Monarchy in Asia and Europe. Danger of Constantinople and the Greek Empire.

FROM the petty quarrels of a city and her suburbs, from the cowardice and discord of the falling Greeks, I shall now ascend to the victorious Turks; whose domestic slavery was ennobled by martial discipline, religious enthusiasm, and the energy of the national character. The rise and progress of the Ottomans, the present sovereigns of Constantinople, are connected with the most important scenes of modern history; but they are founded on a previous knowledge of the great eruption of the Moguls and Tartars, whose rapid conquests may be compared with the primitive convulsions of nature, which have agitated and altered the surface of the globe. I have long since asserted my claim to introduce the nations, the immediate or remote authors of the fall of the Roman empire; nor can I refuse myself to those events which, from their uncommon magnitude, will interest a philosophic mind in the history of blood.[1]

From the spacious highlands between China, Siberia, and the Caspian Sea the tide of emigration and war has repeatedly been poured. These ancient seats of the Huns and Turks were occupied in the twelfth century by many pastoral tribes, of the same descent and similar manners, which were united and led to conquest by the formidable Zingis. In his ascent to greatness that barbarian (whose private appellation was Temugin) had trampled on the necks of his equals. His birth was noble; but it was in the pride of victory that the prince or people deduced his seventh ancestor from the immaculate conception of a virgin. His father had reigned over thirteen hordes, which composed about thirty or forty thousand families: above two-thirds refused to pay tithes or obedience to his infant son; and at the age of thirteen Temugin fought a battle against his rebellious subjects. The future conqueror of Asia was reduced to fly and to obey; but he rose superior to his fortune, and in his fortieth year he had established his fame and dominion over the circumjacent tribes. In a state of society in which policy is rude and valour is universal, the ascendant of one man must be founded on his power and resolution to punish his enemies and recompense his friends. His first military league was ratified by the simple rites of sacrificing a horse and tasting of a running stream: Temugin pledged himself to divide with his followers the sweets and bitters of life; and when he had shared among them his horses and apparel, he was rich in their gratitude and his own hopes. After his first victory he placed seventy caldrons on the fire, and seventy of the most guilty rebels were cast headlong into the boiling water. The sphere of his attraction was continually enlarged by the ruin of the proud and the submission of the prudent; and the boldest chieftains might tremble when they beheld, enchased in silver, the skull of the khan of the Keraites;[2] who, under the name of Prester John, had corresponded with the Roman pontiff and the princes of Europe. The ambition of Temugin condescended to employ the arts of superstition; and it was from a naked prophet, who could ascend to heaven on a white horse, that he accepted the title of Zingis,[3] the *most great*; and a divine right to the conquest and dominion of the earth. In a general *couroultai*, or diet, he was seated on a felt, which was long afterwards revered as a relic, and solemnly proclaimed great khan or emperor of the Moguls[4] and Tartars.[5] Of these kindred, though rival, names, the former had given birth to the imperial race, and the latter has been extended by accident or error over the spacious wilderness of the north.

The code of laws which Zingis dictated to his subjects was adapted to the preservation of domestic peace and the exercise of foreign hostility. The punishment of death was inflicted on the crimes of adultery, murder, perjury, and the capital thefts of a horse or ox; and the fiercest of men were mild and just in their intercourse with each other. The future election of the great khan was vested in the princes of his family and the heads of the tribes; and the regulations of the chase were essential to the pleasures and plenty of a Tartar camp. The victorious nation was held sacred from all servile labours, which were abandoned to slaves and strangers; and every labour was servile except the profession of arms. The service and discipline of the troops, who were armed with bows, scimitars, and iron maces, and divided by hundreds, thousands, and ten thousands, were the institutions of a veteran commander. Each officer and soldier was made responsible, under pain of death, for the safety and honour of his companions; and the spirit of conquest breathed in the law that peace should never be granted unless to a vanquished and suppliant enemy. But it is the religion of Zingis that best deserves our wonder and applause. The Catholic inquisitors of Europe, who defended nonsense by cruelty, might have been confounded by the example of a barbarian, who anticipated the lessons of philosophy,[6] and established by his laws a system of pure theism and perfect toleration. His first and only article of faith was the existence of one God, the Author of all good, who fills by his presence the heavens and earth, which he has created by his power. The Tartars and Moguls were addicted to the idols of their peculiar tribes; and many of them had been converted by the foreign missionaries to the religions of Moses, of Mohammed, and of Christ. These various systems in freedom and concord were taught and practised within the precincts of the same camp; and the Bonze, the Imam, the Rabbi, the Nestorian, and the Latin priest, enjoyed the same honourable exemption from ervice and tribute: in the mosque of Bochara the insolent victor might trample the Koran under his horse's feet, but the calm legislator respected the prophets and pontiffs of the most hostile sects. The reason of Zingis was not informed by books: the khan could neither read nor write; and, except the tribe of the Igours, the greatest part of the Moguls and Tartars were as illiterate as their sovereign. The memory of their exploits was preserved by tradition: sixty-eight years after the death of Zingis these traditions were collected and transcribed;[7] the brevity of their domestic annals may be supplied by the Chinese,[8] Persians,[9] Armenians,[10] Syrians,[11] Arabians,[12] Greeks,[13] Russians,[14] Poles,[15] Hungarians,[16] and Latins;[17] and each nation will deserve credit in the relation of their own disasters and defeats.[18]

The arms of Zingis and his lieutenants successively reduced the hordes of the desert, who pitched their tents between the wall of China and the Volga; and the Mogul emperor became the monarch of the pastoral world, the lord of many millions of shepherds and soldiers, who felt their united strength, and were impatient to rush on the mild and wealthy climates of the south. His ancestors had been the tributaries of the Chinese emperors; and Temugin himself had been disgraced by a title of honour and servitude. The court of Pekin was astonished by an embassy from its former vassal, who, in the tone of the king of nations, exacted the tribute and obedience which he had paid, and who affected to treat the *son of heaven* as the most contemptible of mankind. A haughty answer disguised their secret apprehensions; and their fears were soon justified by the march of innumerable squadrons, who pierced on all sides the feeble rampart of the great wall. Ninety cities were stormed, or starved, by the Moguls; ten only escaped; and Zingis, from a knowledge of the filial piety of the Chinese, covered his vanguard with their captive parents; an unworthy, and by degrees a fruitless, abuse of the virtue of his enemies. His invasion was supported by the revolt of a hundred thousand Khitans, who guarded the frontier: yet he listened to a treaty; and a princess of China, three thousand horses, five hundred youths and as many virgins, and a tribute of gold and silk, were the price of his retreat. In his second expedition he compelled the Chinese emperor to retire beyond the Yellow River to a more southern residence. The siege of Pekin[19] was long and laborious: the inhabitants were reduced by famine to decimate and devour their fellow-citizens; when their ammunition was spent, they discharged ingots of gold and silver from their engines; but the Moguls introduced a mine to the centre of the capital; and the conflagration of the palace burnt above thirty days. China was desolated by Tartar war and domestic faction; and the five northern provinces were added to the empire of Zingis.

In the West he touched the dominions of Mohammed sultan of Carizme, who reigned from the Persian Gulf to the borders of India and Turkestan; and who, in the proud imitation of Alexander the Great, forgot the servitude and ingratitude of his fathers to the house of Seljuk. It was the wish of Zingis to establish a friendly and commercial intercourse with the most powerful of the Moslem princes; nor could he be tempted by the secret solicitations of the caliph of Bagdad, who sacrificed to his personal wrongs the safety of the church and state. A rash and inhuman deed provoked and justified the Tartar arms in the invasion of the southern Asia. A caravan of three ambassadors and one hundred and fifty merchants was arrested and murdered at Otrar, by the command of Mohammed; nor was it till after a demand and denial of justice, till he had prayed and fasted three nights on a mountain, that the Mogul emperor appealed to the judgment of God and his sword. Our European battles, says a philosophic writer,[20] are petty skirmishes, if compared to the numbers that have fought and fallen in the fields of Asia. Seven hundred thousand Moguls and Tartars are said to have marched under the standard of Zingis and his four sons. In the vast plains that extend to the north of the Sihon or Jaxartes they were encountered by four hundred thousand soldiers of the sultan; and in the first battle, which was suspended by the night, one hundred and sixty thousand Carizmians were slain. Mohammed was astonished by the multitude and valour of his enemies; he withdrew from the scene of danger, and distributed his troops in the frontier towns; trusting that the barbarians, invincible in the field, would be repulsed by the length and difficulty of so many regular sieges. But the prudence of Zingis had formed a body of Chinese engineers, skilled in the mechanic arts; informed perhaps of the secret of gunpowder, and capable, under his discipline, of attacking a foreign country with more vigour and success than they had defended their own. The Persian historians will relate the sieges and reduction of Otrar, Cogende, Bochara, Samarcand, Carizme, Herat, Merou, Nisabour, Balch, and Candahar; and the conquest of the rich and populous countries of Transoxiana, Carizme, and Chorazan. The destructive hostilities of Attila and the Huns have long since been elucidated by the example of Zingis and the Moguls; and in this more proper place I shall be content to observe, that, from the Caspian to the Indus, they ruined a tract of many hundred miles, which was adorned with the habitations and labours of mankind, and that five centuries have not been sufficient to repair the ravages of four years. The Mogul emperor encouraged or indulged the fury of his troops: the hope of future possession was lost in the ardour of rapine and slaughter; and the cause of the war exasperated their native fierceness by the pretence of justice and revenge. The downfall and death of the sultan Mohammed, who expired, unpitied and alone, in a desert island of the Caspian Sea, is a poor atonement for the calamities of which he was the author. Could the Carizmian empire have been saved by a single hero, it would have been saved by his son Gelaleddin, whose active valour repeatedly checked the Moguls in the career of victory. Retreating, as he fought, to the banks of the Indus, he was oppressed by their innumerable host, till, in the last moment of despair, Gelaleddin spurred his horse into the waves, swam one of the broadest and most rapid rivers of Asia, and extorted the admiration and applause of Zingis himself. It was in this camp that the Mogul conqueror yielded with reluctance to the murmurs of his weary and wealthy troops, who sighed for the enjoyment of their native land. Incumbered with the spoils of Asia, he slowly measured back his footsteps, betrayed some pity for the misery of the vanquished, and declared his intention of rebuilding the cities which had been swept away by the tempest of his arms. After he had repassed the Oxus and Jaxartes he was joined by two generals whom he had detached with thirty thousand horse to subdue the western provinces of Persia. They had trampled on the nations which opposed their passage, penetrated through the gates of Derbend, traversed the Volga and the desert, and accomplished the circuit of the Caspian Sea, by an expedition which had never been attempted, and has never been repeated. The return of Zingis was signalised by the overthrow of the rebellious or independent kingdoms of Tartary; and he died in the fulness of years and glory, with his last breath exhorting and instructing his sons to achieve the conquest of the Chinese empire.

The harem of Zingis was composed of five hundred wives and concubines; and of his numerous progeny, four sons, illustrious by their birth and merit, exercised under their father the principal offices of peace and war. Toushi was his great huntsman, Zagatai[21] his judge Octai his minister, and Tuli his general; and their names and actions are often conspicuous in the history of his conquests. Firmly united for their own and the public interest, the three brothers and their families were content with dependent sceptres; and Octai, by general consent, was proclaimed great khan, or emperor of the Moguls and Tartars. He was succeeded by his son Gayuk, after whose death the empire devolved to his cousins Mangou and Cublai the sons of Tuli, and the grandsons of Zingis In the sixty-eight years of his four first successors, the Mogul subdued almost all Asia and a large portion of Europe. Without confining myself to the order of time, without expatiating on the detail of events, I shall present a general picture of the progress of their arms; I. In the East, II. In the South; III. In the West; and IV. In the North.

I. Before the invasion of Zingis, China was divided into two empires or dynasties of the North and South;[22] and the difference of origin and interest was smoothed by a general conformity of laws, language, and national manners. The Northern empire, which had been dismembered by Zingis, was finally subdued seven years after his death. After the loss of Pekin, the emperor had fixed his residence at Kaifong, a city many leagues in circumference, and which contained, according to the Chinese annals, fourteen hundred thousand families of inhabitants and fugitives. He escaped from thence with only seven horsemen, and made his last stand in a third capital, till at length the hopeless monarch, protesting his innocence and accusing his fortune, ascended a funeral pile, and gave orders that, as soon as he had stabbed himself, the fire should be kindled by his attendants. The dynasty of the *Song*, the native and ancient sovereigns of the whole empire, survived about forty-five years the fall of the Northern usurpers; and the perfect conquest was reserved for the arms of Cublai. During this interval the Moguls were often diverted by foreign wars; and, if the Chinese seldom dared to meet their victors in the field, their passive courage presented an endless succession of cities to storm and of millions to slaughter. In the attack and defence of places the engines of antiquity and the Greek fire were alternately employed: the use of gunpowder in cannon and bombs appears as a familiar practice;[23] and the sieges were conducted by the Mohammedans and Franks, who had been liberally invited into the service of Cublai. After passing the great river the troops and artillery were conveyed along a series of canals, till they invested the royal residence of Hamcheu, or Quinsay, in the country of silk, the most delicious climate of China. The emperor, a defenceless youth, surrendered his person and sceptre; and before he was sent in exile into Tartary he struck nine times the ground with his forehead, to adore in prayer or thanksgiving the mercy of the great khan. Yet the war (it was now styled a rebellion) was still maintained in the southern provinces from Hamcheu to Canton; and the obstinate remnant of independence and hostility was transported from the land to the sea. But when the fleet of the *Song* was surrounded and oppressed by a superior armament, their last champion leaped into the waves with his infant emperor in his arms. "It is more glorious," he cried, "to die a prince than to live a slave." A hundred thousand Chinese imitated his example; and the whole empire, from Tonkin to the great wall, submitted to the dominion of Cublai. His boundless ambition aspired to the conquest of Japan: his fleet was twice shipwrecked; and the lives of a hundred thousand Moguls and Chinese were sacrificed in the fruitless expedition. But the circumjacent kingdoms, Corea, Tonkin, Cochin-china, Pegu, Bengal, and Thibet, were reduced in different degrees of tribute and obedience by the effort or terror of his arms. He explored the Indian Ocean with a fleet of a thousand ships: they sailed in sixty-eight days most probably to the isle of Borneo, under the equinoctial line; and though they returned not without spoil or glory, the emperor was dissatisfied that the savage king had escaped from their hands.

II. The conquest of Hindostan by the Moguls was reserved in a later period for the house of Timour; but that of Iran, or Persia, was achieved by Holagou Khan, the grandson of Zingis, the brother and lieutenant of the two successive emperors, Mangou and Cublai. I shall not enumerate the crowd of sultans, emirs, and atabeks whom he trampled into dust; but the extirpation of the *Assassins*, or Ismaelians[24] of Persia, may be considered as a service to mankind. Among the hills to the south of the Caspian these odious sectaries had reigned with impunity above a hundred and sixty years; and their prince, or imam, established his lieu-tenant to lead and govern the colony of Mount Libanus, so famous and formidable in the history of the crusades.[25] With the fanaticism of the Koran the Ismaelians had blended the Indian transmigration and the visions of their own prophets; and it was their first duty to devote their souls and bodies in blind obedience to the vicar of God. The daggers of his missionaries were felt both in the East and West: the Christians and the Moslems enumerate, and perhaps multiply, the illustrious victims that were sacrificed to the zeal, avarice, or resentment of *the old man* (as he was corruptly styled) *of the mountain*. But these daggers, his only arms, were broken by the sword of Holagou, and not a vestige is left of the enemies of mankind, except the word *assassin*, which, in the most odious sense, has been adopted in the languages of Europe. The extinction of the Abbassides cannot be indifferent to the spectators of their greatness and decline. Since the fall of their Seljukian tyrants the caliphs had recovered their lawful dominion of Bagdad and the Arabian Irak; but the city was distracted by theological factions, and the commander of the faithful was lost in a harem of seven hundred concubines. The invasion of the Moguls he encountered with feeble arms and haughty embassies. "On the divine decree," said the caliph Mostasem, "is founded the throne of the sons of Abbas: and their foes shall surely be destroyed in this world and in the next. Who is this Holagou that dares to rise against them? If he be desirous of peace, let him instantly depart from the sacred territory; and perhaps he may obtain from our clemency the pardon of his fault." This presumption was cherished by a perfidious vizir, who assured his master that, even if the barbarians had entered the city, the women and children from the terraces would be sufficient to overwhelm them with stones. But when Holagou touched the phantom, it instantly vanished into smoke. After a siege of two months Bagdad was stormed and sacked by the Moguls; and their savage commander pronounced the death of the caliph Mostasem, the last of the temporal successors of Mohammed; whose noble kinsmen, of the race of Abbas, had reigned in Asia above five hundred years. Whatever might be the designs of the conqueror, the holy cities of Mecca and Medina[26] were protected by the Arabian desert; but the Moguls spread beyond the Tigris and Euphrates, pillaged Aleppo and Damascus, and threatened to join the Franks in the deliverance of Jerusalem. Egypt was lost had she been defended only by her feeble offspring; but the Mamalukes had breathed in their infancy the keenness of a Scythian air: equal in valour, superior in discipline, they met the Moguls in many a well-fought field; and drove back the stream of hostility to the eastward of the Euphrates. But it overflowed with resistless violence the kingdoms of Armenia and Anatolia, of which the former was possessed by the Christians and the latter by the Turks. The sultans of Iconium opposed some resistance to the Mogul arms till Azzadin sought a refuge among the Greeks of Constantinople, and his feeble successors, the last of the Seljukian dynasty, were finally extirpated by the khans of Persia.

III. No sooner had Octai subverted the northern empire of China than he resolved to visit with his arms the most remote countries of the West. Fifteen hundred thousand Moguls and Tartars were inscribed on the military roll: of these the great khan selected a third, which he intrusted to the command of his nephew Batou, the son of Tuli; who reigned over his father's conquests to the north of the Caspian Sea. After a festival of forty days Batou set forwards on this great expedition; and such was the speed and ardour of his innumerable squadrons, that in less than six years they had measured a line of ninety degrees of longitude, a fourth part of the circumference of the globe. The great rivers of Asia and Europe, the Volga and Kama, the Don and Borysthenes, the Vistula and Danube, they either swam with their horses or passed on the ice, or traversed in leathern boats, which followed the camp and transported their waggons and artillery. By the first victories of Batou the remains of national freedom were eradicated in the immense plains of Turkestan and Kipzak.[27] In his rapid progress he overran the kingdoms, as they are now styled, of Astracan and Cazan; and the troops which he detached towards Mount Caucasus explored the most secret recesses of Georgia and Circassia. The civil discord of the great dukes, or princes, of Russia betrayed their country to the Tartars. They spread from Livonia to the Black Sea, and both Moscow and Kiow, the modern and the ancient capitals, were reduced to ashes; a temporary ruin, less fatal than the deep, and perhaps indelible, mark which a servitude of two hundred years has imprinted on the character of the Russians. The Tartars ravaged with equal fury the countries which they hoped to possess and those which they were hastening to leave. From the permanent conquest of Russia they made a deadly, though transient, inroad into the heart of Poland, and as far as the borders of Germany. The cities of Lublin and Cracow were obliterated: they approached the shores of the Baltic; and in the battle of Lignitz they defeated the dukes of Silesia, the Polish palatines, and the great master of the Teutonic order, and filled nine sacks with the right ears of the slain. From Lignitz, the extreme point of their western march, they turned aside to the invasion of Hungary; and the presence or spirit of Batou inspired the host of five hundred thousand men: the Carpathian hills could not be long impervious to their divided columns; and their approach had been fondly disbelieved till it was irresistibly felt. The king, Bela the Fourth, assembled the military force of his counts and bishops; but he had alienated the nation by adopting a vagrant horde of forty thousand families of Comans, and these savage guests were provoked to revolt by the suspicion of treachery and the murder of their prince. The whole country north of the Danube was lost in a day and depopulated in a summer; and the ruins of cities and churches were overspread with the bones of the natives who expiated the sins of their Turkish ancestors. An ecclesiastic who fled from the sack of Waradin describes the calamities which he had seen or suffered; and the sanguinary rage of sieges and battles is far less atrocious than the treatment of the fugitives, who had been allured from the woods under a promise of peace and pardon, and who were coolly slaughtered as soon as they had performed the labours of the harvest and vintage. In the winter the Tartars passed the Danube on the ice and advanced to Gran or Strigonium, a German colony, and the metropolis of the kingdom. Thirty engines were planted against the walls; the ditches were filled with sacks of earth and dead bodies; and after a promiscuous massacre, three hundred noble matrons were slain in the presence of the khan. Of all the cities and fortresses of Hungary three alone survived the Tartar invasion, and the unfortunate Bela hid his head among the islands of the Adriatic.

The Latin world was darkened by this cloud of savage hostility: a Russian fugitive carried the alarm to Sweden; and the remote nations of the Baltic and the ocean trembled at the approach of the Tartars,[28] whom their fear and ignorance were inclined to separate from the human species. Since the invasion of the Arabs in the eighth century Europe had never been exposed to a similar calamity; and if the disciples of Mohammed would have oppressed her religion and liberty, it might be apprehended that the shepherds of Scythia would extinguish her cities, her arts, and all the institutions of civil society. The Roman pontiff attempted to appease and convert these invincible pagans by a mission of Franciscan and Dominican friars; but he was astonished by the reply of the khan, that the sons of God and of Zingis were invested with a divine power to subdue or extirpate the nations; and that the pope would be involved in the universal destruction, unless he visited in person and as a suppliant the royal horde. The emperor Frederic the Second embraced a more generous mode of defence; and his letters to the kings of France and England and the princes of Germany represented the common danger, and urged them to arm their vassals in this just and rational crusade.[29] The Tartars themselves were awed by the fame and valour of the Franks: the town of Neustadt in Austria was bravely defended against them by fifty knights and twenty cross-bows; and they raised the siege on the appearance of a German army. After wasting the adjacent kingdoms of Servia, Bosnia, and Bulgaria, Batou slowly retreated from the Danube to the Volga to enjoy the rewards of victory in the city and palace of Serai, which started at his command from the midst of the desert.

IV. Even the poor and frozen regions of the north attracted the arms of the Moguls: Shei-bani khan, the brother of the great Batou, led a horde of fifteen thousand families into the wilds of Siberia; and his descendants reigned at Tobolskoi above three centuries till the Russian conquest. The spirit of enterprise which pursued the course of the Oby and Yenisei must have led to the discovery of the Icy Sea. After brushing away the monstrous fables of men with dogs' heads and cloven feet, we shall find that, fifteen years after the death of Zingis, the Moguls were informed of the name and manners of the Samoyedes in the neighbourhood of the polar circle, who dwelt in subterraneous huts and derived their furs and their food from the sole occupation of hunting.[30]

While China, Syria, and Poland were invaded at the same time by the Moguls and Tartars, the authors of the mighty mischief were content with the knowledge and declaration that their word was the sword of death. Like the first caliphs, the first successors of Zingis seldom appeared in person at the head of their victorious armies. On the banks of the Onon and Selinga, the royal or *golden horde* exhibited the contrast of simplicity and greatness; of the roasted sheep and mare's milk which composed their banquets; and of a distribution in one day of five hundred waggons of gold and silver. The ambassadors and princes of Europe and Asia were compelled to undertake this distant and laborious pilgrimage; and the life and reign of the great dukes of Russia, the kings of Georgia and Armenia, the sultans of Iconium, and the emirs of Persia, were decided by the frown or smile of the great khan. The sons and grandsons of Zingis had been accustomed to the pastoral life; but the village of Caracorum[31] was gradually ennobled by their election and residence. A change of manners is implied in the removal of Octai and Mangou from a tent to a house; and their example was imitated by the princes of their family and the great officers of the empire. Instead of the boundless forest, the enclosure of a park afforded the more indolent pleasures of the chase; their new habitations were decorated with painting and sculpture; their superfluous treasures were cast in fountains, and basins, and statues of massy silver; and the artists of China and Paris vied with each other in the service of the great khan.[32] Caracorum contained two streets, the one of Chinese mechanics, the other of Mohammedan traders; and the places of religious worship, one Nestorian church, two mosques, and twelve temples of various idols, may represent in some degree the number and division of inhabitants. Yet a French missionary declares that the town of St. Denys, near Paris, was more considerable than the Tartar capital; and that the whole palace of Mangou was scarcely equal to a tenth part of that Benedictine abbey. The conquests of Russia and Syria might amuse the vanity of the great khans; but they were seated on the borders of China; the acquisition of that empire was the nearest and most interesting object; and they might learn from their pastoral economy that it is for the advantage of the shepherd to protect and propagate his flock. I have already celebrated the wisdom and virtue of a mandarin who prevented the desolation of five populous and cultivated provinces. In a spotless administration of thirty years this friend of his country and of mankind continually laboured to mitigate, or suspend, the havoc of war; to save the monuments, and to rekindle the flame, of science; to restrain the military commander by the restoration of civil magistrates; and to instil the love of peace and justice into the minds of the Moguls. He struggled with the barbarism of the first conquerors; but his salutary lessons produced a rich harvest in the second generation. The northern, and by degrees the southern, empire acquiesced in the government of Cublai, the lieutenant, and afterwards the successor, of Mangou; and the nation was loyal to a prince who had been educated in the manners of China. He restored the forms of her venerable constitution; and the victors submitted to the laws, the fashions, and even the prejudices, of the vanquished people. This peaceful triumph, which has been more than once repeated, may be ascribed, in a great measure, to the numbers and servitude of the Chinese. The Mogul army was dissolved in a vast and populous country; and their emperors adopted with pleasure a political system which gives to the prince the solid substance of despotism, and leaves to the subject the empty names of philosophy, freedom, and filial obedience. Under the reign of Cublai, letters and commerce, peace and justice, were restored; the great canal of five hundred miles was opened from Nankin to the capital; he fixed his residence at Pekin; and displayed in his court the magnificence of the greatest monarch of Asia. Yet this learned prince declined from the pure and simple religion of his great ancestor: he sacrificed to the idol Fo; and his blind attachment to the lamas of Thibet and the bonzes of China[33] provoked the censure of the disciples of Confucius. His successors polluted the palace with a crowd of eunuchs, physicians, and astrologers, while thirteen millions of their subjects were consumed in the provinces by famine. One hundred and forty years after the death of Zingis, his degenerate race, the dynasty of the Yuen, was expelled by a revolt of the native Chinese; and the Mogul emperors were lost in the oblivion of the desert. Before this revolution they had forfeited their supremacy over the dependent branches of their house, the khans of Kipzak and Russia, the khans of Zagatai or Transoxiana, and the khans of Iran or Persia. By their distance and power these royal lieutenants had soon been released from the duties of obedience; and after the death of Cublai they scorned to accept a sceptre or a title from his unworthy successors. According to their respective situation, they maintained the simplicity of the pastoral life, or assumed the luxury of the cities of Asia; but the princes and their hordes were alike disposed for the reception of a foreign worship. After some hesitation between the Gospel and the Koran, they conformed to the religion of Mohammed; and while they adopted for their brethren the Arabs and Persians, they renounced all intercourse with the ancient Moguls, the idolaters of China.

In this shipwreck of nations some surprise may be excited by the escape of the Roman empire, whose relics, at the time of the Mogul invasion, were dismembered by the Greeks and Latins. Less potent than Alexander, they were pressed, like the Macedonian, both in Europe and Asia, by the shepherds of Scythia; and had the Tartars undertaken the siege, Constantinople must have yielded to the fate of Pekin, Samarcand, and Bagdad. The glorious and voluntary retreat of Batou from the Danube was insulted by the vain triumph of the Franks and Greeks;[34] and in a second expedition death surprised him in full march to attack the capital of the Cæsars. His brother Borga carried the Tartar arms into Bulgaria and Thrace; but he was diverted from the Byzantine war by a visit to Novogorod, in the fifty-seventh degree of latitude, where he numbered the inhabitants and regulated the tributes, of Russia. The Mogul khan formed an alliance with the Mamalukes against his brethren of Persia: three hundred thousand horse penetrated through the gates of Derbend, and the Greeks might rejoice in the first example of domestic war. After the recovery of Constantinople, Michael Palæologus,[35] at a distance from his court and army, was surprised and surrounded in a Thracian castle by twenty thousand Tartars. But the object of their march was a private interest: they came to the deliverance of Azzadin the Turkish sultan, and were content with his person and the treasure of the emperor. Their general Noga, whose name is perpetuated in the hordes of Astracan, raised a formidable rebellion against Mengo Timour, the third of the kahns of Kipzak, obtained in marriage Maria the natural daughter of Palæologus, and guarded the dominions of his friend and father. The subsequent invasions of a Scythian cast were those of outlaws and fugitives; and some thousands of Alani and Comans, who had been driven from their native seats, were reclaimed from a vagrant life and enlisted in the service of the empire. Such was the influence in Europe of the invasion of the Moguls. The first terror of their arms secured rather than disturbed the peace of the Roman Asia. The sultan of Iconium solicited a personal interview with John Vataces; and his artful policy encouraged the Turks to defend their barrier against the common enemy.[36] That barrier indeed was soon overthrown, and the servitude and ruin of the Seljukians exposed the nakedness of the Greeks. The formidable Holagou threatened to march to Constantinople at the head of four hundred thousand men; and the groundless panic of the citizens of Nice will present an image of the terror which he had inspired. The accident of a procession, and the sound of a doleful litany, "From the fury of the Tartars, good Lord, deliver us," had scattered the hasty report of an assault and massacre. In the blind credulity of fear the streets of Nice were crowded with thousands of both sexes, who knew not from what or to whom they fled; and some hours elapsed before the firmness of the military officers could relieve the city from this imaginary foe. But the ambition of Hola-gou and his successors was fortunately diverted by the conquest of Bagdad and a long vicissitude of Syrian wars; their hostility to the Moslems inclined them to unite with the Greeks and Franks;[37] and their generosity or contempt had offered the kingdom of Anatolia as the reward of an Armenian vassal. The fragments of the Seljukian monarchy were disputed by the emirs who had occupied the cities or the mountains; but they all confessed the supremacy of the khans of Persia; and he often interposed his authority, and sometimes his arms, to check their depredations, and to preserve the peace and balance of his Turkish frontier. The death of Cazan,[38] one of the greatest and most accomplished princes of the house of Zingis, removed this salutary control; and the decline of the Moguls gave a free scope to the rise and progress of the OTTOMAN EMPIRE.[39]

After the retreat of Zingis the sultan Gela-leddin of Carizme had returned from India to the possession and defence of his Persian kingdoms. In the peace of eleven years that hero fought in person fourteen battles; and such was his activity that he led his cavalry in seventeen days from Teflis to Kerman, a march of a thousand miles. Yet he was oppressed by the jealousy of the Moslem princes and the innumerable armies of the Moguls; and after his last defeat Gelaleddin perished ignobly in the mountains of Curdistan. His death dissolved a veteran and adventurous army, which included under the name of Carizmians or Corasmins many Turkman hordes that had attached themselves to the sultan's fortune. The bolder and more powerful chiefs invaded Syria, and violated the holy sepulchre of Jerusalem: the more humble engaged in the service of Aladin sultan of Iconium, and among these were the obscure fathers of the Ottoman line. They had formerly pitched their tents near the southern banks of the Oxus, in the plains of Mahan and Nesa; and it is somewhat remarkable that the same spot should have produced the first authors of the Parthian and Turkish empires. At the head, or in the rear, of a Carizmian army, Soliman Shah was drowned in the passage of the Euphrates: his son Orthogrul became the soldier and subject of Aladin, and established at Sur-gut, on the banks of the Sangar, a camp of four hundred families or tents, whom he governed fifty-two years both in peace and war. He was the father of Thaman, or Athman, whose Turkish name has been melted into the appellation of the caliph Othman: and if we describe that pastoral chief as a shepherd and a robber, we must separate from those characters all idea of ignominy and baseness. Othman possessed, and perhaps surpassed, the ordinary virtues of a soldier; and the circumstances of time and place were propitious to his independence and success. The Seljukian dynasty was no more, and the distance and decline of the Mogul khans soon enfranchised him from the control of a superior. He was situate on the verge of the Greek empire: the Koran sanctified his *gazi*, or holy war, against the infidels; and their political errors unlocked the passes of Mount Olympus, and invited him to descend into the plains of Bithynia. Till the reign of Palæologus these passes had been vigilantly guarded by the militia of the country, who were repaid by their own safety and an exemption from taxes. The emperor abolished their privilege and assumed their office; but the tribute was rigorously collected, the custody of the passes was neglected, and the hardy mountaineers degenerated into a trembling crowd of peasants without spirit or discipline. It was on the twenty-seventh of July, in the year twelve hundred and ninety-nine of the Christian era, that Othman first invaded the territory of Nicodemia;[40] and the singular accuracy of the date seems to disclose some foresight of the rapid and destructive growth of the monster. The annals of the twenty-seven years of his reign would exhibit a repetition of the same inroads; and his hereditary troops were multiplied in each campaign by the accession of captives and volunteers. Instead of retreating to the hills, he maintained the most useful and defensible posts, fortified the towns and castles which he had first pillaged, and renounced the pastoral life for the baths and palaces of his infant capitals. But it was not till Othman was oppressed by age and infirmities that he received the welcome news of the conquest of Prusa, which had been surrendered by famine or treachery to the arms of his son Orchan. The glory of Othman is chiefly founded on that of his descendants; but the Turks have transcribed or composed a royal testament of his last counsels of justice and moderation.[41]

From the conquest of Prusa we may date the true era of the Ottoman empire. The lives and possessions of the Christian subjects were redeemed by a tribute or ransom of thirty thousand crowns of gold; and the city, by the labours of Orchan, assumed the aspect of a Mohammedan capital; Prusa was decorated with a mosque, a college, and an hospital, of royal foundation; the Seljukian coin was changed for the name and impression of the new dynasty; and the most skilful professors of human and divine knowledge attracted the Persian and Arabian students from the ancient schools of Oriental learning. The office of vizir was instituted for Aladin, the brother of Orchan; and a different habit distinguished the citizens from the peasants, the Moslems from the infidels. All the troops of Othman had consisted of loose squadrons of Turkman cavalry, who served without pay and fought without discipline; but a regular body of infantry was first established and trained by the prudence of his son. A great number of volunteers was enrolled with a small stipend, but with the permission of living at home, unless they were summoned to the field: their rude manners and seditious temper disposed Orchan to educate his young captives as his soldiers and those of the prophet; but the Turkish peasants were still allowed to mount on horseback and follow his standard, with the appellation and the hopes of *freebooters*. By these arts he formed an army of twenty-five thousand Moslems: a train of battering engines was framed for the use of sieges; and the first successful experiment was made on the cities of Nice and Nicomedia. Orchan granted a safe-conduct to all who were desirous of departing with their families and effects; but the widows of the slain were given in marriage to the conquerors; and the sacrilegious plunder, the books, the vases, and the images, were sold or ransomed at Constantinople. The emperor Andronicus the Younger was vanquished and wounded by the son of Othman:[42] he subdued the whole province or kingdom of Bithynia as far as the shores of the Bosphorus and Hellespont; and the Christians confessed the justice and clemency of a reign which claimed the voluntary attachment of the Turks of Asia. Yet Orchan was content with the modest title of emir; and in the list of his compeers, the princes of Roum or Anatolia,[43] his military forces were surpassed by the emirs of Ghermian and Caramania, each of whom could bring into the field an army of forty thousand men. Their dominions were situate in the heart of the Seljukian kingdom: but the holy warriors, though of inferior note, who formed new principalities on the Greek empire, are more conspicuous in the light of history. The maritime country from the Propontis to the Mæander and the isle of Rhodes, so long threatened and so often pillaged, was finally lost about the thirtieth year of Andronicus the Elder.[44] Two Turkish chieftains, Sarukhan and Aidin, left their names to their conquests, and their conquests to their posterity. The captivity or ruin of the *seven* churches of Asia was consummated; and the barbarous lords of Ionia and Lydia still trample on the monuments of classic and Christian antiquity. In the loss of Ephesus the Christians deplored the fall of the first angel, the extinction of the first candlestick, of the Revelations;[45] the desolation is complete; and the temple of Diana or the church of Mary will equally elude the search of the curious traveller. The circus and three stately theatres of Laodicea are now peopled with wolves and foxes; Sardes is reduced to a miserable village; the God of Mohammed, without a rival or a son, is invoked in the mosques of Thyatira and Pergamus; and the populousness of Smyrna is supported by the foreign trade of the Franks and Armenians. Philadelphia alone has been saved by prophecy, or courage. At a distance from the sea, forgotten by the emperors, encompassed on all sides by the Turks, her valiant citizens defended their religion and freedom above fourscore years, and at length capitulated with the proudest of the Ottomans. Among the Greek colonies and churches of Asia, Philadelphia is still erect—a column in a scene of ruins—a pleasing example that the paths of honour and safety may sometimes be the same. The servitude of Rhodes was delayed above two centuries by the establishment of the knights of St. John of Jerusalem:[46] under the discipline of the order that island emerged into fame and opulence; the noble and warlike monks were renowned by land and sea; and the bulwark of Christendom provoked and repelled the arms of the Turks and Saracens.

The Greeks, by their intestine divisions, were the authors of their final ruin. During the civil wars of the elder and younger Andronicus, the son of Othman achieved, almost without resistance, the conquest of Bithynia; and the same disorders encouraged the Turkish emirs of Lydia and Ionia to build a fleet, and to pillage the adjacent islands and the sea-coast of Europe. In the defence of his life and honour,

Cantacuzene was tempted to prevent, or imitate, his adversaries, by calling to his aid the public enemies of his religion and country. Amir, the son of Aidin, concealed under a Turkish garb the humanity and politeness of a Greek; he was united with the great domestic by mutual esteem and reciprocal services; and their friendship is compared, in the vain rhetoric of the times, to the perfect union of Orestes and Pylades.[47] On the report of the danger of his friend, who was persecuted by an ungrateful court, the prince of Ionia assembled at Smyrna a fleet of three hundred vessels, with an army of twenty-nine thousand men; sailed in the depth of winter, and cast anchor at the mouth of the Hebrus. From thence, with a chosen band of two thousand Turks, he marched along the banks of the river, and rescued the empress, who was besieged in Demotica by the wild Bulgarians. At that disastrous moment the life or death of his beloved Cantacuzene was concealed by his flight into Servia; but the grateful Irene, impatient to behold her deliverer, invited him to enter the city, and accompanied her message with a present of rich apparel and a hundred horses. By a peculiar strain of delicacy, the gentle barbarian refused, in the absence of an unfortunate friend, to visit his wife, or to taste the luxuries of the palace; sustained in his tent the rigour of the winter; and rejected the hospitable gift, that he might share the hardships of two thousand companions, all as deserving as himself of that honour and distinction. Necessity and revenge might justify his predatory excursions by sea and land; he left nine thousand five hundred men for the guard of his fleet; and persevered in the fruitless search of Cantacuzene, till his embarkation was hastened by a fictitious letter, the severity of the season, the clamours of his independent troops, and the weight of his spoil and captives. In the prosecution of the civil war, the prince of Ionia twice returned to Europe, joined his arms with those of the emperor, besieged Thessalonica, and threatened Constantinople. Calumny might affix some reproach on his imperfect aid, his hasty departure, and a bribe of ten thousand crowns which he accepted from the Byzantine court; but his friend was satisfied; and the conduct of Amir is excused by the more sacred duty of defending against the Latins his hereditary dominions. The maritime power of the Turks had united the pope, the king of Cyprus, the republic of Venice, and the order of St. John, in a laudable crusade; their galleys invaded the coast of Ionia; and Amir was slain with an arrow, in the attempt to wrest from the Rhodian knights the citadel of Smyrna.[48] Before his death he generously recommended another ally of his own nation, not more sincere or zealous than himself, but more able to afford a prompt and abundant succour, by his situation along the Propontis and in front of Constantinople. By the prospect of a more advantageous treaty, the Turkish prince of Bithynia was detached from his engagements with Anne of Savoy; and the pride of Orchan dictated the most solemn protestations, that, if he could obtain the daughter of Cantacuzene, he would invariably fulfil the duties of a subject and a son. Parental tenderness was silenced by the voice of ambition: the Greek clergy connived at the marriage of a Christian princess with a sectary of Mohammed; and the father of Theodora describes, with shameful satisfaction, the dishonour of the purple.[49] A body of Turkish cavalry attended the ambassadors, who disembarked from thirty vessels, before his camp of Selymbria. A stately pavilion was erected, in which the empress Irene passed the night with her daughters. In the morning Theodora ascended a throne, which was surrounded with curtains of silk and gold: the troops were under arms; but the emperor alone was on horseback. At a signal the curtains were suddenly withdrawn, to disclose the bride, or the victim, encircled by kneeling eunuchs and hymeneal torches: the sound of flutes and trumpets proclaimed the joyful event; and her pretended happiness was the theme of the nuptial song, which was chanted by such poets as the age could produce. Without the rites of the church, Theodora was delivered to her barbarous lord: but it had been stipulated that she should preserve her religion in the harem of Bursa; and her father celebrates her charity and devotion in this ambiguous situation. After his peaceful establishment on the throne of Constantinople, the Greek emperor visited his Turkish ally, who, with four sons, by various wives, expected him at Scutari, on the Asiatic shore. The two princes partook, with seeming cordiality, of the pleasures of the banquet and the chase; and Theodora was permitted to repass the Bosphorus, and to enjoy some days in the society of her mother. But the friendship of Orchan was subservient to his religion and interest; and in the Genoese war he joined without a blush the enemies of Cantacuzene.

In the treaty with the empress Anne the Ottoman prince had inserted a singular condition, that it should be lawful for him to sell his prisoners at Constantinople, or transport them into Asia. A naked crowd of Christians of both sexes and every age, of priests and monks, of matrons and virgins, was exposed in the public market; the whip was frequently used to quicken the charity of redemption; and the indigent Greeks deplored the fate of their brethren, who were led away to the worst evils of temporal and spiritual bondage.[50] Cantacuzene was reduced to subscribe the same terms; and their execution must have been still more pernicious to the empire: a body of ten thousand Turks had been detached to the assistance of the empress Anne; but the entire forces of Orchan were exerted in the service of his father. Yet these calamities were of a transient nature; as soon as the storm had passed away, the fugitives might return to their habitations; and at the conclusion of the civil and foreign wars Europe was completely evacuated by the Moslems of Asia. It was in his last quarrel with his pupil that Cantacuzene inflicted the deep and deadly wound which could never be healed by his successors, and which is poorly expiated by his theological dialogues against the prophet Mohammed. Ignorant of their own history, the modern Turks confound their first and their final passage of the Hellespont,[51] and describe the son of Orchan as a nocturnal robber, who, with eighty companions, explores by stratagem a hostile and unknown shore. Soliman, at the head of ten thousand horse, was transported in the vessels, and entertained as the friend, of the Greek emperor. In the civil wars of Romania he performed some service and perpetrated more mischief; but the Chersonesus was insensibly filled with a Turkish colony; and the Byzantine court solicited in vain the restitution of the fortresses of Thrace. After some artful delays between the Ottoman prince and his son, their ransom was valued at sixty thousand crowns, and the first payment had been made when an earthquake shook the walls and cities of the provinces; the dismantled places were occupied by the Turks; and Gallipoli, the key of the Hellespont, was rebuilt and repeopled by the policy of Soliman. The abdication of Cantacuzene dissolved the feeble bands of domestic alliance; and his last advice admonished his countrymen to decline a rash contest, and to compare their own weakness with the numbers and valour, the discipline and enthusiasm, of the Moslems. His prudent counsels were despised by the headstrong vanity of youth, and soon justified by the victories of the Ottomans. But as he practised in the field the exercise of the *jerid*,

Soliman was killed by a fall from his horse; and the aged Orchan wept and expired on the tomb of his valiant son.

But the Greeks had not time to rejoice in the death of their enemies; and the Turkish scimitar was wielded with the same spirit by Amurath the First, the son of Orchan, and the brother of Soliman. By the pale and fainting light of the Byzantine annals[52] we can discern that he subdued without resistance the whole province of Romania or Thrace, from the Hellespont to Mount Hæmus and the verge of the capital; and that Adrianople was chosen for the royal seat of his government and religion in Europe. Constantinople, whose decline is almost coeval with her foundation, had often, in the lapse of a thousand years, been assaulted by the barbarians of the East and West; but never till this fatal hour had the Greeks been surrounded, both in Asia and Europe, by the arms of the same hostile monarchy. Yet the prudence or generosity of Amurath postponed for a while this easy conquest; and his pride was satisfied with the frequent and humble attendance of the emperor John Palæologus and his four sons who followed at his summons the court and camp of the Ottoman prince. He marched against the Sclavonian nations between the Danube and the Adriatic, the Bulgarians, Servians, Bosnians, and Albanians; and these warlike tribes, who had so often insulted the majesty of the empire, were repeatedly broken by the destructive inroads. Their countries did not abound either in gold or silver; nor were their rustic hamlets and townships enriched by commerce or decorated by the arts of luxury. But the natives of the soil have been distinguished in every age by their hardiness of mind and body; and they were converted by a prudent institution into the firmest and most faithful supporters of the Ottoman greatness.[53] The vizir of Amurath reminded his sovereign that, according to the Mohammedan law, he was entitled to a fifth part of the spoil and captives; and that this duty might easily be levied, if vigilant officers were stationed at Gallipoli, to watch the passage, and to select for his use the stoutest and most beautiful of the Christian youth. This advice was followed: the edict was proclaimed; many thousands of the European captives were educated in religion and arms; and the new militia was consecrated and named by a celebrated dervish. Standing in the front of their ranks, he stretched the sleeve of his gown over the head of the foremost soldier, and his blessing was delivered in these words: "Let them be called Janizaries (*Yengi cheri*, or new soldiers); may their countenance be ever bright! their hand victorious! their sword keen! may their spear always hang over the heads of their enemies; and wheresoever they go, may they return with a *white face*!"[54] Such was the origin of these haughty troops, the terror of the nations, and sometimes of the sultans themselves. Their valour has declined, their discipline is relaxed, and their tumultuary array is incapable of contending with the order and weapons of modern tactics; but at the time of their institution they possessed a decisive superiority in war; since a regular body of infantry, in constant exercise and pay, was not maintained by any of the princes of Christendom. The Janizaries fought with the zeal of proselytes against their *idolatrous* countrymen; and in the battle of Cossova the league and independence of the Sclavonian tribes was finally crushed. As the conqueror walked over the field, he observed that the greatest part of the slain consisted of beardless youths; and listened to the flattering reply of his vizir, that age and wisdom would have taught them not to oppose his irresistible arms. But the sword of his Janizaries could not defend him from the dagger of despair; a Servian soldier started from the crowd of dead bodies, and Amurath was pierced to the belly with a mortal wound. The grandson of Othman was mild in his temper, modest in his apparel, and a lover of learning and virtue; but the Moslems were scandalised at his absence from public worship; and he was corrected by the firmness of the mufti, who dared to reject his testimony in a civil cause; a mixture of servitude and freedom not unfrequent in Oriental history.[55]

The character of Bajazet, the son and successor of Amurath, is strongly expressed in his surname of *Ilderim*, or the lightning; and he might glory in an epithet which was drawn from the fiery energy of his soul and the rapidity of his destructive march. In the fourteen years of his reign[56] he incessantly moved at the head of his armies, from Boursa to Adrianople, from the Danube to the Euphrates; and, though he strenuously laboured for the propagation of the law, he invaded, with impartial ambition, the Christian and Mohammedan princes of Europe and Asia. From Angora to Amasia and Erzeroum, the northern regions of Anatolia were reduced to his obedience: he stripped of their hereditary possessions his brother emirs of Ghermian and Caramania, of Aidin and Sarukhan; and after the conquest of Iconium the ancient kingdom of the Seljukians again revived in the Ottoman dynasty. Nor were the conquests of Bajazet less rapid or important in Europe. No sooner had he imposed a regular form of servitude on the Servians and Bulgarians than he passed the Danube to seek new enemies and new subjects in the heart of Moldavia.[57] Whatever yet adhered to the Greek empire in Thrace, Macedonia, and Thessaly, acknowledged a Turkish master: an obsequious bishop led him through the gates of Thermopylæ into Greece; and we may observe, as a singular fact, that the widow of a Spanish chief, who possessed the ancient seat of the oracle of Delphi, deserved his favour by the sacrifice of a beauteous daughter. The Turkish communication between Europe and Asia had been dangerous and doubtful, till he stationed at Gallipoli a fleet of galleys, to command the Hellespont and intercept the Latin succours of Constantinople. While the monarch indulged his passions in a boundless range of injustice and cruelty, he imposed on his soldiers the most rigid laws of modesty and abstinence; and the harvest was peaceably reaped and sold within the precincts of his camp. Provoked by the loose and corrupt administration of justice, he collected in a house the judges and lawyers of his dominions, who expected that in a few moments the fire would be kindled to reduce them to ashes. His ministers trembled in silence: but an Æthiopian buffoon presumed to insinuate the true cause of the evil; and future venality was left without excuse by annexing an adequate salary to the office of cadhi.[58] The humble title of emir was no longer suitable to the Ottoman greatness; and Bajazet condescended to accept a patent of sultan from the caliphs who served in Egypt under the yoke of the Mamalukes:[59] a last and frivolous homage that was yielded by force to opinion; by the Turkish conquerors to the house of Abbas and the successors of the Arabian prophet. The ambition of the sultan was inflamed by the obligation of deserving this august title; and he turned his arms against the kingdom of Hungary, the perpetual theatre of the Turkish victories and defeats. Sigismond, the Hungarian king, was the son and brother of the emperors of the West: his cause was that of Europe and the church; and, on the report of his danger, the bravest knights of France and Germany were eager to march under his standard and that of the cross. In the battle of Nicopolis Bajazet defeated a confederate army of a hundred thousand Christians, who had proudly boasted that if the sky should fall they could uphold it on their lances. The far greater part were slain or driven into the Danube; and Sigismond, escaping to Constantinople by the river and the Black Sea, returned after a long circuit to his exhausted kingdom.[60] In the pride of victory Bajazet threatened that he would besiege Buda; that he would subdue the adjacent countries of Germany and Italy; and that he would feed his horse with a bushel of oats on the altar of St. Peter at Rome. His progress was checked, not by the miraculous interposition of the apostle, not by a crusade of the Christian powers, but by a long and painful fit of the gout. The disorders of the moral are sometimes corrected by those of the physical world; and an acrimonious humour falling on a single fibre of one man may prevent or suspend the misery of nations.

Such is the general idea of the Hungarian war; but the disastrous adventure of the French has procured us some memorials which illustrate the victory and character of Bajazet.[61] The duke of Burgundy, sovereign of Flanders and uncle of Charles the Sixth, yielded to the ardour of his son, John count of Nevers; and the fearless youth was accompanied by four princes, *his* cousins, and those of the French monarch. Their inexperience was guided by the Sire de Coucy, one of the best and oldest captains of Christendom;[62] but the constable, admiral, and marshal of France[63] commanded an army which did not exceed the number of a thousand knights and squires. These splendid names were the source of presumption and the bane of discipline. So many might aspire to command, that none were willing to obey; their national spirit despised both their enemies and their allies; and in the persuasion that Bajazet *would* fly, or *must* fall, they began to compute how soon they should visit Constantinople and deliver the holy sepulchre. When their scouts announced the approach of the Turks, the gay and thoughtless youths were at table, already heated with wine: they instantly clasped their armour, mounted their horses, rode full speed to the vanguard, and resented as an affront the advice of Sigismond, which would have deprived them of the right and honour of the foremost attack. The battle of Nicopolis would not have been lost if the French would have obeyed the prudence of the Hungarians: but it might have been gloriously won had the Hungarians imitated the valour of the French. They dispersed the first line, consisting of the troops of Asia; forced a rampart of stakes which had been planted against the cavalry; broke, after a bloody conflict, the Janizaries themselves; and

were at length overwhelmed by the numerous squadrons that issued from the woods and charged on all sides this handful of intrepid warriors. In the speed and secrecy of his march, in the order and evolutions of the battle, his enemies felt and admired the military talents of Bajazet. They accuse his cruelty in the use of victory. After reserving the count of Nevers and four-and-twenty lords, whose birth and riches were attested by his Latin interpreters, the remainder of the French captives, who had survived the slaughter of the day, were led before his throne; and, as they refused to abjure their faith, were successively beheaded in his presence. The sultan was exasperated by the loss of his bravest Janizaries; and if it be true that, on the eve of the engagement, the French had massacred their Turkish prisoners,[64] they might impute to themselves the consequences of a just retaliation. A knight, whose life had been spared, was permitted to return to Paris, that he might relate the deplorable tale, and solicit the ransom of the noble captives. In the meanwhile the count of Nevers, with the princes and barons of France, were dragged along in the marches of the Turkish camp, exposed as a grateful trophy to the Moslems of Europe and Asia, and strictly confined at Boursa as often as Bajazet resided in his capital. The sultan was pressed each day to expiate with their blood the blood of his martyrs; but he had pronounced that they should live, and either for mercy or destruction his word was irrevocable. He was assured of their value and importance by the return of the messenger, and the gifts and intercessions of the kings of France and of Cyprus. Lusignan presented him with a gold saltcellar of curious workmanship, and of the price of ten thousand ducats; and Charles the Sixth despatched by the way of Hungary a cast of Norwegian hawks, and six horse-loads of scarlet cloth, of fine linen of Rheims, and of Arras tapestry, representing the battles of the great Alexander. After much delay, the effect of distance rather than of art, Bajazet agreed to accept a ransom of two hundred thousand ducats for the count of Nevers and the surviving princes and barons: the marshal Boucicault, a famous warrior, was of the number of the fortunate; but the admiral of France had been slain in the battle; and the constable, with the Sire de Coucy, died in the prison of Boursa. This heavy demand, which was doubled by incidental costs, fell chiefly on the duke of Burgundy, or rather on his Flemish subjects, who were bound by the feudal laws to contribute for the knightood and captivity of the eldest son of their ord. For the faithful discharge of the debt some merchants of Genoa gave security to the amount of five times the sum; a lesson to those warlike times, that commerce and credit are the links of the society of nations. It had been stipulated in the treaty that the French captives should wear never to bear arms against the person of their conqueror; but the ungenerous restraint was abolished by Bajazet himself. "I despise," said he to the heir of Burgundy, "thy oaths and thy arms. Thou art young, and mayest be ambitious of effacing the disgrace or misfortune of thy first chivalry. Assemble thy powers, proclaim thy design, and be assured that Bajazet will rejoice to meet thee a second time in a field of battle." Before their departure they were indulged in the freedom and hospitality of the court of Boursa. The French princes admired the magnificence of the Ottoman, whose hunting and hawking equipage was composed of seven thousand huntsmen and seven thousand falconers.[65] In their presence, and at his command, the belly of one of his chamberlains was cut open, on a complaint against him for drinking the goat's milk of a poor woman. The strangers were astonished by this act of justice; but it was the justice of a sultan who disdains to balance the weight of evidence or to measure the degrees of guilt.

After his enfranchisement from an oppressive guardian, John Palæologus remained thirty-six years the helpless, and, as it should seem, the careless, spectator of the public ruin.[66] Love, or rather lust, was his only vigorous passion; and in the embraces of the wives and virgins of the city the Turkish slave forgot the dishonour of the emperor of the *Romans*. Andronicus, his eldest son, had formed, at Adrianople, an intimate and guilty friendship with Sauzes, the son of Amurath; and the two youths conspired against the authority and lives of their parents. The presence of Amurath in Europe soon discovered and dissipated their rash counsels; and, after depriving Sauzes of his sight, the Ottoman threatened his vassal with the treatment of an accomplice and an enemy unless he inflicted a similar punishment on his own son. Palæologus trembled and obeyed, and a cruel precaution involved in the same sentence the childhood and innocence of John the son of the criminal. But the operation was so mildly or so unskilfully performed that the one retained the sight of an eye, and the other was afflicted only with the infirmity of squinting. Thus excluded from the succession, the two princes were confined in the tower of Anema; and the piety of Manuel, the second son of the reigning monarch, was rewarded with the gift of the Imperial crown. But at the end of two years the turbulence of the Latins and the levity of the Greeks produced a revolution, and the two emperors were buried in the tower from whence the two prisoners were exalted to the throne. Another period of two years afforded Palæologus and Manuel the means of escape; it was contrived by the magic or subtlety of a monk, who was alternately named the angel or the devil; they fled to Scutari; their adherents armed in their cause, and the two Byzantine factions displayed the ambition and animosity with which Cæsar and Pompey had disputed the empire of the world. The Roman world was now contracted to a corner of Thrace, between the Propontis and the Black Sea, about fifty miles in length and thirty in breadth: a space of ground not more extensive than the lesser principalities of Germany or Italy, if the remains of Constantinople had not still represented the wealth and populousness of a kingdom. To restore the public peace it was found necessary to divide this fragment of the empire; and while Palæologus and Manuel were left in possession of the capital, almost all that lay without the walls was ceded to the blind princes, who fixed their residence at Rhodosto and Selymbria. In the tranquil slumber of royalty the passions of John Palæologus survived his reason and his strength: he deprived his favourite and heir of a blooming princess of Trebizond; and while the feeble emperor laboured to consummate his nuptials, Manuel, with a hundred of the noblest Greeks, was sent on a peremptory summons to the Ottoman *Porte*. They served with honour in the wars of Bajazet; but a plan of fortifying Constantinople excited his jealousy; he threatened their lives; the new works were instantly demolished; and we shall bestow a praise, perhaps above the merit of Palæologus, if we impute this last humiliation as the cause of his death.

The earliest intelligence of that event was communicated to Manuel, who escaped with speed and secrecy from the palace of Boursa to the Byzantine throne. Bajazet affected a proud indifference at the loss of this valuable pledge; and while he pursued his conquests in Europe and Asia, he left the emperor to struggle with his blind cousin John of Selymbria, who, in eight years of civil war, asserted his right of primogeniture. At length the ambition of the victorious sultan pointed to the conquest of

Constantinople: but he listened to the advice of his vizir, who represented that such an enterprise might unite the powers of Christendom in a second and more formidable crusade. His epistle to the emperor was conceived in these words:—"By the divine clemency, our invincible scimitar has reduced to our obedience almost all Asia, with many and large countries in Europe, excepting only the city of Constantinople; for beyond the walls thou hast nothing left. Resign that city; stipulate thy reward; or tremble, for thyself and thy unhappy people, at the consequences of a rash refusal." But his ambassadors were instructed to soften their tone, and to propose a treaty, which was subscribed with submission and gratitude. A truce of ten years was purchased by an annual tribute of thirty thousand crowns of gold; the Greeks deplored the public toleration of the law of Mohammed; and Bajazet enjoyed the glory of establishing a Turkish cadhi, and founding a royal mosque, in the metropolis of the Eastern church.[67] Yet this truce was soon violated by the restless sultan; in the cause of the prince of Selymbria, the lawful emperor, an army of Ottomans again threatened Constantinople, and the distress of Manuel implored the protection of the king of France. His plaintive embassy obtained much pity and some relief, and the conduct of the succour was intrusted to the marshal Boucicault,[68] whose religious chivalry was inflamed by the desire of revenging his captivity on the infidels. He sailed, with four ships of war, from Aiguesmortes to the Hellespont; forced the passage, which was guarded by seventeen Turkish galleys; landed at Constantinople a supply of six hundred men-at-arms and sixteen hundred archers, and reviewed them in the adjacent plain without condescending to number or array the multitude of Greeks. By his presence the blockade was raised both by sea and land; the flying squadrons of Bajazet were driven to a more respectful distance; and several castles in Europe and Asia were stormed by the emperor and the marshal, who fought with equal valour by each other's side. But the Ottomans soon returned with an increase of numbers; and the intrepid Boucicault, after a year's struggle, resolved to evacuate a country which could no longer afford either pay or provisions for his soldiers. The marshal offered to conduct Manuel to the French court, where he might solicit in person a supply of men and money; and advised, in the meanwhile, that to extinguish all domestic discord, he should leave his blind competitor on the throne. The proposal was embraced: the prince of Selymbria was introduced to the capital; and such was the public misery that the lot of the exile seemed more fortunate than that of the sovereign. Instead of applauding the success of his vassal, the Turkish sultan claimed the city as his own; and, on the refusal of the emperor John, Constantinople was more closely pressed by the calamities of war and famine. Against such an enemy prayers and resistance were alike unavailing; and the savage would have devoured his prey if, in the fatal moment, he had not been overthrown by another savage stronger than himself. By the victory of Timour or Tamerlane the fall of Constantinople was delayed about fifty years; and this important though accidental service may justly introduce the life and character of the Mogul conqueror.

CHAPTER LXV

Elevation of Timour or Tamerlane to the Throne of Samarcand. His Conquests in Persia, Georgia, Tartary, Russia, India, Syria, and Anatolia. His Turkish War. Defeat and Captivity of Bajazet. Death to Timour. Civil War of the Sons of Bajazet. Restoration of the Turkish Monarchy by Mohammed the First. Siege of Constantinople by Amurath the Second.

THE conquest and monarchy of the world was the first object of the ambition of Timour. To live in the memory and esteem of future ages was the second wish of his magnanimous spirit. All the civil and military transactions of his reign were diligently recorded in the journals of his secretaries:[1] the authentic narrative was revised by the persons best informed of each particular transaction; and it is believed in the empire and family of Timour that the monarch himself composed the *commentaries*[2] of his life and the *institutions*[3] of his government.[4] But these cares were ineffectual for the preservation of his fame, and these precious memorials in the Mogul or Persian language were concealed from the world, or, at least, from the knowledge of Europe. The nations which he vanquished exercised a base and impotent revenge; and ignorance has long repeated the tale of calumny[5] which had disfigured the birth and character, the person, and even the name, of *Tamerlane*.[6] Yet his real merit would be enhanced rather than debased by the elevation of a peasant to the throne of Asia; nor can his lameness be a theme of reproach, unless he had the weakness to blush at a natural, or perhaps an honourable, infirmity.

In the eyes of the Moguls, who held the indefeasible succession of the house of Zingis, he was doubtless a rebel subject; yet he sprang from the noble tribe of Berlass: his fifth ancestor, Carashar Nevian, had been the vizir of Zagatai, in his realm of Transoxiana; and in the ascent of some generations, the branch of Timour is confounded, at least by the females,[7] with the Imperial stem.[8] He was born forty miles to the south of Samarcand, in the village of Sebzar, in the fruitful territory of Cash, of which his fathers were the hereditary chiefs, as well as of a toman of ten thousand horse.[9] His birth[10] was cast on one of those periods of anarchy which announce the fall of the Asiatic dynasties, and open a new field to adventurous ambition. The khans of Zagatai were extinct; the emirs aspired to independence, and their domestic feuds could only be suspended by the conquest and tyranny of the khans of Kashgar, who, with an army of Getes or Calmucks,[11] invaded the Transoxian kingdom. From the twelfth year of his age Timour had entered the field of action; in the twenty-fifth he stood forth as the deliverer of his country, and the eyes and wishes of the people were turned towards a hero who suffered in their cause. The chiefs of the law and of the army had pledged their salvation to support him with their lives and fortunes, but in the hour of danger they were silent and afraid; and, after waiting seven days on the hills of Samarcand, he retreated to the desert with only sixty horsemen. The fugitives were overtaken by a thousand Getes, whom he repulsed with incredible slaughter; and his enemies were forced to exclaim, "Timour is a wonderful man: fortune and the divine favour are with him." But in this bloody action his own followers were reduced to ten, a number which was soon diminished by the desertion of three Carizmians. He wandered in the desert with his wife, seven companions, and four horses; and sixty-two days was he plunged in a loathsome dungeon,

from whence he escaped by his own courage and the remorse of the oppressor. After swimming the broad and rapid stream of the Jihoon or Oxus, he led, during some months, the life of a vagrant and outlaw on the borders of the adjacent states. But his fame shone brighter in adversity; he learned to distinguish the friends of his person, the associates of his fortune, and to apply the various characters of men for their advantage, and, above all, for his own. On his return to his native country Timour was successively joined by the parties of his confederates, who anxiously sought him in the desert; nor can I refuse to describe, in his pathetic simplicity, one of their fortunate encounters. He presented himself as a guide to three chiefs, who were at the head of seventy horse. "When their eyes fell upon me," says Timour, "they were overwhelmed with joy, and they alighted from their horses, and they came and kneeled, and they kissed my stirrup. I also came down from my horse, and took each of them in my arms. And I put my turban on the head of the first chief; and my girdle, rich in jewels and wrought with gold, I bound on the loins of the second; and the third I clothed in my own coat. And they wept, and I wept also; and the hour of prayer was arrived, and we prayed. And we mounted our horses, and came to my dwelling; and I collected my people, and made a feast." His trusty bands were soon increased by the bravest of the tribes; he led them against a superior foe, and, after some vicissitudes of war, the Getes were finally driven from the kingdom of Transoxiana. He had done much for his own glory; but much remained to be done, much art to be exerted, and some blood to be spilt, before he could teach his equals to obey him as their master. The birth and power of emir Houssein compelled him to accept a vicious and unworthy colleague, whose sister was the best beloved of his wives. Their union was short and jealous; but the policy of Timour, in their frequent quarrels, exposed his rival to the reproach of injustice and perfidy, and, after a final defeat, Houssein was slain by some sagacious friends, who presumed, for the last time, to disobey the commands of their lord. At the age of thirty-four,[12] and in a general diet or *couroultai*, he was invested with *Imperial* command; but he affected to revere the house of Zingis; and while the emir Timour reigned over Zagatai and the East, a nominal khan served as a private officer in the armies of his servant. A fertile kingdom, five hundred miles in length and in breadth, might have satisfied the ambition of a subject;

but Timour aspired to the dominion of the world, and before his death the crown of Zagatai was one of the twenty-seven crowns which he had placed on his head. Without expatiating on the victories of thirty-five campaigns; without describing the lines of march which he repeatedly traced over the continent of Asia; I shall briefly represent his conquests in, I. Persia, II. Tartary, and III. India,[13] and from thence proceed to the more interesting narrative of his Ottoman war.

I. For every war a motive of safety or revenge, of honour or zeal, of right or convenience, may be readily found in the jurisprudence of conquerors. No sooner had Timour re-united to the patrimony of Zagatai the dependent countries of Carizme and Candahar, than he turned his eyes towards the kingdoms of Iran or Persia. From the Oxus to the Tigris that extensive country was left without a lawful sovereign since the death of Abousaid, the last of the descendants of the great Holacou. Peace and justice had been banished from the land above forty years, and the Mogul invader might seem to listen to the cries of an oppressed people. Their petty tyrants might have opposed him with confederate arms: they separately stood, and successively fell; and the difference of their fate was only marked by the promptitude of submission or the obstinacy of resistance. Ibrahim, prince of Shirwan or Albania, kissed the footstool of the Imperial throne. His peace-offerings of silks, horses, and jewels, were composed, according to the Tartar fashion, each article of nine pieces; but a critical spectator observed that there were only eight slaves. "I myself am the ninth," replied Ibrahim, who was prepared for the remark, and his flattery was rewarded by the smile of Timour.[14] Shah Mansour, prince of Fars, or the proper Persia, was one of the least powerful, but most dangerous, of his enemies. In a battle, under the walls of Shiraz, he broke, with three or four thousand soldiers, the *coul* or main-body of thirty thousand horse, where the emperor fought in person. No more than fourteen or fifteen guards remained near the standard of Timour; he stood firm as a rock, and received on his helmet two weighty strokes of a scimitar;[15] the Moguls rallied; the head of Mansour was thrown at his feet; and he declared his esteem of the valour of a foe by extirpating all the males of so intrepid a race. From Shiraz his troops advanced to the Persian Gulf, and the richness and weakness of Ormuz[16] were displayed in an annual tribute of six hundred thousand dinars

of gold. Bagdad was no longer the city of peace, the seat of the caliphs; but the noblest conquest of Holacou could not be overlooked by his ambitious successor. The whole course of the Tigris and Euphrates, from the mouth to the sources of those rivers, was reduced to his obedience; he entered Edessa; and the Turkmans of the black sheep were chastised for the sacrilegious pillage of a caravan of Mecca. In the mountains of Georgia the native Christians still braved the law and the sword of Mohammed; by three expeditions he obtained the merit of the *gazie*, or holy war; and the prince of Teflis became his proselyte and friend.

II. A just retaliation might be urged for the invasion of Turkestan, or the Eastern Tartary. The dignity of Timour could not endure the impunity of the Getes: he passed the Sihoon, subdued the kingdom of Kashgar, and marched seven times into the heart of their country. His most distant camp was two months' journey, or four hundred and eighty leagues, to the northeast of Samarcand; and his emirs, who traversed the river Irtish, engraved in the forests of Siberia a rude memorial of their exploits. The conquest of Kipzak, or the western Tartary,[17] was founded on the double motive of aiding the distressed, and chastising the ungrateful. Toctamish, a fugitive prince, was entertained and protected in his court: the ambassadors of Auruss Khan were dismissed with a haughty denial, and followed on the same day by the armies of Zagatai; and their success established Toctamish in the Mogul empire of the North. But, after a reign of ten years, the new khan forgot the merits and the strength of his benefactor; the base usurper, as he deemed him, of the sacred rights of the house of Zingis. Through the gates of Derbend he entered Persia at the head of ninety thousand horse: with the innumerable forces of Kipzak, Bulgaria, Circassia, and Russia, he passed the Sihoon, burnt the palaces of Timour, and compelled him, amidst the winter snows, to contend for Samarcand and his life. After a mild expostulation, and a glorious victory, the emperor resolved on revenge: and by the east, and the west, of the Caspian, and the Volga, he twice invaded Kipzak with such mighty powers, that thirteen miles were measured from his right to his left wing. In a march of five months they rarely beheld the footsteps of man: and their daily subsistence was often trusted to the fortune of the chase. At length the armies encountered each other; but the treachery of the standard-bearer, who, in the heat of action, reversed the Imerial standard of Kipzak determined the victory of the Zagatais; and Toctamish (I speak the language of the Institutions) gave the tribe of Toushi to the wind of desolation.[18] He fled to the Christian duke of Lithuania; again returned to the banks of the Volga; and, after fifteen battles with a domestic rival, at last perished in the wilds of Siberia. The pursuit of a flying enemy carried Timour into the tributary provinces of Russia: a duke of the reigning family was made prisoner amidst the ruins of his capital; and Yeletz, by the pride and ignorance of the Orientals, might easily be confounded with the genuine metropolis of the nation. Moscow trembled at the approach of the Tartar, and the resistance would have been feeble, since the hopes of the Russians were placed in a miraculous image of the Virgin, to whose protection they ascribed the casual and voluntary retreat of the conqueror. Ambition and prudence recalled him to the South, the desolate country was exhausted, and the Mogul soldiers were enriched with an immense spoil of precious furs, of linen of Antioch,[19] and of ingots of gold and silver.[20] On the banks of the Don, or Tanais, he received a humble deputation from the consuls and merchants of Egypt,[21] Venice, Genoa, Catalonia, and Biscay, who occupied the commerce and city of Tana, or Azoph, at the mouth of the river. They offered their gifts, admired his magnificence, and trusted his royal word. But the peaceful visit of an emir, who explored the state of the magazines and harbour, was speedily followed by the destructive presence of the Tartars. The city was reduced to ashes; the Moslems were pillaged and dismissed; but all the Christians who had not fled to their ships were condemned either to death or slavery.[22] Revenge prompted him to burn the cities of Serai and Astrachan, the monuments of rising civilisation; and his vanity proclaimed that he had penetrated to the region of perpetual daylight, a strange phenomenon, which authorised his Mohammedan doctors to dispense with the obligation of evening prayer.[23]

III. When Timour first proposed to his princes and emirs the invasion of India or Hindostan,[24] he was answered by a murmur of discontent: "The rivers! and the mountains and deserts! and the soldiers clad in armour! and the elephants, destroyers of men!" But the displeasure of the emperor was more dreadful than all these terrors; and his superior reason was convinced that an enterprise of such tremendous aspect was safe and easy in the execution. He was informed by his spies of the weakness and anarchy of Hindostan: the soubahs of the provinces had erected the standard of rebellion: and the perpetual infancy of sultan Mahmoud was despised even in the harem of Delhi. The Mogul army moved in three great divisions; and Timour observes with pleasure that the ninety-two squadrons of a thousand horse most fortunately corresponded with the ninety-two names or epithets of the prophet Mohammed. Between the Jihoon and the Indus they crossed one of the ridges of mountains which are styled by the Arabian geographers The Stony Girdles of the Earth. The highland robbers were subdued or extirpated; but great numbers of men and horses perished in the snow; the emperor himself was let down a precipice on a portable scaffold—the ropes were one hundred and fifty cubits in length; and before he could reach the bottom, this dangerous operation was five times repeated. Timour crossed the Indus at the ordinary passage of Attok; and successively traversed, in the footsteps of Alexander, the *Punjab*, or five rivers,[25] that fall into the master stream. From Attok to Delhi the high road measures no more than six hundred miles; but the two conquerors deviated to the south-east; and the motive of Timour was to join his grandson, who had achieved by his command the conquest of Moultan. On the eastern bank of the Hyphasis, on the edge of the desert, the Macedonian hero halted and wept: the Mogul entered the desert, reduced the fortress of Batnir, and stood in arms before the gates of Delhi, a great and flourishing city, which had subsisted three centuries under the dominion of the Mohammedan kings. The siege, more especially of the castle, might have been a work of time; but he tempted, by the appearance of weakness, the sultan Mahmoud and his vizir to descend into the plain, with ten thousand cuirassiers, forty thousand of his foot-guards, and one hundred and twenty elephants, whose tusks are said to have been armed with sharp and poisoned daggers. Against these monsters, or rather against the imagination of his troops, he condescended to use some extraordinary precautions of fire and a ditch, of iron spikes and a rampart of bucklers; but the event taught the Moguls to smile at their own fears; and as soon as these unwieldy animals were routed, the inferior species (the men of India) disappeared from the field. Timour made his triumphal entry into the capital of Hindostan; and admired, with a view to imitate, the architecture of the stately mosque; but the order or licence of a general pillage and massacre polluted the festival of his victory. He resolved to purify his soldiers in the blood of the idolators, or Gentoos, who still surpass, in the proportion of ten to one, the numbers of the Moslems. In this pious design he advanced one hundred miles to the north-east of Delhi, passed the Ganges, fought several battles by land and water, and penetrated to the famous rock of Coupele, the statue of the cow, that *seems* to discharge the mighty river, whose source is far distant among the mountains of Thibet.[26] His return was along the skirts of the northern hills; nor could this rapid campaign of one year justify the strange foresight of his emirs, that their children in a warm climate would degenerate into a race of Hindoos.

It was on the banks of the Ganges that Timour was informed, by his speedy messengers, of the disturbances which had arisen on the confines of Georgia and Anatolia, of the revolt of the Christians, and the ambitious designs of the sultan Bajazet. His vigour of mind and body was not impaired by sixty-three years and innumerable fatigues; and, after enjoying some tranquil months in the palace of Samarcand, he proclaimed a new expedition of seven years into the western countries of Asia.[27] To the soldiers who had served in the Indian war he granted the choice of remaining at home, or following their prince; but the troops of all the provinces and kingdoms of Persia were commanded to assemble at Ispahan, and wait the arrival of the Imperial standard. It was first directed against the Christians of Georgia, who were strong only in their rocks, their castles, and the winter season; but these obstacles were overcome by the zeal and perseverance of Timour: the rebels submitted to the tribute or the Koran; and if both religions boasted of their martyrs, that name is more justly due to the Christian prisoners, who were offered the choice of abjuration or death. On his descent from the hills, the emperor gave audience to the first ambassadors of Bajazet, and opened the hostile correspondence of complaints and menaces which fermented two years before the final explosion. Between two jealous and haughty neighbours, the motives of quarrel will seldom be wanting. The Mogul and Ottoman conquests now touched each other in the neighbourhood of Erzeroum and the Euphrates; nor had the doubtful limit been ascertained by time and treaty. Each of these ambitious monarchs might accuse his rival of violating his territory, of threatening his vassals, and protecting his rebels; and by the name of rebels each understood the fugitive

princes whose kingdoms he had usurped, and whose life or liberty he implacably pursued. The resemblance of character was still more dangerous than the opposition of interest; and in their victorious career, Timour was impatient of an equal, and Bajazet was ignorant of a superior. The first epistle[28] of the Mogul emperor must have provoked, instead of reconciling, the Turkish sultan, whose family and nation he affected to despise.[29] "Dost thou not know that the greatest part of Asia is subject to our arms and our laws? that our invincible forces extend from one sea to the other? that the potentates of the earth form a line before our gate? and that we have compelled Fortune herself to watch over the prosperity of our empire? What is the foundation of thy insolence and folly? Thou hast fought some battles in the woods of Anatolia; contemptible trophies! Thou hast obtained some victories over the Christians of Europe; thy sword was blessed by the apostle of God; and thy obedience to the precept of the Koran, in waging war against the infidels, is the sole consideration that prevents us from destroying thy country, the frontier and bulwark of the Moslem world. Be wise in time; reflect; repent; and avert the thunder of our vengeance, which is yet suspended over thy head. Thou art no more than a pismire; why wilt thou seek to provoke the elephants? Alas! they will trample thee under their feet." In his replies Bajazet poured forth the indignation of a soul which was deeply stung by such unusual contempt. After retorting the basest reproaches on the thief and rebel of the desert, the Ottoman recapitulates his boasted victories in Iran, Touran, and the Indies; and labours to prove that Timour had never triumphed unless by his own perfidy and the vices of his foes. "Thy armies are innumerable: be they so; but what are the arrows of the flying Tartar against the scimitars and battle-axes of my firm and invincible Janizaries? I will guard the princes who have implored my protection: seek them in my tents. The cities of Arzingan and Erzeroum are mine; and unless the tribute be duly paid, I will demand the arrears under the walls of Tauris and Sultania." The ungovernable rage of the sultan at length betrayed him to an insult of a more domestic kind. "If I fly from thy arms," said he, "may *my* wives be thrice divorced from my bed: but if thou hast not courage to meet me in the field, mayest thou again receive *thy* wives after they have thrice endured the embraces of a stranger."[30] Any violation by word or deed of the secrecy of the harem is an unpardonable offence among the Turkish nations;[31] and the political quarrel of the two monarchs was embittered by private and personal resentment. Yet in his first expedition Timour was satisfied with the siege and destruction of Suvas or Sebaste, a strong city on the borders of Anatolia; and he revenged the indiscretion of the Ottoman on a garrison of four thousand Armenians, who were buried alive for the brave and faithful discharge of their duty. As a Musulman he seemed to respect the pious occupation of Bajazet, who was still engaged in the blockade of Constantinople; and after this salutary lesson the Mogul conqueror checked his pursuit, and turned aside to the invasion of Syria and Egypt. In these transactions, the Ottoman prince, by the Orientals, and even by Timour, is styled the *Kaissar of Roum*, the Cæsar of the Romans; a title which, by a small anticipation, might be given to a monarch who possessed the provinces, and threatened the city, of the successors of Constantine.[32]

The military republic of the Mamalukes still reigned in Egypt and Syria: but the dynasty of the Turks was overthrown by that of the Circassians;[33] and their favourite Barkok, from a slave and a prisoner, was raised and restored to the throne. In the midst of rebellion and discord, he braved the menaces, corresponded with the enemies, and detained the ambassadors, of the Mogul, who patiently expected his decease, to revenge the crimes of the father on the feeble reign of his son Farage. The Syrian emirs[34] were assembled at Aleppo to repel the invasion: they confided in the fame and discipline of the Mamalukes, in the temper of their swords and lances of the purest steel of Damascus, in the strength of their walled cities, and in the populousness of sixty thousand villages; and instead of sustaining a siege, they threw open their gates, and arrayed their forces in the plain. But these forces were not cemented by virtue and union; and some powerful emirs had been seduced to desert or betray their more loyal companions. Timour's front was covered with a line of Indian elephants, whose turrets were filled with archers and Greek fire: the rapid evolutions of his cavalry completed the dismay and disorder; the Syrian crowds fell back on each other; many thousands were stifled or slaughtered in the entrance of the great street; the Moguls entered with the fugitives; and after a short defence, the citadel, the impregnable citadel of Aleppo, was surrendered by cowardice or treachery. Among the suppliants and captives Timour distinguished the doctors of the law, whom he invited to the dangerous honour of a personal conference.[35] The Mogul prince was a zealous Musulman; but his Persian schools had taught him to revere the memory of Ali and Hosein; and he had imbibed a deep prejudice against the Syrians, as the enemies of the son of the daughter of the apostle of God. To these doctors he proposed a captious question, which the casuists of Bochara, Samarcand, and Herat were incapable of resolving. "Who are the true martyrs, of those who are slain on my side, or on that of my enemies?" But he was silenced, or satisfied, by the dexterity of one of the cadhis of Aleppo, who replied, in the words of Mohammed himself, that the motive, not the ensign, constitutes the martyr; and that the Moslems of either party, who fight only for the glory of God, may deserve that sacred appellation. The true succession of the caliphs was a controversy of a still more delicate nature; and the frankness of a doctor, too honest for his situation, provoked the emperor to exclaim, "Ye are as false as those of Damascus: Moawiyah was a usurper, Yezid a tyrant, and Ali alone is the lawful successor of the prophet." A prudent explanation restored his tranquillity; and he passed to a more familiar topic of conversation. "What is your age?" said he to the cadhi. "Fifty years."—"It would be the age of my eldest son. You see me here (continued Timour) a poor, lame, decrepit mortal. Yet by my arm has the Almighty been pleased to subdue the kingdoms of Iran, Touran, and the Indies. I am not a man of blood; and God is my witness that in all my wars I have never been the aggressor, and that my enemies have always been the authors of their own calamity." During this peaceful conversation the streets of Aleppo streamed with blood, and re-echoed with the cries of mothers and children, with the shrieks of violated virgins. The rich plunder that was abandoned to his soldiers might stimulate their avarice; but their cruelty was enforced by the peremptory command of producing an adequate number of heads, which, according to his custom, were curiously piled in columns and pyramids: the Moguls celebrated the feast of victory, while the surviving Moslems passed the night in tears and in chains. I shall not dwell on the march of the destroyer from Aleppo to Damascus, where he was rudely encountered, and almost overthrown, by the armies of Egypt. A retrograde motion was imputed to his distress and despair: one of his nephews deserted to the enemy; and Syria rejoiced in the tale of his defeat, when the sultan was driven by the revolt of the Mamalukes to escape with precipitation and shame to his palace of Cairo. Abandoned by their prince, the inhabitants of Damascus still defended their walls; and Timour consented to raise the siege, if they would adorn his retreat with a gift or ransom; each article of nine pieces. But no sooner had he introduced himself into the city, under colour of a truce, than he perfidiously violated the treaty; imposed a contribution of ten millions of gold; and animated his troops to chastise the posterity of those Syrians who had executed, or approved, the murder of the grandson of Mohammed. A family which had given honourable burial to the head of Hosein, and a colony of artificers whom he sent to labour at Samarcand, were alone reserved in the general massacre; and after a period of seven centuries Damascus was reduced to ashes, because a Tartar was moved by religious zeal to avenge the blood of an Arab. The losses and fatigues of the campaign obliged Timour to renounce the conquest of Palestine and Egypt; but in his return to the Euphrates he delivered Aleppo to the flames; and justified his pious motive by the pardon and reward of two thousand sectaries of Ali, who were desirous to visit the tomb of his son. I have expatiated on the personal anecdotes which mark the character of the Mogul hero; but I shall briefly mention[36] that he erected on the ruins of Bagdad a pyramid of ninety thousand heads; again visited Georgia; encamped on the banks of the Araxes; and proclaimed his resolution of marching against the Ottoman emperor. Conscious of the importance of the war, he collected his forces from every province: eight hundred thousand men were enrolled on his military list;[37] but the splendid commands of five and ten thousand horse may be rather expressive of the rank and pension of the chiefs than of the genuine number of effective soldiers.[38] In the pillage of Syria the Moguls had acquired immense riches; but the delivery of their pay and arrears for seven years more firmly attached them to the Imperial standard.

During this diversion of the Mogul arms, Bajazet had two years to collect his forces for a more serious encounter. They consisted of four hundred thousand horse and foot,[39] whose merit and fidelity were of an unequal complexion. We may discriminate the Janizaries, who have been gradually raised to an establishment of forty thousand men; a national cavalry, the Spahis of modern times; twenty thousand cuirassiers of Europe, clad in black and impenetrable armour; the troops of Anatolia, whose princes had taken refuge in the camp of Timour and a colony of Tartars, whom he had driven from Kipzak, and to whom Bajazet had assigned a settlement in the plains of Adrianople The fearless confidence of the sultan urged him to meet his antagonist; and, as if he had chosen that spot for revenge, he displayed his banner near the ruins of the unfortunate Suvas. In the meanwhile Timour moved from the Araxes through the countries of Armenia and Anatolia his boldness was secured by the wisest precautions; his speed was guided by order and discipline; and the woods, the mountains, and the rivers were diligently explored by the flying squadrons who marked his road and preceded his standard. Firm in his plan of fighting in the heart of the Ottoman kingdom, he avoided their camp, dexterously inclined to the left, occupied Cæsarea, traversed the salt desert and the river Halys, and invested Angora; while the sultan, immovable and ignorant in his post, compared the Tartar swiftness to the crawling of a snail;[40] he returned on the wings of indignation to the relief of Angora; and as both generals were alike impatient for action, the plains round that city were the scene of a memorable battle, which has immortalised the glory of Timour and the shame of Bajazet. For this signal victory the Mogul emperor was indebted to himself, to the genius of the moment, and the discipline of thirty years. He had improved the tactics, without violating the manners, of his nation,[41] whose force still consisted in the missile weapons and rapid evolutions of a numerous cavalry. From a single troop to a great army the mode of attack was the same: a foremost line first advanced to the charge, and was supported in a just order by the squadrons of the great vanguard. The general's eye watched over the field, and at his command the front and rear of the right and left wings successively moved forwards in their several divisions, and in a direct or oblique line; the enemy was pressed by eighteen or twenty attacks, and each attack afforded a chance of victory. If they all proved fruitless or unsuccessful, the occasion was worthy of the emperor himself, who gave the signal of advancing to the standard and main body, which he led in person.[42] But in the battle of Angora the main body itself was supported, on the flanks and in the rear, by the bravest squadrons of the reserve, commanded by the sons and grandsons of Timour. The conqueror of Hindostan ostentatiously showed a line of elephants, the trophies rather than the instruments of victory: the use of the Greek fire was familiar to the Moguls and Ottomans; but had they borrowed from Europe the recent invention of gunpowder and cannon, the artificial thunder, in the hands of either nation, must have turned the fortune of the day.[43] In that day Bajazet displayed the qualities of a soldier and a chief; but his genius sunk under a stronger ascendant, and, from various motives, the greatest part of his troops failed him in the decisive moment. His rigour and avarice had provoked a mutiny among the Turks, and even his son Soliman too hastily withdrew from the field. The forces of Anatolia, loyal in their revolt, were drawn away to the banners of their lawful princes. His Tartar allies had been tempted by the letters and emissaries of Timour,[44] who reproached their ignoble servitude under the slaves of their fathers, and offered to their hopes the dominion of their new or the liberty of their ancient country. In the right wing of Bajazet the cuirassiers of Europe charged, with faithful hearts and irresistible arms; but these men of iron were soon broken by an artful flight and headlong pursuit; and the Janizaries alone, without cavalry or missile weapons, were encompassed by the circle of the Mogul hunters. Their valour was at length oppressed by heat, thirst, and the weight of numbers; and the unfortunate sultan, afflicted with the gout in his hands and feet, was transported from the field on the fleetest of his horses. He was pursued and taken by the titular khan of Zagatai; and, after his capture and the defeat of the Ottoman powers, the kingdom of Anatolia submitted to the conqueror, who planted his standard at Kiotahia, and dispersed on all sides the ministers of rapine and destruction. Mirza Mehemmed Sultan, the eldest and best beloved of his grandsons, was despatched to Boursa with thirty thousand horse; and such was his youthful ardour, that he arrived with only four thousand at the gates of the capital, after performing in five days a march of two hundred and thirty miles. Yet fear is still more rapid in its course; and Soliman, the son of Bajazet, had already passed over to Europe with the royal treasure. The spoil, however, of the palace and city was immense: the inhabitants had escaped; but the buildings, for the most part of wood, were reduced to ashes. From Boursa the grandson of Timour advanced to Nice, even yet a fair and flourishing city; and the Mogul squadrons were only stopped by the waves of the Propontis. The same success attended the other mirzas and emirs in their excursions; and Smyrna, defended by the zeal and courage of the Rhodian knights, alone deserved the presence of the emperor himself. After an obstinate defence the place was taken by storm: all that breathed was put to the sword; and the heads of the Christian heroes were launched from the engines, on board of two carracks or great ships of Europe that rode at anchor in the harbour. The Moslems of Asia rejoiced in their deliverance from a dangerous and domestic foe; and a parallel was drawn between the two rivals by observing that Timour, in fourteen days, had reduced a fortress which had sustained seven years the siege, or at least the blockade, of Bajazet.[45]

The *iron cage* in which Bajazet was imprisoned by Tamerlane, so long and so often repeated as a moral lesson, is now rejected as a fable by the modern writers, who smile at the vulgar credulity.[46] They appeal with confidence to the Persian history of Sherefeddin Ali, which has been given to our curiosity in a French version, and from which I shall collect and abridge a more specious narrative of this memorable transaction. No sooner was Timour informed that the captive Ottoman was at the door of his tent than he graciously stepped forward to receive him, seated him by his side, and mingled with just reproaches a soothing pity for his rank and misfortune. "Alas!" said the emperor, "the decree of fate is now accomplished by your own fault; it is the web which you have woven, the thorns of the tree which yourself have planted. I wished to spare, and even to assist, the champion of the Moslems: you braved our threats; you despised our friendship; you forced us to enter your kingdom with our invincible armies. Behold the event. Had you vanquished, I am not ignorant of the fate which you reserved for myself and my troops. But I disdain to retaliate: your life and honour are secure; and I shall express my gratitude to God by my clemency to man." The royal captive showed some signs of repentance, accepted the humiliation of a robe of honour, and embraced with tears his son Mousa, who, at his request, was sought and found among the captives of the field. The Ottoman princes were lodged in a splendid pavilion, and the respect of the guards could be surpassed only by their vigilance. On the arrival of the harem from Boursa, Timour restored the queen Despina and her daughter to their father and husband; but he piously required that the Servian princess, who had hitherto been indulged in the profession of Christianity, should embrace without delay the religion of the prophet. In the feast of victory, to which Bajazet was invited, the Mogul emperor placed a crown on his head and a sceptre in his hand, with a solemn assurance of restoring him with an increase of glory to the throne of his ancestors. But the effect of this promise was disappointed by the sultan's untimely death; amidst the care of the most skilful physicians he expired of an apoplexy at Akshehr, the Antioch of Pisidia, about nine months after his defeat. The victor dropped a tear over his grave: his body, with royal pomp, was conveyed to the mausoleum which he had erected at Boursa; and his son Mousa, after receiving a rich present of gold and jewels, of horses and arms, was invested by a patent in red ink with the kingdom of Anatolia.

Such is the portrait of a generous conqueror, which has been extracted from his own memorials, and dedicated to his son and grandson, nineteen years after his decease;[47] and, at a time when the truth was remembered by thousands, a manifest falsehood would have implied a satire on his real conduct. Weighty indeed is this evidence, adopted by all the Persian histories;[48] yet flattery, more especially in the East, is base and audacious; and the harsh and ignominious treatment of Bajazet is attested by a chain of witnesses, some of whom shall be produced in the order of their time and country. 1. The reader has not forgot the garrison of French whom the marshal Boucicault left behind him for the defence of Constantinople. They were on the spot to receive the earliest and most faithful intelligence of the overthrow of their great adversary, and it is more than probable that some of them accompanied the Greek embassy to the camp of Tamerlane. From their account, the *hardships* of the prison and death of Bajazet are affirmed by the marshal's servant and historian, within the distance of seven years.[49] 2. The name of Poggius the Italian[50] is deservedly famous among the revivers of learning in the fifteenth century. His elegant dialogue on the vicissitudes of fortune[51] was composed in his fiftieth year, twenty-eight years after the Turkish victory of Tamerlane,[52] whom he celebrates as not inferior to the illustrious barbarians of antiquity. Of his exploits and discipline Poggius was informed by several ocular witnesses: nor does he forget an example so apposite to his theme as the Ottoman monarch, whom the Scythian confined like a wild beast in an iron cage, and exhibited a spectacle to Asia. I might add the authority of two Italian chronicles, perhaps of an earlier date, which would prove at least that the same story,

whether false or true, was imported into Europe with the first tidings of the revolution.[53] 3. At the time when Poggius flourished at Rome, Ahmed Ebn Arabshah composed at Damascus the florid and malevolent history of Timour, for which he had collected materials in his journeys over Turkey and Tartary.[54] Without any possible correspondence between the Latin and the Arabian writer, they agree in the fact of the iron cage; and their agreement is a striking proof of their common veracity. Ahmed Arabshah likewise relates another outrage which Bajazet endured, of a more domestic and tender nature. His indiscreet mention of women and divorces was deeply resented by the jealous Tartar: in the feast of victory the wine was served by female cupbearers, and the sultan beheld his own concubines and wives confounded among the slaves, and exposed without a veil to the eyes of intemperance. To escape a similar indignity, it is said that his successors, except in a single instance, have abstained from legitimate nuptials; and the Ottoman practice and belief, at least in the sixteenth century, is attested by the observing Busbequius,[55] ambassador from the court of Vienna to the great Soliman. 4. Such is the separation of language, that the testimony of a Greek is not less independent than that of a Latin or an Arab. I suppress the names of Chalcocondyles and Ducas, who flourished in a later period, and who speak in a less positive tone; but more attention is due to George Phranza,[56] protovestiare of the last emperors, and who was born a year before the battle of Angora. Twenty-two years after that event he was sent ambassador to Amurath the Second; and the historian might converse with some veteran Janizaries, who had been made prisoners with the sultan, and had themselves seen him in his iron cage. 5. The last evidence, in every sense, is that of the Turkish annals, which have been consulted or transcribed by Leunclavius, Pocock, and Cantemir.[57] They unanimously deplore the captivity of the iron cage; and some credit may be allowed to national historians, who cannot stigmatise the Tartar without uncovering the shame of their king and country.

From these opposite premises a fair and moderate conclusion may be deduced. I am satisfied that Sherefeddin Ali has faithfully described the first ostentatious interview, in which the conqueror, whose spirits were harmonised by success, affected the character of generosity. But his mind was insensibly alienated by the unseasonable arrogance of Bajazet; the complaints of his enemies, the Anatolian princes, were just and vehement; and Timour betrayed a design of leading his royal captive in triumph to Samarcand. An attempt to facilitate his escape, by digging a mine under the tent, provoked the Mogul emperor to impose a harsher restraint; and in his perpetual marches an iron cage on a waggon might be invented, not as a wanton insult, but as a rigorous precaution. Timour had read in some fabulous history a similar treatment of one of his predecessors, a king of Persia; and Bajazet was condemned to represent the person and expiate the guilt of the Roman Cæsar.[58] But the strength of his mind and body fainted under the trial, and his premature death might, without injustice, be ascribed to the severity of Timour. He warred not with the dead: a tear and a sepulchre were all that he could bestow on a captive who was delivered from his power; and if Mousa, the son of Bajazet, was permitted to reign over the ruins of Boursa, the greatest part of the provinces of Anatolia had been restored by the conqueror to their lawful sovereigns.

From the Irtish and Volga to the Persian Gulf, and from the Ganges to Damascus and the Archipelago, Asia was in the hand of Timour: his armies were invincible, his ambition was boundless, and his zeal might aspire to conquer and convert the Christian kingdoms of the West, which already trembled at his name. He touched the utmost verge of the land; but an insuperable, though narrow sea, rolled between the two continents of Europe and Asia,[59] but the lord of so many *tomans* or myriads of horse was not master of a single galley. The two passages of the Bosphorus and Hellespont, of Constantinople and Gallipoli, were possessed, the one by the Christians, the other by the Turks. On this great occasion they forgot the difference of religion, to act with union and firmness in the common cause: the double straits were guarded with ships and fortifications, and they separately withheld the transports which Timour demanded of either nation, under the pretence of attacking their enemy. At the same time they soothed his pride with tributary gifts and suppliant embassies, and prudently tempted him to retreat with the honours of victory. Soliman, the son of Bajazet, implored his clemency for his father and himself; accepted, by a red patent, the investiture of the kingdom of Romania, which he already held by the sword, and reiterated his ardent wish of casting himself in person at the feet of the king of the world. The Greek emperor[60] (either John or Manuel) submitted to pay the same tribute which he had stipulated with the Turkish sultan, and ratified the treaty by an oath of allegiance, from which he could absolve his conscience so soon as the Mogul arms had retired from Anatolia. But the fears and fancy of nations ascribed to the ambitious Tamerlane a new design of vast and romantic compass; a design of subduing Egypt and Africa, marching from the Nile to the Atlantic Ocean, entering Europe by the Straits of Gibraltar, and, after imposing his yoke on the kingdoms of Christendom, of returning home by the deserts of Russia and Tartary. This remote, and perhaps imaginary danger, was averted by the submission of the sultan of Egypt: the honours of the prayer and the coin attested at Cairo the supremacy of Timour; and a rare gift of a *giraffe* or camelopard, and nine ostriches, represented at Samarcand the tribute of the African world. Our imagination is not less astonished by the portrait of a Mogul, who, in his camp before Smyrna, meditates and almost accomplishes the invasion of the Chinese empire.[61] Timour was urged to this enterprise by national honour and religious zeal. The torrents which he had shed of Musulman blood could be expiated only by an equal destruction of the infidels; and as he now stood at the gates of paradise, he might best secure his glorious entrance by demolishing the idols of China, founding mosques in every city, and establishing the profession of faith in one God and his prophet Mohammed. The recent expulsion of the house of Zingis was an insult on the Mogul name, and the disorders of the empire afforded the fairest opportunity for revenge. The illustrious Hongvou, founder of the dynasty of *Ming*, died four years before the battle of Angora, and his grandson, a weak and unfortunate youth, was burnt in his palace, after a million of Chinese had perished in the civil war.[62] Before he evacuated Anatolia, Timour despatched beyond the Sihoon a numerous army, or rather colony, of his old and new subjects, to open the road, to subdue the pagan Calmucks and Mungals, and to found cities and magazines in the desert, and, by the diligence of his lieutenant, he soon received a perfect map and description of the unknown regions, from the source of the Irtish to the wall of China. During these preparations the emperor achieved the final conquest of Georgia, passed the winter on the banks of the Araxes, appeased the troubles of Persia, and slowly returned to his capital after a campaign of four years and nine months.

On the throne of Samarcand[63] he displayed, in a short repose, his magnificence and power; listened to the complaints of the people; distributed a just measure of rewards and punishments; employed his riches in the architecture of palaces and temples; and gave audience to the ambassadors of Egypt, Arabia, India, Tartary, Russia, and Spain, the last of whom presented a suit of tapestry which eclipsed the pencil of the Oriental artists. The marriage of six of the emperor's grandsons was esteemed an act of religion as well as of paternal tenderness; and the pomp of the ancient caliphs was revived in their nuptials. They were celebrated in the gardens of Canighul, decorated with innumerable tents and pavilions, which displayed the luxury of a great city and the spoils of a victorious camp. Whole forests were cut down to supply fuel for the kitchens; the plain was spread with pyramids of meat and vases of every liquor, to which thousands of guests were courteously invited: the orders of the state and the nations of the earth were marshalled at the royal banquet; nor were the ambassadors of Europe (says the haughty Persian) excluded from the feast; since even the *casses*, the smallest of fish, find their place in the ocean.[64] The public joy was testified by illuminations and masquerades; the trades of Samarcand passed in review; and every trade was emulous to execute some quaint device, some marvellous pageant, with the materials of their peculiar art. After the marriage-contracts had been ratified by the cadhis, the bridegrooms and their brides retired to the nuptial chambers: nine times, according to the Asiatic fashion, they were dressed and undressed; and at each change of apparel pearls and rubies were showered on their heads, and contemptuously abandoned to their attendants. A general indulgence was proclaimed: every law was relaxed, every pleasure was allowed; the people was free, the sovereign was idle; and the historian of Timour may remark, that, after devoting fifty years to the attainment of empire, the only happy period of his life were the two months in which he ceased to exercise his power. But he was soon awakened to the cares of government and war. The standard was unfurled for the invasion of China: the emirs made their report of two hundred thousand, the select and veteran soldiers of Iran and Touran: their baggage and provisions were transported by five hundred great waggons and an immense train of horses and camels; and the troops might prepare for a long absence, since more than six months were employed in the tranquil journey of a caravan from Samarcand to Pekin. Neither age nor the severity of the winter could retard the impatience of Timour; he mounted on horseback, passed the Sihoon on the ice, marched seventy-six parasangs, three hundred miles, from his capital, and pitched his last camp in the neighbourhood of Otrar, where he was expected by the angel of death. Fatigue, and the indiscreet use of iced water, accelerated the progress of his fever; and the conqueror of Asia expired in the seventieth year of his age, thirty-five years after he had ascended the throne of Zagatai. His designs were lost; his armies were disbanded; China was saved; and fourteen years after his decease, the most powerful of his children sent an embassy of friendship and commerce to the court of Pekin.[65]

The fame of Timour has pervaded the East and West: his posterity is still invested with the Imperial *title*; and the admiration of his subjects, who revered him almost as a deity, may be justified in some degree by the praise or confession of his bitterest enemies.[66] Although he was lame of a hand and foot, his form and stature were not unworthy of his rank; and his vigorous health, so essential to himself and to the world, was corroborated by temperance and exercise. In his familiar discourse he was grave and modest; and if he was ignorant of the Arabic language, he spoke with fluency and elegance the Persian and Turkish idioms. It was his delight to converse with the learned on topics of history and science; and the amusement of his leisure hours was the game of chess, which he improved or corrupted with new refinements.[67] In his religion he was a zealous, though not perhaps an orthodox, Musulman;[68] but his sound understanding may tempt us to believe that a superstitious reverence for omens and prophecies, for saints and astrologers, was only affected as an instrument of policy. In the government of a vast empire he stood alone and absolute, without a rebel to oppose his power, a favourite to seduce his affections, or a minister to mislead his judgment. It was his firmest maxim, that, whatever might be the consequence, the word of the prince should never be disputed or recalled; but his foes have maliciously observed that the commands of anger and destruction were more strictly executed than those of beneficence and favour. His sons and grandsons, of whom Timour left six-and-thirty at his decease, were his first and most submissive subjects; and whenever they deviated from their duty, they were corrected, according to the laws of Zingis, with the bastonade, and afterwards restored to honour and command. Perhaps his heart was not devoid of the social virtues; perhaps he was not incapable of loving his friends and pardoning his enemies; but the rules of morality are founded on the public interest; and it may be sufficient to applaud the *wisdom* of a monarch, for the liberality by which he is not impoverished, and for the justice by which he is strengthened and enriched. To maintain the harmony of authority and obedience, to chastise the proud, to protect the weak, to reward the deserving, to banish vice and idleness from his dominions, to secure the traveller and merchant, to restrain the depredations of the soldier, to cherish the labours of the husbandman, to encourage industry and learning, and, by an equal and moderate assessment, to increase the revenue without increasing the taxes, are indeed the duties of a prince; but, in the discharge of these duties, he finds an ample and immediate recompense. Timour might boast that, at his accession to the throne, Asia was the prey to anarchy and rapine, whilst under his prosperous monarchy a child, fearless and unhurt, might carry a purse of gold from the East to the West. Such was his confidence of merit, that from this reformation he derived an excuse for his victories and a title to universal dominion. The four following observations will serve to appreciate his claim to the public gratitude; and perhaps we shall conclude that the Mogul emperor was rather the scourge than the benefactor of mankind. 1. If some partial disorders, some local oppressions, were healed by the sword of Timour, the remedy was far more pernicious than the disease. By their rapine, cruelty, and discord, the petty tyrants of Persia might afflict their subjects; but whole nations were crushed under the footsteps of the reformer. The ground which had been occupied by flourishing cities was often marked by his abominable trophies, by columns, or pyramids, of human heads. Astracan, Carizme, Delhi, Ispahan, Bagdad, Aleppo, Damascus, Boursa, Smyrna, and a thousand others, were sacked, or burnt, or utterly destroyed, in his presence and by his troops: and perhaps his conscience would have been startled if a priest or philosopher had dared to number the millions of victims whom he had sacrificed to the establishment of peace and order.[69] 2. His most destructive wars were rather inroads than conquests. He invaded Turkestan, Kipzak, Russia, Hindostan, Syria, Anatolia, Armenia, and Georgia, without a hope or a desire of preserving those distant provinces. From thence he departed laden with

spoil; but he left behind him neither troops to awe the contumacious, nor magistrates to protect the obedient, natives. When he had broken the fabric of their ancient government he abandoned them to the evils which his invasion had aggravated or caused; nor were these evils compensated by any present or possible benefits. 3. The kingdoms of Transoxiana and Persia were the proper field which he laboured to cultivate and adorn as the perpetual inheritance of his family. But his peaceful labours were often interrupted, and sometimes blasted, by the absence of the conqueror. While he triumphed on the Volga or the Ganges, his servants, and even his sons, forgot their master and their duty. The public and private injuries were poorly redressed by the tardy rigour of inquiry and punishment; and we must be content to praise the *Institutions* of Timour as the specious idea of a perfect monarchy. 4. Whatsoever might be the blessings of his administration, they evaporated with his life. To reign, rather than to govern, was the ambition of his children and grandchildren,[70] the enemies of each other and of the people. A fragment of the empire was upheld with some glory by Sharokh, his youngest son; but after *his* decease the scene was again involved in darkness and blood; and before the end of a century Transoxiana and Persia were trampled by the Uzbeks from the north, and the Turkmans of the black and white sheep. The race of Timour would have been extinct if a hero, his descendant in the fifth degree, had not fled before the Uzbek arms to the conquest of Hindostan. His successors (the great Moguls[71]) extended their sway from the mountains of Cashmir to Cape Comorin, and from Candahar to the gulf of Bengal. Since the reign of Aurungzebe their empire has been dissolved; their treasures of Delhi have been rifled by a Persian robber; and the richest of their kingdoms is now possessed by a company of Christian merchants of a remote island in the Northern Ocean.

Far different was the fate of the Ottoman monarchy. The massy trunk was bent to the ground, but no sooner did the hurricane pass away than it again rose with fresh vigour and more lively vegetation. When Timour in every sense had evacuated Anatolia, he left the cities without a palace, a treasure, or a king. The open country was overspread with hordes of shepherds and robbers of Tartar or Turkman origin; the recent conquests of Bajazet were restored to the emirs, one of whom, in base revenge, demolished his sepulchre; and his five sons were eager, by civil discord, to consume the remnant of their patrimony. I shall enumerate their names in the order of their age and actions.[72] 1. It is doubtful whether I relate the story of the true *Mustapha*, or of an impostor who personated that lost prince. He fought by his father's side in the battle of Angora: but when the captive sultan was permitted to inquire for his children, Mousa alone could be found; and the Turkish historians, the slaves of the triumphant faction, are persuaded that his brother was confounded among the slain. If Mustapha escaped from that disastrous field, he was concealed twelve years from his friends and enemies, till he emerged in Thessaly, and was hailed by a numerous party as the son and successor of Bajazet. His first defeat would have been his last, had not the true or false Mustapha been saved by the Greeks, and restored, after the decease of his brother Mohammed, to liberty and empire. A degenerate mind seemed to argue his spurious birth; and if, on the throne of Adrianople, he was adored as the Ottoman sultan, his flight, his fetters, and an ignominious gibbet delivered the impostor to popular contempt. A similar character and claim was asserted by several rival pretenders: thirty persons are said to have suffered under the name of Mustapha; and these frequent executions may perhaps insinuate that the Turkish court was not perfectly secure of the death of the lawful prince. 2. After his father's captivity Isa[73] reigned for some time in the neighbourhood of Angora, Sinope, and the Black Sea; and his ambassadors were dismissed from the presence of Timour with fair promises and honourable gifts. But their master was soon deprived of his province and life by a jealous brother, the sovereign of Amasia; and the final event suggested a pious allusion that the law of Moses and Jesus, of *Isa* and *Mousa*, had been abrogated by the greater *Mohammed*. 3. *Soliman* is not numbered in the list of the Turkish emperors: yet he checked the victorious progress of the Moguls, and, after their departure, united for a while the thrones of Adrianople and Boursa. In war he was brave, active, and fortunate: his courage was softened by clemency; but it was likewise inflamed by presumption, and corrupted by intemperance and idleness. He relaxed the nerves of discipline in a government where either the subject or the sovereign must continually tremble: his vices alienated the chiefs of the army and the law; and his daily drunkenness, so contemptible in a prince and a man, was doubly odious in a disciple of the prophet.

In the slumber of intoxication he was surprised by his brother Mousa; and as he fled from Adrianople towards the Byzantine capital, Soliman was overtaken and slain in a bath, after a reign of seven years and ten months. 4. The investiture of Mousa degraded him as the slave of the Moguls: his tributary kingdom of Anatolia was confined within a narrow limit, nor could his broken militia and empty treasury contend with the hardy and veteran bands of the sovereign of Romania. Mousa fled in disguise from the palace of Boursa; traversed the Propontis in an open boat; wandered over the Wallachian and Servian hills; and after some vain attempts, ascended the throne of Adrianople, so recently stained with the blood of Soliman. In a reign of three years and a half his troops were victorious against the Christians of Hungary and the Morea; but Mousa was ruined by his timorous disposition and unseasonable clemency. After resigning the sovereignty of Anatolia he fell a victim to the perfidy of his ministers and the superior ascendant of his brother Mohammed. 5. The final victory of Mohammed was the just recompense of his prudence and moderation. Before his father's captivity the royal youth had been intrusted with the government of Amasia, thirty days' journey from Constantinople, and the Turkish frontier against the Christians of Trebizond and Georgia. The castle in Asiatic warfare was esteemed impregnable; and the city of Amasia,[74] which is equally divided by the river Iris, rises on either side in the form of an amphitheatre, and represents on a smaller scale the image of Bagdad. In his rapid career Timour appears to have overlooked this obscure and contumacious angle of Anatolia; and Mohammed, without provoking the conqueror, maintained his silent independence, and chased from the province the last stragglers of the Tartar host. He relieved himself from the dangerous neighbourhood of Isa; but in the contests of their more powerful brethren his firm neutrality was respected, till, after the triumph of Mousa, he stood forth the heir and avenger of the unfortunate Soliman. Mohammed obtained Anatolia by treaty and Romania by arms; and the soldier who presented him with the head of Mousa was rewarded as the benefactor of his king and country. The eight years of his sole and peaceful reign were usefully employed in banishing the vices of civil discord, and restoring on a firmer basis the fabric of the Ottoman monarchy. His last care was the choice of two viziers, Bajazet and Ibrahim,[75] who might guide the youth of his son Amurath; and such was their union and prudence, that they concealed above forty days the emperor's death till the arrival of his successor in the palace of Boursa. A new war was kindled in Europe by the prince, or impostor, Mustapha; the first vizir lost his army and his head; but the more fortunate Ibrahim, whose name and family are still revered, extinguished the last pretender to the throne of Bajazet, and closed the scene of domestic hostility.

In these conflicts the wisest Turks, and indeed the body of the nation, were strongly attached to the unity of the empire; and Romania and Anatolia, so often torn asunder by private ambition, were animated by a strong and invincible tendency of cohesion. Their efforts might have instructed the Christian powers; and had they occupied, with a confederate fleet, the straits of Gallipoli, the Ottomans, at least in Europe, must have been speedily annihilated. But the schism of the West, and the factions and wars of France and England, diverted the Latins from this generous enterprise: they enjoyed the present respite, without a thought of futurity; and were often tempted by a momentary interest to serve the common enemy of their religion. A colony of Genoese,[76] which had been planted at Phocaea[77] on the Ionian coast, was enriched by the lucrative monopoly of alum;[78] and their tranquillity, under the Turkish empire, was secured by the annual payment of tribute. In the last civil war of the Ottomans, the Genoese governor, Adorno, a bold and ambitious youth, embraced the party of Amurath; and undertook, with seven stout galleys, to transport him from Asia to Europe. The sultan and five hundred guards embarked on board the admiral's ship; which was manned by eight hundred of the bravest Franks. His life and liberty were in their hands; nor can we, without reluctance, applaud the fidelity of Adorno, who, in the midst of the passage, knelt before him, and gratefully accepted a discharge of his arrears of tribute. They landed in sight of Mustapha and Gallipoli; two thousand Italians, armed with lances and battle-axes, attended Amurath to the conquest of Adrianople; and this venal service was soon repaid by the ruin of the commerce and colony of Phocaea.

If Timour had generously marched at the request, and to the relief, of the Greek emperor, he might be entitled to the praise and gratitude of the Christians.[79] But a Musulman who carried into Georgia the sword of persecution, and respected the holy warfare of Bajazet, was not disposed to pity or succour the *idolaters* of Europe. The Tartar followed the impulse of ambition; and the deliverance of Constantinople was the accidental consequence. When Manuel abdicated the government, it was his prayer, rather than his hope, that the ruin of the church and state might be delayed beyond his unhappy days; and after his return from a western pilgrimage, he expected every hour the news of a sad catastrophe. On a sudden he was astonished and rejoiced by the intelligence of the retreat, the overthrow, and the captivity of the Ottoman. Manuel[80] immediately sailed from Modon in the Morea; ascended the throne of Constantinople, and dismissed his blind competitor to an easy exile in the isle of Lesbos. The ambassadors of the son of Bajazet were soon introduced to his presence; but their pride was fallen, their tone was modest: they were awed by the just apprehension lest the Greeks should open to the Moguls the gates of Europe. Soliman saluted the emperor by the name of father; solicited at his hands the government or gift of Romania; and promised to deserve his favour by inviolable friendship, and the restitution of Thessalonica, with the most important places along the Strymon, the Propontis, and the Black Sea. The alliance of Soliman exposed the emperor to the enmity and revenge of Mousa: the Turks appeared in arms before the gates of Constantinople; but they were repulsed by sea and land; and unless the city was guarded by some foreign mercenaries, the Greeks must have wondered at their own triumph. But, instead of prolonging the division of the Ottoman powers, the policy or passion of Manuel was tempted to assist the most formidable of the sons of Bajazet. He concluded a treaty with Mohammed, whose progress was checked by the insuperable barrier of Gallipoli: the sultan and his troops were transported over the Bosphorus; he was hospitably entertained in the capital; and his successful sally was the first step to the conquest of Romania. The ruin was suspended by the prudence and moderation of the conqueror: he faithfully discharged his own obligations and those of Soliman; respected the laws of gratitude and peace; and left the emperor guardian of his two younger sons, in the vain hope of saving them from the jealous cruelty of their brother Amurath. But the execution of his last testament would have offended the national honour and religion; and the divan unanimously pronounced that the royal youths should never be abandoned to the custody and education of a Christian dog. On this refusal the Byzantine councils were divided: but the age and caution of Manuel yielded to the presumption of his son John; and they unsheathed a dangerous weapon of revenge, by dismissing the true or false Mustapha, who had long been detained as a captive and hostage, and for whose maintenance they received an annual pension of three hundred thousand aspers.[81] At the door of his prison, Mustapha subscribed to every proposal; and the keys of Gallipoli, or rather of Europe, were stipulated as the price of his deliverance. But no sooner was he seated on the throne of Romania than he dismissed the Greek ambassadors with a smile of contempt, declaring, in a pious tone, that, at the day of judgment, he would rather answer for the violation of an oath, than for the surrender of a Musulman city into the hands of the infidels. The emperor was at once the enemy of the two rivals, from whom he had sustained, and to whom he had offered, an injury; and the victory of Amurath was followed, in the ensuing spring, by the siege of Constantinople.[82]

The religious merit of subduing the city of the Cæsars attracted from Asia a crowd of volunteers, who aspired to the crown of martyrdom; their military ardour was inflamed by the promise of rich spoils and beautiful females; and the sultan's ambition was consecrated by the presence and prediction of Seid Bechar, a descendant of the prophet,[83] who arrived in the camp, on a mule, with a venerable train of five hundred disciples. But he might blush, if a fanatic could blush, at the failure of his assurances. The strength of the walls resisted an army of two hundred thousand Turks: their assaults were repelled by the sallies of the Greeks and their foreign mercenaries; the old resources of defence were opposed to the new engines of attack; and the enthusiasm of the dervish, who was snatched to heaven in visionary converse with Mohammed, was answered by the credulity of the Christians, who *beheld* the Virgin Mary, in a violet garment, walking on the rampart and animating their courage.[84] After a siege of two months Amurath was recalled to Boursa by a domestic revolt, which had been kindled by Greek treachery, and was soon extinguished by the death of a guiltless brother. While he led his Janizaries to new conquests in Europe and Asia, the Byzantine empire was indulged in a servile and precarious respite of thirty years. Manuel sank into the grave; and John Palæologus was permitted to reign, for an annual tribute of three hundred thousand aspers, and the dereliction of almost all that he held beyond the suburbs of Constantinople

In the establishment and restoration of the Turkish empire the first merit must doubtless be assigned to the personal qualities of the sultans; since, in human life, the most important scenes will depend on the character of a single actor. By some shades of wisdom and virtue they may be discriminated from each other; but, except in a single instance, a period of nine reigns, and two hundred and sixty-five years, is occupied, from the elevation of Othman to the death of Soliman, by a rare series of warlike and active princes, who impressed their subjects with obedience and their enemies with terror. Instead of the slothful luxury of the seraglio, the heirs of royalty were educated in the council and the field: from early youth they were entrusted by their fathers with the command of provinces and armies; and this manly institution, which was often productive of civil war must have essentially contributed to the discipline and vigour, of the monarchy. The Ottomans cannot style themselves, like the Arabian caliphs, the descendants or successors of the apostle of God; and the kindred which they claim with the Tartar khans of the house of Zingis appears to be founded in flattery rather than in truth.[85] Their origin is obscure; but their sacred and indefeasible right, which no time can erase, and no violence can fringe, was soon and unalterably implanted in the minds of their subjects. A weak or vicious sultan may be deposed and strangled; but his inheritance devolves to an infant or an idiot: nor has the most daring rebel presumed to ascend the throne of his lawful sovereign.[86]

While the transient dynasties of Asia have been continually subverted by a crafty vizir in the palace or a victorious general in the camp, the Ottoman succession has been confirmed by the practice of five centuries, and is now incorporated with the vital principle of the Turkish nation.

To the spirit and constitution of that nation a strong and singular influence may however be ascribed. The primitive subjects of Othman were the four hundred families of wandering Turkmans who had followed his ancestors from the Oxus to the Sangar; and the plains of Anatolia are still covered with the white and black tents of their rustic brethren. But this original drop was dissolved in the mass of voluntary and vanquished subjects, who, under the name of Turks, are united by the common ties of religion, language, and manners. In the cities from Erzeroum to Belgrade, that national appellation is common to all the Moslems, the first and most honourable inhabitants; but they have abandoned, at least in Romania, the villages and the cultivation of the land to the Christian peasants. In the vigorous age of the Ottoman government the Turks were themselves excluded from all civil and military honours; and a servile class, an artificial people, was raised by the discipline of education to obey, to conquer, and to command.[87] From the time of Orchan and the first Amurath the sultans were persuaded that a government of the sword must be renewed in each generation with new soldiers; and that such soldiers must be sought, not in effeminate Asia, but among the hardy and warlike natives of Europe. The provinces of Thrace, Macedonia, Albania, Bulgaria, and Servia became the perpetual seminary of the Turkish army; and when the royal fifth of the captives was diminished by conquest, an inhuman tax of the fifth child, or of every fifth year, was rigorously levied on the Christian families. At the age of twelve or fourteen years the most robust youths were torn from their parents; their names were enrolled in a book; and from that moment they were clothed, taught, and maintained for the public service. According to the promise of their appearance, they were selected for the royal schools of Boursa, Pera, and Adrianople, intrusted to the care of the bashaws, or dispersed in the houses of the Anatolian peasantry. It was the first care of their masters to instruct them in the Turkish language: their bodies were exercised by every labour that could fortify their strength; they learned to wrestle, to leap, to run, to shoot with the bow, and afterwards with the musket; till they were drafted into the chambers and companies of the Janizaries, and severely trained in the military or monastic discipline of the order. The youths most conspicuous for birth, talents, and beauty, were admitted into the inferior class of *Agiamoglans*, or the more liberal rank of *Ichoglans*, of whom the former were attached to the palace, and the latter to the person of the prince. In four successive schools, under the rod of the white eunuchs, the arts of horsemanship and of darting the javelin were their daily exercise, while those of a more studious cast applied themselves to the study of the Koran, and the knowledge of the Arabic and Persian tongues. As they advanced in seniority and merit, they were gradually dismissed to military, civil, and even ecclesiastical employments: the longer their stay, the higher was their expectation; till, at a mature period, they were admitted into the number of the forty agas, who stood before the sultan, and were promoted by his choice to the government of provinces and the first honours of the empire.[88] Such a mode of institution was admirably adapted to the form and spirit of a despotic monarchy. The ministers and generals were, in the strictest sense, the slaves of the emperor, to whose bounty they were indebted for their instruction and support. When they left the seraglio, and suffered their beards to grow as the symbol of enfranchisement, they found themselves in an important office, without faction or friendship, without parents and without heirs, dependent on the hand which had raised them from the dust, and which, on the slightest displeasure, could break in pieces these statues of glass, as they are aptly termed by the Turkish proverb.[89] In the slow and painful steps of education, their characters and talents were unfolded to a discerning eye: the *man*, naked and alone, was reduced to the standard of his personal merit; and, if the sovereign had wisdom to choose, he possessed a pure and boundless liberty of choice. The Ottoman candidates were trained by the virtues of abstinence to those of action; by the habits of submission to those of command. A similar spirit was diffused among the troops; and their silence and sobriety, their patience and modesty, have extorted the reluctant praise of their Christian enemies.[90] Nor can the victory appear doubtful, if we compare the discipline and exercise of the Janizaries with the pride of birth, the independence of chivalry, the ignorance of the new levies, the mutinous temper of the veterans, and the vices of intemperance and disorder which so long contaminated the armies of Europe.

The only hope of salvation for the Greek empire and the adjacent kingdoms would have been some more powerful weapon, some discovery in the art of war, that should give them a decisive superiority over their Turkish foes. Such a weapon was in their hands; such a discovery had been made in the critical moment of their fate. The chemists of China or Europe had found, by casual or elaborate experiments, that a mixture of saltpetre, sulphur, and charcoal produces, with a spark of fire, a tremendous explosion. It was soon observed that, if the expansive force were compressed in a strong tube, a ball of stone or iron might be expelled with irresistible and destructive velocity. The precise era of the invention and application of gunpowder[91] is involved in doubtful traditions and equivocal language; yet we may clearly discern that it was known before the middle of the fourteenth century, and that before the end of the same the use of artillery in battles and sieges by sea and land was familiar to the states of Germany, Italy, Spain, France, and England.[92] The priority of nations is of small account; none could derive any exclusive benefit from their previous or superior knowledge; and in the common improvement they stood on the same level of relative power and military science. Nor was it possible to circumscribe the secret within the pale of the church; it was disclosed to the Turks by the treachery of apostates and the selfish policy of rivals; and the sultans had sense to adopt, and wealth to reward, the talents of a Christian engineer. The Genoese, who transported Amurath into Europe, must be accused as his preceptors; and it was probably by their hands that his cannon was cast and directed at the siege of Constantinople.[93] The first attempt was indeed unsuccessful; but

in the general warfare of the age the advantage was on *their* side who were most commonly the assailants; for a while the proportion of the attack and defence was suspended, and this thundering artillery was pointed against the walls and towers which had been erected only to resist the less potent engines of antiquity. By the Venetians the use of gunpowder was communicated without reproach to the sultans of Egypt and Persia, their allies against the Ottoman power; the secret was soon propagated to the extremities of Asia; and the advantage of the European was confined to his easy victories over the savages of the new world. If we contrast the rapid progress of this mischievous discovery with the slow and laborious advances of reason, science, and the arts of peace, a philosopher, according to his temper, will laugh or weep at the folly of mankind.

CHAPTER LXVI

Applications of the Eastern Emperors to the Popes. Visits to the West of John the First, Manuel, and John the Second, Palæologus. Union of the Greek and Latin Churches promoted by the Council of Basil, and concluded at Ferrara and Florence. State of Literature at Constantinople. Its Revival in Italy by the Greek Fugitives. Curiosity and Emulation of the Latins.

IN the four last centuries of the Greek emperors their friendly or hostile aspect towards the pope and the Latins may be observed as the thermometer of their prosperity or distress—as the scale of the rise and fall of the barbarian dynasties. When the Turks of the house of Seljuk pervaded Asia, and threatened Constantinople, we have seen at the council of Placentia the suppliant ambassadors of Alexius imploring the protection of the common father of the Christians. No sooner had the arms of the French pilgrims removed the sultan from Nice to Iconium than the Greek princes resumed, or avowed, their genuine hatred and contempt for the schismatics of the West, which precipitated the first downfall of their empire. The date of the Mogul invasion is marked in the soft and charitable language of John Vataces. After the recovery of Constantinople the throne of the first Palæologus was encompassed by foreign and domestic enemies: as long as the sword of Charles was suspended over his head he basely courted the favour of the Roman pontiff, and sacrificed to the present danger his faith, his virtue, and the affection of his subjects. On the de-

cease of Michael the prince and people asserted the independence of their church and the purity of their creed: the elder Andronicus neither feared nor loved the Latins; in his last distress pride was the safeguard of superstition; nor could he decently retract in his age the firm and orthodox declarations of his youth. His grandson, the younger Andronicus, was less a slave in his temper and situation; and the conquest of Bithynia by the Turks admonished him to seek a temporal and spiritual alliance with the Western princes. After a separation and silence of fifty years a secret agent, the monk Barlaam, was despatched to Pope Benedict the Twelfth; and his artful instructions appear to have been drawn by the master-hand of the great domestic.[1] "Most holy father," was he commissioned to say, "the emperor is not less desirous than yourself of a union between the two churches; but in this delicate transaction he is obliged to respect his own dignity and the prejudices of his subjects. The ways of union are twofold, force and persuasion. Of force, the inefficacy has been already tried, since the Latins have subdued the empire without subduing the minds of the

Greeks. The method of persuasion, though slow, is sure and permanent. A deputation of thirty or forty of our doctors would probably agree with those of the Vatican in the love of truth and the unity of belief; but on their return, what would be the use, the recompense, of such agreement? the scorn of their brethren, and the reproaches of a blind and obstinate nation. Yet that nation is accustomed to reverence the general councils which have fixed the articles of our faith; and if they reprobate the decrees of Lyons, it is because the Eastern churches were neither heard nor represented in that arbitrary meeting. For this salutary end it will be expedient, and even necessary, that a well-chosen legate should be sent into Greece to convene the patriarchs of Constantinople, Alexandria, Antioch, and Jerusalem, and with their aid to prepare a free and universal synod. But at this moment," continued the subtle agent, "the empire is assaulted and endangered by the Turks, who have occupied four of the greatest cities of Anatolia. The Christian inhabitants have expressed a wish of returning to their allegiance and religion; but the forces and revenues of the emperor are insufficient for their deliverance: and the Roman legate must be accompanied or preceded by an army of Franks to expel the infidels, and open a way to the holy sepulchre." If the suspicious Latins should require some pledge, some previous effect of the sincerity of the Greeks, the answers of Barlaam were perspicuous and rational. "1. A general synod can alone consummate the union of the churches; nor can such a synod be held till the three Oriental patriarchs and a great number of bishops are enfranchised from the Mohammedan yoke. 2. The Greeks are alienated by a long series of oppression and injury: they must be reconciled by some act of brotherly love, some effectual succour, which may fortify the authority and arguments of the emperor and the friends of the union. 3. If some difference of faith or ceremonies should be found incurable, the Greeks however are the disciples of Christ, and the Turks are the common enemies of the Christian name. The Armenians, Cyprians, and Rhodians are equally attacked; and it will become the piety of the French princes to draw their swords in the general defence of religion. 4. Should the subjects of Andronicus be treated as the worst of schismatics, of heretics, of pagans, a judicious policy may yet instruct the powers of the West to embrace a useful ally, to uphold a sinking empire, to guard the confines of Europe, and rather to join the Greeks against the Turks than

to expect the union of the Turkish arms with the troops and treasures of captive Greece." The reasons, the offers, and the demands of Andronicus were eluded with cold and stately indifference. The kings of France and Naples declined the dangers and glory of a crusade: the pope refused to call a new synod to determine old articles of faith; and his regard for the obsolete claims of the Latin emperor and clergy engaged him to use an offensive superscription— "To the *moderator*[2] of the Greeks, and the persons who style themselves the patriarchs of the Eastern churches." For such an embassy a time and character less propitious could not easily have been found. Benedict the Twelfth[3] was a dull peasant, perplexed with scruples, and immersed in sloth and wine: his pride might enrich with a third crown the papal tiara, but he was alike unfit for the regal and the pastoral office.

After the decease of Andronicus, while the Greeks were distracted by intestine war, they could not presume to agitate a general union of the Christians. But as soon as Cantacuzene had subdued and pardoned his enemies, he was anxious to justify, or at least to extenuate, the introduction of the Turks into Europe and the nuptials of his daughter with a Musulman prince. Two officers of state, with a Latin interpreter, were sent in his name to the Roman court, which was transplanted to Avignon, on the banks of the Rhône, during a period of seventy years: they represented the hard necessity which had urged him to embrace the alliance of the miscreants, and pronounced by his command the specious and edifying sounds of union and crusade. Pope Clement the Sixth,[4] the successor of Benedict, received them with hospitality and honour, acknowledged the innocence of their sovereign, excused his distress, applauded his magnanimity, and displayed a clear knowledge of the state and revolutions of the Greek empire, which he had imbibed from the honest accounts of a Savoyard lady, an attendant of the empress Anne.[5] If Clement was ill endowed with the virtues of a priest, he possessed however the spirit and magnificence of a prince whose liberal hand distributed benefices and kingdoms with equal facility. Under his reign Avignon was the seat of pomp and pleasure: in his youth he had surpassed the licentiousness of a baron; and the palace, nay the bed-chamber of the pope, was adorned, or polluted, by the visits of his female favourites. The wars of France and England were adverse to the holy enterprise; but his vanity was amused by the splendid idea; and the Greek ambassadors returned with two Latin bishops, the ministers of the pontiff. On their arrival at Constantinople the emperor and the nuncios admired each other's piety and eloquence; and their frequent conferences were filled with mutual praises and promises, by which both parties were amused, and neither could be deceived. "I am delighted," said the devout Cantacuzene, "with the project of our holy war, which must redound to my personal glory as well as to the public benefit of Christendom. My dominions will give a free passage to the armies of France: my troops, my galleys, my treasures, shall be consecrated to the common cause; and happy would be my fate could I deserve and obtain the crown of martyrdom. Words are insufficient to express the ardour with which I sigh for the reunion of the scattered members of Christ. If my death could avail, I would gladly present my sword and my neck: if the spiritual phœnix could arise from my ashes, I would erect the pile and kindle the flame with my own hands." Yet the Greek emperor presumed to observe that the articles of faith which divided the two churches had been introduced by the pride and precipitation of the Latins: he disclaimed the servile and arbitrary steps of the first Palæologus, and firmly declared that he would never submit his conscience unless to the decrees of a free and universal synod. "The situation of the times," continued he, "will not allow the pope and myself to meet either at Rome or Constantinople; but some maritime city may be chosen on the verge of the two empires, to unite the bishops, and to instruct the faithful of the East and West." The nuncios seemed content with the proposition; and Cantacuzene affects to deplore the failure of his hopes, which were soon overthrown by the death of Clement, and the different temper of his successor. His own life was prolonged, but it was prolonged in a cloister; and, except by his prayers, the humble monk was incapable of directing the counsels of his pupil or the state.[6]

Yet of all the Byzantine princes, that pupil, John Palæologus, was the best disposed to embrace, to believe, and to obey the shepherd of the West. His mother, Anne of Savoy, was baptised in the bosom of the Latin church: her marriage with Andronicus imposed a change of name, of apparel, and of worship, but her heart was still faithful to her country and religion: she had formed the infancy of her son, and she governed the emperor after his mind, or at least his stature, was enlarged to the size of man. In the first year of his deliverance and restoration the Turks were still masters of the Hellespont; the son of Cantacuzene was in arms at Adrianople, and Palæologus could depend neither on himself nor on his people. By his mother's advice, and in the hope of foreign aid, he abjured the rights both of the church and state; and the act of slavery,[7] subscribed in purple ink, and sealed with the *golden* bull, was privately intrusted to an Italian agent. The first article of the treaty is an oath of fidelity and obedience to Innocent the Sixth and his successors, the supreme pontiffs of the Roman and Catholic church. The emperor promises to entertain with due reverence their legates and nuncios, to assign a palace for their residence and a temple for their worship, and to deliver his second son Manuel as the hostage of his faith. For these condescensions he requires a prompt succour of fifteen galleys, with five hundred men-at-arms and a thousand archers, to serve against his Christian and Musulman enemies. Palæologus engages to impose on his clergy and people the same spiritual yoke; but as the resistance of the Greeks might be justly foreseen, he adopts the two effectual methods of corruption and education. The legate was empowered to distribute the vacant benefices among the ecclesiastics who should subscribe the creed of the Vatican: three schools were instituted to instruct the youth of Constantinople in the language and doctrine of the Latins; and the name of Andronicus, the heir of the empire, was enrolled as the first student. Should he fail in the measures of persuasion or force, Palæologus declares himself unworthy to reign, transfers to the pope all regal and paternal authority, and invests Innocent with full power to regulate the family, the government, and the marriage of his son and successor. But this treaty was neither executed nor published: the Roman galleys were as vain and imaginary as the submission of the Greeks; and it was only by the secrecy that their sovereign escaped the dishonour of this fruitless humiliation.

The tempest of the Turkish arms soon burst on his head; and after the loss of Adrianople and Romania he was enclosed in his capital, the vassal of the haughty Amurath, with the miserable hope of being the last devoured by the savage. In this abject state Palæologus embraced the resolution of embarking for Venice, and casting himself at the feet of the pope: he was the first of the Byzantine princes who had ever visited the unknown regions of the West, yet in them alone he could seek consolation or relief; and with less violation of his dignity he might appear in the sacred college than at the Ottoman *Porte*. After a long absence the Roman pontiffs were returning from Avignon to the banks of the Tiber: Urban the Fifth,[8] of a mild and virtuous character, encouraged or allowed the pilgrimage of the Greek prince, and, within the same year, enjoyed the glory of receiving in the Vatican the two Imperial shadows who represented the majesty of Constantine and Charlemagne. In this suppliant visit the emperor of Constantinople, whose vanity was lost in his distress, gave more than could be expected of empty sounds and formal submissions. A previous trial was imposed; and in the presence of four cardinals he acknowledged, as a true Catholic, the supremacy of the pope, and the double procession of the Holy Ghost. After this purification he was introduced to a public audience in the church of St. Peter: Urban, in the midst of the cardinals, was seated on his throne; the Greek monarch, after three genuflexions, devoutly kissed the feet, the hands, and at length the mouth of the holy father, who celebrated high mass in his presence, allowed him to lead the bridle of his mule, and treated him with a sumptuous banquet in the Vatican. The entertainment of Palæologus was friendly and honourable, yet some difference was observed between the emperors of the East and West;[9] nor could the former be entitled to the rare privilege of chanting the Gospel in the rank of a deacon.[10] In favour of his proselyte, Urban strove to rekindle the zeal of the French king and the other powers of the West; but he found them cold in the general cause, and active only in their domestic quarrels. The last hope of the emperor was in an English mercenary, John Hawkwood,[11] or Acuto, who, with a band of adventurers, the White Brotherhood, had ravaged Italy from the Alps to Calabria, sold his services to the hostile states, and incurred a just excommunication by shooting his arrows against the papal residence. A special licence was granted to negotiate with the outlaw, but the forces, or the spirit, of Hawkwood were unequal to the enterprise: and it was for the advantage perhaps of Palæologus to be disappointed of a succour that must have been costly, that could not be effectual, and which might have been dangerous.[12] The disconsolate Greek[13] prepared for his return, but even his return was impeded by a most ignominious obstacle. On his arrival at Venice he had borrowed large sums at exorbitant usury; but his coffers were empty, his creditors were impatient,

and his person was detained as the best security for the payment. His eldest son Andronicus, the regent of Constantinople, was repeatedly urged to exhaust every resource, and, even by stripping the churches, to extricate his father from captivity and disgrace. But the unnatural youth was insensible of the disgrace, and secretly pleased with the captivity of the emperor: the state was poor, the clergy was obstinate; nor could some religious scruple be wanting to excuse the guilt of his indifference and delay. Such undutiful neglect was severely reproved by the piety of his brother Manuel, who instantly sold or mortgaged all that he possessed, embarked for Venice, relieved his father, and pledged his own freedom to be responsible for the debt. On his return to Constantinople the parent and king distinguished his two sons with suitable rewards; but the faith and manners of the slothful Palæologus had not been improved by his Roman pilgrimage; and his apostasy or conversion, devoid of any spiritual or temporal effects, was speedily forgotten by the Greeks and Latins.[14]

Thirty years after the return of Palæologus, his son and successor Manuel, from a similar motive, but on a larger scale, again visited the countries of the West. In a preceding chapter I have related his treaty with Bajazet, the violation of that treaty, the siege or blockade of Constantinople, and the French succour under the command of the gallant Boucicault.[15] By his ambassadors Manuel had solicited the Latin powers; but it was thought that the presence of a distressed monarch would draw tears and supplies from the hardest barbarians,[16] and the marshal who advised the journey prepared the reception of the Byzantine prince. The land was occupied by the Turks; but the navigation of Venice was safe and open: Italy received him as the first, or at least as the second, of the Christian princes; Manuel was pitied as the champion and confessor of the faith, and the dignity of his behaviour prevented that pity from sinking into contempt. From Venice he proceeded to Padua and Pavia; and even the Duke of Milan, a secret ally of Bajazet, gave him safe and honourable conduct to the verge of his dominions.[17] On the confines of France[18] the royal officers undertook the care of his person, journey, and expenses; and two thousand of the richest citizens, in arms and on horseback, came forth to meet him as far as Charenton, in the neighbourhood of the capital. At the gates of Paris he was saluted by the chancellor and the parliament; and Charles the Sixth, attended by his princes and nobles, welcomed his brother with a cordial embrace. The successor of Constantine was clothed in a robe of white silk and mounted on a milk-white steed, a circumstance, in the French ceremonial, of singular importance: the white colour is considered as the symbol of sovereignty; and in a late visit the German emperor, after a haughty demand and a peevish refusal, had been reduced to content himself with a black courser. Manuel was lodged in the Louvre: a succession of feasts and balls, the pleasures of the banquet and the chase, were ingeniously varied by the politeness of the French to display their magnificence and amuse his grief; he was indulged in the liberty of his chapel, and the doctors of the Sorbonne were astonished, and possibly scandalised, by the language, the rites, and the vestments of his Greek clergy. But the slightest glance on the state of the kingdom must teach him to despair of any effectual assistance. The unfortunate Charles, though he enjoyed some lucid intervals, continually relapsed into furious or stupid insanity; the reigns of government were alternately seized by his brother and uncle, the dukes of Orleans and Burgundy, whose factious competition prepared the miseries of civil war. The former was a gay youth, dissolved in luxury and love: the latter was the father of John count of Nevers, who had so lately been ransomed from Turkish captivity; and, if the fearless son was ardent to revenge his defeat, the more prudent Burgundy was content with the cost and peril of the first experiment. When Manuel had satiated the curiosity, and perhaps fatigued the patience of the French, he resolved on a visit to the adjacent island. In his progress from Dover he was entertained at Canterbury with due reverence by the prior and monks of St. Austin, and, on Blackheath, king Henry the Fourth, with the English court, saluted the Greek hero (I copy our old historian), who, during many days, was lodged and treated in London as emperor of the East.[19] But the state of England was still more adverse to the design of the holy war. In the same year the hereditary sovereign had been deposed and murdered: the reigning prince was a successful usurper, whose ambition was punished by jealousy and remorse; nor could Henry of Lancaster withdraw his person or forces from the defence of a throne incessantly shaken by conspiracy and rebellion. He pitied, he praised, he feasted, the emperor of Constantinople; but if the English monarch assumed the cross, it was only to appease his people, and perhaps his conscience, by the merit

or semblance of this pious intention.[20] Satisfied, however, with gifts and honours, Manuel returned to Paris; and, after a residence of two years in the West, shaped his course through Germany and Italy, embarked at Venice, and patiently expected, in the Morea, the moment of his ruin or deliverance. Yet he had escaped the ignominious necessity of offering his religion to public or private sale. The Latin church was distracted by the great schism: the kings, the nations, the universities of Europe, were divided in their obedience between the popes of Rome and Avignon; and the emperor, anxious to conciliate the friendship of both parties, abstained from any correspondence with the indigent and unpopular rivals. His journey coincided with the year of the jubilee; but he passed through Italy without desiring or deserving the plenary indulgence which abolished the guilt or penance of the sins of the faithful. The Roman pope was offended by this neglect, accused him of irreverence to an image of Christ, and exhorted the princes of Italy to reject and abandon the obstinate schismatic.[21]

During the period of the crusades the Greeks beheld with astonishment and terror the perpetual stream of emigration that flowed, and continued to flow, from the unknown climates of the West. The visits of their last emperors removed the veil of separation, and they disclosed to their eyes the powerful nations of Europe, whom they no longer presumed to brand with the name of barbarians. The observations of Manuel and his more inquisitive followers have been preserved by a Byzantine historian of the times:[22] his scattered ideas I shall collect and abridge; and it may be amusing enough, perhaps instructive, to contemplate the rude pictures of Germany, France, and England, whose ancient and modern state are so familiar to our minds. I. GERMANY (says the Greek Chalcocondyles) is of ample latitude from Vienna to the Ocean, and it stretches (a strange geography) from Prague, in Bohemia, to the river Tartessus and the Pyrenæan mountains.[23] The soil, except in figs and olives, is sufficiently fruitful; the air is salubrious, the bodies of the natives are robust and healthy, and these cold regions are seldom visited with the calamities of pestilence or earthquakes. After the Scythians or Tartars, the Germans are the most numerous of nations: they are brave and patient, and, were they united under a single head, their force would be irresistible. By the gift of the pope, they have acquired the privilege of choosing the Roman emperor;[24] nor is any people more devoutly atached to the faith and obedience of the Latin patriarch. The greatest part of the country is divided among the princes and prelates; but Strasburg, Cologne, Hamburg, and more than two hundred free cities, are governed by sage and equal laws, according to the will and for the advantage of the whole community. The use of duels, or single combats on foot, prevails among them in peace and war; their industry excels in all the mechanic arts; and the Germans may boast of the invention of gunpowder and cannon, which is now diffused over the greatest part of the world. II. The kingdom of FRANCE is spread above fifteen or twenty days' journey from Germany to Spain, and from the Alps to the British Ocean, containing many flourishing cities, and among these Paris, the seat of the king, which surpasses the rest in riches and luxury. Many princes and lords alternately wait in his palace and acknowledge him as their sovereign: the most powerful are the dukes of Bretagne and Burgundy, of whom the latter possesses the wealthy province of Flanders, whose harbours are frequented by the ships and merchants of our own and the more remote seas. The French are an ancient and opulent people, and their language and manners, though somewhat different, are not dissimilar from those of the Italians. Vain of the Imperial dignity of Charlemagne, of their victories over the Saracens, and of the exploits of their heroes Oliver and Rowland,[25] they esteem themselves the first of the western nations; but this foolish arrogance has been recently humbled by the unfortunate events of their wars against the English, the inhabitants of the British island. III. BRITAIN, in the ocean and opposite to the shores of Flanders, may be considered either as one or as three islands; but the whole is united by a common interest, by the same manners, and by a similar government. The measure of its circumference is five thousand stadia: the land is overspread with towns and villages; though destitute of wine, and not abounding in fruit-trees, it is fertile in wheat and barley, in honey and wool, and much cloth is manufactured by the inhabitants. In populousness and power, in riches and luxury, London,[26] the metropolis of the isle, may claim a pre-eminence over all the cities of the West. It is situate on the Thames, a broad and rapid river, which at the distance of thirty miles falls into the Gallic Sea; and the daily flow and ebb of the tide affords a safe entrance and departure to the vessels of commerce. The king is the head of a powerful and turbulent aristocracy: his principal vassals hold their estates by a free and unalterable tenure, and the laws define the limits of his authority and their obedience. The kingdom has been often afflicted by foreign conquest and domestic sedition; but the natives are bold and hardy, renowned in arms and victorious in war. The form of their shields or targets is derived from the Italians, that of their swords from the Greeks; the use of the long bow is the peculiar and decisive advantage of the English. Their language bears no affinity to the idioms of the continent: in the habits of domestic life they are not easily distinguished from their neighbours of France; but the most singular circumstance of their manners is their disregard of conjugal honour and of female chastity. In their mutual visits, as the first act of hospitality, the guest is welcomed in the embraces of their wives and daughters: among friends they are lent and borrowed without shame; nor are the islanders offended at this strange commerce and its inevitable consequences.[27] Informed as we are of the customs of old England, and assured of the virtue of our mothers, we may smile at the credulity, or resent the injustice, of the Greek, who must have confounded a modest salute[28] with a criminal embrace. But his credulity and injustice may teach an important lesson, to distrust the accounts of foreign and remote nations, and to suspend our belief of every tale that deviates from the laws of nature and the character of man.[29]

After his return, and the victory of Timour, Manuel reigned many years in prosperity and peace. As long as the sons of Bajazet solicited his friendship and spared his dominions, he was satisfied with the national religion; and his leisure was employed in composing twenty theological dialogues for its defence. The appearance of the Byzantine ambassadors at the council of Constance[30] announces the restoration of the Turkish power, as well as of the Latin church: the conquest of the sultans, Mohammed and Amurath, reconciled the emperor to the Vatican; and the siege of Constantinople almost tempted him to acquiesce in the double procession of the Holy Ghost. When Martin the Fifth ascended without a rival the chair of St. Peter, a friendly intercourse of letters and embassies was revived between the East and West. Ambition on one side, and distress on the other, dictated the same decent language of charity and peace: the artful Greek expressed a desire of marrying his six sons to Italian princesses; and the Roman, not less artful, despatched the daughter of the marquis of Montferrat, with a company of noble virgins, to soften, by their charms, the obstinacy of the schismatics. Yet under this mask of zeal a discerning eye will perceive that all was hollow and insincere in the court and church of Constantinople. According to the vicissitudes of danger and repose, the emperor advanced or retreated; alternately instructed and disavowed his ministers; and escaped from an importunate pressure by urging the duty of inquiry, the obligation of collecting the sense of his patriarchs and bishops, and the impossibility of convening them at a time when the Turkish arms were at the gates of his capital. From a review of the public transactions it will appear that the Greeks insisted on three successive measures, a succour, a council, and a final reunion, while the Latins eluded the second, and only promised the first as a consequential and voluntary reward of the third. But we have an opportunity of unfolding the most secret intentions of Manuel, as he explained them in a private conversation without artifice or disguise. In his declining age the emperor had associated John Palæologus, the second of the name, and the eldest of his sons, on whom he devolved the greatest part of the authority and weight of government. One day, in the presence only of the historian Phranza,[31] his favourite chamberlain, he opened to his colleague and successor the true principle of his negotiations with the pope.[32] "Our last resource," said Manuel, "against the Turks is their fear of our union with the Latins, of the warlike nations of the West, who may arm for our relief and for their destruction. As often as you are threatened by the miscreants, present this danger before their eyes. Propose a council; consult on the means; but ever delay and avoid the convocation of an assembly, which cannot tend either to our spiritual or temporal emolument. The Latins are proud; the Greeks are obstinate; neither party will recede or retract; and the attempt of a perfect union will confirm the schism, alienate the churches, and leave us, without hope or defence, at the mercy of the barbarians." Impatient of this salutary lesson, the royal youth arose from his seat and departed in silence; and the wise monarch (continues Phranza), casting his eyes on me, thus resumed his discourse: "My son deems himself a great and heroic prince; but, alas! our miserable age does not afford scope for heroism or greatness. His daring spirit might have suited the happier times of our ancestors; but the present state requires not an emperor, but a cautious steward of the last relics of our fortunes. Well do I remember the

lofty expectations which he built on our alliance with Mustapha; and much do I fear that his rash courage will urge the ruin of our house, and that even religion may precipitate our downfall." Yet the experience and authority of Manuel preserved the peace and eluded the council; till, in the seventy-eighth year of his age, and in the habit of a monk, he terminated his career, dividing his precious movables among his children and the poor, his physicians and his favourite servants. Of his six sons,[33] Andronicus the Second was invested with the principality of Thessalonica, and died of a leprosy soon after the sale of that city to the Venetians and its final conquest by the Turks. Some fortunate incidents had restored Peloponnesus, or the Morea, to the empire; and in his more prosperous days, Manuel had fortified the narrow isthmus of six miles[34] with a stone wall and one hundred and fifty-three towers. The wall was overthrown by the first blast of the Ottomans; the fertile peninsula might have been sufficient for the four younger brothers, Theodore and Constantine, Demetrius and Thomas; but they wasted in domestic contests the remains of their strength; and the least successful of the rivals were reduced to a life of dependence in the Byzantine palace.

The eldest of the sons of Manuel, John Palæologus the Second, was acknowledged, after his father's death, as the sole emperor of the Greeks. He immediately proceeded to repudiate his wife, and to contract a new marriage with the princess of Trebizond: beauty was in his eyes the first qualification of an empress; and the clergy had yielded to his firm assurance, that, unless he might be indulged in a divorce, he would retire to a cloister and leave the throne to his brother Constantine. The first, and in truth the only victory of Palæologus, was over a Jew,[35] whom, after a long and learned dispute, he converted to the Christian faith; and this momentous conquest is carefully recorded in the history of the times. But he soon resumed the design of uniting the East and the West; and, regardless of his father's advice, listened, as it should seem with sincerity, to the proposal of meeting the pope in a general council beyond the Adriatic. This dangerous project was encouraged by Martin the Fifth, and coldly entertained by his successor Eugenius, till, after a tedious negotiation, the emperor received a summons from a Latin assembly of a new character, the independent prelates of Basil, who styled themselves the representatives and judges of the Catholic church.

The Roman pontiff had fought and conquered in the cause of ecclesiastical freedom; but the victorious clergy were soon exposed to the tyranny of their deliverer; and his sacred character was invulnerable to those arms which they found so keen and effectual against the civil magistrate. Their great charter, the right of election, was annihilated by appeals, evaded by trusts or commendams, disappointed by reversionary grants, and superseded by previous and arbitrary reservations.[36] A public auction was instituted in the court of Rome; the cardinals and favourites were enriched with the spoils of nations; and every country might complain that the most important and valuable benefices were accumulated on the heads of aliens and absentees. During their residence at Avignon, the ambition of the popes subsided in the meaner passions of avarice[37] and luxury: they rigorously imposed on the clergy the tributes of first-fruits and tenths; but they freely tolerated the impunity of vice, disorder, and corruption. These manifold scandals were aggravated by the great schism of the West, which continued above fifty years. In the furious conflicts of Rome and Avignon, the vices of the rivals were mutually exposed; and their precarious situation degraded their authority, relaxed their discipline, and multiplied their wants and exactions. To heal the wounds, and restore the monarchy, of the church, the synods of Pisa and Constance[38] were successively convened; but these great assemblies, conscious of their strength, resolved to vindicate the privileges of the Christian aristocracy. From a personal sentence against two pontiffs whom they rejected, and a third, their acknowledged sovereign, whom they deposed, the fathers of Constance proceeded to examine the nature and limits of the Roman supremacy; nor did they separate till they had established the authority, above the pope, of a general council. It was enacted, that, for the government and reformation of the church, such assemblies should be held at regular intervals; and that each synod, before its dissolution, should appoint the time and place of the subsequent meeting. By the influence of the court of Rome, the next convocation at Sienna was easily eluded; but the bold and vigorous proceedings of the council of Basil[39] had almost been fatal to the reigning pontiff, Eugenius the Fourth. A just suspicion of his design prompted the fathers to hasten the promulgation of their first decree, that the representatives of the church-militant on earth were invested with a divine and spiritual jurisdiction over all Christians, without excepting the pope; and that a general council could not be dissolved, prorogued, or transferred, unless by their free deliberation and consent. On the notice that Eugenius had fulminated a bull for that purpose, they ventured to summon, to admonish, to threaten, to censure, the contumacious successor of St. Peter. After many delays, to allow time for repentance, they finally declared, that, unless he submitted within the term of sixty days, he was suspended from the exercise of all temporal and ecclesiastical authority. And to mark their jurisdiction over the prince as well as the priest, they assumed the government of Avignon, annulled the alienation of the sacred patrimony, and protected Rome from the imposition of new taxes. Their boldness was justified, not only by the general opinion of the clergy, but by the support and power of the first monarchs of Christendom: the emperor Sigismond declared himself the servant and protector of the synod; Germany and France adhered to their cause; the duke of Milan was the enemy of Eugenius; and he was driven from the Vatican by an insurrection of the Roman people. Rejected at the same time by his temporal and spiritual subjects, submission was his only choice: by a most humiliating bull, the pope repealed his own acts, and ratified those of the council; incorporated his legates and cardinals with that venerable body; and *seemed* to resign himself to the decrees of the supreme legislature. Their fame pervaded the countries of the East: and it was in their presence that Sigismond received the ambassadors of the Turkish sultan,[40] who laid at his feet twelve large vases filled with robes of silk and pieces of gold. The fathers of Basil aspired to the glory of reducing the Greeks, as well as the Bohemians, within the pale of the church; and their deputies invited the emperor and patriarch of Constantinople to unite with an assembly which possessed the confidence of the Western nations. Palæologus was not averse to the proposal; and his ambassadors were introduced with due honours into the Catholic senate. But the choice of the place appeared to be an insuperable obstacle, since he refused to pass the Alps, or the sea of Sicily, and positively required that the synod should be adjourned to some convenient city in Italy, or at least on the Danube. The other articles of this treaty were more readily stipulated: it was agreed to defray the travelling expenses of the emperor, with a train of seven hundred persons,[41] to remit an immediate sum of eight thousand ducats[42] for the accommodation of the

Greek clergy; and in his absence to grant a supply of ten thousand ducats, with three hundred archers and some galleys for the protection of Constantinople. The city of Avignon advanced the funds for the preliminary expenses; and the embarkation was prepared at Marseilles with some difficulty and delay.

In his distress the friendship of Palæologus was disputed by the ecclesiastical powers of the West; but the dexterous activity of a monarch prevailed over the slow debates and inflexible temper of a republic. The decrees of Basil continually tended to circumscribe the despotism of the pope, and to erect a supreme and perpetual tribunal in the church. Eugenius was impatient of the yoke; and the union of the Greeks might afford a decent pretence for translating a rebellious synod from the Rhine to the Po. The independence of the fathers was lost if they passed the Alps: Savoy or Avignon, to which they acceded with reluctance, were described at Constantinople as situate far beyond the Pillars of Hercules;[43] the emperor and his clergy were apprehensive of the dangers of a long navigation; they were offended by a haughty declaration, that, after suppressing the *new* heresy of the Bohemians, the council would soon eradicate the *old* heresy of the Greeks.[44] On the side of Eugenius all was smooth, and yielding, and respectful; and he invited the Byzantine monarch to heal by his presence the schism of the Latin, as well as of the Eastern, church. Ferrara, near the coast of the Adriatic, was proposed for their amicable interview: and with some indulgence of forgery and theft, a surreptitious decree was procured, which transferred the synod, with its own consent, to that Italian city. Nine galleys were equipped for this service at Venice and in the isle of Candia; their diligence anticipated the slower vessels of Basil: the Roman admiral was commissioned to burn, sink, and destroy;[45] and these priestly squadrons might have encountered each other in the same seas where Athens and Sparta had formerly contended for the pre-eminence of glory. Assaulted by the inportunity of the factions, who were ready to fight for the possession of his person, Palæologus hesitated before he left his palace and country on a perilous experiment. His father's advice still dwelt on his memory; and reason must suggest, that, since the Latins were divided among themselves, they could never unite in a foreign cause. Sigismond dissuaded the unseasonable adventure; his advice was impartial, since he adhered to the council; and it was enforced by the strange belief that

the German Cæsar would nominate a Greek his heir and successor in the empire of the West.[46] Even the Turkish sultan was a counsellor whom it might be unsafe to trust, but whom it was dangerous to offend. Amurath was unskilled in the disputes, but he was apprehensive of the union, of the Christians. From his own treasures he offered to relieve the wants of the Byzantine court; yet he declared with seeming magnanimity that Constantinople should be secure and inviolate in the absence of her sovereign.[47] The resolution of Palæologus was decided by the most splendid gifts and the most specious promises: he wished to escape for a while from a scene of danger and distress; and after dismissing with an ambiguous answer the messengers of the council, he declared his intention of embarking in the Roman galleys. The age of the patriarch Joseph was more susceptible of fear than of hope; he trembled at the perils of the sea, and expressed his apprehension that his feeble voice, with thirty perhaps of his orthodox brethren, would be oppressed in a foreign land by the power and numbers of a Latin synod. He yielded to the royal mandate, to the flattering assurance that he would be heard as the oracle of nations, and to the secret wish of learning from his brother of the West to deliver the church from the yoke of kings.[48] The five *crossbearers*, or dignitaries, of St. Sophia, were bound to attend his person; and one of these, the great ecclesiarch or preacher, Sylvester Syropulus,[49] has composed a free and curious history[50] of the *false* union.[51] Of the clergy that reluctantly obeyed the summons of the emperor and the patriarch, submission was the first duty, and patience the most useful virtue. In a chosen list of twenty bishops we discover the metropolitan titles of Heraclea and Cyzicus, Nice and Nicomedia, Ephesus and Trebizond, and the personal merit of Mark and Bessarion, who, in the confidence of their learning and eloquence, were promoted to the episcopal rank. Some monks and philosophers were named to display the science and sanctity of the Greek church; and the service of the choir was performed by a select band of singers and musicians. The patriarchs of Alexandria, Antioch, and Jerusalem appeared by their genuine or fictitious deputies; the primate of Russia represented a national church, and the Greeks might contend with the Latins in the extent of their spiritual empire. The precious vases of St. Sophia were exposed to the winds and waves, that the patriarch might officiate with becoming splendour: whatever gold the emperor could procure was expended in the massy ornaments of his bed and chariot;[52] and while they affected to maintain the prosperity of their ancient fortune, they quarrelled for the division of fifteen thousand ducats, the first alms of the Roman pontiff. After the necessary preparations, John Palæologus, with a numerous train, accompanied by his brother Demetrius and the most respectable persons of the church and state, embarked in eight vessels with sails and oars, which steered through the Turkish straits of Gallipoli to the Archipelago, the Morea, and the Adriatic Gulf.[53]

After a tedious and troublesome navigation of seventy-seven days, this religious squadron cast anchor before Venice; and their reception proclaimed the joy and magnificence of that powerful republic. In the command of the world the modest Augustus had never claimed such honours from his subjects as were paid to his feeble successor by an independent state. Seated on the poop, on a lofty throne, he received the visit, or, in the Greek style, the *adoration*, of the doge and senators.[54] They sailed in the Bucentaur, which was accompanied by twelve stately galleys: the sea was overspread with innumerable gondolas of pomp and pleasure; the air resounded with music and acclamations; the mariners, and even the vessels, were dressed in silk and gold; and in all the emblems and pageants the Roman eagles were blended with the lions of St. Mark. The triumphal procession, ascending the great canal, passed under the bridge of the Rialto; and the Eastern strangers gazed with admiration on the palaces, the churches, and the populousness of a city that seems to float on the bosom of the waves.[55] They sighed to behold the spoils and trophies with which it had been decorated after the sack of Constantinople. After an hospitable entertainment of fifteen days, Palæologus pursued his journey by land and water from Venice to Ferrara; and on this occasion the pride of the Vatican was tempered by policy to indulge the ancient dignity of the emperor of the East. He made his entry on a *black* horse; but a milk-white steed, whose trappings were embroidered with golden eagles, was led before him; and the canopy was borne over his head by the princes of Este, the sons or kinsmen of Nicholas, marquis of the city, and a sovereign more powerful than himself.[56] Palæologus did not alight till he reached the bottom of the staircase: the pope advanced to the door of the apartment; refused his proffered genuflexion; and, after a paternal embrace, conducted the emperor to a seat on his left hand. Nor would the patriarch descend from his galley till a ceremony, almost equal, had been stipulated between the bishops of Rome and Constantinople. The latter was saluted by his brother with a kiss of union and charity; nor would any of the Greek ecclesiastics submit to kiss the feet of the Western primate. On the opening of the synod, the place of honour in the centre was claimed by the temporal and ecclesiastical chiefs; and it was only by alleging that his predecessors had not assisted in person at Nice or Chalcedon that Eugenius could evade the ancient precedents of Constantine and Marcian. After much debate it was agreed that the right and left sides of the church should be occupied by the two nations; that the solitary chair of St. Peter should be raised the first of the Latin line; and that the throne of the Greek emperor, at the head of his clergy, should be equal and opposite to the second place, the vacant seat of the emperor of the West.[57]

But as soon as festivity and form had given place to a more serious treaty, the Greeks were dissatisfied with their journey, with themselves, and with the pope. The artful pencil of his emissaries had painted him in a prosperous state, at the head of the princes and prelates of Europe, obedient at his voice to believe and to arm. The thin appearance of the universal synod of Ferrara betrayed his weakness; and the Latins opened the first session with only five archbishops, eighteen bishops, and ten abbots, the greatest part of whom were the subjects or countrymen of the Italian pontiff. Except the duke of Burgundy, none of the potentates of the West condescended to appear in person, or by their ambassadors; nor was it possible to suppress the judicial acts of Basil against the dignity and person of Eugenius, which were finally concluded by a new election. Under these circumstances a truce or delay was asked and granted, till Palæologus could expect from the consent of the Latins some temporal reward for an unpopular union; and, after the first session, the public proceedings were adjourned above six months. The emperor, with a chosen band of his favourites and *Janizaries*, fixed his summer residence at a pleasant spacious monastery, six miles from Ferrara; forgot, in the pleasures of the chase, the distress of the church and state; and persisted in destroying the game, without listening to the just complaints of the marquis or the husbandmen.[58] In the meanwhile his unfortunate Greeks were exposed to all the miseries of exile and poverty; for the support of each stranger a monthly allowance was assigned of three or four gold florins, and, although the entire sum did not amount to seven hundred florins, a long arrear was repeatedly incurred by the indigence or policy of the Roman court.[59] They sighed for a speedy deliverance, but their escape was prevented by a triple chain; a passport from their superiors was required at the gates of Ferrara; the government of Venice had engaged to arrest and send back the fugitives, and inevitable punishment awaited them at Constantinople; excommunication, fines, and a sentence, which did not respect the sacerdotal dignity, that they should be stripped naked and publicly whipped.[60] It was only by the alternative of hunger or dispute that the Greeks could be persuaded to open the first conference, and they yielded with extreme reluctance to attend from Ferrara to Florence the rear of a flying synod. This new translation was urged by inevitable necessity: the city was visited by the plague; the fidelity of the marquis might be suspected; the mercenary troops of the duke of Milan were at the gates, and, as they occupied Romagna, it was not without difficulty and danger that the pope, the emperor, and the bishops explored their way through the unfrequented paths of the Apennine.[61]

Yet all these obstacles were surmounted by time and policy. The violence of the fathers of Basil rather promoted than injured the cause of Eugenius: the nations of Europe abhorred the schism, and disowned the election, of Felix the Fifth, who was successively a duke of Savoy, a hermit, and a pope; and the great princes were gradually reclaimed by his competitor to a favourable neutrality and a firm attachment. The legates, with some respectable members, deserted to the Roman army, which insensibly rose in numbers and reputation; the council of Basil was reduced to thirty-nine bishops and three hundred of the inferior clergy;[62] while the Latins of Florence could produce the subscriptions of the pope himself, eight cardinals, two patriarchs, eight archbishops, fifty-two bishops, and forty-five abbots or chiefs of religious orders. After the labour of nine months and the debates of twenty-five sessions, they attained the advantage and glory of the reunion of the Greeks. Four principal questions had been agitated between the two churches: 1. The use of unleavened bread in the communion of Christ's body. 2. The nature of purgatory. 3. The supremacy of the pope. And, 4. The single or double procession of the Holy Ghost. The cause of either nation was managed by ten theological champions: the Latins were supported by the inexhaustible eloquence of Cardinal Julian, and Mark of Ephesus and Bessarion of Nice were the bold and able leaders of the Greek forces. We may bestow some praise on the progress of human reason, by observing that the first of these questions was *now* treated as an immaterial rite, which might innocently vary with the fashion of the age and country. With regard to the second, both parties were agreed in the belief of an intermediate state of purgation for the venial sins of the faithful; and whether their souls were purified by elemental fire was a doubtful point, which in a few years might be conveniently settled on the spot by the disputants. The claims of supremacy appeared of a more weighty and substantial kind, yet by the Orientals the Roman bishop had ever been respected as the first of the five patriarchs; nor did they scruple to admit that his jurisdiction should be exercised agreeably to the holy canons: a vague allowance, which might be defined or eluded by occasional convenience. The procession of the Holy Ghost from the Father alone, or from the Father and the Son, was an article of faith which had sunk much deeper into the minds of men; and in the sessions of Ferrara and Florence the Latin addition of *filioque* was subdivided into two questions, whether it were legal, and whether it were orthodox. Perhaps it may not be necessary to boast on this subject of my own impartial indifference: but I must think that the Greeks were strongly supported by the prohibition of the council of Chalcedon against adding any article whatsoever to the creed of Nice, or rather of Constantinople.[63] In earthly affairs it is not easy to conceive how an assembly of legislators can bind their successors invested with powers equal to their own. But the dictates of inspiration must be true and unchangeable; nor should a private bishop or a provincial synod have presumed to innovate against the judgment of the Catholic church. On the substance of the doctrine the controversy was equal and endless; the reason is confounded by the procession of a deity; the Gospel, which lay on the altar, was silent; the various texts of the fathers might be corrupted by fraud or entangled by sophistry; and the Greeks were ignorant of the characters and writings of the Latin saints.[64] Of this at least we may be sure, that neither side could be convinced by the arguments of their opponents. Prejudice may be enlightened by reason, and a superficial glance may be rectified by a clear and more perfect view of an object adapted to our faculties. But the bishops and monks had been taught from their infancy to repeat a form of mysterious words: their national and personal honour depended on the repetition of the same sounds, and their narrow minds were hardened and inflamed by the acrimony of a public dispute.

While they were lost in a cloud of dust and darkness, the pope and emperor were desirous of a seeming union, which could alone accomplish the purposes of their interview; and the obstinacy of public dispute was softened by the arts of private and personal negotiation. The patriarch Joseph had sunk under the weight of age and infirmities; his dying voice breathed the counsels of charity and concord, and his vacant benefice might tempt the hopes of the ambitious clergy. The ready and active obedience of the archbishops of Russia and Nice, of Isidore and Bessarion, was prompted and recompensed by their speedy promotion to the dignity of cardinals. Bessarion, in the first debates, had stood forth the most strenuous and eloquent champion of the Greek church; and if the apostate, the bastard, was reprobated by his country,[65] he appears in ecclesiastical story a rare example of a patriot who was recommended to court favour by loud opposition and well-timed compliance. With the aid of his two spiritual coadjutors, the emperor applied his arguments to the general situation and personal characters of the bishops, and each was successively moved by authority and example. Their revenues were in the hands of the Turks, their persons in those of the Latins; an episcopal treasure, three robes and forty ducats, was soon exhausted;[66] the hopes of their return still depended on the ships of Venice and the alms of Rome; and such was their indigence, that their arrears, the payment of a debt, would be accepted as a favour, and might operate as a bribe.[67] The danger and relief of Constantinople might excuse some prudent and pious dissimulation; and it was insinuated that the obstinate heretics who should resist the consent of the East and West would be abandoned in a hostile land to the revenge or justice of the Roman pontiff.[68] In the first private assembly of the Greeks the formulary of union was approved by twenty-four, and rejected by twelve, members; but the five crossbearers of St. Sophia, who aspired to represent the patriarch, were disqualified by ancient discipline, and their right of voting was transferred to an obsequious train of monks, grammarians, and profane laymen. The will of the monarch produced a false and servile unanimity, and no more than two patriots had courage to speak their own sentiments and those of

their country. Demetrius, the emperor's brother, retired to Venice, that he might not be witness of the union; and Mark of Ephesus, mistaking perhaps his pride for his conscience, disclaimed all communion with the Latin heretics, and avowed himself the champion and confessor of the orthodox creed.[69] In the treaty between the two nations several forms of consent were proposed, such as might satisfy the Latins without dishonouring the Greeks; and they weighed the scruples of words and syllables till the theological balance trembled with a slight preponderance in favour of the Vatican. It was agreed (I must entreat the attention of the reader) that the Holy Ghost proceeds from the Father *and* the Son, as from one principle and one substance; that he proceeds *by* the Son, being of the same nature and substance; and that he proceeds from the Father *and* the Son, by one *spiration* and production. It is less difficult to understand the articles of the preliminary treaty: that the pope should defray all the expenses of the Greeks in their return home; that he should annually maintain two galleys and three hundred soldiers for the defence of Constantinople; that all the ships which transported pilgrims to Jerusalem should be obliged to touch at that port; that as often as they were required, the pope should furnish ten galleys for a year, or twenty for six months; and that he should powerfully solicit the princes of Europe, if the emperor had occasion for land-forces.

The same year, and almost the same day, were marked by the deposition of Eugenius at Basil, and, at Florence, by his reunion of the Greeks and Latins. In the former synod (which he styled indeed an assembly of demons) the pope was branded with the guilt of simony, perjury, tyranny, heresy, and schism;[70] and declared to be incorrigible in his vices, unworthy of any title, and incapable of holding any ecclesiastical office. In the latter he was revered as the true and holy vicar of Christ, who, after a separation of six hundred years, had reconciled the Catholics of the East and West in one fold, and under one shepherd. The act of union was subscribed by the pope, the emperor, and the principal members of both churches; even by those who, like Syropulus,[71] had been deprived of the right of voting. Two copies might have sufficed for the East and West; but Eugenius was not satisfied unless four authentic and similar transcripts were signed and attested as the monuments of his victory.[72] On a memorable day, the sixth of July, the successors of St. Peter and Constantine ascended their thrones; the two nations assembled in the cathedral of Florence; their representatives, Cardinal Julian, and Bessarion archbishop of Nice, appeared in the pulpit, and, after reading in their respective tongues the act of union, they mutually embraced in the name and the presence of their applauding brethren. The pope and his ministers then officiated according to the Roman liturgy; the creed was chanted with the addition of *filioque*; the acquiescence of the Greeks was poorly excused by their ignorance of the harmonious but inarticulate sounds;[73] and the more scrupulous Latins refused any public celebration of the Byzantine rite. Yet the emperor and his clergy were not totally unmindful of national honour. The treaty was ratified by their consent: it was tacitly agreed that no innovation should be attempted in their creed or ceremonies; they spared and secretly respected the generous firmness of Mark of Ephesus, and, on the decease of the patriarch, they refused to elect his successor, except in the cathedral of St. Sophia. In the distribution of public and private rewards the liberal pontiff exceeded their hopes and his promises: the Greeks, with less pomp and pride, returned by the same road of Ferrara and Venice; and their reception at Constantinople was such as will be described in the following chapter.[74] The success of the first trial encouraged Eugenius to repeat the same edifying scenes, and the deputies of the Armenians, the Maronites, the Jacobites of Syria and Egypt, the Nestorians, and the Æthiopians, were successively introduced to kiss the feet of the Roman pontiff, and to announce the obedience and the orthodoxy of the East. These Oriental embassies, unknown in the countries which they presumed to represent,[75] diffused over the West the fame of Eugenius; and a clamour was artfully propagated against the remnant of a schism in Switzerland and Savoy which alone impeded the harmony of the Christian world. The vigour of opposition was succeeded by the lassitude of despair; the council of Basil was silently dissolved; and Felix, renouncing the tiara, again withdrew to the devout or delicious hermitage of Ripaille.[76] A general peace was secured by mutual acts of oblivion and indemnity: all ideas of reformation subsided; the popes continued to exercise and abuse their ecclesiastical despotism; nor has Rome been since disturbed by the mischiefs of a contested election.[77]

The journeys of three emperors were unavailing for their temporal, or perhaps their spiritual, salvation; but they were productive of a beneficial consequence, the revival of the Greek learning in Italy, from whence it was propagated to the last nations of the West and North. In their lowest servitude and depression, the subjects of the Byzantine throne were still possessed of a golden key that could unlock the treasures of antiquity, of a musical and prolific language that gives a soul to the objects of sense, and a body to the abstractions of philosophy. Since the barriers of the monarchy, and even of the capital, had been trampled under foot, the various barbarians had doubtless corrupted the form and substance of the national dialect; and ample glossaries have been composed, to interpret a multitude of words, of Arabic, Turkish, Sclavonian, Latin, or French origin.[78] But a purer idiom was spoken in the court and taught in the college, and the flourishing state of the language is described, and perhaps embellished, by a learned Italian,[79] who, by a long residence and noble marriage,[80] was naturalised at Constantinople about thirty years before the Turkish conquest. "The vulgar speech," says Philephus,[81] "has been depraved by the people, and infected by the multitude of strangers and merchants, who every day flock to the city and mingle with the inhabitants. It is from the disciples of such a school that the Latin language received the versions of Aristotle and Plato, so obscure in sense, and in spirit so poor. But the Greeks, who have escaped the contagion, are those whom *we* follow, and they alone are worthy of our imitation. In familiar discourse they still speak the tongue of Aristophanes and Euripides, of the historians and philosophers of Athens; and the style of their writings is still more elaborate and correct. The persons who, by their birth and offices, are attached to the Byzantine court, are those who maintain, with the least alloy, the ancient standard of elegance and purity; and the native graces of language most conspicuously shine among the noble matrons, who are excluded from all intercourse with foreigners. With foreigners do I say? They live retired and sequestered from the eyes of their fellow-citizens. Seldom are they seen in the streets; and when they leave their houses, it is in the dusk of evening, on visits to the churches and their nearest kindred. On these occasions they are on horseback, covered with a veil, and encompassed by their parents, their husbands, or their servants.[82]

Among the Greeks a numerous and opulent clergy was dedicated to the service of religion; their monks and bishops have ever been distinguished by the gravity and austerity of their manners, nor were they diverted, like the Latin priests, by the pursuits and pleasures of a secular and even military life. After a large deduction for the time and talents that were lost in the devotion, the laziness, and the discord of the church and cloister, the more inquisitive and ambitious minds would explore the sacred and profane erudition of their native language. The ecclesiastics presided over the education of youth: the schools of philosophy and eloquence were perpetuated till the fall of the empire; and it may be affirmed that more books and more knowledge were included within the walls of Constantinople than could be dispersed over the extensive countries of the West.[83] But an important distinction has been already noticed: the Greeks were stationary or retrograde, while the Latins were advancing with a rapid and progressive motion. The nations were excited by the spirit of independence and emulation; and even the little world of the Italian states contained more people and industry than the decreasing circle of the Byzantine empire. In Europe the lower ranks of society were relieved from the yoke of feudal servitude; and freedom is the first step to curiosity and knowledge. The use, however rude and corrupt, of the Latin tongue had been preserved by superstition; the universities, from Bologna to Oxford,[84] were peopled with thousands of scholars; and their misguided ardour might be directed to more liberal and manly studies. In the resurrection of science Italy was the first that cast away her shroud; and the eloquent Petrarch, by his lessons and his example, may justly be applauded as the first harbinger of day. A purer style of composition, a more generous and rational strain of sentiment, flowed from the study and imitation of the writers of ancient Rome; and the disciples of Cicero and Virgil approached, with reverence and love, the sanctuary of their Grecian masters. In the sack of Constantinople, the French, and even the Venetians, had despised and destroyed the works of Lysippus and Homer; the monuments of art may be annihilated by a single blow, but the immortal mind is renewed and multiplied by the copies of the pen, and such copies it was the ambition of Petrarch and his friends to possess and understand. The arms of the Turks undoubtedly pressed the flight of the Muses: yet we may tremble at the thought that Greece might have been overwhelmed, with her schools and libraries, before Europe had emerged from the deluge of barbarism; that the seeds of science might have been scattered by the winds before

the Italian soil was prepared for their cultivation.

The most learned Italians of the fifteenth century have confessed and applauded the restoration of Greek literature, after a long oblivion of many hundred years.[85] Yet in that country, and beyond the Alps, some names are quoted; some profound scholars who, in the darker ages, were honourably distinguished by their knowledge of the Greek tongue; and national vanity has been loud in the praise of such rare examples of erudition. Without scrutinising the merit of individuals, truth must observe that their science is without a cause and without an effect; that it was easy for them to satisfy themselves and their more ignorant contemporaries; and that the idiom, which they had so marvellously acquired, was transcribed in few manuscripts, and was not taught in any university of the West. In a corner of Italy it faintly existed as the popular, or at least as the ecclesiastical, dialect.[86] The first impression of the Doric and Ionic colonies has never been completely erased; the Calabrian churches were long attached to the throne of Constantinople; and the monks of St. Basil pursued their studies in Mount Athos and the schools of the East. Calabria was the native country of Barlaam, who has already appeared as a sectary and an ambassador; and Barlaam was the first who revived, beyond the Alps, the memory, or at least the writings, of Homer.[87] He is described, by Petrarch and Boccace,[88] as a man of a diminutive stature, though truly great in the measure of learning and genius: of a piercing discernment, though of a slow and painful elocution. For many ages (as they affirm) Greece had not produced his equal in the knowledge of history, grammar, and philosophy; and his merit was celebrated in the attestations of the princes and doctors of Constantinople. One of these attestations is still extant; and the emperor Cantacuzene, the protector of his adversaries, is forced to allow that Euclid, Aristotle, and Plato were familiar to that profound and subtle logician.[89] In the court of Avignon he formed an intimate connection with Petrarch[90] the first of the Latin scholars; and the desire of mutual instruction was the principle of their literary commerce. The Tuscan applied himself with eager curiosity and assiduous diligence to the study of the Greek language, and in a laborious struggle with the dryness and difficulty of the first rudiments he began to reach the sense, and to feel the spirit, of poets and philosophers whose minds were congenial to his own. But he was soon deprived of the society and lessons of this

useful assistant; Barlaam relinquished his fruitless embassy, and, on his return to Greece, he
rashly provoked the swarms of fanatic monks,
by attempting to substitute the light of reason
to that of their navel. After a separation of three
years the two friends again met in the court of
Naples; but the generous pupil renounced the
fairest occasion of improvement; and by his
recommendation Barlaam was finally settled in
a small bishopric of his native Calabria.[91] The
manifold avocations of Petrarch, love and
friendship, his various correspondence and frequent journeys, the Roman laurel, and his
elaborate compositions in prose and verse, in
Latin and Italian, diverted him from a foreign
idiom; and as he advanced in life the attainment of the Greek language was the object of
his wishes rather than of his hopes. When he
was about fifty years of age, a Byzantine ambassador, his friend, and a master of both tongues,
presented him with a copy of Homer, and the
answer of Petrarch is at once expressive of his
eloquence, gratitude, and regret. After celebrating the generosity of the donor, and the
value of a gift more precious in his estimation
than gold or rubies, he thus proceeds:—"Your
present of the genuine and original text of the
divine poet, the fountain of all invention, is worthy of yourself and of me; you have fulfilled
your promise, and satisfied my desires. Yet your
liberality is still imperfect: with Homer you
should have given me yourself; a guide who
could lead me into the fields of light, and disclose to my wondering eyes the specious miracles of the Iliad and Odyssey. But, alas! Homer
is dumb, or I am deaf; nor is it in my power to
enjoy the beauty which I possess. I have seated
him by the side of Plato, the prince of poets
near the prince of philosophers, and I glory in
the sight of my illustrious guests. Of their immortal writings, whatever had been translated
into the Latin idiom I had already acquired;
but if there be no profit, there is some pleasure,
in beholding these venerable Greeks in their
proper and national habit. I am delighted with
the aspect of Homer; and as often as I embrace
the silent volume, I exclaim with a sigh, Illustrious bard! with what pleasure should I listen
to thy song, if my sense of hearing were not obstructed and lost by the death of one friend, and
in the much lamented absence of another! Nor
do I yet despair, and the example of Cato suggests some comfort and hope, since it was in the
last period of age that he attained the knowledge
of the Greek letters."[92]

The prize which eluded the efforts of Petrarch was obtained by the fortune and industry of his friend Boccace,[93] the father of the Tuscan prose. That particular writer, who derived
his reputation from the Decameron, a hundred
novels of pleasantry and love, may aspire to the
more serious praise of restoring in Italy the
study of the Greek language. In the year one
thousand three hundred and sixty a disciple of
Barlaam, whose name was Leo or Leontius Pilatus, was detained in his way to Avignon by
the advice and hospitality of Boccace, who
lodged the stranger in his house, prevailed on
the republic of Florence to allow him an annual
stipend, and devoted his leisure to the first
Greek professor, who taught that language in
the Western countries of Europe. The appearance of Leo might disgust the most eager disciple: he was clothed in the mantle of a philosopher or a mendicant; his countenance was hide-
ous; his face was overshadowed with black hair;
his beard long and uncombed; his deportment
rustic; his temper gloomy and inconstant; nor
could he grace his discourse with the ornaments or even the perspicuity of Latin elocution. But his mind was stored with a treasure of
Greek learning: history and fable, philosophy
and grammar, were alike at his command; and
he read the poems of Homer in the schools of
Florence. It was from his explanation that Boccace composed and transcribed a literal prose
version of the Iliad and Odyssey, which satisfied
the thirst of his friend Petrarch, and which,
perhaps in the succeeding century, was clan-
destinely used by Laurentius Valla, the Latin
interpreter. It was from his narratives that the
same Boccace collected the materials for his
treatise on the genealogy of the heathen gods, a
work, in that age, of stupendous erudition, and
which he ostentatiously sprinkled with Greek
characters and passages, to excite the wonder
and applause of his more ignorant readers.[94]
The first steps of learning are slow and laborious; no more than ten votaries of Homer could
be enumerated in all Italy, and neither Rome
nor Venice, nor Naples, could add a single
name to this studious catalogue. But their numbers would have multiplied, their progress
would have been accelerated, if the inconstant
Leo, at the end of three years, had not relinquished an honourable and beneficial station.
In his passage Petrarch entertained him at Padua a short time: he enjoyed the scholar, but
was justly offended with the gloomy and unso-
cial temper of the man. Discontented with the
world and with himself, Leo depreciated his
present enjoyments, while absent persons and

objects were dear to his imagination. In Italy he was a Thessalian, in Greece a native of Calabria; in the company of the Latins he disdained their language, religion, and manners: no sooner was he landed at Constantinople than he again sighed for the wealth of Venice and the elegance of Florence. His Italian friends were deaf to his importunity: he depended on their curiosity and indulgence, and embarked on a second voyage; but on his entrance into the Adriatic the ship was assailed by a tempest, and the unfortunate teacher, who like Ulysses had fastened himself to the mast, was struck dead by a flash of lightning. The humane Petrarch dropped a tear on his disaster; but he was most anxious to learn whether some copy of Euripides or Sophocles might not be saved from the hands of the mariners.[95]

But the faint rudiments of Greek learning, which Petrarch had encouraged and Boccace had planted, soon withered and expired. The succeeding generation was content for a while with the improvement of Latin eloquence; nor was it before the end of the fourteenth century that a new and perpetual flame was rekindled in Italy.[96] Previous to his own journey, the emperor Manuel despatched his envoys and orators to implore the compassion of the Western princes. Of these envoys the most conspicuous, or the most learned, was Manuel Chrysoloras,[97] of noble birth, and whose Roman ancestors are supposed to have migrated with the great Constantine. After visiting the courts of France and England, where he obtained some contributions and more promises, the envoy was invited to assume the office of a professor; and Florence had again the honour of this second invitation. By his knowledge, not only of the Greek but of the Latin tongue, Chrysoloras deserved the stipend and surpassed the expectation of the republic. His school was frequented by a crowd of disciples of every rank and age; and one of these, in a general history, has described his motives and his success. "At that time," says Leonard Aretin,[98] "I was a student of the civil law; but my soul was inflamed with the love of letters, and I bestowed some application on the sciences of logic and rhetoric. On the arrival of Manuel I hesitated whether I should desert my legal studies or relinquish this golden opportunity; and thus, in the ardour of youth, I communed with my own mind—Wilt thou be wanting to thyself and thy fortune? Wilt thou refuse to be introduced to a familiar converse with Homer, Plato, and Demosthenes? with those poets, philosophers, and orators, of whom such wonders are related, and who are celebrated by every age as the great masters of human science? Of professors and scholars in civil law, a sufficient supply will always be found in our universities; but a teacher, and such a teacher of the Greek language, if he once be suffered to escape, may never afterwards be retrieved. Convinced by these reasons, I gave myself to Chrysoloras, and so strong was my passion, that the lessons which I had imbibed in the day were the constant subject of my nightly dreams."[99] At the same time and place the Latin classics were explained by John of Ravenna, the domestic pupil of Petrarch:[100] the Italians, who illustrated their age and country, were formed in this double school, and Florence became the fruitful seminary of Greek and Roman erudition.[101] The presence of the emperor recalled Chrysoloras from the college to the court; but he afterwards taught at Pavia and Rome with equal industry and applause. The remainder of his life, about fifteen years, was divided between embassies and lessons. In the noble office of enlightening a foreign nation, the grammarian was not unmindful of a more sacred duty to his prince and country; and Emanuel Chrysoloras died at Constance on a public mission from the emperor to the council.

After his example, the restoration of the Greek letters in Italy was prosecuted by a series of emigrants who were destitute of fortune and endowed with learning, or at least with language. From the terror or oppression of the Turkish arms, the natives of Thessalonica and Constantinople escaped to a land of freedom, curiosity, and wealth. The synod introduced into Florence the lights of the Greek church and the oracles of the Platonic philosophy; and the fugitives who adhered to the union had the double merit of renouncing their country, not only for the Christian but for the Catholic cause. A patriot, who sacrifices his party and conscience to the allurements of favour, may be possessed however of the private and social virtues: he no longer hears the reproachful epithets of slave and apostate, and the consideration which he acquires among his new associates will restore in his own eyes the dignity of his character. The prudent conformity of Bessarion was rewarded with the Roman purple: he fixed his residence in Italy, and the Greek cardinal, the titular patriarch of Constantinople, was respected as the chief and protector of his nation:[102] his abilities were exercised in the legations of Bologna, Venice, Germany, and France; and his election to the chair of St. Peter floated for a moment on the uncertain breath of a conclave.[103] His ecclesiastical honours diffused a splendour and pre-eminence over his literary merit and service: his palace was a school; as often as the cardinal visited the Vatican he was attended by a learned train of both nations;[104] of men applauded by themselves and the public, and whose writings, now overspread with dust, were popular and useful in their own times. I shall not attempt to enumerate the restorers of Grecian literature in the fifteenth century; and it may be sufficient to mention with gratitude the names of Theodore Gaza, of George of Trebizond, of John Argyropulus, and Demetrius Chalcocondyles, who taught their native language in the schools of Florence and Rome. Their labours were not inferior to those of Bessarion, whose purple they revered, and whose fortune was the secret object of their envy. But the lives of these grammarians were humble and obscure: they had declined the lucrative paths of the church; their dress and manners secluded them from the commerce of the world; and since they were confined to the merit, they might be content with the rewards of learning. From this character Janus Lascaris[105] will deserve an exception. His eloquence, politeness, and Imperial descent, recommended him to the French monarchs; and in the same cities he was alternately employed to teach and to negotiate. Duty and interest prompted them to cultivate the study of the Latin language, and the most successful attained the faculty of writing and speaking with fluency and elegance in a foreign idiom. But they ever retained the inveterate vanity of their country: their praise, or at least their esteem, was reserved for the national writers to whom they owed their fame and subsistence; and they sometimes betrayed their contempt in licentious criticism or satire on Virgil's poetry and the oratory of Tully.[106] The superiority of these masters arose from the familiar use of a living language; and their first disciples were incapable of discerning how far they had degenerated from the knowledge and even the practice of their ancestors. A vicious pronunciation,[107] which they introduced, was banished from the schools by the reason of the succeeding age. Of the power of the Greek accents they were ignorant; and those muscial notes, which, from an Attic tongue and to an Attic ear, must have been the secret soul of harmony, were to their eyes, as to our own, no more than mute and unmeaning marks, in prose superfluous and troublesome in verse. The art of grammar they truly possessed; the valuable fragments of Apollonius

and Herodian were transfused into their lessons; and their treatises of syntax and etymology, though devoid of philosophic spirit, are still useful to the Greek student. In the shipwreck of the Byzantine libraries each fugitive seized a fragment of treasure, a copy of some author, who, without his industry, might have perished: the transcripts were multiplied by an assiduous and sometimes an elegant pen, and the text was corrected and explained by their own comments or those of the elder scholiasts The sense, though not the spirit, of the Greek classics was interpreted to the Latin world: the beauties of style evaporate in a version; but the judgment of Theodore Gaza selected the more solid works of Aristotle and Theophrastus, and their natural histories of animals and plants opened a rich fund of genuine and experimental science.

Yet the fleeting shadows of metaphysics were pursued with more curiosity and ardour. After a long oblivion, Plato was revived in Italy by a venerable Greek,[108] who taught in the house of Cosmo of Medicis. While the synod of Florence was involved in theological debate, some beneficial consequences might flow from the study of his elegant philosophy: his style is the purest standard of the Attic dialect, and his sublime thoughts are sometimes adapted to familiar conversation, and sometimes adorned with the richest colours of poetry and eloquence. The dialogues of Plato are a dramatic picture of the life and death of a sage; and, as often as he descends from the clouds, his moral system inculcates the love of truth, of our country, and of mankind. The precept and example of Socrates recommended a modest doubt and liberal inquiry; and if the Platonists, with blind devotion, adored the visions and errors of their divine master, their enthusiasm might correct the dry, dogmatic method of the Peripatetic school. So equal, yet so opposite, are the merits of Plato and Aristotle, that they may be balanced in endless controversy; but some spark of freedom may be produced by the collision of adverse servitude. The modern Greeks were divided between the two sects: with more fury than skill they fought under the banner of their leaders, and the field of battle was removed in their flight from Constantinople to Rome. But this philosophical debate soon degenerated into an angry and personal quarrel of grammarians; and Bessarion, though an advocate for Plato, protected the national honour by interposing the advice and authority of a mediator. In the gardens of the Medici the academical doctrine was enjoyed by the polite and learned; but their philosophic society was quickly dissolved; and if the writings of the Attic sage were perused in the closet, the more powerful Stagyrite continued to reign the oracle of the church and school.[109]

I have fairly represented the literary merits of the Greeks; yet it must be confessed that they were seconded and surpassed by the ardour of the Latins. Italy was divided into many independent states; and at that time it was the ambition of princes and republics to vie with each other in the encouragement and reward of literature. The fame of Nicholas the Fifth[110] has not been adequate to his merits. From a plebeian origin he raised himself by his virtue and learning: the character of the man prevailed over the interest of the pope, and he sharpened those weapons which were soon pointed against the Roman church.[111] He had been the friend of the most eminent scholars of the age: he became their patron; and such was the humility of his manners, that the change was scarcely discernible either to them or to himself. If he pressed the acceptance of a liberal gift, it was not as the measure of desert, but as the proof of benevolence; and when modest merit declined his bounty, "Accept it," would he say, with a consciousness of his own worth: "you will not always have a Nicholas among ye." The influence of the holy see pervaded Christendom; and he exerted that influence in the search, not of benefices, but of books. From the ruins of the Byzantine libraries, from the darkest monasteries of Germany and Britain, he collected the dusty manuscripts of the writers of antiquity; and wherever the original could not be removed, a faithful copy was transcribed and transmitted for his use. The Vatican, the old repository for bulls and legends, for superstition and forgery, was daily replenished with more precious furniture; and such was the industry of Nicholas, that in a reign of eight years he formed a library of five thousand volumes. To his munificence the Latin world was indebted for the versions of Xenophon, Diodorus, Polybius, Thucydides, Herodotus, and Appian; of Strabo's Geography, of the Iliad, of the most valuable works of Plato and Aristotle, of Ptolemy and Theophrastus, and of the fathers of the Greek church. The example of the Roman pontiff was preceded or imitated by a Florentine merchant, who governed the republic without arms, and without a title. Cosmo of Medicis[112] was the father of a line of princes whose name and age are almost synonymous

with the restoration of learning: his credit was ennobled into fame; his riches were dedicated to the service of mankind; he corresponded at once with Cairo and London; and a cargo of Indian spices and Greek books was often imported in the same vessel. The genius and education of his grandson Lorenzo rendered him not only a patron but a judge and candidate in the literary race. In his palace, distress was entitled to relief, and merit to reward: his leisure hours were delightfully spent in the Platonic academy; he encouraged the emulation of Demetrius Chalcocondyles and Angelo Politian; and his active missionary Janus Lascaris returned from the East with a treasure of two hundred manuscripts, fourscore of which were as yet unknown in the libraries of Europe.[113] The rest of Italy was animated by a similar spirit, and the progress of the nation repaid the liberality of her princes. The Latins held the exclusive property of their own literature and these disciples of Greece were soon capable of transmitting and improving the lessons which they had imbibed. After a short succession of foreign teachers, the tide of emigration subsided; but the language of Constantinople was spread beyond the Alps, and the natives of France, Germany, and England[114] imparted to their country the sacred fire which they had kindled in the schools of Florence and Rome.[115] In the productions of the mind, as in those of the soil, the gifts of nature are excelled by industry and skill; the Greek authors, forgotten on the banks of the Ilissus, have been illustrated on those of the Elbe and the Thames; and Bessarion or Gaza might have envied the superior science of the barbarians, the accuracy of Budæus, the taste of Erasmus, the copiousness of Stephens, the erudition of Scaliger, the discernment of Reiske or of Bentley. On the side of the Latins the discovery of printing was a casual advantage; but this useful art has been applied by Aldus and his innumerable successors to perpetuate and multiply the works of antiquity.[116] A single manuscript imported from Greece is revived in ten thousand copies, and each copy is fairer than the original. In this form Homer and Plato would peruse with more satisfaction their own writings; and their scholiasts must resign the prize to the labours of our Western editors.

Before the arrival of classic literature the barbarians in Europe were immersed in ignorance; and their vulgar tongues were marked with the rudeness and poverty of their manners. The students of the more perfect idioms of Rome and Greece were introduced to a new world of light and science; to the society of the free and polished nations of antiquity; and to a familiar converse with those immortal men who spoke the sublime language of eloquence and reason. Such an intercourse must tend to refine the taste and to elevate the genius of the moderns; and yet, from the first experiment, it might appear that the study of the ancients had given fetters, rather than wings, to the human mind. However laudable, the spirit of imitation is of a servile cast; and the first disciples of the Greeks and Romans were a colony of strangers in the midst of their age and country. The minute and laborious diligence which explored the antiquities of remote times might have improved or adorned the present state of society; the critic and metaphysician were the slaves of Aristotle; the poets, historians, and orators were proud to repeat the thoughts and words of the Augustan age: the works of nature were observed with the eyes of Pliny and Theophrastus; and some Pagan votaries professed a secret devotion to the gods of Homer and Plato.[117] The Italians were oppressed by the strength and number of their ancient auxiliaries: the century after the deaths of Petrarch and Boccace was filled with a crowd of Latin imitators, who decently repose on our shelves; but in that era of learning it will not be easy to discern a real discovery of science, a work of invention or eloquence, in the popular language of the country.[118] But as soon as it had been deeply saturated with the celestial dew, the soil was quickened into vegetation and life; the modern idioms were refined; the classics of Athens and Rome inspired a pure taste and a generous emulation; and in Italy, as afterward in France and England, the pleasing reign of poetry and fiction was succeeded by the light of speculative and experimental philosophy. Genius may anticipate the season of maturity; but in the education of a people, as in that of an individual, memory must be exercised before the powers of reason and fancy can be expanded; nor may the artist hope to equal or surpass, till he has learned to imitate, the works of his predecessors.

CHAPTER LXVII

Schism of the Greeks and Latins. Reign and Character of Amurath the Second. Crusade of Ladislaus, King of Hungary. His Defeat and Death. John Huniades. Scanderbeg. Constantine Palæologus, last Emperor of the East.

THE respective merits of Rome and Constantinople are compared and celebrated by an eloquent Greek, the father of the Italian schools.[1] The view of the ancient capital, the seat of his ancestors, surpassed the most sanguine expectations of Manuel Chrysoloras; and he no longer blamed the exclamation of an old sophist, that Rome was the habitation, not of men, but of gods. Those gods, and those men, had long since vanished; but, to the eye of liberal enthusiasm, the majesty of ruin restored the image of her ancient prosperity. The monuments of the consuls and Cæsars, of the martyrs and apostles, engaged on all sides the curiosity of the philosopher and the Christian; and he confessed that in every age the arms and the religion of Rome were destined to reign over the earth. While Chrysoloras admired the venerable beauties of the mother, he was not forgetful of his native country, her fairest daughter, her Imperial colony; and the Byzantine patriot expatiates with zeal and truth on the eternal advantages of nature, and the more transitory glories of art and dominion, which adorned, or had adorned, the city of Constantine. Yet the perfection of the copy still redounds (as he modestly observes) to the honour of the original, and parents are delighted to be renewed, and even excelled, by the superior merit of their children. "Constantinople," says the orator, "is situate on a commanding point between Europe and Asia, between the Archipelago and the Euxine. By her interposition the two seas and the two continents are united for the common benefit of nations; and the gates of commerce may be shut or opened at her command. The harbour, encompassed on all sides by the sea and the continent, is the most secure and capacious in the world. The walls and gates of Constantinople may be compared with those of Babylon: the towers are many; each tower is a solid and lofty structure; and the second wall, the outer fortification, would be sufficient for the defence and dignity of an ordinary capital. A broad and rapid stream may be introduced into the ditches; and the artificial island may be encompassed, like Athens[2], by land or water." Two strong and natural causes are alleged for the perfection of the model of new Rome. The royal founder reigned over the most illustrious nations of the globe; and in the accomplishment of his designs the power of the Romans was combined with the art and science of the Greeks. Other cities have been reared to maturity by accident and time: their beauties are mingled with disorder and deformity; and the inhabitants, unwilling to remove from their natal spot, are incapable of correcting the errors of their ancestors and the original vices of situation or climate. But the free idea of Constantinople was formed and executed by a single mind: and the primitive model was improved by the obedient zeal of the subjects and successors of the first monarch. The adjacent isles were stored with an inexhaustible supply of marble; but the various materials were transported from the most remote shores of Europe and Asia; and the public and private buildings, the palaces, churches, aqueducts, cisterns, porticoes, columns, baths, and hippodromes, were adapted to the greatness of the capital of the East. The superfluity of wealth was spread along the shores of Europe and Asia; and the Byzantine territory, as far as the Euxine, the Hellespont, and the long wall, might be considered as a populous suburb and a perpetual garden. In this flattering picture, the past and the present, the times of prosperity and decay, are artfully confounded; but a sigh and a confession escape from the orator, that his wretched country was the shadow and sepulchre of its former self. The works of ancient sculpture had been defaced by Christian zeal or barbaric violence; the fairest structures were demolished; and the marbles of Paros or Numidia were burnt for lime, or applied to the meanest uses. Of many a statue, the place was marked by an empty pedestal; of many a column, the size was determined by a broken capital; the tombs of the emperors were scattered on the ground; the stroke of time was accelerated by storms and earthquakes; and the vacant space was adorned by vulgar tradition with fabulous monuments of gold and silver. From these wonders, which lived only in memory or belief, he distinguishes, however, the porphyry pillar, the column and colossus of Justinian,[3] and the church, more especially the dome, of St. Sophia; the best conclusion, since it could not be described according to its merits, and after it no other object could deserve to be mentioned. But he forgets that, a century before, the trembling fabrics of the colossus and the church had been saved and supported by the timely care of Andronicus the Elder. Thirty years after the emperor had fortified St. Sophia with two new buttresses or pyramids, the eastern hemisphere suddenly gave way; and the images, the altars, and the sanctuary were crushed by the falling ruin. The mischief indeed was speedily repaired; the rubbish was cleared by the incessant labour of every rank and age; and the poor remains of riches and industry were consecrated by the Greeks to the most stately and venerable temple of the East.[4]

The last hope of the falling city and empire was placed in the harmony of the mother and daughter, in the maternal tenderness of Rome, and the filial obedience of Constantinople. In the synod of Florence, the Greeks and Latins had embraced, and subscribed, and promised; but these signs of friendship were perfidious or fruitless;[5] and the baseless fabric of the union vanished like a dream.[6] The emperor and his prelates returned home in the Venetian galleys; but as they touched at the Morea and the isles of Corfu and Lesbos, the subjects of the Latins complained that the pretended union would be an instrument of oppression. No sooner did they land on the Byzantine shore, than they were saluted, or rather assailed, with a general murmur of zeal and discontent. During their absence, above two years, the capital had been deprived of its civil and ecclesiastical rulers; fanaticism fermented in anarchy; the most furious monks reigned over the conscience of women and bigots; and the hatred of the Latin name was the first principle of nature and religion. Before his departure for Italy the emperor had flattered the city with the assurance of a prompt relief and a powerful succour; and the clergy, confident in their orthodoxy and science, had promised themselves and their flocks an easy victory over the blind shepherds of the West. The double disappointment exasperated the Greeks; the conscience of the subscribing prelates was awakened; the hour of temptation was past; and they had more to dread from the public resentment than they could hope from the favour of the emperor or the pope. Instead of justifying their conduct, they deplored their weakness, professed their contrition, and cast themselves on the mercy of God and of their brethren. To the reproachful question, what had been the event or the use of their Italian synod? they answered, with sighs and tears, "Alas! we have made a new faith; we have exchanged piety for impiety; we have betrayed the immaculate sacrifice; and we are become *Azymites*." (The Azymites were those who celebrated the communion with unleavened bread; and I must retract or qualify the praise which I have bestowed on the growing philosophy of the times.) "Alas! we have been seduced by distress, by fraud, and by the hopes and fears of a transitory life. The hand that has signed the union should be cut off; and the tongue that has pronounced the Latin creed deserves to be torn from the root." The best proof of their repentance was an increase of zeal for the most trivial rites and the most incomprehensible doctrines; and an absolute separation from all, without excepting their prince, who preserved some regard for honour and consistency. After the decease of the patriarch Joseph, the archbishops of Heraclea and Trebizond had courage to refuse the vacant office; and Cardinal Bessarion preferred the warm and comfortable shelter of the Vatican. The choice of the emperor and his clergy was confined to Metrophanes of Cyzicus: he was consecrated in St. Sophia, but the temple was vacant. The crossbearers abdicated their service; the infection spread from the city to the villages; and Metrophanes discharged, without effect, some ecclesiastical thunders against a nation of schismatics. The eyes of the Greeks were directed to Mark of Ephesus, the champion of his country; and the sufferings of the holy confessor were repaid with a tribute of admiration and applause. His example and writings propagated the flame of religious discord; age and infirmity soon removed him from the world; but the gospel of Mark was not a law of forgiveness; and he requested with his dying breath that none of the adherents of Rome might attend his obsequies or pray for his soul.

The schism was not confined to the narrow limits of the Byzantine empire. Secure under the Mamaluke sceptre, the three patriarchs of Alexandria, Antioch, and Jerusalem assembled a numerous synod; disowned their representatives at Ferrara and Florence; condemned the creed and council of the Latins; and threatened the emperor of Constantinople with the censures of the Eastern church. Of the sectaries of the Greek communion, the Russians were the most powerful, ignorant, and superstitious. Their primate, the cardinal Isidore, hastened from Florence to Moscow,[7] to reduce the independent nation under the Roman yoke. But the Russian bishops had been educated at Mount Athos; and the prince and people embraced the theology of their priests. They were scandalised by the title, the pomp, the Latin cross of the legate, the friend of those impious men who shaved their beards, and performed the divine office with gloves on their hands and rings on their fingers: Isidore was condemned by a synod; his person was imprisoned in a monastery; and it was with extreme difficulty that the cardinal could escape from the hands of a fierce and fanatic people.[8] The Russians refused a passage to the missionaries of Rome who aspired to convert the Pagans beyond the Tanais;[9] and their refusal was justified by the maxim that the guilt of idolatry is less damnable than that of schism. The errors of the Bohemians were excused by their abhorrence for the pope; and a deputation of the Greek clergy solicited the friendship of those sanguinary enthusiasts.[10] While Eugenius triumphed in the union and orthodoxy of the Greeks, his party was contracted to the walls, or rather to the palace, of Constantinople. The zeal of Palæologus had been excited by interest; it was soon cooled by opposition: an attempt to violate the national belief might endanger his life and crown; nor could the pious rebels be destitute of foreign and domestic aid. The sword of his brother Demetrius, who in Italy had maintained a prudent and popular silence, was half unsheathed in the cause of religion; and Amurath, the Turkish sultan, was displeased and alarmed by the seeming friendship of the Greeks and Latins.

"Sultan Murad, or Amurath, lived fortynine, and reigned thirty years, six months, and eight days. He was a just and valiant prince, of a great soul, patient of labours, learned, merciful, religious, charitable; a lover and encourager of the studious, and of all who excelled in any art or science; a good emperor, and a great general. No man obtained more or greater victories than Amurath; Belgrade alone withstood his attacks. Under his reign the soldier was ever victorious, the citizen rich and secure. If he subdued any country, his first care was to build mosques and caravanseras, hospitals and colleges. Every year he gave a thousand pieces of gold to the sons of the Prophet, and sent two thousand five hundred to the religious persons of Mecca, Medina, and Jerusalem."[11] This portrait is transcribed from the historian of the Othman empire: but the applause of a servile and superstitious people has been lavished on the worst of tyrants; and the virtues of a sultan are often the vices most useful to himself, or most agreeable to his subjects. A nation ignorant of the equal benefits of liberty and law must be awed by the flashes of arbitrary power: the cruelty of a despot will assume the character of justice; his profusion, of liberality; his obstinacy, of firmness. If the most reasonable excuse be rejected, few acts of obedience will be found impossible; and guilt must tremble, where innocence cannot always be secure. The tranquillity of the people, and the discipline of the troops, were best maintained by perpetual action in the field: war was the trade of the Janizaries; and those who survived the peril, and divided the spoil, applauded the generous ambition of their sovereign. To propagate the true religion was the duty of a faithful Musulman: the unbelievers were *his* enemies, and those of the Prophet; and, in the hands of the Turks, the scimitar was the only instrument of conversion. Under these circumstances, however, the justice and moderation of Amurath are attested by his conduct, and acknowledged by the Christians themselves, who consider a prosperous reign and a peaceful death as the reward of his singular merits. In the vigour of his age and military power he seldom engaged in war till he was justified by a previous and adequate provocation: the victorious sultan was disarmed by submission; and in the observance of treaties, his word was inviolate and sacred.[12] The Hungarians were commonly the aggressors; he was provoked by the revolt of Scanderbeg; and the perfidious Caramanian was twice vanquished, and twice pardoned, by the Ottoman monarch. Before he invaded the Morea, Thebes had been surprised by the despot: in the conquest of Thessalonica the grandson of Bajazet might dispute the recent purchase of the Venetians; and after the first siege of Constantinople, the sultan was never tempted, by the distress, the absence, or the injuries of Palæologus, to extinguish the dying light of the Byzantine empire.

But the most striking feature in the life and character of Amurath is the double abdication of the Turkish throne; and, were not his motives debased by an alloy of superstition, we must praise the royal philosopher,[13] who at the age of forty could discern the vanity of human greatness. Resigning the sceptre to his son, he retired to the pleasant residence of Magnesia; but he retired to the society of saints and hermits. It was not till the fourth century of the Hegira that the religion of Mohammed had been corrupted by an institution so adverse to his genius; but in the age of the crusades the various orders of dervishes were multiplied by the example of the Christian, and even the Latin, monks.[14] The lord of nations submitted to fast, and pray, and turn round in endless rotation with the fanatics, who mistook the giddiness of the head for the illumination of the spirit.[15] But he was soon awakened from this dream of enthusiasm by the Hungarian invasion; and his obedient son was the foremost to urge the public danger and the wishes of the people. Under the banner of their veteran leader, the Janizaries fought and conquered; but he withdrew from the field of Varna, again to pray, to fast, and to turn round with the Magnesian brethren. These pious occupations were again interrupted by the danger of the state. A victorious army disdained the inexperience of their youthful ruler: the city of Adrianople was abandoned to rapine and slaughter; and the unanimous divan implored his presence to appease the tumult, and prevent the rebellion, of the Janizaries. At the well-known voice of their master they trembled and obeyed; and the reluctant sultan was compelled to support his splendid servitude, till, at the end of four years, he was relieved by the angel of death. Age or disease, misfortune or caprice, have tempted several princes to descend from the throne; and they have had leisure to repent of their irretrievable step. But Amurath alone, in the full liberty of choice, after the trial of empire and solitude, has *repeated* his preference of a private life.

After the departure of his Greek brethren, Eugenius had not been unmindful of their temporal interest; and his tender regard for the Byzantine empire was animated by a just apprehension of the Turks, who approached, and might soon invade, the borders of Italy. But the spirit of the crusades had expired; and the coldness of the Franks was not less unreasonable than their headlong passion. In the eleventh century a fanatic monk could precipitate Europe on Asia for the recovery of the holy sepulchre: but in the fifteenth, the most pressing motives of religion and policy were insufficient to unite the Latins in the defence of Christendom. Germany was an inexhaustible storehouse of men and arms:[16] but that complex and languid body required the impulse of a vigorous hand; and Frederic the Third was alike impotent in his personal character and his Imperial dignity. A long war had impaired the strength, without satiating the animosity, of France and England;[17] but Philip duke of Burgundy was a vain and magnificent prince; and he enjoyed, without danger or expense, the adventurous piety of his subjects, who sailed, in a gallant fleet, from the coast of Flanders to the Hellespont. The maritime republics of Venice and Genoa were less remote from the scene of action; and their hostile fleets were associated under the standard of St. Peter. The kingdoms of Hungary and Poland, which covered as it were the interior pale of the Latin church, were the most nearly concerned to oppose the progress of the Turks. Arms were the patrimony of the Scythians and Sarmatians; and these nations might appear equal to the contest, could they point, against the common foe, those swords that were so wantonly drawn in bloody and domestic quarrels. But the same spirit was adverse to concord and obedience: a poor country and a limited monarch are incapable of maintaining a standing force; and the loose bodies of Polish and Hungarian horse were not armed with the sentiments and weapons which, on some occasions, have given irresistible weight to the French chivalry. Yet, on this side, the designs of the Roman pontiff, and the eloquence of Cardinal Julian, his legate, were promoted by the circumstances of the times;[18] by the union of the two crowns on the head of Ladislaus,[19] a young and ambitious soldier; by the valour of a hero, whose name, the name of John Huniades, was already popular among the Christians, and formidable to the Turks. An endless treasure of pardons and indulgences was scattered by the legate; many private warriors of France and Germany enlisted under the holy banner; and the crusade derived some strength, or at least some reputation, from the new allies both of Europe and Asia. A fugitive despot of Servia exaggerated the distress and ardour of the Christians beyond the Danube, who would unanimously rise to vindicate their religion and liberty. The Greek emperor,[20] with a spirit unknown to his fathers, engaged to guard the Bosphorus, and to sally from Constantinople at the head of his national and mercenary troops. The sultan of Caramania[21] announced the retreat of Amurath, and a powerful diversion in the heart of Anatolia; and if the fleets of the West could occupy at the same moment the straits of the Hellespont, the Ottoman monarchy would be dissevered and destroyed. Heaven and earth must rejoice in the perdition of the miscreants; and the legate, with prudent ambiguity, instilled the opinion of the invisible, perhaps the visible, aid of the Son of God and his divine mother.

Of the Polish and Hungarian diets a religious war was the unanimous cry; and Ladislaus, after passing the Danube, led an army of his confederate subjects as far as Sophia, the capital of the Bulgarian kingdom. In this expedition they obtained two signal victories, which were justly ascribed to the valour and conduct of Huniades. In the first, with a vanguard of ten thousand men, he surprised the Turkish camp; in the second, he vanquished and made prisoner the most renowned of their generals, who possessed the double advantage of ground and numbers. The approach of winter, and the natural and artificial obstacles of Mount Hæmus, arrested the progress of the hero, who measured a narrow interval of six days' march from the foot of the mountains to the hostile towers of Adrianople and the friendly capital of the Greek empire. The retreat was undisturbed; and the entrance into Buda was at once a military and religious triumph. An ecclesiastical procession was followed by the king and his warriors on foot: he nicely balanced the merits and rewards of the two nations; and the pride of conquest was blended with the humble temper of Christianity. Thirteen bashaws, nine standards, and four thousand captives, were unquestionable trophies; and as all were willing to believe, and none were present to contradict, the crusaders multiplied, with unblushing confidence, the myriads of Turks whom they had left on the field of battle.[22] The most solid proof, and the most salutary consequence, of victory, was a deputation from the divan to solicit peace, to restore Servia, to ransom the prisoners, and to evacuate the Hungarian frontier. By this treaty the rational objects of the war were obtained: the king, the despot, and Huniades himself, in the diet of Segedin, were satisfied with public and private emolument; a truce of ten years was concluded; and the followers of Jesus and Mohammed, who swore on the Gospel and the Koran, attested the word of God as the guardian of truth and the avenger of perfidy. In the place of the Gospel the Turkish ministers had proposed to substitute the Eucharist, the real presence of the Catholic Deity; but the Christians refused to profane their holy mysteries; and a superstitious conscience is less forcibly bound by the spiritual energy than by the outward and visible symbols of an oath.[23]

During the whole transaction the cardinal legate had observed a sullen silence, unwilling to approve, and unable to oppose, the consent of the king and people. But the diet was not dissolved before Julian was fortified by the welcome intelligence that Anatolia was invaded by the Caramanian, and Thrace by the Greek emperor; that the fleets of Genoa, Venice, and Burgundy were masters of the Hellespont; and that the allies, informed of the victory, and ignorant of the treaty, of Ladislaus, impatiently waited for the return of his victorious army.

And is it thus," exclaimed the cardinal,[24] that you will desert their expectations and our own fortune? It is to them, to your God, and your fellow-Christians, that you have pledged your faith; and that prior obligation annihilates a rash and sacrilegious oath to the enemies of Christ. His vicar on earth is the Roman pontiff; without whose sanction you can neither promise nor perform. In his name I absolve your perjury and sanctify your arms: follow my footsteps in the paths of glory and salvation; and if still you have scruples, devolve on my head the punishment and the sin." This mischievous casuistry was seconded by his respectable character and the levity of popular assemblies: war was resolved on the same spot where peace had so lately been sworn; and, in the execution of the treaty, the Turks were assaulted by the Christians, to whom, with some reason, they might apply the epithet of Infidels. The falsehood of Ladislaus to his word and oath was palliated by the religion of the times: the most perfect, or at least the most popular, excuse would have been the success of his arms and the deliverance of the Eastern church. But the same treaty which should have bound his conscience had diminished his strength. On the proclamation of the peace the French and German volunteers departed with indignant murmurs: the Poles were exhausted by distant warfare, and perhaps disgusted with foreign command; and their palatines accepted the first licence, and hastily retired to their provinces and castles. Even Hungary was divided by faction, or restrained by a laudable scruple; and the relics of the crusade that marched in the second expedition were reduced to an inadequate force of twenty thousand men. A Walachian chief, who joined the royal standard with his vassals, presumed to remark that their numbers did not exceed the hunting retinue that sometimes attended the sultan; and the gift of two horses of matchless speed might admonish Ladislaus of his secret foresight of the event. But the despot of Servia, after the restoration of his country and children, was tempted by the promise of new realms; and the inexperience of the king, the enthusiasm of the legate, and the martial presumption of Huniades himself, were persuaded that every obstacle must yield to the invincible virtue of the sword and the cross. After the passage of the Danube two roads might lead to Constantinople and the Hellespont; the one direct, abrupt, and difficult, through the mountains of Hæmus; the other more tedious and secure, over a level

country, and along the shores of the Euxine; in which their flanks, according to the Scythian discipline, might always be covered by a movable fortification of waggons. The latter was judiciously preferred: the Catholics marched through the plains of Bulgaria, burning, with wanton cruelty, the churches and villages of the Christian natives; and their last station was at Varna, near the sea-shore; on which the defeat and death of Ladislaus have bestowed a memorable name.[25]

It was on this fatal spot that, instead of finding a confederate fleet to second their operations, they were alarmed by the approach of Amurath himself, who had issued from his Magnesian solitude and transported the forces of Asia to the defence of Europe. According to some writers the Greek emperor had been awed, or seduced, to grant the passage of the Bosphorus; and an indelible stain of corruption is fixed on the Genoese, or the pope's nephew, the Catholic admiral, whose mercenary connivance betrayed the guard of the Hellespont. From Adrianople the sultan advanced by hasty marches at the head of sixty thousand men; and when the cardinal and Huniades had taken a nearer survey of the numbers and order of the Turks, these ardent warriors proposed the tardy and impracticable measure of a retreat. The king alone was resolved to conquer or die; and his resolution had almost been crowned with a glorious and salutary victory. The princes were opposite to each other in the centre; and the Beglerbegs, or generals of Anatolia and Romania, commanded on the right and left against the adverse divisions of the despot and Huniades. The Turkish wings were broken on the first onset: but the advantage was fatal; and the rash victors, in the heat of the pursuit, were carried away far from the annoyance of the enemy or the support of their friends. When Amurath beheld the flight of his squadrons, he despaired of his fortune and that of the empire: a veteran Janizary seized his horse's bridle; and he had magnanimity to pardon and reward the soldier who dared to perceive the terror, and arrest the flight, of his sovereign. A copy of the treaty, the monument of Christian perfidy, had been displayed in the front of battle; and it is said that the sultan in his distress, lifting his eyes and his hands to heaven, implored the protection of the God of truth; and called on the prophet Jesus himself to avenge the impious mockery of his name and religion.[26] With inferior numbers and disordered ranks the king of Hungary rushed forwards in the confidence of victory, till his career was stopped by the impenetrable phalanx of the Janizaries. If we may credit the Ottoman annals, his horse was pierced by the javelin of Amurath;[27] he fell among the spears of the infantry; and a Turkish soldier proclaimed with a loud voice, "Hungarians, behold the head of your king!" The death of Ladislaus was the signal of their defeat. On his return from an intemperate pursuit, Huniades deplored his error and the public loss: he strove to rescue the royal body, till he was overwhelmed by the tumultuous crowd of the victors and vanquished; and the last efforts of his courage and conduct were exerted to save the remnant of his Wallachian cavalry. Ten thousand Christians were slain in the disastrous battle of Varna: the loss of the Turks, more considerable in numbers, bore a smaller proportion to their total strength; yet the philosophic sultan was not ashamed to confess that his ruin must be the consequence of a second and similar victory. At his command a column was erected on the spot where Ladislaus had fallen; but the modest inscription, instead of accusing the rashness, recorded the valour and bewailed the misfortune of the Hungarian youth.[28]

Before I lose sight of the field of Varna I am tempted to pause on the character and story of two principal actors, the cardinal Julian and John Huniades. Julian[29] Cæsarini was born of a noble family of Rome: his studies had embraced both the Latin and Greek learning, both the sciences of divinity and law; and his versatile genius was equally adapted to the schools, the camp, and the court. No sooner had he been invested with the Roman purple than he was sent into Germany to arm the empire against the rebels and heretics of Bohemia. The spirit of persecution is unworthy of a Christian; the military profession ill becomes a priest; but the former is excused by the times; and the latter was ennobled by the courage of Julian, who stood dauntless and alone in the disgraceful flight of the German host. As the pope's legate he opened the council of Basil; but the president soon appeared the most strenuous champion of ecclesiastical freedom; and an opposition of seven years was conducted by his ability and zeal. After promoting the strongest measures against the authority and person of Eugenius, some secret motive of interest or conscience engaged him to desert on a sudden the popular party. The cardinal withdrew himself from Basil to Ferrara; and, in the debates of the Greeks and Latins, the two nations admired the dexterity of his arguments and the depth of his theological erudition.[30] In his Hungarian embassy we have already seen the mischievous effects of his sophistry and eloquence, of which Julian himself was the first victim. The cardinal, who performed the duties of a priest and a soldier, was lost in the defeat of Varna. The circumstances of his death are variously related but it is believed that a weighty incumbrance of gold impeded his flight, and tempted the cruel avarice of some Christian fugitives.

From a humble, or at least a doubtful, origin the merit of John Huniades promoted him to the command of the Hungarian armies. His father was a Wallachian, his mother a Greek: her unknown race might possibly ascend to the emperors of Constantinople; and the claims of the Wallachians, with the surname of Corvinus from the place of his nativity, might suggest a thin pretence for mingling his blood with the patricians of ancient Rome.[31] In his youth he served in the wars of Italy, and was retained with twelve horsemen, by the bishop of Zagrab: the valour of the *white knight*[32] was soon conspicuous; he increased his fortunes by a noble and wealthy marriage; and in the defence of the Hungarian borders he won in the same year three battles against the Turks. By his influence Ladislaus of Poland obtained the crown of Hungary; and the important service was rewarded by the title and office of Waivod of Transylvania. The first of Julian's crusades added two Turkish laurels on his brow; and in the public distress the fatal errors of Varna were forgotten. During the absence and minority of Ladislaus of Austria, the titular king, Huniades was elected supreme captain and governor of Hungary; and if envy at first was silenced by terror, a reign of twelve years supposes the arts of policy as well as of war. Yet the idea of a consummate general is not delineated in his campaigns; the white knight fought with the hand rather than the head, as the chief of desultory barbarians, who attack without fear and fly without shame; and his military life is composed of a romantic alternative of victories and escapes. By the Turks, who employed his name to frighten their perverse children, he was corruptly denominated *Jancus Lain*, or the Wicked: their hatred is the proof of their esteem; the kingdom which he guarded was inaccessible to their arms; and they felt him most daring and formidable when they fondly believed the captain and his country irrecoverably lost. Instead of confining himself to a defensive war, four years after the defeat of Varna he again penetrated into the heart of Bulgaria, and in the plain of Cossova sustained, till the third day, the shock of the Ottoman army, four times more numerous than his own. As he fled alone through the woods of Wallachia, the hero was surprised by two robbers; but while they disputed a gold chain that hung at his neck, he recovered his sword, slew the one, terrified the other, and, after new perils of captivity or death, consoled by his presence an afflicted kingdom. But the last and most glorious action of his life was the defence of Belgrade against the powers of Mohammed the Second in person. After a siege of forty days the Turks, who had already entered the town, were compelled to retreat; and the joyful nations celebrated Huniades and Belgrade as the bulwarks of Christendom.[33] About a month after this great deliverance the champion expired; and his most splendid epitaph is the regret of the Ottoman prince, who sighed that he could no longer hope for revenge against the single antagonist who had triumphed over his arms. On the first vacancy of the throne Matthias Corvinus, a youth of eighteen years of age, was elected and crowned by the grateful Hungarians. His reign was prosperous and long: Matthias aspired to the glory of a conqueror and a saint; but his purest merit is the encouragement of learning; and the Latin orators and historians, who were invited from Italy by the son, have shed the lustre of their eloquence on the father's character.[34]

In the list of heroes John Huniades and Scanderberg are commonly associated;[35] and they are both entitled to our notice, since their occupation of the Ottoman arms delayed the ruin of the Greek empire. John Castriot, the father of Scanderbeg,[36] was the hereditary prince of a small district of Epirus, or Albania, between the mountains and the Adriatic Sea. Unable to contend with the sultan's power, Castriot submitted to the hard conditions of peace and tribute: he delivered his four sons as the pledges of his fidelity; and the Christian youths, after receiving the mark of circumcision, were instructed in the Mohammedan religion and trained in the arms and arts of Turkish policy.[37] The three elder brothers were confounded in the crowd of slaves; and the poison to which their deaths are ascribed cannot be verified or disproved by any positive evidence. Yet the suspicion is in a great measure removed by the kind and paternal treatment of George Castriot, the fourth brother, who, from his tender youth, displayed the strength and spirit of a soldier. The successive overthrow of a Tartar and two

Persians, who carried a proud defiance to the Turkish court, recommended him to the favour of Amurath, and his Turkish appellation of Scanderberg (*Iskender beg*), or the lord Alexander, is an indelible memorial of his glory and servitude. His father's principality was reduced into a province; but the loss was compensated by the rank and title of Sanjiak, a command of five thousand horse, and the prospect of the first dignities of the empire. He served with honour in the wars of Europe and Asia; and we may smile at the art or credulity of the historian, who supposes that in every encounter he spared the Christians, while he fell with a thundering arm on his Musulman foes. The glory of Huniades is without reproach: he fought in the defence of his religion and country; but the enemies who applaud the patriot have branded his rival with the name of traitor and apostate. In the eyes of the Christians the rebellion of Scanderbeg is justified by his father's wrongs, the ambiguous death of his three brothers, his own degradation, and the slavery of his country; and they adore the generous, though tardy, zeal with which he asserted the faith and independence of his ancestors. But he had imbibed from his ninth year the doctrines of the Koran: he was ignorant of the Gospel; the religion of a soldier is determined by authority and habit; nor is it easy to conceive what new illumination at the age of forty[38] could be poured into his soul. His motives would be less exposed to the suspicion of interest or revenge, had he broken his chain from the moment that he was sensible of its weight: but a long oblivion had surely impaired his original right; and every year of obedience and reward had cemented the mutual bond of the sultan and his subject. If Scanderbeg had long harboured the belief of Christianity and the intention of revolt, a worthy mind must condemn the base dissimulation that could serve only to betray, that could promise only to be forsworn, that could actively join in the temporal and spiritual perdition of so many thousands of his unhappy brethren. Shall we praise a secret correspondence with Huniades while he commanded the vanguard of the Turkish army? Shall we excuse the desertion of his standard, a treacherous desertion which abandoned the victory to the enemies of his benefactor? In the confusion of a defeat, the eye of Scanderberg was fixed on the Reis Effendi, or principal secretary: with the dagger at his breast, he extorted a firman or patent for the government of Albania; and the murder of the guiltless scribe and his train prevented the consequences of an immediate discovery. With some bold companions, to whom he had revealed his design, he escaped in the night by rapid marches from the field of battle to his paternal mountains. The gates of Croya were opened to the royal mandate; and no sooner did he command the fortress than George Castriot dropped the mask of dissimulation, abjured the prophet and the sultan, and proclaimed himself the avenger of his family and country. The names of religion and liberty provoked a general revolt: the Albanians, a martial race, were unanimous to live and die with their hereditary prince; and the Ottoman garrisons were indulged in the choice of martyrdom or baptism. In the assembly of the states of Epirus, Scanderbeg was elected general of the Turkish war; and each of the allies engaged to furnish his respective proportion of men and money. From these contributions, from his patrimonial estate, and from the valuable salt-pits of Selina, he drew an annual revenue of two hundred thousand ducats;[39] and the entire sum, exempt from the demands of luxury, was strictly appropriated to the public use. His manners were popular; but his discipline was severe; and every superfluous vice was banished from his camp: his example strengthened his command and under his conduct the Albanians were invincible in their own opinion and that of their enemies. The bravest adventurers of France and Germany were allured by his fame and retained in his service: his standing militia consisted of eight thousand horse and seven thousand foot; the horses were small, the men were active: but he viewed with a discerning eye the difficulties and resources of the mountains; and, at the blaze of the beacons, the whole nation was distributed in the strongest posts. With such unequal arms Scanderbeg resisted twenty-three years the powers of the Ottoman empire; and two conquerors, Amurath the Second and his greater son, were repeatedly baffled by a rebel whom they pursued with seeming contempt and implacable resentment. At the head of sixty thousand horse and forty thousand Janizaries, Amurath entered Albania: he might ravage the open country, occupy the defenceless towns, convert the churches into mosques, circumcise the Christian youths, and punish with death his adult and obstinate captives: but the conquests of the sultan were confined to the petty fortress of Sfetigrade; and the garrison, invincible to his arms, was oppressed by a paltry artifice and a superstitious scruple.[40] Amurath retired with shame and loss from the walls of Croya, the

castle and residence of the Castriots; the march, the siege, the retreat, were harassed by a vexatious, and almost invisible, adversary;[41] and the disappointment might tend to embitter, perhaps to shorten, the last days of the sultan.[42] In the fulness of conquest Mohammed the Second still felt at his bosom this domestic thorn; his lieutenants were permitted to negotiate a truce, and the Albanian prince may justly be praised as a firm and able champion of his national independence. The enthusiasm of chivalry and religion has ranked him with the names of Alexander and Pyrrhus; nor would they blush to acknowledge their intrepid countryman: but his narrow dominion and slender powers must leave him at a humble distance below the heroes of antiquity, who triumphed over the East and the Roman legions. His splendid achievements, the bashaws whom he encountered, the armies that he discomfited, and the three thousand Turks who were slain by his single hand, must be weighed in the scales of suspicious criticism. Against an illiterate enemy, and in the dark solitude of Epirus, his partial biographers may safely indulge the latitude of romance; but their fictions are exposed by the light of Italian history, and they afford a strong presumption against their own truth by a fabulous tale of his exploits, when he passed the Adriatic with eight hundred horse to the succour of the king of Naples.[43] Without disparagement to his fame, they might have owned that he was finally oppressed by the Ottoman powers; in his extreme danger he applied to pope Pius the Second for a refuge in the ecclesiastical state; and his resources were almost exhausted, since Scanderbeg died a fugitive at Lissus, on the Venetian territory.[44] His sepulchre was soon violated by the Turkish conquerors; but the Janizaries, who wore his bones enchased in a bracelet, declared by this superstitious amulet their involuntary reverence for his valour. The instant ruin of his country may redound to the hero's glory; yet, had he balanced the consequences of submission and resistance, a patriot perhaps would have declined the unequal contest which must depend on the life and genius of one man. Scanderbeg might indeed be supported by the rational, though fallacious, hope that the pope, the king of Naples, and the Venetian republic would join in the defence of a free and Christian people, who guarded the seacoast of the Adriatic and the narrow passage from Greece to Italy. His infant son was saved from the national shipwreck; the Castriots[45] were invested with a Neapolitan dukedom, and eir blood continues to flow in the noblest amilies of the realm. A colony of Albanian fugives obtained a settlement in Calabria, and hey preserve at this day the language and maners of their ancestors.[46]

In the long career of the decline and fall of he Roman empire, I have reached at length he last reign of the princes of Constantinople, vho so feebly sustained the name and majesty f the Cæsars. On the decease of John Palæ-logus, who survived about four years the Hun-arian crusade,[47] the royal family, by the death f Andronicus and the monastic profession of sidore, was reduced to three princes, Constan-ine, Demetrius, and Thomas, the surviving ons of the emperor Manuel. Of these, the first nd the last were far distant in the Morea; but Demetrius, who possessed the domain of Selym-ria, was in the suburbs, at the head of a party; iis ambition was not chilled by the public dis-ress, and his conspiracy with the Turks and the schismatics had already disturbed the peace of his country. The funeral of the late emperor was accelerated with singular and even sus-picious haste; the claim of Demetrius to the vacant throne was justified by a trite and flimsy sophism, that he was born in the purple, the eldest son of his father's reign. But the empress-mother, the senate and soldiers, the clergy and people, were unanimous in the cause of the lawful successor; and the despot Thomas, who, ignorant of the change, accidentally returned to the capital, asserted with becoming zeal the interest of his absent brother. An ambassador, the historian Phranza, was immediately des-patched to the court of Adrianople. Amurath received him with honour and dismissed him with gifts; but the gracious approbation of the Turkish sultan announced his supremacy, and the approaching downfall of the Eastern em-pire. By the hands of two illustrious deputies the Imperial crown was placed at Sparta on the head of Constantine. In the spring he sailed from the Morea, escaped the encounter of a Turkish squadron, enjoyed the acclamations of his subjects, celebrated the festival of a new reign, and exhausted by his donatives the treasure, or rather the indigence, of the state. The emperor immediately resigned to his brothers the possession of the Morea; and the brittle friendship of the two princes, Demetrius and Thomas, was confirmed in their mother's presence by the frail security of oaths and em-braces. His next occupation was the choice of a consort. A daughter of the doge of Venice had been proposed, but the Byzantine nobles ob-jected the distance between an hereditary mon-arch and an elective magistrate; and in their subsequent distress the chief of that powerful republic was not unmindful of the affront. Con-stantine afterwards hesitated between the royal families of Trebizond and Georgia; and the em-bassy of Phranza represents in his public and private life the last days of the Byzantine em-pire.[48]

The *protovestiare*, or great chamberlain, Phranza, sailed from Constantinople as the minister of a bridegroom, and the relics of wealth and luxury were applied to his pompous appearance. His numerous retinue consisted of nobles and guards, of physicians and monks: he was attended by a band of music; and the term of his costly embassy was protracted above two years. On his arrival in Georgia or Iberia the natives from the towns and villages flocked around the strangers; and such was their sim-plicity that they were delighted with the effects, without understanding the cause, of musical harmony. Among the crowd was an old man above a hundred years of age, who had former-ly been carried away a captive by the bar-barians,[49] and who amused his hearers with a tale of the wonders of India,[50] from whence he had returned to Portugal by an unknown sea.[51] From this hospitable land Phranza proceeded to the court of Trebizond, where he was in-formed by the Greek prince of the recent de-cease of Amurath. Instead of rejoicing in the deliverance, the experienced statesman ex-pressed his apprehension that an ambitious youth would not long adhere to the sage and pacific system of his father. After the sultan's decease his Christian wife, Maria,[52] the daugh-ter of the Servian despot, had been honourably restored to her parents; on the fame of her beauty and merit she was recommended by the ambassador as the most worthy object of the royal choice; and Phranza recapitulates and refutes the specious objections that might be raised against the proposal. The majesty of the purple would ennoble an unequal alliance; the bar of affinity might be removed by liberal alms and the dispensation of the church; the disgrace of Turkish nuptials had been repeatedly over-looked; and, though the fair Maria was near fifty years of age, she might yet hope to give an heir to the empire. Constantine listened to the advice, which was transmitted in the first ship that sailed from Trebizond; but the factions of the court opposed his marriage, and it was fi-nally prevented by the pious vow of the sultana, who ended her days in the monastic profession.

Reduced to the first alternative, the choice of Phranza was decided in favour of a Georgian princess; and the vanity of her father was dazzled by the glorious alliance. Instead of demanding, according to the primitive and national custom, a price for his daughter,[53] he offered a portion of fifty-six thousand, with an annual pension of five thousand, ducats; and the services of the ambassador were repaid by an assurance that, as his son had been adopted in baptism by the emperor, the establishment of his daughter should be the peculiar care of the empress of Constantinople. On the return of Phranza the treaty was ratified by the Greek monarch, who with his own hand impressed three vermilion crosses on the golden bull, and assured the Georgian envoy that in the spring his galleys should conduct the bride to her Imperial palace. But Constantine embraced his faithful servant, not with the cold approbation of a sovereign, but with the warm confidence of a friend, who, after a long absence, is impatient to pour his secrets into the bosom of his friend. "Since the death of my mother and of Cantacuzene, who alone advised me without interest or passion,[54] I am surrounded," said the emperor, "by men whom I can neither love, nor trust, nor esteem. You are not a stranger to Lucas Notaras, the great admiral: obstinately attached to his own sentiments, he declares, both in private and public, that his sentiments are the absolute measure of my thoughts and actions. The rest of the courtiers are swayed by their personal or factious views; and how can I consult the monks on questions of policy and marriage? I have yet much employment for your diligence and fidelity. In the spring you shall engage one of my brothers to solicit the succour of the Western powers; from the Morea you shall sail to Cyprus on a particular commission, and from thence proceed to Georgia to receive and conduct the future empress." "Your commands," replied Phranza, "are irresistible; but deign, great sir," he added, with a serious smile, "to consider that, if I am thus perpetually absent from my family, my wife may be tempted either to seek another husband, or to throw herself into a monastery." After laughing at his apprehensions, the emperor more gravely consoled him by the pleasing assurance that *this* should be his last service abroad, and that he destined for his son a wealthy and noble heiress; for himself, the important office of great logothete, or principal minister of state. The marriage was immediately stipulated: but the office, however incompatible with his own, had been usurped by the ambition of the admiral. Some delay was requisite to negotiate a consent and an equivalent; and the nomination of Phranza was half declared and half suppressed, lest it might be displeasing to an insolent and powerful favourite. The winter was spent in the preparations of his embassy; and Phranza had resolved that the youth his son should embrace this opportunity of foreign travel, and be left, on the appearance of danger, with his maternal kindred on the Morea. Such were the private and public designs, which were interrupted by a Turkish war, and finally buried in the ruins of the empire.

CHAPTER LXVIII

Reign and Character of Mohammed the Second. Siege, Assault, and Final Conquest of Constantinople by the Turks. Death of Constantine Palæologus. Servitude of the Greeks. Extinction of the Roman Empire in the East. Consternation of Europe. Conquests and Death of Mohammed the Second.

THE siege of Constantinople by the Turks attracts our first attention to the person and character of the great destroyer. Mohammed the Second[1] was the son of the second Amurath; and though his mother has been decorated with the titles of Christian and princess, she is more probably confounded with the numerous concubines who peopled from every climate the harem of the sultan. His first education and sentiments were those of a devout Musulman; and as often as he conversed with an infidel he purified his hands and face by the legal rites of ablution. Age and empire appear to have relaxed this narrow bigotry: his aspiring genius disdained to acknowledge a power above his own; and in his looser hours he presumed (it is said) to brand the prophet of Mecca as a robber and impostor. Yet the sultan persevered in a decent reverence for the doctrine and discipline of the Koran:[2] his private indiscretion must have been sacred from the vulgar ear; and we should suspect the credulity of strangers and sectaries, so prone to believe that a mind which is hardened against truth must be armed with superior contempt for absurdity and error. Under the tuition of the most skilful masters Mohammed advanced with an early and rapid progress in the paths of knowledge; and besides his native tongue it is affirmed that he spoke or understood five languages,[3] the Arabic, the Persian, the Chaldæan or Hebrew, the Latin, and the Greek. The Persian might indeed contribute to his amusement, and the Arabic to his edification; and such studies are familiar to the Oriental youth. In the intercourse of the Greeks and Turks a conqueror might wish to converse with the people over whom he was ambitious to reign: his own praises in Latin poetry[4] or prose[5] might find a passage to the royal ear; but what use or merit could recommend to the statesman or the scholar the uncouth dialect of his Hebrew slaves? The history and geography of the world were familiar to his memory: the lives of the heroes of the East, perhaps of the West,[6] excited his emulation: his skill in astrology is excused by the folly of the times, and supposes some rudiments of mathematical science; and a profane taste for the arts is betrayed in his liberal invitation and reward of the painters of Italy.[7] But the influence of religion and learning were employed without effect on his savage and licentious nature. I will not transcribe, nor do I firmly believe, the stories of his fourteen pages whose bellies were ripped open in search of a stolen melon, or of the beauteous slave whose head he severed from her body to convince the Janizaries that their master was not the votary of love. His sobriety is attested by the silence of the Turkish annals, which accuse three, and three only, of the Ottoman line of the vice of drunkenness.[8] But it cannot be denied that his passions were at once furious and inexorable; that in the palace, as in the field, a torrent of blood was spilt on the slightest provocation; and that the noblest of the captive youth were often dishonoured by his unnatural lust. In the Albanian war he studied the lessons, and soon surpassed the example, of his father; and the conquest of two empires, twelve kingdoms, and two hundred cities, a vain and flattering account, is ascribed to his invincible sword. He was doubtless a soldier, and possibly a general; Constantinople has sealed his glory; but if we compare the means, the obstacles, and the achievements, Mohammed the Second must blush to sustain a parallel with Alexander or Timour. Under his command the Ottoman forces were always more numerous than their enemies, yet their progress was bounded by the Euphrates and the Adriatic, and his arms were checked by Huniades and Scanderbeg, by the Rhodian knights, and by the Persian king.

In the reign of Amurath he twice tasted of royalty, and twice descended from the throne: his tender age was incapable of opposing his father's restoration, but never could he forgive the vizirs who had recommended that salutary measure. His nuptials were celebrated with the daughter of a Turkman emir; and, after a festival of two months, he departed from Adrianople with his bride to reside in the government of Magnesia. Before the end of six weeks he was recalled by a sudden message from the divan which announced the decease of Amurath and the mutinous spirit of the Janizaries. His speed and vigour commanded their obedience: he passed the Hellespont with a chosen guard: and at the distance of a mile from Adrianople the vizirs and emirs, the imams and cadhis, the soldiers and the people, fell prostrate before the new sultan. They affected to weep, they affected to rejoice: he ascended the throne at the age of twenty-one years, and removed the cause of sedition by the death, the inevitable death, of his infant brothers.[9] The ambassadors of Europe and Asia soon appeared to congratulate his accession and solicit his friendship, and to all he spoke the language of moderation and peace. The confidence of the Greek emperor was revived by the solemn oaths and fair assurances with which he sealed the ratification of the treaty: and a rich domain on the banks of the Strymon was assigned for the annual payment of three hundred thousand aspers, the pension of an Ottoman prince who was detained at his request in the Byzantine court. Yet the neighbours of Mohammed might tremble at the severity with which a youthful monarch reformed the pomp of his father's household: the expenses of luxury were applied to those of ambition, and a useless train of seven thousand falconers was either dismissed from his service or enlisted in his troops. In the first summer of his reign he visited with an army the Asiatic provinces; but after humbling the pride Mohammed accepted the submission of the Caramanian, that he might not be diverted by the smallest obstacle from the execution of his great design.[10]

The Mohammedan, and more especially the Turkish casuists, have pronounced that no promise can bind the faithful against the interest and duty of their religion, and that the sultan may abrogate his own treaties and those of his predecessors. The justice and magnanimity of Amurath had scorned this immoral privilege; but his son, though the proudest of men, could stoop from ambition to the basest arts of dissimulation and deceit. Peace was on his lips while war was in his heart: he incessantly sighed for the possession of Constantinople; and the Greeks, by their own indiscretion, afforded the first pretence of the fatal rupture.[11] Instead of labouring to be forgotten, their ambassadors pursued his camp to demand the payment, and even the increase, of their annual stipend: the divan was importuned by their complaints; and the vizir, a secret friend of the Christians, was constrained to deliver the sense of his brethren. "Ye foolish and miserable Romans," said Calil, "we know your devices, and ye are ignorant of your own danger! the scrupulous Amurath is no more; his throne is occupied by a young conqueror whom no laws can bind, and no obstacles can resist: and if you escape from his hands, give praise to the divine clemency, which yet delays the chastisement of your sins. Why do you seek to affright us by vain and indirect menaces? Release the fugitive Orchan, crown him sultan of Romania, call the Hungarians from beyond the Danube, arm against us the nations of the West, and be assured that you will only provoke and precipitate your ruin." But if the fears of the ambassadors were alarmed by the stern language of the vizir, they were soothed by the courteous audience and friendly speeches of the Ottoman prince; and Mohammed assured them that on his return to Adrianople he would redress the grievances, and consult the true interests of the Greeks. No sooner had he repassed the Hellespont than he issued a mandate to suppress their pension, and to expel their officers from the banks of the Strymon: in this measure he betrayed a hostile mind; and the second order announced, and in some degree commenced, the siege of Constantinople. In the narrow pass of the Bosphorus an Asiatic fortress had formerly been raised by his grandfather; in the opposite situation, on the European side, he resolved to erect a more formidable castle, and a thousand masons were commanded to assemble in the spring on a spot named Asomaton, about five miles from the Greek metropolis.[12] Persuasion is the resource of the feeble; and the feeble can seldom persuade: the ambassadors of the emperor attempted, without success, to divert Mohammed from the execution of his design. They represented that his grandfather had solicited the permission of Manuel to build a castle on his own territories; but that this double fortification, which would command the strait, could only tend to violate the alliance of the nations, to intercept the Latins who traded in the Black Sea, and perhaps to annihilate the subsistence of the city. "I form no enterprise," replied the perfidious sultan, "against the city; but the empire of Constantinople is measured by her walls. Have you forgot the distress to which my father was reduced when you formed a league with the Hungarians, when they invaded our country by land, and the Hellespont was occupied by the French galleys? Amurath was compelled to force the passage of the Bosphorus; and your strength was not equal to your malevolence. I was then a child at Adrianople; the Moslems trembled, and for a while the *Gabours*[13] insulted our disgrace. But when my father had triumphed in the field of Varna, he vowed to erect a fort on the western shore, and that vow it is my duty to accomplish. Have ye the right, have ye the power, to control my actions on my own ground? For that ground *is* my own: as far as the shores of the Bosphorus Asia is inhabited by the Turks, and Europe is deserted by the Romans. Return, and inform your king that the present Ottoman is far different from his predecessors, that *his* resolutions surpass *their* wishes, and that *he* performs more than *they* could resolve. Return in safety; but the next who delivers a similar message may expect to be flayed alive." After this declaration, Constantine, the first of the Greeks in spirit as in rank,[14] had determined to unsheathe the sword, and to resist the approach and establishment of the Turks on the Bosphorus. He was disarmed by the advice of his civil and ecclesiastical ministers, who recommended a system less generous, and even less prudent, than his own, to approve their patience and long-suffering, to brand the Ottoman with the name and guilt of an aggressor, and to depend on chance and time for their own safety, and the destruction of a fort which could not long be maintained in the neighbourhood of a great and populous city. Amidst hope and fear, the fears of the wise and the hopes of the credulous, the winter rolled away; the proper business of each man and each hour was postponed; and the Greeks shut their eyes against the impending danger, till the arrival of the spring and the sultan decided the assurance of their ruin.

Of a master who never forgives, the orders are seldom disobeyed. On the twenty-sixth of

March the appointed spot of Asomaton was covered with an active swarm of Turkish artificers; and the materials by sea and land were diligently transported from Europe and Asia.[15] The lime had been burnt in Cataphrygia, the timber was cut down in the woods of Heraclea and Nicomedia, and the stones were dug from the Anatolian quarries. Each of the thousand masons was assisted by two workmen; and a measure of two cubits was marked for their daily task. The fortress[16] was built in a triangular form; each angle was flanked by a strong and massy tower, one on the declivity of the hill, two along the sea-shore; a thickness of twenty-two feet was assigned for the walls, thirty for the towers; and the whole building was covered with a solid platform of lead. Mohammed himself pressed and directed the work with indefatigable ardour: his three viziers claimed the honour of finishing their respective towers; the zeal of the cadhis emulated that of the Janizaries; the meanest labour was ennobled by the service of God and the sultan; and the diligence of the multitude was quickened by the eye of a despot whose smile was the hope of fortune, and whose frown was the messenger of death. The Greek emperor beheld with terror the irresistible progress of the work, and vainly strove by flattery and gifts to assuage an implacable foe, who sought, and secretly fomented, the slightest occasion of a quarrel. Such occasions must soon and inevitably be found. The ruins of stately churches, and even the marble columns which had been consecrated to Saint Michael the archangel, were employed without scruple by the profane and rapacious Moslems; and some Christians, who presumed to oppose the removal, received from their hands the crown of martyrdom. Constantine had solicited a Turkish guard to protect the fields and harvests of his subjects: the guard was fixed; but their first order was to allow free pasture to the mules and horses of the camp, and to defend their brethren if they should be molested by the natives. The retinue of an Ottoman chief had left their horses to pass the night among the ripe corn: the damage was felt, the insult was resented, and several of both nations were slain in a tumultuous conflict. Mohammed listened with joy to the complaint; and a detachment was commanded to exterminate the guilty village: the guilty had fled; but forty innocent and unsuspecting reapers were massacred by the soldiers. Till this provocation Constantinople had been open to the visits of commerce and curiosity: on the first alarm the gates were shut;

but the emperor, still anxious for peace, released on the third day his Turkish captives,[17] and expressed, in a last message, the firm resignation of a Christian and a soldier. "Since neither oaths, nor treaty, nor submission can secure peace, pursue," said he to Mohammed, "your impious warfare. My trust is in God alone: if it should please him to mollify your heart, I shall rejoice in the happy change; if he delivers the city into your hands, I submit without a murmur to his holy will. But until the Judge of the earth shall pronounce between us, it is my duty to live and die in the defence of my people." The sultan's answer was hostile and decisive: his fortifications were completed; and before his departure for Adrianople he stationed a vigilant Aga and four hundred Janizaries to levy a tribute on the ships of every nation that should pass within the reach of their cannon. A Venetian vessel, refusing obedience to the new lords of the Bosphorus, was sunk with a single bullet. The master and thirty sailors escaped in the boat; but they were dragged in chains to the *Porte*: the chief was impaled, his companions were beheaded; and the historian Ducas[18] beheld, at Demotica, their bodies exposed to the wild beasts. The siege of Constantinople was deferred till the ensuing spring; but an Ottoman army marched into the Morea to divert the force of the brothers of Constantine. At this era of calamity one of these princes, the despot Thomas, was blessed or afflicted with the birth of a son—"the last heir," says the plaintive Phranza, "of the last spark of the Roman empire."[19]

The Greeks and the Turks passed an anxious and sleepless winter: the former were kept awake by their fears, the latter by their hopes; both by the preparations of defence and attack; and the two emperors, who had the most to lose or to gain, were the most deeply affected by the national sentiment. In Mohammed that sentiment was inflamed by the ardour of his youth and temper: he amused his leisure with building at Adrianople[20] the lofty palace of Jehan Numa (the watchtower of the world); but his serious thoughts were irrevocably bent on the conquest of the city of Cæsar. At the dead of night, about the second watch, he started from his bed, and commanded the instant attendance of his prime vizir. The message, the hour, the prince, and his own situation, alarmed the guilty conscience of Calil Basha; who had possessed the confidence, and advised the restoration, of Amurath. On the accession of the son the vizir was confirmed in his office and the appearances of favour; but the veteran statesman was not insensible that he trod on a thin and slippery ice, which might break under his footsteps and plunge him in the abyss. His friendship for the Christians, which might be innocent under the late reign, had stigmatised him with the name of Gabour Ortachi, or foster-brother of the infidels;[21] and his avarice entertained a venal and treasonable correspondence, which was detected and punished after the conclusion of the war. On receiving the royal mandate, he embraced, perhaps for the last time, his wife and children; filled a cup with pieces of gold, hastened to the palace, adored the sultan, and offered, according to the Oriental custom, the slight tribute of his duty and gratitude.[22] "It is not my wish," said Mohammed "to resume my gifts, but rather to heap and multiply them on thy head. In my turn I ask a present far more valuable and important—Constantinople." As soon as the vizir had recovered from his surprise, "The same God," said he, "who has already given thee so large a portion of the Roman empire, will not deny the remnant and the capital. His providence, and thy power, assure thy success; and myself, with the rest of thy faithful slaves, will sacrifice our lives and fortunes."—"Lala"[23] (or preceptor), continued the sultan, "do you see this pillow? all the night, in my agitation, I have pulled it on one side and the other; I have risen from my bed, again have I lain down, yet sleep has not visited these weary eyes. Beware of the gold and silver of the Romans: in arms we are superior; and with the aid of God, and the prayers of the prophet, we shall speedily become masters of Constantinople." To sound the disposition of his soldiers, he often wandered through the streets alone and in disguise; and it was fatal to discover the sultan when he wished to escape from the vulgar eye. His hours were spent in delineating the plan of the hostile city; in debating with his generals and engineers on what spot he should erect his batteries; on which side he should assault the walls; where he should spring his mines; to what place he should apply his scaling-ladders: and the exercises of the day repeated and proved the lucubrations of the night.

Among the implements of destruction, he studied with peculiar care the recent and tremendous discovery of the Latins; and his artillery surpassed whatever had yet appeared in the world. A founder of cannon, a Dane or Hungarian, who had been almost starved in the Greek service, deserted to the Moslems, and was liberally entertained by the Turkish sultan.

Mohammed was satisfied with the answer to h first question, which he eagerly pressed on th artist. "Am I able to cast a cannon capable throwing a ball or stone of sufficient size to ba ter the walls of Constantinople? I am not i norant of their strength; but were they mor solid than those of Babylon, I could oppose a engine of superior power; the position an management of that engine must be left to you engineers." On this assurance a foundry wa established at Adrianople: the metal was pre pared; and at the end of three months Urba produced a piece of brass ordnance of stupen dous and almost incredible magnitude; measure of twelve palms is assigned to the bore and the stone bullet weighed above six hundre pounds.[24] A vacant place before the new palac was chosen for the first experiment; but to pre vent the sudden and mischievous effects of as tonishment and fear, a proclamation was issue that the cannon would be discharged the en suing day. The explosion was felt or heard in circuit of a hundred furlongs: the ball, by th force of gunpowder, was driven above a mile and on the spot where it fell, it buried itself fathom deep in the ground. For the conveyanc of this destructive engine, a frame or carriage c thirty waggons was linked together and draw along by a team of sixty oxen: two hundre men on both sides were stationed to poise an support the rolling weight; two hundred an fifty workmen marched before to smooth th way and repair the bridges; and near two month were employed in a laborious journey of on hundred and fifty miles. A lively philosopher derides on this occasion the credulity of th Greeks, and observes, with much reason, tha we should always distrust the exaggerations of vanquished people. He calculates that a ball even of two hundred pounds, would require charge of one hundred and fifty pounds o powder; and that the stroke would be feeble and impotent, since not a fifteenth part of the mass could be inflamed at the same moment. A stranger as I am to the art of destruction, I can discern that the modern improvements of artillery prefer the number of pieces to the weight of metal; the quickness of the fire to the sound, or even the consequences, of a single explosion. Yet I dare not reject the positive and unanimous evidence of contemporary writers; nor can it seem improbable that the first artists, in their rude and ambitious efforts, should have transgressed the standard of moderation. A Turkish cannon, more enormous than that of Mohammed, still guards the entrance of the

Dardanelles; and if the use be inconvenient, it has been found on a late trial that the effect was far from contemptible. A stone bullet of *eleven* hundred pounds' weight was once discharged with three hundred and thirty pounds of powder: at the distance of six hundred yards it shivered into three rocky fragments; traversed the strait; and, leaving the waters in a foam, again rose and bounded against the opposite hill.[26]

While Mohammed threatened the capital of the East, the Greek emperor implored with fervent prayers the assistance of earth and Heaven. But the invisible powers were deaf to his supplications; and Christendom beheld with indifference the fall of Constantinople, while she derived at least some promise of supply from the jealous and temporal policy of the sultan of Egypt. Some states were too weak and others too remote; by some the danger was considered as imaginary, by others as inevitable: the Western princes were involved in their endless and domestic quarrels; and the Roman pontiff was exasperated by the falsehood or obstinacy of the Greeks. Instead of employing in their favour the arms and treasures of Italy, Nicholas the Fifth had foretold their approaching ruin; and his honour was engaged in the accomplishment of his prophecy. Perhaps he was softened by the last extremity of their distress; but his compassion was tardy; his efforts were faint and unavailing; and Constantinople had fallen before the squadrons of Genoa and Venice could sail from their harbours.[27] Even the princes of the Morea and of the Greek islands affected a cold neutrality: the Genoese colony of Galata negotiated a private treaty; and the sultan indulged them in the delusive hope that by his clemency they might survive the ruin of the empire. A plebeian crowd and some Byzantine nobles basely withdrew from the danger of their country; and the avarice of the rich denied the emperor, and reserved for the Turks, the secret treasures which might have raised in their defence whole armies of mercenaries.[28] The indigent and solitary prince prepared however to sustain his formidable adversary; but if his courage were equal to the peril, his strength was inadequate to the contest. In the beginning of the spring the Turkish vanguard swept the towns and villages as far as the gates of Constantinople: submission was spared and protected; whatever presumed to resist was exterminated with fire and sword. The Greek places on the Black Sea, Mesembria, Acheloum, and Bizon, surrendered on the first summons; Selymbria alone deserved the honours of a siege or blockade; and the bold inhabitants, while they were invested by land, launched their boats, pillaged the opposite coast of Cyzicus, and sold their captives in the public market. But on the approach of Mohammed himself all was silent and prostrate: he first halted at the distance of five miles; and, from thence advancing in battle array, planted before the gate of St. Romanus the Imperial standard; and on the sixth day of April formed the memorable siege of Constantinople.

The troops of Asia and Europe extended on the right and left from the Propontis to the harbour; the Janizaries in the front were stationed before the sultan's tent; the Ottoman line was covered by a deep intrenchment; and a subordinate army enclosed the suburb of Galata, and watched the doubtful faith of the Genoese. The inquisitive Philelphus, who resided in Greece about thirty years before the siege, is confident that all the Turkish forces of any name or value could not exceed the number of sixty thousand horse and twenty thousand foot; and he upbraids the pusillanimity of the nations who had tamely yielded to a handful of barbarians. Such indeed might be the regular establishment of the *Capiculi*,[29] the troops of the Porte who marched with the prince, and were paid from his royal treasury. But the bashaws, in their respective governments, maintained or levied a provincial militia; many lands were held by a military tenure; many volunteers were attracted by the hope of spoil; and the sound of the holy trumpet invited a swarm of hungry and fearless fanatics, who might contribute at least to multiply the terrors, and in a first attack to blunt the swords of the Christians. The whole mass of the Turkish powers is magnified by Ducas, Chalcocondyles, and Leonard of Chios, to the amount of three or four hundred thousand men; but Phranza was a less remote and more accurate judge; and his precise definition of two hundred and fifty-eight thousand does not exceed the measure of experience and probability.[30] The navy of the besiegers was less formidable: the Propontis was overspread with three hundred and twenty sail; but of these no more than eighteen could be rated as galleys of war; and the far greater part must be degraded to the condition of store-ships and transports, which poured into the camp fresh supplies of men, ammunition, and provisions. In her last decay Constantinople was still peopled with more than a hundred thousand inhabitants; but these numbers are found in the accounts, not of war, but of captivity; and they mostly consisted of mechanics, of priests, of women, and of men devoid of that spirit which even women have sometimes exerted for the common safety. I can suppose, I could almost excuse, the reluctance of subjects to serve on a distant frontier, at the will of a tyrant; but the man who dares not expose his life in the defence of his children and his property has lost in society the first and most active energies of nature. By the emperor's command a particular inquiry had been made through the streets and houses, how many of the citizens, or even of the monks, were able and willing to bear arms for their country. The lists were intrusted to Phranza;[31] and after a diligent addition he informed his master, with grief and surprise, that the national defence was reduced to four thousand nine hundred and seventy *Romans*. Between Constantine and his faithful minister this comfortless secret was preserved; and a sufficient proportion of shields, cross-bows, and muskets, was distributed from the arsenal to the city bands. They derived some accession from a body of two thousand strangers, under the command of John Justiniani, a noble Genoese; a liberal donative was advanced to these auxiliaries; and a princely recompense, the isle of Lemnos, was promised to the valour and victory of their chief. A strong chain was drawn across the mouth of the harbour: it was supported by some Greek and Italian vessels of war and merchandise; and the ships of every Christian nation, that successively arrived from Candia and the Black Sea, were detained for the public service. Against the powers of the Ottoman empire, a city of the extent of thirteen, perhaps of sixteen, miles was defended by a scanty garrison of seven or eight thousand soldiers. Europe and Asia were open to the besiegers; but the strength and provisions of the Greeks must sustain a daily decrease; nor could they indulge the expectation of any foreign succour or supply.

The primitive Romans would have drawn their swords in the resolution of death or conquest. The primitive Christians might have embraced each other, and awaited in patience and charity the stroke of martyrdom. But the Greeks of Constantinople were animated only by the spirit of religion, and that spirit was productive only of animosity and discord. Before his death the emperor John Palæologus had renounced the unpopular measure of a union with the Latins; nor was the idea revived till the distress of his brother Constantine imposed a last trial of flattery and dissimulation.[32] With the demand of temporal aid his ambassadors were instructed to mingle the assurance of spiritual obedience: his neglect of the church was excused by the urgent cares of the state; and his orthodox wishes solicited the presence of a Roman legate. The Vatican had been too often deluded; yet the signs of repentance could not decently be overlooked; a legate was more easily granted than an army; and about six months before the final destruction, the cardinal Isidore of Russia appeared in that character with a retinue of priests and soldiers. The emperor saluted him as a friend and father; respectfully listened to his public and private sermons; and with the most obsequious of the clergy and laymen subscribed the act of union, as it had been ratified in the council of Florence. On the twelfth of December the two nations, in the church of St. Sophia, joined in the communion of sacrifice and prayer; and the names of the two pontiffs were solemnly commemorated; the names of Nicholas the Fifth, the vicar of Christ, and of the patriarch Gregory, who had been driven into exile by a rebellious people.

But the dress and language of the Latin priest who officiated at the altar were an object of scandal; and it was observed with horror that he consecrated a cake or wafer of *unleavened* bread, and poured cold water into the cup of the sacrament. A national historian acknowledges with a blush that none of his countrymen, not the emperor himself, were sincere in this occasional conformity.[33] Their hasty and unconditional submission was palliated by a promise of future revisal; but the best, or the worst, of their excuses was the confession of their own perjury. When they were pressed by the reproaches of their honest brethren, "Have patience," they whispered, "have patience till God shall have delivered the city from the great dragon who seeks to devour us. You shall then perceive whether we are truly reconciled with the Azymites." But patience is not the attribute of zeal; nor can the arts of a court be adapted to the freedom and violence of popular enthusiasm. From the dome of St. Sophia the inhabitants of either sex, and of every degree, rushed in crowds to the cell of the monk Gennadius,[34] to consult the oracle of the church. The holy man was invisible; entranced, as it should seem, in deep meditation, or divine rapture: but he had exposed on the door of his cell a speaking tablet; and they successively withdrew, after reading these tremendous words: "O miserable Romans, why will ye abandon

e truth; and why, instead of confiding in God
ill ye put your trust in the Italians? In losing
our faith you will lose your city. Have mercy
a me, O Lord! I protest in thy presence that I
n innocent of the crime. O miserable Romans,
insider, pause, and repent. At the same mo-
ent that you renounce the religion of your
thers, by embracing impiety, you submit to a
reign servitude." According to the advice of
ennadius, the religious virgins, as pure as
igels, and as proud as demons, rejected the act
' union, and abjured all communion with the
resent and future associates of the Latins; and
eir example was applauded and imitated by
ie greatest part of the clergy and people. From
ie monastery the devout Greeks dispersed
iemselves in the taverns; drank confusion to
ie slaves of the pope; emptied their glasses in
onour of the image of the holy Virgin; and
esought her to defend against Mohammed the
ity which she had formerly saved from Chos-
oes and the Chagan. In the double intoxica-
on of zeal and wine, they valiantly exclaimed,
What occasion have we for succour, or union,
r Latins? far from us be the worship of the
azymites!" During the winter that preceded
he Turkish conquest the nation was distracted
by this epidemical frenzy; and the season of
Lent, the approach of Easter, instead of breath-
ng charity and love, served only to fortify the
bstinacy and influence of the zealots. The
onfessors scrutinised and alarmed the con-
cience of their votaries, and a rigorous penance
vas imposed on those who had received the
ommunion from a priest who had given an
xpress or tacit consent to the union. His service
t the altar propagated the infection to the
nute and simple spectators of the ceremony:
hey forfeited, by the impure spectacle, the
virtue of the sacerdotal character; nor was it
awful, even in danger of sudden death, to in-
roke the assistance of their prayers or absolu-
ion. No sooner had the church of St. Sophia
oeen polluted by the Latin sacrifice than it was
leserted as a Jewish synagogue, or a heathen
emple, by the clergy and people; and a vast
and gloomy silence prevailed in that venerable
Iome, which had so often smoked with a cloud
of incense, blazed with innumerable lights, and
resounded with the voice of prayer and thanksgiving. The Latins were the most odious of
neretics and infidels; and the first minister of
the empire, the great duke, was heard to declare
that he had rather behold in Constantinople
the turban of Mohammed than the pope's tiara
or a cardinal's hat.[35] A sentiment so unworthy

of Christians and patriots was familiar and fatal
to the Greeks: the emperor was deprived of the
affection and support of his subjects; and their
native cowardice was sanctified by resignation
to the divine decree or the visionary hope of a
miraculous deliverance.

Of the triangle which composes the figure of
Constantinople the two sides along the sea were
made inaccessible to an enemy; the Propontis
by nature, and the harbour by art. Between the
two waters, the basis of the triangle, the land
side was protected by a double wall and a deep
ditch of the depth of one hundred feet. Against
this line of fortification, which Phranza, an eye
witness, prolongs to the measure of six miles,[36]
the Ottomans directed their principal attack;
and the emperor, after distributing the service
and command of the most perilous stations,
undertook the defence of the external wall. In
the first days of the siege the Greek soldiers descended into the ditch, or sallied into the field;
but they soon discovered that, in the proportion
of their numbers, one Christian was of more
value than twenty Turks; and, after these bold
preludes, they were prudently content to maintain the rampart with their missile weapons.
Nor should this prudence be accused of pusillanimity. The nation was indeed pusillanimous
and base; but the last Constantine deserves the
name of a hero: his noble band of volunteers
was inspired with Roman virtue; and the foreign auxiliaries supported the honour of the
Western chivalry. The incessant volleys of
lances and arrows were accompanied with the
smoke, the sound, and the fire of their musketry
and cannon. Their small arms discharged at
the same time either five, or even ten, balls of
lead, of the size of a walnut; and, according to
the closeness of the ranks and the force of the
powder, several breastplates and bodies were
transpierced by the same shot. But the Turkish
approaches were soon sunk in trenches or covered with ruins. Each day added to the science
of the Christians; but their inadequate stock of
gunpowder was wasted in the operations of each
day. Their ordnance was not powerful either in
size or number; and if they possessed some
heavy cannon, they feared to plant them on the
walls, lest the aged structure should be shaken
and overthrown by the explosion.[37] The same
destructive secret had been revealed to the
Moslems; by whom it was employed with the
superior energy of zeal, riches, and despotism.
The great cannon of Mohammed has been separately noticed; an important and visible object in the history of the times: but that enor-

mous engine was flanked by two fellows almost of equal magnitude:[38] the long order of the Turkish artillery was pointed against the walls; fourteen batteries thundered at once on the most accessible places; and of one of these it is ambiguously expressed that it was mounted with one hundred and thirty guns, or that it discharged one hundred and thirty bullets. Yet in the power and activity of the sultan we may discern the infancy of the new science. Under a master who counted the moments the great cannon could be loaded and fired no more than seven times in one day.[39] The heated metal unfortunately burst; several workmen were destroyed, and the skill of an artist was admired who bethought himself of preventing the danger and the accident, by pouring oil, after each explosion, into the mouth of the cannon.

The first random shots were productive of more sound than effect; and it was by the advice of a Christian that the engineers were taught to level their aim against the two opposite sides of the salient angles of a bastion. However imperfect, the weight and repetition of the fire made some impression on the walls; and the Turks, pushing their approaches to the edge of the ditch, attempted to fill the enormous chasm and to build a road to the assault.[40] Innumerable fascines, and hogsheads, and trunks of trees, were heaped on each other; and such was the impetuosity of the throng, that the foremost and the weakest were pushed headlong down the precipice and instantly buried under the accumulated mass. To fill the ditch was the toil of the besiegers; to clear away the rubbish was the safety of the besieged; and, after a long and bloody conflict, the web that had been woven in the day was still unravelled in the night. The next resource of Mohammed was the practice of mines; but the soil was rocky; in every attempt he was stopped and undermined by the Christian engineers; nor had the art been yet invented of replenishing those subterraneous passages with gunpowder and blowing whole towers and cities into the air.[41] A circumstance that distinguishes the siege of Constantinople is the reunion of the ancient and modern artillery. The cannon were intermingled with the mechanical engines for casting stones and darts; the bullet and the battering-ram were directed against the same walls; nor had the discovery of gunpowder superseded the use of the liquid and unextinguishable fire. A wooden turret of the largest size was advanced on rollers: this portable magazine of ammunition and fascines was protected by a threefold covering of bulls'

hides; incessant volleys were securely discharged from the loopholes; in the front three doors were contrived for the alternate sally and retreat of the soldiers and workmen. They ascended by a staircase to the upper platform, and, as high as the level of that platform, a scaling-ladder could be raised by pulleys to form a bridge and grapple with the adverse rampart. By these various arts of annoyance, some as new as they were pernicious to the Greeks, the tower of St. Romanus was at length overturned: after a severe struggle the Turks were repulsed from the breach and interrupted by darkness; but they trusted that with the return of light they should renew the attack with fresh vigour and decisive success. Of this pause of action, this interval of hope, each moment was improved by the activity of the emperor and Justiniani, who passed the night on the spot, and urged the labours which involved the safety of the church and city. At the dawn of day the impatient sultan perceived, with astonishment and grief, that his wooden turret had been reduced to ashes: the ditch was cleared and restored, and the tower of St. Romanus was again strong and entire. He deplored the failure of his design, and uttered a profane exclamation, that the word of the thirty-seven thousand prophets should not have compelled him to believe that such a work, in so short a time, could have been accomplished by the infidels.

The generosity of the Christian princes was cold and tardy; but in the first apprehension of a siege Constantine had negotiated, in the isles of the Archipelago, the Morea, and Sicily, the most indispensable supplies. As early as the beginning of April, five[42] great ships, equipped for merchandise and war, would have sailed from the harbour of Chios, had not the wind blown obstinately from the north.[43] One of these ships bore the Imperial flag; the remaining four belonged to the Genoese; and they were laden with wheat and barley, with wine, oil, and vegetables, and, above all, with soldiers and mariners, for the service of the capital. After a tedious delay a gentle breeze, and on the second day a strong gale from the south, carried them through the Hellespont and the Propontis; but the city was already invested by sea and land, and the Turkish fleet, at the entrance of the Bosphorus, was stretched from shore to shore, in the form of a crescent, to intercept, or at least to repel, these bold auxiliaries. The reader who has present to his mind the geographical picture of Constantinople will conceive and admire the greatness of the spectacle. The five Christian hips continued to advance with joyful shouts, and a full press both of sails and oars, against the hostile fleet of three hundred vessels; and the rampart, the camp, the coasts of Europe and Asia, were lined with innumerable spectators, who anxiously awaited the event of this momentous succour. At the first view that event could not appear doubtful; the superiority of the Moslems was beyond all measure or account, and, in a calm, their numbers and valour must inevitably have prevailed. But their hasty and imperfect navy had been created, not by the genius of the people, but by the will of the sultan: in the height of their prosperity the Turks have acknowledged that, if God had given them the earth, he had left the sea to the infidels;[44] and a series of defeats, a rapid progress of decay, had established the truth of their modest confession. Except eighteen galleys of some force, the rest of their fleet consisted of open boats, rudely constructed and awkwardly managed, crowded with troops, and destitute of cannon; and since courage arises in a great measure from the consciousness of strength, the bravest of the Janizaries might tremble on a new element. In the Christian squadron five stout and lofty ships were guided by skilful pilots, and manned with the veterans of Italy and Greece, long practised in the arts and perils of the sea. Their weight was directed to sink or scatter the weak obstacles that impeded their passage: their artillery swept the waters; their liquid fire was poured on the heads of the adversaries, who, with the design of boarding, presumed to approach them; and the winds and waves are always on the side of the ablest navigators. In this conflict the Imperial vessel, which had been almost overpowered, was rescued by the Genoese; but the Turks, in a distant and a closer attack, were twice repulsed with considerable loss. Mohammed himself sat on horseback on the beach, to encourage their valour by his voice and presence, by the promise of reward, and by fear more potent than the fear of the enemy. The passions of his soul, and even the gestures of his body,[45] seemed to imitate the actions of the combatants; and, as if he had been the lord of nature, he spurred his horse with a fearless and impotent effort into the sea. His loud reproaches, and the clamours of the camp, urged the Ottomans to a third attack, more fatal and bloody than the two former; and I must repeat, though I cannot credit, the evidence of Phranza, who affirms, from their own mouth, that they lost above twelve thousand men in the slaughter of the day. They fled in disorder to the shores of Europe and Asia, while the Christian squadron, triumphant and unhurt, steered along the Bosphorus, and securely anchored within the chain of the harbour. In the confidence of victory, they boasted that the whole Turkish power must have yielded to their arms; but the admiral, or captain bashaw, found some consolation for a painful wound in his eye, by representing that accident as the cause of his defeat. Baltha Ogli was a renegade of the race of the Bulgarian princes: his military character was tainted with the unpopular vice of avarice; and under the despotism of the prince or people, misfortune is a sufficient evidence of guilt. His rank and services were annihilated by the displeasure of Mohammed. In the royal presence, the captain bashaw was extended on the ground by four slaves, and received one hundred strokes with a golden rod:[46] his death had been pronounced, and he adored the clemency of the sultan, who was satisfied with the milder punishment of confiscation and exile. The introduction of this supply revived the hopes of the Greeks, and accused the supineness of their Western allies. Amidst the deserts of Anatolia and the rocks of Palestine, the millions of the crusades had buried themselves in a voluntary and inevitable grave; but the situation of the Imperial city was strong against her enemies, and accessible to her friends; and a rational and moderate armament of the maritime states might have saved the relics of the Roman name, and maintained a Christian fortress in the heart of the Ottoman empire. Yet this was the sole and feeble attempt for the deliverance of Constantinople: the more distant powers were insensible of its danger; and the ambassador of Hungary, or at least of Huniades, resided in the Turkish camp, to remove the fears and to direct the operations of the sultan.[47]

It was difficult for the Greeks to penetrate the secret of the divan; yet the Greeks are persuaded that a resistance so obstinate and surprising had fatigued the perseverance of Mohammed. He began to meditate a retreat; and the siege would have been speedily raised, if the ambition and jealousy of the second vizir had not opposed the perfidious advice of Calil Bashaw, who still maintained a secret correspondence with the Byzantine court. The reduction of the city appeared to be hopeless, unless a double attack could be made from the harbour as well as from the land; but the harbour was inaccessible: an impenetrable chain was now defended by eight large ships, more than twenty of a smaller size, with several galleys and sloops; and, instead of forcing this barrier, the Turk might apprehend a naval sally and a second encounter in the open sea. In this perplexity the genius of Mohammed conceived and executed a plan of a bold and marvellous cast, of transporting by land his lighter vessels and military stores from the Bosphorus into the higher part of the harbour. The distance is about ten miles; the ground is uneven, and was overspread with thickets; and, as the road must be opened behind the suburb of Galata, their free passage or total destruction must depend on the option of the Genoese. But these selfish merchants were ambitious of the favour of being the last devoured, and the deficiency of art was supplied by the strength of obedient myriads. A level way was covered with a broad platform of strong and solid planks; and to render them more slippery and smooth, they were anointed with the fat of sheep and oxen. Fourscore light galleys and brigantines of fifty and thirty oars were disembarked on the Bosphorus shore, arranged successively on rollers, and drawn forwards by the power of men and pulleys. Two guides or pilots were stationed at the helm and the prow of each vessel: the sails were unfurled to the winds, and the labour was cheered by song and acclamation. In the course of a single night this Turkish fleet painfully climbed the hill, steered over the plain, and was launched from the declivity into the shallow waters of the harbour, far above the molestation of the deeper vessels of the Greeks. The real importance of this operation was magnified by the consternation and confidence which it inspired; but the notorious, unquestionable fact was displayed before the eyes, and is recorded by the pens, of the two nations.[48] A similar stratagem had been repeatedly practised by the ancients;[49] the Ottoman galleys (I must again repeat) should be considered as large boats; and, if we compare the magnitude and the distance, the obstacles and the means, the boasted miracle[50] has perhaps been equalled by the industry of our own times.[51] As soon as Mohammed had occupied the upper harbour with a fleet and army, he constructed in the narrowest part a bridge, or rather mole, of fifty cubits in breadth and one hundred in length: it was formed of casks and hogsheads, joined with rafters, linked with iron, and covered with a solid floor. On this floating battery he planted one of his largest cannon, while the fourscore galleys, with troops and scaling-ladders, approached the most accessible side, which had formerly been stormed by

the Latin conquerors. The indolence of the Christians has been accused for not destroying these unfinished works; but their fire, by a superior fire, was controlled and silenced; nor were they wanting in a nocturnal attempt to burn the vessels as well as the bridge of the sultan. His vigilance prevented their approach: their foremost galliots were sunk or taken; forty youths, the bravest of Italy and Greece, were inhumanly massacred at his command: nor could the emperor's grief be assuaged by the just though cruel retaliation of exposing from the walls the heads of two hundred and sixty Musulman captives. After a siege of forty days the fate of Constantinople could no longer be averted. The diminutive garrison was exhausted by a double attack: the fortifications, which had stood for ages against hostile violence, were dismantled on all sides by the Ottoman cannon; many breaches were opened, and near the gate of St. Romanus four towers had been levelled with the ground. For the payment of his feeble and mutinous troops, Constantine was compelled to despoil the churches with the promise of fourfold restitution; and his sacrilege offered a new reproach to the enemies of the union. A spirit of discord impaired the remnant of the Christian strength: the Genoese and Venetian auxiliaries asserted the pre-eminence of their respective service; and Justiniani and the great duke, whose ambition was not extinguished by the common danger, accused each other of treachery and cowardice.

During the siege of Constantinople the words of peace and capitulation had been sometimes pronounced; and several embassies had passed between the camp and the city.[52] The Greek emperor was humbled by adversity; and would have yielded to any terms compatible with religion and royalty. The Turkish sultan was desirous of sparing the blood of his soldiers; still more desirous of securing for his own use the Byzantine treasures; and he accomplished a sacred duty in presenting to the *Gabours* the choice of circumcision, of tribute, or of death. The avarice of Mohammed might have been satisfied with an annual sum of one hundred thousand ducats; but his ambition grasped the capital of the East: to the prince he offered a rich equivalent, to the people a free toleration, or a safe departure: but after some fruitless treaty, he declared his resolution of finding either a throne or a grave under the walls of Constantinople. A sense of honour, and the fear of universal reproach, forbade Palæologus to resign the city into the hands of the Ottomans.

and he determined to abide the last extremities of war. Several days were employed by the sultan in the preparations of the assault; and a respite was granted by his favourite science of astrology, which had fixed on the twenty-ninth of May as the fortunate and fatal hour. On the evening of the twenty-seventh he issued his final orders; assembled in his presence the military chiefs; and dispersed his heralds through the camp to proclaim the duty and the motives of the perilous enterprise. Fear is the first principle of a despotic government; and his menaces were expressed in the Oriental style, that the fugitives and deserters, had they the wings of a bird,[53] should not escape from his inexorable justice. The greatest part of his bashaws and Janizaries were the offspring of Christian parents: but the glories of the Turkish name were perpetuated by successive adoption; and in the gradual change of individuals, the spirit of a legion, a regiment, or an *oda*, is kept alive by imitation and discipline. In this holy warfare the Moslems were exhorted to purify their minds with prayer, their bodies with seven ablutions; and to abstain from food till the close of the ensuing day. A crowd of dervishes visited the tents, to instil the desire of martyrdom, and the assurance of spending an immortal youth amidst the rivers and gardens of paradise, and in the embraces of the black-eyed virgins. Yet Mohammed principally trusted to the efficacy of temporal and visible rewards. A double pay was promised to the victorious troops; "The city and the buildings," said Mohammed, "are mine; but I resign to your valour the captives and the spoil, the treasures of gold and beauty; be rich and be happy. Many are the provinces of my empire: the intrepid soldier who first ascends the walls of Constantinople shall be rewarded with the government of the fairest and most wealthy; and my gratitude shall accumulate his honours and fortunes above the measure of his own hopes." Such various and potent motives diffused among the Turks a general ardour, regardless of life and impatient for action: the camp re-echoed with the Moslem shouts of "God is God: there is but one God, and Mohammed is the apostle of God;"[54] and the sea and land, from Galata to the seven towers, were illuminated by the blaze of their nocturnal fires.

Far different was the state of the Christians; who, with loud and impotent complaints, deplored the guilt, or the punishment, of their sins. The celestial image of the Virgin had been exposed in solemn procession; but their divine patroness was deaf to their entreaties: they accused the obstinacy of the emperor for refusing a timely surrender; anticipated the horrors of their fate; and sighed for the repose and security of Turkish servitude. The noblest of the Greeks and the bravest of the allies, were summoned to the palace, to prepare them, on the evening of the twenty-eighth, for the duties and dangers of the general assault. The last speech of Palæologus was the funeral oration of the Roman empire:[55] he promised, he conjured, and he vainly attempted to infuse the hope which was extinguished in his own mind. In this world all was comfortless and gloomy; and neither the Gospel nor the church have proposed any conspicuous recompense to the heroes who fall in the service of their country. But the example of their prince, and the confinement of a siege, had armed these warriors with the courage of despair; and the pathetic scene is described by the feelings of the historian Phranza, who was himself present at this mournful assembly. They wept, they embraced: regardless of their families and fortunes, they devoted their lives; and each commander, departing to his station, maintained all night a vigilant and anxious watch on the rampart. The emperor, and some faithful companions, entered the dome of St. Sophia, which in a few hours was to be converted into a mosque; and devoutly received, with tears and prayers, the sacrament of the holy communion. He reposed some moments in the palace, which resounded with cries and lamentations; solicited the pardon of all whom he might have injured;[56] and mounted on horseback to visit the guards, and explore the motions of the enemy. The distress and fall of the last Constantine are more glorious than the long prosperity of the Byzantine Cæsars.

In the confusion of darkness an assailant may sometimes succeed; but in this great and general attack, the military judgment and astrological knowledge of Mohammed advised him to expect the morning, the memorable twenty-ninth of May, in the fourteen hundred and fifty-third year of the Christian era. The preceding night had been strenuously employed: the troops, the cannon, and the fascines were advanced to the edge of the ditch, which in many parts presented a smooth and level passage to the breach; and his fourscore galleys almost touched, with the prows and their scaling ladders, the less defensible walls of the harbour. Under pain of death, silence was enjoined; but the physical laws of motion and sound are not obedient to discipline or fear: each individual might suppress his voice and measure his footsteps; but the march and labour of thousands must inevitably produce a strange confusion of dissonant clamours, which reached the ears of the watchmen of the towers. At daybreak, without the customary signal of the morning gun, the Turks assaulted the city by sea and land; and the similitude of a twined or twisted thread has been applied to the closeness and continuity of their line of attack.[57] The foremost ranks consisted of the refuse of the host, a voluntary crowd who fought without order or command; of the feebleness of age or childhood, of peasants and vagrants, and of all who had joined the camp in the blind hope of plunder and martyrdom. The common impulse drove them onwards to the wall; the most audacious to climb were instantly precipitated; and not a dart, not a bullet, of the Christians, was idly wasted on the accumulated throng. But their strength and ammunition were exhausted in this laborious defence: the ditch was filled with the bodies of the slain; they supported the footsteps of their companions; and of this devoted vanguard the death was more serviceable than the life. Under their respective bashaws and sanjaks, the troops of Anatolia and Romania were successively led to the charge: their progress was various and doubtful; but, after a conflict of two hours, the Greeks still maintained and improved their advantage; and the voice of the emperor was heard, encouraging his soldiers to achieve, by a last effort, the deliverance of their country. In that fatal moment the Janizaries arose, fresh, vigorous, and invincible. The sultan himself on horseback, with an iron mace in his hand, was the spectator and judge of their valour; he was surrounded by ten thousand of his domestic troops, whom he reserved for the decisive occasion; and the tide of battle was directed and impelled by his voice and eye. His numerous ministers of justice were posted behind the line, to urge, to restrain, and to punish; and if danger was in the front, shame and inevitable death were in the rear, of the fugitives. The cries of fear and of pain were drowned in the martial music of drums, trumpets, and attaballs; and experience has proved that the mechanical operation of sounds, by quickening the circulation of the blood and spirits, will act on the human machine more forcibly than the eloquence of reason and honour. From the lines, the galleys, and the bridge, the Ottoman artillery thundered on all sides; and the camp and city, the Greeks and the Turks, were involved in a cloud of smoke, which

could only be dispelled by the final deliverance or destruction of the Roman empire. The single combats of the heroes of history or fable amuse our fancy and engage our affections: the skilful evolutions of war may inform the mind, and improve a necessary, though pernicious, science. But in the uniform and odious pictures of a general assault, all is blood, and horror, and confusion; nor shall I strive, at the distance of three centuries and a thousand miles, to delineate a scene of which there could be no spectators, and of which the actors themselves were incapable of forming any just or adequate idea.

The immediate loss of Constantinople may be ascribed to the bullet, or arrow, which pierced the gauntlet of John Justiniani. The sight of his blood, and the exquisite pain, appalled the courage of the chief, whose arms and counsels were the firmest rampart of the city. As he withdrew from his station in quest of a surgeon, his flight was perceived and stopped by the indefatigable emperor. "Your wound," exclaimed Palæologus, "is slight; the danger is pressing: your presence is necessary; and whither will you retire?"—"I will retire," said the trembling Genoese, "by the same road which God has opened to the Turks;" and at these words he hastily passed through one of the breaches of the inner wall. By this pusillanimous act he stained the honours of a military life; and the few days which he survived in Galata, or the isle of Chios, were embittered by his own and the public reproach.[58] His example was imitated by the greatest part of the Latin auxiliaries, and the defence began to slacken when the attack was pressed with redoubled vigour. The number of the Ottomans was fifty, perhaps a hundred, times superior to that of the Christians; the double walls were reduced by the cannon to a heap of ruins: in a circuit of several miles some places must be found more easy of access, or more feebly guarded; and if the besiegers could penetrate in a single point, the whole city was irrecoverably lost. The first who deserved the sultan's reward was Hassan the Janizary, of gigantic stature and strength. With his scimitar in one hand and his buckler in the other, he ascended the outward fortification: of the thirty Janizaries who were emulous of his valour, eighteen perished in the bold adventure. Hassan and his twelve companions had reached the summit: the giant was precipitated from the rampart: he rose on one knee, and was again oppressed by a shower of darts and stones. But his success had proved that the achievement was possible: the walls and towers were instantly covered with a swarm of Turks; and the Greeks, now driven from the vantage ground, were overwhelmed by increasing multitudes. Amidst these multitudes, the emperor,[59] who accomplished all the duties of a general and a soldier, was long seen and finally lost. The nobles, who fought round his person, sustained, till their last breath, the honourable names of Palæologus and Cantacuzene: his mournful exclamation was heard, "Cannot there be found Christian to cut off my head?"[60] and his last fear was that of falling alive into the hands of the infidels.[61] The prudent despair of Constantine cast away the purple: amidst the tumult he fell by an unknown hand, and his body was buried under a mountain of the slain. After his death resistance and order were no more: the Greeks fled towards the city; and many were pressed and stifled in the narrow pass of the gate of St. Romanus. The victorious Turks rushed through the breaches of the inner wall; and as they advanced into the streets, they were soon joined by their brethren, who had forced the gate Phenar on the side of the harbour.[62] In the first heat of the pursuit about two thousand Christians were put to the sword; but avarice soon prevailed over cruelty; and the victors acknowledged that they should immediately have given quarter, if the valour of the emperor and his chosen bands had not prepared them for a similar opposition in every part of the capital. It was thus, after a siege of fifty-three days, that Constantinople, which had defied the power of Chosroes, the Chagan, and the caliphs, was irretrievably subdued by the arms of Mohammed the Second. Her empire only had been suberted by the Latins: her religion was trampled in the dust by the Moslem conquerors.[63]

The tidings of misfortune fly with a rapid wing; yet such was the extent of Constantinople, that the more distant quarters might prolong, some moments, the happy ignorance of their ruin.[64] But in the general consternation, in the feelings of selfish or social anxiety, in the tumult and thunder of the assault, a *sleepless* night and morning must have elapsed; nor can I believe that many Grecian ladies were awakened by the Janizaries from a sound and tranquil slumber. On the assurance of the public calamity, the houses and convents were instantly deserted; and the trembling inhabitants flocked together in the streets, like a herd of timid animals, as if accumulated weakness could be productive of strength, or in the vain hope that amid the crowd each individual might be safe and invisible. From every part of the capital they flowed into the church of St. Sophia: in the space of an hour, the sanctuary, the choir, the nave, the upper and lower galleries, were filled with the multitudes of fathers and husbands, of women and children, of priests, monks, and religious virgins: the doors were barred on the inside, and they sought protection from the sacred dome which they had so lately abhorred as a profane and polluted edifice. Their confidence was founded on the prophecy of an enthusiast or impostor, that one day the Turks would enter Constantinople, and pursue the Romans as far as the column of Constantine in the square before St. Sophia: but that this would be the term of their calamities; that an angel would descend from heaven with a sword in his hand, and would deliver the empire, with that celestial weapon, to a poor man seated at the foot of the column. "Take this sword," would he say, "and avenge the people of the Lord." At these animating words the Turks would instantly fly, and the victorious Romans would drive them from the West, and from all Anatolia, as far as the frontiers of Persia. It is on this occasion that Ducas, with some fancy and much truth, upbraids the discord and obstinacy of the Greeks. "Had that angel appeared," exclaims the historian, "had he offered to exterminate your foes if you would consent to the union of the church, even then, in that fatal moment, you would have rejected your safety, or have deceived your God."[65]

While they expected the descent of the tardy angel, the doors were broken with axes; and as the Turks encountered no resistance, their bloodless hands were employed in selecting and securing the multitude of their prisoners. Youth, beauty, and the appearance of wealth, attracted their choice; and the right of property was decided among themselves by a prior seizure, by personal strength, and by the authority of command. In the space of an hour the male captives were bound with cords, the females with their veils and girdles. The senators were linked with their slaves; the prelates with the porters of the church; and young men of a plebeian class with noble maids whose faces had been invisible to the sun and their nearest kindred. In this common captivity the ranks of society were confounded; the ties of nature were cut asunder; and the inexorable soldier was careless of the father's groans, the tears of the mother, and the lamentations of the children. The loudest in their wailings were the nuns, who were torn from the altar with naked bosoms, outstretched hands, and dishevelled hair; and we should piously believe that few could be tempted to prefer the vigils of the harem to those of the monastery. Of these unfortunate Greeks, of these domestic animals, whole strings were rudely driven through the streets; and as the conquerors were eager to return for more prey, their trembling pace was quickened with menaces and blows. At the same hour a similar rapine was exercised in all the churches and monasteries, in all the palaces and habitations, of the capital; nor could any place, however sacred or sequestered, protect the persons or the property of the Greeks. Above sixty thousand of this devoted people were transported from the city to the camp and fleet; exchanged or sold according to the caprice or interest of their masters, and dispersed in remote servitude through the provinces of the Ottoman empire. Among these we may notice some remarkable characters. The historian Phranza, first chamberlain and principal secretary, was involved with his family in the common lot. After suffering four months the hardships of slavery, he recovered his freedom: in the ensuing winter he ventured to Adrianople, and ransomed his wife from the *mir bashi*, or master of the horse; but his two children, in the flower of youth and beauty, had been seized for the use of Mohammed himself. The daughter of Phranza died in the seraglio, perhaps a virgin: his son, in the fifteenth year of his age, preferred death to infamy, and was stabbed by the hand of the royal lover.[66] A deed thus inhuman cannot surely be expiated by the taste and liberality with which he released a Grecian matron and her two daughters, on receiving a Latin ode from Philelphus, who had chosen a wife in that noble family.[67] The pride or cruelty of Mohammed would have been most sensibly gratified by the capture of a Roman legate; but the dexterity of Cardinal Isidore eluded the search, and he escaped from Galata in a plebeian habit.[68] The chain and entrance of the outward harbour was still occupied by the Italian ships of merchandise and war. They had signalised their valour in the siege: they embraced the moment of retreat, while the Turkish mariners were dissipated in the pillage of the city. When they hoisted sail, the beach was covered with a suppliant and lamentable crowd; but the means of transportation were scanty; the Venetians and Genoese selected their countrymen; and, notwithstanding the fairest promises of the sultan, the inhabitants of Galata evacuated their houses, and embarked with their most precious effects.

In the fall and the sack of great cities an historian is condemned to repeat the tale of uni form calamity: the same effects must be pro duced by the same passions; and when thos passions may be indulged without control, smal alas! is the difference between civilised an savage man. Amidst the vague exclamations o bigotry and hatred, the Turks are not accuse of a wanton or immoderate effusion of Christia blood: but according to their maxims (th maxims of antiquity), the lives of the van quished were forfeited; and the legitimate re ward of the conqueror was derived from th service, the sale, or the ransom of his captives both sexes.[69] The wealth of Constantinople ha been granted by the sultan to his victoriou troops; and the rapine of an hour is more pr ductive than the industry of years. But as n regular division was attempted of the spoil, th respective shares were not determined by merit and the rewards of valour were stolen away b the followers of the camp, who had declined th toil and danger of the battle. The narrative their depredations could not afford eithe amusement or instruction: the total amount, i the last poverty of the empire, has been value at four millions of ducats;[70] and of this sum small part was the property of the Venetian the Genoese, the Florentines, and the merchan of Ancona. Of these foreigners the stock wa improved in quick and perpetual circulation but the riches of the Greeks were displayed i the idle ostentation of palaces and wardrobe or deeply buried in treasures of ingots and o coin, lest it should be demanded at their hand for the defence of their country. The profana tion and plunder of the monasteries an churches excited the most tragic complaint The dome of St. Sophia itself, the earthl heaven, the second firmament, the vehicle the cherubim, the throne of the glory of God, was despoiled of the oblations of ages; and th gold and silver, the pearls and jewels, the vas and sacerdotal ornaments, were most wickedl converted to the service of mankind. After th divine images had been stripped of all tha could be valuable to a profane eye, the canva or the wood, was torn, or broken, or burnt, trod under foot, or applied, in the stables or th kitchen, to the vilest uses. The example of sa rilege was imitated, however, from the Lati conquerors of Constantinople; and the trea ment which Christ, the Virgin, and the sain had sustained from the guilty Catholic, migh be inflicted by the zealous Musulman on th monuments of idolatry. Perhaps, instead joining the public clamour, a philosopher wi observe that in the decline of the arts the workmanship could not be more valuable than the work, and that a fresh supply of visions and miracles would speedily be renewed by the craft of the priest and the credulity of the people. He will more seriously deplore the loss of the Byzantine libraries, which were destroyed or scattered in the general confusion: one hundred and twenty thousand manuscripts are said to have disappeared;[72] ten volumes might be purchased for a single ducat; and the same ignominious price, too high perhaps for a shelf of theology, included the whole works of Aristotle and Homer, the noblest productions of the science and literature of ancient Greece. We may reflect with pleasure that an inestimable portion of our classic treasures was safely deposited in Italy; and that the mechanics of a German town had invented an art which derides the havoc of time and barbarism.

From the first hour[73] of the memorable twenty-ninth of May, disorder and rapine prevailed in Constantinople till the eighth hour of the same day, when the sultan himself passed in triumph through the gate of St. Romanus. He was attended by his viziers, bashaws, and guards, each of whom (says a Byzantine historian) was robust as Hercules, dexterous as Apollo, and equal in battle to any ten of the race of ordinary mortals. The conqueror[74] gazed with satisfaction and wonder on the strange though splendid appearance of the domes and palaces, so dissimilar from the style of Oriental architecture. In the hippodrome, or *atmeidan*, his eye was attracted by the twisted column of the three serpents; and, as a trial of his strength, he shattered with his iron mace or battle-axe the under jaw of one of these monsters,[75] which in the eyes of the Turks were the idols or talismans of the city. At the principal door of St. Sophia he alighted from his horse and entered the dome; and such was his jealous regard for that monument of his glory, that, on observing a zealous Musulman in the act of breaking the marble pavement, he admonished him with his scimitar that, if the spoil and captives were granted to the soldiers, the public and private buildings had been reserved for the prince. By his command the metropolis of the Eastern church was transformed into a mosque: the rich and portable instruments of superstition had been removed; the crosses were thrown down; and the walls, which were covered with images and mosaics, were washed and purified, and restored to a state of naked simplicity. On the same day, or on the ensuing Friday, the *muezin*, or crier,

ascended the most lofty turret, and proclaimed the *ezan*, or public invitation, in the name of God and his prophet; the imam preached; and Mohammed the Second performed the *namaz* of prayer and thanksgiving on the great altar, where the Christian mysteries had so lately been celebrated before the last of the Cæsars.[76] From St. Sophia he proceeded to the august but desolate mansion of a hundred successors of the great Constantine, but which in a few hours had been stripped of the pomp of royalty. A melancholy reflection on the vicissitudes of human greatness forced itself on his mind, and he repeated an elegant distich of Persian poetry: "The spider has wove his web in the Imperial palace, and the owl hath sung her watch-song on the towers of Afrasiab."[77]

Yet his mind was not satisfied, nor did the victory seem complete, till he was informed of the fate of Constantine—whether he had escaped, or been made prisoner, or had fallen in the battle. Two Janizaries claimed the honour and reward of his death: the body, under a heap of slain, was discovered by the golden eagles embroidered on his shoes; the Greeks acknowledged with tears the head of their late emperor; and, after exposing the bloody trophy,[78] Mohammed bestowed on his rival the honours of a decent funeral. After his decease Lucas Notaras, great duke[79] and first minister of the empire, was the most important prisoner. When he offered his person and his treasures at the foot of the throne, "And why," said the indignant sultan, "did you not employ these treasures in the defence of your prince and country?"—"They were yours," answered the slave; "God had reserved them for your hands."—"If he reserved them for me," replied the despot, "how have you presumed to withhold them so long by a fruitless and fatal resistance?" The great duke alleged the obstinacy of the strangers, and some secret encouragement from the Turkish vizir; and from this perilous interview he was at length dismissed with the assurance of pardon and protection. Mohammed condescended to visit his wife, a venerable princess oppressed with sickness and grief; and his consolation for her misfortunes was in the most tender strain of humanity and filial reverence. A similar clemency was extended to the principal officers of state, of whom several were ransomed at his expense; and during some days he declared himself the friend and father of the vanquished people. But the scene was soon changed, and before his departure the hippodrome streamed with the blood of his noblest captives. His perfidious cruelty is execrated by the Christians: they adorn with the colours of heroic martyrdom the execution of the great duke and his two sons, and his death is ascribed to the generous refusal of delivering his children to the tyrant's lust. Yet a Byzantine historian has dropped an unguarded word of conspiracy, deliverance, and Italian succour: such treason may be glorious; but the rebel who bravely ventures, has justly forfeited his life; nor should we blame a conqueror for destroying the enemies whom he can no longer trust. On the eighteenth of June the victorious sultan returned to Adrianople, and smiled at the base and hollow embassies of the Christian princes, who viewed their approaching ruin in the fall of the Eastern empire.

Constantinople had been left naked and desolate, without a prince or a people. But she could not be despoiled of the incomparable situation which marks her for the metropolis of a great empire; and the genius of the place will ever triumph over the accidents of time and fortune. Boursa and Adrianople, the ancient seats of the Ottomans, sunk into provincial towns; and Mohammed the Second established his own residence and that of his successors on the same commanding spot which had been chosen by Constantine.[80] The fortifications of Galata, which might afford a shelter to the Latins, were prudently destroyed; but the damage of the Turkish cannon was soon repaired, and before the month of August great quantities of lime had been burnt for the restoration of the walls of the capital. As the entire property of the soil and buildings, whether public or private, or profane or sacred, was now transferred to the conqueror, he first separated a space of eight furlongs from the point of the triangle for the establishment of his seraglio or palace. It is here, in the bosom of luxury, that the *Grand Signor* (as he has been emphatically named by the Italians) appears to reign over Europe and Asia; but his person on the shores of the Bosphorus may not always be secure from the insults of a hostile navy. In the new character of a mosque, the cathedral of St. Sophia was endowed with an ample revenue, crowned with lofty minarets, and surrounded with groves and fountains for the devotion and refreshment of the Moslems. The same model was imitated in the *jami*, or royal mosques; and the first of these was built by Mohammed himself, on the ruins of the church of the holy apostles and the tombs of the Greek emperors. On the third day after the conquest the grave of Abou Ayub, or Job, who had fallen in the first siege of the Arabs, was revealed in a vision; and it is before the sepulchre of the martyr that the new sultans are girded with the sword of empire.[81] Constantinople no longer appertains to the Roman historian; nor shall I enumerate the civil and religious edifices that were profaned or erected by its Turkish masters: the population was speedily renewed, and before the end of September five thousand families of Anatolia and Romania had obeyed the royal mandate, which enjoined them, under pain of death, to occupy their new habitations in the capital. The throne of Mohammed was guarded by the numbers and fidelity of his Moslem subjects; but his rational policy aspired to collect the remnant of the Greeks, and they returned in crowds as soon as they were assured of their lives, their liberties, and the free exercise of their religion. In the election and investiture of a patriarch the ceremonial of the Byzantine court was revived and imitated. With a mixture of satisfaction and horror, they beheld the sultan on his throne, who delivered into the hands of Gennadius the crosier or pastoral staff, the symbol of his ecclesiastical office; who conducted the patriarch to the gate of the seraglio, presented him with a horse richly caparisoned, and directed the vizirs and bashaws to lead him to the palace which had been allotted for his residence.[82] The churches of Constantinople were shared between the two religions: their limits were marked; and, till it was infringed by Selim, the grandson of Mohammed, the Greeks[83] enjoyed above sixty years the benefit of this equal partition. Encouraged by the ministers of the divan, who wished to elude the fanaticism of the sultan, the Christian advocates presumed to allege that this division had been an act, not of generosity, but of justice; not a concession, but a compact; and that, if one-half of the city had been taken by storm, the other moiety had surrendered on the faith of a sacred capitulation. The original grant had indeed been consumed by fire; but the loss was supplied by the testimony of three aged Janizaries who remembered the transaction, and their venal oaths are of more weight in the opinion of Cantemir than the positive and unanimous consent of the history of the times.[84]

The remaining fragments of the Greek kingdom in Europe and Asia I shall abandon to the Turkish arms; but the final extinction of the two last dynasties[85] which have reigned in Constantinople should terminate the decline and fall of the Roman empire in the East. The despots of the Morea, Demetrius and Thomas,[86] the two surviving brothers of the name of PA-LÆOLOGUS, were astonished by the death of the emperor Constantine and the ruin of the monarchy. Hopeless of defence, they prepared, with the noble Greeks who adhered to their fortune, to seek a refuge in Italy, beyond the reach of the Ottoman thunder. Their first apprehensions were dispelled by the victorious sultan, who contented himself with a tribute of twelve thousand ducats; and while his ambition explored the continent and the islands in search of prey, he indulged the Morea in a respite of seven years. But this respite was a period of grief, discord, and misery. The *hexamilion*, the rampart of the isthmus, so often raised and so often subverted, could not long be defended by three hundred Italian archers: the keys of Corinth were seized by the Turks; they returned from their summer excursions with a train of captives and spoil, and the complaints of the injured Greeks were heard with indifference and disdain. The Albanians, a vagrant tribe of shepherds and robbers, filled the peninsula with rapine and murder: the two despots implored the dangerous and humiliating aid of a neighbouring bashaw; and when he had quelled the revolt, his lessons inculcated the rule of their future conduct. Neither the ties of blood, nor the oaths which they repeatedly pledged in the communion and before the altar, nor the stronger pressure of necessity, could reconcile or suspend their domestic quarrels. They ravaged each other's patrimony with fire and sword; the alms and succours of the West were consumed in civil hostility, and their power was only exerted in savage and arbitrary executions. The distress and revenge of the weaker rival invoked their supreme lord; and, in the season of maturity and revenge, Mohammed declared himself the friend of Demetrius, and marched into the Morea with an irresistible force. When he had taken possession of Sparta, "You are too weak," said the sultan, "to control this turbulent province; I will take your daughter to my bed, and you shall pass the remainder of your life in security and honour." Demetrius sighed and obeyed; surrendered his daughter and his castles, followed to Adrianople his sovereign and son, and received for his own maintenance and that of his followers a city in Thrace, and the adjacent isles of Imbros, Lemnos, and Samothrace. He was joined the next year by a companion of misfortune, the last of the COMNENIAN race, who, after the taking of Constantinople by the Latins, had founded a new empire on the coast of the Black Sea.[87] In the progress of his Anatolian conquests, Mohammed invested with a fleet and army the capital of David, who presumed to style himself emperor of Trebizond;[88] and the negotiation was comprised in a short and peremptory question. "Will you secure your life and treasures by resigning your kingdom? or had you rather forfeit your kingdom, your treasures, and your life?" The feeble Comnenus was subdued by his own fears, and the example of a Musulman neighbour, the prince of Sinope,[89] who, on a similar summons, had yielded a fortified city with four hundred cannon and ten or twelve thousand soldiers. The capitulation of Trebizond was faithfully performed, and the emperor, with his family, was transported to a castle in Romania; but on a slight suspicion of corresponding with the Persian king, David, and the whole Comnenian race, were sacrificed to the jealousy or avarice of the conqueror. Nor could the name of father long protect the unfortunate Demetrius from exile and confiscation: his abject submission moved the pity and contempt of the sultan, his followers were transplanted to Constantinople, and his poverty was alleviated by a pension of fifty thousand aspers, till a monastic habit and a tardy death released Palæologus from an earthly master. It is not easy to pronounce whether the servitude of Demetrius or the exile of his brother Thomas,[90] be the most inglorious. On the conquest of the Morea the despot escaped to Corfu, and from thence to Italy, with some naked adherents: his name, his sufferings, and the head of the apostle St. Andrew entitled him to the hospitality of the Vatican; and his misery was prolonged by a pension of six thousand ducats from the pope and cardinals. His two sons, Andrew and Manuel, were educated in Italy; but the eldest, contemptible to his enemies and burdensome to his friends, was degraded by the baseness of his life and marriage. A title was his sole inheritance; and that inheritance he successively sold to the kings of France and Arragon.[91] During his transient prosperity, Charles the Eighth was ambitious of joining the empire of the East with the kingdom of Naples: in a public festival he assumed the appellation and the purple of *Augustus*; the Greeks rejoiced, and the Ottoman already trembled, at the approach of the French chivalry.[92] Manuel Palæologus, the second son, was tempted to revisit his native country: his return might be grateful, and could not be dangerous, to the Porte; he was maintained at Constantinople in safety and ease, and an honourable train of Christians and Moslems attended him to the grave. If there be some animals of so generous a nature that they refuse to propagate in a domestic state, the last of the Imperial race must be ascribed to an inferior kind; he accepted from the sultan's liberality two beautiful females, and his surviving son was lost in the habit and religion of a Turkish slave.

The importance of Constantinople was felt and magnified in its loss: the pontificate of Nicholas the Fifth, however peaceful and prosperous, was dishonoured by the fall of the Eastern empire; and the grief and terror of the Latins revived, or seemed to revive, the old enthusiasm of the crusades. In one of the most distant countries of the West, Philip duke of Burgundy entertained, at Lisle in Flanders, an assembly of his nobles; and the pompous pageants of the feast were skilfully adapted to their fancy and feelings.[93] In the midst of the banquet a gigantic Saracen entered the hall, leading a fictitious elephant with a castle on his back: a matron in a mourning robe, the symbol of religion, was seen to issue from the castle: she deplored her oppression, and accused the slowness of her champions: the principal herald of the golden fleece advanced, bearing on his fist a live pheasant, which, according to the rites of chivalry, he presented to the duke. At this extraordinary summons Philip, a wise and aged prince, engaged his person and powers in the holy war against the Turks: his example was imitated by the barons and knights of the assembly: they swore to God, the Virgin, the ladies, and the *pheasant*; and their particular vows were not less extravagant than the general sanction of their oath. But the performance was made to depend on some future and foreign contingency; and during twelve years, till the last hour of his life, the duke of Burgundy might be scrupulously, and perhaps sincerely, on the eve of his departure. Had every breast glowed with the same ardour; had the union of the Christians corresponded with their bravery; had every country from Sweden[94] to Naples supplied a just proportion of cavalry and infantry, of men and money, it is indeed probable that Constantinople would have been delivered, and that the Turks might have been chased beyond the Hellespont or the Euphrates. But the secretary of the emperor, who composed every epistle, and attended every meeting, Æneas Sylvius,[95] a statesman and orator, describes from his own experience the repug-

nant state and spirit of Christendom. "It is a body," says he, "without a head; a republic without laws or magistrates. The pope and the emperor may shine as lofty titles, as splendid images; but *they* are unable to command. and none are willing to obey: every state has a separate prince, and every prince has a separate interest. What eloquence could unite so many discordant and hostile powers under the same standard? Could they be assembled in arms, who would dare to assume the office of general? What order could be maintained?—what military discipline? Who would undertake to feed such an enormous multitude? Who would understand their various languages, or direct their stranger and incompatible manners? What mortal could reconcile the English with the French, Genoa with Arragon, the Germans with the natives of Hungary and Bohemia? If a small number enlisted in the holy war, they must be overthrown by the infidels: if many, by their own weight and confusion." Yet the same Æneas, when he was raised to the papal throne, under the name of Pius the Second, devoted his life to the prosecution of the Turkish war. In the council of Mantua he excited some sparks of a false or feeble enthusiasm; but when the pontiff appeared at Ancona, to embark in person with the troops, engagements vanished in excuses; a precise day was adjourned to an indefinite term; and his effective army consisted of some German pilgrims, whom he was obliged to disband with indulgences and alms. Regardless of futurity, his successors and the powers of Italy were involved in the schemes of present and domestic ambition; and the distance or proximity of each object determined in their eyes its apparent magnitude. A more enlarged view of their interest would have taught them to maintain a defensive and naval war against the common enemy; and the support of Scanderbeg and his brave Albanians might have prevented the subsequent invasion of the kingdom of Naples. The siege and sack of Otranto by the Turks diffused a general consternation; and Pope Sixtus was preparing to fly beyond the Alps, when the storm was instantly dispelled by the death of Mohammed the Second, in the fifty-first year of his age.[96] His lofty genius aspired to the conquest of Italy: he was possessed of a strong city and a capacious harbour; and the same reign might have been decorated with the trophies of the NEW and the ANCIENT ROME.[97]

State of Rome from the Twelfth Century. Temporal Dominion of the Popes. Seditions of the City. Political Heresy of Arnold of Brescia. Restoration of the Republic. The Senators. Pride of the Romans. Their Wars. They are deprived of the Election and Presence of the Popes, who retire to Avignon. The Jubilee. Noble Families of Rome. Feud of the Colonna and Ursini.

IN the first ages of the decline and fall of the Roman empire our eye is invariably fixed on the royal city, which had given laws to the fairest portion of the globe. We contemplate her fortunes, at first with admiration, at length with pity, always with attention; and when that attention is diverted from the Capitol to the provinces, they are considered as so many branches which have been successively severed from the Imperial trunk. The foundation of a second Rome, on the shores of the Bosphorus, has compelled the historian to follow the successors of Constantine; and our curiosity has been tempted to visit the most remote countries of Europe and Asia, to explore the causes and the authors of the long decay of the Byzantine monarchy. By the conquests of Justinian we have been recalled to the banks of the Tiber, to the deliverance of the ancient metropolis; but that deliverance was a change, or perhaps an aggravation, of servitude. Rome had been already stripped of her trophies, her gods, and her Cæsars; nor was the Gothic dominion more inglorious and oppressive than the tyranny of the Greeks. In the eighth century of the Christian era a religious quarrel, the worship of images, provoked the Romans to assert their independence: their bishop became the temporal, as well as the spiritual, father of a free people; and of the Westem empire, which was restored by Charlemagne, the title and image still decorate the singular constitution of modern Germany. The name of Rome must yet command our involuntary respect: the climate (whatsoever may be its influence) was no longer the same:[1] the purity of blood had been contaminated through a thousand channels; but the venerable aspect of her ruins, and the memory of past greatness, rekindled a spark of the national character. The darkness of the middle ages exhibits some scenes not unworthy of our notice. Nor shall I dismiss the present work till I have reviewed the state and revolutions of the ROMAN CITY, which acquiesced under the absolute dominion of the popes about the same time that Constantinople was enslaved by the Turkish arms.

In the beginning of the twelfth century,[2] the era of the first crusade, Rome was revered by the Latins as the metropolis of the world, as the throne of the pope and the emperor, who, from the eternal city derived their title, their honours, and the right or exercise of temporal dominion. After so long an interruption it may not be useless to repeat that the successors of Charlemagne and the Othos were chosen beyond the Rhine in a national diet; but that these princes were content with the humble names of kings of Germany and Italy till they had passed the Alps and the Apennine, to seek their Imperial crown on the banks of the Tiber.[3] At some distance from the city their approach was saluted by a long procession of the clergy and people with palms and crosses; and the terrific emblems of wolves and lions, of dragons and eagles, that floated in the military banners, represented the departed legions and cohorts of the republic. The royal oath to maintain the liberties of Rome was thrice reiterated, at the bridge, the gate, and on the stairs of the Vatican; and the distribution of a customary donative feebly imitated the magnificence of the first Cæsars. In the church of St. Peter the coronation was performed by his successor: the voice of God was confounded with that of the people; and the public consent was declared in the acclamations of "Long life and victory to our lord the pope! long life and victory to our lord the emperor; long life and victory to the Roman and Teutonic armies!"[4] The names of Cæsar and Augustus, the laws of Constantine and Justinian, the example of Charlemagne and Otho, established the supreme dominion of the emperors: their title and image was engraved on the papal coins;[5] and their jurisdiction was marked by the sword of justice, which they delivered to the præfect of the city. But every Roman prejudice was awakened by the name, the language, and the manners of a barbarian lord. The Cæsars of Saxony or Franconia were the

557

chiefs of a feudal aristocracy; nor could they exercise the discipline of civil and military power, which alone secures the obedience of a distant people, impatient of servitude, though perhaps incapable of freedom. Once, and once only, in his life, each emperor, with an army of Teutonic vassals, descended from the Alps. I have described the peaceful order of his entry and coronation; but that order was commonly disturbed by the clamour and sedition of the Romans, who encountered their sovereign as a foreign invader: his departure was always speedy, and often shameful; and, in the absence of a long reign, his authority was insulted and his name was forgotten. The progress of independence in Germany and Italy undermined the foundations of the Imperial sovereignty, and the triumph of the popes was the deliverance of Rome.

Of her two sovereigns, the emperor had precariously reigned by the right of conquest; but the authority of the pope was founded on the soft though more solid basis of opinion and habit. The removal of a foreign influence restored and endeared the shepherd to his flock. Instead of the arbitrary or venal nomination of a German court, the vicar of Christ was freely chosen by the college of cardinals, most of whom were either natives or inhabitants of the city. The applause of the magistrates and people confirmed his election; and the ecclesiastical power that was obeyed in Sweden and Britain had been ultimately derived from the suffrage of the Romans. The same suffrage gave a prince, as well as a pontiff, to the capital. It was universally believed that Constantine had invested the popes with the temporal dominion of Rome; and the boldest civilians, the most profane sceptics, were satisfied with disputing the right of the emperor and the validity of his gift. The truth of the fact, the authenticity of his donation, was deeply rooted in the ignorance and tradition of four centuries; and the fabulous origin was lost in the real and permanent effects. The name of *Dominus*, or Lord, was inscribed on the coin of the bishops: their title was acknowledged by acclamations and oaths of allegiance, and, with the free or reluctant consent of the German Cæsars, they had long exercised a supreme or subordinate jurisdiction over the city and patrimony of St. Peter. The reign of the popes, which gratified the prejudices of Rome, was not incompatible with the liberties of Rome; and a more critical inquiry would have revealed a still nobler source of their power—the gratitude of a nation whom they had rescued from the

heresy and oppression of the Greek tyrant. In an age of superstition it should seem that the union of the royal and sacerdotal character would mutually fortify each other, and that the keys of Paradise would be the surest pledge of earthly obedience. The sanctity of the office might indeed be degraded by the personal vices of the man. But the scandals of the tenth century were obliterated by the austere and more dangerous virtues of Gregory the Seventh and his successors; and in the ambitious contests which they maintained for the rights of the church, their sufferings or their success must equally tend to increase the popular veneration They sometimes wandered in poverty and exile the victims of persecution; and the apostolic zeal with which they offered themselves to martyrdom must engage the favour and sympathy of every Catholic breast. And sometimes, thundering from the Vatican, they created, judged and deposed the kings of the world; nor could the proudest Roman be disgraced by submitting to a priest whose feet were kissed and whose stirrup was held by the successors of Charlemagne.[6] Even the temporal interest of the city should have protected in peace and honour the residence of the popes, from whence a vain and lazy people derived the greatest part of their subsistence and riches. The fixed revenue of the popes was probably impaired: many of the old patrimonial estates, both in Italy and the provinces, had been invaded by sacrilegious hands nor could the loss be compensated by the claim rather than the possession, of the more ample gifts of Pepin and his descendants. But the Vatican and Capitol were nourished by the incessant and increasing swarms of pilgrims and suppliants: the pale of Christianity was enlarged, and the pope and cardinals were overwhelmed by the judgment of ecclesiastical and secular causes. A new jurisprudence had established in the Latin church the right and practice of appeals;[7] and from the North and West the bishops and abbots were invited or summoned to solicit, to complain, to accuse, or to justify, before the threshold of the apostles. A rare prodigy is once recorded, that two horses, belonging to the archbishops of Mentz and Cologne, repassed the Alps, yet laden with gold and silver; but it was soon understood that the success, both of the pilgrims and clients, depended much less on the justice of their cause than on the value of their offering. The wealth and piety of these strangers were ostentatiously displayed, and their expenses, sacred or profane, circulated in various channels for the emolument of the Romans

Such powerful motives should have firmly attached the voluntary and pious obedience of the Roman people to their spiritual and temporal father. But the operation of prejudice and interest is often disturbed by the sallies of ungovernable passion. The Indian who fells the tree that he may gather the fruit,[9] and the Arab who plunders the caravans of commerce, are actuated by the same impulse of savage nature, which overlooks the future in the present, and relinquishes for momentary rapine the long and secure possession of the most important blessings. And it was thus that the shrine of St. Peter was profaned by the thoughtless Romans, who pillaged the offerings and wounded the pilgrims, without computing the number and value of similar visits, which they prevented by their inhospitable sacrilege. Even the influence of superstition is fluctuating and precarious; and the slave, whose reason is subdued, will often be delivered by his avarice or pride. A credulous devotion for the fables and oracles of the priesthood most powerfully acts on the mind of a barbarian; yet such a mind is the least capable of preferring imagination to sense, of sacrificing to a distant motive, to an invisible, perhaps an ideal object, the appetites and interests of the present world. In the vigour of health and youth, his practice will perpetually contradict his belief, till the pressure of age, or sickness, or calamity, awakens his terrors, and compels him to satisfy the double debt of piety and remorse. I have already observed that the modern times of religious indifference are the most favourable to the peace and security of the clergy. Under the reign of superstition they had much to hope from the ignorance, and much to fear from the violence, of mankind. The wealth, whose constant increase must have rendered them the sole proprietors of the earth, was alternately bestowed by the repentant father and plundered by the rapacious son: their persons were adored or violated; and the same idol, by the hands of the same votaries, was placed on the altar or trampled in the dust. In the feudal system of Europe, arms were the title of distinction and the measure of allegiance; and amidst their tumult the still voice of law and reason was seldom heard or obeyed. The turbulent Romans disdained the yoke and insulted the impotence of their bishop;[10] nor would his education or character allow him to exercise, with decency or effect, the power of the sword. The motives of his election and the frailties of his life were exposed to their familiar observation; and proximity must diminish the reverence which

his name and his decrees impressed on a barbarous world. This difference has not escaped the notice of our philosophic historian: "Though the name and authority of the court of Rome were so terrible in the remote countries of Europe, which were sunk in profound ignorance and were entirely unacquainted with its character and conduct, the pope was so little revered at home, that his inveterate enemies surrounded the gates of Rome itself, and even controlled his government in that city; and the ambassadors, who from a distant extremity of Europe carried to him the humble, or rather abject, submissions of the greatest potentate of the age, found the utmost difficulty to make their way to him and to throw themselves at his feet."[11]

Since the primitive times the wealth of the popes was exposed to envy, their power to opposition, and their persons to violence. But the long hostility of the mitre and the crown increased the numbers and inflamed the passions of their enemies. The deadly factions of the Guelphs and Ghibelines, so fatal to Italy, could never be embraced with truth or constancy by the Romans, the subjects and adversaries both of the bishop and emperor; but their support was solicited by both parties, and they alternately displayed in their banners the keys of St. Peter and the German eagle. Gregory the Seventh who may be adored or detested as the founder of the papal monarchy, was driven from Rome, and died in exile at Salerno. Six-and-thirty of his successors,[12] till their retreat to Avignon, maintained an unequal contest with the Romans: their age and dignity were often violated; and the churches, in the solemn rites of religion, were polluted with sedition and murder. A repetition[13] of such capricious brutality, without connection or design, would be tedious and disgusting; and I shall content myself with some events of the twelfth century which represent the state of the popes and the city. On Holy Thursday, while Paschal officiated before the altar, he was interrupted by the clamours of the multitude, who imperiously demanded the confirmation of a favourite magistrate. His silence exasperated their fury: his pious refusal to mingle the affairs of earth and heaven was encountered with menaces and oaths that he should be the cause and the witness of the public ruin. During the festival of Easter, while the bishop and the clergy, barefoot and in procession, visited the tombs of the martyrs, they were twice assaulted, at the bridge of St. Angelo and before the Capitol, with volleys of stones and darts. The houses of his adherents were levelled with the ground: Paschal escaped with difficulty and danger; he levied an army in the patrimony of St. Peter, and his last days were embittered by suffering and inflicting the calamities of civil war. The scenes that followed the election of his successor Gelasius the Second were still more scandalous to the church and city. Cencio Frangipani,[14] a potent and factious baron, burst into the assembly furious and in arms: the cardinals were stripped, beaten, and trampled under foot; and he seized, without pity or respect, the vicar of Christ by the throat. Gelasius was dragged by his hair along the ground, buffeted with blows, wounded with spurs, and bound with an iron chain in the house of his brutal tyrant. An insurrection of the people delivered their bishop: the rival families opposed the violence of the Frangipani; and Cencio, who sued for pardon, repented of the failure, rather than of the guilt, of his enterprise. Not many days had elapsed when the pope was again assaulted at the altar. While his friends and enemies were engaged in a bloody contest, he escaped in his sacerdotal garments. In this unworthy flight, which excited the compassion of the Roman matrons, his attendants were scattered or unhorsed; and, in the fields behind the church of St. Peter, his successor was found alone and half dead with fear and fatigue. Shaking the dust from his feet, the *apostle* withdrew from a city in which his dignity was insulted and his person was endangered; and the vanity of sacerdotal ambition is revealed in the involuntary confession that one emperor was more tolerable than twenty.[15] These examples might suffice; but I cannot forget the sufferings of two pontiffs of the same age, the second and third of the name of Lucius. The former, as he ascended in battle-array to assault the Capitol, was struck on the temple by a stone, and expired in a few days; the latter was severely wounded in the persons of his servants. In a civil commotion several of his priests had been made prisoners; and the inhuman Romans, reserving one as a guide for his brethren, put out their eyes, crowned them with ludicrous mitres, mounted them on asses with their faces to the tail, and extorted on oath that, in this wretched condition, they should offer themselves as a lesson to the head of the church. Hope or fear, lassitude or remorse, the characters of the men and the circumstances of the times, might sometimes obtain an interval of peace and obedience; and the pope was restored with joyful acclamations to the Lateran

or Vatican, from whence he had been driven with threats and violence. But the root of mischief was deep and perennial; and a momentary calm was preceded and followed by such tempests as had almost sunk the bark of St. Peter. Rome continually presented the aspect of war and discord: the churches and palaces were fortified and assaulted by the factions and families; and, after giving peace to Europe, Calistus the Second alone had resolution and power to prohibit the use of private arms in the metropolis. Among the nations who revered the apostolic throne, the tumults of Rome provoked a general indignation; and, in a letter to his disciple Eugenius the Third, St. Bernard, with the sharpness of his wit and zeal, has stigmatised the vices of the rebellious people.[16] "Who is ignorant," says the monk of Clairvaux, "of the vanity and arrogance of the Romans? a nation nursed in sedition, cruel, untractable, and scorning to obey, unless they are too feeble to resist. When they promise to serve, they aspire to reign; if they swear allegiance, they watch the opportunity of revolt; yet they vent their discontent in loud clamours if your doors or your counsels are shut against them. Dexterous in mischief, they have never learnt the science of doing good. Odious to earth and heaven, impious to God, seditious among themselves, jealous of their neighbours, inhuman to strangers, they love no one, by no one are they beloved; and while they wish to inspire fear, they live in base and continual apprehension. They will not submit: they know not how to govern; faithless to their superiors, intolerable to their equals, ungrateful to their benefactors, and alike impudent in their demands and their refusals. Lofty in promise, poor in execution: adulation and calumny, perfidy and treason, are the familiar arts of their policy." Surely this dark portrait is not coloured by the pencil of Christian charity;[17] yet the features, however harsh and ugly, express a lively resemblance of the Romans of the twelfth century.[18]

The Jews had rejected the Christ when he appeared among them in a plebeian character; and the Romans might plead their ignorance of his vicar when he assumed the pomp and pride of a temporal sovereign. In the busy age of the crusades some sparks of curiosity and reason were rekindled in the Western world: the heresy of Bulgaria, the Paulician sect, was successfully transplanted into the soil of Italy and France, the Gnostic visions were mingled with the simplicity of the Gospel; and the enemies of the lergy reconciled their passions with their con-cience, the desire of freedom with the profes-ion of piety.[19] The trumpet of Roman liberty vas first sounded by Arnold of Brescia,[20] whose promotion in the church was confined to the owest rank, and who wore the monastic habit ather as a garb of poverty than as a uniform of obedience. His adversaries could not deny the wit and eloquence which they severely felt: hey confess with reluctance the specious purity of his morals; and his errors were recommended o the public by a mixture of important and beneficial truths. In his theological studies he had been the disciple of the famous and unfor-unate Abelard,[21] who was likewise involved in he suspicion of heresy: but the lover of Eloisa vas of a soft and flexible nature; and his eccle-iastic judges were edified and disarmed by the humility of his repentance. From this master Arnold most probably imbibed some meta-physical definitions of the Trinity, repugnant to he taste of the times; his ideas of baptism and he eucharist are loosely censured; but a *political* heresy was the source of his fame and misfor-unes. He presumed to quote the declaration of Christ, that his kingdom is not of this world: he boldly maintained that the sword and the ceptre were intrusted to the civil magistrate; hat temporal honours and possessions were awfully vested in secular persons; that the abbots, the bishops, and the pope himself, must renounce either their state or their salvation; and that, after the loss of their revenues, the voluntary tithes and oblations of the faithful would suffice, not indeed for luxury and ava-ice, but for a frugal life in the exercise of spir-itual labours. During a short time the preacher vas revered as a patriot; and the discontent, or evolt, of Brescia against her bishop, was the irst fruits of his dangerous lessons. But the favour of the people is less permanent than the resentment of the priest; and after the heresy of Arnold had been condemned by Innocent the second,[22] in the general council of the Lateran, he magistrates themselves were urged by preju-dice and fear to execute the sentence of the church. Italy could no longer afford a refuge; and the disciple of Abelard escaped beyond the Alps, till he found a safe and hospitable shelter n Zürich, now the first of the Swiss cantons. From a Roman station,[23] a royal villa, a chap-er of noble virgins, Zürich had gradually in-reased to a free and flourishing city; where the ppeals of the Milanese were sometimes tried y the Imperial commissaries.[24] In an age less ripe for reformation the precursor of Zuinglius

was heard with applause: a brave and simple people imbibed, and long retained, the colour of his opinions; and his art, or merit, seduced the bishop of Constance, and even the pope's legate, who forgot, for his sake, the interest of their master and their order. Their tardy zeal was quickened by the fierce exhortations of St. Bernard;[25] and the enemy of the church was driven by persecution to the desperate measure of erecting his standard in Rome itself, in the face of the successor of St. Peter.

Yet the courage of Arnold was not devoid of discretion: he was protected, and had perhaps been invited, by the nobles and people; and in the service of freedom his eloquence thundered over the seven hills. Blending in the same dis-course the texts of Livy and St. Paul, uniting the motives of Gospel and of classic enthusiasm, he admonished the Romans how strangely their patience and the vices of the clergy had degen-erated from the primitive times of the church and the city. He exhorted them to assert the inalienable rights of men and Christians; to re-store the laws and magistrates of the republic; to respect the *name* of the emperor; but to con-fine their shepherd to the spiritual government of his flock.[26] Nor could his spiritual govern-ment escape the censure and control of the re-former; and the inferior clergy were taught by his lessons to resist the cardinals, who had usurped a despotic command over the twenty-eight regions or parishes of Rome.[27] The revo-lution was not accomplished without rapine and violence, the effusion of blood and the dem-olition of houses: the victorious faction was en-riched with the spoils of the clergy and the adverse nobles. Arnold of Brescia enjoyed, or deplored, the effects of his mission: his reign continued above ten years, while two popes, Innocent the Second and Anastasius the Fourth, either trembled in the Vatican or wandered as exiles in the adjacent cities. They were suc-ceeded by a more vigorous and fortunate pon-tiff, Adrian the Fourth,[28] the only Englishman who has ascended the throne of St. Peter; and whose merit emerged from the mean condition of a monk, and almost a beggar, in the monas-tery of St. Albans. On the first provocation, of a cardinal killed or wounded in the streets, he cast an interdict on the guilty people: and from Christmas to Easter Rome was deprived of the real or imaginary comforts of religious worship. The Romans had despised their temporal prince; they submitted with grief and terror to the cen-sures of their spiritual father; their guilt was expiated by penance, and the banishment of the seditious preacher was the price of their absolution. But the revenge of Adrian was yet unsatisfied, and the approaching coronation of Frederic Barbarossa was fatal to the bold reformer, who had offended, though not in an equal degree, the heads of the church and state. In their interview at Viterbo, the pope represented to the emperor the furious, ungovernable spirit of the Romans: the insults, the injuries, the fears, to which his person and his clergy were continually exposed; and the pernicious tendency of the heresy of Arnold, which must subvert the principles of civil, as well as ecclesiastical, subordination. Frederic was convinced by these arguments, or tempted by the desire of the Imperial crown; in the balance of ambition the innocence or life of an individual is of small account; and their common enemy was sacrificed to a moment of political concord. After his retreat from Rome, Arnold had been protected by the viscounts of Campania, from whom he was extorted by the power of Cæsar: the præfect of the city pronounced his sentence: the martyr of freedom was burnt alive in the presence of a careless and ungrateful people; and his ashes were cast into the Tiber, lest the heretics should collect and worship the relics of their master.[29] The clergy triumphed in his death: with his ashes his sect was dispersed; his memory still lived in the minds of the Romans. From his school they had probably derived a new article of faith, that the metropolis of the Catholic church is exempt from the penalties of excommunication and interdict. Their bishops might argue that the supreme jurisdiction, which they exercised over kings and nations, more specially embraced the city and diocese of the prince of the apostles. But they preached to the winds, and the same principle that weakened the effect, must temper the abuse, of the thunders of the Vatican.

The love of ancient freedom has encouraged a belief that as early as the tenth century, in their first struggles against the Saxon Othos, the commonwealth was vindicated and restored by the senate and people of Rome; that two consuls were annually elected among the nobles and that ten or twelve plebeian magistrates revived the name and office of the tribunes of the commons.[30] But this venerable structure disappears before the light of criticism. In the darkness of the middle ages the appellations of senators, of consuls, of the sons of consuls, may sometimes be discovered.[31] They were bestowed by the emperors, or assumed by the most powerful citizens, to denote their rank, their honours,[32] and perhaps the claim of a pure and patrician descent: but they float on the surface without a series or a substance, the titles of men not the orders of government;[33] and it is only from the year of Christ one thousand one hundred and forty-four that the establishment of the senate is dated, as a glorious era, in the acts of the city. A new constitution was hastily framed by private ambition or popular enthusiasm; nor could Rome, in the twelfth century, produce an antiquary to explain, or a legislator to restore, the harmony and proportions of the ancient model. The assembly of a free, or an armed, people, will ever speak in loud and weighty acclamations. But the regular distribution of the thirty-five tribes, the nice balance of the wealth and numbers of the centuries, the debates of the adverse orators, and the slow operation of votes and ballots, could not easily be adapted by a blind multitude, ignorant of the arts, and insensible of the benefits of legal government. It was proposed by Arnold to revive and discriminate the equestrian order, but what could be the motive or measure of such distinction?[34] The pecuniary qualification of the knights must have been reduced to the poverty of the times: those times no longer required their civil functions of judges and farmers of the revenue; and their primitive duty, their military service on horseback, was more nobly supplied by feudal tenures and the spirit of chivalry. The jurisprudence of the republic was useless and unknown; the nations and families of Italy who lived under the Roman and barbaric laws were insensibly mingled in a common mass; and some faint tradition, some imperfect fragments, preserved the memory of the Code and Pandects of Justinian. With their liberty the Romans might doubtless have restored the appellation and office of consuls, had they not disdained a title so promiscuously adopted in the Italian cities, that it has finally settled on the humble station of the agents of commerce in a foreign land. But the rights of the tribunes, the formidable word that arrested the public counsels, suppose or must produce a legitimate democracy. The old patricians were the subjects, the modern barons the tyrants, of the state; nor would the enemies of peace and order, who insulted the vicar of Christ, have long respected the unarmed sanctity of a plebeian magistrate.[35]

In the revolution of the twelfth century which gave a new existence and era to Rome, we may observe the real and important events that marked or confirmed her political indeendence. I. The Capitoline hill, one of her seven eminences,[36] is about four hundred yards in length, and two hundred in breadth. A flight of a hundred steps led to the summit of the Tarpeian rock; and far steeper was the ascent before the declivities had been smoothed and the precipices filled by the ruins of fallen edifices. From the earliest ages the Capitol had been used as a temple in peace, a fortress in war: after the loss of the city it maintained a siege against the victorious Gauls; and the sanctuary of the empire was occupied, assaulted, and burnt, in the civil wars of Vitellius and Vespasian.[37] The temples of Jupiter and his kindred deities had crumbled into dust; their place was supplied by monasteries and houses; and the solid walls, the long and shelving porticoes, were decayed or ruined by the lapse of time. It was the first act of the Romans, an act of freedom, to restore the strength, though not the beauty, of the Capitol; to fortify the seat of their arms and counsels; and as often as they ascended the hill, the coldest minds must have glowed with the remembrance of their ancestors. II. The first Cæsars had been invested with the exclusive coinage of the gold and silver; to the senate they abandoned the baser metal of bronze or copper:[38] the emblems and legends were inscribed on a more ample field by the genius of flattery; and the prince was relieved from the care of celebrating his own virtues. The successors of Diocletian despised even the flattery of the senate: their royal officers at Rome, and in the provinces, assumed the sole direction of the mint; and the same prerogative was inherited by the Gothic kings of Italy, and the long series of the Greek, the French, and the German dynasties. After an abdication of eight hundred years the Roman senate asserted this honourable and lucrative privilege; which was tacitly renounced by the popes, from Paschal the Second to the establishment of their residence beyond the Alps. Some of these republican coins of the twelfth and thirteenth centuries are shown in the cabinets of the curious. On one of these, a gold medal, Christ is depictured holding in his left hand a book with this inscription: "THE VOW OF THE ROMAN SENATE AND PEOPLE: ROME THE CAPITAL OF THE WORLD;" on the reverse, St. Peter delivering a banner to a kneeling senator in his cap and gown, with the name and arms of his family impressed on a shield.[39] III. With the empire, the præfect of the city had declined to a municipal officer; yet he still exercised in the last appeal the civil and criminal jurisdiction; and a drawn sword, which he received from the successors of Otho, was the mode of his investiture and the emblem of his functions.[40] The dignity was confined to the noble families of Rome: the choice of the people was ratified by the pope; but a triple oath of fidelity must have often embarrassed the præfect in the conflict of adverse duties.[41] A servant, in whom they possessed but a third share, was dismissed by the independent Romans: in his place they elected a patrician; but this title, which Charlemagne had not disdained, was too lofty for a citizen or a subject; and after the first fervour of rebellion, they consented without reluctance to the restoration of the præfect. About fifty years after this event, Innocent the Third, the most ambitious or at least the most fortunate of the pontiffs, delivered the Romans and himself from this badge of foreign dominion: he invested the præfect with a banner instead of a sword, and absolved him from all dependence of oaths or service to the German emperors.[42] In his place an ecclesiastic, a present or future cardinal, was named by the pope to the civil government of Rome; but his jurisdiction has been reduced to a narrow compass; and in the days of freedom the right or exercise was derived from the senate and people. IV. After the revival of the senate,[43] the conscript fathers (if I may use the expression) were invested with the legislative and executive power; but their views seldom reached beyond the present day; and that day was most frequently disturbed by violence and tumult. In its utmost plenitude the order or assembly consisted of fifty-six senators,[44] the most eminent of whom were distinguished by the title of counsellors: they were nominated, perhaps annually, by the people; and a previous choice of their electors, ten persons in each region, or parish, might afford a basis for a free and permanent constitution. The popes, who in this tempest submitted rather to bend than to break, confirmed by treaty the establishment and privileges of the senate, and expected from time, peace, and religion, the restoration of their government. The motives of public and private interest might sometimes draw from the Romans an occasional and temporary sacrifice of their claims; and they renewed their oath of allegiance to the successor of St. Peter and Constantine, the lawful head of the church and the republic.[45]

The union and vigour of a public council was dissolved in a lawless city; and the Romans soon adopted a more strong and simple mode of administration. They condensed the name and authority of the senate in a single magistrate or two colleagues; and as they were changed at the end of a year, or of six months, the greatness of the trust was compensated by the shortness of the term. But in this transient reign the senators of Rome indulged their avarice and ambition: their justice was perverted by the interest of their family and faction; and as they punished only their enemies, they were obeyed only by their adherents. Anarchy, no longer tempered by the pastoral care of their bishop, admonished the Romans that they were incapable of governing themselves; and they sought abroad those blessings which they were hopeless of finding at home. In the same age, and from the same motives, most of the Italian republics were prompted to embrace a measure which, however strange it may seem, was adapted to their situation, and productive of the most salutary effects.[46] They chose, in some foreign but friendly city, an impartial magistrate of noble birth and unblemished character, a soldier and a statesman, recommended by the voice of fame and his country, to whom they delegated for a time the supreme administration of peace and war. The compact between the governor and the governed was sealed with oaths and subscriptions; and the duration of his power, the measure of his stipend, the nature of their mutual obligations, were defined with scrupulous precision. They swore to obey him as their lawful superior: he pledged his faith to unite the indifference of a stranger with the zeal of a patriot. At his choice, four or six knights and civilians, his assessors in arms and justice, attended the *Podestà*,[47] who maintained at his own expense a decent retinue of servants and horses: his wife, his son, his brother, who might bias the affections of the judge, were left behind: during the exercise of his office he was not permitted to purchase land, to contract an alliance, or even to accept an invitation in the house of a citizen; nor could he honourably depart till he had satisfied the complaints that might be urged against his government.

It was thus, about the middle of the thirteenth century, that the Romans called from Bologna the senator Brancaleone,[48] whose fame and merit have been rescued from oblivion by the pen of an English historian. A just anxiety for his reputation, a clear foresight of the difficulties of the task, had engaged him to refuse the honour of their choice: the statutes of Rome were suspended, and his office prolonged to the term of three years. By the guilty and licentious he was accused as cruel; by the clergy he was

suspected as partial; but the friends of peace and order applauded the firm and upright magistrate by whom those blessings were restored. No criminals were so powerful as to brave, so obscure as to elude, the justice of the senator. By his sentence two nobles of the Annibaldi family were executed on a gibbet; and he inexorably demolished, in the city and neighbourhood, one hundred and forty towers, the strong shelters of rapine and mischief. The bishop, as a simple bishop, was compelled to reside in his diocese; and the standard of Brancaleone was displayed in the field with terror and effect. His services were repaid by the ingratitude of a people unworthy of the happiness which they enjoyed. By the public robbers whom he had provoked for their sake, the Romans were excited to depose and imprison their benefactor; nor would his life have been spared if Bologna had not possessed a pledge for his safety. Before his departure the prudent senator had required the exchange of thirty hostages of the noblest families of Rome: on the news of his danger, and at the prayer of his wife they were more strictly guarded; and Bologna in the cause of honour, sustained the thunder of a papal interdict. This generous resistance allowed the Romans to compare the present with the past; and Brancaleone was conducted from the prison to the Capitol amidst the acclamations of a repentant people. The remainder of his government was firm and fortunate; and as soon as envy was appeased by death, his head, enclosed in a precious vase, was deposited on a lofty column of marble.[49]

The impotence of reason and virtue recommended in Italy a more effectual choice: instead of a private citizen, to whom they yielded a voluntary and precarious obedience, the Romans elected for their senator some prince of independent power, who could defend them from their enemies and themselves. Charles of Anjou and Provence, the most ambitious and warlike monarch of the age, accepted at the same time the kingdom of Naples from the pope and the office of senator from the Roman people.[50] As he passed through the city in his road to victory he received their oath of allegiance, lodged in the Lateran palace, and smoothed in a short visit the harsh features of his despotic character. Yet even Charles was exposed to the inconstancy of the people, who saluted with the same acclamations the passage of his rival, the unfortunate Conradin; and a powerful avenger, who reigned in the Capitol, alarmed the fears and jealousy of the popes.

The absolute term of his life was superseded by a renewal every third year; and the enmity of Nicholas the Third obliged the Sicilian king to abdicate the government of Rome. In his bull, a perpetual law, the imperious pontiff asserts the truth, validity, and use of the donation of Constantine, not less essential to the peace of the city than to the independence of the church; establishes the annual election of the senator, and formally disqualifies all emperors, kings, princes, and persons of an eminent and conspicuous rank.[51] This prohibitory clause was repealed in his own behalf by Martin the Fourth, who humbly solicited the suffrage of the Romans. In the presence, and by the authority, of the people two electors conferred, not on the pope, but on the noble and faithful Martin, the dignity of senator and the supreme administration of the republic,[52] to hold during his natural life, and to exercise at pleasure by himself or his deputies. About fifty years afterwards the same title was granted to the emperor Lewis of Bavaria; and the liberty of Rome was acknowledged by her two sovereigns, who accepted a municipal office in the government of their own metropolis.

In the first moments of rebellion, when Arnold of Brescia had inflamed their minds against the church, the Romans artfully laboured to conciliate the favour of the empire, and to recommend their merit and services in the cause of Cæsar. The style of their ambassadors to Conrad the Third and Frederic the First is a mixture of flattery and pride, the tradition and the ignorance of their own history.[53] After some complaint of his silence and neglect, they exhort the former of these princes to pass the Alps, and assume from their hands the Imperial crown. "We beseech your majesty not to disdain the humility of your sons and vassals, not to listen to the accusations of our common enemies, who calumniate the senate as hostile to your throne, who sow the seeds of discord that they may reap the harvest of destruction. The pope and the *Sicilian* are united in an impious league to oppose *our* liberty and *your* coronation. With the blessing of God our zeal and courage has hitherto defeated their attempts. Of their powerful and factious adherents, more especially the Frangipani, we have taken by assault the houses and turrets: some of these are occupied by our troops, and some are levelled with the ground. The Milvian bridge, which they had broken, is restored and fortified for your safe passage, and your army may enter the city without being annoyed from the castle of St. Angelo. All that we have done, and all that we design, is for your honour and service, in the loyal hope that you will speedily appear in person to vindicate those rights which have been invaded by the clergy, to revive the dignity of the empire, and to surpass the fame and glory of your predecessors. May you fix your residence in Rome, the capital of the world; give laws to Italy and the Teutonic kingdom; and imitate the example of Constantine and Justinian,[54] who, by the vigour of the senate and people, obtained the sceptre of the earth."[55] But these splendid and fallacious wishes were not cherished by Conrad the Franconian, whose eyes were fixed on the Holy Land, and who died without visiting Rome soon after his return from the Holy Land.

His nephew and successor, Frederic Barbarossa, was more ambitious of the Imperial crown; nor had any of the successors of Otho acquired such absolute sway over the kingdom of Italy. Surrounded by his ecclesiastical and secular princes, he gave audience in his camp at Sutri to the ambassadors of Rome, who thus addressed him in a free and florid oration: "Incline your ear to the queen of cities; approach with a peaceful and friendly mind the precincts of Rome, which has cast away the yoke of the clergy, and is impatient to crown her legitimate emperor. Under your auspicious influence may the primitive times be restored. Assert the prerogatives of the eternal city, and reduce under her monarchy the insolence of the world. You are not ignorant that in former ages, by the wisdom of the senate, by the valour and discipline of the equestrian order, she extended her victorious arms to the East and West, beyond the Alps, and over the islands of the ocean. By our sins, in the absence of our princes, the noble institution of the senate has sunk in oblivion; and with our prudence our strength has likewise decreased. We have revived the senate and the equestrian order: the counsels of the one, the arms of the other, will be devoted to your person and the service of the empire. Do you not hear the language of the Roman matron? You were a guest, I have adopted you as a citizen; a Transalpine stranger, I have elected you for my sovereign,[56] and given you myself, and all that is mine. Your first and most sacred duty is to swear and subscribe that you will shed your blood for the republic; that you will maintain in peace and justice the laws of the city and the charters of your predecessors; and that you will reward with five thousand pounds of silver the faithful senators who shall proclaim your titles in the Capitol. With the name assume the character of Augustus." The flowers of Latin rhetoric were not yet exhausted; but Frederic, impatient of their vanity, interrupted the orators in the high tone of royalty and conquest. "Famous indeed have been the fortitude and wisdom of the ancient Romans; but your speech is not seasoned with wisdom, and I could wish that fortitude were conspicuous in your actions. Like all sublunary things, Rome has felt the vicissitudes of time and fortune. Your noblest families were translated to the East, to the royal city of Constantine; and the remains of your strength and freedom have long since been exhausted by the Greeks and Franks. Are you desirous of beholding the ancient glory of Rome, the gravity of the senate, the spirit of the knights, the discipline of the camp, the valour of the legions? you will find them in the German republic. It is not empire, naked and alone; the ornaments and virtues of empire have likewise migrated beyond the Alps to a more deserving people:[57] they will be employed in your defence, but they claim your obedience. You pretend that myself or my predecessors have been invited by the Romans: you mistake the word; they were not invited, they were implored. From its foreign and domestic tyrants the city was rescued by Charlemagne and Otho, whose ashes repose in our country; and their dominion was the price of your deliverance. Under that dominion your ancestors lived and died. I claim by the right of inheritance and possession, and who shall dare to extort you from my hands? Is the hand of the Franks[58] and Germans enfeebled by age? Am I vanquished? Am I a captive? Am I not encompassed with the banners of a potent and invincible army? You impose conditions on your master; you require oaths: if the conditions are just, an oath is superfluous; if unjust, it is criminal. Can you doubt my equity? It is extended to the meanest of my subjects. Will not my sword be unsheathed in the defence of the Capitol? By that sword the northern kingdom of Denmark has been restored to the Roman empire. You prescribe the measure and the objects of my bounty, which flows in a copious but a voluntary stream. All will be given to patient merit; all will be denied to rude importunity."[59] Neither the emperor nor the senate could maintain these lofty pretensions of dominion and liberty. United with the pope, and suspicious of the Romans, Frederic continued his march to the Vatican; his coronation was disturbed by a sally from the Capitol; and if the numbers and valour of the Germans prevailed in the bloody conflict, he could not safely encamp in the presence of a city of which he styled himself the sovereign. About twelve years afterwards he besieged Rome, to seat an antipope in the chair of St. Peter; and twelve Pisan galleys were introduced into the Tiber; but the senate and people were saved by the arts of negotiation and the progress of disease; nor did Frederic or his successors reiterate the hostile attempt. Their laborious reigns were exercised by the popes, the crusades, and the independence of Lombardy and Germany: they courted the alliance of the Romans; and Frederic the Second offered in the Capitol the great standard, the *Caroccio* of Milan.[60] After the extinction of the house of Swabia, they were banished beyond the Alps; and their last coronations betrayed the impotence and poverty of the Teutonic Cæsars.[61]

Under the reign of Hadrian, when the empire extended from the Euphrates to the ocean, from Mount Atlas to the Grampian hills, a fanciful historian[62] amused the Romans with the picture of their infant wars. "There was a time," says Florus, "when Tibur and Præneste, our summer retreats, were the objects of hostile vows in the Capitol, when we dreaded the shades of the Arician groves, when we could triumph without a blush over the nameless villages of the Sabines and Latins, and even Corioli could afford a title not unworthy of a victorious general." The pride of his contemporaries was gratified by the contrast of the past and the present: they would have been humbled by the prospect of futurity; by the prediction that, after a thousand years, Rome, despoiled of empire and contracted to her primæval limits, would renew the same hostilities, on the same ground which was then decorated with her villas and gardens. The adjacent territory on either side of the Tiber was always claimed, and sometimes possessed, as the patrimony of St. Peter; but the barons assumed a lawless independence, and the cities too faithfully copied the revolt and discord of the metropolis. In the twelfth and thirteenth centuries the Romans incessantly laboured to reduce or destroy the contumacious vassals of the church and senate; and if their headstrong and selfish ambition was moderated by the pope, he often encouraged their zeal by the alliance of his spiritual arms. Their warfare was that of the first consuls and dictators, who were taken from the plough. They assembled in arms at the foot of the Capitol; sallied from the gates, plundered or burnt he harvests of their neighbours, engaged in tumultuary conflict, and returned home after an expedition of fifteen or twenty days. Their sieges were tedious and unskilful: in the use of victory they indulged the meaner passions of jealousy and revenge; and instead of adopting the valour, they trampled on the misfortunes, of their adversaries. The captives, in their shirts, with a rope round their necks, solicited their pardon: the fortifications, and even the buildings, of the rival cities were demolished, and the inhabitants were scattered in the adjacent villages. It was thus that the seats of the cardinal bishops, Porto, Ostia, Albanum, Tusculum, Præneste, and Tibur or Tivoli, were successively overthrown by the ferocious hostility of the Romans.[63] Of these,[64] Porto and Ostia, the two keys of the Tiber, are still vacant and desolate: the marshy and unwholesome banks are peopled with herds of buffaloes, and the river is lost to every purpose of navigation and trade. The hills, which afford a shady retirement from the autumnal heats, have again smiled with the blessings of peace; Frascati has arisen near the ruins of Tusculum; Tibur or Tivoli has resumed the honours of a city;[65] and the meaner towns of Albano and Palestrina are decorated with the villas of the cardinals and princes of Rome. In the work of destruction, the ambition of the Romans was often checked and repulsed by the neighbouring cities and their allies: in the first siege of Tibur they were driven from their camp; and the battles of Tusculum[66] and Viterbo[67] might be compared in their relative state to the memorable fields of Thrasymene and Cannæ. In the first of these petty wars thirty thousand Romans were overthrown by a thousand German horse, whom Frederic Barbarossa had detached to the relief of Tusculum; and if we number the slain at three, the prisoners at two, thousand, we shall embrace the most authentic and moderate account. Sixty-eight years afterwards they marched against Viterbo in the ecclesiastical state with the whole force of the city; by a rare coalition the Teutonic eagle was blended, in the adverse banners, with the keys of St. Peter; and the pope's auxiliaries were commanded by a count of Toulouse and a bishop of Winchester. The Romans were discomfited with shame and slaughter; but the English prelate must have indulged the vanity of a pilgrim, if he multiplied their numbers to one hundred, and their loss in the field to thirty, thousand men. Had the policy of the senate and the discipline of the legions been restored with the Capitol, the divided condition of Italy would have offered the fairest opportunity of a second conquest. But in arms the modern Romans were not *above*, and in arts they were far *below*, the common level of the neighbouring republics. Nor was their warlike spirit of any long continuance: after some irregular sallies they subsided in the national apathy, in the neglect of military institutions, and in the disgraceful and dangerous use of foreign mercenaries.

Ambition is a weed of quick and early vegetation in the vineyard of Christ. Under the first Christian princes the chair of St. Peter was disputed by the votes, the venality, the violence, of a popular election: the sanctuaries of Rome were polluted with blood; and, from the third to the twelfth century, the church was distracted by the mischief of frequent schisms. As long as the final appeal was determined by the civil magistrate, these mischiefs were transient and local: the merits were tried by equity or favour; nor could the unsuccessful competitor long disturb the triumph of his rival. But after the emperors had been divested of their prerogatives, after a maxim had been established that the vicar of Christ is amenable to no earthly tribunal, each vacancy of the holy see might involve Christendom in controversy and war. The claims of the cardinals and inferior clergy, of the nobles and people, were vague and litigious: the freedom of choice was overruled by the tumults of a city that no longer owned or obeyed a superior. On the decease of a pope, two factions proceeded in different churches to a double election: the number and weight of votes, the priority of time, the merit of the candidates, might balance each other: the most respectable of the clergy were divided; and the distant princes, who bowed before the spiritual throne, could not distinguish the spurious from the legitimate idol. The emperors were often the authors of the schism, from the political motive of opposing a friendly to a hostile pontiff; and each of the competitors was reduced to suffer the insults of his enemies, who were not awed by conscience, and to purchase the support of his adherents, who were instigated by avarice or ambition. A peaceful and perpetual succession was ascertained by Alexander the Third,[68] who finally abolished the tumultuary votes of the clergy and people, and defined the right of election in the sole college of cardinals.[69] The three orders of bishops, priests, and deacons, were assimilated to each other by this important privilege; the parochial clergy of Rome obtained the first rank in the hierarchy: they were indifferently chosen among the nations of Christendom; and the possession of the richest benefices, of the most important bishoprics, was not incompatible with their title and office. The senators of the Catholic church, the coadjutors and legates of the supreme pontiff, were robed in purple, the symbol of martyrdom or royalty; they claimed a proud equality with kings; and their dignity was enhanced by the smallness of their number, which, till the reign of Leo the Tenth, seldom exceeded twenty or twenty-five persons. By this wise regulation all doubt and scandal were removed, and the root of schism was so effectually destroyed, that in a period of six hundred years a double choice has only once divided the unity of the sacred college. But as the concurrence of two-thirds of the votes had been made necessary, the election was often delayed by the private interest and passions of the cardinals; and while they prolonged their independent reign, the Christian world was left destitute of a head. A vacancy of almost three years had preceded the elevation of Gregory the Tenth, who resolved to prevent the future abuse; and his bull, after some opposition, has been consecrated in the code of the canon law.[70] Nine days are allowed for the obsequies of the deceased pope, and the arrival of the absent cardinals; on the tenth, they are imprisoned, each with one domestic, in a common apartment or *conclave*, without any separation of walls or curtains; a small window is reserved for the introduction of necessaries; but the door is locked on both sides, and guarded by the magistrates of the city, to seclude them from all correspondence with the world. If the election be not consummated in three days, the luxury of their table is contracted to a single dish at dinner and supper; and after the eighth day they are reduced to a scanty allowance of bread, water, and wine. During the vacancy of the holy see the cardinals are prohibited from touching the revenues, or assuming, unless in some rare emergency, the government of the church: all agreements and promises among the electors are formally annulled; and their integrity is fortified by their solemn oath and the prayers of the Catholics. Some articles of inconvenient or superfluous rigour have been gradually relaxed, but the principle of confinement is vigorous and entire: they are still urged, by the personal motives of health and freedom, to accelerate the moment of their deliverance; and the improvement of ballot or secret votes has wrapped the struggles of the conclave[71] in the silky veil of charity and po-

liteness.[72] By these institutions the Romans were excluded from the election of their prince and bishop; and in the fever of wild and precarious liberty, they seemed insensible of the loss of this inestimable privilege. The emperor Lewis of Bavaria revived the example of the great Otho. After some negotiation with the magistrates, the Roman people was assembled[73] in the square before St. Peter's: the pope of Avignon, John the Twenty-second, was deposed: the choice of his successor was ratified by their consent and applause. They freely voted for a new law, that their bishop should never be absent more than three months in the year, and two days' journey from the city; and that, if he neglected to return on the third summons, the public servant should be degraded and dismissed.[74] But Lewis forgot his own debility and the prejudices of the times: beyond the precincts of a German camp, his useless phantom was rejected; the Romans despised their own workmanship; the antipope implored the mercy of his lawful sovereign;[75] and the exclusive right of the cardinals was more firmly established by this unseasonable attack.

Had the election been always held in the Vatican, the rights of the senate and people would not have been violated with impunity. But the Romans forgot, and were forgotten, in the absence of the successors of Gregory the Seventh, who did not keep as a divine precept their ordinary residence in the city and diocese. The care of that diocese was less important than the government of the universal church; nor could the popes delight in a city in which their authority was always opposed, and their person was often endangered. From the persecution of the emperors, and the wars of Italy, they escaped beyond the Alps into the hospitable bosom of France; from the tumults of Rome they prudently withdrew to live and die in the more tranquil stations of Anagni, Perugia, Viterbo, and the adjacent cities. When the flock was offended or impoverished by the absence of the shepherd, they were recalled by a stern admonition, that St. Peter had fixed his chair, not in an obscure village, but in the capital of the world; by a ferocious menace that the Romans would march in arms to destroy the place and people that should dare to afford them a retreat. They returned with timorous obedience; and were saluted with the account of a heavy debt, of all the losses which their desertion had occasioned, the hire of lodgings, the sale of provisions, and the various expenses of servants and strangers who attended the court.[76] After a short interval of peace, and perhaps of authority, they were again banished by new tumults, and again summoned by the imperious or respectful invitation of the senate. In these occasional retreats the exiles and fugitives of the Vatican were seldom long, or far, distant from the metropolis; but in the beginning of the fourteenth century the apostolic throne was transported, as it might seem for ever, from the Tiber to the Rhône; and the cause of the transmigration may be deduced from the furious contest between Boniface the Eighth and the king of France.[77] The spiritual arms of excommunication and interdict were repulsed by the union of the three estates, and the privileges of the Gallican church; but the pope was not prepared against the carnal weapons which Philip the Fair had courage to employ. As the pope resided at Anagni, without the suspicion of danger, his place and person were assaulted by three hundred horse, who had been secretly levied by William of Nogaret, a French minister, and Sciarra Colonna, of a noble but hostile family of Rome. The cardinals fled; the inhabitants of Anagni were seduced from their allegiance and gratitude; but the dauntless Boniface, unarmed and alone, seated himself in his chair, and awaited, like the conscript fathers of old, the swords of the Gauls. Nogaret, a foreign adversary, was content to execute the orders of his master: by the domestic enmity of Colonna, he was insulted with words and blows; and during a confinement of three days his life was threatened by the hardships which they inflicted on the obstinacy which they provoked. Their strange delay gave time and courage to the adherents of the church, who rescued him from sacrilegious violence; but his imperious soul was wounded in a vital part; and Boniface expired at Rome in a frenzy of rage and revenge. His memory is stained with the glaring vices of avarice and pride; nor has the courage of a martyr promoted this ecclesiastical champion to the honours of a saint; a magnanimous sinner (say the chronicles of the times), who entered like a fox, reigned like a lion, and died like a dog. He was succeeded by Benedict the Eleventh, the mildest of mankind. Yet he excommunicated the impious emissaries of Philip, and devoted the city and people of Anagni by a tremendous curse, whose effects are still visible to the eyes of superstition.[78]

After his decease, the tedious and equal suspense of the conclave was fixed by the dexterity of the French faction. A specious offer was made and accepted, that, in the term of forty days, they would elect one of the three candidates who should be named by their opponents. The archbishop of Bordeaux, a furious enemy of his king and country, was the first on the list; but his ambition was known; and his conscience obeyed the calls of fortune and the commands of a benefactor, who had been informed by a swift messenger that the choice of a pope was now in his hands. The terms were regulated in a private interview; and with such speed and secrecy was the business transacted, that the unanimous conclave applauded the elevation of Clement the Fifth.[79] The cardinals of both parties were soon astonished by a summons to attend him beyond the Alps; from whence, as they soon discovered, they must never hope to return. He was engaged by promise and affection to prefer the residence of France; and, after dragging his court through Poitou and Gascony, and devouring, by his expense, the cities and convents on the road, he finally reposed at Avignon,[80] which flourished above seventy years[81] the seat of the Roman pontiff and the metropolis of Christendom. By land, by sea, by the Rhône, the position of Avignon was on all sides accessible; the southern provinces of France do not yield to Italy itself; new palaces arose for the accommodation of the pope and cardinals; and the arts of luxury were soon attracted by the treasures of the church. They were already possessed of the adjacent territory, the Venaissin county,[82] a populous and fertile spot; and the sovereignty of Avignon was afterwards purchased from the youth and distress of Jane, the first queen of Naples, and countess of Provence, for the inadequate price of fourscore thousand florins.[83] Under the shadow of the French monarchy, amidst an obedient people, the popes enjoyed an honourable and tranquil state, to which they long had been strangers: but Italy deplored their absence; and Rome, in solitude and poverty, might repent of the ungovernable freedom which had driven from the Vatican the successor of St. Peter. Her repentance was tardy and fruitless: after the death of the old members, the sacred college was filled with French cardinals,[84] who beheld Rome and Italy with abhorrence and contempt, and perpetuated a series of national, and even provincial, popes, attached by the most indissoluble ties to their native country.

The progress of industry had produced and enriched the Italian republics: the era of their liberty is the most flourishing period of population and agriculture, of manufactures and commerce; and their mechanic labours were gradually refined into the arts of elegance and genius. But the position of Rome was less favourable, the territory less fruitful: the character of the inhabitants was debased by indolence and elated by pride; and they fondly conceived that the tribute of subjects must for ever nourish the metropolis of the church and empire. This prejudice was encouraged in some degree by the resort of pilgrims to the shrines of the apostles; and the last legacy of the popes, the institution of the HOLY YEAR,[85] was not less beneficial to the people than to the clergy. Since the loss of Palestine, the gift of plenary indulgences, which had been applied to the crusades, remained without an object; and the most valuable treasure of the church was sequestered above eight years from public circulation. A new channel was opened by the diligence of Boniface the Eighth, who reconciled the vices of ambition and avarice; and the pope had sufficient learning to recollect and revive the secular games which were celebrated in Rome at the conclusion of every century. To sound without danger the depth of popular credulity, a sermon was seasonably pronounced, a report was artfully scattered, some aged witnesses were produced; and on the first of January of the year thirteen hundred the church of St. Peter was crowded with the faithful, who demanded the *customary* indulgence of the holy time. The pontiff, who watched and irritated their devout impatience, was soon persuaded by ancient testimony of the justice of their claim; and he proclaimed a plenary absolution to all Catholics who, in the course of that year, and at every similar period, should respectfully visit the apostolic churches of St. Peter and St. Paul. The welcome sound was propagated through Christendom; and at first from the nearest provinces of Italy, and at length from the remote kingdoms of Hungary and Britain, the highways were thronged with a swarm of pilgrims who sought to expiate their sins in a journey, however costly or laborious, which was exempt from the perils of military service. All exceptions of rank or sex, of age or infirmity, were forgotten in the common transport; and in the streets and churches many persons were trampled to death by the eagerness of devotion. The calculation of their numbers could not be easy nor accurate; and they have probably been magnified by a dexterous clergy, well apprised of the contagion of example: yet we are assured by a judicious historian, who assisted at the ceremony, that Rome was never replenished with less than two hundred thousand strangers; and another spectator has fixed at two millions the total concourse of the year. A trifling oblation from each individual would accumulate a royal treasure; and two priests stood night and day, with rakes in their hands, to collect, without counting, the heaps of gold and silver that were poured on the altar of St. Paul.[86] It was fortunately a season of peace and plenty; and if forage was scarce, if inns and lodgings were extravagantly dear, an inexhaustible supply of bread and wine, of meat and fish, was provided by the policy of Boniface and the venal hospitality of the Romans. From a city without trade or industry all casual riches will speedily evaporate: but the avarice and envy of the next generation solicited Clement the Sixth[87] to anticipate the distant period of the century. The gracious pontiff complied with their wishes; afforded Rome this poor consolation for his loss; and justified the change by the name and practice of the Mosaic Jubilee.[88] His summons was obeyed; and the number, zeal, and liberality of the pilgrims did not yield to the primitive festival. But they encountered the triple scourge of war, pestilence, and famine: many wives and virgins were violated in the castles of Italy; and many strangers were pillaged or murdered by the savage Romans, no longer moderated by the presence of their bishop.[89] To the impatience of the popes we may ascribe the successive reduction to fifty, thirty-three, and twenty-five years; although the second of these terms is commensurate with the life of Christ. The profusion of indulgences, the revolt of the Protestants, and the decline of superstition, have much diminished the value of the jubilee; yet even the nineteenth and last festival was a year of pleasure and profit to the Romans; and a philosophic smile will not disturb the triumph of the priest or the happiness of the people.[90]

In the beginning of the eleventh century Italy was exposed to the feudal tyranny, alike oppressive to the sovereign and the people. The rights of human nature were vindicated by her numerous republics, who soon extended their liberty and dominion from the city to the adjacent country. The sword of the nobles was broken; their slaves were enfranchised; their castles were demolished; they assumed the habits of society and obedience; their ambition was confined to municipal honours; and in the proudest aristocracy of Venice or Genoa, each patrician was subject to the laws.[91] But the feeble and disorderly government of Rome was unequal to the task of curbing her rebellious sons, who scorned the authority of the magistrate within and without the walls. It was no longer a civil contention between the nobles and plebeians for the government of the state: the barons asserted in arms their personal independence; their palaces and castles were fortified against a siege; and their private quarrels were maintained by the numbers of their vassals and retainers. In origin and affection they were aliens to their country:[92] and a genuine Roman, could such have been produced, might have renounced these haughty strangers, who disdained the appellation of citizens, and proudly styled themselves the princes of Rome.[93] After a dark series of revolutions all records of pedigree were lost; the distinction of surnames was abolished; the blood of the nations was mingled in a thousand channels; and the Goths and Lombards, the Greeks and Franks, the Germans and Normans, had obtained the fairest possessions by royal bounty, or the prerogative of valour. These examples might be readily presumed; but the elevation of a Hebrew race to the rank of senators and consuls is an event without a parallel in the long captivity of these miserable exiles.[94] In the time of Leo the Ninth a wealthy and learned Jew was converted to Christianity; and honoured at his baptism with the name of his godfather, the reigning pope. The zeal and courage of Peter the son of Leo were signalised in the cause of Gregory the Seventh, who intrusted his faithful adherents with the government of Hadrian's mole, the tower of Crescentius, or, as it is now called, the castle of St. Angelo. Both the father and the son were the parents of a numerous progeny: their riches, the fruits of usury, were shared with the noblest families of the city; and so extensive was their alliance, that the grandson of the proselyte was exalted by the weight of his kindred to the throne of St. Peter. A majority of the clergy and people supported his cause: he reigned several years in the Vatican; and it is only the eloquence of St. Bernard, and the final triumph of Innocent the Second, that has branded Anacletus with the epithet of antipope. After his defeat and death the posterity of Leo is no longer conspicuous; and none will be found of the modern nobles ambitious of descending from a Jewish stock. It is not my design to enumerate the Roman families which have failed at different periods, or those which are continued in different degrees of splendour to the present time.[95] The old consular line of the *Frangipani* discover their name in the generous

act of *breaking* or dividing bread in a time of famine; and such benevolence is more truly glorious than to have enclosed, with their allies the *Corsi*, a spacious quarter of the city in the chains of their fortifications; the *Savelli*, as it should seem a Sabine race, have maintained their original dignity; the obsolete surname of the *Capizucchi* is inscribed on the coins of the first senators; the *Conti* preserve the honour, without the estate, of the counts of Signia; and the *Annibaldi* must have been very ignorant, or very modest, if they had not descended from the Carthaginian hero.[96]

But among, perhaps above, the peers and princes of the city, I distinguish the rival houses of COLONNA and URSINI, whose private story is an essential part of the annals of modern Rome. I. The name and arms of Colonna[97] have been the theme of much doubtful etymology; nor have the orators and antiquarians overlooked either Trajan's pillar, or the columns of Hercules, or the pillar of Christ's flagellation, or the luminous column that guided the Israelites in the desert. Their first historical appearance in the year eleven hundred and four attests the power and antiquity, while it explains the simple meaning, of the name. By the usurpation of Cavæ the Colonna provoked the arms of Paschal the Second; but they lawfully held in the Campagna of Rome the hereditary fiefs of Zagarola and *Colonna*; and the latter of these towns was probably adorned with some lofty pillar, the relic of a villa or temple.[98] They likewise possessed one moiety of the neighbouring city of Tusculum; a strong presumption of their descent from the counts of Tusculum, who in the tenth century were the tyrants of the apostolic see. According to their own and the public opinion, the primitive and remote source was derived from the banks of the Rhine;[99] and the sovereigns of Germany were not ashamed of a real or fabulous affinity with a noble race, which in the revolutions of seven hundred years has been often illustrated by merit and always by fortune.[100] About the end of the thirteenth century the most powerful branch was composed of an uncle and six brothers, all conspicuous in arms or in the honours of the church. Of these, Peter was elected senator of Rome, introduced to the Capitol in a triumphant car, and hailed in some vain acclamations with the title of Cæsar; while John and Stephen were declared marquis of Ancona and count of Romagna, by Nicholas the Fourth, a patron so partial to their family, that he has been delineated in satirical portraits, imprisoned as it were in a hollow pillar.[101] After his decease their haughty behaviour provoked the displeasure of the most implacable of mankind. The two cardinals, the uncle and the nephew, denied the election of Boniface the Eighth; and the Colonna were oppressed for a moment by his temporal and spiritual arms.[102] He proclaimed a crusade against his personal enemies; their estates were confiscated; their fortresses on either side of the Tiber were besieged by the troops of St. Peter and those of the rival nobles; and after the ruin of Palestrina or Præneste, their principal seat, the ground was marked with a ploughshare, the emblem of perpetual desolation. Degraded, banished, proscribed, the six brothers, in disguise and danger, wandered over Europe without renouncing the hope of deliverance and revenge. In this double hope the French court was their surest asylum: they prompted and directed the enterprise of Philip; and I should praise their magnanimity had they respected the misfortune and courage of the captive tyrant. His civil acts were annulled by the Roman people, who restored the honours and possessions of the Colonna; and some estimate may be formed of their wealth by their losses, of their losses by the damages of one hundred thousand gold florins which were granted them against the accomplices and heirs of the deceased pope. All the spiritual censures and disqualifications were abolished[103] by his prudent successors; and the fortune of the house was more firmly established by this transient hurricane. The boldness of Sciarra Colonna was signalised in the captivity of Boniface, and long afterwards in the coronation of Lewis of Bavaria; and by the gratitude of the emperor the pillar in their arms was encircled with a royal crown. But the first of the family in fame and merit was the elder Stephen, whom Petrarch loved and esteemed as a hero superior to his own times and not unworthy of ancient Rome. Persecution and exile displayed to the nations his abilities in peace and war; in his distress he was an object, not of pity but of reverence; the aspect of danger provoked him to avow his name and country; and when he was asked, "Where is now your fortress?" he laid his hand on his heart, and answered, "Here." He supported with the same virtue the return of prosperity; and, till the ruin of his declining age, the ancestors, the character, and the children of Stephen Colonna exalted his dignity in the Roman republic and at the court of Avignon. II. The Ursini migrated from Spoleto;[104] the

sons of Ursus, as they are styled in the twelfth century, from some eminent person who is only known as the father of their race. But they were soon distinguished among the nobles of Rome by the number and bravery of their kinsmen, the strength of their towers, the honours of the senate and sacred college, and the elevation of two popes, Celestin the Third and Nicholas the Third, of their name and lineage.[105] Their riches may be accused as an early abuse of nepotism: the estates of St. Peter were alienated in their favour by the liberal Celestin;[106] and Nicholas was ambitious for their sake to solicit the alliance of monarchs; to found new kingdoms in Lombardy and Tuscany; and to invest them with the perpetual office of senators of Rome. All that has been observed of the greatness of the Colonna will likewise redound to the glory of the Ursini, their constant and equal antagonists in the long hereditary feud which distracted above two hundred and fifty years the ecclesiastical state. The jealousy of preeminence and power was the true ground of their quarrel; but as a specious badge of distinction, the Colonna embraced the name of Ghibelines and the party of the empire; the Ursini espoused the title of Guelphs and the cause of the church. The eagle and the keys were displayed in their adverse banners; and the two factions of Italy most furiously raged when the origin and nature of the dispute were long since forgotten.[107] After the retreat of the popes to Avignon they disputed in arms the vacant republic; and the mischiefs of discord were perpetuated by the wretched compromise of electing each year two rival senators. By their private hostilities the city and country were desolated, and the fluctuating balance inclined with their alternate success. But none of either family had fallen by the sword till the most renowned champion of the Ursini was surprised and slain by the younger Stephen Colonna.[108] His triumph is stained with the reproach of violating the truce; their defeat was basely avenged by the assassination, before the church door, of an innocent boy and his two servants. Yet the victorious Colonna, with an annual colleague, was declared senator of Rome during the term of five years. And the muse of Petrarch inspired a wish, a hope, a prediction, that the generous youth, the son of his venerable hero, would restore Rome and Italy to their pristine glory; that his justice would extirpate the wolves and lions, the serpents and *bears*, who laboured to subvert the eternal basis of the marble COLUMN.[109]

CHAPTER LXX

Character and Coronation of Petrarch. Restoration of the Freedom and Government of Rome by the Tribune Rienzi. His Virtues and Vices, his Expulsion and Death. Return of the Popes from Avignon. Great Schism of the West. Reunion of the Latin Church. Last Struggles of Roman Liberty. Statutes of Rome. Final Settlement of the Ecclesiastical State.

In the apprehension of modern times Petrarch[1] is the Italian songster of Laura and love. In the harmony of his Tuscan rhymes Italy applauds, or rather adores, the father of her lyric poetry; and his verse, or at least his name, is repeated by the enthusiasm or affectation of amorous sensibility. Whatever may be the private taste of a stranger, his slight and superficial knowledge should humbly acquiesce in the judgment of a learned nation; yet I may hope or presume that the Italians do not compare the tedious uniformity of sonnets and elegies with the sublime compositions of their epic muse, the original wildness of Dante, the regular beauties of Tasso, and the boundless variety of the incomparable Ariosto. The merits of the lover I am still less qualified to appreciate: nor am I deeply interested in a metaphysical passion for a nymph so shadowy, that her existence has been questioned;[2] for a matron so prolific,[3] that she was delivered of eleven legitimate children,[4] while her amorous swain sighed and sung at the fountain of Vaucluse.[5] But in the eyes of Petrarch and those of his graver contemporaries his love was a sin, and Italian verse a frivolous amusement. His Latin works of philosophy, poetry, and eloquence established his serious reputation, which was soon diffused from Avignon over France and Italy: his friends and disciples were multiplied in every city; and if the ponderous volume of his writings[6] be now abandoned to a long repose, our gratitude must applaud the man who, by precept and example, revived the spirit and study of the Augustan age. From his earliest youth Petrarch aspired to the poetic crown. The academical honours of the three faculties had introduced a royal degree of master or doctor in the art of poetry;[7] and the title of poet-laureate, which custom, rather than vanity, perpetuates in the English court,[8] was first invented by the Cæsars of Germany. In the musical games of antiquity a prize was bestowed on the victor:[9] the belief that Virgil and Horace had been crowned in the Capitol inflamed the emulation of a Latin bard;[10]

and the laurel was endeared to the lover by a verbal resemblance with the name of his mistress.[11] The value of either object was enhanced by the difficulties of the pursuit; and if the virtue or prudence of Laura was inexorable,[12] he enjoyed, and might boast of enjoying the nymph of poetry. His vanity was not of the most delicate kind, since he applauds the success of his own *labours*; his name was popular; his friends were active; the open or secret opposition of envy or prejudice was surmounted by the dexterity of patient merit. In the thirty-sixth year of his age he was solicited to accept the object of his wishes; and on the same day, in the solitude of Vaucluse, he received a similar and solemn invitation from the senate of Rome and the university of Paris. The learning of a theological school, and the ignorance of a lawless city, were alike unqualified to bestow the ideal though immortal wreath which genius may obtain from the free applause of the public and of posterity: but the candidate dismissed this troublesome reflection; and, after some moments of complacency and suspense, preferred the summons of the metropolis of the world.

The ceremony of his coronation[13] was performed in the Capitol, by his friend and patron the supreme magistrate of the republic. Twelve patrician youths were arrayed in scarlet; six representatives of the most illustrious families, in green robes, with garlands of flowers, accompanied the procession; in the midst of the princes and nobles, the senator, count of Anguillara, a kinsman of the Colonna, assumed his throne; and at the voice of a herald Petrarch arose. After discoursing on a text of Virgil, and thrice repeating his vows for the prosperity of Rome, he knelt before the throne and received from the senator a laurel crown, with a more precious declaration, "This is the reward of merit." The people shouted, "Long life to the Capitol and the poet!" A sonnet in praise of Rome was accepted as the effusion of genius and gratitude; and after the whole procession had visited the Vatican the profane wreath was suspended before the shrine of St. Peter. In the act or diploma[14] which was presented to Petrarch, the title and prerogatives of poet-laureate are revived in the Capitol after the lapse of thirteen hundred years; and he receives the perpetual privilege of wearing, at his choice, a crown of laurel, ivy, or myrtle, of assuming the poetic habit, and of teaching, disputing, interpreting, and composing, in all places whatsoever, and on all subjects of literature. The grant was ratified by the authority of the senate and people; and the character of citizen was the recompense of his affection for the Roman name. They did him honour, but they did him justice. In the familiar society of Cicero and Livy he had imbibed the ideas of an ancient patriot; and his ardent fancy kindled every idea to a sentiment, and every sentiment to a passion. The aspect of the seven hills and their majestic ruins confirmed these lively impressions; and he loved a country by whose liberal spirit he had been crowned and adopted. The poverty and debasement of Rome excited the indignation and pity of her grateful son: he dissembled the faults of his fellow-citizens; applauded with partial fondness the last of their heroes and matrons; and in the remembrance of the past, in the hope of the future, was pleased to forget the miseries of the present time. Rome was still the lawful mistress of the world; the pope and the emperor, her bishop and general, had abdicated their station by an inglorious retreat to the Rhône and the Danube; but if she could resume her virtue, the republic might again vindicate her liberty and dominion. Amidst the indulgence of enthusiasm and eloquence,[15] Petrarch, Italy, and Europe were astonished by a revolution which realised for a moment his most splendid visions. The rise and fall of the tribune Rienzi will occupy the following pages:[16] the subject is interesting, the materials are rich, and the glance of a patriot bard[17] will sometimes vivify the copious, but simple, narrative of the Florentine,[18] and more especially of the Roman,[19] historian.

In a quarter of the city which was inhabited only by mechanics and Jews, the marriage of an innkeeper and a washerwoman produced the future deliverer of Rome.[20] From such parents Nicholas Rienzi Gabrini could inherit neither dignity nor fortune; and the gift of a liberal education, which they painfully bestowed, was the cause of his glory and untimely end. The study of history and eloquence, the writings of Cicero, Seneca, Livy, Cæsar, and Valerius Maximus, elevated above his equals and contemporaries the genius of the young plebeian: he perused

with indefatigable diligence the manuscripts and marbles of antiquity; loved to dispense his knowledge in familiar language, and was often provoked to exclaim, "Where are now these Romans? their virtue, their justice, their power? why was I not born in those happy times?"[21] When the republic addressed to the throne of Avignon an embassy of the three orders, the spirit and eloquence of Rienzi recommended him to a place among the thirteen deputies of the commons. The orator had the honour of haranguing Pope Clement the Sixth, and the satisfaction of conversing with Petrarch, a congenial mind; but his aspiring hopes were chilled by disgrace and poverty, and the patriot was reduced to a single garment and the charity of the hospital. From this misery he was relieved by the sense of merit or the smile of favour; and the employment of apostolic notary afforded him a daily stipend of five gold florins, a more honourable and extensive connection, and the right of contrasting both in words and actions, his own integrity with the vices of the state. The eloquence of Rienzi was prompt and persuasive: the multitude is always prone to envy and censure: he was stimulated by the loss of a brother and the impunity of the assassins; nor was it possible to excuse or exaggerate the public calamities. The blessings of peace and justice, for which civil society has been instituted, were banished from Rome: the jealous citizens, who might have endured every personal or pecuniary injury, were most deeply wounded in the dishonour of their wives and daughters;[22] they were equally oppressed by the arrogance of the nobles and the corruption of the magistrates; and the abuse of arms or of laws was the only circumstance that distinguished the lions from the dogs and serpents of the Capitol. These allegorical emblems were variously repeated in the pictures which Rienzi exhibited in the streets and churches; and while the spectators gazed with curious wonder, the bold and ready orator unfolded the meaning, applied the satire, inflamed their passions, and announced a distant hope of comfort and deliverance. The privileges of Rome, her eternal sovereignty over her princes and provinces, was the theme of his public and private discourse; and a monument of servitude became in his hands a title and incentive of liberty. The decree of the senate, which granted the most ample prerogatives to the emperor Vespasian, had been inscribed on a copper-plate still extant in the choir of the church of St. John Lateran.[23] A numerous assembly of nobles and plebeians was invited to his political lecture, and a convenient theatre was erected for their reception. The notary appeared in a magnificent and mysterious habit, explained the inscription by a version and commentary,[24] and descanted with eloquence and zeal on the ancient glories of the senate and people, from whom all legal authority was derived. The supine ignorance of the nobles was incapable of discerning the serious tendency of such representations: they might sometimes chastise with words and blows the plebeian reformer; but he was often suffered in the Colonna palace to amuse the company with his threats and predictions; and the modern Brutus[25] was concealed under the mask of folly and the character of a buffoon. While they indulged their contempt, the restoration of the *good estate*, his favourite expression, was entertained among the people as a desirable, a possible, and at length as an approaching, event; and while all had the disposition to applaud, some had the courage to assist, their promised deliverer.

A prophecy, or rather a summons, affixed on the church door of St. George, was the first public evidence of his designs—a nocturnal assembly of a hundred citizens on Mount Aventine, the first step to their execution. After an oath of secrecy and aid, he represented to the conspirators the importance and facility of their enterprise; that the nobles, without union or resources, were strong only in the fear of their imaginary strength; that all power, as well as right, was in the hands of the people; that the revenues of the apostolical chamber might relieve the public distress; and that the pope himself would approve their victory over the common enemies of government and freedom. After securing a faithful band to protect this first declaration, he proclaimed through the city, by sound of trumpet, that on the evening of the following day all persons should assemble without arms before the church of St. Angelo, to provide for the re-establishment of the good estate. The whole night was employed in the celebration of thirty masses of the Holy Ghost; and in the morning Rienzi, bareheaded, but in complete armour, issued from the church, encompassed by the hundred conspirators. The pope's vicar, the simple bishop of Orvieto, who had been persuaded to sustain a part in this singular ceremony, marched on his right hand, and three great standards were borne aloft as the emblems of their design. In the first, the banner of *liberty*, Rome was seated on two lions, with a palm in one hand and a globe in the other; St. Paul, with a drawn sword, was delineated in the banner of *justice*; and in the third, St. Peter held the keys of *concord* and *peace*. Rienzi was encouraged by the presence and applause of an innumerable crowd, who understood little and hoped much; and the procession slowly rolled forwards from the castle of St. Angelo to the Capitol. His triumph was disturbed by some secret emotions which he laboured to suppress: he ascended without opposition, and with seeming confidence, the citadel of the republic; harangued the people from the balcony, and received the most flattering confirmation of his acts and laws. The nobles, as if destitute of arms and counsels, beheld in silent consternation this strange revolution; and the moment had been prudently chosen when the most formidable, Stephen Colonna, was absent from the city. On the first rumour he returned to his palace, affected to despise this plebeian tumult, and declared to the messenger of Rienzi that at his leisure he would cast the madman from the windows of the Capitol. The great bell instantly rang an alarm, and so rapid was the tide, so urgent was the danger, that Colonna escaped with precipitation to the suburb of St. Laurence: from thence, after a moment's refreshment, he continued the same speedy career till he reached in safety his castle of Palestrina, lamenting his own imprudence, which had not trampled the spark of this mighty conflagration. A general and peremptory order was issued from the Capitol to all the nobles that they should peaceably retire to their estates: they obeyed, and their departure secured the tranquillity of the free and obedient citizens of Rome.

But such voluntary obedience evaporates with the first transports of zeal; and Rienzi felt the importance of justifying his usurpation by a regular form and a legal title. At his own choice, the Roman people would have displayed their attachment and authority by lavishing on his head the names of senator or consul, of king or emperor: he preferred the ancient and modest appellation of tribune; the protection of the commons was the essence of that sacred office, and they were ignorant that it had never been invested with any share in the legislative or executive powers of the republic. In this character, and with the consent of the Romans, the tribune enacted the most salutary laws for the restoration and maintenance of the good estate. By the first he fulfils the wish of honesty and inexperience, that no civil suit should be protracted beyond the term of fifteen days. The danger of frequent perjury might justify the pronouncing against a false accuser the same penalty which his evidence would have inflicted: the disorders of the times might compel the legislator to punish every homicide with death and every injury with equal retaliation. But the execution of justice was hopeless till he had previously abolished the tyranny of the nobles. It was formally provided that none, except the supreme magistrate, should possess or command the gates, bridges, or towers of the state; that no private garrisons should be introduced into the towns or castles of the Roman territory; that none should bear arms or presume to fortify their houses in the city or country; that the barons should be responsible for the safety of the highways and the free passage of provisions; and that the protection of malefactors and robbers should be expiated by a fine of a thousand marks of silver. But these regulations would have been impotent and nugatory, had not the licentious nobles been awed by the sword of the civil power. A sudden alarm from the bell of the Capitol could still summon to the standard above twenty thousand volunteers: the support of the tribune and the laws required a more regular and permanent force. In each harbour of the coast a vessel was stationed for the assurance of commerce: a standing militia of three hundred and sixty horse and thirteen hundred foot was levied, clothed, and paid in the thirteen quarters of the city; and the spirit of a commonwealth may be traced in the grateful allowance of one hundred florins, or pounds, to the heirs of every soldier who lost his life in the service of his country. For the maintenance of the public defence, for the establishment of granaries, for the relief of widows, orphans, and indigent convents, Rienzi applied, without fear of sacrilege, the revenues of the apostolic chamber: the three branches of hearth-money, the salt-duty, and the customs were each of the annual produce of one hundred thousand florins;[26] and scandalous were the abuses, if in four or five months the amount of the salt-duty could be trebled by his judicious economy. After thus restoring the forces and finances of the republic, the tribune recalled the nobles from their solitary independence, required their personal appearance in the Capitol, and imposed an oath of allegiance to the new government, and of submission to the laws of the good estate. Apprehensive for their safety, but still more apprehensive of the danger of a refusal, the princes and barons returned to their houses at Rome in the garb of simple and peaceful citizens; the Colonna and Ursini, the Savelli and Frangipani, were confounded before the tribunal of a

plebeian, of the vile buffoon whom they had so often derided, and their disgrace was aggravated by the indignation which they vainly struggled to disguise. The same oath was successively pronounced by the several orders of society, the clergy and gentlemen, the judge and notaries, the merchants and artisans, and the gradual descent was marked by the increase of sincerity and zeal. They swore to live and die with the republic and the church, whose interest was artfully united by the nominal association of the bishop of Orvieto, the pope's vicar, to the office of tribune. It was the boast of Rienzi that he had delivered the throne and patrimony of St. Peter from a rebellious aristocracy; and Clement the Sixth, who rejoiced in its fall, affected to believe the professions, to applaud the merits, and to confirm the title of his trusty servant. The speech, perhaps the mind, of the tribune, was inspired with a lively regard for the purity of the faith: he insinuated his claim to a supernatural mission from the Holy Ghost; enforced by a heavy forfeiture the annual duty of confession and communion; and strictly guarded the spiritual as well as temporal welfare of his faithful people.[27]

Never perhaps has the energy and effect of a single mind been more remarkably felt than in the sudden, though transient, reformation of Rome by the tribune Rienzi. A den of robbers was converted to the discipline of a camp or convent: patient to hear, swift to redress, inexorable to punish, his tribunal was always accessible to the poor and stranger; nor could birth, or dignity, or the immunities of the church, protect the offender or his accomplices. The privileged houses, the private sanctuaries in Rome, on which no officer of justice would presume to trespass, were abolished; and he applied the timber and iron of their barricades in the fortifications of the Capitol. The venerable father of the Colonna was exposed in his own palace to the double shame of being desirous and of being unable to protect a criminal. A mule, with a jar of oil, had been stolen near Capranica; and the lord of the Ursini family was condemned to restore the damage and to discharge a fine of four hundred florins for his negligence in guarding the highways. Nor were the persons of the barons more inviolate than their lands or houses; and, either from accident or design, the same impartial rigour was exercised against the heads of the adverse factions. Peter Agapet Colonna, who had himself been senator of Rome, was arrested in the street for injury or debt; and justice was appeased by the tardy execution of

Martin Ursini, who, among his various acts of violence and rapine, had pillaged a shipwrecked vessel at the mouth of the Tiber.[28] His name, the purple of two cardinals his uncles, a recent marriage, and a mortal disease, were disregarded by the inflexible tribune, who had chosen his victim. The public officers dragged him from his palace and nuptial bed: his trial was short and satisfactory; the bell of the Capitol convened the people: stripped of his mantle, on his knees, with his hands bound behind his back, he heard the sentence of death, and, after a brief confession, Ursini was led away to the gallows. After such an example, none who were conscious of guilt could hope for impunity, and the flight of the wicked, the licentious, and the idle, soon purified the city and territory of Rome. In this time (says the historian) the woods began to rejoice that they were no longer infested with robbers; the oxen began to plough; the pilgrims visited the sanctuaries; the roads and inns were replenished with travellers; trade, plenty, and good faith were restored in the markets; and a purse of gold might be exposed without danger in the midst of the highway. As soon as the life and property of the subject are secure, the labours and rewards of industry spontaneously revive: Rome was still the metropolis of the Christian world, and the fame and fortunes of the tribune were diffused in every country by the strangers who had enjoyed the blessings of his government.

The deliverance of his country inspired Rienzi with a vast and perhaps visionary idea of uniting Italy in a great federative republic, of which Rome should be the ancient and lawful head, and the free cities and princes the members and associates. His pen was not less eloquent than his tongue, and his numerous epistles were delivered to swift and trusty messengers. On foot, with a white wand in their hand, they traversed the forests and mountains; enjoyed, in the most hostile states, the sacred security of ambassadors; and reported, in the style of flattery or truth, that the highways along their passage were lined with kneeling multitudes, who implored Heaven for the success of their undertaking. Could passion have listened to reason, could private interest have yielded to the public welfare, the supreme tribunal and confederate union of the Italian republic might have healed their intestine discord, and closed the Alps against the barbarians of the North. But the propitious season had elapsed; and if Venice, Florence, Sienna, Perugia, and many inferior cities, offered their lives and fortunes to the good estate, the tyrants of Lombardy and Tuscany must despise or hate the plebeian author of a free constitution. From them, however, and from every part of Italy, the tribune received the most friendly and respectful answers: they were followed by the ambassadors of the princes and republics; and in this foreign conflux, on all the occasions of pleasure or business, the low-born notary could assume the familiar or majestic courtesy of a sovereign.[29] The most glorious circumstance of his reign was an appeal to his justice from Lewis king of Hungary, who complained that his brother and her husband had been perfidiously strangled by Jane queen of Naples:[30] her guilt or innocence was pleaded in a solemn trial at Rome; but after hearing the advocates,[31] the tribune adjourned this weighty and invidious cause, which was soon determined by the sword of the Hungarian. Beyond the Alps, more especially at Avignon, the revolution was the theme of curiosity, wonder, and applause. Petrarch had been the private friend, perhaps the secret counsellor, of Rienzi: his writings breathe the most ardent spirit of patriotism and joy; and all respect for the pope, all gratitude for the Colonna, was lost in the superior duties of a Roman citizen. The poet-laureate of the Capitol maintains the act, applauds the hero, and mingles with some apprehension and advice the most lofty hopes of the permanent and rising greatness of the republic.[32]

While Petrarch indulged these prophetic visions, the Roman hero was fast declining from the meridian of fame and power; and the people, who gazed with astonishment on the ascending meteor, began to mark the irregularity of its course, and the vicissitudes of light and obscurity. More eloquent than judicious, more enterprising than resolute, the faculties of Rienzi were not balanced by cool and commanding reason; he magnified in a tenfold proportion the objects of hope and fear; and prudence, which could not have erected, did not presume to fortify, his throne. In the blaze of prosperity, his virtues were insensibly tinctured with the adjacent vices; justice with cruelty, liberality with profusion, and the desire of fame with puerile and ostentatious vanity. He might have learned that the ancient tribunes, so strong and sacred in the public opinion, were not distinguished in style, habit, or appearance, from an ordinary plebeian;[33] and that, as often as they visited the city on foot, a single viator, or beadle, attended the exercise of their office. The Gracchi would have frowned or smiled, could they have read the sonorous titles and epithets of their successor—"NICHOLAS, SEVERE AND MERCIFUL; DELIVERER OF ROME; DEFENDER OF ITALY;[34] FRIEND OF MANKIND, AND OF LIBERTY, PEACE, AND JUSTICE; TRIBUNE AUGUST:" his theatrical pageants had prepared the revolution; but Rienzi abused, in luxury and pride, the political maxim of speaking to the eyes, as well as the understanding, of the multitude. From nature he had received the gift of a handsome person,[35] till it was swelled and disfigured by intemperance: and his propensity to laughter was corrected in the magistrate by the affectation of gravity and sternness. He was clothed, at least on public occasions, in a parti-coloured robe of velvet or satin, lined with fur, and embroidered with gold: the rod of justice, which he carried in his hand, was a sceptre of polished steel, crowned with a globe and cross of gold, and enclosing a small fragment of the true and holy wood. In his civil and religious processions through the city, he rode on a white steed, the symbol of royalty: the great banner of the republic, a sun with a circle of stars, a dove with an olive-branch, was displayed over his head; a shower of gold and silver was scattered among the populace; fifty guards with halberds encompassed his person; a troop of horse preceded his march; and their tymbals and trumpets were of massy silver.

The ambition of the honours of chivalry[36] betrayed the meanness of his birth and degraded the importance of his office; and the equestrian tribune was not less odious to the nobles, whom he adopted, than to the plebeians, whom he deserted. All that yet remained of treasure, or luxury, or art, was exhausted on that solemn day. Rienzi led the procession from the Capitol to the Lateran; the tediousness of the way was relieved with decorations and games; the ecclesiastical, civil, and military orders marched under their various banners; the Roman ladies attended his wife; and the ambassadors of Italy might loudly applaud or secretly deride the novelty of the pomp. In the evening, when they had reached the church and palace of Constantine, he thanked and dismissed the numerous assembly, with an invitation to the festival of the ensuing day. From the hands of a venerable knight he received the order of the Holy Ghost; the purification of the bath was a previous ceremony; but in no step of his life did Rienzi excite such scandal and censure as by the profane use of the porphyry vase in which Constantine (a foolish legend) had been healed of his leprosy by Pope Sylvester.[37] With equal pre-

sumption the tribune watched or reposed within the consecrated precincts of the baptistery; and the failure of his statebed was interpreted as an omen of his approaching downfall. At the hour of worship he showed himself to the returning crowds in a majestic attitude, with a robe of purple, his sword, and gilt spurs; but the holy rites were soon interrupted by his levity and insolence. Rising from his throne, and advancing towards the congregation, he proclaimed in a loud voice, "We summon to our tribunal Pope Clement, and command him to reside in his diocese of Rome: we also summon the sacred college of cardinals.[38] We again summon the two pretenders, Charles of Bohemia and Lewis of Bavaria, who style themselves emperors: we likewise summon all the electors of Germany to inform us on what pretence they have usurped the inalienable right of the Roman people, the ancient and lawful sovereigns of the empire."[39] Unsheathing his maiden sword, he thrice brandished it to the three parts of the world, and thrice repeated the extravagant declaration, "And this too is mine!" The pope's vicar, the bishop of Orvieto, attempted to check this career of folly; but his feeble protest was silenced by martial music; and instead of withdrawing from the assembly, he consented to dine with his brother tribune at a table which had hitherto been reserved for the supreme pontiff. A banquet, such as the Cæsars had given, was prepared for the Romans. The apartments, porticoes, and courts of the Lateran were spread with innumerable tables for either sex and every condition; a stream of wine flowed from the nostrils of Constantine's brazen horse; no complaint, except of the scarcity of water, could be heard; and the licentiousness of the multitude was curbed by discipline and fear. A subsequent day was appointed for the coronation of Rienzi;[40] seven crowns of different leaves or metals were successively placed on his head by the most eminent of the Roman clergy; they represented the seven gifts of the Holy Ghost; and he still professed to imitate the example of the ancient tribunes. These extraordinary spectacles might deceive or flatter the people; and their own vanity was gratified in the vanity of their leader. But in his private life he soon deviated from the strict rule of frugality and abstinence; and the plebeians, who were awed by the splendour of the nobles, were provoked by the luxury of their equal. His wife, his son, his uncle (a barber in name and profession), exposed the contrast of vulgar manners and princely expense; and without acquiring the majesty, Rienzi degenerated into the vices, of a king.

A simple citizen describes with pity, or perhaps with pleasure, the humiliation of the barons of Rome. "Bareheaded, their hands crossed on their breast, they stood with downcast looks in the presence of the tribune; and they trembled, good God, how they trembled!"[41] As long as the yoke of Rienzi was that of justice and their country, their conscience forced them to esteem the man whom pride and interest provoked them to hate: his extravagant conduct soon fortified their hatred by contempt; and they conceived the hope of subverting a power which was no longer so deeply rooted in the public confidence. The old animosity of the Colonna and Ursini was suspended for a moment by their common disgrace: they associated their wishes, and perhaps their designs; an assassin was seized and tortured; he accused the nobles; and as soon as Rienzi deserved the fate, he adopted the suspicions and maxims, of a tyrant. On the same day, under various pretences, he invited to the Capitol his principal enemies, among whom were five members of the Ursini and three of the Colonna name. But instead of a council or a banquet, they found themselves prisoners under the sword of despotism or justice; and the consciousness of innocence or guilt might inspire them with equal apprehensions of danger. At the sound of the great bell the people assembled; they were arraigned for a conspiracy against the tribune's life; and though some might sympathise in their distress, not a hand nor a voice was raised to rescue the first of the nobility from their impending doom. Their apparent boldness was prompted by despair; they passed in separate chambers a sleepless and painful night; and the venerable hero, Stephen Colonna, striking against the door of his prison, repeatedly urged his guards to deliver him by a speedy death from such ignominious servitude. In the morning they understood their sentence from the visit of a confessor and the tolling of the bell. The great hall of the Capitol had been decorated for the bloody scene with red and white hangings: the countenance of the tribune was dark and severe; the swords of the executioners were unsheathed; and the barons were interrupted in their dying speeches by the sound of trumpets. But in this decisive moment Rienzi was not less anxious or apprehensive than his captives: he dreaded the splendour of their names, their surviving kinsmen, the inconstancy of the people, the reproaches of the world; and, after rashly offering a mortal injury, he vainly presumed that, if he could forgive, he might himself be forgiven. His elaborate oration was that of a Christian and a suppliant; and, as the humble minister of the commons, he entreated his masters to pardon these noble criminals, for whose repentance and future service he pledged his faith and authority. "If you are spared," said the tribune, "by the mercy of the Romans, will you not promise to support the good estate with your lives and fortunes?" Astonished by this marvelous clemency, the barons bowed their heads; and while they devoutly repeated the oath of allegiance, might whisper a secret, and more sincere, assurance of revenge. A priest, in the name of the people, pronounced their absolution; they received the communion with the tribune, assisted at the banquet, followed the procession; and, after every spiritual and temporal sign of reconciliation, were dismissed in safety to their respective homes, with the new honours and titles of generals, consuls, and patricians.[42]

During some weeks they were checked by the memory of their danger, rather than of their deliverance, till the most powerful of the Ursini, escaping with the Colonna from the city, erected at Marino the standard of rebellion. The fortifications of the castle were hastily restored; the vassals attended their lord; the outlaws armed against the magistrate; the flocks and herds, the harvests and vineyards from Marino to the gates of Rome, were swept away or destroyed; and the people arraigned Rienzi as the author of the calamities which his government had taught them to forget. In the camp Rienzi appeared to less advantage than in the rostrum; and he neglected the progress of the rebel barons till their numbers were strong, and their castles impregnable. From the pages of Livy he had not imbibed the art, or even the courage, of a general: an army of twenty thousand Romans returned without honour or effect from the attack of Marino; and his vengeance was amused by painting his enemies, their heads downwards, and drowning two dogs (at least they should have been bears) as the representatives of the Ursini. The belief of his incapacity encouraged their operations: they were invited by their secret adherents; and the barons attempted, with four thousand foot and sixteen hundred horse, to enter Rome by force or surprise. The city was prepared for their reception; the alarm-bell rung all night; the gates were strictly guarded, or insolently open; and after some hesitation they sounded a retreat. The two first divisions had passed along the walls, but the prospect of a free entrance tempted the head-strong valour of the nobles in the rear; and after a successful skirmish, they were overthrown and massacred without quarter by the crowds of the Roman people. Stephen Colonna the younger, the noble spirit to whom Petrarch ascribed the restoration of Italy, was preceded or accompanied in death by his son John, a gallant youth, by his brother Peter, who might regret the ease and honours of the church, by a nephew of legitimate birth, and by two bastards of the Colonna race; and the number of seven, the seven crowns, as Rienzi styled them, of the Holy Ghost, was completed by the agony of the deplorable parent, of the veteran chief, who had survived the hope and fortune of his house. The vision and prophecies of St. Martin and Pope Boniface had been used by the tribune to animate his troops:[43] he displayed, at least in the pursuit, the spirit of a hero; but he forgot the maxims of the ancient Romans, who abhorred the triumphs of civil war. The conqueror ascended the Capitol; deposited his crown and sceptre on the altar; and boasted, with some truth, that he had cut off an ear which neither pope nor emperor had been able to amputate.[44] His base and implacable revenge denied the honours of burial; and the bodies of the Colonna, which he threatened to expose with those of the vilest malefactors, were secretly interred by the holy virgins of their name and family.[45] The people sympathised in their grief, repented of their own fury, and detested the indecent joy of Rienzi, who visited the spot where these illustrious victims had fallen. It was on that fatal spot that he conferred on his son the honour of knighthood: and the ceremony was accomplished by a slight blow from each of the horsemen of the guard, and by a ridiculous and inhuman ablution from a pool of water, which was yet polluted with patrician blood.[46]

A short delay would have saved the Colonna, the delay of a single month, which elapsed between the triumph and the exile of Rienzi. In the pride of victory he forfeited what yet remained of his civil virtues, without acquiring the fame of military prowess. A free and vigorous opposition was formed in the city; and when the tribune proposed in the public council[47] to impose a new tax, and to regulate the government of Perugia, thirty-nine members voted against his measures, repelled the injurious charge of treachery and corruption, and urged him to prove, by their forcible exclusion, that, if the populace adhered to his cause, it was already disclaimed by the most respectable citizens. The pope and the sacred college had never been dazzled by his specious professions; they were justly offended by the insolence of his conduct; a cardinal legate was sent to Italy, and after some fruitless treaty, and two personal interviews, he fulminated a bull of excommunication, in which the tribune is degraded from his office, and branded with the guilt of rebellion, sacrilege, and heresy.[48] The surviving barons of Rome were now humbled to a sense of allegiance; their interest and revenge engaged them in the service of the church; but as the fate of the Colonna was before their eyes, they abandoned to a private adventurer the peril and glory of the revolution. John Pepin, count of Minorbino,[49] in the kingdom of Naples, had been condemned for his crimes, or his riches, to perpetual imprisonment; and Petrarch, by soliciting his release, indirectly contributed to the ruin of his friend. At the head of one hundred and fifty soldiers the count of Minorbino introduced himself into Rome, barricaded the quarter of the Colonna, and found the enterprise as easy as it had seemed impossible. From the first alarm the bell of the Capitol incessantly tolled; but instead of repairing to the well-known sound, the people were silent and inactive; and the pusillanimous Rienzi, deploring their ingratitude with sighs and tears, abdicated the government and palace of the republic.

Without drawing his sword, Count Pepin restored the aristocracy and the church; three senators were chosen, and the legate, assuming the first rank, accepted his two colleagues from the rival families of Colonna and Ursini. The acts of the tribune were abolished, his head was proscribed; yet such was the terror of his name, that the barons hesitated three days before they would trust themselves in the city, and Rienzi was left above a month in the castle of St. Angelo, from whence he peaceably withdrew, after labouring, without effect, to revive the affection and courage of the Romans. The vision of freedom and empire had vanished: their fallen spirit would have acquiesced in servitude, had it been smoothed by tranquillity and order; and it was scarcely observed that the new senators derived their authority from the Apostolic See, that four cardinals were appointed to reform, with dictatorial power, the state of the republic. Rome was again agitated by the bloody feuds of the barons, who detested each other and despised the commons: their hostile fortresses, both in town and country, again rose, and were again demolished: and the peaceful citizens, a flock of sheep, were devoured, says the Florenine historian, by these rapacious wolves. But when their pride and avarice had exhausted the patience of the Romans, a confraternity of the Virgin Mary protected or avenged the republic: the bell of the Capitol was again tolled, the nobles in arms trembled in the presence of an unarmed multitude; and of the two senators, Colonna escaped from the window of the palace, and Ursini was stoned at the foot of the altar. The dangerous office of tribune was successively occupied by two plebeians, Cerroni and Baroncelli. The mildness of Cerroni was unequal to the times, and after a faint struggle he retired with a fair reputation and a decent fortune to the comforts of rural life. Devoid of eloquence or genius, Baroncelli was distinguished by a resolute spirit: he spoke the language of a patriot, and trod in the footsteps of tyrants; his suspicion was a sentence of death, and his own death was the reward of his cruelties. Amidst the public misfortunes the faults of Rienzi were forgotten, and the Romans sighed for the peace and prosperity of the good estate.[50]

After an exile of seven years, the first deliverer was again restored to his country. In the disguise of a monk or a pilgrim he escaped from the castle of St. Angelo, implored the friendship of the king of Hungary at Naples, tempted the ambition of every bold adventurer, mingled at Rome with the pilgrims of the jubilee, lay concealed among the hermits of the Apennine, and wandered through the cities of Italy, Germany, and Bohemia. His person was invisible, his name was yet formidable; and the anxiety of the court of Avignon supposes, and even magnifies, his personal merit. The emperor Charles the Fourth gave audience to a stranger, who frankly revealed himself as the tribune of the republic, and astonished an assembly of ambassadors and princes by the eloquence of a patriot and the visions of a prophet, the downfall of tyranny and the kingdom of the Holy Ghost.[51] Whatever had been his hopes, Rienzi found himself a captive; but he supported a character of independence and dignity, and obeyed, as his own choice, the irresistible summons of the supreme pontiff. The zeal of Petrarch, which had been cooled by the unworthy conduct, was rekindled by the sufferings and the presence of his friend; and he boldly complains of the times in which the saviour of Rome was delivered by her emperor into the hands of her bishop. Rienzi was transported slowly but in safe custody from Prague to Avignon: his entrance into the city was that of a malefactor; in his prison he was chained by the leg, and four cardinals were named to inquire into the crimes of heresy and rebellion. But his trial and condemnation would have involved some questions which it was more prudent to leave under the veil of mystery: the temporal supremacy of the popes, the duty of residence, the civil and ecclesiastical privileges of the clergy and people of Rome. The reigning pontiff well deserved the appellation of *Clement*: the strange vicissitudes and magnanimous spirit of the captive excited his pity and esteem; and Petrarch believes that he respected in the hero the name and sacred character of a poet.[52] Rienzi was indulged with an easy confinement and the use of books; and in the assiduous study of Livy and the Bible he sought the cause and the consolation of his misfortunes.

The succeeding pontificate of Innocent the Sixth opened a new prospect of his deliverance and restoration; and the court of Avignon was persuaded that the successful rebel could alone appease and reform the anarchy of the metropolis. After a solemn profession of fidelity, the Roman tribune was sent into Italy with the title of senator; but the death of Baroncelli appeared to supersede the use of his mission; and the legate, Cardinal Albornoz,[53] a consummate statesman, allowed him with reluctance, and without aid, to undertake the perilous experiment. His first reception was equal to his wishes: the day of his entrance was a public festival, and his eloquence and authority revived the laws of the good estate. But this momentary sunshine was soon clouded by his own vices and those of the people: in the Capitol he might often regret the prison of Avignon; and after a second administration of four months Rienzi was massacred in a tumult which had been fomented by the Roman barons. In the society of the Germans and Bohemians he is said to have contracted the habits of intemperance and cruelty: adversity had chilled his enthusiasm without fortifying his reason or virtue; and that youthful hope, that lively assurance, which is the pledge of success, was now succeeded by the cold impotence of distrust and despair. The tribune had reigned with absolute dominion, by the choice, and in the hearts, of the Romans; the senator was the servile minister of a foreign court; and while he was suspected by the people, he was abandoned by the prince. The legate Albornoz, who seemed desirous of his ruin, inflexibly refused all supplies of men and money: a faithful subject could no longer presume to touch the revenues of the apostolical chamber; and the first idea of a tax was the signal of clamour and sedition. Even his justice was tainted with the guilt or reproach of selfish cruelty: the most virtuous citizen of Rome was sacrificed to his jealousy; and in the execution of a public robber, from whose purse he had been assisted, the magistrate too much forgot, or too much remembered, the obligations of the debtor.[54] A civil war exhausted his treasures and the patience of the city: the Colonna maintained their hostile station at Palestrina; and his mercenaries soon despised a leader whose ignorance and fear were envious of all subordinate merit. In the death, as in the life, of Rienzi, the hero and the coward were strangely mingled. When the Capitol was invested by a furious multitude, when he was basely deserted by his civil and military servants, the intrepid senator, waving the banner of liberty, presented himself on the balcony, addressed his eloquence to the various passions of the Romans, and laboured to persuade them that in the same cause himself and the republic must either stand or fall. His oration was interrupted by a volley of imprecations and stones; and after an arrow had transpierced his hand, he sunk into abject despair, and fled weeping to the inner chambers, from whence he was let down by a sheet before the windows of the prison. Destitute of aid or hope, he was besieged till the evening; the doors of the Capitol were destroyed with axes and fire; and while the senator attempted to escape in a plebeian habit, he was discovered and dragged to the platform of the palace, the fatal scene of his judgments and executions. A whole hour, without voice or motion, he stood amidst the multitude half naked and half dead: their rage was hushed into curiosity and wonder: the last feelings of reverence and compassion yet struggled in his favour; and they might have prevailed, if a bold assassin had not plunged a dagger in his breast. He fell senseless with the first stroke; the impotent revenge of his enemies inflicted a thousand wounds; and the senator's body was abandoned to the dogs, to the Jews, and to the flames. Posterity will compare the virtues and failings of this extraordinary man; but in a long period of anarchy and servitude, the name of Rienzi has often been celebrated as the deliverer of his country, and the last of the Roman patriots.[55]

The first and most generous wish of Petrarch was the restoration of a free republic; but after the exile and death of his plebeian hero, he turned his eyes from the tribune to the king of the Romans. The Capitol was yet stained with the blood of Rienzi when Charles the Fourth descended from the Alps to obtain the Italian and Imperial crowns. In his passage through Milan he received the visit, and repaid the flattery, of the poet laureat; accepted a medal of Augustus; and promised, without a smile, to imitate the founder of the Roman monarchy. A false application of the names and maxims of antiquity was the source of the hopes and disappointments of Petrarch; yet he could not overlook the difference of times and characters; the immeasurable distance between the first Cæsars and a Bohemian prince, who by the favour of the clergy had been elected the titular head of the German aristocracy. Instead of restoring to Rome her glory and her provinces, he had bound himself by a secret treaty with the pope to evacuate the city on the day of his coronation; and his shameful retreat was pursued by the reproaches of the patriot bard.[56]

After the loss of liberty and empire, his third and more humble wish was to reconcile the shepherd with his flock; to recall the Roman bishop to his ancient and peculiar diocese. In the fervour of youth, with the authority of age, Petrarch addressed his exhortations to five successive popes, and his eloquence was always inspired by the enthusiasm of sentiment and the freedom of language.[57] The son of a citizen of Florence invariably preferred the country of his birth to that of his education; and Italy, in his eyes, was the queen and garden of the world. Amidst her domestic factions she was doubtless superior to France both in art and science, in wealth and politeness; but the difference could scarcely support the epithet of barbarous, which he promiscuously bestows on the countries beyond the Alps. Avignon, the mystic Babylon, the sink of vice and corruption, was the object of his hatred and contempt; but he forgets that her scandalous vices were not the growth of the soil, and that in every residence they would adhere to the power and luxury of the papal court. He confesses that the successor of St. Peter is the bishop of the universal church; yet it was not on the banks of the Rhône, but of the Tiber, that the apostle had fixed his everlasting throne: and while every city in the Christian world was blessed with a bishop, the metropolis alone was desolate and forlorn. Since the removal of the Holy See the sacred buildings of the Lateran and the Vatican, their altars and their saints, were left in a state of poverty and decay; and Rome was often painted under the image of a disconsolate matron, as if the wandering husband could be reclaimed by the homely portrait of the age and infirmities of his weeping spouse.[58] But the cloud which hung over the seven hills would be dispelled by the presence of

heir lawful sovereign: eternal fame, the prosperity of Rome, and the peace of Italy, would
be the recompense of the pope who should dare
to embrace this generous resolution. Of the five
whom Petrarch exhorted, the three first, John
the Twenty-second, Benedict the Twelfth, and
Clement the Sixth, were importuned or amused
by the boldness of the orator; but the memorable change which had been attempted by Urban the Fifth was finally accomplished by Gregory the Eleventh. The execution of their design
was opposed by weighty and almost insuperable
obstacles. A king of France, who has deserved
the epithet of wise, was unwilling to release
them from a local dependence: the cardinals,
for the most part his subjects, were attached to
the language, manners, and climate of Avignon; to their stately palaces; above all, to the
vines of Burgundy. In their eyes Italy was foreign or hostile; and they reluctantly embarked
at Marseilles, as if they had been sold or banished into the land of the Saracens. Urban the
Fifth resided three years in the Vatican with
safety and honour; his sanctity was protected
by a guard of two thousand horse; and the king
of Cyprus, the queen of Naples, and the emperors of the East and West, devoutly saluted their
common father in the chair of St. Peter. But the
joy of Petrarch and the Italians was soon turned
into grief and indignation. Some reasons of public or private moment, his own impatience or
the prayers of the cardinals, recalled Urban to
France; and the approaching election was saved
from the tyrannic patriotism of the Romans.
The powers of heaven were interested in their
cause: Bridget of Sweden, a saint and pilgrim,
disapproved the return, and foretold the death,
of Urban the Fifth; the migration of Gregory
the Eleventh was encouraged by St. Catherine
of Sienna, the spouse of Christ and ambassa-
dress of the Florentines; and the popes themselves, the great masters of human credulity,
appear to have listened to these visionary females.[59] Yet those celestial admonitions were
supported by some arguments of temporal policy. The residence of Avignon had been invaded by hostile violence: at the head of thirty
thousand robbers a hero had extorted ransom
and absolution from the vicar of Christ and the
sacred college; and the maxim of the French
warriors, to spare the people and plunder the
church, was a new heresy of the most dangerous
import.[60] While the pope was driven from Avignon, he was strenuously invited to Rome. The
senate and people acknowledged him as their
lawful sovereign, and laid at his feet the keys of
the gates, the bridges, and the fortresses;[61] of the
quarter at least beyond the Tiber. But this loyal
offer was accompanied by a declaration that
they could no longer suffer the scandal and
calamity of his absence; and that his obstinacy
would finally provoke them to revive and assert
the primitive right of election. The abbot of
Mount Cassin had been consulted whether he
would accept the triple crown[62] from the clergy
and people: "I am a citizen of Rome,"[63] replied
that venerable ecclesiastic, "and my first law is
the voice of my country."[64]

If superstition will interpret an untimely
death;[65] if the merit of counsels be judged from
the event; the heavens may seem to frown on a
measure of such apparent reason and propriety.
Gregory the Eleventh did not survive above
fourteen months his return to the Vatican; and
his decease was followed by the great schism of
the West, which distracted the Latin church
above forty years. The sacred college was then
composed of twenty-two cardinals: six of these
had remained at Avignon; eleven Frenchmen,
one Spaniard, and four Italians, entered the
conclave in the usual form. Their choice was
not yet limited to the purple; and their unanimous votes acquiesced in the archbishop of
Bari, a subject of Naples, conspicuous for his
zeal and learning, who ascended the throne of
St. Peter under the name of Urban the Sixth.
The epistle of the sacred college affirms his free
and regular election, which had been inspired
as usual by the Holy Ghost; he was adored, invested, and crowned, with the customary rites;
his temporal authority was obeyed at Rome
and Avignon, and his ecclesiastical supremacy
was acknowledged in the Latin world. During
several weeks the cardinals attended their new
master with the fairest professions of attachment and loyalty, till the summer heats permitted a decent escape from the city. But as
soon as they were united at Anagni and Fundi,
in a place of security, they cast aside the mask,
accused their own falsehood and hypocrisy, excommunicated the apostate the antichrist of
Rome, and proceeded to a new election of
Robert of Geneva, Clement the Seventh, whom
they announced to the nations as the true and
rightful vicar of Christ. Their first choice, an involuntary and illegal act, was annulled by the
fear of death and the menaces of the Romans;
and their complaint is justified by the strong
evidence of probability and fact. The twelve
French cardinals, above two-thirds of the votes,
were masters of the election; and whatever
might be their provincial jealousies, it cannot

fairly be presumed that they would have sacrificed their right and interest to a foreign candidate, who would never restore them to their native country. In the various, and often inconsistent, narratives,[66] the shades of popular violence are more darkly or faintly coloured: but the licentiousness of the seditious Romans was inflamed by a sense of their privileges, and the danger of a second emigration. The conclave was intimidated by the shouts, and encompassed by the arms, of thirty thousand rebels; the bells of the Capitol and St. Peter's rang an alarm; "Death, or an Italian pope!" was the universal cry; the same threat was repeated by the twelve bannerets or chiefs of the quarters, in the form of charitable advice; some preparations were made for burning the obstinate cardinals; and had they chosen a Transalpine subject, it is probable that they would never have departed alive from the Vatican. The same constraint imposed the necessity of dissembling in the eyes of Rome and of the world; the pride and cruelty of Urban presented a more inevitable danger; and they soon discovered the features of the tyrant, who could walk in his garden and recite his breviary while he heard from an adjacent chamber six cardinals groaning on the rack. His inflexible zeal, which loudly censured their luxury and vice, would have attached them to the stations and duties of their parishes at Rome; and had he not fatally delayed a new promotion, the French cardinals would have been reduced to a helpless minority in the sacred college. For these reasons, and in the hope of repassing the Alps, they rashly violated the peace and unity of the church; and the merits of their double choice are yet agitated in the Catholic schools.[67] The vanity, rather than the interest of the nation, determined the court and clergy of France.[68] The states of Savoy, Sicily, Cyprus, Arragon, Castile, Navarre, and Scotland, were inclined by their example and authority to the obedience of Clement the Seventh, and, after his decease, of Benedict the Thirteenth. Rome and the principal states of Italy, Germany, Portugal, England,[69] the Low Countries, and the kingdoms of the North, adhered to the prior election of Urban the Sixth, who was succeeded by Boniface the Ninth, Innocent the Seventh, and Gregory the Twelfth.

From the banks of the Tiber and the Rhône the hostile pontiffs encountered each other with the pen and the sword: the civil and ecclesiastical order of society was disturbed; and the Romans had their full share of the mischiefs of which they may be arraigned as the primary authors.[70] They had vainly flattered themselves with the hope of restoring the seat of the ecclesiastical monarchy, and of relieving their poverty with the tributes and offerings of the nations; but the separation of France and Spain diverted the stream of lucrative devotion; nor could the loss be compensated by the two jubilees which were crowded into the space of ten years. By the avocations of the schism, by foreign arms, and popular tumults, Urban the Sixth and his three successors were often compelled to interrupt their residence in the Vatican. The Colonna and Ursini still exercised their deadly feuds: the bannerets of Rome asserted and abused the privileges of a republic: the vicars of Christ, who had levied a military force, chastised their rebellion with the gibbet, the sword, and the dagger; and, in a friendly conference, eleven deputies of the people were perfidiously murdered and cast into the street. Since the invasion of Robert the Norman, the Romans had pursued their domestic quarrels without the dangerous interposition of a stranger. But in the disorders of the schism, an aspiring neighbour, Ladislaus king of Naples, alternately supported and betrayed the pope and the people; by the former he was declared *gonfalonier*, or general, of the church, while the latter submitted to his choice the nomination of their magistrates. Besieging Rome by land and water, he thrice entered the gates as a barbarian conqueror; profaned the altars, violated the virgins, pillaged the merchants, performed his devotions at St. Peter's, and left a garrison in the castle of St. Angelo. His arms were sometimes unfortunate, and to a delay of three days he was indebted for his life and crown: but Ladislaus triumphed in his turn; and it was only his premature death that could save the metropolis and the ecclesiastical state from the ambitious conqueror, who had assumed the title, or at least the powers, of King of Rome.[71]

I have not undertaken the ecclesiastical history of the schism; but Rome, the object of these last chapters, is deeply interested in the disputed succession of her sovereigns. The first counsels for the peace and union of Christendom arose from the university of Paris, from the faculty of the Sorbonne, whose doctors were esteemed, at least in the Gallican church, as the most consummate masters of theological science.[72] Prudently waiving all invidious inquiry into the origin and merits of the dispute, they proposed, as a healing measure, that the two pretenders of Rome and Avignon should abdi-

ate at the same time, after qualifying the cardi-
als of the adverse factions to join in a legitimate election; and that the nations should *sub-
act*[73] their obedience, if either of the competi-
ors preferred his own interest to that of the pub-
c. At each vacancy these physicians of the
church deprecated the mischiefs of a hasty
choice; but the policy of the conclave and the
mbition of its members were deaf to reason
nd entreaties; and whatsoever promises were
made, the pope could never be bound by the
aths of the cardinal. During fifteen years the
acific designs of the university were eluded by
he arts of the rival pontiffs, the scruples or pas-
ons of their adherents, and the vicissitudes of
rench factions, that ruled the insanity of
Charles the Sixth. At length a vigorous resolu-
ion was embraced; and a solemn embassy, of
he titular patriarch of Alexandria, two arch-
ishops, five bishops, five abbots, three knights,
nd twenty doctors, was sent to the courts of
Avignon and Rome, to require, in the name of
he church and king, the abdication of the two
retenders, of Peter de Luna, who styled him-
elf Benedict the Thirteenth, and of Angelo
Corrario, who assumed the name of Gregory
he Twelfth. For the ancient honour of Rome,
nd the success of their commission, the ambas-
adors solicited a conference with the magis-
rates of the city, whom they gratified by a
ositive declaration that the most Christian
ing did not entertain a wish of transporting
he holy see from the Vatican, which he con-
dered as the genuine and proper seat of the
uccessor of St. Peter. In the name of the senate
nd people, an eloquent Roman asserted their
esire to co-operate in the union of the church,
eplored the temporal and spiritual calamities
f the long schism, and requested the protec-
ion of France against the arms of the king of
Naples. The answers of Benedict and Gregory
vere alike edifying and alike deceitful; and, in
vading the demand of their abdication, the
wo rivals were animated by a common spirit.
They agreed on the necessity of a previous in-
erview; but the time, the place, and the man-
er, could never be ascertained by mutual coni-
ent. "If the one advances," says a servant of
Gregory, "the other retreats; the one appears
n animal fearful of the land, the other a crea-
ure apprehensive of the water. And thus, for a
hort remnant of life and power, will these aged
riests endanger the peace and salvation of the
Christian world."[74]

The Christian world was at length provoked
y their obstinacy and fraud: they were deserted by their cardinals, who embraced each
other as friends and colleagues; and their revolt was supported by a numerous assembly of
prelates and ambassadors. With equal justice,
the council of Pisa deposed the popes of Rome
and Avignon; the conclave was unanimous in
the choice of Alexander the Fifth, and his vacant seat was soon filled by a similar election of
John the Twenty-third, the most profligate of
mankind. But instead of extinguishing the
schism, the rashness of the French and Italians
had given a third pretender to the chair of St.
Peter. Such new claims of the synod and conclave were disputed; three kings, of Germany,
Hungary, and Naples, adhered to the cause of
Gregory the Twelfth: and Benedict the Thirteenth, himself a Spaniard, was acknowledged
by the devotion and patriotism of that powerful
nation. The rash proceedings of Pisa were corrected by the council of Constance; the emperor
Sigismond acted a conspicuous part as the advocate or protector of the Catholic church; and
the number and weight of civil and ecclesiastical members might seem to constitute the states-
general of Europe. Of the three popes, John the
Twenty-third was the first victim: he fled and
was brought back a prisoner: the most scandalous charges were suppressed; the vicar of Christ
was only accused of piracy, murder, rape, sodomy, and incest; and after subscribing his own
condemnation, he expiated in prison the imprudence of trusting his person to a free city beyond the Alps. Gregory the Twelfth, whose
obedience was reduced to the narrow precincts
of Rimini, descended with more honour from
the throne; and his ambassador convened the
session in which he renounced the title and authority of lawful pope. To vanquish the obstinacy of Benedict the Thirteenth or his adherents, the emperor in person undertook a journey from Constance to Perpignan. The kings of
Castile, Arragon, Navarre, and Scotland, obtained an equal and honourable treaty: with
the concurrence of the Spaniards, Benedict was
deposed by the council; but the harmless old
man was left in a solitary castle to excommuni-
cate twice each day the rebel kingdoms which
had deserted his cause. After thus eradicating
the remains of the schism, the synod of Constance proceeded with slow and cautious steps
to elect the sovereign of Rome and the head of
the church. On this momentous occasion the
college of twenty-three cardinals was fortified
with thirty deputies; six of whom were chosen
in each of the five great nations of Christendom
—the Italian, the German, the French, the

Spanish, and the *English*:[75] the interference of strangers was softened by their generous preference of an Italian and a Roman; and the hereditary, as well as personal, merit of Otho Colonna recommended him to the conclave. Rome accepted with joy and obedience the noblest of her sons; the ecclesiastical state was defended by his powerful family; and the elevation of Martin the Fifth is the era of the restoration and establishment of the popes in the Vatican.[76]

The royal prerogative of coining money, which had been exercised near three hundred years by the senate, was *first* resumed by Martin the Fifth,[77] and his image and superscription introduce the series of the papal medals. Of his two immediate successors, Eugenius the Fourth was the *last* pope expelled by the tumults of the Roman people,[78] and Nicholas the Fifth, the *last* who was importuned by the presence of a Roman emperor.[79] I. The conflict of Eugenius with the fathers of Basil, and the weight or apprehension of a new excise, emboldened and provoked the Romans to usurp the temporal government of the city. They rose in arms; elected seven governors of the republic, and a constable of the Capitol; imprisoned the pope's nephew; besieged his person in the palace; and shot volleys of arrows into his bark as he escaped down the Tiber in the habit of a monk. But he still possessed in the castle of St. Angelo a faithful garrison and a train of artillery: their batteries incessantly thundered on the city, and a bullet more dexterously pointed broke down the barricade of the bridge, and scattered with a single shot the heroes of the republic. Their constancy was exhausted by a rebellion of five months. Under the tyranny of the Ghibeline nobles, the wisest patriots regretted the dominion of the church; and their repentance was unanimous and effectual. The troops of St. Peter again occupied the Capitol; the magistrates departed to their homes; the most guilty were executed or exiled; and the legate, at the head of two thousand foot and four thousand horse, was saluted as the father of the city. The synods of Ferrara and Florence, the fear or resentment of Eugenius, prolonged his absence: he was received by a submissive people; but the pontiff understood, from the acclamations of his triumphal entry, that, to secure their loyalty and his own repose, he must grant without delay the abolition of the odious excise. II. Rome was restored, adorned, and enlightened, by the peaceful reign of Nicholas the Fifth. In the midst of these laudable occupations, the pope was alarmed by the approach of Frederic the Third

of Austria; though his fears could not be justified by the character or the power of the Imperial candidate. After drawing his military force to the metropolis, and imposing the best security of oaths[80] and treaties, Nicholas received with a smiling countenance the faithful advocate and vassal of the church. So tame were the times, so feeble was the Austrian, that the pomp of his coronation was accomplished with order and harmony: but the superfluous honour was so disgraceful to an independent nation, that his successors have excused themselves from the toilsome pilgrimage to the Vatican, and rest their Imperial title on the choice of the electors of Germany.

A citizen has remarked, with pride and pleasure, that the king of the Romans, after passing with a slight salute the cardinals and prelates who met him at the gate, distinguished the dress and person of the senator of Rome; and in this last farewell, the pageants of the empire and the republic were clasped in a friendly embrace.[81] According to the laws of Rome[82] her first magistrate was required to be a doctor of laws, an alien, of a place at least forty miles from the city, with whose inhabitants he must not be connected in the third canonical degree of blood or alliance. The election was annual: a severe scrutiny was instituted into the conduct of the departing senator; nor could he be recalled to the same office till after the expiration of two years. A liberal salary of three thousand florins was assigned for his expense and reward; and his public appearance represented the majesty of the republic. His robes were of gold brocade or crimson velvet, or in the summer season of a lighter silk: he bore in his hand an ivory sceptre; the sound of trumpets announced his approach; and his solemn steps were preceded at least by four lictors or attendants, whose red wands were enveloped with bands or streamers of the golden colour or livery of the city. His oath in the Capitol proclaims his right and duty, to observe and assert the laws, to control the proud, to protect the poor, and to exercise justice and mercy within the extent of his jurisdiction. In these useful functions he was assisted by three learned strangers; the two *collateral*, and the judge of criminal appeals: their frequent trials of robberies, rapes, and murders are attested by the laws; and the weakness of these laws connives at the licentiousness of private feuds and armed associations for mutual defence. But the senator was confined to the administration of justice: the Capitol, the treasury, and the government of the city and its ter itory were intrusted to the three *conservators*, who were changed four times in each year: the militia of the thirteen regions assembled under the banners of their respective chiefs, or *capoioni*; and the first of these was distinguished by the name and dignity of the *prior*. The popular legislature consisted of the secret and the common councils of the Romans. The former was composed of the magistrates and their immediate predecessors, with some fiscal and legal officers, and three classes of thirteen, twenty-six, and forty counsellors; amounting in the whole to about one hundred and twenty persons. In the common council all male citizens had a right to vote; and the value of their privilege was enhanced by the care with which any foreigners were prevented from usurping the title and character of Romans. The tumult of a democracy was checked by wise and jealous precautions: except the magistrates, none could propose a question; none were permitted to speak, except from an open pulpit or tribunal; all disorderly acclamations were suppressed; the sense of the majority was decided by a secret ballot; and their decrees were promulgated in the venerable name of the Roman senate and people. It would not be easy to assign a period in which this theory of government has been reduced to accurate and constant practice, since the establishment of order has been gradually connected with the decay of liberty. But in the year one thousand five hundred and eighty the ancient statutes were collected, methodised in three books, and adapted to present use, under the pontificate, and with the approbation, of Gregory the Thirteenth:[83] this civil and criminal code is the modern law of the city; and, if the popular assemblies have been abolished, a foreign senator, with the three conservators, still resides in the palace of the Capitol.[84] The policy of the Cæsars has been repeated by the popes; and the bishop of Rome affected to maintain the form of a republic, while he reigned with the absolute powers of a temporal, as well as spiritual, monarch.

It is an obvious truth that the times must be suited to extraordinary characters, and that the genius of Cromwell or Retz might now expire in obscurity. The political enthusiasm of Rienzi had exalted him to a throne; the same enthusiasm, in the next century, conducted his imitator to the gallows. The birth of Stephen Porcaro was noble, his reputation spotless: his tongue was armed with eloquence, his mind was enlightened with learning; and he aspired, beyond the aim of vulgar ambition, to free his country and immortalise his name. The dominion of priests is most odious to a liberal spirit: every scruple was removed by the recent knowledge of the fable and forgery of Constantine's donation; Petrarch was now the oracle of the Italians; and as often as Porcaro revolved the ode which describes the patriot and hero of Rome, he applied to himself the visions of the prophetic bard. His first trial of the popular feelings was at the funeral of Eugenius the Fourth: in an elaborate speech he called the Romans to liberty and arms; and they listened with apparent pleasure till Porcaro was interrupted and answered by a grave advocate, who pleaded for the church and state. By every law the seditious orator was guilty of treason; but the benevolence of the new pontiff, who viewed his character with pity and esteem, attempted by an honourable office to convert the patriot into a friend. The inflexible Roman returned from Anagni with an increase of reputation and zeal; and, on the first opportunity, the games of the place Navona, he tried to inflame the casual dispute of some boys and mechanics into a general rising of the people. Yet the humane Nicholas was still averse to accept the forfeit of his life; and the traitor was removed from the scene of temptation to Bologna, with a liberal allowance for his support, and the easy obligation of presenting himself each day before the governor of the city. But Porcaro had learned from the younger Brutus that with tyrants no faith or gratitude should be observed: the exile disclaimed against the arbitrary sentence; a party and a conspiracy was gradually formed; his nephew, a daring youth, assembled a band of volunteers; and on the appointed evening a feast was prepared at his house for the friends of the republic. Their leader, who had escaped from Bologna, appeared among them in a robe of purple and gold: his voice, his countenance, his gestures, bespoke the man who had devoted his life or death to the glorious cause. In a studied oration he expatiated on the motives and the means of their enterprise; the name and liberties of Rome; the sloth and pride of their ecclesiastical tyrants; the active or passive consent of their fellow-citizens; three hundred soldiers and four hundred exiles, long exercised in arms or in wrongs; the license of revenge to edge their swords, and a million of ducats to reward their victory. It would be easy (he said) on the next day, the festival of the Epiphany, to seize the pope and his cardinals before the doors or at the altar of St. Peter's; to lead them in chains under the walls of St. Angelo; to extort by the threat of their instant death, a surrender of the castle; to ascend the vacant Capitol; to ring the alarm-bell; and to restore in a popular assembly the ancient republic of Rome. While he triumphed, he was already betrayed. The senator, with a strong guard, invested the house: the nephew of Porcaro cut his way through the crowd; but the unfortunate Stephen was drawn from a chest, lamenting that his enemies had anticipated by three hours the execution of his design. After such manifest and repeated guilt even the mercy of Nicholas was silent. Porcaro, and nine of his accomplices, were hanged without the benefit of the sacraments; and, amidst the fears and invectives of the papal court, the Romans pitied, and almost applauded, these martyrs of their country.[85] But their applause was mute, their pity ineffectual, their liberty for ever extinct; and, if they have since risen in a vacancy of the throne or a scarcity of bread, such accidental tumults may be found in the bosom of the most abject servitude.

But the independence of the nobles, which was fomented by discord, survived the freedom of the commons, which must be founded in union. A privilege of rapine and oppression was long maintained by the barons of Rome: their houses were a fortress and a sanctuary; and the ferocious train of banditti and criminals, whom they protected from the law, repaid the hospitality with the service of their swords and daggers. The private interest of the pontiffs, or their nephews, sometimes involved them in these domestic feuds. Under the reign of Sixtus the Fourth, Rome was distracted by the battles and sieges of the rival houses: after the conflagration of his palace, the protonotary Colonna was tortured and beheaded; and Savelli, his captive friend, was murdered on the spot for refusing to join in the acclamations of the victorious Ursini.[86] But the popes no longer trembled in the Vatican: they had strength to command, if they had resolution to claim, the obedience of their subjects; and the strangers who observed these partial disorders admired the easy taxes and wise administration of the ecclesiastical state.[87]

The spiritual thunders of the Vatican depend on the force of opinion; and if that opinion be supplanted by reason or passion, the sound may idly waste itself in the air; and the helpless priest is exposed to the brutal violence of a noble or a plebeian adversary. But after their return from Avignon, the keys of St. Peter were guarded by the sword of St. Paul. Rome was commanded by an impregnable citadel: the use of cannon is a powerful engine against popular seditions: a regular force of cavalry and infantry was enlisted under the banners of the pope: his ample revenues supplied the resources of war; and, from the extent of his domain, he could bring down on a rebellious city an army of hostile neighbours and loyal subjects.[88] Since the union of the duchies of Ferrara and Urbino the ecclesiastical state extends from the Mediterranean to the Adriatic, and from the confines of Naples to the banks of the Po; and as early as the sixteenth century the greater part of that spacious and fruitful country acknowledged the lawful claims and temporal sovereignty of the Roman pontiffs. Their claims were readily deduced from the genuine or fabulous donation of the darker ages: the successive steps of their final settlement would engage us too far in the transactions of Italy, and even of Europe; the crimes of Alexander the Sixth, the martial operations of Julius the Second, and the liberal policy of Leo the Tenth, a theme which has been adorned by the pens of the noblest historians of the times.[89] In the first period of their conquests, till the expedition of Charles the Eighth, the popes might successfully wrestle with the adjacent princes and states, whose military force was equal or inferior to their own. But as soon as the monarchs of France, Germany, and Spain contended with gigantic arms for the dominion of Italy, they supplied with art the deficiency of strength, and concealed, in a labyrinth of wars and treaties, their aspiring views and the immortal hope of chasing the barbarians beyond the Alps. The nice balance of the Vatican was often subverted by the soldiers of the North and West, who were united under the standard of Charles the Fifth: the feeble and fluctuating policy of Clement the Seventh exposed his person and dominions to the conqueror; and Rome was abandoned seven months to a lawless army more cruel and rapacious than the Goths and Vandals.[90] After this severe lesson the popes contracted their ambition, which was almost satisfied, resumed the character of a common parent, and abstained from all offensive hostilities, except in a hasty quarrel, when the vicar of Christ and the Turkish sultan were armed at the same time against the kingdom of Naples.[9] The French and Germans at length withdrew from the field of battle: Milan, Naples, Sicily, Sardinia, and the sea-coast of Tuscany, were firmly possessed by the Spaniards; and it became their interest to maintain the peace and dependence of Italy, which continued almost without disturbance from the middle of the sixeenth to the opening of the eighteenth century. The Vatican was swayed and protected by the religious policy of the Catholic king: his prejudice and interest disposed him in every dispute to support the prince against the people; and instead of the encouragement, the aid, and the asylum which they obtained from the adjacent states, the friends of liberty, or the enemies of law were enclosed on all sides within the iron circle of despotism. The long habits of obedience and education subdued the turbulent spirit of the nobles and commons of Rome. The barons forgot the arms and factions of their ancestors, and insensibly became the servants of luxury and government. Instead of maintaining a crowd of tenants and followers, the produce of their estates was consumed in the private expenses which multiply the pleasures and diminish the power of the lord.[92] The Colonna and Ursini vied with each other in the decoration of their palaces and chapels; and their antique splendour was rivalled or surpassed by the sudden opulence of the papal families. In Rome the voice of freedom and discord is no longer heard; and, instead of the foaming torrent, a smooth and stagnant lake reflects the image of idleness and servitude.

A Christian, a philosopher,[93] and a patriot, will be equally scandalised by the temporal kingdom of the clergy; and the local majesty of Rome, the remembrance of her consuls and triumphs, may seem to embitter the sense and aggravate the shame of her slavery. If we calmly weigh the merits and defects of the ecclesiastical government, it may be praised in its present state as a mild, decent, and tranquil system, exempt from the dangers of a minority, the sallies of youth, the expenses of luxury, and the calamities of war. But these advantages are overbalanced by a frequent, perhaps a septennial, election of a sovereign, who is seldom a native of the country: the reign of a *young* statesman of threescore, in the decline of his life and abilities, without hope to accomplish, and without children to inherit, the labours of his transitory reign. The successful candidate is drawn from

the church, and even the convent—from the mode of education and life the most adverse to reason, humanity, and freedom. In the trammels of servile faith he has learned to believe because it is absurd, to revere all that is contemptible, and to despise whatever might deserve the esteem of a rational being; to punish error as a crime, to reward mortification and celibacy as the first of virtues; to place the saints of the calendar[94] above the heroes of Rome and the sages of Athens; and to consider the missal, or the crucifix, as more useful instruments than the plough or the loom. In the office of nuncio, or the rank of cardinal, he may acquire some knowledge of the world; but the primitive stain will adhere to his mind and manners: from study and experience he may suspect the mystery of his profession; but the sacerdotal artist will imbibe some portion of the bigotry which he inculcates. The genius of Sixtus the Fifth[95] burst from the gloom of a Franciscan cloister. In a reign of five years he exterminated the outlaws and banditti, abolished the *profane* sanctuaries of Rome,[96] formed a naval and military force, restored and emulated the monuments of antiquity, and, after a liberal use and large increase of the revenue, left five millions of crowns in the castle of St. Angelo. But his justice was sullied with cruelty, his activity was prompted by the ambition of conquest: after his decease the abuses revived; the treasure was dissipated; he entailed on posterity thirty-five new taxes and the venality of offices; and, after his death, his statue was demolished by an ungrateful or an injured people.[97] The wild and original character of Sixtus the Fifth stands alone in the series of the pontiffs: the maxims and effects of their temporal government may be collected from the positive and comparative view of the arts and philosophy, the agriculture and trade, the wealth and population, of the ecclesiastical state. For myself, it is my wish to depart in charity with all mankind, nor am I willing, in these last moments, to offend even the pope and clergy of Rome.[98]

CHAPTER LXXI

Prospect of the Ruins of Rome in the Fifteenth Century. Four Causes of Decay and Destruction. Example of the Coliseum. Renovation of the City. Conclusion of the Whole Work.

IN the last days of Pope Eugenius the Fourth, two of his servants. the learned Poggius[1] and a friend, ascended the Capitoline hill, reposed themselves among the ruins of columns and temples, and viewed from that commanding spot the wide and various prospect of desolation.[2] The place and the object gave ample scope for moralising on the vicissitudes of fortune, which spares neither man nor the proudest of his works, which buries empires and cities in a common grave; and it was agreed that, in proportion to her former greatness, the fall of Rome was the more awful and deplorable. "Her primeval state, such as she might appear in a remote age, when Evander entertained the stranger of Troy,[3] has been delineated by the fancy of Virgil. This Tarpeian rock was then a savage and solitary thicket: in the time of the poet it was crowned with the golden roofs of a temple; the temple is overthrown, the gold has been pillaged, the wheel of fortune has accomplished her revolution, and the sacred ground is again disfigured with thorns and brambles. The hill of the Capitol, on which we sit, was formerly the head of the Roman empire, the citadel of the earth, the terror of kings; illustrated by the footsteps of so many triumphs, enriched with the spoils and tributes of so many nations. This spectacle of the world, how is it fallen! how changed! how defaced! the path of victory is obliterated by vines, and the benches of the senators are concealed by a dunghill. Cast your eyes on the Palatine hill, and seek among the shapeless and enormous fragments the marble theatre, the obelisks, the colossal statues, the porticoes of Nero's palace: survey the other hills of the city, the vacant space is interrupted only by ruins and gardens. The forum of the Roman people, where they assembled to enact their laws and elect their magistrates, is now enclosed for the cultivation of pot-herbs, or thrown open for the reception of swine and buffaloes. The public and private edifices, that were founded for eternity, lie prostrate, naked, and broken, like the limbs of a mighty giant; and the ruin is the more visible, from the stupendous relics that have survived the injuries of time and fortune."[4]

These relics are minutely described by Poggius, one of the first who raised his eyes from the monuments of legendary to those of classic superstition.[5] 1. Besides a bridge, an arch, a sepulchre, and the pyramid of Cestius, he could discern, of the age of the republic, a double row of vaults in the salt-office of the Capitol, which were inscribed with the name and munificence of Catulus. 2. Eleven temples were visible in some degree, from the perfect form of the Pantheon to the three arches and a marble column of the temple of Peace, which Vespasian erected after the civil wars and the Jewish triumph. 3. Of the number, which he rashly defines, of seven *thermæ*, or public baths, none were sufficiently entire to represent the use and distribution of the several baths; but those of Diocletian and Antoninus Caracalla still retained the titles of the founders, and astonished the curious spectator, who, in observing their solidity and extent, the variety of marbles, the size and multitude of the columns, compared the labour and expense with the use and importance. Of the baths of Constantine, of Alexander, of Domitian, or rather of Titus, some vestige might yet be found. 4. The triumphal arches of Titus, Severus, and Constantine, were entire, both the structure and the inscriptions: a falling fragment was honoured with the name of Trajan; and two arches, then extant, in the Flaminian way, have been ascribed to the base memory of Faustina and Gallienus. 5. After the wonder of the Coliseum, Poggius might have overlooked a small amphitheatre of brick, most probably for the use of the prætorian camp: the theatres of Marcellus and Pompey were occupied in a great measure by public and private buildings; and in the Circus, Agonalis and Maximus, little more than the situation and the form could be investigated. 6. The columns of Trajan and Antonine were still erect; but the Egyptian obelisks were broken or buried. A people of gods and heroes, the workmanship of art, was reduced to one equestrian figure of gilt brass and to five marble statues, of which the most conspicuous were the two horses of Phidias and Praxiteles. 7. The two mausoleums or seplchres of Augustus and Hadrian could not otally be lost; but the former was only visible s a mound of earth, and the latter, the castle of St. Angelo, had acquired the name and appearance of a modern fortress. With the addition of ome separate and nameless columns, such were he remains of the ancient city; for the marks of a more recent structure might be detected in he walls, which formed a circumference of ten miles, included three hundred and seventy-nine turrets, and opened into the country by thirteen gates.

This melancholy picture was drawn above nine hundred years after the fall of the Western empire, and even of the Gothic kingdom of Italy. A long period of distress and anarchy, in which empire, and arts. and riches had migrated from the banks of the Tiber, was incapable of restoring or adorning the city; and, as all that is human must retrograde if it do not advance, every successive age must have hastened the ruin of the work of antiquity. To measure the progress of decay, and to ascertain, at each era, the state of each edifice, would be an endless and a useless labour; and I shall content myself with two observations which will introduce a short inquiry into the general causes and effects. 1. Two hundred years before the eloquent complaint of Poggius, an anonymous writer composed a description of Rome.[6] His ignorance may repeat the same objects under strange and fabulous names. Yet this barbarous topographer had eyes and ears; he could observe the visible remains; he could listen to the tradition of the people; and he distinctly enumerates seven theatres, eleven baths, twelve arches, and eighteen palaces, of which many had disappeared before the time of Poggius. It is apparent that many stately monuments of antiquity survived till a late period,[7] and that the principles of destruction acted with vigorous and increasing energy in the thirteenth and fourteenth centuries. 2. The same reflection must be applied to the last three ages; and we should vainly seek the Septizonium of Severus,[8] which is celebrated by Petrarch and the antiquarians of the sixteenth century. While the Roman edifices were still entire, the first blows, however weighty and impetuous, were resisted by the solidity of the mass and the harmony of the parts; but the slightest touch would precipitate the fragments of arches and columns, that already nodded to their fall.

After a diligent inquiry I can discern four principal causes of the ruin of Rome, which continued to operate in a period of more than a thousand years. I. The injuries of time and nature. II. The hostile attacks of the barbarians and Christians. III. The use and abuse of the materials. And, IV. The domestic quarrels of the Romans.

I. The art of man is able to construct monuments far more permanent than the narrow span of his own existence: yet these monuments, like himself, are perishable and frail; and in the boundless annals of time his life and his labours must equally be measured as a fleeting moment. Of a simple and solid edifice it is not easy however to circumscribe the duration. As the wonders of ancient days, the pyramids[9] attracted the curiosity of the ancients: a hundred generations, the leaves of autumn,[10] have dropped into the grave; and after the fall of the Pharaohs and Ptolemies, the Cæsars and caliphs, the same pyramids stand erect and unshaken above the floods of the Nile. A complex figure of various and minute parts is more accessible to injury and decay; and the silent lapse of time is often accelerated by hurricanes and earthquakes, by fires and inundations. The air and earth have doubtless been shaken; and the lofty turrets of Rome have tottered from their foundations; but the seven hills do not appear to be placed on the great cavities of the globe; nor has the city, in any age, been exposed to the convulsions of nature, which, in the climate of Antioch, Lisbon, or Lima, have crumbled in a few moments the works of ages into dust. Fire is the most powerful agent of life and death: the rapid mischief may be kindled and propagated by the industry or negligence of mankind; and every period of the Roman annals is marked by the repetition of similar calamities. A memorable conflagration, the guilt or misfortune of Nero's reign, continued, though with unequal fury, either six or nine days.[11] Innumerable buildings, crowded in close and crooked streets, supplied perpetual fuel for the flames; and when they ceased, four only of the fourteen regions were left entire; three were totally destroyed, and seven were deformed by the relics of smoking and lacerated edifices.[12] In the full meridian of empire the metropolis arose with fresh beauty from her ashes; yet the memory of the old deplored their irreparable losses, the arts of Greece, the trophies of victory, the monuments of primitive or fabulous antiquity. In the days of distress and anarchy every wound is mortal, every fall irretrievable; nor can the damage be restored either by the public care of government, or the activity of private interest. Yet two causes may be alleged which render the calamity of fire more destructive to a flourishing than a decayed city. 1. The more combustible materials of brick, timber, and metals, are first melted or consumed; but the flames may play without injury or effect on the naked walls and massy arches that have been despoiled of their ornaments. 2. It is among the common and plebeian habitations that a mischievous spark is most easily blown to a conflagration; but as soon as they are devoured, the greater edifices which have resisted or escaped are left as so many islands in a state of solitude and safety. From her situation, Rome is exposed to the danger of frequent inundations. Without excepting the Tiber, the rivers that descend from either side of the Apennine have a short and irregular course; a shallow stream in the summer heats; an impetuous torrent when it is swelled in the spring or winter, by the fall of rain and the melting of the snows. When the current is repelled from the sea by adverse winds, when the ordinary bed is inadequate to the weight of waters, they rise above the banks, and overspread, without limits or control, the plains and cities of the adjacent country. Soon after the triumph of the first Punic war the Tiber was increased by unusual rains; and the inundation, surpassing all former measure of time and place, destroyed all the buildings that were situate below the hills of Rome. According to the variety of ground, the same mischief was produced by different means; and the edifices were either swept away by the sudden impulse, or dissolved and undermined by the long continuance, of the flood.[13] Under the reign of Augustus the same calamity was renewed: the lawless river overturned the palaces and temples on its banks;[14] and, after the labours of the emperor in cleansing and widening the bed that was encumbered with ruins,[15] the vigilance of his successors was exercised by similar dangers and designs. The project of diverting into new channels the Tiber itself, or some of the dependent streams, was long opposed by superstition and local interests;[16] nor did the use compensate the toil and cost of the tardy and imperfect execution. The servitude of rivers is the noblest and most important victory which man has obtained over the licentiousness of nature;[17] and if such were the ravages of the Tiber under a firm and active government, what could oppose, or who can enumerate, the injuries of the city after the fall of the Western empire? A remedy was at length produced by the evil itself: the accumulation of rubbish and the earth that has been washed down from the

hills is supposed to have elevated the plain of Rome fourteen or fifteen feet, perhaps, above the ancient level;[18] and the modern city is less accessible to the attacks of the river.[19]

II. The crowd of writers of every nation, who impute the destruction of the Roman monuments to the Goths and the Christians, have neglected to inquire how far they were animated by a hostile principle, and how far they possessed the means and the leisure to satiate their enmity. In the preceding volumes of this History I have described the triumph of barbarism and religion; and I can only resume, in a few words, their real or imaginary connection with the ruin of ancient Rome. Our fancy may create, or adopt, a pleasing romance, that the Goths and Vandals sallied from Scandinavia, ardent to avenge the flight of Odin;[20] to break the chains, and to chastise the oppressors, of mankind; that they wished to burn the records of classic literature, and to found their national architecture on the broken members of the Tuscan and Corinthian orders. But in simple truth, the northern conquerors were neither sufficiently savage, nor sufficiently refined, to entertain such aspiring ideas of destruction and revenge. The shepherds of Scythia and Germany had been educated in the armies of the empire, whose discipline they acquired, and whose weakness they invaded: with the familiar use of the Latin tongue they had learned to reverence the name and titles of Rome; and though incapable of emulating, they were more inclined to admire than to abolish the arts and studies of a brighter period. In the transient possession of a rich and unresisting capital, the soldiers of Alaric and Genseric were stimulated by the passions of a victorious army; amidst the wanton indulgence of lust or cruelty, portable wealth was the object of their search: nor could they derive either pride or pleasure from the unprofitable reflection that they had battered to the ground the works of the consuls and Cæsars. Their moments were indeed precious the Goths evacuated Rome on the sixth,[21] the Vandals on the fifteenth day;[22] and, though it be far more difficult to build than to destroy, their hasty assault would have made a slight impression on the solid piles of antiquity. We may remember that both Alaric and Genseric affected to spare the buildings of the city; that they subsisted in strength and beauty under the auspicious government of Theodoric;[23] and that the momentary resentment of Totila[24] was disarmed by his own temper and the advice of his friends and enemies. From these innocent barbarians the reproach may be transferred to the Catholics of Rome. The statues, altars, and houses of the demons were an abomination in their eyes; and in the absolute command of the city, they might labour with zeal and perseverance to erase the idolatry of their ancestors. The demolition of the temples in the East[25] affords to *them* an example of conduct, and to *us* an argument of belief; and it is probable that a portion of guilt or merit may be imputed with justice to the Roman proselytes. Yet their abhorrence was confined to the monuments of heathen superstition; and the civil structures that were dedicated to the business or pleasure of society might be preserved without injury or scandal. The change of religion was accomplished, not by a popular tumult, but by the decrees of the emperors, of the senate, and of time. Of the Christian hierarchy the bishops of Rome were commonly the most prudent and least fanatic; nor can any positive charge be opposed to the meritorious act of saving and converting the majestic structure of the Pantheon.[26]

III. The value of any object that supplies the wants or pleasures of mankind is compounded of its substance and its form, of the materials and the manufacture. Its price must depend on the number of persons by whom it may be acquired and used; on the extent of the market; and consequently on the ease or difficulty of remote exportation, according to the nature of the commodity, its local situation, and the temporary circumstances of the world. The barbarian conquerors of Rome usurped in a moment the toil and treasure of successive ages; but, except the luxuries of immediate consumption, they must view without desire all that could not be removed from the city in the Gothic waggons or the fleet of the Vandals.[27] Gold and silver were the first objects of their avarice; as in every country, and in the smallest compass, they represent the most ample command of the industry and possessions of mankind. A vase or a statue of those precious metals might tempt the vanity of some barbarian chief; but the grosser multitude, regardless of the form, was tenacious only of the substance; and the melted ingots might be readily divided and stamped into the current coin of the empire. The less active or less fortunate robbers were reduced to the baser plunder of brass, lead, iron, and copper: whatever had escaped the Goths and Vandals was pillaged by the Greek tyrants; and the emperor Constans, in his rapacious visit, stripped the bronze tiles from the roof of the Pantheon.[28] The edifices of Rome might be considered as a vast and various mine; the first labour of extracting the materials was already performed; the metals were purified and cast; the marbles were hewn and polished; and after foreign and domestic rapine had been satiated, the remains of the city, could a purchaser have been found, were still venal. The monuments of antiquity had been left naked of their precious ornaments; but the Romans would demolish with their own hands the arches and walls, if the hope of profit could surpass the cost of the labour and exportation. If Charlemagne had fixed in Italy the seat of the Western empire, his genius would have aspired to restore, rather than to violate, the works of the Cæsars; but policy confined the French monarch to the forests of Germany; his taste could be gratified only by destruction; and the new palace of Aix-la-Chapelle was decorated with the marbles of Ravenna[29] and Rome.[30] Five hundred years after Charlemagne, a king of Sicily, Robert, the wisest and most liberal sovereign of the age, was supplied with the same materials by the easy navigation of the Tiber and the sea; and Petrarch sighs in indignant complaint, that the ancient capital of the world should adorn from her own bowels the slothful luxury of Naples.[31] But these examples of plunder or purchase were rare in the darker ages; and the Romans, alone and unenvied, might have applied to their private or public use the remaining structures of antiquity, if in their present form and situation they had not been useless in a great measure to the city and its inhabitants. The walls still described the old circumference, but the city had descended from the seven hills into the Campus Martius; and some of the noblest monuments which had braved the injuries of time were left in a desert far remote from the habitations of mankind. The palaces of the senators were no longer adapted to the manners or fortunes of their indigent successors: the use of baths[32] and porticoes was forgotten: in the sixth century the games of the theatre, amphitheatre, and circus had been interrupted: some temples were devoted to the prevailing worship; but the Christian churches preferred the holy figure of the cross; and fashion, or reason, had distributed after a peculiar model the cells and offices of the cloister. Under the ecclesiastical reign the number of these pious foundations was enormously multiplied: and the city was crowded with forty monasteries of men, twenty of women, and sixty chapters and colleges of canons and priests,[33] who aggravated, instead of relieving, the depopulation of the tenth century. But if the forms of ancient architecture were disregarded by a people insensible of their use and beauty, the plentiful materials were applied to every call of necessity or superstition; till the fairest columns of the Ionic and Corinthian orders, the richest marbles of Paros and Numidia, were degraded, perhaps to the support of a convent or a stable. The daily havoc which is perpetrated by the Turks in the cities of Greece and Asia may afford a melancholy example; and in the gradual destruction of the monuments of Rome, Sixtus the Fifth may alone be excused for employing the stones of the Septizonium in the glorious edifice of St. Peter's.[34] A fragment, a ruin, howsoever mangled or profaned, may be viewed with pleasure and regret; but the greater part of the marble was deprived of substance, as well as of place and proportion; it was burnt to lime for the purpose of cement. Since the arrival of Poggius the temple of Concord[35] and many capital structures had vanished from his eyes; and an epigram of the same age expresses a just and pious fear that the continuance of this practice would finally annihilate all the monuments of antiquity.[36] The smallness of their numbers was the sole check on the demands and depredations of the Romans. The imagination of Petrarch might create the presence of a mighty people;[37] and I hesitate to believe that, even in the fourteenth century, they could be reduced to a contemptible list of thirty-three thousand inhabitants. From that period to the reign of Leo the Tenth, if they multiplied to the amount of eighty-five thousand,[38] the increase of citizens was in some degree pernicious to the ancient city.

IV. I have reserved for the last the most potent and forcible cause of destruction, the domestic hostilities of the Romans themselves. Under the dominion of the Greek and French emperors the peace of the city was disturbed by accidental, though frequent, seditions: it is from the decline of the latter, from the beginning of the tenth century, that we may date the licentiousness of private war, which violated with impunity the laws of the Code and the Gospel, without respecting the majesty of the absent sovereign, or the presence and person of the vicar of Christ. In a dark period of five hundred years Rome was perpetually afflicted by the sanguinary quarrels of the nobles and the people, the Guelphs and Ghibelines, the Colonna and Ursini; and if much has escaped the knowledge, and much is unworthy of the notice, of history, I have exposed in the two preceding chapters the causes and effects of the public disorders. At such a time, when every quarrel was decided by the sword, and none could trust their lives or properties to the impotence of law, the powerful citizens were armed for safety, or offence, against the domestic enemies whom they feared or hated. Except Venice alone, the same dangers and designs were common to all the free republics of Italy; and the nobles usurped the prerogative of fortifying their houses, and erecting strong towers[39] that were capable of resisting a sudden attack. The cities were filled with these hostile edifices; and the example of Lucca, which contained three hundred towers; her law, which confined their height to the measure of fourscore feet, may be extended with suitable latitude to the more opulent and populous states. The first step of the senator Brancaleone in the establishment of peace and justice was to demolish (as we have already seen) one hundred and forty of the towers of Rome; and, in the last days of anarchy and discord, as late as the reign of Martin the Fifth, forty-four still stood in one of the thirteen or fourteen regions of the city. To this mischievous purpose the remains of antiquity were most readily adapted: the temples and arches afforded a broad and solid basis for the new structures of brick and stone; and we can name the modern turrets that were raised on the triumphal monuments of Julius Cæsar, Titus, and the Antonines.[40] With some slight alterations, a theatre, an amphitheatre, a mausoleum, was transformed into a strong and spacious citadel. I need not repeat that the mole of Hadrian has assumed the title and form of the castle of St. Angelo[41] the Septizonium of Severus was capable of standing against a royal army;[42] the sepulchre of Metella has sunk under its outworks;[43] the theatres of Pompey and Marcellus were occupied by the Savelli and Ursini families;[44] and the rough fortress has been gradually softened to the splendour and elegance of an Italian palace. Even the churches were encompassed with arms and bulwarks, and the military engines on the roof of St. Peter's were the terror of the Vatican and the scandal of the Christian world. Whatever is fortified will be attacked; and whatever is attacked may be destroyed. Could the Romans have wrested from the popes the castle of St. Angelo, they had resolved by a public decree to annihilate that monument of servitude. Every building of defence was exposed to a siege; and in every siege the arts and engines of destruction were laboriously employed. After the death of Nicholas the Fourth, Rome, without a sovereign or a senate, was abandoned six months to the fury of civil war. "The houses," says a cardinal and poet of the times,[45] "were crushed by the weight and velocity of enormous stones;[46] the walls were perforated by the strokes of the battering-ram; the towers were involved in fire and smoke; and the assailants were stimulated by rapine and revenge." The work was consummated by the tyranny of the laws; and the factions of Italy alternately exercised a blind and thoughtless vengeance on their adversaries, whose houses and castles they razed to the ground.[47] In comparing the *days* of foreign with the *ages* of domestic hostility, we must pronounce that the latter have been far more ruinous to the city; and our opinion is confirmed by the evidence of Petrarch. "Behold," says the laureate, "the relics of Rome, the image of her pristine greatness! neither time nor the barbarian can boast the merit of this stupendous destruction: it was perpetrated by her own citizens, by the most illustrious of her sons; and your ancestors (he writes to a noble Annibaldi) have done with the battering-ram what the Punic hero could not accomplish with the sword."[48] The influence of the two last principles of decay must in some degree be multiplied by each other; since the houses and towers which were subverted by civil war required a new and perpetual supply from the monuments of antiquity.

These general observations may be separately applied to the amphitheatre of Titus, which has obtained the name of the COLISEUM,[49] either from its magnitude, or from Nero's colossal statue: an edifice, had it been left to time and nature, which might perhaps have claimed an eternal duration. The curious antiquaries, who have computed the numbers and seats, are disposed to believe that above the upper row of stone steps the amphitheatre was encircled and elevated with several stages of wooden galleries, which were repeatedly consumed by fire, and restored by the emperors. Whatever was precious, or portable, or profane, the statues of gods and heroes, and the costly ornaments of sculpture, which were cast in brass, or overspread with leaves of silver and gold, became the first prey of conquest or fanaticism, of the avarice of the barbarians or the Christians. In the massy stones of the Coliseum many holes are discerned; and the two most probable conjectures represent the various accidents of its decay. These stones were connected by solid links of brass or iron, nor had the eye of rapine overlooked the value of the baser metals;[50] the vacant space was converted into a fair or market; the artisans of the Coliseum are mentioned in an ancient survey; and the chasms were perforated or enlarged to receive the poles that supported the shops or tents of the mechanic trades.[51] Reduced to its naked majesty, the Flavian amphitheatre was contemplated with awe and admiration by the pilgrims of the North; and their rude enthusiasm broke forth in a sublime proverbial expression, which is recorded in the eighth century, in the fragments of the venerable Bede: "As long as the Coliseum stands, Rome shall stand; when the Coliseum falls, Rome shall fall; when Rome falls, the world will fall."[52] In the modern system of war, a situation commanded by three hills would not be chosen for a fortress; but the strength of the walls and arches could resist the engines of assault; a numerous garrison might be lodged in the enclosure; and while one faction occupied the Vatican and the Capitol, the other was intrenched in the Lateran and the Coliseum.[53]

The abolition at Rome of the ancient games must be understood with some latitude; and the carnival sports, of the Testacean mount and the Circus Agonalis,[54] were regulated by the law[55] or custom of the city. The senator presided with dignity and pomp to adjudge and distribute the prizes, the gold ring, or the *pallium*,[56] as it was styled, of cloth or silk. A tribute on the Jews supplied the annual expense;[57] and the races, on foot, on horseback, or in chariots, were ennobled by a tilt and tournament of seventy-two of the Roman youth. In the year one thousand three hundred and thirty-two, a bull-feast, after the fashion of the Moors and Spaniards, was celebrated in the Coliseum itself; and the living manners are painted in a diary of the times.[58] A convenient order of benches was restored; and a general proclamation as far as Rimini and Ravenna, invited the nobles to exercise their skill and courage in this perilous adventure. The Roman ladies were marshalled in three squadrons, and seated in three balconies, which on this day, the third of September, were lined with scarlet cloth. The fair Jacova di Rovere led the matrons from beyond the Tiber, a pure and native race, who still represent the features and character of antiquity. The remainder of the city was divided as usual between the Colonna and Ursini: the two factions were proud of the number and beauty of their female bands: the charms of Savella Ursini are mentioned with praise; and the Colonna regretted the absence of the youngest of their house, who had sprained her ankle in the garden of Nero's tower. The lots of the champions were drawn by an old and respectable citizen; and they descended into the arena, or pit, to encounter the wild bulls, on foot as it should seem, with a single spear. Amidst the crowd, our annalist has selected the names, colours, and devices of twenty of the most conspicuous knights. Several of the names are the most illustrious of Rome and the ecclesiastical state: Malatesta, Polenta, della Valle, Cafarello, Savelli, Capoccio, Conti, Annibaldi, Altieri, Corsi: the colours were adapted to their taste and situation; the devices are expressive of hope or despair, and breathe the spirit of gallantry and arms. "I am alone, like the youngest of the Horatii," the confidence of an intrepid stranger: "I live disconsolate," a weeping widower: "I burn under the ashes," a discreet lover: "I adore Lavinia, or Lucretia," the ambiguous declaration of a modern passion: "My faith is as pure," the motto of a white livery: "Who is stronger than myself?" of a lion's hide: "If I am drowned in blood, what a pleasant death!" the wish of ferocious courage. The pride or prudence of the Ursini restrained them from the field, which was occupied by three of their hereditary rivals, whose inscriptions denoted the lofty greatness of the Colonna name: "Though sad, I am strong:" "Strong as I am great:" "If I fall," addressing himself to the spectators, "you fall with me"—intimating (says the contemporary writer) that, while the other families were the subjects of the Vatican, they alone were the supporters of the Capitol. The combats of the amphitheatre were dangerous and bloody. Every champion successively encountered a wild bull; and the victory may be ascribed to the quadrupeds, since no more than eleven were left on the field, with the loss of nine wounded and eighteen killed on the side of their adversaries. Some of the noblest families might mourn, but the pomp of the funerals, in the churches of St. John Lateran and Sta. Maria Maggiore, afforded a second holiday to the people. Doubtless it was not in such conflicts that the blood of the Romans should have been shed; yet, in blaming their rashness, we are compelled to applaud their gallantry; and the noble volunteers, who display their magnificence, and risk their lives, under the balconies of the fair, excite a more generous sympathy than the thousands of captives and malefactors who were reluctantly dragged to the scene of slaughter.[59]

This use of the amphitheatre was a rare, perhaps a singular, festival: the demand for the materials was a daily and continual want, which the citizens could gratify without restraint or remorse. In the fourteenth century a scandalous act of concord secured to both factions the privilege of extracting stones from the free and common quarry of the Coliseum;[60] and Poggius laments that the greater part of these stones had been burnt to lime by the folly of the Romans.[61] To check this abuse, and to prevent the nocturnal crimes that might be perpetrated in the vast and gloomy recess, Eugenius the Fourth surrounded it with a wall and, by a charter, long extant, granted both the ground and edifice to the monks of an adjacent convent.[62] After his death the wall was overthrown in a tumult of the people; and had they themselves respected the noblest monument of their fathers, they might have justified the resolve that it should never be degraded to private property. The inside was damaged; but in the middle of the sixteenth century, an era of taste and learning, the exterior circumference of one thousand six hundred and twelve feet was still entire and inviolate; a triple elevation of fourscore arches, which rose to the height of one hundred and eight feet. Of the present ruin the nephews of Paul the Third are the guilty agents; and every traveller who views the Farnese palace may curse the sacrilege and luxury of these upstart princes.[63] A similar reproach is applied to the Barberini; and the repetition of injury might be dreaded from every reign, till the Coliseum was placed under the safeguard of religion by the most liberal of the pontiffs, Benedict the Fourteenth, who consecrated a spot which persecution and fable had stained with the blood of so many Christian martyrs.[64]

When Petrarch first gratified his eyes with a view of those monuments whose scattered fragments so far surpass the most eloquent descriptions, he was astonished at the supine indifference[65] of the Romans themselves;[66] he was humbled rather than elated by the discovery that, except his friend Rienzi, and one of the Colonna, a stranger of the Rhône was more conversant with these antiquities than the nobles and natives of the metropolis.[67] The ignorance and credulity of the Romans are elaborately displayed in the old survey of the city which was composed about the beginning of the thirteenth century; and, without dwelling on the manifold errors of name and place, the legend of the Capitol[68] may provoke a smile of contempt and indignation. "The Capitol," ays the anonymous writer, "is so named as being the head of the world; where the consuls and senators formerly resided for the government of the city and the globe. The strong and lofty walls were covered with glass and gold, and crowned with a roof of the richest and most curious carving. Below the citadel stood a palace, of gold for the greatest part, decorated with precious stones, and whose value might be esteemed at one third of the world itself. The statues of all the provinces were arranged in order; each with a small bell suspended from its neck; and such was the contrivance of art magic,[69] that, if the province rebelled against Rome, the statue turned round to that quarter of the heavens, the bell rang, the prophet of the Capitol reported the prodigy, and the senate was admonished of the impending danger." A second example, of less importance, though of equal absurdity, may be drawn from the two marble horses, led by two naked youths, which have since been transported from the baths of Constantine to the Quirinal hill. The groundless application of the names of Phidias and Praxiteles may perhaps be excused; but these Grecian sculptors should not have been removed above four hundred years from the age of Pericles to that of Tiberius; they should not have been transformed into two philosophers or magicians, whose nakedness was the symbol of truth and knowledge, who revealed to the emperor his most secret actions; and, after refusing all pecuniary recompense, solicited the honour of leaving this eternal monument of themselves.[70] Thus awake to the power of magic, the Romans were insensible to the beauties of art: no more than five statues were visible to the eyes of Poggius; and of the multitudes which chance or design had buried under the ruins, the resurrection was fortunately delayed till a safer and more enlightened age.[71] The Nile, which now adorns the Vatican, had been explored by some labourers, in digging a vineyard near the temple, or convent, of the Minerva; but the impatient proprietor, who was tormented by some visits of curiosity, restored the unprofitable marble to its former grave.[72] The discovery of a statue of Pompey, ten feet in length, was the occasion of a lawsuit. It had been found under a partition wall: the equitable judge had pronounced, that the head should be separated from the body to satisfy the claims of the contiguous owners; and the sentence would have been executed if the intercession of a cardinal, and the liberality of a pope, had not rescued the Roman hero from the hands of his barbarous countrymen.[73]

But the clouds of barbarism were gradually dispelled; and the peaceful authority of Martin the Fifth and his successors restored the ornaments of the city as well as the order of the ecclesiastical state. The improvements of Rome, since the fifteenth century, have not been the spontaneous produce of freedom and industry. The first and most natural root of a great city is the labour and populousness of the adjacent country, which supplies the materials of subsistence, of manufactures, and of foreign trade. But the greater part of the Campagna of Rome is reduced to a dreary and desolate wilderness: the overgrown estates of the princes and the clergy are cultivated by the lazy hands of indigent and hopeless vassals; and the scanty harvests are confined or exported for the benefit of a monopoly. A second and more artificial cause of the growth of a metropolis is the residence of a monarch, the expense of a luxurious court, and the tributes of dependent provinces. Those provinces and tributes had been lost in the fall of the empire; and if some streams of the silver of Peru and the gold of Brazil have been attracted by the Vatican, the revenues of the cardinals, the fees of office, the oblations of pilgrims and clients, and the remnant of ecclesiastical taxes, afford a poor and precarious supply, which maintains, however, the idleness of the court and city. The population of Rome, far below the measure of the great capitals of Europe, does not exceed one hundred and seventy thousand inhabitants;[74] and within the spacious enclosure of the walls, the largest portion of the seven hills is overspread with vineyards and ruins. The beauty and splendour of the modern city may be ascribed to the abuses of the government, to the influence of superstition. Each reign (the exceptions are rare) has been marked by the rapid elevation of a new family, enriched by the childless pontiff at the expense of the church and country. The palaces of these fortunate nephews are the most costly monuments of elegance and servitude: the perfect arts of architecture, painting, and sculpture, have been prostituted in their service; and their galleries and gardens are decorated with the most precious works of antiquity, which taste or vanity has prompted them to collect. The ecclesiastical revenues were more decently employed by the popes themselves in the pomp of the Catholic worship; but it is superfluous to enumerate their pious foundations of altars, chapels, and churches, since these lesser stars are eclipsed by the sun of the Vatican, by the dome of St. Peter, the most glorious structure that ever has been applied to the use of religion. The fame of Julius the Second, Leo the Tenth, and Sixtus the Fifth, is accompanied by the superior merit of Bramante and Fontana, of Raphael and Michael Angelo; and the same munificence which had been displayed in palaces and temples was directed with equal zeal to revive and emulate the labours of antiquity. Prostrate obelisks were raised from the ground, and erected in the most conspicuous places; of the eleven aqueducts of the Cæsars and consuls, three were restored; the artificial rivers were conducted over a long series of old or of new arches, to discharge into marble basins a flood of salubrious and refreshing waters: and the spectator, impatient to ascend the steps of St. Peter's, is detained by a column of Egyptian granite, which rises between two lofty and perpetual fountains to the height of one hundred and twenty feet. The map, the description, the monuments of ancient Rome, have been elucidated by the diligence of the antiquarian and the student;[75] and the footsteps of heroes, the relics, not of superstition, but of empire, are devoutly visited by a new race of pilgrims from the remote and once savage countries of the North.

Of these pilgrims, and of every reader, the attention will be excited by a History of the Decline and Fall of the Roman Empire; the greatest, perhaps, and most awful scene in the history of mankind. The various causes and progressive effects are connected with many of the events most interesting in human annals: the artful policy of the Cæsars, who long maintained the name and image of a free republic; the disorders of military despotism; the rise, establishment, and sects of Christianity; the foundation of Constantinople; the division of the monarchy; the invasion and settlements of the barbarians of Germany and Scythia; the institutions of the civil law; the character and religion of Mohammed; the temporal sovereignty of the popes; the restoration and decay of the Western empire of Charlemagne; the crusades of the Latins in the East; the conquests of the Saracens and Turks; the ruin of the Greek empire; the state and revolutions of Rome in the middle age. The historian may applaud the importance and variety of his subject; but, while he is conscious of his own imperfections, he must often accuse the deficiency of his materials. It was among the ruins of the Capitol that I first conceived the idea of a work which has amused and exercised near twenty years of my life, and which, however inadequate to my own wishes, I finally deliver to the curiosity and candour of the public.

LAUSANNE, *June* 27, 1787.

Chapter XLI

1. The complete series of the Vandal war is related by Procopius in a regular and elegant narrative (l. i. c. 9–25, l. ii. c. 1–13); and happy would be my lot, could I always tread in the footsteps of such a guide. From the entire and diligent perusal of the Greek text I have a right to pronounce that the Latin and French versions of Grotius and Cousin may not be implicitly trusted; yet the President Cousin has been often praised, and Hugo Grotius was the first scholar of a learned age.

2. See Ruinart, Hist. Persecut. Vandal. c. xii. p. 589 [ed. Par. 1694]. His best evidence is drawn from the Life of St. Fulgentius, composed by one of his disciples, transcribed in a great measure in the Annals of Baronius, and printed in several great collections (Catalog. Bibliot. Bunavianæ, tom. i. vol. ii. p. 1258).

3. For what quality of the mind or body? For speed, or beauty, or valour?—In what language did the Vandals read Homer?—Did he speak German?—The Latins had four versions (Fabric. tom. i. l. ii. c. 3, p. 297): yet, in spite of the praises of Seneca (Consol. [ad Polyb.] c. 26), they appear to have been more successful in imitating than in translating the Greek poets. But the name of Achilles might be famous and popular, even among the illiterate barbarians.

4. *A year*—absurd exaggeration! The conquest of Africa may be dated A.D. 533, September 14. It is celebrated by Justinian in the preface to his Institutes, which were published November 21 of the same year. Including the voyage and return, such a computation might be truly applied to *our* Indian empire.

5. Ὥρμητο δὲ ὁ Βελισάριος ἐκ Γερμανίας, ἣ Θρα-κῶντε καὶ Ἰλλυρῶν μεταξὺ κεῖται (Procop. Vandal. l. i. c. 11 [tom. i. p. 361, ed. Bonn]). Aleman. (Not. ad Anecdot. p. 5), an Italian, could easily reject the German vanity of Giphanius and Velserus, who wished to claim the hero; but his Germania, a metropolis of Thrace, I cannot find in any civil or ecclesiastical lists of the provinces and cities.

6. The two first Persian campaigns of Belisarius are fairly and copiously related by his secretary (Persic. l. i. c. 12–18).

7. See the birth and character of Antonina, in the Anecdotes, c. 1, and the notes of Alemannus, p. 3.

8. See the preface of Procopius [Bell. Pers. c. 1]. The enemies of archery might quote the reproaches of Diomede (Iliad, xi. 385, etc.) and the permittere vulnera ventis of Lucan (viii. 383): yet the Romans could not despise the arrows of the Parthians; and in the siege of Troy, Pandarus, Paris, and Teucer pierced those haughty warriors who insulted them as women or children.

9. Νευρὴν μὲν μαζῷ πέλασεν, τόξῳ δὲ σίδηρον (Iliad, iv, 123). How concise—how just—how beautiful is the whole picture! I see the attitudes of the archer —I hear the twanging of the bow:—

Λίγξε βιός, νευρὴ δὲ μέγ' ἴαχεν, ἇλτο δ' ὀϊστός.

10. The text appears to allow for the largest vessels 50,000 medimni, or 3000 tons (since the *medimnus* weighed 160 Roman, or 120 avoirdupois, pounds). I have given a more rational interpretation, by supposing that the Attic style of Procopius conceals the legal and popular *modius*, a sixth part of the *medimnus* (Hooper's Ancient Measures, p. 152, etc.). A contrary, and indeed a stranger, mistake has crept into an oration of Dinarchus (contra Demosthenem, in Reiske Orator. Græc. tom. iv. P. ii. p. 34). By reducing the *number* of ships from 500 to 50, and translating μεδίμνοι by *mines*, or pounds, Cousin has generously allowed 500 tons for the whole of the Imperial fleet?—Did he never think?

11. I have read of a Greek legislator who inflicted a *double* penalty on the crimes committed in a state of intoxication; but it seems agreed that this was rather a political than a moral law.

12. Or even in three days, since they anchored the first evening in the neighbouring isle of Tenedos: the second day they sailed to Lesbos, the third to the promontory of Eubœa, and on the fourth they reached Argos (Homer. Odyss. iii, 130–183; Wood's Essay on Homer, p. 40–46). A pirate sailed from the Hellespont to the seaport of Sparta in three days (Xenophon. Hellen. l. ii. c. 1).

13. Caucana, near Camarina, is at least 50 miles (350 or 400 stadia) from Syracuse (Cluver. Sicilia Antiqua, p. 191).

14. Procopius, Gothic. l. i. c. 3. Tibi tollit hinnitum apta quadrigis equa, in the Sicilian pastures of Grosphus (Horat. Carm. ii. 16). Acragas . . . magnanimûm quondam generator equorum (Virg. Æneid. iii. 704). Thero's horses, whose victories are immortalised by Pindar, were bred in this country.

15. The Caput Vada of Procopius (where Justinian afterwards founded a city—De Ædific. l. vi. c. 6) is the promontory of Ammon in Strabo, the Brachodes of Ptolemy, the Capaudia of the moderns, a long narrow slip that runs into the sea (Shaw's Travels, p. 111).

16. A centurion of Mark Antony expressed, though in a more manly strain, the same dislike to the sea and to naval combats (Plutarch in the life of Antony).

17. Sullecte is perhaps the Turris Hannibalis, an old building, now as large as the Tower of London. The march of Belisarius to Leptis, Adrumetum, etc., is illustrated by the campaign of Cæsar (Hirtius de Bello Africano, with the Analyse of Guichardt), and Shaw's Travels (p. 105–113) in the same country.

18. Παράδεισος κάλλιστος ἀπάντων ὧν ἡμεῖς ἴσμεν. The paradises, a name and fashion adopted from Persia, may be represented by the royal garden of Ispahan (Voyage d'Olearius, p. 774). See, in the Greek romances, their most perfect model (Longus, Pastoral. l. iv. p. 99–101; Achilles Tatius, l. i. p. 22, 23).

19. The neighbourhood of Carthage, the sea, the land, and the rivers, are changed almost as much as the works of man. The isthmus, or neck, of the city is now confounded with the continent; the harbour is a dry plain; and the lake, or stagnum, no more than a morass, with six or seven feet water in the mid-channel. See D'Anville (Géographie Ancienne, tom. iii. p. 82), Shaw (Travels, p. 77–84), Marmol (Description de l'Afrique, tom. ii. p. 465), and Thuanus (lviii. 12, tom. iii. p. 334).

20. From Delphi, the name of Delphicum was given, both in Greek and Latin, to a tripod; and, by an easy analogy, the same appellation was extended at Rome, Constantinople, and Carthage to the royal banqueting-room. (Procopius. Vandal. l. i. c. 21. Ducange, Gloss. Græc. p. 277. Δέλφικον, ad Alexiad. 412.)

21. These orations always express the sense of the times, and sometimes of the actors. I have condensed that sense, and thrown away declamation.

22. The relics of St. Augustin were carried by the African bishops to their Sardinian exile (A.D. 500); and it was believed, in the eighth century, that Liutprand, king of the Lombards, transported them (A.D. 721) from Sardinia to Pavia. In the year 1695 the Augustin friars of that city *found* a brick arch, marble coffin, silver case, silk wrapper, bones, blood, etc., and perhaps an inscription of Agostino in Gothic letters. But this useful discovery has been disputed by reason and jealousy. (Baronius, Annal. A.D. 725, No. 2–9. Tillemont, Mém. Ecclés. tom. xiii. p. 944. Montfaucon, Diarium Ital. p. 26–30. Muratori, Antiq. Ital. Medii Ævi. tom. v. dissert. lviii. p. 9, who had composed a separate treatise before the decree of the bishop of Pavia, and pope Benedict XIII.)

23. Τὰ τῆς πολιτείας προοίμια, is the expression of Procopius (de Ædific. l. vi. c. 7). Ceuta, which has been defaced by the Portuguese, flourished in nobles and palaces, in agriculture and manufactures, under the more prosperous reign of the Arabs (l'Afrique de Marmol, tom. ii. p. 236).

24. See the second and third preambles to the Digest, or Pandects, promulgated A.D. 533, December 16. To the titles of *Vandalicus* and *Africanus*, Justinian, or rather Belisarius, had acquired a just claim; *Gothicus* was premature, and *Francicus* false, and offensive to a great nation.

25. See the original acts in Baronius (A.D. 535, No. 21–54). The emperor applauds his own clemency to the heretics, cum sifficiat eis vivere.

26. Dupin (Geograph. Sacra Africana, p. lix. ad Optat. Milev.) observes and bewails this episcopal decay. In the more prosperous age of the church, he had noticed 690 bishoprics; but however minute were the dioceses, it is not probable that they all existed at the same time.

27. The African laws of Justinian are illustrated by his German biographer (Cod. l. i. tit. 27. Novell. 36, 37, 131. Vit. Justinian. p. 349–377).

28. Mount Papua is placed by D'Anville (tom. iii. p. 92, and Tabul. Imp. Rom. Occident.) near Hippo Regius and the sea; yet this situation ill agrees with the long pursuit beyond Hippo, and the words of Procopius (l. ii. c. 4 [tom. i. p. 427, ed Bonn]), ἐν τοῖς Νουμιδίας ἐσχάτοις.

29. Shaw (Travels, p. 220) most accurately represents the manners of the Bedoweens and Kabyles, the last of whom, by their language, are the remnant of the Moors; yet how changed—how civilised are these modern savages!—provisions are plenty among them, and bread is common.

30. By Procopius it is styled a *lyre;* perhaps *harp* would have been more national. The instruments of music are thus distinguished by Venantius Fortunatus:—

> Romanusque *lyrâ* tibi plaudat, Barbarus *harpâ.*

31. Herodotus elegantly describes the strange effects of grief in another royal captive, Psammetichus [Psammenitus] of Egypt, who wept at the lesser and was silent at the greatest of his calamities (l. iii. c. 14). In the interview of Paulus Æmilius and Perses, Belisarius might study his part: but it is probable that he never read either Livy or Plutarch; and it is certain that his generosity did not need a tutor.

32. After the title of *imperator* had lost the old military sense, and the Roman *auspices* were abolished by Christianity (see La Bléterie, Mém. de l'Académie, tom. xxi. p. 302–332), a triumph might be given with less inconsistency to a private general.

33. If the Ecclesiastes be truly a work of Solomon, and not, like Prior's poem, a pious and moral composition of more recent times, in his name, and on the subject of his repentance. The latter is the opinion of the learned and free-spirited Grotius (Opp. Theolog. tom. i. p. 258); and indeed the Ecclesiastes and Proverbs display a larger compass of thought and experience than seem to belong either to a Jew or a king.

34. In the Bélisaire of Marmontel the king and the conqueror of Africa meet, sup, and converse, without recollecting each other. It is surely a fault of that romance, that not only the hero, but all to whom he had been so conspicuously known, appear to have lost their eyes or their memory.

35. Shaw, p. 59. Yet since Procopius (l. ii. c. 13 [tom. i. p. 466, ed. Bonn]) speaks of a people of Mount Atlas, as already distinguished by white

odies and yellow hair, the phenomenon (which likewise visible in the Andes of Peru, Buffon, om. iii. p. 504) may naturally be ascribed to the elevation of the ground and the temperature of he air.

36. The geographer of Ravenna (l. iii. c. xi. p. 29, 130, 131; Paris, 1688) describes the Mauriania *Gaditana* (opposite to Cadiz), ubi gens Vanalorum, a Belisario devicta in Africâ, fugit, et unquam comparuit.

37. A single voice had protested, and Genseric dismissed, without a formal answer, the Vandals of Germany: but those of Africa derided his prudence, and affected to despise the poverty of their orests (Procopius, Vandal. l. i. c. 22).

38. From the mouth of the great Elector (in 687) Tollius describes the secret royalty and rebellious spirit of the Vandals of Brandenburgh, who could muster five or six thousand soldiers, who had procured some cannon, etc. (Itinerar. Hungar. p. 42, apud Dubos, Hist. de la Monarchie Françoise, tom. i. p. 182, 183). The veracity, not of the elector, but of Tollius himself, may justly be suspected.

39. Procopius (l. i. c. 22 [tom. i. p. 400, ed. Bonn]) was in total darkness—οὔτε μνήμη τις οὔτε ὄνομα ἐς ἐμὲ σωζέται. Under the reign of Dagobert (A.D. 630) the Sclavonian tribes of the Sorbi and Venedi already bordered on Thuringia (Mascou, Hist. of the Germans, xv. 3, 4, 5).

40. Sallust represents the Moors as a remnant of the army of Heracles (de Bell. Jugurth. c. 21 [18]), and Procopius (Vandal. l. ii. c. 10 [tom. ii. p. 450, ed. Bonn]) as the posterity of the Cananæans who fled from the robber Joshua (λῃστὴς). He quotes two columns, with a Phœnician inscription. I believe in the columns—I doubt the inscription—and I reject the pedigree.

41. Virgil (Georgic. iii. 339) and Pomponius Mela (i. 8) describe the wandering life of the African shepherds, similar to that of the Arabs and Tartars; and Shaw (p. 222) is the best commentator on the poet and the geographer.

42. The customary gifts were a sceptre, a crown or cap, a white cloak, a figured tunic, and shoes, all adorned with gold and silver; nor were these precious metals less acceptable in the shape of coin (Procop. Vandal. l. i. c. 25).

43. See the African government and warfare of Solomon in Procopius (Vandal. l. ii. c. 10, 11, 12, 13, 19, 20). He was recalled and again restored; and his last victory dates in the thirteenth year of Justinian (A.D. 539). An accident in his childhood had rendered him an eunuch (l. i. c. 11): the other Roman generals were amply furnished with beards, πώγωνος ἐμπιπλάμενοι (l. ii. c. 8).

44. This natural antipathy of the horse for the camel is affirmed by the ancients (Xenophon. Cyropæd. l. vi. [c. 2.] p. 438; l. vii. [c. 1] p. 483, 492, edit. Hutchinson; Polyæn. Stratagem. vii. 6 [§ 6]; Plin. Hist. Nat. viii. 26; Ælian de Natur. Animal. l. iii. c. 7); but it is disproved by daily experience,

and derided by the best judges, the Orientals (Voyage d'Olearius, p. 553).

45. Procopius is the first who describes Mount Aurasius (Vandal. l. ii. c. 13; De Ædific. l. vi. c. 7). He may be compared with Leo Africanus (dell' Africa, parte v. in Ramusio, tom. i. fol. 77, recto), Marmol (tom. ii. p. 430), and Shaw (p. 56–59).

46. Isidor. Chron. p. 722, edit. Grot. Mariana, Hist. Hispan. l. v. c. 8, p. 173. Yet, according to Isidore, the siege of Ceuta and the death of Theudes happened, A. Æ. H. 586–A.D. 548; and the place was defended, not by the Vandals, but by the Romans.

47. Procopius, Vandal. l. i. c. 24.

48. See the original Chronicle of Isidore and the fifth and sixth books of the History of Spain by Mariana. The Romans were finally expelled by Suintila king of the Visigoths (A.D. 621–626), after their re-union to the catholic church.

49. See the marriage and fate of Amalafrida in Procopius (Vandal. l. i. c. 8, 9), and in Cassiodorus (Var. ix. 1) the expostulation of her royal brother. Compare likewise the Chronicle of Victor Tunnunensis.

50. Lilybæum was built by the Carthaginians, Olymp. xcv. 4; and in the first Punic war a strong situation and excellent harbour rendered that place an important object to both nations.

51. Compare the different passages of Procopius (Vandal. l. ii. c. 5; Gothic. l. i. c. 3).

52. For the reign and character of Amalasontha see Procopius (Gothic. l. i. c. 2, 3, 4, and Anecdot. c. 16, with the Notes of Alemannus), Cassiodorus (Var. viii. ix. x. and xi. 1), and Jornandes (de Rebus Geticis, c. 59, and De Successione Regnorum, in Muratori, tom. i. p. 241).

53. The marriage of Theodoric with Audefleda, the sister of Clovis, may be placed in the year 495, soon after the conquest of Italy (De Buat, Hist. des Peuples, tom. ix. p. 213). The nuptials of Eutharic and Amalasontha were celebrated in 515 (Cassiodor. in Chron. p. 453 [tom. i. p. 395, ed. Rotom.]).

54. At the death of Theodoric his grandson Athalaric is described by Procopius as a boy about eight years old—ὀκτὼ γεγονὼς ἔτη. Cassiodorus, with authority and reason, adds two years to his age—infantulum adhuc vix decennem.

55. The lake, from the neighbouring towns of Etruria, was styled either Vulsiniensis (now of Bolsena) or Tarquiniensis. It is surrounded with white rocks, and stored with fish and wild-fowl. The younger Pliny (Epist. ii. 96 [95]) celebrates two woody islands that floated on its waters: if a fable, how credulous the ancients! If a fact, how careless the moderns! Yet, since Pliny, the islands may have been fixed by new and gradual accessions.

56. Yet Procopius discredits his own evidence (Anecdot. c. 16), by confessing that in his public history he had not spoken the truth. See the Epistles from queen Gundelina to the empress Theodora (Var. x. 20, 21, 23, and observe a suspicious word, de illâ personâ, etc.), with the elab-

orate Commentary of Buat (tom. x. p. 177–185).

57. For the conquest of Sicily compare the narrative of Procopius with the complaints of Totila (Gothic. l. i. c. 5; l. iii. c. 16). The Gothic queen had lately relieved that thankless island (Var. iv. 10, 11).

58. The ancient magnitude and splendour of the five quarters of Syracuse are delineated by Cicero (in Varrem, actio ii. l. iv. c. 52, 53), Strabo (l. vi. p. 415 [p. 270, ed. Casaub.]), and D'Orville Sicula (tom. ii. p. 174–202). The new city, restored by Augustus, shrunk towards the island.

59. Procopius (Vandal. l. ii. c. 14, 15) so clearly relates the return of Belisarius into Sicily (p. 146, edit. Hoeschelii [tom. i. p. 481, ed. Bonn]), that I am astonished at the strange misapprehension and reproaches of a learned critic (Œuvres de la Mothe le Vayer, tom. viii. p. 162, 163).

60. The ancient Alba was ruined in the first age of Rome. On the same spot, or at least in the neighbourhood, successively arose, 1. The villa of Pompey, etc. 2. A camp of the Prætorian cohorts. 3. The modern episcopal city of Albanum or Albano (Procop. Goth. l. ii. c. 4. Cluver. Ital. Antiq. tom. ii. p. 914).

61. A Sibylline oracle was ready to pronounce —Africâ captâ *mundus* cum nato peribit; a sentence of portentous ambiguity (Gothic. l. i. c. 7), which has been published in unknown characters by Opsopæus, an editor of the oracles. The Père Maltret has promised a commentary; but all his promises have been vain and fruitless.

62. In his chronology, imitated in some degree from Thucydides, Procopius begins each spring the years of Justinian and of the Gothic war; and his first era coincides with the first of April, 535, and not 536, according to the Annals of Baronius (Pagi Crit. tom. ii. p. 555, who is followed by Muratori and the editors of Sigonius). Yet in some passages we are at a loss to reconcile the dates of Procopius with himself, and with the Chronicle of Marcellinus.

63. The series of the first Gothic war is represented by Procopius (l. i. c. 5–29, l. ii. c. 1–30, l. iii. c. 1) till the captivity of Vitiges. With the aid of Sigonius (Opp. tom. i. de Imp. Occident. l. xvii., xviii.) and Muratori (Annali d'Italia, tom. v.), I have gleaned some few additional facts.

64. Jornandes, de Rebus Geticis, c. 60, p. 702, edit. Grot., and tom. i. p. 221, Muratori. de Success. Regn. [ib.] p. 241.

65. Nero (says Tacitus, Annal. xv. 33) Neapolim quasi Græcum urbem delegit. One hundred and fifty years afterwards, in the time of Septimius Severus, the *Hellenism* of the Neapolitans is praised by Philostratus:γένος Ἕλληνες καὶ ἀστυκοί, ὅθεν καὶ τὰς σπουδὰς τῶν λόγων Ἑλληνικοί εἰσι (Icon. l. i. p. 763, edit. Olear.).

66. The otium of Naples is praised by the Roman poets, by Virgil, Horace, Silius Italicus, and Statius (Cluver. Ital. Ant. l. iv. p. 1149, 1150). In an elegant epistle (Silv. l. iii. 5. p. 94–98, edit.

Markland) Statius undertakes the difficult task of drawing his wife from the pleasures of Rome to that calm retreat.

67. This measure was taken by Roger I. after the conquest of Naples (A.D. 1139), which he made the capital of his new kingdom (Giannone, Istoria Civile, tom. ii. p. 169). That city, the third in Christian Europe, is now at least twelve miles in circumference (Jul. Cæsar. Capaccii Hist. Neapol. l. i. p. 47), and contains more inhabitants (350,000) in a given space than any other spot in the known world.

68. Not geometrical, but common, paces or steps, of 22 French inches (D'Anville, Mesures Itinéraires, p. 7, 8): the 2363 do not make an English mile.

69. Belisarius was reproved by pope Sylverius for the massacre. He repeopled Naples, and imported colonies of African captives into Sicily, Calabria, and Apulia (Hist. Miscell. l. xvi. in Muratori, tom. i. p. 106, 107).

70. Beneventum was built by Diomede, the nephew of Meleager (Cluver. tom. ii. p. 1195, 1196). The Calydonian hunt is a picture of savage life (Ovid, Metamorph. l. viii.). Thirty or forty heroes were leagued against a hog: the brutes (not the hog) quarrelled with a lady for the head.

71. The *Decennovium* is strangely confounded by Cluverius (tom. ii. p. 1007) with the river Ufens. It was in truth a canal of nineteen miles, from Forum Appii to Terracina, on which Horace embarked in the night. The Decennovium which is mentioned by Lucan, Dion Cassius, and Cassiodorus, has been successively ruined, restored, and obliterated (D'Anville, Analyse de l'Italie, p. 185, etc.).

72. A Jew gratified his contempt and hatred for *all* the Christians, by enclosing three bands, each of ten hogs, and discriminated by the names of Goths, Greeks, and Romans. Of the first, almost all were found dead—almost all of the second were alive—of the third, half died, and the rest lost their bristles. No unsuitable emblem of the event.

73. Bergier (Hist. des Grands Chemins des Romains, tom. i. p. 221–228, 440–444) examines the structure and materials, while D'Anville (Analyse de l'Italie, p. 200–213) defines the geographical line.

74. Of the first recovery of Rome, the *year* (536) is certain, from the series of events, rather than from the corrupt, or interpolated, text of Procopius: the *month* (December) is ascertained by Evagrius (l. iv. c. 19); and the *day* (the *tenth*) may be admitted on the slight evidence of Nicephorus Callistus (l. xvii. c. 13). For this accurate chronology we are indebted to the diligence and judgment of Pagi (tom. ii. p. 559, 560).

75. A horse of a bay or red colour was styled φάλιος by the Greeks, balan by the barbarians, and spadix by the Romans. Honesti spadices, says Virgil (Georgic. l. iii. 81, with the Observations of Martin and Heyne). Σπαδίξ, or βαίον, signifies a

branch of the palm-tree, whose name, φοινίξ, is synonymous to *red* (Aulus Gellius, ii. 26).

76. I interpret βανδαλάριος, not as a proper name, but an office, standard-bearer, from *bandum* (vexillum), a barbaric word adopted by the Greeks and Romans (Paul Diacon. l. i. c. 20, p. 760). Grot. Nomina Gothica, p. 575. (Ducange, Gloss. Latin. tom. i. p. 539, 540.)

77. M. D'Anville has given, in the Memoirs of the Academy for the year 1756 (tom. xxx. p. 198–236), a plan of Rome on a smaller scale, but far more accurate, than that which he had delineated in 1738 for Rollin's history. Experience had improved his knowledge; and instead of Rossi's topography he used the new and excellent map of Nolli. Pliny's old measure of xiii must be reduced to viii miles. It is easier to alter a text than to remove hills or buildings.

78. In the year 1709 Labat (Voyages en Italie, tom. iii. p. 218) reckoned 138,568 Christian souls, besides 8000 or 10,000 Jews—without souls?—In the year 1763 the numbers exceeded 160,000.

79. The accurate eye of Nardini (Roma Antica, l. i. c. viii. p. 31) could distinguish the tumultuarie opere di Belisario.

80. The fissure and leaning in the upper part of the wall, which Procopius observed (Goth. l. i. c. 14 [tom. ii. p. 76, ed. Bonn]), is visible to the present hour (Donat. Roma Vetus, l. i. c. 17, p. 53, 54).

81. Lipsius (Opp. tom. iii. Poliorcet. l. iii.) was ignorant of this clear and conspicuous passage of Procopius (Goth. l. i. c. 21 [p. 104, ed. Bonn]). The engine was named ὄναγρος, the wild ass, a calcitrando (Hen. Steph. Thesaur. Linguæ Græc. tom. ii. p. 1340, 1341, tom. iii. p. 877). I have seen an ingenious model, contrived and executed by General Melville, which imitates or surpasses the art of antiquity.

82. The description of this mausoleum, or mole, in Procopius (l. i. c. 22 [tom. i. p. 106, ed. Bonn]), is the first and best. The height above the walls σχεδόν τι ἐς λίθου βολήν. On Nolli's great plan, the sides measure 260 English feet.

83. Praxiteles excelled in Fauns, and that of Athens was his own masterpiece. Rome now contains above thirty of the same character. When the ditch of St. Angelo was cleansed under Urban VIII. the workmen found the sleeping Faun of the Barberini palace; but a leg, a thigh, and the right arm had been broken from that beautiful statue (Winckelman, Hist. de l'Art, tom. ii. p. 52, 53, tom. iii. p. 265).

84. Procopius has given the best description of the temple of Janus [Goth. l. i. c. 25], a national deity of Latium (Heyne, Excurs. v. ad l. vii. Æneid). It was once a gate in the primitive city of Romulus and Numa (Nardini, p. 13, 256, 329). Virgil has described the ancient rite like a poet and an antiquarian.

85. *Vivarium* was an angle in the new wall enclosed for wild beasts (Procopius, Goth. l. i. c. 23 [tom. ii. p. 111, ed. Bonn]). The spot is still visible in Nardini (l. iv. c. 2, p. 159, 160) and Nolli's great plan of Rome.

86. For the Roman trumpet and its various notes, consult Lipsius, de Militiâ Romanâ (Opp. tom. iii. l. iv. dialog. x. p. 125–129). A mode of distinguishing the *charge* by the horse-trumpet of solid brass, and the *retreat* by the foot-trumpet of leather and light wood, was recommended by Procopius, and adopted by Belisarius (Goth. l. ii. c. 23 [tom. ii. p. 241, ed. Bonn]).

87. Procopius (Goth. l. ii. c. 3 [p. 154, ed. Bonn]) has forgot to name these aqueducts; nor can such a double intersection, at such a distance from Rome, be clearly ascertained from the writings of Frontinus, Fabretti, and Eschinard, de Aquis and de Agro Romano, or from the local maps of Lameti and Cingolani. Seven or eight miles from the city (50 stadia), on the road to Albano, between the Latin and Appian ways, I discern the remains of an aqueduct (probably the Septimian), a series (630 paces) of arches twenty-five feet high (ὑψηλὼ ἐς ἄγαν).

88. They made sausages, ἀλλᾶντας, of mule's flesh: unwholesome, if the animals had died of the plague. Otherwise the famous Bologna sausages are said to be made of ass-flesh (Voyages de Labat, tom. ii. p. 218).

89. The name of the palace, the hill, and the adjoining gate were all derived from the senator Pincius. Some recent vestiges of temples and churches are now smoothed in the garden of the Minims of the Trinità del Monte (Nardini, l. iv. c. 7, p. 196; Eschinard, p. 209, 210; the old plan of Buffalino; and the great plan of Nolli). Belisarius had fixed his station between the *Pincian* and Salarian gates (Procop. Goth. l. i. c. 19 [tom. ii. p. 97, ed. Bonn]).

90. From the mention of the primum et secundum velum, it should seem that Belisarius, even in a siege, represented the emperor, and maintained the proud ceremonial of the Byzantine palace.

91. Of this act of sacrilege, Procopius (Goth. l. i. c. 25 [tom. ii. p. 121, ed. Bonn]) is a dry and reluctant witness. The narratives of Liberatus (Breviarum, c. 22), and Anastasius (de Vit. Pont. p. 39 [ap. Murat. tom. iii. p. 130]) are characteristic, but passionate. Hear the execrations of Cardinal Baronius (A.D. 536, No. 123; A.D. 538, No. 4–20): portentum, facinus omni execratione dignum.

92. The old Capena was removed by Aurelian to, or near, the modern gate of St. Sebastian (see Nolli's plan). That memorable spot has been consecrated by the Egerian grove, the memory of Numa, triumphal arches, the sepulchres of the Scipios, Metelli, etc.

93. The expression of Procopius has an invidious cast—τύχην ἐκ τοῦ ἀσφήλους τὴν σφίσι ξυμβησομένην καραδοκεῖν (Goth. l. ii. c. 4 [tom. ii. p. 160, ed. Bonn]). Yet he is speaking of a woman.

94. Anastasius (p. 40 [tom. iii. p. 130, ed. Murat.]) has preserved this epithet of *Sanguinarius*, which might do honour to a tiger.

95. This transaction is related in the public history (Goth. l. ii. c. 8 [p. 180, ed. Bonn]) with candour or caution; in the Anecdotes (c. 7 [c. i. p. 16, ed. Bonn]) with malevolence or freedom; but Marcellinus, or rather his continuator (in Chron.), casts a shade of premeditated assassination over the death of Constantine. He had performed good service at Rome and Spoleto (Procop. Goth. l. i. c. 7, 16 [tom. ii. p. 81, ed. Bonn]); but Alemannus confounds him with a Constantianus comes stabuli.

96. They refused to serve after his departure; sold their captives and cattle to the Goths; and swore never to fight against them. Procopius introduces a curious digression on the manners and adventures of this wandering nation, a part of whom finally emigrated to Thule or Scandinavia (Goth. l. ii. c. 14, 15).

97 This national reproach of perfidy (Procop. Goth. l. ii. c. 25 [tom. ii. p. 247, ed. Bonn]) offends the ear of La Mothe le Vayer (tom. viii. p. 163–165), who criticises, as if he had not read, the Greek historian.

98. Baronius applauds his treason, and justifies the catholic bishops—qui ne sub heretico principe degant omnem lapidem movent—a useful caution. The more rational Muratori (Annali d'Italia, tom. v. p. 54) hints at the guilt of perjury, and blames at least the *imprudence* of Datius.

99. St. Datius was more successful against devils than against barbarians. He travelled with a numerous retinue, and occupied at Corinth a large house (Baronius, A.D. 538, No. 89; A.D. 539, No. 20).

100. Μυριάδες τριάκοντα (compare Procopius, Goth. l. ii. c. 7, 21 [tom. ii. p. 234, ed. Bonn]). Yet such population is incredible; and the second or third city of Italy need not repine if we only decimate the numbers of the present text. Both Milan and Genoa revived in less than thirty years (Paul Diacon. de Gestis Langobard. l. ii. c. 38 [16 or 22?]).

101. Besides Procopius, perhaps too Roman, see the Chronicles of Marius and Marcellinus, Jornandes (in Success. Regn. in Muratori, tom. i. p. 241), and Gregory of Tours (l. iii. c. 32, in tom. ii. of the Historians of France). Gregory supposes a defeat of Belisarius, who, in Aimoin (de Gestis Franc. l. ii. c. 23, in tom. iii. p. 59), is slain by the Franks.

102. Agathias, l. i. [c. 4], p. 14, 15 [ed. Par.; p. 20, 21, ed. Bonn]. Could he have seduced or subdued the Gepidæ or Lombards of Pannonia, the Greek historian is confident that he must have been destroyed in Thrace.

103. The king pointed his spear—the bull overturned a tree on his head—he expired the same day. Such is the story of Agathias; but the original historians of France (tom. ii. p. 202, 403, 558, 667) impute his death to a fever.

104. Without losing myself in a labyrinth of species and names—the aurochs, urus, bisons, bubalus, bonasus, buffalo, etc. (Buffon, Hist. Nat.

tom. xi. and Supplement, tom. iii. vi.), it is certain that in the sixth century a large wild species of horned cattle was hunted in the great forests of the Vosges in Lorraine, and the Ardennes (Greg. Turon. tom. ii. l. x. c. 10, p. 369).

105. In the siege of Auximum, he first laboured to demolish an old aqueduct, and then cast into the stream, 1. dead bodies; 2. mischievous herbs; and 3. quick lime, which is named (says Procopius, l. ii. c. 27) τίτανος by the ancients; by the moderns ἄσβεστος. Yet both words are used as synonymous in Galen, Dioscorides, and Lucian (Hen. Steph. Thesaur. Ling. Græc. tom. iii. p. 748).

106. The Goths suspected Mathasuenta as an accomplice in the mischief, which perhaps was occasioned by accidental lightning.

107. In strict philosophy, a limitation of the rights of war seems to imply nonsense and contradiction. Grotius himself is lost in an idle distinction between the jus naturæ and the jus gentium, between poison and infection. He balances in one scale the passages of Homer (Odyss. i, 259, etc.) and Florus (l. ii. c. 20, No. 7, ult.); and in the other, the examples of Solon (Pausanias, l. x. c. 37) and Belisarius. See his great work De Jure Belli et Pacis (l. iii. c. 4, s. 15, 16, 17, and in Barbeyrac's version, tom. ii. p. 257, etc.). Yet I can understand the benefit and validity of an agreement, tacit or express, mutually to abstain from certain modes of hostility. See the Amphictyonic oath in Æschines, de Falsâ Legatione.

108. Ravenna was taken, not in the year 540, but in the latter end of 539; and Pagi (tom. ii. p. 569) is rectified by Muratori (Annali d'Italia, tom. v. p. 62), who proves, from an original act on papyrus (Antiquit. Italiæ Medii Ævi, tom. ii. dissert. xxxii. p. 999–1007; Maffei, Istoria Diplomat. p. 155–160), that before the third of January, 540, peace and free correspondence were restored between Ravenna and Faenza.

109. He was seized by John the Sanguinary, but an oath or sacrament was pledged for his safety in the Basilica Julii (Hist. Miscell. l. xvi. in Muratori, tom. i. p. 107). Anastasius (in Vit. Pont. p. 40 [t. iii. p. 130, ed. Murat.]) gives a dark but probable account. Montfaucon is quoted by Mascou (Hist. of the Germans, xii. 21) for a votive shield representing the captivity of Vitiges, and now in the collection of Signor Landi at Rome.

110. Vitiges lived two years at Constantinople, and imperatoris in affectû *convictus* (or conjunctus) rebus excessit humanis. His widow, *Mathasuenta*, the wife and mother of the patricians, the elder and younger Germanus, united the streams of Anician and Amali blood. (Jornandes, c. 60, p. 221, in Muratori, tom. i.)

111. Procopius, Goth. l. iii. c. 1 [p. 283, ed. Bonn]. Aimoin, a French monk of the eleventh century, who had obtained, and has disfigured, some authentic information of Belisarius, mentions, in his name, 12,000 *pueri* or slaves—quopropriis alimus stipendiis—besides 18,000 soldiers

Historians of France, tom. iii. De Gestis Franc. l. . c. 6, p. 48).

112. The diligence of Alemannus could add but ttle to the four first and most curious chapters of ie Anecdotes. Of these strange Anecdotes, a part iay be true, because probable; and a part true, ecause improbable. Procopius must have *known* ie former, and the latter he could scarcely *invent*.

113. Procopius insinuates (Anecdot. c. 4 [tom. i. p. 35, ed. Bonn]), that, when Belisarius re- irned to Italy (A.D. 543), Antonina was sixty ears of age. A forced, but more polite construc- ion, which refers that date to the moment when e was writing (A.D. 559), would be compatible /ith the manhood of Photius (Gothic. l. i. c. 10) 1 536.

114. Compare the Vandalic War (l. i. c. 12) /ith the Anecdotes (c. i. [tom. iii. p. 14, ed. Bonn]

and Alemannus (p. 2, 3). This mode of baptismal adoption was revived by Leo the philosopher.

115. In November, 537, Photius arrested the pope (Liberat. Brev. c. 22; Pagi, tom. ii. p. 562). About the end of 539 Belisarius sent Theodosius— τὸν τῇ οἰκίᾳ τῇ αὐτοῦ ἐφέστωτα—on an important and lucrative commission to Ravenna (Goth. l. ii. c. 28 [tom. ii. p. 261, ed. Bonn]).

116. Theophanes (Chronograph. p. 204 [ed. Par.; tom. i. p. 373, ed. Bonn]) styles him *Photinus*, the son-in-law of Belisarius; and he is copied by the Historia Miscella and Anastasius.

117. The continuator of the Chronicle of Mar- cellinus gives, in a few decent words, the substance of the Anecdotes: Belisarius de Oriente evocatus, in offensam periculumque incurrens grave et, invidiæ subjacens rursus remittitur in Italiam (p. 54).

Chapter XLII

1. It will be a pleasure, not a task, to read He- odotus (l. vii. c. 104, 134). The conversation f Xerxes and Demaratus at Thermopylæ is ne of the most interesting and moral scenes in .istory. It was the torture of the royal Spartan to iehold, with anguish and remorse, the virtue of .is country.

2. See this proud inscription in Pliny (Hist. Vatur. vii. 27). Few men have more exquisitely asted of glory and disgrace; nor could Juvenal Satir. x.) produce a more striking example of the icissitudes of fortune, and the vanity of human vishes.

3. Γραικοὺς ... ἐξ ὧν τὰ πρότερα οὐδένα ἐς Ἰταλίαν κοντα εἶδον, ὅτι μὴ τραγῳδοὺς, καὶ ναύτας λωποδύτας Goth. i. 18, tom. ii. p. 93, ed. Bonn]. This last epi- het of Procopius is too nobly translated by pirates; iaval thieves is the proper word: strippers of gar- nents, either for injury or insult (Demosthenes ontra Canon. in Reiske, Orator. Græc. tom. ii.). 1264).

4. See the third and fourth books of the Gothic Var: the writer of the Anecdotes cannot aggravate hese abuses.

5. Agathias, l. v. [c. 14] p. 157, 158 [p. 306, ed. Bonn]. He confines this weakness of the emperor ind the empire to the old age of Justinian; but, ilas! he was never young.

6. This mischievous policy, which Procopius Anecdot. c. 19 [tom. iii. p. 113, ed. Bonn]) im- iutes to the emperor, is revealed in his epistle to a Scythian prince who was capable of understanding t. Ἄγαν προμηθῆ καὶ ἀγχινούστατον, says Agathias l. v. [c. 5] p. 170, 171 [p. 331, ed. Bonn]).

7. Gens Germanâ feritate ferocior, says Velleius Paterculus of the Lombards (ii. 106). Langobardos iaucitas nobilitat. Plurimis ac valentissimis na- ionibus cincti non per obsequium, sed prœliis et iericlitando, tuti sunt (Tacit. de Moribus Ger-

man, c. 40). See likewise Strabo (l. vii. p. 446 [p. 290, 291, ed. Casaub.]). The best geographers place them beyond the Elbe, in the bishopric of Magdeburg and the middle march of Branden- burg; and their situation will agree with the patri- otic remark of the Count de Hertzeberg, that most of the barbarian conquerors issued from the same countries which still produce the armies of Prussia.

8. The Scandinavian origin of the Goths and Lombards, as stated by Paul Warnefrid [l. i. c. 2], surnamed the Deacon, is attacked by Cluverius (Germania Antiq. l. iii. c. 26, p. 102, etc.), a na- tive of Prussia, and defended by Grotius (Pro- legom. ad Hist. Goth. p. 38, etc.), the Swedish ambassador.

9. Two facts in the narrative of Paul Diaconus (l. i. c. 20) are expressive of national manners: 1. Dum *ad tabulam* luderet—while he played at draughts. 2. Camporum viridantia *lina*. The culti- vation of flax supposes property, commerce, agri- culture, and manufactures.

10. I have used, without undertaking to recon- cile, the facts in Procopius (Goth. l. ii. c. 14, l. iii c. 33, 34, l. iv. c. 18, 25), Paul Diaconus (de Gestis Langobard. l. i. c. 1–23, in Muratori, Script. Rerum Italicarum, tom. i. p. 405–419), and Jor- nandes (de Success. Regnorum, p. 242). The pa- tient reader may draw some light from Mascou (Hist. of the Germans, and Annotat. xxiii.) and De Buat (Hist. des Peuples, etc., tom. ix. x. xi.).

11. I adopt the appellation of Bulgarians from Ennodius (in Panegyr. Theodorici, Opp. Sirmond, tom. i. p. 1598, 1599), Jornandes (de Rebus Get- icis, c. 5, p. 194, et de Regn. Successione, p. 242), Theophanes (p. 185 [tom. i. p. 338, ed. Bonn]), and the Chronicles of Cassiodorus and Marcel- linus. The name of Huns is too vague; the tribes of the Cutturgurians and Utturgurians are too mi- nute and too harsh.

12. Procopius (Goth. l. iv. c. 19 [tom. ii. p. 556, ed. Bonn]). His verbal message (he owns himself an illiterate barbarian) is delivered as an epistle. The style is savage, figurative, and original.

13. This sum is the result of a particular list, in a curious MS. fragment of the year 550, found in the library of Milan. The obscure geography of the times provokes and exercises the patience of the Count de Buat (tom. xi. p. 69–189). The French minister often loses himself in a wilderness which requires a Saxon and Polish guide.

14. *Panicum, milium.* See Columella, l. ii. c. 9, p. 430, edit. Gesner. Plin. Hist. Natur. xviii. 24, 25. The Sarmatians made a pap of millet, mingled with mare's milk or blood. In the wealth of modern husbandry, our millet feeds poultry, and not heroes. See the dictionaries of Bomare and Miller.

15. For the name and nation, the situation and manners, of the Sclavonians, see the original evidence of the sixth century, in Procopius (Goth. l. ii. c. 26, l. iii. c. 14), and the emperor Mauritius or Maurice (Stratagemat. l. xi. c. 5, apud Mascou, Annotat. xxxi.). The Stratagems of Maurice have been printed only, as I understand, at the end of Scheffer's edition of Arrian's Tactics, at Upsal, 1664 (Fabric. Bibliot. Græc. l. iv. c. 8, tom. iii. p. 278), a scarce, and hitherto, to me, an inaccessible book.

16. Antes eorum fortissimi . . . Taysis [Tausis] qui rapidus et verticosus in Histri fluenta furens devolvitur (Jornandes, c. 5, p. 194, edit. Murator. Procopius, Goth. l. iii. c. 14, et de Ædific. l. iv. c. 7). Yet the same Procopius mentions the Goths and Huns as neighbours, γειτονοῦντα, to the Danube (de Ædific. l. iv. c. 1).

17. The national title of *Anticus*, in the laws and inscriptions of Justinian, was adopted by his successors, and is justified by the pious Ludewig (in Vit. Justinian. p. 515). It had strangely puzzled the civilians of the middle age.

18. Procopius, Goth. l. iv. c. 15 [tom. ii. p. 592, ed. Bonn].

19. An inroad of the Huns is connected by Procopius with a comet; perhaps that of 531 (Persic. l. ii. c. 4). Agathias (l. v. [c. 11] p. 154, 155 [p. 300, ed. Bonn]) borrows from his predecessor some early facts.

20. The cruelties of the Sclavonians are related or magnified by Procopius (Goth. l. iii. c. 29, 38). For their mild and liberal behaviour to their prisoners we may appeal to the authority, somewhat more recent, of the emperor Maurice (Stratagem. l. xi. c. 5 [p. 272, *sqq.*]).

21. Topirus was situate near Philippi in Thrace, or Macedonia, opposite to the isle of Thasos, twelve days' journey from Constantinople (Cellarius, tom. i. p. 676, 840).

22. According to the malevolent testimony of the Anecdotes (c. 18 [tom. iii. p. 108, ed. Bonn]) these inroads had reduced the provinces south of the Danube to the state of a Scythian wilderness.

23. From Caf to Caf; which a more rational geography would interpret, from Imaus, perhaps to Mount Atlas. According to the religious philosophy of the Mahometans the basis of Mount Caf is an emerald, whose reflection produces the azure of the sky. The mountain is endowed with a sensitive action in its roots or nerves; and their vibration, at the command of God, is the cause of earthquakes (D'Herbelot, p. 230, 231).

24. The Siberian iron is the best and most plentiful in the world: and in the southern parts above sixty mines are now worked by the industry of the Russians (Strahlenberg, Hist. of Siberia, p. 342 387; Voyage en Sibérie, par l'Abbé Chappe d'Auteroche, p. 603–608, edit. in 12mo. Amsterdam, 1770). The Turks offered iron for sale; yet the Roman ambassadors, with strange obstinacy, persisted in believing that it was all a trick, and that their country produced none (Menander in Excerpt. Leg. p. 152 [ed. Par.; p. 380, ed Bonn]).

25. Of Irgana-kon (Abulghazi Khan, Hist. Généalogique des Tatars, P. ii. c. 5, p. 71–77, c. 15, p. 155). The tradition of the Moguls, of the 450 years which they passed in the mountains, agrees with the Chinese periods of the history of the Huns and Turks (De Guignes, tom. i. part ii. p. 376), and the twenty generations from their restoration to Zingis.

26. The country of the Turks, now of the Calmucks, is well described in the Genealogical History, p. 521–562. The curious notes of the French translator are enlarged and digested in the second volume of the English version.

27. Visdelou, p. 141, 151. The fact, though it strictly belongs to a subordinate and successive tribe, may be introduced here.

28. Procopius (Persic. l. i. c. 12, l. ii. c. 3; Peyssonel, Observations sur les Peuples Barbares, p. 99, 100) defines the distance between Caffa and the old Bosphorus at xvi long Tartar leagues.

29. See, in a Mémoire of M. de Boze (Mém. de l'Académie des Inscriptions, tom. vi. p. 549–565), the ancient kings and medals of the Cimmerian Bosphorus; and the gratitude of Athens, in the Oration of Demosthenes against Leptines (in Reiske, Orator. Græc. tom. i. p. 466, 467).

30. For the origin and revolutions of the first Turkish empire, the Chinese details are borrowed from De Guignes (Hist. des Huns, tom. i. P. ii. p. 367–462) and Visdelou (Supplément à la Bibliothèque Orient. d'Herbelot, p. 82–114). The Greek or Roman hints are gathered in Menander (p. 108–164 [p. 298, 404, ed. Bonn]), and Theophylact Simocatta (l. vii. c. 7, 8).

31. The river Til, or Tula, according to the geography of De Guignes (tom. i. part ii. p. lviii. and 352), is a small, though grateful, stream of the desert, that falls into the Orhon, Selinga, etc. See Bell, Journey from Petersburg to Pekin (vol. ii. p. 124); yet his own description of the Keat, down which he sailed into the Oby, represents the name and attributes of the *black river* (p. 139).

32. Theophylact, l. vii. c. 7, 8. And yet his *true* Avars are invisible even to the eyes of M. de Guignes; and what can be more illustrious than the *false?* The right of the fugitive Ogors to that national appellation is confessed by the Turks themselves (Menander, p. 108).

33. The Alani are still found in the Genealogical History of the Tartars (p. 617), and in D'Anville's maps. They opposed the march of the generals of Zingis round the Caspian Sea, and were over-thrown in a great battle (Hist. de Gengiscan, l. iv. c. 9, p. 447).

34. The embassies and first conquests of the Avars may be read in Menander (Excerpt. Legat. p. 99, 100, 101, 154, 155 [p. 282–287, 385–388, ed. Bonn]), Theophanes (p. 196 [tom. i. p. 359, ed. Bonn]), the Historia Miscella (l. xvi. p. 109), and Gregory of Tours (l. iv. c. 23, 29, in the Historians of France, tom. ii. p. 214, 217).

35. Theophanes (Chron. p. 204) and the Hist. Miscella (l. xvi. p. 110), as understood by De Guignes (tom. i. part ii. p. 354), *appear* to speak of a Turkish embassy to Justinian himself; but that of Maniach, in the fourth year of his successor Justin, is positively the first that reached Con-stantinople (Menander, p. 108).

36. The Russians have found characters, rude hieroglyphics, on the Irtish and Yenisei, on medals, tombs, idols, rocks, obelisks, etc. (Strahlenberg, Hist. of Siberia, p. 324, 346, 406, 429). Dr. Hyde (de Religione Veterum Persarum, p. 521, etc.) has given two alphabets of Thibet and of the Eygours. I have long harboured a suspicion that *all* the Scythian, and *some*, perhaps *much*, of the Indian science, was derived from the Greeks of Bactriana.

37. All the details of these Turkish and Roman embassies, so curious in the history of human man-ners, are drawn from the Extracts of Menander p. 106–110, 151–154, 161–164 [295–303, 380–385, 397–405, ed. Bonn]), in which we often regret the want of order and connection.

38. See D'Herbelot (Bibliot. Orient. p. 568, 929); Hyde (de Religione Vet. Persarum, c. 21, p. 290, 291); Pocock (Specimen Hist. Arab. p. 70, 71); Eutychius (Annal. tom. ii. p. 176); Texeira (in Stevens, Hist. of Persia, l. i. c. 34).

39. The fame of the new law for the community of women was soon propagated in Syria (Asseman. Biblioth. Orient. tom. iii. p. 402) and Greece (Pro-cop. Persic. l. i. c. 5).

40. He offered his own wife and sister to the prophet; but the prayers of Nushirvan saved his mother, and the indignant monarch never forgave the humiliation to which his filial piety had stooped: pedes tuos deosculatus (said he to Maz-dak) cujus fœtor adhuc nares occupat (Pocock, Specimen Hist. Arab. p. 71).

41. Procopius, Persic. l. i. c. 11. Was not Proclus over-wise? Was not the danger imaginary?—The excuse, at least, was injurious to a nation not ig-norant of letters: οὐ γράμμασιν οἱ βάρβαροι τοὺς παῖδας ποιοῦνται ἀλλ' ὅπλων κενῇ. Whether any mode

of adoption was practised in Persia I much doubt.

42. From Procopius and Agathias, Pagi (tom. ii. p. 543, 626) has proved that Chosroes Nushir-van ascended the throne in the fifth year of Jus-tinian (A.D. 531, April 1—A.D. 532, April 1). But the true chronology, which harmonises with the Greeks and Orientals, is ascertained by John Ma-lala (tom. ii. 211 [ed. Oxon.; p. 471, ed. Bonn]). Cabades, or Kobad, after a reign of forty-three years and two months, sickened the 8th, and died the 13th of September, A.D. 531, aged eighty-two years. According to the Annals of Eutychius, Nu-shirvan reigned forty-seven years and six months; and his death must consequently be placed in March, A.D. 579.

43. Procopius, Persic. l. i. c. 23 [tom. i. p. 118, ed. Bonn]. Brisson de Regn. Pers. p. 494. The gate of the palace of Ispahan is, or was, the fatal scene of disgrace or death (Chardin, Voyage en Perse, tom. iv. p. 312, 313).

44. In Persia the prince of the waters is an officer of state. The number of wells and subterraneous channels is much diminished, and with it the fer-tility of the soil: 400 wells have been recently lost near Tauris, and 42,000 were once reckoned in the province of Khorasan (Chardin, tom. iii. p. 99, 100; Tavernier, tom. i. p. 416).

45. The character and government of Nushir-van is represented sometimes in the words of D'Her-belot (Bibliot. Orient. p. 680, etc., from Khon-demir), Eutychius (Annal. tom. ii. p. 179, 180—very rich), Abulpharagius (Dynast. vii. p. 94, 95—very poor), Tarikh Schikard (p. 144–150), Tex-eira (in Stevens, l. i. c. 35), Asseman (Bibliot. Orient. tom. iii. p. 404–410), and the Abbé Four-mont (Hist. de l'Acad. des Inscriptions, tom. vii. p. 325–334), who has translated a spurious or genuine testament of Nushirvan.

46. A thousand years before his birth, the judges of Persia had given a solemn opinion—τῷ βασιλεύοντι Περσέων ἐξεῖναι ποιέειν τὸ ἂν βούληται (Herodot. l. iii. c. 31). Nor had this constitu-tional maxim been neglected as a useless and barren theory.

47. On the literary state of Persia, the Greek versions, philosophers, sophists, the learning or ig-norance of Chosroes, Agathias (l. ii. [c. 28 *sq.*] p. 66–71 [p. 126 *sqq.*, ed. Bonn]) displays much in-formation and strong prejudices.

48. Asseman. Bibliot. Orient. tom. iv. p. DCCXLV. vi. vii.

49. The Shah Nameh, or Book of Kings, is per-haps the original record of history which was translated into Greek by the interpreter Sergius (Agathias, l. iv. [c. 30] p. 141 [p. 273, ed. Bonn]), preserved after the Mahometan conquest, and versified, in the year 994, by the national poet Fer-doussi. See D'Anquetil (Mém. de l'Académie, tom. xxxi. p. 379) and Sir William Jones (Hist. of Nadir Shah, p. 161).

50. In the fifth century, the name of Restom, or Rostam, a hero who equalled the strength of

twelve [120?] elephants, was familiar to the Armenians (Moses Chorenensis, Hist. Armen. l. ii. c. 7, p. 96, edit. Whiston). In the beginning of the seventh, the Persian romance of Rostam and Isfendiar was applauded at Mecca (Sale's Koran, c. xxxi. p. 335). Yet this exposition of ludicrum novæ historiæ is not given by Maracci Refutat. Alcoran. p. 544–548).

51. Procop. (Goth. l. iv. c. 10 [tom. ii. p. 505, ed. Bonn]). Kobad had a favourite Greek physician, Stephen of Edessa (Persic. l. ii. c. 26 [tom. i. p. 271, ed. Bonn]). The practice was ancient; and Herodotus relates the adventures of Democedes of Crotona (l. iii. c. 125–137).

52. See Pagi, tom. ii. p. 626. In one of the treaties an honourable article was inserted for the toleration and burial of the catholics (Menander, in Excerpt. Legat. p. 142 [p. 363, sq., ed. Bonn]). Nushizad, a son of Nushirvan, was a Christian, a rebel, and—a martyr? (D'Herbelot, p. 681.)

53. On the Persian language, and its three dialects, consult D'Anquetil (p. 339–343) and Jones (p. 153–185): ἀγρία τινὶ γλώττη καὶ ἀμουσοτάτη, is the character which Agathias (l. ii. [c. 28] p. 67 [p. 126, ed. Bonn]) ascribes to an idiom renowned in the East for poetical softness.

54. Agathias [l. c.] specifies the Gorgias, Phædo, Parmenides, and Timæus. Renaudot (Fabricius, Biblioth. Græc. tom. xii. p. 246–261) does not mention this barbaric version of Aristotle.

55. Of these fables I have seen three copies in three different languages: 1. In *Greek*, translated by Simeon Seth (A.D. 1100) from the Arabic, and published by Starck at Berlin in 1697, in 12mo. 2. In *Latin*, a version from the Greek, Sapientia Indorum, inserted by Père Poussin at the end of his edition of Pachymer (p. 547–620, edit. Roman.). 3. In *French*, from the Turkish, dedicated, in 1540, to Sultan Soliman. Contes et Fables Indiennes de Bidpai et de Lokman, par MM. Galland et Cardonne, Paris, 1778, 3 vols. in 12mo. Mr. Warton (History of English Poetry, vol. i. p. 129–131) takes a larger scope.

56. See the Historia Shahiludii of Dr. Hyde (Syntagm. Dissertat. tom. ii. p. 61–69).

57. The endless peace (Procopius, Persic. l. i. c. 22 [tom. i. p. 114, ed. Bonn]) was concluded or ratified in the sixth year, and third consulship, of Justinian (A.D. 533, between January 1 and April 1; Pagi, tom. ii. p. 550). Marcellinus, in his Chronicle, uses the style of Medes and Persians.

58. Procopius, Persic. l. i. c. 26 [p. 137, ed. Bonn].

59. Almondar, king of Hira, was deposed by Kobad, and restored by Nushirvan. His mother from her beauty, was surnamed *Celestial Water*, an appellation which became hereditary, and was extended for a more noble cause (liberality in famine) to the Arab princes of Syria (Pocock, Specimen Hist. Arab. p. 69, 70).

60. Procopius, Persic. l. ii. c. 1 [tom. i. p. 154, ed. Bonn]. We are ignorant of the origin and ob-

ject of this *strata*, a paved road of ten days' journey from Auranitis to Babylonia. (See a Latin note in Delisle's Map Imp. Orient.) Wesseling and D'Anville are silent.

61. I have blended, in a short speech, the two orations of the Arsacides of Armenia and the Gothic ambassadors. Procopius, in his public history, feels, and makes us feel, that Justinian was the true author of the war (Persic. l. ii. c. 2, 3).

62. The invasion of Syria, the ruin of Antioch, etc., are related in a full and regular series by Procopius (Persic. l. ii. c. 5–14). Small collateral aid can be drawn from the Orientals: yet not they, but D'Herbelot himself (p. 680), should blush, when he blames them for making Justinian and Nushirvan contemporaries. On the geography of the seat of war, D'Anville (l'Euphrate et le Tigre) is sufficient and satisfactory.

63. In the public history of Procopius (Persic. l. ii. c. 16, 18, 19, 20, 21, 24, 25, 26, 27, 28); and with some slight exceptions, we may reasonably shut our ears against the malevolent whisper of the Anecdotes (c. 2, 3, with the Notes, as usual, of Alemannus).

64. The Lazic war, the contest of Rome and Persia on the Phasis, is tediously spun through many a page of Procopius (Persic. l. ii. c. 15, 17, 28, 29, 30; Gothic. l. iv. c. 7–16) and Agathias (l. ii., iii., and iv. p. 55–132, 141).

65. The *Periplus*, or circumnavigation of the Euxine Sea, was described in Latin by Sallust, and in Greek by Arrian: 1. The former work, which no longer exists, has been restored by the *singular* diligence of M. de Brosses, first president of the parliament of Dijon (Hist. de la République Romaine, tom. ii. l. iii. p. 199–298), who ventures to assume the character of the Roman historian. His description of the Euxine is ingeniously formed of *all* the fragments of the original, and of *all* the Greeks and Latins whom Sallust might copy, or by whom he might be copied; and the merit of the execution atones for the whimsical design. 2. The Periplus of Arrian is addressed to the emperor Hadrian (in Geograph. Minor. Hudson, tom. i.), and contains whatever the governor of Pontus had seen from Trebizond to Dioscurias; whatever he had heard from Dioscurias to the Danube; and whatever he knew from the Danube to Trebizond.

66. Besides the many occasional hints from the poets, historians, etc., of antiquity, we may consult the geographical descriptions of Colchis by Strabo (l. xi. p. 760–765 [p. 497–501, ed. Casaub.]) and Pliny (Hist. Natur. vi. 5, 19, etc.).

67. I shall quote, and have used, three modern descriptions of Mingrelia and the adjacent countries. 1. Of the Père Archangeli Lamberti (Relations de Thevenot, part i. p. 31–52, with a map), who has all the knowledge and prejudices of a missionary. 2. Of Chardin (Voyages en Perse, tom. i. p. 54, 68–168): his observations are judicious; and his own adventures in the country are still more instructive than his observations. 3. Of Peys-

onel (Observations sur les Peuples Barbares, p.
9, 50, 51, 58, 62, 64, 65, 71, etc., and a more
ecent treatise, Sur le Commerce de la Mer Noire,
om. ii. p. 1–53): he had long resided at Caffa, as
onsul of France; and his erudition is less valuable
han his experience.

68. Pliny, Hist. Natur. l. xxxiii. 15. The gold
nd silver mines of Colchis attracted the Argo-
auts (Strab. l. i. p. 77 [p. 45, ed. Casaub.]). The
agacious Chardin could find no gold in mines,
ivers, or elsewhere. Yet a Mingrelian lost his hand
nd foot for showing some specimens at Constan-
inople of native gold.

69. Herodot. l. ii. c. 104, 105; Diodor. Sicul.
. i. [c. 28] p. 33, edit. Wesseling; Dionys. Perieget.
89; and Eustath. ad loc Scholiast. ad Apollo-
ium Argonaut. l. iv. 282–291.

70. Montesquieu, The Spirit of Laws, l. xxi. c. 6.
'Isthme . . . couvert de villes et nations qui ne
ont plus.

71. Bougainville, Mémoires de l'Académie des
nscriptions, tom. xxvi. p. 33, on the African
oyage of Hanno and the commerce of antiquity.

72. A Greek historian, Timosthenes, had af-
irmed, in eam ccc nationes dissimilibus linguis
lescendere; and the modest Pliny is content to
dd, et postea a nostris cxxx interpretibus negotia
bi gesta (vi. 5): but the words nunc deserta cover
 multitude of past fictions.

73. Buffon (Hist. Nat tom. iii. p. 433–437) col-
ects the unanimous suffrage of naturalists and
ravellers. If, in the time of Herodotus, they were
n truth μελάγχροες and οὐλότριχες (and he had ob-
erved them with care), this precious fact is an ex-
mple of the influence of climate on a foreign
olony.

74. The Mingrelian ambassador arrived at Con-
tantinople with two hundred persons; but he ate
(sold) them day by day, till his retinue was dimin-
shed to a secretary and two valets (Tavernier,
om. i. p. 365). To purchase his mistress, a Mingrelian gentleman sold twelve priests and his wife
o the Turks (Chardin, tom. i. p. 66).

75. Strabo, l. xi. p. 763 [p. 499, ed. Casaub.].
Lamberti, Relation de la Mingrelie. Yet we must
avoid the contrary extreme of Chardin, who al-
ows no more than 20,000 inhabitants to supply an
annual exportation of 12,000 slaves; an absurdity
inworthy of that judicious traveller.

76. Herodot. l. iii. c. 97. See, in l. vii. c. 79,
heir arms and service in the expedition of Xerxes
against Greece.

77. Xenophon, who had encountered the Colchians in his retreat (Anabasis. l. iv. [c. 8] p. 320,
343, 348, edit. Hutchinson; and Foster's Disserta-
ion, p. liii.–lviii., in Spelman's English version,
vol. ii), styles them αὐτόνομοι. Before the conquest
of Mithridates they are named by Appian ἔθνος
ἱρειμανὲς (de Bell. Mithridatico, c. 15, tom. i. p.
561, of the last and best edition, by John Schweig-
хаeuser, Lipsiæ, 1785, 3 vols· large octavo).

78. The conquest of Colchis by Mithridates and
Pompey is marked by Appian (de Bell. Mithridat.
[l. c.]) and Plutarch (in Pompey).

79. We may trace the rise and fall of the family
of Polemo, in Strabo (l. xi. p. 755; l. xii. p. 867 [p.
493 and 578, ed. Casaub.]), Dion Cassius or Xiphilin (p. 588, 593, 601, 719, 754, 915, 946, edit.
Reimar [l. xlix. c. 25, 33, 44; l. liii. c. 25; l. liv. c.
24; l. lix. c. 12; l. lx. c. 8]), Suetonius (in Neron. c.
18, in Vespasian. c. 8), Eutropius (vii. 14 [9], Josephus (Antiq. Judiac. l. xx. c. 6, p. 970, edit.
Havercamp), and Eusebius (Chron. with Scaliger,
Animadvers. p. 196).

80. In the time of Procopius there were no Roman forts on the Phasis. Pityus and Sebastopolis
were evacuated on the rumour of the Persians
(Goth. l. iv. c. 4); but the latter was afterwards restored by Justinian (de Ædif. l. iii. c. 7 [tom. iii. p.
261, ed. Bonn]).

81. In the time of Pliny, Arrian, and Ptolemy,
the Lazi were a particular tribe on the northern
skirts of Colchis (Cellarius, Geograph. Antiq. tom.
ii. p. 222). In the age of Justinian they spread, or
at least reigned, over the whole country. At present
they have migrated along the coast towards Trebizond, and compose a rude seafaring people, with
a peculiar language (Chardin, p. 149; Peyssonel,
p. 64).

82. John Malala, Chron. tom. ii. p. 134–137
[ed. Oxon.; p. 412–414, ed. Bonn]; Theophanes,
p. 144 [tom. i. p. 259, ed Bonn]; Hist. Miscell. l.
xv. p. 103. The fact is authentic, but the date
seems too recent. In speaking of their Persian alliance, the Lazi contemporaries of Justinian employ
the most obsolete words—ἐν γράμμασι μνημεῖα,
πρόγονοι, etc. Could they belong to a connection
which had not been dissolved above twenty years?

83. The sole vestige of Petra subsists in the
writings of Procopius and Agathias. Most of the
towns and castles of Lazica may be found by comparing their names and position with the map of
Mingrelia, in Lamberti.

84. See the amusing letters of Pietro della Valle,
the Roman traveller (Viaggi, tom. ii. 207, 209,
213, 215, 266, 286, 300; tom. iii. p. 54, 127). In
the years 1618, 1619, and 1620, he conversed with
Shah Abbas, and strongly encouraged a design
which might have united Persia and Europe
against their common enemy the Turk.

85. See Herodotus (l. i. c. 140), who speaks
with diffidence, Lacher tom. i. p. 399–401; Notes
sur Herodote), Procopius (Persic. l. i. c. 11 [tom. i.
p. 56, ed. Bonn]), and Agathias (l. ii. p. 61, 62 [ed.
Par.; p. 113 sq., ed. Bonn]). This practice, agreeable to the Zendavesta (Hyde, de Relig. Pers. c.
34, p. 414–421), demonstrates that the burial of
the Persian kings (Xenophon, Cyropæd. l. viii.
[c. 7] p. 658), τί γὰρ τούτου μακαριώτερον τοῦ τῇ γῇ
μιχθῆναι, is a Greek fiction, and that their tombs
could be no more than cenotaphs.

86. The punishment of flaying alive could not
be introduced into Persia by Sapor (Brisson, de
Regn. Pers. l. ii. p. 578), nor could it be copied

from the foolish tale of Marsyas the Phrygian piper, most foolishly quoted as a precedent by Agathias (l. iv. p. 132, 133).

87. In the palace of Constantinople there were thirty silentiaries, who are styled hastati ante fores cubiculi, τῆς [ἀμφὶ τόν βασιλέα] σιγῆς ἐπιστάται, an honourable title which conferred the rank, without imposing the duties, of a senator (Cod. Theodos. l. vi. tit. 23; Gothofred. Comment. tom. ii. p. 129).

88. On these judicial orations Agathias (l. iii. p. 81–89; l. iv. p. 108–119 [p. 155–170, 206–230, ed. Bonn]) lavishes eighteen or twenty pages of false and florid rhetoric. His ignorance or carelessness overlooks the strongest argument against the king of Lazica—his former revolt.

89. Procopius represents the practice of the Gothic court of Ravenna (Goth. l. i. c. 7 [tom. ii. p. 34, ed. Bonn]); and foreign ambassadors have been treated with the same jealousy and rigour in Turkey (Busbequius, Epist. iii. p. 149, 242, etc.), Russia (Voyage d'Olearius), and China (Narrative of M. de Lange, in Bell's Travels, vol. ii. p. 189–311).

90. The negotiations and treaties between Justinian and Chosroes are copiously explained by Procopius (Persic. l. ii. c. 10, 13, 26, 27, 28; Gothic. l. ii. c. 11, 15; Agathias, l. iv. p. 141, 142 [ed. Par.; p. 274 sq., ed. Bonn]), and Menander (in Excerpt. Legat. p. 132–147 [p. 346 sqq., ed. Bonn]). Consult Barbeyrac, Hist. des Anciens Traités, tom. ii. p. 154, 181–184, 193–200.

91. D'Herbelot, Biblioth. Orient. p. 680, 681, 294, 295.

92. See Buffon, Hist. Naturelle, tom. iii. p. 449. This Arab cast of features and complexion, which has continued 3400 years (Ludolph. Hist. et Comment. Æthiopic. l. i. c. 4) in the colony of Abyssinia, will justify the suspicion that race, as well as climate, must have contributed to form the negroes of the adjacent and similar regions.

93. The Portuguese missionaries, Alvarez (Ramusio, tom. i. fol. 204, rect. 274, vers.), Bermudez (Purchas's Pilgrims, vol. ii. l. v. c. 7, p. 1149–1188), Lobo (Relation, etc., par M. le Grand, with xv Dissertations, Paris, 1728), and Tellez (Relations de Thevenot, part iv.), could only relate of modern Abyssinia what they had seen or invented. The erudition of Ludolphus (Hist. Æthiopica, Francofurt. 1681; Commentarius, 1691; Appendix, 1694), in twenty-five languages, could add little concerning its ancient history. Yet the fame of

Caled, or Ellisthæus, the conqueror of Yemen, is celebrated in national songs and legends.

94. The negotiations of Justinian with the Axumites, or Æthiopians, are recorded by Procopius (Persic. l. i. c. 19, 20) and John Malala (tom. ii. p 163–165, 193–196 [p. 433, 434–457, 459, ed Bonn]). The historian of Antioch quotes the original narrative of the ambassador Nonnosus, of which Photius (Biblioth. Cod. iii.) has preserved a curious extract.

95. The trade of the Axumites to the coast of India and Africa and the isle of Ceylon is curiously represented by Cosmas Indicopleustes (Topograph. Christian. l. ii. p. 132, 138, 139, 140; l. xi p. 338, 339).

96. Ludolph. Hist. et Comment. Æthiop. l. ii c. 3.

97. The city of Negra, or Nag'ran, in Yemen, is surrounded with palm-trees, and stands in the high road between Saana, the capital, and Mecca; from the former ten, from the latter twenty days' journey of a caravan of camels (Abulfeda, Descript. Arabiæ, p. 52).

98. The martyrdom of St. Arethas, prince of Negra, and his three hundred and forty companions, is embellished in the legends of Metaphrastes and Nicephorus Callistus, copied by Baronius (A.D. 522, No. 22–66; A.D. 523, No. 16–29), and refuted, with obscure diligence, by Basnage (Hist. des Juifs, tom. xii. l. viii. c.ii. p. 333–348), who investigates the state of the Jews in Arabia and Æthiopia.

99. Alvarez (in Ramusio, tom. i. fol. 219, vers. 221, vers.) saw the flourishing state of Axume in the year 1520—luogo molto buono e grande. It was ruined in the same century by the Turkish invasion. No more than one hundred houses remain; but the memory of its past greatness is preserved by the regal coronation (Ludolph. Hist. et Comment. l. ii. c. 11).

100. The revolutions of Yemen in the sixth century must be collected from Procopius (Persic. l. i. c. 19, 20), Theophanes Byzant. (apud Phot. cod. lxiv. p. 80 [p. 26, ed. Bekk.]), St. Theophanes (in Chronograph. p. 144, 145, 188, 189, 206, 207 [tom. i. p. 259, 260, 377, 378, ed. Bonn], who is full of strange blunders), Pocock (Specimen Hist. Arab. p. 62, 65), D'Herbelot (Bibliot. Orientale, p. 12, 477), and Sale's Preliminary Discourse and Koran (c. 105). The revolt of Abrahah is mentioned by Procopius; and his fall, though clouded with miracles, is an historical fact.

Chapter XLIII

1. For the troubles of Africa I neither have nor desire another guide than Procopius, whose eye contemplated the image, and whose ear collected the reports, of the memorable events of his own times. In the second book of the Vandalic War he

relates the revolt of Stoza (c. 14–24), the return of Belisarius (c. 15), the victory of Germanus (c. 16, 17, 18), the second administration of Solomon (c. 19, 20, 21), the government of Sergius (c. 22, 23), of Areobindus (c. 24), the tyranny and death of

Gontharis (c. 25, 26, 27, 28); nor can I discern any symptoms of flattery or malevolence in his various portraits.

2. Yet I must not refuse him the merit of painting, in lively colours, the murder of Gontharis. One of the assassins uttered a sentiment not unworthy of a Roman patriot: "If I fail," says Artasires, "in the first stroke, kill me on the spot, lest the rack should extort a discovery of my accomplices." [Vand. ii. 28, tom. i. p. 529, ed. Bonn.]

3. The Moorish wars are occasionally introduced into the narrative of Procopius (Vandal. l. ii. c. 19–23, 25, 27, 28; Gothic, l. iv. c. 17); and Theophanes adds some prosperous and adverse events in the last years of Justinian.

4. Now Tibesh, in the kingdom of Algiers. It is watered by a river, the Sujerass, which falls into the Mejerda (*Bagradas*). Tibesh is still remarkable for its walls of large stones (like the Coliseum of Rome), a fountain, and a grove of walnut-trees: the country is fruitful, and the neighbouring Bereberes are warlike. It appears from an inscription, that, under the reign of Hadrian, the road from Carthage to Tebeste was constructed by the third legion (Marmol, Description de l'Afrique, tom. ii. p. 442, 443; Shaw's Travels, p. 64, 65, 66).

5. Procopius, Anecdot. c. 18 [tom. iii. p. 107, ed. Bonn]. The series of the African history attests this melancholy truth.

6. In the second (c. 30) and third books (c. 1–40), Procopius continues the history of the Gothic war from the fifth to the fifteenth year of Justinian. As the events are less interesting than in the former period, he allots only half the space to double the time. Jornandes, and the Chronicle of Marcellinus, afford some collateral hints. Sigonius, Pagi, Muratori, Mascou, and De Buat are useful, and have been used.

7. Sylverius, bishop of Rome, was first transported to Patara, in Lycia, and at length starved (sub eorum custodiâ inedia confectus) in the isle of Palmaria, A.D. 538, June 20 (Liberat. in Breviar. c. 22; Anastasius, in Sylverio; Baronius, A.D. 540, No. 2, 3; Pagi, in Vit. Pont. tom. i. p. 285, 286). Procopius (Anecdot. c. 1) accuses only the empress and Antonina.

8. Palmaria, a small island, opposite to Terracina and the coast of the Volsci (Cluver. Ital. Antiq. l. iii. c. 7, p. 1014).

9. As the Logothete Alexander, and most of his civil and military colleagues, were either disgraced or despised, the ink of the Anecdotes (c. 4, 5, 18) is scarcely blacker than that of the Gothic History (l. iii. c. 1, 3, 4, 9, 20, 21, etc.).

10. Procopius (l. iii. c. 2, 8, etc.) does ample and willing justice to the merit of Totila. The Roman historians, from Sallust and Tacitus, were happy to forget the vices of their countrymen in the contemplation of barbaric virtue.

11. Procopius, l. iii. c. 12. The soul of a hero is deeply impressed on the letter; nor can we confound such genuine and original acts with the elaborate and often empty speeches of the Byzantine historians.

12. The avarice of Bessas is not dissembled by Procopius (l. iii. c. 17, 20). He expiated the loss of Rome by the glorious conquest of Petræa (Goth. l. iv. c. 12); but the same vices followed him from the Tiber to the Phasis (c. 13); and the historian is equally true to the merits and defects of his character. The chastisement which the author of the romance of *Belisaire* has inflicted on the oppressor of Rome is more agreeable to justice than to history.

13. During the long exile, and after the death of Vigilius, the Roman church was governed, at first by the archdeacon, and at length (A.D. 555) by the pope Pelagius, who was not thought guiltless of the sufferings of his predecessor. See the original Lives of the popes under the name of Anastasius (Muratori, Script. Rer. Italicarum, tom. iii. P. i. p. 130, 131), who relates several curious incidents of the sieges of Rome and the wars of Italy.

14. Mount Garganus, now Monte St. Angelo, in the kingdom of Naples, runs three hundred stadia into the Hadriatic Sea (Strab. l. vi. p. 436 [p. 284, ed. Casaub.]), and in the darker ages was illustrated by the apparition, miracles, and church of St. Michael the archangel. Horace, a native of Apulia or Lucania, had seen the elms and oaks of Garganus labouring and bellowing with the north wind that blew on that lofty coast (Carm. ii. 9; Epist. ii. i. 202).

15. I cannot ascertain this particular camp of Hannibal; but the Punic quarters were long and often in the neighbourhood of Arpi (T. Liv. xxii. 9, 12; xxiv. 3, etc.).

16. Totila . . . Romam ingreditur . . . ac evertit muros, domos aliquantas igni comburens, ac omnes Romanorum res in prædam accepit, hos ipsos Romanos in Campaniam captivos abduxit. Post quam devastationem, xl aut amplius dies, Roma fuit ita desolata, ut nemo ibi hominum, nisi (*nullæ?*) bestiæ morarentur (Marcellin. in Chron. p. 54).

17. The *tribuli* are small engines with four spikes, one fixed in the ground the three others erect or adverse (Procopius, Gothic. l. iii. c. 24 [tom. ii. p. 379, ed. Bonn]; Just. Lipsius, Poliorcet ων, l. v. c. 3). The metaphor was borrowed from the tribuli (*land-caltrops*), an herb with a prickly fruit, common in Italy (Martin, ad Virgil. Georgic. i. 153, vol. ii. p. 33).

18. Ruscia, the *navale Thuriorum*, was transferred to the distance of sixty stadia to Ruscianum, Rossano, an archbishopric without suffragans. The republic of Sybaris is now the estate of the Duke of Corigliano (Riedesel, Travels into Magna Græcia and Sicily, p. 166–171).

19. This conspiracy is related by Procopius (Gothic. l. iii. c. 31, 32) with such freedom and candour that the liberty of the Anecdotes gives him nothing to add.

20. The honours of Belisarius are gladly com-

memorated by his secretary (Procop. Goth. l. iii. c. 35; l. iv. c. 21). The title of Στράτηγος is ill translated, at least in this instance, by præfectus prætorio; and to a military character, magister militum is more proper and applicable (Ducange, Gloss. Græc. p. 1458, 1459).

21. Alemannus (ad Hist. Arcanam, p. 68 [tom. iii. p. 418, ed. Bonn]), Ducange (Familiæ Byzant. p. 98), and Heineccius (Hist. Juris Civilis, p. 434), all three represent Anastasius as the son of the daughter of Theodora; and their opinion firmly reposes on the unambiguous testimony of Procopius (Anecdot. c. 4, 5—θυγατρίδῳ twice repeated). And yet I will remark, 1. That in the year 547 Theodora could scarcely have a grandson at the age of puberty; 2. That we are totally ignorant of this daughter and her husband; and 3. That Theodora concealed her bastards, and that her grandson by Justinian would have been heir-apparent of the empire.

22. The ἁμαρτήματα, or sins, of the hero in Italy and after his return, are manifested ἀπαρακαλύπτως, and most probably swelled, by the author of the Anecdotes (c. 4, 5). The designs of Antonina were favoured by the fluctuating jurisprudence of Justinian. On the law of marriage and divorce, that emperor was trocho versatilior (Heineccius, Element. Juris Civil. ad Ordinem Pandect. P. iv. No. 233).

23. The Romans were still attached to the monuments of their ancestors; and according to Procopius (Goth. l. iv. c. 22 [tom. ii. p. 573, ed. Bonn]), the galley of Æneas, of a single rank of oars, 25 feet in breadth, 120 in length, was preserved entire in the *navalia*, near Monte Testaceo, at the foot of the Aventine (Nardini, Roma Antica, l. vii. c. 9, p. 466; Donatus, Roma Antiqua, l. iv. c. 13, p. 334). But all antiquity is ignorant of this relic.

24. In these seas Procopius searched without success for the isle of Calypso. He was shown, at Phæacia or Corcyra, the petrified ship of Ulysses (Odyss. xiii. 163); but he found it a recent fabric of many stones, dedicated by a merchant to Jupiter Casius (l. iv. c. 22 [tom. ii. p. 575, ed. Bonn]). Eustathius had supposed it to be the fanciful likeness of a rock.

25. M. D'Anville (Mémoires de l'Acad. tom. xxxii. p. 513–528) illustrates the gulf of Ambracia; but he cannot ascertain the situation of Dodona. A country in sight of Italy is less known than the wilds of America.

26. See the acts of Germanus in the public (Vandal. l. ii. c. 16, 17, 18; Goth. l. iii. c. 31, 32) and private history (Anecdot. c. 5), and those of his son Justin, in Agathias (l. iv. p. 130, 131 [p. 250 sq., ed. Bonn]). Notwithstanding an ambiguous expression of Jornandes, fratri suo, Alemannus has proved that he was the son of the emperor's brother.

27. Conjuncta Aniciorum gens cum Amalâ stirpe spem adhuc utriusque generis promittit (Jornan-des, c. 60, p. 703). He wrote at Ravenna befor. the death of Totila.

28. The third book of Procopius is terminate. by the death of Germanus (Add. l. iv. c. 23, 24 25, 26).

29. Procopius relates the whole series of thi. second Gothic war and the victory of Narses (l. iv c. 21, 26–35). A splendid scene! Among the si. subjects of epic poetry which Tasso revolved in hi mind, he hesitated between the conquests of Ital. by Belisarius and by Narses (Hayley's Works, vo. iv. p. 70).

30. The country of Narses is unknown, since h. must not be confounded with the Persarmenian. Procopius styles him (Goth. l. ii. c. 13 [tom. ii. p. 199, ed. Bonn]) βασιλικῶν χρημάτων ταμίας; Pau. Warnefrid (l. ii. c. 3, p. 776), Chartularius: Mar. cellinus adds the name of Cubicularius. In an in. scription on the Salarian bridge he is entitled Ex consul, Ex-præpositus, Cubiculi Patricius (Mas. cou, Hist. of the Germans, l. xiii. c. 25). The lav. of Theodosius against eunuchs was obsolete o. abolished (Annotation xx.), but the foolish proph. ecy of the Romans subsisted in full vigour (Procop. l. iv. c. 21 [tom. ii. p. 571, ed. Bonn]).

31. Paul Warnefrid, the Lombard, records with complacency the succour, service, and honourable dismission of his countrymen—Romanæ reipubli. cæ adversum æmulos adjutores fuerunt (l. ii. c. i. p. 774, edit. Grot.). I am surprised that Alboin. their martial king, did not lead his subjects i. person.

32. He was, if not an impostor, the sun of th. blind Zames, saved by compassion and educate. in the Byzantine court by the various motives o. policy, pride, and generosity (Procop. Persic. l. i. c. 23 [tom. i. p. 115, ed. Bonn]).

33. In the time of Augustus and in the middl. ages the whole waste from Aquileia to Ravenn. was covered with woods, lakes, and morasses. Mar. has subdued nature, and the land has been culti. vated, since the waters are confined and embanked. See the learned researches of Muratori (Antiqui. tat. Italiæ Medii Ævi, tom. i. dissert. xxi. p. 253. 254), from Vitruvius, Strabo, Herodian, old char. ters, and local knowledge.

34. The Flaminian way, as it is corrected from the Itineraries, and the best modern maps, b. D'Anville (Analyse de l'Italie, p. 147–162), may. be thus stated: ROME to Narni, 51 Roman miles. Terni, 57; Spoleto, 75; Foligno, 88; Nocera, 103. Cagli, 142; Intercisa, 157; Fossombrone, 160. Fano, 176; Pesaro, 184; RIMINI, 208—about 18. English miles. He takes no notice of the death o. Totila; but Wesseling (Itinerar. p. 614) exchanges. for the field of *Taginas*, the unknown appellatior. of *Ptanias*, eight miles from Nocera.

35. Taginæ, or rather Tadinæ, is mentioned by. Pliny [iii. 19]; but the bishopric of that obscur. town, a mile from Gualdo, in the plain, was united. in the year 1007, with that of Nocera. The signs o. antiquity are preserved in the local appellations

Fossato, the camp; *Capraia*, Caprea; *Bastia*, Busta Gallorum. See Cluverius (Italia Antiqua, l. ii. c. 6, p. 615, 616, 617), Lucas Holstenius (Annotat. ad Cluver. p. 85, 86), Guazzesi (Dissertat. p. 177–217, a professed inquiry), and the maps of the ecclesiastical state and the march of Ancona, by Le Maire and Magini.

36. The battle was fought in the year of Rome 458; and the consul Decius, by devoting his own life, assured the triumph of his country and his colleague Fabius (T. Liv. x. 28, 29). Procopius ascribes to Camillus the victory of the *Busta Gallorum* [tom. ii. p. 610, ed. Bonn]; and his error is branded by Cluverius with the national reproach of Græcorum nugamenta.

37. Theophanes, Chron. p. 193 [tom. i. p. 354, ed. Bonn]. Hist. Miscell. l. xvi. p. 108.

38. Evagrius, l. iv. c. 24. The inspiration of the Virgin revealed to Narses the day, and the word, of battle (Paul Diacon. l. ii. c. 3, p. 776).

39. Ἐπὶ τούτου βασιλεύοντος τὸ πέμπτον ἑάλω. [Procop. Goth. lib. iv. c. 33; tom. ii. p. 632, ed. Bonn.] In the year 536 by Belisarius, in 546 by Totila, in 547 by Belisarius, in 549 by Totila, and in 552 by Narses. Maltretus had inadvertently translated *sextum*; a mistake which he afterwards retracts: but the mischief was done; and Cousin, with a train of French and Latin readers, have fallen into the snare.

40. Compare two passages of Procopius (l. iii. c. 26, l. iv. c. 34 [tom. ii. p. 389 and 633, ed. Bonn]), which, with some collateral hints from Marcellinus and Jornandes, illustrate the state of the expiring senate.

41. See, in the example of Prusias, as it is delivered in the fragments of Polybius (Excerpt. Legat. xcvii. p. 927, 928), a curious picture of a royal slave.

42. The Δράκων of Procopius (Goth. l. iv. c. 35) is evidently the Sarnus. The text is accused or altered by the rash violence of Cluverius (l. iv. c. 3, p. 1156): but Camillo Pellegrini of Naples (Discorsi sopra la Campania Felice, p. 330, 331) has proved from old records that as early as the year 822 that river was called the Dracontio, or Draconcello.

43. Galen (de Method. Medendi, l. v. apud Cluver. l. iv. c. 3, p. 1159, 1160) describes the lofty site, pure air, and rich milk of Mount Lactarius, whose medicinal benefits were equally known and sought in the time of Symmachus (l. vi. Epist. 18 [17?]), and Cassiodorus (Var. xi. 10). Nothing is now left except the name of the town of *Lettere*.

44. Buat (tom. xi. p. 2, etc.) conveys to his favourite Bavaria this remnant of Goths, who by others are buried in the mountains of Uri, or restored to their native isle of Gothland (Mascou, Annot. xxi.).

45. I leave Scaliger (Animadvers. in Euseb. p. 59) and Salmasius (Exercitat. Plinian. p. 51, 52) to quarrel about the origin of Cumæ, the oldest of the Greek colonies in Italy (Strab. l. v. p. 372 [p.

243, ed. Casaub.]; Velleius Paterculus, l. i. c. 4), already vacant in Juvenal's time (Satir. iii. [v. 2]), and now in ruins.

46. Agathias (l. i. p. 21 [c. 10, p. 34, ed. Bonn]) settles the Sibyl's cave under the wall of Cumæ: he agrees with Servius (ad l. vi. Æneid.); nor can I perceive why their opinion should be rejected by Heyne, the excellent editor of Virgil (tom. ii. p. 650, 651). In urbe mediâ secreta religio! But Cumæ was not yet built; and the lines (l. vi. 96, 97) would become ridiculous if Æneas were actually in a Greek city.

47. There is some difficulty in connecting the 35th chapter of the fourth book of the Gothic War of Procopius with the first book of the history of Agathias. We must now relinquish a statesman and soldier to attend the footsteps of a poet and rhetorician (l. i. p. 11, l. ii. p. 51, edit. Louvre).

48. Among the fabulous exploits of Buccelin, he discomfited and slew Belisarius, subdued Italy and *Sicily*, etc. See in the Historians of France, Gregory of Tours (tom. ii. l. iii. c. 32, p. 201), and Aimoin (tom. iii. l. ii. de Gestis Francorum, c. 23, p. 59).

49. Agathias notices their superstition in a philosophic tone (l. i. p. 18 [c. 28, *sq.*, ed. Bonn]). At Zug, in Switzerland, idolatry still prevailed in the year 613: St. Columban and St. Gall were the apostles of that rude country; and the latter founded an hermitage, which has swelled into an ecclesiastical principality and a populous city, the seat of freedom and commerce.

50. See the death of Lothaire in Agathias (l. ii. p. 38 [p. 70, ed. Bonn]) and Paul Warnefrid, surnamed Diaconus (l. ii. c. 2, p. 775). The Greek makes him rave and tear his flesh. He had plundered churches.

51. Père Daniel (Hist. de la Milice Françoise, tom. i. p. 17–21) has exhibited a fanciful representation of this battle, somewhat in the manner of the Chevalier Folard, the once famous editor of Polybius, who fashioned to his own habits and opinions all the military operations of antiquity.

52. Agathias (l. ii. p. 47 [p. 87, ed. Bonn]) has produced a Greek epigram of six lines on this victory of Narses, which is favourably compared to the battles of Marathon and Platæa. The chief difference is indeed in their consequences—so trivial in the former instance—so permanent and glorious in the latter.

53. The Beroia and Brincas of Theophanes or his transcriber (p. 201 [tom. i. p. 367, ed. Bonn]) must be read or understood Verona and Brixia.

54. Ἐλείπετο γὰρ, οἶμαι, αὐτοῖς ὑπὸ ἀβελτερίας τὰς ἀσπίδας τυχὸν καὶ τὰ κράνη ἀμφορέως οἴνου ἢ καὶ βαρβίτου ἀποδόσθαι. (Agathias, l. ii. [c. 11] p. 48 [p. 88, ed. Bonn]). In the first scene of Richard III. our English poet has beautifully enlarged on this idea, for which, however, he was not indebted to the Byzantine historian.

55. Maffei has proved (Verona Illustrata, P. i. l. x. p. 257, 289), against the common opinion, that the dukes of Italy were instituted before the con-

quest of the Lombards, by Narses himself. In the Pragmatic Sanction (No. 23) Justinian restrains the judices militares.

56. See Paulus Diaconus, l. iii. c. 3, p. 776. Menander (in Excerpt. Legat. p. 133 [p. 345, ed. Bonn]) mentions some risings in Italy by the Franks, and Theophanes (p. 201 [tom. i. p. 367, ed. Bonn]) hints at some Gothic rebellions.

57. The Pragmatic Sanction of Justinian, which restores and regulates the civil state of Italy, consists of xxvii. articles: it is dated August 15, A.D. 554; is addressed to Narses, V. J. Præpositus Sacri Cubiculi, and to Antiochus Præfectus Prætorio Italiæ; and has been preserved by Julian Antecessor, and in the Corpus Juris Civilis, after the novels and edicts of Justinian, Justin, and Tiberius.

58. A still greater number was consumed by famine in the southern provinces, without (ἔκτος) the Ionian Gulf. Acorns were used in the place of bread. Procopius had seen a deserted orphan suckled by a she-goat [Goth. ii. c. 17]. Seventeen passengers were lodged, murdered, and eaten, by two women, who were detected and slain by the eighteenth, etc.

59. Quinta regio Piceni est; quondam uberrimæ multitudinis, ccclx millia Picentium in fidem P. R. venere (Plin. Hist. Natur. iii. 18). In the time of Vespasian this ancient population was already diminished.

60. Perhaps fifteen or sixteen millions. Procopius (Anecdot. c. 18) computes that Africa lost five millions, that Italy was thrice as extensive, and that the depopulation was in a larger proportion. But his reckoning is inflamed by passion, and clouded with uncertainty.

61. In the decay of these military schools, the satire of Procopius (Anecdot. c. 24 [tom. iii. p. 135, ed. Bonn]; Aleman. p. 102, 103) is confirmed and illustrated by Agathias (l. v. p. 159 [p. 310, ed. Bonn]), who cannot be rejected as an hostile witness.

62. The distance from Constantinople to Melanthias, Villa Cæsariana (Ammian. Marcellin. xxxi. 11), is variously fixed at 120 or 140 stadia (Suidas, tom. ii. p. 522, 523; Agathias, l. v. [c. 14] p. 158 [p. 308, ed. Bonn]), or xviii or xix miles (Itineraria, p. 138, 230, 323, 332, and Wesseling's Observations). The first xii miles, as far as Rhegium, were paved by Justinian, who built a bridge over a morass or gullet between a lake and the sea (Procop. de Ædif. l. iv. c. 8).

63. The Atyras (Pompon. Mela, l. ii. c. 2, p. 169, edit. Voss.). At the river's mouth a town or castle of the same name was fortified by Justinian (Procop. de Ædif. l. iv. c. 2; Itinerar. p. 570; and Wesseling).

64. The Bulgarian war, and the last victory of Belisarius, are imperfectly represented in the prolix declamation of Agathias (l. v. p. 154-174 [p. 299 sqq., ed. Bonn]) and the dry Chronicle of Theophanes (p. 197, 198 [tom. i. p. 360 sq., ed. Bonn]).

65. Ἰνδοὺς. They could scarcely be real Indians; and the Æthiopians, sometimes known by that name, were never used by the ancients as guards or followers: they were the trifling, though costly, objects of female and royal luxury (Terent. Eunuch. act i. scene ii. [v. 88]; Sueton. in August. c. 83, with a good note of Casaubon, in Caligulâ, c. 57).

66. The Sergius (Vandal. l. ii. c. 21, 22, Anecdot. c. 5) and Marcellus (Goth. l. iii. c. 32) are mentioned by Procopius. See Theophanes, p. 197, 201 [tom. i. p. 360, 367, ed. Bonn].

67. Alemannus (p. 3) quotes an old Byzantine MS., which has been printed in the Imperium Orientale of Banduri [tom. iii. p. 349, ed. Bonn].

68. Of the disgrace and restoration of Belisarius, the genuine original record is preserved in the Fragment of John Malala (tom. ii. p. 234-243 [p. 494 sq., ed. Bonn]) and the exact Chronicle of Theophanes (p. 194-204 [tom. i. p. 368 and Zonaras (tom. ii. l. xiv. [c. 9] p. 69) seem to hesitate between the obsolete truth and the growing falsehood.

69. The source of this idle fable may be derived from a miscellaneous work of the twelfth century, the Chiliads of John Tzetzes, a monk (Basil. 1546, ad calcem Lycophront. Colon. Allobrog. 1614, in Corp. Poet. Græc.). He relates the blindness and beggary of Belisarius in ten vulgar or *political* verses (Chiliad iii. No. 88, 339-348, in Corp. Poet. Græc tom. ii. p. 311).

Ἔκπωμα ξύλινον κρατῶν, ἐβόα τῷ μιλίῳ,
Βελισαρίῳ ὀβολὸν δότε τῷ στρατηλάτῃ
Ὅν τύχη μὲν ἐδόξασεν, ἀποτυφλοῖ δ' ὁ φθόνος.

This moral or romantic tale was imported into Italy with the language and manuscripts of Greece, repeated before the end of the fifteenth century by Crinitus, Pontanus, and Volaterranus; attacked by Alciat, for the honour of the law; and defended by Baronius (A.D. 561, No. 2, etc.), for the honour of the church. Yet Tzetzes himself had read in *other* chronicles that Belisarius did not lose his sight, and that he recovered his fame and fortunes.

70. The statue in the villa Borghese at Rome, in a sitting posture, with an open hand, which is vulgarly given to Belisarius, may be ascribed with more dignity to Augustus in the act of propitiating Nemesis (Winckelman, Hist. de l'Art, tom. iii. p. 266). Ex nocturno visû etiam stipem, quotannis, die certo emendicabat a populo, cavam manum asses porrigentibus præbens (Sueton. in August. c. 91, with an excellent note of Casaubon).

71. The *rubor* of Domitian is stigmatised, quaintly enough, by the pen of Tacitus (in Vit. Agricol. c. 45), and has been likewise noticed by the younger Pliny (Panegyr. c. 48) and Suetonius (in Domitian, c. 18, and Casaubon ad locum). Procopius (Anecdot. c. 8 [tom. iii. p. 55, ed. Bonn]) foolishly believes that only *one* bust of Domitian had reached the sixth century.

72. The studies and science of Justinian are attested by the confession (Anecdot. c. 8, 13), still more than by the praises (Gothic. l. iii. c. 31, de Ædific. l. i. Proem. c. 7) of Procopius. Consult the

opious index of Alemannus, and read the Life of ustinian by Ludewig (p. 135–142).

73. See in the C. P. Christiana of Ducange (l. i. , 24, No. 1) a chain of original testimonies, from rocopius in the sixth, to Gyllius in the sixteenth, entury.

74. The first comet is mentioned by John Malala tom. ii. p. 190, 219 [p. 454, 477, ed. Bonn]) and Theophanes (p. 154 [tom. i. p. 278, ed. Bonn]); he second by Procopius (Persic. l. ii. c. 4). Yet I trongly suspect their identity. The paleness of the un (Vandal. l. ii. c. 14) is applied by Theophanes p. 158) to a different year.

75. Seneca's seventh book of Natural Questions isplays in the theory of comets a philosophic hind. Yet should we not too candidly confound a ague prediction, a venient tempus, etc., with the herit of real discoveries.

76. Astronomers may study Newton and Halley. draw my humble science from the article Comète, n the French Encyclopédie, by M. d'Alembert.

77. Whiston, the honest, pious, visionary Whis- on, had fancied, for the era of Noah's flood (2242 ears before Christ), a prior apparition of the same omet which drowned the earth with its tail.

78. A dissertation of Fréret (Mémoires de l'Aca- lémie des Inscriptions, tom. x. p. 357–377) affords happy union of philosophy and erudition. The henomenon in the time of Ogyges was preserved by Varro (apud Augustine, The City of God, xxi.), who quotes Castor, Dion of Naples, and Adrastus f Cyzicus—nobiles mathematici. The two sub- equent periods are preserved by the Greek hythologists and the spurious books of Sibylline erses.

79. Pliny (Hist. Nat. ii. 23) has transcribed the riginal memorial of Augustus. Mairan, in his host ingenious letters to the P. Parennin, mis- ionary in China, removes the games and the omet of September from the year 44 to the year 3 before the Christian era; but I am not totally ubdued by the criticism of the astronomer (Opus- ules, p. 275–351).

80. This last comet was visible in the month of December, 1680. Bayle, who began his Pensées ur la Comète in January, 1681 (Œuvres, tom. iii.), vas forced to argue that a *supernatural* comet would have confirmed the ancients in their idolatry. Ber- houlli (see his *Eloge*, in Fontenelle, tom. v. p. 99) vas forced to allow that the tail, though not the head, was a *sign* of the wrath of God.

81. Paradise Lost was published in the year 667; and the famous lines (l. ii. 708, etc.), which tartled the licenser, may allude to the recent omet of 1664, observed by Cassini at Rome in the presence of queen Christina (Fontenelle, in his *Eloge*, tom. v. p. 338). Had Charles II. betrayed hy symptoms of curiosity or fear?

82. For the cause of earthquakes see Buffon tom. i. p. 502–536; Supplément à l'Hist. Natu- elle, tom. v. p. 382–390, edition in 4to), Valmont le Bomare (Dictionnarie d'Histoire Naturelle,

Tremblemens de Terre, *Pyrites*), Watson (Chemical Essays, tom. i. p. 181–209).

83. The earthquakes that shook the Roman world in the reign of Justinian are described or mentioned by Procopius (Goth. l. iv. c. 25 [tom. ii. p. 594, ed. Bonn]; Anecdot. c. 18), Agathias (l. ii. p. 52, 53, 54; l. v. p. 145–152 [p. 96–101, 281– 294, ed. Bonn]), John Malala (Chron. tom. ii. p. 140–146, 176, 177, 183, 193, 220, 229, 231, 233, 234 [p. 419, *sq.*, 442 *sq.*, 448, 456, 478, 485 *sq.*, 488 *sq.*, ed. Bonn]), and Theophanes (p. 151, 183 189, 191–196 [tom. i. p. 272, 336, 347, 350, 357, ed. Bonn]).

84. An abrupt height, a perpendicular cape, between Aradus and Botrys, named by the Greeks θεῶν πρόσωπον, and εὐπρόσωπον or λιθοπρόσωπον by the scrupulous Christians (Polyb. l. v. [c. 68] p. 411; Pompon. Mela, l. i. c. 12, p. 87, cum Isaac Voss. Observat. Maundrell, Journey, p. 32, 33; Pocock's Description, vol. ii. p. 99).

85. Botrys was founded (ann. ante Christ. 935– 903) by Ithobal, king of Tyre (Marsham, Canon Chron. p. 387, 388). Its poor representative, the village of Patrone, is now destitute of an harbour.

86. The university, splendour, and ruin of Be- rytus are celebrated by Heineccius (p. 351–356) as an essential part of the history of the Roman law. It was overthrown in the twenty-fifth year of Justinian, A.D. 551, July 9 (Theophanes, p. 192); but Agathias (l. ii. p. 51, 52 [p. 95 *sq.*, ed. Bonn]) suspends the earthquake till he has achieved the Italian war.

87. I have read with pleasure Mead's short, but elegant, treatise concerning Pestilential Disorders, the seventh edition, London, 1722.

88. The great plague which raged in 542 and the following years (Pagi, Critica, tom. ii. p. 518) must be traced in Procopius (Persic. l. ii. c. 22, 23), Agathias (l. v. p. 153, 154 [p. 297 *sq.*, ed. Bonn]), Evagrius (l. iv. c. 29), Paul Diaconus (l. ii. c. 4, p. 776, 777), Gregory of Tours (tom. ii. l. iv. c. 5, p. 205), who styles it *Lues Inguinaria*, and the Chron- icles of Victor Tunnunensis (p. 9 in Thesaur. Tem- porum), of Marcellinus (p. 54), and of Theoph- anes (p. 153).

89. Dr. Friend (Hist. Medicin. in Opp. p. 416– 420, Lond. 1733) is satisfied that Procopius must have studied physic, from his knowledge and use of the technical words. Yet many words that are now scientific were common and popular in the Greek idiom.

90. See Thucydides, l. ii. c. 47–54, and poetical description of the same plague by Lucretius (l. vi. 1136–1284). I was indebted to Dr. Hunter for an elaborate commentary on this part of Thucydides, a quarto of 600 pages (Venet. 1603, apud Juntas), which was pronounced in St. Mark's library by Fabius Paullinus Utinensis, a physician and phi- losopher.

91. Thucydides (c. 51) affirms that the infection could only be once taken; but Evagrius, who had family experience of the plague, observes that some

persons, who had escaped the first, sunk under the second attack; and this repetition is confirmed by Fabius Paullinus (p. 588). I observe that on this head physicians are divided; and the nature and operation of the disease may not always be similar.

92. It was thus that Socrates had been saved by his temperance, in the plague of Athens (Aul. Gellius, Noct. Attic. ii. 1). Dr. Mead accounts for the peculiar salubrity of religious houses by the two advantages of seclusion and abstinence (p. 18, 19).

93. Mead proves that the plague is contagious, from Thucydides, Lucretius, Aristotle, Galen, and common experience (p. 10–20); and he refutes (Preface, p. ii.–xiii.) the contrary opinion of the French physicians who visited Marseilles in the year 1720. Yet these were the recent and enlightened spectators of a plague which, in a few months, swept away 50,000 inhabitants (sur la Peste de Marseille, Paris, 1786), of a city that, in the present hour of prosperity and trade, contains no more than 90,000 souls (Necker, sur les Finances, tom. p. 231).

94. The strong assertions of Procopius—οὔτε γὰ ἰατρῷ οὔτε ἰδιώτῃ—are overthrown by the sub sequent experience of Evagrius.

95. After some figures of rhetoric, the sands the sea, etc., Procopius (Anecdot. c. 18) attempt a more definite account; that μυριάδας μυριάδω μυρίας had been exterminated under the reign the Imperial demon. The expression is obscure i grammar and arithmetic; and a literal interpreta tion would produce several millions of millions Alemannus (p. 80) and Cousin (tom. iii. p. 178 translate this passage "two hundred millions;" bu I am ignorant of their motives. If we drop th μυριάδας, the remaining μυριάδων μυριάς, a myria of myriads, would furnish one hundred millions, number not wholly inadmissible.

Chapter XLIV

1. The civilians of the darker ages have established an absurd and incomprehensible mode of quotation, which is supported by authority and custom. In their references to the Code, the Pandects, and the Institutes, they mention the number, not of the *book*, but only of the *law*; and content themselves with reciting the first words of the *title* to which it belongs; and of these titles there are more than a thousand. Ludewig (Vit. Justiniani, p. 268) wishes to shake off this pedantic yoke; and I have dared to adopt the simple and rational method of numbering the book, the title, and the law.

2. Germany, Bohemia, Hungary, Poland, and Scotland, have received them as common law or reason; in France, Italy, etc., they possess a direct or indirect influence; and they were respected in England from Stephen to Edward I., our national Justinian (Duck. de Usû et Auctoritate Juris Civilis, l. ii. c. 1, 8–15; Heineccius, Hist. Juris Germanici, c. 3, 4, No. 55–124, and the legal historians of each country).

3. Francis Hottoman, a learned and acute lawyer of the sixteenth century, wished to mortify Cujacius and to please the Chancellor de l'Hôpital. His Anti-Tribonianus (which I have never been able to procure) was published in French in 1609; and his sect was propagated in Germany (Heineccius, Op. tom. iii. sylloge iii. p. 171–183).

4. At the head of these guides I shall respectfully place the learned and perspicuous Heineccius, a German professor, who died at Halle in the year 1741 (see his Eloge in the Nouvelle Bibliothèque Germanique, tom. ii. p. 51–64). His ample works have been collected in eight volumes in 4to, Geneva, 1743–1748. The treatises which I have separately used are, 1. Historia Juris Romani et Germanici, Lugd. Batav. 1740, in 8vo. 2. Syn tagma Antiquitatum Romanum Jurisprudentiam illustrantum, 2 vols. in 8vo. Traject. ad Rhenum 3. Elementa Juris Civilis secundum Ordinem In stitutionum, Lugd. Bat. 1751, in 8vo. 4. Element. J. C. secundum Ordinem Pandectarum, Traject 1772, in 8vo, 2 vols.

5. Our original text is a fragment de Origin Juris (Pandect. l. i. tit. ii.) of Pomponius, a Roma lawyer, who lived under the Antonines (Heinecc tom. iii. syl. iii. p. 66–126). It has been abridged and probably corrupted, by Tribonian, and sinc restored by Bynkershoek (Opp. tom. i. p. 279–304)

6. The constitutional history of the kings Rome may be studied in the first book of Livy, more copiously in Dionysius Halicarnassensis (l. ii [c. 4–25] p. 80–96, 119–130 [c. 57–70]; l. iv. [c. 1 etc.] p. 198–220), who sometimes betrays the char acter of a rhetorician and a Greek.

7. This threefold division of the law was applie to the three Roman kings by Justus Lipsius (Opp tom. iv. p. 279); is adopted by Gravina (Origine Juris Civilis, p. 28, edit. Lips. 1737); and is reluc tantly admitted by Mascou, his German editor.

8. The most ancient Code or Digest was style *Jus Papirianum*, from the first compiler, Papirius who flourished somewhat before or after the *Reg fugium* (Pandect. l. i. tit. ii.). The best judicia critics, even Bynkershoek (tom. i. p. 284, 285) an Heineccius (Hist. J. C. R. l. i. c. 16, 17, and Opp tom. iii. sylloge iv. p. 1–8), give credit to this tal of Pomponius, without sufficiently adverting t the value and rarity of such a monument of th third century of the *illiterate* city. I much suspec that the Caius Papirius, the Pontifex Maximus who revived the laws of Numa (Dionys. Hal. l. iii [c. 36] p. 171), left only an oral tradition; and tha

the Jus Papirianum of Granius Flaccus (Pandect. l. l. tit. xvi. leg. 144) was not a commentary, but an original work, compiled in the time of Cæsar (Censorin. de Die Natali, c. iii. p. 13; Duker de Latinitate J. C. p. 157).

9. A pompous, though feeble, attempt to restore the original, is made in the Histoire de la Jurisprudence Romaine of Terrasson, p. 22–72; Paris, 1750, in folio; a work of more promise than performance.

10. In the year 1444 seven or eight tables of brass were dug up between Cortona and Gubbio. A part of these, for the rest is Etruscan, represents the primitive state of the Pelasgic letters and language, which are ascribed by Herodotus to that district of Italy (l. i. c. 56, 57, 58); though this difficult passage may be explained of a Crestona in Thrace (Notes de Larcher, tom. i. p. 256–261). The savage dialect of the Eugubine Tables has exercised, and may still elude, the divination of criticism; but the root is undoubtedly Latin, of the same age and character as the Saliare Carmen, which, in the time of Horace, none could understand. The Roman idiom, by an infusion of Doric and Æolic Greek, was gradually ripened into the style of the twelve tables, of the Duilian column, of Ennius, of Terence, and of Cicero (Gruter. Inscript. tom. i. p. cxlii.; Scipion Maffei, Istoria Diplomatica, p. 241–258; Bibliothèque Italique, tom. iii. p. 30–41, 174–205, tom. xiv. p. 1–52).

11. Compare Livy (l. iii. c. 31–59) with Dionysius Halicarnassensis (l. x. [c. 55] p. 644—xi. [c. 1, sqq.] p. 691). How concise and animated is the Roman—how prolix and lifeless the Greek! Yet he has admirably judged the masters, and defined the rules, of historical composition.

12. From the historians, Heineccius (Hist. J. R. l. i. No. 26) maintains that the twelve tables were of brass: æreas: in the text of Pomponius we read eboreas; for which Scaliger has substituted roboreas (Bynkershoek, p. 286). Wood, brass, and ivory, might be successively employed.

13. His exile is mentioned by Cicero (Tusculan. Quæstion. v. 36); his statue by Pliny (Hist. Nat. xxxiv. 11). The letter, dream, and prophecy of Heraclitus are alike spurious (Epistolæ Græc. Divers. p. 337).

14. This intricate subject of the Sicilian and Roman money is ably discussed by Dr. Bentley (Dissertation on the Epistles of Phalaris, p. 427–479), whose powers in this controversy were called forth by honour and resentment.

15. The Romans, or their allies, sailed as far as the fair promontory of Africa (Polyb. l. iii. [c. 22] p. 177, edit. Casaubon, in folio). Their voyages to Cumæ, etc., are noticed by Livy and Dionysius.

16. This circumstance would alone prove the antiquity of Charondas, the legislator of Rhegium and Catana, who, by a strange error of Diodorus Siculus (tom. i. l. xii. [c. 11 sq.] p. 485–492), is celebrated long afterwards as the author of the policy of Thurium.

17. Zaleucus, whose existence has been rashly attacked, had the merit and glory of converting a band of outlaws (the Locrians) into the most virtuous and orderly of the Greek republics. (See two Mémoires of the Baron de St. Croix, sur la Législation de la Grande Grèce; Mém. de l'Académie, tom. xlii. p. 276–333.) But the laws of Zaleucus and Charondas, which imposed on Diodorus and Strobæus, are the spurious composition of a Pythagorean sophist, whose fraud has been detected by the critical sagacity of Bentley, p. 335–377.

18. I seize the opportunity of tracing the progress of this national intercourse: 1. Herodotus and Thucydides (A.U.C. 300–350) appear ignorant of the name and existence of Rome (Joseph. contra Apion. tom. ii. l. i. c. 12, p. 444, edit. Havercamp.). 2. Theopompus (A.U.C. 400, Plin. iii. 9) mentions the invasion of the Gauls, which is noticed in looser terms by Heraclides Ponticus (Plutarch in Camillus [c. 15], p. 292, edit. H. Stephan.). 3. The real or fabulous embassy of the Romans to Alexander (A.U.C. 430) is attested by Clitarchus (Plin. iii. 9), by Aristus and Asclepiades (Arrian, l. vii. [c. 15] p. 294, 295), and by Memnon of Heraclea (apud Photium, cod. ccxxiv. p. 725 [p. 229, ed. Bekker]), though tacitly denied by Livy. 4. Theophrastus (A.U.C. 440) primus externorum aliqua de Romanis diligentius scripsit (Plin. iii. 9). 5. Lycophron (A.U.C. 480–500) scattered the first seed of a Trojan colony and the fable of the Æneid (Cassandra, 1226–1280):

Γῆς καὶ θαλάσσης σκῆπτρα καὶ μοναρχίαν
Λαβόντες.

A bold prediction before the end of the first Punic war.

19. The tenth table, de modo sepulturæ, was borrowed from Solon (Cicero de Legibus, ii. 23–26): the furtum per lancem et licium conceptum is derived by Heineccius from the manners of Athens (Antiquitat. Rom. tom. ii. p. 167–175). The right of killing a nocturnal thief was declared by Moses, Solon, and the Decemvirs (Exodus xxii. 2; Demosthenes contra Timocratem, tom. i. p. 736, edit. Reiske; Macrob. Saturnalia, l. i. c. 4; Collatio Legum Mosaicarum et Romanarum, tit. vii. No. i. p. 218, edit. Cannegieter [Lugd. Bat. 1774]).

20. Βραχέως καὶ ἀπερίττως is the praise of Diodorus (tom. i. l. xii. [c. 26] p. 494), which may be fairly translated by the eleganti atque absolutâ brevitate verborum of Aulus Gellius (Noct. Attic. xx. 1).

21. Listen to Cicero (de Legibus, ii. 23) and his representative Crassus (de Oratore, i. 43, 44).

22. See Heineccius (Hist. J. R. No. 29–33). I have followed the restoration of the twelve tables by Gravina (Origines J. C. p. 280–307) and Terrasson (Hist. de la Jurisprudence Romaine, p. 94–205).

23. Finis æqui juris (Tacit. Annal. iii. 27). Fons omnis publici et privati juris (T. Liv. iii. 34).

24. De principiis juris, et quibus modis ad hanc multitudinem infinitam ac varietatem legum per-

ventum sit *altius* disseram (Tacit. Annal. iii. 25). This deep disquisition fills only two pages, but they are the pages of Tacitus. With equal sense, but with less energy, Livy (iii. 34) had complained, in hoc immenso aliarum super alias acervataruɱ legum cumulo, etc.

25. Suetonius in Vespasiano, c. 8.

26. Cicero ad Familiares, viii. 8.

27. Dionysius, with Arbuthnot, and most of the moderns (except Eisenschmidt de Ponderibus, etc., p. 137–140), represent the 100,000 *asses* by 10,000 Attic drachmæ, or somewhat more than 300 pounds sterling. But their calculation can apply only to the later times, when the *as* was diminished to 1-24th of its ancient weight: nor can I believe that in the first ages, however destitute of the precious metals, a single ounce of silver could have been exchanged for seventy pounds of copper or brass. A more simple and rational method is to value the copper itself according to the present rate, and, after comparing the mint and the market-price, the Roman and avoirdupois weight, the primitive *as* or Roman pound of copper may be appreciated at one English shilling, and the 100,000 *asses* of the first class amounted to 5000 pounds sterling. It will appear from the same reckoning that an ox was sold at Rome for five pounds, a sheep for ten shillings, and a quarter of wheat for one pound ten shillings (Festus, p. 330, edit. Dacier; Plin. Hist. Natur. xviii. 4): nor do I see any reason to reject these consequences, which moderate our ideas of the poverty of the first Romans.

28. Consult the common writers on the Roman Comitia, especially Sigonius and Beaufort. Spanheim (de Præstantiâ et Usû Numismatum, tom. ii. dissert. x. p. 192, 193) shows, on a curious medal, the Cista, Pontes, Septa, Diribitor, etc.

29. Cicero (de Legibus, iii. 16, 17, 18) debates this constitutional question, and assigns to his brother Quintus the most unpopular side.

30. Præ tumultu recusantium perferre non potuit (Sueton. in August. c. 34). See Propertius, l. ii. eleg. 6 [or 7]. Heineccius, in a separate history, has exhausted the whole subject of the Julian and Papian-Poppæan laws (Opp. tom. vii. P. i. p. 1–479).

31. Tacit. Annal. i. 15; Lipsius, Excursus E, in Tacitum.

32. Non ambigitur senatum jus facere posse, is the decision of Ulpian (l. xvi. ad Edict. in Pandect. l. i. tit. iii. leg. 9). Pomponius taxes the *comitia* of the people as a turba hominum (Pandect. l. i. tit. ii. leg. 9).

33. The jus honorarium of the prætors and other magistrates is strictly defined in the Latin text of the Institutes (l. i. tit. ii. No. 7), and more loosely explained in the Greek paraphrase of Theophilus (p. 33–38, edit. Reitz), who drops the important word *honorarium*.

34. Dion Cassius (tom. i. l. xxxvi. [c. 23] p. 100) fixes the perpetual edicts in the year of Rome 686.

Their institution, however, is ascribed to the yea 585 in the Acta Diurna, which have been publishe from the papers of Ludovicus Vives. Their au thenticity is supported or allowed by Pighius (Ar nal. Roman. tom. ii. p. 377, 378), Grævius (a Sueton. p. 778), Dodwell (Prælection. Cambder p. 665), and Heineccius: but a single word, Scu tum *Cimbricum*, detects the forgery (Moyle's Works vol. i. p. 303).

35. The history of edicts is composed, and th text of the perpetual edict is restored, by the mas ter-hand of Heineccius (Opp. tom. vii. P. ii. p 1–564); in whose researches I might safely ac quiesce. In the Academy of Inscriptions, M. Bou chaud has given a series of memoirs to this inter esting subject of law and literature.

36. His laws are the first in the Code. See Dod well (Prælect. Cambden, p. 319–340), who wan ders from the subject in confused reading an feeble paradox.

37. Totam illam veterem et squalentem silvar legum novis principalium rescriptorum et edic torum securibus truncatis et cæditis (Apologet. 4, p. 50, edit. Havercamp.). He proceeds to prais the recent firmness of Severus, who repealed th useless or pernicious laws, without any regard t their age or authority.

38. The constitutional style of *Legibus solutus* misinterpreted by the art or ignorance of Dio Cassius (tom. i. l. liii. [c. 18] p. 713). On this oc casion his editor, Reimar, joins the universal cen sure which freedom and criticism have pronounce against that slavish historian.

39. The *word* (*Lex Regia*) was still more recer than the *thing*. The slaves of Commodus or Cara calla would have started at the name of royalty.

40. See Gravina (Opp. p. 501–512) and Beau fort (République Romaine, tom. i. p. 255–274 He has made a proper use of two dissertations b John Frederick Gronovius and Noodt, both trans lated, with valuable notes, by Barbeyrac, 2 vols. i 12mo, 1731.

41. Institut. l. i. tit. ii. No. 6; Pandect. l. i. tit iv. leg. 1; Cod. Justinian. l. i. tit. xvii. leg. 1, No 7. In his Antiquities and Elements, Heineccius ha amply treated de constitutionibus principum which are illustrated by Godefroy (Comment ac Cod. Theodos. l. i. tit. i. ii. iii.) and Gravina (p 87–90).

42. Theophilus, in Paraphras. Græc. Institu p. 33, 34, edit. Reitz. For his person, time, writing see the Theophilus of J. H. Mylius, Excurs. iii. p 1034–1073.

43. There is more envy than reason in the com plaint of Macrinus (Jul. Capitolin. c. 13). Nefa esse leges videri Commodi et Caracallæ et homi num imperitorum voluntates. Commodus wa made a Divus by Severus (Dodwell, Prælect. viii p. 324, 325). Yet he occurs only twice in th Pandects.

44. Of Antoninus Caracalla alone 200 constitu tions are extant in the Code, and with his fathe

60. These two princes are quoted fifty times in he Pandects and eight in the Institutes (Terrason, p. 265).

45. Plin. Secund. Epistol. x. 66; Sueton. in Domitian, c. 23.

46. It was a maxim of Constantine, contra jus escripta non valeant (Cod. Theodos. l. i. tit. ii. eg. 1). The emperors reluctantly allow some scruiny into the law and the fact, some delay, petition, tc.; but these insufficient remedies are too much n the discretion and at the peril of the judge.

47. A compound of vermilion and cinnabar, which marks the Imperial diplomas from Leo I. (A.D. 470) to the fall of the Greek empire (Bibliohèque Raisonnée de la Diplomatique, tom. i. p. 509–514; Lami, de Eruditione Apostolorum, tom. i. p. 720–726).

48. Schulting, Jurisprudentia Ante-Justinianea, p. 681–718. Cujacius assigned to Gregory the eigns from Hadrian to Gallienus, and the continuation to his fellow-labourer Hermogenes. This general division may be just, but they often trespassed on each other's ground.

49. Scævola, most probably Q. Cervidius Scævola, the master of Papinian, considers this acceptance of fire and water as the essence of marriage Pandect. l. xxiv. tit. 1, leg. 66. See Heineccius, Hist. J. R. No. 317).

50. Cicero (de Officiis, iii. 19) may state an ideal case, but St. Ambrose (de Officiis, iii. 2) appeals to the practice of his own times, which he understood as a lawyer and a magistrate (Schuling ad Ulpian. Fragment. tit. xxii. No. 28, p. 643, 644 [Jurispr. Ante-Justin.]).

51. The furtum lance licioque conceptum was no longer understood in the time of the Antonines Aulus Gellius, xvi. 10). The Attic derivation of Heinecius (Antiquitat. Rom. l. iv. tit. i. No. 13– 21) is supported by the evidence of Aristophanes, his scholiast, and Pollux.

52. In his Oration for Murena (c. 9–13) Cicero urns into ridicule the forms and mysteries of the ivilians, which are represented with more candour by Aulus Gellius (Noct. Attic. xx. 10), Gravina (Opp. p. 265, 266, 267), and Heineccius, Antiquitat. l. iv. tit. vi.).

53. The series of the civil lawyers is deduced by Pomponius (de Origine Juris Pandect. l. i. tit. ii. § 35 sqq.]). The moderns have discussed, with earning and criticism, this branch of literary hisory; and among these I have chiefly been guided by Gravina (p. 41–79) and Heineccius (Hist. J. R. No. 113–351). Cicero, more especially in his books de Oratore, de Claris Oratoribus, de Legibus, and he Clavis Ciceroniana of Ernesti (under the names of Mucius, etc.), afford much genuine and pleasing nformation. Horace often alludes to the morning labours of the civilians (Serm. I. i. 10, Epist. II. i. 03, etc.).

Agricolam laudat juris legumque peritus,
Sub galli cantum consultor ubi ostia pulast.

· · · · · ·

Romæ dulce diu fuit et solemne, reclusâ
Mane domo vigilare, clienti promere jura.

54. Crassus, or rather Cicero himself, proposes (de Oratore, i. 41, 42) an idea of the art or science of jurisprudence, which the eloquent, but illiterate, Antonius (i. 58) affects to deride. It was partly executed by Servius Sulpicius (in Bruto, c. 41), whose praises are elegantly varied in the classic Latinity of the Roman Gravina (p. 60).

55. Perturbatricem autem omnium harum rerum Academiam, hanc ab Arcesila et Carneade recentem, exoremus ut sileat, name si invaserit in hæc, quæ satis scite instructa et composita videntur, nimias edet ruinas, quam quidem ego placare cupio, submovere non audeo (de Legibus, i. 13). From this passage alone, Bentley (Remarks on Freethinking, p. 250) might have learned how firmly Cicero believed in the specious doctrines which he has adorned.

56. The stoic philosophy was first taught at Rome by Panætius, the friend of the younger Scipio (see his Life in the Mém. de l'Académie des Inscriptions, tom. x. p. 75–89).

57. As he is quoted by Ulpian (leg. 40 ad Sabinum in Pandect. l. xlvii. tit. ii. leg. 21). Yet Trebatius, after he was a leading civilian, qui [quod] familiam duxit, became an epicurean (Cicero ad Fam. vii. 5). Perhaps he was not constant or sincere in his new sect.

58. See Gravina (p. 45–51) and the ineffectual cavils of Mascou. Heineccius (Hist. J. R. No. 125) quotes and approves a dissertation of Everard Otto, de Stoicâ Jurisconsultorum Philosophiâ.

59. We have heard of the Catonion rule, the Aquilian stipulation, and the Manilian forms, of 211 maxims, and of 247 definitions (Pandect. l. L. tit. xvi. xvii.).

60. Read Cicero, l. i. de Oratore, Topica, pro Murena.

61. See Pomponius (de Origine Juris Pandect. l. i. tit. ii. leg. 2, No. 47), Heineccius (ad Institut. l. i. tit. ii. No. 8, l. ii. tit. xxv. in Element. et Antiquitat.), and Gravina (p. 41–45). Yet the monopoly of Augustus, a harsh measure, would appear with some softening in contemporary evidence; and it was probably veiled by a decree of the senate.

62. I have perused the Diatribe of Gotfridus Mascovius, the learned Mascou, de Sectis Jurisconsultorum (Lipsiæ, 1728, in 12mo. p. 276), a learned treatise on a narrow and barren ground.

63. See the character of Antistius Labeo in Tacitus (Annal. iii. 75) and in an epistle of Ateius Capito (Aul. Gellius, xiii. 12), who accuses his rival of libertas nimia et vecors. Yet Horace would not have lashed a virtuous and respectable senator; and I must adopt the emendation of Bentley, who reads Labieno insanior (Serm. I. iii. 82). See Mascou, de Sectis (c. i. p. 1–24).

64. Justinian (Institut. l. iii. tit. 23, and Theophil. Vers. Græc. p. 677, 680) has commemorated this weighty dispute, and the verses of Homer that were alleged on either side as legal authorities. It

was decided by Paul (leg. 33, ad Edict. in Pandect. l. xviii. tit. i. leg. 1), since, in a simple exchange, the buyer could not be discriminated from the seller.

65. This controversy was likewise given for the Proculians, to supersede the indecency of a search, and to comply with the aphorism of Hippocrates, who was attached to the septenary number of two weeks of years, or 700 of days (Institut. l. i. tit. xxii.). Plutarch and the Stoics (de Placit. Philosoph. l. v. c. 24) assign a more natural reason. Fourteen years is the age—περὶ ἣν ὁ σπερματικὸς κρίψεται ἀῤῥός. See the vestigia of the sects in Mascou, c. ix. p. 145–276.

66. The series and conclusion of the sects are described by Mascou (c. ii.–vii. p. 24–120); and it would be almost ridiculous to praise his equal justice to these obsolete sects.

67. At the first summons he flies to the turbot-council; yet Juvenal (Satir. iv. 75–80) styles the præfect or bailiff of Rome sanctissimus legum interpres. From his science, says the old scholiast, he was called, not a man but a book. He derived the singular name of Pegasus from the galley which his father commanded.

68. Tacit. Annal. xvi. 7. Sueton. in Nerone, c. xxxvii.

69. Mascou, de Sectis, c. viii. p. 120–144, de Herciscundis, a legal term which was applied to these eclectic lawyers: herciscere is synonymous to dividere.

70. See the Theodosian Code, l. i. tit. iv. with Godefroy's Commentary, tom. i. p. 31–35. This decree might give occasion to Jesuitical disputes like those in the Lettres Provinciales, whether a judge was obliged to follow the opinion of Papinian, or of a majority, against his judgment, against his conscience, etc. Yet a legislator might give that opinion, however false, the validity, not of truth, but of law.

71. For the legal labours of Justinian, I have studied the Preface to the Institutes; the 1st, 2nd, and 3rd Prefaces to the Pandects; the 1st and 2nd Preface to the Code; and the Code itself (l. i. tit. xvii. de Veteri Jure enucleando). After these original testimonies, I have consulted, among the moderns, Heineccius (Hist. J. R. No. 383–404), Terrasson (Hist. de la Jurisprudence Romaine, p. 295–356), Gravina (Opp. p. 93–100), and Ludewig, in his Life of Justinian (p. 19–123, 318–321; for the Code and Novels, p. 209–261; for the Digest or Pandects, p. 262–317).

72. For the character of Tribonian, see the testimonies of Procopius (Persic. l. i. c. 23, 24 [24, 25]; Anecdot. c. 13, 20 [and Suidas (tom. iii. p. 501, edit. Kuster). Ludewig (in Vit. Justinian. p. 175–209) works hard, very hard, to whitewash—the blackamoor.

73. I apply the two passages of Suidas to the same man; every circumstance so exactly tallies. Yet the lawyers appear ignorant; and Fabricius is inclined to separate the two characters (Biblioth.

Græc. tom. i. p. 341, ii. p. 518, iii. p. 418, xii. p. 346, 353, 474).

74. This story is related by Hesychius (de Viris Illustribus), Procopius (Anecdot. c. 13 [tom. iii. p. 84, ed. Bonn]), and Suidas (tom. iii. p. 501). Such flattery is incredible!

——Nihil est quod credere de se

Non possit, cum laudatur Diis æqua potestas.

Fontenelle (tom. i. p. 32–39) has ridiculed the impudence of the modest Virgil. But the same Fontenelle places his king above the divine Augustus; and the sage Boileau has not blushed to say, "Le destin à ses yeux n'oseroit balancer." Yet neither Augustus nor Louis XIV. were fools.

75. Πάνδεκται (general receivers) was a common title of the Greek miscellanies (Plin. Præfat. ad Hist. Natur.). The Digesta of Scævola, Marcellinus, Celsus, were already familiar to the civilians: but Justinian was in the wrong when he used the two appellations as synonymous. Is the word Pandects Greek or Latin—masculine or feminine? The diligent Brenckman will not presume to decide these momentous controversies (Hist. Pandect. Florentin. p. 300–304).

76. Angelus Politianus (l. v. Epist. ult.) reckons thirty-seven (p. 192–200) civilians quoted in the Pandects—a learned, and for his times, an extraordinary list. The Greek index to the Pandects enumerates thirty-nine, and forty are produced by the indefatigable Fabricius (Biblioth. Græc. tom. iii. p. 488–502). Antoninus Augustus [Antonius Augustinus] (de Nominibus Propriis Pandect. apud Ludewig, p. 283) is said to have added fifty-four names; but they must be vague or secondhand references.

77. The Στίχοι of the ancient MSS. may be strictly defined as sentences or periods of a complete sense, which, on the breadth of the parchment rolls or volumes, composed as many lines of unequal length. The number of Στίχοι in each book served as a check on the errors of the scribes (Ludewig, p. 211–215; and his original author Suicer. Thesaur. Ecclesiast. tom. i. p. 1021–1036).

78. An ingenious and learned oration of Schultinguis (Jurisprudentia Ante-Justinianea, p. 883–907) justifies the choice of Tribonian against the passionate charges of Francis Hottoman and his sectaries.

79. Strip away the crust of Tribonian, and allow for the use of technical words, and the Latin of the Pandects will be found not unworthy of the silver age. It has been vehemently attacked by Laurentius Valla, a fastidious grammarian of the fifteenth century, and by his apologist Floridus Sabinus. It has been defended by Alciat, and a nameless advocate (most probably James Capellus). Their various treatises are collected by Duker (Opuscula de Latinitate veterum Jurisconsultorum, Lugd. Bat. 1721, in 12mo).

80. Nomina quidem veteribus servavimus, legum autem veritatem nostram fecimus. Itaque siquid erat in illis seditiosum, multa autem talia

rant ibi reposita, hoc decisum est et definitum, et a perspicuum finem deducta est quæque lex (Cod. Justinian. l. i. tit. xvii. leg. 3, No. 10). A frank confession!

81. The number of these *emblemata* (a polite name for forgeries) is much reduced by Bynkershoek (in the four last books of his Observations), who poorly maintains the right of Justinian and the duty of Tribonian.

82. The *antinomies*, or opposite laws of the Code and Pandects, are sometimes the cause, and often the excuse, of the glorious uncertainty of the civil law which so often affords what Montaigne calls "Questions pour l'Ami." See a fine passage of Franciscus Balduinus in Justinian (l. ii. p. 259, etc., apud Ludewig, p. 305, 306).

83. When Fust, or Faustus, sold at Paris his first printed Bibles as manuscripts, the price of a parchment copy was reduced from four or five hundred to sixty, fifty, and forty crowns. The public was at first pleased with the cheapness, and at length provoked by the discovery of the fraud (Mattaire, Annal. Typograph. tom. i. p. 12; first edition).

84. This execrable practice prevailed from the eighth, and more especially from the twelfth century, when it became almost universal (Montfaucon, in the Mémoires de l'Académie, tom. vi. p. 606, etc.; Bibliothèque Raisonnée de la Diplomatique, tom. i. p. 176).

85. Pomponius (Pandect. l. i. tit. ii. leg. 2 [§ 39]) observes, that of the three founders of the civil law, Mucius, Brutus, and Manilius, extant volumina, [in-] scripta Manilii monumenta; that of some old republican lawyers, hæc versantur eorum scripta inter manus hominum. Eight of the Augustan sages were reduced to a compendium: of Cascellus, scripta non extant sed unus liber, etc. [§ 45]; of Trebatius, minus frequentatur [ib.]; of Tubero, libri parum grati sunt [§ 46]. Many quotations in the Pandects are derived from books which Tribonian never saw; and, in the long period from the seventh to the thirteenth century of Rome, the *apparent* reading of the moderns successively depends on the knowledge and veracity of their predecessors.

86. *All*, in several instances, repeat the errors of the scribe and the transpositions of some leaves in the Florentine Pandects. This fact, if it be true, is decisive. Yet the Pandects are quoted by Ivo of Chartres (who died in 1117), by Theobald, archbishop of Canterbury, and by Vacarius, our first professor, in the year 1140 (Selden ad Fletam, c. 7, tom. ii. p. 1080–1085). Have our British MSS. of the Pandects been collated?

87. See the description of this original in Brenckman (Hist. Pandect. Florent. l. i. c. 2, 3, p. 4–17, and l. ii.). Politian, an enthusiast, revered it as the authentic standard of Justinian himself (p. 407, 408); but this paradox is refuted by the abbreviations of the Florentine MS. (l. ii. c. 3, p. 117–130). It is composed of two quarto volumes, with large margins, on a thin parchment, and the Latin characters betray the hand of a Greek scribe.

88. Brenckman, at the end of his history, has inserted two dissertations on the republic of Amalphi, and the Pisan war in the year 1135, etc.

89. The discovery of the Pandects at Amalphi (A.D. 1137) is first noticed (in 1501) by Ludovicus Bologninus (Brenckman, l. i. c. 11, p. 73, 74; l. iv. c. 2, p. 417–425), on the faith of a Pisan chronicle (p. 409, 410) without a name or a date. The whole story, though unknown to the twelfth century, embellished by ignorant ages, and suspected by rigid criticism, is not, however, destitute of much internal probability (l. i. c. 4–8, p. 17–50). The Liber Pandectarum of Pisa was undoubtedly consulted in the fourteenth century by the great Bartolus (p. 406, 407. See l. i. c. 9, p. 50–62).

90. Pisa was taken by the Florentines in the year 1406; and in 1411 the Pandects were transported to the capital. These events are authentic and famous.

91. They were new bound in purple, deposited in a rich casket, and shown to curious travellers by the monks and magistrates bare-headed, and with lighted tapers (Brenckman, l. i. c. 10, 11, 12, p. 62–93).

92. After the collations of Politian, Bologninus, and Antoninus Augustinus, and the splendid edition of the Pandects by Taurellus (in 1551), Henry Brenckman, a Dutchman, undertook a pilgrimage to Florence, where he employed several years in the study of a single manuscript. His Historia Pandectarum Florentinorum (Utrecht, 1722, in 4to), though a monument of industry, is a small portion of his original design. [The Pandects were edited by Taurellius, not Taurellus, and in 1553. The name of the third collator should be Antonius Augustinus.]

93. Χρύσεα χαλκείων, ἑκατόμβοι ἐννεαβοίων, apud Homerum patrem omnis virtutis (1st Præfat. ad Pandect.). A line of Milton or Tasso would surprise us in an act of parliament. Quæ omnia obtinere sancimus in omne ævum. Of the first Code he says (2nd Præfat.) in æternum valiturum. Man and for ever!

94. *Novellæ* is a classic adjective, but a barbarous substantive (Ludewig, p. 245). Justinian never collected them himself; the nine collations, the legal standard of modern tribunals, consists of ninety-eight Novels; but the number was increased by the diligence of Julian, Haloander, and Contius (Ludewig, p. 249, 258; Aleman. Not. in Anecdot. p. 98).

95. Montesquieu, Considérations sur la Grandeur et la Décadence des Romains, c. 20, tom. iii. p. 501, in 4to. On this occasion he throws aside the gown and cap of a President à Mortier.

96. Procopius, Anecdot. c. 28 [tom. iii. p. 155, ed. Bonn]. A similar privilege was granted to the church of Rome (Novel. ix.). For the general repeal of these mischievous indulgences, see Novel. cxi. and Edict. v.

97. Lactantius, in his Institutes of Christianity, an elegant and specious work, proposes to imitate the title and method of the civilians. Quidam prudentes et arbitri æquitatis Institutiones Civilis Juris compositas ediderunt (Institut. Divin. l. i. c. 1). Such as Ulpian, Paul, Florentinus, Marcian.

98. The emperor Justinian calls him *suum*, though he died before the end of the second century. His Institutes are quoted by Servius, Boethius, Priscian, etc.; and the Epitome by Arrian is still extant. (See the Prolegomena and notes to the edition of Schulting, in the Jurisprudentia Ante-Justinianea, Lugd. Bat. 1717; Heineccius, Hist. J. R. No. 313; Ludewig, in Vit. Just. p. 199.)

99. See the Annales Politiques de l'Abbé de St. Pierre, tom. i. p. 25, who dates in the year 1735. The most ancient families claim the immemorial possession of arms and fiefs. Since the Crusades, some, the most truly respectable, have been created by the king for merit and services. The recent and vulgar crowd is derived from the multitude of venal offices, without trust or dignity, which continually ennoble the wealthy plebeians.

100. If the option of a slave was bequeathed to several legatees, they drew lots, and the losers were entitled to their share of his value: ten pieces of gold for a common servant or maid under ten years; if above that age, twenty; if they knew a trade, thirty; notaries or writers, fifty; midwives or *physicians*, sixty; eunuchs under ten years, thirty pieces; above, fifty; if tradesmen, seventy (Cod. l. vi. tit. xliii. leg. 3). These legal prices are generally below those of the market.

101. For the state of slaves and freedmen see Institutes, l. i. tit. iii.–viii., l. ii. tit. ix., l. iii. tit. viii. ix. [vii. viii.]; Pandects or Digest, l. i. tit. v. vi., l. xxxviii. tit. i.–iv., and the whole of the fortieth book; Code, l. vi. tit. iv. v., l. vii. tit. i.–xxiii. Be it henceforward understood that, with the original text of the Institutes and Pandects, the correspondent articles in the Antiquities and Elements of Heineccius are implicitly quoted; and with the twenty-seven first books of the Pandects, the learned and rational Commentaries of Gerard Noodt (Opera, tom. ii. p. 1–590, the end, Lugd. Bat. 1724).

102. See the patria potestas in the Institutes (l. i. tit. ix.), the Pandects (l. i. tit. vi. vii.), and the Code (l. viii. tit. xlvii. xlviii. xlix. [tit. xlvi. xlvii. xlviii.]). Jus potestatis quod in liberos habemus proprium est civium Romanorum. Nulli enim alii sunt homines, qui talem in liberos habeant potestatem qualem nos habemus.

103. Dionysius Hal. l. ii. [c. 26] p. 94. 95. Gravina (Opp. p. 286) produces the words of the twelve tables. Papinian (in Collatione Legum Roman. et Mosaicarum, tit. iv. p. 204 [ed. Cannegieter, 1774]) styles this patria potestas, lex regia: Ulpian (ad Sabin. l. xxvi. in Pandect. l. i. tit. vi. leg. 8) says, just potestatis moribus receptum; and furiosus filium in potestate nabetit. How sacred— or rather, how absurd!

104. Pandect. l. xlvii. tit. ii. leg. 14, No. 13, leg 38, No. 1. Such was the decision of Ulpian an Paul.

105. The trina mancipatio is most clearly de fined by Ulpian (Fragment. x. p. 591, 592, edit Schulting); and best illustrated in the Antiquitie of Heineccius.

106. By Justinian, the old law, the jus necis c the Roman father (Institut. l. iv. tit. ix. [viii.] No 7), is reported and reprobated. Some legal ves tiges are left in the Pandects (l. xliii. tit. xxix. leg 3, No. 4) and the Collatio Legum Romanarum e Mosaicarum (tit. ii. No. 3, p. 189).

107. Except on public occasions and in th actual exercise of his office. In publicis locis atqu muneribus, atque actionibus patrum, jura cun filiorum qui in magistratû sunt, potestatibus co lata interquiescere paullulum et connivere, etc (Aul. Gellius, Noctes Atticæ, ii. 2). The Lessons o the philosopher Taurus were justified by the ol and memorable example of Fabius; and we ma contemplate the same story in the style of Liv (xxiv. 44) and the homely idiom of Claudiu Quadrigarius the annalist.

108. See the gradual enlargement and securit of the filial *peculium* in the Institutes (l. ii. tit. ix.) the Pandects (l. xv. tit. i., l. xli. tit. i.), and th Code (l. iv. tit. xxvi. xxvii.).

109. The examples of Erixo and Arius are re lated by Seneca (de Clementia, i. 14, 15), th former with horror, the latter with applause.

110. Quod latronis magis quam patris jure eun interfecisset, nam patria potestas in pietate debe non in atrocitate consistere (Marcian, Institut. l xiv. in Pandect. l. xlviii. tit. ix. leg. 5).

111. The Pompeian and Cornelian laws de sic ariis and *parricidis*, are repeated, or rather abridged with the last supplements of Alexander Severus Constantine, and Valentinian, in the Pandects (l xlviii. tit. viii. ix.), and Code (l. ix. tit. xvi. xvii.) See likewise the Theodosian Code (l. ix. tit. xiv xv.), with Godefroy's Commentary (tom. iii. p 84–113), who pours a flood of ancient and moder learning over these penal laws.

112. When the Chremes of Terence reproache his wife for not obeying his orders and exposin their infant, he speaks like a father and a master and silences the scruples of a foolish woman. Se Apuleius (Metamorph. l. x. p. 337, edit. Delphin.)

113. The opinion of the lawyers, and the dis cretion of the magistrates, had introduced in th time of Tacitus some legal restraints, which migh support his contrast of the boni mores of the Ger mans to the bonæ leges alibi—that is to say, a Rome (de Moribus Germanorum, c. 19). Ter tullian (ad Nationes, l. i. c. 15) refutes his ow charges, and those of his brethren, against th heathen jurisprudence.

114. The wise and humane sentence of th civilian Paul (l. ii. Sententiarum in Pandect. l xxv. tit. iii. leg. 4) is represented as a mere mora precept by Gerard Noodt (Opp. tom. i. in Juliu

Paulus, p. 567–588, and Amica Responsio, p. 591–606), who maintains the opinion of Justus Lipsius (Opp. tom. ii. p. 409, ad Belgas, cent. i. epist. 85), and as a positive binding law by Bynkershoek (de Jure occidendi Liberos, Opp. tom. i. p. 318–340; Curæ Secundæ, p. 391–427). In a learned but angry controversy the two friends deviated into the opposite extremes.

115. Dionys. Hal. l. ii. p. 92, 93; Plutarch, in the life of Numa. Τὸ σῶμα καὶ τὸ ἦθος κάθαρον καὶ ἄθικτον ἐπὶ τῷ γαμοῦντι γένεσθαι. [Comp. Lycurg. cum Numâ, tom. i. p. 310, ed. Reiske.]

116. Among the winter *frumenta*, the *triticum*, or bearded wheat; the *siligo*, or the unbearded; the *far*, *adorea*, *oryza*, whose description perfectly tallies with the rice of Spain and Italy. I adopt this identity on the credit of M. Paucton in his useful and laborious Métrologie (p. 517–529).

117. Aulus Gellius (Noctes Atticæ, xviii. 6) gives a ridiculous definition of Ælius Melissus, Matrona, quæ semel, *materfamilias* quæ sæpius peperit, as porcetra, and scropha in the sow kind. He then adds the genuine meaning, quæ in matrimonium vel in manum convenisset.

118. It was enough to have tasted wine, or to have stolen the key of the cellar (Plin. Hist. Nat. xiv. 14).

119. Solon requires three payments per month. By the Misna, a daily debt was imposed on an idle, vigorous, young husband; twice a week on a citizen; once on a peasant; once in thirty days on a camel-driver; once in six months on a seaman. But the student or doctor was free from tribute; and *no* wife, if she received a *weekly* sustenance, could sue for a divorce; for one week a vow of abstinence was allowed. Polygamy divided, without multiplying, the duties of the husband (Selden, Uxor Ebraica, l. iii. c. 6, in his works, vol. ii. p. 717–720).

120. On the Oppian law we may hear the mitigating speech of Valerius Flaccus and the severe censorial oration of the elder Cato (Liv. xxxiv. 1–8). But we shall rather hear the polished historian of the eighth, than the rough orators of the sixth, century of Rome. The principles, and even the style, of Cato are more accurately preserved by Aulus Gellius (x. 23).

121. For the system of Jewish and Catholic matrimony, see Selden (Uxor Ebraica, Opp. vol. ii. p. 529–860), Bingham (Christian Antiquities, l. xxii.), and Chardon (Hist. des Sacremens, tom. vi.).

122. The civil laws of marriage are exposed in the Institutes (l. i. tit. x.), the Pandects (l. xxiii. xxiv. xxv.), and the Code (l. v.); but as the title de ritû nuptiarum is yet imperfect, we are obliged to explore the fragments of Ulpian (tit. ix. p. 590, 591), and the Collatio Legum Mosaicarum (tit. xvi. p. 790, 791) with the notes of Pithæus and Schulting [Jurispr. Ante-Justin.]. They find, in the Commentary of Servius (on the 1st Georgic and the 4th Æneid), two curious passages.

123. According to Plutarch Romulus allowed only three grounds of a divorce, drunkenness, adultery, and false keys. Otherwise, the husband who abused his supremacy forfeited half his goods to the wife, and half to the goddess Ceres, and offered a sacrifice (with the remainder?) to the terrestrial deities. This strange law was either imaginary or transient.

124. In the year of Rome 523, Spurius Cavilius Ruga repudiated a fair, a good, but a barren wife (Dionysius Hal. l. ii. [c. 25] p. 93; Plutarch, in Numa [Lycurgus and Numa compared]; Valerius Maximus, l. ii. c. 1 [§ 4]; Aulus Gellius, iv. 3). He was questioned by the censors, and hated by the people; but his divorce stood unimpeached in law.

125. ——Sic fiunt octo mariti
Quinque per autumnos.
(Juvenal, Satir. vi. 229.)
A rapid succession, which may yet be credible, as well as the non consulum numero, sed maritorum annos suos computant, of Seneca (de Beneficiis, iii. 16). Jerom saw at Rome a triumphant husband bury his twenty-first wife, who had interred twenty-two of his less sturdy predecessors (Opp. tom. i. p. 90, ad Gerontiam). But the ten husbands in a month of the poet Martial is an extravagant hyperbole (l. vi. epigram 7).

126. Sacellum Viriplacæ (Valerius Maximus, l. ii. c. 1 [§ 6], in the Palatine region, appears in the time of Theodosius, in the description of Rome by Publius Victor.

127. Valerius Maximus, l. ii. c. 9 [§ 2]. With some propriety he judges divorce more criminal than celibacy: illo namque conjugalia sacra spreta tantum, hoc etiam injuriose tractata.

128. See the laws of Augustus and his successors, in Heineccius, ad Legem Papiam-Poppæam, c. 19, in Opp. tom. vi. P. i. p. 323–333.

129. Aliæ sunt leges Cæsarum, aliæ Christi; aliud Papinianus, aliud Paulus *noster* præcipit (Jerom, tom. i. p. 198; Selden, Uxor Ebraica, l. iii. c. 31, p. 847–853).

130. The Institutes are silent; but we may consult the Codes of Theodosius (l. iii. tit. xvi. with Godefroy's Commentary, tom. i. p. 311–313) and Justinian (l. v. tit. xvii.), the Pandects (l. xxiv. tit. ii.) and the Novels (xxii. cxvii. cxxvii. cxxxiv. cxl.). Justinian fluctuated to the last between civil and ecclesiastical law.

131. In pure Greek, πορνεία is not a common word; nor can the proper meaning, fornication, be strictly applied to matrimonial sin. In a figurative sense, how far, and to what offences, may it be extended? Did Christ speak the Rabbinical or Syriac tongue? Of what original word is πορνεία the translation? How variously is that Greek word translated in the versions ancient and modern! There are two (Mark x. 11, Luke xvi. 18) to one (Matthew xix. 9) that such ground of divorce was not excepted by Jesus. Some critics have presumed to think, by an evasive answer, he avoided the giving offence either to the school of Sammai or to

that of Hillel (Selden, Uxor Ebraica, l. iii. c. 18-22, 28, 31).

132. The principles of the Roman jurisprudence are exposed by Justinian (Institut. l. i. tit. x.); and the laws and manners of the different nations of antiquity concerning forbidden degrees, etc., are copiously explained by Dr. Taylor in his Elements of Civil Law (p. 108, 314-339), a work of amusing though various reading, but which cannot be praised for philosophical precision.

133. When her father Agrippa died (A.D. 44), Berenice was sixteen years of age (Joseph. tom. i. Antiquit. Judaic. l. xix. c. 9, p. 952, edit. Havercamp.). She was therefore above fifty years old when Titus (A.D. 79) invitus invitam invisit. This date would not have adorned the tragedy or pastoral of the tender Racine.

134. The *Ægyptia conjux* of Virgil (Æneid, viii. 688) seems to be numbered among the monsters who warred with Mark Antony against Augustus, the senate, and the gods of Italy.

135. The humble but legal rights of concubines and natural children are stated in the Institutes (l. i. tit. x.), the Pandects (l. i. tit. vii.), the Code (l. v. tit. xxv.), and the Novels (lxxiv. lxxxix.). The researches of Heineccius and Giannone (ad Legem Juliam et Papiam-Poppæam, c. iv. p. 164-175, Opere Posthume, p. 108-158) illustrate this interesting and domestic subject.

136. See the article of guardians and wards in the Institutes (l. i. tit. xiii.-xxvi.), the Pandects (l. xxvi. xxvii.), and the Code (l. v. tit. xxviii.-lxx.).

137. Institut. l. ii. tit. i. ii. Compare the pure and precise reasoning of Caius and Heineccius (l. ii. tit. i. p. 69-91) with the loose prolixity of Theophilus (p. 207-265). The opinions of Ulpian are preserved in the Pandects (l. i. tit. viii. leg. 41, No. 1).

138. The *heredium* of the first Romans is defined by Varro (de Re Rusticâ, l. i. c. ii. p. 141, c. x. p. 160, 161, edit. Gesner), and clouded by Pliny's declamation (Hist. Natur. xviii. 2). A just and learned comment is given in the Administration des Terres chez les Romains (p. 12-66).

139. The *res mancipi* is explained from faint and remote lights by Ulpian (Fragment. tit. xviii. [xix.] p. 618, 619) and Bynkershoek (Opp. tom. i. p. 306-315). The definition is somewhat arbitrary; and as none except myself have assigned a reason, I am diffident of my own.

140. From this short prescription, Hume (Essays, vol. i. p. 423) infers that there could not *then* be more order and settlement in Italy than *now* amongst the Tartars. By the civilian of his adversary Wallace he is reproached, and not without reason, for overlooking the conditions (Institut. l. ii. tit. vi.).

141. See the Institutes (l. i. [ii.] tit. iv. v.) and the Pandects (l. vii.). Noodt has composed a learned and distinct treatise de Usufructû (Opp. tom. i. p. 387-478).

142. The questions de Servitutibus are discussed in the Institutes (l. ii. tit. iii.) and Pandects (l. viii.). Cicero (pro Murenâ, c. 9) and Lactantius (Institut. Divin. l. i. c. i.) affect to laugh at the insignificant doctrine, de aquâ pluviâ arcendâ, etc. Yet it might be of frequent use among litigious neighbours, both in town and country.

143. Among the patriarchs, the first-born enjoyed a mystic and spiritual primogeniture (Genesis xxv. 31). In the land of Canaan he was entitled to a double portion of inheritance (Deuteronomy xxi. 17, with Le Clerc's judicious Commentary).

144. At Athens the sons were equal; but the poor daughters were endowed at the discretion of their brothers. See the κληρικοί pleadings of Isæus (in the seventh volume of the Greek Orators), illustrated by the version and comment of Sir William Jones, a scholar, a lawyer, and a man of genius.

145. In England, the eldest son alone inherits *all* the land; a law, says the orthodox Judge Blackstone (Commentaries on the Laws of England, vol. ii. p. 215), unjust only in the opinion of younger brothers. It may be of some political use in sharpening their industry.

146. Blackstone's Tables (vol. ii. p. 202) represent and compare the decrees of the civil with those of the canon and common law. A separate tract of Julius Paulus, de gradibus et affinibus, is inserted or abridged in the Pandects (l. xxxviii. tit. x. [leg. 10]). In the seventh degrees he computes (No. 18) 1024 persons.

147. The Voconian law was enacted in the year of Rome 584. The younger Scipio, who was then 17 years of age (Freinsheimius, Supplement. Livian. xlvi. 44), found an occasion of exercising his generosity to his mother, sisters, etc. (Polybius, tom. ii. l. xxxi. p. 1453-1464, edit. Gronov. [xxxii. 12], a domestic witness.)

148. Legem Voconiam (Ernesti, Clavis Ciceroniana) voce magnâ bonis lateribus (at sixty-five years of age) suasissem, says old Cato (de Senectute, c. 5). Aulus Gellius (vii. 13, xvii. 6) has saved some passages.

149. See the law of succession in the Institutes of Caius (l. ii. tit. viii. p. 130-144, [Schulting, Jurispr. Ante-Justin. Lips. 1737]) and Justinian (l. iii. tit. i.-vi. with the Greek version of Theophilus, p. 515-575, 588-600), the Pandects (l. xxxviii. tit. vi-xvii.), the Code (l. vi. tit. lv.-lx.), and the Novels (cxviii.).

150. That succession was the *rule*, testament the *exception*, is proved by Taylor (Elements of Civil Law, p. 519-527), a learned, rambling, spirited writer. In the second and third books the method of the Institutes is doubtless preposterous; and the chancellor Daguesseau (Œuvres, tom. i. p. 275) wishes his countryman Domat in the place of Tribonian. Yet *covenants* before *successions* is not surely *the natural order of the civil laws.*

151. Prior examples of testaments are perhaps fabulous. At Athens a *childless* father only could

make a will (Plutarch. in Solon. See Isæus and ones).

152. The testament of Augustus is specified by Suetonius (in August. c. 101, in Neron. c. 4), who may be studied as a code of Roman antiquities. Plutarch (Opuscul. tom. ii. p. 976) is surprised ταν δὲ διαθήκας γράθωσιν, ἑτέρους μὲν ἀπολείπουσι ληρονόμους, ἕτεροι δὲ πωλοῦσι τὰς οὐσίας. The language of Ulpian (Fragment. tit. xx. [§ 2] p. 627, edit. Schulting) is almost too exclusive—solum in isû est.

153. Justinian (Novell. cxv. c. 3, 4) enumerates only the public and private crimes, for which a son might likewise disinherit his father.

154. The *substitutions fidei-commissaires* of the modern civil law is a feudal idea grafted on the Roman jurisprudence, and bears scarcely any resemblance to the ancient fidei-commissa (Institutions du Droit François, tom. i. p. 347–383; Denissart, Décisions de Jurisprudence, tom. iv. p. 577–604). They were stretched to the fourth degree by an abuse of the clix. Novel; a partial, perplexed, declamatory law.

155. Dion Cassius (tom. ii. l. lvi. [c. 10] p. 814, with Reimar's Notes) specifies in Greek money the sum of 25,000 drachms.

156. The revolutions of the Roman laws of inheritance are finely, though sometimes fancifully, deduced by Montesquieu (The Spirit of Laws, l. xxvii.)

157. Of the civil jurisprudence of successions, testaments, codicils, legacies, and trusts, the principals are ascertained in the Institutes of Caius (l. ii. tit. ii.–viii. p. 91–144), Justinian (l. ii. tit. x.–xv.), and Theophilus (p. 328, 514); and the immense detail occupies twelve books (xxviii.–xxxix.) of the Pandects.

158. The Institutes of Caius (l. ii. tit. ix. x. p. 144–214), of Justinian (l. iii. tit. xiv.–xxx. [xiii.–xix.] l. iv. tit. i.–vi.), and of Theophilus (p. 616–637), distinguish four sorts of obligations—aut *re*, aut *verbis*, aut *literis*, aut *consensû:* but I confess myself partial to my own division.

159. How much is the cool, rational evidence of Polybius (l. vi. [c. 56] p. 693, l. xxxi. p. 1459, 460) superior to vague, indiscriminate applause —omnium maxime et præcipue fidem coluit (A. Gellius, xx. 1 [tom. ii. p. 289, ed. Bipont.]).

160. The Jus Prætorium de Pactis et Transactionibus is a separate and satisfactory treatise of Gerard Noodt (Opp. tom. i. p. 483–564). And I will here observe that the universities of Holland and Brandenburg, in the beginning of the present century, appear to have studied the civil law on the most just and liberal principles.

161. The nice and various subject of contracts by consent is spread over four books (xvii.–xx.) of the Pandects, and is one of the parts best deserving of the attention of an English student.

162. The covenants of rent are defined in the Pandects (l. xix.) and the Code (l. iv. tit. lxv.). The quinquennium, or term of five years, appears to have been a custom rather than a law; but in France all leases of land were determined in nine years. This limitation was removed only in the year 1775 (Encyclopédie Méthodique, tom. i. de la Jurisprudence, p. 668, 669); and I am sorry to observe that it yet prevails in the beauteous and happy country where I am permitted to reside.

163. I might implicitly acquiesce in the sense and learning of the three books of G. Noodt, de fœnore et usuris (Opp. tom. i. p. 175–268). The interpretation of the *asses* or *centesimæ usuræ* at twelve, the *unciariæ* at one per cent., is maintained by the best critics and civilians: Noodt (l. ii. c. 2, p. 207), Gravina (Opp. p. 205, etc., 210), Heineccius (Antiquitat. ad Institut. l. iii. tit. xv.), Montesquieu (The Spirit of Laws, l. xxii. c. 22; Défense de l'Esprit des Loix, tom. iii. p. 478, etc.), and above all John Frederic Gronovius (de Pecunia Veteri, l. iii. c. 13, p. 213–227, and his three Antexegeses, p. 455–655), the founder, or at least the champion, of this probable opinion, which is, however, perplexed with some difficulties.

164. Primo xii Tabulis sancitum est ne quis unciario fœnore amplius exerceret (Tacit. Annal. vi. 16). Pour peu (says Montesquieu, The Spirit of Laws, l. xxii. c. 22) qu'on soit versé dans l'histoire de Rome, on verra qu'une pareille loi ne devoit pas être l'ouvrage des décemvirs. Was Tacitus ignorant—or stupid? But the wiser and more virtuous patricians might sacrifice their avarice to their ambition, and might attempt to check the odious practice by such interest as no lender would accept, and such penalties as no debtor would incur.

165. Justinian has not condescended to give usury a place in his Institutes; but the necessary rules and restrictions are inserted in the Pandects (l. xxii. tit. i. ii.) and the Code (l. iv. tit. xxxii. xxxiii.).

166. The fathers are unanimous (Barbeyrac, Morale des Pères, p. 144, etc.): Cyprian, Lactantius, Basil, Chrysostom (see his frivolous arguments in Noodt, l. i. c. 7, p. 188), Gregory of Nyssa, Ambrose, Jerom, Augustin, and a host of councils and casuists.

167. Cato, Seneca, Plutarch, have loudly condemned the practice or abuse of usury. According to the etymology of *fœnus* and γοκὸς the principal is supposed to *generate* the interest: a breed of barren metal, exclaims Shakspeare—and the stage is the echo of the public voice.

168. Sir William Jones has given an ingenious and rational Essay on the Law of Bailment (London, 1781, p. 127, in 8vo.). He is perhaps the only lawyer equally conversant with the year-books of Westminster, the Commentaries of Ulpian, the Attic pleadings of Isæus, and the sentences of Arabian and Persian cadhis.

169. Noodt (Opp. tom. i. p. 137–172) has composed a separate treatise, ad Legem Aquiliam (Pandect. l. ix. tit. ii.).

170. Aulus Gellius (Noct. Attic. xx. 1 [tom. ii. p. 284]) borrowed this story from the Commentaries of Q. Labeo on the twelve tables.

171. The narrative of Livy (i. 28) is weighty and solemn. At tu dictis, Albane, maneres, is a harsh reflection, unworthy of Virgil's humanity (Æneid. viii. 643). Heyne, with his usual good taste, observes that the subject was too horrid for the shield of Æneas (tom. iii. p. 229).

172. The age of Draco (Olympiad xxxix. 1) is fixed by Sir John Marsham (Canon Chronicus, p. 593–596) and Corsini (Fasti Attici, tom. iii. p. 62). For his laws, see the writers on the government of Athens, Sigonius, Meursius, Potter, etc.

173. The seventh, de delictis, of the twelve tables is delineated by Gravina (Opp. p. 292, 293, with a commentary, p. 214–230). Aulus Gellius (xx. 1) and the Collatio Legum Mosaicarum et Romanarum afford much original information.

174. Livy mentions two remarkable and flagitious eras, of 3000 persons accused, and of 190 noble matrons convicted, of the crime of poisoning (xl. 43, viii. 18). Mr. Hume discriminates the ages of private and public virtue (Essays, vol. i. p. 22, 23). I would rather say that such ebullitions of mischief (as in France in the year 1680) are accidents and prodigies which leave no marks on the manners of a nation.

175. The twelve tables and Cicero (pro Roscio Amerino, c. 25, 26) are content with the sack; Seneca (Excerpt. Controvers. v. 4) adorns it with serpents; Juvenal pities the guiltless monkey (innoxia simia—Satir. xiii. 156). Adrian (apud Dositheum Magistrum, l. iii. c. 16, p. 874–876, with Schulting's Note), Modestinus (Pandect. xlviii. tit. ix. leg. 9), Constantine (Cod. l. ix. tit. xvii.), and Justinian (Institut. l. iv. tit. xviii.), enumerate all the companions of the parricide. But this fanciful execution was simplified in practice. Hodie tamen vivi exuruntur vel ad bestias dantur (Paul. Sentent. Recept. l. v. tit. xxiv. p. 512, edit. Schulting [Jurispr. Ante-Justin.]).

176. The first parricide at Rome was L. Ostius, after the second Punic war (Plutarch in the life of Romulus). During the Cimbric, P. Malleolus was guilty of the first matricide (Liv. Epitom. l. lxviii.).

177. Horace talks of the formidine fustis (l. ii. Epist. i. 154), but Cicero (de Republicâ, l. iv. apud Augustine, The City of God, ii. 9, in Fragment. Philosoph. tom. iii. p. 393, edit. Olivet) affirms that the decemvirs made libels a capital offence: cum perpaucas res capite sanxissent—perpaucas!

178. Bynkershoek (Observat. Juris Rom. l. i. c. 1, in Opp. tom. i. p. 9, 10, 11) labours to prove that the creditors divided not the body, but the price, of the insolvent debtor. Yet his interpretation is one perpetual harsh metaphor; nor can he surmount the Roman authorities of Quintilian, Cæcilius, Favonius, and Tertullian. See Aulus Gellius, Noct. Attic. xx. 1 [tom. ii. p. 285].

179. The first speech of Lysias (Reiske, Orator. Græc. tom. v. p. 2–48) is in defence of a husband who had killed the adulterer. The rights of husbands and fathers at Rome and Athens are dis-

cussed with much learning by Dr. Taylor (Lectiones Lysiacæ, c. xi. in Reiske, tom. vi. p. 301–308).

180. See Casaubon ad Athenæum, l. i. c. 5, p. 19. Percurrent raphanique mugilesque (Catull. [xv. 18] p. 41, 42, edit. Vossian.). Hunc mugilis intrat (Juvenal. Satir. x. 317). Hunc perminxere calones (Horat. l. i. Satir. ii. 44). Familiæ stuprandum dedit [objecit] . . . fraudi non fuit (Val. Maxim. l. vi. c. 1, No. 13).

181. This law is noticed by Livy (ii. 8) and Plutarch (in the life of Poblicola), and it fully justifies the public opinion on the death of Cæsar, which Suetonius could publish under the Imperial government. Jure cæsus existimatur (in Julio, c. 76). Read the letters that passed between Cicero and Matius a few months after the ides of March (ad Fam. xi. 27, 28).

182. Πρῶτοι δὲ Ἀθηναῖοι τόν τε σίδηρον κατέθεντο. Thucydid. l. i. c. 6. The historian who considers this circumstance as the test of civilisation would disdain the barbarism of a European court.

183. He first rated at millies (£800,000) the damages of Sicily (Divinatio in Cæcilium, c. 5), which he afterwards reduced to quadringenties (£320,000 —1 Actio in Verrem, c. 18), and was finally content with tricies (£24,000). Plutarch (in the life of Cicero) has not dissembled the popular suspicion and report.

184. Verres lived near thirty years after his trial, till the second triumvirate, when he was proscribed by the taste of Mark Antony for the sake of his Corinthian plate (Plin. Hist. Natur. xxxiv. 3).

185. Such is the number assigned by Valerius Maximus (l. ix. c. 2, No. 1). Florus (iii. 21) distinguishes 2000 senators and knights. Appian (de Bell. Civil. l. i. c. 95, tom. ii. p. 133, edit. Schweighäuser) more accurately computes 40 victims of the senatorian rank and 1600 of the equestrian census or order.

186. For the penal laws (Leges Corneliæ, Pompeiæ, Juliæ, of Sulla, Pompey, and the Cæsars), see the sentences of Paulus (l. iv. tit. xviii.–xxx. p. 497–528, edit. Schulting), the Gregorian Code (Fragment. l. xix. p. 705, 706, in Schulting), the Collatio Legum Mosaicarum et Romanarum (tit. i.–xv.), the Theodosian Code (l. ix.), the Code of Justinian (l. ix.), the Pandects (xlviii.), the Institutes (l. iv. tit. xviii.), and the Greek version of Theophilus (p. 917–926).

187. It was a guardian who had poisoned his ward. The crime was atrocious: yet the punishment is reckoned by Suetonius (c. 9) among the acts in which Galba showed himself acer, vehemens, et in delictis coercendis immodicus.

188. The abactores or abigeatores, who drove one horse, or two mares or oxen, or five hogs, or ten goats, were subject to capital punishment. (Paul. Sentent. Recept. l. iv. tit. xviii. p. 497, 498). Hadrian (ad Concil. Bæticæ), most severe where the offence was most frequent, condemns the criminals, ad gladium, ludi damnationem (Ulpian, de Officio Proconsulis, l. viii. in Collatione

_egum Mosaic. et Rom. tit. xi. p. 236 [ed. Can-\
_egieter, 1774]).

189. Till the publication of the Julius Paulus of\
Schulting (l. ii. tit. xxvi. p. 317-323), it was af-\
firmed and believed that the Julian laws punished\
adultery with death; and the mistake arose from\
the fraud or error of Tribonian. Yet Lipsius had\
suspected the truth from the narratives of Tacitus\
(Annal. ii. 50, iii. 24, iv. 42), and even from the\
practice of Augustus, who distinguished the _trea-\
sonable_ frailties of his female kindred.

190. In cases of adultery Severus confined to\
the husband the right of public accusation (Cod.\
Justinian. l. ix. tit. ix. leg. 1). Nor is this privilege\
unjust—so different are the effects of male or\
female infidelity.

191. Timon [Timæus] (l. i.) and Theopompus\
(l. xliii. apud Athenæum, l. xii. p. 517 [c. 14, tom.\
v. p. 422, ed. Schweigh.]) describe the luxury and\
lust of the Etruscans: πολὺ μέν τοι γε χαίρουσι\
συνόντες τοῖς παισὶ καὶ τοῖς πειρακίοις. About the same\
period (A.U.C. 445) the Roman youth studied in\
Etruria (liv. ix. 36).

192. The Persians had been corrupted in the\
same school: ἀπ᾽ Ἑλλήνων μαθόντες παισὶ μίσγονται\
(Herodot. l. i. c. 135). A curious dissertation might\
be formed on the introduction of pæderasty after\
the time of Homer, its progress among the Greeks\
of Asia and Europe, the vehemence of their pas-\
sions, and the thin device of virtue and friendship\
which amused the philosophers of Athens. But,\
scelera ostendi oportet dum puniuntur, abscondi\
flagitia.

193. The name, the date, and the provisions of\
this law are equally doubtful (Gravina, Opp. p.\
432, 433; Heineccius, Hist. Jur. Rom. No. 108;\
Ernesti, Clav. Ciceron. in Indice Legum). But I\
will observe that the _nefanda_ Venus of the honest\
German is styled _aversa_ by the more polite Italian.

194. See the oration of Æschines against the\
catamite Timarchus (in Reiske, Orator. Græc.\
tom. iii. p. 21-184).

195. A crowd of disgraceful passages will force\
themselves on the memory of the classic reader: I\
will only remind him of the cool declaration of\
Ovid:—

Odi concubitus qui non utrumque resolvunt.\
Hoc est quod puerûm tangar amore _minus_.

196. Ælius Lampridius, in Vit. Heliogabal. in\
Hist. August. p. 112. Aurelius Victor, in Philippo\
[de Cæsar. c. 28],' Codex Theodos. l. ix. tit. vii.\
leg. 6, and Godefroy's Commentary, tom. iii. p.\
63. Theodosius abolished the subterraneous brothels\
of Rome, in which the prostitution of both sexes\
was acted with impunity.

197. See the laws of Constantine and his suc-\
cessors against adultery, sodomy, etc., in the The-\
odosian (l. ix. tit. vii. leg. 7, l. xi. tit. xxxvi. leg. 1,\
4) and Justinian Codes (l. ix. tit. ix. leg. 30, 31).\
These princes speak the language of passion as\
well as of justice, and fraudulently ascribe their\
own severity to the first Cæsars.

198. Justinian, Novel. lxxvii. cxxxiv. cxli.; Pro-\
copius in Anecdot. c. 11, 16 [tom. iii. p. 76, 99, ed.\
Bonn], with the notes of Alemannus; Theophanes,\
p. 151 [ed. Par;. tom. i. p. 271, ed. Bonn]; Ced-\
renus, p. 368 [ed. Par.; tom. i. p. 645, ed. Bonn];\
Zonaras, l. xiv. [c. 7] p. 64.

199. Montesquieu, The Spirit of Laws, l. xii. c.\
6. That eloquent philosopher conciliates the rights of\
liberty and of nature, which should never be\
placed in opposition to each other.

200. For the corruption of Palestine, 2000 years\
before the Christian era, see the history and laws\
of Moses. Ancient Gaul is stigmatised by Diodorus\
Siculus (tom. i. l. v. [c. 32] p. 356), China by the\
Mahometan and Christian travellers (Ancient Re-\
lations of India and China, p. 34, translated by\
Renaudot, and his bitter critic the Père Premare,\
Lettres Edifiantes, tom. xix. p. 435), and native\
America by the Spanish historians (Garcilasso de\
la Vega, l. iii. c. 13, Rycaut's translation; and\
Dictionnaire de Bayle, tom. iii. p. 88). I believe,\
and hope, that the negroes, in their own country,\
were exempt from this moral pestilence.

201. The important subject of the public ques-\
tions and judgments at Rome is explained with\
much learning, and in a classic style, by Charles\
Sigonius (l. iii. de Judiciis, in Opp. tom. iii. p.\
679-864); and a good abridgment may be found\
in the République Romaine of Beaufort (tom. ii. l.\
v. p. 1-121). Those who wish for more abstruse\
law may study Noodt (de Jurisdictione et Imperio\
Libri duo, tom. i. p. 93-134), Heineccius (ad Pan-\
dect. l. i. et ii. ad Institut. l. iv. tit. xvii. Element.\
ad Antiquitat.), and Gravina (Opp. 230-251).

202. The office, both at Rome and in England,\
must be considered as an occasional duty, and not\
a magistracy or profession. But the obligation of a\
unanimous verdict is peculiar to our laws, which\
condemn the juryman to undergo the torture from\
whence they have exempted the criminal.

203. We are indebted for this interesting fact to\
a fragment of Asconius Pedianus, who flourished\
under the reign of Tiberius. The loss of his Com-\
mentaries on the Orations of Cicero has deprived\
us of a valuable fund of historical and legal\
knowledge.

204. Polyb. l. vi. [c. 14] p. 643. The extension of\
the empire and _city_ of Rome obliged the exile to\
seek a more distant place of retirement.

205. Qui de se statuebant, humabantur corpora,\
manebant testamenta; pretium festinandi. Tacit.\
Annal. vi. 29, with the Notes of Lipsius.

206. Julius Paulus (Sentent. Recept. l. v. tit.\
xii. p. 476), the Pandects (l. xlviii. tit. xxi.), the\
Code (l. ix. tit. L.), Bynkershoek (tom. i. p. 59,\
Observat. J. C. R. iv. 4), and Montesquieu (The\
Spirit of Laws, l. xxix. c. 9), define the civil limita-\
tions of the liberty and privileges of suicide. The\
criminal penalties are the production of a later\
and darker age.

207. Plin. Hist. Natur. xxxvi. 24. When he fa-\
tigued his subjects in building the Capitol, many

of the labourers were provoked to despatch themselves: he nailed their dead bodies to crosses.

208. The sole resemblance of a violent and premature death has engaged Virgil (Æneid. vi. 434-

439) to confound suicides with infants, lovers, an persons unjustly condemned. Heyne, the best of his editors, is at a loss to deduce the idea, or ascer tain the jurisprudence, of the Roman poet.

Chapter XLV

1. See the family of Justin and Justinian in the Familiæ Byzantinæ of Ducange, p. 89–101. The devout civilians, Ludewig (in Vit. Justinian. p. 131) and Heineccius (Hist. Juris Roman. p. 374) have since illustrated the genealogy of their favourite prince.

2. In the story of Justin's elevation I have translated into simple and concise prose the eight hundred verses of the two first books of Corippus, De Laudibus Justini, Appendix Hist. Byzant. p. 401–416, Rome, 1777 [p. 166–187, ed. Bonn].

3. It is surprising how Pagi (Critica, in Annal. Baron. tom. ii. p. 639) could be tempted by any chronicles to contradict the plain and decisive text of Corippus (vicina dona, l. ii. 354, vicina dies, l. iv. 1), and to postpone, till A.D. 567, the consulship of Justin.

4. Theophan. Chronograph. p. 205 [tom. i. p. 374, ed. Bonn]. Whenever Cedrenus or Zonaras are mere transcribers, it is superfluous to allege their testimony.

5. Corippus, l. iii. 390. The unquestionable sense relates to the Turks, the conquerors of the Avars; but the word scultor has no apparent meaning, and the sole MS. of Corippus, from whence the first edition (1581, apud Plantin) was printed, is no longer visible. The last editor, Foggini of Rome, has inserted the conjectural emendation of soldan: but the proofs of Ducange (Joinville, Dissert. xvi. p. 238– 240), for the early use of this title among the Turks and Persians, are weak or ambiguous. And I must incline to the authority of D'Herbelot (Bibliothèque Orient. p. 825), who ascribes the word to the Arabic and Chaldæan tongues, and the date to the beginning of the eleventh century, when it was bestowed by the khalif of Bagdad on Mahmud, prince of Gazna, and conqueror of India.

6. For these characteristic speeches, compare the verse of Corippus (l. iii. 266–401) with the prose of Menander (Excerpt. Legation. p. 102, 103 [ed. Par.; p. 287 sq., ed. Bonn]). Their diversity proves that they did not copy each other; their resemblance, that they drew from a common original.

7. For the Austrasian war, see Menander (Excerpt. Legat. p. 110 [c. 11, p. 303, ed. Bonn]), Gregory of Tours (Hist. Franc. l. iv. c. 29), and Paul the Deacon (de Gest. Langobard. l. ii. c. 10).

8. Paul Warnefrid, the deacon of Friuli, de Gest. Langobard. l. i. c. 23, 24. His pictures of national manners, though rudely sketched, are more lively and faithful than those of Bede or Gregory of Tours.

9. The story is told by an impostor (Theophy lact. Simocat. l. vi. c. 10 [p. 261, ed. Bonn]); bu he had art enough to build his fictions on publi and notorious facts.

10. It appears from Strabo [l. vii.], Pliny [l. vi c. 11], and Ammianus Marcellinus [l. xxvii.], tha the same practice was common among the Scythia tribes (Muratori, Scriptores Rer. Italic. tom. i. p 424). The scalps of North America are likewis trophies of valour. The skull of Cunimund wa preserved above two hundred years among th Lombards; and Paul himself was one of the guest to whom Duke Ratchis exhibited this cup on high festival (l. ii. c. 28).

11. Paul, l. i. c. 27. Menander, in Excerpt. Le gat. p. 110, 111 [p. 303, 304, ed. Bonn].

12. Ut hactenus etiam tam apud Bajoarioruɪ gentem, quam et Saxonum, sed et alios ejusdeɪ linguæ homines . . . in eorum carminibus cele bretur. Paul. l. i. c. 27. He died A.D. 799 (Mura tori, in Præfat. tom. i. p. 397). These German songs some of which might be as old as Tacitus (de Mor ibus Germ. c. 2), were compiled and transcribeɪ by Charlemagne. Barbara et antiquissima car mina, quibus veterum regum actus et bella cane bantur scripsit memoriæque mandavit (Eginarɪ in Vit. Carol. Magn. c. 29, p. 130, 131). Th poems, which Goldast commends (Animadvers ad Eginard. p. 207), appear to be recent and con temptible romances.

13. The other nations are rehearsed by Paul (l ii. c. 6, 26). Muratori (Antichità Italiane, tom. i dissert. i. p. 4) has discovered the village of the Bavarians, three miles from Modena.

14. Gregory the Roman (Dialog. l. iii. c. 27, 28 apud Baron. Annal. Eccles. A.D. 579, No. 10) sup poses that they likewise adored this she-goat. I know but of one religion in which the god and the victim are the same.

15. The charge of the deacon against Narses (l ii. c. 5) may be groundless; but the weak apolog of the cardinal (Baron. Annal. Eccles. A.D. 567 No. 8–12) is rejected by the best critics—Pag (tom. ii. p. 639, 640), Muratori (Annali d'Italia tom. v. p. 160–163), and the last editors, Horatiu Blancus (Script. Rerum Italic. tom. i. p. 427, 428 and Philip Argelatus (Sigon. Opera, tom. ii. p. 11 12). The Narses who assisted at the coronation o Justin (Corippus, l. iii. 221) is clearly understoo to be a different person.

16. The death of Narses is mentioned by Paul l. ii. c. 11. Anastas. in Vit. Johan. iii. p. 43. Ag nellus, Liber Pontifical. Raven. [c. 3 fin] in Script

Rer. Italicarum, tom. ii. part i. p. 114, 124. Yet I cannot believe with Agnellus that Narses was ninety-five years of age. Is it probable that all his exploits were performed at fourscore?

17. The designs of Narses and of the Lombards for the invasion of Italy are exposed in the last chapter of the first book, and the seven first chapters of the second book, of Paul the Deacon.

18. Which from this translation was called New Aquileia (Chron. Venet. p. 3). The patriarch of Grado soon became the first citizen of the republic (p. 9, etc.), but his seat was not removed to Venice till the year 1450. He is now decorated with titles and honours; but the genius of the church has bowed to that of the state, and the government of a catholic city is strictly presbyterian. Thomassin, Discipline de l'Eglise, tom. i. p. 156, 157, 161–165. Amelot de la Houssaye, Gouvernement de Venise, tom. i. p. 256–261.

19. Paul has given a description of Italy, as it was then divided, into eighteen regions (l. ii. c. 14–24). The Dissertatio Chorographica de Italia Medii Ævi, by Father Beretti, a Benedictine monk, and regius professor at Pavia, has been usefully consulted.

20. For the conquest of Italy, see the original materials of Paul (l. ii. c. 7–10, 12, 14, 25, 26, 27), the eloquent narrative of Sigonius (tom. ii. de Regno Italiæ, l. i. p. 13–19), and the correct and critical review of Muratori (Annali d'Italia, tom. v. p. 164–180).

21. The classical reader will recollect the wife and murder of Candaules, so agreeably told in the first book of Herodotus [c. 8, *sqq.*]. The choice of Gyges, αἱρέεται αὐτὸς περιεῖναι, may serve as the excuse of Precedeus; and this soft insinuation of an odious idea has been imitated by the best writers of antiquity (Grævius, ad Ciceron. Orat. pro Milone, c. 10).

22. See the history of Paul, l. ii. c. 28–32. I have borrowed some interesting circumstances from the Liber Pontificalis of Agnellus [c. 4] in Script. Rer. Ital. tom. ii. p. 124. Of all chronological guides Muratori is the safest.

23. The original authors for the reign of Justin the younger are Evagrius, Hist. Eccles. l. v. c. 1–12; Theophanes, in Chronograph. p. 204–210 [tom. i. p. 373, *sqq.*, ed. Bonn]; Zonaras, tom. ii. l. xiv. [c. 10] p. 70–72; Cedrenus, in Compend. p. 388–392 [tom. i. p. 680–688, ed. Bonn].

23a. Dispositor que novus sacræ Baduarius aulæ.
Successor soceri mox factus Cura-palatî.
—Corippus.
Baduarius is enumerated among the descendants and allies of the house of Justinian. A family of noble Venetians (Casa *Badoero*) built churches and gave dukes to the republic as early as the ninth century; and, if their descent be admitted, no kings in Europe can produce a pedigree so ancient and illustrious. Ducange, Fam. Byzantin. p. 99.

Amelot de la Houssaye, Gouvernement de Venise, tom. ii. p. 555.

24. The praise bestowed on princes before their elevation is the purest and most weighty. Corippus has celebrated Tiberius at the time of the accession of Justin (l. i. 212–222). Yet even a captain of the guards might attract the flattery of an African exile.

25. Evagrius (l. v. c. 13) has added the reproach to his ministers. He applies this speech to the ceremony when Tiberius was invested with the rank of Cæsar. The loose expression, rather than the positive error, of Theophanes, etc., has delayed it to his *Augustan* investiture, immediately before the death of Justin.

26. Theophylact Simocatta (l. iii. c. 11 [p. 136, ed. Bonn]) declares that he shall give to posterity the speech of Justin as it was pronounced, without attempting to correct the imperfections of language or rhetoric. Perhaps the vain sophist would have been incapable of producing such sentiments.

27. For the character and reign of Tiberius see Evagrius, l. v. c. 13; Theophylact. l. iii. c. 12, etc.; Theophanes, in Chron. p. 210–213 [ed. Par.; tom. i. p. 382–388, ed. Bonn]; Zonaras, tom. ii. l. xiv. [c. 11] p. 72; Cedrenus, p. 392 [tom. i. p. 688, ed. Bonn]; Paul Warnefrid, de Gestis Langobard. l. iii. c. 11, 12. The deacon of Forum Julii appears to have possessed some curious and authentic facts.

28. It is therefore singular enough that Paul (l. iii. c. 15) should distinguish him as the first Greek emperor—primus ex Græcorum genere in Imperio constitutus [confirmatus]. His immediate predecessors had indeed been born in the Latin provinces of Europe: and a various reading, in Græcorum Imperio, would apply the expression to the empire rather than the prince.

29. Consult, for the character and reign of Maurice, the fifth and sixth books of Evagrius, particularly l. vi. c. 1; the eight books of his prolix and florid history by Theophylact Simocatta; Theophanes, p. 213, etc. [tom. i. p. 288, *sqq.*, ed. Bonn]; Zonaras, tom. ii. l. xiv. [c. 12] p. 73; Cedrenus, p. 394 [tom. i. p. 691, ed. Bonn].

30. Αὐτοκράτωρ ὄντως γενόμενος τὴν μὲν ὀχλοκρατείαν τῶν παθῶν ἐκ τῆς οἰκείας ἐξενηλάτησε ψυχῆς· ἀριστοκρατείαν δὲ ἐν τοῖς ἑαυτοῦ λογισμοῖς καταστησάμενος [l. vi. c. 1]. Evagrius composed his history in the twelfth year of Maurice; and he had been so wisely indiscreet that the emperor knew and rewarded his favourable opinion (l. vi. c. 24).

31. The Columna Rhegina, in the narrowest part of the Faro of Messina, one hundred stadia from Rhegium itself, is frequently mentioned in ancient geography. Cluver. Ital. Antiq. tom. ii. p. 1295; Lucas Holsten. Annotat. ad Cluver. p. 301; Wesseling, Itinerar. p. 106.

32. The Greek historians afford some faint hints of the wars of Italy (Menander, in Excerpt. Legat. p. 124, 126 [p. 327, 331, ed. Bonn]; Theophylact, l. iii. c. 4 [p. 120, ed. Bonn]). The Latins are more

satisfactory; and especially Paul Warnefrid (l. iii. c. 13–34), who had read the more ancient histories of Secundus and Gregory of Tours. Baronius produces some letters of the popes, etc.; and the times are measured by the accurate scale of Pagi and Muratori.

33. The papal advocates, Zacagni and Fontanini, might justly claim the valley or morass of Commachio as a part of the exarchate. But the ambition of including Modena, Reggio, Parma, and Placentia, has darkened a geographical question somewhat doubtful and obscure. Even Muratori, as the servant of the house of Este, is not free from partiality and prejudice.

34. See Brenckman, Dissert. Ima. de Republicâ Amalphitanâ, p. 1–42, ad calcem Hist. Pandect. Florent.

35. Gregor. Magn. l. iii. Epist. 23, 25, 26, 27.

36. I have described the state of Italy from the excellent Dissertation of Beretti. Giannone (Istoria Civile, tom. i. p. 374–387) has followed the learned Camillo Pellegrini in the geography of the kingdom of Naples. After the loss of the true Calabria the vanity of the Greeks substituted that name instead of the more ignoble appellation of Bruttium; and the change appears to have taken place before the time of Charlemagne (Eginard, p. 75 [c. 15]).

37. Maffei (Verona Illustrata, part i. p. 310–321) and Muratori (Antichità Italiane, tom. ii. Dissertazione xxxii. xxxiii. p. 71–365) have asserted the native claims of the Italian idiom: the former with enthusiasm, the latter with discretion: both with learning, ingenuity, and truth.

38. Paul, de Gest. Langobard. l. iii. c. 5, 6, 7.

39. Paul, l. ii. c. 9. He calls these families or generations by the Teutonic name of Faras, which is likewise used in the Lombard laws. The humble deacon was not insensible of the nobility of his own race. See l. iv. c. 39.

40. Compare No. 3 and 177 of the Laws of Rotharis.

41. Paul, l. ii. c. 31, 32, l. iii. c. 16. The Laws of Rotharis, promulgated A.D. 643, do not contain the smallest vestige of this payment of thirds; but they preserve many curious circumstances of the state of Italy and the manners of the Lombards.

42. The studs of Dionysius of Syracuse, and his frequent victories in the Olympic games, had diffused among the Greeks the fame of the Venetian horses; but the breed was extinct in the time of Strabo (l. v. p. 325 [p. 212, ed. Casaub.]). Gisulf obtained from his uncle generosarum equarum greges. Paul, l. ii. c. 9. The Lombards afterwards introduced caballi silvatici—wild horses. Paul, l. iv. c. 11.

43. Tunc (A.D. 596) primum, bubali in Italiam delati Italiæ populis miracula fuere (Paul Warnefrid, l. iv. c. 11). The buffaloes, whose native climate appears to be Africa and India, are unknown to Europe, except in Italy, where they are numerous and useful. The ancients were ignorant of these animals, unless Aristotle (History of Animals,

ii. 1. 499ª 4) has described them as the wild oxen of Arachosia. See Buffon, Hist. Naturelle, tom. xi. and Supplement, tom. vi. Hist. Générale des Voyages, tom. i. p. 7, 481, ii. 105, iii. 291, iv. 234, 461, v. 193, vi. 491, viii. 400, x. 666; Pennant's Quadrupedes, p. 24; Dictionnaire d'Hist. Naturelle, par Valmont de Bomare, tom. ii. p. 74. Yet I must not conceal the suspicion that Paul, by a vulgar error, may have applied the name of bubalus to the aurochs, or wild bull, of ancient Germany.

44. Consult the twenty-first Dissertation of Muratori.

45. Their ignorance is proved by the silence even of those who professedly treat of the arts of hunting and the history of animals. Aristotle (History of Animals, ix. 36. 620ª 33 ff., and the Notes of his last editor, M. Camus, tom. ii. p. 314), Pliny (Hist. Natur. l. x. c. 10), Ælian (de Natur. Animal. l. ii. c. 42), and perhaps Homer (Odyss. xxii. 302–306), describe with astonishment a tacit league and common chase between the hawks and the Thracian fowlers.

46. Particularly the gerfaut, or gyrfalcon, of the size of a small eagle. See the animated description of M. de Buffon, Hist. Naturelle, tom. xvi. p. 239, etc.

47. Script. Rerum Italicarum, tom. i. part ii. p. 129. This is the sixteenth law of the emperor Lewis the Pious. His father Charlemagne had falconers in his household as well as huntsmen (Mémoires sur l'Ancienne Chevalerie, par M. de St. Palaye, tom. iii. p. 175). I observe in the Laws of Rotharis a more early mention of the art of hawking (No. 322); and in Gaul, in the fifth century, it is celebrated by Sidonius Apollinaris among the talents of Avitus (202–207).

48. The epitaph of Droctulf (Paul, l. iii. c. 19) may be applied to many of his countrymen:—

Terribilis visu facies, sed mente benignus
Longaque robusto pectore barba fuit.

The portraits of the old Lombards might still be seen in the palace of Monza, twelve miles from Milan, which had been founded or restored by queen Theudelinda (l. iv. 22, 23). See Muratori, tom. i. dissertaz. xxiii. p. 300.

49. The story of Autharis and Theudelinda is related by Paul, l. iii. c. 29, 34; and any fragment of Bavarian antiquity excites the indefatigable diligence of the Count de Buat, Hist. des Peuples de l'Europe, tom. xi. p. 595-635, tom. xii. p. 1-53.

50. Giannone (Istoria Civile di Napoli, tom. i. p. 263) has justly censured the impertinence of Boccaccio (Gio. iii. Novel. 2), who without right or truth, or pretence, has given the pious queen Theudelinda to the arms of a muleteer.

51. Paul, l. iii. c. 16. The first dissertations of Muratori, and the first volume of Giannone's history, may be consulted for the state of the kingdom of Italy.

52. The most accurate edition of the Laws of the Lombards is to be found in the Scriptores Re-

'um Italicarum, tom. i. part ii. p. 1–181, collated 'rom the most ancient MSS., and illustrated by the critical notes of Muratori.

53. Montesquieu, The Spirit of Laws, l. xxviii. c. . Les loix des Bourguignons sont assez judicieuses; celles de Rotharis et des autres princes Lombards e sont encore plus.

54. See Leges Rotharis, No. 379, p. 47. Striga is used as the name of a witch. It is of the purest classic origin (Horat. epod. v. 20; Petron. c. 134); and from the words of Petronius (quæ striges comederunt nervos tuos?) it may be inferred that the prejudice was of Italian rather than barbaric extraction.

55. Quia incerti sumas de judicio Dei, et multos audivimus per pugnam sine justâ causâ suam causam perdere. Sed propter consuetudinem gentem nostram Langobardorum legem impiam vetare non possumus. See p. 74, No. 65, of the Laws of Liutprand, promulgated A.D. 724.

56. Read the history of Paul Warnefrid; particularly l. iii. c. 16. Baronius rejects the praise, which appears to contradict the invectives, of pope Gregory the Great; but Muratori (Annali d'Italia, tom. v. p. 217) presumes to insinuate that the saint may have magnified the faults of Arians and enemies.

57. The passages of the homilies of Gregory which represent the miserable state of the city and country are transcribed in the Annals of Baronius, A.D. 590, No. 16, A.D. 595, No. 2, etc. etc.

58. The inundation and plague were reported by a deacon, whom his bishop, Gregory of Tours, had despatched to Rome for some relics. The ingenious messenger embellished his tale and the river with a great dragon and a train of little serpents (Greg. Turon. l. x. c. 1).

59. Gregory of Rome (Dialog. l. ii. c. 15) relates a memorable prediction of St. Benedict. Roma à Gentilibus [gentibus] non exterminabitur sed tempestatibus, coruscis turbinibus ac terræ motû [fatigata] in semetipsa marcescet. Such a prophecy melts into true history, and becomes the evidence of the fact after which it was invented.

60. Quia in uno se ore cum Jovis laudibus, Christi laudes non capiunt, et quam grave nefandumque sit episcopis canere quod nec laico religioso conveniat, ipse considera (l. ix. Ep. 4). The writings of Gregory himself attest his innocence of any classic taste or literature.

61. Bayle (Dictionnaire Critique, tom. ii. p. 598, 599), in a very good article of Grégoire I., has quoted, for the buildings and statues, Platina in Gregorio I.; for the Palatine library, John of Salisbury (de Nugis Curialium, l. ii. c. 26); and for Livy, Antoninus of Florence: the oldest of the three lived in the twelfth century.

62. Gregor. l. iii. Epist. 24, Indict. 12, etc. [l. iv. Ep. 30, ed. Bened.]. From the Epistles of Gregory, and the eighth volume of the Annals of Baronius, the pious reader may collect the particles of holy iron which were inserted in keys or crosses of gold, and distributed in Britain, Gaul, Spain, Africa, Constantinople, and Egypt. The pontifical smith who handled the file must have understood the miracles which it was in his own power to operate or withhold; a circumstance which abates the superstition of Gregory at the expense of his veracity.

63. Besides the Epistles of Gregory himself, which are methodised by Dupin (Bibliothèque Ecclés. tom. v. p. 103–126), we have three Lives of the pope; the two first written in the eighth and ninth centuries (de Triplici Vita St. Greg. Preface to the fourth volume of the Benedictine edition) by the deacons Paul (p. 1–18) and John (p. 19–188), and containing much original, though doubtful, evidence; the third, a long and laboured compilation by the Benedictine editors (p. 199–305). The Annals of Baronius are a copious but partial history. His papal prejudices are tempered by the good sense of Fleury (Hist. Ecclés. tom. viii.), and his chronology has been rectified by the criticism of Pagi and Muratori.

64. John the deacon has described them like an eye-witness (l. iv. c. 83, 84); and his description is illustrated by Angelo Rocca, a Roman antiquary (St. Greg. Opera, tom. iv. p. 312–326), who observes that some mosaics of the popes of the seventh century are still preserved in the old churches of Rome (p. 321–323). The same walls which represented Gregory's family are now decorated with the martyrdom of St. Andrew, the noble contest of Domenichino and Guido.

65. Disciplinis vero liberalibus, hoc est grammaticâ, rhetoricâ, dialecticâ ita a puero est institutus, ut quamvis eo tempore florerent adhuc Romæ studia literarum, tamen nulli in urbe ipsâ secundus putaretur. Paul. Diacon. in Vit. S. Gregor. c. 2.

66. The Benedictines (Vit. Greg. l. i. 205–208) labour to reduce the monasteries of Gregory within the rule of their own order; but, as the question is confessed to be doubtful, it is clear that these powerful monks are in the wrong. See Butler's Lives of the Saints, vol. iii. p. 145; a work of merit: the sense and learning belong to the author—his prejudices are those of his profession.

67. Monasterium Gregorianum in ejusdem Beati Gregorii ædibus ad clivum Scauri prope ecclesiam SS. Johannis et Pauli in honorem St. Andræ (John, in Vit. Greg. l. i. c. 6; Greg. l. vii. Epist. 13). This house and monastery were situate on the side of the Cælian hill which fronts the Palatine; they are now occupied by the Camaldoli: San Gregorio triumphs, and St. Andrew has retired to a small chapel. Nardini, Roma Antica, l. iii. c. 6, p. 100; Descrizione di Roma, tom. i. p. 442–446.

68. The Lord's prayer consists of half a dozen lines; the Sacramentarius and Antiphonarius of Gregory fill 880 folio pages (tom. iii. P. i. p. 1–880); yet these only constitute a part of the Ordo Romanus, which Mabillon has illustrated and Fleury has abridged (Hist. Ecclés. tom. viii. p. 139–152).

69. I learn from the Abbé Dubos (Réflexions sur la Poésie et la Peinture, tom. iii. p. 174, 175) that the simplicity of the Ambrosian chant was confined to four *modes*, while the more perfect harmony of the Gregorian comprised the eight modes or fifteen chords of the ancient music. He observes (p. 332) that the connoisseurs admire the preface and many passages of the Gregorian office.

70. John the deacon (in Vit. Greg. l. ii. c. 7) expresses the early contempt of the Italians for tramontane singing. Alpina scilicet corpora vocum suarum tonitruis altisone perstrepentia, susceptæ modulationis dulcedinem proprie non resultant: quia bibuli gutturis barbara feritas dum inflexionibus et repercussionibus mitem nititur edere cantilenam, naturali quodam fragore, quasi plaustra per gradus confuse sonantia, rigidas voces jactat, etc. In the time of Charlemagne, the Franks, though with some reluctance, admitted the justice of the reproach. Muratori, Dissert. xxv.

71. A French critic (Petrus Gussanvillus, Opera, tom. ii. p. 105–112) has vindicated the right of Gregory to the entire nonsense of the Dialogues.

Dupin (tom. v. p. 138) does not think that any one will vouch for the truth of all these miracles: should like to know *how many* of them he believes himself.

72. Baronius is unwilling to expatiate on the care of the patrimonies, lest he should betray that they consisted not of *kingdoms* but *farms*. The French writers, the Benedictine editor (tom. iv. l. iii. p. 272, etc.), and Fleury (tom. viii. p. 29, etc.), are not afraid of entering into these humble, though useful, details; and the humanity of Fleury dwells on the social virtues of Gregory.

73. I much suspect that this pecuniary fine on the marriages of villains produced the famous, and often fabulous, right, *de cuissage*, *de marquette*, etc. With the consent of her husband, a handsome bride might commute the payment in the arms of a young landlord, and the mutual favour might afford a precedent of local rather than legal tyranny.

74. The temporal reign of Gregory I. is ably exposed by Sigonius in the first book, de Regno Italiæ. See his works, tom. ii. p. 44–75.

Chapter XLVI

1. Missisqui ... reposcerent ... veteres Persarum ac Macedonum terminos, seque invasurum possessa Cyro et post Alexandro, per vaniloquentiam ac minas jaciebat. Tacit. Annal. vi. 31. Such was the language of the *Arsacides:* I have repeatedly marked the lofty claims of the *Sassanians.*

2. See the embassies of Menander, extracted and preserved in the tenth century by the order of Constantine Porphyrogenitus.

3. The general independence of the Arabs, which cannot be admitted without many limitations, is blindly asserted in a separate dissertation of the authors of the Universal History, vol. xx. p. 196–250. A perpetual miracle is supposed to have guarded the prophecy in favour of the posterity of Ishmael; and these learned bigots are not afraid to risk the truth of Christianity on this frail and slippery foundation.

4. D'Herbelot, Biblioth. Orient. p. 477; Pocock, Specimen Hist. Arabum, p. 64, 65. Father Pagi (Critica, tom. ii. p. 646) has proved that, after ten years' peace, the Persian war, which continued twenty years, was renewed A.D. 571. Mahomet was born A.D. 569, in the year of the elephant, or the defeat of Abrahah (Gagnier, Vie de Mahomet, tom. i. p. 89, 90, 98); and this account allows two years for the conquest of Yemen.

5. He had vanquished the Albanians, who brought into the field 12,000 horse and 60,000 foot; but he dreaded the multitude of venomous reptiles, whose existence may admit of some doubt, as well as that of the neighbouring Amazons. Plutarch, in [The Lives of the Noble Grecians and Romans] Pompey.

6. In the history of the world I can only perceive two navies on the Caspian: 1. Of the Macedonians when Patrocles, the admiral of the kings of Syria Seleucus and Antiochus, descended most probably the river Oxus, from the confines of India (Plin Hist. Natur. vi. 21). 2. Of the Russians, when Peter the First conducted a fleet and army from the neighbourhood of Moscow to the coast of Persia (Bell's Travels, vol. ii. p. 325–352). He justly observes that such martial pomp had never been displayed on the Volga.

7. For these Persian wars and treaties, see Menander, in Excerpt. Legat. p. 113–125 [p. 311–331, ed. Bonn]; Theophanes Byzant. apud Photium, cod. lxiv. p. 77, 80, 81 [p. 26, 27, ed. Bekk.]; Evagrius, l. v. c. 7–15; Theophylact, l. iii. c. 9–16; Agathias, l. iv. [c. 29] p. 140 [p. 271, ed. Bonn].

8. Buzurg Mihir may be considered, in his character and station, as the Seneca of the East; but his virtues, and perhaps his faults, are less known than those of the Roman, who appears to have been much more loquacious. The Persian sage was the person who imported from India the game of chess and the fables of Pilpay. Such has been the fame of his wisdom and virtues, that the Christians claim him as a believer in the Gospel; and the Mohammedans revere Buzurg as a premature Musulman. D'Herbelot, Bibliothèque Orientale, p. 218.

9. See the imitation of Scipio in Theophylact, l. i. c. 14; the image of Christ, l. ii. c. 3. Hereafter I shall speak more amply of the Christian *images*—I had almost said *idols.* This, if I am not mistaken, is the oldest ἀχειροποίητος of divine manufacture; but

in the next thousand years, many others issued from the same workshop.

10. Ragæ, or Rei, is mentioned in the apocryphal book of Tobit as already flourishing 700 years before Christ, under the Assyrian empire. Under the foreign names of Europus and Arsacia, this city, 500 stadia to the south of the Caspian gates, was successively embellished by the Macedonians and Parthians (Strabo, l. xi. p. 796 [p. 524, ed. Casaub.]). Its grandeur and populousness in the ninth century is exaggerated beyond the bounds of credibility; but Rei has been since ruined by wars and the unwholesomeness of the air. Chardin, Voyage en Perse, tom. i. p. 279, 280; D'Herbelot, Biblioth. Oriental. p. 714.

11. Theophylact, l. iii. c. 18 [p. 153, ed. Bonn]. The story of the seven Persians is told in the third book of Herodotus; and their noble descendants are often mentioned, especially in the fragments of Ctesias. Yet the independence of Otanes (Herodot. l. iii. c. 83, 84) is hostile to the spirit of despotism, and it may not seem probable that the seven families could survive the revolutions of eleven hundred years. They might however be represented by the seven ministers (Brisson, de Regno Persico, l. i. p. 190); and some Persian nobles, like the kings of Pontus (Polyb. l. v. [c. 43] p. 540) and Cappadocia (Diodor. Sicul. l. xxxi. [c. 19] tom. ii. p. 517), might claim their descent from the bold companions of Darius.

12. See an accurate description of this mountain by Olearius (Voyage en Perse, p. 997, 998), who ascended it with much difficulty and danger in his return from Ispahan to the Caspian Sea.

13. The Orientals suppose that Bahram convened this assembly and proclaimed Chosroes; but Theophylact is, in this instance, more distinct and credible.

14. See the words of Theophylact, l. iv. c. 7 [p. 173, ed. Bonn]. Βαράμ φίλος τοῖς θεοῖς, νικητής, ἐπιφανής, τυράννων ἐχθρός, σατράπης μεγιστάνων τῆς Περσικῆς ἄρχων δυνάμεως, etc. In his answer Chosroes styles himself τῇνυκτὶ χαριζόμενος ὄμματα . . . ὁ τοὺς ἥΑσωνας (the genii) μισθούμενος [p. 175]. This is genuine Oriental bombast.

15. Theophylact (l. iv. c. 7 [p. 173, ed. Bonn]) imputes the death of Hormouz to his son, by whose command he was beaten to death with clubs. I have followed the milder account of Khondemir and Eutychius, and shall always be content with the slightest evidence to extenuate the crime of parricide.

16. After the battle of Pharsalia, the Pompey of Lucan (l. viii. 256–455) holds a similar debate. He was himself desirous of seeking the Parthians: but his companions abhorred the unnatural alliance; and the adverse prejudices might operate as forcibly on Chosroes and his companions, who could describe, with the same vehemence, the contrast of laws, religion, and manners, between the East and West.

17. In this age there were three warriors of the name of Narses, who have been often confounded (Pagi, Critica, tom. ii. p. 640); 1. A Persarmenian, the brother of Isaac and Armatius, who, after a successful action against Belisarius, deserted from his Persian sovereign, and afterwards served in the Italian war. 2. The eunuch who conquered Italy. 3. The restorer of Chosroes, who is celebrated in the poem of Corippus (l. iii. 220–227) as excelsus super omnia vertice agmina . . . habitu modestus . . . morum probitate placens, virtute verendus; fulmineus, cautus, vigilans, etc.

18. Experimentis cognitum est barbaros malle Româ petere reges quam habere. These experiments are admirably represented in the invitation and expulsion of Vonones (Annal. ii. 1–3), Tiridates (Annal. vi. 32–44), and Meherdates (Annal. xi. 10, xii. 10–14). The eye of Tacitus seems to have transpierced the camp of the Parthians and the walls of the harem.

19. Sergius and his companion Bacchus, who are said to have suffered in the persecution of Maximian, obtained divine honour in France, Italy, Constantinople, and the East. Their tomb at Rasaphe was famous for miracles, and that Syrian town acquired the more honourable name of Sergiopolis. Tillemont, Mém. Ecclés. tom. v. p. 491–496; Butler's Saints, vol. x. p. 155.

20. Evagrius (l. vi. c. 21) and Theophylact (l. v. c. 13, 14 [p. 230, sqq., ed. Bonn]) have preserved the original letters of Chosroes, written in Greek, signed with his own hand, and afterwards inscribed on crosses and tables of gold, which were deposited in the church of Sergiopolis. They had been sent to the bishop of Antioch, as primate of Syria.

21. The Greeks only describe her as a Roman by birth, a Christian by religion; but she is represented as the daughter of the emperor Maurice in the Persian and Turkish romances which celebrate the love of Khosrou for Schirin, of Schirin for Ferhad, the most beautiful youth of the East. D'Herbelot, Biblioth. Orient. p. 789 997, 998.

22. The whole series of the tyranny of Hormouz, the revolt of Bahram, and the flight and restoration of Chosroes, is related by two contemporary Greeks—more concisely by Evagrius (l. vi. c. 16, 17, 18, 19), and most diffusely by Theophylact Simocatta (l. iii. c. 6–18, l. iv. c. 1–16, l. v. c. 1–15): succeeding compilers, Zonaras and Cedrenus, can only transcribe and abridge. The Christian Arabs, Eutychius (Annal. tom. ii. p. 200–208) and Abulpharagius (Dynast. p. 96–98), appear to have consulted some particular memoirs. The great Persian historians of the fifteenth century, Mirkhond and Khondemir, are only known to me by the imperfect extracts of Schikard (Tarikh, p. 150–155), Texeira, or rather Stevens (Hist. of Persia, p. 182–186), a Turkish MS. translated by the Abbé Fourmont (Hist. de l'Académie des Inscriptions, tom. vii. p. 325–334), and D'Herbelot (aux mots, Hormouz, p. 457–459; Bahram, p. 174; Khosrou Parviz, p. 996). Were I perfectly satisfied

of their authority, I could wish these Oriental materials had been more copious.

23. A general idea of the pride and power of the chagan may be taken from Menander (Excerpt. Legat. p. 113, etc. [p. 308, *sq.*, ed. Bonn]), and Theophylact (l. i. c. 3, l. vii. c. 15), whose eight books are much more honourable to the Avar than to the Roman prince. The predecessors of Baian had tasted the liberality of Rome, and *he* survived the reign of Maurice (Buat, Hist. des Peuples Barbares, tom. xi. p. 545). The chagan who invaded Italy A.D. 611 (Muratori, Annali, tom. v. p. 305) was then juvenili ætate florentem (Paul Warnefrid, de Gest. Langobard. l. iv. c. 38), the son, perhaps, or the grandson, of Baian.

24. Theophylact, l. i. c. 5, 6.

25. Even in the field the chagan delighted in the use of these aromatics. He solicited, as a gift, Ἰνδικὰς καρυκείας, and received πέπερι καὶ φύλλον Ἰνδῶν, κασίαν τε καὶ τόν λεγόμενον κόστον. Theophylact, l. vii. c. 13 [p. 294, ed. Bonn]. The Europeans of the ruder ages consumed more spices in their meat and drink than is compatible with the delicacy of a modern palate. Vie Privée des François, tom. ii. p. 162, 163.

26. Theophylact, l. vi. c. 6, l. vii. c. 15 [p. 251, 299, ed. Bonn]. The Greek historian confesses the truth and justice of his reproach.

27. Menander (in Excerpt. Legat. p. 126–132, 174, 175 [p. 332–342, 424, 425, ed. Bonn]) describes the perjury of Baian and the surrender of Sirmium. We have lost his account of the siege, which is commended by Theophylact, l. i. c. 3. Τὸ δ' ὅπως Μενάνδρῳ τῷ περιφανεῖ σαφῶς διηγόρευται [p. 38, ed. Bonn]).

28. See D'Anville, in the Mémoires de l'Acad. des Inscriptions, tom. xxviii. p. 412–443. The Sclavonic name of *Belgrade* is mentioned in the tenth century by Constantine Porphyrogenitus: the Latin appellation of *Alba Græca* is used by the Franks in the beginning of the ninth (p. 414).

29. Baron. Annal. Eccles. A.D. 600, No. 1. Paul Warnefrid (l. iv. c. 38) relates their irruption into Friuli, and (c. 39) the captivity of his ancestors, about A.D. 632. The Sclavi traversed the Hadriatic cum multitudine navium, and made a descent in the territory of Sipontum (c. 47).

30. Even the helepolis, or movable turret. Theophylact, l. ii. 16, 17.

31. The arms and alliances of the chagan reached to the neighbourhood of a western sea, fifteen months' journey from Constantinople. The emperor Maurice conversed with some itinerant harpers from that remote country, and only seems to have mistaken a trade for a nation. Theophylact, l. vi. c. 2 [p. 243, *sq.*, ed. Bonn].

32. This is one of the most probable and luminous conjectures of the learned Count de Buat (Hist. des Peuples Barbares, tom. xi. p. 546–568). The Tzechi and Serbi are found together near Mount Caucasus, in Illyricum, and on the lower Elbe. Even the wildest traditions of the Bohemians, etc., afford some colour to his hypothesis.

33. See Fredegarius, in the Historians of France, tom. ii. p. 432. Baian did not conceal his proud insensibility. Ὅτι τοιουτοὺς (not τοσουτους, according to a foolish emendation) ἐπαφήσω τῇ Ῥωμαϊκῇ, ὡς εἰ καὶ συμβαίη γε σφισί θανατῷ ἀλῶναι, ἀλλ᾿ ἐμοὶ γε μὴ γένεσθαι συναίσθησιν.

34. See the march and return of Maurice, in Theophylact, l. v. c. 16, l. vi. c. 1, 2, 3. If he were a writer of taste or genius, we might suspect him of an elegant irony; but Theophylact is surely harmless.

35. Εἷς οἰωνὸς ἄριστος ἀμύνεσθαι περὶ πάτρης. Iliad, xii. 243.
This noble verse, which unites the spirit of a hero with the reason of a sage, may prove that Homer was in every light superior to his age and country.

36. Theophylact, l. vii. c. 3 [p. 274, ed. Bonn]. On the evidence of this fact, which had not occurred to my memory, the candid reader will correct and excuse a note in Chapter XXXIV., vol. i. p. 853, of this History, which hastens the decay of Asimus, or Azimuntium: another century of patriotism and valour is cheaply purchased by such a confession.

37. See the shameful conduct of Commentiolus, in Theophylact, l. ii. c. 10–15, l. vii. c. 13, 14, l. viii. c. 2, 4.

38. See the exploits of Priscus, l. viii. c. 2, 3.

39. The general detail of the war against the Avars may be traced in the first, second, sixth, seventh, and eighth books of the History of the Emperor Maurice, by Theophylact Simocatta. As he wrote in the reign of Heraclius, he had no temptation to flatter; but his want of judgment renders him diffuse in trifles, and concise in the most interesting facts.

40. Maurice himself composed twelve books on the military art, which are still extant, and have been published (Upsal, 1664) by John Scheffer, at the end of the Tactics of Arrian (Fabricius, Biblioth. Græca, l. iv. c. 8, tom. iii. p. 278), who promises to speak more fully of his work in its proper place.

41. See the mutinies under the reign of Maurice, in Theophylact, l. iii. c. 1–4, l. vi. c. 7, 8, 10, l. vii. c. 1, l. viii. c. 6, etc.

42. Theophylact and Theophanes seem ignorant of the conspiracy and avarice of Maurice. These charges, so unfavourable to the memory of that emperor, are first mentioned by the author of the Paschal Chronicle (p. 379, 380 [ed. Par.; tom. i. p. 695, ed. Bonn]); from whence Zonaras (tom. ii. l. xiv. [c. 13] p. 77, 78) has transcribed them. Cedrenus (p. 399 [tom. i. p. 700, ed. Bonn]) has followed another computation of the ransom.

43. In their clamours against Maurice the people of Constantinople branded him with the name of Marcionite or Marcionist: a heresy (says Theophylact, l. viii. c. 9 [p. 331, ed. Bonn]) μετά τινος μωρᾶς εὐλαβείας, εὐήθης τε καὶ καταγέλαστος.

Did they only cast out a vague reproach—or had the emperor really listened to some obscure teacher of those ancient Gnostics?

44. The church of St. Autonomus (whom I have not the honour to know) was 150 stadia from Constantinople (Theophylact, l. viii. c. 9). The port of Eutropius, where Maurice and his children were murdered, is described by Gyllius (de Bosphoro Thracio, l. iii. c. xi) as one of the two harbours of Chalcedon.

45. The inhabitants of Constantinople were generally subject to the νόσοι ἀρθρίτιδες; and Theophylact insinuates (l. viii. c. 9 [p. 332, ed. Bonn], that, if it were consistent with the rules of history, he could assign the medical cause. Yet such a digression would not have been more impertinent than his inquiry (l. vii. c. 16, 17) into the annual inundations of the Nile, and all the opinions of the Greek philosophers on that subject.

46. From this generous attempt Corneille has deduced the intricate web of his tragedy of *Heraclius*, which requires more than one representation to be clearly understood (Corneille de Voltaire, tom. v. p. 300); and which, after an interval of some years, is said to have puzzled the author himself (Anecdotes Dramatiques, tom. i. p. 422).

47. The revolt of Phocas and death of Maurice are told by Theophylact Simocatta (l. viii. c. 7–12), the Paschal Chronicle (p. 379, 380 [tom. i. p. 694, *sq.*, ed. Bonn]), Theophanes (Chronograph. p. 238–244 [tom. i. p. 432–448, ed. Bonn]), Zonaras (tom. ii. l. xiv. [c. 13, 14] p. 77–80), and Cedrenus (p. 399–404 [tom. i. p. 700–708, ed. Bonn]).

48. Gregor. l. xi. Epist. 38 [l. xiii. Ep. 31, ed. Bened.] indict. vi. Benignitatem vestræ pietatis ad Imperiale fastigium pervenisse gaudemus. Lætentur cœli et evultet terra, et de vestris benignis actibus universæ reipublicæ populus nunc usque vehementer afflictus hilarescat, etc. This base flattery, the topic of Protestant invective, is justly censured by the philosopher Bayle (Dictionnaire Critique, Grégoire I. Not. H. tom. ii. p. 597, 598). Cardinal Baronius justifies the pope at the expense of the fallen emperor.

49. The images of Phocas were destroyed; but even the malice of his enemies would suffer one copy of such a portrait or caricature (Cedrenus, p. 404 [tom. i. p. 708, ed. Bonn]) to escape the flames.

50. The family of Maurice is represented by Ducange (Familiæ Byzantinæ, p. 106, 107, 108): his eldest son Theodosius had been crowned emperor when he was no more than four years and a half old, and he is always joined with his father in the salutations of Gregory. With the Christian daughters, Anastasia and Theocteste, I am surprised to find the Pagan name of Cleopatra.

51. Some of the cruelties of Phocas are marked by Theophylact, l. viii. c. 13, 14, 15. George of Pisidia, the poet of Heraclius, styles him (Bell. Abaricum, p. 46, Rome, 1777) τῆς τυραννίδος ὁ δυσκάθεκτος καὶ βιοφθόρος δράκων [v. 49]. The latter epithet is just—but the corrupter of life was easily vanquished.

52. In the writers, and in the copies of those writers, there is such hesitation between the names of *Priscus* and *Crispus* (Ducange, Fam. Byzant. p. 111), that I have been tempted to identify the son-in-law of Phocas with the hero five times victorious over the Avars.

53. According to Theophanes [tom. i. p. 459, ed. Bonn], κιβώτια and εἰκόνας [τῆς] θεομήτορος. Cedrenus adds an ἀχειροποίητον εἴκονα τοῦ κυρίου, which Heraclius bore as a banner in the first Persian expedition [tom. i. p. 719]. See George Pisid. Acroas. i. 140. The manufacture seems to have flourished, but Foggini, the Roman editor (p. 26), is at a loss to determine whether this picture was an original or a copy.

54. See the tyranny of Phocas and the elevation of Heraclius, in Chron. Paschal. p. 380–383 [tom. i. p. 694–701, ed. Bonn]; Theophanes, p. 242–250 [tom. i. p. 446–459, ed. Bonn]; Nicephorus, p. 3–7 [ed. Par. 1648]; Cedrenus, p. 404–407 [tom. i. p. 708–714, ed. Bonn]; Zonaras, tom. ii. l. xiv. [c. 14, 15] p. 80–82.

55. Theophylact, l. viii. c. 15 [p. 346, ed. Bonn]. The Life of Maurice was composed about the year 628 (l. viii. c. 13) by Theophylact Simocatta, expræfect, a native of Egypt. Photius, who gives an ample extract of the work (cod. lxv. p. 81–100 [p. 27–33, ed. Bekk.]), gently reproves the affectation and allegory of the style. His preface is a dialogue between Philosophy and History; they seat themselves under a plane-tree, and the latter touches her lyre.

56. Christianis nec pactum esse, nec fidem nec fœdus . . . quod si ulla ipsis fides fuisset, regem suum non occidissent. Eutych. Annales, tom. ii. p. 211, vers. Pocock.

57. We must now, for some ages, take our leave of contemporary historians, and descend, if it be a descent, from the affectation of rhetoric to the rude simplicity of chronicles and abridgments. Those of Theophanes (Chronograph. p. 244–279 [tom. i. p. 449–516, ed. Bonn] and Nicephorus (p. 3–16) supply a regular, but imperfect, series of the Persian war; and for any additional facts I quote my special authorities. Theophanes, a courtier who became a monk, was born A.D. 748; Nicephorus, patriarch of Constantinople, who died A.D. 829, was somewhat younger: they both suffered in the cause of images. Hankius, de Scriptoribus Byzantinis, p. 200–246.

58. The Persian historians have been themselves deceived; but Theophanes (p. 244 [tom. i. p. 449, ed. Bonn]) accuses Chosroes of the fraud and falsehood; and Eutychius believes (Annal. tom. ii. p. 211) that the son of Maurice, who was saved from the assassins, lived and died a monk on Mount Sinai.

59. Eutychius dates all the losses of the empire under the reign of Phocas; an error which saves the honour of Heraclius, whom he brings not from

Carthage, but Salonica, with a fleet laden with vegetables for the relief of Constantinople (Annal. tom. ii. p. 223, 224). The other Christians of the East, Barhebræus (apud Asseman, Bibliothec. Oriental. tom. iii. p. 412, 413), Elmacin (Hist. Saracen. p. 13–16), Abulpharagius (Dynast. p. 98, 99), are more sincere and accurate. The years of the Persian war are disposed in the chronology of Pagi.

60. On the conquest of Jerusalem, an event so interesting to the church, see the Annals of Eutychius (tom. ii. p. 212–223), and the lamentations of the monk Antiochus (apud Baronium, Annal. Eccles. A.D. 614, No. 16–26), whose one hundred and twenty-nine homilies are still extant, if what no one reads may be said to be extant.

61. The Life of this worthy saint is composed by Leontius, a contemporary bishop; and I find in Baronius (Annal. Eccles. A.D. 610, No. 10, etc.) and Fleury (tom. viii. p. 235–242) sufficient extracts of this edifying work.

62. The error of Baronius, and many others who have carried the arms of Chosroes to Carthage instead of Chalcedon, is founded on the near resemblance of the Greek words Καλχήδονα and Καρχήδονα, in the text of Theophanes, etc., which have been sometimes confounded by transcribers, and sometimes by critics.

63. The *genuine* acts of St. Anastasius are published in those of the seventh general council, from whence Baronius (Annal. Eccles. A.D. 614, 626, 627) and Butler (Lives of the Saints, vol. i. p. 242–248) have taken their accounts. The holy martyr deserted from the Persian to the Roman army, became a monk at Jerusalem, and insulted the worship of the Magi, which was then established at Cæsarea in Palestine.

64. Abulpharagius, Dynast. p. 99; Elmacin, Hist. Saracen. p. 14.

65. D'Anville, Mém. de l'Académie des Inscriptions, tom. xxxii. p. 568–571.

66. The difference between the two races consists in one or two humps; the dromedary has only one; the size of the proper camel is larger; the country he comes from, Turkistan or Bactriana; the dromedary is confined to Arabia and Africa. Buffon, Hist. Naturelle, tom. xi. p. 211, etc.; Aristot. Hist. Animal. tom. i. l. ii. c. 1, tom. ii. p. 185.

67. Theophanes, Chronograph. p. 268 [tom. i. p. 494, ed. Bonn]. D'Herbelot, Bibliothèque Orientale, p. 997. The Greeks describe the decay, the Persians the splendour, of Dastagerd; but the former speak from the modest witness of the eye, the latter from the vague report of the ear.

68. The historians of Mohammed, Abulfeda (in Vit. Mohammed, p. 92, 93) and Gagnier (Vie de Mohammed, tom. ii. p. 247), date this embassy in the seventh year of the Hegira, which commences A.D. 628, May 11. Their chronology is erroneous, since Chosroes died in the month of February of the same year (Pagi, Critica, tom. ii. p. 779). The Count de Boulainvilliers (Vie de Mahomed, p.

327, 328) places this embassy about A.D. 615, soon after the conquest of Palestine. Yet Mohammed would scarcely have ventured so soon on so bold a step.

69. See the thirtieth chapter of the Koran, entitled *the Greeks*. Out honest and learned translator, Sale (p. 330, 331), fairly states this conjecture, guess, wager, of Mohammed; but Boulainvilliers (p. 329–344), with wicked intentions, labours to establish this evident prophecy of a future event, which must, in his opinion, embarrass the Christian polemics.

70. Paul Warnefrid, de Gestis Langobardorum, l. iv. c. 38, 42; Muratori, Annali d'Italia, tom. v. p. 305, etc.

71. The Paschal Chronicle, which sometimes introduces fragments of history into a barren list of names and dates, gives the best account of the treason of the Avars, p. 389, 390 [tom. i. p. 712 *sq.*, ed. Bonn]. The number of captives is added by Nicephorus.

72. Some original pieces, such as the speech or letter of the Roman ambassadors (p. 386–388 [ed. Par.; tom. i. p. 707–709, ed. Bonn]), likewise constitute the merit of the Paschal Chronicle, which was composed, perhaps at Alexandria, under the reign of Heraclius.

73. Nicephorus (p. 10, 11), who brands this marriage with the names of ἄθεσμον and ἀθέμιτον, is happy to observe, that of two sons, its incestuous fruit, the elder was marked by Providence with a stiff neck, the younger with the loss of hearing.

74. George of Pisidia (Acroas. i. 112–125, p. 5), who states the opinions, acquits the pusillanimous counsellors of any sinister views. Would he have excused the proud and contemptuous admonition of Crispus? Ἐπιθωπτάζων οὐκ ἔξον βασιλεῖ ἔφασκε καταλιμπάνειν βασίλεια, καὶ τοῖς πόρρω ἐπιχωριάζειν δυνάμεσιν.

75. Εἰ τὰς ἐπ' ἄκρον ἠρμένας εὐεξίας
   Ἐσφαλμένας λέγουσιν οὐκ ἀπεικότως,
    Κείσθω τὸ λοιπὸν ἐν κακοῖς τὰ Πέρσιδος,
   Ἀντιστρόψως δὲ, etc.

     George Pisid. Acroas. i. 51, etc., p. 4. The Orientals are not less fond of remarking this strange vicissitude; and I remember some story of Khosrou Parviz, not very unlike the ring of Polycrates of Samos.

76. Baronius gravely relates this discovery, or rather transmutation, of barrels, not of honey, but of gold (Annal. Eccles. A.D. 620, No. 3, etc.). Yet the loan was arbitrary, since it was collected by soldiers, who were ordered to leave the patriarch of Alexandria no more than one hundred pounds of gold. Nicephorus (p. 11), two hundred years afterwards, speaks with ill-humour of this contribution, which the church of Constantinople might still feel.

77. Theophylact Simocatta, l. viii. c. 12 [p. 340, ed. Bonn]. This circumstance need not excite our surprise. The muster-roll of a regiment, even in

time of peace, is renewed in less than twenty or twenty-five years.

78. He changed his *purple*, for *black*, buskins, and dyed them *red* in the blood of the Persians (George. Pisid. Acroas. iii. 118, 121, 122. See the Notes of Foggini, p. 35).

79. George of Pisidia (Acroas. ii. 10, p. 8) has fixed this important point of the Syrian and Cilician gates. They are elegantly described by Xenophon, who marched through them a thousand years before. A narrow pass of three stadia, between steep high rocks (πέτραι ἠλίβατοι) and the Mediterranean, was closed at each end by strong gates, impregnable to the land (παρελθεῖν οὐκ ἦν βίᾳ), accessible by sea (Anabasis, l. i. [c. 4] p. 35, 36, with Hutchinson's Geographical Dissertation, p. vi.). The gates were thirty-five parasangs, or leagues, from Tarsus (Anabasis, l. i. [c. 4] p. 33, 34), and eight or ten from Antioch. Compare Itinerar. Wesseling. p. 580, 581; Schultens, Index Geograph. ad calcem Vit. Saladin. p. 9; Voyage en Turquie et en Perse, par M. Otter, tom. i. p. 78, 79.

80. Heraclius might write to a friend in the modest words of Cicero: "Castra habuimus ea ipsa quæ contra Darium habuerat apud Issum Alexander, imperator haud paulo melior quam aut tu aut ego." Ad Atticum, v. 20. Issus, a rich and flourishing city in the time of Xenophon, was ruined by the prosperity of Alexandria or Scanderoon, on the other side of the bay.

81. Foggini (Annotat. p. 31) suspects that the Persians were deceived by the φάλαγξ πεπληγμένη of Ælian (Tactic. c. 48), an intricate spiral motion of the army. He observes (p. 28) that the military descriptions of George of Pisidia are transcribed in the Tactics of the emperor Leo.

82. George of Pisidia, an eye-witness (Acroas. ii. 122, etc.), described, in three *acroaseis* or cantos, the first expedition of Heraclius. The poem has been lately (1777) published at Rome; but such vague and declamatory praise is far from corresponding with the sanguine hopes of Pagi, D'Anville, etc.

83. Theophanes (p. 256) carries Heraclius swiftly (κατά ταχός) into Armenia. Nicephorus (p. 11), though he confounds the two expeditions, defines the province of Lazica. Eutychius (Annal. tom. ii. p. 231) has given the 5000 men, with the more probable station of Trebizond.

84. From Constantinople to Trebizond, with a fair wind, four or five days; from thence to Erzerom, five; to Erivan, twelve; to Tauris, ten: in all, thirty-two. Such is the Itinerary of Tavernier (Voyages, tom. i. p. 12–56), who was perfectly conversant with the roads of Asia. Tournefort, who travelled with a pasha, spent ten or twelve days between Trebizond and Erzerom (Voyage du Levant, tom. iii. lettre xviii.); and Chardin (Voyages, tom. i. p. 249–254) gives the more correct distance of fifty-three parasangs, each of 5000 paces (what paces?), between Erivan and Tauris.

85. The expedition of Heraclius into Persia is finely illustrated by M. D'Anville (Mémoires de l'Académie des Inscriptions, tom. xxviii. p. 559–573). He discovers the situation of Gandzaca, Thebarma, Dastagerd, etc., with admirable skill and learning; but the obscure campaign of 624 he passes over in silence.

86. Et pontem indignatus Araxes.
    —Virgil, Æneid, viii. 728.

The river Araxes is noisy, rapid, vehement, and, with the melting of the snows, irresistible; and the strongest and most massy bridges are swept away by the current; and its *indignation* is attested by the ruins of many arches near the old town of Zulfa. Voyages de Chardin, tom. i. p. 252.

87. Chardin, tom. i. p. 255–259. With the Orientals (D'Herbelot, Biblioth. Orient. p. 834), he ascribes the foundation of Tauris, or Tebris, to Zobeide, the wife of the famous Khalif Haroun Alrashid; but it appears to have been more ancient; and the names of Gandzaca, Gazaca, Gaza, are expressive of the royal treasure. The number of 550,000 inhabitants is reduced by Chardin from 1,100,000, the popular estimate.

88. He opened the Gospel and applied or interpreted the first casual passage to the name and situation of Albania. Theophanes, p. 258 [tom. i. p. 474, ed. Bonn].

89. The heath of Mogan, between the Cyrus and the Araxes, is sixty parasangs in length and twenty in breadth (Olearius, p. 1023, 1024), abounding in waters and fruitful pastures (Hist. de Nadir Shah, translated by Mr. Jones from a Persian MS. part ii. p. 2, 3). See the encampments of Timur (Hist. par Sherefeddin Ali, l. v. c. 37, l. vi. c. 13) and the coronation of Nadir Shah (Hist. Persanne, p. 3–13, and the English Life by Mr. Jones, p. 64, 65).

90. Thebarma and Ormia, near the lake Spauta, are proved to be the same city by D'Anville (Mémoires de l'Académie, tom. xxviii. p. 564, 565). It is honoured as the birthplace of Zoroaster, according to the Persians (Schultens, Index Geograph. p. 48); and their tradition is fortified by M. Perron d'Anquetil (Mém. de l'Acad. des Inscript. tom. xxxi. p. 375), with some texts from *his*, or *their*, Zendavesta.

91. I cannot find, and (what is much more) M. D'Anville does not attempt to seek, the Salban, Tarantum, territory of the Huns, etc., mentioned by Theophanes (p. 260–262). Eutychius (Annal. tom. ii. p. 231, 232), an insufficient author, names Asphahan; and Casbin is most probably the city of Sapor. Ispahan is twenty-four days' journey from Tauris, and Casbin half way between them (Voyages de Tavernier, tom. i. p. 63–82).

92. At ten parasangs from Tarsus the army of the younger Cyrus passed the Sarus, three plethra in breadth: the Pyramus, a stadium in breadth, ran five parasangs farther to the east (Xenophon, Anabas. l. i. p. 33, 34 [c. 4 *init.*]).

93. George of Pisidia (Bell. Abaricum, 246–265,

p. 49) celebrates with truth the persevering courage of the three campaigns (τρεις περιδρόμους) against the Persians.

94. Petavius (Annotationes ad Nicephorum, p. 62, 63, 64) discriminates the names and actions of five Persian generals who were successively sent against Heraclius.

95. This number of eight myriads is specified by George of Pisidia (Bell. Abar. 219). The poet (50–88) clearly indicates that the old chagan lived till the reign of Heraclius, and that his son and successor was born of a foreign mother. Yet Foggini (Annotat. p. 57) has given another interpretation to this passage.

96. A bird, a frog, a mouse, and five arrows, had been the present of the Scythian king to Darius (Herodot. l. iv. c. 131, 132). Substituez une lettre à ces signes (says Rousseau, with much good taste), plus elle sera menaçante moins elle effrayera: ce ne sera qu'une fanfaronnade dont Darius n'eut fait que rire (Emile, tom. iii. p. 146). Yet I much question whether the senate and people of Constantinople *laughed* at this message of the chagan.

97. The Paschal Chronicle (p. 392–397 [tom. i. p. 716–726, ed. Bonn]) gives a minute and authentic narrative of the siege and deliverance of Constantinople. Theophanes (p. 264) adds some circumstances; and a faint light may be obtained from the smoke of George of Pisidia, who has composed a poem (de Bello Abarico, p. 45–54) to commemorate this auspicious event.

98. The power of the Chozars prevailed in the seventh, eighth, and ninth centuries. They were known to the Greeks, the Arabs, and, under the name of *Kosa*, to the Chinese themselves. De Guignes, Hist. des Huns, tom. ii. part ii. p. 507–509.

99. Epiphania, or Eudocia, the only daughter of Heraclius and his first wife Eudocia, was born at Constantinople on the 7th of July A.D. 611, baptised the 15th of August, and crowned (in the oratory of St. Stephen in the palace) the 4th of October of the same year. At this time she was about fifteen. Eudocia was afterwards sent to her Turkish husband, but the news of his death stopped her journey, and prevented the consummation (Ducange, Familiæ Byzantin. p. 118).

100. Elmacin (Hist. Saracen. p. 13–16) gives some curious and probable facts; but his numbers are rather too high—300,000 Romans assembled at Edessa—500,000 Persians killed at Nineveh. The abatement of a cipher is scarcely enough to restore his sanity.

101. Ctesias (apud Diodor. Sicul. tom. i. l. ii. [c. 3] p. 115, edit. Wesseling) assigns 480 stadia (perhaps only 32 miles) for the circumference of Nineveh. Jonas talks of three days' journey: the 120,000 persons described by the prophet as incapable of discerning their right hand from their left may afford about 700,000 persons of all ages for the inhabitants of that ancient capital (Goguet,

Origines des Loix, etc., tom. iii. part i. p. 92, 93), which ceased to exist 600 years before Christ. The western suburb still subsisted, and is mentioned under the name of Mosul, in the first age of the Arabian khalifs.

102. Niebuhr (Voyage en Arabie, etc., tom. ii. p. 286) passed over Nineveh without perceiving it. He mistook for a ridge of hills the old rampart of brick or earth. It is said to have been 100 feet high, flanked with 1500 towers, each of the height of 200 feet.

103. Rex regia arma fero (says Romulus, in the first consecration) . . . bina postca (continues Livy, i. 10) inter tot bella, opima parta sunt spolia, adeo rara ejus fortuna decoris. If Varro (apud Pomp. Festum, p. 306, edit. Dacier) could justify his liberality in granting the *opime* spoils even to a common soldier who had slain the king or general of the enemy, the honour would have been much more cheap and common.

104. In describing this last expedition of Heraclius, the facts, the places, and the dates of Theophanes (p. 265–271 [tom. i. p. 487–502, ed. Bonn]) are so accurate and authentic, that he must have followed the original letters of the emperor, of which the Paschal Chronicle has preserved (p. 398–402 [tom. i. p. 727–734, ed. Bonn]) a very curious specimen.

105. The words of Theophanes are remarkable: εἰσῆλθεν Χοσρόης εἰς οἶκον γεωργοῦ μεδαμινοῦ μεῖναι, μόλις χωρηθεὶς ἐν τῇ τούτου θύρᾳ, ἣν ἰδὼν ἔσχατον Ἡράκλειος ἐθαύμασεν (p. 269 [p. 496, ed. Bonn]). Young princes who discover a propensity to war should repeatedly transcribe and translate such salutary texts.

106. The authentic narrative of the fall of Chosroes is contained in the letter of Heraclius (Chron. Paschal. p. 398 [tom. i. p. 727, ed. Bonn]) and the history of Theophanes (p. 271 [tom. i. p. 500, *sq.*, ed. Bonn]).

107. On the first rumour of the death of Chosroes, an Heracliad in two cantos was instantly published at Constantinople by George of Pisida (p. 97–105). A priest and a poet might very properly exult in the damnation of the public enemy (ἐμπεσὼν τῷ Ταρτάρῳ, v. 56): but such mean revenge is unworthy of a king and a conqueror; and I am sorry to find so much black superstition (θεομάχος Χοσρόης ἔπεσεν καὶ ἐππωματίσθη εἰς τὰ καταχθόνια . . . εἰς τὸ πῦρ τὸ ἀκατάσβεστον, etc.) in the letter of Heraclius [Chron. Pasch. p. 728 *sq.*, ed. Bonn]: he almost applauds the parricide of Siroes as an act of piety and justice.

108. The best Oriental accounts of this last period of the Sassanian kings are found in Eutychius (Annal. tom. ii. p. 251–256), who dissembles the parricide of Siroes, D'Herbelot (Bibliothèque Orientale, p. 789), and Assemanni (Bibliothec. Oriental. tom. iii. p. 415–420).

109. The letter of Siroes in the Paschal Chronicle (p. 402 [tom. i. p. 735, ed. Bonn]) unfortunately ends before he proceeds to business. The treaty

appears in its execution in the histories of Theophanes and Nicephorus.

110. The burthen of Corneille's song,

"Montrez Heraclius au peuple qui l'attend,"

is much better suited to the present occasion. See his triumph in Theophanes (p. 272, 273 [tom. i. p. 503, sq., ed. Bonn]) and Nicephorus (p. 15, 16). The life of the mother and tenderness of the son are attested by George of Pisidia (Bell. Abar. 255, etc. p. 49). The metaphor of the Sabbath is used, somewhat profanely, by these Byzantine Christians.

111. See Baronius (Annal. Eccles. A.D. 628, No. 1-4), Eutychius (Annal. tom. ii. p. 240-248), Nicephorus (Brev. p. 15). The seals of the case had never been broken; and this preservation of the cross is ascribed (under God) to the devotion of queen Sira.

112. George of Pisidia, Acroas. iii. de Expedit. contra Persas, 415, etc. [p. 21], and Heracliad. Acroas. i. 65-138. I neglect the meaner parallels of Daniel, Timotheus, etc.; Chosroes and the chagan were of course compared to Belshazzar, Pharaoh, the old serpent, etc.

113. Suidas (in Excerpt. Hist. Byzant. p. 46) gives this number; but either the *Persian* must be read for the *Isaurian* war, or this passage does not belong to the *emperor* Heraclius.

Chapter XLVII

1. By what means shall I authenticate this previous inquiry, which I have studied to circumscribe and compress?—If I persist in supporting each fact or reflection by its proper and special evidence, every line would demand a string of testimonies, and every note would swell to a critical dissertation. But the numberless passages of antiquity which I have seen with my own eyes are compiled, digested, and illustrated by *Petavius* and *Le Clerc*, by *Beausobre* and *Mosheim*. I shall be content to fortify my narrative by the names and characters of these respectable guides; and in the contemplation of a minute or remote object, I am not ashamed to borrow the aid of the strongest glasses:—1. The *Dogmata Theologica* of Petavius are a work of incredible labour and compass; the volumes which relate solely to the Incarnation (two folios, fifth and sixth, of 837 pages) are divided into sixteen books—the first of history, the remainder of controversy and doctrine. The Jesuit's learning is copious and correct; his Latinity is pure, his method clear, his argument profound and well connected; but he is the slave of the fathers, the scourge of heretics, and the enemy of truth and candour, as often as *they* are inimical to the Catholic cause. 2. The Armenian Le Clerc, who has composed in a quarto volume (Amsterdam, 1716) the ecclesiastical history of the two first centuries, was free both in his temper and situation; his sense is clear, but his thoughts are narrow; he reduces the reason or folly of ages to the standard of his private judgment, and his impartiality is sometimes quickened, and sometimes tainted, by his opposition to the fathers. See the heretics (Cerinthians, lxxx.; Ebionites, ciii.; Carpocratians, cxx.; Valentinians, cxxi.; Basilidians, cxxiii.; Marcionites, cxli., etc.) under their proper dates. 3. The Histoire Critique du Manichéisme (Amsterdam, 1734, 1739, in two vols. in 4to, with a posthumous dissertation sur les Nazarènes, Lausanne, 1745) of M. de Beausobre, is a treasure of ancient philosophy and theology. The learned historian spins with incomparable art the systematic thread of opinion, and transforms himself by turns into the person of a saint, a sage, or an heretic. Yet his refinement is sometimes excessive: he betrays an amiable partiality in favour of the weaker side, and, while he guards against calumny, he does not allow sufficient scope for superstition and fanaticism. A copious table of contents will direct the reader to any point that he wishes to examine. 4. Less profound than Petavius, less independent than Le Clerc, less ingenious than Beausobre, the historian Mosheim is full, rational, correct, and moderate. In his learned work, De Rebus Christianis ante Constantinum (Helmstadt, 1753, in 4to), see the *Nazarenes* and *Ebionites*, p. 172-179, 328-332; the Gnostics in general, p. 179, etc.; *Cerinthus*, p. 196-202; Basilides, p. 352-361; Carpocrates, p. 363-367; Valentinus, p. 371-389; Marcion, p. 404-410; the Manichæans, p. 829-837, etc.

2. Καὶ γὰρ πάντες ἡμεῖς τὸν Χριστὸν ἄνθρωπον ἐξ ἀνθρώπων προσδοκῶμεν γενήσεσθαι, says the Jew Tryphon (Justin. Dialog. p. 207 [p. 142, ed. Jebb]), in the name of his countrymen; and the modern Jews, the few who divert their thoughts from money to religion, still hold the same language, and allege the literal sense of the prophets.

3. Chrysostom (Basnage, Hist. des Juifs, tom. v. c. 9, p. 183) and Athanasius (Petav. Dogmat. Theolog. tom. v. l. i. c. 2, p. 3) are obliged to confess that the divinity of Christ is rarely mentioned by himself or his apostles.

4. The two first chapters of St. Matthew did not exist in the Ebionite copies (Epiphan. Hæres. xxx. 13); and the miraculous conception is one of the last articles which Dr. Priestley has curtailed from his scanty creed.

5. It is probable enough that the first of the gospels for the use of the Jewish converts was composed in the Hebrew or Syriac idiom: the fact is attested by a chain of fathers—Papias, Irenæus, Origen, Jerom, etc. It is devoutly believed by the Catholics, and admitted by Casaubon, Grotius, and Isaac Vossius, among the Protestant critics.

But this Hebrew Gospel of St. Matthew is most unaccountably lost; and we may accuse the diligence or fidelity of the primitive churches, who have preferred the unauthorized version of some nameless Greek. Erasmus and his followers, who respect our Greek text as the original gospel, deprived themselves of the evidence which declares it to be the work of an apostle. See Simon, Hist. Critique, etc., tom. iii. c. 5–9, p. 47–101, and the Prolegomena of Mill and Wetstein to the New Testament.

6. The metaphysics of the soul are disengaged by Cicero (Tusculan. l. i.) and Maximus of Tyre (Dissertat. xvi.) from the intricacies of dialogue, which sometimes amuse, and often perplex, the readers of the *Phædrus*, the *Phædo*, and the *Laws* of Plato.

7. The disciples of Jesus were persuaded that a man might have sinned before he was born (John ix. 2), and the Pharisees held the transmigration of virtuous souls (Joseph. de Bell. Judaico, l. ii. c. 7 [c. 8, § 14]); and a modern Rabbi is modestly assured that Hermes, Pythagoras, Plato, etc., derived their metaphysics from his illustrious countrymen.

8. Four different opinions have been entertained concerning the origin of human souls. 1. That they are external and divine. 2. That they were created, in a separate state of existence, before their union with the body. 3. That they have been propagated from the original stock of Adam, who contained in himself the mental as well as the corporeal seed of his posterity. 4. That each soul is occasionally created and embodied in the moment of conception.—The last of these sentiments appears to have prevailed among the moderns; and our spiritual history is grown less sublime, without becoming more intelligible.

9. Ὅτι ἡ τοῦ Σωτῆρος ψυχὴ, ἡ τοῦ Ἀδὰμ ἦν, was one of the fifteen heresies imputed to Origen, and denied by his apologist (Photius, Bibliothec. cod. cxvii. p. 296 [p. 92, ed. Bekk.]). Some of the Rabbis attribute one and the same soul to the persons of Adam, David, and the Messiah.

10. Apostolis adhuc in seculo superstitibus, apud Judæam Christi sanguine recente, PHANTASMA domini corpus asserebatur. Hieronym. advers. Lucifer. c. 8. The epistle of Ignatius to the Smyrnæans, and even the Gospel according to St. John, are levelled against the growing error of the Docetes, who had obtained too much credit in the world (1 John iv. 1–5).

11. About the year 200 of the Christian era, Irenæus and Hippolytus refuted the thirty-two sects, τῆς ψευδωνύμου γνωσέως, which had multiplied to fourscore in the time of Epiphanius (Phot. Biblioth. cod. cxx. cxxi. cxxii.). The five books of Irenæus exist only in barbarous Latin; but the original might perhaps be found in some monastery of Greece.

12. The pilgrim Cassian, who visited Egypt in the beginning of the fifth century, observes and laments the reign of anthropomorphism among the monks, who were not conscious that they embraced the system of Epicurus (Cicero, de Nat. Deorum, i. 18, 49). Ab universo propemodum genere monarchorum, qui per totam provinciam Egypti morabantur, pro simplicitatis errore susceptum est, ut e contrario memoratum pontificem (*Theophilus*) velut hæresi gravissimâ depravatum, pars maxima seniorum ab universo fraternitatis corpore decerneret detestandum (Cassian. Collation. x. 1). As long as St. Augustin remained a Manichæan, he was scandalised by the anthropomorphism of the vulgar Catholics.

13. Ita est in oratione senex mente confusus, eo quod illam ἀνθρωπόμορφον imaginem Deitatis, quam proponere sibi in oratione consueverat, aboleri de suo corde sentiret, ut in amarissimos fletus, crebrosque singultus repente prorumpens, in terram prostratus, cum ejulatû validissimo proclamaret; "Heu me miserum! tulerunt a me Deum meum, et quem nunc teneam non habeo, vel quem adorem, aut interpellam jam nescio." Cassian, Collat. x. 2.

14. St. John and Cerinthus (A.D. 80, Cleric. Hist. Eccles. p. 493) accidentally met in the public bath of Ephesus; but the apostle fled from the heretic lest the building should tumble on their heads. This foolish story, reprobated by Dr. Middleton (Miscellaneous Works, vol. ii.), is related however by Irenæus (iii. 3), on the evidence of Polycarp, and was probably suited to the time and residence of Cerinthus. The obsolete, yet probably the true, reading of 1 John iv. 3—ὃ λύει τὸν Ἰησοῦν —alludes to the double nature of that primitive heretic.

15. The Valentinians embraced a complex and almost incoherent system. 1. Both Christ and Jesus were æons, though of different degrees; the one acting as the rational soul, the other as the divine spirit of the Saviour. 2. At the time of the passion they both retired, and left only a sensitive soul and a human body. 3. Even that body was ethereal, and perhaps apparent.—Such are the laborious conclusions of Mosheim. But I much doubt whether the Latin translator understood Irenæus, and whether Irenæus and the Valentinians understood themselves.

16. The heretics abused the passionate exclamations of "My God, my God, why hast thou *forsaken* me?" Rousseau, who has drawn an eloquent but indecent parallel between Christ and Socrates, forgets that not a word of impatience or despair escaped from the mouth of the dying philosopher. In the Messiah such sentiments could be only apparent; and such ill-sounding words are properly explained as the application of a psalm and prophecy.

17. This strong expression might be justified by the language of St. Paul (1 Tim. iii. 16); but we are deceived by our modern Bibles. The word ὃ (*which*) was altered to θεὸς (*God*) at Constantinople in the beginning of the sixth century: the true

reading, which is visible in the Latin and Syriac versions, still exists in the reasoning of the Greek as well as of the Latin fathers; and this fraud, with that of the *three witnesses of St. John*, is admirably detected by Sir Isaac Newton. (See his two letters translated by M. de Missy, in the Journal Britannique, tom. xv. p. 148-190, 351-390.) I have weighed the arguments, and may yield to the authority of the first of philosophers, who was deeply skilled in critical and theological studies.

18. For Apollinaris and his sect, see Socrates, l. ii. c. 46, l. iii. c. 16; Sozomen, l. v. c. 18, l. vi. c. 25, 27; Theodoret, l. v. 3, 10, 11; Tillemont, Mémoires Ecclésiastiques, tom. vii. p. 602-638; Not., p. 789-794, in 4to, Venice, 1732. The contemporary saints always mention the bishop of Laodicea as a friend and brother. The style of the more recent historians is harsh and hostile; yet Philostorgius compares him (l. viii. c. 11-15) to Basil and Gregory.

19. I appeal to the confession of two Oriental prelates, Gregory Abulpharagius the Jacobite primate of the East, and Elias the Nestorian metropolitan of Damascus (see Asseman, Bibliothec. Oriental. tom. ii. p. 291; tom. iii. p. 514, etc.), that the Melchites, Jacobites, Nestorians, etc., agree in the *doctrine*, and differ only in the *expression*. Our most learned and rational divines—Bassnage, Le Clerc, Beausobre, La Croze, Mosheim, Jablonski—are inclined to favour this charitable judgment; but the zeal of Petavius is loud and angry, and the moderation of Dupin is conveyed in a whisper.

20. La Croze (Hist. du Christianisme des Indes, tom. i. p. 24) avows his contempt for the genius and writings of Cyril—De tous les ouvrages des anciens, il y en a peu qu'on lise avec moins d'utilité: and Dupin (Bibliothèque Ecclésiastique, tom. iv. p. 42-52), in words of respect, teaches us to despise them.

21. Of Isidore of Pelusium (l. i. Epist. 25, p. 8). As the letter is not of the most creditable sort, Tillemont, less sincere than the Bollandists, affects a doubt whether *this* Cyril is the nephew of Theophilus (Mém. Ecclés. tom. xiv. p. 268).

22. A grammarian is named by Socrates (l. vii. c. 13) διάπυρος δὲ ἀκροατὴς τοῦ ἐπισκόπου Κυρίλλου καθεστὼς, καὶ περὶ τὸ κρότους ἐν ταῖς διδασκαλίαις αὐτοῦ ἐγείρειν ἦν σπουδαιότατος.

23. See the youth and promotion of Cyril, in Socrates (l. vii. c. 7) and Renaudot (Hist. Patriarch. Alexandrin. p. 106, 108). The Abbé Renaudot drew his materials from the Arabic history of Severus, bishop of Hermopolis Magna, or Ashmunein, in the tenth century, who can never be trusted, unless our assent is extorted by the internal evidence of facts.

24. The *Parabolani* of Alexandria were a charitable corporation, instituted during the plague of Gallienus, to visit the sick and to bury the dead. They gradually enlarged, abused, and sold the privileges of their order. Their outrageous conduct during the reign of Cyril provoked the emperor to deprive the patriarch of their nomination, and to restrain their number to five or six hundred. But these restraints were transient and ineffectual. See the Theodosian Code, l. xvi. tit. ii. [leg. 42], and Tillemont, Mém. Ecclés. tom. xiv. p. 276-278.

25. For Theon and his daughter Hypatia, see Fabricius, Bibliothec. tom. viii. p. 210, 211. Her article in the Lexicon of Suidas is curious and original. Hesychius (Meursii Opera, tom. vii. p. 295, 296) observes that she was persecuted διὰ τὴν ὑπερβάλλουσαν σοφίαν; and an epigram in the Greek Anthology (l. i. c. 76, p. 159, edit. Brodæi) celebrates her knowledge and eloquence. She is honourably mentioned (Epist. 10, 15, 16, 33-80, 124, 135, 153) by her friend and disciple the philosophic bishop Synesius.

26. Ὀστράκοις ἀνεῖλον, καὶ μεληδὸν διασπάσαντες, etc. Oyster-shells were plentifully strewed on the sea-beach before the Cæsareum. I may therefore prefer the literal sense without rejecting the metaphorical version of *tegulæ*, tiles, which is used by M. de Valois. I am ignorant, and the assassins were probably regardless, whether their victim was yet alive.

27. These exploits of St. Cyril are recorded by Socrates (l. vii. c. 13, 14, 15); and the most reluctant bigotry is compelled to copy an historian who coolly styles the murderers of Hypatia ἄνδρες τὸ φρόνημα ἔνθερμοι. At the mention of that injured name, I am pleased to observe a blush even on the cheek of Baronius (A.D. 415, No. 48).

28. He was deaf to the entreaties of Atticus of Constantinople, and of Isidore of Pelusium, and yielded only (if we may believe Nicephorus, l. xiv. c. 18) to the personal intercession of the Virgin. Yet in his last years he still muttered that John Chrysostom had been justly condemned (Tillemont, Mém. Ecclés. tom. xiv. p. 278-282; Baronius, Annal. Eccles. A.D. 412, No. 46-64).

29. See their characters in the history of Socrates (l. vii. c. 25-28); their power and pretensions in the huge compilation of Thomassin (Discipline de l'Eglise, tom. i. p. 80-91).

30. His elevation and conduct are described by Socrates (l. vii. c. 29, 31); and Marcellinus seems to have applied the eloquentiæ satis, sapientiæ parum, of Sallust.

31. Cod. Theodos. l. xvi. tit. v. leg. 65; with the illustrations of Baronius (A.D. 428, No. 25, etc.), Godefroy (ad locum), and Pagi Critica, tom. ii. p 208.

32. Isidore of Pelusium (l. iv. Epist. 57). His words are strong and scandalous—τί θαυμάζεις, εἰ καὶ νῦν περὶ πρᾶγμα θεῖον καὶ λόγου κρεῖττον διαφωνεῖν προσποιοῦνται ὑπὸ φιλαρχίας ἐκβακχευόμενοι. Isidore is a saint, but he never became a bishop; and I half suspect that the pride of Diogenes trampled on the pride of Plato.

33. La Croze (Christianisme des Indes, tom. i. p. 44-53; Thesaurus Epistolicus La Crozianus, tom. iii. p. 276-280) has detected the use of ὁ δεσπότης and ὁ κύριος Ἰησοῦς, which, in the fourth,

fifth, and sixth centuries, discriminates the school of Diodorus of Tarsus and his Nestorian disciples.

34. Θεοτόκος—*Deipara:* as in zoology we familiarly speak of oviparous and viviparous animals. It is not easy to fix the invention of this word, which La Croze (Christianisme des Indes, tom. i. p. 16) ascribes to Eusebius of Cæsarea and the Arians. The orthodox testimonies are produced by Cyril and Petavius (Dogmat. Theolog. tom. v. l. v. c. 15, p. 254, etc.); but the veracity of the saint is questionable, and the epithet of θ εοτόκος so easily slides from the margin to the text of a Catholic MS.

35. Basnage, in the Histoire de l'Eglise, a work of controversy (tom. i. p. 505), justifies the mother, by the blood, of God (Acts xx. 28, with Mill's various readings). But the Greek MSS. are far from unanimous; and the primitive style of the blood of Christ is preserved in the Syriac version, even in those copies which were used by the Christians of St. Thomas on the coast of Malabar (La Croze, Christianisme des Indes, tom. i. p. 347). The jealousy of the Nestorians and Monophysites has guarded the purity of their text.

36. The pagans of Egypt already laughed at the new Cybele of the Christians (Isidor. l. i. Epist. 54); a letter was forged in the name of Hypatia, to ridicule the theology of her assassin (Synodicon, c. 216, in iv. tom. Concil. p. 484). In the article of Nestorius, Bayle has scattered some loose philosophy on the worship of the Virgin Mary.

37. The ἀντίδοσις of the Greeks, a mutual loan or transfer of the idioms or properties of each nature to the other—of infinity to man, possibility to God, etc. Twelve rules on this nicest of subjects compose the Theological Grammar of Petavius (Dogmata Theolog. tom. v. l. iv. c. 14, 15, p. 209, etc.).

38. See Ducange, C. P. Christiana, l. i. p. 30, etc.

39. Concil. tom. iii. p. 943. They have never been *directly* approved by the church (Tillemont. Mém. Ecclés. tom. xiv. p. 368–372). I almost pity the agony of rage and sophistry with which Petavius seems to be agitated in the sixth book of his Dogmata Theologica.

40. Such as the rational Basnage (ad tom. i.; Variar. Lection. Canisii in Præfat. c. 2, p. 11–23) and La Croze, the universal scholar (Christianisme des Indes, tom. i. p. 16–20; De l'Ethiopie, p. 26, 27; Thesaur. Epist. p. 176, etc., 283, 285). His free sentence is confirmed by that of his friends Jablonski (Thesaur. Epist. tom. i. p. 193–201) and Mosheim (idem, p. 304: Nestorium crimine caruisse est et mea sententia); and three more respectable judges will not easily be found. Asseman, a learned and modest slave, can *hardly* discern (Bibliothec. Orient. tom. iv. p. 190–224) the guilt and error of the Nestorians.

41. The origin and progress of the Nestorian controversy, till the synod of Ephesus, may be found in Socrates (l. vii. c. 32), Evagrius (l. i. c. 1, 2), Liberatus (Brev. c. 1–4), the original Acts (Concil. tom. iii. p. 551–991, edit. Venice, 1728), the Annals of Baronius and Pagi, and the faithful collections of Tillemont (Mém. Ecclés. tom. xiv. p. 283–377).

42. The Christians of the four first centuries were ignorant of the death and burial of Mary. The tradition of Ephesus is affirmed by the synod (ἔνθα ὁ θεολόγος Ἰωάννης, καὶ ἡ θεοτόκος παρθένος ἡ ἁγία Μαρία—Concil. tom. iii. p. 1102); yet it has been superseded by the claim of Jerusalem; and her *empty* sepulchre, as it was shown to the pilgrims, produced the fable of her resurrection and assumption, in which the Greek and Latin churches have piously acquiesced. See Baronius (Annal. Eccles. A.D. 48, No. 6, etc.) and Tillemont (Mém. Ecclés. tom. i. p. 467–477).

43. The Acts of Chalcedon (Concil. tom. iv. p. 1405, 1408) exhibit a lively picture of the blind, obstinate servitude of the bishops of Egypt to their patriarch.

44. Civil or ecclesiastical business detained the bishops at Antioch till the 18th of May. Ephesus was at the distance of thirty days' journey; and ten days more may be fairly allowed for accidents and repose. The march of Xenophon over the same ground enumerates above 260 parasangs or leagues; and this measure might be illustrated from ancient and modern itineraries, if I knew how to compare the speed of an army, a synod, and a caravan. John of Antioch is reluctantly acquitted by Tillemont himself (Mém. Ecclés. tom. xiv. p. 386–389).

45. Μεμφόμενον μὴ κατὰ τὸ δέον τὰ ἐν Ἐφέσῳ συντεθῆναι ὑπομνήματα, πανουργία δὲ καί τινι ἀθέσμῳ καινοτομία Κυρίλλου τεχνάζοντος. Evagrius, l. i. c. 7. The same imputation was urged by Count Irenæus (tom. iii. p. 1249); and the orthodox critics do not find it an easy task to defend the purity of the Greek or Latin copies of the Acts.

46. Ὁ δὲ ἐπ' ὀλέθρῳ τῶν ἐκκλησιῶν τεχθεὶς καὶ τραφείς. After the coalition of John and Cyril these invectives were mutually forgotten. The style of declamation must never be confounded with the genuine sense which respectable enemies entertain of each other's merit (Concil. tom. iii. p. 1244).

47. See the Acts of the Synod of Ephesus in the original Greek, and a Latin version almost contemporary (Concil. tom. iii. p. 991–1339, with the Synodicon adversus Tragœdiam Irenæi, tom. iv. p. 235–497), the Ecclesiastical Histories of Socrates (l. vii. c. 34) and Evagrius (l. i. c. 3, 4, 5), and the Breviary of Liberatus (in Concil. tom. vi. p. 419–459, c. 5, 6), and the Mémoires Ecclés. of Tillemont (tom. xiv. p. 377–487).

48. Ταραχὴν (says the emperor in pointed language) τό γε ἐπὶ σαυτῷ καὶ χωρισμὸν ταῖς ἐκκλησίαις ἐμβέβληκας . . . ὡς θρασυτέρας ὁρμῆς πρεπούσης μᾶλλον ἢ ἀκριβείας . . . καὶ ποικιλίας μᾶλλον τούτων ἡμῖν ἀρκούσης ἥπερ ἁπλότητος . . . παντὸς μᾶλλον ἢ ἱέρεως . . . τά τε τῶν ἐκκλησιῶν, τά τε τῶν βασιλέων μέλλειν χωρίζειν βούλεσθαι, ὡς οὐκ οὔσης ἀφορμῆς ἑτέρας εὐδοκιμήσεως. I should be curious to know how much Nestorius paid for these expressions, so mortifying to his rival.

49. Eutyches, the heresiarch Eutyches, is honourably named by Cyril as a friend, a saint, and the strenuous defender of the faith. His brother, the abbot Dalmatius, is likewise employed to bind the emperor and all his chamberlains *terribili conjuratione*. Synodicon, c. 203, in Concil. tom. iv. p. 467.

50. Clerici qui hic sunt contristantur, quod ecclesia Alexandrina nudata sit hujus causâ turbelæ: et debet præter illa quæ hinc transmissa sint *auri libras mille quingentas*. Et nunc ei scriptum est ut præstet; sed de tuâ ecclesiâ præsta avaritiæ quorum nosti, etc. This curious and original letter, from Cyril's archdeacon to his creature the new bishop of Constantinople, has been unaccountably preserved in an old Latin version (Synodicon, c. 203, Concil. tom. iv. p. 465–468). The mask is almost dropped, and the saints speak the honest language of interest and confederacy.

51. The tedious negotiations that succeeded the synod of Ephesus are diffusely related in the original Acts (Concil. tom. iii. p. 1339–1771) ad fin. vol. and the Synodicon, in tom. iv.), Socrates (l. vii. c. 28, 35, 40, 41), Evagrius (l. i. c. 6, 7, 8, 12), Liberatus (c. 7–10), Tillemont (Mém. Ecclés. tom. xiv. p. 487–676). The most patient reader will thank me for compressing so much nonsense and falsehood in a few lines.

52. Αὐτοῦ τε αὖ δεηθέντος, ἐπετράπη κατὰ τὸ οἰκεῖον ἐπαναζεῦξαι μοναστήριον. Evagrius, l. i. c. 7. The original letters in the Synodicon (c. 15, 24, 25, 26) justify the *appearance* of a voluntary resignation, which is asserted by Ebed-Jesu, a Nestorian writer, apud Asseman. Biblioth. Oriental. tom. iii. p. 299, 302.

53. See the Imperial letters in the Acts of the Synod of Ephesus (Concil. tom. iii. p. 1730–1735). The odious name of *Simonians*, which was affixed to the disciples of this τερατώδους διδασκαλίας, was designed ὡς ἀν ὀνείδεσι προβληθέντες αἰώνιον ὑπομένοιεν τιμωρίαν τῶν ἁμαρτημάτων, καὶ μήτε ζῶντας τιμωρίας, μήτε θανόντας ἀτιμίας ἐκτὸς ὑπάρχειν. Yet these were Christians! who differed only in names and in shadows.

54. The metaphor of islands is applied by the grave civilians (Pandect. l. xlviii. tit. 22, leg. 7 [§ 5]) to those happy spots which are discriminated by water and verdure from the Libyan sands. Three of these under the common name of Oasis, or Alvahat: 1. The temple of Jupiter Ammon. 2. The middle Oasis, three days' journey to the west of Lycopolis. 3. The southern, where Nestorius was banished, in the first climate, and only three days' journey from the confines of Nubia. See a learned Note of Michaelis (ad Descript. Ægypt. Abulfedæ, p. 21–34).

55. The invitation of Nestorius to the synod of Chalcedon is related by Zacharias, bishop of Melitene (Evagrius, l. ii. c. 2; Asseman. Biblioth. Orient. tom. ii. p. 55), and the famous Xenaias or Philoxenus, bishop of Hierapolis (Asseman. Biblioth. Orient. tom. ii. p. 40, etc.), denied by Evag-

rius and Asseman, and stoutly maintained by La Croze (Thesaur. Epistol. tom. iii. p. 181, etc.). The fact is not improbable; yet it was the interest of the Monophysites to spread the invidious report; and Eutychius (tom. ii. p. 12) affirms that Nestorius died after an exile of seven years, and consequently ten years before the synod of Chalcedon.

56. Consult D'Anville (Mémoire sur l'Egypt, p. 191), Pocock (Description of the East, vol. i. p. 76) Abulfeda (Descript. Ægypt. p. 14), and his commentator Michaelis (Not. p. 78–83), and the Nubian Geographer (p. 42), who mentions, in the twelfth century, the ruins and the sugar-canes of Akmim.

57. Eutychius (Annal. tom. ii. p. 12) and Gregory Bar-Hebræus, or Abulpharagius (Asseman. tom. ii. p. 316), represent the credulity of the tenth and thirteenth centuries.

58. We are obliged to Evagrius (l. i. c. 7) for some extracts from the letters of Nestorius; but the lively picture of his sufferings is treated with insult by the hard and stupid fanatic.

59. Dixi Cyrillum dum viveret, auctoritate suâ effecisse, ne Eutychianismus et Monophysitarum error in nervum erumperet: idque verum puto . . . aliquo . . . honesto modo παλινῳδίαν cecinerat. The learned but cautious Jablonski did not always speak the whole truth. Cum Cyrillo lenius omnino egi, quam si tecum aut cum aliis rei hujus probe gnaris et æquis rerum æstimatoribus sermones privatos conferrum (Thesaur. Epistol. La Crozian. tom. i. p. 197, 198); an excellent key to his dissertations on the Nestorian controversy!

60. Ἡ ἁγία σύνοδος εἶπεν, ἆρον, καῦσον Εὐσέβιον, οὗτος ζῶν καῇ, οὗτος εἰς δύο γένηται, ὡς ἐμέρισε, μερισθῇ . . . εἴ τις λέγει δύο, ἀνάθεμα. At the request of Dioscorus, those who were not able to roar (βοῆσαι), stretched out their hands. At Chalcedon, the Orientals disclaimed these exclamations: but the Egyptians more consistently declared ταῦτα καὶ τότε εἴπομεν καὶ νῦν λέγομεν. (Concil. tom. iv. p. 1012.)

61. Ἔλεγε δὲ (Eusebius, bishop of Dorylæum) τὸν Φλαβιανόν τε δειλαίως ἀναιρεθῆναι πρὸς Διοσκόρου ὠθούμενόν τε καὶ λακτιζόμενον: and this testimony of Evagrius (l. ii. c. 2) is amplified by the historian Zonaras (tom. ii. l. xiii. [c. 23] p. 44), who affirms that Dioscorus kicked like a wild ass. But the language of Liberatus (Brev. c. 12, in Concil. tom. vi. p. 438) is more cautious; and the Acts of Chalcedon, which lavish the names of *homicide*, *Cain*, etc., do not justify so pointed a charge. The monk Barsumas is more particularly accused—ἔσφαξε τὸν μακάριον Φλαυιανόν· αὐτὸς ἔστηκε καὶ ἔλεγε, σφάξον. (Concil. tom. iv. p. 1413.)

62. The acts of the Council of Chalcedon (Concil. tom. iv. p. 761–2071) comprehend those of Ephesus (p. 890–1189), which again comprise the synod of Constantinople under Flavian (p. 930–1072); and it requires some attention to disengage this double involution. The whole business of Eutyches, Flavian, and Dioscorus, is related by Evag-

rius (l. i. c. 9-12, and l. ii. c. 1, 2, 3, 4) and Liberatus (Brev. c. 11, 12, 13, 14). Once more, and almost for the last time, I appeal to the diligence of Tillemont (Mém. Ecclés. tom. xv. p. 479-719). The annals of Baronius and Pagi will accompany me much further on my long and laborious journey.

63. Μάλιστα ἡ περιβόητος Πανσοφία, ἡ καλουμένη Ὀρεινή (perhaps Εἰρηνή), περὶ ἧς καὶ ὁ πολυάνθρωπος τῆς Ἀλεξανδρέων δῆμος ἀφῆκε φωνήν, αὐτῆς τε καὶ τοῦ ἐραστοῦ μεμνημένος (Concil. tom. iv. p. 1276). A specimen of the wit and malice of the people is preserved in the Greek Anthology (l. ii. c. 5, p. 188, edit. Wechel), although the application was unknown to the editor Brodæus. The nameless epigrammatist raises a tolerable pun, by confounding the episcopal salutation of "Peace be to all!" with the genuine or corrupted name of the bishop's concubine:—

Εἰρήνη πάντεσσιν, ἐπίσκοπος εἶπεν ἐπελθών.
Πῶς δύναται πᾶσιν, ἣν μόνος ἔνδον ἔχει;

I am ignorant whether the patriarch, who seems to have been a jealous lover, is the Cimon of a preceding epigram, whose πέος ἐστηκός was viewed with envy and wonder by Priapus himself.

64. Those who reverence the infallibility of synods may try to ascertain their sense. The leading bishops were attended by partial or careless scribes, who dispersed their copies round the world. Our Greek MSS. are sullied with the false and proscribed reading of ἐκ τῶν φύσεων (Concil. tom. iii. p. 1460): the authentic translation of Pope Leo I. does not seem to have been executed, and the old Latin versions materially differ from the present Vulgate, which was revised (A.D. 550) by Rusticus, a Roman priest, from the best MSS. of the Ἀκοίμητοι at Constantinople (Ducange, C. P. Christiana, l. iv. p. 151), a famous monastery of Latins, Greeks, and Syrians. See Concil. tom. iv. p. 1959-2049, and Pagi, Critica, tom. ii. p. 326, etc.

65. It is darkly represented in the microscope of Petavius (tom. v. l. iii. c. 5); yet the subtle theologian is himself afraid—ne quis fortasse supervacaneam, et nimis anxiam putet hujusmodi vocularum inquisitionem, et ab instituti theologici gravitate alienam (p. 124).

66. Ἐβόησαν, ἢ ὁ ὅρος κρατείτω, ἢ ἀπερχόμεθα . . . οἱ ἀντιλέγοντες φανεροὶ γένωνται, οἱ ἀντιλέγοντες Νεστοριανοί εἰσιν, οἱ ἀντιλέγοντες εἰς Ῥώμην ἀπέλθωσιν (Concil. tom. iv. p. 1449). Evagrius and Liberatus present only the placid face of the synod, and discreetly slide over these embers, suppositos cineri doloso.

67. See, in the Appendix to the Acts of Chalcedon, the confirmation of the synod by Marcian (Concil. tom. iv. p. 1781, 1783); his letters to the monks of Alexandria (p. 1791), of Mount Sinai (p. 1793), of Jerusalem and Palestine (p. 1798); his laws against the Eutychians (p. 1809, 1811, 1831); the correspondence of Leo with the provincial synods on the revolution of Alexandria (p. 1835-1930).

68. Photius (or rather Eulogius of Alexandria) confesses, in a fine passage, the specious colour of this double charge against pope Leo and his synod of Chalcedon (Biblioth. cod. ccxxv. p. 768 [p. 243, ed. Bekk.]). He waged a double war against the enemies of the church, and wounded either foe with the darts of his adversary—καταλλήλοις βέλεσι τοὺς ἀντιπάλους ἐτίτρωσκε. Against Nestorius he seemed to introduce the σύγχυσις of the Monophysites; against Eutyches he appeared to countenance the ὑποστάσεων διάφορα of the Nestorians. The apologist claims a charitable interpretation for the saints: if the same had been extended to the heretics, the *sound* of the controversy would have been lost in the air.

69. Αἴλουρος, from his nocturnal expeditions. In darkness and disguise he crept round the cells of the monastery, and whispered the revelation to his slumbering brethren (Theodor. Lector. l. i. [c. 8]).

70. Φόνους τε τολμηθῆναι μυρίους, [καὶ] αἱμάτων πλήθει πολυνθῆναι μὴ μόνον τὴν γῆν ἀλλὰ καὶ αὐτὸν τὸν ἀέρα. Such is the hyperbolic language of the Henoticon.

71. See the Chronicle of Victor Tunnunensis, in the Lectiones Antiquæ of Canisius, republished by Basnage, tom. i. p. 326.

72. The Henoticon is transcribed by Evagrius (l. iii. c. 13 [14]), and translated by Liberatus (Brev. c. 18). Pagi (Critica, tom. ii. p. 411) and Asseman (Biblioth. Orient. tom. i. p. 343) are satisfied that it is free from heresy; but Petavius (Dogmat. Theolog. tom. v. l. i. c. 13, p. 40) most unaccountably affirms Chalcedonensem ascivit. An adversary would prove that he had never read the Henoticon.

73. See Renaudot (Hist. Patriarch. Alex. p. 123, 131, 145, 195, 247). They were reconciled by the care of Mark I. (A.D. 799-819): he promoted their chiefs to the bishoprics of Athribis and Talba (perhaps Tava: see D'Anville, p. 82), and supplied the sacraments, which had failed for want of an episcopal ordination.

74. De his quos baptizavit, quos ordinavit Acacius, majorum traditione confectam et veram, præcipue religiosæ solicitudini congruam præbemus sine difficultate medicinam (Galasius, in Epist. i. ad Euphemium, Concil. tom. v. p. 286). The offer of a medicine proves the disease, and numbers must have perished before the arrival of the Roman physician. Tillemont himself (Mém. Ecclés. tom. xvi. p. 372, 642, etc.) is shocked at the proud, uncharitable temper of the popes: they are now glad, says he, to invoke St. Flavian of Antioch, St. Elias of Jerusalem, etc., to whom they refused communion whilst upon earth. But Cardinal Baronius is firm and hard as the rock of St. Peter.

75. Their names were erased from the diptych of the church: ex venerabili diptycho, in quo piæ memoriæ transitum ad cœlum habentium episcoporum vocabula continentur (Concil. tom. iv. p. 1846). This ecclesiastical record was therefore equivalent to the book of life.

76. Petavius (Dogmat. Theolog. tom. v. l. v. c. ?, 3, 4, p. 217–225) and Tillemont (Mém. Ecclés. om. xiv. p. 713, etc., 799) represent the history and doctrine of the Trisagion. In the twelve centuries between Isaiah and St. Proclus's boy, who was taken up into heaven before the bishop and people of Constantinople, the song was considerably improved. The boy heard the angels sing, 'Holy God! Holy strong! Holy immortal!"

77. Peter Gnapheus, the *fuller* (a trade which he had exercised in his monastery), patriarch of Antioch. His tedious story is discussed in the Annals of Pagi (A.D. 477–490) and a dissertation of M. de Valois at the end of his Evagrius.

78. The troubles under the reign of Anastasius must be gathered from the Chronicles of Victor, Marcellinus, and Theophanes. As the last was not published in the time of Baronius, his critic Pagi is more copious, as well as more correct.

79. The general history, from the council of Chalcedon to the death of Anastasius, may be found in the Breviary of Liberatus (c. 14–19), the second and third books of Evagrius, the abstract of the two books of Theodore the Reader, the Acts of the Synods, and the Epistles of the Popes (Concil. tom. v.). The series is continued with some disorder in the fifteenth and sixteenth tomes of the Mémoires Ecclésiastiques of Tillemont. And here I must take leave for ever of that incomparable guide, whose bigotry is overbalanced by the merits of erudition, diligence, veracity, and scrupulous minuteness. He was prevented by death from completing, as he designed, the sixth century of the church and empire.

80. The strain of the Anecdotes of Procopius (c. 11, 13, 18, 27, 28) with the learned remarks of Alemannus is confirmed, rather than contradicted, by the Acts of the Councils, the fourth book of Evagrius, and the complaints of the African Facundus, in his twelfth book—de tribus capitulis, "cum videri doctus appetit importune . . . spontaneis quæstionibus ecclesiam turbat." See Procop. de Bell. Goth. l. iii. c. 35 [tom. ii. p. 429, ed. Bonn].

81. Procop. de Ædificiis, l. i. c. 6, 7, etc., passim.

82. Ὃς δὴ κάθηται ἀφύλακτος ἐς ἀεὶ ἐπὶ λέοχης τινὸς ἀωρὶ νυκτῶν, ὁμοῦ τοῖς τῶν ἱερέων ἔσχατον γέρουσιν [ἐσχατογέρουσιν] ἀνακυκλεῖν τὰ Χριστιανῶν λόγια σπουδὴν ἔχων. Procop. de Bell. Goth. l. iii. c. 32 [tom. ii. p. 409, ed. Bonn]. In the Life of St. Eutychius (apud Aleman. ad Procop. Arcan. c. 18 [tom. iii. p. 439, ed. Bonn]) the same character is given with a design to praise Justinian.

83. For these wise and moderate sentiments Procopius (de Bell. Goth. l. i. c. 3) is scourged in the preface of Alemannus, who ranks him among the *political* Christians—sed longe verius hæresium omnium sentinas, prorsusque Atheos—abominable Atheists, who preached the imitation of God's mercy to man (ad Hist. Arcan. c. 13).

84. This alternative, a precious circumstance, is preserved by John Malala (tom. ii. p. 63, edit. Venet. 1733 [p. 449, ed. Bonn]), who deserves more credit as he draws towards his end. After numbering the heretics, Nestorians, Eutychians, etc., ne expectent, says Justinian, ut digni veniâ judicentur: jubemus enim ut . . . convicti et aperti hæretici justæ et idoneæ animadversioni subjiciantur. Baronius copies and applauds this edict of the Code (A.D. 527, No. 39, 40).

85. See the character and principles of the Montanists, in Mosheim, de Rebus Christ. ante Constantinum, p. 410–424.

86. Theophan. Chron. p. 153 [tom. i. p. 276, ed. Bonn]. John, the Monophysite bishop of Asia, is a more authentic witness of this transaction, in which he was himself employed by the emperor (Asseman. Bib. Orient. tom. ii. p. 85).

87. Compare Procopius (Hist. Arcan. c. 28 [tom. iii. p. 156, ed. Bonn] and Aleman's Notes) with Theophanes (Chron. p. 190 [tom. i. p. 340, ed. Bonn]). The council of Nice has intrusted the patriarch, or rather the astronomers, of Alexandria, with the annual proclamation of Easter; and we still read, or rather we do not read, many of the Paschal epistles of St. Cyril. Since the reign of Monophytism in Egypt, the Catholics were perplexed by such a foolish prejudice as that which so long opposed, among the Protestants, the reception of the Gregorian style.

88. For the religion and history of the Samaritans, consult Basnage, Histoire des Juifs, a learned and impartial work.

89. Sichem, Neapolis, Naplous, the ancient and modern seat of the Samaritans, is situate in a valley between the barren Ebal, the mountain of cursing to the north, and the fruitful *Garizim*, or mountain of cursing to the south, ten or eleven hours' travel from Jerusalem. See Maundrell, Journey from Aleppo, etc., p. 59–63.

90. Procop. Anecdot. c. 11 [p. 75, ed. Bonn]; Theophan. Chron. p. 122 [vol. i. p. 274, ed. Bonn]; John Malala, Chron. tom. ii. p. 62 [p. 447, ed. Bonn]. I remember an observation, half philosophical, half superstitious, that the province which had been ruined by the bigotry of Justinian was the same through which the Mohammedans penetrated into the empire.

91. The expression of Procopius is remarkable: οὐ γὰρ οἱ ἐδόκει φόνος ἀνθρώπων εἶναι, ἥν γε μὴ τῆς αὐτοῦ δόξης οἱ τελευτῶντες τύξοιεν ὄντες. Anecdot. c. 13 [p. 84, ed. Bonn].

92. See the Chronicle of Victor, p. 328, and the original evidence of the laws of Justinian. During the first years of his reign, Baronius himself is in extreme good humour with the emperor, who courted the popes, till he got them into his power.

93. Procopius, Anecdot. c. 13; Evagrius, l. iv. c. 10. If the ecclesiastical never read the secret historian, their common suspicion proves at least the general hatred.

94. On the subject of the three chapters, the original acts of the fifth general council of Constantinople supply much useless though authentic

knowledge (Concil. tom. vi. p. 1–419). The *Greek*
Evagrius is less copious and correct (l. iv. c. 38)
than the three zealous *Africans*, Facundus (in his
twelve books, de tribus capitulis, which are most
correctly published by Sirmond), Liberatus (in
his Breviarium, c. 22, 23, 24), and Victor Tunu-
nensis in his Chronicle (in tom. i. Antiq. Lect.
Canisii, p. 330–334). The Liber Pontificalis, or
Anastasius (in Vigilio, Pelagio, etc.), is original
Italian evidence. The modern reader will derive
some information from Dupin (Biblioth. Ecclés.
tom. v. p. 189–207) and Basnage (Hist. de l'Eglise,
tom. i. p. 519–541); yet the latter is too firmly resolved to depreciate the authority and character
of the popes.

95. Origen had indeed too great a propensity to
imitate the πλάνη and δυσσέβεια of the old philosophers (Justinian, ad Mennam, in Concil. tom. vi.
p. 356). His moderate opinions were too repugnant to the zeal of the church, and he was found
guilty of the heresy of reason.

96. Basnage (Præfat. p. 11–14, ad tom. i. Antiq.
Lect. Canis.) has fairly weighed the guilt and innocence of Theodore of Mopsuestia. If he composed 10,000 volumes, as many errors would be a
charitable allowance. In all the subsequent cata-
logues of heresiarchs, he alone, without his two
brethren, is included; and it is the duty of Asseman
(Biblioth. Orient. tom. iv. p. 203–207) to justify
the sentence.

97. See the complaints of Liberatus and Victor,
and the exhortations of pope Pelagius to the conqueror and exarch of Italy. Schisma . . . per po-
testates publicas opprimatur, etc. (Concil. tom. vi.
p. 467, etc.). An army was detained to suppress
the sedition of an Illyrian city. See Procopius (de
Bell. Goth. l. iv. c. 25 [tom. iii. p. 594, ed. Bonn]):
ὥνπερ ἕνεκα σφίσιν αὐτοῖς οἱ Χριστιανοὶ διαμάχονται.
He seems to promise an ecclesiastical history. It
would have been curious and impartial.

98. The bishops of the patriarchate of Aquileia
were reconciled by pope Honorius A.D. 638 (Muratori, Annali d'Italia, tom. v. p. 376); but they
again relapsed, and the schism was not finally extinguished till 698. Fourteen years before, the
church of Spain had overlooked the fifth general
council with contemptuous silence (xiii. Concil.
Toletan. in Concil. tom. vii. p. 487–494).

99. Nicetius, bishop of Trèves (Concil. tom. vi.
p. 511–513): he himself, like most of the Gallican
prelates (Gregor. Epist. l. vii. Ep. 5, in Concil.
tom. vi. p. 1007), was separated from the communion of the four patriarchs by his refusal to condemn the three chapters. Baronius almost pronounces the damnation of Justinian (A.D. 565,
No. 6).

100. After relating the last heresy of Justinian
(l. iv. c. 39, 40, 41) and the edict of his successor
(l. v. c. 3 [4]), the remainder of the history of
Evagrius is filled with civil, instead of ecclesiastical,
events.

101. This extraordinary, and perhaps inconsis-

tent, doctrine of the Nestorians, had been observed
by La Croze (Christianisme des Indes, tom. i. p.
19, 20), and is more fully exposed by Abulpharagius (Biblioth. Orient. tom. ii. p. 292; Hist. Dynast. p. 91, vers. Latin. Pocock), and Asseman
himself (tom. iv. p. 218). They seem ignorant that
they might allege the positive authority of the
ecthesis. Ὁ μίαρος Νεστόριος καίπερ διαίρων τὴν θείαν
τοῦ Κυρίου ἐνανθρώπησιν, καὶ δύο εἰσάγων υἱοὺς (the
common reproach of the Monophysites), δύο θελήμ-
ατα τούτων εἴπειν οὐκ ἐτόλμησε, τουναντίον δὲ τοῦτο
βουλίαν τῶν. . . . δύο πρόσωπων ἐδόξασε (Concil. tom.
vii. p. 205).

102. See the orthodox faith in Petavius (Dogmata Theolog. tom. v. l. ix. c. 6–10, p. 433–447):
all the depths of this controversy are sounded in
the Greek dialogue between Maximus and Pyrrhus
(ad calcem, tom. viii. Annal. Baron. p. 755–794),
which relates a real conference, and produced a
short-lived conversion.

103. Impiissimam ecthesim . . . scelerosum ty-
pum (Concil. tom. vii. p. 366) diabolicæ opera-
tionis genimina (fors. *germina*, or else the Greek
γενήματα, in the original—Concil. p. 363, 364) are
the expressions of the eighteenth anathema. The
epistle of pope Martin to Amandus, a Gallican
bishop, stigmatises the Monothelites and their
heresy with equal virulence (p. 392).

104. The sufferings of Martin and Maximus are
described with pathetic simplicity in their original
letters and acts (Concil. tom. vii. p. 63–78; Baron.
Annal. Eccles. A.D. 656, No. 2, et annos subsequent.). Yet the chastisement of their disobedience, ἐξόρια and σώματος αἴκισμος, had been previously announced in the Type of Constans (Concil. tom. vii. p. 240).

105. Eutychius (Annal. tom. ii. p. 348) most
erroneously supposes that the 124 bishops of the
Roman synod transported themselves to Constantinople; and by adding them to the 168
Greeks, thus composes the sixth council of 292
fathers.

106. The Monothelite Constans was hated by
all, διὰ τοι ταῦτα (says Theophanes, Chron. p. 292
[ed. Par.; tom. i. p. 538, ed. Bonn]) ἐμισήθη σφόδρως
παρὰ πάντων. When the Monothelite monk
failed in his miracle, the people shouted, ὁ λαὸς
ἀνεβόησε (Concil. tom. vii. p. 1032). But this was a
natural and transient emotion; and I much fear
that the latter is an anticipation of orthodoxy in
the good people of Constantinople.

107. The history of Monothelitism may be
found in the Acts of the Synods of Rome (tom. vii.
p. 77–395, 601–608) and Constantinople (p. 609–
1429). Baronius extracted some original documents from the Vatican library; and his chronology is rectified by the diligence of Pagi. Even
Dupin (Bibliothèque Ecclés. tom. vi. p. 57–71)
and Basnage (Hist. de l'Eglise, tom. i. p. 541–555)
afford a tolerable abridgment.

108. In the Lateran synod of 679, Wilfrid, an
Anglo-Saxon bishop, subscribed pro omni Aqui-

lonari parte Britanniæ et Hiberniæ, quæ ab An-
glorum et Brittonum, necnon Scotorum et Pic-
torum gentibus colebantur (Eddius, in Vit. St.
Wilfrid, c. 31, apud Pagi, Critica, tom. iii. p. 88).
Theodore (magnæ insulæ Britanniæ archiepisco-
pus et philosophus) was long expected at Rome
(Concil. tom. vii. p. 714), but he contented himself with holding (A.D. 680) his provincial synod of
Hatfield, in which he received the decrees of pope
Martin and the first Lateran council against the
Monothelites (Concil. tom. vii. p. 597, etc.). Theodore, a monk of Tarsus in Cilicia, had been named
to the primacy of Britain by pope Vitalian (A.D.
668, see Baronius and Pagi), whose esteem for his
learning and piety was tainted by some distrust of
his national character—ne quid contrarium veri-
tati fidei, Græcorum more, in ecclesiam cui præ-
esset introduceret. The Cilician was sent from
Rome to Canterbury under the tuition of an African guide (Bedæ Hist. Eccles. Anglorum, l. iv. c
1). He adhered to the Roman doctrine; and the
same creed of the incarnation has been uniformly
transmitted from Theodore to the modern primates, whose sound understanding is perhaps seldom engaged with that abstruse mystery.

109. This name, unknown till the tenth century, appears to be of Syriac origin. It was invented by the Jacobites, and eagerly adopted by
the Nestorians and Mahometans; but it was accepted without shame by the Catholics, and is
frequently used in the Annals of Eutychius (Asseman. Biblioth. Orient. tom. ii. p. 507, etc., tom.
iii. p. 355; Renaudot, Hist. Patriarch. Alexandrin.
p. 119). Ἡμεῖς δοῦλοι τοῦ Βασιλέως, was the acclamation of the fathers of Constantinople (Concil.
tom. vii. p. 765).

110. The Syriac, which the natives revere as the
primitive language, was divided into three dialects. 1. The *Aramæan*, as it was refined at Edessa
and the cities of Mesopotamia; 2. The *Palestine*,
which was used in Jerusalem, Damascus, and the
rest of Syria; 3. The *Nabathæan*, the rustic idiom of
the mountains of Assyria and the villages of Irak
(Gregor. Abulpharag. Hist. Dynast. p. 11). On
the Syriac, see Ebed-Jesu (Asseman. tom. iii. p.
326, etc.), whose prejudice alone could prefer it to
the Arabic.

111. I shall not enrich my ignorance with the
spoils of Simon, Walton, Mill, Wetstein, Assemannus, Ludolphus, La Croze, whom I have consulted with some care. It appears, 1. *That*, of all
the versions which are celebrated by the fathers, it
is doubtful whether any are now extant in their
pristine integrity. 2. *That* the Syriac has the best
claim, and that the consent of the Oriental sects is
a proof that it is more ancient than their schism.

112. In the account of the Monophysites and
Nestorians I am deeply indebted to the Bibliotheca
Orientalis Clementino-Vaticana of Joseph Simon
Assemannus. That learned Maronite was de-
spatched in the year 1715 by pope Clement XI. to
visit the monasteries of Egypt and Syria, in search

of MSS. His four folio volumes, published at Rome
1719–1728, contain a part only, though perhaps
the most valuable, of his extensive project. As a
native and as a scholar, he possessed the Syriac
literature; and, though a dependent of Rome, he
wishes to be moderate and candid.

113. See the Arabic canons of Nice in the translation of Abraham Ecchelensis, No. 37, 38, 39, 40.
Concil. tom. ii. p. 335, 336, edit. Venet. These
vulgar titles, *Nicene* and *Arabic*, are both apocryphal. The council of Nice enacted no more than
twenty canons (Theodoret, Hist. Eccles. l. i. c. 8);
and the remainder, seventy or eighty, were collected from the synods of the Greek church. The
Syriac edition of Maruthas is no longer extant
(Asseman. Biblioth. Oriental. tom. i. p. 195, tom.
iii. p. 74), and the Arabic version is marked with
many recent interpolations. Yet this Code contains many curious relics of ecclesiastical discipline; and since it is equally revered by all the
Eastern communions, it was probably finished before the schism of the Nestorians and Jacobites
(Fabric. Biblioth. Græc. tom. xi. p. 363–367).

114. Theodore the Reader (l. ii. c. 5, 49, ad
calcem Hist. Eccles.) has noticed this Persian
school of Edessa. Its ancient splendour and the
two eras of its downfall (A.D. 431 and 489) are
clearly discussed by Assemanni (Biblioth. Orient.
tom. ii. p. 402, iii. p. 376, 378, iv. p. 70, 924).

115. A dissertation on the state of the Nestorians
has swelled in the hands of Assemanni to a folio
volume of 950 pages, and his learned researches
are digested in the most lucid order. Besides this
fourth volume of the *Bibliotheca Orientalis*, the extracts in the three preceding tomes (tom. i. p. 203,
ii. p. 321–463, iii. 64–70, 378–395, etc., 403–408,
580–589) may be usefully consulted.

116. See the Topographia Christiana of Cosmos,
surnamed Indicopleustes, or the Indian navigator,
l. iii. p. 178, 179; l. xi. p. 337. The entire work, of
which some curious extracts may be found in
Photius (cod. xxxvi. p. 9, 10, edit. Hoeschel),
Thevenot (in the 1st part of his Relation des
Voyages, etc.), and Fabricius (Biblioth. Græc. l.
iii. c. 25, tom. ii. p. 603–617), has been published
by Father Montfaucon at Paris, 1707, in the Nova
Collectio Patrum (tom. ii. p. 113–346). It was the
design of the author to confute the impious heresy
of those who maintained that the earth is a globe,
and not a flat oblong table, as it is represented in
the Scriptures (l. ii. p. 138 [125, sq.]). But the nonsense of the monk is mingled with the practical
knowledge of the traveller, who performed his
voyage, A.D. 522, and published his book at Alexandria, A.D. 547 (l. ii. p. 140, 141; Montfaucon,
Præfat. c. 1). The Nestorianism of Cosmas, unknown to his learned editor, was detected by La
Croze (Christianisme des Indes, tom. i. p. 40–55),
and is confirmed by Assemanni (Biblioth. Orient.
tom. iv. p. 605, 606).

117. In its long progress to Mosul, Jerusalem,
Rome, etc., the story of Prester John evaporated

in a monstrous fable, of which some features have been borrowed from the Lama of Thibet (Hist. Généalogique des Tatares, P. ii. p. 42; Hist. de Gengiscan, p. 31, etc.), and were ignorantly transferred by the Portuguese to the emperor of Abyssinia (Ludolph. Hist. Æthiop. Comment. l. ii. c. 1). Yet it is probable that in the eleventh and twelfth centuries Nestorian Christianity was professed in the horde of the Keraites (D'Herbelot, p. 256, 915, 959; Assemanni, tom. iv. p. 468–504).

118. The Christianity of China, between the seventh and the thirteenth century, is invincibly proved by the consent of Chinese, Arabian, Syriac, and Latin evidence (Assemanni. Biblioth. Orient. tom. iv. p. 502–552; Mém. de l'Académie des Inscript. tom. xxx. p. 802–819). The inscription of Siganfu, which describes the fortunes of the Nestorian church, from the first mission, A.D. 636, to the current year 781, is accused of forgery by La Croze, Voltaire, etc., who become the dupes of their own cunning, while they are afraid of a Jesuitical fraud.

119. Jacobitæ et Nestorianæ plures quam Græci et Latini. Jacob a Vitriaco, Hist. Hierosol. l. ii. c. 76, p. 1093, in the Gesta Dei per Francos. The numbers are given by Thomassin, Discipline de l'Eglise, tom. i. p. 172.

120. The division of the patriarchate may be traced in the Bibliotheca Orient. of Assemanni, tom. i. p. 523–549, tom. ii. p. 457, etc., tom. iii. p. 603, 621–623, tom. iv. p. 164–169, 423, 622–629, etc.

121. The pompous language of Rome, on the submission of a Nestorian patriarch, is elegantly represented in the seventh book of Fra-Paolo, Babylon, Nineveh, Arbela, and the trophies of Alexander, Tauris and Ecbatana, the Tigris and Indus.

122. The Indian missionary, St. Thomas, an apostle, a Manichæan, or an Armenian merchant (La Croze, Christianisme des Indes, tom. i. p. 57–70), was famous, however, as early as the time of Jerom (ad Marcellam, Epist. 148 [Ep. 59, p. 328, ed., Vallars.]). Marco Polo was informed on the spot that he suffered martyrdom in the city of Maabar, or Meliapour, a league only from Madras (D'Anville, Eclaircissimens sur l'Inde, p. 125), where the Portuguese founded an episcopal church under the name of St. Thomé, and where the saint performed an annual miracle, till he was silenced by the profane neighbourhood of the English (La Croze, tom. ii. p. 7–16).

123. Neither the author of the Saxon Chronicle (A.D. 883) nor William of Malmesbury (de Gestis Regum Angliæ, l. ii. c. 4, p. 44) were capable, in the twelfth century, of inventing this extraordinary fact; they are incapable of explaining the motives and measures of Alfred, and their hasty notice serves only to provoke our curiosity. William of Malmesbury feels the difficulties of the enterprise, quod quivis in hoc sæculo miretur; and I almost suspect that the English ambassadors collected

their cargo and legend in Egypt. The royal author has not enriched his Orosius (see Barrington's Miscellanies) with an Indian as well as a Scandinavian voyage.

124. Concerning the Christians of St. Thomas, see Assemann. Biblioth. Orient. tom. iv. p. 391–407, 435–451; Geddes's Church History of Malabar; and, above all, La Croze, Histoire du Christianisme des Indes, in two vols. 12mo, La Haye, 1758—a learned and agreeable work. They have drawn from the same source the Portuguese and Italian narratives; and the prejudices of the Jesuits are sufficiently corrected by those of the Protestants.

125. Οἷον εἰπεῖν ψευδαλήθης is the expression of Theodore, in his Treatise of the Incarnation, p. 245, 247, as he is quoted by La Croze (Hist. du Christianisme d'Ethiopie et d'Arménie, p. 35), who exclaims, perhaps too hastily, "Quel pitoyable raisonnement!" Renaudot has touched (Hist. Patriarch. Alex. p. 127–138) the Oriental accounts of Severus; and his authentic creed may be found in the epistle of John the Jacobite patriarch of Antioch, in the tenth century, to his brother Mennas of Alexandria (Asseman. Biblioth. Orient. tom. ii. p. 132–141).

126. Epist. Archimandritarum et Monachorum Syriæ Secundæ ad Papam Hormisdam, Concil. tom. v. p. 598–602. The courage of St. Sabas, ut leo animosus, will justify the suspicion that the arms of these monks were not always spiritual or defensive (Baronius, A.D. 513, No. 7, etc.).

127. Assemanni (Biblioth. Orient. tom. ii. p. 10–46) and La Croze (Christianisme d'Ethiopie, p. 36–40) will supply the history of Xenaias, or Philoxenus, bishop of Mabug, or Hierapolis, in Syria. He was a perfect master of the Syriac language, and the author or editor of a version of the New Testament.

128. The names and titles of fifty-four bishops who were exiled by Justin are preserved in the Chronicle of Dionysius (apud Asseman. tom. ii. p. 54). Severus was personally summoned to Constantinople—for his trial, says Liberatus (Brev. c. 19)—that his tongue might be cut out, says Evagrius (l. iv. c. 4). The prudent patriarch did not stay to examine the difference. This ecclesiastical revolution is fixed by Pagi to the month of September of the year 518 (Critica, tom. ii. p. 506).

129. The obscure history of James, or Jacobus Baradæus, or Zanzalus, may be gathered from Eutychius (Annal. tom. ii. p. 144, 147), Renaudot (Hist. Patriarch. Alex. p. 133), and Assemannus (Biblioth. Orient. tom. i. p. 424; tom. ii. p. 62–69, 324–332, 414; tom. iii. p. 385–388). He seems to be unknown to the Greeks. The Jacobites themselves had rather deduce their name and pedigree from St. James the apostle.

130. The account of his person and writings is perhaps the most curious article in the Bibliotheca of Assemannus (tom. ii. p. 244–321, under the name of Gregorius Bar-Hebræus). La Croze (Christianisme d'Ethiopie, p. 53–63) ridicules the prej-

udice of the Spaniards against the Jewish blood which secretly defiles their church and state.

131. This *excessive* abstinence is censured by La Croze (p. 352), and even by the Syrian Assemannus (tom. i. p. 226; tom. ii. p. 304, 305).

132. The state of the Monophysites is excellently illustrated in a dissertation at the beginning of the second volume of Assemannus, which contains 142 pages. The Syriac Chronicle of Gregory Bar-Hebræus, or Abulpharagius (Biblioth. Orient. tom. ii. p. 321–463), pursues the double series of the Nestorian *Catholics* and the *Maphrians* of the Jacobites.

133. The synonymous use of the two words may be proved from Eutychius (Annal. tom. ii. p. 191, 267, 332), and many similar passages which may be found in the methodical table of Pocock. He was not actuated by any prejudice against the Maronites of the tenth century; and we may believe a Melchite, whose testimony is confirmed by the Jacobites and Latins.

134. Concil. tom. vii. p. 780. The Monothelite cause was supported with firmness and subtlety by Constantine, a *Syrian* priest of Apamea (p. 1040, etc.).

135. Theophanes (Chron. p. 295, 296, 300, 302, 306 [tom. i. p. 542 *sq.*, 552, 555, 561, ed. Bonn]) and Cedrenus (p. 437, 440 (ed. Par.; tom. i. p. 765 *sqq.*, ed. Bonn]) relate the exploits of the Mardaites: the name (*Mard*, in Syriac *rebellavit*) is explained by La Roque (Voyage de la Syrie, tom. ii. p. 53); the dates are fixed by Pagi (A.D. 676, No. 4–14; A.D. 685, No. 3, 4); and even the obscure story of the patriarch John Maron (Asseman. Biblioth. Orient. tom. i. p. 496–520) illustrates, from the year 686 to 707, the troubles of Mount Libanus.

136. In the last century twenty large cedars still remained (Voyage de La Roque, tom. i. p. 68–76); at present they are reduced to four or five (Volney, tom. i. p. 264). These trees, so famous in Scripture, were guarded by excommunication: the wood was sparingly borrowed for small crosses, etc.; an annual mass was chanted under their shade; and they were endowed by the Syrians with a sensitive power of erecting their branches to repel the snow, to which Mount Libanus is less faithful than it is painted by Tacitus: inter ardores opacum fidumque nivibus—a daring metaphor (Hist. v. 6).

137. The evidence of William of Tyre (Hist. in Gestis Dei per Francos, l. xxii. c. 8, p. 1022 [fol. Hanov. 1611]) is copied or confirmed by Jacques de Vitra (Hist. Hierosolym. l. ii. c. 77, p. 1093, 1094). But this unnatural league expired with the power of the Franks; and Abulpharagius (who died in 1286) considers the Maronites as a sect of Monothelites (Biblioth. Orient. tom. ii. p. 292).

138. I find a description and history of the Maronites in the Voyage de la Syrie et du Mont Liban par La Roque (2 vols. in 12mo, Amsterdam, 1723; particularly tom. i. p. 42–47, 174–184, tom. ii. p. 10–120). In the ancient part he copies the prejudices of Nairon and the other Maronites of Rome,

which Assemannus is afraid to renounce and ashamed to support. Jablonski (Institut. Hist. Christ. tom. iii. p. 186), Niebuhr (Voyage de l'Arabie, etc., tom. ii. p. 346, 370–381), and, above all, the judicious Volney (Voyage en Egypte et en Syrie, tom. ii. p. 8–31, Paris, 1787), may be consulted.

139. The religion of the Armenians is briefly described by La Croze (Hist. du Christ. de l'Ethiopie et de l'Arménie, p. 269–402). He refers to the great Armenian History of Galanus (3 vols. in fol. Rome, 1650–1661), and commends the state of Armenia in the third volume of the Nouveaux Mémoires des Missions du Levant. The work of a Jesuit must have sterling merit when it is praised by La Croze.

140. The schism of the Armenians is placed eighty-four years after the council of Chalcedon (Pagi, Critica, ad A.D. 535). It was consummated at the end of seventeen years; and it is from the year of Christ 552 that we date the era of the Armenians (l'Art de vérifier les Dates, p. xxxv.).

141. The sentiments and success of Julian of Halicarnassus may be seen in Liberatus (Brev. c. 19), Renaudot (Hist. Patriarch. Alex. p. 132, 303), and Assemannus (Biblioth. Orient. tom. ii. Dissertat. de Monophysitis, p. viii. p. 286).

142. See a remarkable fact of the twelfth century in the History of Nicetas Choniates (p. 258). Yet three hundred years before, Photius (Epistol. ii. p. 49, edit. Montacut.) had gloried in the conversion of the Armenians—λατρεύει σήμερον ὀρθοδόξως [τὴν χριστιάνων λατρείαν].

143. The travelling Armenians are in the way of every traveller, and their mother church is on the high road between Constantinople and Ispahan: for their present state, see Fabricius (Lux Evangelii, etc., c. xxxviii. p. 40–51), Olearius (l. iv. c. 40), Chardin (vol. ii. p. 232), Tournefort (lettre xx.), and, above all, Tavernier (tom. i. p. 28–37, 510–518), that rambling jeweller, who had read nothing, but had seen so much and so well.

144. The history of the Alexandrian patriarchs, from Dioscorus to Benjamin, is taken from Renaudot (p. 114–164), and the second tome of the Annals of Eutychius.

145. Liberat. Brev. c. 20, 23; Victor. Chron. p. 329, 330; Procop. Anecdot. c. 26, 27.

146. Eulogius, who had been a monk of Antioch, was more conspicuous for subtlety than eloquence. He proves that the enemies of the faith, the Gaianites and Theodosians, ought not to be reconciled; that the same proposition may be orthodox in the mouth of St. Cyril, heretical in that of Severus; that the opposite assertions of St. Leo are equally true, etc. His writings are no longer extant, except in the Extracts of Photius, who had perused them with care and satisfaction, cod. ccviii. ccxxv., ccxxvi., ccxxvii., ccxxx., cclxxx.

147. See the Life of John the Eleemosynary by his contemporary Leontius, bishop of Neapolis in Cyprus, whose Greek text, either lost or hidden, is reflected in the Latin version of Baronius (A.D.

610, No. 9, A.D. 620, No. 8). Pagi (Critica, tom. ii. p. 763) and Fabricius (l. v. c. 11, tom. vii. p. 454) have made some critical observations.

148. This number is taken from the curious Recherches sur les Egyptiens et les Chinois (tom. ii. p. 192, 193); and appears more probable than the 600,000 ancient or 15,000 modern Copts of Gemelli Carreri. Cyril Lucar, the Protestant patriarch of Constantinople, laments that those heretics were ten times more numerous than his orthodox Greeks, ingeniously applying the πολλαί κεν δεκάδες δευοίατο οἰνοχόοιο of Homer (Iliad. ii. 128), the most perfect expression of contempt (Fabric. Lux Evangelii, 740).

149. The history of the Copts, their religion, manners, etc., may be found in the Abbé Renaudot's motley work, neither a translation nor an original; the Chronicon Orientale of Peter, a Jacobite; in the two versions of Abraham Ecchellensis, Paris, 1651; and John Simon Asseman, Venet. 1729. These annals descend no lower than the thirteenth century. The more recent accounts must be searched for in the travellers into Egypt, and the Nouveaux Mémoires des Missions du Levant. In the last century Joseph Abudacnus, a native of Cairo, published at Oxford, in thirty pages, a slight Historia Jacobitarum, 147, post. 150.

150. About the year 737. See Renaudot, Hist. Patriarch. Alex. p. 221, 222; Elmacin, Hist. Saracen, p. 99.

151. Ludolph. Hist. Æthiopic. et Comment. l. i. c. 8; Renaudot, Hist. Patriarch. Alex. p. 480, etc. This opinion, introduced into Egypt and Europe by the artifice of the Copts, the pride of the Abyssinians, the fear and ignorance of the Turks and Arabs, has not even the semblance of truth. The rains of Æthiopia do not, in the increase of the Nile, consult the will of the monarch. If the river approaches at Napata within three days' journey of the Red Sea (see D'Anville's Maps), a canal that should divert its course would demand, and most probably surpass, the power of the Cæsars.

152. The Abyssinians, who still preserve the features and olive complexion of the Arabs, afford a proof that two thousand years are not sufficient to change the colour of the human race. The Nubians, an African race, are pure negroes, as black as those of Senegal or Congo, with flat noses, thick lips, and woolly hair (Buffon, Hist. Naturelle, tom. v. p. 117, 143, 144, 166, 219, edit. in 12mo, Paris, 1769). The ancients beheld, without much attention, the extraordinary phenomenon which has exercised the philosophers and theologians of modern times.

153. Asseman. Biblioth. Orient. tom. i. p. 329.

154. The Christianity of the Nubians, A.D. 1153, is attested by the sheriff al Edrisi, falsely described under the name of the Nubian geographer (p. 18), who represents them as a nation of Jacobites. The rays of historical light that twinkle in the history of Renaudot (p. 178, 220-224, 281-286, 405, 434,

451, 464), are all previous to this era. See the modern state in the Lettres Edifiantes (Recueil, iv.) and Busching (tom. ix. p. 152-159, par Berenger).

155. The abuna is improperly dignified by the Latins with the title of patriarch. The Abyssinians acknowledge only the four patriarchs, and their chief is no more than a metropolitan or national primate (Ludolph. Hist. Æthiopic. et Comment. l. iii. c. 7). The seven bishops of Renaudot (p. 511), who existed A.D. 1131, are unknown to the historian.

156. I know not why Assemannus (Biblioth. Orient. tom. ii. p. 384) should call in question these probable missions of Theodora into Nubia and Æthiopia. The slight notices of Abyssinia till the year 1500 are supplied by Renaudot (p. 336-341, 381, 382, 405, 443, etc., 452, 456, 463, 475, 480, 511, 525, 559-564) from the Coptic writers. The mind of Ludolphus was a perfect blank.

157. Ludolph. Hist. Æthiop. l. iv. c. 5. The most necessary arts are now exercised by the Jews, and the foreign trade is in the hands of the Armenians. What Gregory principally admired and envied was the industry of Europe—artes et opificia.

158. John Bermudez, whose relation, printed at Lisbon, 1569, was translated into English by Purchas (Pilgrims, l. vii. c. 7, p. 1149, etc.), and from thence into French by La Croze (Christianisme d'Ethiopie, p. 92-265). The piece is curious; but the author may be suspected of deceiving Abyssinia, Rome, and Portugal. His title to the rank of patriarch is dark and doubtful (Ludolph. Comment. No. 101, p. 473).

159. Religio Romana . . . nec precibus patrum nec miraculis ab ipsis editis suffulciebatur, is the uncontradicted assurance of the devout emperor Susneus to his patriarch Mendez (Ludolph. Comment. No. 126, p. 529); and such assurances should be preciously kept, as an antidote against any marvellous legends.

160. I am aware how tender is the question of circumcision. Yet I will affirm, 1. That the Æthiopians have a physical reason for the circumcision of males, and even of females (Recherches Philosophiques sur les Américains, tom. ii.). 2. That it was practised in Æthiopia long before the introduction of Judaism or Christianity (Herodot. l. ii. c. 104; Marsham, Canon Chron. p. 72, 73). "Infantes circumcidunt ob consuetudinem non ob Judaismum," says Gregory the Abyssinian priest (apud Fabric. Lux Christiana, p. 720). Yet, in the heat of dispute, the Portuguese were sometimes branded with the name of uncircumcised (La Croze, p. 80; Ludolph. Hist. and Comment. l. iii. c. 1).

161. The three Protestant historians, Ludolphus (Hist. Æthiopica, Francofurt, 1681; Commentarius, 1691; Relatio Nova, etc., 1693, in folio), Geddes (Church History of Æthiopia, London, 1696, in 8vo), and La Croze (Hist. du Christianisme d'Ethiopie et d'Arménie, La Haye, 1739, in 12mo), have drawn their principal materials from the Jesuits, especially from the General History of Tellez, published in Portuguese at Coimbra,

1660. We might be surprised at their frankness; but their most flagitious vice, the spirit of persecution, was in their eyes the most meritorious virtue. Ludolphus possessed some, though a slight, advantage from the Æthiopic language, and the personal conversation of Gregory, a free-spirited Abyssinian priest, whom he invited from Rome to the court of Saxe-Gotha. See the Theologia Æthiopica of Gregory, in Fabricius, Lux Evangelii, p. 716–734.

Chapter XLIX

1. The learned Selden has given the history of transubstantiation in a comprehensive and pithy sentence: "This opinion is only rhetoric turned into logic." (His Works, vol. iii. p. 2073, in his Table-Talk.)

2. Nec intelligunt homines ineptissimi, quôd si sentire simulacra et moveri possent, [ultro] adoratura hominem fuissent à quo sunt expolita. (Divin. Institut. l. ii. c. 2.) Lactantius is the last, as well as the most eloquent, of the Latin apologists. Their raillery of idols attacks not only the object, but the form and matter.

3. See Irenæus, Epiphanius, and Augustin (Basnage, Hist. des Eglises Réformées, tom. ii. p. 1313). This Gnostic practice has a singular affinity with the private worship of Alexander Severus (Lampridius, c. 29; Lardner, Heathen Testimonies, vol. iii. p. 34).

4. See this History, vol. i. p. 294, 353 and 465 seq.

5. Οὐ γὰρ τὸ Θεῖον ἁπλοῦν ὕπαρχου καὶ ἄληπτον μορφαῖς τισι καὶ σχήμασιν ἀπεικάζομεν, οὔτε κηρῷ καὶ ξύλοις τὴν ὑπερούσιον καὶ προάναρχον οὐσίαν τιμᾶν ἥμεις διεγνώκαμεν. (Concilium Nicenum, ii. in Collect. Labb. tom. viii. p. 1025, edit. Venet.) Il seroit peut-être à-propos de ne point souffrir d'images de la Trinité ou de la Divinité; les défenseurs les plus zélés des images ayant condamné celles-ci, et le concile de Trente ne parlant que des images de Jésus-Christ et des Saints (Dupin, Biblioth. Ecclés. tom. vi. p. 154).

6. This general history of images is drawn from the twenty-second book of the Hist. des Eglises Réformées of Basnage, tom. ii. p. 1310-1337. He was a Protestant, but of a manly spirit; and on this head the Protestants are so notoriously in the right, that they can venture to be impartial. See the perplexity of poor Friar Pagi, Critica, tom. i. p. 42.

7. After removing some rubbish of miracle and inconsistency, it may be allowed that, as late as the year 300, Paneas in Palestine was decorated with a bronze statue, representing a grave personage wrapped in a cloak, with a grateful or suppliant female kneeling before him, and that an inscription—τῷ Σῶτηρι, τῷ εὐεργέτῃ—was perhaps inscribed on the pedestal. By the Christians this group was foolishly explained of their founder and the *poor* woman whom he had cured of the bloody flux (Euseb. vii. 18; Philostorg. vii. 3, etc.). M. de Beausobre more reasonably conjectures the philosopher Apollonius, or the emperor Vespasian; in the latter supposition the female is a city, a prov-ince, or perhaps the queen Berenice (Bibliothèque Germanique, tom. xiii. p. 1–92).

8. Euseb. Hist. Ecclés. l. i. c. 13. The learned Assemannus has brought up the collateral aid of three Syrians, St. Ephrem, Josua Stylites, and James bishop of Sarug; but I do not find any notice of the Syriac orinal or the archives of Edessa (Biblioth. Orient. tom. i. p. 318, 420, 554); their vague belief is probably derived from the Greeks.

9. The evidence for these epistles is stated and rejected by the candid Lardner (Heathen Testimonies, vol. i. p. 297–309). Among the herd of bigots who are forcibly driven from this convenient but untenable post, I am ashamed—with the Grabes, Caves, Tillemonts, etc., to discover Mr. Addison, an English gentleman (His Works, vol. i. p. 528, Baskerville's edition); but his superficial tract on the Christian religion owes its credit to his name, his style, and the interested applause of our clergy.

10. From the silence of James of Sarug (Asseman. Biblioth. Orient. p. 289, 318), and the testimony of Evagrius (Hist. Ecclés. l. iv. c. 27), I conclude that this fable was invented between the years 521 and 594, most probably after the siege of Edessa in 540 (Asseman. tom. i. p. 416; Procopius, de Bell. Persic. l. ii. [c. 12, tom. i. p. 208 sq., ed. Bonn]). It is the sword and buckler of Gregory II. (in Epist. i. ad Leon. Isaur. Concil. tom. viii. p. 656, 657), of John Damascenus (Opera, tom. i. p. 281, edit. Lequien [De Fide Orthod. l. iv. c. 16]), and of the second Nicene Council (Actio v. p. 1030). The most perfect edition may be found in Cedrenus (Compend. p. 175-178 [ed. Par.; tom. i. p. 308-314, ed. Bonn]).

11. Ἀχειροποίητος. See Ducange, in Gloss. Græc. et Lat. The subject is treated with equal learning and bigotry by the Jesuit Gretser (Syntagma de Imaginibus non Manû factis, ad calcem Codini de Officiis, p. 289-330), the ass, or rather the fox, of Ingoldstadt (see the Scaligerana); with equal reason and wit by the Protestant Beausobre, in the ironical controversy which he has spread through many volumes of the Bibliothèque Germanique (tom. xviii. p. 1-50; xx. p. 27-68; xxv. p. 1-36; xxvii. p. 85-118; xxviii. p. 1-33; xxxi. p. 111-148; xxxii. p. 75-107; xxxiv. p. 67-96).

12. Theophylact. Simocatta (l. ii. c. 3, p. 34 [ed. Par.; p. 70, ed. Bonn]; l. iii. c. 1, p. 63 [p. 114, ed. Bonn]) celebrates the θεανδρικὸν εἴκασμα, which he styles ἀχειροποίητον; yet it was no more than a

copy, since he adds, ἀρχέτυπον γὰρ ἐκεῖνο (of Edessa) θρησκεύουσι 'Ρωμαῖοί τι ἄρρητον. See Pagi, tom. ii. A.D. 586, No. 11.

13. See, in the genuine or supposed works of John Damascenus, two passages on the Virgin and St. Luke, which have not been noticed by Gretser, nor consequently by Beausobre (Opera Joh. Damascen. tom. i. p. 618, 631 [Adv. Constantinum Cabal. c. 6; Epist. ad Theophilum Imp. c. 4]).

14. "Your scandalous figures stand quite out from the canvas: they are as bad as a group of statues!" It was thus that the ignorance and bigotry of a Greek priest applauded the pictures of Titian, which he had ordered, and refused to accept.

15. By Cedrenus, Zonaras, Glycas, and Manasses, the origin of the Iconoclasts is imputed to the caliph Yezid and two Jews, who promised the empire to Leo; and the reproaches of these hostile sectaries are turned into an absurd conspiracy for restoring the purity of the Christian worship (see Spanheim, Hist. Imag. c. 2).

16. See Elmacin (Hist. Saracen. p. 267), Abulpharagius (Dynast. p. 201), and Abulfeda (Annal. Moslem. p. 264), and the criticisms of Pagi (tom. iii A.D. 944). The prudent Franciscan refuses to determine whether the image of Edessa now reposes at Rome or Genoa; but its repose is inglorious, and this ancient object of worship is no longer famous or fashionable.

17. 'Αρμενίοις καὶ 'Αλαμανοῖς ἐπ' ἴσης ἡ τῶν ἁγίων εἰκόνων προσκύνησις ἀπηγόρευται (Nicetas, l. ii. p. 258 [ed. Par.; p. 527, ed. Bonn]). The Armenian churches are still content with the Cross (Missions du Levant, tom. iii. p. 148); but surely the superstitious Greek is unjust to the superstition of the Germans of the twelfth century.

18. Our original but not impartial monuments of the Iconoclasts must be drawn from the Acts of the Councils, tom. viii. and ix. Collect. Labbé, edit. Venet., and the historical writings of Theophanes, Nicephorus, Manasses, Cedrenus, Zonaras, etc. Of the modern Catholics, Baronius, Pagi, Natalis Alexander (Hist. Eccles. Seculum viii. and ix.), and Maimbourg (Hist. des Iconoclastes), have treated the subject with learning, passion, and credulity. The Protestant labours of Frederick Spanheim (Historia Imaginum restituta) and James Basnage (Hist. des Eglises Réformées, tom. ii. l. xxiii. p. 1339–1385) are cast into the Iconoclast scale. With this mutual aid and opposite tendency it is easy for us to poise the balance with philosophic indifference.

19. Some flowers of rhetoric are Σύνοδον παράνομον καὶ ἄθεον, and the bishops τοῖς ματαιόφροσιν. By Damascenus it is styled ἄκυρος καὶ ἄδεκτος (Opera, tom. i. p. 623 [Adv. Constant. Cabal. c. 16]). Spanheim's Apology for the Synod of Constantinople (p. 171, etc.) is worked up with truth and ingenuity from such materials as he could find in the Nicene Acts (p. 1046, etc.). The witty John of Damascus converts ἐπισκόπους into ἐπισκότους;

makes them κοιλιοδούλους, slaves of their belly, etc. Opera, tom. i. p. 306.

20. He is accused of proscribing the title of saint; styling the Virgin, Mother of Christ; comparing her after her delivery to an empty purse; of Arianism, Nestorianism, etc. In his defence, Spanheim (c. iv. p. 207) is somewhat embarrassed between the interest of a Protestant and the duty of an orthodox divine.

21. The holy confessor Theophanes approves the principle of their rebellion, θείῳ κινούμενοι ζήλῳ (p. 339). Gregory II. (in Epist. i. ad imp. Leon. Concil. Tom. viii. p. 661, 664) applauds the zeal of the Byzantine women who killed the Imperial officers.

22. John, or Mansur, was a noble Christian of Damascus, who held a considerable office in the service of the caliph. His zeal in the cause of images exposed him to the resentment and treachery of the Greek emperor; and, on the suspicion of a treasonable correspondence, he was deprived of his right hand, which was miraculously restored by the Virgin. After this deliverance he resigned his office, distributed his wealth, and buried himself in the monastery of St. Sabas, between Jerusalem and the Dead Sea. The legend is famous; but his learned editor, Father Lequien, has unluckily proved that St. John Damascenus was already a monk before the Iconoclast dispute (Opera, tom. i. Vit. St. Joan. Damascen. p. 10–13, et Notas ad loc.).

23. After sending Leo to the devil, he introduces his heir—τὸ μιαρὸν αὐτοῦ γέννημα, καὶ τῆς κακίας αὐτοῦ κληρονόμος ἐν διπλῷ γενόμενος (Opera Damascen. tom. i. p. 625 [Adv. Constant. Cabal. c. 20]). If the authenticity of this piece be suspicious, we are sure that in other works, no longer extant, Damascenus bestowed on Constantine the titles of νέον Μωαμέθ, Χριστομάχον, μισάγιον (tom. i. p. 306).

24. In the narrative of this persecution from Theophanes and Cedrenus, Spanheim (p. 235–238) is happy to compare the Draco of Leo with the dragoons (Dracones) of Louis XIV., and highly solaces himself with this controversial pun.

25. Πρόγραμμα γὰρ ἐξεπέμψε κατὰ πᾶσαν ἐξαρχίαν τὴν ὑπὸ τῆς χειρὸς αὐτοῦ, πάντας ὑπογράψαι καὶ ὀμνύναι· τοῦ ἀθετῆσαι τὴν προσκύνησιν τῶν σεπτῶν εἰκόνων (Damascen. Op. tom. i. p. 625 [Adv. Constant. Cabal. c. 21]). This oath and subscription I do not remember to have seen in any modern compilation.

26. Καὶ τὴν 'Ρώμην σὺν πάσῃ [τῇ] 'Ιταλίᾳ τῆς βασιλείας αὐτοῦ ἀπέστησε, says Theophanes (Chronograph. p. 343 [tom. i. p. 630, ed. Bonn]). For this Gregory is styled by Cedrenus ἀνὴρ ἀποστολικός (p. 450). Zonaras specifies the thunder, ἀναθέματι συνοδικῷ (tom. ii. l. xv. [c. 4] p. 104, 105). It may be observed that the Greeks are apt to confound the times and actions of two Gregories.

27. See Baronius, Annal. Eccles. A.D. 730, No. 4, 5: dignum exemplum! Bellarmin. de Romano Pontifice, l. v. c. 8: mulctavit eum parte imperii.

Sigonius, de Regno Italiæ, l. iii. Opera, tom. ii. p. 169. Yet such is the change of Italy, that Sigonius is corrected by the editor of Milan, Philippus Argelatus, a Bolognese, and subject of the pope.

28. Quod si Christiani olim non deposuerunt Neronem aut Julianum, id fuit quia deerant vires temporales Christianis (honest Bellarmine, de Rom. Pont. l. v. c. 7). Cardinal Perron adds a distinction more honourable to the first Christians, but not more satisfactory to modern princes—the *treason* of heretics and apostates, who break their oath, belie their coin, and renounce their allegiance to Christ and his vicar (Perroniana, p. 89).

29. Take, as a specimen, the cautious Basnage (Hist. de l'Eglise, p. 1350, 1351) and the vehement Spanheim (Hist. Imaginum), who, with a hundred more, tread in the footsteps of the centuriators of Magdeburg.

30. See Launoy (Opera, tom. v. pars ii. Epist. vii. 7, p. 456–474), Natalis Alexander (Hist. Nov. Testamenti, secul. viii. dissert. i. p. 92–96), Pagi (Critica, tom. iii. p. 215, 216), and Giannone (Istoria Civile di Napoli, tom. i. p. 317–320), a disciple of the Gallican school. In the field of controversy I always pity the moderate party, who stand on the open middle ground exposed to the fire of both sides.

31. They appeal to Paul Warnefrid, or Diaconus (de Gestis Langobard. l. vi. c. 49, p. 506, 507, in Script. Ital. Muratori, tom. i. pars i.), and the nominal Anastasius (de Vit. Pont. in Muratori, tom. iii. pars. i.; Gregorius II., p. 154; Gregorius III., p. 158; Zacharias, p. 161; Stephanus III., p. 165; Paulus, p. 172; Stephanus IV., p. 174; Hadrianus, p. 179; Leo III., p. 195). Yet I may remark that the true Anastasius (Hist. Eccles. p. 134, edit. Reg.) and the Historia Miscella (l. xxi. p. 151, in tom. i. Script. Ital.), both of the ninth century, translate and approve the Greek text of Theophanes.

32. With some minute difference, the most learned critics, Lucas Holstenius, Schelestrate, Ciampini, Bianchini, Muratori (Prolegomena ad tom. iii. pars. i.), are agreed that the Liber Pontificalis was composed and continued by the apostolical librarians and notaries of the eighth and ninth centuries, and that the last and smallest part is the work of Anastasius, whose name it bears. The style is barbarous, the narrative partial, the details are trifling; yet it must be read as a curious and authentic record of the times. The epistles of the popes are dispersed in the volumes of Councils.

33. The two epistles of Gregory II. have been preserved in the Acts of the Nicene Council (tom. viii. p. 651–674). They are without a date, which is variously fixed—by Baronius in the year 726, by Muratori (Annali d'Italia, tom. vi. p. 120) in 729, and by Pagi in 730. Such is the force of prejudice, that some *papists* have praised the good sense and moderation of these letters.

34. Εἴκοσι τέσσαρα στάδια ὑποχωρήσει ὁ Ἀρχιερεὺς Ῥώμης εἰς τὴν χώραν Καμπανίας, καὶ ὕπαγε δίωξον τοὺς ἀνέμους (Epist. i. p. 664). This proximity of the Lombards is hard of digestion. Camillo Pellegrini (Dissert. iv. de Ducatû Beneventi, in the Script. Ital. tom. v. p. 172, 173) forcibly reckons the twenty-fourth stadia, not from Rome, but from the limits of the Roman duchy, to the first fortress, perhaps Sora, of the Lombards. I rather believe that Gregory, with the pedantry of the age, employs *stadia* for miles, without much inquiry into the genuine measure.

35. Ὃν αἱ πᾶσαι βασιλεῖαι τῆς δύσεως ὡς Θεὸν ἐπίγειον ἔχουσι.

36. Ἀπὸ τῆς ἐσωτέρου δύσεως τοῦ λεγομένου Σεπτετοῦ (p. 665). The Pope appears to have imposed on the ignorance of the Greeks: he lived and died in the Lateran, and in his time all the kingdoms of the West had embraced Christianity. May not this unknown *Septetus* have some reference to the chief of the Saxon *Heptarchy*, to Ina king of Wessex, who, in the pontificate of Gregory the Second, visited Rome for the purpose, not of baptism, but of pilgrimage (Pagi, A.D. 689, No. 2; A.D. 726, No. 15)?

37. I shall transcribe the important and decisive passage of the Liber Pontificalis. Respiciens ergo pius vir profanam principis jussionem, jam contra Imperatorem quasi contra *hostem* se armavit, renuens hæresim ejus, scribens ubique se cavere Christianos, eo quod orta fuisset impietas talis. *Igitur* permoti omnes Pentapolenses, atque Venetiarum exercitus contra Imperatoris jussionem restiterunt: dicentes se nunquam in ejusdem pontificis condescendere necem, sed pro ejus magis defensione viriliter decertare (p. 156).

38. A *census*, or capitation, says Anastasius (p. 156): a most cruel tax, unknown to the Saracens themselves, exclaims the zealous Maimbourg (Hist. des Iconoclastes, l. i.), and Theophanes (p. 344 [tom. i. p. 631, ed. Bonn]), who talks of Pharaoh's numbering the male children of Israel. This mode of taxation was familiar to the Saracens; and, most unluckily for the historian, it was imposed a few years afterwards in France by his patron Louis XIV.

39. See the Liber Pontificalis of Agnellus (in the Scriptores Rerum Italicarum of Muratori, tom. ii. pars. i.), whose deeper shade of barbarism marks the difference between Rome and Ravenna. Yet we are indebted to him for some curious and domestic facts—the quarters and factions of Ravenna (p. 154), the revenge of Justinian II. (p. 160, 161), the defeat of the Greeks (p. 170, 171), etc.

40. Yet Leo was undoubtedly comprised in the si quis . . . imaginum sacrarum . . . destructor . . . extiterit, sit extorris a corpore D.N. Jesu Christi vel totius ecclesiæ unitate. The canonists may decide whether the guilt or the name constitutes the excommunication; and the decision is of the last importance of their safety, since, according to the oracle (Gratian, Caus. xxiii. q. 5, c. 47, apud Spanheim, Hist. Imag. p. 112), homicidas non esse qui excommunicatos trucidant.

41. Compescuit tale consilium Pontifex, sperans conversionem principis (Anastas. p. 156). Sed ne desisterent ab amore et fide R.J. admonebat (p. 157). The popes style Leo and Constantine Copronymus, Imperatores et Domini, with the strange epithet of *Piissimi*. A famous mosaic of the Lateran (A.D. 798) represents Christ, who delivers the keys to St. Peter and the banner to Constantine V. (Muratori, Annali d'Italia, tom. vi. p. 337).

42. I have traced the Roman duchy according to the maps, and the maps according to the excellent dissertation of Father Beretti (de Chorographia Italiæ Medii Ævi, sect. xx. p. 216–232). Yet I must nicely observe that Viterbo is of Lombard foundation (p. 211), and that Terracina was usurped by the Greeks.

43. On the extent, population, etc., of the Roman kingdom, the reader may peruse with pleasure the *Discours Préliminaire* to the République Romaine of M. de Beaufort (tom. i.), who will not be accused of too much credulity for the early ages of Rome.

44. Quos (*Romanos*) nos, Longobardi scilicet, Saxones, Franci, Lotharingi, Bajoarii, Suevi, Burgundiones, tanto dedignamur ut inimicos nostros commoti, nil aliud contumeliarum nisi Romane, dicamus: hoc solo, id est Romanorum nomine, quicquid ignobilitatis, quicquid timiditatis, quicquid avaritiæ, quicquid luxuriæ, quicquid mendacii, immo quicquid vitiorum est comprehendentes (Liutprand, in Legat. Script. Ital. tom. ii. pars. i. p. 481). For the sins of Cato or Tully, Minos might have imposed as a fit penance the daily perusal of this barbarous passage.

45. Pipino regi Francorum [et Patricio Romanorum] omnis senatus atque universa populi generalitas a Deo servatæ Romanæ urbis. Codex Carolin. epist. 36 in Script. Ital. tom. iii. pars ii. p. 160. The names of senatus and senator were never totally extinct (Dissert. Chorograph. p. 216, 217); but in the middle ages they signified little more than nobiles, optimates, etc. (Ducange, Gloss. Latin.).

46. See Muratori, Antiquit. Italiæ Medii Ævi, tom. ii. Dissertat. xxvii. p. 548. On one of these coins we read Hadrianus Papa (A.D. 772); on the reverse, Vict. DDNN. with the word *CONOB*, which the Père Joubert (Science des Médailles, tom. ii. p. 42) explains by *CON*stantinopoli *O*fficina *B* (*secunda*).

47. See West's Dissertation on the Olympic Games (Pindar, vol. ii. p. 32–36, edition in 12mo) and the judicious reflections of Polybius (tom. i. l. iv. [c. 73] p. 466, edit. Gronov.).

48. The speech of Gregory to the Lombard is finely composed by Sigonius (de Regno Italiæ, l. iii. Opera, tom. ii. p. 173), who imitates the licence and the spirit of Sallust or Livy.

49. The Venetian historians, John Sagorninus (Chron. Venet. p. 13) and the doge, Andrew Dandolo (Scriptores Rer. Ital. tom. xii. p. 135), have preserved this epistle of Gregory. The loss

and recovery of Ravenna are mentioned by Paulus Diaconus (de Gest. Langobard. l. vi. c. 49, 54, in Script. Ital. tom. i. pars. i. p. 506, 508); but our chronologists, Pagi, Muratori, etc., cannot ascertain the date or circumstances.

50. The option will depend on the various readings of the MSS. of Anastasius—*deceperat*, or *decerpserat* (Script. Ital. tom. iii. pars. i. p. 167).

51. The Codex Carolinus is a collection of the epistles of the popes to Charles Martel (whom they style *Subregulus*), Pepin, and Charlemagne, as far as the year 791, when it was formed by the last of these princes. His original and authentic MS (Bibliothecæ Cubicularis) is now in the Imperial library of Vienna, and has been published by Lambecius and Muratori (Script. Rerum Ital. tom. iii. pars. ii. p. 75, etc.).

52. See this most extraordinary letter in the Codex Carolinus, epist. iii. p. 92. The enemies of the popes have charged them with fraud and blasphemy; yet they surely meant to persuade rather than deceive. This introduction of the dead, or of immortals, was familiar to the ancient orators, though it is executed on this occasion in the rude fashion of the age.

53. Except in the divorce of the daughter of Desiderius, whom Charlemagne repudiated sine aliquo crimine. Pope Stephen IV. had most furiously opposed the alliance of a noble Frank—cum perfidâ, horridâ, nec dicendâ, fœtentissimâ natione Longobardorum—to whom he imputes the first stain of leprosy (Cod. Carolin. epist. 45, p. 178, 179). Another reason against the marriage was the existence of a first wife (Muratori, Annali d'Italia, tom. vi. p. 232, 233, 236, 237). But Charlemagne indulged himself in the freedom of polygamy or concubinage.

54. See the Annali d'Italia of Muratori, tom. vi., and the three first Dissertations of his Antiquitates Italiæ Medii Ævi, tom. i.

55. Besides the common historians, three French critics, Launoy (Opera, tom. v. pars ii. l. vii. epist. 9, p. 477–487), Pagi (Critica, A.D. 751, No. 1–6, A.D. 752, No. 1–10), and Natalis Alexander (Hist. Novi Testamenti, dissertat. ii. p. 96–107), have treated this subject of the deposition of Childeric with learning and attention, but with a strong bias to save the independence of the crown. Yet they are hard pressed by the texts which they produce of Eginhard, Theophanes, and the old annals, Laureshamenses, Fuldenses, Loisielani.

56. Not absolutely for the first time. On a less conspicuous theatre it had been used, in the sixth and seventh centuries, by the provincial bishops of Britain and Spain. The royal unction of Constantinople was borrowed from the Latins in the last age of the empire. Constantine Manasses mentions that of Charlemagne as a foreign, Jewish, incomprehensible ceremony. See Selden's Titles of Honour, in his Works, vol. iii. part i. p. 234–249.

57. See Eginhard, in Vitâ Caroli Magni, c. i. p. 9, etc., c. iii. p. 24 [ed. Schminck]. Childeric was

deposed—*jussû*, the Carlovingians were established —*auctoritate*, Pontificis Romani. Launoy, etc., pretend that these strong words are susceptible of a very soft interpretation. Be it so; yet Eginhard understood the world, the court, and the Latin language.

58. For the title and powers of patrician of Rome, see Ducange (Gloss. Latin. tom. v. p. 149–151), Pagi (Critica, A.D. 740, No. 6–11), Muratori (Annali d'Italia, tom. vi. p. 308–329), and St. Marc (Abrégé Chronologique de l'Italie, tom. i. p. 379–382). Of these the Franciscan Pagi is the most disposed to make the patrician a lieutenant of the church, rather than of the empire.

59. The papal advocates can soften the symbolic meaning of the banner and the keys; but the style of ad *regnum* dimisimus, or direximus (Codex Carolin. epist. i. tom. iii. pars ii. p. 76), seems to allow of no palliation or escape. In the MS. of the Vienna library, they read, instead of *regnum*, *rogum*, prayer or request (see Ducange); and the royalty of Charles Martel is subverted by this important correction (Catalani, in his Critical Prefaces, Annali d'Italia, tom. xvii. p. 95–99).

60. In the authentic narrative of this reception, the Liber Pontificalis observes—obviam illi ejus sanctitas dirigens venerabiles [venerandas] cruces, id est signa; sicut mos est ad exarchum, aut patricium suscipiendum, eum cum ingenti honore suscipi fecit (tom. iii. pars. i. p. 185).

61. Paulus Diaconus, who wrote before the *empire* of Charlemagne, describes Rome as his subject city—vestræ civitates (ad Pompeium Festum), suis addidit sceptris (de Metensis Ecclesiæ Episcopis). Some Carlovingian medals, struck at Rome, have engaged Le Blanc to write an elaborate, though partial, dissertation on their authority at Rome, both as patricians and emperors (Amsterdam, 1692, in 4to).

62. Mosheim (Institution Hist. Eccles. p. 263) weighs this donation with fair and deliberate prudence. The original act has never been produced; but the Liber Pontificalis represents (p. 171), and the Codex Carolinus supposes, this ample gift. Both are contemporary records; and the latter is the more authentic, since it has been preserved, not in the Papal, but the Imperial, library.

63. Between the exorbitant claims, and narrow concessions, of interest and prejudice, from which even Muratori (Antiquitat. tom. i. p. 63–68) is not exempt, I have been guided, in the limits of the Exarchate and Pentapolis, by the Dissertatio Chorographica Italiæ Medii Ævi, tom. x. p. 160–180.

64. Spoletini deprecati sunt, ut eos in servitio B. Petri reciperet et more Romanorum tonsurari faceret (Anastasius, p. 185). Yet it may be a question whether they gave their own persons or their country.

65. The policy and donations of Charlemagne are carefully examined by St. Marc (Abrégé, tom. i. p. 390–408), who has well studied the Codex Carolinus. I believe, with him, that they were only verbal. The most ancient act of donation that pretends to be extant is that of the emperor Lewis the Pious (Sigonius, de Regno Italiæ, l. iv. Opera, tom. ii. p. 267–270). Its authenticity, or at least its integrity, are much questioned (Pagi, A.D. 817, No. 7, etc.; Muratori, Annali, tom. vi. p. 432, etc.; Dissertat. Chorographica, p. 33, 34); but I see no reasonable objection to these princes so freely disposing of what was not their own.

66. Charlemagne solicited and obtained from the proprietor, Adrian I., the mosaics of the palace of Ravenna, for the decoration of Aix-la-Chapelle (Cod. Carolin. epist. 67, p. 223).

67. The popes often complain of the usurpations of Leo of Ravenna (Codex Carolin. epist. 51, 52, 53, p. 200–205). Si corpus St. Andreæ germani St. Petri hîc humasset, nequaquam nos Romani pontifices sic subjugassent (Agnellus, Liber Pontificalis, in Scriptores Rerum Ital. tom. ii. pars. i. p. 107).

68. Piissimo Constantino magno, per ejus largitatem S. R. Ecclesia elevata et exaltata est, et potestatem in his Hesperiæ partibus largiri dignatus est. . . . Quia ecce novus Constantinus his temporibus, etc. (Codex Carolin. epist. 49, in tom. iii. part. ii. p. 195). Pagi (Critica, A.D. 324, No. 16) ascribes them to an imposter of the eighth century, who borrowed the name of St. Isidore: his humble title of *Peccator* was ignorantly, but aptly, turned into *Mercator;* his merchandise was indeed profitable, and a few sheets of paper were sold for much wealth and power.

69. Fabricius (Biblioth. Græc. tom. vi. p. 4–7) has enumerated the several editions of this Act, in Greek and Latin. The copy which Laurentius Valla recites and refutes appears to be taken either from the spurious Acts of St. Silvester or from Gratian's Decree, to which, according to him and others, it has been surreptitiously tacked.

70. In the year 1059 it was believed (was it believed?) by Pope Leo IX., Cardinal Peter Damianus, etc. Muratori places (Annali d'Italia, tom. ix. p. 23, 24) the fictitious donations of Lewis the Pious, the Othos, etc., de Donatione Constantini. See a Dissertation of Natalis Alexander, seculum iv. diss. 25, p. 335–350.

71. See a large account of the controversy (A.D. 1105), which arose from a private lawsuit, in the Chronicon Farsense (Script. Rerum Italicarum, tom. ii. pars. ii. p. 637, etc.), a copious extract from the archives of that Benedictine abbey. They were formerly accessible to curious foreigners (Le Blanc and Mabillon), and would have enriched the first volume of the Historia Monastica Italiæ of Quirini. But they are now imprisoned (Muratori, Scriptores R. I. tom. ii. pars ii. p. 269) by the timid policy of the court of Rome; and the future cardinal yielded to the voice of authority and the whispers of ambition (Quirini, Comment. pars ii. p. 123–136).

72. I have read in the collection of Schardius (de Potestate Imperiali Ecclesiasticâ, p. 734–780)

this animated discourse, which was composed by the author A.D. 1440, six years after the flight of Pope Eugenius IV. It is a most vehement party pamphlet; Valla justifies and animates the revolt of the Romans, and would even approve the use of a dagger against their sacerdotal tyrant. Such a critic might expect the persecution of the clergy; yet he made his peace, and is buried in the Lateran (Bayle, Dictionnaire Critique, VALLA; Vossius, de Historicis Latinis, p. 580).

73. See Guicciardini, a servant of the popes, in that long and valuable digression, which has resumed its place in the last edition, correctly published from the author's MS., and printed in four volumes in quarto, under the name of Friburgo, 1775 (Istoria d'Italia, tom. i. p. 385-395).

74. The Paladin Astolpho found it in the moon, among the things that were lost upon earth (Orlando Furioso, xxxiv. 80).

Di vari fiori ad un gran monte passa,
Ch' ebbe già buono odore, or puzza forte:
Questo era il dono (se però dir lece)
Che Constantino al buon Silvestro fece.

Yet this incomparable poem has been approved by a bull of Leo X.

75. See Baronius, A.D. 324, No. 117-123; A.D. 1191, No. 51, etc. The cardinal wishes to suppose that Rome was offered by Constantine, and *refused* by Silvester. The act of donation he considers, strangely enough, as a forgery of the Greeks.

76. Baronius n'en dit guères contre; encore en a-t-il trop dit, et l'on vouloit sans moi (*Cardinal du Perron*), qui l'empêchai, censurer cette partie de son histoire. J'en devisai un jour avec le Pape, et il ne me répondit autre chose "che volete? i Canonici la tengono," il le disoit *en riant* (Perroniana, p. 77).

77. The remaining history of images, from Irene to Theodora, is collected for the Catholics by Baronius and Pagi (A.D. 780-840), Natalis Alexander (Hist. N. T. seculum viii.; Panoplia adversus Hæreticos, p. 118-178), and Dupin (Biblioth. Ecclés. tom. vi. p. 136-154); for the Protestants, by Spanheim (Hist. Imag. p. 305-639), Basnage (Hist. de l'Eglise, tom. i. p. 556-572; tom. ii. p. 1362-1385), and Mosheim (Institut. Hist. Eccles. secul. viii. et ix.). The Protestants, except Mosheim, are soured with controversy; but the Catholics, except Dupin, are inflamed by the fury and superstition of the monks; and even Le Beau (Hist. du Bas Empire), a gentleman and a scholar, is infected by the odious contagion.

78. See the Acts, in Greek and Latin, of the second Council of Nice, with a number of relative pieces, in the eighth volume of the Councils, p. 645-1600. A faithful version, with some critical notes, would provoke, in different readers, a sigh or a smile.

79. The pope's legates were casual messengers, two priests without any special commission, and who were disavowed on their return. Some vagabond monks were persuaded by the Catholics to

represent the Oriental patriarchs. This curious anecdote is revealed by Theodore Studites (Epist. i. 38, in Sirmond. Opp. tom. v. p. 1319), one of the warmest Iconoclasts of the age.

80. Συμφέρει δέ σοι μὴ καταλιπεῖν ἐν τῇ πόλει ταύτῃ πορνεῖον εἰς ὃ μὴ εἰσέλθῃς, ἢ ἵνα ἀρνήσῃ τὸ προσκύνειν τὸν κύριον ἡμῶν καὶ θεὸν Ἰησοῦν Χριστὸν μετὰ τῆς ἰδίας αὐτοῦ μήτρος ἐν εἰκόνι. These visits could not be innocent, since the Δαίμων πορνείας (the demon of fornication) ἐπολέμει δὲ αὐτὸν . . . ἐν μιᾷ οὖν ὡς ἐπέκειτο αὐτῷ σφόδρα, etc. Actio iv. p. 901; Actio v. p. 1031.

81. See an account of this controversy in the Alexias of Anna Comnena (l. v. p. 129 [ed. Par.; c. 2, p. 229, ed. Bonn]) and Mosheim (Institut. Hist. Eccles. p. 371, 372).

82. The Libri Carolini (Spanheim, p. 443-529), composed in the palace or winter quarters of Charlemagne, at Worms, A.D. 790, and sent by Engebert to Pope Adrian I., who answered them by a grandis et verbosa epistola (Concil. tom. viii. p. 1553). The Carolines propose 120 objections against the Nicene synod, and such words as these are the flowers of their rhetoric—Dementiam . . . priscæ Gentilitatis obsoletum errorem . . . argumenta insanissima et absurdissima . . . derisione dignas nænias, etc. etc.

83. The assemblies of Charlemagne were political as well as ecclesiastical; and the three hundred members (Nat. Alexander, sect. viii. p. 53) who sat and voted at Frankfort must include not only the bishops, but the abbots, and even the principal laymen.

84. Qui supra sanctissima patres nostri (episcopi et sacerdotes) *omnimodis* servitium et adorationem imaginum renuentes contempserunt, atque consentientes condemnaverunt (Concil. tom. ix. p. 101; Canon ii. Franckfurd). A polemic must be hard-hearted indeed who does not pity the efforts of Baronius, Pagi, Alexander, Maimbourg, etc., to elude this unlucky sentence.

85. Theophanes (p. 343 [tom. i. p. 631, ed. Bonn]) specifies those of Sicily and Calabria, which yielded an annual rent of three talents and a half of gold (perhaps £7000 sterling). Liutprand more pompously enumerates the patrimonies of the Roman church in Greece, Judæa, Persia, Mesopotamia, Babylonia, Egypt, and Libya, which were detained by the injustice of the Greek emperor (Legat. ad Nicephorum, in Script. Rerum Italicarum, tom. ii. pars. i. p. 481).

86. The great diocese of the Eastern Illyricum, with Apulia, Calabria, and Sicily (Thomassin, Discipline de l'Eglise, tom. i. p. 145). By the confession of the Greeks, the patriarch of Constantinople had detached from Rome the metropolitans of Thessalonica, Athens, Corinth, Nicopolis, and Patræ (Luc. Holsten. Geograph. Sacra, p. 22); and his spiritual conquests extended to Naples and Amalfi (Giannone, Istoria Civile di Napoli, tom. i. p. 517-524; Pagi, A.D. 730, No. 11).

87. In hoc ostenditur, quia ex uno capitulo ab

errore reversis, in aliis duobus, in *eodem* (was it the same?) permaneant errore . . . de diocesi S. R. E. seu de patrimoniis iterum increpantes commonemus, ut si ea restituere noluerit hereticum eum pro hujusmodi errore perseverantiâ decernemus (Epist. Hadrian. Papæ ad Carolum Magnum, in Concil. tom. viii. p. 1598); to which he adds a reason most directly opposite to his conduct, that he preferred the salvation of souls and rule of faith to the goods of this transitory world.

88. Fontanini considers the emperors as no more than the advocates of the church (advocatus et defensor S. R. E. See Ducange, Gloss. Lat. tom. i. p. 97). His antagonist Muratori reduces the popes to be no more than the exarchs of the emperor. In the more equitable view of Mosheim (Institut. Hist. Eccles. p. 264, 265), they held Rome under the empire as the most honourable species of fief or benefice—premuntur nocte caliginosâ!

89. His merits and hopes are summed up in an epitaph of thirty-eight verses, of which Charlemagne declares himself the author (Concil. tom. viii. p. 520).

> Post patrem lacrymans Carolus hæc carmina scripsi.
>
> Tu mihi dulcis amor, te modo plango pater . . .
> Nomina jungo simul titulis, clarissime, nostra
> Adrianus, Carolus, rex ego, tuque pater.

The poetry might be supplied by Alcuin; but the tears, the most glorious tribute, can only belong to Charlemagne.

90. Every new pope is admonished—"Sancte Pater, non videbis annos Petri," twenty-five years. On the whole series the average is about eight years—a short hope for an ambitious cardinal.

91. The assurance of Anastasius (tom. iii. pars i. p. 197, 198) is supported by the credulity of some French annalists; but Eginhard, and other writers of the same age, are more natural and sincere. "Unus ei oculus paululum est læsus," says John the deacon of Naples (Vit. Episcop. Napol. in Scriptores Muratori, tom. i. pars ii. p. 312). Theodolphus, a contemporary bishop of Orleans, observes with prudence (l. iii. carm. 3):—

> Reddita sunt? mirum est: mirum est auferre nequisse.
>
> Est tamen in dubio, hinc mirer an inde magis.

92. Twice, at the request of Adrian and Leo, he appeared at Rome—longâ tunicâ et chlamyde amictus, et calceamentis quoque Romano more formatis. Eginhard (c. xxiii. p. 109-113) describes, like Suetonius, the simplicity of his dress, so popular in the nation, that, when Charles the Bald returned to France in a foreign habit, the patriotic dogs barked at the apostate (Gaillard, Vie de Charlemagne, tom. iv. p. 109).

93. See Anastasius (p. 199) and Eginhard (c. xxviii. p. 124-128). The unction is mentioned by Theophanes (p. 399 [tom. i. p. 733, ed. Bonn]), the oath by Sigonius (from the Ordo Romanus), and the pope's adoration, more antiquorum principum, by the Annales Bertiniani (Script. Murator. tom. ii. pars ii. p. 505).

94. This great event of the translation or restoration of the empire is related and discussed by Natalis Alexander (secul. ix. dissert. i. p. 390-397), Pagi (tom. iii. p. 418), Muratori (Annali d'Italia, tom. vi. p. 339-352), Sigonius (de Regno Italiæ, l. iv. Opp. tom. ii. p. 247-251), Spanheim (de fictâ Translatione Imperii), Giannone (tom. i. p. 395-405), St. Marc (Abrégé Chronologique, tom. i. p. 438-450), Gaillard (Hist. de Charlemagne, tom. ii. p. 386-446). Almost all these moderns have some religious or national bias.

95. By Mably (Observations sur l'Histoire de France), Voltaire (Histoire Générale), Robertson (History of Charles V.), and Montesquieu (Esprit des Loix, l. xxxi. c. 18). In the year 1782 M. Gaillard published his Histoire de Charlemagne (in 4 vols. in 12mo), which I have freely and profitably used. The author is a man of sense and humanity, and his work is laboured with industry and elegance. But I have likewise examined the original monuments of the reigns of Pepin and Charlemagne, in the fifth volume of the Historians of France.

96. The vision of Weltin, composed by a monk eleven years after the death of Charlemagne, shows him in purgatory, with a vulture, who is perpetually gnawing the guilty member, while the rest of his body, the emblem of his virtues, is sound and perfect (see Gaillard, tom. ii. p. 317-360).

97. The marriage of Eginhard with Imma, daughter of Charlemagne, is, in my opinion, sufficiently refuted by the *probrum* and *suspicio* that sullied these fair damsels, without excepting his own wife (c. xix. p. 98-100, cum Notis Schmincke). The husband must have been too strong for the historian.

98. Besides the massacres and transmigrations, the pain of death was pronounced against the following crimes:—1. The refusal of baptism. 2. The false pretence of baptism. 3. A relapse to idolatry. 4. The murder of a priest or bishop. 5. Human sacrifices. 6. Eating meat in Lent. But every crime might be expiated by baptism or penance (Gaillard, tom. ii. p. 241-247); and the Christian Saxons became the friends and equals of the Franks (Struv. Corpus Hist. Germanicæ p. 133).

99. In this action the famous Rutland, Rolando, Orlando, was slain—cum compluribus aliis. See the truth in Eginhard (c. 9, p. 51-56), and the fable in an ingenious Supplement of M. Gaillard (tom. iii. p. 474). The Spaniards are too proud of a victory which history ascribes to the Gascons, and romance to the Saracens.

100. Yet Schmidt, from the best authorities, represents the interior disorders and oppression of his reign (Hist. des Allemands, tom. ii. p. 45-49).

101. Omnis homo ex suâ proprietate legitimam decimam ad ecclesiam conferat. Experimento enim didicimus, in anno, quo illa valida fames irrepsit,

ebullire vacuas annonas à dæmonibus devoratas, et voces exprobrationis auditas. Such is the decree and assertion of the great Council of Frankfort (Canon xxv. tom. ix. p. 105). Both Selden (Hist. of Tithes; Works, vol. iii. part ii. p. 1146) and Montesquieu (The Spirit of Laws, l. xxxi. c. 12) represent Charlemagne as the first *legal* author of tithes. Such obligations have country gentlemen to his memory!

102. Eginhard (c. 25, p. 119) clearly affirms tentabat et scribere . . . sed parum prospere successit labor præposterus et sero inchoatus. The moderns have perverted and corrected this obvious meaning, and the title of M. Gaillard's Dissertation (tom. iii. p. 247-260) betrays his partiality.

103. See Gaillard, tom. iii. p. 138-176, and Schmidt, tom. ii. p. 121-129.

104. M. Gaillard (tom. iii. p. 372) fixes the true stature of Charlemagne (see a Dissertation of Marquard Freher ad calcem Eginhard, p. 220, etc.) at five feet nine inches of French, about six feet one inch and a fourth English, measure. The romance-writers have increased it to eight feet, and the giant was endowed with matchless strength and appetite: at a single stroke of his good sword *Joyeuse*, he cut asunder a horseman and his horse; at a single repast he devoured a goose, two fowls, a quarter of mutton, etc.

105. See the concise, but correct and original, work of D'Anville (Etats formés en Europe après la Chute de l'Empire Romain en Occident, Paris, 1771, in 4to), whose map includes the empire of Charlemagne; the different parts are illustrated—by Valesius (Notitia Galliarum) for France, Beretti (Dissertatio Chorographica) for Italy, De Marca (Marca Hispanica) for Spain. For the middle geography of Germany I confess myself poor and destitute.

106. After a brief relation of his wars and conquests (Vit. Carol. c. 5-14), Eginhard recapitulates, in a few words (c. 15), the countries subject to his empire. Struvius (Corpus Hist. German. p. 118-149) has inserted in his Notes the texts of the old Chronicles.

107. Of a charter granted to the monastery of Alaon (A.D. 845) by Charles the Bald, which deduces this royal pedigree. I doubt whether some subsequent links of the ninth and tenth centuries are equally firm; yet the whole is approved and defended by M. Gaillard (tom. ii. p. 60-81, 203-206), who affirms that the family of Montesquieo (not of the President de Montesquieu) is descended, in the female line, from Clotaire and Clovis—an innocent pretension!

108. The governors or counts of the Spanish march revolted from Charles the Simple about the year 900; and a poor pittance, the Rousillon, has been recovered in 1642 by the kings of France (Longuerue, Description de la France, tom. i. p. 220-222). Yet the Rousillon contains 188,900 subjects, and annually pays 2,600,000 livres (Necker,

Administration des Finances, tom. i. p. 278, 279); more people, perhaps, and doubtless more money, than the march of Charlemagne.

109. Schmidt, Hist. des Allemands, tom. ii. p. 200, etc.

110. See Giannone, tom. i. p. 374, 375, and the Annals of Muratori.

111. Quot prælia in eo gesta! quantum sanguinis effusum sit! Testatur vacua omni habitatione Pannonia, et locus in quo regia Cagani fuit ita desertus ut ne vestigium quidem humanæ habitationis appar t. Tota in hoc bello Hunnorum nobilitas periit, tota gloria decidit, omnis pecunia et congesti ex longo tempore thesauri direpti sunt. Eginhard, c. 13.

112. The junction of the Rhine and Danube was undertaken only for the service of the Pannonian war (Gaillard, Vie de Charlemagne, tom. ii. p. 312-315). The canal, which would have been only two leagues in length, and of which some traces are still extant in Swabia, was interrupted by excessive rains, military avocations, and superstitious fears (Schæpflin, Hist. de l'Académie des Inscriptions, tom. xviii. p. 256; Molimina fluviorum, etc., jungendorum, p. 59-62).

113. See Eginhard, c. 16; and Gaillard, tom. ii. p. 361-385, who mentions with a loose reference, the intercourse of Charlemagne and Egbert, the emperor's gift of his own sword, and the modest answer of his Saxon disciple. The anecdote, if genuine, would have adorned our English histories.

114. The correspondence is mentioned only in the French annals, and the Orientals are ignorant of the caliph's friendship for the *Christian dog*—a polite appellation, which Harun bestows on the emperor of the Greeks.

115. Gaillard, tom. ii. p. 361-365, 471-476, 492. I have borrowed his judicious remarks on Charlemagne's plan of conquest, and the judicious distinction of his enemies of the first and second *enceinte* (tom. ii. p. 184, 509, etc.).

116. Thegan, the biographer of Lewis, relates this coronation; and Baronius has honestly transcribed it (A.D. 813, No. 13, etc.; see Gaillard, tom. ii. p. 506, 507, 508), howsoever adverse to the claims of the popes. For the series of the Carlovingians, see the historians of France, Italy, and Germany; Pfeffel, Schmidt, Velly, Muratori, and even Voltaire, whose pictures are sometimes just, and always pleasing.

117. He was the son of Otho, the son of Ludolph, in whose favour the duchy of Saxony had been instituted, A.D. 858. Ruotgerus, the biographer of a St. Bruno (Biblioth. Bunavianæ Catalog. tom. iii. vol. ii. p. 679), gives a splendid character of his family. Atavorum atavi usque ad hominum memoriam omnes nobilissimi; nullus in eorum stirpe ignotus, nullus degener facile reperitur (apud Struvium, Corp. Hist. German. p. 216). Yet Gundling (in Henrico Aucupe) is not satisfied of his descent from Witikind.

118. See the treatise of Conringius (de Finibus

Imperii Germanici, Francofurt. 1680, in 4to); he rejects the extravagant and improper scale of the Roman and Carlovingian empires, and discusses with moderation the rights of Germany, her vassals, and her neighbours.

119. The power of custom forces me to number Conrad I. and Henry I., the Fowler, in the list of emperors, a title which was never assumed by those kings of Germany. The Italians, Muratori for instance, are more scrupulous and correct, and only reckon the princes who have been crowned at Rome.

120. Invidiam tamen suscepti nominis (C. P. imperatoribus super hoc indignantibus) magnâ tulit patientiâ, vicitque eorum contumaciam . . . mittendo ad eos crebras legationes, et in epistolis fratres eos appellando. Eginhard, c. 28, p. 128. Perhaps it was on their account that, like Augustus, he affected some reluctance to receive the empire.

121. Theophanes speaks of the coronation and unction of Charles, κάρουλος (Chronograph. p. 399 [tom. i. p. 733, ed. Bonn]), and of his treaty of marriage with Irene (p. 402 [p. 737, ed. Bonn]), which is unknown to the Latins. Gaillard relates his transactions with the Greek empire (tom. ii. p. 446-468).

122. Gaillard very properly observes that this pageant was a farce suitable to children only; but that it was indeed represented in the presence, and for the benefit, of children of a larger growth.

123. Compare in the original texts collected by Pagi (tom. iii. A.D. 812, No. 7, A.D. 824, No. 10, etc.) the contrast of Charlemagne and his son: to the former the ambassadors of Michael (who were indeed disavowed) more suo, id est linguâ Græcâ laudes dixerunt, imperatorem eum et Βασιλέα appellantes; to the latter, Vocato imperatori Francorum, etc.

124. See the epistle, in Paralipomena, of the anonymous writer of Salerno (Script. Ital. tom. ii. pars ii. p. 243-254, c. 93-107), whom Baronius (A.D. 871, No. 51-71) mistook for Erchempert, when he transcribed it in his Annals.

125. Ipse enim vos, non imperatorem, id est Βασιλέα suâ linguâ, sed ob indignationem 'Ρῆγα id est regem nostrâ vocabat (Liutprand, in Legat. in Script. Ital. tom. ii. pars i. p. 479). The pope had exhorted Nicephorus, emperor of the Greeks, to make peace with Otho, the august emperor of the Romans—quæ inscriptio secundum Græcos peccatoria [peccatrix] et temeraria . . . imperatorem inquiunt, universalem Romanorum, Augustum, magnum, solum, Nicephorum (ib. p. 486).

126. The origin and progress of the title of cardinal may be found in Thomassin (Discipline de l'Eglise, tom. i. p. 1261-1298), Muratori (Antiquitat. Italiæ Medii Ævi, tom. vi. Dissert. lxi. p. 159-182), and Mosheim (Institut. Hist. Eccles. p. 345-347), who accurately remarks the forms and changes of the election. The cardinal-bishops, so highly exalted by Peter Damianus, are sunk to a level with the rest of the sacred college.

127. Firmiter jurantes, nunquam se papam electuros aut ordinaturos, præter consensum et electionem Othonis et filii sui (Liutprand, l. vi. c. 6, p. 472). This important concession may either supply or confirm the decree of the clergy and people of Rome, so fiercely rejected by Baronius, Pagi, and Muratori (A.D. 964), and so well defended and explained by St. Marc (Abrégé, tom. ii. p. 808-816, tom. iv. p. 1167-1185). Consult that historical critic, and the Annals of Muratori, for the election and confirmation of each pope.

128. The oppression and vices of the Roman church in the tenth century are strongly painted in the history and legation of Liutprand (see p. 440, 450, 471-476, 479, etc.); and it is whimsical enough to observe Muratori tempering the invectives of Baronius against the popes. But these popes had been chosen, not by the cardinals, but by lay-patrons.

129. The time of Pope Joan (papissa Joanna) is placed somewhat earlier than Theodora or Marozia; and the two years of her imaginary reign are forcibly inserted between Leo IV. and Benedict III. But the contemporary Anastasius indissolubly links the death of Leo and the elevation of Benedict (illico, mox, p. 247); and the accurate chronology of Pagi, Muratori, and Leibnitz fixes both events to the year 857.

130. The advocates for Pope Joan produce one hundred and fifty witnesses, or rather echoes, of the fourteenth, fifteenth, and sixteenth centuries. They bear testimony against themselves and the legend, by multiplying the proof that so curious a story must have been repeated by writers of every description to whom it was known. On those of the ninth and tenth centuries the recent event would have flashed with a double force. Would Photius have spared such a reproach? Could Liutprand have missed such scandal? It is scarcely worth while to discuss the various readings of Martinus Polonus, Sigebert of Gemblours, or even Marianus Scotus; but a most palpable forgery is the passage of Pope Joan which has been foisted into some MSS. and editions of the Roman Anastasius.

131. As false, it deserves that name; but I would not pronounce it incredible. Suppose a famous French chevalier of our own times to have been born in Italy, and educated in the church, instead of the army: her merit or fortune might have raised her to St. Peter's chair; her amours would have been natural; her delivery in the streets unlucky, but not improbable.

132. Till the Reformation the tale was repeated and believed without offence: and Joan's female statue long occupied her place among the popes in the cathedral of Sienna (Pagi, Critica, tom. iii. p. 624-626). She has been annihilated by two learned Protestants, Blondel and Bayle (Dictionnaire Critique, PAPESSE, POLONUS, BLONDEL): but their brethren were scandalised by this equitable and generous criticism. Spanheim and Lenfant attempt to save this poor engine of controversy; and

even Mosheim condescends to cherish some doubt and suspicion (p. 289).

133. Lateranense palatium ... prostibulum meretricum ... Testis omnium gentium, præterquam Romanorum, absentia mulierum, quæ sanctorum apostolorum limina orandi gratiâ timent visere, cum nonnullas ante dies paucos, hunc audierint conjugatas, viduas, virgines vi oppressisse (Liutprand, Hist. l. vi. c. 6, p. 471. See the whole affair of John XII. p. 471–476).

134. A new example of the mischief of equivocation is the *beneficium* (Ducange, tom. i. p. 617, etc.), which the pope conferred on the emperor Frederic I., since the Latin word may signify either a legal fief, or a simple favour, an obligation (we want the word *bienfait*). (See Schmidt, Hist. des Allemands, tom. iii. p. 393–408. Pfeffel, Abrégé Chronologique, tom. i. p. 229, 296, 317, 324, 420, 430, 500, 505, 509, etc.)

135. For the history of the emperors in Rome and Italy, see Sigonius, de Regno Italiæ, Opp. tom. ii., with the Notes of Saxius, and the Annals of Muratori, who might refer more distinctly to the authors of his great collection.

136. See the Dissertation of Le Blanc at the end of his treatise des Monnoyes de France, in which he produces some Roman coins of the French emperors.

137. Romanorum aliquando servi, scilicet Burgundiones, Romanis imperent? . . . Romanæ urbis dignitas ad tantam est stultitiam ducta, ut meretricum etiam imperio pareat? (Liutprand, l. iii. c. 12, p. 450.) Sigonius (l. vi. p. 400) positively affirms the renovation of the consulship; but in the old writers Albericus is more frequently styled princeps Romanorum.

138. Ditmar, p. 354, apud Schmidt, tom. iii. p. 439.

139. This bloody feast is described in Leonine verse in the Pantheon of Godfrey of Viterbo (Script. Ital. tom. vii. p. 436, 437), who flourished towards the end of the twelfth century (Fabricius, Biblioth. lat. med. et infimi Ævi, tom. iii. p. 69, edit. Mansi); but his evidence, which imposed on Sigonius, is reasonably suspected by Muratori (Annali, tom. viii. p. 177).

140. The coronation of the emperor, and some original ceremonies of the tenth century, are preserved in the Panegyric on Berengarius (Script. Ital. tom. ii. pars i. p. 405–414), illustrated by the Notes of Hadrian Valesius and Leibnitz. Sigonius has related the whole process of the Roman expedition, in good Latin, but with some errors of time and fact (l. vii. p. 441–446).

141. In a quarrel at the coronation of Conrad II. Muratori takes leave to observe—doveano ben essere allora indisciplinati, barbari, e *bestiali* i Tedeschi. Annal. tom. viii. p. 368.

142. After boiling away the flesh. The caldrons for that purpose were a necessary piece of travelling furniture; and a German, who was using it for his brother, promised it to a friend, after it should

have been employed for himself (Schmidt, tom. iii. p. 423, 424). The same author observes that the whole Saxon line was extinguished in Italy (tom. ii. p. 440).

143. Otho, bishop of Frisingen, has left an important passage on the Italian cities (l. ii. c. 13, in Script. Ital. tom. vi. p. 707–710): and the rise, progress, and government of these republics are perfectly illustrated by Muratori (Antiquitat. Ital. Medii Ævi, tom. iv. dissert. xlv.–liii. p. 1–675; Annal tom. viii. ix. x.).

144. For these titles, see Selden (Titles of Honour, vol. iii. part i. p. 488), Ducange (Gloss. Latin. tom. ii. p. 140, tom. vi. p. 776), and St. Marc (Abrégé Chronologique, tom. ii. p. 719).

145. The Lombards invented and used the *carocium*, a standard planted on a car or waggon, drawn by a team of oxen (Ducange, tom. ii. p. 194, 195; Muratori, Antiquitat. tom. ii. diss. xxvi. p. 489–493).

146. Gunther Ligurinus, l. viii. 584, et seq. apud Schmidt, tom. iii. p. 399.

147. Solus imperator faciem suam firmavit ut petram (Burcard. de Excidio Mediolani, Script. Ital. tom. vi. p. 917). This volume of Muratori contains the originals of the history of Frederic the First, which must be compared with due regard to the circumstances and prejudices of each German or Lombard writer.

148. For the history of Frederic II. and the House of Swabia at Naples, see Giannone, Istoria Civile, tom. ii. l. xiv.–xix.

149. In the immense labyrinth of the *jus publicum* of Germany, I must either quote one writer or a thousand; and I had rather trust to one faithful guide than transcribe, on credit, a multitude of names and passages. That guide is M. Pfeffel, the author of the best legal and constitutional history that I know of any country (Nouvel Abrégé Chronologique de l'Histoire et du Droit Public d'Allemagne; Paris, 1776, 2 vols. in 4to). His learning and judgment have discerned the most interesting facts; his simple brevity comprises them in a narrow space; his chronological order distributes them under the proper dates; and an elaborate index collects them under their respective heads. To this work, in a less perfect state, Dr. Robertson was gratefully indebted for that masterly sketch which traces even the modern changes of the Germanic body. The Corpus Historiæ Germanicæ of Struvius has been likewise consulted, the more usefully, as that huge compilation is fortified in every page with the original texts.

150. Yet, *personally*, Charles IV. must not be considered as a barbarian. After his education at Paris, he recovered the use of the Bohemian, his native, idiom; and the emperor conversed and wrote with equal facility in French, Latin, Italian, and German (Struvius, p. 615, 616). Petrarch always represents him as a polite and learned prince.

151. Besides the German and Italian historians,

the expedition of Charles IV. is painted in lively and original colours in the curious Mémoires sur la Vie de Petrarque, tom. iii. p. 376-430, by the Abbé de Sade, whose prolixity has never been blamed by any reader of taste and curiosity.

152. See the whole ceremony, in Struvius, p. 629.

153. The republic of Europe, with the pope and emperor at its head, was never represented with more dignity than in the council of Constance. See Lenfant's History of that assembly.

154. Gravina, Origines Juris Civilis, p. 108.

155. Six thousand urns have been discovered of the slaves and freedmen of Augustus and Livia. So minute was the division of office, that one slave was appointed to weigh the wool which was spun by the empress's maids, another for the care of her lapdog, etc. (Camere Sepolchrale, etc., by Bianchini. Extract of his work, in the Bibliotheque Italique, tom. iv. p. 175. His Eloge, by Fontenelle, tom. vi. p. 356.) But these servants were of the same rank, and possibly not more numerous than those of Pollio or Lentulus. They only prove the general riches of the city.

Chapter L

1. As in this and the following chapter I shall display much Arabic learning, I must profess my total ignorance of the Oriental tongues, and my gratitude to the learned interpreters, who have transfused their science into the Latin, French, and English languages. Their collections, versions, and histories, I shall occasionally notice.

2. The geographers of Arabia may be divided into three classes:— 1. The *Greeks* and *Latins*, whose progressive knowledge may be traced in Agatharchides (de Mari Rubro, in Hudson, Geograph. Minor. tom. i.), Diodorus Siculus (tom. i. l. ii. [c. 48-54] p. 159-167; l. iii. [c. 14 *sqq.*] p. 211-216, edit. Wesseling), Strabo (l. xvi. p. 1112-1114 [p. 767-769, ed. Casaub.], from Eratosthenes, p. 1122-1132 [776-785, ed. Casaub.], from Artemidorus), Dionysius (Periegesis, v. 927-969), Pliny (Hist. Natur. v. 12; vi. 32), and Ptolemy (Descript. et Tabulæ Urbium, in Hudson, tom. iii.). 2. The *Arabic writers*, who have treated the subject with the zeal of patriotism or devotion: the extracts of Pocock (Specimen Hist. Arabum, p. 125-128) from the Geography of the Sherif al Edrissi, render us still more dissatisfied with the version or abridgment (p. 24-27, 44-56, 108, etc., 119, etc.) which the Maronites have published under the absurd title of Geographia Nubiensis (Paris, 1619); but the Latin and French translators, Greaves (in Hudson, tom. iii.) and Galland (Voyage de la Palestine par la Roque, p. 265-346), have opened to us the Arabia of Abulfeda, the most copious and correct account of the peninsula, which may be enriched, however, from the Bibliothèque Orientale of D'Herbelot, p. 120, et alibi passim. 3. The *European travellers*, among whom Shaw (p. 438-455) and Niebuhr (Description, 1773; Voyages, tom. i. 1776) deserve an honourable distinction: Busching (Géographie par Berenger, tom. viii. p. 416-510) has compiled with judgment; and D'Anville's Maps (Orbis Veteribus Notus, and 1re Partie de l'Asie) should lie before the reader, with his Géographie Ancienne, tom. ii. p. 208-231.

3. Abulfed. Descript. Arabiæ, p. 1; D'Anville, l'Euphrate et le Tigre, p. 19, 20. It was in this place, the paradise or garden of a satrap, that Xenophon and the Greeks first passed the Euphrates (Anabasis, l. i. c. 10 [c. 4, § 10] p. 29, edit. Wells).

4. Reland has proved, with much superfluous learning, 1. That our Red Sea (the Arabian Gulf) is no more than a part of the *Mare Rubrum*, the Ἐρυθρὰ θαλάσση of the ancients, which was extended to the indefinite space of the Indian Ocean. 2. That the synonymous words ἐρυθρος, αἰθίοψ, allude to the colour of the blacks or negroes (Dissert. Miscell. tom. i. p. 59-117).

5. In the thirty days, or stations, between Cairo and Mecca, there are fifteen destitute of good water. See the route of the Hadjees, in Shaw's Travels, p. 477.

6. The aromatics, especially the *thus* or frankincense, of Arabia, occupy the twelfth book of Pliny. Our great poet (Paradise Lost, l. iv.) introduces, in a simile, the spicy odours that are blown by the north-east wind from the Sabæan coast:—

——Many a league,
    Pleas'd with the grateful scent, old Ocean
    smiles.

(Plin. Hist. Natur. xii. 42.)

7. Agatharchides affirms that lumps of pure gold were found from the size of an olive to that of a nut; that iron was twice, and silver ten times, the value of gold (de Mari Rubro, p. 60 [Hudson, Geogr. M., tom. i.]). These real or imaginary treasures are vanished; and no gold-mines are at present known in Arabia (Niebuhr, Description, p. 124).

8. Consult, peruse, and study the Specimen Historiæ Arabum of Pocock (Oxon. 1650, in 4to). The thirty pages of text and version are extracted from the Dynasties of Gregory Abulpharagius, which Pocock afterwards translated (Oxon. 1663, in 4to): the three hundred and fifty-eight notes form a classic and original work on the Arabian antiquities.

9. Arrian remarks the Ichthyophagi of the coast of Hejaz (Periplus Maris Erythræi, p. 12) and beyond Aden (p. 15 [Hudson, Geogr. M., t. i.]). It seems probable that the shores of the Red Sea (in the largest sense) were occupied by these savages

in the time perhaps of Cyrus; but I can hardly believe that any cannibals were left among the savages in the reign of Justinian (Procop. de Bell. Persic. l. i. c. 19 [t. i. p. 100, ed. Bonn]).

10. See the Specimen Historiæ Arabum of Pocock, p. 2, 5, 86, etc. The journey of M. d'Arvieux, in 1664, to the camp of the emir of Mount Carmel (Voyage de la Palestine, Amsterdam, 1718) exhibits a pleasing and original picture of the life of the Bedoweens, which may be illustrated from Niebuhr (Description de l'Arabie, p. 327–344), and Volney (tom. i. p. 343–385), the last and most judicious of our Syrian travellers.

11. Read (it is no unpleasing task) the incomparable articles of the *Horse* and the *Camel*, in the Natural History of M. de Buffon.

12. For the Arabian horses, see D'Arvieux (p. 159–173) and Niebuhr (p. 142–144). At the end of the thirteenth century the horses of Neged were esteemed sure-footed, those of Yemen strong and serviceable, those of Hejaz most noble. The horses of Europe, the tenth and last class, were generally despised as having too much body and too little spirit (D'Herbelot, Biblioth. Orient. p. 339): their strength was requisite to bear the weight of the knight and his armour.

13. Qui carnibus camelorum vesci solent odii tenaces sunt, was the opinion of an Arabian physician (Pocock, Specimen, p. 88). Mohammed himself, who was fond of milk, prefers the cow, and does not even mention the camel; but the diet of Mecca and Medina was already more luxurious (Gagnier, Vie de Mahomet, tom. iii. p. 404).

14. Yet Marcian of Heraclea (in Periplo, p. 16, in tom. i. Hudson, Minor Geograph.) reckons one hundred and sixty-four towns in Arabia Felix. The size of the towns might be small, the faith of the writer might be large.

15. It is compared by Abulfeda (in Hudson, tom. iii. p. 54) to Damascus, and is still the residence of the Imam of Yemen (Voyages de Niebuhr, tom. i. p. 331–342). Saana is twenty-four parasangs from Dafar (Abulfeda, p. 51) and sixty-eight from Aden (p. 53).

16. Pocock, Specimen, p. 57; Geograph. Nubiensis, p. 52. Mariaba, or Merab, six miles in circumference, was destroyed by the legions of Augustus (Plin. Hist. Nat. vi. 32), and had not revived in the fourteenth century (Abulfed. Descript. Arab. p. 58).

17. The name of *city*, Medina, was appropriated, κατ' ἐξόχην, to Yatreb (the Iatrippa of the Greeks), the seat of the prophet. The distances from Medina are reckoned by Abulfeda in stations, or days' journey of a caravan (p. 15): to Bahrein, fifteen; to Bassora, eighteen; to Cufah, twenty; to Damascus or Palestine, twenty; to Cairo, twenty-five; to Mecca, ten; from Mecca to Saana (p. 52) or Aden, thirty; to Cairo, thirty-one days, or 412 hours (Shaw's Travels, p. 477); which, according to the estimate of D'Anville (Mesures Itinéraires, p. 99), allows about twenty-five English miles for a day's journey. From the land of frankincense (Hadramaut, in Yemen, between Aden and Cape Fartasch) to Gaza, in Syria, Pliny (Hist. Nat. xii. 32) computes sixty-five mansions of camels. These measures may assist fancy and elucidate facts.

18. Our notions of Mecca must be drawn from the Arabians (D'Herbelot, Bibliothèque Orientale, p. 368–371; Pocock, Specimen, p. 125–128; Abulfeda, p. 11–40). As no unbeliever is permitted to enter the city, our travellers are silent; and the short hints of Thevenot (Voyages du Levant, part i. 490) are taken from the suspicious mouth of an African renagado. Some Persians counted 6000 houses (Chardin, tom. iv. p. 167).

19. Strabo, l. xvi. p. 1110 [p. 766, ed. Casaub.]. See one of these salt houses near Bassora, in D'Herbelot, Biblioth. Orient. p. 6.

20. Mirum dictû ex innumeris populis pars æqua in *commerciis* aut in latrociniis degit (Plin. Hist. Nat. vi. 32). See Sale's Koran, Sûra. cvi. p. 503; Pocock, Specimen, p. 2; D'Herbelot, Biblioth. Orient. p. 361; Prideaux's Life of Mahomet, p. 5; Gagnier, Vie de Mahomet, tom. i. p. 72, 120, 126, etc.

21. A nameless doctor (Universal Hist. vol. xx. octavo edition) has formerly *demonstrated* the truth of Christianity by the independence of the Arabs. A critic, besides the exceptions of fact, might dispute the meaning of the text (Gen. xvi. 12), the extent of the application, and the foundation of the pedigree.

22. It was subdued, A.D. 1173, by a brother of the great Saladin, who founded a dynasty of Curds or Ayoubites (Guignes, Hist. des Huns, tom. i. p. 425; D'Herbelot, p. 477).

23. By the lieutenant of Soliman I. (A.D. 1538) and Selim II. (1568). See Cantemir's Hist. of the Othman Empire, p. 201, 221. The pasha, who resided at Saana, commanded twenty-one beys; but no revenue was ever remitted to the Porte (Marsigli, Stato Militare dell' Imperio Ottomanno, p. 124), and the Turks were expelled about the year 1630 (Niebuhr, p. 167, 168).

24. Of the Roman province, under the name of Arabia and the third Palestine, the principal cities were Bostra and Petra, which dated their era from the year 105, when they were subdued by Palma, a lieutenant of Trajan (Dion Cassius, l. lxviii. [c. 14]). Petra was the capital of the Nabathæans, whose name is derived from the eldest of the sons of Ismael (Gen. xxv. 12, etc., with the Commentaries of Jerom, Le Clerc, and Calmet). Justinian relinquished a palm country of ten days' journey to the south of Ælah (Procop. de Bell. Persic. l. i. c. 19 [t. i. p. 101, ed. Bonn]), and the Romans maintained a centurion and a custom-house (Arrian in Periplo Maris Erythræi, p. 11, in Hudson, tom. i.) at a place (λεύκη κώμη, Pagus Albus, Hawara) in the territory of Medina (D'Anville, Mémoire sur l'Egypte, p. 243). These real possessions, and some naval inroads of Trajan (Peripl. p. 14, 15), are

magnified by history and medals into the Roman conquest of Arabia.

25. Niebuhr (Description de l'Arabie, p. 302, 303, 329–331) affords the most recent and authentic intelligence of the Turkish empire in Arabia.

26. Diodorus Siculus (tom. ii. l. xix. [c. 94] p. 390–393, edit. Wesseling) has clearly exposed the freedom of the Nabathæan Arabs, who resisted the arms of Antigonus and his son.

27. Strabo, l. xvi. p. 1127–1129 [p. 781 sq. ed. Casaub.]; Plin. Hist. Natur. vi. 32. Ælius Gallus landed near Medina, and marched near a thousand miles into the part of Yemen between Mareb and the ocean. The non ante devictis Sabææ regibus (Od. i. 29) and the intacti Arabum thesauri (Od. iii. 24) of Horace, attest the virgin purity of Arabia.

28. See the imperfect history of Yemen in Pocock, Specimen, p. 55–66; of Hira, p. 66–74; of Gassan, p. 75–78; as far as it could be known or preserved in the time of ignorance.

29. The Σαρακηνικὰ φῦλα, μυριάδες ταῦτα, καὶ τὸ πλεῖστον αὐτῶν ἐρημονόμοι καὶ ἀδέσποτοι, are described by Menander (Excerpt. Legation. p. 149 [ed. Par.; p.375, ed. Bonn]), Procopius (de Bell. Persic. l. i. c. 17, 19; l. ii. c. 10), and in the most lively colours by Ammianus Marcellinus (l. xiv. c. 4), who had spoken of them as early as the reign of Marcus.

30. The name which, used by Ptolemy and Pliny in a more confined, by Ammianus and Procopius in a larger, sense, has been derived, ridiculously, from Sarah, the wife of Abraham, obscurely from the village of Saraka (μετὰ τοὺς Ναβαταίους, Stephan. de Urbibus [s. v. Σάρακα]), more plausibly from the Arabic words, which signify a thievish character, or Oriental situation (Hottinger, Hist. Oriental. l. i. c. i. p. 7, 8; Pocock, Specimen, p. 33–35; Asseman. Biblioth. Orient. tom. iv. p. 567). Yet the last and most popular of these etymologies is refuted by Ptolemy (Arabia, p. 2, 18, in Hudson, tom. iii.), who expressly remarks the western and southern position of the Saracens, then an obscure tribe on the borders of Egypt. The appellation cannot therefore allude to any national character; and, since it was imposed by strangers, it must be found, not in the Arabic, but in a foreign language.

31. Saraceni . . . mulieres aiunt in eos regnare (Expositio totius Mundi, p. 3, in Hudson, tom. iii.). The reign of Mavia is famous in ecclesiastical story. Pocock, Specimen, p. 69, 83.

32. Ἐκ τῶν βασιλείων μὴ ἐξελθεῖν is the report of Agatharchides (de Mari Rubro, p. 63, 64, in Hudson, tom. i.), Diodorus Siculus (tom. i. l. iii. c. 47, p. 215), and Strabo (l. xvi. p. 1124 [p. 778, ed. Casaub.]). But I much suspect that this is one of the popular tales, or extraordinary accidents, which the credulity of travellers so often transforms into a fact, a custom, and a law.

33. Non gloriabantur antiquitus Arabes, nisi gladio, hospite, et eloquentiâ (Sephadius apud Pocock, Specimen, p. 161, 162). This gift of speech they shared only with the Persians; and the sententious Arabs would probably have disdained the simple and sublime logic of Demosthenes.

34. I must remind the reader that D'Arvieux, D'Herbelot, and Niebuhr represent in the most lively colours the manners and government of the Arabs, which are illustrated by many incidental passages in the Life of Mahomet.

35. Observe the first chapter of Job, and the long wall of 1500 stadia which Sesostris built from Pelusium to Heliopolis (Diodor. Sicul. tom. i. l. i. [c. 57] p. 67). Under the name of Hycsos, the shepherd kings, they had formerly subdued Egypt (Marsham, Canon. Chron. p. 98–163, etc.).

36. Or, according to another account, 1200 (D'Herbelot, Bibliothèque Orientale, p. 75): the two historians who wrote of the Ayam al Arab, the battles of the Arabs, lived in the ninth and tenth century. The famous war of Dahes and Gabrah was occasioned by two horses, lasted forty years, and ended in a proverb (Pocock, Specimen, p. 48).

37. The modern theory and practice of the Arabs in the revenge of murder are described by Niebuhr (Description, p. 26–31). The harsher features of antiquity may be traced in the Koran, c. 2, p. 20, c. 17, p. 230, with Sale's Observations.

38. Procopius (de Bell. Persic. l. i. c. 16) places the two holy months about the summer solstice. The Arabians consecrate four months of the year—the first, seventh, eleventh, and twelfth; and pretend that, in a long series of ages, the truce was infringed only four or six times (Sale's Preliminary Discourse, p. 147–150, and Notes on the ninth chapter of the Koran, p. 154, etc.; Casiri, Biblioth. Hispano-Arabica, tom. ii. p. 20, 21).

39. Arrian, in the second century, remarks (in Periplo Maris Erythræi, p. 12 [Hudson, Geog. M., t. i.]) the partial or total difference of the dialects of the Arabs. Their language and letters are copiously treated by Pocock (Specimen, p. 150–154), Casiri (Biblioth. Hispano-Arabica, tom. i. p. 1, 83, 292; tom. ii. p. 25, etc.), and Niebuhr (Description de l'Arabie, p. 72–86), I pass slightly; I am not fond of repeating words like a parrot.

40. A familiar tale in Voltaire's Zadig (le Chien et le Cheval) is related to prove the natural sagacity of the Arabs (D'Herbelot, Biblioth. Orient. p. 120, 121; Gagnier, Vie de Mahomet, tom. i. p. 37–46); but D'Arvieux, or rather La Roque (Voyage de Palestine, p. 92), denies the boasted superiority of the Bedoweens. The one hundred and sixty-nine sentences of Ali (translated by Ockley, London, 1718) afford a just and favourable specimen of Arabian wit.

41. Pocock (Specimen, p. 158–161) and Casiri (Biblioth. Hispano-Arabica, tom. i. p. 48, 84, etc., 119, tom. ii. p. 17, etc.) speak of the Arabian poets before Mohammed: the seven poems of the Caaba have been published in English by Sir William Jones; but his honourable mission to India has

deprived us of his own notes, far more interesting than the obscure and obsolete text.

42. Sale's Preliminary Discourse, p. 29, 30.

43. D'Herbelot, Biblioth. Orient. p. 458; Gagnier, Vie de Mahomet, tom. iii. p. 118; Caab and Hesnus (Pocock, Specimen, p. 43, 46, 48) were likewise conspicuous for their liberality; and the latter is elegantly praised by an Arabian poet: "Videbis eum cum accesseris exultantem, ac si dares illi quod ab illo petis."

44. Whatever can now be known of the idolatry of the ancient Arabians may be found in Pocock (Specimen, p. 89–136, 163, 164). His profound erudition is more clearly and concisely interpreted by Sale (Preliminary Discourse, p. 14–24); and Assemanni (Biblioth. Orient. tom. iv. p. 580–590) has added some valuable remarks.

45. Ἱερὸν ἁγιώτατον ἴδρυται τιμώμενον ὑπὸ πάντων Ἀράβων περιττότερον (Diodor. Sicul. tom. i. l. iii. [c. 43] p. 211). The character and position are so correctly apposite, that I am surprised how this curious passage should have been read without notice or application. Yet this famous temple had been overlooked by Agatharchides (de Mari Rubro, p. 58, in Hudson, tom. i.), whom Diodorus copies in the rest of the description. Was the Sicilian more knowing than the Egyptian? Or was the Caaba built between the years of Rome 650 and 746, the dates of their respective histories? (Dodwell, in Dissert. ad tom. i. Hudson. p. 72; Fabricius, Biblioth. Græc. tom. ii. p. 770).

46. Pocock, Specimen, p. 60, 61. From the death of Mohammed we ascend to 68, from his birth to 129, years before the Christian era. The veil or curtain, which is now of silk and gold, was no more than a piece of Egyptian linen (Abulfeda, in Vit. Mohammed. c. 6, p. 14 [ed. Gagnier, Oxon. 1723]).

47. The original plan of the Caaba (which is servilely copied in Sale, the Universal History, etc.) was a Turkish draught, which Reland (de Religione Mohammedicâ, p. 113–123) has corrected and explained from the best authorities. For the description and legend of the Caaba, consult Pocock (Specimen, p. 115–122), the Bibliothèque Orientale of D'Herbelot (Caaba, Hagiar, Zemzem, etc.), and Sale (Preliminary Discourse, p. 114–122).

48. Cosa [Kussai], the fifth ancestor of Mohammed, must have usurped the Caaba A.D. 440; but the story is differently told by Jannabi (Gagnier, Vie de Mahomet, tom. i. p. 65–69) and by Abulfeda (in Vit. Moham. c. 6, p. 13).

49. In the second century, Maximus of Tyre attributes to the Arabs the worship of a stone— Ἀράβιοι σέβουσι μὲν, ὄντινα δὲ οὐκ οἶδα, τὸ δὲ ἄγαλμα [ὃ] εἶδον λίθος ἦν τετράγωνος (Dissert. viii. tom. i. p. 142, edit. Reiske); and the reproach is furiously re-echoed by the Christians (Clemens Alex. in Protreptico, p. 40 [ed. Oxon. 1715]; Arnobius contra Gentes, l. vi. p. 246 [t. i. p. 196, ed. Lugd. B. 1651]). Yet these stones were no other than the βαίτυλα of Syria and Greece, so renowned in sacred and profane antiquity (Euseb. Præp. Evangel. l. i. p. 37; Marsham, Canon. Chron. p. 54–56).

50. The two horrid subjects of Ἀνδροθυσία and Παιδοθυσία are accurately discussed by the learned Sir John Marsham (Canon. Chron. p. 76–78, 301–304). Sanchoniatho derives the Phœnician sacrifices from the example of Chronus; but we are ignorant whether Chronus lived before or after Abraham, or indeed whether he lived at all.

51. Κατ' ἐτὸς ἕκαστον παῖδα ἔθυον, is the reproach of Porphyry; but he likewise imputes to the Romans the same barbarous custom, which, A.U.C. 657, had been finally abolished. Dumætha, Daumat al Gendal, is noticed by Ptolemy (Tabul. p. 37, Arabia, p. 9–29) and Abulfeda (p. 57); and may be found in D'Anville's maps, in the mid-desert between Chaibar and Tadmor.

52. Procopius (de Bell. Persico, l. ii. c. 28), Evagrius (l. vi. c. 21), and Pocock (Specimen, p. 72, 86) attest the human sacrifices of the Arabs in the sixth century. The danger and escape of Abdallah is a tradition rather than a fact (Gagnier, Vie de Mahomet, tom. i. p. 82–84).

53. Suillis carnibus abstinent, says Solinus (Polyhistor. c. 33), who copies Pliny (l. viii. c. 78) in the strange supposition that hogs cannot live in Arabia. The Egyptians were actuated by a natural and superstitious horror for that unclean beast (Marsham, Canon. p. 205). The old Arabians likewise practised, post coitum, the rite of ablution (Herodot. l. i. c. 189), which is sanctified by the Mohammedan law (Reland, p. 75, etc.; Chardin, or rather the Mollah of Shah Abbas, tom. iv. p. 71, etc.).

54. The Mohammedan doctors are not fond of the subject; yet they hold circumcision necessary to salvation, and even pretend that Mohammed was miraculously born without a foreskin (Pocock, Specimen, p. 319, 320; Sale's Preliminary Discourse, p. 106, 107).

55. Diodorus Siculus (tom. i. l. ii. [c. 29 sqq.] p. 142–145) has cast on their religion the curious but superficial glance of a Greek. Their astronomy would be far more valuable; they had looked through the telescope of reason, since they could doubt whether the sun were in the number of the planets or of the fixed stars.

56. Simplicius (who quotes Porphyry), de Cœlo, l. ii. com. xlvi. p. 123, lin. 18, apud Marsham, Canon. Chron. p. 474, who doubts the fact, because it is adverse to his systems. The earliest date of the Chaldæan observations is the year 2234 before Christ. After the conquest of Babylon by Alexander, they were communicated, at the request of Aristotle, to the astronomer Hipparchus. What a moment in the annals of science!

57. Pocock (Specimen, p. 138–146), Hottinger (Hist. Orient. p. 162–203), Hyde (de Religione Vet. Persarum, p. 124, 128, etc.), D'Herbelot (Sabi, p. 725, 726), and Sale (Preliminary Discourse, p. 14, 15), rather excite than gratify our

curiosity; and the last of these writers confounds Sabianism with the primitive religion of the Arabs.

58. D'Anville (l'Euphrate et le Tigre, p. 130–147) will fix the position of these ambiguous Christians; Assemannus (Biblioth. Oriental. tom. iv. p. 607–614) may explain their tenets. But it is a slippery task to ascertain the creed of an ignorant people, afraid and ashamed to disclose their secret traditions.

59. The Magi were fixed in the province of Bahrein (Gagnier, Vie de Mahomet, tom. iii. p. 114), and mingled with the old Arabians (Pocock, Specimen, p. 146–150).

60. The state of the Jews and Christians in Arabia is described by Pocock from Sharestani, etc. (Specimen, p. 60, 134, etc.), Hottinger (Hist. Orient. p. 212–238), D'Herbelot (Biblioth. Orient. p. 474–476), Basnage (Hist. des Juifs, tom. vii. p. 185; tom. viii. p. 280), and Sale (Preliminary Discourse, p. 22, etc., 33, etc.).

61. In their offerings it was a maxim to defraud God for the profit of the idol—not a more potent, but a more irritable, patron (Pocock, Specimen, p. 108, 109).

62. Our versions now extant, whether Jewish or Christian, appear more recent than the Koran; but the existence of a prior translation may be fairly inferred—1. From the perpetual practice of the synagogue, of expounding the Hebrew lesson by a paraphrase in the vulgar tongue of the country. 2. From the analogy of the Armenian, Persian, Æthiopic versions expressly quoted by the fathers of the fifth century, who assert that the Scriptures were translated into all the barbaric languages (Walton, Prolegomena ad Biblia Polyglot, p. 34, 93–97; Simon, Hist. Critique du V. et du N. Testament, tom. i. p. 180, 181, 282–286, 293, 305, 306, tom. iv. p. 206).

63. In eo conveniunt omnes, ut plebeio vilique genere ortum, etc. (Hottinger, Hist. Orient. p. 136). Yet Theophanes, the most ancient of the Greeks, and the father of many a lie, confesses that Mohammed was of the race of Ismael, ἐκ μιᾶς γενικωτάτης φυλῆς (Chronograph. p. 277 [ed. Par.; tom. i. p. 512, ed. Bonn]).

64. Abulfeda (in Vit. Mohammed. c. 1, 2) and Gagnier (Vie de Mahomet, p. 25–97) describe the popular and approved genealogy of the prophet. At Mecca, I would not dispute its authenticity: at Lausanne, I will venture to observe—1. That, from Ismael to Mohammed, a period of 2500 years, they reckon thirty, instead of seventy-five, generations. 2. That the modern Bedoweens are ignorant of their history, and careless of their pedigree (Voyage de D'Arvieux, p. 100, 103).

65. The seed of this history, or fable, is contained in the cv. chapter of the Koran; and Gagnier (in Præfat. ad Vit. Moham. p. 18, etc.) has translated the historical narrative of Abulfeda, which may be illustrated from D'Herbelot (Biblioth. Orientale, p. 12) and Pocock (Specimen, p. 64). Prideaux (Life of Mahomet, p. 48) calls it a

lie of the coinage of Mohammed; but Sale (Koran, p. 501–503), who is half a Musulman, attacks the inconsistent faith of the Doctor for believing the miracles of the Delphic Apollo. Maracci (Alcoran, tom. i. part ii. p. 14; tom. ii. p. 823) ascribes the miracle to the devil, and extorts from the Mohammedans the confession that God would not have defended against the Christians the idols of the Caaba.

66. The safest eras of Abulfeda (in Vit. c. i. p. 2), of Alexander, or the Greeks, 882, of Bocht Naser, or Nabonassar, 1316, equally lead us to the year 569. The old Arabian calendar is too dark and uncertain to support the Benedictines (Art de vérifier les Dates, p. 15), who, from the day of the month and week, deduce a new mode of calculation, and remove the birth of Mohammed to the year of Christ 570, the 10th of November. Yet this date would agree with the year 882 of the Greeks, which is assigned by Elmacin (Hist. Saracen. p. 5) and Abulpharagius (Dynast. p. 101; and Errata, Pocock's version). While we refine our chronology, it is possible that the illiterate prophet was ignorant of his own age.

67. [Mohammed's father died two months before his birth.]

68. I copy the honourable testimony of Abu Taleb to his family and nephew. Laus Deo, qui nos a stirpe Abrahami et semine Ismaelis constituit, et nobis regionem sacram dedit, et nos judices hominibus statuit. Porro Mohammed filius Abdollahi nepotis mei (nepos meus) quo cum [non] ex æquo librabitur e Koraishidis quispiam cui non præponderaturus est bonitate, et excellentiâ, et intellectû, et gloriâ, et acumine, etsi opum inops fuerit (et certe opes umbra transiens sunt et depositum quod reddi debet), desiderio Chadijæ filiæ Chowailedi tenetur, et illa vicissim ipsius, quicquid autem dotis vice petieritis, ego in me suscipiam (Pocock, Specimen, e septimâ parte libri Ebn Hamduni [p. 171]).

69. The private life of Mohammed, from his birth to his mission, is preserved by Abulfeda (in Vit. c. 3–7), and the Arabian writers of genuine or apocryphal note, who are alleged by Hottinger (Hist. Orient. p. 204–211), Maracci (tom. i. p. 10–14), and Gagnier (Vie de Mahomet, tom. i. p. 97–134).

70. Abulfeda, in Vit. c. 65, 66; Gagnier, Vie de Mahomet, tom. iii. p. 272–289; the best traditions of the person and conversation of the prophet are derived from Ayesha, Ali, and Abu Horaira (Gagnier, tom. ii. p. 267; Ockley's Hist. of the Saracens, vol. ii. p. 149), surnamed the Father of a Cat, who died in the year 59 of the Hegira.

71. Those who believe that Mohammed could read or write are incapable of reading what is written, with another pen, in the Suras, or chapters of the Koran, vii. xxix. xcvi. These texts, and the tradition of the Sonna, are admitted, without doubt, by Abulfeda (in Vit. c. 7), Gagnier (Not. ad Abulfed. p. 15), Pocock (Specimen, p. 151),

Reland (de Religione Mohammedicâ, p. 236), and Sale (Preliminary Discourse, p. 42). Mr. White, almost alone, denies the ignorance, to accuse the imposture, of the prophet. His arguments are far from satisfactory. Two short trading journeys to the fairs of Syria were surely not sufficient to infuse a science so rare among the citizens of Mecca: it was not in the cool, deliberate act of a treaty that Mohammed would have dropped the mask; nor can any conclusion be drawn from the words of disease and delirium. The *lettered* youth, before he aspired to the prophetic character, must have often exercised, in private life, the arts of reading and writing; and his first converts, of his own family, would have been the first to detect and upbraid his scandalous hypocrisy (White's Sermons, p. 203, 204, Notes, p. xxxvi.-xxxviii.).

72. The Count de Boulainvilliers (Vie de Mahomet, p. 202-228) leads his Arabian pupil, like the Telemachus of Fénelon, or the Cyrus of Ramsay. His journey to the court of Persia is probably a fiction, nor can I trace the origin of his exclamation, "Les Grecs sont pourtant des hommes." The two Syrian journeys are expressed by almost all the Arabian writers, both Mohammedans and Christians (Gagnier, ad. Abulfed. p. 10).

73. I am not at leisure to pursue the fables or conjectures which name the strangers accused or suspected by the infidels of Mecca (Koran, c. 16, p. 223, c. 35, p. 297, with Sale's Remarks; Prideaux's Life of Mahomet, p. 22-27; Gagnier, Not. ad Abulfed. p. 11, 74; Maracci, tom. ii. p. 400). Even Prideaux has observed that the transaction must have been secret, and that the scene lay in the heart of Arabia.

74. Abulfeda in Vit. c. 7, p. 15; Gagnier, tom. i. p. 133, 135. The situation of Mount Hera is remarked by Abulfeda (Geograph. Arab. p. 4). Yet Mohammed had never read of the cave of Egeria, ubi nocturnæ Numa constituebat amicæ, of the Idæan mount, where Minos conversed with Jove, etc.

75. Koran, c. 9, p. 153. Al Beidawi, and the other commentators quoted by Sale, adhere to the charge; but I do not understand that it is coloured by the most obscure or absurd tradition of the Talmudists.

76. Hottinger, Hist. Orient. p. 225-228. The Collyridian heresy was carried from Thrace to Arabia by some women, and the name was borrowed from the κόλλυρις, or cake, which they offered to the goddess. This example, that of Beryllus bishop of Bostra (Euseb. Hist. Eccles. l. vi. c. 33), and several others, may excuse the reproach, Arabia hæreseων ferax.

77. The three gods in the Koran (c. 4, p. 81, c. 5, p. 92) are obviously directed against our Catholic mystery: but the Arabic commentators understand them of the Father, the Son, and the Virgin Mary, an heretical Trinity, maintained, as it is said, by some barbarians at the Council of Nice (Eutych. Annal. tom. i. p. 440). But the existence of the *Marianites* is denied by the candid Beausobre (Hist. de Manichéisme, tom. i. p. 532); and he derives the mistake from the word *Rouah*, the Holy Ghost, which in some Oriental tongues is of the feminine gender, and is figuratively styled the mother of Christ in the gospel of the Nazarenes.

78. This train of thought is philosophically exemplified in the character of Abraham, who opposed in Chaldæa the first introduction of idolatry (Koran, c. 6, p. 106; D'Herbelot, Biblioth. Orient. p. 13).

79. See the Koran, particularly the second (p. 30), the fifty-seventh (p. 437), the fifty-eighth (p. 441) chapters, which proclaim the omnipotence of the Creator.

80. The most orthodox creeds are translated by Pocock (Specimen, p. 274, 284-292), Ockley (Hist. of the Saracens, vol. ii. p. lxxxii.-xcv.), Reland (de Religion. Moham. l. i. p. 7-13), and Chardin (Voyages en Perse, tom. iv. p. 4-28). The great truth, that God is without similitude, is foolishly criticised by Maracci (Alcoran, tom. i. part iii. p. 87-94), because he made man after his own image.

81. Reland, de Relig. Moham. l. i. p. 17-47; Sale's Preliminary Discourse, p. 73-76; Voyages de Chardin, tom. iv. p. 28-37 and 37-47, for the Persian addition, "Ali is the Vicar of God!" Yet the precise number of prophets is not an article of faith.

82. For the apocryphal books of Adam, see Fabricius, Codex Pseudepigraphus V. T. p. 27-29; of Seth, p. 154-157; of Enoch, p. 160-219. But the book of Enoch is consecrated, in some measure, by the quotation of the apostle St. Jude; and a long legendary fragment is alleged by Syncellus and Scaliger.

83. The seven precepts of Noah are explained by Marsham (Canon. Chronicus, p. 154-180) who adopts, on this occasion, the learning and credulity of Selden.

84. The articles of *Adam, Noah, Abraham, Moses,* etc., in the Bibliothèque of D'Herbelot, are gaily bedecked with the fanciful legends of the Mohammedans, who have built on the groundwork of Scripture and the Talmud.

85. Koran, c. 7, p. 128, etc., c. 10, p. 173, etc.; D'Herbelot, p. 647, etc.

86. Koran, c. 3, p. 40, c. 4, p. 80; D'Herbelot, p. 399, etc.

87. See the gospel of St. Thomas, or of the Infancy, in the Codex Apocryphus N. T. of Fabricius, who collects the various testimonies concerning it (p. 128-158). It was published in Greek by Cotelier, and in Arabic by Sike, who thinks our present copy more recent than Mohammed. Yet his quotations agree with the original about the speech of Christ in his cradle, his living birds of clay, etc. (*Sike,* c. i. p. 168, 169, c. 36, p. 198, 199, c. 46, p. 206; *Cotelier,* c. 2, p. 160, 161).

88. It is darkly hinted in the Koran (c. 3, p. 39), and more clearly explained by the tradition of the

Sonnites (Sale's Note, and Maracci, tom. ii. p. 112). In the twelfth century, the immaculate conception was condemned by St. Bernard as a presumptuous novelty (Fra Paolo, Istoria del Concilio di Trento, l. ii.).

89. See the Koran, c. 3, v. 53, and c. 4, v. 156, of Maracci's edition. Deus est præstantissimus dolose agentium (an odd praise) . . . nec crucifixerunt eum, sed objecta est eis similitudo: an expression that may suit with the system of the Docetes; but the commentators believe (Maracci, tom. ii. p. 113-115, 173; Sale, p. 42, 43, 79) that another man, a friend or an enemy, was crucified in the likeness of Jesus; a fable which they had read in the gospel of St. Barnabas, and which had been started as early as the time of Irenæus, by some Ebionite heretics (Beausobre, Hist. du Manichéisme, tom. ii. p. 25; Mosheim de Reb. Christ. p. 353).

90. This charge is obscurely urged in the Koran (c. 3, p. 45); but neither Mohammed nor his followers are sufficiently versed in languages and criticism to give any weight or colour to their suspicions. Yet the Arians and Nestorians could relate some stories, and the illiterate prophet might listen to the bold assertions of the Manichæans. See Beausobre, tom. i. p. 291-305.

91. Among the prophecies of the Old and New Testament, which are perverted by the fraud or ignorance of the Musulmans, they apply to the prophet the promise of the *Paraclete*, or Comforter, which had been already usurped by the Montanists and Manichæans (Beausobre, Hist. Critique du Manichéisme, tom. i. p. 263, etc.); and the easy change of letters, περικλυτὸς for παράκλητος, affords the etymology of the name of Mohammed (Maracci, tom. i. part i. p. 15-28).

92. For the Koran, see D'Herbelot, p. 85-88; Maracci, tom. i. in Vit. Mohammed. p. 32-45; Sale, Preliminary Discourse, p. 56-70.

93. Koran, c. 17, v. 89. In Sale, p. 235, 236. In Maracci, p. 410.

94. Yet a sect of Arabians was persuaded that it might be equalled or surpassed by a human pen (Pocock, Specimen, p. 221, etc.); and Maracci (the polemic is too hard for the translator) derides the rhyming affectation of the most applauded passage (tom. i. part ii. p. 69-75).

95. Colloquia (whether real or fabulous) in mediâ Arabiâ atque ab Arabibus habita (Lowth, de Poesi Hebræorum Prælect. xxxii. xxxiii. xxxiv. with his German editor Michaelis, Epimetron iv.). Yet Michaelis (p. 671-673) has detected many Egyptian images, the elephantiasis, papyrus, Nile, crocodile, etc. The language is ambiguously styled *Arabico-Hebræa*. The resemblance of the sister dialects was much more visible in their childhood than in their mature age (Michaelis, p. 682; Schultens, in Præfat. Job).

96. Al Bochari died A.H. 224. See D'Herbelot, p. 208, 416, 827; Gagnier, Not. ad Abulfed. c. 19, p. 33.

97. See, more remarkably, Koran, c. 2, 6, 12, 13, 17. Prideaux (Life of Mahomet, p. 18, 19) has confounded the impostor. Maracci, with a more learned apparatus, has shown that the passages which deny his miracles are clear and positive (Alcoran, tom. i. part ii. p. 7-12), and those which seem to assert them are ambiguous and insufficient (p. 12-22).

98. See the Specimen Hist. Arabum, the text of Abulpharagius, p. 17; the notes of Pocock, p. 187-190; D'Herbelot, Bibliothèque Orientale, p. 76, 77; Voyages de Chardin, tom. iv. p. 200-203; Maracci (Alcoran, tom. i. p. 22-64) has most laboriously collected and confuted the miracles and prophecies of Mohammed, which, according to some writers, amount to three thousand.

99. The nocturnal journey is circumstantially related by Abulfeda (in Vit. Mohammed. c. 19, p. 33), who wishes to think it a vision; by Prideaux (p. 31-40), who aggravates the absurdities; and by Gagnier (tom. i. p. 252-343), who declares, from the zealous Al Jannabi, that to deny this journey is to disbelieve the Koran. Yet the Koran, without naming either heaven, or Jerusalem, or Mecca, has only dropped a mysterious hint: Laus illi qui transtulit servum suum ab oratorio Haram ad oratorium remotissimum (Koran, c. 17, v. 1; in Maracci, tom. ii. p. 407; for Sale's version is more licentious). A slender basis for the aërial structure of tradition.

100. In the prophetic style, which uses the present or past for the future, Mohammed had said, Approprinquavit hora et scissa est luna (Koran, c. 54, v. 1; in Maracci, tom. ii. p. 688). This figure of rhetoric has been converted into a fact, which is said to be attested by the most respectable eyewitnesses (Maracci, tom. ii. p. 690). The festival is still celebrated by the Persians (Chardin, tom. iv. p. 201); and the legend is tediously spun out by Gagnier (Vie de Mahomet, tom. i. p. 183-234), on the faith, as it should seem, of the credulous Al Jannabi. Yet a Mohammedan doctor has arraigned the credit of the principal witness (apud Pocock, Specimen, p. 187); the best interpreters are content with the simple sense of the Koran (Al Beidawi, apud Hottinger, Hist. Orient. l. ii. p. 302), and the silence of Abulfeda is worthy of a prince and a philosopher.

101. Abulpharagius, in Specimen Hist. Arab. p. 17; and his scepticism is justified in the notes of Pocock, p. 190-194, from the purest authorities.

102. The most authentic account of these precepts, pilgrimage, prayer, fasting, alms, and ablutions, is extracted from the Persian and Arabian theologians by Maracci (Prodrom. part iv. p. 9-24), Reland (in his excellent treatise de Religione Mohammedicâ, Utrecht, 1717, p. 67-123), and Chardin (Voyages en Perse, tom. iv. p. 47-195). Maracci is a partial accuser; but the jeweller, Chardin, had the eyes of a philosopher; and Reland, a judicious student, had travelled over the East in his closet at Utrecht. The fourteenth letter

of Tournefort (Voyage du Levant, tom. ii. p. 325–360, in octavo) describes what he had seen of the religion of the Turks.

103. Mohammed (Sale's Koran, c. 9, p. 153) reproaches the Christians with taking their priests and monks for their lords, besides God. Yet Maracci (Prodromus, part iii. p. 69, 70) excuses the worship, especially of the pope, and quotes, from the Koran itself, the case of Eblis, or Satan, who was cast from heaven for refusing to adore Adam.

104. Koran, c. 5, p. 94, and Sale's note, which refers to the authority of Jallaloddin and Al Beidawi. D'Herbelot declares the Mohammed condemned *la vie religieuse*, and that the first swarms of fakirs, dervises, etc., did not appear till after the year 300 of the Hegira (Biblioth. Orient. p. 292, 718).

105. See the double prohibition (Koran, c. 2, p. 25, c. 5, p. 94); the one in the style of a legislator, the other in that of a fanatic. The public and private motives of Mohammed are investigated by Prideaux (Life of Mahomet, p. 62, 64) and Sale (Preliminary Discourse, p. 124).

106. The jealousy of Maracci (Prodromus, part iv. p. 33) prompts him to enumerate the more liberal alms of the Catholics of Rome. Fifteen great hospitals are open to many thousand patients and pilgrims; fifteen hundred maidens are annually portioned; fifty-six charity-schools are founded for both sexes; one hundred and twenty confraternities relieve the wants of their brethren, etc. The benevolence of London is still more extensive; but I am afraid that much more is to be ascribed to the humanity than to the religion of the people.

107. See Herodotus (l. ii. c. 123) and our learned countryman Sir John Marsham (Canon. Chronicus, p. 46). The Ἅδης of the same writer (p. 254–274) is an elaborate sketch of the infernal regions, as they were painted by the fancy of the Egyptians and Greeks, of the poets and philosophers of antiquity.

108. The Koran (c. 2, p. 259, etc.; of Sale, p. 32; of Maracci, p. 97) relates an ingenious miracle, which satisfied the curiosity and confirmed the faith of Abraham.

109. The candid Reland has demonstrated that Mohammed damns all unbelievers (de Religione Moham. p. 128–142); that devils will not be finally saved (p. 196–199); that paradise will not *solely* consist of corporeal delights (p. 199–205); and that women's souls are immortal (p. 205–209).

110. Al Beidawi, apud Sale, Koran, c. 9, p. 164. The refusal to pray for an unbelieving kindred is justified, according to Mohammed, by the duty of a prophet, and the example of Abraham, who reprobated his own father as an enemy of God. Yet Abraham (he adds, c. 9, v. 116; Maracci, tom. ii. p. 317) fuit sane pius, mitis.

111. For the day of judgment, hell, paradise, etc., consult the Koran (c. 2, v. 25, c. 56, 78, etc.),

with Maracci's virulent but learned refutation (in his notes, and in the Prodromus, part iv. p. 78, 120, 122, etc.); D'Herbelot (Bibliothèque Orientale, p. 368, 375); Reland (p. 47–61); and Sale (p. 76–103). The original ideas of the Magi are darkly and doubtfully explored by their apologist Dr. Hyde (Hist. Religionis Persarum, c. 33, p. 402–412, Oxon. 1760). In the article of Mohammed, Bayle has shown how indifferently wit and philosophy supply the absence of genuine information.

112. Before I enter on the history of the prophet, it is incumbent on me to produce my evidence. The Latin, French, and English versions of the Koran are preceded by historical discourses, and the three translators, Maracci (tom. i. p. 10–32), Savary (tom. i. p. 1–248), and Sale (Preliminary Discourse, p. 33–56), had accurately studied the language and character of their author. Two professed Lives of Mahomet have been composed by Dr. Prideaux (Life of Mahomet, seventh edition, London, 1718, in octavo) and the Count de Boulainvilliers (Vie de Mahomet, Londres, 1730, in octavo); but the adverse wish of finding an impostor or a hero has too often corrupted the learning of the Doctor and the ingenuity of the Count. The article in D'Herbelot (Biblioth. Orient. p. 598–603) is chiefly drawn from Novairi and Mirkond; but the best and most authentic of our guides is M. Gagnier, a Frenchman by birth, and professor at Oxford of the Oriental tongues. In two elaborate works (Ismael Abulfeda de Vita et Rebus gestis Mohammedis, etc., Latine vertit, Præfatione et Notis illustravit Johannes Gagnier, Oxon. 1723, in folio; La Vie de Mahomet traduite et compilée de l'Alcoran, des Traditions Authentiques de la Sonna et des meilleurs Auteurs Arabes, Amsterdam, 1748, 3 vols. in 12mo) he has interpreted, illustrated, and supplied the Arabic text of Abulfeda and Al Jannabi; the first an enlightened prince, who reigned at Hamah, in Syria, A.D. 1310–1332 (see Gagnier, Præfat. ad Abulfed.); the second a credulous doctor, who visited Mecca A.D. 1556. (D'Herbelot, p. 397; Gagnier, tom. iii. p. 209, 210). These are my general vouchers, and the inquisitive reader may follow the order of time and the division of chapters. Yet I must observe that both Abulfeda and Al Jannabi are modern historians, and that they cannot appeal to any writers of the first century of the Hegira.

113. After the Greeks, Prideaux (p. 8) discloses the secret doubts of the wife of Mohammed. As if he had been a privy counsellor of the prophet, Boulainvilliers (p. 272, etc.) unfolds the sublime and patriotic views of Cadijah and the first disciples.

114. *Vezirus, portitor, bajulus, onus ferens:* and this plebeian name was transferred by an apt metaphor to the pillars of the state (Gagnier, Not. ad Abulfed. p. 19). I endeavour to preserve the Arabian idiom, as far as I can feel it myself in a Latin or French translation.

115. The passages of the Koran in behalf of

toleration are strong and numerous: c. 2, v. 257, c. 16, 129, c. 17, 54, c. 45, 15, c. 50, 39, c. 88, 21, etc., with the notes of Maracci and Sale. This character alone may generally decide the doubts of the learned, whether a chapter was revealed at Mecca or Medina.

116. See the Koran (passim, and especially c. 7, p. 123, 124, etc.), and the tradition of the Arabs (Pocock, Specimen, p. 35-37). The caverns of the tribe of Thamud, fit for men of the ordinary stature, were shown in the midway between Medina and Damascus (Abulfed. Arabiæ Descript. p. 43, 44), and may be probably ascribed to the Troglodytes of the primitive world (Michaelis, ad Lowth de Poesi Hebræor. p. 131-134; Recherches sur les Egyptiens, tom. ii. p. 48, etc.).

117. In the time of Job the crime of impiety was punished by the Arabian magistrate (c. 31, v. 26, 27, 28). I blush for a respectable prelate (de Poesi Hebræorum, p. 650, 651, edit. Michaelis; and a letter of a late professor in the university of Oxford, p. 15-53), who justifies and applauds this patriarchal inquisition.

118. D'Herbelot, Biblioth. Orient. p. 445. He quotes a particular history of the flight of Mohammed.

119. The *Hegira* was instituted by Omar, the second caliph, in imitation of the era of the martyrs of the Christians (D'Herbelot, p. 444); and properly commenced sixty-eight days before the flight of Mohammed, with the first of Moharren, or first day of that Arabian year, which coincides with Friday, July 16th, A.D. 622 (Abulfeda, Vit. Moham. c. 22, 23, p. 45-50; and Greaves's edition of Ullug Beg's Epochæ Arabum, etc., c. 1, p. 8, 10, etc.).

120. Mohammed's life, from his mission to the Hegira, may be found in Abulfeda (p. 14-45) and Gagnier (tom. i. p. 134-251, 342-383). The legend from p. 187-234 is vouched by Al Jannabi, and disdained by Abulfeda.

121. The triple inauguration of Mohammed is described by Abulfeda (p. 30, 33, 40, 86), and Gagnier (tom. i. p. 342, etc., 349, etc., tom. ii. p. 223, etc.).

122. Prideaux (Life of Mahomet, p. 44) reviles the wickedness of the impostor, who despoiled two poor orphans, the sons of a carpenter; a reproach which he drew from the Disputatio contra Saracenos, composed in Arabic before the year 1130; but the honest Gagnier (ad Abulfed. p. 53) has shown that they were deceived by the word *Al Nagjar*, which signifies, in this place, not an obscure trade, but a noble tribe of Arabs. The desolate state of the ground is described by Abulfeda; and his worthy interpreter has proved, from Al Bochari, the offer of a price; from Al Jannabi, the fair purchase; and from Ahmed Ben Joseph, the payment of the money by the generous Abubeker. On these grounds the prophet must be honourably acquitted.

123. Al Jannabi (apud Gagnier, tom. ii. p. 246, 324) describes the seal and pulpit as two venerable relics of the apostle of God; and the portrait of his court is taken from Abulfeda (c. 44, p. 85).

124. The eighth and ninth chapters of the Koran are the loudest and most vehement; and Maracci (Prodromus, part iv. p. 59-64) has inveighed with more justice than discretion against the double dealing of the impostor.

125. The tenth and twentieth chapters of Deuteronomy, with the practical comments of Joshua, David, etc., are read with more awe than satisfaction by the pious Christians of the present age. But the bishops, as well as the rabbis of former times, have beat the drum-ecclesiastic with pleasure and success. (Sale's Preliminary Discourse, p. 142, 143.)

126. Abulfeda, in Vit. Moham. p. 156. The private arsenal of the apostle consisted of nine swords, three lances, seven pikes or half-pikes, a quiver and three bows, seven cuirasses, three shields, and two helmets (Gagnier, tom. iii. p. 328-334), with a large white standard, a black banner (p. 335), twenty horses (p. 322), etc. Two of his martial sayings are recorded by tradition (Gagnier, tom. ii. p. 88, 337).

127. The whole subject de jure belli Mohammedanorum is exhausted in a separate dissertation by the learned Reland (Dissertationes Miscellaneæ, tom. iii. Dissertat. x. p. 3-53).

128. The doctrine of absolute predestination, on which few religions can reproach each other, is sternly exposed in the Koran (c. 3, p. 52, 53, c. 4, p. 70, etc., with the notes of Sale, and c. 17, p. 413, with those of Maracci). Reland (de Relig. Moham. p. 61-64) and Sale (Prelim. Discourse, p. 103) represent the opinions of the doctors, and our modern travellers the confidence, the fading confidence, of the Turks.

129. Al Jannabi (apud Gagnier, tom. ii. p. 9) allows him seventy or eighty horse; and on two other occasions, prior to the battle of Ohud, he enlists a body of thirty (p. 10) and of 500 (p. 66) troopers. Yet the Musulmans, in the field of Ohud, had no more than two horses, according to the better sense of Abulfeda (in Vit. Mohamm. c. 31, p. 65). In the *Stony* province the camels were numerous; but the horse appears to have been less common than in the *Happy* or the *Desert* Arabia.

130. Bedder Houneene, twenty miles from Medina, and forty from Mecca, is on the high road of the caravan of Egypt; and the pilgrims annually commemorate the prophet's victory by illuminations, rockets, etc. Shaw's Travels, p. 477.

131. The place to which Mohammed retired during the action is styled by Gagnier (in Abulfeda, c. 27, p. 58; Vie de Mahomet, tom. ii. p. 30, 33) *Umbraculum, une loge de bois avec une porte.* The same Arabic word is rendered by Resike (Annales Moslemici Abulfedæ, p. 23) by *Solium, Suggestus editior;* and the difference is of the utmost moment for the honour both of the interpreter and of the

hero, I am sorry to observe the pride and acrimony with which Reiske chastises his fellow-labourer. Sæpe sic vertit, ut integræ paginæ nequeant nisi unâ liturâ corrigi: Arabice non satis callebat, et carebat judicio critico. J. J. Reiske, Prodidagmata ad Hagji Chalisæ Tabulas, p. 228, ad calcem Abulfedæ Syriæ Tabulæ; Lipsiæ, 1766, in 4to.

132. The loose expressions of the Koran (c. 3, p. 124, 125, c. 8, p. 9) allow the commentators to fluctuate between the numbers of 1000, 3000, or 9000 angels; and the smallest of these might suffice for the slaughter of seventy of the Koreish (Maracci, Alcoran, tom. ii. p. 131). Yet the same scholiasts confess that this angelic band was not visible to any mortal eye (Maracci, p. 297). They refine on the words (c. 8, 16), "not thou, but God," etc. (D'Herbelot, Biblioth. Orientale, p. 600, 601).

133. Geograph. Nubiensis, p. 47.

134. In the third chapter of the Koran (p. 50-53, with Sale's notes) the prophet alleges some poor excuses for the defeat of Ohud.

135. For the detail of the three Koreish wars, of Beder, of Ohud, and of the ditch, peruse Abulfeda (p. 56-61, 64-69, 73-77), Gagnier (tom. ii. p. 23-45, 70-96, 120-139), with the proper articles of D'Herbelot, and the abridgments of Elmacin (Hist. Saracen. p. 6, 7) and Abulpharagius (Dynast. p. 102).

136. The wars of Mohammed against the Jewish tribes of Kainoka, the Nadhirites, Koraidha, and Chaibar, are related by Abulfeda (p. 61, 71, 77, 87, etc.) and Gagnier (tom. ii. p. 61-65, 107-112, 139-148, 268-294).

137. Abu Rafe, the servant of Mohammed, is said to affirm that he himself and seven other men afterwards tried, without success, to move the same gate from the ground (Abulfeda, p. 90). Abu Rafe was an eye-witness, but who will be witness for Abu Rafe?

138. The banishment of the Jews is attested by Elmacin (Hist. Saracen. p. 9) and the great Al Zabari (Gagnier, tom. ii. p. 285), Yet Niebuhr (Description de l'Arabie, p. 324) believes that the Jewish religion and Karaite sect are still professed by the tribe of Chaibar; and that, in the plunder of the caravans, the disciples of Moses are the confederates of those of Mohammed.

139. The successive steps of the reduction of Mecca are related by Abulfeda (p. 84-87, 97-100, 102-111) and Gagnier (tom. ii. p. 209-245, 309-322; tom. iii. p. 1-58), Elmacin (Hist. Saracen. p. 8, 9, 10), Abulpharagius (Dynast. p. 103).

140. After the conquest of Mecca, the Mohammed of Voltaire imagines and perpetrates the most horrid crimes. The poet confesses that he is not supported by the truth of history, and can only allege, que celui qui fait la guerre à sa patrie au nom Dieu est capable de tout (Œuvres de Voltaire, tom. xv. p. 282). The maxim is neither charitable nor philosophic; and some reverence is surely due to the fame of heroes and the religion of nations. I am informed that a Turkish ambassador

at Paris was much scandalised at the representation of this tragedy.

141. The Mohammedan doctors still dispute whether Mecca was reduced by force or consent (Abulfeda, p. 107, et Gagnier ad locum); and this verbal controversy is of as much moment as our own about William the Conqueror.

142. In excluding the Christians from the peninsula of Arabia, the province of Hejaz, or the navigation of the Red Sea, Chardin (Voyages en Perse, tom. iv. p. 166) and Reland (Dissertat. Miscell. tom. iii. p. 51) are more rigid than the Musulmans themselves. The Christians are received without scruple into the ports of Mocha, and even of Gedda; and it is only the city and precincts of Mecca that are inaccessible to the profane (Niebuhr, Description de l'Arabie, p. 308, 309; Voyage en Arabie, tom. i. p. 205, 248, etc.).

143. Abulfeda, p. 112-115; Gagnier, tom. iii. p. 67-88; D'Herbelot MOHAMMED.

144. The siege of Tayef, division of the spoil, etc., are related by Abulfeda (p. 117-123) and Gagnier (tom. iii. p. 88-111). It is Al Jannabi who mentions the engines and engineers of the tribe of Daws. The fertile spot of Tayef was supposed to be a piece of the land of Syria detached and dropped in the general deluge.

145. The last conquests and pilgrimage of Mohammed are contained in Abulfeda (p. 121-133), Gagnier (tom. iii. p. 119-219), Elmacin (p. 10, 11 [4to ed., Lugd. Bat. 1625]), Abulpharagius (p. 103). The ninth of the Hegira was styled the Year of Embassies (Gagnier, Not. ad Abulfed. p. 121).

146. Compare the bigoted Al Jannabi (apud Gagnier, tom. ii. p. 232-255) with the no less bigoted Greeks, Theophanes (p. 276-278 [tom. i. p. 511-514, ed. Bonn]), Zonaras (tom. ii. l. xiv. [c. 16] p. 86), and Cedrenus (p. 421 [tom. i. p. 737, ed. Bonn]).

147. For the battle of Muta, and its consequences, see Abulfeda (p. 100-102) and Gagnier (tom. ii. p. 327-343). Χάλεδος (says Theophanes) ὃν λέγουσι μάχαιραν τοῦ Θεοῦ [t. i. p. 515, ed. Bonn].

148. The expedition of Tabuc is recorded by our ordinary historians, Abulfeda (Vit. Moham. p. 123-127) and Gagnier (Vie de Mahomet, tom. iii. p. 147-163); but we have the advantage of appealing to the original evidence of the Koran (c. 9, p. 154, 165), with Sale's learned and rational notes.

149. The Diploma securitatis Ailensibus is attested by Ahmed Ben Joseph, and the author Libri Splendorum (Gagnier, Not. ad Abulfedam, p. 125); but Abulfeda himself, as well as Elmacin (Hist. Saracen. p. 11), though he owns Mohammed's regard for the Christians (p. 13), only mention peace and tribute. In the year 1630 Sionita published at Paris the text and version of Mohammed's patent in favour of the Christians; which was admitted and reprobated by the opposite taste of Salmasius and Grotius (Bayle, MAHOMET, Rem. AA). Hot-

tinger doubts of its authenticity (Hist. Orient. p. 237); Renaudot urges the consent of the Mohammedans (Hist. Patriarch. Alex. p. 169); but Mosheim (Hist. Eccles. p. 244) shows the futility of their opinion, and inclines to believe it spurious. Yet Abulpharagius quotes the impostor's treaty with the Nestorian patriarch (Asseman. Biblioth. Orient. tom. ii. p. 418); but Abulpharagius was primate of the Jacobites.

150. The epilepsy, or falling sickness of Mohammed, is asserted by Theophanes, Zonaras, and the rest of the Greeks; and is greedily swallowed by the gross bigotry of Hottinger (Hist. Orient. p. 10, 11), Prideaux (Life of Mahomet, p. 12), and Maracci (tom. ii. Alcoran, p. 762, 763). The titles (the wrapped-up, the covered) of two chapters of the Koran (73, 74) can hardly be strained to such an interpretation: the silence, the ignorance of the Mohammedan commentators, is more conclusive than the most peremptory denial; and the charitable side is espoused by Ockley (Hist. of the Saracens, tom. i. p. 301), Gagnier (ad Abulfedam, p. 9; Vie de Mahomet, tom. i. p. 118), and Sale (Koran, p. 469-474).

151. This poison (more ignominious since it was offered as a test of his prophetic knowledge) is frankly confessed by his zealous votaries, Abulfeda (p. 92) and Al Jannabi (apud Gagnier, tom. ii. p. 286-288).

152. The Greeks and Latins have invented and propagated the vulgar and ridiculous story that Mohammed's iron tomb is suspended in the air at *Mecca* (σῆμα μετεωριζόμενον. Laonicus Chalcocondyles de Rebus Turcicis, l. iii. p. 66 [ed. Par.; p. 126, ed. Bonn.]), by the action of equal and potent loadstones (Dictionnaire de Bayle, MAHOMET, Rem. EE. FF.). Without any philosophical inquiries, it may suffice, that, 1. The prophet was not buried at Mecca; and, 2. That his tomb at Medina, which has been visited by millions, is placed on the ground (Reland, de Relig. Moham. l. ii. c. 19, p. 209-211; Gagnier, Vie de Mahomet, tom. iii. p. 263-268).

153. Al Jannabi enumerates (Vie de Mahomet, tom. iii. p. 372-391) the multifarious duties of a pilgrim who visits the tombs of the prophet and his companions; and the learned casuist decides that this act of devotion is nearest in obligation and merit to a divine precept. The doctors are divided which, of Mecca or Medina, be the most excellent (p. 391-394).

154. The last sickness, death, and burial of Mohammed are described by Abulfeda and Gagnier (Vit. Moham. p. 133-142; Vie de Mahomet, tom. iii. p. 220-271). The most private and interesting circumstances were originally received from Ayesha, Ali, the sons of Abbas, etc.; and as they dwelt at Medina, and survived the prophet many years, they might repeat the pious tale to a second or third generation of pilgrims.

155. The Christians, rashly enough, have assigned to Mohammed a tame pigeon, that seemed to descend from heaven and whisper in his ear. As this pretended miracle is urged by Grotius (de Veritate Religionis Christianæ), his Arabic translator, the learned Pocock, inquired of him the names of his authors; and Grotius confessed that it is unknown to the Mohammedans themselves. Lest it should provoke their indignation and laughter, the pious *lie* is suppressed in the Arabic version; but it has maintained an edifying place in the numerous editions of the Latin text (Pocock, Specimen Hist. Arabum, p. 186, 187; Reland, de Religion. Moham. l. ii. c. 39, p. 259-262).

156. Ἐμοὶ δὲ τοῦτό ἐστιν ἐκ παιδὸς ἀρξάμενον, φωνή τις γιγνομένη; ἣ ὅταν γένηται ἀεὶ ἀποτρέπει με τούτου ὃ ἂν μέλλω πράττειν, προτρέπει δὲ οὔποτε (Plato, Apology, 31).

The familiar examples which Socrates urges in his Dialogue with Theages (Platon. Opera, tom. i. p. 128, 129, edit. Hen. Stephan.) are beyond the reach of human foresight; and the divine inspiration (the Δαιμόνιου) of the philosopher is clearly taught in the Memorabilia of Xenophon. The ideas of the most rational Platonists are expressed by Cicero (de Divinat. i. 54), and in the fourteenth and fifteenth Dissertations of Maximus of Tyre (p. 153-172, edit. Davis).

157. In some passage of his voluminous writings, Voltaire compares the prophet, in his old age, to a fakir "qui détache la chaîne de son cou pour en donner sur les oreilles à ses confrères."

158. Gagnier relates, with the same impartial pen, this humane law of the prophet, and the murders of Caab and Sophian, which he prompted and approved (Vie de Mahomet, tom. ii. p. 69, 97, 208).

159. For the domestic life of Mohammed, consult Gagnier, and the corresponding chapters of Abulfeda; for his diet (tom. iii. p. 285-288); his children (p. 189, 289); his wives (p. 290-303); his marriage with Zeineb (tom. ii. p. 152-160); his amour with Mary (p. 303-309); the false accusation of Ayesha (p. 186-199). The most original evidence of the three last transactions is contained in the twenty-fourth, thirty-third, and sixty-sixth chapters of the Koran, with Sale's Commentary. Prideaux (Life of Mahomet, p. 80-90) and Maracci (Prodrom. Alcoran, part iv. p. 49-59) have maliciously exaggerated the frailties of Mohammed.

160. Incredibile est quo ardore apud eos in Venerem uterque solvitur sexus (Ammian. Marcellin. l. xiv. c. 4).

161. Sale (Preliminary Discourse, p. 133-137) has recapitulated the laws of marriage, divorce, etc.; and the curious reader of Selden's Uxor Hebraica will recognise many Jewish ordinances.

162. In a memorable case, the Caliph Omar decided that all presumptive evidence was of no avail; and that all the four witnesses must have actually seen stylum in pyxide (Abulfedæ Annales Moslemici, p. 71, vers. Reiske [Lip. 1754]).

163. Sibi robur ad generationem, quantum triginta viri habent, inesse jactaret: ita ut unicâ horâ

posset undecim fœminis *satisfacere*, ut ex Arabum libris refert Stus. Petrus Paschasius, c. 2 (Maracci, Prodromus Alcoran, p. iv. p. 55. See likewise Observations de Belon, l. iii. c. 10, fol. 179, recto). Al Jannabi (Gagnier, tom. iii. p. 287) records his own testimony, that he surpassed all men in conjugal vigour; and Abulfeda mentions the exclamation of Ali, who washed his body after his death, "O propheta, certa penis tuus cœlum versus erectus est," in Vit. Mohammed, p. 140.

164. I borrow the style of a father of the church, ἐναθλεύων Ἡρακλῆς τρισκαιδέκατου ἄθλον (Greg. Nazianzen, Orat. iii. p. 108 [ed. Par. 1609]).

165. The common and most glorious legend includes, in a single night, the fifty victories of Hercules over the virgin daughters of Thestius (Diodor. Sicul. tom. i. l. iv. [c. 29] p. 274; Pausanias, l. ix. [c. 27, § 6] p. 763; Statius Silv. l. i. eleg. iii. v. 42). But Athenæus allows seven nights (Deipnosophist, l. xiii. [c. 4] p. 556), and Apollodorus fifty, for this arduous achievement of Hercules, who was then no more than eighteen years of age (Biblioth. l. ii. c. 4 [§ 10] p. 111, cum notis Heyne, part i. p. 332).

166. Abulfeda in Vit. Moham. p. 12, 13, 16, 17, cum notis Gagnier.

167. This outline of the Arabian history is drawn from the Bibliothèque Orientale of D'Herbelot (under the names of *Aboubecre, Omar, Othman, Ali*, etc.), from the Annals of Abulfeda, Abulpharagius, and Elmacin (under the proper years of the *Hegira*), and especially from Ockley's History of the Saracens (vol. i. p. 1–10, 115–122, 229, 249, 363–372, 378–391, and almost the whole of the second volume). Yet we should weigh with caution the traditions of the hostile sects; a stream which becomes still more muddy as it flows farther from the source. Sir John Chardin has too faithfully copied the fables and errors of the modern Persians (Voyages, tom. ii. p. 235–250, etc.).

168. Ockley (at the end of his second volume) has given an English version of 169 sentences, which he ascribes, with some hesitation, to Ali, the son of Abu Taleb. His preface is coloured by the enthusiasm of a translator; yet these sentences delineate a characteristic, though dark, picture of human life.

169. Ockley (Hist. of the Saracens, vol. i. p. 5, 6) from an Arabian MS. represents Ayesha as adverse to the substitution of her father in the place of the apostle. This fact, so improbable in itself, is unnoticed by Abulfeda, Al Jannabi, and Al Bochari, the last of whom quotes the tradition of Ayesha herself (Vit. Mohammed, p. 136; Vie de Mahomet, tom. iii. p. 236).

170. Particularly by his friend and cousin Abdallah, the son of Abbas, who died A.D. 687, with the title of grand doctor of the Moslems. In Abulfeda [Ann. Moslem.] he recapitulates the important occasions in which Ali had neglected his salutary advice (p. 76, vers. Reiske); and concludes (p. 85), O princeps fidelium, absque controversia tu quidem vere [vir] fortis es, at inops boni consilii, et rerum gerendarum parum callens.

171. I suspect that the two seniors (Abulpharagius, p. 115; Ockley, tom. i. p. 371) may signify not two actual counsellors, but his two predecessors, Abubeker and Omar.

172. The schism of the Persians is explained by all our travellers of the last century, especially in the second and fourth volumes of their master Chardin. Niebuhr, though of inferior merit, has the advantage of writing so late as the year 1764 (Voyages en Arabie, etc., tom. ii. p. 208–233), since the ineffectual attempt of Nadir Shah to change the religion of the nation (see his Persian History translated into French by Sir William Jones, tom. ii. p. 5, 6, 47, 48, 144–155).

173. Omar is the name of the devil; his murderer is a saint. When the Persians shoot with the bow, they frequently cry, "May this arrow go to the heart of Omar!" (Voyages de Chardin, tom. ii. p. 239, 240, 259, etc.)

174. This gradation of merit is distinctly marked in a creed illustrated by Reland (de Relig. Mohamm. l. i. p. 37); and a Sonnite argument inserted by Ockley (Hist. of the Saracens, tom. ii. p. 230). The practice of cursing the memory of Ali was abolished, after forty years, by the Ommiades themselves (D'Herbelot, p. 690); and there are few among the Turks who presume to revile him as an infidel (Voyages de Chardin, tom. iv. p. 46).

175. The plain of Siffin is determined by D'Anville (l'Euphrate et le Tigre, p. 29) to be the Campus Barbaricus of Procopius.

176. Abulfeda, a moderate Sonnite, relates the different opinions concerning the burial of Ali, but adopts the sepulchre of Cufa, hodie famâ numeroque religiose frequentantium celebratum. This number is reckoned by Niebuhr to amount annually to 2000 of the dead and 5000 of the living (tom. ii. p. 208, 209).

177. All the tyrants of Persia, from Adhad el Dowlat (A.D. 977, D'Herbelot, p. 58, 59, 95) to Nadir Shah (A.D. 1743, Hist. de Nadir Shah, tom. ii. p. 155), have enriched the tomb of Ali with the spoils of the people. The dome is copper, with a bright and massy gilding, which glitters to the sun at the distance of many a mile.

178. The city of Meshed Ali, five or six miles from the ruins of Cufa, and one hundred and twenty to the south of Bagdad, is of the size and form of the modern Jerusalem. Meshed Hosein, larger and more populous, is at the distance of thirty miles.

179. I borrow, on this occasion, the strong sense and expression of Tacitus (Hist. i. 4): Evulgato imperii arcano, posse imperatorem [principem] alibi quam Romæ fieri.

180. I have abridged the interesting narrative of Ockley (tom. ii. p. 170–231). It is long and minute; but the pathetic, almost always, consists in the detail of little circumstances.

181. Niebuhr the Dane (Voyages en Arabie,

etc., tom. ii. p. 208, etc.) is, perhaps, the only European traveller who has dared to visit Meshed Ali and Meshed Hosein. The two sepulchres are in the hands of the Turks, who tolerate and tax the devotion of the Persian heretics. The festival of the death of Hosein is amply described by Sir John Chardin, a traveller whom I have often praised.

182. The general article of *Imam*, in D'Herbelot's Bibliothèque, will indicate the succession, and the lives of the *twelve* are given under their respective names.

183. The name of *Antichrist* may seem ridiculous, but the Mohammedans have liberally borrowed the fables of every religion (Sale's Preliminary Discourse, p. 80, 82). In the royal stable of Ispahan two horses were always kept saddled, one for the Mahadi himself, the other for his lieutenant, Jesus the son of Mary.

184. In the year of the Hegira 200 (A.D. 815). See D'Herbelot, p. 546.

185. D'Herbelot, p. 342. The enemies of the Fatimites disgraced them by a Jewish origin. Yet they accurately deduced their genealogy from Jaafar, the sixth Imam; and the impartial Abulfeda allows (Annal. Moslem. p. 230) that they were owned by many, qui absque controversiâ genuini sunt Alidarum, homines propaginum suæ gentis exacte callentes. He quotes some lines from the celebrated *Scherif* or *Radhi*, Egone humilitatem induam in terris hostium? (I suspect him to be an Edrissite of Sicily) cum in Ægypto sit Chalifa de gente Alii, quocum ego communem habeo patrem et vindicem.

186. The kings of Persia of the last dynasty are descended from Sheik Sefi, a saint of the fourteenth century, and, through him, from Moussa Cassem, the son of Hosein, the son of Ali (Olearius, p. 957; Chardin, tom. iii. p. 288). But I cannot trace the intermediate degrees in any genuine or fabulous pedigree. If they were truly Fatimites, they might draw their origin from the princes of Mazanderan, who reigned in the ninth century (D'Herbelot, p. 96).

187. The present state of the family of Mohammed and Ali is most accurately described by Demetrius Cantemir (Hist. of the Othman Empire, p. 94) and Niebuhr (Description de l'Arabie, p. 9-16, 317, etc.). It is much to be lamented that the Danish traveller was unable to purchase the chronicles of Arabia.

188. The writers of the Modern Universal History (vols. i. and ii.) have compiled in 850 folio pages the life of Mohammed and the annals of the caliphs. They enjoyed the advantage of reading, and sometimes correcting, the Arabic text; yet, notwithstanding their high-sounding boasts, I cannot find, after the conclusion of my work, that they have afforded me much (if any) additional information. The dull mass is not quickened by a spark of philosophy or taste; and the compilers indulge the criticism of acrimonious bigotry against Boulainvilliers, Sale, Gagnier, and all who have treated Mohammed with favour, or even justice.

Chapter LI

1. See the description of the city and country of Al Yamanah, in Abulfeda, Descript. Arabiæ, p. 60, 61. In the thirteenth century there were some ruins and a few palms; but in the present century the same ground is occupied by the visions and arms of a modern prophet, whose tenets are imperfectly known (Niebuhr, Description de l'Arabie, p. 296-302).

2. Their first salutation may be transcribed, but cannot be translated. It was thus that Moseilama said or sung:—

Surge tandem itaque strenue permolenda; nam stratus tibi thorus est.

Aut in propatulo tentorio si velis, aut in abditiore cubiculo si malis;

Aut supinam te humi exporrectam fustigabo, si velis, aut si malis manibus pedibusque nixam.

Aut si velis ejus (*Priapi*) gemino triente, aut si malis totus veniam.

Imo, totus venito, O Apostole Dei, clamabat fœmina. Id ipsum, dicebat

Moseilama, mihi quoque suggessit Deus.

The prophetess Segjah, after the fall of her lover, returned to idolatry; but, under the reign of Moawiyah, she became a Musulman, and died at Bassora (Abulfeda, Annal. vers. Reiske, p. 63).

3. See this text, which demonstrates a God from the work of generation, in Abulpharagius (Specimen Hist. Arabum, p. 13; and Dynast. p. 103) and Abulfeda (Annal. p. 63).

4. His reign in Eutychius, tom. ii. p. 251. Elmacin, p. 18. Abulpharagius, p. 108. Abulfeda, p. 60. D'Herbelot, p. 58.

5. His reign in Eutychius, p. 264. Elmacin, p. 24. Abulpharagius, p. 110. Abulfeda, p. 66. D'Herbelot, p. 686.

6. His reign in Eutychius, p. 323. Elmacin, p. 36. Abulpharagius, p. 115. Abulfeda, p. 75. D'Herbelot, p. 695.

7. His reign in Eutychius, p. 343. Elmacin, p. 51. Abulpharagius, p. 117. Abulfeda, p. 83. D'Herbelot, p. 89.

8. His reign in Eutychius, p. 344. Elmacin, p. 54. Abulpharagius, p. 123. Abulfeda, p. 101. D'Herbelot, p. 586.

9. Their reigns in Eutychius, tom. ii. p. 360-395. Elmacin, p. 59-108. Abulpharagius, Dynast. ix. p. 124-139. Abulfeda, p. 111-141. D'Herbelot,

Bibliothèque Orientale, p. 691, and the particular articles of the Ommiades.

10. For the seventh and eighth century, we have scarcely any original evidence of the Byzantine historians, except the chronicles of Theophanes (Theophanis Confessoris Chronographia, Gr. et Lat. cum notis Jacobi Goar. Paris, 1655, in folio), and the Abridgment of Nicephorus (Nicephori Patriarchæ C. P. Breviarium Historicum, Gr. et Lat. Paris, 1648, in folio), who both lived in the beginning of the ninth century (see Hanckius de Scriptor. Byzant. p. 200-246). Their contemporary, Photius, does not seem to be more opulent. After praising the style of Nicephorus, he adds, Καὶ ὅλως πολλοὺς ἐστιτῶν πρὸ αὐτοῦ ἀποκρυπτόμενος τῇδὲ τῆς ἱστορίας τῇ συγγραφῇ, and only complains of his extreme brevity (Phot. Biblioth. Cod. lxvi. p. 100 [p. 33, ed. Bekk.]). Some additions may be gleaned from the more recent histories of Cedrenus and Zonaras of the twelfth century.

11. Tabari, or Al Tabari, a native of Taborestan, a famous Imam of Bagdad, and the Livy of the Arabians, finished his general history in the year of the Hegira 302 (A.D. 914). At the request of his friends he reduced a work of 30,000 sheets to a more reasonable size. But his Arabic original is known only by the Persian and Turkish versions. The Saracenic history of Ebn Amid, or Elmacin, is said to be an abridgment of the great Tabari (Ockley's Hist. of the Saracens, vol. ii. preface, p. xxxix.; and, list of authors, D'Herbelot, p. 866, 870, 1014).

12. Besides the lists of authors framed by Prideaux (Life of Mahomet, p. 179-189), Ockley (at the end of his second volume), and Petit de la Croix (Hist. de Gengiscan, p. 525-550), we find in the Bibliothèque Orientale Tarikh, a catalogue of two or three hundred histories or chronicles of the East, of which not more than three or four are older than Tabari. A lively sketch of Oriental literature is given by Reiske (in his Prodidagmata ad Hagji Chalifæ librum memorialem ad calcem Abulfedæ Tabulæ Syriæ, Lipsiæ, 1766); but his project and the French version of Petit de la Croix (Hist. de Timur Bec, tom. i. preface, p. xlv.) have fallen to the ground.

13. The particular historians and geographers will be occasionally introduced. The four following titles represent the Annals which have guided me in this general narrative:—1. *Annales Eutychii, Patriarchæ Alexandrini, ab Edwardo Pocockio*, Oxon. 1656, 2 vols. in 4to. A pompous edition of an indifferent author, translated by Pocock to gratify the presbyterian prejudices of his friend Selden. 2. *Historia Saracenica Georgii Elmacini, operâ et studio Thomæ Erpenii*, in 4to, Lugd. Batavorum, 1625. He is said to have hastily translated a corrupt MS., and his version is often deficient in style and sense. 3. *Historia compendiosa Dynastiarum a Gregorio Abulpharagio, interprete Edwardo Pocockio*, in 4to, Oxon. 1663. More useful for the literary than the civil history of the East. 4. *Abulfedæ Annales Moslemici ad Ann. Hegiræ ccccvi. a Jo. Jac. Reiske*, in 4to Lipsiæ, 1754. The best of our chronicles, both for the original and version, yet how far below the name of Abulfeda! We know that he wrote at Hamah in the fourteenth century. The three former were Christians of the tenth, twelfth, and thirteenth centuries; the two first, natives of Egypt —a Melchite patriarch, and a Jacobite scribe.

14. M. de Guignes (Hist. des Huns, tom. i. pref. p. xix. xx.) has characterised, with truth and knowledge, the two sorts of Arabian historians— the dry annalist, and the tumid and flowery orator.

15. Bibliothèque Orientale, par M. D'Herbelot, in folio, Paris, 1697. For the character of the respectable author consult his friend Thevenot (Voyages du Levant, part i. chap. 1). His work is an agreeable miscellany which must gratify every taste; but I never can digest the alphabetical order; and I find him more satisfactory in the Persian than the Arabic history. The recent supplement from the papers of MM. Visdelou and Galland (in folio, La Haye, 1779) is of a different cast, a medley of tales, proverbs, and Chinese antiquities.

16. Pocock will explain the chronology (Specimen Hist. Arabum, p. 66-74), and D'Anville the geography (l'Euphrate et le Tigre, p. 125), of the dynasty of the Almondars. The English scholar understood more Arabic than the mufti of Aleppo (Ockley, vol. ii. p. 34); the French geographer is equally at home in every age and every climate of the world.

17. Fecit et Chaled plurima in hoc anno prælia, in quibus vicerunt Muslimi, et *infidelium* immensâ multitudine occisâ spolia infinita et innumera sunt nacti (Hist. Saracenica, p. 20). The Christian annalist slides into the national and compendious term of *infidels*, and I often adopt (I hope without scandal) this characteristic mode of expression.

18. A cycle of 120 years, at the end of which an intercalary month of 30 days supplied the use of our Bissextile, and restored the integrity of the solar year. In a great revolution of 1440 years this intercalation was successively removed from the first to the twelfth month; but Hyde and Freret are involved in a profound controversy, whether the twelve, or only eight of these changes were accomplished before the era of Yezdegerd, which is unanimously fixed to the 16th of June, A.D. 632. How laboriously does the curious spirit of Europe explore the darkest and most distant antiquities (Hyde, de Religione Persarum, c. 14-18, p. 181-211; Freret in the Mém. de l'Académie des Inscriptions, tom. xvi. p. 233-267)!

19. Nine days after the death of Mahomet (7th June, A.D. 632) we find the era of Yezdegerd (16th June, A.D. 632), and his accession cannot be postponed beyond the end of the first year. His predecessors could not therefore resist the arms of the caliph Omar; and these unquestionable dates overthrow the thoughtless chronology of Abulpharagius. See Ockley's Hist. of the Saracens, vol. i. p. 130.

20. Cadesia, says the Nubian geographer (p. 121), is, in margine solitudinis, 61 leagues from Bagdad, and two stations from Cufa. Otter (Voyage, tom. i. p. 163) reckons 15 leagues, and observes that the place is supplied with dates and water.

21. Atrox, contumax, plus semel renovatum, are the well-chosen expressions of the translator of Abulfeda (Reiske, p. 69).

22. D'Herbelot, Bibliothèque Orientale, p. 297, 348.

23. The reader may satisfy himself on the subject of Bassora by consulting the following writers: —Geograph. Nubiens. p. 121; D'Herbelot, Bibliothèque Orientale, p. 192; D'Anville, L'Euphrate et le Tigre, p. 130, 133, 145; Raynal, Hist. Philosophique des deux Indes, tom. ii. p. 92-100; Voyages di Pietro della Valle, tom. iv. p. 370-391; De Tavernier, tom. i. p. 240-247; De Thevenot, tom. ii. p. 545-584; D'Otter, tom. ii. p. 45-78; De Niebuhr, tom. ii. p. 172-199.

24. Mente vix potest numerove comprehendi quanta spolia . . . nostris cesserint. Abulfeda, p. 69. Yet I still suspect that the extravagant numbers of Elmacin may be the error, not of the text, but of the version. The best translators from the Greek, for instance, I find to be very poor arithmeticians.

25. The camphire-tree grows in China and Japan, but many hundredweight of those meaner sorts are exchanged for a single pound of the more precious gum of Borneo and Sumatra (Raynal, Hist. Philosoph. tom. i. p. 362-365; Dictionnaire d'Hist. Naturelle par Bomare; Miller's Gardener's Dictionary). These may be the islands of the first climate from whence the Arabians imported their camphire (Geograph. Nub. p. 34, 35; D'Herbelot, p. 232).

26. See Gagnier, Vie de Mahomet, tom. i. p. 376, 377. I may credit the fact without believing the prophecy.

27. The most considerable ruins of Assyria are the tower of Belus, at Babylon, and the hall of Chosroes, at Ctesiphon: they have been visited by that vain and curious traveller Pietro della Valle (tom. i. p. 713-718, 731-735).

28. Consult the article of Coufah in the Bibliothèque of D'Herbelot (p. 277, 278), and the second volume of Ockley's History, particularly p. 40 and 153.

29. See the article of Nehavena, in D'Herbelot p. 667, 668; and Voyages en Turquie et en Perse, par Otter, tom. i. p. 191.

30. It is in such a style of ignorance and wonder that the Athenian orator describes the Arctic conquests of Alexander, who never advanced beyond the shores of the Caspian. Ἀλέξανδρος ἔξω τῆς ἄρκτου καὶ τῆς οἰκουμένης, ὀλίγου δεῖν, πάσης μεθειστήκει. Æschines contra Ctesiphontem, tom. iii. p. 554, edit. Græc. Orator. Reiske. This memorable cause was pleaded at Athens, Olymp. cxii. 3 (before Christ 330), in the autumn (Taylor, præfat. p. 370, etc.), about a year after the battle of Arbela;

and Alexander, in the pursuit of Darius, was marching towards Hyrcania and Bactriana.

31. We are indebted for this curious particular to the Dynasties of Abulpharagius, p. 116; but it is needless to prove the identity of Estachar and Persepolis (D'Herbelot, p. 327); and still more needless to copy the drawings and descriptions of Sir John Chardin, or Corneille le Bruyn.

32. After the conquest of Persia, Theophanes adds, αὐτῷ δὲ τῷ χρόνῳ ἐκέλευσεν Οὔμαρος ἀναγραφῆναι πᾶσαν τὴν ὑπ' αὐτὸν οἰκουμένην · ἐγένετο δὲ ἡ ἀναγραθὴ καὶ ἀνθρώπων καὶ κτηνῶν καὶ θυτῶν (Chronograph. p. 283 [tom. i. p. 522, ed. Bonn]).

33. Amidst our meagre relations, I must regret that D'Herbelot has not found and used a Persian translation of Tabari, enriched, as he says, with many extracts from the native historians of the Ghebers or Magi (Bibliothèque Orientale, p. 1014).

34. The most authentic accounts of the two rivers, the Sihon (Jaxartes) and the Gihon (Oxus), may be found in Sherif al Edrisi (Geograph. Nubiens. p. 138); Abulfeda (Descript. Chorasan. in Hudson, tom. iii. p. 23); Abulghazi Kahn, who reigned on their banks (Hist. Généalogique des Tatars, p. 32, 57, 766); and the Turkish Geographer, a MS. in the king of France's library (Examen Critique des Historiens d'Alexandre, p. 194-360).

35. The territory of Fargana is described by Abulfeda, p. 76, 77.

36. Eo redegit angustiarum eundem regem exsulem, ut Turcici regis, et Sogdiani, et Sinensis, auxilia missis literis imploraret (Abulfed. Annal. p. 74). The connection of the Persian and Chinese history is illustrated by Freret (Mém. de l'Académie, tom. xvi. p. 245-255), and De Guignes (Hist. des Huns, tom. i. p. 54-59; and for the geography of the borders, tom. ii. p. 1-43).

37. Hist. Sinica, p. 41-46, in the third part of the Relations Curieuses of Thevenot.

38. I have endeavoured to harmonise the various narratives of Elmacin (Hist. Saracen. p. 37), Abulpharagius (Dynast. p. 116), Abulfeda (Annal. p. 74, 79), and D'Herbelot (p. 485). The end of Yezdegerd was not only unfortunate, but obscure.

39. The two daughters of Yezdegerd married Hassan, the son of Ali, and Mohammed, the son of Abubeker; and the first of these was the father of a numerous progeny. The daughter of Phirouz became the wife of the caliph Walid, and their son Yezid derived his genuine or fabulous descent from the Chosroes of Persia, the Cæsars of Rome, and the Chagans of the Turks or Avars (D'Herbelot, Biblioth. Orientale, p. 96, 487).

40. It was valued at 2000 pieces of gold, and was the prize of Obeidollah, the son of Ziyad, a name afterwards infamous by the murder of Hosein (Ockley's History of the Saracens, vol. ii. p. 142, 143). His brother Salem was accompanied by his wife, the first Arabian woman (A.D. 680) who passed the Oxus: she borrowed, or rather

stole, the crown and jewels of the princess of the Sogdians (p. 231, 232).

41. A part of Abulfeda's geography is translated by Greaves, inserted in Hudson's collection of the minor geographers (tom. iii.), and entitled, Descriptio Chorasmiæ et *Mawaralnahræ*, id est, regionum extra fluvium, Oxum, p. 80. The name of *Transoxiana*, softer in sound, equivalent in sense, is aptly used by Petit de la Croix (Hist. de Gengiscan, etc.) and some modern Orientalists, but they are mistaken in ascribing it to the writers of antiquity.

42. The conquests of Cutibah are faintly marked by Elmacin (Hist. Saracen. p. 84), D'Herbelot (Biblioth. Orient. *Catbah, Samarcand Valid.*), and De Guignes (Hist. des Huns, tom. i. p. 58, 59).

43. A curious description of Samarcand is inserted in the Bibliotheca Arabico-Hispana, tom. i. p. 208, etc. The librarian Casiri (tom. ii. 9) relates from credible testimony that paper was first imported from China to Samarcand, A.H. 30, and *invented*, or rather introduced, at Mecca, A.H. 88. The Escurial library contains paper MSS. as old as the fourth or fifth century of the Hegira.

44. A separate history of the conquest of Syria has been composed by Al Wakidi, cadi of Bagdad, who was born A.D. 748, and died A.D. 822: he likewise wrote the conquest of Egypt, of Diarbekir, etc. Above the meagre and recent chronicles of the Arabians, Al Wakidi has the double merit of antiquity and copiousness. His tales and traditions afford an artless picture of the men and the times. Yet his narrative is too often defective, trifling, and improbable. Till something better shall be found, his learned and spirited interpreter (Ockley, in his History of the Saracens, vol. i. p. 21–342) will not deserve the petulant animadversion of Reiske (Prodidagmata ad Hagji Chalifæ Tabulas, p. 236). I am sorry to think that the labours of Ockley were consummated in a jail (see his two prefaces to the first vol. A.D. 1708, to the second, 1718, with the list of authors at the end).

45. The instructions, etc., of the Syrian war are described by Al Wakidi and Ockley, tom. i. p. 22–27, etc. In the sequel it is necessary to contract, and needless to quote, their circumstantial narrative. My obligations to others shall be noticed.

46. Notwithstanding this precept, M. Pauw (Recherches sur les Egyptiens, tom. ii. p. 192, edit. Lausanne) represents the Bedoweens as the implacable enemies of the Christian monks. For my own part, I am more inclined to suspect the avarice of the Arabian robbers and the prejudices of the German philosopher.

47. Even in the seventh century the monks were generally laymen: they wore their hair long and dishevelled, and shaved their heads when they were ordained priests. The circular tonsure was sacred and mysterious: it was the crown of thorns; but it was likewise a royal diadem, and every priest was a king, etc. (Thomassin, Discipline de l'Eglise, tom. i. p. 721–758, especially p. 737, 738.)

48. Huic Arabia est conserta, ex alio latere Nabathæis contigua; opima varietate commerciorum castrisque oppleta validis et castellis, quæ ad repellendos gentium vicinarum excursus, solicitudo per vigil veterum per opportunos saltus erexit e cautos. Ammian. Marcellin. xiv. 8; Reland, Palestin. tom. i. p. 85, 86.

49. With Gerasa and Philadelphia, Ammianu praises the fortifications of Bosra [murorum] firmitate cautissimas. They deserved the same praise in the time of Abulfeda (Tabul. Syriæ, p. 99), whe describes this city, the metropolis of Hawran (Auranitis), four days' journey from Damascus. The Hebrew etymology I learn from Reland, Palestin. tom. ii. p. 666.

50. The apostle of a desert and an army wa obliged to allow this ready succedaneum for wate (Koran, c. iii. p. 66; c. v. p. 83); but the Arabia and Persian casuists have embarrassed his fre permission with many niceties and distinction (Reland, de Relig. Mohammed. l. i. p. 82, 83 Chardin, Voyages en Perse, tom. iv.).

51. *The bells rung!* Ockley, vol. i. p. 38. Yet I much doubt whether this expression can be justi fied by the text of Al Wakidi, or the practice of the times. Ad Græcos, says the learned Ducange (Glossar. med. et infim. Græcitat. tom. i. p. 774 campanarum usus serius transit et etiamnum rarissimus est. The oldest example which he can find in the Byzantine writers is of the year 1040; but the Venetians pretend that they introduced bells a Constantinople in the ninth century.

52. Damascus is amply described by the Sheri al Edrisi (Geograph. Nub. p. 116, 117), and hi translator, Sionita (Appendix, c. 4); Abulfeda (Tabula Syriæ, p. 100); Schultens (Index Geograph. ad Vit. Saladin.); D'Herbelot (Biblioth. Orient. p. 291); Thevenot (Voyage du Levant, part i. p. 688, 698); Maundrell (Journey from Aleppo to Jerusalem, p. 122–130); and Pocock (Description of the East, vol. ii. p. 117–127).

53. Nobilissima civitas, says Justin. According to the Oriental traditions, it was older than Abraham or Semiramis. Joseph. Antiq. Jud. l. i. c. 6 [§ 4], 7 [§ 2], p. 24, 29, edit. Havercamp. Justin xxxvi. 2.

54. Ἔδει γὰρ, οἶμαι, τὴν Διὸς πόλιν ἀληθῶς, καὶ τὸ τῆς Ἐώας ἀπάσης ὀφθαλμόν, τὴν ἱερὰν καὶ μεγίστην Δάμασκον λέγω, τοῖς τε ἄλλοις σύμπασιν, οἷον ἱερῶ κάλλει, καὶ νεῶν μεγέθει, καὶ ὡρῶν εὐκαιρίᾳ, καὶ πηγῶ ἀγλαΐα, καὶ ποταμῶν πλήθει, καὶ γῆς εὐφορίᾳ νικῶσαν, etc. Julian. Epist. xxiv. p. 392. These splendid epithets are occasioned by the figs of Damascus, o which the author sends a hundred to his friend Serapion, and this rhetorical theme is inserted by Petavius, Spanheim, etc. (p. 390–396), among the genuine epistles of Julian. How could they overlook that the writer is an inhabitant of Damascus (he thrice affirms that this peculiar fig grows only (παρ' ἡμῖν), a city which Julian never entered or approached?

55. Voltaire, who casts a keen and lively glance

over the surface of history, has been struck with the resemblance of the first Moslems and the heroes of the Iliad—the siege of Troy and that of Damascus (Hist. Générale, tom. i. p. 348).

56. These words are a text of the Koran, c. ix. 32, lxi. 8. Like our fanatics of the last century, the Moslems, on every familiar or important occasion, spoke the language of *their* Scriptures—a style more natural in their mouths than the Hebrew idiom, transplanted into the climate and dialect of Britain.

57. The name of Werdan is unknown to Theophanes; and, though it might belong to an Armenian chief, has very little of a Greek aspect or sound. If the Byzantine historians have mangled the Oriental names, the Arabs, in this instance, likewise have taken ample revenge on their enemies. In transposing the Greek character from right to left, might they not produce, from the familiar appellation of *Andrew*, something like the anagram *Werdan?*

58. Vanity prompted the Arabs to believe that Thomas was the son-in-law of the emperor. We know the children of Heraclius by his two wives; and his *august* daughter would not have married in exile at Damascus (see Ducange, Fam. Byzantin. p. 118, 119). Had he been less religious, I might only suspect the legitimacy of the damsel.

59. Al Wakidi (Ockley, p. 101) says, "with poisoned arrows"; but this savage invention is so repugnant to the practice of the Greeks and Romans, that I must suspect on this occasion the malevolent credulity of the Saracens.

60. Abulfeda allows only seventy days for the siege of Damascus (Annal. Moslem. p. 67, vers. Reiske); but Elmacin, who mentions this opinion, prolongs the term to six months, and notices the use of *balistæ* by the Saracens (Hist. Saracen. p. 25, 32). Even this longer period is insufficient to fill the interval between the battle of Aiznadin (July, A.D. 633) and the accession of Omar (24th July, A.D. 634), to whose reign the conquest of Damascus is unanimously ascribed (Al Wakidi, apud Ockley, vol. i. p. 115; Abulpharagius, Dynast. p. 112, vers. Pocock). Perhaps, as in the Trojan war, the operations were interrupted by excursions and detachments till the last seventy days of the siege.

61. It appears from Abulfeda (p. 125) and Elmacin (p. 32) that this distinction of the two parts of Damascus was long remembered, though not always respected, by the Mohammedan sovereigns. See likewise Eutychius (Annal. tom. ii. p. 379, 380, 383).

62. On the fate of these lovers, whom he names Phocyas and Eudocia, Mr. Hughes has built the Siege of Damascus, one of our most popular tragedies, and which possesses the rare merit of blending nature and history, the manners of the times and the feelings of the heart. The foolish delicacy of the players compelled him to soften the guilt of the hero and the despair of the heroine. Instead of a base renegado, Phocyas serves the Arabs as an honourable ally; instead of prompting their pursuit, he flies to the succour of his countrymen, and, after killing Caled and Derar, is himself mortally wounded, and expires in the presence of Eudocia, who professes her resolution to take the veil at Constantinople. A frigid catastrophe!

63. The towns of Gabala and Laodicea, which the Arabs passed, still exist in a state of decay (Maundrell, p. 11, 12; Pocock, vol. ii. p. 13). Had not the Christians been overtaken, they must have crossed the Orontes on some bridge in the sixteen miles between Antioch and the sea, and might have rejoined the high road of Constantinople at Alexandria. The Itineraries will represent the directions and distances (p. 146, 148, 581, 582, edit. Wesseling).

64. *Dair Abil Kodos.* After retrenching the last word, the epithet *holy*, I discover the Abila of Lysanias between Damascus and Heliopolis: the name (*Abil* signifies a vineyard) concurs with the situation to justify my conjecture (Reland, Palestin. tom. i. p. 317, tom. ii. p. 525, 527).

65. I am bolder than Mr. Ockley (vol. i. p. 164), who dares not insert this figurative expression in the text, though he observes in a marginal note that the Arabians often borrow their similes from that useful and familiar animal. The reindeer may be equally famous in the songs of the Laplanders.

66. We heard the *tecbir;* so the Arabs call
     Their shout of onset, when with loud appeal
     They challenge heaven, as if demanding conquest.

This word, so formidable in their holy wars, is a verb active (says Ockley in his index) of the second conjugation, from *Kabbara*, which signifies saying *Alla Acbar*, God is most mighty.

67. In the Geography of Abulfeda, the description of Syria, his native country, is the most interresting and authentic portion. It was published in Arabic and Latin, Lipsiæ, 1766, in quarto, with the learned notes of Kochler and Reiske, and some extracts of geography and natural history from Ibn Ol Wardii. Among the modern travels, Pocock's Description of the East (of Syria and Mesopotamia, vol. ii. p. 88–209) is a work of superior learning and dignity; but the author too often confounds what he had seen and what he had read.

68. The praises of Dionysius are just and lively. Καὶ τὴν μὲν (Syria) πολλοί τε καὶ ὄλβιοι ἄνδρες ἔχουσιν (in Periegesi, v. 902, in tom. iv. Geograph. Minor. Hudson). In another place he styles the country πολύπτολιν αἶαν (v. 898). He proceeds to say,

Πᾶσα δέ τοι λιπαρή τε καὶ εὔβοτος ἔπλετο χώρη,
Μῆλά τε φερβέμεναι καὶ δένδρεσι καρπὸν ἀέξειν.

v. 921, 922.

This poetical geographer lived in the age of Augustus, and his description of the world is illustrated by the Greek commentary of Eustathius, who paid the same compliment to Homer and

Dionysius (Fabric. Biblioth. Græc. l. iv. c. 2. tom. iii. p. 21, etc.).

69. The topography of the Libanus and Anti-Libanus is excellently described by the learning and sense of Reland (Palestin. tom. i. p. 311–326).

70. _____Emesæ fastigia celsa renident.

Nam diffusa solo latus explicat, ac subit auras

Turribus in cœlum nitentibus: incola claris

Cor studiis acuit . . .

Denique flammicomo devoti pectora soli

Vitam agitant:—Libanus frondosa cacumina turget,

Et tamen his celsi certant fastigia templi.

These verses of the Latin version of Rufus Avienus [vv. 1085, seq.] are wanting in the Greek original of Dionysius; and since they are likewise unnoticed by Eustathius, I must, with Fabricius (Biblioth. Latin. tom. iii. p. 153, edit. Ernesti), and against Salmasius (ad Vopiscum, p. 366, 367, in Hist. August.), ascribe them to the fancy, rather than the MSS., of Avienus.

71. I am much better satisfied with Maundrell's slight octavo (Journey, p. 134–139) than with the pompous folio of Dr. Pocock (Description of the East, vol. ii. p. 106–113); but every preceding account is eclipsed by the magnificent description and drawings of MM. Dawkins and Wood, who have transported into England the ruins of Palmyra and Baalbec.

72. The Orientals explain the prodigy by a never-failing expedient. The edifices of Baalbec were constructed by the fairies or the genii (Hist. de Timour Bec, tom. iii. l. v. c. 23, p. 311, 312; Voyage d'Otter, tom. i. p. 83). With less absurdity, but with equal ignorance, Abulfeda and Ibn Chaukel ascribe them to the Sabæans or Aadites. Non sunt in omni Syria ædificia magnificentiora his (Tabula Syriæ, p. 103).

73. I have read somewhere in Tacitus, or Grotius, Subjectos habent tanquam suos, viles tanquam alienos. Some Greek officers ravished the wife, and murdered the child, of their Syrian landlord; and Manuel smiled at his undutiful complaint.

74. See Reland, Palestin. tom. i. p. 272, 283, tom. ii. p. 773, 775. This learned professor was equal to the task of describing the Holy Land, since he was alike conversant with Greek and Latin, with Hebrew and Arabian literature. The Yermuk, or Hieromax, is noticed by Cellarius (Geograph. Antiq. tom. ii. p. 392) and D'Anville (Géographie Ancienne, tom. ii. p. 185). The Arabs, and even Abulfeda himself, do not seem to recognise the scene of their victory.

75. These women were of the tribe of the Hamyarites, who derived their origin from the ancient Amalekites. Their females were accustomed to ride on horseback, and to fight like the Amazons of old (Ockley, vol. i. p. 67).

76. We killed of them, says Abu Obeidah to the caliph, one hundred and fifty thousand, and made prisoners of forty thousand (Ockley, vol. i. p. 241). As I cannot doubt his veracity, nor believe his computation, I must suspect that the Arabic historians indulged themselves in the practice of composing speeches and letters for their heroes.

77. After deploring the sins of the Christians, Theophanes adds (Chronograph. p. 276 [tom. i. p. 510, ed. Bonn]), ἀνέστη ὁ ἐρημικὸς [ἐρημικώτατος] Ἀμαλὴκ τύπτων ἡμᾶς τὸν λαὸν τοῦ Χριστοῦ, καὶ γίνεται πρώτη φορᾷ πτῶσις τοῦ Ῥωμαϊκοῦ στρατοῦ ἡ κατὰ τὸ Γαβιθὰν [Γαβιθᾶ] λέγω (does he mean Aiznadin?) καὶ Ἰερμουχὰν, καὶ τὴν ἄθεσμον αἱματοχυσίαν. His account is brief and obscure, but he accuses the numbers of the enemy, the adverse wind, and the cloud of dust: μὴ δυνηθέντες (the Romans) ἀντιπροσωπῆσαι [ἀντωπῆσαι] ἐχθροῖς διὰ τὸν κονιορτὸν ἡττῶνται· καὶ ἑαυτοὺς βάλλοντες εἰς τὰς στενόδους τοῦ Ἰερμοχθοῦ ποταμοῦ ἐκεῖ ἀπώλοντο ἄρδην (Chronograph. p. 280 [t. i. p. 518, ed. Bonn]).

78. See Abulfeda (Annal. Moslem. p. 70, 71), who transcribes the poetical complaint of Jabalah himself, and some panegyrical strains of an Arabian poet, to whom the chief of Gassan sent from Constantinople a gift of five hundred pieces of gold by the hands of the ambassador of Omar.

79. In the name of the city, the profane prevailed over the sacred: Jerusalem was known to the devout Christians (Euseb. de Martyr. Palest. c. xi.); but the legal and popular appellation of Ælia (the colony of Ælius Hadrianus) has passed from the Romans to the Arabs. (Reland, Palestin. tom. i. p. 207, tom. ii. p. 835; D'Herbelot, Bibliothèque Orientale, Cods, p. 269; Ilia, p. 420). The epithet of Al Cods, the Holy, is used as the proper name of Jerusalem.

80. The singular journey and equipage of Omar are described (besides Ockley, vol. i. p. 250) by Murtadi (Merveilles de l'Egypte, p. 200–202).

81. The Arabs boast of an old prophecy preserved at Jerusalem, and describing the name, the religion, and the person of Omar, the future conqueror. By such arts the Jews are said to have soothed the pride of their foreign masters, Cyrus and Alexander (Joseph. Ant. Jud. l. xi. c. 1 [§ 1, 2], 8 [§ 5], p. 547, 579–582).

82. Τὸ βδέλυγμα τῆς ἐρημώσεως τὸ ῥηθὲν διὰ Δανιὴλ τοῦ προφήτου ἑστὼς ἐν τόπῳ ἁγίῳ. Theophan. Chronograph. p. 281 [tom. i. p. 520, ed. Bonn]. This prediction, which had already served for Antiochus and the Romans, was again refitted for the present occasion, by the economy of Sophronius, one of the deepest theologians of the Monothelite controversy.

83. According to the accurate survey of D'Anville (Dissertation sur l'ancienne Jerusalem, p. 42–54), the mosch of Omar, enlarged and embellished by succeeding caliphs, covered the ground of the ancient temple (πάλαιον τοῦ μεγάλου ναὸν δάπεδον, says Phocas), a length of 215, a breadth of 172, toises. The Nubian geographer declares that this magnificent structure was second only in size and

beauty to the great mosch of Cordova (p. 113), whose present state Mr. Swinburne has so elegantly represented (Travels into Spain, p. 296–302).

84. Of the many Arabic tarikhs or chronicles of Jerusalem (D'Herbelot, p. 867), Ockley found one among the Pocock MSS. of Oxford (vol. i. p. 257), which he has used to supply the defective narrative of Al Wakidi.

85. The Persian historian of Timur (tom. iii. l. v. c. 21, p. 300) describes the castle of Aleppo as founded on a rock one hundred cubits in height; a proof, says the French translator, that he had never visited the place. It is now in the midst of the city, of no strength, with a single gate, the circuit is about 500 or 600 paces, and the ditch half full of stagnant water (Voyages de Tavernier, tom. i. p. 149; Pocock, vol. ii. part i. p. 150). The fortresses of the East are contemptible to a European eye.

86. The date of the conquest of Antioch by the Arabs is of some importance. By comparing the years of the world in the Chronography of Theophanes with the years of the Hegira in the history of Elmacin, we shall determine that it was taken between January 23rd and September 1st of the year of Christ 638 (Pagi, Critica, in Baron. Annal. tom. ii. p. 812, 813). Al Wakidi (Ockley, vol. i. p. 314) assigns that event to Tuesday, August 21st, an inconsistent date; since Easter fell that year on April 5th, the 21st of August must have been a Friday (see the Tables of the Art de Vérifier les Dates).

87. His bounteous edict, which tempted the grateful city to assume the victory of Pharsalia for a perpetual era, is given ἐν Ἀντιοχείᾳ τῇ μητροπόλει, ἱερᾷ καὶ ἀσύλῳ καὶ αὐτονόμῳ, καὶ ἀρχούσῃ καὶ προκαθεμένῃ τῆς ἀνατολῆς. John Malala, in Chron. p. 91, edit. Venet. [p. 216, ed. Bonn.]. We may distinguish his authentic information of domestic facts from his gross ignorance of general history.

88. See Ockley (vol. i. p. 308, 312), who laughs at the credulity of his author. When Heraclius bade farewell to Syria, Vale Syria et ultimum vale, he prophesied that the Romans should never reenter the province till the birth of an inauspicious child, the future scourge of the empire. Abulfeda, p. 68. I am perfectly ignorant of the mystic sense, or nonsense, of this prediction.

89. In the loose and obscure chronology of the times, I am guided by an authentic record (in the book of ceremonies of Constantine Porphyrogenitus), which certifies that June 4, A.D. 638, the emperor crowned his younger son Heraclius, in the presence of his eldest, Constantine, and in the palace of Constantinople; that January 1, A.D. 639, the royal procession visited the great church, and, on the 4th of the same month, the hippodrome.

90. Sixty-five years before Christ, Syria Pontusque Cn. Pompeii virtutis monumenta sunt (Vell. Patercul. ii. 38), rather of his fortune and power; he adjudged Syria to be a Roman province,

and the last of the Seleucides were incapable of drawing a sword in the defence of their patrimony (see the original texts collected by Usher, Annal. p. 420).

91. Abulfeda, Annal. Moslem. p. 73. Mohammed could artfully vary the praises of his disciples. Of Omar he was accustomed to say, that, if a prophet could arise after himself, it would be Omar, and that in a general calamity Omar would be accepted by the divine justice (Ockley, vol. i. p. 221.)

92. Al Wakidi had likewise written a history of the conquest of Diarbekir, or Mesopotamia (Ockley, at the end of the second vol.), which our interpreters do not appear to have seen. The Chronicle of Dionysius of Telmar, the Jacobite patriarch, records the taking of Edessa A.D. 637, and of Dara A.D. 641 (Asseman. Biblioth. Orient. tom. ii. p. 103); and the attentive may glean some doubtful information from the Chronography of Theophanes (p. 285–287 [t. i. p. 526, sqq. ed. Bonn]). Most of the towns of Mesopotamia yielded by surrender (Abulpharag. p. 112).

93. He dreamt that he was at Thessalonica, a harmless and unmeaning vision; but his soothsayer, or his cowardice, understood the sure omen of a defeat concealed in that inauspicious word θὲς ἄλλῳ νίκην, Give to another the victory (Theoph. p. 287 [vol. i. p. 529, ed Bonn.]; Zonaras, tom. ii. l. xiv. [c. 19] p. 88).

94. Every passage and every fact that relates to the isle, the city, and the colossus of Rhodes, are compiled in the laborious treatise of Meursius, who has bestowed the same diligence on the two larger islands of Crete and Cyprus. See, in the third vol. of his works, the Rhodus of Meursius (l. i. c. 15, p. 715–719). The Byzantine writers, Theophanes and Constantine, have ignorantly prolonged the term to 1360 years, and ridiculously divide the weight among 30,000 camels.

95. Centum colossi alium nobilitaturi locum, says Pliny, with his usual spirit. Hist. Natur. xxxiv. 18.

96. We learn this anecdote from a spirited old woman, who reviled to their faces the caliph and his friend. She was encouraged by the silence of Amrou and the liberality of Moawiyah (Abulfeda, Annal. Moslem. p. 111).

97. Gagnier, Vie de Mahomet, tom. ii. p. 46, etc., who quotes the Abyssinian history, or romance, of Abdel Balcides. Yet the fact of the embassy and ambassador may be allowed.

98. This saying is preserved by Pocock (Not. ad Carmen Tograi, p. 184), and justly applauded by Mr. Harris (Philosophical Arrangements, p. 350).

99. For the life and character of Amrou, see Ockley (Hist. of the Saracens, vol. i. p. 28, 63, 94, 328, 342, 344, and to the end of the volume; vol. ii. p. 51, 55, 57, 74, 110–112, 162) and Otter (Mém. de l'Académie des Inscriptions, tom. xxi. p. 131, 132). The readers of Tacitus may aptly compare Vespasian and Mucianus with Moawiyah and

Amrou. Yet the resemblance is still more in the situation, than in the characters, of the men.

100. Al Wakidi had likewise composed a separate history of the conquest of Egypt, which Mr. Ockley could never procure; and his own inquiries (vol. i. p. 344–362) have added very little to the original text of Eutychius (Annal. tom. ii. p. 296–323, vers. Pocock), the Melchite patriarch of Alexandria, who lived three hundred years after the revolution.

101. Strabo, an accurate and attentive spectator, observes of Heliopolis νυνὶ μὲν οὖν ἐστι πανέρημος ἡ πόλις (Geograph. l. xvii. p. 1158 [p. 805, ed. Casaub.]); but of Memphis he declares πόλις δ' ἐστὶ μεγαλή τε καὶ εὔανδρος, δευτέρα μετ' Ἀλεξάνδειαν (p. 1161 [p. 807, ed. Casaub.]): he notices, however, the mixture of inhabitants, and the ruin of the palaces. In the proper Egypt, Ammianus enumerates Memphis among the four cities, maximus urbibus quibus provincia nitet (xxii. 16); and the name of Memphis appears with distinction in the Roman Itinerary and episcopal lists.

102. These rare and curious facts, the breadth (2946 feet) and the bridge of the Nile, are only to be found in the Danish traveller and the Nubian geographer (p. 98).

103. From the month of April the Nile begins imperceptibly to rise; the swell becomes strong and visible in the moon after the summer solstice (Plin. Hist. Nat. v. 10), and is usually proclaimed at Cairo on St. Peter's day (June 29). A register of thirty successive years marks the greatest height of the waters between July 25 and August 18 (Maillet, Description de l'Egypte, lettre xi. p. 67, etc.; Pocock's Description of the East, vol. i. p. 200; Shaw's Travels, p. 383).

104. Murtadi, Merveilles de l'Egypte, p. 243–259. He expatiates on the subject with the zeal and minuteness of a citizen and a bigot, and his local traditions have a strong air of truth and accuracy.

105. D'Herbelot, Bibliothèque Orientale, p. 233.

106. The position of New and Old Cairo is well known, and has been often described. Two writers who were intimately acquainted with ancient and modern Egypt have fixed, after a learned inquiry, the city of Memphis at *Gizeh*, directly opposite the Old Cairo (Sicard, Nouveaux Mémoires des Missions du Levant, tom. vi. p. 5, 6; Shaw's Observations and Travels, p. 296–304). Yet we may not disregard the authority or the arguments of Pocock (vol. i. p. 25–41), Niebuhr (Voyage, tom. i. p. 77–106), and, above all, of D'Anville (Description de l'Egypte, p. 111, 112, 130–149), who have removed Memphis towards the village of Mohannah, some miles farther to the south. In their heat the disputants have forgot that the ample space of a metropolis covers and annihilates the far greater part of the controversy.

107. See Herodotus, l. iii. c. 27, 28, 29; Ælian. Hist. Var. l. iv. c. 8; Suidas in Ωχος, tom. ii. p. 774; Diodor. Sicul. tom. ii. l. xvii. [c. 49] p. 197, ed.

Wesseling. Τῶν Περσῶν ἠσεβηκότων εἰς τὰ ἱερά, says the last of these historians.

108. Mokawkas sent the prophet two Coptic damsels, with two maids and one eunuch, an alabaster vase, an ingot of pure gold, oil, honey, and the finest white linen of Egypt, with a horse, a mule, and an ass, distinguished by their respective qualifications. The embassy of Mohammed was despatched from Medina in the seventh year of the Hegira (A.D. 628). See Gagnier (Vie de Mahomet, tom. ii. p. 255, 256, 303), from Al Jannabi.

109. The præfecture of Egypt, and the conduct of the war, had been trusted by Heraclius to the patriarch Cyrus (Theophan. p. 280, 281, [t. i. p. 518, 519, ed. Bonn.]). "In Spain," said James II., "do you not consult your priests?" "We do," replied the Catholic ambassador, "and our affairs succeed accordingly." I know not how to relate the plans of Cyrus, of paying tribute without impairing the revenue, and of converting Omar by his marriage with the emperor's daughter (Nicephor. Breviar. p. 17, 18 [ed. Par. 1648]).

110. See the Life of Benjamin, in Renaudot (Hist. Patriarch. Alexandrin. p. 156–172), who has enriched the conquest of Egypt with some facts from the Arabic text of Severus the Jacobite historian.

111. The local description of Alexandria is perfectly ascertained by the master-hand of the first of geographers (D'Anville, Mémoire sur l'Egypte, p. 52–63); but we may borrow the eyes of the modern travellers, more especially of Thevenot (Voyage au Levant, part i. p. 381–395), Pocock (vol. i. p. 2–13), and Niebuhr (Voyage en Arabie, tom. i. p. 34–43). Of the two modern rivals, Savary and Volney, the one may amuse, the other will instruct.

112. Both Eutychius (Annal. tom. ii. p. 319) and Elmacin (Hist. Saracen. p. 28) concur in fixing the taking of Alexandria to Friday of the new moon of Moharram of the twentieth year of the Hegira (December 22, A.D. 640). In reckoning backwards fourteen months spent before Alexandria, seven months before Babylon, etc., Amrou might have invaded Egypt about the end of the year 638: but we are assured that he entered the country the 12th of Bayni, 6th of June (Murtardi, Merveilles de l'Egypte, p. 164; Severus, apud Renaudot, p. 162). The Saracen, and afterwards Lewis IX. of France, halted at Pelusium, or Damietta, during the season of the inundation of the Nile.

113. Eutych. Annal. tom. ii. p. 316, 319.

114. Notwithstanding some inconsistencies of Theophanes and Cedrenus, the accuracy of Pagi (Critica, tom. ii. p. 824) has extracted from Nicephorus and the Chronicon Orientale the true date of the death of Heraclius, February 11th, A.D. 641, fifty days after the loss of Alexandria. A fourth of that time was sufficient to convey the intelligence.

115. Many treatises of this lover of labour (φιλόπονος) are still extant; but for readers of the

present age, the printed and unpublished are nearly in the same predicament. Moses and Aristotle are the chief objects of his verbose commentaries, one of which is dated as early as May 10th, A.D. 617 (Fabric. Biblioth. Græc. tom. ix. p. 458–468). A modern (John Le Clerc), who sometimes assumed the same name, was equal to old Philoponus in diligence, and far superior in good sense and real knowledge.

116. Abulpharag. Dynast. p. 114, vers. Pocock. Audi quid factum sit et mirare. It would be endless to enumerate the moderns who have wondered and believed, but I may distinguish with honour the rational scepticism of Renaudot (Hist. Alex. Patriarch. p. 170): historia . . . habet aliquid ἄπιστον ut Arabibus familiare est.

117. This curious anecdote will be vainly sought in the annals of Eutychius, and the Saracenic history of Elmacin. The silence of Abulfeda, Murtadi, and a crowd of Moslems, is less conclusive, from their ignorance of Christian literature.

118. See Reland, de Jure Militari Mohammedanorum, in his third volume of Dissertations, p. 37. The reason for not burning the religious books of the Jews or Christians is derived from the respect that is due to the *name* of God.

119. Consult the collections of Frensheim (Supplement. Livian. c. 12, 43) and Usher (Annal. p. 469). Livy himself had styled the Alexandrian library, elegantiæ regum curæque egregium opus —a liberal encomium, for which he is pertly criticised by the narrow stoicism of Seneca (De Tranquillitate Animi, c. 9), whose wisdom on this occasion deviates into nonsense.

120. See this History, vol. i. p. 462.

121. Aulus Gellius (Noctes Atticæ, vi. 17), Ammianus Marcellinus (xxii. 16), and Orosius (l. vi. c. 15 [p. 421]). They all speak in the *past* tense, and the words of Ammanius are remarkably strong: fuerunt Bibliothecæ innumerabiles [inæstimabiles]; et loquitur monumentorum veterum concinens fides, etc.

122. Renaudot answers for versions of the Bible, Hexapla, *Catenæ Patrum*, Commentaries, etc. (p. 170). Our Alexandrian MS., if it came from Egypt, and not from Constantinople or Mount Athos Wetstein, Prolegom. ad. N. T. p. 8, etc.), might *possibly* be among them.

123. I have often perused with pleasure a chapter of Quintilian (Institut. Orator. x. 1) in which that judicious critic enumerates and appreciates the series of Greek and Latin classics.

124. Such as Galen, Pliny, Aristotle, etc. On this subject Wotton (Reflections on Ancient and Modern Learning, p. 85–95) argues with solid sense against the lively exotic fancies of Sir William Temple. The contempt of the Greeks for *barbaric* science would scarcely admit the Indian or Æthiopic books into the library of Alexandria; nor is it proved that philosophy has sustained any real loss from their exclusion.

125. This curious and authentic intelligence of

Murtadi (p. 284–289) has not been discovered either by Mr. Ockley or by the self-sufficient compilers of the Modern Universal History.

126. Eutychius, Annal. tom. ii. p. 320. Elmacin, Hist. Saracen. p. 35.

127. On these *obscure* canals the reader may try to satisfy himself from D'Anville (Mém. sur l'Egypte, p. 108–110, 124, 132), and a learned thesis, maintained and printed at Strasburg in the year 1770 (Jungendorum marium fluviorumque molimina, p. 39–47, 68–70). Even the supine Turks have agitated the old project of joining the two seas (Mémoires du Baron de Tott, tom. iv.).

128. A small volume, des Merveilles, etc., de l'Egypte, composed in the thirteenth century by Murtadi of Cairo, and translated from an Arabic MS. of Cardinal Mazarin, was published by Pierre Vatier, Paris, 1666. The antiquities of Egypt are wild and legendary; but the writer deserves credit and esteem for his account of the conquest and geography of his native country (see the Correspondence of Amrou and Omar, p. 279–289).

129. In a twenty years' residence at Cairo, the consul Maillet had contemplated that varying scene—the Nile (Lettre ii., particularly p. 70, 75); the fertility of the land (Lettre ix.). From a college at Cambridge the poetic eye of Gray had *seen* the same objects with a keener glance:—

> What wonder in the sultry climes that spread,
> Where Nile, redundant o'er his summer bed,
> From his broad bosom life and verdure flings,
> And broods o'er Egypt with his wat'ry wings,
> If with advent'rous oar, and ready sail,
> The dusky people drive before the gale,
> Or on frail floats to neighbouring cities ride,
> That rise and glitter o'er the ambient tide.
> (Mason's Works and Memoirs of Gray,
> p. 199, 200.)

130. Murtadi, p. 164–167. The reader will not easily credit a human sacrifice under the Christian emperors, or a miracle of the successors of Mohammed.

131. Maillet, Description de l'Egypte, p. 22. He mentions this number as the *common* opinion; and adds that the generality of these villages contain two or three thousand persons, and that many of them are more populous than our large cities.

132. Eutych. Annal. tom. ii. p. 308, 311. The twenty millions are computed from the following *data:* one-twelfth of mankind above sixty, one-third below sixteen, the proportion of men to women as seventeen to sixteen (Recherches sur la Population de la France, p. 71, 72). The president Goguet (Origine des Arts, etc. tom. iii. p. 26, etc.) bestows twenty-seven millions on ancient Egypt, because the seventeen hundred companions of Sesostris were born on the same day.

133. Elmacin, Hist. Saracen. p. 218; and this gross lump is swallowed without scruple by D'Herbelot (Biblioth. Orient. p. 1031), Arbuthnot (Tables of Ancient Coins, p. 262), and De Guignes (Hist. des Huns, tom. iii. p. 135). They might

allege the not less extravagant liberality of Appian in favour of the Ptolemies (in præfat.) of seventy-four myriads, 740,000 talents, an annual income of 185, or near 300, millions of pounds sterling, according as we reckon by the Egyptian or the Alexandrian talent (Bernard de Ponderibus Antiq. p. 186).

134. See the measurement of D'Anville (Mém. sur l'Egypte, p. 23, etc.). After some peevish cavils, M. Pauw (Recherches sur les Egyptiens, tom. i. p. 118-121) can only enlarge his reckoning to 2250 square leagues.

135. Renaudot, Hist. Patriarch. Alexand. p. 334, who calls the common reading or version of Elmacin *error librarii*. His own emendation, of 4,300,000 pieces, in the ninth century, maintains a probable medium between the 3,000,000 which the Arabs acquired by the conquest of Egypt (idem, p. 168), and the 2,400,000 which the sultan of Constantinople levied in the last century (Pietro della Valle, tom. i. p. 352; Thevenot, part i. p. 824). Pauw (Recherches, tom. ii. p. 365-373) gradually raises the revenue of the Pharaohs, the Ptolemies, and the Cæsars, from six to fifteen millions of German crowns.

136. The list of Schultens (Index Geograph. ad calcem Vit. Saladin. p. 5) contains 2396 places; that of D'Anville (Mém. sur l'Egypte, p. 29), from the divan of Cairo, enumerates 2696.

137. See Maillet (Description de l'Egypte, p. 28), who seems to argue with candour and judgment. I am much better satisfied with the observations than with the reading of the French consul. He was ignorant of Greek and Latin literature, and his fancy is too much delighted with the fictions of the Arabs. Their best knowledge is collected by Abulfeda (Descript. Ægypt. Arab. et Lat. à Joh. David Michaelis, Göttingæ, in 4to, 1776); and in two recent voyages into Egypt, we are amused by Savary, and instructed by Volney. I wish the latter could travel over the globe.

138. My conquest of Africa is drawn from two French interpreters of Arabic literature, Cardonne (Hist. de l'Afrique et de l'Espagne sous la Domination des Arabes, tom. i. p. 8-55) and Otter (Hist. de l'Académie des Inscriptions, tom. xxi. p. 111-125 and 136). They derive their principal information from Novairi, who composed, A.D. 1331, an Encyclopædia in more than twenty volumes. The five general parts successively treat of, 1. Physics; 2. Man; 3. Animals; 4. Plants; and 5. History; and the African affairs are discussed in the sixth chapter of the fifth section of this last part (Reiske, Prodidagmata ad Hagji Chalifæ Tabulas, p. 232-234). Among the older historians who are quoted by Novairi we may distinguish the original narrative of a soldier who led the van of the Moslems.

139. See the history of Abdallah, in Abulfeda (Vit. Mohammed, p. 109) and Gagnier (Vie de Mahomet, tom. iii. p. 45-48).

140. The province and city of Tripoli are de-scribed by Leo Africanus (in Navigatione et Viaggi di Ramusio, tom. i. Venetia, 1550, fol. 76 *verso*) and Marmol (Description de l'Afrique, tom. ii. p. 562). The first of these writers was a Moor, a scholar, and a traveller, who composed or trans-lated his African geography in a state of captivity at Rome, where he had assumed the name and religion of Pope Leo X. In a similar captivity among the Moors, the Spaniard Marmol, a soldier of Charles V., compiled his Description of Africa, translated by D'Ablancourt into French (Paris, 1667, 3 vols. in 4to). Marmol had read and seen, but he is destitute of the curious and extensive observation which abounds in the original work of Leo the African.

141. Theophanes, who mentions the defeat, rather than the death, of Gregory. He brands the præfect with the name of Τύραννος: he had prob-ably assumed the purple (Chronograph. p. 285 [tom. i. p. 525, ed. Bonn.]).

142. See in Ockley (Hist. of the Saracens, vol. ii. p. 45) the death of Zobeir, which was honoured with the tears of Ali, against whom he had rebelled *His* valour at the siege of Babylon, if indeed it be the same person, is mentioned by Eutychius (An-nal. tom. ii. p. 308).

143. Shaw's Travels, p. 118, 119.

144. Mimica emptio, says Abulfeda, erat hæc, et mira donatio; quando-quidem Othman, ejus nomine nummos ex ærario prius ablatos ærario præstabat (Annal. Moslem. p. 78). Elmacin (in his cloudy version, p. 39) seems to report the same job. When the Arabs besieged the palace of Oth-man, it stood high in their catalogue of grievances.

145. Ἐπεστράτευσαν Σαρακηνοὶ τὴν Ἀφρικήν, καὶ συμβάλοντες τῷ τυράννῳ Γρηγορίῳ τοῖτον τρέπουσι, καὶ τοὺς σὺν αὐτῷ κτείνουσι, καὶ στοιχήσαντες φόρους μετὰ τῳν Ἄφρων ὑπέστρεψαν. Theophan. Chrono-graph. p. 285, edit. Paris [vol. i. p. 525, ed. Bonn] His chronology is loose and inaccurate.

146. Theophanes (in Chronograph. p. 293 [vol. i. p. 539]) inserts the vague rumours that might reach Constantinople of the Western conquests of the Arabs; and I learn from Paul Warnefrid, deacon of Aquileia (de Gestis Langobard. l. v. c 13), that at this time they sent a fleet from Alex-andria into the Sicilian and African seas.

147. See Novairi (apud Otter, p. 118), Leo Africanus (fol. 81, *verso*), who reckons only cinque città e infinite casale, Marmol (Description de l'Afrique, tom. iii. p. 33), and Shaw (Travels, p. 57, 65-68).

148. Leo African. fol. 58, *verso;* 59, *recto;* Mar-mol, tom. ii. p. 415; Shaw, p. 43.

149. Leo African. fol. 52; Marmol, tom. ii. p. 228.

150. Regio ignobilis, et vix quicquam illustre sortita, parvis oppidis habitatur, parva flumina emittit, solo quam viris melior, et segnitie gentis obscura. Pomponius Mela, i. 5; iii. 10. Mela de-serves the more credit, since his own Phœnician ancestors had migrated from Tingitana to Spain

see, in ii. 6, a passage of that geographer so cru-lly tortured by Salmasius, Isaac Vossius, and the most virulent of critics, James Gronovius). He ved at the time of the final reduction of that ountry by the emperor Claudius; yet, almost nirty years afterwards, Pliny (Hist. Nat. v. i.) omplains of his authors, too lazy to inquire, too roud to confess their ignorance of that wild and emote province.

151. The foolish fashion of this citron-wood pre-ailed at Rome among the men, as much as the aste for pearls among the women. A round board r table, four or five feet in diameter, sold for the rice of an estate (latifundii taxatione), eight, ten, r twelve thousand pounds sterling (Plin. Hist. Natur. xiii. 29). I conceive that I must not con-ound the tree *citrus* with that of the fruit *citrum*. Sut I am not botanist enough to define the former it is like the wild cypress) by the vulgar or Lin-æan name; nor will I decide whether the *citrum* be the orange or the lemon. Salmasius appears to xhaust the subject, but he too often involves him-elf in the web of his disorderly erudition (Plinian. Exercitat. tom. ii. p. 666, etc.).

152. Leo African. fol. 16, *verso*. Marmol. tom. ii. o. 28. This province, the first scene of the exploits and greatness of the *cherifs*, is often mentioned in he curious history of that dynasty at the end of the hird volume of Marmol, Description de l'Afrique. The third volume of the Recherches Historiques ur les Maures (lately published at Paris) illus-rates the history and geography of the kingdoms of Fez and Morocco.

153. Otter (p. 119) has given the strong tone of anaticism to this exclamation, which Cardonne p. 37) has softened to a pious wish of *preaching* the Koran. Yet they had both the same text of No-airi before their eyes.

154. The foundation of Cairoan is mentioned by Ockley (Hist. of the Saracens, vol. ii. p. 129, 30); and the situation, mosch, etc., of the city are lescribed by Leo Africanus (fol. 75), Marmol tom. ii. p. 532), and Shaw (p. 115).

155. A portentous though frequent, mistake nas been the confounding, from a slight similitude of name, the *Cyrene* of the Greeks and the *Cairoan* of he Arabs, two cities which are separated by an nterval of a thousand miles along the sea-coast. The great Thuanus has not escaped this fault, the ess excusable as it is connected with a formal and elaborate description of Africa (Historiar. l. vii. c. 2, in tom. i. p. 240, edit. Buckley).

156. Besides the Arabic chronicles of Abulfeda, Elmacin, and Abulpharagius, under the seventy-hird year of the Hegira, we may consult D'Her-belot (Biblioth. Orient. p. 7) and Ockley (Hist. of he Saracens, vol. ii. p. 339–349). The latter has given the last and pathetic dialogue between Ab-lallah and his mother, but he has forgot a physical effect of *her* grief for his death, the return, at the age of ninety, and fatal consequences of her *menses*.

157. Λεόντιος . . . ἅπαντα τὰ Ῥωμαϊκὰ ἐξώπλισε πλόϊμα, στρατηγόν τε ἐπ' αὐτοῖς Ἰωάννην τὸν Πατ-ρίκιον ἔμπειρον τῶν πολεμίων προχειρισάμενος πρὸς Καρχηδόνα κατὰ τῶν Σαρακηνῶν ἐξέπεμψεν. Nice-phori Constantinopolitani Breviar. p. 26. The patriarch of Constantinople, with Theophanes (Chronograph. p. 309 [vol. i. p. 566, *sq.*, ed. Bonn]), have slightly mentioned this last attempt for the relief of Africa. Pagi (Critica, tom. iii. p. 129, 141) has nicely ascertained the chronology by a strict comparison of the Arabic and Byzantine historians, who often disagree both in time and fact. See like-wise a note of Otter (p. 121).

158. Dove s'erano ridotti i nobili Romani e i *Gotti;* and afterwards, i Romani fuggirono e i *Gotti* lasciarono Carthagine (Leo African. fol. 72, *recto*.). I know not from what Arabic writer the African derived his Goths; but the fact, though new, is so interesting and so probable, that I will accept it on the slightest authority.

159. This commander is styled by Nicephorus Βασιλεὺς Σαρακηνῶν, a vague though not improper definition of the caliph. Theophanes introduces the strange appellation of Πρωτοσύμβολος, which his interpreter Goar explains by *Vizir Azem*. They may approach the truth, in assigning the active part to the minister rather than the prince; but they forget that the Ommiades had only a *kateb*, or secretary, and that the office of Vizir was not re-vived or instituted till the 132nd year of the Hegira (D'Herbelot, p. 912).

160. According to Solinus (c. 27 [§ 11], p. 36, edit. Salmas.), the Carthage of Dido stood either 677 or 737 years—a various reading, which pro-ceeds from the difference of MSS. or editions (Sal-mas. Plin. Exercit. tom. i. p. 228). The former of these accounts, which gives 823 years before Christ, is more consistent with the well-weighed testimony of Velleius Paterculus; but the latter is preferred by our chronologist (Marsham, Canon. Chron. p. 398) as more agreeable to the Hebrew and Tyrian annals.

161. Leo African. fol. 71, *verso*; 72, *recto*. Mar-mol. tom. ii. p. 445–447. Shaw, p. 80.

162. The history of the word *Barbar* may be classed under four periods. 1. In the time of Homer, when the Greeks and Asiatics might probably use a common idiom, the imitative sound of Bar-bar was applied to the ruder tribes, whose pronunciation was most harsh, whose grammar was most defective. Κάρες Βαρβαρόφωνοι (Iliad, ii. 867, with the Oxford Scholiast Clarke's Anno-tation, and Henry Stephens's Greek Thesaurus, tom. i. p. 720). 2. From the time, at least, of He-rodotus, it was extended to *all* the nations who were strangers to the language and manners of the Greeks. 3. In the age of Plautus, the Romans sub-mitted to the insult (Pompeius Festus, l. ii. p. 48, edit. Dacier), and freely gave themselves the name of barbarians. They insensibly claimed an exemp-tion for Italy and her subject provinces; and at length removed the disgraceful appellation to the savage or hostile nations beyond the pale of the

empire. 4. In every sense it was due to the Moors: the familiar word was borrowed from the Latin provincials by the Arabian conquerors, and has justly settled as a local denomination (Barbary) along the northern coast of Africa.

163. The first book of Leo Africanus, and the observations of Dr. Shaw (p. 220, 223, 227, 247, etc.), will throw some light on the roving tribes of Barbary, of Arabian or Moorish descent. But Shaw had seen these savages with distant terror; and Leo, a captive in the Vatican, appears to have lost more of his Arabic than he could acquire of Greek or Roman learning. Many of his gross mistakes might be detected in the first period of the Mohammedan history.

164. In a conference with a prince of the Greeks, Amrou observed that their religion was different; upon which score it was lawful for brothers to quarrel. Ockley's History of the Saracens, vol. i. p. 328.

165. Abulfeda, Annal. Moslem. p. 78, vers. Reiske.

166. The name of Andalusia is applied by the Arabs not only to the modern province, but to the whole peninsula of Spain (Geograph. Nub. p. 151; D'Herbelot, Biblioth. Orient. p. 114, 115). The etymology has been most improbably deduced from Vandalusia, country of the Vandals (D'Anville, Etats de l'Europe, p. 146, 147, etc.). But the Handalusia of Casiri, which signifies, in Arabic, the region of the evening, of the West, in a word, the Hesperia of the Greeks, is perfectly apposite (Biblioth. Arabico-Hispana, tom. ii. p. 327, etc.).

167. The fall and resurrection of the Gothic monarchy are related by Mariana (tom. i. p. 238–260; l. vi. c. 19–26; l. vii. c. 1, 2). That historian has infused into his noble work (Historiæ de Rebus Hispaniæ, libri xxx.; Hagæ Comitum, 1733, in four volumes in folio, with the Continuation of Miniana) the style and spirit of a Roman classic; and, after the twelfth century, his knowledge and judgment may be safely trusted. But the Jesuit is not exempt from the prejudices of his order; he adopts and adorns, like his rival Buchanan, the most absurd of the national legends; he is too careless of criticism and chronology, and supplies, from a lively fancy, the chasms of historical evidence. These chasms are large and frequent; Roderic, archbishop of Toledo, the father of the Spanish history, lived five hundred years after the conquest of the Arabs; and the more early accounts are comprised in some meagre lines of the blind chronicles of Isidore of Badajoz (Pacensis) and of Alphonso III, king of Leon, which I have seen only in the annals of Pagi.

168. Le viol (says Voltaire) est aussi difficile à faire qu'à prouver. Des Evêques se seroient-ils ligués pour une fille? (Hist. Générale, c. xxvi.) His argument is not logically conclusive.

169. In the story of Cava, Mariana (l. vi. c. 21, p. 241, 242) seems to vie with the Lucretia of Livy. Like the ancients, he seldom quotes; and the oldest testimony of Baronius (Annal. Eccles. A.D. 713, N 19), that of Lucas Tudensis, a Gallician deacon the thirteenth century, only says, Cava quam p concubinâ utebatur.

170. The Orientals, Elmacin, Abulpharagiu Abulfeda, pass over the conquest of Spain in s lence, or with a single word. The text of Novai and the other Arabian writers, is represented though with some foreign alloy, by M. de Ca donne (Hist. de l'Afrique et de l'Espagne sous Domination des Arabes, Paris, 1765, 3 vols. 12mo, tom. i. p. 55–114), and more concisely b M. de Guignes (Hist. des Huns, tom. i. p. 347 350). The librarian of the Escurial has not satisfie my hopes: yet he appears to have searched wit diligence his broken materials; and the history the conquest is illustrated by some valuable fra ments of the *genuine* Razis (who wrote at Cordub A.H. 300) of Ben Hazil, etc. See Biblioth. Arabic Hispana, tom. ii. p. 32, 105, 106, 182, 252, 31 332. On this occasion the industry of Pagi has bee aided by the Arabic learning of his friend the Abb de Longuerue, and to their joint labours I a deeply indebted.

171. A mistake of Roderic of Toledo, in cor paring the lunar years of the Hegira with th Julian years of the Era, has determined Baroniu Mariana, and the crowd of Spanish historians place the first invasion in the year 713, and th battle of Xeres in November, 714. This anach ronism of three years has been detected by th more correct industry of modern chronologist above all, of Pagi (Critica, tom. iii. p. 169, 171 174), who have restored the genuine date of th revolution. At the present time an Arabian schola like Cardonne, who adopts the ancient error (ton i. p. 75), is inexcusably ignorant or careless.

172. The Era of Cæsar, which in Spain was i legal and popular use till the fourteenth centur begins thirty-eight years before the birth of Chris I would refer the origin to the general peace b sea and land, which confirmed the power an *partition* of the Triumvirs (Dion Cassius, l. xlviii. 547, 553 [c. 28 and 36]. Appian de Bell. Civil. l. [c. 72] p. 1034, edit. fol.). Spain was a province Cæsar Octavian; and Tarragona, which raise the first temple to Augustus (Tacit. Annal. i. 78 might borrow from the Orientals this mode flattery.

173. The road, the country, the old castle Count Julian, and the superstitious belief of th Spaniards of hidden treasures, etc., are describe by Père Labat (Voyages en Espagne et en Itali tom. i. p. 207–217) with his usual pleasantry.

174. The Nubian Geographer (p. 154) explai the topography of the war; but it is highly incred ible that the lieutenant of Musa should execut the desperate and useless measure of burning hi ships.

175. Xeres (the Roman colony of Asta Regia is only two leagues from Cadiz. In the sixteent century it was a granary of corn; and the wine o

Xeres is familiar to the nations of Europe (Lud. Nonii Hispania, c. 13, p. 54–56, a work of correct and concise knowledge; D'Anville, Etats de l'Europe, etc. p. 154).

176. Id sane infortunii regibus pedem ex acie referentibus sæpe contingit. Ben Hazil of Granada, in Biblioth. Arabico-Hispana, tom. ii. p. 327. Some credulous Spaniards believe that king Roderic, or Rodrigo, escaped to a hermit's cell; and others, that he was cast alive into a tub full of serpents, from whence he exclaimed, with a lamentable voice, "They devour the part with which I have so grievously sinned." (Don Quixote, part ii. ch. 33.)

177. The direct road from Corduba to Toledo was measured by Mr. Swinburne's mules in 72½ hours; but a larger computation must be adopted for the slow and devious marches of an army. The Arabs traversed the province of La Mancha, which the pen of Cervantes has transformed into classic ground to the readers of every nation.

178. The antiquities of Toledo, *Urbs Parva* in the Punic wars, *Urbs Regia* in the sixth century, are briefly described by Nonius (Hispania, c. 59, p. 181–186). He borrows from Roderic the *fatale palatium* of Moorish portraits, but modestly insinuates that it was no more than a Roman amphitheatre.

179. In the Historia Arabum (c. 9, p. 17, ad calcem Elmacin), Roderic of Toledo describes the emerald tables, and inserts the name of Medinat Almeyda, in Arabic words and letters. He appears to be conversant with the Mohammedan writers; but I cannot agree with M. de Guignes (Hist. des Huns, tom. i. p. 350), that he had read and transcribed Novairi; because he was dead a hundred years before Novairi composed his history. This mistake is founded on a still grosser error. M. de Guignes confounds the historian Roderic Ximenes archbishop of Toledo in the thirteenth century, with Cardinal Ximenes who governed Spain in the beginning of the sixteenth, and was the subject, not the author, of historical compositions.

180. Tarik might have inscribed on the last rock the boast of Regnard and his companions in their Lapland journey:

"Hic tandem stetimus, nobis ubi defuit orbis."

181. Such was the argument of the traitor Oppas, and every chief to whom it was addressed did not answer with the spirit of Pelagius: Omnis Hispania dudum sub uno regimine Gothorum, omnis exercitus Hispaniæ in uno congregatus Ismaelitarum non valuit sustinere impetum. Chron. Alphonsi Regis, apud Pagi, tom. iii. p. 177.

182. The revival of the Gothic kingdom in the Asturias is distinctly though concisely noticed by D'Anville (Etats de l'Europe, p. 159).

183. The honourable relics of the Cantabrian war (Dion Cassius, l. liii. [c. 26] p. 720) were planted in this metropolis of Lusitania, perhaps of Spain (submittit cui tota suos Hispania fasces). Nonius (Hispania, c. 31, p. 106–110) enumerates

the ancient structures, but concludes with a sigh: Urbs hæc olim nobilissima ad magnam incolarum infrequentiam delapsa est, et prætor priscæ claritatis ruinas nihil ostendit.

184. Both the interpreters of Novairi, De Guignes (Hist. des Huns, tom. i. p. 349) and Cardonne (Hist. de l'Afrique et de l'Espagne, tom. i. p. 93, 94, 104, 105), lead Musa into the Narbonnese Gaul. But I find no mention of this enterprise, either in Roderic of Toledo, or the MSS. of the Escurial, and the invasion of the Saracens is postponed by a French chronicle till the ninth year after the conquest of Spain, A.D. 721 (Pagi, Critica, tom. iii. p. 177, 195; Historians of France, tom. iii.). I much question whether Musa ever passed the Pyrenees.

185. Four hundred years after Theodemir, his territories of Murcia and Carthagena retain in the Nubian geographer Edrisi (p. 154, 161) the name of Tadmir (D'Anville, Etats de l'Europe, p. 156; Pagi, tom. iii. p. 174). In the present decay of Spanish agriculture Mr. Swinburne (Travels into Spain, p. 119) surveyed with pleasure the delicious valley from Murcia to Orihuela, four leagues and a half of the finest corn, pulse, lucern, oranges, etc.

186. See the treaty in Arabic and Latin, in the Bibliotheca Arabico-Hispana, tom. ii. p. 105, 106. It is signed the 4th of the month of Regeb, A.H. 94, the 5th of April, A.D. 713; a date which seems to prolong the resistance of Theodemir, and the government of Musa.

187. From the history of Sandoval, p. 87. Fleury (Hist. Ecclés. tom. ix. p. 261) has given the substance of another treaty concluded A.Æ.C. 782, A.D. 734, between an Arabian chief and the Goths and Romans, of the territory of Coimbra in Portugal. The tax of the churches is fixed at twenty-five pounds of gold; of the monasteries, fifty; of the cathedrals, one hundred: the Christians are judged by their count, but in capital cases he must consult the alcaide. The church doors must be shut, and they must respect the name of Mohammed. I have not the original before me; it would confirm or destroy a dark suspicion that the piece has been forged to introduce the immunity of a neighbouring convent.

188. This design, which is attested by *several* Arabian historians (Cardonne, tom. i. p. 95, 96), may be compared with that of Mithridates, to march from the Crimea to Rome; or with that of Cæsar, to conquer the East and return home by the North; and all three are perhaps surpassed by the *real* and successful enterprise of Hannibal.

189. I much regret our loss, or my ignorance, of two Arabic works of the eighth century, a Life of Musa, and a Poem on the exploits of Tarik. Of these authentic pieces, the former was composed by a grandson of Musa, who had escaped from the massacre of his kindred; the latter by the Vizir of the first Abdalrahman, caliph of Spain, who might have conversed with some of the veterans of the

conqueror (Biblioth. Arabico-Hispana, tom. ii. p. 36, 139).

190. Biblioth. Arab.-Hispana, tom. ii. p. 32, 252. The former of these quotations is taken from a *Biographia Hispanica*, by an Arabian of Valentia (see the copious Extracts of Casiri, tom. ii. p. 30–121); and the latter from a general Chronology of the Caliphs, and of the African and Spanish Dynasties, with a particular History of the kingdom of Granada, of which Casiri has given almost an entire version (Biblioth. Arabico-Hispana, tom. ii. p. 177–319). The author, Ebn Khateb, a native of Granada, and a contemporary of Novairi and Abulfeda (born A.D. 1313, died A.D. 1374), was an historian, geographer, physician, poet, etc. (tom. ii. p. 71, 72).

191. Cardonne, Hist. de l'Afrique et de l'Espagne, tom. i. p. 116, 117.

192. A copious treatise of husbandry, by an Arabian of Seville, in the twelfth century, is in the Escurial library, and Casiri had some thoughts of translating it. He gives a list of the authors quoted, Arabs as well as Greeks, Latins, etc.; but it is much if the Andalusian saw these strangers through the medium of his countryman Columella (Casiri, Biblioth. Arabico-Hispana, tom. i. p. 323–338).

193. Biblioth. Arabico-Hispana, tom. ii. p. 104. Casiri translates the original testimony of the historian Rasis, as it is alleged in the Arabic Biographia Hispanica, pars ix. But I am most exceedingly surprised at the address, Principibus cæterisque Christianis Hispanis suis *Castellæ*. The name of Castellæ was unknown in the eighth century; the kingdom was not erected till the year 1022, an hundred years after the time of Rasis (Biblioth. tom. ii. p. 330), and the appellation was always expressive, not of a tributary province, but of a line of *castles* independent of the Moorish yoke (D'Anville, Etats de l'Europe, p. 166–170). Had Casiri been a critic, he would have cleared a difficulty, perhaps of his own making.

194. Cardonne, tom. i. p. 337, 338. He computes the revenue at 130,000,000 of French livres. The entire picture of peace and prosperity relieves the bloody uniformity of the Moorish annals.

195. I am happy enough to possess a splendid and interesting work, which has only been distributed in presents by the court of Madrid: *Bibliotheca Arabico-Hispana Escurialensis, operâ et studio Michaelis Casiri, Syro Maronitæ. Matriti, in folio, tomus prior*, 1760; *tomus posterior*, 1770. The execution of this work does honour to the Spanish press; the MSS. to the number of MDCCCLI, are judiciously classed by the editor, and his copious extracts throw *some* light on the Mohammedan literature and history of Spain. These relics are now secure, but the task has been supinely delayed, till, in the year 1671, a fire consumed the greatest part of the Escurial library, rich in the spoils of Granada and Morocco.

196. The *Harbii*, as they are styled, qui tolerari nequeunt, are, 1. Those who, *besides* God, worship the sun, moon, or idols. 2. Atheists. Utrique, quamdiu princeps aliquis inter Mohammedanos superest, oppugnari debent donec religionem amplectantur, nec requies iis concedenda est, nec pretium acceptandum pro obtinendâ conscientiæ libertate (Reland, Dissertat. x. de Jure Militari Mohammedan. tom. iii. p. 14): a rigid theory!

197. The distinction between a proscribed and a tolerated sect, between the *Harbii* and the people of the Book, the believers in some divine revelation, is correctly defined in the conversation of the caliph Al Mamun with the idolaters or Sabæans of Charræ. Hottinger, Hist. Orient. p. 107, 108.

198. The Zend or Pazend, the Bible of the Ghebers, is reckoned by themselves, or at least by the Mohammedans, among the ten books which Abraham received from heaven; and their religion is honourably styled the religion of Abraham (D'Herbelot, Biblioth. Orient. p. 701; Hyde, de Religione veterum Persarum, c. iii. p. 27, 28, etc.). I much fear that we do not possess any pure and *free* description of the system of Zoroaster. Dr. Prideaux (Connection, vol. i. p. 300, octavo) adopts the opinion that he had been the slave and scholar of some Jewish prophet in the captivity of Babylon. Perhaps the Persians, who have been the masters of the Jews, would assert the honour—a poor honour—of being *their* masters.

199. The Arabian Nights, a faithful and amusing picture of the Oriental world, represent in the most odious colours the Magians, or worshippers of fire, to whom they attribute the annual sacrifice of a Musulman. The religion of Zoroaster has not the least affinity with that of the Hindoos, yet they are often confounded by the Mohammedans; and the sword of Timour was sharpened by this mistake (Hist. de Timour Bec, par Cherefeddin Ali Yezdi, l. v.).

200. Vie de Mahomet, par Gagnier, tom. iii. p. 114, 115.

201. Hæ tres sectæ, Judæi, Christiani, et qui inter Persas Magorum institutis addicti sunt κατ' ἐξοχήν, *populi libri* dicuntur (Reland, Dissertat. tom. iii. p. 15). The caliph Al Mamun confirms this honourable distinction in favour of the three sects, with the vague and equivocal religion of the Sabæans, under which the ancient polytheists of Charræ were allowed to shelter their idolatrous worship (Hottinger, Hist. Orient. p. 167, 168).

202. This singular story is related by D'Herbelot (Biblioth. Orient. p. 448, 449) on the faith of Khondemir, and by Mirchond himself (Hist. priorum Regum Persarum, etc., p. 9, 10, not. p. 88, 89).

203. Mirchond (Mohammed Emir Khoondah Shah), a native of Herat, composed in the Persian language a general history of the East, from the creation to the year of the Hegira 875 (A.D. 1471). In the year 904 (A.D. 1498) the historian obtained the command of a princely library, and his applauded work, in seven or twelve parts, was abbreviated in three volumes by his son Khondemir,

A.H. 927 (A.D. 1520). The two writers, most accurately distinguished by Petit de la Croix (Hist. de Genghizcan, p. 537, 538, 544, 545), are loosely confounded by D'Herbelot (p. 358, 410, 994, 995); but his numerous extracts, under the improper name of Khondemir, belong to the father rather than the son. The historian of Genghizcan refers to a MS. of Mirchond, which he received from the hands of his friend D'Herbelot himself. A curious fragment (the Taherian and Soffarian Dynasties) has been lately published in Persic and Latin (Viennæ, 1782, in 4to, cum notis Bernard de Jenisch); and the editor allows us to hope for a continuation of Mirchond.

204. Quo testimonio boni se quidpiam præstitisse opinabantur. Yet Mirchond must have condemned their zeal, since he approved the legal toleration of the Magi, cui (the fire temple) peracto singulis annis censû, uti sacra Mohammedis lege cautum, ab omnibus molestiis ac oneribus libero esse licuit.

205. The last Magian of name and power appears to be Mardavige the Dilemite, who, in the beginning of the tenth century, reigned in the northern provinces of Persia, near the Caspian Sea (D'Herbelot, Biblioth. Orient. p. 355). But his soldiers and successors, the *Bowides*, either professed or embraced the Mohammedan faith; and under their dynasty (A.D. 933–1020) I should place the fall of the religion of Zoroaster.

206. The present state of the Ghebers in Persia is taken from Sir John Chardin, not indeed the most learned, but the most judicious and inquisitive, of our modern travellers (Voyages en Perse, tom. ii. p. 109, 179–187, in 4to). His brethren, Pietro della Valle, Olearius, Thevenot, Tavernier, etc., whom I have fruitlessly searched, had neither eyes nor attention for this interesting people.

207. The letter of Abdoulrahman, governor or tyrant of Africa, to the caliph Aboul Abbas, the first of the Abbassides, is dated A.H. 132 (Cardonne, Hist. de l'Afrique et de l'Espagne, tom. i. p. 168).

208. Bibliothèque Orientale, p. 66; Renaudot, Hist. Patriarch. Alex. p. 287, 288.

209. Among the Epistles of the Popes, see Leo IX. Epist. 3; Gregor. VII. l. i. Epist. 22, 23, l. iii. Epist. 19, 20, 21; and the criticisms of Pagi (tom. iv. A.D. 1053, No. 14, A.D. 1073, No. 13), who investigates the name and family of the Moorish prince with whom the proudest of the Roman pontiffs so politely corresponds.

210. Mozarabes, or Mostarabes, *adscititii*, as it is interpreted in Latin (Pocock, Specimen Hist. Arabum, p. 39, 40; Biblioth. Arabico-Hispana, tom. ii. p. 18). The Mozarabic liturgy, the ancient ritual of the church of Toledo, has been attacked by the popes, and exposed to the doubtful trials of the sword and of fire (Marian. Hist. Hispan. tom. i. l. ix. c. 18, p. 378). It was, or rather it is, in the Latin tongue; yet in the eleventh century it was found necessary (A.Æ.C. 1087—A.D.1039) to transcribe an Arabic version of the canons of the councils of Spain (Biblioth. Arab. Hisp. tom. i. p. 547), for the use of the bishops and clergy in the Moorish kingdoms.

211. About the middle of the tenth century the clergy of Cordova was reproached with this criminal compliance by the intrepid envoy of the emperor Otho I. (Vit. Johan. Gorz, in Secul. Benedict. V. No. 115, apud Fleury, Hist. Ecclés. tom. xii. p. 91).

212. Pagi, Critica, tom. iv. A.D. 1149, No. 8, 9. He justly observes that, when Seville, etc., were taken by Ferdinand of Castille, no Christians, except captives, were found in the place; and that the Mozarabic churches of Africa and Spain, described by James à Vitriaco, A.D. 1218 (Hist. Hierosol. c. 80, p. 1095, in Gest. Dei per Francos), are copied from some older book. I shall add that the date of the Hegira 677 (A.D. 1278) must apply to the copy, not the composition, of a treatise of jurisprudence, which states the civil rights of the Christians of Cordova (Biblioth. Arab. Hisp. tom. i. p. 471), and that the Jews were the only dissenters whom Abul Waled, king of Granada, (A.D. 1313), could either discountenance or tolerate (tom. ii. p. 288).

213. Renaudot, Hist. Patriarch. Alex. p. 288. Leo Africanus would have flattered his Roman masters, could he have discovered any latent relics of the Christianity of Africa.

214. Absit (said the Catholic to the Vizir of Bagdad) ut pari loco habeas Nestorianos, quorum præter Arabas nullus alius rex est, et Græcos quorum reges amovendo Arabibus bello non desistunt, etc. See in the Collections of Assemannus (Biblioth. Orient. tom. iv. p. 94–101) the state of the Nestorians under the caliphs. That of the Jacobites is more concisely exposed in the Preliminary Dissertation of the second volume of Assemannus.

215. Eutych. Annal. tom. ii. p. 384, 387, 388. Renaudot, Hist. Patriarch. Alex. p. 205, 206, 257, 332. A taint of the Monothelite heresy might render the first of these Greek patriarchs less loyal to the emperors and less obnoxious to the Arabs.

216. Motadhed, who reigned from A.D. 892 to 902. The Magians still held their name and rank among the religions of the empire (Assemanni, Biblioth. Orient. tom. iv. p. 97).

217. Reland explains the general restraints of the Mohammedan policy and jurisprudence (Dissertat. tom. iii. p. 16–20). The oppressive edicts of the caliph Motawakkel (A.D. 847–861), which are still in force, are noticed by Eutychius (Annal. tom. ii. p. 448) and D'Herbelot (Biblioth. Orient. p. 640). A persecution of the caliph Omar II. is related, and most probably magnified, by the Greek Theophanes (Chron. p. 334 [vol. i. p. 614, ed. Bonn]).

218. The martyrs of Cordova (A.D. 850, etc.) are commemorated and justified by St. Eulogius,

who at length fell a victim himself. A synod, convened by the caliph, ambiguously censured their
rashness. The moderate Fleury cannot reconcile
their conduct with the discipline of antiquity,
toutefois l'autorité de l'église, etc. (Fleury, Hist.
Ecclés. tom. x. p. 415-522, particularly p. 451,
508, 509). Their authentic acts throw a strong,
though transient, light on the Spanish church in
the ninth century.

219. See the article *Eslamiah* (as we say Christendom), in the Bibliothèque Orientale (p. 325).
This chart of the Mohammedan world is suited by
the author, Ebn Alwardi, to the year of the Hegira
385 (A.D. 995). Since that time the losses in Spain
have been overbalanced by the conquests in India
Tartary, and the European Turkey.

220. The Arabic of the Koran is taught as a
dead language in the college of Mecca. By the
Danish traveller this ancient idiom is compared to
the Latin; the vulgar tongue of Hejaz and Yemen
to the Italian; and the Arabian dialects of Syria
Egypt, Africa, etc., to the Provençal, Spanish, and
Portuguese (Niebuhr, Description de l'Arabie, p.
74, etc.).

Chapter LII

1. Theophanes places the *seven* years of the siege
of Constantinople in the year of *our* Christian era
673 (of the Alexandrian 665, Sept. 1), and the
peace of the Saracens four years afterwards; a
glaring inconsistency! which Petavius, Goar, and
Pagi (Critica, tom. iv. p. 63, 64) have struggled to
remove. Of the Arabians, the Hegira 52 (A.D. 672,
January 8) is assigned by Elmacin [p. 56], the
year 48 (A.D. 668, Feb. 20) by Abulfeda, whose
testimony I esteem the most convenient and creditable.

2. For this first siege of Constantinople see Nicephorus (Breviar. p. 21, 22 [ed. Par.]); Theophanes (Chronograph. p. 294 [t. i. p. 541, ed.
Bonn]); Cedrenus (Compend. p. 437 [ed. Par.;
tom. i. p. 764, ed. Bonn]); Zonaras (Hist. tom. ii.
l. xiv. [c. 20] p. 89); Elmacin (Hist. Saracen. p. 56,
57); Abulfeda (Annal. Moslem. p. 107, 108, vers.
Reiske); D'Herbelot (Biblioth. Orient. Constan-
tinah); Ockley's History of the Saracens, vol. ii. p.
127, 128.

3. The state and defence of the Dardanelles is
exposed in the Memoirs of the Baron de Tott (tom.
iii. p. 39-97), who was sent to fortify them against
the Russians. From a principal actor I should have
expected more accurate details; but he seems to
write for the amusement, rather than the instruction, of his reader. Perhaps, on the approach of the
enemy, the minister of Constantine was occupied,
like that of Mustapha, in finding two Canary-
birds who should sing precisely the same note.

4. Demetrius Cantemir's Hist. of the Othman
Empire, p. 105, 106; Rycaut's State of the Ottoman Empire, p. 10, 11; Voyages de Thevenot,
part i. p. 189. The Christians, who suppose that
the martyr of Abu Ayub is vulgarly confounded
with the patriarch Job, betray their own ignorance
rather than that of the Turks.

5. Theophanes, though a Greek, deserves credit
for these tributes (Chronograph. p. 295, 296, 300,
301 [vol. i. p. 543, 552, ed. Bonn]), which are confirmed, with some variation, by the Arabic History
of Abulpharagius (Dynast. p. 128, vers. Pocock).

6. The censure of Theophanes is just and pointed,
τὴν Ῥωμαϊκὴν δυναστείαν ἀκρωτηριάσας . . . πάνδεινα

κακὰ πέπονθεν ἡ Ῥωμανία ὑπὸ τῶν Ἀράβων μεχρὶ τοῦ
νῦν (Chronograph. p. 302, 303 [vol. i. p. 555, 556,
ed. Bonn]). The series of these events may be
traced in the Annals of Theophanes, and in the
Abridgment of the Patriarch Nicephorus, p. 22, 24.

7. These domestic revolutions are related in a
clear and natural style, in the second volume of
Ockley's History of the Saracens, p. 253-370. Besides our printed authors, he draws his materials
from the Arabic MSS. of Oxford, which he would
have more deeply searched had he been confined
to the Bodleian library instead of the city jail; a
fate how unworthy of the man and of his country!

8. Elmacin, who dates the first coinage A.H. 76,
A.D. 695, five or six years later than the Greek historians, has compared the weight of the best or
common gold dinar to the drachm or dirhem of
Egypt (p. 77), which may be equal to two pennies
(48 grains) of our Troy weight (Hooper's Enquiry
into Ancient Measures, p. 24-36), and equivalent
to eight shillings of our sterling money. From the
same Elmacin and the Arabian physicians some
dinars as high as two dirhems, as low as half a
dirhem, may be deduced. The piece of silver was
the dirhem, both in value and weight: but an old,
though fair coin, struck at Waset, A.H. 88, and preserved in the Bodleian library, wants four grains of
the Cairo standard (see the Modern Universal
History, tom. i. p. 548, of the French translation).

9. Καὶ ἐκώλυσε γράφεσθαι Ἑλληνιστὶ τοὺς δημοσίους
τῶν λογοθεσίων κώδικας, ἀλλ' Ἀραβίοις αὐτὰ παρασημαίνεσθαι, χωρὶς τῶν ψήφων, ἐπειδὴ ἀδύνατον, τῇ ἐκείνων γλώσσῃ μονάδα, ἢ δυάδα, ἢ τριάδα, ἢ ὀκτὼ ἥμισυ ἢ
τρία γράφεσθαι. Theophan. Chronograph. p. 314
[t. i. p. 575, ed. Bonn]. This defect, if it really
existed, must have stimulated the ingenuity of the
Arabs to invent or borrow.

10. According to a new, though probable, notion, maintained by M. de Villoison (Anecdota
Græca, tom. ii. p. 152-157), our ciphers are not of
Indian or Arabic invention. They were used by
the Greek and Latin arithmeticians long before
the age of Boethius. After the extinction of science
in the West, they were adopted by the Arabic

versions from the original MSS., and *restored* to the Latins about the eleventh century.

11. In the division of the *Themes*, or provinces described by Constantine Porphyrogenitus (de Thematibus, l. i. p. 9, 10 [ed. Par.; vol. iii. p. 24, *sqq.*, ed. Bonn]), the *Obsequium*, a Latin appellation of the army and palace, was the fourth in the public order. Nice was the metropolis, and its jurisdiction extended from the Hellespont over the adjacent parts of Bithynia and Phrygia (see the two maps prefixed by Delisle to the Imperium Orientale of Banduri).

12. The caliph had emptied two baskets of eggs and of figs, which he swallowed alternately, and the repast was concluded with marrow and sugar. In one of his pilgrimages to Mecca, Soliman ate, at a single meal, seventy pomegranates, a kid, six fowls, and a huge quantity of the grapes of Tayef. If the bill of fare be correct, we must admire the appetite, rather than the luxury, of the sovereign of Asia (Abulfeda, Annal. Moslem. p. 126).

13. See the article of Omar Ben Abdalaziz, in the Bibliothèque Orientale (p. 689, 690), præferens, says Elmacin (p. 91), religionem suam rebus suis mundanis. He was so desirous of being with God, that he would not have anointed his ear (his own saying) to obtain a perfect cure of his last malady. The caliph had only one shirt, and in an age of luxury his annual expense was no more than two drachms (Abulpharagius, p. 131). Haud diu gavisus eo principe fuit orbis Moslemus (Abulfeda, p. 127).

14. Both Nicephorus [p. 36] and Theophanes agree that the siege of Constantinople was raised the 15th of August (A.D. 718); but as the former, our best witness, affirms that it continued thirteen months [p. 35], the latter must be mistaken in supposing that it began on the same day of the preceding year. I do not find that Pagi has remarked this inconsistency.

15. In the second siege of Constantinople I have followed Nicephorus (Brev. p. 33–36), Theophanes (Chronograph. p. 324–334 [t. i. p. 593, *sqq.* ed. Bonn]), Cedrenus (Compend. p. 449–452 [p. 787–791, ed. Bonn]), Zonaras (tom. ii. [l. xiv. c. 27, l. xv. c. 3] p. 98–102), Elmacin (Hist. Saracen. p. 88), Abulfeda (Annal. Moslem. p. 126), and Abulpharagius (Dynast. p. 130), the most satisfactory of the Arabs.

16. Our sure and indefatigable guide in the middle ages and Byzantine history, Charles du Fresne du Cange, has treated in several places of the Greek fire, and his collections leave few gleanings behind. See particularly Glossar. Med. et Infim. Græcitat. p. 1275, sub voce Πυρ θαλάσσιον, ὑγρον; Glossar. Med. et Infim. Latinitat. *Ignis Græcus;* Observations sur Villehardouin, p. 305, 306; Observations sur Joinville, p. 71, 72.

17. Theophanes styles him ἀρχιτεκτών (p. 295 [t. i. p. 542, ed. Bonn]). Cedrenus (p. 437 [tom. i. p. 765, ed. Bonn]) brings this artist from (the ruins of) Heliopolis in Egypt; and chemistry was indeed the peculiar science of the Egyptians.

18. The naphtha, the oleum incendiarium of the history of Jerusalem (Gest. Dei per Francos, p. 1167), the Oriental fountain of James de Vitry (l. iii. c. 84 [p. 1098]), is introduced on slight evidence and strong probability. Cinnamus (l. vi. p. 165 [c. 10, p. 283, ed. Bonn]) calls the Greek fire πῦρ Μήδικον: and the naphtha is known to abound between the Tigris and the Caspian Sea. According to Pliny (Hist. Natur. ii. 109), it was subservient to the revenge of Medea, and in either etymology the ἔλαιον Μηδίας, or Μηδείας (Procop. de Bell. Gothic. l. iv. c. 11 [t. ii. p. 512, ed. Bonn]), may fairly signify this liquid bitumen.

19. On the different sorts of oils and bitumens see Dr. Watson's (the present Bishop of Llandaff's) Chemical Essays, vol. iii. essay i., a classic book, the best adapted to infuse the taste and knowledge of chemistry. The less perfect ideas of the ancients may be found in Strabo (Geograph. l. xvi. p. 1078 [p. 743, ed. Casaub.]) and Pliny (Hist. Natur. ii. 108, 109). Huic (*Naphthæ*) magna cognatio est ignium, transiliuntque protinus in eam undecunque visam. Of our travellers I am best pleased with Otter (tom. i. p. 153, 158).

20. Anna Comnena has partly drawn aside the curtain. Ἀπὸ τῆς πεύκης, καὶ ἄλλων τινῶν τοιούτων δένδρων ἀειθάλων συνάγεται δάκρυον ἄκαυστον. Τοῦτο μετὰ θείου τριβόμενον ἐμβάλλεται εἰς αὐλίσκους καλάμων, καὶ ἐμφύσαται παρὰ τοῦ παίζοντος λάβρῳ καὶ συνεχεῖ πνεύματι (Alexiad. l. xiii. p. 383). Elsewhere (l. xi. p. 336) she mentions the property of burning, κατὰ τὸ πρανὲς καὶ ἐφ' ἑκάτερα. Leo, in the nineteenth chapter [§ 51] of his Tactics (Opera Meursii, tom. vi. p. 841, edit. Lami, Florent. 1745), speaks of the new invention of πῦρ μετὰ βροντῆς καὶ κάπνου. These are genuine and *Imperial* testimonies.

21. Constantin. Porphyrogenit. de Administrat. Imperii, c. xiii. p. 64, 65 [ed. Par.; tom. iii. p. 84, *sq.*, ed. Bonn].

22. Histoire de St. Louis, p. 39; Paris, 1668, p. 44; Paris, de l'Imprimerie Royale, 1761. The former of these editions is precious for the observations of Ducange; the latter for the pure and original text of Joinville. We must have recourse to that text to discover that the feu Gregeois was shot with a pile or javelin from an engine that acted like a sling.

23. The vanity, or envy, of shaking the established property of Fame, has tempted some moderns to carry gunpowder above the fourteenth (see Sir William Temple, Dutens, etc.), and the Greek fire above the seventh century (see the Saluste du Président des Brosses, tom. ii. p. 381). But their evidence, which precedes the vulgar era of the invention, is seldom clear or satisfactory, and subsequent writers may be suspected of fraud or credulity. In the earliest sieges some combustibles of oil and sulphur have been used, and the Greek fire has *some* affinities with gunpowder both in its nature and effects: for the antiquity of the first, a

passage of Procopius (de Bell. Goth. l. iv. c. 11 [t. ii. p. 512, ed. Bonn]); for that of the second, some facts in the Arabic history of Spain (A.D. 1249, 1312, 1332; Biblioth. Arab. Hisp. tom. ii. p. 6, 7, 8) are the most difficult to elude.

24. That extraordinary man, Friar Bacon, reveals two of the ingredients, saltpetre and sulphur, and conceals the third in a sentence of mysterious gibberish, as if he dreaded the consequences of his own discovery (Biog. Brit. vol. i. p. 430, new edition).

25. For the invasion of France, and the defeat of the Arabs by Charles Martel, see the Historia Arabum (c. 11, 12, 13, 14) of Roderic Ximenes, archbishop of Toledo, who had before him the Christian Chronicle of Isidore Pacensis, and the Mohammedan history of Novairi. The Moslems are silent or concise in the account of their losses, but M. Cardonne (tom. i. p. 129, 130, 131) has given a *pure* and simple account of all that he could collect from Ibn Halikan, Hidjazi, and an anonymous writer. The texts of the chronicles of France, and lives of saints, are inserted in the Collection of Bouquet (tom. iii.) and the Annals of Pagi, who (tom. iii. under the proper years) has restored the chronology, which is anticipated six years in the Annals of Baronius. The Dictionary of Bayle (*Abderame* and *Munuza*) has more merit for lively reflection than original research.

26. Eginhart, de Vita Caroli Magni, c. ii. p. 13-18, edit. Schmink, Utrecht, 1711. Some modern critics accuse the minister of Charlemagne of exaggerating the weakness of the Merovingians; but the general outline is just, and the French reader will for ever repeat the beautiful lines of Boileau's Lutrin.

27. *Mamaccæ*, on the Oise, between Compiègne and Noyon, which Eginhart calls preparvi reditús villam (see the notes, and the map of ancient France for Dom. Bouquet's Collection). Compendium, or Compiègne, was a palace of more dignity (Hadrian. Valesii Notitia Galliarum, p. 152); and that laughing philosopher, the Abbé Galliani (Dialogues sur le Commerce des Bleds), may truly affirm that it was the residence of the rois très Chrétiens et très chevelûs.

28. Even before that colony, A.U.C. 630 (Velleius Patercul. i. 15), in the time of Polybius (Hist. l. iii. [c. 37] p. 265, edit. Gronov.) Narbonne was a Celtic town of the first eminence, and one of the most northern places of the known world (D'Anville, Notice de l'Ancienne Gaule, p. 473).

29. With regard to the sanctuary of St. Martin of Tours, Roderic Ximenes accuses the Saracens of the *deed*. Turonis civitatem, ecclesiam et palatia vastatione et incendio simili diruit et consumpsit. The continuator of Fredegarius imputes to them no more than the *intention*. Ad domum beatissimi Martini evertendam destinant. At Carolus, etc. The French annalist was more jealous of the honour of the saint.

30. Yet I sincerely doubt whether the Oxford mosch would have produced a volume of controversy so elegant and ingenious as the sermons lately preached by Mr. White, the Arabic professor, at Mr. Bampton's lecture. His observations on the character and religion of Mohammed are always adapted to his argument, and generally founded in truth and reason. He sustains the part of a lively and eloquent advocate, and sometimes rises to the merit of an historian and philosopher.

31. Gens Austriæ membrorum pre-eminentiâ valida, et gens Germana corde et corpore præstantissima, quasi in ictû oculi, manû ferreâ, et pectore arduo, Arabes extinxerunt (Roderic. Toletan. c. xiv.).

32. These numbers are stated by Paul Warnefrid, the deacon of Aquileia (de Gestis Langobard. l. vi. [c. 46] p. 921, edit. Grot.), and Anastasius, the librarian of the Roman church (in Vit. Gregorii II. [ap. Muratori Scrip. R. I. vol. iii. p. 155]), who tells a miraculous story of three consecrated sponges, which rendered invulnerable the French soldiers among whom they had been shared. It should seem that, in his letters to the pope, Eudes usurped the honour of the victory, for which he is chastised by the French annalists, who, with equal falsehood, accuse him of inviting the Saracens.

33. Narbonne and the rest of Septimania was recovered by Pepin, the son of Charles Martel, A.D. 755 (Pagi, Critica, tom. iii. p. 300). Thirty-seven years afterwards it was pillaged by a sudden inroad of the Arabs, who employed the captives in the construction of the mosch of Cordova (De Guignes, Hist. des Huns, tom. i. p. 354).

34. This pastoral letter, addressed to Lewis the Germanic, the grandson of Charlemagne, and most probably composed by the pen of the artful Hincmar, is dated in the year 858, and signed by the bishops of the provinces of Rheims and Rouen (Baronius, Annal. Eccles. A.D. 741; Fleury, Hist. Ecclés. tom. x. p. 514-516). Yet Baronius himself and the French critics reject with contempt this episcopal fiction.

35. The steed and the saddle which had carried any of his wives were instantly killed or burnt, lest they should be afterwards mounted by a male. Twelve hundred mules or camels were required for his kitchen furniture; and the daily consumption amounted to three thousand cakes, a hundred sheep, besides oxen, poultry, etc. (Abulpharagius, Hist. Dynast. p. 140).

36. *Al Hemar.* He had been governor of Mesopotamia, and the Arabic proverb praises the courage of that warlike breed of asses who never fly from an enemy. The surname of Mervan may justify the comparison of Homer (Iliad xi, 557, etc.), and both will silence the moderns, who consider the ass as a stupid and ignoble emblem (D'Herbelot, Biblioth. Orient. p. 558).

37. Four several places, all in Egypt, bore the name of Busir, or Busiris, so famous in Greek fable. The first, where Mervan was slain, was to the west of the Nile, in the province of Fium, or Arsinoe:

the second in the Delta, in the Sebennytic nome; the third near the Pyramids; the fourth, which was destroyed by Diocletian (see above, vol. i. p. 314), in the Thebais. I shall here transcribe a note of the learned and orthodox Michaelis: Videntur in pluribus Ægypti superioris urbibus Busiri, Copto [Esne], arma sumpsisse Christiani, libertatemque de religione sentiendi defendisse, sed succubuisse, quo in bello Coptus et Busiris diruta, et circa Esnam magna strages edita. Bellum narrant sed causam belli ignorant scriptores Byzantini, alioqui Coptum et Busirin non rebellasse dicturi sed causam Christianorum suscepturi (Not. 211, p. 100). For the geography of the four Busirs, see Abulfeda (Descript. Ægypt. p. 9, vers. Michaelis, Gottingæ, 1776, in 4to), Michaelis (Not. 122–127, p. 58–63), and D'Anville (Mémoire sur l'Egypte, p. 85, 147, 205)

38. See Abulfeda (Annal. Moslem. p. 136–145), Eutychius (Annal. tom. ii. p. 392, vers. Pocock), Elmacin (Hist. Saracen. p. 109–121), Abulpharagius (Hist. Dynast. p. 134–140), Roderic of Toledo (Hist. Arabum, c. xviii. p. 33), Theophanes (Chronograph. p. 356, 357 [vol. i. p. 654, ed. Bonn], who speaks of the Abbassides under the name of Χωρασάνιται and Μαυροφόροι), and the Bibliothèque of D'Herbelot, in the articles *Ommiades, Abbassides, Mærvan, Ibrahim, Saffah, Abou Moslem.*

39. For the revolution of Spain, consult Roderic of Toledo (c. xviii. p. 34, etc.), the Bibliotheca Arabico-Hispana (tom. ii. p. 30, 198), and Cardonne (Hist. de l'Afrique et de l'Espagne, tom. i. p. 180–197, 205, 272, 323, etc.)

40. I shall not stop to refute the strange errors and fancies of Sir William Temple (his Works, vol. iii. p. 371–374, octavo edition) and Voltaire (Histoire Générale, c. xxviii. tom. ii. p. 124, 125, édition de Lausanne), concerning the division of the Saracen empire. The mistakes of Voltaire proceeded from the want of knowledge or reflection; but Sir William was deceived by a Spanish impostor, who has framed an apocryphal history of the conquest of Spain by the Arabs.

41. The geographer D'Anville (l'Euphrate et le Tigre, p. 121–123), and the Orientalist D'Herbelot (Bibliothèque, p. 167, 168), may suffice for the knowledge of Bagdad. Our travellers, Pietro della Valle (tom. i. p. 688–698), Tavernier (tom. i. p. 230–238), Thevenot (part ii. p. 209–212), Otter (tom. i. p. 162–168), and Niebuhr (Voyage en Arabie, tom. ii. p. 239–271), have seen only its decay; and the Nubian geographer (p. 204), and the travelling Jew, Benjamin of Tudela (Itinerarium, p. 112–123, à Const. l'Empereur, apud Elzevir, 1633), are the only writers of my acquaintance who have known Bagdad under the reign of the Abbassides.

42. The foundations of Bagdad were laid A.H. 145, A.D. 762. Mostasem, the last of the Abbassides, was taken and put to death by the Tartars, A.H. 656, A.D. 1258, the 20th of February.

43. Medinat al Salam, Dar al Salem. Urbs pacis, or, as it is more neatly compounded by the Byzantine writers, Εἰρηνόπολις (Irenopolis). There is some dispute concerning the etymology of Bagdad, but the first syllable is allowed to signify a garden in the Persian tongue; the garden of Dad, a Christian hermit, whose cell had been the only habitation on the spot.

44. Reliquit in ærario sexcenties millies mille stateres, et quater et vicies millies mille aureos aureos. Elmacin, Hist. Saracen. p. 126. I have reckoned the gold pieces at eight shillings, and the proportion to the silver as twelve to one. But I will never answer for the numbers of Erpenius; and the Latins are scarcely above the savages in the language of arithmetic.

45. D'Herbelot, p. 530; Abulfeda, p. 154. Nivem Meccam apportavit, rem ibi aut nunquam aut rarissime visam.

46. Abulfeda, p. 184, 189, describes the splendour and liberality of Almamon. Milton has alluded to this Oriental custom:

—Or where the gorgeous East, with richest hand,

Showers on her kings barbaric pearls and gold.

I have used the modern word *lottery* to express the *Missilia* of the Roman emperors, which entitled to some prize the person who caught them, as they were thrown among the crowd.

47. When Bell of Antermony (Travels, vol. i. p. 99) accompanied the Russian ambassador to the audience of the unfortunate Shah Hussein of Persia, *two* lions were introduced, to denote the power of the king over the fiercest animals.

48. Abulfeda, p. 237; D'Herbelot, p. 590. This embassy was received at Bagdad, A.H. 305, A.D. 917. In the passage of Abulfeda, I have used, with some variations, the English translation of the learned and amiable Mr. Harris of Salisbury (Philological Enquiries, p. 363, 364).

49. Cardonne, Histoire de l'Afrique et de l'Espagne, tom. i. p. 330–336. A just idea of the taste and architecture of the Arabians of Spain may be conceived from the description and plates of the Alhambra of Granada (Swinburne's Travels, p. 171–188).

50. Cardonne, tom. i. p. 329, 330. This confession, the complaints of Solomon of the vanity of this world (read Prior's verbose but eloquent poem), and the happy ten days of the emperor Seghed (Rambler, No. 204, 205), will be triumphantly quoted by the detractors of human life. Their expectations are commonly immoderate, their estimates are seldom impartial. If I may speak of myself (the only person of whom I can speak with certainty), *my* happy hours have far exceeded and far exceed, the scanty numbers of the caliph of Spain; and I shall not scruple to add, that many of them are due to the pleasing labour of the present composition.

51. The Gulistan (p. 239) relates the conversation of Mohammed and a physician (Epistol. Re-

naudot. in Fabricius, Biblioth. Græc. tom. i. p. 814). The prophet himself was skilled in the art of medicine; and Gagnier (Vie de Mahomet, tom. iii. p. 394–405) has given an extract of the aphorisms which are extant under his name.

52. See their curious architecture in Reaumur (Hist. des Insectes, tom. v. Mémoire viii.). These hexagons are closed by a pyramid; the angles of the three sides of a similar pyramid, such as would accomplish the given end with the smallest quantity possible of materials, were determined by a mathematician, at 109 degrees 26 minutes for the larger, 70 degrees 34 minutes for the smaller. The actual measure is 109 degrees 28 minutes, 70 degrees 32 minutes. Yet this perfect harmony raises the work at the expense of the artist: the bees are not masters of transcendent geometry.

53. Said Ebn Ahmed, cadhi of Toledo, who died A.H. 462, A.D. 1069, has furnished Abulpharagius (Dynast. p. 160) with this curious passage, as well as with the text of Pocock's Specimen Historiæ Arabum. A number of literary anecdotes of philosophers, physicians, etc., who have flourished under each caliph, form the principal merit of the Dynasties of Abulpharagius.

54. These literary anecdotes are borrowed from the Bibliotheca Arabico-Hispana (tom. ii. p. 38, 71, 201, 202), Leo Africanus (de Arab. Medicis et Philosophis, in Fabric. Biblioth. Græc. tom. xiii. p. 259–298, particularly p. 274), and Renaudot (Hist. Patriarch. Alex. p. 274, 275, 536, 537), besides the chronological remarks of Abulpharagius.

55. The Arabic catalogue of the Escurial will give a just idea of the proportion of the classes. In the library of Cairo the MSS. of astronomy and medicine amounted to 6500, with two fair globes, the one of brass, the other of silver (Biblioth. Arab. Hisp. tom. i. p. 417).

56. As for instance, the fifth, sixth, and seventh books (the eighth is still wanting) of the Conic Sections of Apollonius Pergæus, which were printed from the Florence MS. 1661 (Fabric. Biblioth. Græc. tom. ii. p. 559). Yet the fifth book had been previously restored by the mathematical divination of Viviani (see his Eloge in Fontenelle, tom. v. p. 59, etc.).

57. The merit of these Arabic versions is freely discussed by Renaudot (Fabric. Biblioth. Græc. tom. i. p. 812–816), and piously defended by Casiri (Biblioth. Arab. Hispana, tom. i. p. 238–240). Most of the versions of Plato, Aristotle, Hippocrates, Galen, etc., are ascribed to Honain, a physician of the Nestorian sect, who flourished at Bagdad in the court of the caliphs, and died A.D. 876. He was at the head of a school or manufacture of translations, and the works of his sons and disciples were published under his name. See Abulpharagius (Dynast. p. 88, 115, 171–174, and apud Asseman. Biblioth. Orient. tom. ii. p. 438), D'Herbelot (Biblioth. Orientale, p. 456), Asseman. (Biblioth. Orient. tom. iii. p. 164), and Casiri (Biblioth.

Arab. Hispana, tom. i. p. 238, etc. 251, 286–290, 302, 304, etc.).

58. See Mosheim, Institut. Hist. Eccles. p. 181, 214, 236, 257, 315, 338, 396, 438, etc.

59. The most elegant commentary on the Categories or Predicaments of Aristotle may be found in the Philosophical Arrangements of Mr. James Harris (London, 1775, in octavo), who laboured to revive the studies of Grecian literature and philosophy.

60. Abulpharagius, Dynast. p. 81, 222; Biblioth. Arab. Hisp. tom. i. p. 370, 371. In quem (says the primate of the Jacobites) si immiserit se lector, oceanum hoc in genere (*Algebræ*) inveniet. The time of Diophantus of Alexandria is unknown; but his six books are still extant, and have been illustrated by the Greek Planudes and the Frenchman Meziriac (Fabric. Biblioth. Græc. tom. iv. p. 12–15).

61. Abulfeda (Annal. Moslem. p. 210, 211, vers. Reiske) describes this operation according to Ibn Challecan and the best historians. This degree most accurately contains 200,000 royal or Hashemite cubits, which Arabia had derived from the sacred and legal practice both of Palestine and Egypt. This ancient cubit is repeated 400 times in each basis of the great pyramid, and seems to indicate the primitive and universal measures of the East. See the Métrologie of the laborious M. Paucton, p. 101–195.

62. See the Astronomical Tables of Ulugh Begh, with the preface of Dr. Hyde, in the first volume of his Syntagma Dissertationum, Oxon. 1767.

63. The truth of astrology was allowed by Albumazar, and the best of the Arabian astronomers, who drew their most certain predictions, not from Venus and Mercury, but from Jupiter and the sun (Abulpharag. Dynast. p. 161–163). For the state and science of the Persian astronomers, see Chardin (Voyages en Perse, tom. iii. p. 162–203).

64. Biblioth. Arabico-Hispana, tom. i. p. 438. The original relates a pleasant tale of an ignorant, but harmless, practitioner.

65. In the year 956 Sancho the Fat, king of Leon, was cured by the physicians of Cordova (Mariana, l. viii. c. 7, tom. i. p. 318).

66. The school of Salerno, and the introduction of the Arabian sciences into Italy, are discussed with learning and judgment by Muratori (Antiquitat. Italiæ Medii Ævi, tom. iii. p. 932–940) and Giannone (Istoria Civile di Napoli, tom. ii. p. 119–127).

67. See a good view of the progress of anatomy in Wotton (Reflections on Ancient and Modern Learning, p. 208–256). His reputation has been unworthily depreciated by the wits in the controversy of Boyle and Bentley.

68. Biblioth. Arab. Hispana, tom. i. p. 275. Al Beithar, of Malaga, their greatest botanist, had travelled into Africa, Persia, and India.

69. Dr. Watson (Elements of Chemistry, vol. i. p. 17, etc.) allows the *original* merit of the Arabians.

Yet he quotes the modest confession of the famous Geber of the ninth century (D'Herbelot, p. 387), that he had drawn most of his science, perhaps of the transmutation of metals, from the ancient sages. Whatever might be the origin or extent of their knowledge, the arts of chemistry and alchymy appear to have been known in Egypt at least three hundred years before Mohammed (Wotton's Reflections, p. 121–133; Pauw, Recherches sur les Egyptiens et les Chinois, tom. i. p. 376–429).

70. Abulpharagius (Dynast. p. 26, 148) mentions a *Syriac* version of Homer's two poems, by Theophilus, a Christian Maronite of Mount Libanus, who professed astronomy at Roha or Edessa towards the end of the eighth century. His work would be a literary curiosity. I have read somewhere, but I do not believe, that Plutarch's Lives were translated into Turkish for the use of Mohammed the Second.

71. I have perused with much pleasure Sir William Jones's Latin Commentary on Asiatic Poetry (London, 1774, in octavo), which was composed in the youth of that wonderful linguist. At present, in the maturity of his taste and judgment, he would perhaps abate of the fervent and even partial praise which he has bestowed on the Orientals.

72. Among the Arabian philosophers, Averroes has been accused of despising the religions of the Jews, the Christians, and the Mohammedans (see his article in Bayle's Dictionary). Each of these sects would agree that, in two instances out of three, his contempt was reasonable.

73. D'Herbelot, Bibliothèque Orientale, p. 546.

74. Θεόφιλος ἄτοπον κρίνας εἰ τὴν τῶν ὄντων γνῶσιν, δι᾽ ἣν τὸ Ῥωμαίων γένος θαυμάζεται, ἔκδοτον ποιήσει τοῖς ἔθνεσι, etc. Cedrenus, p. 548 [vol. ii. p. 169, ed. Bonn], who relates how manfully the emperor refused a mathematician to the instances and offers of the caliph Almamon. This absurd scruple is expressed almost in the same words by the continuator of Theophanes (Scriptores post Theophanem, p. 118 [ed. Par.; p. 190, ed. Bonn]).

75. See the reign and character of Harun al Rashid in the Bibliothèque Orientale, p. 431–433, under his proper title, and in the relative articles to which M. D'Herbelot refers. That learned collector has shown much taste in stripping the Oriental chronicles of their instructive and amusing anecdotes.

76. For the situation of Racca, the old Nicephorium, consult D'Anville (l'Euphrate et le Tigre, p. 24–27). The Arabian Nights represent Harun al Rashid as almost stationary in Bagdad. He respected the royal seat of the Abbassides; but the vices of the inhabitants had driven him from the city (Abulfed. Annal. p. 167).

77. M. de Tournefort, in his coasting voyage from Constantinople to Trebizond, passed a night at Heraclea or Eregri. His eye surveyed the present state, his reading collected the antiquities, of the city (Voyage du Levant, tom. iii. lettre xvi. p. 23–35). We have a separate history of Heraclea in the fragments of Memnon, which are preserved by Photius.

78. The wars of Harun al Rashid against the Roman empire are related by Theophanes (p. 384, 385, 391, 396, 407, 408 [tom. i. p. 705, 717, 727, 748, *sq.*, ed. Bonn]), Zonaras (tom. ii. l. xv. [c. 10–15], p. 115, 124), Cedrenus (p. 477, 478 [tom. ii. p. 34, *sq.*, ed. Bonn]), Eutychius (Annal. tom. ii. p. 407), Elmacin (Hist. Saracen. p. 136, 151, 152), Abulpharagius (Dynast. p. 147, 151), and Abulfeda (p. 156, 166–168).

79. The authors from whom I have learned the most of the ancient and modern state of Crete are Belon (Observations, etc., c. 3–20, Paris, 1555), Tournefort (Voyage du Levant, tom. i. lettre ii. et iii.), and Meursius (CRETA, in his works, tom. iii. p. 343–544). Although Crete is styled by Homer πίειρα, by Dionysius λιπάρη τε καὶ εὔβοτος, I cannot conceive that mountainous island to surpass, or even to equal, in fertility the greater part of Spain.

80. The most authentic and circumstantial intelligence is obtained from the four books of the Continuation of Theophanes, compiled by the pen or the command of Constantine Porphyrogenitus, with the Life of his father Basil the Macedonian (Scriptores post Theophanem, p. 1–162, à Francisc. Combefis, Paris, 1685 [p. 4–260, ed. Bonn]). The loss of Crete and Sicily is related, l. ii. p. 46–52 [ed. Par.; p. 74–83, ed. Bonn]. To these we may add the secondary evidence of Joseph Genesius (l. ii. p. 21, Venet. 1733), George Cedrenus (Compend. p. 506–508 [p. 509–512, ed. Par.; p. 92–99, ed. Bonn]), and John Scylitzes Curopalata (apud Baron. Annal. Eccles. A.D. 827, No. 24, etc.). But the modern Greeks are such notorious plagiaries, that I should only quote a plurality of names.

81. Renaudot (Hist. Patriarch. Alex. p. 251–256, 268–270) has described the ravages of the Andalusian Arabs in Egypt, but has forgot to connect them with the conquest of Crete.

82. Δηλοῖ (says the continuator of Theophanes, l. ii. p. 51 [p. 82, ed. Bonn]), δὲ ταῦτα σαφέστατα καὶ πλατικώτερον ἡ τότε γραφεῖσα Θεογνώστῳ καὶ εἰς χεῖρας ἐλθοῦσα ἡμῶν. This history of the loss of Sicily is no longer extant. Muratori (Annali d'Italia, tom. vii. p. 719, 721, etc.) has added some circumstances from the Italian chronicles.

83. The splendid and interesting tragedy of *Tancrede* would adapt itself much better to this epoch than to the date (A.D. 1005) which Voltaire himself has chosen. But I must gently reproach the poet for infusing into the Greek subjects the spirit of modern knights and ancient republicans.

84. The narrative or lamentation of Theodosius is transcribed and illustrated by Pagi (Critica, tom. iii. p. 719, etc.). Constantine Porphyrogenitus (in Vit. Basil. c. 69, 70, p. 190–192 [Theoph. Cont. p. 309, *sq.*, ed. Bonn]) mentions the loss of Syracuse and the triumph of the demons.

85. The extracts from the Arabic histories of Sicily are given in Abulfeda (Annal. Moslem. p.

271–273), and in the first volume of Muratori's Scriptores Rerum Italicarum. M. de Guignes (Hist. des Huns, tom. i. p. 363, 364) has added some important facts.

86. One of the most eminent Romans (Gratianus, magister militum et Romani palatii superista) was accused of declaring, Quia Franci nihil nobis boni faciunt, neque adjutorium præbent, sed magis quæ nostra sunt violenter tollunt. Quare non advocamus Græcos, et cum eis fœdus pacis componentes, Francorum regem et gentem de nostro regno et dominatione expellimus? Anastasius in Leone IV. p. 199 [ap. Muratori, Script. R. I. iii. p. 246].

87. Voltaire (Hist. Générale, tom. ii. c. 38, p. 124) appears to be remarkably struck with the character of Pope Leo IV. I have borrowed his general expression, but the sight of the forum has furnished me with a more distinct and lively image.

88. De Guignes, Hist. Générale des Huns, tom. i. p. 363, 364; Cardonne, Hist. de l'Afrique et de l'Espagne sous la Domination des Arabes, tom. ii. p. 24, 25. I observe, and cannot reconcile, the difference of these writers in the succession of the Aglabites.

89. Beretti (Chorographia Italiæ Medii Ævi, p. 106, 108) has illustrated Centumcellæ, Leopolis, Civitas Leonina, and the other places of the Roman duchy.

90. The Arabs and the Greeks are alike silent concerning the invasion of Rome by the Africans. The Latin chronicles do not afford much instruction (see the Annals of Baronius and Pagi). Our authentic and contemporary guide for the Popes of the ninth century is Anastasius, librarian of the Roman church. His Life of Leo IV. contains twenty-four pages (p. 175–199, edit. Paris); and if a great part consists of superstitious trifles, we must blame or commend his hero, who was much oftener in a church than in a camp.

91. The same number was applied to the following circumstances in the life of Motassem: he was the *eighth* of the Abbassides; he reigned *eight* years, *eight* months, and *eight* days; left *eight* sons, *eight* daughters, *eight* thousand slaves, *eight* millions of gold.

92. Amorium is seldom mentioned by the old geographers, and totally forgotten in the Roman Itineraries. After the sixth century it became an episcopal see, and at length the metropolis of the new Galatia (Carol. Scto. Paulo, Geograph. Sacra. p. 234). The city rose again from its ruins, if we should read *Ammuria*, not *Anguria*, in the text of the Nubian geographer (p. 236).

93. In the East he was styled Δυστυχὴς (Continuator Theophan. l. iii. p. 84 [p. 135, ed. Bonn]): but such was the ignorance of the West, that his ambassadors, in public discourse, might boldly narrate, de victoriis, quas adversus exteras bellando gentes cœlitus fuerat assecutus (Annalist. Bertinian. apud Pagi, tom. iii. p. 720).

94. Abulpharagius (Dynast. p. 167, 168) relates

one of these singular transactions on the bridge of the river Lamus in Cilicia, the limit of the two empires, and one day's journey westward of Tarsus (D'Anville, Géographie Ancienne, tom. ii. p. 91) Four thousand four hundred and sixty Moslems eight hundred women and children, one hundred confederates, were exchanged for an equal number of Greeks. They passed each other in the middle of the bridge, and when they reached their respective friends they shouted *Allah Acbar*, and *Kyrie Eleison* Many of the prisoners of Amorium were probably among them, but in the same year (A.H. 231) the most illustrious of them, the forty-two martyrs, were beheaded by the caliph's orders.

95. Constantin. Porphyrogenitus, in Vit. Basil. c. 61, p. 186 [p. 301, ed. Bonn]. These Saracens were indeed treated with peculiar severity as pirates and renegadoes.

96. For Theophilus, Motassem, and the Amorian war, see the Continuator of Theophanes (l. iii. p. 77–84 [p. 124–135, ed. Bonn]), Genesius (l. iii. p. 24–34), Cedrenus (p. 528–532 [tom. ii. p. 129–137, ed. Bonn]), Elmacin (Hist. Saracen. p. 180), Abulpharagius (Dynast. p. 165, 166), Abulfeda (Annal. Moslem. p. 191), D'Herbelot (Biblioth. Orientale, p. 639, 640).

97. M. de Guignes, who sometimes leaps, and sometimes stumbles, in the gulf between Chinese and Mohammedan story, thinks he can see that these Turks are the *Hoei-ke*, alias the *Kao-tche*, or *high-waggons;* that they were divided into fifteen hordes, from China and Siberia to the dominions of the caliphs and Samanides, etc. (Hist. des Huns, tom. iii. p. 1–33, 124–131).

98. He changed the old name of Sumere, or Samara, into the fanciful title of *Ser-menrai*, that which gives pleasure at first sight (D'Herbelot, Bibliothèque Orientale, p. 808; D'Anville, l'Euphrate et le Tigre, p. 97, 98).

99. Take a specimen, the death of the caliph Motaz: Correptum pedibus pertrahunt, et sudibus probe permulcant, et spoliatum laceris vestibus in sole collocant, præ cujus acerrimo æstú pedes alternos attolebat et demittebat. Adstantium aliquis misero colaphos continuo ingerebat, quos ille objectis manibus avertere studebat. . . . Quo facto traditus tortori fuit, totoque triduo cibo potuque prohibitus. . . . Suffocatus, etc. (Abulfeda, p. 206). Of the caliph Mohtadi, he says, cervices ipsi perpetuis ictibus contundebant, testiculosque pedibus conculcabant (p. 208).

100. See under the reigns of Motassem, Motawakkel, Montasser, Mostain, Motaz, Mohtadi, and Motamed, in the Bibliothèque of D'Herbelot, and the now familiar Annals of Elmacin, Abulpharagius, and Abulfeda.

101. For the sect of the Carmathians, consult Elmacin (Hist. Saracen, p. 219, 224, 229, 231, 238, 241, 243), Abulpharagius (Dynast. p. 179–182), Abulfeda (Annal. Moslem. p. 218, 219, etc. 245, 265, 274), and D'Herbelot (Bibliothèque Orientale, p. 256–258, 635). I find some inconsistencies

of theology and chronology, which it would not be easy nor of much importance to reconcile.

102. Hyde, Syntagma Dissertat. tom. ii. p. 57, in Hist. Shahiludii.

103. The dynasties of the Arabian empire may be studied in the Annals of Elmacin, Abulpharagius, and Abulfeda, under the *proper* years; in the dictionary of D'Herbelot, under the *proper* names. The tables of M. de Guignes (Hist. des Huns, tom. i.) exhibit a general chronology of the East, interspersed with some historical anecdotes; but his attachment to national blood has sometimes confounded the order of time and place.

104. The Aglabites and Edrisites are the professed subject of M. de Cardonne (Hist. de l'Afrique et de l'Espagne sous la Domination des Arabes, tom. ii. p. 1–63).

105. To escape the reproach of error, I must criticise the inaccuracies of M. de Guignes (tom. i. p. 359) concerning the Edrisites. 1. The dynasty and city of Fez could not be founded in the year of the Hegira 173, since the founder was a *posthumous* child of a descendant of Ali, who fled from Mecca in the year 168. 2. This founder, Edris, the son of Edris, instead of living to the improbable age of 120 years, A.H. 313, died A.H. 214, in the prime of manhood. 3. The dynasty ended A.H. 307, twenty-three years sooner than it is fixed by the historian of the Huns. See the accurate Annals of Abulfeda, p. 158, 159, 185, 238.

106. The dynasties of the Taherites and Soffarides, with the rise of that of the Samanides, are described in the original history and Latin version of Mirchond: yet the most interesting facts had already been drained by the diligence of M. D'Herbelot.

107. M. de Guignes (Hist. des Huns, tom. iii. p. 124–154) has exhausted the Toulunides and Ikshidites of Egypt, and thrown some light on the Carmathians and Hamadanites.

108. Hic est ultimus chalifah qui multum atque sæpius pro concione peroraret. . . . Fuit etiam ultimus qui otium cum eruditis et facetis hominibus fallere hilariterque agere soleret. Ultimus tandem chalifarum cui sumtus, stipendia, reditus, et thesauri, culinæ, cæteraque omnis aulica pompa priorum chalifarum ad instar comparata fuerint. Videbimus enim paullo post quem indignis et servilibus ludibriis exagitati, quam ad humilem fortunam altimumque contempti abjecti fuerint hi quondam potentissimi totius terrarum Orientalium orbis domini. Abulfed. Annal. Moslem. p. 261. I have given this passage as the manner and tone of Abulfeda, but the cast of Latin eloquence belongs more properly to Reiske. The Arabian historian (p. 255, 257, 261–269, 283, etc.) has supplied me with the most interesting facts of this paragraph.

109. Their master, on a similar occasion, showed himself of a more indulgent and tolerating spirit. Ahmed Ebn Hanbal, the head of one of the four orthodox sects, was born at Bagdad A.H. 164, and died there A.H. 241. He fought and suffered in the dispute concerning the creation of the Koran.

110. The office of vizir was superseded by the emir al Omra, Imperator Imperatorum, a title first instituted by Rahdi, and which merged at length in the Bowides and Seljukides: vectigalibus, et tributis, et curiis per omnes regiones præfecit, jussitque in omnibus suggestis nominis ejus in concionibus mentionem fieri (Abulpharagius, Dynast. p. 199). It is likewise mentioned by Elmacin (p. 254, 255).

111. Liutprand, whose choleric temper was embittered by his uneasy situation, suggests the names of reproach and contempt more applicable to Nicephorus than the vain titles of the Greeks, Ecce venit stella matutina, surgit Eous, reverberat obtutū solis radios, pallida Saracenorum mors, Nicephorus μεδων.

112. Notwithstanding the insinuation of Zonaras, καὶ εἰ μὴ, etc. (tom. ii. l. xvi. [c. 23] p. 197), it is an undoubted fact that Crete was completely and finally subdued by Nicephorus Phocas (Pagi, Critica, tom. iii. p. 873–875; Meursius, Creta, l. iii. c. 7, tom. iii. p. 464, 465).

113. A Greek Life of St. Nicon the Armenian was found in the Sforza library, and translated into Latin by the Jesuit Sirmond, for the use of Cardinal Baronius. This contemporary legend casts a ray of light on Crete and Peloponnesus in the tenth century. He found the newly-recovered island, fœdis detestandæ Agarenorum superstitionis vestigiis adhuc plenam ac refertam . . . but the victorious missionary, perhaps with some carnal aid, ad baptismum omnes veræque fidei disciplinam pepulit. Ecclesiis per totam insulam ædificatis, etc. (Annal. Eccles. A.D. 961).

114. Elmacin, Hist. Saracen. p. 278, 279. Liutprand was disposed to depreciate the Greek power, yet he owns that Nicephorus led against Assyria an army of eighty thousand men.

115. Ducenta fere millia hominum numerabat urbs (Abulfeda, Annal. Moslem. p. 281) of Mopsuestia, or Masifa, Mampsysta, Mansista, Mamista, as it is corruptly, or perhaps more correctly, styled in the middle ages (Wesseling, Itinerar. p. 580). Yet I cannot credit this extreme populousness a few years after the testimony of the emperor Leo, οὐ γὰρ πολυπληθία στρατοῦ τοῖς Κίλιξι βαρβάροις ἐστὶν (Tactica, c. xviii. [§ 139] in Meursii Oper. tom. vi. p. 817).

116. The text of Leo the Deacon, in the corrupt names of Emeta and Myctarsim, reveals the cities of Amida and Martyropolis (Miafarekin; see Abulfeda, Geograph. p. 245, vers. Reiske). Of the former, Leo observes, urbs munita et illustris; of the latter, clara atque conspicua opibusque et pecore, reliquis ejus provinciis urbibus atque oppidis longe præstans.

117. Ut et Ecbatana pergeret Agarenorumque regiam everteret . . . aiunt enim urbium quæ usquam sunt ac toto orbe existunt felicissimam esse auroque ditissimam (Leo Diacon. apud Pagium,

tom. iv. p. 34). This splendid description suits only with Bagdad, and cannot possibly apply either to Hamadan, the true Ecbatana (D'Anville, Géog. Ancienne, tom. ii. p. 237), or Tauris, which has been commonly mistaken for that city. The name of Ecbatana, in the same indefinite sense, is transferred by a more classic authority (Cicero pro Lege Maniliâ, c. 4) to the royal seat of Mithridates, king of Pontus.

118. See the Annals of Elmacin, Abulpharagius,

and Abulfeda, from A.H. 351 to A.H. 361; and the reigns of Nicephorus Phocas and John Zimisces, in the Chronicles of Zonaras (tom. ii. l. xvi. [c. 24] p. 199; l. xvii. [c. 4] 215) and Cedrenus (Compend. p. 649-684 [tom. ii. p. 351-415, ed. Bonn]). Their manifold defects are partly supplied by the MS. history of Leo the Deacon, which Pagi obtained from the Benedictines, and has inserted almost entire, in a Latin version (Critica, tom. iii. p. 873; tom. iv. p. 37).

Chapter LIII

1. The epithet of Πορφυρογένητος, Porphyrogenitus, born in the purple, is elegantly defined by Claudian:—

Ardua privatos nescit fortuna Penates;
Et regnum cum luce dedit. Cognata potestas
Excepit Tyrio venerabile pignus in ostro.

And Ducange, in his Greek and Latin Glossaries produces many passages expressive of the same idea.

2. A splendid MS. of Constantine, de Cæremoniis Aulæ et Ecclesiæ Byzantinæ, wandered from Constantinople to Buda, Frankfort, and Leipsic, where it was published in a splendid edition by Leich and Reiske (A.D. 1751, in folio), with such lavish praise as editors never fail to bestow on the worthy or worthless object of their toil.

3. See, in the first volume of Banduri's Imperium Orientale, Constantinus de Thematibus, p. 1-24 [tom. iii. p. 11-64, ed. Bonn]; de Administrando Imperio, p. 45-127, edit. Venet. [t. iii. p. 65-270, ed. Bonn]. The text of the old edition of Meursius is corrected from a MS. of the royal library of Paris, which Isaac Casaubon had formerly seen (Epist. ad Polybium, p. 10), and the sense is illustrated by two maps of William Deslisle, the prince of geographers till the appearance of the greater D'Anville.

4. The Tactics of Leo and Constantine are published with the aid of some new MSS. in the great edition of the works of Meursius, by the learned John Lami (tom. vi. p. 531-920, 1211-1417, Florent. 1745), yet the text is still corrupt and mutilated, the version is still obscure and faulty. The Imperial library of Vienna would afford some valuable materials to a new editor (Fabric. Biblioth. Græc. tom. vi. p. 369, 370).

5. On the subject of the *Basilics*, Fabricius (Biblioth. Græc. tom. xii. p. 425-514), and Heineccius (Hist. Juris Romani, p. 396-499), and Giannone (Istoria Civile di Napoli, tom. i. p. 450-458), as historical civilians, may be usefully consulted. Forty-one books of this Greek code have been published, with a Latin version, by Charles Annibal Fabrottus (Paris, 1647), in seven tomes in folio; four other books have been since discovered, and are inserted in Gerard Meerman's Novus Thesaurus Juris Civ. et Canon. tom. v. Of the whole work, the sixty books, John Leunclavius has

printed (Basil, 1575) an *eclogue* or synopsis. The 113 novels, or new laws, of Leo, may be found in the Corpus Juris Civilis.

6. I have used the last and best edition of the Geoponics (by Nicolas Niclas, Lipsiæ, 1781, 2 vols. in octavo). I read in the preface that the same emperor restored the long-forgotten systems of rhetoric and philosophy; and his two books of *Hippiatrica*, or Horse-physic, were published at Paris, 1530, in folio (Fabric. Biblioth. Græc. tom. vi. p. 493-500).

7. Of these fifty-three books, or titles, only two have been preserved and printed—de Legationibus (by Fulvius Ursinus, Antwerp, 1582, and Daniel Hœschelius, August. Vindel. 1603) and de Virtutibus et Vitiis (by Henry Valesius, or de Valois, Paris, 1634).

8. The life and writings of Simeon Metaphrastes are described by Hankius (de Scriptoribus Byzant. p. 418-460). This biographer of the saints indulged himself in a loose paraphrase of the sense or nonsense of more ancient acts. His Greek rhetoric is again paraphrased in the Latin version of Surius, and scarcely a thread can be now visible of the original texture.

9. According to the first book of the Cyropædia, professors of tactics, a small part of the science of war, were already instituted in Persia, by which Greece must be understood. A good edition of all the Scriptores Tactici would be a task not unworthy of a scholar. His industry might discover some new MSS., and his learning might illustrate the military history of the ancients. But this scholar should be likewise a soldier; and, alas! Quintus Icilius is no more.

10. After observing that the demerit of the Cappadocians rose in proportion to their rank and riches, he inserts a more pointed epigram, which is ascribed to Demodocus:—

Καππαδόκην ποτ' ἔχιδνα κατὴ δάκεν, ἀλλὰ καὶ αὐτὴ
Κάτθανε, γευσαμένη αἵματος ἰοβόλου.

The sting is precisely the same with the French epigram against Fréron: Un serpent mordit Jean Fréron—Eh bien? Le serpent en mourut. But, as the Paris wits are seldom read in the Anthology, I should be curious to learn through what channel it was conveyed for their imitation (Constantin. Porphyrogen. de Temat. c. ii. [tom. iii. p. 21, ed.

Bonn]; Brunck, Analect. Græc. tom. ii. p. 56; Brodæi Anthologia, l. ii. p. 244).

11. The Legatio Liutprandi Episcopi Cremonensis ad Nicephorum Phocam is inserted in Muratori, Scriptores Rerum Italicarum, tom. ii. pars. i.

12. See Constantine de Thematibus, in Banduri, tom. i. p. 1–30, who owns that the word is οὐκ παλαιά. Θέμα is used by Maurice (Stratagem. l. ii. c. 2) for a legion, from whence the name was easily transferred to its post or province (Ducange, Gloss. Græc. tom. i. p. 487, 488). Some etymologies are attempted for the Opsician, Optimatian, Thracesian, themes.

13. Ἅγιος πέλαγὸς, as it is styled by the modern Greeks, from which the corrupt names of Archipelago, l'Archipel, and the Arches have been transformed by geographers and seamen (D'Anville, Géographie Ancienne, tom. i. p. 281; Analyse de la Carte de la Grèce, p. 60). The numbers of monks or caloyers in all the islands and the adjacent mountain of Athos (Observations de Belon, fol. 32, verso), Monte Santo, might justify the epithet of holy, ἅγιος, a slight alteration from the original αἴγαιος, imposed by the Dorians, who, in their dialect, gave the figurative name of αἴγες, or goats, to the bounding waves (Vossius, apud Cellarium, Geograph. Antiq. tom. i. p. 829).

14. According to the Jewish traveller who had visited Europe and Asia, Constantinople was equalled only by Bagdad, the great city of the Ismaelites (Voyage de Benjamin de Tudèle, par Baratier, tom. i. c. 5, p. 46).

15. Ἐσθλαβώθη δὲ πᾶσα ἡ χώρα καὶ γέγονε βάρβαρος, says Constantine (Thematibus, l. ii. c. 6, p. 25 [tom. iii. p. 53, ed. Bonn]), in a style as barbarous as the idea, which he confirms, as usual, by a foolish epigram. The epitomiser of Strabo likewise observes, καὶ νῦν δὲ πᾶσαν Ἤπειρον, καὶ Ἑλλάδα σχεδὸν, καὶ Πελοπόννησον, καὶ Μακεδονίαν, Σκύθαι Σκλάβοι νέμονται (l. vii. p. 98, edit. Hudson.; p. 1251, edit. Casaub. [Almel.]): a passage which leads Dodwell a weary dance (Geograph. Minor. tom. ii. dissert. vi. p. 170–191), to enumerate the inroads of the Sclavi, and to fix the date (A.D. 980) of this petty geographer.

16. Strabon. Geograph. l. viii. p. 562 [p. 366, ed. Casaub.]; Pausanias, Græc. Descriptio, l. iii. c. 21, p. 264, 265; Plin. Hist. Natur. l. iv. c. 8.

17. Constantin. de Administrando Imperio [de Thematibus], l. ii. c. 50, 51, 52 [tom. iii. p. 52, ed. Bonn].

18. The rock of Leucate was the southern promontory of his island and diocese. Had he been the exclusive guardian of the Lover's Leap, so well known to the readers of Ovid (Epist. Sappho) and the Spectator, he might have been the richest prelate of the Greek church.

19. Leucatensis mihi juravit episcopus, quotannis ecclesiam suam debere Nicephoro aureos centum persolvere, similiter et ceteras plus minusve secundum vires suas. (Liutprand in Legat. p. 489 [Murat. Scrip. R. I. tom. ii.]).

20. See Constantine (in Vit. Basil. c. 74, 75, 76, p. 195, 197 [p. 317–320, ed. Bonn], in Script. post Theophanem), who allows himself to use many technical or barbarous words: barbarous, says he, τῇ τῶν πολλῶν ἀμαθίᾳ, καλὸν γὰρ ἐπὶ τούτοις κοινολεκτεῖν. Ducange labours on some; but he was not a weaver.

21. The manufactures of Palermo, as they are described by Hugo Falcandus (Hist. Sicula in proem. in Muratori Script. Rerum Italicarum, tom. vii. p. 256), are a copy of those of Greece. Without transcribing his declamatory sentences, which I have softened in the text, I shall observe that in this passage the strange word *exarentasmata* is very properly changed for *exanthemata* by Carusius, the first editor. Falcandus lived about the year 1190.

22. Inde ad interiora Græciæ progressi, Corinthum, Thebas, Athenas, antiquâ nobilitate celebres, expugnant; et, maximâ ibidem prædâ direptâ, opifices etiam, qui Sericos pannos texere solent, ob ignominiam Imperatoris illius, suique principis gloriam, captivos deducunt. Quos Rogerius, in Palermo Siciliæ metropoli collocans, artem texendi suos edocere præcepit; et exhinc prædicta ars illa, prius à Græcis tantum inter Christianos habita, Romanis patere cœpit ingeniis. (Otho Frisingen. de Gestis Frederici I. l. i. c. 33, in Muratori Script. Ital. tom. vi. p. 668). This exception allows the bishop to celebrate Lisbon and Almeria in sericorum pannorum opificio prænobilissimæ (in Chron. apud Muratori, Annali d'Italia, tom. ix. p. 415).

23. Nicetas in Manuel, l. ii. c. 8, p. 65 [p. 129, 130, ed. Bonn]. He describes these Greeks as skilled εὐητρίους ὀθόνας ὑφαίνειν, as ἱστῷ προσανέχοντας τῶν ἐξαμίτων καὶ χρισοπάστων στολῶν.

24. Hugo Falcandus styles them nobiles officinas. The Arabs had not introduced silk, though they had planted canes and made sugar in the plain of Palermo.

25. See the Life of Castruccio Casticani, not by Machiavel, but by his more authentic biographer Nicholas Tegrimi. Muratori, who has inserted it in the eleventh volume of his Scriptores, quotes this curious passage in his Italian Antiquities (tom. i. dissert. xxv. p. 378).

26. From the MS. statutes, as they are quoted by Muratori in his Italian Antiquities (tom. ii. dissert. xxx. p. 46–48).

27. The broad silk manufacture was established in England in the year 1620 (Anderson's Chronological Deduction, vol. ii. p. 4): but it is to the revocation of the Edict of Nantes that we owe the Spitalfields colony.

28. Voyage de Benjamin de Tudèle, tom. i. c. 5, p. 44–52. The Hebrew text has been translated into French by that marvellous child Baratier, who has added a volume of crude learning. The errors and fictions of the Jewish rabbi are not a sufficient ground to deny the reality of his travels.

29. See the continuator of Theophanes (l. iv. p.

107 [ed. Par.; p. 172, ed. Bonn]), Cedrenus (p. 544 [tom. ii. p. 158, ed. Bonn]), and Zonaras (tom. ii. l. xvi. [c. 2] p. 157).

30. Zonaras (tom. ii. l. xvii. [c. 8] p. 225), instead of pounds, uses the more classic appellation of talents, which, in a literal sense and strict computation, would multiply sixty-fold the treasure of Basil.

31. For a copious and minute description of the Imperial palace, see the Constantinop. Christiana (l. ii. c. 4, p. 113–123) of Ducange, the Tillemont of the middle ages. Never has laborious Germany produced two antiquarians more laborious and accurate than these two natives of lively France.

32. The Byzantine palace surpasses the Capitol, the palace of Pergamus, the Rufinian wood (φαιδρὸν ὄγαλμα), the temple of Hadrian at Cyzicus, the Pyramids, the Pharus, etc., according to an epigram (Antholog. Græc. l. iv. p. 498, 499; Brodæi, apud Wechel) ascribed to Julian, ex-præfect of Egypt. Seventy-one of his epigrams, some lively, are collected in Brunck (Analect. Græc. tom. ii. p. 493–510); but this is wanting.

33. Constantinopolitanum Palatium non pulchritudine solum, verum etiam fortitudine, omnibus quas unquam viderim munitionibus præstat (Liutprand, Hist. l. v. c. 9, p. 465).

34. See the anonymous continuator of Theophanes (p. 59, 61, 86 [p. 94, 98, 139, ed. Bonn]), whom I have followed in the neat and concise abstract of Le Beau (Hist. du Bas Empire, tom. xiv. p. 436, 438).

35. In aureo triclinio quæ præstantior est pars potentissime degens (the usurper Romanus), cæteras partes (filiis) distribuerat (Liutprand. Hist. l. v. c. 9, p. 465). For this lax signification of Triclinium (ædificium tria vel plura κλίνη scilicet στέγη complectens), see Ducange (Gloss. Græc. et Observations sur Joinville, p. 240) and Reiske (ad Constantinum de Ceremoniis, p. 7).

36. In equis vecti (says Benjamin of Tudela) regum filiis videntur persimiles. I prefer the Latin version of Constantine l'Empereur (p. 46) to the French of Baratier (tom. i. p. 49).

37. See the account of her journey, munificence, and testament, in the Life of Basil, by his grandson Constantine (c. 74, 75, 76, p. 195–197 [Theophan. Contin. p. 227, sqq., 317 sqq., ed. Bonn]).

38. Carsamatium (καρξιμαδες, Ducange, Gloss.) Græci vocant, amputatis virilibus et virgâ, puerum eunuchum: quos Verdunenses mercatores ob immensum lucrum facere solent et in Hispaniam ducere (Liutprand, l. vi. c. 3, p. 470). The last abomination of the abominable slave-trade! Yet I am surprised to find in the tenth century such active speculations of commerce in Lorraine.

39. See the Alexiad (l. iii. p. 78, 79 [ed. Par.; tom. i. p. 147, sq., ed. Bonn]) of Anna Comnena, who, except in filial piety, may be compared to Mademoiselle de Montpensier. In her awful reverence for titles and forms, she styles her father

'Επιστημονάρχης, the inventor of this royal art, the τέχνη τεχνῶν, and ἐπιστήμη ἐπιστημῶν.

40. Στέμμα, στέφανος, διάδημα; see Reiske, ad Ceremoniale, p. 14, 15. Ducange has given a learned dissertation on the crowns of Constantinople, Rome, France, etc. (sur Joinville, xxv. p. 289–303); but of his thirty-four models none exactly tally with Anna's description.

41.   Pars exstans curis, solo diademate dispar
       Ordine pro rerum vocitatus Cura-Palati;
says the African Corippus (de Laudibus Justini, l. i. 136); and in the same century (the sixth) Cassiodorus represents him, who, virgâ aureâ decoratus, inter obsequia numerosa, ante pedes Regios primus incederet (Variar. vii. 5). But this great officer (unknown) ἀνεπίγνωστος, exercising no function, νῦν δὲ οὐδεμίαν was cast down by the modern Greeks to the fifteenth rank (Codin. c. 5, p. 65 [ed. Par.; p. 35, ed. Bonn]).

42. Nicetas (in Manuel, l. vii. c. i. [p. 262, ed. Bonn]) defines him ὡς ἡ Λατίνων [βούλεται] φωνὴ Καγκελάριον, ὡς δ' Ἕλληνες εἴποιεν Λογοθέτην. Yet the epithet of μέγας was added by the elder Andronicus (Ducange, tom. i. p. 822, 823).

43. From Leo I. (A.D. 470) the Imperial ink, which is still visible on some original acts, was a mixture of vermilion and cinnabar, or purple. The emperor's guardians, who shared in this prerogative, always marked in green ink the indiction and and the month. See the Dictionnaire Diplomatique (tom. i. p. 511–513), a valuable abridgment.

44. The sultan sent a Σιαοὺς to Alexius (Anna Comnena, l. vi. p. 170 [tom. i. p. 301, ed. Bonn]; Ducange ad loc.); and Pachymer often speaks of the μέγας τξαούς (l. vii. c. 1, l. xii. c. 30, l. xiii. c. 22). The Chiaoush basha is now at the head of 700 officers (Rycaut's Ottoman Empire, p. 349, octavo edition).

45. Tagerman is the Arabic name of an interpreter (D'Herbelot, p. 854, 855); πρῶτος τῶν ἑρμηνέων, οὓς κοινῶς ὀνομάζουσι δραγομάνους, says Codinus (c. v. No. 70, p. 67 [p. 40, ed. Bonn]). See Villehardouin (No. 96), Busbequius (Epist. iv. p. 338), and Ducange (Observations sur Villehardouin, and Gloss. Græc. et Latin.).

46. Κονόσταυλος, or κοντόσταυλος, a corruption from the Latin Comes stabuli, or the French Connétable. In a military sense it was used by the Greeks in the eleventh century, at least as early as in France.

47. It was directly borrowed from the Normans. In the twelfth century Giannone reckons the admiral of Sicily among the great officers.

48. This sketch of honours and offices is drawn from George Codinus Curopalata, who survived the taking of Constantinople by the Turks: his elaborate, though trifling, work (de Officiis Ecclesiæ et Aulæ C. P.) has been illustrated by the notes of Goar, and the three books of Gretser, a learned Jesuit.

49. The respectful salutation of carrying the hand to the mouth, ad os, is the root of the Latin

word *adoro, adorare*. See our learned Selden (vol. iii. p. 143–145, 942), in his Titles of Honour. It seems, from the first book of Herodotus, to be of Persian origin.

50. The two embassies of Liutprand to Constantinople, all that he saw or suffered in the Greek capital, are pleasantly described by himself (Hist. l. vi. c. 1–4, p. 469–471; Legatio ad Nicephorum Phocam, p. 479–489).

51. Among the amusements of the feast, a boy balanced, on his forehead, a pike or pole, twenty-four feet long, with a cross bar of two cubits a little below the top. Two boys, naked, though cinctured (*campestrati*), together, and singly, climbed, stood, played, descended, etc., ita me stupidum reddidit: utrum mirabilius nescio (p. 470 [Liutpr. Hist. vi. c. 4]). At another repast an homily of Chrysostom on the Acts of the Apostles was read elatâ voce non Latine (p. 483 [Murat. S. I. t. ii.]).

52. *Gala* is not improbably derived from Cala, or Caloat, in Arabic a robe of honour (Reiske, Not. in Ceremon. p. 84).

53. Πολυχρονίζειν is explained by εὐφημίζειν (Codin. c. 7 [c. 6, p. 53, ed. Bonn]; Ducange, Gloss. Græc. tom. i. p. 1199).

54. Κονσέρβετ Δέους ἡμπέριουμ βέστρουμ — βίκτωρ σῆς σέμπερ — βήβητε Δόμηνι 'Ημεράτορες, ἠν μοῦλτος ἄννος (Ceremon. c. 75, p. 215 [tom. i. p. 370, ed. Bonn]). The want of the Latin V obliged the Greeks to employ their β; nor do they regard quantity. Till he recollected the true language, these strange sentences might puzzle a professor.

55. Πολυχρονίζουσι Βάραγγοι, κατὰ τὴν πάτριον καὶ οὗτοι γλῶσσαν αὐτῶν, ἤγουν 'Ιγκλινιστὶ (Codin. p. 90 [p. 57, ed. Bonn]). I wish he had preserved the words, however corrupt, of their English acclamation.

56. For all these ceremonies see the professed work of Constantine Porphyrogenitus, with the notes, or rather dissertations, of his German editors, Leich and Reiske. For the rank of the *standing* courtiers, p. 80 [ed. Lips.; tom. i. p. 136, ed. Bonn], not. 23, 62; for the adoration, except on Sundays, p. 95, 240 [p. 162, 414, ed. Bonn], not. 131; the processions, p. 2 [p. 5, ed. Bonn], etc., not. p. 3, etc.; the acclamations passim, not. 25, etc.; the factions and Hippodrome, p. 177–214 [c. 68–73, p. 303–369, ed. Bonn], not. 9, 93, etc.; the Gothic games, p. 221 [p. 381, ed. Bonn], not. 111; vintage, p. 217 [c. 78, p. 373, ed. Bonn], not. 109: much more information is scattered over the work.

57. Et privato Othoni nuper atque eadem dicenti nota adulatio (Tacit. Hist. i. 85).

58. The thirteenth chapter, de Administratione Imperii, may be explained and rectified by the Familiæ Byzantinæ of Ducange.

59. Sequiturque nefas! Ægyptia conjunx (Virgil, Æneid viii. 686). Yet this Egyptian wife was the daughter of a long line of kings. Quid te mutavit? (says Antony in a private letter to Augustus) an quod reginam ineo? Uxor mea est (Sueton. in August. c. 69). Yet I much question (for I cannot

stay to inquire) whether the triumvir ever dared to celebrate his marriage either with Roman or Egyptian rites.

60. Berenicem invitus invitam dimisit (Suetonius in Tito, c. 7). Have I observed elsewhere that this Jewish beauty was at this time above fifty years of age? The judicious Racine has most discreetly suppressed both her age and her country.

61. Constantine was made to praise the εὐγενεία and περιφανεία of the Franks, with whom he claimed a private and public alliance. The French writers (Isaac Casaubon in Dedicat. Polybii) are highly delighted with these compliments.

62. Constantine Porphyrogenitus (de Administrat. Imp. c. 26) exhibits a pedigree and Life of the illustrious king Hugo (περιβλέπτου ρηγὸς Οὔγωνος). A more correct idea may be formed from the Criticism of Pagi, the Annals of Muratori, and the Abridgment of St. Marc. A.D. 925–946.

63. After the mention of the three goddesses, Liutprand very naturally adds, et quoniam non rex solus iis abutebatur, earum nati ex incertir patribus originem ducunt (Hist. l. iv. c. 6): for the marriage of the younger Bertha, see Hist. l. v. c. 5; for the incontinence of the elder, dulcis exercitio Hymenæi, l. ii. c. 15; for the virtues and vices of Hugo, l. iii. c. 5. Yet it must not be forgot that the bishop of Cremona was a lover of scandal.

64. Licet illa Imperatrix Græca sibi et aliis fuisset satis utilis et optima, etc., is the preamble of an inimical writer, apud Pagi, tom. iv. A.D. 989, No. 3. Her marriage and principal actions may be found in Muratori, Pagi, and St. Marc, under the proper years.

65. Cedrenus, tom. ii. p. 699 [p. 444, ed. Bonn]; Zonaras, tom. ii. p. 221 [l. xvii. c. 7]; Elmacin, Hist. Saracenica, l. iii. c. 6; Nestor apud Levesque, tom. ii. p. 112; Pagi, Critica, A.D. 987, No. 6: a singular concourse! Wolodomir and Anne are ranked among the saints of the Russian church. Yet we know his vices, and are ignorant of her virtues.

66. Henricus Primus duxit uxorem Scythicam [et] Russam, filiam regis Jeroslai. An embassy of bishops was sent into Russia, and the father gratanter filiam cum multis donis misit. This event happened in the year 1051. See the passages of the original chronicles in Bouquet's Historians of France (tom. xi. p. 29, 159, 161, 319, 384, 481). Voltaire might wonder at this alliance; but he should not have owned his ignorance of the country, religion, etc., of Jeroslaus—a name so conspicuous in the Russian annals.

67. A constitution of Leo the Philosopher (lxxviii.) ne senatus-consulta amplius fiant, speaks the language of naked despotism, ἐξ οὗ τὸ μόναρχον κράτος τὴν τουτῶν ἄνηπται διοίκησιν, καὶ ἄκαιρον καὶ μάταιον τὸ ἄχρηστον μετὰ τῶν χρείαν παρεχομένων συνάπτεσθαι.

68. Codinus (de Officiis, c. xvii. p. 120, 121 [p. 87, ed. Bonn]) gives an idea of this oath, so strong to the church, πιστὸς καὶ γνήσιος δοῦλος καὶ υἱὸς τῆς

ἀγίας ἐκκλησιας, so weak to the people, καὶ ἀπέχεσθαι φόνων καὶ ἀκρωτηριασμῶν καὶ τῶν ὁμοίων τούτοις κατὰ τὸ δυνατόν.

69. If we listen to the threats of Nicephorus to the ambassador of Otho, Nec est in mari domino tuo classium numerus. Navigantium fortitudo mihi soli inest, qui eum classibus aggrediar, bello maritimas ejus civitates demoliar; et quæ flumi.ibus sunt vicina redigam in favillam. (Liutprand in Legat. ad Nicephorum Phocam, in Muratori Scriptores Rerum Italicarum, tom. ii. pars. i. p 481). He observes, in another place, qui cæteris præstant Venetici sunt et Amalphitani.

70. Nec ipsa capiet eum (the emperor Otho) in quâ ortus est pauper et pellicea Saxonia: pecuniâ quâ pollemus omnes nationes super eum invitabimus; et quasi Keramicum [id est, vas fictile] confringemus (Liutprand in Legat. p. 487). The two books, de Administrando Imperio, perpetually inculcate the same policy.

71. The nineteenth chapter of the Tactics of Leo (Meurs. Opera, tom. vi. p. 825-848), which is given more correct from a manuscript of Gudius, by the laborious Fabricius (Biblioth. Græc. tom. vi. p. 372-379), relates to the *Naumachia* or naval war.

72. Even of fifteen and sixteen rows of oars, in the navy of Demetrius Poliorcetes. These were for real use: the forty rows of Ptolemy Philadelphus were applied to a floating palace, whose tonnage, according to Dr. Arbuthnot (Tables of Ancient Coins, etc. p. 231-236), is compared as 4½ to 1, with an English 100-gun ship.

73. The Dromones of Leo, etc., are so clearly described with two tier of oars, that I must censure the version of Meursius and Fabricius, who pervert the sense by a blind attachment to the classic appellation of *Triremes*. The Byzantine historians are sometimes guilty of the same inaccuracy.

74. Constantin. Porphyrogen. in Vit. Basil. c. lxi. p. 185. He calmly praises the stratagem as a βουλὴν συνετὴν καὶ σοφὴν; but the sailing round Peloponnesus is described by his terrified fancy as a circumnavigation of a thousand miles.

75. The Continuator of Theophanes (l. iv. p. 122, 123 [p. 197, ed. Bonn]) names the successive stations, the castle of Lulum near Tarsus, Mount Argæus, Isamus, Ægilus, the hill of Mamas, Cyrisus, Mocilus, the hill of Auxentius, the sun-dial of the Pharus of the great palace. He affirms that the news were transmitted ἐν ἀκάρει, in an indivisible moment of time. Miserable amplification, which, by saying too much, says nothing. How much more forcible and instructive would have been the definition of three, or six or twelve hours!

76. See the Ceremoniale of Constantine Porphyrogenitus, l. ii. c. 44, p. 376-392 [tom. i. p. 651, sqq., ed. Bonn]. A critical reader will discern some inconsistencies in different parts of this account; but they are not more obscure or more stubborn than the establishment and effectives, the present and fit for duty, the rank and file and the private,

of a modern return, which retain in proper hands the knowledge of these profitable mysteries.

77. See the fifth, sixth, and seventh chapters, περὶ ὅπλων, περὶ ὁπλίσεως, and περὶ γυμνασίας, in the Tactics of Leo, with the corresponding passages in those of Constantine.

78. They observe τῆς γὰρ τοξείας παντελῶς ἀμελ- ηθείσης . . . ἐν τοῖς Ρωμαίοις τὰ πολλὰ νῦν εἴωθε σφάλ- ματα γένεσθαι. (Leo, Tactic. p. 581 [c. vi. § 5]; Con- stantin. p. 1216). Yet such were not the maxims of the Greeks and Romans, who despised the loose and distant practice of archery.

79. Compare the passages of the Tactics, p. 669 and 721, and the twelfth with the eighteenth chapter.

80. In the preface to his Tactics, Leo very freely deplores the loss of discipline and the calamities of the times, and repeats, without scruple (Proem. p. 357), the reproaches of ἀμέλεια, ἀταξία, ἀγυμνασία, δειλία etc., nor does it appear that the same censures were less deserved in the next generation by the disciples of Constantine.

81. See in the Ceremonial (l. ii. c. 19, p. 353 [tom. i. p. 610, sq., ed. Bonn]) the form of the emperor's trampling on the necks of the captive Saracens, while the singers chanted "Thou hast made my enemies my footstool!" and the people shouted forty times the kyrie eleison.

82. Leo observes (Tactic. p. 668) that a fair open battle against any nation whatsoever is ἐπισφαλὲς and ἐπικινδυνόν: the words are strong, and the remark is true; yet if such had been the opinion of the old Romans, Leo had never reigned on the shores of the Thracian Bosphorus.

83. Zonaras (tom. ii. l. xvi. [c. 25] p. 202, 203) and Cedrenus (Compend. p. 668 [p. 658, ed. Par.; tom. ii. p. 369, ed. Bonn]), who relate the design of Nicephorus, must unfortunately apply the epi- thet of γενναίως to the opposition of the patriarch.

84. The eighth chapter of the tactics of the dif- ferent nations is the most historical and useful of the whole collection of Leo. The manners and arms of the Saracens (Tactic. p. 809-817, and a fragment from the Medicean MS. in the preface of the sixth volume of Meursius) the Roman em- peror was too frequently called upon to study.

85. Παντὸς δὲ καὶ κακοῦ ἔργου τὸν Θεὸν εἶναι αἴτιον ὑποτίθενται, καὶ πολέμοις χαίρειν λέγουσι τὸν Θεὸν, τὸν διασκορπίζοντα ἔθνη τὰ τοὺς πολέμους θέλοντα. Leon. Tactic. p. 809 [c. 18, § 111].

86. Liutprand (p. 484, 485) relates and inter- prets the oracles of the Greeks and Saracens, in which, after the fashion of prophecy, the past is clear and historical, the future is dark, enigmatical, and erroneous. From this boundary of light and shade an impartial critic may commonly determine the date of the composition.

87. The sense of this distinction is expressed by Abulpharagius (Dynast. p. 2, 62, 101); but I can- not recollect the passage in which it is conveyed by this lively apophthegm.

88. Ex Francis, quo nomine tam Latinos quam

Teutones comprehendit, ludum habuit (Liutprand in Legat. ad Imp. Nicephorum, p. 483, 484). This extension of the name may be confirmed from Constantine (de Administrando Imperio, l. ii. c. 27, 28) and Eutychius (Annal. tom. i. p. 55, 56), who both lived before the Crusades. The testimonies of Abulpharagius (Dynast. p. 69) and Abulfeda (Præfat. ad Geograph.) are more recent.

89. On this subject of ecclesiastical and beneficiary discipline, Father Thomassin (tom. iii. l. i. c. 40, 45, 46, 47) may be usefully consulted. A general law of Charlemagne exempted the bishops from personal service; but the opposite practice, which prevailed from the ninth to the fifteenth century, is countenanced by the example or silence of saints and doctors. . . . You justify your cowardice by the holy canons, says Ratherius of Verona; the canons likewise forbid you to whore, and yet—

90. In the eighteenth chapter of his Tactics, the emperor Leo has fairly stated the military vices and virtues of the Franks (whom Meursius ridiculously translates by *Galli*) and the Lombards or Langobards. See likewise the twenty-sixth Dissertation of Muratori de Antiquitatibus Italiæ medii Ævi.

91. Domini tui milites (says the proud Nicephorus) equitandi ignari, pedestris pugnæ sunt inscii: scutorum magnitudo, loricarum gravitudo, ensium longitudo, galearumque pondus neutrâ parte pugnare eos sinit; ac subridens, impedit, inquit, et eos gastrimargia, hoc est ventris ingluvies, etc. Liutprand in Legat. p. 480, 481.

92. In Saxonia certo scio . . . decentius ensibus pugnare quam calamis et prius mortem obire quam hostibus terga dare (Liutprand, p. 482).

93. Φραγγοὶ τοίνυν καὶ Λογίβαρδοι λόγον ἐλευθερίας περὶ πολλοῦ ποιοῦνται, ἀλλ᾿ οἱ μὲν Λογίβαρδοι τὸ πλέον τῆς τοιαύτης ἀρετης νῦν ἀπώλεσαν. Leonis Tactica, c. 18, p. 804. The emperor Leo died A.D. 911: an historical poem, which ends in 916, and appears to have been composed in 940, by a native of Venetia, discriminates in these verses the manners of Italy and France:

　　　—Quid inertia bello
Pectora (Ubertus ait) duris prætenditis armis,
O Itali? Potius vobis sacra pocula cordi;
Sæpius et stomachum nitidis laxare saginis
Elatasque domos rutilo fulcire metallo.
Non eadem Gallos similis vel cura remordet;
Vicinas quibus est studium devincere terras,
Depressumque larem spoliis hinc inde coactis
Sustentare——
(Anonym. Carmen Panegyricum de Laudibus Berengarii Augusti, l. ii. in Muratori Script. Rerum Italic. tom. ii. pars i. p. 395).

94. Justinian, says the historian Agathias (l. v. p. 157 [ed. Par.; p. 306, ed. Bonn]), πρῶτος Ῥωμαίων αὐτοκράτωρ ὀνόματί τε καὶ πράγματι. Yet the specific title of Emperor of the Romans was not used at Constantinople till it had been claimed by the French and German emperors of old Rome.

95. Constantine Manasses reprobates this design in his barbarous verse:

Τὴν πόλιν τὴν βασίλειαν ἀποκοσμῆσαι θέλων,
Καὶ τὴν ἀρχὴν χαρίσασθαι τῇ τριπεμπέλῳ Ῥώμῃ,
Ὡς εἴτις ἀβροστόλιστον ἀποκοσμήσει νύμφην,
Καὶ γραῦν τινὰ τρικόρωνον ὡς κόρην ὡράϊσει·
　　　　　　[v. 3836, p. 165, ed. Bonn.]
and it is confirmed by Theophanes, Zonaras, Cedrenus, and the Historia Miscella: voluit in urbem Romam Imperium transferre (l. xix. p. 137, in tom. i. pars i. of the Scriptores Rer. Ital. of Muratori).

96. Paul. Diacon. l. v. c. 11, p. 480; Anastasius in Vitis Pontificum, in Muratori's Collection, tom. iii. pars i. p. 141.

97. Consult the preface of Ducange (ad Gloss. Græc. medii Ævi) and the Novels of Justinian (vii. lxvi.). The Greek language was κοίνος, the Latin was πάτριος to himself, κυριώτατος to the πολιτείας σχῆμα, the system of government.

98. Οὐ μὴν ἀλλὰ καὶ Λατινική λέξις καὶ φράσις εἰσέτι τοὺς νόμους κρύπτουσα τοὺς συνεῖναι ταύτην μὴ δυναμένους ἰσχυρῶς ἀπετείχιζε (Matth. Blastares, Hist. Juris, apud Fabric. Biblioth. Græc. tom. xii. p. 369 [ed. Hamb. 1724]). The Code and Pandects (the latter by Thalelæus) were translated in the time of Justinian (p. 358, 366). Theophilus, one of the original triumvirs, has left an elegant, though diffuse, paraphrase of the Institutes. On the other hand, Julian, antecessor of Constantinople (A.D. 570), 120 Novellas Græcas eleganti Latinitate donavit (Heineccius, Hist. J. R. p. 396) for the use of Italy and Africa.

90. Abulpharagius assigns the seventh Dynasty to the Franks or Romans, the eighth to the Greeks, the ninth to the Arabs. A tempore Augusti Cæsaris donec imperaret Tiberius Cæsar spatio circiter annorum 600 fuerunt (Imperatores C. P. Patricii, et præcipua pars exercitûs Roman [i.e. Franci]: extra quod, consiliarii, scribæ et populus, omnes Græci fuerunt: deinde regnum etiam Græcanicum factum est (p. 95, vers. Pocock). The Christian and ecclesiastical studies of Abulpharagius gave him some advantage over the more ignorant *Moslems*.

100. Primus ex Græcorum genere in Imperio confirmatus est; or, according to another MS. of Paulus Diaconus (l. iii. c. 15, p. 443), in Græcorum Imperio.

101. Quia linguam, mores, vestesque mutâstis, putavit Sanctissimus Papa (an audacious irony), ita vobis displicere Romanorum nomen. His nuncios, rogabant Nicephorum Imperatorem Græcorum, ut cum Othone Imperatore Romanorum amicitiam faceret (Liutprand in Legatione, p. 486).

102. By Laonicus Chalcocondyles, who survived the last siege of Constantinople, the account is thus stated (l. i. p. 3 [p. 6, ed. Bonn]). Constantine transplanted his Latins of Italy to a Greek city of Thrace: they adopted the language and manners of the natives, who were confounded with them under the name of Romans. The kings of Constantinople, says the historian, ἐπὶ τῷ σφᾶς αὐτοὺς

Ρωμαίων βασιλεῖς τε καὶ αὐτοκράτορας σεμνύνεσθαι ἀποκαλεῖν, Ἑλλήνων δὲ βασιλεῖς οὐκέτι οὐδαμῇ ἀξιοῦν.

103. See Ducange (C. P. Christiana, l. ii. p. 150, 151), who collects the testimonies, not of Theophanes, but at least of Zonaras (tom. ii. l. xv. [c. 3] p. 104), Cedrenus (p. 454 [tom. i. p. 795, sq., ed. Bonn]), Michael Glycas (p. 281 [p. 522, ed. Bonn]), Constantine Manasses (p. 87 [v. 4257, p. 182, ed. Bonn]). After refuting the absurd charge against the emperor, Spanheim (Hist. Imaginum, p. 99–111), like a true advocate, proceeds to doubt or deny the reality of the fire, and almost of the library.

104. According to Malchus (apud Zonar. l. xiv. p. 53), this Homer was burnt in the time of Basiliscus. The MS. might be renewed—but on a serpent's skin? Most strange and incredible!

105. The ἀλογία of Zonaras, the ἀγρία καὶ ἀμαθία of Cedrenus, are strong words, perhaps not ill-suited to these reigns.

106. See Zonaras (l. xvi. [c. 4] p. 160, 161) and Cedrenus (p. 549, 550 [tom. ii. p. 168, sqq., ed. Bonn]). Like Friar Bacon, the philosopher Leo has been transformed by ignorance into a conjurer; yet not so undeservedly, if he be the author of the oracles more commonly ascribed to the emperor of the same name. The physics of Leo in MS. are in the library of Vienna (Fabricius, Biblioth. Græc. tom. vi. p. 366; tom. xii. p. 781). Quiescant!

107. The ecclesiastical and literary character of Photius is copiously discussed by Hanckius (de Scriptoribus Byzant. p. 269–396) and Fabricius.

108. Εἰς Ἀσσυρίους can only mean Bagdad, the seat of the caliph; and the relation of his embassy might have been curious and instructive. But how did he procure his books? A library so numerous could neither be found at Bagdad, nor transported with his baggage, nor preserved in his memory. Yet the last, however incredible, seems to be affirmed by Photius himself, ὅσας αὐτῶν ἡ μνήμη διέσωζε. Camusat (Hist. Critique des Journaux, p. 87–94) gives a good account of the Myriobiblon.

109. Of these modern Greeks, see the respective articles in the Bibliotheca Græca of Fabricius; a laborious work, yet susceptible of a better method

and many improvements: of Eustathius (tom. i. p. 289–292, 306–329), of the Pselli (a diatribe of Leo Allatius, ad calcem tom. v.), of Constantine Porphyrogenitus (tom. vi. p. 486–509), and of John Strobæus (tom. viii. 665–728), of Suidas (tom. ix. p. 620–827), John Tzetzes (tom. xii. p. 245–273). Mr. Harris, in his Philological Arrangements, opus senile, has given a sketch of this Byzantine learning (p. 287–300).

110. From obscure and hearsay evidence, Gerard Vossius (de Poetis Græcis, c. 6) and Le Clerc (Bibliothèque Choisie, tom. xix. p. 285) mention a commentary of Michael Psellus on twenty-four plays of Menander, still extant in MS. at Constantinople. Yet such classic studies seem incompatible with the gravity or dulness of a schoolman who pored over the categories (de Psellis, p. 42); and Michael has probably been confounded with Homerus *Sellius*, who wrote arguments to the comedies of Menander. In the tenth century Suidas quotes fifty plays, but he often transcribes the old scholiast of Aristophanes.

111. Anna Comnena may boast of her Greek style (τὸ Ἑλληνίζειν ἐς ἄκρον ἐσπουδακυῖα), and Zonaras, her contemporary, but not her flatterer, may add with truth, γλῶτταν εἶχεν ἀκριβῶς Ἀττικίζουσαν. The princess was conversant with the artful dialogues of Plato, and had studied the τετρακτὺς, or *quadrivium* of astrology, geometry, arithmetic, and music (see her preface to the Alexiad, with Ducange's notes).

112. To censure the Byzantine taste, Ducange (Præfat. Gloss. Græc. p. 17) strings the authorities of Aulus Gellius, Jerom, Petronius, George Hamartolus, Longinus, who give at once the precept and the example.

113. The *versus politici*, those common prostitutes, as, from their easiness, they are styled by Leo Allatius, usually consist of fifteen syllables. They are used by Constantine Manasses, John Tzetzes, etc. (Ducange, Gloss. Latin. tom. iii. p. i. p. 345, 346, edit. Basil. 1762).

114. As St. Bernard of the Latin, so St. John Damascenus, in the eighth century, is revered as the last father of the Greek, church.

115. Hume's Essays, vol. i. p. 125.

Chapter LIV

1. The errors and virtues of the Paulicians are weighed, with his usual judgment and candour, by the learned Mosheim (Hist. Ecclesiast. seculum ix. p. 311, etc.). He draws his original intelligence from Photius (contra Manichæos, l. i.) and Peter Siculus (Hist. Manichæorum). The first of these accounts has not fallen into my hands; the second, which Mosheim prefers, I have read in a Latin version inserted in the Maxima Bibliotheca Patrum (tom. xvi. p. 754–764) from the edition of the Jesuit Raderus (Ingolstadii, 1604, in 4to).

2. In the time of Theodoret, the diocese of Cyrrhus, in Syria, contained eight hundred villages. Of these, two were inhabited by Arians and Eunomians, and eight by *Marcionites*, whom the laborious bishop reconciled to the Catholic church (Dupin, Biblioth. Ecclésiastique, tom. iv. p. 81, 82).

3. Nobis profanis ista (*sacra Evangelia*) legere non licet sacerdotibus duntaxat, was the first scruple of a Catholic when he was advised to read the Bible (Petr. Sicul. p. 761).

4. In rejecting the *second* Epistle of St. Peter, the Paulicians are justified by some of the most respectable of the ancients and moderns (see Wetstein ad loc., Simon, Hist. Critique du Nouveau Testament, c. 17). They likewise overlooked the Apocalypse (Petr. Sicul. p. 756); but as such neglect is not imputed as a crime, the Greeks of the ninth century must have been careless of the credit and honour of the Revelations.

5. This contention, which has not escaped the malice of Porphyry, supposes some error and passion in one or both of the apostles. By Chrysostom, Jerome, and Erasmus, it is represented as a sham quarrel, a pious fraud, for the benefit of the Gentiles and the correction of the Jews (Middleton's Works, vol. ii. p. 1–20).

6. Those who are curious of this heterodox library may consult the researches of Beausobre (Hist. Critique du Manichéisme, tom. i. p. 305–437). Even in Africa, St. Austin could describe the Manichæan books, tam multi, tam grandes, tam pretiosi codices (contra Faust. xiii. 14); but he adds, without pity, Incendite omnes illas membranas: and his advice has been rigorously followed.

7. The six capital errors of the Paulicians are defined by Peter Siculus (p. 756) with much prejudice and passion.

8. Primum illorum axioma est, duo rerum esse principia; Deum malum et Deum bonum, aliumque hujus mundi conditorem et principem, et alium futuri ævi (Petr. Sicul. p. 756).

9. Two learned critics, Beausobre (Hist. Critique du Manichéisme, l. i. iv. v. vi.) and Mosheim (Institut. Hist. Eccles. and de Rebus Christianis ante Constantinum, sec. i. ii. iii.), have laboured to explore and discriminate the various systems of the Gnostics on the subject of the two principles.

10. The countries between the Euphrates and the Halys were possessed above 350 years by the Medes (Herodot. l. i. c. 103) and Persians; and the kings of Pontus were of the royal race of the Achæmenides (Sallust. Fragment, l. iii. with the French supplement and notes of the President de Brosses).

11. Most probably founded by Pompey after the conquest of Pontus. This Colonia, on the Lycus above Neo-Cæsarea, is named by the Turks Couleihisar, or Chonac, a populous town in a strong country (D'Anville, Géographie Ancienne, tom. ii. p. 34; Tournefort, Voyage du Levant, tom. iii. lettre xxi. p. 293).

12. The temple of Bellona, at Comana in Pontus, was a powerful and wealthy foundation, and the high priest was respected as the second person in the kingdom. As the sacerdotal office had been occupied by his mother's family, Strabo (l. xii. p. 809, 835, 836, 837 [p. 535, 557, sqq., ed. Casaub.]) dwells with peculiar complacency on the temple, the worship, and festival, which was twice celebrated every year. But the Bellona of Pontus had the features and character of the goddess, not of war, but of love.

13. Gregory, bishop of Neo-Cæsarea (A.D. 240–265), surnamed Thaumaturgus, or the Wonderworker. A hundred years afterwards, the history or romance of his life was composed by Gregory of Nyssa, his namesake and countryman, the brother of the great St. Basil.

14. Hoc cæterum ad sua egregia facinora, divini atque orthodoxi Imperatores addiderunt, ut Manichæos Montanosque capitali puniri sententiâ juberent, eorumque libros, quocunque in loco inventi essent, flammis tradi; quod siquis uspiam eosdem occultasse deprehenderetur, hunc eundem morits pœnæ addici, ejusque bona in fiscum inferri (Petr. Sicul. p. 759). What more could bigotry and persecution desire?

15. It should seem that the Paulicians allowed themselves some latitude of equivocation and mental reservation, till the Catholics discovered the pressing questions which reduced them to the alternative of apostacy or martyrdom (Petr. Sicul. p. 760).

16. The persecution is told by Petrus Siculus (p. 579–763) with satisfaction and pleasantry. Justus *justa* persolvit. Simeon was not τιτος but κῆτος (the pronunciation of the two vowels must have been nearly the same), a great whale that drowned the mariners who mistook him for an island. See likewise Cedrenus (p. 432–435 [tom. i. p. 756–761, ed. Bonn]).

17. Petrus Siculus (p. 763, 764), the continuator of Theophanes (l. iv. c. 4 [c. 16], p. 103, 104 [p. 165–167, ed. Bonn]), Cedrenus (p. 541, 542, 545 [tom. ii. p. 153 sqq.]), and Zonaras (tom. ii. l. xvi. [c. 2] p. 156), describe the revolt and exploits of Carbeas and his Paulicians.

18. Otter (Voyage en Turquie et en Perse, tom. ii.) is probably the only Frank who has visited the independent barbarians of Tephrice, now Divrigni, from whom he fortunately escaped in the train of a Turkish officer.

19. In the history of Chrysocheir, Genesius (Chron. p. 67–70, edit. Venet.) has exposed the nakedness of the empire. Constantine Porphyrogenitus (in Vit. Basil. c. 37–43, p. 166–171 [p. 266–276, ed. Bonn]) has displayed the glory of his grandfather. Cedrenus (p. 570–573 [tom. ii. p. 209–212, ed. Bonn]) is without their passions or their knowledge.

20. Συναπεμαράνθη πᾶσα ἡ ἀνθοῦσα τῆς Τεφρικῆς εὐανδρία [p. 212]. How elegant is the Greek tongue, even in the mouth of Cedrenus!

21. Copronymus transported his συγγενεῖς heretics; and thus ἐπλατύνθη ἡ αἵρεσις τῶν Παυλικιανῶν, says Cedrenus (p. 463 [tom. ii. p. 10, ed. Bonn]), who has copied the annals of Theophanes.

22. Petrus Siculus, who resided nine months at Tephrice (A.D. 870) for the ransom of captives (p. 764), was informed of their intended mission, and addressed his preservative, the Historia Manichæorum, to the new archbishop of the Bulgarians (p. 754).

23. The colony of Paulicians and Jacobites

transplanted by John Zimisces (A.D. 970) from
Armenia to Thrace is mentioned by Zonaras (tom.
ii. l. xvii. [c. 1] p. 209) and Anna Comnena
(Alexiad, l. xiv. p. 450, etc. [ed. Par. 1651]).

24. The Alexiad of Anna Comnena (l. v. p. 131
[t. i. p. 232, ed. Bonn], l. vi. p. 154, 155 [p. 272 *sq.*,
ed. Bonn], l. xiv. p. 450–457 [ed. Par. 1651], with
the Annotations of Ducange) records the transactions of her apostolic father with the Manichæans whose abominable heresy she was desirous
of refuting.

25. Basil, a monk, and the author of the Bogo-
miles, a sect of Gnostics who soon vanished (Anna
Comnena, Alexiad, l. xv. p. 486–494 [ed. Par.];
Mosheim, Hist. Ecclesiastica, p. 420).

26. Matt. Paris, Hist. Major, p. 267. This passage of our English historian is alleged by Ducange
in an excellent note on Villehardouin (No. 208),
who found the Paulicians at Philippopolis the
friends of the Bulgarians.

27. See Marsigli, Stato Militare dell' Imperio
Ottomano, p. 24.

28. The introduction of the Paulicians into Italy
and France is amply discussed by Muratori (Antiquitat. Italiæ medii Ævi, tom. v. dissert. lx. p.
81–152) and Mosheim (p. 379–382, 419–422). Yet
both have overlooked a curious passage of William
the Apulian, who clearly describes them in a battle
between the Greeks and Normans, A.D. 1040 (in
Muratori, Script. Rerum Ital. tom. v. p. 256):

Cum Græcis aderant quidam, quos pessimus
      error
Fecerat amentes, et ab ipso nomen habebant.

But he is so ignorant of their doctrine as to make
them a kind of Sabellians or Patripassians.

29. *Bulgari, Boulgres, Bougres*, a national apella-
tion, has been applied by the French as a term of
reproach to usurers and unnatural sinners. The
Paterini, or *Patelini*, has been made to signify a
smooth and flattering hypocrite, such as *l'Avocat
Patelin* of that original and pleasant farce (Ducange, Gloss. Latinitat. medii et infimi Ævi). The
Manichæans were likewise named *Cathari*, or the
pure, by corruption, *Gazari*, etc.

30. Of the laws, crusade, and persecution against
the Albigeois, a just, though general, idea is expressed by Mosheim (p. 447–481). The detail may
be found in the ecclesiastical historians, ancient
and modern, Catholics and Protestants; and among
these Fleury is the most impartial and moderate.

31. The Acts (Liber Sententiarum) of the Inquisition of Toulouse (A.D. 1307–1323) have been
published by Limborch (Amstelodami, 1692),
with a previous History of the Inquisition in general. They deserved a more learned and critical
editor. As we must not calumniate even Satan, or
the Holy Office, I will observe that, of a list of
criminals which fills nineteen folio pages, only fifteen men and four women were delivered to the
secular arm.

32. The opinions and proceedings of the reformers are exposed in the second part of the gen-

eral history of Mosheim; but the balance, which
he has held with so clear an eye and so steady a
hand, begins to incline in favour of his Lutheran
brethren.

33. Under Edward VI. our reformation was
more bold and perfect: but in the fundamental
articles of the church of England, a strong and
explicit declaration against the real presence was
obliterated in the original copy, to please the
people, or the Lutherans, or Queen Elizabeth
(Burnet's History of the Reformation, vol. ii. p.
82, 128, 302).

34. "Had it not been for such men as Luther
and myself," said the fanatic Whiston to Halley
the philosopher, "you would now be kneeling before an image of St. Winifred."

35. The article of *Servet* in the Dictionnaire Critique of Chauffepié is the best account which I
have seen of this shameful transaction. See likewise
the Abbé d'Artigny, Nouveaux Mémoires d'Histoire, etc., tom. ii. p. 55–154.

36. I am more deeply scandalised at the single
execution of Servetus than at the hecatombs which
have blazed in the Auto da Fès of Spain and
Portugal. 1. The zeal of Calvin seems to have been
envenomed by personal malice, and perhaps envy.
He accused his adversary before their common
enemies, the judges of Vienne, and betrayed, for
his destruction, the sacred trust of a private correspondence. 2. The deed of cruelty was not varnished
by the pretence of danger to the church or state.
In his passage through Geneva Servetus was a
harmless stranger, who neither preached, nor
printed, nor made proselytes. 3. A Catholic inquisitor yields the same obedience which he requires,
but Calvin violated the golden rule of doing as he
would be done by; a rule which I read in a moral
treatise of Isocrates (in Nicocle, tom. i. p. 93, edit.
Battie), four hundred years before the publication
of the Gospel. "Ἃ πάσχοντες ὑφ' ἑτέρων ὀργίζεσθε,
ταῦτα τοῖς ἄλλοις μὴ ποιεῖτε."

37. See Burnet, vol. ii. p. 84–86. The sense and
humanity of the young king were oppressed by
the authority of the primate.

38. Erasmus may be considered as the father of
rational theology. After a slumber of a hundred
years, it was revived by the Arminians of Holland,
Grotius, Limborch, and Le Clerc: in England by
Chillingworth, the latitudinarians of Cambridge
(Burnet, Hist. of own Times, vol. i. p. 261–268,
octavo edition), Tillotson, Clarke, Hoadley, etc.

39. I am sorry to observe that the three writers
of the last age, by whom the rights of toleration
have been so nobly defended, Bayle, Leibnitz, and
Locke, are all laymen and philosophers.

40. See the excellent chapter of Sir William
Temple on the Religion of the United Provinces.
I am not satisfied with Grotius (de Rebus Belgicis,
Annal. l. i. p. 13, 14, edit. in 12mo), who approves
the Imperial laws of persecution, and only con-
demns the bloody tribunal of the Inquisition.

41. Sir William Blackstone (Commentaries, vol.

iv. p. 53, 54) explains the law of England as it was fixed at the Revolution. The exceptions of Papists, and of those who deny the Trinity, would still leave a tolerable scope for persecution, if the national spirit were not more effectual than a hundred statutes.

42. I shall recommend to public animadversion two passages in Dr. Priestley which betray the ultimate tendency of his opinions. At the first of these (Hist. of the Corruptions of Christianity, vol. i. p. 275, 276) the priest, at the second (vol. ii. p. 484) the magistrate, may tremble!

Chapter LV

1. *All* the passages of the Byzantine history which relate to the barbarians are compiled, methodised, and transcribed, in a Latin version, by the laborious John Gotthelf Stritter, in his "Memoriæ Populorum, ad Danubium, Pontum Euxinum, Paludem Mæotidem, Caucasum, Mare Caspium, et inde magis ad Septemtriones incolentium." Petropoli, 1771–1779; in four tomes, or six volumes, in 4to. But the fashion has not enhanced the price of these raw materials.

2. Hist. vol. v. p. 8.

3. Theophanes, p. 296–299 [tom. i. p. 544–550, ed. Bonn]; Anastasius, p. 113; Nicephorus, C. P. p. 22, 23. Theophanes places the old Bulgaria on the banks of the Atell or Volga; but he deprives himself of all geographical credit by discharging that river into the Euxine Sea.

4. Paul. Diacon. de Gestis Langobard. l. v. c. 29, p. 881, 882. The apparent difference between the Lombard historian and the above-mentioned Greeks is easily reconciled by Camillo Pellegrino (de Ducatû Beneventano, dissert. vii. in the Scriptores Rerum Ital. tom. v. p. 186, 187) and Beretti (Chorograph. Italiæ medii Ævi. p. 273, etc.). This Bulgarian colony was planted in a vacant district of Samnium, and learned the Latin without forgetting their native language.

5. These provinces of the Greek idiom and empire are assigned to the Bulgarian kingdom in the dispute of ecclesiastical jurisdiction between the patriarchs of Rome and Constantinople (Baronius, Annal. Eccles. A.D. 869, No. 75).

6. The situation and royalty of Lychnidus, or Achrida, are clearly expressed in Cedrenus (p. 713 [tom. ii. p. 468, ed. Bonn]). The removal of an archbishop or patriarch from Justinianea prima to Lychnidus, and at length to Ternovo, has produced some perplexity in the ideas or language of the Greeks (Nicephorus Gregoras, l. ii. c. 2, p. 14, 15 [tom. i. p. 27, ed. Bonn]; Thomassin, Discipline de l'Eglise, tom. i. l. i. c. 19, 23); and a Frenchman (D'Anville) is more accurately skilled in the geography of their own country (Hist. de l'Académie des Inscriptions, tom. xxxi.).

7. Chalcocondyles, a competent judge, affirms the identity of the language of the Dalmatians, Bosnians, Servians, *Bulgarians*, Poles (de Rebus Turcisis, l. x. p. 283 [ed. Par.; p. 530, ed. Bonn]), and elsewhere of the Bohemians (l. ii. p. 38 [p. 73, ed. Bonn]). The same author has marked the separate idiom of the Hungarians. [Gibbon's assertion that the Bulgarians are Slavonic in origin contradicts his statement in chapter xlii., where he had correctly identified the Bulgarians and the Huns as belonging to the Turkish and not to the Slavonic race.]

8. See the work of John Christopher de Jordan, de Originibus Sclavicis, Vindobonæ, 1745, in four parts, or two volumes in folio. His collections and researches are useful to elucidate the antiquities of Bohemia and the adjacent countries; but his plan is narrow, his style barbarous, his criticism shallow, and the Aulic counsellor is not free from the prejudices of a Bohemian. [The Wallachians are a Romance people, of Illyrian origin, speaking a language derived from Latin.]

9. Jordan subscribes to the well-known and probable derivation from *Slava, laus, gloria*, a word of familiar use in the different dialects and parts of speech, and which forms the termination of the most illustrious names (de Originibus Sclavicis, pars i. p. 40, pars iv. p. 101, 102).

10. This conversion of a national into an appellative name appears to have arisen in the eighth century, in the Oriental France, where the princes and bishops were rich in Sclavonian captives, not of the Bohemian (exclaims Jordan), but of Sorabian race. From thence the word was extended to general use, to the modern languages, and even to the style of the last Byzantines (see the Greek and Latin Glossaries of Ducange). The confusion of the Σερβλοι or Servians, with the Latin *Servi*, was still more fortunate and familiar (Constant. Porphyr. de Administrando Imperio, c. 32, p. 99 [tom. iii. p. 152, ed. Bonn]).

11. The emperor Constantine Porphyrogenitus, most accurate for his own times, most fabulous for preceding ages, describes the Sclavonians of Dalmatia ([de Admin. Imp.] c. 29–36).

12. See the anonymous Chronicle of the eleventh century, ascribed to John Sagorninus (p. 94–102), and that composed in the fourteenth by the Doge Andrew Dandolo (Script. Rerum Ital. tom. xii. p. 227–230)—the two oldest monuments of the history of Venice.

13. The first kingdom of the Bulgarians may be found, under the proper dates, in the Annals of Cedrenus and Zonaras. The Byzantine materials are collected by Stritter (Memoriæ Populorum, tom. ii. pars. ii. p. 441–647); and the series of their kings is disposed and settled by Ducange (Fam. Byzant. p. 305–318).

14. Simeonem semi-Græcum esse aiebant, eo quod à pueritiâ Byzantii Demosthenis rhetoricam et Aristotelis syllogismos didicerat. Liutprand, l. iii. c. 8. He says, in another place, Simeon, fortis bellator, Bulgariæ [Bulgaris] præerat; Christianus, sed vicinis Græcis valde inimicus (l. i. c. 2).

15. ——Rigidum fera dextera cornu
Dum tenet infregit, truncâque à fronte revellit.

Ovid (Metamorph. ix. 1–100) has boldly painted the combat of the river-god and the hero—the native and the stranger. [The Greeks were defeated by the Servians not on the banks of the Achelous in Greece, but at a place of the same name in Bulgaria.]

16. The ambassador of Otho was provoked by the Greek excuses, cum Christophori filiam Petrus Bulgarorum *Vasileus* conjugem duceret, *Symphona*, id est consonantia, scripto juramento firmata sunt, ut omnium gentium *Apostolis*, id est nunciis, penes nos Bulgarorum Apostoli præponantur, honorentur, diligantur (Liutprand in Legatione, p. 482). See the Ceremoniale of Constantine Porphyrogenitus, tom. i. p. 82 [p. 139, ed. Bonn], tom. ii. p. 429, 430, 434, 435, 443, 444, 446, 447 [tom. i. p. 740–743, 749–752, 767, *sqq.*, ed. Bonn], with the annotations of Reiske.

17. A bishop of Wurtzburg submitted this opinion to a reverend abbot; but *he* more gravely decided that Gog and Magog were the spiritual persecutors of the church; since Gog signifies the roof, the pride of the heresiarchs, and Magog what comes from the roof, the propagation of their sects. Yet these men once commanded the respect of mankind (Fleury, Hist. Eccles. tom. xi. p. 594, etc.).

18. The two national authors from whom I have derived the most assistance are George Pray (Dissertationes ad Annales veterum Hungarorum, etc., Vindobonæ, 1775, in folio) and Stephen Katona (Hist. Critica Ducum et Regum Hungariæ stirpis Arpadianæ, Pæstini, 1778–1781, 5 vols. in octavo). The first embraces a large and often conjectural space; the latter, by his learning, judgment, and perspicuity, deserves the name of a critical historian.

19. The author of this Chronicle is styled the notary of king Bela. Katona has assigned him to the twelfth century, and defends his character against the hypercriticism of Pray. This rude annalist must have transcribed some historical records, since he could affirm with dignity, rejectis falsis fabulis rusticorum, et garrulo cantû joculatorum. In the fifteenth century these fables were collected by Thurotzius, and embellished by the Italian Bonfinius. See the Preliminary Discourse in the Hist. Critica Ducum, p. 7–33.

20. See Constantine de Administrando Imperio, c. 3, 4, 13, 38–42. Katona has nicely fixed the composition of this work to the years 949, 950, 951 (p. 4–7). The critical historian (p. 34–107) endeavours to prove the existence, and to relate the actions, of a first duke *Almus*, the father of Arpad, who is tacitly rejected by Constantine.

21. Pray (Dissert. p. 37–39, etc.) produces and illustrates the original passages of the Hungarian missionaries, Bonfinius and Æneas Sylvius.

22. Fischer, in the Quæstiones Petropolitanæ, de Origine Ungrorum, and Pray, Dissertat. i. ii. iii., etc., have drawn up several comparative tables of the Hungarian with the Fennic dialects. The affinity is indeed striking, but the lists are short; the words are purposely chosen; and I read in the learned Bayer (Comment. Academ. Petropol. tom. x. p. 374) that, although the Hungarian has adopted many Fennic words (innumeras voces), it essentially differs toto genio et naturâ.

23. In the region of Turfan, which is clearly and minutely described by the Chinese geographers (Gaubil, Hist. du Grand Gengiscan, p. 13; De Guignes, Hist. des Huns, tom. ii. p. 31, etc.).

24. Hist. Généalogique des Tartars, par Abulghazi Bahadur Khan, partie ii. p. 90–98.

25. In their journey to Pekin, both Isbrand Ives (Harris's Collection of Voyages and Travels, vol. ii. p. 920, 921) and Bell (Travels, vol. i. p. 174) found the Vogulitz in the neighbourhood of Tobolsky. By the tortures of the etymological art, *Ugur* and *Vogul* are reduced to the same name; the circumjacent mountains really bear the appellation of *Ugrian;* and of all the Fennic dialects, the Vogulian is the nearest to the Hungarian (Fischer, Dissert. i. p. 20–30; Pray, Dissert. ii. p. 31–34).

26. The eight tribes of the Fennic race are described in the curious work of M. levêque (Hist. des Peuples soumis à la Domination de la Russie, tom. i. p. 361–561).

27. This picture of the Hungarians and Bulgarians is chiefly drawn from the Tactics of Leo, p. 796–801, and the Latin Annals, which are alleged by Baronius, Pagi, and Muratori, A.D. 889, etc.

28. Buffon, Hist. Naturelle, tom. v. p. 6, in 12mo. Gustavus Adolphus attempted, without success, to form a regiment of Laplanders. Grotius says of these Arctic tribes, arma arcus et pharetra, sed adversus feras (Annal. l. iv. p. 236); and attempts, after the manner of Tacitus, to varnish with philosophy their brutal ignorance.

29. Leo has observed that the government of the Turks was monarchical, and that their punishments were rigorous. (Tactic. p. 796 [c. xviii. § 46] ἀπεινεῖς καὶ βαρείας.) Rhegino (in Chron. A.D. 889) mentions theft as a capital crime, and his jurisprudence is confirmed by the original code of St. Stephen (A.D. 1016). If a slave were guilty, he was chastised, for the first time, with the loss of his nose, or a fine of five heifers; for the second, with the loss of his ears, or a similar fine; for the third, with death; which the freeman did not incur till the fourth offence, as his first penalty was the loss of liberty (Katona, Hist. Regum Hungar. tom. i. p. 231, 232).

30. See Katona, Hist. Ducum Hungar. p. 321–352.

31. Hungarorum gens, cujus omnes fere nationes

expertæ sævitium, etc., is the preface of Liutprand (l. i. c. 2), who frequently expatiates on the calamities of his own times. See l. i. c. 5, l. ii. c. 1, 2, 4, 5, 6, 7, l. iii. c. 1, etc., l. v. c. 8, 15, in Legat. p. 485. His colours are glaring, but his chronology must be rectified by Pagi and Muratori.

32. The three bloody reigns of Arpad, Zoltan, and Toxus are critically illustrated by Katona (Hist. Ducum, etc., p. 107-499). His diligence has searched both natives and foreigners; yet to the deeds of mischief, or glory, I have been able to add the destruction of Bremen (Adam Bremensis, i. 43).

33. Muratori has considered with patriotic care the danger and resources of Modena. The citizens besought St. Germinianus, their patron, to avert, by his intercession, the *rabies, flagellum*, etc.

Nunc to rogamus, licet servi pessimi,
Ab Ungerorum nos defendas jaculis.

The bishop erected walls for the public defence, not contra dominos serenos (Antiquitat. Ital. med. Ævi, tom. i. dissertat. i. p. 21, 22), and the song of the nightly watch is not without elegance or use (tom. iii. diss. xl. p. 709). The Italian annalist has accurately traced the series of their inroads (Annali d'Italia, tom. vii. p. 365, 367, 393, 401, 437, 440; tom. viii. p. 19, 41, 52, etc.).

34. Both the Hungarian and Russian annals suppose that they besieged, or attacked, or insulted Constantinople (Pray, dissertat. x. p. 239; Katona, Hist. Ducum, p. 354-360); and the fact is *almost* confessed by the Byzantine historians (Leo Grammaticus, p. 506 [ed. Par.; p. 322, ed. Bonn]; Cedrenus, tom. ii. p. 629 [tom. ii. p. 316, ed. Bonn]); yet, however glorious to the nation, it is denied or doubted by the critical historian, and even by the notary of Bela. Their scepticism is meritorious; they could not safely transcribe or believe the rusticorum fabulas; but Katona might have given due attention to the evidence of Liutprand, Bulgarorum gentem atque *Græcorum* tributariam fecerant (Hist. l. ii. c. 4, p. 435).

35. ———— λεονθ' ὡς, δηρινθήτην,
"Ωτ' ὄρεος κορυφῇσι περὶ κταμένης ἐλάφοιο,
Ἄμφω πεινάοντε, μέγα φρονέοντε μάχεσθον.
—Iliad. xvi. 756.

36. They are amply and critically discussed by Katona (Hist. Ducum, p. 360-368, 427-470). Liutprand (l. ii. c. 8, 9) is the best evidence for the former, and Witichind (Annal. Saxon. l. iii.) of the latter; but the critical historian will not even overlook the horn of a warrior, which is said to be preserved at Jaz-berin.

37. Hunc vero triumphum, tam laude quam memoriâ dignum, ad Meresburgum rex in superiori cœnaculo domûs per ζωγραφίαν, id est, picturam, notari præcepit, adeo ut rem veram potius quam verisimilem videas: a high encomium (Liutprand, l. ii. c. 9). Another palace in Germany had been painted with holy subjects by the order of Charlemagne; and Muratori may justly affirm, nulla sæcula fuere in quibus pictores desiderati fuerint (Antiquitat. Ital. medii Ævi, tom. ii. dis-

sert. xxiv. p. 360, 361). Our domestic claims to antiquity of ignorance and original imperfection (Mr. Walpole's lively words) are of a much more recent date (Anecdotes of Painting, vol. i. p. 2, etc.).

38. See Baronius, Annal. Eccles., A.D. 929, No. 2-5. The lance of Christ is taken from the best evidence—Liutprand (l. iv. c. 12), Sigebert, and the Acts of St. Gerard; but the other military relics depend on the faith of the Gesta Anglorum post Bedam, l. ii. c. 8.

39. Katona, Hist. Ducum Hungariæ, p. 500, etc.

40. Among these colonies we may distinguish—1. The Chazars, or Cabari, who joined the Hungarians on their march (Constant. de Admin. Imp. c. 39, 40, p. 108, 109 [tom. iii. p. 171, *seqq.*, ed. Bonn]). 2. The Jazyges, Moravians, and Siculi, whom they found in the land; the last were *perhaps* a remnant of the Huns of Attila, and were intrusted with the guard of the borders. 3. The Russians, who, like the Swiss in France, imparted a general name to the royal porters. 4. The Bulgarians, whose chiefs (A.D. 956) were invited, cum magnâ multitudine Hismahelitarum. Had any of these Sclavonians embraced the Mohammedan religion? 5. The Bisseni and Cumans, a mixed multitude of Patzinacites, Uzi, Chazars, etc., who had spread to the lower Danube. The last colony of 40,000 Cumans, A.D. 1239, was received and converted by the kings of Hungary, who derived from that tribe a new regal appellation (Pray, dissert. vi. vii. p. 109-173; Katona, Hist. Ducum, p. 95-99, 259-264, 476, 479-483, etc.).

41. Christiani autem, quorum pars major populi est, qui ex omni parte mundi illuc tracti sunt captivi, etc. Such was the language of Piligrinus, the first missionary who entered Hungary, A.D. 973. Pars major is strong. Hist. Ducum, p. 517.

42. The fideles Teutonici of Geisa are authenticated in old charters; and Katona, with his usual industry, has made a fair estimate of these colonies, which had been so loosely magnified by the Italian Ranzanus (Hist. Critic Ducum, p. 667-681).

43. Among the Greeks, this national appellation has a singular form, 'ρῶς, as an undeclinable word, of which many fanciful etymologies have been suggested. I have perused, with pleasure and profit, a dissertation de Origine Russorum (Comment. Academ. Petropolitanæ, tom. viii. p. 388-436) by Theophilus Sigefrid Bayer, a learned German, who spent his life and labours in the service of Russia. A geographical tract of D'Anville, de l'Empire de Russie, son Origine, et ses Accroissemens (Paris, 1772, in 12mo), has likewise been of use.

44. See the entire passage (dignum, says Bayer, ut aureis in tabulis figatur) in the Annales Bertiniani Francorum (in Script. Ital. Muratori. tom. ii. pars i. p. 525), A.D. 839, twenty-two years before the era of Ruric. In the tenth century Liutprand (Hist. l. v. c. 6) speaks of the Russians and Nor-

mans as the same Aquilonares homines of a red complexion.

45. My knowledge of these annals is drawn from M. Levêque, Histoire de Russie. Nestor, the first and best of these ancient annalists, was a monk of Kiow, who died in the beginning of the twelfth century; but his Chronicle was obscure till it was published at Petersburgh, 1767, in 4to; Levêque, Hist. de Russie, tom. i. p. xvi.; Coxe's Travels, vol. ii. p. 184.

46. Theophil. Sig. Bayer de Varagis (for the name is differently spelt), in Comment. Academ. Petropolitanæ, tom. iv. p. 275-311.

47. Yet, as late as the year 1018, Kiow and Russia were still guarded ex fugitivorum servorum robore, confluentium et maxime Danorum. Bayer, who quotes (p. 292) the Chronicle of Ditmar of Merseburg, observes that it was unusual for the Germans to enlist in a foreign service.

48. Ducange has collected from the original authors the state and history of the Varangi at Constantinople (Glossar. Med. et Infimæ Græcitatis, sub voce Βάραγγοι; Med. et Infimæ Latinitatis, sub voce *Vagri;* Not. ad Alexiad. Annæ Comnenæ, p. 256, 257, 258; Notes sur Villehardouin, p. 296-299). See likewise the annotations of Reiske to the Ceremoniale Aulæ Byzant. of Constantine, tom. ii. p. 149, 150. Saxo Grammaticus affirms that they spoke Danish; but Codinus maintains them till the fifteenth century in the use of their native English: Πολυχρονίζουσι οἱ Βάραγγοι κατὰ τὴν πάτριον γλῶσσαν αὐτῶν, ἤγουν Ἰγκλινιστί [p. 57, ed. Bonn].

49. The original record of the geography and trade of Russia is produced by the emperor Constantine Porphyrogenitus (de Administrat. Imperii, c. 2, p. 55, 56, c. 9, p. 59-61, c. 13, p. 63-67, c. 37, p. 106, c. 42, p. 112, 113 [tom. iii. p. 59, *sq.,* p. 74-79, p. 82-90, p. 165, p. 177, *sqq.,* ed. Bonn]), and illustrated by the diligence of Bayer (de Geographiâ Russiæ vicinarumque Regionum circiter A.C. 948, in Comment. Academ. Petropol. tom. ix. p. 367-422, tom. x. p. 371-421), with the aid of the chronicles and traditions of Russia, Scandinavia, etc.

50. The haughty proverb, "Who can resist God and the great Novogorod?" is applied by M. Levêque (Hist. de Russie, tom. i. p. 60) even to the times that preceded the reign of Ruric. In the course of his history he frequently celebrates this republic, which was suppressed A.D. 1475 (tom. ii. p. 252-266). That accurate traveller, Adam Olearius, describes (in 1635) the remains of Novogorod, and the route by sea and land of the Holstein ambassadors, tom. i. p. 123-129.

51. In hac magnâ civitate, quæ est caput regni, plus trecentæ ecclesiæ habentur et nundinæ octo, populi etiam ignota manus (Eggehardus ad A.D. 1018, apud Bayer, tom. ix. p. 412). He likewise quotes (tom. x. p. 397) the words of the Saxon annalist, Cujus (*Russiæ*) metropolis est Chive, æmula sceptri Constantinopolitani, quæ est clarissimum

decus Græciæ. The fame of Kiow, especially in the eleventh century, had reached the German and the Arabian geographers.

52. In Odoræ ostio quâ Scythicas alluit paludes, nobilissima civitas Julinum, celeberrimam Barbaris et Græcis, qui sunt in circuitû, præstans stationem. Est sane maxima omnium quas Europa claudit civitatum (Adam Bremensis, Hist. Eccles. p. 19 [l. ii. c. 12]). A strange exaggeration even in the eleventh century. The trade of the Baltic, and the Hanseatic League, are carefully treated in Anderson's Historical Deduction of Commerce; at least, in *our* languages, I am not acquainted with any book so satisfactory.

53. According to Adam of Bremen (de Sitû Daniæ, p. 58 [c. 223, p. 146, ed. Maderi]), the old Curland extended eight days' journey along the coast; and by Peter Teutoburgicus (p. 68, A.D. 1326) Memel is defined as the common frontier of Russia, Curland, and Prussia. Aurum ibi plurimum (says Adam), divinis, auguribus, atque necromanticis omnes domus sunt plenæ . . . a toto orbe ibi responsa petuntur, maxime ab Hispanis (forsan *Zupanis,* id est regulis Lettoviæ) et Græcis. The name of Greeks was applied to the Russians even before their conversion; an imperfect conversion, if they still consulted the wizards of Curland (Bayer, tom. x. p. 378, 402, etc.; Grotius, Prolegomen. ad Hist. Goth. p. 99).

54. Constantine only reckons seven cataracts, of which he gives the Russian and Sclavonic names; but thirteen are enumerated by the Sieur de Beauplan, a French engineer, who had surveyed the course and navigation of the Dnieper or Borysthenes (Description de l'Ukraine, Rouen, 1660, a thin quarto); but the map is unluckily wanting in my copy.

55. Nestor, apud Levêque, Hist. de Russie, tom. i. p. 78-80. From the Dnieper or Borysthenes, the Russians went to Black Bulgaria, Chazaria, and Syria. To Syria, how? where? when? May we not, instead of Συρία, read Συανία (de Administrat. Imp. c. 42, p. 113)? The alteration is slight; the position of Suania, between Chazaria and Lazica, is perfectly suitable; and the name was still used in the eleventh century (Cedren. tom. ii. p. 770 [p. 573, ed. Bonn]).

56. The wars of the Russians and Greeks in the ninth, tenth, and eleventh centuries, are related in the Byzantine annals, especially those of Zonaras and Cedrenus; and all their testimonies are collected in the *Russica* of Stritter, tom. ii. pars ii. p. 939-1044.

57. Προσεταιρισάμενος δὲ καὶ συμμαχικὸν οὐκ ὀλίγον ἀπὸ τῶν κατοικούντων ἐν ταῖς προσαρκτίοις τοῦ Ὠκεανοῦ νήσοις ἐθνῶν. Cedrenus in Compend. p. 758 [tom. ii. p. 551, ed. Bonn].

58. See Beauplan (Description de l'Ukraine, p. 54-61); his descriptions are lively, his plans accurate, and, except the circumstance of fire-arms, we may read old Russians for modern Cosacks.

59. It is to be lamented that Bayer has only

given a Dissertation de Russorum *primâ* Expeditione Constantinopolitanâ (Comment. Academ. Petropol. tom. vi. p. 365–391). After disentangling some chronological intricacies, he fixes it in the years 864 or 865, a date which might have smoothed some doubts and difficulties in the beginning of M. Levêque's history.

60. When Photius wrote his encyclic epistle on the conversion of the Russians, the miracle was not yet sufficiently ripe; he reproaches the nation as εἰς ὠμότητα καὶ μιαιφονίαν πάντας δευτέρους ταττόμενον.

61. Leo Grammaticus, p. 463, 464 [p. 241, ed. Bonn]; Constantini Continuator, in Script. post Theophanem, p. 121, 122 [p. 196, 197, ed. Bonn]; Symeon Logothet. p. 445, 446 [p. 674, 675, ed. Bonn]; Georg. Monach. p. 535, 536 [p. 826, 827, ed. Bonn]; Cedrenus, tom. ii. p. 551 [p. 173, ed. Bonn]; Zonaras, tom. ii. p. 162 [l. xvi. c. 5].

62. See Nestor and Nicon, in Levêque's Hist. de Russie, tom. i. p. 74–80. Katona (Hist. Ducum, p. 75–79) uses his advantage to disprove this Russian victory, which would cloud the siege of Kiow by the Hungarians.

63. Leo Grammaticus, p. 506, 507 [p. 323, 324, ed. Bonn]; Incert. Contin. p. 263, 264 [p. 424, *sqq.*, ed. Bonn]; Symeon Logothet. p. 490, 491; Georg. Monach. p. 588, 589 [p. 914, 915, ed. Bonn]; Cedren. tom. ii. p. 629 [p. 316, ed. Bonn]; Zonaras, tom. ii. p. 190, 191 [l. xvi. c. 19]; and Liutprand, l. v. c. 6, who writes from the narratives of his father-in-law, then ambassador at Constantinople, and corrects the vain exaggeration of the Greeks.

64. I can only appeal to Cedrenus (tom. ii. p. 758, 759 [p. 551, *sq.*, ed. Bonn]) and Zonaras (tom. ii. p. 253, 254 [l. xvii. c. 24]); but they grow more weighty and credible as they draw near to their own times.

65. Nestor, apud Levêque, Hist. de Russie, tom. i. p. 87.

66. This brazen statue, which had been brought from Antioch, and was melted down by the Latins, was supposed to represent either Joshua or Bellerophon—an odd dilemma. See Nicetas Choniates (p. 413, 414 [ed. Par.; p. 848, 849, ed. Bonn]), Codinus (de Originibus, C. P. p. 24), and the anonymous writer de Antiquitat. C. P. (Banduri, Imp. Orient. tom. i. p. 17, 18), who lived about the year 1100. They witness the belief of the prophecy; the rest is immaterial.

67. The life of Swatoslaus, or Sviatoslaf, or Sphendosthlabus, is extracted from the Russian Chronicles by M. Levêque (Hist. de Russie, tom. i. p. 94–107).

68. This resemblance may be clearly seen in the ninth book of the Iliad (205–221) in the minute detail of the cookery of Achilles. By such a picture a modern epic poet would disgrace his work and disgust his reader; but the Greek verses are harmonious—a dead language can seldom appear low or familiar; and, at the distance of two thousand seven hundred years, we are amused with the primitive manners of antiquity.

69. This singular epithet is derived from the Armenian language, and Τζιμισκῆς is interpreted in Greek by μουζακίτζης or μοιρακίτζης. As I profess myself equally ignorant of *these* words, I may be indulged in the question in the play, "Pray, which of you is the interpreter?" From the context, they seem to signify *Adolescentulus* (Leo Diacon. l. iv. MS. apud Ducange, Glossar. Græc. p. 1570).

70. In the Sclavonic tongue the name of Peristhlaba implied the great or illustrious city, μεγάλη καὶ οὖσα καὶ λεγομένη, says Anna Comnena (Alexiad, l. vii. p. 194). From its position between Mount Hæmus and the Lower Danube, it appears to fill the ground, or at least the station, of Marcianopolis. The situation of Durostolus, or Dristra, is well known and conspicuous (Comment. Academ. Petropol. tom. ix. p. 415, 416; D'Anville, Géographie Ancienne, tom. i. p. 307, 311).

71. The political management of the Greeks, more especially with the Patzinacites, is explained in the seven first chapters, de Administratione Imperii.

72. In the narrative of this war Leo the Deacon (apud Pagi, Critica, tom. iv. A.D. 968–973) is more authentic and circumstantial than Cedrenus (tom. ii. p. 660–683) and Zonaras (tom. ii. p. 205–214). These declaimers have multiplied to 308,000 and 330,000 men those Russian forces of which the contemporary had given a moderate and consistent account.

73. Phot. Epistol. ii. No. 35, p. 58, edit. Montacut. It was unworthy of the learning of the editor to mistake the Russian nation, τὸ 'Ρῶς, for a war-cry of the Bulgarians; nor did it become the enlightened patriarch to accuse the Sclavonian idolaters τῆς Ελληνικῆς καὶ ἀθέου δόξης. They were neither Greeks nor atheists.

74. M. Levêque has extracted, from old chronicles and modern researches, the most satisfactory account of the religion of the *Slavi* and the conversion of Russia (Hist. de Russie, tom. i. p. 35–54, 59, 92, 93, 113–121, 124–129, 148, 149, etc.).

75. See the Ceremoniale Aulæ Byzant. tom. ii. c. 15, p. 343–345: the style of Olga, or Elga, is Ἀρχόντισσα 'Ρωσίας. For the chief of barbarians the Greeks whimsically borrowed the title of an Athenian magistrate, with a female termination, which would have astonished the ear of Demosthenes.

76. See an anonymous fragment, published by Banduri (Imperium Orientale, tom. ii. p. 112, 113), de Conversione Russorum.

77. Cherson, or Corsun, is mentioned by Herberstein (apud Pagi, tom. iv. p. 56) as the place of Wolodomir's baptism and marriage; and both the tradition and the gates are still preserved at Novogorod. Yet an observing traveller transports the brazen gates from Magdeburg in Germany (Coxe's Travels into Russia, etc., vol. i. p. 452), and quotes an inscription which seems to justify his opinion. The modern reader must not confound this old Cherson of the Tauric or Crimæan peninsula with

a new city of the same name which has arisen near the mouth of the Borysthenes, and was lately honoured by the memorable interview of the empress of Russia with the emperor of the West.

78. Consult the Latin text, or English version, of Mosheim's excellent History of the Church, under the first head or section of each of these centuries.

79. In the year 1000 the ambassadors of St. Stephen received from Pope Silvester the title of King of Hungary, with a diadem of Greek workmanship. It had been designed for the duke of Poland; but the Poles, by their own confession, were yet too barbarous to deserve an *angelical* and *apostolical* crown. (Katona, Hist. Critic. Regum Stirpis Arpadianæ, tom. i. p. 1-20).

80. Listen to the exultations of Adam of Bremen (A.D. 1080), of which the substance is agreeable to truth: Ecce illa ferocissima Danorum, etc., natio ... jamdudum novit in Dei laudibus Alleluia resonare. Ecce populus ille piraticus ... suis nunc

finibus contentus est. ... Ecce patria horribilis semper inaccessa propter cultum idolorum ... prædicatores veritatis ubique certatim admittit, etc., etc. (de Sitú Daniæ, etc., p. 40, 41, edit. Elzevir [c. 251, p. 161, ed. Maderi]: a curious and original prospect of the north of Europe, and the introduction of Christianity).

81. The great princes removed in 1156 from Kiow, which was ruined by the Tartars in 1240. Moscow became the seat of empire in the fourteenth century. See the first and second volumes of Levêque's History, and Mr. Coxe's Travels into the North, tom. i. p. 241, etc.

82. The ambassadors of St. Stephen had used the reverential expressions of *regnum oblatum*, *debitam obedientiam*, etc., which were most rigorously interpreted by Gregory VII.; and the Hungarian Catholics are distressed between the sanctity of the pope and the independence of the crown (Katona, Hist. Critica, tom. i. p. 20-25; tom. ii. p. 304, 346, 360, etc.).

Chapter LVI

1. For the general history of Italy in the ninth and tenth centuries I may properly refer to the fifth, sixth, and seventh books of Sigonius de Regno Italiæ (in the second volume of his works, Milan, 1732); the Annals of Baronius, with the Criticism of Pagi; the seventh and eighth books of the Istoria Civile del Regno di Napoli of Giannone; the seventh and eighth volumes (the octavo edition) of the Annali d'Italia of Muratori, and the second volume of the Abrégé Chronologique of M. de St. Marc, a work which, under a superficial title, contains much genuine learning and industry. But my long-accustomed reader will give me credit for saying that I myself have ascended to the fountainhead as often as such ascent could be either profitable or possible; and that I have diligently turned over the originals in the first volumes of Muratori's great collection of the *Scriptores Rerum Italicarum*.

2. Camillo Pellegrino, a learned Capuan of the last century, has illustrated the history of the duchy of Beneventum, in his two books, Historia Principum Longobardorum, in the Scriptores of Muratori, tom. ii. pars. i. p. 221-345, and tom. v. p. 159-245.

3. See Constantin. Porphyrogen. de Thematibus, l. ii. c. xi. [tom. iii. p. 62, ed. Bonn] in Vit. Basil. c. 55, p. 181.

4. The original epistle of the emperor Lewis II. to the emperor Basil, a curious record of the age, was first published by Baronius (Annal. Eccles. A.D. 871, No. 51-71), from the Vatican MS. of Erchempert, or rather of the anonymous historian of Salerno.

5. See an excellent Dissertation de Republicâ Amalphitanâ, in the Appendix (p. 1-42) of Henry

Brenckmann's Historia Pandectarum (Trajecti ad Rhenum, 1722, in 4to).

6. Your master, says Nicephorus, has given aid and protection principibus Capuano et Beneventano, servis meis, quos oppugnare dispono. ... Nova (potius *nota*) res est quòd eorum patres et avi nostro Imperio tributa dederunt (Liutprand, in Legat. p. 484). Salerno is not mentioned, yet the prince changed his party about the same time, and Camillo Pellegrino (Script. Rer. Ital. tom. ii. pars i. p. 285) has nicely discerned this change in the style of the anonymous Chronicle. On the rational ground of history and language, Liutprand (p. 480) had asserted the Latin claim to Apulia and Calabria.

7. See the Greek and Latin Glossaries of Ducange (Κατεπανω, catapanus), and his notes on the Alexias (p. 275). Against the contemporary notion, which derives it from Κατὰ πᾶν, *juxta omne*, he treats it as a corruption of the Latin *capitaneus*. Yet M. de St. Marc has accurately observed (Abrégé Chronologique, tom. ii. p. 924) that in this age the capitanei were not *captains*, but only nobles of the first rank, the great valvassors of Italy.

8. Οὐ μόνον διὰ πολέμων ἀκριβῶς τεταγμένων τὸ τοιοῦτον ὑπήγαγε τὸ ἔθνος (the Lombards) ἀλλὰ καὶ ἀγχινοίᾳ χρησάμενος, καὶ δικαιοσύνῃ καὶ χρηστότητι ἐπιεικῶς τε τοῖς προσερχομένοις προσφερόμενος (Leon. Tactic. c. xv. [§ 38] p. 741). The little Chronicle of Beneventum (tom. ii. pars i. p. 280) gives a far different character of the Greeks during the five years (A.D. 891-896) that Leo was master of the city.

9. Calabriam adeunt, eamque inter se divisam reperientes funditus depopulati sunt (or depopu-

larunt), ita ut deserta sit velut in diluvio. Such is the text of Herempert, or Erchempert, according to the two editions of Carraccioli (Rer. Italic. Script. tom. v. p. 23) and of Camillo Pellegrino (tom. ii. pars i. p. 246). Both were extremely scarce when they were reprinted by Muratori.

10. Baronius (Annal. Eccles. A.D. 874, No. 2) has drawn this story from a MS. of Erchempert, who died at Capua only fifteen years after the event. But the Cardinal was deceived by a false title, and we can only quote the anonymous Chronicle of Salerno (Paralipomena, c. 110), composed towards the end of the tenth century, and published in the second volume of Muratori's Collection. See the Dissertations of Camillo Pellegrino, tom. ii. pars i. p. 231–281, etc.

11. Constantine Porphyrogenitus (in Vit. Basil. c. 58, p. 183 [p. 296, ed. Bonn]) is the original author of this story. He places it under the reigns of Basil and Lewis II.; yet the reduction of Beneventum by the Greeks is dated A.D. 891, after the decease of both of those princes.

12. In the year 663 the same tragedy is described by Paul the Deacon (de Gestis Langobard. l. v. c. 7, 8, p. 870, 871, edit. Grot.), under the walls of the same city of Beneventum. But the actors are different, and the guilt is imputed to the Greeks themselves, which in the Byzantine edition is applied to the Saracens. In the late war in Germany, M. d'Assas, a French officer of the regiment of Auvergne, is said to have devoted himself in a similar manner. His behaviour is the more heroic, as mere silence was required by the enemy who had made him prisoner (Voltaire, Siècle de Louis XV. c. 33, tom. ix. p. 172).

13. Theobald, who is styled *Heros* by Liutprand, was properly duke of Spoleto and marquis of Camerino, from the year 926 to 935. The title and office of marquis (commander of the march or frontier) was introduced into Italy by the French emperors (Abrégé Chronologique, tom. ii. p. 645–732, etc.).

14. Liutprand, Hist. l. iv. c. 4, in the Rerum Italic. Script. tom. ii. pars i. p. 453, 454. Should the licentiousness of the tale be questioned, I may exclaim, with poor Sterne, that it is hard if I may not transcribe with caution what a bishop could write without scruple. What if I had translated, ut viris certetis testiculos amputare, in quibus nostri corporis refocillatio, etc?

15. The original monuments of the Normans in Italy are collected in the fifth volume of Muratori; and among these we may distinguish the poem of William Appulus (p. 245–278) and the history of Galfridus (*Jeffrey*) Malaterra (p. 537–607). Both were natives of France, but they wrote on the spot, in the age of the first conquerors (before A.D. 1100), and with the spirit of freemen. It is needless to recapitulate the compilers and critics of Italian history, Sigonius, Baronius, Pagi, Giannone, Muratori, St. Marc, etc., whom I have always consulted, and never copied.

16. Some of the first converts were baptised ten or twelve times, for the sake of the white garment usually given at this ceremony. At the funeral of Rollo, the gifts to monasteries for the repose of his soul were accompanied by a sacrifice of one hundred captives. But in a generation or two the national change was pure and general.

17. The Danish language was still spoken by the Normans of Bayeux on the sea-coast, at a time (A.D. 940) when it was already forgotten at Rouen, in the court and capital. Quem (Richard I.) confestim pater Baiocas mittens Botoni militiæ suæ principi nutriendum tradidit, ut, ibi *linguâ* eruditus *Danicâ*, suis exterisque hominibus sciret aperte dare responsa (Wilhelm. Gemeticensis de Ducibus Normannis, l. iii. c. 8, p. 623, edit. Camden). Of the vernacular and favourite idiom of William the Conqueror (A.D. 1035), Selden (Opera, tom. ii. p. 1640–1656) has given a specimen, obsolete and obscure even to antiquarians and lawyers.

18. See Leandro Alberti (Descrizione d'Italia, p. 250) and Baronius (A.D. 493, No. 43). If the archangel inherited the temple and oracle, perhaps the cavern, of old Calchas the soothsayer (Strab. Geograph. l. vi. p. 435, 436 [p. 284, ed. Casaub.]), the Catholics (on this occasion) have surpassed the Greeks in the elegance of their superstition.

19. See the first book of William Appulus. His words are applicable to every swarm of barbarians and freebooters:—

Si vicinorum quis *pernitiosus* ad illos
Confugiebat, eum gratanter suscipiebant:
Moribus et linguâ quoscumque venire vide-
    bant
Informant propriâ; gens efficiatur ut una.
[p. 255.]

And elsewhere, of the native adventurers of Normandy:—

Pars parat, exiguæ vel opes aderant quia
    nullæ:
Pars, quia de magnis majora subire volebant.
[p. 254.]

20. Liutprand in Legatione, p. 485. Pagi has illustrated this event from the MS. history of the deacon Leo (tom. iv. A.D. 965, No. 17–19).

21. See the Arabian Chronicle of Sicily, apud Muratori, Script. Rerum Ital. tom. i. p. 253.

22. Jeffrey Malaterra, who relates the Sicilian war and the conquest of Apulia (l. i. c. 7, 8, 9, 19). The same events are described by Cedrenus (tom. ii. p. 741–743, 755, 756) and Zonaras (tom. ii. p. 237, 238 [l. xvii. c. 15]); and the Greeks are so hardened to disgrace, that their narratives are impartial enough.

23. Cedrenus specifies the τάγμα of the Obsequium (Phrygia), and the μέρος of the Thracesians (Lydia: consult Constantine de Thematibus, i. 3, 4 [tom. iii. p. 22 sqq., ed. Bonn], with Delisle's map); and afterwards names the Pisidians and Lycaonians with the fœderati.

24.   Omnes conveniunt; et bis sex nobiliores,
    Quos genus et gravitas morum decorabat
        et ætas,

Elegere duces. Provectis ad comitatum
  His alii parent; comitatus nomen honoris
Quo donantur, erat. Hi totas undique
  terras
Divisere sibi, ni sors inimica repugnet;
Singula proponunt loca quæ contingere
  sorte
Cuique duci debent, et quæque tributa
  locorum. [p. 255.]

And after speaking of Melphi, William Appulus adds,

  Pro numero comitum bis sex statuere
    plateas,
  Atque domus comitum totidem fabri-
    cantur in urbe. [p. 256.]

Leo Ostiensis (l. ii. c. 67) enumerates the divisions of the Apulian cities, which it is needless to repeat.

25. Gulielm. Appulus, l. ii. c. 12, according to the reference of Giannone (Istoria Civile di Napoli, tom. ii. p. 31), which I cannot verify in the original. The Apulian praises indeed his *validas vires, probitas animi,* and *vivida virtus;* and declares that, had he lived, no poet could have equalled his merits (l. i. p. 258, l. ii. p. 259). He was bewailed by the Normans, quippe qui tanti consilii virum (says Malaterra, l. i. c. 12, p. 552), tam armis strenuum, tam sibi munificum, affabilem, morigeratum ulterius se habere diffidebant.

26. The gens astutissima, injuriarum ultrix . . . adulari sciens . . . eloquentiis inserviens, of Malaterra (l. i. c. 3, p. 550), are expressive of the popular and proverbial character of the Normans.

27. The hunting and hawking more properly belong to the *descendants* of the Norwegian sailors; though they might import from Norway and Iceland the finest casts of falcons.

28. We may compare this portrait with that of William of Malmesbury (de Gestis Anglorum, l. iii. p. 101, 102), who appreciates, like a philosophic historian, the vices and virtues of the Saxons and Normans. England was assuredly a gainer by the conquest.

29. The biographer of St. Leo IX. pours his holy venom on the Normans. Videns indisciplinatam et alienam gentem Normannorum, crudeli et inauditâ rabie et plusquam Paganâ impietate adversus ecclesias Dei insurgere, passim Christianos trucidare, etc. (Wibert, c. 6). The honest Apulian (l. ii. p. 259) says calmly of their accuser, Veris commiscens fallacia.

30. The policy of the Greeks, revolt of Maniaces, etc., must be collected from Cedrenus (tom. ii. p. 757, 758 [p. 548, *sq.*, ed. Bonn]), William Appulus (l. i. p. 257, 258, l. ii. p. 259), and the two Chronicles of Bari, by Lupus Protospata (Muratori, Script. Ital. tom. v. p. 42, 43, 44), and an anonymous writer (Antiquitat. Italiæ medii Ævi, tom. i. p. 31-35). This last is a fragment of some value.

31. Argyrus received, says the anonymous Chronicle of Bari, imperial letters, Fœderatûs et Patriciatûs, et Catapani et Vestatûs. In his Annals Muratori (tom. viii. p. 426) very properly reads, or interprets, *Sevestatus,* the title of Sebastos or Augustus. But in his Antiquities he was taught by Ducange to make it a palatine office, master of the wardrobe.

32. A Life of St. Leo IX., deeply tinged with the passions and prejudices of the age, has been composed by Wibert, printed at Paris, 1615, in octavo, and since inserted in the Collections of the Bollandists, of Mabillon, and of Muratori. The public and private history of that pope is diligently treated by M. de St. Marc (Abrégé, tom. ii. p. 140-210, and p. 25-95, second column.)

33. See the expedition of Leo IX. against the Normans. See William Appulus (l. ii. p. 259-261) and Jeffrey Malaterra (l. i. c. 13, 14, 15, p. 253). They are impartial, as the national is counterbalanced by the clerical prejudice.

34. Teutonici, quia cæsaries et forma decoros
    Fecerat egregie proceri corporis illos,
  Corpora derident Normannica, quæ breviora
    Esse videbantur. [p. 259.]

The verses of the Apulian are commonly in this strain, though he heats himself a little in the battle. Two of his similes from hawking and sorcery are descriptive of manners.

35. Several respectable censures or complaints are produced by M. de St. Marc (tom. ii. p. 200-204). As Peter Damianus, the oracle of the times, had denied the popes the right of making war, the hermit (lugens eremi incola) is arraigned by the cardinal, and Baronius (Annal. Eccles. A.D. 1053, No. 10-17) most strenuously asserts the two swords of St. Peter.

36. The origin and nature of the papal investitures are ably discussed by Giannone (Istoria Civile di Napoli, tom. ii. p. 37-49, 57-66) as a lawyer and antiquarian. Yet he vainly strives to reconcile the duties of patriot and Catholic, adopts an empty distinction of "Ecclesia Romana non dedit sed accepit," and shrinks from an honest but dangerous confession of the truth.

37. The birth, character, and first actions of Robert Guiscard may be found in Jeffrey Malaterra (l. i. c. 3, 4, 11, 16, 17, 18, 38, 39, 40), William Appulus (l. ii. p. 260-262), William Gemeticensis or of Jumieges (l. xi. c. 30, p. 663, 664, edit. Camden), and Anna Comnena (Alexiad, l. i. p. 23-27, l. vi. p. 165, 166 [tom. i. p. 49-56, 293-295, ed. Bonn]), with the annotations of Ducange (Not. in Alexiad. p. 230-232, 320), who has swept all the French and Latin Chronicles for supplemental intelligence.

38. Ὁ δὲ Ῥομπέρτος (a Greek corruption) οὗτος Νορμάννος τὸ γένος, τὴν τύχην ἄσημος [tom. i. p. 50]. . . . Again, ἐξ ἀφανοῦς πανὺ τύχης περιφάνης. And elsewhere (l. iv. p. 84 [ed. Ven.; p. 104, ed. Par.; tom. i. p. 190, ed. Bonn]), ἀπὸ ἐσχάτης πενίας καὶ τύχης ἀφανοῦς Anna Comnena was born in the purple; yet her father was no more than a private

though illustrious subject, who raised himself to the empire.

39. Giannone (tom. ii. p. 2) forgets all his original authors, and rests this princely descent on the credit of Inveges, an Augustine monk of Palermo in the last century. They continue the succession of dukes from Rollo to William II. the Bastard or Conqueror, whom they hold (communemente si tiene) to be the father of Tancred of Hauteville: a most strange and stupendous blunder! The sons of Tancred fought in Apulia before William II. was three years old (A.D. 1037).

40. The judgment of Ducange is just and moderate: Certè humilis fuit ac tenuis Roberti familia, si ducalem et regium spectemus apicem, ad quem postea pervenit; quæ honesta tamen et præter nobilium vulgarium statum et conditionem illustris habita est, "quæ nec humi reperet nec altum quid tumeret." (Wilhelm. Malmsbur. de Gestis Anglorum, l. iii. p. 107; Not. ad Alexiad. p. 230.)

41. I shall quote with pleasure some of the best lines of the Apulian (l. ii. p. 260).

Pugnat utrâque manû, nec lancea cassa, nec ensis
Cassus erat, quocunque manû deducere vellet.
Ter dejectus equo, ter viribus ipse resumptis
Major in arma redit: stimulos furor ipse ministrat.
Ut Leo cum frendens, etc.

.   .   .   .   .   .

Nullus in hoc bello sicuti post bella probatum est
Victor vel victus, tam magnos edidit ictus.

42. The Norman writers and editors most conversant with their own idiom interpret Guiscard or Wiscard by Callidus, a cunning man. The root (wise) is familiar to our ear; and in the old word Wiseacre I can discern something of a similar sense and termination. Τὴν ψύχην πανουργότατος is no bad translation of the surname and character of Robert.

43. The acquisition of the ducal title by Robert Guiscard is a nice and obscure business. With the good advice of Giannone, Muratori, and St. Marc, I have endeavoured to form a consistent and probable narrative.

44. Baronius (Annal. Eccles. A.D. 1059, No. 69) has published the original act. He professes to have copied it from the Liber Censuum, a Vatican MS. Yet a Liber Censuum of the twelfth century has been printed by Muratori (Antiquit. medii Ævi, tom. v. p. 851–908); and the names of Vatican and Cardinal awaken the suspicions of a Protestant, and even of a philosopher.

45. Read the Life of Guiscard in the second and third books of the Apulian, the first and second books of Malaterra.

46. The conquests of Robert Guiscard and Roger I., the exemption of Benevento and the twelve provinces of the kingdom, are fairly exposed by Giannone in the second volume of his Istoria Civile, l. ix. x. xi., and l. xvii. p. 460–470. This modern division was not established before the time of Frederick II.

47. Giannone (tom. ii. p. 119–127), Muratori (Antiquitat. medii Ævi, tom. iii. dissert. xliv. p. 935, 936), and Tiraboschi (Istoria della Letteratura Italiana), have given an historical account of these physicians; their medical knowledge and practice must be left to our physicians.

48. At the end of the Historia Pandectarum of Henry Brenckmann (Trajecti ad Rhenum, 1722, in 4to) the indefatigable author has inserted two dissertations—de Republicâ Amalphitanâ, and de Amalphi à Pisanis direptâ, which are built on the testimonies of one hundred and forty writers. Yet he has forgotten two most important passages of the embassy of Liutprand (A.D. 969), which compare the trade and navigation of Amalphi with that of Venice.

49. Urbs Latii non est hâc delitiosior urbe,
Frugibus, arboribus, vinoque redundat; et unde
Non tibi poma, nuces, non pulchra palatia desunt,
Non species muliebris abest probitasque virorum.
Gulielmus Appulus, l. iii. p. 267.

50. Muratori carries their antiquity above the year (1066) of the death of Edward the Confessor, the rex Anglorum to whom they are addressed. Nor is this date affected by the opinion, or rather mistake, of Pasquier (Recherches de la France, l. vii. c. 2) and Ducange (Glossar. Latin.). The practice of rhyming, as early as the seventh century, was borrowed from the languages of the North and East (Muratori, Antiquitat. tom. iii. dissert. xl. p. 686–708).

51. The description of Amalphi, by William the Apulian (l. iii. p. 267,) contains much truth and some poetry, and the third line may be applied to the sailor's compass:—

Nulla magis locuples argento, vestibus, auro
Partibus innumeris: hâc [ac] plurimus urbe moratur
Nauta maris cælique vias aperire peritus.
Huc et Alexandri diversa feruntur ab urbe
Regis, et Antiochi. Gens hæc freta plurima transit.
His [Huic] Arabes, Indi, Siculi noscuntur et Afri.
Hæc gens est totum prope nobilitata per orbem,
Et mercando ferens, et amans mercata referre.

52. Latrocinio armigerorum suorum in multis sustentabatur, quod quidem ad ejus ignominiam non dicimus; sed ipso ita præcipiente adhuc viliora et reprehensibiliora dicturi sumus [de ipso scripturi sumus] ut pluribus patescat, quam laboriose et cum quantâ angustiâ a profundâ paupertate ad summum culmen divitiarum vel honoris attigerit. Such is the preface of Malaterra (l. i. c. 25) to the horse-stealing. From the moment (l. i. c. 19) that

he has mentioned his patron Roger, the elder brother sinks into the second character. Something similar in Velleius Paterculus may be observed of Augustus and Tiberius.

53. Duo sibi proficua deputans, animæ scilicet et corporis, si terram idolis deditam ad cultum divinum revocaret (Galfrid Malaterra, l. ii. c. 1). The conquest of Sicily is related in the three last books, and he himself has given an accurate summary of the chapters (p. 544–546).

54. See the word *Milites* in the Latin Glossary of Ducange.

55. Of odd particulars, I learn from Malaterra that the Arabs had introduced into Sicily the use of camels (l. ii. c. 33) and of carrier-pigeons (c. 42); and that the bite of the tarantula provokes a windy disposition, quæ per anum inhoneste crepitando emergit—a symptom most ridiculously felt by the whole Norman army in their camp near Palermo (c. 36). I shall add an etymology not unworthy of the eleventh century: *Messana* is derived from *Messis*, the place from whence the harvests of the isle were sent in tribute to Rome (l. ii. c. 1).

56. See the capitulation of Palermo in Malaterra, l. ii. c. 45, and Giannone, who remarks the general toleration of the Saracens (tom. ii. p. 72).

57. John Leo Afer, de Medicis et Philosophis Arabibus, c. 14, apud Fabric. Biblioth. Græc. tom. xiii. p. 278, 279. This philosopher is named Esseriph Essachalli, and he died in Africa, A.H. 516—A.D. 1122. Yet this story bears a strange resemblance to the Sherif al Edrissi, who presented his book (Geographia Nubiensis, see preface, p. 88, 90, 170) to Roger king of Sicily, A.H. 548—A.D. 1153 (D'Herbelot, Bibliothèque Orientale, p. 786; Prideaux's Life of Mahomet, p. 188; Petit de la Croix, Hist. de Gengiscan, p. 535, 536; Casiri, Biblioth. Arab. Hispan. tom. ii. p. 9–13); and I am afraid of some mistake.

58. Malaterra remarks the foundation of the bishoprics (l. iv. c. 7), and produces the original of the bull (l. iv. c. 29). Giannone gives a rational idea of this privilege, and the tribunal of the monarchy of Sicily (tom. ii. p. 95–102); and St. Marc (Abrégé, tom. iii. p. 217–301, first column) labours the case with the diligence of a Sicilian lawyer.

59. In the first expedition of Robert against the Greeks, I follow Anna Comnena (the first, third, fourth, and fifth books of the Alexiad), William Appulus (l. iv. and v., p. 270–275), and Jeffrey Malaterra (l. iii. c. 13, 14, 24–29, 39). Their information is contemporary and authentic, but none of them were eye-witnesses of the war.

60. One of them was married to Hugh, the son of Azzo, or Axo, a marquis of Lombardy, rich, powerful, and *noble* (Gulielm. Appul. l. iii. p. 267) in the eleventh century, and whose ancestors in the tenth and ninth are explored by the critical industry of Leibnitz and Muratori. From the two elder sons of the marquis Azzo are derived the illustrious lines of Brunswick and Este. See Muratori, Antichità Estense.

61. Anna Comnena somewhat too wantonly praises and bewails that handsome boy, who, after the rupture of his barbaric nuptials (l. i. p. 23 [tom. i. p. 49, ed. Bonn]), was betrothed as her husband; he was ἄγαλμα φύσεως . . . Θεοῦ χειρῶν φιλοτίμημα . . . χρυσοῦ γένους ἄπορρον, etc. (p. 27 [tom. i. p. 57, ed. Bonn]). Elsewhere she describes the red and white of his skin, his hawk's eyes, etc., l. iii. p. 71 [tom. i. p. 135, ed. Bonn].

62. Anna Comnena, l. i. p. 28, 29 [tom. i. p. 58, sq., ed. Bonn]; Gulielm. Appul. l. iv. p. 271; Galfrid Malaterra, l. iii. c. 13, p. 579, 580. Malaterra is more cautious in his style; but the Apulian is bold and positive.

——Mentitus se Michaelem

Venerat a Danais quidam seductor ad illum.

As Gregory VII. had believed, Baronius, almost alone, recognises the emperor Michael (A.D. 1080, No. 44).

63. Ipse armatæ militiæ non plusquam MCCC milites secum habuisse, ab eis qui eidem negotio interfuerunt attestatur (Malaterra, l. iii. c. 24, p. 583). These are the same whom the Apulian (l. iv. p. 273) styles the equestris gensducis, equites de gente ducis.

64. Εἰς τριάκοντα χιλιάδας, says Anna Comnena (Alexias, l. i. p. 37 [tom. i. p. 75, ed. Bonn]); and her account tallies with the number and lading of the ships. Ivit in [contra] Dyrrachium cum xv millibus hominum, says the Chronicon Breve Normannicum (Muratori, Scriptores, tom. v. p. 278). I have endeavoured to reconcile these reckonings.

65. The Itinerary of Jerusalem (p. 609, edit. Wesseling) gives a true and reasonable space of a thousand stadia, or one hundred miles, which is strangely doubled by Strabo (l. vi. p. 433 [p. 283, ed. Casaub.]) and Pliny (Hist. Natur. iii. 16).

66. Pliny (Hist. Nat. iii. 6, 16) allows *quinquaginta* millia for this brevissimus cursus, and agrees with the real distance from Otranto to La Vallona, or Aulon (D'Anville, Analyse de la Carte des Côtes de la Grèce, etc., p. 3–6). Hermolaus Barbarus, who substitutes *centum* (Hardiun, Not. lxvi. in Plin. l. iii.), might have been corrected by every Venetian pilot who had sailed out of the gulf.

67. Infames scopulos Acroceraunia, Horat. carm. i. 3. The præcipitem Africum decertantem Aquilonibus et rabiem Noti, and the monstra natantia of the Adriatic, are somewhat enlarged; but Horace trembling for the life of Virgil is an interesting moment in the history of poetry and friendship.

68. Τῶν δὲ εἰς τὸν πώγωνα αὐτοῦ ἐφυβρισάντων (Alexias, l. iv. p. 106 [tom. i. p. 193, ed. Bonn]). Yet the Normans shaved, and the Venetians wore their beards: they must have derided the *no* beard of Bohemond; a harsh interpretation! (Ducange, Not. ad Alexiad. p. 283).

69. Muratori (Annali d'Italia, tom. ix. p. 136,

137) observes that some authors (Petrus Diacon. Chron. Casinen. l. iii. c. 49) compose the Greek army of 170,000 men, but that the *hundred* may be struck off, and that Malaterra reckons only 70,000: a slight inattention. The passage to which he alludes is in the Chronicle of Lupus Protospata (Script. Ital. tom. v. p. 45). Malaterra (l. iii. c. 27) speaks in high but indefinite terms of the emperor, cum copiis innumerabilibus: like the Apulian poet (l. iv. p. 272):—

More locustarum montes et plana teguntur.

70. See William of Malmesbury de Gestis Anglorum, l. ii. p. 92. Alexius fidem Anglorum suspiciens præcipuis familiaritatibus suis eos applicabat, amorem eorum filio transcribens. Ordericus Vitalis (Hist. Eccles. l. iv. p. 508, l. vii. p. 641) relates their emigration from England and their service in Greece.

71. See the Apulian (l. i. p. 256). The character and story of these Manichæans has been the subject of the fifty-fourth chapter.

72. See the simple and masterly narrative of Cæsar himself (Comment. de Bell. Civil. iii. 41–75). It is a pity that Quintus Icilius (M. Guischard) did not live to analyse these operations, as he has done the campaigns of Africa and Spain.

73. Παλλὰς ἄλλη κἂν μὴ 'Αθήνη, which is very properly translated by the President Cousin (Hist. de Constantinople, tom. iv. p. 131, in 12mo), qui combattoit comme une Pallas, quoiqu'elle ne fût pas aussi savante que celle d'Athènes. The Grecian goddess was composed of two discordant characters—of Neith, the workwoman of Sais in Egypt, and of a virgin Amazon of the Tritonian lake in Libya (Banier, Mythologie, tom. iv. p. 1–31, in 12mo).

74. Anna Comnena (l. iv. p. 116 [tom. i. p. 210, ed. Bonn]) admires, with some degree of terror, her masculine virtues. They were more familiar to the Latins; and though the Apulian (l. iv. p. 273) mentions her presence and her wound, he represents her as far less intrepid.

Uxor in hoc bello Roberti forte sagittâ
Quâdam læsa fuit: quo vulnere *territa*, nullam
Dum sperabat opem, se pœne *subegerat* hosti.
The last is an unlucky word for a female prisoner.

75. 'Απὸ τῆς τοῦ 'Ρομπερτοῦ προηγησαυένης μάχης γινώσκων τὴν πρώτην κατὰ τῶν ἐναντίων ἱππασίαν τῶν Κελτῶν ἀνύποιστον (Anna, l. v. p. 133 [tom. i. p. 137, ed. Bonn]); and elsewhere καὶ γὰρ Κελτὸς ἀνὴρ πᾶς ἐποχούμενος μὲν ἀνύποιστος τὴν ὁρμὴν καὶ τὴν δέαν ἐστίν (p. 140 [tom. i. p. 251, ed. Bonn]). The pedantry of the princess in the choice of classic appellations encouraged Ducange to apply to his countrymen the characters of the ancient Gauls.

76. Lupus Protospata (tom. v. p. 45) says 6000; William the Apulian more than 5000 (l. iv. p. 273). Their modesty is singular and laudable: they might with so little trouble have slain two or three myriads of schismatics and infidels!

77. The Romans had changed the inauspicious name of *Epi-damnus* to Dyrrachium (Plin. iii. 26); and the vulgar corruption of Duracium (see Malaterra) bore some affinity to *hardness*. One of Robert's names was Durand, *à durando:* poor wit! (Alberic. Monach. in Chron. apud Muratori, Annali d'Italia, tom. ix. p. 137.)

78. Βρούχους καὶ ἀκρίδας εἶπεν ἄν τις αὐτοὺς, [τὸν] πατέρα καὶ [τὸν] υἱον (Anna, l. i. p. 35 [tom. i. p. 70, ed. Bonn]). By these similes, so different from those of Homer, she wishes to inspire contempt as well as horror for the little noxious animal, a conqueror. Most unfortunately, the common sense, or common nonsense, of mankind, resists her laudable design.

79. Prodiit hâc auctor Trojanæ cladis Achilles. The supposition of the Apulian (l. v. p. 275) may be excused by the more classic poetry of Virgil (Æneid II. 197), Larissæus Achilles, but it is not justified by the geography of Homer.

80. The τῶν πεδίλων προάλματα, which encumbered the knights on foot, have been ignorantly translated spurs (Anna Comnena, Alexias, l. v. p. 140 [tom. i. p. 251, ed. Bonn]). Ducange has explained the true sense by a ridiculous and inconvenient fashion, which lasted from the eleventh to the fifteenth century. These peaks, in the form of a scorpion, were sometimes two feet, and fastened to the knee with a silver chain.

81. The epistle itself (Alexias, l. iii. p. 93, 94, 95 [tom. i. p. 174–177, ed. Bonn]) well deserves to be read. There is one expression, ἀστροπέλεκυν δεδεμένον μετὰ χρυσαφίου [p. 177], which Ducange does not understand. I have endeavoured to grope out a tolerable meaning: χρυσάφιον is a golden crown; ἀστροπελεκυς is explained by Simon Portius (in Lexico Græco-Barbar.), by κεραυνὸς, πρηστὴρ, a flash of lightning.

82. For these general events I must refer to the general historians Sigonius, Baronius, Muratori, Mosheim, St. Marc, etc.

83. The lives of Gregory VII. are either legends or invectives (St. Marc, Abrégé, tom. iii. p. 235, etc.); and his miraculous or magical performances are alike incredible to a modern reader. He will, as usual, find some instruction in Le Clerc (Vie de Hildebrand, Biblioth. ancienne et moderne, tom. viii.), and much amusement in Bayle (Dictionnaire Critique, *Grégoire* VII.). That pope was undoubtedly a great man, a second Athanasius, in a more fortunate age of the church. May I presume to add that the portrait of Athanasius is one of the passages of my history (vol. i. p. 697, *seq.*) with which I am the least dissatisfied?

84. Anna, with the rancour of a Greek schismatic, calls him κατάπτυστος οὗτος Πάπας (l. i. p. 32 [tom. i. p. 66, ed. Bonn]), a pope, or priest, worthy to be spit upon; and accuses him of scourging, shaving, and perhaps of castrating, the ambassadors of Henry (p. 31, 33). But this outrage is improbable and doubtful (see the sensible preface of Cousin).

85.   Sic uno tempore victi
       Sunt terræ Domini duo: rex Alemannicus
             iste,
       Imperii rector Romani maximus ille.
       Alter ad arma ruens armis superatur; et
             alter
       Nominis auditi solâ formidine cessit.

It is singular enough, that the Apulian, a Latin,
should distinguish the Greek as the ruler of the
Roman empire (l. iv. p. 274).

86. The narrative of Malaterra (l. iii. c. 37, p.
587, 588) is authentic, circumstantial, and fair.
Dux ignem exclamans urbe incensa, etc. The
Apulian softens the mischief (inde *quibusdam* ædibus exustis), which is again exaggerated in some
partial chronicles (Muratori Annali, tom. ix. p.
147).

87. After mentioning this devastation, the Jesuit
Donatus (de Româ veteri et novâ, l. iv. c. 8, p.
489) prettily adds, Duraret hodieque in Cœlio
monte, interque ipsum et capitolium, miserabilis
facies prostratæ urbis, nisi in hortorum vinetor-
umque amœnitatem Roma resurrexisset, ut per-
petuâ viriditate contegeret vulnera et ruinas suas.

88. The royalty of Robert, either promised or
bestowed by the pope (Anna, l. i. p. 32 [tom. i. p.
65, ed. Bonn]), is sufficiently confirmed by the
Apulian (l. iv. p. 270).

       Romani regni sibi promisisse coronam
       Papa ferebatur.

Nor can I understand why Gretser and the other
papal advocates should be displeased with this
new instance of apostolic jurisdiction.

89. See Homer, Iliad B (I hate this pedantic
mode of quotation by the letters of the Greek alphabet), 87, etc. His bees are the image of a disorderly
crowd; their discipline and public works seem to
be the ideas of a later age (Virgil. Æneid. l. i. [v.
430, *sqq.*]).

90. Gulielm. Appulus, l. v. p. 276. The admirable port of Brundusium was double; the outward
harbour was a gulf covered by an island, and narrowing by degrees, till it communicated by a small
gullet with the inner harbour, which embraced
the city on both sides. Cæsar and nature have
laboured for its ruin; and against such agents
what are the feeble efforts of the Neapolitan government? (Swinburne's Travels in the Two Sicilies, vol. i. p. 384–390.)

91. William of Apulia (l. v. p. 276) describes
the victory of the Normans, and forgets the two
previous defeats, which are diligently recorded by
Anna Comnena (l. vi. p. 159, 160, 161 [p. 282–
285, ed. Bonn]). In her turn, she invents or magnifies a fourth action, to give the Venetians revenge and rewards. Their own feelings were far
different, since they deposed their doge, propter
excidium stoli (Dandulus in Chron. in Muratori,
Script. Rerum Italicarum, tom. xii. p. 249).

92. The most authentic writers, William of
Apulia (l. v. 277), Jeffrey Malaterra (l. iii. c. 41,
p. 589), and Romuald of Salerno (Chron. in Mu-

ratori, Script. Rerum Ital. tom. vii.), are ignorant
of this crime, so apparent to our countrymen
William of Malmesbury (l. iii. p. 107) and Roger
de Hoveden (p. 710, in Script. post Bedam); and
the latter can tell how the just Alexius married,
crowned, and burnt alive, his female accomplice.
The English historian is indeed so blind, that he
ranks Robert Guiscard, or Wiscard, among the
knights of Henry I., who ascended the throne fifteen years after the duke of Apulia's death.

93. The joyful Anna Comnena scatters some
flowers over the grave of an enemy (Alexiad, l. v.
[vi.] p. 162–166 [tom. i. p. 288–295, ed. Bonn]);
and his best praise is the esteem and envy of William the Conqueror, the sovereign of his family.
Græcia (says Malaterra) hostibus recedentibus
libera læta quievit: Apulia tota sive Calabria
turbatur.

94.   Urbs Venusina nitet tantis decorata sep-
             ulchris,

is one of the last lines of the Apulian's poem (l. v.
p. 278). William of Malmesbury (l. iii. p. 107) inserts an epitaph on Guiscard, which is not worth
transcribing.

95. Yet Horace had few obligations to Venusia:
he was carried to Rome in his childhood (Serm. i.
6 [v. 76]); and his repeated allusions to the doubtful limit of Apulia and Lucania (Carm. iii. 4;
Serm. ii. 1 [v. 34, *sqq.*]) are unworthy of his age
and genius.

96. See Giannone (tom. ii. p. 88–93) and the
historians of the first crusade.

97. The reign of Roger and the Norman kings
of Sicily fills four books of the Istoria Civile of Giannone (tom. ii. l. xi.–xiv. p. 136–340), and is
spread over the ninth and tenth volumes of the
Italian Annals of Muratori. In the Bibliothèque
Italique (tom. i. p. 175–222) I find a useful abstract of Capecelatro, a modern Neapolitan, who
has composed, in two volumes, the history of his
country from Roger I. to Frederic II. inclusive.

98. According to the testimony of Philistus and
Diodorus, the tyrant Dionysius of Syracuse could
maintain a standing force of 10,000 horse, 100,000
foot, and 400 galleys. Compare Hume (Essays, vol.
i. p. 268, 435) and his adversary Wallace (Numbers of Mankind, p. 306, 307). The ruins of Agrigentum are the theme of every traveller, D'Orville, Reidesel, Swinburne, etc.

99. A contemporary historian of the acts of
Roger from the year 1127 to 1135 founds his title
on merit and power, the consent of the barons,
and the ancient royalty of Sicily and Palermo,
without introducing pope Anacletus (Alexand.
Cœnobii Telesini Abbatis de Rebus Gestis Regis
Rogerii, lib. iv. in Muratori, Script. Rerum Ital.
tom. v. p. 607–645).

100. The kings of France, England, Scotland,
Castille, Arragon, Navarre, Sweden, Denmark,
and Hungary. The three first were more ancient
than Charlemagne; the three next were created by
their sword; the three last by their baptism; and of

these the king of Hungary alone was honoured or debased by a papal crown.

101. Fazellus and a crowd of Sicilians had imagined a more early and independent coronation (A.D. 1130, May 1), which Giannone unwillingly rejects (tom. ii. p. 137-144). This fiction is disproved by the silence of contemporaries; nor can it be restored by a spurious charter of Messina (Muratori, Annali d'Italia, tom. ix. p. 340; Pagi, Critica, tom. iv. p. 467, 468).

102. Roger corrupted the second person of Lothaire's army, who sounded, or rather cried, a retreat; for the Germans (says Cinnamus, l. iii. c. i. p. 52 [ed. Par.; p. 90, ed. Bonn]) are ignorant of the use of trumpets. Most ignorant himself!

103. See De Guignes, Hist. Générale des Huns, tom. i. p. 369-373, and Cardonne, Hist. de l'Afrique, etc., sous la Domination des Arabes, tom. ii. p. 70-144. Their common original appears to be Novairi.

104. Tripoli (says the Nubian geographer, or, more properly, the Sherif al Edrisi) urbs fortis, saxeo muro vallata, sita prope litus maris. Hanc expugnavit Rogerius, qui mulieribus captivis ductis, viros peremit.

105. See the geography of Leo Africanus (in Ramusio, tom. i. fol. 74 verso, fol. 75 recto) and Shaw's Travels (p. 110), the seventh book of Thuanus, and the eleventh of the Abbé de Vertot. The possession and defence of the place was offered by Charles V. and wisely declined by the knights of Malta.

106. Pagi has accurately marked the African conquests of Roger; and his criticism was supplied by his friend the Abbé de Longuerue, with some Arabic memorials (A.D. 1147, No. 26, 27; A.D. 1148, No. 16; A.D. 1153, No. 16).

107. Appulus et Calaber, Siculus mihi servit et Afer.
A proud inscription, which denotes that the Norman conquerors were still discriminated from their Christian and Moslem subjects.

108. Hugo Falcandus (Hist. Sicula, in Muratori Script. tom. vii. p. 270, 271) ascribes these losses to the neglect or treachery of the admiral Majo.

109. The silence of the Sicilian historians, who end too soon or begin too late, must be supplied by Otho of Frisingen, a German (de Gestis Frederici I. l. i. c. 33, in Muratori Script. tom. vi. p. 668), the Venetian Andrew Dandulus (Id. tom. xii. p. 282, 283), and the Greek writers Cinnamus (l. iii. c. 2-5) and Nicetas (in Manuel. l. iii. c. 1-6 [p. 131, sqq., ed. Bonn]).

110. To this imperfect capture and speedy rescue I apply the παρ' ὀλίγον ἦλθε τοῦ ἁλῶναι of Cinnamus, l. ii. c. 19, p. 49 [p. 87, ed. Bonn]. Muratori, on tolerable evidence (Annali d'Italia, tom. ix. p. 420, 421), laughs at the delicacy of the French, who maintain, marisque nullo impediente periculo ad regnum proprium reversum esse; yet I observe that their advocate, Ducange, is less positive as the

commentator on Cinnamus than as the editor of Joinville.

111. In palatium regium sagittas igneas injecti, says Dandulus; but Nicetas, l. ii. c. 8, p. 66 [p. 130, ed. Bonn], transforms them into βέλη ἀργυρέους ἔχοντα ἀτράκτους, and adds that Manuel styled this insult παίγνιον and γέλωτα ... λῃστεύοντα. These arrows, by the compiler, Vincent de Beauvais, are again transmuted into gold.

112. For the invasion of Italy, which is almost overlooked by Nicetas, see the more polite history of Cinnamus (l. iv. c. 1-15, p. 78-101 [p. 134-175, ed. Bonn]), who introduces a diffuse narrative by a lofty profession, περὶ τε Σικελίας, καὶ τῆς 'Ιταλῶν ἐσκέπτετο γῆς, ὡς καὶ ταύτας ‛Ρωμαίοις ἀνασώσαιτο, iii. 5 [p. 101, ed. Bonn].

113. The Latin, Otho (de Gestis Frederici I. l. ii. c. 30, p. 734), attests the forgery; the Greek, Cinnamus (l. iv. c. 1, p. 78 [p. 135, ed. Bonn]), claims a promise of restitution from Conrad and Frederic. An act of fraud is always credible when it is told of the Greeks.

114. Quod Anconitani Græcum imperium nimis diligerent ... Veneti speciali odio Anconam oderunt. The cause of love, perhaps of envy, were the beneficia, flumen aureum of the emperor; and the Latin narrative is confirmed by Cinnamus (l. iv. c. 14, p. 98 [p. 170, ed. Bonn]).

115. Muratori mentions the two sieges of Ancona; the first, in 1167, against Frederic I. in person (Annali, tom. x. p. 39, etc.); the second, in 1173, against his lieutenant Christian, Archbishop of Mentz, a man unworthy of his name and office (p. 76, etc.). It is of the second siege that we possess an original narrative, which he has published in his great collection (tom. vi. p. 921-946).

116. We derive this anecdote from an anonymous chronicle of Fossa Nova, published by Muratori (Script. Ital. tom. vii. p. 874).

117. The Βασίλειον σημεῖον of Cinnamus (l. iv. c. 14, p. 99 [p. 171, ed. Bonn]) is susceptible of this double sense. A standard is more Latin, an image more Greek.

118. Nihilominus quoque petebat, ut quia occasio justa et tempus opportunum et acceptabile se obtulerant, Romani corona imperii a sancto apostolo sibi redderetur; quoniam non ad Frederici Alamanni, sed ad suum jus asseruit pertinere (Vit. Alexandri III. a Cardinal. Arragoniæ, in Script. Rerum Ital. tom. iii. par. i. p. 458). His second embassy was accompanied cum immensa multitudine pecuniarum.

119. Nimis alta et perplexa sunt (Vit. Alexandri III. p. 460, 461) says the cautious pope.

120. Μηδὲν μετὸν εἶναι λέγων ‛Ρώμῃ τῇ νεωτέρᾳ πρὸς τὴν πρεσβυτέραν, πάλαι ἀπορραγεισῶν (Cinnamus, l. iv. c. 14, p. 99 [p. 171, ed. Bonn]).

121. In his sixth book, Cinnamus describes the Venetian war, which Nicetas has not thought worthy of his attention. The Italian accounts, which do not satisfy our curiosity, are reported by the annalist Muratori, under the years 1171, etc.

122. This victory is mentioned by Romuald of Salerno (in Muratori, Script. Ital. tom. vii. p. 198). It is whimsical enough that, in the praise of the king of Sicily, Cinnamus (l. iv. c. 13, p. 97, 98 [p. 168, ed. Bonn]) is much warmer and more copious than Falcandus (p. 268, 270). But the Greek is fond of description, and the Latin historian is not fond of William the Bad.

123. For the epistle of William I. see Cinnamus (l. iv. c. 15, p. 101, 102 [p. 173-175, ed. Bonn]) and Nicetas (l. ii. c. 8 [p. 128, ed. Bonn]). It is difficult to affirm whether these Greeks deceived themselves or the public in these flattering portraits of the grandeur of the empire.

124. I can only quote of original evidence the poor chronicles of Sicard of Cremona (p. 603), and of Fossa Nova (p. 875), as they are published in the seventh tome of Muratori's historians. The king of Sicily sent his troops contra nequitiam Andronici . . . ad acquirendum imperium C. P. They were capti aut confusi . . . decepti captique, by Isaac.

125. By the failure of Cinnamus, we are now reduced to Nicetas (in Andronico, l. i. c. 7, 8, 9, l. ii. c. 1, in Isaac Angelo, l. i. c. 1-4), who now becomes a respectable contemporary. As he survived the emperor and the empire, he is above flattery: but the fall of Constantinople exasperated his prejudices against the Latins. For the honour of learning I shall observe that Homer's great commentator, Eustathius, archbishop of Thessalonica, refused to desert his flock.

126. The Historia Sicula of Hugo Falcandus, which properly extends from 1154 to 1169, is inserted in the seventh volume of Muratori's Collection (tom. vii. p. 259-344), and preceded by an eloquent preface or epistle (p. 251-258, de Calamitatibus Siciliæ). Falcandus has been styled the Tacitus of Sicily; and, after a just, but immense, abatement, from the first to the twelfth century, from a senator to a monk, I would not strip him of his title: his narrative is rapid and perspicuous, his style bold and elegant, his observation keen; he had studied mankind, and feels like a man. I can only regret the narrow and barren field on which his labours have been cast.

127. The laborious Benedictines (l'Art de vérifier les Dates, p. 896), are of opinion that the true name of Falcandus is Fulcandus or Foucault. According to them, Hugues Foucault, a Frenchman by birth, and at length Abbot of St. Denys, had followed into Sicily his patron Stephen de la Perche, uncle to the mother of William II., archbishop of Palermo, and great chancellor of the kingdom. Yet Falcandus has all the feelings of a Sicilian; and the title of *Alumnus* (which he bestows on himself) appears to indicate that he was born, or at least educated, in the island.

128. Falcand. p. 303. Richard de St. Germano begins his history from the death and praises of William II. After some unmeaning epithets, he thus continues: Legis et justitiæ cultus tempore suo vigebat in regno; suâ erat quilibet sorte contentus; (were they mortals?) ubique pax, ubique securitas, nec latronum metuebat viator insidias, nec maris nauta offendicula piratarum (Script. Rerum Ital. tom. vii. p. 969).

129. Constantia, primis a cunabulis in deliciarum tuarum affluentiâ diutius educata, tuisque institutis, doctrinis et moribus informata, tandem opibus tuis Barbaros delatura discessit: et nunc cum ingentibus copiis revertitur, ut pulcherrimæ nutricis ornamenta barbaricâ fœditate contaminet . . . Intueri mihi jam videor turbulentas barbarorum acies . . . civitates opulentas et loca diuturnâ pace florentia metû concutere, cæde vastare, rapinis atterere, et fœdare luxuriâ: [occurrunt] hinc cives aut gladiis intercepti, aut servitute depressi, virgines constupratæ, matronæ, etc. [p. 253 and 254.]

130. Certe si regem [sibi] non dubiæ virtutis elegerint, nec a Saracenis Christiani dissentiant, poterit rex creatus rebus licet quasi desperatis et perditis subvenire, et incursus hostium, si prudenter egerit, propulsare. [p. 253 and 254.]

131. In Apulis, qui, semper novitate gaudentes, novarum rerum studiis aguntur, nihil arbitror spei aut fiduciæ reponendum. [ib.]

132. Si civium tuorum virtutem et audaciam attendas, . . . murorum etiam ambitum densis turribus circumseptum. [ib.]

133. Cum crudelitate piraticâ Theutonum confligat atrocitas, et inter ambustos lapides, et Ethnæ flagrantis incendia, etc. [ib.]

134. Eam partem, quam nobilissimarum civitatum fulgor illustrat, quæ et toti regno singulari meruit privilegio præminere nefarium esset . . . vel barbarorum ingressû pollui. I wish to transcribe his florid, but curious, description of the palace, city, and luxuriant plain of Palermo. [ib.]

135. Vires non suppetunt, et conatus tuos tam inopia civium, quam paucitas bellatorum elidunt. [ib.]

136. At vero, quia difficile est Christianos in tanto rerum turbine, sublato regis timore Saracenos non opprimere, si Saraceni injuriis fatigati ab eis cœperint dissidere, et castella forte maritima vel montanas munitiones occupaverint; ut hinc cum Theutonicis summâ [sit] virtute pugnandum, illinc Saracenis crebris insultibus occurrendum, quid putas acturi sunt Siculi inter has depressi augustias, et velut inter malleum et incudem multo cum discrimine constituti? hoc utique agent quod poterunt, ut se Barbaris miserabili conditione dedentes, in eorum se conferant potestatem. O utinam plebis et procerum Christianorum et Saracenorum vota conveniant; ut regem sibi concorditer eligentes, [irruentes] barbaros totis viribus, toto conamine, totisque desideriis proturbare contendant [p. 254]. The Normans and Sicilians appear to be confounded.

137. The testimony of an Englishman, of Roger de Hoveden (p. 689), will lightly weigh against the silence of German and Italian history (Mura-

tori, Annali d'Italia, tom. x. p. 156). The priests and pilgrims, who returned from Rome, exalted, by every tale, the omnipotence of the holy father.

138. Ego enim in eo cum Teutonicis manere non debeo (Caffari, Annal. Genuenses, in Muratori, Script. Rerum Italicarum, tom. vi. p. 367, 368).

139. For the Saracens of Sicily and Nocera, see the Annals of Muratori (tom. x. p. 149, and A.D. 1223, 1247), Giannone (tom. ii. p. 385), and of the originals, in Muratori's Collection, Richard de St. Germano (tom. vii. p. 996), Matteo Spinelli de Giovenazzo (tom. vii. p. 1064), Nicholas de Jamsilla (tom. x. 494), and Matteo Villani (tom. xiv.

l. vii. p. 103). The last of these insinuates, that, in reducing the Saracens of Nocera, Charles II. of Anjou employed rather artifice than violence.

140. Muratori quotes a passage from Arnold of Lubec (l. iv. c. 20): Reperit thesauros absconditos, et omnem lapidum pretiosorum et gemmarum gloriam, ita ut oneratis 160 somariis, gloriose ad terram suam redierit. Roger de Hoveden, who mentions the violation of the royal tombs and corpses, computes the spoil of Salerno at 200,000 ounces of gold (p. 476). On these occasions I am almost tempted to exclaim with the listening maid in La Fontaine, "Je voudrois bien avoir ce qui manque."

Chapter LVII

1. I am indebted for his character and history to D'Herbelot (Bibliothèque Orientale, *Mahmud*, p. 533–537), M. de Guignes (Histoire des Huns, tom. iii. p. 155–173), and our countryman Colonel Alexander Dow (vol. i. p. 23–83). In the two first volumes of his History of Hindostan he styles himself the translator of the Persian Ferishta; but in his florid text it is not easy to distinguish the version and the original.

2. The dynasty of the Samanides continued 125 years, A.D. 874–999, under ten princes. See their succession and ruin in the Tables of M. de Guignes (Hist. des Huns, tom. i. p. 404–406). They were followed by the Gaznevides, A.D. 999–1183 (see tom. i. p. 239, 240). His division of nations often disturbs the series of time and place.

3. Gaznah hortos non habet: est emporium et domicilium mercaturæ Indicæ. Abulfedæ Geograph. Reiske, tab. xxiii. p. 349; D'Herbelot, p. 364. It has not been visited by any modern traveller.

4. By the ambassador of the caliph of Bagdad, who employed an Arabian or Chaldaic word that signifies *lord* and *master* (D'Herbelot, p. 825). It is interpreted Αὐτοκράτωρ, Βασιλεὺς, Βασιλέων, by the Byzantine writers of the eleventh century; and the name (Σουλτανὸς, Soldanus) is familiarly employed in the Greek and Latin languages, after it had passed from the Gaznevides to the Seljukides, and other emirs of Asia and Egypt. Ducange (Dissertation xvi. sur Joinville, p. 238–240, Gloss. Græc. et Latin.) labours to find the title of Sultan in the ancient kingdom of Persia: but his proofs are mere shadows; a proper name in the Themes of Constantine (ii. 11 [tom. iii. p. 61, ed. Bonn]), an anticipation of Zonaras, etc., and a manual of Kai Khosrou, not (as he believes) the Sassanide of the sixth, but the Seljukide of Iconium of the thirteenth century (De Guignes, Hist. des Huns, tom. i. p. 246).

5. Ferishta (apud Dow, Hist. of Hindostan, vol. i. p. 49) mentions the report of a *gun* in the Indian army. But as I am slow in believing this premature

(A.D. 1008) use of artillery, I must desire to scrutinise first the text and then the authority of Ferishta, who lived in the Mogul court in the last century.

6. Kinoge, or Canouge (the old Palimbothra), is marked in latitude 27° 3′, longitude 80° 13′. See D'Anville (Antiquité de l'Inde, p. 60–62), corrected by the local knowledge of Major Rennell (in his excellent Memoir on his Map of Hindostan, p. 37–43): 300 jewellers, 30,000 shops for the areca nut, 60,000 bands of musicians, etc. (Abulfed. Geograph. tab. xv. p. 274; Dow, vol. i. p. 16), will allow an ample deduction.

7. The idolaters of Europe, says Ferishta (Dow, vol. i. p. 66). Consult Abulfeda (p. 272) and Rennell's Map of Hindostan.

8. D'Herbelot, Bibliothèque Orientale, p. 527. Yet these letters, apophthegms, etc., are rarely the language of the heart, or the motives of public action.

9. For instance, a ruby of four hundred and fifty miskals (Dow, vol. i. p. 53), or six pounds three ounces: the largest in the treasury of Delhi weighed seventeen miskals (Voyages de Tavernier, partie ii. p. 280). It is true that in the East all coloured stones are called rubies (p. 355), and that Tavernier saw three larger and more precious among the jewels de notre grand roi, le plus puissant et plus magnifique de tous les rois de la terre (p. 376).

10. Dow, vol. i. p. 65. The sovereign of Kinoge is said to have possessed 2500 elephants (Abulfed. Geograph. tab. xv. p. 274). From these Indian stories the reader may correct a note in my first volume; or from that note he may correct these stories.

11. See a just and natural picture of these pastoral manners, in the history of William Archbishop of Tyre (l. i. c. vii. in the Gesta Dei per Francos, p. 633, 634), and a valuable note by the editor of the Histoire Généalogique des Tatars, p. 535–538.

12. The first emigrations of the Turkmans, and doubtful origin of the Seljukians, may be traced in

the laborious History of the Huns, by M. de Guignes (tom. i. Tables Chronologiques, l. v. tom. iii. l. vii. ix. x.), and the Bibliothèque Orientale of D'Herbelot (p. 799–802, 897–901), Elmacin (Hist. Saracen. p. 331–333 [4to ed., Lugd. B., 1625]), and Abulpharagius (Dynast. p. 221, 222).

13. Dow, Hist. of Hindostan, vol. i. p. 89, 95–98. I have copied this passage as a specimen of the Persian manner; but I suspect that, by some odd fatality, the style of Ferishta has been improved by that of Ossian.

14. The Zendekan of D'Herbelot (p. 1028), the Dindaka of Dow (vol. i. p. 97), is probably the Dandanekan of Abulfeda (Geograph. p. 345, Reiske), a small town of Chorasan, two days' journey from Marû, and renowned through the East for the production and manufacture of cotton.

15. The Byzantine historians (Cedrenus, tom. ii. p. 766, 767 [p. 566, sq., ed. Bonn], Zonaras, tom. ii. p. 255 [l. xvii. c. 25]; Nicephorus Bryennius, p. 21 [p. 26, ed. Bonn]) have confounded in this revolution the truth of time and place, of names and persons, of causes and events. The ignorance and errors of these Greeks (which I shall not stop to unravel) may inspire some distrust of the story of Cyaxares and Cyrus, as it is told by their most eloquent predecessors.

16. Willerm. Tyr. l. i. c. 7, p. 633. [In Gesta Dei per Franc. tom. i. fol. Hanov. 1611.] The divination by arrows is ancient and famous in the East.

17. D'Herbelot, p. 801. Yet after the fortune of his posterity, Seljuk became the thirty-fourth in lineal descent from the great Afrasiab emperor of Touran (p. 800). The Tartar pedigree of the house of Zingis gave a different cast to flattery and fable; and the historian Mirkhond derives the Seljukides from Alankavah, the virgin mother (p. 801, col. 2). If they be the same as the *Zalzuts* of Abulghazi Bahadur Khan (Hist. Généalogique, p. 148), we quote in their favour the most weighty evidence of a Tartar prince himself, the descendant of Zingis, Alankavah, or Alancu, and Oguz Khan.

18. By a slight corruption Togrul Beg is the Tangroli-pix of the Greeks. His reign and character are faithfully exhibited by D'Herbelot (Bibliothèque Orientale, p. 1027, 1028) and De Guignes (Hist. des Huns, tom. iii. p. 189–201).

19. Cedrenus, tom. ii. p. 774, 775 [p. 580, sq., ed. Bonn]; Zonaras, tom. ii. p. 257 [l. xvii. c. 25]. With their usual knowledge of Oriental affairs, they describe the ambassador as a *sherif*, who, like the syncellus of the patriarch, was the vicar and successor of the caliph.

20. From William of Tyre I have borrowed this distinction of Turks and Turkmans, which at least is popular and convenient. The names are the same, and the addition of *man* is of the same import in the Persic and Teutonic idioms. Few critics will adopt the etymology of James de Vitry (Hist. Hierosol. l. i. c. 11, p. 1061 [Gesta Dei p. Franc.]), of Turcomani, quasi *Turci et Comani*, a mixed people.

21. Hist. Générale des Huns, tom. iii. p. 165, 166, 167. M. de Guignes quotes Abulmahasen, an historian of Egypt.

22. Consult the Bibliothèque Orientale, in the articles of the *Abbassides*, *Caher*, and *Caiem*, and the Annals of Elmacin and Abulpharagius.

23. For this curious ceremony I am indebted to M. de Guignes (tom. iii. p. 197, 198), and that learned author is obliged to Bondari, who composed in Arabic the history of the Seljukides (tom. v. p. 365). I am ignorant of his age, country, and character.

24. Eodem anno (A.H. 455) obiit princeps Togrulbecus . . . rex fuit clemens, prudens, et peritus regnandi, cujus terror corda mortalium invaserat, ita ut obedirent ei reges atque ad ipsum scriberent. Elmacin, Hist. Saracen. p. 342, vers. Erpenii [4to ed.].

25. For these wars of the Turks and Romans, see in general the Byzantine histories of Zonaras and Cedrenus, Scylitzes the continuator of Cedrenus and Nicephorus Bryennius Cæsar. The two first of these were monks, the two latter statesmen; yet such were the Greeks, that the difference of style and character is scarcely discernible. For the Orientals, I draw as usual on the wealth of D'Herbelot (see titles of the first Seljukides) and the accuracy of De Guignes (Hist. des Huns, tom. iii. l. x.).

26. Ἐφέρετο γὰρ ἐν Τούρκοις λόγος, ὡς εἴη πεπρωμένον καταστραφῆναι τὸ Τούρκων γένος ὑπὸ τῆς τοιαύτης δυνάμεως, ὁποίαν ὁ Μακεδὼν Ἀγέξανδρος ἔχων κατεστρέψατο Πέρσας. Cedrenus, tom. ii. p. 791 [p. 611, ed. Bonn]. The credulity of the vulgar is always probable; and the Turks had learned from the Arabs the history or legend of Escander Dulcarnein (D'Herbelot, p. 317, etc.).

27. Οἳ τὴν Ἰβηρίαν καὶ Μεσοποταμίαν, καὶ τὴν παρακειμένην οἰκοῦσιν Ἀρμενίαν καὶ οἳ τὴν Ἰουδαϊκὴν τοῦ Νεστορίου καὶ τῶν Ἀκεφάλων θρησκεύουσιν αἵρεσιν (Scylitzes, ad calcem Cedreni, tom. ii. p. 834 [p. 687, ed. Bonn], whose ambiguous construction shall not tempt me to suspect that he confounded the Nestorian and Monophysite heresies). He familiarly talks of the μῆνις, χολος, ὀργὴ, Θεοῦ, qualities, as I should apprehend, very foreign to the perfect Being; but his bigotry is forced to confess that they were soon afterwards discharged on the orthodox Romans.

28. Had the name of Georgians been known to the Greeks (Stritter, Memoriæ Byzant. tom. iv. *Iberica*), I should derive it from their agriculture, as the Σκυθαὶ γεωργοὶ of Herodotus (l. iv. c. 18, p. 289, edit. Wesseling). But it appears only since the crusades, among the Latins (Jac. a Vitriaco, Hist. Hierosol. c. 79, p. 1095) and Orientals (D'Herbelot, p. 407), and was devoutly borrowed from St. George of Cappadocia.

29. Mosheim, Institut. Hist. Eccles. p. 632. See, in Chardin's Travels (tom. i. p. 171–174), the manners and religion of this handsome but worthless nation. See the pedigree of their princes from

Adam to the present century, in the Tables of M. de Guignes (tom. i. p. 433–438).

30. This city is mentioned by Constantine Porphyrogenitus (de Administrat. Imperii, l. ii. c. 44, p. 119 [tom. iii. p. 192, ed. Bonn]) and the Byzantines of the eleventh century, under the name of Mantzikierte, and by some is confounded with Theodosiopolis; but Deslisle, in his notes and maps, has very properly fixed the situation. Abulfeda (Geograph. tab. xviii. p. 310) describes Malasgerd as a small town, built with black stone, supplied with water, without trees, etc.

31. The Uzi of the Greeks (Stritter, Memor. Byzant., tom. iii. p. 923–948) are the Gozz of the Orientals (Hist. des Huns, tom. ii. p. 522; tom. iii. p. 133, etc.). They appear on the Danube and the Volga, in Armenia, Syria, and Chorasan, and the name seems to have been extended to the whole Turkman race.

32. Urselius [Ursellus] (the Russelius of Zonaras) is distinguished by Jeffrey Malaterra (l. ii. c. 33) among the Norman conquerors of Sicily, and with the surname of *Baliol:* and our own historians will tell how the Baliols came from Normandy to Durham, built Bernard's castle on the Tees, married an heiress of Scotland, etc. Ducange (Not. ad Nicephor. Bryennium, l. ii. No. 4) has laboured the subject in honour of the President de Bailleul, whose father had exchanged the sword for the gown.

33. Elmacin (p. 343, 344) assigns this probable number which is reduced by Abulpharagius to 15,000 (p. 227), and by D'Herbelot (p. 102) to 12,000 horse. But the same Elmacin gives 300,000 men to the emperor, of whom Abulpharagius says, Cum centum hominum millibus, multisque equis et magnâ pompâ instructus. The Greeks abstain from any definition of numbers.

34. The Byzantine writers do not speak so distinctly of the presence of the sultan; he committed his forces to a eunuch, had retired to a distance, etc. Is it ignorance, or jealousy, or truth?

35. He was the son of the Cæsar John Ducas, brother of the emperor Constantine (Ducange, Fam. Byzant. p. 165). Nicephorus Bryennius applauds his virtues and extenuates his faults (l. i. p. 30, 38 [p. 41, 54, ed. Bonn]; l. ii. p. 53 [p. 76, ed. Bonn]). Yet he owns his enmity to Romanus, οὐ πάνυ δὲ φιλίως ἔχων πρὸς Βασιλέα. Scylitzes speaks more explicitly of his treason.

36. This circumstance, which we read and doubt in Scylitzes and Constantine Manasses, is more prudently omitted by Nicephorus and Zonaras.

37. The ransom and tribute are attested by reason and the Orientals. The other Greeks are modestly silent; but Nicephorus Bryennius dares to affirm that the terms were οὐκ ἀνάξιας Ῥωμαίων [p. 44, ed. Bonn], and that the emperor would have preferred death to a shameful treaty.

38. The defeat and captivity of Romanus Diogenes may be found in John Scylitzes ad calcem

Cedreni, tom. ii. p. 835–843 [p. 689–704, ed. Bonn]; Zonaras, tom. ii. p. 281–284 [l. xvii. c. 13–15]; Nicephorus Bryennius, l. i. p. 25–32 [p. 33–44, ed. Bonn]; Glycas, p. 325–327 [p. 607–611, ed. Bonn]; Constantine Manasses, p. 134 [v. 6594, p. 280, ed. Bonn]; Elmacin, Hist. Saracen. p. 343, 344; Abulpharag. Dynast. p. 227; D'Herbelot, p. 102, 103; De Guignes, tom. iii. p. 207–211. Besides my old acquaintance Elmacin and Abulpharagius, the historian of the Huns has consulted Abulfeda, and his epitomiser Benschounah, a Chronicle of the Caliphs, by Soyouthi, Abulmahasen of Egypt, and Novairi of Africa.

39. This interesting death is told by D'Herbelot (p. 103, 104) and M. de Guignes (tom. iii. p. 212, 213), from their Oriental writers; but neither of them have transfused the spirit of Elmacin (Hist. Saracen. p. 344, 345).

40. A critic of high renown (the late Dr. Johnson), who has severely scrutinised the epitaphs of Pope, might cavil in this sublime inscription at the words "repair to Maru," since the reader must already be at Maru before he could peruse the inscription.

41. The Bibliothèque Orientale has given the text of the reign of Malek (p. 542, 543, 544, 654, 655); and the Histoire Générale des Huns (tom. iii. p. 214–224) has added the usual measure of repetition, emendation, and supplement. Without those two learned Frenchmen I should be blind indeed in the Eastern world.

42. See an excellent discourse at the end of Sir William Jones's History of Nadir Shah, and the articles of the poets Amak, Anvari, Raschidi, etc., in the Bibliothèque Orientale.

43. His name was Kheder Khan. Four bags were placed round his sofa, and, as he listened to the song, he cast handfuls of gold and silver to the poets (D'Herbelot, p. 107). All this may be true; but I do not understand how he could reign in Transoxiana in the time of Malek Shah, and much less how Kheder could surpass him in power and pomp. I suspect that the beginning, not the end, of the eleventh century is the true era of his reign.

44. See Chardin, Voyages en Perse, tom. ii. p. 235.

45. The Gelalæan era (Gelaleddin, Glory of the Faith, was one of the names or titles of Malek Shah) is fixed to the fifteenth of March, A.H. 471 — A.D. 1079. Dr. Hyde has produced the original testimonies of the Persians and Arabians (de Religione veterum Persarum, c. 16, p. 200–211).

46. She speaks of this Persian royalty as ἁπάσης κακοδαιμονέστερον πενίας. Anna Comnena was only nine years old at the end of the reign of Malek Shah (A.D. 1092), and when she speaks of his assassination she confounds the sultan with the vizir (Alexias, l. vi. p. 177, 178 [tom. i. p. 314–317, ed. Bonn]).

47. So obscure, that the industry of M. de Guignes could only copy (tom. i. p. 244; tom. iii. part i. p. 269, etc.) the history, or rather list, of the

Seljukides of Kerman, in Bibliothèque Orientale. They were extinguished before the end of the twelfth century.

48. Tavernier, perhaps the only traveller who has visited Kerman, describes the capital as a great ruinous village, twenty-five days' journey from Ispahan, and twenty-seven from Ormus, in the midst of a fertile country (Voyages en Turquie et en Perse, p. 107, 110).

49. It appears from Anna Comnena that the Turks of Asia Minor obeyed the signet and chiauss of the great sultan (Alexias, l. vi. p. 170 [tom. i. p. 302, ed. Bonn]), and that the two sons of Soliman were detained in his court (p. 180 [p. 319, ib.]).

50. This expression is quoted by Petit de la Croix (Vie de Gengiscan, p. 161) from some poet, most probably a Persian.

51. On the conquest of Asia Minor, M. de Guignes has derived no assistance from the Turkish or Arabian writers, who produce a naked list of the Seljukides of Roum. The Greeks are unwilling to expose their shame, and we must extort some hints from Scylitzes (p. 860, 863 [p. 731, 736, ed. Bonn]), Nicephorus Bryennius (p. 88, 91, 92, etc., 103, 104 [p. 130, 136, sqq., 158 sqq., ed. Bonn]), and Anna Comnena (Alexias, p. 91, 92, etc., 168, etc. [tom. i. p. 169, sqq., 299, sqq., ed. Bonn]).

52. Such is the description of Roum by Haiton, the Armenian, whose Tartar history may be found in the collections of Ramusio and Bergeron (see Abulfeda, Geograph. climat. xvii. p. 310–305).

53. Dicit eos quendam abusione Sodomitica intervertisse episcopum (Guibert. Abbat. Hist. Hierosol. l. i. p. 468). It is odd enough that we should find a parallel passage of the same people in the present age. "Il n'est point d'horreur que ces Turcs n'aient commis; et semblables aux soldats effrénés, qui dans le sac d'une ville, non contens de disposer de tout à leur gré, prétendent encore aux succès les moins désirables, quelques Siphais ont porté leurs attentats sur la personne du vieux rabbi de la synagogue, et celle de l'Archevêque Grec." (Mémoirs du Baron de Tott, tom. ii. p. 193.)

54. The emperor, or abbot, describe the scenes of a Turkish camp as if they had been present. Matres correptæ in conspectû filiarum multipliciter repetitis diversorum coitibus vexabantur (is that the true reading?); cum filiæ assistentes carmina præcinere saltando cogerentur. Mox eadem passio ad filias, etc.

55. See Antioch, and the death of Soliman, in Anna Comnena (Alexias, l. vi. p. 168, 169 [tom. i. p. 299–301, ed. Bonn]), with the notes of Ducange.

56. William of Tyre (l. i. c. 9, 10, p. 635) gives the most authentic and deplorable account of these Turkish conquests.

57. In his epistle to the count of Flanders, Alexius seems to fall too low beneath his character and dignity; yet it is approved by Ducange (Not. ad Alexiad. p. 335, etc.), and paraphrased by the Abbot Guibert, a contemporary historian. The Greek text no longer exists; and each translator and scribe might say with Guibert (p. 475), verbis vestita meis—a privilege of most indefinite latitude.

58. Our best fund for the history of Jerusalem from Heraclius to the crusades is contained in two large and original passages of William archbishop of Tyre (l. i. c. 1–10; l. xviii. c. 5, 6), the principal author of the Gesta Dei per Francos. M. de Guignes has composed a very learned Mémoire sur the Commerce des François dans le Levant avant les Croisades, etc. (Mém. de l'Académie des Inscriptions, tom. xxxvii. p. 467–500.)

59. Secundum Dominorum dispositionem plerumque lucida plerumque nubila recepit intervalla, et ægrotantis more temporum præsentium gravabatur aut respirabat qualitate (l. i. c. 3, p. 630). The Latinity of William of Tyre is by no means contemptible; but in his account of 490 years, from the loss to the recovery of Jerusalem, he exceeds the true account by thirty years.

60. For the transactions of Charlemagne with the Holy Land, see Eginhard (de Vitâ Caroli Magni, c. 16, p. 79–82), Constantine Porphyrogenitus (de Administratione Imperii, l. ii. c. 26, p. 80 [tom. iii. p. 115, ed. Bonn]), and Pagi (Critica, tom. iii. A.D. 800, No. 13, 14, 15).

61. The caliph granted his privileges, Amalphitanis viris amicis et utilium introductoribus (Gesta Dei, p. 934 [Willerm. Tyr. lib. xviii. c. 5]). The trade of Venice to Egypt and Palestine cannot produce so old a title, unless we adopt the laughable translation of a Frenchman who mistook the two factions of the circus (Veneti et Prasini) for the Venetians and Parisians.

62. An Arabic chronicle of Jerusalem (apud Asseman. Biblioth. Orient. tom. i. p. 628, tom. iv. p. 368) attests the unbelief of the caliph and the historian; yet Cantacuzene presumes to appeal to the Mohammedans themselves for the truth of this perpetual miracle.

63. In his Dissertations on Ecclesiastical History the learned Mosheim has separately discussed this pretended miracle (tom. ii. p. 214–306), de lumine sancti sepulchri.

64. William of Malmesbury (l. iv. c. ii. p. 209) quotes the Itinerary of the monk Bernard, an eyewitness, who visited Jerusalem A.D. 870. The miracle is confirmed by another pilgrim some years older; and Mosheim ascribes the invention to the Franks soon after the decease of Charlemagne.

65. Our travellers, Sandys (p. 134), Thevenot (p. 621–627), Maundrell (p. 94, 95), etc., describe this extravagant farce. The Catholics are puzzled to decide *when* the miracle ended and the trick began.

66. The Orientals themselves confess the fraud, and plead necessity and edification (Mémoires du Chevalier D'Arvieux, tom. ii. p. 140; Joseph Abudacni, Hist. Copt. c. 20); but I will not attempt, with Mosheim, to explain the mode. Our travellers have failed with the blood of St. Januarius at Naples.

67. See D'Herbelot (Biblioth. Orientale, p. 411), Renaudot (Hist. Patriarch. Alex. p. 390, 397, 400, 401), Elmacin (Hist. Saracen. p. 321–323), and Marei (p. 384–386), an historian of Egypt, translated by Reiske from Arabic into German, and verbally interpreted to me by a friend.

68. The religion of the Druses is concealed by their ignorance and hypocrisy. Their secret doctrines are confined to the elect who profess a contemplative life; and the vulgar Druses, the most indifferent of men, occasionally conform to the worship of the Mohammedans and Christians of their neighbourhood. The little that is, or deserves to be known, may be seen in the industrious Niebuhr (Voyages, tom. ii. p. 354–357), and the second volume of the recent and instructive Travels of M. de Volney.

69. See Glaber, l. iii. c. 7, and the Annals of Baronius and Pagi, A.D. 1009.

70. Per idem tempus ex universo orbe tam innumerabilis multitudo cœpit confluere ad sepulchrum Salvatoris Hierosolymis, quantum nullus hominum prius sperare poterat. Ordo inferioris plebis . . . mediocres . . . reges et comites . . . præsules . . . mulieres multæ nobiles cum pauperioribus. . . . Pluribus enim erat mentis desiderium mori priusquam ad propria reverterentur (Glaber, l. iv. c. 6; Bouquet, Historians of France, tom. x. p. 50).

71. Glaber, l. iii. c. 1. Katona (Hist. Critic. Regum Hungariæ, tom. i. p. 304–311) examines whether St. Stephen founded a monastery at Jerusalem.

72. Baronius (A.D. 1064, No. 43–56) has transcribed the greater part of the original narratives of Ingulphus, Marianus, and Lambertus.

73. See Elmacin (Hist. Saracen. p. 349, 350) and Abulpharagius (Dynast. p. 237, vers. Pocock). M. de Guignes (Hist. des Huns, tom. iii. part i. p. 215, 216) adds the testimonies, or rather the names, of Abulfeda and Novairi.

74. From the expedition of Isar Atsiz (A.H. 469 —A.D. 1076) to the expulsion of the Ortokides (A.D. 1096). Yet William of Tyre (l. i. c. 6, p. 633) asserts that Jerusalem was thirty-eight years in the hands of the Turks; and an Arabic chronicle, quoted by Pagi (tom. iv. p. 202,) supposes that the city was reduced by a Carizmian general to the obedience of the caliph of Bagdad, A.H. 463—A.D. 1070. These early dates are not very compatible with the general history of Asia; and I am sure that, as late as A.D. 1064, the regnum Babylonicum (of Cairo) still prevailed in Palestine (Baronius, A.D. 1064, No. 56).

75. De Guignes, Hist. des Huns, tom. i. p. 249–252.

76. Willerm. Tyr. l. i. c. 8, p. 634, who strives hard to magnify the Christian grievances. The Turks exacted an *aureus* from each pilgrim! The *caphar* of the Franks is now fourteen dollars: and Europe does not complain of this voluntary tax.

Chapter LVIII

1. Whimsical enough is the origin of the name of *Picards*, and from thence of *Picardie*, which does not date earlier than A.D. 1200. It was an academical joke, an epithet first applied to the quarrelsome humour of those students, in the University of Paris, who came from the frontier of France and Flanders (Valesii Notitia Galliarum, p. 447; Longuerue, Description de la France, p. 54).

2. William of Tyre (l. i. c. 11, p. 637, 638) thus describes the hermit: Pusillus, persona contemptibilis, vivacis ingenii, et oculum habens perspicacem gratumque, et sponte fluens ei non deerat eloquium. See Albert Aquensis, p. 185; Guibert, p. 482 [l. ii. c. 8]; Anna Comnena in Alexiad. l. x. p. 284, etc., with Ducange's notes, p. 349.

3. Ultra quinquaginta millia, si me possunt in expeditione pro duce at pontifice habere, armatâ manú volunt in inimicos Dei insurgere et ad sepulchrum Domini ipso ducente pervenire (Gregor. VII. epist. ii. 31, in tom. xii. p. 322, concil.).

4. See the original lives of Urban II. by Pandulphus Pisanus and Bernardus Guido, in Muratori, Rer. Ital. Script. tom. iii. pars i. p. 352, 353.

5. She is known by the different names of Praxes, Eupræcia, Eufrasia, and Adelais; and was the daughter of a Russian prince, and the widow of a margrave of Brandenburg. Struv. Corpus Hist. Germanicæ, p. 340.

6. Henricus odio eam cœpit habere: ideo incarceravit eam, et concessit ut plerique vim ei inferrent; immo filium hortans ut eam subagitaret (Dodechin, Continuat. Marian. Scot. apud Baron. A.D. 1093, No. 4). In the synod of Constance she is described by Bertholdus, rerum inspector: quæ se tantas et tam inauditas fornicationum spurcitias, et a tantis passam fuisse conquesta est, etc.; and again at Placentia: satis misericorditer suscepit, eo quòd ipsam tantas spurcitias non tam commisisse quam invitam pertulisse pro certo cognoverit papa cum sanctâ synodo. Apud Baron. A.D. 1093, No. 4, 1094, No. 3. A rare subject for the infallible decision of a pope and council. These abominations are repugnant to every principle of human nature, which is not altered by a dispute about rings and crosiers. Yet it should seem that the wretched woman was tempted by the priests to relate or subscribe some infamous stories of herself and her husband.

7. See the narrative and acts of the synod of Placentia, Concil. tom. xii. p. 821, etc.

8. Guibert, himself a Frenchman, praises the piety and valour of the French nation, the author

and example of the crusades: Gens nobilis, prudens, bellicosa, dapsilis et nitida. . . . Quos enim Britones, *Anglos*, Ligures, si bonis eos moribus videamus, non illico *Francos homines* appellemus? (p. 478 [l. ii. c. 1]). He owns, however, that the vivacity of the French degenerates into petulance among foreigners (p. 483 [l. ii. c. 10]) and vain loquaciousness (p. 502 [l. iv. c. 9]).

9. Per viam quam jamdudum Carolus Magnus mirificus rex Francorum aptari fecit usque C. P. (Gesta Francorum, p. 1; Robert. Monach. Hist. Hieros. l. i. p. 33), etc.

10. John Tilpinus, or Turpinus, was Archbishop of Rheims, A.D. 773. After the year 1000 this romance was composed in his name, by a monk of the borders of France and Spain; and such was the idea of ecclesiastical merit, that he describes himself as a fighting and drinking priest! Yet the book of lies was pronounced authentic by Pope Calixtus II. (A.D. 1122), and is respectfully quoted by the abbot Suger, in the great Chronicles of St. Denys (Fabric. Biblioth. Latin. medii Ævi, edit. Mansi, tom. iv. p. 161).

11. See Etat de la France, by the Count de Boulainvilliers, tom. i. p. 180–182, and the second volume of the Observations sur l'Histoire de France, by the Abbé de Mably.

12. In the provinces to the south of the Loire, the first *Capetians* were scarcely allowed a feudal supremacy. On all sides, Normandy, Bretagne, Aquitain, Burgundy, Lorraine, and Flanders, contracted the name and limits of the *proper* France. See Hadrian Vales. Notitia Galliarum.

13. These counts, a younger branch of the dukes of Aquitain, were at length despoiled of the greatest part of their country by Philip Augustus. The bishops of Clermont gradually became princes of the city. Mélanges tirés d'une Grande Bibliothèque, tom. xxxvi. p. 288, etc.

14. See the Acts of the Council of Clermont, Concil. tom. xii. p. 829, etc.

15. Confluxerant ad concilium e multis regionibus, viri potentes, et honorati, innumeri, quamvis cingulo laicalis militiæ superbi (Baldric, an eyewitness, p. 86–88; Robert. Mon. p. 31, 32; Will. Tyr. i. 14, 15, p. 639–641; Guibert, p. 478–480 [l. ii. c. 2–4]; Fulcher. Carnot. p. 382).

16. The Truce of God (Treva, or Treuga Dei) was first invented in Aquitain, A.D. 1032; blamed by some bishops as an occasion of perjury, and rejected by the Normans as contrary to their privileges (Ducange, Gloss. Latin. tom. vi. p. 682–685).

17. *Deus vult, Deus vult*! was the pure acclamation of the clergy who understood Latin (Robert. Mon. l. i. p. 32). By the illiterate laity, who spoke the *Provincial* or *Limousin* idiom, it was corrupted to *Deus lo volt*, or *Diex el volt*. See Chron. Casinense, l. iv. c. 11, p. 497, in Muratori, Script. Rerum Ital. tom. iv., and Ducange (Dissertat. xi. p. 207, sur Joinville, and Gloss. Latin. tom. ii. p. 690), who, in his preface, produces a very difficult specimen of the dialect of Rovergue, A.D. 1100, very near,

both in time and place, to the Council of Clermont (p. 15, 16).

18. Most commonly on their shoulders, in gold, or silk, or cloth, sewed on their garments. In the first crusade all were red; in the third the French alone preserved that colour, while green crosses were adopted by the Flemings, and white by the English (Ducange, tom. ii. p. 651). Yet in England the red ever appears the favourite, and, as it were, the national colour of our military ensigns and uniforms.

19. Bongarsius, who has published the original writers of the crusades, adopts, with much complacency, the fanatic title of Guibertus, Gesta DEI per Francos; though some critics propose to read Gesta *Diaboli* per Francos (Hanoviæ, 1611, two vols. in folio). I shall briefly enumerate, as they stand in this collection, the authors whom I have used for the first crusade. I. Gesta Francorum. II. Robertus Monachus. III. Baldricus. IV. Raimundus de Agiles. V. Albertus Aquensis. VI. Fulcherius Carnotensis. VII. Guibertus. VIII. Willielmus Tyriensis. Muratori has given us, IX. Radulphus Cadomensis de Gestis Tancredi (Script. Rer. Ital. tom. v. p. 285–333), and, X. Bernardus Thesaurarius de Acquisitione Terræ Sanctæ (tom. vii. p. 664–848). The last of these was unknown to a late French historian, who has given a large and critical list of the writers of the crusades (Esprit des Croisades, tom. i. p. 13–141), and most of whose judgments my own experience will allow me to ratify. It was late before I could obtain a sight of the French historians collected by Duchesne. I. Petri Tudebodi Sacerdotis Sivracensis Historia de Hierosolymitano Itinere (tom. iv. p. 773–815) has been transfused into the first anonymous writer of Bongarsius. II. The Metrical History of the First Crusade, in seven books (p. 890–912), is of small value or account.

20. If the reader will turn to the first scene of the First Part of Henry the Fourth, he will see in the text of Shakspeare the natural feelings of enthusiasm; and in the notes of Dr. Johnson the workings of a bigoted, though vigorous, mind, greedy of every pretence to hate and persecute those who dissent from his creed.

21. The sixth Discourse of Fleury on Ecclesiastical History (p. 223–261) contains an accurate and rational view of the causes and effects of the crusades.

22. The penance, indulgences, etc., of the middle ages are amply discussed by Muratori (Antiquitat. Italiæ medii Ævi, tom. v. dissert. lxviii. p. 709–768) and by M. Chais (Lettres sur les Jubilés et les Indulgences, tom. ii. lettres 21 and 22, p. 478–556), with this difference, that the abuses of superstition are mildly, perhaps faintly, exposed by the learned Italian, and peevishly magnified by the Dutch minister.

23. Schmidt (Histoire des Allemands, tom. ii. p. 211–220, 452–462) gives an abstract of the Penitential of Rhegino in the ninth, and of Burchard

in the tenth, century. In one year five-and-thirty murders were perpetrated at Worms.

24. Till the twelfth century we may support the clear account of twelve *denarii*, or pence, to the *solidus*, or shilling; and twenty *solidi* to the pound weight of silver, about the pound sterling. Our money is diminished to a third, and the French to a fiftieth, of this primitive standard.

25. Each century of lashes was sanctified with the recital of a psalm; and the whole Psalter, with the accompaniment of 15,000 stripes, was equivalent to five years.

26. The Life and Achievements of St. Dominic Loricatus was composed by his friend and admirer, Peter Damianus. See Fleury, Hist. Ecclés. tom. xiii. p. 96-104; Baronius, A.D. 1056, No. 7, who observes, from Damianus, how fashionable, even among ladies of quality (sublimis generis), this expiation (purgatorii genus) was grown.

27. At a quarter, or even half, a rial a lash, Sancho Panza was a cheaper, and possibly not a more dishonest, workman. I remember in Père Labat (Voyages en Italie, tom. vii. p. 16-29) a very lively picture of the *dexterity* of one of these artists.

28. Quicunque pro solâ devotione, non pro honoris vel pecuniæ adeptione, ad liberandam ecclesiam Dei Jerusalem profectus fuerit, iter illud pro omni pœnitentia reputetur. Canon. Concil. Claromont. ii. p. 829. Guibert styles it novum salutis genus (p. 471 [l. i. c. 1]) and is almost philosophical on the subject.

29. Such at least was the belief of the crusaders, and such is the uniform style of the historians (Esprit des Croisades, tom. iii. p. 477); but the prayers for the repose of their souls are inconsistent in orthodox theology with the merits of martyrdom.

30. The same hopes were displayed in the letters of the adventurers ad animandos qui in Francia resederant. Hugh de Reiteste could boast that his share amounted to one abbey and ten castles, of the yearly value of 1500 marks, and that he should acquire a hundred castles by the conquest of Aleppo (Guibert, p. 554, 555 [l. vii. c. 35]).

31. In his genuine or fictitious letter to the Count of Flanders, Alexius mingles with the danger of the church, and the relics of saints, the auri et argenti amor, and pulcherrimarum fœminarum voluptas (p. 476 [l. i. c. 4]); as if, says the indignant Guibert, the Greek women were handsomer than those of France.

32. See the privileges of the *Crucesignati*—freedom from debt, usury, injury, secular justice, etc. The pope was their perpetual guardian (Ducange, tom. ii. p. 651, 652).

33. Guibert (p. 481 [l. ii. c. 6]) paints in lively colours this general emotion. He was one of the few contemporaries who had genius enough to feel the astonishing scenes that were passing before their eyes. Erat itaque videre miraculum, caro omnes emere, atque vili vendere, etc.

34. Some instances of these *stigmata* are given in the Esprit des Croisades (tom. iii. p. 169, etc.) from authors whom I have not seen.

35. Fuit et aliud scelus detestabile in hac congregatione pedestris populi stulti et vesanæ levitatis . . . *anserem* quendam divino spiritû asserebant afflatum, et *capellam* non minus eodem repletam, et has sibi duces [hujus] secundæ viæ fecerant, etc. (Albert. Aquensis, l. i. c. 31, p. 196). Had these peasants founded an empire, they might have introduced, as in Egypt, the worship of animals, which their philosophic descendants would have glossed over with some specious and subtle allegory.

36. Benjamin of Tudela describes the state of his Jewish brethren from Cologne along the Rhine: they were rich, generous, learned, hospitable, and lived in the eager hope of the Messiah (Voyage, tom. i. p. 243-245, par Baratier). In seventy years (he wrote about A.D. 1170) they had recovered from these massacres.

37. These massacres and depredations on the Jews, which were renewed at each crusade, are *coolly* related. It is true that St. Bernard (Epist. 363, tom. i. p. 329 [p. 328, ed. Bened.]) admonishes the Oriental Franks, non sunt persequendi Judæi, non sunt trucidandi. The contrary doctrine had been preached by a *rival* monk.

38. See the contemporary description of Hungary in Otho of Frisingen, l. i. c. 31, in Muratori, Script. Rerum Italicarum, tom. vi. p. 665, 666.

39. The old Hungarians, without excepting Turotzius, are ill-informed of the first crusade, which they involve in a single passage. Katona, like ourselves, can only quote the writers of France; but he compares with local science the ancient and modern geography. *Ante portam Cyperon* is Sopron or Poson; *Mallevilla*, Zemlin; *Fluvius Maroe*, Savus; *Lintax*, Leith; *Mesebroch*, or *Merseburg*, Ouar, or Moson; *Tollenburg*, Pragg (de Reg. Hung., iii. p. 19-53).

40. Anna Comnena (Alexias, l. x. p. 287) describes this ὀστῶν κολωνὸς as a mountain ὑψηλὸν καὶ βάθος καὶ πλάτος ἀξιολογώτατον. In the siege of Nice such were used by the Franks themselves as the materials of a wall.

41. See pp. 726-727 below.

42. The author of the Esprit des Croisades has doubted, and might have disbelieved, the crusade and tragic death of Prince Sueno, with 1500 or 15,000 Danes, who was cut off by Sultan Soliman in Cappadocia, but who still lives in the poem of Tasso (tom. iv. p. 111-115).

43. The fragments of the kingdoms of Lotharingia, or Lorraine, were broken into the two duchies, of the Moselle, and of the Meuse: the first has preserved its name, which, in the latter, has been changed into that of Brabant (Vales. Notit. Gall. p. 283-288).

44. See, in the Description of France, by the Abbé de Longuerue, the articles of *Boulogne*, part i. p. 54; *Brabant*, part ii. p. 47, 48; *Bouillon*, p. 134. On his departure Godfrey sold or pawned Bouillon to the church for 1300 marks.

41. To save time and space, I shall represent, in a short table, the

	The Crowd.	The Chiefs.	The Road to Constantinople.	Alexius.	Nice and Asia Minor.
I. Gesta Francorum	p. 1, 2.	p. 2.	p. 2, 3.	p. 4, 5.	p. 5–7.
II. Robertus Monachus	p. 33, 34.	p.35, 36.	p. 36, 37.	p. 37, 38.	p. 39–45.
III. Baldricus	p. 89.	—	p. 91–93.	p. 91–94.	p. 94–101.
IV. Raimundus de Agiles	—	—	p. 139, 140.	p. 140, 141.	p. 142.
V. Albertus Aquensis	l. i. c. 7–31.	—	l. ii. c. 1–8.	l. ii. c. 9–19.	l. ii. c. 20–43; l. iii. c. 1–4.
VI. Fulcherius Carnotensis	p. 384.	—	p. 385, 386.	p. 386.	p. 387–389.
VII. Guibertus	p. 482, 485.	—	p. 485, 489.	p. 485–490.	p. 491–493, 498.
VIII. Willermus Tyrensis	l. i. c. 18–30.	l. i. c. 17.	l. ii. c. 1–4, 13, 17, 22.	l. ii. c. 5–23.	l. iii. c. 1–12; l. iv.c. 13–25.
IX. Radulphus Cadomensis	—	c. 1–3, 15.	c. 4–7, 17.	c. 8–13, 18, 19.	c. 14–16, 21–47.
X. Bernardus Thesaurarius	c. 7–11	—	c. 11–20	c. 11–20	c. 21–25

45. See the family character of Godfrey in William of Tyre, l. ix. c. 5–8; his previous design in Guibert (p. 485 [l. ii. c. 12]); his sickness and vow in Bernard. Thesaur. (c. 78).

46. Anna Comnena supposes that Hugh was proud of his nobility, riches, and power (l. x. p. 288): the two last articles appear more equivocal; but an ἐυγενεία, which seven hundred years ago was famous in the palace of Constantinople, attests the ancient dignity of the Capetian family of France.

47. Will. Gemeticensis, l. vii. c. 7, p. 672, 673, in Camden. Normanicis [ed. Frankf. 1603]. He pawned the duchy for one hundredth part of the present yearly revenue. Ten thousand marks may be equal to five hundred thousand livres, and Normandy annually yields fifty-seven millions to the king (Necker, Administration des Finances, tom. i. p. 287).

48. His original letter to his wife is inserted in the Spicilegium of Dom. Luc. d'Acheri, tom. iv., and quoted in the Esprit des Croisades, tom. i. p. 63.

49. Unius enim, duúm, trium seu quatuor oppidorum dominos quis numeret? quorum tanta fuit copia, ut vix totidem Trojana obsidio coegisse putetur. (Ever the lively and interesting Guibert, p. 486 [l. ii. c. 17]).

50. It is singular enough that Raymond of St. Giles, a second character in the genuine history of the crusades, should shine as the first of heroes in the writings of the Greeks (Anna Comnen. Alexiad. l. x. xi.) and the Arabians (Longueruana, p. 129).

51. Omnes de Burgundiâ, et Alverniâ, et Vasconiâ, et Gothi (of *Languedoc*), provinciales appellabantur, cæteri vero Francigenæ; et hoc in exercitu; inter hostes autem Franci dicebantur. Raymond de Agiles, p. 144.

52. The town of his birth, or first appanage, was consecrated to St. Ægidius, whose name, as early as the first crusade, was corrupted by the French into St. Gilles, or St. Giles. It is situate in the Lower Languedoc, between Nismes and the Rhône, and still boasts a collegiate church of the foundation of Raymond (Mélanges tirés d'une Grande Bibliothèque, tom. xxxvii. p. 51).

53. The mother of Tancred was Emma, sister of the great Robert Guiscard; his father, the marquis Odo the Good. It is singular enough that the family and country of so illustrious a person should be unknown; but Muratori reasonably conjectures that he was an Italian, and perhaps of the race of the marquises of Montferrat in Piedmont (Script. tom. v. p. 281, 282).

54. To gratify the childish vanity of the house of Este, Tasso has inserted in his poem, and in the first crusade, a fabulous hero, the brave and amorous Rinaldo (x. 75, xvii. 66–94). He might borrow his name from a Rinaldo, with the Aquila bianca Estense, who vanquished, as the standard-bearer of the Roman church, the emperor Frederic I. (Storia Imperiale di Ricobaldo, in Muratori Script. Ital. tom. ix. p. 360; Ariosto, Orlando Furioso, iii. 30). But, 1. The distance of sixty years between the youth of the two Rinaldos destroys their identity. 2. The Storia Imperiale is a forgery of the Conte Boyardo, at the end of the fifteenth century (Muratori, p. 281–289). 3. This Rinaldo, and his exploits, are not less chimerical than the

particular references to the great events of the first crusade.

Edessa.	Antioch.	The Battle.	The Holy Lance.	Conquest of Jerusalem.
—	p. 9–15.	p. 15–22.	p. 18–20.	p. 26–29.
—	p. 45–55.	p. 56–66.	p. 61, 62.	p. 74–81.
—	p. 101, 111.	p. 111–122.	p. 116–119.	p. 130–138.
—	p. 142–149.	p. 149–155.	p. 150, 152, 156.	p. 173–183.
{l. iii. c. 5–32; l. iv. 9, 12; l. v. 15–22.	{l. iii. c. 33–66; iv. 1–26.	l. iv. c. 7–56.	l. iv. c. 43.	{l. v. c. 45, 46; l. vi. c. 1–50.
p. 389, 390.	p. 390–392.	p. 392–395.	p. 392.	p. 396–400.
p. 496, 497.	p. 498, 506, 512.	p. 512–523.	p. 520, 530, 533.	p. 523–537.
l. iv. c. 1–6	{l. iv. 9–24; l. v. 1–23.	l. vi. c. 1–23.	l. vi. c. 14.	{l. vii. c. 1–25; l. vii. c. 1–24.
—	c. 48–71.	c. 72–91.	c. 100–109.	c. 111–138.
c. c. 26.	c. 27–38.	c. 39–52.	c. 45.	c. 54–77.

hero of Tasso (Muratori, Antichità Estense, tom. i. p. 350).

55. Of the words *gentilis*, *gentilhomme*, *gentleman*, two etymologies are produced: 1. From the barbarians of the fifth century, the soldiers, and at length the conquerors, of the Roman empire, who were vain of their foreign nobility; and, 2. From the sense of the civilians, who consider *gentilis* as synonymous with *ingenuus*. Selden inclines to the first, but the latter is more pure, as well as probable.

56. Framea scutoque juvenem ornant. Tacitus, Germania, c. 13.

57. The athletic exercises, particularly the cestus and pancratium, were condemned by Lycurgus, Philopœmen, and Galen, a lawgiver, a general, and a physician. Against their authority and reasons, the reader may weigh the apology of Lucian, in the character of Solon. See West on the Olympic Games, in his Pindar, vol. ii. p. 86–96, 245–248.

58. On the curious subjects of knighthood, knights-service, nobility, arms, cry of war, banners, and tournaments, an ample fund of information may be sought in Selden (Opera, tom. iii. part i.; Titles of Honour, part ii. c. 1, 3, 5, 8), Ducange (Gloss. Latin. tom. iv. p. 398–412, etc.), Dissertations sur Joinville (i. vi.–xii. p. 127–142, p. 165–222), and M. de St. Palaye (Mémoires sur la Chevalerie).

59. The Familiæ Dalmaticæ of Ducange are meagre and imperfect; the national historians are recent and fabulous, the Greeks remote and careless. In the year 1104 Coloman reduced the maritime country as far as Trau and Salona (Katona, Hist. Crit. tom. iii. p. 195–207).

60. Scodras appears in Livy as the capital and fortress of Gentius king of the Illyrians, arx munitissima, afterwards a Roman colony (Cellarius, tom. i. p. 393, 394). It is now called Iscodar, or Scutari (D'Anville, Géographie Ancienne, tom. i. p. 164). The sanjiak (now a pasha) of Scutari, or Schendeire, was the eighth under the Beglerbeg of Romania, and furnished 600 soldiers on a revenue of 78,787 rix-dollars (Marsigli, Stato Militare del Imperio Ottomano, p. 128).

61. In Pelagonia castrum hæreticûm . . . spoliatum cum suis habitatoribus igne combussere. *Nec id eis injuriâ contigit:* quia illorum detestabilis sermo et [ut] cancer serpebat, jamque circumjacentes regiones suo pravo dogmate fœdaverat (Robert. Mon. p. 36, 37). After coolly relating the fact, the archbishop Baldric adds, as a praise, Omnes siquidem illi viatores, Judæos, hæreticos, Saracenos æqualiter habent exosos; quos omnes appellant inimicos Dei (p. 92).

62. Ἀναλαβόμενος ἀπὸ Ῥώμης τὴν χρυσῆν τοῦ Ἁγίου Πέτρου σημαίαν (Alexiad. l. x. p. 288).

63. Ὁ Βασιλεὺς τῶν βασιλέων, καὶ ἄρχηγος τοῦ Φραγγίκου στρατεύματος ἄπαντος [Alexiad. l. x. p. 288]. This Oriental pomp is extravagant in a count of Vermandois; but the patriot Ducange repeats with much complacency (Not. ad Alexiad. p. 352, 353; Dissert. xxvii. sur Joinville, p. 315) the passages of Matthew Paris (A.D. 1254) and Froissard (vol. iv. p. 201) which style the king of France rex regum, and chef de tous les rois Chrétiens.

64. Anna Comnena was born the 1st of December, A.D. 1083, indiction vii. (Alexiad. l. vi. p. 166, 167 [ed. Par.; tom. i. p. 295, 296, ed. Bonn]). At

thirteen, the time of the first crusade, she was nubile, and perhaps married to the younger Nicephorus Bryennius, whom she fondly styles τὸν ἐμὸν Καίσαρα (l. x. p. 295, 296). Some moderns have *imagined* that her enmity to Bohemond was the fruit of disappointed love. In the transactions of Constantinople and Nice her partial accounts (Alex. l. x. xi. p. 283–317) may be opposed to the partiality of the Latins, but in their subsequent exploits she is brief and ignorant.

65. In their views of the character and conduct of Alexius, Maimbourg has favoured the *Catholic* Franks, and Voltaire has been partial to the *schismatic* Greeks. The prejudice of a philosopher is less excusable than that of a Jesuit.

66. Between the Black Sea, the Bosphorus, and the river Barbyses, which is deep in summer, and runs fifteen miles through a flat meadow. Its communication with Europe and Constantinople is by the stone bridge of the *Blachernæ*, which in successive ages was restored by Justinian and Basil (Gyllius de Bosphoro Thracio, l. ii. c. 3; Ducange, C. P. Christiana, l. iv c. 2, p. 179).

67. There were two sorts of adoption, the one by arms, the other by introducing the son between the shirt and skin of his father. Ducange (sur Joinville, diss. xxii. p. 270) supposes Godfrey's adoption to have been of the latter sort.

68. After his return Robert of Flanders became the *man* of the king of England, for a pension of four hundred marks. See the first act in Rymer's Fœdera.

69. Sensit vetus regnandi, falsos in amore, odia non fingere. Tacit. [Ann.] vi. 44.

70. The proud historians of the crusades slide and stumble over this humiliating step. Yet, since the heroes knelt to salute the emperor as he sat motionless on his throne, it is clear that they must have kissed either his feet or knees. It is only singular that Anna should not have amply supplied the silence or ambiguity of the Latins. The abasement of their princes would have added a fine chapter to the Ceremoniale Aulæ Byzantinæ.

71. He called himself Φραγγὸς κάθαρος τῶν εὐγένων (Alexias, l. x. p. 301). What a title of *noblesse* of the eleventh century, if any one could now prove his inheritance! Anna relates, with visible pleasure, that the swelling barbarian, Λατινὸς τετυφωμένος, was killed, or wounded, after fighting in the front in the battle of Dorylæum (l. xi. p. 317). This circumstance may justify the suspicion of Ducange (Not. p. 362), that he was no other than Robert of Paris, of the district most peculiarly styled the Duchy or Island of France (*L'Isle de France*).

72. With the same penetration, Ducange discovers his church to be that of St. Drausus, or Drosin, of Soissons, quem duello dimicaturi solent invocare: pugiles qui ad memoriam ejus (*his tomb*) pernoctant invictos reddit, ut et de Burgundiâ et Italiâ tali necessitate confugiatur ad eum. Joan. Sariberiensis, epist. 139.

73. There is some diversity on the numbers of his army; but no authority can be compared with that of Ptolemy, who states it at five thousand horse and thirty thousand foot (see Usher's Annales, p. 152).

74. Fulcher. Carnotensis, p. 387. He enumerates nineteen nations of different names and languages (p. 389); but I do not clearly apprehend his difference between the *Franci* and *Galli*, *Itali* and *Apuli*. Elsewhere (p. 385) he contemptuously brands the deserters.

75. Guibert, p. 556 [l. vii. c. 39]. Yet even his gentle opposition implies an immense multitude. By Urban II., in the fervour of his zeal, it is only rated at 300,000 pilgrims (Epist. xvi. Concil. tom. xii. p. 731).

76. Alexias, l. x. p. 283, 305. Her fastidious delicacy complains of their strange and inarticulate names, and indeed there is scarcely one that she has not contrived to disfigure with the proud ignorance so dear and familiar to a polished people. I shall select only one example, *Sangeles*, for the count of St. Giles.

77. William of Malmesbury (who wrote about the year 1130) has inserted in his history (l. iv. p. 130–154 [Script. post Bedam]) a narrative of the first crusade: but I wish that, instead of listening to the tenue murmur which had passed the British ocean (p. 143), he had confined himself to the numbers, families, and adventures of his countrymen. I find in Dugdale, that an English Norman, Stephen earl of Albemarle and Holdernesse, led the rear-guard with duke Robert at the battle of Antioch (Baronage, part i. p. 61).

78. Videres Scotorum apud se ferocium alias imbellium cuneos (Guibert, p. 471): the *crus intectum* and *hispida chlamys* may suit the Highlanders, but the finibus uliginosis may rather apply to the Irish bogs. William of Malmesbury expressly mentions the Welsh and Scots, etc. (l. iv. p. 133), who quitted, the former venationem saltuum, the latter familiaritatem pulicum.

79. This cannibal hunger, sometimes real, more frequently an artifice or a lie, may be found in Anna Comnena (Alexias, l. x. p. 288), Guibert (p. 546), Radulph. Cadom. (c. 97). The stratagem is related by the author of the Gesta Francorum, the monk Robert Baldric, and Raymond de Agiles, in the siege and famine of Antioch.

80. His Musulman appellation of Soliman is used by the Latins, and his character is highly embellished by Tasso. His Turkish name of Kilidge-Arslan (A.H. 485–500, A.D. 1192–1206: see De Guignes's Tables, tom. i. p. 245) is employed by the Orientals, and with some corruption by the Greeks; but little more than his name can be found in the Mohammedan writers, who are dry and sulky on the subject of the first crusade (De Guignes, tom. iii. p. ii. p. 10–30).

81. On the fortifications, engines, and sieges of the middle ages, see Muratori (Antiquitat. Italiæ, tom. ii. dissert. xxvi. p. 452–524). The *belfredus*,

from whence our belfry, was the movable tower of the ancients (Ducange, tom. i. p. 608).

82. I cannot forbear remarking the resemblance between the siege and lake of Nice with the operations of Hernan Cortez before Mexico. See Dr. Robertson, Hist. of America, l. v.

83. *Mécréant*, a word invented by the French crusaders, and confined in that language to its primitive sense. It should seem that the zeal of our ancestors boiled higher, and that they branded every unbeliever as a rascal. A similar prejudice still lurks in the minds of many who think themselves Christians.

84. Baronius has produced a very doubtful letter to his brother Roger (A.D. 1098, No. 15). The enemies consisted of Medes, Persians, Chaldæans: be it so. The first attack was cum nostro incommodo; true and tender. But why Godfrey of Bouillon and Hugh *brothers?* Tancred is styled *filius*—of whom? certainly not of Roger, nor of Bohemond.

85. Verumtamen dicunt se esse de Francorum generatione; et quia nullus homo naturaliter debet esse miles nisi Franci et Turci (Gesta Francorum, p. 7). The same community of blood and valour is attested by archbishop Baldric (p. 99).

86. *Balista, Balestra, Arbalestre*. See Muratori, Antiq. tom. ii. p. 517–524; Ducange, Gloss. Latin. tom. i. p. 531, 532. In the time of Anna Comnena, this weapon, which she describes under the name of *tzangra*, was unknown in the East (l. x. p. 291). By a humane inconsistency, the pope strove to prohibit it in Christian wars.

87. The curious reader may compare the classic learning of Cellarius and the geographical science of D'Anville. William of Tyre is the only historian of the crusades who has any knowledge of antiquity; and M. Otter trod almost in the footsteps of the Franks from Constantinople to Antioch (Voyage en Turquie et en Perse, tom. i. p. 35–88).

88. This detached conquest of Edessa is best represented by Fulcherius Carnotensis, or of Chartres (in the collections of Bongarsius, Duchesne, and Martenne), the valiant chaplain of Count Baldwin (Esprit des Croisades, tom. i. p. 13, 14). In the disputes of that prince with Tancred, his partiality is encountered by the partiality of Radulphus Cadomensis, the soldier and historian of the gallant marquis.

89. See De Guignes, Hist. des Huns, tom. i. p. 456.

90. For Antioch, see Pocock (Description of the East, vol. ii. p. i. p. 188–193), Otter (Voyage en Turquie, etc. tom. i. p. 81, etc.), the Turkish geographer (in Otter's notes), the Index Geographicus of Schultens (ad calcem Bohadin. Vit. Saladin.), and Abulfeda (Tabula Syriæ, p. 115, 116, vers. Reiske).

91. Ensem elevat, eumque à sinistrâ parte scapularum tantâ virtute intorsit, quòd pectus medium disjunxit, spinam et vitalia interrupit, et sic lubricus ensis super crus dextrum integer exivit; sicque caput integrum cum dextrâ parte corporis immersit gurgite, partemque quæ equo præsidebat remisit civitati (Robert. Mon. p. 50). Cujus ense trajectus, Turcus duo factus est Turci; ut inferior alter in urbem equitaret, alter arcitenens in flumine nataret (Radulph. Cadom. c. 53, p. 304). Yet he justifies the deed by the *stupendis* viribus of Godfrey; and William of Tyre covers it by obstupuit populus facti novitate . . . mirabilis (l. v. c. 6, p. 701). Yet it must not have appeared incredible to the knights of that age.

92. See the exploits of Robert, Raymond, and the modest Tancred, who imposed silence on his squire (Radulph. Cadom. c. 53).

93. After mentioning the distress and humble petition of the Franks, Abulpharagius adds the haughty reply of Codbuka, or Kerboga: "Non evasuri estis nisi per gladium" (Dynast. p. 242).

94. In describing the host of Kerboga, most of the Latin historians, the author of the Gesta (p. 17), Robert Monachus (p. 56), Baldric (p. 111), Fulcherius Carnotensis (p. 392), Guibert (p. 512), William of Tyre (l. vi. c. 3, p. 714), Bernard Thesaurarius (c. 39, p. 695), are content with the vague expressions of infinita multitudo, immensum agmen, innumeræ copiæ or gentes, which correspond with the μετὰ ἀναριθμήτων χιλιάδων of Anna Comnena (Alexias, l. xi. p. 318–320). The numbers of the Turks are fixed by Albert Aquensis at 200,000 (l. iv. c. 10, p. 242), and by Radulphus Cadomensis at 400,000 horse (c. 72, p. 309).

95. See the tragic and scandalous fate of an archdeacon of royal birth, who was slain by the Turks as he reposed in an orchard, playing at dice with a Syrian concubine.

96. The value of an ox rose from five solidi (fifteen shillings) at Christmas to two marks (four pounds), and afterwards much higher; a kid or lamb, from one shilling to eighteen of our present money: in the second famine, a loaf of bread, or the head of an animal, sold for a piece of gold. More examples might be produced; but it is the ordinary, not the extraordinary, prices that deserve the notice of the philosopher.

97. Alii multi, quorum nomina non tenemus; quia, deleta de libro vitæ, præsenti operi non sunt inserenda (Will. Tyr. l. vi. c. 5, p. 715). Guibert (p. 518, 523 [l. v. c. 25; l. vi. c. 11]) attempts to excuse Hugh the Great, and even Stephen of Chartres.

98. See the progress of the crusade, the retreat of Alexius, the victory of Antioch, and the conquest of Jerusalem, in the Alexiad. l. xi. p. 317–327. Anna was so prone to exaggeration, that she magnifies the exploits of the Latins.

99. The Mohammedan Aboulmahasen (apud De Guignes, tom. ii. p. ii. p. 95) is more correct in his account of the holy lance than the Christians, Anna Comnena and Abulpharagius: the Greek princess confounds it with the nail of the cross (l. xi. p. 326); the Jacobite primate, with St. Peter's staff (p. 242).

100. The two antagonists who express the most

intimate knowledge and the strongest conviction of the *miracle* and of the *fraud* are Raymond de Agiles and Radulphus Cadomensis, the one attached to the count of Toulouse, the other to the Norman prince. Fulcherius Carnotensis presumes to say, Audite fraudem et non fraudem! and afterwards, Invenit lanceam, fallaciter occultatam forsitan. The rest of the herd are loud and strenuous.

101. See M. de Guignes, tom. ii. p. ii. p. 223, etc.; and the articles of *Barkiarok, Mohammed, Sangiar,* in D'Herbelot.

102. The emir, or sultan Aphdal, recovered Jerusalem and Tyre, A.H. 489 (Renaudot, Hist. Patriarch. Alexandrin. p. 478; De Guignes, tom. i. p. 249, from Abulfeda and Ben Schounah). Jerusalem ante adventum vestrum recuperavimus, Turcos ejecimus, say the Fatimite ambassadors.

103. See the transactions between the caliph of Egypt and the crusaders in William of Tyre (l. iv. c. 24, l. vi. c. 19) and Albert Aquensis (l. iii. c. 59 [p. 234]), who are more sensible of their importance than the contemporary writers.

104. The greatest part of the march of the Franks is traced, and most accurately traced, in Maundrell's Journey from Aleppo to Jerusalem (p. 11–67); un des meilleurs morçeaux, sans contredit, qu'on ait dans ce genre (D'Anville, Mémoire sur Jérusalem, p. 27).

105. See the masterly description of Tacitus (Hist. v. 11, 12, 13), who supposes that the Jewish lawgivers had provided for a perpetual state of hostility against the rest of mankind.

106. The lively scepticism of Voltaire is balanced with sense and erudition by the French author of the Esprit des Croisades (tom. iv. p. 386–388), who observes, that, according to the Arabians, the inhabitants of Jerusalem must have exceeded 200,000; that, in the siege of Titus, Josephus collects 1,300,000 Jews; that they are stated by Tacitus himself at 600,000; and that the largest defalcation that his *accepimus* can justify will still leave them more numerous than the Roman army.

107. Maundrell, who diligently perambulated the walls, found a circuit of 4630 paces, or 4167 English yards (p. 109, 110): from an authentic plan D'Anville concludes a measure nearly similar, of 1960 French *toises* (p. 23–29), in his scarce and valuable tract. For the topography of Jerusalem, see Reland (Palestina, tom. ii. p. 832–860).

108. Jerusalem was possessed only of the torrent of Kedron, dry in summer, and of the little spring or brook of Siloe (Reland, tom. i. p. 294, 300). Both strangers and natives complained of the want of water, which, in time of war, was studiously aggravated. Within the city, Tacitus mentions a perennial fountain, an aqueduct and cisterns for rain-water. The aqueduct was conveyed from the rivulet Tekoe or Etham, which is likewise mentioned by Bohadin (in Vit. Saladin. p. 238).

109. Gierusalemme Liberata, canto xiii. It is pleasant enough to observe how Tasso has copied

and embellished the minutest details of the siege.

110. Besides the Latins, who are not ashamed of the massacre, see Elmacin (Hist. Saracen. p. 363), Abulpharagius (Dynast. p. 243), and M. de Guignes (tom. ii. p. ii. p. 99), from Aboulmahasen.

111. The old tower Psephina, in the middle ages Neblosa, was named Castellum Pisanum, from the patriarch Daimbert. It is still the citadel, the residence of the Turkish aga, and commands a prospect of the Dead Sea, Judea, and Arabia (D'Anville, p. 19–23). It was likewise called the Tower of David, πυργὸς παμμεγέθέστατος.

112. Hume, in his History of England, vol. i. p. 311, 312, octavo edition.

113. Voltaire, in his Essai sur l'Histoire Générale, tom. ii. c. 54, p. 345, 346.

114. The English ascribe to Robert of Normandy, and the Provincials to Raymond of Toulouse, the glory of refusing the crown; but the honest voice of tradition has preserved the memory of the ambition and revenge (Villehardouin, No. 136) of the count of St. Giles. He died at the siege of Tripoli, which was possessed by his descendants.

115. See the election, the battle of Ascalon, etc., in William of Tyre, l. ix. c. 1–12, and in the conclusion of the Latin historians of the first crusade.

116. Renaudot, Hist. Patriarch. Alex. p. 479.

117. See the claims of the patriarch Daimbert, in William of Tyre (l. ix. c. 15–18, x. 4, 7, 9), who asserts with marvellous candour the independence of the conquerors and kings of Jerusalem.

118. Willerm. Tyr. l. x. 19. The Historia Hierosolimitana of Jacobus à Vitriaco (l. i. c. 21–50), and the Secreta Fidelium Crucis of Marinus Sanutus (l. iii. p. 1 [7?]), describe the state and conquests of the Latin kingdom of Jerusalem.

119. An actual muster, not including the tribes of Levi and Benjamin, gave David an army of 1,300,000 or 1,574,000 fighting men; which, with the addition of women, children, and slaves, may imply a population of thirteen millions, in a country sixty leagues in length and thirty broad. The honest and rational Le Clerc (Comment. on 2nd Samuel, xxiv. and 1st Chronicles, xxi.) æstuat augusto in limite, and mutters his suspicion of a false transcript; a dangerous suspicion!

120. These sieges are related, each in its proper place, in the great history of William of Tyre, from the ninth to the eighteenth book, and more briefly told by Bernardus Thesaurarius (de Acquisitione Terræ Sanctæ, c. 87–98, p. 732–740). Some domestic facts are celebrated in the Chronicles of Pisa, Genoa, and Venice, in the sixth, ninth, and twelfth tomes of Muratori.

121. Quidam populus de insulis occidentis egressus, et maxime de eâ parte quæ Norvegia dicitur. William of Tyre (l. xi. c. 14, p. 804) marks their course per Britannicum mare et Calpen to the siege of Sidon.

122. Benelathir, apud De Guignes, Hist. des

Huns, tom. ii. part ii. p. 150, 151, A.D. 1127. He must speak of the inland country.

123. Sanut very sensibly descants on the mischiefs of female succession in a land hostibus circumdata, ubi cuncta virilia et virtuosa esse deberent. Yet, at the summons and with the approbation of her feudal lord, a noble damsel was obliged to choose a husband and champion (Assises de Jérusalem, c. 242, etc.). See in M. de Guignes (tom. i. p. 441-471) the accurate and useful tables of these dynasties, which are chiefly drawn from the *Lignages d'Outremer.*

124. They were called by derision *Poullains, Pullani,* and their name is never pronounced without contempt (Ducange, Gloss. Latin. tom. v. p. 535; and Observations sur Joinville, p. 84, 85; Jacob. à Vitriaco, Hist. Hierosol. l. i. c. 67, 72; and Sanut, l. iii. p. viii. c. 2, p. 182). Illustrium virorum qui ad Terræ Sanctæ . . . liberationem in ipsâ manserunt degeneres filii . . . in deliciis enutriti, molles et effeminati, etc.

125. This authentic detail is extracted from the Assises de Jérusalem (c. 324, 326-331). Sanut (l. iii. p. viii. c. 1, p. 174) reckons only 518 knights and 5775 followers.

126. The sum total, and the division, ascertain the service of the three great baronies at 100 knights each; and the text of the Assises, which extends the number to 500, can only be justified by this supposition.

127. Yet on great emergencies (says Sanut) the barons brought a voluntary aid; decentem comitivam militum juxta statum suum.

128. William of Tyre (l. xviii. c. 3, 4, 5) relates the noble origin and early insolence of the Hospitalers, who soon deserted their humble patron, St. John the Eleemosynary, for the more august character of St. John the Baptist (see the ineffectual struggles of Pagi, Critica, A.D. 1099, No. 14-18). They assumed the profession of arms about the year 1120; the Hospital was *mater;* the Temple *filia;* the Teutonic order was founded A.D. 1190, at the siege of Acre (Mosheim, Institut. p. 389, 390).

129. See St. Bernard de Laude Novæ Militiæ Templi, composed A.D. 1132-1136, in Opp. tom. i. p. ii. p. 547-563, edit. Mabillon, Venet. 1750. Such an encomium, which is thrown away on the dead Templars, would be highly valued by the historians of Malta.

130. Matthew Paris, Hist. Major, p. 544. He assigns to the Hospitalers 19,000, to the Templars 9000 *maneria,* a word of much higher import (as Ducange has rightly observed) in the English than in the French idiom. *Manor* is a lordship, *manoir* a dwelling.

131. In the three first books of the Histoire des Chevaliers de Malthe, par l'Abbé de Vertot, the reader may amuse himself with a fair, and sometimes flattering, picture of the order, while it was employed for the defence of Palestine. The subsequent books pursue their emigrations to Rhodes and Malta.

132. The Assises de Jérusalem, in old law French, were printed with Beaumanoir's Coûtumes de Beauvoisis (Bourges and Paris, 1690, in folio), and illustrated by Gaspard Thaumas de la Thaumassière with a comment and glossary. An Italian version had been published in 1535, at Venice, for the use of the kingdom of Cyprus.

133. A la terre perdue, tout fut perdû, is the vigorous expression of the Assise (c. 281). Yet Jerusalem capitulated with Saladin; the queen and the principal Christians departed in peace; and a code so precious and so portable could not provoke the avarice of the conquerors. I have sometimes suspected the existence of this original copy of the Holy Sepulchre, which might be invented to sanctify and authenticate the traditionary customs of the French in Palestine.

134. A noble lawyer, Raoul de Tabarie, denied the prayer of king Amauri (A.D. 1195-1205), that he would commit his knowledge to writing, and frankly declared, que de ce qu'il savoit ne feroit-il ja nul borjois son pareill, ne nul sage homme lettré (c. 281).

135. The compiler of this work, Jean d'Ibelin, was count of Jaffa and Ascalon, lord of Baruth (Berytus) and Rames, and died A.D. 1266 (Sanut. l. iii. p. xii. c. 5, 8 [p. 220, 222]). The family of Ibelin, which descended from a younger brother of a count of Chartres in France, long flourished in Palestine and Cyprus (see the Lignages de deça Mer, or d'Outremer, c. 6, at the end of the Assises de Jérusalem, an original book, which records the pedigrees of the French adventurers).

136. By sixteen commissioners chosen in the states of the island: the work was finished the 3rd of November, 1369, sealed with four seals, and deposited in the cathedral of Nicosia (see the preface to the Assises).

137. The cautious John d'Ibelin argues, rather than affirms, that Tripoli is the fourth barony, and expresses some doubt concerning the right or pretension of the constable and marshal ([Assises de Jérus.] c. 324).

138. Entre seignor et homme n'a que la foi; . . . mais tant que l'homme doit à son seignor reverence en toutes choses (c. 206). Tous les hommes dudit royaume sont par ladite Assise tenus les uns as autres . . . et en celle maniere que le seignor mette main ou face mettre au cors ou au fié d'aucun d'yaus sans esgard et sans connoissance de court, que tous les autres doivent venir devant le seignor, etc. (212). The form of their remonstrances is conceived with the noble simplicity of freedom.

139. See The Spirit of Laws, l. xxviii. In the forty years since its publication, no work has been more read and criticised; and the spirit of inquiry which it has excited is not the least of our obligations to the author.

140. For the intelligence of this obscure and obsolete jurisprudence (c. 80-111) I am deeply indebted to the friendship of a learned lord, who,

with an accurate and discerning eye, has surveyed the philosophic history of law. By his studies posterity might be enriched: the merit of the orator and the judge can be *felt* only by his contemporaries.

141. Louis le Gros, who is considered as the father of this institution in France, did not begin his reign till nine years (A.D. 1108) after Godfrey of Bouillon (Assises, c. 2, 324). For its origin and effects see the judicious remarks of Dr. Robertson (History of Charles V. vol. i. p. 30–36, 251–265, quarto edition).

142. Every reader conversant with the historians of the crusades will understand, by the peuple des Suriens, the Oriental Christians, Melchites, Jacobites, or Nestorians, who had all adopted the use of the Arabic language (vol. iv. p. 593).

143. See the Assises de Jérusalem (c. 310, 311, 312). These laws were enacted as late as the year 1350, in the kingdom of Cyprus. In the same century, in the reign of Edward I., I understand, from a late publication (of his Book of Account), that the price of a war-horse was not less exorbitant in England.

Chapter LIX

1. Anna Comnena relates her father's conquests in Asia Minor, Alexiad, l. xi. p. 321–325, l. xiv. p. 419; his Cilician war against Tancred and Bohemond, p. 328–342; the war of Epirus, with tedious prolixity, l. xii. xiii. p. 345–406; the death of Bohemond, l. xiv. p. 419.

2. The kings of Jerusalem submitted however to a nominal dependence, and in the dates of their inscriptions (one is still legible in the church of Bethlehem) they respectfully placed before their own the name of the reigning emperor (Ducange, Dissertations sur Joinville, xxvii. p. 319).

3. Anna Comnena adds [l. xi. p. 341], that, to complete the imitation, he was shut up with a dead cock; and condescends to wonder how the barbarian could endure the confinement and putrefaction. This absurd tale is unknown to the Latins.

4. Ἀπὸ Θύλης, in the Byzantine geography, must mean England; yet we are more credibly informed that our Henry I. would not suffer him to levy any troops in his kingdom (Ducange, Not. ad Alexiad. p. 41).

5. The copy of the treaty (Alexiad, l. xiii. p. 406–416) is an original and curious piece, which would require, and might afford, a good map of the principality of Antioch.

6. See in the learned work of M. de Guignes (tom. ii. part ii.) the history of the Seljukians of Iconium, Aleppo, and Damascus, as far as it may be collected from the Greeks, Latins, and Arabians. The last are ignorant or regardless of the affairs of *Roum*.

7. Iconium is mentioned as a station by Xenophon, and by Strabo with the ambiguous title of Κωμόπολις (Cellarius, tom. ii. p. 121). Yet St. Paul found in that place a multitude (πλῆθος) of Jews and Gentiles. Under the corrupt name of *Kunijah*, it is described as a great city, with a river and gardens, three leagues from the mountains, and decorated (I know not why) with Plato's tomb (Abulfeda, tabul. xvii. p. 303, vers. Reiske; and the Index Geographicus of Schultens from Ibn Said).

8. For this supplement to the first crusade see Anna Comnena (Alexias, l. xi. p. 331, etc., and the eighth book of Albert Aquensis).

9. For the second crusade, of Conrad III. and Louis VII. see William of Tyre (l. xvi. c. 18–29), Otho of Frisingen (l. i. c. 34–45, 59, 60), Matthew Paris (Hist. Major. p. 68), Struvius (Corpus Hist. Germanicæ, p. 372, 373), Scriptores Rerum Francicarum à Duchesne, tom. iv.; Nicetas, in Vit. Manuel, l. i. c. 4, 5, 6, p. 41–48 [p. 80–96, ed. Bonn]; Cinnamus, l. ii. p. 41–49 [ed. Par.; p. 73–89, ed. Bonn].

10. For the third crusade of Frederic Barbarossa, see Nicetas in Isaac. Angel. l. ii. c. 3–8, p. 257–266 [p. 524–544, ed. Bonn]; Struv. (Corpus Hist. Germ. p. 414); and two historians, who probably were spectators, Tagino (in Scriptor. Freher. tom. i. p. 406–416, edit. Struv.), and the Anonymous de Expeditione Asiaticâ Fred. I. (in Canisii Antiq. Lection. tom. iii. p. ii. p. 498–526, edit. Basnage).

11. Anna, who states these later swarms at 40,000 horse and 100,000 foot, calls them Normans, and places at their head two brothers of Flanders. The Greeks were strangely ignorant of the names, families, and possessions of the Latin princes.

12. William of Tyre, and Matthew Paris, reckon 70,000 loricati in each of the armies.

13. The imperfect enumeration is mentioned by Cinnamus (ἐννενήοντα μυριάδες [p. 69, ed. Bonn]), and confirmed by Odo de Diogilo apud Ducange with the more precise sum of 900,556. Why must therefore the version and comment suppose the modest and insufficient reckoning of 90,000? Does not Godfrey of Viterbo (Pantheon, p. xix. in Muratori, tom. vii. p. 462) exclaim—

——Numerum si noscere quæras,
Millia millena militis agmen erat.

14. This extravagant account is given by Albert of Stade (apud Struvium, p. 414); my calculation is borrowed from Godfrey of Viterbo, Arnold of Lubeck, apud eundem, and Bernard Thesaur. (c. 169, p. 804). The original writers are silent. The Mohammedans gave him 200,000 or 260,000 men

(Bohadin, in Vit. Saladin. p. 110 [P. ii. c. 61]).

15. I must observe that, in the second and third crusades, the subjects of Conrad and Frederic are styled by the Greeks and Orientals *Alamanni*. The Lechi and Tzechi of Cinnamus are the Poles and Bohemians; and it is for the French that he reserves the ancient appellation of Germans. He likewise names the Βρίττιοι, or Βριτavvoí.

16. Nicetas was a child at the second crusade, but in the third he commanded against the Franks the important post of Philippopolis. Cinnamus is infected with national prejudice and pride.

17. The conduct of the Philadelphians is blamed by Nicetas, while the anonymous German accuses the rudeness of his countrymen (culpâ nostrâ). History would be pleasant if we were embarrassed only by *such* contradictions. It is likewise from Nicetas that we learn the pious and humane sorrow of Frederic.

18. Χθαμάλη ἕδρα, which Cinnamus translates into Latin by the word Σέλλιον [p. 83, ed. Bonn]. Ducange works very hard to save his king and country from such ignominy (sur Joinville, dissertat. xxvii. p. 317–320). Louis afterwards insisted on a meeting in mari ex æquo, not ex equo, according to the laughable readings of some MSS.

19. Ego Romanorum imperator sum, ille Romaniorum (Anonym. Canis. p. 512). The public and historical style of the Greeks was Ρὴξ . . . *princeps*. Yet Cinnamus owns that Ἰμπεράτωρ is synonymous to Βασιλεύς [p. 69, ed. Bonn].

20. In the Epistles of Innocent III. (xiii. p. 184), and the History of Bohadin (p. 129, 130), see the views of a pope and a cadhi on this *singular* toleration.

21. As counts of Vexin, the kings of France were the vassals and advocates of the monastery of St. Denys. The saint's peculiar banner, which they received from the abbot, was of a square form, and a red or *flaming* colour. The *oriflamme* appeared at the head of the French armies from the twelfth to the fifteenth century (Ducange sur Joinville, dissert. xviii. p. 244–253).

22. The original French histories of the second crusade are the Gesta Ludovici VII., published in the fourth volume of Duchesne's collection. The same volume contains many original letters of the king, of Suger his minister, etc., the best documents of authentic history.

23. Terram horroris et salsuginis, terram siccam, sterilem, inamœnam. Anonym. Canis. p. 517. The emphatic language of a sufferer.

24. Gens innumera, sylvestris, indomita, prædones sine ductore. The sultan of Cogni might sincerely rejoice in their defeat. Anonym. Canis. p. 517, 518.

25. See in the anonymous writer in the Collection of Canisius, Tagino, and Bohadin (Vit. Saladin. p. 119, 120 [P. ii. c. 69]), the ambiguous conduct of Kilidge Arslan, sultan of Cogni, who hated and feared both Saladin and Frederic.

26. The desire of comparing two great men has tempted many writers to drown Frederic in the river Cydnus, in which Alexander so imprudently bathed (Q. Curt. l. iii. c. 4, 5). But, from the march of the emperor, I rather judge that his Saleph is the Calycadnus, a stream of less fame, but of a longer course.

27. Marianus Sanutus, A.D. 1321, lays it down as a precept, Quod stolus ecclesiæ per terram nullatenus est ducenda. He resolves, by the Divine aid, the objection, or rather exception, of the first crusade (Secreta Fidelium Crucis, l. ii. pars. ii. c. i. p. 37).

28. The most authentic information of St. Bernard must be drawn from his own writings, published in a correct edition by Père Mabillon, and reprinted at Venice, 1750, in six volumes in folio. Whatever friendship could recollect, or superstition could add, is contained in the two lives, by his disciples, in the sixth volume: whatever learning and criticism could ascertain, may be found in the prefaces of the Benedictine editor.

29. Clairvaux, surnamed the Valley of Absynth, is situate among the woods near Bar sur Aube in Champagne. St. Bernard would blush at the pomp of the church and monastery; he would ask for the library, and I know not whether he would be much edified by a tun of 800 muids (914 1-7th hogsheads), which almost rivals that of Heidelberg (Mélanges tirés d'une Grande Bibliothèque, tom. xlvi. p. 15–20).

30. The disciples of the saint (Vit. ima. l. iii. c. 2, p. 1232; Vit. iida. c. 16, No. 45, p. 1383) record a marvelous example of his pious apathy. Juxta lacum etiam Lausannensem totius diei itinere pergens, penitus non attendit aut se videre non vidit. Cum enim vespere facto de eodem lacú socii colloquerentur, interrogabat eos ubi lacus ille esset; et mirati sunt universi. To admire or despise St. Bernard as he ought, the reader, like myself, should have before the windows of his library the beauties of that incomparable landscape.

31. Otho Frising. l. i. c. 4 [34]; Bernard. Epist. 363, ad Francos Orientales; Opp. tom. i. p. 328; Vit. ima. l. iii. c. 4, tom. vi. p. 1235.

32. Mandastis et obedivi . . . multiplicati sunt super numerum; vacuantur urbes et castella; et *pene* jam non inveniunt quem apprehendant septem mulieres unum virum; adeo ubique viduæ vivis remanent viris. Bernard, Epist. 247 [p. 246, ed. Bened.]. We must be careful not to construe *pene* as a substantive.

33. Quis ego sum ut disponam acies, ut egrediar ante facies armatorum? aut quid tam remotum a professione meâ, [etiam] si vires, [suppeterent, etiam] si peritia [non deesset], etc. Epist. 256, tom. i. p. 259 [p. 258, ed. Bened.]. He speaks with contempt of the hermit Peter, vir quidam. Epist. 363.

34. Sic [sed] dicunt forsitan isti, unde scimus quod a Domino sermo egresssus sit? Quæ signa tu facis ut credamus tibi? Non est quod ad ista ipse respondeam; parcendum verecundiæ meæ. Res-

ponde tu pro me, et pro te ipso, secundum quæ vidisti et audisti, et [aut certe] secundum quod te [tibi] inspiraverit Deus. Consolat. [De Considerat.] l. ii. c. 1; Opp. tom. ii. p. 421–423 [p. 417, ed. Bened.].

35. See the testimonies in Vita ima. l. iv. c. 5, 6; Opp. tom. vi. p. 1258–1261, l. vi. c. 1–17, p. 1286–1314.

36. Abulmahasen apud De Guignes, Hist. des Huns, tom. ii. p. ii. p. 99.

37. See his *article* in the Bibliothèque Orientale of D'Herbelot, and De Guignes, tom. ii. p. i. p. 230–261. Such was his valour, that he was styled the second Alexander; and such the extravagant love of his subjects, that they prayed for the sultan a year after his decease. Yet Sangiar might have been made prisoner by the Franks, as well as by the Uzes. He reigned near fifty years (A.D. 1103–1152), and was a munificent patron of Persian poetry.

38. See the Chronology of the Atabeks of Irak and Syria, in De Guignes, tom. i. p. 254; and the reigns of Zenghi and Noureddin in the same writer (tom. ii. p. ii. p. 147–221), who uses the Arabic text of Benelathir, Ben Schounah, and Abulfeda; the Bibliothèque Orientale, under the articles *Atabeks* and *Noureddin*, and the Dynasties of Abulpharagius, p. 250–267, vers. Pocock.

39. William of Tyre (l. xvi. c. 4, 5, 7) describes the loss of Edessa, and the death of Zenghi. The corruption of his name into *Sanguin* afforded the Latins a comfortable allusion to his *sanguinary* character and end, fit sanguine sanguinolentus.

40. Noradinus (says William of Tyre, l. xx. 33 [p. 995]) maximus nominis et fidei Christianæ persecutor; princeps tamen justus, vafer, providus, et secundum gentis suæ traditiones religiosus. To this Catholic witness we may add the primate of the Jacobites (Abulpharag. p. 267), quo non alter erat inter reges vitæ ratione magis laudabili, aut quæ pluribus justitiæ experimentis abundaret. The true praise of kings is after their death, and from the mouth of their enemies.

41. From the ambassador, William of Tyre (l. xix. c. 17, 18) describes the palace of Cairo. In the caliph's treasure were found a pearl as large as a pigeon's egg, a ruby weighing seventeen Egyptian drachms, an emerald a palm and a half in length, and many vases of crystal and porcelain of China (Renaudot, p. 526).

42. *Mamluc*, plur. *Mamalic*, is defined by Pocock (Prolegom. ad Abulpharag. p. 7) and D'Herbelot (p. 545), servum emptitium, seu qui pretio numerato in domini possessionem cedit. They frequently occur in the wars of Saladin (Bohadin, p. 236, etc.); and it was only the *Bahartie* Mamalukes that were first introduced into Egypt by his descendants.

43. Jacobus à Vitriaco (p. 1116) gives the king of Jerusalem no more than 370 knights. Both the Franks and the Moslems report the superior numbers of the enemy—a difference which may be solved by counting or omitting the unwarlike Egyptians.

44. It was the Alexandria of the Arabs, a middle term in extent and riches between the period of the Greeks and Romans and that of the Turks (Savary, Lettres sur l'Egypte, tom. i. p. 25, 26).

45. For this great revolution of Egypt, see William of Tyre (l. xix. 5, 6, 7, 12–31; xx. 5–12), Bohadin (in Vit. Saladin. p. 30–39), Abulfeda (in Excerpt. Schultens, p. 1–12), D'Herbelot (Biblioth. Orient. *Adhed, Fathemah*, but very incorrect), Renaudot (Hist. Patriarch. Alex. p. 522–525, 532–537), Vertot (Hist. des Chevaliers de Malthe, tom. i. p. 141–163, in 4to), and M. de Guignes (tom. ii. p. ii. p. 185–215).

46. For the Curds, see De Guignes, tom. i. p. 416, 417; the Index Geographicus of Schultens; and Tavernier, Voyages, p. i. p. 308, 309. The Ayoubites descended from the tribe of the Rawadiæi, one of the noblest; but as *they* were infected with the heresy of the Metempsychosis, the orthodox sultans insinuated that their descent was only on the mother's side, and that their ancestor was a stranger who settled among the Curds.

47. See the fourth book of the Anabasis of Xenophon. The ten thousand suffered more from the arrows of the free Carduchians than from the splendid weakness of the Great King.

48. We are indebted to the Professor Schultens (Lugd. Bat. 1755, in folio) for the richest and most authentic materials, a Life of Saladin by his friend and minister the Cadhi Bohadin, and copious extracts from the history of his kinsman the prince Abulfeda of Hamah. To these we may add the article of *Salaheddin* in the Bibliothèque Orientale, and all that may be gleaned from the Dynasties of Abulpharagius.

49. Since Abulfeda was himself an Ayoubite, he may share the praise for imitating, at least tacitly, the modesty of the founder.

50. Hist. Hierosol. in the Gesta Dei per Francos, p. 1152. A similar example may be found in Joinville (p. 42, édition du Louvre); but the pious St. Louis refused to dignify infidels with the order of Christian knighthood (Ducange, Observations, p. 70).

51. In these Arabic titles *religionis* must always be understood; *Noureddin*, lumen r.; *Ezzodin*, decus; *Amadoddin*, columen: our hero's proper name was Joseph, and he was styled *Salahoddin*, salus; *Al Malichus, Al Nasirus*, rex defensor; *Abu Modaffir*, pater victoriæ. Schultens, Præfat.

52. Abulfeda, who descended from a brother of Saladin, observes, from many examples, that the founders of dynasties took the guilt for themselves, and left the reward to their innocent collaterals (Excerpt. p. 10).

53. See his life and character in Renaudot, p.

54. His civil and religious virtues are celebrated in the first chapter of Bohadin (p. 4–30), himself an eye-witness and an honest bigot.

55. In many works, particularly Joseph's well in

the castle of Cairo, the sultan and the patriarch have been confounded by the ignorance of natives and travellers.

56. Anonym. Canisii, tom. iii. p. ii. p. 504.

57. Bohadin, p. 129, 130.

58. For the Latin kingdom of Jerusalem, see William of Tyre, from the ninth to the twenty-second book; Jacob. à Vitriaco, Hist. Hierosolem. l. i.; and Sanutus, Secreta Fidelium Crucis, l. iii. p. vi. vii. viii. ix.

59. Templarii ut apes bombatant et Hospitalarii ut venti stridebant, et barones se exitio offerebant, et Turcopuli (the Christian light troops) semet ipsi in ignem injiciebant (Ispahani de Expugnatione Kudsiticâ, p. 18, apud Schultens)—a specimen of Arabian eloquence somewhat different from the style of Xenophon!

60. The Latins affirm, the Arabians insinuate, the treason of Raymond; but, had he really embraced their religion, he would have been a saint and a hero in the eyes of the latter.

61. Renaud, Reginald, or Arnold de Châtillon, is celebrated by the Latins in his life and death; but the circumstances of the latter are more distinctly related by Bohadin and Abulfeda; and Joinville (Hist. de St. Louis, p. 70) alludes to the practice of Saladin, of never putting to death a prisoner who had tasted his bread and salt. Some of the companions of Arnold had been slaughtered, and almost sacrificed, in a valley of Mecca, ubi sacrificia mactantur (Abulfeda, p. 32).

62. Vertot, who well describes the loss of the kingdom and city (Hist. des Chevaliers de Malthe, tom. i. l. ii. p. 226–278), inserts two original epistles of a knight templar.

63. Renaudot, Hist. Patriarch. Alex. p. 545.

64. For the conquest of Jerusalem, Bohadin (p. 67–75 [P. ii. c. 35, 36] and Abulfeda (p. 40–43) are our Moslem witnesses. Of the Christian, Bernard Thesaurarius (c. 151–167) is the most copious and authentic; see likewise Matthew Paris (p. 120–124).

65. The sieges of Tyre and Acre are most copiously described by Bernard Thesaurarius (de Acquisitione Terræ Sanctæ, c. 167–179), the author of the Historia Hierosolymitana (p. 1150–1172, in Bongarsius), Abulfeda (p. 43–50) and Bohadin (p. 75–179).

66. I have followed a moderate and probable representation of the fact: by Vertot, who adopts without reluctance a romantic tale, the old marquis is actually exposed to the darts of the besieged.

67. Northmanni et Gothi, et cæteri populi insularum quæ inter occidentem et septemtrionem sitæ sunt, gentes bellicosæ, corporis proceri, mortis intrepidæ, bipennibus armatæ, navibus rotundis, quæ Ysnachiæ dicuntur, advectæ.

68. The historian of Jerusalem (p. 1168) adds the nations of the East from the Tigris to India, and the swarthy tribes of Moors and Getulians, so that Asia and Africa fought against Europe.

69. Bohadin, p. 183 [P. ii. c. 115]; and this mas-

sacre is neither denied nor blamed by the Christian historians. Alacriter jussa complentes (the English soldiers), says Galfridus à Vinesauf (l. iv. c. 4, p. 346), who fixes at 2700 the number of victims, who are multiplied to 5000 by Roger Hoveden (p. 697, 698). The humanity or avarice of Philip Augustus was persuaded to ransom his prisoners (Jacob à Vitriaco, l. i. c. 99, p. 1122).

70. Bohadin, p. 14. He quotes the judgment of Balianus and the prince of Sidon, and adds, ex illo mundo quasi hominum paucissimi redierunt. Among the Christians who died before St. John d'Acre, I find the English names of De Ferres earl of Derby (Dugdale, Baronage, part i. p. 260), Mowbray (idem. p. 124), De Mandevil, De Fiennes, St. John, Scrope, Pigot, Talbot, etc.

71. Magnus hic apud eos, interque reges eorum tum virtute, tum majestate eminens . . . summus rerum arbiter (Bohadin, p. 159 [P. ii. c. 95]). He does not seem to have known the names either of Philip or Richard.

72. Rex Angliæ, præstrenuus . . . rege Gallorum minor apud eos censebatur ratione regni atque dignitatis; sed tum divitiis florentior, tum bellicâ virtute multo erat celebrior (Bohadin, p. 161 [P. ii. c. 97]). A stranger might admire those riches; the national historians will tell with what lawless and wasteful oppression they were collected.

73. Joinville, p. 17. Cuides-tu que ce soit le roi Richart?

74. Yet he was guilty in the opinion of the Moslems, who attest the confession of the assassins that they were sent by the king of England (Bohadin, p. 225 [P. ii. c. 144]); and his only defence is an absurd and palpable forgery (Hist. de l'Académie des Inscriptions, tom. xvi. p. 155–163), a pretended letter from the prince of the assassins, the Sheich, or old man of the mountain, who justified Richard, by assuming to himself the guilt or merit of the murder.

75. See the distress and pious firmness of Saladin, as they are described by Bohadin (p. 7–9, 235–237), who himself harangued the defenders of Jerusalem; their fears were unknown to the enemy (Jacob. à Vitriaco, l. i. c. 100, p. 1123; Vinisauf, l. v. c. 50, p. 399).

76. Yet, unless the sultan, or an Ayoubite prince, remained in Jerusalem, nec Curdi Turcis, nec Turci essent obtemperaturi Curdis (Bohadin, p. 236 [P. ii. c. 156]). He draws aside a corner of the political curtain.

77. Bohadin (p. 237), and even Jeffrey de Vinisauf (l. vi. c. 1–8, p. 403–409), ascribe the retreat to Richard himself; and Jacobus à Vitriaco observes that, in his impatience to depart, in alterum virum mutatus est (p. 1123). Yet Joinville, a French knight, accuses the envy of Hugh duke of Burgundy (p. 116), without supposing, like Matthew Paris, that he was bribed by Saladin.

78. The expeditions to Ascalon, Jerusalem, and Jaffa, are related by Bohadin (p. 184–249) and Abulfeda (p. 51, 52). The author of the Itinerary,

or the monk of St. Alban's, cannot exaggerate the cadhi's account of the prowess of Richard (Vinisauf, l. vi. c. 14–24, p. 412–421; Hist. Major, p. 137–143); and on the whole of this war there is a marvellous agreement between the Christian and Mohammedan writers, who mutually praise the virtues of their enemies.

79. See the progress of negotiation and hostility in Bohadin (p. 207–260), who was himself an actor in the treaty. Richard declared his intention of returning with new armies to the conquest of the Holy Land; and Saladin answered the menace with a civil compliment (Vinisauf, l. vi. c. 28, p. 423).

80. The most copious and original account of this holy war is Galfridi à Vinisauf, Itinerarium Regis Anglorum Richardi et aliorum in Terram Hierosolymorum, in six books, published in the second volume of Gale's Scriptores Hist. Anglicanæ (p. 247–429). Roger Hoveden and Matthew Paris afford likewise many valuable materials; and the former describes with accuracy the discipline and navigation of the English fleet.

81. Even Vertot (tom. i. p. 251) adopts the foolish notion of the indifference of Saladin, who professed the Koran with his last breath.

82. See the succession of the Ayoubites, in Abulpharagius (Dynast. p. 277, etc.), and the tables of M. de Guignes, l'Art de Vérifier les Dates, and the Bibliothèque Orientale.

83. Thomassin (Discipline de l'Eglise, tom. iii. p. 311–374) has copiously treated of the origin, abuses, and restrictions of these *tenths*. A theory was started, but not pursued, that they were rightfully due to the pope, a tenth of the Levite's tenth to the high priest (Selden on Tithes; see his Works, vol. iii. p. ii. p. 1083).

84. See the Gesta Innocentii III. in Muratori, Script. Rer. Ital. (tom. iii. p. i. p. 486–568).

85. See the fifth crusade, and the siege of Damietta, in Jacobus à Vitriaco (l. iii. p. 1125–1149, in the Gesta Dei of Bongarsius), an eye-witness; Bernard Thesaurarius (in Script. Muratori, tom. vii. p. 825–846, c. 194–207), a contemporary; and Sanutus (Secreta Fidel. Crucis, l. iii. p. xi. c. 4–9), a diligent compiler; and of the Arabians, Abulpharagius (Dynast. p. 294), and the Extracts at the end of Joinville (p. 533, 537, 540, 547, etc.).

86. To those who took the cross against Mainfroy, the pope (A.D. 1255) granted plenissimam peccatorum remissionem. Fidelis mirabantur quod tantum eis promitteret pro sanguine Christianorum effundendo quantum pro cruore infidelium aliquando (Matthew Paris, p. 785). A high flight for the reason of the thirteenth century.

87. This simple idea is agreeable to the good sense of Mosheim (Institut. Hist. Eccles. p. 332) and the fine philosophy of Hume (Hist. of England, vol. i. p. 330).

88. The original materials for the crusade of Frederic II. may be drawn from Richard de St. Germano (in Muratori, Script. Rerum Ital. tom.

vii. p. 1002–1013) and Matthew Paris (p. 286, 291, 300, 302, 304). The most rational moderns are Fleury (Hist. Eccles. tom. xvi.), Vertot (Chevaliers de Malthe, tom. i. l. iii.), Giannone (Istoria Civile di Napoli, tom. ii. l. xvi.), and Muratori (Annali d'Italia, tom. x.).

89. Poor Muratori knows what to think, but knows not what to say: "Chino qui il capo," etc., p. 322.

90. The clergy artfully confounded the mosque or church of the temple with the holy sepulchre, and their wilful error has deceived both Vertot and Muratori.

91. The irruption of the Carizmians, or Corasmins, is related by Matthew Paris (p. 546, 547), and by Joinville, Nangis, and the Arabians (p. 111, 112, 191, 192, 528, 530).

92. Read, if you can, the Life and Miracles of St. Louis, by the confessor of Queen Margaret (p. 291–523, Joinville, du Louvre).

93. He believed all that mother-church taught (Joinville, p. 10), but he cautioned Joinville against disputing with infidels. "L'omme lay (said he in his old language), quand il ot medire de la loy Crestienne, ne doit pas deffendre la loy Crestienne ne mais que de l'espée, dequoi il doit donner parmi le ventre dedens, tant comme elle y peut entrer" (p. 12).

94. I have two editions of Joinville: the one (Paris, 1668) most valuable for the observations of Ducange; the other (Paris au Louvre, 1761) most precious for the pure and authentic text, a MS. of which has been recently discovered. The last editor proves that the history of St. Louis was finished A.D. 1309, without explaining, or even admiring, the age of the author, which must have exceeded ninety years (Preface, p. xi.; Observations de Ducange, p. 17).

95. Joinville, p. 32; Arabic Extracts. p. 549.

96. The last editors have enriched their Joinville with large and curious extracts from the Arabic historians, Macrizi, Abulfeda, etc. See likewise Abulpharagius (Dynast. p. 322–325), who calls him by the corrupt name of *Redefrans*. Matthew Paris (p. 683, 684) has described the rival folly of the French and English who fought and fell at Massoura.

97. Savary, in his agreeable Lettres sur l'Egypte, has given a description of Damietta (tom. i. lettre xxiii. p. 274–290), and a narrative of the expedition of St. Louis (xxv. p. 306–350).

98. For the ransom of St. Louis a million of byzants was asked and granted; but the sultan's generosity reduced that sum to 800,000 byzants, which are valued by Joinville at 400,000 French livres of his own time, and expressed by Matthew Paris by 100,000 marks of silver (Ducange, Dissertation xx. sur Joinville).

99. The idea of the emirs to choose Louis for their sultan is seriously attested by Joinville (p. 77, 78), and does not appear to me so absurd as to M. de Voltaire (Hist. Générale, tom. ii. p. 386,

387). The Mamalukes themselves were strangers, rebels, and equals: they had felt his valour, they hoped his conversion; and such a motion, which was not seconded, might be made perhaps by a secret Christian in their tumultuous assembly.

100. See the expedition in the Annals of St. Louis, by William de Nangis, p. 270-287; and the Arabic Extracts, p. 545, 555, of the Louvre edition of Joinville.

101. Voltaire, Hist. Générale, tom. ii. p. 391.

102. The chronology of the two dynasties of Mamalukes, the Baharites, Turks or Tartars of Kipzak, and the Borgites, Circassians, is given by Pocock (Prolegom. ad Abulpharag. p. 6-31) and De Guignes (tom. i. p. 264-270); their history from Abulfeda, Macrizi, etc., to the beginning of the fifteenth century, by the same M. de Guignes (tom. iv. p. 110-328).

103. Savary, Lettres sur l'Egypte, tom. ii. lettre xv. p. 189-208. I much question the authenticity of this copy; yet it is true that sultan Selim concluded a treaty with the Circassians or Mamalukes of Egypt, and left them in possession of arms, riches, and power. See a new Abrégé de l'Histoire Ottomane, composed in Egypt, and translated by M. Digeon (tom. i. p. 55-58; Paris, 1781), a curious, authentic, and national history.

104. Si totum quo regnum occupârunt tempus respicias, præsertim quod fini propius, reperies illud bellis, pugnis, injuriis, ac rapinis refertum (Al Jannabi, apud Pocock, p. 31). The reign of Mohammed (A.D. 1311-1341) affords an happy exception (De Guignes, tom. iv. p. 208-210).

105. They are now reduced to 8500: but the expense of each Mamaluke may be rated at 100 louis: and Egypt groans under the avarice and insolence of these strangers (Voyages de Volney, tom. i. p. 89-187).

106. See Carte's History of England, vol. ii. p. 165-175, and his original authors, Thomas Wikes and Walter Hemingford (l. iii. c. 34, 35), in Gale's Collection (tom. ii. p. 97, 589-592). They are both ignorant of the princess Eleanor's piety in sucking the poisoned wound, and saving her husband at the risk of her own life.

107. Sanutus, Secret. Fidelium Crucis, l. iii. p. xii. c. 9, and De Guignes, Hist. des Huns, tom. iv. p. 143, from the Arabic historians.

108. The state of Acre is represented in all the chronicles of the times, and most accurately in John Villani, l. vii. c. 144, in Muratori, Scriptores Rerum Italicarum, tom. xiii. p. 337, 338.

109. See the final expulsion of the Franks in Sanutus, l. iii. p. xii. c. 11-22; Abulfeda, Macrizi, etc., in De Guignes, tom. iv. p. 162, 164; and Vertot, tom. i. l. iii. p. 407-428.

Chapter LX

1. In the successive centuries, from the ninth to the eighteenth, Mosheim traces the schism of the Greeks with learning, clearness, and impartiality: the *filioque* (Institut. Hist. Eccles. p. 277), Leo III. p. 303; Photius, p. 307, 308; Michael Cerularius, p. 370, 371, etc.

2. Ἄνδρες δυσσεβεῖς καὶ ἀποτρόπαιοι, ἄνδρες ἐκ σκότους ἀνάδυντες, τῆς γὰρ Ἑσπέριου μοῖρας ὑπῆρχον γεννήματα (Phot. Epist. p. 47, edit. Montacut.). The Oriental patriarch continues to apply the images of thunder, earthquake, hail, wild boar, precursors of Antichrist, etc., etc.

3. The mysterious subject of the procession of the Holy Ghost is discussed in the historical, theological, and controversial sense, or nonsense, by the Jesuit Petavius. (Dogmata Theologica, tom. ii. l. vii. p. 362-440.)

4. Before the shrine of St. Peter he placed two shields of the weight of 94½ pounds of pure silver; on which he inscribed the text of both creeds (utroque symbolo) pro amore et *cautelâ* orthodoxæ fidei (Anastas. in Leon. III. in Muratori, tom. iii. pars. i. p. 208). His language most clearly proves that neither the *filioque* nor the Athanasian creed were received at Rome about the year 830.

5. The Missi of Charlemagne pressed him to declare that all who rejected the filioque, at least the doctrine, must be damned. All, replies the pope, are not capable of reaching the altiora mysteria; qui potuerit, et non voluerit, salvus esse non potest (Collect. Concil. tom. ix. p. 277-286). The *potuerit* would leave a large loophole of salvation!

6. In France, after some harsher laws, the ecclesiastical discipline is now relaxed: milk, cheese, and butter are become a perpetual, and eggs an annual, indulgence in Lent (Vie privée des François, tom. ii. p. 27-38).

7. The original monuments of the schism, of the charges of the Greeks against the Latins, are deposited in the epistles of Photius (Epist. Encyclica, ii. p. 47-61) and of Michael Cerularius (Canisii Antiq. Lectiones, tom. iii. p. i. p. 281-324, edit. Basnage, with the prolix answer of Cardinal Humbert).

8. The tenth volume of the Venice edition of the Councils contains all the acts of the synods, and history of Photius: they are abridged, with a faint tinge of prejudice or prudence, by Dupin and Fleury.

9. The synod of Constantinople, held in the year 869, is the eighth of the general councils, the last assembly of the East which is recognised by the Roman church. She rejects the synods of Constantinople of the years 867 and 879, which were, however, equally numerous and noisy; but they were favourable to Photius.

10. See this anathema in the Councils, tom. xi. p. 1457-1460.

11. Anna Comnena (Alexiad, l. i. p. 31–33 [tom. i. p. 63–68, ed. Bonn]) represents the abhorrence, not only of the church, but of the palace, for Gregory VII., the popes, and the Latin communion. The style of Cinnamus and Nicetas is still more vehement. Yet how calm is the voice of history compared with that of polemics!

12. His anonymous historian (de Expedit. Asiat. Fred. I. in Canisii Lection. Antiq. tom. iii. pars ii. p. 511, edit. Basnage) mentions the sermons of the Greek patriarch, quomodo Græcis injunxerat in remissionem peccatorum peregrinos occidere et delere de terrâ. Tagino observes (in Scriptores Freher. tom. i. p. 409, edit. Struv.), Græci hæreticos nos appellant: clerici et monachi dictis et factis persequuntur. We may add the declaration of the emperor Baldwin fifteen years afterwards: Hæc est (gens) quæ Latinos omnes non hominum nomine, sed canum dignabatur; quorum sangiunem effundere penè inter merita reputabant (Gesta Innocent. III. c. 92, in Muratori, Script. Rerum Italicarum, tom. iii. pars i. p. 536). There may be some exaggeration, but it was as effectual for the action and re-action of hatred.

13. See Anna Comnena (Alexiad. l. vi. p. 161, 162 [tom. i. p. 286, sq., ed. Bonn]) and a remarkable passage of Nicetas (in Manuel. l. v. c. 9 [p. 223, ed. Bonn]), who observes of the Venetians, κατὰ σμήνη καὶ φρατρίας τὴν Κωνσταντίνου πόλιν τῆς οἰκείας ἠλλάξαντο, etc.

14. Ducange, Fam. Byzant. p. 186, 187.

15. Nicetas in Manuel. l. vii. c. 2 [p. 267, ed. Bonn]. Regnante enim (Manuele) . . . apud eum tantam Latinus populus repererat gratiam ut neglectis Græculis suis tanquam viris mollibus et effeminatis, . . . solis Latinis grandia committeret negotia . . . erga eos profusâ liberalitate abundabat, ex omni orbe ad eum tanquam ad benefactorem nobiles et ignobiles concurrebant. Willelm. Tyr. xxii. c. 10.

16. The suspicions of the Greeks would have been confirmed, if they had seen the political epistles of Manuel to pope Alexander III., the enemy of his enemy Frederic I., in which the emperor declares his wish of uniting the Greeks and Latins as one flock under one shepherd, etc. (See Fleury, Hist. Ecclés. tom. xv. p. 187, 213, 243.)

17. See the Greek and Latin narratives in Nicetas (in Alexio Comneno, c. 10 [p. 320, ed. Bonn]) and William of Tyre (l. xxii. c. 10, 11, 12, 13); the first soft and concise, the second loud, copious, and tragical.

18. The history of the reign of Isaac Angelus is composed in three books, by the senator Nicetas (p. 228–290); and his offices of logothete, or principal secretary, and judge of the veil or palace, could not bribe the impartiality of the historian. He wrote, it is true, after the fall and death of his benefactor.

19. See Bohadin, Vit. Saladin. p. 129–131, 226, vers. Schultens. The ambassador of Isaac was equally versed in the Greek, French, and Arabic languages; a rare instance in those times. His embassies were received with honour, dismissed without effect, and reported with scandal in the West.

20. Ducange, Familiæ Dalmaticæ, p. 318, 319, 320. The original correspondence of the Bulgarian king and the Roman pontiff is inscribed in the Gesta Innocent. III. c. 66–82, p. 513–525.

21. The pope acknowledges his pedigree, a nobili urbis Romæ prosapiâ genitores tui originem traxerunt. This tradition, and the strong resemblance of the Latin and Wallachian idioms, are explained by M. D'Anville (Etats de l'Europe, p. 258–262). The Italian colonies of the Dacia of Trajan were swept away by the tide of emigration from the Danube to the Volga, and brought back by another wave from the Volga to the Danube. Possible, but strange!

22. This parable is in the best savage style; but I wish the Wallach had not introduced the classic name of Mysians, the experiment of the magnet or loadstone, and the passage of an old comic poet (Nicetas, in Alex. Comneno, l. i. p. 299, 300 [ed. Par.; p. 613, ed. Bonn]).

23. The Latins aggravate the ingratitude of Alexius, by supposing that he had been released by his brother Isaac from Turkish captivity. This pathetic tale had doubtless been repeated at Venice and Zara; but I do not readily discover its grounds in the Greek historians.

24. See the reign of Alexius Angelus, or Comnenus, in the three books of Nicetas, p. 291–352.

25. See Fleury, Hist. Ecclés. tom. xvi. p. 26, etc., and Villehardouin, No. 1, with the observations of Ducange, which I always mean to quote with the original text.

26. The contemporary life of Pope Innocent III., published by Baluze and Muratori (Scriptores Rerum Italicarum, tom. iii. pars i. p. 486–568), is most valuable for the important and original documents which are inserted in the text. The bull of the crusade may be read, c. 84, 85 [p. 526].

27. Por-ce que cil pardon fut issi gran, si s'en esmeurent mult li cuers des genz, et mult s'en croisierent, porce que li pardons ere si gran. Villehardouin, No. 1. Our philosophers may refine on the causes of the crusades, but such were the genuine feelings of a French knight.

28. This number of fiefs (of which 1800 owed liege homage) was enrolled in the church of St. Stephen at Troyes, and attested, A.D. 1213, by the marshal and butler of Champagne (Ducange, Observ. p. 254).

29. Campania . . . militiæ privilegio singularius excellit . . . in tyrociniis . . . prolusione armorum, etc. Ducange, p. 249, from the old Chronicle of Jerusalem, A.D. 1177–1199.

30. The name of Villehardouin was taken from a village and castle in the diocese of Troyes, near the river Aube, between Bar and Arcis. The family was ancient and noble: the elder branch of our historian existed after the year 1400; the younger,

which acquired the principality of Achaia, merged in the house of Savoy (Ducange, p. 235–245).

31. This office was held by his father and his descendants; but Ducange has not hunted it with his usual sagacity. I find that, in the year 1356, it was in the family of Conflans; but these provincial have been long since eclipsed by the national marshals of France.

32. This language, of which I shall produce some specimens, is explained by Vigenere and Ducange, in a version and glossary. The President Des Brosses (Méchanisme des Langues, tom. ii. p. 83) gives it as the example of a language which has ceased to be French, and is understood only by grammarians.

33. His age, and his own expression, moi qui ceste œuvre *dicta* (No. 62, etc.), may justify the suspicion (more probable than Mr. Wood's on Homer) that he could neither read nor write. Yet Champagne may boast of the two first historians, the noble authors of French prose, Villehardouin and Joinville.

34. The crusade and reigns of the counts of Flanders, Baldwin and his brother Henry, are the subject of a particular history by the Jesuit Doutremens (Constantinopolis Belgica; Turnaci, 1638, in 4to), which I have only seen with the eyes of Ducange.

35. History, etc., vol. i. p. 567.

36. The foundation and independence of Venice, and Pepin's invasion, are discussed by Pagi (Critica, tom. iii. A.D. 810, No. 4, etc.) and Beretti (Dissert. Chorograph. Italiæ medii Ævi, in Muratori, Script. tom. x. p. 153). The two critics have a slight bias, the Frenchman adverse, the Italian favourable, to the republic.

37. When the son of Charlemagne asserted his right of sovereignty, he was answered by the loyal Venetians, ὅτι ἡμεῖς δοῦλοι θέλομεν εἶναι τοῦ 'Ρωμαίων Βασιλέως (Constantin. Porphyrogenit. de Administrat. Imperii, pars ii. c. 28, p. 85); and the report of the ninth establishes the fact of the tenth century, which is confirmed by the embassy of Liutprand of Cremona. The annual tribute, which the emperor allows them to pay to the king of Italy, alleviates, by doubling, their servitude; but the hateful word δοῦλοι must be translated, as in the charter of 827 (Laugier, Hist. de Venise, tom. i. p. 67, etc.), by the softer appellation of *subditi*, or *fideles*.

38. See the twenty-fifth and thirtieth dissertations of the Antiquitates medii Ævi of Muratori. From Anderson's History of Commerce, I understand that the Venetians did not trade to England before the year 1323. The most flourishing state of their wealth and commerce in the beginning of the fifteenth century is agreeably described by the Abbé Dubos (Hist. de la Ligue de Cambray, tom. ii. p. 443–480).

39. The Venetians have been slow in writing and publishing their history. Their most ancient monuments are, 1. The rude Chronicle (perhaps) of John Sagorninus (Venezia, 1765, in octavo) which represents the state and manners of Venice in the year 1008. 2. The larger history of the doge (1342–1354) Andrew Dandolo, published for the first time in the twelfth tom. of Muratori, A.D. 1728. The History of Venice by the Abbé Laugier (Paris, 1728) is a work of some merit, which I have chiefly used for the constitutional part.

40. Henry Dandolo was eighty-four at his election (A.D. 1192), and ninety-seven at his death (A.D. 1205). See the Observations of Ducange sur Villehardouin, No. 204. But this *extraordinary* longevity is not observed by the original writers, nor does there exist another example of a hero near a hundred years of age. Theophrastus might afford an instance of a writer of ninety-nine; but instead of ἐννενήκοντα (Procem. ad Character.), I am much inclined to read ἑβδομήκοντα, with his last editor Fischer, and the first thoughts of Casaubon. It is scarcely possible that the powers of the mind and body should support themselves till such a period of life.

41. The modern Venetians (Laugier, tom. ii. p. 119) accuse the emperor Manuel; but the calumny is refuted by Villehardouin and the older writers, who suppose that Dandolo lost his eyes by a wound (No. 34, and Ducange).

42. See the original treaty in the Chronicle of Andrew Dandolo, p. 323–326 [Murat. Script. Ital. t. xii.].

43. A reader of Villehardouin must observe the frequent tears of the marshal and his brother knights. Sachiez que la ot mainte lerme plorée de pitié (No. 17); mult plorant (ibid.); mainte lerme plorée (No. 34); si orent mult pitié et plorerent mult durement (No. 60); i ot mainte lerme plorée de pitié (No. 202). They weep on every occasion of grief, joy, or devotion.

44. By a victory (A.D. 1191) over the citizens of Asti, by a crusade to Palestine, and by an embassy from the pope to the German princes (Muratori, Annali d'Italia, tom. x. p. 163, 202).

45. See the crusade of the Germans in the Historia C. P. of Gunther (Canisii Antiq. Lect. tom. iv. p. v.–viii.), who celebrates the pilgrimage of his abbot Martin, one of the preaching rivals of Fulk of Neuilly. His monastery, of the Cistercian order, was situate in the diocese of Basil.

46. Jadera, now Zara, was a Roman colony, which acknowledged Augustus for its parent. It is now only two miles round, and contains five or six thousand inhabitants; but the fortifications are strong, and it is joined to the main land by a bridge. See the Travels of the two companions Spon and Wheeler (Voyage de Dalmatie, de Grèce, etc., tom. i. p. 64–70; Journey into Greece, p. 8–14); the last of whom, by mistaking *Sestertia* for *Sestertii*, values an arch with statues and columns at twelve pounds. If, in his time, there were no trees near Zara, the cherry-trees were not yet planted which produce our incomparable *marasquin*.

47. Katona (Hist. Critica Reg. Hungariæ, Stir-

pis Arpad. tom. iv. p. 536–558) collects all the facts and testimonies most adverse to the conquerors of Zara.

48. See the whole transaction, and the sentiments of the pope, in the Epistles of Innocent III. Gesta, c. 86, 87, 88.

49. A modern reader is surprised to hear of the valet de Constantinople, as applied to young Alexius, on account of his youth, like the *infants* of Spain, and the *nobilissimus puer* of the Romans. The pages and *valets* of the knights were as noble as themselves (Villehardouin and Ducange, No. 36).

50. The emperor Isaac is styled by Villehardouin *Sursac* (No. 35, etc.), which may be derived from the French *Sire*, or the Greek Κυρ (κίριος) melted into his proper name; the farther corruptions of Tursac and Conserac will instruct us what licence may have been used in the old dynasties of Assyria and Egypt.

51. Reinier and Conrad: the former married Maria, daughter of the emperor Manuel Comnenus; the latter was the husband of Theodora Angela, sister of the emperors Isaac and Alexius. Conrad abandoned the Greek court and princess for the glory of defending Tyre against Saladin (Ducange, Fam. Byzant. p. 187, 203).

52. Nicetas (in Alexio Comneno, l. iii. c. 9 [p. 715, ed. Bonn]) accuses the doge and Venetians as the first authors of the war against Constantinople, and considers only as a κῦμα ἐπὶ κύματι the arrival and shameful offers of the royal exile.

53. Villehardouin and Gunther represent the sentiments of the two parties. The abbot Martin left the army at Zara, proceeded to Palestine, was sent ambassador to Constantinople, and became a reluctant witness of the second siege.

54. The birth and dignity of Andrew Dandolo gave him the motive and the means of searching in the archives of Venice the memorable story of his ancestor. His brevity seems to accuse the copious and more recent narratives of Sanudo (in Muratori, Script. Rerum Italicarum, tom. xxii.), Blondus, Sabellicus, and Rhamnusius.

55. Villehardouin, No. 62. His feelings and expressions are original: he often weeps, but he rejoices in the glories and perils of war with a spirit unknown to a sedentary writer.

56. In this voyage almost all the geographical names are corrupted by the Latins. The modern appellation of Chalcis, and all Euboea, is derived from its *Euripus, Evripo, Negri-po, Negropont*, which dishonours our maps (D'Anville, Géographie Ancienne, tom. i. p. 263).

57. Et sachiez que il ni ot si hardi cui le cuer ne fremist (c. 66). . . . Chascuns regardoit ses armes . . . que par tems en arons mestier (c. 67). Such is the honesty of courage.

58. Eandem urbem plus in solis navibus piscatorum abundare, quam illos in toto navigio. Habebat enim mille et sexcentas piscatorias naves. . . . Bellicas autem sive mercatorias habebant infinitæ multitudinis et portum tutissimum. Gunther, Hist. C. P. c. 8, p. 10 [in Canisus. Ant. Lect. t. iv.].

59. Καθάπερ ἱερῶν ἀλσέων, εἰπεῖν δὲ καὶ θεοφυτεύτων παραδείσων ἐφείδοντο τουτωνί. Nicetas in Alex. Comneno, l. iii. c. 9, p. 348 [p. 716, ed. Bonn].

60. From the version of Vigenere I adopt the well-sounding word *palander*, which is still used, I believe, in the Mediterranean. But had I written in French, I should have preferred the original and expressive denomination of *vessiers* or *huissiers*, from the *huis*, or door, which was let down as a drawbridge; but which, at sea, was closed into the side of the ship. (See Ducange au Villehardouin, No. 14, and Joinville, p. 27, 28, édit. du Louvre.)

61. To avoid the vague expressions of followers, etc., I use, after Villehardouin, the word serjeants for all horsemen who were not knights. There were serjeants at arms and serjeants at law; and if we visit the parade and Westminster Hall, we may observe the strange result of the distinction (Ducange, Glossar. Latin. *Servientes*, etc., tom. vi. p. 226–231).

62. It is needless to observe that on the subject of Galata, the chain, etc., Ducange is accurate and full. Consult likewise the proper chapters of the C. P. Christiana of the same author. The inhabitants of Galata were so vain and ignorant, that they applied to themselves St. Paul's Epistle to the Galatians.

63. The vessel that broke the chain was named the Eagle, Aquila (Dandol. Chronicon, p. 322), which Blondus (de Gestis Venet.) has changed into Aquilo, the north-wind. Ducange, Observations, No. 83, maintains the latter reading; but he had not seen the respectable text of Dandolo, nor did he enough consider the topography of the harbour. The south-east would have been a more effectual wind.

64. Quatre cens mil homes ou plus (Villehardouin, No. 133) must be understood of *men* of a military age. Le Beau (Hist. du Bas Empire, tom. xx. p. 417) allows Constantinople a million of inhabitants, of whom 60,000 horse, and an infinite number of foot soldiers. In its present decay, the capital of the Ottoman empire may contain 400,000 souls (Bell's Travels, vol. ii. p. 410, 402); but as the Turks keep no registers, and as circumstances are fallacious, it is impossible to ascertain (Niebuhr, Voyage en Arabie, tom. i. p. 18, 19) the real populousness of their cities.

65. On the most correct plans of Constantinople, I know not how to measure more than 4000 paces. Yet Villehardouin computes the space at three leagues (No. 86). If his eye were not deceived, he must reckon by the old Gallic league of 1500 paces, which might still be used in Champagne.

66. The guards, the Varangi, are styled by Villehardouin (No. 89, 95, etc.) Englois et Danois avec leurs haches. Whatever had been their origin, a French pilgrim could not be mistaken in the nations of which they were at that time composed.

67. For the first siege and conquest of Con-

stantinople, we may read the original letter of the crusaders to Innocent III., Gesta, c. 91, p. 533, 534; Villehardouin, No. 75–99; Nicetas, in Alexio Comnen. l. iii. c. 10, p. 349–352 [p. 718–725, ed. Bonn]; Dandolo, in Chron. p. 322. Gunther and his abbot Martin were not yet returned from their obstinate pilgrimage to Jerusalem, or St. John d'Acre, where the greatest part of the company had died of the plague.

68. Compare, in the rude energy of Villehardouin (No. 66, 100), the inside and outside views of Constantinople, and their impression on the minds of the pilgrims: cette ville (says he) que de totes les autres ére souveraine. See the parallel passages of Fulcherius Carnotensis, Hist. Hierosol. l. i. c. 4 [p. 386], and Will. Tyr. ii. 3, xx. 26.

69. As they played at dice, the Latins took off his diadem, and clapped on his head a woollen or hairy cap, τὸ μεγαλοπρεπὲς καὶ παγκλέϊστον κατερρύπαινεν ὄνομα (Nicetas, p. 358 [p. 736, ed. Bonn]). If these merry companions were Venetians, it was the insolence of trade and a commonwealth.

70. Villehardouin, No. 101; Dandolo, p. 322. The doge affirms that the Venetians were paid more slowly than the French; but he owns that the histories of the two nations differed on that subject. Had he read Villehardouin? The Greeks complained, however, quòd totius Graeciæ opes transtulisset (Gunther, Hist. C. P. c. 13). See the lamentations and invectives of Nicetas (p. 355 [p. 729, ed. Bonn]).

71. The reign of Alexius Comnenus occupies three books in Nicetas, p. 291–352. The short restoration of Isaac and his son is despatched in five chapters, p. 352–362.

72. When Nicetas reproaches Alexius for his impious league, he bestows the harshest names on the pope's new religion, μεῖζον καὶ ἀτοπώτατον . . . παρεκτροπὴν πίστεως . . . τῶν τοῦ Πάπα προνομίων καινισμὸν, μετάθεσίν τε καὶ μεταποίησιν τῶν παλαιῶν Ῥωμαίοις ἐθῶν (p. 348 [p. 715, ed. Bonn]). Such was the sincere language of every Greek to the last gasp of the empire.

73. Nicetas (p. 355 [p. 731, ed. Bonn]) is positive in the charge, and specifies the Flemings (Φλαμίονες), though he is wrong in supposing it an ancient name. Villehardouin (No. 107) exculpates the barons, and is ignorant (perhaps affectedly ignorant) of the names of the guilty.

74. Compare the suspicions and complaints of Nicetas (p. 359–362 [p. 740–747, ed. Bonn]) with the blunt charges of Baldwin of Flanders (Gesta Innocent. III. c. 92, p. 534), cum patriarcha et mole nobilium, nobis promissis perjurus et mendax.

75. His name was Nicholas Canabus: he deserved the praise of Nicetas and the vengeance of Mourzoufle (p. 362 [p. 744, ed. Bonn]).

76. Villehardouin (No. 116) speaks of him as a favourite, without knowing that he was a prince of the blood, Angelus and Ducas. Ducange, who pries into every corner, believes him to be the son of

Isaac Ducas Sebastocrator, and second cousin of young Alexius.

77. This negotiation, probable in itself, and attested by Nicetas (p. 365 [p. 751, ed. Bonn]), is omitted as scandalous by the delicacy of Dandolo and Villehardouin.

78. Baldwin mentions both attempts to fire the fleet (Gest. c. 92, p. 534, 535); Villehardouin (No. 113–115) only describes the first. It is remarkable that neither of these warriors observe any peculiar properties in the Greek fire.

79. Ducange (No. 119) pours forth a torrent of learning on the Gonfanon Imperial. This banner of the Virgin is shown at Venice as a trophy and relic: if it be genuine, the pious doge must have cheated the monks of Citeaux.

80. Villehardouin (No. 126) confesses that mult ere grant peril; and Guntherus (Hist. C. P. c. 13 [c. 14, p. xiv.]) affirms that nulla spes victoriæ arridere poterat. Yet the knight despises those who thought of flight, and the monk praises his countrymen who were resolved on death.

81. Baldwin and all the writers honour the names of these two galleys, felici auspicio.

82. With an allusion to Homer, Nicetas calls him ἐννεόργυιος, nine orgyæ, or eighteen yards, high—a stature which would, indeed, have excused the terror of the Greek. On this occasion the historian seems fonder of the marvellous than of his country, or perhaps of truth. Baldwin exclaims, in the words of the psalmist, persequitur unus ex nobis centum alienos.

83. Villehardouin (No. 130) is again ignorant of the authors of this more legitimate fire, which is ascribed by Gunther to a quidam comes Teutonicus (c. 14 [c. 17, p. xv.]). They seem ashamed, the incendiaries!

84. For the second siege and conquest of Constantinople, see Villehardouin (No. 113–132), Baldwin's second Epistle to Innocent III. (Gesta, c. 92, p. 534–537), with the whole reign of Mourzoufle, in Nicetas (p. 363–375 [p. 748–770, ed. Bonn]), and borrow some hints from Dandolo (Chron. Venet. p. 323–330) and Gunther (Hist. C. P. c. 14–18), who add the decorations of prophecy and vision. The former produces an oracle of the Erythræan sibyl, of a great armament on the Adriatic, under a blind chief, against Byzantium, etc. Curious enough, were the prediction anterior to the fact.

85. Ceciderunt tamen eâ die civium quasi duo millia, etc. (Gunther, c. 18.) Arithmetic is an excellent touchstone to try the amplifications of passion and rhetoric.

86. Quidam (says Innocent III., Gesta, c. 94, p. 538) nec religioni, nec ætati, nec sexui pepercerunt: sed fornicationes, adulteria, et incestus in oculis omnium exercentes, non solùm maritatas et viduas, sed et matronas et virgines Deoque dicatas, exposuerunt spurcitiis garcionum. Villehardouin takes notice of these common incidents.

87. Nicetas saved, and afterwards married, a

noble virgin (p. 380 [p. 781, ed. Bonn]), whom a soldier, ἐπὶ μάρτυσι πολλοῖς ὀνηδὸν ἐπιβρωμώμενος, had almost violated, in spite of the ἔντολαι, ἐντάλματα εὖ γεγονότων.

88. Of the general mass of wealth, Gunther observes, ut de pauperibus et advenis cives ditissimi redderentur (Hist. C. P. c. 18); Villehardouin (No. 132), that since the creation, ne fu tant gaaignié en une ville: Baldwin (Gesta, c. 92), ut tantum tota non videatur possidere Latinitas [p. 535].

89. Villehardouin, No. 133–135. Instead of 400,000, there is a various reading of 500,000. The Venetians had offered to take the whole booty, and to give 400 marks to each knight, 200 to each priest and horseman, and 100 to each foot soldier: they would have been great losers (Le Beau, Hist. du Bas-Empire, tom. xx. p. 506: I know not from whence).

90. At the council of Lyons (A.D. 1245) the English ambassadors stated the revenue of the crown as below that of the foreign clergy, which amounted to 60,000 marks a-year (Matthew Paris, p. 451; Hume's History of England, vol. ii. p. 170).

91. The disorders of the sack of Constantinople, and his own adventures, are feelingly described by Nicetas, p. 367–369 [p. 757–761, ed. Bonn], and in the Status Urb. C. P. p. 375–384 [p. 771–790, ed. Bonn]. His complaints, even of sacrilege, are justified by Innocent III. (Gesta, c. 92); but Villehardouin does not betray a symptom of pity or remorse.

92. If I rightly apprehend the Greek of Nicetas's receipts, their favourite dishes were boiled buttocks of beef, salt pork and peas, and soup made of garlic and sharp or sour herbs (p. 382 [p. 786, ed. Bonn]).

93. Nicetas uses very harsh expressions, παρ' ἀγραμμάτοις Βαρβάροις, καὶ τέλεον ἀναλφαβήτοις (Fragment. apud Fabric. Biblioth. Græc. tom. vi. p. 414). This reproach, it is true, applies most strongly to their ignorance of Greek and of Homer. In their own language, the Latins of the twelfth and thirteenth centuries were not destitute of literature. See Harris's Philological Inquiries, p. iii. c 9, 10, 11.

94. Nicetas was of Chonæ in Phrygia (the old Colossæ of St. Paul): he raised himself to the honours of senator, judge of the veil, and great logothete; beheld the fall of the empire, retired to Nice, and composed an elaborate history from the death of Alexius Comnenus to the reign of Henry.

95. A manuscript of Nicetas in the Bodleian library contains this curious fragment on the statues of Constantinople, which fraud, or shame, or rather carelessness, has dropped in the common editions. It is published by Fabricius (Biblioth.

Græc. tom. vi. p. 405–416), and immoderately praised by the late ingenious Mr. Harris of Salisbury (Philological Inquiries, p. iii. c. 5, p. 301–312).

96. To illustrate the statue of Hercules, Mr. Harris quotes a Greek epigram, and engraves a beautiful gem, which does not, however, copy the attitude of the statue: in the latter, Hercules had not his club, and his right leg and arm were extended.

97. I transcribe these proportions, which appear to me inconsistent with each other, and may possibly show that the boasted taste of Nicetas was no more than affectation and vanity.

98. Nicetas in Isaaco Angelo et Alexio, c. 3, p. 359 [p. 738, ed. Bonn]. The Latin editor very properly observes that the historian, in his bombast style, produces ex pulice elephantem.

99. In two passages of Nicetas (edit. Paris, p. 360; Fabric. p. 408) the Latins are branded with the lively reproach of οἱ τοῦ καλοῦ ἀνέραστοι βάρβαροι, and their avarice of brass is clearly expressed. Yet the Venetians had the merit of removing four bronze horses from Constantinople to the place of St. Mark (Sanuto, Vite de' Dogi, in Muratori, Script. Rerum Italicarum, tom. xxii. p. 534).

100. Winckelman, Hist. de l'Art, tom. iii. p. 269, 270.

101. See the pious robbery of the abbot Martin, who transferred a rich cargo to his monastery of Paris, diocese of Basil (Gunther, Hist. C. P. c. 19, 23, 24). Yet, in secreting this booty, the saint incurred an excommunication, and perhaps broke his oath. [Compare Wilken, vol. v. p. 308.—M.]

102. Fleury, Hist. Ecclés. tom. xvi. p. 139–145.

103. I shall conclude this chapter with the notice of a modern history, which illustrates the taking of Constantinople by the Latins, but which has fallen somewhat late into my hands. Paolo Ramusio, the son of the compiler of Voyages, was directed by the senate of Venice to write the history of the conquest; and this order, which he received in his youth, he executed in a mature age, by an elegant Latin work, de Bello Constantinopolitano et Imperatoribus Comnenis per Gallos et Venetos restitutis (Venet. 1635, in folio). Ramusio, or Rhamnusius, transcribes and translates, sequitur ad unguem, a MS. of Villehardouin, which he possessed; but he enriches his narrative with Greek and Latin materials, and we are indebted to him for a correct state of the fleet, the names of the fifty Venetian nobles who commanded the galleys of the republic, and the patriot opposition of Pantaleon Barbus to the choice of the doge for emperor.

Chapter LXI

1. See the original treaty of partition in the Venetian Chronicle of Andrew Dandolo, p. 326–330, and the subsequent election in Villehardouin, No. 136–140, with Ducange in his Observations, and the 1st book of his Histoire de Constantinople sous l'Empire des François.

2. After mentioning the nomination of the doge by a French elector, his kinsman Andrew Dandolo approves his exclusion, quidam Venetorum fidelis et nobilis senex, usus oratione satis probabili, etc. [p. 330], which has been embroidered by modern writers from Blondus to Le Beau.

3. Nicetas (p. 384 [p. 789, ed. Bonn]), with the vain ignorance of a Greek, describes the marquis of Montferrat as a *maritime* power. Λαμπαρδίαν δὲ οἰκεῖσθαι παράλιον. Was he deceived by the Byzantine theme of Lombardy, which extended along the coast of Calabria?

4. They exacted an oath from Thomas Morosini to appoint no canons of St. Sophia the lawful electors, except Venetians who had lived ten years at Venice, etc. But the foreign clergy was envious, the pope disapproved this national monopoly, and of the six Latin patriarchs of Constantinople only the first and the last were Venetians.

5. Nicetas, p. 383 [p. 788, ed. Bonn].

6. The Epistles of Innocent III. are a rich fund for the ecclesiastical and civil institution of the Latin empire of Constantinople; and the most important of these epistles (of which the collection in 2 vols. in folio is published by Stephen Baluze) are inserted in his Gesta, in Muratori, Script. Rerum Italicarum, tom. iii. p. 1, c. 94–105.

7. In the treaty of partition most of the names are corrupted by the scribes: they might be restored, and a good map, suited to the last age of the Byzantine empire, would be an improvement of geography. But, alas! D'Anville is no more!

8. Their style was dominus quartæ partis et dimidiæ [cum dimidio totius] imperii Romani, till Giovanni Dolfino, who was elected doge in the year 1356 (Sanuto, p. 530, 641). For the government of Constantinople see Ducange, Histoire de C. P. i. 37.

9. Ducange (Hist. de C. P. ii. 6) has marked the conquests made by the state or nobles of Venice of the islands of Candia, Corfu, Cephalonia, Zante, Naxos, Paros, Melos, Andros, Mycone, Scyro, Cea, and Lemnos.

10. Boniface sold the isle of Candia, August 12, A.D. 1204. See the act in Sanuto, p. 533: but I cannot understand how it could be his mother's portion, or how she could be the daughter of an emperor Alexius.

11. In the year 1212 the doge Peter Zani sent a colony to Candia, drawn from every quarter of Venice. But in their savage manners and frequent rebellions the Candiots may be compared to the Corsicans under the yoke of Genoa; and when I compare the accounts of Belon and Tournefort, I cannot discern much difference between the Venetian and the Turkish island.

12. Villehardouin (No. 159, 160, 173–177) and Nicetas (p. 387–394) describe the expedition into Greece of the marquis Boniface. The Choniate might derive his information from his brother Michael, archbishop of Athens, whom he paints as an orator, a statesman, and a saint. His encomium of Athens, and the description of Tempe, should be published from the Bodleian MS. of Nicetas (Fabric. Biblioth. Græc. tom. vi. p. 405), and would have deserved Mr. Harris's inquiries.

13. Napoli di Romania, or Nauplia, the ancient seaport of Argos, is still a place of strength and consideration, situate on a rocky peninsula, with a good harbour (Chandler's Travels into Greece, p. 227).

14. I have softened the expression of Nicetas, who strives to expose the presumption of the Franks. See de Rebus C. P. expugnatam, p. 375–384.

15. A city surrounded by the river Hebrus, and six leagues to the south of Adrianople, received from its double wall the Greek name of Didymoteichos, insensibly corrupted into Demotica and Dimot. I have preferred the more convenient and modern appellation of Demotica. This place was the last Turkish residence of Charles XII.

16. Their quarrel is told by Villehardouin (No. 146–158) with the spirit of freedom. The merit and reputation of the marshal are acknowledged by the Greek historian (p. 387 [p. 794, ed. Bonn]), μέγα παρὰ τοῖς τῶν Λατίνων δυναμένου στρατεύμασι; unlike some modern heroes, whose exploits are only visible in their own memoirs.

17. See the fate of Mourzoufle, in Nicetas (p. 392 [p. 804, ed. Bonn]), Villehardouin (No. 141–145, 163), and Guntherus (c. 20, 21). Neither the marshal nor the monk afford a grain of pity for a tyrant or rebel, whose punishment, however, was more unexampled than his crime.

18. The column of Arcadius, which represents in basso relievo his victories, or those of his father Theodosius, is still extant at Constantinople. It is described and measured, Gyllius (Topograph. iv. 7), Banduri (ad. l. i. Antiquit. C. P. p. 507, etc.), and Tournefort (Voyage du Levant, tom. ii. lettre xii. p. 231).

19. The nonsense of Gunther and the modern Greeks concerning this *columna fatidica* is unworthy of notice; but it is singular enough, that, fifty years before the Latin conquest, the poet Tzetzes (Chiliad, ix. 277) relates the dream of a matron, who saw an army in the forum, and a man sitting on the column, clapping his hands and uttering a loud exclamation.

20. The dynasties of Nice, Trebizond, and Epirus (of which Nicetas saw the origin without much pleasure or hope), are learnedly explored, and clearly represented, in the Familiæ Byzantinæ of Ducange.

21. Except some facts in Pachymer and Nicephorus Gregoras, which will hereafter be used, the Byzantine writers disdain to speak of the empire of Trebizond, or principality of the *Lazi;* and among the Latins it is conspicuous only in the romances of the fourteenth or fifteenth centuries. Yet the indefatigable Ducange has dug out (Fam. Byz. p. 192) two authentic passages in Vincent of Beauvais (l. xxxi. c. 144), and the protonotary Ogerius (apud Wading, A.D. 1279, No. 4).

22. The portrait of the French Latins is drawn in Nicetas by the hand of prejudice and resentment: οὐδὲν τῶν ἄλλων ἐθνῶν εἰς Ἄρεος ἔργα παρασυμβεβλῆσθαι σφισιν ἠνείχοντο· ἀλλ' οὐδέ τις τῶν Χαρίτων ἢ τῶν Μουσῶν παρὰ τοῖς βαρβάροις τούτοις ἐπεξενίζετο καὶ παρὰ τοῦτο οἶμαι τὴν φύσιν ἦσαν ἀνήμεροι, καὶ τὸν χόλον εἶχον τοῦ λόγου προτρέχοντα [P. 791, ed. Bonn.]

23. I here begin to use, with freedom and confidence, the eight books of the Histoire de C. P. sous l'Empire des François, which Ducange has given as a supplement to Villehardouin; and which, in a barbarous style, deserves the praise of an original and classic work.

24. In Calo-John's answer to the pope we may find his claims and complaints (Gesta Innocent. III. c. 108, 109): he was cherished at Rome as the prodigal son.

25. The Comans were a Tartar or Turkman horde, which encamped in the twelfth and thirteenth centuries on the verge of Moldavia. The greater part were pagans, but some were Mohammedans, and the whole horde was converted to Christianity (A.D. 1370) by Lewis, king of Hungary.

26. Nicetas, from ignorance or malice, imputes the defeat to the cowardice of Dandolo (p. 383 [p. 397, ed. Par.; p. 814, ed. Bonn]): but Villehardouin shares his own glory with his venerable friend, qui viels home ére et gote ne veoit, mais mult ére sages et preus et vigueros (No. 193).

27. The truth of geography, and the original text of Villehardouin (No. 194), place Rodosto three days' journey (trois jornées) from Adrianople: but Vigenere, in his version, has most absurdly substituted *trois heures* [lieuës]; and this error, which is not corrected by Ducange, has entrapped several moderns, whose names I shall spare.

28. The reign and end of Baldwin are related by Villehardouin and Nicetas (p. 386-416 [p. 791-853, ed. Bonn]); and their omissions are supplied by Ducange in his Observations, and to the end of his first book.

29. After brushing away all doubtful and improbable circumstances, we may prove the death of Baldwin—1. By the firm belief of the French barons (Villehardouin, No. 230); 2. By the decla-

ration of Calo-John himself, who excuses his not releasing the captive emperor, quia debitum carnis exsolverat cum carcere teneretur (Gesta Innocent III. c. 109 [p. 550]).

30. See the story of this impostor from the French and Flemish writers, in Ducange, Hist. de C. P. iii. 9; and the ridiculous fables that were believed by the monks of St. Alban's, in Matthew Paris, Hist. Major, p. 271, 272.

31. Villehardouin, No. 257. I quote, with regret, this lamentable conclusion, where we lose at once the original history, and the rich illustrations of Ducange. The last pages may derive some light from Henry's two epistles to Innocent III. (Gesta, c. 106, 107).

32. The marshal was alive in 1212, but he probably died soon afterwards, without returning to France (Ducange, Observations sur Villehardouin, p. 238). His fief of Messinople, the gift of Boniface, was the ancient Maximianopolis, which flourished in the time of Ammianus Marcellinus among the cities of Thrace. (No. 141.)

33. The church of this patron of Thessalonica was served by the canons of the holy sepulchre, and contained a divine ointment which distilled daily and stupendous miracles (Ducange, Hist. de C. P. ii. 4).

34. Acropolita (c. 17) observes the persecution of the legate, and the toleration of Henry (Ερη, as he calls him), κλύδωνα κατεστόρεσε.

35. See the reign of HENRY, in Ducange (Hist. de C. P. l. i. c. 35-41, l. ii. c. 1-22), who is much indebted to the Epistles of the Popes. Le Beau (Hist. du Bas Empire, tom. xxi. p. 120-122) has found, perhaps in Doutreman, some laws of Henry which determined the service of fiefs and the prerogatives of the emperor.

36. Acropolita (c. 14) affirms that Peter of Courtenay died by the sword (ἔργον μαχαίρας γενέσθαι); but from his dark expressions I should conclude a previous captivity, ὡς πάντας ἄρδην δεσμώτας ποιῆσαι σὺν πᾶσι σκεύεσι. The Chronicle of Auxerre delays the emperor's death till the year 1219; and Auxerre is in the neighbourhood of Courtenay.

37. See the reign and death of Peter of Courtenay, in Ducange (Hist. de C. P. l. ii. c. 22-28), who feebly strives to excuse the neglect of the emperor by Honorius III.

38. Marinus Sanutus (Secreta Fidelium Crucis, l. ii. p. 4, c. 18, p. 73) is so much delighted with this bloody deed, that he has transcribed it in his margin as a bonum exemplum. Yet he acknowledges the damsel for the lawful wife of Robert.

39. See the reign of Robert, in Ducange (Hist. de C. P. l. iii. c. 1-12).

40. Rex igitur Franciæ, deliberatione habitâ, respondit nuntiis, se daturum hominem Syriæ partibus aptum; in armis probum (*preux*), in bellis securum, in agendis providum, Johannem comitem Brennensem. Sanut. Secret. Fidelium, l. iii. p. xi. c. 4, p. 205; Matthew Paris, p. 159.

41. Giannone (Istoria Civile, tom. ii. l. xvi. p. 380–385) discusses the marriage of Frederic II. with the daughter of John of Brienne, and the double union of the crowns of Naples and Jerusalem.

42. Acropolita, c. 27. The historian was at that time a boy, and educated at Constantinople. In 1233, when he was eleven years old, his father broke the Latin chain, left a splendid fortune, and escaped to the Greek court of Nice, where his son was raised to the highest honours.

43. Philip Mouskes, bishop of Tournay (A.D. 1274–1282), has composed a poem, or rather a string of verses, in bad old Flemish French, on the Latin emperors of Constantinople, which Ducange has published at the end of Villehardouin; see p. 224, for the prowess of John of Brienne.

N'Aie, Ector, Roll' ne Ogiers
Ne Judas Machabeus li fiers
Tant ne fit d'armes en estors
Com fist li Rois Jehans cel jors
Et il defors et il dedans
La paru sa force et ses sens
Et li hardiment qu'il avoit.

44. See the reign of John de Brienne, in Ducange, Hist. de C. P. l. iii. c. 13–26.

45. See the reign of Baldwin II. till his expulsion from Constantinople, in Ducange, Hist. de C. P. l. iv. c. 1–34; the end, l. v. c. 1–33.

46. Matthew Paris relates the two visits of Baldwin II. to the English court, p. 396, 637; his return to Greece armatâ manû, p. 407; his letters of his nomen formidabile, etc., p. 481 (a passage which had escaped Ducange); his expulsion, p. 850.

47. Louis IX. disapproved and stopped the alienation of Courtenay (Ducange, l. iv. c. 23). It is now annexed to the royal demesne, but granted for a term (engagé) to the family of Boulainvilliers. Courtenay, in the election of Nemours in the Isle de France, is a town of 900 inhabitants, with the remains of a castle (Mélanges tirés d'une Grande Bibliothèque, tom. xlv. p. 74–77).

48. Joinville, p. 104, édit. du Louvre. A Coman prince, who died without baptism, was buried at the gates of Constantinople with a live retinue of slaves and horses.

49. Sanut. Secret. Fidel. Crucis, l. ii. p. iv. c. 18, p. 73.

50. Under the words Perparus, Perpera, Hyperperum, Ducange is short and vague: Monetæ genus. From a corrupt passage of Guntherus (Hist. C. P. c. 8, p. 10) I guess that the Perpera was the nummus aureus, the fourth part of a mark of silver, or about ten shillings sterling in value. In lead it would be too contemptible.

51. For the translation of the holy crown, etc., from Constantinople to Paris, see Ducange (Hist. de C. P. l. iv. c. 11–14, 24, 35) and Fleury (Hist. Ecclés. tom. xvii. p. 201–204).

52. Mélanges tirés d'une Grande Bibliothèque, tom. xliii. p. 201–205. The Lutrin of Boileau exhibits the inside, the soul and manners of the Sainte Chapelle: and many facts relative to the institution are collected and explained by his commentators, Brosset and De St. Marc.

53. It was performed A.D. 1656, March 24, on the niece of Pascal; and that superior genius, with Arnauld, Nicole, etc., were on the spot, to believe and attest a miracle which confounded the Jesuits and saved Port Royal (Œuvres de Racine, tom. vi. p. 176–187, in his eloquent History of Port Royal).

54. Voltaire (Siècle de Louis XIV. c. 37; Œuvres, tom. ix. p. 178, 179) strives to invalidate the fact: but Hume (Essays, vol. ii. p. 483, 484), with more skill and success, seizes the battery, and turns the cannon against his enemies.

55. The gradual losses of the Latins may be traced in the third, fourth, and fifth books of the compilation of Ducange: but of the Greek conquests he has dropped many circumstances which may be recovered from the larger history of George Acropolita and the three first books of Nicephorus Gregoras, two writers of the Byzantine series who have had the good fortune to meet with learned editors, Leo Allatius at Rome, and John Voivin in the Academy of Inscriptions of Paris.

56. George Acropolita, c. 78, p. 89, 90, edit. Paris [p. 171 sq. ed. Bonn].

57. The Greeks, ashamed of any foreign aid, disguise the alliance and succour of the Genoese; but the fact is proved by the testimony of J. Villani (Chron. l. vi. c. 71, in Muratori, Script. Rerum Italicarum, tom. xiii. p. 202, 203) and William de Nangis (Annales de St. Louis, p. 248, in the Louvre Joinville), two impartial foreigners; and Urban IV. threatened to deprive Genoa of her archbishop.

58. Some precautions must be used in reconciling the discordant numbers; the 800 soldiers of Nicetas, the 15,000 of Spandugino (apud Ducange, l. v. c. 24); the Greeks and Scythians of Acropolita; and the numerous army of Michael, in the Epistles of pope Urban IV. (i. 129.)

59. Θεληματάριοι. They are described and named by Pachymer (l. ii. c. 14).

60. It is needless to seek these Comans in the deserts of Tartary, or even of Moldavia. A part of the horde had submitted to John Vataces, and was probably settled as a nursery of soldiers on some waste lands of Thrace Cantacuzen (l. i. c. 2).

61. The loss of Constantinople is briefly told by the Latins: the conquest is described with more satisfaction by the Greeks; by Acropolita (c. 85), Pachymer (l. ii. c. 26, 27), Nicephorus Gregoras (l. iv. c. 1, 2). See Ducange, Hist. de C. P. l. v. c. 19–27.

62. See the three last books (l. v.–viii.) and the genealogical tables of Ducange. In the year 1382 the titular emperor of Constantinople was James de Baux, duke of Andria in the kingdom of Naples, the son of Margaret, daughter of Catherine de Valois, daughter of Catherine, daughter of Philip, son of Baldwin II. (Ducange, l. viii. c. 37, 38). It is uncertain whether he left any posterity.

63. Abulfeda, who saw the conclusion of the

crusades, speaks of the kingdoms of the Franks and those of the Negroes as equally unknown (Prolegom. ad Geograph.). Had he not disdained the Latin language, how easily might the Syrian prince have found books and interpreters!

64. A short and superficial account of these versions from Latin into Greek is given by Huet (de Interpretatione et de claris Interpretibus, p. 131–135). Maximus Planudes, a monk of Constantinople (A.D. 1327–1353), has translated Cæsar's Commentaries, the Somnium Scipionis, the Metamorphoses and Heroides of Ovid, etc. (Fabric. Bib. Græc. tom. x. p. 533).

65. Windmills, first invented in the dry country of Asia Minor, were used in Normandy as early as the year 1105 (Vie privée des François, tom. i. p. 42, 43; Ducange, Gloss. Latin. tom. iv. p. 474).

66. See the complaints of Roger Bacon (Biographia Britannica, vol. i. p. 418, Kippis's edition). If Bacon himself, or Gerbert, understood *some* Greek, they were prodigies, and owed nothing to the commerce of the East.

67. Such was the opinion of the great Leibnitz (Œuvres de Fontenelle, tom. v. p. 458), a master of the history of the middle ages. I shall only instance the pedigree of the Carmelites and the flight of the house of Loretto, which were both derived from Palestine.

68. If I rank the Saracens with the barbarians, it is only relative to their wars, or rather inroads, in Italy and France, where their sole purpose was to plunder and destroy.

69. On this interesting subject, the progress of society in Europe, a strong ray of philosophic light has broke from Scotland in our own times; and it is with private, as well as public regard, that I repeat the names of Hume, Robertson, and Adam Smith.

70. I have applied but not confined myself to *A Genealogical History of the noble and illustrious Family of Courtenay, by Ezra Cleaveland, Tutor to Sir William Courtenay, and Rector of Honiton: Oxon.* 1735, *in folio*. The first part is extracted from William of Tyre; the second from Bouchet's French history; and the third from various memorials, public, provincial, and private, of the Courtenays of Devonshire. The rector of Honiton has more gratitude than industry, and more industry than criticism.

71. The primitive record of the family is a passage of the continuator of Aimoin, a monk of Fleury, who wrote in the twelfth century. See his Chronicle, in the Historians of France (tom. xi. p. 276).

72. Turbessel, or, as it is now styled, Telbesher, is fixed by D'Anville four-and-twenty miles from the great passage over the Euphrates at Zeugma.

73. His possessions are distinguished in the Assises of Jerusalem (c. 326) among the feudal tenures of the kingdom, which must therefore have been collected between the years 1153 and 1187. His pedigree may be found in the Lignages d'Outremer, c. 16.

74. The rapine and satisfaction of Reginald de Courtenay are preposterously arranged in the Epistles of the abbot and regent Suger (cxiv. cxvi.), the best memorials of the age (Duchesne, Scriptores Hist. Franc. tom. iv. p. 530).

75. In the beginning of the eleventh century, after naming the father and grandfather of Hugh Capet, the monk Glaber is obliged to add, cujus genus valde in-ante reperitur obscurum. Yet we are assured that the great-grandfather of Hugh Capet was Robert the Strong, count of Anjou (A.D. 863–873), a noble Frank of Neustria, Neustricus . . . generosæ stirpis, who was slain in the defence of his country against the Normans, dum patriæ fines tuebatur. Beyond Robert all is conjecture or fable. It is a probable conjecture that the third race descended from the second by Childebrand, the brother of Charles Martel. It is an absurd fable that the second was allied to the first by the marriage of Ansbert, a Roman senator and the ancestor of St. Arnoul, with Blitilde, a daughter of Clotaire I. The Saxon origin of the house of France is an ancient but incredible opinion. See a judicious memoir of M. de Foncemagne (Mémoires de l'Académie des Inscriptions, tom. xx. p. 548–579). He had promised to declare his own opinion in a second memoir, which has never appeared.

76. Of the various petitions, apologies, etc., published by the *princes* of Courtenay, I have seen the three following, all in octavo:—1. De Stirpe et Origine Domus de Courtenay: addita sunt Responsa celeberrimorum Europæ Jurisconsultorum: Paris, 1607. 2. Representation du Procedé tenû a l'instance faicte devant le Roi, par Messieurs de Courtenay, pour la conservation de l'Honneur et Dignité de leur Maison, branche de la royaile Maison de France: à Paris, 1613. 3. Representation du subject qui a porté Messieurs de Salles et de Fraville, de la Maison de Courtenay, se retirer hors du Royaume, 1614. It was a homicide, for which the Courtenays expected to be pardoned, or tried, as princes of the blood.

77. The sense of the parliaments is thus expressed by Thuanus: Principis nomen nusquam in Galliâ tributum, nisi iis qui per mares e regibus nostris originem repetunt; qui nunc tantum a Ludovico Nono beatæ memoriæ numerantur; nam *Cortinæi* et Drocenses, a Ludovico crasso genus ducentes, hodie inter eos minime recensentur—a distinction of expediency rather than justice. The sanctity of Louis IX. could not invest him with any special prerogative, and all the descendants of Hugh Capet must be included in his original compact with the French nation.

78. The last male of the Courtenays was Charles Roger, who died in the year 1730, without leaving any sons. The last female was Hélène de Courtenay, who married Louis de Beaufremont. Her title of Princess du Sang Royal de France was suppressed (February 7th, 1737) by an *arret* of the parliament of Paris.

79. The singular anecdote to which I allude is related in the Recueil des Pièces interessantes et peu connues (Maestricht, 1786, in 4 vols. 12mo); and the unknown editor quotes his author, who had received it from Hélène de Courtenay, marquise de Beaufremont.

80. Dugdale, Monasticon Anglicanum, vol. i. p. 786. Yet this fable must have been invented before the reign of Edward III. The profuse devotion of the three first generations to Ford Abbey was followed by oppression on one side and ingratitude on the other; and in the sixth generation the monks ceased to register the births, actions, and deaths of their patrons.

81. In his Britannia, in the list of the earls of Devonshire. His expression, e regio sanguine ortos credunt, betrays, however, some doubt or suspicion.

82. In his Baronage, P. i. p. 634, he refers to his own Monasticon. Should he not have corrected the register of Ford Abbey, and annihilated the phantom Florus, by the unquestionable evidence of the French historians?

83. Besides the third and most valuable book of Cleaveland's History, I have consulted Dugdale, the father of our genealogical science (Baronage, P. i. p. 634–643).

84. This great family, de Ripuariis, de Redvers, de Rivers, ended, in Edward the First's time, in Isabella de Fortibus, a famous and potent dowager, who long survived her brother and husband (Dugdale, Baronage, P. i. p. 254–257).

85. Cleaveland, p. 142. By some it is assigned to a Rivers earl of Devon; but the English denotes the fifteenth rather than the thirteenth century.

86. *Ubi lapsusé Quid feciè* a motto which was probably adopted by the Powderham branch after the loss of the earldom of Devonshire, etc. The primitive arms of the Courtenays were *Or, three torteaux, Gules*, which seem to denote their affinity with Godfrey of Bouillon and the ancient counts of Boulogne.

Chapter LXII

1. For the reigns of the Nicene emperors, more especially of John Vataces and his son, their minister, George Acropolita, is the only genuine contemporary; but George Pachymer returned to Constantinople with the Greeks at the age of nineteen (Hanckius de Script. Byzant. c. 33, 34, p. 564–578; Fabric. Biblioth. Græc. tom. vi. p. 448–460). Yet the history of Nicephorus Gregoras, though of the fourteenth century, is a valuable narrative from the taking of Constantinople by the Latins.

2. Nicephorus Gregoras (l. ii. c. 1) distinguishes between the ὀξεῖα ὁρμη of Lascaris and the εὐστάθεια of Vataces. The two portraits are in a very good style.

3. Pachymer, l. i. c. 23, 24; Nic. Greg. l. ii. c. 6 [tom. i. p. 42, ed. Bonn]. The reader of the Byzantines must observe how rarely we are indulged with such precious details.

4. Μόνοι γὰρ ἁπάντων ἀνθρώπων ὀνομαστότατοι βασιλεὺς καὶ φιλόσοφος (Greg. Acropol. c. 32). The emperor, in a familiar conversation, examined and encouraged the studies of his future logothete.

5. Compare Acropolita (c. 18, 52), and the two first books of Nicephorus Gregoras.

6. A Persian saying, that Cyrus was the *father*, and Darius the *master*, of his subjects, was applied to Vataces and his son. But Pachymer (l. i. c. 23) has mistaken the mild Darius for the cruel Cambyses, despot or tyrant of his people. By the institution of taxes, Darius had incurred the less odious, but more contemptible, name of Κάπηλος, merchant or broker (Herodotus, iii. 89).

7. Acropolita (c. 63) seems to admire his own firmness in sustaining a beating, and not returning to council till he was called. He relates the exploits of Theodore, and his own services, from c. 53 to c. 74 of his history. See the third book of Nicephorus Gregoras.

8. Pachymer (l. i. c. 21 [tom. i. p. 65, ed. Bonn]) names and discriminates fifteen or twenty Greek families, καὶ ὅσοι ἄλλοι, οἷς ἡ μεγαλογενὴς σειρὰ καὶ χρυσῆ συγκεκρότητο. Does he mean, by this decoration, a figurative or a real golden chain? Perhaps both.

9. The old geographers, with Cellarius and D'Anville, and our travellers, particularly Pocock and Chandler, will teach us to distinguish the two Magnesias of Asia Minor, of the Mæander and of Sipylus. The latter, our present object, is still flourishing for a Turkish city, and lies eight hours, or leagues, to the north-east of Smyrna (Tournefort, Voyage du Levant, tom. iii. lettre xxii. p. 365–370; Chandler's Travels into Asia Minor, p. 267).

10. See Acropolita (c. 75, 76, etc.), who lived too near the times; Pachymer (l. i. c. 13–25); Gregoras (l. iii. c. 3, 4, 5).

11. The pedigree of Palæologus is explained by Ducange (Famil. Byzant. p. 230, etc.): the events of his private life are related by Pachymer (l. i. c. 7–12) and Gregoras (l. ii. c. 8; l. iii. 2, 4; l. iv. 1) with visible favour to the father of the reigning dynasty.

12. Acropolita (c. 50) relates the circumstances of this curious adventure, which seem to have escaped the more recent writers.

13. Pachymer (l. i. c. 12 [tom. i. p. 33, ed. Bonn]), who speaks with proper contempt of this barbarous trial, affirms that he had seen in his youth many persons who had sustained, without injury, the fiery ordeal. As a Greek, he is credulous; but the ingenuity of the Greeks might furnish

some remedies of art or fraud against their own superstition or that of their tyrant.

14. Without comparing Pachymer to Thucydides or Tacitus, I will praise his narrative (l. i. c. 13-32, l. ii. c. 1-9), which pursues the ascent of Palæologus with eloquence, perspicuity, and tolerable freedom. Acropolita is more cautious, and Gregoras more concise.

15. The judicial combat was abolished by St. Louis in his own territories; and his example and authority were at length prevalent in France (Esprit des Loix, l. xxviii. c. 29).

16. In civil cases Henry II. gave an option to the defendant: Glanvile prefers the proof by evidence; and that by judicial combat is reprobated in the Fleta. Yet the trial by battle has never been abrogated in the English law, and it was ordered by the judges as late as the beginning of the last century.

17. Yet an ingenious friend has urged to me in mitigation of this practice, 1. *That* in nations emerging from barbarism it moderates the licence of private war and arbitrary revenge. 2. *That* it is less absurd than the trials by the ordeal, or boiling water, or the cross, which it has contributed to abolish. 3. *That* it served at least as a test of personal courage; a quality so seldom united with a base disposition, that the danger of a trial might be some check to a malicious prosecutor, and a useful barrier against injustice supported by power. The gallant and unfortunate earl of Surrey might probably have escaped his unmerited fate, had not his demand of the combat against his accuser been overruled.

18. The site of Nymphæum is not clearly defined in ancient or modern geography. But from the last hours of Vataces (Acropolita, c. 52), it is evident the palace and gardens of his favourite residence were in the neighbourhood of Smyrna. Nymphæum might be loosely placed in Lydia (Gregoras, l. vi. 6 [tom. i. p. 190, ed. Bonn]).

19. This sceptre, the emblem of justice and power, was a long staff, such as was used by the heroes in Homer. By the latter Greeks it was named *Dicanice*, and the Imperial sceptre was distinguished as usual by the red or purple colour.

20. Acropolita affirms (c. 87) that this bonnet was after the French fashion; but from the ruby at the point or summit, Ducange (Hist. de C. P. l. v. c. 28, 29) believes that it was the high-crowned hat of the Greeks. Could Acropolita mistake the dress of his own court?

21. See Pachymer (l. ii. c. 28-33), Acropolita (c. 88), Nicephorus Gregoras l. iv. 7); and for the treatment of the subject Latins, Ducange (l. v. c. 30, 31).

22. This milder invention for extinguishing the sight was tried by the philosopher Democritus on himself, when he sought to withdraw his mind from the visible world: a foolish story! The word *abacinare*, in Latin and Italian, has furnished Ducange (Gloss. Latin.) with an opportunity to review the various modes of blinding: the more violent were scooping, burning with an iron or hot vinegar, and binding the head with a strong cord till the eyes burst from their sockets. Ingenious tyrants!

23. See the first retreat and restoration of Arsenius, in Pachymer (l. ii. c. 15, l. iii. c. 1, 2) and Nicephorus Gregoras (l. iii. c. 1, l. iv. c. 1). Posterity justly accused the ἀφέλεια and ῥαθυμία of Arsenius, the virtues of a hermit, the vices of a minister (l. xii. c. 2).

24. The crime and excommunication of Michael are fairly told by Pachymer (l. iii. c. 10, 14, 19, etc.) and Gregoras (l. iv. c. 4). His confession and penance restored their freedom.

25. Pachymer relates the exile of Arsenius (l. iv. c. 1-16): he was one of the commissaries who visited him in the desert island. The last testament of the unforgiving patriarch is still extant (Dupin, Bibliothèque Ecclésiastique, tom. x. p. 95).

26. Pachymer (l. vii. c. 22 [tom. ii. p. 60, ed. Bonn]) relates this miraculous trial like a philosopher, and treats with similar contempt a plot of the Arsenites, to hide a revelation in the coffin of some old saint (l. vii. c. 13 [tom. ii. p. 40, ed. Bonn]). He compensates this incredulity by an image that weeps, another that bleeds (l. vii. c. 30 [tom. ii. p. 82, ed. Bonn]), and the miraculous cures of a deaf and a mute patient (l. xi. c. 32 [tom. ii. p. 453, ed. Bonn]).

27. The story of the Arsenites is spread through the thirteen books of Pachymer. Their union and triumph are reserved for Nicephorus Gregoras (l. vii. c. 9 [tom. i. p. 262, ed. Bonn]), who neither loves nor esteems these sectaries.

28. Of the thirteen books of Pachymer, the first six (as the fourth and fifth of Nicephorus Gregoras) contain the reign of Michael, at the time of whose death he was forty years of age. Instead of breaking, like his editor the Père Poussin, his history into two parts, I follow Ducange and Cousin, who number the thirteen books in one series.

29. Ducange, Hist. de C. P. l. v. c. 33, etc., from the Epistles of Urban IV.

30. From their mercantile intercourse with the Venetians and Genoese, they branded the Latins as κάπηλοι and βάναυσοι (Pachymer, l. v. c. 10). "Some are heretics in name; others, like the Latins, in fact," said the learned Veccus (l. v. c. 12), who soon afterwards became a convert (c. 15, 16) and a patriarch (c. 24).

31. In this class we may place Pachymer himself, whose copious and candid narrative occupies the fifth and sixth books of his history. Yet the Greek is silent on the council of Lyons, and seems to believe that the popes always resided in Rome and Italy (l. v. c. 17, 21).

32. See the acts of the council of Lyons in the year 1274; Fleury, Hist. Ecclésiastique, tom. xviii. p. 181-199; Dupin, Biblioth. Ecclés. tom. x. p. 135.

33. This curious instruction, which has been

drawn with more or less honesty by Wading and Leo Allatius from the archives of the Vatican, is given in an abstract or version by Fleury (tom. xviii. p. 252-258).

34. This frank and authentic confession of Michael's distress is exhibited in barbarous Latin by Ogerius, who signs himself Protonotarius Interpretum, and transcribed by Wading from the MSS. of the Vatican (A.D. 1278, No. 3). His annals of the Franciscan order, the Fratres Minores, in seventeen volumes in folio (Rome, 1741), I have now accidentally seen among the waste paper of a bookseller.

35. See the sixth book of Pachymer, particularly the chapters 1, 11, 16, 18, 24-27. He is the more credible, as he speaks of this persecution with less anger than sorrow.

36. Pachymer, l. vii. c. 1, 11, 17 [tom. ii. p. 11, 36, 50, ed. Bonn]. The speech of Andronicus the Elder (lib. xii. c. 2) is a curious record which proves that, if the Greeks were the slaves of the emperor, was not less the slave of superstition and the clergy.

37. The best accounts, the nearest the time, the most full and entertaining, of the conquest of Naples by Charles of Anjou, may be found in the Florentine Chronicles of Ricordano Malespina (c. 175-193) and Giovanni Villani (l. vii. c. 1-10, 25-30), which are published by Muratori in the eighth and thirteenth volumes of the Historians of Italy. In his Annals (tom. xi. p. 56-72), he has abridged these great events, which are likewise described in the Istoria Civile of Giannone, tom. ii. l. xix., tom. iii. l. xx.

38. Ducange, Hist. de C. P. l. v. c. 49-56, l. vi. c. 1-13. See Pachymer, l. iv. c. 29, l. v. c. 7-10, 25, l. vi. c. 30, 32, 33; and Nicephorus Gregoras, l. iv. 5, l. v. 1, 6.

39. The reader of Herodotus will recollect how miraculously the Assyrian host of Sennacherib was disarmed and destroyed (l. ii. c. 141).

40. According to Sabas Malaspina (Hist. Sicula, l. iii. c. 16, in Muratori, tom. viii. p. 832), a zealous Guelph, the subjects of Charles, who had reviled Mainfroy as a wolf, began to regret him as a lamb; and he justifies their discontent by the oppressions of the French government (l. vi. c. 2, 7). See the Sicilian manifesto in Nicholas Specialis (l. i. c. 11, in Muratori, tom. x. p. 930).

41. See the character and counsels of Peter king of Arragon, in Mariana (Hist. Hispan. l. xiv. c. 6, tom. ii. p. 133). The reader forgives the Jesuit's defects, in favour, always of his style, and often of his sense.

42. After enumerating the sufferings of his country, Nicholas Specialis adds, in the true spirit of Italian jealousy, Quæ omnia et graviora quidem, ut arbitror, patienti animo Siculi tolerassent, nisi (quod primum cunctis dominantibus cavendum est) alienas feminas in vasissent (l. i. c. 2, p. 924).

43. The French were long taught to remember this bloody lesson: "If I am provoked (said Henry the Fourth), I will breakfast at Milan, and dine at Naples." "Your majesty (replied the Spanish ambassador) may perhaps arrive in Sicily for vespers."

44. This revolt, with the subsequent victory, are related by two national writers, Bartholemy à Neocastro (in Muratori, tom. xiii.) and Nicholas Specialis (in Muratori, tom. x.), the one a contemporary, the other of the next century. The patriot Specialis disclaims the name of rebellion, and all previous correspondence with Peter of Arragon (nullo communicato consilio), who happened to be with a fleet and army on the African coast (l. i. c. 4, 9).

45. Nicephorus Gregoras (l. v. c. 6) admires the wisdom of Providence in this equal balance of states and princes. For the honour of Palæologus I had rather this balance had been observed by an Italian writer.

46. See the Chronicle of Villani, the eleventh volume of the Annali d'Italia of Muratori, and the twentieth and twenty-first books of the Istoria Civile of Giannone.

47. In this motley multitude the Catalans and Spaniards, the bravest of the soldiery, were styled by themselves and the Greeks Amogavares. Moncada derives their origin from the Goths, and Pachymer (l. xi. c. 22 [tom. ii. p. 416, ed. Bonn]) from the Arabs, and, in spite of national and religious pride, I am afraid the latter is in the right.

48. Some idea may be formed of the population of these cities from the 36,000 inhabitants of Tralles, which, in the preceding reign, was rebuilt by the emperor, and ruined by the Turks. (Pachymer, l. vi. c. 20, 21.)

49. I have collected these pecuniary circumstances from Pachymer (l. xi. c. 21, l. xii. c. 4, 5, 8, 14, 19 [tom. ii. p. 493, 494, ed. Bonn]), who describes the progressive degradation of the gold coin. Even in the prosperous times of John Ducas Vataces, the byzants were composed in equal proportions of the pure and the baser metal. The poverty of Michael Palæologus compelled him to strike a new coin, with nine parts, or carats, of gold, and fifteen of copper alloy. After his death the standard rose to ten carats, till in the public distress it was reduced to the moiety. The prince was relieved for a moment, while credit and commerce were for ever blasted. In France the gold coin is of twenty-two carats (one twelfth alloy), and the standard of England and Holland is still higher.

50. The Catalan war is most copiously related by Pachymer, in the eleventh, twelfth, and thirteenth books, till he breaks off in the year 1308. Nicephorus Gregoras (l. vii. 3-6) is more concise and complete. Ducange, who adopts these adventurers as French, has hunted their footsteps with his usual diligence (Hist. de C. P. l. vi. c. 22-46). He quotes an Arragonese history, which I have read with pleasure, and which the Spaniards extol as a model of style and composition (Expedicion de los Catalanes y Arragoneses contra Turcos y

Griegos: Barcelona, 1623, in quarto: Madrid, 1777, in octavo). Don Francisco de Moncada, Conde de Osona, may imitate Cæsar or Sallust; he may transcribe the Greek or Italian contemporaries: but he never quotes his authorities, and I cannot discern any national records of the exploits of his countrymen.

51. See the laborious history of Ducange, whose accurate table of the French dynasties recapitulates the thirty-five passages in which he mentions the dukes of Athens.

52. He is twice mentioned by Villehardouin with honour (No. 151, 235); and under the first passage Ducange observes all that can be known of his person and family.

53. From these Latin princes of the fourteenth century, Boccace, Chaucer, and Shakspeare have borrowed their Theseus *duke* of Athens. An ignorant age transfers its own language and manners to the most distant times.

54. The same Constantine gave to Sicily a king, to Russia the *magnus dapifer* of the empire, to Thebes the *primicerius;* and these absurd fables are properly lashed by Ducange (ad Nicephor. Greg. l. vii. c. 5). By the Latins the lord of Thebes was styled, by corruption, the Megas Kurios, or Grand Sire!

55. *Quodam miraculo,* says Alberic. He was probably received by Michael Choniates, the archbishop who had defended Athens against the ty-

rant Leo Sgurus (Nicetas urbs capta, p. 805, ed. Bek.). Michael was the brother of the historian Nicetas; and his encomium of Athens is still extant in MS. in the Bodleian library (Fabric. Biblioth. Græc. tom. vi. p. 405).

56. The modern account of Athens and the Athenians is extracted from Spon (Voyage en Grèce, tom. ii. p. 79-199) and Wheeler (Travels into Greece, p. 337-414), Stuart (Antiquities of Athens, passim) and Chandler (Travels into Greece, p. 23-172). The first of these travellers visited Greece in the year 1676; the last 1765; and ninety years had not produced much difference in the tranquil scene.

57. The ancients, or at least the Athenians, believed that all the bees in the world had been propagated from Mount Hymettus. They taught that health might be preserved, and life prolonged, by the external use of oil and the internal use of honey (Geoponica, l. xv. c. 7, p. 1089-1094, edit. Niclas.).

58. Ducange, Glossar. Græc. Præfat. p. 8, who quotes for his author Theodosius Zygomalas, a modern grammarian. Yet Spon (tom. ii. p. 194) and Wheeler (p. 355), no incompetent judges, entertain a more favourable opinion of the Attic dialect.

59. Yet we must not accuse them of corrupting the name of Athens, which they still call Athini. From the εἰς τὴν Ἀθήνην we have formed our own barbarism of *Setines.*

Chapter LXIII

1. Andronicus himself will justify our freedom in the invective (Nicephorus Gregoras, l. i. c. 1) which he pronounced against historic falsehood. It is true that his censure is more pointedly urged against calumny than against adulation.

2. For the anathema in the pigeon's nest, see Pachymer (l. ix. c. 24 [tom. ii. p. 249, ed. Bonn]), who relates the general history of Athanasius (l. viii. c. 13-16, 20-24, l. x. c. 27-29, 31-36, l. xi. c. 1-3, 5, 6, l. xiii. c. 8, 10, 23, 35), and is followed by Nicephorus Gregoras (l. vi. c. 5, 7, l. vii. c. 1, 9), who includes the second retreat of this second Chrysostom.

3. Pachymer, in seven books, 377 folio pages, describes the first twenty-six years of Andronicus the Elder; and marks the date of his composition by the current news or lie of the day (A.D. 1308). Either death or disgust prevented him from resuming the pen.

4. After an interval of twelve years from the conclusion of Pachymer, Cantacuzenus takes up the pen; and his first book (c. 1-59, p. 9-150 [ed. Ven.]) relates the civil war and the eight last years of the elder Andronicus. The ingenious comparison with Moses and Cæsar is fancied by his French translator, the president Cousin.

5. Nicephorus Gregoras more briefly includes

the entire life and reign of Andronicus the Elder (l. vi. c. 1—l. x. c. 1, p. 96-291). This is the part of which Cantacuzene complains as a false and malicious representation of his conduct.

6. He was crowned May 21st, 1295, and died October 12th, 1320 (Ducange, Fam. Byz. p. 239). His brother Theodore, by a second marriage, inherited the marquisate of Montferrat, apostatised to the religion and manners of the Latins (ὅτι καὶ γνώμη καὶ πίστει καὶ σχήματι, καὶ γενείων κουρᾷ καὶ πᾶσιν ἔθεσιν Λατῖνος ἦν ἀκραιφνής. Nic. Greg. l. ix. c. 1), and founded a dynasty of Italian princes, which was extinguished A.D. 1533 (Ducange, Fam. Byz. p. 249-253).

7. We are indebted to Nicephorus Gregoras (l. viii. c. 1) for the knowledge of this tragic adventure; while Cantacuzene more discreetly conceals the vices of Andronicus the Younger, of which he was the witness, and perhaps the associate (l. i. c. 1, etc.).

8. His destined heir was Michael Catharus, the bastard of Constantine his second son. In this project of excluding his grandson Andronicus, Nicephorus Gregoras (l. viiii. c. 3 [6?]) agrees with Cantacuzene (l. i. c. 1, 2).

9. See Nicephorus Gregoras, l. viii. c. 6 [tom. i. p. 317, ed. Bonn]. The younger Andronicus com-

plained that in four years and four months a sum of 350,000 byzants of gold was due to him for the expenses of his household (Cantacuzen. l. i. c. 48 [tom. i. p. 237, ed. Bonn]). Yet he would have remitted the debt, if he might have been allowed to squeeze the farmers of the revenue.

10. I follow the chronology of Nicephorus Gregoras, who is remarkably exact. It is proved that Cantacuzene has mistaken the dates of his own actions, or rather that his text has been corrupted by ignorant transcribers.

11. I have endeavoured to reconcile the 24,000 pieces of Cantacuzene (l. ii. c. 1) with the 10,000 of Nicephorus Gregoras (l. ix. c. 2); the one of whom wished to soften, the other to magnify, the hardships of the old emperor.

12. See Nicephorus Gregoras (l. ix. 6, 7, 8, 10, 14, l. x. c. 1). The historian had tasted of the prosperity, and shared the retreat, of his benefactor; and that friendship which "waits or to the scaffold or the cell" should not lightly be accused as "a hireling, a prostitute to praise."

13. The sole reign of Andronicus the younger is described by Cantacuzene (l. ii. c. 1-40, p. 191-339 [ed. Par.]), and Nicephorus Gregoras (l. ix. c. 7—l. xi. c. 11, p. 262-351).

14. Agnes, or Irene, was the daughter of duke Henry the Wonderful, the chief of the house of Brunswick, and the fourth in descent from the famous Henry the Lion, duke of Saxony and Bavaria, and conqueror of the Slavi on the Baltic coast. Her brother Henry was surnamed the *Greek*, from his two journeys into the East: but these journeys were subsequent to his sister's marriage; and I am ignorant *how* Agnes was discovered in the heart of Germany, and recommended to the Byzantine court. (Rimius, Memoirs of the House of Brunswick, p. 126-137.)

15. Henry the Wonderful was the founder of the branch of Grubenhagen, extinct in the year 1596. (Rimius, p. 287.) He resided in the castle of Wolfenbüttel, and possessed no more than a sixth part of the allodial estates of Brunswick and Luneburg, which the Guelph family had saved from the confiscation of their great fiefs. The frequent partitions among brothers had almost ruined the princely houses of Germany, till that just, but pernicious, law was slowly superseded by the right of primogeniture. The principality of Grubenhagen, one of the last remains of the Hercynian forest, is a woody, mountainous, and barren tract. (Busching's Geography, vol. vi. p. 270-286, English translation.)

16. The royal author of the Memoirs of Brandenburg will teach us how justly, in a much later period, the north of Germany deserved the epithets of poor and barbarous. (Essai sur les Mœurs, etc.) In the year 1306, in the woods of Luneburg, some wild people of the Vened race were allowed to bury alive their infirm and useless parents. (Rimius, p. 136.)

17. The assertion of Tacitus, that Germany was destitute of the precious metals, must be taken, even in his own time, with some limitation. (Germania, c. 5; Annal. xi. 20.) According to Spener (Hist. Germaniæ Pragmatica, tom. i. p. 351), *Argentifodinæ* in Hercyniis montibus, imperante Othone magno (A.D. 968) primum apertæ, largam etiam opes augendi dederunt copiam: but Rimius (p. 258, 259) defers till the year 1016 the discovery of the silver-mines of Grubenhagen, or the Upper Hartz, which were productive in the beginning of the fourteenth century, and which still yield a considerable revenue to the house of Brunswick.

18. Cantacuzene has given a most honourable testimony, ἥνδ᾿ ἐκ Γερμανῶν αὕτη θυγάτηρ δουκὸς ντὶ Μπρουζουὴκ (the modern Greeks employ the ντ for the δ, and the μπ for the β, and the whole will read in the Italian idiom di Brunzuic), τοῦ παρ᾿ αὐτοῖς ἐπιφανεστάτου, καὶ λαμπρότητι πάντας τοὺς ὁμοφύλους ὑπερβ ἀλλόντος τοῦ γένους [l. i. c. 10, tom. i. p. 52, ed. Bonn]. The praise is just in itself, and pleasing to an English ear.

19. Anne, or Jane, was one of the four daughters of Amedêe the Great, by a second marriage, and half sister of his successor Edward count of Savoy (Anderson's Tables, p. 650). See Cantacuzene (l. i. c. 40-41).

20. That king, if the fact be true, must have been Charles the Fair, who in five years (1321-1326) was married to three wives (Anderson, p. 628). Anne of Savoy arrived at Constantinople in February 1326.

21. The noble race of the Cantacuzeni (illustrious from the eleventh century in the Byzantine annals) was drawn from the Paladins of France, the heroes of those romances which, in the thirteenth century, were translated and read by the Greeks (Ducange, Fam. Byzant. p. 258).

22. See Cantacuzene (l. iii. c. 24, 30, 36).

23. Saserna in Gaul, and Columella in Italy or Spain, allow two yoke of oxen, two drivers, and six labourers, for two hundred jugera (125 English acres) of arable land, and three more men must be added if there be much underwood (Columella de Re Rusticâ, l. ii. c. 13, p. 441, edit. Gesner).

24. In this enumeration (l. iii. c. 30) the French translation of the president Cousin is blotted with three palpable and essential errors. 1. He omits the 1000 yoke of working oxen. 2. He interprets the πεντακόσιαι πρὸς δισχιλίαις by the number of fifteen hundred. 3. He confounds myriads with chiliads, and gives Cantacuzene no more than 5000 hogs. Put not your trust in translations!

25. See the regency and reign of John Cantacuzenus, and the whole progress of the civil war, in his own history (l. iii. c. 1-100, p. 348-700 [ed. Par.]), and in that of Nicephorus Gregoras (l. xii. c. 1—l. xv. c. 9, p. 353-492).

26. He assumed the royal privilege of red shoes or buskins; placed on his head a mitre of silk and gold; subscribed his epistles with hyacinth or green ink; and claimed for the new whatever Constantine had given to the ancient Rome (Canta-

cuzen. l. iii. c. 26 [tom. ii. p. 162, ed. Bonn]; Nic. Gregoras, l. xiv. c. 3).

27. Nic. Gregoras (l. xii. c. 5) confesses the innocence and virtues of Cantacuzenus, the guilt and flagitious vices of Apocaucus; nor does he dissemble the motive of his personal and religious enmity to the former; νυν δὲ διά κακίαν ἄλλων, αἴτιος ὁ πραότατος τῆς τῶν ὅλων ἔδοξεν εἶναι φθορᾶς [tom. ii. p. 590, ed. Bonn].

28. The princes of Servia (Ducange, Famil. Dalmaticæ, etc., c. 2, 3, 4, 9) were styled Despots in Greek, and Cral in their native idiom. (Ducange, Gloss. Græc. p. 751). That title, the equivalent of king, appears to be of Sclavonic origin, from whence it has been borrowed by the Hungarians, the modern Greeks, and even by the Turks (Leunclavius, Pandect. Turc. p. 422), who reserve the name of Padishah for the emperor. To obtain the latter instead of the former is the ambition of the French at Constantinople (Avertissement à l'Histoire de Timur Bec, p. 39).

29. Nic. Gregoras, l. xii. c. 14 [tom. ii. p. 622, ed. Bonn]. It is surprising that Cantacuzene has not inserted this just and lively image in his own writings.

30. The two avengers were both Palæologi, who might resent, with royal indignation, the shame of their chains. The tragedy of Apocaucus may deserve a peculiar reference to Cantacuzene (l. iii. c. 88) and Nic. Gregoras (l. xiv. c. 10).

31. Cantacuzene accuses the patriarch, and spares the empress, the mother of his sovereign (l. iii. 33, 34), against whom Nic. Gregoras expresses a particular animosity (l. xiv. 10, 11; xv. 5). It is true that they do not speak exactly of the same time.

32. The traitor and treason are revealed by Nic. Gregoras (l. xv. c. 8); but the name is more discreetly suppressed by his great accomplice (Cantacuzen. l. iii. c. 99).

33. Nic. Greg. l. xv. 11 [tom. ii. p. 788, ed. Bonn]. There were, however, some true pearls, but very thinly sprinkled. The rest of the stones had only παντοδαπὴν χροιὰν πρὸς τὸ διαυγές.

34. From his return to Constantinople, Cantacuzene continues his history and that of the empire one year beyond the abdication of his son Matthew, A.D. 1357 (l. iv. c. 1–50, p. 705–911). Nicephorus Gregoras ends with the synod of Constantinople, in the year 1351 (l. xxii. c. 3, p. 660; the rest, to the conclusion of the twenty-fourth book, p. 717, is all controversy); and his fourteen last books are still MSS. in the king of France's library.

35. The emperor (Cantacuzen. l. iv. c. 1) represents his own virtues, and Nic. Gregoras (l. xv. c. 11) the complaints of his friends, who suffered by its effects. I have lent them the words of our poor cavaliers after the Restoration.

36. The awkward apology of Cantacuzene (l. iv. c. 39–41), who relates, with visible confusion, his own downfall, may be supplied by the less accurate, but more honest, narratives of Matthew

Villani (l. iv. c. 46, in the Script. Rerum Ital. tom. xiv. p. 268) and Ducas (c. 10, 11).

37. Cantacuzene, in the year 1375, was honoured with a letter from the pope (Fleury, Hist. Ecclés. tom. xx. p. 250). His death is placed by a respectable authority on the 20th of November, 1411 (Ducange, Fam. Byzant. p. 260). But if he were of the age of his companion Andronicus the Younger, he must have lived 116 years—a rare instance of longevity, which in so illustrious a person would have attracted universal notice.

38. His four discourses, or books, were printed at Basil 1543 (Fabric. Biblioth. Græc. tom. vi. p. 473). He composed them to satisfy a proselyte who was assaulted with letters from his friends of Ispahan. Cantacuzene had read the Koran; but I understand from Maracci that he adopts the vulgar prejudices and fables against Mohammed and his religion.

39. See the Voyages de Bernier, tom. i. p. 127.

40. Mosheim, Institut. Hist. Eccles. p. 522, 523; Fleury, Hist. Ecclés. tom. xx. p. 22, 24, 107–114, etc. The former unfolds the causes with the judgment of a philosopher, the latter transcribes and translates with the prejudices of a Catholic priest.

41. Basnage (in Canisii Antiq. Lectiones, tom. iv. p. 363–368) has investigated the character and story of Barlaam. The duplicity of his opinions had inspired some doubts of the identity of his person. See likewise Fabricius (Biblioth. Græc. tom. x. p. 427–432).

42. See Cantacuzene (l. ii. c. 39, 40; l. iv. c. 3, 23, 24, 25) and Nic. Gregoras (l. xi. c. 10; l. xv. 3, 7, etc.), whose last books, from the nineteenth to the twenty-fourth, are almost confined to a subject so interesting to the authors. Boivin (in Vit. Nic. Gregoræ), from the unpublished books, and Fabricius (Biblioth. Græc. tom. x. p. 462–473), or rather Montfaucon, from the MSS. of the Coislin library, have added some facts and documents.

43. Pachymer (l. v. c. 10 [tom. i. p. 366, ed. Bonn]) very properly explains λυζίους (ligios) by ἰδίους. The use of these words in the Greek and Latin of the feudal times may be amply understood from the Glossaries of Ducange (Græc. p. 811, 812; Latin. tom. iv. p. 109–111).

44. The establishment and progress of the Genoese at Pera, or Galata, is described by Ducange (C. P. Christiana, l. i. p. 68, 69) from the Byzantine historians, Pachymer (l. ii. c. 35; l. v. 10, 30; l. ix. 15; l. xii. 6, 9), Nicephorus Gregoras (l. v. c. 4; l. vi. c. 11; l. ix. c. 5; l. xi. c. 1; l. xv. c. 1, 6), and Cantacuzene (l. i. c. 12; l. ii. c. 29, etc.).

45. Both Pachymer (l. iii. c. 3, 4, 5) and Nic. Greg. (l. iv. c. 7) understand and deplore the effects of this dangerous indulgence. Bibars, sultan of Egypt, himself a Tartar, but a devout Musulman, obtained from the children of Zingis the permission to build a stately mosque in the capital of Crimea (De Guignes, Hist. des Huns, tom. iii. p. 343).

46. Chardin (Voyages en Perse, tom. i. p. 48)

was assured at Caffa that these fishes were sometimes twenty-four or twenty-six feet long, weighed eight or nine hundred pounds, and yielded three or four quintals of caviar. The corn of the Bosphorus had supplied the Athenians in the time of Demosthenes.

47. De Guignes, Hist. des Huns, tom. iii. p. 343, 344; Viaggi di Ramusiol tom. i. fol. 400. But this land or water carriage could only be practicable when Tartary was united under a wise and powerful monarch.

48. Nic. Gregoras (l. xiii. c. 12) is judicious and well-informed on the trade and colonies of the Black Sea. Chardin describes the present ruins of Caffa, where, in forty days, he saw above 400 sail employed in the corn and fish trade (Voyages en Perse, tom. i. p. 46–48).

49. See Nic. Gregoras, l. xvii. c. 1.

50. The events of this war are related by Cantacuzene (l. iv. c. 11) with obscurity and confusion, and by Nic. Gregoras (l. xvii. c. 1–7) in a clear and honest narrative. The priest was less respon-sible than the prince for the defeat of the fleet.

51. This second war is darkly told by Cantacuzene (l. iv. c. 18, 24, 25, 28–32), who wishes to disguise what he dares not deny. I regret this part of Nic. Gregoras, which is still in MS. at Paris.

52. Muratori (Annali d'Italia, tom. xii. p. 144) refers to the most ancient Chronicles of Venice (Caresinus, the continuator of Andrew Dandulus, tom. xii. p. 421, 422) and Genoa (George Stella, Annales Genuenses, tom. xvii. p. 1091, 1092), both which I have diligently consulted in his great Collection of the Historians of Italy.

53. See the Chronicle of Matteo Villani of Florence, l. ii. c. 59, 60, p. 145–147; c. 74, 75, p. 156, 157, in Muratori's Collection, tom. xiv.

54. The Abbé de Sade (Mémoires sur la Vie de Pétrarque, tom. iii. p. 257–263) translates this letter, which he had copied from a MS. in the king of France's library. Though a servant of the duke of Milan, Petrarch pours forth his astonishment and grief at the defeat and despair of the Genoese in the following year (p. 323–332).

Chapter LXIV

1. The reader is invited to review chapters xxii. to xxvi. and xxxiii. to xxxviii., the manners of pastoral nations, the conquests of Attila and the Huns, which were composed at a time when I entertained the wish, rather than the hope, of concluding my history.

2. The khans of the Keraites were most probably incapable of reading the pompous epistles composed in their name by the Nestorian missionaries, who endowed them with the fabulous wonders of an Indian kingdom. Perhaps these Tartars (the Presbyter or Priest John) had submitted to the rites of baptism and ordination (Asseman. Biblioth. Orient. tom. iii. p. ii. p. 487–503).

3. Since the history and tragedy of Voltaire, *Gengis*, at least in French, seems to be the more fashionable spelling; but Abulghazi Khan must have known the true name of his ancestor. His etymology appears just: *Zin*, in the Mogul tongue, signifies *great*, and *gis* is the superlative termination (Hist. Généalogique des Tatars, part iii. p. 194, 195). From the same idea of magnitude the appellation of *Zingis* is bestowed on the ocean.

4. The name of Moguls has prevailed among the Orientals, and still adheres to the titular sovereign, the Great Mogul of Hindostan.

5. The Tartars (more properly Tatars) were descended from Tatar Khan, the brother of Mogul Khan (see Abulghazi, parts i. and ii.), and once formed a horde of 70,000 families on the borders of Kitay (p. 103–112). In the great invasion of Europe (A.D. 1238) they seem to have led the vanguard; and the similitude of the name of *Tartarei* recommended that of Tartars to the Latins (Matt. Paris, p. 398 [p. 546, ed. Lond. 1640], etc.).

6. A singular conformity may be found between the religious laws of Zingis Khan and of Mr. Locke (Constitutions of Carolina, in his works, vol. iv. p. 535, 4to edition, 1777).

7. In the year 1294, by the command of Cazan, khan of Persia, the fourth in descent from Zingis. From these traditions his vizir Fadlallah composed a Mogul history in the Persian language, which has been used by Petit de la Croix (Hist. de Genghizcan, p. 537–539). The Histoire Généalogique des Tatars (à Leyde, 1726, in 12mo, 2 tomes) was translated by the Swedish prisoners in Siberia from the Mogul MS. of Abulgasi Bahadur Khan, a descendant of Zingis, who reigned over the Usbeks of Charasm, or Carizme (A.D. 1644–1663). He is of most value and credit for the names, pedigrees, and manners of his nation. Of his nine parts, the first descends from Adam to Mogul Khan; the second, from Mogul to Zingis; the third is the life of Zingis; the fourth, fifth, sixth, and seventh, the general history of his four sons and their posterity; the eighth and ninth, the particular history of the descendants of Sheibani Khan, who reigned in Maurenahar and Charasm. [The Igours were Turks, not Mongols.]

8. Histoire de Gentchiscan, et de toute la Dinastie des Mongous ses Successeurs, Conquérans de la Chine; tirée de l'Histoire de la Chine par le R. P. Gaubil, de la Société de Jésus, Missionaire à Peking; à Paris, 1739, in 4to. This translation is stamped with the Chinese character of domestic accuracy and foreign ignorance.

9. See the Histoire du Grand Genghizcan, premier Empereur des Moguls et Tartares, par M. Petit de la Croix, à Paris, 1710, in 12mo: a work

of ten years' labour, chiefly drawn from the Persian writers, among whom Nisavi, the secretary of sultan Gelaleddin, has the merit and prejudices of a contemporary. A slight air of romance is the fault of the originals, or the compiler. See likewise the articles of *Genghizcan, Mohammed, Gelaleddin,* etc., in the Bibliothèque Orientale of D'Herbelot.

10. Haithonus, or Aithonus, an Armenian prince, and afterwards a monk of Premontré (Fabric. Biblioth, Lat. medii Ævi, tom. i. p. 34), dictated in the French language his book *de Tartaris*, his old fellow-soldiers. It was immediately translated into Latin, and is inserted in the Novus Orbis of Simon Grynæus (Basil, 1555, in folio).

11. Zingis Khan, and his first successors, occupy the conclusion of the ninth Dynasty of Abulpharagius (vers. Pocock, Oxon. 1663, in 4to); and his tenth Dynasty is that of the Moguls of Persia. Assemannus (Biblioth. Orient. tom. ii.) has extracted some facts from his Syriac writings, and the lives of the Jacobite maphrians, or primates of the East.

12. Among the Arabians, in language and religion, we may distinguish Abulfeda, sultan of Hamah in Syria, who fought in person, under the Mameluke standard, against the Moguls.

13. Nicephorus Gregoras (l. ii. c. 5, 6) has felt the necessity of connecting the Scythian and Byzantine histories. He describes with truth and elegance the settlement and manners of the Moguls of Persia, but he is ignorant of their origin, and corrupts the names of Zingis and his sons.

14. M. Levesque (Histoire de Russie, tom. ii.) has described the conquest of Russia by the Tartars, from the patriarch Nicon and the old chronicles.

15. For Poland I am content with the Sarmatia Asiatica et Europæa of Matthew à Michou, or De Michoviâ, a canon and physician of Cracow (A.D. 1506), inserted in the Novus Orbis of Grynæus Fabric. Biblioth. Latin. mediæ et infimæ Ætatis, tom. v. p. 56.

16. I should quote Thuroczius, the oldest general historian (pars ii. c. 74, p. 150), in the first volume of the Scriptores Rerum Hungaricarum, did not the same volume contain the original narrative of a contemporary, an eye-witness, and a sufferer (M. Rogerii, Hungari, Varadiensis Capituli Canonici, Carmen miserabile, seu Historia super Destructione Regni Hungariæ Temporibus Belæ IV. Regis per Tartaros facta, p. 292–321); the best picture that I have ever seen of all the circumstances of a barbaric invasion.

17. Matthew Paris has represented, from authentic documents, the danger and distress of Europe (consult the word *Tartari* in his copious Index). From motives of zeal and curiosity, the court of the great khan in the thirteenth century was visited by two friars, John de Plano Carpini, and William Rubruquis, and by Marco Polo, a Venetian gentleman. The Latin relations of the two former are inserted in the first volume of Hakluyt; the Italian original or version of the third (Fabric. Biblioth. Latin. medii Ævi, tom. ii. p. 198, tom. v. p. 25) may be found in the second tome of Ramusio.

18. In his great History of the Huns M. de Guignes has most amply treated of Zingis Khan and his successors. See tom. iii. l. xv.–xix. and in the collateral articles of the Seljukians of Roum, tom. ii. l. xi.; the Carizmians, l. xiv.; and the Mamelukes, tom. iv. l. xxi.: consult likewise the tables of the first volume. He is ever learned and accurate; yet I am only indebted to him for a general view, and some passages of Abulfeda, which are still latent in the Arabic text.

19. More properly *Yen-king*, an ancient city, whose ruins still appear some furlongs to the southeast of the modern *Pekin*, which was built by Cublai Khan (Gaubil, p. 146). Pe-king and Nan-king are vague titles, the courts of the north and of the south. The identity and change of names perplex the most skilful readers of the Chinese geography (p. 177).

20. M. de Voltaire, Essai sur l'Histoire Générale, tom. iii. c. 60, p. 8. His account of Zingis and the Moguls contains, as usual, much general sense and truth, with some particular errors.

21. Zagatai gave his name to his dominions of Maurenahar, or Transoxiana; and the Moguls of Hindostan, who emigrated from that country, are styled Zagatais by the Persians. This certain etymology, and the similar example of Uzbek, Nogai, etc., may warn us not absolutely to reject the derivations of a national, from a personal, name.

22. In Marco Polo, and the Oriental geographers, the names of Cathay and Mangi distinguish the northern and southern empires, which, from A.D. 1234 to 1279, were those of the great khan and of the Chinese. The search of Cathay, after China had been found, excited and misled our navigators of the sixteenth century in their attempts to discover the north-east passage.

23. I depend on the knowledge and fidelity of the Père Gaubil, who translates the Chinese text of the annals of the Moguls or Yuen (p. 71, 93, 153); but I am ignorant at what time these annals were composed and published. The two uncles of Marco Polo, who served as engineers at the siege of Siengyangfou (l. ii. c. 61, in Ramusio, tom. ii.; see Gaubil, p. 155, 157), must have felt and related the effects of this destructive powder; and their silence is a weighty, and almost decisive, objection. I entertain a suspicion that the recent discovery was carried from Europe to China by the caravans of the fifteenth century, and falsely adopted as an old national discovery before the arrival of the Portuguese and Jesuits in the sixteenth. Yet the Père Gaubil affirms that the use of gunpowder has been known to the Chinese above 1600 years.

24. All that can be known of the Assassins of Persia and Syria is poured from the copious, and even profuse, erudition of M. Falconet, in two *Mémoires* read before the Academy of Inscriptions (tom. xvii. p. 127–170).

25. The Ismaelians of Syria, 40,000 Assassins, had acquired or founded ten castles in the hills above Tortosa. About the year 1280 they were extirpated by the Mamalukes.

26. As a proof of the ignorance of the Chinese in foreign transactions, I must observe that some of their historians extend the conquests of Zingis himself to Medina, the country of Mohammed (Gaubil, p. 42).

27. The *Dashté Kipzak*, or plain of Kipzak, extends on either side of the Volga, in a boundless space towards the Jaik and Borysthenes, and is supposed to contain the primitive name and nation of the Cosacks.

28. In the year 1238 the inhabitants of Gothia (*Sweden*) and Frise were prevented, by their fear of the Tartars, from sending, as usual, their ships to the herring-fishery on the coast of England; and, as there was no exportation, forty or fifty of these fish were sold for a shilling (Matthew Paris, p. 396). It is whimsical enough that the orders of a Mogul khan, who reigned on the borders of China, should have lowered the price of herrings in the English market.

29. I shall copy his characteristic or flattering epithets of the different countries of Europe: Furens ac fervens ad arma Germania, strenuæ militiæ genitrix et alumna Francia, bellicosa et audax Hispania, virtuosa viris et classe munita fertilis Anglia, impetuosis bellatoribus referta Alemannia, navalis Dacia, indomita Italia, pacis ignara Burgundia, inquieta, Apulia, cum maris Græci, Adriatici et Tyrrheni insulis pyraticis et invictis, Cretâ, Cypro, Siciliâ, cum Oceano conterminis insulis, et regionibus, cruenta Hybernia, cum agili Wallia, palustris Scotia, glacialis Norwegia, suam electam militiam sub vexillo Crucis destinabunt, etc. (Matthew Paris, p. 498.)

30. See Carpin's relation in Hakluyt, vol. i. p. 30. The pedigree of the khans of Siberia is given by Abulghazi (part viii. p. 485–495). Have the Russians found no Tartar chronicles at Tobolskoi?

31. The Map of D'Anville and the Chinese Itineraries (De Guignes, tom. i. part ii. p. 57) seem to mark the position of Holin, or Caracorum, about six hundred miles to the north-west of Pekin. The distance between Selinginsky and Pekin is near 2000 Russian versts, between 1300 and 1400 English miles (Bell's Travels, vol. ii. p. 67).

32. Rubruquis found at Caracorum his countryman *Guillaume Boucher, orfèvre de Paris*, who had executed for the khan a silver tree, supported by four lions, and ejecting four different liquors. Abulghazi (part iv. p. 366) mentions the painters of Kitay or China.

33. The attachment of the khans, and the hatred of the mandarins, to the bonzes and lamas (Duhalde, Hist. de la Chine, tom. i. p. 502, 503) seems to represent them as the priests of the same god, of the Indian *Fo*, whose worship prevails among the sects of Hindostan, Siam, Thibet, China, and Japan. But this mysterious subject is still lost in a cloud, which the researches of our Asiatic Society may gradually dispel.

34. Some repulse of the Moguls in Hungary (Matthew Paris, p. 545, 546) might propagate and colour the report of the union and victory of the kings of the Franks on the confines of Bulgaria. Abulpharagius (Dynast. p. 310), after forty years beyond the Tigris, might be easily deceived.

35. See Pachymer, l. iii. c. 25, and l. ix. c. 26, 27; and the false alarm at Nice, l. iii. c. 27 [c. 28, tom. i. p. 244, ed. Bonn]; Nicephorus Gregoras, l. iv. c. 6.

36. G. Acropolita, p. 36, 37; Nic. Greg. l. ii. c. 6, l. iv. c. 5.

37. Abulpharagius, who wrote in the year 1284, declares that the Moguls, since the fabulous defeat of Batou, had not attacked either the Franks or Greeks; and of this he is a competent witness. Hayton likewise, the Armeniac prince, celebrates their friendship for himself and his nation.

38. Pachymer gives a splendid character of Cazan Khan, the rival of Cyrus and Alexander (l. xii. c. 1). In the conclusion of his history (l. xiii. c. 36 [tom. ii. p. 651, ed. Bonn]), he *hopes* much from the arrival of 30,000 Tochars, or Tartars, who were ordered by the successor of Cazan to restrain the Turks of Bithynia, A.D. 1308.

39. The origin of the Ottoman dynasty is illustrated by the critical learning of MM. de Guignes (Hist. des Huns, tom. iv. p. 329–337) and D'Anville (Empire Turc, p. 14–22), two inhabitants of Paris, from whom the Orientals may learn the history and geography of their own country.

40. See Pachymer, l. x. c. 25, 26, l. xiii. c. 33, 34, 36, and concerning the guard of the mountains, l. i. c. 3–6; Nicephorus Gregoras, l. vii. c. 1; and the first book of Laonicus Chalcocondyles, the Athenian.

41. I am ignorant whether the Turks have any writers older than Mohammed II., nor can I reach beyond a meagre chronicle (Annales Turcici ad Annum 1550), translated by John Gaudier, and published by Leunclavius (ad calcem Laonic. Chalcocond. p. 311–350), with copious pandects, or commentaries. The History of the Growth and Decay (A.D. 1300–1683) of the Othman Empire was translated into English from the Latin MS. of Demetrius Cantemir, prince of Moldavia (London, 1734, in folio). The author is guilty of strange blunders in Oriental history; but he was conversant with the language, the annals, and institutions of the Turks. Cantemir partly draws his materials from the Synopsis of Saadi Effendi of Larissa, dedicated in the year 1696 to sultan Mustapha, and a valuable abridgment of the original historians. In one of the Ramblers Dr. Johnson praises Knolles (A General History of the Turks to the present Year: London, 1603) as the first of historians, unhappy only in the choice of his subject. Yet I much doubt whether a partial and verbose compilation from Latin writers, thirteen hundred folio pages of speeches and battles, can either instruct or

amuse an enlightened age, which requires from the historian some tincture of philosophy and criticism.

42. Cantacuzene, though he relates the battle and heroic flight of the younger Andronicus (l. ii. c. 6, 7, 8), dissembles by his silence the loss of Prusa, Nice, and Nicomedia, which are fairly confessed by Nicephorus Gregoras (l. viii. 15; ix. 9, 13; xi. 6). It appears that Nice was taken by Orchan in 1330, and Nicomedia in 1339, which are somewhat different from the Turkish dates.

43. The partition of the Turkish emirs is extracted from two contemporaries, the Greek Nicephorus Gregoras (l. vii. 1) and the Arabian Marakeschi (De Guignes, tom. ii. P. ii. p. 76, 77). See likewise the first book of Laonicus Chalcocondyles.

44. Pachymer, l. xiii. c. 13.

45. See the Travels of Wheeler and Spon, of Pocock and Chandler, and more particularly Smith's Survey of the Seven Churches of Asia, p. 205-276. The more pious antiquaries labour to reconcile the promises and threats of the author of the Revelations with the *present* state of the seven cities. Perhaps it would be more prudent to confine his predictions to the characters and events of his own times.

46. Consult the fourth book of the Histoire de l'Ordre de Malthe, par l'Abbé de Vertot. That pleasing writer betrays his ignorance in supposing that Othman, a freebooter of the Bithynian hills, could besiege Rhodes by sea and land.

47. Nicephorus Gregoras has expatiated with pleasure on this amiable character (l. xii. 7; xiii. 4, 10; xiv. 1, 9; xvi. 6). Cantacuzene speaks with honour and esteem of his ally (l. iii. c. 56, 57, 63, 64, 66, 67, 68, 86, 89, 95, 96), but he seems ignorant of his own sentimental passion for the Turk, and indirectly denies the possibility of such unnatural friendship (l. iv. c. 40 [tom. iii. p. 297, ed. Bonn]).

48. After the conquest of Smyrna by the Latins, the defence of this fortress was imposed by Pope Gregory XI. on the knights of Rhodes (see Vertot, l. v.).

49. See Cantacuzenus, l. iii. c. 95 [tom. ii. p. 586, ed. Bonn]. Nicephorus Gregoras, who, for the light of Mount Thabor, brands the emperor with the names of tyrant and Herod, excuses, rather than blames, this Turkish marriage, and alleges the passion and power of Orchan, ἐγγύτατος, καὶ τῇ δυνάμει τοὺς κατ' αὐτὸν ἤδη Περσικοὺς (*Turkish*) ὑπεραίρων Σατράπας (l. xv. 5). He afterwards celebrates his kingdom and armies. See his reign in Cantemir, p. 24-30.

50. The most lively and concise picture of this captivity may be found in the history of Ducas (c. 8 [p. 32, ed. Bonn]), who fairly describes what Cantacuzene confesses with a guilty blush!

51. In this passage, and the first conquests in Europe, Cantemir (p. 27, etc.) gives a miserable idea of his Turkish guides; nor am I much better

satisfied with Chalcocondyles (l. i. p. 12, etc. [ed. Par.; p. 25, ed. Bonn]). They forget to consult the most authentic record, the fourth book of Cantacuzene. I likewise regret the last books, which are still manuscript, of Nicephorus Gregoras.

52. After the conclusion of Cantacuzene and Gregoras there follows a dark interval of a hundred years. George Phranza, Michael Ducas, and Laonicus Chalcocondyles, all three wrote after the taking of Constantinople.

53. See Cantemir, p. 37-41, with his own large and curious annotations.

54. *White* and *black* face are common and proverbial expressions of praise and reproach in the Turkish language. Hic *niger* est, hunc tu Romane caveto, was likewise a Latin sentence.

55. See the life and death of Morad, or Amurath I., in Cantemir (p. 33-45), the first book of Chalcocondyles, and the Annales Turcici of Leunclavius. According to another story, the sultan was stabbed by a Croat in his tent; and this accident was alleged to Busbequius (Epist. i. p. 98) as an excuse for the unworthy precaution of pinioning, as it were, between two attendants, an ambassador's arms, when he is introduced to the royal presence.

56. The reign of Bajazet I., or Ilderim Bayazid, is contained in Cantemir (p. 46), the second book of Chalcocondyles, and the Annales Turcici. The surname of Ilderim, or lightning, is an example that the conquerors and poets of every age have *felt* the truth of a system which derives the sublime from the principle of terror.

57. Cantemir, who celebrates the victories of the great Stephen over the Turks (p. 47), had composed the ancient and modern state of his principality of Moldavia, which has been long promised, and is still unpublished.

58. Leunclav. Annal. Turcici, p. 318, 319. The venality of the cadhis has long been an object of scandal and satire; and, if we distrust the observations of our travellers, we may consult the feeling of the Turks themselves (D'Herbelot, Biblioth. Orientale, p. 216, 217, 229, 230).

59. The fact, which is attested by the Arabic history of Ben Schounah, a contemporary Syrian (De Guignes, Hist. des Huns, tom. iv. p. 336), destroys the testimony of Saad Effendi and Cantemir (p. 14, 15), of the election of Othman to the dignity of sultan.

60. See the Decades Rerum Hungaricarum (Dec. iii. l. ii. p. 379) of Bonfinius, an Italian, who, in the fifteenth century, was invited into Hungary to compose an eloquent history of that kingdom. Yet, if it be extant and accessible, I should give the preference to some homely chronicle of the time and country.

61. I should not complain of the labour of this work, if my materials were always derived from such books as the Chronicle of honest Froissard (vol. iv. c. 67, 69, 72, 74, 79-83, 85, 87, 89), who read little, inquired much, and believed all. The

original Mémoires of the Maréchal de Boucicault (partie i. c. 22–28) add some facts, but they are dry and deficient, if compared with the pleasant garrulity of Froissard.

62. An accurate Memoir on the Life of Enguerrand VII., Sire de Coucy, has been given by the Baron de Zurlauben (Hist. de l'Académie des Inscriptions, tom. xxv.). His rank and possessions were equally considerable in France and England; and, in 1375, he led an army of adventurers into Switzerland, to recover a large patrimony which he claimed in right of his grandmother, the daughter of the emperor Albert I. of Austria (Sinner, Voyage dans la Suisse Occidentale, tom. i. p. 118–124).

63. That military office, so respectable at present, was still more conspicuous when it was divided between two persons (Daniel, Hist. de la Milice Françoise, tom. ii. p. 5). One of these, the marshal of the crusade, was the famous Boucicault, who afterwards defended Constantinople, governed Genoa, invaded the coast of Asia, and died in the field of Azincour.

64. For this odious fact, the Abbé de Vertot quotes the Hist. Anonyme de St. Denys, l. xvi. c. 10, 11. (Ordre de Malthe, tom. ii. p. 310.)

65. Sherefeddin Ali (Hist. de Timour Bec, l. v. c. 13) allows Bajazet a round number of 12,000 officers and servants of the chase. A part of his spoils was afterwards displayed in a hunting-match of Timour:—1, hounds with satin housings; 2, leopards with collars set with jewels; 3, Grecian greyhounds; and 4, dogs from Europe, as strong as African lions (idem, l. vi. c. 15). Bajazet was particularly fond of flying his hawks at cranes (Chalcocondyles, l. ii. p. 35 [p. 67, ed. Bonn]).

66. For the reigns of John Palæologus and his son Manuel, from 1354 to 1402, see Ducas, c. 9–15; Phranza, l. i. c. 16–21; and the first and second books of Chalcocondyles, whose proper subject is drowned in a sea of episode.

67. Cantemir, p. 50–53. Of the Greeks, Ducas alone (c. 13, 15) acknowledges the Turkish cadhi at Constantinople. Yet even Ducas dissembles the mosque.

68. Mémoires du bon Messire Jean le Maingre, dit *Boucicault*, Maréchal de France, partie ire., c. 30–35.

Chapter LXV

1. These journals were communicated to Sherefeddin, or Cherefeddin, Ali, a native of Yezd, who composed in the Persian language a history of Timour Beg, which has been translated into French by M. Petit de la Croix (Paris, 1722, in 4 vols. 12mo), and has always been my faithful guide. His geography and chronology are wonderfully accurate; and he may be trusted for public facts, though he servilely praises the virtue and fortune of the hero. Timour's attention to procure intelligence from his own and foreign countries may be seen in the Institutions, p. 215, 217, 349, 351.

2. These Commentaries are yet unknown in Europe: but Mr. White gives some hope that they may be imported and translated by his friend Major Davy, who had read in the East this "minute and faithful narrative of an interesting and eventful period."

3. I am ignorant whether the original institution, in the Turki or Mogul language, be still extant. The Persic version, with an English translation, and most valuable index, was published (Oxford, 1783, in 4to) by the joint labours of Major Davy and Mr. White the Arabic professor. This work has been since translated from the Persic into French (Paris, 1787) by M. Langlès, a learned Orientalist, who has added the Life of Timour and many curious notes.

4. Shaw Allum, the present Mogul, reads, values, but cannot imitate, the institutions of his great ancestor. The English translator relies on their internal evidence; but if any suspicion should arise of fraud and fiction, they will not be dispelled by Major Davy's letter. The Orientals have never cultivated the art of criticism; the patronage of a prince, less honourable perhaps, is not less lucrative than that of a bookseller; nor can it be deemed incredible that a Persian, the *real* author, should renounce the credit, to raise the value and price, of the work.

5. The original of the tale is found in the following work, which is much esteemed for its florid elegance of style: *Ahmedis Arabsiadæ* (Ahmed Ebn Arabshah) *Vitæ et Rerum Gestarum Timuri. Arabice et Latine. Edidit Samuel Henricus Manger. Franequeræ*, 1767, 2 tom. in 4to. This Syrian author is ever a malicious, and often an ignorant, enemy: the very titles of his chapters are injurious; as how the wicked, as how the impious, as how the viper, etc. The copious article of TIMUR, in Bibliothèque Orientale, is of a mixed nature, as D'Herbelot indifferently draws his materials (p. 877–888) from Khondemir, Ebn Schounah, and the Lebtarikh.

6. *Demir* or *Timour* signifies, in the Turkish language, Iron; and *Beg* is the appellation of a lord or prince. By the change of a letter or accent it is changed into *Lenc* or Lame; and a European corruption confounds the two words in the name of Tamerlane.

7. After relating some false and foolish tales of Timour *Lenc*, Arabshah is compelled to speak truth, and to own him for a kinsman of Zingis, per mulieres (as he peevishly adds) laqueos Satanæ (pars i. c. i. p. 25). The testimony of Abulghazi Khan (P. ii. c. 5, P. v. c. 4) is clear, unquestionable, and decisive.

8. According to one of the pedigrees, the fourth ancestor of Zingis, and the ninth of Timour, were brothers; and they agreed that the posterity of the elder should succeed to the dignity of khan, and that the descendants of the younger should fill the office of their minister and general. This tradition was at least convenient to justify the *first* steps of Timour's ambition (Institutions, p. 24, 25, from the MS. fragments of Timour's History).

9. See the preface of Sherefeddin, and Abulfeda's Geography (Chorasmiæ, etc., Descriptio, p. 60, 61), in the third volume of Hudson's Minor Greek Geographers.

10. See his nativity in Dr. Hyde (Syntagma Dissertat. tom. ii. p. 466) as it was cast by the astrologers of his grandson Ulugh Beg. He was born A.D. 1336, April 9, 11° 57′ P.M. lat. 36. I know not whether they can prove the great conjunction of the planets from whence, like other conquerors and prophets, Timour derived the surname of Saheb Keran, or master of the conjunctions (Biblioth. Orient. p. 878).

11. In the Institutions of Timour, these subjects of the khan of Kashgar are most improperly styled Ouzbegs or Uzbeks, a name which belongs to another branch and country of Tartars (Abulghazi, P. v. c. v. 5; P. vii. c. 5). Could I be sure that this word is in the Turkish original, I would boldly pronounce that the Institutions were framed a century after the death of Timour, since the establishment of the Uzbeks in Transoxiana.

12. The first book of Sherefeddin is employed on the private life of the hero; and he himself, or his secretary (Institutions, p. 3–77), enlarges with pleasure on the thirteen designs and enterprises which most truly constitute his *personal* merit. It even shines through the dark colouring of Arabshah (P. i. c. 1–12).

13. The conquests of Persia, Tartary, and India are represented in the second and third books of Sherefeddin, and by Arabshah (c. 13–55). Consult the excellent Indexes to the Institutions.

14. The reverence of the Tartars for the mysterious number of *nine* is declared by Abulghazi Khan, who, for that reason, divides his Genealogical History into nine parts.

15. According to Arabshah (P. i. c. 28, p. 183), the coward Timour ran away to his tent, and hid himself from the pursuit of Shah Mansour under the women's garments. Perhaps Sherefeddin (l. iii. c. 25) has magnified his courage.

16. The history of Ormuz is not unlike that of Tyre. The old city, on the continent, was destroyed by the Tartars, and renewed in a neighbouring island without fresh water or vegetation. The kings of Ormuz, rich in the Indian trade and the pearl fishery, possessed large territories both in Persia and Arabia; but they were at first the tributaries of the sultans of Kerman, and at last were delivered (A.D. 1505) by the Portuguese tyrants from the tyranny of their own vizirs (Marco Polo, l. i. c. 15, 16, fol. 7, 8; Abulfeda, Geograph. tabul.

xi. p. 261, 262; an original Chronicle of Ormuz, in Texeira, or Stevens' History of Persia, p. 376–416; and the Itineraries inserted in the first volume of Ramusio; of Ludovico Barthema, 1503, fol. 167; of Andrea Corsali, 1517, fol. 202, 203; and of Odoardo Barbessa, in 1516, fol. 315–318).

17. Arabshah had travelled into Kipzak, and acquired a singular knowledge of the geography, cities, and revolutions of that northern region (P. i. c. 45–49).

18. Institutions of Timour, p. 123, 125. Mr. White, the editor, bestows some animadversion on the superficial account of Sherefeddin (l. iii. c. 12, 13, 14), who was ignorant of the designs of Timour and the true springs of action.

19. The furs of Russia are more credible than the ingots. But the linen of Antioch has never been famous; and Antioch was in ruins. I suspect that it was some manufacture of Europe, which the Hanse merchants had imported by the way of Novogorod.

20. M. Levesque (Hist. de Russie, tom. ii. p. 247; Vie de Timour, p. 64–67, before the French version of the Institutes) has corrected the error of Sherefeddin, and marked the true limit of Timour's conquests. His arguments are superfluous; and a simple appeal to the Russian annals is sufficient to prove that Moscow, which six years before had been taken by Toctamish, escaped the arms of a more formidable invader.

21. An Egyptian consul from Grand Cairo is mentioned in Barbaro's Voyage to Tana in 1436, after the city had been rebuilt (Ramusio, tom. ii. fol. 92).

22. The sack of Azoph is described by Sherefeddin (l. iii. c. 55), and much more particularly by the author of an Italian chronicle (Andreas de Redusiis de Quero, in Chron. Tarvisiano, in Muratori, Script. Rerum Italicarum, tom. xix. p. 802–805). He had conversed with the Mianis, two Venetian brothers, one of whom had been sent a deputy to the camp of Timour, and the other had lost at Azoph three sons and 12,000 ducats.

23. Sherefeddin only says (l. iii. c. 13) that the rays of the setting, and those of the rising sun, were scarcely separated by any interval; a problem which may be solved, in the latitude of Moscow (the 56th degree), with the aid of the Aurora Borealis and a long summer twilight. But a *day* of forty days (Khondemir apud D'Herbelot, p. 880) would rigorously confine us within the polar circle.

24. For the Indian war, see the Institutions (p. 129–139), the fourth book of Sherefeddin, and the history of Ferishta (in Dow, vol. ii. p. 1–20), which throws a general light on the affairs of Hindostan.

25. The rivers of the Punjab, the five eastern branches of the Indus, have been laid down for the first time with truth and accuracy in Major Rennell's incomparable map of Hindostan. In his Critical Memoir he illustrates with judgment and learning the marches of Alexander and Timour.

26. The two great rivers, the Ganges and Bur-

rampooter, rise in Thibet, from the opposite ridges of the same hills, separate from each other to the distance of 1200 miles, and, after a winding course of 2000 miles, again meet in one point near the gulf of Bengal. Yet so capricious is Fame, that the Burrampooter is a late discovery, while his brother Ganges has been the theme of ancient and modern story. Coupele, the scene of Timour's last victory, must be situate near Loldong, 1100 miles from Calcutta; and, in 1774, a British camp! (Rennell's Memoir, p. 7, 59, 90, 91, 99.)

27. See the Institutions, p. 141, to the end of the first book, and Sherefeddin (l. v. c. 1–16) to the entrance of Timour into Syria.

28. We have three copies of these hostile epistles in the Institutions (p. 147), in Sherefeddin (l. v. c. 14), and in Arabshah (tom. ii. c. 19, p. 183–201); which agree with each other in the spirit and substance rather than in the style. It is probable that they have been translated, with various latitude, from the Turkish original into the Arabic and Persian tongues.

29. The Mogul emir distinguishes himself and his countrymen by the name of *Turks*, and stigmatises the race and nation of Bajazet with the less honourable epithet of *Turkmans*. Yet I do not understand how the Ottomans could be descended from a Turkman sailor; those inland shepherds were so remote from the sea and all maritime affairs.

30. According to the Koran (c. ii. p. 27, and Sale's Discourses, p. 134), a Musulman who had thrice divorced his wife (who had thrice repeated the words of a divorce) could not take her again till after she had been married *to*, and repudiated *by*, another husband; an ignominious transaction, which is needless to aggravate by supposing that the first husband must see her enjoyed by a second before his face (Rycaut's State of the Ottoman Empire, l. ii. c. 21).

31. The common delicacy of the Orientals, in never speaking of their women, is ascribed in a much higher degree by Arabshah to the Turkish nations; and it is remarkable enough that Chalcocondyles (l. ii. p. 55 [p. 105, ed. Bonn]) had some knowledge of the prejudice and the insult.

32. For the style of the Moguls see the Institutions (p. 131, 147), and for the Persians the Bibliothèque Orientale (p. 882); but I do not find that the title of Cæsar has been applied by the Arabians, or assumed by the Ottomans themselves.

33. See the reigns of Barkok and Faradge, in M. de Guignes (tom. iv. l. xxii.), who, from the Arabic texts of Aboulmahasen, Ebn Schounah, and Aintabi, has added some facts to our common stock of materials.

34. For these recent and domestic transactions, Arabshah, though a partial, is a credible, witness (tom. i. c. 64–68, tom. ii. c. 1–14). Timour must have been odious to a Syrian; but the notoriety of facts would have obliged him, in some measure, to respect his enemy and himself. His bitters may correct the luscious sweets of Sherefeddin (l. v. c 17–29).

35. These interesting conversations appear to have been copied by Arabshah (tom. i. c. 68, p. 625–645) from the cadhi and historian Ebn Schounah, a principal actor. Yet how could he be alive seventy-five years afterwards (D'Herbelot, p. 792)?

36. The marches and occupations of Timour between the Syrian and Ottoman wars are represented by Sherefeddin (l. v.c. 29–43) and Arabshah (tom. ii. c. 15–18).

37. This number of 800,000 was extracted by Arabshah, or rather by Ebn Schounah, ex rationario Timuri, in the faith of a Carizmian officer (tom. i. c. 68, p. 617); and it is remarkable enough that a Greek historian (Phranza, l. i. c. 29) adds no more than 20,000 men. Poggius reckons 1,000,000; another Latin contemporary (Chron. Tarvisianum, apud Muratori, tom. xix. p. 800) 1,100,000; and the enormous sum of 1,600,000 is attested by a German soldier who was present at the battle of Angora (Leunclav. ad Chalcocondyl. l. iii. p. 82). Timour, in his Institutions, has not deigned to calculate his troops, his subjects, or his revenues.

38. A wide latitude of non-effectives was allowed by the Great Mogul for his own pride and the benefit of his officers. Bernier's patron was Penge-Hazari, commander of 5000 horse; of which he maintained no more than 500 (Voyages, tom. i. p. 288, 289).

39. Timour himself fixes at 400,000 men the Ottoman army (Institutions, p. 153), which is reduced to 150,000 by Phranza (l. i. c. 29), and swelled by the German soldier to 1,400,000. It is evident that the Moguls were the more numerous.

40. It may not be useless to mark the distances between Angora and the neighbouring cities by the journeys of the caravans, each of twenty or twenty-five miles; to Smyrna twenty, to Kiotahia ten, to Boursa ten, to Cæsarea eight, to Sinope ten, to Nicomedia nine, to Constantinople twelve or thirteen (see Tournefort, Voyage au Levant, tom. ii. lettre xxi.).

41. See the Systems of Tactics in the Institutions, which the English editors have illustrated with elaborate plans (p. 373–407).

42. The sultan himself (says Timour) must then put the foot of courage into the stirrup of patience. A Tartar metaphor, which is lost in the English, but preserved in the French, version of the Institutes (p. 156, 157).

43. The Greek fire, on Timour's side, is attested by Sherefeddin (l. v. c. 47); but Voltaire's strange suspicion that some cannon, inscribed with strange characters, must have been sent by that monarch to Delhi, is refuted by the universal silence of contemporaries.

44. Timour has dissembled this secret and important negotiation with the Tartars, which is indisputably proved by the joint evidence of the Arabian (tom. i. c. 47, p. 391), Turkish (Annal.

Leunclav. p. 321), and Persian historians (Khon-demir apud D'Herbelot, p. 882).

45. For the war of Anatolia or Roum, I add some hints in the Institutions to the copious narratives of Sherefeddin (l. v. c. 44–65) and Arabshah (tom. ii. c. 20–35). On this part only of Timour's history it is lawful to quote the Turks (Cantemir, p. 53–55; Annal. Leunclav. p. 320–322) and the Greeks (Phranza, l. i. c. 29; Ducas, c. 15–17; Chalco-condyles, l. iii.).

46. The scepticism of Voltaire (Essai sur l'His-toire Générale, c. 88) is ready on this, as on every occasion, to reject a popular tale, and to diminish the magnitude of vice and virtue; and on most oc-casions his incredulity is reasonable.

47. See the History of Sherefeddin (l. v. c. 49, 52, 53, 59, 60). This work was finished at Shiraz, in the year 1424, and dedicated to sultan Ibrahim, the son of Sharokh, the son of Timour, who reigned in Farsistan in his father's lifetime.

48. After the perusal of Khondemir, Ebn Schou-nah, etc., the learned D'Herbelot (Biblioth. Ori-entale, p. 882) may affirm that this fable is not mentioned in the most authentic histories; but his denial of the visible testimony of Arabshah leaves some room to suspect his accuracy.

49. Et fut lui-même (*Bajazet*) pris, et menê en prison, en laquelle mourut de *dure mort!* Mémoires de Boucicault, P. i. c. 37. These memoirs were composed while the marshal was still governor of Genoa, from whence he was expelled, in the year 1409, by a popular insurrection (Muratori, Annali d'Italia, tom. xii. p. 473, 474).

50. The reader will find a satisfactory account of the life and writings of Poggius in the Poggiana, an entertaining work of M. Lenfant, and in the Bibliotheca Latina mediæ et infimæ Ætatis of Fabricius (tom. v. p. 305–308). Poggius was born in the year 1380, and died in 1459.

51. The dialogue de Varietate Fortunæ (of which a complete and elegant edition has been published at Paris in 1723, in 4to) was composed a short time before the death of pope Martin V. (p. 5), and consequently about the end of the year 1430.

52. See a splendid and eloquent encomium of Tamerlane, p. 36–39, ipse enim novi (says Pog-gius) qui uere in ejus castris. . . . Regem vivum cepit, caveâque in modum feræ inclusum per om-nem Asiam circumtulit egregium admirandumque spectaculum fortunæ.

53. The Chronicon Tarvisianum (in Muratori, Script. Rerum Italicarum, tom. xix. p. 800), and the Annales Estenses (tom. xviii. p. 974). The two authors, Andrea de Redusiis de Quero, and James de Delayto, were both contemporaries, and both chancellors, the one of Trevigi, the other of Fer-rara. The evidence of the former is the most positive.

54. See Arabshah, tom. ii. c. 28, 34. He travelled in regiones Rumæas, A.H. 839 (A.D. 1435, July 27), tom. ii. c. 2, p. 13.

55. Busbequius in Legatione Turcicâ, epist. i. p.

52. Yet his respectable authority is somewhat shaken by the subsequent marriages of Amurath II. with a Servian, and of Mohammed II. with an Asiatic princess Cantemir, p. 83, 93).

56. See the testimony of George Phranza (l. i. c. 26 [p. 85, ed. Bonn]), and his life in Hanckius (de Script. Byzant. P. i. c. 40). Chalcocondyles and Ducas speak in general terms of Bajazet's *chains*.

57. Annales Leunclav. p. 321; Pocock, Proleg-omen. ad Abulpharag. Dynast. Cantemir, p. 55.

58. A Sapor, king of Persia, had been made prisoner, and enclosed in the figure of a cow's hide, by Maximian or Galerius Cæsar. Such is the fable related by Eutychius (Annal. tom. i. p. 421, vers. Pocock). The recollection of the true history (Decline and Fall, etc., vol. i. p. 149–150) will teach us to appreciate the knowledge of the Ori-entals of the ages which precede the Hegira.

59. Arabshah (tom. ii. c. 25) describes, like a curious traveller, the straits of Gallipoli and Con-stantinople. To acquire a just idea of these events I have compared the narratives and prejudices of the Moguls, Turks, Greeks, and Arabians. The Spanish ambassador mentions this hostile union of the Christians and Ottomans (Vie de Timour, p. 96).

60. Since the name of Cæsar had been trans-ferred to the sultans of Roum, the Greek princes of Constantinople (Sherefeddin, l. v. c. 54) were con-founded with the Christian *lords* of Gallipoli, Thessalonica, etc., under the title of *Tekkur*, which is derived by corruption from the genitive τοῦ κυρίου (Cantemir, p. 51).

61. See Sherefeddin, l. v. c. 4, who marks, in a just itinerary, the road to China, which Arabshah (tom. ii. c. 33) paints in vague and rhetorical colours.

62. Synopsis Hist. Sinicæ, p. 74–76 (in the fourth part of the Relations de Thevenot); Du-halde, Hist. de la Chine (tom. i. p. 507, 508, folio edition); and for the chronology of the Chinese emperors. De Guignes. Hist. des Huns, tom. i. p. 71, 72.

63. For the return, triumph, and death of Ti-mour, see Sherefeddin (l. vi. c. 1–30) and Arab-shah (tom. ii. c. 35–47).

64. Sherefeddin (l. vi. c. 24) mentions the am-bassadors of one of the most potent sovereigns of Europe. We know that it was Henry III. king of Castile; and the curious relation of his two em-bassies is still extant (Mariana, Hist. Hispan. l. xix. c. 11, tom. ii. p. 329, 330; Avertissement à l'Hist. de Timur Bec, p. 28–33). There appears likewise to have been some correspondence between the Mogul emperor and the court of Charles VII. king of France (Histoire de France, par Velly et Villaret, tom. xii. p. 336).

65. See the translation of the Persian account of their embassy, a curious and original piece (in the fourth part of the Relations de Thevenot). They presented the emperor of China with an old horse which Timour had formerly rode. It was in the

year 1419 that they departed from the court of Herat, to which place they returned in 1422 from Pekin.

66. From Arabshah, tom. ii. c. 96. The bright or softer colours are borrowed from Sherefeddin, D'Herbelot, and the Institutions.

67. His new system was multiplied from 32 pieces and 64 squares to 56 pieces and 110 or 130 squares: but, except in his court, the old game has been thought sufficiently elaborate. The Mogul emperor was rather pleased than hurt with the victory of a subject: a chess-player will feel the value of this encomium!

68. See Sherefeddin, l. v. c. 15, 25. Arabshah (tom. ii. c. 96, p. 801, 803) reproves the impiety of Timour and the Moguls, who almost preferred to the Koran the *Yacsa*, or Law of Zingis (cui Deus maledicat); nor will he believe that Sharokh had abolished the use and authority of that pagan code.

69. Besides the bloody passages of this narrative, I must refer to an anticipation in the first volume of the Decline and Fall, which in a single note (p. 852, note 25) accumulates near 300,000 heads of the monuments of his cruelty. Except in Rowe's play on the fifth of November, I did not expect to hear of Timour's amiable moderation (White's preface, p. 7). Yet I can excuse a generous enthusiasm in the reader, and still more in the editor, of the *Institutions*.

70. Consult the last chapters of Sherefeddin and Arabshah, and M. de Guignes (Hist. des Huns, tom. iv. l. xx.). Fraser's History of Nadir Shah (p. 1–62). The story of Timour's descendants is imperfectly told; and the second and third parts of Sherefeddin are unknown.

71. Shah Allum, the present Mogul, is in the fourteenth degree from Timour, by Miran Shah his third son. See the second volume of Dow's History of Hindostan.

72. The civil wars, from the death of Bajazet to that of Mustapha, are related, according to the Turks, by Demetrius Cantemir (p. 58–82). Of the Greeks, Chalcocondyles (l. iv. and v.), Phranza (l. i. c. 30–32), and Ducas (c. 18–27), the last is the most copious and best informed.

73. Arabshah, tom. ii. c. 26, whose testimony on this occasion is weighty and valuable. The existence of Isa (unknown to the Turks) is likewise confirmed by Sherefeddin (l. v. c. 57).

74. Arabshah, loc. citat. Abulfeda, Geograph. tab. xvii. p. 302; Busbequius, epist. i. p. 96, 97, in Itinere C. P. et Amasiano.

75. The virtues of Ibrahim are praised by a contemporary Greek (Ducas, c. 25). His descendants are the sole nobles in Turkey: they content themselves with the administration of his pious foundations, are excused from public offices, and receive two annual visits from the sultan (Cantemir, p. 76).

76. See Pachymer (l. v. c. 29 [c. 30, tom. i. p. 420, ed. Bonn]), Nicephorus Gregoras (l. ii. c. 1 [xv. 7? vol. ii. p. 766, ed. Bonn]), Sherefeddin (l. v. c. 57), and Ducas (c. 25). The last of these, a

curious and careful observer, is entitled, from his birth and station, to particular credit in all that concerns Ionia and the islands. Among the nations that resorted to New Phocæa, he mentions the English ('Ιγγλῆνοι [p. 161, ed. Bonn]); an early evidence of Mediterranean trade.

77. For the spirit of navigation and freedom of ancient Phocæa, or rather of the Phocæans, consult the first book of Herodotus, and the Geographical Index of his last and learned French translator, M. Larcher (tom. vii. p. 299).

78. Phocæa is not enumerated by Pliny (Hist. Nat. xxxv. 52) among the places productive of alum: he reckons Egypt as the first, and for the second the isle of Melos, whose alum-mines are described by Tournefort (tom. i. lettre iv.), a traveller and a naturalist. After the loss of Phocæa, the Genoese, in 1459, found that useful mineral in the isle of Ischia (Ismael. Bouillaud, ad Ducam, c. 25).

79. The writer who has the most abused this fabulous generosity is our ingenious Sir William Temple (his Works, vol. iii. p. 349, 350, octavo edition), that lover of exotic virtue. After the conquest of Russia, etc., and the passage of the Danube, his Tartar hero relieves, visits, admires, and refuses the city of Constantine. His flattering pencil deviates in every line from the truth of history; yet his pleasing fictions are more excusable than the gross errors of Cantemir.

80. For the reigns of Manuel and John, of Mohammed I. and Amurath II., see the Othman history of Cantemir (p. 70–95), and the three Greeks, Chalcocondyles, Phranza, and Ducas, who is still superior to his rivals.

81. The Turkish asper (from the Greek ἀσπρὸς) is, or was, a piece of *white* or silver money, at present much debased, but which was formerly equivalent to the fifty-fourth part, at least, of a Venetian ducat or sequin; and the 300,000 aspers, a princely allowance or royal tribute, may be computed at £2500 sterling (Leunclav. Pandect. Turc. p. 406–408).

82. For the siege of Constantinople in 1422, see the particular and contemporary narrative of John Cananus, published by Leo Allatius, at the end of his edition of Acropolita (p. 188–199).

83. Cantemir, p. 80. Cananus, who describes Seid Bechar without naming him, supposes that the friend of Mohammed assumed in his amours the privilege of a prophet, and that the fairest of the Greek nuns were promised to the saint and his disciples.

84. For this miraculous apparition Cananus appeals to the Musulman saint; but who will bear testimony for Seid Bechar?

85. See Rycaut (l. i. c. 13). The Turkish sultans assume the title of khan. Yet Abulghazi is ignorant of his Ottoman cousins.

86. The third grand vizir of the name of Kiuperli, who was slain at the battle of Salankanen in 1691 (Cantemir, p. 382), presumed to say that all the successors of Soliman had been fools or tyrants,

and that it was time to abolish the race (Marsigli, Stato Militare, etc., p. 28). This political heretic was a good Whig, and justified against the French embassador the revolution of England (Mignot, Hist. des Ottomans, tom. iii. p. 434). His presumption condemns the singular exception of continuing offices in the same family.

87. Chalcocondyles (l. v.) and Ducas (c. 23) exhibit the rude lineaments of the Ottoman policy, and the transmutation of Christian children into Turkish soldiers.

88. This sketch of the Turkish education and discipline is chiefly borrowed from Rycaut's State of the Ottoman Empire, the Stato Militare del' Imperio Ottomanno of Count Marsigli (in Haya, 1732, in folio), and a Description of the Seraglio, approved by Mr. Greaves himself, a curious traveller, and inserted in the second volume of his works.

89. From the series of 115 vizirs, till the siege of Vienna (Marsigli, p. 13), their place may be valued at three years and a half purchase.

90. See the entertaining and judicious letters of Busbequius.

91. The first and second volumes of Dr. Watson's Chemical Essays contain two valuable discourses on the discovery and composition of gunpowder.

92. On this subject modern testimonies cannot be trusted. The original passages are collected by Ducange (Gloss. Latin. tom. i. p. 675, *Bombarda*). But in the early doubtful twilight, the name, sound, fire, and effect, that seem to express *our* artillery, may be fairly interpreted of the old engines and the Greek fire. For the English cannon at Crecy, the authority of John Villani (Chron. l. xii. c. 65) must be weighed against the silence of Froissard. Yet Muratori (Antiquit. Italiæ medii Ævi, tom. ii. Dissert. xxvi. p. 514, 515) has produced a decisive passage from Petrarch (De Remediis utriusque Fortunæ Dialog.), who, before the year 1344, execrates this terrestrial thunder, *nuper* rara, *nunc* communis.

93. The Turkish cannon, which Ducas (c. 30 [p. 211, ed. Bonn]) first introduces before Belgrade (A.D. 1436), is mentioned by Chalcocondyles (l. v. p. 123 [p. 231, ed. Bonn]) in 1422, at the siege of Constantinople.

Chapter LXVI

1. This curious instruction was transcribed (I believe) from the Vatican archives by Odoricus Raynaldus, in his Continuation of the Annals of Baronius (Romæ, 1646-1677, in ten volumes in folio). I have contented myself with the abbé Fleury (Hist. Ecclésiastique, tom. xx. p. 1-8), whose abstracts I have always found to be clear, accurate, and impartial.

2. The ambiguity of this title is happy or ingenious; and *moderator*, as synonymous to *rector*, *gubernator*, is a word of classical, and even Circeronian, Latinity, which may be found, not in the Glossary of Ducange, but in the Thesaurus of Robert Stephens.

3. The first epistle (sine titulo) of Petrarch exposes the danger of the *bark* and the incapacity of the *pilot*. Hæc inter, vino madidus, ævo gravis, ac soporifero rore perfusus, jamjam nutitat, dormitat, jam somno præceps, atque (utinam solus) ruit. . . . Heu quanto felicius patrio terram sulcasset aratro, quam scalmum piscatorium ascendisset! This satire engages his biographer to weigh the virtues and vices of Benedict XII., which have been exaggerated by Guelphs and Ghibelines, by Papists and Protestants (see Mémoires sur la Vie de Pétrarque, tom. i. p. 259; ii. not. xv. p. 13-16). He gave occasion to the saying, Bibamus papaliter.

4. See the original Lives of Clement VI. in Muratori (Script. Rerum Italicarum, tom. iii. P. ii. p. 550-589); Matteo Villani (Chron. l. iii. c. 43, in Muratori, tom. xiv. p. 186), who styles him molto cavallaresco, poco religioso; Fleury (Hist. Ecclés. tom. xx. p. 126); and the Vie de Pétrarque

(tom. ii. p. 42-45). The abbé de Sade treats him with the most indulgence; but *he* is a gentleman as well as a priest.

5. Her name (most probably corrupted) was Zampea. She had accompanied and alone remained with her mistress at Constantinople, where her prudence, erudition, and politeness deserved the praises of the Greeks themselves (Cantacuzen. l. i. c. 42 [tom. i. p. 205, ed. Bonn]).

6. See this whole negotiation in Cantacuzene (l. iv. c. 9), who, amidst the praises and virtues which he bestows on himself, reveals the uneasiness of a guilty conscience.

7. See this ignominious treaty in Fleury (Hist. Ecclés. p. 151-154), from Raynaldus, who drew it from the Vatican archives. It was not worth the trouble of a pious forgery.

8. See the two first original Lives of Urban V. (in Muratori, Script. Rerum Italicarum, tom. iii. P. ii. p. 623, 635), and the Ecclesiastical Annals of Spondanus (tom. i. p. 573, A.D. 1369, No. 7), and Raynaldus (Fleury, Hist. Ecclés. tom. xx. p. 223, 224). Yet, from some variations, I suspect the papal writers of slightly magnifying the genuflexions of Palæologus.

9. Paullo minus quam si fuisset Imperator Romanorum. Yet his title of Imperator Græcorum was no longer disputed (Vit. Urban V., p. 623).

10. It was confined to the successors of Charlemagne, and to them only on Christmas Day. On all other festivals these Imperial deacons were content to serve the pope, as he said mass, with the book and the *corporal*. Yet the abbé de Sade gen-

erously thinks that the merits of Charles IV. might have entitled him, though not on the proper day (A.D. 1368, November 1), to the whole privilege. He seems to affix a just value on the privilege and the man (Vie de Pétrarque, tom. iii. p. 735).

11. Through some Italian corruptions, the etymology of *Falcone in bosco* (Matteo [Filippo] Villani, l. xi. c. 79, in Muratori, tom. xiv. p. 746) suggests the English word *Hawkwood*, the true name of our adventurous countryman (Thomas Walsingham, Hist. Anglican. inter Scriptores Camdeni, p. 184). After two-and-twenty victories and one defeat, he died, in 1394, general of the Florentines, and was buried with such honours as the republic has not paid to Dante or Petrarch (Muratori, Annali d'Italia, tom. xii. p. 212–371).

12. This torrent of English (by birth or service) overflowed from France into Italy after the peace of Bretigny in 1360. Yet the exclamation of Muratori (Annali, tom. xii. p. 197) is rather true than civil. "Ci mancava ancor questo, che dopo essere calpestrata l'Italia da tanti masnadieri Tedeschi ed Ungheri, venissero fin dall' Inghliterra nuovi *cani* a finire di divorarla."

13. Chalcocondyles, l. i. p. 25, 26 [p. 50, *sq.*, ed. Bonn]. The Greek supposes his journey to the king of France, which is sufficiently refuted by the silence of the national historians. Nor am I much more inclined to believe that Palæologus departed from Italy, valde bene consolatus et contentus (Vit. Urban V. p. 623).

14. His return in 1370, and the coronation of Manuel, Sept. 25, 1373 (Ducange, Fam. Byzant. p. 241), leaves some intermediate era for the conspiracy and punishment of Andronicus.

15. Mémoires de Boucicault, P. i. c. 35, 36.

16. His journey into the west of Europe is slightly, and I believe reluctantly, noticed by Chalcocondyles (l. ii. p. 44–50 [p. 84–97, ed. Bonn]) and Ducas (c. 14).

17. Muratori, Annali d'Italia, tom. xii. p. 406. John Galeazzo was the first and most powerful duke of Milan. His connection with Bajazet is attested by Froissard, and he contributed to save and deliver the French captives of Nicopolis.

18. For the reception of Manuel at Paris, see Spondanus (Annal. Eccles. tom. i. p. 676, 677 A.D. 1400, No. 5), who quotes Juvenal des Ursins, and the monk of St. Denys; and Villaret (Hist. de France, tom. xii. p. 331–334), who quotes nobody, according to the last fashion of the French writers.

19. A short note of Manuel in England is extracted by Dr. Hody from a MS. at Lambeth (de Græcis illustribus, p. 14), C. P. Imperator, diu variisque et horrendis Paganorum insultibus coarctatus, ut pro eisdem resistentiam triumphalem perquireret, Anglorum Regem visitare decrevit, etc. Rex (says Walsingham, p. 364 [cum] nobili apparatû . . . suscepit (ut decuit) tantum Heroa, duxitque Londonias, et per multos dies exhibuit gloriose, pro expensis hospitii sui solvens, et eum respiciens [dignis] tanto fastigo donativis. He repeats the same in his Upodigma Neustriæ (p. 556).

20. Shakespeare begins and ends the play of Henry IV. with that prince's vow of a crusade, and his belief that he should die in Jerusalem.

21. This fact is preserved in the Historia Politica, A.D. 1391–1478, published by Martin Crusius (Turco-Græcia, p. 1–43). The image of Christ, which the Greek emperor refused to worship, was probably a work of sculpture.

22. The Greek and Turkish history of Laonicus Chalcocondyles ends with the winter of 1463, and the abrupt conclusion seems to mark that he laid down his pen in the same year. We know that he was an Athenian, and that some contemporaries of the same name contributed to the revival of the Greek language in Italy. But in his numerous digressions the modest historian has never introduced himself; and his editor Leunclavius, as well as Fabricius (Biblioth. Græc. tom. vi. p. 474), seems ignorant of his life and character. For his descriptions of Germany, France, and England, see l. ii. p. 36, 37, 44–50 [p. 70–72, 85–96, ed. Bonn].

23. I shall not animadvert on the geographical errors of Chalcocondyles. In this instance he perhaps followed, and mistook, Herodotus (l. ii. c. 33), whose text may be explained (Herodote de Larcher, tom. ii. p. 219, 220), or whose ignorance may be excused. Had these modern Greeks never read Strabo, or any of their lesser geographers?

24. A citizen of new Rome, while new Rome survived, would have scorned to dignify the German Ῥήξ with the titles of Βασιλεύς or Αὐτοκράτωρ Ῥωμαίων; but all pride was extinct in the bosom of Chalcocondyles, and he describes the Byzantine prince and his subject by the proper, though humble, names of Ἕλληνες and Βασιλεὺς Ἑλλήνων.

25. Most of the old romances were translated in the fourteenth century into French prose, and soon became the favourite amusement of the knights and ladies in the court of Charles VI. If a Greek believed in the exploits of Rowland and Oliver, he may surely be excused, since the monks of St. Denys, the national historians, have inserted the fables of Archbishop Turpin in their Chronicles of France.

26. Λονδρῶν δὲ ἡ πόλις δυνάμει τε προέχουσα τῶν ἐν τῇ νήσῳ ταύτῃ πασῶν πόλεων, ὄλβῳ τε καὶ τῇ ἄλλῃ εὐδαιμονίᾳ οὐδεμιᾶς τῶν πρὸς ἑσπέραν λειπομένη [l. ii. p. 93, ed. Bonn]. Even since the time of Fitzstephen (the twelfth century), London appears to have maintained this pre-eminence of wealth and magnitude; and her gradual increase has, at least, kept pace with the general improvement of Europe.

27. If the double sense of the verb κύω (osculor, and in utero gero) be equivocal, the context and pious horror of Chalcocondyles can leave no doubt of his meaning and mistake (p. 49 [p. 93, ed. Bonn]).

28. Erasmus (Epist. Fausto Andrelino) has a pretty passage on the English fashion of kissing strangers on their arrival and departure, from

whence, however, he draws no scandalous inferences.

29. Perhaps we may apply this remark to the community of wives among the old Britons, as it is supposed by Cæsar [Bell. Gall. l. v. c. 14] and Dion (Dion Cassius, l. lxii. tom. ii. [c. 6] p. 1007), with Reimar's judicious annotation. The *Arreoy* of Otaheite, so certain at first, is become less visible and scandalous in proportion as we have studied the manners of that gentle and amorous people.

30. See Lenfant, Hist. du Concile de Constance, tom. ii. p. 576; and, for the ecclesiastical history of the times, the Annals of Spondanus, the Bibliothèque of Dupin, tom. xii. and twenty-first and twenty-second volumes of the History, or rather the Continuation, of Fleury.

31. From his early youth, George Phranza, or Phranzes, was employed in the service of the state and palace; and Hanckius (de Script. Byzant. P. i. c. 40) has collected his life from his own writings. He was no more than four-and-twenty years of age at the death of Manuel, who recommended him in the strongest terms to his successor: Imprimis vero hunc Phranzen tibi commendo, qui ministravit mihi fideliter et diligenter (Phranzes, l. ii. c. 1 [p. 125, ed. Bonn]). Yet the emperor John was cold, and he preferred the service of the despots of Peloponnesus.

32. See Phranzes, l. ii. c. 13 [p. 178, ed. Bonn]. While so many manuscripts of the Greek original are extant in the libraries of Rome, Milan, the Escurial, etc., it is a matter of shame and reproach that we should be reduced to the Latin version, or abstract, of James Pontanus (ad calcem Theophylact. Simocattæ: Ingolstadt, 1604), so deficient in accuracy and elegance (Fabric. Biblioth. Græc. tom. vi. p. 615–620).

33. See Ducange, Fam. Byzant. p. 243–248.

34. The exact measure of the Hexamilion, from sea to sea, was 3800 orgyiæ, or *toises*, of six Greek feet (Phranzes, l. i. c. 35 [p. 108, ed. Bonn]), which would produce a Greek mile still smaller than that of 660 French *toises*, which is assigned by D'Anville as still in use in Turkey. Five miles are commonly reckoned for the breadth of the isthmus. See the Travels of Spon, Wheeler, and Chandler.

35. The first objection of the Jews is on the death of Christ: if it were voluntary, Christ was a suicide: which the emperor parries with a mystery. They then dispute on the conception of the Virgin, the sense of the prophecies, etc. (Phranzes, l. ii. c. 12, a whole chapter.)

36. In the treatise delle Materie Beneficiarie of Fra Paolo (in the fourth volume of the last, and best, edition of his works) the papal system is deeply studied and freely described. Should Rome and her religion be annihilated, this golden volume may still survive, a philosophical history and a salutary warning.

37. Pope John XXII. (in 1334) left behind him, at Avignon, eighteen millions of gold florins, and the value of seven millions more in plate and jewels. See the Chronicle of John Villani (l. xi. c. 20, in Muratori's Collection, tom. xiii. p. 765), whose brother received the account from the papal treasurers. A treasure of six or eight millions sterling in the fourteenth century is enormous, and almost incredible.

38. A learned and liberal Protestant, M. Lenfant, has given a fair history of the councils of Pisa, Constance, and Basil, in six volumes in quarto; but the last part is the most hasty and imperfect except in the account of the troubles of Bohemia.

39. The original acts or minutes of the council of Basil are preserved in the public library, in twelve volumes in folio. Basil was a free city, conveniently situate on the Rhine, and guarded by the arms of the neighbouring and confederate Swiss. In 1459 the university was founded by pope Pius II. (Æneas Sylvius), who had been secretary to the council. But what is a council, or a university, to the presses of Froben and the studies of Erasmus?

40. This Turkish embassy, attested only by Crantzius, is related with some doubt by the annalist Spondanus, A.D. 1433, No. 25, tom. i. p. 824.

41. Syropulus, p. 19. In this list the Greeks appear to have exceeded the real numbers of the clergy and laity which afterwards attended the emperor and patriarch, but which are not clearly specified by the great ecclesiarch. The 75,000 florins which they asked in this negotiation of the pope (p. 9) were more than they could hope or want.

42. I use indifferently the words *ducat* and *florin*, which derive their names, the former from the *dukes* of Milan, the latter from the republic of *Florence*. These gold pieces, the first that were coined in Italy, perhaps in the Latin world, may be compared in weight and value to one-third of the English guinea.

43. At the end of the Latin version of Phranzes we read a long Greek epistle or declamation of George of Trebizond, who advises the emperor to prefer Eugenius and Italy. He treats with contempt the schismatic assembly of Basil, the barbarians of Gaul and Germany, who had conspired to transport the chair of St. Peter beyond the Alps; οἱ ἄθλιοι (says he) σε καὶ τὴν μετὰ σου σύνοδον ἔξω τῶν Ἡρακλείων στηλῶν καὶ περὰ Γαδήρων ἐξάξουσι. Was Constantinople unprovided with a map?

44. Syropulus (p. 26–31) attests his own indignation, and that of his countrymen; and the Basil deputies, who excused the rash declaration, could neither deny nor alter an act of the council.

45. Condolmieri, the pope's nephew and admiral, expressly declared, ὅτι ὁρισμον ἔχει παρὰ τοῦ Πάπα ἵνα πολεμήσῃ ὁποῦ ἀν εὕρῃ τὰ κάτεργα τῆς Συνόδου, καὶ εἰ δυνήθῃ, καταδύσῃ, καὶ ἀφανίσῃ. The naval orders of the synod were less peremptory, and, till the hostile squadrons appeared, both parties tried to conceal their quarrel from the Greeks.

46. Syropulus mentions the hopes of Palæologus (p. 36), and the last advice of Sigismond (p. 57).

At Corfu the Greek emperor was informed of his friend's death; had he known it sooner, he would have returned home (p. 79).

47. Phranzes himself, though from different motives, was of the advice of Amurath (l. ii. c. 13). Utinam ne synodus ista unquam fuisset, si tantas offensiones et detrimenta paritura erat. This Turkish embassy is likewise mentioned by Syropulus (p. 58); and Amurath kept his word. He might threaten (p. 125, 219), but he never attacked, the city.

48. The reader will smile at the simplicity with which he imparted these hopes to his favourites: τοιαύτην πληροφορίαν σχήσειν ἤλπιζε καὶ διὰ ροῦ Πάπα ἐθάρρει ἐλευθερῶσαι τὴν ἐκκλησίαν ἀπὸ τῆς ἀποτεθείσης αὐτοῦ δουλείας παρὰ τοῦ βασιλέως(p. 92). Yet it would have been difficult for him to have practised the lessons of Gregory VII.

49. The Christian name of Sylvester is borrowed from the Latin calendar. In modern Greek, πουλός, as a diminutive, is added to the end of words: nor can any reasoning of Creyghton, the editor, excuse his changing into *Sguro*pulus (Sguros, fuscus) the Syropulus of his own manuscript, whose name is subscribed with his own hand in the acts of the council of Florence. Why might not the author be of Syrian extraction?

50. From the conclusion of the history I should fix the date to the year 1444, four years after the synod, when the great ecclesiarch had abdicated his office (sectio xii. p. 330–350). His passions were cooled by time and retirement; and, although Syropulus is often partial, he is never intemperate.

51. *Vera historia unionis non veræ inter Græcos et Latinos* (*Hagæ Comitis*, 1660, in folio) was first published with a loose and florid version, by Robert Creyghton, chaplain to Charles II. in his exile. The zeal of the editor has prefixed a polemic title, for the beginning of the original is wanting. Syropulus may be ranked with the best of the Byzantine writers for the merit of his narration, and even of his style; but he is excluded from the orthodox collections of the councils.

52. Syropulus (p. 63) simply expresses his intention ἐν' οὕτω πομπάων ἐν' Ἰτάλοις μεγὰς βασιλεὺς παρ' ἐκεινῶν νομίζοιτο; and the Latin of Creyghton may afford a specimen of his florid paraphrase. Ut pompâ circumductus noster Imperator Italiæ populis aliquis deauratus Jupiter crederetur, aut Crœsus ex opulentâ Lydiâ.

53. Although I cannot stop to quote Syropulus for every fact, I will observe that the navigation of the Greeks from Constantinople to Venice and Ferrara is contained in the fourth section (p. 67–100), and that the historian has the uncommon talent of placing each scene before the reader's eye.

54. At the time of the synod Phranzes was in Peloponnesus: but he received from the despot Demetrius a faithful account of the honourable reception of the emperor and patriarch both at Venice and Ferrara (Dux . . . sedentem Imperatorem *adorat*), which are more slightly mentioned by the Latins (l. ii. c. 14, 15, 16).

55. The astonishment of a Greek prince and a French ambassador (Mémoires de Philippe de Comines, l. vii. c. 18) at the sight of Venice, abundantly proves that in the fifteenth century it was the first and most splendid of the Christian cities. For the spoils of Constantinople at Venice see Syropulus (p. 87).

56. Nicholas III. of Este reigned forty-eight years (A.D. 1393–1441), and was lord of Ferrara, Modena, Reggio, Parma, Rovigo, and Commachio. See his Life in Muratori (Antichità Estense, tom. ii. p. 159–201).

57. The Latin vulgar was provoked to laughter at the strange dresses of the Greeks, and especially the length of their garments, their sleeves, and their beards; nor was the emperor distinguished, except by the purple colour, and his diadem or tiara with a jewel on the top (Hody de Græcis Illustribus, p. 31). Yet another spectator confesses that the Greek fashion was più grave e più degna than the Italian (Vespasiano, in Vit. Eugen. IV. in Muratori, tom. xxv. p. 261).

58. For the emperor's hunting see Syropulus (p. 143, 144, 191). The pope had sent him eleven miserable hacks; but he bought a strong and swift horse that came from Russia. The name of *Janizaries* may surprise; but the name, rather than the institution, had passed from the Ottoman to the Byzantine court, and is often used in the last age of the empire.

59. The Greeks obtained, with much difficulty, that, instead of provisions, money should be distributed, four florins *per* month to the persons of honourable rank, and three florins to their servants, with an addition of thirty more to the emperor, twenty-five to the patriarch, and twenty to the prince, or despot, Demetrius. The payment of the first month amounted to 691 florins, a sum which will not allow us to reckon above 200 Greeks of every condition (Syropulus, p. 104, 105). On the 20th October, 1438, there was an arrear of four months; in April, 1439, of three; and of five and a half in July, at the time of the union (p. 172, 225, 271).

60. Syropulus (p. 141, 142, 204, 221) deplores the imprisonment of the Greeks and the tyranny of the emperor and patriarch.

61. The wars of Italy are most clearly represented in the thirteenth volume of the Annals of Muratori. The schismatic Greek, Syropulus (p. 145), appears to have exaggerated the fear and disorder of the pope in his retreat from Ferrara to Florence, which is proved by the acts to have been somewhat more decent and deliberate.

62. Syropulus is pleased to reckon seven hundred prelates in the council of Basil. The error is manifest, and perhaps voluntary. That extravagant number could not be supplied by *all* the ecclesiastics of every degree who were present at the council, nor by *all* the absent bishops of the West, who, expressly or tacitly, might adhere to its decrees.

63. The Greeks, who disliked the union, were unwilling to sally from this strong fortress (p. 178, 193, 195, 202, of Syropulus). The shame of the Latins was aggravated by their producing an old MS. of the second council of Nice, with *filioque* in the Nicene creed. A palpable forgery! (p. 173).

64. Ὡς ἔγω (said an eminent Greek) ὅταν εἰς νάον εἰσέλθω Λατίνων οὐ προσκυνῶ τινα τῶν ἔκεισε ἁγίων, ἔπει οὐδε γνωρίζω τινα (Syropulus, p. 109). See the perplexity of the Greeks (p. 217, 218, 252, 253, 273).

65. See the polite altercation of Mark and Bessarion in Syropulus (p. 257), who never dissembles the vices of his own party, and fairly praises the virtues of the Latins.

66. For the poverty of the Greek bishops, see a remarkable passage of Ducas (c. 31 [p. 216, ed. Bonn]). One had possessed, for his whole property, three old gowns, etc. By teaching one-and-twenty years in his monastery, Bessarion himself had collected forty gold florins; but of these the archbishop had expended twenty-eight in his voyage from Peloponnesus, and the remainder at Constantinople (Syropulus, p. 127).

67. Syropulus denies that the Greeks received any money before they had subscribed the act of union (p. 283): yet he relates some suspicious circumstances; and their bribery and corruption are positively affirmed by the historian Ducas [loc. cit.].

68. The Greeks most piteously express their own fears of exile and perpetual slavery (Syropul. p. 196); and they were strongly moved by the emperor's threats (p. 260).

69. I had forgot another popular and orthodox protester: a favourite hound, who usually lay quiet on the foot-cloth of the emperor's throne, but who barked most furiously while the act of union was reading, without being silenced by the soothing or the lashes of the royal attendants (Syropul. p. 265, 266).

70. From the original Lives of the Popes, in Muratori's Collection (tom. iii. P. ii. tom. xxv.), the manners of Eugenius IV. appear to have been decent, and even exemplary. His situation, exposed to the world and to his enemies, was a restraint, and is a pledge.

71. Syropulus, rather than subscribe, would have assisted, as the least evil, at the ceremony of the union. He was compelled to do both; and the great ecclesiarch poorly excuses his submission to the emperor (p. 290-292).

72. None of these original acts of union can at present be produced. Of the ten MSS. that are preserved (five at Rome, and the remainder at Florence, Bologna, Venice, Paris, and London), nine have been examined by an accurate critic (M. de Brequigny), who condemns them for the variety and imperfections of the Greek signatures. Yet several of these may be esteemed as authentic copies, which were subscribed at Florence, before (26th of August, 1439) the final separation of the pope and emperor (Mémoires de l'Académie des Inscriptions, tom. xliii. p. 287-311).

73. Ἥμιν δὲ ὡς ἀσήμοι ἐδοκοῦν φώναι (Syropul. p. 297).

74. In their return the Greeks conversed at Bologna with the ambassadors of England; and after some questions and answers these impartial strangers laughed at the pretended union of Florence (Syropul. p. 307).

75. So nugatory, or rather so fabulous, are these reunions of the Nestorians, Jacobites, etc., that I have turned over, without success, the Bibliotheca Orientalis of Assemannus, a faithful slave of the Vatican.

76. Ripaille is situate near Thonon, in Savoy, on the southern side of the lake of Geneva. It is now a Carthusian abbey; and Mr. Addison (Travels into Italy, vol. ii. p. 147, 148, of Baskerville's edition of his works) has celebrated the place and the founder. Æneas Sylvius, and the fathers of Basil, applaud the austere life of the ducal hermit; but the French and Italian proverbs most unluckily attest the popular opinion of his luxury.

77. In this account of the councils of Basil, Ferrara, and Florence, I have consulted the original acts, which fill the seventeenth and eighteenth tomes of the edition of Venice, and are closed by the perspicuous, though partial, history of Augustin Patricius, an Italian of the fifteenth century. They are digested and abridged by Dupin (Bibliothèque Ecclés. tom. xii.), and the continuator of Fleury (tom. xxii.); and the respect of the Gallican church for the adverse parties confines their members to an awkward moderation.

78. In the first attempt Meursius collected 3600 Græco-barbarous words, to which, in a second edition, he subjoined 1800 more; yet what plenteous gleanings did he leave to Portius, Ducange, Fabrotti, the Bollandists, etc.! (Fabric. Biblioth. Græc. tom. x. p. 101, etc.). Some Persic words may be found in Xenophon, and some Latin ones in Plutarch; and such is the inevitable effect of war and commerce; but the form and substance of the language were not affected by this slight alloy.

79. The life of Francis Philelphus, a sophist, proud, restless, and rapacious, has been diligently composed by Lancelot (Mémoires de l'Academie des Inscriptions, tom. x. p. 691-751) and Tiraboschi (Istoria della Letteratura Italiana, tom. vii. p. 282-294), for the most part from his own letters. His elaborate writings, and those of his contemporaries, are forgotten: but their familiar epistles still describe the men and the times.

80. He married, and had perhaps debauched, the daughter of John, and the granddaughter of Manuel Chrysoloras. She was young, beautiful, and wealthy; and her noble family was allied to the Dorias of Genoa and the emperors of Constantinople.

81. Græci quibus lingua depravata non sit ... ita loquuntur vulgo hâc etiam tempestate ut Aristophanes comicus, aut Euripides tragicus, ut ora-

tores omnes, ut historiographi, ut philosophi . . litterati autem homines et doctius et emendatius. . . . Nam viri aulici veterem sermonis dignitatem atque elegantiam retinebant in primisque ipsæ nobiles mulieres; quibus cum nullum esset omnino cum viris peregrinis commercium, merus ille ac purus Græcorum sermo servabatur intactus (Philelph. Epist. ad ann. 1451, apud Hodium, p. 188, 189). He observes in another passage, uxor illa mea Theodora locutione erat abmodum moderatâ et suavi et maxime Atticâ.

82. Philelphus, absurdly enough, derives this Greek or Oriental jealousy from the manners of ancient Rome.

83. See the state of learning in the thirteenth and fourteenth centuries in the learned and judicious Mosheim (Institut. Hist. Eccles. p. 434–440, 490–494).

84. At the end of the fifteenth century there existed in Europe about fifty universities, and of these the foundation of ten or twelve is prior to the year 1300. They were crowded in proportion to their scarcity. Bologna contained 10,000 students, chiefly of the civil law. In the year 1357 the number at Oxford had decreased from 30,000 to 6000 scholars (Henry's History of Great Britain, vol. iv. p. 478). Yet even this decrease is much superior to the present list of the members of the university.

85. Of those writers who professedly treat of the restoration of the Greek learning in Italy, the two principal are Hodius, Dr. Humphrey Hody (de Græcis Illustribus, Linguæ Græcæ Literarumque humaniorum Instauratoribus; Londini, 1742, in large octavo), and Tiraboschi (Istoria della Letteratura Italiana, tom. v. p. 364–377, tom. vii. p. 112–143). The Oxford professor is a laborious scholar, but the librarian of Modena enjoys the superiority of a modern and national historian.

86. In Calabria quæ olim Magna Græcia dicebatur, coloniis Græcis repleta, remansit quædam linguæ veteris cognitio (Hodius, p. 2). If it were eradicated by the Romans, it was revived and perpetuated by the monks of St. Basil, who possessed seven convents at Rossano alone (Giannone, Istoria di Napoli, tom. i. p. 520).

87. Ii Barbari (says Petrarch, the French and Germans) vix, non dicam libros sed nomen Homeri audiverunt. Perhaps in that respect the thirteenth century was less happy than the age of Charlemagne.

88. See the character of Barlaam, in Boccace de Genealog. Deorum, l. xv. c. 6.

89. Cantacuzen. l. ii. c. 36 [c. 39, tom. i. p. 543, ed. Bonn].

90. For the connection of Petrarch and Barlaam, and the two interviews, at Avignon in 1339, and at Naples in 1342, see the excellent Mémoires sur la Vie de Pétrarque, tom. i. p. 406–410; tom. ii. p. 75–77.

91. The bishopric to which Barlaam retired was the old Locri, in the middle ages Scta. Cyriaca, and by corruption Hieracium, Gerace (Dissert.

Chorographica Italiæ medii Ævi, p. 312). The dives opum of the Norman times soon lapsed into poverty, since even the church was poor: yet the town still contains 3000 inhabitants (Swinburne, p. 340).

92. I will transcribe a passage from this epistle of Petrarch (Famil. ix. 2): Donasti Homerum non in alienum sermonem violento alveo derivatum, sed ex ipsis Græci eloquii scatebris, et qualis divino illi profluxit ingenio. . . . Sine tuâ voce Homerus tuus apud me mutus, immo vero ego apud illum surdus sum. Gaudeo tamen vel adspectû solo, ac sæpe illum amplexus atque suspirans dico, O magne vir, etc.

93. For the life and writings of Boccace, who was born in 1313, and died in 1375, Fabricius (Biblioth. Latin. medii Ævi, tom. i. p. 248, etc.) and Tiraboschi (tom. v. p. 83, 439–451) may be consulted. The editions, versions, imitations of his novels, are innumerable. Yet he was ashamed to communicate that trifling, and perhaps scandalous, work to Petrarch, his respectable friend, in whose letters and memoirs he conspicuously appears.

94. Boccace indulges an honest vanity: Ostentationis causâ Græca carmina adscripsi . . . jure utor meo; meum est hoc decus, mea gloria scilicet inter Etruscos Græcis uti carminibus. Nonne ego fui qui Leontium Pilatum, etc. (de Genealogiâ Deorum, l. xv. c. 7, a work which, though now forgotten, has run through thirteen or fourteen editions).

95. Leontius, or Leo Pilatus, is sufficiently made known by Hody (p. 2–11) and the abbé de Sade (Vie de Pétrarque, tom. iii. p. 625–634, 670–673), who has very happily caught the lively and dramatic manner of his original.

96. Dr. Hody (p. 54) is angry with Leonard Aretin, Guarinus, Paulus Jovius, etc., for affirming that the Greek letters were restored in Italy post septingentos annos; as if, says he, they had flourished till the end of the seventh century. These writers most probably reckoned from the last period of the exarchate; and the presence of the Greek magistrates and troops at Ravenna and Rome must have preserved, in some degree, the use of their native tongue.

97. See the article of Emanuel, or Manuel Chrysoloras, in Hody (p. 12–54) and Tiraboschi (tom. vii. p. 113–118). The precise date of his arrival floats between the years 1390 and 1400, and is only confined by the reign of Boniface IX.

98. The name of Aretinus has been assumed by five or six natives of Arezzo in Tuscany, of whom the most famous and the most worthless lived in the sixteenth century. Leonardus Brunus Aretinus, the disciple of Chrysoloras, was a linguist, an orator, and an historian, the secretary of four successive popes, and the chancellor of the republic of Florence, where he died A.D. 1444, at the age of seventy-five (Fabric. Biblioth. medii Ævi, tom. i. p. 190, etc.; Tiraboschi, tom. vii. p. 33–38).

99. See the passage in Aretin. Commentario

Rerum suo Tempore in Italia Gestarum, apud Hodium, p. 28–30.

100. In this domestic discipline, Petrarch, who loved the youth, often complains of the eager curiosity, restless temper, and proud feelings, which announce the genius and glory of a riper age (Mémoires sur Pétrarque, tom. iii. p. 700–709).

101. Hinc Græcæ Latinæque scholæ exortæ sunt, Guarino Philelpho, Leonardo Aretino, Caroloque, ac plerisque aliis tanquam ex equo Trojano prodeuntibus, quorum emulatione multa ingenia deinceps ad laudem excitata sunt (Platina in Bonifacio IX.). Another Italian writer adds the names of Paulus Petrus Vergerius, Omnibonus Vincentius, Poggius, Franciscus Barbarus, etc. But I question whether a rigid chronology would allow Chrysoloras all these eminent scholars (Hodius, p. 25–27, etc.).

102. See in Hody the article of Bessarion (p. 136–177). Theodore Gaza, George of Trebizond, and the rest of the Greeks whom I have named or omitted, are inserted in their proper chapters of his learned work. See likewise Tiraboschi, in the first and second parts of the sixth tome.

103. The cardinals knocked at his door, but his conclavist refused to interrupt the studies of Bessarion; "Nicholas," said he, "thy respect has cost thee a hat, and me the tiara."

104. Such as George of Trebizond, Theodore Gaza, Argyropulus, Andronicus of Thessalonica, Philelphus, Poggius, Blondus, Nicholas Perrot, Valla, Campanus, Platina, etc. Viri (says Hody, with the pious zeal of a scholar) nullo ævo perituri (p. 156).

105. He was born before the taking of Constantinople, but his honourable life was stretched far into the sixteenth century (A.D. 1535). Leo X. and Francis I. were his noblest patrons, under whose auspices he founded the Greek colleges of Rome and Paris (Hody, p. 247–275). He left posterity in France; but the counts de Vintimille, and their numerous branches, derive the name of Lascaris from a doubtful marriage in the thirteenth century with the daughter of a Greek emperor (Ducange, Fam. Byzant. p. 224–230).

106. Two of his epigrams against Virgil, and three against Tully, are preserved and refuted by Franciscus Floridus, who can find no better names than Græculus ineptus et impudens (Hody, p. 274). In our own times an English critic has accused the Æneid of containing multa languida, nugatoria, spiritû et majestate carminis heroici defecta; many such verses as he, the said Jeremiah Markland, would have been ashamed of owning (præfat. ad. Statii Sylvas, p. 21, 22).

107. Manuel Chrysoloras and his colleagues are accused of ignorance, envy, or avarice (Sylloge, etc., tom. ii. p. 235). The modern Greeks pronounce the β as a V consonant, and confound three vowels (η ι υ) and several diphthongs. Such was the vulgar pronunciation which the stern Gardiner maintained by penal statutes in the university of Cambridge; but the monosyllable βη represented to an Attic ear the bleating of sheep, and a bellwether is better evidence than a bishop or a chancellor. The treatises of those scholars, particularly Erasmus, who asserted a more classical pronunciation, are collected in the Sylloge of Havercamp (2 vols. in octavo, Lugd. Bat. 1736, 1740); but it is difficult to paint sounds by words; and, in their reference to modern use, they can be understood only by their respective countrymen. We may observe that our peculiar pronunciation of the θ, th, is approved by Erasmus (tom. ii. p. 130).

108. George Gemistus Pletho, a various and voluminous writer, the master of Bessarion, and all the Platonists of the times. He visited Italy in his old age, and soon returned to end his days in Peloponnesus. See the curious Diatribe of Leo Allatius de Georgiis, in Fabricius (Biblioth. Græc. tom. x. p. 739–756).

109. The state of the Platonic philosophy in Italy is illustrated by Boivin (Mém. de l'Acad. des Inscriptions, tom. ii. p. 715–729) and Tiraboschi (tom. vi. P. i. p. 259–288).

110. See the Life of Nicholas V. by two contemporary authors, Janottus Manettus (tom. iii. P. ii. p. 905–962) and Vespasian of Florence (tom. xxv. p. 267–290, in the collection of Muratori; and consult Tiraboschi (tom. vi. P. i. p. 46–52, 109) and Hody, in the articles of Theodore Gaza, George of Trebizond, etc.

111. Lord Bolingbroke observes, with truth and spirit, that the popes in this instance were worse politicians than the muftis, and that the charm which had bound mankind for so many ages was broken by the magicians themselves (Letters on the Study of History, l. vi. p. 165, 166, octavo edition, 1779).

112. See the literary history of Cosmo and Lorenzo of Medicis, in Tiraboschi (tom. vi. P. i. l. i. c. 2), who bestows a due measure of praise on Alphonso of Arragon, king of Naples, the dukes of Milan, Ferrara, Urbino, etc. The republic of Venice has deserved the least from the gratitude of scholars.

113. Tiraboschi (tom. vi. P. i. p. 104), from the preface of Janus Lascaris to the Greek Anthology, printed at Florence 1494; Latebant (says Aldus, in his preface to the Greek orators, apud Hodium, p. 249) in Atho Thraciæ monte. Eas Lascaris . . . in Italiam reportavit. Miserat enim ipsum Laurentius ille Medices in Græciam ad inquirendos simul, et quantovis emendos pretio bonos libros. It is remarkable enough that the research was facilitated by sultan Bajazet II.

114. The Greek language was introduced into the university of Oxford in the last years of the fifteenth century by Grocyn, Linacer, and Latimer, who had all studied at Florence under Demetrius Chalcocondyles. See Dr. Knight's curious Life of Erasmus. Although a stout academical patriot, he is forced to acknowledge that Erasmus learned Greek at Oxford, and taught it at Cambridge.

115. The jealous Italians were desirous of keeping a monopoly of Greek learning. When Aldus was about to publish the Greek scholiasts on Sophocles and Euripides, Cave (said they), cave hoc facias, ne *Barbari* istis adjuti domi maneant, et pauciores in Italiam ventitent (Dr. Knight, in his Life of Erasmus, p. 365, from Beatus Rhenanus).

116. The press of Aldus Manutius, a Roman, was established at Venice about the year 1494: he printed above sixty considerable works of Greek literature, almost all for the first time; several containing different treatises and authors, and of several authors two, three, or four editions (Fabric. Biblioth. Græc. tom. xiii. p. 605, etc.). Yet his glory must not tempt us to forget that the first Greek book, the Grammar of Constantine Lascaris, was printed at Milan in 1476, and that the Florence Homer of 1488 displays all the luxury of the typographical art. See the Annales Typographici of Mattaire, and the Bibliographie Instructive of De Bure, a knowing bookseller of Paris.

117. I will select three singular examples of this classic enthusiasm. 1. At the synod of Florence, Gemistus Pletho said, in familiar conversation, to George of Trebizond, that in a short time mankind would unanimously renounce the Gospel and the Koran for a religion similar to that of the Gentiles (Leo Allatius, apud Fabricium, tom. x. p. 751). 2. Paul II. persecuted the Roman academy, which had been founded by Pomponius Lætus; and the principal members were accused of heresy, impiety, and *paganism* (Tiraboschi, tom. vi. P. i. p. 81, 82). 3. In the next century some scholars and poets in France celebrated the success of Jodelle's tragedy of Cleopatra by a festival of Bacchus, and, as it is said, by the sacrifice of a goat (Bayle, Dictionnaire, JODELLE; Fontenelle, tom. iii. p. 56–61). Yet the spirit of bigotry might often discern a serious impiety in the sportive play of fancy and learning.

118. The survivor Boccace died in the year 1375; and we cannot place before 1480 the composition of the Morgante Maggiore of Pulci, and the Orlando Inamorato of Boiardo (Tiraboschi, tom. vi. P. ii. p. 174–177).

Chapter LXVII

1. The epistle of Manuel Chrysoloras to the emperor John Palæologus will not offend the eye or ear of a classical student (ad calcem Codini de Antiquitatibus C. P. p. 107–126). The superscription suggests a chronological remark, that John Palæologus II. was associated in the empire before the year 1414, the date of Chrysoloras's death. A still earlier date, at least 1408, is deduced from the age of his youngest sons, Demetrius and Thomas, who were both *Porphyrogeniti* (Ducange, Fam. Byzant. p. 244, 247).

2. Somebody observed that the city of Athens might be circumnavigated (τις εἶπεν τὴν πόλιν τῶν Ἀθηναίων δύνασθαι καὶ παραπλεῖν καὶ περιπλεῖν). But what may be true in a rhetorical sense of Constantinople, cannot be applied to the situation of Athens, five miles from the sea, and not intersected or surrounded by any navigable streams.

3. Nicephorus Gregoras has described the colossus of Justinian (l. vii. 12): but his measures are false and inconsistent. The editor Boivin consulted his friend Girardon; and the sculptor gave him the true proportions of an equestrian statue. That of Justinian was still visible to Peter Gyllius, not on the column, but in the outward court of the seraglio; and he was at Constantinople when it was melted down, and cast into a brass cannon (de Topograph. C. P. l. ii. c. 17).

4. See the decay and repairs of St. Sophia, in Nicephorus Gregoras (l. vii. 12, l. xv. 2). The building was propped by Andronicus in 1317, the eastern hemisphere fell in 1345. The Greeks, in their pompous rhetoric, exalt the beauty and holiness of the church, an earthly heaven, the abode of angels, and of God himself, etc.

5. The genuine and original narrative of Syropulus (p. 312–351) opens the schism from the first *office* of the Greeks at Venice to the general opposition at Constantinople of the clergy and people.

6. On the schism of Constantinople, see Phranza (l. ii. c. 17), Laonicus Chalcocondyles (l. vi. p. 155, 156 [p. 292–295, ed. Bonn]), and Ducas (c. 31); the last of whom writes with truth and freedom. Among the moderns we may distinguish the continuator of Fleury (tom. xxii. p. 338, etc., 401, 420, etc.) and Spondanus (A.D. 1440–50). The sense of the latter is drowned in prejudice and passion as soon as Rome and religion are concerned.

7. Isidore was metropolitan of Kiow, but the Greeks subject to Poland have removed that see from the ruins of Kiow to Lemberg, or Leopold (Herbestein, in Ramusio, tom. ii. p. 127). On the other hand, the Russians transferred their spiritual obedience to the archbishop, who became, in 1588, the patriarch of Moscow (Levesque, Hist. de Russie, tom. iii. p. 188, 190, from a Greek MS. at Turin, Iter et labores Archiepiscopi Arsenii).

8. The curious narrative of Levesque (Hist. de Russie, tom. ii. p. 242–247) is extracted from the patriarchal archives. The scenes of Ferrara and Florence are described by ignorance and passion; but the Russians are credible in the account of their own prejudices.

9. The Shamanism, the ancient religion of the Samanæans and Gymnosophists, has been driven by the more popular Bramins from India into the northern deserts: the naked philosophers were

compelled to wrap themselves in fur; but they insensibly sunk into wizards and physicians. The Mordvans and Tcheremisses in the European Russia adhere to this religion, which is formed on the earthly model of one king or God, his ministers or angels, and the rebellious spirits who oppose his government. As these tribes of the Volga have no images, they might more justly retort on the Latin missionaries the name of idolaters (Levesque, Hist. des Peuples soumis à la Domination des Russes, tom. i. p. 194–237, 423–460).

10. Spondanus, Annal. Eccles. tom. ii. A.D. 1451, No. 13. The epistle of the Greeks, with a Latin version, is extant in the college library at Prague.

11. See Cantemir, History of the Othman Empire, p. 94. Murad, or Morad, may be more correct: but I have preferred the popular name to that obscure diligence which is rarely successful in translating an Oriental, into the Roman, alphabet.

12. See Chalcocondyles (l. vii. p. 186, 198 [p. 375, ed. Bonn]), Ducas (c. 33 [p. 228, ed. Bonn]), and Marinus Barletius (in Vit. Scanderbeg, p. 145, 146). In his good faith towards the garrison of Sfetigrade, he was a lesson and example to his son Mohammed.

13. Voltaire (Essai sur l'Histoire Générale, c. 89, p. 283, 284) admires le Philosophe Turc: would he have bestowed the same praise on a Christian prince for retiring to a monastery? In his way, Voltaire was a bigot, an intolerant bigot.

14. See the articles Dervische, Fakir, Nasser, Rohbaniat, in D'Herbelot's Bibliothèque Orientale. Yet the subject is superficially treated from the Persian and Arabian writers. It is among the Turks that these orders have principally flourished.

15. Rycaut (in the Present State of the Ottoman Empire, p. 242–268) affords much information, which he drew from his personal conversation with the heads of the dervishes, most of whom ascribed their origin to the time of Orchan. He does not mention the Zichidæ of Chalcocondyles (l. vii. p. 186 [p. 352, ed. Bonn]), among whom Amurath retired: the Seids of that author are the descendants of Mohammed.

16. In the year 1431 Germany raised 40,000 horse, men-at-arms, against the Hussites of Bohemia (Lenfant, Hist. du Concile de Basle, tom. i. p. 318). At the siege of Nuys, on the Rhine, in 1474, the princes, prelates, and cities sent their respective quotas; and the bishop of Munster (qui n'est pas des plus grands) furnished 1400 horse, 6000 foot, all in green, with 1200 waggons. The united armies of the king of England and the duke of Burgundy scarcely equalled one-third of this German host (Mémoires de Philippe de Comines, l. iv. c. 2). At present, six or seven hundred thousand men are maintained in constant pay and admirable discipline by the powers of Germany.

17. It was not till the year 1444 that France and England could agree on a truce of some months. (See Rymer's Fœdera, and the chronicles of both nations.)

18. In the Hungarian crusade, Spondanus (Annal. Eccles. A.D. 1443, 1444) has been my leading guide. He has diligently read, and critically compared, the Greek and Turkish materials, the historians of Hungary, Poland, and the West. His narrative is perspicuous; and where he can be free from a religious bias, the judgment of Spondanus is not contemptible.

19. I have curtailed the harsh letter (Wladislaus) which most writers affix to his name, either in compliance with the Polish pronunciation, or to distinguish him from his rival the infant Ladislaus of Austria. Their competition for the crown of Hungary is described by Callimachus (l. i. ii. p. 447–486), Bonfinius (Decad. iii. l. iv.), Spondanus, and Lenfant.

20. The Greek historians, Phranza, Chalcocondyles, and Ducas, do not ascribe to their prince a very active part in this crusade, which he seems to have promoted by his wishes, and injured by his fears.

21. Cantemir (p. 88) ascribes to his policy the original plan, and transcribes his animating epistle to the king of Hungary. But the Mohammedan powers are seldom informed of the state of Christendom; and the situation and correspondence of the knights of Rhodes must connect them with the sultan of Caramania.

22. In their letters to the emperor Frederic III. the Hungarians slay 30,000 Turks in one battle; but the modest Julian reduces the slaughter to 6000 or even 2000 infidels (Æneas Sylvius in Europ. c. 5, and epist. 44, 81, apud Spondanum).

23. See the origin of the Turkish war, and the first expedition of Ladislaus, in the fifth and sixth books of the third decad of Bonfinius, who, in his division and style, copies Livy with tolerable success. Callimachus (l. ii. p. 487–496) is still more pure and authentic.

24. I do not pretend to warrant the literal accuracy of Julian's speech, which is variously worded by Callimachus (l. iii. p. 505–507), Bonfinius (dec. iii. l. vi. p. 457, 458), and other historians, who might indulge their own eloquence, while they represent one of the orators of the age. But they all agree in the advice and arguments for perjury, which in the field of controversy are fiercely attacked by the Protestants, and feebly defended by the Catholics. The latter are discouraged by the misfortune of Varna.

25. Varna, under the Grecian name of Odessus, was a colony of the Milesians, which they denominated from the hero Ulysses (Cellarius, tom. i. p. 374; D'Anville, tom. i. p. 312). According to Arrian's Periplus of the Euxine (p. 24, 25, in the first volume of Hudson's Geographers), it was situate 1740 stadia, or furlongs, from the mouth of the Danube, 2140 from Byzantium, and 360 to the north of a ridge or promontory of Mount Hæmus, which advances into the sea.

26. Some Christian writers affirm that he drew from his bosom the host or wafer on which the

treaty had *not* been sworn. The Moslems suppose, with more simplicity, an appeal to God and his prophet Jesus, which is likewise insinuated by Callimachus (l. iii. p. 516; Spondan. A.D. 1444, No. 8).

27. A critic will always distrust these *spolia opima* of a victorious general, so difficult for valour to obtain, so easy for flattery to invent (Cantemir, p. 90, 91). Callimachus (l. iii. p. 517) more simply and probably affirms, supervenientibus Janizaris, telorum multitudine, non tam confossus est, quam obrutus.

28. Besides some valuable hints from Æneas Sylvius, which are diligently collected by Spondanus, our best authorities are three historians of the fifteenth century, Philippus Callimachus (de Rebus a Vladislao Polonorum atque Hungarorum Rege gestis, libri iii. in Bell. Script. Rerum Hungaricarum, tom. i. p. 433–518), Bonfinius (decad iii. l. v. p. 460–467), and Chalcocondyles (l. vii. p. 165–179 [p. 312, seq. ed. Bonn]). The two first were Italians, but they passed their lives in Poland and Hungary (Fabric. Biblioth. Latin. med. et infimæ Ætatis, tom. i. p. 324; Vossius, de Hist. Latin. l. iii. c. 8, 11; Bayle, Dictionnaire, BONFINIUS). A small tract of Fælix Petancius, chancellor of Segnia (ad calcem Cuspinian. de Cæsaribus, p. 716, 722), represents the theatre of the war in the fifteenth century.

29. M. Lenfant has described the origin (Hist. du Concile de Basle, tom. i. p. 247, etc.) and Bohemian campaign (p. 315, etc.) of Cardinal Julian. His services at Basil and Ferrara, and his unfortunate end, are occasionally related by Spondanus and the continuator of Fleury.

30. Syropulus honourably praises the talents of an enemy (p. 117): τοιαυτα τινα εἶπεν ὁ Ἰουλιανός, πεπλατυσμένως ἀγὰν καὶ λογίκως, καὶ μετ᾽ἐπιστήμης καὶ δεινότητος ῥητορίκης.

31. See Bonfinius, decad iii. l. iv. p. 423. Could the Italian historian pronounce, or the king of Hungary hear, without a blush, the absurd flattery which confounded the name of a Wallachian village with the casual, though glorious, epithet of a single branch of the Valerian family at Rome?

32. Philip de Comines (Mémoires, l. vi. c. 13), from the tradition of the times, mentions him with high encomiums, but under the whimsical name of the Chevalier Blanc de Valaigne (Vallachia). The Greek Chalcocondyles, and the Turkish annals of Leunclavius, presume to accuse his fidelity or valour.

33. See Bonfinius (decad iii. l. viii. p. 492) and Spondanus (A.D. 1456, No. 1–7). Huniades shared the glory of the defence of Belgrade with Capistran, a Franciscan friar; and in their respective narratives, neither the saint nor the hero condescends to take notice of his rival's merit.

34. See Bonfinius, decad iii. l. viii.—decad iv. l. viii. The observations of Spondanus on the life and character of Matthias Corvinus are curious and critical (A.D. 1464, No. 1; 1475, No. 6; 1476, No. 14–16; 1490, No. 4, 5). Italian fame was the

object of his vanity. His actions are celebrated in the Epitome Rerum Hungaricarum (p. 322–412) of Peter Ranzanus, a Sicilian. His wise and facetious sayings are registered by Galestus Martius of Narni (528–568), and we have a particular narrative of his wedding and coronation. These three tracts are all contained in the first vol. of Bel's Scriptores Rerum Hungaricarum.

35. They are ranked by Sir William Temple, in his pleasing Essay on Heroic Virtue (Works, vol. iii. p. 385), among the seven chiefs who have deserved, without wearing, a royal crown: Belisarius, Narses, Gonsalvo of Cordova, William first prince of Orange, Alexander duke of Parma, John Huniades, and George Castriot, or Scanderbeg.

36. I could wish for some simple, authentic memoirs of a friend of Scanderbeg, which would introduce me to the man, the time, and the place. In the old and national history of Marinus Barletius, a priest of Scodra (de Vitâ, Moribus, et Rebus gestis Georgii Castrioti, etc., libri xiii. pp. 367, Argentorat. 1537, in fol.), his gaudy and cumbersome robes are stuck with many false jewels. See likewise Chalcocondyles, l. vii. p. 185, l. viii. p. 229 [p. 350 and 432, ed. Bonn].

37. His circumcision, education, etc., are marked by Marinus with brevity and reluctance (l. i. p. 6, 7).

38. Since Scanderbeg died A.D. 1466, in the sixty-third year of his age (Marinus, l. xiii. p. 370), he was born in 1403; since he was torn from his parents by the Turks when he was *novennis* (Marinus, l. i. p. 1, 6), that event must have happened in 1412, nine years before the accession of Amurath II., who must have inherited, not acquired, the Albanian slave. Spondanus has remarked this inconsistency, A.D. 1431, No. 31; 1443, No. 14.

39. His revenue and forces are luckily given by Marinus (l. ii. p. 44).

40. There were two Dibras, the upper and lower, the Bulgarian and Albanian: the former, 70 miles from Croya (l. i. p. 17), was contiguous to the fortress of Sfetigrade, whose inhabitants refused to drink from a well into which a dead dog had traitorously been cast (l. v. p. 139, 140). We want a good map of Epirus.

41. Compare the Turkish narrative of Cantemir (p. 92) with the pompous and prolix declamation in the fourth, fifth, and sixth books of the Albanian priest, who has been copied by the tribe of strangers and moderns.

42. In honour of his hero, Barletius (l. vi. p. 188–192) kills the sultan, by disease indeed, under the walls of Croya. But this audacious fiction is disproved by the Greeks and Turks, who agree in the time and manner of Amurath's death at Adrianople.

43. See the marvels of his Calabrian expedition in the ninth and tenth books of Marinus Barletius, which may be rectified by the testimony or silence of Muratori (Annali d'Italia, tom. xiii. p. 291), and his original authors (Joh. Simonetta de Rebus

Francisci Sfortiæ, in Muratori, Script. Rerum Ital. tom. xxi. p. 728, et alios). The Albanian cavalry, under the name of *Stradiots*, soon became famous in the wars of Italy (Mémoires de Comines, l. viii. c. 5).

44. Spondanus, from the best evidence and the most rational criticism, has reduced the giant Scanderbeg to the human size (A.D. 1461, No. 20; 1463, No. 9; 1465, No. 12, 13; 1467, No. 1). His own letter to the pope, and the testimony of Phranza (l. iii. c. 28), a refugee in the neighbouring isle of Corfu, demonstrate his last distress, which is awkwardly concealed by Marinus Barletius (l. x.).

45. See the family of the Castriots, in Ducange (Fam. Dalmaticæ, etc., xviii. p. 348–350).

46. This colony of Albanese is mentioned by Mr. Swinburne (Travels into the Two Sicilies, vol. i. p. 350–354).

47. The chronology of Phranza is clear and authentic; but instead of four years and seven months, Spondanus (A.D. 1445, No. 7) assigns seven or eight years to the reign of the last Constantine, which he deduces from a spurious epistle of Eugenius IV. to the king of Æthiopia.

48. Phranza (l. iii. c. 1–6) deserves credit and esteem.

49. Suppose him to have been captured in 1394, in Timour's first war in Georgia (Sherefeddin, l. iii. c. 50), he might follow his Tartar master into Hindostan in 1398, and from thence sail to the Spice islands.

50. The happy and pious Indians lived a hundred and fifty years, and enjoyed the most perfect productions of the vegetable and mineral kingdoms. The animals were on a large scale: dragons seventy cubits, ants (the *formica Indica*) nine inches long, sheep like elephants, elephants like sheep. Quidlibet audendi, etc.

51. He sailed in a country vessel from the Spice islands to one of the ports of the exterior India; invenitque navem grandem *Ibericam*, quâ in *Portugalliam* est delatus. This passage, composed in 1477 (Phranza, l. iii. c. 30), twenty years before the discovery of the Cape of Good Hope, is spurious or wonderful. But this new geography is sullied by the old and incompatible error which places the source of the Nile in India.

52. Cantemir (p. 83), who styles her the daughter of Lazarus Ogli, and the Helen of the Servians, places her marriage with Amurath in the year 1424. It will not easily be believed that, in six-and-twenty years' cohabitation, the sultan corpus ejus non tetigit. After the taking of Constantinople she fled to Mohammed II. (Phranza, l. iii. c. 22.)

53. The classical reader will recollect the offers of Agamemnon (Iliad. I. v. 144), and the general practice of antiquity.

54. Cantacuzene (I am ignorant of his relation to the emperor of that name) was a great domestic, a firm asserter of the Greek creed, and a brother of the queen of Servia, whom he visited with the character of ambassador. (Syropulus, p. 37, 38, 45.)

Chapter LXVIII

1. For the character of Mohammed II. it is dangerous to trust either the Turks or the Christians. The most moderate picture appears to be drawn by Phranza (l. i. c. 32 [p. 93, ed. Bonn]), whose resentment had cooled in age and solitude. See likewise Spondanus (A.D. 1451, No. 11), and the continuator of Fleury (tom. xxii. p. 552), the *Elogia* of Paulus Jovius (l. iii. p. 164–166), and the Dictionnaire de Bayle (tom. iii. p. 272–279).

2. Cantemir (p. 115), and the mosques which he founded, attest his public regard for religion. Mohammed freely disputed with the patriarch Gennadius on the two religions (Spond. A.D. 1453, No. 22).

3. Quinque linguas præter suam noverat, Græcam, Latinam, Chaldaicam, Persicam. The Latin translator of Phranza has dropped the Arabic, which the Koran must recommend to every Musulman.

4. Philelphus, by a Latin ode, requested and obtained the liberty of his wife's mother and sisters from the conqueror of Constantinople. It was delivered into the sultan's hands by the envoys of the duke of Milan. Philelphus himself was suspected of a design of retiring to Constantinople; yet the

orator often sounded the trumpet of holy war (see his Life by M. Lancelot, in the Mémoires de l'Académie des Inscriptions, tom. x. p. 718, 724, etc.).

5. Robert Valturio published at Verona, in 1483, his twelve books de Re Militari, in which he first mentions the use of bombs. By his patron Sigismond Malatesta, prince of Rimini, it had been addressed with a Latin epistle to Mohammed II.

6. According to Phranza, he assiduously studied the lives and actions of Alexander, Augustus, Constantine, and Theodosius. I have read somewhere that Plutarch's Lives were translated by his orders into the Turkish language. If the sultan himself understood Greek, it must have been for the benefit of his subjects. Yet these Lives are a school of freedom as well as of valour.

7. The famous Gentile Bellino, whom he had invited from Venice, was dismissed with a chain and collar of gold and a purse of 3000 ducats. With Voltaire I laugh at the foolish story of a slave purposely beheaded to instruct the painter in the action of the muscles.

8. These Imperial drunkards were Soliman I., Selim II., and Amurath IV. (Cantemir, p. 61).

The sophis of Persia can produce a more regular succession; and in the last age our European travellers were the witnesses and companions of their revels.

9. Calapin, one of these royal infants, was saved from his cruel brother, and baptised at Rome under the name of Callistus Othomannus. The emperor Frederic III. presented him with an estate in Austria, where he ended his life; and Cuspinian, who in his youth conversed with the aged prince at Vienna, applauds his piety and wisdom (de Cæsaribus, p. 672, 673).

10. See the accession of Mohammed II. in Ducas (c. 33), Phranza (l. i. c. 33; l. iii. c. 2), Chalcocondyles (l. vii. p. 199 [p. 376, ed. Bonn]), and Cantemir (p. 96).

11. Before I enter on the siege of Constantinople I shall observe that, except the short hints of Cantemir and Leunclavius, I have not been able to obtain any Turkish account of this conquest—such an account as we possess of the siege of Rhodes by Soliman II. (Mémoires de l'Académie des Inscriptions, tom. xxvi. p. 723–769). I must therefore depend on the Greeks, whose prejudices, in some degree, are subdued by their distress. Our standard texts are those of Ducas (c. 34–42), Phranza (l. iii. c. 7–20), Chalcocondyles (l. viii. p. 201–214 [p 380–403, ed. Bonn]), and Leonardus Chiensis (Historia C. P. a Turco expugnatæ; Norimberghæ, 1544, in 4to, 20 leaves). The last of these narratives is the earliest in date, since it was composed in the isle of Chios, the 16th of August, 1453, only seventy-nine days after the loss of the city, and in the first confusion of ideas and passions. Some hints may be added from an epistle of Cardinal Isidore (in Farragine Rerum Turcicarum, ad calcem Chalcocondyl. Clauseri, Basil, 1556) to Pope Nicholas V., and a tract of Theodosius Zygomala, which he addressed in the year 1581 to Martin Crusius (Turco-Græcia, l. i. p. 74–98, Basil, 1584). The various facts and materials are briefly, though critically, reviewed by Spondanus (A.D. 1453, No. 1–27). The hearsay relations of Monstrelet and the distant Latins I shall take leave to disregard.

12. The situation of the fortress and the topography of the Bosphorus are best learned from Peter Gyllius (de Bosphoro Thracio, l. ii. c. 13), Leunclavius (Pandect. p. 445), and Tournefort (Voyage dans le Levant, tom. ii. lettre xv. p. 443, 444); but I must regret the map or plan which Tournefort sent to the French minister of the marine. The reader may turn back to chap. xvii. of this History.

13. The opprobrious name which the Turks bestow on the infidels is expressed καβουρ by Ducas, and Giaour by Leunclavius and the moderns. The former term is derived by Ducange (Gloss. Græc. tom. i. p. 530) from καβουρον, in vulgar Greek a tortoise, as denoting a retrograde motion from the faith. But, alas! Gabour is no more than Gheber, which was transferred from the Persian to the Turkish language, from the worshippers of fire to those of the crucifix (D'Herbelot, Biblioth. Orient. p. 375).

14. Phranza does justice to his master's sense and courage—Calliditatem hominis non ignorans Imperator prior arma movere constituit; and stigmatises the folly of the cum sacri tum profani proceres, which he had heard, amentes spe vanâ pasci. Ducas was not a privy counsellor.

15. Instead of this clear and consistent account, the Turkish Annals (Cantemir, p. 97) revived the foolish tale of the ox's hide, and Dido's stratagem in the foundation of Carthage. These annals (unless we are swayed by an anti-Christian prejudice) are far less valuable than the Greek historians.

16. In the dimensions of this fortress, the old castle of Europe, Phranza does not exactly agree with Chalcocondyles, whose description has been verified on the spot by his editor Leunclavius.

17. Among these were some pages of Mohammed, so conscious of his inexorable rigour, that they begged to lose their heads in the city unless they could return before sunset.

18. Ducas, c. 35 [p. 248, ed. Bonn]. Phranza (l. iii. c. 3), who had sailed in his vessel, commemorates the Venetian pilot as a martyr.

19. Auctum est Palæologorum genus, et Imperii successor, parvæque Romanorum scintillæ hæres natus, Andreas, etc. (Phranza, l. iii. c. 3 [p. 236, ed. Bonn]). The strong expression was inspired by his feelings.

20. Cantemir, p. 97, 98. The sultan was either doubtful of his conquest or ignorant of the superior merits of Constantinople. A city or a kingdom may sometimes be ruined by the Imperial fortune of their sovereign.

21. Συντροφός, by the president Cousin, is translated père nourricier, most correctly indeed from the Latin version; but in his haste he has overlooked the note by which Ismael Boillaud (ad Ducam, c. 35 [p. 251, ed. Bonn]) acknowledges and rectifies his own error.

22. The Oriental custom of never appearing without gifts before a sovereign or a superior is of high antiquity, and seems analogous with the idea of sacrifice, still more ancient and universal. See the examples of such Persian gifts, Ælian, Hist. Var. l. i. c. 31, 32, 33.

23. The Lala of the Turks (Cantemir, p. 34) and the Tata of the Greeks (Ducas, c. 35) are derived from the natural language of children; and it may be observed that all such primitive words which denote their parents are the simple repetition of one syllable, composed of a labial or dental consonant and an open vowel (Des Brosses, Méchanisme des Langues, tom. i. p. 231–247).

24. The Attic talent weighed about sixty minæ, or avoirdupois pounds (see Hooper on Ancient Weights, Measures, etc.); but among the modern Greeks that classic appellation was extended to a weight of one hundred, or one hundred and twenty-five pounds (Ducange, τάλαντον). Leonardus Chiensis measured the ball or stone of the *second*

cannon: Lapidem, qui palmis undecim ex meis ambibat in gyro.

25. See Voltaire (Hist. Générale, c. xci. p. 294, 295). He was ambitious of universal monarchy; and the poet frequently aspires to the name and style of an astronomer, a chemist, etc.

26. The Baron de Tott (tom. iii. p. 85-89), who fortified the Dardanelles against the Russians, describes in a lively, and even comic, strain his own prowess, and the consternation of the Turks. But that adventurous traveller does not possess the art of gaining our confidence.

27. Non audivit, indignum ducens, says the honest Antoninus; but, as the Roman court was afterwards grieved and ashamed, we find the more courtly expression of Platina, in animo fuisse pontifici juvare Græcos, and the positive assertion of Æneas Sylvius, structam classem, etc. (Spond. A.D. 1453, No. 3.)

28. Antonin. in Proem.—Epist. Cardinal. Isidor. apud Spondanum; and Dr. Johnson, in the tragedy of Irene, has happily seized this characteristic circumstance:—

The groaning Greeks dig up the golden caverns,

The accumulated wealth of hoarding ages;

That wealth which, granted to their weeping prince,

Had rang'd embattled nations at their gates.

29. The palatine troops are styled *Capiculi;* the provincials, *Seratculi;* and most of the names and institutions of the Turkish militia existed before the *Canon Nameh* of Soliman II., from which, and his own experience, Count Marsigli has composed his Military State of the Ottoman Empire.

30. The observation of Philelphus is approved by Cuspinian in the year 1508 (de Cæsaribus, in Epilog. de Militiâ Turcicâ, p. 697). Marsigli proves that the effective armies of the Turks are much less numerous than they appear. In the army that besieged Constantinople Leonardus Chiensis reckons no more than 15,000 Janizaries.

31. Ego, eidem (Imp.) tabellas extribui non absque dolore et mœstitia, mansitque apud nos duos aliis occultus numerus (Phranza, l. iii. c. 3 [p. 241, ed. Bonn]). With some indulgence for national prejudices, we cannot desire a more authentic witness, not only of public facts, but of private counsels.

32. In Spondanus the narrative of the union is not only partial, but imperfect. The bishop of Pamiers died in 1642, and the history of Ducas, which represents these scenes (c. 36, 37) with such truth and spirit, was not printed till the year 1649.

33. Phranza, one of the conforming Greeks, acknowledges that the measure was adopted only propter spem auxilii; he affirms with pleasure that those who refused to perform their devotions in St. Sophia, extra culpam et in pace essent (l. iii. c. 20).

34. His primitive and secular name was George Scholarius, which he changed for that of Gennadius, either when he became a monk or a patri-arch. His defence, at Florence, of the same union which he so furiously attacked at Constantinople, has tempted Leo Allatius (Diatrib. de Georgiis, in Fabric. Biblioth. Græc. tom. x. p. 760-786) to divide him into two men; but Renaudot (p. 343-383) has restored the identity of his person and the duplicity of his character.

35. Φακιόλιον, κάλυπτρα, may be fairly translated a cardinal's hat. The difference of the Greek and Latin habits embittered the schism.

36. We are obliged to reduce the Greek miles to the smallest measure which is preserved in the wersts of Russia, of 547 French *toises*, and of 1042/5 to a degree. The six miles of Phranza do not exceed four English miles (D'Anville, Mesures Itinéraires, p. 61, 123, etc.).

37 At indies doctiores nostri facti paravere contra hostes machinamenta, quæ tamen avare dabantur. Pulvis erat nitri modica, exigua; tela modica; bombardæ si aderant incommoditate loci primum hostes offendere, macieriebus alveisque tectos, non poterant. Nam si quæ magnæ erant, ne murus concuteretur noster, quiescebant. This passage of Leonardus Chiensis is curious and important.

38. According to Chalcocondyles and Phranza the great cannon burst; an accident which, according to Ducas, was prevented by the artist's skill. It is evident that they do not speak of the same gun.

39. Near a hundred years after the siege of Constantinople the French and English fleets in the Channel were proud of firing 300 shot in an engagement of two hours (Mémoires de Martin du Bellay, l. x. in the Collection Générale, tom. xxi. p. 239).

40. I have selected some curious facts, without striving to emulate the bloody and obstinate eloquence of the Abbé de Vertot, in his prolix descriptions of the sieges of Rhodes, Malta, etc. But that agreeable historian had a turn for romance; and as he wrote to please the Order, he has adopted the same spirit of enthusiasm and chivalry.

41. The first theory of mines with gunpowder appears in 1480, in a MS. of George of Sienna (Tiraboschi, tom. vi. P. i. p. 324). They were first practised at Sarzanella, in 1487; but the honour and improvement in 1503 is ascribed to Peter of Navarre, who used them with success in the wars of Italy (Hist. de la Ligue de Cambray, tom. ii. p. 93-97).

42. It is singular that the Greeks should not agree in the number of these illustrious vessels; the *five* of Ducas, the *four* of Phranza and Leonardus, and the *two* of Chalcocondyles, must be extended to the smaller, or confined to larger, size. Voltaire, in giving one of these ships to Frederic III., confounds the emperors of the East and West.

43. In bold defiance, or rather in gross ignorance, of language and geography, the president Cousin detains them at Chios with a south, and wafts them to Constantinople with a north, wind.

44. The perpetual decay and weakness of the Turkish navy may be observed in Rycaut (State of the Ottoman Empire, p. 372–378), Thévenot (Voyages, P. i. p. 229–242), and Tott (Mémoires, tom. iii.); the last of whom is always solicitous to amuse and amaze his reader.

45. I must confess that I have before my eyes the living picture which Thucydides (vii. 71) has drawn of the passions and gestures of the Athenians in a naval engagement in the great harbour of Syracuse.

46. According to the exaggeration or corrupt text of Ducas (c. 38 [p. 270, ed. Bonn]) this golden bar was of the enormous and incredible weight of 500 libræ, or pounds. Bouillaud's reading of 500 drachms, or five pounds, is sufficient to exercise the arm of Mohammed, and bruise the back of his admiral.

47. Ducas, who confesses himself ill informed of the affairs of Hungary, assigns a motive of superstition, a fatal belief that Constantinople would be the term of the Turkish conquests. See Phranza (l. iii. c. 20) and Spondanus.

48. The unanimous testimony of the four Greeks is confirmed by Cantemir (p. 96) from the Turkish annals; but I could wish to contract the distance of *ten* miles, and to prolong the term of *one* night.

49. Phranza relates two examples of a similar transportation over the six miles of the isthmus of Corinth; the one fabulous, of Augustus after the battle of Actium; the other true, of Nicetas, a Greek general in the tenth century. To these he might have added a bold enterprise of Hannibal to introduce his vessels into the harbour of Tarentum (Polybius, l. viii. [c. 36] p. 749, edit. Gronov.).

50. A Greek of Candia, who had served the Venetians in a similar undertaking (Spond. A.D. 1438, No. 37), might possibly be the adviser and agent of Mohammed.

51. I particularly allude to our own embarkations on the lakes of Canada in the years 1776 and 1777, so great in the labour, so fruitless in the event.

52. Chalcocondyles and Ducas differ in the time and circumstances of the negotiation; and as it was neither glorious nor salutary, the faithful Phranza spares his prince even the thought of a surrender.

53. These wings (Chalcocondyles, l. viii. p. 208 [p. 393, ed. Bonn]) are no more than an Oriental figure: but in the tragedy of Irene Mohammed's passion soars above sense and reason:—

Should the fierce North, upon his frozen wings,
Bear him aloft above the wondering clouds,
And seat him in the Pleiads' golden chariot—
Thence should my fury drag him down to
        tortures.

Besides the extravagance of the rant, I must observe, 1. That the operation of the winds must be confined to the *lower* region of the air. 2. That the name, etymology, and fable of the Pleiads are purely Greek (Scholiast ad Homer, Σ. 686; Eudocia in Ioniâ, p. 339; Apollodor. l. iii. c. 10; Heyne, p. 229; Not. 682), and had no affinity with the astronomy of the East (Hyde ad Ulugbeg, Tabul. in Syntagma Dissert. tom. i. p. 40, 42; Goguet, Origine des Arts, etc., tom. vi. p. 73–78; Gebelin, Hist. du Calendrier, p. 73), which Mohammed had studied. 3. The golden chariot does not exist either in science or fiction; but I much fear that Dr. Johnson has confounded the Pleiads with the great bear or waggon, the zodiac with a northern constellation:—

Ἄρκτον θ' ἥν καὶ ἄμαξαν ἐπίκλησιν καλέουσιν.
                                    Il. xviii. 487.

54. Phranza quarrels with these Moslem acclamations, not for the name of God, but for that of the prophet: the pious zeal of Voltaire is excessive, and even ridiculous.

55. I am afraid that this discourse was composed by Phranza himself; and it smells so grossly of the sermon and the convent, that I almost doubt whether it was pronounced by Constantine. Leonardus assigns him another speech, in which he addresses himself more respectfully to the Latin auxiliaries.

56. This abasement, which devotion has sometimes extorted from dying princes, is an improvement of the Gospel doctrine of the forgiveness of injuries: it is more easy to forgive 490 times than once to ask pardon of an inferior.

57. Besides the 10,000 guards, and the sailors and the marines, Ducas numbers in this general assault 250,000 Turks, both horse and foot [c. 39, p. 283, ed. Bonn].

58. In the severe censure of the flight of Justiniani, Phranza expresses his own feelings and those of the public. For some private reasons he is treated with more lenity and respect by Ducas; but the words of Leonardus Chiensis express his strong and recent indignation, gloriæ salutis suique oblitus. In the whole series of their Eastern policy, his countrymen, the Genoese, were always suspected, and often guilty.

59. Ducas kills him with two blows of Turkish soldiers; Chalcocondyles wounds him in the shoulder, and then tramples him in the gate. The grief of Phranza, carrying him among the enemy, escapes from the precise image of his death; but we may, without flattery, apply these noble lines of Dryden:—

As to Sebastian, let them search the field;
And, where they find a mountain of the slain,
Send one to climb, and, looking down beneath,
There they will find him at his manly length,
With his face up to heaven, in that red monument
Which his good sword had digg'd.

60. Spondanus (A.D. 1453, No. 10), who has hopes of his salvation, wishes to absolve this demand from the guilt of suicide.

61. Leonardus Chiensis very properly observes that the Turks, had they known the emperor, would have laboured to save and secure a captive so acceptable to the sultan.

62. Cantemir, p. 96. The Christian ships in the

mouth of the harbour had flanked and retarded this naval attack.

63. Chalcocondyles most absurdly supposes that Constantinople was sacked by the Asiatics in revenge for the ancient calamities of Troy [l. viii. p. 403, ed. Bonn]; and the grammarians of the fifteenth century are happy to melt down the uncouth appellation of Turks into the more classical name of *Teucri.*

64. When Cyrus surprised Babylon during the celebration of a festival, so vast was the city, and so careless were the inhabitants, that much time elapsed before the distant quarters knew that they were captives. Herodotus (l. i. c. 191), and Usher (Annal. p. 78), who has quoted from the prophet Jeremiah a passage of similar import.

65. This lively description is extracted from Ducas (c.39 [p. 291, ed. Bonn]), who, two years afterwards, was sent ambassador from the prince of Lesbos to the sultan (c. 44). Till Lesbos was subdued in 1463 (Phranza, l. iii. c. 27), that island must have been full of the fugitives of Constantinople, who delighted to repeat, perhaps to adorn, the tale of their misery.

66. See Phranza, l. iii. c. 20, 21. His expressions are positive: Ameras suâ manú jugulavit . . . volebat enim eo turpiter et nefarie abuti. Me miserum et infelicem! Yet he could only learn from report the bloody or impure scenes that were acted in the dark recesses of the seraglio.

67. See Tiraboschi (tom. vi. P. i. p. 290) and Lancelot (Mém. de l'Académie des Inscriptions, tom. x. p. 718). I should be curious to learn how he could praise the public enemy, whom he so often reviles as the most corrupt and inhuman of tyrants.

68. The Commentaries of Pius II. suppose that he craftily placed his cardinal's hat on the head of a corpse which was cut off and exposed in triumph, while the legate himself was bought and delivered as a captive of no value. The great Belgic Chronicle adorns his escape with new adventures, which he suppressed (says Spondanus, A.D. 1453, No. 15) in his own letters, lest he should lose the merit and reward of suffering for Christ.

69. Busbequius expatiates with pleasure and applause on the rights of war and the use of slavery among the ancients and the Turks (de Legat. Turcicâ, Epist. iii. p. 161).

70. This sum is specified in a marginal note of Leunclavius (Chalcocondyles, l. viii. p. 211); but, in the distribution to Venice, Genoa, Florence, and Ancona, of 50, 20, 20, and 15,000 ducats, I suspect that a figure has been dropped. Even with the restitution, the foreign property would scarcely exceed one-fourth.

71. See the enthusiastic praises and lamentations of Phranza (l. iii. c. 17).

72. See Ducas (c. 42 [p. 312, ed. Bonn]), and an epistle, July 15th, 1453, from Laurus Quirinus to Pope Nicholas V. (Hody de Græcis, p. 192, from a MS. in the Cotton library).

73. The Julian calendar, which reckons the days and hours from midnight, was used at Constantinople. But Ducas seems to understand the natural hours from sunrise.

74. See the Turkish Annals, p. 329, and the Pandects of Leunclavius, p. 448.

75. I have had occasion (vol. i. p. 238) to mention this curious relic of Grecian antiquity.

76. We are obliged to Cantemir (p. 102) for the Turkish account of the conversion of St. Sophia, so bitterly deplored by Phranza and Ducas. It is amusing enough to observe in what opposite lights the same object appears to a Musulman and a Christian eye.

77. This distich, which Cantemir gives in the original, derives new beauties from the application. It was thus that Scipio repeated, in the sack of Carthage, the famous prophecy of Homer. The same generous feeling carried the mind of the conqueror to the past or the future.

78. I cannot believe with Ducas (see Spondanus, A.D. 1453, No. 13) that Mohammed sent round Persia, Arabia, etc., the head of the Greek emperor: he would surely content himself with a trophy less inhuman.

79. Phranza was the personal enemy of the great duke; nor could time, or death, or his own retreat to a monastery, extort a feeling of sympathy or forgiveness. Ducas is inclined to praise and pity the martyr; Chalcocondyles is neuter, but we are indebted to him for the hint of the Greek conspiracy.

80. For the restitution of Constantinople and the Turkish foundations, see Cantemir (p. 102–109), Ducas (c. 42 [p. 317, ed. Bonn]), with Thévenot, Tournefort, and the rest of our modern travellers. From a gigantic picture of the greatness, population, etc., of Constantinople and the Ottoman empire (Abrégé de l'Histoire Ottomane, tom. i. p. 16–21), we may learn that, in the year 1586, the Moslems were less numerous in the capital than the Christians, or even the Jews.

81. The *Turbé*, or sepulchral monument of Abou Ayub, is described and engraved in the Tableau Générale de l'Empire Ottoman (Paris, 1787, in large folio), a work of less use, perhaps, than magnificence (tom. i. p. 305, 306).

82. Phranza (l. iii. c. 19) relates the ceremony, which has possibly been adorned in the Greek reports to each other, and to the Latins. The fact is confirmed by Emanuel Malaxus, who wrote, in vulgar Greek, the History of the Patriarchs after the taking of Constantinople, inserted in the Turco-Græcia of Crusius (l. v. p. 106–184). But the most patient reader will not believe that Mohammed adopted the Catholic form, "Sancta Trinitas quæ mihi donavit imperium te in patriarcham novæ Romæ deligit."

83. From the Turco-Græcia of Crusius, etc., Spondanus (A.D. 1453, No. 21; 1458, No. 16) describes the slavery and domestic quarrels of the Greek church. The patriarch who succeeded Gennadius threw himself in despair into a well.

84. Cantemir (p. 101–105) insists on the unanimous consent of the Turkish historians, ancient as well as modern, and argues that they would not have violated the truth to diminish their national glory, since it is esteemed more honourable to take a city by force than by composition. But, 1. I doubt this consent, since he quotes no particular historian; and the Turkish Annals of Leunclavius affirm, without exception, that Mohammed took Constantinople *per vim* (p. 329). 2. The same argument may be turned in favour of the Greeks of the times, who would not have forgotten this honourable and salutary treaty. Voltaire, as usual, prefers the Turks to the Christians.

85. For the genealogy and fall of the Comneni of Trebizond, see Ducange (Fam. Byzant. p. 195); for the last Palæologi, the same accurate antiquarian (p. 244, 247, 248). The Palæologi of Montferrat were not extinct till the next century, but they had forgotten their Greek origin and kindred.

86. In the worthless story of the disputes and misfortunes of the two brothers, Phranza (l. iii. c. 21–30) is too partial on the side of Thomas; Ducas (c. 44, 45) is too brief, and Chalcocondyles (l. viii. ix. x.) too diffuse and digressive.

87. See the loss or conquest of Trebizond in Chalcocondyles (l. ix. p. 263–266 [p. 494–498, ed. Bonn]), Ducas (c. 45 [p. 343, ed. Bonn]), Phranza (l. iii. c. 27), and Cantemir (p. 107).

88. Though Tournefort (tom. iii. lettre xvii. p. 179) speaks of Trebizond as mal peuplée, Peyssonel, the latest and most accurate observer, can find 100,000 inhabitants (Commerce de la Mer Noire, tom. ii. p. 72; and, for the province, p. 53–90). Its prosperity and trade are perpetually disturbed by the factious quarrels of two *odas* of Janizaries, in one of which 30,000 Lazi are commonly enrolled (Mémoires de Tott, tom. iii. p. 16, 17).

89. Ismael Beg, prince of Sinope or Sinople, was possessed (chiefly from his copper-mines) of a revenue of 200,000 ducats (Chalcocond. l. ix. p. 258, 259 [p. 489, ed. Bonn]). Peyssonel (Commerce de la Mer Noire, tom. ii. p. 100) ascribes to the modern city 60,000 inhabitants. This account seems enormous; yet it is by trading with a people that we become acquainted with their wealth and numbers.

90. Spondanus (from Gobelin Comment. Pii II. l. v.) relates the arrival and reception of the despot Thomas at Rome (A.D. 1461, No. 3).

91. By an act dated A.D. 1494, Sept. 6, and lately transmitted from the archives of the Capitol to the royal library of Paris, the despot Andrew Palæologus, reserving the Morea, and stipulating some private advantages, conveys to Charles VIII. king of France the empires of Constantinople and Trebizond (Spondanus, A.D. 1495, No. 2). M. de Foncemagne (Mém. de l'Académie des Inscriptions, tom. xvii. p. 539–578) has bestowed a dissertation on this national title, of which he had obtained a copy from Rome.

92. See Philippe de Comines (l. vii. c. 14), who reckons with pleasure the number of Greeks who were prepared to rise, 60 miles of an easy navigation, eighteen days' journey from Valona to Constantinople, etc. On this occasion the Turkish empire was saved by the policy of Venice.

93. See the original feast in Olivier de la Marche (Mémoires, P. i. c. 29, 30), with the abstract and observations of M. de Ste. Palaye (Mémoires sur la Chevalerie, tom. i. P. iii. p. 182–185). The peacock and the pheasant were distinguished as royal birds.

94. It was found, by an actual enumeration, that Sweden, Gothland, and Finland contained 1,800,000 fighting men, and consequently were far more populous than at present.

95. In the year 1454 Spondanus has given, from Æneas Sylvius, a view of the state of Europe, enriched with his own observations. That valuable annalist, and the Italian Muratori, will continue the series of events from the year 1453 to 1481, the end of Mohammed's life and of this chapter.

96. Besides the two annalists, the reader may consult Giannone (Istoria Civile, tom. iii. p. 449–455) for the Turkish invasion of the kingdom of Naples. For the reign and conquests of Mohammed II. I have occasionally used the Memorie Istoriche de' Monarchi Ottomanni di Giovanni Sagredo (Venezia, 1677, in 4to). In peace and war the Turks have ever engaged the attention of the republic of Venice. All her despatches and archives were open to a procurator of St. Mark, and Sagredo is not contemptible either in sense or style. Yet he too bitterly hates the infidels: he is ignorant of their language and manners; and his narrative, which allows only seventy pages to Mohammed II. (p. 69–140), becomes more copious and authentic as he approaches the years 1640 and 1644, the term of the historic labours of John Sagredo.

97. As I am now taking an everlasting farewell of the Greek empire, I shall briefly mention the great collection of Byzantine writers whose names and testimonies have been successively repeated in this work. The Greek presses of Aldus and the Italians were confined to the classics of a better age; and the first rude editions of Procopius, Agathias, Cedrenus, Zonaras, etc., were published by the learned diligence of the Germans. The whole Byzantine series (thirty-six volumes in folio) has gradually issued (A.D. 1648, etc.) from the royal press of the Louvre, with some collateral aid from Rome and Leipsic; but the Venetian edition (A.D. 1729), though cheaper and more copious, is not less inferior in correctness than in magnificence to that of Paris. The merits of the French editors are various; but the value of Anna Comnena, Cinnamus, Villehardouin, etc., is enhanced by the historical notes of Charles du Fresne du Cange. His supplemental works, the Greek Glossary, the Constantinopolis Christiana, the Familiæ Byzantinæ, diffuse a steady light over the darkness of the Lower Empire.

Chapter LXIX

1. The abbé Dubos, who, with less genius than his successor Montesquieu, has asserted and magnified the influence of climate, objects to himself the degeneracy of the Romans and Batavians. To the first of these examples he replies, 1. That the change is less real than apparent, and that the modern Romans prudently conceal in themselves the virtues of their ancestors. 2. That the air, the soil, and the climate of Rome have suffered a great and visible alteration (Réflexions sur la Poësie et sur la Peinture, part ii. sect. 16).

2. The reader has been so long absent from Rome that I would advise him to recollect or review the xlix. chapter of this History.

3. The coronation of the German emperors at Rome, more especially in the eleventh century, is best represented from the original monuments by Muratori (Antiquitat. Italiæ medii Ævi, tom. i. dissertat. ii. p. 99, etc.) and Cenni (Monument. Domin. Pontif. tom. ii. diss. vi. p. 261), the latter of whom I only know from the copious extract of Schmidt (Hist. des Allemands, tom. iii. p. 255–266).

4. Exercitui Romano et Teutonico! The latter was both seen and felt; but the former was no more than magni nominis umbra.

5. Muratori has given the series of the papal coins (Antiquitat. tom. ii. diss. xxvii. p. 548–554). He finds only two more early than the year 800: fifty are still extant from Leo III. to Leo IX. with the addition of the reigning emperor; none remain of Gregory VII. or Urban II.; but in those of Paschal II. he seems to have renounced this badge of dependence.

6. See Ducange, Gloss. mediæ et infimæ Latinitat. tom. vi. p. 364, 365, Staffa. This homage was paid by kings to archbishops, and by vassals to their lords (Schmidt, tom. iii. p. 262); and it was the nicest policy of Rome to confound the marks of filial and of feudal subjection.

7. The appeals from all the churches to the Roman pontiff are deplored by the zeal of St. Bernard (de Consideratione, l. iii. tom. ii. p. 431–442, edit. Mabillon, Venet. 1750) and the judgment of Fleury (Discours sur l'Hist. Ecclésiastique, iv. et vii.). But the saint, who believed in the false decretals, condemns only the abuse of these appeals; the more enlightened historian investigates the origin and rejects the principles of this new jurisprudence.

8. Germanici . . . summarii non levatis sarcinis onusti nihilominus repatriant inviti. Nova res! quando hactenus aurum Roma refudit? Et nunc Romanorum consilio id usurpatum non credimus (Bernard de Consideratione, l. iii. c. 3, p. 437). The first words of the passage are obscure, and probably corrupt.

9. Quand les sauvages de la Louisiane veulent avoir du fruit, ils coupent l'arbre au pied et cueillent le fruit. Voilà le gouvernement despotique (The Spirit of Laws, l. v. c. 13); and passion and ignorance are always despotic.

10. In a free conversation with his countryman Adrian IV., John of Salisbury accuses the avarice of the pope and clergy: Provinciarum diripiunt spolia, ac si thesauros Crœsi studeant reparare. Sed recte cum eis agit Altissimus, quoniam et ipsi aliis et sæpe vilissimis hominibus dati sunt in direptionem (de Nugis Curialium, l. vi. c. 24, p. 387). In the next page he blames the rashness and infidelity of the Romans, whom their bishops vainly strove to conciliate by gifts instead of virtues. It is pity that this miscellaneous writer has not given us less morality and erudition, and more pictures of himself and the times.

11. Hume's History of England, vol. i. p. 419. The same writer has given us from Fitz-Stephen a singular act of cruelty perpetrated on the clergy by Geoffrey, the father of Henry II. "When he was master of Normandy the chapter of Seez presumed, without his consent, to proceed to the election of a bishop: upon which he ordered all of them, with the bishop elect, to be castrated, and made all their testicles be brought him in a platter." Of the pain and danger they might justly complain; yet, since they had vowed chastity he deprived them of a superfluous treasure.

12. From Leo IX. and Gregory VII, an authentic and contemporary series of the lives of the popes by the Cardinal of Arragon, Pandulphus Pisanus, Bernard Guido, etc., is inserted in the Italian Historians of Muratori (tom. iii. P. i. p. 277–685), and has been always before my eyes.

13. Throughout this chapter the Annals of Muratori have been my ordinary and excellent guide. Muratori uses, and indeed quotes with the freedom of a master, his great Collection of the Italian Historians in twenty-eight volumes; and as that treasure is in my library, I have thought it an amusement, if not a duty, to consult the originals.

14. I cannot refrain from transcribing the high-coloured words of Pandulphus Pisanus (p. 384): Hoc audiens inimicus pacis atque turbator jam fatus Centius Frajapane, more draconis immanissimi sibilans, et ab imis pectoribus trahens longa suspiria, accinctus retro gladio sine more cucurrit, valvas ac fores confregit. Ecclesiam furibundus introiit, inde custode remoto papam per gulam accepit, distraxit, pugnis calcibusque percussit, et tanquam brutum animal intra limen ecclesiæ acriter calcaribus cruentavit; et latro tantum dominum per capillos et brachia, Jesú bono interim dormiente, detraxit, ad domum usque deduxit, inibi catenavit et inclusit.

15. Ego coram Deo et Ecclesiâ dico, si unquam possibile esset, mallem unum imperatorem quam tot dominos (Vit. Gelas. II. p. 398).

16. Quid tam notum seculis quam protervia et cervicositas Romanorum? Gens insueta paci, tumultui assueta, gens immitis et intractabilis usque adhuc, subdi nescia, nisi cum non valet resistere (de Considerat. l. iv. c. 2, p. 441). The saint takes breath, and then begins again: Hi, invisi terræ et cœlo, utrique injecere manus, etc. (p. 443).

17. As a Roman citizen, Petrarch takes leave to observe that Bernard, though a saint, was a man; that he might be provoked by resentment, and possibly repent of his hasty passion, etc. (Mémoires sur la Vie de Pétrarque, tom. i. p. 330.)

18. Baronius, in his index to the twelfth volume of his Annals, has found a fair and easy excuse. He makes two heads, of Romani *Catholici* and *Schismatici*: to the former he applies all the good, to the latter all the evil, that is told of the city.

19. The heresies of the twelfth century may be found in Mosheim (Institut. Hist. Eccles. p. 419–427), who entertains a favourable opinion of Arnold of Brescia. I have already described the sect of the Paulicians, and followed their migration from Armenia to Thrace and Bulgaria, Italy and France.

20. The original pictures of Arnold of Brescia are drawn by Otho bishop of Frisingen (Chron. l. vii. c. 31, de Gestis Frederici I. l. i. c. 27, l. ii. c. 21), and in the third book of the Ligurinus, a poem of Gunther, who flourished A.D. 1200, in the monastery of Paris near Basil (Fabric. Biblioth. Latin. med. et infimæ Ætatis, tom. iii. p. 174, 175). The long passage that relates to Arnold is produced by Guilliman (de Rebus Helveticus, l. iii. c. 5, p. 108).

21. The wicked wit of Bayle was amused in composing, with much levity and learning, the articles of ABELARD, FOULQUES, HELOISE, in his Dictionnaire Critique. The dispute of Abelard and St. Bernard, of scholastic and positive divinity, is well understood by Mosheim (Institut. Hist. Eccles. p. 412–415).

22.   ——Damnatus ab illo
        Præsule, qui numeros vetitum contingere
        nostros
    Nomen ab *innocuâ* ducit laudabile vitâ.
We may applaud the dexterity and correctness of Ligurinus, who turns the unpoetical name of Innocent II. into a compliment.

23. A Roman inscription of Statio Turicensis has been found at Zürich (D'Anville, Notice de l'Ancienne Gaul, p. 642–644); but it is without sufficient warrant that the city and canton have usurped, and even monopolised, the names of Tigurum and Pagus Tigurinus.

24. Guilliman (de Rebus Helveticis l. iii. c. 5, p. 106) recapitulates the donation (A.D. 833) of the emperor Lewis the Pious to his daughter the Abbess Hildegardis. Curtim nostram Turegum in ducatú Alamanniæ in pago Durgaugensi, with villages, woods, meadows, waters, slaves, churches, etc.—a noble gift. Charles the Bald gave the jus monetæ, the city was walled under Otho I., and the line of the bishop of Frisingen,

Nobile Turegum multarum copiâ rerum,
is repeated with pleasure by the antiquaries of Zürich.

25. Bernard, Epistol. cxcv. cxcvi. tom. i. p. 187–190. Amidst his invectives he drops a precious acknowledgement, qui, utinam quam sanæ esset doctrinæ quam districtæ est vitæ. He owns that Arnold would be a valuable acquisition for the church.

26. He advised the Romans,
    Consiliis armisque sua moderamina summa
    Arbitrio tractare suo: nil juris in hâc re
    Pontifici summo, modicum concedere regi
    Suadebat populo. Sic læsâ stultus utrâque
    Majestate, reum geminæ se fecerat aulæ.
Nor is the poetry of Gunther different from the prose of Otho.

27. See Baronius (A.D. 1148, No. 38, 39) from the Vatican MSS. He loudly condemns Arnold (A.D. 1141, No. 3) as the father of the political heretics, whose influence then hurt him in France.

28. The English reader may consult the Biographia Britannica, ADRIAN IV.; but our own writers have added nothing to the fame or merits of their countryman.

29. Besides the historian and poet already quoted, the last adventures of Arnold are related by the biographer of Adrian IV. (Muratori, Script. Rerum Ital. tom. iii. P. i. p. 441, 442.)

30. Ducange (Gloss. Latinitatis mediæ et infimæ Ætatis, DECARCHONES, tom. ii. p. 726) gives me a quotation from Blondus (Decad. ii. l. ii.): Duo consules ex nobilitate quotannis fiebant, qui ad vetustum consulum exemplar summæ rerum præessent. And in Sigonius (de Regno Italiæ, l. vi. Opp. tom. ii. p. 400) I read of the consuls and tribunes of the tenth century. Both Blondus and even Sigonius too freely copied the classic method of supplying from reason or fancy the deficiency of records.

31. In the panegyric of Berengarius (Muratori, Script. Rer. Ital. tom. ii. P. i. p. 408) a Roman is mentioned as consulis natus in the beginning of the tenth century. Muratori (Dissert. v.) discovers, in the years 952 and 956, Gratianus in Dei nomine consul et dux, Georgius consul et dux; and in 1015, Romanus, brother of Gregory VIII., proudly, but vaguely, styles himself consul et dux et omnium Romanorum senator.

32. As late as the tenth century the Greek emperors conferred on the dukes of Venice, Naples, Amalphi, etc., the title of ὕπατος or consuls (see Chron. Sagornini, *passim*); and the successors of Charlemagne would not abdicate any of their prerogative. But in general the names of *consul* and *senator*, which may be found among the French and Germans, signify no more than count and lord (*Signeur*, Ducange, Glossar.). The monkish writers are often ambitious of fine classic words.

33. The most constitutional form is a diploma of Otho III. (A.D. 998), Consulibus senatús populique Romani; but the act is probably spurious. At

the coronation of Henry I., A.D. 1014, the historian Dithmar (apud Muratori, Dissert. xxiii.) describes him, a senatoribus duodecim vallatum, quorum sex rasi barbâ, alii prolixâ, mystice incedebant cum baculis. The senate is mentioned in the panegyric of Berengarius (p. 406).

34. In the ancient Rome the equestrian order was not ranked with the senate and people as a third branch of the republic till the consulship of Cicero, who assumes the merit of the establishment (Plin. Hist. Natur. xxxiii. 3 [8]; Beaufort, République Romaine, tom. i. p. 144–155).

35. The republican plan of Arnold of Brescia is thus stated by Gunther:—

Quin etiam titulos urbis renovare vetustos;
Nomine plebeio secernere nomen equestre,
Jura tribunorum, sanctum reparare senatum,
Et senio fessas mutasque reponere leges.
Lapsa ruinosis, et adhuc pendentia muris
Reddere primævo Capitolia prisca nitori.

But of these reformations some were no more than ideas, others no more than words.

36. After many disputes among the antiquaries of Rome, it seems determined that the summit of the Capitoline hill next the river is strictly the Mons Tarpeius, the Arx; and that on the other summit, the church and convent of Araceli, the barefoot friars of St. Francis occupy the temple of Jupiter (Nardini, Roma Antica, l. v. c. 11–16).

37. Tacit. Hist. iii. 69, 70.

38. This partition of the noble and baser metals between the emperor and senate must however be adopted, not as a positive fact, but as the probable opinion of the best antiquaries (see the Science des Médailles of the Père Joubert, tom. ii. p. 208–211, in the improved and scarce edition of the Baron de la Bastie).

39. In his twenty-seventh dissertation on the Antiquities of Italy (tom. ii. p. 559–569), Muratori exhibits a series of the senatorian coins, which bore the obscure names of Affortiati, Infortiati, Provisini, Paparini. During this period, all the popes, without excepting Boniface VIII., abstained from the right of coining, which was resumed by his successor Benedict XI. and regularly exercised in the court of Avignon.

40. A German historian, Gerard of Reicherspeg (in Baluz. Miscell. tom. v. p. 64, apud Schmidt, Hist. des Allemands, tom. iii. p. 265), thus describes the constitution of Rome in the eleventh century: Grandiora urbis et orbis negotia spectant ad Romanum pontificem itemque ad Romanum Imperatorem, sive illius vicarium urbis præfectum, qui de suâ dignitate respicit utrumque, videlicet dominum papam cui facit hominium, et dominum imperatorem a quo accipit suæ potestatis insigne, scilicet gladium exertum.

41. The words of a contemporary writer (Pandulph. Pisan. in Vit. Paschal. II. p. 357, 358) describe the election and oath of the præfect in 1118, inconsultis patribus . . . loca præfectoria . . . Laudes præfectoriæ . . . comitiorum applausum

. . . juraturum populo in ambonem sublevant . . . confirmari eum in urbe præfectum petunt.

42. Urbis præfectum ad ligiam fidelitatem recepit, et per mantum quod illi donavit de præfecturâ eum publice investivit, qui usque ad id tempus juramento fidelitatis imperatori fuit obligatus et ab eo præfecturæ tenuit honorem (Gesta Innocent. III. in Muratori, tom. iii. P. i. p. 487).

43. See Otho Frising. Chron. vii. 31, de Gest. Frederic. I., l. i. c. 27.

44. Our countryman, Roger Hoveden, speaks of the single senators, of the Capuzzi family, etc., quorum temporibus melius regebatur Roma quam nunc (A.D. 1194) est temporibus lvi. senatorum (Ducange, Gloss. tom. vi. p. 191, SENATORES).

45. Muratori (dissert. xlii. tom. iii. p. 785–788) has published an original treaty: Concordia inter D. nostrum papam Clementem III. et senatores populi Romani super regalibus et aliis dignitatibus urbis, etc., anno 44° senatús. The senate speaks, and speaks with authority: Reddimus ad præsens . . . habebimus . . . dabitis presbyteria . . . jurabimus pacem et fidelitatem, etc. A chartula de Tenimentis Tusculani, dated in the forty-seventh year of the same era, and confirmed decreto amplissimi ordinis senatús, acclamatione P. R. publice Capitolio consistentis. It is there we find the difference of senatores consiliarii and simple senators (Muratori dissert. xlii. tom. iii. p. 787–789).

46. Muratori (dissert. xlv. tom. iv. p. 64–92) has fully explained this mode of government; and the Occulus Pastoralis, which he has given at the end, is a treatise or sermon on the duties of these foreign magistrates.

47. In the Latin writers, at least of the silver age, the title of Potestas was transferred from the office to the magistrate:—

Hujus qui trahitur prætextam sumere mavis;
An Fidenarum Gabiorumque esse Potestas.
(Juvenal. Satir. x. 99.)

48. See the life and death of Brancaleone, in the Historia Major of Matthew Paris, p. 741, 757, 792, 797, 799, 810, 823, 833, 836, 840. The multitude of pilgrims and suitors connected Rome and St. Alban's, and the resentment of the English clergy prompted them to rejoice whenever the popes were humbled and oppressed.

49. Matthew Paris thus ends his account: Caput vero ipsius Brancaleonis in vase pretioso super marmoream columnam collocatum, in signum sui valoris et probitatis, quasi reliquias, superstitiose nimis et pompose sustulerunt. Fuerat enim superborum potentum et malefactorum urbis malleus et exstirpator, et populi protector et defensor, veritatis et justitiæ imitator et amator (p. 840). A biographer of Innocent IV. (Muratori, Script. tom. iii. P. i. p. 591, 592) draws a less favourable portrait of this Ghibeline senator.

50. The election of Charles of Anjou to the office of perpetual senator of Rome is mentioned by the historians in the eighth volume of the Collection of Muratori, by Nicholas de Jamsilla (p. 592), the

monk of Padua (p. 724), Sabas Malaspina (l. ii. c. 9, p. 808), and Ricordano Malespini (c. 177, p. 999).

51. The high-sounding bull of Nicholas III., which founds his temporal sovereignty on the donation of Constantine, is still extant; and as it has been inserted by Boniface VIII. in the *Sexte* of the Decretals, it must be received by the Catholics, or at least by the Papists, as a sacred and perpetual law.

52. I am indebted to Fleury (Hist. Ecclés. tom. xviii. p. 306) for an extract of this Roman act, which he has taken from the Ecclesiastical Annals of Odericus Raynaldus, A.D. 1281, No. 14, 15.

53. These letters and speeches are preserved by Otho bishop of Frisingen (Fabric. Biblioth. Lat. med. et infim. tom. v. p. 186, 187), perhaps the noblest of historians: he was son of Leopold marquis of Austria; his mother, Agnes, was daughter of the emperor Henry IV.; and he was half-brother and uncle to Conrad III. and Frederic I. He has left, in seven books, a Chronicle of the Times; in two, the Gesta Frederici I., the last of which is inserted in the sixth volume of Muratori's Historians.

54. We desire (said the ignorant Romans) to restore the empire in eum statum, quo fuit tempore Constantini et Justiniani, qui totum orbem vigore senatûs et populi Romani suis tenuere manibus.

55. Otho Frising. de Gestis Frederici I., l. i. c. 28, p. 662-664.

56. Hospes eras, civem feci. Advena fuisti ex Transalpinis partibus; principem constitui.

57. Non cessit nobis nudum imperium, virtute sua amictum venit, ornamenta sua secum traxit. Penes nos sunt consules tui, etc. Cicero or Livy would not have rejected these images, the eloquence of a barbarian born and educated in the Hercynian forest.

58. Otho of Frisingen, who surely understood the language of the court and diet of Germany, speaks of the Franks in the twelfth century as the reigning nation (Proceres Franci, equites Franci, manus Francorum): he adds, however, the epithet of *Teutonici*.

59. Otho Frising. de Gestis Frederici I., l. ii. c. 22, p. 720-723. These original and authentic acts I have translated and abridged with freedom, yet with fidelity.

60. From the chronicles of Ricobaldo and Francis Pipin, Muratori (dissert. xxvi. tom. ii. p. 492) has transcribed this curious fact with the doggerel verses that accompanied the gift:—

Ave decus orbis, ave! victus tibi destinor, ave!
Currus ab Augusto Frederico Cæsare justo.
Væ Mediolanum! jam sentis spernere vanum
Imperii vires, proprias tibi tollere vires.
Ergo triumphorum urbs potes memor esse
    priorum
Quos tibi mittebant reges qui bella gerebant.

Ne si dee tacere (I now use the Italian Dissertations, tom. i. p. 444) che nell' anno 1727, una

copia desso Caroccio in marmo dianzi ignoto si scopri, nel Campidoglio, presso alle carcere di quel luogo, dove Sisto V. l' avea falto rinchiudere. Stava esso posto sopra quatro colonne di marmo fino colla sequente inscrizione, etc.; to the same purpose as the old inscription.

61. The decline of the Imperial arms and authority in Italy is related with impartial learning in the Annals of Muratori (tom. x. xi. xii.): and the reader may compare his narrative with the Histoire des Allemands (tom. iii. iv.) by Schmidt, who has deserved the esteem of his countrymen.

62. Tibur nunc suburbanum, et æstivæ Præneste deliciæ, nuncupatis in Capitolio votis petebantur. The whole passage of Florus (l. i. c. 11) may be read with pleasure, and has deserved the praise of a man of genius (Œuvres de Montesquieu, tom. iii. p. 634, 635, quarto edition).

63. Ne a feritate Romanorum, sicut fuerant Hostienses, Portuenses, Tuscalanenses, Albanenses, Labicenses, et nuper Tiburtini destruerentur (Matthew Paris, p. 757). These events are marked in the Annals and Index (the eighteenth volume) of Muratori.

64. For the state or ruin of these suburban cities, the banks of the Tiber, etc., see the lively picture of the P. Labat (Voyage en Espagne et en Italie), who had long resided in the neighbourhood of Rome; and the more accurate description of which P. Eschinard (Roma, 1750, in octavo) has added to the topographical map of Cingolani.

65. Labat (tom. iii. p. 233) mentions a recent decree of the Roman government, which has severely mortified the pride and poverty of Tivoli: in civitate Tiburtinâ non vivitur civiliter.

66. I depart from my usual method of quoting only by the date the Annals of Muratori, in consideration of the critical balance in which he has weighed nine contemporary writers who mention the battle of Tusculum (tom. x. p. 42-44).

67. Matthew Paris, p. 345. This bishop of Winchester was Peter de Rupibus, who occupied the see thirty-two years (A.D. 1206-1238), and is described, by the English historian, as a soldier and a statesman (p. 178, 399).

68. See Mosheim, Institut. Histor. Ecclesiast. p. 401, 403. Alexander himself had nearly been the victim of a contested election; and the doubtful merits of Innocent had only preponderated by the weight of genius and learning which St. Bernard cast into the scale (see his life and writings).

69. The origin, titles, importance, dress, precedency, etc., of the Roman cardinals, are very ably discussed by Thomassin (Discipline de l'Eglise, tom. i. p. 1262-1287); but their purple is now much faded. The sacred college was raised to the definite number of seventy-two, to represent, under his vicar, the disciples of Christ.

70. See the bull of Gregory X., approbante sacro concilio, in the *Sexte* of the Canon Law (l. i. tit. 6, c. 3), a supplement to the Decretals, which Boniface VIII. promulgated at Rome in 1298,

and addressed to all the universities of Europe.

71. The genius of Cardinal de Retz had a right to paint a conclave (of 1655) in which he was a spectator and an actor (Mémoires, tom. iv. p. 15-57); but I am at a loss to appreciate the knowledge or authority of an anonymous Italian, whose history (Conclavi de' Pontifici Romani, in 4to, 1667) has been continued since the reign of Alexander VII. The accidental form of the work furnishes a lesson, though not an antidote, to ambition. From a labyrinth of intrigues we emerge to the adoration of the successful candidate; but the next page opens with his funeral.

72. The expressions of Cardinal de Retz are positive and picturesque: On y vécut toujours ensemble avec le même respect et la même civilité que l'on observe dans le cabinet des rois, avec la même politesse qu'on avoit dans la cour de Henri III., avec la même familiarité que l'on voit dans les collèges; avec la même modestie qui se remarque dans les noviciats; et avec la même charité, du moins en apparence, qui pourroit être entre des frères parfaitement unis.

73. Richiesti per bando (says John Villani) sanatori di Roma, e 52 del popolo, et capitani de' 25, e consoli (consoli?), et 13 buone huomini, uno per rione. Our knowledge is too imperfect to pronounce how much of this constitution was temporary, and how much ordinary and permanent. Yet it is faintly illustrated by the ancient statutes of Rome.

74. Villani (l. x. c. 68-71, in Muratori, Script. tom. xiii. p. 641-645) relates this law, and the whole transaction, with much less abhorrence than the prudent Muratori. Any one conversant with the darker ages must have observed how much the sense (I mean the nonsense) of superstition is fluctuating and inconsistent.

75. In the first volume of the Popes of Avignon, see the second original Life of John XXII. p. 142-145; the confession of the antipope, p. 145-152; and the laborious notes of Baluze, p. 714, 715.

76. Romani autem non valentes nec volentes ultra suam celare cupiditatem gravissimam, contra papam movere cœperunt questionem, exigentes ab eo urgentissime omnia quæ subierant per ejus absentiam damna et jacturas, videlicet in hospitiis locandis, in mercimoniis, in usuris, in redditibus, in provisionibus, et in aliis modis innumerabilibus. Quòd cum audisset papa, præcordialiter ingemuit, et se comperiens muscipulatum, etc. Matt. Paris, p. 757. For the ordinary history of the popes, their life and death, their residence and absence, it is enough to refer to the ecclesiastical annalists, Spondanus and Fleury.

77. Besides the general historians of the church of Italy and of France, we possess a valuable treatise composed by a learned friend of Thuanus, which his last and best editors have published in the appendix (Histoire particulière du grand Différend entre Boniface VIII. et Philippe le Bel, par Pierre du Puis, tom. vii. P. xi. p. 61-82).

78. It is difficult to know whether Labat (tom. iv. p. 53-57) be in jest or in earnest, when he supposes that Anagni still feels the weight of this curse, and that the corn-fields, or vineyards, or olive-trees, are annually blasted by Nature, the obsequious handmaid of the popes.

79. See in the Chronicle of Giovanni Villani (l. viii. c. 63, 64, 80, in Muratori, tom. xiii.) the imprisonment of Boniface VIII. and the election of Clement V., the last of which, like most anecdotes, is embarrassed with some difficulties.

80. The original lives of the eight popes of Avignon—Clement V., John XXII., Benedict XII., Clement VI., Innocent VI., Urban V., Gregory XI., and Clement VII.—are published by Stephen Baluze (Vitæ Paparum Avenionensium; Paris, 1693, 2 vols. in 4to) with copious and elaborate notes, and a second volume of acts and documents. With the true zeal of an editor and a patriot, he devoutly justifies or excuses the characters of his countrymen.

81. The exile of Avignon is compared by the Italians with Babylon, and the Babylonish captivity. Such furious metaphors, more suitable to the ardour of Petrarch than to the judgment of Muratori, are gravely refuted in Baluze's preface. The abbé de Sade is distracted between the love of Petrarch and of his country. Yet he modestly pleads that many of the local inconveniences of Avignon are now removed; and many of the vices against which the poet declaims had been imported with the Roman court by the strangers of Italy (tom. i. p. 23-28).

82. The comtat Venaissin was ceded to the popes in 1273 by Philip III., king of France, after he had inherited the dominions of the count of Toulouse. Forty years before, the heresy of Count Raymond had given them a pretence of seizure, and they derived some obscure claim from the eleventh century to some lands citra Rhodanum (Valesii Notitia Galliarum, p. 459, 610; Longuerue, Description de la France, tom. i. p. 376-381).

83. If a possession of four centuries were not itself a title, such objection might annul the bargain; but the purchase-money must be refunded, for indeed it was paid. Civitatem Avenionem emit ... per ejusmodi venditionem pecuniâ redundates, etc. (iida. Vita Clement. VI. in Baluz. tom. i. p. 272; Muratori, Script. tom. iii. P. ii. p. 565). The only temptation for Jane and her second husband was ready money, and without it they could not have returned to the throne of Naples.

84. Clement V. immediately promoted ten cardinals, nine French and one English (Vita, ivta, p. 63, et Baluz. p. 625, etc.). In 1331 the pope refused two candidates recommended by the king of France, quod xx. cardinales, de quibus xvii. de regno Franciæ originem traxisse noscuntur in memorato collegio existant (Thomassin, Discipline de l'Eglise, tom. i. p. 1281).

85. Our primitive account is from Cardinal James Caietan (Maxima Biblioth. Patrum, tom.

xxv.); and I am at a loss to determine whether the nephew of Boniface VIII. be a fool or a knave: the uncle is a much clearer character.

86. See John Villani (l. viii. c. 36) in the twelfth, and the Chronicon Astense in the eleventh volume (p. 191, 192) of Muratori's Collection. Papa innumerabilem pecuniam ab eisdem accepit, nam duo clerici, cum rastris, etc.

87. The two bulls of Boniface VIII. and Clement VI. are inserted in the Corpus Juris Canonici (Extravagant. Commun. l. v. tit. ix. c. 1, 2).

88. The sabbatic years and jubilees of the Mosaic law (Car. Sigon. de Republicâ Hebræorum, Opp. tom. iv. l. iii. c. 14, 15, p. 151, 152), the suspension of all care and labour, the periodical release of lands, debts, servitude, etc., may seem a noble idea, but the execution would be impracticable in a *profane* republic; and I should be glad to learn that this ruinous festival was observed by the Jewish people.

89. See the Chronicle of Matteo Villani (l. i. c. 56) in the fourteenth volume of Muratori, and the Mémoires sur la Vie de Pétrarque, tom. iii. p. 75–89.

90. The subject is exhausted by M. Chais, a French minister at the Hague, in his Lettres Historiques et Dogmatiques sur les Jubilés et les Indulgences; la Haye, 1751, 3 vols. in 12mo; an elaborate and pleasing work, had not the author preferred the character of a polemic to that of a philosopher.

91. Muratori (Dissert. xlvii.) alleges the Annals of Florence, Padua, Genoa, etc., the analogy of the rest, the evidence of Otho of Frisingen (de Gest. Fred. I. l. ii. c. 13), and the submission of the marquis of Este.

92. As early as the year 824 the emperor Lothaire I. found it expedient to interrogate the Roman people, to learn from each individual by what national law he chose to be governed (Muratori, Dissert. xxii.).

93. Petrarch attacks these foreigners, the tyrants of Rome, in a declamation or epistle, full of bold truths and absurd pedantry, in which he applies the maxims and even prejudices of the old republic to the state of the fourteenth century (Mémoires, tom. iii. p. 157–169).

94. The origin and adventures of this Jewish family are noticed by Pagi (Critica, tom. iv. p. 435, A.D. 1124, No. 3, 4), who draws his information from the Chronographus Maurigniacensis, and Arnulphus Sagiensis de Schismate (in Muratori, Script. Ital. tom. iii. P. i. p. 423–432). The fact must in some degree be true; yet I could wish that it had been coolly related before it was turned into a reproach against the antipope.

95. Muratori has given two dissertations (xli. and xlii.) to the names, surnames, and families of Italy. Some nobles, who glory in their domestic fables, may be offended with his firm and temperate criticism; yet surely some ounces of pure gold are of more value than many pounds of base metal.

96. The cardinal of St. George, in his poetical, or rather metrical, history of the election and coronation of Boniface VIII. (Muratori, Script. Ital. tom. iii. P. i. p. 641, etc.), describes the state and families of Rome at the coronation of Boniface VIII. (A.D. 1295):—

Interea titulis redimiti sanguine et armis
Illustresque viri Romanâ a stirpe trahentes
Nomen in emeritos tantæ virtutis honores
Intulerant sese medios festumque colebant
Auratâ fulgentes togâ sociante catervâ.
Ex ipsis devota domus præstantis ab *Ursâ*
Ecclesiæ, vultumque gerens demissius altum
Festa *Columna* jocis, necnon *Sabellia* mitis;
Stephanides senior, *Comites, Annibalica* proles,
Præfectusque urbis magnum sine viribus nomen.

(l. ii. c. 5, 100, p. 647, 648.)

The ancient statutes of Rome (l. iii. c. 59, p. 174, 175) distinguish eleven families of barons, who are obliged to swear in concilio communi, before the senator, that they would not harbour or protect any malefactors, outlaws, etc.—a feeble security!

97. It is a pity that the Colonna themselves have not favoured the world with a complete and critical history of their illustrious house. I adhere to Muratori (Dissert. xlii. tom. iii. p. 647, 648).

98. Pandulph. Pisan. in Vit. Paschal. II. in Muratori, Script. Ital. tom. iii. P. i. p. 335. The family has still great possessions in the Campagna of Rome; but they have alienated to the Rospigliosi this original fief of *Colonna* (Eschinard, p. 258, 259).

99. Te longinqua dedit tellus et pascua Rheni, says Petrarch; and in 1417 a duke of Guelders and Juliers acknowledges (Lenfant, Hist. du Concile de Constance, tom. ii. p. 539) his descent from the ancestors of Martin V. (Otho Colonna): but the royal author of the Memoirs of Brandenburg observes that the sceptre in his arms has been confounded with the column. To maintain the Roman origin of the Colonna it was ingeniously supposed (Diario di Monaldeschi, in the Script. Ital. tom. xii. p. 533) that a cousin of the emperor Nero escaped from the city and founded Mentz in Germany.

100. I cannot overlook the Roman triumph or ovation of Marco Antonio Colonna, who had commanded the pope's galleys at the naval victory of Lepanto (Thuan. Hist. l. 7, tom. iii. p. 55, 56; Muret. Oratio x. Opp. i. p. 180–190).

101. Muratori, Annali d'Italia, tom. x. p. 216, 220.

102. Petrarch's attachment to the Colonna has authorised the abbé de Sade to expatiate on the state of the family in the fourteenth century, the persecution of Boniface VIII., the character of Stephen and his sons, their quarrels with the Ursini, etc. (Mémoires sur Pétrarque, tom. i. p. 98–110, 146–148, 174–176, 222–230, 275–280.) His criticism often rectifies the hearsay stories of Villani, and the errors of the less diligent moderns. I

understand the branch of Stephen to be now extinct.

103. Alexander III. had declared the Colonna who adhered to the emperor Frederic I. incapable of holding any ecclesiastical benefice (Villani, l. v. c. 1); and the last stains of annual excommunication were purified by Sixtus V. (Vita di Sisto V. tom. iii. p. 416). Treason, sacrilege, and proscription are often the best titles of ancient nobility.

104. ————Vallis te proxima misit,
    Appenninigenæ quâ prata virentia sylvæ
    Spoletana metunt armenta gregesque
    protervi.

Monaldeschi (tom. xii. Script. Ital. p. 533) gives the Ursini a French origin which may be remotely true.

105. In the metrical life of Celestin V. by the Cardinal of St. George (Muratori, tom. iii. P. i. p. 613, etc.) we find a luminous and not inelegant passage (l. i. c. 3, p. 203, etc.):—

————genuit quem nobilis Ursæ (*Ursi?*)
Progenies, Romana domus, veterataque mag-
   nis
Fascibus in clero, pompasque experta senatûs,
Bellorumque manu grandi stipata parentum

Cardineos apices necnon fastigia dudum
Papatûs *iterata* tenens.

Muratori (Dissert. xlii. tom. iii.) observes that the first Ursini pontificate of Celestin III. was unknown: he is inclined to read *Ursi* progenies.

106. Filii Ursi, quondam Cœlestini papæ nepotes, de bonis ecclesiæ Romanæ ditati (Vit. Innocent. III. in Muratori, Script. tom. iii. P. I.). The partial prodigality of Nicholas III. is more conspicuous in Villani and Muratori. Yet the Ursini would disdain the nephews of a *modern* pope.

107. In his fifty-first Dissertation on the Italian Antiquities Muratori explains the factions of the Guelphs and Ghibelines.

108. Petrarch (tom. i. p. 222–230) has celebrated this victory according to the Colonna; but two contemporaries, a Florentine (Giovanni Villani l. x. c. 220) and a Roman (Ludovico Monaldeschi, p. 533, 534), are less favourable to their arms.

109. The Abbé de Sade (tom. i. Notes, p. 61–66) has applied the sixth Canzone of Petrarch, *Spirto Gentil*, etc., to Stephen Colonna the younger:—

Orsi, lupi, leoni, aquile e serpi
Ad una gran marmorea *colonna*
Fanno noja sovente e à se danno.

Chapter LXX

1. The Mémoires sur la Vie de François Pétrarque (Amsterdam, 1764, 1767, 3 vols. in 4to) form a copious, original, and entertaining work, a labour of love, composed from the accurate study of Petrarch and his contemporaries; but the hero is too often lost in the general history of the age, and the author too often languishes in the affectation of politeness and gallantry. In the preface to his first volume he enumerates and weighs twenty Italian biographers, who have professedly treated of the same subject.

2. The allegorical interpretation prevailed in the fifteenth century; but the wise commentators were not agreed whether they should understand, by Laura, religion, or virtue, or the blessed Virgin, or ————. See the prefaces to the first and second volume.

3. Laure de Noves, born about the year 1307, was married in January, 1325, to Hugues de Sade, a noble citizen of Avignon, whose jealousy was not the effect of love, since he married a second wife within seven months of her death, which happened the 6th of April, 1348, precisely one-and-twenty years after Petrarch had seen and loved her.

4. Corpus crebris partubus exhaustum: from one of these is issued, in the tenth degree, the abbé de Sade, the fond and grateful biographer of Petrarch; and this domestic motive most probably suggested the idea of his work, and urged him to inquire into every circumstance that could affect the history and character of his grandmother (see

particularly tom. i. p. 122–133, notes, p. 7–58; tom. ii. p. 455–495, not. p. 76–82).

5. Vaucluse, so familiar to our English travellers, is described from the writings of Petrarch, and the local knowledge of his biographer (Mémoires, tom. i. p. 340–359). It was, in truth, the retreat of a hermit; and the moderns are much mistaken if they place Laura and a happy lover in the grotto.

6. Of 1250 pages, in a close print, at Basil in the sixteenth century, but without the date of the year. The abbé de Sade calls aloud for a new edition of Petrarch's Latin works; but I much doubt whether it would redound to the profit of the bookseller or the amusement of the public.

7. Consult Selden's Titles of Honour, in his works (vol. iii. p. 457–466). A hundred years before Petrarch, St. Francis received the visit of a poet qui ab imperatore fuerat coronatus et exinde rex versuum dictus.

8. From Augustus to Louis the muse has too often been false and venal; but I much doubt whether any age or court can produce a similar establishment of a stipendiary poet, who, in every reign and at all events, is bound to furnish twice a-year a measure of praise and verse, such as may be sung in the chapel, and, I believe, in the presence, of the sovereign. I speak the more freely, as the best time for abolishing this ridiculous custom is while the prince is a man of virtue, and the poet a man of genius.

9. Isocrates (in Panegyrico, tom. i. p. 116, 117,

edit. Battie, Cantab. 1729) claims for his native Athens the glory of first instituting and recommending the ἀλῶνας—καὶ τὰ ἄθλα μέγιστα—μὴ μόνον τάχους καὶ ῥώμης, ἀλλὰ καὶ λόγων καὶ γνώμης. The example of the Panathenæa was imitated at Delphi; but the Olympic games were ignorant of a musical crown, till it was extorted by the vain tyranny of Nero (Sueton. in Nerone, c. 23; Philostrat. apud Casaubon ad locum; Dion Cassius, or Xiphilin, l. lxiii. [c. 9, 20] p. 1032, 1041; Potter's Greek Antiquities. vol. i. p. 445, 450).

10. The Capitoline games (certamen quinquennale, *musicum*, equestre, gymnicum) were instituted by Domitian (Sueton. c. 4) in the year of Christ 86 (Censorin. de Die Natali, c. 18, p. 100, edit. Havercamp.), and were not abolished in the fourth century (Ausonius de Professoribus Burdegal. V.). If the crown were given to superior merit, the exclusion of Statius (Capitolia nostræ inficiata lyræ, Silv. l. iii. v. 31) may do honour to the games of the Capitol; but the Latin poets who lived before Domitian were crowned only in the public opinion.

11. Petrarch and the senators of Rome were ignorant that the laurel was not the Capitoline, but the Delphic, crown (Plin. Hist. Natur. xv. 39; Hist. Critique de la République des Lettres, tom. i. p. 150-220). The victors in the Capitol were crowned with a garland of oak-leaves (Martial, l. iv. epigram 54).

12. The pious grandson of Laura has laboured, and not without success, to vindicate her immaculate chastity against the censures of the grave and the sneers of the profane (tom. ii. notes, p. 76-82).

13. The whole process of Petrarch's coronation is accurately described by the abbé de Sade (tom. i. p. 425-435; tom. ii. p. 1-6, notes, p. 1-13) from his own writings, and the Roman diary of Ludovico Monaldeschi, without mixing in this authentic narrative the more recent fables of Sannuccio Delbene.

14. The original act is printed among the Pièces Justificatives in the Mémoires sur Pétrarque, tom. iii. p. 50-53.

15. To find the proofs of his enthusiasm for Rome, I need only request that the reader would open, by chance, either Petrarch or his French biographer. The latter has described the poet's first visit to Rome (tom. i. p. 323-335). But, in the place of much idle rhetoric and morality, Petrarch might have amused the present and future age with an original account of the city and his coronation.

16. It has been treated by the pen of a Jesuit, the P. du Cerçeau, whose posthumous work (Conjuration de Nicolas Gabrini, dit de Rienzi, Tyran de Rome, en 1347) was published at Paris, 1748, in 12mo. I am indebted to him for some facts and documents in John Hocsemius, canon of Liege, a contemporary historian (Fabricius, Biblioth. Lat. med. Ævi, tom. iii. p. 273; tom. iv. p. 85).

17. The abbé de Sade, who so freely expatiates on the history of the fourteenth century, might treat, as his proper subject, a revolution in which the heart of Petrarch was so deeply engaged (Mémoires, tom. ii. p. 50, 51, 320-417, notes, p. 70-76; tom. iii. p. 221-243, 366-375). Not an idea or a fact in the writings of Petrarch has probably escaped him.

18. Giovanni Villani, l. xii. c. 89, 104, in Muratori, Rerum Italicarum Scriptores, tom. xiii. p. 969, 970, 981-983.

19. In his third volume of Italian Antiquities (p. 249-548) Muratori has inserted the Fragmenta Historiæ Romanæ ab Anno 1327 usque ad Annum 1354, in the original dialect of Rome or Naples in the fourteenth century, and a Latin version for the benefit of strangers. It contains the most particular and authentic life of Colà (Nicholas) di Rienzi, which had been printed at Bracciano, 1627, in 4to, under the name of Tomaso Fortifiocca, who is only mentioned in this work as having been punished by the tribune for forgery. Human nature is scarcely capable of such sublime or stupid impartiality; but whosoever is the author of these Fragments, he wrote on the spot and at the time, and paints, without design or art, the manners of Rome and the character of the tribune.

20. The first and splendid period of Rienzi, his tribunitian government, is contained in the eighteenth chapter of the Fragments (p. 399-479), which, in the new division, forms the second book of the history in thirty-eight smaller chapters or sections.

21. The reader may be pleased with a specimen of the original idiom: Fò da soa juventutine nutricato di latte de eloquentia, bono gramatico, megliore rettuorico, autorista bravo. Deh como et quanto era veloce leitore! moito usava Tito Livio, Seneca, et Tullio, et Balerio Massimo, moito li dilettava le magnificientie di Julio Cesare raccontare. Tutta la die se speculava negl' intagli di marmo lequali iaccio intorno Roma. Non era altri che esso, che sapesse lejere li antichi pataffii. Tutte scritture antiche vulgarizzava; quesse fiure di marmo justamente interpretava. Oh come spesso diceva, "Dove suono quelli buoni Romani? dove ene loro somma justitia? poleramme trovare in tempo che quessi fiuriano!"

22. Petrarch compares the jealousy of the Romans with the easy temper of the husbands of Avignon (Mémoires, tom. i. p. 330).

23. The fragments of the Lex regia may be found in the Inscriptions of Gruter, tom. i. p. 242, and at the end of the Tacitus of Ernesti, with some learned notes of the editor, tom. ii.

24. I cannot overlook a stupendous and laughable blunder of Rienzi. The Lex regia empowers Vespasian to enlarge the Pomœrium, a word familiar to every antiquary. It was not so to the tribune; he confounds it with pomarium, an orchard, translates lo Jardino de Roma cioene Italia, and is copied by the less excusable ignorance of the Latin translator (p. 406) and the French his-

torian (p. 33). Even the learning of Muratori has slumbered over the passage.

25. Priori (*Bruto*) tamen similior, juvenis uterque, longe ingenio quam cujus simulationem induerat, ut sub hoc obtentû liberator ille P. R. aperiretur tempore suo. . . . Ille regibus, hic tyrannis contemptus (Opp. p. 536).

26. In one MS. I read (l. ii. c. 4, p. 409) perfumante quatro *solli;* in another, quatro *fiorini*—an important variety, since the florin was worth ten Roman *solidi* (Muratori, dissert. xxviii.). The former reading would give us a population of 25,000, the latter of 250,000, families; and I much fear that the former is more consistent with the decay of Rome and her territory.

27. Hocsemius, p. 398, apud du Cerçeau, Hist. de Rienzi, p. 194. The fifteen tribunitian laws may be found in the Roman historian (whom for brevity I shall name) Fortifiocca, l. ii. c. 4.

28. Fortifiocca, l. ii. c. 11. From the account of this shipwreck we learn some circumstances of the trade and navigation of the age. 1. The ship was built and freighted at Naples for the ports of Marseilles and Avignon. 2. The sailors were of Naples and the isle of Œnaria, less skilful than those of Sicily and Genoa. 3. The navigation from Marseilles was a coasting voyage to the mouth of the Tiber, where they took shelter in a storm; but, instead of finding the current, unfortunately ran on a shoal: the vessel was stranded, the mariners escaped. 4. The cargo, which was pillaged, consisted of the revenue of Provence for the royal treasury, many bags of pepper and cinnamon, and bales of French cloth, to the value of 20,000 florins: a rich prize.

29. It was thus that Oliver Cromwell's old acquaintance, who remembered his vulgar and ungracious entrance into the House of Commons, were astonished at the ease and majesty of the Protector on his throne (see Harris's Life of Cromwell, p. 27–34, from Clarendon, Warwick, Whitelocke, Waller, etc.). The consciousness of merit and power will sometimes elevate the manners to the station.

30. See the causes, circumstances, and effects of the death of Andrew, in Giannone (tom. iii. l. xxiii. p. 220-229), and the Life of Petrarch (Mémoires, tom. ii. p. 143–148, 245–250, 375–379, notes, p. 21–37). The abbé de Sade *wishes* to extenuate her guilt.

31. The advocate who pleaded against Jane could add nothing to the logical force and brevity of his master's epistle. Johanna! inordinata vita præcedens, retentio potestatis in regno, neglecta vindicta, vir alter susceptus, et excusatio subsequens, necis viri tui te probant fuisse participem et consortem. Jane of Naples and Mary of Scotland have a singular conformity.

32. See the Epistola Hortatoria de Capessenda Republica, from Petrarch to Nicholas Rienzi (Opp. p. 535–540), and the fifth eclogue or pastoral, a perpetual and obscure allegory.

33. In his Roman Questions, Plutarch ([c. 81] Opuscul. tom. i. p. 505, 506, edit. Græc. Hen. Steph.) states, on the most constitutional principles, the simple greatness of the tribunes, who were not properly magistrates, but a check on magistracy. It was their duty and interest ὁμοιοῦσθαι καὶ σχήματι καὶ σρολῇ καὶ διαίτῃ τοῖς ἐπιτυγχάνουσι τῶν πολιτῶν . . . . καταπατεῖσθα δεῖ (a saying of C. Curio) καὶ μὴ σεμνὸν εἶναι τῇ ὕψει μηδὲ δυσπρόσοδου . . . ὅσῳ δὲ μᾶλλον ἐκταπεινοῦται τῷ σώματι, τοσούτῳ μᾶλλον αὔξεται τῇ δυνάμει, etc. Rienzi, and Petrarch himself, were incapable perhaps of reading a Greek philosopher; but they might have imbibed the same modest doctrines from their favourite Latins, Livy and Valerius Maximus.

34. I could not express in English the forcible, though barbarous, title of *Zelator* Italiæ, which Rienzi assumed.

35. Era bell' homo (l. ii. c. 1, p. 399). It is remarkable that the riso sarcastico of the Bracciano edition is wanting in the Roman MS. from which Muratori has given the text. In his second reign, when he is painted almost as a monster, Rienzi travea una ventresca tonna trionfale, a modo de uno Abbate Asiano, or Asinino (l. iii. c. 18, p. 523).

36. Strange as it may seem, this festival was not without a precedent. In the year 1327, two barons, a Colonna and an Ursini, the usual balance, were created knights by the Roman people: their bath was of rose-water, their beds were decked with royal magnificence, and they were served at St. Maria of Araceli in the Capitol by the twenty-eight *buoni huomini*. They afterwards received from Robert king of Naples the sword of chivalry (Hist. Rom. l. i. c. 2, p. 259).

37. All parties believed in the leprosy and bath of Constantine (Petrarch, Epist. Famil. vi. 2), and Rienzi justified his own conduct by observing to the court of Avignon, that a vase which had been used by a pagan could not be profaned by a pious Christian. Yet this crime is specified in the bull of excommunication (Hocsemius, apud du Cerçeau, p. 189, 190).

38. This *verbal* summons of Pope Clement VI., which rests on the authority of the Roman historian and a Vatican MS., is disputed by the biographer of Petrarch (tom. ii. not. p. 70–76) with arguments rather of decency than of weight. The court of Avignon might not choose to agitate this delicate question.

39. The summons of the two rival emperors, a monument of freedom and folly, is extant in Hocsemius (Cerçeau, p. 163–166).

40. It is singular that the Roman historian should have overlooked this sevenfold coronation, which is sufficiently proved by internal evidence, and the testimony of Hocsemius, and even of Rienzi (Cerçeau, p. 167–170, 229).

41. Puoi se faceva stare denante a se, mentre sedeva, li baroni tutti in piedi ritti co le vraccia piecate, e co li capucci tratti. Deh como stavano

paurosi! (Hist. Rom. l. ii. c. 20, p. 439.) He saw them, and we see them.

42. The original letter, in which Rienzi justifies his treatment of the Colonna (Hocsemius, apud Du Cerçeau, p. 222–229), displays, in genuine colours, the mixture of the knave and the madman.

43. Rienzi, in the above-mentioned letter, ascribes to St. Martin the tribune, Boniface VIII. the enemy of Colonna, himself, and the Roman people, the glory of the day, which Villani likewise (l. xii. c. 104) describes as a regular battle. The disorderly skirmish, the flight of the Romans, and the cowardice of Rienzi, are painted in the simple and minute narrative of Fortifiocca, or the anonymous citizen (l. ii. c. 34–37).

44. In describing the fall of the Colonna, I speak only of the family of Stephen the elder, who is often confounded by the P. du Cerçeau with his son. That family was extinguished, but the house has been perpetuated in the collateral branches, of which I have not a very accurate knowledge. Circumspice (says Petrarch) familiæ tuæ statum. Columniensium *domos:* solito pauciores habeat columnas. Quid ad rem? modo fundamentum stabile, solidumque permaneat.

45. The convent of St. Silvester was founded, endowed, and protected by the Colonna cardinals, for the daughters of the family who embraced a monastic life, and who, in the year 1318, were twelve in number. The others were allowed to marry with their kinsmen in the fourth degree, and the dispensation was justified by the small number and close alliances of the noble families of Rome (Mémoires sur Pétrarque, tom. i. p. 110, tom. ii. p. 401).

46. Petrarch wrote a stiff and pedantic letter of consolation (Fam. l. vii. epist. 13, p. 682, 683). The friend was lost in the patriot. Nulla toto orbe principum familia carior; carior tamen respublica, carior Roma, carior Italia.

> Je rends grâces aux Dieux de n'être pas Romain.

47. This council and opposition is obscurely mentioned by Pollistore, a contemporary writer, who has preserved some curious and original facts. (Rer. Italicarum, tom. xxv. c. 31, p. 798–804).

48. The briefs and bulls of Clement VI. against Rienzi are translated by the P. du Cerçeau (p. 196, 232) from the ecclesiastical Annals of Odericus Raynaldus (A.D. 1347, No. 15, 17, 21, etc.), who found them in the archives of the Vatican.

49. Matteo Villani describes the origin, character, and death of this count of Minorbino, a man da natura inconstante e senza fede, whose grandfather, a crafty notary, was enriched and ennobled by the spoils of the Saracens of Nocera (l. vii. c. 102, 103). See his imprisonment, and the efforts of Petrarch, tom. ii. p. 149–151.

50. The troubles of Rome, from the departure to the return of Rienzi, are related by Matteo Villani (l. ii c. 47, l. iii. c. 33, 57, 78) and Thomas Fortifiocca (l. iii. c. 1–4). I have slightly passed over these secondary characters, who imitated the original tribune.

51. These visions, of which the friends and enemies of Rienzi seem alike ignorant, are surely magnified by the zeal of Pollistore, a Dominican inquisitor (Rer. Ital. tom. xxv. c. 36, p. 819). Had the tribune taught that Christ was succeeded by the Holy Ghost, that the tyranny of the pope would be abolished, he might have been convicted of heresy and treason, without offending the Roman people.

52. The astonishment, the envy almost, of Petrarch, is a proof, if not of the truth of this incredible fact, at least of his own veracity. The abbé de Sade (Mémoires, tom. iii. p. 242) quotes the sixth epistle of the thirteenth book of Petrarch, but it is of the royal MS. which he consulted, and not of the ordinary Basil edition (p. 920).

53. Ægidius, or Giles Albornoz, a noble Spaniard, archbishop of Toledo, and cardinal legate in Italy (A.D. 1353–1367), restored, by his arms and counsels, the temporal dominion of the popes. His life has been separately written by Sepulveda; but Dryden could not reasonably suppose that his name, or that of Wolsey, had reached the ears of the Mufti in Don Sebastian.

54. From Matteo Villani and Fortifiocca, the P. du Cerçeau (p. 344–394) has extracted the life and death of the Chevalier Montreal, the life of a robber and the death of a hero. At the head of a free company, the first that desolated Italy, he became rich and formidable: he had money in all the banks—60,000 ducats in Padua alone.

55. The exile, second government, and death of Rienzi, are minutely related by the anonymous Roman, who appears neither his friend nor his enemy (l. iii. c. 12–25). Petrarch, who loved the *tribune*, was indifferent to the fate of the *senator*.

56. The hopes and the disappointment of Petrarch are agreeably described in his own words by the French biographer (Mémoires, tom. iii. p. 375–413); but the deep, though secret, wound was the coronation of Zanubi, the poet laureat, by Charles IV.

57. See, in his accurate and amusing biographer, the application of Petrarch and Rome to Benedict XII. in the year 1334 (Mémoires, tom. i. p. 261–265), to Clement VI. in 1342 (tom. ii. p. 45–47), and to Urban V. in 1366 (tom. iii. p. 677–691): his praise (p. 711–715) and excuse (p. 771) of the last of these pontiffs. His angry controversy on the respective merits of France and Italy may be found Opp. p. 1068–1085.

58.   Squalida sed quoniam facies, neglectaque cultú
    Cæsaries; multisque malis lassata senectus
    Eripuit solitam effigiem: vetus accipe nomen;
    Roma vocor.   (Carm. l. ii. p. 77.)

He spins this allegory beyond all measure or patience. The Epistles to Urban V. in prose are more simple and persuasive (Senilium, l. vii. p. 811–827; l. ix. epist. i. p. 844–854).

59. I have not leisure to expatiate on the legends of St. Bridget or St. Catherine, the last of which might furnish some amusing stories. Their effect on the mind of Gregory XI. is attested by the last solemn words of the dying pope, who admonished the assistants, ut caverant ab hominibus, sive viris, sive mulieribus, sub specie religionis loquentibus visiones sui capitis, quia per tales ipse seductus, etc. (Baluz. Not. ad Vit. Pap. Avenionensium, tom. i. p. 1223).

60. This predatory expedition is related by Froissard (Chronique, tom. i. p. 230), and in the Life of Du Guesclin (Collection Générale des Mémoires Historiques, tom. iv. c. 16, p. 107–113). As early as the year 1361 the court of Avignon had been molested by similar freebooters, who afterwards passed the Alps (Mémoires sur Pétrarque, tom. iii. p. 563–569).

61. Fleury alleges, from the annals of Odericus Raynaldus, the original treaty which was signed the 21st of December, 1376, between Gregory XI. and the Romans (Hist. Eccles. tom. xx. p. 275).

62. The first crown or regnum (Ducange, Gloss. Latin. tom. v. p. 701) on the episcopal mitre of the popes is ascribed to the gift of Constantine, or Clovis. The second was added by Boniface VIII., as the emblem not only of a spiritual, but of a temporal kingdom. The three states of the church are represented by the triple crown, which was introduced by John XXII. or Benedict XII. (Mémoires sur Pétrarque, tom. i. p. 258, 259).

63. Baluze (Not. ad Pap. Avenion. tom. i. p. 1194, 1195) produces the original evidence which attests the threats of the Roman ambassadors, and the resignation of the abbot of Mount Cassin, qui, ultro se offerens, respondit se civem Romanum esse, et illud velle quod ipsi vellent.

64. The return of the popes from Avignon to Rome, and their reception by the people, are related in the original Lives of Urban V. and Gregory XI. in Baluze (Vit. Paparum Avenionensium, tom. i. p. 363–486) and Muratori (Script. Rer. Italicarum, tom. iii. P. i. p. 610–712). In the disputes of the schism every circumstance was severely, though partially, scrutinised; more especially in the great inquest which decided the obedience of Castile, and to which Baluze, in his notes, so often and so largely appeals from a MS. volume in the Harley library (p. 1281, etc.).

65. Can the death of a good man be esteemed a punishment by those who believe in the immortality of the soul? They betray the instability of their faith. Yet as a mere philosopher, I cannot agree with the Greeks, ὃν οἱ θέοι φιλοῦσιν ἀποθνῄσκει νέος (Brunck, Poetæ Gnomici, p. 231). See in Herodotus (l. i. c. 31) the moral and pleasing tale of the Argive youths.

66. In the first book of the Histoire du Concile de Pise, M. Lenfant has abridged and compared the original narratives of the adherents of Urban and Clement, of the Italians and Germans, the French and Spaniards. The latter appear to be the most active and loquacious, and every fact and word in the original lives of Gregory XI. and Clement VII. are supported in the notes of their editor Baluze.

67. The ordinal numbers of the popes seem to decide the question against Clement VII. and Benedict XIII., who are boldly stigmatised as antipopes by the Italians, while the French are content with authorities and reasons to plead the cause of doubt and toleration (Baluz. in Præfat.). It is singular, or rather it is not singular, that saints, visions, and miracles should be common to both parties.

68. Baluze strenuously labours (Not. p. 1271–1280) to justify the pure and pious motives of Charles V., king of France: he refused to hear the arguments of Urban; but were not the Urbanists equally deaf to the reasons of Clement, etc.?

69. An epistle, or declamation, in the name of Edward III. (Baluz. Vit. Pap. Avenion. tom. i. p. 553) displays the zeal of the English nation against the Clementines. Nor was their zeal confined to words: the bishop of Norwich led a crusade of 60,000 bigots beyond sea (Hume's History, vol. iii. p. 57, 58).

70. Besides the general historians, the Diaries of Delphinus Gentilis, Peter Antonius, and Stephen Infessura, in the great Collection of Muratori, represent the state and misfortunes of Rome.

71. It is supposed by Giannone (tom. iii. p. 292) that he styled himself Rex Romæ, a title unknown to the world since the expulsion of Tarquin. But a nearer inspection has justified the reading of Rex Ramæ, of Rama, an obscure kingdom annexed to the crown of Hungary.

72. The leading and decisive part which France assumed in the schism is stated by Peter du Puis in a separate history, extracted from authentic records, and inserted in the seventh volume of the last and best edition of his friend Thuanus (P. xi. p. 110–184).

73. Of this measure, John Gerson, a stout doctor, was the author or the champion. The proceedings of the university of Paris and the Gallican church were often prompted by his advice, and are copiously displayed in his theological writings, of which Le Clerc (Bibliothèque Choisie, tom. x. p. 1–78) has given a valuable extract. John Gerson acted an important part in the councils of Pisa and Constance.

74. Leonardus Brunus Aretinus, one of the revivers of classic learning in Italy, who, after serving many years as secretary in the Roman court, retired to the honourable office of chancellor of the republic of Florence (Fabric. Biblioth. medii Ævi, tom. i. p. 290). Lenfant has given the version of this curious epistle (Concile de Pise, tom. i. p. 192–195).

75. I cannot overlook this great national cause, which was vigorously maintained by the English

ambassadors against those of France. The latter contended that Christendom was essentially distributed into the four great nations and votes of Italy, Germany, France, and Spain; and that the lesser kingdoms (such as England, Denmark, Portugal, etc.) were comprehended under one or other of these great divisions. The English asserted that the British islands, of which they were the head, should be considered as a fifth and co-ordinate nation, with an equal vote; and every argument of truth or fable was introduced to exalt the dignity of their country. Including England, Scotland, Wales, the four kingdoms of Ireland, and the Orkneys, the British islands are decorated with eight royal crowns, and discriminated by four or five languages, English, Welsh, Cornish, Scotch, Irish, etc. The greater island from north to south measures 800 miles, or 40 days' journey; and England alone contains 32 counties and 52,000 parish churches (a bold account!) besides cathedrals, colleges, priories, and hospitals. They celebrate the mission of St. Joseph of Arimathea, the birth of Constantine, and the legatine powers of the two primates, without forgetting the testimony of Bartholemy de Glanville (A.D. 1360), who reckons only four Christian kingdoms—1, of Rome; 2, of Constantinople; 3, of Ireland, which had been transferred to the English monarchs; and, 4, of Spain. Our countrymen prevailed in the council, but the victories of Henry V. added much weight to their arguments. The adverse pleadings were found at Constance by Sir Robert Wingfield, ambassador from Henry VIII. to the emperor Maximilian I., and by him printed in 1517 at Louvain. From a Leipsic MS. they are more correctly published in the Collection of Von der Hardt, tom. v.; but I have only seen Lenfant's abstract of these acts (Concile de Constance, tom. ii. p. 447, 453, etc.).

76. The histories of the three successive councils, Pisa, Constance, and Basil, have been written with a tolerable degree of candour, industry, and elegance, by a Protestant minister, M. Lenfant, who retired from France to Berlin. They form six volumes in quarto; and as Basil is the worst, so Constance is the best, part of the Collection.

77. See the twenty-seventh Dissertation of the Antiquities of Muratori, and the first Instruction of the Science des Médailles of the Père Joubert and the Baron de la Bastie. The Metallic History of Martin V. and his successors has been composed by two monks, Moulinet a Frenchman, and Bonanni an Italian: but I understand that the first part of the series is restored from more recent coins.

78. Besides the Lives of Eugenius IV. (Rerum Italic. tom. iii. P. i. p. 869, and tom. xxv. p. 256), the Diaries of Paul Petroni and Stephen Infessura are the best original evidence for the revolt of the Romans against Eugenius IV. The former, who lived at the time and on the spot, speaks the language of a citizen, equally afraid of priestly and popular tyranny.

79. The coronation of Frederic III. is described by Lenfant (Concile de Basle, tom. ii. p. 276–288) from Æneas Sylvius, a spectator and actor in that splendid scene.

80. The oath of fidelity imposed on the emperor by the pope is recorded and sanctified in the Clementines (l. ii. tit. ix.); and Æneas Sylvius, who objects to this new demand, could not foresee that in a few years he should ascend the throne and imbibe the maxims of Boniface VIII.

81. Lo senatore di Roma, vestito di brocarto con quella beretta, e con quelle maniche, et ornamenti di pelle, co' quali va alle feste di Testaccio e Nagone, might escape the eye of Æneas Sylvius, but he is viewed with admiration and complacency by the Roman citizen (Diario di Stephano Infessura, p. 1133).

82. See in the statutes of Rome the *senator and three judges* (l. i. c. 3–14), the *conservators* (l. i. c. 15, 16, 17, l. iii. c. 4), the *caporioni* (l. i. c. 18, l. iii. c. 8), the *secret council* (l. iii. c. 2), the *common council* (l. iii. c. 3). The title of *feuds, defiances, acts of violence*, etc., is spread through many a chapter (c. 14–40) of the second book.

83. *Statuta almæ Urbis Romæ Auctoritate S. D. N. Gregorii XIII. Pont. Max. a Senatû Populoque Rom. reformata et edita. Romæ,* 1580, *in folio.* The obsolete, repugnant statutes of antiquity were confounded in five books, and Lucas Pætus, a lawyer and antiquarian, was appointed to act as the modern Tribonian. Yet I regret the old code, with the rugged crust of freedom and barbarism.

84. In my time (1765), and in M. Grosley's (Observations sur l'Italie, tom. ii. p. 361), the senator of Rome was M. Bielke, a noble Swede, and a proselyte to the Catholic faith. The pope's right to appoint the senator and the conservator is implied, rather than affirmed, in the statutes.

85. Besides the curious, though concise, narrative of Machiavel (Istoria Fiorentina, l. vi. Opere, tom. i. p. 210, 211, edit. Londra, 1747, in 4to), the Porcarian conspiracy is related in the Diary of Stephen Infessura (Rer. Ital. tom. iii. P. ii. p. 1134, 1135), and in a separate tract by Leo Baptista Alberti (Rer. Ital. tom. xxv. p. 609–614). It is amusing to compare the style and sentiments of the courtier and citizen. Facinus profecto quo . . . neque periculo horribilius, neque audaciâ detestabilius, neque crudelitate tetrius, a quoquam perditissimo uspiam excogitatum sit. . . . Perdette la vita quell' huomo da bene, e amatore dello bene e libertà di Roma.

86. The disorders of Rome, which were much inflamed by the partiality of Sixtus IV., are exposed in the Diaries of two spectators, Stephen Infessura and an anonymous citizen. See the troubles of the year 1484, and the death of the protonotary Colonna, in tom. iii. P. ii. p. 1083, 1158.

87. Est toute la terre de l'église troublée pour cette partialité (des Colonnes et des Ursins), comme nous dirions Luce et Grammont, ou en Hollande Houc et Caballan; et quand ce ne seroit

ce différend la terre de l'église seroit la plus heureuse habitation pour les sujets qui soit dans tout le monde (car ils ne payent ni tailles ni guères autres choses), et seroient toujours bien conduits (car toujours les papes sont sages et bien conseillés); mais très souvent en advient de grands et cruels meurtres et pilleries.

88. By the economy of Sixtus V. the revenue of the ecclesiastical state was raised to two millions and a half of Roman crowns (Vita, tom. ii. p. 291–296); and so regular was the military establishment, that in one month Clement VIII. could invade the duchy of Ferrara with three thousand horse and twenty thousand foot (tom. iii. p. 64). Since that time (A.D. 1597) the papal arms are happily rusted, but the revenue must have gained some nominal increase.

89. More especially by Guicciardini and Machiavel; in the general history of the former; in the Florentine history, the "Prince," and the political discourses of the latter. These, with their worthy successors, Fra-Paolo and Davila, were justly esteemed the first historians of modern languages, till, in the present age, Scotland arose to dispute the prize with Italy herself.

90. In the history of the Gothic siege I have compared the barbarians with the subjects of Charles V (vol. i. p. 1125)—an anticipation which, like that of the Tartar conquests, I indulged with the less scruple, as I could scarcely hope to reach the conclusion of my work.

91. The ambitious and feeble hostilities of the Caraffa pope, Paul IV., may be seen in Thuanus (l. xvi.–xviii.) and Giannone (tom. iv. p. 149–163). Those Catholic bigots, Philip II. and the duke of Alva, presumed to separate the Roman prince from the vicar of Christ; yet the holy character, which would have sanctified his victory, was decently applied to protect his defeat.

92. This gradual change of manners and expense is admirably explained by Dr. Adam Smith (Wealth of Nations, Bk. iii, ch. 4), who proves, perhaps too severely, that the most salutary effects have flowed from the meanest and most selfish causes.

93. Mr. Hume (Hist. of England, vol. i. p. 389) too hastily concludes that, if the civil and ecclesiastical powers be united in the same person, it is of little moment whether he be styled prince or prelate, since the temporal character will always predominate.

94. A Protestant may disdain the unworthy preference of St. Francis or St. Dominic, but he will not rashly condemn the zeal or judgment of Sixtus V., who placed the statues of the apostles St. Peter and St. Paul on the vacant columns of Trajan and Antonine.

95. A wandering Italian, Gregorio Leti, has given the Vita di Sisto Quinto (Amstel. 1721, three vols. in 12mo), a copious and amusing work, but which does not command our absolute confidence. Yet the character of the man, and the principal facts, are supported by the annals of Spondanus and Muratori (A.D. 1585–1590) and the contemporary history of the great Thuanus l. lxxxii. c. 1, 2; l. lxxxiv. c. 10; l. c. c. 8).

96. These privileged places, the *quartieri* or *franchises*, were adopted from the Roman nobles by the foreign ministers. Julius II. had once abolished the abominandum et detestandum franchitiarum hujusmodi nomen; and after Sixtus V. they again revived. I cannot discern either the justice or magnanimity of Louis XIV., who, in 1687, sent his ambassador, the marquis de Lavardin, to Rome, with an armed force of a thousand officers, guards, and domestics, to maintain this iniquitous claim, and insult Pope Innocent XI. in the heart of his capital (Vita di Sisto V. tom. iii. p. 260–278; Muratori, Annali d'Italia, tom. xv. p. 494–496; and Voltaire, Siècle de Louis XIV. tom. ii. c. 14, p. 58, 59).

97. This outrage produced a decree, which was inscribed on marble, and placed in the Capitol. It is expressed in a style of manly simplicity and freedom: Si quis, sive privatus, sive magistratum gerens de collocandâ *vivo* pontifici statuâ mentionem facere ausit, legitimo S. P. Q. R. decreto in perpetuum infamis et publicorum munerum expers esto. MDXC. mense Augusto (Vita di Sisto V. tom. iii. p. 469). I believe that this decree is still observed, and I know that every monarch who deserves a statue should himself impose the prohibition.

98. The histories of the church, Italy, and Christendom, have contributed to the chapter which I now conclude. In the original Lives of the Popes we often discover the city and republic of Rome; and the events of the fourteenth and fifteenth centuries are preserved in the rude and domestic chronicles which I have carefully inspected, and shall recapitulate in the order of time.

1. Monaldeschi (Ludovici Boncomitis) Fragmenta Annalium Roman. (A.D. 1328), in the Scriptores Rerum Italicarum of Muratori, tom. xii. p. 525. N.B. The credit of this fragment is somewhat hurt by a singular interpolation, in which the author relates *his own death* at the age of 115 years.

2. Fragmenta Historiæ Romanæ (vulgo Thomas Fortifioccæ), in Romana dialecto vulgari (A.D. 1327–1354, in Muratori, Antiquitat. medii Ævi Italiæ, tom. iii. p. 247–548); the authentic groundwork of the history of Rienzi.

3. Delphini (Gentilis) Diarium Romanum (A.D. 1370–1410), in the Rerum Italicarum, tom. iii. P. ii. p. 846.

4. Antonii (Petri) *Diarium* Rom. (A.D. 1404–1417), tom. xxiv. p. 969.

5. Petroni (Pauli) Miscellanea Historica Romana (A.D. 1433–1446), tom. xxiv. p. 1011.

6. Volaterrani (Jacob.) Diarium Rom. (A.D. 1472–1484), tom. xxiii. p. 81.

7. Anonymi Diarum Urbis Romæ (A.D. 1481–1492), tom. iii. P. ii. p. 1069.

8. Infessuræ (Stephani) Diarium Romanum (A.D. 1294, or 1378–1494), tom. iii. P. ii. p. 1109.

9. Historia Arcana Alexandri VI. sive Excerpta ex Diario Joh. Burcardi (A.D. 1492–1503), edita a Godefr. Gulielm. Leibnizio, Hanover, 1697, in 4to. The large and valuable Journal of Burcard might be completed from the MSS. in different libraries of Italy and France (M. de Fonce-magne, in the Mémoires de l'Acad. des Inscrip. tom. xvii. p. 597–606).

Except the last, all these fragments and diaries are inserted in the Collections of Muratori, my guide and master in the history of Italy. His country, and the public, are indebted to him for the following works on that subject:—1. *Rerum Italicarum Scriptores* (A.D. 500–1500), *quorum potissima pars nunc primum in lucem prodit*, etc., twenty-eight vols. in folio, Milan, 1723–1738, 1751. A volume of chronological and alphabetical tables is still wanting as a key to this great work, which is yet in a disorderly and defective state. 2. *Antiquitates Italiæ medii Ævi*, six vols., in folio, Milan, 1738–1743, in seventy-five curious dissertations, on the manners, government, religion, etc., of the Italians of the darker ages, with a large supplement of charters, chronicles, etc. 3. *Dissertazioni sopra le Antiquità Italiane*, three vols. in 4to, Milano, 1751, a free version by the author, which may be quoted with the same confidence as the Latin text of the Antiquities. 4. *Annali d'Italia*, eighteen vols. in octavo, Milan, 1753–1756, a dry, though accurate and useful, abridgment of the history of Italy, from the birth of Christ to the middle of the eighteenth century. 5. *Dell' Antichità Estense ed Italiane*, two vols. in folio, Modena, 1717, 1740. In the history of this illustrious race, the parent of our Brunswick kings, the critic is not seduced by the loyalty or gratitude of the subject. In all his works Muratori approves himself a diligent and laborious writer, who aspires above the prejudices of a Catholic priest. He was born in the year 1672, and died in the year 1750, after passing near sixty years in the libraries of Milan and Modena (Vita del Proposto Ludovico Antonio Muratori, by his nephew and successor Gian. Francesco Soli Muratori, Venezia, 1756, in 4to).

Chapter LXXI

1. I have already (notes 50 and 51, p. 760, vol. ii.) mentioned the age, character, and writings of Poggius; and particularly noticed the date of this elegant moral lecture on the varieties of fortune.

2. Consedimus in ipsis Tarpeiæ arcis ruinis, pone ingens portæ cujusdam, ut puto, templi, marmoreum limen, plurimasque passim confractas columnas, unde magnâ ex parte prospectus urbis patet (p. 5).

3. Æneid viii. 97–369. This ancient picture, so artfully introduced, and so exquisitely finished, must have been highly interesting to an inhabitant of Rome; and our early studies allow us to sympathise in the feelings of a Roman.

4. Capitolium adeo ... immutatum ut vineæ in senatorum subsellia successerint, stercorum ac purgamentorum receptaculum factum. Respice ad Palatinum montem ... vasta rudera ... cæteros colles perlustra omnia vacua ædificiis, ruinis vineisque oppleta conspicies (Poggius de Varietat. Fortunæ, p. 21).

5. See Poggius, p. 8–22.

6. Liber de Mirabilibus Romæ, ex Registro Nicolai Cardinalis de Arragoniâ, in Bibliothecâ St. Isidori Armario IV. No. 69. This treatise, with some short but pertinent notes, has been published by Montfaucon (Diarium Italicum, p. 283–301), who thus delivers his own critical opinion: Scriptor xiiimi. circiter sæculi, ut ibidem notatur; antiquariæ rei imperitus, et, ut ab illo ævo, nugis et anilibus fabellis refertus: sed, quia monumenta quæ iis temporibus Romæ supererant pro modulo recenset, non parum inde lucis mutuabitur qui Romanis antiquitatibus indagandis operam navabit (p. 283).

7. The Père Mabillon (Analecta, tom. iv. p. 502) has published an anonymous pilgrim of the ninth century, who, in his visit round the churches and holy places of Rome, touches on several buildings, especially porticoes, which had disappeared before the thirteenth century.

8. On the Septizonium, see the Mémoires sur Pétrarque (tom. i. p. 325), Donatus (p. 338), and Nardini (p. 117, 414).

9. The age of the pyramids is remote and unknown, since Diodorus Siculus (tom. i. l. i. c. 44, p. 72) is unable to decide whether they were constructed 1000 or 3400 years before the clxxx. Olympiad. Sir John Marsham's contracted scale of the Egyptian dynasties would fix them about 2000 years before Christ (Canon. Chronicus, p. 47).

10. See the speech of Glaucus in the Iliad (vi. 146). This natural but melancholy image is familiar to Homer.

11. The learning and criticism of M. des Vignoles (Histoire Critique de la République des Lettres, tom. viii. p. 74–118; ix. p. 172–187) dates the fire of Rome from A.D. 64, July 19, and the subsequent persecution of the Christians from November 15 of the same year.

12. Quippe in regiones quatuordecim Roma dividitur, quarum quatuo integræ manebant, tres solo tenus dejectæ: septem reliquis pauca tectorum vestigia supererant, lacera et semiusta. Among the old relics that were irreparably lost, Tacitus enumerates the temple of the Moon of Servius Tullius;

the fane and altar consecrated by Evander præsenti Herculi; the temple of Jupiter Stator, a vow of Romulus; the palace of Numa; the temple of Vesta cum Penatibus populi Romani. He then deplores the opes tot victoriis quæsitæ et Græcarum artium decora ... multa quæ seniores meminerant, quæ reparari nequibant (Annal. xv. 40, 41).

13. A.U.C. 507, repentina subversio ipsius Romæ prævenit triumphum Romanorum ... diversæ ignium aquarumque clades pene absumsere urbem. Nam Tiberis insolitis auctus imbribus et ultra opinionem, vel diuturnitate vel magnitudine redundans, omnia Romæ ædificia in plano posita delevit. Diversæ qualitates locorum ad unam convenere perniciem: quoniam et quæ segnior inundatio tenuit madefacta dissolvit, et quæ cursus torrentis invenit impulsa dejecit (Orosius, Hist. l. iv. c. 11, p. 244, edit. Havercamp). Yet we may observe that it is the plan and study of the Christian apologist to magnify the calamities of the pagan world.

14. Vidimus flavum Tiberim, retortis
    Littore Etrusco violenter undis,
Ire dejectum monumenta Regis
    Templaque Vestæ.
            (Horat. Carm. i. 2.)

If the palace of Numa and temple of Vesta were thrown down in Horace's time, what was consumed of those buildings by Nero's fire could hardly deserve the epithets of vetustissima or incorrupta.

15. Ad coercendas inundationes alveum Tiberis laxavit ac repurgavit, completum olim ruderibus, et ædificiorum prolapsionibus coarctatum (Suetonius in Augusto, c. 30).

16. Tacitus (Annal. i. 79) reports the petitions of the different towns of Italy to the senate against the measure; and we may applaud the progress of reason. On a similar occasion local interests would undoubtedly be consulted; but an English House of Commons would reject with contempt the arguments of superstition, "that nature had assigned to the rivers their proper course," etc.

17. See the Epoques de la Nature of the eloquent and philosophic Buffon. His picture of Guyana, in South America, is that of a new and savage land, in which the waters are abandoned to themselves, without being regulated by human industry (p. 212, 561, quarto edition).

18. In his Travels in Italy, Mr. Addison (his Works, vol. ii. p. 98, Baskerville's edition) has observed this curious and unquestionable fact.

19. Yet in modern times the Tiber has sometimes damaged the city, and in the years 1530, 1557, 1598, the Annals of Muratori record three mischievous and memorable inundations (tom. xiv. p. 268, 429; tom. xv. p. 99, etc.).

20. I take this opportunity of declaring that, in the course of twelve years, I have forgotten, or renounced, the flight of Odin from Azoph to Sweden, which I never very seriously believed. The Goths are apparently Germans; but all beyond

Cæsar and Tacitus is darkness or fable in the antiquities of Germany.

21. History of the Decline, etc., vol. i. p. 512.

22. Ibid. vol. i. p. 573.

23. Ibid. vol. i. p. 641.

24. Ibid. vol. ii. p. 57.

25. Ibid. vol. i. p. 460–461.

26. Eodem tempore petiit a Phocate principe templum, quod appellatur Pantheon, in quo fecit ecclesiam Sanctæ Mariæ semper Virginis, et omnium martyrum; in quâ ecclesiæ princeps multa bona obtulit (Anastasius vel potius Liber Pontificalis in Bonifacio IV. in Muratori, Script. Rerum Italicarum, tom. iii. P. i. p. 135). According to the anonymous writer in Montfaucon, the Pantheon had been vowed by Agrippa to Cybele and Neptune, and was dedicated by Boniface IV. on the calends of November to the Virgin, quæ est mater omnium sanctorum (p. 297, 298).

27. Flaminius Vacca (apud Montfaucon, p. 155, 156: his memoir is likewise printed, p. 21, at the end of the Roma Antica of Nardini) and several Romans, doctrinâ graves, were persuaded that the Goths buried their tresaures at Rome, and bequeathed the secret marks filiis nepotibusque. He relates some anecdotes to prove that, in his own time, these places were visited and rifled by the Transalpine pilgrims, the heirs of the Gothic conquerors.

28. Omnia quæ erant in ære ad ornatum civitatis deposuit; sed et ecclesiam B. Mariæ ad martyres quæ de tegulis æreis cooperta discooperuit (Anast. in Vitalian. p. 141). The base and sacrilegious Greek had not even the poor pretence of plundering a heathen temple; the Pantheon was already a Catholic church.

29. For the spoils of Ravenna (musiva atque marmora) see the original grant of Pope Adrian I. to Charlemagne (Codex Carolin. epist. lxvii. in Muratori, Script. Ital. tom. iii. P. ii. p. 223).

30. I shall quote the authentic testimony of the Saxon poet (A.D. 887–899), de Rebus gestis Caroli Magni, l. v. 437–440, in the Historians of France (tom. v. p. 180):—

Ad quæ marmoreas præstabat ROMA columnas,
    Quasdam præcipuas pulchra Ravenna
    dedit.
De tam longinquâ poterit regione vetustas
    Illius ornatum, Francia, ferre tibi.

And I shall add, from the chronicle of Sigebert (Historians of France, tom. v. p. 378) extruxit etiam Aquisgrani basilicam plurimæ pulchritudinis, ad cujus structuram a ROMA et Ravenna columnas et marmora devehi fecit.

31. I cannot refuse to transcribe a long passage of Petrarch (Opp. p. 536, 537) in Epistolâ hortatoriâ ad Nicolaum Laurentium; it is so strong and full to the point: Nec pudor aut pietas continuit quominus impii spoliata Dei templa, occupatas arces, opes publicas, regiones urbis, atque honores magistratúum inter se divisos; (habeant?) quam unâ

in re, turbulenti ac seditiosi homines et totius reliquæ vitæ consiliis et rationibus discordes, inhumani fœderis studendâ societate convenirent, in pontes et mœnia atque immeritos lapides desævirent. Denique post vi vel senio collapsa palatia, quæ quondam ingentes tenuerunt viri, post diruptos arcus triumphales (unde majores horum forsitan corruerunt), de ipsius vetustatis ac propriæ impietatis fragminibus vilem quæstum turpi mercimonio captare non puduit. Itaque nunc, heu dolor! heu scelus indignum! de vestris marmoreis columnis, de liminibus templorum (ad quæ nuper ex orbe toto concursus devotissimus fiebat), de imaginibus sepulchrorum sub quibus patrum vestrorum venerabilis civis (*cinis?*) erat, ut reliquas sileam, desidiosa Neapolis adornatur. Sic paullatim ruinæ ipsæ deficiunt. Yet king Robert was the friend of Petrarch.

32. Yet Charlemagne washed and swam at Aixla-Chapelle with a hundred of his courtiers (Eginhart, c. 22, p. 108, 109); and Muratori describes, as late as the year 814, the public baths which were built at Spoleto in Italy (Annali, tom. vi. p. 416).

33. See the Annals of Italy, A.D. 988. For this and the preceding fact Muratori himself is indebted to the Benedictine history of Père Mabillon.

34. Vita di Sisto Quinto, da Gregorio Leti, tom. iii. p. 50.

35. Porticus ædis Concordiæ, quam cum primum ad urbem accessi vidi fere integram opere marmoreo admodum specioso: Romani postmodum ad calcem ædem totam et porticûs partem disjectis columnis sunt demoliti (p. 12). The temple of Concord was therefore *not* destroyed by a sedition in the thirteenth century, as I have read in a MS. treatise del' Governo civile di Roma, lent me formerly at Rome, and ascribed (I believe falsely) to the celebrated Gravina. Poggius likewise affirms that the sepulchre of Cæcilia Metella was burnt for lime (p. 19, 20).

36. Composed by Æneas Sylvius, afterwards Pope Pius II., and published by Mabillon, from a MS. of the queen of Sweden (Musæum Italicum, tom. i. p. 97).

Oblectat me, Roma, tuas spectare ruinas;
Ex cujus lapsú gloria prisca patet.
Sed tuus hic populus muris defossa vetustis
Calcis in obsequium marmora dura coquit.
Impia tercentum si sic gens egerit annos
Nullum hinc indicium nobilitatis erit.

37. Vagabamur pariter in illâ urbe tam magnâ; quæ, cum propter spatium vacua videretur, populum habet immensum (Opp. p. 605, Epist. Familiares, ii. 14).

38. These states of the population of Rome at different periods are derived from an ingenious treatise of the physician Lancisi, de Romani Cœli Qualitatibus (p. 122).

39. All the facts that relate to the towers at Rome, and in other free cities of Italy, may be found in the laborious and entertaining compilation of Muratori, Antiquitates Italiæ medii Ævi, dissertat. xxvi. (tom. ii. p. 493–496, of the Latin; tom. i. p. 446, of the Italian work).

40. As for instance, Templum Jani nunc dicitur turris Centii Frangapanis; et sane Jano impositæ turris lateritiæ conspicua hodieque vestigia supersunt (Montfaucon Diarium Italicum, p. 186). The anonymous writer (p. 285) enumerates arcus Titi, turris Cartularia; arcus Julii Cæsaris et Senatorum, turres de Bratis; arcus Antonini, turris de Cosectis, etc.

41. Hadriani molem . . . magna ex parte Romanorum injuria . . . disturbavit: quod certe funditus evertissent, si eorum manibus pervia, absumptis grandibus saxis, reliqua moles exstitisset (Poggius de Varietate Fortunæ, p. 12).

42. Against the emperor Henry IV. (Muratori, Annali d'Italia, tom. ix. p. 147).

43. I must copy an important passage of Montfaucon: Turris ingens rotunda . . . Cæciliæ Metellæ . . . sepulchrum erat, cujus muri tam solidi, ut spatium perquam minimum intus vacuum supersit: et *Torre di Bove* dicitur, a boum capitibus muro inscriptis. Huic sequiori ævo, tempore intestinorum bellorum, ceu urbecula adjuncta fuit, cujus mœnia et turres etiamnum visuntur; ita ut sepulchrum Metellæ quasi arx oppiduli fuerit. Ferventibus in urbe partibus, cum Ursini atque Columnenses mutuis cladibus perniciem inferrent civitati, in utriusve partis ditionem cederet magni momenti erat (p. 142).

44. See the testimonies of Donatus, Nardini, and Montfaucon. In the Savelli palace the remains of the theatre of Marcellus are still great and conspicuous.

45. James, cardinal of St. George, ad velum aureum, in his metrical Life of Pope Celestin V. (Muratori, Script. Ital. tom. i. P. iii. p. 621, l. i. c. 1, ver. 132, etc).

Hoc dixisse sat est, Romam caruisse Senatû
Mensibus exactis heu sex; belloque vocatum
(*vocatos*)
In scelus, in socios fraternaque vulnera patres;
Tormentis jecisse viros immania saxa;
Perfodisse domus trabibus, fecisse ruinas
Ignibus; incensas turres, obscuraque fumo
Lumina vicino, quo sit spoliata supellex.

46. Muratori (Dissertazione sopra le Antiquità Italiane, tom. i. p. 427–431) finds that stone bullets of two or three hundred pounds' weight were not uncommon; and they are sometimes computed at twelve or eighteen *cantari* of Genoa, each *cantaro* weighing 150 pounds.

47. The sixth law of the Visconti prohibits this common and mischievous practice; and strictly enjoins that the houses of banished citizens should be preserved pro communi utilitate (Gualvaneus de la Flamma, in Muratori, Script. Rerum Italicarum, tom. xii. p. 1041).

48. Petrarch thus addresses his friend, who, with shame and tears, had shown him the mœnia, laceræ specimen miserabile Romæ, and declared

his own intention of restoring them (Carmina Latina, l. ii. epist. Paulo Annibalensi, xii. p. 97, 98).

> Nec te parva manet servatis fama ruinis
> Quanta quod integræ fuit olim gloria Romæ
> Reliquiæ testantur adhuc; quas longior ætas
> Frangere non valuit; non vis aut ira cruenti
> Hostis, ab egregiis franguntur civibus, heu! heu!
> ———Quod *ille* nequivit (*Hannibal*)
> Perficit hic aries.

49. The fourth part of the Verona Illustrata of the Marquis Maffei professedly treats of amphitheatres, particularly those of Rome and Verona, of their dimensions, wooden galleries, etc. It is from magnitude that he derives the name of *Colosseum*, or *Coliseum:* since the same appellation was applied to the amphitheatre of Capua, without the aid of a colossal statue; since that of Nero was erected in the court (*in atrio*) of his palace, and not in the Coliseum (p. iv. p. 15–19, l. i. c. 4).

50. Joseph Maria Suarés, a learned bishop, and the author of a history of Præneste, has composed a separate dissertation on the seven or eight probable causes of these holes, which has been since reprinted in the Roman Thesaurus of Sallengre. Montfaucon (Diarium, p. 233) pronounces the rapine of the barbarians to be the unam germanamque causam foraminum.

51. Donatus, Roma Vetus et Nova, p. 285.

52. Quamdiu stabit Colyseus, stabit et Roma; quando cadet Colyseus, cadet Roma; quando cadet Roma, cadet et mundus (Beda in Excerptis seu Collectaneis apud Ducange Glossar. med. et infimæ Latinitatis, tom. ii. p. 407, edit. Basil). This saying must be ascribed to the Anglo-Saxon pilgrims who visited Rome before the year 735, the era of Bede's death; for I do not believe that our venerable monk ever passed the sea.

53. I cannot recover, in Muratori's original Lives of the Popes (Script. Rerum Italicarum, tom. iii. P. I.), the passage that attests this hostile partition, which must be applied to the end of the eleventh or the beginning of the twelfth century.

54. Although the structure of the Circus Agonalis be destroyed, it still retains its form and name (Abona, Nagona, Navona); and the interior space affords a sufficient level for the purpose of racing. But the Monte Testaceo, that strange pile of broken pottery, seems only adapted for the annual practice of hurling from top to bottom some waggon-loads of live hogs for the diversion of the populace (Statuta Urbis Romæ, p. 186).

55. See the Statuta Urbis Romæ, l. iii. c. 87, 88, 89, p. 185, 186. I have already given an idea of this municipal code. The races of Nagona and Monte Testaceo are likewise mentioned in the Diary of Peter Antonius from 1404 to 1417 (Muratori, Script. Rerum Italicarum, tom. xxiv. p. 1124).

56. The *Pallium*, which Menage so foolishly derives from *Palmarium*, is an easy extension of the idea and the words, from the robe or cloak to the materials, and from thence to their application as a prize (Muratori, dissert. xxxiii.).

57. For these expenses the Jews of Rome paid each year 1130 florins, of which the odd thirty represented the pieces of silver for which Judas had betrayed his Master to their ancestors. There was a foot-race of Jewish as well as of Christian youths (Statuta Urbis, ibidem).

58. This extraordinary bull-feast in the Coliseum is described, from tradition rather than memory, by Ludovico Buonconte Monaldesco, in the most ancient fragments of Roman annals (Muratori, Script. Rerum Italicarum, tom. xii. p. 535, 536); and however fanciful they may seem, they are deeply marked with the colours of truth and nature.

59. Muratori has given a separate dissertation (the xxixth) to the games of the Italians in the middle ages.

60. In a concise but instructive memoir, the abbé Barthelemy (Mémoires de l'Académie des Inscriptions, tom. xxviii. p. 585) has mentioned this agreement of the factions of the fourteenth century de Tiburtino faciendo in the Coliseum, from an original act in the archives of Rome.

61. Coliseum . . . ob stultitiam Romanorum *majori ex parte* ad calcem deletum, says the indignant Poggius (p. 17): but his expression, too strong for the present age, must be very tenderly applied to the fifteenth century.

62. Of the Olivetan monks. Montfaucon (p. 142) affirms this fact from the memorials of Flaminius Vacca (No. 72). They still hoped, on some future occasion, to revive and vindicate their grant.

63. After measuring the priscus amphitheatri gyrus, Montfaucon (p. 142) only adds that it was entire under Paul III.; tacendo clamat. Muratori (Annali d'Italia, tom. xiv. p. 371) more freely reports the guilt of the Farnese pope, and the indignation of the Roman people. Against the nephews of Urban VIII. I have no other evidence than the vulgar saying, "Quod non fecerunt Barbari, fecere Barberini," which was perhaps suggested by the resemblance of the words.

64. As an antiquarian and a priest, Montfaucon thus deprecates the ruin of the Coliseum: Quòd si non suopte merito atque pulchritudine dignum fuisset quod improbas arceret manus, indigna res utique in locum tot martyrum cruore sacrum tantopere sævitum esse.

65. Yet the Statutes of Rome (l. iii. c. 81, p. 182) impose a fine of 500 *aurei* on whosoever shall demolish any ancient edifice, ne ruinis civitas deformetur, et ut antiqua ædificia decorem urbis perpetuo repræsentent.

66. In his first visit to Rome (A.D. 1337; see Mémoires sur Pétrarque, tom. i. p. 322, etc.) Petrarch is struck mute miraculo rerum tantarum, et stuporis mole obrutus. . . . Præsentia vero, mirum dictú, nihil imminuit: vere major fuit Roma ma-

joresque sunt reliquiæ quam rebar. Jam non orbem ab hâc urbe domitum, sed tam sero domitum, miror (Opp. p. 605, Familiares, ii. 14, Joanni Columnæ).

67. He excepts and praises the *rare* knowledge of John Colonna. Qui enim hodie magis ignari rerum Romanarum, quam Romani cives? Invitus dico, nusquam minus Roma cognoscitur quam Romæ.

68. After the description of the Capitol, he adds, statuæ erant quot sunt mundi provinciæ; et habebat quælibet tintinnabulum ad collum. Et erant ita per magicam artem dispositæ, ut quando aliqua regio Romano Imperio rebellis erat, statim imago illius provinciæ vertebat se contra illam; unde tintinnabulum resonabat quod pendebat ad collum; tuncque vates Capitolii qui erant custodes senatui, etc. He mentions an example of the Saxons and Suevi, who, after they had been subdued by Agrippa, again rebelled: tintinnabulum sonuit; sacerdos qui erat in speculo in hebdomadâ senatoribus nuntiavit: Agrippa marched back and reduced the —— Persians (Anonym. in Montfaucon, p. 297, 298).

69. The same writer affirms that Virgil captus a Romanis invisibiliter exiit, ivitque Neapolim. A Roman magician, in the eleventh century, is introduced by William of Malmesbury (de Gestis Regum Anglorum, l. ii. p. 86); and in the time of Flaminius Vacca (No. 81, 103) it was the vulgar belief that the strangers (the *Goths*) invoked the demons for the discovery of hidden treasures.

70. Anonym. p. 289. Montfaucon (p. 191) justly observes that, if Alexander be represented, these statues cannot be the work of Phidias (Olympiad lxxxiii.) or Praxiteles (Olympiad civ.), who lived before that conqueror (Plin. Hist. Natur. xxxiv. 19).

71. William of Malmesbury (l. ii. p. 86, 87) relates a marvellous discovery (A.D. 1046) of Pallas, the son of Evander, who had been slain by Turnus; the perpetual light in his sepulchre, a Latin epitaph, the corpse, yet entire, of a young giant, the enormous wound in his breast (pectus perforat ingens), etc. If this fable rests on the slightest foundation, we may pity the bodies, as well as the statues, that were exposed to the air in a barbarous age.

72. Prope porticum Minervæ, statua est recubantis, cujus caput integrâ effigie tantæ magnitudinis, ut signa omnia excedat. Quidam ad plantandas arbores scrobes faciens detexit. Ad hoc visendum cum plures in dies magis concurrerent, strepitum adeuntium fastidiumque pertæsus, horti patronus congestâ humo texit (Poggius de Varietate Fortunæ, p. 12).

73. See the memorials of Flaminius Vacca, No. 57, p. 11, 12, at the end of the Roma Antica of Nardini (1704, in 4to).

74. In the year 1709 the inhabitants of Rome (without including eight or ten thousand Jews) amounted to 138,568 souls (Labat, Voyages en Espagne et en Italie, tom. iii. p. 217, 218). In 1740 they had increased to 146,080; and in 1765 I left them, without the Jews, 161,899. I am ignorant whether they have since continued in a progressive state.

75. The Père Montfaucon distributes his own observations into twenty days, he should have styled them weeks, or months, of his visits to the different parts of the city (Diarium Italicum, c. 8–20, p. 104–301). That learned Benedictine reviews the topographers of ancient Rome; the first efforts of Blondus, Fulvius, Martianus, and Faunus, the superior labours of Pyrrhus Ligorius, had his learning been equal to his labours; the writings of Onuphrius Panvinius, qui omnes obscuravit, and the recent but imperfect books of Donatus and Nardini. Yet Montfaucon still sighs for a more complete plan and description of the old city, which must be attained by the three following methods:—1. The measurement of the space and intervals of the ruins. 2. The study of inscriptions and the places where they were found. 3. The investigation of all the acts, charters, diaries of the middle ages, which name any spot or building of Rome. The laborious work, such as Montfaucon desired, must be promoted by princely or public munificence: but the great modern plan of Nolli (A.D. 1748) would furnish a solid and accurate basis for the ancient topography of Rome.

MAPS: VOLUME II

VIII. THE CAROLINGIAN EMPIRE

IX. THE EMPIRE OF THE CALIPHS

X. THE LATIN STATES
IN SYRIA

KINGDOM OF HUNGARY

Halicz

Dniester R.

Prut R.

Danube R.

CUMANS OR POLOVZIANS

KHAZARS

Dnieper R.

Rostov

ALANS

SEA OF AZOV

Kuban R.

Bosporus

Cherson

BLACK SEA

Sinope

Trebizond

Neocaesarea

Erzerum

Amasia

Sivas

Halys R.

SELJUKS OF ROUM

Angora

Meletene

Amida

Edessa

Harran

Euphrates R.

Zemlin
Belgrade

SERVIA

Nissa
Sardica

BULGARIANS

Philippopolis

Adrianople

Demotika

Constantinople

Chalcedon

Nicomedia

Nicaea

GODFREY OF BOUILLON 1096

Caesarea

Marash (Germanjicia)

Aleppo

CONRAD III & LOUIS VII 1148

BYZANTINE

Durazzo

Okhrida

Devol

Thessalonica

1096

Gallipoli

Larissa

EMPIRE

Thebes

Athens

Adramyttium

Pergamum

Sardis

Smyrna

Ephesus

CONRAD III

Dorylaeum

Philadelphia

Laodicea

LOUIS VII 1148

Philomelium

Antioch

Iconium

PISIDIA

Heraclea

Tarsus

LESSER ARMENIA

Seleucia

Antioch

Homs

Đamascus

FREDERICK II 1228

FLEET 1191

1191

SEA

CRETE

Candia

Attalia

Myra

FREDERICK II 1148

RICHARD & FLEET 1191

PHILIP II 1191

CYPRUS

Famagusta

Limasol

1228

Tripoli

Beirut

Sidon

Tyre

Acre

GODFREY OF BOUILLON 1096

LOUIS IX 1248

Barca

Alexandria

Damietta

El Arish

Gaza

Ascalon

Jaffa

JERUSALEM

KINGDOM OF JERUSALEM

DOMINIONS OF SALADIN

Cairo

·V·R·

XI. THE CRUSADES

XII. THE OTTOMAN EMPIRE: 1481

KHANATE OF CRIMEA

SEA OF AZOV

CRIMEA

Azov

Taman

Kertch

Kaffa

Bakchiserai

KURDS

DIARBEKR

Euphrates R.

BLACK SEA

Trebizond

Tejin

Karahissar

Amasia

Sivas

Samsun

Caessea

DOMINION OF THE MAMELUKES

Sinope

Kizil R.

Angora

Archelaus

KARAMAN

Konia

Karaman

Selefke

Adana

Tarsus

Antioch

Tripoli

Amastris

Nicomedia

Scutari

Constantinople

Nicea

Dorylaeum

Sangarius R.

Philomelium

Attalia

KINGDOM OF CYPRUS

Nicosia

Famagusta

MOLDAVIA

DOBRUJA

Braila

WALLACHIA

Bukharest

Aluta R.

Tergovist

Giurgevo

Silistra

Nicopolis

Danube R.

Vidin

KINGDOM OF HUNGARY

Temesvar

Mohacs

Drave R.

Save R.

Semlin

Belgrade

Smederevo

Mitrovitza

SERVIA

Nishi

Prishtina

Kossovopolje

Uskub

BOSNIA

HERZEGOVINA

Jaicè

Mostar

Scutari

ALBANIA

Durazzo

Prevesa

Buttrinto

Corfu

Otranto

ITALY

ADRIATIC SEA

IONIAN SEA

Cephalonia

Zante

MOREA

Modon

Coron

Corinth

Patras

Lepanto

Arta

Prevesa

MACEDONIA

Ochrida

Kastoria

THESSALY

Yanina

Larissa

Corinth

Argos

Cerigo

Napoli

Napoli di Romania

CYCLADES

Candia

CRETE

AEGEAN SEA

Lesbos

Chios

Smyrna

Ephesus

Magnesia

Maeander R.

Philadelphia

Miletus

Rhodes

Mt. Athos

Lemnos

Thasos

SEA OF MARMORA

Gallipoli

Rodosto

Adrianople

Chirmen

Moritza R.

Philippopolis

Sofia

BULGARIA

Timova

Sistova

Seres

Thessalonica

RUMELIA

Varna

Vidin

Brusa

0   100   200   300 MILES

.VR.

Yildiz Kiosk

COSMIDION

Mosque of Ayyub

GOLDEN HORN

Palace of Blachernae

Palace of the Porphyrogenitus

Gate of Charisius   Greek Patriarchate

PHANARIOT QUARTER

Route used to drag ships of Mohammed II

PERA

Tomb of
Khair-ed-Din Barbarossa   Cheragan Palace

Dolma
Baghcheh

BOSPORUS

Wall of   Mediaeval Galata
Christ Tower

Old   GALATA
Bridge

New

Bridge

"Tower of
Leander"

SCUTARI

Gate of St. Romanus

Constantine   Wall of

OLD JANIZARY
QUARTER

Wall of   Theodosius I

Double

Gate of Rhegium

Gate of the Pegé

Holy Apostles

Grave of the
last Byzantine emperor

Sheik-ul-Islam

Mosque of
Suleiman

Aqueduct
of Valens

Lycus R.

Mosque of Bajazet

OLD SERAGLIO

Column of
Arcadius

Port of
Theodosius

Barrier   Chain

Seraglio Point

Mosque of
Sultan Valideh

New Seraglio

Sublime Porte

NEW SERAGLIO

Acropolis of Greek Byzantium

Burnt Column

Forum of Constantine   St. Sophia
Statue of Justinian   Bucoleon Palace
Serpent Column
Hippodrome   Imperial
Palace

SEA OF MARMORA

CHALCEDON

Golden Gate
Castle of the Seven Towers

0   ½   1   2 MILES

·V·R·

XIII. CONSTANTINOPLE AND VICINITY

XIV. MEDIAEVAL TRADE ROUTES

INDEX

Index

813

Baiæ, I, 129, 642
Baian, chagan of the Avars, II, 117-20
Baikal, Lake, I, 414
Bail (Regent), II, 441
Bajazet I (Ilderim Bayazid), Sultan, II, 491-4, 498-503, 756
Bajazet, vizir of Amurath II, II, 506
Balbatus, see Vaballathus
Balbinus (D. Caelius Calvius), I, 74, 76-7
Balbus, Cornelius, I, 691
Balch, I, 80, 82; II, 257, 481
Baldwin I (Count of Flanders), Emperor of the East, II, 427, 429-30, 432, 434, 437, 440-1, 444-5
Baldwin II, Emperor of the East, II, 447-51, 454, 460
Baldwin I, brother of Godfrey of Bouillon, II, 388, 396, 400, 402
Baldwin II, King of Jerusalem, II, 402
Baldwin III, King of Jerusalem, II, 413
Baldwin IV, King of Jerusalem, II, 413
Baldwin V, King of Jerusalem, II, 413
Baldwin, hermit, pretender to the Empire of the East, II, 445
Balearic Islands, I, 11
Balik, horde of, II, 370
Baliol, Urselius (Ursellus, Russelius), II, 721
Baliols, II, 721
Balista, II, 20
Balista, Emperor, I, 111
Balti (Baltha), I, 478, 517
Baltic Sea, I, 22
Banchor, Monastery of, I, 595
Bannerets, II, 353; see Valvassors
Baptism, I, 191, 297-8, 306, 326, 438, 604, 606, 724; II, 711
Baradeus, James (Jacobus Zanzalus), II, 155
Barbalissus, II, 42
Barbarus, Franciscus, II, 768
Barbatio, I, 275, 285
Barberini, family of, II, 596
Barbus, Pantaleon, II, 742
Barca, I, 11
Barcelona, I, 519; II, 283
Barchochebas, I, 208
Bardanes, rebel, II, 172
Bardanes, surnamed Philippicus, II, 167-8, 172
Bardas Phocas, II, 181
Bardas Sclerus, II, 181
Bardas, uncle of Michael III, II, 176, 326, 423
Bards, I, 94, 398, 627, 629
Bargus, I, 525
Bar-Hebræus, see Abulpharagius
Bari, II, 346, 351, 354, 364
Barid, II, 125
Barkok, Circassian (Mamaluke), II, 499
Barlaam, Calabrian monk, II, 476-7, 510-11, 523-4
Barmecides, II, 300
Barnabas, St., Gospel of, II, 667
Baroncelli, II, 581
Barsumas, II, 143-4
Bartholemy, Peter, II, 398-9
Bartolus, II, 219
Basic and Cursic, I, 548
Basil, St., I, 765, 787-8, 797, 815
Basil I, the Macedonian, II, 175-7, 326, 331-2, 336, 348, 423
Basil II, Emperor, II, 179-81, 315, 337
Basil, Archbishop of Cæsarea, I, 392, 439
Basil the monk, I, 594; II, 704

Basil, city of, I, 8, 285; II, 516-18, 521-2
Basilacius, II, 185, 373-4
Basileus, title of, I, 154; II, 214, 337
Basilics, II, 177, 311
Basilides, II, 161
Basilides the Gnostic, II, 136
Basilidians, I, 184
Basilina, I, 797
Basiliscus, I, 584-5, 635
Basilius, consul, I, 592
Basilius, delator of Boethius, I, 890
Basilius, Roman Patrician, II, 57
Basilius, senator, I, 504, 858
Basina, I, 609
Basra, I, 367; see Bassora
Bassi, I, 459
Bassianus (Cæsar), I, 174, 714
Bassianus, name of Caracalla, I, 686
Bassianus, name of Elagabalus, I, 58-9
Bassora (Basra, Bussorah), II, 227, 248, 256, 306, 673
Bastarnae, I, 99, 135, 147, 472
Batavians, I, 95, 133, 283, 331, 609, 674; horse-guards, 122, 683; legion, 383, 394, 399; war, 92
Bath (Aquæ Sulis), I, 20, 626
Batnae, I, 365
Batnir, II, 497
Batou, II, 484-6
Bau (Pabau), I, 868
Bauto, I, 470
Baux, de, James, II, 745
Baux, name corrupted from Baltha, I, 824; Lords of, near Arles, 824
Bavaria, I, 9; II, 339
Bavarians, I, 538, 546, 616; II, 211, 340
Beatrice, II, 464
Beaune, I, 679
Becket, Thomas, I, 732
Bede, the Venerable, I, 190, 398, 624
Beder, II, 238
Bederiana, I, 891
Bedoweens, II, 221-3, 225, 241, 306, 600
Beglerbegs, II, 533
Beineddin, II, 409
Bela IV, King of Hungary, II, 484
Bela (Alexius), Hungarian prince, II, 188-9
Belenus, I, 75
Beles (Balis), II, 220
Belfry (Belfridus), II, 728
Belgae, I, 9
Belgic Gaul, I, 8, 559, 562
Belgrade, see Singidunum
Belisarius, I, 603, 648, 655, 661, 861; II, 2-13, 16-32, 43, 52, 55-60, 65-7
Bellini, Gentile, II, 772
Bellona, temple of, II, 330
Beltis, I, 745
Belus, I, 705; tower of, II, 675
Benacus, I, 568; II, 64
Bender, I, 3
Benedict XI, Pope, II, 569, 780
Benedict XII, Pope, II, 510-11, 583, 787-8
Benedict XIII (Peter de Luna), Pope, II, 584-5
Benedict XIV, Pope, II, 596
Benedict Anianinus, I, 869
Benefice, I, 619; II, 215, 218
Benevento, II, 347, 355, 362, 464
Beneventum, II, 18, 211, 349-50, 355
Bengal, II, 483
Benjamin of Tudela, II, 315

THE GREAT IDEAS, Volumes 2 and 3